Are you frightened of speaking in public?

Here are some strategies to make public speaking easier and more effective.

Pages 244–265

Are you being held back from success because you are a poor reader?

Find out how to improve your speed, comprehension, and enjoyment of reading.
Learn how to read memos, reports, and technical books in order to get ahead.

Pages 302–327

Do you believe your memory is not good enough?

Find out how you can improve your memory. Learn how not to forget a person's name.

Pages 180–205

Do people often use words you do not understand?

Build a powerful vocabulary in order to do better at school or on the job.

Pages 206–243

Are you thinking of purchasing a personal computer?

Learn what you need to know to make a wise decision.

Pages 2–21

Are you going abroad this year? Or do you need to know another language at work?

Profit from a review of the French, German, or Spanish you learned in school.

Pages 352–437

Are you beginning to think about retiring?

Learn how to plan for your retirement so it will be as rewarding as you have always hoped.

Pages 127–130

Student Handbook

with

Roget's University Thesaurus

Volume **3**

Student Handbook

with

Roget's University Thesaurus

Volume 3

THE SOUTHWESTERN COMPANY
Nashville, Tennessee

Roget's University Thesaurus
was originally published under the title
Roget's International Thesaurus of English Words and Phrases.

Preface

This volume of the *Student Handbook with Roget's University Thesaurus* is the most practical reference book ever designed for use by the American family. All members of the family—students looking ahead to advanced schooling or that important first job, those out of school and wanting to advance their careers, parents concerned with the organization and management of their lives, senior citizens wishing to remain active—will discover essential information about increasing their enjoyment from life by becoming healthier, wealthier, and wiser. *Student Handbook,* Volume 3, covers in a single volume subjects that ordinarily require an entire shelf of books. Thus, it is an indispensable home reference book to be kept next to the other, more specialized books you may already have: cookbooks, telephone books, the Bible, etc.

Though this *Student Handbook* is completely independent and can be consulted separately, it is expressly designed to be the third volume in the well-known and popular *Student Handbook* set. The *Student Handbooks* are intended to help students improve at school. They assemble in an easy-to-learn way the many subjects taught in elementary, junior high, and high schools.

Volume 3, on the other hand, offers help to the whole family in its everyday activities. It is especially useful for those who are looking for a job or who want to move ahead in their careers, and for those who are retired and want new ways to make life more interesting and productive. Thus, Volume 3 is a lifelong resource. It will be as useful to you decades from now as it will be the first time you consult it.

This volume is in two major parts: PART ONE covers all practical aspects of home management, such as finances, health, and the law; and all aspects of career advancement, such as computers, letter writing, memory improvement, speaking, and writing. If published separately, each of these topics would be a book in itself.

PART TWO is a world-famous thesaurus, a treasury of words that will help you find exactly the right one to express your every thought.

The 15 sections of PART ONE are:

1. *Understanding Computers*—You too can be knowledgeable about computers.
2. *Advancing Your Career*—How to get a job, get along in your job, change careers, or start your own business.
3. *Health and Fitness*—How to eat well and stay healthy, with good advice for every family member, even senior citizens.
4. *You and Modern Medicine*—What to do when you are sick; how to choose a doctor; generic drugs; your hospital stay; medical payments.
5. *Managing the Family's Money*—Credit, banking, investment, shopping, vacationing, retirement, money-saving ideas.
6. *You and the Law*—Wills and estates, consumers' rights, criminal law, finding a lawyer.
7. *Improving Your Memory*—A tested and successful way to learn how to remember anything: names, numbers, essential facts, school subjects, on-the-job information.
8. *Building Your Vocabulary*—How to learn new words and their meanings; 15 days to a more forceful vocabulary; vocabulary tests; words you should know.
9. *Improving Your Speech*—How to say what you want clearly and effectively; public speaking made easy; Robert's Rules of Order.
10. *Writing Effective Letters*—Social letters, business letters, hard-to-write letters, postal information, scores of examples for every need.
11. *Improving Your Reading*—How to read better and faster; learning to read special kinds of texts; reading lists.

12. *Taking Major Tests*—How to prepare for tests; sample questions from those all-important General Educational Development Tests (GED's), Scholastic Assessment Tests (SAT's), American College Testing (ACT's), and Graduate Record Examinations (GRE's).
13. *Review of French Grammar*—Parts of speech, rules governing their use, verb tables, sample sentences, important expressions, plus a concise French-English dictionary and English-French dictionary.
14. *Review of German Grammar*—Parts of speech, rules governing their use, verb tables, sample sentences, important expressions, plus a concise German-English dictionary and English-German dictionary.
15. *Review of Spanish Grammar*—All parts of speech, rules governing their use, verb tables, sample sentences, important expressions, plus a concise Spanish-English dictionary and English-Spanish dictionary.

PART TWO is the complete, newly revised publication of the famous *Roget's University Thesaurus,* printed here for the first time in two colors to make it easier and quicker to use. This thesaurus, though it has been modernized, is based on the family word book devised over a hundred years ago by Peter Mark Roget. It has proven so useful that it has been in print continuously ever since. Your family will find it helpful in writing letters, student papers, and reports.

Note that each section of this volume begins with its own table of contents, including page numbers, so that you can turn immediately to the particular subject that interests you most. Each section offers charts, checklists, and boxes of special information that you will use again and again. Learn how the famous *Roget's University Thesaurus* will help you find the word you need and assist you in building your vocabulary, simply and quickly. Are you intimidated by the world of computers? Have a look at the very first section for an introduction to these marvelous machines that every member of your family can use with ease. Are you interested in brushing up on your French, German, or Spanish? Note, finally, that there is a general index that gives you quick access to every topic in the book.

We are certain you will find the *Student Handbook,* Volume 3 of lasting value for the whole family.

—Gorton Carruth, Editor-in-Chief

Table of Contents

Part 1
Student Handbook

Managing the Family's Money 110

You and the Law 140

Part 2
Roget's
University
Thesaurus

Editorial development of the Student Handbook was directed by
The Hudson Group, Inc., Pleasantville, New York 10570

Administrative editors:	Eugene Ehrlich
Editors-in-chief:	Gorton Carruth
Managing editor:	Hayden Carruth
Administrative assistant:	Nicole Grandjean
Copy-editing and indexing:	Felice Levy/AEIOU, Inc.
Contributors:	Renni Browne/The Editorial Department
	Frances E. Barth, Else Behrendt, Marietta Burrowes,
	Delia Bye, Gisele Carruth, Karl Friese,
	John Harrington, Sylvia Helm, Lawrence Heyl, Jr.,
	Helene Isaac, Naomi Katz, Seymour Levine,
	John Maloney, Elizabeth Rich
Special advisor:	"Improving Your Memory," Harry Lorayne
Design and art direction:	Pam Forde Graphics
Production:	Rachelle Engelman, Kathleen Marks
Illustrations and maps:	Ric Del Rossi/Mulvey Associates, Bill Colrus/Mulvey Associates,
	H. Peter Loewer/Graphos Studio,
	Leslie Dunlap/Publishers' Graphics, Inc.
Photo researchers:	Lenore Weber, Carousel Research

Part 1

Student
Handbook

Understanding Computers

Today, computers are everywhere you look, even in places where you might be surprised to find them. Nearly all of us use computers every day, whether we realize it or not.

Computers process your checks at the bank by reading the computer-scannable numbers on the bottom left-hand corner of your check. Computers in automated cash or teller machines let you withdraw and deposit money regardless of banking hours. Airline ticketing and reservation agents book you on a flight by using a computerized system that keeps track of routes, fares, and seats.

Computers scan the Universal Product Code on your groceries, tally your bill, and adjust the store's inventory. Computers tune the radio, pump gas, set thermostats, and control or monitor engine emissions and fuel economy.

Computers are on your wrist (digital watches) and in your pocket (calculators). If you have a microwave oven, you have a computer. When you press the "redial" button on a telephone receiver, a computer remembers and dials the number you last called.

Computers have had an enormous impact on the job market. Almost every job soon may require some level of computer use. In addition, there are computer-related careers that did not even exist a generation ago. These careers are found not only in the computer industry itself, but in government, banking, manufacturing, publishing—in fact, in every sector of the economy.

The computer age is *your* age. You have the right to live in it comfortably, without feeling threatened by this pervasive new technology. A computer is just another tool for you to use.

Numerous tasks at home can be performed by a computer. You can bank at home, shop at home, and read newspapers on the computer; you can even use your computer as a library. You can also monitor your health and advance your education by means of a computer.

The computer also makes it possible to bring work home. Some companies allow employees to work on company-owned computers placed in employees' homes and connected via telephone lines to the office.

In our schools, the push is on to make children "computer literate." This means learning more about computers themselves, and being able to use a computer to learn about other subjects. Many parents and teachers fear that those students who are not familiar with computers will be left behind. They know that long after youngsters leave school, computers will remain a powerful tool in their lives.

This chapter will explain what a computer is, and what it can and cannot do. It will tell you how you can use one in your home to improve your job skills, earn extra income, and enjoy more leisure time.

What is a computer?

Historically, a computer, broadly defined, was a device that helped in computation—counting, calculating, adding, subtracting, multiplying, dividing, etc.—as you might guess from the root of the word *computer*. Today the word computer is used to describe an electronic device that stores, manipulates, and analyzes information. Computers no longer simply perform mathematical calculations; they can perform a much wider range of tasks, as described in the second half of this chapter.

The first computers. Stonehenge, the prehistoric circular stone monuments in Great Britain, and the abacus are two examples of early computers. Stonehenge is a man-made device used to *calculate* the movement of the stars and planets in order to *measure* the seasons and *predict* seasonal change. The abacus, although it is associated almost exclusively with the Chinese, was also used in some version by early Romans, Greeks, and Egyptians to *count* and *calculate*.

Gottfried Leibniz (b. 1646) and Blaise Pascal (b. 1623) each invented calculating machines in the 17th century. Leibniz also developed the system of using the base-two (binary) number system that computers use today.

How computers work

The computing process has four steps:
1. **Input:** A program or data are entered into the computer.
2. **Processing:** The computer executes the program or processes the data.
3. **Output:** The computer delivers the results of its operations to the user on a monitor, and on paper via a printer.
4. **Storage:** The computer saves programs and data for further use.

The shrinking computer. Although Pascal's simple calculator (which could add and subtract) came before that of Charles Babbage, Babbage is considered the father of the modern computer. An early 19th-century Englishman, Babbage developed the principles on which modern computers are based.

The Difference Engine. Babbage started by inventing a small machine, the Difference Engine, in 1822. The machine computed algebraic expressions with many terms (polynomials), but it did only that. Babbage decided to build a machine that could solve virtually any mathematical problem and perform any kind of mathematical calculation.

The Analytical Engine. Babbage's design—a general-purpose computing machine—encompassed the main elements of a modern computer: it had input, storage, control, and output mechanisms. It was controlled by punched cards and was digital. (Think of a digital computer as a machine that counts on its fingers, or digits.)

Babbage planned for his Analytical Engine to be capable of storing thousands of figures, but as with many modern computer designs, his plans and his machine were never fully realized.

Hollerith's tabulating machine. Across the Atlantic Ocean, about 50 years after Babbage's work, the U.S. Census Bureau was having trouble tabulating the 1880 census, even though the next one was fast approaching. Herman Hollerith, a census agent, was asked to invent a mechanized tabulating system for the 1890 census.

Hollerith's system used paper tape initially, but punched cards worked better. Census takers punched holes in census cards to record data. The cards were fed into Hollerith's device, which had pins that stuck through the punched holes to form a closed electrical circuit, causing the information in each census category to be recorded.

The machine was a success. Hollerith went on to form his own concern, the Tabulating Machine Company, which became the International Business Machines Corporation (IBM) in 1924.

Mark I. The next major advance was the development of Mark I. It was assembled at Harvard University in 1943, under the direction of mathematician Howard Aiken and with funding from IBM. Mark I used electric relay switches instead of punched cards, and punched paper tape for input. Mark I was used by the U.S. Army during World War II to compute ballistic data.

ENIAC. The world's first *electronic* digital computer was ENIAC—the *E*lectronic *N*umerical *I*ntegrator *a*nd *C*alculator. Until ENIAC was developed, computers were mechanical.

ENIAC was room-sized, taking up 15,000 square feet. It was built of 18,000 vacuum tubes, and it weighed 30 tons. Developed by a U.S. government team and completed in 1946, it was 17 times faster than Mark I, performing 5000 additions per second. It was used to design the hydrogen bomb.

UNIVAC. Business first computerized with UNIVAC, the *Univ*ersal *A*utomatic *C*omputer, which was smaller than its predecessors in size. UNIVAC, introduced in 1951, correctly tabulated the results of the 1952 presidential election.

Transistors. The invention of the transistor at Bell Laboratories in 1947 quickly made possible a miniature world of transistor radios, hearing aids, and electronic equipment of all kinds. The transistor was smaller than a thimble. The first transistorized computers were introduced in 1957 and 1958. They were smaller, faster, more reliable, and much more powerful than vacuum-tube computers. They also cost much less.

Integrated Circuits. The next step in the evolution of computers was the development in 1958 of integrated circuits. An integrated circuit consists of a number of transistors, switches, connecting wires, and other components of circuits—all engraved onto a small flat silicon surface called a chip. A single integrated circuit can do the same work as thousands of transistors.

Commercial computers with integrated circuits began appearing in the mid-1960's. Computers that once took up an entire floor of a building could now fit in the corner of an office. The next major development in computer technology, the *microchip,* would make possible computers small enough to sit on a desk or rest on your lap.

Common questions about computers

Q: Do I need to know a lot about computers in order to use one?

A: No. Here is what you *do not need* to know. You do not need to know how to program a computer. You do not need to know programming languages. You do not have to possess scientific or mathematical aptitude. In fact, you do not have to know any math at all. You do not even have to know how the computer works. Most users do not.

Q: What should I know about my computer's disk operating system (DOS)?

A: All you have to know about a computer's DOS is which kind it is: common types include Apple DOS, MS-DOS, OS/2, and UNIX. The operating system manages and controls everything the computer does. All the software and hardware you buy has to run on your operating system, or you cannot use it. Think of your operating system as speaking French—unable to "read" German or Russian.

Q: Do I have to be computer-literate in order to use a computer?

A: You may be intimidated by what is called computer literacy. There is no need to be. Other than the experience of using a computer and a software program or two, nothing is required to join the ranks of the computer qualified.

Why do you want a computer?

How do you translate the things a computer does well into the kinds of things *you* might want a computer to do?

Some common reasons for wanting a computer are listed here to get you started. Look at this list and check off the things you want your computer to do.

_____Balance the checkbook
_____Chat with other computer users
_____Do calculations in class, at meetings, on trips
_____Do taxes
_____Draw pictures/graphs/charts
_____Improve job skills
_____Keep addresses
_____Keep Christmas mailing list
_____Keep personal records
_____Keep recipes
_____Keep the family budget
_____Learn more about computers
_____Organize records and tapes
_____Play games
_____Start or run a small business
_____Teach programming languages
_____Teach spelling, math, or other subjects
_____Tie into computer data banks
_____Track the stock market
_____Write music
_____Write term papers or reports

The microcomputer

A *microcomputer* is a computer that is very much smaller in size than other computers. Microcomputers are also commonly called *micros* and *personal computers*. Some inexpensive models, such as the type people use to play games, are called *home computers*. Lightweight models that operate on batteries and can be carried from one place to another are called *portables, laptops,* and *notebook computers* (or simply notebooks).

The microchip.
The core of the microcomputer is the *microprocessor,* sometimes called a computer on a chip. Although no larger than a baby's thumbnail, a microprocessor contains all the electronic circuits that make up the central processing unit of a computer. It serves the same function as did the relay switches and vacuum tubes of the older, larger computers.

The first microprocessor, introduced by Intel in late 1970, had 2250 transistors. It could process four bits of data at a time and carry out about 60,000 operations a second—more than ten times the speed of ENIAC at a fraction of the cost. By 1990 microprocessors holding 1 million transistors and able to process 64 bits of data at a time were on the market.

In order to examine the circuitry on a chip, you would have to use a microscope. To "remember" 16K (store in memory 16 kilobytes, or about 16,000 pieces of data), a computer memory bank of the 1950's had to be taller and larger than an average adult standing up. With modern technology that same amount of memory can now be stored on a tiny 16K memory chip.

The technology that put so many transistors on a chip has also reduced drastically the price of computers. Today, personal computers with power and capabilities that rival those once available only to government and big business can be purchased by private individuals and families.

Development of the microchip made possible ever smaller computers, from the room-size ENIAC to the notebook-size portable.

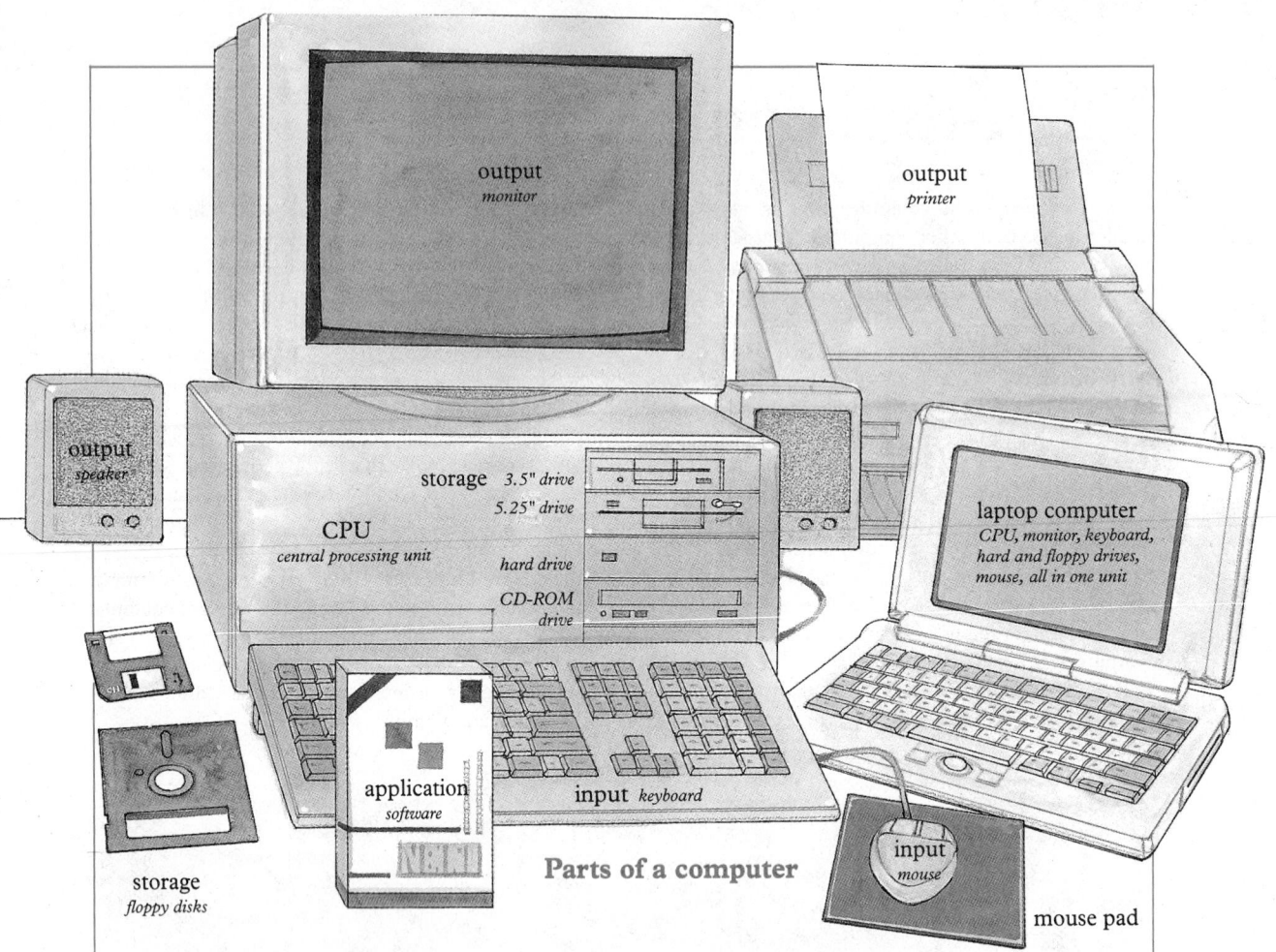

monitor

printer

speaker

storage   3.5" drive
          5.25" drive

CPU
central processing unit

          hard drive

CD-ROM
drive

laptop computer
*CPU, monitor, keyboard,
hard and floppy drives,
mouse, all in one unit*

application
software

input *keyboard*

Parts of a computer

input
mouse

storage
floppy disks

mouse pad

The main part of the computer is the central processing unit (CPU). Though the CPU is the "brains" of the computer, you cannot do anything with a CPU by itself. You need some way to communicate with it.

The computer's ears. The computer has to "hear" what you say. This is accomplished with *input devices,* such as game controls, a keyboard, or a mouse.

You use *game controls* to communicate with your computer. These controls, sometimes called joy sticks, come with or without a number pad. The stick moves up, down, right, and left in a two-dimensional axis and controls the movements of the game (your space ship, your hero, etc.) on the screen. Or the stick is a trigger that fires a weapon or, perhaps, a Ping-Pong ball at your command.

A more advanced way of communicating with your computer is to use a typewriterlike *keyboard.* The keys may include a number pad similar to that on a calculator.

A mouse is a hand-operated device that can be used to select data or commands. You use the mouse to "point" to an object on the screen and then press one of its buttons to execute a command. It is faster than a keyboard and easier to master since it does not require that you know how to type.

The computer's mouth. The computer tells you what it has done and is doing through *output devices.*

A *monitor,* or video screen similar to that on a television set, is one form of output device. It enables you to see instantaneously what is occurring inside the computer in response to your input (from the keyboard, game control, mouse, etc.). A *printer* is an output device that records what the computer has done on paper. *Multimedia speakers* add a new dimension to computing—stereophonic sound.

Storage devices, such as floppy disk drives and hard disk drives, enable you to store, or save, what you did on a computer. Another type of storage device, the CD-ROM drive, enables you to gain access to programs and files that already have been stored on *compact discs,* or CD's. You cannot store new information on the discs, however, which is what the "ROM" tells you—the disc is read only memory.

Some low-priced computers turn out to be, upon closer investigation, next to useless without add-ons like monitors, disk drives, and printers, which can end up being more expensive than the computer itself.

Bit/Byte

How does a bit differ from a byte?

Bit is a contraction of "*b*inary dig*it*" and refers to the smallest unit of information a computer can process. Everything a computer does is done with electric circuitry, and electric current has two states: on and off. These two states are represented by the base two, or binary, number system, which has two symbols (0 and 1) to represent all numbers.

A byte is a group of bits, usually eight, forming a character, letter, number, punctuation mark, etc.

Here are some examples:

letter:	*byte:*
The letter A is	01000001
The letter B is	01000010
The letter C is	01000011

It is never too late to learn!

Many people feel intimidated by computers or believe they are too old to learn how to use one. However, for those out of work or seeking a new job, experience in using a computer will provide new opportunities. Even if you have been out of school for a long time, it is not too late to learn how the computer can help you at home or on the job. There are many training programs aimed at reluctant computer users. Adult education programs and community colleges frequently offer classes in basic computer skills.

Computer stores frequently provide some kind of training on the equipment and software they sell. In addition, many computer programs are designed with on-screen selection "buttons" and drop-down menus that make it easier for an inexperienced user to get to work quickly.

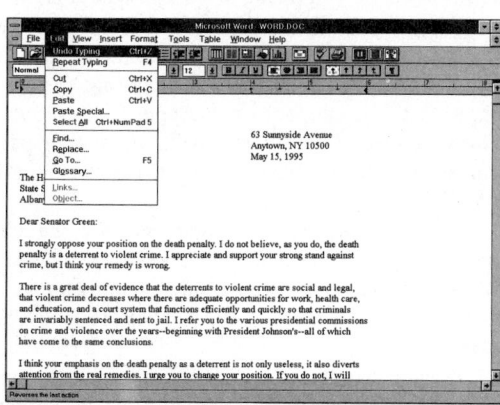

Computer programs. The computer that you use to play video games on your television set is dedicated to one task: playing games. You tell your computer what to do (play a game) by inserting a game cartridge. More expensive, sophisticated computers also need instructions to tell them what to do. These instructions are called programs, or *software*.

You can write a program yourself, but you certainly do not have to. Some computer owners hire someone to write a program for them. Businesses and some professionals (doctors, accountants, etc.) tailor programming to the exact requirements of their offices. Although you, too, could hire someone to write a program for your computer, the cost would probably exceed the price of the computer itself.

Most likely, you will buy programs the same way you buy books or tape cassettes: in a store or by mail. These are programs designed for use by many people, although they may allow you to make modifications for personal preferences. A set of instructions, called documentation, comes with each program. It explains what the program does and how to use it.

There are two broad categories of software: *system* and *applications.*

System software. This category includes operating systems, utilities (software programs of a specific type), and languages.

A *disk operating system* (DOS) is what the computer uses to run itself. It directs the transfer of information from one part of the computer to another, and controls its storage in memory and on disk. It consists of a supervisory core and a collection of utility programs.

Utilities give the operating system additional features. The programmers of operating systems cannot foresee all user needs so utilities are added to perform functions not included in the operating system. Two of the most common utilities include one that copies files from one disk drive to another and one that lets you specify exactly how you want something to be printed. Some of the more exotic utilities can examine and change specific bytes or groups of bytes in memory.

Languages let you program the computer. Computers are machines that work with electrical impulses; computer languages let you "speak" to the computer without knowing anything about the machine's internal processes. The language is your interpreter.

Applications software. This term describes the task-oriented software programs that your computer uses to run your business, play games, type term papers, teach you or your family how to program, etc.

Applications software uses the operating system to interact with the computer. Although basic understanding of the operating system is necessary when using a computer, much applications software today is

---

---

written to "hide" the operating system from the user. Detailed knowledge of the operating system's capabilities is becoming less needed.

The applications software (other than games) that you are most likely to use are programs in the fields of

- business/financial
- education
- health
- word processing

Later in this chapter you will learn more about software categories and how to use them.

Compatibility. The computer's disk operating system (DOS) determines the kinds of software that will or will not work on your computer. Applications software is run (made to work) by the computer's operating system. For example, if the operating system of a computer is PC-DOS, then the computer can only run PC-DOS software. If the operating system is Apple-DOS, it can only run Apple-DOS software. This is similar to the situation with automobile parts: you cannot put a Cadillac El Dorado carburetor in the Honda Civic.

When different types of computers use the same operating system, the computers are said to be *compatible.* Many companies manufacture computers that are compatible with either the IBM PC or the IBM PS/2 series.

Software manufacturers often make different versions of their programs for different operating systems. For example, a certain game or accounting program

---

may be available in both Apple-DOS and PC-DOS versions. But this is not always the case. Some operating systems have had much more software written for them than have other operating systems. Therefore, it is important to know what you want your computer to do before you make any purchases. Pick out the software first, before you buy hardware (the computer, printer, etc.). Then choose hardware that works well with the software.

Buying software.
Take your list to a computer store—or to any large retail store that sells computers—and ask to see a demonstration of software that will perform the tasks you want. In addition, look through computer magazines for the names of software programs that do the tasks you have selected. Ask the advice of people who are using their computers to do the kinds of tasks you plan to do. Teachers may be helpful in suggesting educational programs for your children.

While you are trying out software, you will also get a chance to see different types of computers. The best way to begin selecting a computer is to actually try it out, watching it do what you want it to.

Shop around for the best price for both software and hardware.

Selecting hardware.
To select the right computer for you—the hardware—go back to the list of things you want your computer to do.

Once you have a list of applications, make a list of computers that run the software you will be using. Next, consider the following:

Price range. How much money are you able and willing to spend on your computer system?

Necessary features. How much memory is needed to run the programs you plan to use? What peripherals are needed? If you want a computer only for games, you do not need a printer. But a printer is essential if you plan to do word processing. On the other hand, games may require a graphics card, which is not needed for word processing.

Space requirements. How much space do you have for the computer? Will you need special furniture for it? Will you want to move the computer between your home and your office? If space is limited or if you expect to move the computer frequently, you may wish to consider a portable model.

Expandability. Perhaps at the present time you want a computer just for games and simple educational programs. But soon your children may be old enough to use word-processing programs. You may decide to computerize your taxes and other financial data. Being able to communicate with other computers via telephone may also sound appealing, though you probably

Video game or personal computer?

Today's personal computers and video games have powerful microprocessors. Most of them offer dazzling graphics, but the personal computer is the more versatile of the two types of machines becase it can run more different types of software. With CD-ROM, modem, and multimedia capabilities, a personal computer can be used for work and play, and for communicating with other computer users. No video game can do all that!

aren't ready to try that right now. Expandability means that a computer system can be upgraded or improved. New features can be added at a fraction of the cost it would take to replace the entire system. Some inexpensive computers cannot be expanded, thus limiting their versatility.

Quality, maintenance, and service. Check the terms of the warranty. Does the retailer provide training and maintenance services? How easy is it to fix the computer—or a peripheral—if it breaks down? How much will repairs cost? Where—and how quickly—will this work be done? Do you have to ship the computer somewhere at your own expense?

Storing your data.
One fact of computer life that people often forget (with sometimes tragic results) is that when you turn off the computer, or the power fails, you lose any information that was stored only in the internal electronic memory of the computer. If you want to keep records, balance the checkbook, plan the budget, keep recipe files, or organize your record collection, then you want your computer to remember what you did the last time you used it. This requires a *storage device.*

Some inexpensive computers, particularly game machines, use programs stored on cartridges that are easily inserted into the computers. Some portables weighing no more than a pound have credit-card-size storage cards. Large business computers use reels of tape. Videodisks and CD-ROM (*C*ompact *D*isk-*R*ead *O*nly *M*emory) are also used. But the most commonly used storage devices are disks.

Disks and disk drives. There are two types of disks: floppy and hard. A device called a disk drive is needed to store information on a disk and to read, or retrieve, that information.

The floppy disk—a flexible, flat platter that is enclosed in a protective jacket—is the standard external storage device that is used for most personal computers. Almost all computers today come with hard disk drives that store the operating system and applications software.

Both floppy disk drives and hard disk drives are usually a physical part of the main computer housing.

The essential difference between them is that a floppy disk can be removed from its drive, while a hard disk is permanently fixed in its drive.

Floppy disks come in two sizes: 5.25 inch and 3.5 inch. The 5.25-inch disks can hold up to 1.2MB (megabytes or millions of bytes) and are flexible and easily damaged if handled carelessly. The 3.5-inch disks hold up to 1.44MB and are encased in rigid plastic cases, making them far more durable. Hard disks generally have storage capacities of between 85MB and 540MB, although capacities of more than 2GB (gigabytes or billions of bytes) are available.

The storage capacity that you need will be determined for the most part by the applications you intend using the computer for. Some applications programs are very large and can only be stored on several high capacity disks or, more commonly, a hard disk. If you intend to use your computer to create a very large database, you may need a hard disk. Discuss your storage needs with your computer salesman.

What about those expensive add-ons?

The following are extra features that can be bought as add-on, peripheral (side) devices or can be built into the computer. Not everyone has a use for them, and in some cases they are quite expensive.

Touch screens	Some computers allow you to tell them what to do by touching the video display screen instead of the keyboard.
Voice	Some computers recognize voice commands. Speech recognition is rudimentary right now, but it is an important feature for those who cannot use a keyboard.
CD-ROM	CD-ROM is the result of a "marriage" between the compact disk (CD) and the personal computer. Words and other data are recorded on the CD, in much the same way that the Beatles are recorded on the CDs that have revolutionized the music industry. Huge amounts of data can be stored on a CD-ROM. For example, an encyclopedia that fills 20 volumes can be put on a single CD. A special CD-ROM player must be attached to the computer to read the information on the disk.
Graphics tablets	These have a flat surface on which you can draw. Depending on the model, you draw with a special stylus, an ordinary pen, or even a finger. Your drawing is entered into the computer's memory and appears on the screen.
Modems	These devices let a computer talk over telephone lines to other computers. Sometimes a modem is built-in, most commonly in portable or transportable computers. More often, however, you have to buy the modem. You need a modem to tap into the information services that carry stock quotes, airline guides, and user bulletin boards. If you do not want your computer to communicate with other computers, you do not need a modem.
Sound synthesizers	These plug into the computer and create sounds, including spoken words and music. You can compose and play music on your computer with special extras you plug in or add on to it, although some computers do come with this ability built-in.

Understanding Computers

Printers

Certain uses you may have for your computer—writing letters or research papers, keeping your budget, running a business from your home—will require putting the output of your computer on paper. This is called hard copy and it requires a printer.

There are several kinds of printers. Three popular choices are the laser, inkjet, and dot matrix printers. Their names describe the kind of printing element that produces their distinctive type of character. Each has advantages (+) and disadvantages (−).

Laser printers. These printers use a highly focused beam of light to form an image on a charged cylinder that then transfers a powder called toner onto the paper, in much the same way that a copier machine does. Laser printers

+ come in a wide range of prices ($400 and up).
+ are extremely quiet.
+ print high-quality text suitable for professional-looking documents.
+ can produce graphics (bar graphs, charts, pictures, tables, etc.). Some higher priced models can print in color.
+ are able to produce multiple type styles and sizes.
+ are very fast, printing 4 to 18 pages per minute.
− cost more per page to operate than inkjet or dot matrix printers.
− cannot be used to print multiple-copy forms.

Inkjet printers. These printers spray ink through nozzles in the print head onto the paper, depositing an extremely fine pattern of dots to produce characters and graphics. Most color inkjets use three colored inks—red (magenta), yellow, and blue (cyan)—as well as the black ink used by monochrome inkjets, but some use just the three colors to produce black. Inkjet printers

+ are relatively inexpensive (starting at under $300 for monochrome, under $500 for color).
+ are extremely quiet.
+ produce high-quality text and graphics.
+ are fast (4 to 6 pages a minute).
− cost more per page to operate than dot matrix printers.
− cannot be used to print multiple-copy forms.

Dot matrix printers. These printers have a printing element that produces letters, numbers, and punctuation, plus graphs and pictures, by "drawing" them with a series of tiny dots at a speed of 80 to 350 characters per second. The "matrix" may consist of a grid of five rows of seven dots (5 × 7), nine rows of nine dots (9 × 9), and so on. The greater the number of dots, the higher the quality of character produced. Dot matrix printers

+ are lowest in cost of the three types of printers ($100 to $600).
+ cost least per page to operate.
+ can be used to print multiple-copy forms.
− are much noisier than laser or inkjet printers.
− do not print as fast as laser or inkjet printers.
− do not produce letter-quality characters (as sharp and well formed as those printed by a typewriter).

Which printer is for you? Quality is in the eye of the beholder. You have to look at the print and decide if it is what you want.

A 24-pin dot matrix printer is considered close to laser print quality. The print head contains a total of 24 pins and produces characters that are clear and well delineated. A 9-pin printer, on the other hand, may not print the tails of descenders (*j, q, p, y,* and *g*) deeply enough.

While you are looking at the print, listen to the printer. Any dot matrix printer is noisy, and you should take this into consideration when deciding which type of printer to buy. Laser and inkjet printers are much quieter and offer better print quality, but they are more expensive, cost more per page to operate, and cannot print multiple-copy forms.

If you decide on a dot matrix printer, check the features that are available. Many dot matrix printers offer both *pin-feed* (or *tractor-feed*) paper advance mechanisms, which use "pins" on the platen to advance the paper through the printer, and *friction-feed* advance, in which the paper is gripped between the platen and roller, as in a typewriter. Having both features means you can use continuous-feed printer paper and standard sheet paper, such as letterhead.

Some dot matrix printers offer "paper parking," which enables you to temporarily switch from continuous-feed paper to standard sheet paper without actually removing the continuous-feed paper from the printer. Laser and inkjet printers use friction feed and print on sheet paper.

Computers and education

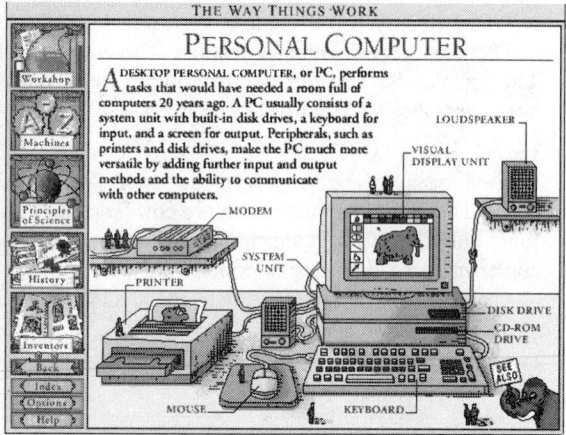

Educational software for children that is also fun to use can be an important learning aid. Of course, there is software available to help students with such basic school subjects as arithmetic, but there are also many programs that help children—and adults—explore the world around them.

Why are computers good for learning new things? Computers can entertain as they educate, with engaging graphics, colors, sounds, movement, and simulations. Computer learning can be fun.

Computers can force one-to-one attention (one person, teacher, or computer to one student), which is known to speed learning.

Unlike a textbook, computers can encourage you when you have grasped the material. By making a sound or by flashing a message on the screen ("GREAT WORK!"), they can congratulate you on a job well done.

Computers are endlessly patient when you are wrong, going over and over the material until you get it right. No harsh words, no lost tempers.

Young children are especially good candidates for computer education because they are fascinated with how a computer works. Early education software takes advantage of a child's natural delight with games, and combines games with learning to produce a painless teaching environment.

Educational software. A wide variety of educational software is now available for use on home computers. They range in difficulty from the very basic educational software for preschool children to complex math or problem-solving programs for older children.

Some inexpensive game computers that use plug-in cartridges instead of floppy disks to load programs have educational titles. This is an especially attractive option for those with very young children who have no need for an expensive personal computer. It has the added advantage of enabling children to plug in and run programs themselves.

Evaluating the software. Some educational software consists of nothing more than expensive flash cards, such as those you used in school to learn multiplication and addition. Such software does not take advantage of the full potential of your computer.

How can you tell a good educational software program from a bad one? How do you go about finding a good one?

1. **For children, start in the school.** If your child's school has computers, ask the teacher what kind of software they use. You may wish to duplicate or complement the software your child is already using. Or you may want to use the next, more advanced program in a series.

2. **Next, go to a computer store and try out some programs.** If you are buying the software for children, take them into the store to try it out with you. The software should be labeled with suggested age levels, but a test run will ensure that the software is appropriate for your children. Let them use it.

3. **Read the manual** (the documentation, or instructions that go with the program). Are the instructions easy to read? Good instructions are written in plain English. There is a clear explanation of how to use the program, and all of the program's options are described. Often, manuals contain suggestions for follow-up activities that reinforce the skills taught by the software. In some software, the documentation is actually part of the program. If this is true, can the instructions be skipped once your child is familiar with the program?

4. **When you test-run the program,** look for these features:

Understanding Computers

Two educational software examples

Speed reading. Speed-reading courses outside the home are often quite expensive, and they require you to spend hours in a classroom that may be far from home. With a computer, you can learn to increase your reading speed, at home, much more economically. You can buy a speed-reading software program for about $70. More than one member of your family can take the same "course," which brings the cost down even further.

The computer is an especially effective tool for learning speed reading. It can train your eye movements to extend your peripheral (side) vision, so that you read larger groups of words at a time instead of one or two at a time. It can flash individual words on the screen at faster and faster rates, enabling you to build up your comprehension. It can also roll text across the screen at increasingly faster rates to train you to read actual running text more and more quickly.

Some of these techniques are the same ones used in speed-reading courses given outside the home. But when you are working on your own computer, you can insert your own reading material so that the selections you use for practice are the kinds of material you enjoy reading.

History. How does history take shape? Instead of memorizing names and dates of famous people and wars, you can use the computer to study factors that influence the way history unfolds. Some history programs trace the interplay of economic, political, religious, and other influences. The programs use the software to present a "model" that allows for the random selection of events within the established limits (historical period, countries, etc.).

Instead of reading the names of kings and generals and the locations of the major wars, for example, you could put yourself in tenth-century Spain or the American Civil War. Then, you could manipulate the historical, economic, and human factors as variables on the computer. The result is a model of theoretical history.

The program is unique each time it runs, although it preserves the broad historical overview. Color displays are used to show maps and graphic detail for the time period, as well as political or religious areas of influence.

The models offer information you might also get from books or a course, but learning through models allows you to make choices and participate in the process.

* *Friendliness.* Is the structure of the program non-threatening and easy to use? It should be. This does not mean that the course content of the program should be something your child can breeze through, thereby learning nothing. It means that the program itself should be something you and your child can use on the computer without major problems.

In addition, the content of the program, the actual material to be learned, should be neither above nor below your child's ability. Just because the package says "Ages 5–8" does not mean that your seven-year-old will find the program useful. Your child may not be ready, or may be too advanced, for that particular program.

* *Usefulness.* What does this program purport to do? Read the claims on the package or brochure. It should clearly state what the program will teach your child. Is this what your child wants or needs? Do not waste money on programs that your child cannot, or will not, benefit from.

* *Encouragement.* The software should assess your child's progress. If an answer is incorrect, does the program just move on, or does it offer help, and review the material when an answer is incorrect? Better yet, does it rephrase the original explanation,

presenting the material in a new way for those who did not understand it the first time? A program that simply indicates wrong answers is not as good as one that offers feedback and encouragement.

* *Flexibility.* A good program has the flexibility to adjust to progress. If the child grasps the material with no difficulty (three answers right in a row, for example), the program should adjust accordingly: it should become progressively more challenging. Some programs are flexible enough to let you add new material—for example, extra passages for reading comprehension, additional vocabulary, or a whole new text with questions. When the original content has been mastered, such programs remain useful so long as you continue making additions to them.

* *Entertainment.* Finally, the software should take full advantage of the computer's ability to enhance the learning experience with movement, color, sound, interesting displays, simulations, etc. If the program simply presents screen after screen of straight text, followed by multiple choice questions, it offers no advantages over a textbook. Do not buy it. You do not need a computer to read a book, unless you are learning how to speed read.

Financial and business programs

- Are you thinking of starting an income-producing business at home?
- Do you run a small business?
- Do you take work home from the office frequently?
- Do you want tighter control over the family budget?

Using a personal computer for financial or business applications will probably justify the cost. For simply balancing your checkbook, a pocket calculator is more cost-effective than a computer, and it is more time-efficient. But if you also want to set up a small business in your home, then a computer is a wise purchase.

The computer offers invaluable assistance for business-oriented tasks, such as:

- maintaining inventory records
- keeping a customer file for billings or advertising
- accounting

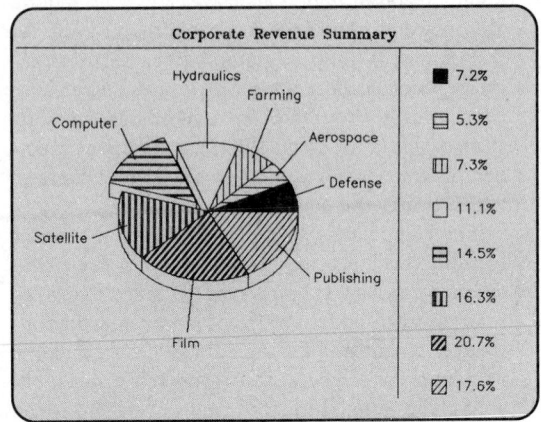

Computer-drawn illustrations can be instantly revised. Changing the percentages will automatically cause the pie to be redrawn.

Applications

Word processing. Writing on a computer—word processing—is discussed on page 16. If you prepare long or repetitive documents on a typewriter, a computer with word processing software can make you more productive.

Number crunching. Simple addition, subtraction, multiplication, and division—the kind you do to balance the checkbook—do not require a computer. Figuring out how much a mortgage would cost at five different interest rates, for five different down payments, over a $20,000 range in housing prices, is, however, the kind of complicated calculation made easier and quicker by a computer. Computers perform these kinds of math gymnastics, called "crunching," with electronic spreadsheet software.

Database management. Also called information management, this software allows multiple arrangements of files of data. For a business, a database management program could sort your customer list by zip code for cheaper mailing rates, or target the big spenders for advertising promotions, or select them by any other category you enter into the computer.

Graphics. Do you make sales presentations? You can turn numbers into charts, graphs, and other visual displays with a computer and a graphics printer.

Desktop publishing. You can use your computer and printer to create professional-looking newsletters, forms, advertisements, sales presentations, and other printed materials, complete with catchy graphics.

Project management. Are you handling a large project, such as a company reorganization, a new-product introduction, the construction of a house, or a wedding? Project-management software can help you plan and manage the job more effectively. It helps you schedule people and resources and break down a project into a series of smaller activities, each with its own deadline. It also lets you compare actual versus planned schedules, costs, and resources.

What is integrated software? An
integrated software package contains several different applications, such as a word processor, a data base, a graphics program, and an electronic spreadsheet. Data can easily be shared among the applications. And all the applications use the same standard commands, eliminating the need to master the intricacies of different programs.

With a typical integrated package, you can do financial projections on the spreadsheet, then use the data to create charts. Or you can incorporate the financial data you have prepared directly into a memo written with the word processor.

Some programs and operating systems allow you to split the display screen into sections, called *windows.* This permits you to view material from several different applications at the same time.

Software titles for your business

Lotus 1-2-3	*Microsoft Word*
Excel	*dBase IV*
WordPerfect	*Paradox*
PageMaker	*XyWrite*

The electronic spreadsheet

The software most used in business is the spreadsheet program. In fact, it is the electronic spreadsheet that made microcomputers popular. It was invented by a student at the Harvard Business School in 1978. He knew there had to be an easier way to do the recalculations required every time one element changed in accounting or recordkeeping. His invention made it possible for the recalculations to be done on a microcomputer.

What is a spreadsheet? Think of an electronic spreadsheet as a computer program that duplicates the rows and columns printed on accounting graph paper and does all the arithmetic you would have to do to fill in all those rows and columns.

To do an accounting or recordkeeping spreadsheet by hand often means doing not one spreadsheet but many, each one different, each involving a multitude of complicated, repetitive calculations. Changing one figure requires changing related figures. A mistake in one figure produces a chain of mistakes in related figures.

Unlike people, the computer thrives on doing things over and over again, and it does not make mathematical errors. It does all its calculations in seconds. You simply enter the figures, or in a few places change them, and the entire spreadsheet is recalculated in an instant with no mistakes.

What can you use a spreadsheet to do? You can analyze a business or personal budget using a spreadsheet program. You can see the effect of changes in income or of different deductions on your taxes; you can keep track of your investments; you can control your cash flow; or you can project your profits.

You can, to use a more specific example, make use of "what if " scenarios. Suppose you want to buy a new house. Into a spreadsheet you could enter figures for varying

- down payments: $5000 $7500 $10,000 $15,000 $20,000
- purchase prices: $30,000 $50,000 $80,000 $100,000
- interest rates: 9% 10% 12% 14%

Now you can find out how much house you can afford if interest rates go up, or if you put down a larger or smaller down payment, or if you buy a more or less expensive house.

In business the electronic spreadsheet can help answer questions like these:

- Should you build or buy? What would the difference in cost be?
- How much should you charge for a new product in order to recoup your cost?
- How much should you charge to make a profit?
- What would your financial situation be if you gave every employee a raise?
- What would the impact on your business be if sales fell by 10 percent next quarter?
- How much new business will you have to generate to recoup the cost of advertising?
  The problem-solving capabilities of the spreadsheet are nearly limitless.

By using a spreadsheet program you can automatically revise a whole table to reflect a change in only one number. In this example the sales figure in October for the Marina was corrected, resulting in instant recalculation of the totals in three places.

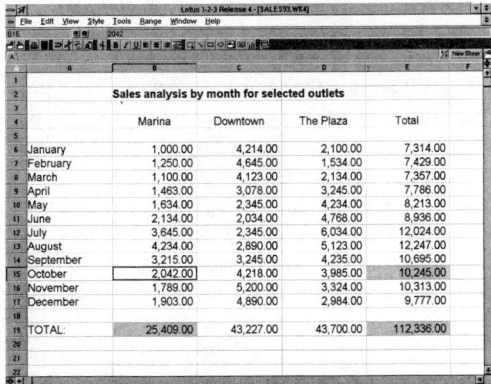

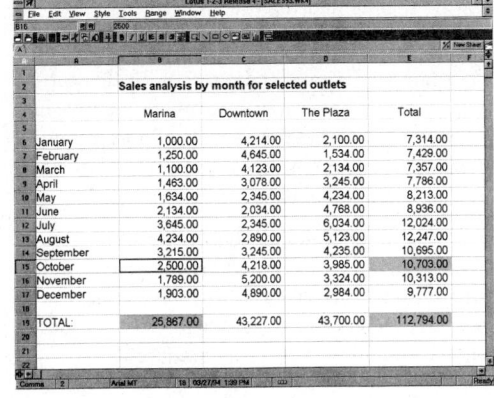

Word processing

If you want to use your computer for running a home-based business, improving your job skills, or writing long research papers, word processing is the applications software for you. In fact, word processing has become the most important use for most people who have computers in the home.

Word processing: how it works.

Word processing is typing by computer, with a big plus. Word processing software can turn your computer into a typewriter, a typesetter, a printer, a dictionary, a thesaurus, an editor, and a secretary.

Instead of using paper to try out your ideas, you use the computer's memory. Instead of typing and retyping on paper, you type a first draft of a document into the computer. The computer lets you correct or revise it without retyping the whole document.

What can word processing do?

If you can type, you can do word processing. Using a computer instead of a typewriter for reports, memos, letters, etc., has important advantages:

1. **It can justify margins** automatically. That means that everything on the right and left side of the page or column will be lined up evenly.
2. **It can rearrange the order** of anything you have typed. You can move sentences, words, and paragraphs up or down on the page without retyping them.

Related software

A spelling checker. A spelling checker automatically looks through your typed document for spelling errors. Any word that is misspelled will be highlighted for you to correct.

An electronic thesaurus. Do you keep using the same words over and over? With this software, you can be creative instead of repetitive in your word choice. At the stroke of a key, synonyms for the word you want to replace appear on the computer screen.

Mailing lists. You can coordinate word processing software with programs that can handle any mailing list—your Christmas cards, your business clients. Each letter will carry an individual salutation with its own address.

---

3. **It can copy automatically** any part of the document, or even another document, and deposit it at another location using one key.
4. **It can change the format** of material. You can make the margins much wider, or you can make them much narrower if you prefer. Without any retyping.
   You can center material
   with one keystroke.
You can <u>underline</u>, highlight, number and renumber the pages, insert footnotes automatically, type ^{above} or below the line, **use bold type for emphasis.**
5. **It can help you save time** because you do not have to retype. Also, because you do not have to retype the whole document, you reduce the possibility of introducing new errors while correcting old ones. If you are sending one letter, manuscript, or document to several people, the computer saves you even more time.

What equipment do you need?

A keyboard. If you intend to do a lot of typing (whether of words or numbers), you should have a computer with a typewriterlike keyboard to make your typing easier. Instead of such a keyboard, some computers have a membrane with the letters and symbols painted on; some have thin little keys somewhat like those on pocket calculators. Neither is adequate for heavy word processing.

A printer. You will need some kind of printer for the output of your typing.

A word processing program. Many different programs are available, ranging in price from a few dollars to hundreds of dollars. Most home and small business users will find that programs costing less than $100 will meet their needs. There is no reason to pay for features that you will never use. However, if you are planning to bring home work from the office, your word processor should be compatible with the program used in the office. Either buy the same program or have a program that can convert the files from your home word processor into files that can be read by the word processor at work.

A monitor, or video display screen. Although some early home computers were designed so that a television set could be used to view copy, the quality and detail of the picture left much to be desired. You will want to buy a monitor with your home computer. If you are going to use it for long periods, it is important to choose a monitor that provides a bright, clear, sharp picture.

Understanding Computers

Staying healthy with computers

From improving the hearing to monitoring heart disease, computer-based health aids are helping people live longer and better. A computer can affect your health and well-being in two major ways.

Staying healthy.
If you are already in good health, or simply need a little push to get there, there are computer programs that monitor your lifestyle to make sure you stay healthy.

Programs you may want include the following:
Computerized medical records keep track of doctor visits, immunizations, and health problems. They schedule checkups and record the health history for every member of your family.

Exercise programs monitor the quality of your exercise. Some exercise devices have their own built-in computer.

Diet software translates your meals into the nutrients and calories you get from them. The programs typically use the U.S. Department of Agriculture's nutritional data values, focusing on 24 nutrients in 1000 foods. Some programs combine diet and exercise, analyzing your exercise and your food intake to see if you have met a weight-loss or weight-maintaining goal.

Computerized meal-planning programs range from gourmet cookbooks to simple menu planners that analyze and plan meals so that all nutritional needs are covered. Such programs can recalculate calories and nutrients for reduced servings or substitutions ("What if I use cottage cheese instead of sour cream?").

Handling a health impairment.
Microcomputers are also used in a variety of devices designed to help people with various disabilities. They improve the quality of life. They can make the difference between idleness and productivity, or between dependence and independence. Here are some of the many devices and inventions that are already helping disabled people:

- *Bio-ears,* implanted behind the ear, offer hearing for the severely impaired.
- *Prostheses* (artificial limbs) can be electronically activated by computer circuitry.
- *Electronic reading aids* for the visually impaired include devices that translate a printed word into a vibrating tactile form.
- *Alternate input devices* such as mouth switches, eye trackers, and expanded keyboards help physically impaired users.
- *Speech synthesizers* are an aid for mute individuals.

- *Microprocessors for Braille* combine computers and Braille communication.
- *Microcomputer-based devices* allow the hearing-impaired to send and receive messages over the telephone.
- *Sonar-guided wheelchairs* and *voice-operated robot arms* are two sophisticated computer aids. The wheelchair uses a microcomputer for steering and speed control.
- *Blood pressure monitors* that you can wear during your normal day-to-day activities have an electronic memory and use a computer display. They are more likely to reflect a normal blood pressure reading than the inflated reading a visit to the doctor's office sometimes produces.

Also in development is a computer aid to help the blind to see: a small television camera attached to an even smaller computer.

For more information about disabilities and personal computers, see the list of books on page 21.

A microcomputer, which is carried over the shoulder, can be tuned to adjust a prosthetic knee joint for different gaits: normal walking, running, or climbing stairs.

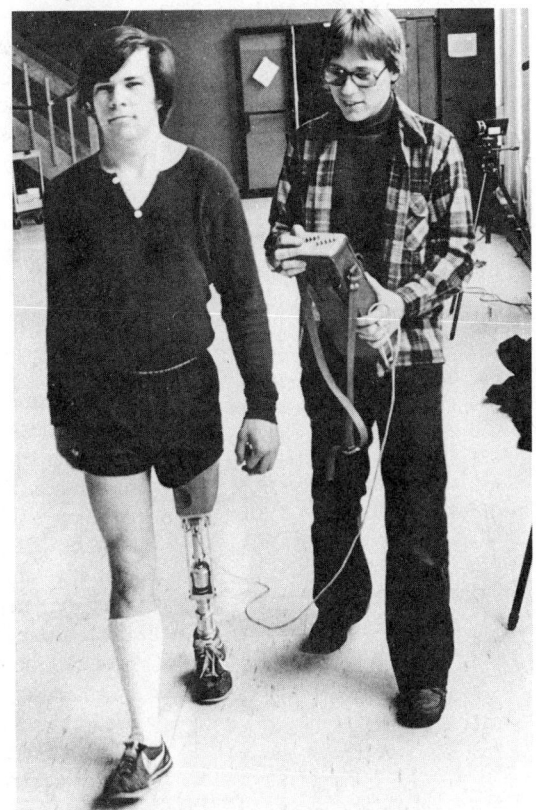

Dow Jones averages
from online database

Glossary of computer terms

Some standard keyboard characters with their ASCII equivalents

033 !	063 ?	093]
034 "	064 @	094 ∧
035 #	065 A	095 —
036 $	066 B	096 '
037 %	067 C	097 a
038 &	068 D	098 b
039 '	069 E	099 c
040 (	070 F	100 d
041)	071 G	101 e
042 *	072 H	102 f
043 +	073 I	103 g
044 ,	074 J	104 h
045 -	075 K	105 i
046 .	076 L	106 j
047 /	077 M	107 k
048 0	078 N	108 l
049 1	079 O	109 m
050 2	080 P	110 n
051 3	081 Q	111 o
052 4	082 R	112 p
053 5	083 S	113 q
054 6	084 T	114 r
055 7	085 U	115 s
056 8	086 V	116 t
057 9	087 W	117 u
058 :	088 X	118 v
059 ;	089 Y	119 w
060 <	090 Z	120 x
061 =	091 [	121 y
062 >	092 \	122 z

AI (artificial intelligence). The field or study of computer use to reproduce human intelligence. Also describes the ability of computers to simulate human intelligence and reasoning, as well as attempts to make computers "think."

algorithm. The mathematical or logical steps needed to solve a problem.

applications software. Computer programs that enable a computer to do specific tasks, such as accounting, graphics, and word processing.

ASCII (the *A*merican *S*tandard *C*ode for *I*nformation *I*nterchange). An internationally used coding scheme for representing character information. With ASCII, any two computers—regardless of operating system or brand—can communicate. ASCII uses 128 numbers to represent the letters of the alphabet, the numbers 0 through 9, and punctuation marks. For example, the lower-case letter "a" is represented by the ASCII code 97.

BASIC (*B*eginner's *A*ll-purpose *S*ymbolic *I*nstruction *C*ode). A widely used, easy-to-learn programming language that uses familiar words, such as *print, read,* and *let. See also* language.

baud. A unit of measurement that indicates the speed at which data are transferred via a modem from one computer to another. Usually calculated in bits per second (bps). Thus 1200 bps means that data are sent at a rate of about 120 characters per second.

binary, binary system. The base-two number system used by computers. The two digits used in base two, and in the binary system, are 0 and 1. Each successive digit to the left is a progressive power of two.

Base two is used in computers because it represents the basis of computer operations: on-off or high-low electric current.

bit, binary digit. The basic unit of encoded computer data. A bit is one unit of storage space in a computer. Each electric pulse is one bit. Generally, eight bits form one byte.

boot. Start up a computer by loading essential information, such as an operating system, usually from a disk. Boot can also mean loading a program into computer memory.

Bps. Bits per second. A way of measuring the speed at which a computer sends information. *See also* baud.

buffer. A section of memory used for the temporary storage of information.

bug. An error in the computer or its programming software. The origin of "bug" is interesting. Legend has it that an early large mainframe computer malfunctioned because of an insect trapped somewhere in the computer's tubes. The insect was discovered and removed. Since then, the word "bug" has come to describe general computer problems. Getting rid of the problems is called debugging.

byte. Eight bits, the number required to encode one letter or number or symbol.

character. Any information that can be stored in one byte. Examples are letters of the alphabet.

chip. A tiny piece of silicon or other semiconductor material that contains thousands of transistors joined by microscopic circuits. A computer has one or more chips.

clone. A computer that is compatible with an IBM computer. It can run the same software as the IBM computer.

Understanding Computers

command. Any instruction given to a computer. Commands are frequently preset by the software program you use.

computer piracy. The unauthorized copying of software.

CPU (central processing unit). The part of the computer that interprets and carries out instructions and sends the results to the user, the computer's memory, or both.

cursor. A spot of light on a computer screen that indicates the place to enter data or give commands to the computer.

database. An organized collection of related information, such as a mailing list, a hospital's medical records, or a library's card catalog.

disk/diskette. The magnetic-coated flexible disk on which software programs are stored, and on which you can store your own data. Disks come in various types and sizes. *See also* hard disk.

disk drive. A device that records data on and retrieves data from a spinning disk (see above).

documentation. The instructions for using a computer or software.

expansion slot. The place in a computer where a circuit board with additional memory or other capabilities can be inserted.

floppy disk. *See* disk/diskette.

hard disk. A rigid magnetic disk sealed in a hard disk drive, used for storing computer programs and data.

hardware. The computer and related machine equipment, such as the printer.

home computer. *See* personal computer.

information utility. An organization that offers access to computerized databases and other information services.

Computer communicating

Your computer can communicate. You can use it like a telephone, to call and chat, using the keyboard and monitor, with other computer users. You can program it to send calls to other computer owners late at night, when rates are cheap.

You can also use your computer to gain access to libraries of books, newspapers, and magazines through computer information services and bibliographic databases.

How it works. Your computer can talk to another computer any distance away over telephone lines. To use normal phone lines, you have to convert the binary or digital signals your computer makes into the voice-frequency signals telephone lines carry.

Modems do that, among other things. They translate digital signals produced by your computer into oscillating signals, and vice versa (when in the receiving mode). That process is one of *mo*dulation and *dem*odulation, hence the name modem.

Equipment. There are two popular types of modems that are used with microcomputers.

Internal modems consist of a board inside the computer that connects to a phone line directly.

External modems connect to the computer with a cable.

Many modems can also send documents directly to fax machines. These devices, known as *faxmodems,* have become extremely popular with microcomputer users.

What must you buy? Some computers are sold with built-in telecommunications ability. But many microcomputers do not have this capability, which means you will need additional hardware and peripheral equipment:

- an asynchronous board with RS-232C port and cable for an external modem, and the modem itself, or
- an internal modem,
- and a telephone line to connect the modem (external or internal) to a telephone wall jack.

You also will need *communications software:* programming on a disk telling your computer how to interact with other computers. You may find modem hardware and communications software sold together.

You can buy good programs for under $200—sometimes well under. Procomm is a shareware program that is highly regarded, with good features and documentation. You can find shareware and public domain software in magazines, through computer clubs, etc.

Online services. Once you have installed your modem and have become familiar with your communications software, you will probably want to become a subscriber to one or more of the computer information services. These provide access to numerous databases and electronic bulletin board systems (bbs's), enable you to send electronic letters, or e-mail, to other subscribers, and even provide entry to the international linkup of computer networks known as the Internet (see page 20). Among the most popular online services are CompuServe, Prodigy, GEnie, and America Online.

To tap into it, you need a computer, communications software, a modem, and a telephone line.

input/output (I/O). What goes in and what comes out of the computer.

Internet. A worldwide linkup of computer networks, electronic databases, and on-line services.

K (kilobyte). A unit of computer memory equal to approximately 1000 bytes.

language. A special set of vocabulary and rules used to write programs. It allows communication within and between computers or between computers and their users. Examples include BASIC, C, LOGO, and PASCAL.

laptop. A small, portable computer. It is battery powered and has a built-in keyboard and display screen.

load. To enter data or programs into the computer.

LOGO. An easy-to-learn and easy-to-use computer language. Popular in schools, especially with young children.

mainframe. A large, powerful computer that can store huge amounts of data and do many tasks at the same time. It can be connected to and used by smaller computers.

MB (megabyte). A unit of computer memory equal to about 1 million bytes.

memory. Holds the program or data to be worked on. *See also* RAM *and* ROM.

menu. A list of functions or commands for a program. They are displayed on the computer screen for you to indicate the option you want.

merge. Combine data from two or more computer files.

microcomputer. A computer that uses a microprocessor as its central processing unit. A personal computer.

---

microprocessor. A chip that contains the "brains," or CPU, of a microcomputer.

modem. A device that lets computers communicate with each other by telephone. It changes computer signals into audio signals that can be carried over telephone lines. It also changes audio signals back into computer signals. The word is derived from the term *mo*dulator-*dem*odulator.

monitor. A unit that looks like a television screen. It has a video screen to display information produced by the computer.

mouse. A hand-held pointer used with a computer for word processing, graphics, etc. It is used as a means of telling the computer what to do.

network. A system for connecting computers. A network can be within a limited area, such as a building, or over a wide area or long distances.

on-line. Connected to another computer through the use of a modem and a telephone line.

operating system. A program that controls the operation of a computer system. It handles such tasks as loading programs and storing data. Common operating systems include MS-DOS, OS/2, and UNIX.

Pascal. A programming language named after the French philosopher, mathematician, and inventor Blaise Pascal.

peripheral. Any hardware connected to a computer, such as printers, modems, and joysticks.

personal computer. A microcomputer, designed for personal use by an individual at home or in a business.

pixel. One of the tiny dots of light on a computer screen. The greater the number of pixels per square inch, the higher the picture resolution.

port. The place on a computer or peripheral where connecting cables can be attached.

program. Any instructions telling the computer what to do. *See also* software.

public domain software. Software that is uncopyrighted and available free of charge.

RAM (*r*andom *a*ccess *m*emory). Temporary computer memory used to hold software and data. It "forgets" whatever is in it when you turn off the computer.

ROM (*r*ead *o*nly *m*emory). Permanent memory built into the computer during manufacture.

RS-232, 232C. A standard interface for computers and peripheral devices, such as a modems.

save. To store a program or data on a storage device, such as a disk, so it can be used again.

scroll. To move text on a screen vertically or horizontally.

semiconductor. A material that transmits electricity better than a resistor or an insulator but not as well as a true conductor.

Understanding Computers

The ability of a semiconductor to conduct electricity can be changed by temperature variation or by adding impurities. Used to make memory chips and other computer circuits.

shareware. Software that is made available on a try-before-you-buy basis. You agree to pay only after you have made a firm decision to continue using the program.

software. The instructions telling a computer what to do. Also called programs. There are two main types of software: system and applications.

spreadsheet program. A tool used for budgeting, accounting, and other financial tasks. Like a paper spreadsheet, an electronic spreadsheet consists of rows and columns.

supercomputer. The fastest type of computer. Used to design bridges and airplanes, do basic research in science, forecast weather, etc.

telecommunications. The transmission of data from one computer to another via telephone lines and other communications links.

user friendly. A term that indicates that a computer or piece of software is easy to use.

user groups. Clubs of computer owners, usually organized around one particular type of computer or software. Some user groups have software libraries—programs members can try out, copy, and use.

virus. A computer program or part of a program made to reproduce itself, like a biological virus, and spread from one program or computer to another. The virus may destroy data and programs or damage equipment.

word processing software. A program that enables you to write and edit text.

For further reference

General
Blasko, Larry
ABCs of Computers: A Plain-English Guide
Computing

Bradbeer, Robin, De Bono, Peter, and Laurie, Peter
The Beginner's Guide to Computers
Addison-Wesley

Holtz, Herman
How to Make Money with Your Micro
John Wiley

Makower, Ernest
Personal Computers A–Z
Doubleday

Roberts, Ralph
Computer Viruses
Compute!

Wang, Wally
101 Computer Business Ideas
Computer Publishing Enterprises

Weintraub, Joseph
Exploring Careers in the Computer Field
Rosen Publishing Group

How to buy a computer
Consumer Guide
Computer Buying Guide
Publications International

Gookin, Dan
How to Understand and Buy Computers
Computer Publishing Enterprises

Children and computers
Gebhart-Seele, Peter A.
Computers and the Child: A Montessori Approach
Computer Science

Pagnoni, Mario
Computers and Small Fries
Avery Publishing Group

Computer history
Augarten, Stan
Bit by Bit: An Illustrated History of Computers
Ticknor & Fields

Kidder, Tracy
The Soul of a New Machine
Little, Brown

Ritchie, David
The Computer Pioneers: The Making of a Modern Computer
Simon & Schuster

Slater, Robert
Portraits in Silicon
MIT Press

Computer programming
Crookall, Philip
Computer Programming for Real Beginners
Arco

Downing, Douglas
Computer Programming in Basic the Easy Way
Barron's Educational Series

Hartnell, Tim
Creating Adventure Games on Your Computer
Ballantine

Lammers, Susan
Programmers at Work
Microsoft

Lampton, Christopher
Basic for Beginners
Franklin Watts

Special applications
Brand, Stewart
The Whole Earth Computer Catalogue
Doubleday

Hsu, Jeffrey
Guide to Commercial Telecommunications Services
Prentice-Hall

McWilliams, Peter
Computers and the Disabled
Doubleday

Noble, David F. and Noble, Virginia
Improve Your writing with Word Processing
Que

Parker, Roger C.
Looking Good in Print: A Guide to Basic Design for Desktop Publishing
Ventana

Townsend, Carl
Electronic Mail and Beyond
Wadsworth

Advancing Your Career

Whether you are interested in part-time work or a lifetime career commitment, careful reading of this chapter will inform you of the many possibilities before you. If you have already chosen your career, the information will help prepare you for promotion. It will also help those who simply want to ensure that they keep their jobs. Starting a new career in mid-life or after retirement calls for special advice and encouragement.

Here are some of the forecasts worth considering before making any new career decisions:

- About 131 million men and women are expected to comprise the 1995 labor force—3.8 million more than the figure named in earlier projections.
- Nearly two-thirds of the increase will be among women. Already, two-income families are the norm rather than the exception in today's economy.
- Job growth in the service industries (such as transportation, communications, public utilities, trade, finance, insurance, real estate, fast food, and government) is expected to account for nearly 75 percent of all new jobs between 1985 and 1995.
- By 1990, over 4.3 million senior citizens will have retired. Many of them will be taking advantage of the 1984 Social Security amendments that allow them to earn additional income (from $6400 to $8400, depending on age and yearly cost-index adjustments).
- High-school graduates are quickly entering the job market, often foregoing college in favor of computer schools and vocational training institutions.
- A shortage of college graduates is starting to show up in such fields as computer engineering and telecommunications.
- The demand for typists will decrease as the use of word processors creates openings for computer operators and programmers.
- Two of the fastest growing occupations will be repairmen for the computers and electrical equipment being produced, and health technicians to operate the new medical equipment being developed.
- Employment of teachers for preschool children is expected to surge in the next ten years, increasing by more than 40 percent. This demand will be created in part by the children of those born during the baby boom.

Specific, practical advice follows in each of the following sections.

Job opportunities in rapidly growing fields

Fastest growing industry	Fastest growing occupation	Jobs with most openings	Annual openings
Medical and dental instruments and other medical services	occupational therapists physical therapists physical therapy assistants medical insurance clerks	nurses' aides, orderlies, and attendants registered nurses licensed practical nurses	94,000 85,000 60,000
Business services	legal assistants office machine repairers banking and insurance credit clerks employment interviewers	secretaries and stenographers cashiers bookkeepers accountants typists real estate agents and brokers bank clerks receptionists	305,000 119,000 96,000 61,000 59,000 50,000 45,000 41,000
Computers and peripheral equipment and scientific and controlling equipment	computer systems analysts computer programmers computer operators peripheral EDP equipment operators	fast growing but small industry engineers	
Radio and television broadcasting	electrical engineers electrical and electronic technicians	engineers	total in engineering occupations: 46,500
Electronic components	electronic engineers electrical and electronic technicians	engineers	
New construction	surveyors' helpers mechanical engineers mechanical engineering technicians	blue-collar workers and supervisors local truck drivers carpenters construction laborers	69,000 64,000 58,000 49,500
Plastics products	compression and injection mold plastics machine operators	industrial assemblers machinery repairers	77,000 58,000

Preparing for the job search

Assessing your abilities.

When preparing for a job search, take the time to sit quietly and assess what you have done with your life. In addition to any work experience, what abilities do you have that qualify you for the job market? If you look closely at your past experiences, you may be surprised at the possibilities they point to for your future.

Take a pencil and paper and list all the skills and talents you have taken for granted all your life. What abilities do you use in your nonpaid activities? Can you cook, drive a car, write letters, sing in the church choir? See how you might apply the skills that you enjoy using most to a job situation.

How to start. To draw up your success chart, start as far back in your life as you wish. For instance, you may have had to recite a soliloquy from Shakespeare in tenth grade, or a poem in Sunday school when you were even younger. Whatever your age at the time, recitation in front of a group indicates poise, some public speaking ability, commitment—and courage.

Divide your life into five-year intervals. List each success or accomplishment in the first column, the skills or experience gained in a second column. It is also a good idea to consider negative experiences. Perhaps you hated selling Girl Scout cookies. You should ask yourself if this typifies your attitude toward selling

Matching yourself with the World of Work

	1. Leadership/Persuasion	2. Helping/Instructing others	3. Problem-solving/Creativity	4. Initiative	5. Work as part of team	6. Frequent public contacts	7. Manual dexterity	8. Physical stamina	9. Hazardous	10. Outdoors	11. Confined
Automobile mechanics			•		•	•	•	•			•
Bank clerks				•							•
Bank tellers					•	•					•
Blue-collar supervisors		•	•	•	•		•		•		
Dental hygienists		•			•	•	•	•			
Dieticians	•	•	•	•	•	•					
Drafters					•		•				•
Employment counselors	•	•	•	•	•						•
Firefighters		•	•		•		•	•	•	•	
Landscape architects			•	•		•	•				
Librarians	•	•	•	•	•	•					
Mail carriers						•	•	•		•	
Market research analysts	•		•		•						
Police officers	•	•	•	•	•		•	•	•	•	
Photographic process workers							•				•
Secondary school teachers	•	•	•	•	•	•					
Secretaries				•	•		•				
Waiters, waitresses				•		•	•	•			

Advancing Your Career

and, if so, remind yourself to stay out of that field.

Stick to your positive experiences when making an entry on the success chart. Consider what satisfactions and rewards came out of each experience. List these in a third column.

Matching your skills with work. Your success chart will give you the information about your marketable skills that you will need to apply to the Department of Labor *World of Work* chart. A sample from this chart is shown on page 24; you will find the entire chart on page 52.

The average person's length of time at the same job is 4.8 years. Although your career decisions are important, they are not necessarily meant to last forever. Once you have developed some experience at self-assessment, you will be able to go through the process more efficiently five years hence if need be. It would be wise to keep all you paperwork filed away for future reference.

The two examples shown on this page and on page 26 show the success charts of Julie Parsons, a homemaker who wants to reenter the work force, and Edward Stubbs, a hospital administrator who wants to start his own business (with his wife, Alice) after he retires. The amount of your work experience will determine where you start your success chart.

Julie Parsons started her chart back in childhood, which increased her confidence for job-hunting because she saw the range of her own experience. Edward and Alice Stubbs started with adult work experience. Though the Stubbses had tested most of their abilities, they wanted to develop a full profile of themselves because going into business on their own was a big and somewhat risky step for them.

Broad experience is useful in business

Edward and Alice Stubbs's catering business is a perfect example of a business formed from skills that are most enjoyed. Their access to advertising in their community theater program enabled them to reach exactly the right market at a low cost. Their big old house was well suited to their business needs and activities.

Past social and volunteer participation gave them the opportunity to show off their talents to the community and to gain experience and a good reputation.

CATERING SERVICE	Finance budgeting	Public Relations	Organizational ability	Communication	Working with people	Leadership	Cooperation	Dexterity, cooking	Creativity	Risk	
Edward Stubbs age 65	•	•	•	•	•	•	•	•	•		Alice Stubbs age 63
Hospital Administrator 35 yrs.	•	•	•	•	•	•			•		
Gourmet cook 40 yrs.							•	•			Gourmet Club Secretary 10 yrs.
Budget chairman 15 yrs. Finance committee	•	•	•								
Board of Directors community theater 7 yrs.	•	•	•	•	•	•			•	•	Board of Directors community theater 15 yrs.
Co-chairman social committee 8 yrs.			•	•	•	•	•	•			Co-chairman social committee 14 yrs.
Member of Chamber of commerce 30 yrs.		•		•	•						
Church Deacon 30 yrs.			•	•	•	•					Deaconess of Church 30 yrs.
			•	•	•	•		•			Publicity chairman community theater 14 yrs.
			•	•	•						Subscription Drive 8 yrs.
	•	•	•	•	•						Secretary of Church choir 13 yrs.
		•	•	•	•	•	•				Volunteer at hospital cafeteria 25 yrs.

JULIE PARSONS' SUCCESS CHART

Age	Successes	Skills used/acquired	Enjoyment/rewards
5-10	Recited poem at school assembly	Courage, poise, following directions, public speaking	Public acclaim, applause, approval
	Learned to swim	Physical fitness, athletic dexterity	Feeling of fitness, prize for diving
	Won spelling contest	Competition, self-motivation	Prize, public acclaim
11-15	Sold most Scout cookies	Salesmanship, competition, teamwork, self-motivation	Prize, personal satisfaction, helped troop
	Babysitting	Dependability, trust, child care	Approval, earning money
16-19	Editor of yearbook	Typing, design, layout, organization, photography, public relations, dependability, leadership	Concrete proof of accomplishment: book, name in print; problem-solving
	Lead in school musical	Teamwork, poise, following directions, dependability	Public acclaim, approval, using talent
	Class treasurer for 3 years	Mathematical ability, leadership, dependability	Problem-solving, public approval, trust, popularity
	Graduation	Intelligence, public relations, leadership	Diploma, feeling of accomplishment
20-25	Job as library assistant	Public relations, mathematical ability	Feeling of independence, earning money
	Church choir	Musical talent, teamwork, dependability	Public approval, using talent
	Marriage	Economics, math, sewing, teamwork, budget management, public relations	Personal acceptance, independence, trust, love
	Mother	Nursing, laundress, instructor, chef, counselor, public relations, arbitrator, flexibility	Trust, approval, love, problem-solving
26-30	Cub Scout leader and Sunday school teacher	Organization, leadership, fund-raising, trust, commitment	Public approval, teamwork, problem-solving
	Treasurer of church fair and fund-raising drive	Mathematical ability, trust, popularity	Teamwork, public approval, leadership
	Treasurer of reading club, member of library board of directors	Mathematical ability, trust, leadership, knowledge of books	Working with books and math again

Advancing Your Career

Career goals

Ultimate goals. Carefully consider your success chart and see what patterns show up. On Julie Parsons' chart, two interests keep reappearing: math/accounting and books/publishing. These patterns caused Julie to list "comptroller of her local newspaper" as her ultimate goal.

Edward Stubbs found the confidence to begin his own catering business after reviewing his success chart. He saw that throughout their 40 years of marriage, he and his wife had gained great satisfaction and given great pleasure to others through cooking, a joint hobby.

Now is the time to let yourself think about your ideal job. Refer to your success chart and ask yourself what you would most like to do with the remainder of your working years. Consider what contribution your work could make to society and make sure that your goal fits your values. A sample goal statement is shown at the top of this page.

Intermediate goals. With your goal statement in front of you, consider what intermediate goals you can set for yourself that will logically lead to your ideal job. If you want to be a teacher, education courses would be one of your intermediate goals. An even shorter range intermediate goal would be finding out about available courses. The point is to break your tasks down into manageable steps so that you can embark enthusiastically on taking the first one.

GOAL STATEMENT	PAUL CARTER
1. Career goal:	Chief computer programmer in medical diagnostics
2. Preparation:	B.S. electrical engineering and computer programming
3. Company:	High-tech industries
4. Social value:	Contributing to medical research

If you find yourself procrastinating, you may have made your intermediate goals too general. Rework them until you have made them so specific that at least one of them can be accomplished immediately. Making a list is an important visual aid, and you have the added pleasure of checking off each step that you complete. Below you will find an intermediate goal scoreboard used by a young man preparing for a job interview.

Paul Carter's scoreboard illustrates one way of setting down intermediate steps. Set up your own scoreboard any way that works for you, as long as it is

Paul Carter's monthly plan

SUN	MON	TUES	WED	THUR	FRI	SAT
	1 SEND FOR HI-TECH ANNUAL REPORT	2 CHECK LIBRARY FOR RECENT ARTICLES ABOUT HI-TECH; LOOK FOR NAMES	3 Call Friends who might know someone in HI-TECH field	4	5	6
7	8 See College Placement officer Ask For References	9	10 FIND NAME TO WRITE TO IN ANNUAL REPORT	11 Talk with Professors in Related courses; Ask For References	12 CHECK COLLEGE DIRECTORY FOR ALUMNAE IN HI-TECH JOBS; TELL THEM OF PLANNED VISIT	13 CHECK ALL MATERIAL FOR JOB DESCRIPTIONS
14	15 Begin work on résumé	16	17	18 FINISH RÉSUMÉ	19 HAVE RÉSUMÉ PRINTED PROFESSIONALLY	20
21	22 VISIT HI-TECH FIRMS; SPEAK WITH CONTACTS; TAKE NOTES FOR INTERVIEW	23 PICK UP RÉSUMÉ	24 WRITE FOR INTERVIEW; SEND RÉSUMÉ AND COVER LETTER OF INTRODUCTION	25 SEND THANK YOU NOTES TO ALL CONTACTS	26 Plan questions for interview	27
28	29	30 Follow up Letter with call for appointment GET APPOINTMENT!!	31			

specific. Some useful questions to ask yourself are:

- Keeping in mind your ultimate goal, what skills must you develop? How?
- What are the available jobs in your area and how do your qualifications fit their needs? How do *your* needs fit their requirements?
- What are the priorities among the steps you must take to qualify for your ideal job?
- What resources are necessary—money, education, equipment, uniforms, etc.?
- What reasonable time limits can you set for accomplishing each intermediate goal?

If the intermediate goal is a course, when can the course be completed? If it is an interview, when will you set that up? Be realistic, write everything down, and then do your best to stick to your timetable.

If unexpected delays occur, rewrite your scoreboard so that it is once more realistic and manageable. If you face long-term career preparation, such as completing a course, serving an apprenticeship, or getting an advanced degree, divide your goals into yearly steps until they can be broken down into monthly or weekly tasks, as Paul Carter has done.

What schooling do you need?

To school or not to school? If you have been out of the job market for a while, you may immediately think of additional schooling as a solution to your dilemma. Often it is the appropriate first step to embarking on a new or different career. Nevertheless, make sure you do not rush to the registrar's office before taking an inventory of your skills. Lack of confidence rather than lack of education may be your problem.

The essential diploma. There is only one diploma that should not be questioned—your high school diploma. If your high school career was interrupted, there is a basic exam you may take to earn your General Equivalency Diploma (GED). This certificate will make you eligible for jobs requiring the completion of high school.

Your local high school guidance office will refer you to the nearest adult learning center where you can find out what steps are necessary to obtain your GED. Often you can study independently at home and pass your exam without having to go back into the classroom. You may take the exam as many times as necessary to earn your GED.

Going back to school?

Pros and cons. If you are undecided about the necessity of additional schooling, consider these arguments for and against. Applying such arguments to your own situation can help you make the right decision.

PROS

- An additional degree may advance your career in a specific way.
- A particular course of study may guarantee you a job.
- A master's degree may guarantee you a higher salary in your field.
- You may need more education to break into the field of your choice.
- All education is useful and may be applied in unexpected ways in the future.

CONS

- A liberal arts degree does not guarantee a job.
- Most people do not end up working in their field of study.
- Approximately 80 percent of the new jobs (see chart on next page) do not require a degree, though they may require vocational training.
- Many companies prefer to do their own training.
- You may price yourself out of the job market with more degrees, especially in the field of education.

Checklist: Getting the most out of additional training

Recall your previous educational experience. Consider each of the following and check one.

1. You prefer:
   ( ) Studying by yourself
   ( ) Studying with others

2. What suits you best is:
   ( ) Learning at your own speed
   ( ) Learning at the speed of a group

3. You learn best:
   ( ) In a lecture course taking notes
   ( ) In a course where you learn by doing

4. You prefer having material presented:
   ( ) By using words and ideas
   ( ) By sounds, pictures, and objects

Try to tailor any courses you take to fit the choices checked above. You will learn more easily in a situation that suits your educational preferences.

More school = more pay

Earnings: L = $145 – 225, M = $225 – 360, H = $360 –

Degree jobs

Administration
Buyers	H
City managers	H
FBI agents	H
Secondary school administrators	H

Clergy
Ministers	M
Priests	M
Rabbis	H

Education
Counselors	M

Engineering and science
Oceanographers	H
Physicists	H

Professional, technical
Chemists	H
Computer systems analysts	H
Dentists	H
Laboratory technicians	H
Lawyers	H
Librarians	M
Registered nurses	M

Social scientists
Psychologists	H
Social workers	L

Teachers
College and university	H
Elementary	M

Technicians
Airplane pilots	H
Radio and TV announcers	L

Writers, artists, entertainers
Painters	M
Publicity writers	H
Reporters	H

Nondegree jobs

Clerical-type workers
Bank tellers	L
Bookkeepers	M
Counter clerks	L
Insurance adjusters	H
Mail carriers	H
Payroll clerks	M
Receptionists	L
Secretaries, medical	M
Teachers' aides	L
Telephone operators	H

Craft-type workers
Bakers	M
Carpenters	M
Electricians	H
Heavy equipment mechanics	H
Painters, maintenance workers	M
Radio/TV repairpersons	M
Tool and die makers	H

Food service
Bartenders	L
Waiters, waitresses	L

Health and personal service workers
Child care workers	L
Hairdressers	M

Operatives
Bottlers and canners	L
Earth drillers	H

Selling
Insurance agents, brokers	H
Real estate agents	H
Sales clerks	M

Transportation
Taxi drivers	M
Truck drivers	M

Lifetime earnings estimates by education and age

male female
college graduates
high school graduates

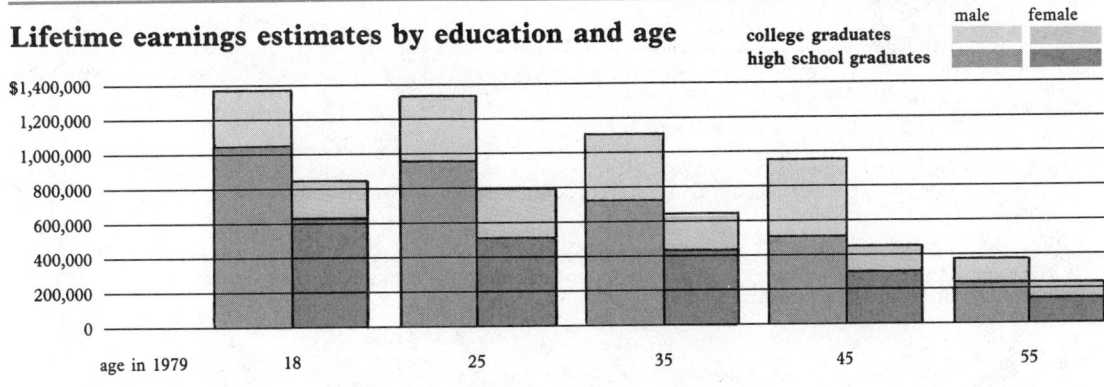

Weighing the alternatives. Julie Parsons, the homemaker who filled out one of the success charts shown earlier, wants to reenter the job market now that her children are in high school. As is the case with many families, the Parsons will find an additional salary more than welcome when the time comes to put two children through college.

How should Julie Parsons go about qualifying for a job in the field of her choice? Although she has had very little paid job experience, the skills she discovered from her success chart affirm her enjoyment of and talent for math and her interest in the field of publishing. Matching her skills to the Department of Labor occupational charts, Julie has decided on a career in public accounting and publishing. Her ultimate goal—her ideal job—is to be the comptroller of her town newspaper. Does Julie need to go back to school?

Julie Parsons has many responsibilities to juggle while preparing herself for a career. She cannot abandon her role of homemaker to become a full-time student. She still wants to participate in activities with her children, and knows she must find a way to advance her knowledge and expertise in the field of public accounting. Can she do all of these?

Educational alternatives. Getting a Bachelor of Arts or Bachelor of Science (B.A. or B.S.) degree usually involves a four-year commitment, a luxury many people cannot afford. Fortunately, there are other options that still will allow you to advance your career. Listed on the next page are a series of alternatives to a four-year degree. Evaluate each one in the light of your particular career situation and needs.

Going for the college degree

Deciding on the institution. Colleges and universities will send catalogs on request, but your local library may have copies of the ones you are interested in.

SHOULD JULIE PARSONS GO TO COLLEGE?

```
ULTIMATE GOAL:      Treasurer of town paper

JOB DESCRIPTION:    Position requires excellent bookkeeping and accounting
                    skills, ability to deal directly with the public, and the
                    leadership qualities necessary to supervise a business
                    office.

                    QUALIFICATIONS                   JULIE'S EXPERIENCE

                    Knowledge of newspaper business  Editor of yearbook
                                                        organizational skills
                    Experience                         leadership
                      bookkeeping                      initiative
                      budgeting
                      accounting                     Treasurer—various organizations
                                                        problem-solving
                                                        bookkeeping
                                                        budgeting
                    Skills
                      problem-solving
                      leadership
                      initiative                     History of public relations
                      administrative                    dependability


                    LACKING: accounting; administrative

JULIE'S CHOICE:     Community College

In a community college Julie could take her courses while the children were
in school during the day. Vacations would coincide with their school
vacations.

In two years she completed a course in business administration in a classroom
situation that allowed her to learn and experience leadership roles again in
a setting best suited to her.
```

Advancing Your Career

Make an appointment with your local high school guidance counselor, who has all the information you need—and, probably, some helpful advice. These guidance services are available to any taxpayer, no matter how long ago or where you received your high school diploma. The counselor will help you choose a college and make out the application.

How do you pay for college? When Paul Carter, the graduating high school student interested in a job in computer programming, decided to go to the state university, his family could not afford to support him throughout his college career. Paul was an exceptionally bright student and he earned a scholarship. This helped but did not entirely solve his financial problems. His guidance counselor referred him to *College Financial Aid*, a book edited by John Schwartz (College Research Group, Prentice-Hall, NY). Another good book prepared by the College Research Group is the *College Financial Aid Annual*.

"How to Get Credit for What You Know"
(alternative routes to educational credit)
This pamphlet is intended for both men and women.

Contact: Women's Bureau
Department of Labor
200 Constitution Avenue, NW
Washington, DC 20210

For veterans:
Read *The Guide to the Evaluation of Educational Experiences in the Armed Services*, published by the American Council on Education, which is available in some libraries and at many Veterans' Affairs offices.

Alternatives to a four-year degree

Community colleges: Most of these colleges vary their courses to fit the needs of the community where they are located. Usually, courses in both vocational training and management are offered. Specific training courses (hotel and restaurant management, accounting, nursing, hairstyling, dental hygiene, etc.) generally take two years to complete. Associate degrees in applied arts and sciences are often awarded for the completion of a two-year course of study. The academic courses are similar to those given at four-year colleges, and credits are transferable for those who wish to continue their education.

Vocational training schools: Courses are offered full- or part-time to prepare you for a particular occupation. The placement rate for these schools is high, and the costs are reasonable.

Correspondence and evening courses: These courses may take longer to complete than those in which attendance is required, but they make the exploration of new fields available to everyone, no matter where they live. People who cannot attend classes regularly may continue their education or job advancement at their own pace without putting a strain on their financial resources.

Apprenticeship programs: These are offered by many companies or, in some instances, by master craftsmen. Usually the company or craftsman will pay the apprentice and guarantee a job if the program is successfully completed.

Employee training programs: Many companies prefer to train their own personnel (airlines, for example). The training may be considered part of the job in that it requires a full-time commitment and is paid at the same rate as the base salary of the job itself. Often it is regarded as on-the-job training.

Armed services: The U.S. government offers training in marketable skills applicable to civilian life in return for an armed-service career commitment of two to four years.

Temporary services: There are many temporary services throughout the country that offer part-time work, mainly in clerical jobs. Working for one or more of them can be a productive way for a person who has been out of the job market a long time to become familiar with office procedures, earn a salary, and get an idea of what work is available. Getting some experience in a field unfamiliar to you may reveal talents you did not know you had. In addition, working for a company as a temporary employee may lead to a permanent job offer.

Going after the job

Résumés. Résumés are a useful if overrated tool in a job search. Sending out résumés is not an effective way of seeking job interviews. In fact, statistics show that you will receive a response on the average of one out of every 40 to 50 résumés; depending on the competition in the field you want to enter, the response could be as low as one out of every thousand. You could end up very discouraged if you depend on your résumé to launch you. You will, however, need a résumé at some point before being employed.

An important function of your résumé is to serve as a reminder to a prospective employer of your suitability for the job available. A résumé can also serve to notify the company that you have skills or abilities they may wish to call upon in the future. The wisest course is to carry your résumé with you to interviews rather than send it on ahead to be thrown away, or to be filed away, with dozens of other résumés.

Some experts advise writing the résumé *after* the interview, tailoring it to the job. You would then send the résumé along with a thank-you letter. Some people use a heavy beige or cream-colored paper for their résumé so that it will stand out from all the rest. Those sending out a great many résumés should use a professional copying machine or service.

The short form. Anyone faced with writing a résumé knows the frustration of trying to stretch the relevant information to a full page—or to cut it down to fit just one page. The most important thing to remember is that the résumé must point out a special talent or interest you have that matches the job desired. Although the rule is to make your résumé precise and concise, keeping it to one page if possible, you should never crowd the information so that it is hard to read. Special circumstances may necessitate a two- or even three-page résumé. Just make sure that it is neatly typed, correctly spelled, and attractively arranged on the paper. If your typing is inadequate or nonexistent, professional résumé services are available at a small cost. Since a messy, badly typed résumé will represent you very poorly indeed, this expenditure is well worth the investment.

Job search detective work. Once you have prepared yourself for a career in the field of your choice, you need to become a detective dedicated to finding the best job for you. Unless you are lucky enough to have the right job offered to you early in your job search, finding it in the shortest possible time is—and should be—a full-time occupation in itself.

```
JEROME DAY
56 Cash Street
Catersville, Kansas 09376
(814)773-5791

JOB OBJECTIVE
Electrician

WORK EXPERIENCE   Tom's Small Engines
1986-Present      Catersville, Kansas
                  Repaired electrical equipment
                  and parts of engines,
                  hand-crafted parts for
                  obsolete machines.

1981-1985         Jansen Tool and Electrical Parts
                  56 Center Street
                  Evansville, Kansas
                  Apprenticed and worked up
                  to position of foreman of ten men
                  doing industrial wiring.

EDUCATION
1981-1984         Electrician's Apprenticeship
                  Completed all courses
                  including blueprint reading.

1979              General Equivalency Diploma

ARMED SERVICES    U.S. Army. Private to Sergeant.
1979-1981         Served in California and Alaska.
                  Inventoried electrical parts.

PERSONAL          Excellent health. Free to travel.

REFERENCES        Furnished upon request.
```

```
JULIE PARSONS
Halfbend Road
Turnston, Indiana 32557
(702) 560-1422

JOB OBJECTIVE
Accountant, Administrative Assistant

WORK EXPERIENCE   Turnston Standard Journal
1980-Present      45 Main Street
                  Turnston, Indiana
                  Sold classified advertising.
1965-1980         Retired to raise family.
1964-1966         Assistant in Turnston Library.
EDUCATION
1980-1985         Part-time courses in Accounting
                  and Business Administration
                  Turnston Community College
                  Certificate of Completion
                  with distinction.

VOLUNTEER WORK    Served as treasurer of community
Accounting        organizations for 15 years
and               (Parent-Teachers Assn., Reading Club,
Budgeting         church fund-raising campaign and fairs).
Public Relations  Appeared on local radio and TV
and               during fund-raising campaigns,
Communications    promoting church fair and shows.
Publishing        Editor of high school yearbook;
                  in charge of layout, editing,
                  financing, printing, and bookkeeping.

PERSONAL          Mature, in good health,
                  own and drive a car.
REFERENCES        Furnished upon request.
```

Your future is worth your concentrated attention to the details that could make the difference between earning your salary in a boring, dead-end job or advancing over the years in a satisfying and rewarding career.

Looking for valuable clues. You have chosen your field and identified geographically where you are likely to be most successful in your job search. The next step is to target the companies or institutions that could actually offer you the job you want. Your local library and magazine stand are logical places to begin your research.

Magazines covering business generally or concentrating on the particular field you hope to enter will give you an idea about the successful companies, the future trends, and even the openings in new areas. A search through the periodical (newspaper and magazine) catalogs in your library can provide valuable information about any company you are interested in working for.

When you have narrowed down your choice of places to apply, your detective work should focus on learning everything you can about those companies. Ask people in the field for information about the company's future, its problems, its new products, its expansion plans, and, of course, any expected layoffs. Sending for the company's newsletter and promotional material will add bits and pieces to the overall picture of your potential employer. No clue you find to a possible job should be overlooked.

Organizing the job search

Networking. Much has been written on the "old boy network"—a seemingly closed club of powerful men making executive decisions among themselves. Though most of us do not qualify for chairperson of the board, we can thank the "old boys" for a good idea. Realize the power of networking, and create your own network. Enlist the help of people you know or meet in your job search. Tell them what your goals are and ask them to help you in any way they can.

You will be surprised at the way useful bits of information turn up if you keep asking friends and acquaintances what they know about your field or company of choice.

Your butcher, your minister, your car mechanic—do not hesitate to let everyone with whom you are on friendly terms know that you are job hunting. Your mechanic may service a manager in the company where you want to work and may have overheard him mention a problem or an opening. You never know.

Another way to create your own network is to go to conventions or civic interest groups frequented by the personnel of a company you have targeted as a prospect. Make yourself known to these people and listen to any advice they have. There is, of course, a fine line between showing enthusiasm for your job search and making a nuisance of yourself. Watch people's faces, listen to their tone of voice, and politely withdraw if you feel a chill.

Checklist for writing your résumé

1. **Your name, address, and phone number** should be typed at the top of the page.

2. **Your job objective** comes next. Be as specific as you can. Your research should have informed you of the job that the company has available or the area that you want to pursue for your career.

3. **List your work experience and education,** along with any special experience (volunteer work, avocations) that enhances your qualifications for the job. There is no need to list jobs or bosses that were a career mistake for you.

4. **Add personal information** if you wish. Personal information should never be negative (such as "Divorced"). In fact, all the information on your résumé should be positive. Do not lie, but do omit any negative information, such as being fired, or negative preferences, such as "Hate to type."

5. **References** need only be furnished on request; however, you should have your references readily available should they be called upon. Everyone (friends and past employers alike) appreciates advance notice that a stranger may be calling to ask questions about you. This consideration will keep your source from being embarrassed and caught off-guard, and will probably result in a better recommendation for you.

Suggested reading

Résumés that get jobs
Résumé Service
Jane Reed, Editor
Arco Publishing Co., N.Y.

What Color Is Your Parachute: A Practical Manual for Job and Career Changers
Richard Nelson Bolles
Ten Speed Press

Introduction to the Job Hunt Success Kit
Center for Career Development
Phyllis Martin
11385 Landon Lane
Cincinnati, Ohio 45246

Resources for researching careers

For information about particular fields:
A Guide to Special Book Collections in Libraries
Lee Ash and Denis Lorenz, editors
New York: Bowker

For information about organizations:
Annual reports, house organs, stock reports, public relations offices, newspapers, historical societies

For information about occupations:
Directory of Professional and Trade Organizations
(check local societies)

For information about people:
Who's Who in America;
Who's Who in the East;
Who's Who in the West
Professional directories

Let Uncle Sam help you in your search

The federal government has agencies engaged in continuous research on careers. This work is funded by your tax dollars. Let them work for you. Here are a few places to write for assistance:

Director, Office of Plans, Policies, and Design
Employment Service
Employment and Training Administration
Department of Labor
601 D Street NW
Washington, DC 20213

Job seekers and employers will be sent a list of placement related services funded by the government.

Division of Applicant Services
Office of Program Services
Employment Service
Employment and Training Administration
Department of Labor
601 D Street NW
Washington, DC 20213

This job information service is located within local employment centers. The office provides a *Job Bank Book* that enables the applicant to conduct his own search.

Department of Labor
601 D Street NW
Washington, DC 20213

For any questions regarding the job possibilities in your area or forecasts with respect to employment, an inquiry to this agency will prove useful.

Your letter will be directed to the proper office, which will send you the information you have requested.

Computerized Placement System
Automated Matching System Division
Office of Program Services
Employment Service
Employment and Training Administration
601 D Street NW
Washington, DC 20213

This office provides a daily printout of all jobs listed with the employment service in your area and distributes it to local employment service offices. Automated Matching System uses computers to identify registered jobs for which a particular applicant is qualified.

Where to look for job openings

- Local Chamber of Commerce
- Local Better Business Bureau
- *Commerce and Industry Directory*
  (Contacts Influential
  Market Research and Development Services
  321 Bush Street
  San Francisco CA 94014
  Check your library first.)
- *Career Guide to Professional Associations*
  Garrett Park Press
  Garrett Park, MD 20766
- *National Trade and Professional Associations of the United States and Canada and Labor Unions*
  Garrett Park Press
  Garrett Park, MD 20766

- *How to Reach Anyone Who's Anyone*
  by Michel Levine
  Price/Stern/Sloan Publications, Inc.
  410 North La Cienega Blvd.
  Los Angeles, CA 90048
- *What Color Is Your Parachute?: A Practical Manual for Job-Hunters & Career-Changers*
  by Richard Nelson Bolles
  Ten Speed Press
  P.O. Box 7123
  Berkeley, CA 94707
  Published annually, this book is an invaluable source for job-hunters.

Reading want ads

Quite a bit of time may be required to go through want ad columns. You must read enough of each ad to discover whether it interest you, whether you are qualified for the job offered, and—most important—whether you should apply. This is time well spent. With experience, you will be able to read the ads faster because the wording used will become familiar. You will learn, for example, that EOE means equal opportunity employer, a term indicating that the firm offering the job does not discriminate against women or minority groups. FEE PAID or F/PD means that the firm offering the job will pay the employment agency's fee. EXPD F/T means experienced, full-time.

Most important, however, is the caution you develop in deciding whether a job offered in an ad is realistic. Can one really believe a claim that an untrained person can make $35,000 a year at a job? Incidentally, ads that make such claims often do not mention what the job is. Other ads offer work at home for unrealistically high rates of pay. It is wise to be careful.

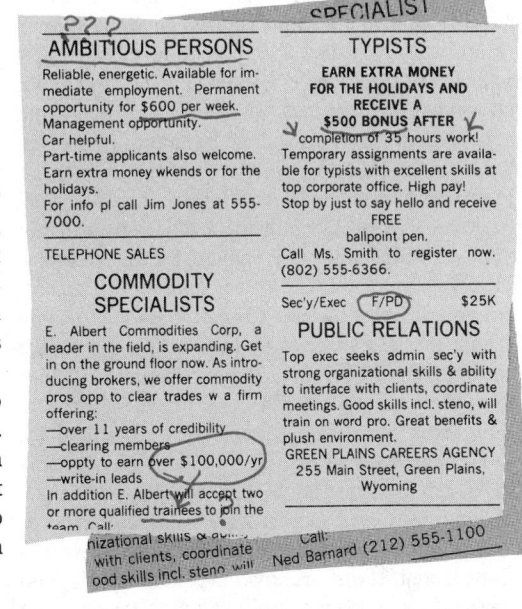

Know your salary range

Before you go to an interview, you should know the salary range for the job you want. Money is always an intimidating subject, so prepare yourself with as much knowledge as possible. Here are some sources to consult for information.

- **Visit your library.** You will find a number of books listed in the card catalogs under "salaries" and under the occupations you are interested in.

- **Write to the Department of Labor,** Bureau of Labor Statistics, Washington, DC 20212. Ask for Area Wage Surveys and the Bureau of Labor Statistics News Releases.

- **Consult the professional organization that serves your chosen field.** The Encyclopedia of Associations (at your local library) will tell you where to write.

- **Call the personnel office of the company you want to interview.** Tell them you are doing research on various careers and ask about their salary range for the job or jobs you are interested in. Such a call should, of course, be made well before any interview letter is sent or appointment made.

- **Inquire at your college placement office.** Here you can find up-to-date material on professional and higher level careers.

- **Check the want ads.** These newspaper advertisements are good for learning about salaries offered for entry-level jobs.

Know the value of fringe benefits

Find out whether the salary includes such fringe benefits as insurance, health plans, vacation, education, and retirement programs. *These benefits can add as much as 25 percent to the value of a salary.* A salary of $1000 a month with maximum benefits is really $1250.

The job interview

Writing for an interview. Consult the letter-writing section of this volume for samples of interview letters. What you want to say about yourself in the letter will be more important than the form. You should know specifically to whom you are writing and be clear about what you have to offer in the job you want. You should conclude the letter by informing the employer that you will phone the following week for an appointment.

If you have briefly referred to experience, education, or training that qualify you for a job, you need not include a résumé with your request for an interview. Even if you have no friend or acquaintance to recommend you, it helps to refer to some reputable person of whom the interviewer may have heard: "Professor Johnson of State University Biology Department suggested that I write to you" is a reasonable approach.

Your letter must make the interviewer want to see you. Think of ways you can contribute to the company even though there may not be a job opening at the time. Your letter may even suggest ways to increase sales or solve a problem or meet a challenge that your research has uncovered. If you are inventive, enthusiastic, and organized in your presentation, you may convince the interviewer to create a job for you. This happens more often than you might imagine, but it takes research, confidence, and imagination to prepare yourself with a solid proposal. On the other hand, you have nothing to lose if the company you want to work for has no openings. Making a good impression on interviewers may serve you well at some future time, when jobs you are suited for do fall open.

How to avoid preinterview jitters. The day of the interview, make sure you allow enough time to make your appearance impeccable. Get up an hour earlier or cancel other appointments. Make sure your appearance matches the appropriate points on the checklist and the drawings on the next page. For instance, if you have a heavy beard growth and your interview is scheduled for late afternoon, allow time for a fresh shave. Confronting your five o'clock shadow in the revolving door as you go into a building for an interview can throw you off balance and ruin your composure. These checkpoints are only guidelines, of course. Showing a clean appearance is obvious to most of us. Yet every one of us has forgotten the obvious under stress, and job interviews may certainly qualify as stressful situations. You should check every detail before you leave for your appointment.

Conservative dress is the recommendation of all experts in the employment field. Loud colors and flamboyant styles are not appropriate when interviewing for most jobs. Nevertheless, the ultimate judge of appropriate dress is you. If you are interviewing for a job as a construction worker, you may decide that clean

Preinterview checklist

Once your research and detective work are completed, check off these next steps:

1. Make sure you have used *all* your contacts and resources to inform yourself thoroughly about the company. Have you been able to identify the person who is in a position to hire you?

2. Ask yourself if you have done everything you can to have an interview arranged by someone in your network. All it takes is one sentence—"A good friend of mine asked me to recommend that you see a young journalism graduate"—and there you have an interview, thanks to the intervention of a stranger. But *you* have to set the process in motion and follow up.

3. Deal with personnel departments when you must. They are useful for entry-level jobs and are sometimes a necessary channel in setting up interviews with the department head you want to see. You may walk into most personnel departments without telephoning in advance. Have with you (in your head or on paper) a list of questions you wish to have answered, and leave with copies of any informational material (annual reports, benefit plan pamphlets, etc.) that may be useful to you.

4. Make use of employment agencies. They can sometimes be the fastest route to a job for which you are qualified. Use them if you feel you are bogging down in your own efforts. Every interview is a learning experience, and your ideal job can turn up through any channel.

5. If none of these approaches is successful, write a letter asking for an interview.

---

work clothes would be most appropriate. Surveys have shown, however, that even in occupations where a certain type of clothing is necessary on the job, taking the care to dress up instead of down for the interview impresses the employer and may even lead to an offer of a job at a higher level than the one you seek.

It never hurts to present yourself properly dressed. It is the first signal to the interviewer that you are concerned with detail. He will certainly see it as a sign of respect for him and your serious intent about the job.

Finally, write down and memorize the name of the person who will be interviewing you. If possible, find out and write down the names of any company personnel you will be dealing with before or after the interview.

Checklist for night before interview

1. **Hair** trimmed. Check supplies of shampoo, deodorant, toothpaste, etc., for morning shower.

2. **Fingernails** filed conservatively and cleaned. For women, polish should be neutral or coordinated to blend with your clothes and makeup.

3. **Clothes** freshly cleaned and pressed.

4. **Two pairs of hose** ready (one pair for your handbag) is a good idea for women. A sudden unsightly run need not be the cause for panic.

5. **A clean handkerchief** or a packet of tissues. Nervousness often makes the nose run; snuffling your way through an interview is likely to make both you and the interviewer uncomfortable.

6. **A small notebook and pen** for taking notes, such as names of secretaries, assistants, and receptionists. Make sure the notebook already contains the list of questions you want to ask, and the names of the people you will be seeing.

Looking good

clean, neatly trimmed hair

teeth cleaned, breath freshened

no strong perfume

face shaved recently

well knotted, plain tie

fresh, pressed shirt

fresh handkerchief, pen, small pad inside pocket

conservative suit

clean hands and fingernails

plain earrings, classic style

makeup applied conservatively

classic blouse and skirt, dress, or suit

tissues or handkerchief, pen, pad or paper

hem to knees or below

hose well fitted, extra pair in handbag

classic pumps with moderate heel

Checklist for arrival at interview

1. **Arrive early enough** to visit the rest room and check your appearance.

2. **Consult your notebook** to refresh your memory on the questions and names you have written down.

3. **Focus your attention** on what is happening around you. Be alert to people's expressions, the atmosphere of the office, and any clues as to how smoothly things are functioning. If what you notice is positive, say so in the interview: "The atmosphere here is electric. It must be an exciting place to work. . . . I find I do my best work in a calm environment like this one. . . . I like the way everything is neat and organized. . . . Your employees seem so cheerful and friendly. . . . I work best in a busy, fast-paced office like this one."

4. **Comment only on what is true and positive.** Negative thoughts should be kept to yourself and noted for your private consideration in accepting or rejecting the job. If noisy, chaotic work areas disturb you, do not think you are going to change the atmosphere. A better decision would be to turn down the job if it is offered.

Tips for the interview

1. **Always knock** on doors before entering.

2. **Use the interviewer's name** when acknowledging the introduction *and* when saying goodby. Introduce yourself by name if there is no one to perform the introduction. Be prepared to shake hands but do not initiate the gesture.

3. **Speak clearly and slowly.**

4. **Do not smoke or chew gum.**

5. **Listen well:**
   - Face the person squarely.
   - Establish eye contact.
   - Sit upright with straight but relaxed posture.
   - Keep hands away from face, preferably resting in your lap.
   - Lean forward to show interest.

6. **Do not use slang** or questionable language.

7. **Be prepared for leading questions:** "Tell me about yourself."
   Have clear, brief answers rehearsed. "What do you think you could do for this job?"
   "Why are you interested in us?"

8. **Ask open questions** as much as possible:
   "I would like to know more about the qualifications for the job."
   "What do you think Hi Tech's future [production, sales] will hold in the next few years?"
   This sort of question leads to more information and a chance for you to participate by pointing out ways in which your qualifications fit the job description or the company's goals.

9. **When appropriate, ask questions or make comments that reveal your knowledge of the company:** "Hi Tech chose one of my favorite architects to design their executive offices. . . . I am very impressed with SeaLinks' support of the Olympics (or involvement in the community)."

10. **Do not interrupt;** always let the interviewer be the guide. Eye contact will enable you to tell if the interviewer expects you to fill in a silence. If he looks down at something on his desk, he may be thinking a point over. Wait until he looks up again before continuing the conversation.

11. **Do not get flustered** when asked a question you have no answer for. This is an opportunity to show your presence of mind and composure. Simply say, "I don't have the answer right now, but I will get back to you tomorrow." Make an entry on your note pad and follow through.

12. **Do not volunteer negative information.** If you left a previous job because you hated it, a positive but truthful comment might be that you wanted to move on to something more challenging. If you were fired, do not lie about it if asked, but do not volunteer the information. "My previous job was terminated," is just as truthful and less negative-sounding than "I was fired."

13. **Describe yourself by your skills** ("I have good secretarial skills") instead of letting your skills describe you ("I am a secretary"). The message thus conveyed is that you are not limited to a certain job category but can apply your skills to different jobs.

14. **Be alert to signs that the interview is over.** If the interviewer does not seem to know how to conclude, you might say, "I know your time is valuable. Thank you for seeing me. Is there anything more you would like to know about me?"

15. **Say goodby and thank you** (when appropriate) **to assistants, secretaries, and receptionists.** Use their names whenever possible.

16. **Always write a thank-you note.** Include any new information you think relevant, or any responses to unanswered questions. Attach your résumé (tailored to fit the job and preferably on beige or cream-colored paper).

Advancing Your Career

A job search may begin (left) *at a state employment office. A warm handshake* (right) *may signal successful conclusion of a search and the start of a promising career.*

Interviewers are people too. Most people who conduct interviews do not think they are very good at it. It is unlikely to be their main occupation. In fact, they may dread the interviewing process more than you do.

Interviewers fear they will fail to screen out applicants who are:
1. Chronic abusers of sick time.
2. Too passive to take any initiative or too headstrong to take instruction.
3. Abrasive or disruptive around coworkers.
4. Dishonest, incompetent, or irresponsible.

Any of these defects showing up in an employee would reflect badly on the interviewer's judgment and represent an expensive mistake for the company. In other words, hiring you could end up costing the interviewer his or her job.

It is up to you to address these silent questions and real fears by conveying the message that you will not turn out to be a problem. Here are some possible ways to do this:

Character: The interviewer is looking for signs that you are honest, trustworthy, and responsible. A mention of charitable activities, volunteer work, personal recommendations, or awards you have received may be appropriate.

Competence: How to handle this subject depends on your previous experience and the type of work you are seeking. The hardest situation is when you want to convey your ability to perform effectively in a job where you have no experience. Your enthusiasm and confidence will have to convince the interviewer. "I'm a quick learner and know I have abilities in this area from [mention avocational experience]. . . . I particularly enjoy mastering new skills. . . . I have always taken pride in my work. . . . I have always had a knack for detail work. . . . I'm good at working with people."

Health: "I never used up my sick time in my previous job," or simply, "I keep myself fit by regular exercise." Or, "My feeling is that if I'm home sick, I'm not doing the job I'm being paid to do."

Your interview rights

Federal law prohibits a hiring decision based on race, color, national origin, religion, sex, pregnancy, marital status, parenthood, age, height, weight, or criminal record.

There are rare exceptions in which an employer is entitled to demand a certain race or sex as a bona fide occupational qualification, as in a job for an actress.

Finally, the law prohibits asking personal questions or questions irrelevant to the position for which you are applying.

How to handle illegal questions

1. Answer politely with a question: "Is this relevant to the requirements of the job?"

2. Answer the question and ignore the fact that it is illegal if the job is important enough to you, or if you think the question is actually innocent of discriminatory intent.

3. Contact the nearest Equal Employment Opportunity Commission Office and file a complaint if you believe you have been discriminated against.

Getting the job

The job offer. Finally your search comes to a successful conclusion. You are offered a job, or perhaps several jobs. At this point, take time to consider before accepting a job.

Show your appreciation for the job offer and ask when your decision is expected. If the employer says immediately, then you must give an answer unless you can use your negotiating skills to convince him or her that you need some time to reflect. You certainly can indicate that you are very interested while postponing your decision for a few days to allow consideration.

Evaluating the job offer. Often a series of interviews is necessary before a job is offered. This gives your prospective employers the opportunity to find out more about you and to observe you at different times; it also gives you the same opportunity. Take the time to consider these questions:

Challenge: Will the work keep you motivated and enthusiastic?

Personalities: Do you like what you have seen of your coworkers? Do you think you can work well with them?

Environment: Is the work space acceptable to you; for example, if you are allergic to smoke, will you be surrounded by chain smokers? Have you observed any safety violation?

Job security: Have you investigated the future of this company? What is the long-range economic outlook for the industry?

Reputation: Do the values of this company come up to your standards? Will you be asked to do anything that would compromise your integrity? (One job applicant thought she had found a job selling by phone until the employer informed her she must lie and say that her husband is a paraplegic.) Save yourself embarrassment by finding these things out ahead of time.

Never sell yourself short. Your research will have given you an idea of the salary range for the job offered. Where you fall in that range will depend on your negotiating ability. There can be as much as a $2000 to $3000 difference in your salary. Your employer wants to save the company that dollar difference as much as you want to earn it.

One negotiating expert has suggested the following tactic for securing the highest salary. Suppose the salary range is $22,000 to $25,000. When the employer asks you what salary you are thinking about, say that you are thinking about $26,000 as fairly representing your abilities, but that you cannot consider an offer under $23,500. Your lowest salary consideration falls

---

What is your bottom line?

To arrive at a salary figure you can live with, list all your necessary **monthly** expenses:

rent	_____
food	_____
gas/electricity	_____
transportation	_____
clothes	_____
miscellaneous	_____
subtotal	_____
__% of city, state, and federal taxes*	_____
add another 15% for emergencies and inflation	_____
monthly salary	_____
multiply subtotal by 12 for yearly salary	_____
divide by 52 for weekly	_____

This is your bottom line—weekly, monthly, and yearly. You cannot accept a job paying less without changing your lifestyle.

*Find the approximate percentage of taxes on the income you have arrived at by calling your local tax office.

Can you afford *this* job?

1. **Are there hidden expenses,** such as transportation, day care/babysitting, or nursing for elderly members of your family? Are you required to buy equipment or uniforms?

2. **What is the travel time** to and from the work place? Is employee parking provided?

3. **How much overtime is expected?** Is it reimbursed? At what rate? If you are required to work late hours, will you be safe returning home?

4. **Do you need flexible hours** occasionally if children or elderly relations living at home become sick? Will your employer agree to them?

5. **Is it possible to do some of your work at home?**

6. **Are the fringe benefits** (medical, insurance, retirement, vacation, sick days) acceptable to you? If not provided, how much additional salary will you need in order to assume the cost of these benefits?

---

within their range but is well above the bottom. And if you have impressed them with your abilities enough to make them stretch their salary offer above their range limit, you are on your way to a resounding success.

This is also the time to clarify the company's policy on raises, fringe benefits, and vacations. Often these items are negotiable. It is up to you to put the highest value on yourself. If you know what is possible, your employer can only respect you for wanting to secure the best offer possible. He may even envision your using your negotiating skill on behalf of the company.

Once terms are agreed upon, you should get them in writing. A good way to protect yourself is to write a letter to your boss immediately after these face-to-face negotiations, formally accepting the job. Include a run-down of your verbal agreements and ask him to inform you if you have misunderstood any point. Keep a copy of the letter and of any response to it in case a misunderstanding develops in the future.

Job descriptions

Unless your duties are self-evident or absolutely cut and dried, you should ask for a written copy of your job description when you accept the position. It will save both you and your boss a lot of time in the long run, and it serves as a protection for both of you.

Remember, your job description is a guideline, not a law written in stone. When you see things that need to be done that do not come under your job description, you have a choice. If you choose to take on additional work, your job description will verify your initiative. If you refuse (because of overwork or distaste for the extra work), the job description is your proof that these tasks were not to be expected of you.

Moving up the ladder

Work rules. Every organization has work rules. It is a great mistake to assume that they do not apply to you. Find out from the start what the basic rules are and show your cooperation. Remember, there is usually a good reason for every rule. Employers expect that their employees will live up to work rules.

Common rules of employment

Attendance: You are expected to work a certain number of days or hours for your salary. Most businesses allow you sick leave; some give you days for personal leave, such as funerals; nearly all grant vacation time. Find out *exactly* what is allowed and stick to the rules.

Punctuality: You will be told what time you are expected to be at work each day. Plan accordingly, taking traffic and weather into account. There is seldom a good excuse for being late. Coffee breaks and lunches have set time frames: observe them.

Dress: If you have any questions about what the dress codes are for your job, do not hesitate to ask. Some jobs require dress rules to meet safety standards, such as hard hats, safety glasses, long-sleeved shirts, etc. Do not wear strong perfume or after-shave lotion. Your chewing gum should be left at home.

Safety: Many companies have weekly safety meetings. For instance, public service companies have standards dealing with the parking of their trucks, wearing apparel, the handling of equipment in private homes, the backing out of driveways, etc. Safety rules will be prominently posted. It is your responsibility to observe them for the protection of everyone.

Protocol: Leave your personal business at home. Make personal phone calls *only* in emergencies. Give the respect due a superior. Bypassing the next in line or going over someone's head could cost you your job. Take the time to find out who is in charge and take the care to go through proper channels. These practices are good job insurance.

Communicating on the job.

As a new employee, you will be busy mastering your job. Establishing good relations with your coworkers can provide you with much-needed advice and support.

Avoid the pitfalls of participating in office gossip and taking sides in disputes. Your early communications should be especially friendly and courteous. Your curiosity should be focused on ways to perform your job as efficiently and thoroughly as possible.

Be helpful to your fellow workers but not at the expense of your own job performance. If you have any complaints, direct them to the proper person to solve the problem. Be observant of what is going on around you, but avoid jumping to conclusions. If you are patient and stay uninvolved in any potentially explosive situation, your options will eventually become clear to you. Your long-range assessment of the situation will probably be quite different from your immediate reactions during the first few weeks on the job.

Making suggestions

Suggestion box. As a relatively new employee, you may bring a fresh approach to solving company problems. Many companies have a suggestion box. Unless you have been hired specifically as a troubleshooter, the suggestion box is the best place to direct your ideas. Such initiative often pays off in the form of a bonus or even a promotion.

Direct suggestions. You may soon develop a close enough relationship with your superior to make a written memo to him an appropriate way to make a suggestion. If you can relate the inspiration of the suggestion to your superior ("something you mentioned made me think of the possibility of . . ." or "in keeping with your work philosophy, I would like to suggest . . ."), you have expressed support for your superior and created a positive atmosphere for your suggestion.

Suggesting changes can be risky without the support and enthusiasm of the decision-makers. Sharing the credit by allowing them to feel that they were in part the source of the idea allows them to join you in carrying out a constructive suggestion. Learning to communicate diplomatically is a major key to success.

How to be supportive to your employer

1. **Have a positive attitude:** Take note of your superior's contributions, acknowledge the good ones, and keep quiet about the bad ones.

2. **Know your boss:** Learn his or her working methods and adjust your own to harmonize with them. Be clear on your boss's priorities.

3. **Be informed:** Do your homework by keeping up to date in your field. Read carefully all memos and annual reports.

4. **Become a team worker:** Cooperate with coworkers; contribute whatever you can to a pleasant working environment.

5. **Be honest:** The best way to be supportive to your boss is to be honest, responsible, and trustworthy.

The art of listening.

One of the more satisfying rewards of teaching is the profound silence of someone listening. If you can give this attention to your boss, he will not fail to notice.

Most new employees want to impress everyone with how much they know, their speed in catching on, and their enthusiasm. They are much more concerned with feedback ("How am I doing?") than with giving appreciation to their boss or mentor.

Remember, it may be lonely at the top. Your boss needs appreciation for his contributions as much as you do. In fact, directing your attention to listening and acknowledging him can open blocked channels of communication for everyone.

Yearly job assessments. Many companies now make it a practice to require their employees to turn in statements of their yearly goals and assessments of their past job performances. This exercise can be very helpful. Even though your company may not require it, you

---

Tips for getting along on the job	Checklist for making suggestions
1. Make your job performance your top priority.	1. Examine your suggestion carefully before you submit it.
2. Become a team worker.	2. Make sure you do not imply criticism of a superior or jeopardize anyone's job.
3. Be willing to accept more responsibility.	3. Phrase you suggestion positively.
4. Be loyal to your boss or keep quiet if you are not.	4. Check it from all angles for clarity and detail.
5. Treat everyone with courtesy.	5. Leave no chance for misinterpretation.
6. Avoid office gossip.	
7. Avoid making personal phone calls.	

Advancing Your Career

could celebrate your yearly anniversary by reflecting on your progress. Experience can change your direction. Yearly assessments will clarify your focus on future progress and serve as a useful guide for making changes if you are dissatisfied. And reviewing your progress can be an enormous help when you are asking for a raise.

Shifts in responsibility

Asking for a lighter load. Sometimes your success on the job can create a situation in which it is wise to request a decrease in responsibility. For example, maybe your workload has increased to the point where you cannot possibly keep up with your work or perform it to your (or anyone else's) satisfaction. Or perhaps a classroom teacher has been promoted to assistant principal, a logical next step up the ladder of success. But that promotion may have robbed her of her greatest pleasure, teaching her students, and may have put her in an administrative position where she has no particular skills.

Awareness of your strengths, preferences, and limitations when a well-intentioned promotion is offered is important. If you are competent and enthusiastic in a job, think twice before accepting a promotion that does not feel right to you. More money and prestige are seldom worth the giving up of duties you love for those you dislike or cannot perform well.

If union membership is mandatory

1. Become familiar with union rules on payment of dues, work, and behavior.

2. Use your union's services responsibly. It exists to improve your working conditions and salary, and to protect you.

3. Do not discuss union business with nonunion employees or with members of other unions.

4. Work for changes if you are dissatisfied with your union leadership. Complaining without constructive suggestions is counterproductive. On the other hand, constructive suggestions may be welcomed and result in improved organizational procedures.

5. Look for a job in another field if you cannot support your union and are unwilling to change it.

Increasing responsibilities. As you become more experienced in your job, responsibilities may be assigned to you that are not in your job description. If you are ambitious and like the challenge, you may

---

Asking for a promotion

1. Do you have the necessary qualifications, including experience, to do your present job well?
2. Have you been on your present job long enough to warrant a promotion?
3. Where do you stand in line for a promotion?
4. Do you have a clear understanding of the new position and all it involves?
5. Are you willing to make the necessary commitment to the new job?
6. Does your employer know what your expectations are?
7. Are you on good terms with fellow workers?

Steps in asking for a raise

1. **Check company policy:** Some companies have automatic raises that go into effect at scheduled intervals; some use a merit system. Others will grant increases for merit in addition to regularly scheduled increases.

2. **Use good judgment:** Check salaries for jobs in companies similar to yours. Make sure your own company is in a financial position to grant an increase at this time.

3. **Review your record:** Read over your yearly assessments if you have made them. Have firmly in mind your contributions as an employee—from good attendance and/or productivity to increasing the efficiency of your department.

4. **Be assertive:** Tie your request for a raise to the specific factors most appropriate in your case: your time on the job, comparable salaries in the field, your career goals, your contributions to the company, etc. Asking for a raise is difficult for all of us; taking the first three steps will make this one easier for you—and make you more likely to succeed.

---

welcome the extra work. After proving yourself sufficiently, you should take the opportunity to review your job description with your superior.

It is a good idea to bring two copies of your old job description with you, plus a new description of your present job as you see it. If you have been assigned more work than you can handle efficiently, make constructive suggestions for dealing with the problem. If you think additional training is necessary, present your request for it along with a specific plan. If you need to hire an assistant, back up your request with facts about productivity and costs.

This is a good time to ask for a raise. It is certainly reasonable to ask for confirmation of your new job description and to inquire what increase in salary accompanies the increase in your responsibilities.

Changing careers

Case history.
Paul Carter's mother, Carol, has taught English at the local high school for 15 years. Although she enjoys her work, she has always dreamed of becoming a travel agent: she loves travel, and has a real aptitude for learning foreign languages. For the past four years, while Paul has been at college, Carol has been researching her dream job. She has worked part-time in a friend's travel agency every summer, and is now ready to resign from teaching and take a full-time job with the agency.

One of the reasons Carol Carter can afford to give up the superior fringe benefits and security of teaching is that her husband, Jeffrey, has been promoted from his job as sports equipment buyer for a local department store.

It was Jeffrey Carter who came up with the idea of expanding the sports department into a separate facility to include a health club and restaurant. He presented his expansion plan so convincingly that he was made a vice president of the store and put in charge of the entire new operation.

When to make a change.
Unlike Carol Carter, who considered her career change for a number of years before she came to a decision, some people wake up one morning and experience a moment

---

Carol Carter consulted this list from the *Department of Labor Occupational Outlook Quarterly* and was pleased to find her background in English related to skills needed in her new career choice.

Occupations related to English

High school graduate

Actor or actress	Insurance agent	Secretary
Claims adjuster	Printer	Service representative
Court clerk	Proofreader	Telephone operator
Court reporter	Receptionist	Travel guide or agent
Flight attendant	Reservation/ticket passenger agent	Typesetter
	Salesperson	Typist

Two years of college

Computer operator	Library technician and assistant	Medical secretary
Film editor	Licensed practical nurse	Paralegal
Legal secretary	Maitre d'hotel	Police officer

College graduate +

Administrator	Employment counselor	Psychologist
Advertising executive	Executive	Public relations worker
Advertising writer	Job analyst	Publisher
Announcer–radio, TV	Journalist	Registrar–college and university
Archivist	Librarian	School counselor
Buyer	Market research analyst	Script writer–radio, TV, movies
Criminologist	Missionary/minister/rabbi/priest	Social worker
Drama coach	Personnel and labor relations worker	Speech pathologist/clinician
Editor	Physician	Teacher
Editorial assistant	Political scientist	Translator
Education and public affairs director	Producer–TV, films, plays	Tutor
Educator	Program director–radio/TV	Writer

of truth: their job is no longer challenging or satisfying, and no money or benefits are worth so much dissatisfaction.

If this happens to you, do not quit your present job or even start discreetly exploring other possibilities immediately. First, make yourself a plan.

Jeffrey Carter was bored with his job when he got an inspiration from observing the health-club boom spreading across the country. Having always been a fitness addict, Jeffrey now dreamed of opening a health club. He had to restrain himself from putting in his resignation so that he could work full-time on financing his dream.

Instead, he used his spare time to work out a plan, researching it thoroughly and devising a presentation that was practical and specific. Jeffrey was prepared to resign and launch the venture on his own if his proposal met with a negative response. As it was, he got his health club, a big raise and promotion.

Every employee experiences some job dissatisfaction some of the time. If yours is serious and pervasive, however, a change may be indicated. Before you do anything, look at your situation from every possible angle. Sometimes a well-thought-out plan or even a single good idea can make it possible for you to change jobs within your organization.

Changing jobs: what to consider

1. Can you make a job change within your present company?
2. Would you increase your chances of getting a job you like better by staying where you are?
3. Have you done everything you can to increase the rewards in your present job?
4. Are you using the abilities you enjoy most? Are you learning skills important to your career advancement?
5. Are you fulfilling a need for yourself or the community in your present job?
6. Are you willing to risk the loss of security and/or your present benefits if you make a change?
7. Is your family supportive of your desire to change?
8. Can you financially afford to make a change?
9. Would a change involve a geographic move?
10. Is it possible to work part-time in another job to see how well it suits you before leaving your present job?

If you decide to quit

If you are certain that there will be no openings for advancement at your present job, give the boss the proper notice when you decide to leave. He or she should honor your good record with a letter of recommendation. The usual required notice is two weeks, but check your work rules.

Where the jobs are

American workers have always shown an enthusiasm for going after the job if the job will not come to them. If your occupation is threatened with extinction, or if jobs are scarce in your area, you may choose to make a geographic as well as a career move. Consult these charts before you decide.

10 Best Areas	Nonfarm employees in thousands 1980	1993	Percent change
Nevada	400	670	+68
Florida	3,576	5,567	+56
Arizona	1,014	1,571	+55
Alaska	169	253	+50
Utah	551	810	+47
Georgia	2,159	3,106	+44
Washington	1,608	2,250	+40
North Carolina	2,380	3,245	+36
Virginia	2,157	2,920	+34
Delaware	259	348	+34

10 Worst Areas	Nonfarm employees in thousands 1980	1993	Percent change
Wyoming	210	210	0
West Virginia	646	652	+1
Louisiana	1,579	1,643	+4
Connecticut	1,427	1,529	+7
Massachusetts	2,652	2,842	+7
New York	7,207	7,736	+7
Pennsylvania	4,753	5,110	+7
Rhode Island	398	429	+8
Washington, D.C.	616	670	+9
Oklahoma	1,138	1,240	+9

If you lose your job. If you have been fired, ask questions if you do not know why. The truth may be difficult to face; but only if you know the truth, can you make constructive use of your experience. If you were fired for unreliability, you can try to avoid making the same mistakes next time. If you were dismissed because your company or field is in trouble, you can try to avoid putting yourself in a similar situation next time. Ask for a letter of recommendation.

There is no need to panic, or to rush into a new job you do not want. If you were fired or laid off, you automatically qualify for unemployment insurance to assist you in your search for another job (your local unemployment office will give you all the information you need).

Your time between jobs offers an opportunity to consider carefully where you were, what you have learned, where you are now, and where you want to go.

Warning signs!

1. The company is suffering unusual losses.
2. People are getting laid off.
3. You are not invited to the usual meetings.
4. You feel uninformed.
5. People seem to be avoiding you.
6. You were passed over for a promotion.
7. Your boss shows continued dissatisfaction and impatience with your performance.
8. Your boss leaves.
9. The new boss starts bringing in his own people.
10. Little by little, your responsibilities are being assigned to other people.

You are fired. Why?

1. Were you qualified for the job? Did you honestly represent your skills before you were hired?
2. Were you truly suited for the job?
3. Should you have taken additional courses to keep you up to date?
4. Did you make costly mistakes?
5. Did you get along with your fellow workers?
6. Did you participate in office gossip and politics?
7. Were you given warnings before being fired? Did you make constructive use of criticism from superiors?
8. Did you often find yourself making excuses for work not finished, getting to work late, leaving early, taking excessive sick leave?
9. Have you been fired before? If so, why?
10. Do you see a pattern forming? For example, do you always become bored in your jobs?

Taking an unflinching look at what went wrong can be invaluable for finding the right job in the future and for recognizing how you can perform that job more effectively.

Applying for unemployment insurance

Go *immediately* to your nearest office of unemployment with two forms of identification (driver's license, birth certificate, passport, etc.) and your Social Security number (your Social Security card does not qualify as identification). Pride is *not* a factor: get in line and sign up.

How to survive until the first unemployment check comes

1. Call or visit your local office of Human Services for information about:
   a. food stamps   b. rent allowances   c. fuel assistance

2. An employee laid off or fired will normally receive at least two weeks' severance pay.

3. Look in the first few pages of your telephone book for a special section commonly called Community Service Numbers. There you will find the local telephone number for job services, unemployment, food stamps, and other social services that can help you.

Advancing Your Career

Getting back into the work force

Opportunities for retirees.
Many companies have a mandatory retirement age, as do certain occupations (pilots must retire at age 60, for example). Some retirees are surprised to find that they do not adjust well to so much leisure time and are not happy unless they are in a work-related environment. For others, continuing to work for pay is not a matter of choice but of simple economics: Social Security and pension checks are often inadequate to provide a comfortable or even a reasonable standard of living.

There are many opportunities for older people to get back into the work force or work-related activities. For those who are not concerned with more income, programs such as ACTION, Retired Senior Volunteer Program (RSVP), VISTA, Peace Corps, Foster Grandparents, and Senior Companion urgently need older Americans who are willing to share their concern and expertise. See pages 296-297 for more information.

If you discover that your retirement income will be inadequate before you have actually retired, you may be able to arrange with your employer for part-time work as a consultant or during vacation or peak periods. You may even find that full- or part-time work in an entirely different capacity from your present job can be arranged. The fact that you still work for the company gives you more leverage than you would have as a former employee in the months after retirement.

Retirement often allows people the security to take the risk of trying to make money out of a new activity or one formerly considered recreational. America is the home of success stories like those of Ray Kroc and Colonel Harland Sanders, who came out of retirement to start McDonald's and Kentucky Fried Chicken. It is also the home of thousands of cottage industries started all over the country by retirees who turned their hobbies into profit-making ventures.

If you cannot find any work in your field, the JTPS (Job Training Partnership Act) is a state-funded program that assists low-income people over 55 who need job training and placement.

Other areas to investigate are local churches, YMCA and YWCA occupational services, professional or trade associations, labor union employment services, and Forty-Plus Clubs. Ample help and counseling are available if you know where to look.

Another avenue to explore is the office of your state representative or senator. Their local offices have workers who collect information in all problem areas, especially unemployment. Upon request they will provide this information and assist you in any other way they can.

Odd jobs can solve problems

For retirees, there are many ways to make money without actually working at a regular job. Here are some ideas to start you thinking:

1. Retired teachers or anyone with expertise in a particular area (in a foreign language, for example) can tutor at home. An ad in your local paper, a call or visit to a school or college in your area, even a notice on a supermarket or shopping-mall bulletin board can help attract this kind of business.

2. In most communities, those qualified to supply music, art, or drama coaching can attract willing students.

3. Anyone who can sew or tailor is likely to find a ready supply of customers.

4. Those who have no specific area of expertise can make money running errands, chauffering, house-sitting, babysitting, or assisting the elderly and infirm.

5. Gardening can be profitable to those who sell their own vegetables, flowers, or fruits. Tending other people's gardens while they are traveling can be enjoyable and profitable. Landscaping can supplement your income even more.

6. There is a market in most communities for hand-crafted items, from dolls and pillows to furniture. Homemade baked goods are easy to sell, and can be the start of a home catering business.

7. For more ideas write for an eight-page fact sheet compiled by the government telling where to look for both paid and unpaid jobs:
   Consumer Information Center
   Pueblo, Colorado 81009

Women who work. Approximately 131.4 million people will make up the 1995 labor force—3.8 million more than originally projected. Job growth for women is expected to continue. For example, according to the Department of Labor, the employment of preschool teachers (nearly all of them women) is expected to increase some 54 percent between 1992 and 2005.

The majority of people reentering the work force are also women. In 1960, slightly more than 23 million women held paying jobs. Today, the number is more than twice that, and rising every year. Women comprise over 45 percent of the work force in America today. Many of these women are supplementing the family income or working their way up in a chosen career. The majority of them are in the work force because of economic necessity. Over 50 percent of women reentering the work force are single parents.

Far-reaching social changes have contributed to the surge of women workers. Many women have chosen to defer marriage and/or motherhood. Equal pay and antidiscrimination laws, along with new tax allowances for child-care expenses, have opened up the job choices available to women. It is still true that many more women are employed in service rather than goods-producing industries; but it is also true that the service industries are expanding while manufacturing is on the decrease. Service-related industries (public relations, transportation, communications, finance, insurance, real estate, etc.) are projected to account for nearly 75 percent of all jobs in 2005.

Over half of women with children under six are now in the work force. Lack of adequate child care remains the most significant problem for working mothers, although the picture is considerably brighter than it was a few years ago. Federally funded day-care centers, where tuition is scaled to income, are still on the increase. Many corporations, and some local schools, are now providing day-care centers.

About three out of four employed adult American women work full time. Forty-five percent of American mothers with infants are employed outside the home. Sixty percent of American mothers with children between ages three and five are employed outside the home.

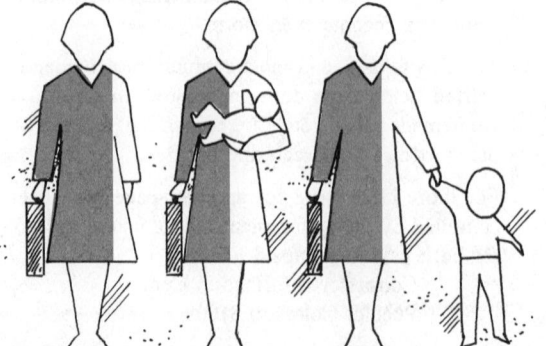

Alternative work patterns

For information on part-time work, flexible work schedules, and shared jobs, write to:

New Ways to Work Newsletter
   New Ways to Work
   149 Ninth Street
   San Francisco, CA 944103

Alternative Work Patterns: Changing Approaches to Work Scheduling, by David Robinson
   Work in America Institute, Inc.
   700 White Plains Road
   Scarsdale, NY 10583

First National Directory on Part-Time and Flexitime Programs
   National Council for Alternative Work Programs
   1925 K Street NW, Suite 308A
   Washington, DC 20036

Many companies now offer flexible hours in certain jobs. This trend is a great boon to working mothers, who can arrange their assigned number of hours per week to accommodate their children's schedules. For example, a parent need not miss a child's graduation or school play: the hours can be made up before or after the normal working day, or on the weekend.

Job-sharing is another trend in meeting the special needs of working women. Two people can share the same job, working out their hours and finances between them along whatever lines seem fair to both parties. So long as they get the job done satisfactorily, it does not matter to the employer which worker does what. This arrangement can allow each employee to hold a more challenging or better paying job than part-time work could offer either of them.

Help is as near as your mailbox

The U.S. government spends millions of dollars each year printing information invaluable to women in—or entering—the work force. Write to:
   Information Office
   Women's Bureau
   Department of Labor
   200 Constitution Ave. NW
   Washington, DC 20210
Ask for a list of their publications. There is likely to be one pertaining to any problem you may have or supplying any information you seek.

Advancing Your Career

Starting your own business

Starting your own *successful* business can be best described as turning your passion into your profession. The secret ingredient in the formula for a successful small business is likely to be an obsessed owner—one willing to put in the time needed to get the job done (often well over eight hours a day) and full of unflagging enthusiasm.

It is likely that running your own business will be harder than working at a regular job. Studies have demonstrated that most entrepreneurs are not motivated primarily by the desire to make money. The satisfactions lie more in the areas of independence, power over the future, and the pleasure of doing a good job.

Whether a business succeeds or fails most often depends on a simple thing called "cash flow." If there is not enough cash coming in or reserved to pay the expenses of running the business, the business will soon fail. It does not matter how much money is owed to you (debtors may also be suffering a cash flow problem); what counts is *cash in hand.*

Smart entrepreneurs reserve every bit of cash they can for unexpected expenses or dry periods. Giving in to the temptation to expand too quickly or display the fruits of sudden profits can turn an apparent success into a sudden failure.

Here are some questions to ask yourself before you embark on any business venture of your own. Answering them thoughtfully will help you decide whether starting your own business is right for you.

Starting your own business

1. Do you have a clear idea of the business you would like to start in terms of the product or service?
2. Do you have (or can you acquire) the necessary knowhow to run that type of business?
3. Have you gained experience in that field or in a related field?
4. Do you have any necessary equipment, or the money to acquire it?
5. Do you have the kind of contacts you will need to launch your business—bankers, accountants, potential customers, promoters, etc.?
6. Do you have the time and energy necessary to commit to a new business? (Remember, this may mean 18-hour work days and seven-day work weeks.)
7. Does your family support your endeavor?
8. Do you have the temperament for taking risks?
9. Are you practical enough to implement your ideas?
10. Are you capable of picking the right people to help you?
11. Do you have a good supply of self-confidence?
12. Are you willing to admit your mistakes and learn from them?
13. Can you tolerate the uncertainty that characterizes any new business?
14. Do you have a plan to provide for you and your family if the business fails?
15. Do you have plans to expand where necessary if the business succeeds?

Advantages and disadvantages of starting your own business

ADVANTAGES
- You are totally responsible for any success.
- You can work at your own speed.
- Your schedule will be flexible.
- You will reap the profits of your hard work and have many tax advantages.
- Your business may provide security and even jobs for your family.
- You will not face forced retirement.

DISADVANTAGES
- You are totally responsible for any failure.
- You may work during all your waking hours.
- You will have no paid vacation; you may have no vacation at all.
- You will have no weekly paycheck or fringe benefits.
- You may go deeply into debt; you may have almost no time to spend with your family.
- If the business fails, your savings and property can be eaten up by debts, leaving nothing for your retirement.

The birth of a small business.

Edward and Alice Stubbs, whose success chart appears on page 25, want to start a catering business now that Edward is retired. They have had many years of volunteer catering experience at their church and community theater. More important, they both love to cook and have ample kitchen facilities in a large house with plenty of storage space.

If you want to start your own business, make an analysis similar to the Stubbs's. Think of every contingency for success and failure. Write everything down. Consult anyone who might have valuable advice or experience, including people operating a similar business far enough out of your area to be noncompetitive. Visit or write to the Small Business Administration, whose retired business people are available for free consultation. Inform yourself about your proposed business from all sources mentioned in this section. It is particularly important to get help in arriving at the right profit margin for your product or services (many businesses fail because they are priced too low). If you are thinking about opening a retail shop, for example, you will probably find that doubling the cost to you of items for sale will not be adequate. Finally, make sure you have enough cash to carry you until the business can carry itself.

Stubbs's catering service: An analysis

Market: Their initial market already existed, since their reputation as splendid cooks was well established in the community.

Pricing: After doing research at the library and drawing from their own knowledge about the actual cost of preparing dishes, they marked up the price of their ingredients three times in order to ensure a profit. Dishes or meals especially time-consuming to prepare were marked up five times.

Competition: The only catering service in their community was a firm that catered for guest lists of 50 or more. The Stubbses were interested in providing a small, personal service.

Goods and overhead: Because they operated out of their own large kitchen, relatively little initial investment was required. They needed trays and some large pots and platters, but their expenditures were minimal. They used their own station wagon for deliveries, making it a company car and a tax deduction.

Regulations: The Stubbses worked out of their home, so there was no need for health department inspections (although theoretically there could have been).

Risk: Relatively little risk was involved. The Stubbs's policy was to ask for one-third to one-half of their fee in advance, which covered their costs. They either sent a bill for the remainder or collected upon delivery, depending on the customer. After consulting a lawyer, they had a legal form drawn up that each customer signed upon ordering. They consulted their insurance agent and took out a liability policy that covered them in the event of a lawsuit from a customer. These precautions protected the Stubbses from unanticipated threats to their business and personal investment and property, and, more important to their everyday business, ensured their cash flow.

Time commitment: At first, the Stubbses were capable of handling all of the business themselves. They worked long hours to keep overhead to a minimum, not minding because theirs was a labor of love. Eventually, the volume of business became too much for them and they hired an assistant.

Start-up expenses checklist

1. Do you need printed business cards, stationery, invoices, wrapping paper, shopping bags, etc.?
2. Do you need to buy a mailing list or lists?
3. Do you need to rent work space, furniture, typewriters, cash registers, etc.?
4. Do you need a separate phone line for the business?
5. What are the advertising rates in the local newspapers? Can you arrange to have a promotional article written about your new business?
6. Will you need a telephone answering service or machine?
7. Do you need to file the name of your business in your state? Do you need to incorporate?

Think of every hidden expense and write it down. Talk with people in similar businesses and ask them what expenses, including unexpected ones, are likely to come up. Then draw up a budget and compare it with your cash on hand to estimate how much money you will have to raise.

How your government can help

Some of the best information is supported by your tax dollars. It is yours for the asking. Write to:

> Office of Small Business Development Centers
> Management Assistance
> Small Business Administration
> 1441 L Street NW
> Washington, DC 20416

Ask for their complete kit of information. Write to the Office of Management Counseling Services, Management Assistance, at the Small Business Administration for free personal counseling.

Special help for women. Helping women become successful entrepreneurs is a special goal of the Small Business Administration. Write to:

> Office of Women's Business Enterprise Division
> Small Business Administration
> 1441 L Street NW
> Washington, DC 20416

If you want to start a business out of your home, write to: National Alliance of Homebased Businesswomen
P.O. Box 95
Norwood, New Jersey 07648

Starting out

Starting Out Series publications are available free from the Small Business Administration Washington District Office, 1111 18th Street NW, 6th Floor, Washington, DC 20417. Tel. (202) 634-6156.

101 Building Service Contracting	118 The Nursery Business	135 Printing
102 Service Stations	119 The Wholesale Nursery Business	136 Fabricare
103 Catering	120 The Garden Center Business	137 The Bookstore
104 Radio-Television Repair Shop	121 The Landscaping Business	138 Home Furnishings
105 Retail Florist	122 Apparel Store	139 Handbags
106 Franchise Businesses	123 Pharmacies	140 Bake Shops
107 Hardware Store or Home Center	124 Retail Photography Store	141 Portable Sanitation
108 Home Building, Small Volume	125 Office Products	142 Ice Cream
109 Travel Agency	126 Automotive Parts & Accessories	143 Recreational Vehicles
110 Restaurants	127 Motels	144 Real Estate
111 Sporting Goods Stores	128 Paint & Decorating Store	145 Sewing Centers
112 Dry Cleaning	129 Interior Design Services	146 Exhibit Design and Production
113 Car Wash	130 Fish Farming	147 Electric Vehicles
114 Beauty Salon	131 Day-Care Centers–Preschoolers	148 Personnel Referral Service
115 Pest Control	132 Men's Outerwear	149 Selling by Mail Order
116 Marine Retailers	133 Bicycles	150 Solar Energy
117 Retail Grocery Stores	134 Roofing Contractors	201 Breakeven Point for Independent Truckers

A hobby developed into a marketable skill and eventually became a promising small business (left) for an ambitious couple. Another innovative entrepreneur (right) saw a big future in a commodity that always is in demand.

Matching yourself to the World of Work

L = lowest level
M = middle level
H = highest level

[1] Estimates not available.
[2] Vary, depending on job.

Job requirements — 1. Leadership/persuasion; 2. Helping/instructing others; 3. Problem-solving/creativity; 4. Initiative; 5. Work as part of a team; 6. Frequent public contacts; 7. Manual dexterity; 8. Physical stamina; 9. Hazardous; 10. Outdoors; 11. Confined; 12. Jobs concentrated geographically; 13. Part-time
Work environs / Occupational characteristics — 14. Earnings; 15. Employment growth; 16. Entry requirements

Occupation	1	2	3	4	5	6	7	8	9	10	11	12	13	14 Earnings	15 Empl. growth	16 Entry req.
Administrative and Managerial Occupations																
Accountants and auditors		•	•		•	•						•		M	M	H
Bank officers and managers	•	•	•	•	•	•						•		H	M	H
Buyers	•		•	•										M	M	H
College student personnel workers	•	•	•	•		•								1	1	H
Construction inspectors (government)		•	•	•	•		•			•				M	H	M
Credit managers	•	•	•		•	•						•		M	L	H
Health services administrators	•		•		•	•								H	H	H
Hotel managers and assistants	•	•	•	•		•								1	H	M
Medical record administrators	•		•	•										H	H	H
Occupational safety and health workers		•	•	•		•				•				H	1	H
Personnel and labor relations specialists	•	•	•	•		•								M	L	H
Purchasing agents	•		•		•									1	L	H
School administrators	•	•	•	•	•	•								H	L	H
Engineers, Surveyors, and Architects																
Architects		•	•	•	•	•								H	H	H
Landscape architects		•	•		•	•								1	H	H
Surveyors and surveying technicians				•		•	•			•				L	M	M
Engineers																
Agricultural engineers			•	•	•									H	H	H
Chemical engineers			•	•	•									H	M	H
Civil engineers and electrical engineers			•	•	•									H	H	H
Electrical engineers			•	•	•									H	H	H
Industrial and mechanical engineers			•	•	•									H	H	H
Metallurgical and mining engineers			•	•	•									H	H	H
Natural Scientists and Mathematicians																
Mathematical scientists and systems analysts																
Mathematicians			•	•										H	L	H
Statisticians			•	•										M	M	H
Systems analysts	•		•	•	•							•		H	H	H
Physical scientists																
Astronomers			•	•										H	L	H
Chemists			•	•										H	M	H
Geographers			•	•	•									H	M	H
Geologists and geophysicists			•	•	•					•				H	H	H
Meteorologists			•	•	•									H	L	H
Oceanographers			•	•	•					•	•			H	M	H
Physicists			•	•										H	L	H

	Job requirements											Work environs		Occupational characteristics		
	1. Leadership/persuasion	2. Helping/instructing others	3. Problem-solving/creativity	4. Initiative	5. Work as part of a team	6. Frequent public contacts	7. Manual dexterity	8. Physical stamina	9. Hazardous	10. Outdoors	11. Confined	12. Jobs concentrated geographically	13. Part-time	14. Earnings	15. Employment growth	16. Entry requirements
Life scientists																
Agricultural and biological scientists			•	•										1	M	H
Biochemists			•	•										H	M	H
Food technologists			•	•										H	L	H
Foresters			•	•	•			•	•	•				M	L	H
Soil conservationists		•	•	•						•				H	L	H
Social Scientists, Social Workers, Religious Workers, and Lawyers																
Lawyers	•	•	•	•	•	•								H	M	H
Social scientists																
Anthropologists			•	•	•									H	M	H
Economists			•	•										H	H	H
Historians			•	•										H	L	H
Political scientists			•	•	•	•								H	L	H
Psychologists		•	•	•	•		•							H	M	H
Sociologists			•	•			•							H	L	H
Social and recreation workers																
Recreation workers	•	•	•	•	•	•	•	•		•		•		L	M	M
Social workers	•	•	•	•	•	•								L	M	H
Religious workers																
Ministers and priests	•	•	•	•	•	•								L	1	H
Rabbis	•	•	•	•	•	•								H	1	H
Teachers, Librarians, and Counselors																
College career counselors	•	•	•	•	•	•								M	1	H
College and university faculty	•	•	•	•	•	•						•		H	L	H
Employment counselors	•	•	•	•	•	•					•			1	1	H
Kindergarten, school teachers	•	•	•	•	•	•	•	•				•		M	M	H
Librarians	•	•	•	•	•	•						•		M	L	H
Rehabilitation counselors	•	•	•	•	•	•								1	1	H
School counselors	•	•	•	•	•	•								M	L	H
Secondary school teachers	•	•	•	•	•	•								M	L	H
Health Diagnosing and Treating Practitioners																
Chiropractors	•	•	•	•	•	•	•	•				•		H	M	H
Dentists	•	•	•	•	•	•	•	•						H	M	H
Optometrists	•	•	•	•	•	•	•	•				•		H	M	H
Physicians	•	•	•	•	•	•	•	•	•					H	H	H
Veterinarians	•	•	•	•	•	•	•	•	•					H	H	H
Registered Nurses, Pharmacists, Dietitians, etc.																
Dietitians	•	•	•	•	•	•						•		L	H	H
Occupational therapists	•	•	•	•	•	•	•	•						1	H	H
Pharmacists	•	•	•	•	•	•					•	•		H	L	H
Physical therapists	•	•	•	•	•	•	•	•	•					M	H	H
Physician assistants	•	•	•	•	•	•	•	•	•					M	1	H
Registered nurses	•	•	•	•	•	•	•	•				•		M	H	M

Job requirements | Work environs | Occupational characteristics

Column key:
1. Leadership/persuasion
2. Helping/instructing others
3. Problem-solving/creativity
4. Initiative
5. Work as part of a team
6. Frequent public contacts
7. Manual dexterity
8. Physical stamina
9. Hazardous
10. Outdoors
11. Confined
12. Jobs concentrated geographically
13. Part-time
14. Earnings
15. Employment growth
16. Entry requirements

Occupation	1	2	3	4	5	6	7	8	9	10	11	12	13	14	15	16
Health Technologists and Technicians																
Dental hygienists		•		•	•	•	•				•		•	L	H	M
Electrocardiograph technicians		•		•	•								•	1	H	M
Emergency medical technicians		•	•		•	•	•	•	•					L	M	M
Licensed practical nurses		•			•	•	•						•	L	H	M
Medical laboratory workers					•		•		•		•			L	H	2
Radiologic (x-ray) technicians		•			•		•		•				•	L	H	M
Surgical technicians		•			•	•	•							L	H	M
Writers, Artists, and Entertainers																
Communications occupations																
Public relations workers	•		•	•	•	•								M	M	H
Radio and television announcers and newscasters	•	•		•	•	•						•		L	H	H
Reporters and correspondents	•		•	•	•	•								1	M	H
Writers and editors	•		•	•	•							•	•	1	M	H
Design occupations																
Commercial, graphic designers			•	•	•		•						•	1	L	M
Display workers	•		•	•			•		•					L	M	L
Floral designers			•			•	•					•		1	L	L
Industrial designers			•	•	•		•							1	L	H
Interior designers			•	•	•		•							1	M	M
Photographers			•	•	•		•						•	L	L	M
Performing artists																
Actors and actresses			•	•	•	•	•				•		•	L	M	M
Dancers and musicians			•	•	•	•	•	•					•	L	M	M
Singers			•	•	•	•	•	•			•		•	1	L	M
Technologists and Technicians, Except Health																
Air-traffic controllers		•	•	•	•		•					•		H	L	H
Broadcast technicians			•		•		•					•		L	L	M
Drafters				•			•					•		M	H	M
Forestry technicians						•	•	•	•					1	H	M
Engineering, science technicians			•		•		•	2	2			2		M	M	M
Legal assistants			2	•	2									M	H	L
Programmers			•		•							•		M	H	H
Technical writers			•	•	•							•		1	H	M
Marketing and Sales Occupations																
Advertising workers	•		•	•										1	1	H
Automobile parts counter workers		•				•		•						L	M	M
Automobile salesworkers	•			•		•								M	H	L
Cashiers						•	•					•		L	H	L
Insurance agents and brokers	•	•	•	•		•							•	M	M	M
Models						•	•		•		•		•	1	1	L
Real estate agents and brokers	•	•	•	•		•				•			•	M	H	M
Retail trade salesworkers	•					•		•						L	M	L
Travel agents	•	•	•	•		•								1	H	M

Advancing Your Career

Column key:
1. Leadership/persuasion
2. Helping/instructing others
3. Problem-solving/creativity
4. Initiative
5. Work as part of a team
6. Frequent public contacts
7. Manual dexterity
8. Physical stamina
9. Hazardous
10. Outdoors
11. Confined
12. Jobs concentrated geographically
13. Part-time
14. Earnings
15. Employment growth
16. Entry requirements

Occupation	1	2	3	4	5	6	7	8	9	10	11	12	13	14	15	16
Administrative Support Occupations, Including Clerical																
Airline reservation, ticket agents		•	•		•	•				•				M	L	L
Bank clerks					•					•			•	L	H	L
Bank tellers					•	•				•			•	L	M	L
Bookkeepers and accounting clerks					•					•			•	L	L	L
Collection workers	•			•	•	•				•				L	M	L
Computer operating personnel			•		•		•			•				L	M	M
Mail carriers						•	•	•		•				M	L	L
Postal clerks					•	•	•	•		•		•		M	L	L
Receptionists		•			•	•				•			•	L	M	L
Secretaries and stenographers			•	•			•							L	H	L
Teacher aides	•	•			•	•	•						•	L	L	L
Telephone operators		•				•							•	L	M	L
Typists							•						•	L	M	L
Service Occupations																
Protective service occupations																
Correction officers	•	•			•			•	•		•			1	H	L
Firefighters		•	•		•	•	•	•	•	•			•	M	M	L
Guards						•	•	•	•		•		•	L	M	L
Police officers	•	•	•	•	•	•	•	•	•					M	M	L
Food and beverage preparation and service occupations																
Bartenders			•		•	•	•			•			•	L	M	M
Cooks and chefs			•		•	•	•			•			•	L	M	M
Food and counterworkers			•		•	•	•			•			•	L	H	L
Waiters and waitresses			•		•	•	•						•	L	M	L
Kitchen helpers			•			•	•						•	L	H	L
Health service occupations																
Dental assistants				•	•	•	•						•	L	H	L
Medical assistants				•	•	•								L	H	L
Occupational and physical therapy assistants		•		•	•	•	•						•	1	H	M
Cleaning and building service occupations																
Hotel housekeepers and assistants						•	•	•						L	M	L
Personal service occupations																
Barbers					•	•	•			•			•	L	L	M
Bellhops and bell captains				•	•	•	•						•	L	L	L
Cosmetologists					•	•	•				•		•	L	L	M
Flight attendants		•			•	•	•							M	L	L
Mechanics and Repairers																
Vehicle and mobile equipment mechanics and repairers																
Aircraft mechanics			•	•			•	•	•	•				H	L	M
Automobile body repairers			•				•	•			•			M	M	M
Automobile mechanics			•			•	•	•			•			L	M	M
Farm equipment mechanics			•				•	•	•		•			L	M	M
Truck and bus mechanics			•				•	•			•			M	M	M

Electrical and electronic equipment repairers

	1	2	3	4	5	6	7	8	9	10	11	12	13	14	15	16
Appliance repairers			•	•		•	•							L	M	M
Central office craft occupations			•		•		•	•	•					1	L	L
Computer service technicians			•	•		•	•							M	H	M
Line installers and cable splicers			•			•	•	•	•					M	L	L
Maintenance electricians			•	•		•	•	•	•					M	M	M
Telephone installers, repairers			•		•	•	•							M	L	L
Television, radio technicians			•	•		•	•		•			•		M	H	M

Other mechanics and repairers

	1	2	3	4	5	6	7	8	9	10	11	12	13	14	15	16
Air-conditioning, refrigeration, and heating mechanics			•			•		•						M	M	M
Business machine repairers			•	•	•	•								M	H	M
Industrial machinery repairers			•			•	•	•						M	M	M
Piano and organ tuners and repairers						•								L	L	M
Watch repairers			•	•	•	•					•		•	L	L	M

Construction and Extractive Occupations

Construction occupations

	1	2	3	4	5	6	7	8	9	10	11	12	13	14	15	16
Bricklayers and stonemasons			•			•	•	•	•					M	H	M
Carpenters			•			•	•	•	•					M	M	M
Electricians (construction)			•			•	•	•	•					H	M	M
Floorcovering installers					•	•	•							L	M	M
Glaziers				•		•	•	•	•					L	M	M
Insulation workers						•	•	•						M	L	M
Ironworkers					•	•	•	•	•					H	M	M
Painters and paperhangers					•	•	•	•	•					L	L	M
Plasterers						•	•							M	L	M
Plumbers and pipefitters			•		•	•	•	•	•					H	M	M
Roofers					•	•	•	•	•					L	L	M
Sheet-metal workers			•			•	•	•						M	M	M

Extractive occupations

	1	2	3	4	5	6	7	8	9	10	11	12	13	14	15	16
Coal mining operatives						•		•	•	•	•			M	H	L

Production Occupations

	1	2	3	4	5	6	7	8	9	10	11	12	13	14	15	16
Blue-collar worker supervisors	•	•	•	•		•		•						M	L	M

Precision production occupations

	1	2	3	4	5	6	7	8	9	10	11	12	13	14	15	16
Bookbinders and bindery workers		2				•	•	•			•		2	L	L	M
Dental and laboratory technicians						•								L	H	M
Furniture upholsterers						•	•	•			•	•		L	L	M
Instrument makers (mechanical)			•	•	•	•					•	•		M	M	M
Jewelers			•	•	•	•					•		•	L	M	M
Lithographers						•					•			H	H	M
Machinists			•			•	•	•			•			M	M	M
Molders (foundry)						•	•	•			•			M	L	M
Patternmakers (foundry)						•	•				•			H	L	M
Photoengravers						•					•			1	L	M
Tool-and-die makers			•			•	•	•			•			H	L	M

Column key (Job requirements): 1. Leadership/persuasion — 2. Helping/instructing others — 3. Problem-solving/creativity — 4. Initiative — 5. Work as part of a team — 6. Frequent public contacts — 7. Manual dexterity — 8. Physical stamina — 9. Hazardous — 10. Outdoors — 11. Confined — 12. Jobs concentrated geographically — 13. Part-time. **Work environs:** 14. Earnings. **Occupational characteristics:** 15. Employment growth — 16. Entry requirements

| | Job requirements | | | | | | | | | | Work environs | | | Occupational characteristics | | |
	1. Leadership/persuasion	2. Helping/instructing others	3. Problem-solving/creativity	4. Initiative	5. Work as part of a team	6. Frequent public contacts	7. Manual dexterity	8. Physical stamina	9. Hazardous	10. Outdoors	11. Confined	12. Jobs concentrated geographically	13. Part-time	14. Earnings	15. Employment growth	16. Entry requirements
Plant and system operators																
Stationary engineers			•				•	•	•					M	L	M
Water treatment operators			•	•			•		•	•				L	L	M
Machine operators, tenders, and setup workers																
Boiler tenders							•	•	•					M	L	M
Forge shop occupations							•	•	•		•			M	L	M
Machine tool operators			•				•	•	•		•			M	M	M
Machine tool setup workers			•				•	•	•		•			M	M	M
Printing press operators							•	•	•		•			M	L	M
Fabricators, assemblers, and hand-working occupations																
Assemblers				•			•			•				L	M	L
Automotive painters							•	•	•	•				H	H	M
Welders and flamecutters							•	•	•	•				M	M	M
Transportation and Material Moving Occupations																
Motor vehicle operators																
Bus drivers			•		•	•	•			•		•		H	L	M
Truck drivers			•			•	•			•				M	M	L
Other transportation and material moving occupations																
Airplane pilots			•	•	•		•			•				H	L	M
Merchant marine sailors				•			•	•	•	•	•	•		M	L	M
Operating engineers							•		•	•				M	L	M

For further reference

Barth, George Francis
  Your Aptitudes
  Lothrop, Lee & Shepard
Bolles, Richard Nelson
  What Color Is Your Parachute: A Practical Manual for Job and Career Changers
  Ten Speed Press
Brown, Denver
  The Entrepreneur's Guide
  Ballantine
Figler, Howard
  The Complete Job-Search Handbook
  Holt, Rinehart & Winston
Guide to Federal Career Literature
  Superintendent of Documents
  U.S. Government Printing Office
  Washington, DC 20402

Jablonski, Donna M.
  How to Find Information About Companies
  Washington Research
  918 16th Street NW
  Washington, DC 20006
Jawin, Ann J.
  A Woman's Guide to Career Preparation: Scholarships, Grants, and Loans
  Doubleday/Anchor Press
Lieberoff, Allen
  Climb Your Own Ladder
  Simon & Schuster
Martin, Phyllis
  Introduction to the Job Hunt Success Kit
  Center for Career Development
  11385 Landon Lane
  Cincinnati, Ohio 45246
Reed, Jane
  Résumés That Get Jobs
  Arco

Health and Fitness

During the past few decades, a great change has taken place in the attitude of the general public and professionals toward the maintenance of good health. A growing number of individuals are concerned about their own health care and that of members of their family. Doctors, as well as other medical and health professionals, are placing greater emphasis on *preventive medicine:* the use of appropriate measures to help prevent illness.

A century ago, human effort accounted for one-third of all the energy needed to run the factories, farms, businesses, and homes in the United States. However, in the late 20th century, human effort provides only one-half of one percent of the energy needed. We lead softer lives physically, but the pace of life has been stepped up to the point where unbridled stress has become a common problem. The harmful effects of stress contribute to our foremost health concerns: heart disease, stroke, cancer, and high blood pressure.

These degenerative diseases can be controlled and to some extent prevented by your habits and lifestyle. If these diseases were wiped out, the average current life expectancy of 74.5 years would be raised to 90.5 years. This statistical projection, made by the U.S. Public Health Service, is not unrealistic. It can be attained with changes in lifestyle, nutrition and diet, the handling of stress, weight control, and physical activity. Preventive medicine can not only add years to your life, it can put more life into those years.

In this chapter, you will find useful information on nutrition, stress, exercise, and other essentials that can provide preventive health care for your entire family. The highlighted *Health Care Alert* boxes, listing signals of major diseases, are intended to help you in recognizing early symptoms of disease and in reporting them in detail to your doctor. Because there are still so many myths and misconceptions about various health issues, we have included another feature, *Fact or Fiction,* which separates false notions from factual information.

Many such notions are obtained from articles appearing in popular magazines and from product advertising that is misleading in the presentation, or lacks factual information. The Food and Drug Administration advises everyone to review carefully all advertisements, especially those making claims for medical remedies. Bogus medical products include certain weight reduction pills or diets, arthritis and cancer cures, and panaceas for whatever ails you.

Answers to specific medical questions, or medical treatment, should be sought from a reputable doctor. While a majority of medical professionals are trustworthy, there are still many quack doctors who make promises of quick cures to unsuspecting victims of such serious diseases as cancer and arthritis. Choose your doctor carefully and know the drugs you use. For helpful suggestions, see You and Modern Medicine on page 78. See also the section on Health and Safety in volume 1.

Fatigue

Fatigue is a common complaint, one for which you yourself can often pinpoint the reason quite readily: a sleepless night, on-the-job frustration, frazzled nerves from trying to run a busy household.

There are many other less obvious, but equally plausible, explanations for a feeling of tiredness. All too often, people fail to see the connection between poor nutrition and fatigue. A lack of B vitamins or an inadequate intake of carbohydrates may interfere with the production of body energy. Too little activity may result in too little oxygen reaching the tissues.

Unless your tired feeling is related to a specific disease or medical problem, you can fight it with some simple changes in your daily routine. However, before you decide how to deal with fatigue, it is important for you to know what is causing it. Under any circumstances, if tiredness continues for more than a few weeks, you should check with a doctor. Such fatigue may be due to an illness that needs medical treatment.

Basically, fatigue may be placed into three major categories: physical (of the body), pathological (from a disease), psychological (of the mind).

Physical.
This fatigue may be brought on by strenuous activity such as jogging or heavy housework. It may also be caused by such factors as poor muscle tone or bad posture.

Pathological.
A tired feeling is often one symptom present in such conditions as iron-deficiency anemia, heart disease, cancer, arthritis, and diabetes; however, other and even more specific symptoms are also usually in evidence.

Certain prescription drugs (for example, tranquilizers and allergy remedies) may induce fatigue. If medication you are taking seems to rob you of vital energy, ask your doctor to prescribe an alternate drug. Excessive use of alcohol or caffeine, cigarette smoking, and poor eating habits are other factors that may result in fatigue.

Psychological.
Severe emotional stress, tension, anxiety, and other psychogenic factors are predominant in causing a feeling of constant tiredness. The person who feels trapped in a job situation or a marriage, for example, is bound to suffer from a persistent fatigue and lack of energy.

There are any number of ways in which you can fight that tired feeling. Take stock of your lifestyle, and see what you can do to take out the monotony, the frustration, or the stress in your day-to-day routines.

A working couple may need to share household responsibilities more equally; a "workaholic" may need to fit in some time for relaxation; and a weary housewife may need to hire a babysitter and join an exercise or art group. Make certain, too, that you include the essential nutrients in your daily diet; they are all needed for top performance by your body. Get enough exercise and rest, and try not to undertake too many demanding activities at one time.

Fact or fiction?

Exercise will make you feel more tired.
Fiction. Exercise releases tensions, improves sleep patterns, and promotes fitness. Those who exercise regularly get more done with less effort.

A sweet snack will *not* give you energy.
Fact. You will probably feel even more tired an hour or so after a sweet snack between meals. Have some fresh fruit instead.

Coffee or colas will give you energy.
Fiction. Caffeinated drinks may keep you awake, but too much can interfere with sleep and simply add to that tired feeling.

A light supper helps you sleep.
Fact. A high protein meal induces wakefulness; supper should be a low-protein, high-carbohydrate meal.

Energy-boosters to fight fatigue

- **Eat three well-balanced meals a day.** Include the four basic food groups (milk, meat, vegetables and fruits, breads and cereals).

- **Choose a conditioning exercise that you enjoy.** Aerobic exercises (increasing the heart rate and flow of oxygen to the blood) are especially beneficial. Jogging, bicycling, aerobic dancing, and brisk walking fall into this category.

- **Be certain to get as many hours of sleep as *you* need.** Different people require different amounts of sleep.

- **Plan activities according to your natural body rhythms.** If you have more energy in the morning, do your most demanding work at that time, and keep lesser tasks for another time of day.

- **Pace yourself, balancing out your work demands and social activities.** Take revitalizing breaks throughout the day.

- **Cut down, or avoid, the use of caffeine, alcoholic substances, and tobacco.**

- **Do not use over-the-counter drugs to pep you up;** do not become dependent upon sleeping pills (they have a bad effect upon the quality of sleep).

Stress

Stress is an essential part of our lives, and we would not want to be without it. Many types of stress provide the impetus that makes us excel at a chosen task, or at reaching a desired personal goal. Other kinds of stress, however, particularly that arising from the complexities of modern life, can have a disturbing effect upon those who do not know how to handle it.

Simply defined, stress is the total response of your body (physical, mental, and chemical) to events that irritate, frighten, endanger, confuse, or excite you. Some stress is of your own making, as when you enter college, embark on a new career, or get married. Other pressures are forced upon you, such as nerve-wracking job or home situations, or sudden injury or illness. Whatever the nature of the stress, the important thing is how you come to grips with it.

There is no one foolproof way of dealing with stress, but learning to identify the "stressor," or stressful event, can be the first step in turning your stress into positive energy. Stressful situations can help you to be receptive to changes and challenges, and to think and act clearly. On the other hand, if not handled right, stress can thwart clear thinking and decisive action and become a threat to good health. It can add to the likelihood of developing such high stress conditions as anxiety, chronic headaches, ulcers, arthritis, high blood pressure, asthma, and heart disorders.

Remember: Experiencing stress is normal. But sometimes stress can be a real problem. The trick is to turn it from a destructive to a positive force.

Body protection against stress.

The father of modern research on stress, Hans Selye, described stress in terms of a syndrome—the adaptive energy syndrome. Dr. Selye believed that each one of us is born with an individualized amount of adaptive energy and that we use up some of this supply every time we draw upon it.

There are three stages to the adaptive energy syndrome: 1) the alarm reaction, 2) the resistance stage, and 3) the exhaustion stage.

In the alarm reaction, the body is subjected to stress and it responds with a significant drop in its level of resistance. Adrenalin (the stress hormone) is pumped into the bloodstream, the pulse races, and breathing speeds up. The blood supply is promptly redirected from the internal organs to other parts of the body, particularly the muscles, where it is needed to respond during the emergency.

The resistance stage represents the continuing attempt of the body to develop defenses in combatting the stressor. During this period, the body works hard to raise its level of resistance well above normal. Gradually, the distinctive indicators of the alarm reaction disappear and the body seemingly returns to normal. However, if the body remains mobilized for an over-long period of time, the above normal level of resistance will not continue and will drop below normal. At this point, the exhaustion stage sets in, making the body increasingly vulnerable to disease related to stress, organic dysfunction, and even death.

Health and Fitness

STRESS

Signals of badly channeled stress

Many commonly experienced stress reactions signal potential stress damage to the body. These reactions may include heart palpitations or a pounding pulse, nagging headaches, irritability, and a feeling of tightness in the chest, neck, or shoulders. Other symptoms may be difficulty in falling asleep, back pain, upset stomach, loss of appetite, lack of concentration, and fatigue.

With increased stress, the stress reactions intensify and signal possible greater damage to the body. A person may find it impossible to unwind or enjoy physical relaxation, become impatient or depressed, do more drinking or smoking than usual, spend sleepless nights, or have frequent headaches and stomach disturbances.

Eventually, if negatively channeled stress continues for a long time, the accumulated effects can contribute to such serious ailments as asthma, heart disease, migraine headaches, high blood pressure, stomach ulcers, alcoholism, and drug addiction.

Executives should have hobbies sufficiently different from their office routines to help relieve the stresses of the work day. Gourmet cooking is relaxing and fun.

Some common stressors

Stressors mean different things to different people. What is high stress to one person may cause no reaction in another.

Day-to-day living: being stuck in traffic; standing on long supermarket or bank lines; a rough day at home or at work; marital discord.

Emotional: negative feelings such as anger, fear, or worry; positive feelings such as profound joy, love, or excitement.

Environmental: intense noise or air pollution; bright blinking lights; exposure to extremes of heat or cold.

Health: allergies or chemotherapy; serious illness; accidents or physical injury; excesses of drugs, alcohol, caffeine, or nicotine.

Life cycle: adolescent's struggle for independence and identity; pregnancy and motherhood; oldsters adjusting to physical limitations of aging.

Life milestones: start of formal education; graduating from school; getting married; embarking on a new career.

Social: overcrowding or unpleasant surroundings; unsuccessful interpersonal relationships at work or at home.

Some ways to beat stress

Basically, a good stress skill is anything that can help *you* deal with the stress you feel. There is little help to be found in the use of alcohol or drugs, or "stress-formula" products bought at the drugstore. If a situation becomes too difficult for you to handle, see a doctor or therapist.

- **Change your attitude.** Either decide to work out or get out of a stressful situation.
- **Give yourself a break.** Get away from yourself and your problems. Take 10-minute breaks during the day; get away for a day, a week, or longer if possible.
- **Eat sensibly.** Eat plenty of high-energy foods each day. Avoid, or greatly limit, the use of sugar, salt, coffee, and alcohol.
- **Exercise regularly.** Keep physically active: walk, run, swim, bicycle to keep trim and strong, and to relieve pent-up feelings.
- **Get moral support.** At times, talking over a problem with family or friends can be of help in deciding how best to deal with it.
- **Learn to relax.** Take up a hobby: art or music, vegetable gardening or flower arranging, handicrafts or photography.

Eye care

It has been estimated that no less than 50,000 Americans become blind each year. *This number could be reduced by one-half if people took proper measures to guard against accident and disease.* By taking simple common-sense precautions, you can help to preserve your sight.

Proper lighting

Reading or close work. A room should have at least 200 watts of general lighting or 100 watts of general lighting and 75 to 100 watts of direct lighting.

Glare. Arrange lighting so that it is not reflected by a book or other reading material. Make certain, too, that no shadows fall upon the reading material.

Television. To avoid eyestrain, a child should sit at least 6 feet from the TV set and at about the same level as the screen. Some other light in the room is necessary, but the TV set should be located where it cannot reflect light from a lamp. Video games are especially tiring for the eyes as children tend to stay closer to the screen and watch it more steadily than when watching TV. Home computers may cause similar problems.

Eye changes in children. Vision problems occur in 5 percent of all preschool children and 25 percent of all school-age youngsters. Ophthalmologists advise a first test when the child is six months, and again at three or four years of age.

Parents can help their children maintain healthy eyes by being alert to various changes in the eye, and by having their children's eyes examined periodically. **Appearance:** an eye that turns in, out, up, or down. Red-rimmed, encrusted, or swollen lids. Inflamed or watery eyes, recurring sties, an enlarged eye, an eye that appears cloudy, or a white spot in the pupil. **Behavior:** excessive rubbing of the eyes, shutting or covering of one eye. Tilting or thrusting the head forward. Difficulty in reading or doing close work. Blinking more than usual or irritability when doing close work. Inability to see distant objects clearly, squinting, or frowning. **Complaints:** itching, burning, or scratchy feeling. Inability to see well, dizziness, headaches, or nausea following close work. Blurred or double vision.

Health hints on eye care

Rubbing and poking 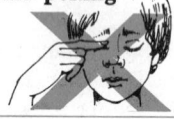	Children especially need to be reminded not to put their fingers into their eyes, particularly if their hands are soiled or if they have touched an open infectious cold sore or wound. Spread of a virus infection to the eye can ulcerate and scar the cornea, a primary cause of blindness.
Safety goggles	These should be worn to protect the eyes from accident or injury. For example, wear goggles when using electric tools such as saws and drills, lawn mowers, and hedge clippers; chemicals such as pesticidal or herbicidal sprays and household cleaning products; and in sports, particularly squash and racketball. An optician can help you choose proper goggles.
Sunglasses	Use sunglasses in reflected sunlight (on the water or the beach). Do not wear sunglasses indoors or for night driving. When selecting sunglasses, check the label to see that they filter out ultraviolet rays. Ask an optician for help, if necessary.
Drugs	At times, prescription drugs may cause complications. If you are taking a medication to control a condition such as high blood pressure, ask your doctor if the drug you are taking can affect the eye in any way.
Visits to the eye doctor	See your eye doctor (ophthalmologist) about any injury to the eye so that he or she can make sure that there is no damage. Check out any eye symptoms such as sudden pain or extreme sensitivity to light. After age 40, eyes should be checked for glaucoma (increased pressure in the eye) every two or three years. Begin checking after age 30 if there is a family history of glaucoma.

Ear care

Together with your eyes, your ears are the most vital sense organs. They are the lines of communication with the world around you.

Wax in the ear. Sometimes wax accumulates in the outer auditory canal; this can impede hearing. Do not remove the wax by using a hairpin, matchstick, or other sharp object. You may cause damage by scratching or perforating the eardrum. If you have a wax plug, an insect, or any foreign body in your ear, keep in mind the advice not to put anything in your ear smaller than your elbow. See your doctor for proper treatment.

Hearing problems. Some people are born deaf. Many others suffer hearing loss as a result of an accident or an infection. When the delicate inner ear structure has been damaged by meningitis or scarlet fever, "nerve deafness" occurs, and very little, if anything, can be done to relieve the condition.

Children who seem to be inattentive at school and who have learning disabilities are often afflicted with hearing problems. To avoid such difficulties, a child's hearing should be checked regularly. The value of good hearing can hardly be overestimated, and any change in hearing ability calls for prompt examination by an ear doctor.

Foot care

Foot problems afflict at least 75 percent of the American adult population. The most common problems are corns and bunions. Proper care of the feet will help keep feet strong and healthy. The most important protective measure is to keep your feet clean and dry. Take soothing foot baths as needed to relieve soreness. Allow toenails to grow to the tip of the toe; then cut straight across, not on a curve. Exercise your feet to keep them flexible and to strengthen the arches.

A large number of foot problems (flat feet, corns, bunions, calluses, and ingrown toenails) are caused by poorly fitted shoes. Select shoes with sensible heels and plenty of toe room. Always try on *both* shoes of a pair for size (one foot is usually larger than the other). Make certain that the back of the shoe fits snugly, and that the shoe has an inner or outer cushioning sole.

Simple care for minor foot problems

Bunions (hallux valgus)	Some people, such as diabetics, need special foot care. Any foot problems that are troublesome should be checked with your doctor or podiatrist (foot specialist). To avoid bunion pain, pressure on the prominent joint must be eliminated. Chiefly, this is a matter of wearing sensible shoes with plenty of toe room.
Calluses and corns (clavus)	After your bath or shower, gently rub your feet with a piece of pumice smeared with soap to remove excess calluses. Use of an emery board a few times a week will help reduce a hard corn. Medicated corn drops must be used very carefully so that there is no damage to good skin. The use of doughnut-shaped corn pads may also afford some relief.
Ingrown toenail (onyxia)	Try to wedge a small piece of cotton (soaked in castor oil) under the edge of the embedded nail. Apply a clean gauze pad to protect the nail from pressure. Soak the foot in water daily.
Athlete's foot (tinea pedis)	To help avoid this infection, keep feet clean and thoroughly dry, especially between the toes. Dusting with a medicated or other foot powder can help keep feet free of moisture.

Important nutrients

There are about 50 different nutrients that your body needs to stay healthy, including vitamins, minerals, carbohydrates, proteins, and fats. In this section, you will find out more about fiber, trace minerals, vitamins, and water.

On the whole, the American diet is thought to be relatively low in fiber. Most experts agree that the average person could probably double the amount of dietary fiber consumed, increasing intake to about 30 to 40 grams a day.

Mainly, there are two forms of minerals: macrominerals (needed in comparatively large amounts by the body) and microminerals (needed by the body in only very small amounts). There are some additional minerals, such as cobalt and nickel, which may take on greater nutritional importance as research determines the full extent of their usefulness in the human body.

Vitamins, organic substances derived from plants and animals, are required in the diet in very small amounts for normal health and growth. Although vitamins do not supply energy, they do help to trigger biochemical reactions that convert food into usable substances by the body.

In a listing of important nutrients, water is not always mentioned, yet the entire body mechanism needs water to function properly. Active people often fail to drink enough fluids; this may result in muscle fatigue, even upon moderate exertion. During strenuous exertion, as when running a marathon, an inadequate amount of water may be scarcely tolerable and even life-threatening.

Eat more high in fiber foods. To
get enough fiber in your diet, eat whole-grain breads and cereals, nuts, fruits, and vegetables. Some good

You should eat some foods high in fiber each day, but beware of high-fiber diets. Eating too much fiber may interfere with the body's absorption of essential nutrients. Regular servings of whole wheat bread, vegetables, and fruit should provide enough fiber for most people.

sources are found in dried figs and apricots, avocados, and apples with their skins, green beans and peas, broccoli, Brussels sprouts, turnips, lentils, black beans, whole-wheat breads, and crackers. Adding fiber to foods that contain fiber is of no value.

All fibers are not the same, which is why you must include some of the various available types in your daily diet. Most fibers prove beneficial in weight control, and whole grains may help tighten a flabby stomach. But pectins and gums are needed for the proper body use of fats, cholesterol, and carbohydrates. A *high-fiber* diet, compared with one that is *adequate* in fiber, can interfere with intestinal absorption, which may result in the loss of essential nutrients. You will probably get enough fiber in your diet by eating two servings of vegetables and two servings of whole grains (whole-wheat bread, for instance) each day.

How to add fiber to your diet

DO'S

- Make certain to eat a wide variety of foods in reasonable amounts.
- Be sure to drink adequate liquids when you eat fiber to avoid constipation.
- Look for the words "whole grain," "whole wheat," or "whole oats" on breads and cereals. Generally, coarse fiber is more effective than the same fiber ground fine.
- Include fresh fruits and raw vegetables in your diet. Their fiber content is more useful than peeled, cooked, or puréed fruits and vegetables.

DON'TS

- Do not depend upon fiber pills or tablets. You would have to take a whole bottle to get any benefit.
- Do not use fiber as a food additive. Change the kinds of foods you eat *gradually* to avoid a bloated feeling, diarrhea, or gas.
- Do not cut out all refined carbohydrates at one time. Replace them slowly with natural, whole-grain foods.
- Do not concentrate on one or another type of fiber; consider them all.

Trace minerals. Mineral elements account for only about four percent of total body weight. However, the body holds enough iron to make a good size nail, and enough sodium to fill a small salt shaker.

More needs to be learned about the exact daily requirements of trace minerals, but a diet with a sufficient amount of natural foods should be adequate to maintain good health.

Food sources and body functions

Trace mineral	Chief food sources	Chief body functions
Chromium	Liver, beef, dried beans, cheese, whole-grain breads and cereals, peanuts, brewer's yeast, molasses, and beets.	Aids the body, together with insulin, in deriving energy from glucose (blood sugar). Plays an important role in the synthesis of fatty acids and cholesterol in the liver.
Copper	Oysters, fish, nuts, dried peas, beans, beef and pork liver, organ meats, eggs, spinach, asparagus, and corn-oil margarine.	Aids in the manufacture of red blood cells, and helps the body store iron. A component of several respiratory enzymes, copper is also part of the enzyme that helps make melanin (the pigment in the skin).
Fluorine (Fluoride)	Fish, tea, most animal foods, fluoridated water, and foods grown with or cooked in fluoridated water.	Helps form strong teeth and resistance to decay. Aids in maintenance of bone strength.
Iodine	Seafood, saltwater fish, seaweed, sea salt, and iodized salt.	A component of thyroid hormones that control the body's metabolism. Aids in the development and functioning of the thyroid gland, and in the prevention of goiter.
Iron	Liver (especially pork, followed by calf, beef, and chicken), kidneys, red meat, egg yolks, green leafy vegetables, dried raisins, apricots, prunes, dried beans, peas, potatoes, blackstrap molasses; enriched, whole-grain cereals.	Helps form red blood cells and myoglobin in muscles that supply oxygen in cells. Found in enzyme systems, including one that works to produce energy in the body.
Manganese	Nuts, whole grains, fruits, vegetables, tea, instant coffee, and cocoa powder.	Aids in proper function of the nervous system, normal bone structure, and reproduction. Extremely important in many vital enzyme systems in the body. Needed for utilization of iron.
Molybdenum	Legumes, cereal grains, liver, kidney, some dark green vegetables.	Required by three important enzymes. May aid in prevention of tooth decay. Associated with carbohydrate metabolism.
Selenium	Seafood, whole-grain cereals, meat, egg yolks, chicken, and milk.	Antioxidant, preventing breakdown of fats and other body chemicals. Interacts with Vitamin E in protecting cell membranes.
Zinc	Beef, liver, eggs, poultry, seafood, especially oysters, peas, carrots, whole grains, and pure maple syrup.	A component of as many as 100 enzymes in the body. Involved in normal wound healing. Needed for growth and development.

Know your vitamins. There are 13 compounds considered to be vitamins. Four—A, D, E, and K—are soluble in fat. The eight B vitamins and C are soluble in water. The fat-soluble vitamins, stored in body fat, are not readily excreted and therefore do not need to be replaced as often as the water-soluble

How vitamins can keep you healthy

Vitamin	Food sources	How they help you
Vitamin A Retinol (discovered 1913)	Yellow, orange, and dark green vegetables, liver, cheese, milk, eggs, and butter.	Known as the growth vitamin, Vitamin A is essential in maintaining healthy skin, hair, mucous membranes, and bone. It provides visual pigments that allow you to see.
Vitamin B$_1$ Thiamin (discovered 1936)	Whole-wheat grains, wheat germ, liver and kidney, pork, peas, beans, peanuts, oranges, and many other fruits and vegetables.	All B vitamins play a similar role in the body: they help enzymes to do their job. B$_1$ acts as a cofactor for 24 enzymes, aiding cells to utilize carbohydrates. It assists in the proper functioning of the nervous system and digestive tract.
Vitamin B$_2$ Riboflavin (discovered 1935)	Liver, kidney, lamb, beef, veal, eggs, whole-wheat products, yeast, asparagus, beets, peas, and dark green vegetables.	A cofactor in enzymes helping cells to use carbohydrates, proteins, and fats, and producing energy. Promotes growth, healthy skin, and mucous membranes.
Vitamin B$_3$ Niacin Nicotinamide Nicotinic acid (discovered 1867)	Lean meat, fish, liver, yeast, eggs, whole-grain breads and cereals, peas, beans, and nuts.	An essential component of enzymes that contribute to the production of energy in cells. Also assists in the breakdown of fats.
Vitamin B$_6$ Pyridoxine Pyridoxal (discovered 1934)	Poultry, fish, liver, whole grains, cereals, breads, tomatoes, yellow corn, spinach, green beans, bananas, and yogurt.	An essential activator of many enzymes, pyridoxine aids in breaking down protein, carbohydrates, and fat, and in forming hormones such as adrenalin and insulin. It also helps to regenerate red blood cells and produce antibodies.
Folic acid Folicin (discovered 1946)	Liver, kidneys, green leafy vegetables, and dried legumes.	Necessary for formation of red and white cells. Aids in protein metabolism and in creating some components of the DNA molecule.
Vitamin C Ascorbic acid (discovered 1919)	Abundant in most fruits and vegetables, especially citrus fruits, tomatoes, potatoes, green peppers, and dark green vegetables.	Enhances the activity of certain enzymes. Aids body use of iron and blood clotting as needed. Helps formation of teeth, gums, and bones; aids in healing of bone fractures and wounds.
Vitamin D Calciferol (discovered 1925)	Egg yolks, butter, fortified milk, liver, fish liver oils, tuna, salmon, herring, sardines, and oysters.	Known as the "sunshine vitamin." Aids in the normal growth and development of bones and teeth. Important in the intestinal absorption of calcium and phosphorus. Affords antirachitic activity.
Vitamin E Alpha tocopherol (discovered 1936)	Lettuce and other leafy green vegetables, seed oils, whole grains, dried beans, and liver.	Helps in the production of red blood cells and in the strengthening of muscles and other tissues. An antioxidant, it protects Vitamin A and fats from reacting with oxygen.

Health and Fitness

vitamins. These must be included in your daily diet in adequate amounts. On the whole, vitamins can be used and reused by the body, which explains why you need only small amounts to replace those lost in the urine or feces. Studying this table will help you choose the right foods for a balanced diet.

Research indications

In animal tests, some researchers found that a lack of Vitamin A can increase the toxicity of aflatoxin (a natural poison produced by a fungus living in peanuts and grains), and with it the chance of getting cancer of the colon. It is also becoming more evident that Vitamin A may play an important part in preventing epithelial cancers, such as are produced by smoking cigarettes.

Vitamin B_1 deficiency is implicated in all stages of alcoholism; a diet rich in B_1 will help prevent polyneuritis in alcoholics. There has been some success in treating children suffering repeated episodes of fever and gland swellings (unresponsive to conventional therapy) with B_1 supplementation.

Vitamin B_2 helps the body obtain energy from food. One study has shown that women who exercise vigorously and regularly may need almost twice as much riboflavin as those who are less active. This may be owed to the part Vitamin B_2 has in producing energy.

Niacin has been used effectively to lower high cholesterol levels associated with familial hypercholesterolemia, which cannot be controlled by diet alone and which quintuples the risk of heart disease.

In test animals, a diet lacking pyridoxine and other B vitamins, and with exposure to aflatoxin, increased the likelihood of cancer of the liver. Pyridoxine has been used medically to treat the toxic effects of carbon disulfide. A diet rich in pyridoxine may help prevent cirrhosis in alcoholics.

Preliminary British studies with pregnant women indicate that a large dose (4 mg daily) of this vitamin may help prevent such congenital defects as spina bifida (a defect in the wall of the spinal canal) and encephalocele (a defect involving the brain). An American study indicates that a megadose (10 mg daily) may lower the risk of cervical cancer in women on the pill who show cervical cell abnormalities.

In animal studies, Vitamin C has shown a possible activity against gum disease. Research shows that large doses of Vitamin C may be able to help the body detoxify such poisonous substances as malathion, lead, and cancer-causing nitrosamines.

Rickets and osteomalacia due to a lack of Vitamin D can be effectively treated with a form of Vitamin D known as 25-hydroxy-cholecalciferol. It has been found that Vitamin D breaks down in the body into compounds that may act as hormones. A synthetic compound, 1-25 Vitamin D, has been approved for use as an agent to promote bone growth.

Animal tests have shown that Vitamin E can lessen the damage that two air pollutants, ozone and nitrogen dioxide, can have on the lungs. Vitamin E, together with Vitamin C and zinc, may reduce toxicity to cadmium. Reportedly, Vitamin E may relieve chronic cystic mastitis in many cases; also, nighttime leg cramps.

Vitamin C is a cure for the common cold.
Fiction. To date, there is no accepted medical evidence to support such a claim. Excessive doses, many times higher than the recommended 30 to 60 milligrams a day, may cause health problems in some people, such as the formation of kidney or bladder stones.

Vitamin D should be used carefully.
Fact. Too high doses of Vitamin D can result in nausea, loss of appetite, excessive thirst, and excessive urination. The heart, lungs, kidneys, and joints may develop calcium deposits, while the bones may become fragile.

Laxatives can cause vitamin deficiencies.
Fact. For example, the frequent use of mineral oil can rob your body of vitamins A, D, and K. Vitamin deficiencies due to overuse of laxatives make the user more susceptible to many toxic substances and to carcinogens.

There is no danger in taking large amounts of Vitamin A.
Fiction. A form of Vitamin A, retinol, taken in very high doses, can be quite toxic. If too much is taken, retinol can cause various conditions, including headaches, fatigue, blurred vision, intestinal disturbances, liver and kidney damage, hair loss, and brain damage.

OSTEOPOROSIS

Signs of brittle bones

In the United States, women over 45 suffer a million fractures each year. Most are associated with a condition in which there is a degenerative thinning of the bones.

Detection in the early stages is difficult. X-rays, for example, will not show bone loss until there is a loss of 30 to 50 percent. There are a few simple signs that may alert a person to the presence of osteoporosis.

Decrease in height may give the earliest detectable sign, and it is one that often goes unnoticed. It is suggested that people at high risk of osteoporosis (such as menopausal women, alcoholics, and the elderly) keep a record of their height and check it every six to twelve months. Any height loss should be reported to a doctor.

Another sign is tooth loss brought on by periodontal (gum) disease. Gum inflammation, attributed to the formation of plaque on teeth, can also be due to bone degeneration. Regular visits to the dentist will prevent the development of gum disease.

To help avoid brittle bones, women over 35 should get an adequate amount of calcium, magnesium, and vitamins C and D in their diet. Regular exercise, such as walking and stretching, is most important, as it improves calcium absorption and stimulates bone formation. Excessive intake of coffee and alcohol, and smoking, add to bone loss and should be avoided.

Water is a vital nutrient.
Your body is about two-thirds water, and contains about 40 to 50 quarts of water. In women, water content averages 55 to 65 percent, while it is around 65 to 75 percent in men.

Every living body cell needs water to perform its vital function. Water aids in the digestion and absorption of nutrients, such as vitamins. It transports oxygen to the cells and removes both liquid and solid wastes. It helps the body maintain a normal temperature, and lubricates the joints. It provides a protective cushion for the tissues, and keeps skin from drying out.

How much water should you drink? Most people drink far less water than the six to eight 8-ounce glasses considered nutritionally adequate even though the fluid requirement includes fruit juices, soft drinks, milk, coffee, and tea as well as plain water. Even greater amounts of liquid are needed during periods of increased water loss in hot weather, strenuous exercise, and illness accompanied by fever. Infants and child-bearing women also require extra fluids.

Water forms the larger part of most solid foods. Fruits and vegetables are about 80 percent water, green beans 89 percent, and lettuce 95 percent. Even milk is 87 percent water, and fish foods around 75 percent. Meat is half water, while bread is about one-third water by weight.

The body excretes about 2 quarts of water a day, most of it as urine. Water may also be lost in sizeable amounts through the skin by sweating, through the lungs in the process of breathing, and upon extreme exertion in strenuous exercise.

Good nutrition

Eating less meat and other high cholesterol foods will reduce deaths caused by heart disease, from which 555,000 die each year.

Most Americans eat too much. There is too much fat, refined sugar, and salt in our diets. On the whole, our diets consist of about 50 percent nonessential foods. You can, however, easily improve your eating habits for the better. Start by cutting down on fats and using polyunsaturated for saturated fats. Eat more lean meats and poultry, and fewer dairy products. Instead of overloading your diet with foods high in sugar, substitute fresh fruits and vegetables. Use low-calorie for high-calorie foods whenever possible. Limit your salt intake, using herbs to flavor food.

Types of fats

Saturated	butter	meat
Avoid use of	cheese	milk chocolate
(tend to raise	coconut,	palm oil
blood cholesterol)	coconut oil	vegetable
	egg yolks	shortening
	lard	whole milk
Monounsaturated	avocados	peanuts
Use occasionally	cashews	peanut butter
(have no effect on	olives,	peanut oil
blood cholesterol)	olive oil	
Polyunsaturated	almonds	pecans
Good to use	corn oil	safflower oil
(tend to lower	cottonseed oil	salad dressing
blood cholesterol)	filberts	soybean oil
	fish	sunflower oil
	margarine	walnuts

Heart attacks. The average American, eating a diet high in saturated fats and cholesterol, is at greater risk of having a heart attack than other populations consuming diets low in fat and cholesterol. In the opinion of the American Heart Association, reduction of fat intake is one of the most important steps a person can take to lower the risk of heart disease. Most people obtain their total daily calories from fat. It is recommended that fat intake be cut to 30 percent, and that fats in the diet be equally divided among saturated, polyunsaturated, and monounsaturated fats.

Cancer.

Faulty diets, according to a report from the National Academy of Sciences, account for 30 to 40 percent of all cancers in men and as high as 60 percent in women. The cancers most exclusively linked to diet are cancers of the stomach, colon, breast, and, to a lesser extent, the lung and prostate.

Eat more fruits, vegetables, fiber. Fresh dark green, orange, and yellow vegetables (broccoli, carrots, and others) are rich in a substance called beta-carotene, which the body converts into Vitamin A. Cabbage-family vegetables (Brussels sprouts, cabbages, and others) contain several chemicals that have been found to inhibit cancer in animals. Their plentiful use is associated with a reduced risk of certain cancers, especially of the colon.

Get plenty of foods rich in Vitamin C, especially citrus and red fruits and dark green vegetables. Laboratory studies have shown that Vitamin C stops the formation of certain chemicals causing cancer. In studies of persons at high risk of cancer, Vitamin C reduced the incidence of stomach or esophageal cancer.

When dietary fiber (whole grains, fresh fruits, and vegetables) intake amounts to 20 to 40 grams a day, there is possible protection against colon and rectal cancer.

Eat less fats, smoked foods. Avoid or limit intake of dietary fats. Both saturated (for example, animal fats, butter fat, palm oil, coconut oil) and unsaturated fats (mostly vegetable oils) have been linked with increased cancer, in particular, of the breast and colon. A 25 percent reduction in *all* dietary fats is recommended.

Fact or fiction?

Cow's milk is a perfect food.
Fiction. Cow's milk may be a relatively good food for young children, but most infants fare better on mother's milk. Milk is a good food but does not contain enough of some important nutrients, especially iron, copper, and Vitamin C.

Enriched breads are nutritious.
Fact. Important vitamins and minerals (thiamin, riboflavin, niacin, and iron) are partially removed in the milling of flour. By enrichment, these substances are replaced to a level equivalent to those in whole-wheat flour or bread.

Vegetarians often develop severe nutritional deficiencies.
Fact. Strict vegetarians do not get enough Vitamin D or Vitamin B_{12} (the only B vitamin not found in any vegetable). For good sources of these vitamins, as well as calcium and protein, we must depend upon foods of animal origin.

Eating out . . . healthily and enjoyably

Be in control of your diet, no matter where you eat or what the occasion.

- **Ask that dishes be prepared as you wish:** with reduced salt or no salt at all; with margarine instead of butter; with entrees broiled, roasted, or baked.
- **Avoid rich sauces,** or ask that sauces be served on the side. Spoon off as much sauce as you can when you are served a precooked dish with a rich sauce. Also, pass up such salads as shrimp and tuna.
- **Trim off all fat and skin** from served meats.
- **If high sodium seasonings,** such as soy sauce, monosodium glutamate (MSG), and salt are used, ask that they be used sparingly, or not at all.
- **Snack on nonfattening foods** at a buffet party and leave the patés, dips, smoked fish, and the like.

Smoked, salt-cured, or pickled foods should be used sparingly. In smoking and curing, foods are exposed to certain compounds, such as the nitrosamines. These compounds cause cancer in animals and are suspect in humans.

The consumption of alcohol should be limited to one or two drinks a day, or eliminated. More than a few drinks a day has been linked to cancer of the mouth, larynx, esophagus, and respiratory tract, and beer drinking has been linked to cancer of the colon and rectum. The risk is increased with cigarette smoking.

HEALTH CARE ALERT

CANCER

Seven signals

1. Change in bowel or bladder habits.
2. A sore that does not heal.
3. Unusual bleeding or discharge.
4. Thickening or lump in the breast or any other part of the body.
5. Indigestion or difficulty in swallowing.
6. Obvious change in wart or mole.
7. Nagging cough or hoarseness.

If you have any of these signals, it does not necessarily mean that you have cancer. It does mean that something is wrong in your body, and you need to check with your doctor.

Cigarette smoking is a major cause of lung cancer. For more than a decade, the number of women smokers has been increasing steadily. Today, lung cancer will kill more women than breast cancer.

Fast foods. Probably nothing has changed the eating habits of millions of Americans more than the fast-food eateries found nearly everywhere and the introduction of convenience foods, which are steadily increasing in number and variety.

Many of these foods are labeled junk foods. They provide few or no nutrients other than sugar calories. These are rightly called empty calories because they are mostly carbohydrate and contain no proteins, minerals, or vitamins. Most popular soft drinks, pastries, candies, and ice creams contain as much as 100 percent of sugar calories.

While fast foods do not fall into the junk food category, they supply either too little or too much of one or more essential nutrients. Even pizza, which contains more protein and less fat than most other fast foods, has a rather high calorie and salt content. *The average American consumes nearly 10 grams of salt a day, which is more than three times the recommended daily allowance.* This excessive use of salt has led health authorities to suggest that salt intake be restricted to 5 grams a day.

It pays to read food labels. You can readily check packaged foods for their sugar, sodium, or fat content by reading the labels. In general, the ingredient with the highest amount of a given substance is listed first, followed by others in descending order of content.

Familiarize yourself with other names for sugar, sodium, or fat content in packaged foods. Sugar may be listed as sucrose, glucose, zylose, fructose, mannose, and disaccharides or monosaccharides. Sodium is the main ingredient in monosodium glutamate (MSG), phosphates, nitrites, and baking soda as well as in table salt. Some manufacturers give the milligram content of sodium per serving. A product is considered high in sodium if it contains more than 350 to 500 milligrams per serving.

In general, the term "shortening," either animal or vegetable, implies that the fat is saturated, and the term "liquid vegetable oil" suggests a polyunsaturated fat. If the label lists "vegetable oil" as a main ingredient but does not specify the kind, or if it lists coconut or palm oil (high in saturated fat), it is best to avoid use of the product.

Food values of fast foods

Fast food	Calories	Protein (grams)	Carbohydrates (grams)	Fats (grams)	Sodium (mg)
Burger King Hamburger	260	14	28	10	500
Burger King French Fries (medium)	400	5	43	20	240
Burger King Vanilla Shake (medium)	310	9	53	7	230
Burger King Big Fish Sandwich	720	25	59	43	1090
Burger King Whopper	630	27	45	39	850
Dairy Queen Banana Split	610	9	93	11	250
Dairy Queen Cheese Dog	330	12	24	21	920
Dairy Queen Onion Rings	240	4	29	12	135
Kentucky Fried Chicken Extra Tasty Crispy Chicken (breast)	470	31	25	28	930
Kentucky Fried Chicken Original Recipe (breast)	360	33	12	20	870
Long John Silver's Fish (2 pieces)	318	19	19	19	N.A.*
McDonald's Apple Pie	290	3	37	15	220
McDonald's Big Mac	510	25	46	26	930
McDonald's Chocolate Shake (small)	350	13	62	6	240
McDonald's Egg McMuffin	290	17	27	13	730
McDonald's Filet-o-Fish	360	14	41	16	710
Pizza Hut Chunky Meat Pizza (hand tossed crust, 1 medium slice)	325	17	28	16	970
Pizza Hut Personal Pan Pizza (pepperoni)	675	29	76	30	1335
Taco Bell Taco	180	10	N.A.*	11	276
Arthur Treacher's Coleslaw	123	1	11	8	266
Arthur Treacher's Fish Sandwich	440	16	39	24	836

Source: Data supplied by Burger King Corporation; International Dairy Queen, Inc.; KFC Corporation; McDonalds' Corporation; Pizza Hut, Inc.; Taco Bell Corporation. Other companies' data supplied by the companies to the Senate Select Committee on Nutrition and Human Needs.
*N.A.—not available.

Watch your weight

As a nation we are becoming more obese, with the typical American adult male averaging 20 to 30 pounds of excess weight, and the typical female carrying 15 to 30 extra pounds. Overweight people are more likely to run the risk of high blood pressure, diabetes, high blood cholesterol, and heart disease.

To maintain ideal weight, it is necessary to keep your body energy needs in balance. Take in *more* energy than is needed and your body will store it as excess fat and you will gain weight. Take in *less* energy than is used up, and your body will withdraw some from the stored fat and you will lose weight. For the average person, it takes about 3500 extra calories to produce a pound of fat and, conversely, about 3500 fewer calories to use up a pound of stored fat. The easiest way to keep your weight constant is to lose any weight gain promptly, even if it is only 1 pound.

Ideal body weight may be determined by checking a table of suggested body weights. Such tables give no absolute answers on what constitutes ideal weight, but they can be helpful in determining your weight range.

Cut calories, not nutrients. There are almost as many diet plans as there are dieters. They embrace a variety of weight-loss theories: crash diets, liquid protein diets, cleansing and no-food diets, fruit juice, vegetable, or meat diets, high-fat and low-carbohydrate diets, low-fat and high-carbohydrate diets, to mention a few. To this list must be added the numerous reducing drugs that can be bought at the drugstore.

Many diet plans are nutritionally unbalanced. Most are disappointing as they seldom result in permanent weight loss. The repeated gaining, losing, and regaining of weight is considered by some health professionals to have a more damaging effect upon health than being consistently and moderately overweight. In sensible weight loss, you reduce your calorie intake without depriving your body of the nutrients needed for good health.

In the long run, the only diet that can do you real good is one that changes your bad eating habits for the better. The need is not for a 7-, or 10- or 21-day reducing plan, but a lifetime diet that includes all the

---

Metropolitan Life height and weight tables

Compared with figures as revised in 1959, this latest update on height and weight tables issued by the Metropolitan Life Insurance Company shows that adults can now weigh more than previously. There is an average increase in weight of 13 pounds for short men and 10 pounds for short women; 7 pounds for men of medium height, and 3 pounds for women of medium height; and 2 pounds for tall men, and 3 pounds for tall women. These tables apply to people from ages 25 to 59. The weight is stated in pounds, according to body frame size and the wearing of indoor clothing (5 pounds for men and 3 pounds for women in shoes with 1-inch heels).

Men Height	Small frame	Medium frame	Large frame	Women Height	Small frame	Medium frame	Large frame
5' 2"	128–134	131–141	138–150	4' 10"	102–111	109–121	118–131
5' 3"	130–136	133–143	140–153	4' 11"	103–113	111–123	120–134
5' 4"	132–138	135–145	142–156	5' 0"	104–115	113–126	122–137
5' 5"	134–140	137–148	144–160	5' 1"	106–118	115–129	125–140
5' 6"	136–142	139–151	146–164	5' 2"	108–121	118–132	128–143
5' 7"	138–145	142–154	149–168	5' 3"	111–124	121–135	131–147
5' 8"	140–148	145–157	152–172	5' 4"	114–127	124–138	134–151
5' 9"	142–151	148–160	155–176	5' 5"	117–130	127–141	137–155
5' 10"	144–154	151–163	158–180	5' 6"	120–133	130–144	140–159
5' 11"	146–157	154–166	161–184	5' 7"	123–136	133–147	143–163
6' 0"	149–160	157–170	164–188	5' 8"	126–139	136–150	146–167
6' 1"	152–164	160–174	168–192	5' 9"	129–142	139–153	149–170
6' 2"	155–168	164–178	172–197	5' 10"	132–145	142–156	152–173
6' 3"	158–172	167–182	176–202	5' 11"	135–148	145–159	155–176
6' 4"	162–176	171–187	181–207	6' 0"	138–151	148–162	158–179

© 1983 Metropolitan Life Insurance Company/Source of basic data 1979 Build Study, Society of Actuaries and Association of Life Insurance Medical Directors of America, 1980.

essential nutrients obtained from a variety of foods. It is never too late to correct faulty eating habits, and by doing so you can help children learn good eating habits as they grow up.

To gain weight, add calories.

To those who are forever fighting the battle of the midriff bulge, putting on extra pounds may seem to be an easy task. Such, however, is not always the case. Some people are naturally thin because of their inherited body build; others cannot put on weight no matter how much food rich in calories they consume. In some cases, medical problems such as hyperthyroidism or diabetes must be corrected before considering a program to gain weight.

If you are underweight, it may be due to faulty eating habits, or just eating too little food. You may not have a good appetite, which in itself may signal an underlying illness, and you may also suffer from poor digestion and absorption of food. A physical checkup may be needed to determine the cause of being underweight, or having continued weight loss, before deciding on the measures necessary to assure weight gain.

In general, a person who desires to gain weight needs to eat more nutritious food and to increase the total number of calories in the daily diet. Proper living habits are important, too: eat regular meals, take mild exercise, get sufficient sleep, and avoid tension.

Fact or fiction?

You can shed pounds by skipping breakfast. *Fiction.* Breakfast should be your first meal of the day, providing essential nutrients to assure body function at a high level of energy. Without breakfast, you may be tempted to snack between meals, or eat too much at the next meal.

The more exercise, the bigger the appetite. *Fiction.* You will not only use up calories with regular moderate exercise, but you will keep physically fit. In many cases, inactivity is a main reason for obesity in children as well as adults.

You can lose ten pounds in ten days. *Fact.* This is possible, but it will probably be mostly a water loss, which will be quickly replaced once you go off the crash diet. A sound weight loss program recommends a slow, sure loss of 1 or 2 pounds a week.

With determination, everyone can reduce. *Fact.* People who claim they cannot lose weight are usually themselves at fault. Many persons do not eat to appease hunger, but to satisfy a craving. Hunger signals the body's need for food; appetite, based on remembered eating pleasures, is a desire for certain types of food.

Food for thought

If you eat . . .	you add on . . .	to lose, you must walk
2 strips of bacon	100 calories	20 minutes
10 potato chips	100 calories	20 minutes
1 doughnut	150 calories	29 minutes
1 piece cake	358 calories	68 minutes
1 slice apple pie	375 calories	73 minutes
1 malted milk shake	500 calories	97 minutes

Substitute . . . burn off more calories. By substituting one ingredient for another in the preparation of food, and eating one type of food for another, you can reduce your total calorie intake. An ounce of pure protein or carbohydrate will produce 110 calories; an ounce of fat will supply 250 calories. These figures may help you calculate your own calorie intake from a meal or dietary plan.

Food preparation		Food consumption		Saved
Instead of . . .	Substitute	Instead of . . .	Substitute . . .	calories
whole milk	skim milk	2 tbsp. regular mayonnaise	2 tbsp. diet mayonnaise	about 150
cream	evaporated milk	1 cup ice cream	1 cup ice milk	about 90
sour cream	yogurt	1 regular hamburger	1 lean hamburger	about 76
cream cheese	low-fat cottage cheese	1 serving French fries	1 baked potato	about 200
whole milk cheese	skim-milk or low-fat cheese	1 can (6½ oz.) tuna, oil-packed, drained	1 can (6½ oz.) tuna water-packed, drained	about 100

Get back into shape

Moderate and regular exercise, which is good for you at any time of life, is doubly important when losing weight. It can help your body burn up unwanted fat faster while firming up muscles and flattening out bulges. Physical activity can also keep your body flexible, and help maintain muscle tone, stimulate body functions, especially the circulatory and respiratory systems, and help relieve tension.

To keep physically fit, you need not take up strenuous exercise or a demanding sport. If you make a conscious effort, you can even find plenty of opportunity to stretch and bend while you are doing some everyday task—dusting, sweeping, making the beds, weeding the garden, doing small repair jobs around the house.

Choose an exercise that you enjoy, and one suited to your physical condition, body build, age, and lifestyle. While you will benefit little from doing exercise in a lax manner, you should not overexercise to the point of physical pain or injury.

Exercise works. Walking is an excellent
form of exercise, considered by health authorities to be the best overall nonstrenuous activity for the heart and legs. All you need is a comfortable pair of walking shoes. *A brisk 20- to 30-minute walk each day can help you take weight off and keep it off.*

Swimming, jogging, or bicycling are exercises that develop a strong heart, while calisthenics and gymnastics improve strength, agility, and muscle tone. Whatever your choice of activity, it is important to remember that it will only be beneficial and improve your state of health if you stick with it.

Energy expenditures

This table gives approximate energy expenditures by a 150-pound person in various activities.

Activity	Calories per hour
Bicycling, 5½ mph	210
Bicycling, 13 mph	660
Bowling	270
Domestic work	180
Driving an automobile	120
Gardening	220
Golf	250
Lawn mowing (power mower)	250
Lying down or sleeping	80
Roller skating	350
Running, 10 mph	900
Sitting	100
Skiing, 10 mph	600
Square dancing	350
Squash and handball	600
Standing	140
Swimming, ¼ mph	300
Tennis	420
Volleyball	350
Walking, 2½ mph	210
Walking, 3¾ mph	300
Wood chopping or sawing	400

Source: Based on material prepared by Robert E. Johnson, M.D., Ph.D., and colleagues, University of Illinois.

HEALTH CARE ALERT

ARTHRITIS

There are many forms of arthritis but, in general, sufferers are afflicted with either osteoarthritis or rheumatoid arthritis. Osteoarthritis takes a decade or longer to develop, so most sufferers are at least middle-aged. In this condition, the protective cartilage normally cushioning a joint begins to break down, causing pain and stiffness, and inflammation in some cases.

Rheumatoid arthritis (RA), unlike osteoarthritis, strikes children and young adults as well as older adults. In this arthritic disorder, the body's immune system (defense network) goes haywire and turns on the body itself. There is pain and recurrent inflammation. RA can be severely crippling.

Do not ignore these signals.
Medical care in the early stages of arthritis can often lessen the permanent damage to diseased joints. If you experience any of the symptoms listed below for more than two weeks, check with your physician.
- Swelling in one or more joints.
- Recurring pain or tenderness in any body joint.
- Inability to move a joint properly, or to perform normal activities.
- Obvious redness and warmth in one of the joints.
- Persistent early morning pain and stiffness in joints. Unexplained weight loss, fever, weakness, or fatigue combined with joint pain.

Home medical testing

Medical tests help to determine the cause of pain or disease, and in themselves become meaningful only after your physician has studied them in the light of your complete medical history. There are any number of medical tests that can be performed at home. Some require nothing more than close observation, while others, such as various urine tests, require certain medical supplies (which can be purchased at a local pharmacy), and a knowledge of how the tests should be performed. Still others, such as taking your blood pressure, call for the purchase of special equipment and must be carefully performed to be useful. Before buying medical supplies or equipment, it is advisable to check with your doctor to see if there is any drawback to home testing and to obtain detailed instructions on performing a test correctly.

Home medical testing should not be regarded as a means of making a self-diagnosis, or instituting self-treatment. Any body signals, such as persistent pain, unexplained bleeding, skin or other growths, difficulties in breathing, seeing, or hearing, or uncoordinated movements, should be promptly brought to the attention of your physician.

The tests included in this discussion do not call for the purchase of special supplies or equipment. They are intended to help you learn more about your own or your family's health, and to communicate more effectively with your doctor if a medical problem arises.

Two important tests

Taking your pulse. Pulse measurements generally consist of rate, rhythm, and character. The most frequently used location is the wrist. With the palm up, place two or three fingers of the examining hand on the thumb side of the wrist being examined. Do *not* use the thumb, and be careful not to apply too much pressure.

Rest for ten minutes before taking your pulse, and then take it in a sitting position. To begin with, you may want to count the pulse beats for a full minute, timing them by the second hand of a watch. As you become more experienced, you can shorten the time to half a minute, and then 15 seconds, multiplying the result by four. Normal pulse rates may range from 60 to 70 beats per minute for men and from 70 to 80 beats per minute for women. Wide variations in pulse rate, or a weak or irregular pulse, should be checked out with your doctor. Pulse rhythm may be observed at the

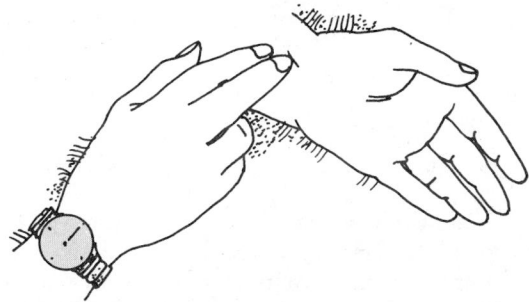

same time that the pulse rate is being counted. It should be regular without pauses; that is, there should be no skipped beats or extra beats between normal beats. Pulse character is determined by the smoothness of the beat: no beat should be any stronger or weaker than any of the others.

Testing your sense of smell. This type of test is more useful than it may seem at first. There are many people who live in danger of serious harm because they are unable to detect the odor that accompanies spoiled or contaminated foods, smoke from fire, escaping gas from a heating apparatus, and lethal chemical fumes.

Gather together at least three items with familiar odors, such as an onion or garlic, milk chocolate, turpentine, fresh flowers with a distinctive scent (roses, lilacs), and a burning paper match, or burning paper in an ashtray. With the exception of the burning match and paper, the items are best tested by being enclosed in a tightly closed container, and then opened for a few seconds when the test is being made.

Before starting, make certain that your nasal passages are clear. Then, begin the test by closing one nostril (apply pressure to it with a finger). Close your eyes, and smell the odor being tested through the open nostril; repeat with the other nostril. Both sides of the nose should be able to smell the tested odors with equal efficiency.

Glossary

fructose sources

For definitions of additional medical terms, see Glossary on page 96.

angina pectoris. Painful oppression about the heart which is usually severe and radiates from the heart to the shoulder and down the left arm.

antioxidant. An agent inhibiting oxidation and thereby preventing oils or fats from becoming rancid through the process of oxidation.

aromatic. The series of carbon compounds in which the carbon atoms form closed rings, such as benzene.

arthritis. An inflammatory condition of the joints in which there is usually pain and changes in structure.

asthma. A term generally used to mean bronchial asthma, which is a condition of the lungs having widespread narrowing of the airways.

calorie. The energy value of foods, calculated by the amount of heat needed to raise one kilogram of water through 1° C, a kilocalorie.

carbohydrates. Sugar; saccharides. A class of organic compounds in which hydrogen and oxygen are in the same ratio as they are in water.

cells. Minute structures that are the physical basis of all plant and animal life processes.

cellulose. A plant fiber, or fibrous form of carbohydrate, which aids peristaltic stimulation and intestinal elimination.

cholesterol. A sterol (fatlike substance) widely distributed in animal tissues, and occurring in egg yolk, various oils, fats, and nerve tissue (brain and spinal cord).

cornea. A transparent membrane that is part of the outer coat of the eyeball.

degenerative. The state in which a body part or organ becomes impaired or deteriorates.

disaccharides. One of a group of carbohydrates, dissacharose is a complex sugar that may be split into two molecules of monosaccharides.

DNA (deoxyribonucleic acid). A nucleic acid that is found in chromosomes of the nuclei of cells. It is considered to be the carrier of genetic information and the chemical basis of heredity.

enzymes. Complex proteins that are capable of inducing chemical changes in other substances without themselves becoming altered in the process.

fructose. Levulose; a fruit sugar found in corn syrup, honey, and fruit juices. Produces glycogen and maintains normal glucose content in the blood.

glaucoma. Eye disease marked by increased pressure in the eye that results in atrophy of the optic nerve and blindness.

glucose. A sugar that is formed during digestion. It is the most important carbohydrate in body metabolism.

glycogen. A polysaccharide, it is the main carbohydrate reserve in the body that is readily converted into sugar.

goiter. An enlargement of the thyroid gland.

hydrocarbon. A compound made up only of hydrogen and carbon.

hydrogenation. Adding hydrogen to a compound, especially to an unsaturated fat. In this way, soft fats or oils are solidified or "hardened."

hypertension. Condition in which a person has higher blood pressure than is considered to be normal.

mannose. An aldohexose (sugar) obtained from various plant sources: mannons (various legumes).

Health and Fitness

monosaccharide. A simple sugar (fructose, galactose, glucose) that is absorbed directly. It maintains the glucose content of the blood and aids in the production of glycogen.

monosodium glutamate. Sodium salt of glutamic acid; a white crystalline substance with a meatlike taste. It is used to flavor foods.

myoglobin. Muscle protein that transports oxygen, similar in function to blood hemoglobin.

nitrosamines. A combination of nitrites with a type of organic chemical in food known as amines. Nitrosamines are potent cancer-causing substances.

nutrient. A food supplying the body with essential elements. Carbohydrates, proteins, and alcohol provide energy. Water, electrolytes (acids, bases, salts), minerals, and vitamins are needed for metabolism.

nutrition. The taking in and utilization of food substances for body growth, repair, and maintenance. Successive stages are known as digestion, absorption, metabolism (assimilation), and excretion.

osteomalacia. A disease that is marked by increased softening of the bone. This makes bone flexible and brittle, resulting in deformities.

pectin. Plant carbohydrate that forms a gelatinous mass in the cooking of fruits and vegetables, causing them to jell.

polysaccharide. One of a group of carbohydrates that, upon hydrolysis, yields more than two molecules of simple sugars.

polyunsaturated. Refers to long-chain carbon compounds, especially fats that have many carbon atoms joined by double or triple bonds.

saccharides. A group of carbohydrates (including sugars) that is divided into these classifications: monosaccharides,

---

─HEALTH CARE ALERT─

DIABETES

In this disorder, the body does not make proper use of sugar. Sugar, derived from the food we eat, is an important fuel needed by the body to supply energy. Normally, insulin (a substance made in the pancreas) allows sugar to reach the muscles, fat, and other tissues and be burned to produce energy. In diabetes, there is not enough insulin; consequently, the sugar cannot enter the tissues.

Diabetes is found most often in persons who have a relative with diabetes, are overweight, or elderly. In some cases, adults become diabetic without developing any symptoms.

Signals of diabetes
Check with your doctor if you notice any of the following symptoms:
1. Excessive thirst
2. Increased appetite
3. Frequent urination
4. Itching of the skin, especially the genital area
5. Weakness and tiredness
6. Weight loss
7. Pain, numbness, or tingling in the hands and feet
8. Disturbances of vision
9. Irritability, nervousness, or nausea

---

disaccharides, trisaccharides, and polysaccharides.

saturated. Carbon compounds in which all the atoms are linked by single bonds.

sodium. Sodium salts are found in body fluids, serum, blood, lymph, and tissues. These salts are needed to maintain a balance between calcium and potassium for normal heart function, and for equilibrium of the body.

synthesis. In general, this is the process involved in the formation of a complex substance from simpler elements or compounds; for example, the synthesis of proteins from amino acids.

For further reference

Bright, Deborah
  Creative Relaxation: Turning Your Stress Into Positive Energy
  Harcourt Brace Jovanovich
Brody, Jane
  Nutrition Book: A Lifetime Guide
  W. W. Norton & Company
Calabrese, E. J. and Dorsey, Michael W.
  Healthy Living in an Unhealthy World
  Simon & Schuster
Davis, Adelle
  Let's Stay Healthy: A Guide to Lifelong Nutrition
  Harcourt Brace Jovanovich

Schroeder, Henry A.
  The Trace Minerals and Man: Some Positive and Negative Aspects
  The Devin-Adair Company
Tubesing, D.A.
  Kicking Your Stress Habits: A Do-It-Yourself Guide for Coping With Stress
  Whole Person Associates
Wenck, D. A.
  A Supermarket Nutrition
  Reston Publishing Company
Wentzler, R.
  The Vitamin Book: A Complete Guide to Vitamins, Minerals and Essential Nutrients
  Gramercy Publishing Company

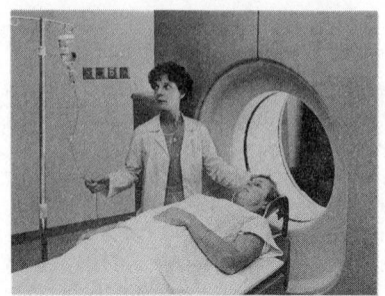

You and Modern Medicine

There are doctors practicing today who have never seen a case of polio, smallpox, typhoid, childbed fever, or any number of other diseases that devastated human society in the past. As a generation, our life expectancy is longer than that of any other generation in history. Organ transplants and miraculous surgical techniques seem to promise an even brighter future.

We also live in a time when technology has outrun man's ability to absorb its implications or to use it safely and wisely. Life-saving devices are frequently perverted into death-prolonging machinery. Drugs proliferate at a rate beyond the ordinary doctor's capability to use them. Medical costs have skyrocketed, giving us the most expensive system in the world, with many of us living in dread of a catastrophic illness that could bankrupt us.

The average American is caught in the middle. This chapter is a guide for those consumers of medical services who wish to take better control of their lives and to use the medical system to their advantage.

You and the doctor

A doctor is an ordinary human being, highly and expensively trained to treat disease. He sees himself as a saver of lives. All of his training has led him to expect unquestioning obedience from his own staff, hospital personnel, and his patients.

In the past, most patients agreed that "doctor knows best," but as specialization and technology have eroded the patient-doctor relationship, many have begun to ask questions.

Recent court decisions have affirmed patients' right to know and right to informed consent. Informed consent means that the doctor must not only tell his pa-

tient what he proposes as treatment, but must make sure that the patient truly understands. A consent form, read and signed, is not enough.

Not all doctors are comfortable with this arrangement, and not all patients are ready to give up a dependent relationship.

When to look for a doctor. The key to good medical care is having a competent, knowledgeable, well-trained primary care physician. Many people postpone finding such a doctor for years. They use an orthopedist if they break a bone, or consult a dermatologist for skin problems. It is only when they become seriously ill that they begin the search. This is the very worst time to look.

A primary care physician has the opportunity to know his patients, their families, and their lifestyles. He is the logical keeper of medical records, an invaluable go-between in the mystifying world of specialists, an important member of the hospital treatment team, and more likely to treat the whole person than just the disease.

The hole left by the disappearing general practitioner is being filled by a growing number of young doctors who choose "family practice" as their specialty. The general internist also serves as a primary care physician. Pediatricians are primary care doctors for children.

How to find a doctor. Talking to as

many people as possible is a good beginning in finding the right doctor. Since other doctors and medical associations are rarely frank about their fellow professionals, the most reliable source of information about doctors are friends, neighbors, storekeepers, pharmacists, and nurses.

Once a tentative list of names is compiled, *The American Medical Directory* (available in libraries) and your local medical association can be consulted about medical schools, medical degrees, board certification, and hospital affiliations.

Particular attention should be paid to the hospital affiliations of doctors under consideration. You should be sure that the doctor you choose is entitled to admit patients to the hospital you determine to be the best in your community.

When the list of doctors has been narrowed to one or two, it is time to make an appointment with the doctor who sounds most promising.

A good strategy is to make a list of things you wish to observe and learn. Time and extent of office hours, who takes over when the doctor is not available, and how he can be reached in an emergency should be among the items on the list. You will want to inquire about fees, and how and when they are payable. Women will ask whether the doctor handles routine gynecological matters, and people with children will ask at what age their children will be accepted as patients.

How a doctor's office is run can affect the quality of medical care. A crowded waiting room may mean poor scheduling. The amount of time you are kept waiting on your first visit probably will not change. Only you can decide what your limits are.

A concerned, courteous, and helpful office staff is an important link between patient and doctor. An arrogant, disinterested, or rude staff can put a real stumbling block in the way of your getting the most for your medical dollar.

Getting the most from a doctor.

A successful patient is one who has reasonable expectations from his doctor; who learns as much as he can

---

Do not lie to the doctor

Many people have things in their lives that they do not want anyone to know about. These things should not be kept from the doctor. Drinking more than just occasionally is a habit he needs to know about—not only because of its possible effect on physical health, but because it can influence the kinds of medications he may safely prescribe. A three-pack-a-day smoker should own up, as should users of drugs, even recreationally. Venereal diseases are treatable but not if you are too embarrassed to describe your symptoms. If you are not comfortable discussing such things with your doctor, you should not hesitate to change to someone you are comfortable with.

It is not uncommon for a patient to accept a prescription and then, for some reason, not use it. The doctor should know about this, too. Consulting another doctor when not satisfied is a mistake only when you fail to tell your own doctor in advance.

You and your doctor are partners in the enterprise of recovering your health. Like all successful partnerships, it requires mutual trust.

about his own illness and treatment; and who follows instructions or informs his doctor when he is not doing so and why. He gets to know the office nurse and talks frankly and openly to her about why he is calling and what he expects from the phone call. He learns to be explicit and insistent with the answering service, and he also learns the value of an early call when he is feeling ill (perhaps making it easier for him to place a call in the middle of the night). A combination of assertiveness and consideration is as effective in dealing with a doctor as it is in dealing with the rest of the world.

When to change doctors. A continuing feeling of dissatisfaction is a valid reason for changing doctors. The frequent changing of doctors is deplored by the medical profession, and may be an indication that the patient has unrealistic expectations;

When to call the doctor

People are often reluctant to call the doctor for fear of being either a nuisance or an alarmist. There are symptoms that call for an immediate call to the doctor and an immediate response from him.

Symptoms to take seriously
- Chest pain; sudden rapid or irregular pulse
- Difficulty in breathing
- Sudden coughing up of blood
- Severe nosebleed
- Inability to urinate or defecate
- Sudden and profuse vaginal bleeding
- Severe abdominal pain
- Blood in the stool
- Uncontrollable vomiting or diarrhea
- Inability to swallow
- Sudden loss of vision
- Eye pain or double vision
- Loss of balance, hearing, or sudden weakness
- Mental confusion, fainting, or vertigo
- Headache accompanied by stiff neck
- Very high or very low temperature

GET A SECOND OPINION!

Surgery is not always the only effective treatment. Check with another qualified surgeon before agreeing to even minor surgery.

however, when needs are not being met, it is time for a change.

In the case of doctor error, each case should be decided on its own merits. A mistake that is freely acknowledged and does not represent a pattern of carelessness is not necessarily a reason for change. An error that is life-threatening may permanently shake our confidence, however, and make a change advisable.

Do you need a specialist? The decision to consult a specialist should always be made after consultation with your primary care doctor. A referral from him will insure that you are seeing someone whose competence he trusts, and that your care will continue in the hands of someone *you* trust.

A consultation with a specialist does not mean that you will continue to see him on an extended basis. Although your internist may wish you to see a cardiologist for diagnosis of a heart problem, he is quite capable of monitoring and managing heart conditions himself. Not only will this make you more comfortable; it will save you money as well because internists' fees are usually lower than those of specialists.

What about surgery? Surgeons not only save lives but improve the quality of life for many people. They also are rather single-minded in that they are inclined to think only in terms of surgical procedures, frequently rejecting alternative methods of treatment. Since even minor surgery can be hazardous, the patient and his primary care doctor must be on guard against unnecessary surgery.

Many insurance companies now require and pay for a second opinion when surgery is recommended. There are certain operations that are widely considered to be overperformed. If any of the operations listed below are advised, it is wise to ask for a second opinion.

Overused surgical procedures. These operations, which used to be considered more or less routine, are often thought to be unnecessary today. As with any operation, be sure you get the very best advice before proceeding with:

Hysterectomy	Gallbladder removal
Oophorectomy	Radical mastectomy
(removal of ovaries)	Dilation and curettage
Tonsillectomy	Caesarean section

Doctors: Who they are and what they do

Primary care

Family Practitioner. Receives additional training in family medicine. Replaces old general practitioner. Provides care from birth to death.

Internist. Not to be confused with intern, a recent medical school graduate. Practices "internal medicine." Training qualifies him to care for adult patients in all matters that do not require surgery.

Pediatrician. Trained to deliver primary care to children from infancy to adolescence.

Specialists

Allergist. Treats such diseases as asthma, hay fever, or skin allergy.

Anesthesiologist. Administers anesthetics, or pain killers, during an operation.

Cardiologist. Highly trained to treat complicated diseases of the heart and blood vessels.

Dermatologist. Specializes in diseases of the skin.

Endocrinologist. Deals with disorders of the glandular system.

Gastroenterologist. Treats diseases of the digestive organs—esophagus, stomach, bowels, liver, and pancreas.

Gerontologist. Deals with aging and the problems of old people.

Hematologist. Expert in diseases of the blood.

Infectious Disease Specialist. Helps treat patients with serious or baffling diseases.

Nephrologist. Specializes in diseases of the kidney.

Neurologist. Qualified to treat illnesses of the nervous system.

Obstetrician/Gynecologist. Manages pregnancies, delivers babies, and handles problems concerning the reproductive organs of women.

Oculist. Deals with diseases of the eye.

Oncologist. Treats malignancies; decides on appropriate treatment and administers it.

Pulmonary Specialist. Treats diseases of the lungs; performs pulmonary function tests and bronchoscopy.

Radiologist. Gives and interprets x-ray photographs.

Rheumatologist. Cares for patients with diseases of the joints, and treats diseases such as rheumatoid arthritis, systemic lupus erythematosus, and scleroderma.

Nonmedical Specialists

Osteopath. Licensed to practice medicine and perform surgery, specializes in musculoskeletal manipulation.

Chiropractor. Licensed in most states to practice a system of manipulation of the spine.

Optometrist. Tests the eye for defective vision in order to prescribe corrective lenses.

Podiatrist. Trained in a four-year program as a specialist in disorders of the feet. Admitted to practice in many hospitals, but usually treat and operate on an outpatient basis.

Surgeons

General. Trained to perform abdominal, gynecological, and vascular surgery. In most urban areas, removes gallbladders, appendixes, moles, and cysts. Performs hysterectomies and repairs hernias.

Cardiac. Performs heart surgery such as coronary bypass and grafts. Removes aortic aneurysms.

Neurosurgeon. Operates on brain and spinal tumors, performs back surgery, repairs carotid arteries.

Obstetric/Gynecologic. Performs surgery related to the female reproductive system.

Ophthalmologic. Eye surgeons. Will also treat diseases of the eye.

Orthopedic. Sets bones, replaces joints, pins hips, and cares for traumatic injuries.

Otolaryngologic. Ear, nose, and throat.

Plastic. Performs both cosmetic and reconstructive surgery.

Urologic. Operates on the prostate, scrotum, bladder, and kidneys.

You and the hospital

The modern hospital is a remarkable place. It is a scene of human drama, where lives are saved, pain is eased, babies are born, and people die. The hospital is also a place where serious errors in treatment may be made, where unnecessary surgery may be performed, where technology may prolong life when there is no hope for survival, and where even strong-minded individuals are reduced to childlike dependency.

Increasingly, doctors and insurance companies recognize the advantages of limiting hospital stays, not only to save money for the patient and his insurer, but to assure the ultimate well-being of the individual.

Before you go. When the doctor recommends putting you in the hospital, it is time to ask serious questions and to make sure they are answered satisfactorily. Are there alternatives? What are the benefits? What are the risks? Is it an emergency? Can it be postponed? Is a second opinion advisable? How long will I be there?

Frequently, hospitalization is suggested by a specialist, and it may be wise to postpone decisions until you have discussed the situation with your primary care doctor.

Which hospital to choose. Factors such as what is available in the community, where your doctor has admission privileges, or where an ambulance takes you after an accident often limit your choices. Large and famous is not always better. Open heart surgery is probably best performed in a large medical center where there is a concentration of specific skills and experience; the gallbladder patient, however, may actually receive better care in a small community hospital.

Although differences may be blurred in specific cases, the kinds of hospitals can be categorized:

Teaching hospitals are connected with medical schools, are usually large, and are staffed by students, residents, and doctors who both teach and attend patients.

Public hospitals are the large institutions funded by local, county, state, or federal governments. They also have interns, residents, and a permanent medical staff.

Private and community hospitals are usually operated on a not-for-profit basis. They may or may not have a house staff, and they are operated for the convenience of the doctors who admit patients.

Nursing and convalescent homes are designed for patients who no longer need full medical facilities and who cannot be cared for at home.

There are no simple guidelines, but a little research into available facilities, before they are needed, will help a great deal. Nursing homes, particularly, should be investigated in advance. When you visit, talk with patients and their families. Ask your own doctor if a particular home is a place he recommends.

Your decision is made. Before packing a bag and finding your health insurance card, choose a member of your family or a close friend to act as your personal advocate during your stay in the hospital. When the person in the admitting office asks for "next of kin," give the name of the person you wish to serve as advocate. If the hospital requires further authorization, you will be informed at that time. Your advocate will be able to keep track of your treatment, ask questions on your behalf, register legitimate complaints, and stand between you and hospital bureaucracy.

Defend against hospital error. Most people emerge from the hospital in better health than when they went in. Usually, their most serious complaints deal with the food or difficulty in sleeping.

Can you stay out of the hospital?	How to help yourself in the hospital
1. Not all surgery requires hospitalization.	*Ask questions!* *Do not remain ignorant of what is being done for you.*
2. Many tests and procedures can be performed on an outpatient basis.	1. Make sure you get the right medication.
3. Many kinds of medical care can be delivered at home through the use of community services.	2. Make sure you get your medication on time.
4. Families of the terminally ill have more options as a result of the hospice movement and changing attitudes toward care of the dying.	3. Make sure you get the right tests—not someone else's tests.
	4. Make sure you get the food your doctor ordered for you.

However, wrong medications, wrong tests, and needless exposure to invasive procedures are all hazards.

Patients are not helpless. The person who constantly asks questions or has his personal advocate ask them in his behalf is putting up a good defense against error. No procedure, test, or medication should come as a surprise—it could be meant for someone else. Make a point of knowing your medication schedule; if medication does not come on time, ask for it. If it is new or unfamiliar, make sure that it is intended for you.

If you have been told to take nothing by mouth prior to surgery or a diagnostic test, do not assume that the arrival of your breakfast tray means that someone has changed his mind.

Be sure to take some of your personal belongings to the hospital. Do not forget your eye glasses so that you can read or watch television.

What to pack for your stay.
As an antidote to the loss of identity that usually occurs when you walk through hospital doors, take part of your home with you: snapshots, a favorite bathrobe, even if it is old, your own cosmetics, deodorant, shaving cream, and toothpaste. Leave valuables at home, but you may want to take a small battery-run radio with earphones. Arrange to have your favorite newspaper delivered. Maintaining a sense of your own personality will help you to stand up for yourself and to make the best use of the facilities that exist to restore you to health.

When you get there.
Checking into a hospital used to be an interminable ordeal. Today, many hospitals arrange for blood tests, x-rays, urine analyses, and many diagnostic tests to be done well in advance of admission. The vast amount of preadmission paperwork is handled by the admitting office before you arrive. This has worked to shorten hospital stays and has nearly eliminated those weekend admissions that once resulted in a patient's being tucked into a very expensive hospital bed days in advance of his need for it.

The Patient's Bill of Rights

The patient has a right to:

- **Complete, current information** concerning his diagnosis, treatment, and prognosis in terms he can understand.

- **Information necessary to give informed consent** prior to any medical procedures, except in emergencies, including knowledge of significant risks, duration of incapacitation, alternatives for care or treatment, and the names of persons who will perform the procedures.

- **Refuse treatment** to the extent permitted by law, and to be informed of the medical consequences of refusal.

- **Privacy** concerning medical care, diagnosis, and records.

- **Reasonable response** to requests for services.

- **Not be transferred** to another facility without his permission.

- **Be advised** if treatment involves human experimentation.

- **Refuse** such experimentation.

- **Continuity** of care following discharge.

- **Examine** and receive an explanation of charges regardless of source of payment.

—excerpted from a document prepared by the American Hospital Association

What about all those tests?

As diagnostic techniques have improved and expanded, and words like "CAT scan" and "sonogram" have entered ordinary language, doctors have an increasingly difficult time knowing when to stop testing. Hospitals have enormous sums of money invested in machinery; the way to pay for them is to charge for their use.

Another factor in overtesting is the doctor's real fear of malpractice suits. This seems to be a byproduct of overspecialization on the part of the medical profession. A patient who has developed a comfortable and trusting relationship with his doctor rarely sues, even when things go wrong.

You and your primary doctor can work together to ensure that you get only those tests that are absolutely necessary. High-risk, invasive procedures, such as arteriograms or surgical biopsies, require especially careful consideration. They will not be performed without your consent, but before giving that consent be sure to ask about benefits, risks, and alternatives.

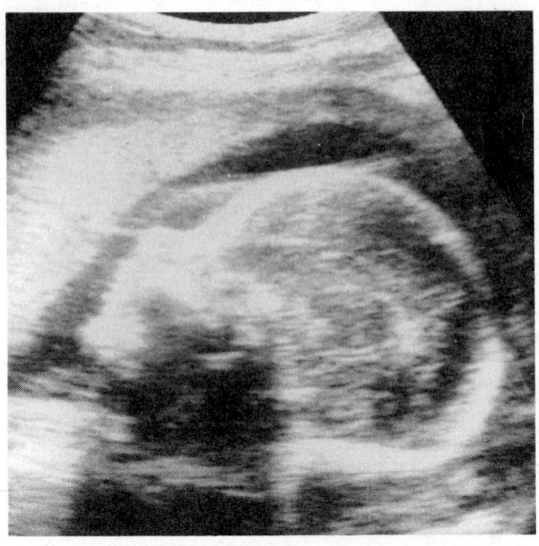

Computer-aided imaging has increased the reliability of medical diagnosis. This ultrasound image shows the head of a fetus.

What they mean when they say . . .

CAT scan	(Computerized tomography) An x-ray technique that photographs cross-sections of the body. Normal x-rays produce pictures that are flat, like a photograph; the CAT scan sends rays through the body that are picked up by a scanner, fed into a computer, and visualized on a screen. This procedure has eliminated many complicated and high-risk tests.
Sonogram	(Ultrasound examination) High-frequency sound waves are directed at the body; the echoes are received on a TV screen and recorded photographically. This procedure is often performed in the last trimester of pregnancy to determine the position and health of the fetus.
EEG	(Electroencephalogram) Electrodes are glued to the scalp, and the electrical activity of the brain is painlessly recorded.
EKG	(Electrocardiogram) A machine records the electrical activity of the heart. It gives information about heartbeat, the strength of the heart, and the location of any injury. A stress test is an EKG given while the patient is exercising.
Spinal tap	(Lumbar puncture) A small amount of fluid is drawn from the spinal column to test the internal pressure or to provide a sample for laboratory testing.
Biopsy	A surgical procedure, often performed under a local anesthetic, in which a small amount of tissue is obtained for laboratory study.
GI series	(Upper and lower) X-ray pictures are taken of the digestive tract after the introduction of barium, by mouth or by enema, to make the tract visible.
Amniocentesis	Fluid is drawn from the amniotic sac surrounding the fetus during the end of the first trimester of pregnancy. Cells grown in the laboratory provide information about such genetic defects as Down's syndrome.

You and emergency rooms

Some emergency rooms are little more than first-aid stations with a nurse on duty and a doctor on call; others are full-scale trauma centers attached to major medical centers. The average emergency room falls somewhere in between. Locating and evaluating emergency rooms in your immediate area could save a life. The closest place to go is not always the best place to go in a true emergency.

What to look for. A well-run emergency room is staffed around the clock by doctors trained in emergency medicine. If there is not a permanent house staff, specialists are on call. Emergency rooms attached to good hospitals have access to cardiac and intensive care units; these can assume great importance for patients needing such care.

A talk with your doctor about nearby facilities should prove helpful; your choice will be governed by his hospital affiliations whenever possible.

Before you go. No matter how serious the emergency, a cool head is essential. A call to your own doctor for his help in evaluating the seriousness of the emergency is wise. His call to the emergency room—warning them that you are on the way and ordering whatever tests or treatments he thinks necessary—will cut a lot of red tape and assure fast attention. If you cannot reach your doctor before leaving, have the hospital call him on arrival.

In the face of an emergency, calling an ambulance is almost a reflex action. When there is a suspected heart attack, poisoning, severe pain, impaired breathing, or any condition in which rapid medical help is

---

True emergencies

- Severe and uncontrolled bleeding
- Serious difficulty in breathing
- Choking
- Poisoning
- Severe chest pain
- Convulsions
- Heat stroke
- Unconsciousness
- Severe injuries
- Stabbing or bullet wounds, severe burns
- Diabetic acidosis or shock from hypoglycemia
- Hypothermia

DO NOT BE TIMID!

Remember to leave tact and good manners at home. An emergency room is no place to assume automatically that somebody else knows best or to let consideration of other people sway your judgment. If you know that the condition is serious, do whatever is necessary to make sure that the doctor and nurses know it too.

---

essential, it is best to use whatever transportation is available—personal car, taxi, or police car. Many police departments have trained their officers in basic first aid and equipped their cars with life-saving apparatuses.

If there is time, locate insurance cards, regular medication, and, in the case of poisoning or drug overdose, the original container the substance came in. If there is not enough time, a neighbor or a friend can follow soon after with the appropriate information.

When you get there. At a glance, the average emergency room looks like a scene of total chaos. Despite appearances, there *is* a system functioning called "triage." This means that a nurse, a doctor, or other emergency room personnel will determine who will have first call on limited facilities and personnel. Top priority is assigned to patients with suspected heart attacks, seriously injured accident victims, cases of poisoning or drug overdose, or those in need of immediate attention.

Although many people tell horror stories about interminable hours spent waiting for attention, as a rule those who need help the most get it the quickest. To the parent of an hysterical child who has suffered a non-life-threatening injury, the system may seem unfair and insensitive. But remember, the person in charge must balance urgent need against discomfort and inconvenience.

Children and emergencies. Mothers of large families may, when the children are grown up, swear that they spent most of their children's younger years in one emergency room or another. The most common reasons for these trips are accidents, poisoning, and difficulties in breathing.

Often there seems to be a conflict of interest between medical personnel and parents. No child should be left unattended by a familiar adult or made to go through any procedure alone. Parents are often asked to leave the room in the interest of the child's welfare. The answer to that request is an emphatic "No!" Keep quiet and calm, but stay. Your leaving may be better for the doctors and nurses, but it is not better for the child.

The elderly and emergencies.

Fractures are the most common reason for trips by the elderly to emergency rooms. Pseudo-dementia is a close second. If an elderly person becomes suddenly disoriented, hallucinates, or shows signs of paranoia, he may be suffering from a drug reaction. If the attending doctor has a list of all the prescription and nonprescription drugs that the patient is taking, it may save time, money, and discomfort. The tests to determine organic causes, such as those in Alzheimer's disease, stroke, etc., are complicated, upsetting, and expensive.

The emergency room doctor. If

the emergency room does not have a permanent medical staff, it does have a list of doctors who are on call. Make clear to the admitting desk, and to the doctor you see, that you do have your own doctor and that you do wish to have him informed as soon as possible. Although you may receive excellent care from the available doctor, if hospital admission is indicated, you may not welcome the discovery that you have inadvertently changed doctors. It is better to be clear in the beginning than to try to sort things out later.

Misusing the emergency room.

The hospital emergency room has become a substitute for a personal doctor in many people's lives. Families often postpone finding a doctor when they move to a new community and fall into the habit of going to the nearest emergency room whenever anyone in the family needs medical care. Tetanus shots, medication for sore throats, or examination of a sick child are very expensive when delivered by an emergency room.

Other people have a very low tolerance for suffering, their own as well as that of other people. A bump on the head when there is no loss of consciousness, a minor cut that bleeds profusely, mild muscle sprains or strains, and vomiting when there is no indication of poisoning are not reasons for taking up valuable time and space in a busy emergency room. A course in first aid at the local Red Cross—and a greater use of your doctor's telephone number—will save money.

Should you be admitted? Admission

to the hospital is not necessarily the outcome of a visit to an emergency room. If your own doctor is on hand or on the other end of a telephone, this decision should be made under his guidance.

If your own doctor is not available, the discussion will need to be carried on with the attending physician. No one would think of taking a suspected heart attack victim home until his condition has been verified, but a bump on the head may be a different matter. Careful questioning, followed by the use of your own common sense, should resolve the matter.

Unless you are far from home or have been taken by an ambulance to a hospital where your doctor does not have admitting privileges, try to make sure that the hospital has the name of your primary care doctor. If your doctor is not available, you are entitled to be admitted by a private doctor of your choice.

If you are not admitted to the hospital, you should inquire about follow-up care. For example, who will remove the stitches?

Post a note by the telephone

Display prominently the telephone number of your local police and your own street address. Emergency police cars can arrive at your house in minutes. Also, households with young children or elderly parents should place a notice near the telephone for use by babysitters or caretakers.

> POLICE • FIRE
> AMBULANCE
> **555-7000**
> Compliments of
> Your Volunteer Fire Department

- If you have found a primary care doctor, investigated local hospitals and emergency rooms, and located a pharmacist you can rely on, this information should be readily available when you are out of the house.

- Current medications, how they are taken, and for what conditions should be noted.

- If children are likely to have croup or experience allergic reactions, the measures to take in case of an attack should be described.

- Working mothers with regular, reliable babysitters or housekeepers should make certain that the doctor knows their names and whether or not they are empowered to act in your behalf.

You and drugs

Most drugs simply alleviate symptoms, modify the course of an illness, or assist the body to achieve normal functioning. Our own bodies fight most illnesses better than most drugs. Given time, many conditions improve without any treatment. For example, early diabetes can often be controlled by diet alone. And drugs used to control high blood pressure need assistance from a modified diet and appropriate exercise.

Otherwise sensible people cling to the notion that all they need to recover from any illness, from a cold to cancer, are the right words written on a prescription blank, or the right bottle of nonprescription medicine brought home from the drugstore.

Any drug powerful enough to have a significant effect on a disease also has the potential to cause harm. The risks range from slight to major, and it is the job of the patient and his doctor to weigh risks against benefits. Powerful drugs are to be reserved for serious illnesses.

No one should refuse medication that is thoughtfully and knowledgeably prescribed, but the wise person guards against misuse and overuse of medication by assuming personal responsibility for knowing as much as possible and for following directions.

Doctors are human. Most of us have
nagged our doctors for a prescription that we think we need to make us feel better, and most doctors have written unnecessary prescriptions for the same reason. In the past, doctors had a very limited number of effective drugs they could use, so they sometimes offered their patients "sugar pills" to make them feel better.

Today, however, modern pharmacology has made a bewildering number of drugs available to doctors, making it difficult for them to keep up with their names, much less their efficacy and side effects. When today's physician reaches for his copy of the *Physician's Desk Reference* to look up a drug he is about to prescribe, he is demonstrating sound medical sense and taking care to prescribe the right drug for the right condition.

The smart patient should not hesitate to use the same reference book, which is available in libraries and pharmacies, before starting a new medicine. Although the information may seem too extensive and too technical, it will provide a basis for asking further questions of your doctor. Understanding all you can about your medication should make it easier to follow instructions and to make the most effective use of it.

Doctors complain that their patients accept prescriptions that they never fill, fill prescriptions that

Warning signs when taking medication

- Rash, nausea, swelling, muscle cramps
- Trouble with urination, heart, breathing, circulation, headaches, vision
- Yellowing of skin or eyes
- Depression or exhilaration
- Weight gain or loss
- Stomach upset, constipation, or diarrhea
- Feeling worse or showing no sign of improvement

they never take, and take medication only until they feel better. If the goal is to form a full partnership with a doctor, thus ensuring better care, such quirks on the part of a patient get in the way. A doctor needs to know about the course of a disease—what worked and what did not, why a patient seemed to recover and then had a relapse, etc. Good information is one way to ensure good care.

How to use your pharmacist.
Pharmacists are highly trained professionals who are well informed on the use, composition, and effects of drugs. They are qualified not only to advise the consumer, but the doctor as well. They are not allowed to prescribe medications, make a diagnosis, or refuse to fill a prescription. They can offer advice about nonprescription medicines and are usually willing to take the time to answer questions about prescription drugs.

Many good pharmacists keep a complete drug record on each customer; as more and more stores are computerized, this information is stored for instant retrieval.

In an effort to save money, many people use the discount drug stores and chain stores. The pharmacists in these large operations are inaccessible to customers and do not keep personal drug profiles. It is advisable to balance the advantages and disadvantages in making a choice between a well-stocked neighborhood pharmacy and a large commercial operation.

Over-the-counter drugs. After this
category of drugs was studied by the Food and Drug Administration (FDA), many over-the-counter drugs were taken off the market because they were judged to be ineffective.

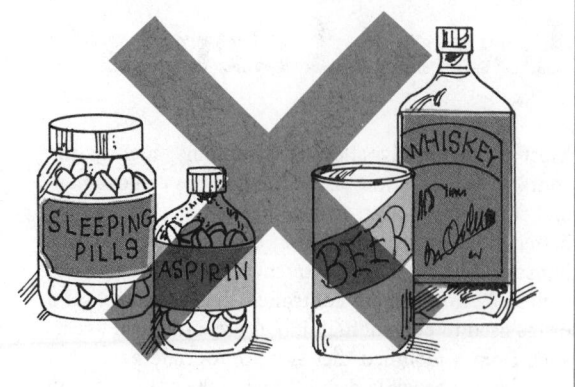

Some drugs do not mix safely

(see drug chart on pages 90-91)

Do not take even an aspirin without consulting your doctor or pharmacist if you are taking prescription medication. Aspirin, for example, taken with anticoagulants, increases the anticoagulant effect of the aspirin and internal bleeding can result.

Alcohol, even in small quantities, can have fatal effects when combined with barbituates.

It is reasonably safe to use nonprescription drugs for such conditions as a bad cold, headache, mild allergic reaction, constipation, mild diarrhea, or any condition that is self-limiting—so long as you receive some guidance from a doctor or pharmacist.

Elderly people, young children, pregnant women, or people who are taking prescription medication should exercise particular care.

Make sure to read the label, avoiding medications that contain more than two active ingredients. Make sure *not* to use these preparations to put off a visit to the doctor for a condition that might be serious.

Brand name vs. generic. Achromycin

is a brand name antibiotic that costs just under $10. Tetracycline is its generic equivalent; it costs about half that amount. The drugs are equally effective and pharmacists in all states are permitted to fill a prescription with either drug, providing the doctor has not specifically forbidden it.

Unfortunately for the consumer, not all brand-name drugs have a generic equivalent available. Some are still protected by patent. Until recently, the Food and Drug Administration (FDA) made approval of generic copies so complicated and expensive that there was no

Darvon is one of a half-dozen brands, all relatively expensive, for the common generic analgesic Propoxyphene Hydrochloride, which costs much less.

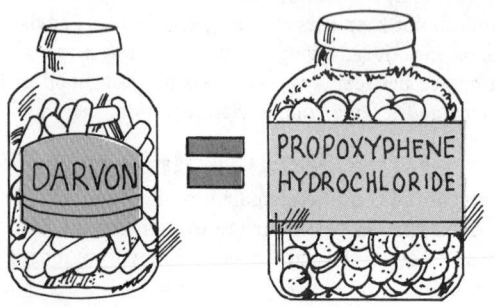

real incentive for other drug companies to manufacture copies, even when the patent expired.

But now, under a recent FDA ruling, drug companies will be able to issue generic copies so long as they demonstrate that the generic drugs are chemically the same and that they perform in the same way as the brand-name drugs. Any FDA-approved generic drug is as safe and effective as any brand-name drug. The saving to the consumer should be enormous.

Medicine and high-risk groups.

These three groups are at particular risk, and extra precautions must be taken to ensure that medications are effective and do no harm.

Children. Children not only require smaller doses of drugs than adults, but they frequently react in opposite ways. Sedatives may stimulate, and stimulants may sedate. Children should be given only those medicines prescribed for them by their own doctor.

Adults should make their own medicine-taking a very private affair. Many doctors and psychologists feel that children who observe their parents taking drugs for any discomfort are getting a message that could pave the way for drug abuse at a later age.

Pregnant women. Extraordinary care must be exercised when taking medication during pregnancy. Nursing mothers should practice the same restraint. The fetus was once considered totally secure while in the womb. The tragic thalidomide babies were a testament to the fallacy of that perception.

Not all pregnant women can forego all medication, but they must cooperate closely with an obstetrician who is sensitive to the possible dangers.

The elderly. This group can present their doctors, their caretakers, and even themselves with troublesome medication problems. They complain of lack of sleep, lose their appetites, develop aches and pains, break bones, lose their sharpness of sight and hearing, and find that their vital organs have slowed in their

You and Modern Medicine

functioning. As a result, many of them become doctor shoppers and enthusiastic consumers of vast quantities of prescription and over-the-counter drugs. To add to their problems, many old people swap drugs with each other. The result may be a drug-induced nightmare for those who love the elderly and care for them.

A single primary care physician—a gerontologist or an internist—can act as a deterrent to freewheeling drug use. Not only will one doctor have a record of all the drugs taken, but the patient can be encouraged to substitute exercise, relaxation, and good nutrition for some of the medication. An introduction to commonly prescribed drugs, their generic names, and a guide to possible problems appears on the next page.

The home medicine cabinet

The bathroom medicine cabinet is often a disorderly jumble of deodorants, toothpaste, expired prescriptions, cosmetics, dried-up cough syrups, and empty Band-Aid boxes. This may lead to a small child's being rushed to the emergency room after eating a bottle of aspirin.

The smart thing to do is to clean up and lock up. Medications belong in a locked cabinet, preferably located in a cool, dry place. All out-of-date medications should be discarded. The pharmacist will usually be willing to make recommendations about what to keep and what to flush down the toilet.

Home remedies should be confined to a few reliable kinds, and first-aid supplies should be kept organized and ready to use.

A well-ordered medicine cabinet will reduce the temptation to self-medicate with leftover prescription drugs.

Suggestions for the home pharmacy

Keep	For
Aspirin or nonaspirin pain reliever	Pain or fever
Antacid	Upset stomach
Adhesive tape and bandages	Covering minor wounds
Hydrogen peroxide	Antiseptic
Sodium bicarbonate	For soaking
Syrup of ipecac	To induce vomiting
Milk of magnesia	Constipation
Kaopectate	Diarrhea
Eyedrops	Simple irritation
Hydrocortisone ointment	Poison ivy, other rashes

Home remedies and first-aid supplies should be kept in one place. Teach children not to open the cabinet doors, which should be kept locked. Do not give old medicines to friends. Destroy them by flushing them down the toilet.

A sample listing of frequently prescribed drugs

Brand name	Generic	Possible problems
Pain killers		
Darvon	Propoxyphene hydrochloride	Habit forming; avoid alcohol, muscle relaxants, tranquilizers, nervous system depressants
Percodan	Oxycodone, aspirin, phenacetin, caffeine	Avoid alcohol, sedatives, antihistamines, oral diabetes drugs, muscle relaxants
Antibiotics		
Achromycin V, SK-Tetracycline, Sumycin	Tetracycline	Avoid milk, dairy products, exposure to sun; oral anticoagulants may have increased effects
Amcill, Omnipen, SK-Ampicillin	Ampicillin	Avoid other antibiotics and antacids
E. E. S., E-Mycin, Erypar, Erythrocin, Ethril	Erythromycin	Avoid other antibiotics and alcohol
Penicillin, SK-Penicillin VK, Pen-Vee K	Penicillin	Avoid if you have a past history of allergy to any penicillin; to be taken for full treatment on empty stomach; do not take with fruit juice; avoid antacids
Anticoagulants		
Coumadin, Panwarfin	Warfarin	Avoid if pregnant or a nursing mother
Antihypertensives		
Aldactatone	Spirionolactone plus hydrochlorothiazide	This group of drugs, used to control high blood pressure, must be taken under regular supervision of the doctor with attention to high or low potassium levels; before any surgical procedure, the surgeon and anesthetist must know about the medication (this includes dental surgery); Regroton can cause sensitivity to sunlight
Apresoline	Hydralazine plus hydrochloride	
Inderal	Propranolol plus hydrochloride	
Lopressor	Metoprolol plus tartrate	
Regroton	Resperine plus chlorthalidone	
Oral antidiabetics		
Diabinese	Chlorpropamide	Avoid taking anticoagulants, aspirin, diuretics, or any other medication without consulting a doctor
Ulcer medication		
Cogentin	Benztropine mesylate	Can cause sensitivity to sunlight; do not take within an hour of antacid or diarrhea medication
Tagamet	Cimetidine	Avoid anticoagulants, some penicillins, Valium, Librium, etc., and alcohol and caffeine

You and Modern Medicine

Brand name	Generic	Possible problems
Major tranquilizers and antipsychotic medications		
Thorazine	Chlorpromazine	These are important drugs used in controlling serious mental illness; they have many side effects when taken over an extended period of time; many patients discontinue medication when they feel better or because of side effects; taking these drugs can mean the difference between being hospitalized or being able to live in the community; cooperation on the part of the patient and careful management on the part of the doctor are essential
Prolixin	Fluphenazine	
Mellaril	Thioridazine hydrochloride	
Stelazine	Trifluoperazine	
Haldol	Haloperidol	
Navane	Thiothixene	
Clozaril	Clozapine	
Other tranquilizers and antidepressants		
Librium	Chlordiazepoxide	No other medication should be taken without consulting a doctor; alcohol can be highly dangerous
Valium	Diazepam	
Equanil	Meprobamate	
Serax	Oxazepam	
Tranxene	Clorazepate	
Xanax	Alprazolam	
Prozac	Fluoxetine hydrachloride	
MAO inhibitor antidepressants		
Marplan	Isocarboxazid	Aged cheese, aged meat, pods of broad beans, beer, wine, pickled herring, yogurt, liver, yeast extract, heavy amounts of caffeine, bananas, soy sauce, anchovies, avocados, and sour cream (all with high tramine content) must be avoided; can cause dangerous rise in blood pressure
Nardil	Phenelezine	
Parnate	Transylcypromine sulfate	
Tricyclic antidepressants		
Tofranil	Imipramine	Take two to six weeks to become effective; do not combine with other medication except on doctor's specific instruction; avoid alcohol; may have side effects like dry mouth or constipation; people over 60 years of age should have heart and blood pressure checked before beginning medication and regularly thereafter
Norpramin	Desipramine	
Elavil	Amitriptyline	
Sleeping pills		
Seconal	Secobarbital	Tolerance develops very quickly and physical addiction can occur from extended use; withdrawal can be dangerous if not undergone slowly; absolutely avoid combining with alcohol
Nembutal	Phenobarbital	
Sodium Amytal	Amobarbital	

You and your mental health

Many people are uncomfortable with discussions of mental illness. A persistent stomach ache sends us to the doctor at once, yet the pain from a deep depression may be endured for months or years out of fear or shame. We talk freely of triple bypass heart surgery or kidney dialysis, but speak of schizophrenia in whispers. Alcoholism or drug addiction may be fervently denied in the face of incontrovertible evidence.

What is mental illness? Mental ill-
nesses fall roughly into two categories: neuroses and psychoses. Neurotic symptoms may become disabling, but they respond well to psychotherapy. Psychosis is a term for serious organic mental illness often thought to be caused by a disruption in the brain's chemistry. These illnesses, such as schizophrenia and manic-depression, are treated by a combination of hospitalization, medication, and supportive therapy for both the patient and his family.

When to go for help. Few people escape
periodic feelings of depression. Death, job loss, broken marriages or relationships, and major illness all make normal people feel sad, angry, or unhappy. But when those feelings persist over an extended period of time, even when the situation changes, or when there seems to be no rational explanation for the feelings, it is time to look for outside help. Researchers have found that therapy helps most people to some extent, no matter who delivers it.

Depression is the most common reason for people to seek help. Anxiety attacks, eating disorders, marital conflict, phobias, and some psychosomatic illnesses are all responsive to psychotherapy.

Depression checklist

- Sad moods and crying spells
- Feelings of despair
- Recurring guilt feelings
- Loss of pleasure
- Forgetfulness and lack of concentration
- Insomnia or abnormal amounts of sleep
- Loss of appetite or abnormal hunger
- Loss of interest in sex
- Suicidal thoughts
- Vague or actual physical complaints
- Irritability

Other mental illnesses, such as psychoses, alcoholism, and drug addition, are rarely helped by psychotherapy alone.

How to get help. The phone book is a good
place to begin for mental health centers, Alcoholics Anonymous, and drug and alcohol treatment centers, but it is probably the very worst way to locate a psychotherapist.

Although proper credentials are important, they are not as vital as a sense of caring and warmth. A recommendation from a primary care doctor is useful, but word of mouth is also valuable. Talking to people who have been in therapy and who have been helped can put you on the right track.

Many clergymen are trained as counselors. For some people, this help is the most accessible and the least expensive.

Who are the mentally ill?

One out of ten American families has a member who is seriously mentally ill. If you do not have a victim in your own family, the family down the block probably does. It is particularly important not to dismiss a "blue Monday" teenager as just going through an adolescent stage. Seek professional advice if your daughter or son seems persistently depressed.

Understanding alcoholism.

Alcoholism is defined by the American Medical Association as a disease that, if not checked, leads to death. Yet the image of the alcoholic as the town drunk sleeping it off on a park bench fades slowly. Since most people in our society drink safely, it is easy to view alcoholism as the result of moral weakness and poor self-control.

Alcoholism is a leading cause of death and is implicated in 90 percent of physical assaults, 50 percent of murders, and 25 percent of suicides. Drunken drivers account for 25,000 deaths on the highway each year.

The causes of alcoholism are still obscure, although recent research points toward a genetic predisposition in many cases. Young people who combine alcohol with drugs account for a new phenomenon—17- and 18-year-olds who are as physically and mentally ill as older alcoholics who have been drinking for 30 or 40 years.

Who are the alcoholics? Despite the popular stereotype, alcoholics are found in corporate board rooms, on the police force, in the classroom, in the medical profession, among priests, ministers, and rabbis, and in suburban homes. Alcoholism permeates our entire society.

Because the progress of the disease is often slow, many people cross the line into alcoholism without being aware of it. Any wife who has tried to convince her husband that he is drinking too much knows how difficult it is for someone else to make an alcoholic recognize his own problem.

Can an alcoholic be helped? Very real help is available to the alcoholic who is able to recognize his need for it. Lifelong abstinence sounds like a grim sentence in a society that celebrates all occasions with alcohol. However, many people considered "hopeless" by their families, employers, and doctors have recovered through participation in Alcoholics Anonymous (A.A.), the self-help group with the best track record. Many people combine A.A. with alcohol counseling.

Many large corporations now have outreach programs for their employees, often financing extended treatment. Local governments are establishing alcohol treatment centers, and in many states, insurance companies are required by state law to provide coverage for both in-hospital and outpatient treatment.

Are you in trouble with alcohol?

- Do you need a drink to make you feel relaxed? Self-confident? To have a good time?
- Do you drink every day?
- Do you look forward all day to your first drink?
- Are you drinking more than you used to? More than you want to?
- Do you have a drink before going to a party?
- Have you changed your favorite drink lately to help you cut down?
- Have friends, family, or your employer mentioned your drinking?
- Do you frequently plan to stop drinking?
- Do you ever hide bottles or lie about the amount you drink?
- Do you drink in the morning, alone, or at work?
- Do you ever carry liquor in your breast pocket or pocketbook?
- Do you have blackouts, severe hangovers, or guilt feelings?
- Are you proud of being able to hold your liquor?
- Are most of your friends heavy drinkers?

There is no passing grade for this quiz. If you answer "yes" to more than one question, it is probably time to take a hard look at your "social" drinking.

Understanding drug addiction.

The drug addict is as poorly understood as the alcoholic. Although alcohol is available at the corner liquor store, drugs are available only from illegal sources—which puts the drug user at odds with the law.

Some drugs, such as heroin and morphine, are truly addictive. Others are considered to be "habituating." The effect is frequently the same. It is not uncommon for someone to try "recreational" drugs as an experiment at a party, to like the effect, and in time to become as addicted as the heroin user.

Prescription drug abusers are a hidden element in the drug addiction picture. Many people start taking tranquilizers or sleeping pills as recommended by their doctor and find themselves not only addicted but forced to seek illegal sources if they do not have a compliant doctor.

Can the drug addict be helped? The same conditions prevail for the drug addict as for the alcoholic. He must want to stop and be willing to turn to appropriate channels for assistance. Detoxification is almost always essential in the case of such drugs as heroin, amphetamines, barbiturates, and some tranquilizers. "Cold turkey" withdrawal from heroin is merely painful, but with some other drugs, it can cause convulsions and even death.

Chapters of Narcotics Anonymous are appearing all over the country, as are fine drug rehabilitation centers. Although addiction is seemingly intractable, many people do recover from its effects and go on to lead normal, drug-free, productive lives.

What about mental patients?

The discovery of major tranquilizers promised a new era in the treatment of the mentally ill. The hospitals were emptied of long-term patients, and promises were made to support their existence in the community. Those promises were not kept, and many communities find heavily medicated former patients wandering the streets, frequently with no place to live. Some are leading sad and dreary lives, with no supervision, as residents of shamefully inadequate rooming houses.

If serious mental illness strikes someone in your family, becoming informed about treatment, medication, and management is vital for your family's survival and for the well-being of your sick family member. Joining advocacy groups, support groups, and becoming active in your community mental health center will provide a focus.

Schizophrenics who learn to manage their illness, who are properly medicated, and who receive family and community support are often able to lead nearly normal lives, spending most of their time outside a hospital setting.

What are psychiatric medications? Psychotropic (psychiatric) medicines are tools used by psychiatrists in treating many kinds of mental illnesses. These medicines do not cure; they ease symptoms or, in the case of psychotic illnesses, control the disease.

As with any other medication, these drugs carry risks that have to be balanced against benefits. The major tranquilizers, for example, carry the potential for serious, permanent side effects; yet they can make the difference between long-term hospitalization and the possibility of living independently.

Managing medication—whether it involves an antidepressant or a major tranquilizer—should be a joint effort on the part of the therapist, the patient, and the patient's family. See page 91 for a chart of psychiatric drugs, their uses and side effects.

Methadone stations like this one exist all over the United States. Methadone helps the addict to overcome his or her dependence on heroin.

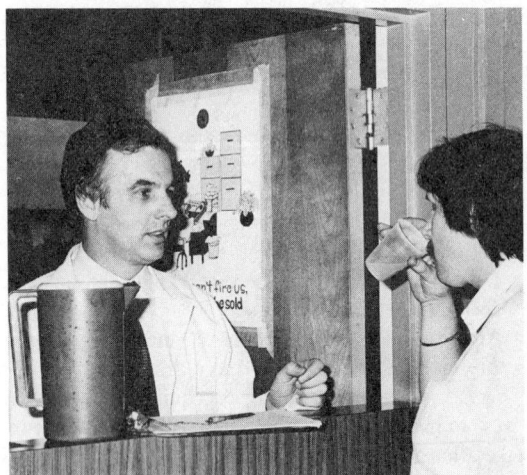

Former mental patients often live in group homes where they gain support from each other and live constructive lives.

Who are the therapists?

Psychiatrist (M.D.)
A medical doctor who is trained in diagnosis and therapy. He or she is the only choice when medication is necessary as an adjunct to therapy.

Psychologist (Ph.D.)
A nonmedical doctor trained in therapeutic techniques, skilled at helping people who do not suffer from psychosis. Cannot prescribe medication. Fees are generally lower than those of a psychiatrist.

Psychiatric Social Worker (M.S.W.)
Trained in counseling and particularly effective in family therapy.

Medical payments

Health insurance is a major element in a family's economic security. Many people are insured through their employers and have only a vague idea of their coverage until a sudden, major illness strikes. Sometimes the extent of that coverage comes as a painful and expensive surprise. It is also not uncommon to forget that health coverage stops unless converted to a personal policy when an employee is dismissed.

Get to know your health policy.
If your policy is difficult to understand, consult the person in your company who handles the coverage.

Here are some important things to know: Is there coverage for office visits? What about prescription drugs? Out-of-hospital tests? Pregnancy? Newborns? Premature births? What are the dollar limits and when does the insurance company begin to pay? Do you pay in advance and get reimbursed later? Are doctors and surgeons fees paid in full or according to an established fee schedule? When does coverage run out?

Major medical insurance. Many
people who are self-employed or who have minimal coverage turn to major medical insurance. Basically, this insurance either picks up when primary insurance stops or provides full coverage when medical expenses pass a predetermined amount, the deductible.

How does your doctor get paid?
The day of doctors' bills being sent to the home seems to be passing. It is quite common, today, to be expected to pay as you go. If this is not possible, discuss it with the doctor. Price is often negotiable.

Specialists' fees. Specialists and surgeons
set their own fees, sometimes at a scale that has made many patients gasp upon hearing them. This is a very sound reason for using specialists only when your primary care doctor thinks it absolutely necessary. If a surgeon's fee is beyond your ability to pay immediately, make arrangements in advance to pay it over an extended period of time.

Managed care. This fast-growing sector of
the health care industry attempts to control medical costs by emphasizing preventive care, eliminating unnecessary tests and procedures, and reducing the number of doctor referrals to specialists or hospital care. Subscribers to a managed care plan pay a standard premium, which covers almost all of their medical costs. Their choice of doctors, however, is limited to those physicians participating in the plan.

Medicaid and Medicare. The sim-
plest thing to remember about these two government-subsidized health benefits is this: Medicaid is linked to income and/or disability; Medicare is linked to age and/or permanent disability.

A doctor must accept the standard of fees set by Medicaid. He or she is not bound to a fee schedule for Medicare, under which patients pay part of their bills.

Many retired persons choose to supplement their Medicare coverage with additional private coverage.

Further information is contained in the chapter *Managing the Family's Money* on page 110, or in the government pamphlet on the subject listed at the end of this chapter.

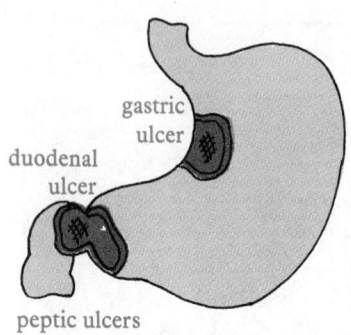

gastric ulcer

duodenal ulcer

peptic ulcers

Glossary

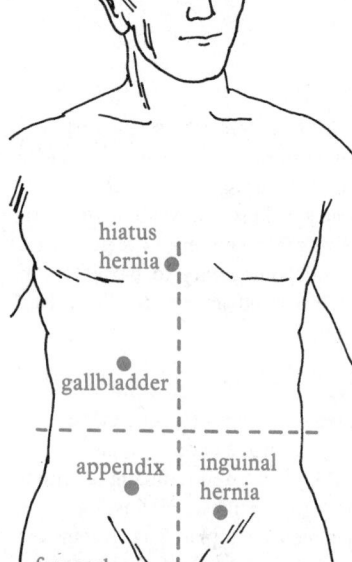

hiatus hernia

gallbladder

appendix

inguinal hernia

femoral hernia

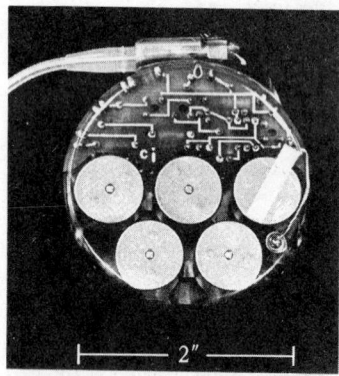

pacemaker

abdominal distention. Condition that may be due to overeating or to gross enlargement of any abdominal organ. Other causes include fluid in the abdomen and gas in the bowels.

abscess. A localized collection of pus (dead cell debris) that can develop in any part of the body. Commonly, abscesses are caused by bacteria, but fungi, yeasts, and amoebae may also be involved.

acromegaly. Slowly progressive disease that produces a characteristic appearance: enlarged bones, a protruding jaw, and a coarsening and thickening of all features.

addiction. Medically, the habitual use of alcohol or drugs.

Addison's disease. Condition caused by inadequate secretion of the adrenal glands. Early symptoms include weakness, loss of energy, and muscular aches.

aerophagia. The habitual swallowing of air as while eating fast, drinking large amounts of carbonated beverages, or chewing gum. In severe cases, there may be abdominal distention, difficult breathing, and palpitations.

alcoholism. The compulsive abuse of alcohol, with resultant extreme nervousness, loss of appetite, vitamin deficiencies, nausea, and vomiting. When chronic, there is liver and kidney dysfunction, and DTs (delirium tremens).

allergy. An unusual reaction in an individual to a substance that usually does not affect other people. Most often, dust, feathers, animal hair, cosmetics, some foods and drugs, and fabrics are involved.

Alzheimer's disease. Generally noted between the ages of 40 and 60. It is associated with gradual memory loss, disorientation, and apathy, and is caused by a disorder of the cells of the brain.

amenorrhea. The absence of menstrual flow. Occurs most commonly during pregnancy and the menopause. Menstruation not started by age 18 is termed primary amenorrhea, while cessation of periods after they have begun is called secondary amenorrhea.

amniocentesis. Diagnostic procedure used to assess various genetic defects and some hereditary disorders of the fetus.

anaphylaxis. A potentially life-threatening type of allergic reaction that can result from the injection of some drugs or diagnostic agents. It may also be caused by wasp stings or such foods as shellfish and strawberries.

anemia. A variety of conditions marked by excessive loss, destruction, or faulty production of red blood cells. Iron-deficiency anemia, the most common form, is often due to a lack of dietary iron.

aneurysm. A swelling or localized bulging of a weakened arterial wall, particularly dangerous when it involves the aorta or arteries in the brain. If ruptured, it can lead to massive internal bleeding that may prove fatal.

angina pectoris. A condition marked by sudden pain in the chest. Generally occurs during strenuous exertion, such as shoveling snow or climbing stairs, which makes the heart work harder.

angiography. X-ray technique in which blood vessels are made visible by injection of a radiopaque substance. The test is useful in detecting the presence of tumors, atherosclerosis, and aneurysms.

You and Modern Medicine

anorexia nervosa. A condition that mainly affects adolescent girls and younger women who eat less and less food. As food intake and weight continue to drop, severe nutritional deficiencies and even death by starvation may occur.

antibiotics. Various natural and synthetic substances widely used to treat infectious diseases. If bactericidal, an antibiotic kills organisms; if bacteriostatic, it prevents their growth.

anticoagulant. Term used to describe the prevention of blood coagulation, or an agent that prevents coagulation.

appendicitis. An inflammation of the worm-shaped (vermiform) appendix, which is located at the tip of the cecum (part of the large bowel). A perforated appendix is a serious complication with the potential of peritonitis.

arrhythmia. An alteration in the regular rhythm of the heart, either in the formation or conduction of heart impulses. Such disturbances may be functional or due to disease.

arteriogram. An x-ray picture of an artery after it has been injected with a contrast medium.

arteriosclerosis. Commonly referred to as hardening of the arteries. Involves thickening, hardening, and loss of elasticity of the artery walls.

arthritis. An inflammation of the joints. Rheumatoid arthritis is a chronic and generally progressive inflammatory disease marked by pain and swelling of the joints. Osteoarthritis is a chronic degenerative disease mainly of weight-bearing joints. See also *Still's disease*.

asthma. A condition marked by difficult breathing and wheezing, chronic or episodic. Three major contributory factors are allergy, respiratory infection, and emotional stress.

atherosclerosis. A form of arteriosclerosis in which fatty substances are deposited in the arteries and their inner layers become tough and sinewy.

athlete's foot (tinea pedis). An infection caused by a fungus that thrives on dead skin cells between the toes. It is commonly found in locker rooms, public showers, and swimming pool walkways.

beta blockers. Drugs that reduce the workload of the heart and thereby lower the demand of the coronary arteries for blood. Beta-blocking agents are prescribed for the treatment of angina pectoris, hypertension, and cardiac arrhythmias.

biopsy. The excision and microscopic examination of tissue samples and cells to determine abnormalities. Indicated when cancer, or certain liver or kidney diseases, are suspected.

bone marrow. The soft red (in spongy bones) or yellow (in long bones) tissue filling the interior cavities of bones. Red marrow is the site of production of the red and white blood cells and the platelets.

brain death. Condition in which there is irreversible coma and evidence of irreparable brain damage. There is lack of electrical activity for a prolonged period, no response to external stimuli, fixed pupils, and absence of spontaneous breathing.

brain scan. Diagnostic technique in which a radioactive isotope or tracer is injected into a vein, usually the arm. A scintillation scanner is used to detect the tiny radioactive emissions as the tracer flows through the blood vessels in the brain.

bronchitis. An acute inflammatory condition usually due to exposure to cold and dampness. When chronic and uncontrolled, bronchitis can create serious lung problems.

bronchoscopy. A diagnostic procedure that permits inspection of the interior of the tracheobronchial tree through a bronchoscope. The technique is helpful in obtaining biopsy specimens and removing obstructions.

bursitis. A painful inflammation of the bursa, which are small fluid-filled sacs that facilitate movement of body joints. Most commonly, the shoulder, elbow, hip, and knee are involved.

Caesarean section. A technique in which the fetus is removed by means of an incision into the uterus, usually via the abdominal wall. Generally, it is employed when there is an overly large fetus or an abnormally small pelvis.

cancer. Many diseases, all characterized by an irregular and uncontrolled growth of body cells. These malignant cells may remain in the area where they formed or may spread via the blood and lymph to other parts of the body.

candidiasis. A yeastlike fungus. *Candida albicans* is responsible for this infection, called thrush when it is localized in the mouth or throat, vaginitis when it affects the vaginal walls.

cardiac arrest. A sudden cessation of heartbeat and breathing. This is a medical emergency calling for immediate attention. Cardio-pulmonary resuscitation (CPR) is potentially life-saving, but can only be performed by a person trained in the technique.

CAT scan. See *computerized axial tomography*.

chemotherapy. The use of drugs or chemical agents that have a specific and toxic effect upon disease-causing microorganisms. The term is often applied to potent drugs that destroy cancer cells.

chicken pox (varicella). A highly contagious infectious disease that occurs mostly in children. Symptoms include fever, headache, malaise, and at times a sore throat. A red rash that crusts develops.

childbed fever (puerpural fever). Occurs after a prolonged or difficult childbirth and is marked by septicemia. There is absorption of septic products into blood and tissues, or disease-causing organisms that may multiply in these areas.

cholecystitis. Inflammation of the gallbladder, either acute or chronic, often due to obstruction of the bile duct by gallstones. Symptoms include pain, nausea, vomiting, and fever.

cholecystography. The examination of the gallbladder by x-ray study. Useful in detecting gallstones or gallbladder dysfunction.

cholesterol. A sterol, this fatlike substance is found in animal fats and oils, nerve tissue, bile, blood, and egg yolk. A normal constituent of bile, cholesterol can also be manufactured in the liver.

chromosome. A microscopic J- or V-shaped body present in all living cells. Chromosomes contain genes, the particles responsible for determining hereditary characteristics. The normal number of chromosomes in each human cell is 46, arranged in 23 pairs.

cirrhosis. Chronic condition in which there are degenerative changes in the liver cells and thickening of surrounding tissue; interferes with normal liver function. Often associated with advanced alcoholism.

collagen. An insoluble protein that represents about 30

percent of total body protein. Found in the white fibers of connective tissue, cartilage, and bone.

collagen diseases. Various conditions causing cellular changes affecting the body's connective tissue. Diseases include lupus erythematosus, rheumatoid arthritis, and scleroderma.

colonoscopy. Permits examination of the upper portion of the rectum with an elongated speculum. May also be useful in removing polyps and obtaining tissue samples for biopsy.

colostomy. Temporary or permanent surgical opening made from the colon through the abdominal wall. Creates an artificial passage for the elimination of solid wastes to the outside of the body.

computerized axial tomography (CAT scan). A computer-aided x-ray system that can be used with safety and effectiveness, exposing a person to about the same amount of radiation as obtained from a chest x-ray. Provides highly detailed imaging of internal structures of the brain, lungs, pancreas, and kidneys.

concussion. Commonly the result of a severe blow to the head. Brain concussion may be accompanied by temporary or prolonged unconsciousness. Recovery may be gradual, depending upon age, damage, and care given.

congestive heart failure. Impaired circulation when the heart cannot pump sufficient blood to supply the body's needs. Congestion, or fluid accumulation, may develop in the lungs, legs, or abdomen.

conjunctivitis. Refers to inflammation of the conjunctiva, the mucous membrane

lining the eyelids and white of the eye. Causative factors include allergy, bacterial and viral infections, smoke, dust, or wind.

convulsions. Condition marked by involuntary jerking movements, often with momentary unconsciousness. Some possible causes may be epilepsy, stroke, meningitis, hypoglycemia, skull fracture, brain tumor, and drug reactions.

coronary bypass. A major operative procedure in which a blocked coronary artery is bypassed with a section of vein taken from the leg and grafted into position. Double, triple, and quadruple bypass can be performed.

coronary occlusion. Blockage of vessels supplying blood to the myocardium (heart muscle). May be produced by growth of plaque (fatty materials), or by growth of a thrombus (blood clot) plugging the artery.

corpus luteum. Ovarian follicle after it has released its ovum. Produces the hormone progesterone, which prepares the uterine lining for possible implantation of the ovum.

crib death. See *sudden infant death.*

cross-eye. See *strabismus.*

croup. An acute viral infection that occurs most often in infants and young children. Marked by difficult breathing and a hoarse cough.

cryosurgery. Surgical procedure in which cells are destroyed by the application of extreme cold (the tissue is usually cooled to below 0° F (−20° C). Used in the treatment of malignant tumors and certain precancerous conditions.

culdoscopy. Examination of the female internal organs and pelvic cavity with an endoscope. Used in cases of suspected abnormal uterine tissue growth, infertility, and pelvic disorders.

curettage. Scraping of a cavity with a curette. In uterine curettage, scraping is done to remove contents of the uterus, obtain diagnostic specimens, or remove growths.

cyst. An abnormal sac or swelling filled with fluid or a semisolid material; may occur anywhere in the body. Sebaceous cysts, often forming on the scalp, consist of a small sac containing a yellowish-white caseous matter.

cystocele. A hernia sometimes associated with childbirth, where part of the bladder protrudes into the vagina. The condition may be accompanied by bladder incontinence or infection.

cystoscopy. An examination of the inside of the bladder and urethra with a cystoscope. Indicated when there is a suspicion of bladder or urinary tract cancer or polyps.

D&C (dilation and curettage). Procedure in which the cervix is enlarged (dilated) to facilitate scraping of the uterine walls. Undertaken to remove unwanted tissue from the uterus, remove growths, or obtain tissue for examination.

decubitus ulcers. Bedsores caused by poor circulation in the area under pressure. Common in bedridden patients who must lie in one position. Buttocks, shoulders, elbows, and heels are often involved.

dermatitis. An inflammation of the skin which, in extremely sensitive persons, may be due to contact with such skin irritants as acids and alkalis, cosmetics, fabrics, and animal hair. Marked by itching, redness, and skin lesions.

diabetes insipidus. Form of diabetes in which there is a chronic excretion of very large amounts of urine, accompanied by extreme thirst. Ordinarily results from an insufficient production of the antidiuretic hormone by the pituitary gland.

diabetes mellitus. A metabolic disorder in which the body is unable to utilize carbohydrates, primarily due to the inadequate production of insulin by the pancreas. It is detected by the presence of sugar in the blood and urine.

diagnosis. The use of various methods to determine the cause and nature of a disease. Among the methods are study of the signs and symptoms of a disease, laboratory data, and special tests.

dialysis. A process employed to separate or extract certain substances in solution by diffusion through a porous membrane. Used to purify the blood (hemodialysis) in persons with one or both kidneys defective or absent.

diarrhea. A condition that is marked by the frequent passage of loose, watery stools. May be caused by infection, food poisoning, overeating, or certain drugs.

diverticular disease. Condition marked by diarrhea, colic, and abdominal pain. Diverticula are pouches or pockets that form on the large bowel. In diverticulosis, the colon contains dozens of these pouches.

DNA (deoxyribonucleic acid). A nucleic acid present in chromosomes of the nuclei of cells. Considered the chemical basis of heredity, and the carrier of genetic information.

Down's syndrome. Congenital abnormality, also known as mongolism, marked by moderate to severe mental retardation. Children born with Down's have a sloping forehead, low-set ears, slanted eyes, and a generally dwarfed physique.

dysmenorrhea. Painful or difficult menstruation. Discomfort is usually felt in the lower abdomen and sometimes the lower back. Often the condition improves with age and may disappear after childbirth.

dysplasia. Abnormal tissue development that can occur in the cervix, lungs, and other parts of the body. Women with cervical dysplasia must be examined regularly as it may become cancerous.

electrocardiogram (ECG or EKG). A graphic record of the electrical activity of the heart. Can indicate whether electrical conduction is normal and whether there is dead tissue due to a previous heart attack.

electroencephalogram (EEG). Graphic recording of the electric activity of the brain. May be used for a number of different purposes, such as diagnosing epilepsy and for research into sleep and dream patterns.

embolism. An obstruction of a blood vessel by a transported solid (an embolus): a blood clot, bacterial mass, or other foreign material. The severity of the condition is in direct relationship to the size and location of the blocked vessel.

emphysema. A chronic lung disease. The alveoli (air sacs) become greatly distended, bronchioles become thinned, and, eventually, the architecture of the lungs is destroyed. Chronic bronchitis or bronchial asthma, smoking, and air pollution may be implicated.

endocardiography. Method used to record the size, motion, and composition of various cardiac structures. Indicated in heart valve problems that are difficult to diagnose.

endocarditis. An inflammation of the heart lining (endocardium). Persons with damaged heart valves are most vulnerable. The condition is often observed in young adults and the middle-aged.

endometriosis. A nonmalignant condition in which tissue normally located in the lining of the uterus (endometrium) begins to grow elsewhere. Often seen in the ovaries, the Fallopian tubes, the bladder, or between the rectum and vagina.

enzyme. One of various complex proteins produced by living cells. Enzymes alter the chemical reactions in other substances while remaining unchanged in the process, and help break down food particles into simple, more readily absorbed compounds.

epilepsy. Includes a group of nervous disorders characterized by either convulsive or nonconvulsive seizures and, generally, a temporary loss of consciousness. Seizures are associated with a sudden unruly pattern of brain waves.

epistaxis (nosebleed). Included among the causes are high blood pressure, injury, infection, foreign bodies, and a direct blow to the nose. If severe or uncontrolled, nosebleed requires medical attention.

erythrocyte sedimentation rate. A laboratory test that determines how fast red blood cells (erythrocytes) in a blood specimen settle to the bottom of a long narrow tube. The speed of settling is increased in various infections, pregnancy, and cancer.

fever (pyrexia). A body temperature above the normal, which, taken orally, is 98.6° F (37° C). Generally, a fever of 101° F (39° C) calls for medical attention.

fibroma. A benign tumor derived from fibrous tissue. May vary in size from a millet seed to large enough to fill the entire abdominal cavity. May be single or multiple in number.

fistula. An abnormal tubelike passage that leads from a normal cavity or tube to the free surface, or to another cavity. Fistulae may be congenital or result from abscesses, injuries, or inflammatory processes.

flatulence. An excessive amount of gas in the stomach and intestine. May be due to habitual air swallowing or indigestion. If it is worse after eating fatty foods, there may be gallstones.

flu. See *influenza*.

fluoroscopy. A technique that permits examination of inner parts of the body by means of the fluoroscope. In the upper body, there is x-ray visualization of the esophagus, stomach, and duodenum; in the lower body, the large intestine is visualized.

gallstones. Concretions or stonelike masses that form in the gallbladder or bile ducts. May not cause much distress or may be associated with painful attacks.

gamma globulin. Various proteins found in the lymphatic system, bone marrow, and spleen, associated with the production of antibodies. They circulate in the blood and help the body to resist infection.

gastritis. Inflammation of the mucous membrane of the stomach. May be due to viral infection, hot spicy food, food poisoning, or overindulgence in alcoholic beverages.

gastroscopy. Inspection of the inner surface of the stomach by the use of an endoscope.

Useful in confirming stomach ulcers, unexplained bleeding, or other abnormalities.

genetics. The branch of science that is concerned with heredity.

German measles (rubella). An acute contagious disease similar to measles and scarlet fever. Women who have not had rubella in childhood should be protected against this disease before considering pregnancy.

glandular. Relates to the nature of a gland, a secreting organ or structure. There are many types of glands, and they serve different purposes throughout the body.

glaucoma. A disease of the eye marked by an unaccountable rise in fluid pressure within the eyeball. If unrelieved, it can cause permanent damage to the eye and result in partial or total blindness.

glossitis. Inflammation of the tongue, which may be associated with stomatitis (inflammation of the mouth). The tongue becomes tender and painful; thick saliva makes swallowing difficult.

goiter. An enlarged thyroid. Due to overactivity of the gland in secreting an excessive amount of hormones. In severe cases, the thyroid gland may swell to several times its normal size and be observable as a large growth on the front of the throat.

gonorrhea. A sexually transmitted disease that, if untreated, can lead to serious damage. In the male, it can cause epididymitis; in women, it may result in painful infection of the Fallopian tubes, often causing sterility.

graft. Insertion of skin or other living substance into similar substance for the purpose of overcoming a defect. In skin graft, a piece of skin is removed from one part of the body to another to cover a large superficial burn.

gynecology. A branch of medicine that deals with diseases of women, in particular, the genital tract and the female endocrine and reproductive systems.

habituation. The act of becoming accustomed to something by frequent use. In general, it refers to the psychological dependence that develops with the continued use of a drug, eventually resulting in drug addiction.

Hashimoto's disease. A chronic form of thyroiditis (inflammation of the thyroid gland) manifested by a particular type of goiter.

headache (cephalalgia). A symptom that is associated with a great many diseases and emotional states. Infection and tension are among the causes.

heart attack. See *myocardial infarction*.

heartburn. An abnormal return of acid liquid from the stomach into the esophagus. Produces a burning sensation deep in the chest together with an oppressive tightening sensation.

hematoma. A localized mass of blood that has escaped from a vessel into the tissues, occurring at the site of an injury where the blood vessels have broken.

hemodialysis. A procedure that is used to purify the blood in persons with kidney failure; usually requires 20 hours a week; 10 hours twice a week; or 6½ hours three times a week.

hemophilia. An hereditary blood disease in which the blood fails to clot and there is an abnormal tendency to bleed from a cut or other injury. Transmitted from mother to son as a sex-linked recessive condition.

hemorrhoids (piles). Varicose (enlarged or swollen) veins of the anal and rectal area. External hemorrhoids occur on the outside of the anal sphincter; internal hemorrhoids develop within the anal canal.

hepatitis (infectious). Acute disease of the liver. Viral hepatitis type A is transmitted by the oral-fecal route. It is spread from person to person by infected food handlers or contaminated food, water, feces, or bedpans.

hepatitis (serum). Viral hepatitis type B. Transmitted by injection of infected blood or by the use of contaminated needles or instruments. Similar to type A, it is caused by a virus found in blood and tissues rather than in the feces.

hepatitis (toxic). An inflammation of the liver caused by exposure to certain chemicals (carbon tetrachloride, insecticides, solvents). In those overly sensitive to such drugs as ioniazid and bromates, liver damage may result.

hernia. A weak point in the abdominal wall through which a part of the intestine can protrude. Commonly seen types are inguinal (groin), umbilical (navel), and femoral (thigh).

hernia (hiatus). Protrusion of the upper part of the stomach into the chest cavity. This condition is associated with weakness in the area where the esophagus opens up into the diaphragm. This impairment permits leakage of acid stomach contents into the esophagus.

herpes smplex. A virus infection that causes painful fluid-filled blisters, called cold sores or fever blisters. Other forms of herpes simplex are denoted according to site; for example, herpes genitalis.

herpes zoster (shingles). A completely different disease from herpes simplex, this painful vesicular eruption occurs along the course of a nerve. It is due to the same virus, herpes varicella, as that causing chicken pox.

Hodgkin's disease. A malignant disease that mostly afflicts men. It is marked by painless and progressive swelling of the lymph glands with enlargement of the spleen. Some symptoms are anemia, fever, and fatigue.

hydrocephalus. An increased accumulation of cerebrospinal fluid within the hollow spaces (ventricles) of the brain. It may result from a malformation, infection, injury, or a brain tumor.

hypertension. High blood pressure denoting arterial pressure that is consistently elevated. Added pressure on the blood vessel walls makes the heart work harder; untreated, it can cause organ damage.

hyperthyroidism (Graves' disease). The result of an overproduction of hormones by the thyroid gland. Besides exophthalmos goiter, symptoms include increased nervousness and heart rate, weight loss, and heat intolerance.

hypoglycemia. An abnormally low concentration of sugar in circulating blood. May be due to an insulin overdose or a missed meal by a diabetic. In nondiabetics, poor diet may be a cause.

hypothermia. A technique used to lower body temperature and so reduce the need for oxygen during surgery. It is especially useful when the heart and the nerves are involved.

hypothyroidism (myxedema). Condition in which the thyroid gland is underactive, failing to secrete an adequate amount of hormones. As the condition progresses, there is slowed pulse rate, sluggish movement, facial puffiness, and muscle weakness.

hysterectomy. An operative procedure that involves removal of the uterus. It is usually indicated when tumors are present, whether benign or malignant.

immunosuppressive agent. Belonging to a group of drugs that interfere with the body's natural immune system. Used before surgical transplant of a foreign organ, such as a kidney, to avert body rejection.

indigestion. Often caused by eating too much too fast, not chewing food well, eating when emotionally upset, or swallowing large amounts of air. Symptoms may be heartburn, gas, and belching.

infarction (infarct). Condition in which there is death of tissue and consequent scarring in an organ deprived of an adequate supply of blood. Myocardial infarction describes such an occurrence in the heart.

influenza (flu). A respiratory infection caused by one of several related, yet distinct, viruses. It strikes suddenly with chills, fever, headache, muscle aches, and a dry cough, most of which subside after a few days.

insomnia. Inability to sleep. In itself, not a disease, but it may be a symptom of disease, either of a slight or serious nature. Most often due to pain or anxiety.

insulin shock. A low blood sugar reaction that can be caused by an insulin overdose. Often the result of lowered blood sugar brought on by a break in normal routine or emotional upset.

irritable bowel syndrome. A common gastric disorder marked by abdominal pain, diarrhea, and/or constipation.

In general, the problem is not organic but stems from the nature of a person's personality, particularly an inability to deal with stress.

jaundice. An excessive amount of bile pigment in the blood and a yellowish discoloration of the skin. Associated with diseases of the liver, gallbladder, bile ducts, and certain blood diseases.

laryngitis. An inflammation of the larynx. May be due to improper use or overuse of the voice. May also be caused by upper respiratory infections, the inhalation of irritating vapors or dust, or tobacco smoke.

lead poisoning. Results from the ingestion of lead, as during prolonged exposure to lead dust in the workplace, when using lead vessels for eating or drinking, or when chewing on lead toys.

legionnaires' disease. Applies to a severe pneumonialike disease that felled 249 American Legion conventioneers in Philadelphia (July, 1976). Marked by fever, cough, and bloody sputum. Additional symptoms may not be distinguishable from other types of pneumonia.

leukemia. A form of cancer in which there is a rapid increase of white blood cells in the bloodstream. The cells infiltrate body tissues and, in particular, bone marrow. This condition leads to anemia, hemorrhaging, and infection.

lumpectomy. Surgical procedure in which only a primary tumor and a varying amount of surrounding breast tissue is removed. Radiation therapy is used postoperatively.

lupus erythematoses. Systemic, and possibly chronic, disease in which a skin rash spreads across the bridge of the nose

and face in a butterfly pattern. The disease affects the blood vessels.

lymphatic vessels. Vessels that transport lymph (the clear fluid bathing all body tissues), lymphocytes (a type of white blood cell), and other substances needed for the body's immune system. These vessels are part of the lymph system along with the lacteals, lymph capillaries, ducts, and nodes.

malignancy. Term that describes a condition occurring in severe form, growing worse, and resisting treatment. In cancer, it denotes uncontrollable growth and dissemination, or recurrence after removal of a tumor, or both.

mammography. Specialized x-ray technique for detecting breast abnormalities, especially early cancers. Recent improvements assure more accurate information and smaller amounts of radiation.

manic-depressive psychoses. A major mental disorder in which a person displays severe changes of mood: overelation and excessive activity during the manic state; depression and anxiety while in the depressed state.

mastectomy. A surgical procedure that involves removal of the breast. If simple, only breast tissue is excised; if major, the underlying chest muscles and the lymph nodes in the armpit are also removed.

mastoiditis. Infection that spreads through the ear to the mastoid process (part of the temporal bone). When acute, symptoms include chills, fever, malaise, and headache. When chronic, mastoid tissue is destroyed and there is loss of hearing.

measles. A highly communicable viral disease that usually occurs in early childhood. Marked by nasal discharge, fever, cough, and reddening of the eyes; also, a blotchy rash and fine white spots inside the mouth.

medication. A medicinal substance that is a medicine or remedy. Also refers to treatment with a remedy. (See pages 90-91 for a list of prescription drugs.)

Ménierè's disease. An impairment of the balancing mechanism of the inner ear. Attacks often come on with alarming suddenness. Symptoms include vertigo, ringing or other disturbing noises in the ear, and progressive loss of hearing.

meningitis. An inflammation of the meninges, the delicate membranes covering the layers of the brain. A local infection of the ears, sinuses, or tonsils may spread the infection to the meninges, or be carried into the bloodstream.

menopause. The cessation of menstruation that brings to a close the reproductive life of a woman. Natural menopause may occur as early as age 35, and as late as 58. Usually, it takes place between the ages of 47 and 52.

metabolism. The sum of chemical changes affecting the function of nutrition. Two fundamental processes are involved: anabolism—converting small molecules into large; and catabolism—converting large molecules into small.

microorganisms. Living organisms too small to be seen with the naked eye. Only a relatively small number are pathogenic (capable of causing disease). Protozoa, bacteria, fungi, rickettsiae, and viruses are all microorganisms.

migraine. A severe, periodic, vascular type of headache, usually one-sided. It may be

preceded or accompanied by various symptoms: visual disturbances, extreme sensitivity to light, and nausea.

mole. A congenital discolored spot raised above the skin surface. Generally, moles are harmless unless there is irritation in the area.

mongolism. See *Down's syndrome*.

mononucleosis (infectious). An acute infection, also called glandular fever, believed to be due to a virus. It is manifested by a sore throat, fever, swollen lymph nodes, headache, and a faintly red eruption.

multiple sclerosis (MS). A chronic disease of the central nervous system in which there is degeneration of the myelin (a fatlike substance) sheath in the brain and spinal cord. Symptoms may come and go for years, but incapacitation worsens with progress of the disease.

mumps (epidemic parotitis). An acute febrile disease marked by inflammation of the parotid salivary glands (just below the ears). Although not as communicable as chicken pox or measles, mumps are quite contagious.

muscular dystrophy (Duchenne's disease). A hereditary disorder that primarily affects boys. There is progressive weakness and wasting of muscles, first affecting the abdomen and buttocks, then the chest and other body parts.

musculoskeletal. Relates to the muscles and the skeleton.

myasthenia gravis. A chronic neuromuscular disorder caused by a defective transmission of nerve impulse to the muscles. Marked by extreme muscular weakness, but no wasting of muscles.

myelitis. An inflammation of the spinal cord or of bone marrow. A potentially serious condition

that calls for prompt diagnosis and treatment. If the spinal nerves are involved, there may be partial or total paralysis.

myocardial infarction (heart attack). Condition in which part of the heart muscle is deprived of blood and dies, being gradually replaced by a fibrous scar (infarct).

nephritis. Inflammation of the kidneys. Denotes a group of noninfectious diseases involving widespread kidney damage. The glomeruli (filtering units of the kidney) or the tubules may be affected.

nephrolithiasis. Condition in which calculi, or stones, are formed in the kidney and urinary bladder. Many kidney stones eventually pass out; others must be removed surgically.

neuritis. May be inflammation of a nerve (mononeuritis) or nerves (polyneuritis), usually characterized by pain. May be caused by injury, infection, metallic poisoning, or a metabolic disturbance.

neurosis. A psychological or behavioral disorder with the chief underlying factor being anxiety. In contrast with psychosis, persons with neurosis maintain contact with reality and undergo no major personality changes.

nonspecific urethritis. Condition in which the specific organism causing inflammation of the urethra is unknown. May be due to Chlamydia trachomatis, the same microbe that causes the eye disease trachoma.

nosebleed. See *epistaxis*.

oophorectomy. Surgical procedure in which an ovary or a portion of it is removed; also called ovariectomy.

osteoarthritis. Form of arthritis in which there is chronic degeneration of the joints, especially the weight-bearing (spinal column, hip, and knee) joints. Swelling may appear at the sides of each finger joint (Heberden's nodes).

osteomalacia. Disease in which bones gradually become soft due to bonelike tissue that fails to calcify. Bones become flexible and brittle, resulting in pain and deformation.

osteomyelitis. An inflammation of bone marrow and adjacent bone involving sudden pain, fever, and bone tenderness. Movement is painful and restricted, with subsequent swelling over the bone and often the nearby joint.

osteoporosis. A disorder characterized by the loss of bone mass. Increases the potential for fractures, particularly of the weight-bearing vertebrae. With compression of vertebrae, there is loss of height and, at times, kyphosis (humpback).

otitis. Inflammation of the ear differentiated by the part of the ear affected: otitis externa, the outer ear; otitis media, the middle ear; and otitis interna, the inner ear.

otosclerosis. Formation of spongy bone around the stapes (a small bone in the middle ear) that results in progressively worsening deafness. This hearing loss can be corrected surgically or with a hearing aid.

ovarian cyst. An abnormal fluid-filled sac that develops within an ovary. It afflicts many women between the ages of 30 and 60. Enlarged, painful cysts are removed surgically.

pacemaker. Defines any rhythmic center that controls heart rhythm; normally, the sinus node. An artificial pacemaker is a device that substitutes for the normal pacemaker and controls heart rhythm.

Paget's disease (osteitis deformans). Generalized skeletal disease seen mainly in older persons. It is marked by an increased breakdown and reforming of bone that leads to abnormal thickening and softening of the bones.

pancreatitis. Condition in which there is inflammation of the pancreas. In the acute form, may lead to areas of tissue destruction and scattered hemorrhages. Complaints include abdominal pain, nausea, vomiting, and fever.

paralysis. A temporary or permanent loss of voluntary muscular movement in a part of the body. There are many different causes, including injury, infection, and stroke.

paraplegia. Paralysis caused by injury to the spinal cord. Paraplegics suffer paralysis in both legs and, usually, the lower trunk. Quadriplegics have paralysis in all four limbs.

paratyphoid fever. Similar to but less severe than typhoid fever. Caused by an infection of Salmonella bacteria. The infection is transmitted by contaminated food, milk, or water.

Parkinson's disease (paralysis agitans). A chronic, progressive disease involving the brain. Symptoms include a masklike face, muscular tremor of the head and extremities, and muscular stiffness with slowed voluntary movement.

pediculosis. An infestation of the body with lice. The infection is spread by direct contact with an infected person, or by the use of infected clothing or objects. There are three kinds of lice: head, body, and pubic.

pellagra. Chiefly a B vitamin deficiency (nicotinic acid). May also be caused by intestinal diseases or alcoholism. In severe cases, there is inflamed

mouth and tongue, skin rash, diarrhea, and anemia.

peptic ulcer. May be a stomach ulcer (gastric) or of the duodenum (duodenal). It is associated with a decreased ability of the organ to withstand bathing by the acid gastric juices (pepsin and hydrochloric acid).

pericarditis. Condition in which there is inflammation of the pericardium, the membranous sac enveloping the heart. It is often accompanied by shortness of breath and chest pains that may be aggravated on coughing or deep breathing.

peritonitis. Inflammation of the peritoneum, the membrane lining the abdominal cavity. Acute peritonitis is caused by infection, such as that caused by a ruptured appendix, which requires immediate hospitalization and treatment.

pheochromocytoma. A disorder caused by a tumor of the adrenal gland. Usually manifested by sustained high blood pressure. Symptoms, varying widely from person to person, include nausea, headache, palpitations, and weakness.

phlebitis. Inflammation of a vein, most often noted in a leg. May involve injury to the vein, obesity, infection, or a problem related to blood circulation.

pleurisy (pleuritis). Inflammation of the membrane covering the lungs. Usually due to a bacterial or viral infection. In acute cases, there is stabbing pain in the affected side, high fever, and a dry cough.

pneumonia. An inflammatory condition of the lungs, marked by cough, chest pains, and fever. Causative agents are bacteria or viruses, but mostly the pneumococcus— *Diplococcus pneumoniae*—is involved.

You and Modern Medicine

pneumothorax. A condition in which air or gas escapes into the pleural cavity. It usually results from a penetrating chest wound, or may be due to various lung diseases. In either case, the lung or parts of the lung collapse.

poliomyelitis (infantile paralysis). A viral infection that attacks the gray matter of the spinal cord. This can lead to muscular paralysis, especially of the limbs and of the muscles involved with breathing.

polyarteritis. Condition marked by widespread inflammation of the smaller arteries. Often leads to complications, such as kidney disease and high blood pressure.

polyp. An abnormal, often benign, stalklike growth. Usually occurs in vascular organs, such as the nose, uterus, and rectum. If there is any sign of malignancy, polyps should be removed surgically.

Pontiac fever. A pneumonialike disease first noted in Pontiac, Michigan (1968). The bacteria are believed to be slightly different strains of the same bacteria as those causing legionnaires' disease.

positron emission tomography (PET). A scanner that makes images of the body from radioactive isotopes; the images are deciphered by computers. It is an invasive means of visualizing brain sites to detect neuropsychiatric disorders.

Pott's disease. Spinal tuberculosis. The condition may also affect the hips and knees. It occurs mainly in children and adults up to 40 years of age.

preeclampsia and eclampsia. Conditions commonly referred to as toxemias of pregnancy. Preeclampsia is often marked by fluid retention and high blood pressure. In eclampsia, convulsions occur and pregnancy must be terminated.

pregnancy tests.
Slide test. Simple test that involves mixing urine with a solution on a slide and examining results. It is most accurate when done at least seven weeks after the last menstrual period.
Tube (hemagglutination inhibition) test. Typical of home pregnancy tests, urine is mixed with a testing solution in a tube. It is slightly more accurate and can be done about a week earlier than the slide test.
Radioreceptor assay (RRA) blood test; beta-HCG (human chorionic gonadotropin) test; monoclonal antibodies test. The newest of available tests with which accurate positive results can be obtained as early as the time of the first missed period.

prognosis. Foretelling of the probable course and outcome of a disease.

prolapse. Downward or forward displacement of a part of the body. Most often used in denoting a displaced or "fallen" uterus.

prostaglandins. A group of fatty acid derivatives present in many body tissues. They can lower blood pressure, stimulate uterine contractions, and regulate body temperatures.

prostatitis. Inflammation of the prostate. In the acute bacterial form, marked by fever, chills, and back pain. There is usually accompanying difficulty in urination, as well as pain in muscles and joints.

prothrombin time (PT). Test that measures the time needed for a fibrin (a protein formed by the action of thrombin on fibrinogen) clot to form in a treated blood sample.

pseudodementia. Condition in which a person experiences an exaggerated indifference to his surroundings. However, there is no actual impairment of mental capacity.

psittacosis. A viral disease that may be transmitted to humans by infected birds, especially parrots, parakeets, love birds, and canaries. It is generally acquired by breathing in the dust from the cage contents or feathers of the infected birds.

psoriasis. A skin condition marked by formation of unsightly reddish, silvery-scaled patches. In general, the elbows, knees, legs, lower back, chest, and scalp are affected.

psychiatry. A medical specialty that deals with the diagnosis and treatment of mental illness. Psychotherapy employs mental rather than physical means.

psychosis. Mental disorders in which there is disturbed thought, disintegration of personality, and lack of touch with reality. Schizophrenia is the most common psychosis.

psychosomatic. The influence of the mind (emotions, fears, desires) upon the body functions, especially as it pertains to disease.

psychotropic. All that affects the mind and its processes. Also refers to psychotropic drugs, which have an effect on psychic function, behavior, and experience.

pulmonary embolism. A clot in an artery of the lungs, often due to a detached clot from a leg vein. Those most vulnerable are the bedridden or those with heart or lung disease, cancer, or hip fractures.

purpura. A group of bleeding disorders due to various causes. Characterized by bleeding into the skin and other tissues, mucous membranes, and internal organs.

pyelography. X-ray examination of the renal pelvis and ureter.

It is indicated in cases of recurrent kidney or bladder infection, or severe symptoms of prostate enlargement.

pyelonephritis. Inflammation of the kidney as well as the renal pelvis, commonly caused by an ascending bacterial infection. When chronic, the kidney suffers irreversible changes.

Q fever (query fever, Balkan grippe). An acute infective disease. When first noted, its cause was unknown and the Q stood for "query." The organism is carried by livestock and transmitted to humans by inhalation of infected dusts, or by drinking of contaminated milk of infected animals.

radiation sickness. An illness resulting from chronic exposure to or excessive amounts of high-energy radiation. Symptoms may be mild or may result in serious disturbances in blood cell formation, leukemia, and other changes.

radioisotope scanning. The study of the function and condition of internal organs, vessels, or body fluids with radioactive forms of chemicals, such as iodine.

radiotherapy (radiation, roentgenography). Treatment of disease by the use of roentgen rays (x-rays), radium, ultraviolet, and other radiations. It may be used alone or in combination with surgery or drugs.

Raynaud's disease. Condition in which there is spasm in the blood vessels of the extremities, especially in response to cold temperatures that would not normally affect a person. Most often, the fingers are affected.

reticular activating system (RAS). A complex system of nerve cells and fibers in the brain stem, hypothalamus, and adjacent areas. It plays an important part in maintaining alertness or wakefulness.

retinitis pigmentosa. Chronic and progressive disease that usually starts in childhood. It is marked by retinal degeneration, widespread changes in retinal pigmentation, wasting of the optic nerve, and defective night vision.

Reye's syndrome. Potentially fatal disorder that usually afflicts children under 18 following a viral infection such as chicken pox. It is marked by increased pressure on the brain and fatty degeneration of the liver.

Rh blood factor (Rhesus factor). A factor discovered in red blood cells of the rhesus monkey. It is present in about 85 percent of the human population who are said to be Rh positive (Rh+). Those not having this substance in the blood are Rh negative (Rh−).

rheumatic fever. A disease of childhood and adolescence that often follows symptoms of throat infection. If untreated, it can lead to heart damage.

rheumatoid arthritis. A chronic and usually progressive inflammatory disease of the joints that affects women more than men. Pain and swelling of the joints result in restricted movement.

rickets. A childhood disease primarily due to a lack of dietary Vitamin D, or inadequate exposure to sunlight, or both. Rickets interferes with the normal deposition of calcium.

RNA (ribonucleic acid). The "message" molecule that carries information from the nucleus (the vital body in cell protoplasm) to cytoplasma (cell protoplasm outside the nucleus) sites.

Rocky Mountain spotted fever. An infectious disease caused by a species of rickettsia. Usually acquired in man from the bite of infected ticks. Marked by high fever, muscle and bone pain, and rash.

Salmonellosis. The most common form of food poisoning, caused by ingestion of food contaminated with bacteria of the genus Salmonella. There is severe inflammation of the stomach lining and intestines.

salpingitis. Inflammatory condition of a Fallopian tube usually caused by a bacterial infection spreading upward from the uterus, cervix, or vagina.

sarcoma. A general term for cancer. Composed of cells from connective tissues of the body, such as bone or muscle. The bladder, kidneys, lungs, liver, spleen, and nearby tissues may be involved.

scabies. Highly infectious skin disease caused by the itch mite, *Sarcoptes scabiei*, and spread by close contact with infected persons. Most often, the hands, wrists, armpits, breasts, and thighs are affected.

scarlet fever. Acute contagious disease caused by a bacterial infection. Marked by sore throat, fever, and a scarlet rash. The infection is spread by the breath or cough of an infected person, or by handling contaminated objects.

schistosomiasis (snail fever). Parasitic infestation due to blood flukes (a type of worm) belonging to a species of Schistosoma. Man becomes infected by bathing in water containing parasitic worms issued from snails.

schizophrenia. A group of mental disorders in which there are disturbances in thinking, mood, and behavior. In some cases, there is an altered sense of reality, delusions, and hallucinations.

sciatica. A severe pain involving the sciatic nerve, which extends from the back of the thigh down through the inside of the leg. The pain is sharp, usually more intense when standing, and often accompanied by tingling, numbness, and tenderness.

scleroderma. Progressive skin disease involving collagen tissue. There is widespread hardening of the skin due to swelling and thickening of fibrous tissue. This may be followed by skin atrophy and pigmentation.

scoliosis. An abnormal sideways curvature of the spine. There may be just one curve or a compensatory curve in the opposite direction. It may be due to a congenital defect, injury, disease, or poor posture.

senile dementia (senility, senile psychosis). A wide variety of mental and emotional changes affecting the elderly. Symptoms of this condition include loss of recent memory, short attention span, and irritability.

shingles. See *herpes zoster.*

shock. A state of deep mental and physical depression after receiving severe physical injury or undergoing emotional stress. Some causes are heart failure, hemorrhage, drug reaction, or poisoning.

sickle-cell anemia. An inherited blood disorder marked by a genetic abnormality of the red blood cells in which the cells become crescent or sickle-shaped.

sigmoidoscopy. A technique that permits inspection, through a tubular speculum called a sigmoidscope, of the interior of the sigmoid colon. It is indicated for detection of polyps, cancer, and bowel abnormalities.

sinusitis. Inflammation of the lining membrane of any sinus, but especially the nasal sinus. Most often, the condition occurs as an extension of nasal infections.

sleeping sickness. See *trypanosomiasis.*

slipped disk (prolapsed disk). Herniation or rupture of part of the intervertebral disk, which is normally held in place by fibrous tissues. When fibers weaken, protrusion from between the vertebrae occurs.

smallpox (variola). An acute, contagious, febrile disease that begins with chills, high fever, backache, and headache. Symptoms subside within five days and a skin eruption appears, ending up in dry scabs that fall off and mark the skin.

snail fever. See *schistosomiasis.*

specialist. A physician who, on completion of specialized postgraduate training, is able to practice a particular branch of medicine, such as surgery or obstetrics. (See page 81 for a description of various specialists.)

spinal tap. Involves lumbar puncture, which is used in cases of suspected meningitis and in certain types of spinal cord or brain damage.

Still's disease (juvenile rheumatoid arthritis). Similar to rheumatoid arthritis found in adults; however, children are affected much more severely during the development of the disease and less so in the later stages.

Stokes-Adams syndrome. Characterized by light-headedness or sudden loss of consciousness. Condition is associated with various disorders of the heart that disrupt its normal pumping action and consequent output of blood.

strabismus (cross-eye, squint). Condition in which the eyes fail to point in the same direction. Involves one or more muscles controlling eyeball movement.

stroke (apoplexy). Sudden loss of consciousness and paralysis on one side due to blockage of a cerebral artery by an embolus or thrombus or rupture of a blood vessel in the brain.

sudden infant death (SIDS; crib death). Unexplained death of an apparently well infant occurring most often between the second week and the first year of life. About 10 percent of cases are associated with cardiovascular or central nervous systems.

symptom. Any noticeable change in the body or its functions that indicates the presence of an illness or disease. May be of a general nature or pertain to the part of the body affected.

syphilis. A venereal disease caused by bacterial infection of the species *Treponema pallidum.* Spread almost exclusively by sexual intercourse with an infected partner.

tachycardia. Condition in which there is an abnormally fast heartbeat, especially over 100 beats per minute. May result from an overactive thyroid gland or some form of heart disease.

tapes dorsalis (locomotor ataxia). A late manifestation of syphilis involving the spinal cord. Occurs in persons having had inadequate or no treatment during early stages of syphilis.

Tay-Sachs disease. An hereditary disease caused by transmission of an abnormal gene. It results in a specific enzyme deficiency and is marked by progressive mental and physical retardation, paralysis, spasticity, and blindness.

telangiectasia. Dilation of capillaries, or a group of small blood vessels, which causes a small dark red elevation on the skin. May appear as a birthmark or become noticeable in young children.

temporal arteritis. Inflammation of the arteries that supply the sides of the scalp. Of unknown origin, it is becoming increasingly recognized in the elderly.

tetanus. An acute infection caused by the bacteria *Clostridium tetani.* These bacteria enter the body through a scratch or wound, where they release their poison (toxin) by growth and multiplication.

tetany. Nervous disorder in which there are intermittent tonic spasms involving the extremities. It can occur after a critical drop in the amount of calcium circulating in the blood.

thalassemia. An hereditary form of anemia characterized by the development of abnormally thin and fragile red blood cells. There are several variants of the disease, but no specific treatment is obtainable.

thalidomide. A hypnotic drug widely used in European countries as a sleeping pill in the early 1960's. Use of the drug was discontinued when it was found to cause severe limb deformities in developing fetuses.

therapeutic. The treatment of disease, or the results obtained from treatment. It may also pertain to a healing agent, or having healing properties.

thermography. A technique used to detect, record by a sensitive scanner, and interpret the significance of radiant heat thrown off by tissues affected by disease. It is used to study blood flow in limbs and to detect cancer.

thrombocytopenia. An abnormal decrease in the number of platelets (thrombocytes) in the circulating blood. It results in an inability of the blood to clot efficiently.

tinnitus. Condition in which a person experiences in one or both ears the sensation of noises that are not caused by external sound vibrations. It may be nothing more serious than impacted wax, or it may be an early sign of inner ear disease.

tonsillitis. An inflammation of tonsillar tissue. Tonsils appear enlarged and red, and are painful on swallowing. There may also be high fever, chills, and headache. It is more frequent in children than in adults.

toxic. A poisonous substance, a condition caused by a poison, or pertaining to a toxin. A toxin is a poisonous substance of animal or plant origin.

toxic shock syndrome. A fast-spreading, often deadly form of toxic reaction that sometimes kills or permanently disables a person within hours. About 80 percent of the cases occur in menstruating women using tampons.

toxoplasmosis. An infection caused by a parasite. Usually transmitted to humans through cat litter or from raw or uncooked meat. In pregnant women, the infectious organism can be transmitted to the fetus and cause jaundice, anemia, or nerve damage.

tranquilizer. Drug that acts to reduce mental tension and anxiety without causing depression in the user. Such drugs have facilitated treatment of certain severely disturbed psychiatric patients.

trichinosis. A parasitic disease caused by eating raw or inadequately cooked or processed pork or pork products infected with *Trichinella spiralis.* Symptoms may be absent or there may be pain, nausea, and diarrhea.

trichomoniasis vaginitis. One of the most common vaginal diseases, it is caused by a single-celled organism. Sometimes, it produces no symptoms, but often there is discharge and itching. Untreated, it can cause urinary problems.

trypanosomiasis (sleeping sickness). May be one of several diseases occurring in man and domestic animals caused by a trypanosome. The infection is marked by drowsiness, lethargy, muscular weakness, and cerebral symptoms.

tuberculosis. Three types of tubercle bacillus cause this infection: human, bovine, and avian. The human type is most responsible for the infection in man. Generally, contact is with an infected person or with contaminated milk from an infected cow.

typhoid fever. A bacterial infection caused by ingesting contaminated food, milk, or water. The bacteria responsible, *Salmonella typhosa*, are excreted in the feces and sometimes the urine of infected persons or carriers of the disease.

ulcerative colitis. Inflammation combined with ulceration of the mucous membrane lining the large intestine. Marked by acute abdominal pain, tenderness, and watery stools.

ultrasonography. The use of sound waves to produce an image or photograph of an organ or tissue. It is indicated where there is a suspicion of thyroid or gallbladder dysfunction, in certain heart problems, and in the last trimester of pregnancy to determine size and position of fetus.

ultrasound (sonogram). Procedure that produces velocities in tissues that differ in density and elasticity from others. Outlines the shape of various body tissues and organs.

uremia. A toxic condition in which the kidneys fail to filter out various nitrogen-containing waste products in the blood, especially urea.

urticaria. An allergic skin reaction, more commonly called hives or nettle rash. Produces an eruption of wheals (red or white raised patches on the skin) that is accompanied by intense itching.

vaginitis. An inflammation of the vagina that may be caused by a bacterial, fungal, or protozoan infection. May also be due to irritation from chemical douches or foreign bodies, or poor hygiene of the vulval area.

varicose veins. Enlarged, twisted veins, usually in the leg, caused by damage to their one-way valves (which normally prevent a backward flow of blood); stretching of their relatively thin walls results.

vascular. The blood vessels. Collectively, the blood vessels together with the heart and lymph vessels constitute the vascular system.

vertigo. A sensation of whirling about, either of oneself or external objects, associated with difficulty in keeping one's balance. May be due to drug reactions, middle ear disease, or infection.

volvulus. A twisting upon itself of a section of intestine, causing a serious obstruction. Signs and symptoms include severe, sudden abdominal pain followed by vomiting and distention.

wart (verruca). A small skin tumor caused by papilloma viruses. They are usually benign, and may disappear spontaneously. Warts may form on fingers, elbows, face, soles of feet, or genitalia.

whooping cough (pertussis). An acute infectious disease caused by *Bordetella pertussis* and spread in the air by the cough of an infected person. Highly contagious, it is a serious childhood disease.

xanthema. Condition in which a yellow pigment, carotene, is present in the blood. Marked by yellowing of the skin and a pseudo, rather than a true, jaundice, as there is no yellow discoloration of eye whites.

x-rays. Electromagnetic radiation of a wavelength shorter than visible light or ultraviolet radiation. X-rays have the ability to penetrate the body and most other solids, and to act on photographic film, making them valuable in diagnosing diseases.

yeast infection. A popular term for several fungal infections: candidiasis, thrush, and some forms of vaginitis. Yeasts, which reproduce by budding, are unicellar fungi of the genus *Saccharomyces.*

Zollinger-Ellison syndrome. A condition characterized by tumors of the pancreas, about 60 percent of which are malignant. With the secretion of too much hydrochloric acid and pepsin, there is eventual ulceration of the intestinal lining and the stomach.

For further reference

The American Medical Directory
American Medical Association
Angel, Jack E.
 Physicians Desk Reference
 Medical Economics Company
Belsky, Marvin S., M.D.
 How to Choose Your Doctor
 Arbor House
Berkow, Robert, M.D.
 The Merck Manual (Diagnosis and Therapy)
 Merck & Company
Directory of Medical Specialists
 A.N. Marquis Company
It's Good to Know About Mental Health
 U.S. Government Printing Office
 1724-0037
Medicaid-Medicare, Which Is Which?
 U.S. Government Printing Office
 MSA-901-70

Mindell, Earl
 Earl Mindell's Pill Bible
 Bantam Books
Sehnert, Keith W., M.D.
 How to Be Your Own Doctor
 Grosset & Dunlap
Someone Close to You Drinks Too Much
 U.S. Government Printing Office
 HE 20.8302:D 83 (SB) $2
Vickery, Donald, M.D. and Fries, James F., M.D.
 Take Care of Yourself: A Consumer's Guide to Medical Care
 Addison-Wesley Publishing Company
Wolfe, Sidney and Coley, Christopher
 Pills That Don't Work
 Farrar Strauss & Giroux

Information resources:
American Hospital Association
 840 North Lake Shore Drive
 Chicago, IL 60611
Joint Commission on Accreditation of Hospitals
 875 N. Michigan Avenue
 Chicago, IL 60611

The National Cancer Institute
 Building 31, Room 10 A
 Bethesda, MD 20205
The American Heart Association
 44 East 23rd Street
 New York, NY 10010
The U.S. Government Printing Office
 Washington, DC 20402

Managing the Family's Money

When most of us think about money, it is either about how it comes in or how it goes out. This section will not tell you how to make more money come in—except through prudent investing. It will tell you some of the ways you can control the way money goes out. Managing the family's money means keeping track of it and making sure you put it to the best use in the ways you spend and save it.

In this age of inflation, changing interest rates, and wide-ranging opportunities for saving and investing, money management has captured the interest of people everywhere. People who never spent much time thinking about the subject before are now paying for the advice of professional financial planners.

There are many paths on the financial landscape, and not all of them lead where we might hope. But there are some basic facts that can help us make sensible choices. This section sets many of them forth.

The information here is generally correct for the entire United States, but state laws do vary in some cases. If you think your state requirements might differ, ask your elected representative to check them for you.

The seven ages of your economic life

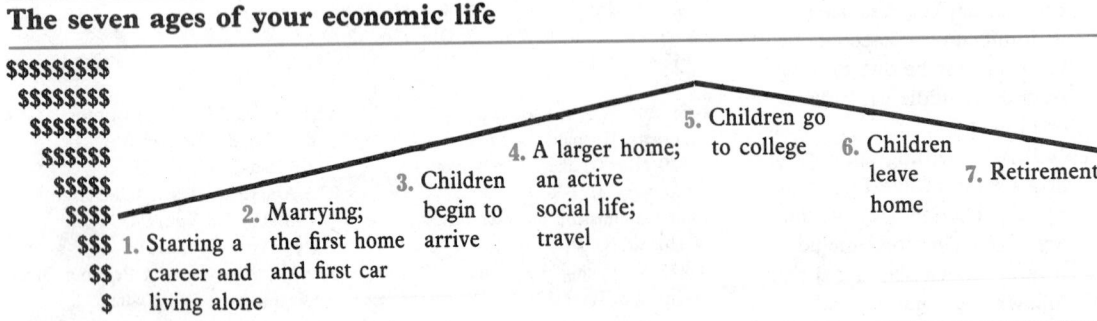

1. Starting a career and living alone
2. Marrying; the first home and first car
3. Children begin to arrive
4. A larger home; an active social life; travel
5. Children go to college
6. Children leave home
7. Retirement

Planning and record-keeping

Dwight D. Eisenhower is said to have remarked when he was a general, "It's not the plan that counts, it's the planning." What he meant, of course, was that the very act of planning—setting goals, gathering facts, deciding what is important, figuring out how to get where you want to go—is worthwhile in itself. It helps you to understand what you are doing and why you are doing it. The particular plan you come up with may have to be changed or discarded in favor of a better one, but the discipline and knowledge that come from working up a plan will always be to your advantage.

Managing the family's money begins with planning. You set your goals for the kind of life you want to lead and the things you want your family to have. You get all the facts you can about how much you will need to save, to spend, and to invest. You also need to know how to make the best use of credit, the services that are available, and the potential pitfalls.

Good record-keeping is essential. You must keep receipts for important items and make note of important cash outlays. To do this, you must find a way to keep records that suits you. For one person, it might be a ledger book with neatly written entries. For another, a shoebox would be just right for keeping records on separate pieces of paper. There is nothing wrong with a shoebox provided you use it consistently and start a new one at regular intervals—every six months or a year—putting each important sales slip or receipt into it and making sure that each item is identified on the slip. Include gifts to charity, interest expense items, sales tax, and all other items you would not find recorded in your checkbook.

Planning also means keeping permanent records of basic information (such as that suggested on the next page). This information can be useful to you and your family at various times throughout the year and is absolutely essential when a family member dies. The mere act of filling out the form may suggest ideas to you. Perhaps you have partly overlapping insurance policies, or not enough coverage. As you review the

record at least once a year, changing conditions will suggest other revisions.

Your financial plan should start with your estimate of how much you are worth. Use the chart on page 112 as your guide.

Your net worth at any one time does not mean very much by itself. But if you go through the exercise of figuring out your net worth every year and you find that it is going down, this is a clear signal that something is wrong.

Next it is time to work up a budget, based on how much you earn and how much you should reasonably

Paying for college

Some schools offer tuition budget plans. You make monthly payments while your son or daughter is in college.

The Stafford Loan Program enables eligible freshmen to borrow up to $2625 a year, sophomores up to $3500, and juniors and seniors up to $5000 at low interest rates. Repayment begins on completion of studies. Parent Loans to Undergraduate Students (PLUS) are also available, as are Supplemental Loans for Students (SLS) up to $4000 a year.

The College Work-Study Program (CWS) provides jobs for students who need financial aid and want to extra money to pay for expenses.

Students who show exceptional need can get Federal Supplemental Educational Opportunity Grants (FSEOG) up to $4000 a year.

Unusually needy students borrowing for the first time can get loans at 5 percent from the Carl D. Perkins National Direct Student Loan program. The Pell Grant program provides grants based on need up to $2300 a year (1994).

spend. Before you draw up a budget, have your family keep an informal record of expenses for a month. Then estimate how much you spend on once-a-year events like a vacation and Christmas, dividing such expenses by twelve. Make sure you take into account all other outlays that come up during the year, such as quarterly tax payments. Then summarize all your income during the year, including interest payments from the bank and dividends on life insurance. With this information on inflow and outgo, you have the basis for your budget.

If the figures show that there is not much left over for savings, review your expense items with your family and decide on what can be cut back or eliminated. Be sure to make some provision for unexpected expenses. A budget will soon fail if it is too tightly drawn up.

$1 × 10 years = 50¢

The problem of our time

Underlying all your planning, there should be an awareness of the recurring problem of our time—inflation. Remember this rule of thumb: a 7 percent increase each year would mean a doubling in ten years, which means that you would need $1 ten years from now to buy what 50 cents buys today.

When you see an advertisement for an investment that claims, for example, that $2000 a year may grow to a million dollars at your time of retirement, remember that a million dollars in the 2030's would be worth $125,000 in today's dollars, assuming 6 percent inflation.

How much are you worth?

Like a business, a family that manages its money effectively starts with a balance sheet. The difference between the assets and the liabilities is what cost accountants call *net worth*.

Assets
Cash and marketable securities
Cash in checking and
   savings accounts   _____
Certificates of deposit   _____
Mutual fund shares   _____
U.S. Savings Bonds   _____
Life insurance cash value
   (obtainable from your
   insurance agent)   _____

Other assets
Real estate (including
   your home)   _____
Pension value   _____
IRA and Keogh accounts   _____
★ Automobiles   _____
★ Furniture and appliances   _____
★ Personal possessions   _____
        Total assets   _____

Liabilities
Current liabilities
Bills payable   _____
Installment loans   _____

Long-term liabilities
Mortgage   _____
Bank loans   _____
        Total liabilities   _____

*Depreciated   Net worth   _____

The family budget

No budget format would be right for all families, but here are typical items that should be included in an annual budget.

Income
Salaries   _____
Interest   _____
Dividends   _____
Sale of securities or property
   (these should be recognized
   as unusual items unless you
   sell securities every year)   _____
Bonuses
   (also to be treated as
   unusual items)   _____
        Total income   _____

Outgo
Food   _____
Clothing   _____
Automobile operating costs   _____
Shelter costs, including
   mortgage payments   _____
Miscellaneous purchases   _____
Health care   _____
Entertainment   _____
Vacation   _____
Education   _____
Interest expense   _____
Insurance premiums   _____
Charitable contributions   _____
Taxes   _____
        Total outgo   _____
Balance available for
   saving and investing   _____

The family record

Information related to money management that should be available to everyone in your family.

Your name: | Date and place of birth:
Your Social Security number:

Your spouse's name: | Date and place of birth:
Spouse's Social Security number:

First child's name: | Date and place of birth:
Social Security number:

Same information for each additional child:

Your employer's name and address:
Name and telephone number of your supervisor:

Spouse's employer's name and address:
Name and telephone number of supervisor:

Your attorney's name and telephone number:

Your accountant's, or tax advisor's, name and telephone number:

Your insurance agent's name and telephone number:

Your bank or savings institution officer:

Date and location of your will:
Your executor:

Numbers of bank checking and savings accounts and certificates of deposit:

Interest income:

Location of check recordbooks, passbooks, and certificates:

Your safe deposit box location and number:
Location of keys:
Description of valuable possessions and serial numbers (of such items as cameras):

Description of real estate you own:
Date and cost of purchase:
Name and address of mortgage holder:

Descriptions of investments, such as mutual fund shares:
Income from investments: | Dates investments were made:
Name of investment company, bank or broker,
and numbers of the accounts:

Name of life insurance company:
Numbers and face values of the policies on your life: | Loans against the policies:
Same information for policies on your spouse's life: | Premium due dates:

Name of automobile insurance company:
Number and amount of the policy: | Premium due date:

Name of health and disability insurance company:
Number and amount of the policy: | Premium due date:

Name of home-owner's insurance company:
Number and amount of the policy:

Loans outstanding: | Interest payment dates:
Repayment dates:
Mortgage balance and monthly payment:
Installment loans: | Payments due:

Credit card account numbers:
Address of issuer to be notified:

Your Social Security benefit (if applicable):

Using credit wisely

Like fire and water, credit is a good servant but a poor master. The nation's economy runs on credit, and most of us have come to depend on it every day of our lives.

For most people, credit is not difficult to obtain, whether in the form of a charge account or installment credit at a store, a credit card from a bank, or a loan from a credit union.

Applying for credit. When you apply for credit, you will be asked questions about your stability in society and your ability to pay off loans. How long have you been with your present employer? Do you own your own home? If not, how long have you rented the space where you now live? Do you have checking and savings accounts? Do you have a history of paying your bills on time?

There is no fixed credit rating that follows you wherever you go. Lenders judge you by their own standards. **Credit at a store.** When you open a charge account at a department store, you may be offered a revolving account. This has a set limit on how much you can owe the store at one time, with interest to be paid every month on the unpaid balance.

If you want to buy something on the installment plan, ask yourself these two questions first: Would I pay cash for this if I had the cash available? Is what I am buying going to last longer than it will take me to pay off this loan?

Before you sign the installment contract, ask the seller for the annual percentage rate (APR). The APR, which is the total finance charge expressed as a percentage of the amount you are borrowing, is the true interest cost, and it may be higher than you realize. For example, if you paid off a loan of $100 with twelve equal monthly installments totaling $110, your true interest was not 10 percent; it was 18 percent. The amount you owed kept declining while you continued to pay interest on the total loan.

Also ask the seller for the total cost of the loan, including payments and principal, the cost of late charges, and the penalties, if any, for paying off early.

Credit unions. If you live in an area where there are few banks or savings institutions competing with each other, an economical source of credit is a local credit union. Members purchase shares in the association, and loan applications are reviewed by a committee of members. Since members do much of the administrative work with the help of a small paid staff, a credit union can give its members better value.

Credit card tips

- Be sure to sign your credit card promptly.
- Do not carry more cards than you absolutely need.
- Do not give your card to a salesperson without making sure that you get your own card back.
- When your card expires and a new one is issued, cut the old card in half before you discard it.
- When you get your credit card receipt, ask for and then destroy both of the little pieces of carbon paper. Wastebaskets are searched by credit card defrauders, who can copy your number and signature from the carbon paper, or even manufacture a fake card with your name and number.
- Do not give your credit card number to strangers who telephone you.
- Keep the numbers and issue dates of your cards with your personal records.
- Report the loss of your card immediately, even if someone telephones you to say he has found it and will return it. He may be stalling for time in which to run up charges in your name. You are not liable for any charges if you report the loss promptly.

"Plastic" from the bank. Credit cards issued by banks, such as Visa and MasterCharge, are by far the most widely used form of credit. If you have "plastic," the best rule is to think of it not as a *credit* card but as a *charge* card—a convenience that you have with you to avoid the trouble and risk of carrying cash. A card also saves you money by enabling you to take advantage of unexpected sales and bargains. In addition, it offers the great convenience of shopping by telephone.

With many bank cards, it has been possible to obtain free credit by paying the bill in full before the monthly due date. Increasingly, however, banks are charging interest from the day they receive each charge slip from the participating establishment.

If you let your balance accumulate, you are paying interest at the rate of 18 to about 20 percent a year, although some banks introduce credit cards with rates as low as approximately 10.5 percent. Your bank will not object if you take your time paying off the balance, provided you pay the relatively small monthly minimum—a sure sign that this arrangement is to the bank's advantage, not yours. By paying off more than the minimum, you significantly reduce your interest costs.

Dealing with your bank

Do not choose a bank on the basis of its giveaways. Instead read the bank's fine print about its interest rates and service charges.

A bank borrows at wholesale and lends at retail. Besides paying you interest on money you deposit and charging you higher interest on money you borrow, a commercial—or full-service—bank offers a wide range of services.

In addition to checking and savings accounts, banks offer money market accounts, Individual Retirement Accounts (IRA's), Keogh accounts, certificates of deposit (CD's), home improvement loans, home mortgages, automobile loans, personal loans, and credit cards. They also provide such services as automatic teller machines (ATM's), safe deposit boxes, purchasing government bonds on your behalf, paying utility bills out of your account, and automatically depositing your paychecks or Social Security checks. Savings institutions offer some of these services, including negotiable orders of withdrawal (NOW) accounts, which are interest-bearing checking accounts.

Choosing your bank. In selecting your bank or savings institution, remember that no service is truly free. Compare the rates and service charges with those of their competitor institutions and look at the details of the various savings plans, including certificates of deposit and money market accounts.

Ask about savings plans. Among the questions you should ask about savings plans are these: How frequently is interest compounded? What is the effective annual yield, not just the interest rate? Is interest compounded from day of deposit to day of withdrawal? Is there an interest penalty for early or frequent withdrawal? Are deposits insured? How quickly do funds become available?

You should have no difficulty obtaining the answers to such questions. A law passed in 1991 requires financial institutions to provide a great deal more information to depositors than they did in the past.

The checking account. The greatest convenience a bank or savings institution offers is the checking account. A check is essentially theftproof and, once it has been paid and returned to you, indisputable proof that payment was made. Your check recordbook gives you a dependable and up-to-the-minute record of your cash inflow and outgo.

Banks typically offer several kinds of checking accounts. Find out if the checking services in the bank you are considering are competitive on interest paid (if any), number of checks allowed, service charges, and minimum balance required.

Special checking usually involves a fee but no minimum balance; it is best suited to someone who writes less than half a dozen checks a month. *Regular checking,* for people who write more checks, is likely to require a minimum balance or service charge. A *NOW account,* at either a bank or savings institution, pays interest close to savings account rates. A *Super NOW account* pays higher rates, but it may require a minimum balance of $1000 or more, and it imposes relatively high service charges. Instead of separate NOW and Super NOW accounts, many banks simply have interest-paying checking accounts.

A *joint checking account* is a convenience for a couple, provided they both enter all their transactions in the same recordbook, which the bank provides along with the blank checks. A couple should be aware that any money in a joint account belongs legally to either person and can be completely withdrawn without the other's knowledge. Since some states freeze a joint account when one of the co-owners dies, it is essential for the survivor to have access to other funds at such a time.

Do not make out a check to "cash" unless you immediately give it to the recipient, because you have thereby turned your check into cash. If your checkbook is stolen, notify the bank immediately so that your account can be frozen. The bank will honor only those checks that you have written.

If you write a check and then decide you do not want it honored, call the bank's stop-payment department. It will stop payment for a fee, provided there would have been enough in your account to pay the check anyway. Notify the person to whom you issued the check.

When you make a deposit into your checking account, your bank is required by law to credit the account with at least $100 on the next business day; the full amount of a local bank check on the second business day; and the full amount of any out-of-town check by the fifth business day. Always deposit a check as soon as you receive it.

Balancing your checkbook.

After you receive your checking account statement from the bank, balance your check recordbook against the statement within a few days. If you wait longer and find an error in the bank's statement, it may be too late for them to locate their error speedily.

Although it should be a simple matter to balance your check recordbook, some people find it confusing because not all of the checks that have been written clear the bank by the time a statement is completed.

The figure on the last line of your table should equal the balance on the bank statement. If it is off by a significant amount, check your arithmetic, making sure you did not add when you should have subtracted, or vice versa. If your balance is off by an insignificant amount, assume the bank statement to be correct and make a compensating entry on the first open line of your check recordbook.

How to balance your checkbook	Do's and don'ts of writing a check
1. Arrange the canceled checks in numerical order.	**Face of check**
2. Check them off in pencil against the debit column of the bank's statement.	1. Name and address printed on check make it easier to cash.
3. Go through the canceled checks again, this time checking them off in pencil against the entries in your check recordbook. The lowest-numbered checks will probably include a few that did not clear before the previous statement.	2. Number your checks if they are not already numbered.
	3. Date properly; never postdate. It *is* legal to date a check on a Sunday or holiday.
	4. Do not use Mr., Mrs., Ms., or Miss.
4. When you come to a check in your recordbook that has not yet cleared the bank, draw a circle in red around the number of that check in the recordbook.	5. Do not leave a space between $ and the first digit.
	6. Start writing at the end of the line. The written figure with the fraction is the amount the bank pays.
5. Go through the same two procedures with your deposit slips. If you have entered a deposit in your check recordbook that does not show up on the bank statement, draw a red circle around it in the recordbook.	7. Draw a line between the fraction and "dollars."
	8. The memo entry is for your convenience only.
	9. Sign the same way every time. Do not write in pencil, even though it is legal. If you make a mistake, tear up the check and cross out the check number in your check recordbook.
6. Draw a red line underneath the last check in your recordbook that is also shown on the bank statement. This is the cutoff point.	**Back of check**
7. Enter in your recordbook the bank's debit for charges and credit for interest (if any), so that these amounts will be reflected in your own balance before the next statement comes from the bank.	10. Endorse on back of left end.
	11. Endorse exactly as your name appears on the face of the check as payee. Write your regular name underneath in parentheses.
8. Draw up a simple table on a piece of paper like this:	12. Writing "for deposit only" will prevent the check from being cashed by someone else.

Your recordbook balance

	(the last balance above the red line you drew)	_____
Plus	Total of outstanding checks (those you circled in red)	+ _____
Plus	Any interest credited to your statement (if it is an interest-bearing account)	+ _____
	Total	
Minus	Recent deposits entered by you but not yet credited by the bank (circled in red)	− _____
	Difference	_____
Minus	Service charges shown on the bank statement	− _____
	Difference: Your balance	

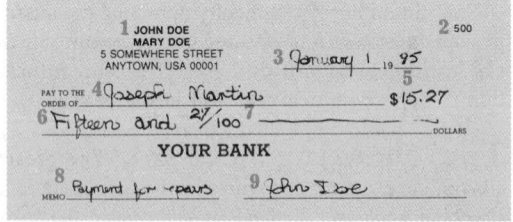

Managing the Family's Money

Other kinds of checks. For an unusual transaction, you may be asked to pay with a certified check. In this case, you write your own check for a specific amount to a specific payee and take it to your bank, where it will be signed and stamped by a bank officer. At the same time, the officer will reserve that amount from your account so that there will be enough to pay the check when it comes in, regardless of what other checks you write. At this point, your certified check is as good as cash and should be given directly to the payee. Avoid sending it by mail or messenger.

A cashier's check has similar uses. It is made out and signed by an officer of the bank in return for a payment by you to the bank. It is best to have it made out to your name so that there is a record that the payment is going through your hands. You can then endorse it, photocopy it, hand it over to the payee, and ask for a receipt.

Most banks provide traveler's checks, which are issued by a few large banks or other financial institutions known around the world. Traveler's checks are useful when you are traveling or moving because they are usually accepted everywhere while personal checks are not. If lost, traveler's checks can be replaced and the money returned. But they should not be held for a long time. When you buy one, you are in effect lending the bank your money at no interest, and at a small charge to you. Always carry one or two traveler's checks for emergencies.

A place for your savings. Banks compete vigorously for your savings. In addition to the traditional passbook savings account, many banks and savings institutions now offer time deposit accounts with fixed interest. Usually referred to as CD's, these insured accounts have minimum periods of deposit ranging from thirty days to as long as ten years, with penalties for early withdrawal.

Banks also offer money market deposit accounts, which pay interest that is adjusted periodically in line with interest rates in the money market. This is the market where short-term debt securities are traded. Some banks require a minimum deposit in a money market account.

A place to borrow. On the other side of the banking business, there is at least as much competition to lend you money.

One of the simplest and most economical ways to borrow at a bank or savings institution is to borrow against your own passbook. The interest rate is lower than on a regular loan, and you continue to earn interest on your entire deposit. Some banks, however, have discontinued passbook accounts.

Many banks also offer overdraft checking accounts under various names. You activate your account sim-

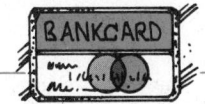

Do not carry your ATM number

- Be sure *not* to write your ATM identification number on anything you carry or keep at your place of work. Keep the only record of the number in a safe place at home.
- Always check your receipt before leaving.
- Make sure the machine is back to its original setting.
- As soon as you get home, enter your ATM transaction in your recordbook.
- If you lose your ATM access card, call the bank immediately. If the card is used by someone who has found out your ATM identification number, you will have to file a report with the police.

ply by writing one of the special checks for that account given to you by the bank. Each month you receive a statement specifying the part of the loan to be paid back that month and the high interest rate charges you have to pay.

You can obtain loans at banks for a variety of specific needs. In applying for such a loan, be sure to ask the annual percentage rate. This is the total finance charge—more than simple interest—expressed as a percentage of the amount borrowed.

Some banks also offer debt consolidation loans, for people who are unable to keep up with their bills. The idea sounds appealing because your monthly payment for the loan can be less than the monthly total for all your bills. The bank achieves this sleight-of-hand by stretching out the payments over a long period of time; thus, the total interest you pay is very high.

Other bank services. *Automatic teller machines (ATM's)* enable you to make deposits or withdrawals at any hour of the day, including weekends and holidays. This means you can make a deposit without carrying cash or checks around, and you can begin earning interest immediately. It also means you can obtain cash whenever you need it.

Safe deposit boxes are useful for storing items difficult to replace. These include securities; the deed to your house; the title to your automobile; birth and marriage certificates; your home-owner's insurance policy; an inventory of possessions in your house; and a copy—not the original—of your will. Since some states seal safe deposit boxes on the death of the owner, do not store any items that would be needed right after your death. Keep a list at home of the contents of your box. The bank is not responsible for the loss of the contents.

Saving and investing

Everyone knows it is wise to put something aside regularly. Everyone also knows of good uses for the money saved.

Clearly, some ways of saving are easier than others, and some investments are safer than others. U.S. Savings Bonds purchased through the payroll savings plan and mutual fund shares acquired with regular monthly payments offer good investment and good savings.

Savings bonds. U.S. Savings Bonds, Series EE, once considered an unappealing investment choice in a time of high interest rates, are now more attractive. The most secure of all savings or investments, because they are backed by the U.S. government, they now offer—when held for five years or more—an annual interest rate that equals 85 percent of the average yield on U.S. Treasury five-year notes over the period, with a guaranteed minimum of 4.0 percent. They can be bought in multiples of $25 and can be redeemed at any time between the fifth and tenth years. After ten years, an EE bond purchased for $25 can be worth $50 or more, depending on how much interest has been accumulated; it will continue to earn interest until 40 years after the issue date if issued before December, 1965; 30 years if issued after November, 1965. Federal income taxes do not have to be paid on any of the interest until the bonds are redeemed. The interest may be tax free if used to pay college tuition for you or your dependents. Like other U.S. government securities, EE bonds are never subject to state and local income tax.

Great American tax shelters. In recent years, three forms of investment have been introduced through changes in the tax laws. They have made it highly attractive for employed and self-employed people to save for their retirement.

Investment Retirement Accounts (IRA's). An IRA offers any man or woman earning at least $2000 a year who is not covered by an employer pension plan or, if covered, has an adjusted gross income of less than $25,000 (single person) or $40,000 (joint return), an opportunity to make a tax-deductible contribution of $2000 to an IRA account. You can take this deduction even if you do not itemize deductions on your tax return. More important in the long run, any income earned in the IRA account is sheltered from income tax until you withdraw it after the age of 59½. This has a powerful multiplier effect, since tax-sheltered income on your original investment can be reinvested to produce further income that is also tax-sheltered.

Compounding makes the difference

Always ask for the effective annual yield when you are planning to deposit money in a bank or savings institution.

Here is why. Simple interest—that is, without compounding—on $10,000 at 7.15 percent would be $715 for a year.

With daily compounding, the interest would be $26 more.

SAVINGS BANK RATES (not typical of all savings banks) Compounded Daily		
Account	Annual rate %	Annual yield %
1 year	6.20	6.40
2 years	6.65	6.88
4 years	7.15	7.41

No tax is due until you begin withdrawals, which can be as early as age 59½. At age 70½, withdrawals must begin according to a schedule based on your life expectancy.

If you need to, you may borrow the funds needed to deposit in your IRA; it could be to your advantage to borrow for this purpose in view of the tax benefits. Your deposit can be made as late as April 15 in the year following the year for which you want to take the deduction on your income tax. The sooner you make the deposit, however, the sooner it will begin earning tax-sheltered income for you.

IRA accounts at banks, savings institutions, and credit unions are all insured up to $100,000. If your account is with a mutual fund company, it will have more potential for gain at possibly greater risk than in a bank or savings institution, and it will not be federally insured. Insurance companies also offer IRA's, but they tend to charge higher fees for opening accounts.

If only one member of your family is earning income, a joint IRA account can be opened with an annual deposit and tax deduction of $2250. For a working couple not covered by employer pension plans (or with an adjusted gross income of less than $40,000 if filing jointly and if either is covered by an employer pension plan), the amount would be $4000.

Keogh accounts. Self-employed people can invest not only in IRA's but also in Keogh accounts, which work in a similar way.

If you are self-employed, you can invest in a profit-sharing Keogh plan and claim a deduction each year for as much as 13.04 percent of your net earnings up to a maximum of $30,000. This would be in addition to the $2000 that you can invest in an IRA if your adjusted gross income is below $25,000 (single person) or $40,000 (joint return). The deposit can be made as late as the due date of your tax return. You can begin withdrawals as early as age 59½ without a tax penalty, and you must begin withdrawing by 70½.

401 (k) savings plans. Following the reduction of tax benefits from IRAs for middle- and upper-income earners, employees planning for retirement have been attracted to tax-deferred savings plans, principally the 401 (k). Available from many large employers and some smaller ones, a 401 (k) shelters part of your current income from tax by permitting you to defer part of your salary. The limit on how much you can defer, which was $8475 in 1991, increases with inflation.

Your employer may match at least part of every dollar you set aside, and this addition to your income is also exempt from current tax. Income earned by your investment builds up—also free of tax—until you withdraw your funds. Payroll deduction makes saving attractive.

Your investment choices.
Many people look for opportunities for investment, but few have the expert knowledge to select from the many choices offered by the financial markets. Except for the wealthy person who can pay for expert advice, it is nearly impossible for an investor to obtain professional, unbiased recommendations on which stocks or bonds to buy and, sometimes more important, when to sell.

Mutual funds. Many investors meet the problem of obtaining expert advice by purchasing shares in mutual funds. Owning large, diversified portfolios of stocks or bonds selected and continuously reviewed by professional managers, mutual funds spread the risk, and they can be bought and sold easily.

Many mutual funds have a sales charge as high as 8.5 percent of the investment. These are called "load" funds. "No-load" funds, so called because they have no sales commission and charge only a management fee of typically no more than 1 percent a year, perform in many cases as well as the load funds or better.

In either case, you can select a fund according to its investment objective—income (from high-dividend stocks and corporate or government bonds); growth (with investments in stocks that involve more than average risk); or balance (offering both income and growth). Funds are rated according to their performance every year in magazines that you will find at your library, including *Forbes* and *Money*.

Mutual funds can be purchased under various plans. If you do not have a large sum to invest at once, you might consider the contractual plan, under which you pay a fixed amount each month.

Dividends are paid every quarter from the income on the fund's portfolio of investments. Once a year, the fund makes a capital gain distribution based on any increase in the value of the shares of the stocks it owns.

Money market funds. Many investment companies that manage mutual funds also offer money market funds. These funds are directly competitive with banks' money market accounts, and tend to have somewhat higher returns on investment. Unlike the banks' accounts, money market funds are not insured by the government; but you can, if you wish, select a fund that invests only in U.S. Treasury securities, which is as good as insurance.

A family of funds. If you have not invested in mutual funds before, you could pick an investment company with a family of funds and start in their money market fund until you build up a substantial amount of cash. Then you could switch all or part of that money to one or more of the other funds in the same group.

Real estate.
A completely different kind of investment—and, in the view of many, a hedge against inflation—is real estate. Before the Tax Reform Act of 1986 took effect, real estate investments offered significant tax advantages to people in higher income brackets. But tax considerations aside, there are some disadvantages to real estate for investors to keep in mind.

If the neighborhood deteriorates, you may have to sell at a sacrifice. In a time of depression, any real estate value is likely to suffer. If your property stays undeveloped, it produces no income but still gets taxed. Values are no longer rising as they did in the early 1980's, and in many areas they have fallen.

If you are, nevertheless, persuaded by the argument that the supply of land is fixed while the number of people keeps growing, limit your real estate investing to opportunities in your own area. Then you can see for yourself what is happening to values. Experts say the best residential real estate investment, whether you live in it or not, is a medium-priced house in a neighborhood that is desirable or improving. Typical buyers consider three bedrooms and two baths essential.

An investment that's sure to pay off

Looking for a risk-free investment with a good return? If your credit card debt is piling up, think about paying it all off at once. The return will be equivalent to the interest charge you no longer have to pay—as high as 20 percent.

Looking ahead to tax time

Income tax instructions have been simplified in recent years, and several inexpensive books are available to help you prepare your return. Whether you do your own return or have it done for you, it is essential to keep good records throughout the year. These include
- property tax receipts;
- canceled checks for gifts to charity, tax payments, and other deductible items;
- receipted bills for moving expenses;
- medical bills;
- bills for expenses in connection with your job, such as safety equipment, for which you have not been reimbursed.

The Internal Revenue Service (IRS) urges you to continue keeping such records three years after a return is filed, after which the statute of limitations runs out for that return.

The IRS also suggests that you read the tax form when you receive it at the beginning of the year and make sure that you understand it; collect all your records early; begin to work on the sample sheets; and call the nearest IRS office if you have any questions. The earlier in the year you do this, the easier it will be to get their attention.

After you have filled out your return, wait until just before April 15 to mail it. The funds that you have to provide with the return can be earning money for you at the bank until the filing date. More important, you are likely to pick up an error you may have made if you give yourself plenty of time to review the figures. The IRS says that people who prepare their returns just before the deadline make the most errors.

Income you do not have to report

- Accident and health insurance benefits
- Benefits from disability insurance you purchased yourself
- Federal income tax refunds
- Gifts to you
- Life insurance dividends (unless they include interest on reinvested dividends)
- Life insurance proceeds
- Sick pay (if permanently and totally disabled)
- Social Security benefits (unless your adjusted gross income [1994]—including half of Social Security retirement benefits—is more than $34,000 for you alone or $44,000 for you and your spouse filing jointly)
- Veterans' benefits
- Welfare payments
- Workmen's compensation

Start work on completing your tax return early, but wait until the last minute before returning it with your check.

Confusing income tax terms

exemption: gives every taxpayer and dependent (except those with high incomes) a deduction ($2450 for 1994).

deduction: an amount that you are allowed to subtract from your income *before* computing your tax.

credit: an amount that you subtract from your tax *after* computing it; thus it is worth more than a deduction.

deferral: a tax obligation that you do not have to pay as long as the income is sheltered.

exclusion: an option to avoid a tax—such as on profits from selling a house or on income earned abroad.

Do you like to get a big refund?

If you like to get a big refund on your income tax, you are not managing your money the best way.

Getting a refund means you have given the government the use of your money for nothing, because a refund comes to you with absolutely no interest.

If you got a big refund last year, try doing an estimate of what your tax is going to be for the current year. If you find that too much of your income is being withheld, ask your employer for a W-4 form. Using the formula on the form, figure out how many allowances to request in order to bring your total withholding for the year close to your estimated tax.

You will not have a nice refund to look forward to, but you will have the use of funds to invest yourself.

Tax facts

Loss on sale. You cannot deduct a loss on a sale of property or goods to close relatives—grandparents, parents, children, brothers, sisters, spouse.

Working at home. If you are unable to set aside a whole room as an office for a business that you carry on at home, you can meet the IRS test for a home office by setting up a partition to separate the office area from the rest of the room.

Selling your house. If you sell your house when you are 55 or older, you can avoid tax on up to $125,000 of the profit on the sale. But you can do this only once, and, if the profit is less than $125,000, you cannot save the balance for another tax-exempt sale. The $125,000 allowance must also include any deferred profits on sales of houses you made before you were 55. (If you sold a house at a profit before 55, the capital gain was deferred for tax purposes if you bought another house costing at least as much.)

Job deductions. You can deduct the cost of looking for a new job *in the same line of work* as you are currently in, along with the cost of courses to maintain or improve your job skills.

Marriage penalty. A working married couple is penalized in comparison with two single people with the same income, and the couple can no longer take a deduction to minimize the penalty.

Itemizing deductions. Nearly all home owners save taxes by itemizing deductions instead of taking the standard deduction, chiefly because of interest costs on the mortgage.

State tax deduction. Your deduction for state income taxes should be the actual cash outlay for the tax year, not the amount shown on your latest state tax return.

Moving costs. Moving costs and unreimbursed employee business expenses can be subtracted from your income as an itemized deduction. The moving deduction is allowed only if a change in your work place has added at least 35 miles to the distance from your previous home to the new work place.

Travel expenses. Although daily travel expenses from home to work are definitely not deductible, you can deduct travel expenses from one regular job to another.

Child care credit. If you work full- or part-time, you may qualify for a tax credit for the expenses of caring for children—or other dependents—while you are at work. The credit is 20 to 30 percent of as much as $2400 of care expenses for one dependent or $4800 for two or more dependents.

Baby exemption. A baby born on December 31 counts as an exemption for the whole year.

Deceased spouse. If your spouse dies during the year, you may file a joint return for that year and continue to do so for two more years, provided you have at least one dependent child and do not remarry during that time.

Estate taxes. Not to be confused with income taxes, these are paid out of the estate of a deceased person. In no case do heirs pay *income* taxes on money they inherit. (Income tax, however, is paid out of the estate if the deceased had taxable income in the final year.

"Quarterly" intervals. If you file an estimated return, remember that payments are not due at regular three-month intervals. Starting with the April 15 filing, succeeding intervals are two, three, four, and three months.

Buying insurance

When you take out an insurance policy, you are betting that something unfortunate will happen to you at some time. The insurance company is betting it will not happen, at least for quite a while. If nothing happens to you for many years, you and the insurance company both win—in different ways. If something does happen to you, nobody wins, but the insurance coverage helps protect you or your family from financial disaster.

The rates you pay for insurance reflect to some degree the odds of something happening to you. But there is clearly more to buying insurance than knowing the odds. In each field—life, health, home owners, and automobile—you have to make your choice from many types of policies offered by many companies at different prices. Some kinds of coverage are far more economical and effective than others.

Life insurance.
The first rule about life insurance is not to buy it until someone is dependent on the earning power of the insured person. That is why it makes no sense to buy it when you are just out of college, or to insure the life of a child, as some do.

A rule of thumb many people follow is to buy enough life insurance to make up for five years of the breadwinner's take-home pay. You should also find out how much your family would receive in Social Security survivors' benefits if the breadwinner died now. Your local Social Security office will figure this out for you if you make it clear that you are not asking them to estimate how much you will get in retirement benefits at a future date.

After you have decided how much coverage you need, it is time to select an insurance company. Do not wait for an agent to call on you; he or she will come primed with all the reasons why you should buy from a particular company. If you have a good library nearby, ask to see a copy of *Best's Insurance Reports,* which rates the quality of companies from A++ to C−, the lowest passing grade. No matter where you live, make sure the company is licensed to write insurance in New York State, which has unusually strict standards.

There are two basic kinds of life insurance policy—whole life (also called straight, ordinary, or permanent) and term insurance.

Whole life. This is a combination of insurance and savings, since it eventually builds up a cash value that you can borrow against or cash in. Insurance companies will not tell you how much of your whole life premium is going for savings. Purely from a savings point of view, you would probably do almost as well to

Insurance-buying strategy

Whether you are buying major medical, homeowner's, or automobile liability insurance, a simple strategy can give you the most effective coverage and help protect you from being financially wiped out.

The strategy is to *accept the highest deductible you think you can handle.* Then, using the money you save, buy the highest coverage you can afford. In exchange for the temporary hardship that a high deductible may cause, you will be buying protection against a financial disaster that could impoverish you and your family for life.

For example, if you increased the deductible on your automobile collision insurance from $200 to $500, you would save up to a quarter of your premium. It would cost you only a small part of that savings to increase your automobile liability insurance from maximum coverage of $300,000 for all the people in one accident to $1,000,000 coverage.

save money in a passbook loan account. In fact, the return on your investment in a whole life policy is negative for about the first ten years.

When you take out a whole life policy, the premiums are fixed for life. Since the cost of one company's coverage is hard to compare with that of another, ask your agent to show you the interest adjusted cost index for the policy. This takes into account dividends, cash value, and interest you would have earned if you had invested elsewhere. The lower the index figure, the more favorable the comparison.

Some companies also offer whole life without dividends, which means lower premiums. In any case, ask whether the policy has a waiver of premium in the event of your total and permanent disability, and double indemnity in the event of your accidental death. Also ask about discounts for nonsmokers and people who exercise regularly.

The head of a family needs the most insurance when he or she is young and with dependents. Thus, there may come a time when it no longer seems necessary to continue paying premiums on whole life insurance. At that time, take the cash value, which is roughly two-thirds of the face value after 25 to 30 years, or accept reduced coverage without further premiums. Or convert to term insurance, with the same coverage for a limited time.

When you have built up cash value in a whole life policy, it is the most accessible source of funds for borrowing, short of a passbook loan. Insurance companies charge in the range of 6 to 8 percent annual interest for loans against whole life policies. If you choose not to pay the interest, the insurance company simply adds the unpaid interest to your outstanding loan. Because there is no time limit on a policy loan—it is really your own money you are borrowing—there is a great temptation not to pay it back. Some investors deliberately do not pay it back because they do so much better by putting the funds elsewhere. If you do this, of course, there would be less coverage for your heirs, or less value for you if you decided to cash in the policy. The interest on a life insurance loan is not tax-deductible in most cases.

Term insurance. This is life insurance pure and simple, without any savings feature. It starts off in the early years with premiums as low as one-fifth of whole life. That is why insurance agents make lower commissions selling term and thus have far less enthusiasm for it than they do for whole life. Like whole life, term insurance can be bought without dividends, which makes the premiums even lower.

The early years of marriage, when you have children and your spouse may be dependent on you, are not only the years when you need a lot of coverage. They are also the years during which you are less able to pay high premiums, hence, the great appeal of term insurance. The most popular way to buy term is called "annual, renewable, and convertible." This means that the rates go up every year on a fixed schedule; you have the right to renew at the end of each term (generally five years) until you are in your sixties or older; you can convert without a physical examination to whole life whenever you choose. Future premiums are stated in the contract and cannot be changed. But term insurance has no cash value and coverage lasts only as long as you pay premiums.

Since term premiums rise sharply as you get older, you may wish to convert to whole life, with its fixed rates. The time to make this conversion is before one's late forties, after which rates go up significantly.

Universal life. A third basic type of life insurance, universal life, combines term insurance with savings that earn bond-market rates. You are told, moreover, how much of your premiums are going into savings, which is not the case with whole life. Because of administrative fees, universal life is not economical in policies of less than about $50,000.

Mail order life insurance. Some life insurance is sold by mail to members of associations or such groups as users of an oil company credit card. This is generally an economical way to buy insurance, provided the company is well rated by Best's and licensed in New York State, and you cannot be turned down when you apply. Bear in mind, however, that premium rates are not guaranteed and you lose the coverage if you happen to leave the group.

Health insurance. Every one needs three kinds of health insurance, and a wage-earner needs a fourth as well.

The three kinds are for hospitalization; other basic medical expenses, including surgery and doctors' fees; and major medical fees, in the event of a lengthy or catastrophic illness. The fourth kind, which most wage-earners tend to skimp on, is for disability coverage, to make up for loss of income if a breadwinner is disabled for a long time.

Some private companies offer comprehensive insurance, which combines the first three types. Such a policy is not necessarily the most economical. Compared with private companies, Blue Cross and Blue Shield, which are not-for-profit organizations with great economies of scale, pay out a very high proportion of each dollar they take in. Blue Cross is available through group plans at places of employment or on an individual basis and covers hospitalization. Blue Shield covers the other basic medical expenses. Both provide major medical coverage, mainly to groups.

The Blues have different plans for different areas of the country, with rates based on where you live and how many people are covered, rather than on age, sex,

---

Life insurance over 55?

Advertisements on TV may sound appealing: life insurance for people over 55 with no medical examination and a monthly premium of a few dollars. But the premium is likely to be for $1000 of coverage. Multiply that by twelve months and the number of thousands you want, and the annual premium may not seem a bargain. Finally, it makes no sense to buy life insurance unless someone is dependent on your earning power.

Is an HMO best for you and your family?

If your company offers health benefits, you probably have the option of joining a Health Maintenance Organization (HMO). You can also join one if you are not employed by such a company.

Bringing the physician, the laboratory, and the clinic together, an HMO provides—for a flat fee paid in advance—virtually all the medical services you might need, except dental and long-term psychiatric care.

The largest HMOs include programs run in some states by Blue Cross/Blue Shield in addition to their other operations.

Although HMOs save you money, the services and choices they offer may be less than you want. A variation on the HMO that you might consider includes the IPA (independent practice arrangement), which pays doctors set fees for treating you in their own offices.

---

or health. The family rate covers a family of any size, a particular attraction for large families. The hospital and the other providers of service are paid directly, saving you the need to have cash available. The policies are guaranteed renewable, and any one may sign up during the annual open enrollment period. The Blues may, however, exclude coverage for a preexisting condition for a certain period. As economical and dependable as Blue Cross/Blue Shield coverage is, you may want to consider purchasing additional major medical coverage from a private company to supplement your coverage from the Blues.

When you purchase major medical coverage, accept a high deductible and buy maximum coverage. Ask whether the maximum applies to each illness or injury, or whether it is merely a lifetime total. The latter is clearly less desirable. Also find out whether the "internal limits" of coverage are adequate—the hospital day rate, for example.

When you purchase disability insurance, the amount of income it would pay should be enough to make up for your loss of wages until you are, say, 65. Make sure the policy is not cancelable and that there is no question about the company's definition of disability: you are unable to work at the occupation for which you have been trained. Premiums will be cheaper if you buy coverage that does not begin until a certain period, such as 90 days after you are disabled. Many wage-earners who buy life insurance have never seriously considered disability insurance, not realizing how much of a burden to a family a disabled person would be.

Home-owner's insurance. This is the insurance that covers damage to your home and belongings, and provides liability coverage for injury to others on your property. It also covers damage to other people's property *accidentally* caused by you or your family, or by accidents originating on your property, such as falling trees.

Two particular points to remember about this insurance are that it does not include damage from floods or earthquakes and that the coverage you buy should be at least 80 percent of the replacement cost—not the market value—of your house. Again, accept a high deductible and use the savings to buy liability coverage that will keep you from being wiped out. Awards by juries of a million dollars are not uncommon. "Umbrella liability" insurance to cover you up to that amount can be purchased as a wrap-around for adequate home-owner's and automobile policies for not much more than $100.

Home-owner's insurance comes in various packages. The most popular, called Home-Owner's 3 (HO-3), includes all-risk coverage on your dwelling—for everything except floods, earthquakes, wars, nuclear accidents, and anything else specified—plus limited risk coverage on your personal belongings.

When you insure your house for 80 percent or more of its replacement cost, damage to any part of the house, such as a bathroom, will be covered at full replacement cost. If the entire house is destroyed, you will receive only 80 percent of the total replacement cost. If you can afford it, you should consider 100 percent coverage on the house.

Your belongings are generally covered for 50 percent of the insured value of the house, which you may want to increase if you have unusually valuable possessions. Your home-owner's policy will also pay your additional temporary living expenses if your house is too damaged to live in, and it will cover losses away from home of belongings up to certain limits for various items. Home-owner's will also pay *up to* $500 if you lose your credit card. The standard personal liability coverage for a home-owner's policy is $100,000, making it highly desirable to purchase additional coverage at a small cost.

Because replacement costs increase every year although the market value of a house may not, it is essential to keep your coverage in step with inflation. You can have an "inflation-guard" provision added to a new or existing policy. This will provide for automatic increases in coverage and save you from having to review your policy each year.

Flood and earthquake coverage

Flood and earthquake coverage, not included in home-owner's policies, can be obtained under separate policies.

For information about flood coverage, which is written by local insurance agents and guaranteed by the federal government, call the National Flood Insurance Program, 800-638-6620.

Automobile insurance. As with health and home-owner's insurance, accept a high deductible and buy extra liability coverage. A rule of thumb for a deductible on automobile insurance is slightly more than a week's take-home pay.

Automobile insurance includes five different kinds:
Liability. Typical coverage is called 100/300/50: $100,000 for injury to one person; $300,000 maximum for all the people in one accident; $50,000 for property damage. If you own a house and other assets and even have umbrella coverage, consider increasing your liability coverage to 250/500/100 or more. The additional coverage costs little more.

Insurance planning worksheet: a checklist

To find out if you have enough insurance—or more than you need—it pays to look through your policies.

Life insurance

What is the total coverage you have (including group coverage by your employer)?

What is the value of each policy and what is the annual premium and dividend?

Do the policies have double indemnity (double payment in case of death by accident)?

What do you estimate to be the cash value? (Your agent can help you.)

What loans have you made against any of the policies?

What assets would your heirs receive in addition to Social Security survivors' benefits?

How long would you expect your survivors to need to adjust to the loss of your income?

Health and disability insurance

How much coverage do your various policies provide?

What is the cost to you?

How much could you afford to pay yourself in case of an extended illness?

How much disability insurance coverage do you have from your employer?

Home-owner's insurance

What do you estimate is the replacement cost of your home?

How much of that cost could you assume in the event the house was totally destroyed?

What is the value of your personal possessions?

If a valuable possession were lost, how much of the replacement cost would you be able to assume?

Automobile insurance

How much coverage does your policy provide for injury to one person?

What is the maximum for all the people in one accident?

How much coverage do you have for collision insurance? Could you afford a larger deductible?

When will your car be five years old and thus no longer worth covering with collision insurance?

Would your uninsured driver coverage be adequate if the breadwinner in your family were seriously injured?

Umbrella insurance

Do you have umbrella insurance to increase your protection against damage awards not adequately covered by home-owner's or automobile insurance? Is your umbrella coverage adequate in light of the million-dollar-or-more awards frequently granted?

Collision. The most expensive automobile insurance, this covers damage you yourself cause to your car. It should be dropped when a car is four to five years old.
Comprehensive. Also expensive, this covers damage other than that caused by collisions.
Uninsured driver. Cheap and highly desirable, this insurance covers injuries caused by an uninsured or insufficiently insured driver, or a hit-and-run driver.

Medical. This automobile insurance covers treatment for you and your passengers. It is included in your basic coverage except in certain states that have no-fault insurance.

It is worth shopping around for automobile insurance, since rates and quality of service vary widely. Some companies have lower rates for people over 65 no longer driving to work.

Putting your affairs in order

Your estate is what you leave when you die. It consists of all your property, including real estate, investments, bank accounts, life insurance proceeds, personal possessions, and any interests you might have in business ventures. From the total value of your estate are deducted funeral expenses, fees for executors and lawyers, state inheritance taxes, and any outstanding debts.

What is left is subject to federal *estate* taxes—not income taxes. As a result of changes in the tax laws in recent years, few estates are subject to federal taxes. No tax return has to be filed for a gross estate (before deductions) of less than $600,000. Moreover, you can leave any amount in any year to your spouse without incurring a federal estate tax. If your estate will be large enough to be subject to federal tax, you should consult your lawyer or accountant on the best way to

keep your tax to a minimum.

After a person dies, his or her will is probated. Probate is the process of filing a will with the appropriate court and having it declared valid; this process can take several months. Certain property, however, passes directly to the beneficiaries without their having to wait for probate. This includes life insurance proceeds (which are paid directly by the insurance company when notified by your agent); pension benefits to a beneficiary named by the pensioner (although not all pension arrangements call for the survivor to receive benefits); U.S. Savings Bonds (if jointly held or if solely held with a designated beneficiary named on the face of the bond); property held in joint tenancy (that is, with the survivor having the right to receive the property); and joint bank accounts.

Your heirs do not have to pay any *income* taxes on life insurance proceeds or anything else they receive from your estate, whether written into the will or not.

In some states, joint bank accounts may be frozen and safe deposit vaults sealed until the state is satisfied that state taxes have been paid for the year in which the person died. That is why it is important for your survivors to have access to funds outside of joint bank accounts—and why your vault should not contain any document, such as a life insurance policy, that would be needed right after your death.

Funeral arrangements should be made clear in the instructions you leave for survivors. A federal law requires funeral directors to break down the costs of the various services they provide when quoting a price for a funeral.

There are certain facts a funeral director might not mention unless asked. No state requires embalming unless a body is to be shipped, but funeral directors do it routinely. Burial vaults required for caskets by certain cemeteries can be simpler and far less costly than the ones recommended by many funeral directors. Caskets usually are not required for cremation. Cremation costs far less than burial.

What to do
when the head of the family dies

- Notify employer.
- Notify lawyer who drew up the will.
- Notify life insurance agent.
- Cancel all credit cards, or convert them to the name of the surviving spouse.
- Notify the local Social Security office, which will arrange for a funeral benefit of $255 and advise on possible benefits for survivors.
- Notify the nearest Veterans Administration (VA) office if the deceased was in the armed services. The VA will provide for a wartime veteran or any veteran who suffered a disability a $300 funeral allowance, a $150 allowance if the burial is not in a national cemetery, and a flag for the casket. (Burial in a national cemetery is free for any veteran and for his or her spouse and children in the same grave.)

Managing the Family's Money

Planning for retirement

The time to start planning for retirement is when you still have many paychecks ahead of you.

Social Security and, for those who have them, pensions are only a base on which to build a satisfactory retirement income. To achieve an income at the desirable level of two-thirds of your preretirement income, you clearly need your own savings and investments. The sooner you start setting aside a certain amount for retirement out of every paycheck, the smaller the monthly amount will have to be.

Your retirement needs. Allowing for continued inflation, you can project how much income you are likely to need after you retire. Some of your needs, such as transportation, may end. Taxes will be lower. Some of your costs, such as your mortgage, will remain fixed and thus insulated from inflation. Your savings are likely to earn higher interest as inflation continues, and your Social Security benefits will be indexed for inflation.

On this page is a table that suggests how you can go

In planning your retirement income, consider a variety of investments because your Social Security and pension benefits may not be adequate.

about estimating your retirement living costs. If you are still many years away from retirement, it is too early to work out a close estimate of your income from Social Security; in addition, your local Social Security office will be reluctant to help you until you get much closer to retirement. Your pension would also be difficult to estimate many years ahead. But it is still worth trying to get some idea of your retirement needs so that you can plan your savings and investment program wisely.

How much retirement income will you need?

Item	What each item costs you now per month*	What it would cost you in retirement today (current dollars)	What it would cost you in future retirement (inflated dollars)
Food	____	____	____
Shelter (including mortgage, maintenance, fuel, and utilities)	____	____	____
Transportation	____	____	____
Clothing	____	____	____
Medical	____	____	____
Insurance	____	____	____
Vacation	____	____	____
Entertainment	____	____	____
Savings and investments	____	____	____
Total	____	____	____

To calculate for inflation, use a compound interest table from your local library to see how much one dollar of expense would increase over the number of years until you retire. For example, at 5 percent annual inflation for ten years, it would increase to $1.63. Multiply the current figure by that amount to get an inflation-adjusted total.

*For items that do not come up every month, such as a vacation, divide the total yearly cost by 12.

Social Security.

Your Social Security benefits are based on the number of years you have been paying Social Security taxes and your earnings over certain of those years. No one has to work more than the equivalent of ten years, or 40 quarters, to qualify for retirement benefits. Earnings are credited regardless of how much of the year you actually worked. (For 1994 each $620 earned at any time in the year counted as credit for one quarter, up to a maximum of four quarters.) The amount of your Social Security check will depend not on your quarterly credits but on how much you earn over the years (see table below).

Inequities in the system. Families with similar incomes often receive different benefits. For example, a family in which only the husband was a wage-earner will receive higher benefits than a family in which both husband and wife worked with a combined income equal to the husband's income in the first family.

This is one of various inequities embedded in a system that originated half a century ago, when attitudes and social conditions were different. With all the problems Social Security now faces, such inequities are unlikely to be removed. Social Security is not a fund into which people make "contributions" that they withdraw after retirement. It is a pay-as-you-go system under which working people and their employers are taxed in order to provide benefits for retired people, survivors, and the disabled.

Although you are eligible for full retirement benefits when you reach 65 if you were born before 1938 (67 if born after 1959), you can, if you choose, begin receiving benefits as early as 62. Monthly benefits in that case will be 80 percent of regular benefits (or a prorated percentage for any age between 62 and full retirement age) and will be fixed at that percentage for the rest of your life.

If you delay starting benefits until after full retirement, your monthly benefits will be higher than the basic full rate by 3 percent for each year you delay if you were born before 1925, rising to 8 percent a year for people born after 1942.

When a married man is receiving Social Security benefits, his wife can begin receiving *her* benefits at 50 percent of his rate when she reaches full retirement age. She never receives more than 50 percent of his benefits while he is alive. If she chooses to begin receiving benefits at any age between 62 and full retirement age, she will get between 37½ percent and 50 percent of her husband's retirement check. This lower rate will continue until her husband dies, after which she would receive a survivor's benefit, explained below.

If the wife has been working and paying Social Security taxes herself, she can receive either a spouse's benefit or a benefit based on her own Social Security taxes, but she cannot receive both.

If the husband dies first, the wife can receive 100 percent of his benefit beginning at full retirement age, or 71 percent beginning at age 60.

How big will your Social Security check be?

If you would like an estimate of what your Social Security payments will be when you retire, call the toll-free number 1-800-772-1213 and ask for a "Request for Earnings and Benefit Estimate" form. After you fill out this simple form and mail it in, Social Security will send you your complete earnings history; estimates of your retirement benefits at three ages—age 62, full retirement age (65 until the year 2000, after which it gradually increases to 67), and age 70; and estimates of disability or survivors' benefits that might be payable. To get a general idea of the range of your benefits, check the table below. It assumes that you will retire at full retirement age; your spouse is the same age as you; your spouse will not earn enough to receive a benefit higher than 50 percent of yours; and you will have steady lifetime earnings. (The total benefits for a couple could be higher depending on the spouse's work record.) The accuracy of these estimates depends on your actual earnings in the past and future.

Approximate monthly benefits if you retire at full retirement age

Your age in 1994	Receiver of benefits	Your Earnings in 1993			
		$20,000	$30,000	$40,000	$50,000
45	You	$777	$1,044	$1,177	$1,301
	or You and your spouse	1,165	1,566	1,765	1,953
55	You	777	1,043	1,157	1,244
	or You and your spouse	1,165	1,564	1,735	1,866
65	You	752	998	1,076	1,027
	or You and your spouse	1,128	1,497	1,616	1,690

If the husband dies before the wife reaches 60, and after the youngest child reaches 16, the wife receives no benefits as a survivor until age 60. The child receives benefits until age 18.

All of these examples assume that the husband is the principal wage earner. If the wife is, the figures would be the same in reverse.

Applying for benefits. To apply for benefits, you must visit your Social Security office three months before the date that you will become eligible, or the date when you choose to begin receiving your retirement checks, if that is later.

When the husband applies for his social security benefits, it is not necessary for the wife to be there, unless she is also applying for her benefits. Take the following documents with you: Social Security card and proof of age (birth certificate or baptismal papers); marriage certificate (if applying as a spouse); copy of W-2 form showing the latest year's earnings, or a copy of the latest income tax return.

Medicare coverage. Apply for Medicare at the same time that you apply for retirement benefits. If you have already begun receiving Social Security payments before 65, you will automatically get your Medicare card in the mail by your 65th birthday, which is when Medicare coverage begins.

If you plan to delay the start of retirement checks past age 65, you and your spouse must each remember to apply for Medicare three months before each of you is 65.

Medicare consists of two parts—A and B. Part A, which costs you nothing, pays for your hospital bills. Part B, medical insurance, pays doctors' bills and a number of other items not covered by Part A. For Part B, you pay a monthly premium that covers your spouse and eligible dependents. This premium, which is deducted from your retirement check, is the same for everybody and increases every year.

Part B is optional. If you do not enroll when you become eligible, you have another chance to sign up in the first quarter of each year, but your monthly premium for medical insurance will be 10 percent higher for each twelve-month period that you could have been enrolled but were not.

Part A helps pay for up to 90 days in each benefit period at any participating hospital. A benefit period runs from the first day of hospital treatment to the 60th day after release from a hospital or nursing home. After that, if you have to go in again, a new 90-day benefit period starts. (In 1991 the deductible for the first 60 days in the hospital was a total of $628, and for the last 30 days, *$157 a day.*)

Part B generally pays 80 percent of approved medical charges after a deductible that you pay once a year.

You can buy Medicare Supplement policies and Major Medical Expense policies to cover costs not

covered by Medicare. If you decide to buy such a policy, make sure it does not duplicate any part of Medicare.

(Medicaid, not to be confused with Medicare, is completely separate. It is a program run by your state government primarily to help people with low incomes and little or no resources.)

Your pension. For many employed people, a pension offers additional retirement income. Most pensions are based, to some extent, on Social Security benefits. The employer usually takes your Social Security benefits into account in deciding how much of a pension to provide for you.

If you die before early retirement age, benefits for your spouse are not likely unless you have contributed to the pension plan yourself.

When you retire, you can choose to have your pension cover your spouse in the event that you die first. In that case, your own monthly payments are reduced while you are living. Depending on your spouse's age, benefits after your death could be as little as 50 percent of your own benefits.

Some pension plans give you a choice of receiving your benefits in monthly payments or in a lump sum. Monthly payments are guaranteed for life but are not adjusted for inflation, unless your employer volunteers to do so. A lump sum can be invested by you, most likely in a rollover Individual Retirement Account, into which you can deposit the entire sum without paying taxes at the time. Unlike a conventional IRA, there is no tax deduction for making the investment, but there are very large tax savings because the income from the investment is sheltered from tax until you make withdrawals, which must begin at age 70½. Assuming that you or your spouse do not draw out all the funds in the account, there would still be money left for your heirs, in contrast to a pension.

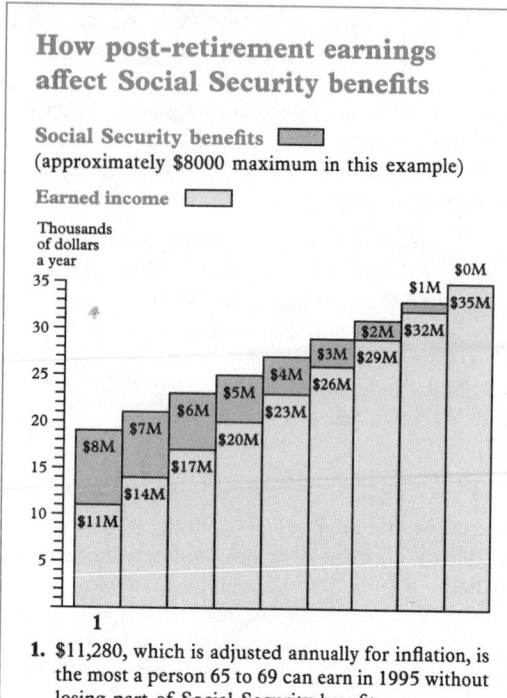

How post-retirement earnings affect Social Security benefits

Social Security benefits ▨
(approximately $8000 maximum in this example)

Earned income ▧

Thousands
of dollars
a year

1. $11,280, which is adjusted annually for inflation, is the most a person 65 to 69 can earn in 1995 without losing part of Social Security benefits.

Working for yourself. In these inflationary times, many people augment their retirement income by continuing to work.

If you are self-employed and use part of your home as a business, you are allowed significant deductions on your income tax. Check with your local Internal Revenue Service office.

But as long as you work, you will be required to pay self-employment tax to help support the Social Security system, even though you may already be drawing Social Security benefits. Regardless of age, you must pay the tax if you have net income of $400 or more from your own business or profession. The tax also applies if you have income from providing services such as baby-sitting, nursing, selling door to door, or working as a real estate agent.

The self-employment tax rate is over 15 percent of a "taxable base" equal to almost all your net self-employment income, if that figure is no more than $61,200, in 1995. (If it is over that limit, the tax rate is a little under 3 percent on the part of the taxable base over $61,200.)

When self-employed people receive Social Security payments, any amount they earn over a certain level reduces their Social Security benefits by one dollar for every three earned. The deduction is made from Social Security benefits at the beginning of the calendar year. In 1995, a retired person age 65 to 69 could earn up to $11,280 a year without losing any Social Security retirement benefits. This limit has been increasing every year. From age 70 on, under present regulations, you can earn as much as you want without losing any Social Security benefits.

Managing your shopping

Shopping is where management of the family's money begins. Planning what you are going to buy and following simple rules when you shop can mean the difference between just making ends meet and having money to save.

Going to the supermarket. At least once a week or so, someone in the family has to shop for food and other household needs. Here are some guidelines that can bring considerable savings.

- Do not shop more than once a week. Read the newspaper ads on Wednesdays and Thursdays and plan where you will shop and what you will buy each week. Jot down several menus featuring the specials advertised and note the staples on sale—unperishable items you can stock up on for weeks ahead. Make a shopping list to take with you.
- Go to the supermarket shortly after you have eaten so that you will not have an appetite for expensive

treats. Try to shop early in the morning, when stocks of produce and fresh meats and fish offer the greatest choice. Just before a long weekend, you might try shopping late in the day to take advantage of last-minute markdowns. Schedule your shopping trip without your children. Their impulses can wipe out your economies.

- Do not overstock on produce, the most profitable line for most supermarkets. Do not buy the first of a new crop of fruit or vegetables; prices should come down later. Remember that frozen food prices also go up and down with the season, so try stocking up on a frozen vegetable when the same vegetable is as good a buy as fresh produce. Buy canned fruits and vegetables at the end of summer, when many prices are reduced before the fresh packs come in.
- Keep portions in mind when you are buying meat. Steaks and chops will serve for only one meal; a roast can last for several days.

- Read labels and note how much you are paying per ounce. The large size is not always the economy size.
- Try buying day-old bakery products. After you freeze and thaw them, most people cannot tell them from fresh.
- Remember that junk food is costly, apart from its lack of nourishment.
- Think hard about convenience foods. Instant coffee can be more economical than regular, but does it make sense to pay someone to make your iced tea for you?
- Soft drinks in cans and bottles are an expensive way to buy water—with tiny percentages of artificial flavor. For about the same cost as two 12-ounce cans of soft drink, you can make a sparkling genuine fruit drink by adding store-brand carbonated water to a 6-ounce can of frozen concentrated fruit juice.

Shopping in other stores.

In your other shopping, it is important to time certain purchases according to the seasons and to take advantage of sales. Not all sales, however, are what they appear to be. Some, such as department store white sales, feature items that may have been especially manufactured for the sale. Certain goods ordered by mail are not manufactured until after your order has been received. When a sale is announced, look for words that mean the goods have been marked down from a quoted figure. If the ad uses terms like "special purchase" or "comparable value," the prices may not be genuine reductions.

When you purchase a big-ticket item such as a refrigerator or a television set, you will probably be urged to buy a service contract, which provides that repairs will be made at no additional cost for the life of the contract. What some stores do not tell you is that the service contract may partly duplicate the coverage already offered in the warranty, such as parts and repairs at no cost for a full year. Service contracts, moreover, are usually sold for the early years of the life of your purchase, when a problem is less likely to develop. A study at Cornell University concluded that most service contracts are not good buys.

Those glossy catalogs.

Unsolicited catalogs that come in the mail have become a popular way to shop for clothes, gifts, and a broad range of unusual items. Catalogs offer convenience and, for people away from large cities, a wide choice of high-priced items. But shipping costs can be high.

Some catalogs do offer sales from time to time, but most catalog prices are not competitive, not even with other catalogs. If an item in a catalog catches your eye, watch for it in other catalogs and in your local stores, since prices vary widely. If you do order an item, be prepared to wait a few weeks. According to federal regulations, you have the right to receive any mail-order item within 30 days unless the seller has specified a longer delivery time. If the deadline is not met, you have the right to cancel and get all your money back.

Returns may be a problem unless your catalog is from a nearby department store.

Clubs, outlets, and co-ops

Two recent entries in the retailing business—membership warehouse clubs and factory outlet stores—are offering shoppers in heavily populated areas opportunities to buy quality merchandise at significant savings. A third kind of money-saving institution, the co-op, has been around since the Great Depression of the 1930's.

With prices as much as 40 percent below retail prices elsewhere, the warehouse clubs may charge a membership fee of $25. If you have a chance to join one, spend some time visiting it before you sign up.

Outlet stores, often located in shopping centers of their own, may offer top-of-the-line products at discounts of about half of retail prices.

If there is a co-op in your area, you might try it for dairy products, meat, produce, and various staples, on which big savings are possible. If you would like to start a co-op, write for information to:

National Cooperative Business Association
1401 New York Avenue NW
Washington DC, 20005.

A shopper's calendar

As retailing becomes increasingly competitive, sales on various items are being held more frequently throughout the year. But this calendar of traditional sales periods for department stores may be useful.

January–February	White sales (and other household goods)
After Easter	Storewide clearance sales
Late June	Men's clothing
After July 4	Storewide clearance sales
August	Children's clothing Camping equipment
Autumn	China, glassware, silver
October–November	Women's coats
After Christmas	Women's dressy clothes Men's clothing Storewide clearance sales

---

Your shelter dollar

The American ideal of owning a one-family home has become difficult for many to achieve. Young families seeking a home for the first time find that they have to settle for far less space than they wanted at a cost that takes a disproportionate share of their income.

The principal question to be answered is how much home can you afford. As the table below indicates, your gross annual income needs to be at least a third of the price of the house, assuming you can get a mortgage as low as 8 percent. With a 12 percent mortgage, it should be half the price of the house.

The figures that are shown here do not include closing costs, which are identified in the adjoining table. Closing costs can vary from as low as 2 percent of the amount of the loan to around 7 percent.

Although a 30-year loan has long been the typical mortgage, people who want to save money over the life of the loan have been signing up for 15-year mortgages, when their near-term income permits. On a 10 percent mortgage, they pay back less than twice the price of a $100,000 house over 15 years instead of more than three times the price over 30 years. They are also likely to get a more attractive interest rate.

Partly offsetting the high cost of interest payments is the tax advantage of owning your home, since interest as well as property taxes are deductible from federal income tax.

Lenders' smorgasbord.
Lending institutions have come up with a smorgasbord of alternatives to the traditional fixed mortgage. When you select a lender—a bank, savings institution, mortgage banker, or credit union—find out first if mortgages are fairly easy to obtain at that institution. Do they charge a fee for originating the mortgage? (This consists of a one-time charge called "points," explained in the glossary.) Do they offer a choice of mortgage plans? Is there a prepayment penalty?

Traditional fixed rate. This type of mortgage, on which the figures in the table are based, appears at first glance to be the most expensive. That is because the interest rate is higher than starting rates for other kinds of mortgage now being offered. But this appearance is deceptive. The fixed rate mortgage is not only the most certain, it is likely to be the most economical in a time of rising interest rates.

Adjustable rate. The most common of the other types of mortgage available is the adjustable rate mortgage (ARM). Starting at a lower rate than the fixed rate mortgage, the ARM can be adjusted at any time, with 30 days' notice, to reflect changes in interest rates. The change could affect your monthly payment, or the outstanding principal, or the length of the mortgage. There is, however, no penalty for prepayment.

If the terms of an ARM include a cap on the

What can you afford to buy?

Here are some approximate figures that should give you some idea of how much house you can afford. They are based on a down payment of 15 percent, with property taxes and insurance coming to just under a third of your monthly payment.

Following the general rule of thumb, monthly payments assumed here are no more than 28 percent of gross income—essentially the regular income your family has had for at least a year.

House price	$100,000	$150,000	$200,000
Mortgage rate	*Annual gross income you need*		
8 percent	$33,000	$52,000	$70,000
10 percent	$41,000	$62,000	$83,000
12 percent	$48,000	$73,000	$98,000

(Figures in between those shown can be prorated.)

Checklist of closing costs

When you buy the house, you will encounter a whole battery of additional costs, called closing costs. Buyers can expect to pay most or all of these charges, in addition to the purchase price of the house. Actual costs vary from locality to locality; get an estimate from your lawyer or a local real estate man.

- Appraisal
- Title search fees
- Judgment search fees
- Title insurance policy fee
- Survey costs
- Attorney's fee
- Loan origination fee for mortgage
- Mortgage insurance
- Credit report fee
- Fee for bank's lawyer
- Home-owner's insurance premium
- Taxes, recording fees
- Adjustment for costs paid by seller (fuel, water, etc.)

Borrowing on your house

To home owners who have paid a large part or all of their mortgages, lending institutions are actively offering equity conversion. This is a loan with your equity in your house as collateral. Another form is a line of credit, on which you can draw by writing checks.

Unlike other kinds of interest payments, mortgage interest is deductible under the 1986 Tax Reform Act; the interest on home equity loans of up to $100,000 is also deductible.

But equity conversion advertising does not always make it clear that your monthly payments may be for interest only, with the original amount of the loan to be paid off in a "balloon" at the end of the

term. Nor do the ads always tell you that you have to pay closing costs as well as interest.

monthly amount you pay, a rise in interest rates could result in negative amortization. When your payments are not sufficient to cover interest charges at current rates, the lender can make up the difference by increasing the principal—the amount of your loan. This is the opposite of building up equity under a conventional mortgage. To avoid negative amortization, the term of an ARM could be extended, but to no more than 40 years.

Graduated payment. In the Graduated Payment Mortgage (GPM), the rates begin low and build up on a fixed schedule, ending at a higher level than rates on a conventional fixed mortgage.

Buy-down. Still another choice is the buy-down, offered as an incentive to the buyer by house builders. The builder turns over to the lending institution part of the money he receives for the house. This money is used to reduce your interest payments for a limited number of years.

Reverse. This type of mortgage enables senior citizens or others on a fixed income to receive a monthly payment using the equity of their home as security. The mortgage is paid off when the homeowner sells the home, or when the homeowner dies and the property is sold in settlement of the homeowner's estate.

For any kind of mortgage, the lender is likely to urge you to take out mortgage insurance. Like other life insurance on credit purchases, this is more for the convenience and protection of the lender than for yours, since you could probably purchase term insurance more economically on your own. If you do find it convenient to take out mortgage insurance, make sure the policy is *not* made out to the lender; your family might prefer to keep the mortgage and invest the insurance proceeds.

Ways to save energy in your home

Everyone knows that you can save energy by insulating a home and turning off the lights, but here are some points you may not have thought about:

- In cold weather, use the sun's heat by opening blinds or curtains; in summer keep them closed as much as possible.
- When the outside temperature is 78° or cooler, turn off the air conditioner and open the windows.
- Run the dishwasher and clothes washer only with full loads. In the clothes washer, use warm or cold water cycles when you can.
- A shower uses about half as much hot water as a tub bath.
- Clean the condenser coils on the back or bottom of your refrigerator with a vacuum or brush at least once a year.
- Check the gasket on the refrigerator door by seeing if it will resist letting you pull out a slip of paper. Replace it if necessary.
- Do not open the refrigerator or oven doors more than necessary. Opening the oven door lowers the temperature about 25°.
- Check the refrigerator temperature to make sure the settings are correct. The refrigerator compartment should be about 40° and the freezer should be 0°.
- The refrigerator should have enough space around food to let air circulate, but the freezer should be solidly packed, even if it means filling a milk carton with water and freezing it to take up space.
- One 100-watt incandescent bulb gives more light with less energy than two 60-watt bulbs.

Managing your car

How long a car loan?

If you take out a loan for a period of more than three years, there could be a span of well over a year when the car is worth less than the loan still to be paid off. If you trade in the car during that period, or if it is stolen or wrecked, you will not receive enough to pay off the loan.

Best time to buy

If you decide to buy a new car, and you are thinking of a domestic make, plan to buy it just before the new models come out. The next best time is mid-December to late February—especially Christmas week—when salesmen spend a lot of time looking out of the showroom window.

The most economical way to own a car, according to a study made by the U.S. Department of Transportation, is to keep driving it until it cannot go anymore.

Most drivers would prefer not to put that proposition to the test, but there is no question that it is less expensive to keep running an old car that is in tolerably good condition than to buy a new one.

Nearly half the depreciation of a new car occurs in the first two years of ownership. In fact, a new car depreciates by as much as a third as soon as you drive it out of the showroom. Repairs and maintenance tend to be at their highest level in the fourth to seventh years, when the original parts begin to fail. That is why many people who could afford new cars used to trade them in after three years. More recently, as car prices have soared, drivers keep their new cars longer, which means fewer choices for used-car buyers.

Buying a new car.
Before you go to the showroom, you can find out what the dealer paid for the car you have your eye on. The figure is shown as the base price in one of the guidebooks to new automobile prices available in paperback or at your public library. The sticker on a showroom model will tell you the charges for optional equipment, freight, and dealer preparation. Add those to the base price in the book and you will know how much leeway you have for bargaining on the dealer's price to you.

You should also know the value of the old car you are trading in. Ask your bank lending officer, to whom you will be returning after you buy the car, to let you see his Red Book of Official Used Car Market Values. Knowing the old-car value will alert you to a fairly common practice among dealers—"highballing," or offering a high trade-in to attract the customer while making the price of the new car correspondingly higher.

When the dealer offers you a package of options, remember that his profit margin on them is higher than on the car itself. The most expensive option is factory-installed air conditioning.

Your dealer will be more than happy to arrange financing for your car, because that is likely to be another source of profit for him. In many cases, you can probably get a better deal by financing through your bank.

Buying a used car.
A used car is estimated, on an average, to be about 40 percent less expensive than a comparable new one. In selecting a dealer, it is usually wise to go to a well-regarded new car dealer; he has a reputation to protect and hopes to sell you a new car some day. Insist on being allowed to give the car a road test—more than just around the block. You might take it to an automobile diagnostic service listed in the yellow pages under that heading.

Tips for economical driving

- Do not leave the motor idling if you are stopping for more than a minute. It is more economical to turn off the engine and restart it later than to let it run.
- Speed kills economy. Remember that wind resistance cuts mileage above 50 mph, and the most economical speed is about 45 to 50. Tire treads wear twice as fast at 70 as they do at 45.
- Switch wheels every 5000 miles so that tires wear evenly.
- Maintain tire pressure, and check it only when the tires are cool.
- Check wheel alignment regularly.
- Avoid sudden stops as well as sudden starts. If you have to brake hard at a traffic light or a toll booth, you were using too much gasoline to get to that point.
- Do not try to maintain speed going up a long grade.

An economical vacation

Camping. Certainly the most economical way to vacation and, in many ways, the most rewarding, is to take the family camping.

You have many camping areas to choose from. If you write to the National Park Service, P.O. Box 37127, Washington, DC 37127, you will receive free of charge: a 50-state map of national parks; admission prices and facility charges at camping areas; a price list of booklets about individual areas; and addresses of all the state government travel offices. Admission for a single visit ranges from $1 to $4 per person or $3 to $10 per carload.

If you plan to visit in one year several places maintained by the federal government, send $25 to the address above for a Golden Eagle Passport, or buy it in person at any National Park Service area where entrance fees are charged. This will entitle you and your family to visit, in your private vehicle, any federal outdoor recreation area that charges an entrance fee, as well as historical houses and museums in federal areas. It does not cover fees such as those charged for camping, and it is good only for the calendar year when issued.

National park areas are generally open every day of the year except Christmas and New Year's, but the Park Service suggests you consider making your visit in the spring or fall, when visitors are fewer. It also recommends a booklet, "The National Parks: Lesser-Known Areas," available for $1.50 postpaid from the Superintendent of Documents, U.S. Government Printing Office, Washington, DC 20402 (stock number 024-005-00911-6).

You can also order a Department of the Interior booklet, "Camps in the National Park System," from: Consumer Information Center Y, P.O. Box 100, Pueblo, CO 81002 (50 cents postpaid). To make camping reservations en route, call the toll-free number 1-800-365-CAMP (2267).

Sleeping indoors. If you prefer to sleep indoors on your vacation, there are still ways to hold down costs.

Two people traveling a considerable distance may find that a fly-and-drive trip can be more economical than driving the whole way. To take advantage of airfare bargains, however, you may not be able to leave and return at the time when you would most like to. Moreover, the economical car rental services are not as conveniently located at airports as the well-known ones. But the savings on gasoline and en route motel costs could make this kind of trip worthwhile.

Finally, plan your route carefully. Do not try to cover too many miles in one day; this would necessitate wasteful and tiring high-speed driving. Try also to avoid urban and resort areas, where prices are higher.

Trimming vacation expenses

- Schedule your trip just before or just after the busy season, generally from Memorial Day to Labor Day, when rates are likely to be lower in vacation areas.
- If you are in a hot climate, start driving quite early in the morning and stop around mid-afternoon. This will save on use of the air conditioner and give you a better choice of economical accommodations.
- Do not carry a container on the roof, where it will increase wind resistance.
- Take along a small heating coil so that you can make your own coffee or tea. With fruit juice and pastry picked up the day before, you can have breakfast in your room. Save on lunch as well by taking along a simple picnic kit. Buy fruit, cold cuts, and other easy-to-eat items in small quantities along the way.

For senior citizens

People 62 and older may obtain free of charge from the National Park Service a lifetime permit that admits them, and anyone accompanying them in a private vehicle, to federal recreation areas that charge fees. It also provides a 50 percent discount on use fees in park areas, but not on prices charged by concessionaires.

The Golden Age Passport must be obtained in person with suitable identification (not a Medicare card) and is available at most federally operated recreation areas.

GOLDEN AGE PASSPORT

A Lifetime Admission Permit

Signature

Valid for the lifetime of the permittee   Nº 3029306

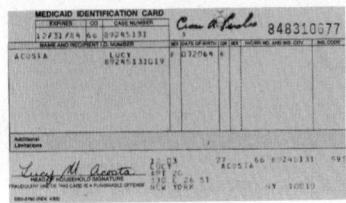

Medicaid identification card

Glossary

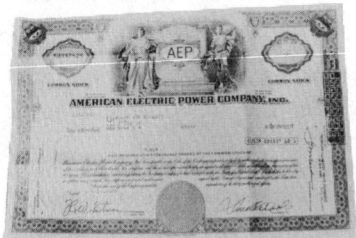

one share of common stock

Invest like a pro

- Get all the information you can—from books in your library, trade publications, newspapers, and TV programs on business-related topics.
- Talk to people who have done a lot of investing about what they have done right and what they have done wrong.
- Draw up a list of your investment objectives, and decide how much risk you can accept at your age.
- Do not get into collectibles unless you know a great deal about them.
- Do not agree to buy anything from a stranger who telephones you.

amortize. To reduce the principal of a loan by regular payments.

annual percentage rate (APR). The true interest cost of an installment payment, as distinct from simple interest; true interest takes into account the fact that the debt is being paid off during the time the interest is paid.

balance. The difference in an account between debits and credits.

balloon payment. The unpaid part of a mortgage that is due at one time (not typical of most mortgage arrangements).

bankruptcy. The condition of being insolvent and thus unable to meet one's obligations.

binder. A temporary contract issued by an insurance agent that covers the insured until the policy is prepared and executed; it is customary for fire insurance and other insurance protecting property.

blue chip stocks. Stocks issued by leading companies known for a continuing record of good earnings and dividend payments.

bond. An IOU or promissory note of a corporation or government, with a promise to pay a specified amount of interest for a specified length of time, and to repay the face value of the bond when it matures.

bottom line. The net income, which is the last line on an income statement.

bracket creep. A slang term referring to the way inflation pushes salaries and wages into higher tax brackets.

buy-down. Money offered by a builder as an inducement, which reduces monthly mortgage payments.

cash surrender value. Amount for which you can cash in your whole life insurance policy.

certificate of deposit (CD). A savings certificate with a fixed interest rate and a fixed maturity from 30 days to 10 years.

closing. The conclusion of a real estate transaction when all documents are signed and the deed is transferred to the new owner.

co-insurance. Condition, usually in major medical, in which you and the insurance company share costs; typically, the insurer pays 80 percent and you pay the rest.

collateral. Anything you own of value against which you can borrow money.

common stock. Securities that represent an ownership interest in a corporation.

compound interest. Interest that is computed on both the principal and the previously earned interest; in a savings account, interest left on deposit will itself earn interest.

condominium. Individually owned real estate consisting of a dwelling unit and an undivided interest in joint facilities and areas that serve the multi-unit complex.

consumer price index. A measure of the relative change in prices paid for a "market basket" of consumer goods by a typical wage-earner.

contractual plan. In mutual funds, a plan under which the total amount you intend to invest is stated, with a commitment to invest regular amounts monthly.

convertibles. Securities, such as bonds, that can be converted into other securities, such as stocks, at a certain price.

co-operative. Real estate ownership in which each person owns stock in a corporation, which owns and administers the residential units.

debenture. A debt certificate issued by a company that is not secured by a specific asset but by the company's credit in general.

deductible. In insurance, the sum you must pay before insurance coverage begins.

defined benefit pension. A type of pension in which a worker is guaranteed a certain amount of retirement income.

demand deposit. A bank deposit, such as in a passbook or checking account, that is payable to the depositor on demand (unlike a certificate of deposit).

discretionary income. The part of an individual's income that is left after paying taxes and buying necessities.

disposable income. The part of an individual's income that is left after paying taxes.

dividend. A payment made from earnings to the stockholders of a corporation; a payment made by an insurance company to holders of ordinary life or term insurance (if they choose a dividend-paying policy).

double indemnity. A policy rider that provides for double the face amount of the policy in the event of death by accident.

earnings per share. The after-tax earnings of a company divided by the number of shares outstanding.

effective annual interest rate. The total amount, expressed as a percentage, that one dollar will earn in one year; it is higher than the nominal rate when interest is compounded during the year.

equity. The residual value of a business or property beyond any remaining debt.

equity conversion. A loan for which your equity in your house serves as collateral.

escrow. Deposit of money with a neutral third party, as during the sale of a home.

estate tax. A tax imposed by the federal government and some state governments on the value of property transferred at death.

extended coverage. In insurance, extension of a policy to provide coverage against hazards not covered by the basic policy.

face value. In investing, the principal of a debt instrument, such as a bond or certificate of deposit, on which interest is computed and which is payable at maturity; in life insurance, the amount of the death benefit (as opposed to the cash value, which is less).

fee simple. Comprehensive ownership of real estate, with the right to pass it on to one's heirs.

float. In banking, the value of checks that have been written by you but not yet paid by the bank; in credit cards, the value of charges made to the account but not yet paid by the cardholder; in travelers' checks, the value of checks purchased but not yet cashed (in the second case, the cardholder benefits; in the third case, the bank benefits).

government bonds. Obligations of the U.S. government, considered the highest-grade bonds anywhere.

guaranty. A promise that merchandise will perform as claimed; differs from a warranty in that the latter is absolute assurance and failure to perform may void the basic contract; a guaranty merely provides that the guarantor will be liable (the two terms are often used interchangeably).

head of family. A person who maintains a family unit (not necessarily a father or husband).

Individual Retirement Account (IRA). A retirement program for anyone with earned income under which they may benefit from tax deferrals and in some cases from tax deductions while investing for retirement.

insufficient funds. A statement stamped on a check by a bank when the account does not have enough funds to cover that check.

interest. Money paid for the use of borrowed money.

investment company. A company that invests in stocks or bonds of other companies and sells shares to the public.

joint tenancy. The holding of property by two or more persons in such a manner that, upon the death of one, the survivor or survivors take the entire property.

Keogh plan. A retirement program for self-employed people under which they may benefit from tax deferrals and in some cases tax deductions while investing for retirement.

lien. A claim against a person's property.

liquid assets. Cash, or assets that can readily be converted into cash without any serious loss.

major medical. Protection against the expenses of a catastrophic illness.

market value. The value in a free market transaction agreed to by a willing seller and a willing buyer.

Medicaid. Combined federal-state program that pays for many medical expenses of the poor.

Medicare. The comprehensive federal health and medical insurance program that covers almost all people over 65.

money market account. An account offered by a bank with funds invested in short-term securities in the money market; the deposit is federally insured.

money market funds. Mutual funds that trade in short-term securities in the money market.

money markets. Financial markets where short-term debt securities are traded.

mutual fund. An investment managed by a company that pools the money of individual investors and buys a diversity of securities, such as stocks and bonds, to reduce risk.

net income. Also called net earnings or net profit, it is the difference between a company's sales and its expenses, before payment of dividends.

over the counter. Trading in securities that are not listed on major exchanges such as the New York Stock Exchange or the American Exchange.

payroll tax. The tax that an employee and employer each pay to support the Social Security program.

points. A one-time charge by a lending institution for originating a mortgage; one point equals 1 percent of the value of the loan.

price-earnings ratio. The market price of a company's common stock divided by its earnings per share.

prime rate. The interest rate that commercial banks charge their most creditworthy customers (lower than rates charged for loans to most individuals).

promissory note. A written promise to pay a debt.

rate of return. The annual percentage of an investment that is returned to the investor.

recipient. A person who receives public assistance or welfare payments, as distinguished from a "beneficiary," who works in covered employment and pays Social Security taxes.

rollover IRA. A special kind of Individual Retirement Account in which an employee deposits

a lump-sum pension, paying no taxes on the lump sum or on the income it earns until starting to withdraw the money after age 59½.

simple interest. The interest earned by the principal only, and thus not compounded.

term life insurance. Insurance without any cash value that provides coverage for a limited term; it can be renewed at specified increasing rates; it is considerably cheaper than ordinary life in the early years but more expensive in later years.

treasury bill. A short-term obligation of the U.S. Treasury that is issued at a discount without interest.

treasury bond. A U.S. Treasury obligation that pays interest and matures in more than seven years.

treasury note. A U.S. Treasury obligation that pays interest, with a maturity of from one to seven years.

vesting. The acquisition by an employee of an interest in the contributions made by the employer to the pension fund, or to other employee-benefit funds.

warranty. A statement that merchandise is as represented; a false warranty is cause for legal action.

yield. Dividends on a stock or interest on a bond expressed as a percentage of current price.

For further reference

Abromovitz, Les
  Family Insurance Handbook: The Complete Guide for the 1990's
  Liberty Hall Press
Annual Buying Guide Issue
  Consumer Reports magazine
Bamford, Janet, et al.
  Complete Guide to Managing Your Money
  Consumers Union
Cheeks, James E.
  The Dow Jones-Irwin Guide to Keoghs
  Dow Jones-Irwin
Klott, Gary L.
  The Complete Financial Guide to the 1990s
  Times Books
Kunes, Ellen
  Living Well—or Even Better—on Less
  Perigee
J. K. Lasser Tax Institute
  J. K. Lasser's Your Income Tax
  Prentice-Hall
Lieberman, Trudy
  Life Insurance
  Consumers Union
Loeb, Marshall
  Marshall Loeb's 1992 Money Guide
  Little, Brown

Martin, Renee, and Don M.
  The Survival Guide for Women
  Regnery Gateway
Mobil Travel Guide (seven area editions)
  Prentice-Hall
Passell, Peter
  The Money Manual 1992
  Simon & Schuster
Quinn, Jane Bryant
  Making the Most of Your Money
  Simon & Schuster
Ross, Charles
  The Best of Your Personal Finance
  FMS Publishing
Savage, Terry
  Terry Savage Talks Money
  HarperCollins
Schlayer, Mary Elizabeth
  How to Be a Financially Secure Woman
  Ballantine

Booklets on request (free unless otherwise noted)

College	"Federal Student Aid Programs" Department DEA—88 Pueblo, CO 81009	
Investing	"The Investor's Guide to Low-Cost Mutual Funds" (about 500 funds) Mutual Fund Education Alliance 1900 Erie Street, Suite 120 Kansas City, MO 64116 ($5 postpaid)	
Income tax	"Your Federal Income Tax" Write the I.R.S. Forms Distribution Center for your area (address is in the last section of Federal Income Tax Forms and Instructions).	Tax information publications and forms are available for reference and photocopying at your public library. "Tax Benefits for Older Americans" I.R.S. Publication 554 U.S. Government Printing Office Washington, DC 20402
Insurance	"Buyers' Guide to Insurance" National Insurance Consumer Organization 121 North Payne Street Alexandria, VA 22314 (send self-addressed envelope with $3)	
Vacation	"Travel Tips for Senior Citizens" Superintendent of Documents U.S. Government Printing Office Department 33 Washington, DC 20402 (send $1)	
Retirement	"Understanding Social Security" "Retirement" "Survivors" "Disability" "Supplemental Security Income" "Medicare" "Guide to Health Insurance for People with Medicare" (includes information on private health insurance) From your Social Security office.	Catalog of Publications (C-48) American Association of Retired Persons 601 E Street NW Washington, DC 20049
Shopping	Subject bibliography "Consumer Information" of booklets Superintendent of Documents U. S. Government Printing Office Washington, DC 20402 (includes guides to buying food and managing personal finances)	"Consumer Information Catalog" Consumer Information Center—Z P.O. Box 100 Pueblo, CO 81002

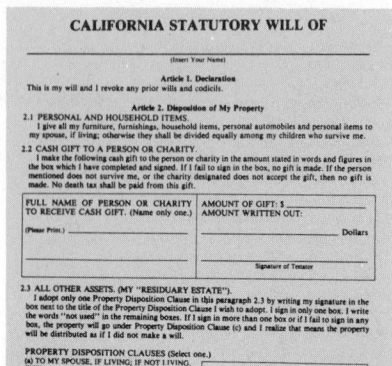

You and the Law

What is the law? Basically, the law is the set of rules that enables the members of a society to live and work together in reasonable harmony and to settle their disputes without violence. Some laws are in the form of written constitutions or statutes; others are legal principles that have arisen over the years from custom, experience, and common acceptance. Law is not confined to courts and legislatures. It pervades

our day-to-day relationships with our families, our neighbors, the people we deal with on our jobs, and the members of our community.

When you pick up the phone and order something from a store, you make a contract governed by the law of sales. When you drive your car, you are subject to traffic laws and the laws of negligence and liability. Your wages and working conditions depend on your contract with your employer, perhaps a union contract, and federal and state labor laws. When a couple marries or a child is born, the law establishes the rights and duties of family members. When a person dies, the law determines who gets his or her property and who will care for the children. Even as you sleep at night, you are protected by laws against burglary and trespass— and perhaps by zoning laws that prevent a boiler factory from being built next door.

Most of the time we attend to our everyday affairs without running into any legal problems. Inevitably, though, conflicts arise. The goods we order fail to arrive, or they are unsatisfactory. Accidents happen and people are injured. Disputes arise between employers and employees, or between landlords and tenants. Families break up, or fight among themselves about inheritance or other rights. The person with no knowledge of the law may find that he has put himself in a weak legal position or incurred legal obligations that he never intended. Unscrupulous persons may take advantage of him, or he may simply not know what his rights are or what to do about them.

The purpose of this chapter is to help you deal with legal situations and, if possible, prepare for them. Reading the chapter will not make you a legal expert, but it may help you to recognize the problems most likely to arise in everyday situations, the pitfalls to look out for and errors to avoid, and the means by which you can protect and enforce your legal rights.

This chapter deals with general legal principles; but each state has its own special rules, which may differ from other states. Always check your own state and local law before making any important decisions.

The *Glossary* at the end of this chapter defines some technical terms you may come across in the newspaper or in other reading. *For further reference* lists a number of nontechnical books on law. Many more can be found at your local library, always a good source of information. For more technical information, try the courthouse library. If you are not familiar with using a law library, do not be afraid to ask the librarian for help.

Your family and the law

Marriage. Marriage is a contract, but not an ordinary one. Because of the importance of the family, society sets rules and imposes duties and obligations that usually do not apply to purely private agreements.

A marriage is valid everywhere if valid in the state where it takes place. *Each state sets its own rules,* which usually include a license, a blood test, a waiting period, and a ceremony performed by a clergyman or judge. Some marriages are prohibited because of blood relationship, age, prior marriage, or physical or mental incapacity.

Annulments. Marriages that do not conform to the rules are not automatically void. Unless incestuous or bigamous, a marriage will be valid unless one or both parties takes legal action and has it annulled within a reasonable time. (If an underage person marries, the child's parents can have the marriage annulled.) Annulments may also be obtained on grounds of fraud if, for example, one party expressed a desire for children knowing that he or she could not or would not have any.

Each state sets its own rules.

Common law marriage. Newspapers often use the term "common law marriage" to refer to the state of any couple living together; such use of the phrase is not accurate. A common law marriage is an agreement to marry and live together as man and wife without going through a ceremony. In states where they are permitted, common law marriages are exactly the same, legally, as any other marriage. The difficulty lies in proving the agreement and the intention of the parties, especially if one or both is dead and there is a dispute over inheritance.

Most states no longer recognize common law marriages. However, they will recognize a common law marriage that was valid at the time it was entered into, or one made in a state that does recognize them.

Changing your name

A married woman often wants to continue using her maiden name; she may, for example, have established a useful professional reputation under that name. Using a maiden name is perfectly legal. In fact, anyone can use any name he or she wants, so long as there is no intent to defraud. (You could not, for example, use the name of a well-known person in order to borrow money.) Getting a court order to change your name makes it official; but it is not necessary.

State laws. Some states do require women to use their married names on drivers' licenses or other documents. The state can do this, as it is responsible for public records. In these states, a woman must either comply or go to court and have her name officially changed.

Updating records. Most women do take their husbands' names. Those women should immediately notify the Social Security Administration to avoid any possible confusion in the records, as well as employers, insurance companies, department stores where they have charge accounts, and anyone else whose records should be changed.

141

Children. A child born to a married woman is presumed to be legitimate, even if the marriage turns out to be invalid. Illegitimate children become legitimate if their parents later marry each other.

Scientific developments, such as artificial insemination and "test-tube babies," pose new legal problems. Many states have passed laws requiring the consent of both husband and wife to these methods of conception or birth. If the law is complied with, the children are legitimate.

Illegitimate children. With respect to their mother, illegitimate children have full legal rights. They also have the right to support from their father; it may, however, take a lawsuit and a court order to establish paternity. Inheritance rights of illegitimate children from their fathers vary from state to state. Many states allow illegitimate children to inherit if the father has acknowledged the child in writing.

Abortion. The U.S. Supreme Court has ruled it unconstitutional to forbid abortion during the first three months of pregnancy. In other situations, each state can set its own abortion laws, and they vary widely.

Adopted children. Adopted children have the same legal relationship to their parents as natural children. In some states, an adopted child may also inherit from his or her natural parents, but in no state can natural parents inherit from the child. The right of adopted children to inherit from the adopting parents' relatives (where there is no will) varies widely from state to state. The trend is toward allowing inheritance rights.

How to adopt a child

Learn your state's law and follow it to the letter. Consent must be obtained from the natural parents unless they have been legally deprived of custody. Consent may also be required from the child, if above a certain age.

The rules vary. Some states allow adoptions by single persons, but singles usually find it hard to get approval. Religious requirements are not absolute but the state may give preference to adoptive parents of the same religion as the child's natural parents.

The essential point. You must satisfy a court, at a hearing, that you are of good moral character, able to provide a good home, and financially responsible. The court usually accepts the recommendation of the social agency in charge, but if it is unfavorable, you can introduce evidence to overturn it. A deaf couple, for instance, overcame an unfavorable report by showing that they had successfully raised their own children, who had normal hearing.

Adults may be adopted. The practice is uncommon, but it has sometimes been done to establish inheritance rights.

Legal status of minors

Contracts	Minors cannot be held to a contract or agreement while underage. Moreover, they can repudiate and cancel a contract at any time. (*Exception:* Real estate contracts cannot be repudiated while the minor is underage.) If the minor does not repudiate and cancel the contract before coming of age or within a reasonable time afterward, the contract will be valid.
	A minor can cancel a sale and get his money back. This rule does not apply to food, clothing, medical care, or other necessities. However, a minor who bought a car was able to get his money back, even though he had cracked it up. As a general rule, anyone who deals with a minor acts at his own risk, even if he does not know that the person is underage.
Liability for damages	Minors are responsible for injuries they cause to other people or to their property. They can be sued for damages; the damages can be paid from property owned or later acquired by the minor. Parents are usually not liable for the acts of their children, but some states have changed this rule.
Crimes	Under traditional law, a minor over seven could be tried as an adult. Today, children under 16 are charged with juvenile delinquency, not crime, to keep them from being encumbered by a criminal record. (The age may vary in some states.) Minors charged with juvenile delinquency have the right to a trial, a lawyer, and all constitutional safeguards.

Since an underage teenager can not be held to a contract, his father must cosign a car loan and become legally responsible for making the payments. But the son can be held responsible for the damage he does with his car.

Legal capacity

Children. Children do not have full legal rights and duties until they reach the *age of majority*. Traditionally, this age was 21, but many states have lowered it to 18, along with the voting age. Most states also have age limits for specific privileges, such as buying alcoholic beverages or obtaining a driver's license.

Incompetent adults. Adults are presumed to have full legal rights and capacities unless declared incompetent by a court after a full hearing. This proce-

dure has severe drawbacks:

- It stigmatizes the person as mentally unsound.
- It is not appropriate for physical disabilities or mental difficulties, such as forgetfulness, that fall far short of mental unsoundness.
- The incompetent loses most of his or her legal rights, including the right to vote, make contracts, buy or sell, lend or borrow money, make gifts, marry, travel, or choose a place of residence. The incompetent may even be committed to a mental hospital.

Property	Minors can own property of all types, but it must be managed by a parent or guardian. A child's earnings legally belong to his father (or mother), unless the child is "emancipated"—no longer dependent upon his parents for support. Examples of emancipated minors are those in the armed forces, those who have married, and those whose parents will not support them.
Right to sue	Lawsuits may be brought on a child's behalf by a parent, guardian, or person appointed by a court. Children can sue parents for intentional injuries, but not for negligence (auto accidents, for example). Some states allow negligence suits against a parent who does not have custody.
School rights	Children have a right to an education, but parents cannot be compelled to send them to public schools. Many states recognize the right of handicapped or retarded children to special education; parents can participate in the decision to send or not send their children to special classes. Schools have the right to maintain reasonable discipline, but a child cannot be expelled or suspended without a hearing, except in emergencies. Parents have a right to see their children's records and correct any misinformation. The records cannot be shown to others without the parents' consent (except to school officials or to protect a child's health or safety).

A gift belongs legally to the person who receives it. But household furnishings usually belong to the husband, except in those states that have community property laws. A paycheck belongs to the person who earned it.

In some states it is possible to appoint a conservator to manage a person's property simply by showing that he is unable to handle it himself due to mental or physical disability. The usual proof is a doctor's statement. The person has the right to contest the proceeding, but is less likely to do so because he is not declared incompetent and does not lose his other legal rights.

Aliens. Resident aliens have the same rights as citizens, except that they cannot vote or hold elective office. They must register and must get a permit to work in the United States. In some states, they are ineligible for public employment. Illegal aliens may be deported.

Legal rights and duties.

At one time, married women could not manage their own property; in fact, their legal status was almost that of children. These laws are a thing of the past. Husbands and wives have equal legal rights and powers.

Property. Except in community property states, wages and salaries belong to the person who earns them. Income from property belongs to the person who owns it. Property belongs to the person who bought it or in whose name it is placed. Household furnishings belong to the husband unless proven otherwise.

Gifts, including gifts between husband and wife, belong to the person who receives them. However, a man

Planning for old age, illness, or incapacity

Old age is not necessarily incapacity. Elderly people lose none of their legal rights, but the infirmities of age may make it difficult for some to handle their legal affairs. There are ways to plan against possible incapacity without the need for court proceedings; the same methods can be used by persons who simply want to be relieved of business responsibilities, and by people who wish to have someone else take care of their affairs.

Power of attorney	A power of attorney, which must be in writing, gives someone else the power to act on your behalf. It can be a *general* power to handle your affairs, or a *special* power, limited as you see fit. It can be revoked at any time and ends at your death. In some states, you may provide that the power of attorney is to take effect only if your physician certifies you are no longer able to handle your own affairs.
Trusts	You can put your money or property in a trust (see *Glossary*), and appoint a trustee to manage it for your benefit. The trust can be set up to take effect only on your doctor's certification that you are incapacitated; another way is to appoint yourself as trustee and name a co-trustee to take over automatically if you are incapacitated. You can put whatever you want into the trust, impose any limitations you want on the trustee, and reserve the right to cancel the trust at any time and take back the property.
Married couples	Do not keep everything in one spouse's name. If that spouse becomes incapacitated, the other will be in a financial bind. Legal proceedings to straighten things out may be time consuming. Each spouse should have at least enough money or separate property to provide for emergency situations.

who "gave" his wife money to save for his old age was able to get it back by proving no gift was intended. Contrary to popular belief, wedding gifts do not belong to the bride; they belong to both partners, unless clearly intended for just one (a necklace, for example).

Joint bank accounts and other joint property are owned equally by husband and wife; if one dies, the other gets the property. Some states recognize a special form of real estate ownership called "tenancy by the entireties." It is similar to joint ownership, but neither party can sell or mortgage his or her share without consent of the other. Also, creditors cannot get at the property except for debts owed jointly by husband and wife. This form of ownership ends if the parties are divorced; they become ordinary co-owners. See also "Community property laws," page 146.

Antenuptial agreements. Husband and wife can make a property agreement before marriage; each can give up any right to inherit from the other. Agreements are common among people with children from prior marriages; they assure that the children get their property free of any claims from a second spouse. These agreements are enforced by the courts unless grossly unfair. One was set aside because the husband, who had only a moderate income when he married, later became rich.

Husband and wife. Despite the trend toward equality, the husband is still "head of the family" in most states. He can decide where the family is to live. If his wife refuses to accompany him, she cannot charge him with desertion or abandonment. The husband also has the right to direct the children's education and religious upbringing.

Duty to support. A husband has a duty to support his wife and children, even if they have money of their own. If the husband is unable to support the family, the duty passes to the wife.

Support means the provision of "necessaries," but this includes more than the bare necessities of life. It means providing a standard of living in keeping with the father's financial condition. Some courts have held that a father must give his children a college education if he is financially able.

Purchases. A wife can buy necessities for the family and charge them to her husband; she is acting as his agent. A merchant can assume she is acting for the family unless the husband has notified him not to extend credit. A newspaper announcement, such as "I will not be responsible for debts incurred by my wife," is sufficient, but *only if the merchant knows of it.*

There are limits to the rule. It applies to purchases that are reasonable—not to sable coats or Rolls-Royces. If, however, the couple has a joint charge account or credit card, either is entitled to make purchases on it.

Indigent parents. Some states require adult children to support their parents if the parents cannot support themselves and would otherwise have to apply for public assistance.

Divorce and separation. Tradition-

ally, a divorce could be granted only for an offense committed by one spouse against the other. The "guilty party" was often barred from remarrying and from receiving alimony, which is why most divorce actions were brought by the wife.

Grounds for divorce include adultery, desertion, cruelty, conviction of crime, and habitual drunkenness or drug addiction. Defenses to a lawsuit for divorce include "condonation" (forgiveness of the offense), collusion, and justification (for instance, abandonment by the wife might be justified by the cruelty of the husband).

No-fault divorce. Most states now permit divorces for incompatibility, irreconcilable differences, or separation for a long period of time. No one need be at fault.

"Quickie" divorces. Most divorces, even those granted from foreign countries, will be recognized if both parties have appeared in court, either personally or through an attorney. But "mail-order" divorces and divorces where the defendant was not notified will be set aside if challenged.

Separation. A separated couple can make an agreement between themselves or go to court for a legal separation. The rules are similar to the rules in divorce cases, but a separation does not dissolve the marriage or change the parties' legal status as married persons.

A newspaper ad may not always protect a person from a spouse's debts. Consult a lawyer before placing an ad.

I, CHRISTOPHER SMARTS, also known professionally and publicly as CHRIS MILLS, do hereby declare that I am not responsible for any debts incurred by MISS BETTY WHITE or BETTY SMARTS as of June 15, 1985. I am in the process of challenging the legality of this marriage in Nevada and at no time did Miss White or myself establish residence in Boston or any other city in the United States.

Alimony and property settlements. Courts today base their decisions on equity and fairness, not on set rules or formulas. For instance, wives have been awarded alimony for a period of time while attending college or taking training courses to enable them to support themselves. In a few cases, alimony has been awarded to the husband. If the parties can agree to a settlement between themselves, the court will usually accept it and make it a part of the court order.

Property settlements are permanent, but alimony or child support orders can be modified. Alimony normally ends if the wife remarries, but a father's duty to support his children is not ended by the remarriage. A support order may continue even after the child comes of age. For example, the court may find that the father is financially able to help the child through college or to help support a child who is incompetent. The amount, however, can always be modified to reflect changes in the parents' financial status.

Enforcement. A husband who fails to pay is guilty of contempt of court and can be punished by being sent to jail. This is done rarely, but the threat is always there.

Child custody. The welfare of the child is the primary consideration; but, in practice, the mother is almost always awarded custody (unless clearly unfit), with visitation rights for the husband. Recently, there has been a trend toward shared custody.

Custody fights are the bitterest of all lawsuits. One study showed that, even in uncontested divorces, over half the couples with children wound up in court later in custody battles. Couples would be well advised to settle their differences, perhaps with the help of a clergyman or social worker, before engaging in neverending court battles. Such custody suits can do great harm to children.

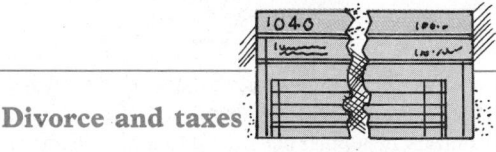

Divorce and taxes

While uncontested divorces can be handled by a legal clinic at low fees—or even with a do-it-yourself divorce kit—you should be sure to talk with your tax adviser. There are some tricky income tax points that may depend on the wording of the divorce decree.

Alimony is deductible. Alimony payments are deductible from the husband's income; they are taxable income to the wife. Child support payments are not deductible, and are not income to the wife. Payments are considered alimony if they meet the following rules:

- They are made under a written agreement or court order.
- They are scheduled to continue for at least six years.
- They are to terminate at the death of the wife.
- They are not specifically designated as something other than alimony (such as child support).
- They do not depend on the status of a child (for example, if payments are scheduled to end when a child reaches 18, they are considered child support, not alimony).

Other payments. Property settlements are not taxable to either spouse, but later sales may be taxable. Payments under oral agreements are considered gifts and are not tax deductible.

Fees. Legal fees for getting a divorce are not deductible. Fees for tax advice are. Get separate bills.

Community property laws

Eight states—Arizona, California, Idaho, Louisiana, Nevada, New Mexico, Texas, and Washington—have community property laws for married couples. The laws vary, but the basic features of community property are these:

Anything owned before marriage remains the property of the person who owns it.

Gifts and inheritances, before or after marriage, are the property of the person who receives them.

All other property acquired after marriage (including wages, salaries, and other earnings) is community property shared equally by husband and wife, no matter how the property was acquired or whose name it is in.

If the couple is divorced, the property is split between them. If one dies, community property does *not* automatically go to the survivor. It goes to the person named in the deceased spouse's will, or to the next of kin if there is no will.

If you are moving into or out of a community property state, it may be a good idea to check on any problems that might arise. Talk to a lawyer in the community property state; lawyers in other states often know little about community property law.

Your home and the law

Buying a home. This may be the biggest financial deal of your life, and the one most important to the happiness of your family. Do not let yourself be rushed or pressured. You should probably consult a lawyer as early as possible, before you commit yourself to anything.

Land and buildings are called *real property*. All contracts for the sale of real property *must* be in writing, and cannot be changed except in writing. Never sign anything on the assurance that "It doesn't really mean anything" or "We'll change that later if you don't like it." *You are legally bound by anything you sign, and an oral agreement to change it is worthless.*

You are bound by anything you sign.

If you buy through a real estate broker, he or she may ask you to leave a deposit and sign a binder agreement to hold the property until you can get together with the seller. Do not sign unless you have spoken to a lawyer. And get a receipt for any deposit.

Down payments. When you sign the sales contract, or before, you will have to put down a deposit. Make sure

Questions to ask *before* signing a contract

About the property	Exactly what is included in the sale? Stoves, refrigerators, ovens? Carpets, shelves, Venetian blinds, storm windows, screens? Awnings? TV antennas? Is a survey needed? Who pays for it? Are there any old mortgages on the house, judgments against the seller, or payments due to contractors or repairmen?
About the sale	When will the sale be completed? When can I take possession? Are any delays likely? Are there penalties for delays? Who is to pay escrow fees, taxes, insurance, etc.? Are there any hidden fees?
About the mortgage	Can I cancel the contract if I cannot get the kind of mortgage I want? Under what conditions? How much time do I have?
About inspection	Do I have the right to inspect? What if the inspection shows damage from termites or other causes? Suppose the house needs repair? Who pays for it? Can I cancel the contract if the inspection shows the house is unsatisfactory?
About restrictions	Are there any restrictions on building or on the use of the property? What are the zoning regulations? Does the town have a building code? Can I build a tennis court? Put in a swimming pool? Keep a horse? Other pets? Store my old car in the backyard? Practice with my band? Can I run a business out of my home? What kind?
About the neighborhood	What kind of neighborhood is the house in? Who are my neighbors? What school will my children go to? Where can I do my shopping? Is the neighborhood entirely residential, or are there some businesses? What kind? Are there any plans to build a factory in the neighborhood, or run a highway through it?

the contract states when you are entitled to get it back. For example, the contract may take effect only if you can get a "satisfactory" mortgage. The bank offers a mortgage, but the interest rate is too high. The seller might argue that the mortgage was "satisfactory," in which case you would have to go to court to get your money back. You might not succeed. The contract should have defined exactly what, in this particular case, is meant by "satisfactory."

The sales contract. To be valid, the contract must contain all essential terms of the agreement, including enough information to identify the property, the buyer, the seller, the date of sale, the price, and how the money is to be paid.

Some tips to the buyer

- **Make sure of the identity of the seller.** Swindlers usually pass themselves off as someone else.

- **Insist that the seller's spouse sign,** in case he or she has any claim on the property.

- **Beware of printed forms.** They favor the seller.

- **Do not sign without having the house and property inspected,** unless the contract gives you the right to cancel if an inspection shows the place to be unsatisfactory.

Contract clauses of importance to buyers. Make sure your lawyer covers them.

Type of deed	A *quitclaim* deed simply releases all right, title, and interest that the seller has in the property. A *warranty* deed also guarantees that he actually does have the right, title, and interest that he claims to have. Buyers should insist on a warranty deed. If the contract does not specify, the seller only has to give a quitclaim deed.
Date of sale	If it is absolutely imperative that you have the house by a certain date (for example, you have to move from your old house), you can request a clause saying "time is of the essence." This makes the seller responsible for any financial loss you suffer from delay. If such a clause is too strict to be accepted, the seller may at least agree to a clause imposing monetary penalties for each day's delay.
Encumbrances	Property may be "encumbered" by unpaid taxes, old mortgages, court judgments against the seller, claims of third parties, etc. Such encumbrances are what the title insurance company looks for when searching the records. Until the search is made, do not sign any agreement to buy "subject to all encumbrances" unless they are listed specifically. (Title insurance protects you against any unknown or undiscovered encumbrances that turn up in the future.)
Fixtures	Items permanently affixed to the property, such as furnaces or plumbing, are part of the real property. Movables, such as tables or chairs, are not. Many other items, such as storm windows, are borderline. The contract should state exactly what goes with the house and what does not.
Risk of loss	Be sure to include a clause canceling the sale if the house is lost by fire or other disaster before the sale is completed.

How the contract is enforced. What if the seller refuses to go through with the deal? The buyer can sue for any damages and can also sue for "specific performance," which is a court order directing the seller to complete the sale. The seller has the same remedies if the buyer backs out. Most likely, though, he will just keep the down payment and sell the house to someone else.

Title closing. The sale is completed and the deed transferred at the closing. Usually, the buyer, the seller, their lawyers, a representative of the bank or other mortgage lender, and a lawyer from the title insurance company are present. Costs and fees are settled, including the buyer's share of costs already paid by the seller, such as taxes, insurance, fuel, etc.

Escrow. If there are encumbrances on the land, such as judgments or unpaid taxes, part of the purchase price may be put in escrow. This means that a neutral third party will hold the money until the seller removes the encumbrances.

When the sale is complete. Finally, the seller gets his money and the buyer gets his home. Besides the deed, the buyer should receive all insurance policies, tax receipts, and a bill of sale for any personal property, such as furniture, that has been purchased along with the house. The buyer will also receive a title insurance policy and a mortgage statement from the bank.

It is important to have the deed recorded immediately to protect your title. Dishonest persons sometimes sell property to more than one buyer. If the first buyer has not recorded his deed, a person who buys later but is first to record his deed may have a valid claim to the property.

Get it in writing.

Building a home. Contracts to build should be in writing, though it is not legally required. The best way to avoid legal disputes with contractors is to make the contract and specifications as exact and detailed as possible, including types and quality of materials and equipment, colors, and brand names. Any changes should require your written approval.

Method of payment. Partial payments are usually made at various stages of construction, with final payment due when the house is completed. If an architect drew the plans, you might hire him to supervise construction and make payment to the contractor subject to his approval. At the very least, you should have periodic inspections by someone who knows the construction business.

The contract may provide for penalties if the contractor does not finish on time, except in the case of causes beyond his control.

Liens. Serious problems can arise if the contractor does not pay his workmen, suppliers, or subcontractors. Even though you did not deal with them directly, they can file liens, or claims, against the property for the amount owed them. The legal status of these liens depends on your state's law, but they are encumbrances on the property and have roughly the same effect as unpaid mortgages. The contractor is liable for

The home owner should always exercise caution when coming to terms with a contractor. The slip shown below is an estimate, not a contract. It does not bind the contractor to do the work for the stated price.

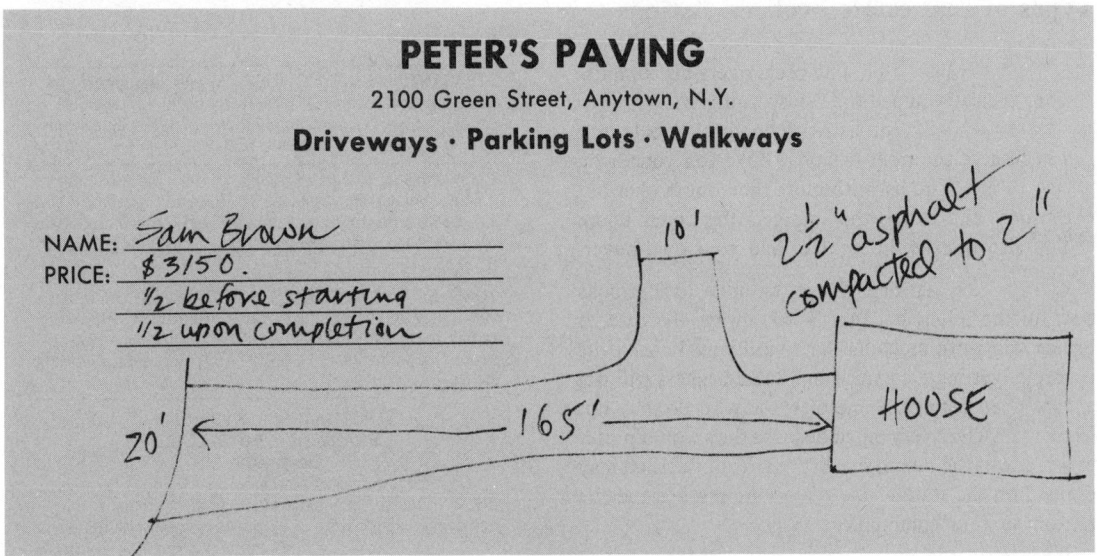

satisfying these claims, but that will not help if he becomes bankrupt or cannot pay.

If you get notice of a lien, do not make any further payments to the contractor until he removes the lien by paying the claim.

One way to protect yourself. You might require the contractor to post a bond to guarantee payment of any claims. Bonds can be obtained from insurance companies; they are common in big commercial projects. There are drawbacks. The premium charged by the insurance company will probably add to the cost of the house, and the insurance company will have a voice in any changes you want to make in the plans or specifications.

Selling your home. Sellers have the same

legal problems as buyers—but in reverse. If a sales contract is conditional on the buyer's obtaining a mortgage or having an inspection made, be sure to set a time limit, or the sale may be held up indefinitely. Also, stipulate that the buyer relies *solely* on the inspection, not on any promises or statements made by you.

If the buyer cannot get a mortgage, you may be willing to finance all or part of the price by a *purchase money mortgage.* This means you agree to be paid in installments and you retain a mortgage on the property, just like a bank, in case the buyer does not pay.

Real estate brokers. If you sell through a real estate broker, the broker is entitled to his commission if he produces a buyer who is "ready, willing, and able" to buy at your price. Even if the buyer backs out or cannot get a mortgage, the broker may be entitled to his commission unless you protect yourself by a clause in the contract with the broker.

How to save on taxes when you sell

If you sell your house, you normally have to pay capital gains tax on the profit. But you can postpone the tax by purchasing or building a new house within two years before or after you sell the old one. The postponed tax will become due if you sell the second house, but you can postpone again by buying still another house. There is no limit on the number of postponements. The tax may never become due.

Tax break for the elderly. If you have reached age 55, you can sell your home and pay no tax on up to $125,000 of profit. If spouses own the home jointly, the rule applies if either has reached age 55. This tax option is permitted only once in your lifetime.

Figuring your tax correctly. If you do not qualify for these tax breaks, you can keep taxes to a minimum by remembering to deduct the following costs from your profit:

- Costs of buying and selling, such as legal fees, brokers' commissions, and recording fees.
- Costs of any capital improvements, such as additional rooms, air-conditioning systems, swimming pools, and landscaping (but not ordinary repairs).
- "Fixing-up costs" to put the house in shape to sell.

Keep records. Be sure to keep all bills, records, and documents *permanently.* You can never tell when you might need them.

Types of real estate brokers' listings

Exclusive right to sell. The broker gets his commission, even if you sell the house yourself.

Exclusive listing. You list with one broker only, but you reserve the right to find a buyer on your own.

Open listing. You list with more than one broker but the one who makes the sale gets the commission. You also reserve the right to find your own buyer.

Which is best? At first glance, an open listing looks best for the seller, but that is not always the case. A broker will work much harder to sell your house if he is sure of getting a commission. Some brokers will not accept open listings. Some of those who do may not exert themselves very much because they would prefer to sell one of their exclusive listings. Your decision may depend on the state of the real estate market and the custom in your community.

Brokers' contracts. Contracts are normally in writing, and should have a time limit, such as six months. When the contract expires, get a list of persons to whom the broker has shown the property. Otherwise, one of those persons may come back later and buy the property. You would then owe the broker a commission because he first produced the buyer.

Look out for the fine print. As always, beware of printed contracts. They favor the broker.

Owners' rights and duties. Your

use of your property may be subject to restrictions for the benefit of other persons or the public in general. Here are some of the most common restrictions.

Covenants and conditions. Deeds often contain restrictions on property, such as a ban on commercial use or rules on the type and size of buildings. Developers often put these rules in deeds to maintain the character of the development. The restrictions are binding on future buyers. If the property has passed through several hands, a thorough search of the records may be needed to discover the restrictions.

If a restriction is made a *condition* of ownership, a violation could cost the owner the title to the property. Most restrictions, however, are *covenants* (promises); if they are violated, nothing happens automatically, but persons who are affected, such as neighbors, can get a court order (injunction) requiring the owner to comply with the covenant. Courts may refuse to enforce covenants if they make no sense because the neighborhood has changed. If in doubt, a landowner can ask for a court ruling in advance. Some covenants are illegal, such as restrictions based on race or religion.

BUILDING PERMIT

No._____

HAS BEEN ISSUED FOR THIS CONSTRUCTION

Dated_____

TOM JONES
BUILDING DEPARTMENT
TOWN OF MOUNT PLEASANT
14 Sunny Lane
Anytown, N.Y. 10000

This card must be conspicuously posted on premises until completion of building operations.

An "Application for Zoning & Building Permit" must be filed with the building department of your local government. The application usually requires specifications about the proposed renovation or new building and may require a survey or architectural drawings.

Public laws. Most communities have zoning laws restricting land use, but they normally do not apply to land or buildings already constructed or in use when the law is passed. Most towns also have building codes and require a permit before building. If you want an *exception* or *variance* from the zoning laws, you have to apply to the zoning board and show good cause. It is very important to show that your neighbors have no objection to the proposed use or construction.

Co-ownership of property

Ownership of property of any kind may be shared by two or more persons. Co-owners are either *tenants in common* or *joint tenants.* (Married couples may also be "tenants by the entirety" or share "community property"—see pages 144–145.)

Do not be confused by the word "tenants." It usually refers to renters of property, but here it means owners.

Tenants in common. Each owns a *fractional* share in the entire property; no one owns any specific part. Each may sell or mortgage his share; creditors may reach it for payment of debt. When a tenant in common dies, his share does not go to the co-owners, but to the person named in his will, or to his next of kin.

Joint tenants. Each owns an *equal* share in the property. Each can sell or mortgage his share, and creditors can reach it. When a joint tenant dies, his share goes to the survivor or survivors. If a joint tenant sells his share, the survivorship feature ends, and the new owner is a tenant in common.

Is co-ownership desirable? Except possibly for married couples or business partners, co-ownership is usually not a good idea. The owners may disagree on what to do with the property. A sale may be missed if one co-owner holds out, as the buyer may be unwilling to take less than full ownership. Even if owners agree on managing the property, one may die or sell out, in which case there would be a new owner to deal with. If the new owner is a minor, the property can be tied up for years.

If the owners are deadlocked, the only solution may be a court order of "partition," which will physically divide the property among the owners.

Neighbors have duties to each other. One cannot create a nuisance to the other, such as by polluting a stream or continuously making a loud noise. Local laws vary, so be careful about taking action on your own. Consult a lawyer.

Easements. Other persons may have the right to use your property or pass through it. Such easements and rights of way may be purchased, or they may arise from continuous use over a long period of time. If one neighbor has an easement or right of way in the property of another, it will continue even if either or both properties are sold.

Condemnation. The government has the power (eminent domain) to take all or part of your property for public purposes, such as for highways or schools. The power may also be exercised on behalf of public utilities; for example, an electric company may need to run power lines over the land. Landowners are entitled to reasonable compensation, which is decided at a condemnation proceeding, where there is presented evidence from appraisers and experts. You may also be entitled to compensation if the use of your land is interfered with, even if it is not actually taken; for example, low-flying planes from a nearby airport may lessen the value of the property.

Mortgages. If you fail to make mortgage payments, the bank cannot just take your home; it must go to court in a *foreclosure* proceeding. In every state, you are given a period of time (usually a year or more) to make the payments and *redeem* your house—or else work out a new arrangement with the bank, such as smaller payments over a longer period of time.

If you are unable to pay and the mortgage is foreclosed, the property will be sold at auction. If the price does not cover the mortgage, you still owe the balance. If the price is higher than the mortgage, you are entitled to the difference.

Air, water, and mineral rights. You own the air over your land (subject to reasonable use by airplanes) and the minerals beneath it. Air and mineral rights can be sold separately from the land itself, and can be ex-

tremely valuable; if you get an offer, see a lawyer.

You own any body of water entirely on your property, such as a pond. But rivers and streams flowing through your land or next to it are subject to the rights of downstream owners. You may not pollute the river, dam it up, or divert it from its course. (Navigable bodies of water are under the jurisdiction of the federal government.)

Neighbors' rights. Neighbors owe each other a duty of *lateral support;* this means they cannot make excavations that would weaken the other's land. If their buildings share a *party wall,* neither can weaken the wall.

Neighbors may not use their land in such a way as to create a *nuisance,* such as loud noise or foul odors. The remedy is to get an injunction banning the nuisance. Overhanging branches from a neighbor's tree may constitute a nuisance, and a landowner has the right to cut them down, but check local laws first.

Insurance. If you have a mortgage, the bank will insist you have fire insurance, but the bank only requires enough insurance to cover the mortgage. You may want to buy more. The cost of replacing a home is likely to be more than the original price because of inflation.

Homeowners should also have liability insurance, in case anyone is injured on the premises. Property owners' liability for injuries is a complicated subject. If you buy insurance, the insurance company will take care of all claims. Some companies sell *comprehensive* policies, which cover most or all kinds of insurance a homeowner wants.

Renting a home.
A contract to rent is a *lease.* Most leases are in a writing, but an oral lease is valid. If no period of time is specified, either the landlord or the tenant can cancel at any time, usually by

You and the Law

one giving a month's notice to the other.

Most written leases specify how long they are to last, usually a year or more. A tenant who stays on after the lease has run out is called a holdover tenant. The landlord has the choice of evicting him, or of regarding the lease as renewed for another term.

Unless the lease states otherwise, the tenant can sublet or assign (transfer) the lease. Most leases, however, ban or restrict the right to assign or sublet, except with the owner's consent.

Landlord's duties. The landlord is responsible for keeping the building structurally sound. The old rule held the tenant responsible for ordinary repairs, but in many states, the landlord is now considered responsible for repairs in residential property, unless otherwise provided in the lease. (In commercial property, the tenant usually makes repairs.) In apartment buildings, the landlord is responsible for maintaining hallways, staircases, driveways, laundry rooms, and other areas used by all the tenants.

A *constructive eviction* occurs if the landlord lets the building run down to the point where it is not fit for use. The tenant can move out, does not have to pay any more rent, and can sue the landlord.

Tenant's duties. The tenant's main obligation is to pay rent. If he moves before the lease expires, he must continue to pay rent until the end of the lease or until the landlord rents the property to someone else. Under traditional law, the tenant had to pay the rent even if the landlord violated his part of the agreement—or even if the house burned down. This rule has been modified in many states.

Some states recognize an "implied warranty of habitability," which means the landlord is regarded as promising that the property is fit for the tenant to live in, even if the lease contains no actual promise or guarantee. Tenants can sue for violation of the implied promise or withhold payment of the rent. How serious does a violation have to be to justify not paying the rent? That depends on the rules of the state. Check with a lawyer or with a tenants' group before trying it.

Tenants are liable for any damage they do to the property. Landlords usually require a security deposit when the lease is signed. The tenant gets the deposit back when he leaves, if he has not damaged the property and does not owe any rent. Sometimes the deposit serves in place of the final month's rent. Some states require the landlord to pay interest on the security deposit.

Government regulations. Many state and local governments have passed laws that extensively regulate the relationship between landlords and tenants, especially in communities with housing shortages; some have rent control. Landlords' associations and tenants' groups will provide members with information and, sometimes, legal counsel.

Co-operatives and condominiums

"Co-ops" and "condos" are the fastest growing type of housing in the United States.

Co-ops. A co-operative apartment house is owned by a corporation. The residents are the stockholders; they own shares in proportion to the value of their apartments. Each has the exclusive use of his own apartment and the right to use common areas: stairways, halls, basement, grounds, driveways. The mortgage covers the entire building; stockholders are not personally liable for payment, but must make up the difference if any stockholder defaults, or risk foreclosure of the mortgage. Anyone who wants to sell must get approval from the other stockholders, who rule on the desirability of the proposed new resident.

Condos. Each condominium resident actually *owns* his apartment and shares ownership of the common areas. Each separate apartment can be mortgaged. This sometimes makes condos easier to buy and sell than co-ops, as banks are more willing to lend money if they can get a mortgage on the owner's apartment. (Co-op owners have only their shares of stock to pledge as security for a loan; the primary mortgage is on the whole building.) Condos are also easier to sell because approval of the other owners is not required (though owners may reserve the right to buy the condo themselves if they do not like a proposed owner).

Both co-ops and condos are run by a committee of residents; often, they hire a professional manager. Residents pay a monthly fee, which often includes maintenance, taxes, mortgage payments, etc. The ground floor is sometimes rented to commercial tenants, but there are legal limitations on how much of the building can be rented.

Advantages of co-ops and condos over renting:
- The residents actually own property. They can sell it or raise money on it. Tenants own nothing.
- Owners usually take better care of property than tenants do.
- Property owners get valuable tax breaks that renters do not, including tax deductions for mortgage interest and real estate taxes.

Wills and estates

What is a will?

A will is a way for a person (the testator) to direct who will get his property (estate) after his death. The will has no effect before death and can be changed or revoked at any time. A will is valid even if it does not dispose of *all* the testator's property; anything not mentioned in the will goes to the next of kin under state law. Normally, a will contains a "residuary clause" naming a person or persons to get everything not specifically left to someone else.

Why do you need a will? If you have no will, your property will be distributed according to state law, regardless of your wishes or your family's needs. The court will appoint an administrator (and a guardian if you leave children). They will have to post bond, which will be payable from your estate, along with their fees. If any money or property goes to minors, it will be tied up until they come of age. The guardian will not be able to touch it, even for education or medical costs, without getting a special court order.

If you have a will, you can be sure your property will go to the persons of your choice. You can appoint an executor to handle the estate, and guardians or trustees for the property of children. You can give the persons you appoint any powers that you see fit, or impose any limitations. You can direct what is to happen if you and your spouse (or other heirs) should die at the same time —in an auto accident, for example.

You can also appoint a personal guardian for your minor children; the appointment is not binding, but the court will usually follow your wishes.

How to make a will.

The testator must be at least 18 years old and of sound mind. The will must be in writing and signed in the presence of two witnesses (three, in some states); the witnesses should also sign. Witnesses cannot inherit under a will, so do not pick as a witness anyone you are leaving anything to.

If you die without a will . . .

- **If you leave a spouse and children,** they get your estate. In some states, it is divided half and half; in others the children take two-thirds and the spouse one-third. If you leave no spouse, the children get it all. If any of your children die before you, their children take what would have been their share. If you leave no children, the spouse either gets everything or, in some states, divides the estate with your parents, brothers, and sisters.

- **If you leave no wife or descendants,** your parents take the estate; if they are not alive, your brothers and sisters (or their children, if they are deceased) divide the estate.

- **If you leave no close relatives,** you can figure out who is your next of kin by counting generations to and from a common ancestor. For example, you and your first cousins have a common grandparent; so you count back two generations to the grandparent, and two generations down to your cousins. They are of the fourth degree of relationship. Their children would be of the fifth degree. Your estate will be split equally among all those of the nearest degree of relationship. Some states do not allow relatives beyond a specified degree to inherit.

- **If you leave no next of kin,** everything goes to the state.

Degrees of blood relationships under the civil law. They all stem from the box labeled "decedent."

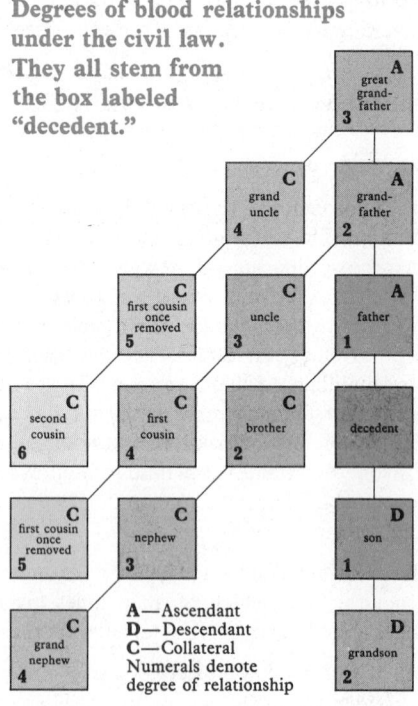

A—Ascendant
D—Descendant
C—Collateral
Numerals denote degree of relationship

There are exceptions. Some states require no witnesses to a *holographic* will, one entirely in the testator's handwriting. Some states allow *oral* wills in special circumstances, such as on a deathbed or when a serviceman is going overseas. Holographic or oral wills should be used only in emergencies, and replaced by a regular will as soon as possible.

Changes to a will (codicils) must also be in writing, signed, and witnessed.

A will may be declared invalid if the testator was of such unsound mind that he did not understand what he was doing, or if the will was made because of force, duress, fraud, mistake, or undue influence.

Revoking a will. A will can be revoked by another will or written document, signed and witnessed. It can also be revoked by physical destruction, such as tearing it up or burning it; but this is *not* a good idea. If you die and your will is not found, no one will know whether it was destroyed or just lost. A lost will, however, can be given effect if there is a copy, or some other proof of what was in it.

A will may be revoked by a later marriage or the birth or adoption of a child. In some states, the revocation is only partial. The wife or child gets what he or she would have inherited if there were no will; the balance, if any, is distributed according to the will.

Your rights to your body

You do not have an absolute right to decide where you will be buried or what service will be performed. The right belongs to the next of kin. Normally, however, your wishes will be respected.

You do have the right to leave your body to a hospital, college, or medical school for scientific purposes, or to donate any parts of your body for organ transplants. You can do this in your will or by using a special form; one common form is called a "Universal Donor Card." (Using a will may be too slow, especially in the case of transplants.)

Make your decision known. If you are donating your body, be sure to notify your family, your doctor, and any hospital you are in. You should also keep a copy of the donor card with you, in your wallet or purse, in case you die in an accident or away from home.

Sample will clauses

Specific bequests	I bequeath to my niece Jane Roberts, now residing at 4 Main Street, Centerville, IL, the sum of three thousand dollars ($3,000.00).
	I bequeath to my son John Jones, now residing at 2 Main Street, Centerville, IL, all my jewelry and any other personal effects and mementos which he may desire.
Residuary clause	I give, devise, and bequeath all of the rest, residue, and remainder of my estate to my wife Mary Jones if she survives me. If she fails to survive me, then I give the remainder of my estate to my friend William Brown, now residing at 10 Elm Street, Centerville, IL.
Common disaster clause	In the event that my wife Mary Jones and I die under circumstances where it cannot be established who died first, it shall be presumed that I survived my wife and this will and all dispositions contained herein shall be interpreted on the basis of that presumption.
Appointment of executor	I nominate my son John Jones as executor of my estate, to serve without bond. If my son predeceases me or is for any reason unable or unwilling to serve, then I appoint the First National Bank of Centerville, IL, as executor.
Appointment of guardian	Should my son John Jones be under the age of 18 years when I die, then I nominate my brother Thomas Jones and his wife Ann Jones, now residing at 12 Elm Street, Centerville, IL, to be guardians of his person. I appoint the First National Bank of Centerville to be guardian of all my son's property, subject to the following rules (enumerate powers and limitations on guardian).

Limitations on wills. You can disinherit any relative, including children, but you cannot totally disinherit a spouse. All states require that a certain minimum be left to the spouse. If it is not, the spouse can elect to get the share he or she would have received had the testator died without a will.

Some states limit the amount you can leave to charity if you are survived by a spouse, children, or other close relatives.

Mutual wills. Contracts to make wills or leave property to specific persons are enforceable. Sometimes, husbands and wives make mutual wills. Each leaves his or her property to the other, with the entire property to go to named beneficiaries (such as children) upon the death of the survivor. If the wills are made by agreement, the surviving spouse cannot change his or her will. But the agreement should be stated clearly in the will or in a separate written document. The mere fact that the two wills are the same does not prove that they were made by contractual agreement.

Probate and how to avoid it.

Court proceedings to establish your will and settle the estate (probate) are usually necessary, even if you die without a will. The court will appoint an administrator, usually your next of kin. Some property, however, need not go through court. Joint property goes directly to the joint owner. Insurance proceeds are paid directly to the beneficiary.

Some people want to avoid court proceedings to save costs and delay, and to maintain privacy (court records are open to the public). The best way is to put all your property in a trust (see *Glossary*), naming yourself as beneficiary for life and designating the persons you want to receive the property at your death, just as in a will. You should still have a will, however, as you may own property at your death without realizing it. For example, if you die in an accident, your estate may have a claim against the person responsible. Or you may have inherited property that has not yet been distributed.

Consumers' rights

You may have heard of the old legal rule Caveat emptor, Latin for "Let the buyer beware." If a buyer purchased shoddy goods, paid exorbitant prices, or failed to read the fine print in a contract, any problem was considered to be his own fault. This is still the law in the case of some business deals, but state and federal laws protect consumers in most transactions.

A consumer loan or transaction is for the purchase of goods or services for personal, family, or household purposes, and sometimes for agricultural purposes.

Getting out of bad deals. Federal and

state laws ban false, fraudulent, and deceptive advertising. Not only outright falsehoods are banned, but also deceptive practices such as "bait and switch" advertising, in which a merchant advertises a bargain to get you into his store (the bait), then tells you the bargain item is sold out and talks you into buying something more expensive (the switch).

You may be able to cancel a sale or a contract on grounds of fraudulent advertising, but it is hard to

---

**"Caveat emptor."
Let the buyer beware.**

---

prove. Mere sales talk or exaggeration about a product is not enough; and if a salesman does tell an outright lie, he will probably deny it. The best course is not to be taken in by tricky advertising in the first place. Many agencies have published pamphlets and booklets telling consumers what to look out for. Write your state consumer agency, or the Consumer Information Center, Pueblo, CO 81009.

Mail-order sales. If you buy something by mail, you can cancel the order and get your money back if the goods are not shipped within 30 days.

You absolutely do not have to pay for unsolicited goods sent through the mail. You do not have to send them back either. Just treat them as a gift.

Door-to-door sales. If you sign a contract with a door-to-door salesman, you have three business days to think it over. Within this period, you can cancel the sale and get back any payments just by giving written notice to the seller. However, if you request immediate delivery, you lose this right.

Warranties. A warranty is a guarantee or

promise about the quality or condition of goods and products; sometimes it includes a promise to repair. An express warranty is one actually made by the manufacturer or seller. Whether or not he makes an express warranty, the law regards him as making an implied warranty that the goods are fit for the purpose they are

LIMITED ONE-YEAR WARRANTY

Name _____

Address _____

City _____ State ____ Zip code _____

Date purchased _____ Store name _____

Product name _____ Model number _____

A warranty gives you specific legal rights, but you may also have other rights that vary from state to state. Consult your lawyer.

being purchased for. The seller can avoid this, however, by specifically stating that he makes no warranties whatsoever; this statement is called a disclaimer.

If the goods do not live up to the warranty, the buyer can sue for damages or get his money back.

Federal law. A seller who makes a written warranty must designate the warranty as *full* or *limited.* Under a full warranty, if repeated attempts to repair a product fail, the consumer must be given the choice of a replacement or his money back.

Defective products. What redress is available if someone is injured by an exploding bottle, contaminated food, or an appliance that catches fire? The buyer can sue under the product warranty. But suppose someone else is hurt, or the seller has specifically disclaimed any warranties?

In the past, it was necessary to prove the injury was caused by negligent or improper manufacture or handling of the product. Sometimes negligence is obvious (a dead mouse is found in a bottle of soda). But in many cases it may be difficult to prove negligence in manufacture, or to determine just who was at fault.

The modern trend. Today, many states impose *strict liability* on anyone who sells a consumer product, from the manufacturer to the retailer. The injured person need only prove that the product was defective and caused the injury. The rule of strict liability is applied in most cases involving food, drugs and medicines, clothing, cosmetics, and other products intended for bodily use, and products inherently dangerous, such as automobiles. In other cases, it may still be necessary to prove negligence in manufacturing. It depends on state law.

Credit.

Anyone who makes a loan or extends credit for consumer purposes must disclose all terms and conditions in clear, understandable language, including the annual interest rate, any other charges, and what happens if there is a dispute or if the consumer fails to pay. Credit may not be denied because of race, religion, national origin, age, sex, marital status, or receipt of public assistance. If you are denied credit (a loan, a charge account, a credit card) you must be told why—in writing.

Protecting your credit rating. If you are turned down because of an unfavorable report from a credit rating bureau or agency, you must be told which agency. Upon request, the agency must tell you the nature and source of the unfavorable information (but it does not have to show you its file). It must also disclose the names and addresses of all persons who have been given the information within the past six months (two years if the information was given for employment purposes).

If you disagree, you may insist that the agency reinvestigate. If you still disagree, you may put a brief statement of your own in the file (up to 100 words) telling your side of the story.

Small claims court

All states have small claims courts to handle cases involving less than a maximum amount set by state law. The federal Tax Court has a Small Case Division to handle tax disputes up to $10,000. Small claims courts provide a speedy, inexpensive way for people to assert their legal rights without the time, trouble, and cost of a major lawsuit.

Bringing a lawsuit. The court clerk will help you fill out the forms to start the case. There is a small fee, which the other side will pay if you win. The other party will be notified. Often, this will be enough to get him to settle. If not, you will be notified of the time and place of trial.

Caution: If the other party pays up, you can just drop the case. But if he only *promises* to pay, be sure to show up on the trial date and tell the judge. The case will then be held open, to make sure that you get paid.

Trials are informal. You can have a lawyer, but you do not need one. Here are some tips on how to behave:

- Dress well, but do not dress up.
- Stand when you talk to the judge. Call him or her "Your Honor."
- Describe your case in a general way before going into detail. Be sure to bring with you all documentary evidence, such as bills, canceled checks, letters, forms, etc.
- Testify yourself and call any witnesses.
- Do not fight or argue with the other party. Do not act like a lawyer. Do not ever argue with the judge.
- Do what the judge says. If he or she asks you a question, answer it. If he or she tells you not to say anything, be silent.

Credit cards.

If your card is lost or stolen, you should notify the credit card company at once. But even if someone has used the card before you notify the company, you can be held liable for no more than $50.

If you find an error on your monthly statement, you must notify the company within 60 days, in writing, stating your name, address, card number, and the nature and amount of the mistake. *A phone call is not sufficient, nor is a note written on the monthly bill.* Write a separate letter. The company must investigate and give you a written answer within two billing periods, but not longer than 90 days.

Until then, the company may not try to collect the disputed amount; it may not revoke your card; and it may not report you as a delinquent payer to anyone, such as a credit rating bureau.

If the company, after investigation, still insists that you owe the money, it must furnish you with documentary evidence upon your request. If you still disagree, you should protect your credit rating by writing to the company again. If the company then reports you to anyone as delinquent, it must also report that the matter is in dispute and must notify you of the report.

Defective goods. If you buy merchandise that turns out to be defective or worthless, you do not have to pay the credit card company, provided:

* The transaction was for more than $50.

* It was made in your home state or within 100 miles of your home.
* You made an honest attempt to settle the dispute with the merchant.

The rule applies only to the unpaid balance. You cannot get back payments already made. Of course, you can try to get your money back from the merchant.

Bill collectors.

Bill collection agencies operate under federal restrictions. The law does not apply, however, to persons or companies trying to collect their own debts. The following practices by collection agencies are forbidden:

* Telling anyone, including your employer, that you owe a debt (but they may ask for your address).
* Contacting you at unreasonable times or places (no middle-of-the-night phone calls).
* Using forms or envelopes that look official.
* Sending collection notices on postcards that other people might read.
* Using any abusive, deceptive, or unfair methods.

Moreover, the agency must stop *all* bill collection efforts if you notify them in writing to stop, or tell them you dispute the debt, or hire a lawyer.

If the agency violates the law, you can sue for actual damages, plus up to $1000 additional damages (if the court so decides), plus costs and attorneys' fees.

Are your debts too big?

Although you should always exercise care not to accumulate too many debts, it may happen that you become overwhelmed by the amount of money you owe. Declaring bankruptcy is the solution of last resort. Prudent management of your money will not only help you avoid bankruptcy, it can often get you out of your overwhelming debt. Read carefully "Managing the Family's Money," pages 110-139, for good advice on how not to overextend yourself. Sometimes it makes sense to consolidate your debts in order to avoid high monthly payments (see page 117 for more information). In order to get a fresh start, however, you may have to file for personal bankruptcy in a federal court.

How it works. You give the court a list of everything you own, the debts you owe, and any debts owed to you. The court appoints a trustee to collect your assets and distribute them to creditors. Mortgaged property or property pledged as security (collateral) goes to the particular creditor involved; the rest is distributed proportionately to all. If you have not misrepresented or concealed anything, your debts will be canceled (discharged) except for taxes, alimony, and child support.

Caution: Judges have the power to deny discharges if they find that the debtor *can* pay his debts and is improperly trying to take advantage of the bankruptcy law.

What you keep. Not everything you own can be taken. You can keep personal belongings, most household goods, your car (up to $1200 in value), the tools of your trade, and a certain amount of cash. But if you own a home, you could be in danger of losing it. There is a "homestead exemption" of $7500, but if your house is worth more, it will be sold, and you will receive only the $7500.

Wage earner plans. The bankruptcy law provides another alternative, under which you submit to the court a plan to pay a specified amount each month, depending on your income, how much you owe, and the needs of your family. If the court approves the plan and you make the monthly payments, your creditors are not allowed to demand more. Eventually, you will be free of debt.

Personal property

Your neighbor is responsible for your lawnmower if he borrows it for his own use, but you are not responsible for his car if you let him park in your garage.

Land and buildings are *real* property. All other property is *personal* property, including cash, movable goods, stocks, bonds, and intangible legal rights.

Abandoned property belongs to the finder. *Lost* property belongs to the finder only if the real owner cannot be found. Many states require that anything over a certain value be turned over to the police; the finder gets it if the owner fails to turn up within a specified period. *Stolen* property continues to belong to the owner; he can get it back, even from people who bought it without knowing that it was stolen. The exception is *cash*. If cash is stolen, you can recover it only if it is still in the possession of the thief.

Owners and possessors

Bailments. Temporary transfers of possession, but not ownership, of property are called bailments. If someone borrows property for his own use (your neighbor borrows your lawnmower), he is normally required to return it or pay for any loss or damage. If the bailment is for the benefit of the owner (you let someone keep his car in your garage), you, the possessor, are responsible only for intentional damage or gross negligence.

Most bailments are business transactions for mutual benefit (you take your TV set to the repair shop, or leave your jewelry as security for a loan). The possessor must use reasonable care, and is responsible for loss or damage that results from his negligence.

Some special cases. Hotels and motels are usually protected by state laws limiting liability to a small amount—and then only if the property is put in the hotel safe. Common carriers, such as railroads or trucking companies, are held to a high standard of care. They are generally liable for all loss or damage, unless caused by improper packing or an act of God, such as lightning, a flood, or a hurricane.

Liens. Repairmen, hotelkeepers, and others have a lien on goods in their possession; they can keep them until their bill is paid. If you want your property back, you have no choice but to pay—or go to court. (If you are

overcharged, consider suing in small claims court—see page 157.)

Ideas as property. You cannot "own" an idea. If you have a business idea you think is worth money, do not divulge it to anyone unless you get an agreement to pay for its use, or to keep it confidential.

Copyrights protect writing, music, works of art, and computer programs. What is protected is not the idea, but the form in which it is expressed. The copyright belongs to the producer of the work (or to his employer, if the work was done for hire). Copyrights can be registered, but need not be.

Patents are issued by the U.S. Patent Office to protect inventors. No one else may copy or manufacture the invention for a period of years. There is an exception, however. The inventor's employer may own the invention or have rights in it if it was invented during the course of employment.

Trademarks are names, designs, or slogans associated with a company or product; they may not be copied by competing companies. Trademarks may be registered or may simply arise from long use and association.

Installment sales. Sales of autos, furniture, and the like are often *conditional sales*. The buyer takes possession, but the seller remains legal owner until the goods are paid for. He can repossess the goods (if this can be accomplished without violence) or get them back from third parties if the buyer has sold or transferred them.

Watch out for this trap. An installment buyer usually signs a *promissory note* for the amount due. If a merchant sells the note to a finance company, the buyer will find himself in debt to the finance company even if the goods are defective or worthless. The finance company is a "holder in due course," not responsible for the condition of the goods. Many states have modified this rule. If you find yourself in this spot, talk to a lawyer or consumers' rights agency.

Your car. Legally, buying a car is no different from buying any other consumer product, but mistakes can be more costly. (For the law of conditional sales, see page 159; for the law of warranty, see page 156.) Be sure to read the warranty you get with your car. It tells you what rights you have if anything goes wrong.
"Lemon" laws. Many states have laws, stronger than the federal law, protecting consumers who buy cars that turn sour. The laws vary, but most work like this: If, within a year (or the warranty period, if less than a year), the dealer or manufacturer has been unable to repair a defect after four tries, or if the car has been out of commission for 30 days or more, the buyer is entitled to a new car or his money back.
Used cars. If you buy from a used car dealer, you are probably buying at your own risk, except for whatever warranty the dealer may give you. This holds even more so when you buy from a private party, unless you can show that you were defrauded.
Registration. A dealer will probably handle the registration of the car. If you buy privately, you may have to handle it yourself, and you may have to pay a sales tax to get the car registered. Contact your local motor vehicle bureau.
Insurance. Most states require car owners to carry liability insurance to cover any claims arising from auto accidents. Other types of insurance, such as fire, theft, or collision, are not required. You can buy them or not, as you choose.

If your new car does not work properly, you may be able, under the laws of your state, to get another car or your money back.

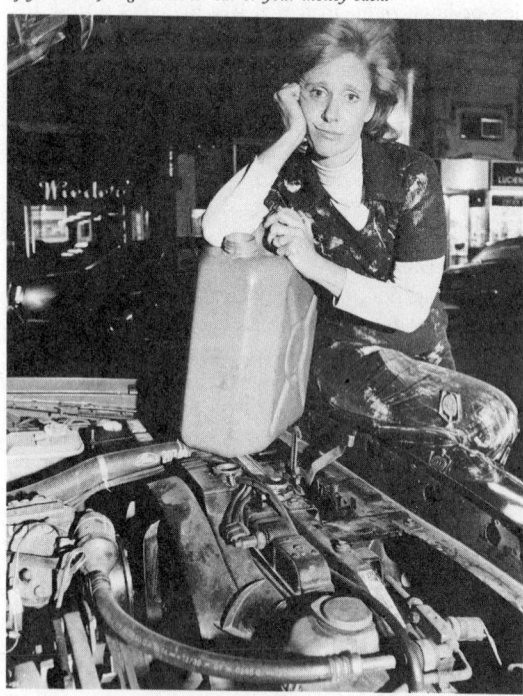

Accidents. More lawsuits arise from auto accidents than from any other single cause. If you are involved in one, notify your insurance company immediately. The company will handle any claim against you, provide a lawyer if you are sued, and pay any judgment. If the judgment is for more than your insurance coverage, you are liable for the balance. You are required to cooperate with the insurance company in the defense of the case.
If you are injured. You may wish to make a claim for personal injuries or property damage. Write to the owner or driver of the other car, stating that you are making a claim, and asking him to turn it over to his insurance company, which will probably contact you. *Do not give the opposing insurance company any written statement about the accident;* it can be used against you. If you do not have a lawyer, you will have to communicate the nature of your claim and provide evidence, such as doctors' reports and repair bills. Do not give more evidence than is necessary, and never make any admissions. (If you have a lawyer, he will handle all this; it would be improper for the other side to contact you personally.)
Should you get a lawyer? A lawyer can probably get more than you can from the insurance company, but he will take part of it for his fee. Most accident cases are on a *contingent fee* basis. The lawyer gets nothing if you lose; but if you win he gets a percentage, which may run from a third to a half. It may even be more for small claims, as the lawyer may have to do as much paperwork in a small case as a large one. If the percentage seems too high, you might try to settle the claim yourself. You can call in a lawyer later, if necessary.
Evaluating a claim. You are entitled to be paid for actual losses, such as lost wages, repair bills, and medical costs (even if paid by insurance). These are called special damages. You are also entitled to damages for pain and suffering. As a general rule, a settlement should run from two to four times the amount of special damages. If there is doubt as to who was at fault in the accident, the settlement may be less. If there are permanent injuries, it will be much more, since future losses, expenses, and pain and suffering must be taken into account.

The law of negligence. Except in states with no-fault insurance, you can recover damages only from a person who has caused an accident through negligence (carelessness). Negligence means the failure to use the ordinary care that could be expected of a reasonable person. Violation of the traffic laws is evidence of negligence, but a driver may be negligent without violating any law.
Who may recover? In some states, the injured person may not recover damages if he has also been guilty of

You and the Law

negligence, even in the slightest degree. This is called contributory negligence. Other states follow a rule of comparative negligence. The injured party can recover, but the amount he gets will be reduced in proportion to the extent he was at fault for the accident. A jury, for example, might find that the injured party was 20 percent responsible, and reduce his damages by that percentage.

Owner's liability. The driver is liable for his negligence. Under traditional law, the owner of the vehicle was liable only if the driver was his employee or was acting on the owner's behalf. In some states, it was presumed that any member of the owner's family was acting on his behalf (family purpose rule).

Many states now hold the owner responsible whenever the car is being driven with his consent.

Uninsured motorist laws. Many states have passed laws and established funds to pay persons injured by stolen cars, cars that do not carry insurance, and hit-and-run drivers who cannot be identified.

Who can sue? In most states, one spouse cannot sue the other for negligence, nor can a minor child sue a parent for negligence. Some states allow a child to sue if the parent does not have custody.

Some states have "guest statutes" that ban a guest in an automobile from suing the owner. The guest can, of course, sue the driver of the other car.

No-fault insurance

A growing number of states are adopting no-fault insurance laws, under which persons injured in auto accidents are paid for their economic losses no matter who was at fault, including lost wages and out-of-pocket medical expenses (not covered by medical insurance). Under this system, you apply to your own insurance company for payment instead of suing the other driver. Passengers in your car also apply to your company. Injured pedestrians apply to the company carrying insurance on the car that hit them.

Lawsuits are still possible. In serious cases, you can also sue the other driver for damages, including pain and suffering. A serious case is one involving death or permanent injury, or medical expenses above a threshold amount, which is set by state law.

A good idea? Advocates of no-fault insurance claim that it speeds payments, avoids lawsuits, and cuts the cost of insurance. Some claimants receive smaller amounts than under the old system, but they save the cost of a lawyer.

What to do if you are involved in an accident

1. Get help
First of all, get medical help for anyone who is injured. If the accident is at all serious, call the police.

2. Exchange information
Exchange information with the other driver. Get his name, address, phone number, license number, and the make and license number of his car. If the driver does not own the car, get the owner's name, address, and phone number.

Do not admit you were at fault. Do not get into any argument about who was at fault. Stay calm and simply exchange information.

3. Get evidence
Get names, addresses, and phone numbers of passengers and witnesses. If the police come to the scene, get the officers' names and badge numbers, and the address and phone number of their station.

If you have a camera with you, take pictures of the scene. Otherwise, get photographs as soon after the accident as possible. Write down the details of the accident as soon as you get the chance, while you still remember them clearly. Include all details, such as the weather, time of day, and visibility.

4. Give notice
All states require a report to the police if anyone was injured. It is also required for property damage beyond a certain amount, set by state law. If in doubt, play it safe and file a report.

Notify your insurance company as soon as you possibly can. Failure to report, or unnecessary delay, could jeopardize your insurance coverage.

Injuries and damages

Property owners must exercise reasonable care that customers or guests are not injured on their property.

A wrongful act that injures another person or his property is called a tort. Torts are classified as intentional or negligent. Auto accidents are the most common examples of negligent tort; another is malpractice by doctors, lawyers, or other professionals.

Property owners' liability.
Many lawsuits arise over injuries on someone else's property; for example, someone trips and falls. Whether the property owner is liable may depend on who is injured. Here are the rules:

- **Invitees** are invited on the premises for business purposes; an example is customers in a store. The owner owes them a duty of reasonable care and is liable for any negligence.
- **Licensees** are persons allowed on the premises who are not business invitees. Social guests generally fall into this category. Licensees are on the premises at their own risk, but owners are under a duty to warn of hidden dangers, such as a loose floorboard.
- **Trespassers** have no right on the premises, and owners owe them no duty except to refrain from intentional harm. However, if the trespassers are children, and the owner knows that some building, structure, condition, or object on the property is likely to attract children, he may be held liable for any failure to exercise reasonable care.

Intentional torts.
The word "intentional" does not necessarily imply an intention to hurt anyone. For example, if you slap someone on the back, thinking he is an old friend, and he turns out to be a stranger with a heart condition, you are liable for any damage.

Intention to harm (malice) is necessary to recover *punitive damages*. Punitive damages, over and above any actual damages, may be awarded to punish the wrongdoer and deter him (and others) from repeating the wrongful act.

Assault and battery. Assault is a threat of violence that puts someone in fear of bodily harm. Battery is the actual physical contact. Either (or both) is grounds for a lawsuit.

Self-defense is the only legal excuse. Insults or provocative language do not excuse assault and battery; but the jury may consider them in awarding damages.

Illegal confinement. This term includes any interference with personal liberty, including false arrest, false imprisonment, or any detention by physical barriers, force, or the threat of force. Normally, no one may be detained against his will. But most states permit shopkeepers and others to detain persons suspected of theft, provided they have reasonable grounds for suspicion and do not use excessive force or make unnecessary false public accusations.

Private citizens who make citizen's arrests do so at their own risk. If the arrested person is released or acquitted, he may sue. (For police arrests, see pages 167-168.)

Defamation of character. Defamation is the communication of false statements that injure the reputation of a living person. False statements about the dead, or about groups in general, are not defamation, no matter how offensive.

Libel is written defamation; slander is spoken defamation. Traditionally, libel was more serious, as the written word can be more widely circulated. Radio and TV have made the distinction less important. Pictures or other communications may be defamatory, as well as words.

A statement is automatically defamatory if it accuses a person of crime, immoral or unethical conduct, loathsome disease, unfitness for one's trade or profession, or unchastity (if female). Even if there is no financial damage, a person may sue to vindicate his reputation. For other statements, a person must show in what way they were defamatory and what damages were suffered.

162

Publication. To be defamatory, a statement must be communicated to a third person; private insults do not count. But communication to even one other person is enough to constitute publication. Anyone who repeats or republishes a defamation also commits defamation.

Defenses. If you are sued for defamation, there are several ways to defend yourself.

- By showing the statement was *true.*
- By proving the person gave *consent* to the statement.
- By showing the statement was *fair comment* on a matter of public interest. (A fair comment is one based on fact, or an honest expression of belief or opinion, and not made from malice or dishonorable motives.)
- By showing you had a *privilege* to make the statement. Any statement is absolutely privileged if made between husband and wife, or if made in court, legislative, or other government proceedings.

There is also a *qualified privilege* for statements by an employer who is asked about an employee, and for statements by newspapers or other media about public figures. But the privilege is lost if the statement was made with malice and with either a knowledge of its falsity or a reckless disregard for the truth.

Invasion of privacy. No one may use your name or picture for commercial or advertising purposes without your consent. You can sue for damages and can also get a court order stopping such use.

There has been much discussion of the right of privacy and the danger of computerized data banks that hold information about private lives and personal affairs. So far, however, there are few laws on the subject, except for laws prohibiting government employees from disclosing confidential information.

Trespass. Anybody who goes on someone else's land (or enters their buildings) without permission, or places or throws anything on the property, is a trespasser and can be sued for any damage to the property. Even if no damage is done, the owner may want to sue, to establish his right to keep the person off the property.

Conversion. Trespass applies to real property; the term conversion applies to personal property. Anyone who takes another's personal property or uses it without permission, or obtains it by fraud or trickery, or destroys or damages it, or disposes of it without permission by sale, gift, lease, or other means, has committed a conversion (meaning he "converted" the property to his own purposes). Even if someone has legal possession of another's property, he commits conversion if he damages it, loses it, gives it to someone else, or refuses to return it to its owner. The owner can sue for any damage to the property, or the full value, if it is lost or destroyed.

A lawsuit for conversion is a lawsuit for money. If

Jacqueline Onassis charged that her civil rights were violated when this photo, used in an ad, showed her look-alike in the background.

the owner wants the actual property back, he may file a lawsuit known as replevin. This is appropriate for property that is unique in some way—such as a work of art or a family heirloom.

Emotional damages

Courts are reluctant to award damages when the only injury is emotional. There is too much chance of fraud or of exaggerated claims for hurt feelings. But where there has been actual physical injury, the court or jury may award additional damages for emotional harm. The physical injury proves the claim is not a fraud and that it involves more than hurt feelings.

Recent trends. Recently, there has been a trend toward allowing damages solely for emotional harm where it is obvious that the harm is real. For instance, a mother who watched her child run down by a car recovered emotional damages from the driver. Damages will also be awarded if they result from some illegal act.

There has also been a trend toward allowing damages for *intentional* infliction of emotional harm. Examples would include vicious harassment by bill collectors, and obscene phone calls.

A special case. Common carriers, such as railroads and bus lines, are obligated to provide passengers with courteous service. Therefore, they can be sued for insulting behavior on the part of their employees.

Earning a living

Your job. At one time, employers could hire, fire, and set the terms and conditions of work almost at will. About all an employee could do was quit or accept the conditions. Today, employees' rights are protected by federal and state laws, enforced by government agencies. Some laws give employees the right to sue on their own, but it is usually better to go to an agency and take advantage of its services. Some important laws and agencies are in the chart below.

Who are employees? If your boss has the right to control the manner and means by which you do your job, you are an employee. If not, you are an independent contractor. A good example of an independent contractor is your doctor; you hire him to cure your illness, but you do not tell him how to examine you or

PLACEMENT SUPERVISOR: (Work-site) to provide vocational training to handicapped adults for job placement in area business & industry. Community work-site position working with handicapped people. Related Bachelor's Degree required. Prior experience in rehabilitation desirable. Reply Box 204 EOE, M/F.

An Equal Opportunity Employer will not discriminate when hiring on the grounds of race, age, sex, religion, or national origin.

what medicine to prescribe. Some occupations are borderline cases; some commission salesmen are employees, some are not.

Persons working at home may be employees: an example would be women hired by clothing manufacturers to do sewing. Some office workers now work at home, with a computer tie-in to the office.

Officers of a corporation are employees, but partners are not employees of the partnership.

Laws protecting employees rights and the agencies that enforce them

Union activity	Protected and regulated for nonsupervisory employees by National Labor Relations Act. *Contact:* National Labor Relations Board.
Racial, ethnic, or religious discrimination	Banned by Civil Rights Act of 1964. *Contact:* Equal Employment Opportunity Commission (EEOC).
Sex discrimination	Banned by Civil Rights Act of 1964. *Contact:* EEOC. Wage discrimination banned by Equal Pay Act. *Contact:* U.S. Labor Department, Wage and Hour Division.
Age discrimination	Banned, for persons aged 40 to 69, by the Age Discrimination in Employment Act. *Contact:* U.S. Labor Department, Wage and Hour Division.
Safety and health	Occupational Safety and Health Administration sets workplace and industry standards and conducts inspections. Special laws apply for coal miners and other hazardous occupations.
Wages and salaries	Fair Labor Standards Act guarantees a minimum wage and time and a half for hours worked over 40 a week to most nonsupervisory employees. *Contact:* U.S. Labor Department, Wage and Hour Division. Consumer Credit Protection Act limits the amount of wages and salaries a creditor can seize for payment of a debt.
Veterans	Right to reemployment at previous job. *Contact:* Department of Veterans Affairs.
Child labor	Limited and restricted by Fair Labor Standards Act. *Contact:* U.S. Department of Labor, Wage and Hour Division.
Disability	The Americans with Disabilities Act of 1990 prohibits employers from discriminating against any qualified person with a disability and requires most employers to make existing facilities accessible to the disabled. *Contact:* EEOC.

Employment is a contract. Except

in union plants, the contract is usually oral, and either employer or employee can end it at will, with or without notice. But as long as the contract lasts, both parties must comply with its terms. Your employer, for example, cannot cut your salary for work already done.

Some courts have ruled that company manuals, employee handbooks, and the like are to be considered part of the contract; employees are entitled to all benefits described in them. Many companies, however, now put a specific statement in company publications reserving the right to make changes at any time.

Unlawful discharge. Traditionally, employers had an absolute right to fire at will, subject only to antidiscrimination laws and union contracts. Recent court decisions cast doubt on the old rule. Courts have awarded damages to employees dismissed for refusing to give false testimony at a hearing, and to employees dismissed for filing workers' compensation claims. Employees have sued when fired for opposing company practices or products they considered unethical or against public policy—such as products harmful to the environment. Some won, some lost. The law is changing in the direction of greater employee rights; but no one knows how far the change will go.

Union contracts. Employers must deal with unions representing a majority of workers in a bargaining unit, which may be the whole company, a division, or some group of employees. The National Labor Relations Board (or a state board) decides the proper bargaining unit and holds elections, if necessary. In a union shop, you must join the union or, at least, pay dues (except in a minority of states, which have right-to-work laws).

Wages and conditions of employment are set by a written collective bargaining agreement between company and union. Most contain grievance or arbitration procedures for resolving disputes. If you have a grievance or dispute with your employer, you must go through the union; if it decides not to press your claim, you have no remedy. There is an exception. The union owes a "duty of fair representation" to its members and cannot discriminate against any of them. If the union violates this duty, a member may be able to sue.

Union members have the right to run for union office, vote in union elections, and express their opinions on union matters—subject to reasonable regulations.

Employee benefits. Some benefits are re-

quired by law:

Social Security pays benefits to retired or disabled workers and their families, and families of deceased workers. It includes Medicare. (For details, see pages 95 and 128-130.)

Unemployment insurance pays benefits to workers laid off or unemployed through no fault of their own. They must be ready, willing, and able to work.

Disability insurance is required by a few states (including California, New York, and New Jersey). It is similar to unemployment insurance, but applies to those unable to work because of illness, not unemployment. Some companies carry disability insurance even when not required.

Workers' compensation pays medical bills and sick benefits to workers injured on the job.

Pensions are *not* required by law. But if an employer does have a pension system, it must comply with federal pension law, which sets minimum standards for eligibility, length of service, etc. It also requires that participants be given a summary of the plan, written in language the average man can understand, explaining all the rules and provisions of the plan. It is important to read the summary; if you have any questions, ask the company personnel people for an explanation.

Other benefits. Many companies and union contracts provide other fringe benefits, including highly important ones, such as life insurance and medical insurance. Be sure to learn your rights to these benefits, and find out what will happen if you leave the company or are laid off. How long will the insurance continue? Can you renew it on your own? How much will it cost?

Starting your own business. If you

have the money to set up or buy a full-scale business, you undoubtedly have a lawyer. Many people, though, start out on a small scale, often working from their homes, sometimes as a sideline to their regular jobs. Many housewives do typing at home or run small telephone answering services. Here are some legal problems that may arise with a new business.

How to save on taxes. If you operate from your home, reserve part of the home *exclusively* for business. You can take a percentage of household costs as a home office business deduction, including heat, repairs, maintenance, utilities, depreciation, and rent.

Hobbies, such as photography or woodworking, can often be turned into profitable businesses. But the Internal Revenue Service will be suspicious, especially if you show a loss (as many new business do, at first). If you are just pursuing a hobby, you cannot deduct any losses or home office expenses. To prove you are really in business, you should operate in a businesslike fashion. Keep records of income and expenses. Get business cards. Put out a sign, or advertise. Comply with any licensing or registration laws. You do not have to be making a profit, but you must show that you are trying to. (*Note:* If you make a profit in two years out of five, the law presumes you are in business for profit.)

There may be tax advantages in hiring your spouse and children. Check with your accountant.

Hiring employees. You must comply with all labor laws. You must also withhold taxes and send them in to the government, including Social Security and unemployment. You must buy workers' compensation insurance.

If you need only part-time or occasional help, you can avoid these problems by using free-lance workers or independent contractors, such as public stenographers who do clerical work. Another way is to get your help from a temporary agency. The agency is the legal employer of the employees. You pay a fee to the agency, and the agency pays the employees.

Government regulations. You need a license for some occupations, especially those affecting public health or safety. If your business has anything to do with food or drink, you will certainly be subject to regulation and inspection. If you use a business name (Acme Plumbing Co.), you may have to register it somewhere. For information, contact local authorities or any business group.

Partnerships. Each partner acts as agent for the others. Each is personally liable for all debts of the business; this means that creditors can get at a partner's home, bank account, or other property—not just the property of the partnership. Partners share profits (or losses) in any way they agree on. It is best to have a written agreement, specifying what each partner is entitled to, how much money he is to invest, how much time he is to put in, and any other agreements between the partners.

Every partnership must have at least one *general* partner. It may also have *limited* partners, who put money in the partnership and are entitled to share in the profits, but who have no say in running the business. Limited partners are personally liable for partnership debts only to the extent of their investment.

Buying a franchise. A franchise is the right to use a name or trademark, or to manufacture or sell a product. Fast food chains like McDonald's are well-known examples. Local people own and operate the restau-

---

Should you form a corporation?

A corporation is a legal "person," separate and distinct from the stockholders who own it. Its great advantage is *limited liability.* Stockholders are not personally liable for corporate debts; they may lose their investment, but no more. (Small businesses, however, may find it difficult to get bank loans or credit unless officers or stockholders agree to be personally liable.) Other advantages:

- Corporations can raise money by issuing stock; it is a lot easier to sell shares of stock than a percentage interest in a business.
- Corporations go on, even if individual stockholders die.
- Family corporations can be used to split income among family members to save on taxes.

A disadvantage is double taxation. Corporations pay income tax; then stockholders pay personal income tax when profits are distributed to them. On the other hand, if the corporation grows in value, so does the stock. And if a stockholder sells, he is taxed on only 40 percent of the profit.

Small corporations can avoid double taxation by electing to be taxed as if they were partnerships.

Forming a corporation is simple, legally. What you need more than a lawyer is a good accountant or businessman to advise you.

Doing business with relatives

Your brother has a great idea for a new business, so you stake him to the money to get started. A few months later, he dies in an auto accident. What happens now?

- *If the money was a loan,* you can get it back.
- *If the money was a gift,* you cannot get it back; you may even owe a gift tax.
- *If the money was an investment,* you might be considered your brother's partner, entitled to a share of any business profit. On the other hand, you might be liable for business debts.

You probably have nothing in writing, and you cannot remember exactly what was said. In fact, neither you nor your brother may even have thought about the possibilities. As a result, you may be faced with the trouble of a lawsuit, with no assurance of getting your money.

The moral is, when making a loan to a friend or relative, setting up a partnership, or doing anything with legal consequences, *put it in writing,* just as you would with a stranger. Aside from the possibility of a death, you never know when there may be a falling out in the family. Any lawyer can tell you that family disputes are more bitter than any other.

In addition, the Internal Revenue Service is always suspicious of family deals. If your taxes are ever audited, you may need proof of exactly what transpired.

GARDNER & GARDNER TREE WORK

rants, using the companies' names. Other common franchises are gas stations and automobile dealerships. The owner gets the benefit of the name, the advertising, and a lot of management and financial help. There is a drawback. The franchising company will retain a great deal of control.

Before signing any agreement, have it read by your lawyer. These are important questions to ask: How long will the franchise last? Is it permanent? Can I sell it? Can I lose it? If so, under what circumstances? Do I have to buy only from certain suppliers? What are the restrictions on my right to run the business?

Getting help. The U.S. Small Business Administration gives information, counseling, financial aid, and help in getting bank loans and government contracts. A special division aids minority businesses.

Criminal law and procedure

What is a crime?
A *felony* is a serious crime, such as murder, manslaughter, rape, robbery, arson, burglary, or assault with a weapon. Lesser crimes are *misdemeanors*. Traffic violations or violations of local ordinances are not crimes. An attempt to commit a crime is itself a crime. An *accessory* (one who aids in a crime though not present when it is committed) is guilty of a crime.

No law may make an act a crime, if the act was not a crime when it was performed. Nor may penalties be increased retroactively.

Who can commit a crime?
An insane person cannot commit a crime. Insane means "unable to understand the nature of his act, or unable to know right from wrong." Drunkenness or voluntary use of drugs is not insanity and is not a defense to crime; but a person whose mind is affected by drugs prescribed as medicine may be excused. Children under a specified age set by state law (usually 15 or 16) cannot commit a crime (juvenile delinquency is not a crime). Young people over that age may be treated as "youthful offenders," and their crime later expunged from the record if not repeated.

Defenses. Ignorance of the law is not a defense, but ignorance of the fact may be. For example, a person may take another's property believing it to be his own.

If a person reasonably believes himself to be in danger of death or bodily harm, he may use force and even kill another person in self-defense.

Arrests. A policeman may arrest a person who commits *any* crime in his presence. He may arrest on reasonable suspicion in cases of *felony*. Otherwise, he needs a warrant.

Searches. An officer may make a search in the course of a lawful arrest. He may search a person for weapons if he thinks it is necessary to ensure his own safety. He may search a vehicle if he has reasonable grounds to believe that it contains evidence of a crime and that it may be driven away before he can get a search warrant.

If your child is arrested

If you are ever unlucky enough to get a phone call informing you that your son or daughter has been arrested, *what you do next can affect your child's whole future.* So do not panic, however you may feel. Here is what to do:

- **Get all the information you can,** including the address of the police station, the names and badge numbers of the arresting officers and the desk sergeant, the district attorney's man in charge of the case, and when and where your child will be taken for arraignment (a court hearing to advise the defendant of the charges and set bail).
- **Ask to talk to the desk sergeant and tell him you do not want your child questioned until you or your lawyer get there.** Ask him to write this request down. If your child has medical or emotional problems requiring any special treatment, tell the desk sergeant. (As soon as you can, have the child's doctor call the police.)
- **When you talk to the child, try to calm him down.** If possible, one parent should keep the child on the phone while the other goes to the station. Tell the child to be courteous and polite to the police and not to antagonize them, but not to answer any questions.
- **Do not argue or fight with the child at the station,** no matter how you feel. It is important to show the police a good family relationship. Get the child out on bail; if there is any delay, try to have him held at the station house, not the county jail. Jails are not safe, and can be a harrowing experience for young people.
- **Get a lawyer who is experienced at criminal law,** and do what he says.

**Answer no questions.
Get a lawyer.**

In other cases, he must get a warrant. If a search is unlawful, nothing that is discovered can be admitted as evidence against the person searched.

Rights of accused persons. Anyone

charged with a crime has the right to remain silent. He has the right to a lawyer and a speedy trial before a jury. He has the right to confront and cross-examine his accusers, and he is entitled to be considered innocent until proven guilty "beyond a reasonable doubt." Even if convicted, he may not be subjected to "cruel or unusual punishment."

When a person is arrested, he must be informed of his rights, including the right to a lawyer and the right to remain silent. Otherwise, any admission or confession may not be used as evidence against him. This rule applies only to arrests.

When the police are questioning witnesses or persons at the scene of a crime, they are not required to give any warning, and anything a person says at that time may be used against him.

What to do if you are arrested. There are two basic rules: (1) Do not answer questions, and (2) Get a lawyer. The more serious the charge, the more important these rules are. Most non-criminals have a strong urge to explain themselves. Resist the urge. You can always make a statement later after you have talked to your lawyer.

If you do say anything, tell the truth. Any lies will probably be found out, and no one will believe anything you say after that.

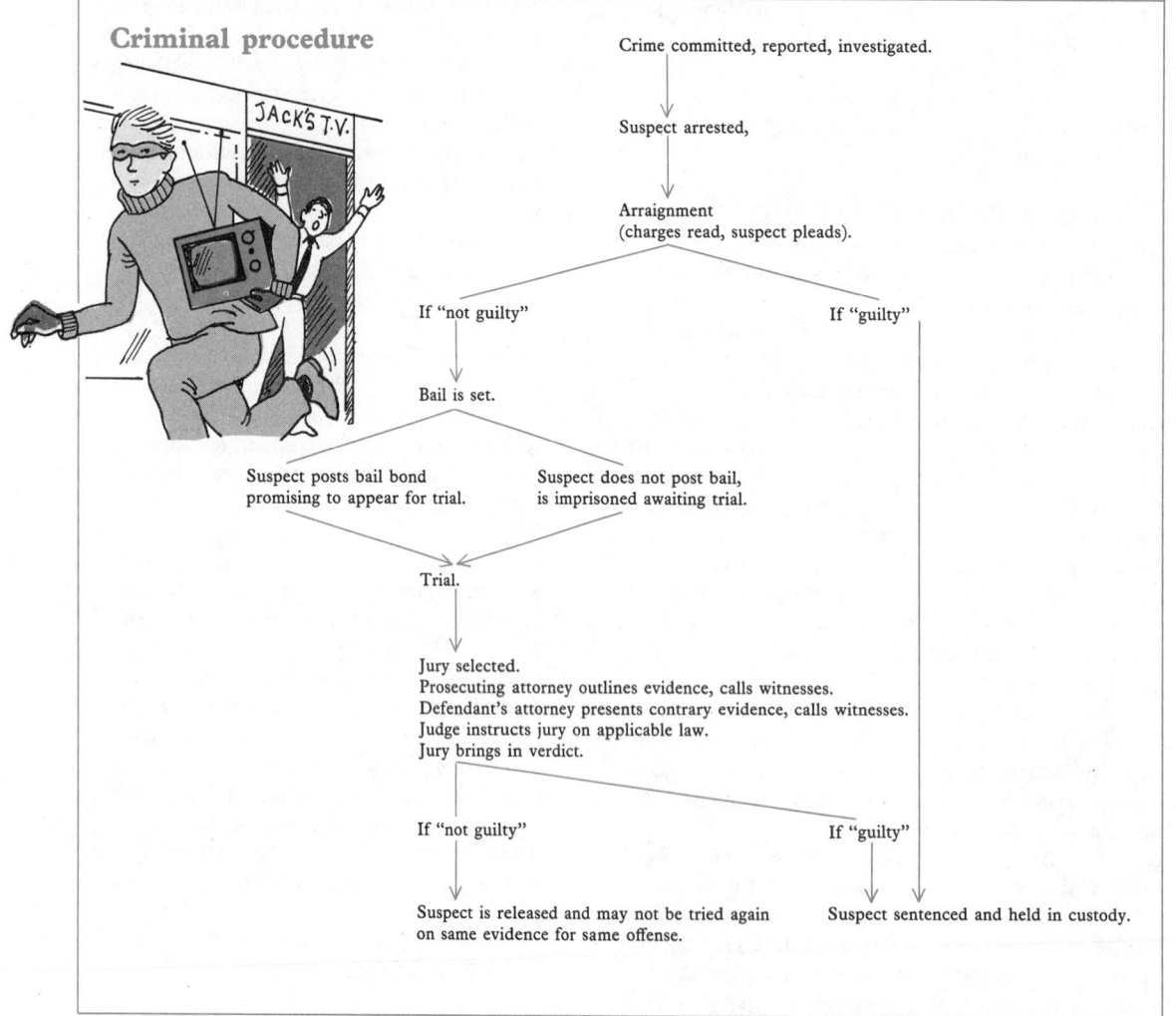

Criminal procedure

Crime committed, reported, investigated.

Suspect arrested,

Arraignment
(charges read, suspect pleads).

If "not guilty"   If "guilty"

Bail is set.

Suspect posts bail bond   Suspect does not post bail,
promising to appear for trial.   is imprisoned awaiting trial.

Trial.

Jury selected.
Prosecuting attorney outlines evidence, calls witnesses.
Defendant's attorney presents contrary evidence, calls witnesses.
Judge instructs jury on applicable law.
Jury brings in verdict.

If "not guilty"   If "guilty"

Suspect is released and may not be tried again   Suspect sentenced and held in custody.
on same evidence for same offense.

How to find a lawyer

Do you need one? Many simple legal matters can be handled without a lawyer. Simple wills, uncontested divorces with no property or custody complications, personal bankruptcies, even settling simple estates often involve nothing more than filling out standard forms available at legal supply stores or from the courts. But be careful not to take legal advice from anyone who is not a lawyer.

Many books contain sample clauses for wills, contracts, leases, etc. You can find them at your library or the law library at the courthouse. Ask the librarian for help.

Here are other inexpensive ways to handle legal matters:

- **Legal clinics** handle routine matters for a small fee. Often the work is done by *paralegals* — nonlawyers trained in specific areas — under a lawyer's supervision.
- **Prepaid legal services,** a form of insurance like medical insurance, are provided by many employers and union contracts. If you need legal help, use a participating lawyer and the insurance pays the fee.
- **Arbitration** is used extensively in labor and commercial disputes, and now in consumer and housing disputes. Arbitration is like an informal court hearing, and the arbitrator's decision is binding. Usually, both sides must agree, in advance, to arbitrate the dispute.

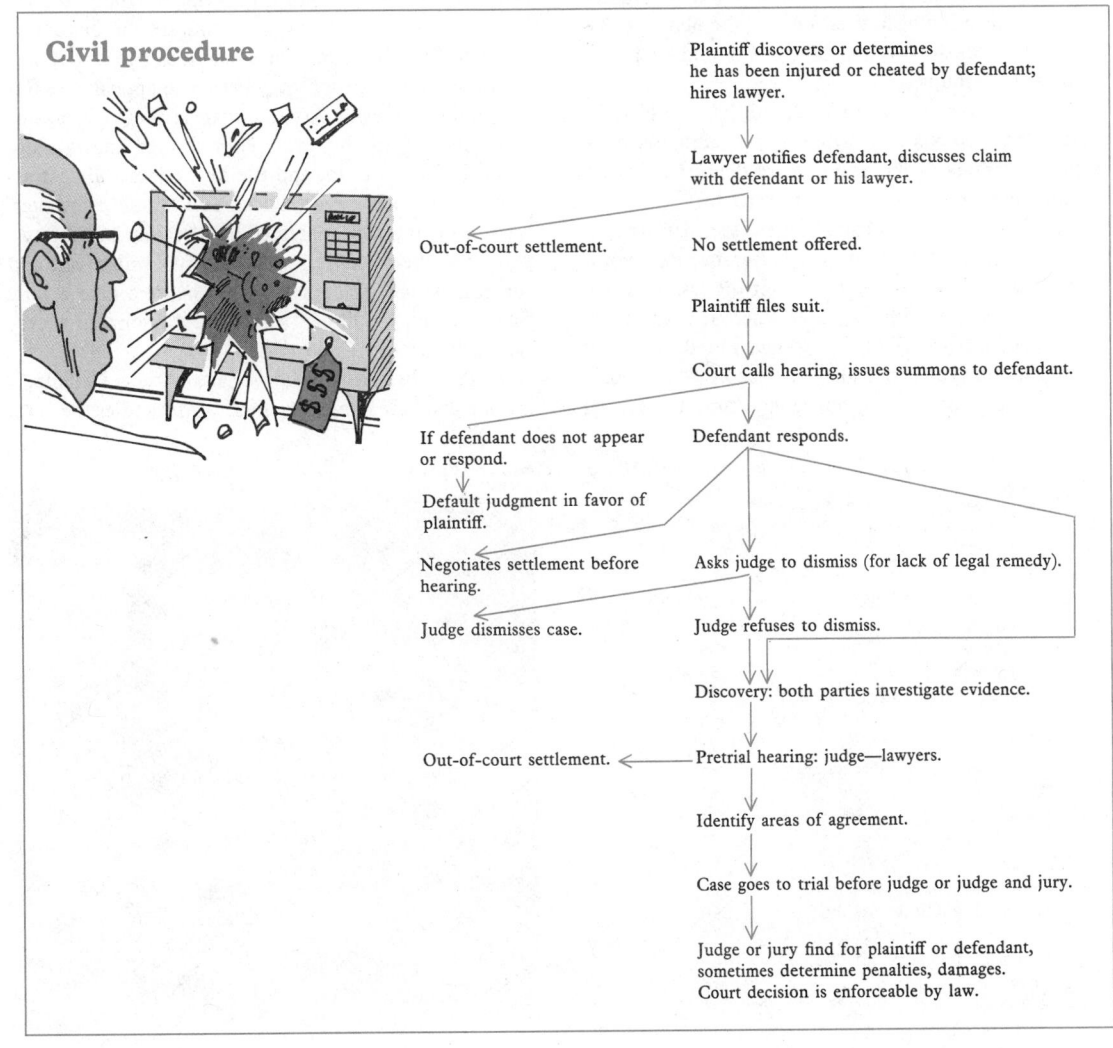

Civil procedure

Plaintiff discovers or determines he has been injured or cheated by defendant; hires lawyer.

Lawyer notifies defendant, discusses claim with defendant or his lawyer.

Out-of-court settlement. ← No settlement offered.

Plaintiff files suit.

Court calls hearing, issues summons to defendant.

If defendant does not appear or respond. — Defendant responds.

Default judgment in favor of plaintiff.

Negotiates settlement before hearing. — Asks judge to dismiss (for lack of legal remedy).

Judge dismisses case. ← Judge refuses to dismiss.

Discovery: both parties investigate evidence.

Out-of-court settlement. ← Pretrial hearing: judge—lawyers.

Identify areas of agreement.

Case goes to trial before judge or judge and jury.

Judge or jury find for plaintiff or defendant, sometimes determine penalties, damages. Court decision is enforceable by law.

If you do need a lawyer, look for someone with experience in your type of case. Many lawyers specialize, particularly in the fields of criminal law, accident and negligence law, domestic relations law, real estate law, tax law, and various kinds of business law. If you do not know any lawyers, here are some people to ask:

- *Friends* who have had a similar legal problem.
- *Your boss,* on business matters.
- *Your union,* on employment matters or questions of your entitlement to benefits.
- *Your clergyman,* or a social worker, on family matters, divorce, child custody, and so on.
- *Your accountant or banker* on financial, tax, or inheritance matters.
- *Your doctor* on injury cases. He has probably been called to testify, and may know a good lawyer.
- *People who work at the courthouse.* They see the lawyers in action.
- *Civic or community groups,* or groups like the American Association of Retired People, the National Association for the Advancement of Colored People, or women's groups.

Interviewing a lawyer. You do not have to hire the first lawyer you talk to; you can shop around. Never be reluctant to talk about fees; you are the one who pays them. There are various ways to set fees:

- *Contingent fees,* in accident cases (see page 160).
- *Statutory fees* may be set by law. For instance, workers' compensation laws may limit the lawyer's fee.
- *Flat fees* are suitable for cases where it is known in advance just what has to be done. The drawback is that the lawyer is not likely to put in extra time.
- *Hourly fees* depend on how much time the lawyer

puts in. That sounds fair, but there is a danger: the longer the case drags on, the higher the fee, so your lawyer may be in no hurry to get anything done. Put a limit, in advance, on how much you can afford to pay.

Other factors affecting fees are the difficulty of the case, the amount of money involved, the skill and experience of the lawyer, and the customary fee charged in your community. (Local bar associations used to set minimum fee schedules. No lawyer who was a member could charge less. The practice has been banned by the U.S. Supreme Court as illegal price-fixing. Unfortunately, it still goes on, though not openly.)

What is a retainer? When you hire a lawyer, you make a down payment on the fee, called a retainer, which binds the lawyer to act in your interests and to accept no business that conflicts with your interests. You should have a written payment schedule, and insist that all bills show just what services were performed, especially if you are paying by the hour.

Working with your lawyer. You are the boss. You make all final decisions, such as whether to settle, how much to offer or to accept, whether to appeal, etc. But it would be foolish to try to dictate strategy or day-to-day handling of the case. Your lawyer knows more about it than you do, and the best course, almost always, is to follow his advice. You should, however, insist on being kept informed on a regular basis. Lawyers, like everybody else, tend to put things off, and sometimes need prodding. Legal matters take a long time anyway; you do not want any additional unnecessary delays.

You can dismiss your lawyer at any time. Usually, it is not a good idea unless he totally mishandles the case.

Usually lawyers charge what is customary in their communities. But if you cannot afford a lawyer, consult a Legal Aid attorney.

LEGAL CLINIC	
FEE SCHEDULE	
Consultation	$ 20
Matrimonial *(uncontested)*	
Divorce	150
Annulment	250
Separation Agreement *(simple)*	95
Adoption	210
Name Change	95
Service of Papers *(if necessary)*	25
All of the above if contested	35 per hour
Personal Bankruptcy *(uncontested, limited assets)*	195
Wills and Estates	
Individual *(simple)*	60
Husband and Wife *(separate wills)*	90
Standard Trust for Children	65
Filing for Probate	150
Incorporation	175
Real Estate	

You have to pay him for work already done, and you will have to pay a new lawyer as well. If a case is already on trial, changing lawyers can make a bad impression on a judge or jury.

Cooperate with your lawyer. Do not lie or conceal anything from him. The more damaging the information, the more the lawyer needs to know it. Anything you tell your lawyer is *absolutely confidential.* He is not allowed to tell anyone else, even if he wants to; the same rule applies to his employees.

Do not try to decide what is important and what is not. That is what you hire a lawyer for. There is no way that he can win a case if the other side comes up with evidence he knows nothing about. This advice is not limited to lawsuits. A lawyer who is drawing a will or a contract has to understand the entire situation. Most lawsuits about the meaning of legal documents arise because something has been left out, or some aspect of the situation has not been covered.

How to complain. You can file a complaint with the bar committee, which can take disciplinary action or even recommend disbarment. If your lawyer has actually stolen or misappropriated your money, you can file a criminal complaint. (Lawyers are supposed to keep clients' money separate from their own; it is entirely improper to mingle the funds.)

You can also sue for malpractice, which means failure to exercise the reasonable care expected of a professional. Making an error of judgment would not be malpractice; but failure to know the elementary principles of law would. So would a failure to file a lawsuit on time, thereby costing the client the right to sue.

Where to go if you cannot afford a lawyer

The Legal Aid Society gives free legal help to those who cannot afford to pay. It does not handle divorces or criminal cases.

Lawyers referral services of local bar associations do not offer free aid, but they may refer you to a lawyer who bases his charges on what the client can afford.

The Legal Services Corporation, federally funded, provides legal help to poor people. Neighborhood Justice Centers try to settle disputes without lawyers.

Government agencies, such as consumer agencies, human rights commissions, and labor departments, will bring legal actions on behalf of people who file complaints.

Law schools sometimes run legal clinics staffed by law students. If not, the school can give you information.

Civil rights groups, such as the NAACP Legal Defense Fund and the American Civil Liberties Union, may handle a case or refer you to someone who can help.

Private organizations, such as landlords' and tenants' groups, trade associations, business groups, and labor unions, may provide legal services for their members.

Questions to ask before hiring a lawyer

Do you handle cases like mine? Ask the lawyer about some of them. How did they come out? How long did they take? What were the costs? Were there any special problems?

Will you actually do the work? If the lawyer's secretary or staff does the work, will the bill be reduced? You do not want to pay high professional rates for a clerk filling out a standard form.

What are your fee arrangements and billing practices? Some lawyers, for instance, bill by the quarter-hour. If they make a two-minute phone call, they bill for the full quarter hour. A few phone calls and your bill starts to mount. You should also check on other costs that may be incurred: Xeroxing of documents, filing fees and other court costs, and the cost of taking depositions from witnesses.

About how long will the whole thing take? You want to know, first, what the total period of time will be, and second, how much time the lawyer will actually put in.

How closely do you work with clients? You want to be kept informed and have some say in what is being done.

What happens if something goes wrong or we disagree? Suppose you have a dispute over fees? If your lawyer mismanages, will he still expect to be paid? Will he agree to submit disputes to an impartial arbitrator other than the bar association? (Bar associations are notorious for favoring lawyers over clients.)

circumstantial evidence

Glossary

encroachment

MAYOR CALLS
POLICE CHIEF
CROOKED

libel

felony

ab initio. From the beginning.

abatement. Reduction or decrease.

accord and satisfaction. An agreement between two persons that settles a claim or lawsuit.

administrative law. The law regulating the procedure to be followed by government agencies.

adverse possession. Acquisition of ownership of land by continuous use for a long period of time, usually 20 years.

affidavit. A written statement made under oath.

agent. One who has authority to act for another (the principal). Acts or promises of the agent are binding on the principal.

alibi. Latin for "elsewhere." Alibi does not mean excuse. It means a person was somewhere else when a crime was committed.

alienate. To transfer ownership of property.

amicus curiae. Friend of the court. A person not a party in a case, but allowed to participate because of some indirect interest.

amortization. Payment of a debt over a period of time, usually a mortgage or bond.

appellant. A person who requests a higher court to review the decision of a lower court. The other party is called the *appellee* or *respondent*.

arraignment. Bringing a person charged with crime before a court to be advised of the charges against him.

assign. Transfer one's right or interest in something to another.

attachment. Seizure of property for payment of debt.

attestation. Witnessing the signature of a will or document.

attorney. One who has power to act for another.

bail. Money or property deposited in court to guarantee the appearance of a criminal defendant at his trial.

bailee. One in legal possession of another's property (has nothing to do with criminal bail; see page 159).

bench warrant. A court order for someone's arrest.

bequest. A gift of personal property in a will.

bill of exchange. A written order directing one person to pay a sum of money to another. The most common bill of exchange is a check, which directs a bank to pay a sum of money to the person named on the check.

bill of lading. A written contract for delivery of goods by freight.

bill of particulars. A written statement of the details of a claim in a lawsuit.

bill of sale. Written transfer of rights for personal property.

bona fide. In good faith; genuine.

breach of the peace. Disturbance of public order, usually by fighting.

brief. Written statement by a lawyer in support of his legal position in a case.

burden of proof. The obligation to produce evidence in support of allegations in a lawsuit. Whoever alleges a fact has the burden of proving it if it is disputed.

burglary. The crime of breaking into and entering property with intention to commit a felony.

capital. The money invested in a business, adjusted each year for the business's profits or losses.

capital crime. A crime punishable by death.

capital stock. The stock issued by a corporation.

causa mortis. "In contemplation of approaching death." Gifts made causa mortis are subject to special legal rules.

cause of action. The legal basis of a lawsuit, such as negligence, debt, breach of contract, or libel.

certiorari. A legal procedure by which a higher court reviews the decision of a lower one.

challenge. An objection to a juror. A juror may be challenged "for cause," if, for example, he is biased in favor of one side. In addition, each side has a certain number of peremptory challenges, for which no reason need be given.

chattel. An item or article of personal property.

chattel mortgage. A loan on which personal property is put up as security; for example, an auto loan or a loan on jewelry.

circumstantial evidence. Evidence from which a fact can be inferred; for example, a person's fingerprint is evidence of his presence at the place the fingerprint was found.

C.O.D. Cash on delivery. A type of sale in which the buyer pays when the goods are delivered to him.

codicil. An amendment to a will (see page 155).

collateral. Property pledged as security for a debt.

collateral relatives. Relatives other than direct ancestors or descendants.

common carrier. A transportation facility, such as a railroad or trucking company, in the business of transporting passengers or goods for a price.

common law. The body of law that has grown up over the centuries from custom and from the decisions of the courts—as opposed to statutory law, which is law passed by legislatures.

common law marriage. Marriage without a formal ceremony (see page 141).

commutation. Reduction in punishment, ordered by the governor or another authority.

complaint. A document in a lawsuit setting forth the claim that is being made.

condemnation. Taking of property by the government (see page 152).

condition. A provision in a contract which *must* be performed, or the contract loses its validity.

condonation. Forgiveness (see page 145).

consanguinity. Blood relationship.

consideration. See *contract*.

consortium. A person's right to the sex, services, and society of his or her spouse. Traditionally, a husband could sue for loss of consortium if his wife were injured. In many states today, a wife can sue for loss of consortium if her husband is injured.

conversion. Misappropriation or misuse of personal property.

convey. To transfer property in writing.

corpus delicti. Latin for "body of the crime." Proof that a crime was committed; it does *not* mean the body of the victim.

co-signer or co-maker. One who signs a note or other

Contract

contract. An agreement by which one person promises to do something in return for the act or promise of another. Contracts usually arise from an *offer* by one person and *acceptance* by the other. An *executory* contract is one consisting of promises that have not yet been *executed*.

Consideration is the legal term for the act or promise of one side that induces the act or promise of the other. For example, I agree to sell you my watch for $100. My promise to sell the watch is the consideration for your promise to pay the $100, and vice versa.

A mere promise, without consideration, is not a contract and cannot be enforced. But a promise given for consideration is binding, even if the consideration is of no benefit to the promisor. *Example:* You promise to give your nephew $1000 if he does not smoke or drink until he is 21. If he performs his side of the bargain, you must give him the $1000 even though his act (not smoking or drinking) is of no material benefit to you.

Contracts may be written or oral, and may be *implied* from conduct or even silence. For example, if you go into a restaurant and eat a meal, you have to pay for it. If you let someone perform services for you knowing that he expects to be paid, you have to pay him. Implied contracts are sometimes called quasicontracts (*quasi* is Latin for "as if"). You accepted the benefit of another's action, so you must pay for it *as if* you had made a contract.

Some contracts, because of their importance, are required to be in writing or they will not be enforced by the courts. The most common are:

- Contracts for the sale of real property.
- Contracts which, by their terms, cannot be performed within one year.
- Contracts holding one responsible for the debt of another.
- Contracts to sell goods for more than a specified amount of money (the amount varies from state to state).

document and makes himself liable to pay if the original signer does not.

counterclaim. A claim made by the defendant in a lawsuit against the plaintiff.

covenant. A promise in a deed (see page 151).

curtesy. A widower's legal right to a share of the lands owned by his wife.

damages. Money awarded to compensate for injury to person or property.

decedent. A person who has died and whose estate is being settled.

decree. Written judgment of a court.

deed. A document transferring ownership of land.

defamation. A false statement that injures a person's reputation (see page 162).

default. Failure to appear for trial. The defaulting party loses unless he can show good reason for not appearing. Also refers to failure to perform a contract or failure to make payments when due—for example, defaulting on a mortgage.

defendant. The person who is being sued. In criminal cases, the person being tried for a crime.

demurrer. A denial by the defendant that there are any legal grounds for the lawsuit.

deposition. A written statement made under oath, generally for use in a lawsuit.

descent and distribution. The law governing the disposition of property of someone who dies without a will.

devise. To transfer real property by will.

dictum. A statement of law made by a judge, but not necessary to decide the case, and therefore not binding.

discovery. See *pretrial procedure*.

dishonor. To refuse to accept an obligation; for example, a bank dishonors a check, if it refuses to pay it.

dispossess. To evict a tenant from the premises he rents.

dividend. Money paid to stockholders of a corporation from the profits of the corporation.

domicile. A person's permanent place of residence.

donee. A person to whom a gift is made.

donor. A person who makes a gift.

double indemnity. A provision in an insurance policy under which the company must pay double the face amount if a person dies by accidental means.

double jeopardy. Trying a person more than once for the same crime; prohibited by the U.S. Constitution.

dower. The right of a widow to a share of her husband's lands.

draft. A written order directing one person to pay a sum of money to another. For example, a person may direct his bank to pay a sum of money to someone.

due process. The constitutional right not to be deprived of life, liberty, or property, except after fair legal proceedings.

duress. Force or threat of force to compel someone to do something against his will.

earnest money. A down payment to make a contract binding.

easement. A right to use the land of another (see page 152).

ejectment. A legal action to remove a person who is wrongfully occupying land.

embezzlement. The crime of misappropriating money by a person to whom it has been entrusted.

eminent domain. The right of the government to take private property for public purposes (see page 152).

encroachment. Something that extends on the land of another, such as part of a building or fence.

encumbrance. Any claim against property that diminishes its value, such as an unpaid mortgage or a lien.

endorsement. Writing one's name on the back of a check or promissory note to cash or transfer it. An endorser normally guarantees the check or note, and is liable if the original signer cannot pay.

enjoin. To direct someone to do something or refrain from doing something.

equity. Court action in a case where money damages are not enough. Examples of equity include a court order directing a person to stop the commission of a nuisance; and an order of specific performance directing a seller to go through with a contract to sell land.

equity of redemption. The right of a landowner to redeem his land by paying the mortgage at any time before it is foreclosed.

escheat. Return of property to the state when there is no one to inherit it.

escrow. Delivery of money or property to a neutral party, to be held until certain conditions are fulfilled.

estate. The property left by a person who has died. (The term may also refer to property in general or any interest in property.)

estoppel. Refusal to allow a person to change his statement or legal position if he has induced people to act on the basis of his previous statement or position.

ex parte. A legal action taken by one side without notice to the other.

ex post facto law. A law making an act a crime, although it was not a crime when it was done;

prohibited by the U.S. Constitution.

executor. The person named in a will to handle and distribute an estate.

exemplary damages. Punitive damages.

extortion. The crime of obtaining money by threats.

extradition. Return of a fugitive from justice to the state in which he is wanted.

false arrest. Unlawful arrest (see page 162).

false imprisonment. Unlawful restraint (see page 162).

fee simple. Absolute ownership.

felony. A serious crime, usually one punishable by imprisonment in the state penitentiary.

fiduciary. One who holds or manages property for another and is held to a high standard of conduct because of his position of trust.

fixture. An item of personal property that becomes real property by being "affixed" to the realty, for example, a furnace.

F.O.B. Free on board. A type of sale in which the seller agrees to deliver the goods to a carrier, such as a railroad, for shipment to the buyer.

foreclosure. Court proceedings to take over property for failure to pay a mortgage.

forgery. The crime of fraudulently making or changing writing or a signature, with intent to deceive.

franchise. The right to vote. A form of business arrangement (see pages 166-167).

fraud. False statement or misrepresentation made to deceive someone into taking an action he would not have taken had he known the truth.

garnishment. Taking all or part of a person's salary in payment of a debt. The amount that can be taken is limited by law.

guaranty. A promise to perform some act or pay some debt on behalf of another if the other fails to perform or pay.

guardian. One legally entrusted with the duty of caring for the person or property of a minor or incompetent adult.

habeas corpus. Latin for "you have the body." A legal proceeding (called a "writ") commanding that a prisoner be brought before a court to decide whether he is legally being held.

hearsay evidence. Evidence of what someone else said, rather than what the witness knows.

heir. One who inherits the property of a person who dies.

holder in due course. A purchaser of a negotiable instrument in good faith without knowledge of any defect (see page 159).

holdover tenant. One who remains on the property after the lease has expired (see page 153).

holographic will. A will entirely in a person's own handwriting (see page 155).

homicide. The killing of one human being by another. "Justifiable" homicide is in self-defense.

impeach. Challenge the truthfulness of a witness. Bring charges against a public official to remove him from office.

implied. Understood from the circumstances, although not directly stated, as an implied promise or an implied contract.

indemnity. An insurance or other agreement guaranteeing payment if a person suffers a loss.

indenture. A formal written contract.

indictment. An accusation of crime made by a grand jury.

infant. A minor. In law, the term refers to any minor, not just a small child.

information. A written accusation of crime by a district attorney or prosecuting officer without a grand jury.

injunction. A court order directing a person to do something or to refrain from doing something.

inquest. Any inquiry by a court to determine a disputed fact. Most commonly, it refers to a coroner's inquest to discover the cause of death.

insolvency. Inability to meet one's debts as they come due.

interest. Any legal right or claim. The amount charged for the use of money.

interlocutory decree. A preliminary decree that does not become final until some further action is taken.

interrogatories. A set of written questions to be proposed to a witness in a pending lawsuit, or to the opposing party.

intestate. Without a will.

joint tenancy. A form of co-ownership (see page 151).

judgment. The decision of a court.

judicial notice. Recognition of certain facts by a court without the need for proof, such as historical events, scientific laws, or geographic facts.

jurisdiction. The authority of a court to decide a case. The jurisdiction of a court is generally set out in the law establishing the court.

jurisprudence. The study of law in general.

kidnapping. The crime of stealing and carrying away a human being.

laches. Excessive delay in asserting a legal right.

larceny. The crime of taking another's property.

leading question. A question that suggests the answer, such as, "Were you walking past Mr. Johnson's house at noon on January 12th?" The proper question would be, "Where were you at noon on January 12th?"

lease. A contract to rent.

legacy. A gift made in a will.

lessee. The tenant under a lease.

lessor. The owner or landlord under a lease.

letters of administration. A court document appointing someone to handle the estate of a person who died without a will.

letters testamentary. A court document authorizing the executor named in a will to take charge of the estate.

levy. A tax. A seizure of property by order of court to pay a judgment.

libel. Written defamation (see page 162).

lien. A claim or charge against property, such as an unpaid mortgage or other debt.

life estate. An interest in property during a person's lifetime ending upon the person's death. For example, a husband's will leaves his house to his wife for her lifetime, and then to his children.

life tenant. A person who owns a life estate in property.

liquidated damages. A specified sum of money agreed on beforehand as damages in case one party to a contract fails to perform.

lis pendens. A notice filed in a county office stating that a lawsuit is pending over a designated piece of real property. Anyone who purchases the property is bound by the result of the lawsuit.

living will. A document by which a person directs whether or not he is to be kept alive by artificial devices if he should fall into an irreversible coma. Living wills are not legally binding in most states, but people often prepare them to inform the family of their wishes.

majority. The age at which a person is considered an adult, with full legal rights and capacities.

malfeasance. Performing an act that is wrong; see also *misfeasance.*

malice. Intention to harm.

malicious mischief. Intentional destruction of property.

malicious prosecution. Knowingly bringing criminal charges that are false.

mandamus. A court order directing a public official to perform his official duty.

manslaughter. The crime of killing a human being without premeditation or malice aforethought.

mayhem. The crime of violently depriving a person of the use of a member, such as an arm, leg, or eye.

mechanic's lien. A claim against property by someone who has done work on it, as a repairman or a workman on a house.

misdemeanor. A crime less serious than a felony.

misfeasance. An act that is not wrong but is improperly performed; see also *malfeasance.*

mistrial. A trial that ends because of some procedural error, or because the jury cannot agree on a verdict.

moot question. A question that is undecided and subject to argument, but is not directly related to a case.

motion. An application to a court for a ruling, decision, or order, usually in connection with some pending case.

murder. The crime of killing a human being, with premeditation or malice aforethought.

naturalization. The process of becoming a citizen. Normally, an alien must reside in the United States for at least five years before he can apply for citizenship; but the period is shortened for aliens married to

or adopted by American citizens. The alien must show that he is mentally and morally fit to become a citizen. Minor children of naturalized citizens also become citizens.

negligence. Failure to use reasonable care, thereby causing an injury to person or property (see pages 160-161).

negotiable instrument. A document, such as a check or promissory note, that can be endorsed and transferred from person to person, almost like cash. Whether an instrument is negotiable depends entirely on how it is worded.

nisi. Latin for "unless." A decree nisi is a court order to take effect on a specified date unless some action is taken in the meantime.

nolle pros. Short for *nolle prosequi,* a decision not to proceed with a prosecution or lawsuit.

nolo contendere. Latin for "I will not contest it." In criminal cases, a plea with the same effect as a plea of guilty, but without actually admitting guilt.

non compos mentis. Latin for "not of sound mind."

nonage. Underage; the period during which a person is a minor.

nonfeasance. Failure to perform an act required by law; for example, nonperformance of duties by a public official.

notary public. An official authorized to administer oaths, witness signatures, and certify to affidavits or other documents.

note. A written promise to pay.

novation. The making of a new contract or agreement to replace one that now exists.

nuncupative will. An oral will (see page 155).

oath. A promise to tell the truth, sworn on one's belief in a

Supreme Being. An *affirmation* is a similar promise by those who have religious or other scruples against taking oaths.

obligee. A person to whom some contractual obligation is owed.

obligor. The person who owes an obligation.

option. The right to buy or sell property at a specified time for a specified price.

palimony. A term applied to lawsuits for payments similar to alimony, brought when an unmarried couple separates after living together. Courts have not recognized any right to such payments, but they have sometimes recognized a contractual right to payment for services rendered, as when a woman gives up her career and provides companionship, assistance, and business help to her male partner. (Note, however, that a contract to pay for sexual relations is against public policy and will not be enforced by a court.)

parol evidence. Oral evidence. The parol evidence rule is that a written document may not be changed or amended by oral testimony.

partition. A court order physically dividing property owned by co-owners who cannot agree on the use to be made of the property. Sometimes the property is sold and the proceeds divided among the owners.

party wall. A common wall shared by two adjoining buildings, providing support to both.

patent. The exclusive right to manufacture and sell an invention.

per capita. In the law of wills, equal division of property among all persons with the same relationship to the deceased. For example, if a will leaves property to grand-children per capita, each grandchild gets an equal share.

per curiam. An opinion by the entire court, rather than an opinion written by one judge.

per stirpes. In the law of wills, division of property by groups rather than individuals. For example, if the deceased had a son who had two children, and a daughter who had three, the two children of the son would get half the property, and the three children of the daughter would get the other half.

perjury. The crime of making false statements under oath.

personal property. Any movable property; anything but land and buildings (see page 159).

petit jury. A jury that decides cases. A *grand jury* decides whether a person should be charged with a crime.

plaintiff. The person who brings a lawsuit.

plea bargaining. An agreement between a prosecutor and a criminal defendant by which the charge is reduced, or a lesser sentence agreed on, in return for the defendant's plea of guilty. Most plea bargaining is unavoidable, as it would be impossible to hold all the trials that would be necessary if most defendants did not plead guilty.

pleadings. The written documents in a lawsuit that state the position of the parties. The usual pleadings are a complaint by the plaintiff and an answer by the defendant. In some cases, further pleadings may be submitted by both sides.

pledge. Delivery of property to a creditor, as security for a debt.

polling the jury. Asking each juror individually for his verdict.

postmortem. Latin for "after death." Usually applied to the medical examination of a dead body to determine the cause of death.

power of attorney. A written authorization giving one person the power to act for another.

precedent. A previous court decision on a case similar to the one being tried.

prescription. A way of acquiring an interest in property by long and continuous use.

presumption. A rule requiring a judge or jury to draw certain conclusions from certain facts. For example, from the fact that a child is born to a married woman, the conclusion must be drawn that the child is legitimate. A *conclusive* presumption is one that cannot be disproven. Other presumptions can be overcome by evidence to the contrary.

pretrial procedure. The process, before a lawsuit comes to trial, of taking depositions, producing documents, conferring with the judge, etc. It is intended to help settle cases or, at least, to make sure that each party is aware of the issues.

prima facie case. Sufficient evidence to win a lawsuit, provided the other side cannot contradict or explain it.

privileged communication. A statement, made in private, which the other party is not allowed to divulge in court, and which cannot be used in evidence. The most common examples are communications between husband and wife, attorney and client, doctor and patient, priest and penitent.

probate. Proving a will. In a wider sense, all the proceedings relating to an estate (see page 156).

probation. In criminal law, a suspended sentence on condition of continued good behavior.

promissory note. A negotiable instrument consisting of a written, unconditional promise to pay a sum of money.

proof. Evidence that is believed by the judge or jury.

protest. A formal notice that a negotiable instrument, such as a check or promissory note, was presented for payment, and that payment was refused.

proximate cause. In the law of torts, an act that directly leads to and results in an injury.

proxy. One entitled to vote on behalf of another; usually applied to meetings of stockholders of a corporation. Proxy marriages were once recognized, but no longer.

public defender. A lawyer hired by the state to defend persons accused of crime who cannot afford their own lawyers.

publication. Making a statement public. In the law of defamation, telling one person constitutes publication.

punitive damages. Damages over and above actual damages, awarded to punish a wrongdoer and deter him from repeating the wrong (see page 162).

quantum meruit. Latin for "amount deserved." A sum of money awarded for services rendered when no specific sum is provided by contract.

quash. To annul or set aside.

quitclaim. A type of deed (see page 148).

quorum. The number of people who must be present at a meeting of a group in order to legally transact business.

rape. The crime of having sexual intercourse with a woman against her will. Statutory rape is the crime of having sexual intercourse with a minor below the age of consent.

ratification. Approval or confirmation of an act already done.

real property. Land and buildings.

rebuttal. Introduction of evidence to contradict a claim made in a lawsuit.

receiver. A person appointed by a court, in a lawsuit about property, to hold and manage the property at the court's direction.

recidivist. A repeater; an habitual criminal.

referee. A person appointed by a court to hear testimony, receive evidence, and report back to the court on his findings.

release. A document giving up a legal claim or right, usually when a case is settled. When an insurance company pays a claim, for example, it will require the claimant to sign a release.

remand. Send back a case from a higher court to a lower one for additional or corrective action.

replevin. A legal action for the return of property (see page 163).

reply. In a lawsuit, the plaintiff's written answer to a counterclaim by the defendant.

res ipsa loquitur. Latin for "the thing speaks for itself." A presumption of negligence, applied when there is no direct proof, but no other explanation makes sense. For example, if something falls from a window sill and injures a passerby, negligence will be presumed, even if it is impossible to prove what caused the accident.

res judicata. A legal or factual dispute that has already been decided by the judgment of a court, and that cannot be disputed any further.

respondent. See *appellant*.

restrictive endorsement. An endorsement when a check or other negotiable instrument is transferred for a specific purpose; for example, "for collection only," or "for deposit only."

retainer. A down payment to a lawyer to retain his services (see page 170).

retroactive. Relating backward in time, as a retroactive pay increase.

reversion. The return of property to its original owner after a trust or a gift for a period of years.

robbery. The crime of taking property by force or threat of force.

royalties. Payments (often a share of profits) to inventors, authors, songwriters, etc., or to owners of mineral or oil rights.

satisfaction piece. A document stating that a recorded mortgage has been paid.

seisin or seizin. The right to possession of real property.

service. Delivery of a summons to a defendant, informing him of a lawsuit against him.

setoff. A claim by the defendant against the plaintiff that reduces or eliminates the plaintiff's claim.

slander. Spoken defamation (see page 162).

specific performance. A court order to perform a contract for the sale of land (see page 149).

statute. A law passed by a legislative body, such as Congress.

statute of limitations. The time limit for bringing a lawsuit (or criminal prosecution). Different types of lawsuits have different limitation periods, but once the particular time limit has passed, no legal action may be taken.

stipulation. An agreement between parties to a lawsuit.

subornation of perjury. Persuading or bribing another to give false testimony.

subpoena. A document commanding a person to appear in court, either as a witness or as a party to a lawsuit.

subpoena duces tecum. A subpoena directing someone to produce documents or records in court.

substantive law. That part of the law that deals with legal rights rather than with legal procedures.

summary judgment. A court decision, made without a trial, when there are no facts in dispute.

summons. The first document in a lawsuit, advising the defendant that the lawsuit is being filed.

surety. One who promises to pay a debt if the original debtor fails to pay.

surrogate's court. A court that handles wills and estates.

tenancy by the entireties. A form of ownership by husband and wife (see pages 145, 151).

tenancy in common. A form of co-ownership (see page 151).

testament. A will.

testator. A person who has made a will or testament.

title. Evidence of one's right to property.

title search. A search of public records to trace the history of ownership of land.

tort. A wrongful act that injures another person (see page 162).

treason. The crime of waging war against the United States or aiding its enemies (treason is the only crime defined in the U.S. Constitution).

trespass. Any wrongful act affecting real property.

true bill. An indictment by a grand jury charging someone with a crime.

usury. Charging more than the legal rate of interest on a loan.

vendee. A purchaser.

vendor. A seller.

venue. The place where a trial is to be held.

verdict. The decision of a jury.

verification. An affidavit swearing that a writing or document is true.

voidable. Anything that can be made void; for example, a contract made by a minor is voidable at the option of the minor.

warrant. A legal document, signed by a judge, authorizing an arrest or a search.

Trust

trust. Money or property legally owned by one person (the trustee) for the benefit of another. The person who establishes the trust, and sets out its terms, conditions, and purposes, is called the *grantor* or *settlor.* The person entitled to the income is the *income beneficiary.* The person who gets the property when the trust comes to an end is the *remainderman,* except when the property is to be returned to the grantor.

A trust may be set up during the grantor's life (living trust) or by his will (testamentary trust). It may be *revocable* or *irrevocable;* in a revocable trust, the grantor reserves the right to cancel the trust and take back the property. In an irrevocable trust, the grantor may not cancel the trust.

The trustee must manage the trust for the sole benefit of the beneficiaries. He may not make any profit for himself, directly or indirectly. He may, however, charge a fee for his services. Many financial institutions, such as banks, have special departments set up for the management of trusts.

Trusts may be set up for many purposes; here are some of the most common:

- To provide an income for children who are minors until they come of age.
- To provide for people who are not good at handling business or financial affairs.
- To provide a lifetime income for someone (such as yourself or your spouse) with the property eventually to revert to someone else (such as your children).
- To provide income to someone for a temporary period.
- To make gifts for charitable purposes.

For further reference

Ashley, Paul P.
You and Your Will
McGraw-Hill

Brown, Robert N.
The Rights of Older Persons
Avon Books

Coughlin, George Gordon
Your Introduction to Law
Barnes & Noble Books

Kling, Samuel G.
The Complete Guide to Everyday Law
Jove Publications, Inc.

Lasson, Kenneth
Representing Yourself
Farrar Straus Giroux

Ross, Martin J. and Steven, Jeffrey
Handbook of Everyday Law
Ballantine Books

Schimmerl, David and Fischer, Louis
Rights of Parents in the Education of Their Children
The National Committee for Citizens in Education

Schwartz, Robert
The Home Owner's Legal Guide
Collier Macmillan

Smith, Robert Ellis
Workrights
E.P. Dutton, Inc.

Improving Your Memory

When you learn something, you practice three skills: *finding* what you need to know, *remembering* what you find, and *applying* that information usefully and effectively. Everyone who attends school, from first grade through college, is drilled over and over in the skills of finding and applying useful information. But without the middle skill—remembering—the other two are short-lived at best. However, most schools do not teach memory skills; they teach you to learn by rote memory—by routine drill—without your necessarily understanding or thinking about the text material. And so, very soon, you tend to forget.

Good memory is not a trick, nor does it require great intellectual resources. It does require systematic mental organization, that is, concentration on what you need to remember. The rest is practice, and the rewards—remembering people, places, and things that you always used to forget—are self-sustaining.

Through the centuries, some of the world's greatest thinkers and philosophers have tried to promote systems of memory improvement. No one system ever caught on; each one turned out to be too personal for general application. In this century mnemonists—memory experts—have shied away from complicated personal systems in favor of simpler methods with everyday applications. You will learn such step-by-step methods in this chapter. "There is memory without learning," writes memory expert Harry Lorayne, "but there is no learning without memory."

Think about that for a moment. How can one say that he has learned something effectively if he cannot recall it when it is needed. This is true whether we are talking about a particular skill or a bit of knowledge or an entire procedure or a religion or a philosophy. True learning puts information, ideas, or systems of thought at one's fingertips, ready for immediate use when needed, ready for direct application, ready for explanation to others, in short, for whatever application is generally called for.

As a result, the process of learning can only be considered complete when you have stored in your memory the subject to be learned. It is for this reason that so much emphasis must be placed on training the memory, especially for those who customarily find difficulty in recalling things they think they have learned, in recalling tasks they must perform, in bringing to mind thoughts they seek to explain to others. The objective of memory training is to make complete the process of learning: *finding*, *remembering*, and *applying* knowledge.

Self-training. No one is born with a poor memory. As you grow up, you develop highly personal habits of awareness and observation. You choose to see and hear, touch and taste certain things, and you choose to ignore most others. Quite likely, you began as a child to organize your daily life around those things you needed most, or were pleased by, or had an interest in. Those meaningful things constitute your earliest memories. Happy childhoods tend to be remembered longer and more fully.

Normally, you pay attention to those things around you that are important, potentially rewarding, and potentially pleasurable, and you teach yourself to remember them. As a child, for instance, your mother may have given you a dime and made you memorize your own phone number ("Always call home if you get lost somewhere"). Now, as an adult, you probably have immediate recall of at least one phone number—your own—even though you may seldom use it. But the memory seed was planted long ago, and you trained yourself to always know your own phone number. It was a start.

Think of how effective your memory is. Besides recalling your telephone number whenever you wish—even though you may hardly ever use it—you also have stored within your memory an enormous number of other bits of information. But you cannot always remember everything you are sure you know. This chapter will help you overcome that problem and greatly improve your recall.

Because your memory is yours alone, you can profitably train yourself to improve what needs improvement. Check your memory out with this list of facts and numbers:

Wait a minute . . . it's on the tip of my tongue

(No peeking, please.
Answer everything from memory.)

1. What is your home phone number?
2. Your license plate number?
3. Your Social Security number?
4. Whose face is on the $20 bill?
5. What is your mother's birthday?
6. How many days are there in June?
7. How many pints are in a gallon?
8. Name the Great Lakes.
9. Name your U.S. congressman.
10. What is your father's birthday?
11. Name your first-grade teacher.
12. Diamond-shaped road signs always indicate what?
13. Top to bottom, name the three colors on a stop light.

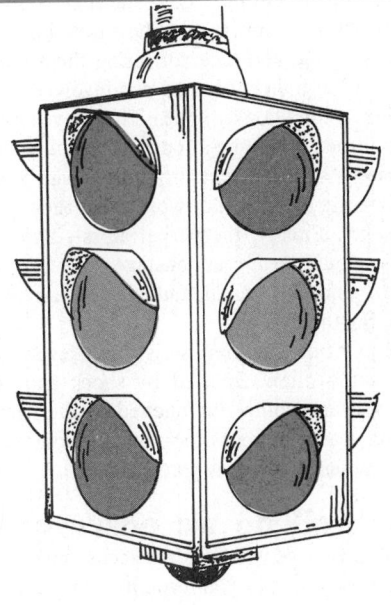

A high-school diploma or a college degree cannot help you answer any of these questions. But the succeeding pages will help you remember all of them.

Observation

Memory—even short-term memory—can be affected by heightened emotions. A studio audience observing a staged struggle cannot be relied on to report just what happened.

How observant are you? How observant do you think you are? Most people assume they are competent eyewitnesses. The fact is, nearly everyone sees the same sequence of events differently.

Testing observation.
TV talk show hosts once were fond of a stunt that included the studio audience in addition to the viewers at home. While the host chatted with his guest onstage, a scuffle would break out in the audience. Angry voices would be raised, stopping the onstage conversation. Members of the audience would look on. Suddenly, one of the combatants would whip out a handgun and shoot one or both of the other participants. Then all the troublemakers would scurry for the exits. Total elapsed time: about one minute.

Of course, the whole drama was staged, and there were no bullets. But the studio audience was taken by surprise. At this point, the TV host would choose four members of the audience and bring them onstage to describe what happened, who was involved, and what the perpetrators looked like. These eyewitness accounts turned out to be at odds. The audience members rarely agreed about anything—who started it, who shot whom, what they wore, what they said, even their sexes. Finally, the perpetrators—two or three actors—would reappear onstage and reenact the "crime," and the studio audience would see it all clearly for the first time.

The point of this exercise is that eyewitness testimony is too often distorted by shock and surprise. Every viewer at home, untouched by the heat of the moment, was a better witness to the crime than the studio audience that was part of it.

How well do we observe?
For the most part, you see what you are accustomed to seeing. You glimpse something, and you have immediate recall of whatever you have trained yourself to expect to see. Your powers of observation, over the years, are restricted to self-imposed limits, to a field of vision that is relevant to your personal or professional life. The television audience was prepared to be entertained. When the unexpected happened, it was a blur.

Whenever there is a dramatic story on the TV news—a violent crime, a fire, or a natural disaster—you are likely to see an interview with a witness or a victim. "How do you feel?" the reporter asks. "Can you tell us what happened?"

The answer rarely makes any sense. The distraught victim may be in shock and is usually too confused to say anything coherent.

Then the same reporter interviews a fireman or a policeman who, with sirens wailing in the background, supplies a precise reconstruction of the tragedy without tears or emotion. The uniformed man is not hardhearted or all-knowing. He is trained to make sense out of what seem to be chaotic events. You, too, can train yourself to observe with detachment what others might recoil from in horror or disgust. Better yet, you can learn to remember anything.

For a moment, think of something completely familiar—your wristwatch. Try to remember: Does it have a six on it? A Roman numeral VI? A dot? An empty space? If yours is a digital watch, how many lines are there in the number eight? Even if you answered correctly, chances are you had to double-check to make sure.

The tests and drills in these pages are designed to get you in the habit of memorizing by stages: observing, paying attention, organizing, forming images, and applying the methods of memory training. All these steps are part of the memory habit and, like most habits, this one can be maintained only through exercise.

Untrained memory is haphazard and unreliable. Trained memory brings all recollections to the surface. **Try this.** The following three exercises are designed to test your native, untrained memory. You may not do well at all, but take heart: in the pages that follow you will learn the techniques for memorizing lists, names, and numbers. And you can gauge your training progress. The tests will be repeated on pages 198-199.

Improving Your Memory

Quick-recall tests

1. Study this 15-digit number for two minutes. Then try to duplicate it exactly on a piece of paper—without looking at the number here

   238158649376914

2. Here are seven phone numbers, each corresponding to a local tradesman or professional. Study the list for six minutes, then copy the seven titles in any order. Finally, without looking, match the memorized numbers to the titles.

Doctor	762-5881	Lawyer	681-9558
Grocer	616-2053	Dentist	386-9156
Plumber	358-0854	Electrician	872-9647
Florist	784-3579		

3. This is an apparently random list of twelve objects found in the home. Study it for just two minutes, then reconstruct the list from memory, in order.

   couch, refrigerator, newspaper, clock, television, mirror, toaster, lamp, toilet, stove, carpet, window

Paying attention

There is nothing wrong with this story, but read it carefully:

> You are driving a bus that contains 50 passengers. At 57th Street, ten people get off and three get on. At 55th, seven get off and two get on. At 53rd and at 51st, four passengers get off each time; three get on at 53rd, no one at 51st. The bus breaks down at 51st, and eight passengers get crosstown transfers and leave. The bus starts up again and proceeds to 49th, where it breaks down once again. The remaining passengers ask for transfers and leave the bus.

Most of us, by paying strict attention, can probably answer several anticipated questions about this bus story (answers below). How many passengers finally got off? How many got transfers? How many stops did the bus make?

But hardly anyone can answer the most obvious question of all: *What is the bus driver's name?*

(Answers in order: 26, 34, 5)

Remember the very first word in the story? *You.* You drove the bus; your own name is the answer. Of course, this was a trick. By misdirection you were led to overlook that critical first word, and to pay close attention to everything else. More important, you tried hard to figure out that story; you were interested in all those bus riders, and you probably had a moving picture in your mind of that bus on its route. The building blocks of memory were all there: concentration plus attention plus image formation—minus misdirection.

Memory needs no notes.
One early step in memory improvement is difficult: *no more note-taking.* If your interest is genuine, part of the drill is to throw away your pencil and paper. As you come to know new memory techniques, you must trust your ability to employ them. Constant list-making, note-taking, and memo-writing betray a lack of self-confidence in your memory and a lack of commitment to memory training. But once you start to remember names and numbers that you never remembered before, you will no longer need to stuff your wallet or pocketbook with little scraps of paper—half of whose messages and numbers make no sense to you when you finally read them.

Memory and high intelligence are not necessarily related. The absent-minded professor knows all there is to know about his academic specialty, but cannot remember to wear two socks of the same color. The professor focuses so hard on one thing that he forgets nearly everything else. At the other end of the spectrum, medical literature contains intriguing case histories of idiots savants—mentally defective people who can play classical piano instinctively, or immediately

Paper slips—and our recollection of what they mean—are rapidly lost.

name the day of the week for any date in history. Like the professor, the idiot savant has a one-track mind: his concentration is perfectly focused and his interest is single-minded. And his memory is pure.

Most of us, in fact, possess a store of useless information that has come to be known as trivia. Boys often have a knack for memorizing the batting averages of hundreds of baseball players. Many women have an astonishing recall of what other women wore, or looked like, when last met. Gamblers stake huge sums on their memory of a single deck of cards. Whatever you are most interested in, you tend to remember best. Memory building, in large part, is a matter of broadening your interests.

Names and faces.
What do you *want* to remember better? Names and faces top the list for most people. Study the faces on the next page for a few minutes, then match them to the names. Cover up the names and see if you can put the right name to the right face. This is rote memorization; even if you can do the match-ups successfully, chances are that the achievement will be short-lived. As you learn better name/face memorization techniques, you may want to refer back to these names and faces and match the memorized names to the anonymous faces on page 195.

In a later section you will learn precise methods for memorizing names and faces. For now, as you study the page, try to isolate a single outstanding feature from each face. These are strangers, after all; trying to memorize an entire new countenance—plus eleven others—is too great a task. Focusing your attention on just one feature (nose, mouth, eyebrows, etc.) will serve your purpose best.

Some of the names may defy rote memorization. They may sound like nothing else you have ever heard, nor look like any word in English. But everyone's name —if you study it hard enough—can be manipulated in sound into *something* else that sticks in your mind. And the mental effort of that transformation has value in itself. When you take the time and trouble to turn O'Bradovich into Over the Bridge, you are not likely to forget that name soon.

For the time being, first names are less important than last names. Concentrate on a distinguishing facial feature, plus a last-name word association, and try to knit them together in your mind. (You can use the same technique later to remember first names, which usually are easier.) This exercise is really just a warm-up to test your capacity to memorize by rote. When you next come across these same names and faces on page 195, you will be much better equipped to remember them. No matter how good your rote memory powers may be, the gains from using them are fleeting. *Trained memory* lasts and lasts.

Vinnie Dodson

Russell Meredith

Eileen Murray

Samantha Kearns

Vicky Seaton

Clinton Montgomery

Sue Young

Neil Keenan

Angelo Rivera

Juan Sanchez

Judy Sommers

Olaf Christenson

Getting organized

Everyone has immediate memory, and almost anyone can get by with a functional short-term memory. But a good long-term memory requires conscious and systematic organizational skills. Foremost among these skills is a technique called *chunking*. Several items (or numbers) worth remembering are grouped together—chunked—for longer and easier recall. A list of nine seems unmanageable unless written down. But three chunks of three, properly organized, can be retained in your head.

Take a grocery shopping list, for instance. Say you need milk, cereal, coffee, lettuce, cheese, sugar, tomatoes, eggs, and celery. Now try to organize your list: three of the items are dairy products (milk, eggs, and cheese); three are dry foods (cereal, coffee, and sugar); and three are vegetables (lettuce, celery, and tomatoes).

Once in the supermarket, you really need only remember dairy (3), dry goods (3), and vegetables (3). Those cues will likely call to mind your specific items. (Similarly, the quantities you need do not have to clutter your mental list.) Of course, if you are thoroughly familiar with the store, you can chunk your purchases according to sections or aisles.

Chunking.
Try the chunking principle on your next shopping expedition. Plan ahead in your mind. Group your purchases into categories, colors, things beginning with the same letter, or goods located in the same part of the store. Put them in chunks of three or four and they become infinitely more memorable—and manageable—than they were in one huge lump. Your list is organized, and so is your brain.

Chunking is made to order for numbers. Many numbers are too big to remember, and no wonder. Memory specialists say that the upper limit for long-term number retention is seven digits—and it is no coincidence that phone numbers are just that long. Nor is it coincidence that, when area codes came into everyday use, the extra three digits were traditionally separated from the original seven by parentheses. Three digits in parentheses happens to be a perfect example of a chunk, set neatly apart from the already memorized number.

Graphically, the memory advantage of chunking is quickly apparent. Consider a twelve-digit number:

 492357168247

Even in mathematical order—492 billion, and so on—it is too big to grasp, much less hold on to. But now try chunking it:

 (492) (357) (168) (247).

Suddenly it becomes comprehensible: you may think of it as four area codes. If you need to know an absurdly long number—a charge account or bank account code, for instance—try using the chunking method. If the number does not break down into neat multiples of three, tack on a one- or two-digit prefix. With practice, and habit, chunking works.

Some useful facts have been imprinted on your memory bank in a peculiarly childish way, through rhymes and ditties that you learned in school or at home. They may be childish, but they save everyone a lot of time and trouble. You probably know these:

(calendar)	Thirty days hath September, April, June, and November . . .
(time change)	Spring forward, fall back
(spelling)	*I* before *E,* except after *C,* Or when sounded like *A* . . .
(treble clef)	*E*very *G*ood *B*oy *D*eserves *F*udge

Mnemonics.
Each of these is an example of a *mnemonic* (nee-MON-ik): a learning aid, often a rhyme, that cues your conscious mind to recall some fact in your long-term memory bank. Some mnemonics are best left to serious memory experts, but many others (supplied in succeeding pages) are accessible to all learners. Each new technique represents a mnemonic progression from some previous level of memory training, and none involves parlor tricks or special intellectual gifts.

Every level of memory building will involve a sustained effort on your part: close *observation*, concentrated *attention*, and mental *organization*. Your progress may be shaky at first, slower than you like, but there will be nothing painful about it, and no one will grade your performance. Best of all, the reward will be considerable: never forgetting names and faces again, no more list-making and note-taking, and the sure self-knowledge that you are more fully aware of everything happening around you.

Image formation

Ridiculous associations can be an aid to memory. For example, you may visualize a dog-food sandwich to help remember dog food and bread.

Image formation, or imaging, is a cornerstone of memory building. You probably do it already, nearly every night, when you dream. Every time you dream, you indulge your natural capacity for forming images. In memory training you teach yourself to dream consciously, on purpose, with your eyes open, in order to make forgettable things memorable.

Any common object can be made memorable by mentally assigning three qualities to it: *detail, color,* and *movement.* Consider something you may frequently misplace. A key is a good example. It is small, dull and much like any other key. Now make your key special in your mind: gleaming, flashing gold in the light, with sharp teeth that might cut you if you are not careful. Next, imagine that this thing is alive and has a mind of its own—if you do not keep track of it, it is likely to jump up and lock you up. You might even give it a name. Once you see this key as somehow distinctive or dangerous, you will be unlikely to lose it again.

Paired images. Remembering two different things is much easier if you pair them in your mind, however improbably. Unpaired, they are readily forgotten. "Oh, and on the way back would you please pick up some dog food and some bread?" On your way home you may vaguely recall something—two things —you were supposed to get at the store, but you are unlikely to recall what they were. But if you had drawn this picture in your mind, you would not soon forget it: a dog-food sandwich, two slices of white bread enclosing three inches of golden brown canine chunks.

In making paired images, it is important to remember that logic, reality, even propriety must be discarded. The idea is to imprint on your mind a truly outrageous and colorful picture, one that takes imagination to come up with. At first this process, like learning to paint, will require time and thought, but soon enough the process will seem easy. In fact, most people find it fun. Image formation is a conscious investment in remembering. Having made that investment, you will be unlikely to give it up easily.

Most lists of things to remember contain more than two or three items. However, your mind picture can accommodate an extensive list, this one, for example:

1. culottes
2. tennis racket
3. rain hat
4. fur-topped boots
5. knee pads
6. bib overalls
7. swim goggles
8. windbreaker
9. ski gloves
10. duck-hunting whistle

Imagine yourself wearing or using all this gear at once, from top to bottom, from the inside out. Silly? Certainly, but not nearly as silly as it could have been— if half your list had been grocery items, for instance.

The primary trick in image formation is to *gather everything together in one room,* or *hang everything on one person.* Construct a situation in which each item belongs with another one, in which unrelated objects become related through the medium of your imagination. By seeing yourself equipped with all ten items in the list, you will be able to remember all ten. Imaging is a useful memory tool.

When trying to remember a long list of items, you might relate each to yourself. Find a way to wear or hold each item on your list.

Peg words

To prepare for the use of peg words in building memory, try to imagine that every number, 0 through 9, *looks like* a certain letter of the alphabet. Here is the version that memory experts use and memory students find most useful. It is sometimes called the number/consonant system or the letter-number alphabet:

Number	Letter/sound	Reason
0	z (*or* s)	zero begins with *z*
1	t (*or* d)	vertical stroke of a *t* looks like number *1*
2	n	printed *n* has *2* downstrokes
3	m	printed *m* has *3* downstrokes
4	r	written-out *4* ends in *r*
5	l	your *5*-fingered left hand, thumb out, forms an *L*
6	ch (j *or* g *or* sh)	turned-around *j* looks like a *6*
7	k (*or* c)	European *7* looks like a *k*
8	f (*or* v)	written *f* looks like a skinny *8*
9	p (*or* b)	mirror-image of *p* is a *9*

Remember one phrase—TeN MoRe LoGiC FiBS—minus the vowels—and you will know 1 through 10. Now you are ready to work with peg words.

The letter-number alphabet, with its single-letter equivalent numbers, is not suitable for all numerical combinations, especially the long ones. The true *memory pegs* for all numbers are pictorial equivalents: 1 = t = a picture (in your mind) of a tie. Tie, of course, begins with t and can be tacked on to almost any word picture you can think up. Each effective pictorial equivalent, or peg, must be short, must begin with the correct letter, and must be readily transferable into picture form. You might think of 1 to 10 this way:

Tie (1) should be a loud necktie or bow tie.
Noah (2) is usually thought of as an old man in robes, with a flowing white beard.
Ma (3) can be your mind's-eye view of your own mother, or any other motherly person.
Rye (4) works well as a loaf of bread.
Law (5) is John Law, a policeman or sheriff.
Shoe (6) stands for a single shoe, preferably a large one.
Cow (7) is the dairy animal. (The hard *c* in cow is the same as phonetic *k*.)
Ivy (8) is the climbing vine, capable of growing on anything. (This is the only exception to the rule that peg words should begin with the correct letter, but ivy is easy to see in your mind and so is remembered easily.)
Bee (9) is the noisy insect.
Toes (10) combine 1 and 0—the *t* sound plus the *z* sound. They stand for your toes.

Peg words for 1–10: TeN MoRe LoGiC FiBS

1 = Tie	2 = Noah	3 = Ma	4 = Rye	5 = Law
6 = Shoe	7 = Cow	8 = Ivy	9 = Bee	10 = Toes

Improving Your Memory

(246)   (3579)

It takes some doing to construct a picture such as this for a telephone number. But once it's done, you'll never forget the number.

The numbers 1 to 10 are enough to learn for now; they include all the basic peg sounds, peg words, and peg pictures. With them alone you can memorize any phone number and itemize any short list in your head. But first you need practice. At every reasonable opportunity, practice using these pegs with phone numbers and street addresses until every number you hear immediately sparks a picture in your mind. Then you can start stringing numbers together in multiples. Your word pictures will become murals. With them, you can start trying to memorize almost any complicated combination. But start modestly.

Peg words are *substitutes* for numbers. Because they are based on the letter-number alphabet, and because they are backed by pictorial equivalents, they are clearly superior to plain numbers as memory builders. (There are peg words for 11 to 100 also, listed in the Appendix, pages 198-199.) By using letter *and* picture substitutes for numbers, every new number takes on two- or three-dimensional significance in your mind's eye.

When you attempt to memorize a phone number, for example, 246-3579, using one-dimensional rote memory, you will usually forget it by the next day. This is because there is nothing memorable about that number. Its letter-number equivalent is a different story. The number 246-3579 becomes *NoRwiCH MiLKuP*, a country scene one can easily remember. Now consider one more version—the pictorial equivalent—of the same phone number:

(246)   Picture old Noah (2), arms outstretched, with a ham on Rye (4) sandwich in one hand and a huge Shoe (6) in the other.

(3579) There goes your Ma (3) riding double with an Officer of the Law (5) on a Cow (7), galloping away from a swarm of Bees (9) in hot pursuit.

That is a picture. More importantly, it is a phone number you will not soon forget. Take your own phone number, fill in the right peg sounds and peg pictures, and see what you come up with. You will soon become good at using letter-number equivalents and peg words.

Link method

The hardest things to remember are those that lack logical association between the items. By contrast, for example, it is easy to remember the multiplication tables—the logic of 1 times 2, 1 times 3, etc. is apparent to all of us. When it comes to remembering to buy shoes, shirts, and soap, the association is missing.

Links are the mortar that holds individual memories together. Links make mental connections between unrelated objects, numbers, or items. Names of objects can be linked in two ways: by placing them one after another in a narrative, or by constructing new words from the first letters of those objects (using the initial method plus connecting vowels, as in *NoRwiCH MiLKuP*).

Initial method.
For example, suppose you want to remember the sites of the last six Olympic Games. Beginning in 1964, they are Tokyo, Mexico City, Munich, Montreal, Moscow, and Los Angeles. You could invent a narrative—a travelogue—that took you to all those cities in order, but you need not do so. It would be better, because there are only six of them, to try the first-initial method. Here is how it might work:

Too	MuCh	M&MMs	LAnguage
(Tokyo)	(Mexico City)	(Munich, Montreal, Moscow)	(Los Angeles)

Many of us enjoy M & M candy, so now we can link together Too MuCh M&MMs LAnguage, not the greatest of thoughts but surely a fine story of someone enjoying candy. When you invent your own link phrase, you become the author of your own memory aid. The phrases are yours alone, and you will remember them.

Narrative method.
The other kind of link association, the narrative method, requires all the imagination you can come up with. Nothing is too outrageous, *if it helps you remember*. As an example, take the nine-item grocery list used earlier (page 186):

> milk, cheese, eggs, cereal, coffee,
> sugar, lettuce, tomatoes, celery

For the sake of demonstration, this is a short and easy list. With practice, the link narrative method will work equally well even for a much longer and more varied shopping list. First, put yourself in the center of the picture: everything that happens will be made to happen by you.

A trip to the supermarket

You are going—in your mind, of course—to the supermarket. You are on a mission of mercy. Some people, you have decided, need groceries more than you do. You commandeer nine shopping carts, tucked into one another, and make your way down the first aisle: Dairy. A young mother is trying to corral her two small youngsters who are sampling everything on the shelves.

"Need some *milk?*" you ask her. She nods. You hand each child a gallon jug of milk—nearly as big as they are—and lift the boys and the milk into the first of your shopping carts. The mother smiles and heads for the check-out counter.

Just then a burly young man comes by with about 15 packages of hamburger buns under each arm.

"*Cheese*burgers?" you ask. He nods, and you heap the second of your carts with dozens of prewrapped packages of assorted cheeses; the young man dumps his hamburger meat on top of it and is on his way, with thanks.

Across the aisle an old lady is painstakingly opening every cardboard *egg* carton in the display to check for breakage. "It would be easier to do that at home," you say pleasantly, and soon the old lady is pushing your third cart filled with 45 dozen eggs. You have made her day.

You come across a little girl in tears, vainly trying to rip open the bottom of a box of *cereal* to get at the prize. No problem: the young lady is packed off in your fourth cart with 24 boxes of cereal, calling out to her mother, "Mommy, I won!"

Improving Your Memory

Hidden in a corner is an enormous aluminum *coffee* urn, steaming from the top, with no sign attached. "The coffee must be free," you conclude. You unplug the coffee-maker and wrestle it into your fifth shopping cart—a perfect fit, with just enough room for three dozen styrofoam cups.

"Take a break, shoppers!" you announce. "Hot coffee. On me." You lead a growing procession to the middle aisle of the store and start dispensing coffee from your cart. More than one shopper remarks that the brew is too bitter.

Not for long: you empty two 5-pound bags of *sugar* into the urn and load your sixth cart with five more bags. Your fellow shoppers are enjoying themselves. But not the store manager, who has been watching you from the moment the coffee urn disappeared. (The coffee was free, but it tasted so bad that the store wanted it hidden.) He is right behind you as you approach your last stop: Produce.

"Pardon me," the manager says, "could I have a word with you in my office?"

"Just a minute," you say. "I'm mixing a salad." You have three shopping carts left. You fill the first with heads of *lettuce,* the second with dozens of *tomatoes,* and the third with every bunch of *celery* in the bin. The shoppers raid each cart and buy out the entire supply, which brings a smile to the store manager's face at last.

"Now, my good man, I believe I owe you for two bags of sugar," you say on your way out, peeling off a five-dollar bill. "Charge the coffee to good customer relations."

Now that is a shopping excursion you will remember—which means, of course, that will also remember your nine-item shopping list. Most shopping lists, however, leave little to the imagination. They are colorless and lifeless. The storytelling method, on the other hand, contains everything a list does not: detail, color, and movement. In addition, of course, you are the star performer in your own story. Like an actor, you have only to remember to follow through the sequence of events. Imagination and the patience to concoct a scenario are the only requirements. After you practice a few times, it will take far less effort to make up a story than it does to write down a list.

Always try to paint your mind pictures in the broadest possible strokes, freely using disproportion, movement, exaggeration, and even substitution. Substitution means using one object in place of another—a potato, say, in place of a prizefighter's broad lumpy nose—because the resemblance is clearly there or because the image is so memorable. Using linked mind pictures, you can learn to memorize lists of 20 or more items that have no apparent relation to one another.

Everyday applications

Even as a beginner in the use of memory systems, you can go a long way with the link method and your ten peg words. Links are used to memorize anything in sequence; pegs help you remember any kind of number, in or out of sequence. Pegs and links can be combined to memorize schedules and appointments.

Using links. Suppose one morning you have eight things to do: (1) phone the vet about your cat; (2) get the car washed; (3) make a deposit at the bank; (4) mail a package at the post office; (5) buy four items at the hardware store (light bulbs, extension cord, duplicate key, and catnip); (6) buy a watchband at the jeweler's; (7) pick up three food items at the convenience store; and (8) stop by a friend's house, where you left your umbrella.

Now for your links. Your movie for the day begins at breakfast, where you imagine yourself milking cows —one cow is sick, call the vet (1). As you get in your car, imagine that it is dripping wet and clean (2). See yourself driving up to the bank teller's drive-in window (3). Your bank deposit slip could be considered postage for your package, which it is time to mail (4). While you are at the post office, study the "Wanted" posters and imagine that you are pictured there as a burglar. You will need tools from the hardware store (5): light bulbs for bright ideas, an extension cord for second-story

work, a skeleton key, and catnip. Right down the street from the hardware store is the jeweler's where you treat yourself to a new watchband (6). The rest is easy. You always pass the convenience store on your way home and you nearly always stop for something. Milk, bread, and eggs (7) are needed this time. So is your umbrella. It always rains when you do not have it. It is raining now—in your mental movie—so you stop at your friend's house to retrieve it (8). Eight errands and eight links, combining to fashion a chain of actions.

Using pegs. The other way to memorize this schedule/list is to peg each stop to its pictorial symbol. You might wear a Tie (1) to talk to the vet. Imagine your car being washed by Noah himself (2). Your Ma (3), wearing an eyeshade, might be the bank teller. Your parcel for mailing might be a loaf of Rye (4) bread. Your imaginary burglar's foray at the hardware store would be thwarted by the Law (5). Your Shoe (6) might be held together by a watchband. Your milk is custom-dispensed by a Cow (7). Finally, your umbrella is found to be upholstered with Ivy (8).

For a short list, the peg method permits a briefer scenario and seems to make more sense. But good sense and good memorability are not always the same. For most students of memory, the link method seems to yield more satisfaction.

Links and pegs

Two surefire ways to memorize the otherwise forgettable:

Link

Peg

Links and pegs in action

Phone numbers
Your task is, of course, very much simplified if you only want to memorize local numbers. You already know the prefix; just deal with the last four numbers. For simplicity, try to make a peg word from those final four numbers; 3819, for example, might become MuFf-Top, which prompts a picture of a fur-topped boot. Link the peg word to the face (or figure) of the person you want to call.

Historical dates
First get rid of the extraneous factors. Replace the names of months with their sequential numbers, 1 to 12. As for years, eliminate the first two century numbers; you already know what century you are dealing with. Thus Lincoln's Gettysburg Address, November 19, 1863, becomes 11 19 63, whose first (peg) initials form TaTTeD SHaM. Picture Mr. Lincoln tatting a sham—that is, stitching a pillowcase—while he tries to memorize the Gettysburg Address.

Playing cards
Think up your own peg words to represent all the cards in the deck, with 13 *s* words in the spade suit, 13 *h* words in hearts, 13 *d* words in diamonds, and 13 *c* words in clubs. Your own one-syllable pegs will be better than a ready-made set, because you will have to memorize them perfectly and practice thoroughly before applying your knowledge of unplayed cards in a game of chance.

Foreign words
This advice is limited to individual words, short expressions, and proper names. Memorization is no substitute for learning a foreign language, but it is a great help in learning useful words. Whatever word gives you trouble can be manipulated, somehow, to approximate an English substitute—a word or name that sounds like the foreign one. Whenever you see or hear the foreign version, a mind picture of your version will give you an instant translation. Pronunciation is not important in this aspect of the work involved in learning a foreign language.

Birthdays
Use the same method as for historical dates, but make a special birthday link between the peg date and the person. If one of your nephews was born on August 2, 1965, for instance, streamline the date—8 2 65—and make a first-letter peg substitution: INSoLe, your nephew's bare foot. The same principle applies to anniversaries, except that you have two people to keep in your mind picture.

Aging and absent-mindedness

Resistance to change is most noticeable when a grandparent or great-grandparent simply stops paying attention; the suspicion sets in that our beloved seniors are finally just too old to function, that senility is taking its toll.

Senility can easily be a misdiagnosis. Old-age mental infirmity, usually called senility, may be the natural product of two maladies of old age: inattention and inactivity. Usually, both are easily reversible, and neither is indicative of true memory loss, which is a clinical condition accompanying physical deterioration. Memory loss rarely shows itself as an isolated symptom.

A leading authority on adult education, Edward L. Thorndike, once stated that "age is no handicap to learning a new trade, profession, or anything you want to do at any time of life." Remember: *anything you want to do.* Your brain can always use exercise. A sedentary brain means a sedentary memory. Absent-mindedness may simply mean not caring.

By practicing the memory-building exercises in this chapter, older people are likely to tap reserves of vitality they thought they had outlived. Memory experts agree: the best memory students are often the oldest. The alertness and involvement you use in practicing a memory system not only sharpen memory but sharpen all your mental faculties as well. Every flex of a memory muscle strengthens it.

Names and faces

If you are like most people, you wish you could remember names and faces better. After all, any man or woman who remembers *your* name is likely to win your respect and attention; it is almost disrespectful if you fail to reply in kind. And when someone knows your name, and assumes you remember his, there is rarely a graceful way out if you do not. First a word of reassurance: do not assume that you are cursed with the inability to remember names. You simply have never gone about it in a systematic way.

Getting a name right.
To begin with, you may have never listened to an introduction properly. On meeting someone—a perfect stranger—at some social function, attend to these ground rules:

- Hear his or her whole name clearly.
- If unclear, ask for the spelling.
- If odd, comment on it.
- Repeat the name during conversation.
- Say the name once more on parting.

Surnames fall into three categories for the purpose of memorization. The first two are easy:

1. Self-descriptive names (Baker, Cook, White, Day, Knight, Brown, Foote, Post, and so on) that in themselves have meaning or spark images.

2. Same-as or sound-like names that duplicate or approximate those of famous people, historical figures, or well-known brand names.

You should have no trouble associating these names with a pictorial equivalent, whether it be a celebrity, an occupation, or a color.

But the third category—meaning 90 percent of all surnames—will require some work. Except to linguists, most names mean nothing by themselves; they defy visualization or definition, perhaps even pronunciation, and they are meaningless as words. The solution: a substitute word or words to stand for the difficult name and to make a picture for deposit in your memory bank. Each syllable in a name will likely add a picture, and then the pictures must be linked. Below are some names, along with suggested pictorial equivalents, to get you started.

After you have practiced this substitution technique, no one's name should be meaningless anymore. But that is only half the battle. It is essential, of course, to memorize someone's name, but it is equally important to match that name to its owner's face. So there is one last association technique to learn. Match your outlandish mind picture (from the name) to *one* outstanding feature of that person's face.

Just as you take pains to get his or her name right, so you must look the other person straight in the face to get it right, too. Almost certainly something will strike you as distinctive—a scar, a hairline (or lack of it), a wide (or pursed) mouth, high cheekbones, a disproportionate nose, a drooping eyelid, a five o'clock shadow, a long chin, squinty eyes or prominent eyeglasses, a long (or dimpled) chin. Then take that one facial feature and combine (link) it with your mind picture of the person's last name. Never mind the ridiculousness of your finished portrait; its lack of logic is what makes it memorable.

Knowing what you have just read, try once more to truly memorize the names and faces on page 185. Then turn back to this page and note your improvement.

Making pictures of names

Name	Phrase	Picture		Name	Phrase	Picture
Cohen	ice cream *cone*			**Kassebaum**	*castle* + *bomb*	
Olzcewski	*old* + *chef* + *ski*ing			**Pottinger**	*pot* + *injure*	
Gordon	vegetable *garden*			**Pfeiffer**	*fife* player	

Improving Your Memory

Suggestions for students

Too many people go through high school and college and adult education courses stuffing themselves with information one day only to disgorge it all the next. They cram for an exam, take it, and emerge with little or no permanent knowledge. Why is all that information forgotten so quickly?

The scholastic method of memory building is rote repetition without regard for meaning. Thus, such students will read something over and over again until it sinks in—for a little while. To memorize something by rote is not really to learn it, and certainly not to understand it. Learning is not a one-shot recital of facts or ideas; it is the informed application of information and ideas. When you build true memory, you absorb facts and ideas in such a way that you store them away, ready to be employed profitably for the rest of your life.

So far you have learned the fundamentals of the peg and link methods of memory, both unsurpassed for the recollection of tangible objects and numbers, and both suitable for translation into mind pictures.

Pegs and links will not work, however, in certain fields of academic study. There is no practical way to conjure up a picture of a French verb, a mathematical equation, or a scientific term. Something else is needed to aid the memory.

Memory techniques for students

English vocabulary
Some words do not look at all like what they mean. In such cases, break the word into separate syllables and give each part a new meaning in a new linkage.
Execrate—to hate, detest. Imagine having to put *eggs* in a *crate* all the time. You would *detest* such a chore.
Hirsute—hairy. Look at that woman in the woolen suit—*her suit* is all covered with *hair*.
Litany—a kind of prayer. Think of yourself *praying* on one knee—praying for mercy because you just *lit* your other *knee* with the votive candle.

English spelling
There is no magical way to become a better speller. The most practical solution is to seize on a habitually misspelled word like "calendar" and write it down five times wrong—c-a-l-e-n-d-e-r—and then cross out the second *e*. Then write it five times correctly and circle the second *a*. Or you might make associations between words you know already and troublesome words you want to know. See *all* lines as par*all*el, *iron* as part of the envi*iron*ment, a *guar*d as *guar*anteeing safety, and *loss* as being co*loss*al.

Mathematics
Your knowledge of peg sounds 1 to 10 (and 1 to 100, on pages 198-199) can be put to good use for learning fractions, formulas, equations, measurements, ratios, and theorems. Use the first-initial link method for individual numbers, then tie them together in a mind picture. The pictures thus formed may be ridiculous in the extreme, but they are intended only to make you familiar with a mathematical concept. When you truly learn it, you will have memorized the concept, not the funny picture.

Biology
Unlike most sciences, biology is well adapted to memory building because most of its terms have direct application to something you can visualize—a human body, an animal, a neural network. Take what you need to know, shorten it to pegs and links, and picture it right on or in the body part to which it belongs.

Chemistry
The language of chemistry is made up of symbols, and symbols are made to order for changing into pegs and links. You can, for instance, treat a subscript—the 2 in H_2O, for example—as its peg sound equivalent. The task is to make something from a chemical formula that illustrates the substance.
H_2SO_4 is sulfuric acid. Using pegs, H_2SO_4 might become HeN SORe. Why is the hen sore? Because it was doused in sulfuric acid.

Improving Your Memory

Substitution. The something else is the *substitution* method. If you are faced with an intangible or abstract nugget of information, find a sound-alike English substitute for it, something you can *picture* in your mind. Here is how substitution works with two French words:

Pont means bridge. In pronunciation it is similar to the English word *pawn*. You might remember both the word and its pronunciation if you make a mind picture of yourself dragging a bridge—the Brooklyn Bridge or the Golden Gate—to a pawnshop.

Pamplemousse means grapefruit. Imagine a big *moose* head on the wall with an enormous *dimple* on its cheek. The dimple is so large that you are able to balance a grapefruit in it.

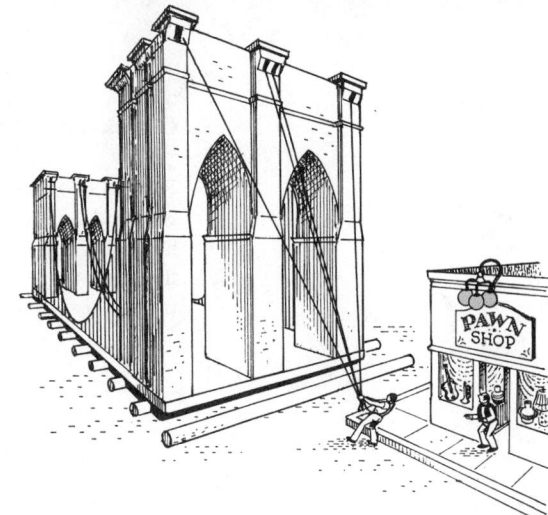

To help remember that the French word pont *means bridge, picture yourself dragging a bridge into a pawnshop.*

Lectures	Your goal is to *stop taking lecture notes* altogether. In lectures you are supposed to be listening and understanding. Remember the memory virtues: close *observation,* strict *attention,* and systematic *organization.* Practice doing these in your head, not your notebook. Lecturers are as eager to make sense to you as you are to make sense of them, so pay attention. In their opening remarks, lecturers will tell you what they will talk about. The lecturers then will talk about their subjects at length. Finally they will usually summarize what they have just said. The middle part—the mental note-taking part—is the most difficult part of a lecture for the audience. The opening remarks and the conclusion, which may last a combined total of five minutes, contain most of what must be retained. Most people, however, are not listening at those times. They are still settling in with note-taking paraphernalia at the start, and they are packing up to leave at the conclusion. A practiced listener should know in advance what the lecture subject is, and write that down. At first, you may need to take minimal notes on paper, as if they were chapter headings. Eventually, with practice, you will be able to take mental notes only.

Reading

As you become more fluent in the construction and use of word pictures, using substitute word pegs, you are likely to find yourself visualizing peculiar mind's-eye views of things you read. Do not be alarmed. This is a sign that pegs, links, and substitutes are becoming part of your conscious memorization process. Without those mind pictures, the reading material might never be recalled at all.

The substitution method is most useful for memorizing quotations and lines of poetry. If the line or passage is a philosophical thought, or simply beautiful language, then make sound-alike substitutions to fix it in your mind. Never forget that it is difficult to memorize anything unless you invest it with *detail, color,* and *movement.* Your aim should be to simplify whatever you read to its memorable essence, and then, through substitutions, to fix it in your mind.

Maps

First consult a map of the United States. From the western border, draw approximately vertical lines southward from the borders of the northernmost states. The West Coast grid, or zone, will take in Washington, Oregon, and California plus Alaska and Hawaii. The East Coast grid, by far the largest, may encompass as many as 17 states under Maine. Try to place all the states within six or eight zones. Then figure out your own substitute word for each state, form a link word picture for each zone, and you will have a six- or eight-chapter mind picture of the map of America.

Appendix

Quick-recall tests

For those readers who had little or no success the first time (page 183), try this test again.

1. Study this 15-digit number for two minutes. Then try to duplicate it exactly on a piece of paper.

   238158649376914

Peg words 1–100

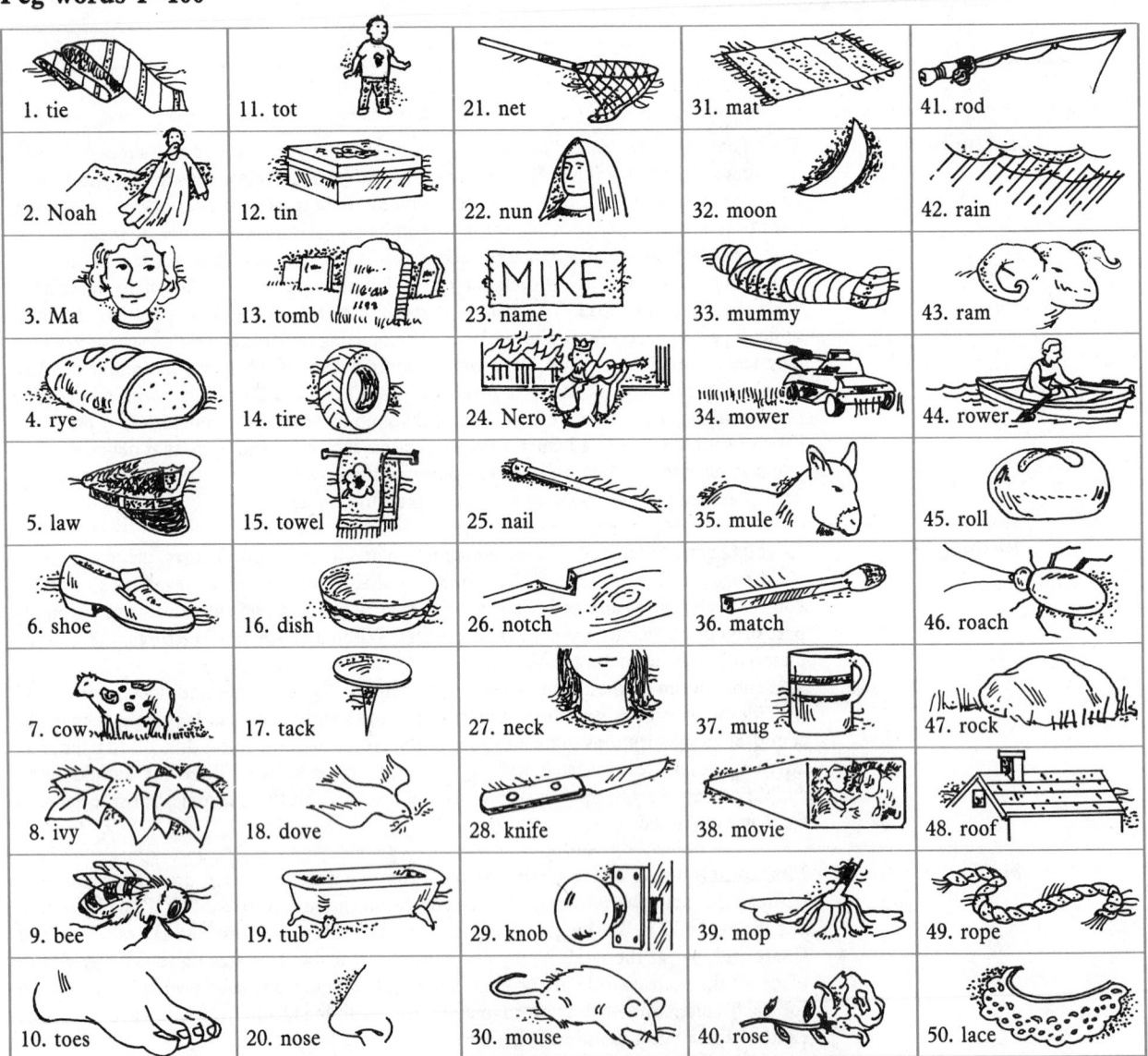

1. tie	11. tot	21. net	31. mat	41. rod
2. Noah	12. tin	22. nun	32. moon	42. rain
3. Ma	13. tomb	23. name	33. mummy	43. ram
4. rye	14. tire	24. Nero	34. mower	44. rower
5. law	15. towel	25. nail	35. mule	45. roll
6. shoe	16. dish	26. notch	36. match	46. roach
7. cow	17. tack	27. neck	37. mug	47. rock
8. ivy	18. dove	28. knife	38. movie	48. roof
9. bee	19. tub	29. knob	39. mop	49. rope
10. toes	20. nose	30. mouse	40. rose	50. lace

2. Here are seven phone numbers, each corresponding to a local tradesman or professional. Study the list for six minutes, then copy the seven titles in any order. Finally, without looking, match the memorized numbers to the titles.

Doctor	762-5881	Lawyer	681-9558
Grocer	616-2053	Dentist	386-3579
Plumber	358-0864	Florist	784-3579
Electrician	872-9647		

3. This is a list of twelve objects found in the home. Study it for just two minutes, then reconstruct the list from memory, in order.

couch, refrigerator, newspaper, clock, mirror, toaster, lamp, toilet, stove, television, carpet, window

51. lot	61. sheet	71. cot	81. fat	91. bat
52. lion	62. chain	72. coin	82. phone	92. bone
53. limb	63. jam	73. comb	83. foam	93. bum
54. lure	64. cherry	74. car	84. fur	94. bear
55. lily	65. jail	75. coal	85. file	95. bell
56. leech	66. choo choo	76. cage	86. fish	96. beach
57. log	67. chalk	77. coke	87. fog	97. book
58. lava	68. chef	78. cave	88. fife	98. puff
59. lip	69. ship	79. cob	89. fob (or fib)	99. pipe
60. cheese	70. case	80. fez	90. bus	100. disease (or dozes)

Names and their pictorial equivalents

Feminine

Abby: abbey, a bee
Abigail: a big ale
Ada: aid her
Addy: add E
Adelaide: a dell aid, addle aid
Adele: a dell
Adeline: add a line
Agatha: agate tore
Agnes: egg nest
Alberta: Al bought her
Alexandra: lick sand raw
Alexis: all ex's, all legs
Alice: blue gown
Alicia: a leash
Aline: lean
Alvira: I'll wire her
Amanda: a man there, amend, a mender
Amelia: a meal yeah
Amy: aim me, hey me
Andrea: hand dryer, angrier
Angela: angel, and Jell-o
Angelina: angel leaner
Anita: anteater, an eater
Annabel: a new bell
Annette: a net
Antoinette: ant turn net
Arlene: I lean
Audrey: all dry, aw dry
Augusta: gust her
Avis: a whiz
Babette: bad bet
Babs: bobs, blabs
Barbara: barber
Becky: bad key, peck E
Bernadette: burn a debt
Bernice: burn niece, burnoose
Bess: best, bass
Beth: bet bath
Beverly: beef early
Bobbie: pin, bob E
Bonnie: bony, bone knee, bonnet
Brenda: bran there
Candace: canned ace, candy
Candy: candy
Carla: car law
Carmen: car men
Caroline: carry line
Carrie: carry
Cecile: says seal
Cecilia: steal ya
Celeste: see less, see last
Celia: seal ya
Charlene: char lean
Cheryl: chair ill
Chrissie: cross E
Christine: pristine, grist in
Cicely: Sicily, sees a lea

Cindy: cinder, sin D
Clara: clearer, clarify
Clarissa: clear as air
Claudia: claw D, clawed ya
Clementine: clam on time
Colleen: call in, coal lean
Conchita: conch eater
Constance: con stands, cons dance
Consuelo: con swallow
Cora: core, corer
Cordelia: core deal ya
Corinne: chlorine, core in
Cornelia: corn kneel
Crystal: crystal, cross tall
Cynthia: send to ya, sin tear
Daphne: deaf knee
Darleen: darling, door lean
Deborah: the borer
Deirdre: deer draw
Delia: deal ya
Denise: the niece, dentist
Diana: piano, die on her, dye Anna
Dinah: diner
Dixie: south, dig sea
Dolly: doll
Dolores: the law is
Dora: door, adore her
Doreen: tureen, door in
Dorothy: adore a tea, door tea
Dot: dot
Eden: eatin', E den
Edith: edict
Edwina: head winner
Eileen: I lean, eye lean
Eleanor: a lean oar
Elena: a loner, a leaner
Elise: a lease, release
Eliza: L icer, he lies t'her
Elizabeth: he lifts a bed
Ellie: alley, a lea
Eloise: hello ease, yellow E's
Elsa: L saw, else
Elsie: L sea, el see
Elva: elf, L where?
Elvira: elf higher, L wirer
Emily: a mill E, M in lea
Emma: hey Ma, hemmer
Enid: he knit, in it
Erica: error car
Ernestine: earnest in, a nest in
Essie: ess sea, S see, I see, icy
Estelle: S tell
Esther: yester(day), yes dear, ess tear
Etta: eater, editor
Eugenia: ewe genius, ewe jeans

Evangeline: evangelist
Eve: eve, heave
Evelyn: evil in, a violin
Faith: faith
Fay: fade, fail
Felicia: full leash
Flo: flow
Flora: flower, floor
Florence: floor ants
Flossie: floor see
Frances: France is
Francesca: France's car
Francine: France seen, ran scene
Freda: freed her
Fritzie: ritzy, frisky
Gabrielle: horn, gabby L
Gail: gale
Genevieve: gem verve
Georgia: gorga ya, gorgeous, gorge
Geraldine: chair old dine
Germaine: German, germane
Gertrude: protrude, go through
Gilda: gill there, gild, guild
Gina: china, gee no
Ginny: gin knee
Gisele: gazelle
Glenda: lender, glen deer
Grace: grace, race
Greta: get her, (re)gretter
Gretchen: retchin', great chin
Griselda: grows older
Gussie: gassy, gust sea
Gwen: when, goin'
Gwendolyn: mandolin, wend all in
Hannah: hand her
Harriet: hurry it, harried
Hattie: had tea, hat tea
Hazel: nut, haze, hassle
Heather: heather, feather
Hedda: header, head her
Hedy: heady
Heidi: hide E, hide
Helen: hellin', hailin'
Helena: hill leaner
Helga: held car
Henrietta: hen reader
Hermione: her my own knee
Hester: S tore, has tear
Hettie: heady
Hilary: hilarious, hill airy
Hilda: builder, hill there
Hildegarde: hill the guard
Holly: holly, holy
Honey: honey
Hope: hope
Hortense: horse sense
Ida: cider

Ilka: ilk, elk, ill car
Ilse: ills, else
Imogene: emergin', in motion
Ina: iron, eye no, I know
Inez: iron S, inn Ess
Ingrid: in grid, ink rid
Irene: eye ran, iron in
Irma: I'm a, her Ma
Isabel: is a bell
Isadora: is a door, adorer
Jackie: jack key
Jacqueline: jackal in, jack line
Jane: jay hen, chain
Janet: chain it, chain net
Janice: chain ice, chain ease
Jean: jeans
Jeannette: gem net, shine it
Jeannie: jean knee, chain knee
Jennifer: chain off her, gem fur
Jenny: jay knee, chain knee
Jessica: sick car, chase a car
Jessie: chase E
Jewel: jewel, chew L
Jill: chill, jail
Jo: show, (G.I.) Joe
Joan: showin', own
Joanna: show Anna, showin' her
Jocelyn: jostlin'
Jody: show D, show tea
Josephine: show sip fine
Joyce: juice, (re)joice, choice
Juanita: one eater, war neater
Judith: showed it, chewed it
Judy: chew D
Julia: jewel, jewel yeah
Juliana: shoe lea Anna
Julie: jewel E
Juliet: balcony, jewel ye
June: chewin'
Justine(ina): just in, just tea
Karen: carryin', carin'
Kate: gate
Katherine: cat run, cat tore in
Kathleen: cat lean
Kathy: cat see
Katie: katydid, K tea
Katrina: cat runner
Kay: K, cake, key
Kim: come, grim
Kirsten: curse tin
Kit: kit, cat
Kitty: kitty, kit E
Laura: lurer
Lauren: lurin', lowerin'
Laurette: lower it, lorgnette
Laurie: lower E, lorry

Laverne: love urn
Lavinia: love in here
Leah: lea ah, leader
Lee: lea, lee (shelter)
Lena: leaner
Leonora: lea and aura, lee and oar
Leslie: less lea
Letitia: the teacher
Letty: let E
Lila: lie low
Lillian: lily in
Linda: lender, lint
Lisa: leaser, lease her
Liza: lies here
Lois: loose
Lola: loller, low lair
Lolita: low lighter, low leader
Loretta: lure a tire, lower it
Lorna: law no, (for)lorn, lawn
Lorraine: low rain
Lottie: lottery, lot tea
Louisa: low icer
Louise: low ice, low ease
Lucia: lose ya'
Lucille: loose sail, low sill
Lucinda: lose cinder, loose in there
Lucy: loose E, low sea
Lulu: tutu, (that's a) lulu, lullaby
Lydia: lid here, lady, lid ya'
Lynne: lin(iment), lean
Mabel: may bell, may bull
Madeleine: mad lean
Madge: mad G, badge
Mae: may(pole)
Magda: make door, nagged her
Magdalena: make door leaner
Maggie: magpie, my key
Maisie: maize, maze E, may see
Malvina: mail wiener
Mamie: maim me
Mandy: mandolin, man D, man handy
Marcella: Ma cellar
Marcy: Ma see
Margie: march E
Margot: Ma go
Marguerite(ta): Ma car eat
Maria: mare here
Marian: marryin'
Marie: marry, mare E
Marietta: marry Etta
Marilyn: merrily, marry lin(iment)
Marion: marryin', carry on
Marjorie: Ma jury

Marsha: marsh, marcher
Mary: marry
Mathilda: mat ill there
Mattie: mat E
Maureen: more in, tureen
Mavis: may whiz
Maxine: Macks(trucks) in
Mehitabel: me hit a bell
Melanie: melody, melon knee
Melissa: me listen, mail a saw
Mercedes: Benz, me say D's, mercy
Meredith: married it, merry dish
Mildred: mill dread
Millicent: mill sent, mini cent
Millie: mill, mill E
Mimi: me me, mime me
Minerva: my nerve
Minnie: my knee
Miranda: veranda, mirror and door
Miriam: mirror him, merry ham
Mitzi: mitt sea
Molly: tropical fish, Ma lea
Mona: moaner
Monica: money car, Monaco
Morna: more no, mourner
Muriel: mural
Myra: my rah, mirer
Myrtle: me tell, more till
Nadine: neigh dine
Nan: nun
Nancy: nun see
Nanette: nun net, no net
Naomi: neigh owe me
Natalie: not tell E, gnat toll E, naturally
Nell: knell, kneel
Nellie: knell E
Nettie: net E, net eel
Nicole: nickel, nick hole
Nicolette: nickel let
Nina: knee no
Nita: neater
Noel: Christmas, no el
Nona: no no
Nora: gnaw her
Noreen: gnaw in, no rain
Norma: no Ma, normal
Octavia: hocked a view
Odette: owed debt
Olga: old car, ogre
Olive: olive
Olivia: oh liver
Opal: opal, old pal
Pam: bam, P ham
Pamela: pummel her
Pandora: box, pan door, panda

Pansy: pansy, pan sea
Pat: pat
Patricia: pat richer
Patty: (meat)patty, pat E
Paula: pull her
Pauline: pull in, poor line
Pearl: pearl
Peg: peg
Peggy: peg E, piggy
Penelope: pen elope
Penny: penny
Philippa: full lip
Philomena: fill meaner
Phoebe: fee bee
Phyllis: fill us
Polly: parrot, pulley
Priscilla: press cellar
Prudence: prude ants
Prue: true, rue, rude
Rachel: ray chill
Ramona: ray moaner, ram owner
Rebecca: ray
Regina: reach in, reachin' her
Rena: rain her
Renee: run hay, grenade
Renni: wren E, runny
Rhoda: road
Rita: reader
Roberta: robe hurt her
Robin: robbin', robin (red breast)
Rochelle: row shell
Rosa: rose
Rosalie: rose lea
Rosaline: rose land
Rosalyn: rose lin(iment)
Rosamund: rose mount
Rose: rose
Rosemarie: rose marry
Rosita: rose eater
Rowena: row wiener
Roxanne: rocks in
Ruby: ruby, rude bee
Ruth: Babe(Ruth), ruth(less)
Sabina: soapin' her, sap eye now
Sadie: say D, lady
Sally: sail E, sally
Salome: veil, salami
Samantha: saw man there
Sandra: sander, sand draw
Sandy: sandy
Sarah: say rah, sharer
Sasha: sash
Saundra: sauna, sundry
Selma: sell Ma
Shari: share E, chair ease
Sharon: chair on
Shawn: shorn
Sheila: shield
Sherry: sherry, cherry

Sheryl: chair ill, share ill
Shirley: surely, surly
Sibyl: see bill
Sidney: sit knee
Sigrid: sea grid, secret
Simone: sea moan
Sonia: sewin' ya', sun ya', sun
Sophia: sew fire, sew fee
Sophie: sew fee
Stacy: stay see
Stella: stellar, cella
Stephanie: staff a knee
Sue: sue
Sue Ann: sue ant
Susan: sues Ann, snoozin', (lazy) Susan
Susannah: sues Anna
Susie: sue sea
Sylvia: silver
Tammy: tan me
Terry: terry(cloth) towel
Tess: toss, test
Tessie: toss E, dressy
Thelma: tell Ma
Theodora: see a door
Theresa: tear easy, terrace
Tilda: tell door
Tillie: till E, dilly
Tina: teeny
Toby: toe bee
Toni: toe knee
Tracey: trace E
Tricia: tree share
Trixie: trick see
Trudy: true D, threw D
Una: owner
Ursula: ice cellar
Valerie: valet read
Vanessa: van a saw
Velma: well Ma
Vera: veer, fear
Verna: firmer
Vicky: icky, V key
Victoria: victory
Vida: feed her
Viola: viola
Violet: violet, file it, violent
Vivian: we win, vivid inn
Wanda: wander
Wendy: wend windy
Wilhelmina: will helm inn
Wilma: will Ma
Winifred: when if red, win if red
Winnie: whinny, win knee
Yetta: yeah tar
Yolanda: you launder
Yvette: he wet, E vet
Yvonne: he won, heave on
Zelda: sell there, seldom
Zoe: sew E

Names and their pictorial equivalents

Masculine

Aaron: air run
Abe: hey bee, ape
Abel: able, a bell
Abner: abnor(mal), nab knee
Abraham: ape ram, a bear ham
Abram: ape ram, a broom, bram(ble)
Adam: atom, at 'em
Adolph: a dolph(in)
Adrian: aid dream, a dream
Alan: a lens, a land
Albert: Prince (Albert)
Alden: all den
Alec: a lick
Alex: all eggs, legs
Alexander: leg sander
Alfred: half red
Algernon: all jaw nun
Alonzo: alone sew
Aloysius: all wishes
Alvin: all win
Ambrose: ham browse
Amos: hey miss
André: hand ray
Andrew: hand drew
Andy: handy
Angelo: angel low
Archibald: arch bald
Archie: archer
Armand: almond
Arnold: arm old
Arthur: author
Ashley: ash lea
Aubrey: orb ray
August: gust
Augustine: gustin'
Augustus: gust us
Austin: awes tin, oars tin
Avery: aviary
Axel: axle
Baldwin: bald one
Barnaby: barn a bee
Barney: bar knee, barn E
Barry: bury
Bart: bought, bart(er)
Bartholomew: bottle anew
Basil: bay sill
Bayard: bay yard
Benedict: benedict(ion)
Benjamin: bend a man
Bennett: bend net
Benny: bend E
Bentley: bent lea
Bernard: burn hard
Bernie: burn knee
Bert: bird
Bertram: bought ram
Bertrand: bird ran
Bobby: bob E
Boris: bore us

Boyd: bird
Bradford: bread ford
Bradley: bread lea
Brandon: brandin'
Brian: brine, buyin'
Bruce: bruise
Bruno: burn O
Burton: buy ton
Byron: buy run
Calvin: cave in
Cameron: camera on
Carlos: car loose
Carter: carter, car tear, cart her
Cary: carry
Casper: cast pear
Cecil: cease ill, see sill
Chad: charred, chat
Charles: quarrels, chars
Charlie: char lea
Charlton: quarrel ton, char ton
Chester: chest, jester
Chet: jet
Chris: cross, kiss, grist
Christian: cross tin
Christopher: grist fur, kissed a fur
Clarence: clearance
Clark: clock
Claude: clawed
Clayton: clay ton
Clement: cement, (in)clement
Clifford: cliff oared, cliff awed
Clifton: cliff ton
Clint: lint
Clinton: clean ton
Clive: alive
Clyde: slide, lied, clod
Cole: coal
Colin: coal in, callin'
Connie: con D, con knee
Conrad: con rat, comrade
Corey: core E
Craig: crack
Curtis: caught us, curt
Cyril: see reel, cereal
Cyrus: sires
Damon: demon
Dana: deign, day, dinner
Daniel: den yell
Danny: den knee
Darren: darin'
Darryl: barrel, dare ill
Dave: dive, gave
David: gave it, save it, slingshot
Davy: day V
Dennis: tennis
Derek: derrick
De Witt: the wit, do it

Dexter: deck stir
Dick: tick, detective
Dirk: dark, dirk, Turk
Dominick: down my neck
Donald: duck, darn old
Douglas: dug glass
Duane: D wane
Dudley: dud lea, deadly
Duke: duke, duck
Duncan: dunkin'
Dustin: dustin'
Dwight: white, D white
Earl: oil
Eddie: eddy, a D, heady
Edgar: headgear
Edmund: head mount
Edward: head ward
Edwin: head win, head wind
Egbert: egg butt
Elbert: el butt
Eldred: el dread
Eli: eel eye
Elias: eel highest
Eliot: L E yacht, eel yacht
Ellery: celery
Elmer: el Ma, el more
Emanuel: manual, he man
Emil: a mill, hem ill
Emmett: hem met, aim it
Enoch: he knock
Ephraim: half ram, F rim
Erasmus: erase most
Erastus: erased us, he razzed us
Eric: a rick(shaw), air egg
Ernest: earnest, her nest, honest
Ernie: earn knee
Errol: error
Ervin: I win, urban
Erwin: her win
Eugene: you jean, ewe jean, huge E
Eustace: used us
Evan: a van, heaven
Everett: ever et (ate), over it
Ezekiel: a Z kill L, seek L
Ezra: S roar, ess raw
Felix: feel eggs
Ferdinand: bull, fur in hand
Fletcher: lecher, fetcher
Floyd: flood
Foster: forced her
Francis: fan sis
Frank: frank(furter)
Franklin: Benjamin (Franklin)
Fred: red, fret
Freddy: ready
Frederick: red rick(shaw)
Fritz: freeze
Gabriel: horn, gave reel
Garrett: garret, carry it

Gary: carry, gory
Gaston: gas ton
Gavin: gave in
Gaylord: gay lord
Gene: jean
George: gorge, judge
Gerald: chair old
Gerard: chair hard
Gideon: Bible, giddy on
Gifford: give Ford
Gil: gill, kill
Gilbert: gill butt
Giles: guiles
Gino: gee no
Godfrey: got free
Godwin: God win, good win
Gordie: gaudy
Graham: cracker, gray ham
Grant: grant, granite
Greg: grog, crack, dreg
Gregory: grog airy, crack gory
Griff: gruff, grip
Griffin: grippin', grip fin
Grover: grove
Gunther: gun tore
Gus: gas, gust
Gustave: gas stove
Hadley: head lea, heady
Hal: hall, hail
Hank: hanky, yank
Hans: hands, hens
Harold: hair old
Harry: hairy
Harvey: hard V
Hector: hick tore
Henry: hen, hen ray
Herb: herb
Herbert: her boot
Herman: her man, ermine
Hilary: hilarious, hill airy
Hiram: hire 'im, eye ram
Homer: homer
Horace: her ace
Horatio: ratio, her ratio
Howard: how ward, coward
Hoyt: hurt
Hubert: you bet, ewe bet
Hugh: you, ewe, hue
Hugo: ewe go, you go
Humphrey: home free
Hy: high
Hyman: high man
Ian: eon, ion
Ignace: egg nice, egg nuts
Ignatius: egg nauseous
Ingram: ink ram
Ira: eye rah, irate
Irving: nerve ink, serving
Irwin: I win
Isaac: eye sack, I sick
Isadore: is a door
Israel: his rail, is real

Ivan: eye van
Ivor: I wore, ivy ore
Jacob: Jacob('s ladder), shake up
Jake: shake
James: aims
Jamie: aim me
Jarvis: jar whiz
Jason: jay son
Jasper: just pair, gasp pear
Jay: jay(bird), jail
Jed: shed
Jeff: shave, shove, chaff, chef
Jeffrey: shove free, chef free
Jeremiah: chair mire
Jeremy: chair on me
Jerome: d'ya' roam?, chair room
Jerry: cherry
Jess: jazz
Jesse: James, d'ya see?, let's see
Jim: gym
Jimmy: jimmy (a door), gimme
Joel: jewel, jowl
Joey: showy, chewy
Johnny: on knee, john
Jonah: whale, show new
Jonas: showin' us
Jonathan: john thin
Jordan: Jordan (River), jaw down
José: oh say, hose
Joseph: shows off
Joshua: josh shoe, josh shower
Juan: one, won, wan
Jud: jut
Jude: chewed
Judson: jut son
Jules: jewels
Julian: jewel in
Julie: jewel, July
Justin: just in, justice
Keith: keys
Kenneth: can it
Kent: can't, canned
Kevin: cave in
Kimball: come bull
Kirk: kick
Lance: lance, lands
Lancelot: lance a lot
Larry: lair E, leery
Lawrence: lower ants
Lemuel: lamb mule
Lenny: lend knee
Leo: lion, lea O
Leon: lean on, lea on
Leonard: lean hard
Leopold: leap old, leap pole
Leroy: lea roil
Leslie: less lea

Lester: less tear
Lionel: lion el, lion L
Lloyd: lewd
Lonny: low knee
Louis: loose
Lowell: low el, lower, loll
Lucas: luke kiss
Ludwig: load wig
Luther: looser
Malcolm: mail come
Manny: many, man E, manly
Marcus: mark us
Mario: marry O
Marmaduke: Mom a duke
Marshall: marshal, marsh ill
Marty: Ma tea
Marvin: Ma win, move in
Mason: mason, my son
Matthew: mat ewe
Maurice: more rice
Maury: more E
Maximilian: makes a million
Maxwell: mix well
Maynard: main yard
Melvin: melt win, delve in
Meredith: married it
Mervin: movin'
Meyer: mire
Michael: my call, mike ill
Mickey: my key
Milton: melt on
Mitchell: mitt shell
Monroe: man row
Montague: mount glue
Montgomery: mount gum airy
Monty: mount tea, mountie
Morgan: more can
Mortimer: morti(fy) Ma, more tea Ma
Morton: more ton
Morty: more tea
Moses: Moseys, Ma says
Murray: more ray
Myron: my run, mire on
Nathan: nay sun
Nathaniel: neigh tan yell
Neil: kneel
Nelson: half nelson
Nero: fiddler, knee row
Neville: never, never ill
Nicholas: nick alas
Niles: miles, Niles (rivers)
Noah: ark, no air
Noel: Christmas, no el
Norbert: no berth
Norman: no man, Norseman
Norton: no ton
Ogden: egg den
Olaf: oh laugh, O laugh
Oliver: olive
Orson: oar sun

Oscar: Academy Award
Otis: elevator
Owen: owin'
Ozzie: ah see, I see
Patrick: pat rick(shaw)
Pattie: (meat) patty
Pedro: pet row
Percy: per se, purse see
Perry: bury, pear E, pair eel
Peter: eater, pea eater
Philip: full lip, fill up
Pierce: pierce
Pierre: pea air
Prescott: press cot
Preston: press ton
Quentin: went in
Quincy: win sea
Ralph: rough
Randall: ran doll
Randolph: ran dolph(in)
Randy: ran D
Raoul: rah oil, roll
Raphael: rah fail
Raymond: ray mount
Reggie: red G
Reginald: red G old
Reuben: ruby in
Rex: king (Latin), wrecks
Reynold: ran old
Richard: rich hard
Richie: rich E
Robbie: rob bee
Robert: robber
Robin: robin (red breast), robbin'
Roddy: ruddy, ready
Roderick: ruddy rick(shaw)
Rodney: rod knee
Roland: row land, rollin'
Rolph: roll off
Ronald: run old
Ronnie: run knee, runny
Rory: roar E
Roscoe: rescue
Ross: roars
Rudolph: rude dolph(in), rude doll off
Rufus: roof us
Rupert: rude pat
Russell: rustle
Sammy: ham me, hammy
Samson: biblical strong man
Samuel: some mule
Sandy: sandy
Schuyler: scholar
Scott: Scott(ish kilt)
Sean: shorn, sh yawn
Sebastian: sea bashed in
Seymour: see more
Shelley: shell E, shell ease
Sherman: sure man, German
Sidney: sit knee

Silas: silence, silo
Silvester: silver vest, investor
Simeon: see me on
Simon: says, sigh man
Sinclair: sin clear, sink lair
Solomon: wise man, solo man
Spence: dispense, pens
Spencer: spend sore
Stanley: stand lea
Stephen: steep hen
Stewart: steward
Teddy: ready, dead E
Terence: tear ants
Terry: terry(-cloth towel)
Theo: see O
Theodore: see a door
Thomas: tom-tom, the miss
Timmy: tinny, dim E
Timothy: dim tea
Titus: tied us
Tobias: toe buy us, bias
Toby: toe bee
Tod: toddy, toward
Tommy: tummy
Tonio: tone E O
Tony: toe knee
Tracy: trace E
Tristan: twistin'
Tyrone: throne, tie rowin'
Upton: uptown
Uriah: you're higher
Valentine: heart, valley dine
Vance: vans
Vergil: verge L
Verne: V earn, fern
Vernon: fur nun
Victor: victor
Vince: wince
Vincent: win cent
Vinnie: fini, V knee
Wade: wade
Waldo: wall dough
Wallace: wall lace, walrus
Wally: wall E
Walter: wall tear
Wayne: wane
Wendell: wend L
Wesley: west lea
Whitney: white knee
Wilbur: will burr, will bear
Wilfred: wolf red
Willard: will lard
William: will yam
Willis: will lace
Willy: willy(-nilly), will E
Winston: wins ton
Winthrop: win troop
Wyatt: Y hat, white
Zachary: sack airy, sack hairy
Zeke: seek

Names and their pictorial equivalents

Surnames

Abbott: abbott, I bought
Abelson: a bell son
Abrams: rams, ape rams
Acheson: hatch a son
Ackerman: hacker man
Addison: add a son
Adler: add law, paddler
Alcott: old cot
Alexander: lick sand, lick sander
Altman: old man
Ambrose: ham browse
Anderson: hand and son
Andrews: Ann draws
Arnold: arm old, darn old
Ashburn: ash burn
Atkins: hat kin
Atkinson: hat kin son
Atwater: at water
Austin: awes tin
Bailey: bale E, bay leaf
Baldwin: bald one, bald win
Ballinger: ball injure
Bankhead: bank head
Barnett: bar net, barn hat
Bartlett: bottle it
Baxter: back stir, backs tear
Begley: beg lea
Benham: bend ham
Benson: bend son
Bentley: band lay, English car
Bergman: (ice)berg man
Bernstein: burn stein
Blum: plum
Borden: milk, boarding
Braddock: bad dock
Bradley: brad lay
Bradshaw: bad shore
Brandt: brand
Brennan: burnin', bran nun
Brent: rent, bent
Brewster: brew stir, rooster
Brock: rock, broke
Brody: broad E
Brophy: trophy
Bryant: buy ant, buoyant
Buchanan: blue cannon
Buckley: buckle
Burgess: purchase
Burke: (ice)berg, perk
Byron: buy run
Cabot: cab butt
Cahill: gay hill
Caldwell: cold well, called well
Callahan: call a hand
Cameron: camera on
Campbell: soup, camp bell
Carlson: call son
Carmichael: car mike call

Carson: car son
Carter: car tear, cart her
Cassidy: cast tea
Cates: gates
Cavanaugh: cave in oar
Chamberlain: chamber lain
Chandler: chandelier
Channing: chaining
Chester: chest tear, jester
Chilton: chill ton
Christenson: Christian son
Clark: clock, clerk
Clinton: clean ton
Colby: cold bee
Coleman: cold man, coal man
Collins: collie, (Tom) Collins
Compton: camped on
Cooper: (chicken) coop, coo pair, barrel maker
Cosgrove: cost grove
Costello: cost hello
Coughlin: coughin'
Cowen: cow in
Crandall: ran doll
Crawford: crawl Ford
Crosby: Bing Crosby
Cunningham: cunning ham
Curtis: curt, caught us
Cushing: cushion
Custer: custard
Dalton: dull ton
Davenport: havin' port
Davis: Davis Cup
Dawson: door son
Delaney: delay knee
Denham: den ham
Denton: dent ton
Devlin: devil in
Diaz: dais
Dillon: tillin', dill on
Dixon: ticks on
Dodson: dud son
Donahue: don a hue (color)
Donaldson: darn old son
Donovan: don a van
Dooley: duel lea
Dougherty: dough in tea
Douglas: dug glass, dug less
Dowling: dowel ink, toweling
Driscoll: drizzle
Drummond: drummin'
Duffy: the fee, toughy
Dugan: do again, due again
Duncan: dunkin'
Dunlap: down lap, down lip
Durant: the rent, tour ant
Durham: door ham
Dutton: button, the ton
Dwyer: wire, dryer
Easley: easy, ease lea, easily

Eastman: yeast man
Eberhardt: ever hard
Eldridge: held ridge
Elliott: yacht, lot, L E hot
Ellsworth: el's worth
Endicott: end a cot
Ericson: a rig son
Ettinger: head injure
Everett: ever et (ate), over it
Farley: far lea
Farrell: far rail, barrel
Faulkner: fork near
Ferguson: fur go son
Findlay: find lea, finned lee
Finney: fishy, fini
Fitzgerald: fits chair old
Fitzpatrick: fits pat rick(shaw)
Flanagan: fan again
Fletcher: fetch her, lecher
Foley: fall E, foal
Forrester: forest, forest tear
Foster: forced her
Fowler: foul law, fouler
Frazer: freezer, raise her
Frederick: red rick(shaw)
Freund: friend, frond
Fuller: full, brush
Fulton: full ton
Galbraith: gal breath
Gaynor: gain her
Geller: gala, gal law, kill her
Gibbons: ribbons
Gilbert: kill bed, gill butt
Gillespie: kills pea
Giordano: jawed an O
Gladstone: glad stone
Gleason: glee son, grease on
Gonzales: guns are less
Gordon: garden
Gorman: gore man
Gould: gold, cooled
Graham: cracker, gray ham
Granger: ranger
Gregory: grog airy
Gulliver: giant, gull over
Gunther: gun tore
Haber: hay bear
Haggerty: haggard tea
Halpern: help urn
Hamilton: hammer ton
Hammond: ham mount
Hanrahan: hen ran
Hansen: hansom (cab), handsome
Harrington: herring ton
Harrison: hairy son
Hartley: heart lea, hardly
Hastings: haste inks
Hathaway: hat away
Hawkins: hawk inns
Hayden: hay den
Haynes: hay nose

Hecht: hacked
Hellman: held man
Henderson: hen son
Hendricks: hen tricks
Herbert: her boot
Hernandez: hurryin' ant is
Higgins: he gains
Hobart: whole bar, hope bard
Hobbs: hops
Hodges: hedges
Hoffman: huff man, half man
Hogan: hoe can, whole can
Holden: hold in, hold den
Hooper: hoop
Hopkins: hop kin
Horton: her ton, hurtin'
Houlihan: hold a hand
Houston: house ton, use ton
Howard: how hard, coward
Hubbard: cupboard
Humphrey: home free
Hutchinson: hutch in son
Hyatt: high hat
Hyman: high man
Ingersoll: anger soul
Ingram: ink ram
Irving: serving
Isaacs: eye sacks, ice axe
Jackson: jack son
Jacobs: cobs, Jacob's (ladder)
Jacobson: shake off son
Jacoby: jack cold bee
Jamison: aim at son
Jarrett: jar it
Jeffers: chef airs
Jeffries: chef freeze
Jenkins: chain cans
Johanson: show hand son
Jonas: showin' us
Jordan: jaw down
Joseph: shows off
Josephson: hose off son
Joyce: juice, choice, joyous
Kaiser: geyser, guy sore
Kaufman: cough man
Kearns: coins
Keenan: keen nun
Keith: keys
Kelleher: killer her
Kelly: call E, kill E
Kemp: camp
Kenny: can knee, penny
Keogh: keyhole
Kessler: cast law, wrestler
Kimball: gamble, come ball
Kingsley: kings lea
Knapp: nap, knap(sack)
Knowles: Noels, knolls
Koenig: king, coin nick
Krakauer: crack hour
Kramer: creamer, gray Ma

Improving Your Memory

Kroger: crow gore
Kruger: crew gore, cruder
Lafferty: laugh tea
Lambert: lamb butt
Landau: land dough
Langer: longer, linger
Larson: larceny, arson
Lawrence: law ants, lower ants
Lawson: law son
Lazarus: lather us
Lederman: leader man, letter man
Lehman: layman
Leonard: lean hard
Leopold: leap old, leap pole
Lester: less tear, jester
Leventhal: lovin' tall
Levinson: level son
Levitt: love it, leave it
Lewis: lose, loose, who is
Lieberman: labor man
Lindsey: lint sea, lindy (hop)
Lindstrom: lint strum
Livingston: living stone
Logan: low again
Loring: low ring, lowering
Loughran: lock ran
Lovell: love el
Lovett: love it
Lowell: low el
Lowenthal: low and tall
Lubin: low bin
McCarthy: Mack cart tea
McCormick: Mack core mike
McDonald: Mack darn old
McGraw: Mack raw
MacGregor: Mack rigor
McKay: Mack hay, my key
McMann: Mack man
Mahoney: Ma hold knee
Maloney: alone knee, baloney
Manning: man ink, manning
Marcus: mark us
Marshall: marshal, Ma shall
Martin: Ma tin, mar tin
Martinez: martinets
Martinson: Ma tin son
Matheson: matter son
Matthew(s): mat ewe(s)
Maxwell: makes well, mix well
Maynard: mane hard
Mercer: mercy
Meredith: married it
Metcalf: met calf
Michaelson: mike call son
Middleton: middle ton
Mitchell: shell, mitt shell
Montgomery: mount gum airy

Morales: morals, more or less
Morgan: more can
Morrison: marry son
Morse: moss
Morton: mutton, more ton
Moynihan: mind a hand
Murray: more ray
Nash: gnash
Nathanson: no tan son
Nichols: nickels
Nicholson: nickel son
Noonan: new nun
Norman: no man, Norseman
Norris: no risk
Norton: no ton, gnaw ton
Nugent: new gent
O'Brien: oh burn, brine
O'Connor: O con her
O'Donnell: ode down hill
Ogden: egg den, egged on
O'Malley: home alley
Oppenheim: open home
O'Reilly: oar oily
O'Rourke: O roar
Ortiz: oared ease
Osborne: is born
Osgood: is good
Otis: elevator
Owen: owin'
Padgett: patch it, page it
Palmer: palm, palm Ma
Papadopoulos: Papa topple us
Patterson: pat a son
Pawley: pulley
Pearce: pierce
Pearson: pierce son
Pendleton: peddle ton
Perlman: pearl man
Peterson: eater son
Phelps: helps
Phillips: full lips
Platt: plate
Poindexter: point egg stir
Pollock: pole lock
Prentiss: parent is, parenthesis

Proctor: doctor
Quentin: went in
Quinn: win
Raleigh: roll lea, raw lea, roll E
Ramirez: ram ear ess (curve)
Randall: ran doll
Randolph: ran dolph(in)
Raymond: ray mount
Reeves: reefs
Reinhard: rain hard
Reynolds: ran old
Richardson: rich son, rich yard son
Rigney: rig knee
Riley: rye lea, rile E
Riordan: rear down, reared on
Rivera: river
Robeson: robe son
Robinson: robbin' son
Romero: roam arrow
Rooney: ruin knee
Rossiter: rose sitter
Rudolph: rude dolph(in)
Rutherford: rode a Ford
Ryan: cryin', rind, Rhine (River)
Samuelson: some mules on
Sanchez: send chest
Sanders: sand, senders
Saunders: sanders, sun doors
Saxon: sacks on
Schultz: shields, shoots
Seaton: see ton, sit on
Sedgwick: search wick
Seiden: side in, sigh den
Seward: steward, seaward
Seymour: see more
Schaeffer: shave four
Shannon: shine on, chainin'
Sheehan: sheen
Shelton: shell ton, shelter
Sheridan: share a den
Sherman: show man, sure man

Simpson: simple son, simper son
Sinclair: sin clear
Slater: slayed her
Sommers: summers
Spaulding: sprawled ink
Spenser: expense her
Stafford: staff ford
Stoddard: stood hard
Sutherland: other land
Sweeney: sweet knee, sweety
Tate: tight, tea ate
Thatcher: that chair, thatcher
Thompson: tom-tom son
Thorpe: tore up
Tompkins: thump kin
Travers: traverse
Tucker: tuck'er
Ullmann: old man
Unger: hunger, hung her
Vance: vans
Vaughn: warn
Vincent: win cent
Wallace: wall lace, wall is, wall ace
Walsh: waltz
Warner: warn her
Warrington: warring ton
Watson: what son
Waverly: wave early, waver lea
Welch: grape juice, welsh
Wesley: west lea
Whalen: whalin', whale, wailing
Whitney: white knee
Whittaker: wit taker, with a car
Wilkinson: milkin' son
Williamson: will yam son
Winston: Churchill
Winthrop: win troop
Woolsey: wool see
Wrightson: write son
York: cork
Young: baby
Zachary: sack airy

For further reference

Cermak, Laird S.
  Improving Your Memory
  McGraw-Hill
Gallant, Roy A.
  Memory: How It Works and How to Improve It
  Four Winds Press
Lorayne, Harry
  How to Develop a Super-Power Memory
  Frederick Fell

Lorayne, Harry
  Remembering People
  Stein and Day
Lorayne, Harry, and Lucas, Jerry
  The Memory Book
  Stein and Day

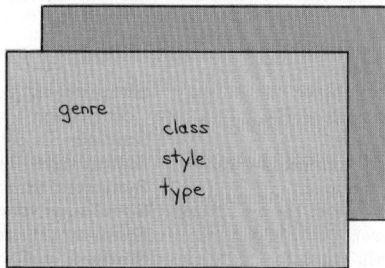

genre
class
style
type

Building Your Vocabulary

"There is a weird power in a spoken word . . . And a word carries far—very far—deals destruction through time as the bullets go flying through space."
Joseph Conrad, 1857–1924

The world recognizes Joseph Conrad as one of the great English novelists. Yet he knew little of the language before he was twenty. A Polish orphan, the teenage Conrad sailed on British ships, where he learned English from his fellow seamen. Conrad was awed by the power of words, and set about becoming a writer. The quotation above is from his masterpiece, *Lord Jim.*

"A powerful agent is the right word. Whenever we come upon one of those intensely right words in a book or a newspaper the resulting effect is physical as well as spiritual, and electrically prompt."
Mark Twain, 1835–1910

Starting his career as a twelve-year-old apprentice newspaper printer, Mark Twain never lost his ambition to be a Mississippi riverboat pilot. Twain, whose real name was Samuel Clemens, used life along the river as background for *The Adventures of Tom Sawyer* and *Adventures of Huckleberry Finn.* Like Joseph Conrad, he was self-taught. Both writers respected the power of words and used them with extreme precision.

A key to success. Those women and men who possess a large vocabulary usually advance more rapidly in their careers and ultimately attain more responsible positions than those whose vocabularies are limited. The Human Engineering Laboratory has studied thousands of successful executives pursuing a wide variety of careers. It found that the only trait the executives held in common was their command of large vocabularies.

What does "to command a large vocabulary" mean? Knowing the meanings of words is part of it; but another part is knowing how to use those words effectively. Other sections in this volume help you learn how to write and speak well. See "Writing Effective Letters," pages 266-301, "Improving Your Reading," pages 302-327, and "Improving Your Speech," pages 244-265. You will also want to consult volume 1, pages 4-77, and volume 2, pages 318-347.

Do not assume that because you know the jargon of your own field, as in accounting, say, or nursing, law, or medicine, that you can communicate successfully. Just think of your own doctor, whom you, as a lay person, may not understand because he uses only incomprehensible medical words. For most people, a vocabulary rich in depth and wide in scope is more useful than one limited to the confines of a particular field. A famous professor at Columbia University once said that graduates from the English department generally ended their careers earning more money and having more responsible positions than graduates from any other field.

So you will gain considerably from the mastery of a large vocabulary. When you are interviewed for a job, or are talking to a manager at your current place of employment, the words you use are an important part of the impression you make.

Even before you are interviewed for a job or a promotion, you may be asked to take a vocabulary test. A passing grade is a necessity. To gain that passing grade, you will want to know the meanings of hundreds of new words. You will learn, and remember, 300 to 400 interesting new words as you read the next three dozen pages. But more than that, you will find three full pages of hints and techniques for passing verbal/vocabulary tests, together with questions similar to the ones you can expect to find in examination booklets.

Memorizing lists of new words and their definitions is not a recommended method for improving your vocabulary. There are several more effective ways to acquire a larger stock of words and the ability to use them correctly.

Those paths to a more powerful vocabulary are explored on the pages of this section. Whichever method you choose to follow, it will work best when you have begun building your own *Word Power* file.

Your Word Power file.
Keep a file card or small notebook in your pocket or handbag. During the day, jot down unknown or puzzling words that you read in newspapers, magazines, or on signs, or hear in conversations or on radio broadcasts. You might even overhear an unknown term as two strangers are talking together near you on a crowded bus.

Wherever you come across it, write the word on your card. If possible, try to include a portion of the way it was used in conversation or a portion of the sentence in which you read it. A typical day's entries might look like the cards at the right.

Using one of the new techniques you have mastered, there is a good chance you will have an approximate idea of the meanings of these new words. But your aim is to use more words with greater accuracy, so approximate meanings are not good enough.

The solution: At the end of each day, write each word on a separate 3×5 card. Put into your own words a dictionary's definition of the word, and enter that on the card. Also add a synonym or two if the dictionary lists them. (A **synonym** is a word that has the *same meaning* as the original word. *Grand* and *magnificent* are synonyms, as are *punish* and *discipline*.)

Keep the cards in alphabetical order. When you add new entries in your *Word Power* file, select a handful of the existing cards at random. Glance at the words but not their meanings. Test yourself. Reinforce the power of your burgeoning vocabulary. (There's a good one to start with: **burgeoning.**)

Keep a notebook in your pocket or purse so you can jot down immediately those new, unknown words you meet in your daily activities.

Building Your Vocabulary

How do you rate?

How much larger will your vocabulary be when you have mastered most of the techniques in this section? That depends on the effort you expend, beginning today. The percentage of your gain can be measured by taking this simple test, recording your score, and a month from now comparing it with your score on the test that appears on page 237.

For each of the questions, select the one term that *most nearly defines* the meaning of the word in dark print. Other readers will be using this book, so please do not write in it; mark your selections on a separate sheet of paper.

1. **acrimony** a) agility; b) court-ordered payments; c) bitterness; d) dryness

2. **adulation** a) growing up; b) adding water; c) hero worship; d) mixture

3. **appellation** a) name; b) maintain; c) small bullet; d) country

4. **capillary** a) form of butterfly; b) slender tube; c) large quantity; d) head, or top

5. **cobalt** a) metallic element; b) African antelope; c) partner; d) garden tool

6. **covert** a) secret; b) ditch, or gutter; c) lid; d) quarrelsome

7. **destitute** a) illegal; b) wicked; c) poverty-stricken; d) enhanced

8. **diffident** a) unlike; b) shy; c) argumentative; d) shining

9. **diurnal** a) under water; b) easily fooled; c) selfish; d) daily

10. **effigy** a) easy task; b) image; c) degree; d) ratio of output to input

11. **exude** a) put away; b) clear out; c) investigate; d) ooze

12. **famished** a) done, completed; b) starved; c) mixed up; d) related, as a cousin or aunt

13. **florid** a) warm; b) ornate; c) damp; d) southern

14. **glean** a) gather bit by bit; b) tilt dangerously; c) flash of light; d) smooth

15. **grotesque** a) bizarre; b) cavelike; c) comical; d) hyacinth

16. **martial** a) art; b) judo; c) general; d) warlike

17. **mendicant** a) remedy; b) ointment; c) beggar; d) prescription

18. **migrant** a) traveler; b) move to another country; c) severe headache; d) worker

19. **natal** a) Asian; b) living under water; c) birth; d) federal

20. **phobia** a) small bird; b) fear; c) drowning; d) falling

21. **pinnacle** a) peak; b) card game; c) evergreen tree; d) sail

22. **sallow** a) empty; b) yellow; c) not deep; d) filled with salt water

23. **tactile** a) crawling; b) touchable; c) pointy; d) cottonlike material

24. **troll** a) streetcar; b) mischievous dwarf; c) drumbeat; d) three of a kind

25. **usury** a) putting on makeup; b) illegal interest rate; c) impersonation; d) counterfeiting

Answers. Score one point for each correct answer. 1, c; 2, c; 3, a; 4, b; 5, a; 6, a; 7, c; 8, b; 9, d; 10, b; 11, d; 12, b; 13, b; 14, a; 15, a; 16, d; 17, c; 18, a; 19, c; 20, b; 21, a; 22, b; 23, b; 24, b; 25, b.

Analyze your score. A score of 25 is perfect (and quite rare), 22 to 24 very good, 18 to 21 above average, and 15 to 18 the score that most adults achieve. With *Word Power* you will gain during the next few weeks. It should be interesting to see how much better you do when you test yourself again.

A permanent memory system

Suppose you are reading a news magazine and come across this sentence: "She attributed the superiority of her tomatoes to the **humus** in which she grew them." You think humus has something to do with the amount of moisture in the gardener's backyard, but you are not sure. You look up the word in your dictionary and learn that it means "organic matter; decayed plants that provide nutriments to soil."

If you merely read a definition in a dictionary, make a mental note of it, and go on with your reading, your chances of retaining the meaning are slim. If you write the new word down, however, you greatly increase the probability that you will remember the meaning of **humus.** Experts in educational psychology say that the act of writing increases a person's ability to remember by as much as 100 percent.

But you are not an ordinary reader who wants to learn the meaning of an occasional new word. You are actively engaged in a campaign to radically increase your *Word Power*. To reinforce your learning process, you require additional techniques to make the new words you encounter every day a part of your working vocabulary.

Review the four-step system that follows.

Four steps to a larger vocabulary

1. **Understand what the word means, in your own terms.** If the dictionary tells you that **perfidy** means "a calculated breach of faith," do not try to add the word and that meaning to your active vocabulary in that form. Instead, read the entire dictionary entry and rephrase it, perhaps as "acts of a traitor; deliberate breaking of trust; spies engage in *perfidious* activities."

2. **Write the meaning on a card.** It requires some discipline to make a habit of the daily transference of words from your pocket notes to a permanent file card. You may be tempted to let it go for the weekend, but weekends often are more crammed with activities than we thought they would be, and file-building may be postponed yet again. The way to guarantee success is to establish a routine: fill out your file cards before you settle down for an evening's television watching or magazine reading. And keep your pocket card with you during those two activities so that any new words you hear or read will be included in the next day's entries.

   If a newspaper or magazine is the source of a word, you may want to clip the sentence from the page; then you can tape the printed sentence right on your *Word Power* card.

3. **Add the new card to your file.** An empty box, any shoebox-sized container, makes a fine storage space for your *Word Power* cards. If you have a special interest or two, you may want to color-code the cards that pertain to it for extra review. Words from the world of law and order, for example, could have green dots in the cards' upper right corners.

   Do you own a home computer? If you do, it will be easy to program a cumulative list of words, definitions, and examples of their use. Prepared software packages for vocabulary building are available, but you will find them less effective than the *Word Power* file you build for yourself.

4. **Systematically use your file.** During your first week of file-building, you may accumulate 20 or more *Word Power* cards. Once you have that many, you are ready to establish a routine that will reinforce your familiarity with the words' meanings.

   All that is required is to take out a handful of cards. Do not shuffle them, or they will have to be repositioned in alphabetical order later. Just lift one card from the pack, glance at the main word, and define it without looking at the printed definition. Then read the definition to see if you remember it correctly. If you do, replace the card and select another word. If you get it wrong, jot down the word on a list you keep for this purpose. A day or two later, look at the list and try to recall the word's meaning. If you remember a new word correctly for several days, in all probability you will remember it for many years.

   By reaching into the box and randomly choosing eight or ten words to test yourself on each day, you are certain to repeat many of the cards. Do not abandon the system. Repetitive practice, as with an athlete's training, brings superior performance.

How words are used

Words, like bricks or shingles, do not have much value when standing alone—a single brick on a patch of bare ground, or a solitary word on a page, is not of much use. But when a number are arranged in a purposeful pattern, both words and bricks are extremely useful.

When you read a newspaper and notice an unfamiliar word, you are seeing it in **context.** That is, you are seeing it in use, among other words. Context can give you clues to an unknown word's meaning. Often, the clues are so strong that you will be able to define the word without **recourse** to a dictionary.

The sense of a sentence. The way in which *recourse* was used in the previous sentence gives you a strong clue as to its meaning. "Without recourse to a dictionary" might mean without returning to a dictionary, or perhaps, without the heaviness of a dictionary. But neither of those possibilities makes much sense. What does make sense is being able to understand the word's meaning without turning to or consulting a dictionary. And that is exactly what *recourse* means in the context of that sentence.

Echo words. At times, the context of an unfamiliar word includes another word that closely duplicates its meaning. "She had never before seen on a tray so many beautiful glasses as she saw on Mrs. March's large **salver.**" In this sentence, it is easily understood that the glasses are, at the same time, on a tray and on a *salver.* The two words have the same meaning; they are *synonyms.*

Easy opposites. Just as echo words, or *synonyms,* are strong context clues, so are opposites, or *antonyms.* "Carl's blueprint specified rigid sheets of plastic, but the ones he brought were **malleable.**" The key clues here are "rigid" and "but." In the context, **malleable** refers to a kind of plastic that is the opposite of rigid. It is correct to assume that the target word means pliable or easily bent.

Read on a bit further. The last of the more common contextual techniques takes you beyond the sentence in which the unknown word appears. If there is no clue to the word's meaning in that sentence—read on. The definition may become clear a sentence or two later. Here is an example: "We recognized those sagging **jowls.** No one else ever had such baggy *jaws.*" There you have a clear definition of the wanted word, right in the next sentence.

On this page and the following pages are paragraphs, each containing several unfamiliar words. Examine those words in the context of their sentences and paragraphs. Then check your conclusions against the ex-

planations printed right below the paragraphs. Of course, you will want to add to your *Word Power* file all words that are new or that you never have used in conversation.

The six-story **edifice** symbolized the values of **bourgeois, bustling** prewar Chicago. The building's solid **facade,** though granite and limestone, had a certain warmth. Built as the **abode** of bankers, it still was **accessible** by trolley car and other public transportation.

In the first two sentences, we learn that the paragraph describes a six-story building. *Edifice,* therefore, means building. *Bourgeois* and *bustling* are harder; you might guess the pair of words refers to busy or businesslike values of prewar Chicago. The precise definition of *bourgeois* is respectable, middle-class, property-owning. *Bustling* means busy, hurrying, or active.

Facade, a form of the word "face," refers to the front of a building. "The *abode* of bankers" can be understood to mean, loosely, their home. And if the building is *accessible* by public transportation, those trolleys have access to it; they can reach it easily.

Though the reason can't be pinned down, Mackey strikes some viewers as a **vaguely** unprofessional anchorman. It might be his slight speech **impediment** (trouble with "r's") or his **wry,** dry sense of humor. Yet, among each night's **welter** of disturbing facts and new worries, Mackey brings comfort to a large audience.

Vaguely tells us something about how or why some viewers think Mackey is unprofessional. Studying the sentence, we see that *vaguely* echoes the "can't be pinned down" quality of their feelings. *Vaguely* means indistinct, or no definite reason. If Mackey has trouble pronouncing "r's," something is standing in the way of clear speech; that is exactly what *impediment* means: an obstacle.

Wry and *dry,* when applied to sense of humor, are synonyms. The two words have the same meaning. *Welter* is not surrounded by enough clues to provide an accurate definition, but it clearly refers to a number of "facts and worries." Later, when you look it up, you will find it means a miscellaneous, hodge-podge grouping; a jumble.

Building Your Vocabulary

Try to visualize the situation, or context, in which new words appear and you may be able to guess their meanings and remember them better.

Her friends at work **twitted** Elaine about her **obsession** with her new grandchild. She was a **caricature** of an adoring grandma, **incessantly recounting** examples of the baby's brilliance. And, of course, she carried **myriad** photographs of the infant.

Her friends probably would not be mean or cruel to Elaine, but they would tease her and make fun of her constant bragging about her granddaughter. *Twitted* means teased. Elaine's mind is occupied with thoughts of the infant: she is *obsessed* with those thoughts. Drawings or actors' portrayals of easily recognizable characters, done in an exaggerated manner, are *caricatures*.

To *recount* a story is to tell it over again, and to do it continually, or without ceasing, is to do it *incessantly*. (Sometimes a story or anecdote is called an "account." Telling it again is to *recount* it.) If you did not know the meaning of *myriad*, you might guess that Elaine would carry very many photographs of the baby. *Myriad* does mean a very large number.

I wondered about Joanne's interest in **exotic** Peruvian shawls. The ancient woolens were harsh and too rough for comfort. The designs were childlike and **rudimentary**, almost primitive. Later, when her husband **confided** that Joanne was a **curator** at the Field Museum, I understood.

It would be difficult, from the context in which it is used, to know exactly what is meant by *exotic*. But the flavor, the general sense, of "exotic Peruvian shawls" indicates that the shawls are strange or foreign in appearance. And that is very close to the exact meaning of *exotic*: unusual, from another part of the world.

Rudimentary designs are described as "childlike" and "primitive." It is clear that the word means basic, elementary, or an early form. You may recognize *confided* as a form of the word *confidential* (secret). When "Joanne's husband *confided*," he made a private, almost secret, statement.

We can associate Joanne's interest in Peruvian weavings, and also the word *curator*, with her work at the museum. Actually, a *curator* is a person who is in charge of a department in a museum, library, or art gallery.

A soccer superstar for a dozen years, Ivor remained an **enigma** to his fans. They could not understand his childlike, stubborn **petulance** and his sudden temper **tantrums.** At the same time, they puzzled over his equally sudden bursts of **altruism.** Within moments, Ivor could be as generous as he had been **irascible** and mean.

If Ivor's fans could not understand his behavior, even after twelve years, *enigma* must refer to his puzzling habits. An *enigma* is a puzzle. Clues to the meaning of *petulance* are the echo words "childlike, stubborn." Ivor is grumpy, with flashes of quick, unreasonable anger. You can assume that his *tantrums* are fits of bad temper. He might kick the ball up into the stands, or shout rude remarks to the fans.

If Ivor has all those unpleasant traits, and *altruism* is strangely different, it might be related to "generous," mentioned in the last sentence. That is exactly right; *altruism* means unselfish help to others. Now, with all we know about Ivor, *irascible* becomes quite clear. It is a form of *irate,* and it means easily angered.

Now that you have seen how the *context method* works when **assessing** the meanings of words, you may be ready to use it with some harder examples. (Did *assessing* stump you? Or did you recognize that it means estimating; forming an opinion of something?) The sample sentences on this page use less of the echo words technique, described on page 210, than the sentences you have worked on so far. But the other techniques for using context clues still **obtain.** (Note the unusual use of *obtain.* Very likely you are familiar only with the meaning to get, or gain possession of. In this instance, *obtain* completes the thought that other techniques exist or are accepted.)

meticulous

Very careful about small details.
Almost too concerned. "Precise."

   experience entering her kitchen. The spices
   were lined up <u>meticulously</u> on a shelf
   carefully lined with heavy white paper.
   Every pot, every pan, was
Syn: fussy; super-careful

Make sure your Word Power *file grows every day. In a short time you will learn many new words. Use them in your conversation and writing.*

Anyone who owns a cat knows that domestic **felines** have certain behavior patterns. They are **unremitting** in their care of their fur. All cats' tails **undulate** gently when cats hunt. And they are **discriminating** eaters, refusing new or suspicious kinds of food.

This short article is about *felines,* the family of animals that includes lions, tigers, and "domestic *felines*"—the ones that live with people. Cats. *Unremitting* has few context clues. You may have guessed, though, that it means unstopping or ceaseless.

If you have ever seen a cat creeping toward an unsuspecting bird, you know its tail waves gently. It *undulates. Discrimination,* as we most commonly use it, means to select or choose certain people, for unfair reasons. But *discriminating* can refer to the careful selection of certain objects. Cats are quite particular—or *discriminating*—about the food they will accept.

The Milwaukee-based sporting goods company is known for its **innovation.** It was the first to develop a safe, **incombustible** tent, and it pioneered an unsinkable, one-hulled **catamaran.** The company's sales are the **cynosure** of the industry.

If the company is first to develop one product and "pioneered" another, it is known for its new ideas. That is what *innovative* means: creative. A safe tent might be one of several kinds, including one that will not blow over. But an *incombustible* tent is one that cannot burn. *Catamarans* almost always are boats with two bottoms, or hulls, so a reference to an *innovative,* unsinkable item of sporting goods with one hull provides a strong context clue to *catamaran's* meaning. *Cynosure* refers to sales that are the envy of the industry; other companies admire and look up to that company's record.

Denizens of towns and cities never **encounter** deer in their natural **habitats.** They **visualize** Bambi or Rudolph, lovable big-eyed creatures. Farmers and **exurbanites,** often **plagued** by deer, see them as **voracious** animals that devour crops and shrubbery. Moreover, the **marauders** never travel alone, but in herds.

Reading all four sentences of the paragraph and then coming back to the target words will make the words' meanings clearer. *Denizens* must be people who are in towns and cities; actually, it means residents or inhabitants—people who live there. *Encounter,* in this context, obviously means to meet or see deer. The exact meaning is to meet unexpectedly. What could be a deer's natural *habitat?* Not towns or cities, but the woods and fields where deer live. (Their *habitation* is their home, or where they are most likely to be found.) You know that *audiovisual* is something you hear and see, and that *invisible* means cannot be seen. *Visualize* is related to those words; it means to see in your mind, or to imagine. City people imagine that deer are big-eyed, lovable creatures.

Urbanites are people who live in cities. *Exurbanites,* together with farmers, live far out from cities. You know that a *plague* is a disaster, generally an epidemic of serious sickness or disease. The word has come to mean any severe annoyance or nuisance. "Animals that devour crops and shrubbery" is a strong clue to the meaning of *voracious*—a huge appetite; greedy; eats great amounts of food.

Marauders is more difficult; you may have seen an athletic team with that name, and recall them using a pirate as their symbol. Like pirates, *marauders* roam around, raiding and stealing others' property. They never travel alone, but in bands.

Test questions. There are two kinds of test questions that often appear in civil service, employment, and college entrance examinations. Both kinds ask you to define words in the context of a sentence. **Supply a synonym.**

Their lawyer, unfortunately, avoided the **salient** issues.

scrupulous   prominent   foreign   childish

You are asked to select the word among the four choices that most closely duplicates the meaning of *salient*.

Starting with *scrupulous*, which means conscientious, or very careful, we see it makes no sense in that sentence. *Prominent*, if we recognize it as meaning standing out or important, does make sense. *Foreign?* Not likely that it would be unfortunate if the lawyer avoided the *foreign* issues. And the last choice, *childish*, makes no sense in the context of the sentence.

In most questions of this kind, the possibilities narrow down to two choices, as the other two words are unlikely or obviously unsuitable. When all four, or three of the four, choices are difficult new words, selecting the right answer becomes considerably harder. You will find some of those difficult questions in the samples on this page. All the words you do not know should be added to your *Word Power* file.

Learning synonyms

1. The Red Cross set up emergency tents in the **devastated** areas of the valley.
   remote   wasted   elevated   largest

   1. *Devastated* means *wasted*. Think about the Red Cross's mission. Few people live in *remote*, or far away, sections of the valley. There is no obvious reason to set up tents in *elevated*, high regions, nor in the *largest* areas of the valley.

2. After failing two inspections, the diner's license was **revoked.**
   revised   released   reissued   recalled

   2. *Revoked* means *recalled*. It is clear that the diner lost its license, so *revised* is inappropriate; it means fixed, or made over. *Released*, a commonly used word, does not fit either. And the license would not be *reissued*, or given out again, if the diner failed to pass inspections.

3. Sharks were seen in the **vicinity**, but all three divers continued their work.
   nearby area   deeper water   emptiness undersea wreck

   3. *Vicinity* means *nearby area*. *Deeper water* and *undersea wreck* might make sense, but *vicinity* is used in everyday language, and should be recognized. *Emptiness* is totally out of place in the context of the sentence.

4. Outraged parents and dog lovers sent **irate** letters to the school board.
   legal   lengthy   angry   questioning

   4. *Irate* means *angry*. "Outraged" is the clue to the tone of the parents' letters. The letters might have been *legal, lengthy,* or *questioning,* but *angry* is the word called for by the context of the sentence.

5. Is the association a **vestige** of times past, when streets were dusty and unpaved?
   trace   memory   religion   raiment

   5. *Vestige* means *trace*, or remnant, of something that has disappeared over the years. *Religion* and *raiment* (clothing) do not make sense. *Memory* comes close, but it would be awkward referring to an association as a *memory* of times past.

6. $700,000 was granted to a **consortium** of four states, to form a defense against tax evaders.
   legislatures   association   treasury   police

   6. A *consortium* is an *association* or grouping together of people or organizations, for a specific purpose. Several churches might form a *consortium* calling for stricter laws against drunk drivers. *Legislatures*, a plural word, should not follow the singular article 'a.' One *treasury* cannot belong to four states. It would be unusual for *police* to deal with tax evaders.

Fill in the blank. The second type of context-based examination question is like the first kind in that you are offered a choice of four words. But it has a slightly different format. Instead of supplying a synonym for the target word as it is used in a sentence, you are asked to fill in the word—from among the four choices—that best completes the sentence.

Your procedure will be much like the one you followed in answering type 1 questions. Try each of the four words. Think how it relates to the central thought of the sentence. Eliminate the one or two impossible selections. Does either of the remaining words conflict with any of the **adjectives** (describing words)? Even if you are unfamiliar with a new word's meaning, does it give you a feeling of belonging—of not destroying the sentence's logic?

Choose the right word

1. It was the same _____ whose advice Julius Caesar had ignored.
   criminal   gesture   soothsayer   cravat

   1. A *soothsayer* reads such signs as cloud formation or tea leaves, and gives advice. He is a fortune teller. (An old term for truth was *sooth;* a soothsayer 'says the truth.') Julius Caesar ignored a fortune teller's advice, not a *criminal* or a *gesture*. A *cravat* is a kind of necktie or scarf.

2. We hear about adolescent _____, yet most teenagers in this town are pleasant and likable.
   translucence   alienation   allegory   viability

   2. *Alienation* is the right word. *Aliens* are foreign; they do not belong to the society in which they find themselves. Adolescents sometimes feel out of place, or isolated: *alienated*. The clue here is knowing that this town's adolescents behave in a manner opposite to *alienation;* they are pleasant and likable.

3. Imagine Joan's _____ after she prepared that marvelous barbecue and only three guests showed up.
   frustration   cuisine   perception   hallucination

   3. *Frustration* is what Joan felt. It means discouragement; a sense of being unable to accomplish one's goal. *Cuisine* is the French word for kitchen; it is an awkward, improper fit. *Perception* means vision or seeing. *Hallucinations* are imaginary sights, nightmares, or the visions of unstable persons.

4. Maria's family was _____, in their sorrow, by a visit from the bishop.
   rewarded   cosseted   controlled   consoled

   4. Maria's family was comforted in their sorrow; they were *consoled* by the bishop's visit. He brought them *consolation,* or sympathy, as well as comfort. There is no reason he would try to *reward* or *control* the family. The fourth choice, *cosseted,* means pampered, petted, or made a great fuss of.

5. When a modern shopping mall opened, the downtown merchants were forced to use strong _____ against it.
   textiles   tactics   statutes   covenants

   5. The merchants used strong *tactics* against their competitor, the shopping mall. Those were maneuvers or actions. Two others of the four choices, *statutes* and *covenants,* are on the right track. They refer to laws. *Textiles* is entirely wrong; it means fabrics or materials, like woven cotton in a dress.

6. Secrecy surrounded the ambassador's plans, and his _____ chef was transferred to another post.
   rustic   perceptive   garrulous   esteemed

   6. The ambassador's chef was *garrulous,* or talkative. *Rustic* refers to country life; rough and simple furniture is called *rustic* furniture. One who sees meanings is called *perceptive*. And though the chef might have been *esteemed*—thought well of, or honored—that would have been no reason for the ambassador to transfer him to another post.

Natural settings for words

A powerful aid to remembering the meanings of new words is to discover them in settings that hold interest for you: in the pages of a magazine or book, or on a television or radio broadcast. Here, where your aim is to come into contact with as many new words as possible, the grouping of target words serves as an effective substitute for those "natural" settings.

On the next few pages you will find such headings as *Health and medicine, Films and theater,* and *Sports.* For each category, there will be a list of six words, followed by six sentences, each containing one blank space. Select the one word from the list that best completes the thought expressed in each sentence. Below the sentences you will find the correct solutions; often, there also will be a brief explanation for the choice.

Note that you will not be able to use the context method for defining all the words in this section, but it can be applied to many of them. Every word here, though, is a perfect one to add to your growing *Word Power* file. Make out a card for each and you will add more than six dozen new words to your vocabulary.

Try creating natural settings of your own and provide new words to fit them. Be sure to make your *Word Power* file grow every day.

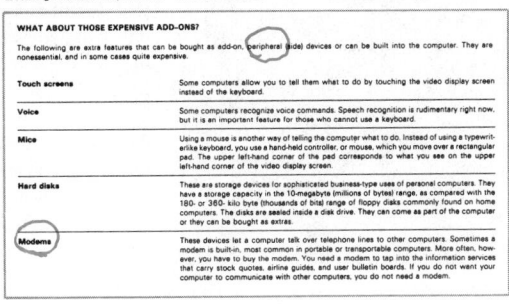

New words in natural settings

Health and medicine

insomnia
intermittently
epidemiology
anatomical
chronic
sedentary

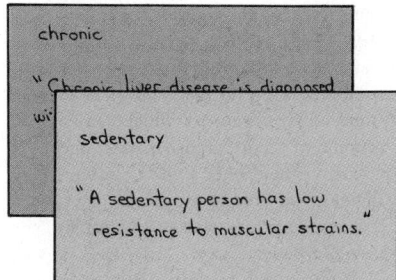

1. _____ liver disease is diagnosed without much difficulty using techniques easily available to most doctors.
2. A _____ person has much lower resistance to muscular strains than one who is active.
3. The symptoms were not present constantly, but appeared _____.
4. Determining rates of disease in population groups, and studying the causes, is what _____ is all about.
5. The amount of sleep necessary for good health varies from person to person, and _____ can cause serious discomfort.
6. Through endless study of the body, Galen, who died in 203 A.D., became known as the father of _____ research.

1. *chronic:* lasting for a long time; continual. It refers to time, as in *chronometer,* a precise clock or watch. **2.** *sedentary:* too much sitting; too little exercise. An active person is exactly the opposite of one who is *sedentary.* **3.** *intermittently:* stopped and started. The symptoms appeared and disappeared, or were *intermittent,* which is why they were not present constantly. **4.** *epidemiology:* the sentence itself is a definition of the word. It is related to *epidemic,* a widespread incidence of disease in a community or territory. **5.** *insomnia:* inability to sleep; unhealthy wakefulness. A *somnolent* person is a sleepy one; *insomnia* is the opposite condition. **6.** *anatomical:* the structure of the body, or any of its parts. *Anatomy* sometimes is used in its wider sense, meaning a general structure: She understood the *anatomy* of company management, and was well paid for her knowledge.

New words in natural settings

Buying a home

prospectus
amortize
condominium
panorama
amenities
modular

1. We decided to buy the house when we stood on the front steps and saw the _____ of autumn leaves.
2. Did you know that your neighbors were musicians before you bought the _____?
3. The description in the _____ was far different from the building we saw when we drove out to the lake.
4. "Are you prepared to _____ this debt in 20 years?" asked the banker.
5. It was a wonderful day for the Kroeger family, for their _____ home was finally delivered from the factory.
6. The _____, including the carpeting, were attractive, but they brought the price up beyond our reach.

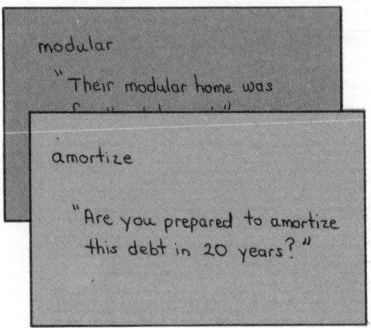

1. *panorama:* unlimited view over a wide area. **2.** *condominium:* apartment or portion of a building owned by its occupants, while the rest of the building, and the grounds around it, are owned in common with other owners. **3.** *prospectus:* a brochure (booklet) that describes a property offered for sale. A *prospect* is an expectation; a *prospectus* tells what you can expect from your purchase of this property. **4.** *amortize:* to pay off a debt in a specified amount of time—in this instance, 20 years. **5.** *modular:* made in parts that are later assembled. A child's building blocks are *modular* toys. A *modular* home, like a block construction, is composed of separate parts that fit together. **6.** *amenities:* things that increase an object's value or comfort. A swimming pool, sun deck, and wall-to-wall carpeting are *amenities.* Another use of the word refers to social courtesies or pleasantries: Charlie overlooked the *amenities,* and Martha never forgave him for his rudeness.

Design and fashion

nonchalant
pretentious
beguiling
intricately
repertoire
hybrid

1. The furniture seemed a _____ of two styles, French provincial and early American.
2. We admired Robert's _____ appearance as he strolled along the boulevard with his fiancée.
3. Doris selected a _____ version of a modern classic, the coatdress.
4. Above the mantel was a mirror with an _____ carved wooden frame.
5. Kate decided not to buy the bracelet, calling it "_____ and showy."
6. After she had attended four sessions of the sewing class, Beverly's _____ of techniques had tripled.

1. *hybrid:* mixture. The word's origin is in the natural sciences, where selected strains of plants and animals are bred to produce *hybrids* with mixed characteristics. **2.** *nonchalant:* a word borrowed from the French, meaning casual, cool, unworried. Robert's carefree appearance could also be described as *debonair.* **3.** *beguiling:* demanding attention, or distracting. At the same time, it means charming or delightful. *Bewitching* is sometimes used as a synonym for *beguiling.* **4.** *intricately:* the frame has many carefully carved details; *intricate* means elaborate, or done with a great deal of skill and effort. **5.** *pretentious:* demanding attention that is not justified. *Showy* is an echo word with almost the same meaning and tone; so is *ostentatious,* which can be added to your *Word Power* file. **6.** *repertoire:* a person's, or group's, range of skills and accomplishments. This word, like *nonchalant* and many others in the world of fashion and design, is borrowed from the French. It originally referred to the songs, plays, or compositions that dramatic or musical groups were able to perform. An English version of the word, used in that theatrical sense, is *repertory.*

hybrid

Building Your Vocabulary

Sports

foiled
caliber
interim
regimen
grimaced
spate

1. No smoking.
2. No beer.
3. No junk food.
4. Regular practice.
5. In bed by 10.

regimen

1. When Dr. Newbold retired, Chris Stanley was named as _____ head coach of the Blue Devils.
2. Josephine had unusual natural ability, but was unwilling to stick to the training _____ demanded of professional athletes.
3. He fell on the field and _____ in intense pain after colliding with Parrish.
4. A _____ of matches against weak opponents gave Miss Yerby a strong boost in the tournament standings.
5. An eighth-inning triple by Hunt _____ pitcher Ken Leslie's attempt at a no-hitter.
6. Reporters agreed Miss Bryant was a superior player, but not quite Olympic _____.

1. *interim:* temporary, or the time between. Chris Stanley's appointment is not permanent. He will act as head coach only between the time that Dr. Newbold resigned and a new coach is appointed. **2.** *regimen:* a system or process; routine procedures. Governments, or *regimes,* control the way many things are done, and *regimen* is formed from that word. **3.** *grimaced:* made a distorted or "scrunched-up" facial expression. A *grimace* usually indicates pain, though sometimes it expresses anger or displeasure. **4.** *spate:* a sudden rush. Miss Yerby had a flood of tennis matches, all during a short time. *Spate's* original meaning was a sudden downpour of heavy rain. **5.** *foiled:* upset, or prevented from being successful. A synonym is *thwarted.* **6.** *caliber:* a measure of worth or quality. The inside of a gun barrel is measured as .22, .38, or some other specific *caliber.* From that single meaning, the measure of a bullet's size, the word has come to mean a measure of any kind.

More sports

climactic
peripheral
disparity
conceded
soared
snared

peripheral

1. "Most of my shots from mid-court are lucky to hit the rim," Anna _____.
2. Jerry Lloyd caught a seemingly impossible pass and trotted away with the _____ six points.
3. The crowd rose to its feet when Thompson _____ a line drive in the third inning.
4. A split second after the ball met her bat, it _____ into the left-field stands.
5. Crowley was paid a star's salary, but was kept in a _____ position all season.
6. Marge acknowledged the _____ in their national rankings, but insisted on first-class travel accommodations.

1. *conceded:* gave, admitted, yielded; acknowledged as true. Anna admitted that most of her shots from mid-court fell short. **2.** *climactic:* refers to a *climax,* the final and most important part of an action. **3.** *snared:* trapped, or caught. A *snare* is a trap for catching animals or birds, but the word has come to have a broader meaning. **4.** *soared:* flew through the air. Hawks *soar* above valleys, and baseballs *soar* when a batter hits a high fly. **5.** *peripheral:* off to one side; not in the center of things. **6.** *disparity:* inequality. Marge may have ranked 34th, but she insisted on the same accommodations (airplane seats and hotel rooms) as the top-ranking players.

New words in natural settings

Films and theater

antagonist
documentary
choreographer
improvise
interlude
genre

1. The city council budgeted $500,000 to make a _____ film about its new mental health center.
2. After a brief musical _____, the curtain rose on the second act of Shakespeare's comedy.
3. "I'm particularly proud to be awarded this Oscar," she said, "because romances are my favorite _____ of film."
4. In those early James Cagney movies, it was usually a G-man or detective who was Jimmy's _____.
5. The brilliant young team of comics rarely work from a script; they _____ nearly every sketch they perform.
6. By the time she had grown too old for an active career as a dancer, she had begun to win notice as a _____.

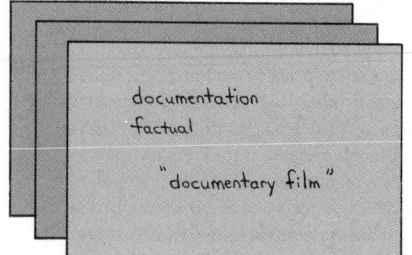

documentation
factual

"documentary film"

1. *documentary:* factual. Most *documentary* films explain a social, historical, or natural event as accurately as possible, using a narrator's (announcer's) voice rather than actors' speeches. **2.** *interlude:* something that comes between the acts of a theatrical entertainment. The word's meaning extends beyond the theater to indicate any in-between period or activity, such as an *interlude* between wars. **3.** *genre:* type, class, or style. The actress may have felt comfortable acting in comedies and mysteries, too, but romances were her favorite type of movie. **4.** *antagonist:* a person who is opposed to another one; an *adversary.* The opposite of *antagonist* is *protagonist,* a person who is friendly—a hero. **5.** *improvise:* invent, or make up as one goes along. **6.** *choreographer:* a person who creates dances or ballets.

Food

piquant
cholesterol
mandatory
ramekin
complement
entails

1. Excess amounts of _____, a substance present in dairy products and animal fats, should be avoided.
2. More and more consumers are taking time to read the _____ information printed on food package labels.
3. Following her aunt's recipes, Molly made some of the most _____ sauces we ever had tasted.
4. Ron has become a popular host ever since he has learned that barbecuing _____ constant, extremely high heat.
5. They ended the meal with a _____ of custard for each guest.
6. In some Near Eastern recipes, raisins are used as a tasty _____ to rice.

1. *cholesterol* is defined in the sentence. A doctor or nurse can advise you about diets that contain normal and excessive amounts of *cholesterol.* **2.** *mandatory:* required by regulations. Laws require food manufacturers to list the ingredients of their products on the packages. *Mandates* are regulations that must be obeyed. **3.** *piquant:* spicy; pleasantly sharp taste. The word is an uncommon one, but would make a fine addition to anyone's vocabulary. **4.** *entails:* is a necessary part of an action or thing. Cooking over extremely high heat is a necessary part of barbecuing. In legal matters, to *entail* has a totally different meaning—to prevent the transfer of property or real estate: The building's title was *entailed,* so the owner was not allowed to sell it. **5.** *ramekin:* a small dish, used for both baking and serving individual portions. **6.** *complement:* something that *completes* a whole, or goes with another thing. To avoid confusing this word with *compliment* (making pleasant or flattering comments), remember that *complement* and *complete* both begin with *comple.*

DIET SODA

USE OF THIS PRODUCT MAY BE HAZ-ARDOUS TO YOUR HEALTH. THIS PRODUCT CONTAINS SACCHARIN, WHICH HAS BEEN DETERMINED TO CAUSE CANCER IN LABORATORY ANIMALS.

mandatory

Law and courtroom procedure

ordinance
warrant
jeopardy
precedent
jurisdiction
arraignment

1. The court issued a search _____, and Sgt. Mellon made the arrest.
2. Within a week, he appeared at his _____ and entered a plea of "not guilty."
3. Mary had never heard of the antinoise _____, but still was ordered to pay the fine.
4. "This court has no _____ over matters in Jefferson County," the judge explained.
5. The Constitution prohibits trials that would put a defendant in double _____.
6. "This may set a _____ for families with similar problems," she told the judge.

1. *warrant:* a certificate authorizing an officer to make an arrest or search or seize property. **2.** *arraignment:* a time at which an accused person is called before a court. *Arraignments* take place before trials are scheduled. **3.** *ordinance:* a law or regulation. A similar word, lacking an "i," is *ordnance;* it has an entirely different meaning— military weapons and ammunition. **4.** *jurisdiction:* the right and power to apply the law; or the territory in which a law is applied. Words that begin with *jur* refer to law —among them are *juror, jury,* and *jurisprudence* (formal study of the law). **5.** *jeopardy:* risk or danger. In courtrooms, *jeopardy* refers to the danger of being found guilty and convicted. The Constitution states that a person can be tried only once for any crime; he cannot be put at risk twice for the same crime. **6.** *precedent:* an action or legal decision that sets an example for similar cases that follow.

jurisdiction

" This court has no jurisdiction over matters in Jefferson County."

Books and reading

creed
squibs
narrative
paraphrase
appendix
prose

1. "To _____ Gertrude Stein," he wrote, "a dog is a dog is a dog."
2. Berryman had gained his reputation as a poet, but _____ seemed beyond his reach.
3. We looked carefully through the _____, but could not find the source of the statistics in chapter 4.
4. The author said that this is her _____: "Never take your writing too seriously—or too lightly."
5. It was a lively _____, but far too long to finish reading in one evening.
6. Young E. B. White got his start writing _____ that were published in newspapers of the day.

1. *paraphrase:* put someone else's writings or thoughts in your own language, or change them somewhat. Gertrude Stein, a noted author of the 1920's, had written ". . . a rose is a rose is a rose." **2.** *prose:* ordinary speech or writing, not poetry. Novels and newspapers are written in *prose.* **3.** *appendix:* additional material that "hangs" at the end of a book. **4.** *creed:* a statement of belief or opinion. **5.** *narrative:* story. A reporter might *narrate* a true story, while a comedian might *narrate* a series of jokes that he made up on his way to the studio. **6.** *squibs:* short, usually humorous, items in a newspaper or magazine. *Squibs* are used by editors to fill the space at the bottom of a column of print.

creed

"*I believe in the supreme worth of the individual and in his right to life, liberty and the pursuit of happiness.*"
—JOHN D. ROCKEFELLER, JR.

New words in natural settings

Music

libretto
uninhibited
syncopated
searing
idiom
ovation

1. Until we got to New Orleans, we had never heard the wonderful tones of rhythmic, _____ riverboat music.
2. Her _____ high notes won Miss Larcher a Golden Recording award.
3. The audience rose to its feet in a wild, frenzied _____.
4. Ray Charles's vocal style was strongly influenced by a modern gospel _____.
5. Once he had the idea for an opera's music, Mozart searched for a poet who could write a suitable _____.
6. Her boisterous, _____ approach to country music made her a great favorite on the West Coast.

1. *syncopated:* music played with a strong beat where it might normally be expected to have a weaker beat. Dixieland music has a toe-tapping, *syncopated* quality. 2. *searing:* literally means scorching or burning. In music, *searing* refers to extremely high notes, sung or played on an instrument. 3. *ovation:* continued, enthusiastic applause. We often hear the phrase standing *ovation* to describe a wildly cheering audience that has risen to its feet in tribute to a performer. (Are you sure about the meaning of "frenzied" in sentence 3? Check it in the dictionary if you have any doubt.) 4. *idiom:* a special style of artistic expression. Singers might be influenced by a gospel *idiom,* an operatic *idiom,* or any of many other schools of singing. The word more often refers to spoken or written language that is not easily understood by anyone who is a foreigner to that language. "Up to snuff" is an *idiomatic* expression. 5. *libretto:* the words that are sung in an opera. 6. *uninhibited:* unrestrained; not held back. A singer who lets herself go is *uninhibited.*

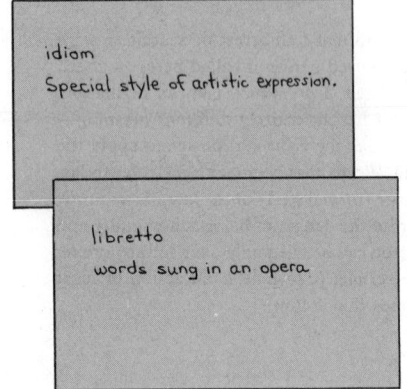

idiom
Special style of artistic expression.

libretto
words sung in an opera

Personalities

contagious
tenacity
affability
skylarking
boisterous
sarcastic

1. Marc's reputation for _____ helped when the vice president was deciding whom to make sales manager.
2. Not everyone appreciated Linda's _____ laughter, but her husband never failed to enjoy it.
3. When Linda laughed, Harry found it _____; it broke him up and left him gasping.
4. "I've had enough of his _____ comments," Hope complained. "He can't say a word without cutting my friends to ribbons."
5. His supervisor made Jess understand that a supermarket was no place for _____ and clowning around.
6. "With all the long faces you see around here," Mr. Watkins said, "Helen's _____ makes her a standout—she's a delight."

1. *tenacity:* holding fast to one's views; persistent. Probably, the aspect of Marc's *tenacity* that appealed most to his boss was Marc's habit of not giving up, even when the competition seemed likely to win. 2. *boisterous:* loud, noisy, uncontrolled. 3. *contagious:* spreading from one person to another; catching. Measles is a *contagious* disease; to Linda's husband, her laughter was a *contagious* emotion. 4. *sarcastic:* remarks intended to be biting, cutting, belittling. *Sarcasm* is usually expressed as humor—but humor that is intended to ridicule someone or something. 5. *skylarking:* frolicking and fooling around. 6. *affability:* friendliness, gentleness.

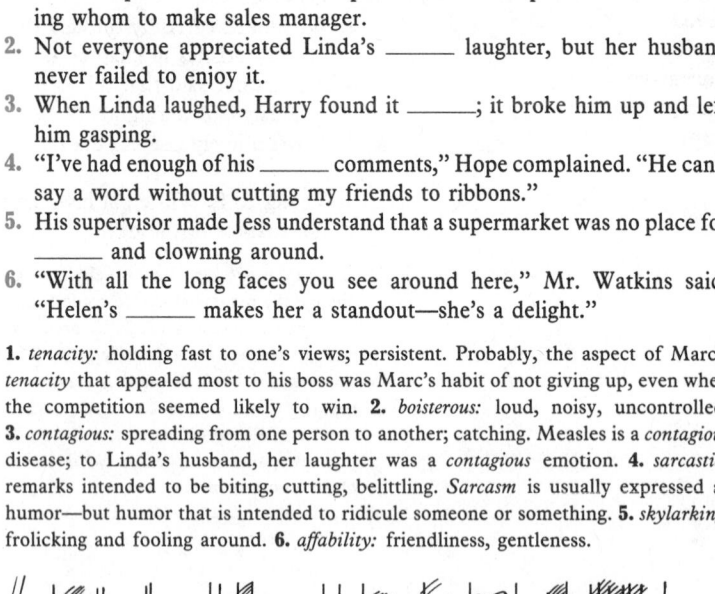

skylarking

Building Your Vocabulary

Gardening

herbicide
lobes
defoliate
prostrate
dormant
variegated

defoliate

1. It was an uncommon type of ivy, with a streaked, _____ leaf.
2. Don paid no attention to the warning on the _____ label, so he killed all the grass in his front yard.
3. "Don't worry," she told me, "these bushes aren't dead. They are _____ in the winter."
4. The rounded _____ of the leaf were the size of half dollars.
5. It resembled a moss, lying low along the soil, but we learned it was a healthy _____ shrub.
6. It took the beetles only four days to completely _____ our entire crop of peas.

1. *variegated:* patches of different color. *Streaked* is an echo word that gives a strong clue to the meaning of *variegated.* **2.** *herbicide:* a substance that kills plants. Words ending in *icide* refer to *death—suicide,* killing oneself; *matricide,* killing one's mother; *fungicide,* killing fungi (mushroomlike plants). **3.** *dormant:* inactive, resting, seemingly asleep. *Dormant* plants grow leaves and become active in the spring. A related word, *dormitory,* means place where people sleep. **4.** *lobes:* rounded parts. You will recall that the rounded, lower part of your ear is called an *earlobe.* **5.** *prostrate:* in plants, growing flat along the ground. People who *prostrate* themselves bow or kneel down before a superior person; sometimes they throw themselves flat on the ground. **6.** *defoliate:* to remove all the leaves from a plant or tree. Leaves are referred to as *foliage;* to remove them is to *defoliate* them, as to remove frost from frozen food is to *defrost* it.

Television

indispensable
vernacular
ennui
eclipsed
absorbed
chide

vernacular

1. In surveys among American families, television has _____ radio in listener-hours per household.
2. It is the one medium _____ by all ages: small children, adolescents, young adults, and the elderly.
3. Politicians find television _____ for getting their messages into voters' households.
4. On newscasts, political candidates gain the opportunity to _____ their opponents and be seen by huge audiences.
5. "We ran my comedy series for five years, and then dropped it before _____ set in," she explained.
6. The newscaster's popularity was due, in part, to his use of the _____.

1. *eclipsed:* we know that as television has become more important over the years, radio has become less so. *Eclipse* originally referred to one star or planet being hidden behind another. It now means any person's or thing's giving way to a more popular one. **2.** *absorbed:* taken up. All ages are totally interested in watching television. A synonym is *engrossed.* **3.** *indispensable:* cannot do without; necessary. **4.** *chide:* scold, reprimand, or express disapproval. **5.** *ennui:* boredom, general dissatisfaction. (A French word, pronounced *ahn-we'.*) **6.** *vernacular:* commonly used language, as opposed to the more formal, literary language used in some books and newspapers.

Pairs, pears

Our language is laced with sets of words that sound alike—or enough alike to confuse many people—yet have entirely different meanings. On these pages we offer some of the most confusing of those pairs of words and their definitions. Be on the lookout, as you read and listen during the coming months, for additional pairs of "confusers." Adding these pairs to your *Word Power* file is a **diverting** way to build your vocabulary.

A military colonel *and a seed or grain called a* kernel *are pronounced the same but spelled very differently.*

annal, annual. An *annal* is a written chronicle or record of events. *The annals of baseball. Annual* means yearly. *We payed our annual taxes.*

arc, ark. An *arc* is a curved or arched shape resembling a rainbow. An *ark* is a boat. In the Old Testament, the *ark* was Noah's boat during the Flood.

ardorous, arduous. A person who is *ardorous* has strong emotions, enthusiasms, or love. An *arduous* task is a difficult one, filled with hardship.

bazaar, bizarre. *Bazaar* refers to one shop, or a street of shops, selling various items. *Bizarre* means odd or extraordinary. *A bizarre costume.*

carat, carrot. A *carat* (also spelled *karat*) is a unit of weight for gems and jewels. *A half-carat diamond. Carrots* are common, orange-colored vegetables.

cite, site. To *cite* is to mention or quote as proof. *Their record was cited in the* World Almanac. A *site* is a place, or the location of a building or group of buildings. *The mayor conducted an on-site inspection.*

colonel, kernel. A military *colonel* (ker'-nell) is an officer ranking above a lieutenant colonel and below a brigadier general. A *kernel* is a grain or seed, usually one that can be eaten.

deceased, diseased. A *deceased* person is a dead person. One who is *diseased* is sick, infected, cannot function normally.

decent, descent. A *decent* appearance or person is modest, not shocking, meeting accepted standards. *A decent rate of pay. Descent* is the act of moving downward. Sometimes it means following from. *She traced the descent of jazz from early 20th-century New Orleans to today.*

demean, demeanor. To *demean* oneself is to act in a way that causes a loss of dignity and respect. *Demeanor* is the manner in which a person conducts himself; a synonym is *deportment.*

flounder, founder. A *flounder* is a flat saltwater fish. To *flounder* means to flop around clumsily, like a fish out of water; to be off balance. To *founder* is to sink. *John quit the foundering company* means that John quit because the company was going under.

flout, flaunt. To *flout* means to disobey openly and scornfully. *He flouted the law.* To *flaunt*, on the other hand, means to display proudly or in a showy way. *She flaunted her new red dress. A man who flaunts his disrespect for women flouts the common courtesies of civilization.*

gauge, gouge. A *gauge* (gayj) is a meter or dial for measuring an activity or amount. It is also the act of measuring or estimating. A *gouge* (gowj) is a chisel-like tool, or the scooping-out action of such a tool.

hawk, hock. A *hawk* is a falcon, or eaglelike, bird. To *hawk* is slang for to sell by calling out. *He hawked programs in the theater lobby.* To *hock* is slang for to pawn—to pledge personal property in return for a cash loan.

impromptu, improper. An *impromptu* speech is one given without preparation or rehearsal. An *improper* action is one that is irregular, not suitable, offensive.

language, languish. *Language* is the spoken words and written symbols that humans use to communicate thoughts. To *languish* is to lose strength, to become feeble and weak; to lie around doing nothing; to be neglected.

lop, lope. To cut off, or trim, part of a bush or tree is to *lop* it off. To *lope* is to run, or to ride a horse, at a steady, even rate.

lucid, ludicrous. *Lucid* writing is easily understood; its meaning is clear. A person who is *lucid* is sane and can make himself understood. *Ludicrous* statements or actions are laughable, ridiculous, or absurd.

lumbar, lumber. *Lumbar* refers to the lower back. *She had a pinched nerve in her lumbar vertebrae. Lumber* is wood in the form of boards or planks.

miller, milliner. A *miller* mills, or grinds, grain into flour or meal. A *milliner* makes or sells women's hats.

morning, mourning. *Morning* is the early part of the day, from sunrise to noon. *Mourning* is grieving for the dead. *Bereavement* is a synonym for *mourning.*

noisome, noisy. A *noisome* odor is one that is foul or disgusting, or giving off dangerous fumes. *Noisy* means making sounds, usually loud and unwanted.

occult, oculist. *Occult* happenings are supernatural, unexplained, ghostly. An *oculist* is an eye doctor—sometimes called an *optometrist*.

pampas, pamper. The *pampas* is a huge grassy area of South America, principally in Argentina, much like our Western prairies. To *pamper* is to pay too much attention to one's own, or another's, desires. *Indulge* and *spoil* are synonyms for *pamper*.

pitfall, pitiful. *Pitfalls* are traps made by digging deep holes, then covering them over lightly. *Pitfall* also means a danger that is not easily seen. *Pitiful* means pathetic; arousing sorrow. Less charitably, it can mean inferior.

quarry. *Quarry* has two entirely different meanings: 1) an open mine or pit, as a gravel *quarry*; 2) a hunted animal, or a person who is pursued.

quota, quote. A *quota* is a number of persons or things. The number is calculated to make the *quota* become a certain share of the whole. To *quote* is to repeat or copy another's words. It also means to state a price.

rouse, ruse. To *rouse* (rhymes with *how's*) someone is to wake him from sleep, or excite him into activity. A *ruse* is a trick, or ploy, meant to mislead someone.

scarce, scares. A *scarce* item is one that is seldom seen or found; it is rare. A dog that *scares* the neighbors is one that frightens them.

several, severance. *Several* means more than two or three, but not many. *She drew several flowers in a bowl.* *Severance* is the act of cutting off or separating. *The company gave Ruth a large amount of severance pay.*

sheik, chic. A *sheik* is the leader of an Arab family or tribe. *Chic* (sheek) is a French word meaning stylish; sophisticated and classy.

slew. *Slew* has two entirely different meanings: 1) killed (the past form of *slay*); 2) a large amount of things or people. *We watched a whole slew of actors perform.*

stake, steak. A wooden or metal *stake* is sharp at one end, which is hammered into the ground. A *steak* is the familiar cut of beef or other meat.

tracked, tract. *Tracked* is the past form of to *track,* to follow footprints or other traces or also to observe. *The police tracked her on their radar.* *Tract* has two meanings: 1) a piece of property or land; 2) a booklet or paper stating a special point of view, such as a political *tract.*

vanish, varnish. To *vanish* is to disappear; to be no longer able to be seen. *Varnish* is a paintlike coating for surfaces, usually wooden. It leaves a hard, smooth finish.

Groups of word parts

In classrooms and textbooks, it has long been the custom to teach vocabulary lessons through *word parts*. This method is also called *derivations,* because many of our English words are *derived* from (*came* from, or *arrived* from) Latin and Greek terms.

In all likelihood, you are not a student of Latin or Greek, so you will **benefit** from the more practical nonderivative techniques for building *Word Power* in this section of your handbook. Yet, you should still know just a few word-source facts.

ben, the first part of *benefit,* is called a *prefix. Ben* means good, and the whole word means good deed or advantage. Other words starting with *ben* are *benediction,* good speech or blessing; and *benevolent,* kindly, or one who is charitable.

Here are four of the hundreds of word parts that form our modern English language.

aud—hear
  audience—people gathered to hear an event
  audition—hear actors or musicians demonstrate their skills
  audiophile—person extremely interested in hearing sounds, particularly electronic reproduction

locut, loqu—to talk, speak
  loquacious—talkative; garrulous
  colloquy—conversation; talking together
  ventriloquist—person who makes his voice "come from his stomach"
  interlocutor—person who speaks between, or interrupts.
  soliloquy—one person's thoughts; a speech by one person in a play

nav—ship
  naval—pertaining to ships or a navy
  navigable—water deep enough to sail on
  navigate—to control the course of a ship or an airplane

pend—to hang, or be inclined toward
  pendulum—hangs from a clock's works
  depend—to hang on, or need, someone or something
  impending—hanging on, or waiting, for an event to take place
  appendage—a connected part, perhaps hanging from the main part

15 days to a forceful vocabulary

Studies have shown that the average American uses relatively few words—about 2000—for normal conversation. That same person may recognize another 12,000 to 13,000 words when he hears or sees them. But he hesitates to try them; he feels uncomfortable because he is not certain of the meanings of the words.

If you have been adding 40 or more words a week to your working vocabulary, you are moving far ahead of the average. Here is a way to boost your rate even higher. In just 15 days, you can add approximately 125 new terms to your working stock. Spend only 15 minutes a day beyond your regular *Word Power* activities and you will have accomplished that gain in less than three weeks!

Each day's activity is designed to be stimulating and enjoyable. Yet, before you start, keep in mind that there is nothing magical about the number "15." If an unexpected drain on your time prevents you from working the plan suggested for day six on the day following day five, do not be concerned. As long as you eventually get back to the routine, and maintain your *Word Power* file at the same time, the plan will work.

DAY 1: A few cents' worth

A daily newspaper is the easiest and least expensive source of new words. For variety and added challenge, get a copy of an out-of-town paper: one from the largest city in your state or a neighboring state. Or get a Washington, D.C., Houston, or New York daily, or *The Wall Street Journal*.

Make a list of eight or ten words that you are not sure about, and the sentences in which you find them. Using your dictionary, add them to your *Word Power* file.

Here are eight sentences, slightly paraphrased, from papers published on the same day in Illinois, Florida, and California.

1. Hungary was the first Soviet **bloc** nation to question the agricultural policy.
2. As he has during much of his **tenure,** Mr. Richards took issue with the district attorney.
3. "We cannot continue to operate on this level, at only half of our full sales **potential**."
4. All except one commander agreed to a **phased** withdrawal of the land forces.
5. Eight more terrorists were seen on the **outskirts** of the city.
6. His manager demanded an aplogy, saying, "They cannot call Sam a **demagogue** and get away with it."
7. The state of Colorado argued that it had not **delegated** that authority to Boulder.
8. "They never actually said we lied, but I do believe the word **prevaricate** was heard."

1. *bloc:* a group of organizations, nations, or persons united for a common purpose. **2.** *tenure:* the time during which a person holds an office or a job. **3.** *potential:* capability for growth that has not yet been realized. **4.** *phased:* done in stages. In *phase* one they pulled out the tanks, in *phase* two the artillery. **5.** *outskirts:* parts away from the central area; the *periphery.* **6.** *demagogue:* an unprincipled political leader who appeals to the emotions of citizens. **7.** *delegated:* a person or organization authorized to act for, or represent, another. **8.** *prevaricate:* to avoid the truth, or twist it to one's purposes.

Soviets deploy cruise missiles on submarines

Nuclear drones —— CAMPAIGN

Double victory vindicates Walsh, Washington High

NEW YORK — George Washington High's football team defeated host Stevenson 14-6 Friday, the ⌐d major win for the team this

that had to be met before the team could resume play.

• A large measure of pride. Friday's triumphant return served as vindication for Walsh and his players.

Building Your Vocabulary

DAY 2: Upping the price slightly

Move upward, in price and degree of specialization, from newspapers to magazines. The periodicals that are most widely read—*People, Time, Cosmopolitan,* and *Reader's Digest,* among others—are good sources of vocabulary-stretching words.

Any single issue is almost sure to provide several useful additions to your *Word Power* file. The sentences to the right were gathered from just three magazines.

1. Reservation services often are **biased** in an airline's favor.
2. Pain caused by bursitis can become **excruciating** with the slightest movement.
3. A mix of traditional English and American styles produced the rich **patina** of years.
4. It was a **premise** stated with authority, but one we had great difficulty accepting.
5. I had become **adept** at using the smaller keyboard.
6. Pat's high school ring had something resembling an **amethyst** at the center.
7. **Trend**-conscious designers abandoned the "layered look."

1. *biased:* prefers one person or thing; prejudiced. 2. *excruciating:* intensely, agonizingly painful. 3. *patina:* appearance of aging. Originally, a thin coating of brown or green on bronze or other metals. 4. *premise:* an underlying or basic statement that can be assumed to be true. 5. *adept:* skillful. 6. *amethyst:* a purple semiprecious stone. 7. *trend:* movement toward a new fashion or style.

DAY 3: Name-words

Late in the 19th century, all across the United States people watched for news of the completion of the Brooklyn Bridge. Knowing it was the focus of so much attention, a publicity-seeking young man called the newspapers, climbed one of the towers, and dived into the East River. He survived the dive, and his name survives in the language as a synonym for "high dive" or "publicity stunt." He was Steve Brody, the originator of "taking a Brody."

Once you know the stories behind some of the names that have become often-used words in our language, it becomes easier to remember their meanings and how they are used. Here is a group of such words—some of them derived from names, others from places.

Annie Oakley: a free pass to a show or concert is called an *Annie Oakley.* Annie was a star of Buffalo Bill Cody's Wild West Show in the 1890's; she shot holes in playing cards and other small targets. A free ticket, punched full of holes, reminded people of her act.

bowdlerize: to take out from, or change, portions of a book that are thought to be offensive. In 1818 an Englishman, Thomas Bowdler, published an edition of Shakespeare's plays "suitable for reading aloud to a family." Bowdlerized versions of stories or plays often are weaker and less effective than the originals.

boycott: to refuse to have anything to do with a person or thing. Captain Boycott was a land agent in Ireland who was shunned by everyone because he bought up the property of evicted farmers.

billingsgate: rude, abusive, often foul language. A fishmarket has been located for centuries near the ancient London tower of Billingsgate. The language used there by fish merchants gave rise to the word.

donnybrook: a brawl or free-for-all commotion. Yearly, in Donnybrook, Ireland, a fair was held. Every year there were said to be blackened eyes, bloodied noses, and many arrests.

Draconian: extremely harsh. Draco was a Greek lawmaker who ruled that death must be the punishment for all crimes, even small ones. A *Draconian* measure is a severe ruling.

gerrymander: to divide a voting district into parts that give an unfair advantage to one party. Elbridge Gerry, 1744–1814, was a governor of Massachusetts who created an odd-shaped election district that looked like a salamander.

malapropism: a comical confusion of words, especially those that sound alike ("a shrewed (for rude) awakening"). The word comes from Mrs. Malaprop in a famous comedy, *The Rivals,* by Richard Sheridan.

gerrymander

DAY 4: Time-words

Hundreds of words in our language have *prefixes,* or parts placed in front of a main stem, that give a special meaning to the word. Some of the most commonly used prefixes indicate *time;* that is, one action's occurrence in relation to another's. Looking at a few examples of the way these prefixes work is the easiest way to understand prefixes that indicate time.

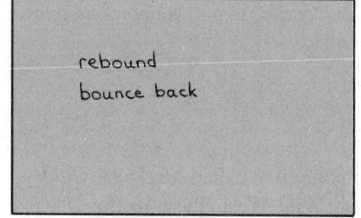

ante (Latin): before
antebellum before the Civil War (*bellum* =war).
antedate at a time before the time mentioned.
archa (Greek): old
archaeology the study of old (ancient) life and culture.
archaic belonging to a much earlier time.
neo (Greek): new
neoclassicism revival of classical form in arts.
neologism a recently invented word or phrase.
neonate a newborn infant.
post (Latin): after
postdate to use a date, as on a check, later than the actual date.
postmeridian afternoon (*meridian* is the highest part of the sun's course across the sky).
pre (Latin): before
preadolescence a child's age, ten to twelve, before adolescence.
predict to say, or make known, before an act happens.
premature growing or existing before the customary time.
re (Latin): again
rebound bounce back again.
recognize know something or someone again.
rehearse practice in preparation for a performance (originally, hear again).

DAY 5: Your lucky number

As a change from yesterday's word-gathering based on formations and derivations from classical languages, try this relaxer. Write down any seven numbers from one to one thousand—roughly, the number of pages in your dictionary. Then turn to each of those numbered pages. Select any unknown words on those pages that come to your notice. Make a *Word Power* card for them, and put the cards in your file.

Here are ten "lucky number words" chosen by one word-collector on a recent evening.

deride *(p. 204 in his dictionary):* to speak with scorn, laughter, or contempt; to ridicule.
astral *(p. 45):* of or about the stars; star-shaped.
nectar *(p. 501):* the drink of the mythic gods; any sweet or delicious drink.
polyp *(p. 579):* a growth in the lining of the stomach, nose, or other body part.
extort *(p. 267):* to gain something by forcing it from another person, often by threats or intimidation.
compunction *(p. 155):* a sense of guilt; uneasiness.
legume *(p. 428):* a plant, eaten as a vegetable, that bears seeds in a pod (as peas or beans).
sobriquet *(p. 709):* a nickname; an alias or assumed name.
triturate *(p. 800):* to grind or crush into a very fine powder; to chew thoroughly.
quadruped *(p. 609):* any animal with four feet.

legroom	428	leprechaun

of mutton: said of a sleeve that puffs out toward the shoulder, etc.
leg·room (leg′rōōm′) *n.* adequate space for the legs while seated, as in a car
leg·ume (leg′yōōm, li gyōōm′) *n.* [< Fr. < L. *legumen* < *legere,* to gather] **1.** any of a large family of plants, including the peas, beans, clovers, etc., with fruit that is a pod splitting along two sutures: many legumes are nitrogen-fixing **2.** the pod or seed of some members of this family, used for food
le·gu·mi·nous (li gyōō′min əs) *adj.* **1.** of, having the nature of, or bearing legumes **2.** of the family of plants to

length·en (-'n) *vt., vi.* to make or become longer —**length′en·er** *n.*
length·wise (-wīz′) *adv., adj.* in the direction of the length: also **length′ways′** (-wāz′)
length·y (-ē) *adj.* **length′i·er, length′i·est** long; esp., too long —**length′i·ly** *adv.* —**length′i·ness** *n.*
le·ni·ent (lē′ni ənt, lēn′yənt) *adj.* [< L. prp. of *lenire,* to soften < *lenis,* soft] not harsh or severe in disciplining, judging, etc.; mild; merciful —**le′ni·en·cy,** *pl.* **-cies, le′ni·ence** *n.* —**le′ni·ent·ly** *adv.*
Len·in (len′in; *Russ.* lye′nyin), **V(ladimir) I(lyich)** (orig. surname *Ulyanov*: also called *Nikolai Lenin*) 1870-1924; *Russ.* Communist revolutionary leader; premier of the

Building Your Vocabulary

DAY 6: The study of studies

Any word that ends in *ology* refers to the study of, or the science of, the subject named in the first part of the word. Since that hard-to-know first part is sometimes a Greek or Latin word, your job is not easy. **Dermatology,** for example, is the study of the skin—and a **dermatologist** is a doctor who specializes in that study.

As your working vocabulary widens, you will find many basic word parts appearing again and again. You will recognize *derm* as part of *hypodermic*—under the skin—and the meaning of *dermatologist* will be reinforced.

For now, here are 14 *study of* words. They will form the **nucleus** (core; center) of this part of your vocabulary.

anthropology: the study of the biologic history and habits of mankind.
archaeology: the study of ancient civilizations through buildings, pottery, and other traces that remain.
biology: the study of life processes and living organisms.
chronology: time-connected studies. The word has come to mean a sequence of events, as they took place in time.
entomology: the study of insects.
etymology: the study of words—how they originated and how they took their present form. (Do not confuse this word with the previous one. There is an "n" in *insect*—and none in *etymology.*)
geology: the study of the structure and development of Earth's crust and its strata.
ichthyology: the study of fish.
meteorology: the study of the atmosphere.
oenology: the study of wine making.
ornithology: the study of birds.
philology: the study of languages and their development.
psychology: the study of the mind, mental processes, and the way humans respond to events around them.
theology: the study of religion.

DAY 7: Words that are *before*

We have already seen two word parts that mean *before* in the sense of time, or when an event happened. One is *ante;* the other is *pre.* Both come to us from Latin and are in common use. Another Latin word part that we use frequently also means before, but in the sense of in front of, concerned with space rather than time. It is *pro,* the first syllable of the following nine words.

proboscis: a long, flexible nose, as of an elephant. Also, an insect's noselike feeding tube. A human nose, if large, is sometimes called a *proboscis.*
proceed: to go before.
prodigal: wasteful, reckless, extravagant. The word's origin is not easily recognized in English, but in Latin it means driving recklessly ahead.
produce: to bring forth, make, or give rise to. Its roots are in *to lead forward.*
profile: the outline of a human head or other object. Also, an essay, graph, or table summarizing an idea or thing; it goes before a full, extended description.
program: a listing of events. It is writing that comes before the event.
progress: movement forward, or toward a goal.
prologue: a short speech or dramatic action presented before a play begins.
promontory: a high ridge of land extending out into the sea.

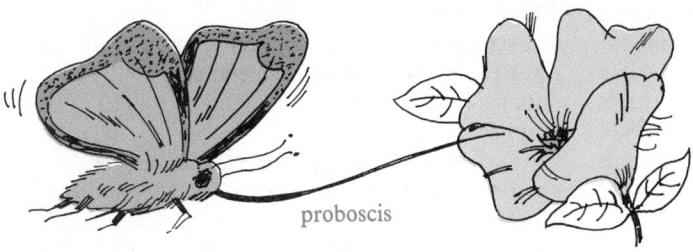

proboscis

DAY 8: Words that are *against,* and some that are *with*

It is possible that this sudden **immersion** (dunking; a teabag is *immersed* in hot water) into the ancient roots of words has proved confusing. So day eight will be used to clarify a few of the ideas that may have bewildered you.

Take **ante,** for example. We saw that it is Latin and that it means before, or earlier, as in *antedate.* But how about **antifreeze?** The answer lies in the spelling. *Ante* with an "e" means before—*anti* with an "i" means against, or opposing. Some of the *opposing* words are **antibacterial, antibody, anticlimax, anticlockwise, antidepressant, antimagnetic, antipoverty,** and **antitrust.**

You may have wondered where, among all those **pro** words, was **con**—as in "they argued *pro and con* the new rent laws." *Con* is short for the Latin *contra,* meaning against. The full *contra* is used in such English words as *contrary, contraband,* and *contravene.*

When you do see *con* at the beginning an English word, it nearly always means together, or with. These are some typical uses of *con* as the first syllable of a word:

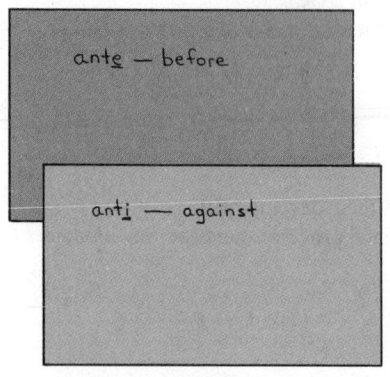

concentrate: to direct or bring together toward a common center.
concert: to work (or produce music) together.
conclave: a secret meeting.
concrete: real, existing things. *A table is a concrete object.* Also, a construction material of mortar or cement mixed together with pebbles or stones.
confabulate: to talk informally, or chat, together.
confederate: an ally, accomplice, or fellow member in a *conspiracy.*
congest: to overfill; bring together too many.
connect: to unite, join, or fasten together.

DAY 9: Culling the classroom

Does a neighbor, or a friend, have a son who is in junior high school? Or does your cousin's daughter go to high school or college not far from where you live? If you know someone who regularly attends school, enlist his or her help in your *Word Power* campaign.

Just ask your helping student to be on the lookout, in the books he reads and the assignments he does, for words he does not recognize. Instead of passing them by, ask him to note them on a piece of paper.

You will notice that the heading for day nine reads "**Culling** the classroom." Is *culling* an unfamiliar term? To *cull* is to select, or gather, from a place; here, to collect new words from the classroom. Here is a typical day's catch.

savant: one who knows many answers; a wise person. (A French word that means knowing.)
perfunctory: done in a routine, uninspired manner; careless; merely getting the job done.
levity: a joking, light manner; frivolity.
matrix: the surrounding environment in which an object is found. *Her ambition must be viewed within the matrix of her family's poverty.*
exacting: making severe demands. *Joan objected to her employer's exacting requirements.*
corpulent: fat; obese.
grapple: to hold or seize something or someone; to struggle, wrestle. A *grappling iron* is a large hook, dragged along a river bottom to seize submerged objects or drowned persons.
jetty: a large pier or wharf that protects a harbor or coastline from damage by the tide.
correlate: to compare or connect in a systematic way.
riposte: a quick retort or counterattack.
fatuous: foolish, silly.
propitious: favorable.
marauding: going in search of plunder or prey.
perverse: obstinately doing something different from what is reasonable or expected.
recondite: refers to an obscure subject, or to writing about an obscure subject.

DAY 10: Largeness

Think about those times when you have tried to describe to someone something you have seen earlier in the day. It was a big accident, or a big crowd, or something else much larger than ordinary. You probably had to hesitate to find exactly the right word—and settled for "huge" or "very big."

That need not happen again. There are dozens of easily used words for expressing *bigness,* and each of them has a distinct, separate meaning. Learn most of them on this list, and you will have made an **imposing** gain in your *Word Power.*

vast: very great area, space, or number of things. *A vast acreage of forest.*

immense: extremely large; so vast it cannot be measured.

substantial: a large number or size; large enough to be worthy of notice.

expansive: open and wide; capable of growing larger or stretching. *We saw an expansive stretch of beach.*

mammoth: huge. *Mammoths* were prehistoric forms of elephants; the word often describes giant animals or people.

monster: actually means "a frightening creature." Has come to mean an abnormally large person or object.

massive: bulky; a very large organism or undertaking. *The Girl Scouts undertook a massive charity drive.*

monumental: outstanding; enduring; remembered; amazing. *She displayed monumental ability to overcome disease.*

towering: higher than all surrounding objects; outstanding in its group or class.

tremendous: extremely large; enormous. Actually means "so large it makes one tremble."

enormous: immense; tremendous. Actually means "so large it is abnormal."

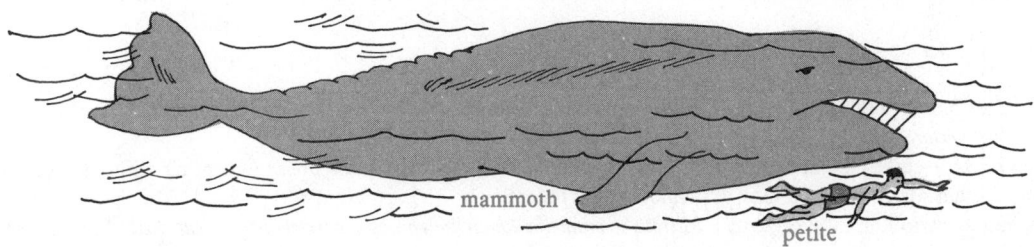

mammoth

petite

DAY 11: Smallness

When it is not the idea of largeness that makes us pause and search for just the right word, it is often the very opposite **concept** (idea)—smallness.

It is not hard to come up with, say, *tiny* when we want to express extreme smallness: The doll's house contained the *tiniest* table and chair I've ever seen.

Sometimes, though, *tiny* and *very small* do not seem exactly right. For those times, here is a collection of words expressing smallness. Some may be ones you know, others may be unfamiliar. All will add strength to your *Word Power* abilities.

diminutive: of very small size. Also, a name that indicates smallness, as *booklet* for "a small book."

minute (min-oot'): exceptionally small; too small for ordinary notice. The Latin *min* in a word almost always indicates smallness, as in *miniature* and *diminish.*

pygmy: an individual or object of unusually small stature (height). Called after a race of African or Asian people who are about 4 feet tall.

infinitesimal: an amount or thing so small it cannot be measured.

insignificant: an amount or thing too small to matter; easily ignored or overlooked.

trace: a barely visible amount.

speck: a very small bit, or spot, or mark.

petite (peh-teet'): dainty, fragile. From the French word for *little.*

bantam: diminuitive, miniature. From a small, domestic fowl.

microscopic: too small to be seen.

midget: extremely small. From midge, a very small, gnatlike insect.

grain: a small particle, such as a *grain of sand.*

mite: a very small quantity, such as *a mite of sympathy.*

DAY 12: Words about words

As you learn more words, you will find it interesting to learn more *about* words. There is, in fact, a whole body of terms that describes specific aspects of word study. Some of those terms you already have added to your *Word Power* file: *etymology* and *neologism* are two. You will rediscover two more in this list.

The word acronym is a good one to learn. Here MADD stands for "Mothers Against Drunken Driving."

lexicography: the work of putting together a dictionary. A person who does this work is a **lexicographer,** and the dictionary itself is a **lexicon.** *Lexicon* also refers to the special terms used in a trade or profession. *The word "quit" was not in the ballplayers' lexicon.*

linguistic: relating to language, or a person who speaks several languages.

locution: a style of speaking; words and phrases used in a style of speaking.

acronym: a word formed by the initial letters of an organization or name, as EPA for Environmental Protection Agency.

provincial: an unsophisticated, heavily rustic word or term, as *taters* instead of *potatoes.*

homonym: a word that sounds like another word: *pail* and *pale,* or *shear* and *sheer.* (You already know the other two terms of the *nym* trio—*antonym* and *synonym.*)

interjection: a word that stands alone and expresses sudden thoughts or emotions. *Darn!* and *Oops!* are interjections. They often come between *(inter)* other thoughts.

usage: the way that a word expresses a thought in a language. See volume 2, pages 336-347 for explanations of correct modern English *usage.*

DAY 13: Free—on the shelves

The fullest, most "official" dictionary—the *Oxford English Dictionary* (O.E.D.)—gives the meanings of more than 500,000 words. Several million words are devoted to those definitions; the complete, multivolume O.E.D. is too heavy for an average man or woman to lift.

Yet right on the nearest shelf of your local library is nearly as good a source of *Word Power*—and easily lifted, too. It is any book that you pick out, skim through—or read fully, if the subject interests you—and from which you select unknown words. Why nearly as good as the OED? Because you see the words in context, actually being used by a writer.

Here, from a book about a scandal in New York City's Department of Water Supply, Gas and Electricity (*A Percentage of the Take,* by Walter Goodman) are a handful of words as they appear, together with their meanings. (The sentences have been shortened for inclusion here.)

That story was **diligently** *reported in the city's newspapers.* Carefully; conscientiously; done with unsparing effort.

What is striking is the **passivity** *of the press.* Accepting without argument, inquiry, or objection.

Marcus's comments about toughness **comprised** *a great deal of the conversation.* Filled.

He was a man whose profession required that a grudge not be lightly **relinquished.** Given up; abandoned; put aside.

This version contains an **inherent implausibility.** *Inherent:* an essential part; without it, the whole could not exist. *Implausibility:* difficulty in believing. (An important part of this version is difficult to believe, so it is difficult to believe the entire story.)

The newspaper commented on Albano's **"adroit** *footwork."* Nimble, agile.

The lawyer had appeals of his own for the **neophyte** *politician, whose hold was* **faltering.** *Neophyte:* beginner or novice. *Faltering:* slipping, missing one's step; beginning to make mistakes.

His stock began a **precipitous** *drop.* Steep; dropping sharply, as when falling off a *precipice* (cliff).

Observers regarded the electric company as highly **paternal** *to its employees.* Like a father. (Providing many of the needs of the employees beyond their salaries.)

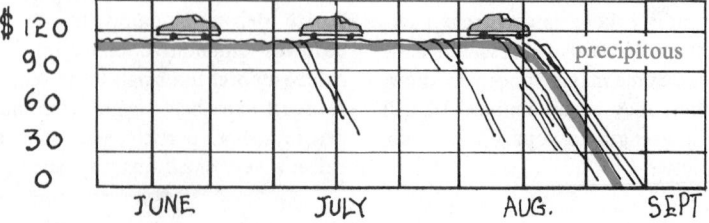

DAY 14: Sending out scouts

Your campaign to improve your vocabulary need not be a **solitary** one (done by one person only —you). It will make your project considerably more interesting if you let others participate in it.

If you have a neighbor who works in an auto showroom, for example, have him or her bring you ten words that are used in the trade. Or your cousin may work for the phone company. What are some new words that he has heard? Here is a sampling of what you might expect from two kinds of "word scouts."

Sheriff's assistant

deterrent: something that prevents or discourages an action. *Increasing the police force would be a deterrent to crime.*

larceny: theft or robbery.

recidivism: slipping back into criminal behavior after being released from prison.

subpoena (suh-peen'-a): an order requiring the receiver to appear in court.

Carpenter/housing contractor

ferrule: a metal ring near the end of a wooden pole or tool handle, to prevent splitting.

shim: a thin wedge of wood or metal, used to level parts or fill spaces.

miter: cutting each of two surfaces at a 45° angle, to form a right angle when they are joined.

rabbet: a groove cut into a piece of wood, in which another piece of wood will be glued or screwed.

DAY 15: Tripling your list

During the past 14 days you have added more than 125 new words to your working vocabulary. No need for you to be modest about it—that is an extraordinary leap beyond the average person's rate of word **accretion** (gradual growth by adding or including new material) and you deserve congratulations.

Better yet, you can triple—or at least double—your number of new words by going back over the 14 formulas and reworking them. Use them to produce two or three sets of all-new words.

Be flexible. If you are not too sure about day six techniques, or if you feel uncomfortable with day eight, skip them. Try to concentrate on those days' plans that interest you the most.

You probably will find a thesaurus extremely helpful, if not essential. Turn now to the *Roget's University Thesaurus* at the back of this book. Study it carefully. Look up some general subjects and add the words you do not know to your *Word Power* file.

Or working at a library—at least in the planning stage of your tripling-up project—may give you just the help you need. You will find the librarian, who works with words all day, a knowledgeable, helpful collaborator.

accord

abutter 199
aby *remain* 141
  endure 821, 826
abysm 198
abysmal *deep* 208
abyss *space* 180
  interval 198
  depth 208
  pitfall 667
  hell 982
acacia 367
academic *theory* 514
  teaching 537, 542
academical *style* 578
academician 492
  Royal–559
academy 542
acanaceous 253
acanthophorous 253
acanthus 847
acariâtre 901
acarpous 169
acatalectic 597
acatastasia 139
acaudal 38
acaudate 38
accede *assent* 488
  submit 725
  consent 762
accelerate *early* 132
  stimulate 173
  velocity 274
  hasten 684
accelerometer 490a
accension 384
accent *sound* 402
  tone of voice 580
  rhythm 597
accentuate 642
accentuated 581
accentuation 580
accept *assent* 488
  consent 762
  receive 785

additive 37
adjunct 39
accompanying 88
aid 707
auxiliary 711
acciaccatura 413
accidence 567
accident *event* 151
  chance 156
  disaster 619
  misfortune 735
  –of an accident 156
  fatal–361
  accidental *extrinsic* 6
  irrelative 10
  occasional 134
  fortuitous 156
  undesigned 621
accidentalism 156
Accipitres 739
acclamation
  assent 488
  approbation 931
  acclam...
acclimat...
  domest...
  inure...
acclivit...
accloy...
accolad...
accom...
  adju...
  aid...
  reco...
  give...
  lenc...
  –one...
  cor...
  acco...
  ki...
  acc...
  (s...
  sj...
  –t...

5. Intrinsicality

[*L.*] etc. (*luminary*) 423; "such stuff as dreams are made on" [*Tempest*]; air, thin air; bubble etc. 353; mockery.

blank; void etc. (*absence*) 187; hollowness.

inanity, fatuity, fool's paradise.

v. **vanish**, evaporate, fade, fleet, sink, fly, dissolve, melt away; die, die away, die out; disappear etc. 449.

adj. **unsubstantial**; baseless, groundless; ungrounded; without foundation, having no foundation.

visionary etc. (*imaginary*) 515; immaterial etc. 317; spectral etc. 980; dreamy; shadowy; ethereal, airy, gaseous, imponderable, tenuous, vague, vaporous, dreamlike, mushroom; cloud...

8. Circumstance

characteristic etc. (*special*) 79, (*indicative*) 550; invariable, incurable, ineradicable, fixed.

adv. **intrinsically** etc. *adj.*; at bottom, in the main, in effect, practically, virtually, substantially, *au fond* [*F.*]; fairly.

6. Extrinsicality

n. **extrinsicality**, objectiveness, *non ego* [*L.*]; extraneousness etc. 57; accident.

adj. **extrinsic**, extrinsical; derived from without; objective; extraneous etc. (*foreign*) 57; modal, adventitious; ascititious, adscititious; incidental, accidental, nonessential, unessential, accessory; contingent, fortuitous, casual, subsidiary.

Preparing for vocabulary tests

Any time you are applying for some step upward—admission to college, or a new job, or a promotion—there seems to be a vocabulary test involved.

That is because a broad vocabulary is recognized as a reliable indicator of intelligence (and, often, education). Also, vocabulary tests are easy to administer and to score: they are right or wrong, pass or fail, with no maybes or gray areas.

Now that you have a significantly improved vocabulary, be sure you know the ins and outs of testing. **Confidence.** For most of us, an attitude of *I'm going to win* goes a long way toward making us actually win.

Salesmen who know they are going to make that sale, even before they walk in the door, are much more likely to get the order.

This will hold true for you when you are faced with a vocabulary test. You have worked on the plans and strategies and projects in these pages. You have built an impressive *Word Power* file. So be confident.

Samples. Know beforehand, as exactly as possible, the kinds of questions you will be asked to answer. There are four commonly used forms of vocabulary questions. They are explained on these pages, and samples are provided for extra practice; see also pages

Four forms of questions

1. Select the appropriate word or term that is most nearly the same in meaning as the capitalized word.

Sample: **ignite**   a) look away   b) put out   c) set fire   d) sleep

There are no context clues, so it is necessary to know or recognize the words themselves in this type of test. Be aware that one or two wrong answers are designed to mislead you. *Look away* might make you think of *ignore,* which could be confused with *ignite;* and *sleep* might relate to the *nite* (night) sound in *ignite.* The right answer is c) *set fire.* Here are some practice questions.

joggle	a) shake slightly	b) run slowly	c) ankle	d) turn a corner
seance	a) after	b) rabbit	c) sofa	d) meeting
buzzard	a) saw	b) fox	c) intestines	d) vulture
evict	a) send to jail	b) put out	c) raise up	d) saying
align	a) line up	b) marker	c) insult	d) press down

answers: joggle, a; seance, d; buzzard, d; evict, b; align, a.

2. For each statement, select the choice that best completes it or answers the question.

Sample: To be **profuse** with compliments means to

a) be obscene   b) give them freely   c) withhold them   d) be vague

Your only clue is the prefix *pro,* which we have seen means *forward* or *in front of.* Among the four choices, all have a negative or backward implication, except b). To be *profuse* means to give freely, even extravagantly. There is no easy way to answer type 2 questions; the more words you know, the better you will do. Practice with these typical questions.

Farmland that is **parched** is	a) elevated	b) dry	c) flooded	d) posted
A **turquoise** would most likely be found in a	a) zoo	b) tunnel	c) bracelet	d) restaurant
A **seamy** neighborhood is	a) sordid	b) morbid	c) elegant	d) hot
The **barrage** consisted of	a) wooden sheds	b) gunfire	c) tiles	d) clear plastic
Who gave the **compress** to Jason?	a) a barber	b) a carpenter	c) a nurse	d) a teacher

answers: parched, b; turquoise, c; seamy, a; barrage, b; compress, c.

Building Your Vocabulary

328-331 for more help on taking tests.

Usually, you can obtain copies of last year's test, or special review copies of tests similar to the one you will be taking. They are in review books and easily obtainable from a guidance counselor, library, or the testing organization itself.

Learn the rules. Should you guess at answers you are not quite sure of? Or are points taken off your score for wrong answers? And what about time? How many minutes will you be allowed?

When you practice for a particular vocabulary test, you will want to do it under conditions that are much like those under which the real test is administered. You should become accustomed to working within a time frame similar to the actual one. If there is no penalty for wrong answers, and there usually is not, you should practice guessing at every question.

The school, government office, or employer that will be testing you will answer your questions well in advance of test day. Phone or drop by in person. Make sure you are talking to someone who really knows the procedures, not a clerk who is only guessing.

Relax. Do not put unnecessary pressure on yourself as you prepare for the test. Cramming until late the night before the test guarantees that you will be groggy on the big day. There is no need for last-minute panic if you have been building *Word Power* day by day, week by week.

Know exactly how you will get to the test place, and plan to arrive ten or fifteen minutes early, with a pocket full of extra pens and pencils. Then relax and let your *Word Power* take over.

---

3. Each question consists of four pairs of words. In one pair among the four, both words have the same meaning: they are synonyms. Select that pair.

Sample: a) magnify-diminish   b) section-partition   c) capitulate-defy   d) encrust-salvage

By looking closely at all four pairs, you may recall that *diminish* means "to make smaller," and is the opposite of *magnify*. *Capitulate* and *defy* are opposites, too; and though you may not be sure about d), you probably will recognize that in b) a *section* and a *part* are the same thing. Your answer is b). See how well you do with these practice questions.

1. a) simile-quote   b) monastery-monograph   c) bisect-divide   d) create-basket
2. a) deprecate-belittle   b) crass-cliff   c) ominous-many   d) biology-oculist
3. a) captain-demagogue   b) curator-bishop   c) fiasco-failure   d) flagrant-tramp
4. a) familiar-intimate   b) recognize-venal   c) proximity-distance   d) thermal-sunshine
5. a) tripod-oyster   b) confide-trust   c) reveal-conceal   d) unite-sever

answers: 1 c; 2 a; 3 c; 4 a; 5 b.

---

4. For each of the following statements, select T if the statement is *true,* F if it is *false.*

Sample: A **parable** is a type of umbrella.   T   F

The question was designed to mislead you slightly. A sunshade, very much like an umbrella, is called a *parasol*. But a *parable* is a story illustrating a religious or moral lesson, so the correct answer is F. Decide if each of these examples is true or false.

1. A **saga** is a long story or report.   T   F
2. A **terminal** is the last car of a railroad train.   T   F
3. To **mediate** is to apply bandages to a wound or a rash.   T   F
4. **Archives** are written records.   T   F
5. **Largesse** is a large, generous gift.   T   F

answers: 1. T; 2. F (a *caboose* is the last car; a *terminal* is a station at the end of the line, or the final portion of a thing); 3. F (to *mediate* is to come between two opposing parties, to resolve their differences); 4. T; 5. T.

American English

American English is made up, to a large extent, of borrowings from the many immigrants who arrived on U.S. shores, each speaking his native tongue. Even the American Indians were immigrants, arriving across a land bridge to Alaska from Asia that no longer exists. And they brought their language with them, too.

American Indian. Among the words that Indians have given to modern American English are **tomahawk; moccasin; wigwam; tepee;** and **cayuse** (horse). Probably, the Indians' most lasting contribution is place names. Consider the following states:

Arkansas: land of south wind people.

Idaho: light on the mountains.

Illinois: warriors (**Chicago,** for some reason, meant place that smells bad).

Iowa: the sleepy people, referring to a local tribe of the Dakota nation.

Kentucky: meadowland.

Minnesota: sky-blue water.

Mississippi: big river.

Spanish. The Indians of the Southwest mingled closely with the Spanish settlers of that territory. The area attracted pioneers from the settled eastern colonies, and the mingled westerners put their own stamp on the language. These cowboy terms are Spanish in origin: **buffalo** (explorer DeSoto's word for our native bison); **chaps** (short for *chaparejos,* a cowboy's leather leg protectors); **cinch; corral; buckaroo** (derived from Spanish *vaquero*); **lariat; lasso; pinto** (spotted horse); **rodeo; pronto; canyon; loco; cabana; fiesta; hombre; siesta; tequila; tortilla; vamoose.** We call a low island a **key** and a common insect pest a **cockroach;** both terms are based on similar Spanish words. If we want someone to leave in a hurry, we tell him to **vamoose**—one more Spanish borrowing.

African. When slaves were shipped to America in chains, they brought with them African words that were converted to the nation's growing language. Among them are **banana; banjo; goober** (peanut); **juke** (to misbehave, much later adapted to mean a tavern music player, or *jukebox*); **tote** (carry).

The various waves of settlers brought with them customs and words they used in their new homes. Dutch, French, English, German, Scandinavian, Italian, and many, many other ethnic groups contributed to the growing language. Here are a few borrowings.

Dutch

bedspread	cookie	sauerkraut
boss	hex	sleigh
bush	landscape	waffle
cole slaw	Santa Claus	Yankee

French

barrage	depot	music
castle	(railroad station)	pantry
chowder	détente	parlor
crime	(easing of tensions)	prairie
dance	manor	procession

Among French place names are **Baton Rouge** (LA), red stick; **Des Moines** (IA), the monks; **Terre Haute** (IN), high ground; **Vermont,** green mountain; and **Louisiana,** for King Louis XIV.

German

and how	dumb	klutz
bub	ecology	(clumsy person)
bum	frankfurter,	phooey
(loafer, tramp)	hamburger	pumpernickel
check	(styles of meat	vampire
(restaurant bill)	served in	("to vamp,"
dachshund	Frankfurt and	bewitch)
delicatessen	Hamburg)	

Italian. A nation of brilliant cooks and dedicated eaters, Italians changed forever the composition of American menus. Among the additions:

espresso	macaroni	spaghetti
lasagna	ravioli	tortoni

And, of course, **pizza.** Contrary to legend, the word does not mean pie. It refers to pinching or plucking the dough, as in the musical term *pizzicato*—to pluck a violin string.

Yiddish. The first large waves of Jewish immigrants from Central and Eastern Europe arrived in the late 1800's. By 1910, 3 million had settled in the United States, mostly in the North Atlantic states. Jews had been colonists in New York, Rhode Island, and Massachusetts since 1654, but their contributions to American English became most significant in the period before and after World War I.

Most American Jews do not speak Hebrew. Their original tongue was Yiddish, a German-based language used by Jews in Central and Eastern Europe. These Yiddish words are common in our language.

bagel: doughnut-shaped hard roll.

chutzpah: audacity; nerve; impudence.

ghetto: living area in which a minority is confined by the majority.

kibitz: give unwanted advice (kibitz at a card game).

kosher: proper, legitimate (derived from special dietary laws observed by Orthodox Jews).

lox: smoked salmon.

mavin: an expert, an authority.

schlemiel: a foolish, clumsy person.

schlep: to drag or carry.

Building Your Vocabulary

Our evolving language. Words you might overhear spoken in Springfield, Massachusetts, or any other American town or city, would be widely different from those you might hear in Peterborough or any other English city or town. We lift the *hood* on our car; they lift the *bonnet*. We might see a *cop* on his *vacation;* an Englishman would see a *bobby* on *holiday.*

Our two languages, of course, started as one. Over a 300-year span, the division has encompassed more than variations in common terms and their usages. Americans have coined their own words and phrases. These are some from various periods in American history:

The Revolutionary War
militia: a reserve force; a citizen army.
redcoats: British soldiers.
rifle: a musket with a spiraled inner barrel.
stockade: a fort protected by a wall of pointed stakes.

The Civil War
carpetbagger: an unscrupulous northerner who went south in 1868 for cheap land; an opportunist.
scalawag: southerner who accepted Reconstruction.

World War I
doughboy: infantry soldier; also used, to a lesser extent, in the Civil War.
goldbrick: to loaf or avoid work (Army term).
rookie: new recruit.

Prohibition
flapper: a "modern," unconventional young woman.
gang wars: battles for supremacy among rival groups of gangsters.
public enemy: notorious criminal, high on the FBI's most-wanted list.
scram: get out of here; leave.
speakeasy: illegal tavern or barroom.
teetotaler: one pledged to total abstinence from intoxicating beverages.

World War II
black market: trafficking in rationed, scarce goods.
Dear John: a letter to a soldier from his sweetheart, calling off their relationship.
GI: an ordinary soldier; based on the term *government issue,* applied to all military materials.
wild blue yonder: the sky, as it applied to the site of aerial battles.

The '50's, '60's, and '70's
dove: one who advocates peaceful overtures, particularly to the Soviets.
game plan: strategy; used in business and politics.
hawk: one who advocates a hard line, particularly against the Soviets; the term was first used, in another context, in Jefferson's era.
leak: disclosure of government papers and plans.
stonewall: resist investigation, as during the Watergate episode of the Nixon Presidency

The '80's
burnout: exhaustion caused by intensive work over an extended period.
computerese: terms used by computer operators; examples are **byte** (unit of information stored in the computer's memory); **glitch** (error); **user-friendly** (program that is easy to operate).

Stud, draw, or deuces wild

Poker is the most American of card games. (Only basketball and baseball have stronger claims to being "the Great American game"—they were invented by Yankees. Poker is an old European card game, and its name is derived from the French *poque.*)

In all parts of the nation, daily, people who do not know a pair of eights from a royal flush use poker terms. Dozens that have become ingrained in our national speech follow.
poker face: a wooden, nonrevealing expression.
on the come, on the blind: hoping or acting as if an event will happen, without really knowing if it will.
go the limit: extend oneself as far as possible.
penny ante: insignificant, petty action or game.
bluff: overblown actions calculated to make an opponent think you are stronger than you are.
wild card: an unexpected factor; may change the outcome.
dead man's hand: two aces and two eights, said to be the hand Wild Bill Hickok was holding when he was murdered.
stand pat: stay with what you have; do not budge.
playing with a short deck: not too bright; dimwitted.
four flusher: cheater; needs five, has only four.

Puzzles and word games

What is good for us is often bad tasting—but there are exceptions. You can enjoy yourself as you progress on several of the paths to a more powerful vocabulary. Word games and puzzles, whether played alone or in competition, are effective learning devices. They really do reinforce your knowledge of new words' meanings, and build considerably your ability to recall those words.

Crossword puzzles. Americans seem to be a nation of crossword puzzlers. Newspapers print daily puzzles; paperback and hardcover books of puzzle collections fill several shelves in most bookstores; crossword puzzle dictionaries and other specialized aids are widely available.

If you are new to the world of crosswords, consider these tips:

1. Search around, while you are still getting the hang of it, for a source of *easy* puzzles. Ones that are difficult are likely to discourage you.
2. Use pencil, write lightly, and do not hesitate to erase guesses that might be wrong.
3. For your first move, skim through the puzzle and insert words you are sure about: names of people or movies; places; facts about games, crafts, or instruments. Then you will have enough letters in place to give you hints for words you are less sure about.

Packaged word games

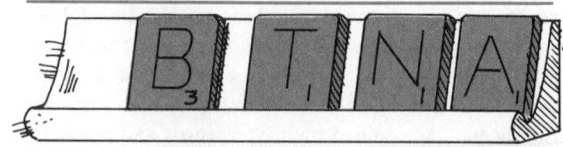

Any bookstore or toy store should be a good source for a half-dozen or more different word games, packaged and ready for spreading out on your table.

Examine the game; read the rules before purchasing it. You may decide it is too specialized or requires too extensive a vocabulary for the people who will be playing it.

Anagrams: the granddaddy of all "take-a-card" or "take-a-tile" word games. Players form their own words, capture opponents' words, and the whole family joins in.

Scrabble: each player forms a word with any number of his seven randomly selected tiles. He lays the letters on the board's marked spaces. Some letters and spaces are good for bonus points. Players add on to, or branch out from, previously laid-down words.

Boggle: 25 letters appear in a square. Players compose hidden lists of all possible words, using only letters that are touching one another. After three minutes, lists are compared and a winner declared.

Ghosts

This age-old game requires two or more players. Each player in turn calls out a letter. If, from the fourth letter on, a player completes a word, he loses that round, and must "carry" letter G.

A new round is begun. If there is a new loser, he too carries letter G. Losers of subsequent rounds must carry G, then H, then O, S, T, and S. When one player has all six letters, he loses. The others play on until one winner remains.

If it is Mary's turn and the letters VAL, for example, have been named, she might call letter I. If she had called E, the word VALE would have been spelled, and she would have lost that round. If the next player cannot think of a word starting VALI, he can challenge Mary, who will say VALISE or VALID. Mary proves she has a word in mind, so the challenger loses that round.

Hangman

This word game requires at least two players. One of the players, the leader, has a word in mind. He tells the other players the number of letters in the word. The other players try to guess the word by calling out letters. When a letter is guessed correctly, the leader tells the others at what position or positions in the word the letter falls.

However, for every letter that is called out that is not in the word, the leader draws a portion of a stick figure. Usually, the figure is made up of a head, eyes, nose, mouth, torso, arms, hands, legs, and feet. If the figure is completed before the word is guessed, then the figure is considered hanged, and the leader has won the game. If someone guesses the word, then that person becomes the next leader.

Building Your Vocabulary

Rate yourself again

Some time ago, when you were setting out to build your *Word Power,* you tested yourself. ("How do you rate?" on page 208.) Now that you nearly have completed the program, it will be interesting to measure your gain over your earlier effort.

To make the comparison valid, you should test your facility with difficult words—ones that you have examined and added to your vocabulary. All of the target words in this self-exam appear and are defined in the preceding pages.

For each of the questions, select the one term that *most nearly defines* the meaning of the word in dark print. Score one point for each correct answer.

If you are determined to improve your vocabulary, but score 17 or under, start over. Work on your *Word Power* file daily. Be certain that you understand the meaning of each word before progressing to the next one. Go back over your new vocabulary. A daily review can go a long way toward cementing new words in your memory.

1. **dubious** a) twin; b) prejudiced; c) doubtful; d) double

2. **humus** a) amateur comedian; b) good feelings; c) bad reputation; d) decayed plants

3. **perfidy** a) smells good; b) large taxes; c) traitor's actions; d) risk

4. **meticulous** a) precise; b) fingernails; c) angry; d) foolish

5. **impediment** a) fooling; b) showing; c) statue; d) blocking

6. **facade** a) front; b) mimic; c) framework; d) mobility

7. **accessible** a) can be captured; b) must leave; c) can be reached; d) too much

8. **curator** a) doctor's assistant; b) museum director; c) bullfighter's sword; d) church official

9. **enigma** a) puzzle; b) birthmark; c) pride; d) energetic

10. **petulance** a) birdlike; b) grumpiness; c) shyness; d) holiday

11. **altruism** a) honesty; b) generosity; c) completion; d) conservatism

12. **irascible** a) held up; b) easily angered; c) ready for action; d) green

13. **felines** a) fish; b) snakes; c) criminals; d) cats

14. **undulate** a) wave; b) chew; c) blink; d) shout

15. **cynosure** a) show; b) deterrent; c) detergent; d) swan

16. **habitat** a) farmyard; b) home; c) unpleasant; d) nun

17. **voracious** a) gets in front; b) eats huge amounts; c) frightening; d) never wins

18. **incombustible** a) untidy; b) unburnable; c) unbreakable; d) can't be equaled

19. **marauders** a) raiders; b) jumpers; c) winners; d) swimmers

20. **gregarious** a) religious; b) young; c) frightened; d) sociable

21. **devastated** a) exasperated; b) humbled; c) wasted; d) enlarged

22. **vestige** a) clothing; b) appropriate; c) persuasion; d) remnant

23. **consoled** a) comforted; b) entertained; c) controlled; d) welcomed

24. **garrulous** a) talkative; b) plump; c) foolish; d) proud

25. **antagonist** a) sufferer; b) opponent; c) follower; d) merchant

Answers. 1, c; 2, d; 3, c; 4, a; 5, d; 6, a; 7, c; 8, b; 9, a; 10, b; 11, b; 12, b; 13, d; 14, a; 15, a; 16, b; 17, b; 18, b; 19, a; 20, d; 21, c; 22, d; 23, a; 24, a; 25, b. A score of 25 is perfect, 22–24 very good, 18–21 above average.

askance

Words you should know

gist
   the main point of a topic.

empirical
   believing things that one has
   observed for oneself.

insouciant
   carefree
   nonchalant
   untroubled

Word Power cards

absolve. To clear or pardon; to pronounce that no blame exists.

abstract. 1. Not concrete or definite (an *abstract* thought). 2. A portion reprinted from a larger book or article.

acerate. Sharpened; pointed at one end.

acquiesce. To agree; consent; to go along with a suggestion.

acrylic. A resin-based synthetic fiber.

acute. 1. Sharp, pointed. 2. Important. 3. Sensitive (an *acute* sense of hearing).

agitate. 1. To move suddenly or violently; to shake up. 2. To disturb. 3. To interest in a cause (*agitated* for higher pay).

albatross. 1. Large sea bird. 2. A burden, handicap, or curse (this meaning is derived from a poem, *The Rime of the Ancient Mariner*, by Coleridge).

alewife. Small, herringlike fish.

anemic. A disease in which too few red blood cells results in weakness and fatigue.

aorta. The largest of the arteries carrying blood from the heart.

apothecary. Druggist; pharmacist.

appalling. Frightening; upsetting (the filth was *appalling*).

askance (a-skans'). Disapproval or distrust; a sidewise glance indicating doubt.

aspect. 1. Appearance. 2. The direction something faces.

assert. To state positively or forcefully.

assuage (a-swaje'). To remedy; make easier, less painful.

badinage (bad-n-ahj'). Playful, joking talk; chitchat.

baste. 1. To sew loosely, temporarily. 2. To keep moist (as with sauce or melted butter) while cooking.

bastion. Fort or strongly held position (the league was a *bastion* of patriotism).

behoove. Necessary or proper (*behooves* us to pay attention).

bellow. To roar or shout; the roar of a large animal, as a buffalo.

benign. Harmless, kindly, mild.

bequeath. To pass on, or leave, as in a will.

bequest. That which has been *bequeathed* (Mary's aunt left her a *bequest* of $50,000).

bigamy. Being married to two persons at one time, a criminal offense.

blackguard (blag'-erd). An unprincipled rascal; a scoundrel.

blanch. To bleach or whiten; to remove the color from an object.

blather. Nonsensical or foolish talk.

blemish. A flaw or spot that spoils the appearance of an object or a person.

blunder. A mistake caused by stupidity or confusion.

bob. To move up and down (Jim *bobbed* alongside the boat).

bolster. 1. A pillow or cushion. 2. To support or prop up (contributions *bolstered* her campaign funds).

bountiful. Plentiful; generous.

Brahmin. Descendant of old, exclusive family (a New England *Brahmin*); derived from Hindu term for *highest rank*.

bravado. A show of false, swaggering bravery.

calligraphy. Handwriting; penmanship.

camber. 1. An arched surface. 2. The way in which automobile wheels are set slanting inward toward their tops.

caster. A small, swiveled wheel under furniture or another heavy object.

cherish. To treat with love and tenderness; to hold dear.

circa. Approximately, about (first used *circa* 1900).

cistern. A tank for holding rainwater.

constrict. To squeeze, compress, make smaller.

Building Your Vocabulary

consummate. 1. To conclude or bring to perfection. 2. Perfect; highly skilled (a *consummate* baker of pastries).

cougar. A mountain lion.

covenant. An agreement or contract that binds two or more persons.

cringe. To move back in fear (synonym: *cower*).

croissant (kwoss-sahn′). A crescent-shaped roll of light, sweet dough.

damsel. A girl or maiden (used in ancient times, but rarely heard today).

decimate. To kill or destroy a large part of something; to kill one-tenth.

desecrate. To disturb something sacred; to profane.

detonate. To explode.

dire. Dreadful, terrible, extreme; having horrible consequences (a *dire* threat).

discord. Tension, strife, lack of agreement.

divan. A backless couch.

dominant. The highest; the one in control, with the most authority.

dominate. To rule or control; to be higher than others.

dub. To apply a nickname (they *dubbed* him "Mr. Careful").

dynasty. A group or family that keeps power for several generations.

edgy. Tense; nervous; anxious.

eject. To throw out; to evict (the noisy couple was *ejected* from the theater).

ember. A dying coal in a fire that is partially out.

embroil. To involve in an argument or contest; to entangle.

empirical. Believing ideas, actions, or things that one has observed for oneself (*empirical* evidence).

epicure. One who has uncommon, highly refined preferences in food and wine.

evince. To demonstrate clearly.

expire. 1. To end; to die; a last breath. 2. To breathe out.

expostulate. To present one's reasons; to argue intelligently.

extol. To praise highly.

extricate. To free or release from an entanglement.

farce. Far-fetched, humorous show; broad, exaggerated comedy.

fastidious. 1. Careful, exacting attention to detail. 2. Overly attentive to good manners.

fervent. Showing great emotional depth; highly enthusiastic.

fetish. 1. Something that is said to have mystic powers. 2. An excessively strong habit or attitude (Tim made a *fetish* of washing his hands).

fickle. Unpredictably changeable in regard to attitudes and affections.

figment. Something made up or invented (the whole story was a *figment* of his imagination).

forage. 1. To look for food. 2. Hay, grain, or other food for domestic animals.

forfeit (for′-fit). Something given up, in punishment for a crime or offense; that which is forfeited.

forlorn. Extreme sadness or loneliness; the appearance of a sad, lonely person.

furl. To roll up a flag.

gabardine. Cotton twill fabric.

gaggle. 1. A flock of geese. 2. A group of silly or cackling people.

gape. To stare, with mouth opened wide in wonderment.

garret. An attic.

genial. Friendly; pleasant; a kindly manner.

gird. 1. To prepare for action. 2. To put on a belt or band.

gist. The main point of a topic; the core, or essence, of a subject.

gnash (nash). To grind one's teeth together.

graphic. Relating to writing, drawing, painting, typesetting, and other representations on paper or a similarly flat surface (*graphic* arts).

grave. 1. Serious, important, dangerous (declaring war was a *grave* decision). 2. A burial place.

guffaw. Coarse, noisy laughter.

gustatory. Relating to the sense of taste (eating at Joe's was a *gustatory* experience).

gyrate. To circle or revolve around a point or axis.

hack. To chop, cut, or break up.

hagiology. Study of the lives of saints.

hale. To drag or pull; to compel someone to go somewhere (*haled* into court). 2. Healthy; not sickly.

hark. To listen carefully.

harridan. Unpleasant, complaining woman.

hearth. The floor of a fireplace, and that part of it extending into a room.

hepatitis (hep′-a-tie-tiss). A serious disease of the liver.

heretic. A person who disagrees with generally accepted opinions, or dissents from religious views.

hexagonal. Six-sided.

hindsight. Noticing the importance and cause of an event after it has happened.

hormone. A chemical substance formed in the body and carried in the bloodstream.

horticulture. The growing of fruits, vegetables, or plants; gardening.

hospice. 1. A place or program that cares for patients who are incurably ill. 2. A shelter for needy travelers.

huckster. 1. A peddler; one who sells merchandise in the street. 2. A writer of advertisements.

hydraulic. Related to water pressure (*hydraulic* pump; *hydraulic* engineer).

iconoclast. One who attacks and destroys popularly held, or traditional, values. (Ancient

Greeks called religious statues *icons. Iconoclasts* were "breakers of statues," or breakers of ideas.)

ignominious. Disgraceful; shameful.

immune. Not affected; excepted from a general condition.

immutable. Unchangeable.

imperial. 1. Relating to an empire or emperor. 2. A nation that maintains control over colonies.

imperturbable. Calm; cannot be shaken or disturbed.

implicit (im-plis'-it). Understood, though stated only indirectly (an *implicit* understanding).

impunity. Will not be punished or harmed (state your opinions with *impunity*).

inception. The beginning; start.

incumbent. Currently holding an office or position (the *incumbent* governor).

inept. Clumsy; foolish; incompetent; not suitable.

influx. Flowing in (an *influx* of immigrants).

inordinate. More than could be expected; an unreasonable amount.

insouciant (in-soo'-see-ont). Carefree, nonchalant, untroubled.

interrogate. Ask questions.

iota. An extremely small amount (we did not care one *iota* what their opinion might be).

itinerant. One who travels from place to place, as part of his work; traveling in such a way.

jamb (jam). The vertical framework of a door or window.

jibe. To agree (your information *jibes* with ours).

jubilant. Joyful; happy enough to sing or laugh aloud.

juxtapose. To put one thing or idea next to another in order to compare them.

kamikaze (ka-me-kah'-zee). A suicidal crash attack (a tactic used by Japanese pilots in World War II).

keynote. Main theme (President Kennedy gave the *keynote* speech at the convention).

koala. An Australian animal, the model for teddy bears.

labyrinth (lab'-a-rinth). Mazelike series of connecting passages and tunnels.

lacerate. To tear, wound, rip, or cut.

laconic (la-kon'-ick). Using few words; short-spoken (Coolidge, who was *laconic*, was called "Silent Cal").

lacuna (la-koo'-nah). An empty space; missing part; gap.

laggard. Straggler; one who falls behind the others.

laity (lay'-ih-tee). People who are not members of a given profession; in churches, those who are not members of the clergy.

lament. To mourn or grieve; to express sorrow; a spoken or written expression of grief.

lapse. 1. To slip or drift backward; to neglect or overlook. 2. A missed opportunity or privilege; the amount of time during which the privilege expired.

late. In addition to the common meaning of coming after the expected time, late also means dead, or recently died (the *late* Mrs. Patterson).

lax. Not strict. Unfirm.

LED. The display of letters or numerals, as on a calculator, furnished by a semiconductor; *LED* is an acronym for Light Emitting Diode.

lenient (lee'-ne-yent). Not inclined to punish; forgiving.

levitate. To rise into the air with no apparent support; a mystical act or illusion that defies gravity.

libation. An alcoholic drink; a drink offered to a god.

limber. Moving easily; supple; working without effort (he sent a more *limber* player into the game).

linear. (linn'-ee-er). Relating to a straight line (a *linear* descendant of the Adams family).

locus. A place or location.

lozenge. A medicated tablet for relief from coughs and colds.

macadam. A type of road made of stone and asphalt or tar.

machination (mack'-in-ayshun). 1. The act of plotting or scheming, usually for an evil purpose; the plot itself.

maculate. Spotted or soiled; to spot or stain (*immaculate* means "without spots," or pure, clean, unstained).

magnate. Powerful person, usually a businessman or industrialist (a lumber *magnate*).

malcontent. Unhappy or discontented; also, a person in that condition (*mal* means bad, or generally negative, as in *malformed* and *malodorous*).

manacle. Handcuff.

mangle. 1. To ruin through clumsiness (Howard *mangled* his speech). 2. To cut, hack, or otherwise physically ruin.

mare's nest. 1. A tangled, complicated situation. 2. A fraud.

marginal. 1. Near the edge or border. 2. Of barely passable quality.

maroon. 1. A color, ranging from reddish brown to reddish purple. 2. To abandon a person; to put him off a boat with little hope of rescue.

martinet. A rigid military leader or taskmaster; one who demands total obedience.

mediate. To settle disputes by acting as a neutral party.

melange (may-lahnj'). A mixture.

menial (mean'-ee-al). 1. A servant. 2. Relating to a job or task that a servant might do.

metamorphosis. A change in shape, appearance, or function (a tadpole's *metamorphosis* into a frog).

Building Your Vocabulary

metropolis. A large city.

microcomputer. A very small computer (*micro* means small or greatly reduced in size).

mien (mean). Facial expression or the way one carries oneself; appearance.

mildew. A fungus, similar to a mold, that grows on leather, plants, cloth, or paper under damp conditions.

minatory. Threatening; fearsome.

minutia (mi-noo'-sha). A very small, unimportant item (we cannot bother with the *minutia* of their complaints).

mode. A way of doing something; a style of action (an unusual *mode* of dress, or of speech).

molest. To harass, bother, or physically disturb.

monarch. A king, emperor, or ruler.

monogram. The initials of a person's name formed into a design.

moot. A matter that can be argued in any of several ways; not easily decided.

mucilage (myoo'-si-laj). Glue.

murky. Dark, gloomy; heavy mist or fog; thick, unclear waters (a *murky* atmosphere).

nape. The back of the neck.

nether. Lower or below (the *nether* regions).

niggling. Fussy; petty; too concerned with unimportant detail.

novel. 1. New, different (Bill's wagon had a *novel* design). 2. A book of fiction; prose narrative.

obfuscate. To hide slightly, or make obscure (he deliberately *obfuscated* the facts about the accident).

Occident. Europe and the western hemisphere (Asia and the Pacific islands are the *Orient*).

offing. Soon, or the near future (a large gift is in the *offing*).

oratory. The skill of public speaking; rhetorical style.

ossify. 1. To become bony. 2. To become set in an unchanging pattern.

ostracize. To shut out or exclude from a group; to banish.

palate. The roof of the mouth.

palette. 1. A hand-held board on which an artist mixes colors. 2. The range of colors used by an artist.

panacea (pan-a-see-a). A cure for all diseases or difficulties, the value of which is doubtful.

paradox. A statement, difficult to believe, that is true (*paradoxically,* the two opponents were brothers).

paragon. A model of excellence.

peccadillo. A small fault; a prank.

pewter. Silver-gray metal used for kitchen and cooking utensils.

pillage. To rob or plunder, as by invading armies in wartime.

poise. 1. To balance, or the state of being balanced. 2. Bearing oneself with dignity and composure (she exhibited *poise* and maturity).

ponder. To think carefully; to consider.

predator. One who preys on others for his own profit, as an animal preys on (kills and eats) weaker animals.

propinquity (pro-pin'-kwi-tee). Nearness (*propinquity* is at the root of most friendships).

quagmire. 1. Swampy, boggy land into which a walker might sink. 2. A predicament or difficult situation that might entrap a person.

quail. 1. To move backward in fear. 2. A small, chickenlike bird; a bobwhite.

quash. To put down; suppress; set aside (the judge *quashed* the motion for appeal).

quiver. 1. To tremble or shake. 2. A case in which an archer's arrows are carried.

radiate. 1. To spread out from a central point (spokes of a wheel *radiate* from the hub). 2. To issue energy—heat, light, or sound.

radical. Carried to an extreme; not moderate.

rail. To speak strongly against; to verbally abuse (Ken *railed* against the new tax collector).

rampart. A fort or defensive position higher than the surrounding ground.

rant. To shout in a violent manner; to rave.

rapport (ra-pour'). A good relationship, marked by mutual trust and admiration.

rationale (rash-a-nal'). A reason (sometimes used as an excuse) for doing something.

redundant. Unnecessarily repeated; not needed.

refute. To disprove; to argue against.

regress. To move backward, usually to a worsened condition (the opposite of *progress*).

reiterate. To say again; repeat.

relent. To soften an attitude; to give up a previously held, harder position.

remonstrate. To protest; object; argue.

repartee (re-par-tay'). Witty, clever conversation, particularly a witty reply.

replete. Plenty, or an oversupply. (a party *replete* with butlers and waitresses).

rife. Appears frequently; often occurs (his work was *rife* with errors).

rook. 1. A crow. 2. To cheat or swindle.

ruminate. 1. To think about something for a long time; to reflect on it. 2. For cattle, to chew and rechew.

Rx. A prescription for medicine or pharmaceutical drugs.

saccharine (sack'-a-rin). Too sweet (*saccharin* is the white, powdery substitute for sugar).

salutation. A greeting, especially at the start of a letter ("Dear Mr. Brenner," for example).

sanctum. A holy place; sacred part of a church or temple.

sarcophagus (sar-kof'-a-gus). A stone coffin.

savvy. *(Slang)* To understand; knowhow (he is *savvy* enough to make a good deal).

scale. Thin, flaky substance on the skins of animals, fishes, or plants. 2. Rate of pay, determined by union schedules, for musicians and other skilled technicians. 3. A device for weighing; a measure.

scant. Meager; a small degree less than a specified amount (a *scant* four miles).

scenario. 1. An outline of a play or book. 2. The probable way in which events will take place, if certain unpredictable circumstances govern the action (here is the *scenario* for our rescue operation, if all the bridges flood out).

scow. A large flat-bottomed boat.

scrawny. Skinny; bony.

scuffle. To grapple or fight with someone in an indeterminate, confused manner.

sealing wax. A soft substance when heated, it hardens to seal bottles and packages.

secondary school. High school.

seethe. 1. To be extremely excited; agitated. 2. To have a motion like that of boiling water.

semantics. The study of the meaning of language.

seminary. 1. A school for the training of religious persons— ministers, priests, rabbis. 2. A school of higher education for young women.

sensor. A machine that receives or sends impulses, like light or heat, not otherwise detected by humans.

sentient. Conscious; able to experience thought and feelings.

sequester. To move away; set apart; place in seclusion (they chose to *sequester* themselves in a far valley).

serrated. Having an edge that is notched or saw-toothed.

servile. Subordinate or submissive in attitude, like a servant.

sham. False, fraudulent; a trick intended to pass off someone or something as other than as it really is.

shear. To remove hair or fleece from an animal (the farmer *sheared* his sheep; the barber *sheared* Don's hair too short).

shoal. Shallow water, sometimes unexpectedly so and a threat to navigators.

shoddy. Inferior; made of poor quality materials.

shortfall. A shortage; an amount below the expected, usually referring to money.

showboating. Showing off; attempting to attract attention.

showdown. An act that forces the outcome of an issue or event (the feud had gone on long enough, so the families arranged a *showdown*).

shrew. 1. A woman who nags and scolds; an unpleasant, constantly criticizing woman. 2. A small, mouselike animal with poor vision.

shrewd. Clever, sharp, cunning; quick-witted.

shrivel. To shrink and dry up, remaining in a wrinkled condition.

shun. To deliberately avoid (Carol walked across the street, *shunning* her nephew).

sickle. A tool with a long, curved blade used for cutting grain, grass, or other tall plants (the Communist flag is known as the hammer and sickle because those two tools are depicted on it).

sidereal. About, or relating to, the stars; stellar.

sidle. To step or move sideways; usually done when trying to avoid another person, or to remain unnoticed.

significant. Having a valuable or important meaning.

silent treatment. To totally ignore an unliked person, as a means of expressing contempt (everyone in the class gave Kim the *silent treatment*).

simper. A silly, childish smile.

simulate. 1. To imitate, or take on the manner and appearance of another person or thing. 2. To pretend (Carl *simulated* interest in Rose's career).

sketchy. Slight; incomplete; leaving out many of the details and finer points.

skimpy. Not enough; too small an amount for the purpose, often due to insufficient money having been spent.

slake. To satisfy; to lessen a condition that had existed (the announcement *slaked* Dan's rage; the water *slaked* Ann's thirst).

snide. Sarcastic; offensive in a rude, superior manner.

solar. Having to do with the sun. (*solar* heat; *solar* rays; *solar* blindness).

sonar. A technique of using sound waves, reflected off objects under water.

sordid. 1. Extremely dirty; filthy; vile. 2. Motivated solely by greed.

souvenir (soo'-va-neer). A memento; something that helps one remember a place or an event (we were given key rings as *souvenirs* of the party).

spectrum. A range of ideas, thoughts, or activities (the whole *spectrum* of medical science).

stalwart. Strong, determined.

stance. One's attitude or position; the way one stands; also, one's thoughts on a controversial issue.

stifle. 1. To smother; suffocate. 2. To cut off opposition.

stunt. To slow or stop the growth of a person or thing.

taboo. A strict rule or custom against an action, imposed by social or religious beliefs.

Building Your Vocabulary

tactful. Sensitive, considerate; taking care not to offend.

taint. To infect; to stain someone's reputation (the *taint* of his dishonorable discharge).

tension. 1. The act of stretching or being stretched. 2. A condition of nervous strain.

thwart. To frustrate; to prevent an action or event desired by another person from taking place.

tirade. A long, angry speech, aimed at an enemy or an enemy's position.

topsy-turvy. Totally confused; upside-down.

torrid. 1. Very hot and dry, parched. 2. Passionate, intense.

touchy. 1. Quick to take offense; too sensitive. 2. A situation that requires delicate handling.

tranquil. Calm and undisturbed.

transitory. Existing only for a brief time; short-lived; an in-between period.

traverse. To move across or through; to travel up or down, or backward and forward, through a place or region.

trounce. To beat, as in a fight.

tumult. Noise and commotion caused by an unruly crowd.

tyrant. A harsh, cruel ruler.

unvailing. Useless.

uncouth. Clumsy, crude, impolite.

unflappable. Calm and unexcited.

ungainly. Awkward; lacking grace; moving clumsily.

unpalatable. Not easily swallowed or accepted; unpleasing; unpleasant.

valor. Bravery; courage (a *valiant* person is one who exhibits *valor*).

vandalism. Meaningless, criminal destruction of property.

veer. To turn in another direction; to move off one's course.

venerable. Honored and respected because of age, position, or reputation.

vicissitudes (vi-siss′-i-toods). Unexpected shifts and changes in one's life; commonly used to mean hardships (the *vicissitudes* of widowhood).

vivid. Bright; strongly experienced; distinct; described in a lifelike manner.

wane. To decline, come to an end, decrease.

wary. Watchful; cautious; on one's guard.

wistful. Vaguely, or sadly, wishful.

word processing. Producing reports, books, and other documents via the use of computers.

wrest. To forcefully pull or grab an object from another person.

For further reference

American language

Boatner, Maxine T. and Gates, J. E.
A Dictionary of American Idioms
Barron's. Four thousand commonly used expressions, including slang, proverbs, and clichés. For each entry, definitions and examples of use in sentences.

Mathews, Mitford M.
Americanisms
Phoenix. A dictionary of words that first came into use in the United States. Includes the earliest recorded use of each word.

Mencken, H. L.
The American Language
(one-volume abridged edition)
Knopf. The enduring classic study of our language: how it evolved and how it is used today. Still as fascinating as when written more than 60 years ago.

Vocabulary building

Davidson, Jessica
How to Improve Your Spelling and Vocabulary
Franklin Watts. Rules, tips, procedures, exercises, and games for students and young adults.

Evans, Bergen
Comfortable Words
Random House. Witty, brief analyses of the origins and accurate meanings of commonly used words and phrases.

Specialized interests

Barnhart, Clarence L., Steinmetz, Sol, and Barnhart, R.
The Second Barnhart Dictionary of New English
Harper & Row. Definitions of new words that appeared in print during the years 1973 to 1979.

Bernstein, Theodore M.
Reverse Dictionary
Quadrangle. Meanings are arranged alphabetically; the word that is defined follows its meaning (for example: "Rope or cable for mooring or towing: HAWSER").

Partridge, Eric
Origins
Macmillan. An etymological dictionary, providing information about the evolution of 12,000 commonly used words.

Pei, Mario
Language of the Specialists
Funk & Wagnalls. Specialists in 20 categories—astronomy, literature, and medicine are typical—each select and define a hundred or more terms.

Webster's New Dictionary of Synonyms
G. & C. Merriam Company. Helpful for finding the right word with precisely the meaning you require.

Games and puzzles

Brandreth, Gyles
The World's Best Indoor Games
Pantheon. Complete rules and explanations for dozens of word games from "Ghosts" to "Guggenheim."

Hill, Norman
How to Solve Crossword Puzzles
Funk & Wagnalls.

Kurzban, Stan and Rosen, Mel
The Compleat Cruciverbalist
Van Nostrand Reinhold. Subtitled "How to solve and compose crossword puzzles for fun and profit." (*Cruciverbalist* is a made-up word meaning "crossword.")

Improving Your Speech

It is said that man is instinctively afraid of only two things: falling and speaking in public. Just a clever remark, you may think, and not one that applies to you. But think a moment longer. Do any of the following cause you anxiety?

- Making an important phone call.
- Being introduced to an important person.
- Trying to convince someone.

Many people are uneasy in such everyday situations, and they betray their anxiety by the way they speak. On the phone, an anxious person may stumble or mumble, and the other party may quickly stop listening. Meeting an influential stranger, an anxious person may launch into a self-promoting one-way conversation—and forget to introduce himself. During a good-natured exchange involving a difference of opinion, an anxious person may undermine his argument by unintentionally bullying or ridiculing his opponent.

What do these situations have to do with public speaking? Most phone calls, many two-way discussions, and all introductions take place between you and a stranger, between you and your "public." Whatever you say is going to leave an indelible first impression; how you speak to a stranger is as memorable to him as your face. For this reason, your private conversation may need improvement before you are ready to go public.

Broadly interpreted, public speaking is the art of communicating effectively. It is a learned skill, always starting at the level of one-to-one communication. By understanding the way people exchange information verbally and symbolically, you can learn to improve the way you speak—to friends, co-workers, and even strangers.

Formal speechmaking is, of course, the highest form of public speaking. But there are virtually no natural public speakers, born to the podium. The great spellbinders in history—politicians, preachers, and actors—were polished and well-rehearsed performers who knew precisely what they were doing. All of them practiced hundreds of times before hundreds of audiences. In fact, every great speaker is likely to remember at least one time when he was terrified: his first time.

Until the basics of speaking are mastered, the best-written speech on Earth will not be truly heard. On the next pages you will find the five keys to effective speech:

1. Pronunciation; 2. Pace; 3. Attention; 4. Eye contact; and 5. Pauses.

Take each key in order, then apply it to your own mannerisms. (Here as elsewhere in this chapter, access to a tape recorder will be highly useful.) The five keys might be called the tools of your private communications trade; all of them together, in order and ready to use, make up your public speaking tool kit. Each of the five is essential if you expect to be a fully effective speaker.

The five keys

Pronunciation. Beginning now, imagine that everything you say is for someone else's consumption. First, ask yourself if you are usually understood when you talk to anyone outside of your immediate family (families sometimes speak in code). Do you make an effort to enunciate each word? Or do you run the words together as if in a hurry to get the sentence over with? Among friends, face to face, you may get by with careless pronunciation. But do you notice any problem in being understood by people who do not know you? By older people? By people with different regional accents?

Your own regional accent or dialect need not concern you; it is part of your personality and may well be part of your charm. Three of the last six U.S. Presidents had pronounced regional accents, and they made no attempt to change them.

Many English words sound similar, but the slightest adjustment between tongue and lips can make the difference between one sound (or word) and another— between *far* and *fire,* for example. One self-test for pronunciation addresses itself to words beginning with *d, t,* and *th.* Try saying *din, tin, thin,* and *then.* Can you hear the difference clearly? If you cannot, perhaps a friend can. Ask other friends if they have any trouble understanding the way you pronounce words. When you read or hear a difficult word or name, write it down and practice saying it. Soon you will develop a highly desirable pronunciation habit: *wanting* to say things right.

Reading from a prepared text, you will have the time to look up the pronunciation of any word about which you feel uncertain—and the time will be well spent. Proper names, too, can be found phonetically notated in large dictionaries. A correctly pronounced proper name or place is always well received by an audience. A mispronounced name is, at best, unnecessary; at worst, it is insulting. Most common mispronunciations arise through constant misuse.

For best results with the following list, cover up the *wrong* and *right* columns and read the words aloud, using a tape recorder if possible. Some of the words on the list are routinely mispronounced by some of the most prominent people in the United States. But no matter who says *new-*cue-ler at a press conference, it is wrong.

Test your pronunciation

	Wrong	*Right*
accidentally	ak-si-*dent*-ly	ak-si-*den*-tal-ly
across	a-*krost*	a-*kross*
anyway	*en*-ee-wayz	*en*-ee-way
anywhere	*en*-ee-wayrze	*en*-ee-ware
asked	axed	asked
burst	bust	burst
drowned	drown-did	drownd
escape	ek-*scape*	es-*cape*
film	*fill*-um	film
government	*guv*-mint	*guh*-vern-ment
heartrending	*hart*-ren-der-ing	*hart*-ren-ding
height	*hite*-th	hite
hold	a-hold	hold
hundred	*hun*-nert	*hun*-drid
incidentally	in-si-*dent*-ly	in-si-*den*-tal-ly
interesting	*in*-nur-es-ting	*in*-tur-es-ting
judgment	*judg*-uh-ment	*judg*-ment
nowhere	*no*-wayrze	*no*-ware
nuclear	*new*-cue-ler	*new*-clee-ur
often	*off*-ten	*off*-en
police	*poh*-leece	poh-*leece*
recur	re-o-*cur*	re-*cur*
regardless	ir-ri-*gard*-liss	ri-*gard*-liss
scared	uh-*scared*	scared
toward	tuh-*ward*	tawrd
unaware	un-uh-*wayrze*	un-uh-*ware*
undoubtedly	un-*dow*-tuh-blee	un-*dow*-tid-lee

Pace. The initial requirement for effective speech is intelligibility. If you are not understood, your thoughts are not conveyed, and if you are to be understood, then you must speak at a pace that enables your listeners to get your message. Rapid-fire speech may be acceptable for comic effect, but it is unacceptable for the purpose of communication.

Most Americans harbor the prejudice that people who speak a foreign language talk too fast. Whatever is unfamiliar, in your own language or another, nearly always seems to be spoken too fast.

Perhaps you have been told that you speak too fast, or too slowly; or perhaps you suspect that your conversational speed is not quite right for public speaking. To test your speaking rate, choose a page from a favorite book and read it aloud, at your normal speed, for three minutes. Then count the number of words you have just read. Fewer than 400 is considered too slow; 450 is the comfortable spoken average; and 500 words or more is too fast.

Most people find after taking this test that they read faster than they thought. Reading aloud takes longer, of course, than normal conversation; your own words are spoken more easily than someone else's. As a starting point, assume that you should try to speak slower in public than in private.

An aid to slower speaking is louder speaking. Trying to talk louder will cause you to slow your pace. Think for a moment about how people respond to fast, soft speech. In a classroom, for example, a student who rattles off an answer in a whispery voice will neither be heard nor understood—even if his answer is correct. The student who speaks deliberately and clearly makes a better impression—even if his facts are not quite right. In terms of public speaking, slower and louder are usually better.

To be sure, you cannot learn effective speaking pace from a book. There are far too many variables in a speech: points of emphasis, pauses for effect, audience responses and interruptions, and catches of breath. Some novices are fearful that they will not have enough to say, or that what they *do* have to say will take up no more than five minutes. (They are often surprised to discover, once they have finished, that they have held forth for ten, even fifteen minutes.) Others are fearful that they will not cover all their points in the time allotted, and speak at a disconcertingly fast pace.

You will find that just a few prepared remarks, or notes for reference, can go a long way in your actual presentation. It is better to have a few well-chosen things to say, and to say them slowly and with conviction, than to overstay your welcome. Remember, once you get started, time goes by much faster for the speaker than for the audience.

This speaker has captured the attention of her audience, but will her message be understood?

For the present, try to get to know the sound of your own voice. Use a tape recorder if possible. Listen to your normal talking speed. Ask yourself if the pace seems unhurried, or slightly frantic. Practice will enable you to speak at a rate that is comfortable for you.

Attention. When speaking to others, your task is to get them to pay attention to *you.* Presumably, standing in front of an audience will give you their attention to begin with. Now you must keep it.

First you must cope with the fear of speaking in public. The best defense against stage fright is an offense. In public speaking, offense usually means loudness. Assuming that you will not use a microphone, you will need to speak louder in performance than you ever did in practice. Most speakers find the process helpful; by concentrating on talking louder than usual, you become less preoccupied with your fear of talking in the first place. Loudness, in its best sense, becomes outspokenness; outspokenness quickly breeds confidence.

Overcoming problems. The most common failing of inexperienced speakers is mumbling—talking too low, not saying things clearly, and sounding apologetic. Consider the way mumblers look when they talk: slouched shoulders, shuffling feet, downward head, eyes darting in every direction except that of the audience. This type of body language will undermine the effectiveness of any spoken language that accompanies it. Clearly the mumbler has no confidence in what he is saying; that message is plain to anyone who sees or hears him. The speaker who mumbles gets sympathy, not attention.

Attention is gotten by a speaker who talks loudly, who stands up straight and leans slightly forward, and who looks as though he believes what he is saying. A loud and forceful delivery also requires more time and energy, thus slowing you down. The extra effort makes

Improving Your Speech

slurpalurp . . . mmm . . . unnastan?

A cigar clenched between one's teeth while talking is a surefire way to obscure one's words.

sounds effortless and natural to the listener. Parrot the words of a newscaster as he reads his copy, using his pauses to supply your own version a split second after his. Compare your sound with the newscaster's. Make adjustments and repeat the process. If you do this exercise often enough, improvement will take place on a subconscious as well as a conscious level.

Going a step further, try this experiment. Turn on a baseball game, a football game, or a tennis match, and turn off the sound on the TV. "Broadcast" the whole game, using a tape recorder. Most top sportscasters have used just such radio/TV exercises to learn their trade. They also started out just like you: unsure of themselves (and their voices) and quite anxious about speaking in public. They conquered their uncertainty and anxiety, and so can you.

How your voice comes across

Many people make value judgments based on the way your voice comes across to them. Using a tape of your normal, conversational speaking voice, monitor yourself for the following:

- **Crispness.** If you slur your words, even unintentionally, your listener is likely to think you are in no condition to talk.

- **Rapidity.** Talking too fast in a conversation gives the listener—particularly a stranger—the idea that he or she will be given no chance to speak at all.

- **Harshness.** A listener or an audience will be put off by harsh, strident tones, which are the verbal equivalent of shaking someone by the arm.

- **Rising inflection.** The habit of ending phrases and sentences on an upward note makes declarations sound like questions. Listeners will question your self-assurance.

- **Falling inflection.** Phrases or sentences that trail off make you sound as if you changed your mind (or lost your conviction) in mid-sentence.

- **Shrillness.** Speaking at too high and sharp a pitch will alienate most listeners. It comes across as over-emotionalism, immaturity, or poor argument.

- **Tenseness.** A slight amount of tension showing up in the voice of a public speaker is quite common and need not concern you. The best cure for a noticeably tense voice, which makes a speaker sound nervous, is practice.

- **Whispering.** Low, "sexy," or whispery tones should be avoided. A whispery voice is hard to hear, and will keep listeners from taking you seriously.

you pay more attention to each word, improving your enunciation. If you are too loud, your audience will signal you quickly by the expressions on their faces. It is far easier to tone down your voice than to raise it.

Before you speak in front of an audience, consider how effective you are—or are not—at holding attention when you speak. Among friends, for instance, do you find it difficult to make yourself heard? Are you accused of making short stories long? Do you have trouble remembering the punch line of a joke or the windup of a story? These are common shortcomings of inexperienced speakers; all are overcome through practice and preparation. When you are thoroughly familiar with what you want to say and how you are going to say it, you will stop worrying about making mistakes. You will speak up. An audience will feel your confidence. You will get—and hold—their attention.

Speech improvement tools. A tape recorder is an invaluable tool for getting to know your best voice level. Most people are surprised and dismayed when they hear themselves for the first time on tape. Both the tone and the volume of your voice sound like someone else's. "I hate the way I sound" is a common reaction. But take heart: the very playback that has dismayed you can help you make truly dramatic improvements. Listen to yourself again and again. Then rerecord your voice, making any adjustments in loudness that seem indicated. You may, for example, find that too many words are being emphasized with volume, creating a strident effect, such as the effect a writer creates who constantly uses italics. Whatever the problem, with loudness or any other aspect of your delivery, a few sessions with a tape recorder can be very revealing.

Another useful aid to self-improvement is the radio. Nearly all radio announcers are chosen for their quality of voice: tone, precise enunciation, and smoothness of delivery. It took years of practice for them to achieve a level of consistency and professionalism that

How to get attention and control of an audience

We all admire speakers who can hold an audience from the time they begin to speak until the moment they finish. No one is born with this talent; experience and the following good practices can build it.

1. Find out how many people will be in your audience. (You can speak less formally in front of a small group.)

2. Determine how many are friends and how many are strangers. (Strangers warrant a different approach than friends.)

3. Decide on what sort of message the audience is likely to appreciate. (Never offend the audience's self-interest.)

4. Keep your ideas and remarks to the intellectual level of the audience.

5. Learn the age level of the audience. (Young people may be unfamiliar with historical references.)

6. Learn how many men and how many women will be in attendance. (Avoid language and examples that are sex-biased.)

7. Find out, approximately, the racial and ethnic composition of the audience. (Giving offense to part of an audience usually affects the whole audience.)

8. Determine beforehand the probable reaction of your audience to your subject. (If you invite controversy, be ready to defend your position.)

9. Eliminate *all* irrelevant material. (A knowledgeable audience will be uninterested in hearing what it knows already, and not at all impressed that you know it, too.)

10. Find out beforehand how well the audience knows *you*. If not at all, take some time at the beginning to introduce yourself, personally and professionally.

Improving Your Speech

Tips for using a microphone

A microphone can frighten even an experienced speaker who has never used one. These tips will help:

- Remember that the microphone will make it possible for for your normal speaking voice to be heard easily by everyone in the room—even a large room. Think of it as a friend.

- If possible, arrive early when you know you will be using a microphone. This will give you time to make sure it is in working order and to test your voice level without an audience.

- Check the height of a stationary microphone before you say anything. If it is uncomfortably high or low, you can adjust the height.

- When you reach the podium, stand at a comfortable speaking distance from the microphone and ask, "Can you hear me?" If your voice is underamplified, the audience will let you know. If it is overamplified, *you* will know. Someone in charge will adjust the mike, or you can take care of the problem yourself by taking a step or two backward or forward.

- Do not lean forward over the microphone. It will be able to pick up your voice from a close but comfortable distance without your bending over.

- Do not touch a stationary microphone, or the head of a hand-held microphone. Your lightest touch can produce a resounding thump or a high, piercing whine.

- If you are given a hand-held microphone, hold it about 6 inches from your mouth and ask, "Can you hear me?" Make any adjustments necessary, moving the mike farther away from or closer to your mouth.

- Stay put behind a podium with a microphone. If you move, you will be moving away from the mike, and you will no longer be heard at the same voice level.

Eye contact.
If you use your voice to get attention, you use your eyes to hold attention. People tend to believe you, trust you, and listen to what you say if you are looking at them. "Shifty-eyed" and "cross-eyed" are not negative adjectives by chance. Direct eye contact is not just preferable; it is essential to effective private conversations and public addresses.

As a tool for public speaking, your eyes are second only to your voice. While you are speaking, you judge your audience to determine how they are reacting to your words. Their eyes, mirrored by the expressions on their faces, tell the story. Even at a distance you can gauge whether your listeners are attentive.

Why look away from someone you are greeting? Lack of eye contact (top) *says, "I do not mean what I'm saying." Good eye contact* (above) *with your audience says, "I mean every word I'm saying."*

Never forget for a moment that your listeners watch your eyes just as intently. How you look at them will determine to a great extent how faithfully they will listen to you. If your eyes never stray from your prepared text, never acknowledge the presence of your live audience, then you might as well hand out copies of your speech instead of delivering it. Without eye contact, you seem to dismiss your audience. Why should they listen if you do not seem to care whether or not you are heard? But when you take pains to establish eye contact with your listeners, they know you mean what you say.

There are three basic ways to use eye contact to your advantage:

Look your listener straight in the eye. Looking someone in the eye while you speak has a similar effect to that of shining your car headlights on a deer: he is transfixed, your captive audience so long as you maintain the beam. The eyes are the meaningful target—

foreheads, lips, and chins are not good enough—and the other person's eyes can tell the difference. Direct eye contact assures your listener that you are sincere, that you care about what you are saying. Direct eye contact enables direct communication to take place.

For contrast, imagine the consequences of these examples of indirect eye contact:

- At a party, you follow the progress of other guests with your eyes while you chat with a friend.
- Standing with a shorter friend, you direct your remarks to the top of his head.
- Making a deal with a business acquaintance, you shake on it—while staring at his shoes.

Look the whole audience straight in the eye. Maintaining eye contact is a simple enough matter when you are face to face with one other person. But what if you are addressing two people? Ten people? Scores of people in a large room?

The answer lies in the target method. For each sentence you speak, zero in on the eyes of a different (target) member of the audience. Use an orderly right-left-center pattern, fixing your gaze on one particular man or woman for each phrase or sentence. The method may sound simplistic, but professional speakers adhere to it with excellent results. The whole audience feels included, cared for, spoken to. Targeting takes some effort to master, but it is worth the effort. **Let your eyes talk for you.** Your eyes are the best indicator of your emotions. If you talk about courage and perseverance while your eyes show fear and indecision, your listeners will probably stop listening, and will certainly stop believing you.

Pauses.
Everyone pauses from time to time in the course of giving a talk. There are good pauses, for an intended effect, and there are bad ones. The bad ones leave you sounding unprepared. There are constructive ways to fill speaking space. First, however, learn to avoid the destructive ways.

An almost universal space filler is hemming and hawing: the all-purpose *uh* and its cousin *um.* These syllables find their way into nearly every phone conversation, where they are simply an irritant if noticed at all by either party. But they can destroy the effectiveness of anyone speaking in public.

Listen again to yourself speaking (not reading) on tape. Just as you may not have realized that you talk too fast, you may be surprised at how many ums and uhs show up in your speech. You do not hear yourself using them, and it is unlikely that anyone else will point them out. Fortunately, the habit is easily broken.

The best cure for such space fillers is the simplest: breathing space. If you find yourself bogging down in mid-sentence, just stop. Pause for a few seconds and collect your thoughts. Once you resume your sentence,

it is likely to end up better than it started out. It will certainly *sound* better, uncluttered by uhs or ums—which tend to make your audience forget what preceded them. Best of all, mid-sentence pauses lend any speaker an aura of thoughtfulness, gravity, and maturity that a space-filling hem or haw cannot match. So take your time. You, the speaker, have the floor.

A particularly irksome space filler is "y'know?" It is not even logical. If your audience already knows, there is no point in telling them. If *you* already know, then "y'know?" cues the audience that you lack the verbal equipment to say what you know. In either case, "y'know?" has no place in good speaking. It may not bother you, and it may not bother your friends, but the average audience reacts to this space filler very poorly indeed. Avoid it.

Grammar counts too. Proper grammar is an essential part of correct speech, particularly since an audience is likely to judge you as much on how you say things as on what you say. The following list consists of common errors in American diction. Do any of them apply to you?

---

25 words and phrases to watch for

Incorrect	Correct
a criteria	a criterion
a phenomena	a phenomenon
Can I go now?	May I go now? (if asking permission)
finalize	complete; finish up
for free	free; for nothing
hardly nothing	hardly anything; almost nothing
hisself	himself
I ain't; it ain't	I am not; it is not
I been	I have been
I can't help but feel	I can't help feeling
I can't hardly	I cannot; I can hardly
I done	I did; I have done
it don't	it does not
off of	off
out loud	aloud
over with	over; finished; done with
quote (as noun)	quotation
reason is because	reason is
snuck	sneaked
supposing I am	suppose I am
theirselves	themselves
the media	the press; a medium
this here	this
this point in time	now; then
thusly	thus

Improving Your Speech

Help yourself

Pronunciation, pace, attention, eye contact, pauses; each of the five keys is an integral part of successful speechmaking; none can be overlooked. To check your progress, try these three self-help exercises:

- Talk to yourself in front of a mirror, with strict emphasis on making eye contact.

- Tape-record yourself—reading from a text and talking extemporaneously—to check your pronunciation, pace, and voice level.

- Listen carefully to the tape playbacks to see how poised you are during pauses.

Tape recorder checklist

You are your own worst judge of your own voice. You simply do not hear yourself accurately. Your ears are misplaced for the purpose, and you need an outside, objective opinion. A tape recorder is the obvious solution, and it makes no judgments at all.

With a tape recorder, you have plenty of time to make adjustments and refinements. Start simply. Talk conversationally into the machine, merely recounting what is on your mind or what you might like to say to somebody else if he were present. Sessions like these teach you what your "normal" voice level is.

As you get more comfortable with self-recording, you can record emotional flare-ups, perhaps, or tiny tantrums. With diligence and patience, you can learn from your tapes just how you sound to everyone else at your best and your worst. Then you can begin to change what you do not like. Remember, this vocal self-improvement is a strictly private matter, between you and your machine.

Here are some tape-playback questions to ask yourself:

1. Do you pronounce each word clearly?
2. Does any of the pronunciation sound uncertain?
3. Do you sometimes run two or more words together?
4. Do you talk too fast to be understood easily?
5. Do you sound tired or bored?
6. Do you speak loudly enough for each word to be heard clearly?
7. Does your speech sound too soft to reach a large audience?
8. Do you sound timid or uncertain?
9. Do you sound angry or belligerent?
10. Is your tone monotonous?
11. Within sentences, do you emphasize certain words?
12. Do you put emphasis on the wrong words?
13. Do you start sentences with the word "well"?
14. Does "y'know?" creep into your speech?
15. Do you handle pauses silently, without hemming or hawing?
16. Are there any grammatical mistakes? Incorrect words?
17. Is your speech marred by slang or profanity?
18. If you were in the audience, would you trust this speaker?
19. Do you sound as if you mean what you are saying?
20. Could you say what you have said on tape to an audience?
21. Do you sound better now than you did when you began taping?

Usually, it is best to listen for one or two speech habits at a time. If you prefer, listen to the tape several times in a row, making notes about whatever you observe. Make adjustments and rerecord. In a surprisingly short time, your answer to Number 21 will be "yes."

Correct speech

Speaking correctly means using the English language correctly. That, necessarily, means paying attention to grammar and word usage. You may have a great deal to say, but if you do not say it right—according to the rules—your listeners will not take you seriously. Sloppy grammar and mispronunciation often go together; the speaker who uses words incorrectly will often mispronounce them as well.

Your basic diction—the way you use and apply words—is probably well grounded as the result of reading, writing, and hearing others talk. But you may be unaware of some common misuses and misapplications of everyday speech. Check your own diction against the following examples. Some of these words are used mistakenly all the time in informal speech.

You may wonder why you should be so careful about your diction. Your friends understand you anyway, and you want to sound like your normal self when you speak in public. But your friends have learned to read between the lines of what you say; you do the same thing when you listen to them. Sometimes, among friends and spouses, almost no words are needed.

This is not so in public speaking. In public, among strangers, the rules of grammar and correct speech are universal. A public speaker wants and needs to be understood the first time—which may be his only time. By learning and using proper diction, you increase your chances of expressing yourself clearly, whoever your audience. However unsophisticated an audience may be, it will understand and respect good diction.

Words commonly confused

affect, effect. *Affect* is a verb meaning to influence. *Effect,* though it can be a verb, usually is a noun meaning result.

compare, contrast. Use *compare* for pointing out similarities *and* differences between things. Use *contrast* only to show differences.

compare to, compare with. Use *compare to* when drawing a comparison between two things that are not really similar: "*Compared to* a glacier, you move quickly." Use *compare with* when drawing a comparison between two things that are similar: "*Compared with* her, you are a fast runner."

each. In formal prose and speech, treat each as meaning *each one* (singular): "*Each* of the soldiers did *his* duty."

either. Always a singular pronoun, meaning *either one:* "*Either* of the teams *is* capable of winning."

exhausting, exhaustive. Use *exhausting* to mean using up completely, especially using up energy, that is, becoming fatigued: "*Exhausting* exercise is not recommended for me." Use *exhaustive* to mean thorough: "My physician gave me an *exhaustive* examination and declared me fit as a fiddle."

farther, further. *Farther* means measurable distance; *further* means intangible distance: "There is no point in talking any *further* if you keep moving *farther* away."

flaunt, flout. Use *flaunt* to mean display conspicuously: "She *flaunted* her new car before all of us." Use *flout* to mean treat with contempt. "Some people *flout* traffic laws."

imply, infer. *Imply* is what the speaker does; *infer* is what the listener does: "The professor *implied* that he was not through yet. I *inferred* that he had yet to conclude his lecture."

it is I, it is me. In strictly formal speech, "It is *I*" is preferred.

kind of, sort of. Use *kind of* and *kinds of* to refer to definite things and commodities. *Sort of* and *sorts of* should be saved for indefinite, imprecise types and categories: "The *kind of* speaker who says he's *kind of* sorry will not be taken seriously." (Note: never use *kind of a* or *sort of a* in formal discourse.)

lay, lie. These are among the most misused verbs in the language. *Lay (laid, lain)* is a transitive verb; it takes an object. *Lie (lay, lain)* is an intransitive verb; it does not take an object: "Are you tired? Why not *lay* down your suitcase." "Thanks, but I need to *lie* down for a while."

learn, teach. *Learn* is intransitive, *teach* is transitive: "I *learned* so much French in a year abroad that I ended up *teaching* it to my classmates this year."

less, few. *Less* refers to amounts measured, and *few* refers to things counted: "We have *less* gas than I thought we had, but just a *few* more miles to go."

like, as. *Like* is a preposition, used for comparisons, and *as* is a conjunction, used to link phrases: "We picked up the suspect just *as* he left the premises. We're sticking to him *like* glue."

slow, slowly. *Slow* is an adjective, *slowly* an adverb: "Can you believe it? Danny ran *slowly* again. I'm afraid he's just a *slow* runner."

Improving Your Speech

**ALWAYS be yourself.
NEVER address your audience
as less intelligent
than yourself.**

Word choice. The best advice to inexperienced speakers is also the oldest: be yourself. Only a trained actor should stand in front of people he does not know and pretend to be Mark Twain, or Emily Dickinson, or Clarence Darrow. Most likely you will be speaking words that you wrote, so you had better use ones that you are comfortable with. Think about the way you would normally use persuasion on another person, or marshal your forces for an argument with that person. Those words are precisely the kind you should choose for a talk before a group. Only this time, your argument will be unopposed. Public speakers have that luxury.

A great deal of specialized jargon has crept into American speech, thanks to television, the press, and rock music. Public speakers who use this jargon—often in an attempt to sound "in"—usually end up sounding phony, presumptuous, or condescending.

Anyone can aspire to be a plain speaker. The chief requirements are telling the truth as you see and know it, telling it simply, and treating your audience as intellectual equals. All of these are healthy underpinnings for any public speaking appearance.

Choosing the right words is often complicated by changing times and fashions. Yesterday's "in" word or phrase is today's cliche. At the right is a list of overworked words. Many of them may remind you of others that you may have fallen into the habit of using. Get rid of them, too.

Choosing the right word

Fad words and phrases. Coming from politics, business, and the social sciences, these words sound pretentious in conversational speech. Some examples are:
bottom line, in context, time frame, viable

Pet words. Most of these words are legacies from adolescence. They say (vaguely) what you feel, but never what you think. They make *you* sound dated. A small sampling:
fabulous, cute, far out, right on, awesome

Extra words. More eloquent than *um* or *uh* (but no more meaningful), these extra words are creatures of habit. A thoughtful pause would be more eloquent than:
you know, frankly, so to speak, well

Slang words. Formal language is always acceptable, colloquial language is generally permissible, but slang usage is risky. When in doubt, use your dictionary. Misused slang sounds vulgar or tasteless.

Exaggeration. Most superlatives should be avoided; they are so overused that they have lost their meaning. Personalize your feelings and value judgments with, I think . . . , In my opinion . . . , etc. Meaningless superlatives include:
great, fantastic, terrific, incredible, the most

Pejorative words. Racial slurs and epithets—you know them all. Avoid them.

Adding -wise. Adding *-wise* to nouns is as unnecessary as it is ill-advised. Try the constructions *as to* or *speaking of.*

Profanity. Despite what you see in current movies, read in novels, and hear from comedians, profanity still has no place at all in formal speech or polite society. Swearing is generally offensive to people who know better ways to express themselves.

Overworked words to avoid

alienated	operative
articulate *(as a verb)*	oppressed
awesome	overreact
concept	paranoid
credibility	posture *(for attitude)*
depersonalization	prioritize
dynamic	rhetoric
elegant	ripoff
enrichment	scenario
holistic	structure *(as a verb)*
involved	substantive
manic	superlative
obscene	veritable

Clichés to avoid

When you say . . .	Do you mean?	When you say . . .	Do you mean?
advance planning	planning	game plan	strategy
as far as	as for; as to	guesstimate	rough guess
as you know	as you may know; let me remind you	head tripping	thinking
		impact (as a verb)	affect
at this/that point in time	now or then	in my opinion	I think
beautiful	good, kind, cooperative	in point of fact	in fact
be that as it may	nonetheless; but	insightful	perceptive
bleep out	censor	learning experience	experience
by the same token	also	love	like; approve; admire
charisma	appeal	meaningful dialogue	discussion
confrontation	meeting	meaningful experience	experience
consciousness-raising	educational	more unique	singular
consensus of opinion	consensus; agreement	my personal opinion	my opinion
curiously enough	curiously	needless to say	obviously
dialogue	conversation; meeting	out of sight	impressive
disadvantaged	poor	out of this world	impressive
due to the fact	because	personal friend	friend
encounter	meet	presently	now
escalate	rise; raise	prior to	before
expertise	knowledge; skill	relationship	friendship; acquaintance
fabulous/ fantastic/ far out	good; excellent; acceptable	underprivileged	poor
		valid	true; genuine
for free	free	validate	confirm
frame of reference	background	with reference to	as to; about

Body language

Your eyes are the most obvious indicator of your attitudes and emotions, but your facial expressions, posture, and gestures—singly or together—can just as surely cue an attentive observer to your state of mind. Your most eloquent words cannot dispel the mistrust that is invited by negative body language.

Just as you can train your eyes to make contact with a single listener as well as an entire audience, you can learn to control the attentiveness of the rest of your body—if you become aware of your body language.

Facial expression. Variety is important. If you smile all the time, you may be considered insincere, perhaps even frivolous. By contrast, an unvarying solemn expression may be interpreted as insensitive, even dangerous. Look at photographs of yourself. Are you characteristically gloomy, grinning, frowning, close-mouthed? Are you noticeably out of step with the occasion? An appropriate variety of facial expressions will encourage an audience to trust you.

Posture. Sitting or standing, you want to look poised. Whether you are sitting behind a table or not, sit up straight. If you are on your feet, do not stand at military attention; it is clearly uncomfortable for most speakers. At the same time, slouching is uncomfortable for most audiences—it signals the speaker's lack of interest or his disrespect. Try to find an intermediate posture, with both feet balanced on the floor, in which you lean slightly *toward* your audience. That alone will focus the audience's attention on your eyes and mouth, which is where you want it.

Gestures. The best advice for novice speakers is to do nothing with your hands—rest them on the podium or clasp them behind your back. Do not fold your arms across your chest; that means, in body language, that you are challenging the audience. Hand gestures to emphasize your words can be highly effective, but they must be learned, usually in performance and often in response to the mood of the moment. Furthermore, hand language must be nearly perfectly synchronized to your spoken words or it will look foolish. Practice before a mirror may be helpful here, but audience feedback—time and time again—is the only sure test.

Body language checklist

Here are some suggestions about silent communication for public and nonpublic speaking occasions:

Fussing with your hair tells your audience your mind is elsewhere.

A sidewise glance says you surely distrust the speaker.

Your eyes and posture can say I do not take you seriously.

Your hands can say I worry about what you are telling me.

Self-assurance can easily become oppressive self-importance.

When neither person looks the other in the eye, who trusts whom?

Close attention is apparent in eyes that stay on the speaker.

Eye contact plus legs crossed toward one another equal rapt attention.

Members of a mature audience are more likely to listen receptively to a speaker whose dress and grooming resemble their own. A younger audience might prefer a speaker less carefully groomed.

Personal appearance.

A speaker needs more than voice plus message to make a good impression. There are silent factors, too, that contribute to your listeners' acceptance or rejection of what you have to say. Your good looks or lack of them are *not* a factor, but your clothes and grooming definitely are. Before you speak a word, they show your opinion of yourself and affect other people's opinion of you—for good or ill.

Department store salespeople know this well. They do significantly more business when they dress up fully for work, even if the weather is hot and the air conditioning inadequate. Customers, they find, are reluctant to buy from salesmen in shirtsleeves or saleswomen in pants. Experienced job seekers know this, too. Applicants who show up for an interview in business clothes increase their chances of being hired, even for blue collar jobs.

For public speaking or for important personal engagements, the rules are the same: dress to show yourself to best advantage. For men, this usually means a pressed suit, shined shoes, a tasteful tie, and a freshly pressed shirt with an unfrayed collar. Good grooming is important, too. The absence of a shave will reflect poorly on any speaker, as will unruly hair or a long-overdue haircut.

Women speakers should take care to avoid being too elaborately dressed, coiffed, or made up. A simple, becoming dress or suit, neatly styled hair, and carefully applied tasteful makeup will increase the speaker's confidence and prevent her audience from being distracted by her appearance. As for accessories, leave attention-drawing jewelry, scarves, etc., at home, and make sure that the shoes you choose are shined or cleaned and not run down at the heels.

If you know the audience you will be addressing, then you can predict with reasonable accuracy how they will be dressed and then dress yourself accordingly. You probably own at least one outfit in which you know you look well. Wear it. You will feel most comfortable in the clothes you like best—which, with very few exceptions, are your best choice for a speaking engagement.

You want to look like your best self, not like someone else. After all, *you* are the one who has been invited to speak. If you pay careful attention to clothes and grooming, you will increase the audience's confidence in you right along with your confidence in yourself.

Improving Your Speech

Preparing to speak

What is needed for a successful outline? A central idea. A clear understanding of the audience that will be addressed. A beginning, middle, and end—all connected and all headed in the same direction.

Why do people make speeches? There are three reasons for speechmaking that will probably never change: the speaker has something special to say; he believes he has an audience receptive to his ideas; and he is confident he can make his case in the allotted time and place. With those reasons in mind, here is a speaker's three-part blueprint for a talk:

1. A receptive audience.
2. A central idea.
3. A beginning, middle, and end.

Unless all three of these fundamentals are present, a speaker probably cannot deliver a successful speech. Why?

—Without a receptive audience, one's points cannot be made.

—Without a central idea, a speech is pointless.

—Without a beginning-to-end structure, very few in the audience will get the point.

These basics of public speaking have not been improved upon in the 2400 years since Aristotle explained them in his great book, *Rhetoric*. Every successful speech, from a three-minute talk to a thirty-minute oration, will adhere to the time-tested formula that states, before you say anything, know your audience and organize your thoughts.

A receptive audience.

Who will be in the audience? In most cases, you will know your listeners or at least be known to them (fellow students, townspeople, club or union members, kindred political spirits, etc.). If this is not the case, find out who will be there, or check with someone likely to know. If you find that your listeners will be older or younger than you expected, better educated or less well informed, all male or all female, then tailor your remarks accordingly. A clear idea of who your audience will be gives you the best possible chance of getting through to them in your speech.

A central idea.

Ask yourself why you are motivated to speak in the first place. What is your point? A central idea is easier to arrive at than you might think. The problem is to distill it, to break it down to *one or two sentences* at the most. That brevity is what will make your central idea memorable. Whenever you can make your point memorably, you know you have succeeded.

A beginning, middle, and end.

Briefly, the *beginning* of your talk should do two things: get your listeners' attention and introduce your central idea. The *middle* portion (the longest by far) will support your central idea and expand on it, with examples or evidence, in some depth. The *end* will restate the central idea, summing up with supporting evidence. Ideally, you will come up with a quotable line, perhaps the central idea itself, that members of the audience can take home with them.

When composing your talk, *begin in the middle*. The bulk of your research and the meat of your argument will be found in the middle portion. No doubt your best ideas will stem from there, too. Try to hold off on composing the beginning of your speech—setting forth your central idea—until you have explored the fertile territory in the middle ground.

Because so many professional speakers do it, you may be tempted to begin or end your talk with a humorous anecdote, a topical or local joke. Resist the temptation. The pros know how to get laughs because they do it all the time. A novice speaker should not risk

FORGET the jokes.
FORGET the big fancy words.

not getting a laugh, which can undermine the effectiveness of a speech at the very beginning.

If you stick to the three basics and honor the beginning–middle–end framework, you will not embarrass yourself—even if you are a first-time speaker. The rest of your preparation will consist of researching your subject matter, writing out your speech (one draft is not enough), and reading it aloud.

The best written speech does not always translate from the page to the podium, just as certain great novels do not read well aloud. Plan to read your text aloud before giving it the final touches. You are likely to make minor alterations that will significantly improve the way your speech "plays."

As in most things, skill is achieved through experience. The first time is the worst by far. Because novice speakers are so apprehensive, they tend to remember, vividly, all their mistakes. Knowing those mistakes, they usually do not repeat them. Members of such organizations as Toastmasters, or Dale Carnegie, or the self-help anonymous groups usually find, after they speak the first time, that they enjoy talking in public. It was only that first time that frightened them, like a plunge into cold water.

You will soon be ready to take that plunge.

Writing a speech.
Speechwriting differs from ordinary prose writing in one crucial respect: speeches are read aloud. Prose is meant to be read silently; it is designed solely for transfer from the printed page directly into the reader's mind. Speechwriting is consciously designed to be transferred by a speaker to a listener; the effect of the spoken word must be emotional as well as intellectual.

Even though you take great pains to write it, a good speech should sound as much like normal conversation as possible, using unadorned language that people can understand. A speech that you write should also conform to the way you normally talk—your tone of voice, choice of words, and cadence. Here is how to begin:

1. Using just one page of a yellow legal pad, outline your talk vertically under the three-part basic framework:

   appeal to audience
   central idea
   beginning–middle–end

   (Allow 80 percent of the page for the last grouping, and most of that for the middle.)

2. Make short notes to "set" each of the three themes above: your informed appeal to a particular audience; a short statement of your central idea; and your beginning–middle–end structure (starting with the middle).

So far your written preparations for speaking will not have taken up more than a page. But you may already have saved hours in wasted time. You now have a clear idea of whom to convince, your intention, and how to hold your argument together.

A first draft of a speech should be written in longhand or typed quickly. Many writers need to use a typewriter or word processor because they need execution that keeps up with their thoughts. It is helpful to get your spontaneous thoughts down, before you start writing like a writer rather than a talker. Here are some time-tested ingredients of an effective speech that should be of help whatever your subject matter:

- **Beginning.** Start by thanking your host or your sponsoring organization. Then introduce your central idea.
- **Middle.** Drawing on your knowledge of the audience, compliment your listeners. If appropriate, suggest ways in which your central idea coincides with certain goals they have or values they believe in.
- **End.** Work toward what salesmen call the *close,* in which the audience becomes persuaded that your central idea, once a hypothesis, is now a given.

When you write your final draft, remember that a typewritten page takes considerably longer to read aloud than you may think. A ten-minute talk translates to five typewritten pages or less. Try to retain most of the unrehearsed scribbled or hastily typed language of your first draft: that is how you really talk. *Given a choice between a big fancy word and a short plain one, take the little one.* Keep your sentences short, too. Long sentences may be artful on paper, but they are deadly when read aloud. Last of all, *never fail to thank the audience* for their attention.

To illustrate a well-written speech, it might be useful to study one of the very best: Lincoln's Gettysburg Address.

For all its deserved fame, for all its renowned eloquence, Lincoln's address was only 280 words long and required only three minutes to deliver. As an accomplished speaker he knew intuitively the appropriate message to deliver at Gettysburg. How would Lincoln have sketched out the Gettysburg Address?

Abraham Lincoln, when he wrote out the Gettysburg Address (supposedly on the back of an envelope), came up with some phrases that will live forever in American prose. He may have memorized the whole speech; he may have read it. But what if he had restricted himself to one small index card for prompting purposes? The card on the next page shows what it might have looked like.

Lincoln's Gettysburg Address

Fourscore and seven years ago our fathers brought forth on this continent a new nation, conceived in liberty, and dedicated to the proposition that all men are created equal. Now we are engaged in a great civil war, testing whether that nation, or any nation so conceived and so dedicated, can long endure. We are met on a great battlefield of that war. We have come to dedicate a portion of that field, as a final resting place for those who here gave their lives that that nation might live. It is altogether fitting and proper that we should do this. But, in a larger sense, we cannot dedicate—we cannot consecrate—we cannot hallow—this ground. The brave men, living and dead, who struggled here, have consecrated it, far above our poor power to add or detract. The world will little note, nor long remember, what we say here, but it can never forget what they did here. It is for us the living, rather, to be dedicated here to the unfinished work which they who fought here have thus far so nobly advanced. It is rather for us to be here dedicated to the great task remaining before us—that from these honored dead we take increased devotion to that cause for which they gave the last full measure of devotion—that we here highly resolve that these dead shall not have died in vain— that this nation, under God, shall have a new birth of freedom—and that government of the people, by the people, for the people, shall not perish from the earth.

How the speech was planned

1. Audience —survivors and mourners of the casualties of Gettysburg. (The occasion is the consecration of the battlefield.)

2. Central idea —Civil war is a dreadful, wasteful undertaking, but in the course of history a noble ideal—an indissoluble union—must on occasion be tested by fire.

3. Rhetorical structure
   a. *Beginning*— the framers of the Constitution foresaw a nation conceived in liberty, in which all men are created equal.
   b. *Middle*—thousands of Americans, from North and South, died at Gettysburg to test the proposition that the nation can endure, at whatever price.
   c. *End*—everyone here today must now profit from the awful witness of Gettysburg: none of these soldiers shall have died in vain; a new nation shall rise from these ashes; the spirit of the Founding Fathers shall somehow transcend the tragic waste and sacrifice of this battlefield.

A card Lincoln might have used

(beginning) Fourscore and seven years ago...
            nation conceived in liberty...
            all men equal

(middle)   world will forget us...
            but not men who died here

(end)   new birth of freedom...
            government of, by, and for people last forever

Reading a speech.
Mark Twain once said, "It usually takes me more than three weeks to prepare a good impromptu speech." He meant it, too. The best speakers, like the best actors, have to practice hard in order to appear natural.

There are three methods for speaking in public: (1) from a written text; (2) extemporaneously (from minimal notes); and (3) impromptu (from no notes at all). At first the alternatives may seem progressively less difficult. But in fact, number three is always the riskiest and often the hardest. A novice speaker should never consider "winging it" in front of a group until he is thoroughly familiar with his own voice, his own style, and his own words—written out. In order, here is how each method works:

Delivery from a written text. Written, as used here, refers to remarks or to a speech that you have written yourself. The first rule is not to read your speech at all—that is, never appear to be reading it word for word. This would necessitate your staring at your text, as if it were an unfamiliar book, and rarely coming up for air. Your audience might conclude that their presence does not matter at all. It would also appear that you have no familiarity with your own words. The only situation in which it is not a mistake to read aloud to a live audience is when broadcasting on the radio. And people who read scripts on the radio are usually professional actors or newscasters. In person you must do more than read; you must communicate.

Never forget that your listeners crave eye contact. You cannot begin to establish whole-room eye contact if your head is buried in your text most of the time. The remedy is twofold. First, practice reading your speech over and over again until the beginning of each section or paragraph is a memory cue to the rest. When you know your material well enough, type your final draft in capital letters, with extra space between words so that you can make it out easily from a distance. Next, underline the crucial first words and phrases of paragraphs and sections—or highlight them in yellow, or type them in red—so that you can be a glancer, not a reader. Glancing is a natural thing to do while speaking; reading is patronizing.

Extemporaneous delivery. When you become sufficiently adept at cuing yourself from first words and phrases, you are but a short step away from making seemingly offhand talks—with careful preparation, but no written-out text. For this method it is best to compose a single-page *master note* (see the Lincoln sample on the previous page). This will include, in digest form, the same information as an outline for a written address: appeal to audience, central idea, and beginning–middle–end linkage.

Impromptu delivery. This method is appropriate for speakers who address audiences frequently and are

---

---

very sure of themselves and their subject matter. Impromptu speaking, in fact, requires more expertise and self-confidence than many experienced speakers are likely to possess. Nonprofessionals are well advised to opt for delivery from a written text, or for extemporaneous delivery.

If proper preparation for speaking involves so much rehearsal and homework, why not simply memorize your remarks? Unless you are a trained actor, this method almost never works. At some time you may have been compelled to memorize stanzas of poetry, or lines from plays, or famous historical orations. Were you pleased with the way you sounded in recitation? Most likely, your version of those great words sounded monotonous, or painfully self-conscious, or both. An entire speech, minus an actor's intonation and dramatic embroidery, would probably sound more awkward still. The moment you memorize something, your delivery stops being spontaneous and genuine. Without spontaneity and sincerity, you cannot persuade anyone of anything.

Practicing a speech.
Most of your speech preparation can be done all by yourself. One crucial part, however, will require the cooperation of another person and the use of a tape recorder, as discussed earlier.

Record a normal conversation with your cooperating friend. When you play the conversation back, note how he or she reacts to whatever you say. Pay even closer attention to your own "performance." Can you be clearly understood? Is your speaking tone monotonous, tired-sounding, markedly accented, or too excitable? Imagine yourself listening to this voice on the tape for the first time. Does the tone make you feel anxious? Bored? Angry?

Practicing for a specific talk, try to simulate difficult conditions for yourself. Turn on a portable fan or a noisy air conditioner; play a radio in the background; train a lamp or two on your face—whatever might disturb your concentration, because something probably will when you actually speak in front of an audience. As you start the tape recorder, make note of the time; however quickly you get through your trial run, your actual speech will almost surely run longer. Do not talk too loudly—only loud enough to overcome your distractions. Wherever you think an audience reaction (laughter, murmurs, applause) is likely or appropriate, pause until the floor is yours again.

Improving Your Speech

Practice under noisy conditions can help you deal with distractions that occur when giving a talk.

Practicing an illustrated talk before giving it can iron out difficulties with visual aids.

If you have a full-length mirror, use it to practice eye contact. Practice your most comfortable speaking stance as well—standing still or shifting slightly, weight on the balls of your feet or on one foot at a time. (Behind a solid lectern, of course, your feet will not be a problem.) If you feel you must use hand gestures, try to limit them to the few that come most naturally to you.

The whole idea here is to get thoroughly comfortable with your text, voice, pace, stance, etc. If you take the care to go through with this rehearsal as many times as seems necessary, there can be few things that will surprise or unnerve you when you are in front of an audience.

Visual aids help. Some rehearsal is essential in situations where visual aids—slides, blackboards, flip charts, etc.—are to be used. Unfamiliarity with blackboard techniques can produce the high, screeching noise that causes most people to shudder. (You might bring your own soft chalk with you.) Botched slide presentations can turn a lecture into an unintended comedy routine. (Insert the slides yourself and run through each of them beforehand.) And someone else's flip chart can too often fall over. Any of these mishaps can become the most memorable aspect of your well-intentioned presentation. But routine rehearsal and practice should forestall all of them.

Most public speakers find that they can quickly remedy their shortcomings. That worst shortcoming of all —dread of the first time out—is largely self-imposed, and all of these tips are designed to do away with it entirely. A well-organized and well-researched speech, thoroughly rehearsed, can actually inspire anticipation rather than dread. All that preparation means that you are ready, that you have every reason to be confident. Look yourself in the mirror one more time, then go out and let the audience know *you* know what you are talking about.

Everyday uses of speech

Telephone speaking. Have you ever tried to determine how much time you spend on the phone each day? The average time is one hour. You may spend more, or less, but telephone conversation is likely to be a significant part of your daily routine. It makes little sense to undermine your phone communications with discourtesy, incoherence, or impatience.

Most people jump to answer the phone when it rings. Perhaps nothing else in your daily or business life commands such instant obedience. Following such a response, it is curious that so many people answer their phone with an ill-tempered snarl. Whoever is calling will not be likely to call again soon. It is, however, remarkably simple to change your telephone etiquette, starting with the way you answer the phone. The best way is the simplest: "Hello? This is [your name]."

Common courtesy and a positive attitude, practiced and maintained, will serve you well in any conceivable at-home telephone conversation. Business calls, however, frequently require another ingredient: patience. When you place a business call, be organized. Know precisely whom you want to reach (or his or her department or assistant), and state that intention.

Telephone pointers

- **Voice.** Unless someone happens to tell you, you may have no idea of how you sound on the phone—too loud perhaps, or too soft, or too fast. Find out. Ask a friend about it or record yourself on tape.

- **Attitude.** When a nervous, inexperienced salesman or fund-raiser calls you, you can tell almost instantly what the call is about. To counteract a bad first impression, try to start every phone conversation as if you really care, as if this call is just the one you were expecting. If it is not, it will not take long to end the conversation.

- **Courtesy.** Before you dial, ask yourself a few questions. Is this an inconvenient time? Is the other person likely to be too busy to talk? Should you call back later? Most of these questions can be answered early in your conversation, before inconsideration sets in. If you reach an answering machine, either hang up or leave a short, straightforward message.

Emotions show through even when you are using a telephone. Bear this in mind when you talk.

If your quarry is "in conference," it means he or she cannot or will not talk to you now. No matter. Leave your number and call back an hour later if your call is not returned. Call back a second time, even a third, if necessary. Your man or woman's secretary will have dropped the conference excuse by this time, and your courteous persistence cannot fail to make an impression. Your name will go to the top of the call-back list. Courtesy, persistence, and patience all have an important place in telephone business transactions.

Every time you talk to a stranger on the phone you are practicing the same arts of persuasion that you use when speaking in public. On-the-phone training is a daily refresher course. Make the most of it, and try your best to be pleasant.

Salesmanship. The art of salesmanship is primarily a one-to-one test of wits between you, the seller, and your listener, the buyer. (See the *Careers* chapter for a discussion of speaking in a job interview.) Before the buyer orders anything, he must be convinced that the salesman means what he says, that his word is his bond regardless of his product. Effective public speaking operates on the same principle. The listener must be persuaded that you, the speaker, are worthy of belief and trust. Persuasiveness, in both selling and speaking, rests on four fundamental precepts:

1. **Knowledge.** Speakers, like salesmen, must know their subjects—particularly their central ideas or selling points—better than their listeners. You may need to anticipate tricky (even mean-spirited) questions and have a ready answer for anything, which is where research and practice come in. The best salesmen always have tailor-made reasons why *anybody* can use their product. The best speakers, especially debaters, always seem capable of summoning a convincing argument on the spot.

2. **Empathy.** Not to be confused with sympathy (feeling *for* the other person), empathy is the ability to step into the other person's shoes, to feel *with* him or her. In terms of public speaking, empathy is the learned talent for saying the right thing in the right words to markedly different listeners. A skilled speaker delivers the same basic message time and time again, simply altering his tone and his style so as not to offend his present audience, and even to flatter them a bit. Top salesmen must do this constantly, of course, trying to convince a housewife, a teenager, and a grandfather that the same car is the right choice for each of them.

3. **Sincerity.** Presumably, you would not choose to talk, publicly, about something you did not believe in. But the moment you decide to stand up and sound off about a subject, your own faith and belief in it is not enough. You must demonstrate, through your delivery technique, that you truly mean what you say. If anything undermines that sincerity—a monotonous tone of voice, shifty eyes, sloppy posture—your credibility will be damaged and may even disappear.

4. **Enthusiasm.** You may not be able to define enthusiasm, but you know it when you see it: excitement, energy, contagious self-confidence. Those who know how to transfer that feeling to others are usually outstanding in their field: successful coaches, teachers, businesspeople, politicians, and religious leaders. Such a talent is too easily passed off as speaking ability. What it really is, when practiced and sustained, is inspirational leadership.

Knowledge, empathy, sincerity, and enthusiasm. All are essential to both selling and speaking in public. Knowledge and enthusiasm are largely a matter of thorough preparation and vigorous delivery; empathy and sincerity are largely determined by your listener's perception of your intentions. Salesmen have a harder time with listeners' misconceptions than speakers do—but not much harder.

Another technique shared by salesmen and speakers is the use of the "grabber" in the first paragraph. In sales, the grabber is the unique selling point; in speaking it is the central idea. Whichever form it takes, it should be mentioned early and often. As a public speaker you must never forget that you are selling *yourself* to whomever you address, just as a politician sells himself in painstakingly crafted 30-second spots on television. You, however, will be "live," not taped. Your only product is yourself. It is important to mean what you say about that product—with your words, your eyes, your body language, and your attitude.

Parliamentary procedure. There

are thousands of community organizations and service groups in the United States. Very few of them would accomplish much of anything unless they depended on *Robert's Rules* for order, decorum, and proper parlia-

Even in an informal meeting, a chairman has the responsibility of conducting proceedings fairly.

mentary procedure. Although every conceivable point of order is covered in *Robert's*, the group chairman is responsible for invoking, enforcing, and interpreting each parliamentary dispute. (A condensed table of *Robert's Rules* may be found on pages 264-265.)

If you know your rules of procedure, local meetings can provide excellent on-the-floor training for self-assertiveness and for making your points aloud and under pressure. If you become disruptive or obstructionist, the chairperson of the meeting will let you know soon enough. When you learn such a lesson in a crowd, you tend to remember it. Here are some examples of ways—within *Robert's Rules*—to influence the course of a public meeting:

Important procedural rules

Adjournment	The chairperson can hold off a hurry-up vote on adjournment until proper consideration is given to the entire scheduled agenda.
Obstructionism	A chairperson is empowered to tell a troublemaker that he will not be recognized to speak —that he is out of order—until he agrees to behave in accordance with the rules.
Recess	As in a courtroom, the chairperson may declare a short recess at a time when feelings are running too high—or when it looks as if an ill-advised vote is in the offing.
Brokering	The chairperson is entitled to interrupt debate and propose a vote whenever he pleases, or to advise postponement of a vote if he does not like the probable outcome.
Quorum	Organizations establish the requirements for a quorum, the minimum number of people that must be present at a meeting before its proceedings can be regarded as valid. If the quorum criterion is not met, the meeting is invalid.

Robert's Rules of order

Table of precedence of parliamentary motions, points of order, and procedural questions

Type of motion		May be debated	May be amended
Privileged category	Fix time of next meeting	yes[1]	yes
	Adjourn	no	no
	Take a recess	yes[1]	no[2]
	Point of privilege (e.g., group comfort)	no	no
	Point of order (refer, agenda)	no	no
Incidental category	Point of order (refer, ruling)	no	no
	Appeal ruling of the chair	yes[4]	no
	Parliamentary inquiry	no	no
	Withdraw motion[6]	no	no
	Suspend the rules (temporary)	no	no
	Object to consideration	no	no
Subsidiary category	Lay on the table (postpone)	no	no
	Close debate (vote previous question)	no	no
	Limit debate	no	yes
	Postpone (to specific time)	yes	yes
	Refer to committee	yes	yes
	Make amendment	no[8]	yes
	Postpone indefinitely	yes	no
Main or unclassified category	Primary motion	yes	yes
	Take up from the table	no	no
	Reconsider[9]	no[8]	no
	Rescind	yes	yes

Improving Your Speech

Type of vote	Needs second	May interrupt speaker
majority	yes	no
majority	yes	no
majority	yes	no
majority[3]	no	yes
no vote	no	yes
majority[3]	no	yes
majority[5]	yes	yes
no vote	no	yes
no vote[7]	no	no
2/3	yes	no
2/3	no	yes
majority	yes	no
2/3	yes	no
2/3	yes	no
majority	yes	no
majority	yes	no
majority	yes	no
majority	yes	no
majority	yes	no
majority	yes	no
majority	yes	yes
2/3[10]	yes	no

Explanatory footnotes

[1] May be debated *except* when another motion is already on the table.

[2] Only the length of the recess may be amended.

[3] The chair decides—but a majority may overrule.

[4] May be debated *except* when it pertains to a rules violation or to indecorum.

[5] A tie vote upholds the chair's ruling.

[6] Only the person who made the motion may withdraw it.

[7] No objection, no vote. If there is an objection, a majority vote is required.

[8] May be debated *only* if the original motion was ruled debatable.

[9] This is complicated. Only a person who voted on the prevailing side may move to reconsider—and that only on the same day that the original vote was taken (or the next day of the same session). The following motions may *not* be reconsidered: adjourn, point of order (agenda), lay on the table (postpone), point of order (ruling), point of privilege, recess, refer to committee, suspend the rules, and take up from the table.

[10] If notice was given at a previous meeting that a vote to rescind would take place, then a majority vote would suffice. Without such notice, a two-thirds vote is required.

For further reference

Braden, Waldo Warder
  Public Speaking: The Essentials
  Harper & Row
Ehrlich, Eugene and Hawes, Gene R.
  Speak for Success
  Bantam Books
Newman, Edwin
  Strictly Speaking
  Bobbs Merrill
Prochnow, Herbert V. and Herbert V., Jr.
  The Toastmaster's Treasure Chest
  Harper & Row

Rogers, Natalie
  Talk-Power
  Dodd, Mead
Stedman, Raymond William
  A Guide to Public Speaking
  Prentice-Hall
Strunk, William, Jr., and White, E.B.
  The Elements of Style
  Macmillan

Letters
mingle souls
Donne   10¢US

Writing Effective Letters

Letters are an important part of life. They can bring you closer to friends and family. They can bring comfort and cheer and inspire affection and love. The right letter can get you a job, sell your products or services, influence others, initiate action, and build goodwill. Knowing how to write the right letter for the right occasion can be a powerful asset in your social and business life, and it is a skill that anyone can learn.

The secret of writing a successful letter is knowing what you want to say and how to say it. Although neither is necessarily difficult, when confronted by a blank piece of paper, *you* may go blank—because, you think, you do not know what to say. In fact, this is rarely the case. You always have at least one reason for writing a letter and need only ask yourself what it is.

More often, the problem is that you do not know *how* to express yourself. The solution to this problem lies in knowing the kind of letter that you wish to write, whether it is a social or a business letter, and, if it is social, whether it is formal or informal and personal. There are specific techniques for each type of letter. Formal letters, such as announcements, invitations, and responses, have a standard form and wording that are simple to follow. Informal or personal letters to friends and relations are like a "visit" on paper; the trick in writing them is to write as you ordinarily talk. Business letters are written with a specific goal in mind, and usually require some advance preparation. You must decide on your goal and organize your supporting material, facts, arguments, requests, or questions *before* you start writing. In this chapter you will find the ways and means of doing this—techniques for organizing your thoughts, correct forms, and samples that you can use as models for the many occasions in your social and business life when you want to say the right thing in the right way.

Social letters

Your personal letters to friends and family can be relaxed and original in form and content. This is not the case, however, for the "letters of etiquette," the communications of social life that have a specific purpose (invitations, announcements, acceptances and re-grets, thank yous, notes of congratulation or condolence). For these, it is important to be correct, to follow the standard social conventions in appearance and content. This section gives valuable help on writing both informal and formal social letters.

Parts of a letter.

This five-part form is standard for all informal letters:

Heading. This is simply your address and the date or, if you have a printed letterhead, just the date. It goes at least an inch from the top, with at least a ¾-inch margin (larger, if you have a short letter) on the right. Cities and street names should be spelled out, but you can abbreviate the states. *You will notice that the date and return address have been omitted from most of the sample letters in this chapter. This was done to save space, but you should always include them in your letters.*

Salutation. This is the greeting. It goes on the left, at least half an inch below the heading, with the left margin equal to the right margin. The standard form is "Dear Sally" or "Dear Mrs. Thomson," depending on how well you know the person you are writing to. In the United States, "My Dear Mr. Jones" is considered more formal, but in England it is less formal. Salutations such as "Dear Friend," "Dear Sir," or "Dear Madam" are impolite for social letters.

Body. This is the message and there is no special form.

Complimentary closing. How you say "goodby" depends on how well you know the person you are writing to. In the past, closings were elaborate, but today's style is short and simple, such as "Yours sincerely" "Sincerely yours." Closing with just "Yours" sounds abrupt; but "Cordially" and "Sincerely" do not. "Respectfully" is usually reserved for writing to employers or customers.

Signature. This goes below the closing, a little to the right, in ink. The social convention is that you never use a title, such as Dr., Mr., Miss, or Mrs. when signing. A married woman would sign Betty Jordan, but she could, and *would* for business correspondence, add Mrs. Donald Jordan underneath her signature in parentheses. A divorced woman, but not a widow, would add Mrs. Betty Jordan.

Addressing the envelope. Use either the block form or indented form. The return address goes in the upper left. The convention is that women use Miss, Mrs., or Ms., but men do not use Mr. A boy under twelve is addressed as Master (that is, Master John Smith). Boys are not addressed as Mister until they are 18 or girls as Miss until they are 16. Use just the boy's full name when he is between the ages of 13 and 17, and the girl's full name when she is under 16. When addressing a husband and wife, the man's name comes first. You may write Mr. and Mrs. John Smith or John and Mary Smith. The address should be complete. Do not abbreviate people's names (unless *they* always do) or words like Street, Road, or Parkway, and do not forget the zip code. This can go on the same line as the town or city and state or on a separate line after the state.

You may add in the lower left corner:

PERSONAL—when you are sending a purely social and confidential letter to someone's office.

PLEASE FORWARD—when you know only the former address.

OPENED BY MISTAKE—when you mistakenly receive and open another person's mail. If you reseal the envelope, write "Opened by Mistake," sign your name, and mail it for the post office to redeliver, you will not be legally liable if the letter is lost.

Heading

63 Glover Street
Pleasantville, CT zip code
March 29, 1995

Salutation
Dear Sally,

Body

    Thank you so much for the lovely weekend. It was wonderful to see you and Jerry again and such a treat for Tom and me to get out of the city. We loved meeting Betty and Jim Henderson. It is always a pleasure to meet fellow sailors. I think it would be wonderful for us all to go sailing together this summer, but I hope you and Jerry will come for a visit way before then. You are such marvelous hosts and I only hope we can show you as good a time.

Closing Affectionately,
Signature *Betty*
          Betty

Stationery. Choose the best quality paper you can afford. Paper comes in different weights: the heavier the weight, the better the quality. A good choice is a 20-pound rag bond.

For formal correspondence (see page 270) that is not printed, the rule is to use plain white paper, a double sheet that folds once into its matching envelope.

For general informal correspondence (everything but personal letters), you have a wide choice, but you will always be in good taste if you stay with subdued shades. The rule used to be, a large sheet of paper, 8 × 10 or 7½ × 10, with matching envelopes in white, cream, or gray for men; and a folded sheet of blue, 5½ × 6½ or 6 × 8, that folds once again into a matching envelope, for women. Today, the larger sizes and a variety of colors are considered suitable for both men and women. For personal letters bright colors are popular and correct now for men and women.

Monograms and letterheads. Stationery printed with your monogram or letterhead costs more but it makes an excellent impression. A monogram is fine for personal letters, but a letterhead (including your telephone number, if you wish) is better for general-purpose letters.

Women have traditionally used the "informal," a folded card of white or off-white with the name engraved in black on the front (Mrs. John Jones, or Harriet Jones if unmarried) for social notes. While this is still correct, today informals can have both the husband's and wife's names, include the address, and be in any color. with printing or engraving in a contrasting color.

Typing vs. writing.
It was once considered bad taste to type personal letters, but this is no longer true. Go ahead and type them, especially if your handwriting is hard to read, but remember to always sign your letters by hand, in ink. Formal invitations and replies, however, are never typed. Although there is no firm rule, it is usually considered more polite, more personal, and more sincere to write short thank-you notes or notes of congratulation or sympathy by hand. (When you type, use larger sheets and do not type on the back of the page.)

Page sequence and folding.
For folded sheets, social notes should be short enough to go on the first page. Longer personal notes are written on pages one and three. A long letter simply follows the natural sequence.

The main point in having matching envelopes is to have as few folds as possible. A double sheet is folded once and put in the envelope fold first, as is a small single sheet. A larger single sheet is folded in three equal sections and inserted with the closed end first in such a way that the letter will be opened right side up.

How to be yourself
- **Visualize the person you are writing to.** Imagine you are face to face. What would you say? What questions would you ask? What questions would the person ask you?
- **Ask, "What would I say to *this* person?"** You would not talk the same way to your dearest friend as you would to a casual acquaintance, your child's school principal, or your boss.
- **Write the way you speak.** Keep thinking about *what* you want to say and do not edit. Your first thought is usually your best. Use the words you normally would in speaking. Most people use contractions (I can't, rather than I cannot) and short, simple words (I *went* to a movie, not I *attended* a movie). Try not to make a special effort to be correct; the result may sound forced and insincere.
- **Use conversational techniques.** You emphasize certain words in conversation by changing your inflection or tone; you can do the same in writing by underlining (Your dinner was *terrific!*), but do not overdo it. You can also occasionally mention the name of the person you are writing to (I wish I could see you, Betty).

Personal letters.
These letters to friends and family can be the most fun to write because they are like a friendly visit. Their purpose is to share experiences and feelings and to give pleasure. Of all the different kinds of letters you write, personal letters give you the best chance to be yourself—which is also the key to writing them well.

Lord Chesterfield, the 18th-century English essayist and social critic, put it very well in this advice to his son: "Write as you speak! Write as though you were seated in a room with me, talking in plain, simple language about the things you have seen and done and thought and experienced since you wrote to me last."

Being yourself or finding your own "voice" is something all good writers must learn. You can tell when you have found your voice because your writing will sound relaxed and easy. Your thoughts and words flow, though this is not always easy to achieve. "Writer's block" can be experienced by letter writers, too. You become tongue-tied, freeze, and feel as though you have nothing to say. That blank piece of paper is intimidating you. The trick to overcoming this, as Lord Chesterfield knew, is to relax and imagine that you are having a conversation with the person you are writing to. Some hints to help you do that are above.

Writing Effective Letters

Letters to friends and relatives

Get well

Dear Uncle Bob,
  I spoke to Margaret last night and she told me about your kidney stone and that you were much better and would be home from the hospital today. Hurrah! I'm sure you'll be just fine again in no time. In the meantime, here's a new book by our favorite, Guy Murtchie, that I hope you'll like. Get well soon!
                                    Cordially,
                                    Hank

Travel

Dearest Sandy,

I'm in Fez at the famous Hotel Jamai, where I stayed 40 years ago when it was about one-sixth the size. In a week I'll be home and eager to see you. I know you'd love Morocco. I'm traveling with Gloria French. Gloria knows a lot about rugs, and we intend to visit all the museums.

There are really impressive Roman ruins of temples, much destroyed, but many stones are standing, one 10 feet high.

As for painting, I've been working—produced three pictures and I've done a lot of work on the book. I'm really on the last lap now. I think of you all the time, for your dear friendship and all of your help on my book.

                                    Much love,
                                    Anne

Christmas letter to a sister

Dearest Sis,

It's so good to be back in Jerome and to have all the children with us after the past few years of being all over the map. It has made it a wonderful Christmas, though we miss you and Jim and wish you could be here with us. Maybe next year!

Of course, there's lots of news. Wes has been working on the pipeline, as you know, and Mike has joined him. Mike is in love with a lovely girl. Her name is Tessie and it looks as though they will get married this summer and settle down in Alaska. Caroline took a job with an engineering firm in Nome—so except for Hank, we're all together again. Hank came up from San Diego in the most incredible van (about a block long). He's joined forces with a friend who manufactures water skis and they're going to promote them on a grand tour of European spas—thus, the van. But you'll see for yourself, as he's coming east in March to ship the van to France and, of course, he'll come and see you.

You can imagine what fun it's been in Jerome. We're staying in the hotel (our house is rented for another year yet). We've been spending lots of time downstairs in the Spirit Room, where Wes threw a gigantic party for our anniversary. Lots of people remember you and Jim from your visit three years ago. Tom and Shirley, Dr. Joe and Margaret, and Burt send their best regards, as do Wes and the kids. Let me hear form you! My love to you and Jim.

                                    With love,
                                    Sarah

When you do not know what to say

If, in spite of everything, you still draw a blank, you can simply say, "I don't know what to say," but say *why.* That's what Michael Faraday, the English physicist famous for his work on electricity, did in this letter written to Sarah Bernard in 1820. Sarah Bernard and Michael Faraday were married soon after this letter was written and had a long and happy life together, a tribute in part, perhaps, to the power of the written word.

My Dear Sarah,

It is astonishing how much the state of the body influences the powers of the mind. I have been thinking all the morning of the very delightful and interesting letter I would send you this evening, and now I am so tired, and yet have so much to do, that my thoughts are quite giddy, and run round your image without any power of themselves to stop and admire it. I want to say a thousand kind and, believe me, heartfelt things to you, but am not master of words fit for the purpose; and still, as I ponder and think on you, chlorides, trials, oil, steel, miscellanea, mercury, and fifty other professional fancies swim before and drive me further and further into the quandry of stupidness.

                                    From your affectionate
                                    Michael

Invitations

Formal vs. informal. A formal event, such as a large church wedding or dinner-dance, requires a formal invitation. An informal invitation can be used for an informal event such as a small at-home wedding or country weekend. Informal invitations are simply handwritten notes in the first person. Formal invitations can be engraved or handwritten, but they have a specific form. They are written in the third person and are centered on the first page of folded white paper. **Acceptances and regrets.** Any invitation should be answered right away. Formal invitations require a handwritten reply that follows the exact form of the invitation.

R.S.V.P. This means "Répondez s'il vous plaît," French for "answer please." It can also be written R.s.v.p. and goes in the lower left with an address beneath on formal invitations, or with a phone number, if you wish, on informal ones. For informal events such as cocktail parties, where you need to know how many people are coming and also want to speed replies, you can write "Regrets only" and your phone number.

Please come to a party to celebrate the publication of Sam Jones's new mystery, A Death in the Afternoon, *at the Little Tor Bookshop, 100 River Road, Grandview, NY.*

Regrets only
555-1212

Formal dinner

John Gordon and Mary Gordon Green
the children of
Henry and Elizabeth Gordon
request the pleasure of your company
at a dinner in honor of their parents'
Golden Wedding Anniversary
on Saturday, the sixteenth of June
at eight o'clock
Tumblebrook Country Club

R.S.V.P.
Mrs. Robert Green
140 Old Mountain Road
West Hartford, CT zip code

Informal dinner

Dear Edith,

My brother John and I are giving a small dinner in honor of our parents' Golden Wedding Anniversary on Saturday, June 16th at eight o'clock at the Tumblebrook Country Club. The celebration wouldn't be complete without you and Harry. I do hope you can come.

Cordially,
Mary Green

Formal acceptance

Mr. and Mrs. Harold Smith
accept with pleasure
the kind invitation of
John Gordon and Mary Gordon Green
to a dinner in honor of
the Golden Wedding Anniversary
of their parents
Henry and Elizabeth Gordon
on Saturday, the sixteenth of June
at eight o'clock
at the Tumblebrook Country Club

Informal acceptance

Dear Mary,

Harry and I will be delighted to come on Saturday at eight to celebrate your parents' Golden Wedding Anniversary. What a wonderful occasion! Thank you so much for asking us.

Yours sincerely,
Edith Smith

Formal regret

Mr. and Mrs. Harold Smith
regret that they are unable to accept
the kind invitation of
John Gordon and Mary Gordon Green
to a dinner in the honor of
the Golden Wedding Anniversary
of their parents
Henry and Elizabeth Gordon
on Saturday, the sixteenth of June
at eight o'clock
at the Tumblebrook Country Club

Informal regret

Dear Mary,

I'm so sorry, but we can't come to what I know will be a wonderful party. We will be away that whole week in Montreal to meet Joe's fiancee and her family, but thank you so much for asking us. Harry and I both wish we could be there.

Yours sincerely,
Edith Smith

Writing Effective Letters

Formal wedding. An invitation to a formal church wedding may include another invitation to the reception afterward. If the reception is held before one o'clock, it is called a breakfast; after one, a reception. If space is limited in the church, guests are also sent an admission card or a card for reserved seating "within the ribbon." Invitations are enclosed in *two* envelopes. The inside envelope is not sealed. It holds the invitation and enclosures and is addressed with only the names of the guests.

Formal reply. Formal wedding invitations do not require a reply, but an invitation to the reception does. You can use the shorter form shown at right, or you can repeat the exact wording of the invitation.

Formal wedding invitation

> Mr. and Mrs. Richard Cameron
> request the honor of your presence
> at the marriage of their daughter
> Nancy Susan
> to
> Mr. Henry McQuiston
> on Saturday morning, the second of June
> at ten o'clock
> Grace Unitarian Church
> Pleasantville, NY

> Mr. and Mrs. Richard Cameron
> request the pleasure of your company
> at breakfast
> Saturday, the second of June
> at twelve o'clock
> Forty-five Riversville Road
> Pleasantville, NY

> The favor of a reply
> is requested

> Please present this card
> at Grace Unitarian Church
> Saturday, June second

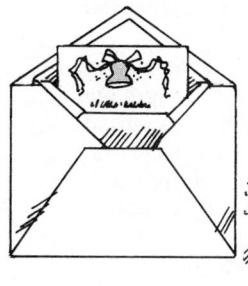

> Mr. and Mrs. Thomas Putnam
> accept with pleasure
> Mr. and Mrs. Richard Cameron's
> kind invitation for
> Saturday, the second of June
> at twelve o'clock

If a husband and wife receive an invitation and only one can attend, the acceptance is stated first, then the regret.

> Mrs. Thomas Putnam
> accepts with pleasure etc.
> Mr. Thomas Putnam
> regrets exceedingly etc.

Informal wedding invitation
Dear Sally,

   Marlene is being married here at home to Ted Smith on Friday, May 25, at four o'clock. We do hope that you and Jack can come and that you will be able to stay for tea after the ceremony.
                                                 Love,
                                                 Helen

Informal reply
Dear Helen,

   We are so happy about Marlene's forthcoming marriage and are delighted to be included. We look forward to seeing you on May 25, at four.
                                                 Love,
                                                 Sally

Formal acceptance

> Mr. and Mrs. Thomas Putnam
> accept with pleasure
> Mr. and Mrs. Richard Cameron's
> kind invitation to be present
> at the marriage of their daughter
> Nancy Susan
> to
> Mr. Henry McQuiston
> on Saturday, the second of June
> at twelve o'clock
> and afterward at the wedding breakfast

Recalling invitations. When a wedding must be postponed or canceled, guests can be notified by telephone, telegram, or, if there is time, by printed cards. The wording is formal, but the style does not have to be indented. Reasons are given for a postponement, but not for a cancellation.

> Mr. and Mrs. Raymond Brown regret that owing to their daughter's illness they are obliged to recall the invitations to her wedding on Sunday, the third of June.

> Mr. and Mrs. Raymond Brown
> announce that the marriage of their daughter
> Suzanne to Mr. Henry Harrison
> will not take place

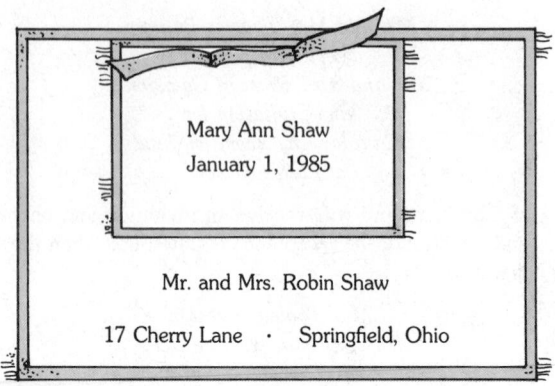

Mary Ann Shaw
January 1, 1985

Mr. and Mrs. Robin Shaw

17 Cherry Lane · Springfield, Ohio

Announcements

Wedding. A wedding is usually announced by calling the society editor of your local paper, but when a wedding is small and private (or when the couple has eloped), formal announcements can be sent out as soon as possible after the event.

> *Mr. and Mrs. Anthony Jerome*
> *announce the marriage of their daughter*
> *Charlotte*
> *to*
> *Mr. Peter Gates*
> *Captain United States Army*
> *on Friday, the fifteenth of June*
> *Saratoga, New York*

NOTE: When the bride or groom is an officer, it is customary to give the military title, but the title can be omitted for a noncommissioned officer or an enlisted person.

Birth. A traditional and formal way to announce a baby's birth is shown above. The baby's card is attached to the parents' joint card with a pink, blue, or white ribbon, or, an engraved card can be sent.

> *Mr. and Mrs. Robin Shaw*
> *announce with joy*
> *the birth of their daughter*
> *Mary Ann*
> *on the first of January, 1985*

Requests and responses

Excuse for absence from school

Dear Mrs. Shepard,

Please excuse Peter's absence from school this past Monday, Tuesday, and Wednesday. He had a bad cold and I thought it would be best (and best for the other children) to keep him home. Could you please tell Peter, or send me a note, if there is any work to be made up?

Thank you.

> *Yours sincerely,*
> *Ruth Jones*

Excuse for lateness

Dear Mrs. Shepard,

Please excuse Peter's lateness this morning. During the storm last night, our electricity must have been off for an hour, as all our clocks and alarms were an hour off, and he missed the school bus. I'm driving him in myself and hope you will forgive his unavoidable lateness.

> *Sincerely,*
> *Ruth Jones*

Excuse for future absence

Dear Miss Costanza,

Sally will be absent from school next Thursday and Friday, October 4th and 5th, as this is an important religious holiday (Yom Kippur) and she will be attending services.

If it's possible to give Sally assignments to make up the class work she will miss, she'll do that over the weekend. Thank you.

> *Very truly yours,*
> *Mary Green*

Apologetic answer to a complaint about a child

Dear Mr. Johnson,

I can certainly understand your being upset about Tommy's hitting a baseball through your windshield. We've told the boys not to play baseball in the street and now they know why.

K & R Auto says the replacement cost would be $40. I've enclosed a check for that amount, which Tommy will make up out of his paper-route money. He is very sorry about what happened and will be over soon to tell you so himself. I am so sorry about the trouble this has caused you.

> *Yours sincerely,*
> *Sally Smith*

Nonapologetic answer to a complaint about a child

Dear Mrs. Henderson,

Billy has told us how upset you were about the noise the children made playing in the vacant lot next to your house over the weekend. I'm sorry that you were disturbed and Billy is, too.

As he explained it, he and his friends have been playing softball in that lot for several years now. The people who used to live in your house, the Jenkins, never objected and it didn't occur to any of the children that you would mind.

He's told me that he and his friends have talked it over and will play future games on the baseball diamond over at the grammar school.

> *Yours very truly,*
> *Hattie Brown*

Writing Effective Letters

Thank you notes.

You are expected to send thank-you notes for wedding and shower gifts and for being entertained for the weekend, but there are many other times when they are appropriate—such as for birthday or Christmas presents or when someone has done you a favor or shown you or your family some particular kindness. Thank-you notes can be quite short, but they should be specific and personal. It is easier, and more polite, to write them right away, while the pleasure of receiving a present, or of having a lovely time, is still fresh in your mind.

For a retirement party and gift

Dear John,

This is just to tell you how much I have enjoyed working with you over the years, and also to thank you for your part in that fine farewell gift. I have always wanted a matched set of golf clubs and these are superb. Thanks again for making my last day at Acme so memorable.

Sincerely,
Henry Maxwell

For the weekend.

When a couple is entertained for the weekend, the "bread and butter" letter is usually written by the wife to the hostess.

Dear Mary Ann,

Thank you so much for an absolutely wonderful weekend. It was such a treat to spend time with you and Jim. Tom hasn't stopped talking about your chocolate soufflé and what a fantastic cook you are. We were especially thrilled with the whale-watching boat trip. How thoughtful of you to know that would be just what we'd love and to arrange it! Thank you again for everything.

Love,
Sarah

For a Christmas gift

Dear Larry,

Thank you so much for the beautiful lamp. It is truly just what I needed. I've clipped it to my drawing board and it not only looks terrific (I love the red color), but it also eliminates the shadows, which is a big help in my work. I feel lucky to have such a wonderful, thoughtful cousin.

Much love,
Sally,

For a wedding gift

Dear Aunt Sarah,

Tom and I are thrilled with your wonderful wedding present. We have always admired Grace Steven's work, and to have an entire dinner set of her beautiful pottery is just fantastic!

I know it will look spendid on our table and I want you and uncle Joe to come for dinner and see for yourselves as soon as we get back from Bermuda. I will call you then to set a date.

Love,
Polly

For a baby gift

Dear Sally,

Angelo doesn't have any words yet, but if he did I know he would thank you for your beautiful present. The baby sack is just what he needed—just the right weight—and the rose and blue stripes make him look so handsome! Thank you so much.

Cordially,
Bianca

Thank you notes from children

For a gift

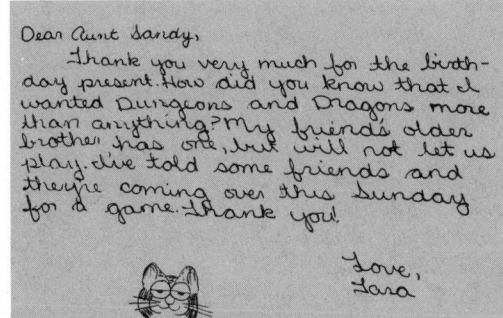

Dear Aunt Sandy,
Thank you very much for the birthday present. How did you know that I wanted Dungeons and Dragons more than anything? My friend's older brother has one, but will not let us play. I've told some friends and they're coming over this Sunday for a game. Thank you!

Love,
Tara

For the weekend

Dear Margie,

Thank you very much for a wonderful time. Your birthday party was great. I loved the treasure hunt (and winning the prize) and I loved staying with you. It was just like old times.

Please thank your Mom for me and ask her to send my Mom her recipe for spaghetti. It's the best I ever tasted. Thanks for everything.

Love,
Tina

Sympathy and condolence.

Writing to someone on the death of a spouse, relative, or friend is difficult for most people and yet there is probably no time when a letter can mean so much and be so deeply appreciated. Your natural feeling of sympathy for someone's loss is what matters here. Your letter can be short, but it should be tactful—not dwelling on the circumstances of the death—and it should be sincere and simple.

To a neighbor

Dear Rose,

I cannot tell you how shocked and sorry I am to learn of Bob's sudden death. He was such a wonderful man and I have such warm memories of his many kindnesses. I know that I will miss him very much and can only imagine what a terrible loss this is to you. Please accept my deepest sympathy.

Most sincerely,
Harriet Jones

To a friend

Dear Margaret,

I have just heard the very sad news that you lost your father and I want you to know how sorry I am. I know how much you loved him and how painful this loss must be for you and your mother.

I wish that words could help, but I know that only time does that. Please know that my loving thoughts and deepest sympathy are with you both.

Love,
Sarah

To an employee

Dear Harry,

I was sorry to hear of your wife's death and can only imagine how terrible this loss must be for you. Although words can do so little, I want you to know that you have my deepest sympathy.

If there is anything that I can do to help in any way, please do not hesitate to call on me.

Yours sincerely,
Franklin Rogers

Acknowledgments.

It is considered correct to send a short thank-you note to everyone who sends a condolence letter. This does not have to be written as promptly as an ordinary thank-you letter, but it should, if possible, be sent within six weeks.

Dear Carol,

I cannot tell you how much your thoughtfulness when my father died meant to me. You are a true and dear friend and I thank you for all your kindness.

Love,
Nancy

Dear Mr. Brown,

Thank you for your very kind and thoughtful letter. It is wonderful to know how well thought of John was among the people he worked with, and I very much appreciate your telling me.

Yours sincerely,
Jane Smith

Lincoln's letter to Mrs. Bixby

One of the most famous letters in American history is Abraham Lincoln's to Mrs. Lydia Bixby after being told by the governor of Massachusetts that she had lost her five sons in the Civil War. That the information turned out to be wrong —that one son survived as a prisoner of war, one went to sea, and one deserted to the Confederate Army—changed the facts upon which the letter was based, but not its substance or its eloquence.

Executive Mansion
Washington, Nov. 21, 1864
To Mrs. Bixby, Boston, Mass.
Dear Madam,
I have been shown in the files of the War Department a statement of the Adjutant General of Massachusetts that you are the mother of five sons who have died gloriously on the field of battle. I feel how weak and fruitless must be any word of mine which should attempt to beguile you from the grief of a loss so overwhelming. But I cannot refrain from tending you the consolation that may be found in the thanks of the republic they died to save. I pray that our Heavenly Father may assuage the anguish of your bereavement, and leave you only the cherished memory of the loved and lost, and the solemn price that must be yours to have laid so costly a sacrifice upon the altar of freedom.
Yours very sincerely and respectfully,
A. Lincoln

Writing Effective Letters

Announcing a death.

Often a member of the family of someone who has died will have to tell other family members or friends the sad news that someone close to them has died. This should be done as gently as possible, with an attempt to lessen the shock. It is hard to find a better example of this kind of letter than the one that Charles Dickens wrote to his wife, who was ill and away from home, to prepare her for finding out that their infant daughter had died. (See below.)

To a relative

Dear Uncle Ben,

I'm so sorry to be writing with some very sad news that I know will be a great shock to you: Uncle Harry passed away last night after having had a stroke two days ago. The funeral will be held at St. Agnes Church on Elm Street in New London, Thursday at two o'clock, and afterward family and friends will go to Aunt Mary's.

Affectionately,
Betty

To a friend of the deceased

Dear Mr. Jones,

I am writing to let you know that my father, Timothy Johnson, died in his sleep last night after a short illness. Father spoke of you so often as a friend that I felt you would want to know.

Yours sincerely,
Fred Johnson

Death and funeral notices

These are prepared by the person in charge of the funeral and are then phoned into the newspaper, either as news or as a paid advertisement. The paper will need the following information:

1. Name of deceased (and maiden name of a married woman)
2. Address
3. Date of death
4. Age
5. Names and relationships of survivors
6. Time and place of funeral and burial
7. Whether services are private or open to the public
8. Whether the family wishes no flowers to be sent or the organization and its address to which a memorial contribution can be sent.

Death notice

HENDERSON, MARY (née Bronson), of 27 Pine Street, Harrison, New York, died suddenly on May 12, in her 55th year, beloved wife of John Henderson. She is also survived by their son Howard Henderson, daughters Alice (Mrs. John Lagrange) and Mary (Mrs. Robert Johnson), and grandchildren Ramond and Susan Lagrange. Funeral services at Community Church, corner of Central and Lafayette Avenues, Harrison, NY, 11 AM Monday, May 14. Interment is private. In lieu of flowers, contributions may be made to the Community Care Society, Box 4000, Harrison, NY zip code.

Dickens' letter to his wife

Often family members or friends will have to be told that someone close to them has died. This should be done as gently as possible. It is hard to find a better example than this letter Charles Dickens wrote to his wife to prepare her for the news that their daughter had died.

Devonshire-terrace
Tuesday morning, 15th April, 1851

My dearest Kate,

Now observe you must read this letter very slowly and carefully. If you have hurried on thus without quite understanding (apprehending some bad news) I rely on your turning back and reading again.

Little Dora, without being in the least pain, is suddenly stricken ill. There is nothing in her appearance but perfect rest— you would suppose her quietly asleep, but I am sure she is very ill, and I cannot encourage myself with much hope of her recovery. I do not (and why should I say I do to you, my dear?) I do not think her recovery at all likely.

I do not like to leave home, I can do no good here, but I think it right to stay. You will not like to be away, I know, and I cannot reconcile it to myself to keep you away. Foster, with his usual affection for us, comes down to bring you this letter and to bring you home, but I cannot close it without putting the strongest entreaty and injunction upon you to come with perfect composure—To remember what I have often told you, that we never can expect to be exempt, as to our many children, from the afflictions of other parents, and that if—if when you come I should even have to say to you, "Our little baby is dead," you are to do your duty to the rest, and to show yourself worthy of the great trust you hold in them.

If you will only read this steadily I have a perfect confidence in your doing what is right.

Ever affectionately,
Charles Dickens

Business letters

A successful business letter is not only grammatically correct and neat, it is also friendly and courteous. It is simple, brief, easy to read, and gets right to the point. Such a letter creates a good impression. It makes your reader feel that you are the kind of person or firm that it is good to do business with. In short, a successful business letter looks good and sounds good. Here are some helpful hints.

Looking good. Business letters are almost always typed on a standard 8½″ × 11″ good quality paper. Most businesses use a letterhead with their name, address, and phone number. The standard formats are shown below. Although some businesses prefer the block form because it saves time for the typist, most use either the modified block or modified semiblock forms.

Basic rules for spacing. Follow these rules no matter which format you use.

1. Place the address two lines below the date, which is two lines below the heading.
2. Place the salutation two lines below the address.
3. Begin the opening sentence or paragraph two lines below the salutation.
4. Single space for the heading, address, and within paragraphs.
5. Double space between paragraphs.
6. Place the complimentary closing two lines below the last paragraph.
7. Place the typed signature four lines below the complimentary closing.
8. Put any additional data (such as enclosures or initials of the writer and typist) two lines below the typed signature, beginning at the left margin.

Styles

Block

ABC Company
100 Main Street
Anytown, Florida zip code
January 1, 1985

Mr. John Smith
12 Broadway
Apple City, New York zip code

Dear Mr. Smith:

This is an example of the block form of business letter. You will notice that the heading, inside address, closing, and signature all line up at the left and the paragraphs are not indented.

This style saves the typist time and that is why some businesses prefer it.

Yours sincerely,

Thomas Rider

Thomas Rider

Modified semiblock

ABC Company
100 Main Street
Anytown, Florida zip code
January 1, 1985

Mr. John Smith
12 Broadway
Apple City, New York zip code

Dear Mr. Smith:

Here is an example of the modified semiblock form. You will notice that the heading, closing, and signature are aligned vertically near the center of the page and that the paragraphs are indented. This last point is the only difference between this and the modified block form shown at the right.

Yours sincerely,

Thomas Rider

Thomas Rider

Parts of a business letter

Modified block format

Heading

Warner Widget Company
100 Marvin Gardins
Centerville, New Jersey zip code
March 10, 19—

Inside address

Mr. Mark Harris
M & H Manufacturing Company
Paradise, Rhode Island zip code

Salutation

Dear Mr. Harris:

Body

Thank you for your letter of February 24 and for your interest in our products. I am sending you our latest brochure describing our entire selection of widgets and particularly refer you to pages 8 and 9, where you will find some widgets well-suited to your needs.

Jack Armstrong, our New England sales representative, will be calling on you soon and will be happy to answer any further questions you may have. I hope that we may soon count you among our many satisfied customers.

Closing

Yours sincerely,

Signature

Frank Jones

Frank Jones, Manager
Product Information

Additional data

FJ/ms
Enclosure

Sounding good. You will be able to write successful business letters by following five basic rules:

1. **Be friendly.** Your letter will build goodwill and be more likely to accomplish its purpose if you maintain a friendly tone. Even if you are angry, avoid sarcasm or insults.
2. **Be specific.** Tell the reader exactly what he or she needs to know. If you have a complaint, say precisely what is wrong and what you want done about it. If you need information, note clearly what you need to know.
3. **Be positive.** Even a letter that must say no can do it in a positive way. Compare, for example, "We regret to inform you that the postal strike makes it impossible to ship your order until . . ." with "Thank you for your order. The merchandise will be shipped to you immediately after the postal strike is settled."
4. **Keep your reader's point of view in mind.** Try to see things from his or her vantage point, not yours. One way to tell whether you have done this is to count the "I's" and the "you's." You want lots of you's and few I's. You can usually get the right effect by rephrasing. Compare these examples:

    I: *I* want to express *my* sincere thanks for the kind words *I* received today from . . .
    You: Thank *you* for *your* very kind words.
    Or:
    I: *We* make four styles in all sizes.
    You: *You* may have *your* choice of four styles in all sizes.

5. **Remember the golden rule.** Write the kind of letter you would like to get if you were in the reader's position.

Anatomy of a letter. You will find it
easier to write a clear, well-organized letter if you think of it as having a basic structure—a beginning, a middle, and an end.

The beginning. The purpose of the first sentence is to get the reader's attention and interest. This can often be done by asking a question. An insurance sales letter might ask: "Do you want to save 40 percent on your auto insurance?" Keep the first sentence short. The rest of the opening paragraph explains it.

The emphasis should be on what the *reader* needs, not what *you* need. This holds true even for a letter of complaint. You might, for example, begin such a letter with, "I know you want to maintain good relationships with your customers, but . . ."

The middle. This is where you state and explain *your* purpose. It is important to present your supporting facts or arguments in order of their importance.

It helps to make notes or an outline (see volume 1, page 56) before you start to write.

Often, you are trying to motivate your reader to take some action, or you may be explaining why you will or will not take some action. Give the facts first and then the conclusion. A tenant might say to an uncooperative landlord, "I have talked to my lawyer about your failure to have my water pipes repaired after my repeated requests and was told that under this jurisdiction I may withhold my rent until repairs are made. I plan to do so unless repairs are made this month."

The end. If the purpose of your letter is to get the reader to take some action, sum up at the end with a direct and positive statement. Sounding tentative or doubtful invites rejection. It is better to say, "Your cooperation in sending a check by return mail will be greatly appreciated," than to say, "We hope you will pay as soon as possible." "Our representative will call for an appointment next week" is better than, "May we send our representative to see you soon?" You should be clear (if you want some action taken), courteous (avoid a cold, curt ending), and complete (the reader should feel you have said everything you have to say).

What's wrong with this letter?

The letter below is a good example of what *not to do* in business writing.

> Dear Sir:
>
> We have the latest edition of your Readers' Complete Bookshelf. After reviewing it very thoroughly with my wife and children, the very best we can find to say about it is that we are completely disgusted with it. We have, however, found that it is very useful in teaching our children how the art of misinformation is being used to deceive Americans. We have found many examples in your book.
>
> Please do not send Volume Three.
>
> *Howard Case*
> Howard Case

The tone of this letter could be improved, but the real problem is that the letter is vague. The writer does not give any concrete examples. A better letter would read,

I have gone over the latest volume of your Readers' Complete Bookshelf and am deeply disappointed with it—particularly in the chapter on the War Between the States. I felt you were unjustly critical of the South and not critical enough of what the North did during Reconstruction. There were also several historical inaccuracies. You have the wrong Confederate commander for the Battle. . .

Job applications. A letter written to apply for a job is really a sales letter. You are selling your own qualifications as a prospective employee. As in any sales letter, you want to get your reader's interest, stress what you can do for the reader, and persuade him or her to take an action—in this case, give you an interview. You would also include a résumé that lists your educational and work experience, but the letter of application has the advantage of being written for *this particular job,* as most résumés do not, and allows you to select and emphasize the experience and abilities that qualify you for that job. (For information on choosing a career and finding the job you want, see Advancing Your Career, page 22.)

A famous letter, written to the Duke of Milan in 1482, is hard to beat as an example of super-salesmanship, but then it was written by an extraordinary man who could do everything he said he could do and more. His name was Leonardo Da Vinci. Below are some excerpts from that letter. Leonardo got the job and he kept it for 16 years, until the French Army marched into Milan and took the Duke prisoner.

"Having, most illustrious lord, seen and considered the experiments of all those who pose as masters in the art of inventing instruments of war, and finding that their inventions differ in no way from those in common use, I am emboldened, without prejudice to anyone, to solicit an appointment of acquainting your Excellency with certain of my secrets.

1. I can construct bridges which are very light and strong and very portable, with which to pursue and defeat the enemy; and others more solid, which resist fire and assault, yet are easily removed and placed in position; and I can also burn and destroy those of the enemy.

2. In case of siege I can cut off water from the trenches and make pontoons and scaling ladders and other similar contrivances. . . .

4. I can also make a kind of cannon which is light and easy of transport, with which to hurl small stones like hail, and of which the smoke causes great terror to the enemy, so that they suffer heavy loss and confusion. . . .

10. In time of peace, I believe that I can give you as complete satisfaction as anyone else in the construction of buildings both public and private, and in conducting water from one place to another.

I can further execute sculpture in marble, bronze or clay, also in painting I can do as much as anyone else, whoever he may be.

And if any of the aforesaid things should seem to anyone impossible or impracticable, I offer myself as ready to make trial of them in your park or in whatever place shall please your Excellency . . . .

If you are looking for your first full-time job, you probably do not have much work experience, but you do have some "life experience." Your letter should emphasize your personal qualities and any relevant work, school, or extracurricular activities:

Letter from a college graduate

354 Hardscrabble Road
Anytown, N.Y. zip code
June 1, 1994

Dear Mr. Johnson:

With my college degree in Business and my strong interest in sales, I believe I could do an excellent job as a management trainee with your company. I have achieved high grades in marketing courses and am sure I could learn to market a product successfully.

I know how valuable successful communication is in business, and feel that being editor of our college newspaper has helped me develop communication skills. You will find a complete résumé of my educational experience and extracurricular activities enclosed. I will call on Monday, June 4th, to arrange an interview so that we may discuss my qualifications for your management-trainee program.

Yours sincerely,
Nancy Graham
Nancy Graham

From prospective high-school graduate

Mr. Harold Long
Personnel Director
Carter Paper Company
52 Broadway
Apple City, New York zip code

Dear Mr. Long:

I will graduate from Centerville High School this June and my guidance counselor, Mr. Herbert Jones, suggested that I write to you about a sales position with your company.

I have worked part-time as an ad salesman for the Centerville Bulletin for the past two years. As advertising manager of our high-school yearbook, I produced a $1500 profit – a first for Centerville High. I've also been manager of the track team for the past two years and organized the successful fund-raising campaign that sent the team to the national meet in Washington this year.

I like sales, think I am good at it and want to make it my career – if possible, with the Carter Paper Company. I will call next Monday for an appointment.

Yours sincerely,
Jack Hudson

278   **Writing Effective Letters**

Putting it the right way. Helpful sentences:

Salary

I would be happy to discuss salary with you when we meet. My range is—, — to —, —.

I will be glad to discuss the matter of salary with you at a personal interview.

Salary considerations are not as important as the career opportunity this position offers. I am sure we can arrive at a satisfactory arrangement.

References

The following people can tell you about my work from several different points of view:

I refer you specifically to the following people with whom I have worked over the past few years.

My former employers and clients will vouch for my integrity and good reputation in the trade. I refer you to the following:

Selling yourself

I would be happy to show you my proposal for increasing your next year's sales by at least 25 percent.

I would like to show you how I can save you money on your company's liability insurance and will call on Monday for an appointment.

I shall phone your secretary next week to arrange for a meeting at your convenience.

I would very much like to discuss my qualifications for your buyer–training program and will call on Monday to set up an appointment.

Experienced worker answering an advertisement

```
        Box 000, Times
        Centerville, NY zip code

        Dear Sir:

           In response to your advertisement in
        this morning's Times for an experienced
        secretary, I would like to apply for that
        position. I have been a secretary for the
        past ten years for three prominent executives
        who will vouch for my efficiency and
        dependability. They are:

           Mr. Harry Ricer, ABC Company,
           Centerville, NY (Hospital Supplies)
           19-- to 19--

           Mr. John Kramer, Consolidated Products,
           Newton, NY (Building Materials)
           19-- to 19--

           Mr. Peter Kent, Hawkins, Smith &
           Barnes, Inc., Centerville, NY
           (Management Consultants) 19-- to 19--

           I have worked for Mr. Kent for the past
        five years. He is being transferred to
        Minneapolis, and so I am looking for another
        position.

           I would like to come in and talk to
        you personally, and have enclosed a self-
        addressed card for you to let me know the
        most convenient time for you. You can also
        call me at work. The number is Hudson 5-1212,
        extension 400.

                          Sincerely yours,
                          Susan Graham
                          Susan Graham
```

Follow-up letter. It is a very good idea to write again *after* an interview to thank the interviewer and remind him or her of your interest and abilities.

Dear Mr. Smith:

I very much enjoyed talking with you and meeting the members of your staff yesterday afternoon.

I am glad you mentioned the importance of budget constraints and feel that my record of cost-effectiveness as a project manager under government contracts would be a definite asset to your organization. I would be happy to discuss this further and will call again in a few days.

Yours sincerely,

Gerald Simms

Thank-you letter. After you get the job, it is a good idea to write thank-you notes to the people who helped you.

Dear Mr. Jones:

I am very happy to be able to tell you that I am now a project manager at Consolidated Technologies. Mr. Smith told me about the fine letter of recommendation you sent and I am sure that that had a lot to do with my getting the job. Thank you very much for your encouragement and help.

Yours sincerely,

Gerald Simms

Getting help. Asking for information or services, particularly from the government or corporate bureaucracy, can be frustrating and time-consuming. Yet you can do it easily by writing the right kind of letter. Here are some hints.

State your reason for writing in the first sentence. This saves your reader time and energy.

Include all reference numbers and dates. If you are writing about a bill, an order, or a missing shipment, you will need to include such things as the invoice number or date of purchase. If a company gives you a reference number to use in writing to them, be sure to use it.

Confine your inquiry or request to one point. Do not confuse your reader by covering several subjects. Write a different letter for each. Be short and specific.

> Gentlemen:
>
> Could you give me an explanation of line 30 of Commerce Department Form 638: Employer Liability. Specifically, does line 30 refer only to office workers or does it cover field representatives?

When you want action, request it clearly. Do this at the end of your letter. Some examples are:

> Please send me a refund.
> Please send me a corrected bill.

Be brief. Keep your letter to one page if possible. Write a draft first, put it aside for a while, then see what you can eliminate.

Write to an individual whenever possible. This will speed a reply. Although you can use just the person's title, a name—which you can usually find out by calling the company—is better. When in doubt, write to the president or department head, who will see that the right person gets it. (For help in finding the right person, see box at top right.)

To a drug company

> Mr. Frank Jones, President
> ABC Vitamin Company
> Deercrossing, Colorado zip code
>
> Dear Mr. Jones:
>
> I am writing to ask about the safety of your special Vitamin x compound, Wondervite. I have been taking this vitamin for some time and have just read in the Health and Science section of the Portland Times that it does not lower cholesterol and that it can cause serious side effects.
>
> I would appreciate your sending me a summary of your laboratory reports on the action and side effects of this vitamin as soon as possible.
>
> Yours sincerely,
>
> Angela Black

Finding the person to write to

Consumer affairs. A pamphlet listing state, city, and county consumer protection offices, Better Business Bureaus, and names and addresses of corporate consumer contacts is available without charge by writing to:

> Consumer Resource Handbook
> Consumer Information Center
> Pueblo, Colorado 81009

U.S. government officials. *The United States Government Manual* is updated regularly to tell you who's who in Congress and all government agencies. You can buy it from the Superintendent of Documents, U.S. Government Printing Office, Washington, D.C. 20402, *but* you must write first for the price (which changes) and the correct order form. You may find it at the public library. *Congressional Staff Directory* is published by Congressional Staff Director, Ltd., Mt. Vernon, Va. 22121. It, too, may be found at the library.

To a company

> John Smith, Sales Manager
> Acme Office Supplies
> Newton, Illinois zip code
>
> Dear Mr. Smith:
>
> Please send me samples and a price quotation for 100 metal paper clips, Product Number 2000 on page 36 of your catalog. I would also like to know the price for an order of 1 million clips.
>
> I would appreciate your sending this information by the end of the week.
>
> Yours sincerely,
>
> Frank Davis

To the Food and Drug Administration

> Gentlemen:
>
> I need to know whether it is safe to use the anti-inflammatory drug, Cureall. The drug is produced by Universal Drug Company, Weaver, Illinois. The code number on the label is Y-8000.
>
> I bought the drug about six months ago from my local druggist, Robert Morley, 200 Main Street, Centerville, New York. I have since heard that the drug has been declared unsafe. Could you let me know the current status of this product?
>
> Yours sincerely,
>
> Helen Smith

Writing Effective Letters

A request for aid

The Reverend Frank E. Roberts
Christ Church
Centerville, New York zip code

Dear Dr. Roberts:

Some of the employees at Consolidated
Industries are repairing broken toys to
be given as Christmas presents to
children in the county. We hoped you
might help us with this project by
setting up a collection depot at the
church and asking parishioners to
contribute broken toys.

I have asked Sandra Smith, an employee
who is one of your parishioners, to speak
to you further about this. Let me just
say that your help would be much
appreciated.

Yours sincerely,

Thomas Brown

Thomas Brown

To a dress company

Manager, Customer Services
Jennie de Woolfe, Inc.
New York, NY zip code

Dear Sir or Madam:

I saw an advertisement for your silk shirtwaist dress on page 35 of the April Vogue magazine and would very much like to buy it.

Could you please tell me if any stores in Marblehead carry the dress or, if not, where I could buy it in Boston?

Yours sincerely,

Barbara Ann Blake

To the Department of Veterans Affairs

Dear Mr. (look up proper person):

Please tell me if you offer educational benefits to children of soldiers killed in action. My husband, Henry Greene, Serial number 000-000, died in Lebanon in 1983. He was a sergeant in the Marine Corps. My son Henry will be ready for college next year and I need to know whether he is eligible for benefits.

Please let me know as soon as possible.

Yours sincerely,

Ruth Greene

Letter of inquiry.

The following letter follows the formula for a letter of inquiry: it gets the reader's attention; states what is wanted, who wants it, and why; motivates action; and expresses appreciation.

Dear Alumna or Alumnus,

Exciting news! The first Address Register of the Alumnae and Alumni of Evergreen College in ten years will be published in 1995. This new volume will contain an alphabetical listing of alumnae/i names and addresses, cross-referenced with name in college, plus class and geographical listings.

We need your help in completing the register. Please check your listing for accuracy, and return the questionnaire in the enclosed envelope by June 1. Please note that the register will be available only to alumnae/i, faculty, and officers of Evergreen College. Your address will not be given out for noncollege use.

An order blank for your copy of the 1995 AAEC Register is attached to the questionnaire. The register is available at the prepublication price of $20. (It will be $25 after June, 1995.)

We hope you will take the time to fill out all of the enclosed questionnaire. If you are one of the 8000 alumnae/i who have joined AAEC's ranks since 1985, do not miss your first chance to tell us about your activities since graduation. If you are one of the 31,000 who were listed in the 1985 directory, this is your chance to bring your record up to date. Information about your current interests and accomplishments helps us in developing our many programs—including our guided travel tours and summer seminars.

Many thanks for your cooperation in filling out this questionnaire. We hope to be flooded by completed answers from all of you!

Yours sincerely,

Annabel Kemp Smith
President, AAEC

Enclosures

Notification of address change

Dear Sir:

Please send all future compensation checks to my new address:

1400 Wharton Avenue
Centerville, New York zip code.

My former address was:

10 Henry Street
Hartsdale, New Jersey zip code.

Yours truly,

Frank Dean

Complaints that get action.

Do not lose your temper if you want to write a letter of complaint that gets results.

People often have a hard time writing an effective letter of complaint because they are angry and they let their anger take over. The anger becomes the important thing. However, what really matters is getting some action that will remedy the situation. This is much more likely if your tone is reasonable and calm. In some situations, it helps to use humor; in others, just to present the facts clearly and briefly. Sometimes it helps to go ahead and write your enraged letter *and put it away*. Then, with you mind clear, you can write the letter you will actually mail. Here are some hints to help you:

Write to the right person. Think carefully about who will be most likely to take action or get action on your complaint. If you are having a problem with the credit department of a store, for example, you will be more likely to get action if you write directly to the store's president, *not* to the credit department. In general, it is always best to write to the boss—you would be surprised how few people do this.

Keep copies of your letters. Knowing when you said what to whom and when may be important to solving the problem.

Do not get personal. Do not be sarcastic or insulting to your reader. You may be angry about the situation, but remember that the person and the situation are different. Try to put yourself in the other person's place and enlist his or her cooperation.

Organize your ideas. It is important to be clear about what you want, why you want it, and how you think you can get it *before* you start to write. A good way to do this is to make a list of your major points. A general list, with examples for a specific case, is given below.

Sending enclosures. You may want to support your complaint or argument by enclosing such items as bills, receipts, canceled checks, previous correspondence, invoices, and newspaper or magazine articles. If you do, be sure to keep the originals for your records and send a copy to the person you are writing to.

How to get organized

Here is how the master list of major points is applied to the specific case of writing a letter of complaint to a state senator about his position on the death penalty. The final letter appears at the right.

Major points	Examples
1. What you want the reader to do in order to remedy what you are complaining about.	1. I want Senator Green to change his mind regarding the death penalty.
2. Your reasons for wanting a remedy—that is, why it is important to *you*.	2. I believe it is morally wrong to take a life and that the government has no right to do this.
3. What information your reader needs in order to act.	3. There is a lot of evidence that the death penalty is not a deterrent to violent crime. Various presidential commissions on crime and violence have found that the real deterrents are social (doing something about such factors as poverty, unemployment, and family disorganization) and legal (having the court system react quickly so that criminals are tried, convicted, and sent to jail in a relatively short time).
4. What is likely to motivate your reader to take action. This includes appealing to your reader's self-interest and any pressure you can bring to bear.	4. I will not vote for Senator Green again unless he changes his position. I will support any opponent of his who is against the death penalty.

Complaint about fraud. The following letter could be sent to the Better Business Bureau and/or the Federal Trade Commission (note that the writer encloses a copy of his receipt, not the original).

Gentlemen:

I am making a complaint about fraudulent pricing. On December 10, I went to Snazzy Sam's Audio Outlet at 81 Spruce Street in Centerville, New York, to buy a CB radio. The salesman claimed that the Star Monitor CB, which he showed me and which I subsequently purchased, was being offered at a special discount price of $89—half the normal retail price. I have enclosed a copy of my receipt. A few days later, at Janes' Department Store in Centerville, I saw the same radio being sold for $69 and was told that this was its normal retail price.

I can only conclude that the salesman at Snazzy Sam's deliberately misrepresented the price of the radio. I am sure you will agree that this store should be investigated and am turning the matter over to you as it involves interstate commerce. Please let me know what action you plan to take.

Yours sincerely,

Arnold Smart

Letter to state senator

63 Sunnyside Avenue
Anytown, N.Y. zip code
May 15, 1994

Dear Senator Green:

I strongly oppose your position on the death penalty. I do not believe, as you do, that the death penalty is a deterrent to violent crime. I appreciate and support your strong stand against crime, but I think your remedy is wrong.

There is a great deal of evidence that the deterrents to violent crime are social and legal, that violent crime decreases where there are adequate opportunities for work, health care, and education, and a court system that functions efficiently and quickly so that criminals are invariably sentenced and sent to jail. I refer you to the various presidential commissions on crime and violence over the years—beginning with President Johnson's—all of which have come to the same conclusions.

I think your emphasis on the death penalty as a deterrent is not only useless, it also diverts attention from the real remedies. I urge you to change your position. If you do not, I will not be able to support your bid for reelection to the State Senate.

Yours very truly,

Lucy Fuller

Lucy Fuller
(Mrs. David Fuller)

Complaint about billing error

Gentlemen:

I have just received my July bill from Universal Utilities and feel that you must have made a mistake. The bill was not only much higher than usual for that month (I have enclosed copies of this and last year's July and August bills), but also our family was away for the entire month.

I always pay my bills promptly and shall continue to do so—as soon as I receive a corrected statement or an explanation of this discrepancy.

Yours sincerely,

Alice Jones
(Mrs. Sidney Jones)

Complaint about a warranty (note that the writer refers to a previous letter and gives the company's file number).

File #6000-B

Dear Mr. Brandt:

I believe you are wrong about the term of my warranty on the Gallactic Food Processor that I bought from your company in June of 1982. Your letter of March 1 says that my warranty expired last year. In fact, it is a five-year warranty and will not expire until 1987. I am therefore sending the Gallactic Food Processor back to you C.O.D., and trust that you will have it repaired and returned postage-paid as your warranty promises.

Yours sincerely,

Ruth Green

Letters to the editor. If you confine your letter to one issue, it will be more forceful.

To the Editor of the Centerville Times:

I strongly disagree with your March 1st editorial recommending that the north end of Wadsworth Park along Central Avenue be used as the site for the new middle school.

Your editorial quotes Mayor Barnes as saying that this use of the land will save the taxpayers' hard-earned money, which it will. But you do not say what this loss of parkland will mean to the citizens of Centerville.

The 40 acres of Wadsworth Park is the last remaining open, green space in Centerville, providing a retreat from our ever-encroaching urban area, a place for relaxation and quiet walks, and a sanctuary for birds and many small wild animals.

Removing even 10 acres of the park would represent a major loss to the city and would set a dangerous precedent. In the long run, it would be uneconomical to lose even a small part of our precious, irreplaceable parkland.

Yours sincerely,

Tom Jones

Answering inquiries. Whether you are answering a personal inquiry or are answering on behalf of your company, your letter should include the following:

- An acknowledgment of the inquiry, mentioning the date and general subject of the letter to you.
- A detailed response to the questions, or an explanation of why you have to refuse.
- Additional information that may be helpful.
- An offer of further help where appropriate.

To an insurance company

Dear Mr. Smith:

Your letter of March 1 asks me to itemize our losses in the flood last month.

As the damage to furniture, carpets, and appliances was extensive, I have prepared the enclosed list with the approximate cost or value of each item. I hope this will be sufficient for your purposes. Please let me know if you need any further information.

Sincerely yours,

Jim Kiley

enc.

To a prospective customer

Dear Mrs. Blake:

In response to your inquiry about the Jennie deWoolfe dress shown in the advertisement in the April Vogue, *you can buy it in Marblehead at Design Research or, in Boston, at Kemp & Co., Market Fair, or Woman's Haberdasher. All these stories regularly carry our line.*

Many thanks for your interest.

Yours sincerely,

Harry Ross
Customer Service

To a mail order company

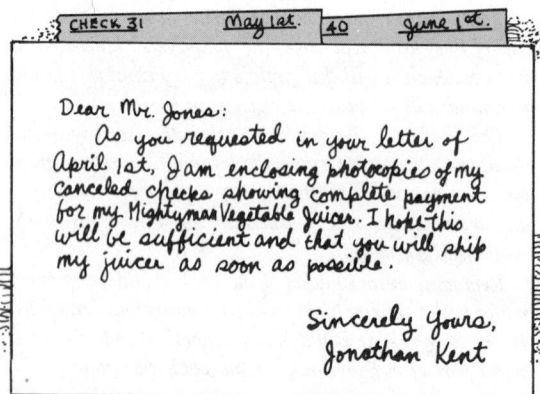

CHECK 31   May 1st.   40   June 1st.

Dear Mr. Jones:
As you requested in your letter of April 1st, I am enclosing photocopies of my canceled checks showing complete payment for my Mightymax Vegetable Juicer. I hope this will be sufficient and that you will ship my juicer as soon as possible.

Sincerely Yours,
Jonathan Kent

Turning inquiries into sales. Answering an inquiry provides a golden opportunity for a company to create goodwill and promote sales. A courteous and helpful reply can be and will be very good for business. See how this works in the following letter to a potential customer:

Dear Mr. Smith:

Many thanks for your inquiry, just received, about our Miracle Re-Circulating Wood Stoves.

As a builder, you know the importance of first-rate equipment. As heating suppliers, we welcome the chance to tell you more about our fine product.

First, it uses a revolutionary design. The curved ducts and chimney fan capture the heat ordinarily lost up the chimney and blow warm air out at floor level, which improves air circulation.

Second, it is efficient. It burns less wood because its airtight construction causes wood to burn slowly.

Third, it is practical. Its small size allows it to fit easily in most existing fireplaces. For new-home construction, it is unobtrusive and easily installed.

Finally, and perhaps most important, it is safe. Our Teflon-coated stovepipe reduces dangerous creosote build-up and does not need to be cleaned as frequently as ordinary stovepipes.

I have enclosed a brochure showing our complete line of stoves and direct your attention particularly to pages 6 and 7, showing models suitable for small summer homes. I would be happy to answer any further questions and arrange for a demonstration. Just call our toll-free number as soon as you are ready.

Yours sincerely,

Ted Jones

enc.

Answering complaints. What if you need to *respond* to a complaint. How you respond depends on the particular situation and on whether or not you feel that you (or your company) is at fault. Whatever the case, it is best to be reasonable and courteous. It will help if you do the following things *before you begin to write:*

Organize your response

- Determine the real nature of the complaint. It is important to know exactly what the complainant thinks is wrong.
- Determine your position. Decide on what you want to accomplish with your letter—that is, if you want to apologize, defend your actions without an apology, or something in between.

Writing Effective Letters

How to get organized

Major points

As in writing most other kinds of letters, setting down the points you want to make in a clear and logical sequence is important in answering complaints effectively.

1. Summarize the complaint in your first sentence or your first paragraph.
2. Make your position clear in your next paragraph. Say whether you are sorry or think the person complaining has made a mistake.
3. Explain your position. Give the information that justifies or at least explains your actions.
4. State what action you plan to take or want your reader to take in your last paragraph.

Example

The following response includes the major points and has a cooperative tone that should gain time until the facts have been determined.

Dear Mr. Jones:

1. *You believe that we have put our driveway across your property line.*
2. *We are having our lawyer check the deed, since we thought we put in the driveway entirely within our own property.*
3. *We realize that many of the old markers are unclear, so we would like to do more research before we come to any conclusions.*
4. *We know you are concerned about this and will be in touch with you as soon as we hear from our lawyer.*

Yours truly,

Harry Green

Responding to customer complaints. In answering complaints, particularly when you have to refuse a request for an adjustment, a company or an individual businessperson wants to keep the goodwill of the customer without acting against the best interests of his or her business. The best way to do this is to avoid an accusatory tone and to present your facts courteously, simply, and clearly so that the customer will find it hard to argue with your conclusion. This is the case in the following letter, in which the service manager refuses to honor his company's warrantee because the damage to the company's product was caused by the owner's misuse.

Dear Mr. Jones:

We do agree with you that your new Easywriter should not have broken down after three months and we were concerned to find out why it did.

That is why we sent it to our laboratory for a thorough examination as soon as we received it. It appears that the machine had been dropped several times and that it must have been left uncovered—a great deal of dust was found inside the motor. Unfortunately, no typewriter can withstand such treatment. If you think it over, we are sure you will agree and will understand why we cannot repair or replace it under the terms of our warranty.

If you have any questions please do not hesitate to call me.

Yours truly,

Howard Smith
Service Manager

When to apologize. This depends on whether you think the complaint has merit. Here are two different responses to slightly different situations:

Apologetic

Dear Mrs. Ashley:

I am very sorry to learn that you are unhappy about the work I did on your house. I want you to be completely satisfied with the job.

I would be glad to come back and touch up the woodwork and window frames as soon as I am available— which should be in about a week. I will call you then to arrange for my completing the work.

Yours truly,

Bob Adams

Nonapologetic

Dear Mrs. Ashley:

I am very sorry that you are unhappy about the completed paint job on your house, particularly the color of the living room and hall.

I would be happy to make any changes you would like, but will have to charge you for the additional time and paint to redo the living room and hall. Under our original agreement, my payment constituted your acceptance of the job.

If you would call me, I would be glad to give you an estimate and arrange for doing the additional work.

Yours truly,

Bob Adams

Collection letters.

Letters asking for money owed are sent after the first bill has not been paid. They include the following points:

- How much is owed (a bill may be enclosed).
- Arguments for payment, including any action you plan (where appropriate).
- Request for payment by a certain date.

A delicate situation. Requests for overdue payments may put you in a somewhat delicate position. You want to get the money owed without antagonizing and losing your customer. You want to convey understanding and tact while remaining firm. Here are some techniques to help you do that.

1. **Put yourself in the other person's place.** Try to see that in most cases the person who owes you money would like to be able to pay on time and is sensitive about being unable. You can make this sensitivity work for you by appealing to his or her self-interest and sense of pride.

2. **Avoid unwarranted threats.** Be careful, you can be held legally liable for threats or insults. Do not accuse your debtor of dishonest behavior or intentions and do not threaten legal action without consulting a lawyer.

3. **Fit the letter to the situation.** Try to think why the payment may be late and use an appropriate approach. It is possible, for example, that the bill was lost or mislaid, that your customer did not understand the terms of sale or credit, or that he or she normally lets small bills accumulate. In such cases, all that is usually needed is a gentle reminder. Here are some examples:

When you opened this letter, I am sure it reminded you of something you meant to do, but forgot—to send us your check. Why not do it now? The amount due is $22.30. Please accept our apologies and thanks if you have already paid.

Perhaps we did not make it clear that our policy is to extend credit for a two-week period only, following the date of purchase.

Your payment of $135.62 was due last week on May 7. We would very much appreciate your sending us your check by return mail.

You may not have noticed that your past-due account with us now totals $236.14. We are trying to clear our books before December 31 and would appreciate your settling your account within the next few days.

Letters in a series. Often collection letters are written in a series, each successive letter getting stronger in tone. It is wise to make sure that your last collection letter reaches the person who owes you money. Send it certified mail, return receipt.

1.

Dear Mrs. Kent:
   We find in checking our accounts that you have an unpaid balance for September of $62.42.
   I thought that you would want us to bring it to your attention. If your check is already in the mail, just disregard this letter.
                Yours truly,

2.

Dear Mrs. Kent:
   As you usually pay your bills on time, we wonder why you have overlooked your September bill. The amount, $62.42, is now more than three months overdue. If there is some reason why you are not paying it, I trust you will let us know.
   If I do not hear from you, I will look forward to getting your check within a few days.
                Yours truly,

3.

Dear Mrs. Kent:
   As you know, we do not usually extend credit for more than a month unless some agreement for partial payment has been made. Your bill for $62.42 is now four months overdue.
   I urge you, therefore, to send us your check right away. If you cannot pay right now or can make only a partial payment, I am sure we could come to some arrangement. Do let me hear from you about this right away.
                Yours truly,

4.

Dear Mrs. Kent:
   I am extremely sorry that you have not responded to any of my letters about your overdue bill of $62.42.
   I am afraid that unless I get your check in a few days, I will have to turn the matter over to our lawyers, Smith, French and Block, for legal action.
                Yours truly,

Family business.

Opening charge accounts, ordering merchandise, paying bills, planning vacations, contracting for work done to the house or yard—there are many occasions in a family's day-to-day life that require the writing of business letters. It is better to write than to telephone because you will not only have a record of your request, but the recipient will have a constant reminder before him. Here are a few examples:

Request for a delay in paying bills

Gentlemen:

Thank you for your recent letter reminding me that my account is long past due and inquiring as to when you can expect to receive payment.

I am enclosing a check for $50 toward the sum of $250, which is currently owed on my account.

Please accept my apologies for being in arrears. Recent medical expenses have placed a severe financial burden on me that I did not expect when I made the purchases at your store last spring.

I can manage to pay you $50 a month and if I do not hear otherwise from you, I will assume that this schedule is satisfactory. Thank you for your patience about this.

> *Yours truly,*
>
> *Mary Snow*
> *(Mrs. Richard Snow)*

enc.

To report a lost credit card

```
                        10 Overlook Drive
                        Essex, CT, zip code

                        May 5, 19--

Galaxy Gas, USA
Credit Card Center
P O Box 1000
Houston, TX, zip code

Gentlemen:

     I wish to make a formal report of the
loss of my Galaxy Credit Card, Number
600-200-000-4 on May 4 in New York City.
I called your 800 number immediately to
report its loss and understand that I am
not liable for any amount over $50 charged
to my card.
     Please send me a new card with a new
charge number.  Thank you.

                   Yours truly,

                   Robert Brown
                   Robert Brown
```

Opening a charge account

Gentlemen:

I would like to open a charge account at your store. I currently have charge accounts at Lord & Taylor, B. Altman, and Saks Fifth Avenue.

If you require further information or references, please let me know.

> *Yours truly,*
>
> *Alice McCoy*
> *(Mrs. Robert McCoy)*

Making a hotel reservation

Gentlemen:

Please reserve a double room with bath for my husband and myself for the week of July 9th through July 15th. We would prefer a room overlooking the lake and, if possible, twin beds.

We will be arriving by train about noon on the 9th and will take a taxi directly to the hotel. Since we will rent a car during our stay, please send us a list of rental fees.

Please confirm and send your rate schedule.

> *Yours sincerely,*
>
> *Harriet Brownly*
> *(Mrs. John Brownly)*

Contract in a letter

```
Dr. Raymond Brown
1 Rolls Plaza
Centerville, New York zip code

Dear Dr. Brown:
    This is to confirm our financial arrangement for
Nancy's orthodontic treatment as explained by you
in your office last week.
    The cost of the treatment is $2080. I agree to
make an initial payment of $400 at the beginning
of the treatment and to pay the balance of $1680
in 24 monthly payments of $70 each. I understand
that there is no finance charge or interest on the
balance due.
    I also understand that the treatment does not
include x-rays, but does include any necessary
fillings or extractions.
    If these arrangements are agreeable to you,
please sign the enclosed copies of this letter and
return one to me.
    I am very pleased that you are going to treat
Nancy and am sure the treatment will be
successful.
                              Yours truly,
                              Henry Graham
                              Henry Graham
enc.
```

Letters that sell

The basic formula. The formula for a successful sales letter, according to an expert on direct mail, is:

INTEREST — DESIRE — CONVICTION — ACTION.

If you can stimulate each of these in your reader, you have made your sale.

An important point that all good salesmen know is this: people are more interested in the "secondary gains" of *what the product or service will do for them* than they are in the product or service itself. As one advertising professional puts it, "You don't sell the steak, you sell the sizzle."

What people want. Experts have compiled lists of the basic reasons why people buy anything from a magazine subscription to a car. The main ones are:

1. Better Health
2. To make money
3. To save money
4. Popularity
5. To look better
6. Security in old age
7. Praise from others
8. Sexual attractiveness
9. Comfort
10. Increased enjoyment
11. Leisure
12. Business advancement
13. Social advancement
14. Cleanliness
15. To escape physical pain
16. To save time

These basic human desires are the "sizzle."

Seven steps that sell the sizzle

Sample sales letter using the 7 steps

Dear Mr. Jones:

1. Capture attention. Pique your reader's interest and get his or her attention with your first sentence. This is the first thing a good business letter does — often by asking a question, such as, "Do you want to improve your memory 100 percent?"

    1. *How would you like to improve your reading speed by 400 percent and remember everything you have read? How would you like to give your children the chance to improve their reading skills and comprehension in the vital early years?*

2. Make an offer. Promise something important that your product can do for the reader and make him or her want to find out more about it.

    2. *We have developed a foolproof programmed course of instruction that will enable the entire Jones family to develop and perfect these essential skills in only four short months.*

3. Appeal to some human need (see checklist).

    3. *There is no better investment you could make in your own career or your wife's, or in your children's future.*

4. Find at least one way that your product is different from similar ones and show how this difference is important.

    4. *Easyreader is different from any other speed-reading program you may have read or heard about because we give you* two complete programs — *one for adults and one for children. The children's program goes from grades 1 through 12. The adults' begins with short stories and ends with market analyses and international relations.*

5. Back up claims with facts. Prove the value of what you are selling. Make your reader agree.

    5. *The Howard Smith family of Brocton, Illinois, wrote us that the Easyreader Program was responsible for their son Tom's getting all A's in his last year of high school. Tom Green from Hanover, New Hampshire, said, "My performance on the job was so improved that I got two raises in one year."*

6. Persuade your reader to take advantage of the opportunity you are offering.

    6. *Do not deprive yourself or your family of this wonderful opportunity to increase your learning and earning power and to enrich your lives. The cost is only $15 a month.*

7. Close with a request for action. Give your reader something specific to do right away, such as telephoning or filling out an enclosed order form.

    7. *So act now. Phone us toll-free (800-100-1000) or fill out the enclosed form. It will be one of the best and most rewarding decisions you ever made!*

    Yours truly,

    Fred Little

enc.

Writing Effective Letters

Magazine subscription renewal. Humor can be an important ingredient in a sales letter. It is a good way to get attention and build goodwill, especially when it is likely that a routine letter would be ignored. This is a common problem for the people who write letters soliciting magazine subscriptions and renewals. The following letter uses humor for a "soft sell" approach.

Dear Reader:

This is to tell you that your future issues of Motor Boat Monthly *are being held captive in the guts of a computer.*

You will never know about the incredible new designs for speed and power, or get a chance to win a family vacation on the Inland Waterway, or read about the amazing race down the Mississippi—unless you send us your check or money order at our special $10 renewal rate, now!

This is no time to hesitate. Act now or you will never see your beloved Motor Boat Monthly *again.*

Yours anonymously,

MBM Subscription Gang

Letter to boss. Here the writer has a new idea that he thinks would be good for business and he wants to "sell" his boss on it. He uses a slightly different approach and does not specifically include steps 3, 4, or 6. But step 5 is particularly important: he backs up his proposal with facts based on a recognized authority.

Milkman's letter for holiday products

Dear Customer:

The holiday season is coming and I'm sure you won't want to run out of all the things you'll need for entertaining friends and family.

Neilson's Dairy is offering two new holiday products this season, which I'm sure you'll enjoy—frozen strawberry cream and frozen lemon soufflé.

Why not use the enclosed form and order everything you'll need in advance?

With best wishes for the holiday season,

George Wilson

Letter promoting winterizing service

Dear Prospective Winter Driver:

Winter is coming. There's a chill in the air that could spell future trouble for your car. Don't wait for signs of trouble. Come in and give your car the attention and cold-weather servicing it needs—right now!

We have the expert mechanics and up-to-date equipment to give your car a thorough inspection and locate any possible difficulties, and repair them. And we are having early-bird specials on replacing coolant, changing oil and oil filters, and putting on snow tires.

Don't put winterizing off and be sorry later. Come in now. You and your car will be glad you did!

Yours truly,

enc.   *Tom Benton*

MEMO

```
TO: Mr. Thomas Grant
FROM: Tony Newman
DATE: August 1, 19—
SUBJECT: Establishing Hang-gliding Training Programs
```

I believe Grant's Glorious Gliders could take advantage of the current surge of interest in hang-gliding to promote our product and build goodwill among a growing group of prospective buyers.

I propose that we initiate a series of hang-gliding training programs and charge an appropriate fee to those who enroll. This would teach many of the inexperienced people who are buying hang-gliders how to use them safely and responsibly, and would enhance our reputation as a company that cares about its products and its customers.

Our expenses in setting up the course would, I believe, represent a sound financial investment in view of the rate at which the sport is growing. Our own sales, as you know, are up 25 percent over the last three months. According to this month's Hang-gliding News, not only is the sport growing nationwide, but enthusiasts are spending up to $2000 on the average for first-time purchases and from $300 to $1000 per year on maintenance and replacement parts. The article goes go on to say that enthusiasts are becoming more aware and concerned about good proceedure and safety.

If you approve of this proposal, I would like to discuss with you my ideas for putting it into practice. I can meet with you whenever it is convenient.

T.N.

Tony Newman

Clubs and organizations

Letters from clubs and organizations can include anything from announcing a meeting to thanking a speaker.

Announcement of meetings.

Include the names, time, date, and place. For a regular meeting, a simple postcard will be quicker and less expensive than a letter.

Monthly Meeting
South Hampton Garden Club
Saturday, May 26
10:00 A.M.
at the home of Mrs. John Jones
32 Job Lane, South Hampton

Judy Greer, Sec.
Tel. 555-1212

A special business meeting would require a letter:

Notice of the 25th Annual Meeting
of the John and Marian Macy Charity Fund

The annual meeting of the trustees of the John and Marian Macy Charity Fund will be held in the Palisades Community Center on March 1, 1995, at 2:00 P.M. for the purpose of considering and acting on the following:

1. Report of the Secretary
2. Report of the Treasurer
3. Report of the Committee on Disbursements
4. Distribution of Income
5. Election of Trustees

Harriet Drew
Secretary

January 15, 1995

Saving money on postage

```
_____  Nonprofit Org
_____  U.S. POSTAGE
_____  PAID
_____  Anytown, State, zip code
_____  PERMIT No. 1
```

Your club or organization may be able to save money by applying to the post office for a third-class mailing permit. If yours is a nonprofit organization, the savings compared with first-class postage can be 75 percent. Even a commercial third-class bulk rate saves about 50 percent. Though there are fees for a permit, the savings can be large on frequent mailings.

Announcement of a special event

Dear Parents:

"Bloomsday" is coming and it's only six weeks away! That is the all-new magic show and musical review being presented by the Bloomfield High School Dramatic Club and Marching Band.

Some of the treats in store for you are:

- A mini-musical comedy with songs, dancing, and lots of laughs in one splendid act.
- Astounding feats of magic by that master magician, School Superintendent Jim Rawson.

It should be a marvelous evening, but that's not all. Proceeds will go to the Bloomfield High School College Scholarship Fund, so the cost of your tickets is tax deductible.

This extraordinary event will take place Friday, June 8, at 8:00 P.M. in the Bloomfield High School Auditorium on North Main Street.

Tickets are $4 each. Just fill out the coupon below and send it to us along with your check and we'll send you your tickets right away—or, for $4.50 each, you may buy them at the door. Come and bring your friends and family. You'll be glad you did.

Yours very truly,

Gertrude Troy

Gertrude Troy
Chairman, Scholarship Fund

- -

Yes, I want to have a wonderful time! Send my tickets at once! Here is my check for $_____
Name _____
Address _____
Phone _____

Note the selling techniques of this letter. Its purpose is to convince the reader to buy a product, which is the ticket, and further, to spend money for the good cause of the scholarship fund. The letter accomplishes its purpose by using the following specific techniques:

- It gets attention and creates interest by giving the event an intriguing name.
- It describes a part of the event to develop the interest further.
- It gives two reasons for buying tickets: the event itself and the scholarship fund, and says that the ticket money is *tax deductible*.
- It does not give the date, time, and place until near the end, *after* the event has been described in an exciting way.
- It suggests an action the reader can take (buying tickets). It provides an easy way to do it (the coupon

at the bottom) and an incentive for doing it (lower price).

* It ends with a final encouragement to come.

Fund raising.
In today's tight economy, many clubs and organizations have to raise funds, either for their own needs or for civic purposes. The following letters might be part of an annual drive.

Fund drive letter to the editor

To the Editor:

Centerville Memorial Hospital needs your help. Some 25,000 new people have come to our town in the past ten years and our hospital has to grow to keep up. We urgently need a new wing with at least 50 beds, additional operating rooms, and diagnostic equipment. This will cost some $3 million and the Centerville Chamber of Commerce is sponsoring a drive for funds.

Very soon you will be receiving letters asking for pledges and contributions. You will see announcements of special sporting events, concerts, and dinners—all to help us reach our $3 million goal. But you can help us get off to a flying start right now by sending your check made out to "Centerville Memorial Hospital Fund." Send it to me today, at the Centerville Chamber of Commerce, 100 Main Street, Centerville, Ohio, zip code. No contribution is too small. All contributions are tax deductible.

> *Yours sincerely,*
>
> *Frank Ross, President*
> *Centerville Chamber*
> *of Commerce*

To the general public

Dear _____ (to be filled in):

Did you know that the population of Centerville has grown by some 25,000 over the past ten years? The people at Centerville Memorial Hospital know this only too well, because the hospital must grow to keep up. An additional 50 beds are badly needed, as are more operating rooms and diagnostic facilities.

This is why the Chamber of Commerce is sponsoring a campaign to raise $3 million for a new wing. Only your dollars will make this possible. Your contribution of $100 or more can buy bricks or a bed or a new piece of equipment. It can be dedicated to whomever you wish, and a memorial plaque will be placed in the lobby upon your request. So please send your check or pledge today in the enclosed return envelope. No amount is too small (or too large) and all contributions are tax deductible.

> *Yours sincerely,*
>
> *Frank Ross, President*
> *Centerville Chamber*
> *of Commerce*

Thanks to a company for their contribution

Dear Mr. Smith:

Your company's generous contribution to the Centerville Memorial Hospital Fund has enabled the hospital to purchase a CAT scanner, which will give it the most modern diagnostic facilities of any hospital in the area. We are deeply grateful.

> *Yours sincerely,*
>
> *Frank Ross, President*
> *Centerville Chamber*

Invitation to speak

Dear Mr. Hunt:

The American Association of Railroads is going to hold its annual convention this year at the Palmer House in Minneapolis from Monday, May 8 through Friday, May 11. We would very much like to have you speak at the May 10 session.

This session is devoted to safety problems in freight handling, an area in which your own contributions are well known throughout the industry. I have enclosed our tentative schedule of speakers and a short list of suggested topics.

The association will, of course, pay your travel expenses to Minneapolis and hotel expenses for two nights. We are happy we can also offer you an honorarium.

I hope you will be able to accept, as your views on solving current safety problems would be of great interest to our membership.

> *Very truly yours,*
>
> *George Brant, Chairman*
> *Organizing Committee*

Acceptance

Dear Mr. Brant:

I would be happy to speak at the May 10 session of the American Association of Railroads' annual convention. Your list of speakers is impressive and I am honored to be included. The suggested topic—the application of systems engineering—is fine. I will send you an outline next week.

> *Yours sincerely,*
>
> *Robert Hunt*

Thanking a speaker

Dear Mr. Hunt:

This year's convention was a big success, due in no small part to your contribution. Many of the people who attended your session told me what a fine and interesting presentation you made. Thank you very much.

> *Yours sincerely,*
>
> *George Brant*

Tips for retired people

Power in numbers. Today more than 26 million Americans are over 65 years old. This group has grown by some 31 percent since the 1970 census and is expected to reach 29 million by the year 2000.

This means that older Americans are an important interest group as consumers and as voters, and a group whose importance can only increase as their numbers grow. So if you have an opinion or complaint, if you need information or assistance—it matters. There are people out there ready to hear from you and ready to help: write to them.

Government agencies. Almost every department of the federal government has policies that affect older people. Special programs on state and local levels were set up by the Older Americans Act and the Older Americans Comprehensive Services Amendments, in such areas as employment, nutrition, recreation, health care, and care of the frail elderly (75 and over).

Finding one's way through the bureaucratic welter can be difficult, but there is a central clearinghouse for information—The Office for the Aging—which also acts as an advocate and mediator between the elderly and various government agencies. There is at least one office in every state. These offices are an invaluable source of information.

Organizations. The number of voluntary organizations of older people who address themselves to a variety of issues on both national and local levels is also growing rapidly. A list of national organizations appears at the end of this section.

You are entitled. If you need help or information in such areas as housing, finance, health, education, travel, recreation, or employment—you are entitled to it. Do not hesitate to ask for it. You can use the telephone, but it is usually better to write a letter. In this section we give you some hints and sample letters to help you do that.

Housing

To a state office for the aging about tax relief

Dear Sir or Madam:

My wife and I are both over 65 and own our own home. I would like to know whether we are eligible for tax abatements, and if so, how we apply.

Yours truly,

John Harris

About eligibility for rent subsidy

```
New York State Office for the Aging
Empire State Plaza
Albany, NY 12230


Gentlemen:

     I would like to know whether I am
eligible for a rent subsidy under any
federal, state, or local program.

     My wife and I are both over 65 and have
been renting the same apartment for 25 years.
We are now living on my pension as a retired
postman and on my wife's Social Security
benefits.  It is sometimes very hard to make
ends meet.  Accordingly, I am eager to know
whether any financial aid is available to
us.  I would appreciate your answer as
soon as possible.

                    Yours truly,

                    Frank Smith
                    Frank Smith
```

About moving to another state

South Carolina Commission on Aging
915 Main Street
Columbia, SC 29201

Dear Sir or Madam:

I plan to retire next year and am very interested in South Carolina as a possible place to live. I need some general information to help me focus on specific towns. I would like to know about the locations of available housing, cost of living and taxes, health care, and special facilities for seniors, including tax exemptions.

My wife and I anticipate a joint income from pensions and Social Security of about $15,000 per year. We plan to sell our house and purchase a small, easily maintained house or apartment for retirement.

I would appreciate any information you can send me on the suitability of South Carolina for retirement, including a list of local Chambers of Commerce to which I can write for more detailed information. Thank you very much.

Yours sincerely,

Henry Crawford

Writing Effective Letters

Finances.

Finances. Finances are of concern to everyone, but never more than to people who are living, or who are about to begin living, on the reduced income that is a fact of life for so many retirees. If you are planning to retire, finding out before you retire about what is likely to be your future financial situation is an excellent idea. The best way to get started is by writing letters.

Some people will be enrolled in private or company pension plans. Some will be entitled to veterans' benefits or survivor benefits. Some will be eligible for food stamps; most for Social Security benefits. Find out about these as soon as possible. There are several ways to go about it:

Send for the Social Security Handbook. You get it without charge by writing to:

Social Security Handbook
U.S. Government Printing Office
Washington, DC 20402

Visit or write to your local Social Security office. Make an appointment to come in and discuss your situation and options.

Get an accounting. There is a credit system for Social Security benefits measured in quarter years, which do not have to be consecutive. What you get depends on your average wages, when you start to collect, and how much you are earning when you put in a claim. If you want to find out where you stand, you can get an accounting of your Social Security earnings at any age, at any time, by writing to:

The Social Security Administration
P.O. Box 57
Baltimore, MD 21203

To make an appointment

Social Security Administration
410 Nanuet Mall
Anytown, NY zip code

Dear Sir or Madam:

I am 64 years old and plan to retire next year. I want to plan for my retirement and need to know what my benefits will be. May I come in and discuss this with you? I can take time off from work any morning, provided I give advance notice. Please let me know when I can come in. I'd appreciate your answer as soon as possible.

Yours truly,

Margaret Green

To request an accounting. Requests should be made on either of two forms which you can get from the Social Security Administration. They are (1) Social Security Request for Detailed Earnings Information, which will provide a year-by-year breakdown, and (2) Request for Statement of Earnings, which will cover a group of years. You should sign your form exactly as you signed your original card. See page 128 for more information.

The Social Security Administration
P.O. Box 57
Baltimore, Md. 21203

Dear Sir or Madam:
    Would you please send me your form, Social Security Request for Detailed Earnings Information, as soon as possible? Thank you.

Yours truly,
Robert Stone

To a local utility

Town Gas and Electric Co.
Town, State zip code

Dear Sir or Madam:

I am writing to inquire about your special rates for senior citizens, and want to know what your eligibility requirements are. I am also interested in any help you could give me on energy conservation and weatherization. I am 70 years old, a widow, and live on a small pension.

Yours truly,

Harriet James

To inquire about food stamps

Department of Social Services
County, State zip code

Dear Sir or Madam:

    I would like to find out if my husband and I are eligible for food stamps. I am 65 and my husband is 72. As it is very hard for us to get to your offices, I wonder if it is possible to conduct an interview in our home or over the telephone. Also, please tell me what material you will need from us to decide whether we are eligible.

        Sincerely yours,

        Jane Duffy
        Jane Duffy
        (Mrs. Thomas Duffy)

Health

Health insurance. Information on *Medicare,* the health insurance program that covers everyone over 65, and on *Medicaid,* the financial assistance program for needy people of all ages who meet their state's requirements, is available from any Social Security office.

Assistance. Your state or county Office for the Aging can also tell you how to arrange for home care, day care, home meals, and medical transportation.

To request information

Office for the Aging
Rockland County Health Center
Pomona, NY zip code

Dear Sir or Madam:

I need transportation from my home to my doctor's office in Pearl River every other month. I am 75 years old and am confined to a wheelchair. Can you provide this service for me on a regular basis?

Yours truly,

Ruth Daley

To apply for Medicaid. You must apply in person, or send a representative if you are unable to come yourself. When you make an appointment, be sure to ask for an application form with its checklist of required information and documents.

```
Department of Social Services
Medicaid Unit
Sanatorium Road
Pomona, NY zip code

Dear Sir or Madam:

   I wish an interview in order
to apply for Medicaid. Please
send me an application form
and a list of what I will need
to prove eligibility. I can
come in any morning.

              Yours truly,

              Ruth Daley
              Ruth Daley
```

Education.

One of the wonderful things you can do with more time is go back to school. You can finish or further your education and explore new interests, taking courses for credit toward a degree.

Write for information about the many programs available for adult and continuing education from your local school district or community college and from state and private colleges. For summer studies in the United States, Canada, and abroad, investigate ELDER-HOSTEL. This program also offers limited fall/winter and winter/spring courses. Write for a catalog (see address on sample letter below).

To a community college

The Institution for Senior Education
Rockland County Community College
Suffern, NY zip code

Dear Sir or Madam:

I have recently retired and would now very much like to finish my college education. Please send me information about your program and about how to apply. I would like to enroll this fall as a sophomore, if that is possible. Please let me hear from you as soon as possible.

Sincerely,

Jane Baker

To inquire about a summer program. There are many special programs open only to retired or elderly people. Here is an example of one:

```
ELDERHOSTEL
100 Boyston Street
Boston, MA 02116

Dear Sir or Madam:

   I am very interested in finding out about
the ELDERHOSTEL program. Please send
me your summer catalog and any other
information you have about the program.

   I do have some special questions:
1) Are there are facilities for the
hearing-impaired?
2) Can you provide any financial
assistance? If so, can you send me the
necessary application forms?
3) Must students make their own travel
arrangements?

   I look forward to hearing from you in
regard to these questions and to receiving
your catalog.

              Yours truly,

              Harry Smith
              Harry Smith
```

Writing Effective Letters

Travel and transportation

Special services. Many municipalities offer transportation to senior centers, doctors and dentists, and grocery stores, but appointments must usually be made well in advance. For information, contact your state or county Office for the Aging.

To request transportation

County Office for the Aging
County Road
City, State zip code

Dear Sir or Madam:

Can you provide transportation from my home to my local senior center and back on Mondays, Thursdays, and Fridays for the next three months? A recent hip operation has confined me to a wheelchair for that period. Thank you.

Yours truly,

John Rudd

To obtain a senior I.D. pass

Rockland County Office for the Aging
Rockland County Health Center
Sanatorium Road
Pomona, NY zip code

Dear Sir or Madam:

I obtained my senior I.D. pass from your office last year and have found it very helpful for my half-fare bus service, and many other discounts. However, I have lost it. Can you send me another or is it necessary for me to come in to your office? Please let me know about this as soon as possible.

Yours truly,

Alice Jones

To a travel agency

Dear Sir or Madam:

I am interested in finding out about group tours on behalf of my Senior Citizens Club. We are interested in spending a week in the White Mountains in New Hampshire. We would need a congenial place that is wheel-chair accessible, with interesting walks (we have quite a few bird watchers), swimming, and golf. There are ten women and eight men in our group.

Could you recommend some hotels that would be appropriate for our needs and send me brochures and rate schedules? We would like to go by chartered bus and would need information on this, as well. I look forward to hearing from you. Thank you.

Yours truly,

Albert Mills

A Guide to U.S. Government Publications, listing many "subject bibliographies" of publications of interest to senior citizens, is available from
U.S. Government Printing Office
Superintendent of Documents
Washington, DC 20402

Recreation.

Recreation. One of the pleasures retired people have is more leisure time. They also have the pleasure of figuring out what to do with it. Local senior centers, which you can find out about from the State or County Office for the Aging, are a valuable source of information.

Inquiry about a senior center

New York State Office for the Aging
Empire State Plaza
Albany, NY 12230

Dear Sir or Madam:

I would like to know which senior center is nearest to my home. Also, please tell me whether noon meals are available at this center, what special programs they offer, and whether transportation is available.

Yours truly,

Frank Parker

To get a recreational pass

National Park Service
Room 1013
U.S. Department of the Interior
18th & C Streets, NW
Washington, DC 20240

Dear Sir or Madam:

Please send me your list of the federal recreational areas where I can obtain a Golden Age Pass. I understand this will provide me with free entrance and a 50 percent discount on fees for all park facilities. Thank you.

Yours truly,

Roger Williams

Requesting a catalog

Sam's Art Supplies
10 Main Street
Centerville, New York zip code

Dear Sir or Madam:

I see from your advertisement that you offer a 10 percent senior citizens discount. Could you please send me your catalog of art supplies? It would be a great convenience to me to be able to order through the mail.

Yours truly,

Harriet Jackson

Employment

Finding work again. The Age Discrimination in Employment Act of 1969 prohibits discrimination against people between the ages of 40 and 65. Nonetheless, finding employment can be difficult for older people.

Remember that you have a lot to offer a prospective employer—the invaluable experience and skills learned over the years, plus the generally excellent record in terms of productivity and dependability that older people have on the job. You need to tell people what you can do, and a very good way to do this is through letters. It usually takes a lot of letters to get a response, but do not get discouraged. You have nothing to lose by trying.

Start a letter campaign. Select a number of companies in the field where you have experience and write directly to them. Explain the type of job you want and that you are not interested in joining a pension plan.

People starting service businesses, such as landscaping and lawn care, catering or real estate, can also use a letter campaign to good advantage. In addition, you can investigate the various government-funded employment programs by writing to the appropriate agency (see table below).

Write to friends and former business associates. Many jobs are found through personal contacts and here, as someone who has been in the business world for many years, you have a definite advantage. Use it.

To a former business associate

> 15 India Street
> Scotch Plains, NJ zip code
> September 3, 1994
>
> Mr. James Morris
> Morris and Burgess, Inc.
> 120 Main Street
> Pleasant Valley, NJ zip code
>
> Dear Jim:
>
> As you know, I retired from McKinsey and Otis last spring when Janet and I moved to Scotch Plains. I find now that I really miss my work as an architectural draftsman (Janet and I miss the income, too) and would very much like to go back to work again.
>
> I wondered, specifically, whether you need additional drafting services in your new office—either full-time or on a free-lance basis. If you don't need anyone right now, do you know of any openings with other architectural firms in our area?
>
> I know you were always pleased with the work I did for you at McKinsey and Otis and I would very much appreciate any help or suggestions you can give me about job possibilities. Again, I would like to work full-time, but would be happy to take on free-lance assignments until I can find something permanent.
>
> I hope to hear from you soon.
>
> Yours truly,
> Henry Scott
> Henry Scott

Write to people that you think might know, or know someone who knows, about job possibilities.

Government employment programs

Action programs. For information about the following programs, write to ACTION, 1100 Vermont Avenue, NW, Washington, DC 20005.

Peace Corps. This international program has no upper age limit. You can also write directly to Senior Citizens Liaison Office of the Peace Corps, Specialized Recruiting, Washington, DC 20525

VISTA (Volunteers in Service to America). This is a domestic Peace Corps which also provides a stipend and living allowance for workers in poor urban and rural areas.

Foster Grandparents. This program pays an hourly wage to low-income people over 60 who care for hospitalized or institutionalized children. Training is provided.

Senior Companion Program. This program is similar to Foster Grandparents, but serves adults with special needs. You visit people who are unable to leave their homes or who are in nursing homes or hospitals.

Department of Labor Programs. This is only a partial listing. Check with the State or County Office for the Aging for other local federally funded programs.

Operation Mainstream. For low-income, unemployed people in about 20 states. Write to U.S.D.A. Forest Service, Manpower Program, P.O. Box 2417, Washington, DC 20013.

Green Thumb. For low-income men over 55. Outdoor work improving public areas. Write to Green Thumb, Inc., National Farmers Union, 2000 North 14th Street, Arlington, VA 22201.

Senior Community Service Aide. Part-time work in Social Security and state employment offices and a variety of service programs. Write to the National Council on the Aging, 409 3rd Street, SW, Washington, DC 20024.

Senior Aides. Part-time work performing a variety of local services such as child care and home health. Write to your State or County Office on the Aging for information.

National organizations

Senior citizens

American Association of Retired Persons (AARP)
601 E Street, NW
Washington, DC 20049

Open to anyone over 55, AARP offers world tours, bimonthly news bulletins, a hospitality house, out-of-hospital major medical insurance (for members 65 and over), life insurance, reduced prices on prescription and nonprescription drugs, a nursing home in California, and Institutes of Lifetime Learning in Long Beach, California, and Washington, D.C. There are almost 500 local chapters.

National Association of Retired Federal Employees (NARFE)
1533 New Hampshire Avenue, NW
Washington, DC 20036

Organized in 1921, NARFE has more than a thousand chapters in the 50 states. NARFE is active in promoting needed legislation and also has separately administered subsidiaries that provide favorable rates in life, casualty, hospital, fire, and automobile insurance. The annual dues include the monthly magazine *Retirement Life.*

National Council of Senior Citizens (NCSC)
1331 F Street, NW
Washington, DC 20004

Established in 1961, NCSC reports a membership of more than 5 million with more than 2000 affiliated clubs in all the states. NCSC is primarily concerned with promoting the general welfare of older people through public understanding and legislation. It also provides low-cost travel, medical, and other services for its members. Its monthly publication is *Senior Citizen News.*

National Council on the Aging (NCOA)
409 3rd Street, SW
Washington, DC 20024

NCOA is a central, national resource. General services include professional consultation, gathering and dissemination of information, a special lending library (largest of its kind), conferences, institutes and seminars, special studies and projects, general liaison with government, and the development and design of funded demonstrations.

National Retired Teachers Association (NRTA)

NRTA was founded in 1947 as a separate organization, but now functions as part of AARP, sharing headquarters, staff, and executive director. It has over 2600 local associations in all the states. Annual membership dues include the bimonthly NRTA edition of *Modern Maturity.*

Retired Officers Association (ROA)
201 North Washington Street
Alexandria, VA 22314

ROA was established in 1929 and reports a membership of more than 380,000 officers from all the services. It encourages legislation that benefits retired military personnel, and provides employment, travel, insurance, and other services for its members. Annual dues include the magazine *The Retired Officer.*

Gray Panthers
2025 Pennsylvania Avenue, NW
Suite 821
Washington, DC 20006

This group was originally called the Coalition of Older and Younger Adults—which is what it is, a loosely knit network of social activists working for change in all areas affecting older people.

Minority groups

National Association for the Spanish Speaking Elderly
3875 Wilshire Boulevard, Suite 401
Los Angeles, CA 90010

National Caucus and Center on Black Aged, Inc.
1424 K Street, NW
Washington, DC 20005

National Hispanic Council on Aging
2713 Ontario Road, NW
Washington, DC 20009

National Indian Council on Aging
6400 Uptown Boulevard, NE
City Centre, Suite 510-W
Albuquerque, NM 87110

You and your post office

The U.S. Postal Service has a lot more to offer than stamps, including many special products and services they would like you to know about. Ask for information at your local post office, or write to:

Consumer Advocate
U.S. Postal Service
Washington, DC 20260-3620

Here is a brief overview:

Classes of mail

Designation	Type of mail	Restrictions	Delivery	Rates
1st class	Letters, documents, postcards	At least 3½″ × 5″ and at least .007″ thick. Must not weigh more than 11 oz.	Usually 2 days, but depends on destination. All 1st-class mail going over 500 miles is delivered by air	32 cents for 1st oz., 23 cents each additional oz., 20 cents for single postcards
Priority mail (1st-class mail over 11 oz.)	Letters, documents, etc.	Same as above, weighing over 11 oz.	Same as above	$3.00 up to 2 lbs; $1.00 additional for each lb. up to 5 lbs.; over 5 lbs., check with post office
2nd class	Newspapers, periodicals		Varies	Ask post office for single and bulk rates
3rd class	Commercial (advertising); parcels	Must weigh under 16 oz.	Varies	Single and bulk rates for advertising mail; single-piece rates are the same as for 1st class up to 13 oz.; 13 to 16 oz. $2.95
4th class	Parcels, printed matter	Weighing over 1 lb.	8–10 days	Rates for most 4th-class mail are determined by zone (check with post office); "book rate" is special 4th-class mail with reduced rates also based on zones (check with post office)

Mailing valuables

Registered mail	Anything of value to you (jewelry, documents, etc.)	Certain kinds of wrapping and envelopes are not accepted	Delivery is according to first class mail. May be insured for up to $25,000 against loss or damage. Return receipt available.	$4.85 and up without postal insurance; $4.95 and up with postal insurance; (up to $100 included in lowest rate)
Insured mail	Same as above	Under $600	Coverage against loss or damage	Varies for different classes of mail
Money orders	Alternative to sending cash	Up to $700	1st class	85 cents
Express mail	See "Fast delivery" section for insurance coverage			

Writing Effective Letters

For fast delivery

Designation	Type of mail	Restrictions	Delivery	Rates
Express mail	Letters, parcels	Check with post office for areas serviced and for daily deadline	Overnight to areas serviced (most zip codes and some foreign countries). Guaranteed (money back) and insured (up to $500 reimbursement for merchandise and up to $50,000 for loss or damage to documents). Includes weekends and holidays	$10.75 up to 8 oz.; $15.00 up to 2 lbs.; $17.25 up to 3 lbs.; $19.40 up to 4 lbs.; $21.55 up to 5 lbs.; $25.40 up to 6 lbs.; $26.45 up to 7 lbs.; consult post office for weights up to 70-lb. limit
Airmail	Letters, packages	Up to 70 lbs. Maximum size: 100 sq. in. Mark "Airmail"	Depends on destination; check with post office	International: 50 cents for half oz., 95 cents for 1 oz. for all foreign countries other than Canada and Mexico (check with post office for complete rate scale)
Aerogram	Lightweight self-mailer	Must have an overseas destination. Self-mailer is single sheet	Depends on destination; check with post office	45 cents to all destinations
Special delivery	Letters, parcels	No bulk 3rd class	Includes evenings, Sundays, and holidays	$9.95 plus postage for 1st class, $10.45 for all others
Mailgrams (night letters)	Letters	Originates with Western Union, Office Telex, or TWX	Postal service delivers next day	$16.95 for 1st 50 words, $5.95 thereafter for each additional group of 50 words
INTEL POST service	Documents	Service only between U.S. and designated foreign countries. Not available at all post offices.	Documents are scanned by a facsimile reader and transmitted via satellite, printed in destination country, and delivered by regular mail (1st class)	$10 for first page, $6 for subsequent pages

Proof of mailing

Certificate of mailing	Letters, parcels	Items of no intrinsic value	According to class of mail. Sender gets a mailing receipt, but post office keeps no record	55-cent fee plus postage according to weight and class of mail
Certified mail	Letters, parcels	1st-class mail only, for items of no intrinsic value	Sender gets a mailing receipt, and post office keeps a record	$1.10 plus postage
Return receipt	Letters, parcels	Given for Certified, Registered, C.O.D., and Express mail, and for any mail insured over $50	According to class/ designation of mail. Receipt, returned to sender, constitutes proof of delivery	$1.10 plus postage

Correct forms of address

Government officials

Person	Address	Salutation
The President	The President The White House Washington, DC 20510	Dear Mr. President or Madam President
The Vice President	The Vice President United States Senate Washington, DC 20510	Dear Mr. Vice President or Madam Vice President
Cabinet Officers	The Honorable John Smith Secretary of the Interior Washington, DC zip code	Dear Mr. Secretary or Madam Secretary
The Attorney General	The Honorable John Smith Attorney General Washington, DC zip code	Dear Mr. Attorney General or Madam Attorney General
Chief Justice of the United States (same applies for a State Supreme Court)	The Chief Justice of the United States The Supreme Court Washington, DC 20543	Dear Mr. Chief Justice or Madam Chief Justice
Associate Justice	Mr. Justice Smith The Supreme Court Washington, DC 20543	Dear Mr. Justice or Madam Justice
U.S. Senator	The Honorable John Smith United States Senate Washington, DC 20510	Dear Senator Smith
U.S. Representative	The Honorable John Smith The United States House of Representatives Washington, DC zip code	Dear Mr. Smith
Governor	The Honorable John Smith Governor of (State) State Capital	Dear Governor Smith
Lieutenant Governor	The Honorable John Smith Lt. Governor of (State) State Capital	Dear Mr. Smith
State Senator	The Honorable John Smith The State Senate State Capital	Dear Senator Smith
State Assemblyman or Representative	The Honorable John Smith State House of Representatives (or Assembly) State Capital	Dear Mr. Smith
Mayors	The Honorable Jane Smith Mayor of (City or Town) Address	Dear Mayor Smith or Dear Madam Mayor
Lawyers	John Smith, Esq. Address	Dear Mr. Smith
Federal Judge	The Honorable John Smith United States District Judge	Dear Judge Smith

For further reference

Adler, Joan
  The Retirement Book
  William Morrow
Amy Vanderbilt's Etiquette
  Doubleday and Company
Blumenthal, Lassor A.
  The Art of Letter Writing
  Grosset & Dunlap
Buckley, Earle C.
  How to Write Better Business Letters
  McGraw-Hill
Mager, N.H. and S.K.
  The Complete Letter Writer
  Pocket Books
Paxson, William C.
  The Business Writing Handbook
  Bantam Books
Schuster, M. Lincoln (ed.)
  A Treasury of the World's Great Letters
  Simon & Schuster
Silverstone, Barbara and Hyman, Helen Kandel
  You and Your Aging Parent
  Pantheon Books
Watson, Lilian Eichler
  The Bantam Book of Correct Letter Writing
  Bantam Books

Members of the clergy	*Person*	*Address*	*Salutation*
	Catholic clergy		
	The Pope	His Holiness, the Pope Vatican City Rome, Italy	Your Holiness
	Cardinals	His Eminence, John Cardinal Smith	Dear Cardinal Smith
	Archbishops and Bishops	The Most Reverend John Smith	Dear Archbishop (Bishop)
	Abbot	The Right Reverend John Smith Abbot of (abbey)	Dear Father Abbot
	Canon	The Very Reverend Canon John Smith	Dear Canon Smith
	Monsignors	The Right (Very or Most)* Reverend Msgr. John Smith	Dear Monsignor Smith
	Priest	The Reverend John Smith	Dear Father Smith
	Brothers	Brother John Smith Name of Community	Dear Brother John
	Sisters	Sister (full religious name) Name of Convent	Dear Sister

*The form of address depends on rank. When in doubt, consult the Official Catholic Directory.

	Protestant clergy		
	Presiding Bishop of the Episcopal Church, U.S.A.	The Most Reverend John Smith, D.D.	Dear Bishop Smith
	Episcopal Bishops	The Right Reverend John Smith, D.D. Bishop of (area)	Dear Bishop Smith
	Dean	The Very Reverend John Smith Dean of (cathedral or seminary)	Dear Dean Smith
	Minister or Priest	The Reverend John Smith	Dear Mr. Smith (or, if the person has a doctorate, Dear Dr. Smith)
	Jewish clergy		
	Rabbi	Rabbi John Smith	Dear Rabbi Smith (or, as above, Dear Dr. Smith)
	Cantor	Cantor John Smith	Dear Cantor Smith

Members of the armed forces

The convention for addressing Army, Navy, Air Force, Coast Guard, and Marine officers and enlisted personnel is: full rank followed by the full name, a comma, and the abbreviation for the branch of service.

The abbreviations for the branches of service are: Army—U.S.A.; Army Reserve—U.S.A.R.; Air Force—U.S.A.F.; Air Force Reserve—U.S.A.F.R.; Navy—U.S.N.; Navy Reserve—U.S.N.R.; Coast Guard—U.S.C.G.; Coast Guard Reserve—U.S.C.G.R.; Marine Corps—U.S.M.C.; Marine Corps Reserve—U.S.M.C.R.

Retired generals and admirals keep their military titles in civilian life. The abbreviation (Ret.) is added after the service initials. Inactive reserve officers or retired officers of lower rank do not keep their titles. A retired brigadier general in the Army Reserve would be addressed as Brigadier General John Smith, U.S.A.R. (Ret.). The salutation would be Dear General Smith. Ensigns, petty officers, and warrant officers would be addressed according to the formula, but the salutation would be written Dear Mr. Smith.

Improving Your Reading

In the world we live in, our everyday actions depend to a great extent on our ability to read. We are always reading, often without even being aware of it: we read traffic signs, recipes, words on a television screen, and billboard advertisements. Surrounded by the printed word, many of us often take reading for granted. We come to think of our reading habits and skills as fixed, unchangeable parts of ourselves.

But good readers have one thing in common—they have *made* themselves good readers, often at a late age. One of the most famous books on reading is Mortimer Adler's *How to Read a Book;* in it he wrote: "I did not discover I could not read until after I had left college." Of course he could read newspapers, magazines, and books. But he discovered that he was not a good reader because he was not getting everything possible out of the things he read, nor was he reading with speed, pleasure, and satisfaction.

This chapter will help any reader become a better one, and it will help make reading more enjoyable. Here you will learn how to improve your reading skills through an effective reading improvement program. You will also learn of the many benefits of good reading skills, which will help you get the most out of the sections How to Study in Volume 1, and Literature and *The Young Reader's Companion* in Volume 2.

Enjoying the benefits of reading

The best reason for improving your reading is one of the most neglected. Reading gives pleasure. Good reading skills make reading even more pleasurable. Most of the books offered by a library or bookstore are for leisure reading, because reading is one of the most stimulating ways people can spend free time. Yet many people avoid reading because they think of it as a kind of chore or a kind of homework that they outgrew when they left school. But think of this: as a reader you have a world of entertainment at your fingertips. You can enjoy reading wherever you find yourself and whenever you wish, without depending on others or on the schedules that control movies and television.

The pleasures of reading are not limited to novels or stories. Good readers enjoy the personal satisfaction of learning more about their fields of interest, such as history or biography or sports, and also the satisfaction of developing new interests. People who enjoy reading usually become engrossed in current events. This gives them the satisfaction of understanding in depth the news of the day that is only skimmed by radio or television. Reading does not prevent activity. It makes people more active. Good readers of all ages use "how to" books on home improvement or hobbies for ideas on improving and broadening their leisure activities. Readers do not dislike parties or sports. In fact, they have more enthusiasm for these activities because they are stimulated by reading to seek more exciting ways to live.

In addition to these personal benefits, good reading skills help promote career advancement. Reading lists of required and recommended books are the heart of any formal education, and the ability to master these books fully and quickly is essential for the success of those planning for college, now in college, or returning to college. Independent reading can also open the doors to occupational advancement or to career changes. Because good readers enjoy reading and do more of it, they are more likely to find the books that will help them to obtain promotions or inspire new job ideas. Reading skills are also closely related to important occupational skills, such as writing and public speaking.

Finally, the benefits of good reading habits are felt by the entire family. Children are more likely to read well if they come from homes where books are valued. Reading is not necessarily a solitary activity. It lends itself to group activities, such as reading aloud or discussing the contents of mutually shared books. Children brought up by people who care about reading benefit from the ideas and discussions stimulated by books. Adults, in turn, can better understand their own reading habits by observing their children and by becoming involved with required school reading. Good reading habits can be learned and relearned by all members of the family together.

Evaluating your reading. To improve your reading, you should first find out where you now stand as a reader. This self-evaluation will enable you to concentrate on areas that need attention. It will also make it possible for you to judge your overall improvement as you work on your reading.

Thus, to benefit from the program in reading improvement described in this chapter, your first task is

> "He that loves reading, has everything within his reach. He has but to desire, and he may possess himself of every species of wisdom to judge and power to perform."
>
> —*William Godwin*

to examine your reading performance for symptoms of a possible problem. Then you will examine individual habits to isolate the ones that can hold you back. Even if your reading performance is acceptable, you can set new, higher goals and achieve them by continuing to work on fundamental habits with the techniques described here.

The most obvious symptom of a reading problem is boredom. No author tries to bore a reader. Rather, most authors spend considerable effort trying to interest their readers. Without knowing it, people who find

The enjoyment of reading is limitless. Reading is not restricted to a particular time or place.

Executives and professionals read for many hours each day to keep up with new developments and advance in their careers.

to keep up with reading as a purposeful activity. They need to renew their sense of reading for specific information, whether to pass a school course, secure a job promotion, or obtain a personal benefit.

Finally, the family benefits of reading are lost by people who make no attempt to master what they read. People who find it difficult to retain what they read can regain this ability by discussing their reading with friends, family members, people who are familiar with the same book, or people who may be interested in hearing about a book.

Boredom, failure to comprehend material, and failure to retain information are only the most general symptoms of reading problems. But these symptoms can help you identify specific reading habits that should be corrected or improved in order to better your overall reading performance. The checklist provided here will help you analyze specific reading habits. These habits are discussed later in this chapter.

themselves bored with books and magazines are working against the benefits of reading. In adults, this is usually because their reading habits have deteriorated since their school years.

The personal benefits of reading for pleasure and information are easily undone by neglecting to keep up with reading as a regular activity. People who pick up a book only when they are bored can hardly hope to be anything but bored while reading it. Good readers plan to read regularly, and they keep material at hand that they look forward to reading.

Similarly, the professional and educational benefits of reading are undone by reading without a purpose. People who have trouble getting started in reading, and who find themselves with only a vague understanding of isolated facts when they have finished, have failed

Essential steps to good reading.

If you are dissatisfied with your present reading ability, if you are unsure of how to improve your reading skills, or if you wish to enjoy reading more, this chapter will give you the practical advice you need. You, in turn, must have the willingness to follow a program of regular practice in special reading skills. You may be asked to break habits caused by years of little or no contact with books. You may also find yourself asked to develop new habits, many of which may seem difficult to adopt. But if you accept the fact that reading is an acquired skill rather than a natural talent, and if you agree that all skills can be sharpened by practice, then you are in an excellent position to begin your own program for reading improvement.

Checklist of reading habits

Answer all questions in this checklist for an inventory of your reading habits.

1. Do you suffer from eyestrain or headaches as you read?
2. Do you find yourself distracted as you read?
3. Do you point at words as you read?
4. Do you audibly or silently say words as you read?
5. Do you frequently reread words or phrases?
6. Do you read everything at a single speed?
7. Do you skip over new words without understanding them?
8. Do you quickly forget what you have read?
9. Do you lack a sense of purpose before you begin reading?
10. Do you find certain kinds of reading especially difficult?
11. Do you go many days without reading at all?
12. Do you read only a single kind of book?
13. Do you lack ideas on what new things you might read?

The questions that you answer "yes" identify your reading habits that need improvement. This chapter provides advice on each of them. Questions 1 through 4 are discussed in the section "What is good reading?"; questions 5 through 8 in the sections on "Reading for speed" and "Reading for comprehension"; 9 and 10 in "Special types of reading"; and 11 through 13 in "Continuing to improve."

Setting realistic goals. We all know of highly advertised schemes for miraculous accomplishments in reading improvement. Most of them concentrate only on reading speed. They advertise success as the ability to skim a novel such as Leo Tolstoy's massive *War and Peace* in a few hours. Such schemes may indeed be able to teach people to turn all 1200 pages of that novel in a short amount of time. But the schemes are flawed on two counts: first, no one can understand that novel in a few hours; second, no one can enjoy that novel in a few hours. A further problem with such promises is the proven fact that superspeed reading ability does not last.

The primary goals of this program are to help you enjoy reading more; to allow you to learn the satisfactions of reading well; and to encourage you to want to read more often for pleasure and self-improvement. You will certainly enjoy reading more if you read faster; this program will help you to double your normal reading speed and beyond. But to increase your enjoyment of books, you must also read better; this program will help you to improve your comprehension so you can enjoy stimulating and challenging books. Both of these goals can be achieved by most people in about eight weeks of daily reading practice for about one hour at a time. This is not an overnight key to superspeed reading. It is a responsible program for achieving long-lasting benefits in reading with only 50 to 60 hours of practice.

To begin, *read every day* for about one hour. If possible, this reading session should be scheduled at the same time each day, but make certain that you avoid a time when you are too tired or too distracted to concentrate. For the first two weeks, read any easy material you find enjoyable. Read at your present natural reading speed. As the days go by, work to improve that reading speed by following the advice on "Reading for speed" given in this chapter. Your goal is to double your natural reading speed within two weeks. Then you will be prepared to develop a repertoire of reading speeds for material of different levels of difficulty. This skill is described in the section of this chapter called "Developing three speeds." From week three to week eight, vary the difficulty of your reading material each day. In this stage you will be taking advantage of the advice in the section on "Reading for comprehension." You will also concentrate on special reading skills, and on reading for special purposes. In this way, you will be developing your ability to read different sorts of books and articles with proficiency. At the end of eight weeks of these daily one-hour reading sessions, compare your initial speed and comprehension with your final speeds and comprehension.

Charting your progress. You will need a record of your daily reading to chart your progress through the eight weeks. The best record is a diary of brief entries recorded after each day's reading. You can keep such a diary in any pad or notebook. The box on this page shows the items of information to record as you complete the program. In the first two weeks, you will be concerned only with the first five items. In later weeks, as you work on special skills, you will want to keep track of all ten questions for a thorough evaluation of your improving skills.

Your reading program

This outline of a good program for reading improvement requires only a single hour each day for a period of eight weeks.

Weeks 1–2: Measure beginning reading speed.
    Read one hour a day.
    Read easy material.
    Check reading speed daily.
    Work to double beginning reading speed.

Weeks 3–8: Measure three reading speeds:
    rapid, normal, and *study.*
    Read one hour a day.
    Alternate readings of easy, average,
        and difficult levels of complexity.
    Check one reading speed daily.
    Review what has been read.
    Keep notes on aspects of reading
        that need work.

A reader's diary

To keep track of your reading, make brief, daily notes in a diary or notebook. The diary sample shown here supplies all the important questions affecting reading plus answers given by one reader.

When you start your diary, only the first questions will be answered in the first weeks. In later weeks, you will answer all these questions.

> Date: 4-6-85
> Words read: 5500
> Reading speed: 360 wpm
> Level of difficulty: average
> Level of speed: normal
> Summary completed: clear presentation of personnel evaluation process
> Special difficulties: none

What is good reading?

Being a competent reader means having a sufficient knowledge of the fundamental habits necessary for success. Poor readers never examine their habits, so they never discover the wasted movements or persistent distractions that prevent them from increasing their speed and comprehension. Good readers scrutinize their basic habits to find ways to improve. Thus, moving toward competent reading begins with self-examination.

Before you read. The eyes are the most important physical tools for reading. Schools regularly check the vision of children, so many minor eye problems are identified early in life. The most common of these are *nearsightedness,* which is clear focus only on close objects, and *farsightedness,* which is clear focus only on more distant ones. Another common problem is *astigmatism,* a blurred perception in one eye that causes eyestrain. All these problems are easily corrected by prescription eyeglasses.

After youth, however, the eyes continue to change, and so adults have as much need as children for regular eye examinations. Because of natural changes in the way the eyes focus, adults may require prescription lenses for the first time or new prescriptions to replace old ones. Adults must also be concerned with diseases of the eyes associated with aging. These include *cataracts,* which cause a clouding of the lens of the eye, and *glaucoma,* which is an increase in the pressure within the eye.

Any weakness in eyesight can lead to eyestrain, headaches, fatigue, and restlessness. But correctly prescribed lenses can correct vision, insuring that reading is both more effective and more pleasant. It is a good habit to have your eyes examined at least once every two years.

Congenial surroundings are another fundamental consideration. Good readers make a habit of reading in an environment conducive to concentration. Poor readers often complain of boredom with books when improper surroundings have made concentration impossible.

First, reading requires proper light. Poor lighting can strain the best of eyes. Reading lamps should throw sufficient light on the printed page without causing glare. Ideally, the light should come from behind the reader—usually over the left shoulder—and be shaded from the reader's eyes. Single bright lights in otherwise dark rooms also cause eyestrain, so make certain that your reading room is also lit by a background lamp.

Second, reading requires the quiet essential for concentration. Many people find some background noise, such as a radio, more conducive to concentration than complete silence. That is because the noise remains in the background, is unobtrusive, and has a soothing effect. Other kinds of noise, however, are specifically designed to attract attention. Television commercials, for example, are designed to draw attention from whatever anyone is doing, including reading. It is important, therefore, to test your tolerance for noise while reading. No one needs a private study or library in order to read well, but readers must control their surroundings in order to eliminate distractions that make concentration difficult.

Finally, reading requires an appropriate seating arrangement. This, too, is largely a matter of personal preference. It may seem too obvious a point to bear repeating, but reading in bed is more conducive to sleeping than to reading effectiveness. Everyone enjoys reading as relaxation, but good readers are aware of their physical posture and choose the one best for a particular reading purpose. A comfortable armchair is best for becoming absorbed in a favorite novel or magazine, but a chair and desk or table are necessary for study. While seated before a desk or table, good readers are able to take notes or reach for a handy dictionary or other reference work without the distraction of moving elsewhere to find the necessary book. Your daily reading for this program should be done at a well lighted desk or table in a quiet room. This promotes alertness and concentration on the reading material itself and the particular reading skill you may be practicing that day.

The act of reading. Reading is primarily a mental activity, requiring only turning pages and moving the eyes. Any other actions are distractions and impediments to understanding. By indulging in bad habits, poor readers often make reading hard for themselves, but good readers free their minds for speedy absorption of written material. To improve your reading, it is important to identify and eliminate physical habits that slow you down while reading.

Eye movements. In reading, the eyes make small, split-second movements across the lines of the page. Only when the eyes stop is vision possible. Thus, only when the eyes stop can reading taking place.

The first person to connect this physical fact with the reading process was the French ophthalmologist Emile Javal. In 1878 he gave the name *saccades* to the jerky jumps of the eye moving across the printed page

Improving Your Reading

Observing eye movements

Most people are unaware of the physical eye movements of reading. Observe the eye movements of another person while reading in order to better understand your own.

1. Have a friend sit in a straight-backed chair.
2. Have the friend hold a book at eye level about 12 inches from the face.
3. As the friend reads, look just over the top of the book at the eyes in motion.
4. Note the movements and pauses of the eyes while reading. Look for regressions and for return eye sweeps from the end of one line to the beginning of the next.

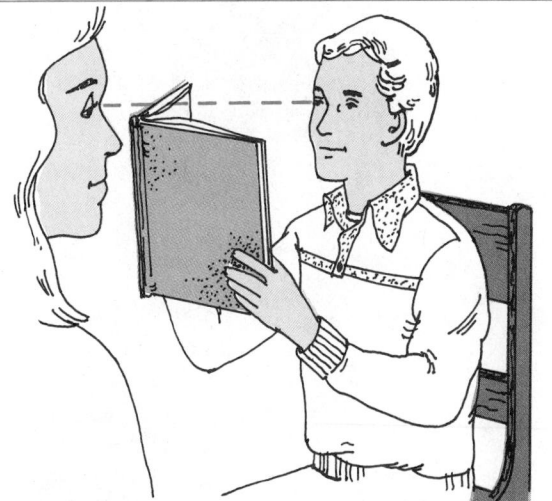

from left to right. He called the pauses between the jumps *fixations*. We are not aware of it as we read, but each line of print is crossed by the eye in a series of these jumps and pauses. For obvious reasons, we cannot observe our own eye movements. But we can observe the eye movements of other people who are reading, and this is a helpful exercise because it demonstrates how our own eyes behave as we read.

During reading, most people fixate on the beginning of a word because their eyes are drawn by the spaces between words. Everyone's reading is a sequence of these fixations. Good readers are able to keep the time of fixation to a minimum, thus speeding the eye along the printed line and on to the next. This increases their interest in the material and their mastery of ideas. Good readers are also able to eliminate *regressions*, the name given to backtracking to words already read. This ensures that they encounter the author's ideas as written and not as a confusing jumble of rearranged and reread words and phrases. As you observe the eye movements of other readers, you can expect to see different numbers of fixations and regressions.

It is important to observe and understand reading eye movement because you can control it. Among the most common bad habits of poor readers are slow or sloppy eye movements and frequent regressions. Both make it harder, not easier, to understand an author's ideas. Both are unnecessary, and both are easy to correct. Prove this to yourself by reading a single page at a slightly faster than normal rate and without any regressions at all. Move your eyes rapidly along the line and do not regress. It takes time to make this a habit, but you will soon notice that the effort increases reading speed and efficiency without any loss in comprehension. (More information on eye movements is provided in the section on "Reading for speed.")

Hand movements. Many young children are instructed to point at words while they are learning to read. Usually these words are in a list, and the exercise is designed to increase vocabulary. Unfortunately, many adult readers are held back because they fail to shed this habit. They read by pointing at words with a finger or a pencil, or even at a whole line of words with a ruler.

The problem with using hand movements is that they not only limit but actually distort reading. Fingers, pencils, and rulers introduce an unnecessary physical act into the reading process—complicating it, slowing it down, and distracting the eye. Habitual hand motions are usually performed at a single speed, making it difficult to achieve the flexibility of speed necessary for efficient reading. Finally, pointers distort reading comprehension because they locate *places on a page* rather than *ideas in a sentence*.

Good readers concentrate on ideas by eliminating the physical distraction of pointing.

Hand movements are a bad reading habit that is easy to correct. Simply refuse to let yourself touch the page when you read. Unless you are taking notes or underlining, place your book on a reading stand or hold it with both hands. A single hour of reading like this will demonstrate that pointing is simply unnecessary. Because a physical hindrance to understanding has been removed, later practice sessions will show improved comprehension.

Lip movements. Although reading is a mental process, many poor readers limit themselves by pronouncing the words they read. This habit is known to specialists as *vocalization*, and it can take several forms. Some people may actually read aloud. Others murmur to themselves. Most vocalizers silently mouth words as they read. These physical actions are the simplest

One can tell that this reader is reading efficiently. She does not distract herself by pointing at the words as she reads, nor does she move her lips. The silent reading she practices is truly silent. Her attention is on the ideas and information she seeks, not on individual words.

forms of vocalization. More often, people have the habit of *subvocalization,* or mentally reproducing the sound of written words without any apparent physical action. These readers are listening to an interior voice rather than seeing words on a page.

Vocalization and subvocalization are not found among good readers because these habits interfere with both comprehension and speed. As in the case of hand movements, these physical or mental actions are a distraction from the ideas of a written work. These habits also substitute sound for meaning, causing a delay or even a loss in understanding. Since good readers focus on ideas, they are not hindered by vocal distractions.

It is easy to prove to yourself how seriously vocalization and subvocalization can slow your reading. Most speakers are able to read a passage aloud at about 125 words per minute. Mentally listening to the sound of printed words produces a reading rate only insignificantly faster. But even slow readers free from vocalizing habits proceed at close to twice this speed. Open any book or magazine you have handy and select two pages with approximately the same number of words. Time yourself while reading the first page aloud. Then time yourself while reading the second page as quickly as you can without any vocalization at all. Do not be surprised if you find you have read the second page a hundred words a minute faster than the first.

Many good readers have cured themselves of the habit of vocalizing. Some have done this merely by resisting the temptation to speak or hear the words they read; they insist, "I will *not* vocalize," and overcome the habit by willpower. But there is another method. You used it already if you did the exercise just described. *Simply force yourself to read faster.* If you work at reading fast, your vocal or subvocal voice will not be able to keep up with your eyes. Continued practice at reading faster with your eyes alone will break the vocalization habit and also improve your ability to read for speed.

How we read. One of the most frequent complaints of poor readers is that they get lost when they begin to read. They get a few pages or paragraphs into a book or article and then find themselves confused. The author seems to be saying something they cannot understand, or the author does not seem to be saying anything at all. The result? Boredom and frustration.

These readers have the bad habit of beginning with the first word of a book or article and treating all the words as if they were of equal importance. These readers have failed to use the signposts provided by writers to help guide readers to the points being made. Good readers make a habit of using these pointers to focus on key ideas.

Prereading. You can preview anything you wish to read, thus locating these pointers before you begin to work your way carefully through the text. This is often called *skimming* or *scanning* the written work. It is a good habit because it helps you to read faster and with better understanding. But it is no substitute for careful reading, and so it is useful to think of this process as *prereading.* You will not want to preread casual leisure reading; few readers of mystery novels, for example, enjoy knowing the outcome of the story in advance. But for all difficult or scholarly reading, you will want to preread the text as a technique that will help you understand the text more completely and more quickly.

Published books and articles include many signposts to help the reader. Some of these signposts are part of the format of the work, for example, chapter titles and subheadings within chapters. Others are part of the organization of the work, such as introductory and summary paragraphs. All are intended to help you get a sense of an author's ideas before you begin to read. Good readers take advantage of these signposts and are not likely to get lost while reading. They already know where they are going.

The first step in prereading is to study titles. Books and magazine articles usually have main titles and subtitles. These indicate both the general subject and the author's special approach to it. When you are reading a book, study the chapter titles in the table of contents. Chapter titles can give you an idea of what to expect

Improving Your Reading

in the book. If you are reading a magazine, look for subheadings within articles. These break up the text just as chapter titles in longer works do. Subheadings provide clues to the ideas in sections of the article and an outline of the contents of each article.

Depending on the kind of material you are reading, you may be given other signposts. Textbooks often include study questions. They should be consulted *before* you read so you know in advance what to look for and concentrate on. Many books also include important illustrations, diagrams, charts, or graphs. These are visual aids to be consulted in prereading for a quick hint about important concepts. Finally, many books and magazines use boxes to set off important quotations, definitions, and key ideas.

In the second stage of prereading, skim the text itself to understand its organization. This can be done with an entire magazine article, but in books you will want to skim each chapter as you come to it. First, examine the opening and closing paragraphs. Opening paragraphs often introduce you to the material, arouse interest, or identify important ideas. Closing paragraphs often restate conclusions or recapitulate the information presented. Then briefly check the interior paragraphs. This can be done by reading only the opening sentences of the paragraphs. These are called topic sentences when they announce the point of the paragraph.

What to preread

Reading material is full of signposts to check *before* you read. These are the kinds of places you can find pointers to the main ideas in any work.

Full titles	Main titles on opening page
Chapter titles	Found in table of contents
Subheadings	Breaks in text
Study questions	At the ends of some chapters
Illustrations	Visual examples with captions
Boxed text	Words in enlarged type
Opening paragraphs	Introduction for all readers
Closing paragraphs	Conclusion in its plainest form
Topic sentences	Informative openings of paragraphs

Prereading, of course, will not answer all of your questions about a work. That can be done only by careful reading according to the principles described later in this chapter. But prereading is a good reading habit because it shows you what writers call the *shape* of the material. This will help you decide what to read, how fast to read it, and what to look for in it.

Prereading

Prereading alerts you to signposts directing attention to important points. Among these signposts are the topic sentences of paragraphs. Scan the passage below by reading only topic sentences, which are printed in boldface. Then read the passage from beginning to end. You will see that your first prereading scan gives you an excellent preliminary idea of the content of the entire passage.

THE SAN FRANCISCO EARTHQUAKE
by Jack London

Within an hour after the earthquake shock, the smoke of San Francisco's burning was a lurid tower visible a hundred miles away. And for three days and nights this lurid tower swayed in the sky, reddening the sun, darkening the day, and filling the land with smoke. **On Wednesday morning at quarter past five came the earthquake.** A minute later the flames were leaping upward. In a dozen different quarters south of Market Street, in the working class ghetto and in the factories, fires started. There was no opposing the flames. There was no organization, no communication. All the cunning adjustments of a twentieth-century city had been smashed by the earthquake. The streets were humped into ridges and depressions, and piled with the debris of fallen walls. The steel rails were twisted into perpendicular and horizontal angles. The telephone and telegraph systems were disrupted. And the great water mains had burst. All the shrewd contrivances and safeguards of man had been thrown out of gear by thirty seconds' twitching of the earth-crust.

By Wednesday afternoon, inside of twelve hours, half the heart of the city was gone. At that time I watched the vast conflagration from out on the bay. It was dead calm. Not a flicker of wind stirred. Yet from every side wind was pouring in upon the city. East, west, north, and south, strong winds were blowing upon the doomed city. The heated air rising made an enormous suck. Thus did the fire of itself build its own colossal chimney through the atmosphere. Day and night this dead calm continued, and yet, near to the flames, the wind was often half a gale, so mighty was the suck.

Wednesday night saw the destruction of the very heart of the city. Dynamite was lavishly used, and many of San Francisco's proudest structures were crumbled by man himself into ruins, but there was no withstanding the onrush of the flames.

Efficient reading

Efficiency in any operation is getting the best results with minimum effort. An efficient machine produces quality work quickly. Should it be too slow, goods cannot be produced economically. But should it be too fast, the loss of quality offsets any gain by speed.

The same can be said of reading, an operation that should produce maximum understanding with minimum time and effort. Read too fast, and you will not understand what you read. Read too slowly, and you risk losing interest.

Good readers are efficient because they balance these dual concerns of speed and comprehension. In this section you will be given instructions on how to read for speed and how to read for comprehension. First you will concentrate on speed, learning how you can double your reading speed with only a few days of practice. Then you will work on comprehension, learning special skills to help you master even difficult study material.

Reading for speed. Most poor readers proceed at about 150 to 200 words a minute. Average readers read about 250 to 300 words a minute. Good readers read from 400 to 500 and even more words a minute. But the most important skill of good readers is that they read at more than a single speed. They have a *repertoire of speeds,* an assortment of speeds for easy,

average, and difficult material. Like the physical mannerisms discussed earlier, reading speeds are habits that can be corrected and improved. With a little practice, you can increase your average reading speed and develop a repertoire for special occasions

Measure your reading speed. The first step in your program for improvement is to measure your present reading speed. This establishes your beginning point; later, you can check your improvement against this original speed.

For this self-assessment you will need a quiet place, a book you consider easy to read, a watch or clock with a second hand, and paper and pencil. Make sure you will be free from interruptions or distractions. Also make sure you choose reading material you like, so you get an accurate measurement of your speed. Time yourself with the watch, and keep a permanent record of the results on paper.

Reading speed is always measured in words per minute. So the first step is to calculate the words on an average page of the book you will use for the test. The simplest way to do this is to count the words on single lines of text. Count the words in each of five full lines of text. Add the total number of words and divide by five. Now you know the average number of words in each line. You can now count the number of lines on a page. All full pages of text in your book will have

---

How to measure your reading speed

To find your average reading speed, first calculate the words on a page of the book you are going to use. When doing this, count both parts of hyphenated words as separate words. Then calculate your reading speed in words per minute (WPM) on a test. To arrive at an accurate figure, you should complete at least five brief tests and combine the results of each to reach your personal average reading speed.

Calculating words per page

Words in first line = ____
Words in second line = ____
Words in third line = ____
Words in fourth line = ____
+   Words in fifth line = ____
Total = ____
Divided by   5
Average words per line = ____
Multiplied by lines per page × ____
Average words per page = ____

Calculating words per minute (WPM)

$$\frac{\text{Total words read} =}{\text{Time in seconds} =} \times 60 = \underline{\quad}\text{WPM}$$

Calculating average reading speed

First test WPM = ____
Second test WPM = ____
Third test WPM = ____
Fourth test WPM = ____
Fifth test WPM = ____
Total = ____
Divided by   5
Average WPM = ____

---

about the same number of lines. You can now multiply the average number of words in a line by the number of lines on a page, thereby obtaining a quick estimate of words per page. Make notes on these counts for later reference. What is the average number of words in a line? What is the average number of lines on a page? What is the average number of words on a page?

Using the same book, test your reading speed. After noting the time, read five pages. Read at your normal speed, making sure you understand the material. Do not rush; you are testing yourself. After five pages, stop and note the elapsed time. You can now calculate your reading speed in words per minute by following the directions in the box on this page.

In this test it is important that you understand what you have read. Rushing to beat the clock is pointless: it makes reading unpleasant and comprehension impossible, and it produces a false estimate of your normal reading speed. After you have finished reading, take a moment to review the main ideas or facts in the pages you have read. If your recall seems poor, you may have read too fast. Another good test is to try to describe what you have read to a family member or friend. If he or she cannot understand the passage from your description of it, then you may not have understood it either. If you do not understand the material, slow down in the next tests and read more carefully.

You will need to conduct five tests in all, for each reading five pages, in order to have an accurate measurement of your average reading speed. After each test, carefully record your speed in words per minute. Relax for a few minutes between tests. It is not necessary to complete all five tests in a single sitting.

After five tests on passages you have understood, average your reading rates for a reliable estimate of your normal reading speed. This is the beginning point for your program to improve your reading speed.

Increasing your reading speed. Your beginning reading speed reflects habits you have developed over a period of years. This means that you cannot expect to increase it dramatically overnight. But it also means that reading speed can be improved by developing new habits.

First, you must focus on the problem of regressions, the backtracking habit you observed while watching the eye movements of another reader. *Regression* is going back to reread a word or, more often, a group of words. For example, suppose a 200-word-per-minute reader regressed five times in a minute to reread five groups of ten words each. In a minute this reader reread 50 words. This reader is actually reading at least 250 words per minute, but all the eye motion is not forward. Eliminating regressions would immediately improve this reader's speed at least 25 percent.

Of course, not all regressions can or even should be eliminated instantly. There are two types of regressions, and it is helpful to distinguish between them. *Voluntary regressions* are necessary searches for key ideas. To read with good comprehension, you must be prepared to reverse occasionally to review information, even at a loss of speed. Remember that speed itself is worthless if it means rushing blindly forward without full understanding. Good readers read for ideas, even if it means some backtracking. If you concentrate and control possible distractions, these voluntary regressions should be infrequent. *Involuntary regressions* are unnecessary. Many poor readers have the bad habit of regressing many times on a page without even being aware that they are doing so.

To correct habitual, unnecessary regressions, do your best to read with concentration and *read forward*. If you feel you are about to go back, ask yourself if it is absolutely necessary. If you have been concentrating, the answer most often will be "no," and you can proceed forward without loss of comprehension. After a few sessions of this exercise, you will find yourself regressing much less often, and so increasing your reading speed.

Another consideration is the *eye return,* the movement of the eye from the end of one line to the beginning of the next. Any typist knows that carriage returns, or the return of the paper for a new line, occupy a surprisingly large portion of typing time. Similarly, eye returns can occupy a large portion of reading time. Lazy eye returns are a bad reading habit, because they also invite distraction and loss of concentration.

To increase your reading speed, you should concentrate on eye returns. Force yourself to move quickly from one line to the next in a swift sweep from right to left without any opportunity for distracting thoughts or daydreams. This is an easily learned good reading habit, one that simultaneously improves both speed and comprehension. Work on eye returns by sweeping from the ends to the beginnings of lines on a page without reading the page at all. Make sure you always sweep to the next line. Readers who do not concentrate may often sweep to the wrong line. Practice demonstrates how fast the return can be if you are conscious of it and its importance.

The key to improved reading speed is practice. Set aside one hour each day. Practice on reading material that is easy and pleasant. Be sure to practice at a well-lit desk in a room free of distractions. As you read, concentrate on eliminating regressions and on speedy return sweeps. This is the way to increase reading speed permanently: practice and force yourself to go faster. Set your goals at a level higher than your present reading speed, and work at achieving them. Push yourself to read faster, eliminate regressions, and concentrate on speedy eye returns. As you achieve one

Regressions

Regressions make reading slower and harder to understand. The two passages printed here are identical except that one shows what a reader sees in making five regressions. You can see that these regressions make the passage longer and far more confusing.

If put to guess his calling and livelihood, I should have taken him for a country schoolmaster as soon as taken him for a country schoolmaster as soon as anything else. He was dressed in a rusty black frock coat and pantaloons, unbrushed, and worn so faithfully that the suit had faithfully that the suit had adapted itself to the curves and angularities of his figure and angularities of his figure, and had grown to be an outer skin of the man. His hair was black, still unmixed with gray, stiff, somewhat bushy, and had apparently been acquainted had apparently been acquainted with neither brush nor comb that morning, after neither brush nor comb that morning, after the disarrangement of the pillow; and as to a nightcap, Uncle Abe probably knows nothing of such effeminacies.
— *Nathaniel Hawthorne, "Abraham Lincoln"*

If put to guess his calling and livelihood, I should have taken him for a country schoolmaster as soon as anything else. He was dressed in a rusty black frock coat and pantaloons, unbrushed, and worn so faithfully that the suit had adapted itself to the curves and angularities of his figure, and had grown to be an outer skin of the man. His hair was black, still unmixed with gray, stiff, somewhat bushy, and had apparently been acquainted with neither brush nor comb that morning, after the disarrangement of the pillow; and as to a nightcap, Uncle Abe probably knows nothing of such effeminacies.
— *Nathaniel Hawthorne, "Abraham Lincoln"*

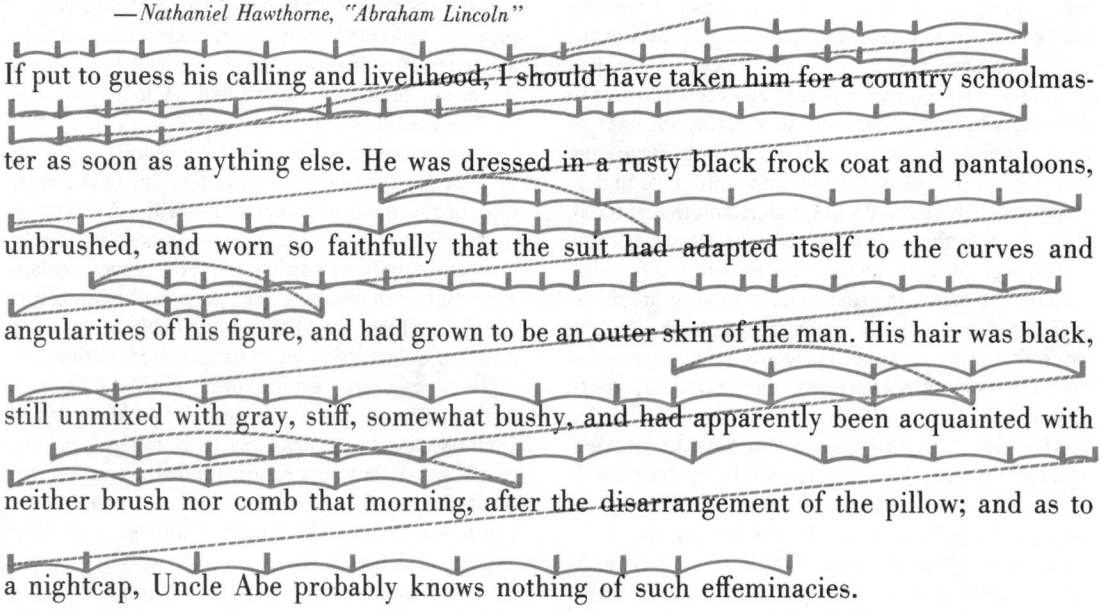

If put to guess his calling and livelihood, I should have taken him for a country schoolmaster as soon as anything else. He was dressed in a rusty black frock coat and pantaloons, unbrushed, and worn so faithfully that the suit had adapted itself to the curves and angularities of his figure, and had grown to be an outer skin of the man. His hair was black, still unmixed with gray, stiff, somewhat bushy, and had apparently been acquainted with neither brush nor comb that morning, after the disarrangement of the pillow; and as to a nightcap, Uncle Abe probably knows nothing of such effeminacies.

WPM (words per minute) goal, it becomes your natural speed. Then you may work on achieving still greater speed.

No matter what your beginning reading speed, you can double it, at least, in only a few days. Continue this daily practice for two weeks. Record your reading speed for each day in your reading diary. Small dips in your reading speed are inevitable because of outside forces such as interruptions or fatigue. With regular practice over two weeks, however, you will soon be reading at your new, faster speed without any special effort or need to slow down.

Developing three reading speeds. As you have already learned, one characteristic of good readers is that they have more than one reading speed. They can shift reading speeds much as a car shifts gears. A car needs different gears for going uphill, downhill, or cruising. Good readers use different speeds for similar reasons. You can prove this to yourself by reading a few pages in a favorite novel and then trying to read a legal document, for example, a mortgage or a lease. One is much less difficult and complex than the other, and so it is neither possible nor desirable to read both at the same speed.

For efficient reading, you should have three speeds. Such a repertoire enables you to get the most out of any material you read and to do so with minimum time and effort. No matter what you read, shifting gears will

Improving Your Reading

keep you from reading so slowly that you become bored or reading so quickly that you lose comprehension. The three speeds are *study reading, normal reading,* and *rapid reading.*

Study reading is the slowest speed. It is used, for example, for textbooks and work manuals, which require you to retain facts and master concepts. Naturally, this takes care and concentration, and it would be foolish to rush headlong through such material. In studying, therefore, you should slow down so that you absorb the material in a single reading. For that reason, good readers study at a rate of about 200 words per minute, or even less.

Normal reading is the middle speed for works of average complexity. It is used for books and magazine articles that require close attention, but not intense study. This speed is suitable for books and articles that present facts without demanding an analysis of concepts, and for novels and general nonfiction read for relaxation. Normal reading speed can also be useful for reviewing difficult material that has already been studied once. Most good readers have a normal reading speed close to twice as fast as their study speed. A good normal reading speed would be anywhere from 300 to 400 words per minute.

Rapid reading is used for easy reading material or for sampling material to find out whether you want to read it completely. Rapid reading is used for magazines, newspapers, and other quick reading for general information. The rapid reading speed is the one you will find it easiest to improve quickly. Good rapid reading proceeds at speeds up to 500 words per minute and sometimes even beyond. The maximum reading speed attainable in easy reading without skipping is about 800 words per minute.

Two considerations will help you choose the speed for any reading material. First ask yourself, what is the level of difficulty? Using your prereading skills, check the material for vocabulary, subject matter, amount of important facts, and complexity of important concepts. Grade the work on a scale from difficult to easy and choose the appropriate reading speed. Then ask yourself, why are you reading it? Decide if your purpose is to study, to be generally informed, or to relax. The answers to these questions usually point to a choice of study, normal, or rapid reading.

After working on your average reading speed for at least two weeks, begin to practice the three reading speeds by varying the kind of material you read. Your first practice was on easy material, at a speed closest to your rapid rate. But in your third week of daily reading, begin to practice with difficult and average as well as easy reading matter. You will quickly find your own beginning speed for each; then work to improve it.

You can now begin to add the level of difficulty to your reading diary and to keep track of three reading speeds. Once you have calculated your beginning speed at all three paces, set personal goals for all three speeds. As always, push yourself to go faster, to eliminate regressions, and to make speedy eye returns. After reading, record your speed and review the passage in your mind to check for comprehension. If you have not understood what you have read, you will have to slow down. But if you continue to practice and to vary your reading material, you will find your words per minute scores at all three speeds beginning to improve.

Reading speeds

Good readers have three reading speeds. They are efficient readers because they can choose the proper speed for any kind of reading material. Here is the basic repertoire of a good reader, illustrating the uses of each speed and the rates attainable with practice. The youth shown here is reading a manual on entomology. Because his purpose is careful analysis, he reads at a slow rate.

Speed	Materials	Purposes	Complexity	WPM
Study	Textbooks Work manuals	Careful analysis Memorization Test preparation	Difficult	200 or less
Normal	Novels Nonfiction	Leisure reading General information	Average	300–400
Rapid	Newspapers Magazines	Locating facts Prereading Sampling	Easy	500 or more

Test your speed and comprehension

Time yourself on this passage. Read at your normal speed. When finished, calculate your reading speed using the information provided at the end of the passage. Then test your comprehension with the questions provided. If you cannot answer most of the questions, you need to slow down and work on comprehension. If you can answer most of them, you are ready to practice reading faster.

Most of us have grown up with unfair stereotypes of those Puritan forefathers we heard so much about in high school. We imagine very joyless people, dressed in black, with little taste for experimentation in life.

In fact, the Puritans were among the most innovative people of all times, and certainly among the most adventurous and daring of any people who came to America in the early days of its colonial history. The very name "Puritan" was once synonymous with experimentation, and those who came to Massachusetts in the 17th century were as contentious a bunch as ever sat in the bistros popularized by the poets of Paris. The origins of the movement can be located in the Protestant Reformation launched in England by Henry VIII, who differed from the Pope on matters of divorce law. Henry founded the Church of England, but some thought that his own church needed to be purified even further of some old traditions, and that is why they became known as Puritans.

The first group to land in the new world were bound, aboard the *Mayflower,* for a place around New York bay. But blown off course, they landed in Massachusetts on December 21, 1620, according to tradition, at Plymouth Rock, near Boston. A group of 103 had left on the voyage that took 64 days; by the time they landed at Plymouth in a snowstorm, two had died and one had been born. Unsure of how to govern themselves, they invented a method: it was called the Mayflower Compact, and it is considered one of the forerunners of the United States Constitution.

Landing in winter was a dreadful mistake. By April of 1621 only 50 of the landing 102 had survived "the great sickness," a combination of scurvy contracted aboard ship and starvation through the winter. As their leader, William Bradford, described it, they arrived in a "howling wilderness" of previously unimaginable proportions. Actually, one key problem on Bradford's mind was the extent of the jungle before him. He imagined a "hideous and desolate wilderness" extending forever, or perhaps to some theoretical "South Sea," or Pacific Ocean, limit, populated only by "savage barbarians ready to fill our sides full of arrows." The Puritans knew this as they huddled in their tents—not log cabins—through that first winter. But when the *Mayflower,* with its shipload of skeptical sailors, left North America for home on April 5, 1621, not one of the surviving Puritans chose to return with the ship.

The Puritans, whom we still think of as rigid and impersonal, made the best of their situation. Three thousand miles by sailing ship from any civilized place, they made what friends they could. They met with Indians—the very people the popular stereotype suggests would most horrify the straight-laced Puritans. Miles Standish, Priscilla Mullins, and the rest of these true pioneers readily sat down and ate with visitors whose names have been recorded, no doubt inaccurately, as Samoset and Squanto. Their Thanksgiving probably never happened on November 24, but the Puritans were open-minded and adventurous enough to celebrate, in the fall of 1621, their own survival with a people completely opposite in culture and personal habit. It was this flexibility, this ability to deal honestly with people whose beliefs were light-years away from their own, that enabled the Puritans, in Bradford's words: "To fit up their houses and dwellings against winter, being all well recovered in health and strength and with all things."

$$\frac{\text{Total words} = 580}{\text{Reading time in seconds} =} \times 60 = \text{\_\_\_\_ WPM}$$

1. The author's major point is:
   a. The Puritans have little to do with modern life.
   b. The Puritans are poorly understood by us.
   c. The Puritans should have emigrated to Virginia.

2. The author appreciates the Puritans for their:
   a. Ability to relate to strangers.
   b. Religious piety.
   c. Political activism.

3. Puritans got their name because they:
   a. Hoped to purify the Church of England.
   b. Hoped to purify the Roman Catholic Church.
   c. Hoped to purify the Presbyterian Church.

4. The Puritans came to Massachusetts in the:
   a. 16th century.
   b. 17th century.
   c. 18th century.

5. This passage to tells us:
   a. Whom the Puritan fought against.
   b. The importance of enduring hardship.
   c. Why the Puritans deserve attention.

Answers: 1 (b); 2 (a); 3 (a); 4 (b); 5 (c).
Being able to answer *most* of these questions means correct responses to 3 or more. If you answered 2 or less correctly, you may have read too fast.

Improving Your Reading

Reading for comprehension.

Reading faster is a physical skill. For the most efficient reading, this physical skill must be matched by an intellectual one. Thus, speed must be based on the ability to comprehend written material quickly. Complete comprehension is easier to manage at slow reading speeds, but efficient readers are able to absorb ideas even when pushing to move through a book at rapid reading speed.

Four basic habits are essential to good comprehension: locating key ideas, marking a book while reading, using reference books, and reviewing what has been read.

Locating key ideas. As you have already learned, prereading is possible because all words on a page are not of equal importance. Prereading establishes this fact. The process of prereading is one of locating key ideas embodied in important words and phrases. Even in difficult material, many words may be read quickly —think of "as," "an," and "the," for example. The important words, however, are crucial terms. They carry specific definitions in any written work, such as the term "prereading" in this chapter. Important words also include words or phrases of transition. They signal the direction of ideas. The word "however" is a good example. Efficient readers are able to comprehend material as they read quickly because they are alert to such important words as they push ahead.

Crucial terms are the heart of any written work, because they contain in single words the focused ideas of the author. For example, government spokesmen in both China and the United States are likely to use the word "propaganda" as a crucial term in their statements. One accepted meaning of propaganda is "promotion of ideas," and the spokesmen of both countries mean this when they use the word in reference to political policies. But by this term the spokesman of one country may mean "important and necessary ideas," while the spokesman from the other may mean "false and misleading ideas." For this reason, recognizing uses of this crucial term is essential to comprehending fully the statements made by spokesmen from competing nations.

Good readers spot a crucial term when they read at any speed, and if necessary they pause to consider the term, to locate its definition in the work, or to check its accepted definition in a dictionary. A crucial term can be located by its frequent recurrence in a work. The appearance of a crucial term may be signaled to the reader through the use of italics or the use of the word in chapter titles or subheadings. Any book on American history, for example, can be expected to use the word "Reconstruction" to refer to the post-Civil War era. Good readers recognize this as a crucial term that the author must define. Having met it for the first

Transition words and phrases

Good readers identify relationships between ideas by spotting transition words and phrases. Pivotal terms, such as those listed here, indicate similarity, difference, or sequence. Paying attention to them helps comprehension at any reading speed.

Similarity	*Difference*	*Sequence*
and	but	then
as well as	although	first, second
also	however	earlier
furthermore	nevertheless	later
likewise	despite	before
similarly	yet	after
in addition	on the other hand	last
another	on the contrary	finally
moreover	instead	as a result
so	though	next

time in a chapter title or important topic sentence to a paragraph, they then look for the definition the author will attach to it—what years are included in "Reconstruction" and what gives the era its significance. This may take a moment, but the pause helps both comprehension and speed because the term can be read confidently and quickly when met again.

Transition words and phrases are another class of important words that indicate key ideas. Transition words and phrases indicate directions and relationships. We are all familiar with the basics of this concept. We all know that the word "and" signals a second action, idea, or fact similar in kind to a first one: "Ulysses S. Grant was a Civil War general *and* a United States President." We know that the word "but" signals a second action or idea different from a first one: "Ulysses S. Grant was an effective Civil War general *but* an ineffective United States President." We also know that the word "then" signals a sequence of ideas or actions: "Ulysses S. Grant was a Civil War general and *then* a United States President." We all know these word indicators of direction, but good readers use this knowledge to their advantage as they read for speed. Good readers look for transition words and phrases that show relationships of ideas.

The transition words and phrases you can look for in your reading all fall into three groups. Some, such as "and," signal *similarity*. Others, such as "but," signal *difference*. The last group, such as "then," signals *sequence*. The table of transition terms shown here provides further examples of the words and phrases that fall into each of these three groups. By looking for transition terms, you can more easily and completely comprehend the relationships between key ideas in your reading.

Marking books. By consciously searching for crucial terms and for transition words or phrases, good readers keep themselves alert and so improve both their speed and comprehension. Another habit they use to make reading an active, conscious process is annotating, or *marking,* their books. Obviously, you cannot mark up a book that does not belong to you, whether it comes from a library or from a friend. Nor will you want to bother with careful annotations on easy material intended to be read at your rapid speed. But for all difficult material that is read at your study speed, and some average material that is read at your normal speed, you will find your comprehension improved if you pause to mark the key ideas in the book. Some people are reluctant to mark up a book because they mistakenly believe that this destroys it. But most books, usually relatively inexpensive, easily replaceable, and salable after use even if marked, are not often heirloom possessions to be preserved in mint condition. Rather, they are objects to be used to acquire knowledge, and good use implies some wear and tear. By marking a book, you make it your own.

Marking books is a good reading habit because it increases concentration and alertness. It also improves your reading ability by reminding you that you are searching for the key ideas that deserve annotation. Marking books also improves your ability to retain what you have read because the physical act of under-lining or circling words or phrases on a page impresses them on your memory. Finally, having the marks on the page makes it easier to review books later on for study purposes or for personal interest.

Many adults still own books they marked up in school. A quick examination of one of them will prove how useful annotations are when studying or reviewing reading material. Many people who mark up their books limit themselves to underlining or coloring over lines of text with a soft-tipped marker. Because good reading distinguishes between ideas, and because you are free to mark books in any way you wish, do not limit yourself to a single kind of marking. Good readers develop a variety of markings to use for different purposes when studying difficult material. While working to improve your reading, develop your own markings, remembering that it is essential to have various marks for a variety of purposes. A typical system might mix circles for crucial terms with underlining for their definitions. It could also use marginal numbers for ideas in a sequence, and stars for important facts.

Using reference books. Good readers often are ambitious. They read for pleasure and relaxation, but they also read to broaden their understanding of various fields of knowledge. In books they discover new interests, and they pursue these new interests in other books. Like any rewarding enterprise, this sort of ambitious reading is a challenge. In pursuing interests through books, you will inevitably encounter works that present challenges in ideas and vocabulary.

No one should make reading an unpleasant chore. If

How to mark a book

Marking your books can help you to understand and review what you are reading. It is helpful, therefore, to develop a system of marking you find useful. The passage below shows how one reader marked it, using circles for crucial terms, underlining for definitions, using numbers for ideas in a sequence and stars for important facts.

Historians undertake to arrange sequences—called stories, or histories—assuming in silence a relation of cause and effect. These assumptions, hidden in the depths of dusty libraries, have been astounding, but commonly unconscious and childlike; so much so, that if any captious critic were to drag them to light, historians would probably reply, with one voice, that they had never supposed themselves required to know what they were talking about. Adams, for one, had toiled in vain to find out what he meant. He had even published a dozen volumes of American history for no other purpose than to satisfy himself whether, by the severest process of stating, with the least possible comment, such facts as seemed sure, in such order as seemed rigorously consequent, he could fix for a familiar moment a necessary sequence of human movement. The result had satisfied him as little as at Har-vard College. Where he saw sequence, other men saw something quite different, and no one saw the same unit of measure. He cared little about his experiments and less about his statesmen, who seemed to him quite as ignorant as himself and, as a rule, no more honest; but he insisted on a relation of sequence, and if he could not reach it by one method, he would try as many methods as science knew. Satisfied that the se- (1) quence of men led to nothing and that the sequence (2) of their society could lead no further, while the mere (3) sequence of time was artificial, and the sequence of (4) thought was chaos, he turned at last to the sequence (5) of force; and thus it happened that, after ten years' pursuit, he found himself lying in the Gallery of Ma-chines at the Great Exposition of 1900, with his histori-cal neck broken by the sudden eruption of forces to-tally new.

a book seems impenetrable, feel free to abandon it. Choose another on the same subject, or switch to another of your interests. However, many good readers get special satisfaction from mastering difficult works. This is because they have the good reading habit of using *reference books,* most often dictionaries and encyclopedias. Many of the advertised methods to quadruple your reading speed overnight actually advise against using reference books. They do this because they are interested only in how *fast* something is read, not in how *well* it is read. Speed is part of good reading, as this section on efficient reading has stressed, but to read something well at any speed, to gain the satisfaction of mastering demanding works, you will surely have to pause occasionally to consult dictionaries and encyclopedias.

Reference works are used because different authors envision different audiences for their books. For example, authors of high-school textbooks on economics write for an audience that is different from that intended by authors of advanced books on United States economy. The difference is that authors of the advanced books assume that the reader will be familiar with certain words and concepts, so there are fewer explanations in advanced books than in textbooks. The authors of textbooks will, for example, provide a complete definition of "capitalism," while authors of advanced works will assume that their readers already understand the definition.

The meanings of words are the domain of the dictionary. Many people mistakenly think that using a dictionary is childish. In fact, most scholars work with a dictionary close at hand. They do this because the dictionary provides precise definitions of its terms. In addition, dictionaries provide information on the pronunciation, derivation, and multiple meanings of a word. With this knowledge, the precise meaning of a word as it is used in context becomes clear.

Facts and ideas are the domain of the encyclopedia. Most encyclopedia entries open with a brief, precise identification of a person, place, or idea, and then move into more detailed explanation. Thus, a quick look at the opening of an encyclopedia entry may be all you need to return to your book confident that you understand a general concept. Also, many encyclopedia entries are pleasurable and informative reading. If you understand a concept mentioned in your reading but want to go deeper into it, you might make a note to consult an encyclopedia when you have finished reading or before you resume again. A final great advantage of consulting an encyclopedia is that it can lead you to other books of interest on the same subject. Many attach bibliographies to their substantial entries.

There are two sorts of reference works. The most common are general encyclopedias and dictionaries.

Keep a dictionary close at hand.

These are all-purpose reference works that cover all fields of knowledge. Southwestern's *Volume Library* and the dictionaries in its *Student Handbooks* are general reference works. The second type of reference works comprises specialized dictionaries and encyclopedias. These cover single fields of knowledge, such as medicine, art, literature, or history. All homes should have general reference works available for use by readers of all ages. Specialized reference works, which are consulted less often, can be used in any local library.

Reviewing what you read. A final consideration in reading for comprehension is the ability to retain information obtained from books. Reading and understanding are not the same thing as memorization. No one is expected to retain everything read in a book. In fact, because reading is a process of understanding and assimilating information, no one should even desire complete recall. Good readers concentrate on ideas, intending to retain the main concepts and facts from whatever they are reading. They help themselves retain this information by developing the habit of reviewing what they have read before going on to another activity. In reviewing material that is difficult, average, or easy, repeat the key ideas to yourself and create a double impression of them in your memory, once in reading and once in reviewing. You should be able to review mentally all reading you do, even leisure reading of easy material. However, reviewing is most important for material that is complex enough to require your normal or study speeds. Reviewing is an important part of any overall program to improve your reading speed and comprehension. If your review suggests lack of comprehension, you will have to slow down and read more carefully.

Good readers review material immediately on finishing their reading. In this way they create that double impression on their memory before the information can slip away.

Questions and sample answers for reviewing what you read

Many readers have only a vague recollection of books they have read. Your comprehension and retention of books and articles can be improved by briefly reviewing what you read soon after finishing it. With a series of general questions, you can focus your reactions. This process will improve both your understanding of books and your ability to remember their content. These five general questions can be asked of any reading material:

1. What was the author's general point?

2. What individual ideas did the author use to support his point?

3. What were the crucial terms discussed by the author?

4. What important facts were cited by the author?

5. What did you like or dislike in this work?

The general questions for review can help you to form a memorable impression of the ideas in your reading. Here is the way a reader might answer those questions, mentally or on paper, for the reading about the Puritans given as a speed test on page 314.

1. The author's general point was to make us interested in what we have to learn from the Puritans.

2. The individual idea used to suggest this was the way the Puritans made friends with the Indians.

3. The name "Puritan" reflects the fact that Puritans hoped to purify their church even more than the English Protestants had already done.

4. The Puritans came to America in 1620. They landed in Massachusetts even though they intended to go to New York.

5. The Puritans may be more interesting than I had thought. I think I will read more about them.

The first step in reviewing is to ask yourself fundamental questions about what you have read. What were the important ideas? What were the important facts? If you have concentrated on locating key ideas by spotting crucial terms and transitions, you should be able to remember these in their proper sequence. If you have taken the time to mark your book, you can use this brief review period to leaf back over the pages you have read, glancing at the key ideas identified by your markings.

The second step in the review process is to summarize the key ideas in your own words. For easy reading material, this can be done mentally. But for difficult material, especially if you have read for study purposes, take the time to summarize on paper what you have read. This can be done in the form of brief notes.

You will find such notes handy for later reference.

Now begin to add this consideration to your reading diary. As described early in this chapter, the diary has space for these new notes on review. First, note whether you have summarized your reading in your mind or on paper. Summarizing readings is always a good habit, but you need not always do so, especially on days when you practice easy reading. Then honestly describe your own sense of your level of comprehension simply by describing your effort at summary as *excellent, mediocre,* or *poor.* As your reading diary grows, you will be able to correlate this information on comprehension against your entries on reading speed. Then you can determine whether you are achieving a balance between speed and comprehension; that is, whether you are progressing toward efficient reading.

Special types of reading

To become a proficient reader, you must learn to vary your reading speed to suit different sorts of reading material. But complete proficiency requires the additional skill of learning how to suit reading methods to reading purposes. If an adult seeking relaxation picks up a classic modern novel, for example, that reader has a reading purpose different from that of a college student reading the same novel for a course in literature.

You should formulate your purposes and expectations before beginning to read. The checklist on this page provides some key questions that can help you do so.

Reading for self-improvement.

Reading for self-improvement requires interest in accumulating general knowledge about a subject. Once you have begun to pursue this interest, your reading purpose should be to add to your fund of knowledge by testing the persuasiveness of different opinions on the subject. An interest in British history, for example, logically begins with some general surveys of events in that long history. But from that point on, you will encounter contradictory accounts and interpretations of the significant movements and periods in British history. Thus, in reading for self-improvement, you should eventually begin to read against your fund of background knowledge, to consider new ideas in the light of older ones.

Reading for this purpose requires regular contact with your chosen subject and careful reading at normal reading speed. Reading for self-improvement also demands the frequent consultation of reference works, which can be counted on to provide relatively objective overviews and impartial summaries of long-standing disputes and differences of opinion. Because this sort of reading constitutes an informal course of study, you probably will not feel it necessary to keep notes on what you read. Another aid to interest and understanding in reading for self-improvement comes from sharing and debating books. That can be done in a reading discussion group, described in the "Continuing to improve" part of this chapter.

Reading for advancement.

No kind of reading provokes a clearer sense of interest and purpose than reading that is intended to develop occupational skills needed for career promotion or change. Here you have a personal interest more intensely felt than that generally found in purely intellectual or leisure pursuits.

Your interest in reading for professional advancement is especially well focused—you want to know what special skill any book or article can teach you. Your purpose in reading is twofold: to determine the relevance of the advice to your position and to master it completely for application to your job or career plans. These two purposes imply two reading strategies. The first demands especially careful prereading so you do not waste your time with irrelevant advice. Most occupational guides are designed to facilitate prereading. Pay close attention to the chapter titles, subtitles, summaries, and questions for review (these are standard features of this sort of reading material). Your second purpose demands that you closely read material of proven relevance at your study speed.

Occupational guides attach special importance to a vocabulary of crucial terms, and mastery of these terms is important in achieving a better job. For that reason, careful note-taking is essential to reading for professional advancement. Be sure to mark your books for later review, and be sure to keep written summaries of especially valuable information. For any occupation, there are likely to be a number of useful guides to advancement. Note-taking can be especially helpful because it makes it possible for you to gather notes on practical advice from many sources.

Reading for pleasure.

Reading for pleasure is the least formal sort of reading endeavor. Your interest in the material might derive from any of the full range of literary pleasures: enjoyment of stories, identification with dynamic characters, or delight in a particular narrative style. Your purpose in reading is a desire for the stimulating and unpredictable entertainment that only books can offer.

But even in reading for pleasure, your repertoire of reading skills is essential for preserving and continually satisfying your desire to read. Reading for enjoyment is best pursued with attention to consciously formulating your interest in the material. Your interest may stem from a particular author's style, the presence of the same interesting character in several novels, or the suspense of a particular kind of plot. Whatever the reason for your interest, you will be led logically to other, similar works that can provide the same enjoyment.

The method of reading for pleasure is as unstructured as the purpose. You should feel free to shift from normal to rapid reading speeds and back again as your interest dictates. Slowing down unnecessarily, however, invites the risk of flagging interest. Brisk reading of works chosen for no interest other than enjoyment can, in fact, intensify delight in them by more quickly and more frequently bringing to the reader the individual features cherished most. No note-taking should intrude on pleasure reading, but you will find it useful to keep some sort of record of your favorite works, either on a shelf that holds your personal library or in a diary of authors and titles.

Study or pleasure? Tailor your approach to your purpose.

Special kinds of reading. Different purposes can change your reading strategy, but differences in reading materials may require special strategies. Technical journals, for example, may rely on complicated charts, graphs, and diagrams to explain ideas discussed in the text or to introduce supplementary ideas. Literary magazines, on the other hand, are rarely broken by any such illustrative material. In the first case, your beginning strategy should be to master the charts, graphs, and diagrams. In the second case, you might begin by prereading titles, subtitles, and topic sentences.

Visual contrasts among kinds of reading materials represent differences of format, both in page arrangements and layouts. But format is indicative of fundamental differences in organization as well. Because a technical journal uses charts, graphs, and diagrams, it may adopt a particular kind of organization.

Kinds of reading

Newspapers. It has been said that no one *reads* newspapers, people just peruse them. There is some truth to this exaggeration. The sheer bulk of your daily newspaper may prohibit careful reading.

Most people read newspapers for quick information on recent events. Newspaper editors know this, and so their news stories feature essential information in the opening paragraphs. There is a journalism school maxim for how to open a news story: Who? What? Where? When? Why? and How? You can see how these important facts find their way into the opening of the sample newspaper story shown on this page. By concentrating only on the opening paragraphs of the news story, you can easily and quickly determine if your are interested enough to read further.

This is true only of news stories. Other parts of the newspaper, such as features and editorials, are organized more along the lines of a magazine article.

Where?
When?
Who?
What?

Why?

How?

MORRISON ELECTION VICTOR

New York City, March 18—Jennifer Morrison was elected president of the new American Federation of Teachers today in a stunning upset over the incumbent, Michael A. Conroy. The vote ended the union's national congress at the convention center here and convincingly demonstrated Ms. Morrison's ability to control the votes of union members disenchanted with the union's pension policies.

The new president made her acceptance speech after midnight from a dais strewn with confetti and streamers. Mr. Conroy, despite losing by a clear margin of 2 to 1, had issued no concession speech.

Magazines. Magazine articles, newspaper editorials, and newspaper features may differ from news stories in at least one important respect: they may be based on opinion rather than fact. For this reason, they are always signed by authors, or, in the case of editorials, they appear on the newspaper's editorial page. Because such articles are not primarily concerned with facts, they open with no recitation of who, what, where, when, why, and how.

Magazines, in particular, tend to pile up as they arrive in the mail. To keep abreast of your magazine reading, you can take advantage of this knowledge of their organization. Preread the table of contents to get an overview of the magazine's contents. Check the full titles and subheadings of individual articles for indications of their special focus. Then go through the opening paragraphs to reach the announcement of the article's purpose and content. If you are interested enough to want to read the entire article, go on. Few good readers ever bother to read all of a magazine.

Mid-Life Career Change: One Man's Story

by Robert Miller

His job had been "obsoleted," as the supervisor said, by new automation that churned out the product faster, better, and cheaper. His daughters, already enrolled in college by then, had been forced to withdraw in mid-semester. His home, carefully reworked for his family's needs over twenty years of amateur handyman projects, had been repossessed by the bank and shown to strangers. Then, hitting rock bottom, William Jameson found himself on an endless line in an overcrowded office filing for welfare benefits.

Last week Congress opened debate on the nation's chronic unemployment problem. The discussion in Washington has to do with hundreds of thousands of workers, but unemployment is also a personal catastrophe. . . .

Recognizing a format and understanding the organization it implies is a matter of knowing facts about the organization of different sorts of publications and of practicing the reading strategy best suited to each. The following pages give you practical facts about several kinds of reading material.

The reading diary you prepared included a final notation for "special difficulties." At this point in your program for reading improvement, you are ready to begin using that notation. Keep track of the single kinds of written material that seem most confusing. Because you are also already varying daily the difficulty of your reading, you should begin to see a pattern emerging. You will be able to recognize potential stumbling blocks in news articles, magazine stories, reference book entries, or visual aids. Then you can consult or review the relevant information given on these pages.

Reference books. Reference books are concise compilations of essential knowledge on a wide variety of subjects. They make this knowledge available in individual entries, organized topically or alphabetically. Each entry begins with a broad statement of the subject's significance. Only then does it proceed to a discussion of individual aspects of the subject.

In the sample biographical entry shown, you can see how a reference book gives easy access to essential information, such as dates and nationality.

In reference books you will also find keys to related articles, such as the cross-reference here to a separate entry on "stream of consciousness." If you were only interested in finding out who James Joyce was, you could have stopped reading this entry after the second paragraph. But if your interest went further, you would have continued to the end, where you would likely have found a bibliography.

JOYCE, JAMES A. (1882–1941). Irish novelist. Although he wrote some poetry (*Chamber Music*, 1907) and one play (*Exiles*, 1918), James Joyce's most important contributions to modern literature were the stories collected in *Dubliners* (1907) and the novels *Portrait of the Artist as a Young Man* (1916), *Ulysses* (1922), and *Finnegans Wake* (1939).

By almost any evaluation, James Joyce ranks as one of the most difficult and most important novelists of the twentieth century. His works have had enormous influence on all subsequent writers because they developed a technique of STREAM OF CONSCIOUSNESS for presentation of the disorganized flow of frequently commonplace thoughts through the minds of their characters.

James Joyce was born in Dublin on. . . .

Tables and graphs. Tables require close study. You should first note the title and the column and row identifications. In this table, for example, it is important to note that the figures are for five-year periods. Notes and explanations attached to tables are crucial. (Here the notes tell you that all figures except the first row are in billions of dollars; they also tell that the statistics have been obtained from the federal government). After acquainting yourself with a table, analyze the figures for trends.

A line graph like the one shown here is read like a grid. To interpret any point on the lines you must move from it to the vertical or horizontal reference points that explain its value. This graph clearly indicates the overall trend of increase in both liabilities and assets of savings and loan associations. It also shows how closely liabilities follow assets, a fact not as obvious in the table on the same subject. Graphs are limited, however, because they can provide only approximate values.

Balance sheet of savings and loan associations
1970–1989
All figures in billions of dollars except number of associations

	1970	1975	1980	1985	1989
Number of associations	5,669	4,931	4,594	3,535	3,011
Total assets	$176.2	$338.2	$632.8	$1,080.1	$1,253.6
Cash	16.5	30.9	58.6	145.3	167.4
Mortgages	150.3	278.6	503.9	652.4	712.1
Other	9.3	28.7	70.3	282.4	374.1
Liabilities	163.8	318.5	599.4	1,032.9	1,229.6
Net worth	$ 12.4	$ 19.7	$ 33.4	$ 47.2	$ 24.0

Source: U.S. Federal Home Loan Bank Board

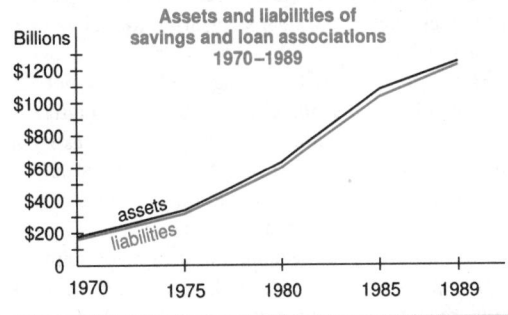

Assets and liabilities of savings and loan associations 1970–1989

Continuing to improve

At the end of eight weeks of daily practice of the principles of good reading, as described in this chapter, you will see a marked improvement in your reading speed and comprehension. Even more important, you will have acquired a new set of reading habits that will make you a better reader and make your reading more enjoyable. You can verify your improvements in speed and comprehension over the eight weeks by comparing the first and the last entries in your reading diary. You can also verify your improvements in reading habits over the same period by answering once again the questions on the "Checklist of reading habits" on page 304.

These improvements will have made you a competent, efficient, and proficient reader by giving you a mastery of important particular skills. But once acquired, the skills must be maintained. People improve their golf or swimming abilities, for example, through a series of lessons. When the lessons are complete, they must practice continually to protect their new abilities at these sports. In the same way, you must practice to protect your new reading skills. This is easier and more enjoyable than learning new habits, because your improved ability will make the practice itself more satisfying and pleasurable.

The checklist for continued improvement shown on this page itemizes the key considerations for maintaining an ongoing reading program of your own. You should periodically review the entire list to protect your new reading skills.

Practice reading.
Daily practice is essential for preserving reading speed and comprehension. You can help yourself with short readings for speed during work breaks. You can mentally summarize your recent reading at virtually any time. Ideally, though, you will continue to set aside a regular reading time each day. Most people find that in addition to keeping their reading skills sharp, regular reading periods become a positive influence on their daily lives, particularly when they choose books of inspirational value or intellectual interest.

Your interest in daily reading can be maintained by varying what you read. There is no need to alternate easy, average, and difficult reading material as rigorously as you did over the eight-week program, but switching from novels to occupational journals or from history books to popular magazines introduces a pleasant variety into your reading and also helps reinforce your repertoire of speeds and your comprehension skills. Even though you may stop thinking about study,

---

My checklist for continuing to improve

1. I read daily.
2. I vary the kinds of things I read.
3. I vary my reading speeds.
4. I test my speed and comprehension regularly.
5. I follow the principles of good reading.
6. I am always conscious of my purpose in reading.
7. I keep interesting things to read at home.
8. I pursue my reading interests.
9. I visit bookstores and libraries.
10. I share my reading with friends and family.

---

normal, and rapid reading speeds, you will find yourself shifting automatically into these speeds if you vary the kinds of things you read.

As a final check on maintaining your new reading speeds and strategies, test yourself periodically. A quick calculation of your reading speed on different sorts of materials every few weeks will remind you of the need to continue to work on your new speeds. Periodic tests will also indicate particular aspects of your reading ability that may still require special attention, such as your high speed reading. A brief review of the advice in this chapter, on any aspect of your reading, along with a few refresher practice sessions, will ensure that you preserve your complete repertoire of reading skills.

Group reading.
One of the best ways to continue your reading improvement is to read as a social activity. Sharing reading with friends has two good effects. It increases your interest in reading, because comments from others force you to think about what you have read and give you ideas for what you might read in the future. Sharing reading with others also helps keep you on a continuing program for improvement by encouraging you to finish books so that you can discuss them intelligently with others.

Reading as a family activity. Many people have fond memories of being read to in their childhood. But family reading is not just a memory from the past. Many families continue to read aloud regularly, and reading is often their only group recreational activity. Reading aloud to others is not just for parents with young children. Sharing readings with one's entire family is a gratifying experience; once introduced, such reading quickly proves its value. Family reading offers a refreshing alternative to television, so anyone seri-

The Oxford Illustrated Literary Guide to the United States by Eugene Ehrlich and Gorton Carruth (Oxford, 464 pages; $29.95). Hawaii? Rupert Brooke went to Oahu in 1913 and wrote the sonnet "Waikiki," which is reprinted in the guide. Whittier, Calif.? Maxwell Anderson became head of the Whittier College English department in 1917. And Samuel Clemens was everywhere. Richly illustrated with photographs and carefully organized by regions, this guide reveals, among other curiosities, the peculiar restlessness of American writers.

Reading is a family activity with lifelong benefits for all members, from the youngest to the most senior. Ideas for books on a wide variety of subjects can often be obtained from book reviews that appear in your local newspaper and in magazines you read.

ously interested in reading should begin to share this activity with the family.

Reading as a social activity. Reading discussion groups are a contagious kind of social activity that can become a regular part of one's life. These discussion groups offer an alternative means of getting together with friends for an evening. Many reading groups thrive for years. Often there is a revolving membership of people of many backgrounds who find that they have much to offer as well as much to learn.

To start a reading group, all you need are a few friends interested in reading the same book. Arrange a time to meet together after everyone has had a chance to finish the book. Most discussions of the book will begin by chatting casually about what the book says and what members of the group have found good or bad about it. Reactions will differ, of course, but different opinions of a book, an author, or a character's worth will enhance the discussion. There is no need to focus on purely intellectual problems, although these may finally become the focus of the discussion.

Reading groups generally vote on the next book to be read. They may also invite additional friends to join the next discussion. Whether the meetings are weekly or monthly, a large membership is useful because it ensures stimulating discussion despite the occasional absence of some regular members.

Keeping in touch with books.

Your reading will be helped by making certain you have an ample supply of books you want to read. More than 40,000 new titles are published in the United States every year. Despite this abundance, many people do not value books highly. While the skill of reading can be acquired through conscious effort, the love of books develops through contact with them.

Bookstores stimulate reading through attractive displays of current books and standard titles that continue to attract readers. Bookstore managers know the books people enjoy reading at any time as well as other works that might match your current reading interests. In comparison with other ages, books in our time are relatively inexpensive. New, hardbound best-sellers may seem difficult to afford, but their worth should be considered in terms of the hours of pleasure or the practical benefits they offer. Almost any reading interest can also be served well by reliance on paperbacks.

Booksellers—often students working their way through college—who come to your door may also offer books of lasting value. Many families fill their bookshelves in this way, establishing reading resources that serve more than a single generation.

Local libraries acquire books they think may be of interest to the taxpayers who support them. A single visit to a library can produce a reading list that will serve for months, and the books may be borrowed at no cost. Libraries, even more than bookstores, keep on hand a variety of books for readers of all ages. Often their books are shelved by age group, so the reading interests of children, young adults, or adults can be fueled simply by browsing along the shelves. All libraries also stock extensive collections of books printed in oversized, especially legible typefaces. These are intended for readers who suffer from poor eyesight. In this way, books become accessible to those who might otherwise be denied.

With bookstores, booksellers, and libraries, you can always keep your home well stocked with books enjoyable to you and all members of your family. Well chosen books, plus attention to the principles of reading discussed in this chapter, can help anyone become and remain a better reader.

THE WORLD-FAMOUS BESTSELLER
ABOUT THE MAN-MADE POLLUTANTS
THAT THREATEN TO DESTROY LIFE
ON THIS EARTH.

Rachel Carson

Silent Spring

Reading lists

The Red Badge of Courage by Stephen Crane

WINNER OF THE PULITZER PRIZE AND THE NATIONAL BOOK CRITICS CIRCLE AWARD

The Stories of John Cheever

"A grand occasion in English literature."
—The New York Times

DASHIELL HAMMETT THE THIN MAN

Making reading a lifelong activity. Books lead to books. This means that one book is likely to lead you to another on the same subject or by the same author. The connections are made in the books themselves, in the topical groupings of library shelves, or in shared displays in bookstores.

What follows is a list of worthwhile books in general fields of interest. Any one of these books can serve as the beginning point in a reading hobby that may travel far from these selections or subject areas, but part of the charm of regular reading is that it takes off in unpredictable directions.

Take full advantage of all available sources of interesting titles: friends who read, your local library, bookstores and booksellers, and the book review columns of magazines and newspapers.

Science and nature

Attenborough, David. *Life on Earth* (1981). Attractively illustrated introduction to natural history.

Bell, Eric. *The Magic of Numbers* (1946). Fascinating demonstrations of the power and allure of mathematics.

Bronowski, Jacob. *The Ascent of Man* (1974). The history of scientific advancement since primitive times.

Carson, Rachel. *Silent Spring* (1962). A classic and harrowing account of the dangers of pollution.

Commoner, Barry. *Science and Survival* (1966). The mixed virtues of science, plainly stated.

Crick, Francis. *Of Molecules and Men* (1966). Narrative account of the Nobelist's achievements in biology.

Eisley, Loren. *The Immense Journey* (1957). Philosophical thoughts on the history of human development.

Freud, Sigmund. *General Introduction to Psychoanalysis* (1920). A general overview of the subject.

Geertz, Clifford. *The Interpretation of Cultures* (1973). Academic introduction to social anthropology.

Jastrow, Robert. *Red Giants and White Dwarfs* (1979). A popular guide to new knowledge of astronomy.

Kidder, Tracy. *The Soul of a New Machine* (1981). Exciting story of the construction of a computer.

McPhee, John. *Basin and Range* (1981). An account of learning geology in the field.

Milgram, Stanley. *Obedience to Authority* (1974). Controversial experiment on our will to obey overwhelming our moral precepts.

Sagan, Carl and Richard Turco. *A Path Where No Man Thought* (1990). A scientific discourse on nuclear winter.

Sears, Paul B. *The Living Landscape* (1967). Elegantly written summation of ecological issues.

Thomas, Lewis. *Lives of a Cell* (1974). Enjoyable essays on the lessons drawn from biology.

Turnbull, Colin. *The Mountain People* (1972). A description of a field anthropologist's work.

Ulam, Stanislaw. *Adventures of a Mathematician* (1976). A scientist's story of his work on the atom bomb.

Watson, James D. *The Double Helix* (1967). Exciting narrative of the discovery of DNA.

Wiener, Norbert. *Cybernetics* (1961). A demanding, groundbreaking discussion of the computer age.

Wilson, Edmund O. *Sociobiology* (1975). Challenging behavioral theory of the dominance of genes over will.

History

Allen, Frederick L. *Only Yesterday* (1931). Engaging, novelistic portrait of the years after World War I.

Boorstin, Daniel. *The Americans* (1958–73). Three-volume popular epic by the librarian of Congress.

Braudel, Fernand. *The Mediterranean* (1972). One of the great modern social histories: life in the 16th century.

Carlyle, Thomas. *The French Revolution* (1832). Dramatic saga of heroes and villains of the uprising.

Catton, Bruce. *The Centennial History of the Civil War* (1961–63). Three eminently readable volumes.

Durant, Will and Ariel. *The Story of Civilization* (1935–75). Eleven volumes of enthusiastic history of ideas.

Fitzgerald, Frances. *Fire on the Lake* (1972). Early prize-winning account of the Vietnam War.

Fussell, Paul. *The Great War and Modern Memory* (1975). Literate and surprising discussion of the special significance of World War I.

Gibbon, Edward. *The Decline and Fall of the Roman Empire* (1776–78). The work that created our image of Rome.

Halberstam, David. *The Best and the Brightest* (1972). How the Kennedy administration slipped toward war in Southeast Asia.

Hamilton, Edith. *The Greek Way* (1930). A persuasive and lucid paean to the merits of ancient Greece.

Hersey, John. *Hiroshima* (1946). The effects of the atomic bomb, focused on the stories of six survivors.

Morison, Samuel Eliot. *The Great Explorers* (1978). A sailor's history of early global navigation.

Plumb, J. H. *The Italian Renaissance* (1965). A beautifully written history of the great flowering.

Shirer, William. *The Rise and Fall of the Third Reich* (1960). A journalist's account of the Hitler years.

Stratton, Joanna L. *Pioneer Women* (1981). Edited diaries of frontier women on the American prairies.

Thomas, Hugh. *A History of the World* (1978). A contemporary overview for background.

Toynbee, Arnold. *A Study of History* (1934–61). A twelve-volume analysis for knowledgeable readers.

Tuchman, Barbara. *A Distant Mirror* (1978). The story of the Middle Ages told through the life of one man.

Tuchman, Barbara. *The March of Folly: From Troy to Vietnam* (1984). Exposé of four historical blunders.

Wills, Garry. *Inventing America* (1978). A journalist's investigation of the Declaration of Independence.

Wills, Garry. *Reagan's America* (1988). A sympathetic account of Ronald Reagan's years in the executive office.

Wood, Gordon S. *The Creation of the American Republic* (1965). A sophisticated political analysis.

Woodham-Smith, Cecil. *The Great Hunger* (1962). Graphic description of the Irish potato famine in 1848.

Places

Abbey, Edward. *Cactus County* (1973). A naturalist's appreciation of the Sonora Desert, with photographs.

Barzini, Luigi. *The Italians* (1964). Native's discursive reflections on the distinctive features of his culture.

Belloc, Hillaire. *The Path to Rome* (1902). A literary critic travels on foot to the Italian capital.

Bellow, Saul. *To Jerusalem and Back* (1976). An American novelist's portrait of Israel.

Benedict, Ruth. *The Chrysanthemum and the Sword* (1946). Noted anthropologist's visit to Japan.

Dos Passos, John. *Brazil on the Move* (1963). Novelist's journalistic account of the South American nation.

Douglas, William O. *My Wilderness* (1960). A distinguished jurist's salute to the Pacific Northwest.

Fisher, M. F. K. *Map of Another Town* (1964). A noted writer on food describes southern France.

Frady, Marshall. *Southerners* (1980). Magazine writer's irreverent look at his native region.

Gornick, Vivian. *In Search of Ali Mahmoud* (1973). Jewish-American feminist meets modern Egypt.

Hoagland, Edward. *Notes of a Century Before* (1969). Compelling journal of frontier British Columbia.

Krutch, Joseph Wood. *The Forgotten Peninsula* (1961). A scholar and naturalist on the Mexican Baja.

Lavender, David. *The Rocky Mountains* (1980). History and lore tied to the modern state of the region.

McGinniss, Joe. *Going to Extremes* (1980). Desperate lives in the magnificent environment of Alaska.

McPhee, John. *Coming Into the Country* (1977). Author describes Alaska and Alaskans.

Mehta, Ved. *Portrait of India* (1970). By an Indian blind since childhood.

Naipaul, V. S. *Among the Believers* (1981). Prominent novelist's exploration of Islamic nations.

Pritchett, V. S. *The Spanish Temper* (1955). An affectionate analysis by a noted English writer and critic.

Smith, Hedrick. *The Russians* (1976). A *New York Times* reporter reflects on his years in Moscow.

Snow, Edgar. *Red Star over China* (1968). One of the first American accounts of life in Communist China.

Steinbeck, John. *Travels with Charley* (1962). The novelist's celebrated cross-country drive, with dog.

Thoreau, Henry David. *The Maine Woods* (1865). Early explorations by the author of *Walden Pond.*

Warner, William W. *Beautiful Swimmers* (1976). Natural history of the Chesapeake.

West, Rebecca. *Black Lamb and Grey Falcon* (1941). A tour of the Balkans in the company of H. G. Wells.

People

Adams, Henry. *The Education of Henry Adams* (1906). Autobiography of a troubled member of a famous family.

Boswell, James. *The Life of Samuel Johnson* (1791). One of the first and finest detailed records of a life.

Caro, Robert. *Means of Ascent* (1990). Biography of Lyndon Johnson's political life.

Curie, Eve. *Madame Curie* (1937). The life of the famous scientist, as told by her daughter.

Ellmann, Richard. *James Joyce* (1982). Revised edition of a great modern biography.

Erikson, Erik H. *Gandhi's Truth* (1969). Theory of identity crisis; portrait of a remarkable man.

Flexner, James Thomas. *Washington: The Indispensable Man* (1979). The author's own condensation of a longer work.

Franklin, Benjamin. *The Autobiography of Benjamin Franklin* (1791). Commonsense and humor, for his son.

Fraser, Antonia. *Cromwell: The Lord Protector* (1973). Best of the author's works on British leaders.

Jones, Ernest. *The Life and Work of Sigmund Freud* (1961). Abridgment of a remarkable life, told by a disciple.

Josephson, Matthew. *Edison* (1963). The inventor's deeds made all the more fascinating by demystification.

Kaplan, Justin. *Walt Whitman: A Life* (1980). The poet in the context of 19th-century American society.

Mabee, Carlton T. *The American Leonardo* (1943). The life of Samuel Morse, painter and inventor.

Malcolm X. *The Autobiography of Malcolm X* (1964). Searing story of ghetto and political life.

Manchester, William. *American Caesar: Douglas MacArthur* (1978). Sumptuous life of the general.

Mizener, Arthur. *The Far Side of Paradise* (1951). The tragic career of F. Scott Fitzgerald.

Muir, John. *Story of My Boyhood* (1913). The naturalist's youth in Scotland and in America.

Murray, K. M. Elizabeth. *Caught in the Web of Words* (1977). Life of the editor of the *Oxford English Dictionary.*

Pais, Abraham. *Subtle Is the Lord* (1982). Portrait of Albert Einstein, physicist and humanist.

Royko, Mike. *Boss: Richard J. Daley of Chicago* (1971). The life of the mayor and his political machine.

Sandburg, Carl. *Abraham Lincoln* (1926). A stately study of the man and President.

Schoenbaum, Samuel. *Shakespeare's Lives* (1970). The

facts and the fiction about the life of the bard.

Strachey, Lytton. *Queen Victoria* (1921). Portrait of the matriarch, by a noted biographer.

Sullivan, J. W. N. *Beethoven* (1927). Convincing links between the man's emotions and the composer's music.

Thurber, James. *The Years with Ross* (1959). Endearing, hilarious life of the first editor of *The New Yorker.*

Literature

Amis, Kingsley. *Lucky Jim* (1954). The most famous of comic novels about professors.

Anderson, Sherwood. *Winesburg, Ohio* (1919). Famous stories of small-town life in the Midwest.

Austen, Jane. *Pride and Prejudice* (1813). Among the wittiest of novels about marriageable ladies.

Baldwin, James. *Go Tell It on the Mountain* (1953). Tense story of black adolescent.

Bellow, Saul. *Henderson The Rain King* (1959). A tragicomedy; traces a man's quest for wisdom.

Bronte, Emily. *Wuthering Heights* (1847). The tempestuous romance of Cathy and Heathcliff.

Burgess, Anthony. *A Clockwork Orange* (1962). Horrific vision of violence in the future.

Caldwell, Erskine. *God's Little Acre* (1933). Folksy story of Georgia mountain families.

Camus, Albert. *The Stranger* (1946). Plainly written novel of modern man's disorientation and loss of self.

Chandler, Raymond. *The Big Sleep* (1939). Philip Marlowe, the archetype of hardboiled detectives.

Cheever, John. *The Stories of John Cheever* (1979). Suburban settings, unpredictable doings, comic tone.

Improving Your Reading

Conrad, Joseph. *Heart of Darkness* (1902). Intricate, enigmatic tale of horrors of African colonization.

Crane, Stephen. *The Red Badge of Courage* (1895). The first, perhaps the best novel of inglorious war.

Dickens, Charles. *David Copperfield* (1850). Poverty and the journey to adulthood in Victorian England.

Dostoevski, Feodor. *The Brothers Karamazov* (1880). Murder, false accusations, moral implications.

Elkin, Stanley. *The Dick Gibson Show* (1971). Almost surreal tale of late-night radio host.

Ellison, Ralph. *Invisible Man* (1952). To many, the best novel ever of black American experience.

Farrell, James T. *Studs Lonigan* (1935). Best of a trilogy of novels about the Irish in Chicago.

Fitzgerald, F. Scott. *The Great Gatsby* (1925). Tragic undoing of a gloriously romantic hero.

Flaubert, Gustave. *Madame Bovary* (1857). Important modern novel of restless wife's petty ambitions.

Garcia-Marquez, Gabriel. *Love in the Time of Cholera* (1988). Love in all its guises during the 20th-century cholera epidemic.

Greene, Graham. *Brighton Rock* (1938). Suspenseful story of gang wars at a British resort.

Hammett, Dashiell. *The Thin Man* (1934). Classic American detective fiction.

Hardy, Thomas. *The Mayor of Casterbridge* (1886). A man doomed by fate and accident.

Heller, Joseph. *Catch-22* (1961). Bleakly humorous novel of combat and red tape in World War II.

Hemingway, Ernest. *A Farewell to Arms* (1929). Terse story of World War I desertion.

Huxley, Aldous. *Brave New World* (1932). Science fiction vision of an impersonal future.

James, Henry. *The Ambassadors* (1902). Complexly told story of American experience in Europe.

Jones, James. *From Here to Eternity* (1951). Military life in Hawaii at the time of Pearl Harbor.

Joyce, James. *Dubliners* (1914). Subtle, deceptive short stories, useful as introduction to his novels.

Kafka, Franz. *The Castle* (1926). Nightmarish vision of personal alienation and social bureaucracy.

Lawrence, D. H. *Sons and Lovers* (1913). Coming of age in the milieu of the English coal mines.

London, Jack. *The Call of the Wild* (1903). The classic animal story, good reading for all ages.

Melville, Herman. *Moby Dick* (1851). The epic sea story, with modernistic digressions on good and evil.

Morrison, Toni. *Beloved* (1988). A spiritual landscape chronicling slavery's legacy in America.

O'Connor, Flannery. *A Good Man Is Hard to Find* (1955). Short stories about the South.

O'Flaherty, Liam. *The Informer* (1926). Study of accidental betrayal during the Irish uprising.

Pasternak, Boris. *Dr. Zhivago* (1958). A man's struggle to preserve personal goals in the midst of the Russian revolution.

Percy, Walker. *The Moviegoer* (1961). Complicated story of film overwhelming reality in the South.

Poe, Edgar Allan. *Tales of the Grotesque* (1840). Unsurpassed stories of Gothic horrors.

Shelley, Mary. *Frankenstein* (1818). The original tale, more chilling than the movies or imitations.

Tolstoy, Leo. *War and Peace* (1866). Expansive panorama of Russian lives disrupted by Napoleonic invasions.

Twain, Mark. *The Adventures of Huckleberry Finn* (1885). Social satire from a boy's perspective.

Walker, Alice. *The Color Purple* (1982). An unusual, moving exchange between two sisters.

Wolfe, Thomas. *Look Homeward, Angel* (1929). An American epic of families and coming of age.

Woolf, Virginia. *To the Lighthouse* (1927). Modern novel told in stream-of-consciousness technique.

For further reference

Adams, W. Royce
Increasing Reading Speed
Macmillan

Agardy, Franklin J.
How to Read Faster and Better
Simon & Schuster

Berger, Gilda
Learning Disabilities and Handicaps
Watts

Cohn, Marvin
Helping Your Teen-age Student: What Parents Can Do to Improve Reading and Study Skills
Dutton & Co.

Ervin, Jane
Your Child Can Read and You Can Help
Doubleday

Lewis, Norman
How to Read Better and Faster
Harper & Row

Miller, William M.
Reading Faster and Understanding More
Little, Brown

Osman, Betty B.
Learning Disabilities: A Family Affair
Random House

Taking Major Tests

Nearly all people who want to advance their educations or careers must at some time take at least one of the major tests. These tests are designed to evaluate general knowledge, aptitude for college, or qualifications for graduate school. All of these tests are developed by nonprofit organizations, and their scores are generally accepted by employers and educators across the United States.

The achievement test called General Educational Development, or GED, is designed to assess whether a person knows as much as a typical high-school graduate. It is administered to people who dropped out of high school or who never entered high school. A passing grade on the GED is accepted by most employers and colleges as the equivalent of a high-school diploma.

Most colleges, however, want students who are better than the typical high-school graduate. They also want to be able to evaluate the best student in a poor high school against an ordinary student in a good high school. While the best students in poor high schools may be at least as good as ordinary students in good schools, they may actually be much better or much worse. By giving the same aptitude test to everyone who applies for admission, college administrators hope to obtain an objective evaluation. Of course, colleges do not rely on tests alone, but the scores provided by standardized tests may indicate whether a student with poor grades in school may have unrealized potential.

Colleges use one of two aptitude tests to acquire the information they need. (Some colleges will accept scores from either.) The test used most in the eastern United States is the Scholastic Assessment Test, or SAT, prepared by the College Entrance Examination Board. The SAT is the grandfather of all the major aptitude tests and many tests have imitated it. Elsewhere in the United States, the American College Testing Program, or ACT, is used more than the SAT. It is important to remember, though, that around the country individual colleges have different requirements. The admissions offices of the colleges to which you are applying should be consulted as to whether you need to take an aptitude test and, if so, which test.

These tests are called *aptitude tests* because they are intended to measure ability, not knowledge. Some colleges also require *achievement tests*, which measure knowledge of specific subjects, such as French or calculus, rather than ability.

Just as college admissions offices want to have standards to judge applicants from different high schools, administrators of graduate schools want to have similar objective standards for college graduates. The Graduate Record Examination, or GRE, is designed to test the kinds of skills needed in graduate school. Not every graduate school requires the GRE, especially where there are programs that lead directly from a college into a specific course of graduate study. Nevertheless, the GRE is frequently required, and failure to pass it can keep a person out of a graduate program.

Improve your test-taking

Though everyone wants to do as well as possible on tests, some students know more than they are ever able to show because they are test-shy. These students often perform more poorly than students who know less than they do. Thus, good test-takers have an advantage over classmates who do not test well. For this reason, you should learn about various tests and try to become "test-wise," that is, comfortable when taking tests and capable of figuring out correct answers even when you do not have firm knowledge to guide you.

Most good test-takers follow a few simple rules that help them get better scores. Some of these rules apply to all tests. Others are specific for multiple-choice tests, or even more specific for a single test, such as the SAT. The first and most important rule, however, is that the better prepared you are, the easier you will find the test and the better your score will be.

Attitude.
Perhaps the most important rule to help you improve your test-taking is to adopt the right attitude. You cannot do well on a test if your mind is blocked by worry. Remember, tests are designed to measure your mastery of a skill or your knowledge of a subject. They are not designed to embarrass you, fool you, or terrify you. In a sense, taking a test should be no harder for you than taking your temperature.

Forget about the students around you—what they do is of no concern. Forget about the teacher, about the plans you have for after the test, and about anything else that may be on your mind. Until the test is over, the only two things that matter are you and the test. With this single-minded attitude, you are ready to concentrate and do your very best. You may feel keyed up, like an athlete before a game. Being keyed up can make you more alert and ready, but you should not feel agitated or worried.

Preparation.
Not less important than attitude is preparation for a test. There are two kinds of preparation for any test, whether it is an end-of-course achievement test or a general aptitude test. The first is study of the subject matter. Even in taking an aptitude test, knowing the subject matter will help you get a high score. If you do not know the subject matter, only your test-wiseness can help you.

Some students study hard but do not master the material. They may read a chapter over and over, desperately trying to memorize hundreds of facts, or they may run in circles, trying over and over again to master a new problem without first understanding it.

If the test is on subject matter from a book, try this approach. Instead of reading the material over and over, read it once. Then spend some time organizing it on paper. What are the major facts or themes of the material? What are the important names or dates or other facts—those necessary to understand the whole? Many of the names and dates may be less important—in fact, some of them can safely be forgotten.

If you are learning a skill, go back to an example, either in the book or in your notes, and follow it step by step, making sure that you see how the right answer was reached. Then take a new problem and follow exactly the same steps. If you still do not understand, ask for help from a classmate or teacher.

There are many aids available to you in preparing for these major tests. The sample items with explanations that are on pages 332–351 are a good place to begin. The box on page 330 lists some other options.

If you are having trouble, it is important that you begin preparing for the test early. Otherwise, there will not be time to ask for help. An early start is a good idea in any case, especially when learning the vocabulary of a foreign language or such basic facts as the multiplication table. The mind needs lots of time and much repetition to fix the information firmly. No amount of cramming on the night before the test is likely to make up for work not done ahead of time. Even if you do manage to remember part of the material for the test, you probably will forget it soon afterward; in that case, you will have to do extra studying for the next test.

Ten ways to improve your test scores

Though the various tests may require differing techniques, here are a few tips that apply to all of them:

1. **Take a course** that will prepare you if you are unsure about your ability to deal with a test. Courses are offered in most major cities and are available by mail or on computer programs. The courses are particularly useful for achievement tests. Although some test-makers believe they cannot improve aptitude test scores, other experts disagree. Books available in most bookstores contain more sample questions than offered here. The testing organizations also publish free or inexpensive booklets that contain sample questions and helpful information.

2. **Take at least one sample test.** This book supplies a few sample questions, but you should obtain a complete sample test, often from your school library or local bookstore. Try to take the test in the same time limit set for the official test. The experience should not only prepare you but will relax you for the actual test. It also might reveal weak areas that require more study.

3. **Be prepared.** Make sure you have whatever is required when you arrive at the testing place. Some tests require an admission ticket, personal identification (such as a driver's license or birth certificate), and Number 2 pencils. Be sure you know what is needed for your test so you do not forfeit your place.

4. **Relax.** Test-takers foul up more often because they are too tense than because they are too calm. The time to stay up nights studying for a test is in the weeks preceding it, when you can use that excess energy for studying. You should be well-rested by the time the test starts. A good night's sleep is better than staying up late and cramming.

5. **Take a moment to look through the whole test** (if allowed) before answering any questions. Read the directions especially carefully. If you do not know exactly what is wanted, you may make mistakes that reduce your score.

6. **Estimate how much time you have** for answering each question. Count quickly how many questions there are altogether, and estimate the time needed for each. If the test has several parts, jot down a rough timetable for handling each part.

7. **Read each question carefully.** If you misunderstand the question, you will probably answer it incorrectly, no matter how much you know about the subject. Some tests have questions with tricky wording just to test your understanding. Especially when a question is complicated, read it a second time to be sure you have it right.

8. **Answer all the easy questions first** and skip questions you are not sure about. Use the remaining time to consider carefully the hard-to-answer questions. Answering easy questions will warm you up and help prevent a mental block, a temporary inability to remember something that you really know. Answering easy questions first also will ensure that you have answered everything you know best before time runs out.

9. **Answer questions first from parts of the test that carry higher scores.** Obviously, if you know which parts count most and have the correct answers, tackling those questions first will help you get the highest possible score.

10. **If you have time left,** use it to read through all the questions and answers. You may find, for example, that you have failed to answer some items whose answers you know. In multiple choice tests with separate answer sheets, take the time to make sure your answers are in the right spaces or columns. Take a moment to determine that each answer seems reasonable, especially in a mathematics test; if an answer is wrong, do not be too lazy to do your calculations again.

The second kind of preparation for any test has nothing at all to do with subject matter. It consists of making sure that you are physically and mentally ready to do well. One important factor is a good night's sleep. The day before a test, remember to take a few minutes now and then to relax. Finish your studying early so that you can get to bed and be ready for sleep at your regular bedtime. In the morning, eat a good breakfast. At the same time, train yourself to put aside any worries or excitement for a few hours, until the test is over. You need all your powers of concentration for the test.

During the test.
Arrive early and have with you the pencils or any other tools you will need. At this point you should be well enough prepared not to think about the test for a moment or two. Do something else if you can, such as chat with a friend.

When the test is handed out, read it through quickly before you answer any of the questions. Be sure you understand *how* you are to provide the answers. Do not, for example, write on the test booklet if a separate answer sheet is required. In fact, it is a good idea to read all the instructions twice—just to make sure. Getting a poor grade because you did not follow the rules is worse than getting a poor grade because you did not know the material. Once you have read through the whole test, do the easy items first. In that way, even if you are short of time, you will make sure you get credit for what you know. After the easy items are done, tackle the items you are not sure of.

Obviously, if you do not know the correct answer to a test item, you will have a more difficult time than if you do know the answer. But you still have many ways to improve your score. For one thing, your unconscious mind usually knows more than your conscious mind does. Although you skip over an item because you do not remember the answer, the answer may pop into your mind later. In addition, if you weed out answers that you know are wrong, you have a good chance of coming up with the correct answer. For example, if you eliminate two of four answers in a multiple choice item, you have a fifty-fifty chance of getting the right answer from the remaining two.

If you are really in trouble, there are other rules you

can use for guessing. Be warned, however, that the people who write the tests know these rules also. For example, correct answers often have to be qualified extensively, which means that the right answer will normally be the longest one. Test-makers know this, of course, so they deliberately try to think of wrong answers that will be longer than the right ones. As a result, the second-longest answer is sometimes the right one. Similarly, absolute qualifiers, such as *always, never,* or *none,* generally apply to incorrect answers, since few things in this world are ever absolute. Test-makers know this also, and sometimes they add absolute qualifiers to correct answers in order to trap the unwary. Finally, the test-makers want there to be about equal numbers of answers labeled A, B, C, D, and E. Each letter should, in this case, get about 20 percent of the answers. While test-makers know that students might exploit this to improve their test scores, most are reluctant to let one answer predominate over the others. Thus, in a multiple choice test, you can use the number of answers for each letter among the items you are sure of as a rough guide to guessing the items of which you are not sure.

Scoring multiple-choice tests.
Multiple-choice tests are used most often to test mastery of facts. Be sure to read each question and its possible answers carefully. Sometimes, more than one answer may seem correct; in that case, choose the one that you think is most accurate.

Short multiple-choice tests usually are graded on the number of right answers. This means that if you do not know the answer to a question, you can guess at answers without being penalized.

On long multiple-choice tests, such as standardized reading and mathematics tests, you are penalized for guessing. For this kind of test you should not guess at an answer if you have no idea what the answer is. You should guess if you can eliminate one or more of the possible answers as surely wrong.

Sample test questions

Sample questions from the four major tests follow. You will notice that the same kinds of questions often appear on more than one test. Each question is accompanied by a short explanation of why one of the answers is correct. Study these explanations carefully; they will reveal techniques of thinking you can use over and over. Note that in multiple-choice questions, the part that sets up the choices is sometimes called the *stem*.

GED

The General Educational Development examination has been developed by the American Council on Education to qualify students who have not finished high school or the equivalent of a secondary school diploma. It is rare for high-school dropouts to make a success of their lives without passing the GED. The GED consists of five parts: writing skills, social studies, science, literature and the arts, and mathematics. The writing skills section is a test of written English, including spelling, capitalization, punctuation, usage, sentence structure, and organization. There is no penalty for guessing, so you should complete all items even if you do not know the correct choice.

Writing skills

Directions: Choose the one best answer to each item. The questions refer to the following paragraphs.

(1)When you are in school, almost any Subject seems a potential area for a good job. (2)But when you are out on your own, you may find it difficult to land a job. (3)When you are told time after time that there are no jobs. (4)And it is time for some creative thinking and acting.

(5)Do your homework before applying for any job. (6)First, you should study the openings posted in the local newspapers—subscribe to all of them if possible, or read it at the public library. (7)Familiarize oneself with the types of jobs most often available, with the various employment offices, and with the skills most in demand.

Sentence 1: When you are in school, almost any Subject seems a potential area for a good job.

What correction should be made to this sentence?

(1) replace you are with one is
(2) remove the comma after school
(3) change Subject to subject
(4) insert a comma after area
(5) no correction is necessary

Choice (3) is correct. The word *subject* is not a proper noun or the first word of a sentence, so it must not be capitalized.

Sentences 3 and 4: When you are told time after time that there are no jobs. And it is time for some creative thinking and acting.

Which of the following is the best way to write the underlined portion of these sentences? If you think the original is the best way, choose option (1).

(1) jobs. And it
(2) jobs, or it
(3) jobs, it
(4) jobs, if it
(5) jobs, and it

Choice (3) is correct. In this form the sentence now consists of a dependent clause and an independent clause, with the clauses separated by a comma.

Sentence 5: Do your homework before applying for any job.

If you rewrote sentence 5 beginning with Be sure that you *the next words should be*

(1) got done your homework
(2) got your homework done
(3) had done your homework
(4) did your homework
(5) have done your homework

Choice (5) is correct. The verb *have done* is in the present perfect tense, so it agrees with the verb *Be,* which is in the present tense.

Sentence 6: First, you should study the openings posted in the local newspapers—subscribe to all of them if possible, or read it at the public library.

What correction should be made to this sentence?

(1) replace you with one
(2) replace you with they
(3) insert a comma after openings
(4) replace it with them
(5) no correction is necessary

Choice (4) is correct. The pronoun has a plural antecedent, *newspapers.* The pronoun must, therefore, also be plural, *them* not *it.*

Sentence 7: Familiarize oneself with the types of jobs most often available, with the various employment offices, and with the skills most in demand.

What correction should be made to this sentence?

(1) change Familiarize to Familiarized
(2) replace oneself with yourself
(3) insert a comma after various
(4) change offices to office
(5) change demand to demanding

Choice (2) is correct. The subject of the verb *Familiarize* does not appear, but it is understood to be the pronoun *you.* The pronoun *yourself* corresponds to the understood subject *you.*

Social studies

<u>Directions:</u> Choose the <u>one</u> best answer to each question.

In the United States, a governor of a state has the power to do all of the following EXCEPT

(1) prepare a budget for the next year
(2) veto a law passed by the state legislature
(3) send an ambassador to a foreign country
(4) campaign for the members of his or her political party
(5) suggest laws he or she would like to see passed

Choices (1), (2), and (5) describe activities that might be performed by the governor of a state. Choice (4) describes an activity common to most elected officials. The correct answer is choice (3). Only the federal government of the United States—the President with the advice and consent of the Senate—can send ambassadors to other countries.

DISTRIBUTION OF POPULATION
IN THE UNITED STATES

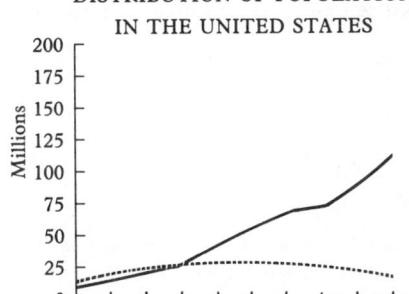

Urban Dwellers——   Farm Dwellers······

According to the graph above, the year the population was evenly distributed between urban and rural areas was approximately

(1) 1880   (2) 1900   (3) 1920   (4) 1940   (5) 1960

First, it is important to understand that "evenly distributed between urban and rural areas" means that the two populations are equal. In a line graph such as the one given here, two quantities are equal when the lines for both quantities cross; that is, because the height of the line above the base represents the quantity, the lines will cross when the heights are the same. The lines for the urban and rural areas cross just once, above the time 1900. Therefore, the correct choice is (2).

**Answer every question on the GED.
There is no penalty for guessing.**

The next two questions refer to the following map.

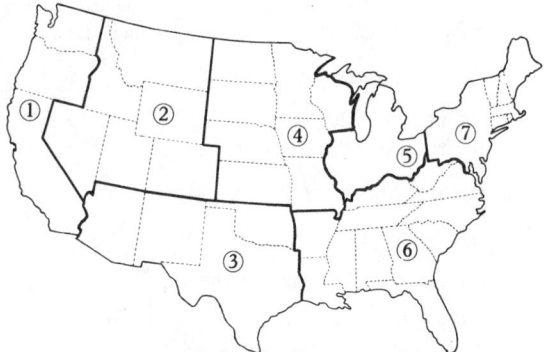

Which area is associated with the Gold Rush of 1849?

(1) 1   (2) 2   (3) 3   (4) 4   (5) 5

Many GED items rely on knowledge that the person taking the test is supposed to have. This is one of them, but you can also eliminate some choices even if you do not remember that the Gold Rush of 1849 brought many people to California. For example, the region east of the Mississippi was filled with people in the 1800's, so choice (5) (region 5) can be ruled out. With only four choices left, you have a better chance of guessing the correct choice, which is (1).

In the middle of the 19th century, American industry was most heavily concentrated in which area?

(1) 1   (2) 3   (3) 4   (4) 6   (5) 7

Make sure that you remember that the 19th century is the same as the 1800's, so this question centers about the years around 1850. As in the previous item, you can eliminate choices (1), (2), and (3) (regions 1, 3, and 4) because these regions did not have enough people to support heavy industry at that time. If you do not remember that heavy industry was concentrated mostly in New England at that time, which is choice (5) (region 7), you still have a fifty-fifty chance of guessing the correct choice.

All of the following are undesirable results of man's efforts to improve his standard of living EXCEPT

(1) erosion of soils
(2) desalination of seawater
(3) destruction of wildlife habitats
(4) exhaustion of mines
(5) pollution of air and water

In this kind of a question, there is a "hidden double negative" that can confuse the person taking the test. The "EXCEPT" in the stem means that you want to find a choice that is not undesirable. "Not undesirable" is not necessarily the same as desirable. It means that you need to reject four choices that *are* undesirable. Choices (1), (3), (4), and (5) all describe results that are undesirable. Choice 2 describes something that can be desirable, so it is correct.

Reading

Directions: Choose the best answer to each question.

What Is Poetry?

What is poetry? Who knows?
Not the rose, but the scent of the rose;

Not the sky, but the light of the sky;

Not the fly, but the gleam of the fly;

Not the sea, but the sound of the sea;

Not myself, but what makes me
See, hear, feel something that prose
Cannot, and what it is, who knows?

Reprinted by permission of Harold Ober Associates Inc. © 1938 by Eleanor Farjeon, renewed.
Copyright 1938, Eleanor Farjeon. Reprinted by permission of J.B. Lippincott Company.

According to the poem, poetry, unlike prose, does which of the following?

(1) relates to feelings rather than to objects
(2) explains things fully and logically
(3) deals with everyday life
(4) concerns itself with things, not people
(5) describes things in simple words

Choice (2) is not generally thought of as relating to poetry, so it can be rejected. The poem does not refer to everyday life (3) or simple words (5), so they can be eliminated. Choice (1) fits better than choice (2) because *scent, light, gleam,* and *sound* involve human *feelings* about the objects that are mentioned.

In a recent survey, three out of four people interviewed said that they liked Soothies better than the other leading pain reliever. Here's what some of those people had to say:

Ms. R. Jones: "Soothies really make me feel better fast. I've told my friends about them."

Mr. L. Smith: "Soothies taste better than the other leading pain reliever. My children chew Soothies like candy. And for the same price, you get more Soothies than pills of the other leading brand."

Dr. Q. Brown: "I recommend Soothies for fast relief. They work best for me."

Soothies cost less than the other leading pain reliever. So get the best for less! Try Soothies.

Dr. Brown recommends Soothies because they

(1) taste good to him   (2) help most people
(3) are inexpensive   (4) bring him relief
(5) are the leading brand

When asked for a specific detail in a reading passage, focus only on the part that contains the information asked for. In this case, you can go directly to what Dr. Brown has said. Choice (4) is the only one with this idea, so it is correct.

Science

Directions: Each of the questions or incomplete statements below is followed by five suggested answers or completions. Select the one that is best in each case and then blacken the corresponding space on the answer sheet.

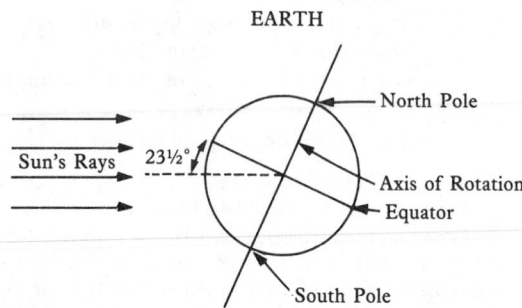

In the diagram above, the sun's rays and the axis of rotation of Earth are both in the plane of the page. The diagram best represents the position of Earth nearest to

(1) March 21
(2) June 21
(3) July 1
(4) September 23
(5) December 21

This is the kind of question that asks you to see something in your mind's eye. As you look at the diagram, picture the time of the year when the northern hemisphere is tilted away from the warming rays of the sun: wintertime. This corresponds to choice (5), which is correct.

Evidence indicates that cigarette smoking results in

(1) cardiovascular stress
(2) hepatitis
(3) whooping cough
(4) pneumonia
(5) pleurisy

Most people think of lung cancer when they think of the effects of cigarette smoking, but lung cancer is not among the choices. Emphysema, another common disease associated with smoking, also is not present. You might think that choices (3), (4), or (5)—all associated with the lungs—might be correct, but this is one of those cases in which the test-maker has been deliberately misleading. If you recognize that choices (2), (3), (4), and (5) all are infectious diseases, then none of them can be caused by cigarette smoking. Therefore, the correct choice must be (1), cardiovascular stress. It is also helpful to know that *cardiovascular* relates to the heart and blood vessels, and smoking is often thought of as being damaging to the heart.

Mathematics

Directions: For all problems choose the one best answer.

During the month of July the Herbert family spent $32.28, $27.39, $37.54, $54.80, and $52.20 for food. How much did they spend on food for the month?

(1) $184.21   (2) $193.11   (3) $193.21
(4) $203.19   (5) $204.21

Speed helps in getting through a test. While this item can be answered by actually adding the amounts, you should notice at once that three of the choices end in 21 cents. Add just the cents: 0.28 + 0.39 + 0.54 + 0.80 + 0.20 = 2.21, so (as could be suspected) the correct choice has to be (1), (3), or (5). Now look at the dollars. Both (2) and (3) have $193. Since (3) is on the possibly correct list and (2) is not, the correct answer is most likely (3). Check by estimating the sum (round off the numbers to whole dollars): $32 + $27 + $38 + $55 + $52 = 204. The correct choice must be (5), not (3). The test-maker was trying to mislead you.

One statute mile is equal to 5280 feet. If one nautical mile is approximately 1.15 statute miles, then one nautical mile is equal to approximately how many feet?

(1) 4590   (2) 5165   (3) 5395
(4) 5545   (5) 6070

With a question such as this one, you may find it easy to perform the indicated multiplication: 1.15 × 5280 = 6072. If multiplication is not easy for you, approach the problem the following way.

The statement that a nautical mile is 1.15 statute miles means that a nautical mile is 15 percent larger than a statute mile. Since a nautical mile is larger than a statute mile, you can eliminate choices (1) and (2) automatically. You also can note that 15 percent is halfway between 10 and 20 percent. It is easy to calculate that 10 percent of 5280 is 528 and that twice 528 is 1056, 20 percent of 5280. Therefore, a nautical mile must be about 700 or 800 feet larger than a statute mile. Only choice (5) is anywhere near correct. The method of estimation is especially good, since the actual product of 1.15 and 5280 is 6072.40, not 6070.

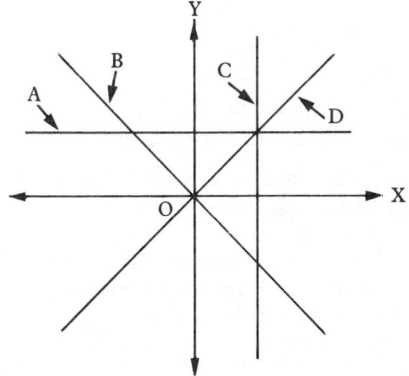

Which of the lines shown in the figure above has zero slope?

(1) A   (2) B   (3) C   (4) D
(5) None of the above

If you have studied slope, it is essential to remember the difference between a slope of zero and no slope. Line A has a slope of zero, while line C has no slope (its slope is undefined). If you have not studied slope, you can still guess that slope refers to the degree of slantedness or steepness of a line. The line that is not slanted, or has zero steepness, is line A. The correct choice is (1).

On the number line above, which lettered point could represent the number $-\frac{9}{8}$?

(1) A   (2) B   (3) C   (4) D   (5) E

From the labels below the number line, it is clear that all the negative numbers are to the left, so you can eliminate points D and E easily. It may help then to think of $-\frac{9}{8}$ as $-1\frac{1}{8}$. Just as $+1\frac{1}{8}$ is a number between $+1$ and $+2$, $-1\frac{1}{8}$ is between -1 and -2, so only A or B could be correct choices. Since $-1\frac{1}{8}$ must be closer to -1 than it is to -2, the correct choice is (2) (point B).

If x + y = 36 and x = 2y, then x =

(1) 9   (2) 12   (3) 18   (4) 24   (5) 27

This problem can be solved by a formal method, but it is probably easier, faster, and just as accurate to treat this as a problem in reasoning, not a problem in algebra. Since x = 2y, the value of x must be twice the value of y, or y must be one half of x. This rules out odd numbers for x, since the sum of x and y would then contain a fraction. Of the remaining choices (2), (3), and (4), choices (2) and (3) are easily seen to be too small, so the correct choice must be (4). Always check problems if you can. If x = 24, then y = 12, and 24 + 12 = 36. (Another approach is to use substitution. Since x = 2y, substitute 2y for x in x + y = 36. This produces 2y + y = 36, or 3y = 36. Therefore, y = $\frac{36}{3}$, or 12. Now go back to x = 2y to see that x is twice 12, or 24.)

SAT

The SAT requires about three hours to complete and consists of two sections, verbal and mathematics. Each section is made up of several subtests. The verbal and mathematics sections are scored individually on a scale of 200 to 800. Guessing is penalized on the SAT. The penalty is so slight, however, that you should guess if you can eliminate even one of the choices.

Verbal

The verbal sections of the SAT contain three types of questions:

- 19 analogies,
- 19 sentence completions, and
- 40 questions based on reading passages.

The analogies usually take the least time per question, followed by sentence completion questions, and, finally, reading comprehension questions. Individual students spend varying amounts of time working on the different types of questions. Some students can answer analogies quickly, but the same students may take more than seven minutes to read a 400-word passage and answer five questions on it.

Analogies. Analogy questions test your ability to see a relationship in a pair of words, to understand the ideas expressed in the relationship, and to recognize a similar or parallel relationship.

For the analogy below, just state the relationship between the original pair of words and then decide which pair of words from choices (A)–(E) has the same relationship.

Remember that a pair of words can have more than one relationship.

Directions: Each question below consists of a related pair of words or phrases, followed by five lettered pairs of words or phrases. Select the lettered pair that best expresses a relationship similar to that expressed in the original pair.

REQUEST : ENTREAT :: (A) control : explode
(B) admire : idolize (C) borrow : steal
(D) repeat : plead (E) cancel : invalidate

The best answer is choice (B). Although both of the capitalized words have similar meanings, they express different degrees of feeling; to (entreat) is to (request) with strong feeling as to (idolize) is to (admire) with strong feeling.

To answer analogy questions, you must think carefully about the precise meanings of words. For instance, if you thought the word *entreat* meant only to ask instead of to ask urgently, you would have trouble establishing the correct relationship between *request* and *entreat*.

AMPLIFIER : HEAR :: (A) turntable : listen
(B) typewriter : spell (C) platter : eat
(D) camera : feel (E) microscope : see

The best answer is choice (E). An (amplifier) magnifies in order to help a person (hear) in the same way that a (microscope) magnifies in order to help a person (see). Note that, in (A), while a *turntable* is part of a larger mechanism that allows a person to *listen,* the choice is not as good an answer as (E) because a *turntable* does not magnify anything. Choice (D) is also wrong for a similar reason: a *camera* produces pictures that may make a person *feel* something, but a *camera* does not magnify in order to help a person to *feel.*

PRIDE : LION :: (A) snake : python
(B) pack : wolf (C) rat : mouse
(D) bird : starling (E) dog : canine

A possible relationship between *pride* and *lion* might be that the first word describes a characteristic of the second (especially in mythology). Using this reasoning, you might look for an answer such as *wisdom : owl,* but none of the given choices has that kind of relationship. Another relationship between *pride* and *lion* is "a group of lions is called a pride"; therefore, the answer is (B) *pack : wolf,* since a group of wolves is called a pack.

KNIFE : INCISION :: (A) bulldozer : excavation
(B) tool : operation (C) pencil : calculation
(D) hose : irrigation (E) plow : agriculture

On the most general level, the relationship between *knife* and *incision* is that the object indicated by the first word is used to perform the action indicated by the second word. Since a (knife) is used to make an (incision), a (bulldozer) is used to make an (excavation), and a (hose) is used for (irrigation), there appear to be two correct answers. You need to go back and state the relationship more precisely. Some aspect of the relationship between the original pair exists in only one of the choices. A more precise relationship between *knife* and *incision* could be expressed as: "a knife cuts into something to make an incision" and "a bulldozer cuts into something to make an excavation." This relationship eliminates *hose : irrigation* as a possible answer. The best answer is choice (A).

Sentence completion. Sentence completion questions test your ability to recognize relationships among parts of a sentence. Each question has a sentence with one or two words missing. You must choose the word or set of words that best fits with the other parts of the sentence. You will find that even if you are not familiar with the topic of a sentence, there is enough information in the sentence for you to find the correct answer from the context of the sentence itself.

For a better understanding of sentence completion questions, read the following sample questions and explanations.

<u>Directions:</u> Each sentence below has one or two blanks, each blank indicating that something has been omitted. Beneath the sentence are five lettered words or sets of words. Choose the word or set of words that <u>best</u> fits the meaning of the sentence as a whole.

Although its publicity has been ----, the film itself is intelligent, well-acted, handsomely produced, and altogether ----.

(A) tasteless . . respectable
(B) extensive . . moderate
(C) sophisticated . . amateur
(D) risqué . . crude
(E) perfect . . spectacular   ● Ⓑ Ⓒ Ⓓ Ⓔ

The word *although* suggests that the publicity gave the wrong impression of the movie, so look for two words that are more or less opposite in meaning. Also, the second word has to fit in with "intelligent, well-acted, handsomely produced." Choices (D) and (E) are not opposites. The words in choice (B) are somewhat opposite in meaning, but do not logically fulfill the expectation set up by the word *although*. Choice (C) can't be the correct answer, even though *sophisticated* and *amateur* are nearly opposites, because an "intelligent, well-acted, handsomely produced" film isn't amateurish. Only choice (A), when inserted in the sentence, makes a logical statement.

She is a skeptic, ---- to believe that the accepted opinion of the majority is generally ----.

(A) prone . . infallible   (B) afraid . . misleading
(C) inclined . . justifiable   (D) quick . . significant
(E) disposed . . erroneous

The words to be inserted in the blank spaces in the question above must result in a statement that is consistent with the definition of a skeptic. Since a skeptic would hardly consider the accepted opinion of the majority as *infallible, justifiable,* or *significant,* you can eliminate choices (A), (C), and (D). A skeptic would not be afraid that the accepted opinion of the majority is misleading; a skeptic would believe that it was. Therefore, choice (B) is not correct. Only choice (E) *disposed . . erroneous* makes a logical sentence.

Nearly all the cultivated plants utilized by the Chinese have been of ---- origin; even rice, though known in China since Neolithic times, came from India.

(A) foreign (B) ancient (C) wild (D) obscure
(E) common

To answer this question, you need to consider the entire sentence—the part that comes after the semicolon as well as the part that comes before it. If you only consider the first part of the question, all five choices seem plausible. The second part of the sentence adds a specific example—that rice came to China from India. This idea of origin supports and clarifies the "origin" mentioned in the first part of the sentence and eliminates (C), (D), and (E) as possible answers. The mention of Neolithic times makes (B) harder to eliminate, but the sentence is not logical when (B) is used to fill in the blank because the emphasis in the second part of the sentence—country of origin—is inconsistent with that in the first—age. Only choice (A) produces a sentence that is logical and consistent.

The excitement does not ---- but ---- his senses, giving him a keener perception of a thousand details.

(A) slow . . diverts
(B) blur . . sharpens
(C) overrule . . constricts
(D) heighten . . aggravates
(E) forewarn . . quickens

Since the sentence has two blanks to be filled, you must make sure that both words make sense in the sentence. If you look for grammatical clues within the sentence, you will see that the word *but* implies that the answer will involve two words that are more or less opposite in meaning. If you keep this in mind, you can eliminate all of the choices except for (B) *blur . . sharpens.* Only the words in choice (B) imply opposition. Also, "sharpens his senses" is consistent with the notion that he has a "keener perception of a thousand details."

They argue that the author was determined to ---- his own conclusion, so he ---- any information that did not support it.

(A) uphold . . ignored
(B) revise . . destroyed
(C) advance . . devised
(D) disprove . . distorted
(E) reverse . . confiscated

The logic of the sentence makes it fairly easy to eliminate choices (B), (D), and (E). The first word in choice (A), *uphold,* and the first word in (C), *advance,* seem all right. However, the second word in choice (C), *devised,* does not make sense in the sentence. Why would an author who wished to advance his theory devise information that did not support it? Only choice (A) makes a logically consistent sentence.

Critical reading. These questions on the SAT test your ability to read and understand a passage. Each passage contains the information you need for the questions that follow it.

Several types of questions are asked about the passage. Some ask about the main idea of a passage. Some questions ask about those ideas that are stated directly in the passage. Some ask you to recognize applications of the author's principles or opinions. In some questions you must make an inference from what you have read. In others you must evaluate the way the author develops and presents the passage.

Following are a sample passage, sample questions, and explanations of each of the questions.

Directions: The passage below is followed by questions based on its content. Answer all questions following the passage on the basis of what is <u>stated</u> or <u>implied</u> in that passage.

Between guilds and modern business firms there is a profound gulf. Unlike modern firms, the purpose of guilds was not first and foremost to make money. Rather, it was to preserve a certain orderly way of life —a way that envisaged a decent income for the master craftsmen but that was certainly not intended to allow any of them to become "big" businessmen. On the contrary, guilds were specifically designed to ward off any such outcome of an uninhibited struggle among their members. The terms of service and wages were fixed by custom. So, too, were the terms of sale: a guild member who cornered the supply of an item or bought wholesale to sell at retail was severely punished. Competition was strictly limited and profits were held to prescribed levels. Advertising was forbidden, and even technical progress in advance of one's fellow guildsmen was considered disloyal.

Surely the guilds represent a more "modern" aspect of feudal life than the manor, but the whole temper of guild life was still far removed from the goals and ideals of modern business enterprise. There was no free competition and no restless probing for advantage. Existing on the margin of a relatively moneyless society, the guilds were organizations that sought to take the risks out of their slender enterprises. As such, they were as drenched in the medieval atmosphere as the manors.

According to the passage, modern business enterprises, compared to the medieval guilds, are

(A) more concerned with increasing profits
(B) influenced more by craftsmen than by tradesmen
(C) more subordinate to the demands of consumers
(D) less progressive in financial dealings
(E) less interested in quantity than quality

SAT reading passages contain all the information you'll need to answer the questions.

Relax.

To answer this question, locate the parts of the passage that compare guilds and modern business—the beginnings of the first and second paragraphs. Lines 2–3 suggest that the foremost purpose of modern firms is to make money. Lines 21–22 indicate that "free competition" and "restless probing for advantage" are central to modern business enterprise. Choice (A) is the most appropriate answer among the choices given. There is no justification in the passage for any of the other choices. Some people might argue from their own experience or opinion that (C) is a possible answer. However, since the question says, "According to the passage . . . ," the answer must be based on what is stated in the passage.

It can be inferred that the guilds were organized as they were because

(A) life on the manors was boring and drab
(B) technical improvements were still improbable
(C) they stressed preservation and stability, not progress
(D) people in medieval times were interested in advancing individual liberty
(E) social status was determined by income

This question is not answered simply and directly in the passage itself, but the passage gives you information to draw on. In the first paragraph, the author notes that the purpose of guilds "was to preserve a certain orderly way of life" and that guilds were specifically designed "to ward off . . . uninhibited struggle among their members." In the second paragraph, the author states that the guilds "were organizations that sought to take the risks out of their slender enterprises." From these statements and the comparisons between guilds and modern business firms that the author makes elsewhere in the passage, choice (C) is the most reasonable conclusion to draw. Choice (A) is not related to the purpose of the organization of the guilds. The statement about technical progress made in lines 16–17 weakens the plausibility of the inference in (B). The passage does not provide enough information to justify the inferences made in (D) and (E). This is a fairly easy and straightforward inference question. You may be asked others that will require somewhat more sophisticated reasoning processes.

There is a slight penalty for guessing on the SAT. If you can eliminate a choice, you should guess.

Mathematics

Three types of questions are used in the mathematical sections of the SAT:

- 35 standard multiple-choice questions,
- 15 quantitative comparison questions,
- 10 student-produced response questions.

Standard multiple-choice

Directions: In this section solve each problem, using any available space on the page for scratch work. Then decide which is the best of the choices given and blacken the corresponding space on the answer sheet.

If $2a + b = 5$, then $4a + 2b =$

(A) $\dfrac{5}{4}$ (B) $\dfrac{5}{2}$ (C) 10 (D) 20 (E) 25

This is an example of a problem that requires realizing that $4a + 2b = 2(2a + b)$. Therefore, $4a + 2b = 2(2a + b) = 2(5) = 10$. The correct answer is (C).

If $16 \cdot 16 \cdot 16 = 8 \cdot 8 \cdot P$, then $P =$

(A) 4 (B) 8 (C) 32 (D) 48 (E) 64

This question can be solved by several methods. A time-consuming method would be to multiply the three 16s and then divide the result by the product of 8 and 8. A quicker approach would be to find what additional factors are needed on the right side of the equation to match those on the left side. These additional factors are two 2's and a 16, the product of which is 64. The correct answer is (E).

If a car travels X kilometers of a trip in H hours, in how many hours can it travel the next Y kilometers at this rate?

(A) $\dfrac{XY}{H}$ (B) $\dfrac{HY}{X}$ (C) $\dfrac{HX}{Y}$ (D) $\dfrac{H + Y}{X}$

(E) $\dfrac{X + Y}{H}$

You can solve this problem by using ratios or by using the distance formula.

Using the ratio method, X kilometers is to H hours as Y kilometers is to $\square$ hours, where $\square$ represents the amount of time required to travel Y kilometers:

$$\frac{X}{H} = \frac{Y}{\square}$$

$$X\,\square = HY$$

$$\square = \frac{HY}{X}$$

The correct answer is (B).

The town of Mason is located on Eagle Lake. The town of Canton is west of Mason. Sinclair is east of Canton, but west of Mason. Dexter is east of Richmond, but west of Sinclair and Canton. Assuming all these towns are in the United States, which town is farthest west?

(A) Mason (B) Dexter (C) Canton
(D) Sinclair (E) Richmond

For this kind of problem, drawing a diagram may help. In this case, a line can be effectively used to locate the relative position of each town. Start with the statement "The town of Canton is west of Mason" and, using abbreviations, draw the following:

From the remaining information, place the other towns in their correct order:

The final sketch shows that the town farthest west is Richmond (R) and the correct answer is (E).

If the symbol $\triangledown$ between two expressions indicates that the expression on the right exceeds the expression on the left by 1, which of the following is (are) true for all real numbers x?

I. $x(x + 2) \triangledown (x + 1)^2$

II. $x^2 \triangledown (x + 1)^2$

III. $\dfrac{x}{y} \triangledown \dfrac{x + 1}{y + 1}$

(A) None (B) I only (C) II only
(D) III only (E) I and III

This kind of problem involves working with a newly defined symbol. One approach is to check the statements one at a time. Statement I reduces to $x^2 + 2x \triangledown x^2 + 2x + 1$, so the expression on the right does exceed the expression on the left by 1. Therefore, statement I is true. Statement II reduces to $x^2 \triangledown x^2 + 2x + 1$, so the right expression exceeds the left expression by $2x + 1$, which is not equal to 1 except when $x = 0$. This makes statement II false. Statement III is more difficult to check, but you can verify by subtraction, or by substituting numbers (for example, $x = 3$, $y = 5$), that the expression on the right does not exceed the expression on the left by 1. Therefore, statement III is false. The only true statement is I, so the correct answer is (B).

In a problem of this kind, if you are able to decide about only one or two statements, you can still eliminate some choices and guess among those remaining. For example, if you can conclude that I is true, then the correct answer is either (B) or (E) because these choices contain statement I.

A number is divisible by 9 if the sum of its digits is divisible by 9. Which of the following numbers is divisible by 45?

(A) 63,345   (B) 72,365
(C) 99,999   (D) 72,144
(E) 98,145

It would be very time-consuming to divide each choice by 45. In order for a number to be divisible by 45 it must be divisible by both 9 and 5. Choices (A), (B), and (E) are divisible by 5, but choices (C) and (D) are not, so you can eliminate choices (C) and (D) immediately. You are given that a number is divisible by 9 if the sum of its digits is divisible by 9. The sums of the digits in choices (A), (B), and (E) are 21, 23, and 27, respectively.

Of these choices only 27 is divisible by 9. The correct answer is (E). Your scratch work for this problem might appear as follows:

(A) 63,345   2̶1̶   (B) 72,365   2̶3̶
(C) ~~99,999~~   (D) ~~72,144~~
(E) 98,145   ㉗

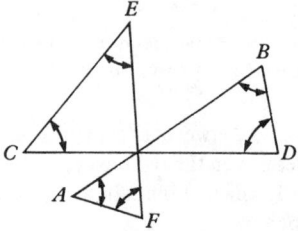

In the triangles above, if AB, CD, and EF are line segments, what is the sum of the measures of the six marked angles?

(A) 180°   (B) 360°   (C) 540°   (D) 720°
(E) It cannot be determined from the information given.

This problem requires a creative problem-solving approach. One solution involves recognizing that the sum of the three unmarked angles in the triangles is 180°.

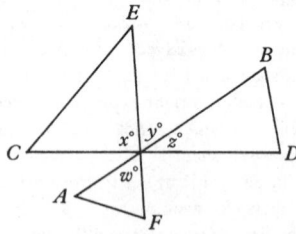

Because CD is a line segment, the sum of angles x, y, and z is 180°. Also, $y = w$ because they are vertical angles. Therefore, $x + w + z = 180$. Since the sum of the measures of all angles in the three triangles is 540° (3 · 180°) and the sum of the unmarked angles of the triangles in the original figure equals 180°, it follows that the sum of the marked angles is 540° − 180° = 360°. The correct answer is (B).

If the average of seven x's is 7, what is the average of fourteen x's?

(A) $\frac{1}{7}$ (B) $\frac{1}{2}$ (C) 1   (D) 7   (E) 14

Do not get caught up in the wording of this problem, which might lead you to choose (E) 14. The average of any number of equal numbers such as x is always x. Since you are given that the average of seven x's is 7, it follows that $x = 7$ and that the average of 14 x's is also 7. The correct answer is (D).

If 90 percent of P is 30 percent of Q, then Q is what percent of P?

(A) 3%   (B) 27%   (C) 30%   (D) 270%
(E) 300%

Writing an algebraic equation for this percent problem not only simplifies the work, it also helps you organize your thoughts. "90 percent of P is 30 percent of Q" can be written as $0.90P = 0.30Q$ (or $\frac{9}{10}P = \frac{3}{10}Q$). "$Q$ is what percent of P" tells you to find $\frac{Q}{P}$ and express it as a percent. $\frac{Q}{P} = 3$; therefore, Q is 300 percent of P and the correct answer is (E).

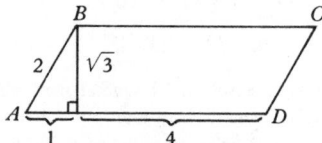

The figure above shows a piece of paper in the shape of a parallelogram with measurements as indicated. If the paper is tacked at its center to a flat surface and then rotated about its center, the points covered by the paper will be a circular region of diameter

(A) $\sqrt{3}$ (B) 2   (C) 5   (D) $\sqrt{28}$ (E) $\sqrt{39}$

The first step in solving the problem is to realize that the center of the parallelogram is the point of intersection of the two diagonals; thus, the diameter you are looking for is the length of the longer diagonal AC. One way to find AC is to think of the additional lines drawn as shown below.

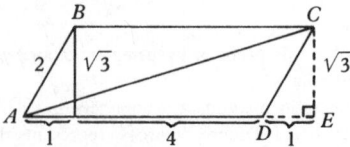

The triangles at each end are congruent (equal in size and shape), so the lengths of DE and CE are 1 and $\sqrt{3}$, respectively. AEC is a right triangle; therefore, the Pythagorean theorem can be used in solving the problem:

$$AC^2 = CE^2 + AE^2$$

$$AC^2 = (\sqrt{3})^2 + (6)^2 = 3 + 36 = 39$$

The diameter AC is $\sqrt{39}$ and the correct answer is (E).

Quantitative comparison. Quantitative comparison questions emphasize the concepts of equalities, inequalities, and estimation. They generally involve less reading, take less time to answer, and require less computation than regular multiple-choice questions. Quantitative comparison questions may not be as familiar to you as other types of questions. Therefore, give special attention to the directions ahead of time. Be careful not to mark answer option E when responding to the four-choice quantitative comparison questions.

To solve a quantitative comparison problem, compare the quantities in the two columns and decide whether one quantity is greater than the other, whether the two quantities are equal, or whether the relationship cannot be determined from the information given.

Problems are clearly separated and the *quantities to be compared are always on the same line as the number of the problem*. Figures and additional information provided for some problems appear *above* the quantities to be compared. The following are some practice problems with explanations to help you understand this type of question.

Directions: Each of the following questions consists of two quantities, one in Column A and one in Column B. You are to compare the two quantities and on the answer sheet blacken space

A if the quantity in Column A is greater;
B if the quantity in Column B is greater;
C if the two quantities are equal;
D if the relationship cannot be determined from the information given.

Notes: 1. In certain questions, information concerning one or both of the quantities to be compared is centered above the two columns.
   2. In a given question, a symbol that appears in both columns represents the same thing in Column A as it does in Column B.
   3. Letters such as x, n, and k stand for real numbers.

Column A	Column B
1. (37) $(\frac{1}{43})$ (58)	(59) $(\frac{1}{43})$ (37)

Because the numbers in this problem are fairly large, it may save time to study the multipliers first before attempting the calculations. Note that (37) and $(\frac{1}{43})$ appear in both quantities; thus, the only numbers left for you to compare are 58 and 59. Since $59 > 58$, the quantity on the right is greater and the correct answer is (B).

Answer the easy questions first.

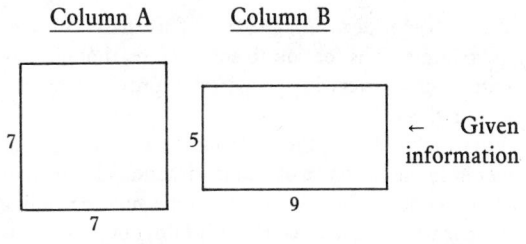

Column A	Column B	
		← Given information
2. The perimeter of the square	The perimeter of the rectangle	← Quantities to be compared

It can be assumed that the units used to indicate measures in a given problem are the same in all figures in that problem unless otherwise stated. The correct answer is (C) because the perimeter of the square is $4 \cdot 7 = 28$ units and the perimeter of the rectangle is $(2 \cdot 5) + (2 \cdot 9) = 28$ units.

Column A	Column B

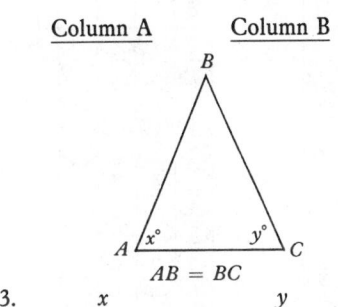

Column A	Column B
3. x	y

Since $AB = BC$, the angles opposite AB and BC are equal; therefore, $x = y$. The correct answer is (C).

Column A	Column B
4. $\sqrt{2} - 1$	$\sqrt{3} - 1$

For any positive number x, the symbol $\sqrt{x}$ denotes the positive square root of x. The fact that $\sqrt{3} > \sqrt{2}$ leads to the conclusion that $\sqrt{3} - 1 > \sqrt{2} - 1$. The correct answer is (B). Note that $x^2 = 9$ has two solutions, $x = 3$ or $x = -3$. However, $\sqrt{9} = 3$, not ± 3.

Column A	Column B

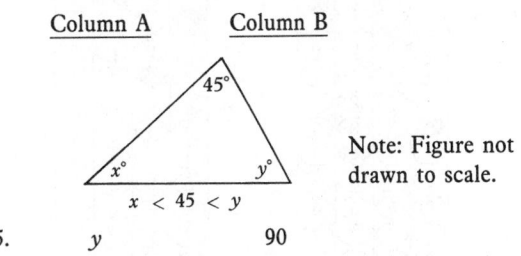

Note: Figure not drawn to scale.

Column A	Column B
5. y	90

Because the sum of the angles of a triangle is 180, $x + y + 45 = 180$ or $x + y = 135$. Since $x < 45$, it follows that $y > 90$. The answer is (A). In this problem, do not try to determine the answer from the appearance of the figure because the note indicates that the figure is not drawn to scale.

Student-produced responses. This part contains just ten questions for you to solve. Here, though, you write your answers in special grids provided on the answer sheet.

For the most part, the grids allow you to write your answer in the form you obtain it—fraction, decimal, or whole number. But spend some time now becoming familiar with all the directions for filling in answers. It will save you precious time during the actual test.

• Write your answer at the top of the grid first, once you are sure it is correct. Then fill in the bubbles, darkening **only one bubble per column.** Remember, your answer counts only if you have filled in the bubbles correctly.

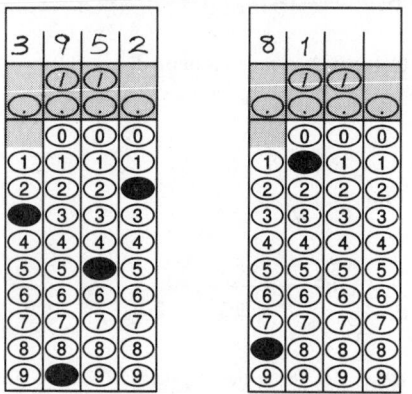

• Start your answer in the left column and, as shown above, do not fill in bubbles in leftover columns.
• For fractions, you must mark a bubble with a slash. For answers with decimals, fill in a bubble with a decimal point. Don't fill in any other bubbles in the column.

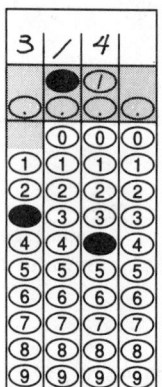 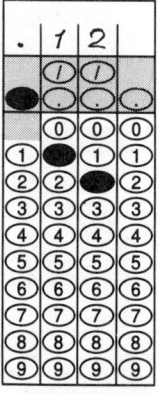

• Where problems have more than one solution, mark only one solution in the answer grid.

• Note that you can enter 0 in any column but the leftmost one (write .61, not 0.61). Also, you cannot use a negative sign. No correct answer in this section will be a negative number.
• Answers with whole numbers and fractions must be converted into a single fraction before entering them on the grid. For example, change $2\frac{1}{4}$ into $\frac{9}{4}$. This is important. If you write in $2\frac{1}{4}$ on the answer grid, the machine will read it as the incorrect answer $\frac{21}{4}$. You could also write $2\frac{1}{4}$ as 2.25.
• Always write in the most accurate decimal you can fit in the answer grid. For example, .88888 . . . can be entered on the grid as .889 or .888. But .88 or .89 would be incorrect.

Suppose you have two lines, one $\frac{1}{5}$ of an inch long and another $\frac{1}{4}$ of an inch. What is the length of a line longer than $\frac{1}{5}$ of an inch but less than $\frac{1}{4}$?

First convert the fractions to 20ths, making them $\frac{4}{20}$ and $\frac{5}{20}$. But you need a length that falls between, so you must use 40ths, or $\frac{8}{40}$ and $\frac{10}{40}$. The intermediate length line then is $\frac{9}{40}$ of an inch. The grid on the left (below) shows how to plot the answer.

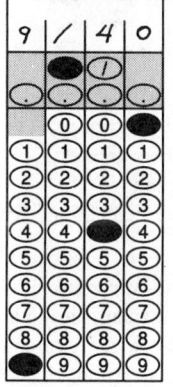 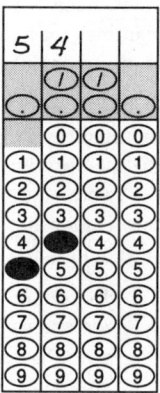

Bob sold 60% of the number of raffle tickets sold by Mary, who topped a school record for one-day ticket sales with 60. The next day, Bob sold 50% more tickets than he had the day before. How many did he sell the second day?

Multiply .60 × 60 to find out how many tickets Bob sold the first day, or 36. The next day Bob's ticket sales were 50% higher, so multiply .50 × 36 = 18. Bob's total sales for the second day amounted to 36 + 18, or 54. The answer is entered on the righthand grid above.

Answer questions even if you are unsure. No points are deducted for incorrect responses.

ACT

The ACT takes about three hours to complete. It consists of four sections: English, mathematics, reading, and science reasoning. The reading and science reasoning tests are based on passages from the social studies, humanities, and sciences, or on a passage of prose fiction. Note that nothing is taken off for wrong answers, so guessing can help when you do not know an answer. Every item should be completed, even if you have no idea of what the right answer is. As the following explanations show, it is often possible to find a helpful clue to the correct answer, or to select the correct answer by eliminating incorrect answers.

English test

<u>Directions</u>: In the passage that follows, certain words and phrases are underlined and numbered. In the right-hand column, you will find alternatives for each underlined part. You are to choose the one that best expresses the idea, makes the statement appropriate for standard written English, or is worded most consistently with the style and tone of the passage as a whole. If you think the original version is best, choose "NO CHANGE." You will also find questions about a section of the passage, or about the passage as a whole. These questions do not refer to an underlined portion of the passage, but rather are identified by a number or numbers in a box. For each question, choose the alternative you consider best and blacken the corresponding oval on your answer sheet. Read the passage through once before you begin to answer the questions that accompany it. You cannot determine most answers without reading several sentences beyond the question. Be sure that you have read far enough ahead each time you choose an alternative.

What teases us with the giddy possibilities of freedom better than a videocassette recorder? There are few things that seem to promise so much for so little effort. Program the right channel, set the timer, and even the late-late-late movie is within grasp. <u>Neither storm nor</u> sleep will keep a
1
well-running VCR from its appointed task.

In fact, a VCR can free us from the tyranny of the television schedule altogether. With video stores almost as prevalent as fast-food <u>restaurants. The</u>
2
desire to finally see the conclusion of a movie can be as readily satisfied as <u>the urge</u> for a burger and fries.
3

[1] Unfortunately, the *us* I've been talking about <u>doesn't including me.</u>
4
[2] For example, I have several versions of Alfred Hitchcock's mystery-comedy *The 39 <u>Steps</u> none of them includes*
5

(continued)

---

1. F. NO CHANGE
   G. Neither, storm nor
   H. Neither storm nor,
   J. Neither storm, nor

F is correct. The phrase *neither storm nor sleep* should not be broken with a comma, so G, H, and J are wrong.

2. A. NO CHANGE
   B. restaurants, the
   C. restaurants; the
   D. restaurants, and the

B is correct. Choice A is wrong because the sentence in question is a fragment. C is wrong because semicolons alone are not used between a dependent clause and an independent clause. D is wrong because the conjunction *and* results in a nonsense sentence.

3. F. NO CHANGE
   G. the urge by one
   H. you can satisfy the urge
   J. the urge can be satisfied by one

F is correct. The words *the urge* and *the desire* are parallel constructions. The other choices upset parallel structure.

4. A. NO CHANGE
   B. doesn't include I.
   C. didn't include me.
   D. doesn't include me.

D is correct. Choice A is wrong because *doesn't including me* is not idiomatic. (Would you say, *it does not including tips?*) B is wrong because *I* cannot be the object of a verb. C is wrong because *didn't* is past tense and does not agree with *I've been talking*, which is present perfect tense.

5. F. NO CHANGE
   G. *Steps,* but
   H. *Steps* which
   J. *Steps,* where

G is correct because it meets the need for a conjunction, *but*, between independent clauses. F is wrong because it lacks a conjunction. H and J are wrong because *which* and *where* cannot act as conjunctions to link independent clauses.

the last fifteen minutes. [3] Either the VCR runs out of tape or the timer clicks off too soon.

[4] The story is building to the climax ₆ the English countryside turns snowy, and the dialogue becomes a steady buzz. [5] Believe me, thirty-eight steps just won't do. [7]

But, I can hear you murmuring, one can always rent a copy of *The 39 Steps,* one that doesn't fade into oblivion. Before the secret of the man ₈ with the missing finger is completely shown and revealed. How much ₉ would it cost? It would cost less than having gone to a movie, in theory ₁₀   ₁₁ that should be a cheap solution, but in practice the result was quite different. You see, I've always had a problem with returning things, from library books to a friend's record. I mean well, but I had tended to ₁₂ procrastinate. With library books I get off lightly—two or three cents per day overdue. With *The 39 Steps,* the bill was a whale, ₁₃ $22.95. It cost me a tidy sum finally to find that last step.

I still consider myself a member of the VCR generation, but if I decide to see it ₁₄ again, I intend to see it at the local theater. The evening will be a bargain even after I pay for my ticket and buy popcorn and a cola.

---

6. A. NO CHANGE
   B. Just when the story is building to the climax,
   C. The story builds to the climax
   D. The story builds to the climax thus

B is correct. The use of *Just when* corrects the run-on sentence by subordinating the first clause to the second. A and C do not. D is wrong because *thus* implies mistakenly that the VCR stops recording because the movie is building to its climax.

---

7. For the sake of unity and coherence, Sentence 2 should be:
   F. placed where it is now.
   G. placed after Sentence 4.
   H. placed after Sentence 5.
   J. OMITTED.

F is correct. The sentence suggests the importance of seeing the final fifteen minutes of the film. Moving or omitting Sentence 2 makes the paragraph less understandable.

---

8. A. NO CHANGE
   B. oblivion before
   C. oblivion! Before
   D. oblivion! Before,

B is correct because it is the only one that repairs the sentence fragment that begins with *Before the secret.*

---

9. F. NO CHANGE
   G. shown and
   H. fully, completely shown and
   J. completely

J is correct. The words *shown* and *revealed* mean the same thing in this sentence, so only one of these words should be used. This makes F, G, and H wrong.

---

10. A. NO CHANGE
    B. being gone
    C. going
    D. having had gone

C is correct. *It* refers to the action of *renting a movie,* which is present tense, so *going* agrees with *renting* in tense. B is present tense but unidiomatic. A and D are past tense.

---

11. F. NO CHANGE
    G. movie, as a
    H. movie in
    J. movie. In

J is correct. It is the only choice that repairs the comma splice—use of a comma without a conjunction to join independent clauses. This makes F, G, and H incorrect.

---

12. A. NO CHANGE
    B. had this tendency
    C. tend
    D. tended

C is correct because the verb *tend,* in the present tense, agrees with *mean.* The verbs of A, B, and D are all in the past tense.

---

13. F. NO CHANGE
    G. *Steps,* the bill was elephantine in its spacious size,
    H. *Steps* the bill came to
    J. *Steps,* the bill came to,

H is correct. It is the most concise and best-punctuated choice. F and J have unnecessary commas. G is especially wordy and stuffy.

---

14. A. NO CHANGE
    B. that
    C. that movie;
    D. *The 39 Steps*

D is correct. It supplies *The 39 Steps,* the antecedent of the pronoun *it,* which would otherwise be too far away, in the previous paragraph. A and B do not supply an antecedent. The semicolon in C is incorrect.

Taking Major Tests

Mathematics test

Directions: Solve each problem, choose the correct answer, and then blacken the corresponding oval on your answer sheet.

Do not linger over problems that take too much time. Solve as many as you can; then return to the others in the time you have left for this test.

Note: Unless otherwise stated, all of the following should be assumed.

1. Illustrative figures are NOT necessarily drawn to scale.
2. Geometric figures lie in a plane.
3. The word *line* indicates a straight line.
4. The word *average* indicates arithmetic mean.

As shown in the figure below, $\triangle ABC$ is isosceles with the length of $\overline{AB}$ equal to the length of $\overline{AC}$. The measure of $\angle A$ is $40°$ and points B, C, and D are collinear. What is the measure of $\angle ACD$?

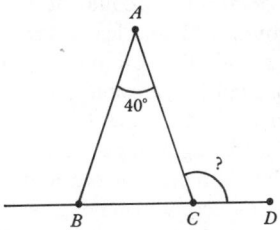

A. $70°$
B. $80°$
C. $110°$
D. $140°$
E. $160°$

The correct choice is C. Knowing that $\overline{AB}$ and $\overline{AC}$ are equal in length, we know that $\angle B$ is equal to $\angle ACB$. Knowing that $\angle A$ is $40°$, the other two angles must total $140°$, because the sum of the angles of a triangle is $180°$. Therefore, since $\angle B + \angle ACB = 140°$, we know that $\angle ACB = 70°$. We also know that $\angle ACB + \angle ACD = 180°$, so $\angle ACD$ is $180° - 70°$, or $110°$.

Read the directions twice.

For additional information about the ACT, inquire at your high school guidance office, or write:

American College Testing Program
P.O. Box 168
Iowa City, Iowa 52243

Mrs. Dorgan's gross monthly income is $1,800. If 15% is withheld for income taxes, 7% for social security, and 2% for insurance, what is her net monthly income (after deducting these expenses)?

F. $ 432
G. $ 630
H. $1,200
J. $1,368
K. $1,530

The correct choice is J. We must deduct 24% (15% + 7% + 2%) from Mrs. Dorgan's gross monthly income to find her net monthly income. In other words, her net monthly income is 100% − 24% = 76% of her gross monthly income. Her net monthly income is, therefore, $1,800 × .76 = $1,368.

Joe has taken 4 tests in his algebra class during the current grading period, earning test scores of 86, 66, 78, and 81. A student needs an average score of 80 on 5 tests to earn a "B" for the class. What is the minimum (integer) score Joe can earn on his next test in order to have an average of at least 80 for the 5 tests?

A. 83
B. 85
C. 87
D. 89
E. 91

The correct choice is D. Joe needs an average score of 80 for each of five tests, so he needs a total of 400 points. Assign the letter X for the unknown test score. Then X + 86 + 66 + 78 + 81 = 400. By subtracting the known scores from each side of the equation, we find that X = 400 − 86 − 66 − 78 − 81 = 400 − 311 = 89.

Which of the following shows the complete factorization of $12a^3b + 26a^2b^2 + 10ab^3$?

A. $2(6ab + 5b^2)(a^2 + ab)$
B. $2(3ab + 5b^2)(2a^2 + ab)$
C. $2ab(2a + 5b)(3a + b)$
D. $2ab(6a + 5b)(a + b)$
E. $2ab(3a + 5b)(2a + b)$

The correct choice is E. Look at the original expression and determine what common elements can be factored from each of the three terms. Each contains the values a and b and each can be divided by 2, so the common factor is $2ab$, which means that choices A and B are incorrect. Factor out $2ab$, and the original expression becomes $2ab(6a^2 + 13ab + 5b^2)$. The part of the expression in parentheses can now be rewritten as the product of two binomials whose cross products add up to $13ab$. The only choice that satisfies this condition is E, in which the cross products are $(5b \times 2a) + (3a \times b) = 10ab + 3ab = 13ab$.

Reading test

Directions: This passage is followed by several questions. After reading the passage, choose the best answer to each question and blacken the corresponding oval on your answer sheet. You may refer to the passage as often as necessary.

I first had to change my ideas about creativity as soon as I began studying people who were positively healthy, highly evolved and matured, self-actualizing. I had first to give up my stereotyped notion that
5 health, genius, talent and productivity were synonymous. A fair proportion of my subjects, though healthy and creative in a special sense that I am going to describe, were *not* productive in the ordinary sense, nor did they have great talent or genius,
10 nor were they poets, composers, inventors, artists or creative intellectuals. It was also obvious that some of the greatest talents of mankind were certainly not psychologically healthy people, Wagner, for example, or Van Gogh or Byron. Some were and some
15 weren't, it was clear. I very soon had to come to the conclusion that great talent was not only more or less independent of goodness or health of character but also that we know little about it. For instance, there is some evidence that great musical talent and
20 mathematical talent are more inherited than acquired. It seemed clear then that health and special talent were separate variables, maybe only slightly correlated, maybe not. We may as well admit at the beginning that psychology knows very little about
25 special talent of the genius type. I shall say nothing more about it, confining myself instead to that more widespread kind of creativeness which is the universal heritage of every human being that is born, and which seems to co-vary with psychological health.
30 Furthermore, I soon discovered that I had, like most other people, been thinking of creativeness in terms of products, and secondly, I had unconsciously confined creativeness to certain conventional areas only of human endeavor, unconsciously
35 assuming that *any* painter, *any* poet, *any* composer was leading a creative life. Theorists, artists, scientists, inventors, writers could be creative. Nobody else could be. Unconsciously I had assumed that creativeness was the prerogative solely of certain
40 professionals.

But these expectations were broken up by various of my subjects. For instance, one woman, uneducated, poor, a full-time housewife and mother, did none of these conventionally creative things and yet
45 was a marvellous cook, mother, wife and homemaker. With little money, her home was somehow always beautiful. She was a perfect hostess. Her meals were banquets. Her taste in linens, silver, glass, crockery and furniture was impeccable. She

50 was in all these areas original, novel, ingenious, unexpected, inventive. I just *had* to call her creative. I learned from her and others like her that a first-rate soup is more creative than a second-rate painting, and that, generally, cooking or parenthood or
55 making a home could be creative while poetry need not be; it could be uncreative. . . .

Another was a psychiatrist, a "pure" clinician who never wrote anything or created any theories or researches but who delighted in his everyday job of
60 helping people to create themselves. This man approached each patient as if he were the only one in the world, without jargon, expectations or presuppositions, with innocence and naivete and yet with great wisdom, in a Taoistic fashion. Each patient
65 was a unique human being and therefore a completely new problem to be understood and solved in a completely novel way. His great success even with very difficult cases validated his "creative" (rather than stereotyped or orthodox) way of doing things.
70 From another man I learned that constructing a business organization could be a creative activity. From a young athlete, I learned that a perfect tackle could be as esthetic a product as a sonnet and could be approached in the same creative spirit.
75 It dawned on me once that a competent cellist I had reflexly thought of as "creative" (because I associated her with creative music? with creative composers?) was actually playing well what someone else had written. She was a mouthpiece. A good
80 cabinetmaker or gardener or dressmaker *could* be more truly creative. I had to make an individual judgment in each instance, since almost any role or job could be either creative or uncreative.

In other words, I learned to apply the word "cre-
85 ative" (and also the word "esthetic") not only to products but also to people in a characterological way, and to activities, processes, and attitudes. And furthermore, I had come to apply the word "creative" to many products other than the standard and
90 conventionally accepted poems, theories, novels, experiments or paintings.

From Abraham H. Maslow, *Toward a Psychology of Being.* © 1968 by Litton Educational Publishing, Inc.

According to the passage, Wagner, Van Gogh, and Byron have in common that they were:

F. psychologically unhealthy.
G. musicians.
H. poets.
J. painters.

F is correct. In the sentence beginning on line 11, the author cites Wagner, Van Gogh, and Byron as examples of talented people who were *certainly not psychologically healthy.* G, H, and J are wrong because Wagner was a musician, Van Gogh was a painter, and Byron was a poet. *(continued)*

As a result of his study of various types of people, the author's previous understanding of creativity has been:

A. confirmed.
B. changed.
C. limited.
D. stereotyped.

B is correct. Choice A is incorrect because in the first sentence of paragraph 1, the author states that he had to change his ideas about creativity. C is incorrect because the last paragraph shows that his understanding of creativity has been broadened. D is incorrect because in paragraph 1 the author tells us that his understanding *was* stereotyped, not that it *has been* stereotyped.

Which of the following opinions about genius would the author most likely reject?

F. Genius is difficult to study.
G. Genius is an interesting phenomenon.
H. Genius is directly related to state of mental health.
J. Genius is much less common than creativity.

H is correct. In lines 14–17 the author states he had concluded that great talent was *more or less independent of goodness or health of character*. In lines 21–22 he states that *health and special talent were separate variables.*

After the first paragraph, how does the author treat the subject of "special talent of the genius type" (line 25)?

A. He considers it the highest type of creativity.
B. He excludes it from his consideration of creativity.
C. He calls all types of creativity indicators of genius.
D. He includes it in his consideration of creativity.

B is correct. The author states in lines 25–28 that he will *say nothing more* about special talent of the genius type. Rather, he will confine himself instead to *that more widespread kind of creativeness which is the universal heritage of every human being that is born.*

The author clearly indicates that he believes genius is:

F. the heritage of each person.
G. a prerequisite for creativity.
H. the product of mental health.
J. not yet explained by psychology.

J is correct. The author states in paragraph 1, lines 24–25, that *psychology knows very little about special talent of the genius type.*

Science reasoning test

Directions: This passage is followed by several questions. After reading the passage, choose the best answer to each question and blacken the corresponding oval on your answer sheet. You may refer to the passage as often as necessary.

Two paleontologists discuss their theories about various characteristics of dinosaurs.

Paleontologist 1

Dinosaurs were large endothermic (warm-blooded) creatures that were physiologically more advanced than the ectothermic (cold-blooded) reptiles. Rather than depending on sunlight or ambient air temperature to warm themselves, as would reptiles, dinosaurs were able to metabolically regulate their body temperatures. Endothermy allowed them to survive in temperatures that would have been lethal to most ectotherms.

Evidence for endothermy includes the discovery of many dinosaur bones in regions of Earth that were arctic during the dinosaur's time. Had the dinosaurs been ectotherms, they would have been forced to constantly sun themselves in order to maintain a stable, warm body temperature. Because this would have been impossible during the dark arctic winter, it seems likely that the dinosaurs were endotherms. Like birds (also endotherms), certain dinosaurs evolved featherlike structures that may have served to insulate them from cold temperatures.

The ratio of predators to prey in some dinosaur communities matches that of fossil mammal communities (low number of predators to high number of prey), indicating that the dinosaurs may have had dietary requirements similar to those of the mammals. Additionally, the bone structure of dinosaurs, with its many blood vessels (highly vascularized), seems virtually identical to that of mammals.

Paleontologist 2

Dinosaurs were large ectothermic reptiles that relied on their enormous mass to act as a heat reservoir and stabilize their body temperature. This forced dinosaurs living in seasonally cold regions to migrate to warmer, sunnier regions for the winter. Likewise, the feather-like structures found on some dinosaurs may have helped shield them from the intense summer sun.

Recent investigations of modern ectothermic communities reveal predator-prey ratios similar to those observed in endotherm communities. In addition, although dinosaur bones exhibit a high degree of vascularization (similar to that of mammals), such a pattern has been observed in the bones of numerous modern reptiles. Also, many small birds and mammals have been found to produce bones that are low in vascularization.

If the theory of Paleontologist 1 is correct, and dinosaurs were alive in Earth's present climate, what geographical distribution on land could be expected for them?

A. They could live only in arctic and antarctic regions.
B. They could live only in temperate to tropical regions.
C. They could live almost anywhere on Earth.
D. They could not survive anywhere on Earth.

C is correct. The theory of Paleontologist 1 states that dinosaurs could regulate their body temperatures. This means that they could live in warm or cold climates, that is, almost anywhere on Earth.

Which of the following would most effectively support the theory of Paleontologist 2?

F. Large, modern reptiles that live year-round in northern Alaska
G. Large, modern reptiles that exhibit seasonal migration
H. Modern endotherms that are capable of lowering their body temperature during periods of hibernation
J. Modern endotherms that have evolved insulating structures

G is correct. The existence of large modern reptiles that migrate seasonally would support the theory that dinosaurs migrated to warmer, sunnier regions in winter. F does not support Paleontologist 2's theory of seasonal migration. H and J describe features that help endotherms to survive. Such features have no bearing on Paleontologist 2's theory that dinosaurs were ectotherms.

When one observes low numbers of predators and high numbers of their prey in a stable community, it can be inferred that the predators are endotherms because endotherms:

A. require more energy to maintain their constant body temperature than do ectotherms of the same size.
B. look for prey only at night when the temperature is lower.
C. store energy as fat for use during hibernation.
D. must run faster than ectotherms to catch their prey.

A is correct. An endotherm (warm-blooded creature) must convert food energy to heat in order to regulate its body temperature. An ectotherm (cold-blooded creature) need not. Therefore, it is reasonable to assume that endotherms require a larger food supply—large numbers of prey—than ectotherms of equal size.

An important concept that underlies both paleontologists' hypotheses is that:

F. endotherms always have a higher body temperature than ectotherms.
G. tropical plants can be artificially grown in cold climates.
H. some characteristics of extinct animals can be determined from their fossil remains.
J. the fossil bone shapes of dinosaurs were similar to those of modern reptiles.

H is correct. Both theories discuss the structure of fossil dinosaur bones and also the featherlike structures developed by some dinosaurs. This implies that something can be learned about extinct animals by studying their fossil remains.

Assuming that dinosaurs were ectotherms, which of the following adaptations might have allowed them to maintain a near-constant body temperature?

A. Regulating their body temperatures by moving back and forth between sunny areas and shady areas
B. Decreasing blood circulation through their bones
C. Having bones that grow only part of the year
D. Increasing blood circulation through their bones

A is correct. The body temperature of an ectotherm is determined by the temperature of its environment. Therefore, by controlling the amount of sunlight that is falling on its body, an ectotherm would be helped in regulating its body temperature.

How would the discovery of many dinosaur bone beds in which very few skeletons of prey occurred affect the two hypotheses?

A. It would support Paleontologist 2, because ectotherms generally require more food than endotherms.
B. It would support Paleontologist 2, because ectotherms generally require less food than endotherms.
C. It would support Paleontologist 1, because endotherms generally require more food than ectotherms.
D. It would refute Paleontologist 1, because ectotherms generally require more food than endotherms.

B is correct. Ectotherms generally require less food than endotherms do, so choices A and D are incorrect. Large numbers of prey would be needed to support endothermic predators, so the small number of fossil prey in the bone beds supports the theory of Paleontologist 2 that dinosaurs were ectotherms. C is wrong because the fossil evidence is that there were *few* prey, indicating that the predators were *less* likely to have been endotherms.

GRE

The GRE takes three and a half hours of actual test time. It consists of a general exam testing verbal skills, analytical ability, and quantitative (mathematical) skills. In addition, test-takers can elect to take one of the 16 subject tests. We cover the general test only, and samples are included below for all types of questions except the reading test. The GRE reading test questions are similar in form to those in the ACT and SAT tests. The GRE can now be taken on computer at over 200 designated test centers nationwide.

Antonyms

Although antonym questions test knowledge of vocabulary more directly than any other verbal questions, the purpose is to measure not merely the strength of one's vocabulary but also the ability to reason from a given concept to its opposite.

Directions: The question below consists of a word printed in capital letters followed by five lettered words or phrases. Choose the lettered word or phrase that is most nearly opposite in meaning to the word in capital letters. Since some of the questions require you to distinguish fine shades of meaning, be sure to consider all the choices before deciding which one is best.

PARSIMONIOUS: (A) initial (B) vegetative (C) prodigal (D) affluent (E) impromptu

The answer to this question is (C); *parsimonious* means "frugal to the point of stinginess," and *prodigal*, which means "extravagant to the point of wastefulness," is the only answer choice opposite in meaning. At first, answer choice (D), *affluent*, may seem plausible in that it may be thought that wealth is an opposite concept to frugality—but it is well known that not all wealthy persons are generous.

Analogies

Analogy questions test the ability to recognize relationships among words and the concepts they represent and to recognize when these relationships are parallel.

Directions: In each of the following questions, a related pair of words or phrases is followed by five lettered pairs of words or phrases. Select the lettered pair that best expresses a relationship similar to that expressed in the original pair.

COLOR : SPECTRUM :: (A) tone : scale (B) sound : waves (C) verse : poem (D) dimension : space (E) cell : organism

The relationship between *color* and *spectrum* is not merely that of part to whole, in which case (E) or even (C) might be defended as correct. A *spectrum* is made up of a progressive, graduated series of colors, as a *scale* is of a progressive, graduated sequence of tones. Thus, (A) is correct. Here, the best answer must be selected from a group of fairly close choices.

Sentence completions

The sentence completion questions measure the ability to recognize words or phrases that both logically and stylistically complete the meaning of a sentence.

Directions: The sentences below have two blanks, each blank indicating that something has been omitted. Choose the word or set of words for each blank that best fits the meaning of the sentence as a whole.

Early ------- of hearing loss is ------- by the fact that the other senses are able to compensate for moderate amounts of loss, so that people frequently do not know that their hearing is imperfect.

(A) discovery . . indicated
(B) development . . prevented
(C) detection . . complicated
(D) treatment . . facilitated
(E) incidence . . corrected

The statement that other senses compensate for partial loss of hearing indicates that hearing loss is not *prevented* or *corrected*, eliminating choices (B) and (E). The ability to compensate for hearing loss does not facilitate early *treatment* (D) or early *discovery* (A) of hearing loss. It is reasonable, however, that early *detection* of hearing loss is *complicated* by the ability to compensate for it. The correct answer is (C).

The ------- science of seismology has grown just enough so that the first overly bold theories have been -------.

(A) magnetic . . accepted
(B) fledgling . . refuted
(C) revolutionary . . analyzed
(D) predictive . . protected
(E) exploratory . . recalled

At first reading, there may appear to be several answer choices that make sense when substituted in the blanks of the sentence. (A) and (D) can be dismissed fairly readily when it is seen that *accepted* and *protected* are not compatible with *overly bold* in the sentence. The sentence yielded by (C) is logically more acceptable but not as strong as the sentences yielded by (B) and (E). Of these two latter choices, (B) is superior on stylistic grounds: theories are not *recalled* (E), and *fledgling* (B) reflects the idea of growth present in the sentence.

Quantitative comparison

The quantitative comparison questions test the ability to reason quickly and accurately about the relative sizes of two quantities or to perceive that not enough information is provided to make such a decision.

Directions: The following question consists of two quantities, one in Column A and one in Column B. You are to compare the two quantities and choose

A if the quantity in Column A is greater;
B if the quantity in Column B is greater;
C if the two quantities are equal;
D if the relationship cannot be determined from the information given.

Note: Since there are only four choices, NEVER MARK (E).

Common
Information: In a question, information concerning one or both of the quantities to be compared is centered under the two columns. A symbol that appears in both columns represents the same thing in Column A as it does in Column B.

Column A	Column B
$(273 \times 87) + q = 29,235$	
$(273 \times 87) + p = 30,063$	
1. p	q

It is unnecessary to do much computation to solve this problem. The sum of a number and q is less than the sum of the same number and p. Therefore $q < p$, and the answer is A.

Column A	Column B
$x^2 = y^2 + 1$	
2. x	y

From the given equation, it can be determined that $x^2 > y^2$; however, the relative sizes of x and y cannot be determined. For example, if $y = 0$, x could be 1 or -1 and, since there is no way to tell which number x is, the answer is D.

Column A	Column B
3. $(-6)^4$	$(-6)^5$

Since $(-6)^4$ is the product of four negative factors and the product of an even number of negative numbers is positive, $(-6)^4$ is positive. Since the product of an odd number of negative numbers is negative, $(-6)^5$ is negative. Therefore $(-6)^4$ is greater than $(-6)^5$ since any positive number is greater than any negative number. The correct answer is A. Do not waste time determining that $(-6)^4 = 1,296$ and that $(-6)^5 = -7,776$. This information is not needed to make the comparison.

Discrete quantitative

Each question contains all information needed for answering it except for the basic mathematical knowledge assumed common to the backgrounds of examinees.

Directions: Each of the following questions has five answer choices. For each of these questions, select the best of the answer choices given.

The average of x and y is 20. If $z = 5$, what is the average of x, y, and z?

(A) $8\frac{1}{3}$ (B) 10   (C) $12\frac{1}{2}$ (D) 15   (E) $17\frac{1}{2}$

Since the average of x and y is 20, $\frac{x+y}{2} = 20$ or $x + y = 40$. Thus $x + y + z = x + y + 5 = 40 + 5 = 45$ and therefore $\frac{x+y+z}{3} = \frac{45}{3} = 15$. The correct answer is (D).

Several years ago, Minnesota produced $\frac{2}{3}$ and Michigan $\frac{1}{6}$ of all the iron ore produced in the United States. If all the other states combined produced 18 million tons in a year, how many million tons did Minnesota produce that year?

(A) 27   (B) 36   (C) 54   (D) 72   (E) 162

Since Minnesota produced $\frac{2}{3}$ and Michigan $\frac{1}{6}$ of all the iron ore produced in the United States, the two states together produced $\frac{5}{6}$ of the iron ore. Therefore, the 18 million tons produced by the rest of the United States was $\frac{1}{6}$ of the total production. Thus, total United States production was $6 \cdot 18 = 108$ million tons, and Minnesota produced $\frac{2}{3}(108) = 72$ million tons. The correct answer is (D).

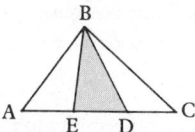

In the figure above, if $AE = ED = DC$ and the area of the shaded region is 5, what is the area of $\triangle ABC$?

(A) 10   (B) 12.5   (C) 15   (D) 20   (E) 25

In this problem, the shaded triangular region has a base that is $\frac{1}{3}$ that of $\triangle ABC$ and has the same height as $\triangle ABC$. Therefore, the area of the shaded region is $\frac{1}{3}$ the area of $\triangle ABC$, and the area of $\triangle ABC = 3(5) = 15$. The answer is (C).

Publications containing current information about the GRE may be obtained from your school guidance office, or from:

Graduate Record Examinations
Educational Testing Service
PO Box 6000
Princeton, NJ 08541-6000

Taking Major Tests

Analytical reasoning

Analytical reasoning questions test the ability to understand a given structure of arbitrary relationships among fictitious persons, places, things, or events; to deduce new information from the relationships given; and to assess the conditions used to establish the structure of relationships.

To apply to college a student must see the school counselor, obtain a transcript at the transcript office, and obtain a recommendation from Teacher A or Teacher B.

A student must see the counselor before obtaining a transcript.

The counselor is available only Friday mornings and Tuesday, Wednesday, and Thursday afternoons.

The transcript office is open only Tuesday and Wednesday mornings, Thursday afternoons, and Friday mornings.

Teacher A is available only Monday and Wednesday mornings.

Teacher B is available only Monday afternoons and Friday mornings.

A student has already seen the counselor and does not care from which teacher she obtains her recommendation. Which of the following is a complete and accurate list of those days when she could possibly complete the application process in one day?

(A) Friday   (B) Monday, Wednesday
(C) Monday, Friday   (D) Wednesday, Friday
(E) Monday, Wednesday, Friday

To complete the application process in one day, the student has to obtain a transcript and a recommendation on the same day. This will be possible on Wednesdays, when both the transcript office and Teacher A are accessible, and on Fridays, when both the transcript office and Teacher B are accessible, and at no other time. The only other day a teacher recommendation can be obtained is Monday, but on Mondays no transcripts can be obtained. Thus, the correct answer is (D).

A student completed his application procedure in one day. Which of the following statements must be true?

  I. He obtained his recommendation from Teacher A.
 II. He obtained his recommendation from Teacher B.
III. He completed the procedure in the morning.

(A) I only   (B) II only   (C) III only
(D) I and III only   (E) II and III only

If a student completed the entire application procedure in a single day, that day must have been a Friday. It could not have been a Monday, since on Mondays neither counselor nor transcript office is accessible. It could not have been either a Tuesday or a Thursday, because on neither of these days would a teacher have been available for a recommendation.

And it could not have been a Wednesday because on Wednesdays one cannot see the counselor before obtaining a transcript. Now, given that the student in question must have done everything on a Friday, I must be false since Teacher A is not available on Fridays, II must be true since Teacher B is both available on Fridays and the only teacher to be so available, and III must also be true since on Fridays all of the relevant business can be conducted only in the morning. Therefore, the correct answer is (E).

Logical reasoning

Logical reasoning questions test the ability to understand, analyze, and evaluate arguments. Some of the abilities tested by specific questions include recognizing the point of an argument, recognizing assumptions on which an argument is based, drawing conclusions from given premises, inferring material missing from given passages, applying principles governing one argument to another, identifying methods of argument, evaluating arguments and counterarguments, and analyzing evidence.

There is no reason to rule out the possibility of life on Uranus. We must, then, undertake the exploration of that planet.

The argument above assumes that

(A) life exists on Uranus
(B) Uranus is the only other planet in the solar system capable of supporting life
(C) Uranian life would be readily recognizable as life
(D) the search for life is a sufficient motive for space exploration
(E) no one has previously proposed the exploration of Uranus

The argument is based on the weak claim that there is a possibility that life may exist on Uranus and not on the stronger claim that life on Uranus actually exists; since logically weak claims do not presuppose logically stronger claims, (A) is not an assumption. (B) is likewise readily eliminated since the author's argument is presented as independent of any comparison of Uranus with other planets. (E) is also clearly not the correct answer: There is no hint in the argument that its author takes it to be a novel one or takes its conclusion to be a novel one. (C) comes closer to being an assumption of the argument: If the mere possibility of the existence of life on Uranus is taken as an impetus for exploration, we can safely conclude that a major aim of any such exploration would be to ascertain whether or not there actually was life on Uranus. But this search for life does not presuppose that the techniques scientists on Earth have for detecting life will be adequate for recognizing possibly alien life forms in every case. Even less is it presupposed that this task will be relatively easy. So (C) cannot be an assumption of the argument. The correct answer is (D), for, if (D) is true, the mere possibility of there being life on Uranus is indeed a compelling reason for the exploration of the planet.

Review of French Grammar

French grammar shares certain characteristics with English grammar, as you may recall from the time when you first studied these languages. For the most part, the names of the parts of speech and the terms used to show how words function in a sentence are the same. If you have any difficulty in recalling the meanings of any words used in this chapter, consult the dictionary in volume 2 of the Student Handbook. No matter how long you have been away from the formal study of French, you will quickly find yourself recalling what you once knew.

Articles

Definite articles

Nouns normally are preceded by a definite or indefinite article or by another introductory word. The uses of the definite article *(le, la, les, l')* are shown in the following examples.

Before a noun used in a general or abstract sense.

L'argent ne fait pas le bonheur.

Money does not make for happiness.

Articles

	Singular		Plural
	Masc.	Fem.	Both genders
Definite	le, l'	la, l'	les
Indefinite	un, de	une, de	des

With a title of office or profession followed by a name, except in direct address.

Le président Mitterrand. President Mitterrand.

With proper nouns that are modified.

La pauvre Louise. Poor Louise.

With the name of a language, except immediately after *parler* and after *en*.

Il apprend l'italien. He is learning Italian.

Il parle italien. He speaks Italian.

en italien in Italian

In the singular, with days of the week, to show regularly repeated action.

Il vient ici le mardi et le jeudi.

He comes here on Tuesdays and Thursdays.

With names of seasons and colors.

L'été est la plus chaude des saisons.

Summer is the hottest of the seasons.

Le rose ne vous va pas bien.

Pink does not suit you.

To express "in" with a part of the day.

Le matin je me lève de bonne heure.

In the morning I get up early.

With nouns of weight and measure to express "a," "an," or "per."

trente-cinq francs le kilo
thirty-five francs a kilo

quinze francs la bouteille
fifteen francs a bottle

Cette soie coûte cent francs le mètre.
This silk costs one hundred francs a meter.

To express frequency of occurrence, *par* is used.

deux fois par an twice a year

With place names, except names of cities.

le Japon, l'Amérique, l'Asie Japan, America, Asia

To express "in," "to," and "from" with names of countries and continents.

For all European countries (except Belgium, Luxembourg, and the Netherlands) and all countries and continents whose names are feminine singular.

For "to" and "in," use *en* and omit the article.

For "from," use *de* and omit the article.

J'ai voyagé en Espagne. I have traveled in Spain.

Je reviens d'Espagne. I am returning from Spain.

With countries whose names are plural and all countries outside of Europe whose names are masculine singular.

For "to" and "in," use *à* and the article (*à le = au*).

For "from," use *de* and the article (*de le = du*).

Nous allons au Canada, au Mexique, au Japon.
We are going to Canada, Mexico, and Japan.

Nous revenons du Canada, du Mexique, du Japon.
We are coming back from Canada, Mexico, and Japan.

With names of parts of the body, and often with articles of clothing, when the possessor is clear.

Elle m'a donné la main.
She gave me her hand.

Il avait le chapeau sur la tête.
He had his hat on his head.

Indefinite articles

The indefinite article (*un, une, de, des*) is omitted before an unmodified noun denoting nationality, profession, religion, etc.

Nationality.

Est-il américain? Is he an American?

Profession.

Il est étudiant et il voudrait devenir acteur.

He is a student and would like to become an actor.

Religion.

Êtes-vous protestant? Are you a Protestant?

Before nouns in apposition.

M. Durand, professeur de français

Mr. Durand, a French teacher

Before the numbers *cent* and *mille*.

cent fois a hundred times

mille baisers a thousand kisses

After an exclamatory adjective (*quel, quelle,* etc.).

Quelle fraise délicieuse!

What a delicious strawberry!

In numerical titles of monarchs.

Henri Quatre Henry the Fourth

If a noun is modified, the article must be used.

C'est un acteur célèbre.

He is a famous actor.

Partitives

A partitive (*de, de la, de l', du, des*) corresponds to "some" or "any," whether expressed or not. *Des* may express either the partitive plural or indefinite plural.

Singular.

Il a un crayon. He has a pencil.

La carotte est un légume. The carrot is a vegetable.

Plural.

Il a des crayons.
He has pencils.

On cultive des légumes de toutes sortes en France.
They grow vegetables of all kinds in France.

Partitive.

Donnez-lui du pain. Give him some bread.

Avez-vous du sucre? Do you have any sugar?

Il a acheté des légumes. He bought vegetables.

Uses of *de*

Without the article after a negative expression.

Elle ne fait pas de fautes.

She does not make mistakes.

When an adjective precedes the noun.

J'ai vu de beaux papillons.

I saw some beautiful butterflies.

After expressions of quantity.

Il a beaucoup de cousins. He has many cousins.

With adverbs of quantity

The following adverbs of quantity, with certain exceptions, take only *de*.

assez	enough
autant	as much, as many
beaucoup	much, many, a lot
combien	how much, how many
moins	less
peu	little, few
plus	more
tant	so much, so many
trop	too much, too many

The partitive is omitted after *sans* and *ni . . . ni.*

Il n'y a pas de rose sans épines.

There are no roses without thorns.

Il n'a ni frères ni soeurs.

He has neither brothers nor sisters.

The partitive is omitted after expressions that normally take *de*: *avoir besoin de* "to need," *se passer de* "to get along without," *se servir de* "to use," *se souvenir de* "to remember," *s'approcher de* "to approach," *remplir de* "to fill with," *couvrir de* "to cover with."

Elle ne peut pas se passer de sucre.

She cannot get along without sugar.

Elle a besoin de secours.

She needs help.

If the noun is omitted, the idea of "some" or "any" is expressed by the pronoun *en*.

Avez-vous des amis? Oui, j'en ai.

Have you any friends? Yes, I have some.

Avez-vous besoin de votre voiture? Oui, j'en ai besoin.

Do you need your car? Yes, I need it.

Pronouns and adjectives

Personal pronouns

Pronoun-verb order

Personal object pronouns directly precede the verb, except in affirmative commands. In the *affirmative imperative*, object pronouns are placed directly after the verb and are linked to it by hyphens. The pronouns *me* and *te* become *moi* and *toi* after the verb, but when followed by *en*, they become *m'* and *t'*.

Me réveillez-vous? Are you waking me up?

Ne les a-t-il pas réveillés? Didn't he wake them up?

Ne les réveillez pas. Do not wake them up.

Réveillons-la. Let's wake her up.

Réveillez-moi. Wake me up.

Double object pronouns, like single object pronouns, as well as *y* and *en*, directly precede the verb, except in the case of the affirmative imperative where they follow the verb.

Je compte la lui raconter. I propose to tell it to him.

Tu me la prêtes. You lend it to me.

Il les y a trouvés. He found them there.

Forms of personal pronouns

| Subject | Conjunctive | | | Disjunctive |
	Direct object	Indirect object	Reflexive	
je (j')	*me (m')*	*me (m')*	*me (m')*	*moi*
tu	*te (t')*	*te (t')*	*te (t')*	*toi*
il	*le (l')*	*lui*	*se (s')*	*lui*
elle	*la (l')*	*lui*	*se (s')*	*elle*
nous	*nous*	*nous*	*nous*	*nous*
vous	*vous*	*vous*	*vous*	*vous*
ils	*les*	*leur*	*se (s')*	*eux*
elles	*les*	*leur*	*se (s')*	*elles*

Order of personal pronouns

me	before	*le*	before	*lui*	before *y* before *en*
te		*la*		*leur*	before verb
se		*les*			
nous					
vous					

Il n'en a pas besoin. He does not need any.
Il nous les a donnés. He gave them to us.
Donnez-le-moi. Give it to me.
Donnez-m'en. Give me some.

Uses of disjunctive pronouns

After a preposition.
avant toi before you
sans lui without him
derrière eux behind them
pour elle for her
When there is no verb.
pas moi not I

Qui l'a dérangé? Elle.
Who disturbed him? She.

Il a plus d'argent qu'eux.
He has more money than they.

As a complement after *être.*
C'est lui. It is he. *C'est moi.* It is I.
C'est elle. It is she. *Ce sont eux.* It is they.
For emphasis.
Lui, il l'a fait. He did it.
Elles ne l'aiment pas, lui. They don't like him.
When a subject or object is separated from its verb.
Lui seul peut le dire. He alone can say it.
Il n'a vu ni lui ni elle. He saw neither him nor her.
With two subjects, objects, or indirect objects.
Lui et moi nous sommes partis hier.
He and I left yesterday.

Je vous ai vus, vous et elle.
I saw you and her.

With *même* or *mêmes* for emphasis.
Je l'ai fait moi-même.
I did it myself.

Ils y sont allés eux-mêmes.
They went there themselves.

Forms of relative pronouns

qui	as subject of the verb: who or which
que	as direct object of the verb: whom, which, or that
lequel, laquelle lesquels, lesquelles	as object of a preposition: whom or which
qui quoi dont	whose, of whom, of which

Relative pronouns

Qui is used as subject of the verb of a relative clause.
C'est l'enfant qui a fait cela.
It is the child that did that.

C'est le livre qui est sur la table.
It is the book that is on the table.

Que is used as direct object of the verb of a relative clause.
C'est la femme que vous connaissez.
It is the woman you know.

Ce sont les livres que vous m'avez donnés.
These are the books you gave me.

Lequel, laquelle, lesquels, and *lesquelles* agree in gender and number with their antecedents. *Lequel, lesquels,* and *lesquelles* contract with the preposition *à* into *auquel, auxquels,* and *auxquelles;* with the preposition *de* into *duquel, desquels,* and *desquelles. Laquelle* does not combine.
For persons, *qui* is generally preferred to *lequel, laquelle,* etc.
Où sont les messieurs avec qui vous parliez?
Where are the gentlemen with whom you were talking?
For things, a form of *lequel* has to be used.
La voiture auprès de laquelle il était lui appartient.
The car he was near belongs to him.
The invariable *dont* combines the sense of *de* plus a relative pronoun (*qui, lequel, quoi*).
le garçon dont le père est médecin
the boy whose father is a doctor

le crayon dont je me sers
the pencil I am using

The order of words in a relative clause is *dont* (or *duquel, de laquelle,* etc.) + subject + verb + object. To avoid mistakes in translation of sentences with the relative "whose," replace "whose" with "of whom," "of which," "from which," "in which."
un livre dont j'ai oublié le titre
a book whose title I have forgotten
Où may serve as an adverb replacing *à, en, dans, sur,* plus *lequel,* when the antecedent is a noun of place.
la maison où j'habite
the house in which I live

le trottoir où la neige tombait
the sidewalk on which the snow was falling

le village d'où je viens
the village from which I come

The words "which," "what," and "that" (= a thing *which,* the thing *which,* that *which*) may be translated as follows:
ce qui, subject of a verb
Ce qui est sur la table est à moi.
What is on the table belongs to me.

ce que, direct object of a verb
> *Ce que tu m'as dit est un secret.*
> What you told me is a secret.

ce dont, used with expressions taking *de*
> *Comprends-tu ce dont il parle?*
> Do you understand what he is talking about?

ce à quoi, used with expressions taking *à*
> *Personne ne pouvait deviner ce à quoi je pensais.*
> No one could guess what I was thinking of.

Interrogatives

> *Qui a cassé la tasse?*
> *Qui est-ce qui a cassé la tasse?*
> Who broke the cup?

> *Qui regardez-vous?*
> *Qui est-ce que vous regardez?*
> Whom are you looking at?

> *Avec qui parle-t-il?*
> *Avec qui est-ce qu'il parle?*
> With whom is he talking?

> *De quoi est-ce qu'il parle?*
> *A quoi pensez-vous?*
> What is he talking about?
> What are you thinking of?

When *à* and *de* are used with forms of *lequel,* the usual contractions take place.
> *Laquelle de ces filles est la vôtre?*
> Which of these girls is yours?

> *Auquel de ces garçons avez-vous parlé?*
> To which one of these boys did you speak?

Quel (quelle, quels, quelles) is the interrogative adjective "which" or "what."
> *Quelle robe as-tu choisie?*
> Which dress did you choose?

> *Quel livre lisez-vous?*
> What book are you reading?

Possessives

Adjectives and pronouns agree in gender and number with the object possessed.
> *Il a pris mon livre et le sien.*
> He took his book and mine.

> *Il emmène sa fille et la mienne.*
> He is taking his daughter and mine.

> *Son père est plus sévère que le nôtre.*
> Her father is stricter than ours.

With parts of the body, the possessive adjective is often replaced by the definite article if the identity of the possessor is clear.
> *Elle s'est coupé le doigt.*
> She cut her finger.

> *Elles se sont lavé les mains.*
> They washed their hands.

The definite article preceding the possessive pronoun contracts after *à* and *de.*
> *Cette valise est-elle aux (not à les) enfants?*
> Is this suitcase the children's?

> *Non, elle est aux filles.*
> No, it's the girls'.

Idiomatic expressions with possessives.
> *un de mes voisins*
> a neighbor of mine

> *bonjour ma tante*
> good morning, aunt

> *une de ses soeurs*
> one of his sisters

> *Dites-leur bonjour de ma part.*
> Say hello to them for me.

> *Serez-vous des nôtres?*
> Will you join us?

The word "own" is expressed by *propre.*
> *Il l'a écrit de sa propre main.*
> He wrote it with his own hand.

Forms of interrogative pronouns

	Subject	Direct object	Object of preposition
persons	*qui* who *qui est-ce qui* who	*qui* whom *qui est-ce que* whom	*qui* whom
things	*qu'est-ce qui* what	*que* what *qu'est-ce que* what	*quoi* what
persons and things	*lequel,* etc. which *and* which one	*lequel,* etc. which *and* which one	*lequel,* etc. which *and* which one
after prepositions	*qui*	*quoi*	

Demonstratives

The following examples illustrate the uses of demonstrative adjectives.

cet avion	this or that	airplane
ce livre		book
cette robe		dress
ces avions	these or those	airplanes
ces livres		books
ces robes		dresses

Uses of *-ci, -là,* etc.

In principle *-ci* refers to the nearest object, *-là* to the farthest, but this distinction is not strictly observed unless objects are contrasted.

> *Comment trouvez-vous ces maisons?*
> How do you like these (those) houses?

> *Je préfère cette maison-ci, celle-là est trop grande.*
> I like this house better; that one is too big.

With demonstrative pronouns, *-ci* or *-là* must be added when the pronoun is not followed by a relative clause or by a prepositional complement. *Celui, celle, ceux,* and *celles* cannot be used alone.

> *Quelle route faut-il prendre?*
> What road must we take?

> *Celle-ci ou celle-là?*
> This one or that one?

> *Prenons celle de droite.*
> Let's take the one on the right.

Ceci, cela, ça, and *ce* are invariable demonstrative pronouns.

ceci	this, it	*ça*	this, that, it
cela	that, it	*ce*	it

> *Ne prenez pas ceci, prenez cela.*
> Do not take this; take that.

> *Ça ne fait rien.*
> It does not matter.

Ceci or *cela* must be used instead of *ce* when emphasis is desired and when "this" and "that" are contrasted

Forms of demonstratives

	Adjectives		Pronouns	
	Singular	*Plural*	*Singular*	*Plural*
Masc.	*ce* (before a consonant) *cet* (before a vowel)	*ces*	*celui*	*ceux*
Fem.	*cette*	*ces*	*celle*	*celles*

and the pronoun is separated from the verb by any word other than *ne.*

> *Ceci est correct, cela ne l'est pas.*
> This is correct; that is not.

> *Cela n'est pas vrai.*
> That is not true.

The neuter demonstrative *ce* is used as the subject of *être* (or *devoir* or *pouvoir être*) only in four instances.

1. When *être* is followed by an adjective, *ce* designates something not previously named, or refers to a thought expressed or understood, or refers to a statement.

> *Paris est une grande ville; c'est la plus belle du monde.*
> Paris is a beautiful city; it is the most beautiful in the world.

> *Ce devait être intéressant.*
> It must have been interesting.

2. When a noun or pronoun follows *être.*

> *Ce doit être celle de mon frère.*
> It must be my brother's.

3. When an antecedent is *ceci* or *cela.*

> *Goûtez ceci. C'est très bon.*
> Taste this. It is very good.

4. When *être* is followed by an adverb or complement.

> *Ce n'est pas assez.* It is not enough.

Forms of possessive adjectives

	Singular		Plural
	Masc.	*Fem.*	
my	*mon*	*ma*	*mes*
your	*ton*	*ta*	*tes*
his, her, its	*son*	*sa*	*ses*
our	*notre*	*notre*	*nos*
your	*votre*	*votre*	*vos*
their	*leur*	*leur*	*leurs*

Note: Use *mon, ton, son* instead of *ma, ta, sa* before a word beginning with a vowel or a silent *h.*

Forms of possessive pronouns

	Singular		Plural	
	Masc.	*Fem.*	*Masc.*	*Fem.*
mine	*le mien*	*la mienne*	*les miens*	*les miennes*
yours	*le tien*	*la tienne*	*les tiens*	*les miennes*
his, hers, its	*le sien*	*la sienne*	*les siens*	*les siennes*
ours	*le nôtre*	*la nôtre*	*les nôtres*	*les nôtres*
yours	*le vôtre*	*la vôtre*	*les vôtres*	*les vôtres*
theirs	*le leur*	*la leur*	*les leurs*	*les leurs*

Le mien...

Indefinites

Uses of *on*

To translate the indefinite "one," "we," "you," "they," or "people" when there is no definite antecedent.

On n'est pas toujours heureux.
One is not always happy.

On ne sait jamais.
You never know.

On ne fait pas cela ici.
People don't do that here.

If faut qu'on se dépêche.
We must hurry.

On ne doit pas toujours parler de soi.
One must not speak always about himself.

On répare notre voiture.
Our car is being repaired.

Ici on ne sera pas dérangés.
Here we will not be disturbed.

Uses of *quelque*

Quelque and *quelques* are adjectives. In using these words there is no agreement in gender or elision of the final *-e* in the singular. *Quelque* and *quelques* are slightly more specific than the partitive.

On va acheter quelques pommes.
We are going to buy some apples.

Quelqu'un, *quelqu'une*, *quelques uns*, and *quelques unes* are the corresponding pronouns.

Quelqu'un l'a cassé.
Someone broke it.

Donnez-moi quelques unes de vos fleurs.
Give me some of your flowers.

Quelque chose, a pronoun meaning "something" or "anything," is followed by *de* before an adjective. It does not require agreement in gender.

Y a-t-il quelque chose qui manque?
Is anything missing?

Oui, il y a quelque chose qui manque.
Yes, something is missing.

Similarly with *pas grand'chose* "little," *autre chose* "something else," and *peu de chose* "little," or "not much."

Common indefinite adjectives and pronouns

Plusieurs, plural adjective and pronoun meaning "several." It shows no agreement for gender.

Nous y sommes allés plusieurs fois.
We went there several times.

J'en ai vu plusieurs.
I saw several of them.

Chaque, singular pronoun meaning "each" or "every." It shows no agreement for gender, no elision.

Chaque artiste est orgueilleux de son oeuvre.
Every artist is proud of his work.

Chacun and *chacune*, singular pronouns meaning "each" or "each one."

Chacun a ses propres traditions.
Each one has its own traditions.

Tout, toute, tous, and *toutes*, pronouns and adjectives meaning "all," "entire," and "every." In the singular (*tout, toute*) without an article, these words mean "every"; with the article, "the whole." In the plural (*tous, toutes*), these words are always accompanied by an article or similar word. As adjectives they precede the noun and the article. These words are never followed by *de*.

Tout chemin mène à Rome.
Every road leads to Rome.

Toutes les bêtes s'étaient sauvées.
All the animals had escaped.

Tous les hommes avaient embarqué.
All the men had embarked.

Tous avaient embarqué.
All had embarked.

Tel, telle, tels, telles, adjectives and pronouns meaning "such," "similar," and "the like." *Tel* as an adjective agrees in gender and number with the noun it modifies. It is preceded by an indefinite article or partitive (*un, une, de*) when *tel* does not introduce a comparison.

Il ne s'attendait pas à une telle chance.
He did not expect such luck.

Tel père tel fils.
Like father like son.

Un and *une* are pronouns only in two constructions:
1. When followed by *de* as one of the objects or persons indicated.
   Une de ces tasses est cassée.
   One of these cups is broken.
2. In contrast with *autre: l'un, l'autre; les uns, les autres.*
   Nous avons besoin l'un de l'autre.
   We need each other.

Même and *mêmes* are used as adjectives meaning "same" before a noun, or "very" or "itself" after a noun; as an adverb meaning "even."

à l'heure même il arrivait à Paris
at the very hour he was arriving in Paris

Ce n'est pas la même chose.
It is not the same thing.

Ce n'est même pas vrai.
It is not even true.

Quiconque, a pronoun meaning "anyone who" or "whoever."

Quiconque le fera sera récompensé.
Whoever does it will be rewarded.

Quelconque, an adjective meaning "any," "of whatever sort," and "no matter what," as an attributive or predicate adjective, meaning "ordinary."

Cette femme est quelconque.
This woman is common.

Donnez-moi un crayon quelconque.
Give me any pencil at all.

Qui que, quoi que, quel que, relative pronouns and adjectives combined with *que* and followed by the subjunctive have an all inclusive sense, and are translated as follows: *qui que ce soit* "whoever it may be," *quoi que*

ce soit "whatever it may be," *quel que soit* "whatever," as in *quel que soit l'heure,* "whatever the time." These expressions are the most emphatic forms of *quelque chose* and *quelqu'un.*

*Si vous dîtes quoi que ce soit à qui que ce soit,
vous le regretterez.*

If you say anything at all (whatever it may be) to anyone (without exception, whoever it may be), you will regret it.

Negation

Negation is expressed by *ne* before the verb plus the second part of a negative expression after it. The principal negative expressions are shown here in two groups.

Group A

ne . . . que	only, none but
ne . . . ni . . . ni	neither . . . nor
ne . . . personne	nobody
ne . . . aucun	no, none, not any

Group B

ne . . . pas	not
ne . . . point	not (less common than *ne . . . pas*)
ne . . . guère	hardly, scarcely
ne . . . plus	no more, no longer
ne . . . jamais	never
ne . . . rien	nothing

Placement of the negative expression

In a declarative sentence with a verb in a simple tense, the two parts of the negative are placed before and after the verb.

Elle ne mange pas. She does not eat.
Il n'est pas ici. He is not here.

With compound tenses, the two parts of the negative of Group A expressions are placed before and after the auxiliary verb *(avoir* or *être).*

Je n'ai jamais fait cela. I have never done that.
Il n'a guère mangé. He scarcely ate.

With compound tenses, the two parts of the negative of Group B expressions are placed before and after the complete verb.

Il n'a lu aucun de ces livres.
He read none of these books.

Il n'a vu personne.
He saw no one.

Additional rules of negation

Only conjunctive and reflexive object pronouns *(me, te, le, lui, nous, vous, les, leur, se, y, en)* can come between *ne* and the verb.

Il ne lui parle pas. He does not speak to him.
Elle ne les a pas vus. She did not see them.

Ne . . . aucun!

Ne . . . jamais!

When the negative is used with an infinitive, both parts come before the infinitive and its pronoun objects, if any.

Il a promis de ne plus la voir.
He promised not to see her again.

The *que* of *ne . . . que* immediately precedes the word it modifies.

Je n'ai acheté que deux livres.
I bought only two books.

Je n'ai parlé qu'à lui seul.
I spoke only to him.

Personne, rien, and *aucun* may be used as subjects and as objects of verbs as well as objects of prepositions. *Ne* must not be omitted.

Personne ne peut faire cela. No one can do that.
Aucun n'est venu. No one came.
Je n'ai rien entendu. I heard nothing.

Ne may sometimes be used without *pas* with the verbs *cesser, oser, savoir,* and *pouvoir,* especially when followed by an infinitive and in some expressions that imply hesitancy rather than definite negation.

Je n'ose le dire. I hardly dare say it.
Je ne saurais vous le dire. I couldn't tell you.
Elle ne cesse de parler. She does not stop talking.

Si must be used instead of *oui* in answering a negative question affirmatively.

Ne l'avez-vous pas vu? Haven't you seen it?
Si, je l'ai vu. Yes, I have.

Jamais used without *ne* means "ever."

A-t-on jamais vu pareille chose?
Has anyone ever seen such a thing?

Rien used without *ne* means "anything."

Y a-t-il rien de plus beau?
Is there anything lovelier?

Verbs

Regular verbs

The infinitives of regular verbs end in *-er, -ir,* or *-re.*
The examples shown here are *donner, finir,* and *rompre.*

Formation of tenses

The simple tenses of all regular verbs and most irregular verbs derive from four forms of the verb.

Conjugation of regular verbs

Formation of tenses

Use the *infinitive* to form:

Future

Infinitive plus -ai, -as, -a, -ons, -ez, -ont.
Example: *donner* ai

Conditional

Infinitive plus -ais, -ais, -ait, -ions, -iez, -aient.
Example: *donner* ais
In the third conjugation the final *e* is dropped.
Example: *rompr* ai

Use the *present participle* to form:

Imperfect indicative

Change *-ant* to -ais, -ais, ait, -ions, -iez, -aient.
Example: *donn* ais

Present subjunctive

Change *-ant* to -e, -es, -e, -ions, -iez, -ent.
Example: *donn* e

Moods

Indicative

		Present I give, finish, break I do give, finish, break			*Imperfect* I was giving, finishing, breaking		
je	donne	finis	romps	donnais	finissais	rompais
tu	donnes	finis	romps	donnais	finissais	rompais
il	donne	finit	romp	donnait	finissait	rompait
nous	donnons	finissons	rompons	donnions	finissions	rompions
vous	donnez	finissez	rompez	donniez	finissiez	rompiez
ils	donnent	finissent	rompent	donnaient	finissaient	rompaient

Conditional

		Present I should give, finish, break		
je	donnerais	finirais	romprais
tu	donnerais	finirais	romprais
il	donnerait	finirait	romprait
nous	donnerions	finirions	romprions
vous	donneriez	finiriez	rompriez
ils	donneraient	finiraient	rompraient

Subjunctive

		Present that I give, finish, break		
que je	donne	finisse	rompe
que tu	donnes	finisses	rompes
qu'il	donne	finisses	rompe
que nous	donnions	finissions	rompions
que vous	donniez	finissiez	rompiez
qu'ils	donnent	finissent	rompent

Don't forget to write

le 5 septembre 1994.

Mon cher George,
  J'avais promis de vous mettre au
courant de tout ce qui m'arriverait
pendant mon séjour à New York. Je ne
sais que trop bien que j'ai manqué
de parole, car je serai de retour à
Paris bientôt. Cependant, je vous
prie de ne pas me tenir rigueur de ma
négligence. J'ai été tellement
occupé que c'est à peine si j'ai eu
le temps d'écrire à mes parents.
  À bientôt.

Ton ami,
Robert

Review of French Grammar

Use the *present indicative* to form:
Imperative
The pronoun subject is dropped from the second person singular and from the first and second person plural. The *-s* of the first conjugation is dropped except before *y* and *en*.
Example: *donne, donnons, donnez*

Use the *past definite* to form:
Imperfect subjunctive
Change the final *-i* or *-s* of the first person singular form to *-sse, -sses, -t, -ssions, -ssiez, -ssent*. A circumflex accent is placed over the last vowel of the third person singular.
Example: *donnât*

Infinitive	-er	-ir	-re
	donner	*finir*	*rompre*
	to give	to finish	to break

Participles

Present			
	giving	finishing	breaking
	donnant	*finissant*	*rompant*
Past			
	given	finished	broken
	donné	*fini*	*rompu*

Imperative

Singular			
	give	finish	break
	donne	*finis*	*romps*
Plural	let's give	let's finish	let's break
	donnons	*finissons*	*rompons*
	give	finish	break
	donnez	*finissez*	*rompez*

Past definite
I gave, finished, broke

donnai	*finis*	*rompis*
donnas	*finis*	*rompis*
donna	*finit*	*rompit*
donnâmes	*finîmes*	*rompîmes*
donnâtes	*finîtes*	*rompîtes*
donnèrent	*finirent*	*rompirent*

Future
I shall give, finish, break

donnerai	*finirai*	*romprai*
donneras	*finiras*	*rompras*
donnera	*finira*	*rompra*
donnerons	*finirons*	*romprons*
donnerez	*finirez*	*romprez*
donneront	*finiront*	*rompront*

September 5, 1985

Dear George,
   I had promised to tell you all the things that happened to me during my visit to New York. I know too well that I have broken my promise, but I shall be back in Paris soon. However, I hope you will not hold this against me. I have been so busy that I have not had time even to write to my parents.
   See you soon.

                    Your friend,
                    Robert

Verbal spelling irregularities

Spelling changes often occur in regular verbs. These changes appear to be needed to retain the original sounds within the infinitive forms. As you will shortly see, for example, by adding a cedilla to *c*, the soft *c* of verbs ending in *cer* is retained before vowels that normally would make the *c* hard.

Spelling irregularities of regular verbs

Verb ending	Change	Example Present participle	Present indicative	Imperfect indicative	Past definite	Imperfect subjunctive
-cer *avancer* to advance	requires the soft *c* sound throughout the conjugation.	*avançant*	*avance* *avançons*	*avançais* *avancions*	*avançai* *avançâmes*	*avançasse* *avançassions*
-ger *manger* to eat	requires the soft *g*, so *g* followed by *a* or *o* becomes *ge*.	*mangeant*	*mange* *mangeons*	*mangeais* *mangions*	*mangeai* *mangeâmes*	*mangeasse* *mangeassions*

Verb ending	Change	Present indicative	Future	Conditional	Present subjunctive
-oyer **-uyer** *netoyer* to clean	*y* changes to *i* before *e* in conjugation, but not elsewhere.	*nettoie*, etc.	*nettoierai*	*nettoierais*	*nettoie*, etc.
-ayer **-eyer** *payer* to clean	may either retain *y* throughout, or change to *i* before *e*.	*paye* *paie*	*payerai* *paierai*	*payerais* *paierais*	*paye* *paie*
-er when unaccented and followed by a single consonant *mener* to lead	*e* changes to *è* when the ending begins with an unstressed *e*	*mène* *mènes* *mène* *menons* *menez* *mènent*	*mènerai* *mèneras* *mènera* *mènerons* *mènerez* *mèneront*	*mènerais* *mènerais* *mènerait* *mènerions* *mèneriez* *mèneraient*	*mène* *mènes* *mène* *menions* *meniez* *mènent*
-eter **-eler** (most verbs) *appeler* to call	the *l* or *t* is doubled to cause the first *e* to be stressed.	*appelle* *appelles* *appelle* *appelons* *appelez* *appellent*	*appellerai* *appelleras* *appellera* *appellerons* *appellerez* *appelleront*	*appellerais* *appellerais* *appellerait* *appellerions* *appelleriez* *appelleraient*	*appelle* *appelles* *appelle* *appelions* *appeliez* *appellent*
jeter to throw		*jette*	*jetterai*	*jetterais*	*jette*
-eter **-eler** (some verbs) *acheter* to buy	follows the rule for unaccented *e*, as in *mener* above.	*achète*	*achèterai*	*achèterais*	*achète*

The auxiliary verbs

Avoir combines with the past participle to form the compound tenses of all transitive verbs and most intransitive verbs. Both *avoir* and *être* themselves are conjugated with *avoir*.

Il a eu besoin d'argent. He needed money.

Il a été malade. He was sick.

Il a acheté des fleurs. He bought some flowers.

Etre is used as the auxiliary to form

1. The compound tenses of all reflexive verbs.
   Elle s'est levée. She got up.
   Elles se sont assises. They sat down.
2. The passive voice.
   Elle est admirée de tous. She is admired by all.
3. The compound tenses of intransitive verbs and their derivatives that indicate motion or change of state:

aller	to go	*venir*	to come
arriver	to arrive	*partir*	to leave
entrer	to go in	*sortir*	to go out
monter	to go up	*descendre*	to go down
naître	to be born	*mourir*	to die
rester	to remain	*retourner*	to go back
tomber	to fall	*devenir*	to become

Certain normally instransitive verbs may also be used transitively, with a corresponding change in meaning. They are conjugated with *avoir* when used transitively.

J'ai descendu ma valise. I took down my suitcase.

Il a sorti les chaises. He took out the chairs.

Il a rentré les chaises. He took in the chairs.

When a verb that is not reflexive is conjugated with *être,* the participle agrees in gender and number with the subject.

Elle est partie ce soir. She left tonight.

When a verb is conjugated with *avoir,* the past participle agrees in gender and number with the direct object, if the direct object precedes the verb.

Il a acheté des fleurs et il les a données à sa mère.

He bought some flowers and gave them to his mother.

Les fleurs qu'il a achetées sont belles.

The flowers he bought are beautiful.

All reflexive verbs are conjugated with *être.* It sometimes is hard to determine whether the reflexive pronoun is the direct object or the indirect object of the verb. In the sentence, *Elle s'est coupée* (she cut herself) the reflexive pronoun, *se,* representing "herself" is the direct object. For this reason there is agreement of the past participle with the direct object. But if the sentence reads *Elle s'est coupé le doigt* (she cut her finger) the direct object is *doigt.* The reflexive pronoun is indirect, merely indicating the possessor. The verb may have but one direct object, so the past participle will not agree with *se.*

As another example, consider the following:

Les chemises qu'il s'est achetées sont belles.

The shirts he bought for himself are pretty.

In this case the preceding direct object is *que* (referring to *chemises,* feminine plural) and *se* is an indirect object. The agreement is with *que: achetées.*

Reflexive verbs may express reciprocal action, that is action which the individuals that are the subject of the verb perform upon each other.

Ils se sont parlé. They spoke to each other.

Auxiliary verbs

		avoir to have	être to be
Infinitives		*avoir* to have	*être* to be
Participles	*Present*	*ayant* having	*étant* being
	Past	*eu* had	*été* been
Indicative	*Present*	*j'ai*	*je suis*
		tu as	*tu es*
		il a	*il est*
		nous avons	*nous sommes*
		vous avez	*vous êtes*
		ils ont	*ils sont*
	Imperfect	*j'avais*	*j'étais*
		tu avais	*tu étais*
		il avait	*il était*
		nous avions	*nous étions*
		vous aviez	*vous étiez*
		ils avaient	*ils étaient*
	Past definite	*j'eus*	*je fus*
		tu eus	*tu fus*
		il eut	*il fut*
		nous eûmes	*nous fûmes*
		vous eûtes	*vous fûtes*
		ils eurent	*ils furent*
	Future	*j'aurai*	*je serai*
		tu auras	*tu seras*
		il aura	*il sera*
		nous aurons	*nous serons*
		vous aurez	*vous serez*
		ils auront	*ils seront*

Uses of verb tenses

Use the past indefinite when expressing simple past tense and when the verb expresses successive actions.

J'ai frappé à la porte et il me l'a ouverte.

I knocked at the door and he opened it for me.

Use the imperfect for past time only when the verb expresses:

1. A mental state.

   Je savais bien que tu connaissais la vie.

   I knew well that you understood life.

2. A condition, continuing action, or an action occurring while another action occurred.

   Je déjeunais quand il est entré.

   I was having lunch when he came in.

3. A repeated or habitual action.

   Je faisais les courses tous les matins.

   I used to do errands every morning.

4. A permanent characteristic.

   Le jardin était plein de fleurs.

   The garden was full of flowers.

The imperfect is used with *depuis* when the verb conveys an action begun in the past and continuing into a later time.

J'étais là depuis trois jours quand il est arrivé.

I had been there for three days when he arrived.

When an action begun in the past is described as continuing up to the present, the present is used with *depuis*.

Elle est ici depuis deux jours.

She has been here for two days.

Conditional sentences

A conditional sentence consists of two parts: a clause expressing a condition, and a clause expressing a result. When the result clause is in the future, the condition clause is in the present.

Si j'étudie, je réussirai à mon examen.

If I study, I will pass my exam.

When the result clause is in the conditional, the condition clause is in the imperfect.

Important irregular verbs

aller   *Present: vais, vas, va, allons, allez, vont*
Imperfect: allais, allais, allait, allions, alliez, allaient
Present participle: allant
Past participle: allé

Conduisez Mlle. Dupont à sa place.

Infinitive	Present indicative	Future	Present participle	Past participle
asseoir	assieds	assierai	asseyant	assis
battre	bats	battrai	battant	battu
conduire	conduis	conduirai	conduisant	conduit
courir	cours	courrai	courant	couru
couvrir	couvre	couvrirai	couvrant	couvert
craindre	crains	craindrai	craignant	craignis
devoir	dois	devrai	devant	dû
dormir	dors	dormirai	dormant	dormi
écrire	écris	écrirai	écrivant	écrit
mentir	mens	mentirai	mentant	menti
mettre	mets	mettrai	mettant	mis
mourir	meurs	mourrai	mourant	mort
offrir	offre	offrirai	offrant	offert
partir	pars	partirai	partant	parti
recevoir	reçois	recevrai	recevant	reçu
sentir	sens	sentirai	sentant	senti
sortir	sors	sortirai	sortant	sorti
souffrir	souffre	souffrirai	souffrant	souffert
venir	viens	viendrai	venant	venu
vêtir	vets	vêtirai	vêtant	vêtu

Si j'étais riche, je voyagerais beaucoup.

If I were rich, I would travel a lot.

The same rule applies to the auxiliaries of compound tenses.

Si je n'étais pas sorti,
je n'aurais pas manqué mes amis.

If I had not gone out,

I would not have missed my friends.

Clauses with *quand* etc.

The future is used after *quand, lorsque, dès que, aussitôt que,* and *tant que* if the action takes place at a future time.

Dès que jaurai écrit cette lettre, je l'enverrai.

As soon as I have written this letter, I will send it.

Quand je parlerai français, j'irai en France.

When I speak French, I will go to France.

Uses of the infinitive

The infinitive may be used as the subject of a verb.

Réussir est très important.

To succeed is very important.

The infinitive may be used as a complement.

Tu n'arriveras pas à faire ce problème.

You will not succeed in working this problem.

The infinitive may be used after many prepositions to express the English present participle.

Il a passé deux jours sans dormir.

He spent two days without sleeping.

The preposition *après* is followed by a past infinitive. The past infinitive has two parts: an auxiliary *(avoir or être)* and the past participle of the verb.

Après avoir diné, je suis allé au cinéma.

After eating, I went to the movies.

Most adjectives and nouns are followed by *de* before an infinitive, but a few common adjectives are followed by *à* before the infinitive: *habile, lent, prêt, premier, dernier,* and *seul.*

Il est prêt à partir.

He is ready to leave.

Elle est toujours la première à finir.

She is always the first one to finish.

When an infinitive is passive in meaning, it is preceded by *à.*

Elle avait encore tout son travail à faire.

She still had all her work to do.

Some verbs are followed directly by the infinitive without a preposition.

aimer mieux	to prefer	*oser*	to dare
aller	to go	*paraître*	to appear
compter	to intend	*pouvoir*	to be able to
croire	to believe	*préférer*	to prefer
désirer	to wish, want	*regarder*	to watch
devoir	to have to	*savoir*	to know
entendre	to hear	*sembler*	to seem

espérer	to hope	*souhaiter*	to wish
faire	to do	*venir*	to come
laisser	to allow, let	*voir*	to see

Some verbs require *à* before the infinitive, as in *apprendre à conduire,* learn to drive.

aider	to help	*renoncer*	to give up
apprendre	to learn	*réussir*	to succeed
arriver	to succeed	*s'amuser*	to enjoy
avoir	to have	*s'attendre*	to expect
chercher	to seek	*se décider*	to decide
commencer	to begin	*se mettre*	to start
enseigner	to teach	*tarder*	to delay
hésiter	to hesitate	*tenir*	to insist on
inviter	to invite	*venir*	to happen

The infinitive preceded by *à* is used with certain nouns to express function or purpose.

une salle à manger a dining room

une machine à laver a washing machine

Subjunctive

The subjunctive mood is used after certain verbs or expressions that indicate desire, doubt, emotion, necessity, or uncertainty. Verbs in the subjunctive are almost always used in dependent clauses. Such clauses are introduced usually by *que* but sometimes by a relative pronoun.

The present subjunctive is formed by dropping the *-ent* of the third person present indicative form and adding *-e, -es, -e, -ions, -iez, -ent*. These endings are the same for all verbs except *avoir* and *être.*

avoir j'aie, tu aies, il ait,
nous ayons, vous ayez, ils aient

être je sois, tu sois, il soit,
nous soyons, vous soyez, ils soient

A few irregular verbs use only one irregular stem for all forms.

faire: je fasse . . . pouvoir: je puisse . . .
falloir: il faille . . . savoir: je sache . . .

Nous cherchons quelqu'un qui puisse faire le travail.

We are looking for someone who can do the work.

Some irregular verbs form the present subjunctive by using one stem for the *nous* and *vous* forms (from the imperfect indicative) and one for the other forms.

The most common verbs of this type are as follows.

aller	*que j'aille, tu ailles, il aille,* *nous allions, vous alliez, ils aillent*
boire	*que je boive, tu boives, il boive,* *nous buvions, vous buviez, ils boivent*
croire	*que je croie, tu croies, il croie,* *nous croyions, vous croyiez, ils croient*
devoir	*que je doive, tu doives, il doive,* *nous devions, vous deviez, ils doivent*
prendre	*que je prenne, tu prennes, il prenne,* *nous prenions, vous preniez, ils prennent*

venir   que je vienne, tu viennes, il vienne,
          nous venions, vous veniez, ils viennent

vouloir que je veuille, tu veuilles, il veuille,
          nous voulions, vous vouliez, ils veuillent

The subjunctive is used in a dependent clause when the subject of the dependent clause is different from the subject of the main clause.

> *Je veux qu'elle fasse sa chambre.*
> I want her to clean her room.

> *Je veux faire ma chambre.*
> I want to clean my room.

The subjunctive is used after certain expressions. Emotion.

avoir peur	to be afraid
craindre	to fear
être content	to be happy
être désolé	to be sorry
être enchanté	to be delighted
être fâché	to be angry
être heureux	to be happy
être surpris	to be surprised
regretter	to be sorry
s'étonner	to be surprised

> *Il est fâché qu'elle ne soit pas rentrée.*
> He is angry that she has not returned.

Verbs of wishing, asking, commanding, permitting, or prohibiting.

aimer mieux	to prefer	*permettre*	to permit
défendre	to forbid	*préférer*	to prefer
demander	to ask	*souhaiter*	to wish
exiger	to demand	*vouloir*	to want
ordonner	to demand		

> *J'aime mieux qu'il fasse ses devoirs maintenant.*
> I prefer that he do his homework now.

> *Je ne crois pas qu'il puisse partir.*
> I do not think he can leave.

The subjunctive is used when the antecedent is modified by a superlative or by *premier, dernier,* or *seul.*

> *C'est le premier livre que nous ayons lu.*
> It is the first book we have read.

The subjunctive is used after certain conjunctions.

afin que	in order that
à moins que	unless
avant que	before
bien que	although
jusqu'à ce que	until
pour que	in order that
pourvu que	provided that
quoique	although

The subjunctive is also used with all conjunctions of condition except *si.*

> *Pourvu qu'il soit là à temps, c'est tout ce que je veux.*
> All I want is for him to be on time.
> (As long as he is on time, that is all I want.)

Interrogation

There are several ways of changing a declarative sentence to an interrogative sentence.

By prefixing *est-ce que.* No change in word order is needed.

> *Ce livre est intéressant.*
> This book is interesting.

> *Est-ce que ce livre est intéressant?*
> Is this book interesting?

By inversion of subject and verb.

When the subject is a personal pronoun or *ce* or *on,* it follows the verb and is joined to it by a hyphen.

> *Est-il chez lui?*
> Is he at home?

> *Est-ce vrai?*
> Is it true?

> *Parle-t-on toujours d'elle?*
> Do people still speak of her?

When the subject is a noun, demonstrative pronoun, possessive pronoun, or indefinite pronoun, the subject precedes the verb and is repeated after it in the form of a pronoun.

> *Votre ami est-il parti?* Has your friend left?
> *Les vôtres sont-ils ici?* Are yours here?
> *Cela est-il vrai?* Is that true?
> *Quel livre choisit-il?* What book does he choose?

The noun subject need not be repeated in pronoun form when three conditions are met: (1) the sentence must be introduced by an interrogative adverb *(combien, comment, où, quand)*; (2) the verb must be in a simple tense: present, imperfect, future, conditional, or past definite; and (3) the verb must have neither an object nor a modifying phrase.

> *Combien coûte ce livre?*
> How much does this book cost?

> *Comment va votre soeur?*
> How is your sister?

When the verb is not a simple tense or has an object or adverbial phrase, subject and verb are inverted or *est-ce que* is used.

> *Pourquoi votre mère a-t-elle acheté ces fruits?*
> Why did your mother buy that fruit?

> *A quelle heure votre ami arrivera-t-il à la gare?*
> When will your friend arrive at the station?

For the traveler

Stores

la bijouterie	jewelry shop
la boucherie	butcher shop
la boulangerie	bakery
le bureau de tabac	tobacco shop
la charcuterie	delicatessen
le coiffeur pour dames	beauty parlor
le grand magasin	department store
la librairie	bookstore
la pâtisserie	pastry shop
la pharmacie	drugstore

English	French
Pardon me, sir, where is the tourist office?	*Pardon, Monsieur, où est le bureau de tourisme?*
It is there, to the right, next to door number 9.	*Il est là-bas, à droite à côté de la porte numéro 9.*
Thank you, sir. Goodbye.	*Merci, Monsieur. Au revoir.*
Good morning, miss. Could you please tell me if there is a good hotel, not very expensive, near here?	*Bonjour Mademoiselle, pourriez-vous m'indiquer un bon hôtel, pas très cher, et près d'ici s'il vous plaît?*
Do you speak English? I do not speak French.	*Parlez-vous anglais? Je ne parle pas français.*
I do not understand. Speak more slowly, please.	*Je ne comprends pas. Parlez plus lentement s'il vous plaît.*
What does that mean?	*Qu'est-ce que ça veut dire?*
A room for two, with bath.	*Une chambre pour deux personnes, avec salle de bain.*
It is expensive.	*C'est très cher.*
Is there a phone?	*Y a-t-il un téléphone?*
What time is breakfast?	*A quelle heure est le petit déjeuner?*
I would like to buy a summer dress.	*Je voudrais acheter une robe d'été.*
How much does it cost?	*Elle coûte combien?*
It is not expensive.	*Elle n'est pas chère.*
Taxi. Are you free? I want to go to the station.	*Taxi. Vous êtes libre? Je veux aller à la gare.*
Can you tell me where there is a good, inexpensive restaurant?	*Pouvez-vous me dire où il y a un bon restaurant pas trop cher?*
A table for two near the window please?	*Une table pour deux, près de la fenêtre, s'il vous plaît.*
Waiter. The menu, please.	*Garçon. La carte, s'il vous plaît.*
I will have antipasto, chicken, and French fries.	*Je prendrais des hors-d'oeuvre variés et ensuite du poulet et des pommes frites.*
The bill, please.	*L'addition, s'il vous plaît.*

Numerals, time, and dates

Cardinal numbers

The word *et* is used in numbers only in 21, 31, 41, 51, 61, and 71. In all other compound numbers through 99, the hyphen is used.

Vingt and *cent* are made plural when multiplied and modifying a noun, but drop the *s* before another number.

> *quatre-vingts garçons*
> eighty boys

> *quatre-vingt-deux garçons*
> eighty-two boys

> *quatre cents mots*
> four hundred words

> *quatre cent cinquante mots*
> four hundred fifty words

Cent and *mille* are not preceded by the indefinite article. Numbers, except *un* and *une,* do not show gender.

> *cent bateaux* a hundred boats
> *six cents bateaux* six hundred boats

Mille does not change in the plural.

> *mille fois* a thousand times
> *six mille plantes* six thousand plants

Periods, not commas, are used with numbers.

> 2.000.000 2,000,000

Ordinal numbers

Ordinals are formed from cardinals by adding *-ième.* Silent *e* is dropped before *-ième.*

> *deuxième* second
> *quatrième* fourth

Exceptions to this rule:

> *premier, première* first
> *second, seconde* second
> *cinquième* (*u* inserted) fifth
> *neuvième* (*f* changes to *v*) ninth
> *quatre-vingtième* (*s* omitted) eightieth

Fractions are formed by combining cardinal and

cardinal numbers

0	*zero*	45	*quarante-cinq*
1	*un, une*	50	*cinquante*
2	*deux*	51	*cinquante et un*
3	*trois*	53	*cinquante-trois*
4	*quatre*	60	*soixante*
5	*cinq*	61	*soixante et un*
6	*six*	64	*soixante-quatre*
7	*sept*	70	*soixante-dix*
8	*huit*	71	*soixante et onze*
9	*neuf*	75	*soixante-quinze*
10	*dix*	78	*soixante-dix-huit*
11	*onze*	80	*quatre-vingts*
12	*douze*	81	*quatre-vingt-un*
13	*treize*	87	*quatre-vingt-sept*
14	*quatorze*	90	*quatre-vingt-dix*
15	*quinze*	91	*quatre-vingt-onze*
16	*seize*	100	*cent*
17	*dix-sept*	101	*cent un*
18	*dix-huit*	122	*cent vingt-deux*
19	*dix-neuf*	200	*deux cents*
20	*vingt*	206	*deux cent-six*
21	*vingt et un*	1000	*mille*
22	*vingt-deux*	1001	*mille un*
30	*trente*	1100	*mille cent*
33	*trente-trois*	3000	*trois mille*
40	*quarante*	1,000,000	*un million*

ordinal numbers. *Quart, moitié,* and *tiers* are irregular. *Moitié* is a noun and must have an article. *Demi,* generally used as an adjective, is connected by a hyphen when it precedes the noun and is invariable. When *demi* follows a noun it modifies, it agrees with it in gender.

> *la moitié de la bouteille* half the bottle
> *une demi-heure* half an hour
> *une heure et demie* an hour and a half

Time

To express time, *heure* (hour) is used for "o'clock." To express time after the hour, the number of minutes is added. The word *et* is used only with *quart* and *demie. Moins* is used to express time before the hour.

In public announcements, such as timetables, the 24-hour system is used. Starting at midnight: *neuf heures* = 9 A.M. 14 heures = 2 P.M.

Quelle heure est-il?	What time is it?
Il est une heure.	It is one o'clock.
Il est deux heures.	It is two o'clock.
Il est dix heures dix.	It is ten past ten.
Il est huit heures et quart.	It is a quarter past eight.
Il est neuf heures et demie.	It is half-past nine.
Il est dix heures moins le quart.	It is quarter of ten.
Il est onze heures moins dix.	It is ten minutes of eleven.
Il est midi.	It is noon.
Il est minuit.	It is midnight.

Dates

The cardinal numbers are used to express dates, except for the first day of a month, week, etc. The masculine definite article always precedes the date.

le premier avril April first
le vingt-cinq décembre December 25th
dix-neuf cent vingt-huit 1928
en dix-sept cent quatre-vingt-neuf in 1789

Months, days, seasons

janvier	January	*lundi*	Monday
février	February	*mardi*	Tuesday
mars	March	*mercredi*	Wednesday
avril	April	*jeudi*	Thursday
mai	May	*vendredi*	Friday
juin	June	*samedi*	Saturday
juillet	July	*dimanche*	Sunday
août	August		
septembre	September	*le printemps*	spring
octobre	October	*l'été*	summer
novembre	November	*l'automne*	autumn
décembre	December	*l'hiver*	winter

Countries

l'Allemagne	Germany
l'Angleterre	England
l'Autriche	Austria
la Belgique	Belgium
l'Espagne	Spain
la Hongrie	Hungary
l'Irlande	Ireland
l'Italie	Italy
les Pays Bas	Netherlands
la Pologne	Poland
le Portugal	Portugal
la Suisse	Switzerland

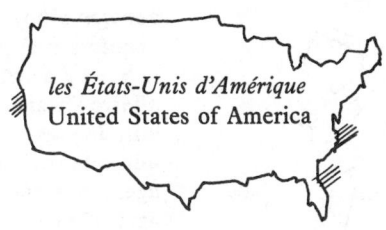

les États-Unis d'Amérique
United States of America

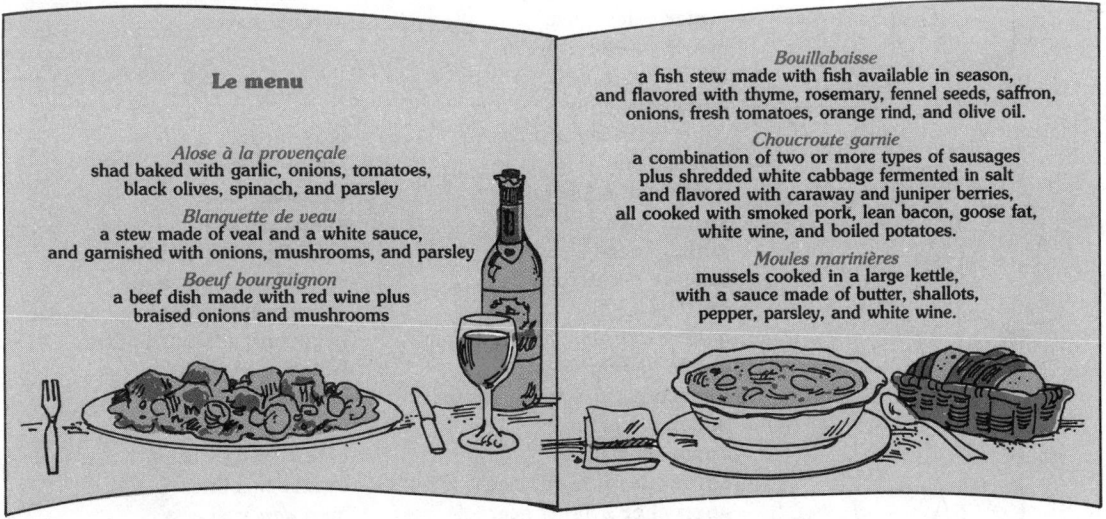

Le menu

Alose à la provençale
shad baked with garlic, onions, tomatoes, black olives, spinach, and parsley

Blanquette de veau
a stew made of veal and a white sauce, and garnished with onions, mushrooms, and parsley

Boeuf bourguignon
a beef dish made with red wine plus braised onions and mushrooms

Bouillabaisse
a fish stew made with fish available in season, and flavored with thyme, rosemary, fennel seeds, saffron, onions, fresh tomatoes, orange rind, and olive oil.

Choucroute garnie
a combination of two or more types of sausages plus shredded white cabbage fermented in salt and flavored with caraway and juniper berries, all cooked with smoked pork, lean bacon, goose fat, white wine, and boiled potatoes.

Moules marinières
mussels cooked in a large kettle, with a sauce made of butter, shallots, pepper, parsley, and white wine.

Talking with a waiter

Une table pour quatre, s'il vous plaît.	A table for four, please.
La carte, s'il vous plaît.	The menu, please.
Une tasse de café avec du pain et du beurre, s'il vous plaît.	A cup of coffee and bread and butter, please.
Je prendrais du boeuf bourguignon.	I will have *boeuf bourguignon.*
Une bouteille de vin du pays, s'il vous plaît.	A bottle of the local wine, please.
Donnez-moi du beurre, s'il vous plaît.	Please give me some butter.
Avez-vous de la crème?	Have you any cream?
L'addition, s'il vous plaît.	The check, please.

les cheveux hair
les yeux eyes
les oreilles ears
le nez nose
les joues cheeks
la bouche mouth
les dents teeth
le menton chin
les lèvres lips

La figure The face

Dictionary

Le corps humain The human body

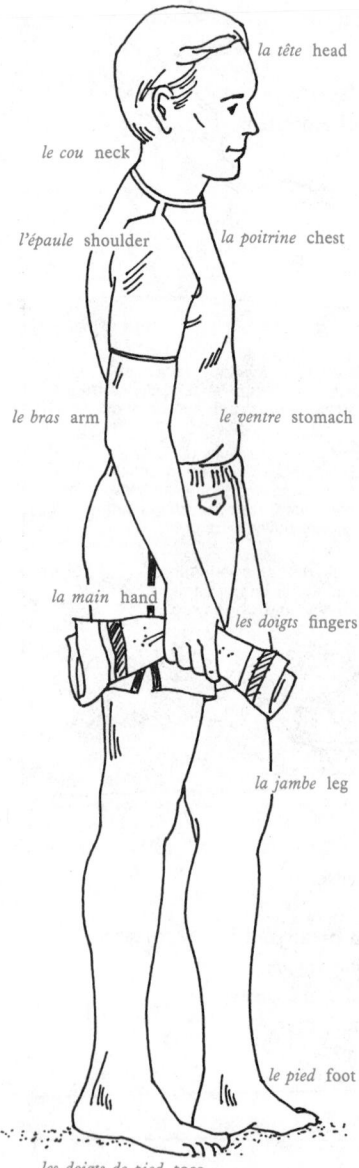

la tête head
le cou neck
l'épaule shoulder
la poitrine chest
le bras arm
le ventre stomach
la main hand
les doigts fingers
la jambe leg
le pied foot

les doigts de pied toes

Dictionary abbreviations. Nouns are identified as masculine *(m)* or feminine *(f)*. Adjectives are identified as *adj*, adverbs as *adv*, conjunctions as *conj*, interjections as *interj*, prepositions as *prep*, pronouns as *pron*, and verbs as *v.* Plurals are identified as *pl.*

French-English

A

à *prep* at, in, to
absence *f* absence
accepter *v* accept
accident *m* accident
accourir *v* run up
accueillir *v* welcome
acheter *v* buy
acquérir *v* acquire, get
activité *f* activity
affaire *f* matter, business
afin de *prep* in order to
afin que *conj* in order that
agent *m* agent
agréable *adj* pleasing
aider *v* help
aimable *adj* friendly, pleasant
aimer *v* love, like
aimer mieux *v* prefer
aller *v* go
amener *v* bring
Américain *adj and noun m* American
Amérique *f* America
ami *m* friend
amie *f* friend
amuser *v* entertain
an *m* year
ancien *adj* old, ancient, former
année *f* year
appartenir *v* belong, pertain
appeler *v* call
apporter *v* bring
apprendre *v* learn, teach
approcher *v* bring near
approuver *v* approve
après *adv* afterward
après *prep* after
après que *conj* after
arbre *m* tree
argent *m* money, silver
arrêter *v* stop
arriver *v* arrive, happen
asseoir *v* seat, **s'asseoir** sit down
assez *adv* enough, **assez de** enough of

attendre *v* wait for, expect
aucun *adj and pron* none, no one, not one, not any
auprès de *prep* near, beside
aussi *adv* also, as, and so
aussitôt *adv* immediately
aussitôt que *conj* as soon as
autant *adv* as much
autant que *conj* as much as
autre *adj* other
autrefois *adv* formerly
avancer *v* move, go forward
avant *adv and prep* before
avertir *v* warn, give notice
avertissement *m* warning
avion *m* plane
avis *m* notice, opinion
avocat *m* lawyer
avoir *v* have

B

bain *m* bath
baiser *m* kiss
bataille *f* battle
bateau *m* boat
battre *v* beat, **se battre** fight
beau, bel *adj m,* **belle** *f* beautiful, handsome, fine, fair
beaucoup *adv* much, many
bénéfice *m* profit
besoin *m* need, **avoir besoin** *v* need
bête *f* animal, beast, brute, fool
beurre *m* butter
bien *adv* well
bien que *conj* although
bière *f* beer
billet *m* ticket
blesser *v* wound, hurt
boire *v* drink
bois *m* wood, forest
boisson *f* drink, beverage
bon *adj m,* **bonne** *f* good
bonheur *m* happiness
bouteille *f* bottle
bruit *m* noise, rumor

Review of French Grammar

brun *adj* brown, brunette
bureau *m* desk, office
but *m* purpose, aim, goal

C

cadeau *m* gift, present
café *m* coffee
carte *f* card, map, chart
casser *v* break
causer *v* chat, cause
céder *v* yield, give in
célèbre *adj* famous
cesser *v* stop, cease
chaise *f* chair
chance *f* luck
chanson *f* song
chanter *v* sing
chapeau *m* hat
chaque *adj* each
charpentier *m* carpenter
chaud *adj* hot
chemin *m* road, path
chemise *f* shirt
chercher *v* seek, look for
chez *prep* at (the home, shop, etc. of . . .)
choisir *v* choose
chose *f* thing, object
clef, clé *f* key
client *m* customer
colère *f* anger, **en colère** angry
colis *m* package
combien *adv* how much, how many
comme *adv* as, how, *conj* as, like
commencer *v* begin, start
comment *adv* how
comprendre *v* understand
compter *v* count, **compter sur** count on
conduire *v* lead, take, drive
conférence *f* lecture, conference
connaissance *f* acquaintance, knowledge
connaître *v* be acquainted with, know
consentir *v* consent
construire *v* build
contenir *v* contain, restrain
content *adj* content, glad
corriger *v* correct
costume *m* suit, costume
coucher *v* put to bed, **se coucher** lie down

coupable *adj* guilty
couper *v* cut
courage *m* courage
courir *v* run
course *f* race, errand
couteau *m* knife
coûter *v* cost
couvrir *v* cover
craindre *v* fear
crainte *f* fear
crayon *m* pencil
croire *v* believe
cueillir *v* gather
cuire *v* cook
cultiver *v* cultivate

D

dame *f* lady
décider *v* decide
déclarer *v* declare, affirm
découvrir *v* discover
décrire *v* describe
défendre *v* defend, forbid
déjeuner *m* lunch, **petit déjeuner** breakfast
délicieux *adj m*, **délicieuse** *f* delicious
demain *adv* tomorrow
demander *v* ask for
demeurer *v* dwell
demi *adj and noun m* half
départ *m* departure
dépit *m* spite, **en dépit de** in spite of
depuis *adv and prep* since
déranger *v* disturb
dernier *adj m* last
dès *prep* since, **dès que** *conj* as soon as
descendre *v* go down, come down
désirer *v* desire, wish
désoler *v* grieve
dessous *m* underside, **au-dessous de,** beneath
dessus *adv* above
devenir *v* become
deviner *v* guess
devoir *m* duty, homework
devoir *v* owe, have to, ought
difficile *adj* difficult, hard
dire *v* say, tell
doigt *m* finger
domestique *m and f* servant

dommage *m* damage, **c'est dommage** that's too bad
donner *v* give
dormir *v* sleep
douter *v* doubt
droit *m* right, law
droit *adj and adv* right, fair
droite *f* right, **à droite** to the right

E

eau *f* water
éblouir *v* dazzle
écarter *v* put aside
échouer *v* fail
écouter *v* listen
écrire *v* write
église *f* church
élève *m or f* pupil
embarquer *v* embark
emmener *v* take away, lead away
empêcher *v* prevent, hinder
encore *adv* again, still, yet
encre *f* ink
endroit *m* place
enfant *m or f* child
enfin *adv* at last, finally
enseigner *v* teach
entendre *v* hear
entrer *v* enter, come in
envie *f* envy, desire, **avoir envie de** feel like
envoyer *v* send, **envoyer chercher** send for
épine *f* thorn, spine
éprouver *v* experience, feel
erreur *f* error, mistake
escalier *m* stairway
espérer *v* hope, await
essuyer *v* wipe
et *conj* and
été *m* summer
éteindre *v* extinguish
étendre *v* extend, stretch out
étonner *v* surprise
étrange *adj* strange, curious
étudiant *m* student
étudier *v* study
évident *adj* evident, obvious
éviter *v* avoid, spare
examen *m* examination, test
exiger *v* require, demand
exprimer *v* express

F

fable *f* fable, story
fabriquer *v* manufacture
fâcher *v* anger, **se fâcher**
  become angry
facile *adj* easy
faim *f* hunger
faire *v* do, make
falloir *v* be necessary
famille *f* family
fatigué *adj* tired
faute *f* fault, mistake
femme *f* woman, wife
fermer *v* close
fête *f* celebration, holiday, party
feuille *f* leaf, sheet
fier *adj* proud
figure *f* face
fille *f* daughter, girl
fils *m* son
fin *f* end
finir *v* finish
fleur *f* flower
fois *f* instance, time
forcer *v* compel, force
fraise *f* strawberry
franc *m* franc, **franc** *adj m*
  frank, open
franche *adj f* frank, open
frapper *v* knock, strike
frère *m* brother
froid *m and adj* cold
fuir *v* flee, shun

G

gagner *v* acquire, gain, win
gant *m* glove
garçon *m* boy, waiter
garder *v* keep, guard
gare *f* station
gêner *v* hinder, bother
goûter *v* taste
grand *adj* large, tall, great
grange *f* barn
guère *adv* hardly
guerre *f* war

H

habile *adj* able, clever
habiller *v* dress, **s'habiller** put
  on one's clothing
habit *m* clothes, coat

habiter *v* inhabit, dwell in
habituer *v* accustom, familiarize
haut *adj* high, **à haute voix**
  aloud, **en haut** upstairs
hésiter *v* hesitate
heure *f* hour, time, **de bonne**
  heure early
heureux *adj m,* **heureuse** *f*
  happy, lucky
hier *adv* yesterday
histoire *f* history, story
homme *m* man
honnête *adj* honest, upright
horloge *f* clock
hôte *m* host, guest

I

ici *adv* here
informer *v* inform, **s'informer**
  make inquiries
ingénieur *m* engineer
intelligent *adj* bright, clever
intéresser *v* interest, concern
interrompre *v* interrupt
inutile *adj* useless, unnecessary
inviter *v* invite

J

jamais *adv* ever, never, **à jamais**
  forever
jardin *m* garden
jaune *adj* yellow
jeter *v* throw, cast
jeune *adj* young
joli *adj* pretty
jouet *m* toy
jour *m* day
jus *m* juice
jusqu'à *prep* up to, as far as,
  until
juste *adj* just, right, exact
juste *adv* just, exactly

K

kilo *m* kilogram

L

lac *m* lake
lacet *m* shoelace
laisser *v* allow
lancer *v* throw

langage *m* language
langue *f* tongue, language
larme *f* tear
laver *v* wash, **se laver** wash
  oneself
leçon *f* lesson
légume *m* vegetable
lent *adj* slow
lettre *f* letter
lever *v* raise
ligne *f* line
lire *v* read
lit *m* bed
livre *m* book, **livre** *f* pound
longtemps *adv* longtime
lorsque *conj* when
louer *v* rent
loyer *m* rent
luire *v* gleam

M

magasin *m* store
main *f* hand
maintenant *adv* now
mais *conj* but
maison *f* house
malade *adj* ill
malle *f* trunk
manger *v* eat
manière *f* manner
manquer *v* miss, fail, lack
marchand *m* merchant
marier *v* marry
matin *m* morning
mauvais *adj* bad
médecin *m* physician, doctor
méfier *v* **se méfier** mistrust
meilleur *adj* better, **le meilleur**
  the best
même *adj* same
mener *v* lead
mentir *v* lie
mère *f* mother
métier *m* trade, craft, loom
mètre *m* meter
mettre *v* put, set
meuble *m* furniture
midi *m* noon, midday
mieux *adv* better, best
mille *m* mile, *adj and noun m*
  thousand
minuit *m* midnight
moins *adv* less, least
mois *m* month

moitié *f* half
monde *m* world, society
monter *v* go up, take up
moquer *v* **se moquer de** make fun of, mock
mourir *v* die

N

nager *v* swim, float
naissance *f* birth
naître *v* be born
négliger *v* neglect
neige *f* snow
nettoyer *v* clean
neuf *adj and noun m* nine
neuf *adj m,* **neuve** *f* new
ni *conj* nor, **ni . . . ni** neither . . . nor
nier *v* deny
nom *m* name, noun
note *f* grade, note
nouvelle *f* news
nuire *v* harm
nuit *f* night

O

obéir *v* obey
observer *v* observe, notice
oeil *m* eye, *pl* **yeux**
oeuvre *f* work, labor
offrir *v* offer, present
or *m* gold
orage *m* storm
ordonner *v* order, command
ordre *m* order
orgueilleux *adj m,* **orgueilleuse** *f* proud, haughty
oser *v* dare
ou *conj* or
où *adv* where, at, on
oublier *v* forget
oui *adv* yes
ouvrir *v* open

P

page *m* pageboy
page *f* page
pain *m* bread
paix *f* peace
pâlir *v* become pale, fade
panne *f* accident, lard
papier *m* paper

papillon *m* butterfly
paraître *v* appear, seem
pardessus *m* overcoat
pardonner *v* pardon
pareil *adj* like
parier *v* bet
parler *v* speak, talk
parmi *prep* among
partager *v* divide, share
partie *f* part, party
partir *v* leave, go away
passer *v* pass, go by
patiner *v* skate
pauvre *adj* poor
pavé *m* pavement
payer *v* pay
pays *m* country
peine *f* pain, penalty
pendant *prep* during
pendant que *conj* while
penser *v* think, **penser à** think of
perdre *v* lose
père *m* father
péril *m* danger
périr *v* perish
permettre *v* allow, permit
personne *f* person
personne *pron* no one, nobody
petit *adj* small, little, petty
peu *m* little, few
peur *f* fear
pièce *f* piece, coin, play
pied *m* foot
pierre *f* stone
plaindre *v* pity
plaire *v* please
plante *f* plant
plein *adj* full
pleurer *v* weep, cry, mourn
pleuvoir *v* rain
plier *v* fold
pluie *f* rain
plume *f* pen, feather
plupart *f* majority, most
plus *adv* more, most
plusieurs *adj and pron* several
poche *f* pocket
pomme *f* apple, **pomme de terre** potato
porte *f* door
porter *v* carry, bear
pourquoi *adv* why
pourvu que *conj* provided that
pouvoir *v* be able, can

préférer *v* prefer
premier *adj* first
prendre *v* take
près *adv* near, **près de** *prep* near
présenter *v* introduce, present
prêt *adj* ready
prêter *v* lend
projet *m* project, plan
promener *v* take out walking
promettre *v* promise
propos *m* talk, subject, **à propos de** with regard to
propre *adj* own, very, same, clean
propriétaire *m* proprietor
protester *v* protest
provoquer *v* provoke
puis *adv* then

Q

qualifier *v* qualify
qualité *f* quality, nature
quand *conj* when
quart *m* quarter, fourth
quelque *adj* some, any, **quelque chose** something
quelquefois *adv* sometimes
quelqu'un *pron* someone, anyone
quitter *v* leave
quoique *conj* although
quotidien *adj* daily

R

raconter *v* tell, narrate
rafraîchir *v* cool, refresh
raison *f* reason, **avoir raison** be right
ralentir *v* slow down, slacken
ramasser *v* pick up
ramener *v* bring back, take back
rapide *adj* swift
rappeler *v* remember
ravi *adj* delighted
recevoir *v* receive
récompense *f* reward
reconnaissance *f* gratitude, recognition
reconnaître *v* recognize
reculer *v* fall back, go back
réfléchir *v* reflect, think
regarder *v* look
règle *f* rule
regretter *v* regret, be sorry for

rejoindre *v* join
relier *v* bind, connect
remarquer *v* notice
remplir *v* fill
remuer *v* move, stir
rencontrer *v* meet
rendre *v* give back
renoncer *v* renounce, give up
rentrer *v* go home, go back
repas *m* meal
répondre *v* reply, answer
reposer *v* rest
résoudre *v* resolve
rester *v* remain, stay
retard *m* delay, **en retard** late
retourner *v* return, turn around
retrouver *v* find again
réussir *v* succeed
rêve *m* dream
réveiller *v* waken
révéler *v* reveal
revenir *v* come back, return
riche *adj* rich
rien *pron* nothing
rire *v* laugh
robe *f* dress
roman *m* novel
rompre *v* break
rond *adj* round
route *f* road, **en route** under way
rue *f* street

S

sable *m* sand
sage *adj* wise
saisir *v* seize
saison *f* season
sale *adj* dirty
salon *m* parlor
sans *prep* without
sauf *prep* except
sauter *v* leap, jump
sauver *v* save, **se sauver** run away
savoir *v* know, know how
savon *m* soap
secours *m* help
selon *prep* according to
semaine *f* week
sembler *v* seem
sentir *v* feel, smell
serviette *f* napkin, towel
servir *v* serve, **se servir de** use

seul *adj* alone, only, single
sévère *adj* strict, severe
si *conj* if, whether
si *adv* so, yes
soeur *f* sister
soie *f* silk
soif *f* thirst
soigner *v* care for
soir *m* evening
soleil *m* sun
sommeil *m* sleep
sonner *v* sound, ring, strike
sorte *f* kind
sortir *v* go out, get out
souffrir *v* suffer, bear
souhaiter *v* wish
soulager *v* relieve
soulever *v* raise, lift up, arouse
sourire *v and n m* smile
souvenir *m* remembrance, **se souvenir de** remember
souvent *adv* often
sucre *m* sugar
suffire *v* suffice
suivre *v* follow
sur *prep* on, upon, over, about
sûr *adj* sure
surtout *adv* above all, especially

T

table *f* table
tableau *m* picture, blackboard
taire *v* keep quiet, **se taire** be silent
tandis que *conj* while, whereas
tant *adv* so many, so much, **tant que** as long as
tante *f* aunt
tard *adv* late
tarder *v* delay, put off
tasse *f* cup
tel *adj* such
temps *m* time, weather
tenir *v* hold, possess
tenter *v* attempt
terre *f* earth, ground, land
tête *f* head
timbre *m* stamp
tirer *v* draw, pull
tomber *v* fall
tort *m* wrong, **avoir tort** be wrong
tôt *adv* soon, early
toucher *v* touch

toujours *adv* always, yet
tourner *v* turn
tout *adj* all, each, every
tout *pron* everything
tranquille *adj* quiet
travailler *v* work
traverser *v* cross
très *adv* very
tromper *v* deceive, **se tromper** make a mistake, be wrong
trop *adv* too much, too
trottoir *m* sidewalk
trouver *v* find

U

usage *m* use
utile *adj* useful
utiliser *v* use

V

vacances *f pl* vacation
vague *f* wave
vaincre *v* conquer
vaisselle *f* dishes
valise *f* suitcase
valoir *v* be worth
vendre *v* sell
verre *m* glass
vêtir *v* dress
viande *f* meat
vide *adj* empty
vie *f* life
vieillard *m* old man
vieille *adj f* old, *noun f* old woman
vieux *adj m* old
village *m* village
ville *f* city, town
vin *m* wine
vite *adv* quick
vivre *v* live
voici *v* here is, here are
voilà *v* there is, there are
voir *v* see
voisin *m* neighbor
voiture *f* car, automobile
voix *f* voice
vouloir *v* wish, want
voyager *v* travel
vrai *adj* true, real

Y

y *adv* there, in it, to it

Dictionary abbreviations. Nouns are identified as masculine *(nm)* or feminine *(nf)*. Adjectives are identified as *adj*, adverbs as *adv*, conjunctions as *conj*, interjections as *interj*, prepositions as *prep*, pronouns as *pron*, and verbs as *v*. Plurals are identified as *pl*.

English-French

A

able *adj* capable, **be able** *v* pouvoir
about *prep* environ, à peu près
above *adv* dessus, au dessus, par dessus
absence *n* absence *f*
accept *v* accepter
accident *n* accident *m*
according to *prep* selon, d'après
accustom *v* habituer
acquaintance *n* connaissance *f*
acquire *v* acquérir
act *v* agir
activity *n* activité *f*
add *v* ajouter, additionner
advise *v* conseiller
afraid *adj* éffrayé
after *adv* après
after *conj* après que
afternoon *n* après-midi *m or f*
afterward *adv* après, ensuite, plus tard
again *adv* encore
agent *n* agent, représentant *m*
ago *adv* il y a, **two days ago** il y a deux jours
agreement *n* accord *m*
aim *n* but *m*
airplane *n* avion *m*
all *adj* tout, tous, toute, toutes
allow *v* laisser, permettre
alone *adj* seul
aloud *adv* à haute voix
already *adv* déjà
also *adv* aussi
although *conj* bien que, quoique
always *adv* toujours
among *prep* parmi, entre
amuse *v* amuser
ancient *adj* ancien, antique
and *conj* et
anger *n* colère *f*
anger *v* fâcher, mettre en colère
animal *n* bête *f*
answer *v* répondre

any *pron* en
anything *pron* quelque chose, **not anything** ne ... rien, **anything at all** n'importe quoi
anyone *pron* quelqu'un, **not ...** personne
anywhere *adv* quelque part, **not ... nulle part**
appear *v* paraître, sembler
apple *n* pomme *f*
approach *v* s'approcher
approve *v* approuver
arrest *v* arrêter
arrive *v* arriver
as *adv* comme, aussi, que
as *conj* comme, en tant que, tel que, **as ... as** aussi ... que
ask *v* demander, **ask a question** poser une question
at *prep* à
attain *v* atteindre
aunt *n* tante *f*
automobile *n* automobile *f*, voiture *f*
avoid *v* éviter
await *v* attendre, espérer
away *adv* absent, loin, au loin

B

bachelor *n* célibataire *m*
back *n* dos *m*, dossier *m*, derrière *m*
back up *v* reculer
bad *adj* mauvais
badly *adv* mal
barely *adv* guère, à peine
barn *n* grange *f*
bath *v* bain *m*
battle *n* bataille *f*
be *v* être
bear *v* porter
beast *n* bête *f*
beat *v* battre, vaincre, frapper
beautiful *adj* beau *and* bel *m*, belle *f*
because *conj* parce que

become *v* devenir
bed *n* lit *m*
beer *n* bière *f*
before *adv* avant, devant
begin *v* commencer, se mettre à
behind *adv* derrière
believe *v* croire
belong *v* appartenir
below *prep* sous, dessous, en bas
bend *v* plier
beside *prep* à côté de, auprès de
besides *adv* d'ailleurs
best *adv* mieux, *adj* le meilleur
bet *v* parier, *n* pari *m*
better *adj* meilleur, *adv* mieux
between *prep* entre
big *adj* grand, gros
bird *n* oiseau *m*
birth *n* naissance *f*
bite *v* mordre
blanket *n* couverture *f*
body *n* corps *m*
book *n* livre *m*
born (be) *v* naître
borrow *v* emprunter
both *adj and pron* les deux
bother *v* déranger, gêner
bottle *n* bouteille *f*
box *n* boîte *f*
bread *n* pain *m*
break *v* casser, rompre, briser
breakfast *n* petit déjeuner *m*
bright *adj* brillant, clair, intelligent
bring *v* amener, apporter
bring back *v* ramener
broad *adj* large
brother *n* frère *m*
build *v* construire
business *n* affaires *f pl*
busy *adj* occupé
but *conj* mais
butter *n* beurre *m*
butterfly *n* papillon *m*
buy *v* acheter
by *prep* par, de, à, près de

C

café *n* café *m*
call *v* appeler
can *v* pouvoir
car *n* voiture *f*

carpenter *n* charpentier *m*
carry *v* porter
cast *v* jeter
cat *n* chat *m*
cause *n* cause *f*
cease *v* cesser, discontinuer
celebration *n* fête *f*
certain *adj* certain
chair *n* chaise *f*
chance *n* chance *f*, hasard *m*
chart *n* carte marine *f*
chat *n* causerie *f*, entretien *m*
cheap *adj* bon marché
child *n* enfant *m or f*
choose *v* choisir
church *n* église *f*
city *n* ville *f*
class *n* classe *f*
clean *adj* propre, *v* nettoyer
clear *adj* clair
clever *adj* habile
climb *v* grimper, monter
clock *n* horloge *f*, pendule *f*
close *v* fermer
clothe *v* habiller, vêtir
clothes *n* habits *m pl*, vêtements
    m pl
cloud *n* nuage *m*
coat *n* habit *m*, manteau *m*
coffee *n* café *m*
cold *adj* froid
come *v* venir
command *v* commander,
    ordonner
company *n* compagnie *f*
compare *v* comparer
compel *v* forcer
complain *v* se plaindre
complaint *n* plainte *f*
concern *v* interesser
conquer *v* vaincre
consent *v* consentir
consider *v* considérer
consist *v* consister
construct *v* construire, fabriquer
contain *v* contenir
contents *n* contenu *m*
continue *v* continuer
convince *v* convaincre
cook *v* cuire
cool *adj* frais *m*, fraîche *f*
cool *v* rafraîchir
correct *v* corriger
cost *v* coûter
costs *n* frais *m pl*

count *v* compter
country *n* pays (nation) *m*,
    patrie (native country) *f*,
    campagne (rural area) *f*
courage *n* courage *m*
course *n* cours *m*
cover *v* couvrir
cross *n* croix *f*
cry *v* pleurer
cultivate *v* cultiver
cup *n* tasse *f*
customer *n* client *m*
cut *v* couper

D

daily *adj* quotidien, tous les jours
damage *n* dommage *m*,
    v endommager
dance *n* danse *f*
dance *v* danser
danger *n* danger *m*, péril *m*
dangerous *adj* dangereux
dare *v* oser
date *n* date *f*
daughter *n* fille *f*
day *n* jour *m*, journée *f*
dazzle *v* éblouir
dealer *n* marchant *m*
deceive *v* tromper
decide *v* décider
declare *v* déclarer
defeat *v* vaincre
delay *v* tarder
delicious *adj* délicieux
delight *n* joie *f*, plaisir *m*
delight *v* ravir
delighted *adj* joyeux, ravi
deny *v* nier
depart *v* s'en aller, partir
descend *v* descendre
describe *v* décrire
deserve *v* mériter
desire *v* désirer, vouloir
desk *n* bureau *m*
despair *v* désespérer
destroy *v* détruire
die *v* mourir
difficult *adj* difficile
dine *v* dîner
dining room *n* salle à manger *f*
direct *v* diriger
dirty *adj* sale
dishes *n* vaisselle *f*
displease *v* déplaire

disturb *v* déranger, troubler
dive *v* plonger
divide *v* diviser, partager
do *v* faire
dog *n* chien *m*
door *n* porte *f*
doubt *n* doute *m*
doubt *v* douter
draw *v* tirer (pull), dessiner
    (sketch)
drawer *n* tiroir *m*
drawing room *n* salon *m*
dress *n* robe *f*
dress *v* vêtir, habiller
drink *n* boisson *f*
drink *v* boire
drive *v* conduire
during *prep* pendant
dust *n* poussière *f*
duty *n* devoir *m*
dwell *v* demeurer, habiter

E

each *adj* chaque, tout
each one *pron* chacun
ear *n* oreille *f*
early *adv* de bonne heure,
    tôt
earn *v* gagner, mériter
earth *n* terre *f*
easy *adj* facile
eat *v* manger
effort *n* effort *m*
egg *n* oeuf *m*
either *adv* ou
else *adv* autrement, ou bien
elsewhere *adv* ailleurs, autre
    part
embark *v* embarquer
employ *v* employer
empty *adj* vide
encourage *v* encourager
end *n* fin *f*
end *v* finir, terminer
engineer *n* ingénieur *m*
enjoy *v* jouir
enough *adv* assez
enter *v* entrer
entire *adj* entier, complet
evening *n* soir *m*
equal *adj* égal
error *n* erreur *f*, faute *f*
especially *adv* surtout
even *adv* même

event *n* événement *m*
ever *adv* jamais
every *adj* tout, chaque
everybody *pron* tout le monde
everything *pron* tout
everywhere *adv* partout
evident *adj* évident, clair
exactly *adv* exactement
examination *n* examen *m*
example *n* exemple *m*
except *prep* excepté, sauf
expect *v* attendre, espérer
expensive *adj* cher, coûteux
experience *v* éprouver
explain *v* expliquer
express *v* exprimer, **express** *adj*
  exprès
extend *v* étendre
extinguish *v* éteindre
eye *n* oeil *m*, yeux *m pl*

F

fable *n* fable *f*
face *n* figure *f*, face *f*
face *v* faire face à, affronter,
  donner sur
fail *v* échouer, manquer
fair *adj* juste
fairly *adv* assez, pas mal,
  honnêtement
faithful *adj* fidèle
fall *v* tomber
false *adj* faux *m*, fausse *f*
familiar *adj* familier
family *n* famille *f*
far *adv* loin
fast *adv* vite
father *n* père *m*
fault *n* faute *f*
fear *n* crainte *f*, peur *f*
fear *v* craindre, avoir peur
feed *v* nourrir
feel *v* sentir, tâter (touch)
feel like *v* avoir envie de
few *adj* peu de, quelques,
  pron peu, quelques-uns
fill *v* remplir
fight *v* se battre
finally *adv* enfin, à la fin
find *v* trouver
find out *v* découvrir
finger *n* doigt *m*
finish *v* finir
fire *n* feu *m*

first *adj* premier, *adv*
  d'abord
fish *n* poisson *m*
fish *v* pêcher
fit *v* aller à, *adj* convenable,
  capable
flee *v* se sauver, s'enfuir
flower *n* fleur *f*
fly *v* voler
fold *v* plier
follow *v* suivre
food *n* nourriture *f*
foot *n* pied *m*
for *prep* pour, *conj* car
forbid *v* défendre
force *n* force *f*, puissance *f*
force *v* force, obliger
forget *v* oublier
former *adj* ancien
free *adj* libre
freeze *v* geler
friend *n* ami *m*, amie *f*
from *prep* de, depuis (since)
full *adj* plein
fun *n* amusement, plaisanterie,
  make fun se moquer
furniture *n* meubles *m pl*
future *n* avenir *m*

G

gain *n* profit *m*, gain *m*,
  avantage *m*
gain *v* gagner
game *n* jeu *m*, gibier
  (hunting) *m*
garden *n* jardin *m*
gate *n* porte *f*, portail *m*,
  barrière *f*
gather *v* cueillir, ramasser, se
  réunir
get *v* prendre, avoir, obtenir,
  gagner, **go and get** aller
  chercher
gift *n* cadeau *m*, présent *m*
girl *n* fille *f*
give *v* donner
give up *v* renoncer à
glad *adj* content
glass *n* verre *m*
glove *n* gant *m*
go *v* aller, se rendre, **go out**
  sortir, **go down** descendre
goal *n* but *m*
gold *n* or *m*

good *adj* bon *m*, bonne *f*, **for**
  good pour de bon
great *adj* grand, gros, **a great**
  deal beaucoup
greet *v* saluer
ground *n* terre *f*, **on the ground**
  par terre
grow *v* grandir, pousser
guard *v* garder
guess *v* deviner
guilty *adj* coupable

H

habit *n* habitude *f*
hair *n* cheveux *m pl*
half *adj* demi, *n* moitié *f*
hall *n* vestibule (entrance) *m*,
  salle (large room) *f*
hand *n* main *m*
happen *v* arriver, se passer
happy *adj* heureux, content
hard *adj* dur
hardly *adv* à peine, ne . . . guère
harm *v* nuire
hat *n* chapeau *m*
hate *v* détester, haïr
haughty *adj* orgueilleux
have *v* avoir
hear *v* entendre
help *n* aide *f*, secours *m*,
  interj au secours!
help *v* aider
here *adv* ici
hesitate *v* hésiter
high *adj* haut
hinder *v* gêner, empêcher
history *n* histoire
hit *v* frapper, battre
hold *v* tenir
holiday *n* fête
home *n* foyer *m*, maison *f*,
  chez soi, à la maison
homework *n* devoir *m*
honest *adj* honnête
hope *v* espérer
hot *adj* chaud
hour *n* heure *f*
house *n* maison *f*
how *adv* comment, comme (in
  exclamation), **how much** combien
however *adv* cependant
hunger *n* faim *f*
hurt *v* blesser, faire mal
husband *n* mari *m*, époux *m*

I

ice *n* glace *f*
idea *n* idée *f*
ill *adv* mal, *adj* malade
in *prep* dans, à, en
incite *v* encourager, provoquer
inform *v* informer, renseigner
inhabitant *n* habitant *m*
ink *n* encre *f*
insist *v* insister, tenir à
instance *n* fois *f*
instead of *prep* au lieu de
intend *v* avoir l'intention de
interest *v* intéresser
interrupt *v* interrompre
introduce *v* introduire, présenter
invite *v* inviter

J

join *v* relier, joindre
joke *v* plaisanter
journey *n* voyage *m*
jump *v* sauter
just *adj* juste, précis
just *adv* justement, donc, **to have just** venir de

K

keep *v* garder, tenir, **keep from** empêcher
key *n* clef *f*
kill *v* tuer
kilogram *n* kilo *m*
kind *adj* aimable, *n* genre *m*, sorte *f*
knife *n* couteau *m*, **pocketknife** canif *m*
knock *v* frapper
know *v* savoir, connaître
knowledge *n* science *f*, connaissances *f pl*

L

lace *n* dentelle *f*, **shoelace** *n* lacet *m*
land *n* terre *f*
land *v* débarquer (ship), atterrir (airplane)
language *n* langage *m*, langue *f*
large *adj* grand, gros
last *adj* dernier, **last night** hier soir

last *v* durer
late *adj* tard, en retard
later *adj* plus tard
laugh *v* rire, **laugh at** se moquer
law *n* droit *m*
lawyer *n* avocat *m*, avoué *m*
lead *n* plomb *m*
lead *v* mener, conduire
leaf *n* feuille *f*
leap *v* sauter
learn *v* apprendre
least *adv, adj, n m* moins
leave *v* quitter, partir, laisser
lecture *n* conférence *f*
leg *n* jambe *f*
lend *v* prêter
less *adv* moins, *adj* moindre, moins de
lesson *n* leçon *f*
let *v* laisser, permettre
letter *n* lettre *f*
lie *v* se coucher
lie *n* mensonge *f*, *v* mentir
life *n* vie *f*, existence *f*
light *n* lumière *f*
light *adj* léger
like *v* aimer
like *adj* comme, pareil, semblable
line *n* ligne *f*
listen *v* écouter
little *adj* petit, *adv* peu
live *v* demeurer, vivre, habiter
living room *n* salon *m*
long *adj* long *m*, longue *f*, *adv* longtemps
look *n* regard *n*
look *v* regarder
look for *v* chercher
look like *v* avoir l'air de
lose *v* perdre
loud *adv* fort, haut
love *v* aimer
luck *n* chance *f*, fortune *f*
lunch *v* déjeuner, *n* déjeuner *m*

M

machine *n* machine *f*
maid *n* bonne à tout faire *f*
main *adj* principal
majority *n* la plupart *f*
make *v* faire, fabriquer
man *n* homme *m*
manner *n* manière *f*

many *adv* beaucoup de
map *n* carte *f*
market *n* marchè *m*
marry *v* se marier, épouser
matter *n* matière *f*, sujet *m*
meal *n* repas *m*
mean *v* vouloir dire, signifier
mean *adj* méchant
meat *n* viande *f*
meet *v* rencontrer, rejoindre
midday *n* midi *m*
midnight *n* minuit *m*
mind *n* esprit *m*, intelligence *f*
mirror *n* miroir *m*
miss *v* manquer
mistake *n* erreur *f*, faute *f*
mistrust *v* se méfier
money *n* argent *m*
month *n* mois *m*
more *pron* en . . . davantage, *adj and adv* plus, encore
morning *n* matin *m*
most *adv* très, bien, *adj* la plupart, *n* le plus *m*
mother *n* mère *f*
mountain *n* montagne *f*
move *v* remuer, avancer
much *adv* beaucoup, **as much** autant
must *v* falloir, devoir

N

name *n* nom *m*
name *v* appeler
napkin *n* serviette *f*
narrate *v* raconter
narrow *adj* étroit
near *adj* proche, *adv* près, *prep* près de
necessary *adj* nécessaire
need *n* besoin *m*
need *v* avoir besoin
neglect *v* négliger
neighbor *n* voisin *m*
never *adv* jamais
new *adj* neuf *m*, nouveau *m*, neuve *f*, nouvelle *f*
news *n* nouvelles *f pl*
newspaper *n* journal *m*
next *adj* prochain
noise *n* bruit *m*
noon *n* midi *m*
note *v* noter, remarquer
nothing *pron* rien

Review of French Grammar

notice *n* avis *m*
notice *v* remarquer
novel *n* roman *m*
novel *adj* nouveau *m*, nouvelle *f*
now *adv* maintenant, à present

O

obey *v* obéir
observe *v* observer
obvious *adj* évident, clair
offend *v* offenser
offer *v* offrir
office *n* bureau *m*
often *adv* souvent
old *adj* vieux *m*, vieil *m*, vieille *f*
once *adv* une fois, autrefois
only *adj* seulement, seul
open *v* ouvrir
opinion *n* avis *m*
or *conj* ou
order *v* commander, ordonner
order *n* ordre *m*
other *adj* autre
out *adv* dehors
outside *adv* au dehors
overcoat *n* pardessus *m*
owe *v* devoir
own *v* posséder

P

package *n* colis *m*
pageboy *n* page *m*
pail *n* seau *m*
pain *n* peine *f*
paper *n* papier *m*
pardon *v* pardonner, faire grâce
part *n* partie *f*
part *v* se séparer
pass *v* passer, réussir
past *adj* passé
path *n* chemin *m*
pay *v* payer
peace *n* paix *f*
pen *n* plume *f*, stylo *m*
pencil *n* crayon *m*
people *n* gens *m*, monde *m*
perish *v* périr
permit *v* permettre
person *n* personne *f*
physician *n* médecin *m*, docteur *m*
pick *v* ceuillir
pick out *v* choisir

picture *n* tableau *m*
pity *v* plaindre
place endroit *m*, lieu *m*
place *v* placer, mettre
plane *n* avion *m*
play *n* pièce *f*, comédie *f*
play *v* jouer
pleasant *adj* agréable
please *v* plaire
pleasure *n* plaisir *m*
pocket *n* poche *f*
pocketknife *n* canif *m*
pond *n* étang *m*
poor *adj* pauvre, mauvais
possess *v* posséder
potato *n* pomme de terre *f*
pound *n* livre *f*
predict *v* deviner
prefer *v* préférer, aimer mieux
prepare *v* préparer
pretty *adj* joli
prevent *v* empêcher
professor *n* professeur *m*
profit *n* bénéfice *m*, profit *m*
project *n* projet *m*
promise *v* promettre
proud *adj* fier
provided that *conj* pourvu que
pull *v* tirer
punish *v* punir
pupil *n* élève *m and f*
put *v* mettre, poser, put out éteindre

Q

qualify *v* qualifier
quality *n* qualité *f*
quantity *n* quantité *f*
quarter *n* quart *m*
question *v* questionner, interroger
quick *adj* rapide, vite
quiet *adj* tranquille, calme
quit *v* quitter
quite *adv* tout à fait, complètement
quiz *n* petit examen *m*

R

race *n* course *f*
rain *v* pleuvoir
rain *n* pluie *f*, rain *v* pleuvoir
raise *v* lever, soulever

reach *v* atteindre
read *v* lire
ready *adj* prêt
real *adj* vrai
realize *v* se rendre compte
really *adv* réellement
reason *n* raison *f*
receive *v* recevoir
recognize *v* reconnaître
reflect *v* réfléchir
refresh *v* rafraîchir
regard *v* considérer
regret *v* regretter
relative *n* parent *m*, *adj* relatif
remain *v* rester
remark *n* remarque *f*, propos *m*
remember *v* se rappeler, se souvenir
renounce *v* renoncer
rent *n* loyer *m*
rent *v* louer
repair *v* réparer
reply *v* répondre, répliquer
require *v* exiger, demander
resolve *v* résoudre
rest *n* repos *m*
rest *v* se reposer
retain *v* garder, retenir
return *v* revenir
reward *n* récompense *f*
rich *adj* riche
right *adj* juste, correct, **be right** avoir raison
ring *v* sonner
road *n* route *f*
room *n* place *f*, chambre *f*, salle *f*
round *adj* rond
rule *n* règlement *m*, règle *f*
rumor *n* bruit *m*
run *v* courir

S

sadden *v* désoler, attrister
safe *adj* sûr, en sûreté
salary *n* salaire *m*
same *adj* même, pareil
sand *n* sable *m*
satisfied *adj* satisfait, content
save *v* sauver (rescue), épargner (economize)
say *v* dire
scarcely *adv* à peine, guère

school *n* école *f*
season *n* saison *f*
seat *v* asseoir
see *v* voir
seek *v* chercher
seem *v* paraître, sembler
sell *v* vendre
send *v* envoyer, **send for**
envoyer chercher
sentence *n* phrase *f*
servant *n* servante *f*, valet *m*,
domestique *m and f*, bonne *f*
serve *v* servir
set *n* serie *f*
set *v* mettre, **set up** monter,
dresser
several *adj* plusieurs
share *v* partager
shine *v* briller, luire
shirt *n* chemise *f*
show *n* spectacle *m*
show *v* montrer, faire voir
sidewalk *n* trottoir *m*
sign *v* signer
silk *n* soie *f*
silver *n* argent *m*
similar *adj* pareil, semblable
since *conj* depuis que, puisque,
since *adv and prep* depuis
sing *v* chanter
sister *n* soeur *f*
sit *v* s'asseoir, **be seated** être
assis
skate *v* patiner
slacken *v* ralentir
sleep *n* sommeil *m*
sleep *v* dormir
slow *adj* lent, tardif, en retard
slow down *v* ralentir
small *adj* petit
smell *v* sentir
smile *n* sourire *m, v*
sourire
smoke *v* fumer
so *adv* si, de telle manière, ainsi
some *adj* quelque, quelques-uns
someone *pron* quelqu'un
something *n* quelque chose *m*
sometimes *adv* quelque fois,
parfois
somewhere *adv* quelque part
son *n* fils *m*
song *n* chanson *f*
soon *adv* bientôt
sorrow *n* peine *f*

sorry *adj* fâché, **be sorry** être
fâché, regretter
sound *v* sonner
spare *v* épargner, ménager,
céder, éviter
speak *v* parler
speech *n* discours *m*
speed *n* vitesse *f*, rapidité *f*
spend *v* dépenser (money),
passer (time)
stairs *n* escalier *m*
stamp *n* timbre *m*
start *v* partir, se mettre en route,
commencer
station *n* gare *f*, station *f*
stay *n* séjour *m*
stay *v* demeurer, rester
still *adv* encore, toujours,
adj tranquille, *conj*
cependant
stir *v* remuer
stone *n* pierre *f*
stop *v* arrêter, cesser
store *n* magasin *m*, boutique *f*
storm *n* orage *m*
story *n* histoire *f*, récit *m*, conte
m, étage (floor) *m*
straight *adj* droit
strange *adj* étrange
strawberry *n* fraise *f*
street *n* rue *f*
stretch *v* tendre, étendre
strict *adj* sévère, étroit, strict
strike *v* frapper, sonner
study *n* étude *f*
study *v* étudier
succeed *v* réussir
such *adj* tel pareil, semblable
suffer *v* souffrir, subir, endurer
suffice *v* suffire, satisfaire
sugar *n* sucre *m*
suit *n* complet *m*, procès (law) *m*
suitcase *n* valise *f*
summer *n* été *m*
sun *n* soleil *m*
sure *adj* sûr
surprise *v* surprendre, étonner
swift *adj* rapide
swim *v* nager

T

table *n* table *f*
take *v* prendre, porter, emporter,
conduire

tale *n* conte *m*
talk *v* parler, causer
tall *adj* grand, haut
task *n* tâche *f*, besogne *f*
taste *n* goût *m*
tea *n* thé *m*
teach *v* enseigner, apprendre
teacher *n* professeur *m*, maître
m, instituteur *m*
tear *n* larme *f*
tear *v* déchirer
tell *v* raconter, dire, annoncer
test *n* épreuve *f*, examen *m*
thank *v* remercier
then *adv* alors, ensuite, puis
there *adv* là, **there is** il y a,
voilà
thing *n* chose *f*, affaire *f*
think *v* penser, croire
thirst *n* soif *f*
thorn *n* épine *f*
throw *v* jeter
ticket *n* billet *m*
tie *v* lier, attacher
till *v* cultiver
time *n* temps *m*, fois *f*, époque *f*
tired *adj* fatigué
today *adv* aujourd'hui
together *adv* ensemble
tomorrow *adv* demain
tongue *n* langue *f*
touch *v* toucher
toward *prep* vers, envers
towel *n* serviette *f*
town *n* ville *f*
trade *n* marché *m*, commerce *m*
travel *v* voyager
tree *n* arbre *m*
trouble *v* déranger, gêner
true *adj* vrai
trunk *n* malle *f*
trust *v* avoir confiance, se fier à
truth *n* vérité *f*
try *v* tâcher, essayer
turn *n* tour *m*
turn *v* tourner
twice *adv* deux fois

U

under *prep* sous, *adv* au-dessous
underneath *adv* en dessous
understand *v* comprendre
unless *conj* à moins que
unnecessary *adj* inutile

unpleasant *adj* désagréable
until *prep* jusqu'à, *conj* jusqu'à
  ce que
up *adj* en haut, **go up** *v* monter
up to *prep* jusqu'à
use *n* emploi *m*
use *v* se servir de, employer
useful *adj* utile
useless *adj* inutile
usually *adv* ordinairement
utensil *n* ustensile *m*
utilize *v* utiliser

V

vacation *n* vacances *f pl*
vaccinate *v* vacciner
vaccine *n* vaccin *m*
valiant *adj* vaillant
valley *n* vallée *f*
vanilla *n* vanille *f*
vanish *v* s'évanouir
variety *n* variété *f*
various *adj* divers
vary *v* varier
vault *n* voûte *f*
vegetable *n* légume *m*
vehicle *n* véhicule *m*
veil *n* voile *m*
vein *n* veine *f*
very *adv* très, bien, fort,
  beaucoup
village *n* village *m*
visit *n* visite *f*
visit *v* faire visite à
voice *n* voix *f*

W

wager *v* parier
wait *v* attendre
waiter *n* garçon *m*
walk *n* promenade *f*, **walk** *v*
  marcher, se promener
wall *n* mur *m*
want *v* vouloir, avoir envie de
war *n* guerre *f*
warm *adj* chaud
warm *v* chauffer
warn *v* avertir
wash *v* laver
watch *n* montre *f*
watch *v* regarder, surveiller
water *n* eau *f*
way *n* route *f*, voie *f*, chemin *m*,
  moyen (means) *m*

wear *v* porter
weather *n* temps *m*
week *n* semaine *f*
weep *v* pleurer
welcome *v* accueillir
well *adv* bien, **as well as** aussi
  bien que
when *conj* quand
where *adv* où
whether *conj* si
while *conj* pendant que, tandis
  que
whole *adj* tout, entier
wide *adj* large
will *v* vouloir
win *v* gagner
wine *n* vin *m*
wipe *v* essuyer
wise *adj* sage
wish *v* vouloir, désirer, souhaiter
with *prep* avec
withdraw *v* se retirer
within *prep* dedans
without *prep* sans

woman *n* femme *f*
wonder *v* se demander
wood *n* bois *m*
word *n* mot *m*, parole *f*
work *n* travail *m*, besogne *f*,
  ouvrage *m*, tâche *f* oeuvre
work *v* travailler, marcher
world *n* monde *m*
worry *n* ennui *m*, souci *m*,
  v préoccuper
worst *adj* pire, *adv* pis
worth *n* valeur *m*, prix *m*
write *v* écrire
wrong *adj* faux, **be wrong** *v*
  avoir tort

Y

year *n* an *m*, année *f*
yellow *adj* jaune
yesterday *adv* hier
yet *conj* pourtant, cependant,
  adv encore, déjà
yield *v* céder
young *adj* jeune

For further reference

Grammars
Barson, John
  La Grammaire à l'oeuvre
  Holt, Rinehart and Winston
Comeau, Raymond F., Bustin
  Normand, Francine L., and
  Lamoureux, L.
  Ensemble: Grammaire
  Holt, Rinehart and Winston
Daudon, René
  French in Review
  Harcourt Brace Jovanovich
Dubois, J., Jouannon, G., and
  Lagane, R.
  La Grammaire Française
  Librairie Larousse

Fraser, Ian Forbes
  French Reviewed
  Holt, Rinehart and Winston
Grevisse, Maurice
  Grammaire Française
  Librairie A. Hatier
Grevisse, Maurice
  Précis de Grammaire Française
  Editions J. Duculot
Jenkins, E. S.
  French Grammar
  David McKay Company

Dictionaries
Deak, Etienne
  Dictionnaire d'américanismes
  Edition du Dauphin
Hanse, Joseph
  *Dictionnaire des difficultés
    grammaticales et lexicologiques*
  Les Editions Scientifiques et
    Littéraires
Levieux, Michel and Eleanor
  Beyond the Dictionary in French
  Cassell

Mansion, J.E.
  *Harrap's New Standard French and
    English Dictionary*
  Charles Scribner's Sons
Micro Robert
  Le Robert
Thomas, Adolphe V. and Toro,
  Michel de
  Dictionnaire de Poche des difficultés
  Librairie Larousse

Review of German Grammar

The grammar of German is closely related to the grammar of English. This is because English, to a large extent, is Germanic in origin, as is obvious from the large number of English words that derive from Germanic sources. Consider *Vater* and father, *Mutter* and mother, *Sohn* and son, to name just a few examples of the many cognates the two languages exhibit.

As you can expect, therefore, German phrases, clauses, and sentences are constructed in somewhat the same way in both languages. The greatest exceptions appear in the relative absence of gender in English nouns, compared with the German noun genders. Another aspect of gender that is missing in English, in contrast with German, is the agreement of adjectives with the gender of the nouns they modify.

To cite an additional difference, German nouns (as well as the adjectives used to modify them) are declined to show their functions in sentences. This means that a noun will change in form to show that it is being used, for example, as the subject of a verb, the object of a verb, or the indirect object of a verb. Yet another form of this linguistic process of declension is the genitive, which we know as the possessive. In English, nouns rarely decline to show function. Instead we show subject, object, and indirect object by placement of the noun within the phrase, clause, or sentence. We do, however, use an apostrophe and the letter *s* to show possession with certain nouns.

Articles

Definite articles

Definite articles agree in gender and number with the nouns they modify: *der* for the masculine singular, *die* for the feminine singular, and *das* for the neuter singular. All three genders have *die* in the plural.

der Mann the man	*die Männer* the men
die Frau the woman	*die Frauen* the women
das Kind the child	*die Kinder* the children

The case of the noun determines the case of the article:

Das Kind sieht den Mann. The child sees the man.
die Frau des Mannes the man's wife
Der Mann gibt dem Kind. The man gives the child.
The dative and the accusative singular of the definite article are often contracted with a preposition. For example, *am* is used instead of *an dem*, at the. Other

Declension of articles:

Case	Definite				Indefinite			
	Singular			Plural	Singular			Plural
	Masc.	Fem.	Neuter		Masc.	Fem.	Neuter	
Nominative	der	die	das	die	ein	eine	ein	einige
Genitive	des	der	des	der	eines	einer	eines	einiger
Dative	dem	der	dem	den	einem	einer	einem	einigen
Accusative	den	die	das	die	einen	eine	ein	einige

contractions for prepositions with articles are:

ans = an das beside the
beim = bei dem at the
im = in dem in the
ins = in das into the
zum = zu dem to the

The definite article is used before abstract nouns.

Es lebe die Demokratie! Long live democracy!

Diminutives formed with the endings *chen* and *lein* are always neuter:

das Mädchen the girl
das Fräulein the miss
das Kindchen the little child

Indefinite articles

Indefinite articles agree in gender with the nouns they modify: *ein* for the masculine singular, *eine* for the feminine singular, and *ein* for the neuter singular. There is no plural for the indefinite article. The word *einige*, some, is used for more than one person or thing.

ein Vater a father   *einige Väter* some fathers
eine Mutter a mother   *einige Mütter* some mothers
ein Kind a child   *einige Kinder* some children

The case of the noun determines the case of the indefinite article:

ein Kind eines Vaters
a child of a father

einer Mutter Kinder
children of a mother

Eine Mutter hat einige Kinder.
A mother has some children.

die Kinder eines Mannes
a man's children

Nouns

Declining singular nouns

Nouns are either masculine, feminine, or neuter. Nouns are declined. In the genitive singular form, for example, most masculine and neuter nouns add *s* to the nominative singular form.

Nominative	*der Bruder*	the brother
Genitive	*des Bruders*	of the brother

Nominative	*das Wetter*	the weather
Genitive	*des Wetters*	of the weather

If a noun is monosyllabic, *es* is added in the genitive singular.

Nominative	*der Sohn*	the son
Genitive	*des Sohnes*	of the son

Nominative	*das Haus*	the house
Genitive	*des Hauses*	of the house

Some nouns ending in *e* add *n* in the genitive singular.

Nominative	*der Verwandte*	the relative
Genitive	*des Verwandten*	of the relative

Der Sohn des Bruders ist der Neffe.
The brother's son is the nephew.

Der Vater des Kindes ist alt.
The child's father is old.

The dative and accusative forms of a masculine or neuter singular noun are usually the same as those of the nominative. If the nominative ends in *e*, however, *n* is added.

Dative	*dem Bruder* to the brother
Accusative	*den Bruder* the brother

Dative	*dem Haus* to the house
Accusative	*das Haus* the house

Feminine singular nouns remain unchanged in all cases.

Die Tochter der Mutter ist schön.
The mother's daughter is beautiful.

Die Frau gibt der Tochter die Birne.
The woman gives the daughter the pear.

Declining plural nouns

The plural of all genders is formed in four ways.
Adding an umlaut to the singular form.

der Bruder the brother   *die Brüder* the brothers

Adding *er* plus an umlaut to the singular form.

der Mann the man   *die Männer* the men

Adding *e* plus an umlaut to the singular form.

die Nacht the night   *die Nächte* the nights

Adding *en* to the singular form.

die Frau the woman   *die Frauen* the women

The nominative, genitive, and accusative of plural nouns are all spelled identically. The dative adds *n* to all plural forms, with the exception of plurals formed by adding *en* to the singular.

	men	brothers	women
Nominative	*die Männer*	*die Brüder*	*die Frauen*
Genitive	*der Männer*	*der Brüder*	*der Frauen*
Dative	*den Männern*	*den Brüdern*	*den Frauen*
Accusative	*die Männer*	*die Brüder*	*die Frauen*

All nouns are capitalized.

Forms of the noun

Certain nouns have two forms, one for masculine gender, the other for feminine gender. For such nouns, the feminine form adds *in* to the masculine form.

Masc.	Fem.	
der Anwalt	*die Anwältin*	the lawyer
der Arzt	*die Ärztin*	the physician
der Künstler	*die Künstlerin*	the artist
der Lehrer	*die Lehrerin*	the teacher
der Wirt	*die Wirtin*	the host, the hostess

Compound nouns take the gender and declension of the last noun.

das Haus + *die Tür* = *die Haustür*
the house + the door = the door to the house

der Schlaf + *das Zimmer* = *das Schlafzimmer*
the sleep + the room = the bedroom

die Tasche + *das Tuch* = *das Taschentuch*
the pocket + the cloth = the handkerchief

Pronouns

Personal pronouns

Personal pronouns agree in number and gender with their antecedents.

	Nominative singular	Nominative plural
1st person	*ich* I	*wir* we
2nd person	*du* you (informal)	*ihr* you (informal)
3rd person	*er, sie, es* he, she, it	*sie* they
		Sie you (formal)

The pronoun *ich* is capitalized only when it is the first word of a sentence. The formal pronoun *Sie* is always capitalized.

Ich sehe dich.
I see you.

Der Tisch ist gross; er ist braun.
The table is big; it is brown.

Die Kinder spielen in dem Haus; sie singen in ihm.
The children play in the house; they sing in it.

Er gibt uns das Brot; er gibt es uns.
He gives us the bread; he gives it to us.

Reflexive pronouns

A reflexive pronoun functions as a direct or indirect object referring to the subject of a verb. It agrees in number and gender with the subject of the verb.

Dieter zieht sich an. Dieter dresses himself.
Wir waschen uns. We wash ourselves.

Ich wasche mir die Hände. I myself wash my hands.

Ihr ärgert euch. You are angry.

Some verbs that are reflexive in German are not reflexive in English.

sich anziehen to dress
sich erinnern to remember
sich freuen to be glad
sich fürchten to be afraid
sich hüten to be careful
sich trennen to separate
sich verbergen to hide
sich verlassen to rely
sich vorsehen to be careful

Declension of pronouns

Personal pronouns

	Singular			Plural		
	First person	*Second person*	*Third person*	*First person*	*Second person*	*Third person*
Nominative	*ich* I	*du* you	*er* he, *sie* she, *es* it	*wir* we	*ihr* you	*sie* they
Genitive	*meiner* of me	*deiner* of you	*seiner* his, *ihrer* her, *seiner* its	*unser* of us	*euer* of you	*ihrer* of them
Dative	*mir* to me	*dir* to you	*ihm* to him, *ihr* to her, *ihm* to it	*uns* to us	*euch* to you	*ihnen* to them
Accusative	*mich* me	*dich* you	*ihn* him, *sie* her, *es* it	*uns* us	*euch* you	*sie* them, *Sie* you (formal)

Reflexive pronouns

Subject	Direct object	Indirect object
ich I	*mich* myself	*mir* (to) myself
du you	*dich* yourself	*dir* (to) yourself
er, sie, es he, she, it	*sich* himself, herself, itself	*sich* (to) himself etc.
wir we	*uns* ourselves	*uns* (to) ourselves
ihr you	*euch* yourselves	*euch* (to) yourselves
sie they	*sich* themselves	*sich* (to) themselves
Sie you (formal)	*sich* yourselves	sich (to) yourselves

Relative pronouns
der who, which, that

	Singular			Plural
	Masc.	*Fem.*	*Neuter*	*All genders*
Nominative	*der*	*die*	*das*	*die*
Genitive	*dessen*	*deren*	*dessen*	*deren*
Dative	*dem*	*der*	*dem*	*denen*
Accusative	*den*	*die*	*das*	*die*

welcher who, which, that

Nominative	*welcher*	*welche*	*welches*	*welche*
Genitive	*dessen*	*deren*	*dessen*	*deren*
Dative	*welchem*	*welcher*	*welchem*	*welchem*
Accusative	*welchen*	*welche*	*welches*	*welche*

Demonstrative pronouns
dieser this

	Singular			Plural
	Masc.	*Fem.*	*Neuter*	*All genders*
Nominative	*dieser*	*diese*	*dieses*	*diese*
Genitive	*dieses*	*dieser*	*dieses*	*dieser*
Dative	*diesem*	*dieser*	*diesem*	*diesen*
Accusative	*diesen*	*diese*	*dieses*	*diese*

jener that

Nominative	*jener*	*jene*	*jenes*	*jene*
Genitive	*jenes*	*jener*	*jenes*	*jener*
Dative	*jenem*	*jener*	*jenem*	*jenen*
Accusative	*jenen*	*jene*	*jedes*	*jede*

Interrogative pronouns
wer who **was** what

	wer	was
Nominative	*wer*	*was*
Genitive	*wessen*	(no form)
Dative	*wem*	(no form)
Accusative	*wen*	*was*

Was gebt ihr?

Demonstrative pronouns

Demonstrative pronouns agree in number and gender with their antecedents. The demonstrative pronouns are *dieser* this, and *jener* that.

Dieses Buch ist besser als jenes.
This book is better than that.

Relative pronouns

Relative pronouns agree with their antecedents in number and gender. The masculine is *der,* who, that, or which; the feminine is *die,* who, that, or which; and the neuter is *das,* who, that, or which.

Der Eimer, der in der Küche ist, ist voll.
The pail that is in the kitchen is full.

Die Tante, die im Garten arbeitet, ist hübsch.
The aunt who is working in the garden is pretty.
Welcher, welche, welches are relative pronouns, with the same meanings as *der, die,* and *das.* They are usually found in the written language.

Dem Schüler, welchem ich das Buch gab, traue ich.
I trust the student to whom I gave the book.

Interrogative pronouns

The interrogative pronouns are *wer* for persons; *was* for things. *Welcher, welche,* and *welches* are used for "which one." There is no plural for *wer* or *was.*

Wer ist das? Who is this?

Was gebt ihr? What are you giving?
English questions introduced by "with what," "from what," etc. are expressed in German by *wo* "where," plus a preposition.

Wovon spricht er? What is he talking about?

Womit schreibt ihr? What do you write with?

Wofür gibt er Geld? What is he giving money for?
Wo becomes *wor* before a vowel.

Woran denkst du?
What do you think about?

Worin liegt die Tugend?
Where is the virtue?

Worüber liegen die Bücher?
What are the books above?

Possessive pronouns

Possessive pronouns are formed in the following ways. By adding *er, e,* or *es* to the possessive adjective. For example, *meiner, meine, meines.*

Wessen Tasse ist das? Es ist meine.
Whose cup is this? It is mine.
By adding *e* to the possessive adjective and employing the definite article. For example, *der deine, die deine, das deine.*

Wessen Glas ist das? Es ist das deine.
Whose glass is this? It is yours.
By adding *ige* to the possessive adjective and employing the definite article. For example, *der seinige, die seinige, das seinige.*

Ist das dein Papier? Nein, es ist das seinige.
Is this your paper? No, it is his.

Prepositions

Prepositions are followed by words in the genitive, dative, or accusative case.

Prepositions taking the genitive

anstatt instead of	*trotz* in spite of
ausserhalb outside of	*während* during
innerhalb inside of	*wegen* on account of
oberhalb above	

wegen des Wetters because of the weather
trotz der Musik in spite of the music

Prepositions taking the dative

aus out of	*nach* after
ausser besides	*seit* since
bei at	*von* from, of
gegenüber opposite of	*zu* at, to
mit with	

Bei mir spricht man deutsch.
At my house everyone speaks German.

Nach der Schule gehe ich nach Hause.
After school I go home.

Prepositions taking the accusative

durch through	*ohne* without
für for	*um* around, about
gegen against, toward	

Ich stimme für den Kandidaten.
I vote for the candidate.

Prepositions taking the dative or the accusative

The following prepositions take the dative case when they answer the question Where? They take the accusative when they answer the question Where to?

an on	*über* over, above
auf on, upon	*unter* under, among
hinter behind	*vor* before
in in, into	*zwischen* between
neben near, beside	

Ich stehe vor der Tür.
I am standing in front of the door.

Ich lege das Buch auf den Tisch.
I put the book on the table.

Adjectives and adverbs

Forms of adjectives

Predicative adjectives never change form.

Der Tiger ist zahm. The tiger is tame.

Das Kind ist frech. The child is impudent.

Attributive adjectives add *e* when they modify a noun preceded by a definite article. They add *er* for the masculine, *e* for the feminine, and *es* for the neuter when they modify a noun preceded by an indefinite article.

der grosse Baum the big tree

das kleine Brot the small bread

ein kleiner Baum a small tree

ein kleines Brot a small bread

The plural adds *en* in all genders and cases.

die schweren Bücher the heavy books

There is no plural form for adjectives used with indefinite articles.

Possessive adjectives

Possessive adjectives agree in number and gender with the nouns they modify and are declined like them.

meine Katze my cat

seines Hundes of his dog

The plural here refers to the number of the noun modified.

deine Bücher your books

ihre Brüder her brothers

Declension of adjectives

with definite article

		Singular	
	Masc.	Fem.	Neuter
Nominative	grosse the big	grosse	grosse
Genitive	grossen of the big	grossen	grossen
Dative	grossen to the big	grossen	grossen
Accusative	grossen the big	grosse	grosse

with indefinite article

Nominative	grosser a big	grosse	grosses
Genitive	grossen of a big	grossen	grossen
Dative	grossen to a big	grossen	grossen
Accusative	grossen a big	grosse	grosses

der grosse Baum

Forms of possessive adjectives

		Singular		Plural
	Masc.	Fem.	Neuter	All genders
my	mein	meine	mein	meine
your	dein	deine	dein	deine
his	sein	seine	sein	seine
her	ihr	ihre	ihr	ihre
its	sein	seine	sein	seine
our	unser	unsere	unser	unsere
your	euer	eure	euer	eure
their	ihr	ihre	ihr	ihre

Declension of possessive adjectives

Nominative	mein	meine	mein	meine
Genitive	meines	meiner	meines	meiner
Dative	meinem	meiner	meinem	meinen
Accusative	meinen	meine	mein	meine
Nominative	dein	deine	dein	deine
Genitive	deines	deiner	deines	deiner
Dative	deinem	deiner	deinem	deinen
Accusative	deinen	deine	dein	deine
Nominative	sein	seine	sein	seine
Genitive	seines	seiner	seines	seiner
Dative	seinem	seiner	seinem	seinen
Accusative	seinen	seine	sein	seine
Nominative	ihr	ihre	ihr	ihre
Genitive	ihres	ihrer	ihres	ihrer
Dative	ihrem	ihrer	ihrem	ihren
Accusative	ihren	ihre	ihr	ihre
Nominative	sein	seine	sein	seine
Genitive	seines	seiner	seines	seiner
Dative	seinem	seiner	seinem	seinen
Accusative	seinen	seine	sein	seine
Nominative	unser	unsere	unser	unsere
Genitive	unseres	unserer	unseres	unserer
Dative	unserem	unserer	unserem	unseren
Accusative	unseren	unsere	unser	unsere
Nominative	euer	eure	euer	eure
Genitive	eures	eurer	eures	eurer
Dative	eurem	eurer	eurem	euren
Accusative	euren	eure	euer	eure
Nominative	ihr	ihre	ihr	ihre
Genitive	ihres	ihrer	ihres	ihrer
Dative	ihrem	ihrer	ihrem	ihren
Accusative	ihren	ihre	ihr	ihre

Adverbs

Adverbs are identical with adjectives but are not declined.

Er geht langsam. He goes slowly.

Comparative forms

The comparative form usually adds *er* to the adjective.

schnell fast   *schneller* faster

Sometimes an umlaut is added before the *er*.

arm poor   *ärmer* poorer

The comparatives of certain adjectives and adverbs are not formed in the conventional way.

gut good	*besser* better	
viel much	*mehr* more	
gern gladly	*lieber* rather	

Ich lese viel aber er liest mehr.
I read much but he reads more.

Superlatives

The superlative is formed by adding *ste* or *este* to the adjective. An umlaut is sometimes added to the vowel preceding the *ste* or *este*.

der ärmste the poorest
die kleinste the smallest
das dümmste the least intelligent
der älteste the oldest

Adjectives with irregular comparative forms also have irregular superlatives.

viel, mehr, am meisten much, more, most
gut, besser, am besten, good, better, best

Verbs

Conjugation of auxiliary verbs

The verbs *sein* to be, *haben* to have, and *werden* to become, are used in the compound tenses of other verbs.

Rules for using verbs

There is only one present tense, but it translates in three ways into English.

Ich gehe zur Schule.
I go to school. I am going to school.
I do go to school.

To form a question, subject and verb are reversed.

Du spielst. You are playing.
Spielst du? Are you playing?

In a negative sentence *nicht* is placed after the verb:

Wir lesen nicht. We do not read.

Conjugation of auxiliary verbs

Infinitive	*sein*	*haben*	*werden*			
	to be	to have	to become			

Indicative	*Present*			*Imperfect*		
ich	*bin*	*habe*	*werde*	*war*	*hatte*	*wurde*
du	*bist*	*hast*	*wirst*	*warst*	*hattest*	*wurdest*
er, sie, es	*ist*	*hat*	*wird*	*war*	*hatte*	*wurde*
wir	*sind*	*haben*	*werden*	*waren*	*hatten*	*wurden*
ihr	*seid*	*habt*	*werdet*	*wart*	*hattet*	*wurdet*
sie	*sind*	*haben*	*werden*	*waren*	*hatten*	*wurden*
(formal) Sie	*sind*	*haben*	*werden*	*waren*	*hatten*	*wurden*

	Perfect			*Future*		
ich	*bin gewesen*	*habe gehabt*	*bin geworden*	*werde sein*	*werde haben*	*werde werden*
du	*bist gewesen*	*hast gehabt*	*bist geworden*	*wirst sein*	*wirst haben*	*wirst werden*
er, sie, es	*ist gewesen*	*hat gehabt*	*ist geworden*	*wird sein*	*wird haben*	*wird werden*
wir	*sind gewesen*	*haben gehabt*	*sind geworden*	*werden sein*	*werden haben*	*werden werden*
ihr	*seid gewesen*	*habt gehabt*	*seid geworden*	*werdet sein*	*werdet haben*	*werdet werden*
sie	*sind gewesen*	*haben gehabt*	*sind geworden*	*werden sein*	*werden haben*	*werden werden*
(formal) Sie	*sind gewesen*	*haben gehabt*	*sind geworden*	*werden sein*	*werden haben*	*werden werden*

Formation of tenses

To form the perfect tense of any verb, the present tense of *haben* or *sein* is used together with the past participle of the verb.

> *Er hat gehabt.* He has had.
>
> *Sie sind gewesen.* They have been.

To form the future tense of any verb, the present tense of *werden* is used with the infinitive of the verb.

> *Du wirst essen.* You will eat.
>
> *Wir werden tanzen.* We shall dance.

Weak and strong verbs

Weak verbs are known in English as regular verbs. The infinitive, past tense, and past participle are shown here for the weak verb *zahlen*.

> *zahlen, zahlte, gezahlt* (to) pay, paid, paid

Strong verbs are known in English as irregular verbs. The infinitive, past tense, and past participle are shown here for the strong verb *singen*.

> *singen, sang, gesungen* (to) sing, sang, sung

Whether weak or strong, all infinitives end in *en*.

> *machen* (to) make   *gehen* (to) go

Dropping the *en* yields the stem of the verb, for example, *mach* for *machen*, *geh* for *gehen*. The endings for the various tenses can then be added to the stem.

Present tense

To form the present tense, the same endings are used for weak verbs and strong verbs: *e, st, t, en, t, en, en.*

Imperfect tense of weak verbs

The imperfect tense of weak verbs is formed by adding the endings *te, test, te, ten, tet, ten* to the stem of the verb.

If the infinitive stem of a verb ends in *d* or *t*, an *e* precedes the endings. In the verb *warten*, for example, the stem is *wart*. The imperfect of *warten*, therefore, is as follows.

ich wartete I waited	*wir warteten* we waited
du wartetest you waited	*ihr wartetet* you waited
er wartete he waited	*sie warteten* they waited

Past participle of weak verbs

The past participle of weak verbs is formed by putting *ge* before the third person singular of the present tense of the verb.

> *(er) spielt* he plays, *gespielt* played
>
> *(er) dankt* he thanks, *gedankt* thanked

Conjugation of weak and strong verbs

Infinitive	weak	strong
	machen	*gehen*
	to make	to go

Indicative	*Present*		*Imperfect*		Imperative	
	I make	I go	I made	I went	(fam. sing.)	*mache*
	I do make	I do go	I did make	I did go	(fam. pl.)	*macht*
	I am making	I am going	I was making	I was going	(formal)	*machen Sie*
ich	*mache*	*gehe*	*machte*	*ging*		
du	*machst*	*gehst*	*machtest*	*gingst*	(fam. sing.)	*gehe*
er, sie, es	*macht*	*geht*	*machte*	*ging*	(fam. pl.)	*geht*
wir	*machen*	*gehen*	*machten*	*gingen*	(formal)	*gehen Sie*
ihr	*macht*	*geht*	*machtet*	*gingt*		
sie	*machen*	*gehen*	*machten*	*gingen*		
(formal) Sie	*machen*	*gehen*	*machten*	*gingen*		

	Perfect		*Future*		Participles	
	I have made	I have gone	I shall make	I shall go	*Past*	*gemacht*
ich	*habe gemacht*	*bin gegangen*	*werde machen*	*werde gehen*	*Present*	*machend*
du	*hast gemacht*	*bist gegangen*	*wirst machen*	*wirst gehen*		
er, sie, es	*hat gemacht*	*ist gegangen*	*wird machen*	*wird gehen*	*Past*	*ist gegangen*
wir	*haben gemacht*	*sind gegangen*	*werden machen*	*werden gehen*	*Present*	*gehend*
ihr	*habt gemacht*	*seid gegangen*	*werdet machen*	*werdet gehen*		
sie	*haben gemacht*	*sind gegangen*	*werden machen*	*werden gehen*		
(formal) Sie	*haben gemacht*	*sind gegangen*	*werden machen*	*werden gehen*		

Perfect tense of weak verbs

The perfect tense of weak verbs is formed by conjugating *sein* to be, or *haben* to have, plus the past participle. Among the verbs forming the perfect with *sein* are verbs of motion.

Ich bin gegangen. I have gone.

Er ist ihm gefolgt. He has followed him.

All reflexive verbs form the perfect with *haben* and the past participle. This is true both for weak and strong verbs.

Sie hat sich gewaschen. She has washed herself.

Wir haben uns gestritten. We have quarreled.

Er hat sich gefreut. He was glad.

Note that past participles are placed at the end of the sentence or independent clause.

Du hast das Buch gelesen. You have read the book.

Imperfect and past participle of strong verbs

Strong verbs form their own imperfect and past participle. Some examples of strong verbs are shown here.

Infinitive	Imperfect	Past participle
fliegen (to) fly	*flog*	*geflogen*
kommen (to) come	*kam*	*gekommen*
lassen (to) let	*liess*	*gelassen*
leiden (to) suffer	*litt*	*gelitten*
rufen (to) call	*rief*	*gerufen*
schlafen (to) sleep	*schlief*	*geschlafen*

Future tense

The future tense of all verbs, whether weak or strong, is formed by conjugating *werden* in the present tense plus the infinitive of the verb.

ich werde halten I shall hold

du wirst halten you will hold

er wird halten he will hold

wir werden halten we will hold

ihr werdet halten you will hold

sie werden halten they will hold

Imperative mood

The imperative with the polite *Sie* is formed by using the infinitive of a verb, followed by *Sie.* To be very polite, the word *bitte* (please) may be added:

Schreiben Sie bitte. Please write.

Gehen Sie bitte. Please go.

The imperative with the *du* form is expressed by deleting the *en* of the infinitive.

Infinitive	Imperative
spielen (to) play	*spiel* play
singen (to) sing	*sing* sing

The imperative for the *ihr,* you plural, form uses the present tense *ihr* form of the verb without the pronoun *ihr.*

ihr geht you go		*geht* go	
ihr nehmt you take		*nehmt* take	

The imperative of the first person plural is expressed by the infinitive followed by *wir* we.

helfen wir let us help   *geben wir* let us give

Forming the passive voice

To form the passive, the auxiliary verb *werden* (to become) is conjugated and followed by the past participle of the main verb:

Sie wird getragen.

She is being carried.

Er wurde gehört.

He was heard.

Wir werden gelobt werden.

We are going to be praised.

Impersonal verbs

Many verbs are used only in the third person singular with the pronoun *es* it. They are used in all tenses. Some examples follow.

es regnet it is raining

es schneit it is snowing

es klopft there is a knock

es gelingt mir I succeed

es gibt there is, there are

wie geht es dir? how are you?

es geht mir gut I am fine

es tut mir leid I am sorry

Verbal prefixes

There are two types of verbal prefixes: inseparable and separable. Although these prefixes may change the meaning of a verb, they do not affect conjugation. Some examples of inseparable verbal prefixes follow.

be as in *besuchen* (to) visit

ent as in *entspannen* (to) relax

er as in *erlangen* (to) get

ge as in *gelingen* (to) succeed

miss as in *misstrauen* (to) mistrust

ver as in *vertrauen* (to) trust

zer as in *zerbrechen* (to) break

Separable verbal prefixes are prefixes that also function as prepositions. Some examples follow.

anhören (to) listen	*an* at, on, to
aufstehen (to) get up	*auf* on, onto
untergehen (to) perish	*unter* under, among
vorstellen (to) introduce	*vor* before

In the simple tenses, the verbal prefix separates from the verb and is placed at the end of the sentence. Consider this example, which uses the verb *untergehen.*

Die Sonne geht unter. The sun sets.

In compound tenses, the verbal prefix does not separate. The *ge* of the past participle appears between the prefix and the verb.

Er hat zugehört. He has listened.

Wir wurden angestellt. We were hired.

Modal auxiliary verbs

Six verbs expressing certain modes of action have a conjugation of their own.

dürfen (to) be allowed to, expressing permission
können (to) be able to, expressing ability
mögen (to) like to, expressing desire
müssen (to) have to, expressing obligation
sollen (to) be obliged to *or* to be said to, expressing obligation
wollen (to) want, expressing intent

The principal forms of the modal auxiliaries follow.

Infinitive	Imperfect	Past participle
dürfen	durfte	gedurft
können	konnte	gekonnt
mögen	mochte	gemocht
müssen	musste	gemusst
sollen	sollte	gesollt
wollen	wollte	gewollt

The following sentences show typical uses of the modal auxiliary verbs. (Modal auxiliaries are used frequently, since they express thoughts commonly needed in situations that arise in the everyday lives of people of all types.)

Willst du nach Hause gehen?
Do you want to go home?

Er darf nicht spielen.
He is not allowed to play.

Wir konnten rennen.
We were able to run.

Sie mag keine Milch.
She does not like milk.

Er hat sprechen gekonnt.
He was able to speak.

Sie muss üben.
She must exercise.

Present tense of modal auxiliary verbs

	dürfen I may	können I can	mögen I may, I like	müssen I must	sollen I should	wollen I want
ich	darf	kann	mag	muss	soll	will
du	darfst	kannst	magst	musst	sollst	willst
er, sie, es	darf	kann	mag	muss	soll	will
wir	dürfen	können	mögen	müssen	sollen	wollen
ihr	dürft	könnt	mögt	müsst	sollt	wollt
sie	dürfen	können	mögen	müssen	sollen	wollen

Conjunctions

There are two types of conjunctions: coordinating conjunctions and subordinating conjunctions.

Coordinating conjunctions

Coordinating conjunctions connect principal clauses and do not affect word order.

Ich trinke Wein, aber Dieter trinkt Bier.
I drink wine but Dieter drinks beer.

Er liest nicht, sondern schläft.
He does not read but sleeps.

Common coordinating conjunctions follow.

aber but
denn for
entweder . . . oder either . . . or
oder or
sondern but (on the contrary)
und and

Subordinating conjunctions

Subordinating conjunctions introduce a dependent clause. Subordinating conjunctions affect the word order.

Er geht langsam, weil er müde ist.
He goes slowly because he is tired.

Sie spielte, obgleich sie müde war.
She was playing although she was tired.

In sentences containing an independent clause and a dependent clause, the auxiliary verb comes last and is preceded by the past participle or an infinitive.

Ich schrieb, nachdem ich angekommen war.
I wrote after I had arrived.

Er trank, weil er durstig gewesen ist.
He drank because he was thirsty.

Common subordinating conjunctions follow.

als when, then	*dass* so that
als ob as if	*obgleich* although
bevor before	*seit, seitdem* since
bis until	*sobald* as soon as
da since, when	*weil* because
damit in order that	

Numbers, time, dates

Cardinal numbers

Cardinal numbers are not declined.

Zehn is added to the numbers three to nine to form thirteen to nineteen. Note the difference in spelling:

  sechs 6, *sechzehn* 16; *sieben* 7, *siebzehn* 17.

Zig is added to the numbers three to nine to form thirty, etc. Note the differences in spelling:

  zwei 2, *zwanzig* 20;
  drei 3, *dreissig* 30;
  sechs 6, *sechzig* 60
  sieben 7, *siebzig* 70.

The numbers from twenty to thirty and so on up to 99 are formed by using the single numbers first and adding *und* and.

Ordinal numbers

Ordinal numbers are declined as adjectives. They are usually formed by adding *te* to the cardinal numbers. With ordinal numbers beginning with *zwanzig* 20, add *ste* to form the cardinal number.

Time of day

The time of day is expressed in two ways.

  Es ist drei Uhr. It is three o'clock.
  um drei Uhr at three o'clock

The progression of time is expressed in two ways. For example, ten-fifteen can be expressed as follows.

  ein Viertel nach zehn a quarter after ten
  ein Viertel elf a quarter past ten

Ten-thirty is *halb elf.* Ten-forty-five is *drei Viertel elf.* The progression of time can also be expressed by employing minutes.

  zehn Minuten vor sieben ten minutes before seven
  zehn Minuten nach sieben ten minutes after seven

In timetables time is expressed on a twenty-four hour basis. From 12 noon to midnight, the hours are 13 to 24 o'clock.

  acht Uhr fünfundzwanzig 8:25 A.M.
  zwanzig Uhr zehn 8:10 P.M.

Cardinal numbers		Ordinal numbers	
1	*eins*	(der, die, das) *erste*	first
2	*zwei*	*zweite*	second
3	*drei*	*dritte*	third
4	*vier*	*vierte*	fourth
5	*fünf*	*fünfte*	fifth
6	*sechs*	*sechste*	sixth
7	*sieben*	*siebente*	seventh
8	*acht*	*achte*	eighth
9	*neun*	*neunte*	ninth
10	*zehn*	*zehnte*	tenth
11	*elf*	*hundertste*	hundredth
12	*zwölf*	*tausendste*	thousandth
13	*dreizehn*	*millionste*	millionth
14	*vierzehn*		
15	*fünfzehn*		
16	*sechzehn*		
17	*siebzehn*		
18	*achtzehn*		
19	*neunzehn*		
20	*zwanzig*		
21	*einundzwanzig*		
22	*zweiundzwanzig*		
30	*dreissig*		
40	*vierzig*		
50	*fünfzig*		
60	*sechzig*		
70	*siebzig*		
80	*achtzig*		
90	*neunzig*		
100	*hundert*		
101	*hunderteins*		
200	*zweihundert*		
1000	*tausend*		
2000	*zweitausend*		
2300	*zweitausenddreihundert*		
4002	*viertausendzwei*		
10900	*zehntausendneunhundert*		
1000000	*eine Million*		

Review of German Grammar

Dates

When numbers are used in expressing dates, they generally are not written out. Instead, a numeral is used and followed by a period.

am 18. Dezember 1983 December 18, 1983
der 19. Mai May 19th

Days

Montag	Monday
Dienstag	Tuesday
Mittwoch	Wednesday
Donnerstag	Thursday
Freitag	Friday
Sonnabend	Saturday
Sonntag	Sunday

Seasons

Frühling	spring
Sommer	summer
Herbst	autumn
Winter	winter

Months

Januar	January	*Juli*	July
Februar	February	*August*	August
März	March	*September*	September
April	April	*Oktober*	October
Mai	May	*November*	November
Juni	June	*Dezember*	December

Arithmetical expressions

Vier und vier ist acht. Four and four are eight.
Instead of *und, plus* can be used.

Acht weniger sechs ist zwei. Eight minus six is two.
Instead of *weniger, minus* can be used.

Drei mal sieben ist einundzwanzig.
Three times seven is twenty-one.

Zehn geteilt durch zwei ist fünf.
Ten divided by two is five.

To indicate a fraction, *tel* is added to the cardinal number.

viertel ¼   *fünftel* ⅕   *sechstel* ⅙

An exception is *ein halb* ½, which is an adjective and is declined.

Er isst einen halben Kuchen. He eats a half a cake.

Another exception is *ein drittel*, which derives from *drei* three.

Indefinite numbers and amounts are not declined.

ein bisschen	a little	*etwas*	some
ein paar	a few	*genug*	enough
ein wenig	a little	*mehr*	more

Note that *ein Paar* means a pair.

Countries

With few exceptions, the names of countries are not preceded by an article. The exceptions follow.

die Niederlande the Netherlands
die Schweiz Switzerland
die Türkei Turkey

Adjectives describing a country or its people are not capitalized.

der deutsche Wein
German wine

die amerikanische Bevölkerung
the American population

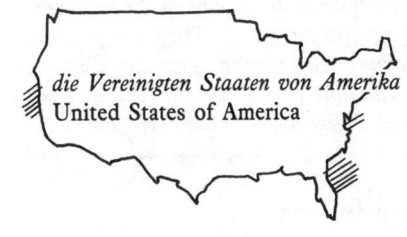

die Vereinigten Staaten von Amerika
United States of America

Country	People	Language
Belgien Belgium	*Belgier* Belgian	*Französisch* French
Dänemark Denmark	*Däne* Dane	*Dänisch* Danish
Deutschland Germany	*Deutsche* German	*Deutsch* German
England England	*Engländer* Englishman	*Englisch* English
Frankreich France	*Franzose* Frenchman	*Französisch* French
Polen Poland	*Pole* Pole	*Polnisch* Polish
Russland Russia	*Russe* Russian	*Russisch* Russian
Schweden Sweden	*Schwede* Swede	*Schwedisch* Swedish
Spanien Spain	*Spanier* Spaniard	*Spanisch* Spanish

Word order

Normal word order

As a rule the word order within a sentence is subject, verb, object.

> *Der Bruder liest das Buch.*
> The brother reads the book.

If a sentence contains a direct and an indirect object, the indirect object precedes the direct object.

> *Der Bruder gibt dem Vater das Buch.*
> The brother gives the father the book.

If the direct object is a pronoun, the direct object precedes the indirect object.

> *Der Bruder gibt es ihm.*
> The brother gives it to him.

> *Der Bruder gibt's dem Vater.*
> The brother gives it to the father.

Inverted word order

Inverted word order is used in forming questions.

> *Kann er lesen?* Does he know how to read?

Inverted word order is used in expressing commands.

> *Kommen Sie her!* Come here!

Inverted word order is used in sentences beginning with expressions of time or place.

> *Heute schlafe ich nicht.*
> Today I do not sleep.

> *In der Stadt gibt es viele Theater.*
> There are many theaters in the city.

In the future tense and with a modal auxiliary verb, an infinitive is placed at the end of the sentence.

> *Sie werden heute spielen.* They will play today.
> *Sie können heute spielen.* They can play today.

A past participle is placed at the end of a sentence.

> *Sie sind angekommen.* They have arrived.

This highway sign illustrates typical German word order: STOPPT (stop) includes the subject "you" understood; the object AUSPUFF-PEST (exhaust pest) follows. Above this message appear the words Unsere Luft (our air).

Participles

A separable prefix becomes inseparable in the past participle.

A past participle precedes the auxiliary verb in sentences containing an independent clause and a dependent clause.

> *Wir wissen, dass er gehört hat.*
> We know that he has heard.

Writing letters

Date

14. August 1984 August 14, 1984

Inside address

The destination is supplied after the name of the addressee. The house number follows the street.

Herrn Max Schulz	Mr. Max Schulz
Düsseldorf	8 Hauptstrasse
Hauptstrasse 8	Düsseldorf

Salutation

(informal)

> *Lieber Herr Schulz* Dear Mr. Schulz

(formal)

> *Sehr geehrter Herr Schulz* Dear Mr. Schulz

Complimentary close

(informal)

> *Mit freundlichen Grüssen*
> With kindest regards

(formal)

> *Hochachtungsvoll* Very truly yours

A letter to friends or family may close in three ways.

> *Mit vielen Grüssen*
> With many regards

> *Mit den besten Grüssen*
> With best regards

> *Viele Grüsse und Küsse*
> With many regards and kisses

For the traveler

Basic expressions and idioms

auf alle Fälle	at any rate
danke	
danke sehr	
danke vielmals	thank you
besten Dank	
vielen Dank	
es tut mir leid	I am sorry
gestern abend	last night
Glück haben	to be lucky
glückliche Reise	have a good trip
herzlichen Glückwunsch	congratulations
heute in acht Tagen	a week from now
Hunger (Durst) haben	to be hungry (thirsty)
ich heisse	my name is
nehmen Sie Platz	please sit down
schönen Gruss an	remember me to
was ist los?	What is going on?
zu Fuss gehen	to walk
zu Hause	at home

A street in West Berlin with many attractions for German shoppers as well as tourists from abroad.

Reading a menu in a German restaurant

Breakfast *Frühstück*

rolls	Brötchen	pancakes	Pfannkuchen	coffee	Kaffee
crescent rolls	Hörnchen	scrambled eggs	Rühreier	cocoa	Kakao
dry toast	Zwieback	fried eggs	Spiegeleier	tea	Tee
		soft-boiled eggs	weichgekochte Eier		

Lunch and dinner *Mittagessen und Abendessen*

cold cuts	Aufschnitt	roast beef	Rinderbraten	potato dumplings	Kartoffelklösse
sandwich	belegtes Brot	roast chicken	Brathuhn	mashed potatoes	Kartoffelpüree
cheese	Käse	roast goose	Gänsebraten	boiled potatoes	Salzkartoffeln
sausage	Wurst	roast veal	Kalbsbraten		
frankfurters	Würstchen	roast pork	Schweinebraten	dessert	Nachtisch
		meatballs	Klopse	ice cream	Eis
consommé	Brühe			stewed fruit	Kompott
noodle soup	Brühe mit Nudeln	fish	Fisch	tarts	Törtchen
soup	Suppe	codfish	Cabeljau	fruit	Obst
		flounder	Flunder		
salad	Salat	halibut	Heilbut		
cucumber salad	Gurkensalat				
tomato salad	Tomatensalat	vegetables	Gemüse		
mixed salad	Gemischter Salat	mushrooms	Champignons		
		peas	Erbsen		
		vegetable plate	Gemüseplatte		
		green beans	grüne Bohnen		
		cabbage	Kohl		
		carrots	Mohrrüben		

die Haare hair
die Augen eyes
die Ohren ears
die Nase nose
die Backen cheeks
der Mund mouth
die Zähne teeth
das Kinn chin
die Lippen lips

das Gesicht The face

Dictionary

der Körper The human body

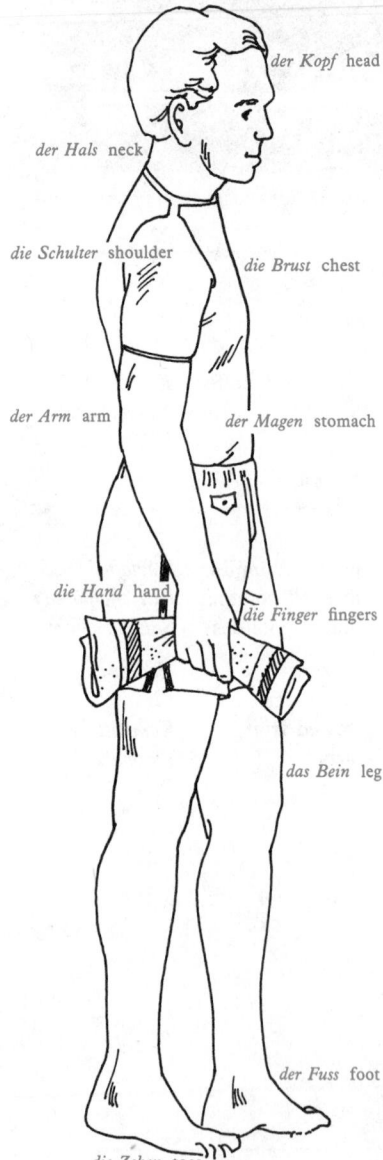

der Kopf head
der Hals neck
die Schulter shoulder
die Brust chest
der Arm arm
der Magen stomach
die Hand hand
die Finger fingers
das Bein leg
der Fuss foot
die Zehen toes

Dictionary abbreviations. Nouns are identified as masculine *(m)*, feminine *(f)*, or neuter *(nt)*. Adjectives are identified as *adj*, adverbs as *adv*, conjunctions as *conj*, interjections as *interj*, prepositions as *prep*, pronouns as *pron*, and verbs as *v*. Plurals are identified as *pl*.

German-English

A

Abend *m* evening
Abenteur *nt* adventure
aber *conj* but
ablehnen *v* decline
ähnlich *adj* similar
also *conj* therefore, so
alt *adj* old
alt werden *v* age
Angina *f* sore throat
Angst *f* fear
Anleihe *f* loan
Ansprache *f* speech
anständig *adj* decent
Antwort *f* reply, answer
antworten *v* answer
Anzug *m* suit
Arbeit *f* work
arbeiten *v* work
Arm *m* arm
arm *adj* poor
Armbanduhr *f* wristwatch
Arzt *m* medical doctor
atmen *v* breathe
auch *conj* also
Aufgabe *f* task
aufpassen *v* watch
aufstehen *v* get up, rise
aufwachen *v* wake up
auf Wiedersehen *interj* goodbye
aufziehen *v* (watch) wind
Auge *nt* eye
Ausflug *m* excursion, outing
Ausgang *m* exit
ausrotten *v* eradicate
ausser *prep* except
Autobahn *f* highway
Autofahrer *m* driver

B

backen *v* bake
Bahnhof *m* station
bald *adv* soon
Ball *m* ball
Bank *f* bench

Bart *m* beard
bauen *v* build, construct
Baum *m* tree
bedeuten *v* mean
beeindrucken *v* impress
behalten *v* keep
Bein *nt* leg
beinahe *adv* almost
bekannt werden *v* become
   acquainted
Belagerung *f* siege
belasten *v* burden
bellen *v* bark
Belohnung *f* reward
benutzen *v* use
beobachten *v* observe
bequem *adj* comfortable
bereit *adj* ready, prepared
berühmt *adj* famous
bescheiden *adj* modest
Bescheidenheit *f* modesty
beschreiben *v* describe
Beschwerde *f* complaint, burden
Besen *m* broom
besonders *adv* particularly
bestechen *v* bribe
Bestechung *f* bribery, graft
bestimmen *v* determine
bestrafen *v* punish
Besuch *m* visit
besuchen *v* visit
beten *v* pray
Bett *nt* bed
Bevölkerung *f* population
bezahlen *v* pay
billig *adj* cheap
bitte *adv* please
blass *adj* pale
blau *adj* blue
bleiben *v* stay
Bleistift *m* pencil
blind *adj* blind
Blinddarm *m* appendix
Blitz *m* lightning
Blume *f* flower
borgen *v* borrow
Brandstiftung *f* arson

brauchen *v* need
braun *adj* brown
Braut *f* bride
Bräutigam *m* bridegroom
Bremse *f* brake
Brief *m* letter
Briefmarke *f* stamp
Briefumschlag *m* envelope
Brot *nt* bread
Brücke *f* bridge
Bruder *m* brother
Buch *nt* book
Bürger *m* citizen

C

Charakter *m* character
Chef *m* boss
Chemie *f* chemistry
Chirurg *m* surgeon
christlich *adj* Christian

D

Dame *f* lady
Dampf *m* steam
Dank *m* gratitude, thanks
danken *v* thank
Daumen *m* thumb
denken *v* think
deswegen *conj* therefore
dichten *v* write poetry
Dichter *m* poet
dick *adj* thick
Dieb *m* thief
Ding *nt* thing
diskutieren *v* discuss
Donner *m* thunder
Draht *m* wire
draussen *adv* outside
dringend *adj* urgent
Druck *m* pressure
dumm *adj* stupid
dunkel *adj* dark
Durst *m* thirst
durstig *adj* thirsty

E

Ecke *f* corner
Efeu *m* ivy
Egoismus *m* egotism
Ehefrau *f* wife
Ehemann *m* husband
Ei *nt* egg

Eid *m* oath
Eigentum *nt* property
einbrechen *v* burglarize
Einbrecher *m* burglar
Eindruck *m* impression
Einfuhr *f* import
einführen *v* introduce
Eingang *m* entrance
Einkommen *nt* income
einladen *v* invite
Einladung *f* invitation
Einschnitt *m* incision
Einwanderer *m* immigrant
Ellbogen *m* elbow
Eltern *pl* parents
Ende *nt* end
endlich *adv* finally
Engel *m* angel
Enkel *m* grandchild
entlassen *v* dismiss
Entlassung *f* dismissal
entwickeln *v* develop
erbärmlich *adj* miserable
erforderlich *adj* necessary
Ergebnis *nt* result
erhalten *v* receive
erinnern *v* remind
erklären *v* explain
erleichtern *v* facilitate, lighten
ernst *adj* earnest
erschöpfen *v* exhaust
ertragen *v* tolerate
essen *v* eat
Europa *nt* Europe
exponieren *v* expose

F

fähig *adj* capable, able
fahren *v* drive, ride
Fahrer *m* driver
Fahrplan *m* timetable
falsch *adj* wrong, false
Familie *f* family
Farbaufnahme *f* color photo
Farbe *f* color
fegen *v* sweep
Fehler *m* mistake
feiern *v* celebrate
Feiertag *m* holiday
Feind *m* enemy
Ferien *pl* vacation
Ferne *f* distance
feucht *adj* damp
Feuchtigkeit *f* dampness

Feuer *nt* fire
finden *v* find
Finger *m* finger
Flasche *f* bottle, flask
fleissig *adj* diligent
Flugzeug *nt* airplane
fordern *v* request
Forderung *f* request
fortfahren *v* continue
Frage *f* question
Frankreich *nt* France
französisch *adj* French
Frau *f* woman, wife
Fräulein *nt* miss
Freiheit *f* liberty
Freund *m* friend
freundlich *adj* kind, friendly
frieren *v* freeze
fröhlich *adj* merry, cheerful
Frucht *f* fruit
früh *adv* early
Frühling *m* spring
Frühstück *nt* breakfast
Fuchs *m* fox
Führerschein *m* driver's license
Funke *m* spark
funkeln *v* spark
funktionieren *v* function, work
für *prep* for
fürchten *v* fear
Fuss *m* foot
Fussboden *m* floor

G

Gabel *f* fork
Gans *f* goose
garantieren *v* vouch for
garnieren *v* adorn
Gast *m* guest
Gastarbeiter *m* foreign worker
Gastgeber *m* host
geben *v* give
Gebirge *nt* mountain range
Gebühr *f* fee
Geburt *f* birth
Geburtstag *m* birthday
Gedächtnis *nt* memory
Gedanke *m* thought, idea
Gedicht *nt* poem
Geduld *f* patience
geduldig *adj* patient
Gefahr *f* danger
gefährlich *adj* dangerous
gegen *prep* against, toward

Gegend *f* area
Gegenwart *f* presence
Gegner *m* adversary
geheim *adj* secret
Geheimnis *nt* secret
gehen *v* go, walk
gehören *v* belong
gehorsam *adj* obedient
Gehorsamkeit *f* obedience
gelb *adj* yellow
Geld *nt* money
Gelegenheit *f* occasion
genau *adv* precisely
genug *adj* enough
geräumig *adj* spacious
Geräusch *nt* noise
Gerüst *nt* scaffolding
Geschenk *nt* present
Gesetz *nt* law
Gesicht *nt* face
Gespenst *nt* ghost
Geständnis *nt* confession
gestehen *v* confess
gestern *adv* yesterday
gesund *adj* healthy
gewaltsam *adj* violent
Gewalttätigkeit *f* violence
gewiss *adv* certainly
Gewissen *nt* conscience
Gewissensbisse *m* remorse
gewissenhaft *adj* conscientious
gewissermassen *adv* so to speak
Gewitter *nt* thunderstorm
Glas *nt* glass
glatt *adj* slippery
Glatze *f* baldness
gleichzeitig *adv* simultaneously
Glocke *f* bell
Glück *nt* luck
Gott *m* god
göttlich *adj* divine
gottlos *adj* godless
Grab *nt* tomb
Graben *m* ditch
graben *v* dig
gratulieren *v* congratulate
Grippe *f* flu
gross *adj* big, tall
grün *adj* green
Grundlage *f* basis
gründlich *adj* profound
Gruppe *f* group
grüssen *v* greet
gültig *adj* valid
gut *adj* good

H

Haar *nt* hair
Hafen *m* harbor
Hagel *m* hail
Hals *m* neck
Hand *f* hand
Handlung *f* action
Handschuh *m* glove
Handtuch *nt* towel
hauptsächlich *adv* chiefly, *adj* principal
Hauptstadt *f* capital
Hauptstrasse *f* main street
Haus *nt* house
Hauswirt *m* landlord
Haut *f* skin
Heide *f* heath
heilen *v* cure, heal
Heiligabend *m* Christmas eve
heiraten *v* marry
helfen *v* help, assist
Hemd *nt* shirt
Herausgeber *m* publisher
Herbst *m* fall, autumn
herrlich *adj* splendid
Herz *nt* heart
herzlich *adj* affectionate
heute *adv* today
heute abend *adv* tonight
hier *adv* here
Hilfe *f* help
hilflos *adj* helpless
Himmel *m* sky, heaven
hinter *prep* behind, beyond
Hintergrund *m* background
hinzufügen *v* add
hoch *adj* high, tall
Hochzeit *f* wedding
hoffen *v* hope
hoffentlich *adv* I hope
Hoffnung *f* hope
höflich *adj* polite
Hölle *f* hell
Holz *nt* wood
hören *v* hear
Hose *f* pants
hübsch *adj* pretty, handsome
Hunger *m* hunger
hungern *v* starve
hungrig *adj* hungry
Husten *m* cough
husten *v* cough
Hut *m* hat
Hütte *f* cabin

I

immer *adv* always
impfen *v* inoculate
Ingenieur *m* engineer
Inhaltsverzeichnis *nt* table of contents
interessant *adj* interesting
Irrtum *m* error

J

Jagd *f* chase
jagen *v* chase
jedoch *conj* nevertheless
jemand *pron* somebody
jenseits *adv* beyond
jetzt *adv* now
Jugend *f* youth
jugendlich *adj* youthful
jung *adj* young

K

kahl *adj* bold
kalt *adj* cold
Kammermusik *f* chamber music
Kampf *m* fight
kämpfen *v* fight
Kapitel *nt* chapter
Karfreitag *m* Good Friday
Kartoffel *f* potato
Käse *m* cheese
Kassier *m* bank teller
kauen *v* chew
kaufen *v* buy
kaum *adv* hardly
Kehle *f* throat
Keim *m* germ
kennenlernen *v* get acquainted, meet
Kern *m* pit
Kind *nt* child
Kirche *f* church
Kissen *nt* pillow
Klasse *f* class
Klatsch *m* gossip
Klavier *nt* piano
Kleid *nt* dress
klein *adj* little, small
klingeln *v* ring
klug *adj* clever
Knie *nt* knee
kochen *v* cook, boil
Koffer *m* suitcase

kommen *v* come
Konditorei *f* coffee shop
Konkurs *m* bankruptcy
Konzept *nt* plan, draft
Kopf *m* head
Kopfschmerz *m* headache
krank *adj* sick, ill
Krankenhaus *n* hospital
Krebs *m* cancer
Krieg *m* war
krumm *adj* crooked
Krüppel *m* cripple
Küche *f* kitchen
Kuchen *m* cake
Kunde *m* customer
Kunst *f* art
Künstler *m* artist
künstlich *adj* artificial
kürzlich *adv* recently
Kusine *f* female cousin
Kuss *m* kiss

L

lächeln *v* smile
lachen *v* laugh
Lachs *m* salmon
Laken *nt* sheet
langsam *adj* slow
Last *f* burden
lästig *adj* burdensome
Leben *nt* life
leben *v* live
ledig *adj* unmarried
leer *adj* empty
Lehrer *m* teacher
Lehrling *m* apprentice
leicht *adj* easy
leider *adv* unfortunately
leihen *v* lend
leise *adv* softly, *adj* soft
lernen *v* learn
lesen *v* read
Leute *pl* people
Licht *nt* light
Liebe *f* love
lieben *v* love
lieber *adv* rather
lieber haben *v* prefer
Literatur *f* literature
Locke *f* curl
Löffel *m* spoon
Luft *f* air
lügen *v* lie
Lust haben *v* like to

M

machen *v* make
Mädchen *nt* girl
Mahlzeit *f* meal
manchmal *adv* sometimes
Mann *m* man, husband
Mantel *m* overcoat
Märchen *nt* fairy tale
Markt *m* market
Maschine *f* machine
Maus *f* mouse
Mehl *nt* flour
mehrere *adj* several
Mensch *m* human being
merken *v* notice
Merkmal *nt* identification mark
messen *v* measure
Messer *nt* knife
Milch *f* milk
mit *prep* with
Mitglied *nt* member
Mittag *m* noon
Mitte *f* middle
Mitternacht *f* midnight
möglich *adj* possible
Monat *m* month
Mord *m* murder
Mörder *m* murderer
morgen *adv* tomorrow
Morgen *m* morning
Motor *m* engine, motor
Muschel *f* shell
Musik *f* music
Mutter *f* mother

N

Nachfolge *f* succession
Nachname *m* last name
Nachricht *f* news
Nacht *f* night
Nachteil *m* disadvantage
Nachtisch *m* dessert
Nadel *f* needle
nahe *adj* near, close
nähren *v* nurse
Nahrung *f* food
Name *m* name
Nase *f* nose
nass *adj* wet
Nässe *f* wetness
Natur *f* nature
natürlich *adj* natural, *adv* of
  course

neben *prep* next to, beside
Neffe *m* nephew
nehmen *v* take
Neid *m* envy
neiden *v* envy
Nichte *f* niece
nichts *pron* nothing
nieder *prep* down
Niedergang *m* decline
niedrig *adj* low
niemand *pron* nobody
Nummer *f* number

O

ob *prep* whether
Ober *m* waiter
obgleich *conj* although
oder *conj* or
Ofen *m* stove
öffnen *v* open
oft *adv* often
ohne *prep* without
ohnegleichen *adv* unequaled
ohnehin *adv* in any case
Ohr *nt* ear
Ohrfeige *f* slap in the face
Onkel *m* uncle
Oper *f* opera
Opfer *nt* sacrifice, victim
Ort *m* spot

P

packen *v* pack
Paket *nt* package
Panne *f* breakdown
Papagei *m* parrot
Papier *nt* paper
Papierkorb *m* wastepaper basket
Park *m* park
Pass *m* passport
Passagier *m* passenger
passieren *v* happen
Person *f* person
Pfeife *f* pipe
Pferd *nt* horse
Platz *m* place
Polizei *f* police
Polizeiwache *f* police station
Priester *m* priest
Programm *nt* program
prüfen *v* examine
Prüfung *f* examination
pünktlich *adj* punctual

Q

Qual *f* torture
quälen *v* torture
Qualitat *f* quality

R

Rabe *m* raven
Rad *nt* wheel
Rauch *m* smoke
rauchen *v* smoke
rechnen *v* calculate, count
Recht *nt* right
recht *adj* right
recht haben *v* be right
rechtzeitig *adv* on time
Regen *m* rain
Regenmantel *m* raincoat
Regenschirm *m* umbrella
Regierung *f* government
regnen *v* rain
Reifen *m* tire
reinigen *v* clean
reisen *v* travel
reissen *v* tear
rennen *v* run
Reservereifen *m* spare tire
Rock *m* skirt
Roman *m* novel
rot *adj* red
Rücken *m* back
Rucksack *m* knapsack
Ruderboot *nt* rowboat
rufen *v* call
ruhig *adj* quiet, calm

S

sammeln *v* collect
Sammlung *f* collection
Sand *m* sand
Satz *m* sentence
schaffen *v* create
Schaffner *m* conductor
Schaffung *f* creation
scharf *adj* sharp
Scheibenwischer *m* windshield wiper
Schere *f* scissors
Schiff *nt* ship
Schinken *m* ham
schlafen *v* sleep
Schlagsahne *f* whipped cream
schlecht *adj* bad

schliessen *v* close
Schlips *m* necktie
Schloss *nt* castle
schmeicheln *v* flatter
schmutzig *adj* dirty
Schnee *m* snow
schneiden *v* cut
schnell *adj* fast, quick
Schokolade *f* chocolate
schön *adj* beautiful
Schornstein *m* chimney
schreiben *v* write
Schuh *m* shoe
Schule *f* school
Schurke *m* villain
schwach *adj* feeble, weak
schwarz *adj* black
Schwein *nt* pig
schwer *adj* heavy
Schwester *f* sister
Schwiegermutter *f* mother-in-law
Schwiegervater *m* father-in-law
sehen *v* to see
sehr *adv* much
seit *prep* since
Seite *f* page
seltsam *adj* strange
senden *v* send
Serviette *f* napkin
sich sorgen *v* worry
sich setzen *v* sit down
singen *v* sing
sitzen *v* sit
sogar *adv* even
Sohn *m* son
Sommer *m* summer
Sonne *f* sun
Sorge *f* worry
sparen *v* save
Speisekarte *f* menu
Spiegel *m* mirror
Spinne *f* spider
spinnen *v* spin
Sprache *f* language
sprechen *v* speak
Sprecher *m* speaker
Stadt *f* city, town
stark *adj* strong
Staub *m* dust
Stein *m* stone
sterben *v* die
steuern *v* conduct, steer
Steuerrad *nt* steering wheel
Stimme *f* voice, vote

Strand *m* beach
Strasse *f* street
streiten *v* quarrel, fight
studieren *v* study
Studium *nt* study
Stuhl *m* chair
Stunde *f* hour
suchen *v* seek, look for
Suppe *f* soup
surren *v* buzz
suspendieren *v* suspend
Szene *f* scene

T

Tag *m* day
Tankstelle *f* gas station
Tante *f* aunt
Tanz *m* dance
tanzen *v* dance
Tasse *f* cup
taub *adj* deaf
Tee *m* tea
teilnehmen *v* take part, participate
Telefon *nt* telephone
telefonieren *v* telephone
telegraphieren *v* telegraph
Teller *m* plate
teuer *adj* expensive
Theater *nt* theater
tief *adj* deep, low
Tier *nt* animal
Tierarzt *m* veterinarian
Tinte *f* ink
Tisch *m* table
Tochter *f* daughter
Topf *m* pot
Torte *f* fancy cake
tot *adj* dead, *n* **Tot** *m*
totmüde *adj* dead tired
tragen *v* carry
trauern *v* mourn
Traum *m* dream
träumen *v* dream
traurig *adj* sad
Treppe *f* staircase
treu *adj* faithful
trinken *v* drink
Trinkgeld *nt* tip
trocken *adj* dry
Trost *m* consolation
trösten *v* comfort
Tür *f* door
Turm *m* tower

U

über *prep* above, over
überraschen *v* surprise
Überraschung *f* surprise
übertreiben *v* exaggerate
Übertreibung *f* exaggeration
Übung *f* exercise
Uhr *f* clock, watch
ungeduldig *adj* impatient
ungefähr *adv* approximately
ungesund *adj* unhealthy
ungewöhnlich *adj* uncommon
unglücklich *adj* unhappy
Universität *f* university
unter *prep* underneath
unterbrechen *v* interrupt
Unterbrechung *f* interruption
Unterhaltung *f* conversation
Unterricht *m* instruction
unterschreiben *v* sign
unverschämt *adj* impudent
unvollendet *adj* unfinished
unzufrieden *adj* dissatisfied
Ursache *f* cause
ursprünglich *adv* originally

V

Vater *m* father
verbessern *v* improve
verbrennen *v* burn
vereinen *v* unite
vergessen *v* forget
verkaufen *v* sell
Verkehr *m* traffic
Verkehrsampel *f* traffic light
verlangen *v* demand
verlieren *v* lose
vermehren *v* increase
veröffentlichen *v* publish
verrückt *adj* crazy
verschwinden *v* disappear
versenden *v* ship
Versicherung *f* insurance
Verspätung *f* delay
verstehen *v* understand
Versuch *m* attempt
verteidigen *v* defend
vertraut *adj* familiar
verwunden *v* wound
verzeihen *v* pardon, forgive
Vetter *m* cousin
viel *adv* much
Vogel *m* bird

Volkslied *nt* folk song
Volksstamm *m* tribe
voll *adj* full
Vorbereitung *f* preparation
vorgestern *adv* day before
  yesterday
vorhaben *v* plan
vorher *adv* before
Vorhersage *f* prediction
vorhersagen *v* predict
vorhersehen *v* anticipate
Vorname *m* first name
Vorschlag *m* proposal
vorschlagen *v* propose
vorsichtig *adj* careful
Vorstadt *f* suburb
Vorstellung *f* performance
Vorteil *m* advantage

W

Waage *f* scale
wachsen *v* grow
wagen *v* risk
Wahl *f* election
wählen *v* choose
während *prep* during
Wahrheit *f* truth
wandern *v* wander
warm *adj* warm
warnen *v* warn
Warnung *f* warning
warten *v* wait
warum *adv and conj* why
Wasser *nt* water
wechseln *v* change
Weg *m* path
weich *adj* soft
weil *conj* because
weinen *v* cry
weiss *adj* white
weit *adj* far
weitergehen *v* go on
Welt *f* world
wenig *adj* little
wetten *v* bet
Wetter *nt* weather
wichtig *adj* important
wieder *adv* again
wiederholen *v* repeat
wiegen *v* weigh
wild *adj* wild
Windel *f* diaper
windig *adj* windy
Windschutzscheibe *f* windshield

Winter *m* winter
Winterfrische *f* winter resort
Wintergarten *m* conservatory
winterlich *adj* wintry
winzig *adj* tiny
wir *pron* we
wirbeln *v* whirl
wirken *v* work
wirklich *adj* actual, real
Wirtshaus *nt* inn
wissen *v* know
Wissenschaft *f* science, learning
Woche *f* week
wöchentlich *adv* weekly
Wolkenkratzer *m* skyscraper
Wörterbuch *n* dictionary
Wunder *nt* miracle
wunderbar *adj* wonderful
Wunderkind *n* prodigy
Wunsch *m* desire, wish
wünschen *v* want

Z

zahlen *v* pay
Zahn *m* tooth
Zahnarzt *m* dentist
Zahnbürste *f* toothbrush
zährtlich *adj* tender
Zehe *f* toe
zeigen *v* show
Zeitalter *nt* age
Zeitung *f* newspaper
Zentrum *nt* center
zerbrechen *v* break
ziehen *v* pull
Ziel *nt* aim
ziemlich *adv* rather
Zimmer *nt* room
zittern *v* tremble
zögernd *adv* reluctantly
Zorn *m* anger
Zucker *m* sugar
Zufall *m* accident
Zug *m* train
zuhören *v* listen
zumachen *v* close
Zündung *f* ignition
Zunge *f* tongue
zurück *adv* back, behind
zurückkommen *v* return
zusammen *adj* together
zwingen *v* force
Zwinger *m* kennel
zwischen *prep* between

Dictionary abbreviations. Nouns are identified as masculine *(nm)*, feminine *(nf)*, or neuter *(nt)*. Adjectives are identified as *adj*, adverbs as *adv*, conjunctions as *conj*, interjections as *interj*, prepositions as *prep*, pronouns as *pron*, and verbs as *v*. Plurals are identified as *pl*.

English-German

A

above *prep* über
action *n* Handlung *f*
add *v* hinzufügen
adorn *v* garnieren
advantage *n* Vorteil *m*
adventure *n* Abenteuer *nt*
adversary *n* Gegner *m*
again *adv* wieder
against *prep* gegen
age *n* Zeitalter *nt*
age *v* altern
air *n* Luft *f*
airplane *n* Flugzeug *nt*
alleviate *v* erleichtern
almost *adv* fast
already *adv* schon
although *conj* obgleich
always *adv* immer
angel *n* Engel *m*
animal *n* Tier *nt*
answer *n* Antwort *f*, *v* antworten
anticipate *v* vorhersehen
appendix *n* (medical)
   Blinddarm *m*
apprentice *n* Lehrling *m*
approximately *adv* ungefähr
arm *n* Arm *m*
arrive *v* ankommen
arson *n* Brandstiftung *f*
art *n* Kunst *f*
artist *n* Künstler *m*
attempt *n* Versuch *m*
attempt *v* versuchen
aunt *n* Tante *f*
autumn *n* Herbst *m*
award *n* Belohnung *f*

B

back *adv* zurück
background *n* Hintergrund *m*
bad *adj* schlecht
bake *v* backen
ball *n* Ball *m*
ban *v* verbannen

bark *v* bellen
beach *n* Strand *m*
beard *n* Bart *m*
beautiful *adj* schön
because *adv* weil
bed *n* Bett *nt*
before *adv* vorher
behind *prep* hinter
bell *n* Glocke *f*
belong *v* gehören
beside *prep* neben
bet *v* wetten
between *prep* zwischen
beyond *adv* jenseits
big *adj* gross
birth *n* Geburt *f*
birthday *n* Geburtstag *m*
bite *v* beissen
black *adj* schwarz
blind *adj* blind
bloom *v* blühen
blue *adj* blau
book *n* Buch *nt*
borrow *v* borgen
boss *n* Chef *m*
bottle *n* Flasche *f*
brake *n* Bremse *f*
bread *n* Brot *nt*
breakdown *n* Panne *f*
breakfast *n* Frühstück *nt*
breath *n* Atem *m*
breathe *v* atmen
bribe *n* Bestechung *f*
bribe *v* bestechen
bride *n* Braut *f*
bridegroom *n* Bräutigam *m*
bridge *n* Brücke *f*
broom *n* Besen *m*
brother *n* Bruder *m*
brown *adj* braun
build *v* bauen
burden *n* Last *f*
burden *v* belasten
burglar *n* Einbrecher *m*
burn *v* brennen
but *conj* aber
buy *v* kaufen

C

cabin *n* Hütte *f*
cake *n* Kuchen *m*
cancer *n* Krebs *m*
capable *adj* fähig
capital *n* Hauptstadt *f*
careful *adj* vorsichtig
carry *v* tragen
castle *n* Schloss *nt*
cause *n* Ursache *f*
cautious *adj* vorsichtig
certainly *adv* gewiss
chair *n* Stuhl *m*
chamber music *n*
   Kammermusik *f*
change *v* wechseln, *n*
   Kleingeld *nt*
character *n* Charakter *m*
chase *v* jagen
cheese *n* Käse *m*
chemistry *n* Chemie *f*
chew *v* kauen
chiefly *adv* hauptsächlich
child *n* Kind *nt*
chimney *n* Schornstein *m*
chocolate *n* Schokolade *f*
choose *v* wählen
Christian *adj* christlich
Christmas eve *n* Heiligabend *m*
church *n* Kirche *f*
citizen *n* Bürger *m*
city *n* Stadt *f*
class *n* Klasse *f*
clean *v* reinigen
clever *adj* klug
close *v* schliessen
coat *n* Mantel *m*
coffee shop *n* Konditorei *f*
cold *adj* kalt
collect *v* sammeln
collection *n* Sammlung *f*
color *n* Farbe *f*
color picture *n* Farbaufnahme *f*
come *v* kommen
comfortable *adj* bequem
compassion *n* Mitleid *nt*
compassionate *adj* mitleidig
complain *v* sich beschweren
complaint *n* Beschwerde *f*
conductor *n* (train) Schaffner *m*
confess *v* gestehen
confession *n* Geständnis *nt*
congratulate *v* gratulieren
conscience *n* Gewissen *m*

Review of German Grammar

consolation *n* Trost *m*
contents *n* Inhalt *m*
continuation *n* Fortsetzung *f*
continue *v* fortfahren
cook *n* Koch *m, v* kochen
corner *n* Ecke *f*
cough *v* husten
courage *n* Mut *m*
cousin *n* Vetter *m*, Kusine *f*
create *v* schaffen
creation *n* Schaffung *f*
cup *n* Tasse *f*
customer *n* Kunde *m*
cut *v* schneiden

D

daily *adj.* täglich
damp *adj* feucht
danger *n* Gefahr *f*
dangerous *adj* gefährlich
dark *adj* dunkel
daughter *n* Tochter *f*
day *n* Tag *m*
dead *adj* tot
dead tired *adj* todmüde
deaf *adj* taub
death *n* Tod *m*
decent *adj* anständig
decline *n* Niedergang *m*
decline *v* ablehnen
deep *adj* tief
defend *v* verteidigen
defense *n* Verteidigung *f*
delay *n* Verzögerung *f*
describe *v* beschreiben
description *n* Beschreibung *f*
desire *n* Wunsch *m*
determine *v* bestimmen
develop *v* entwickeln
dictionary *n* Wörterbuch *nt*
die *v* sterben
difficult *adj* schwierig
dig *v* graben
diligent *adj* fleissig
disadvantage *n* Nachteil *m*
dismiss *v* entlassen
dismissal *n* Entlassung
dissatisfied *adj* unzufrieden
distinguish *v* unterscheiden
ditch *n* Graben *m*
divine *adj* göttlich
doctor *n* Arzt *m*
dog *n* Hund *m*
donkey *n* Esel *m*

door *n* Tür *f*
dream *n* Traum *m*
dress *n* Kleid *n*
drink *v* trinken
driver *n* Fahrer *m*
driver's license *n*
    Führerschein *m*
drugstore *n* Drogerie *f*
dry *adj* trocken
during *prep* während
dust *n* Staub *m*

E

eagle *n* Adler *m*
ear *n* Ohr *nt*
early *adv* früh
easy *adj* leicht
eat *v* essen
egg *n* Ei *nt*
egotism *n* Egoismus *m*
elbow *n* Ellbogen *m*
elect *v* auserwählen
election *n* Wahl *f*
emigrant *n* Auswanderer *m*
empty *adj* leer
end *n* Ende *nt*
enemy *n* Feind *m*
engine *n* Motor *m*
enough *adv* genug
enrich *v* bereichern
entrance *n* Eingang *m*
envelope *n* Umschlag *m*
envoy *n* Gesandte *m*
envy *n* Neid *m*
envy *v* neiden
eradicate *v* ausrotten
error *n* Fehler *m*
Europe *n* Europa *nt*
even *adv* sogar
evening *n* Abend *m*
exaggerate *v* übertreiben
exaggeration *n* Übertreibung *f*
except *prep* ausser
excess *n* Übermass *nt*
excursion *n* Ausflug *m*
exhaust *n* Auspuff *m*
exhaust *v* erschöpfen
exhausted *adj* erschöpft
exhibit *n* Austellung *m*
exhibit *v* ausstellen
exit *n* Ausgang *m*
expensive *adj* teuer
explain *v* erklären
eye *n* Auge *nt*

F

face *n* Gesicht *nt*
facilitate *v* erleichtern
fairy tale *n* Märchen *nt*
faithful *adj* treu
false *adj* falsch
familiar *adj* vertraut
family *n* Familie *f*
famous *adj* berühmt
far *adj* weit
fast *adj* schnell
father *n* Vater *m*
father-in-law *n*
    Schwiegervater *m*
fear *n* Furcht *f, v* fürchten
fee *n* Gebühr *f*
fight *n* Kampf *m, v* kämpfen
finally *adv* endlich
find *v* finden
finger *n* Finger *m*
fire *n* Feuer *nt*
first name *n* Vorname *m*
fish *n* Fisch *m*
fish *v* fischen
flatter *v* schmeicheln
flour *n* Mehl *nt*
flower *n* Blume *f*
flue *n* Grippe *f*
food *n* Nahrung *f*
foot *n* Fuss *m*
for *prep* für
force *v* zwingen
foreign worker *n* Gastarbeiter *m*
forget *v* vergessen
forgive *v* vergeben
fox *n* Fuchs *m*
France *n* Frankreich *nt*
freeze *v* frieren
French *adj* französisch
friend *n* Freund *m*, Freundin *f*
friendly *adj* freundlich
fright *n* Furcht *f*
frog *n* Frosch *m*

G

gas station *n* Tankstelle *f*
get up *v* aufstehen
girl *n* Mädchen *nt*
give *v* geben
glass *n* Glas *nt*
glove *n* Handschuh *m*
go *v* gehen
God *n* Gott *m*

good *adj* gut
goodby *interj* auf Wiedersehen
gossip *n* Klatsch *m*
government *n* Regierung *f*
grandchild *n* Enkel *m*, Enkelin *f*
gratitude *n* Dankbarkeit *f*
green *adj* grün
greet *v* grüssen
greeting *n* Gruss *m*
group *n* Gruppe *f*
grow *v* wachsen
guest *n* Gast *m*

H

hail *n* Hagel *m*, *v* hageln
hair *n* Haar *nt*
ham *n* Schinken *m*
hand *n* Hand *f*
happen *v* passieren
harbor *n* Hafen *m*
hardly *adv* kaum
hat *n* Hut *m*
hay *n* Heu *nt*
head *n* Kopf *m*
headache *n* Kopfschmerz *m*
heal *v* heilen
healthy *adj* gesund
hear *v* hören
heart *n* Herz *nt*
heartily *adv* herzlich
heath *n* Heide *f*
heavy *adj* schwer
hell *n* Hölle *f*
help *n* Hilfe *f*, *v* helfen
helpless *adj* hilflos
here *adv* hier
high *adj* hoch
highlight *n* Höhepunkt *m*
highly *adv* höchst
hilarious *adj* ausgelassen
holiday *n* Feiertag *m*
hope *n* Hoffnung *f*
hope *v* hoffen
horse *n* Pferd *nt*
hospital *n* Krankenhaus *nt*
host *n* Gastgeber *m*
hour *n* Stunde *f*
house *n* Haus *nt*
human being *n* Mensch *m*
hunger *n* Hunger *m*
hungry *adj* hungrig
hunt *n* Jagd *f*
hunt *v* jagen
husband *n* Mann *m*

I

idea *n* Gedanke *m*
ignition *n* Zündung *f*
ill *adj* krank
immigrant *n* Einwanderer *m*
impatient *adj* ungeduldig
import *n* Einfuhr *f*
import *v* einführen
important *adj* wichtig
impress *v* beeindrucken
impression *n* Eindruck *m*
improve *v* verbessern
impudent *adj* unverschämt
incision *n* Einschnitt *m*
income *n* Einkommen *nt*
increase *v* vermehren
inexpensive *adj* billig
ink *n* Tinte *f*
inn *n* Wirtshaus *nt*, Gasthaus *nt*
instead of *conj* anstatt
instruction *n* Unterricht *m*
insurance *n* Versicherung *f*
interesting *adj* interessant
interrupt *v* unterbrechen
interruption *n* Unterbrechung *f*
introduce *v* bekannt machen, einführen
invent *v* erfinden
invention *n* Erfindung *f*
invite *v* einladen
ivy *n* Efeu *m*

K

kennel *n* Zwinger *m*
kind *adj* freundlich, *n* Art *f*
kiss *n* Kuss *m*
kitchen *n* Küche *nt*
knee *n* Knie *nt*
knife *n* Messer *nt*
know *v* wissen

L

lady *n* Dame *f*
landlord *n* Hauswirt *m*
last name *n* Nachname *m*
laugh *n* Lachen *nt*, *v* lachen
law *n* Gesetz *nt*
lazy *adj* faul
learn *v* lernen
leg *n* Bein *nt*
lend *v* leihen
letter *n* Brief *m*

liberty *n* Freiheit *f*
lie *v* (recline) liegen, (tell untruth) lügen, *n* (untruth) Lüge *f*
light *adj* (color) hell, (weight) leicht
lightning *n* Blitz *m*
like to *v* gern
listen *v* zuhören
literature *n* Literatur *f*
little *adj* klein
live *v* leben
living room *n* Wohnzimmer *nt*
loan *n* Anleihe *f*
lock *v* zuschliessen
lose *v* verlieren
loud *adj* laut
love *n* Liebe *f*, *v* lieben
low *adj* niedrig
luck *n* Glück

M

machine *n* Maschine *f*
Main Street *n* Hauptstrasse *f*
majority *n* Mehrheit *f*
make *v* machen
man *n* Mann *m*
many *adj* viel
market *n* Markt *m*
meal *n* Mahlzeit *f*
mean *v* meinen
measure *n* Mass *nt*
measure *v* messen
meet *v* treffen
member *n* Mitglied *nt*
memory *n* Gedächtnis *nt*
menu *n* Speisekarte *f*
merry *adj* fröhlich
middle *n* Mitte *f*
midnight *n* Mitternacht *f*
milk *n* Milch *f*
minority *n* Minderhait *f*
miracle *n* Wunder *n*
mirror *n* Spiegel *m*
miserable *adj* erbärmlich
mistake *n* Fehler *m*
modest *adj* bescheiden
modesty *n* Bescheidenheit *f*
money *n* Geld *nt*
month *n* Monat *m*
mother *n* Mutter *f*
mother-in-law *n* Schwiegermutter *f*
mountain *n* Berg *m*

mourning *n* Trauer *f*
mouse *n* Maus *f*
murder *n* Mord *m*
murderer *n* Mörder *m*
muscle *n* Muskel *m*
music *n* Musik *f*

N

name *n* Name *m*
name *v* ernennen
napkin *n* Serviette *f*
naturally *adv* natürlich
near *adv* nahe
necessary *adj* nötig
neck *n* Nacken *m*
necktie *n* Krawatte *f,* Schlips *m*
needle *n* Nadel *f*
nephew *n* Neffe *m*
never *adv* nie
news *n* Nachricht *f*
next to *prep* neben
niece *n* Nichte *f*
night *n* Nacht *f*
noise *n* Lärm *m*
noon *n* Mittag *m*
no one *pron* niemand
nose *n* Nase *f*
notebook *n* Heft *nt*
nothing *pron* nichts
notice *v* merken
nurse *n* Krankenschwester *f*
nurse *v* nähren

O

oath *n* Eid *m*
obedience *n* Gehorsam *m*
obedient *adj* gehorsam
observation *n* Beobachtung *f*
observe *v* beobachten
occasion *n* Gelegenheit *f*
often *adv* oft
old *adj* alt
on time *adv* rechtzeitig
open *v* öffnen, *adj* offen
opera *n* Oper *f*
or *conj* oder
originally *adv* ursprünglich
otherwise *adv* sonst
outside *adv* draussen

P

pack *v* packen
package *n* Paket *nt*

page *n* Seite *f*
pale *adj* blass
paper *n* Papier *nt*
parents *n* Eltern *pl*
park *n* Park *m*
parrot *n* Papagei *m*
passenger *n* Passagier *m*
passport *n* Pass *m*
patience *n* Geduld *f*
patiently *adv* geduldig
pay *v* zahlen
peculiar *adj* besonders
pea *n* Erbse *f*
peace *n* Friede *m*
pencil *n* Bleistift *m*
people *n* Leute *pl*
person *n* Person *f*
piano *n* Klavier *nt*
pig *n* Schwein *nt*
pillow *n* Kissen *nt*
pipe *n* Pfeife *f*
place *n* Platz *m*
plate *n* Teller *m*
please *interj* bitte, *v* gefallen
poem *n* Gedicht *m*
poet *n* Dichter *m*
police *n* Polizei *f*
police station *n* Polizeiwache *f*
polite *adj* höflich
poor *adj* arm
population *n* Bevölkerung *f*
possible *adj* möglich
pot *n* Topf *m*
potato *n* Kartoffel *f*
pray *v* beten
precisely *adv* genau
predict *v* vorhersagen
prediction *n* Vorhersage *f*
prefer *v* vorziehen
presence *n* Gegenwart *f*
present *n* (gift) Geschenk *nt*
pressure *n* Druck *m*
pretty *adj* hübsch
priest *n* Priester *m*
prison *n* Gefängnis *nt*
profound *adv* gründlich
program *n* Programm *nt*
property *n* Eigentum *nt*
proposal *n* Vorschlag *m*
propose *v* vorschlagen
publish *v* veröffentlichen
publisher *n* Herausgeber *m*
punctual *adj* pünktlich
punish *v* bestrafen
purchase *v* kaufen

Q

quarrel *v* streiten
question *n* Frage *f*
quick *adj* schnell
quiet *adj* ruhig

R

rain *n* Regen *m*, *v* regnen
raincoat *n* Regenmantel *m*
read *v* lesen
ready *adj* bereit
receive *v* erhalten
recently *adv* kürzlich
red *adj* rot
relative *n* Verwandte *m*
reluctant *adj* zögernd
remember *v* sich erinnern an
remorse *n* Gewissensbisse *pl*
request *n* Forderung *f*
request *v* fordern
responsible *adj* verantwortlich
result *n* Ergebnis *nt*
retain *v* zurückbehalten
ride *v* fahren
ring *v* klingeln
rob *v* rauben
robbery *n* Raub *m*
room *n* Zimmer *nt*
runner *n* Läufer *m*

S

sad *adj* traurig
sand *n* Sand *m*
save *v* sparen
scarce *adj* selten
scarcely *adv* kaum
school *n* Schule *f*
science *n* Wissenschaft *f*
scientist *n* Wissenschaftler *m*
scissors *n* Schere *f*
secret *n* Geheimnis *m*
secret *adj* geheim
see *v* sehen
seek *v* suchen
sell *v* verkaufen
send *v* schicken
sentence *n* (grammar) Satz *m,*
  (judgment) Urteil *nt*
serious *adj* ernst
several *adj* mehrere
share *n* Anteil *m*
share *v* teilen

sharp *adj* scharf
sheet *n* Laken *nt*
shell *n* Muschel *f*
ship *n* Schiff *nt*
ship *v* versenden
shirt *n* Hemd *nt*
shoe *n* Schuh *m*
show *v* zeigen
shut *v* schliessen
sick *adj* krank
siege *n* Belagerung *f*
sign *n* Zeichen *nt,*
   v unterschreiben
similar *adj* ähnlich
simultaneously *adv* gleichzeitig
since *prep* seit
sing *v* singen
sit down *v* sich setzen
skin *n* Haut *f*
skirt *n* Rock *m*
sky *n* Himmel *m*
skyscraper *n* Wolkenkratzer *m*
slaughter *v* schlachten
sleep *v* schlafen
slippery *adj* glatt
slow *adj* langsam
smile *n* Lächeln *nt, v* lächeln
smoke *n* Rauch *m, v* rauchen
snow *n* Schnee *m*
soft *adj* weich
softly *adv* leise
soiled *adj* schmutzig
somebody *pron* jemand
sometimes *adv* manchmal
son *n* Sohn *m*
soon *adv* bald
soup *n* Suppe *f*
spacious *adj* geräumig
spare tire *n* Ersatzreifen *m*
spark *n* Funke *m*
spark *v* funkeln
speak *v* sprechen
speaker *n* Sprecher *m*
spider *n* Spinne *f*
splendid *adj* herrlich
spoon *n* Löffel *m*
spring *n* Frühling *m*
stamp *n* Briefmarke *f*
staircase *n* Treppe *f*
starve *v* hungern
station *n* (train) Bahnhof *m*
steam *n* Dampf *m*
steer *v* steuern
steering wheel *n* Steuerrad *nt*
stone *n* Stein *m*

stove *n* Ofen *m*
strange *adj* seltsam
street *n* Strasse *f*
strong *adj* stark
study *n* Studium *nt, v* studieren
succession *n* Nachfolge *f*
suddenly *adv* plötzlich
sugar *n* Zucker *m*
suit *n* Anzug *m*
suitcase *n* Koffer *m*
summer *n* Sommer *m*
sun *n* Sonne *f*
surgeon *n* Chirurg *m*
swallow *n* Schwalbe *f*
swallow *v* schlucken
sweep *v* fegen

T

table *n* Tisch *m*
table of contents *n*
   Inhaltsverzeichnis *nt*
take *v* nehmen
take part *v* teilnehmen
tale *n* Erzählung *f*
tall *adj* gross
task *n* Aufgabe *f*
tea *n* Tee *m*
teacher *n* Lehrer *m,* Lehrerin *f*
telephone *n* Telefon *nt*
telephone *v* telefonieren
tell *v* erzählen
teller *n* (bank) Kassier *m*
temporary *adj* vorübergehend
thank *v* danken
theater *n* Theater *nt*
therefore *adv* also
thick *adj* dick
thief *n* Dieb *m*
thing *n* Ding *nt*
think *v* denken
thirst *n* Durst *m*
thought *n* Gedanke *m*
thumb *n* Daumen *m*
thunder *n* Donner *m*
thunderstorm *n* Gewitter *nt*
time *n* Zeit *f*
timetable *n* Fahrplan *m*
tip *n* Trinkgeld *nt*
tire *n* Reifen *m*
today *adv* heute
together *adv* zusammen
tolerate *v* ertragen
tomorrow *adv* morgen
tongue *n* Zunge *f*

torture *n* Qual *f*
torture *v* quälen
towel *n* Handtuch *nt*
town *n* Stadt *f*
trade *n* Handel *m*
traffic *n* Verkehr *m*
traffic light *n* Verkehrsampel *f*
train *n* Zug *m*
transmission *n* Übertragung *f*
transmit *v* übertragen
travel *v* reisen
tree *n* Baum *m*
tribe *n* Volksstamm *m*
true *adj* wahr
truth *n* Wahrheit *f*

U

umbrella *n* Regenschirm *m*
uncle *n* Onkel *m*
uncommon *adj* ungewöhnlich
under *prep* unter
understand *v* verstehen
unfinished *adj* unvollendet
unfortunately *adv* leider
unhappy *adj* unglücklich
unhealthy *adj* ungesund
university *n* Universität *f*
unmarried *adj* ledig
unusual *adj* ungewöhnlich
urgent *adj* dringend
use *v* benutzen

V

vacation *n* Ferien pl
valid *adj* gültig
very *adv* sehr
veterinarian *n* Tierarzt *m*
victim *n* Opfer *nt*
villain *n* Schurke *m*
violence *n* Gewalttätigkeit *f*
violent *adj* heftig
visit *n* Besuch *m, v* besuchen
voice *n* Stimme *f*
vote *v* wählen
voter *n* Wähler *m*
vouch for *v* garantieren

W

wait *v* warten
waiter *n* Ober *m*
war *n* Krieg *m*
wash *v* waschen

waste basket *n* Papierkorb *m*
watch *v* aufpassen
water *n* Wasser *nt*
waterfall *n* Wasserfall *m*
waterproof *adj* wasserdicht
wave *n* Welle *f*
waver *v* schwanken
wavy *adj* wellig
wax *n* Wachs *nt*
way *n* Weg *m*
we *pron* wir
weak *adj* schwach
weaken *v* schwächen, **feel weak**
    v schwach werden
weakness *n* Schwäche *f*
wealth *n* Reichtum *m*
wealthy *adj* reich
weapon *n* Waffe *f*
wear *v* tragen
wear out *v* abtragen
weary *adj* müde
weather *n* Wetter *nt*
wedding *n* Hochzeit *f*
week *n* Woche *f*
weekly *adv and adj* wöchentlich
weep *v* weinen
weigh *v* wiegen
weight *n* Gewicht *nt*
weird *adj* unheimlich
welcome *n* Willkommen *nt*
welcome *v* bewillkommnen
welfare *n* Wohlergehen *nt*
well *adv* gut, (health) gesund
well *n* Brunnen *m*
well-known *adj* bekannt
west *n* Westen *m*
western *adj* westlich
wet *adj* nass
wetness *n* Nässe *f*
wheel *n* Rad *nt*
when *conj* als, *adv* wann
whether *conj* ob
which *adj and pron* welcher
whichever *adj and pron* welcher
while *conj* während
while *n* Weile *f*
whim *n* Laune *f*
whip *n* Peitsche *f*
whip *v* schlagen
whipped cream *n* Schlagsahne *f*
whirl *v* wirbeln
whirlpool *n* Strudel *m*
whirlwind *n* Wirbelwind *m*
whisker *n* Barthaar *nt*
whiskey *n* Whisky *m*

whisper *v* flüstern
whistle *n* Flöte *f*
whistle *v* flöten
white *adj* weiss
wife *n* Frau *f*
wig *n* Perücke *f*
wild *adj* wild
wilderness *n* Wildnis *f*
will *n* Wille *m*
will *v* (future) werden,
    (bequeath) vermachen, (want
    to) wollen
willful *adj* eigensinnig
willow *n* Weide *f*
wilt *v* welken
wilted *adj* welk
win *v* gewinnen
wind *n* Wind *m*
wind *v* aufziehen
windshield *n*
    Windschutzscheibe *f*
windshield wiper *n*
    Scheibenwischer *m*
windy *adj* windig
winter *n* Winter *m*
wire *n* Draht *m*
wire *v* drahten
wish *n* Wunsch *m*, *v* wünschen
with *prep* mit
within *prep* innerhalb
without *prep* ohne
witness *n* Zeuge *m*
witty *adj* witzig
woe *n* Leid *nt*
wolf *n* Wolf *m*
woman *n* Frau *f*
wood *n* Holz *nt*
woods *n* Wald *m*

word *n* Wort *nt*
work *n* Arbeit *f*, *v* arbeiten
world *n* Welt *f*
worldly *adj* weltlich
worm *n* Wurm *m*
worn-out *adj* abgenutzt
worry *n* Sorge *f*
worry *v* sich sorgen
worse *adj* schlechter
worship *n* Verehrung *f*
worship *v* verehren
worst *adj* schlechtest
worth *n* Wert *m*
worthless *adj* wertlos
worthy *adj* würdig
wound *n* Wunde *f*
wound *v* verwunden
wrap *n* Umhang *m*
wrap *v* wickeln
wrath *n* Zorn *m*
wreath *n* Kranz *m*
wreck *n* Wrack *nt*
wreck *v* demolieren
wrist *n* Handgelenk *nt*
wristwatch *n* Armbanduhr *f*
write *v* schreiben
write poetry *v* dichten

Y

year *n* Jahr *nt*
yell *v* schreien
yellow *adj* gelb
yesterday *adv* gestern
young *adj* jung
youth *n* Jugend *f*
youthful *adj* jugendlich

For further reference

Texts

Huebener, Theodore, and Newmark,
    Maxim
    A First Course in German
    D.C. Heath and Company
Lange, Eva C.
    German in 20 Lessons
    R.D. Cortina

Steinhauer, Harry
    Read, Write, Speak German
    Bantam Books
Steinhauer, Harry, and Sundermeyer,
    William
    Introduction to German
    Macmillan

Dictionaries

Cassell
    German/English; English/German
    Macmillan

Wehrle, Hugo
    Deutscher Wortschatz
    Ernst Klett Verlag.

Review of Spanish Grammar

Spanish grammar shares certain characteristics with English grammar, as you may recall from the time when you first studied these languages. For the most part, the names of the parts of speech and the terms used to show how words function in a sentence are the same. If you have any difficulty in recalling the meanings of any words used in this chapter, consult the dictionary in volume 2 of the *Student Handbooks*. No matter how long you have been away from the formal study of Spanish, you will quickly find yourself recalling what you once learned.

Spanish in Spain and Spanish America

Pronunciation. The *z, ce,* and *ci* are pronounced alike. In southern Spain and Spanish America, they are pronounced like the *s* in *sin.* In central and northern Spain, they are pronounced like the *th* in *thin* and *fifth.*

azúcar sugar
ah-soo-kahr (Spanish America, southern Spain)
ah-thoo-kahr (central and northern Spain)

quince fifteen
keen-say (Spanish America, southern Spain)
keen-thay (central and northern Spain)

hacienda farm
ah-see-en-dah (Spanish America, southern Spain)
ah-thee-en-dah (central and northern Spain)

The *ll* in southern Spain and Spanish America is pronounced like the *y* in *yes.* In central and north- ern Spain, the *ll* is pronounced like the *ly* sound in the second syllable of *million.*

gallo rooster
gah-yoh (Spanish America, southern Spain)
gah-lyoh (central and northern Spain)

Vocabulary. Certain words and expressions differ in Spain and Spanish America, but the differences are minor. A native of one Spanish-speaking country is easily understood by natives of other Spanish-speaking countries.

to drive	*conducir*	(Spain)
	manejar	(Spanish America)
bus	*autobús*	(Spain)
	camión	(Mexico)
peas	*guisantes*	(Spain)
	chícharos	(Spanish America)

The *tortilla* in Spain is an omelet; in Mexico and Guatemala it is a flat corn cake.

Articles

Definite and indefinite articles

	Singular		Plural	
	Masc.	Fem.	Masc.	Fem.
Definite: the	el	la	los	las
Indefinite: a, an	un	una		
some, a few			unos	unas

The neuter article *lo* is used with adjectives and past participles when they are used as nouns.

lo bueno y lo malo the good and the bad

Agreement

Articles agree in number and gender with the nouns they modify.

el niño the boy   *una niña* a girl

El is used instead of *la* before a feminine singular noun that begins with a stressed *a* or *ha*.

el hacha the ax

Contractions of *el*

The prepositions *de* and *a* combine with the masculine article *el* to form *del* and *al*.

Voy al cine. I am going to the movies.

Uses of the definite article

Before each noun in a series.

El padre y el hijo van al centro.
The father and son are going downtown.

Before the names of languages except directly after *hablar*, *en*, or *de*.

El español es importante hoy.
Spanish is important today.

Mi padre habla alemán.
My father speaks German.

Before titles such as *señor*, *doctor*, and *profesor*, except in direct address.

El señor López llegó ayer.
Mr. Lopez arrived yesterday.

¿Cómo está usted, señora Gómez?
How are you, Mrs. Gomez?

Instead of the possessive with clothing and parts of the body.

Me lavo las manos. I wash my hands.

To express "o'clock."

Son las ocho. It is eight o'clock.

Before nouns used in a general or abstract sense.

La medicina es una profesión noble.
Medicine is a noble profession.

Before an infinitive used as a noun.

El comer es necesario. Eating is necessary.

With the names of seasons.

La primavera empieza en marzo.
Spring begins in March.

With days of the week, except after *ser*.

Voy de compras el sábado.
I'm going shopping on Saturday.

Hoy es jueves.
Today is Thursday.

Before certain geographic names such as:

la Argentina Argentina
el Brasil Brazil
los Estados Unidos United States

To express *a* or *an* with weights or measures.

dos pesos el metro two pesos a meter

Omission of the definite article

Before nouns in apposition.

Antonio, criado de los García, llegó tarde.
Anthony, the Garcias' servant, arrived late.

Before numerals expressing numerical order of rulers.

Carlos Quinto Charles the Fifth

Omission of the indefinite article

Before unmodified predicate nouns indicating occupation, profession, or nationality.

Su hermano es médico. His brother is a physician.

Before *cien*, *cierto*, *mil*, *otro*, and *tal*.

cien dólares a hundred dollars
cierto libro a certain book
mil estudiantes a thousand students
otro amigo another friend
tal padre such a father

After the exclamatory *¡que!*

¡Qué mujer! What a woman!

Nouns

Gender

Nouns referring to males and nouns ending in *o* are generally masculine.

el cuaderno the notebook

el abuelo the grandfather

Nouns referring to females and nouns ending in *-a*, *-ión*, *-dad*, *-tad*, *-tud*, or *-umbre* are generally feminine.

la nación the nation   *la madre* the mother

Exceptions

Feminine nouns ending in *o*.

la mano the hand   *la radio* the radio

Masculine nouns ending in *a*.

el drama the drama

el clima the climate

el poeta the poet

el problema the problem

el tranvía the streetcar

el idioma the language

el mapa the map

Plurals

For nouns ending in a vowel, add *s;* for nouns ending in a consonant, add *es*.

el libro, los libros the book, the books

la pared, las paredes the wall, the walls

For nouns ending in *z*, change *z* to *c* before adding *es*.

la luz, las luces the light, the lights

Nouns ending in an unaccented syllable with final *s* remain unchanged in the plural.

el cumpleaños, los cumpleaños

the birthday, the birthdays

For nouns ending in an accented syllable with final *n* or *s*, drop the written accent in the plural.

el jardín, los jardines the garden, the gardens

Nouns indicating rank or relationship may be used in the masculine plural to designate individuals of either sex.

los reyes the kings, or the king and queen

Adjectives and adverbs

Adjectives

Adjectives whose masculine singular forms end in *o* and adjectives of nationality have two singular, two plural forms. All others have one singular, one plural.

Agreement

An adjective agrees in gender and number with the noun modified. An adjective modifying nouns of different genders is generally masculine plural.

Los lápices y las plumas son caros.

The pencils and pens are expensive.

Position

A descriptive adjective usually follows the noun it modifies.

el papel blanco the white paper

A limiting adjective such as a possessive, a demonstrative, or a number, and an adjective of quantity usually precede the noun.

ese vaso that glass

The following adjectives drop the final *o* before a masculine singular noun: *bueno, malo, uno, primero, tercero, alguno, ninguno.*

el primer día the first day

Grande becomes *gran* before a singular noun of either gender.

un gran pintor a great painter

Ciento becomes *cien* immediately before a noun of either gender.

cien vacas one hundred cows

Forms of adjectives

| | Singular | | Plural | |
	Masc.	Fem.	Masc.	Fem.
tall	*alto*	*alta*	*altos*	*altas*
English	*inglés*	*inglesa*	*ingleses*	*inglesas*
poor	*pobre*	*pobre*	*pobres*	*pobres*
easy	*fácil*	*fácil*	*fáciles*	*fáciles*

Common adjectives that change meaning with a change in position

	AFTER *the noun*	BEFORE *the noun*
antiguo	old (ancient)	old (former), old-time
cierto	sure, reliable	a certain
grande	large, big	great, famous
nuevo	new	another, different
pobre	poor	unfortunate
simple	silly, simple-minded	simple, mere

Demonstrative adjectives

	Masc.	Fem.
this	este	esta
these	estos	estas
that	ese	esa
those	esos	esas
that	aquel	aquella
those	aquellos	aquellas

Demonstrative adjectives

Demonstrative adjectives precede the nouns they modify and agree with them in number and gender.

esas manzanas those apples

Este refers to what is near the speaker. *Ese* refers to what is near the person addressed.

Aquel refers to what is remote from both the speaker and the person addressed.

Juan, déme Vd. aquellos libros que están en la sala.
John, give me those books that are in the living room.

Adverbs

Many adverbs are formed by adding the suffix *-mente* to the feminine singular form of the adjective.

un hombre ricamente vestido
a richly dressed man

La tortuga anda lentamente.
The turtle walks slowly.

¡Habla claramente!
Speak clearly!

Maneja cuidadosamente.
He drives carefully.

In a series of two or more adverbs normally formed with *-mente,* the suffix is used only with the last adverb.

Arturo escribió clara y facilmente.
Arthur wrote clearly, and easily.

Comparison

Comparison with adjectives

Superiority	*Juan es más rico que María.*	
	John is richer than Mary.	
Equality	*Juan es tan rico como María.*	
	John is as rich as Mary.	
Inferiority	*Juan es menos rico que María.*	
	John is not as rich as Mary.	

The superlative of an adjective is formed by placing the definite article or possessive adjective before the comparative form.

Miguel es el estudiante más inteligente de la clase.
Michael is the most intelligent student in the class.

Comparison with adverbs

Adverbs are compared as shown in this example.

rápidamente quickly
más (menos) rápidamente more (less) quickly
lo más (menos) rápidamente the most (least) quickly

The article *lo* is used with the superlative form.

The superlative form of the adverb is followed by *de.*

The English word "than" is usually translated as *que.*

Tiene más dinero que Ana.
He has more money than Anna.

Before a number, "than" is translated as *de* if the sentence is affirmative and by *que* if negative.

Recibió más de cien dólares.
He received more than one hundred dollars.

Comparisons of equality are expressed by *tan* plus an adjective or adverb plus *como.*

Manuel es tan alto como Andrés.
Manuel is as tall as Andrew.

Tanto (-a, -os, -as) plus a noun plus *como* is used to express as much (as many) as.

Tengo tantas llaves como tú.
I have as many keys as you.

Tanto (-a, -os, -as) plus *como* is used to express as much (as many) as.

Antonio trabaja tanto como su hermano.
Anthony works as much as his brother.

Comparative forms of adjectives

Positive	Comparative	Superlative
bueno good	*mejor* better	*el mejor* the best
malo bad	*peor* worse	*el peor* the worst
grande great, big	*mayor* greater, older	*el mayor* the greatest, the oldest
	más grande larger	*el más grande* the largest
	menos grande not as large	*el menos grande* the least large
pequeño small	*menor* minor, lesser, younger	*el menor* the least, the youngest
	más pequeño smaller	*el más pequeño* the smallest
	menos pequeño less, small	*el menos pequeño* the least small

Mi pelota!

Possession

Possession is expressed by *de* + the possessor.
> *la cama de mi hermano* my brother's bed

Possessive adjectives

The short form always precedes the noun; the long form always follows the noun. Both forms agree in gender and number with the person or thing possessed.
> *nuestros amigos* our friends
> *las maletas tuyas* your suitcases

Possessive pronouns

A possessive pronoun is formed by the definite article plus the long form of the possessive adjective.
> *el tuyo* yours

A possessive pronoun agrees in number and gender with the noun it replaces.
> *mi pelota y la tuya* my ball and yours

Possessive adjectives

| | Short form | | Long form | | | |
| | Singular | Plural | Singular | | Plural | |
			Masc.	Fem.	Masc.	Fem.
my	mi	mis	mío	mía	míos	mías
your (familiar singular)	tu	tus	tuyo	tuya	tuyos	tuyas
your, his, her, its, their	su	sus	suyo	suya	suyos	suyas
our			nuestro	nuestra	nuestros	nuestras
your (familiar plural)			vuestro	vuestra	vuestros	vuestras

Possessive pronouns

| | Singular | | Plural | |
	Masc.	Fem.	Masc.	Fem.
mine	el mío	la mía	los míos	las mías
yours (familiar singular)	el tuyo	la tuya	los tuyos	las tuyas
your, his, hers, its, theirs	el suyo	la suya	los suyos	las suyas
ours	el nuestro	la nuestra	los nuestros	las nuestras
yours (familiar plural)	el vuestro	la vuestra	los vuestros	las vuestras

Pronouns

Subject pronouns

Subject pronouns are used for clarity, emphasis, or politeness. The English word "it" is not expressed as a subject.
> *Es difícil hacer.* It is difficult to do.

The plural form *vosotros* is used in Spain. In Spanish America, *ustedes* is preferred.

Object pronouns

A pronoun used as the object of a preposition always follows the preposition.

The pronouns *mí, ti* and *sí* combine with the preposition *con* as follows:
> *conmigo* with me
> *contigo* with you (familiar)
> *consigo* with yourself, himself, herself, themselves

These pronoun forms do not change in gender or number.

An object pronoun, whether direct or indirect, is usu- ally placed immediately before the verb. In an affirmative command, infinitive, or present participle, the object pronoun follows and is joined to the verb. In a negative command, the object pronoun precedes the verb. When the object pronoun is joined to an affirmative command or present participle, an accent mark is needed over the vowel of the accented syllable.

Double object pronouns

When a verb has two object pronouns, the indirect object pronoun precedes the direct object pronoun.
> *Me los entregan.* They deliver them to me.

When both object pronouns are in the third person, the indirect object is written as *se*.
> *Se lo digo.* I tell it to her.

The various meanings of *se* may be clarified by adding *a Vd., a Vds., a él, a ella, a ellos, a ellas.*
> *No se la enseñamos a ellos.*
> We don't show it to them.

412   **Review of Spanish Grammar**

Forms of pronouns (see also Possession on page 412)

Subject pronouns

Singular		Plural	
yo	I	*nosotros, -as*	we
tú	you *(familiar)*	*vosotros, -as*	you *(familiar)*
usted (Vd. or Ud.)	you	*ustedes (Vds. or Uds.)*	you
él	he	*ellos*	they
ella	she	*ellas*	they

Pronouns used as objects of prepositions

Singular		Plural	
mí	me	*nosotros, -as*	us
ti	you *(familiar)*	*vosotros, -as*	you *(familiar)*
usted (Vd. or Ud.)	you	*ustedes (Vds. or Uds.)*	you
él	him, it	*ellos*	them *(masc.)*
ella	her, it	*ellas*	them *(fem.)*
sí	yourself, himself, herself, itself	*sí*	yourselves, themselves

Object pronouns

Indirect		Direct		Reflexive	
Singular		*Singular*		*Singular*	
me	to me	*me*	me	*me*	myself
te	to you *(familiar)*	*te*	you *(familiar)*	*te*	yourself *(familiar)*
le	to you, to him, to her, to it	*le*	you *(masc.)*, him	*se*	yourself, himself, herself, itself
		lo	him, it *(masc.)*		
		la	you *(fem.)*, her, it *(fem.)*		
Plural		*Plural*		*Plural*	
nos	to us	*nos*	us	*nos*	ourselves
os	to you *(familiar)*	*os*	you *(familiar)*	*os*	yourselves *(familiar)*
les	to you, to them	*los*	you, them *(masc.)*	*se*	yourselves, themselves
		las	you, them *(fem.)*		

Position of object pronouns

Finite verb	*Les doy el regalo.*	I give them the gift.
Infinitive	*Quieren verlo.*	They want to see it.
	Lo quieren ver.	
Present participle	*Estoy esperándolo.*	I am waiting for it.
	Lo estoy esperando.	
Affirmative command	*Envíelo Vd.*	Send it.
Negative command	*No lo envíe Vd.*	Don't send it.

Relative pronouns and adjectives

que	that, which, who
quien (-es)	who
el (la, los, las) cual (-es)	which, who
lo cual	which
el (la) que	(the one) which, (the one) who, he (she) who
los (las) que	(the ones) which, (the ones) who, those who
lo que	what, which
cuyo (-a, -os, -as)	whose (as relative adjective)

Demonstrative pronouns

	Masc.	Fem.	Neut.
this (one)	*éste*	*ésta*	*esto*
these	*éstos*	*éstas*	
that (one)	*ése*	*ésa*	*eso*
those	*ésos*	*ésas*	
that (one)	*aquél*	*aquélla*	*aquello*
those	*aquéllos*	*aquéllas*	

The placement of double object pronouns is the same as that given above for single object pronouns. Double object pronouns are always kept together.

When both object pronouns are attached to the verb, a written accent mark is used to keep the original stress.

Va a servírselo. He is going to serve it to him.

Demonstrative pronouns

Demonstrative pronouns agree in number and gender with the nouns they represent.

Me gustan estas faldas y aquéllas.

I like these skirts and those (distant).

Neuter forms of demonstrative pronouns indicate things indefinitely referred to, or general ideas and situations.

No haré esto. I shall not do this.

Relative pronouns and adjectives

Relative pronouns and adjectives are never omitted in Spanish.

La revista que compraste es interesante.

The magazine you bought is interesting.

Que refers to both persons and things. After a preposition, however, *que* refers only to things; *quien (-es)* refers to persons.

el chico que jugó   el chico con quien jugué
the boy who played   the boy with whom I played

Negation, interrogatives, and exclamations

Negative words and their opposites

Negative	Affirmative
no no, not	*sí* yes
nadie no one, nobody, not anyone	*alguien* someone, somebody
nada nothing, not anything	*algo* something
nunca, jamás never, not ever	*siempre* always
tampoco neither, not either	*también* also
ninguno (-a) no, none, not any	*alguno (-a)* some, any
ni . . . ni neither . . . nor, not . . . nor	*o . . . o* either . . . or
sin without	*con* with

NO!
NUNCA!

SI!
SIEMPRE!

The negative word *no* precedes the verb.

¿No encontró usted el reloj?

Didn't you find the watch?

If an object pronoun precedes the verb, the negative word precedes the object pronoun.

No lo recibió. He didn't receive it.

All negative sentences must have a negative word preceding the verb. If the negative word follows the verb, then *no* must precede the verb.

Nunca lo haré. I shall never do it.

No lo haré nunca. I shall never do it.

When *nadie* is the object of the verb, it is preceded by the personal *a*.

No veo a nadie. I don't see anyone.

But is expressed as *sino* when the first element is negative and the second is in direct contrast.

No llevaba abrigo negro, sino azul.

He wasn't wearing a black coat, but a blue one.

Interrogative expressions

¿qué? what?

¿quién (-es)? who?

¿cuál (-es)? which, which one(s)?

¿dónde? where?

¿adónde? where? to where? (with verbs of motion)

¿cuándo? when?

¿cuánto (-a)? how much?

¿cuántos (-as)? how many?

¿cómo? how?

¿por qué? why?

Note that all interrogative expressions carry an accent mark.

Exclamations

All exclamatory words carry written accent marks. The most common are:

¡Qué . . . ! What . . . ! What a . . . ! How . . . !

¡Cuánto (a) . . . ! How much . . . !

¡Cuántos (as) . . . ! How many . . . !

Exclamatory sentences have an inverted exclamation point (¡) at the beginning and a regular exclamation point at the end.

¡Qué día! What a day!

Prepositions

Prepositions with infinitives

The infinitive is the only verb form that may follow a preposition.

Después de vestirse, salió.

After getting dressed, he went out.

The infinitive is used after many verbs. In many cases it follows the verb directly.

Quiere salir temprano. He wants to leave early.

In other cases the infinitive is preceded by a preposition. The following common verbs do not require a preposition before an infinitive.

creer	to believe	*necesitar*	to need
deber	ought to, should	*poder*	to be able, can
desear	to wish, desire	*querer*	to wish, want
esperar	to hope	*saber*	to know how to

Verbs expressing beginning, motion, teaching, or learning and several other verbs require the preposition *a* before a following infinitive.

beginning	*comenzar*	motion	*correr* to run
	empezar		*ir* to go
	ponerse		*llegar* to arrive
	principiar		*salir* to go out to
teaching	*enseñar*	other	*invitar* to invite
learning	*aprender*	verbs	*ayudar* to help
			llamar to call

Los niños empezaron a llorar.

The children began to cry.

The following verbs require the preposition *de* before an infinitive.

acabar	to have just	*dejar*	to cease, stop, fail
acordarse	to remember	*olvidarse*	to forget
alegrarse	to be glad to	*tratar*	to try
cesar	to cease, stop		

Trató de esconderse. He tried to hide.

Uses of the personal *a*

The personal *a* is used before direct objects that denote persons or personified things. The personal *a* is not translated.

Visitan a su abuelo They visit their grandfather.

The personal *a* is used before pronouns referring to persons, even when used in a negative sense.

No veo a nadie. I see no one.

The personal *a* is omitted after the verb *tener* with the meaning "to have."

Tiene muchos amigos. He has many friends.

The personal *a* is used with *querer* when it means "to love" and omitted when it means "to want."

El niño quiere su madre.

The child wants his mother.

El niño quiere a su madre.

The child loves his mother.

A striker in Chicago, Illinois, carrying a sign that translates as "On strike for our contract."

Uses of *para*

Purpose:

Como para vivir. I eat in order to live.

Destination:

Saldrá para España. He will leave for Spain.

Use:

Es una caja para dulces. It is a candy box.

Future time:

Estará listo para el sábado.

It will be ready by Saturday.

"Considering the fact that":

Para estudiante, toca muy bien.

For a student, he plays very well.

"Be about to" after *estar:*

Estoy para salir. I am about to leave.

Uses of *por*

"For the sake of":

Lo hizo por su hermano. He did it for his brother.

Price or exchange:

Compró la revista por un peso.

He bought the magazine for a peso.

Length of time:

Quedó en Perú por dos semanas.

He stayed in Peru for two weeks.

"In the morning, afternoon, or night":

Trabajo por la tarde. I work in the afternoon.

"By, through, along":

Dan un paseo por el parque.

They take a walk through the park.

"For" after the verbs *ir, enviar, luchar, llamar,* or *preguntar:*

Fue por el médico. He went for the doctor.

The following verbs are not followed by *para* or *por,* since "for" is part of the meaning of the verb:

buscar to look for,

esperar to wait for,

pedir to ask for.

Buscaron una mesa. They looked for a table.

Verbs

Conjugation of regular verbs

The three conjugations are distinguished by the infinitive endings: *-ar, -er,* and *-ir.*

Conjugation of regular verbs

Simple tenses
Indicative

	Present I take, eat, live / I do take, eat, live			*Imperfect* I was taking, eating, living / I used to take, eat, live		
yo	tomo	como	vivo	tomaba	comía	vivía
tú	tomas	comes	vives	tomabas	comías	vivías
Vd., él, ella	toma	come	vive	tomaba	comía	vivía
nosotros, nosotras	tomamos	comemos	vivimos	tomábamos	comíamos	vivíamos
vosotros, vosotras	tomáis	coméis	vivís	tomabais	comíais	vivíais
Vds., ellos, ellas	toman	comen	viven	tomaban	comían	vivían

Subjunctive

	Present that I may take, eat, live			*Imperfect* that I might take, eat, live / that I should take, eat, live		
yo	tome	coma	viva	tomara or tomase	comiera or comiese	viviera or viviese
tú	tomes	comas	vivas	tomaras or tomases	comieras or comieses	vivieras or vivieses
Vd., él, ella	tome	coma	viva	tomara or tomase	comiera or comiese	viviera or viviese
nosotros, nosotras	tomemos	comamos	vivamos	tomáramos or tomásemos	comiéramos or comiésemos	viviéramos or viviésemos
vosotros, vosotras	toméis	comáis	viváis	tomarais or tomaseis	comierais or comieseis	vivierais or vivieseis
Vds., ellos, ellas	tomen	coman	vivan	tomaran or tomasen	comieran or comiesen	vivieran or viviesen

Compound tenses
Indicative

Present perfect
Present of *haber* plus past participle
I have taken / I have eaten / I have lived
he tomado / *he comido* / *he vivido*

Pluperfect
Imperfect of *haber* plus past participle
I had taken / I had eaten / I had lived
había tomado / *había comido* / *había vivido*

Subjunctive

Present perfect
Present subjunctive of *haber* plus the past participle
that I may have taken / that I may have eaten / that I may have lived
haya tomado / *haya comido* / *haya vivido*

Progressive

The present participle is used with *estar* to denote continuing action.
I am taking / I am eating / I am living
estoy tomando / *estoy comiendo* / *estoy viviendo*

Review of Spanish Grammar

In all but the future and conditional tenses, the inflexional endings are added to the stem of the verb, for example:

tom, *com*, and *viv* for *tomar*, *comer*, and *vivir*. Future and conditional endings are added to the infinitive. These endings are the same for all verbs.

Preterite

I took, ate, lived
I did take, eat, live

tomé	comí	viví
tomaste	comiste	viviste
tomó	comió	vivió
tomamos	comimos	vivimos
tomasteis	comisteis	vivisteis
tomaron	comieron	vivieron

Future

I shall take, eat, live
I will take, eat, live

tomaré	comeré	viviré
tomarás	comerás	vivirás
tomará	comerá	vivirá
tomaremos	comeremos	viviremos
tomaréis	comeréis	viviréis
tomarán	comerán	vivirán

Conditional

I should take, eat, live
I would take, eat, live

tomaría	comería	viviría
tomarías	comerías	vivirías
tomaría	comería	viviría
tomaríamos	comeríamos	viviríamos
tomaríais	comeríais	viviríais
tomarían	comerían	vivirían

Infinitives	*-ar* verb	*-er* verb	*-ir* verb
	tomar	comer	vivir
	to take	to eat	to live

Participles

Present	taking	eating	living
	tomando	comiendo	viviendo
Past	taken	eaten	lived
	tomado	comido	vivido

Imperative	take	eat	live
Familiar s.	toma	come	vive
Familiar pl.	tomad	comed	vivid
Polite s.	tome Vd.	coma Vd.	viva Vd.
Polite pl.	tomen Vds.	coman Vds.	vivan Vds.

Preterite perfect

Preterite of *haber* plus past participle

I had taken	I had eaten	I had lived
hube tomado	hube comido	hube vivido

Future perfect

Future of *haber* plus past participle

I shall have taken	I shall have eaten	I shall have lived
habré tomado	habré comido	habré vivido

Pluperfect

Either form of the imperfect subjunctive of *haber* plus past participle

that I might have taken	that I might have eaten	that I might have lived
hubiera (hubiese) tomado	hubiera (hubiese) comido	hubiera (hubiese) vivido

---

Conditional *perfect*

Conditional of *haber* plus past participle

I should have taken	I should have eaten	I should have lived
habría tomado	habría comido	habría vivido

Stem changing verbs

In conjugating Spanish verbs, we are accustomed to changes in the verb endings, but certain verbs also change the spelling of their stems.

Stem changes are not uncommon in English. Consider the way the verb "eat" changes in English: I eat, I ate. Consider the verb "go": I go, I went. Finally, consider the verb "be": I am, I was.

Conjugation of stem-changing verbs

First class

Certain verbs of the first and second conjugations with stem vowels *e* or *o* change *e* to *ie*, *o* to *ue* when stressed. Note that *jugar*, to play, is conjugated as if it were a first class stem-changing verb with stem vowel *o*.

Examples:

pensar	volver	**Present participle**
to think	to return	*pensando volviendo*

Present indicative		**Present subjunctive**			**Imperative**	
pienso	*vuelvo*	*piense*	*vuelva*			
piensas	*vuelves*	*pienses*	*vuelvas*			
piensa	*vuelve*	*piense*	*vuelva*		*piensa*	*vuelve*
pensamos	*volvemos*	*pensemos*	*volvamos*		*piense*	*vuelva*
pensáis	*volvéis*	*penséis*	*volváis*		*pensemos*	*volvamos*
piensan	*vuelven*	*piensen*	*vuelvan*		*pensad*	*volved*
					piensen	*vuelvan*

Review:
First class verbs
e → ie & o → ue
when stressed.

Second class

Certain verbs of the third conjugation with stem vowels of *e* or *o* change *e* to *ie*, *o* to *ue* when stressed. Changes are the same as those listed above with the addition of *e* changing to *i*, and *o* to *u*, when the following syllable contains a stressed *a*, *ie*, or *io*.

Examples:

(ie) sentir	(ue) dormir	**Present participle**
to feel	to sleep	*sintiendo durmiendo*

Present indicative		**Present subjunctive**		**Preterite**		**Imperfect subjunctive**		**Imperative**	
siento	*duermo*	*sienta*	*duerma*	*sentí*	*dormí*	*sintiera*	*durmiera*		
sientes	*duermes*	*sientas*	*duermas*	*sentiste*	*dormiste*	*sintieras*	*durmieras*	*siente*	*duerme*
siente	*duerme*	*sienta*	*duerma*	*sintió*	*durmió*	*sintiera*	*durmiera*	*sienta*	*duerma*
sentimos	*dormimos*	*sintamos*	*durmamos*	*sentimos*	*dormimos*	*sintiéramos*	*durmiéramos*	*sintamos*	*durmamos*
sentís	*dormís*	*sintáis*	*durmáis*	*sentisteis*	*dormisteis*	*sintierais*	*durmierais*	*sentid*	*dormid*
sienten	*duermen*	*sientan*	*duerman*	*sintieron*	*durmieron*	*sintieran*	*durmieran*	*sientan*	*duerman*

Third class

Certain verbs of the third conjugation with stem vowel *e* change *e* to *i* in all forms affected in the first and second classes of stem-changing verbs.

Example:

(i) pedir	**Present participle**
to ask for	*pidiendo*

Present indicative	**Present subjunctive**	**Preterite**	**Imperfect subjunctive**	**Imperative**
pido	*pida*		*pidiera*	
pides	*pidas*	*pedí*	*pidieras*	
pide	*pida*	*pediste*	*pidiera*	*pide*
pedimos	*pidamos*	*pidió*	*pidiéramos*	*pida*
pedís	*pidáis*	*pedimos*	*pidierais*	*pidamos*
piden	*pidan*	*pedisteis*	*pidieran*	*pedid*
		pidieron		*pidan*

Review of Spanish Grammar

Spelling change verbs

This class of verbs undergoes changes in spelling during conjugation, with the effect of preserving the sound of the consonant found in the infinitive.

The chart below supplies examples of changes in the verbs *buscar* search, *jugar* play, *averiguar* investigate, *vencer* conquer, *conocer* know, *escocer* choose, *leer* read, and *seguir* follow.

Spelling change verbs

Verb ending	Spelling change	Examples
in verbs ending in *car*	*c* changes to *qu* before an *e*	*buscar → busqué*
in verbs ending in *gar*	insert *u* before an *e*	*jugar → jugué*
in verbs ending in *guar*	put dieresis over *u* before an *e*	*averiguar → averigüé*
in verbs ending in *cer* or *cir* preceded by a consonant	replace the *c* by *z* before an *a* or *o*	*vencer → venzo*
in verbs ending in *cer* or *cir* preceded by a vowel	insert *z* before *c* when followed by an *a* or *o*	*conocer → conozco*
in verbs ending in *ger* or *gir*	replace the *g* with *j* before an *a* or *o*	*escoger → escojo*
in verbs ending in *er* or *ir*	change the *i* of the endings *ie* and *io* to *y*	*leer → leyó*
in verbs ending in *guir* when the *u* is silent	drop the *u* before an *a* or *o*	*seguir → sigo*

Correspondencia Correspondence

La carta comercial A business letter

ciudad, fecha city, date	*Miami, 8 de mayo de 19____* Miami, May 8, 19____
destinatario, dirreccion inside address	*Sr. Juan Encina* *Avenida de las Américas 20* *Lima, Perú*
el saludo salutation	*Estimado (a) señor (a):* Dear Sir (Madam):
despedida closing	*Atentamente,* Attentively, *Sinceramente,* Sincerely,
firma signature	José Antonio Rivera

Carta personal A friendly letter

ciudad, fecha city, date	*Nueva York, 20 de julio de 19____* New York, July 20, 19____
saludo salutation	*Querido (a) amigo (a),* Dear friend,
despedida closing	*Cariñosamente,* Lovingly, *Recuerdos,* Regards,
firma signature	José

Irregular verbs

Irregular verbs are the most difficult verbs to learn. Yet, perhaps unfortunately, they describe actions and states of being that are most frequently needed in speaking and writing Spanish. The verb forms given in the chart below and continuing for two more pages take nineteen irregular verbs through nine tenses. As you will see, the verb endings for certain tenses are the same as those you will encounter in conjugating regular verbs.

Conjugation of irregular verbs

Infinitive	Indicative				Conditional	Subjunctive			Imperative
	Present	Imperfect	Preterite	Future	Present	Present	Imperfect (1st form)	(2nd form)	
andar to go, walk	ando	andaba	anduve	andaré	andaría	ande	anduviera	anduviese	
	andas	andabas	anduviste	andaras	andarías	andes	anduvieras	anduvieses	anda
	anda	andaba	anduvo	andará	andaría	ande	anduviera	anduviese	ande
	andamos	andábamos	anduvimos	andaremos	andaríamos	andemos	anduviéramos	anduviésemos	andemos
	andáis	andabais	anduvistei	andaréis	andaríais	andéis	anduvierais	anduvieseis	andad
	andan	andaban	anduvieron	andaran	andarían	anden	anduvieran	anduviesen	anden
dar to give	doy	daba	di	daré	daría	dé	diera	diese	
	das	dabas	diste	darás	darías	des	dieras	dieses	da
	da	daba	dio	dará	daría	dé	diera	diese	dé
	damos	dábamos	dimos	daremos	daríamos	demos	diéramos	diésemos	demos
	dais	dabais	disteis	daréis	daríais	deis	dierais	dieseis	dad
	dan	daban	dieron	darán	darían	den	dieran	diesen	den
decir to say, tell	digo	decía	dije	diré	diría	diga	dijera	dijese	
	dices	decías	dijiste	dirás	dirías	digas	dijeras	dijeses	di
	dice	decía	dijo	dirá	diría	diga	dijera	dijese	diga
	decimos	decíamos	dijimos	diremos	diríamos	digamos	dijéramos	dijésemos	digamos
	decís	decíais	dijisteis	diréis	diríais	digáis	dijerais	dijeseis	decid
	dicen	decían	dijeron	dirán	dirían	digan	dijeran	dijesen	digan
estar to be	estoy	estaba	estuve	estaré	estaría	esté	estuviera	estuviese	
	estás	estabas	estuviste	estarás	estarías	estés	estuvieras	estuvieses	está
	está	estaba	estuvo	estará	estaría	esté	estuviera	estuviese	esté
	estamos	estábamos	estuvimos	estaremos	estaríamos	estemos	estuviéramos	estuviésemos	estemos
	estáis	estabais	estuvisteis	estaréis	estaríais	estéis	estuvierais	estuvieseis	estad
	están	estaban	estuvieron	estarán	estarían	estén	estuvieran	estuviesen	estén
haber to have	he	había	hube	habré	habría	haya	hubiera	hubiese	
	has	habías	hubiste	habrás	habrías	hayas	hubieras	hubieses	he
	ha	había	hubo	habrá	habría	haya	hubiera	hubiese	haya
	hemos	habíamos	hubimos	habremos	habríamos	hayamos	hubiéramos	hubiésemos	hayamos
	habéis	habíais	hubisteis	habréis	habríais	hayáis	hubierais	hubieseis	habed
	han	habían	hubieron	habrán	habrían	hayan	hubieran	hubiesen	hayan
hacer to make, do	hago	hacía	hice	haré	haría	haga	hiciera	hiciese	
	haces	hacías	hiciste	harás	harías	hagas	hicieras	hicieses	haz
	hace	hacía	hizo	hará	haría	haga	hiciera	hiciese	haga
	hacemos	hacíamos	hicimos	haremos	haríamos	hagamos	hiciéramos	hiciésemos	hagamos
	hacéis	hacíais	hicisteis	haréis	haríais	hagáis	hicierais	hicieseis	haced
	hacen	hacían	hicieron	harán	harían	hagan	hicieran	hiciesen	hagan

Conjugation of irregular verbs (continued)

Infinitive	Indicative				Conditional	Subjunctive			Imperative
	Present	Imperfect	Preterite	Future	Present	Present	Imperfect (1st form)	(2nd form)	
ir	voy	iba	fui	iré	iría	vaya	fuera	fuese	
to go	vas	ibas	fuiste	irás	irías	vayas	fueras	fueses	ve
	va	iba	fue	irá	iría	vaya	fuera	fuese	vaya
	vamos	íbamos	fuimos	iremos	iríamos	vayamos	fuéramos	fuésemos	vamos
	vais	ibais	fuisteis	iréis	iríais	vayáis	fuerais	fueseis	id
	van	iban	fueron	irán	irían	vayan	fueran	fuesen	vayan
oír	oigo	oía	oí	oiré	oiría	oiga	oyera	oyese	
to hear	oyes	oías	oíste	oirás	oirías	oigas	oyeras	oyeses	oye
	oye	oía	oyó	oirá	oiría	oiga	oyera	oyese	oiga
	oímos	oíamos	oímos	oiremos	oiríamos	oigamos	oyéramos	oyésemos	oigamos
	oís	oíais	oísteis	oiréis	oiríais	oigáis	oyerais	oyeseis	oíd
	oyen	oían	oyeron	oirán	oirían	oigan	oyeran	oyesen	oigan
poder	puedo	podía	pude	podré	podría	pueda	pudiera	pudiese	
to be able	puedes	podías	pudiste	podrás	podrías	puedas	pudieras	pudieses	puede
	puede	podía	pudo	podrá	podría	pueda	pudiera	pudiese	pueda
	podemos	podíamos	pudimos	podremos	podríamos	podamos	pudiéramos	pudiésemos	podamos
	podéis	podíais	pudisteis	podréis	podríais	podáis	pudierais	pudieseis	poded
	pueden	podían	pudieron	podrán	podrían	puedan	pudieran	pudiesen	puedan
poner	pongo	ponía	puse	pondré	pondría	ponga	pusiera	pusiese	
to put	pones	ponías	pusiste	pondrás	pondrías	pongas	pusieras	pusieses	pon
	pone	ponía	puso	pondrá	pondría	ponga	pusiera	pusiese	ponga
	ponemos	poníamos	pusimos	pondremos	pondríamos	pongamos	pusiéramos	pusiésemos	pongamos
	ponéis	poníais	pusisteis	pondréis	pondríais	pongáis	pusierais	pusieseis	poned
	ponen	ponían	pusieron	pondrán	pondrían	pongan	pusieran	pusiesen	pongan
querer	quiero	quería	quise	querré	querría	quiera	quisiera	quisiese	
to want,	quieres	querías	quisiste	querrás	querrías	quieras	quisieras	quisieses	quiere
love	quiere	quería	quiso	querrá	querría	quiera	quisiera	quisiese	quiera
	queremos	queríamos	quisimos	querremos	querríamos	queramos	quisiéramos	quisiésemos	queramos
	queréis	queríais	quisisteis	querréis	querríais	queráis	quisierais	quisieseis	quered
	quieren	querían	quisieron	querrán	querrían	quieran	quisieran	quisiesen	quieran
saber	sé	sabía	supe	sabré	sabría	sepa	supiera	supiese	
to know	sabes	sabías	supiste	sabrás	sabrías	sepas	supieras	supieses	sabe
	sabe	sabía	supo	sabrá	sabría	sepa	supiera	supiese	sepa
	sabemos	sabíamos	supimos	sabremos	sabríamos	sepamos	supiéramos	supiésemos	sepamos
	sabéis	sabíais	supisteis	sabréis	sabríais	sepáis	supierais	supieseis	sabed
	saben	sabían	supieron	sabrán	sabrían	sepan	supieran	supiesen	sepan

Conjugation of irregular verbs (continued)

Infinitive	Indicative				Conditional	Subjunctive			Imperative
	Present	*Imperfect*	*Preterite*	*Future*	*Present*	*Present*	*Imperfect (1st form)*	*(2nd form)*	
salir to go out	salgo	salía	salí	saldré	saldría	salga	saliera	saliese	
	sales	salías	saliste	saldrás	saldrías	salgas	salieras	salieses	sal
	sale	salía	salió	saldrá	saldría	salga	saliera	saliese	salga
	salimos	salíamos	salimos	saldremos	saldríamos	salgamos	saliéramos	saliésemos	salgamos
	salís	salíais	salisteis	saldréis	saldríais	salgáis	salierais	salieseis	salid
	salen	salían	salieron	saldrán	saldrían	salgan	salieran	saliesen	salgan
ser to be	soy	era	fui	seré	sería	sea	fuera	fuese	
	eres	eras	fuiste	serás	serías	seas	fueras	fueses	sé
	es	era	fue	será	sería	sea	fuera	fuese	sea
	somos	éramos	fuimos	seremos	seríamos	seamos	fuéramos	fuésemos	seamos
	sois	erais	fuisteis	seréis	seríais	seáis	fuerais	fueseis	sed
	son	eran	fueron	serán	serían	sean	fueran	fuesen	sean
tener to have	tengo	tenía	tuve	tendré	tendría	tenga	tuviera	tuviese	
	tienes	tenías	tuviste	tendrás	tendrías	tengas	tuvieras	tuvieses	ten
	tiene	tenía	tuvo	tendrá	tendría	tenga	tuviera	tuviese	tenga
	tenemos	teníamos	tuvimos	tendremos	tendríamos	tengamos	tuviéramos	tuviésemos	tengamos
	tenéis	teníais	tuvisteis	tendréis	tendríais	tengáis	tuvierais	tuvieseis	tened
	tienen	tenían	tuvieron	tendrán	tendrían	tengan	tuvieran	tuviesen	tengan
traer to bring	traigo	traía	traje	traeré	traería	traiga	trajera	trajese	
	traes	traías	trajiste	traerás	traerías	traigas	trajeras	trajeses	trae
	trae	traía	trajo	traerá	traería	traiga	trajera	trajese	traiga
	traemos	traíamos	trajimos	traeremos	traeríamos	traigamos	trajéramos	trajésemos	traigamos
	traéis	traíais	trajisteis	traeréis	traeríais	traigáis	trajerais	trajeseis	traed
	traen	traían	trajeron	traerán	traerían	traigan	trajeran	trajesen	traigan
valer to be worth	valgo	valía	valí	valdré	valdría	valga	valiera	valiese	
	vales	valías	valiste	valdrás	valdrías	valgas	valieras	valieses	val
	vale	valía	valió	valdrá	valdría	valga	valiera	valiese	valga
	valemos	valíamos	valimos	valdremos	valdríamos	valgamos	valiéramos	valiésemos	valgamos
	valéis	valíais	valisteis	valdréis	valdríais	valgáis	valierais	valieseis	valed
	valen	valían	valieron	valdrán	valdrían	valgan	valieran	valiesen	valgan
venir to come	vengo	venía	vine	vendré	vendría	venga	viniera	viniese	
	vienes	venías	viniste	vendrás	vendrías	vengas	vinieras	vinieses	ven
	viene	venía	vino	vendrá	vendría	venga	viniera	viniese	venga
	venimos	veníamos	vinimos	vendremos	vendríamos	vengamos	viniéramos	viniésemos	vengamos
	venís	veníais	vinisteis	vendréis	vendríais	vengáis	vinierais	vinieseis	venid
	vienen	venían	vinieron	vendrán	vendrían	vengan	vinieran	viniesen	vengan
ver to see	veo	veía	vi	veré	vería	vea	viera	viese	
	ves	veías	viste	verás	verías	veas	vieras	vieses	ve
	ve	veía	vio	verá	vería	vea	viera	viese	vea
	vemos	veíamos	vimos	veremos	veríamos	veamos	viéramos	viésemos	veamos
	veis	veíais	visteis	veréis	veríais	veáis	vierais	vieseis	ved
	ven	veían	vieron	verán	verían	vean	vieran	viesen	vean

Review of Spanish Grammar

Uses of *ser* and *estar*

Both *ser* and *estar* mean *to be*. They are used in the following ways: **ser**

With adjectives to express an inherent or permanent quality, such as age, characteristic, color, possession, shape, size, and wealth.

La casa es blanca. The house is white.

With the preposition *de* to express ownership, material, or origin.

La pulsera es de oro. The bracelet is gold.

With a predicate noun or pronoun.

Él es médico. He is a doctor.

With the past participle in a passive construction.

El libro fue escrito por él.

The book was written by him.

In impersonal expressions

Es mejor hacerlo ahora. It is better to do it now.

estar

With adjectives to express an accidental or temporary condition.

La chica está ausente. The girl is absent.

In expressions of location

Barcelona está en España. Barcelona is in Spain.

In expressions of health.

Estaban enfermos. They were sick.

With the past participle used as an adjective to express a condition.

Las ventanas están cerradas.

The windows are closed.

With the present participle to form the present progressive tense.

Estaba durmiendo. He was sleeping.

Gustar

Gustar, which literally means to be pleasing, is used to translate the verb "to like." For example, in the sentence *Me gustan las revistas,* I like the magazines, the subject becomes the indirect object, *me,* and the direct object *revistas,* becomes the subject of the verb *gustar.*

Reflexive verbs

Reflexive verbs are designated by *se* attached to the infinitive so *lavarse* means to wash oneself. Reflexive pronouns are used with reflexive verbs in any tense, so *se lavaron* means they washed themselves.

Uses of the subjunctive mood

The subjunctive is used mainly in certain types of subordinate clauses introduced by *que.* In general, a verb in the subjunctive expresses a feeling or thought in the mind of the speaker rather than an established fact.

After verbs of volition (with a subject change).

Quiero que lo hagas. I want you to do it.

After verbs of emotion (with a subject change).

Se alegra de que venga.

He is happy that I am coming.

After impersonal expressions followd by a definite subject in the subordinate clause.

Es probable que me escriba.

It is likely that he will write to me.

After verbs of doubt and denial in the affirmative.

Dudo que lo sepa. I doubt that he knows it.

After verbs of thinking and believing used in the interrogative or negative.

No creo que tenga razón. I don't think he is right.

In a relative clause modifying a negative or an indefinite antecedent.

No conozco a nadie que hable alemán.

I don't know anyone who speaks German.

After conjunctions of time, purpose, restriction, or result.

Iré con tal que volvamos temprano.

I shall go provided that we return early.

After certain indefinite expressions, such as *dondequiera que* and *cualquier cosa que.*

Dondequiera que viva será feliz.

Wherever she lives, she will be happy.

Idioms

a tiempo on time
Vuelve a tiempo si quieres ver la película.
Return on time if you want to see the movie.

darse prisa to hurry
Date prisa! Ya son las seis.
Hurry up! It's six o'clock.

de repente suddenly
De repente abrió la puerta.
Suddenly he opened the door.

en seguida immediately
Pagó la cuenta y salió en seguida.
He paid the check and left immediately.

estar de vuelta to be back (in a place)
Mi hijo está de vuelta en Nueva York.
My son is back in New York.

hacer frío (calor) of weather: to be cold (warm)
Hace frío hoy.
It is cold today.

hacer un viaje to take a trip
Hice un viaje a España.
I took a trip to Spain.

tener hambre (sed) to be hungry (thirsty)
Tengo mucha hambre.
I am very hungry.

tratar de to try to
Trata de terminar el trabajo.
He tries to finish the work.

Hace frío! **Date prisa!**

Review of Spanish Grammar   423

Numerals, time, and dates

Cardinal numbers

The numbers 16 to 19 and 21 to 29 may be written as single words. Note that as single words, 16, 22, 23, and 26 carry accent marks on the final syllable.

 16 *dieciséis*, 22 *veintidós*

The only numbers that change with gender are *uno* and the compounds of *ciento* from 200 through 900.

 quinientas dos escuelas
 five hundred and two schools

Ciento becomes *cien* before nouns and before the numbers *mil* and *millones*. In all other numbers, the full form *ciento* is used.

 cien soldados one hundred soldiers

Millón requires the preposition *de* before the noun it multiplies.

 tres millones de pesos three million pesos

Un is not used before *ciento* or *mil*. It is used before *millón*.

 ciento doce sillas one hundred and twelve chairs
 un millón de pesos a million pesos

Ordinal numbers

1st *primero*	4th *cuarto*	8th *octavo*
2nd *segundo*	5th *quinto*	9th *noveno*
3rd *tercero*	6th *sexto*	10th *décimo*
	7th *séptimo*	

Ordinal numbers are generally used only through *tenth;* beyond that, the cardinal numbers are used. An ordinal number agrees in number and gender with the noun it modifies.

 la Quinta Avenida Fifth Avenue

The ordinal numbers *primero* and *tercero* drop the final *o* before a masculine singular noun.

 el tercer edificio the third building

Cardinal numbers

0	*cero*	30	*treinta*
1	*uno,*	31	*treinta y uno*
	una	32	*treinta y dos*
2	*dos*	40	*cuarenta*
3	*tres*	41	*cuarenta y uno*
4	*cuatro*	50	*cincuenta*
5	*cinco*	51	*cincuenta y uno*
6	*seis*	60	*sesenta*
7	*siete*	61	*sesenta y uno*
8	*ocho*	70	*setenta*
9	*nueve*	71	*setenta y uno*
10	*diez*	80	*ochenta*
11	*once*	81	*ochenta y uno*
12	*doce*	90	*noventa*
13	*trece*	91	*noventa y uno*
14	*catorce*	100	*ciento (cien)*
15	*quince*	101	*ciento uno*
16	*diez y seis*	102	*ciento dos*
	(dieciséis)	200	*doscientos (-as)*
17	*diez y siete*	201	*doscientos uno*
	(diecisiete)	300	*trescientos (-as)*
18	*diez y ocho*	400	*cuatrocientos (-as)*
	(dieciocho)	500	*quinientos (-as)*
19	*diez y nueve*	600	*seiscientos (-as)*
	(diecinueve)	700	*setecientos (-as)*
20	*veinte*	800	*ochocientos (-as)*
21	*veinte y uno*	900	*novecientos (-as)*
	(veintiuno)	1,000	*mil*
22	*veinte y dos*	2,000	*dos mil*
	(veintidós)	100,000	*cien mil*
23	*veinte y tres*	500,000	*quinientos mil*
	(veintitrés)	1,000,000	*un millón*

Time

The article *la* is always used when expressing *one o'-clock, las* when expressing the other hours.

After or *past* is expressed by *y; to* or *of,* by *menos.* After half past the hour, time is expressed by the following hour minus *(menos)* the minutes.

¿Qué hora es?	What time is it?
Es la una.	It is one o'clock.
Son las dos.	It is two o'clock.
Son las tres y media.	It is three-thirty.
Son las cuatro y cuarto (quince).	It is a quarter past four.
Son las cinco menos cuarto.	It is a quarter to five.
Son las once y diez.	It is ten minutes past eleven.
Son las ocho menos cinco.	It is five minutes to eight.
Son las siete en punto.	It is exactly seven o'clock.
Es mediodía (medianoche).	It is noon (midnight).
¿A qué hora?	At what time?
Las nueve de la mañana.	Nine in the morning.

Dates

¿Cuál es la fecha de hoy?	What is today's date?
¿A cuántos estamos hoy?	
Es el primero de marzo.	It is March 1.
Llegó el dos de junio de mil novecientos cincuenta.	He arrived June 2, 1950.
Salió el cuatro de mayo.	He left on May 4.

Cardinal numbers are used for all dates except *primero* (first).

Months, days, seasons

The names of the months, days of the week, and seasons are written with small letters.

enero	January	*el lunes*	Monday
febrero	February	*el martes*	Tuesday
marzo	March	*el miércoles*	Wednesday
abril	April	*el jueves*	Thursday
mayo	May	*el viernes*	Friday
junio	June	*el sábado*	Saturday
julio	July	*el domingo*	Sunday
agosto	August		
septiembre	September	*la primavera*	spring
octubre	October	*el verano*	summer
noviembre	November	*el otoño*	autumn
diciembre	December	*el invierno*	winter

The English word "on" before a day of the week or a date is expressed by the definite article.

Los sábados voy de compras.

On Saturdays I go shopping.

The years are expressed in thousands and hundreds.

Nació en mil novecientos setenta.

He was born in nineteen seventy.

Age

Age is expressed with the verb *tener.*

¿Cuántos años tienes tú? How old are you?

Tengo once años. I am eleven.

Arithmetic

Sumar Add

Dos y tres son cinco.

Two and three are five.

Restar Subtract

Quince menos ocho son siete.

Fifteen minus eight are seven.

Multiplicar Multiply

Nueve por cuatro son treinta y seis.

Nine times four are thirty six.

Dividir Divide

Sesenta dividido por diez son seis.

Sixty divided by ten are six.

Names of countries

Alemania	Germany	*Inglaterra*	England
Austria	Austria	*Italia*	Italy
Bélgica	Belgium	*Perú*	Peru
Canadá	Canada	*Rusia*	Russia
Dinamarca	Denmark	*Suecia*	Sweden
España	Spain	*Suiza*	Switzerland

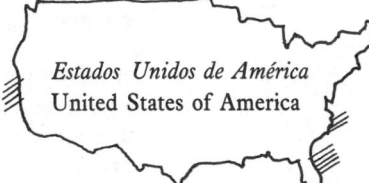

Estados Unidos de América
United States of America

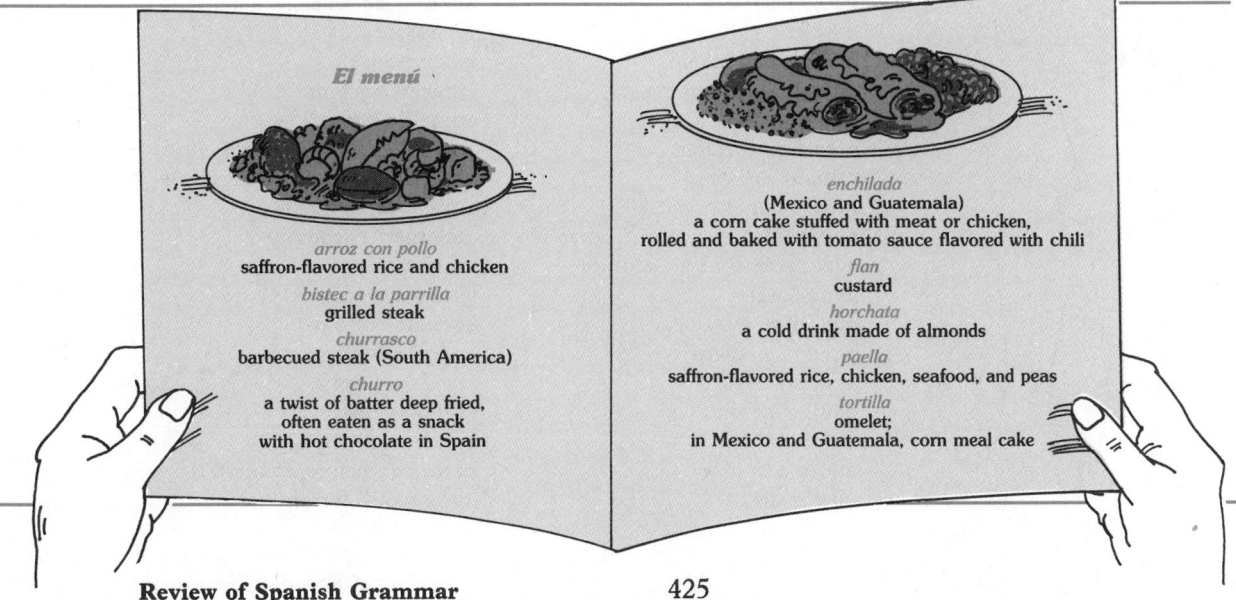

El menú

arroz con pollo
saffron-flavored rice and chicken

bistec a la parrilla
grilled steak

churrasco
barbecued steak (South America)

churro
**a twist of batter deep fried,
often eaten as a snack
with hot chocolate in Spain**

enchilada
**(Mexico and Guatemala)
a corn cake stuffed with meat or chicken,
rolled and baked with tomato sauce flavored with chili**

flan
custard

horchata
a cold drink made of almonds

paella
saffron-flavored rice, chicken, seafood, and peas

tortilla
**omelet;
in Mexico and Guatemala, corn meal cake**

el pelo hair
los ojos eyes
las orejas ears
la nariz nose
las mejillas cheeks
la boca mouth
los dientes teeth
la barba chin
los labios lips

La cara The face

Dictionary

El cuerpo humano The human body

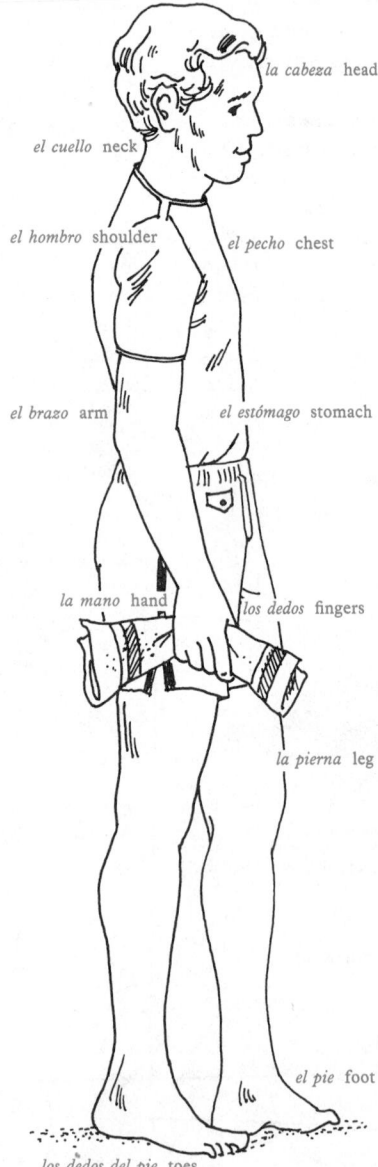

la cabeza head
el cuello neck
el hombro shoulder
el pecho chest
el brazo arm
el estómago stomach
la mano hand
los dedos fingers
la pierna leg
el pie foot
los dedos del pie toes

Spanish-English

A

a *prep* at, to
abajo *adv* below, down
abeja *f* bee
abierto *adj* open
abogado *m* lawyer
abrigo *m* overcoat
abrir *v* open
acá *adv* here
acabar *v* finish, **acabar de** to
  have just . . .
aceite *m* oil
acento *m* accent
aceptar *v* accept
acera *f* sidewalk
acerca de *prep* about, concerning
acercarse *v* approach
acero *m* steel
acompañar *v* accompany
aconsejar *v* advise
acordarse *v* remember
acostarse *v* go to bed
acto *m* act
actual *adj* present
acuerdo *m* agreement
adelante *adv* forward
además *adv* besides
adentro *adv* inside
adiós *interj and m* goodbye
admirar *v* admire
adónde *adv* where
aduana *f* custom house
aeropuerto *m* airport
afecto *m* affection
afilado *adj* sharp
afuera *adv* out, outside
agradable *adj* pleasant, agreeable
agradecer *v* be grateful for
agua *f* water
aguardar *v* wait for
agudo *adj* sharp
águila *f* eagle
aguja *f* needle
ahí *adv* there
ahora *adv* now
aire *m* air

al *prep* to the, at the
albóndiga *f* meatball
alcalde *m* mayor
alcanzar *v* reach, catch
alcoba *f* bedroom
aldea *f* village
alegrarse *v* be glad
alegre *adj* happy
alegría *f* joy
alfiler *m* pin
alfombra *f* carpet, rug
algo *pron* something
algodón *m* cotton
alguien *pron* someone
alguno *adj* some
alimento *m* food
allá *adv* there
allí *adv* there
alma *f* soul
almacén *m* department store
almohada *f* pillow
almorzar *v* lunch
almuerzo *m* lunch
alrededor *adv* around
alto *adj* tall, high
altura *f* height
alumbrar *v* illuminate, light
alumno, -a *n* pupil, student
alzar *v* raise, lift
amable *adj* amiable, kind,
  pleasant
amar *v* love
amargo *adj* bitter
amarillo *adj* yellow
ambos *adj and pron* both
americano *adj and n* American
amigo, -a, *n* friend
amistad *f* friendship
amor *m* love
ancho *adj* wide
anciano *adj* old
andar *v* walk
ángel *m* angel
anillo *m* ring
anoche *adv* last night
antes *adv* before, formerly
antiguo *adj* former

añadir v add
año m year
apagar v extinguish
aparecer v appear, show up
apenas adv hardly
aplicado adj diligent
aprender v learn
aquí adv here
árbol m tree
arena f sand, arena
armario m closet
arreglar v arrange, fix, repair
arriba adv above, up
asar v roast
así adv so, thus
asiento m seat
asistir v attend
asustar v frighten
atar v tie
atrás adv behind
avenida f avenue
averiguar v find out
avisar v inform, notify
ayer adv yesterday
ayudar v help
azul adj blue

B

bailar v dance
bajar v descend, lower
banco m bank, bench
bandera f flag
baño m bath, bathroom
barato adj cheap
barba f beard, chin
barbero m barber
barco m ship
barrio m district
bastante adv and adj enough
beber v drink
bello adj beautiful
beso m kiss
biblioteca f library
bien adv well
billete m ticket
bizcocho m cake, biscuit
blanco adj white
bolígrafo m ballpoint pen
bolsa f purse
bolsillo m pocket
bonito adj pretty
bosque m forest
botella f bottle
bueno adj good

burro m donkey
buscar v look for
butaca f armchair

C

caballero m gentleman
caballo m horse
cabello m hair
cabeza f head
cada adj each, every
cadena f chain
caer v fall
café m coffee, café
caja f box
calentar v heat, warm
caliente adj hot
calle f street
calor m heat
cama f bed
cambio m change, exchange
caminar v walk
camino m road
campo m country
canción f song
cansado adj tired
cantar v sing
cara f face
cariño m affection
caro adj expensive
carro m car
carta f letter
casa f house
casarse v get married
casi adv almost
cena f supper
cepillo m brush
cerca adv near
cerdo m pig, hog
cerrar v close
cerveza f beer
cielo m sky, heaven
cita f appointment
ciudad f city
clavel m carnation
coche m car
cocina f kitchen
cocinar v cook
colina f hill
comedia f comedy, play
comedor m dining room
comenzar v begin
comer v eat
comercio m commerce
comida f food, meal, dinner

como adv and conj as, like
cómo interj how
cómoda f dresser
comprar v buy
comprender v understand
con prep with
conocer v know
conseguir v obtain
contar v count, tell
contento adj happy
contestar v answer
continuar v continue
contra prep against
copa f goblet
correo m mail, post office
correr v run
corrida f race, **corrida de toros**
  bullfight
cortina f curtain
corto adj short
cosa f thing
costar v cost
creer v believe
criada f maid
cristiano m and adj Christian
cuadro m picture
¿cuál? interj which
¿cuándo? interj when
¿cuánto? interj how much?
¿cuántos? interj how many?
cuarto m room, quarter
cuchara f spoon
cuchillo m knife
cuenta f bill
cuero m leather
cuidado m care, caution
cumpleaños m birthday

CH

charla f chat
cheque m check
chico, -a n boy, girl
chiste m joke
choque m collision

D

dama f lady
daño m damage
dar v give
de prep of, from
debajo adv beneath
deber v ought, should, owe
débil adj weak

decir *v* say, tell
dejar *v* leave
delante de *prep* in front of
delgado *adj* thin
demasiado *adv and adj* too much, too many, too
dentista *m* dentist
dentro *adv* within
derecho *adj and adv* straight
desastre *m* disaster
desayunarse *v* breakfast
desayuno *m* breakfast
descansar *v* rest
descubrir *v* discover
desear *v* wish, desire
despacio *adv* slowly
despertar *v* wake
después de *prep* after
detrás de *prep* in back of
devolver *v* return
día *m* day
difícil *adj* difficult
dinero *m* money
Dios *m* God
dolor *m* pain
don, doña *n* titles given to gentlemen and ladies. Used with first names.
dónde *conj and adv* where
dormir *v* sleep
dormitorio *m* bedroom, dormitory
duda *f* doubt
dueño *m* master, owner
dulce *adj* sweet
duro *adj* hard

E

e *conj* and
echar *v* throw
edad *f* age
edificio *m* building
ejemplo *m* example
ejército *m* army
empleado *m* employee
empresa *f* enterprise
empujar *v* push
en *prep* in, on, at
encantador *adj* charming
encontrar *v* find, meet
enfermo *adj* sick
enfrente de *prep* facing
enojado *adj* angry
enseñar *v* teach

entender *v* understand
entero *adj* entire, whole
entonces *adv* then
entrada *f* entrance
entre *prep* between, among
enviar *v* send, ship
equivocado *adj* mistaken
escalera *f* staircase
escoba *f* broom
escoger *v* choose
escribir *v* write
escuchar *v* listen to
escuela *f* school
español *m and adj* Spanish
espejo *m* mirror
esperar *v* hope, wait
esposa *f* wife
esposo *m* husband
esquina *f* corner
estación *f* station, season
estado *m* state, condition
estar *v* be
este *m* east
estrecho *adj* narrow
estrella *f* star
estudiar *v* study
evitar *v* avoid
éxito *m* success
extranjero *m* foreigner

F

fábrica *f* factory
fácil *adj* easy
factura *f* invoice, bill
falda *f* skirt
falta *f* lack, mistake, fault
familia *f* family
fecha *f* date
feliz *adj* happy
feo *adj* ugly
ferrocarril *m* railroad
fiebre *f* fever
fiesta *f* holiday, festival
figurarse *v* imagine
fin *m* end, purpose
fino *adj* fine
firmar *v* sign
flan *m* custard
flor *f* flower
fonda *f* inn
fondo *m* bottom
francés *m and adj* Frenchman, French
frase *f* sentence

frazada *f* blanket
fresco *adj* cool, fresh
frío *m* cold, **tener frío** *v* feel cold
fuego *m* fire
fuente *f* fountain
fuera *adv* outside
fuerte *adj* strong, loud
fumar *v* smoke

G

gallina *f* hen
gallo *m* rooster
ganar *v* earn, win
ganga *f* bargain
gastar *v* spend
gato *m* cat
gemelos *m pl* cufflinks
gente *f* people
golpe *m* blow
gordo *adj* fat
gozar *v* enjoy
gracia *f* grace, wit
gracias *f pl* thanks, thank you
grande *adj* large, great
gritar *v* shout
guapo *adj* handsome
guardar *v* keep, guard
guerra *f* war
gustar *v* please
gusto *m* pleasure, taste

H

haber *v* have
habitación *f* room
hablar *v* speak
hacer *v* do, make
hacia *prep* toward
hallar *v* find
hambre *f* hunger, **tener hambre** be hungry
hasta *prep* until, **hasta luego** until later
hay *v* there is, there are
hecho *m* fact
hermoso *adj* beautiful
hielo *m* ice
hierba *f* grass
hija *f* daughter
hijo *m* son
hilo *m* thread
hoja *f* leaf
hombre *m* man

hora *f* hour, time
hoy *adv* today
hueso *m* bone
huevo *m* egg

I

idioma *m* language
iglesia *f* church
igualmente *adv* equally
inglés *m and adj* Englishman,
   English
inquieto *adj* anxious, worried
ir *v* go
isla *f* island
izquierdo *adj* left

J

jabón *m* soap
jamás *adv* never
jardín *m* garden
jefe *m* chief, boss
joven *adj* young
joya *f* jewel, gem
judío *m and adj* Jew, Jewish
juego *m* game
jugar *v* play
jugo *m* juice
junto *adj* together

L

labio *m* lip
lado *m* side
ladrón *m* thief
lago *m* lake
lágrima *f* tear
lana *f* wool
lápiz *m* pencil
largo *adj* long
lástima *f* pity
lata *f* tin, tin can
lavandería *f* laundry
lavar *v* wash
lectura *f* reading
leer *v* to read
legumbres *f pl* vegetables
lejos *adv* far
lento *adj* slow
levantar *v* raise, lift, **levantarse**
   v get up, rise
ley *f* law
libra *f* pound
libre *adj* free

libro *m* book
ligero *adj* light
limpiar *v* clean, wash
lindo *adj* pretty
listo *adj* clever, ready
lobo *m* wolf
loco *adj* crazy
lograr *v* achieve
lucha *f* fight
luego *adv* then
lugar *m* place
luna *f* moon
luz *f* light

LL

llamar *v* call
llamarse *v* be named
llave *f* key
llegar *v* arrive
lleno *adj* full
llevar *v* carry, wear
llorar *v* cry
llover *v* rain
lluvia *f* rain

M

madera *f* wood
madre *f* mother
maestro *m* teacher
maíz *m* corn
mal *adv* badly
maleta *f* suitcase
malo *adj* bad, sick
mandar *v* send
manga *f* sleeve
mano *f* hand
manta *f* blanket
mantel *m* tablecloth
mar *m and f* sea
marido *m* husband
martillo *m* hammer
más *adj and adv* more
matador *m* bullfighter
matar *v* to kill
mayor *adj* greater, older
medianoche *f* midnight
médico *m* doctor
medio *m* half
mejor *adj* better
menor *adj* smaller, younger
mentira *f* lie
mercado *m* market
mes *m* month

mesa *f* table
metro *m* meter, subway
miedo *m* fear
mientras *conj* while
milla *f* mile
mirar *v* look at
mismo *adj* same
modo *m* manner
molestar *v* trouble, disturb
moneda *f* coin
mono *m* monkey
montar *v* mount, climb
moreno *adj* dark, brunette
morir *v* die
mozo *m* waiter, porter, lad
muchacho, -a *n* boy, girl
mucho *adj* much
mueble *m* furniture
muerte *f* death
mujer *f* woman, wife
mundo *m* world
museo *m* museum
muy *adv* very

N

nacer *v* be born
nada *pron* nothing
nadar *v* swim
nadie *pron* nobody
nariz *f* nose
Navidad *f* Christmas
necesitar *v* need
negar *v* deny
negocio *m* business
negro *adj* black
nevar *v* snow
nieta *f* granddaughter
nieto *m* grandson
nieve *f* snow
niña *f* girl
niño *m* boy
no *interj and adv* no, not
noche *f* night
nombre *m* name, noun
norte *m* north
noticia *f* news
novia *f* sweetheart
novio *m* sweetheart
nube *f* cloud
nubile *adj* marriageable
nublado *adj* cloudy
nuevo *adj* new
número *m* number
nunca *adv* never

O

o *conj* or
obra *f* work
océano *m* ocean
ocupado *adj* busy, occupied
oeste *m* west
oído *m* ear (inner)
oír *v* hear
olor *m* odor
olvidar *v* forget
orar *v* pray
orgulloso *adj* proud
orilla *f* shore
oro *m* gold
oso *m* bear
otro *adj* another, other, **otra vez** *adv* again
oveja *f* sheep

P

pagar *v* pay
país *m* country
pájaro *m* bird
palabra *f* word
paloma *f* dove
pañuelo *m* handkerchief
papel *m* paper
paquete *m* package
par *m* pair, equal
para *prep* for
paraguas *m* umbrella
pardo *adj* brown
parecer *v* seem
pariente *m* relative
parque *m* park
partida *f* departure
pasajero *m* passenger
paseo *m* walk
paso *m* step
paz *f* peace
pedir *v* ask (for)
peinarse *v* comb one's hair
pelota *f* ball
peluquero *m* hairdresser
pena *f* pain, grief, trouble
pensar *v* think
peor *adj* worse
pequeño *adj* small
perder *v* lose
perezoso *adj* lazy
periódico *m* newspaper
pero *conj* but
perro *m* dog

pesado *adj* heavy
piedra *f* stone
pintor *m* painter
pintura *f* painting
piso *m* floor
plata *f* silver
plátano *m* banana
playa *f* beach
pluma *f* pen
pobre *adj* poor
poco *adj and adv* little
poder *v* be able
poner *v* put
por *prep* for, by, through
por favor *adv* please
porque *conj* because
por qué *pron* why
precio *m* price
pregunta *f* question
preguntar *v* ask
prestar *v* lend
primero *adj and adv* first
prisa *f* hurry
probar *v* prove
pronto *adv* soon
propina *f* tip
propio *adj* own, proper
pueblo *m* town, people
puerta *f* door
pulsera *f* bracelet

Q

que *pron* that, than
qué *pron* what
quedar *v* remain
queja *f* complaint
quemar *v* burn
querer *v* want, love
querido *adj* dear, beloved
quien *pron* who
quién *pron* who
quitar *v* remove
quizá *adv* perhaps

R

raíz *f* root
rana *f* frog
rápido *adj* fast
rato *m* while
raya *f* dash, stripe
razón *f* reason
realizar *v* accomplish
recibir *v* receive

recibo *m* receipt
recoger *v* gather
recordar *v* remember
recuerdo *m* remembrance, memory
redondo *adj* round
regalo *m* gift
regla *f* rule
regresar *v* return
reina *f* queen
reír *v* laugh
reloj *m* watch, clock
repetir *v* repeat
resfriado *m* cold (illness)
respirar *v* breathe
responder *v* answer
respuesta *f* answer
resto *m* remainder
resultado *m* result
retrete *m* toilet
reunión *f* meeting
revista *f* magazine
rey *m* king
rezar *v* pray
rico *adj* rich
rincón *m* corner
río *m* river
robar *v* steal
rogar *v* beg
rojo *adj* red
romper *v* break
rubio *adj* blond
rueda *f* wheel
ruido *m* noise

S

sábana *f* sheet
saber *v* know
sabio *adj* wise
sabor *m* flavor
sacar *v* take out
sacerdote *m* priest
sal *f* salt
sala *f* livingroom
salida *f* exit, departure
salir *v* leave
saltar *v* jump
salud *f* health
saludar *v* greet
sandía *f* watermelon
sangre *f* blood
sano *adj* healthy, sane
sastre *m* tailor
satisfecho *adj* satisfied

seco *adj* dry
sed *f* thirst
seda *f* silk
seguida *f* succession, en seguida immediately
seguir *v* follow
seguro *adj* sure
sello *m* stamp
semana *f* week
semejante *adj* similar
señal *f* signal
señor *m* sir, Mr., gentleman
señora *f* madam, Mrs., lady
señorita *f* young lady, Miss
sentarse *v* sit down
sentido *m* meaning, sense
sentir *v* regret, feel, sense
ser *v* be
servicio *m* service
servilleta *f* napkin
servir *v* serve
si *conj* if
sí *interj* yes
siempre *adv* always
sierra *f* mountain range
siglo *m* century
significar *v* mean, signify
siguiente *adj* following
silla *f* chair
simpático *adj* congenial, nice
sin *prep* without
sobre *m* envelope
sobre *prep* on
socio *m* associate, partner
sol *m* sun
solamente *adv* only
solo *adj* alone
sombra *f* shadow
sonar *v* sound
sordo *adj* deaf
sorpresa *f* surprise
subir *v* ascend
suceder *v* happen
sucio *adj* dirty
suelo *m* floor, ground
sueño *m* dream
suerte *f* luck
sur *m* south
susto *m* fright

T

tal *adj* such
tamaño *m* size
también *adv* also

tampoco *adv* neither, either
tan *adv* so
tanto *adj* so much
tarde *f* afternoon
tarjeta *f* card
taza *f* cup
teatro *m* theater
techo *m* ceiling, roof
teléfono *m* telephone
temprano *adv and adj* early
tenedor *m* fork
tener *v* have
terminar *v* end, terminate
tesoro *m* treasure
tiempo *m* time, weather
tienda *f* store
tierra *f* earth, land
tirar *v* throw
tiza *f* chalk
tocar *v* touch, play (instrument)
todo *adj* all
tomar *v* take, drink
tonto *m and adj* fool, foolish
torero *m* bullfighter
toro *m* bull
trabajar *v* work
traducir *v* translate
traer *v* bring
tranvía *m* streetcar
trapo *m* floor, ground
tratar de *v* try to
tren *m* train
trigo *m* wheat
triste *adj* sad
tronco *m* trunk

U

u *conj* or (before *o* or *ho*)
último *adj* last
único *adj* only
unir *v* unite
usar *v* wear, use
útil *adj* useful
uva *f* grape

V

vaca *f* cow
vacaciones *f pl* vacation
vacío *adj* empty
valer *v* be worth
valle *m* valley
vapor *m* steam
varios *adj* several

vaso *m* glass
vecino *m* neighbor
vender *v* sell
venir *v* come
venta *f* sale
ventana *f* window
ver *v* see
veras, de *adv* really
veraz *adj* truthful
verbo *m* verb
verboso *adj* talkative
verdad *f* truth
verde *adj* green
verede *f* path
veredicto *m* verdict
vergonzoso *adj* shameful, shy
vergüenza *f* shame
verificar *v* verify
verja *f* grating
verosímil *adj* likely
vestir *v* dress
vez *f* time, turn
viajar *v* travel
viaje *m* trip
vida *f* life
viejo *adj* old
viento *m* wind
vino *m* wine
visita *f* visit
visitar *v* visit
vista *f* view
viudo, -a *n* widower, widow
vivir *v* live
vivo *adj* living, alive
volar *v* fly
voz *f* voice
vuelta *f* return, turn

Y

y *conj* and
ya *adv* already
yacer *v* lie
yema *f* egg yolk
yerba *f* grass
yerro *m* error

Z

zapatería *f* shoe store
zapato *m* shoe
zarzuela *f* musical comedy
zona *f* zone
zorra *f* vixen
zorro *m* fox

English-Spanish

A

a, an *adj* un, una
able *adj* capaz, **be able** *v* poder
abode *n* residencia *f*
about *prep* acerca de
above *adv* arriba
absent *adj* ausente
accent *n* acento *m*
accept *v* aceptar
accompany *v* acompañar
accomplish *v* realizar
ache *n* dolor *m*
achieve *v* lograr
act *n* acto *m*
add *v* añadir
admire *v* admirar
advantage *n* ventaja *f*
advise *v* consejar
affection *n* afecto *m*, cariño *m*
after *prep* después de
afternoon *n* tarde *f*
again *adv* otra vez
age *n* edad *f*
agreement *n* acuerdo *m*
air *n* aire *m*
airport *n* aeropuerto *m*
all *adj* todo
almost *adv* casi
alone *adv* solo
already *adv* ya
also *adv* también
always *adv* siempre
American *adj and nm* americano
among *prep* entre
and *conj* y, e
angel *n* ángel *m*
angry *adj* enojado
answer *v* responder, contestar
anxious *adj* inquieto
appear *v* aparecer
appointment *n* cita *f*, nombramiento *m*
approach *v* acercarse a
apron *n* delantal *m*
armchair *n* butaca *f*

army *n* ejército *m*
around *adv* alrededor
arrange *v* arreglar
arrive *v* llegar
as *adv and conj* como
ascend *v* subir
ask *v* preguntar
ask for *v* pedir
associate *n* socio *m*
at *prep* a, **at the** al
attend *v* asistir a
aunt *n* tía *f*
author *n* autor *m*
avenue *n* avenida *f*
avoid *v* evitar
awful *adj* horrible, terrible

B

back *adv* atrás, **in back of** detrás de
backward *adj* atrasado
bad *adj* malo
badly *adv* mal
ball *n* pelota *f*
ballpoint pen *n* bolígrato *m*
banana *n* plátano *m*
bank *n* banco *m*
barber *n* barbero *m*
bargain *n* ganga *f*
bath *n* baño *m*
bathroom *n* cuarto de baño *m*
be *v* ser, estar
beach *n* playa *f*
bear *n* oso *m*
beard *n* barba *f*
beautiful *adj* bello, hermoso
because *conj* porque
bed *n* cama *f*, **go to bed** acostarse
bedroom *n* alcoba *f*, dormitorio *m*
bee *n* abeja *f*
beer *n* cerveza *f*
before *adv* antes
beg *v* rogar

begin *v* comenzar, empezar
behind *adv* detrás, *prep* detrás de
believe *v* creer
bell *n* campana *f*
below *adv* abajo
bench *n* banco *m*
beneath *adv* debajo
besides *adv* además
better *adj and adv* mejor
between *prep* entre
bill *n* cuenta *f*, factura *f*
bird *n* pájaro *f*
birthday *n* cumpleaños *m*
bitter *adj* amargo
black *adj* negro
blanket *n* manta *f*, frazada *f*
blind *adj* ciego
blond *adj* rubio
blood *n* sangre *f*
blow *n* golpe *m*
blue *adj* azul
boat *n* barco *m*
bone *n* hueso *m*
book *n* libro *m*
born, be *v* nacer
both *adj and pron* ambos
bottle *n* botella *f*
bottom *n* fondo *m*
box *n* caja *f*
boy *n* niño *m*, chico *m*, muchacho *m*
bracelet *n* pulsera *f*
break *v* romper
breakfast *n* desayuno *m*, *v* desayunar
breathe *v* respirar
bring *v* traer
broom *n* escoba *f*
brother *n* hermano *m*
brown *adj* pardo
brunette *adj and nm* moreno
brush *n* cepillo *m*
building *n* edificio *m*
bull *n* toro *m*
bullfight *n* corrida de toros *f*
bullfighter *n* torero *m*, matador *m*
burn *v* quemar
bus *n* autobús *m*
business *n* negocios *m pl*, comercio *m*
busy *adj* ocupado
butter *n* mantequilla *f*
buy *v* comprar

C

cabin *n* cabaña *f*
cage *n* jaula *f*
cake *n* bizcocho *m*
call *v* llamar
car *n* carro *m*, coche *m*
care *n* cuidado *m*
carnation *n* clavel *m*
carpet *n* alfombra *f*
carry *v* llevar
castle *n* castillo *m*
cat *n* gato *m*
ceiling *n* techo *m*
century *n* siglo *m*
chain *n* cadena *f*
chair *n* silla *f*
chalk *n* tiza *f*
change *n* cambio *m*
charming *adj* encantador
chat *n* charla *f*
cheap *adj* barato
check *n* (banking) cheque *m*
chief *n* jefe *m*
chin *n* barba *f*
choose *v* escoger
Christmas *n* Navidad *f*
church *n* iglesia *f*
city *n* ciudad *f*
clean *v* limpiar
clever *adj* listo
clock *n* reloj *m*
close *v* cerrar
closet *n* armario *m*
cloud *n* nube *f*
coffee *n* café *m*
coin *n* moneda *f*
cold *n* frío *m*,
　(illness) resfriado *m*
collar *n* cuello *m*
collision *n* choque *m*
comb (one's hair) *v* peinarse
come *v* venir
comedy *n* comedia *f*
commerce *n* comercio *m*
concerning *prep* acerca de
congenial *adj* simpático
continue *v* continuar
cool *adj* fresco
corn *n* maíz *m*
corner *n* esquina *f*, rincón *m*
cost *v* costar
cotton *n* algodón *m*
count *v* contar
country *n* campo *m*, país *m*

cow *n* vaca *f*
crash *n* choque *m*
crazy *adj* loco
cry *v* llorar
cufflinks *n* gemelos *m pl*
cup *n* taza *f*
custard *n* flan *m*
custom *n* costumbre *f*
customhouse *n* aduana *f*
cut *v* cortar

D

daily *adj* diario
damage *n* daño *m*
dance *v* bailar
dark *adj* moreno
dash *n* raya *f*
date *n* fecha *f*
daughter *n* hija *f*
day *n* día *m*
dead *adj* muerto
deaf *adj* sordo
dear *adj* querido
death *n* muerte *f*
decide *v* decidir
deep *adj* hondo
dentist *n* dentista *m, f*
deny *v* negar
department store *n* almacén *m*
departure *n* partida *f*, salida *f*
descend *v* bajar
dew *n* rocío *m*
difficult *adj* difícil
diligent *adj* aplicado
dining room *n* comedor *m*
dinner *n* comida *f*
dirty *adj* sucio
disaster *n* desastre *m*
discover *v* descubrir
dish *n* plato *m*
district *n* barrio *m*
disturb *v* molestar
do *v* hacer
doctor *n* médico *m*
dog *n* perro *m*
donkey *n* burro *m*
door *n* puerta *f*
doubt *n* duda *f*
dove *n* paloma *f*
down *adv* abajo
dozen *n* docena *f*
dream *n* sueño *m*, *v* soñar
dress *n* vestido *m*, *v* vestir
dresser *n* cómoda *f*

drink *v* beber
dry *adj* seco
during *prep* durante

E

each cada *adj*
eagle *n* águila *f*
ear *n* (inner) oído *m*, (outer)
　oreja *f*
early *adv and adj* temprano
earn *v* ganar
east *n* este *m*
Easter *n* Pascua Florida *f*
easy *adj* fácil
eat *v* comer
egg *n* huevo *m*
employee *n* empleado *m*
empty *adj* vacío
end *n* fin *m*, *v* terminar
enjoy *v* gozar
enough *adj and adv* bastante
enterprise *n* empresa *f*
entire *adj* entero
entrance *n* entrada *f*
envelope *n* sobre *m*
equally *adv* igualmente
even *adj* igual, *adv* hasta
example *n* ejemplo *m*
exchange *n* cambio *m*
exit *n* salida *f*
expensive *adj* caro
extinguish *v* apagar

F

face *n* cara *f*
facing *prep* enfrente de
fact *n* hecho *m*
factory *n* fábrica *f*
fall *v* caer
false *adj* falso
family *n* familia *f*
far *adv* lejos
farm *n* granja, hacienda *f*
fat *adj* gordo
fear *n* miedo *m*, *v* temer
feel *v* sentir
festival *n* fiesta *f*
fever *n* fiebre *f*
fight *n* lucha *f*
find *v* encontrar, hallar
find out *v* averiguar
fine *adj* fino, *adv* muy bien
finish *v* acabar

fire *n* fuego *m*
first *adj and adv* primero
flavor *n* sabor *m*
floor *n* piso *m*, suelo *m*
flower *n* flor *f*
fly *v* volar, *n* mosca *f*
follow *v* seguir
following *adj* siguiente
food *n* comida *f*
fool *n* tonto *m*
for *prep* por, para
foreigner *n* extranjero *m*
forest *n* bosque *m*
forget *n* olvidar *v*
fork *n* tenedor *m*
former antiguo *adj*
forward adelante *adv*
fountain *n* fuente *f*
frankly *adv* francamente
free libre *adj*
French *adj and nm* francés
fresh fresco *adj*
friend *n* amigo *m*
friendship *n* amistad *f*
fright *n* susto *m*
frighten asustar *v*
frog *n* rana *f*
from *prep* de
front *n* frente *m*, in front of
  delante de
full *adj* lleno
furniture *n* mueble *m*

G

gaiety *n* alegría *f*
game *n* juego *m*
garbage *n* basura *f*
garden *n* jardín *m*
garlic *n* ajo *m*
gasoline *n* gasolina *f*
gather *v* recoger
gem *n* joya *f*
gentleman *n* caballero *m*,
  señor *m*
gift *n* regalo *m*
girl *n* chica *f*, muchacha *f*, niña *f*
give *v* dar
glad *adj* contento, be glad *v*
  alegrarse
glass *n* vaso *m*
glove *n* guante *m*
go *v* ir
go out *v* salir
goblet *n* copa *f*

God *n* Dios *m*
gold *n* oro *m*
goodbye *interj* adiós
grace *n* gracia *f*
granddaughter *n* nieta *f*
grandson *n* nieto *m*
grape *n* uva *f*
grass *n* hierba *f*
grateful *adj* agradecido,
  be grateful for *v* agradecer
great *adj* gran, grande
greater *adj* mayor
green *adj* verde
greet *v* saludar
grief *n* pena *f*
ground *n* suelo *m*
guess *v* advinar

H

hair *n* cabello *m*, pelo *m*
hairdresser *n* peluquero *m*
hammer *n* martillo *m*
hand *n* mano *f*
handkerchief *n* pañuelo *m*
handsome *adj* guapo
happen *v* suceder
happy *adj* alegre, feliz, contento
hard *adj* duro
hardly *adv* apenas
have *v* tener, haber
head *n* cabeza *f*
health *n* salud *f*
healthy *adj* sano
hear *v* oír
heat *n* calor *m*, *v* calentar
heavy *adj* pesado
height *n* altura *f*
help *v* ayudar
hen *n* gallina *f*
here *adv* aquí, acá
hill *n* colina *f*
holiday *n* fiesta *f*
honest *adj* honesto
hope *v* esperar
horse *n* caballo *m*
hot *adj* caliente
hour *n* hora *f*
house *n* casa *f*
how *interj* como
how much, how many *interj*
  cuánto, cuántos
hunger *n* hambre *f*
hurry *n* prisa *f*
husband *n* esposo, marido *m*

I

ice *n* hielo *m*
if *conj* si
illuminate *v* alumbrar
imagine *v* figurarse
immediately *adv* en seguida
in *prep* en
inform *v* avisar
inn *n* fonda *f*
inside *adv* adentro, *adj and nm*
  interior
invoice *n* factura *f*
island *n* isla *f*

J

Jew *n* judio *m*, Jewish *adj* judio
jewel *n* joya *f*
joke *n* chiste *m*, *v* bromear
joy *n* alegría *f*
juice *n* jugo *m*
jump *v* saltar

K

keep *v* guardar
key *n* llave *f*
kill *v* matar
kind *adj* amable
king *n* rey *m*
kitchen *n* cocina *f*
knife *n* cuchillo *m*
know *v* saber, conocer

L

lack *n* falta *f*, *v* faltar
lady *n* dama *f*, señora *f*, young
  lady señorita *f*
lake *n* lago *m*
land *n* tierra *f*
language *n* idioma *m*
large *adj* grande
last *adj* último
last night *adv* anoche
later, see you hasta luego
laugh *v* reír
laundry *n* lavandería *f*
law *n* ley *f*
lawyer *n* abogado *m*
lazy *adj* perezoso
leaf *n* hoja *f*
learn *v* aprender
leather *n* cuero *m*

leave *v* dejar, salir
left *adj* izquierdo
lend *v* prestar
let *v* dejar
letter *n* carta *f*
library *n* biblioteca *f*
lie *n* mentira *f, v* mentir
life *n* vida *f*
light *adj* ligero, *nf* luz
lip *n* labio *m*
listen (to) *v* escuchar
little *adj* poco
live *v* vivir
living *adj* vivo
livingroom *n* sala *f*
look *n* mirada *f,* look at *v* mirar,
   look for buscar
lose *v* perder
love *n* amor *m, v* amar, querer
luck *n* suerte *f*
lunch *n* almuerzo *m, v* almorzar

M

madam *n* señora *f*
magazine *n* revista *f*
maid *n* criada *f*
mail *n* correo *m*
make *v* hacer
man *n* hombre *m*
manner *n* modo *m*
market *n* mercado *m*
marry *v* casarse con
master *n* dueño *m*
mayor *n* alcalde *m*
meal *n* comida *f*
mean *v* significar
meaning *n* sentido *m*
meatball *n* albóndiga *f*
meet *v* encontrar
meeting *n* reunión *f*
meter *n* metro *m*
midnight *n* medianoche *f*
mile *n* milla *f*
mirror *n* espejo *m*
miss *n* señorita *f*
mistake *n* falta *f*
mistaken *adj* equivocado
money *n* dinero *m*
month *n* mes *m*
moon *n* luna *f*
mother *n* madre *f*
mount *v* montar
mountain range *n* sierra *f*
Mr. *n* señor *m*

Mrs. *n* señora *f*
much *adj* mucho, so much
   tanto, too much demasiado
museum *n* museo *m*

N

name *n* nombre *m*
napkin *n* servilleta *f*
narrow *adj* estrecho
near *adv* cerca
need *v* necesitar
needle *n* aguja *f*
neighbor *n* vecino *m*
neither *adv* tampoco
never *adv* jamás, nunca
new *adj* nuevo
news *n* noticias *f pl*
newspaper *n* periódico *m*
night *n* noche *f*
no *adv* no
nobody *pron* nadie
noise *n* ruido *m*
north *n* norte *m*
nose *n* nariz *f*
not *adv* no
nothing nada *pron*
now *adv* ahora
number *n* número *m*

O

obtain *v* conseguir
ocean *n* océano *m*
odor *n* olor *m*
of *prep* de
oil *n* aceite *m*
old *adj* anciano, viejo
older *adj* mayor
on *prep* en, sobre
only *adv* solamente
open *adj* abierto, *v* abrir
or *conj* o, u
other *adj* otro
ought *v* deber
out *adv* afuera
outside *adv* fuera
overcoat *n* abrigo *m*
own *adj* propio
owner *n* dueño *m*

P

package *n* paquete *m*
pain *n* dolor *m*, pena *f*

painter *n* pintor *m*
painting *n* pintura *f,* cuadro *m*
pair *n* par *m*
paper *n* papel *m*
park *n* parque *m, v* estacionar
partner *n* socio *m*
passenger *n* pasajero *m*
pay *v* pagar, *n* pago, salario *m*
pen *n* pluma *f*
pencil *n* lápiz *m*
people *n* gente *f,* pueblo *m*
perhaps *adv* quizá
picture *n* cuadro *m*
pig *n* cerdo *m*
pillow *n* almohada *f*
pin *n* alfiler *m*
place *n* lugar *m*
play *n* comedia *f, v* jugar
pleasant *adj* agradable
please *v* gustar, *adv* por favor
pleasure *n* gusto *m*
pocket *n* bosillo *m*
poor *adj* pobre
porter *n* mozo *m*
post office *n* correo *m*
pound *n* libra *f*
pray *v* rezar, orar
present *adj* actual, presente, *n*
   regalo *m*
pretty *adj* bonito, lindo
price *n* precio *m*
priest *n* sacerdote *m*
proud *adj* orgulloso
prove *v* probar
pupil *n* alumno, -a
purse *n* bolsa *f*
push *v* empujar
put *v* poner

Q

quarter *n* cuarto *m*
queen *n* reina *f*
question *n* pregunta *f*

R

rag *n* trapo *m*
railroad *n* ferrocarril *m*
rain *v* llover, *n* lluvia *f*
raise *v* alzar
reach *v* alcanzar
read *v* leer
reading *n* lectura *f*
ready *adj* listo

reason *n* razón *f*
receipt *n* recibo *m*
receive *v* recibir
red *adj* rojo
regret *v* sentir, *n* pena *f*
relative *n* pariente *m*
remain *v* quedar
remainder *n* resto *m*
remember *v* acordarse, recordar
remembrance *n* recuerdo *m*
remove *v* quitar
repeat *v* repetir
rest *v* descansar, *n* descanso *m*
result resultado *m*
return *v* volver, devolver,
    regresar, *n* vuelta *f*
rich *adj* rico
right *adj and n* derecho *m*
ring *n* anillo *m*
rise *v* levantarse
river *n* río *m*
road *n* camino *m*
roast *v* asar
roof *n* techo *m*
room *n* cuarto *m*, habitación *f*
rooster *n* gallo *m*
root *n* raíz *f*
round *adj* redondo
rule *n* regla *f*
run *v* correr

S

sad *adj* triste
sale *n* venta *f*
salt *n* sal *f*, *v* salar
same *adj and pron* mismo
sand *n* arena *f*
satisfied *adj* satisfecho
say *v* decir
school *n* escuela *f*
sea *n* mar *m and f*
season *n* estación *f*
seat *n* asiento *m*
see *v* ver
seem *v* parecer
sell *v* vender
send *v* enviar, mandar
sentence *n* frase *f*
serve *v* servir
service *n* servicio *m*
shadow *n* sombra *f*
shame *n* vergüenza *f*
sharp *adj* afilado, agudo
sheep *n* oveja *f*

sheet *n* sábana *f*
ship *n* barco *m*
shoe *n* zapato *m*
shoe store *n* zapatería *f*
shore *n* orilla *f*
short *adj* corto
should *v* deber
shout *v* gritar
sick *adj* enfermo, malo
side *n* lado *m*
sidewalk *n* acera *f*
sign *v* firmar
signal *n* señal *f*
silk *n* seda *f*
silver *n* plata *f*
similar *adj* semejante, parecido
sing *v* cantar
sir *title* señor
sit down *v* sentarse
size *n* tamaño *m*
skirt *n* falda *f*
sky *n* cielo *m*
sleep *v* dormir
sleeve *n* manga *f*
slow *adj* lento
slowly *adv* despacio
small *adj* pequeño
smaller *adj* menor
smile *v* sonreír, *n* sonrisa *f*
smoke *v* fumar
snow *v* nevar, *n* nieve *f*
so *adv* tan, así
so much *adj* tanto
soap *n* jabón *m*
some *adj and pron* alguno
someone *pron* alguien
something *pron* algo
song *n* canción *f*
soon *adv* pronto
soul *n* alma *f*
sound *v* sonar, *n* sonido *m*
south *n* sur *m*
Spanish *adj and n m* español
speak *v* hablar
spend *v* gastar
spoon *n* cuchara *f*
staircase *n* escalera *f*
stamp *n* sello *m*
star *n* estrella *f*
state *n* estado *m*
station *n* estación *f*
steal *v* robar
steam *n* vapor *m*
steel *n* acero *m*
step *n* paso *m*

stone *n* piedra *f*
store *n* tienda *f*
straight *adj* derecho
street *n* calle *f*
streetcar *n* tranvía *m*
stripe *n* raya *f*
strong *adj* fuerte
study *v* estudiar
subway *n* metro *m*
success *n* éxito *m*
such *adj* tal
suitcase *n* maleta *f*
sun *n* sol *m*
supper *n* cena *f*
sure *adj* seguro
surprise *n* sorpresa *f*
sweet *adj* dulce
sweetheart *n* novio, -a
swim *v* nadar

T

table *n* mesa *f*
tablecloth *n* mantel *m*
tailor *n* sastre *m*
take *v* tomar
take out *v* sacar
tall *adj* alto
teach *v* enseñar
teacher *n* maestro, -a
tear *n* lágrima *f*
telephone *n* teléfono *m*
tell *v* decir
than *conj* que
that *pron* que
then *adv* entonces, luego
there *adv* ahí, allá, allí
there are hay
there is hay
thief *n* ladrón *m*
thin *adj* delgado
thing *n* cosa *f*
think *v* pensar
thirst *n* sed *f*
thread *n* hilo *m*
throw *v* tirar, echar
thus *adv* así
ticket *n* billete *m*
tie *v* atar
time *n* hora *f*, tiempo *m*, vez *f*
tin *n* lata *f*
tin can *n* lata *f*
tip *n* propina *f*
tired *adj* cansado
to *prep* a

today *adv* hoy
together *adj* junto
toilet *n* retrete *m*
too *adv* demasiado, también
touch *v* tocar
toward *prep* hacia
town *n* pueblo *m*
train *n* tren *m*
translate *v* traducir
travel *v* viajar
treasure *n* tesoro *m*
tree *n* árbol *m*
trip *n* viaje *m*
trouble *v* molestar, *n* apuro *m*, pena *f*
trunk *n* tronco *m*
truth *n* verdad *f*
try to *v* tratar de

U

ugly *adj* feo
umbrella *n* paraguas *m*
understand *v* comprender, entender
unite *v* unir
use *v* usar
useful *adj* útil

V

vacation *n* vacaciones *f pl*
valley *n* valle *m*
view *n* vista *f*
village *n* aldea *f*
visit *n* visita *f*, *v* visitar
voice *n* voz *f*

W

wait for *v* aguadar, esperar
waiter *n* mozo *m*, camarero *m*
wake *v* despertar
walk *v* andar, caminar
want *v* querer
war *n* guerra *f*
wash *v* lavar
watch *n* reloj *m*
water *n* agua *f*
watermelon *n* sandía *f*
weak *adj* débil
weather *n* tiempo *m*
week *n* semana *f*
well *adv* bien, *adj* bueno
west *n* oeste *m*

what *interj pron* qué
wheat *n* trigo *m*
wheel *n* rueda *f*
when *adv* cuándo, *conj* cuando
where *adv* adónde, dónde, *conj* donde
which *pron* cuál
while *conj* mientras, *n* rato *m*
white *adj* blanco
who *pron* quién, quien
whole *adj* entero
why *adv* por qué
wide *adj* ancho
widow *n* viuda *f*
widower *n* viudo *m*
wife *n* esposa *f*
wild *adj* bárbaro
wilderness *n* desierto *m*
wilt *v* marchitar
win *v* ganar
wind *n* viento *m*
window *n* ventana *f*
wine *n* vino *m*
wing *n* ala *f*
winner *n* ganador *m*
winter *n* invierno *m*
wipe *v* limpiar

wise *adj* sabio
wish *v* desear, *n* deseo *m*
wit *n* gracia *f*
with *prep* con
within *adv* dentro
without *prep* sin
wolf *n* lobo *m*
woman *n* mujer *f*
wood *n* madera *f*
wool *n* lana *f*
word *n* palabra *f*
work *n* obra *f*, *v* trabajar
world *n* mundo *m*
worried *adj* inquieto
worse *adv* peor
worth *n* valor *m*, **be worth** *v* valer
write *v* escribir

Y

year *n* año *m*
yellow *adj* amarillo
yes *adv* sí
yesterday *adv* ayer
young *adj* joven
younger *adj* menor

For further reference

Grammars

Greenfield, Eric V.
 Spanish Grammar
 Barnes and Noble
Jarvis, Ana C., Lebredo, Raquel, and
 Mena, Francisco
 Basic Spanish Grammar
 D. C. Heath and Company

Kendris, Christopher
 301 Spanish Verbs
 Barron's

Dictionaries

Castillo, Carlos and Bond, Otto
 *The University of Chicago
 Spanish-English, English-Spanish
 Dictionary*
 Pocket Books
Cuyás, Arturo
 *Appleton's New Cuyás
 English-Spanish, Spanish-English
 Dictionary*
 Prentice-Hall
Dutton, Brian, Harvey, L.P., and
 Walker, Roger M.
 *Cassell's Compact Spanish-English,
 English-Spanish Dictionary*
 Dell Publishing

Velázquez de la Cadena, Mariano,
 Gray, Edward, and Iribas, Juan R.
 *New Revised Velázquez
 Spanish-English, Diccionario
 Inglés-Español*
 New Century Publishers
Williams, Edwin B.
 *The Bantam New College Spanish
 and English Dictionary*
 Bantam Books

Index

How to use the index. The INDEX to this *Student Handbook* is arranged alphabetically acccording to a letter-by-letter system. All entries, regardless of punctuation or spaces between words, are in precise alphabetical order:

> **Cataract**
> **Catering**
> **Catholic Church**
> **CAT scan**

Each entry ends with a period. Following the period is the number of the page or pages on which the term will be found:

> **Lincoln, Abraham.** 258–259, 274, 312

Handy cross-references are provided when a listing may be ambiguous or confusing. Few abbreviations are used in the index, and those that are used are so standard as to eliminate the need for an abbreviations list.

Books, plays, and other titles are not indexed, but authors, artists, composers, etc., are. Monarchs are listed in numerical order:

> **Charles I (King of England)**
> **Charles II (King of England)**
> **Charles V (Holy Roman Emp.)**
> **Charles VII (King of France)**

Part 2

Roget's University Thesaurus

Roget's University Thesaurus

Edited by
Eugene Ehrlich

This work was originally published under the title
Roget's International Thesaurus of English Words and Phrases.

Preface

This edition of *Roget's University Thesaurus* remains true to the original formulation of Peter Mark Roget, followed by all his distinguished successors, including the late C. O. Sylvester Mawson, who edited the first *University Thesaurus*. The distinguishing feature of the present edition is that it responds to the particular needs of all family members, young and old, who are students. The day does not go by when writing or when preparing a speech that an appropriate word or phrase is difficult to recall. It is at those times that the *University Thesaurus* proves invaluable.

The *University Thesaurus* offers its users

1. a large list of synonyms and antonyms;
2. a special grouping of comparisons and related terms;
3. systematic treatment of specialized terminology;
4. a grouping of synonyms in individual paragraphs supplying words more or less related and inter-changeable;
5. characterization of all obsolete, obsolescent, rare, archaic, colloquial, dialectal, and slang words, as well as British, foreign, and special terms;
6. plural forms in all cases of unusual difficulty;
7. numerous phrases and idioms;
8. citations from modern authors.

The words new in the *University Thesaurus* run well into the thousands and embrace all aspects of knowledge, particularly in the sciences and social sciences. The aim has been to suggest ideas and turns of thought. The arrangement of synonyms and antonyms peculiar to the Roget scheme adds to the usefulness of the work: Roget gives *goodness* and *badness*, for example, in sequential entries. There is no need to refer to another part of the book.

Another distinguishing feature of Roget is the inclusion of phrases. Not only does the use of phrases enlarge the group of synonyms for any particular word, but in many instances the phrase furnishes the only possible synonym. Improvement of this feature in the *University Thesaurus* has received painstaking attention.

Our language marches with no frontiers; English is a world possession. Every race and country is reflected in its vocabulary. The *University Thesaurus* is alive to this universality, and, in order to assist writers and speakers in giving local color, the birthplace of every imported word is duly recorded.

Attention must be drawn to the need for using any thesaurus in tandem with a dictionary. Synonyms are often only related words. The dictionary provides precise definitions of individual words, so it must be consulted before using a word or phrase new to the reader.

Eugene Ehrlich

Table of Contents

Abbreviations

abbr. abbreviated, abbreviation
adj. adjective, adjectival expression
adv. adverb, adverbial expression
Afr. Africa
Am. *or* **Amer.** America, American
Am. hist. American history
anat. anatomy
anc. ancient
Anglo-Ind. Anglo-Indian
anon. anonymous
antiq. antiquities
Ar. Arabic
arch. architecture
archaeol. archaeology
arith. arithmetic
A.-S. Anglo-Saxon
astrol. astrology
astron. astronomy
Austral. Australian
Bib. Biblical
biol. biology
bot. botany
Brit. British
Can. Canada, Canadian
Can. F. Canadian French
Celt. Celtic
chem. chemistry
Chin. Chinese
Ch. of Eng. Church of England
class. classical
colloq. colloquial
com. commerce, commercial
conj. conjunction

Du. Dutch
Dan. Danish
derog. derogatory
dial. dialect, dialectal
dim. diminutive
E. East
eccl. ecclesiastical
econ. economics
elec. electricity
Eng. English, England
erron. erroneous, erroneously
esp. especially
exc. except
F. French
fem. feminine
fig. figurative, figuratively
G. *or* **Ger.** German
Gr. Greek
gram. grammar
Gr. Brit. Great Britain
Heb. Hebrew
her. heraldry
Hind. Hindustani
hist. history, historical
Icel. Icelandic
Ind. Indian
Ir. Irish, Ireland
int. interjection
It. Italian
Jap. Japanese
Jew. Jewish
joc. jocular
L. Latin

l.c. lower case
masc. masculine
math. mathematics
Meth. Methodist
Mex. Mexico, Mexican
mil. military
Moham. Mohammedan
myth. mythology
N. North
n. noun
N. Am. North American
naut. nautical
N. E. *or* **New Eng.** New England
neut. neuter
Nfld. Newfoundland
NL. New Latin
Norw. Norwegian
N. W. Northwest, Northwestern
N. Z. New Zealand
obs. obsolete
obsoles. obsolescent
OE. Old English
opp. opposed
orig. original, originally
parl. parliamentary
path. pathology
Per. Persian
Pg. Portuguese
pharm. pharmacy
philos. philosophy
physiol. physiology
P. I. Philippine Islands
pl. plural

Dashes and hyphens are used to avoid the repetition of a term common to each word or phrase in the same group. For example:

"over-, above- the mark;"	= "over the mark," "above the mark"
"on the -verge, -brink, -skirts of;"	= "on the verge of," "on the brink of," "on the skirts of"
"brush-, whisk-, turn-, send- -off, -away;"	= "brush off," "brush away," "whisk off," "whisk away," "turn off," "turn away," "send off," "send away"
"quick-, keen-, clear-, sharp- -eyed, -sighted, -witted;"	= "quick-eyed," "quick-sighted," "quick-witted," "keen-eyed," "keen-sighted," "keen-witted," "clear-eyed," "clear-sighted," "clear-witted," "sharp-eyed," "sharp-sighted," "sharp-witted"
"away from-, foreign to-, beside- the -purpose, -question, -transaction, -point;"	= "away from the purpose," "away from the question," "away from the transaction," "away from the point," "foreign to the purpose," etc., "beside the purpose," etc.
"fall, -to the ground;"	= "fall," "fall to the ground"
"shortness etc. *adj.;*" "shortly etc. *adj.;*" "shortening etc. *v.;*"	= in a similar manner form other words from the groups of *adjectives* or *verbs* in the same category

How to Use the Thesaurus

1. To find a synonym or antonym for any given WORD:

Turn to the Index Guide and find the particular word or any term of kindred meaning; then refer to the category indicated. Under the part of speech sought for [*n., v., adj., adv.*] will be found a wide choice of synonymous and related terms, with their antonyms in the following category or in the preceding category. For example, suppose a synonym is wanted for the word "rare" in the sense of "choice." Turn to the Index Guide, where the following references will be found:

> **rare** *unique* 20
> *exceptional* 83
> *few* 103
> *infrequent* 137
> *underdone* 298
> *tenuous* 322
> *neologic* 563
> *choice* 648

The italicized words denote the general sense of the related terms in the respective categories. Turning to No. 648 (the sense required), we select the most appropriate expression from the comprehensive list presented. To widen the selection, suggested references are given to allied lists; while in No. 649 are grouped the corresponding antonyms. The groups are arranged, not merely to supply synonyms for some special word, but to suggest new lines of thought and to stimulate the imagination.

The writer at a loss for some archaism, colloquialism, or even slang, will find the *University Thesaurus* a veritable mine, such terms being clearly indicated in the text.

2. To find suitable words to express a given IDEA:

Find in the Index Guide some word relating to the idea, and the categories referred to will supply the need. Thus, suppose a writer wishes to use some less hackneyed phrase than "shuffle off this mortal coil," let him look up "die" or even the phrase itself, and reference to No. 360 will immediately furnish a generous list of synonymous phrases.

3. To find appropriate words or new ideas on any given SUBJECT:

Turn to the subject or any branch of it. The Index Guide itself will frequently suggest various lines of thought, while reference to the indicated groups will provide many words and phrases that should prove helpful.

Thus, suppose "philosophy" is the theme, No. 451 will be found most suggestive. Or again, the subject may be "the drama" (599), "music" (415), "zoology" (368), "psychical research" (992a), or "mythology" (979). Writers may perhaps be hazy about the titles of the ruling chiefs of India. The Thesaurus (875) will prevent applying a Hindu title to a Mohammedan prince. The subject may be such an everyday one as "food" (298), "automobiles" (272), "aviation" (267 and 269a), or various kinds of "amusements" (840); whatever it is, the Thesaurus will prove profitable as regards ideas. Writers and speakers who have acquired the Roget habit do not need to be reminded of this valuable aid.

N.B. To grasp the underlying principle of the classification, study the *Tabular Synopsis of Categories,* which begins on the next page. Reference may be made direct from this Synopsis to the body of the work; but it is usually found more convenient to consult the Index Guide first.

The Guide numbers always refer to the *section numbers* in the text and *not* to pages.

Tabular Synopsis of Categories

Class 1. Abstract Relations

Section 1. Existence

1. ABSTRACT	1. Existence	2. Nonexistence
2. CONCRETE	3. Substantiality	4. Unsubstantiality
3. FORMAL	*Internal*	*External*
	5. Intrinsicality	6. Extrinsicality
4. MODAL	*Absolute*	*Relative*
	7. State	8. Circumstance

Section 2. Relation

1. ABSOLUTE	9. Relation	10. Irrelation
	11. Consanguinity	
	12. Correlation	
	13. Identity	14. Contrariety
		15. Difference
2. CONTINUOUS	16. Uniformity	16a. Nonuniformity
3. PARTIAL	17. Similarity	18. Dissimilarity
	19. Imitation	20. Nonimitation
		20a. Variation
	21. Copy	22. Prototype
4. GENERAL	23. Agreement	24. Disagreement

Section 3. Quantity

1. SIMPLE	*Absolute*	*Relative*
	25. Quantity	26. Degree
2. COMPARATIVE	27. Equality	28. Inequality
		29. Mean
		30. Compensation
	By Comparison with a Standard	
	31. Greatness	32. Smallness
	By Comparison with a Similar Object	
	33. Superiority	34. Inferiority
	Changes in Quantity	
	35. Increase	36. Decrease
3. CONJUNCTIVE	37. Addition	38. Nonaddition
		Deduction
	39. Adjunct	40. Remainder
		40a. Decrement
	41. Mixture	42. Simpleness
	43. Junction	44. Disjunction
	45. Vinculum	
	46. Coherence	47. Incoherence
	48. Combination	49. Decomposition
4. CONCRETE	50. Whole	51. Part
	52. Completeness	53. Incompleteness
	54. Composition	55. Exclusion
	56. Component	57. Extraneous

Section 4. Order

1. GENERAL	58. Order	59. Disorder
	60. Arrangement	61. Derangement

x

Roget's
University
Thesaurus

Class 1. Abstract Relations

Section 1. Existence

1. Existence

n. **existence**, being, entity, *ens* [*L.*], *esse* [*L.*], subsistence; quid, hypaxis [*rare*], automaton.

reality, actuality; positiveness etc. *adj.;* fact, matter of fact, sober reality; truth etc. 494; actual existence.

presence etc. (*existence in space*) 186; coexistence etc. 120.

stubborn fact; not a dream etc. 515; no joke.

essence, inmost nature, center of life, inner reality, vital principle.

[science of existence] ontology.

v. **exist**, be; having being etc. *n.;* subsist, live, breathe, stand, obtain, be the case; occur etc. (*event*) 151; have place, rank, prevail; find oneself, pass the time, vegetate.

come into existence etc. *n.;* arise etc. (*begin*) 66; come forth etc. (*appear*) 446.

become etc. (*be converted*) 144; bring into existence etc. 161; coexist, postexist [*rare*], preëxist [*rare*].

consist in, lie in; be comprised in, be contained in, be constituted by.

abide, continue, endure, last, remain.

adj. **existing** etc. *v.;* existent, subsistent, under the sun; in existence etc. *n.;* extant; afloat, on foot, current, prevalent; undestroyed.

real, actual, positive, absolute; factual, veritable, true etc. 494; substantial, substantive; self-existing, self-existent; essential.

well-founded, well-grounded; unideal, unimagined; not potential etc. 2; authentic.

adv. **actually** etc. *adj.;* in fact, in point of fact, in reality; indeed; *de facto* [*L.*], *ipso facto* [*L.*].

2. Nonexistence

n. **nonexistence**, nonsubsistence; inexistence; nonentity, *nil* [*L.*]; negativeness etc. *adj.;* nullity; nihility, nihilism; *tabula rasa* [*L.*], blank; abeyance; absence etc. 187; no such thing etc. 4; nonbeing, nothingness, oblivion, *non esse* [*L.*].

annihilation; extinction etc. (*destruction*) 162; extinguishment, extirpation, Nirvana, obliteration.

v. **not exist** etc. 1; have no existence etc. 1; be null and void; cease to exist etc. 1; pass away, perish; be *or* become extinct etc. *adj.;* die out; disappear etc. 449; melt away, dissolve, leave not a rack behind; go, be no more; die etc. 360.

annihilate, render null, nullify; abrogate etc. 756; destroy etc. 162; take away; remove etc. (*displace*) 185; obliterate, extirpate, deracinate [*rare*].

adj. **inexistent**, nonexistent etc. 1; negative, blank; null, minus, missing, omitted; absent etc. 187; insubstantial, shadowy, spectral, visionary.

unreal, potential, virtual; baseless, *in nubibus* [*L.*]; unsubstantial etc. 4; vain.

unborn, uncreated, unbegotten, unconceived, unproduced, unmade.

perished, annihilated etc. *v.;* extinct, exhausted, gone, lost, departed; defunct etc. (*dead*) 360.

fabulous, ideal etc. (*imaginary*) 515; supposititious etc. 514.

adv. negatively, virtually etc. *adj.*

3. Substantiality

n. **substantiality**, hypostasis; person, thing, object, article; something, a being, an existence; creature, body, substance, flesh and blood, stuff, substratum; matter etc. 316; corporeity, element, essential nature, groundwork, materiality, substantialness, vital part.

[totality of existences] world etc. 318; *plenum* [*L.*].

adj. **substantive**, substantial; hypostatic *or* hypostatical; personal, bodily, practical, effective; tangible etc. (*material*) 316; corporeal; right, sober.

adv. **substantially** etc. *adj.;* bodily, essentially.

4. Unsubstantiality

n. **unsubstantiality**, insubstantiality; nothingness, nihility; no degree, no part, no quantity, no thing.

nothing, naught, *nil* [*L.*], nullity, zero, cipher, no one, nobody; never a one, ne'er a one; no such thing, none in the world; nothing whatever, nothing at all, nothing on earth; not a particle etc. (*smallness*) 32; all talk, all moonshine, all stuff and nonsense; matter of no importance, matter of no consequence.

thing of naught, man of straw, John Doe and Richard Roe, fagot (*or* faggot) voter [*polit. cant, Eng.*]; *nominis umbra* [*L.*], nonentity, cipher, nought, nothing, obscurity, lay figure; flash in the pan, *vox et praeterea nihil* [*L.*].

phantom etc. (*fallacy of vision*) 443; shadow; dream etc. (*imagination*) 515; *ignis fatuus*

[*L.*] etc. (*luminary*) 423; "such stuff as dreams are made on" [*Tempest*]; air, thin air; bubble etc. 353; mockery.

blank; void etc. (*absence*) 187; hollowness.

inanity, fatuity, fool's paradise.

v. **vanish**, evaporate, fade, fleet, sink, fly, dissolve, melt away; die, die away, die out; disappear etc. 449.

adj. **unsubstantial**; baseless, groundless; ungrounded; without foundation, having no foundation.

visionary etc. (*imaginary*) 515; immaterial etc. 317; spectral etc. 980; dreamy; shadowy; ethereal, airy, gaseous, imponderable, tenuous, vague, vaporous, dreamlike, mushroom; cloud-built, cloud-formed; gossamery, illusory, insubstantial, unreal, unsolid [*rare*], slight, bodiless.

vacant, vacuous; empty etc. 187; eviscerated; blank, hollow; nominal; null; inane [*rare*].

5. Intrinsicality

n. **intrinsicality**, intrinsicalness, inbeing, inherence, inhesion, immanence, indwelling; subjectiveness; ego; egohood; essence, quintessence, elixir; essentialness etc. *adj.;* essential part, incarnation, quiddity, gist, pith, core, kernel, marrow, sap, lifeblood, backbone, heart, soul, life, substance, flower; important part etc. (*importance*) 642.

principle, nature, constitution, character, type, quality, crasis, diathesis.

temper, temperament; spirit, humor, grain, nature, vein, mood, frame, cue; disposition; habit.

capacity, endowment; capability etc. (*power*) 157.

aspects, moods, declensions, features; peculiarities etc. (*specialty*) 79; idiosyncrasy; idiocrasy etc. (*tendency*) 176; diagnostics.

v. be in the blood, run in the blood; be born so; be intrinsic etc. *adj.*

adj. **intrinsic**, intrinsical; derived from within, subjective; idiocratic *or* idiocratical, idiosyncratic *or* idiosyncratical; fundamental, normal; implanted, inherent, essential, natural; innate, inborn, inbred, ingrained, indwelling, inwrought; coeval with birth, genetic, genetous, haematobious, syngenic; radical, incarnate, thoroughbred, hereditary, inherited, immanent; congenital, congenite [*obs.*]; connate, running in the blood; ingenerate, ingenit *or* ingenite [*obs.*], ingenita [*obs.*], indigenous; in the grain etc. *n.;* bred in the bone, instinctive; inward, internal etc. 221; to the manner born; virtual.

characteristic etc. (*special*) 79, (*indicative*) 550; invariable, incurable, ineradicable, fixed.

adv. **intrinsically** etc. *adj.;* at bottom, in the main, in effect, practically, virtually, substantially, *au fond* [*F.*]; fairly.

6. Extrinsicality

n. **extrinsicality**, objectiveness, *non ego* [*L.*]; extraneousness etc. 57; accident.

adj. **extrinsic**, extrinsical; derived from without; objective; extraneous etc. (*foreign*) 57; modal, adventitious; ascititious, adscititious; incidental, accidental, nonessential, unessential, accessory; contingent, fortuitous, casual, subsidiary.

implanted, ingrafted; inculcated, infused.

outward etc. (*external*) 220.

adv. **extrinsically** etc. *adj.*

7. State

n. **state**, condition, category, estate, lot, case, trim, mood, temper; aspect etc. (*appearance*) 448.

dilemma, pass, predicament, quandary, corner, hole, *impasse* [*F.*], fix, pickle, plight.

frame, fabric etc. 329; stamp, set, fit, mold *or* mould; constitution, habitude, diathesis.

form, fettle, shape, kilter *or* kelter; tone, tenor, turn; trim, guise, fashion, light, complexion, style, character; build etc. 240; mode, modality, schesis [*obs.*]

v. be in−, possess−, enjoy- a state etc. *n.;* be on a footing, do, fare; come to pass.

adj. **conditional**, modal, formal; structural, organic.

adv. **conditionally** etc. *adj.;* as the matter stands, as things are; such being the case etc. 8; *quae cum ita sint* [*L.*].

8. Circumstance

n. **circumstance**, situation, phase, position, posture, attitude, place, point; terms; *régime* [*F.*]; footing, standing, status.

occasion, juncture, conjuncture; contingency etc. (*event*) 151.

predicament; emergency; exigency, crisis, pinch, pass, plight, push; occurrence; turning point.

bearings, how the land lies.

adj. **circumstantial**; given, conditional, provisional; critical; modal; contingent, incidental; adventitious etc. (*extrinsic*) 6; limitative.

detailed, minute, full, fussy.

adv. **thus**, in such wise; in *or* under the circumstances etc. *n.;* in *or* under the conditions etc. 7.

accordingly; that being the case; such being the case; that being so; since, seeing that.

as matters stand; as things go, as times go.

conditionally, provided, if, in case; if so, if so be, if it be so; if it so happen, if it so turn out; in the event of; in such a contingency, in such a case, in such an event; provisionally, unless, without.

according to circumstances, according to the occasion; as it may happen, as it may turn out, as it may be; as the case may be, as the wind blows.

Section 2. Relation

9. Relation

n. **relation**, bearing, reference, connection, concern, cognation, applicability, apposition, appositeness; correlation etc. 12; analogy; similarity etc. 17; affinity, homology, alliance, nearness, rapport, homogeneity, association; approximation etc. (*nearness*) 197; filiation etc. (*consanguinity*) 11; interest; relevancy etc. 23; dependency, relationship, relative position; correlation, interrelation, interconnection.

ratio, proportion; comparison etc. 464.

link, tie, bond of union, privity [*law*].

v. **be related** etc. *adj.;* have a relation etc. *n.;* relate to, refer to; bear upon, regard, concern, touch, affect, have to do with; pertain to, belong to, appertain to; answer to; interest.

associate, connect; bring into relation with, bring to bear upon; draw a parallel; link etc. 43.

adj. **relative**; correlative etc. 12; relating to etc. *v.;* relative to, in relation with, referrable *or* referable *or* referrible to; belonging to etc. *v.;* appurtenant to, in common with.

related, connected; implicated, associated, affiliated; allied, allied to; collateral, connate [*rare*], cognate, congenerous, connatural, affinitive, paronymous; *en rapport* [*F.*], in touch with.

approximative, approximating; proportional, proportionate, proportionable; allusive, comparable, equiparable [*obs. or rare*].

relevant etc. (*apt*) 23; applicable, equiparant; in the same category etc. 75; like etc. 17.

adv. **relatively** etc. *adj.;* pertinently etc. 23.

thereof; as to, as for, as respects, as regards; about; concerning etc. *v.;* anent; relating to, as relates to; with relation to, with reference to, with respect to, with regard to; in respect of; speaking of, *à propos* [*F.*] of; in connection with; by the way, by the by; whereas; for as much as, in as much as; in point of, as far as;

on the part of, on the score of; under the head of etc. (*class*) 75; in the matter of, *in re* [*L.*].

10. Irrelation
[want or absence of relation]

n. **irrelation**, dissociation; misrelation; inapplicability; inconnection; multifariousness; disconnection etc. (*disjunction*) 44; inconsequence, independence; incommensurability; irreconcilableness etc. (*disagreement*) 24; heterogeneity; unconformity etc. 83; irrelevancy, impertinence, *nihil ad rem* [*L.*]; intrusion etc. 24; nonpertinence.

v. **not concern** etc. 9; have no relation to etc. 9; have no bearing upon, have no concern with etc. 9; have no business with; have nothing to do with, have no business there; intrude etc. 24.

bring–, drag–, lug– in by the head and shoulders.

adj. **irrelative**, irrespective, unrelated, disrelated, irrelate [*rare*]; arbitrary; independent, unallied; disconnected, unconnected, adrift, isolated, insular; extraneous, strange, alien, foreign, outlandish, exotic.

not comparable, incommensurable, heterogeneous; unconformable etc. 83.

irrelevant, inapplicable; not pertinent, not to the purpose; impertinent [*legal*], unessential, inessential, accidental, inapposite, beside the mark; aside from–, away from–, foreign to–, beside the -purpose, –question, –transaction, –point; misplaced etc. (*intrusive*) 24; traveling out of the record.

remote, far-fetched, out-of-the-way, forced, neither here nor there, quite another thing; detached, apart, segregated, segregate; disquiparant.

multifarious; discordant etc. 24.

incidental, parenthetical, *obiter dictum* [*L.*], episodic.

adv. **parenthetically** etc. *adj.;* by the way, by the by; *en passant* [*F.*], incidentally, *obiter* [*L.*]; irrespectively etc. *adj.;* without reference to, without regard to; in the abstract etc. 87; *a se* [*L.*].

11. Consanguinity
[relations of kindred]

n. **consanguinity**, relationship, kindred, blood; parentage etc. (*paternity*) 166; filiation, affiliation; lineage, agnation, connation [*obs.*], cognation, connection, alliance; people [as, my *people*], family, family connection, family tie; ties of blood, blood relation; nepotism.

kinsman, kinsfolk; kith and kin; relation, relative; connection; sib [*rare*]; next of kin; uncle, aunt, nephew, niece; cousin, cousin-german; first cousin, second cousin; cousin once removed, cousin twice removed etc.; near relation, distant relation; brother, sister, one's own flesh and blood.

family, fraternity; brotherhood, sisterhood, cousinhood.

race, stock, generation; sept etc. 166; stirps, side; strain; breed, clan, tribe.

v. be related to etc. *adj.;* claim relationship with etc. *n.*

adj. related, akin, sib [*Scot. or archaic*], consanguineous, of the blood, family, allied, collateral; cognate, agnate, connate [*rare*]; kindred; affiliated; fraternal.

intimately related, nearly related, closely related, remotely related, distantly related; intimately allied, nearly allied, closely allied, remotely allied, distantly allied; affinal, german.

12. Correlation

[double or reciprocal relation]

n. reciprocalness etc. *adj.;* reciprocity, reciprocality, reciprocation; mutuality, correspondence, correlation, interrelation, interconnection, interdependence; interchange etc. 148; exchange, barter, *quid pro quo* [*L.*].

alternation, seesaw, shuttle [*rare*], to-and-fro. reciprocitist.

v. reciprocate, alternate, interact; interchange etc. 148; exchange; counterchange.

adj. reciprocal, mutual, commutual [*rare*], correlative; correspondent, corresponding; alternate; interchangeable; international; complemental, complementary; equivalent.

adv. mutatis mutandis [*L.*]; *vice versa* [*L.*]; each other; by turns etc. 148; reciprocally etc. *adj.*

13. Identity

n. identity, sameness, identicalness, unity, selfsameness, coincidence, coalescence; convertibility; equality etc. 27; selfness, self, oneself; identification.

connaturality, connature, connaturalness, homogeneity.

monotony; tautology etc. (*repetition*) 104.

facsimile etc. (*copy*) 21; homoousia; *alter ego* [*L.*] etc. (*similar*) 17; *ipsissima verba* [*L.*] etc. (*exactness*) 494; same; self-same, very same, one and the same; counterpart; very thing, actual thing; no other.

v. be identical etc. *adj.;* coincide, coalesce.

treat as the same, render the same; treat as identical; render identical; identify; recognize the identity of.

adj. identical; self, ilk [*archaic*]; the identical same etc. *n.;* selfsame, homoousian, one and the same; ditto.

coincident, coinciding, coalescing, coalescent, indistinguishable; one; equivalent etc. (*equal*) 27; much the same, much of a muchness; unaltered.

adv. identically etc. *adj.;* on all fours with; *ibidem* [*L.*], *ibid.*

14. Contrariety

[noncoincidence]

n. contrariety, contrast, foil, antithesis, antipode, counterpole, counterpoint; counterpart; complement; *vis-à-vis* [*F.*], oppositeness; contradiction; antagonism etc. (*opposition*) 708; clashing, repugnance, antipathy.

inversion etc. 218; the opposite, the reverse, the inverse, the converse, the antipodes, the other extreme.

v. be contrary etc. *adj.;* contrast with, oppose, antithesize [*rare*]; differ *toto coelo* [*L.*].

invert, reverse, turn the tables; turn topsy-turvy, turn end for end, turn upside down; retrograde, transpose, invaginate, intussuscept.

contradict, contravene; antagonize etc. 708.

adj. contrary, contrarious [*archaic*], contrariant [*rare*], opposite, counter, dead against; adverse, averse, converse, reverse; opposed, antithetical, contrasted, antipodean, antagonistic, opposing; conflicting, inconsistent, contradictory, at cross purposes; negative; hostile, inimical etc. 703.

differing *toto coelo* [*L.*]; diametrically opposite; as opposite as black and white, as opposite as light and darkness, as opposite as fire and water, as opposite as the poles; "Hyperion to a satyr" [*Hamlet*]; quite the contrary, quite the reverse; no such thing, just the other way, *tout au contraire* [*F.*].

adv. contrarily etc. *adj.;* contra, contrariwise, *per contra* [*L.*], on the contrary, nay rather; *vice versa* [*L.*]; on the other hand etc. (*in compensation*) 30.

15. Difference

n. difference; variance, variation, variety; diversity, divergence, heterogeneity, discongruity, contrast, inconformity, incompatibility, antithesis, antitheticalness, discrepation [*rare*], dissimilarity etc. 18; disagreement etc. 24; disparity etc. (*inequality*) 28; distinction, dissimilitude [*rare*], distinctness, contradiction, contradictoriness, contrariety, contradistinction; alteration.

nice distinction, fine distinction, delicate distinction, subtle distinction; shade of difference, nuance; discrimination etc. 465; differentia.

different thing, something else, apple off another tree, another pair of shoes; this, that, or the other.

modification, commutation [*rare*], moods and tenses.

v.   **be different** etc. *adj.;* differ, vary, ablude [*obs.*], mismatch, contrast; diverge from, depart from, deviate from, disaccord with, discrepate [*rare*]; divaricate; differ *toto coelo* [*L.*], differ *longo intervallo* [*L.*].

vary, modify etc. (*change*) 140.

discriminate etc. 465.

adj. **differing** etc. *v.;* different, diverse, heterogeneous; distinguishable; varied, variant, divergent, contrastive, incongruous, discrepant, dissonant, inharmonious, disparate, inconformable, differential, modified; diversified, various, divers [*archaic*], all manner of; variform etc. 81.

other, another, not the same; unequal etc. 28; unmatched; widely apart.

distinctive, characteristic; discriminative, differentiative, distinguishing; diacritic, diacritical; diagnostic.

adv. **differently** etc. *adj.*

16. Uniformity

n.   **uniformity**; homogeneity, homogeneousness; stability, continuity, permanence, consistency; connature [*rare*], connaturality [*rare*], connaturalness; homology; accordance; conformity etc. 82; agreement etc. 23; consonance, uniformness.

regularity, constancy, evenness, sameness, unity, even tenor, routine; monotony.

v.   **be uniform** etc. *adj.;* accord with etc. 23; run through.

become uniform etc. *adj.;* conform to etc. 82.

render uniform etc. *adj.;* assimilate, level, smooth, dress.

adj. **uniform**; homogeneous, homologous; of a piece, consistent, connatural; singsong, drear [*rare*], drearisome, dreary, monotonous, even, equable, constant, level; invariable; regular, unchanged, undeviating, unvaried, undiversified, unvarying; jog-trot.

adv. **uniformly** etc. *adj.;* uniformly with etc. (*conformably*) 82; in harmony with etc. (*agreeing*) 23; in a rut.

always, ever, evermore, perpetually, forever, everlastingly, invariably, without exception, never otherwise; by clockwork.

16a. Nonuniformity
[absence or want of uniformity]

n.   **diversity**, irregularity, unevenness; multiformity etc. 81; unconformity etc. 83; roughness etc. 256; dissimilarity, dissimilitude, divarication, divergence, heteromorphism, heterogeneity.

adj. **diversified**, varied, irregular, checkered, daedal, uneven, rough etc. 256; multifarious; multiform etc. 81; of various kinds; all manner of, all sorts of, all kinds of.

adv. in all manner of ways; here, there, and everywhere.

17. Similarity

n.   **similarity**, resemblance, likeness, similitude [*rare*], semblance, consimilarity [*rare*]; affinity, approximation, parallelism; agreement etc. 23; analogy, analogicalness; correspondence, homoiousia, parity.

connaturalness, connature [*rare*], connaturality [*rare*]; brotherhood, family likeness.

alliteration, rime *or* rhyme, pun.

repetition etc. 104; sameness etc. (*identity*) 13; uniformity etc. 16; isogamy.

analogue; the like; match, pendant, fellow, companion, pair, mate, twin, double, congener, counterpart, brother, sister; one's second self, *alter ego* [*L.*], chip of the old block, *par nobile fratrum* [*L.*], *Arcades ambo* [*L.*], birds of a feather, *et hoc genus omne* [*L.*]; *gens de même famille* [*F.*].

simile; parallel; type etc. (*metaphor*) 521; image etc. (*representation*) 554; photograph; close–, striking–, speaking–, faithful etc. *adj.* —likeness, –resemblance.

v.   **be similar** etc. *adj.;* look like, resemble, favor [*colloq.*], follow, echo, reproduce, bear resemblance; savor of, smack of; approximate; parallel, match, rime *or* rhyme with; take after; imitate etc. 19; span; hunt in couples, run in couples.

render similar etc. *adj.;* assimilate, approximate, bring near; connaturalize, make alike; rime *or* rhyme, pun.

adj. **similar**; resembling etc. *v.;* like, alike; twin.

analogous, analogical; parallel, of a piece; such as, so; homoiousian.

connatural, correlative, corresponding, cognate, congeneric, congenerous, allied to; akin to etc. (*consanguineous*) 11.

approximate, much the same, near, close, something like, near- [as *near*-silk, *colloq.*], such like; a show of; mock, pseudo, simulating, representing.

exact etc. (*true*) 494; lifelike, faithful; true to nature, true to life; the very image of, the very picture of; for all the world like, *comme deux gouttes d'eau* [*F.*], as like as two peas, as like as it can stare; *instar omnium* [*L.*], cast in the same mold, ridiculously like.

adv. **as if**, so to speak; as it were, as if it were; *quasi* [*L.*], just as.

18. Dissimilarity

n. **dissimilarity**, dissimilitude; unlikeness, diversity, disparity, dissemblance; divergence, variation; difference etc. 15; novelty, originality; creativeness; oögamy.

v. **be unlike** etc. *adj.;* vary etc. (*differ*) 15; bear no resemblance to, differ *toto coelo* [*L.*].
render unlike etc. *adj.;* vary etc. (*diversify*) 140.

adj. **dissimilar**, unlike, disparate; divergent, nonidentical, unidentical; of a different kind etc. (*class*) 75; unmatched, unique; new, novel; unprecedented etc. 83; original.

nothing of the kind; no such thing, quite another thing; far from it, other than, cast in a different mold, *tertium quid* [*L.*], as like a dock as a daisy, "very like a whale" [*Hamlet*]; as different as chalk from cheese, as different as Macedon and Monmouth; *lucus a non lucendo* [*L.*].
diversified etc. 16*a.*

adv. **otherwise**, elsewise; alias.

19. Imitation

n. **imitation**; copying etc. *v.;* transcription; repetition, duplication, reduplication; quotation; reproduction; mimeography.
mockery, apery, mimicking, mimicry.
simulation, personation; parrotism, parrotry; representation etc. 554; semblance, pretense; copy etc. 21; assimilation.
paraphrase, parody etc. 21.
plagiarism; forgery etc. (*falsehood*) 544.
imitator, echo, cuckoo, parrot, ape, monkey, mocking bird, mimic; copyist.

v. **imitate**, copy, mirror, reflect, reproduce, repeat; do like, echo, reëcho, catch; transcribe; match, parallel.
mock, take off, borrow, mimic, ape, simulate, personate; act etc. (*drama*) 599; represent etc. 554; counterfeit, forge, parody, travesty, caricature, burlesque.

follow in the steps of, follow in the footsteps of; follow in the wake of; tread in the steps of, tread in the footsteps of; take pattern by; follow suit [*colloq.*], follow the example of; walk in the shoes of, take a leaf out of another's book, strike in with; take after, model after; emulate.

adj. **imitated** etc. *v.;* mock, mimic; modeled after, molded on.
paraphrastic; literal; imitative; secondhand; imitable; aping, apish, mimicking, borrowed, counterfeit, imitation, false, pseudo, near- [as, *near*-silk, *colloq.*].

adv. **literally**, to the letter, verbatim, *literatim* [*L.*], *sic* [*L.*], *totidem verbis* [*L.*], word for word, *mot à mot* [*F.*], *verbatim et literatim* [*L.*]; exactly, precisely.

20. Nonimitation

n. **nonimitation**, no imitation; originality; creativeness.

adj. **unimitated**, uncopied; unmatched, unparalleled; inimitable etc. 33; unique, original, archetypal, prototypal, prototypical, primordial, creative, untranslated; exceptional, rare, *sui generis* [*L.*], uncommon, unexampled, out-of-the-way, insitate [*rare*], unwonted, *recherché* [*F.*], unordinary [*rare*], supernormal.

20a. Variation

n. **variation**; alteration etc. (*change*) 140.
modification, moods and tenses; discrepance, discrepancy.
divergency etc. 291; deviation etc. 279; aberration; innovation.

v. **vary** etc. (*change*) 140; deviate etc. 279; diverge etc. 291; alternate, swerve.

adj. **varied** etc. *v.;* modified; diversified etc. 16*a;* dissimilar etc. 18.

21. Copy
[result of imitation]

n. **copy**, facsimile, counterpart, *effigies* [*L.*], effigy, form, likeness, similitude, semblance, cast, tracing, ectype, electrotype; imitation etc. 19; model, representation, adumbration, study; "counterfeit presentment" [*Hamlet*]; portrait etc. (*representment*) 554; resemblance.
duplicate; transcript, transcription; counterscript; reflex, reflexion; shadow, echo; chip off the old block; reprint, replica, offprint, transfer, reproduction; second edition etc. (*repetition*) 104; *réchauffé* [*F.*]; apograph, fair copy, revise, rewriting.

matter; manuscript, typescript, flimsy [*cant*].

parody, caricature, burlesque, travesty, *travestie* [*F.*], paraphrase; cartoon.

servile copy, servile imitation; counterfeit etc. (*deception*) 545; *pasticcio* [*It.*].

adj. **faithful**; lifelike etc. (*similar*) 17; close, exact, strict, conscientious.

22. Prototype
[thing copied]

n. **prototype**, original, model, pattern, precedent, standard, scantling [*rare*], type; archetype, antitype; protoplast, protoplasm, plasm [*obs.*], proplasm [*rare*], module, exemplar, example, ensample [*archaic*], paradigm; lay-figure; fugleman, guide.

copy, text, design; keynote.

die, mold; matrix, last, mint, seal, punch, intaglio, negative; stamp.

v. be an example, set an example; set a copy.

23. Agreement

n. **agreement**, accord, accordance; unison, harmony; concord etc. 714; concordance, concert; understanding, mutual understanding; gentleman's agreement, *entente cordiale* [*F.*], consortium; unanimity, consension [*rare*], consentaneity.

conformity etc. 82; conformance; uniformity etc. 16; assonance, consonance, consentaneousness, consistency; congruity, congruence *or* congruency; keeping; congeniality; correspondence, concinnity, parallelism, apposition, union.

fitness, aptness etc. *adj.;* relevancy; pertinence *or* pertinency; sortance [*obs.*]; case in point; aptitude, coaptation, propriety, applicability, admissibility, commensurability, compatibility; cognation etc. (*relation*) 9.

adaptation, adaption, adjustment, graduation, accommodation; reconciliation, reconcilement; assimilation.

consent etc. (*assent*) 488; concurrence etc. 178; consensus, *rapport* [*F.*], meeting of minds, coöperation etc. 709.

right man in the right place, very thing; quite the thing, just the thing.

v. **be accordant** etc. *adj.;* agree, accord, harmonize; correspond, tally, respond; meet, suit, fit, befit, do, adapt itself to; fall in with, chime in with, square with, quadrate with, consort with, comport with; dovetail, assimilate; fit like a glove; fit to a tittle, fit to a T; match etc. 17; become one; homologate.

consent etc. (*assent*) 488.

render accordant etc. *adj.;* fit, suit, adapt, accommodate; graduate; adjust etc. (*render equal*) 27; dress, regulate, readjust; accord, harmonize, reconcile; fadge, dovetail, square.

adj. **agreeing**, suiting etc. *v.;* in accord, accordant, concordant, consonant, congruous, consentaneous [*archaic*], answerable, correspondent, congenial; coherent; becoming; harmonious, reconcilable, conformable; in accordance with, in harmony with, in keeping with, in unison with etc. *n.;* at one with, of one mind, of a piece; consistent, compatible, proportionate; commensurate; on all fours with.

apt, apposite, pertinent, pat; to the point, to the purpose; happy, felicitous, germane, *ad rem* [*L.*], in point, bearing upon, applicable, relevant, admissible.

fit, adapted, *in loco* [*L.*], *à propos* [*F.*], appropriate, seasonable, sortable, suitable, idoneous [*rare*], deft; meet etc. (*expedient*) 646.

at home, in one's proper element.

adv. *à propos* of; pertinently etc. *adj.*

24. Disagreement

n. **disagreement**; discord, discordance, discordancy; dissonance, dissidence, disunity, disunion, discrepancy; unconformity etc. 83; incongruity, incongruence; discongruity, *mésalliance* [*F.*]; jarring etc. *v.;* dissension etc. 713; conflict etc. (*opposition*) 708; bickering, clashing, misunderstanding, wrangle.

disparity, mismatch, disproportion, dissimilitude, inequality; disproportionateness etc. *adj.;* variance, divergence, repugnance.

unfitness etc. *adj.;* inaptitude, impropriety; inapplicability etc. *adj.;* inconsistency, inconcinnity; irrelevancy etc. (*irrelation*) 10.

misjoining, misjoinder; syncretism, intrusion, interference.

fish out of water.

v. **disagree**; clash, conflict, dispute, quarrel, jar etc. (*discord*) 713; interfere, intrude, come amiss; not concern etc. 10; mismatch; *humano capiti cervicem jungere equinam* [*L.*]

adj. **disagreeing** etc. *v.;* discordant, discrepant; at variance, at war; hostile, antagonistic, repugnant, inaccordant, clashing, jarring, factious, dissentient, dissentious, dissident, inacquiescent, incompatible, irreconcilable, inconsistent with; unconformable, exceptional etc. 83; intrusive, incongruent, incongruous; disproportionate, disproportioned; unharmonious; unconsonant; divergent, repugnant to.

inapt, unapt, inappropriate, malappropriate [*rare*], improper; unsuited, unsuitable; inapplicable; unfit, unfitting, unbefitting; unbecoming; ill-timed, ill-adapted, dissuitable [*rare*], infelicitous, unseasonable, *mal à propos* [*F.*], inadmissible; inapposite etc. (*irrelevant*) 10.

uncongenial; ill-assorted, ill-sorted; mismatched, misjoined, misplaced; unaccommodating, irreducible, uncommensurable; unsympathetic.

out of character, out of keeping, out of proportion, out of joint, out of tune, out of place, out of season, out of its element; at odds, at variance with.

adv. in defiance of, in contempt of, in spite of; discordantly etc. *adj.; à tort et à travers* [*F.*].

Section 3. Quantity

25. Quantity
[absolute quantity]

n. **quantity**, magnitude; size etc. (*dimensions*) 192; amplitude, mass, amount, quantum, measure, measurement, substance, strength.
[science of quantity] mathematics, mathesis [*rare*].
[logic] category, general conception, universal predicament.
[definite or finite quantity] armful, handful, mouthful, spoonful, capful; stock, batch, lot, dose; quota, quotiety [*rare*], quotum, pittance, driblet, grist.

v. **quantify**, rate.

adj. **quantitative**, some, any, more or less.

adv. to the tune of.

26. Degree
[relative quantity]

n. **degree**, grade, step, extent, measure, amount, ratio, stint *or* stent, standard, height, pitch; reach, amplitude, range, scope, caliber; gradation, shade; tenor, compass; sphere, station, rank, standing; rate, way, sort.

point, mark, stage etc. (*term*) 71; interval, line [*music*], space [*music*]; intensity, strength etc. (*greatness*) 31.

v. **graduate**, calibrate, measure; rectify.

adj. **comparative**; gradual, gradational, gradatory [*rare*], shading off; within the bounds etc. (*limit*) 233.

adv. **by degrees**, gradually, inasmuch, *pro tanto* [*L.*]; however, howsoever; step by step, bit by bit, little by little, inch by inch, drop by drop;

by inches, by slow degrees, by little and little; in some degree, in some measure; to some extent; *di grado in grado* [*It.*].

27. Equality
[sameness of quantity or degree]

n. **equality**, parity, coextension, symmetry, balance, poise; evenness, monotony, level.

equivalence; equipollence, equipoise, equilibrium, equiponderance; par, quits; not a pin to choose; distinction without a difference, six of one and half a dozen of the other; identity etc. 13; similarity. etc. 17; coequality, coevality [*rare*], isonomy, isopolity, isotropy, parallelism.

equalization, equation; equilibration, coördination, adjustment, readjustment.

tie, dead heat; drawn game, drawn battle; neck-and-neck race.

match, peer, compeer, equal, mate, fellow, brother; equivalent.

v. **be equal** etc. *adj.;* equal, match, reach, keep pace with, run abreast; come to, amount to, come up to; be on a level with, lie on a level with; balance; cope with; come to the same thing, even off.

render equal etc. *adj.;* equalize, level, dress, balance, equate, handicap, give points, trim, adjust, poise; fit, accommodate; adapt etc. (*render accordant*) 23; strike a balance; establish equality, restore equality, establish equilibrium, restore equilibrium; readjust; stretch on the bed of Procrustes.

adj. **equal**, even, level, monotonous, coequal, symmetrical, coördinate; on a par with, on a level with, on a footing with; up to the mark; equiparant, equiparate [*rare*].

equivalent, tantamount; quits; homologous; synonymous etc. 522; resolvable into, convertible, much at one, as broad as long, neither more nor less; much the same as, the same thing as, as good as; all one, all the same; equipollent, equiponderant, equiponderous, equibalanced; equalized etc. *v.;* drawn; half and half; isochronal, isochronous; isoperimetric *or* isoperimetrical; isobath, isobathic.

adv. **equally** etc. *adj.; pari passu* [*L.*], *ad eundem* [*L.*], *caeteris paribus* [*L.*], *in equilibrio* [*L.*]; to all intents and purposes.

28. Inequality
[difference of quantity or degree]

n. **inequality**, inequalness [*rare*]; disparity, imparity [*rare*]; odds; difference etc. 15; unevenness; inclination of the balance, partiality;

shortcoming; casting weight, makeweight; superiority etc. 33; inferiority etc. 34; inequation, inadequation [*archaic*], inadequacy.

v. **be unequal** etc. *adj.;* countervail; have the advantage, give the advantage; turn the scale; kick the beam; topple, topple over; overmatch etc. 33; not come up to etc. 34.

adj. **unequal**, inequal [*rare*], uneven, disparate, partial, inadequate; overbalanced, unbalanced; top-heavy, lopsided; disquiparant; unequaled, unparalleled, fellowless [*rare*], unmatched [*rare*], unrivaled, unique, unapproached, matchless, inimitable, transcendent, peerless, nonpareil, unexampled, unpatterned [*rare*], unpeered [*rare*].

adv. **unequally** etc. *adj.*

29. Mean

n. **mean**, medium, intermedium [*obsoles.*], average, balance, normal, rule, run; mediocrity, generality; golden mean etc. (*mid-course*) 628; middle etc. 68; compromise etc. 774; middle course, middle state; neutrality.

v. **average**, split the difference; take the average etc. *n.;* reduce to a mean etc. *n.;* strike a balance, pair off.

adj. **mean**, intermediate; medial, middle etc. 68; average, normal, standard; neutral.

mediocre, middle-class, *bourgeois* [*F.*], commonplace etc. (*unimportant*) 643.

adv. **on an average**, in the long run; taking one with another, taking all things together, taking it for all in all; *communibus annis* [*L.*], in round numbers.

in the middle, *in medias res* [*L.*].

30. Compensation

n. **compensation**, equation; commutation; indemnification; compromise etc. 774; neutralization, nullification; counteraction etc. 179; reaction; measure for measure; retaliation etc. 718; equalization etc. 27; redemption, recoupment.

set-off, offset; makeweight, casting weight; counterpoise, ballast; indemnity, equivalent, *quid pro quo* [*L.*]; bribe, hush money; gift, donation etc. 784; amends etc. (*atonement*) 952; counterbalance, counterclaim, countervailing; cross debt, cross demand.

pay, payment, reward etc. 973.

v. **compensate**, compense [*obs.*], make compensation, indemnify; counteract, countervail, counterpoise; balance; counterbalance, offset, outbalance, overbalance, set off; hedge, square, give and take; make up for, make leeway; cover,

fill up, neutralize, nullify; equalize etc. 27; make good; recoup, redeem etc. (*atone*) 952; pay, reward etc. 973.

adj. **compensating**, compensatory, compensative, amendatory, indemnificatory, reparative; countervailing etc. *v.;* in the opposite scale; equivalent etc. (*equal*) 27.

adv. **for a consideration**, in return, in consideration.

notwithstanding, but, however, yet, still, nevertheless; although, though; howbeit, albeit; at all events, in spite of, in despite of, despite, at any rate; be that as it may, for all that, even so, on the other hand, at the same time, *quand même* [*F.*], however that may be; after all, after all is said and done; taking one thing with another etc. (*average*) 29.

31. Greatness

n. **greatness** etc. *adj.;* magnitude; size etc. (*dimensions*) 192; multitude etc. (*number*) 102; immensity, enormity, muchness; infinity etc. 105; might, strength, intensity, fullness.

great quantity, quantity, deal [*colloq.*], power [*colloq.*], sight [*colloq.*], pot [*colloq.*], volume, world; mass, heap etc. (*assemblage*) 72; stock etc. (*store*) 636; peck, bushel, load, cargo; cartload, wagonload, shipload; flood, spring tide; abundance etc. (*sufficiency*) 639.

principal part, chief part, main part, greater part, better part, major part, best part, essential part; bulk, mass etc. (*whole*) 50.

fame, distinction, grandeur, dignity; importance etc. 642; generosity.

v. **be great** etc. *adj.;* run high, soar, tower, loom, tower above, rise above, transcend; rise to a great height, carry to a great height; bulk, bulk large; know no bounds; ascend, mount.

enlarge etc. (*increase*) 35, (*expand*) 194.

adj. **great**; greater etc. 33; large, considerable, fair, above par; big, bulky, huge etc. (*large in size*) 192; titanic, Atlantean, Herculean, cyclopean, voluminous; ample; abundant etc. (*enough*) 639; wholesale; many etc. 102; full, intense, strong, sound, passing [*archaic*], heavy, plenary, deep, high; signal, at its height, in the zenith.

worldwide, widespread, far-famed, extensive.

goodly, noble, precious, mighty; sad, grave, serious; far gone, arrant, downright; uttermost; crass, gross, tall, mickle [*archaic*], arch, profound, intense, consummate; rank, unmitigated, red-hot desperate; glaring, flagrant, stark staring; thorough-paced, thorough-going; roaring, whacking [*colloq.*], magnitudinous [*rare*],

11

thumping; extraordinary; important etc. 642; unsurpassed etc. (*supreme*) 33; complete etc. 52.

august, grand dignified, sublime, majestic etc. (*repute*) 873.

vast, immense, enormous, extreme; inordinate, excessive, extravagant, exorbitant, outrageous, preposterous, unconscionable, swinging, monstrous, overgrown; towering, stupendous, prodigious, astonishing, incredible, pronounced, fearful [*colloq.*], thundering [*slang*], terrible [*colloq.*], dreadful [*colloq.*], terrific [*colloq.*]; marvelous etc. (*wonder*) 870.

unlimited etc. (*infinite*) 105; unapproachable, unutterable, indescribable, ineffable, unspeakable, inexpressible, beyond expression, fabulous.

undiminished, unabated, unreduced, unrestricted.

absolute, positive, stark, decided, unequivocal, essential, perfect, finished.

remarkable, of mark, marked, pointed, veriest; notable, noticeable, noteworthy; renowned.

adv. **[in a positive degree]** truly etc. (*truth*) 494; decidedly, unequivocally, purely, absolutely, seriously, essentially, fundamentally, radically, downright, in all conscience; for the most part, in the main.

[in a complete degree] entirely etc. (*completely*) 52; abundantly etc. (*sufficiently*) 639; widely, far and wide.

[in a great or high degree] greatly etc. *adj.;* much, muckle [*archaic*], well, indeed, very, very much, a deal, no end of, most, not a little; pretty, pretty well; enough, in a great measure, no end, passing, richly; to a large extent, to a great extent, to a gigantic extent; on a large scale; so; never so, ever so; ever so much; by wholesale, mighty [*colloq.*], mightily, powerfully; ultra, in the extreme, extremely, exceedingly, intensely, exquisitely, acutely, indefinitely, immeasurably; beyond compare, beyond comparison, beyond measure, beyond all bounds; out of sight [*colloq.*]; incalculably, infinitely.

[in a supreme degree] preëminently, superlatively etc. (*superiority*) 33.

[in a too great degree] immoderately, monstrously, preposterously, inordinately, exorbitantly, excessively, enormously, out of all proportion, with a vengeance.

[in a marked degree] particularly, remarkably, singularly, curiously, uncommonly, unusually, peculiarly, notably, signally, strikingly, pointedly, mainly, chiefly; famously, egregiously, prominently, glaringly, emphatically, strangely, wonderfully, amazingly, surprisingly, astonishingly, incredibly, marvelously, awfully, stupendously.

[in an exceptional degree] peculiarly etc. (*unconformity*) 83.

[in a violent degree] furiously etc. (*violence*) 173; severely, desperately, tremendously, extravagantly, confoundedly, deucedly [*slang*], devilishly [*colloq.*], with a vengeance, à outrance [*F.*], à toute outrance [*F.*].

[in a painful degree] painfully, sadly, grossly, sorely, bitterly, piteously, grievously, miserably, cruelly, woefully, lamentably, shockingly, frightfully, dreadfully, fearfully, terribly, horribly, distressingly, balefully, dolorously.

32.   Smallness

n.   **smallness** etc. *adj.;* littleness etc. (*small size*) 193; tenuity; paucity; fewness etc. (*small number*) 103; meanness, insignificance etc. (*unimportance*) 643; mediocrity, moderation.

small quantity, modicum, minimum; vanishing point; material point, atom, particle, electron, molecule, muon, photon, quark, corpuscle, point, speck, dot, mote, jot, iota, ace; minutiae, details; look, thought, idea, *soupçon* [*F.*], dab, dight [*dial.*], whit, tittle, shade, shadow; spark, scintilla, gleam; touch, cast; grain, scruple, granule, globule, minim, sup, sip, sop, spice, drop, droplet, sprinkling, dash, *morceau* [*F.*], screed [*Scot.*], smack, tinge, tincture; inch, patch, scantling, tatter, cantle, cantlet, flitter, gobbet, dole, mite, bit, morsel, crumb; scrap, shred, tag, splinter, rag; seed, fritter, shive; snip, snippet; snick, snack [*dial.*], snatch, slip; chip, chipping; shiver, sliver, driblet, clipping, paring, shaving, hair.

nutshell; thimbleful, spoonful, handful, capful, mouthful; fragment; fraction etc. (*part*) 51; drop in the ocean.

animalcule etc. 193.

trifle etc. (*unimportant thing*) 643; mere nothing, next to nothing; hardly anything; just enough to swear by; the shadow of a shade.

finiteness, finite quantity.

v.   **be small** etc. *adj.;* lie in a nutshell.

diminish etc. (*decrease*) 36, (*contract*) 195.

adj.   **small,** little; diminutive etc. (*small in size*) 193; minute, miniature, minikin; fine; inconsiderable, dribbling, paltry etc. (*unimportant*) 643; faint etc. (*weak*) 160; slender, light, slight, scanty, scant, limited; meager etc. (*insufficient*) 640; sparing; few etc. 103; low; soso *or* so-so *or* so so [*colloq.*], middling, tolerable, no great shakes [*slang*]; below par, under par, below the mark, under the mark; at a low ebb; halfway; moderate, modest; tender, subtle.

inappreciable, evanescent, infinitesimal, homeopathic, very small; atomic, corpuscular, microscopic, molecular; skin-deep.

mere, simple, sheer, stark, bare; near run.

dull, petty, shallow, stolid, phlegmatic, unintelligent; Boeotian, ungifted etc. 499.

adv. [in a small degree] to a small extent, on a small scale; a little, a wee bit; slightly etc. *adj.;* imperceptibly; miserably, wretchedly; insufficiently etc. 640; imperfectly; faintly etc. 160; passably, pretty well, well enough.

[in a certain or limited degree] partially, in part; in a certain degree, to a certain degree; to a certain extent; comparatively; some, rather, middling [*colloq.*]; in some degree, in some measure; something, somewhat; simply, only, purely, merely; at least, at the least, at most, at the most; ever so little, as little as may be, *tant soit peu* [*F.*], in ever so small a degree; thus far, *pro tanto* [*L.*], within bounds, in a manner, after a fashion.

almost, nearly, well-nigh, short of, not quite, all but; near upon, close upon; *peu s'en faut* [*F.*], near the mark; within an ace of, within an inch of; on the brink of; scarcely, hardly, barely, only just, no more than.

[in an uncertain degree] about, thereabouts, somewhere about, nearly, say; be the same more or less, be the same little more or less.

[in no degree] noway *or* noways, nowise, not at all, not in the least, not a bit, not a bit of it, not a whit, not a jot, not a shadow; in no wise, in no respect; by no means, by no manner of means; on no account, at no hand.

33. Superiority
[supremacy]

n. **superiority,** majority, plurality; greatness etc. 31; advantage; pull [*slang*]; preponderance, preponderation; vantage ground, prevalence, partiality; personal superiority; scepter, sovereignty, sovranty [*poetic*]; nobility etc. (*rank*) 875; Triton among the minnows, *primus inter pares* [*L.*], *nulli secundus* [*L.*]; superman, overman; captain; crackerjack [*slang*].

supremacy, supremeness, supremity [*rare*], primacy, paramountcy, preëminence; lead; maximum, record; crest, climax; culmination etc. (*summit*) 210; transcendence; *ne plus ultra* [*L.*]; lion's share, Benjamin's mess; excess, surplus etc. (*remainder*) 40; redundance etc. 641.

v. **be superior** etc. *adj.;* exceed, excel, transcend; outdo, outbalance, outweigh, outrank, outrival, out-Herod Herod; pass, surpass, get ahead of; overtop, override, overpass, overbalance, overweigh, overmatch; top, o'ertop, cap, beat, cut out [*colloq.*]; beat hollow [*colloq.*]; outstrip etc. 303; eclipse, throw into the shade, take the shine out of [*colloq.*], put one's nose out of joint [*colloq.*]; have the upper hand, have the whip hand of, have the advantage; turn the scale; play first fiddle etc. (*importance*) 642; preponderate, predominate, prevail; precede, take precedence, come first; come to a head, culminate; beat etc. all others, bear the palm; break the record; take the cake [*slang*].

become *or* render larger etc. (*increase*) 35, (*expand*) 194.

adj. **superior,** greater, major, higher; exceeding etc. *v.;* great etc. 31; distinguished, ultra; vaulting; more than a match for.

supreme, greatest, maximal, maximum, utmost, paramount, preëminent, foremost, crowning, hegemonic [*rare*]; first-rate etc. (*important*) 642, (*excellent*) 648; unrivaled; peerless, matchless; second to none, *sans pareil* [*F.*]; unparagoned, unparalleled, unequaled, unapproached, unsurpassed; superlative, inimitable, *facile princeps* [*L.*], incomparable, sovereign, without parallel, *nulli secundus* [*L.*], *ne plus ultra* [*L.*]; beyond compare, beyond comparison; culminating etc (*topmost*) 210; transcendent, transcendental; *plus royaliste que le Roi* [*F.*].

increased etc. (*added to*) 35; enlarged etc. (*expanded*) 194.

adv. **beyond,** more, over; over the mark, above the mark; above par; upwards of, in advance of; over and above; at the top of the scale, at its height.

[in a superior or supreme degree] eminently, egregiously, preëminently, surpassing, prominently, superlatively, supremely, above all, of all things, the most, to crown all, *par excellence* [*F.*], principally, especially, particularly, peculiarly, *a fortiori* [*L.*], even, yea, still more.

34. Inferiority

n. **inferiority,** minority, subordinacy [*obs.*], subordinance [*obs.*]; shortcoming, deficiency; minimum; smallness etc. 32; imperfection; subjacency [*rare*]; lower quality, lower worth; meanness, poorness, baseness, shabbiness.

[personal inferiority] commonalty etc. 876; juniority, subordinacy; subaltern, sub [*colloq.*].

v. **be inferior** etc. *adj.;* fall short of, come short of; not pass, not come up to; want.

become smaller, render smaller etc. (*decrease*), 36, (*contract*) 195; hide its diminished head, retire into the shade, yield the palm, play second fiddle, take a back seat [*colloq.*], kick the beam.

adj. **inferior**, deterior [*rare*], smaller; small etc. 32; minor, less, lesser, deficient, minus, lower, subordinate, secondary, junior, humble; second-rate etc. (*imperfect*) 651; sub-, subaltern.

least, smallest etc. (*see* little, small etc. 193); lowest.

diminished etc. (*decreased*) 36; reduced etc. (*contracted*) 195; unimportant etc. 643.

adv. **less**; under the mark, below the mark, under par, below par; at the bottom of the scale, at a low ebb, at a disadvantage; short of, under.

35. Increase

n. **increase**, augmentation, increasement [*rare*], addition, enlargement, extension; dilatation etc. (*expansion*) 194; increment, accretion; accession etc. 37; development, growth; aggrandizement, accumulation, reënforcement, redoubling, intensification, inflation, enhancement, aggravation; rise; ascent etc. 305; exaggeration, exacerbation; spread etc. (*dispersion*) 73; flood tide, spring tide.

gain, produce, product, profit, gettings [*archaic*], advantage, booty, plunder, superlucration [*rare*], clean-up.

v. **increase**, augment, add to, enlarge; dilate etc. (*expand*) 194; grow, wax, get ahead, gain strength; advance; run up, shoot up; rise; swell, mount, ascend etc. 305; sprout etc. 194.

aggrandize; raise, exalt; deepen, heighten, lengthen, greaten [*archaic*], thicken; eke [*archaic*], inflate; strengthen, intensify, enhance, magnify, redouble, double, triple, etc.; aggravate, exaggerate; exasperate, exacerbate; add fuel to the flame, *oleum addere camino* [*L.*]; superadd etc. (*add*) 37; spread etc. (*disperse*) 73.

adj. **increased** etc. *v.;* on the increase, undiminished; additional etc. (*added*) 37.

increasing, growing, crescent, crescive [*rare*], lengthening, multiplying, intensifying, intensive, intensitive [*rare*], incretionary [*rare*]; crescendo.

adv. crescendo, increasingly.

36. Nonincrease, Decrease

n. **decrease**, diminution, decrescence, decrement, diminishment, lessening etc. *v.;* subtraction etc.

38, reduction, rebatement [*rare*], abatement, declension; shrinkage etc. (*contraction*) 195; coarctation [*obs.*]; curtailment, abridgment etc. (*shortening*) 201; extenuation.

subsidence, wane, ebb, decline; ebb tide, neap tide, ebbing; descent etc. 306; reflux, depreciation, wear and tear, erosion, consumption; deterioration etc. 659; anticlimax; mitigation etc. (*moderation*) 174; catabasis [*med.*].

v. **decrease**, diminish, lessen; abridge etc. (*shorten*) 201; shrink etc. (*contract*) 195; drop off, fall off, tail off; fall away, waste, wear; wane, ebb, decline; descend etc. 306; subside; melt away, die away; retire into the shade, hide its diminished head, fall to a low ebb, run low, languish, decay, crumble, erode, consume away.

bate, abate [*archaic*], dequantitate [*obs.*]; discount, belittle, minify [*rare*], minimize, minish [*rare*], depreciate; extenuate, lower, weaken, attenuate, fritter away; mitigate etc. (*moderate*) 174; dwarf, throw into the shade; reduce etc. 195; shorten etc. 201; subtract etc. 38; deliquesce, ease, remit [*rare*].

adj. **unincreased** etc. (*see* increase etc. 35); decreased, decreasing etc. *v.;* decrescent, reductive; deliquescent, contractive; decrescendo; on the wane etc. *n.*

adv. decrescendo, decreasingly.

37. Addition

n. **addition**, annexation, adjection [*rare*], junction etc. 43; superposition, superaddition, superjunction, superfetation; accession, reënforcement; increase etc. 35; increment.

affix, codicil, subscript, tag, rider, appendage, continuation, equation, postscript, adjunct, etc. 39; supplement; accompaniment etc. 88; interlineation, interposition etc. 228; insertion etc. 300.

computation, footing, totaling, casting, summation.

v. **add**, annex, affix, superadd, subjoin, superpose; clap on, saddle on; tack to, append, tag, adject [*rare*], attach, postfix, adjoin [*rare*], ingraft; saddle with; sprinkle; introduce etc. (*interpose*) 228; insert etc. 300.

compute, foot up, total, cast, sum, count up.

become added, accrue; supervene, advene.

reënforce or reinforce, restrengthen; strengthen, swell the ranks of; augment etc. 35.

adj. **added** etc. *v.;* additional; supplement, supplemental, supplementary; suppletive [*rare*], supervenient [*rare*], suppletory, subjunctive;

adjectitious, adscititious, ascititious; additive, extra, further, fresh, more, new, ulterior, other, remanent [*rare*]; auxiliary, contributory, accessory; spare.

adv. au reste [*F.*]; in addition, more, plus, extra; and, also, likewise, too, furthermore, further, item; and also, and eke [*archaic*]; else, besides, to boot; et cetera, etc.; and so on, and so forth; into the bargain, *cum multis aliis* [*L.*], over and above, moreover.

with, withal; including, inclusive, as well as, not to mention, let alone; together with, along with, coupled with, in conjunction with; conjointly; jointly etc. 43.

38. Nonaddition, Deduction

n. **deduction**, subtraction, subduction; retrenchment; removal; sublation [*rare*], ablation; abstraction etc. (*taking*) 789; garbling etc. *v.;* mutilation, detruncation; amputation; recision, abscision, excision; abrasion; curtailment etc. 201.

rebate etc. (*decrement*) 40*a;* minuend, subtrahend; decrease etc. 36.

v. **subduct**, subtract, deduct, deduce; bate, retrench; remove, withdraw; take from, take away; detract; garble.

mutilate, amputate, detruncate; cut off, cut away, cut out; abscind, excise.

pare, thin, prune, decimate, eliminate, rebate; bant [*colloq.*], reduce; abrade, scrape, file.

geld, castrate, envirate [*rare*], cut, spay (*female*), capon *or* caponize (*a cock*), eunuchize [*rare*], unman, emasculate.

diminish etc. 36; curtail etc. (*shorten*) 201; deprive of etc. (*take*) 789; weaken.

adj. **subtracted** etc. *v.;* subtractive.

tailless, acaudal, acaudate.

adv. **in deduction** etc. *n.;* less; short of; minus, without, except, excepting, with the exception of, barring, bar, save, exclusive of, save and except, with a reservation, ablatitious [*rare*].

39. Adjunct
[thing added]

n. **adjunct**; addition, additament; *additum* [*L.*], affix, appendage, annex; augment, augmentation; increment, reënforcement, supernumerary, accessory, item; garnish, sauce; accompaniment etc. 88; adjective, addendum (*pl.* addenda); complement, supplement; continuation.

rider, offshoot, episode, side issue, corollary, codicil etc. (*addition*) 37.

flap, lug, lapel, apron, tab, fly, tuck, lap, piece, lappet, skirt, embroidery, trappings, cortege *or* cortège [*F.*]; tail, suffix etc. (*sequel*) 65; wing.

v. **add**, annex etc. 37.

adj. **additional** etc. 37.

winged, alate *or* alated.

adv. in addition etc. 37.

40. Remainder
[thing remaining]

n. **remainder**, residue; remains, remanet [*rare*], relict [*rare*], remanence [*rare*], remnant, rest, relic; leavings, heeltap, odds and ends, cheeseparings, candle ends, orts; residuum; dregs etc. (*dirt*) 653; refuse etc. (*useless*) 645; stubble, result, educt; fag-end; ruins, wreck, skeleton, stump, rump; alluvium.

surplus, overplus, excess; balance [*commercial slang*], complement; surplusage; superfluity etc. (*redundance*) 641; survival, survivance [*rare*]; fossil, shadow, *caput mortuum* [*L.*].

v. **remain**; be left etc. *adj.;* exceed, survive; leave.

adj. **remaining**, left; left behind, left over; residual, residuary; over, odd; unconsumed, sedimentary; surviving; net; exceeding, over and above; outlying, outstanding; cast off etc. 782; superfluous etc. (*redundant*) 641.

40a. Decrement
[thing deducted]

n. **decrement**, discount, rebate, rebatement, tare, offtake, drawback, draft, reprise; defect, loss, deduction; afterglow; eduction; waste.

41. Mixture
[forming a whole without coherence]

n. **mixture**, admixture, mixtion [*obs.*], admixtion, commixture, commixtion *or* commixion [*obs.*], intermixture, immixture, minglement, eucrasy [*med.*], interfusion, intertanglement, interlacement, interlacery, intertexture, levigation, alloyage; matrimony; junction etc. 43; combination etc. 48; miscegenation.

impregnation; infusion, diffusion, suffusion, transfusion; infiltration; seasoning, sprinkling, interlarding; interpolation etc. 228; adulteration, sophistication.

[thing mixed] tinge, tincture, touch, dash, smack, sprinkling, spice, seasoning, infusion, *soupçon* [*F.*].

[compound resulting from mixture] alloy, amalgam; brass, chowchow, pewter; magma, half-and-half, *mélange* [*F.*], *tertium quid* [*L.*], miscellany, medley, mess, hash, hodgepodge, hotchpotch, hotchpot, *pasticcio* [*It.*], patch-work, odds and ends, all sorts; jumble etc. (*disorder*) 59; salad, sauce, mash, omnium-gatherum [*colloq.*], gallimaufry, olla-podrida, olio, salmagundi, potpourri, Noah's ark; texture; mingled yarn; mosaic etc. (*variegation*) 440.

half-blood, half-breed, half-caste; mulatto; quarteron *or* quarteroon [*rare*], quintroon *or* quinteron, quadroon, octoroon, sambo *or* zambo; cafuzo; Eurasian; fustee *or* fustie [*W. Ind.*], mestee [*W. Ind.*], mestizo (*fem.* mestiza), griffe, ladino, marabou, sacatra; zebrule; catalo; mule; cross, hybrid, mongrel; cross-breed etc. (*unconformity*) 83.

v. **mix**; join etc. 43; combine etc. 48; commix, immix, intermix; levigate, mix up with, mingle; commingle, intermingle, bemingle; shuffle etc. (*derange*) 61; pound together; hash up, stir up; knead, brew; impregnate with; interlard etc. (*interpolate*) 228; intertwine, interweave etc. 219; associate with; miscegenate.

be mixed etc.; get among, be entangled with.

imbue; infuse, suffuse, transfuse, instill *or* instil, infiltrate, dash, tinge, tincture, season, sprinkle, besprinkle, attemper, medicate, blend, cross; alloy, amalgamate, compound, adulterate, sophisticate, infect.

adj. **mixed** etc. *v.;* implex [*rare*], composite, half-and-half, linsey-woolsey, medley, chowchow, hybrid, mongrel, heterogeneous; motley etc. (*variegated*) 440; miscellaneous, promiscuous, indiscriminate; miscible.

adv. **among**, amongst, amid, amidst; with; in the midst of, in the crowd.

42. Simpleness
[freedom from mixture]

n. **simpleness** etc. *adj.;* purity, homogeneity.
elimination; sifting etc. *v.;* purification etc. (*cleanness*) 652.

v. **render simple** etc. *adj.;* simplify.
sift, winnow, bolt, eliminate; exclude, get rid of; clear; purify etc. (*clean*) 652; disentangle etc. (*disjoin*, 44).

adj. **simple**, uniform, of a piece, homogeneous, Attic, homespun, single, pure, clear, sheer, neat.
unmixed, unmingled, unblended, uncombined, uncompounded; elemental, elementary, undecomposed; unadulterated, unsophisticated, unalloyed, untinged, unfortified; *pur et simple* [*F.*]; incomplex, incomposite [*rare*].
free from, exempt from; exclusive.

adv. **simply** etc. *adj.;* only.

43. Junction

n. **junction**; joining etc. *v.;* joinder, union; connection, conjunction, conjugation; annexion, annexation, annexment [*rare*]; astriction, attachment, compagination [*rare*], subjunction, vincture [*obs.*], ligation, alligation; accouplement; marriage etc. (*wedlock*) 903; infibulation, inosculation, symphysis, anastomosis, confluence, communication, concatenation; meeting, reunion; assemblage etc. 72.

coition, copulation; sexual congress, sexual conjunction, sexual intercourse.

joint, joining, juncture, chiasm, osculature, pivot, hinge, articulation, commissure, seam, gore, gusset, suture, stitch; link etc. 45; miter, mortise.

contingency, emergency, predicament, crisis, concurrence.

closeness, tightness etc. *adj.;* coherence etc. 46; combination etc. 48.

annexationist.

v. **join**, unite; conjoin, connect; associate; put together, lay together, clap together, hang together, lump together, hold together, piece together, tack together, fix together, bind up together; embody, reëmbody; roll into one.

attach, fix, affix, immobilize, saddle on, fasten, bind, secure, clinch, twist, make fast etc. *adj.;* tie, pinion, string, strap, sew, lace, stitch, tack, knit, button, buckle, hitch, lash, truss, bandage, braid, splice, swathe, gird, tether, moor, picket, harness, chain; fetter etc. (*restrain*) 751; lock, latch, belay, brace, hook, grapple, leash, couple, accouple, link, yoke, bracket; marry etc. (*wed*) 903; bridge over, span.

pin, nail, bolt, hasp, clasp, clamp, screw, rivet; impact, solder, braze; cement, set; weld together, fuse together; tighten, trice up, screw up; wedge, rabbet, mortise, miter, jam, dovetail, enchase; graft, ingraft, inosculate.

entwine *or* intwine; interlink, interlace, intertwine, intertwist, interweave; entangle; twine round, belay.

be joined etc.; hang together, hold together; cohere etc. 46.

adj. **joined** etc. *v.;* joint; conjoint, conjunct; corporate, compact; hand in hand.

firm, fast, close, tight, taut *or* taught, secure, set, intervolved [*obs.*]; inseparable, indissoluble, insecable [*obs.*], inseverable.

adv. **jointly** etc. *adj.;* in conjunction with etc. (*in addition to*) 37; fast, firmly, etc. *adj.;* intimately.

44. Disjunction

n. **disjunction**, disconnection, disunity, disunion, disassociation, disengagement, dissociation, disjointure; discontinuity etc. 70; abjunction [*obs.*]; cataclasm; inconnection [*obs.*]; abstraction, abstractedness; isolation; insularity, insulation; oasis; island; separateness etc. *adj.;* severalty; *disjecta membra* [*L.*]; dispersion etc. 73; apportionment etc. 786.

separation; parting etc. *v.;* circumcision, detachment, segregation; divorce, sejunction [*obs.*], seposition [*obs.*], diduction [*rare*], diremption [*rare*], discerption; elision; caesura, division, subdivision, break, fracture, rupture; compartition [*obs.*]; dismemberment, disintegration, dislocation; luxation; severance, disseverance; scission; rescission, abscission; laceration, dilaceration; disruption, abruption; avulsion, divulsion; section, resection, cleavage; fission; partibility, separability, separatism.

fissure, breach, rent, split, rift, crack, slit, incision.

dissection, anatomy; decomposition etc. 49; cutting instrument etc. (*sharpness*) 253; buzz saw, circular saw.

separatist.

v. **be disjoined** etc.; come off, come to pieces, fall off, fall to pieces; peel off; get loose.

disjoin, disconnect, disengage, disunite, dissociate, dispair [*obs.*]; divorce, part, dispart, detach, separate, cut off, rescind, segregate; set apart, keep apart; insulate, isolate; throw out of gear; cut adrift; loose; unloose, undo, unbind, unchain, unlock etc. (*fix*) 43, unpack, unravel; disentangle; set free etc. (*liberate*) 750.

sunder, divide, subdivide, sever, section, sectionize [*rare*], segment, dissever, abscind; circumcise; cut; incide [*obs.*], incise; saw, snip, nib [*obs.*], nip, cleave, rive, rend, slit, split, splinter, chip, crack, snap, break, tear, burst; rend etc., asunder, rend in twain; wrench, rupture, shatter, shiver, crunch, craunch *or* cranch, chop; cut up, rip up; hack, hew, slash; whittle; haggle, hackle, discind [*obs.*], lacerate, scamble [*obs.*], mangle, gash, hash, slice; cut up, carve, quarter, dissect, anatomize; dislimb; take to pieces, pull to pieces, pick to pieces, tear to pieces; tear to tatters, tear piecemeal; divellicate; skin etc. 226.

disintegrate, dismember, disbranch, disband; disperse etc. 73; dislocate, disjoint; break up; mince; comminute etc. (*pulverize*) 330; apportion etc. 786.

partition, parcel, demarcate [*rare*], graduate, district, chapter, canton.

part, part company; separate, leave; alienate, estrange.

adj. **disjoined** etc. *v.;* discontinuous etc. 70; bipartite, biparted [*rare*], multipartite, abstract; disjunctive; secant; isolated etc. *v.;* insular, separate, disparate, discrete, apart, asunder, far between, loose, free; lobate, lobulate, lobulated, lobulose, digitate; unattached, unannexed, unassociated, unconnected; distinct; adrift; straggling; rift, reft, cleft.

[capable of being cut] scissile, divisible, discerptible [*rare*], partible, separable, severable, dividuous [*rare*].

adv. **separately** etc. *adj.;* one by one, severally, apart; adrift, asunder, in twain; in the abstract, abstractedly.

45. Vinculum

[connecting medium]

n. **vinculum**, link; connective, connection; junction etc. 43; bond of union, copula, intermedium, hyphen; bracket; bridge, stepping-stone, isthmus.

bond, tendon, tendril; fiber; cord, cordage; riband, ribbon, rope, guy, cable, line, halser [*obs.*], hawser, painter, moorings, wire, chain; string etc. (*filament*) 205.

fastening, tie; ligament, ligature; strap; tackle, rigging; standing rigging; running rigging; traces, harness; yoke; band, bandage; brace, roller, fillet; inkle; with, withe, withy; thong, braid; girder, tiebeam; girth, girdle, cestus, garter, halter, noose, lasso, surcingle, knot, running knot; *cabestro* [*Sp. Amer.*], cinch, lariat, *legadero* [*Sp. Amer.*], oxreim [*S. Africa*]; suspenders.

pin, corking pin, nail, brad, tack, skewer, staple, clamp; cramp, cramp iron, detent, *larigo* [*Sp. Amer.*], pawl, terret, screw, button, buckle, clasp, hasp, bar, hinge, hank, catch, latch, bolt, latchet, tag; tooth; hook, hook and eye; lock, holdfast, padlock, rivet, couple, coupler, ring; anchor, grappling iron, treenail *or* trennel, stake, post; prop etc. (*support*) 215.

cement, glue, gum, paste, size, wafer, solder, lute, putty, birdlime, mortar, stucco, plaster, grout; viscum.

shackle, rein etc. (*means of restraint*) 752.

v. **bridge over**, span; connect etc. 43; hang etc. 214.

46. Coherence

n. **coherence**, cohesion, cohesiveness, adherence, adhesion, adhesiveness; concretion, accretion;

conglutination, conglomeration, agglutination, agglomeration; aggregation; consolidation, set, cementation; sticking, soldering etc. *v.;* connection; dependence.

tenacity, toughness; stickiness etc. 352; inseparability, inseparableness; bur *or* burr, remora.

conglomerate, concrete etc. *(density)* 321.

v. **cohere,** adhere, coagulate, stick, cling, cleave, hold, take hold of, hold fast, close with, clasp, hug; grow together, hang together; twine round etc. *(join)* 43.

stick like a leech, stick like wax, stick like the paper on the wall; stick closer than a brother; stick close; cling like ivy, cling like a bur; adhere like a remora, adhere like Dejanira's shirt.

glue; agglutinate, conglutinate; cement, lute, belute [*rare*], paste, gum; solder, weld; ferruminate [*archaic*]; cake, consolidate etc. *(solidify)* 321; agglomerate.

adj. **adhesive,** cohesive, adhering, cohering etc. *v.;* tenacious, tough; sticky etc. 352.

united, unseparated, sessile, inseparable, inextricable, infrangible; compact etc. *(dense)* 321.

47. Incoherence

[nonadhesion, immiscibility]

n. **incoherence,** nonadhesion; immiscibility; looseness etc. *adj.;* laxity; relaxation; loosening etc. *v.;* freedom; disjunction etc. 44; rope of sand.

v. **make loose** etc. *adj.;* loosen, slacken, relax; unglue etc. 46; detach etc. *(disjoin)* 44.

adj. **nonadhesive,** immiscible; incoherent, detached, loose, baggy, slack, lax, relaxed, flapping, streaming; disheveled; segregated, like grains of sand; unconsolidated etc. 231; uncombined etc. 48; noncohesive.

48. Combination

n. **combination;** mixture etc. 41; junction etc. 43; union, unification, synthesis, synizesis, syneresis, incorporation, amalgamation, embodiment, coalescence, crasis, fusion, coalescing, blend, blendure [*rare*], blending, absorption, centralization.

alloy, compound, amalgam, composition, *tertium quid* [*L.*]; resultant, impregnation.

v. **combine,** unite, incorporate, inosculate, consubstantiate, alloy, intermix, interfuse, interlard, syncretize, interlace, agglutinate, amalgamate, embody, absorb, reëmbody, blend, merge, fuse, melt into one, consolidate, coalesce, solidify, commix [*archaic*], contemper, centralize, impregnate; put together, lump together.

league, interleague [*rare*], federate, confederate, fraternize, club, associate, amalgamate, cement a union, marry, couple, pair, ally.

adj. **combined** etc. *v.;* wedded; indiscrete, conjunctive, conjugate, conjoint; impregnated with, ingrained; imbued, inoculated.

allied, amalgamated, federate, confederate, corporate, leagued.

49. Decomposition

n. **decomposition,** analysis, dieresis, dissection, resolution, catalysis, dissolution, break-up; dispersion etc. 73; disjunction etc. 44; disintegration.

decay, rot, putrefaction, putrescence, putridity, caries; corruption etc. *(uncleanness)* 653.

electrolysis, electrolyzation, hydrolysis, proteolysis, thermolysis, catalysis.

v. **decompose,** decompound [*rare*]; analyze, disembody, dissolve; resolve into its elements, separate into its elements; dissect, decentralize, break up; disintegrate, disperse etc. 73; unravel etc. *(unroll)* 313; crumble into dust.

corrupt [*archaic*], rot, decay, consume; putrefy, putresce.

electrolyze, hydrolyze, thermolyze, catalyze.

adj. **decomposed** etc. *v.;* catalytic, analytical; resolvent, separative, solvent.

50. Whole

[principal part]

n. **whole,** totality, integrity; totalness etc. *adj.;* entirety, entire [*rare*], *ensemble* [*F.*], collectiveness; unity etc. 87; completeness etc. 52; indivisibility, indiscerptibility; integration, embodiment; integer, integral.

all, general [*archaic*], the whole, total, aggregate, one and all, gross amount, sum, sum total, the altogether [*humorous*], *tout ensemble* [*F.*], length and breadth of, Alpha and Omega, "be all and end all"; complex, *complexus* [*L.*]; lock, stock, and barrel.

bulk, mass, lump, tissue, staple, body, compages; trunk, torso, bole, hull, hulk, skeleton; greater part, major part, best part, principal part, main part; essential part etc. *(importance)* 642; lion's share, Benjamin's mess; the long and the short; nearly all, almost all.

v. **form a whole,** constitute a whole; integrate, embody, amass; aggregate etc. *(assemble)* 72; amount to, come to.

adj. **whole,** total, integral [*rare*], integrate [*rare*], entire; complete etc. 52; one, individual.

unbroken, uncut, undivided, unsevered, unclipped, uncropped, unshorn; seamless; undiminished; undemolished, undissolved, undestroyed, unbruised.

indivisible, indissoluble, indissolvable, indiscerptible.

wholesale, sweeping; comprehensive.

adv. **wholly**, altogether; as a whole, one and indivisible; totally etc. (*completely*) 52; entirely, all, all in all, wholesale, in a body, collectively, all put together; in the aggregate, in the lump, in the mass, in the gross, in the main, in the long run; *en masse* [*F.*], on the whole, bodily, *en bloc* [*F.*], *in extenso* [*L.*], throughout, every inch; substantially.

51. Part

n. **part**, portion; dose, item, particular; aught, any; division; ward, parcel [*law or archaic*], count; sector, segment; fraction, fragment; cantle, cantlet; frustum [*rare*]; detachment, subdivision.

section, chapter, verse; article, clause, phrase, paragraph, passage, number, book, fascicle, fascicule *or* fasciculus, *livraison* [*F.*].

piece, lump, bit, snatch; cut, cutting; chip, chunk, collop, slice, scrap, crumb, scale; lamina etc. 204; small part; morsel, moiety, particle etc. (*smallness*) 32; installment, dividend; share etc. (*allotment*) 786.

oddments, *débris* [*F.*], odds and ends, detritus; *excerpta* [*L.*], excerpt.

member, limb, lobe, lobule, arm, wing, scion, branch, bough, joint, link, offshoot, ramification, twig, bush, spray, sprig; runner, tendril; leaf, leaflet; stump; component part etc. 56; sarmentum.

cue, role, cast; lines, pageant [*archaic*].

compartment; department etc. (*class*) 75; county etc. (*region*) 181.

v. **part**, divide, break etc. (*disjoin*) 44; partition etc. (*apportion*) 786.

adj. **fractional**, fragmentary, portional [*rare*]; sectional, aliquot; divided etc. *v.;* in compartments, multifid; disconnected; incomplete, partial.

divided, broken, cut, severed, clipped, cropped, shorn; seamed.

divisible, dissoluble, dissolvable, discerptible.

adv. **partly**, in part, partially; piecemeal, part by part; by installments, by snatches, by inches, by driblets; bit by bit, inch by inch, foot by foot, drop by drop; in detail, in lots.

52. Completeness

n. **completeness** etc. *adj.;* completion etc. 729; integration; allness [*rare*], totality, integralness, totalness, integrality [*rare*], integrity.

entirety; perfection etc. 650; solidity, solidarity; unity; all; *ne plus ultra* [*L.*], ideal, limit; undividedness, intactness, universality.

complement, supplement, make-weight; filling up etc. *v.*

fill; impletion; saturation, saturity [*obs.*]; high water; high tide, flood tide, springtide; load, bumper, bellyful; brimmer; sufficiency etc. 639.

v. **be complete** etc. *adj.;* come to a head.

render complete etc. *adj.;* complete etc. (*accomplish*) 729; fill, charge, load, stevedore, replenish; make up, make good; piece out, eke out; supply deficiencies; fill up, fill in, fill to the brim, fill the measure of; satiate; saturate.

go the whole hog [*colloq.*], go the whole length; go all lengths; go the limit [*colloq.*].

adj. **complete**, entire; whole etc. 50; perfect etc. 650; full, good, absolute, thorough, plenary; solid, undivided; with all its parts; all-sided.

exhaustive, radical, sweeping, thorough-going; dead.

regular, consummate, unmitigated, sheer, unqualified, unconditional, free; abundant etc. (*sufficient*) 639.

brimming; brimful, topful; chock-full, choke-full; saturated, crammed; replete etc. (*redundant*) 641; fraught, laden; full-laden, full-fraught, full-charged; heavy laden.

completing etc. *v.;* supplemental, supplementary; ascititious.

adv. **completely** etc. *adj.;* altogether, outright, wholly, totally, *in toto* [*L.*], quite; all out; over head and ears; effectually, for good and all, nicely, fully, through thick and thin, head and shoulders, out of sight [*slang*]; neck and heel, neck and crop; in all respects, in every respect; at all points, out and out, to all intents and purposes; *toto coelo* [*L.*]; utterly; clean, clean as a whistle; to the full, to the utmost, to the limit, to the backbone; hollow, stark; heart and soul, root and branch, down to the ground.

to the top of one's bent, as far as possible, *à outrance* [*F.*].

throughout; from first to last, from beginning to end, from end to end, from one end to the other, from Dan to Beersheba, from head to foot, from top to toe, from top to bottom; *de fond en comble* [*F.*]; *à fond* [*F.*]; *a capite ad* *calcem* [*L.*]; *ab ovo usque ad mala* [*L.*]; fore and aft; every whit, every inch; *cap-à-pie* [*F.*], to the end of the chapter; up to the brim, up to the ears, up to the eyes; as . . . as can be.

on all accounts; *sous tous les rapports* [*F.*]; with a vengeance.

53.   Incompleteness

n.   **incompleteness** etc. *adj.;* deficience [*rare*], deficiency, short weight, short measure; shortcoming etc. 304; want, lack, insufficiency etc. 640; imperfection etc. 651; immaturity etc. (*nonpreparation*) 674; half measures.

[part wanting] defect, deficit, defalcation, omission; caret; wantage [*rare*], ullage, shortage; interval etc. 198; break etc. (*discontinuity*) 70; noncompletion etc. 730; missing link.

v.   **be incomplete** etc. *adj.;* fall short of etc. 304; lack etc. (*be insufficient*) 640; neglect etc. 460.

adj.   **incomplete**; imperfect etc. 651; unfinished; uncompleted etc. (*see* complete etc. 729); defective, deficient, wanting, failing; bobtailed; in default, in arrear; short, short of; hollow, meager, jejune, poor, scarce, lame, half-and-half, perfunctory, sketchy; crude etc. (*unprepared*) 674.

mutilated, garbled, hashed, mangled, butchered, docked, lopped, truncated.

in progress, in hand; going on, proceeding.

adv.   **incompletely** etc. *adj.;* by halves.

54.   Composition

n.   **composition**, constitution; crasis, synizesis, syneresis; confection [*rare*], synthesis, compaction [*rare*], make, make-up; combination etc. 48; inclusion, admission, comprehension, reception; embodiment; formation.

authorship, compilation, composition, *recueil* [*F.*], production, inditing *or* inditement, conflation, invention; writing etc. 590.

hymnody, hymnology, instrumentation; opus, aria etc. (*music*) 415.

painting, scenography, etching, design etc. (*painting*) 556; relief, relievo etc. (*sculpture*) 557.

typesetting, typography etc. (*printing*) 591.

v.   **be composed of,** be made of, be formed of, be made up of; consist of, be resolved into.

include etc. (*in a class*) 76; contain, hold, comprehend take in, admit, embrace, embody; involve, implicate; drag into; synthesize.

compose, constitute, form, make; make up, fill up, build up; fabricate, weave, construct; compile, redact, collate, dash off, address, indite,

score, scribble, draw, write; set (*in printing*); enter into the composition of etc. (*be a component*) 56.

adj.   containing, constituting etc. *v.*

55.   Exclusion

n.   **exclusion**, nonadmission, omission, exception, rejection, repudiation; exile etc. (*seclusion*) 893; noninclusion, preclusion, debarrance [*rare*], debarment, lock-out, disfellowship [*rare*], ostracism, prohibition.

separation, segregation, seposition [*obs.*], elimination, expulsion; cofferdam.

v.   be excluded from etc.

exclude, bar; leave out, shut out, bar out; reject, repudiate, blackball, ostracize; lay apart, lay aside, put apart, put aside, set apart, set aside; relegate, segregate; throw overboard; strike off, strike out; neglect etc. 460; banish etc. (*seclude*) 893; separate etc. (*disjoin*) 44.

pass over, omit; garble; eliminate, weed, winnow.

adj.   **excluding** etc. *v.;* exclusive, exclusory; excluded etc. *v.;* unrecounted, not included in; inadmissible, preclusive, preventive, prohibitive.

adv.   exclusive of, barring; except; with the exception of; save; bating.

56.   Component

n.   **component**, integrant; component part, integral part, integrant part; element, constituent, ingredient, leaven; part and parcel; contents; appurtenance; feature; member etc. (*part*) 51; personnel.

v.   **enter into**, enter into the composition of; be a component etc. *n.;* be *or* form part of etc. 51; merge in, be merged in; be implicated in; share in etc. (*participate*) 778; belong to, appertain to; combine, inhere in, unite.

form, make, constitute, compose, precompose, recompose; sonnetize [*rare*]; fabricate etc. 54.

adj.   **forming** etc. *v.;* inherent, intrinsic, essential.

inclusive, all-embracing, compendious, comprehensive, inclusory.

57.   Extraneousness

n.   **extraneousness** etc. *adj.;* extrinsicality etc. 6; exteriority etc. 220; alienage, alienism.

foreign body, foreign substance, foreign element.

alien, stranger, intruder, interloper, foreigner, *novus homo* [*L.*], newcomer, jackaroo [*Australia*], griffin [*Anglo-Ind.*]; recruit, immigrant, emigrant; creole, Africander; outsider, outlander [*archaic*], barbarian, extern [*rare*], tramontane [*rare*], ultramontane; tenderfoot.

adj. **extraneous**, foreign, alien, ulterior, exterior, external, outlandish, outside, outland [*archaic*]; barbaric, barbarian, metic, oversea, tramontane [*rare*], ultramontane.

excluded etc. 55; inadmissible; exceptional.

adv. **abroad**, in foreign parts, in foreign lands; beyond seas; oversea, overseas; on one's travels.

Section 4. Order

---

58. Order

n. **order**, regularity, uniformity, symmetry, *lucidus ordo* [*L.*]; harmony, music of the spheres.

gradation, progression; series etc. (*continuity*) 69.

course, even tenor, routine; method, disposition, arrangement, array, system, economy, discipline; orderliness etc. *adj.;* subordination.

rank, place etc. (*term*) 71.

v. **form**; be *or* become in order etc. *adj.;* fall in, draw up; arrange itself, range itself, place itself; fall into one's place, fall into rank, take one's place, take rank; rally round.

adjust, methodize, regulate, systematize, standardize, normalize; time, police.

adj. **orderly**, regular; in order, in trim, in apple-pie order, in its proper place; neat, tidy, *en règle* [*F.*], well regulated, correct, methodical, uniform, symmetrical, shipshape, businesslike, systematic, systematical, normal, habitual; unconfused etc. (*see* confuse etc. 61); arranged etc. 60.

adv. **in order**; methodically etc. *adj.;* in turn, in its turn; step by step; by regular steps, by regular gradations, by regular stages, by regular intervals; *seriatim* [*NL.*], systematically, by clockwork, gradatim; at stated periods etc. (*periodically*) 138.

59. Disorder

[absence or want of order, etc.]

n. **disorder**; derangement etc. 61; irregularity; deray [*archaic*], deordination [*rare*]; anomaly etc. (*unconformity*) 83; anarchy, anarchism; want of method; untidiness etc. *adj.;* disunion; discord etc. 24.

confusion; confusedness etc. *adj.;* mishmash, mix; disarray, jumble, topsy-turvy, botch, huddle, litter, lumber; *cahotage* [*F.*]; farrago; mess, mash, muddle, muss, hash, hodgepodge, hotchpotch, hotchpot; what the cat brought in [*colloq.*]; imbroglio, chaos, omnium-gatherum [*colloq.*], medley; mere mixture etc. 41; fortuitous concourse of atoms, *disjecta membra* [*L.*].

complexity; complexness etc. *adj.;* complexus, complication, implication; intricacy, intrication [*rare*]; perplexity; network, maze, labyrinth; wilderness, jungle; involution, raveling, entanglement, dishevelment; coil etc. (*convolution*) 248; sleave, tangled skein, knot, Gordian knot, wheels within wheels; kink, gnarl *or* knarl [*obs.*]; webwork.

turmoil; ferment etc. (*agitation*) 315; to-do [*colloq.*], trouble, pudder [*obs. or dial.*], pother, row [*colloq.*], disturbance, convulsion, tumult, uproar, riot, rumpus [*colloq.*], stour [*archaic*], scramble, fracas, embroilment, *mêlée* [*F.*], spill and pelt, rough and tumble; whirlwind etc. 349; bear garden, pandemonium, Babel, Saturnalia, Donnybrook, confusion worse confounded, most admired disorder, *concordia discors* [*L.*]; Bedlam broke loose, hell broke loose; bull in a china shop; all the fat in the fire, *diable à quatre* [*F.*], Devil to pay; pretty kettle of fish; pretty piece of work.

slattern, slut, drab, dowdy, trollop, sloven, draggle-tail [*colloq.*].

v. **be disorderly** etc. *adj.;* ferment, play at cross-purposes.

put out of order; botch, derange etc. 61; drag from under the bed [*colloq.*]; ravel etc. 219; ruffle, rumple.

adj. **disorderly**, orderless; out of order, out of place, out of gear, out of kilter [*colloq.*]; irregular, desultory; anomalous etc. (*unconformable*) 83; acephalous; aimless; disorganized; straggling; unmethodical, immethodical; unsymmetric, unsystematic; untidy, slovenly, messy [*colloq.*], hugger-mugger, dislocated; out of sorts; promiscuous, indiscriminate; chaotic, anarchic, anarchical; unarranged etc. (*see* arrange etc. 60); confused; deranged etc. 61; topsy-turvy etc. (*inverted*) 218; shapeless etc. 241; disjointed, out of joint; gnarled *or* knarled [*obs.*].

complex, complexed; intricate, complicated, perplexed, involved, raveled, entangled, knotted, tangled, inextricable; irreducible.

troublous, tumultuous, turbulent; riotous etc. (*violent*) 173.

adv. **irregularly** etc. *adj.;* by fits, by fits and snatches, by fits and starts; pellmell; higgledy-piggledy; helter-skelter [*colloq.*], harum-scarum [*colloq.*]; in a ferment; at sixes and sevens, at cross-purposes; upside down etc. 218.

60.   Arrangement
[reduction to order]

n.   **arrangement**; plan etc. 626; preparation etc. 673; disposal, disposition, disposure; collocation, allocation; distribution; sorting etc. *v.;* assortment, allotment, apportionment, taxis, taxonomy, syntaxis, graduation, organization, ordination, grouping, groupage.

analysis, classification, division, systematization, categorization, codification, digestion.

[result of arrangement] orderliness, form, lay, array, digest; synopsis etc. (*compendium*) 596, syntagma, table, atlas; register etc. (*record*) 551; cosmos, schematism, organism, architecture; instrumentation, orchestration, score etc. (*music*) 415; stipulation, settlement, *bandobast* or *bundobust* [*Anglo-Ind.*].

[instrument for sorting] sieve, riddle, screen, bolter, colander, grate, grating.

file, card index.

v.   **reduce to order,** bring into order; introduce order into; rally.

arrange, dispose, place, form; put in order, set in order, place in order; set out, collocate, allocate, compose, space, range, pack, marshal, array, size, rank, group, parcel out, allot, distribute, deal; cast the parts, assign the parts; dispose of, assign places to; assort, sort; sift, riddle; put to rights, put into shape, put in trim, put in array, set to rights, set into shape, set in trim, set in array; tidy; apportion.

class, classify; divide; file, list, string together, thread; register etc. (*record*) 551; catalogue, tabulate, index, alphabetize, graduate, digest, grade, codify; orchestrate, score, harmonize.

methodize, regulate, systematize, coördinate, organize, brigade, echelon, seriate [*rare*], settle, fix.

unravel, disentangle, unweave, ravel, card; disembroil; feaze.

adj.   **arrange** etc. *v.;* embattled, in battle array; cut and dried; methodical, orderly, regular, systematic, on file; tabular, tabulate.

61.   Derangement
[subversion of order; bringing into disorder]

n.   **derangement** etc. *v.;* muss, mess, disorder etc. 59; evection, discomposure, disturbance; disorganization, deorganization; dislocation; perturbation, interruption; shuffling etc. *v.;* inversion etc. 218; corrugation etc. (*fold*) 258; involvement; insanity etc. 503.

v.   **derange**; misarrange, disarrange, displace, misplace; mislay, discompose, disorder; disorganize; embroil, unsettle, disturb, confuse, trouble, perturb, jumble, tumble; huddle, shuffle, muddle, toss, hustle, fumble, riot; bring into disorder, put into disorder, throw into disorder etc. 59; muss, mess; break the ranks, disconcert, convulse; break in upon.

unhinge, dislocate, put out of joint, throw out of gear.

turn topsy-turvy etc. (*invert*) 218; bedevil; complicate, involve, perplex, confound; embrangle *or* imbrangle, tangle, entangle, ravel, tousle, dishevel, ruffle; rumple etc. (*fold*) 258; dement, become insane etc. 503.

litter, scatter; mix etc. 41.

adj.   **deranged** etc. *v.;* syncretic, syncretistic; mussy.

62.   Precedence

n.   **precedence**; predecession [*rare*]; coming before etc. *v.;* the lead, *le pas* [*F.*]; superiority etc. 33; importance etc. 642; premise *or* premiss; antecedence *or* antecedency; anteriority etc. (*front*) 234; precursor etc. 64; priority etc. 116; precession [*rare*] etc. 280; anteposition; epacme; preference.

prefix, prefixture [*rare*], prelude, affix, preamble, overture, ritornel, *ritornello* [*It.*], voluntary.

v.   **precede,** forerun, forego [*archaic*], prevene [*rare*]; come before, come first; head, lead, take the lead; lead the way, lead the dance; introduce, prologize [*rare*], usher in; have the *pas* [*F.*]; set the fashion etc. (*influence*) 175; open the ball, lead the cotillion, lead the german; rank, outrank; take precedence, have precedence; have the start etc. (*get before*) 280.

place before; prefix; premise, prelude, preface; affix.

adj.   **preceding** etc. *v.;* precedent, antecedent; anterior; prior etc. 116; before; former, foregoing; before mentioned, above mentioned, aforementioned; aforesaid, said; precursory, precursive; prevenient, preliminary, prefatory, introductory; prelusive, prelusory; proemial, preparatory.

adv.   **before**; in advance etc. (*precession*) 280.

63.   Sequence

n.   **sequence,** train, coming after; pursuance, going after etc. (*following*) 281; consecution, succession; posteriority etc. 117.

continuation, prolongation; mantle of Elijah; order of succession; successiveness; paracme.

secondariness; subordinancy [*obs.*], subordinacy etc. (*inferiority*) 34.

afterbirth, afterburden, afterclap, aftercrop, afterglow, aftergrass, aftermath, afterpain, afterpiece, aftertaste; placenta, secundines; sequelae.

v. **succeed**; come after, come on, come next; follow, ensue, step into the shoes of; alternate.

follow, tag [*colloq.*], heel, dog, dodge, shadow, hound, bedog, hunt; trace, retrace.

place after, suffix, append, subjoin.

adj. **succeeding** etc. *v.;* sequent; subsequent, consequent; sequacious, proximate, next; consecutive etc. (*con*tinuity) 69; alternate, amoebean.

latter; posterior etc. 117.

adv. **after**, subsequently; behind etc. (*rear*) 235.

64. Precursor

n. **precursor**, antecedent, precedent, predecessor; forerunner, apparitor, vancourier [*obs.*]; pioneer, prodrome [*obs.*], *prodromos* [*Gr.*], prodromus [*rare*], outrider; leader, bellwether; herald, harbinger; dawn; bellmare, *avant-coureur* [*F.*], avant-courier, *avant-courrier* [*F.*], forelooper *or* foreloper *or* forelouper [*S. Afr.*], *voorlooper* [*Dutch*], *voortrekker* [*Dutch*].

prelude, preamble, preface, prologue, foreword, *avant-propos* [*F.*], protasis, proemium, prolusion [*rare*], proem, prolepsis, prolegomena, prefix, exordium, introduction; heading, frontispiece, groundwork; preparation etc. 673; overture, voluntary, ritornel, *ritornello* [*It.*], descant, symphony; premises.

prefigurement etc. 511; omen etc. 512.

adj. **precursory**; prelusive, prelusory, preludious; proemial [*rare*], introductory, preludial, prefatory, prodromous [*rare*], inaugural, preliminary; precedent etc. (*prior*) 116.

65. Sequel

n. **sequel**, suffix, successor; tail, queue, train, wake, trail, rear; retinue, suite; appendix, postscript, subscript, postlude, conclusion, epilogue; peroration; codicil; continuation, sequela [*pl.* sequelae]; appendage; tailpiece, heelpiece; tag, more last words; colophon.

follower, successor, sectary, heeler [*slang*], pursuer, adherent, partisan, disciple, client; sycophant, parasite.

aftercome [*Scot.*], aftergrowth, afterpart, afterpiece, after course, aftergame, afterthought; *arrière pensée* [*F.*], second thoughts; outgrowth.

66. Beginning

n. **beginning**, incunabula [*pl.*], commencement, opening, outset, incipience, incipiency, inception, inchoation, inchoacy [*rare*]; introduction etc. (*precursor*) 64; alpha, initial; inauguration, ingress, *début* [*F.*], *le premier pas* [*F.*], embarkation, rising of the curtain; curtain-raiser, maiden speech; exordium; outbreak, onset, brunt; initiative, move, first move; prelude, prime, proem, gambit; narrow *or* thin end of the wedge, fresh start, new departure.

first stage, first blush, first glance, first impression, first sight.

origin etc. (*cause*) 153; source, rise; bud, germ etc. 153; egg, embryo, rudiment; genesis, birth, nativity, cradle, infancy; forefront, outstart, start, starting point etc. 293; dawn etc. (*morning*) 125.

head, heading; title-page; van etc. (*front*) 234; caption, *fatihah* [*Ar.*].

entrance, entry; inlet, orifice, mouth, chops, lips, porch, portal, portico, propylon, door; gate, gateway; postern, wicket, threshold, vestibule; propylaeum; skirts, border etc. (*edge*) 231; tee.

rudiments, elements, principia, outlines, grammar, protasis, alphabet, ABC.

v. **begin**, commence, inchoate, rise, arise, originate, conceive, initiate, open, start, gin [*archaic*], dawn, set in, take its rise, enter upon, enter; set out etc. (*depart*) 293; embark in; incept [*rare*], institute.

usher in; lead off, lead the way, take the lead, take the initiative; inaugurate, auspicate, head; stand at the head, stand first, stand for; lay the foundations etc. (*prepare*) 673; found etc. (*cause*) 153; set up, set on foot, set agoing, set abroach, set the ball in motion; apply the match to a train; launch, broach; open up, open the door to; set about, set to work; make a beginning, make a start; handsel; take the first step, lay the first stone, cut the first turf; break ground, break the ice, break cover; pass the Rubicon, cross the Rubicon; open fire, open the ball; ventilate, air; undertake etc. 676.

come into existence, come into the world; make one's *début* [*F.*], take birth; burst forth, break out; spring up, crop up.

recommence; begin at the beginning, begin *ab ovo* [*L.*], begin again, begin *de novo* [*L.*]; start afresh, make a fresh start, shuffle the cards, resume.

adj. **beginning** etc. *v.;* initial, initiatory, initiative; inceptive, introductory, incipient; proemial [*rare*], inaugural, inauguratory; inchoate, in-choative [*rare*]; embryonic, rudimentary, rudimental; primal, primary, prime, premier [*rare*], primigenial, primigenious *or* primigenous, primogenial; primeval etc. (*old*) 124; aboriginal; natal, nascent.

first, foremost, front, head, leading; maiden.

begun etc. *v.;* just begun etc. *v.*

adv. at *or* in the beginning etc. *n.;* first, in the first place, *imprimis* [*L.*], first and foremost; *in limine* [*L.*]; in the bud, in embryo, in its infancy; from the beginning, from its birth; *ab initio* [*L.*], *ab ovo* [*L.*], *ab incunabilis* [*L.*], *ab origine* [*L.*]; formerly, erst [*archaic*].

67. End

n.   **end**, close, termination; desinence [*rare*], conclusion, finis, finale, period, term, terminus, last, omega; extreme, extremity; gable end, butt end, fag-end; tip, nib, point; tail etc. (*rear*) 235; verge etc. (*edge*) 231; tag, peroration, appendix, epilogue; bottom dollar [*colloq.*], bitter end, tail end [*colloq.*], terminal, apodosis.

consummation, *dénouement* [*F.*]; finish etc. (*completion*) 729; fate; doom, doomsday; crack of doom, day of Judgment, fall of the curtain; goal, destination; limit, stoppage, end-all, wind-up [*colloq.*]; determination; expiration, expiry; dissolution, death etc. 360; end of all things; finality; eschatology.

break up, *commencement de la fin* [*F.*], last stage, evening (*of life*); turning point; *coup de grâce* [*F.*], deathblow; knock-out, knock-out blow; sockdolager [*slang*], K. O. [*slang*].

v.   **end**, close, finish, terminate, conclude, be all over; expire; die etc. 360; come to a close, draw to a close etc. *n.;* perorate; have run its course; run out, pass away.

bring to an end etc. *n.;* put an end to, make an end of; determine; get through; achieve etc. (*complete*) 729; stop etc. (*make to cease*) 142; shut up shop; hang up the fiddle [*colloq.*], hang up the gloves [*colloq.*].

adj.   **ending** etc. *v.;* final, terminal, terminative [*rare*], conclusive, conclusory, determinative, definitive; crowning etc. (*completing*) 729; last, ultimate; hindermost; rear etc. 235; caudal; vergent [*rare*].

conterminate [*obs.*], conterminous, conterminable [*rare*].

ended etc. *v.;* at an end; settled, decided, over, played out, set at rest; conclusive.

penultimate; last but one, last but two, etc.

adv.   **finally** etc. *adj.;* in fine; at the last; once for all.

68. Middle

n.   **middle**, midst, mid [*rare*], thick, midmost, middlemost [*rare*], mediety [*obs.*]; mean etc. 29; medium, middle term; center etc. 222, mid-course etc. 628; *mezzo termine* [*It.*], *mezzo cammin* [*It.*]; *juste milieu* [*F.*] etc. 628; halfway house, nave, navel, omphalos; nucleus, nucleolus.

equidistance, bisection, half distance; equator, diaphragm, midriff; interjacence etc. 228.

adj.   **middle**, medial, mesial, mesian, mean, mid, middlemost, midmost, midway [*rare*], midship, mediate [*rare*]; intermediate etc. (*interjacent*) 228; equidistant; central etc. 222; mediterranean, equatorial; homocentric.

adv.   **midway**, halfway; in the middle; midships, amidships, *in medias res* [*L.*] *meden agan* [*Gr.*].

69. Continuity
[uninterrupted sequence]

n.   **continuity**, continuousness, unbrokenness; consecution, consecutiveness etc. *adj.;* succession, round, suite, progression, series, train, catena, chain; catenation, concatenation; scale; gradation, course; ceaselessness, constant flow, unbroken extent; perpetuity.

procession, column; retinue, *cortège* [*F.*], cavalcade, parade; funeral, ovation, triumph; rank and file, line of battle, array.

pedigree, genealogy, lineage, history, tree, race; ancestry, descent, family, house; line, line of ancestors; strain.

rank, file, line, row, range, tier, string, thread, team; suit; colonnade.

v.   **form a series** etc. *n.;* fall in; follow in a series etc. *n.*

arrange in a series etc. *n.;* string together, file, list, thread, graduate, tabulate.

adj.   **continuous**, continued; consecutive; progressive, gradual; serial, successive; immediate, unbroken, entire; linear; in a line, in a row etc. *n.;* uninterrupted, unintermitting; unremitting; perennial, evergreen; constant.

adv.   **continuously** etc. *adj.;* *seriatim* [*NL.*]; in a line etc. *n.;* in succession, in turn; running, gradually, step by step, gradatim, at a stretch; in file, in column, in single file, in Indian file.

70. Discontinuity
[interrupted sequence]

n.   **discontinuity**, discontinuousness, discreteness, disconnectedness; disjunction [*rare*] etc. 44; anacoluthon; interruption, break, fracture, flaw, fault, crack, cut; gap etc. (*interval*) 198;

solution of continuity, caesura; broken thread; parenthesis, episode, rhapsody, crazy quilt [*colloq.*], patchwork; intermission; alternation etc. (*periodicity*) 138; dropping fire.

v. **be discontinuous** etc. *adj.;* alternate, intermit.

discontinue, pause, interrupt; intervene; break, break in upon, break off; interpose etc. 228; break the thread, snap the thread; disconnect etc. (*disjoin*) 44; dissever.

adj. **discontinuous**, unsuccessive, disconnected, broken, interrupted, *décousu* [*F.*]; disconnected, unconnected; discrete, disjunct [*rare*], disjunctive; fitful etc. (*irregular*) 139; spasmodic, desultory; intermitting etc. *v.,* intermittent; alternate; recurrent etc. (*periodic*) 138.

adv. **at intervals**; by snatches, by jerks, by skips, by catches, by fits and starts; skippingly, *per saltum* [*L.*]; *longo intervallo* [*L.*].

71. Term

n. **term**, rank, station, stage, step; degree etc. 26; scale, remove, grade, link, peg, round of the ladder, status, state, position, place, point, mark, *pas* [*F.*], period, pitch; stand, standing; footing, range.

v. hold a place, occupy a place, find a place, fall into a place etc. *n.;* rank.

72. Assemblage

n. **assemblage**; collection, collocation, colligation; compilation, levy, gathering, ingathering, mobilization, meet, forgathering, muster, *attroupement* [*F.*]; team; concourse, conflux, congregation, contesseration [*obs.*], convergence etc. 290.

meeting, levee, reunion, drawing room, at home; *conversazione* [*It.*] etc. (*social gathering*) 892; assembly, congress, house, senate, legislature, convocation; caucus, séance, eisteddfod, gemot *or* gemote; convention, conventicle; conclave etc. (*council*) 696; Noah's ark.

company, platoon, faction, caravan, claque, posse, *posse comitatus* [*L.*]; watch, squad, corps, troop, troupe; army, regiment etc. (*combatants*) 726; host etc. (*multitude*) 102; populousness.

miscellany, *collectanea* [*L.*]; museum, menagerie etc. (*store*) 636; museology.

crowd, throng; flood, rush, deluge; rabble, mob, rout, press, crush, *cohue* [*F.*], horde, body, tribe; crew, gang, knot, squad, band, party; swarm, shoal, school, covey, flock, herd, drove; kennel; *atajo* [*Sp. Amer.*]; bunch, drive, force, *mulada; remuda* [*Sp.*]; round-up; array, bevy, galaxy.

clan, brotherhood, association etc. (*party*) 712.

group, cluster, Pleiades, clump, pencil; set, batch, lot, pack; budget, assortment, bunch; parcel; packet, package; bundle, fascine, bale, *seron* [*Sp.*], fagot, wisp, truss, tuft; grove, thicket, plump [*archaic*]; shock, rick, fardel, stack, sheaf, haycock, swath; fascicle, fascicule, fasciculus, gavel, hattock [*dial. Eng.*], stook [*dial.*].

volley, shower, storm, cloud.

accumulation etc. (*store*) 636; congeries, heap, lump, pile, rouleau, tissue, mass, pyramid; bing [*obs.*]; drift; snowball, snowdrift; acervation [*rare*], cumulation, amassment; glomeration, agglomeration; conglobation; conglomeration, conglomerate; coacervation [*rare*], coagmentation [*obs.*], aggregation, concentration, congestion, omnium-gatherum [*colloq.*], *spicilegium* [*L.*], Black Hole of Calcutta; quantity etc. (*greatness*) 31.

collector, gatherer; whip, whipper-in.

v. [be or come together] assemble, collect, muster; meet, unite, join, rejoin; cluster, flock, swarm, surge, stream, herd, crowd, throng, associate; congregate, conglomerate, concentrate; center round, rendezvous, resort; come together, flock together, get together, pig together; forgather *or* foregather; huddle; reassemble.

[get or bring together] assemble, muster; bring together, get together, put together, draw together, scrape together, lump together; collect, collocate, colligate; get in, whip in; gather; hold a meeting; convene, convoke, convocate; rake up, dredge, heap, mass, pile; pack, put up, truss, cram; acervate [*rare*]; agglomerate, aggregate; compile; group, aggroup, concentrate, unite; collect into a focus, bring into a focus; amass, accumulate etc. (*store*) 636; collect in a dragnet; heap Ossa upon Pelion.

adj. **assembled** etc. *v.,* closely packed, dense, serried, crowded to suffocation, teeming, swarming, populous; as thick as hops; swarming like maggots; all of a heap, fasciculated; cumulative.

73. Nonassemblage. Dispersion

n. **dispersion**; disjunction etc. 44; divergence etc. 291; aspersion; scattering etc. *v.;* dissemination, diffusion, dissipation, distribution; apportionment etc. 786; spread, respersion [*obs.*], circumfusion, interspersion, spargefaction [*obs.*], affusion.

waifs and estrays, flotsam and jetsam, *disjecta membra; waveson.

v. **disperse**, scatter, sow, disseminate, diffuse, radiate, shed, spread, bestrew, overspread, dispense, disband, disembody, dismember, distribute; apportion etc. 786; blow off, let out, dispel, cast forth, draft (or draught) off; strew, straw [obs.], strow [archaic]; ted; spurtle or spirtle [obs.], cast, sprinkle; issue, deal out, retail, utter; intersperse, resperse [obs.]; set abroach, circumfuse.

spread like wildfire, disperse themselves.

turn adrift, cast adrift; scatter to the winds; sow broadcast.

adj. **unassembled** etc. (see assemble etc. 72); diffuse, disseminated scattered, strown, strewn, dispersed etc. v., dispersive, dissipative, diffusive, dispellent [rare]; sparse, dispread, broadcast, sporadic, widespread; epidemic etc. (general) 78; adrift, stray; disheveled, streaming resolvent, discutient [med.].

adv. sparsim [L.], here and there, passim [L.].

74. Focus

[place of meeting]

n. **focus**; point of convergence etc. 290; corradiation [rare]; center etc. 222; gathering place, resort; haunt; retreat; venue; rendezvous; rallying point, headquarters, home, club; depot etc. (store) 636; tryst, trysting place; place of meeting, place of resort, place of assignation; point de réunion [F.] issue

v. bring to a point, bring to a focus, bring to an issue, focus, corradiate [rare].

75. Class

n. **class**, division, subdivision, category, head, order, section; department, province, domain, sphere.
kind, sort, estate, genus, species, variety, family, race, tribe, caste, sept, phylum, clan, breed; clique, coterie; type, kit, sect, set; assortment; feather [rare], kidney; suit; range; gender, sex, kin.
manner, description, denomination, persuasion, connection, designation, character, stamp; predicament; indication, particularization, selection, specification.
similarity etc. 17.

76. Inclusion

[comprehension under, or reference to, a class]

n. **inclusion**, admission, incorporation, comprisal, comprehension, reception.
composition etc. (inclusion in a compound) 54.

v. **be included** in etc.; come under, fall under, range under; belong to, pertain to; range with; merge in.

include, comprise, comprehend, contain, admit, embrace, subsume, receive, inclose etc. (circumscribe) 229; incorporate, cover, embody, encircle.

reckon among, enumerate among, number among; refer to; place under, place with, arrange under, arrange with; take into account.

adj. **inclusive**, inclusory; included, including etc. v.; congener [rare], congenerous; of the same class etc. 75; comprehensive, sweeping, all-embracing, liberal, unexclusive [rare].

77. Exclusion[1]

n. **exclusion** etc. 55.

[1]The same set of words is used to express *Exclusion from a class* and *Exclusion from a compound*. Reference is therefore made to the former at 55. This identity does not occur with regard to *Inclusion*, which therefore constitutes a separate category.

78. Generality

n. **generality**, generalization; universality; catholicity, catholicism; miscellany, miscellaneousness; dragnet; common run; worldwideness.
Pan-Americanism, Pan-Anglicanism, Pan-Hellenism, Pan-Germanism, Pan-slavism or Pansclavism.
everyone, everybody, tout le monde [F.]; all hands [colloq.], all the world and his wife [humorous]; anybody, N or M, all sorts.
prevalence, rifeness, run.

v. **be general** etc. adj.; prevail, be going about, stalk abroad.
render general etc. adj.; spread, broaden, universalize, generalize.

adj. **general**, generic, collective; current, wide, broad, comprehensive, sweeping; encyclopedic or encyclopedical, panoramic; widespread etc. (dispersed) 73.
universal; catholic, catholical; common, worldwide, nationwide, statewide, heavenwide, ecumenical; prevalent, prevailing, rife, epidemic, besetting; all over [colloq.], covered with.
Pan-American, Pan-Anglican, Pan-Hellenic, Pan-Germanic, Panslavic or Pansclavic, Panslavonic, Panslavonian; panharmonic.
every, all; unspecified, impersonal, indefinite.
customary etc. (habitual) 613.

adv. whatever, whatsoever; to a man, one and all.
generally etc. adj.; always, for better for worse; in general, generally speaking; speaking generally; for the most part; in the long run etc. (on an average) 29; by and large, roughly speaking.

79. Specialty

n. **specialty**, *spécialité* [*F.*]; individuality, individuity [*obs.*]; particularity, peculiarity; *je ne sais quoi* [*F.*], *nescio quid* [*L.*]; idiocrasy etc. (*tendency*) 176; personality, characteristic, mannerism, idiosyncrasy, physiognomic [*rare*], diagnostic; specificness etc. *adj.;* singularity etc. (*unconformity*) 83; reading, version, lection; state; trait; distinctive feature; technicality; differentia.

particulars, details, items, counts; minutiae.

I, self, I myself; myself, himself, herself, itself.

v. **specify**, particularize, individualize, realize, specialize, designate, determine; denote, indicate, point out, select, differentiate, come to the point.

itemize, detail, descend to particulars, enter into detail.

adj. **special**, particular, individual, specific, proper, personal, original, private, respective, definite, determinate, minute, especial, certain, esoteric, endemic, partial, party, peculiar, marked, intimate, appropriate, several, characteristic, diagnostic, exclusive, restricted; singular etc. (*exceptional*) 83; idiomatic; typical, representative.

this, that; yon, yonder.

adv. **specially** etc. *adj.;* in particular, *in propria persona* [*L.*]; *ad hominem* [*L.*]; for my part.

each, apiece, one by one; severally, respectively, each to each; *seriatim* [*NL.*], in detail, bit by bit; *pro hac vice* [*L.*], *pro re nata* [*L.*].

namely, that is to say, *videlicet* [*L.*], viz.; to wit.

80. Rule

n. **regularity**, uniformity, constancy, clockwork precision; punctuality etc. (*exactness*) 494; even tenor, rut; system; routine etc. (*custom*) 613; formula; canon, convention, maxim, rule etc. (*form, regulation*) 697; keynote, standard, model; precedent etc. (*prototype*) 22; conformity etc. 82.

law, capitular *or* capitulary, gnomology [*rare*], *règlement* [*F.*], order of things; normality, normalcy; normal state, normal condition, natural state, natural condition, ordinary state, ordinary condition, model state, model condition; standing dish, standing order; Procrustean law; law of the Medes and Persians; hard and fast rule; nature, principle.

adj. **regular**, uniform, symmetrical, constant, steady; according to rule etc. (*conformable*) 82; normal, habitual, customary etc. 613; methodical, orderly, systematic, systematical.

81. Multiformity

n. **multiformity**, omniformity; variety, diversity; multifariousness etc. *adj.;* varied assortment.

adj. **multiform**, multifold, multifarious, multigenerous, multiplex; variform [*rare*], diversiform, amoebiform, manifold, many-sided; omniform, omnigenous, omnifarious; polymorphic, polymorphous, multiphase, metamorphotic, protean, proteiform, heterogeneous, motley, mosaic; epicene.

indiscriminate, desultory, irregular, diversified, different, divers; all manner of; of every description, of all sorts and kinds; *et hoc genus omne* [*L.*]; and what not?

82. Conformity

n. **conformity**, conformance; observance; habituation; naturalization; conventionality etc. (*custom*) 613; agreement etc. 23.

example, instance, specimen, sample, quotation; exemplification, illustration, case in point; object lesson; elucidation.

pattern etc. (*prototype*) 22.

conventionalist, formalist, bromide [*slang*], Philistine.

v. **conform to**, conform to rule; accommodate oneself to, adapt oneself to; rub off corners.

be regular etc. *adj.;* move in a groove, move in a rut, travel in a rut; follow–, observe–, go by–, bend to–, obey- -rules, –precedents; agree with, comply with, tally with, chime in with, fall in with; be guided by, be regulated by; fall into a custom, fall into a usage; follow the fashion, follow the multitude; assimilate to, shape, harmonize, conventionalize, pass muster, do as others do, *hurler avec les loups* [*F.*]; do in Rome as the Romans do; go with the -stream, –current, –tide; swim with the -stream, –current, –tide; pass current; tread the beaten track etc. (*habit*) 613; keep one in countenance.

exemplify, illustrate, example, sample, type [*rare*], cite, quote, put a case; produce an instance etc. *n.;* elucidate, explain.

adj. **conformable to rule**; adaptable, consistent, agreeable, compliant; regular etc. 80; according to regulation, according to rule, according to Cocker, according to Gunter, according to Hoyle [*all colloq.*]; *en règle* [*F.*], *selon les règles* [*F.*], well regulated, orderly; symmetric etc. 242.

conventional etc. (*customary*) 613; of daily occurrence, of everyday occurrence; in the natural order of things; ordinary, common, habitual, usual, commonplace, prosaic, bromidic, Philistine.

in the order of the day; naturalized.

typical, normal, formal; canonical, orthodox, sound, strict, rigid, positive, uncompromising, Procrustean.

secundum artem [*L.*], shipshape, point-device [*archaic*], technical.

exemplary, illustrative, in point.

adv. **conformably** etc. *adj.;* by rule; agreeably to; in conformity with, in accordance with, in keeping with; according to; consistently with; as usual, *ad instar* [*L.*], *instar omnium* [*L.*]; *more solito* [*L.*], *more majorum* [*L.*].

for the sake of conformity; of course, as a matter of course; *pro forma* [*L.*], for form's sake, by the card.

invariably etc. (*uniformly*) 16.

for example, for instance; *exempli gratia* [*L.*]; *e. g.;* *inter alia* [*L.*].

83. Unconformity

n. **nonconformity** etc. 82; unconformity, disconformity; unconventionality, informality, abnormity, anomaly; anomalousness etc. *adj.;* exception, peculiarity; infraction-, breach-, violation-, infringement- of -law, -custom, -usage; teratism, eccentricity, *bizarrerie* [*F.*], oddity, *je ne sais quoi* [*F.*], monstrosity, rarity; freak of nature.

individuality, idiosyncrasy, singularity, selfness [*rare*], originality, mannerism.

aberration; irregularity; variety; singularity; exemption; *salvo* [*rare*] etc. (*qualification*) 469.

nonconformist, bohemian, nondescript, character [*colloq.*], original, nonesuch [*rare*], freak, crank [*colloq.*], prodigy, wonder, miracle, curiosity, missing link, flying fish, black swan, monster, white blackbird, basilisk, salamander, *lusus naturae* [*L.*], *rara avis* [*L.*], queer fish [*slang*].

mongrel; half-caste, half-blood, half-breed etc. 41; metis, crossbreed, hybrid, mule, mulatto; *tertium quid* [*L.*], hermaphrodite.

monster, phoenix, chimera, hydra, sphinx, minotaur; griffin *or* griffon; centaur; xiphopagus; hippogriff, hippocentaur; sagittary; kraken, cockatrice, wivern *or* wyvern [*obs.*], roc, dragon, sea serpent; mermaid; unicorn; Cyclops, "men whose heads do grow beneath their shoulders" [*Othello*]; teratology.

fish out of water; neither one thing nor another; neither fish, flesh, fowl, nor good red herring; one in a way, one in a thousand.

outcast, outlaw, Ishmael, pariah.

v. **be uncomformable** etc. *adj.;* abnormalize; leave the beaten track, leave the beaten path; infringe-, break-, violate - a -law, -habit, -usage, -custom; stretch a point; have no business there; baffle all description, beggar all description.

adj. **uncomformable**, exceptional; abnormal, abnormous; anomalous, anomalistic; out of order, out of place, out of keeping, out of tune, out of one's element; irregular, arbitrary; teratogenic, teratogenetic; lawless, informal, aberrant, stray, wandering, wanton; peculiar, exclusive, unnatural, eccentric, egregious; out of the beaten track, out of the common, out of the common run, out of the pale of; misplaced; funny [*colloq.*].

unusual, unaccustomed, uncustomary, unordinary, unwonted, uncommon; rare, singular, unique, curious, odd, extraordinary, strange, monstrous; wonderful etc. 870; unexpected, unaccountable; *outré* [*F.*], out of the way, remarkable, noteworthy, *recherché* [*F.*], queer, quaint, nondescript, *sui generis* [*L.*]; original, unconventional, supernormal [*rare*], bohemian, sulphitic [*slang*], unfashionable; undescribed, unprecedented, unparalleled, unexampled, unheard of, unfamiliar; fantastic, newfangled, grotesque, bizarre; outlandish, exotic, *tombé des nues* [*F.*], preternatural; denaturalized.

heterogeneous, heteroclite, amorphous, mongrel, amphibious, epicene, half blood, hybrid; androgynous, androgynal; unsymmetric etc. 243; adelomorphic *or* adelomorphous, gynandrous, bisexual, hermaphrodite, androgynic, androgynous, monoclinous.

adv. **unconformably** etc. *adj.;* except, unless, save, barring, beside, without, save and except, let alone.

however, yet, but.

int. what on earth! what in the world!

Section 5. Number

84. Number

n. **number**, symbol, numeral, figure, cipher, digit, integer; counter; round number; formula; function; series.

sum, difference, complement, subtrahend; product, total, aggregate; multiplicand, multiplier, multiplicator; coefficient, multiple; dividend, divisor, factor, quotient, submultiple, fraction; mixed number; numerator, denominator; decimal, circulating decimal, repetend; common measure, aliquot part; reciprocal; prime number; totient; quota, quotum [*rare*].

figurate numbers, pyramidal numbers, polygonal numbers.

permutation, combination, variation; election.

ratio, proportion; progression; arithmetical progression, geometrical progression, harmonical progression; percentage.

power, root, radix, exponent, index, logarithm, antilogarithm; modulus. differential, integral, fluxion, fluent.

adj. **numeral,** complementary, divisible, aliquot, reciprocal, prime, fractional, decimal, figurate, incommensurable.

proportional, exponential, logarithmic, logometric, differential, fluxional, integral, totitive.

positive, negative; rational, irrational; surd, radical, real, imaginary, impossible.

85. Numeration

n. **numeration;** numbering etc. *v.;* pagination; tale, tally, telling [*archaic*], recension, enumeration, summation, reckoning, computation, supputation [*obs.*]; calculation, calculus; algorithm, rhabdology, dactylonomy; measurement etc. 466; statistics, logistics.

arithmetic, analysis, algebra, fluxions; differential calculus, integral calculus, infinitesimal calculus; calculus of differences.

[statistics] dead reckoning, muster, poll, census, capitation, roll call, recapitulation; account etc. (*list*) 86.

[operations] notation, addition, subtraction, multiplication, division, proportion, rule of three, practice, equations, extraction of roots, reduction, involution, evolution, approximation, interpolation, differentiation, integration, indigitation [*rare*].

[instruments] abacus, calculator, computer, suan pan, logometer, slide rule, tallies, Napier's bones, calculating machine, difference engine; adding machine; cash register.

arithmetician, calculator, geodesist, abacist; algebraist, geometrician, trigonometrician, mathematician, actuary, statistician.

v. **number,** count, tell; call over, run over; take an account of, enumerate, call the roll, muster, poll, recite, recapitulate; sum; sum up, cast up; tell off, score, cipher, reckon, reckon up, tally estimate, make an estimate, furnish an estimate, make up accounts, compute, calculate, suppute [*obs.*], add, subtract, multiply, divide, extract roots, algebraize.

check, prove, demonstrate, balance, audit, overhaul, take stock.

page, affix numbers to, foliate, paginate.

amount to, come to, total.

adj. **numeral,** numerical; arithmetical, analytic, algebraic, statistical, countable, reckonable, numberable, computable, calculable, rhabdological; commensurable, commensurate; incommensurable, incommensurate.

86. List

n. **list,** catalogue *or* catalog, inventory, schedule, calends [*rare*]; register etc. (*record*) 551; account; bill, bill of costs; syllabus; terrier, tally, file; calendar, index, table, atlas, contents; book, ledger; synopsis, *catalogue raisonné* [*F.*]; scroll, brief [*obs.*], screed, manifest, invoice, bill of lading; prospectus, program; bill of fare, menu, carte; score, bulletin, *tableau* [*F.*], census, statistics, returns; Red Book, Blue Book, Domesday Book; directory, gazetteer.

almanac; army list, clergy list, civil service list, navy list; Statesman's Yearbook, Whitaker's Almanack, *Almanach de Gotha,* cadastre *or* cadaster, *cadre* [*F.*], card index; Lloyd's Register, Nautical Almanac, Who's Who.

dictionary, lexicon, glossary, word-book, thesaurus, gloss [*rare*], gradus.

roll; check roll, checker roll, bead roll; muster roll, muster book; roll of honor; roster, slate, rota, poll, panel; chartulary *or* cartulary, diptych.

v. **list,** enroll, schedule, inventorize [*rare*], inventory, register, catalogue *or* catalog, invoice, bill, book, indent, slate, post, manifest, docket; matriculate, empanel, calendar, tally, file, index, tabulate, enter, score, keep score; census.

adj. inventorial, cadastral; listed etc.*v.*

87. Unity

n. **unity;** oneness etc. *adj.;* individuality; solitude etc. (*seclusion*) 893; isolation etc. (*disjunction*) 44; unification etc. 48; completeness etc. 52.

one, unit, ace, monad; individual; none else, no other, nought beside.

integer, item, point, module.

v. **be one,** be alone etc. *adj.*

isolate etc. (*disjoin*) 44.

render one; unite etc. (*join*) 43, (*combine*) 48.

adj. **one,** sole, only-begotten, single, solitary, companionless; individual, apart, alone; kithless.

unaccompanied, unattended; *solus* (*fem.*, *sola*) [*L.*], single-handed; singular, odd, unique, unrepeated, azygous, first and last; isolated etc. (*disjoined*); insular.

monadic, monadical; unific, uniflorous, unilobed, uniglobular, unifoliolate, unigenital, uniliteral, unilocular, unimodular, unitary; monospermous.

inseverable, indiscerptible; compact, irresolvable.

lone, lonely, lonesome; desolate, dreary.

adv. **singly** etc. *adj.;* alone, by itself, *per se* [*L.*], only [*rare*], apart, in the singular number, in the abstract; one by one, one at a time; simply; one and a half, *sesqui-*.

88. Accompaniment

n. **accompaniment**; adjunct etc. 39; context; appendage, appurtenance.

company, association, companionship; coexistence, concomitance; partnership, copartnership; coefficiency.

concomitant, accessory, coefficient; companion, attendant, fellow, associate, *fidus Achates* [*L.*], consort, spouse, colleague; partner, copartner; satellite, hanger-on, shadow; escort, *cortège* [*F.*], suite, train, convoy, follower etc. 65; attribute.

v. **accompany**, coexist, attend, company [*archaic*], convoy, chaperon; hang on, wait on; go hand in hand with; synchronize etc. 120; bear company, keep company; row in the same boat; bring in its train; associate with, couple with.

adj. **accompanying** etc. *v.;* concomitant, fellow, twin, joint; associated with, coupled with; accessory, attendant, comitant [*rare*], obbligato.

adv. **with**, withal; together with, along with, in company with; hand in hand, side by side; cheek by jowl; arm in arm; therewith, herewith; and etc. (*addition*) 37.

together, in a body, collectively, in conjunction.

89. Duality

n. **duality**, dualism; duplicity; biplicity [*rare*], biformity; polarity.

two, deuce, couple, couplet, both, twain, brace, pair, cheeks, twins, Castor and Pollux, gemini, Siamese twins; fellows; yoke, conjugation; dispermy, doublets, dyad, duad, twosome [*rare*], distich, span.

v. [unite in pairs] pair, couple, bracket, yoke; conduplicate; mate, span [*U.S.*]

adj. **two**, twain; dual, dualistic; binary, binomial; twin, biparous; dyadic; conduplicate; duplex etc. 90; biduous, binate, binary, binal [*rare*], diphyletic, dispermic, paired, unijugate; *tête-à-tête* [*F.*].

coupled etc. *v.;* conjugate.

both, both the one and the other.

90. Duplication

n. **duplication**; doubling etc. *v.;* gemination, ingemination; reduplication; iteration etc. (*repetition*) 104; renewal.

duplicate, facsimile, copy, replica, counterpart etc. (*copy*) 21.

v. **double**; redouble, reduplicate; geminate [*rare*]; repeat etc. 104; renew etc. 660.

adj. **double**; doubled etc. *v.;* bicipital, bicephalous, bidental, bilabiate, bivalve, bivalvular, bifold, biform, bilateral, bifarious, bifacial; twofold, twosided; disomatous; duple [*rare*], duplex; double-faced, double-headed; twin, duplicate, geminous [*rare*], geminate, ingeminate; second: dual etc. 89.

adv. **twice**, once more; over again etc. (*repeatedly*) 104; as much again, twofold.

secondly, in the second place, again.

91. Bisection

[division into two parts]

n. **bisection**, bipartition; dichotomy, subdichotomy [*rare*]; halving etc. *v.;* dimidiation.

bifurcation, furcation, forking, branching, ramification, divarication; fork, crotch, furculum, prong; fold.

half, moiety.

v. **bisect**, halve, hemisect [*rare*], divide, split, cut in two, cleave, dimidiate, dichotomize.

go halves, divide with.

separate, fork, bifurcate, furcate, divaricate; branch off *or* out; ramify.

adj. **bisected** etc. *v.;* cloven, cleft; bipartite, dimidiate, divaricate, biconjugate, bicuspid, bifid; bifurcous [*rare*], bifurcate, bifurcated; bigeminate, distichous, distichal, dichotomous, furcular, furcate, lituate [*rare*]; semi-, demi-, hemi-.

92. Triality

n. **triality** [*rare*], trinity, triunity, Trimurti [*Hindu*], triplicity, trialism [*rare*].

three, triad, triplet, ternion, ternary, trine [*rare*], trey, trio, leash; shamrock, tierce, delta, trefoil; triangle, trident, triennium, trigon [*rare*], trinomial, trionym, triplopia *or* triplopy, tripod, trireme, triseme, triskelion *or* triskele, trisul *or* trisula, triumvirate.

third power, cube.

adj. **three**; triform, trinal, trinomial; tertiary; triune; triarch, triadic.

93. Triplication

n. **triplication**, triplicity; trebleness, terza, trine; trilogy.

v. **treble**, triple, triplicate, cube.

adj. **treble**, triple; tern, ternary, ternate, tertiary; triplicate, threefold, trilogistic; triplasic; third; trinal, trine [*rare*].

adv. **three times**, thrice, in the third place, thirdly, threefold, triply, trebly etc. *adj.*

94. Trisection

[division into three parts]

n. **trisection**, tripartition, trichotomy; third, third part.

v. **trisect**, divide into three parts, third.

adj. **trifid**; trisected etc. *v.;* tripartite, trichotomous, trisulcate; ternal, trident, tridental.

triadelphous, triangular, trichotomic, tricuspid, tricapsular, tridental, tridentate *or* tridentated, tridentiferous, trifoliolate, trifurcate *or* trifurcated, trigonoid, trigonous, trigonal, trigrammic *or* trigrammatic, tripedal, trilateral, tripetalous, tripodal, tripodic, triquetral, triquetrous.

95. Quaternity

n. **quaternity** [*rare*], four, tetrad, quartet *or* quartette, quatre [*rare*], quadruplet, quaternion, square, quadrilateral, quadrinomial, biquadrate, quarter, quarto, tetract, tetragon.

quadrangle, quadrature, quadruplet; quatrefoil; tetragram, tetragrammaton; tetrahedron, tetrapody, tetrology, quatrefoil *or* quadrefoil.

v. **square**, biquadrate, reduce to a square.

adj. **four**; quaternary, quaternal; quadratic; quartile, quartic, quadrifid, quadriform, quadric, biquadratic; tetract, tetractine, tetractinal [*zool.*], four-rayed; tetrad, quadrivalent; quadrangular, tetragonal, quadrilateral, tetrahedral.

96. Quadruplication

n. **quadruplication**.

v. **quadruplicate**, biquadrate, multiply by four.

adj. **fourfold**; quadrable, quadruple, quadruplex, quadruplicate, quadrible; fourth.

adv. **four times**; in the fourth place, fourthly.

97. Quadrisection

[division into four parts]

n. **quadrisection**, quadripartition; quartering etc. *v.;* fourth; quart, quarter, quartern; farthing

v. **quarter**, divide into four parts, quadrisect.

adj. **quartered** etc. *v.;* quadrifid, quadripartite [*rare*]; quadrifoliate, quadrigeminal, quadrigeminous, quadrigeminate, quadripennate, quadriplanar, quadriserial, quadrivial, quadrifurcate, quadrumanal, quadrumane, quadrumous.

98. Five, etc.

n. **five**, cinque, quint, quincunx, quintet *or* quintette, quintuple, quintuplet, quinary [*rare*], pentad; pentagon, pentagram, pentameter, pentapody, pentarchy, pentastich, Pentateuch.

six, sise *or* size [*rare*], hexad, sextuplet, hexagon, hexahedron, hexagram, hexameter, hexapod, hexapody, hexastich, Hexateuch, sextet, half-a-dozen.

seven, heptad, septenary [*rare*], heptagon, heptahedron, heptameter, heptarchy, Heptateuch.

eight, octave, octonary, octad, ogdoad, octagon, octahedron, octameter, octastyle, octavo, octet.

nine, novenary [*rare*], ennead, nonary [*rare*]; nonagon, three times three; *novena* [*R. C. Ch.*].

ten, decad [*rare*], decade, dicker; decagon, decagram, decahedron, decapod, decare, decastere, decastyle, decasyllable, decemvir, decemvirate, decennium.

eleven; twelve, dozen; thirteen; long dozen, baker's dozen; twenty, score; twenty-four, four and twenty, two dozen; twenty-five, five and twenty, quarter of a hundred; forty, twoscore; fifty, half a hundred; sixty, sexagenary, threescore; seventy, threescore and ten; eighty, fourscore; ninety, fourscore and ten.

hundred, centenary, hecatomb, century, bicentenary, tercentenary; hundredweight, cwt.; one hundred and forty-four, gross.

thousand, chiliad, milliad [*rare*], millenary [*rare*], millennium; myriad, ten thousand; one hundred thousand, lac *or* lakh [*India*], plum [*obs.*], million; ten million, crore [*India*]; thousand million, billion, milliard.

billion, trillion etc.

v. quintuplicate, sextuple, centuplicate, centuriate [*obs.*].

adj. **five**, fifth, quinary, quintuple; quintuplicate, pentangular, pentagonal, pentastyle.

sixth, senary [*rare*], sextuple, hexagonal, hexangular, hexastyle, hexahedral, sextan.

seventh, septuple, septenary, septimal [*rare*]; heptagonal, heptahedral, heptamerous, heptangular.

eighth, octuple, octonary; octagonal, octahedral, octan, octangular, octastyle.

ninth, ninefold, novenary [*rare*], nonary [*rare*], enneahedral, enneastyle.

tenth, tenfold, decimal, denary, decuple, deca-
gonal, decahedral, decasyllabic.
eleventh, undecennial, undecennary.
twelfth, duodenary, duodenal.
in one's teens, thirteenth, etc.
twentieth, vicenary, vicennial, vigesimal, vicesi-
mal.
sixtieth, sexagesimal, sexagenary.
seventieth, septuagesimal, septuagenary.
centuple, centuplicate, centennial, centenary,
centurial; secular, hundredth; thousandth,
millenary, millennial etc.

99. Quinquesection, etc.

n. **quinquesection** etc.; division by five etc. 98;
decimation; fifth etc.
v. **decimate**; quinquesect; decimalize.
adj. **quinquefid**, quinqueliteral, quinquepartite.
sexpartite; octofid; decimal, tenth, tithe; duodeci-
mal, twelfth; sexagesimal, sexagenary; hundredth, centesimal; millesimal etc.

100. Plurality

[more than one]

n. **plurality**; a number, a certain number; one or
two, two or three etc.; a few, several; multitude
etc. 102; majority.
adj. **plural**, more than one, upwards of, some, certain;
not, not alone etc. 87.
adv. et cetera, etc.

100a. Fraction

[less than one]

n. **fraction**, fractional part; part etc. 51.
adj. **fractional**, fragmentary, inconsiderable, partial,
portional.

101. Zero

n. **zero**, nothing; naught; nought; cipher, none, nobody; *nichts* [*Ger.*], goose egg, nix [*slang*]; not
a soul; absence etc. 187; unsubstantiality etc. 4.
adj. **no**, not one, not any.

102. Multitude

n. **multitude**; multitudinousness, numerousness
etc. *adj.;* numerosity, numerality [*obs.*]; multiplicity; profusion etc. (*plenty*) 639; legion, host;
great number, large number, round number,
enormous number; a quantity, numbers, array,
sight, army, sea, galaxy; scores, peck, bushel,
shoal, oodles [*colloq.*], pile [*colloq.*], heap
[*colloq.*], power [*colloq.*], sight [*colloq.*], lot
[*colloq.*], lots [*colloq.*], swarm, bevy, cloud,
flock, herd, drove, flight, covey, hive, brood,
litter, farrow, fry, nest; mob, crowd etc.

(*assemblage*) 72; all the world and his wife
[*humorous*].
[increase of number] greater number, majority;
multiplication, multiple.
v. **be numerous** etc. *adj.;* swarm with, teem with, be
alive with, creep with; crowd, swarm, come
thick upon; outnumber, multiply; people;
swarm like locusts, swarm like bees.
adj. **many**, several, sundry, divers, various, not a few;
Briarean; a hundred, a thousand, a myriad, a
million, a billion, a quadrillion, a nonillion, a
thousand and one; some ten or a dozen, some
forty or fifty etc.; half a dozen, half a hundred
etc.; alive with; very many, full many, ever so
many; numerous; profuse, in profusion; manifold, multifold, multiplied, multitudinous, multiple, multinomial, teeming, populous, peopled,
outnumbering, crowded, thick, studded; galore
[*colloq.*].
thick coming, many more, more than one can tell,
a world of; no end of, no end to; *cum multis
aliis* [*L.*], thick as hops, thick as hail; plenty as
blackberries; numerous as the stars in the
firmament, numerous as the sands on the seashore, numerous as the hairs on the head; and
what not, and heaven knows what; endless etc.
(*infinite*) 105.

103. Fewness

n. **fewness** etc. *adj.;* paucity, scarcity, sparseness,
sparsity, small number; only a few; small quantity etc. 32; rarity; infrequency etc. 137; handful; minority; exiguity.
[diminution of number] reduction; weeding etc.
v.; elimination, sarculation [*obs.*], decimation;
eradication.
v. **be few** etc. *adj.*
render few etc. *adj.;* reduce, diminish, diminish
the number, weed, eliminate, thin, decimate.
adj. **few**; scant, scanty; thin, rare, scarce, sparse thinly
scattered, few and far between; exiguous; infrequent etc. 137; *rari nantes* [*L.*]; hardly any,
scarcely any; to be counted on one's fingers, to
be counted on the fingers of one hand; reduced
etc. *v.;* unrepeated.
adv. here and there.

104. Repetition

n. **repetition**, iteration, reiteration, iterance [*rare*],
reiterance [*rare*], alliteration, duplication,
reduplication, monotone, harping, recurrence,
succession, run; battology, tautology; monotony, tautophony; rhythm etc. 138; diffuseness,
pleonasm, redundancy.

chimes, repetend, echo, reëcho, encore, dilogy [*rare*], *ritornello* [*It.*], burden of a song, refrain, undersong; rehearsal; *réchauffé* [*F.*], *rifacimento* [*It.*], recapitulation.

cuckoo etc. (*imitation*) 19; reverberation etc. 408; drumming etc. (*roll*) 407; renewal etc. (*restoration*) 660.

twice-told tale, chestnut [*slang*], old stuff [*slang*], old story, old song; second edition, new edition; reappearance, reproduction; periodicity etc. 138.

v. **repeat**, iterate, reiterate, reproduce, echo, reëcho, drum, harp upon, battologize, tautologize, hammer, redouble.

recur, revert, return, reappear; renew etc. (*restore*) 660.

rehearse; do over again, say over again; ring the changes on; harp on the same string; din in the ear, drum in the ear; conjugate in all its moods, tenses and inflexions; begin again, go over the same ground, go the same round, duplicate, reduplicate, never hear the last of; resume, return to, recapitulate, reword.

adj. **repeated** etc. *v.;* warmed up, warmed over, repetitional, repetitionary, repetitive, repetitious, reduplicatory [*rare*], reduplicative, recurrent, recurring; ever recurring, thick coming; frequent, incessant; redundant, pleonastic, tautological, tautologous, tautophonical; inexhaustible, unplumbed.

monotonous, harping, iterative, unvaried; mocking, chiming; retold; habitual etc. 613; another.

aforesaid, aforenamed; above-mentioned, said.

adv. **repeatedly**, often, again, anew, over again, afresh, once more; ditto, encore, *de novo* [*L.*], bis, *da capo* [*It.*].

again and again; over and over, over and over again; many times over; time and again, time after time; times without number; year after year; day by day etc.; many times, several times, a number of times; many a time, full many a time; frequently etc. 136; inexhaustibly, depth beyond depth.

105. Infinity

n. **infinity**, infinitude, infiniteness etc. *adj.;* perpetuity etc. 112; inexhaustibility, immensity, boundlessness.

v. **be infinite** etc. *adj.;* know no limits, know no bounds, have no limits, have no bounds; go on forever.

adj. **infinite**; immense; numberless, countless, sumless, measureless, innumerable, immeasurable, incalculable, illimitable, interminable, unfath-omable, unapproachable; exhaustless, indefinite; without number, without measure, without limit, without end; incomprehensible; limitless, endless, boundless, termless; untold, unnumbered, unmeasured, unbounded, unlimited, illimited; perpetual etc. 112.

adv. **infinitely** etc. *adj.; ad infinitum* [*L.*].

Section 6. Time

106. Time

n. **time**, duration; period, term, stage, space, tide [*archaic*], span, spell, season; the whole time, the whole period; course etc. 109; snap.

intermediate time, while, bit, breathing, interim, interval, pendency; intervention, intermission, intermittence, interregnum, interlude; respite.

era, epoch, Kalpa, eon, cycle; time of life, age, year, date; decade etc. (*period*) 108; point, bell, moment etc. (*instant*) 113; reign etc. 737.

glass of time, ravages of time, whirligig of time, noiseless foot of Time; scythe of Time.

v. **continue**, last, endure, stay, go on, remain, persist, subsist, abide, run, stand, dure [*archaic*], perdure [*rare*], perennate [*rare*], stick [*colloq.*]; intervene; elapse etc. 109; hold out.

take time, take up time, fill time, occupy time.

pass time; pass away time, spend time, while away time, consume time, talk against time; tide over; use time, employ time; seize an opportunity etc. 134; linger on, drag on, drag along, tarry etc. 110; waste time etc. (*be inactive*) 683; procrastinate etc. 133.

adj. **continuing** etc. *v.;* on foot; permanent etc. (*durable*) 110; timely etc. (*opportune*) 134.

adv. **while**, whilst, during, pending; during the time, during the interval; in the course of; for the time being, day by day; in the time of, when; meantime, meanwhile; in the meantime, in the interim; *ad interim* [*L.*], *pendente lite* [*L.*]; *de die in diem* [*L.*]; from day to day, from hour to hour etc.; hourly, always; for a time, for a season; till, until, up to, yet; the whole time, all the time; all along; throughout etc. (*completely*) 52; for good etc. (*diuturnity*) 110.

then, hereupon, thereupon, whereupon; *anno Domini* [*L.*], A.D.; *ante Christum* [*L.*], A.C.; before Christ, B.C.; *anno urbis conditae* [*L.*], A.U.C.; *anno regni* [*L.*], A.R.; once upon a time, one fine morning.

33

107. Neverness

n. **"neverness"**; absence of time, no time; *dies non* [*L.*]; St. Tib's eve; Greek Calends (*or* Kalends).

adv. **never**, ne'er; at no time, at no period; on *or* at the Greek Calends (*or* Kalends); on no occasion, never in all one's born days [*colloq.*], *jamais de ma vie* [*F.*], nevermore, *sine die* [*L.*], in no degree.

108. Period
[definite duration, or portion of time]

n. **period**; second, minute, hour, day, week, month, octave, *novena* [*L.*], semester, quarter, year, decade, decennium, luster *or* lustrum, indication; cycle–, era– of indiction (*or* indictions); quinquennium, lifetime, generation; epoch, era, epact, ghurry *or* ghari [*India*], lunation, moon.
century, age, millennium; *annus magnus* [*L.*], *annus mirabilis* [*L.*].

adj. **horary**; hourly, annual, epochal etc. (*periodical*) 13 ; *ante bellum* [*L.*].

108a. Contingent Duration

adv. during pleasure, during good behavior; *quandiu se bene gesserit* [*L.*].

109. Course
[indefinite duration]

n. corridors of time, sweep of time, vista of time, halls of time, course of time, progress of time, process of time, succession of time, lapse of time, flow of time, flux of time, stream of time, tract of time, current of time, tide of time, march of time, step of time, flight of time; duration etc. 106.
[indefinite time] aeon *or* eon, age, Kalpa; aorist.

v. **elapse**, lapse, flow, run, proceed, advance, pass; roll on, wear on, press on; flit, fly, slip, slide, glide; crawl, drag; run its course, run out; expire; go by, pass by; be past etc. 122.

adj. **elapsing** etc. *v.*; aoristic; transient etc. 111; progressive.

adv. **in time**; in due time, in due season, in due course; in course of time, in process of time, in the fullness of time.

110. Diuturnity
[long duration]

n. **diuturnity** [*rare*]; a long time, length of time; an age, aeon *or* eon, a century, an eternity; slowness etc. 275; coeternity, sempiternity, perpetuity etc. 112; blue moon [*colloq.*], coon's age [*colloq.*], dog's age [*colloq.*].

durableness, durability; persistence, eternalness, lastingness etc. *adj.*; continuance, standing; permanence etc. (*stability*) 150; survival, survivance; longevity etc. (*age*) 128; distance of time.

protraction of time, prolongation of time, extension of time; delay etc. (*lateness*) 133.

v. **last**, endure, stand, remain, abide, continue etc. 106; brave a thousand years.

tarry etc. (*be late*) 133; drag on, drag its slow length along, drag a lengthening chain; protract, prolong; spin out, eke out, draw out, lengthen out; temporize; gain time, make time, talk against time.

outlast, outlive; survive; live to fight again.

adj. **durable**, endurable [*rare*]; lasting etc. *v.*; of long duration, of long standing; permanent, chronic, longstanding; diuturnal [*rare*]; intransient, intransitive; intransmutable, persistent; lifelong, livelong; longeval [*rare*], longevous, endless, fixed, immortal, perdurant [*rare*], perdurable, long-lived, macrobiotic, evergreen, perennial; sempervirent [*rare*], sempervirid; unintermitting, unremitting; perpetual etc. 112.

lingering, protracted, prolonged, spun out etc. *v.*; long-pending, long-winded; slow etc. 275.

adv. **long**; for a long time, for an age, for ages, for ever so long, for many a long day; long ago etc. (*in a past time*) 122; *longo intervallo* [*L.*].
all the day long, all the year round; the livelong day, as the day is long, morning, noon and night; hour after hour, day after day etc.; for good, for good and all; permanently etc. *adj.*; *semper et ubique* [*L.*].

111. Transience
[short duration]

n. **transience**, transiency, ephemerality, transientness [*rare*] etc. *adj.*; evanescence, impermanence *or* impermanency, preterience [*rare*], volatility, fugacity, caducity [*rare*], mortality, span; nine days' wonder, bubble, Mayfly; spurt; temporary arrangement, interregnum, interim.

velocity etc. 274; suddenness etc. 113; changeableness etc. 149.

ephemeron; transient, transient boarder, transient guest, transient rates.

v. **be transient** etc. *adj.*; flit, pass away, fly, gallop, vanish, fleet, sink, melt, fade, evaporate; pass away like a –cloud, –summer cloud, –shadow, –dream.

adj. **transient**, transitory, transitive; passing, evanescent, fleeting; flying etc. *v.*; fugacious, fugitive; transeunt, interim, shifting, slippery; spasmodic.

temporal, temporary; provisional, provisory; cursory, short-lived, ephemeral, ephemerous [*rare*], preterient [*rare*], caducous [*rare*], deciduous; perishable, mortal, precarious; impermanent.

brief, quick, brisk, fleet, cometary, meteoric, volatile, extemporaneous, summary; pressed for time etc. (*haste*) 684; sudden, momentary etc. (*instantaneous*) 113.

adv. **temporarily** etc. *adj.; pro tempore* [*L.*]; for the moment, for a time; awhile, *en passant* [*F.*], *in transitu* [*L.*]; in a short time; soon etc. (*early*) 132; briefly etc. *adj.;* at short notice; on the point of, on the eve of; *in articulo mortis* [*L.*]; between cup and lip.

112. Perpetuity
[endless duration]

n. **perpetuity**, eternity, everness,[1] aye, sempiternity, perenniality [*rare*], coeternity, immortality, athanasy, athanasia; everlastingness etc. *adj.;* perpetuation; continued existence, uninterrupted existence; perennity [*obs.*].

v. **have no end**; last forever, endure forever, go on forever.

eternize, immortalize, eternalize, monumentalize, perpetuate.

adj. **perpetual**, eternal; everduring, everlasting, everliving, everflowing; continual, sempiternal, sempiternous [*rare*], eviternal [*rare*]; coeternal; endless, unending; ceaseless, incessant, uninterrupted, indesinent [*obs.*], unceasing; interminable, eterne [*poetic*], having no end; unfading, evergreen, amaranthine; never-ending, never-dying, never-fading; deathless, immortal, undying, imperishable.

adv. **perpetually** etc. *adj.;* always, ever, evermore [*archaic*], aye; forever, for aye, forevermore, forever and a day, forever and ever; forever and aye, in all ages, from age to age; without end; world without end, time without end; *in secula seculorum* [*L.*]; to the end of time, to the crack of doom, to the "last syllable of recorded time" [*Macbeth*]; till doomsday; constantly etc. (*very frequently*) 136.

113. Instantaneity
[point of time]

n. **instantaneity**, instantaneousness; suddenness, abruptness.

moment, instant, second, minute; twinkling, flash, breath, crack, jiffy [*colloq.*], *coup* [*F.*], burst, flash of lightning, stroke of time.

time; epoch, time of day, time of night; hour, minute; very minute etc., very time, very hour; present time, right time, true time, exact time, correct time.

v. **be instantaneous** etc. *adj.;* twinkle, flash.

adj. **instantaneous**, momentary, extempore, sudden, instant, abrupt; subitaneous [*obs.*], hasty; quick as thought, quick as lightning; rapid as electricity.

adv. **instantaneously** etc. *adj.;* in no time, in less than no time; presto, *subito* [*It. and L.*], instanter, forthright [*archaic*], eftsoon *or* eftsoons [*archaic*], in a trice, in a jiffy [*colloq.*], suddenly, at a stroke, like a shot; in a moment etc. *n.;* in the twinkling of an eye; in one's tracts; right away; *toute à l'heure* [*F.*]; at one jump, in the same breath, *per saltum* [*L.*], *uno saltu* [*L.*]; at once, all at once; plump, slap [*colloq.*]; "at one fell swoop" [*Macbeth*]; at the same instant etc. *n.;* immediately etc. (*early*) 132; extempore, on the moment, on the spot, on the dot [*colloq.*], on the spur of the moment; just then; slapdash etc. (*haste*) 684.

114. Chronometry
[estimation, measurement, and record of time]

n. **chronometry**, horometry, chronology, horology; date, epoch; style, era, age.

almanac, calendar, ephemeris; standard time, daylight-saving time; register, registry; chronicle, annals, journal, diary, chronogram, isochronon.

[instruments for the measurement of time] clock, watch; chronometer, chronoscope, chronograph; repeater; timekeeper, timepiece; dial, sundial, gnomon, horologe, horologium [*rare*], hydroscope, *pendule* [*F.*], hourglass, clepsydra; ghurry *or* ghari [*Hind.*].

chronographer, chronologer, chronologist, horologer; annalist.

v. **fix the time**, mark the time; date, register, chronicle, chronologize; measure time, beat time, mark time; bear date.

adj. **chronologic** *or* chronological, chronometric *or* chronometrical, chronogrammatical; data [*rare*], temporal, isochronous, isochronal, cinquecento, quattrocento, trecento.

adv. o'clock.

115. Anachronism
[false estimate of time]

n. **anachronism**, metachronism, parachronism, prochronism; prolepsis, misdate; anticipation, antichronism [*rare*].

disregard of time, neglect of time, oblivion of time.

intempestivity [*rare*] etc. 135.

v. **misdate**, antedate, postdate, overdate; anticipate; take no note of time; anachronize [*rare*].

adj. **misdated** etc. *v.;* undated; overdue; out of date, anachronous, anachronistic, intempestive, behind time.

116. Priority

n. **priority**, antecedence, anteriority, precedence, preëxistence; precession etc. 280; precursor etc. 64; the past etc. 122; premises.

v. **precede**, come before; forerun; prevent [*rare*], antecede; go before etc. (*lead*) 280; preëxist; dawn; presage etc. 511; herald, usher in, announce.

be beforehand etc. (*be early*) 132; steal a march upon, anticipate, forestall; have the start, gain the start.

adj. **prior**, previous; preceding, precedent [*rare*]; anterior, antecedent; preëxistent; former, aforegoing, aforesighted, aforementioned, aforethought, fore [*obs.*], foregoing; beforementioned, above-mentioned; aforesaid, said; introductory etc. (*precursory*) 64; prodromal.

adv. **before**, prior to; earlier; previously etc. *adj.;* afore [*obs.*], aforehand [*archaic*], ere, theretofore, erewhile; ere then, ere now, before then, before now; already, yet, beforehand; or ever, aforetime; on the eve of.

117. Posteriority

n. **posteriority**; succession, sequence; following etc. 281; subsequence, subsequency, supervention; continuance, prolongation; futurity etc. 121; successor; sequel etc. 65; remainder, reversion.

v. **follow after** etc. 281, come after, go after; succeed, supervene; ensue, attend, emanate [*rare*], occur, result; step into the shoes of.

adj. **subsequent**, posterior, following, after, later, succeeding, sequacious [*rare*], successive, sequential [*rare*], ensuing, consecutive, attendant, sequent, postliminary [*rare*], postnate [*obs.*]; postdiluvial, postdiluvian; posthumous; future etc. 121; after-dinner, postprandial.

adv. **subsequently**, after, afterwards, since, later; at a subsequent period, at a later period; next, in the sequel, close upon, thereafter, thereupon, upon which, eftsoon *or* eftsoons [*archaic*]; from that time, from that moment; after a while, after a time; in process of time.

118. Present Time

n. **the present time**, the present day, the present moment, the present juncture, the present occasion; the times, existing time, time being; twentieth century; crisis, epoch, day, hour. age, time of life.

adj. **present**, actual, instant, current, nonce, latest, existing, that is.

adv. **at this time**, at this moment etc. 113; at the present time etc. *n.;* now, at present; at hand. at this time of day, to-day, now-a-days; already; even now, but now, just now; on the present occasion; for the time being, for the nonce; on the nail, on the spot; on the spur of the moment, on the spur of the occasion.

until now; to this day, to the present day.

119. Different Time

[time different from the present]

n. different time, other time.
[indefinite time] aorist.

adj. aoristic; indefinite.

adv. **then**, at that time, at that moment, at that instant; at which time, at which moment, at which instant; on that occasion, upon.

when; whenever, whensoever; whereupon, upon which, on which occasion; at another time, at a different time, at some other time, at any time; at various times; some of these days, one of these days, some fine morning, one fine morning; some fine day, on divers occasions, sooner or later; some time or other.

once, formerly, once upon a time.

120. Synchronism

n. **synchronism**; coexistence, coincidence; simultaneousness etc. *adj.;* concurrence, concomitance, unity of time, interim.
[having equal times] isochronism.

contemporary, coeval, coetanian [*obs.*].

v. **coexist**, concur, accompany, go hand in hand, keep pace with; synchronize, isochronize.

adj. **synchronous**, synchronal, synchronic *or* synchronical, synchronistic *or* synchronistical, simultaneous, coexisting, coincident, concomitant, concurrent; coeval, coevous [*obs.*]; contemporary, contemporaneous; coetaneous [*rare*], coinstantaneous, coterminous, collateral, coeternal; isochronous.

adv. **at the same time**; simultaneously etc. *adj.;* together, in concert, during the same time; in the same breath; *pari passu* [*L.*]; in the interim.

at the very moment etc. 113; just as, as soon as; meanwhile etc. (*while*) 106.

121. Futurity

[prospective time]

n. **futurity,** futurition [*rare*]; future, hereafter, time to come; approaching—, coming—, subsequent—, after- -time, —age, —days, —hours, —years, —ages, —life; morrow, tomorrow, by and by, the yet [*rare*]; millennium, chiliad [*rare*], millenary, doomsday, day of judgment, crack of doom, remote future.

approach of time, advent, time drawing on, womb of time; destiny etc. 152; eventuality.

heritage, heirs, posterity, descendants.

prospect, anticipation etc. (*expectation*) 507; foresight etc. 510.

v. **look forward;** anticipate etc. (*expect*) 507, (*foresee*) 510; forestall etc. (*be early*) 132.

approach, await, threaten; impend etc. (*be destined*) 152; come on, draw on; draw near.

adj. **future,** to come; coming etc. (*impending*) 152; next, near; near at hand, close at hand; eventual, ulterior; anticipant, expectant, prospective, in prospect etc. (*expectation*) 507; millenary, millennial.

adv. **prospectively,** hereafter, in future; on the knees of the gods; *kal* [*Hind.*], to-morrow, the day after tomorrow; in course of time, in process of time, in the fullness of time; eventually, ultimately, sooner or later; proximo; *paulo post futurum* [*L.*]; in after time; one of these days; after a time, after a while.

from this time; henceforth, henceforwards; thence; thenceforth, thenceforward; whereupon, upon which.

soon etc. (*early*) 132; on the eve of, on the point of, on the brink of; about to; close upon.

122. Preterition

[retrospective time]

n. **preterition;** priority etc. 116; the past, past time; heretofore [*rare*]; days of yore, days of old, days past, days gone by; times of yore, times of old, times past, times gone by; bygone days; old **times,** ancient times, former times; foretime [*rare*]; yesterday, the olden time, good old time; langsyne; eld [*obs. or poetic*].

antiquity, antiqueness, ancientness, *status quo* [*L.*]; time immemorial, distance of time; history, remote age, remote time; remote past; rust of antiquity.

paleontology, paleography, paleology; palaetiology, archaeology; archaism, antiquarianism, medievalism, Pre-Raphaelitism.

retrospection, looking back; memory etc. 505.

antiquary, antiquarian; paleologist, archaeologist etc.; Oldbuck, Dryasdust; *laudator temporis acti* [*L.*]; medievalist, Pre-Raphaelite.

ancestry etc. (*paternity*) 166.

v. **be past** etc. *adj.;* have expired etc. *adj.,* have run its course, have had its day; pass; pass by, pass away, pass off; go by, go away, go off; lapse, blow over.

look back, trace back, cast the eyes back; exhume.

adj. **past,** gone, gone by, over, passed away, bygone, foregone [*archaic*]; elapsed, lapsed, preterlapsed [*rare*], expired, no more, run out, blown over, that has been, bypast, agone [*archaic*], whilom [*archaic*], extinct, never to return, exploded, forgotten, irrecoverable; obsolete etc. (*old*) 124.

former, pristine, quondam, *ci-devant* [*F.*], late; ancestral.

foregoing; last, latter; recent, overnight, preterit *or* preterite, past, plu-perfect, past perfect.

looking back etc. *v.;* retrospective, retroactive; archaeological etc. *n.*

adv. **formerly;** of old, of yore; erst [*archaic or poetic*], erstwhile [*archaic*], whilom [*archaic*], erewhile [*archaic*], time was, ago, over; in the olden time etc. *n.;* anciently, long ago, long since; a long while ago, a long time ago; years ago, ages ago; some time ago, some time since, some time back.

yesterday, the day before yesterday; last year, last season, last month etc.; *ultimo* [*L.*]; lately etc. (*newly*) 123.

retrospectively; ere now, before now, till now; hitherto, heretofore; no longer; once, once upon a time; from time immemorial; in the memory of man; time out of mind; already, yet, up to this time; *ex post facto* [*L.*].

123. Newness

n. **newness** etc. *adj.;* novelty, recency; neology, neologism; immaturity; youth etc. 127; gloss of novelty.

innovation; renovation etc. (*restoration*) 660.

modernist, neoteric; neologist.

upstart, *narikin* [*Jap.*], start-up [*rare*], *nouveau riche* [*F.*], parvenu.

modernism, modernness, modernity; modernization; *dernier cri* [*F.*]; latest fashion; mushroom.

v. **renew** etc. (*restore*) 660; modernize.

adj. **new,** novel, recent, fresh, green; young etc. 127; evergreen; raw, immature; virgin; untried, unhandseled, unheard-of, untrodden, unbeaten; fire-new, span-new.

modern, late, neoteric, neoterical; new-born, new-fashioned, newfangled, newfledged; of yesterday; just out [*colloq.*], brand-new, up-to-date [*colloq.*]; *fin-de-siècle* [*F.*], vernal, renovated; sempervirent [*rare*], sempervirid [*rare*]. fresh as a rose, fresh as a daisy, fresh as paint [*colloq.*]; spick-and-span, spick-and-span-new, unhandled.

adv. **newly** etc. *adj.;* afresh, anew, lately, just now, only yesterday, the other day; latterly, of late. not long ago, a short time ago.

124. Oldness

n. **oldness** etc. *adj.;* age, antiquity, eld [*obs. or poetic*]; cobwebs of antiquity.
maturity, matureness, ripeness.
decline, decay; senility etc. 128.
seniority, eldership, primogeniture.
archaism etc. (*the past*) 122; thing of the past, relic of the past; megatherium; Babylonian, Assyrian, Sanskrit.
tradition, prescription, custom, immemorial usage, common law; folklore.

v. **be old** etc. *adj.;* have had its day, have seen its day.
become old etc. *adj.;* age, fade.

adj. **old**, ancient, olden [*archaic*], eldern [*archaic*], antique; of long standing, time-honored, venerable, hoary, vetust [*obs.*]; elder, eldest; firstborn.
primitive, prime, primeval, primigenous, primigenial, primigenious; paleoanthropic; primordial, primordiate [*rare*]; aboriginal etc. (*beginning*) 66; diluvian, antediluvian, protohistoric, prehistoric, dateless, patriarchal, preadamite; palaeocrystic; fossil, paleozoic, preglacial, antemundane; archaic, Vedic, classic, medieval, Pre-Raphaelite, ancestral; blackletter.
immemorial, traditional, traditive, traditionary [*rare*], prescriptive, customary, unwritten, whereof the memory of man runneth not to the contrary; inveterate, rooted.
antiquated, of other times, old as the hills, of the old school, after-age, obsolete; out-of-date, out-of-fashion; stale, old-fashioned, old-fangled [*rare*], fusty, outworn, moth-eaten [*humorous*], behind the age; old-world; exploded; gone out, gone by, *passé* [*F.*], extinct, dead, disused, past, run out; senile etc. 128; time-worn; crumbling etc. (*deteriorated*) 659; secondhand.

old as the hills, old as Methuselah, old as Adam, old as history.

adv. since the world was made, since the year one, since the days of Methuselah.

125. Morning
[noon]

n. **morning**, morn, matins [*eccl.*], morningtide [*rare or poetic*], forenoon, *a.m.*, prime, dawn, daybreak; dayspring, foreday [*chiefly Scot.*], sun-up, peep of day, break of day; aurora; first blush of the morning, first flush of the morning, prime of the morning; twilight, crepuscle *or* crepuscule, sunrise; daylight, daypeep, cockcrow, cockcrowing; the small hours, the wee sma' hours [*Scot.*].
noon, midday, noonday, noontide, meridian, prime; nooning, noontime.
spring, springtide, springtime, seedtime; vernal equinox.
summer, summertide, summertime, midsummer.

adj. **matin**, matutinal, matinal, matutinary [*rare*]; crepuscular.
noon, noonday, midday, meridional [*rare in this sense*].
spring, vernal, vernant [*obs.*].
summer, aestival *or* estival.

adv. **at sunrise** etc. *n.;* with the lark, when the morning dawns.

126. Evening
[midnight]

n. **evening**, eve; decline of day, fall of day, close of day; candlelight, candlelighting; eventide, evensong [*eccl. or archaic*], vespers [*eccl.*], nighttide [*archaic*], nightfall, curfew, dusk, twilight, eleventh hour; sunset, sundown; going down of the sun, cockshut [*obs.*], dewy eve, gloaming, bedtime.
afternoon, *post meridiem* [*L.*], *p.m.*
midnight; dead of night, witching hour of night, witching time of night, killing-time.
autumn; fall, fall of the leaf; harvest, autumnal equinox; Indian summer, St. Luke's summer, St. Martin's summer.
winter, *hiems* [*L.*].

adj. **vesper**, vespertine, nocturnal; autumnal.
wintry, winterly, brumous, brumal.

127. Youth

n. **youth**; juvenility, juvenescence [*rare*]; juniority; infancy; babyhood, childhood, boyhood, girlhood, youthhood [*archaic*]; incunabula; minority, boyage [*rare*], immaturity, nonage, teens, tender age, bloom.

cradle, nursery, leading strings, puberty, pucelage.

flower of life, springtide of life, seedtime of life, prime of life, golden season of life; heyday of youth, school days; rising generation.

adj. **young**, youthful, juvenile, juvenescent, green, callow, budding, sappy, puisne [*law*], beardless, under age, in one's teens, *in statu pupillari* [*L.*]; younger, junior; hebetic, unfledged, unripe.

128. Age

n. **age**; oldness etc. *adj.* old age, advanced age; senility, senescence; years, anility, gray hairs, climacteric, grand climacteric, declining years, decrepitude, hoary age, caducity [*rare*], eld [*archaic*], superannuation; second childhood, childishness; dotage; vale of years, decline of life, senectitude [*rare*], "sear and yellow leaf" [*Macbeth*]; threescore years and ten; green old age, ripe age; longevity; time of life.

seniority, eldership; elders etc. (*veteran*) 130; firstling; *doyen* [*F.*], dean, father; primogeniture.

[science of old age] nostology; geriatrics *and* gerontology *and* gerocomy [*med.*].

v. **be aged** etc. *adj.;* grow old, get old etc. *adj.;* age; decline, wane, senesce [*rare*].

adj. **aged**; old etc. 124; elderly, eldern [*archaic*], senile; matronly, anile; in years; ripe, mellow, run to seed, declining, waning, past one's prime; gray, grayheaded; hoar, hoary; venerable, time-worn, antiquated, *passé* [*F.*], effete, decrepit, superannuated; advanced in life, advanced in years; stricken in years; wrinkled, marked with the crow's foot; having one foot in the grave; doting etc. (*imbecile*) 499; like the last of pea time.

years old; of a certain age, no chicken [*colloq.*], old as Methuselah; ancestral; patriarchal etc. (*ancient*) 124; gerontic.

older, elder, oldest, eldest; senior; firstborn.

129. Infant

n. **infant**, babe, baby; nursling, suckling, yearling, weanling; papoose, *bambino* [*It.*]; vagitus.

child, bairn [*Scot.*], tot, mite, scrap, chick, kid [*slang*], butcha *or* bacha [*Hind.*]; little one, brat, chit, pickaninny, urchin; bantling, bratling elf.

youth, boy, lad, laddie, slip, sprig, stripling, youngster, younker [*colloq.*], whipster [*rare*], youngling [*rare*], damoiseau [*archaic*], cub, callant [*Scot.*], whippersnapper [*colloq.*], school-

boy, hobbledehoy, hopeful, cadet, minor, master.

scion, sapling, seedling; tendril, olivebranch, nestling, chicken, duckling, larva, chrysalis, tadpole, whelp, cub, pullet, fry, callow [*obs.*], codling *or* codlin; fetus, calf, colt, pup, puppy, foal, kitten; lamb, lambkin; aurelia, caterpillar, cocoon, nymph, nympha, pupa, staddle.

girl, lass, lassie; wench [*dial.*], miss, damsel; damoiselle, damosel *or* damozel [*archaic*]; demoiselle; maid, maiden; virgin; nymph, colleen, girleen, flapper [*slang*], girly [*colloq.*], minx, missy, baggage, hussy; schoolgirl; hoyden, tomboy, romp.

adj. **infantine**, infantile; puerile; boyish, girlish, childish, babyish, kittenish; childly [*rare*], boylike, girllike, kiddish [*colloq.*], dollish [*colloq.*]; youngling, infant, baby; newborn, unfledged, newfledged, callow.

in the cradle, in swaddling clothes, in long clothes, in arms, in leading strings; at the breast; in one's teens; young etc. 127.

130. Veteran

n. **veteran**, old man, reverend sir, seer, patriarch, graybeard; grandfather, grandsire [*archaic*], grisard [*rare*], oldster [*colloq.*], pantaloon [*obs.*]; gaffer, sexagenarian, octogenarian, nonagenarian, centenarian; *doyen* [*F.*], old stager; dotard etc. 501.

granny, grandam *or* grandame [*archaic*], gammer [*dial. Eng.*], crone, hag, oldwife, beldam *or* beldame.

preadamite, Methuselah, Nestor, old Parr; elders; forefathers etc. (*paternity*) 166; Darby and Joan, Philemon and Baucis, "John Anderson, my jo" [Burns].

adj. **veteran**; aged etc. 128.

131. Adolescence

n. **adolescence**, pubescence, majority; adultism; adulthood, adultness etc. *adj.;* manhood, virility; flower of age; full bloom; spring of life.

man etc. 373; woman etc. 374; adult, pubescent, no chicken [*colloq.*].

middle age, *mezzo cammin* [*It.*], maturity, full age, ripe age, prime of life, meridian of life.

v. **come of age**, come to man's estate, come to years of discretion; attain majority, put on long trousers, assume the *toga virilis* [*L.*]; have cut one's eyeteeth [*colloq.*], settle down, have sown one's wild oats.

adj. **adolescent**, pubescent, of age; of full age, of ripe age; out of one's teens, grown up, full-blown, in full bloom, full-grown, manly, manlike, virile, adult; womanly, matronly; marriageable, marriable, nubile.

middle-aged, mature, in one's prime; matronly.

132. Earliness

n. **earliness** etc. *adj.;* morning etc. 125.

punctuality; promptitude etc. (*activity*) 682; haste etc. (*velocity*) 274; suddenness etc. (*instantaneity*) 113.

prematurity, precocity, precipitation, anticipation, prevenience; a stitch in time.

v. **be early** etc. *adj.;* be beforehand etc. *adv.;* keep time, take time by the forelock, anticipate, forestall; have the start, gain the start; steal a march upon; gain time, draw on futurity; bespeak, secure, engage, preëngage.

accelerate; expedite etc. (*quicken*) 274; make haste etc. (*hurry*) 684.

adj. **early**, prime, timely, seasonable, in time, punctual, forward; prompt etc. (*active*) 682; summary.

premature, precipitate, precocious; prevenient, anticipatory; rath *or* rathe [*obs. or poetic*].

sudden etc. (*instantaneous*) 113; unexpected etc. 508; imminent, impending, near, near at hand; immediate.

adv. **early**, soon, anon, betimes, rath *or* rathe [*poetic*]; eftsoon *or* eftsoons [*archaic*]; ere long, before long; punctually etc. *adj.;* to the minute; in time; in good time, in military time, in pudding time [*obs.*], in due time; time enough, on time, on the dot [*slang*].

beforehand; prematurely etc. *adj.;* precipitately etc. (*hastily*) 684; too soon; before its time, before one's time; in anticipation; unexpectedly etc. 508.

suddenly etc. (*instantaneously*) 113; before one can say "Jack Robinson," at short notice, extempore; on the spur of the moment, on the spur of the occasion [Bacon]; at once; on the spot, on the instant; at sight; off hand, out of hand; *à vue d'oeil* [*F.*]; straight, straightway, straightforth; forthwith, incontinently, summarily, instanter, forthright [*archaic*], immediately, briefly, shortly, erewhile [*archaic*], quickly, speedily, apace, before the ink is dry, almost immediately, presently, at the first opportunity, in no long time, by and by, in a while, directly.

133. Lateness

n. **lateness** etc. *adj.;* tardiness etc. (*slowness*) 275.

delay, cunctation [*rare*] tarriance, moration [*rare*], delation [*archaic*], procrastination; def-

erring etc. *v.;* postponement, adjournment, prorogation, retardation, respite; protraction, prolongation; after-time; circumlocution office [*ridicule*], "circumlocution court" [Dickens], chancery suit, Fabian policy, *médecine expectante* [*F.*], moratorium; leeway; high time; truce, reprieve, demurrage; stop, stay, suspension, remand.

v. **be late** etc. *adj.;* tarry, wait, stay, bide, take time; dawdle etc. (*be inactive*) 683; linger, loiter; bide one's time, take one's time; gain time; hang fire; stand over, lie over; hang, hang around *or* about [*colloq.*], hang back [*colloq.*], hang in the balance, hang in the hedge, hang up [*colloq.*], sit up for, stay up for.

put off, defer, delay, lay over, suspend; shift off, stave off; waive, retard, remand, postpone, adjourn; procrastinate; dally; prolong, protract; spin out, draw out, lengthen out; prorogue; keep back; tide over; push to the last, drive to the last; let the matter stand over; table, lay on the table, shelve; respite [*rare*], perendinate [*rare*]; reserve etc. (*store*) 636; temporize, filibuster, stall [*slang*]; consult one's pillow, sleep upon it.

be kept waiting, dance attendance; kick one's heels [*colloq.*], cool one's heels [*colloq.*]; *faire antichambre* [*F.*]; wait impatiently; await etc. (*expect*) 507; sit up, sit up at night; lose an opportunity etc. 135.

adj. **late**, tardy, slow, cunctatious *or* cunctative [*rare*], behindhand, serotine [*rare*], belated, postliminary [*rare*], posthumous, backward, unpunctual, impunctual [*rare*], overdue, moratory; dilatory etc. (*slow*) 275; delayed etc. *v.;* in abeyance.

adv. **late**; backward, lateward [*obs.*], late in the day; at sunset, at the eleventh hour, at length, at last; ultimately; after time, behind time; too late; too late for etc. 135.

slowly, leisurely, deliberately, at one's leisure; *ex post facto* [*L.*]; *sine die* [*L.*].

134. Occasion

n. **occasion**, opportunity, opening, room, scope, space, place, liberty, show [*colloq., U. S.*]; suitable time, suitable season, proper time, proper season; high time; opportuneness etc. *adj.;* tempestivity [*obs.*].

nick of time; golden opportunity, well-timed opportunity, fine opportunity, favorable opportunity; clear stage, fair field; *mollia tempora* [*L.*]; spare time etc. (*leisure*) 685.

crisis, turn, emergency, juncture, conjuncture; turning point, given time.

v. **improve the occasion**; seize etc. (789) an opportunity *or* an occasion; use etc. (677) an opportunity *or* an occasion; give etc. (784) an opportunity *or* an occasion.

suit the occasion etc. (*be expedient*) 646.

strike the iron while it is hot, *battre le fer sur l'enclume* [*F.*], make hay while the sun shines, seize the present hour, take time by the forelock, *prendre la balle au bond* [*F.*].

adj. **opportune**, timely, well-timed, timeful [*obs.*], seasonable, tempestive [*archaic*], timeous [*rare*].

lucky, providential, fortunate, happy, favorable, propitious, auspicious, critical; suitable etc. 23; *obiter dicta* [*L.*].

occasional, accidental, extemporaneous, extemporary; contingent etc. (*uncertain*) 475.

adv. **opportunely** etc. *adj.;* in proper time, in proper course, in proper season; in due time, in due course, in due season; for the nonce; in the nick of time, in the fullness of time; all in good time; just in time, at the eleventh hour, now or never.

by the way, by the by; *en passant* [*F.*], *à propos* [*F.*]; *pro hac vice* [*L.*]; *par parenthèse* [*F.*], parenthetically, by way of parenthesis; while on this subject, speaking of; *par exemple* [*F.*]; extempore; on the spur of the moment, on the spur of the occasion; on the spot etc. (*early*) 132.

135. Intempestivity

n. **intempestivity** [*rare*]; unsuitable time, improper time; unreasonableness etc. *adj.;* evil hour; *contretemps* [*F.*], misventure [*archaic*], misadventure; intrusion; anachronism etc. 115.

v. **be ill-timed** etc. *adj.;* mistime, intrude, come amiss, break in upon; have other fish to fry; be busy, be occupied, be engaged.

lose an opportunity; throw away an opportunity, waste an opportunity, neglect etc. (460) an opportunity; allow *or* suffer the opportunity *or* occasion to -pass, –slip, –go by, –escape, –lapse; waste time etc. (*be inactive*) 683; let slip through the fingers, lock the stable door when the steed is stolen.

adj. **ill-timed**, mistimed; ill-fated, ill-omened, ill-starred; untimely, intrusive, unseasonable; out of date, out of season; inopportune, timeless [*archaic*], inconvenient, intempestive [*rare*], untoward, *mal à propos* [*F.*], unlucky, inauspicious, unpropitious, unfortunate, unfavorable; unsuited etc. 24; inexpedient etc. 647.

unpunctual etc. (*late*) 133; too late for; premature etc. (*early*) 132; too soon for; wise after the event.

adv. **inopportunely** etc. *adj.;* as ill luck would have it, in an evil hour, the time having gone by, a day after the fair.

136. Frequency

n. **frequency**, frequence, oftness [*rare*], oftenness [*rare*], quotiety [*rare*]; repetition etc. 104.

v. **keep**, keep on; recur etc. 104; do nothing but.

adj. **frequent**, often [*archaic*], many, many times, not rare, thickcoming, incessant, perpetual, continual, constant, repeated etc. 104; habitual etc. 613; hourly etc. 138.

adv. **often**, oft, ofttime [*archaic*], ofttimes, oftentimes; oftentime [*rare*], oftentide [*obs.*], not seldom, frequently; repeatedly etc. 104; unseldom, not unfrequently; in quick succession, in rapid succession; many a time and oft; oftly [*rare*], daily, hourly etc.; every day, every hour, every moment etc.

perpetually, continually, constantly, incessantly, unchangingly, steadfastly, without ceasing, at all times, daily and hourly, night and day, day and night, day after day, morning noon and night, ever and anon.

commonly etc. (*habitually*) 613; most often.

sometimes, occasionally, at times, now and then, from time to time, there being times when, *toties quoties* [*L.*], often enough, again and again.

137. Infrequency

n. **infrequency**, infrequence, unfrequency [*rare*], rareness, rarity; sparseness, fewness etc. 103; seldomness; uncommonness.

v. **be rare** etc. *adj.*

adj. **infrequent**, unfrequent [*rare*], seldseen [*archaic*], uncommon, sporadic; rare, rare as a blue diamond; few etc. 103; scarce; almost unheard of, scarce as hen's teeth [*colloq.*], unprecedented, which has not occurred within the memory of the oldest inhabitant, not within one's previous experience.

adv. **seldom**, rarely, scarcely, hardly; not often, unfrequently, infrequently, uncommonly, sparsely, unoften; scarcely ever, hardly ever; once in a blue moon [*colloq.*].

once; once for all, once in a way; *pro hac vice* [*L.*].

138. Regularity of recurrence. Periodicity

n. **periodicity**, intermittence; beat; oscillation etc. 314; pulse, pulsation; systole and diastole; rhythm; alternation, alternateness, alternancy [*rare*], alternativeness, alternity [*rare*].

round, revolution, rotation, bout, turn, say.

anniversary, biennial, triennial, quadrennial, quinquennial, sextennial, septennial, octennial, decennial; tricennial, jubilee, centennial, centenary, bicentennial, bicentenary, tercentenary; birthday, birthright, natal day, fête day, saint's day.

catamenia, courses, menses, menstrual flux.

[regularity of return] rota, cycle, period, stated time, routine; days of the week; Sunday, Monday etc.; months of the year; January etc.; feast, festival, fast etc.; Christmas, Yuletide, New Year's day, Ash Wednesday, Maundy Thursday, Good Friday, Easter; Allhallows, Allhallowmas, All Saints' Day; All Souls' Day; Candlemas, Dewali [*Hindu*], Holi *or* Hoolee [*Hindu*], Memorial *or* Decoration Day, Independence Day, Labor Day, Thanksgiving, ground-hog day, woodchuck day [*U. S.*], Halloween, Hallowmas, Lady Day; leap year, bissextile; Bairam, Ramadan, Muharram [*Mohammedan*]; St. Swithin's Day; Midsummer Day; May Day etc. (*holiday*) 840; yearbook.

punctuality, regularity, steadiness.

v. **return**, revolve; recur in regular -order, –succession; come again, come in its turn; come round, –again; beat, pulsate; alternate; intermit.

adj. **periodic**, periodical; serial, recurrent, cyclic, cyclical, rhythmic *or* rhythmical; recurring etc. *v.;* intermittent, remittent; alternate, every other; every.

hourly; diurnal, daily, quotidian [*rare*]; tertian, weekly; hebdomadal, hebdomadary; biweekly, fortnightly; bimonthly; monthly, catamenial, menstrual; yearly, annual; biennial, triennial etc.; centennial, secular; paschal, lenten etc.

regular, steady, constant, methodical, punctual, regular as clockwork.

adv. **periodically** etc. *adj.;* at regular intervals, at stated times; at fixed periods, at established periods; punctually etc. *adj.; de die in diem* [*L.*]; from day to day, day by day.

by turns; in turn, in rotation; alternately, every other day, off and on, ride and tie, round and round.

139. Irregularity of recurrence

n. **irregularity**, uncertainty, unpunctuality; fitfulness etc. *adj.;* capriciousness, ecrhythmus; acatastasia [*med.*].

adj. **irregular**, uncertain, unpunctual, capricious, erratic, heteroclite, ecrhythmic, ecrhythmous, desultory, fitful, flickering; rambling, rhapsodi-

cal; spasmodic; immethodical, unsystematic, unequal, uneven, variable.

adv. **irregularly** etc. *adj.;* by fits and starts etc. (*discontinuously*) 70.

Section 7. Change

140. Change
[difference at different times]

n. **change**, alteration, mutation, permutation, variation, novation [*rare*], modification, modulation, inflection *or* inflexion, mood, qualification, innovation, eversion, deviation, shift, turn; diversion; break.

transformation, transfiguration, transfigurement; metamorphosis; metabola *or* metabole [*med.*], transmorphism [*rare*], transmutation; deoxidization, deoxidation; transubstantiation; metagenesis, transanimation, transmigration, metempsychosis, version [*rare*]; metasomatism *or* metasomatosis, metathesis; metabolism, metastasis; transmogrification [*colloq.*]; avatar; alterative.

resolution, conversion etc. (*gradual change*) 144; revolution etc. (*sudden or radical change*) 146; inversion etc. (*reversal*) 218; displacement etc. 185; transference etc. 270.

changeableness etc. 149; tergiversation etc. (*change of mind*) 607.

v. **change**, alter, vary, wax and wane; modulate, diversify, qualify, tamper with; turn, shift, veer, gybe *or* jibe, jib, tack, chop, shuffle, swerve, warp, deviate, dodge, tergiversate, turn aside, evert, intervert [*obs.*]; pass to, take a turn, turn the corner, resume.

work a change, modify, vamp, patch, piece, vamp up, superinduce; transform, transfigure, transmute, transmogrify [*colloq.*], transume [*rare*], transverse [*rare*], transshape [*rare*], metabolize, convert, transubstantiate, resolve, revolutionize; chop and change; metamorphose, ring the changes.

innovate, introduce new blood, shuffle the cards; give a turn to, give a color to; influence, turn the scale; shift the scene, turn over a new leaf.

recast etc. 146; reverse etc. 218; disturb etc. 61; convert into etc. 144.

adj. **changed** etc. *v.;* newfangled; eversible; changeable etc. 149; transitional; modifiable; metagenetic; alterative.

adv. *mutatis mutandis* [*L.*].

int. *quantum mutatus!* [*L.*].

141. Permanence
[absence of change]

n. **permanence,** permanency, fixity, persistence, endurance; durableness, durability, lastingness; standing, *status quo* [*L.*]; maintenance, preservation, conservation; conservatism; *laisser faire* [*F.*], *laisser aller* [*F.*]; law of the Medes and Persians; standing dish.

stability etc. 150; quiescence etc. 265; obstinacy etc. 606.

v. **let alone,** let be; persist, remain, stay, tarry, rest; hold, hold on; last, endure, bide, abide, aby *or* abye [*archaic*], dwell, maintain, keep; stand, –still, –fast, –pat [*colloq.*]; subsist, live, outlive, survive; hold–, keep- one's -ground, –footing; hold good.

adj. **permanent;** stable etc. 150; persisting etc. *v.;* established; fixed, irremovable, durable; pucka *or* pukka *or* pakka [*Hind.*]; unchanged etc. (change etc. 140); renewed; intact, inviolate; persistent; monotonous, uncheckered; unfailing, unfading.

undestroyed, unrepealed, unsuppressed; conservative, *qualis ab incepto* [*L.*]; prescriptive etc. (*old*) 124; stationary etc. 265.

adv. **finally;** *in statu quo* [*L.*]; for good, at a stand, at a standstill, *uti possidetis* [*L.*]; without a shadow of turning; as you were!

142. Cessation
[change from action to rest]

n. **cessation,** discontinuance, desistance, desinence. intermission, remission; suspense, suspension; interruption; stop; hitch [*colloq.*]; stopping etc. *v.;* stoppage, halt; arrival etc. 292.

pause, rest, lull, respite, truce, truce of God, armistice, stay, drop; interregnum, abeyance. [in debate] closure, cloture, *clôture* [*F.*].

deadlock, checkmate, backwater, dead water, dead stand, dead stop; end etc. 67; death etc. 360.

punctuation, comma, semicolon, colon, period, full stop, caesura.

v. **cease,** discontinue, desist, stay; break off, leave off; hold, stop, pull up, stop short; check, check in full career, deadlock; stick, hang fire; halt; pause, rest.

come to a -stand, –standstill, –deadlock, –full stop; arrive etc. 292; go out, die away; wear away, wear off; pass away etc. (*be past*) 122; be at an end.

have done with, give over, surcease, shut up shop; give up etc. (*relinquish*) 624.

hold–, stay- one's hand; rest on one's oars, repose on one's laurels.

interrupt, suspend, interpel [*obs.*]; intermit, remit; put an end to, put a stop to, put a period to; derail; bring to a -stand, –standstill; stop, stall, cut short, arrest, stem the -tide, –torrent; pull the check-string.

int. **stop!** hold! enough! avast! [*naut.*], have done! a truce to! soft! leave off! *tenez!* [*F.*], fade away! [*slang*], let up! [*slang*], cut it out! [*slang*].

143. Continuance in action

n. **continuance,** continuation; run, pursuance, maintenance, extension, perpetuation, prolongation; persistence etc. (*perseverance*) 604*a;* repetition etc. 104.

v. **continue,** persist; go on, jog on, keep on, run on, hold on; abide, keep, pursue, stick to; take–, maintain- its course; carry on, keep up, drag on, stick [*colloq.*], persevere, endure, carry on.

sustain, uphold, hold up, keep on foot; follow up, perpetuate, prolong, maintain; preserve etc. 604*a;* harp upon etc. (*repeat*) 104.

keep going, keep alive, keep the pot boiling [*colloq.*], keep up the ball [*colloq.*]; die in harness; plug at it *or* along [*slang*]; keep the field, keep the ball rolling, keep at it, keep up; hold on–, pursue -the even tenor of one's way.

let be; *stare super antiquas vias* [*L.*]; *quieta non movere* [*L.*]; let things take their course.

adj. **continuing** etc. *v.;* uninterrupted, unintermitting, unvarying, persistent, unceasing, unremitting, unshifting; unreversed, unstopped, unrevoked, unvaried; sustained; chronic; undying etc. (*perpetual*) 112; inconvertible.

int. carry on! stand fast!

144. Conversion
[gradual change to something different]

n. **conversion,** reduction, transmutation, resolution, assimilation; chemistry, alchemy; lapse, assumption, growth, progress; naturalization; transportation.

proselytization, regeneration, Catholicization, Protestantization.

passage, transit, transition, transmigration; shifting etc. *v.;* flux; phase; conjugation; convertibility.

laboratory etc. 691; crucible, alembic, caldron, retort, mortar; potter's wheel, anvil, lathe, blowpipe.

convert, neophyte, catechumen, proselyte; pervert, renegade, apostate, turncoat.

v. **be converted into**; become, get, wax; come–, turn- -to, –into; turn out, lapse, shift; run–, fall–, pass–, slide–, glide–, grow–, ripen–, open–, resolve itself–, settle–, merge- into; melt, grow, come round to, mature, mellow; assume the - form, –shape, –state, –nature, character- of; illapse [*rare*]; assume a new phase, undergo a change.

convert into, resolve into; make, render; mold, form etc. 240; remodel, new-model, refound, reform, reorganize; assimilate to, bring to, reduce to.

adj. **converted into** etc. *v.;* convertible, resolvable into; conversible [*rare*], chemical, transitional; naturalized.

adv. gradually etc. (*slowly*) 275; *in transitu* [*L.*] etc. (*transference*) 270.

145. Reversion

n. **reversion**, return; revulsion.

turning point, turn of the tide; *status quo ante bellum* [*L.*]; calm before a storm.

alternation etc. (*periodicity*) 138; inversion etc. 219; recoil etc. 277; retrocession, retrospection, regression etc. 283; restoration etc. 660; relapse etc. 661; atavism, throwback; vicinism; escheat.

v. **revert**, reverse, return, turn back; relapse etc. 661; invert etc. 219; recoil etc. 277; retreat etc. 283; restore etc. 660; undo, unmake; turn the tide, turn the scale; escheat.

adj. **reverting** etc. *v.;* revulsive, reactionary; retrorse.

adv. **revulsively**, retrorsely, on the rebound, *à rebours* [*F.*].

146. Revolution
[sudden or violent change]

n. **revolution**, revolt, *bouleversement* [*F.*], subversion, breakup; destruction etc. 162; sudden–, radical–, sweeping–, organic- change; clean sweep, debacle, *débâcle* [*F.*], overturn, overthrow, *coup d'état* [*F.*], rebellion, rising, uprising, mutiny, sansculottism, bolshevism, counter-revolution.

spasm, convulsion, throe, revulsion; storm, earthquake, eruption, upheaval, cataclysm, transilience *or* transiliency [*rare*], jump, leap, plunge, jerk, start, dash; explosion.

legerdemain etc. (*trick*) 545.

v. **revolutionize**, revolt, rebel, insurrect, rise; new-model, remodel, recast; strike out something new, break with the past; change the face of, unsex.

adj. **unrecognizable**; transilient.

revolutionary, catastrophic, cataclysmic, cataclysmal, convulsionary, insurgent, Red, insurrectional, insurrectionary, mutinous, rebellious, sansculottic, bolshevist *or* bolshevik.

147. Substitution
[change of one thing for another]

n. **substitution**, commutation, subrogation [*law*], surrogation [*rare*]; supplanting etc. *v.*, supersession, supersedence, supersedure; metonymy etc. (*figure of speech*) 521.

[thing substituted] substitute, succedaneum, makeshift, temporary expedient; shift, apology, *pis aller* [*F.*], stopgap, jury mast, *locum tenens* [*L.*], alternate, warming pan [*colloq.*], dummy, scapegoat; double; changeling; *quid pro quo* [*L.*], alternative; representative etc. (*deputy*) 759; palimpsest.

price, purchase money, consideration, equivalent.

v. **substitute**, put in the place of, change for; make way for, give place to; supply–, take- the place of; surrogate [*rare*], subrogate [*law*], supplant, supersede, replace, cut out [*colloq.*], serve as a substitute; step into the shoes of, stand in the shoes of; make a shift with, put up with; borrow of Peter to pay Paul; commute, redeem, compound for.

adj. **substituted** etc. *v.;* vicarious, vicarial, substitutional, subdititious [*rare*].

adv. **instead**; by proxy; in place of, in lieu of, in the stead of, in the room of; *faute de mieux* [*F.*].

148. Interchange
[double or mutual change]

n. **interchange**, exchange; commutation, permutation, intermutation; reciprocation, transposition, transposal, shuffle, shuffling; alternation, reciprocity; castling [at chess]; hocus-pocus; swap [*colloq.*].

barter etc. 794; a Roland for his Oliver; tit for tat etc. (*retaliation*) 718; cross fire, battledore and shuttlecock; *quid pro quo* [*L.*].

interchangeableness, interchangeability.

v. **interchange**, exchange, counterchange; bandy, barter, transpose, shuffle, change hands, swap [*colloq.*], permute, reciprocate, commute; interwork, give and take, return the compliment; play at -puss in the corner, –battledore and shuttlecock; take in one another's washing; retaliate etc. 718; requite.

adj. **reciprocal**, interactive, mutual, commutative, interchangeable; interchanged etc. *v.;* intercurrent [*rare*].

international, interstate, interurban, intercollegiate, intertribal, interdenominational, interscholastic.

adv. **in exchange**, *vice versa* [*L.*], conversely, *mutatis mutandis* [*L.*], backwards and forwards, forward and back, to and fro, back and forth, by turns, turn about, contrariwise, commutatively, turn and turn about; each in his turn, every one in his turn.

149. Changeableness

n. **changeableness** etc. *adj.;* mutability, inconstancy; versatility, mobility; instability, unstable equilibrium; vacillation etc. (*irresolution*) 605; fluctuation, vicissitude; dysphoria; alternation etc. (*oscillation*) 314; transientness etc. 111.

[comparisons] moon, Proteus, kaleidoscope, chameleon, quicksilver, shifting sands, weathercock, vane, weathervane, harlequin, turncoat, Vicar of Bray, Cynthia of the minute, April showers; wheel of Fortune.

restlessness etc. *adj.;* fidgets, disquiet; disquietude, inquietude; unrest; agitation etc. 315.

v. **fluctuate**, vary, waver, flounder, flicker, flitter [*archaic*], flit, flutter, shift, shuffle, shake, totter, tremble, vacillate, wamble [*dial.*], turn and turn about, ring the changes; sway–, shift- to and fro; change and change about; oscillate etc. 314; vibrate–, oscillate- between two extremes; alternate; have as many phases as the moon.

adj. **changeable**, changeful; changing etc. 140; mutable, variable, checkered, ever changing, kaleidoscopic; protean, proteiform; versatile.

inconstant, unstaid, unsteady, unstable, unfixed, unsettled; fluctuating etc. *v.;* restless, uneasy; agitated etc. 315; erratic, fickle; mercurial, irresolute etc. 605; capricious etc. 608; touch and go; inconsonant, fitful, spasmodic; vibratory; vagrant, feathery [*rare*], lightheaded, wayward; desultory; afloat; alternating; alterable, plastic, mobile; transient etc. 111; wavering.

adv. **seesaw** etc. (*oscillation*) 314; off and on.

150. Stability

n. **stability**; immutability etc. *adj.;* unchangeableness etc. *adj.;* constancy; stable equilibrium, immobility, soundness, vitality, stabiliment [*rare*], stabilization; stiffness, ankylosis, solidity, *aplomb* [*F.*]; coherence.

permanence etc. 141; obstinacy etc. 606.

fixture, establishment; rock, pillar, tower, foundation, leopard's spots, Ethiopian's skin; law of the Medes and Persians.

standpatter [*politics*].

v. **be firm** etc. *adj.;* stick fast; stand firm, keep firm, remain firm; stand pat; weather the storm.

establish, settle, stablish [*archaic*], ascertain, fix, set, stabilitate [*obs.*], stabilize; stet [*printing*], retain, keep hold; make good, make sure; fasten etc. (*join*) 43; set on its legs [*colloq.*], set on its feet; float; perpetuate.

settle down; strike root, take root; take up one's abode etc. 184; build one's house on a rock.

adj. **unchangeable**, immutable; unaltered, unalterable; not to be changed, constant; permanent etc. 141; invariable, unyielding, undeviating; stable, durable; perennial etc. (*diuturnal*) 110.

fixed, steadfast, firm, firm as Gibraltar, firm as a rock, on a rock; tethered, anchored, moored, at anchor, firmly -seated, –established etc. *v.;* deep-rooted, ineradicable; fast, steady, balanced; confirmed, inveterate, valid; fiducial; immovable, irremovable, reveted, rooted; stated, settled, stereotyped, established etc. *v.;* obstinate etc. 606; vested; incontrovertible, indeclinable.

stuck fast, transfixed, aground, high and dry, stranded.

incommutable, indefeasible, irretrievable, intransmutable, irresoluble, irrevocable, irreversible, reverseless, inextinguishable, irreducible; indissoluble, indissolvable; indestructible, undying, imperishable, indelible, indeciduous; insusceptible, –of change.

int. stet [*L., printing*].

151. Eventuality

n. **eventuality**, eventuation, event, occurrence, supervention, incident, affair, transaction, proceeding, fact; matter of fact, naked fact; phenomenon: advent.

circumstance, particular, casualty, accident, happening, adventure, passage, crisis, pass, emergency, contingency; concern, business.

consequence, issue, result, termination, conclusion.

affairs, matters; the world, life, things, doings; things–, affairs- in general; the times, state of affairs, order of the day; course–, tide–, stream–, current–, run–, march-of-things, –events; ups and downs of life; chapter of accidents etc. (*chance*) 156; situation etc. (*circumstances*) 8; memorabilia.

v. **happen**, occur; take place, take effect; come, become of; come -off, –about, –round, –into existence, –forth, –to pass, –on; pass, present itself; fall; fall out, turn out; run, be on foot, fall in; befall, betide, bechance; prove, eventuate, draw on; turn up, crop up, spring up, cast up; supervene, survene, [*obs.*] issue, arrive, ensue, result, eventuate, arise, start, hold, take its course; pass off etc. (*be past*) 122.

experience; meet with; fall to the lot of; be one's -chance, –fortune, –lot; find; encounter, un-

45

dergo; pass through, go through; endure etc. (*feel*) 821.

adj. **happening** etc. *v.;* going on, doing, current; in the wind, afloat; on foot, on the carpet, on the tapis; at issue, in question; incidental.

eventful, stirring, bustling, full of incident; memorable, momentous, signal.

adv. **eventually**, ultimately, finally; in the event of, in case; in the course of things; in the natural *or* ordinary course of things; as things go, as times go; as the world -goes, −wags; as the tree falls, as the cat jumps [*colloq.*]; as it may -turn out, −happen.

152. Destiny

n. **destiny** etc. (*necessity*) 601; future existence, postexistence; hereafter; foredoom, future state, next world, world to come, after life; futurity etc. 121; everlasting life, everlasting death; life beyond the grave, life to come, world beyond the grave; prospect etc. (*expectation*) 507.

v. **impend**; hang over, lie over; threaten, loom, await, hover, come on, approach, stare one in the face; foreordain, preordain; predestine, doom, foredoom, have in store for.

adj. **impending** etc. *v.;* destined; about to be, about to happen; coming, in store, to come, going to happen, instant, at hand, near; near at hand, close at hand; overhanging, hanging over one's head, imminent; brewing, preparing, forthcoming; in the wind, in the cards [*colloq.*], in reserve; that will be, that is to be; in prospect etc. (*expected*) 507; looming in the -distance, −horizon, −future; postexistent, unborn, in embryo; in the womb of -time, futurity; on the knees of the gods, in the future; pregnant etc. (*producing*) 161.

adv. **in time**, in the long run; all in good time; eventually etc. 151; whatever may happen etc. (*certainly*) 474; as chance etc. (156) would have it.

Section 8. Causation

153. Cause

[constant antecedent]

n. **cause**, origin, source, principle, element; prime mover, *primum mobile* [*L.*], primordium [*rare*]; *vera causa* [*L.*], ultimate cause, Great First Cause; author etc. (*producer*) 164; mainspring, agent; leaven; groundwork, foundation etc. (*support*) 215.

spring, fountain, well, font; fountainhead, springhead, reservoir, headspring, wellspring,

wellhead; *fons et origo* [*L.*], genesis; descent etc. (*paternity*) 166; remote cause; influence.

pivot, hinge, turning point, lever; key; heart, nucleus, hub, focus; proximate cause, *causa causans* [*L.*]; the straw that breaks the camel's back.

reason, reason why; ground; why and wherefore [*colloq.*], rationale, occasion, derivation; final cause etc. (*intention*) 620; *les dessous des cartes* [*F.*]; undercurrents.

rudiment, egg, germ, embryo, fetus, bud, root, radix, radical, radication [*rare*], etymon, nucleus, seed, stem, stock, stirps, trunk, taproot, gemma, gemmule, radicle, semen, sperm.

nest, cradle, nursery, womb, nidus, birthplace, breeding-place, hotbed.

causality, causation; origination; causative; production etc. 161.

v. **be the cause of** etc. *n.;* originate; give origin to, give rise to, give occasion to; cause, occasion, sow the seeds of, kindle, suscitate [*obs.*]; bring on, bring to pass, bring about; produce; create etc. 161; set up, set afloat, set on foot; found, broach, institute, lay the foundation of; lie at the root of.

procure, induce, draw down, open the door to, superinduce, evoke, entail, operate; elicit, provoke.

contribute; conduce to etc. (*tend to*) 176; have a hand in; have a finger in the pie [*colloq.*]; determine, decide, turn the scale, have the deciding vote, have the final word; have a common origin; derive its origin etc. (*effect*) 154.

adj. **caused** etc. *v.;* causal, aetiological *or* etiological, original; primary, primitive, primordial; aboriginal; originative, generative, inceptive, productive, creative, constitutive, procreative, formative, demiurgic, protogenic, protogenal; radical; in embryo, embryonic, embryotic; *in ovo* [*L.*]; seminal, germinal; at the bottom of; connate, having a common origin.

adv. **from the beginning**, in the first place, before everything; because etc. 155; behind the scenes.

154. Effect

[constant sequent]

n. **effect**, consequence; aftercome [*Scot.*], aftergrowth, afterclap, aftermath, aftercrop, derivative, derivation; result; resultant; upshot, issue, outcome, resultance [*rare*], *dénouement* [*F.*], conclusion; falling action, catastrophe, end etc. 67; impress, impression; development, outgrowth; blossom, bud, ear, fruit, crop, harvest, product.

production, produce, work, handiwork, fabric, performance; creature, creation; offspring, offshoot; first fruits, firstlings; heredity, telegony; premices [*obs.*], primices [*obs.*].

v. **be the effect of** etc. *n.;* be due to, be owing to; originate in *or* from; rise from, arise from, take its rise from, spring from, proceed from, emanate from, come from, grow from, bud from, sprout from, germinate from, issue from, flow from, result from, follow from, derive its origin from, accrue from; come to, come of, come out of; depend upon, hang upon, hinge upon, turn upon.

take the consequences, reap where one has sown, make one's bed and lie on it, sow the wind and reap the whirlwind.

adj. **owing to**; resulting from etc. *v.;* resultant, firstling; derivable from; due to; caused by etc. 153; dependent upon; derived from, evolved from; derivative; hereditary; telegonous.

adv. **consequently**, of course, it follows that, naturally; as a consequence, in consequence; through, necessarily, eventually.

155. Attribution
[assignment of cause]

n. **attribution**, theory, ascription, assignment, reference to, rationale; accounting for etc. *v.;* etiology, imputation, derivation from.

filiation, affiliation; filiality; pedigree etc. (*paternity*) 166.

explanation etc. (*interpretation*) 522; reason why etc. (*cause*) 153.

v. **attribute to**, ascribe to, impute to, refer to, lay to; point to, trace to, bring home to; put down to, set down to; blame; blame upon [*colloq.*]; charge on, ground on; invest with, assign as cause, lay at the door of, father upon, saddle, filiate, affiliate; account for, derive from, point out the reason etc. 153; theorize; tell how it comes; put the saddle on the right horse; find the real culprit.

adj. **attributed** etc. *v.;* attributable etc. *v.;* referable *or* referrible; due to, derivable from; affiliate, derivate [*rare*]; owing to etc. (*effect*) 154; putative; ecbatic.

adv. **hence**, thence, therefore, for, since, on account of, because, owing to; on that account; from this cause, from that cause; thanks to, forasmuch as; whence, *propter hoc* [*L.*].

why? wherefore? whence? how comes it? how is it? how happens it? how come? [*colloq.*] how does it happen? how so?

in some way, in some such way; somehow, somehow or other.

156. Chance[1]
[absence of assignable cause]

n. **chance**, indetermination, accident, fortune, hazard, hap [*rare*], haphazard, chance-medley, random, luck, *raccroc* [*F.*], fluke [*cant*], casualty, fortuity, contingence, adventure, hit; fate etc. (*necessity*) 601; equal chance; lottery; tombola; lotto; toss-up [*colloq.*] etc. 621; turn of the -table, -cards; hazard of the die, chapter of accidents; cast-, throw- of the dice; heads or tails, wheel of Fortune; *sortes* [*L.*], *sortes Virgilianoe* [*L.*].

probability, possibility, contingency, odds, long odds, run of luck; accidentalness, accidentalism, accidentality; main chance.

theory of -probabilities, -chances; bookmaking; assurance; gamble, speculation, gaming etc. 621.

v. **chance**, hap, turn up; fall to one's lot; be one's fate etc. 601; stumble on, light upon; blunder upon, hit, hit upon; take one's chance etc. 621.

adj. **casual**, fortuitous, accidental, chance, chanceable [*archaic*], chanceful [*archaic*], haphazard, random, casual, adventive, adventitious, causeless, incidental, contingent, uncaused, undetermined, indeterminate; possible etc. 470; unintentional etc. 621.

adv. **by chance**, by accident; at random, casually; perchance etc. (*possibly*), 470; for aught one knows; as -good, -bad, -ill-luck etc. *n.*- would have it; as it may -be, -chance, -turn up, -happen; as the case may be.

[1]The word *Chance* has two distinct meanings: the first, the absence of assignable *cause,* as above; and the second, the absence of *design*—for the latter see 621.

157. Power

n. **power**; potency, potentiality; jiva [*theos.*]; puissance, might, force; energy etc. 171; dint; right hand, right arm; ascendancy, sway, control; prepotency, prepollence *or* prepollency [*rare*]; almightiness, omnipotence; *carte blanche* [*F.*], authority etc. 737; strength etc. 159; predominance.

ability; ableness etc. *adj.;* competency; efficiency, efficacy, validity, cogency; enablement; vantage ground; influence etc. 175.

pressure, electromotive force, high pressure; conductivity; elasticity; gravity, electricity, magnetism, magneto-electricity, galvanism, voltaic electricity, voltaism, electromagnetism, electrostatics, electrokinetics, electrodynamics; electromotion, electrification; magnetization, galvanization; attraction, pull; *vis inertiae* [*L.*], *vis mortua* [*L.*], *vis viva* [*L.*]; potential–, dynamic- energy; friction, suction; live-circuit, –rail, –wire; volt, voltage.

[instruments] galvanometer, rheometer; variometer, magnetometer, magnetoscope, electrometer, electroscope, galvanoscope, electrophorus, electrodynamometer, voltameter, ammeter, voltammeter, voltmeter, wattmeter.

capability, capacity; *quid valeant humeri quid ferre recusent* [*L.*]; faculty, quality, attribute, endowment, virtue, gift, property, qualification, susceptibility.

v. **be powerful** etc. *adj.;* gain power etc. *n.*

belong to, pertain to; lie–, be- in one's power; can.

empower; give–, confer–, exercise-power etc. *n.;* enable, invest; indue, endue; endow, arm; strengthen etc. 159; compel etc. 744.

electrify, magnetize, energize, galvanize, attract.

adj. **powerful**, puissant; potent, potential [*rare*]; capable, able; equal to, up to; cogent, valid; effective, effectual; efficient, efficacious, adequate, competent; multipotent [*rare*], plenipotent [*rare*], prepollent [*rare*], predominant; mighty, ascendent, prepotent, omnipotent, armipotent, mightful [*archaic*]; almighty.

forcible etc. *adj.* (*energetic*) 171; influential etc. 175; productive etc. 168.

electric, electrodynamic, electrokinetic, electromagnetic, electrometric, electrometrical, electromotive, electronegative, electropositive, electroscopic; magnetic, magneto-electric *or* magneto-electrical, magnetomotive; voltametric, voltaic; galvanic, galvanometric, galvanoscopic, dynamo-electric *or* dynamo-electrical; dynamic, static, potential.

adv. **powerfully** etc. *adj.;* by virtue of, by dint of.

158. Impotence

n. **impotence**; inability, disability; disablement, impuissance [*rare*], caducity, imbecility; incapacity, incapability; inaptitude, ineptitude; indocility; invalidity, inefficiency, incompetence, disqualification.

telum imbelle [*L.*], *brutum fulmen* [*L.*], blank cartridge, flash in the pan, *vox et praeterea nihil* [*L.*], dead letter, bit of waste paper, dummy; Quaker gun; cripple.

inefficacy etc. (*inutility*) 645; failure etc. 732.

helplessness etc. *adj.;* prostration, paralysis, palsy, apoplexy, syncope, sideration [*obs.*], vin-cibility, vincibleness, deliquium, collapse, exhaustion, softening of the brain, senility, superannuation, atony, decrepitude, imbecility, neurasthenia, invertebracy, inanition; emasculation, orchotomy; eunuch.

mollycoddle, old woman, muff [*colloq.*], tenderling [*rare*], milksop, molly [*colloq.*], sissy [*colloq.*], mother's darling.

v. **be impotent** etc. *adj.;* not have a leg to stand on. *vouloir rompre l'anguille au genou* [*F.*], *vouloir prendre la lune avec les dents* [*F.*].

collapse, faint, swoon, fall into a swoon, drop; go by the board; end in smoke etc. (*fail*) 732.

render powerless etc. *adj.;* depotentiate [*rare*], deprive of power; disable, disenable; disarm, incapacitate, disqualify, unfit, invalidate, disinvigorate [*rare*], undermine, deaden, cramp, tie the hands; double up, prostrate, paralyze, muzzle, cripple, becripple, maim, lame, hamstring, unsinew [*rare*], draw the teeth of; throttle, strangle, garrote *or* garrotte, ratten [*trade-union cant*], silence, sprain, clip the wings of, put *hors de combat* [*F.*], spike the guns; take the wind out of one's sails, scotch the snake, put a spoke in one's wheel; break the -neck, –back; unhinge, unfit; put out of gear.

unman, unnerve, devitalize, effeminize, attenuate, enervate; emasculate, evirate [*rare*], spay, eunuchize [*rare*], caponize, castrate, geld, alter.

shatter, exhaust; weaken etc. 160.

adj. **powerless**, impotent, unable, incapable, incompetent; inefficient, ineffective; inept; unfit, unfitted; unqualified, disqualified; unendowed; doddering [*colloq.*], wambly [*Scot. and dial. Eng.*], inapt, unapt; crippled, disabled etc. *v.;* armless; senile, decrepit, superannuated.

harmless, unarmed, weaponless, defenseless, *sine ictu* [*L.*], unfortified, mightless [*archaic*], indefensible, vincible, pregnable, untenable.

paralytic, paralyzed; palsied, imbecile; nerveless, sinewless, marrowless, pithless, lustless; emasculate, disjointed; out of joint, out of gear; unnerved, unhinged; waterlogged, on one's beam ends, rudderless; laid on one's back; done up [*colloq.*], done for [*colloq.*], done brown [*colloq.*], done [*colloq.*], dead-beat [*colloq.*], exhausted, shattered, atonic, demoralized; graveled [*colloq.*] etc. (*in difficulty*) 704; helpless, unfriended, fatherless; without a leg to stand on, *hors de combat* [*F.*], laid on the shelf.

nugatory, null and void, inoperative, good for nothing, invertebrate, ineffectual etc. (*failing*) 732; inadequate etc. 640; inefficacious etc. (*useless*) 645.

159. Strength

[degree of power]

n. **strength**; power etc. 157; energy etc. 171; vigor, force; main–, physical–, brute- force; spring, elasticity, tone, tension, tonicity.

[comparisons] adamant, steel, iron, oak, heart of oak; iron grip; bone.

virility, vitality; stoutness etc. *adj.;* lustihood, stamina, nerve, muscle, sinew *or* sinews, thews and sinews, physique; grit, pith, pithiness.

athletics, athleticism; gymnastics, acrobatism, agonistics, feats of strength.

athlete, gymnast, pancratiast, acrobat; Atlas, Hercules, Antaeus, Samson, Cyclops, Briareus, Colossus, Polyphemus, Titan, Brobdingnagian, Goliath; tower of strength; giant refreshed

strengthening etc. *v.;* invigoration, refreshment, refocillation [*obs.*].

[science of forces] dynamics, statics.

v. **be strong** etc. *adj.,* be stronger; overmatch.

render strong etc. *adj.;* give strength etc. *n.;* strengthen, invigorate, potentiate [*rare*], brace, nerve, fortify, buttress, sustain, harden, case-harden, steel, gird; screw up, wind up, set up; gird–, brace-up one's loins; recruit, set on one's legs [*colloq.*]; vivify; refresh etc. 689; refect [*archaic*], reinforce *or* reënforce etc. (*restore*) 660.

adj. **strong**, mighty, vigorous, forcible, hard, adamantine, stout, robust, sturdy, husky, doughty, hardy, powerful, potent, puissant, valid.

resistless, irresistible, invincible, proof against, impregnable, unconquerable, indomitable, inextinguishable, unquenchable; incontestable; more than a match for; overpowering, overwhelming; all-powerful, all-sufficient; sovereign.

able-bodied; athletic, gymnastic, carobatic, agonistic, palaestral [*rare*]; Herculean, Briarean, Brobdingnagian, Titanic, Cyclopean, Atlantean; muscular, brawny, wiry, well-knit, broad-shouldered, sinewy, sinewous [*rare*], strapping, stalwart, gigantic.

manly, manlike, manful; masculine, male, virile, in the prime of manhood.

unweakened, unallayed, unwithered, unshaken, unworn, unexhausted; in full force, in full swing; in the plentitude of power.

sound; stubborn, thick-ribbed, made of iron, deep-rooted; strong as -a lion, –an ox, –a horse -brandy; sound as a roach; in fine feather, in high feather [*both colloq.*]; like a giant refreshed.

adv. **strongly** etc. *adj.;* by force etc. *n.;* by main force etc. (*by compulsion*) 744.

160. Weakness

n. **weakness** etc. *adj.;* debility, atony, relaxation, languor, enervation; impotence etc. 158; infirmity, effeminacy, feminality; fragility, flaccidity; inactivity etc. 683.

[comparisons] reed, thread, rope of sand, house of cards, house built on sand.

anemia, bloodlessness, deficiency of blood, poverty of blood.

invalidation; declension–, loss–, failure- of strength; delicacy, decrepitude, asthenia, adynamy [*rare*], cachexia *or* cachexy, sprain, strain.

weakling; softling [*obs.*]; infant etc. 129; youth etc. 127.

v. **be weak** etc. *adj.;* drop, crumble, give way, totter, dodder, tremble, shake, halt, limp, fade, languish, decline, flag, fail, have one foot in the grave.

render weak etc. *adj.;* weaken, enfeeble, debilitate, invalidate, shake, deprive of strength, relax, enervate; unbrace, unnerve; cripple, unman etc. (*render powerless*) 158; cramp, reduce, sprain, strain, blunt the edge of; dilute, impoverish; decimate; extenuate; reduce in strength, reduce the strength of; *mettre de l'eau dans son vin* [*F.*].

adj. **weak**, feeble, debile [*obs.*]; impotent etc. 158; relaxed, unnerved etc. *v.;* sapless, strengthless, powerless; weakly, unstrung, flaccid, adynamic, asthenic; nervous.

soft, effeminate, feminate [*obs.*], womanish.

frail, fragile, shattery; flimsy, sleazy, gossamery, papery, unsubstantial, gimcrack, gingerbread; rickety, jerry-built, *kucha or kachcha* [*Hind.*], cranky; craichy [*dial. Eng.*], drooping, tottering, doddering [*colloq.*] etc. *v.;* broken, lame, withered, shattered, shaken, crazy, shaky, tumbledown; palsied etc. 158; decrepit.

unsound, poor, infirm; faint, faintish; sickly etc. (*disease*) 655; dull, slack, evanid [*obs.*], languid; spent, short-winded, effete; weather-beaten; decayed, rotten, forworn [*archaic*], worn, seedy, languishing, wasted, washy, wishy-washy [*colloq.*], laid low, pulled down, the worse for wear.

unstrengthened etc. 159, unsupported, unaided, unassisted; aidless, defenseless etc. 158.

on its last legs; weak as a -child, –baby, –chicken, –cat, –rat, –rag; weak as -water, –water gruel, –gingerbread, –milk and water; colorless etc. 429.

161. Production

n. **production**, creation, construction, formation, fabrication, manufacture; building, architecture, erection, edification; coinage; disaster; organization; *nisus formativus* [*L.*]; putting together etc. *v.;* establishment; workmanship, performance; achievement etc. (*completion*) 729.

flowering, fructification, fruition; inflorescence.

bringing forth etc. *v.;* parturition, birth, birth throe, childbirth, delivery, confinement, *accouchement* [*F.*], travail, labor, midwifery, obstetrics; geniture [*obs.*]; gestation etc. (*maturation*) 673; assimilation; evolution, development, growth; entelechy; fertilization, gemination, germination, heterogamy, genesis, generation, histogenesis, breeding, begetting, isogamy, epigenesis, procreation, progeneration, propagation; fecundation, impregnation; albumen etc. 357.

spontaneous generation; archigenesis, archebiosis, abiogenesis, biogenesis, biogeny, dysmerogenesis, eumerogenesis, heterogenesis, oögenesis, merogenesis, metogenesis, monogenesis, parthenogenesis, homogenesis, xenogenesis.

dissogeny, digenesis, physiogeny, phylogeny, ontogeny, ontogenesis, mitosis, xenogeny; theogony, tocogony, tocology, vacuolation, vacuolization.

publication; works, *oeuvres* [*F.*], opus (*pl.* opera) [*L.*]; authorship

structure, building, edifice, fabric, erection, pile, tower; flower, fruit, blossom.

v. **produce**, perform, operate, do, make, gar [*obs.*], form, construct, fabricate, frame, contrive, manufacture; weave, forge, coin, carve, chisel; build, raise, edify, rear, erect, put together; set up, run up; establish, constitute, compose, organize, institute; achieve, accomplish etc. (*complete*) 729.

flower, burgeon, blossom, bear fruit, fructify, teem, ean [*obs.*], yean, farrow, drop, pup, whelp, kitten, kindle [*obs.*], spawn, spat; bear, lay, bring forth, give birth to, lie in, be brought to bed of, evolve, pullulate, usher into the world.

make productive etc. 168; create; beget, get, generate, fecundate, impregnate; procreate, progenerate, propagate; engender; bring–, call- into -being, –existence; breed, hatch, develop, bring up.

induce, superinduce; suscitate [*obs.*]; cause etc. 153; acquire etc. 775.

adj. **produced, producing** etc. *v.,* productive of; prolific etc. 168; creative; formative; procreant, generative, genitive, genetic, genial [*rare*], genital; pregnant; *enceinte* [*F.*], big with, fraught with; in the family way [*colloq.*], teeming, parturient, in the straw [*colloq.*], brought to bed of; lying-in; puerperal, puerperous [*rare*].

digenetic, heterogenetic, oögenetic, xenogenetic; ectogenous, gamic, hematobious, sporogenous, sporophorous.

architectonic *or* architectonical, constructive.

162. Destruction
[nonproduction]

n. **destruction**; waste, dissolution, breaking up; disruption; diruption [*obs.*], consumption; disorganization.

fall, downfall, ruin, perdition, debacle, *débâcle* [*F.*], crash, *éboulement* [*F.*], smash [*colloq.*], havoc, *délabrement* [*F.*], breakdown, break-up; prostration, cave-in [*colloq.*]; desolation, *bouleversement* [*F.*], wreck, wrack [*archaic*], shipwreck, cataclysm; washout.

extinction, annihilation; destruction of life etc. 361; knock-out, K. O. [*slang*], knock-out blow, knock-down blow; doom, crack of doom.

destroying etc. *v.;* demolition, demolishment [*rare*], overthrow, subversion, suppression; abolition etc. (*abrogation*) 756; biblioclasm; sacrifice; ravage, devastation, razzia; incendiarism; revolution etc. 146; extirpation etc. (*extraction*) 301; *commencement de la fin* [*F.*], road to ruin; dilapidation etc. (*deterioration*) 659; *sabotage* [*F.*].

v. **be destroyed** etc.; perish; fall, fall to the ground; tumble, topple; go–, fall- to pieces; break up; crumble, –to dust; go to -the dogs, –the wall, –smash, –shivers, –wreck, –pot [*colloq.*], –wrack and ruin; go by the board, go down the drain [*colloq.*]; be all over with, be all up with [*colloq.*], go to glory [*colloq.*], go to pieces, go under, go up the spout [*colloq.*], totter to its fall.

destroy; do–, make- away with nullify; annul etc. 756; sacrifice, demolish; tear up; overturn, overthrow, overwhelm; upset, subvert, put an end to seal the doom of, do for [*colloq.*], dish [*slang*], undo; break up, cut up; break down, cut down, pull down, mow down, blow down, beat down; suppress, quash, put down; cut short, take off, blot out; efface, obliterate, cancel, erase, strike out, expunge, delete, dele; dispel, dissipate, dissolve; consume.

smash, crash, quell, squash [*colloq.*], squelch [*colloq.*], crumple up, shatter, shiver; batter;

tear–, crush–, cut–, shake–, pull–, pick -to pieces; laniate [*rare*]; nip; tear to -rags, –tatters; crush–, knock- to atoms; ruin; strike out; throw down, throw over, knock down, knock over, lay out [*slang*], lay by the heels, fell, sink, swamp, scuttle, wreck, shipwreck, engulf *or* ingulf, submerge; lay in ashes, lay in ruins; sweep away, raze; level, –with the -ground, –dust.

deal destruction, lay waste, ravage, gut; disorganize; dismantle etc. (*render useless*) 645; devour, swallow up, desolate, devastate, sap, mine, blast, confound; exterminate, extinguish, quench, annihilate; snuff out, put out, stamp out, trample out; lay–, trample- in the dust; prostrate; tread–, crush–, trample- under foot; lay the ax to the root of; make short work of, make a clean sweep of, make mincemeat of; cut up root and branch; fling–, scatter- to the winds; throw overboard; strike at the root of, sap the foundations of, spring a mine, blow up; ravage with fire and sword; cast to the dogs; eradicate etc. 301.

adj. **destroyed** etc. *v.;* perishing etc. *v.;* trembling–, nodding–, tottering- to its fall; in course of destruction etc. *n.;* extinct; all-destroying, all-devouring, all-engulfing.

destructive, subversive, ruinous, incendiary, deletory [*obs.*]; destroying etc. *n.;* suicidal; deadly etc. (*killing*) 361.

adv. with crushing effect, with a sledge hammer.

163. Reproduction

n. **reproduction**, renovation; restoration etc. 660; renewal; new edition, reprint etc. (*copy*) 21; revival, regeneration, palingenesis, revivification; apotheosis; resuscitation, reanimation, resurrection, resurgence, reappearance; regrowth; Phoenix.

generation etc. (*production*) 161; multiplication.

v. **reproduce**; restore etc. 660; revive, renovate, renew, regenerate, revivify, resuscitate, reanimate, refashion, stir the embers, put into the crucible; multiply, repeat; resurge.

crop up, crop out, spring up like mushrooms.

adj. **reproduced** etc. *v.;* renascent, resurgent, reappearing; reproductive, proligerous [*rare*], progenitive, proliferous, gametal; hydraheaded; suigenetic.

164. Producer

n. **producer**, originator, inventor, author, founder, generator, mover, architect, grower, raiser, introducer, deviser, constructor, begetter, creator; maker etc. (*agent*) 690; prime mover.

165. Destroyer

n. **destroyer** etc. (*destroy* etc. 162); cankerworm etc. (*bane*) 663; assassin etc. (*killer*) 361; executioner etc. (*punish*) 975; biblioclast; eidoloclast, iconoclast, idoloclast; vandal, destructor [*rare*], Hun, nihilist.

166. Paternity

n. **paternity**; parentage; consanguínity etc. 11.

parent, father, sire, dad, papa, governor [*Engl. slang*], pater [*Engl. colloq.*], daddy [*colloq.*], paterfamilias, abba; genitor [*rare*], progenitor, procreator, begetter; ancestor; grandsire, grandfather; great-grandfather; fathership, fatherhood; *mabap* [*Hind.*].

motherhood, maternity, motherhead [*rare*], mothership; mother, dam, mamma *or* mama, mammy, mam [*colloq.*], motherkin, matriarch, materfamilias; grandmother.

stem, trunk, tree, stock, stirps, pedigree, house, lineage, line, family, tribe, sept, race, clan; genealogy, family tree, descent, extraction, birth, ancestry; forefathers, forbears, patriarchs.

adj. **parental**; paternal; maternal; family, ancestral, linear, patriarchal; racial, phyletic.

167. Posterity

n. **posterity**, progeny, breed, issue, offspring, brood, litter, seed, farrow, spawn, spat; family, children, grandchildren, heirs; great-grandchildren.

child, son, daughter, bairn, baby, kid [*colloq.*], papoose [*Am. Ind.*], imp, brat, moppet [*archaic*], lambkin, cub, cherub, nestling, tot, innocent, urchin, chit [*colloq.*]; infant etc. 129; *butcha or bacha* [*Hind.*]; bantling, scion; acrospire, plumule, shoot, sprout, olive-branch, sprit, branch; offshoot, offset; ramification; descendant; heir, heiress; heir-apparent, heir-presumptive; chip of the old block; heredity; rising generation.

lineage, straight descent, sonship, line, filiation, primogeniture.

adj. **filial**; diphyletic.

168. Productiveness

n. **productiveness** etc. *adj.;* fecundity, fertilization, fertility, luxuriance, uberty [*obs.*].

[comparisons] milch cow, rabbit, hydra, warren, seed plot, land flowing with milk and honey.

aftermath, second crop, aftercrop, aftergrowth, arrish [*dial. Eng.*], eddish [*dial. Eng.*], rowen.

multiplication, multiparity, propagation, procreation; superfetation, pregnancy, pullulation [*rare*], fructification.

v. **make productive** etc. *adj.;* fructify; procreate, pullulate, generate, fertilize, spermatize, impregnate; fecundate, fecundify; teem, spawn, multiply; produce etc. 161; conceive.

adj. **productive**, prolific, copious; teeming, teemful [*dial.*]; fertile, fruitful, frugiferous [*obs.*], fructuous [*rare*], plenteous, proliferous, fructiferous, fruitbearing; fecund, luxuriant; pregnant, uberous.

procreant, procreative; generative, life-giving, spermatic, inceptive, originative; multiparous; omnific; propagable.

parturient etc. (*producing*) 161; profitable etc. (*useful*) 644.

169. Unproductiveness

n. **unproductiveness** etc. *adj.;* infertility, sterility, infecundity; impotence etc. 158; unprofitableness etc. (*inutility*) 645.

waste, desert, Sahara, wild, karoo, wilderness, howling wilderness.

v. **be unproductive** etc. *adj.;* hang fire, flash in the pan, come to nothing.

adj. **unproductive**, acarpous, inoperative, barren, addle, unfertile, unprolific, arid, sterile, unfruitful, infecund, [*rare*], jejune, infertile; useless, otiose; *sine prole* [*L.*]; fallow; teemless, issueless, fruitless, infructuose [*rare*]; unprofitable etc. (*useless*) 645; null and void, of no effect.

170. Agency

n. **agency**, operation, force, working, strain, function, office, maintenance, exercise, work, swing, play; interworking, interaction; procuration procurement.

causation etc. 153; mediation, intermediation, instrumentality etc. 631; conation, influence etc. 175; action etc. (*voluntary*) 680; *modus operandi* [*L.*] etc. 627.

quickening–, maintaining–, sustaining- power; home stroke.

v. **be in action** etc. *adj.;* operate, work; act, act upon; perform, play, support, sustain, strain, maintain, take effect, quicken, strike.

come–, bring- into -operation, –play; have play, have free play; bring to bear upon.

adj. **operative**, operant [*rare*], efficient, efficacious, practical, exertive, conative, effectual.

at work, on foot; acting etc. (*doing*) 680; in operation, in force, in action, in play, in exercise; acted upon, wrought upon.

adv. **by the agency of** etc. *n.;* through etc. (*instrumentality*) 631; by means of etc. 632.

171. Energy

n. **energy**, physical energy, force; keenness etc. *adj.;* intensity, vigor, backbone [*colloq.*], vim [*colloq.*], mettle, *vis viva* [*L.*], *vis vitae* [*L.*], pep [*slang*], ginger [*slang*], go [*colloq.*]; strength, elasticity; high pressure; fire; rush; human dynamo.

activity, agitation, effervescence; ferment, fermentation; ebullition, splutter, perturbation, stir, bustle; voluntary energy etc. 682; quicksilver.

exertion etc. (*effort*) 686; excitation etc. (*mental*) 824; resolution etc. (*mental energy*) 604.

acrimony, acridity, acritude [*obs.*]; causticity, virulence, poignancy; harshness etc. *adj.;* severity, edge, point; pungency etc. 392.

excitant, stimulant; Spanish fly, cantharides; seasoning etc. (*condiment*) 393.

v. **give energy** etc. *n.;* energize, stimulate, kindle, excite, exert; activate, potentialize [*rare*], dynamize, doubleshot; sharpen, intensify; inflame etc. (*render violent*) 173; wind up etc. (*strengthen*) 159.

strike, –into, –hard, –home; make an impression.

adj. **energetic**, strong, forcible, active, strenuous, forceful, mettlesome, enterprising, go-ahead [*colloq.*]; intense, deep-dyed, severe, keen, vivid, sharp, acute, incisive, trenchant, brisk.

rousing, irritating; poignant; virulent, caustic, corrosive, mordant, harsh, stringent; doubleedged, double-shotted, double-distilled; drastic, escharotic; racy etc. (*pungent*) 392; excitant, excitative, excitatory.

potent etc. (*powerful*) 157; radioactive.

adv. **strongly** etc. *adj.;* *fortiter in re* [*L.*]; with telling effect.

172. Inertness

n. **inertness**, physical inertness, inertia, *vis inertiae* [*L.*], inertion, inactivity, torpor, languor; dormancy, *fainéance* [*F.*], quiescence etc. 265; latency, inaction; passivity; stagnation; dullness etc. *adj.*

mental inertness; sloth etc. (*inactivity*) 683; inexcitability etc. 826; irresolution etc. 605; obstinacy etc. 606; permanence etc. 141.

v. **be inert** etc. *adj.;* hang fire, smolder *or* smoulder.

adj. **inert**, inactive, passive; torpid etc. 683; sluggish, stagnant, *fainéant* [*F.*], dull, heavy, flat, slack, tame, slow, blunt; lifeless, dead, uninfluential.

latent, dormant, smoldering *or* smouldering, unexerted.

adv. **inactively** etc. *adj.;* in suspense, in abeyance.

52

173. Violence

n. **violence**, inclemency, vehemence, might, impetuosity, furiosity [*rare*]; boisterousness etc. *adj.;* effervescence, ebullition; turbulence, bluster; uproar, callithump, riot, row [*colloq.*], rumpus, *le diable à quatre* [*F.*], devil to pay [*colloq.*], the fat in the fire [*colloq.*].

ferocity, rage, fury; exacerbation, exasperation, malignity; severity etc. 739.

force, brute force; outrage; *coup de main* [*F.*]; strain, shock, shog [*rare*].

fit, paroxysm, spasm, convulsion, throe; hysterics, passion etc. (*state of excitability*) 825; orgasm, aphrodisia.

outbreak, outburst; debacle; burst, bounce, dissilience [*rare*], discharge, volley, explosion, blow-up, blast, detonation, rush, eruption, displosion [*obs.*], torrent.

turmoil etc. (*disorder*) 59; ferment etc. (*agitation*) 315; storm, tempest, rough weather; squall etc. (*wind*) 349; earthquake, volcano, thunderstorm.

fury, berserk, dragon, demon, tiger, beldam *or* beldame, madcap, wild beast; fire eater [*colloq.*] etc. (*blusterer*) 887; Erinys (*pl.* Erinyes), Eumenides, Tisiphone, Megaera, Alecto.

v. **be violent** etc. *adj.;* run high; ferment, effervesce; romp, rampage; run wild, run riot; break the peace; rush, tear; rush headlong, rush headforemost; run amuck, raise a storm, make a riot; make–, kick up– a row [*colloq.*]; rough-house [*slang*]; bluster, rage, roar, riot, storm; boil, boil over; fume, foam, come in like a lion, wreak, bear down, ride roughshod, out-Herod Herod; spread like wildfire.

explode, go off, displode [*obs.*], detonate, detonize, fulminate, let off, let fly, discharge, thunder, blow up, flash, flare, burst; shock, strain.

break open, force open, prize open, pry open; break out, fly out, burst out.

render violent etc. *adj.;* sharpen, stir up, quicken, excite, incite, urge, lash, stimulate; irritate, inflame, kindle, suscitate [*obs.*], foment; accelerate, aggravate, exasperate, exacerbate, convulse, infuriate, madden, lash into fury; fan the flame, add fuel to the flame; *oleum addere camino* [*L.*].

adj. **violent**, vehement; warm; acute, sharp; rough, tough [*colloq.*], vicious [*colloq.*], rude, ungentle, bluff, boisterous, wild; brusque, abrupt, waspish; impetuous; rampant.

turbulent; disorderly; blustering, towering, raging etc. *v.;* troublous, riotous; tumultuary; tumultuous; obstreperous, uproarious; extravagant; unmitigated, immitigable; ravening, tameless; frenzied etc. (*insane*) 503; desperate etc. (*rash*) 863; infuriate, furious, outrageous, frantic, hysteric, in hysterics.

fiery, flaming, scorching, hot, red-hot, ebullient.

savage, fierce, ferocious, fierce as a tiger.

excited etc. *v.;* unquelled, unquenched, unextinguished, unrepressed, unbridled, unruly; headstrong; ungovernable, unappeasable, unmitigable; uncontrollable, incontrollable; insuppressible, irrepressible; orgastic.

spasmodic, convulsive, explosive; detonating etc. *v.;* volcanic, meteoric; stormy etc. (*wind*) 349.

adv. **violently** etc. *adj.;* amain; by storm, by force, by main force; with might and main; tooth and nail, *vi et armis* [*L.*], at the point of the -sword, –bayonet; at one fell swoop; with a high hand, through thick and thin; in desperation, with a vengeance; *à outrance* [*F.*], *à toute outrance* [*F.*]; headlong, headfirst, headforemost.

aphrodisiac, aphrodisiacal, aphroditous.

174. Moderation

n. **moderation**; lenity etc. 740; temperateness, temperance, passability, passableness, gentleness etc. *adj.;* sobriety; quiet; mental calmness etc. (*inexcitability*) 826.

moderating etc. *v.;* anaphrodisia; relaxation, remission, mitigation, tranquilization, assuagement, alleviation, contemperation [*obs.*], pacification.

mean, measure, *juste milieu* [*F.*], golden mean, *meden agan* [*Gr.*], *ariston metron* [*Gr.*].

moderator; lullaby, sedative, calmative, lenitive, palliative, demulcent, antispasmodic, carminative; laudanum; rose water, balm, poppy, chloroform, opium: soothing sirup, opiate, anodyne, milk.

v. **be moderate** etc. *adj.;* keep within -bounds, -compass; sober down, settle down; keep the peace, remit, relent; take in sail.

moderate, soften, mitigate, temper, accoy [*obs.*]; attemper, contemper [*obs.*], mollify, lenify [*rare*], dulcify, dull, take off the edge, blunt, obtund, sheathe, subdue, chasten; sober down, tone down, smooth down, slow down; weaken etc. 160; lessen etc. (*decrease*) 36; check; palliate.

tranquilize, assuage, appease, suage *or* swage [*dial.*], lull, soothe, compose, still, calm, cool, quiet, hush, quell, sober, pacify, tame, damp, lay, allay, rebate [*archaic*], slacken, smooth, alleviate, rock to sleep, deaden, smother; throw cold water on, throw a wet blanket over; slake; curb etc. (*restrain*) 751; tame etc. (*subjugate*) 749; smooth over; pour oil on the -waves, -troubled waters; pour balm into; *mettre de l'eau dans son vin* [*F.*].

go out like a lamb, "roar you as gently as any sucking dove" [*Midsummer Night's Dream*].

adj. **moderate**; lenient etc. 740; gentle, mild; cool, sober, temperate, reasonable, measured; tempered etc. *v.;* calm, laid back [*slang*], unruffled, quiet, tranquil, still; slow, smooth, untroubled; tame; peaceful, peaceable; pacific, halcyon.

unexciting, unirritating; soft, bland, oily, demulcent, lenitive, anodyne; hypnotic etc. 683; sedative, calmative, assuaging, assuasive, calmant; antiorgastic, anaphrodisiac.

mild as mother's milk, mild as milk, milk and water, gentle as a lamb.

adv. **moderately** etc. *adj.;* gingerly; piano; under easy sail, at half speed, in moderation; within bounds, within compass; in reason.

175. Influence

n. **influence**; importance etc. 642; weight, pressure, preponderance, prevalence, sway; predominance, predominancy; ascendancy; dominance, reign; control, domination, pull [*colloq.*]; authority etc. 737; power, potency, capability etc. (*power*) 157; interest; spell, magic, magnetism.

footing; purchase etc. (*support*) 215; play, leverage, vantage ground, advantage.

tower of strength, host in himself; protection, patronage, auspices; patron etc. (*auxiliary*) 711.

v. **have influence** etc. *n.;* be influential etc. *adj.;* carry weight, sway, bias, actuate, weigh, tell; have a hold upon, magnetize, bear upon, gain a footing, work upon; take root, take hold; strike root in.

pervade, run through; spread like wildfire, be rife etc. *adj.;* rage, gain head.

dominate, subject, predominate; outweigh, overweigh; override, overbear; have-, get-, gain- -the upper hand, -full play; prevail.

be recognized, be listened to; make one's voice heard, gain a hearing; play a -part, -leading part- in; lead, control, rule, manage, master, get the mastery of, get control of, make one's influence felt; take the lead, pull strings; wind round one's finger; turn-, throw one's weight into- the scale; set the fashion, lead the dance.

adj. **influential**, effective, effectual [*rare*], potent; important etc. 642; weighty; prevailing etc. *v.;*

prevalent, rife, rampant, dominant, regnant, predominant, in the ascendant, hegemonical; authoritative, recognized, telling.

adv. with telling effect, with authority.

175a. Absence of Influence

n. **impotence** etc. 158; powerlessness; inertness etc. 172; irrelevancy etc. 10.

v. have no influence etc. 175.

adj. **uninfluential**; unconducing [*rare*], nonconductive, unconductive; forceless, powerless etc. 158; irrelevant etc. 10.

176. Tendency

n. **tendency**; aptness, aptitude; proneness, proclivity, bent, turn, tone, bias, set, warp, leaning (*with* to *or* towards), predisposition, inclination, tendence [*rare*], propensity, susceptibility; conatus, conation [*obs.*], nisus; liability etc. 177; quality, nature, temperament; idiocrasy, idiosyncrasy; cast, vein, grain; humor, mood; trend; drift etc. (*direction*) 278; conduciveness, conducement; applicability etc. (*utility*) 644; subservience etc. (*instrumentality*) 631.

v. **tend**, contribute, conduce, lead, influence, dispose, incline, verge, bend to, warp, turn, work towards, trend, affect, carry, redound to, bid fair to, gravitate towards; promote etc. (*aid*) 707.

adj. **tending** etc. *v.;* conative, conducent [*obs.*], conducive, working towards, in a fair way to, likely to, calculated to; liable etc. 177; subservient etc. (*instrumental*) 631; useful etc. 644; subsidiary etc. (*helping*) 707; idiocratic, indiosyncratic, idiosyncratical.

adv. for, whither; for the purpose of.

177. Liability

n. **liability**, liableness; possibility, contingency; susceptivity, susceptiveness, susceptibility.

v. **be liable** etc. *adj.;* incur, lay oneself open to, be subjected to, run the chance, stand a chance; lie under, expose oneself to, open a door to.

adj. **liable**, subject, susceptive; in danger etc. 665; open to, exposed to, obnoxious to; answerable, responsible, accountable, amenable; unexempt from; apt to; dependent on; incident to.

contingent, incidental, possible, on the cards, within range of, at the mercy of.

178. Concurrence

n. **concurrence**, coöperation, coagency; union; coadunation, coaction [*rare*], coworking [*rare*], synergy, collaboration, conformity, conformableness, agreement etc. 23; consilience;

consent etc. (*assent*) 488; alliance; concert etc. 709; partnership etc. 712.

v. **concur**, conduce, conspire, contribute; agree, unite, harmonize, jibe [*colloq.*], coadunate, combine; hang–, pull- together etc. (*coöperate*) 709; help to etc. (*aid*) 707.

keep pace with, run parallel; go with, go along with, go hand in hand with.

adj. **concurring** etc. *v.;* concurrent, conformable, corresponsive [*rare*], joint, coöperative, concomitant, coincident, concordant, harmonious, consentaneous [*archaic*]; coadunate, coadunative, consilient, in alliance with, banded together, of one mind, at one with.

adv. with one consent.

179. Counteraction

n. **counteraction**, opposition; contrariety etc. 14; antagonism, polarity; clashing etc. *v.;* collision, interference, resistance, renitency, friction;

reaction; retroaction etc. (*recoil*) 277; counterblast; neutralization etc. (*compensation*) 30; *vis inertiae* [*L.*]; check etc. (*hindrance*) 706.

voluntary opposition etc. 708; voluntary resistance etc. 719; repression etc. (*restraint*) 751.

v. **counteract**; run counter, clash, cross; interfere with, conflict with; contravene; jostle; go–, run–, beat–, militate- against; stultify; antagonize, frustrate, oppose etc. 708; traverse; overcome, overpower, withstand etc. (*resist*) 719; impede, hinder etc. 706; repress etc. (*restrain*) 751; react etc. (*recoil*) 277.

undo, neutralize, offset, cancel; counterpoise etc. (*compensate*) 30; overpoise.

adj. **counteracting** etc. *v.;* antagonistic, conflicting, retroactive, renitent, reactionary; contrary etc. 14.

adv. **although** etc. 30; against; mauger, malgre [*obs.*], malgrado [*obs.*], notwithstanding; in spite of etc. 708.

Class 2. Space

Section 1. Space in General

180. Space
[indefinite space]

n. **space**, extension, extent, superficial extent, expanse, stretch; room, accommodation, capacity, scope, range, latitude, field, way, expansion, compass, sweep, play, swing, spread.

spare room, elbowroom, houseroom; leeway, seaway, headway, stowage, roomage [*obs.*], tankage, margin; opening, sphere, arena.

open space, free space; void etc. (*absence*) 187; waste, desert, wild; wildness [*obs.*], wilderness; moor, down, downs, upland, moorland; prairie, steppe, llano [*Sp. Amer.*], campagna.

unlimited space; heavens, ether, plenum, infinity etc. 105; world, wide world; ubiquity etc. (*presence*) 186; length and breadth of the land; abyss etc. (*interval*) 198.

proportions, acreage; acres, –roods and perches; square -inches, –yards etc.; ares, arpents.

adj. **spacious**, roomy, extensive, expansive, capacious, ample; widespread, vast, world-wide, wide, far-flung, vasty [*rare*], uncircumscribed; boundless etc. (*infinite*) 105; shoreless, track-

less, pathless; extended; beyond the verge, far as the eye can see.

adv. **extensively** etc. *adj.;* wherever; everywhere; far and -near, –wide; right and left, all over, all the world over; throughout the world, –length and breadth of the land; under the sun, in every quarter; in all -quarters, –lands; here, there, and everywhere; from pole to pole, from China to Peru [Johnson], from Indus to the pole [Pope], from Dan to Beersheba, from end to end; on the face of the earth, in the wide world, on the face of the waters, "from the four corners of the earth" [*Merchant of Venice*], from all points of the compass; to the four winds, to the uttermost parts of the earth.

180a. Inextension

n. **inextension**, nonextension, point, dot, speck, spot, pinprick, tittle; atom etc. (*small, ness*) 32.

181. Region
[definite space]

n. **region**, sphere, ground, soil, area, realm, hemisphere, quarter, orb, circuit, circle; pale etc. (*limit*) 233; compartment, department; clearing; domain, tract, terrain, dominion, colony, commonwealth, territory, country, fatherland, motherland.

canton, county, shire, province, *arrondissement* [*F.*], mofussil [*India*], parish, diocese, township, commune, ward, wapentake [*hist.*], hundred, riding, soke [*hist.*], tithing, bailiwick; principality, duchy, palatinate, archduchy, dukedom, kingdom, empire.

precinct, arena, *enceinte* [*F.*], walk, march, district, beat; patch, plot, inclosure, close, enclave, field, garth, court; street etc. (*abode*) 189; paddock etc. (*inclosure*) 232.

clime, climate, zone, meridian, latitude.

adj. **territorial**, local, parochial, provincial, regional, insular.

ins and outs; every hole and corner.

adv. **somewhere**, in some place, wherever it may be, here and there, in various places, *passim* [*L.*].

182. Place

[limited space]

n. **place**, lieu, spot, whereabouts, point, dot; niche, nook etc. (*corner*) 244; hole; pigeonhole etc. (*receptacle*) 191; compartment; confine, premises, precinct, station; area, courtyard, square, *place* [*F.*], *piazza* [*It.*], *plaza* [*Sp.*], forum [*L.*], agora [*Gr.*], hamlet, village etc. (*abode*) 189; pen etc. (*inclosure*) 232; countryside, location, site, locality etc. (*situation*) 183.

183. Situation

n. **situation**, position, locality, locale (*properly, local*), status, latitude and longitude; footing, standing, standpoint, post; stage; aspect, attitude, posture, set [*colloq.*], pose.

place, site, situs, station, seat, venue, whereabouts, environment, ground; bearings etc. (*direction*) 278; spot etc. (*limited space*) 182.

topography, geography, chorography; map etc. 554.

v. **be situated**, be situate, be located; lie; have its seat in.

adj. **situate**, situated; local, topical, topographical etc. *n.*

adv. *in situ* [*L.*], *in loco* [*L.*]; here and there, *passim* [*L.*]; hereabouts, thereabouts, whereabouts; in place, here, there.

in-, amidst- such and such- -surroundings, -environs, -*entourage* [*F.*].

184. Location

n. **location**, localization; lodgment; deposition, reposition; stowage; collocation; packing, lad-

ing; establishment, settlement, installation; fixation; insertion etc. 300.

anchorage, roadstead, mooring, encampment.

settlement, plantation, colony, cantonment; situation; quarters, barracks; habitation etc. (*abode*) 189; "a local habitation and a name" [*Midsummer Night's Dream*].

domestication, cohabitation, colonization; endenization [*obs.*], naturalization.

v. **place**, situate, locate, localize, make a place for, put, lay, set, seat, station, lodge, quarter, post, install; house, stow; establish, fix, pin, root; graft; plant etc. (*insert*) 300; shelve, pitch, camp, lay down, deposit, reposit, store, store away, cradle; moor, tether, picket; pack, tuck in; embed, imbed; vest, invest in.

billet on, quarter upon, saddle with.

load, lade, stevedore, freight; pocket, put up, bag.

inhabit etc. (*be present*) 186; domesticate, colonize, found, people; take root, strike root; anchor; cast-, come to an- anchor; sit down, settle down; settle; take up one's -abode, -quarters; plant-, establish-, locate- oneself; have one's legal residence at; hang out one's shingle [*colloq.*]; squat, perch, hive, *se nicher* [*F.*], bivouac, burrow, get a footing; encamp, pitch one's tent; put up -at, -one's horses at; keep house.

naturalize, endenizen [*rare*], adopt.

put back, replace etc. (*restore*) 660.

adj. **placed** etc. *v.;* situate, posited, ensconced, imbedded, embosomed, rooted; domesticated; vested in, unremoved.

moored etc. *v.;* at anchor.

185. Displacement

n. **displacement**, elocation [*obs.*], heterotopy, transposition.

ejectment etc. 297; exile etc. (*banishment*) 893.

removal etc. (*transference*) 270; unshipment, transshipment *or* transshipment, unplacement [*rare*], moving, shift.

misplacement, dislocation etc. 61; fish out of water.

v. **displace**, displant, dislodge, disestablish; misplace, unplace [*rare*], translocate [*rare*], unseat, disturb, disniche; exile etc. (*seclude*) 893; ablegate [*obs.*], set aside, remove; take away, cart away; take off, draft off; lade etc. 184.

unload, empty etc. (*eject*) 297; transfer etc. 270; dispel.

vacate; depart etc. 293.

adj. **displaced** etc. *v.;* unplaced, unhoused, unharbored, unestablished, unsettled; houseless, homeless, harborless [*archaic*]; out of place, out of a situation.

misplaced, out of its element.

186. Presence

n. **presence**, presentness, occupancy, occupation; attendance.

permeation, pervasion; diffusion etc. (*dispersion*) 73.

whereness, ubiety, ubiquity, ubiquitariness; omnipresence.

bystander etc. (*spectator*) 444.

v. **be present** etc. *adj.; assister* [*F.*]; make one -of, –at; look on, attend, remain; find–, present-oneself; show one's face; fall in the way of, occur in a place; exist in space, lie, stand; occupy.

inhabit, dwell, reside, stay, sojourn, live, abide, lodge, bunk, room, nestle, roost [*colloq.*], perch; take up one's abode etc. (*be located*) 184; tenant; people.

frequent, resort to, haunt; revisit.

pervade, permeate; be diffused through, be disseminated through; overspread, overrun; fill, run through; meet one at every turn.

adj. **present**; occupying, inhabiting etc. *v.;* moored etc. 184; resiant [*obs.*], resident, residential, residentiary; domiciled.

ubiquitous, ubiquitary; omnipresent; universally present.

peopled, populous, full of people, inhabited.

adv. here, there, where, everywhere, aboard, on board, at home, afield; on the spot; here there and everywhere etc. (*space*) 180; in presence of, before; under the eyes of, under the nose of; in the face of; *in propria persona* [*L.*].

187. Absence

[nullibicity]

n. **nullibicity**, nullibiety [*rare*], absence; awayness [*rare*], cut [*colloq.*]; inexistence etc. 2; nonresidence, absenteeism; nonattendance, alibi.

emptiness etc. *adj.;* void, vacuum; vacuity [*rare*], vacancy, voidness [*rare*], *tabula rasa* [*L.*]; exemption; hiatus etc. (*interval*) 198; lipotype.

truant, absentee.

nobody; nobody -present, -on earth; not a soul; no man, nix [*slang*].

v. **be absent** etc. *adj.;* keep away, keep out of the way; play truant, absent oneself, stay away; slip off, slip out, slip away; keep–, hold- aloof.

withdraw, make oneself scarce [*colloq.*], retreat, retire, vacate; go away etc. 293.

adj. **absent**, not present, away, nonresident, gone, from home; missing; lost; wanting; omitted; nowhere to be found; inexistent etc. 2.

empty, void; vacant, vacuous; blank, null; untenanted, unoccupied, uninhabited; tenantless; desert, deserted; devoid; unhabitable, uninhabitable.

exempt from, not having.

adv. **without**, minus, nowhere; elsewhere; neither here nor there; in default of; sans; behind one's back.

188. Inhabitant

n. **inhabitant**; resident, residentiary; dweller, indweller, habitant [*rare*]; addressee; occupier, occupant; householder, lodger, roomer, inmate, tenant, incumbent, sojourner, *locum tenens* [*L.*], commorant; settler, squatter, backwoodsman, colonist; islander; denizen, citizen; burgher, oppidan, cockney, cit [*colloq.*], townsman, burgess; villager; cottager, cottier, cotter; compatriot; backsettler, boarder; hotel keeper, innkeeper; habitant; paying guest; planter.

native, indigene [*rare*], aborigines, autochthon (*pl.* autochthones), aboriginal; newcomer etc. (*stranger*) 57.

American; Briton, Englishman, Britisher, John Bull; Canadian, Canuck [*slang*]; downeaster; Scot, Scotchman, Scotsman, Caledonian; Hibernian, Irishman, Paddywhack, Paddy, Mick, Teague, Greek *or* Grecian [*slang*]; Welshman, Cambrian, Taffy; Frenchman, Parleyvoo, Frog *or* Froggy [*slang*]; Chinaman, Celestial; Uncle Sam, Yankee, Brother Jonathan.

people etc. (*mankind*) 372; colony, settlement; household; mir [*Russia*]; garrison, crew; population.

v. **inhabit** etc. (*be present*) 186; endenizen [*rare*] etc. (*locate oneself*) 184.

adj. **indigenous**; native, natal; autochthonal, autochthonous; British, English; American; Canadian; Irish, Hibernian; Scotch, Scottish; Welsh, Cambrian; French, Gallic; Chinese, Celestial, Sinaean, Sinaic *or* Sinic [*rare*]; domestic; domiciliated, domiciled; naturalized, vernacular, domesticated; domiciliary; colonial.

occupied by, in the occupation of; garrisoned by.

189. Abode

[place of habitation, or resort]

n. **abode**, dwelling, lodging, domicile, residence, address, habitation, where one's lot is cast, local habitation, berth, diggings [*colloq.*], seat, lap, sojourn, housing, pad [*slang*], quarters, headquarters, resiance [*obs.*], tabernacle, throne, ark.

home, fatherland, motherland, country; homestead, home stall [*Eng.*], fireside; hearth, hearthstone; chimney corner, ingleside; harem, seraglio, zenana; household gods, *lares et penates* [*L.*], roof, household, housing, *dulce domum* [*L.*], paternal domicile; native soil, native land, "God's country," down home [*colloq.*]

quarter, parish etc. (*region*) 181.

retreat, haunt, resort; nest, nidus, snuggery [*colloq.*], arbor, bower etc. 191; lair, den, cave, hole, hiding place, cell, sanctum sanctorum, aerie, eyrie *or* eyry, rookery, hive; habitat, covert, perch, roost; nidification; *kala jagah* [*Hind.*].

camp, bivouac, encampment, cantonment; castrametation; barrack, casemate, casern *or* caserne; tent etc. 223.

tenement, messuage, farm, farmhouse, grange, hacienda [*Sp. Amer.*], toft [*Scot., and dial. Eng.*].

cot, cabin, hut, chalet *or chalet* [*F.*], croft, shed, booth, stall, hovel, bothy *or* boothy, shanty, dugout [*U.S.*], wigwam; pen etc. (*inclosure*) 232; barn, bawn [*obs.*], kennel, sty, doghole, cote, coop, hutch; byre, cowhouse, cowshed, cowbyre; stable, dovecote, columbary, columbarium; shippen [*dial.*]; igloo *or* iglu [*Eskimo*], jacal; lacustrine–, lake–, pile- dwelling; log cabin, log house; shack [*colloq.*], shebang [*slang*], tepee, topek.

house, mansion, place, villa, cottage, box, lodge, hermitage, *rus in urbe* [*L.*], folly, rotunda, tower, *château* [*F.*], castle, pavilion, hotel, court, manor-house, messuage, hall, palace; kiosk, brownstone, bungalow, chummery [*esp. Anglo-Indian*], *casa* [*Sp., Pg. and It.*], country seat; apartment–, frame–, ranch–, shingle- house; duplex, flat, high-rise, tenement; building etc. (*construction*) 161; room, chamber etc. (*receptacle*) 191; buildings, mews.

hamlet, village, bustee *or* basti [*Hind.*], thorp *or* thrope, dorp, kraal [*S. Africa*], rancho [*Sp. Amer.*].

town, borough, burgh, ham [*now used only in compounds*], city, capital, metropolis; suburb; provincial town, county town, county seat; courthouse; ghetto.

street, place, terrace, parade, esplanade, *alameda* [*Sp.*], board walk, embankment, road, row, lane, alley, court, quadrangle, quad [*colloq.*], wynd [*dial.*], close, yard, passage.

square, polygon, circus, crescent, mall, piazza, arcade, colonnade, peristyle, cloister; gardens, grove, residences; block of buildings, market place, *place* [*F.*], plaza.

anchorage, roadstead, roads; dock, basin, wharf, quay, port, harbor.

assembly room, auditorium, concert hall, armory, gymnasium; cathedral, church, chapel, meetinghouse etc. (*temple*) 1000; parliament etc. (*council*) 696.

inn, hostel [*archaic*], hostelry [*archaic*], hotel, tavern, caravansary *or* caravanserai, xenodochium, dak bungalow [*India*], khan, hospice; public house, alehouse, pothouse, mughouse; gin palace; bar, barroom cocktail lounge; cabaret, chophouse; club, clubhouse; cookshop, dive; grill room, saloon, shebeen [*Irish and Scot.*]; coffee-house, eating-house; canteen, restaurant, buffet, café, *estaminet* [*F.*], *posada* [*Sp.*]

almshouse, flophouse, poorhouse, townhouse.

garden, park, pleasure ground, pleasance *or* plaisance [*archaic*], demesne.

sanatorium. health resort, Hill station *or the* Hills [*India*], health retreat, sanitarium, spa, watering-place, pump room.

v. **inhabit** etc. (*be present*) 186; take up one's abode etc. (*locate oneself*) 184.

adj. **urban,** oppidan [*rare*], metropolitan; suburban; provincial, rural, rustic, agrestic, country, countrified, regional; domestic; cosmopolitan; palatial.

190. Contents

[things contained]

n. **contents;** cargo, lading, freight, shipment, load, bale, burden, jag [*Engl. colloq.*]; cartload, shipload; cup of, basket of etc. (*receptacle*) 191; inside etc. 221; stuffing.

v. **load,** lade, ship, charge, weight, pile, fill, stuff.

191. Receptacle

n. **receptacle,** container; inclosure etc. 232; recipient, receiver, reservatory [*obs.*].

compartment; cell, cellule; follicle; hole, corner, niche, recess, nook; crypt, stall, pigeonhole, cove, oriel; cave etc. (*concavity*) 252; mouth.

capsule, vesicle, cyst, pod, calyx, cancelli, utricle, bladder; pericarp, udder.

stomach, paunch, belly, venter, ventricle, ingluvies, crop, craw, maw, gizzard, breadbasket [*slang*], Little Mary [*slang*]; omasum, manyplies, abomasum, rumen, reticulum.

bag, sac, sack, saccule, wallet, pocket, pouch, fob, sheath, scabbard, socket, cardcase, scrip [*archaic*], poke [*chiefly dial.*], knapsack, haversack, satchel, reticule, budget [*dial.*], net; dittybag, –box; housewife *or* hussif; saddlebags; portfolio; quiver etc. (*magazine*) 636.

case, chest, box, coffer, caddy, casket; pyx *or* pix, monstrance [*R. C. Ch.*]; caisson; desk, bureau, reliquary, shrine; trunk, portmanteau, bandbox, valise, grip *or* gripsack [*colloq.*], suitcase, handbag, Boston bag, school bag, brief case, travelingbag, Gladstone *or* Gladstone bag; skippet, vasculum; boot, imperial [*now rare*]; *vache* [*F.*]; cage, manger, rack.

vessel, vase, bushel, barrel; canister, jar; pottle, basket, pannier; buck basket, clothes basket, hopper, maund [*obs.*], creel, cran *or* crane [*Scot.*], crate, cradle, bassinet, whisket *or* wisket [*dial. Eng.*]; *jardinière* [*F.*], corbeille [*F.*], hamper, dosser *or* dorser, tray, hod, scuttle, utensil; brazier; cuspidor, spittoon.

[for liquids] cistern etc. (*store*) 636; vat, caldron *or* cauldron, barrel, cask, puncheon, keg, rundlet, tun, butt, firkin, kilderkin, carboy, amphora, bottle, jar, decanter, ewer, cruse, carafe, crock, kit [*dial. Eng.*], canteen, flagon; demijohn; flask, flasket; stoup *or* stoop, noggin, vial, phial, cruet, caster; urn, epergne, salver, patella, *tazza* [*It.*], patera; piggin; biggin, percolator, coffeepot, coffee urn, teapot, tea urn, samovar; tig *or* tyg [*dial. Eng.*], nipperkin [*now rare*], pocket pistol [*slang*], tub, bucket, pail, skeel [*dial.*], pot, tankard, jug, pitcher, mug, pipkin; gallipot; matrass *or* mattrass, receiver, retort, alembic, bolthead, capsule, can, kettle; bowl, basin, jorum [*colloq.*], punch bowl, cup, goblet, chalice, tumbler, glass, rummer, horn, saucepan, skillet, posnet [*obs.*], tureen, stein.

bail, beaker, billy [*Australia*], cannikin *or* canakin; catch basin, catch drain; chatti *or* chatty [*India*], lota *or* lotah [*India*], mussuk *or* mussuck [*India*]; schooner, spider, terrine, toby, urceus [*L.*].

plate, platter, dish, trencher, calabash, porringer, potager [*obs.*], saucer, pan, crucible; glassware, tableware; vitrics.

ladle, dipper, tablespoon, spoon; shovel, trowel, spatula.

cupboard, closet, commode, cellaret, chiffonier *or* chiffonnier, *chiffonnière* [*F.*], locker, bin, bunker, buffet, press, clothespress, safe, sideboard, drawer, chest of drawers, till, escritoire, scrutoire [*obs.*], secretary, *secrétaire* [*F.*], dav-

enport, bookcase, cabinet, canterbury; *étagère* [*F.*], vargueno, vitrine.

chamber, apartment, room, cabin; office, court, hall, atrium; suite of rooms, apartment, flat, story; saloon, *salon* [*F.*], parlor; by-room, cubicle; presence chamber; living–, sitting–, drawing–, reception–, state-room; best room [*colloq.*], keeping room [*dial. Eng.*]; gallery, cabinet, closet; pew, box; boudoir; adytum, sanctum; bedroom, dormitory; refectory, dining room, *salle-à-manger* [*F.*]; nursery, schoolroom; library, study; studio; billiard room, bathroom, lavatory, toilet, powder room, smoking room; den; state room, tablinum, tenement.

attic, loft, garret, cockloft, clerestory; cellar, vault, hold, cockpit; cubbyhole; cook house; *entre-sol* [*F.*]; mezzanine *or* mezzanine floor; ground floor, *rez-de-chaussée* [*F.*], basement, kitchen, pantry, *bawarchi-khana* [*Hind.*], scullery, offices; storeroom etc. (*depository*) 636; lumber room; dairy, laundry, coach house; garage; hangar; outhouse, penthouse; lean-to.

portico, porch, stoop [*U.S.*], veranda, lobby, court, hall, vestibule, corridor, passage; anteroom, antechamber; lounge; piazza [= veranda, *U.S.*].

bower, arbor, summerhouse, alcove, grotto, hermitage; conservatory, greenhouse.

lodging etc. (*abode*) 189; bed etc. (*support*) 215.

carriage etc. (*vehicle*) 272.

adj. capsular; saccular, sacculated; recipient; ventricular, cystic, vascular, vesicular, cellular, camerated, locular, multilocular, polygastric; gastric, stomachic, gasteral [*rare*]; marsupial; siliquose, siliquous.

Section 2. Dimensions

192. Size

n. **size,** magnitude, dimension, bulk, volume; largeness etc. *adj.*; greatness etc. (*of quantity*) 31; expanse etc. (*space*) 180; amplitude, mass; proportions.

capacity; tonnage *or* tunnage; cordage; caliber *or* calibre; scantling [*obs.*].

corpulence, obesity; plumpness etc. *adj.*; *embonpoint* [*F.*], corporation [*colloq.*], flesh and blood, lustihood; turgidity etc. (*expansion*) 194.

hugeness etc. *adj.*; enormity, immensity; monstrosity.

giant, Brobdingnagian, Antaeus, Goliath, Polyphemus, Colossus, Titan, Titaness, Briareus,

Norn, Hercules, Cyclops, Gog and Magog, Gargantua, King Kong; monster, mammoth, cachalot, whale, porpoise, behemoth, leviathan, elephant, jumbo, hippopotamus; colossus.

lump, bulk, block, loaf, mass, swad [*slang*], clod, nugget, tun, cord, bushel; thumper [*slang*], whopper *or* whapper [*colloq.*], spanker [*slang*], strapper [*slang*]; "Triton among the minnows" [*Coriolanus*].

mountain, mound; heap etc. (*assemblage*) 72.

full-size, life-size; largest portion etc. 50.

v. **be large** etc. *adj.;* become large etc. (*expand*) 194.

adj. **large**, big; great etc. (*in quantity*) 31; considerable, bulky, voluminous, ample, massive, massy; capacious, comprehensive, spacious etc. 180; mighty, towering, fine, magnificent.

stout, corpulent, fat, plump, squab, full, lusty, strapping [*colloq.*], bouncing; portly, burly, well-fed, full-grown; corn-fed, gram-fed [*Anglo-Ind.*]; stalwart, brawny, fleshy; goodly; in good -case, –condition; in condition, in shape; chopping, jolly; club-faced [*obs.*], chubby-faced.

large as life; plump as a -dumpling, –partridge; fat as -a pig, –a quail, –butter, –brawn, –bacon [*all colloq.*].

hulky, hulking, unwieldy, lumpish, lubberly, gaunt, spanking [*slang.*], whacking [*colloq.*], whopping [*colloq.*], thumping [*colloq.*], thundering [*colloq.*], overgrown; puffy etc. (*swollen*) 194.

huge, immense, enormous, titanic, mighty; vast, vasty [*archaic*]; stupendous; monster, monstrous; gigantic; elephantine; giant, giantlike; colossal, Cyclopean, Brobdingnagian, Gargantuan; infinite etc. 105.

193. Littleness

n. **littleness** etc. *adj.;* smallness etc. (*of quantity*) 32; exiguity, inextension; parvitude [*rare*], parvity [*obs.*]; duodecimo; epitome; microcosm; rudiment; vanishing point; thinness etc. 203.

dwarf, pygmy *or* pigmy, Liliputian, Negrito, Negrillo; chit, fingerling [*rare*], Pigwiggen, pigwidgeon [*rare*], urchin, elf; atomy, dandiprat [*archaic*], doll, puppet; Tom Thumb, hop-o'-my-thumb; manikin *or* mannikin; micromorph [*rare*], homunculus, dapperling.

mite, insect, arthropod, ephemerid, ephemera, bug [*pop.*], larva, emmet, fly, midge, gnat, shrimp, minnow, worm, maggot, grub; tit, tomtit, runt, mouse, small fry; millet seed, mustard seed; barleycorn; pebble, grain of sand; molehill, button, bubble.

atom, monad, animalcule, animalculum (*pl.* animalcula), diatom, dyad, triad, tetrad, pentad, hexad, heptad, octad, molecule, microbe, germ, microörganism, bacterium (*pl.* bacteria), microphyte, microzyme, amoeba, microzoa, entozoön (*pl.* entozoa), phytozoaria, infusoria.

particle etc. (*small quantity*) 32; point, micron; scintilla; fragment etc. (*small part*) 51; powder etc. 330; point of a pin, mathematical point; minutiae etc. (*unimportance*) 643.

micrography; micrometer, microscope, interferometer, vernier; scale.

v. **be little** etc. *adj.;* lie in a nutshell; become small etc. (*decrease*) 36, (*contract*) 195.

adj. **little**; small etc. (*in quantity*) 32; minute, diminutive, microscopic; inconsiderable etc. (*unimportant*) 643; exiguous, puny, runty, tiny, wee [*colloq.*], petty, minikin [*obs.*], miniature, pygmy *or* pigmy, elfin; undersized; dwarf, dwarfed, dwarfish; spare, stunted, limited; cramp, cramped; pollard, Liliputian, Negritic, dapper, pocket; portative, portable; duodecimo; dumpy, squat; short etc. 201.

impalpable, intangible, evanescent, imperceptible, invisible, inappreciable, infinitesimal, homeopathic; rudimentary, rudimental; embryonic, vestigial.

animalcular, amoebic, amoeboid, diatomaceous, diatomic, microzoal, microbial, microbic, molecular, atomic, corpuscular.

scant, weazen [*obs.*], scraggy, scrubby; thin etc. (*narrow*) 203; granular etc. (*powdery*) 330; shrunk etc. 195; brevipennate.

adv. in a small compass, in a nutshell; on a small scale.

194. Expansion

n. **expansion**, dilation, expansibleness; increase etc. 35 -of size; enlargement, extension, augmentation; amplification, ampliation; aggrandizement, spread, increment, growth, development, pullulation [*rare*], swell, dilatation, rarefaction; turgescence *or* turgescency, turgidness, turgidity; dispansion [*obs.*]; obesity etc. (*size*) 192; hydrocephalus, hydrophthalmus; dropsy, tumefaction, intumescence, swelling, tumor, diastole, distension; puffing, puffiness; inflation; pandiculation.

dilatability, expansibility.

growth, upgrowth; accretion etc. 35; germination, budding, gemmation.

bulb etc. (*convexity*) 250; plumper; superiority of size.

overgrowth, overdistension; hypertrophy, tympany.

v. **become larger** etc. (large etc. 192); expand, widen, enlarge, extend, grow, increase, incrassate, swell, gather; fill out; deploy, take open order, dilate, stretch, spread; mantle, wax; grow up, spring up; bud, burgeon *or* bourgeon, shoot, sprout, germinate, put forth, vegetate, pullulate, open, burst forth; gain flesh, gather flesh; outgrow; spread like wildfire, overrun.

be larger than; surpass etc. (*be superior*) 33.

render larger etc. (large etc. 192); expand, spread, extend, aggrandize, distend, develop, amplify, spread out, widen, magnify, rarefy, inflate, puff, blow up, stuff, pad, cram, bloat; exaggerate; fatten.

adj. **expanded** etc. *v.;* larger etc. (large etc. 192); swollen; expansive; wide open, widespread; fan-shaped, flabelliform; overgrown, exaggerated, bloated, fat, turgid, tumid, hypertrophied, dropsical; pot-bellied, swagbellied [*obs.*]; edematous, corpulent, obese, puffy, pursy, blowzy, distended; patulous; bulbous etc. (*convex*) 250; full-blown, full-grown, full-formed; big etc. 192; abdominous, enchymatous, rhipidate; tumefacient, tumefying.

195. Contraction

n. **contraction**, reduction, diminution; decrease etc. 36 -of size; defalcation, decrement; lessening, shrinking etc. *v.;* compaction [*rare*], tabes, collapse, emaciation, attenuation, tabefaction [*rare*], consumption, marasmus, atrophy; systole, syncopation, syncope; neck, hourglass.

compression, condensation, constraint, astriction [*rare*], compactness; compendium etc. 596; squeezing etc. *v.;* strangulation; corrugation; constringency, astringency; astringents, sclerotics; contractibility, contractibleness, contractility, compressibility, compressibleness, coarctation.

inferiority in size.

v. **become small**, become smaller; lessen, decrease etc. 36; grow less, dwindle, shrink, contract, narrow, shrivel, syncopate, collapse, wither, lose flesh, wizen [*dial.*], fall away, waste, wane, ebb; decay etc. (*deteriorate*) 659.

be smaller than, fall short of; not come up to etc. (*be inferior*) 34.

render smaller, lessen, diminish, contract, draw in, narrow, pucker, cockle, coarct *or* coarctate [*rare*]; boil down; deflate, exhaust, empty; constrict, constringe; condense, compress, squeeze, corrugate, crush, crumple up, warp, purse, purse up, pack, stow; pinch, tighten, strangle;

cramp; dwarf, bedwarf; shorten etc. 201; circumscribe etc. 229; restrain etc. 751.

pare, reduce, attenuate, rub down, scrape, file, grind, chip, shave, shear.

adj. **contracting** etc. *v.;* astringent, constringent, shrunk, shrunken, tabescent, tabetic, contractible, contracted etc. *v.;* strangulated, tabid, wizened, weazen, weazeny [*colloq.*], corky, stunted; waning etc. *v.;* neap, compact, compacted.

unexpanded etc. (expand etc. 194); contractile; compressible; smaller etc. (small etc. 193).

196. Distance

n. **distance**; space etc. 180; remoteness, farness; far cry to; longinquity [*rare*], elongation; easting, westing, drift, offing, background; remote region; removedness; parallax; reach, span, stride.

outpost, outskirt; horizon, sky line; aphelion; foreign parts, *ultima Thule* [*L.*], *ne plus ultra* [*L.*], antipodes; jumping-off place [*colloq.*], long range, giant's stride.

dispersion etc. 73.

v. **be distant** etc. *adj.;* extend to, stretch to, reach to, spread to, go to, get to, stretch away to; range, outreach, outlie [*rare*].

remain at a distance; keep–, stand--away, –off, –aloof, –clear of.

adj. **distant**; far off, far away; remote, telescopic, distal, wide of; stretching to etc. *v.;* yon, yonder; ulterior; transmarine, transpontine, transatlantic, transpacific, transoceanic, transalpine; tramontane; ultramontane, ultramundane; hyperborean, antipodean; inaccessible, out-of-the-way, God-forsaken [*colloq.*]; unapproached, unapproachable; incontiguous [*obs.*].

adv. **far off**, far away; afar, –off; off; away; a -long, –great, –good- way off; wide away, beyond range, aloof; wide of, clear of; out of -the way, –reach; abroad, yonder, farther, further, beyond; *outre mer* [*F.*], over the border, far and wide, "over the hills and far away" [Gay]; from pole to pole etc. (*over great space*) 180; to the -uttermost parts, –ends- of the earth; out of range, out of hearing, nobody knows where, *à perte de vue* [*F.*], out of the sphere of, wide of the mark; a far cry to.

apart, asunder; wide apart, wide asunder; *longo intervallo* [*L.*]; at arm's length.

197. Nearness

n. **nearness** etc. *adj.;* proximity, propinquity; vicinity, vicinage; neighborhood, adjacency, nigh-ness [archaic], appropinquity [rare]; contiguity etc. 199.

short -distance, −step, −cut; earshot, close quarters, range, stone's throw; bowshot, gunshot, pistol shot; hair's breadth, span.

purlieus, neighborhood, vicinage, environs, *alentours* [*F.*], suburbs, *faubourg* [*F.*], confines, *banlieue* [*F.*], borderland; whereabouts.

bystander, spectator; neighbor *or* neighbour, borderer.

approach etc. 286; convergence etc. 290; perihelion.

v. **be near** etc. *adj.;* adjoin, abut, neighbor, hang about, trench on; border upon, verge upon; stand by, approximate, tread on the heels of, cling to, clasp, hug; huddle; hang upon the skirts of, hover over; burn [*colloq.*].

bring *or* draw near etc. 286; converge etc. 290; crowd etc. 72; place side by side etc. *adv.*

adj. **near**, nigh; close−, near- at hand; close, neighboring, vicinal, propinquent [rare]; bordering upon, contiguous, adjacent, adjoining; proximate, proximal; at hand, warm [*colloq.*], handy; near the mark, near run; home, intimate.

adv. **near**, nigh; hard by, fast by; close to, close upon; hard upon; at the point of; next door to; within -reach, - call, −hearing, −earshot, −range; within an ace of; but a step, not far from, at no great distance; on the -verge, −brink, −skirts- of; in the environs etc. *n.;* at one's -door, −feet, −elbow, −finger's end, −side; on the tip of one's tongue; under one's nose; within a stone's throw etc. *n.;* in sight of, in presence of; at close quarters; cheek by jowl, cheek to cheek, shoulder to shoulder; beside, alongside, side by side, *tête-à-tête* [*F.*]; in juxtaposition etc. (*touching*) 199; yardarm to yardarm; at the heels of; on the confines of, at the threshold, bordering upon, verging to; in the way.

about; hereabout *or* hereabouts, thereabout *or* thereabouts; roughly, in round numbers; approximately, approximatively; as good as, wellnigh.

198. Interval

n. **interval**, interspace; separation etc. 44; hiatus, caesura; interruption, interregnum; interstice, intersection, lacuna.

parenthesis etc. (*interjacence*) 228; void etc. (*absence*) 187; incompleteness etc. 53.

cleft, break, gap, opening; hole etc. 260; chasm, mesh, crevice, chink, rime [rare], creek, cranny, crack, chap, slit, fissure, scissure, rift, fault,

flaw, breach, fracture, rent, gash, cut, leak, dike, ha-ha.

gorge, defile, ravine, cañon, crevasse, abyss, abysm; gulf; inlet, frith, strait, gully, nullah [*India*]; pass; furrow etc. 259; *abra* [*Sp. Amer.*], barranco [*Sp.*]; clove, gulch, notch, yawning gulf; *hiatus maxime deflendus* [*L.*], *hiatus valde deflendus* [*L.*].

v. **gape** etc. (*open*) 260; separate etc. 44.

adj. with an interval, far between; breachy, rimose, rimous, rimulose.

adv. **at intervals** etc. (*discontinuously*) 70; *longo intervallo* [*L.*].

199. Contiguity

n. **contiguity**, contiguousness, contact, proximity, apposition, abuttal, juxtaposition, touching etc. *v.;* abutment, osculation; meeting, appulse, appulsion, *rencontre* [*F.*], rencounter, syzygy, conjunction, conjugation, coincidence, coexistence; adhesion etc. 46.

borderland; frontier etc. (*limit*) 233; tangent; abutter.

v. **be contiguous** etc. *adj.;* join, adjoin, abut on, neighbor, border, march with; graze, touch, meet, osculate, come in contact, coincide; coexist; adhere etc. 46.

adj. **contiguous**; touching etc. *v.;* in contact etc. *n.;* conterminous, end to end, osculatory; pertingent [*obs.*]; tangential.

hand to hand; close to etc. (*near*) 197; with no interval etc. 198.

200. Length

n. **length**, longitude, longness [rare], extent, span; mileage.

line, bar, rule, stripe, streak, spoke, radius.

lengthening etc. *v.;* prolongation, production, protraction; tension, tensure [*obs.*]; extension.

[measures of length] line, nail, inch, hand, palm, foot, cubit, yard, ell, fathom, rood, pole, furlong, mile, knot, league; chain; arpent, handbreadth, *jornada* [*Sp. Amer.*], kos [*Hind.*], vara [*Sp. & Pg.*]; meter, kilometer, centimeter etc.

pedometer, odometer, odograph, viameter, viatometer, log [*naut.*], speedometer, telemeter, perambulator; scale etc. (*measurement*) 466.

v. **be long** etc. *adj.;* stretch out, sprawl; extend to, reach to, stretch to; make a long arm, "drag its slow length along" [Pope].

render long etc. *adj.;* lengthen, extend, elongate; stretch; prolong, produce [rare], protract; let out, draw out, spin out; drawl.

enfilade, look along, view in perspective.

adj. **long**, longsome [*archaic*]; elongate *or* elongated, longish, lengthy, wiredrawn, outstretched, extended; lengthened etc. *v.;* sesquipedalian etc. (*words*) 577; interminable, no end of [*colloq.*].

linear, lineal; longitudinal, oblong.

lanky, lank, slabsided [*slang*], rangy; tall etc. 206; macrocolous, long-limbed.

as long as -my arm, –to-day and to-morrow; unshortened etc. (shorten etc. 201).

adv. **lengthwise**, at length, longitudinally, endlong [*archaic*], endways, endwise, along; tandem; in a line etc. (*continuously*) 69; in perspective.

from end to end, from stem to stern, from head to foot, from the crown of the head to the sole of the foot, from tip to toe, from top to toe; fore and aft; over all.

201. Shortness

n. **shortness** etc. *adj.;* brevity littleness etc. 193; a span.

shortening etc. *v.;* abbreviation, abbreviature [*obs.*], abridgment, concision, retrenchment, curtailment, decurtation [*obs.*], epitomization, obtruncation [*rare*], condensation; reduction etc. (*contraction*) 195; epitome etc. (*compendium*) 596.

elision, ellipsis; conciseness etc. (*in style*) 572.

abridger, epitomist, epitomizer, obtruncator [*rare*].

v. **be short** etc. *adj.;* **render short** etc. *adj.;* shorten, curtail, abridge, abbreviate, take in, reduce; compress etc. (*contract*) 195; epitomize etc. 596.

cut short, retrench, obtruncate [*rare*], scrimp, cut, chop up, hack, hew; cut down, pare down; clip, dock, lop, prune, shear, shave, mow, reap, crop; snub; truncate, pollard, stunt, nip, check the growth of; foreshorten [*drawing*].

adj. **short**, brief, curt; compendious, compact; stubby, pudgy, tubby [*colloq.*], squatty, squidgy [*rare*], scrimp; shorn, stubbed; stumpy [*colloq.*], thickset, pug; chunky, curtate, curtal [*archaic*], decurtate; *retroussé* [*F.*], turned up; scrub, stocky; squab, squabby; squat, squattish, dumpy; little etc. 193; curtailed of its fair proportions; short by; oblate; abbreviatory; concise etc. 572; summary.

adv. **shortly** etc. *adj.;* in short etc. (*concisely*) 572.

202. Breadth, Thickness

n. **breadth**, width, latitude, amplitude; diameter, bore, caliber, radius; superficial extent etc. (*space*) 180.

thickness, crassitude [*obs.*]; corpulence etc. (*size*) 192; dilatation etc. (*expansion*) 194.

v. **be broad** etc. *adj.;* become *or* render broad etc. *adj.;* expand etc. 194; thicken, widen, calibrate.

adj. **broad**, wide, ample, extended; discous, discoid; fanlike; outspread, outstretched; "wide as a church-door" [*Romeo and Juliet*]; latifoliate [*rare*], latifolious [*rare*].

thick, dumpy, squab, squat, thickset, stubby etc. 201; thick as a rope.

203. Narrowness, Thinness

n. **narrowness** etc. *adj.;* closeness, exility [*rare*]; exiguity etc. (*little*) 193.

line; hair's-, finger's- breadth; strip, streak, vein.

thinness etc. *adj.;* tenuity; emaciation, marcor [*obs.*], macilence *or* macilency [*rare*].

shaving, slip etc. (*filament*) 205; thread paper, skeleton, shadow, scrag, atomy [*obs. or joc.*], anatomy, [*archaic*], study in anatomy [*humorous*], spindle-shanks [*humorous or contemptuous*], bare-bone, lantern jaws, mere skin and bone.

middle constriction, stricture, coarctation [*med.*]; neck, waist, isthmus, wasp, hourglass; ridge, ghat *or* ghaut [*India*], pass; ravine etc. 198.

narrowing, angustation, tapering; contraction etc. 195.

v. be narrow etc. *adj.;* narrow, taper, contract, etc. 195; render narrow etc. *adj.*

adj. **narrow**, close; slender, gracile, thin, fine; threadlike etc. (*filament*) 205; finespun, taper, slim, slight-made; scant, scanty; spare, delicate, incapacious; contracted etc. 195; unexpanded etc. (*expand* etc. 194); slender as a thread.

lean, emaciated, meager *or* meagre, gaunt, macilent; lank, lanky; weedy [*colloq.*], skinny; scrawny, slinky [*dial.*]; starved, starveling; attenuated, shriveled, pinched, poor, peaked [*colloq.*], lathy [*colloq.*], skeletal, flatsided [*colloq.*], slabsided [*slang*]; spindle-legged, spindle-shanked, spindling; coarctate, angustate, tabic, tabelic, tabid, extenuated, marcid [*obs.*], rawboned; herring-gutted [*colloq.*]; worn to a shadow, "lean as a rake" [Chaucer]; thin as a -lath, –whipping post, –wafer; hatchet-faced; lantern-jawed.

204. Layer

n. **layer**, stratum, course, bed, couch, coping, zone, substratum, floor, flag, stage, story, tier, slab, escarpment; table, tablet; dess [*Scot. & dial. Eng.*]; flagstone; board, plank; trencher, platter.

leaf, lamina, lamella, sheet, flake, foil, wafer, scale, coat, peel, pellicle, membrane, film, lap, ply, slice, shive, cut, rasher, shaving, plate; overlay, integument etc. (*covering*) 223; eschar.

stratification, lamination, delamination, foliation; scaliness, nest of boxes, coats of an onion.

v. **slice**, shave, pare, peel, skive; delaminate; plate, coat, veneer; cover etc. 223.

adj. **lamellar**, lamelliferous, lamellate *or* lamellated, lamelliform; laminate *or* laminated, laminiferous; micaceous; schistose, schistous; scaly, filmy, membranous, membranaceous, flaky, squamous; foliated, foliaceous; stratified, stratiform; tabular, discoid; spathic, spathose.

205. Filament

n. **filament**, line; fiber, fibril; funicle, vein, hair, cobweb, capillary, ciliolum, capillament [*rare*], cilium, cirrus, barbel, strand, tendril, gossamer; hair stroke; veinlet, venula, venule.
beard etc. (*roughness*) 256; ramification.

thread, threadlet, harl, yarn, pack-thread, cotton, sewing silk.

string, twine, twist, whipcord, cord, rope, hemp, oakum, jute; tape, ribbon, wire.

strip, shred, slip, spill, list, taenia *or* tenia, band, fillet, fascia; ribbon, ribband *or* riband [*archaic*], roll, lath, splinter, shiver, shaving; ligule *or* ligula.

adj. **filamentous**, filamentiferous, filaceous [*rare*], filiform; fibrous, fibrillous, fibrilliform, fibrilliferous; thread-like, wiry, stringy, ropy; capillary, capilliform; funicular, wire-drawn; anguilliform; flagelliform; barbate, hairy etc. (*rough*) 256; taeniate, taeniform, taenioid; venose, venous; ligulate *or* ligulated.

206. Height

n. **height**, altitude, elevation; eminence, pitch; loftiness etc. *adj.;* sublimity, celsitude [*rare*].

tallness etc. *adj.;* stature, procerity [*rare*]; prominence etc. 250; apex, zenith, culmination.

colossus etc. (*size*) 192; giant, grenadier; giraffe, camelopard.

height, mount, mountain; hill, *alto* [*Sp.*], butte, monticule, monticle [*obs.*], fell [*obs. exc. in proper names*], knap; cape; headland, foreland; promontory; ridge, hogback *or* hog's-back, dune, rising-, vantage- ground; down; moor, moorland; Alp; uplands, highlands; heights etc. (*summit*), 210; knob, *loma, pena, picacho* [*Sp.*], tump [*dial.*]; knoll, hummock, hillock, barrow, mound; steeps, bluff, cliff, craig

[*Scot.*], tor, peak, pike [*dial.*], clough [*obs.*]; escarpment, edge, ledge, brae [*Scot. & dial. Eng.*]; dizzy height.

tower, pillar, column, obelisk, monument, belfry, steeple, spire, minaret, campanile, turret, dome, cupola; pylon, *tourelle* [*F.*], barbican, martello tower; pyramid, pagoda, mole [*Rom. antiq.*],
ceiling etc. (*covering*) 223; upstairs.

pole, pikestaff, maypole, flagstaff; mast, mainmast, topmast, topgallant mast.

high water; high-, flood-, spring-tide.

hypsography, hypsometry, hypsometer, altimeter, altimetry etc. (*angle*) 244; hypsophobia.

v. **be high** etc. *adj.;* tower, soar, command; hover; cap, culminate; overhang, hang over, impend, beetle; bestride, ride, mount; perch, surmount; cover etc. 223; rise above, overtop etc. (*be superior*) 33; stand on tiptoe.

become high etc. *adj.;* grow, grow higher, grow taller; upgrow; rise etc. (*ascend*) 305.

render high etc. *adj.;* heighten etc. (*elevate*) 307.

adj. **high**, elevated, eminent, exalted, lofty; tall; gigantic etc. (*big*) 192; Patagonian; towering, beetling, soaring, mountained, hanging [gardens]; elevated etc. 307; higher, superior, upper, supernal; highest etc. (*topmost*) 210; high-reaching, insessorial, perching; hill-dwelling, monticoline, monticolous.

tall as a -maypole, –popular, –steeple; lanky etc. (*thin*) 203.

upland, moorland; hilly, knobby; mountainous, alpine, subalpine, heaven-kissing; cloud-topt, cloud-capt, cloud-touching; aërial.

overhanging etc. *v.;* incumbent; overlying; superincumbent, supernatant, superimposed; prominent etc. 250.

hypsographic, hypsographical, hypsometric, hypsometrical.

adv. **on high**, high up, aloft, up, above, aloof, overhead; airward; upstairs, above stairs; in the clouds; on tiptoe, on stilts, on the shoulders of; over head and ears; breast high.

over, upwards; from top to bottom etc. (*completely*) 52.

207. Lowness

n. **lowness** etc. *adj.;* debasement; prostration etc. (*horizontal*) 213; depression etc. (*concave*) 252; subjacency; lowlands.

ground floor; *rez de chaussée* [*F.*]; street floor.

basement, basement floor, cellar; hold; base etc. 211.

[comparison] feet, heels; molehill.

low water; low–, ebb–, neap- tide.

v. **be low** etc. *adj.;* lie low, lie flat; underlie; crouch, slouch, wallow, grovel; lower etc. (*depress*) 308.

adj. **low**, neap, debased; lower, inferior, under, nether; lowest, nether-most, lowermost; flat, level with the ground; lying low etc. *v.;* crouched, subjacent, squat, prostrate etc. (*horizontal*) 213; depressed.

adv. **under**; beneath, underneath; below; down, downwards; adown, at the foot of; underfoot, underground; downstairs, belowstairs; at a low ebb; below par.

208. Depth

n. **depth**; deepness etc. *adj.;* profundity, depression etc. (*concavity*) 252.

pit, shaft, hollow, well, crater; gulf etc. 198; deep, abyss, bowels of the earth, bottomless pit, hell.

soundings, depth of water, water, draft *or* draught, submersion; plummet, sound, probe; sounding-rod, –line; lead; bathometer, bathymeter, bathymetry; benthos; submarine, sub [*colloq.*], U-boat; depth bomb.

v. **be deep** etc. *adj.;* render deep etc. *adj.;* deepen.

sound, heave the lead, take soundings; dig etc. (*excavate*) 252; plunge etc. 310.

adj. **deep**, deep-seated, deep-bosomed; profound, sunk, buried; submerged etc. 310; subaqueous, submarine, subterranean, subterrene [*obs.*], subterraneous; underground.

knee-deep, ankle-deep.

bottomless, soundless, fathomless; unfathomed, unfathomable; abysmal; deep as a well; bathycolpian *or* bathukolpic *or* bathukolpian; deep-sea, benthal, benthopelagic; bathymetric, bathymetrical; bathypelagic, bathysmal; down-reaching, yawning.

adv. **out of one's depth**; beyond one's depth; over head and ears.

209. Shallowness

n. **shallowness** etc. *adj.;* shoals; mere scratch.

adj. **shallow**, slight, superficial; skin–, ankle–, knee-deep; depthless, just enough to wet one's feet; shoal, shoaly.

210. Summit

n. **summit**, top, vertex, apex, summit [*obs.*], zenith, pinnacle, acme, culmination, meridian, utmost height, *ne plus ultra* [*L.*], height, pitch, maximum, climax; culminating–, crowning–, turning- point; turn of the tide, fountainhead; watershed, water parting; sky, pole.

tip, tiptoe; crest, crow's nest, cap, truck, peak, nib; end etc. 67; crown, brow; head, nob [*slang*], noddle [*colloq.*], pate [*humorous*]; capsheaf.

high places, heights.

topgallant mast, skyscraper; quarter deck, hurricane deck.

architrave, frieze, cornice, corona, coping, coping stone, zoöphorus, capital, headpiece, capstone, fastigium, larmier, epistyle, sconce, pediment, entablature; tympanum; ceiling etc. (*covering*) 223.

attic, loft, garret, housetop, upper story, roof.

v. **crown**, top, cap, crest, surmount; overtop etc. (*be superior to*) 33; culminate.

adj. **highest** etc. (high etc. 206); top; topmost, overmost, uppermost; tiptop; culminating etc. *v.;* meridian, meridional; capital, head, polar, supreme, supernal, apical, culminate [*rare*], culminal [*rare*], topgallant, skyward.

adv. **atop**, at the top of the tree; *en flûte* [*F.*]; *à fleur d'eau* [*F.*].

211. Base

n. **base**, basement; plinth, dado, wainscot; baseboard, mopboard; bedrock, hardpan; foundation etc. (*support*) 215; substructure, substratum, ground, earth, pavement, floor, paving, flag, carpet, ground floor, deck; footing, ground work, basis; hold, bilge, sump; cullet.

bed, basin, channel, coulee [*Western N. Amer.*], cañon etc. (*interval*) 198.

bottom, nadir, foot, sole, toe, hoof, keel, root; centerboard.

adj. **bottom**, undermost, nethermost; fundamental; founded on, based on, grounded on, built on.

212. Verticality

n. **verticality**; erectness etc. *adj.;* perpendicularity, aplomb; right angle, normal; azimuth circle.

cliff, steep, crag, bluff, palisades; wall, precipice.

elevation, erection; square, plumb line, plummet.

v. **be vertical** etc. *adj.;* stand -up, –on end, –erect, –upright; stick up, cock up.

render vertical etc. *adj.;* set up, stick up, raise up, cock up; erect, rear, raise, pitch, raise on its legs.

adj. **vertical**, upright, erect, perpendicular, unrecumbent [*rare*], plumb, normal, straight, bolt upright; rampant; straight up; standing up etc. *v.;* rectangular orthogonal.

adv. **vertically** etc. *adj.;* up, on end; up–, right- on end; *à plomb* [*F.*], endwise; on one's legs; at right angles.

213. Horizontality

n. **horizontality**; flatness; level, plane; stratum etc. 204; dead level, dead flat; level plane.

recumbency; lying down etc. *v.;* reclination, decumbence *or* decumbency, discumbency [*obs.*]; proneness etc. *adj.;* accubation, supination, resupination, prostration; azimuth.

[level surfaces] plain, floor, platform, bowling green; cricket ground; croquet -ground, –lawn; billiard table, pool table; terrace, estrade [*rare*], esplanade, parterre, table-land, plateau, ledge.

v. **be horizontal** etc. *adj.;* lie, recline, couch; lie -down, –flat, –prostrate; sprawl, loll; sit down.

render horizontal etc. *adj.;* lay, lay down, lay out; level, flatten, even, raze, equalize, smooth, align.

prostrate, knock down, floor, fell, ground, drop, grass [*slang*]; cut–, hew–, mow- down.

adj. **horizontal**, level, even, plane, flush; flat etc. 251; flat as a -billiard table, –bowling green, –pool table, –pancake; alluvial; calm, –as a mill pond; smooth, –as glass.

recumbent, procumbent, accumbent, decumbent [*bot.*]; lying etc. *v.;* prone, supine, couchant, jacent [*rare*], prostrate, recubant [*rare*], resupinate.

adv. **horizontally** etc. *adj.;* on one's back, on all fours, on its beam ends.

214. Pendency

n. **pendency**, dependency; suspension, hanging etc. *v.*

pendant, drop, eardrop, tassel, tippet, lobe, tail, train, flap, skirt, queue, pigtail, pendulum; hangnail.

peg, knob, button, hook, nail, stud, ring, staple, tenterhook; fastening etc. 45; spar, horse.

chandelier, gaselier, electrolier.

v. **be pendent** etc. *adj.;* hang, depend, swing, dangle, lower, droop: swag [*dial.*]; daggle, flap, trail, flow; beetle, jut, overhang.

suspend, hang, sling, hook up, hitch, fasten to, append.

adj. **pendent**, pendulous, pendulant [*rare*], decumbent, penduline [*rare*], pensile; hanging etc. *v.;* beetle; beetling, jutting over, overhanging, projecting; dependent; lowering; suspended etc. *v.;* loose, flowing.

having a pendant etc. *n.;* tailed, caudate.

215. Support

n. **support**, ground, foundation, base, basis; *terra firma* [*L.*], bearing, fulcrum, bait, caudex, crib;

point d'appui [*F.*], *pou sto* [*Gr.*], purchase, footing, hold, *locusstandi* [*L.*]; landing, –stage, –place; stage, platform; block; rest, resting place; groundwork, substratum, riprap, sustentation [*now rare*], sustention [*rare*], subvention; floor etc. (*basement*) 211.

supporter; aid etc. 707; prop, stand, anvil, fulciment [*obs.*]; cue rest, jigger [*slang*], monkey [*builders' slang*], hod; stay, shore, skid, rib, truss, bandage; sleeper; stirrup, stilts, shoe, sole, heel, splint, lap; bar, rod, boom, spirit, outrigger; ratline *or* ratlin *or* ratling.

pedicle, pedicel *or* pedicellus *or* pediculus, peduncle [*all bot.*], stalk.

board, ledge, shelf, hob, bracket, trivet, arbor, rack; mantel, mantelpiece, mantelshelf; slab, console; counter, dresser; flange, corbel; table, trestle; shoulder; perch; horse; easel, desk; clotheshorse, hatrack; retable, predella, teapoy.

staff, stick, crutch, alpenstock, baton, crosier, cross, crook, lituus [*Rom. antiq.*], caduceus, thyrsus, staddle; bourdon, cowlstaff [*archaic*], *lathi* [*Hind.*], maulstick *or* mahlstick.

post, pillar, shaft, thill, column, pilaster; pediment, pedestal; plinth, shank, leg, socle *or* zocle; buttress, jamb, mullion, stile, abutment; baluster, banister, stanchion; balustrade; headstone.

frame, framework; scaffold, skeleton, beam, rafter, girder, lintel, joist, travis *or* traviss [*dial. Eng.*], trave, corner stone, summer, breastsummer *or* bressomer, summertree, transom; rung, round, step, sill; angle-rafter, hip-rafter; cantilever, modillion; crown-post, king-post; vertebra, modiolus.

columella, backbone; keystone; axle, axletree; axis; arch, mainstay.

trunnion, pivot, rowlock; peg etc. (*pendency*) 214; tiebeam etc. (*fastening*) 45; thole pin.

seat, throne, dais; divan, musnud *or* masnad [*Ar.*], guddee *or* gaddi [*Hind.*]; chair, bench, form, sofa, davenport, couch, day-bed, settee, stall; wingchair, armchair, easychair, elbowchair, rocking-chair; *fauteuil* [*F.*], woolsack, ottoman, settle, squab, bench; long chair, long-sleeve chair [*Anglo-Ind.*], *chaise longue* [*F.*], morris chair; *lamba chauki or lamba kursi* [*Hind.*]; saddle, aparejo, panel *or* pannel, pillion; sidesaddle, packsaddle; pommel, horn.

stool, foldstool, *prie-dieu* [*F.*], hassock, footstool; tabouret; tripod.

bed, berth, pallet, tester-bed, crib, cot, hammock, shakedown, truckle-bed, trundle-bed, cradle, litter, stretcher, bedstead; four-poster, French bed; bunk, kip [*dial.*], *palang* [*Hind.*]; roost [*slang*]; bedding, *bichhana* [*Hind.*], mattress, paillasse; pillow, bolster; mat, rug, cushion.

Atlas, Herakles *or* Hercules; tortoise that supports the earth.

[in architecture] atlas (*pl.* atlantes), telamon (*pl.* telamones), caryatid (*pl.* caryatids *or* caryatides).

v. **be supported** etc.; lie–, sit–, recline–, lean–, loll–, rest–, stand–, step–, repose–, abut–, bear–, be based etc.-on; have at one's back; bestride, bestraddle.

support, bear, carry, hold, sustain, shoulder; hold up, back up, bolster up, shore up; uphold, upbear; brace, truss, cradle, pillow, prop; underprop, underpin, underset; riprap; bandage etc. 43.

give–, furnish–, afford–, supply–, lend- -support, –foundations; bottom, found, base, ground, embed, imbed.

maintain, keep on foot; aid etc. 707.

adj. **supporting**, supported, etc. *v.;* Atlantean, columellar, columelliform; sustentative, sustentational; fundamental; dorsigerous.

having a pedicle etc. *n.;* pedunculate, pedicellate.

adv. **straddle**, astride on.

216. Parallelism

n. **parallelism**, coextension, equidistance, concentricity; collimation.

v. **be parallel** etc. *adj.;* parallel, equal; collimate.

adj. **parallel**, coextensive, equidistant, collateral, concentric, concurrent; abreast, aligned, equal, even, alongside.

adv. alongside etc. (*laterally*) 236.

217. Obliquity

n. **obliquity**, inclination, incline, slope, slant, skew, thrawnness [*Scott. & dial. Eng.*]; crookedness etc. *adj.;* slopeness; leaning etc. *v.;* bevel, ramp, pitch, bezel, tilt; bias, list, twist, swag [*prov. Eng.*], sag, cant, lurch; distortion etc. 243; bend etc. (*curve*) 245; tower of Pisa.

acclivity, rise, ascent, gradient [*chiefly Brit.*], grade [*U. S.*], *khudd* [*Hind.*], glacis, rising ground, hill, bank, declivity, downhill, dip, fall, devexity [*obs.*]; gentle–, rapid- slope; easy -ascent, –descent; shelving beach; talus; *montagne Russe* [*F.*]; *facilis descensus Averni* [*L.*].

steepness etc. *adj.;* cliff, precipice etc. (*vertical*) 212; escarpment, scarp; chevron.

[measure of inclination] clinometer; sine, cosine, cotangent, angle, hypothenuse.

diagonal; zigzag.

v. **be oblique** etc. *adj.;* slope, slant, skew, lean, incline, shelve, stoop, decline, descend, bend, keel, careen, sag, swag [*dial.*], seel [*obs.*], slouch, cant, sidle.

render oblique etc. *adj.;* sway, bias; slope, slant; incline, bend, crook; cant, tilt; distort etc. 243.

adj. **oblique**, inclined; sloping etc. *v.;* tilted etc. *v.;* recubant [*rare*], recumbent, clinical, skew, askew, slant, bias, aslant, plagihedral, indirect, wry, awry; agee *or* ajee, thrawn [*both Scot. & dial. Eng.*], crooked; sinuous, zigzag, zigzaggy, chevrony; knock-kneed etc. (*distorted*) 243; bevel, out of the perpendicular; aslope; asquint, backhand *or* backhanded.

uphill, rising, ascending, acclivous.

downhill, falling, descending; hanging (as, *hanging* gardens), declining, declivitous, proclivous [*rare*], declivous, devex [*obs.*], synclinal, anticlinal.

steep, abrupt, precipitous, breakneck.

diagonal; transverse, transversal; athwart, antiparallel; curved etc. 245; loxic, loxotic, loxodromic.

adv. **obliquely** etc. *adj.;* on one side, all on one side; askew, askance *or* askant, awry, skew, skewed, edgewise, at an angle; sidelong, sideways; slopewise, slantwise; by a side wind.

218. Inversion

n. **inversion**, eversion, subversion, reversion, retroversion, introversion; retroflexion; contraposition etc. 237; contrariety etc. 14; reversal; turn of the tide etc. (*reversion*) 145.

overturn; somersault *or* summersault, somerset *or* summerset; *culbute* [*F.*] eversion [*archaic*]; revulsion; pirouette.

transposition, transposal, anastrophy, metastasis, hyperbaton, anastrophe; hysterology, hysteron proteron; hypallage, synchysis, tmesis, parenthesis; metathesis; palindrome; ectropion [*path.*]; invagination, intussusception.

pronation and supination.

v. **be inverted** etc.; turn–, go–, wheel- -round, –about, –to the right-about [*colloq.*]; turn–, go–, tilt–, topple- over; capsize, turn turtle.

invert, subvert, retrovert, introvert; reverse; turn the cat in the pan [*obs*]; upturn, overturn, upset, overset, *bouleverser* [*F.*], evert [*archaic*]; turn topsy-turvy etc. *adj.;* *culbuter* [*F.*]; transpose, put the cart before the horse, turn the tables; invaginate, intussuscept.

adj. **inverted** etc. *v.;* wrong side -out, –up; inside out, upside down; bottom–, keel- upwards; supine, on one's head, topsy-turvy, *sens dessus dessous* [*F.*]; ectropic.

inverse; reverse etc. (*contrary*) 14; opposite etc. 237; palindromic *or* palindromical.

topheavy, unstable.

adv. **inversely** etc. *adj.;* heels over head, head over heels.

219. Crossing

n. **crossing** etc. *v.;* intersection, interdigitation; decussation, transversion; chiasm *or* chiasma; convolution etc. 248; level crossing [*Eng.*], grade crossing.

network, reticulation, cancellation; inosculation, anastomosis, intertexture, mortise.

net, plexus, plexure, web, mesh, twill, skein, Hippocrates' sleeve, sleave [*archaic*]; sieve, sifter, riddle rocker, screen, cradle; felt, lace; wicker; mat, matting; plait, trellis, wattle, lattice, grating, grille, gridiron, tracery, fretwork, filigree, reticle [*obs.*]; tissue, netting, moke [*dial. Eng.*]; rivulation.

cross, chain, wreath, braid, cat's cradle, knot; entanglement etc. (*disorder*) 59.

crucifix, cross, rood, crisscross, christcross, tau; crux.

[woven fabrics] cloth, linen, muslin, cambric, *toile* [*F.*], drill, homespun, silk, satin, broadcloth, tweed etc.

v. **cross**, decussate; intersect, interlace, intertwine, intertwist, interweave, interdigitate, interlink, intercross [*rare*], crisscross, crossbar.

twine, entwine, weave, inweave, twist, wreathe; anastomose, inosculate, dovetail, splice, link.

mat, plait, pleat, plat, braid, felt, twill; tangle, entangle, ravel; net, knot; dishevel, raddle.

adj. **crossing** etc. *v.;* crossed, matted etc. *v.;* transverse; intersected, decussate *or* decussated; chiasmal.

cross, cross-shaped cruciform, crucial; netlike, retiform, reticular, reticulate; areolar, cancellate *or* cancellated, cancellous, latticed, grated, barred, streaked; textile; crossbarred, cruciate, secant; cruciferous; plexal, plexiform; anastomotic; web-footed, palmiped.

adv. **cross**, thwart, athwart, transversely; at grade; crosswise, thwartwise [*rare*].

220. Exteriority

n. **exteriority**; outside, exterior; surface, superficies; skin etc. (*covering*) 223; superstratum; disk *or* disc; face, facet; extrados.

eccentricity; circumjacence etc. 227.

v. **be exterior** etc. *adj.;* lie around etc. 227.

place exteriorly, place outwardly, place outside; put out, turn out.

externalize, objectize [*rare*], objectify, visualize, envisage, actualize.

adj. **exterior**, external, extraneous; outer, outermost; outward, outlying, outside, outdoor, *alfresco* [*It.*]; round about etc. 227; extramural; extralimitary, extramundane, extraterrene, extraterrestrial, extraterritorial, exterritorial; extern [*rare*].

extraregarding; eccentric *or* eccentrical; outstanding; extrinsic etc. 6; ecdemic, exomorphic.

superficial, skin-deep; frontal, discoid.

adv. **externally** etc. *adj.;* out, without, over, outwards, *ab extra* [*L.*], out of doors; *extra muros* [*L.*].

in the open air; *sub Jove* [*L.*], *sub dio* [*L.*]; *à la belle étoile* [*F.*], *alfresco* [*It.*].

221. Interiority

n. **interiority**; inside, interior; interspace, subsoil, substratum; intrados.

contents etc. 190; substance, pith, marrow; backbone etc. (*center*) 222; heart, bosom, breast; abdomen.

vitals, viscera, entrails, bowels, belly, intestines, guts [*vulgar or tech.*], chitterlings, chitlings *or* chitlins, womb, lap [*obs.*], rectum, cecum *or* caecum, ileum, duodenum, jejunum.

gland, glandule [*rare*], gland cell; thyroid, parotid, prostate; liver, kidney.

penetralia, recesses, innermost recesses; cave etc. (*concavity*) 252.

enterology, enterotomy, enteropathy, enteritis, splanchnology; peristalsis, vermiculation.

inmate, intern, inhabitant etc. 188.

v. **be inside** etc. *adj.;* be within etc. *adv.*

inclose etc. (*circumscribe*) 229; intern embed *or* imbed etc. (*insert*) 300; place within, keep within.

adj. **interior**, internal; inner, intern [*archaic*], intraneous [*rare*], intimate, inside, inward, intraregarding; inmost, innermost; deep-seated; intestine, intestinal, visceral, rectal, duodenal, splanchnic; subcutaneous; abdominal, celiac *or* coeliac, endomorphic.

intracanal, intracellular, intralobular, intramarginal, intramolecular, intramundane, intraocular, intraseptal, intratelluric, intrauterine, intravascular, intravenous, intraventricular.

interstitial etc. (*interjacent*) 228; inwrought etc. (*intrinsic*) 5; inclosed etc. *v.*

home, inland, domestic, family, indoor, intramural, vernacular; endemic.

adv. **internally** etc. *adj.;* inwards, within, in, inly; herein, therein, wherein, *ab intra* [*L.*]; indoors, within doors; at home, in the bosom of one's family.

222. Centrality

n. **centrality,** centricalness, centricality, center *or* centre; middle etc. 68; focus etc. 74.

center of -gravity, −pressure, −percussion, −oscillation, −buoyancy etc.; metacenter.

core, kernel; nucleus, nucleolus; heart, pole, axis, bull's-eye, nave, hub, navel, umbilicus; marrow, pith; backbone; vertebra, vertebral column; hotbed.

concentration etc. (*convergence*) 290; centralization; symmetry; metropolis.

v. **be central** etc. *adj.;* converge etc. 290.

render central, centralize, concentrate; bring to a focus.

adj. **central,** centrical; middle etc. 68; axial, pivotal, nuclear, nucleate, centric, focal, umbilical, concentric; middlemost; rachial, rachidial *or* rachidian; spinal, vertebral; metropolitan.

adv. **middle;** midst; centrally etc. *adj.*

223. Covering

n. **covering,** cover, baldachin *or* baldaquin; canopy, *shamianah* [*Hind.*], tilt, awning, tent, marquee, marquise, wigwam, tepee, *tente d'abri* [*F.*], umbrella, parasol, sunshade; veil (*shade*) 424; shield etc. (*defense*) 717.

roof, ceiling, thatch, tile, pantile, tiling, slates, slating, leads, shingles; dome, cupola, mansard, hip roof; barrack, *plafond* [*F.*], planchment, tiling, shed etc. (*abode*) 189.

top, lid, covercle [*obs.*], door, operculum; bulkhead.

wrapping, bandage, dressing, plaster, lint, dossil, pledget, finger stall.

coverlet, counterpane, sheet, quilt, blanket, rug, drugget; housing; tidy, antimacassar, eiderdown quilt *or* eiderdown; comforter *or* comfortable *or* comfort, numdah [*Hind.*], pillowcase, pillowslip; linoleum, oilcloth; tarpaulin; saddle blanket, saddlecloth; tilpah, apishamore, poncho.

tegmen (*pl.* tegmina), integument, tegument; skin, pellicle, fleece, fell, fur, leather, lambskin, sable, miniver, beaver, ermine, shagreen, hide, coat, buff, pelt, peltry [*collective noun*]; cordwain [*archaic*]; robe, buffalo robe.

cuticle, cutis, dermis, corium, scarfskin, epidermis, derm [*rare*], derma; ectoderm, epithelium, ecderon, ecteron, enderon.

exuviae, desquamation, slough, cast, cast-off skin.

clothing etc. 225; mask etc. (*concealment*) 530.

peel, crust, bark, rind. cortex, husk, shell, epicarp, testa; eggshell, glume.

capsule; sheath, sheathing; pod, cod [*dial.*], casing, case, theca; elytron; elytrum; involucrum; wrapping, wrapper; envelope, vesicle; cornhusk, cornshuck.

dermatography, dermatology, dermatogen, dermoplasty, dermatopathy, dermatophyte; conchology; testaceology.

veneer, facing; pavement; imbrication, scale etc. (*layer*) 204; anointing etc. *v.;* ointment etc. (*grease*) 356; inunction; incrustation, superposition, obduction [*obs.*]; coating, paint, stain, engobe; varnish etc. (*resin*) 356*a;* ground, enamel, whitewash, plaster, stucco, roughcast, plasterwork, scagliola, compo; cerement; cerecloth, shroud.

v. **cover;** superpose, superimpose; overlay, overspread; wrap etc. 225; incase, encase, enchase, face, case, veneer, pave, paper; tip, cap, bind; bulkhead, bulkhead in; clapboard, shingle; imbricate.

overlie, overarch; endome [*rare*]; conceal etc. 528.

coat, paint, stain, varnish, flat, incrust, encrust, crust, cement, roughcast, stucco, dab, plaster, tar; wash; besmear; bedaub; anoint, do over; gild, plate, japan, lacquer, lacker, enamel, whitewash; parget; lay it on thick.

adj. **covering** etc. *v.;* cutaneous, dermal, cortical, cuticular, tegumentary, tegumental, tegmental, integumentary, integumental, epidermal *or* epidermic, endermic, epicarpal, testaceous, dermatopathic, dermatological, dermoplastic, dermatophytic, subcutaneous, hypodermic.

scaly, squamate, squamiferous, squamous; covered etc. *v.;* imbricate, imbricated, loricate, loricated, armored, encuirassed, armor-plated, ironclad, under cover.

hooded, cowled, cucullate *or* cucullated, tectiform, rooflike; vaginate.

skinlike, dermic, dermoid, dermatoid, epidermoid, skinny.

224. Lining

n. **lining,** inner coating; coating etc. (*covering*) 223; stalactite, stalagmite.

filling, stuffing, wadding, padding, facing; bushing.

wainscot, parietes, wall, brattice, sheathing.

v. line, stuff, incrust, wad, pad, fill, face, ceil, bush, wainscot, sheathe.

adj. lined etc. v.

225. Investment

n. investment; covering etc. 223; dress, clothing, raiment, drapery, costume, attire, guise, toilet, toilette, trim; habiliment; vesture, vestment; garment, garb, palliament [obs.], apparel, wardrobe, wearing apparel, clothes, things.

array; tailoring, millinery; best bib and tucker [colloq.]; finery etc. (ornament) 847; full dress etc. (show) 882; garniture; theatrical properties.

outfit, equipment, trousseau; uniform, khaki, olive-drab, regimentals; continentals [Am. hist.]; canonicals etc. 999; livery, gear, harness, turnout, accouterment, caparison, suit, rigging, trappings, traps [colloq.], slops, togs [colloq.], toggery [colloq.]; masquerade.

dishabille or deshabille, morning dress, tea gown, wrapper, negligee or négligé [F.], dressing gown, undress; kimono; shooting coat; smoking jacket; mufti [chiefly Eng.]; rags, tatters, old clothes; mourning, weeds; duds [colloq.]; slippers.

robe, tunic, paletot, habit, gown, coat, frock, blouse, middy blouse or middy, jumper, shirt waist, suit; one-piece -, two-piece- suit; toga, smock, frock; Prince Albert coat [colloq.]; frock–, sack–, tail- coat.

dress suit, dress clothes, evening dress, swallow-tailed coat [colloq.], claw-hammer coat [colloq.]; dinner -coat, –jacket; tuxedo, soup-and-fish [colloq.]; glad rags [slang].

cloak, pall [archaic], mantle, mantua, mantelet or mantlet, sagum, shawl, pelisse, wrapper; veil; cape, kirtle [archaic], plaid [Scot.], tippet, muffler, comforter, balaklava helmet, haik, huke [obs.], chlamys, mantilla, tabard, housing, horse cloth, burnoose or burnous, roquelaure; houpland [hist.]; surcoat, overcoat, greatcoat; surtout, spencer, oilskins, slicker, mackintosh, waterproof, ulster, dreadnaught or dreadnought, wraprascal, poncho; pea-coat, pea-jacket; cardinal, pelerine; chuddar or chadar [Hind.], jubbah [Hind.], pullover, pyjamas or pajamas, pilot jacket, sweater, blazer, coatee, cardigan or cardigan jacket; Mackinaw coat or Mackinaw; talma.

jacket, vest, jerkin [hist. or dial.], chaqueta [Sp.], sontag, waistcoat, doublet, gaberdine; stays, corsage, corset, bra, brassière [F.], camisole, corselet, bodice; stomacher.

skirt, petticoat, farthingale, kilt, filibeg or philibeg, jupe, crinoline, bustle, panier, apron, pinafore; bloomer, bloomers; tablier [F.].

loin cloth, dhoti [Hindu], lungi [Burmese]; G string.

trousers, breeches, pantaloons, inexpressibles [humorous], trews [Scot.], innominables [humorous], unmentionables [humorous], continuations [slang], kicks [slang]; overalls, smalls [colloq. or archaic], smallclothes [archaic]; pants [colloq.]; shintiyan; shorts; tights, drawers; knickerbockers, knickers [Engl. colloq.].

headdress, headgear, coiffure [F.], head, head-cloths, chignon [F.]; chapeau [F.], crush hat, opera hat; kaffiyeh [Ar.]; taj, tam-o'-shanter, topee or topi [India], sola topi [India], puggree or pagri [Hind.]; sombrero, sundown, cap, hat, beaver, castor, bonnet, tile [slang], wide-awake, panama, leghorn; derby, bowler [Eng.], billycock [Eng.]; wimple; nightcap, skullcap; mobcap, boudoir cap, Dutch cap; Salvation-Army bonnet; hood, coif, capote, calash, kerchief, snood; crown etc. (circle) 247; pelt, wig, front, peruke, periwig; caftan, turban, fez, tarboosh, shako, busby; kepi, forage cap, campaign hat, overseas cap, bearskin; helmet etc. 717; mask, domino.

body clothes; linen; hickory shirt [U. S.]; shirt, O.-D. (olive-drab) shirt; sark [archaic or dial.], smock, shift, chemise; nightgown, nightshirt; bed-gown, sac de nuit [F.]; jersey; underclothing, underwaistcoat, undershirt, undervest, chemisette, guimpe.

tie, neckerchief, neckcloth; ruff, collar, cravat, stock, handkerchief, scarf, bib, tucker; boa; girdle etc. (circle) 247; cummerbund [India], rumal [Hind.], rabat [F.], rabato.

shoe, pump, sneakers, boot, slipper, sandal, galosh or galoshe, patten, clog; high-low; Blucher–, Wellington–, Hessian–, jack–, top- boot; Oxford -shoe, –tie; Balmoral; arctics, bootee, bootikin, brogan, brogue, chaparajos [Mex. Sp.], chaps [colloq.], chivarras or chivarros [Sp. Amer.]; gums [U. S.], larrigan [N. Amer.], rubbers; snowshoe, ski; stogy, veldtschoen [Dutch], legging, puttee or putty, buskin, greave, galligaskin [dial.], moccasin, gambado, gaiter, spatterdashes, spats, gamashes [archaic or dial. Eng.], gamache [F.]; antigropelos.

stocking, hose, gaskins [obs.], trunk hose, sock; hosiery.

glove, gauntlet, mitten, mitt.

cuff, wristband; sleeve.

baby linen, swaddling clothes, diaper, layette.

[suppliers] clothier, tailor, snip [*slang*], tailoress, milliner, costumer, costumier, seamstress *or* sempstress, dressmaker, *modiste* [*F.*], habit-maker; breeches-maker; shoemaker, Crispin cordwainer, cobbler; hosier, hatter, glover, draper, linen draper, haberdasher, mercer; hair-dresser, *friseur* [*F.*].

v. **invest**; cover etc. 223; envelop, lap, involve; inwrap *or* enwrap; wrap; fold up, wrap up, lap up, muffle up; overlap; sheathe, swathe, swaddle, roll up in, shroud, circumvest [*obs.*].

clothe, vest [*rare*], array, dress, dight [*archaic*], bedight [*archaic*], drape, robe, enrobe, attire, apparel, tire [*archaic*], habilitate [*rare*], garb, enclothe, breech, coat, jacket, gown, accouter, rig, fit out; dizen, bedizen, deck etc. (*ornament*) 847; perk, equip, harness, caparison.

wear; don; put on, huddle on, slip on; mantle.

adj. **invested** etc. *v.;* habited; dight, dighted; barbed, barded; clad, *costumé* [*F.*], shod, *chaussé* [*F.*]; *en grande tenue* [*F.*] etc. (*show*) 882; *décolletée* [*F.*].

sartorial, sartorian [*rare*].

226. Divestment

n. **divestment**; taking off etc. *v.*

nudity; bareness etc. *adj.;* undress; dishabille etc. 225; altogether; *tout ensemble* [*F.*]; nudation [*rare*], denudation; decortication, depilation, excoriation, desquamation, slough etc. 223; molting *or* moulting, exuviation; exfoliation; trichosis.

baldness, hairlessness, alopecia.

v. **divest**; uncover etc. (cover etc. 223); denude, bare, strip; disfurnish; undress, disrobe etc. (dress, enrobe etc. 225); uncoif; dismantle; put off, take off, cast off; doff.

peel, pare, decorticate, desquamate, slough, excoriate, skin, scalp, flay, bark, husk, rind; expose, lay open; exfoliate, molt *or* moult, exuviate, mew [*archaic*]; cast the skin.

adj. **divested** etc. *v.;* bare, naked, nude; undressed, undraped, unclad, ungarmented, unclothed, unappareled, unarrayed; exposed; in dishabille.

in a state of nature, in nature's garb, in the buff, in native buff, in birthday suit; *in puris naturalibus* [*L.*]; with nothing on, stark-naked; bare as the back of one's hand.

out at elbows; threadbare, ragged, callow, roofless; barefoot; bareback, barebacked; leafless, napless, hairless.

bald, hairless, depilous [*rare*], glabrous, glabrate, tonsured, beardless, bald as a coot.

exuvial, sloughy, desquamative, desquamatory.

227. Circumjacence

n. **circumjacence** *or* circumjacency, circumfluence [*rare*], circumambience environment, encompassment; atmosphere, medium; surroundings, *entourage* [*F.*].

outpost; border etc. (*edge*) 231; girdle etc. (*circumference*) 230; outskirts, boulevards, suburbs, purlieus, precincts, *faubourgs* [*F.*], environs, environment, entourage, *banlieue* [*F.*], neighborhood, vicinage, vicinity.

v. **lie around** etc. *adv.;* surround, beset, compass, encompass, environ, inclose *or* enclose, encircle, encincture [*rare*], circle, girdle, ensphere, hedge, embrace, circumvent, lap, gird; belt; begird, engird; skirt; twine round; hem in etc. (*circumscribe*) 229; beleaguer, invest, besiege, beset, blockade.

adj. **circumjacent**, circumambient, circumfluent; ambient; surrounding etc. *v.;* circumferential, suburban.

adv. **around**, about; without; on every side, on all sides; right and left, all round, roundabout.

228. Interjacence

n. **interjacence** *or* interjacency, intercurrence, intervenience *or* interveniency [*rare*], interlocation, interdigitation, interpenetration; permeation.

interjection, interpolation, interlineation, interspersion, intercalation; embolism.

intervention, interference, interposition, intromission, intrusion, obtrusion; insinuation; insertion etc. 300; dovetailing; infiltration.

intermedium, intermediary; go-between, interagent, middleman, intervener, mean, medium, bodkin [*colloq.*], intruder, interloper; parenthesis, episode, flyleaf.

partition, septum, interseptum, phragma, septulum, mediastinum, diaphragm, midriff; dissepiment; party wall, panel, bulkhead, brattice, *cloison* [*F.*], perpend, halfway house.

v. **lie between**, come between, get between; intervene, slide in, interpenetrate, permeate.

put between, introduce, import; throw in, wedge in, edge in, jam in, worm in, foist in, run in, plow in, work in; interpose, interject, intercalate, interpolate, interline, interleave, intersperse, interweave, interlard, interdigitate; let in, dovetail, splice, mortise; insinuate, smuggle; infiltrate, ingrain.

interfere, put in an oar, stick one's nose in; intrude, obtrude; have a finger in the pie; introduce the thin end of the wedge; thrust in etc. (*insert*) 300.

adj. **interjacent**, intervenient [*rare*], intervening etc. *v.;* intercalary, intercolumnar, intercostal, intercurrent, interfacial, intergrowth, interlineal, interlobular, interlocular, intermedial, intermediary, intermediate, intermaxillary, intermolecular, intermundane, internasal, interneural, internodal, interoceanic, interosseal, interosseous, interplanetary, interpolar, interradial, interrenal, interscapular, interseptal, interstellar, interstitial, intervalvular, intervascular, interventricular, intervertebral; septal, embolismal.

parenthetical, episodic; mediterranean; intrusive; embosomed; merged.

mean, medium, mesne, middle, median.

adv. **between**, betwixt; 'twixt; among *or* amongst; amid, amidst; 'mid, 'midst; in the thick of; betwixt and between [*colloq.*]; sandwich-wise; parenthetically, *obiter dictum* [*L.*].

229. Circumscription

n. **circumscription**, limitation, inclosure; confinement etc. (*restraint*) 751; circumvallation; encincture; envelope etc. 232.

v. **circumscribe**, limit, bound, confine, inclose *or* enclose; surround etc. 227; compass about; imprison etc. (*restrain*) 751; hedge in, wall in, rail in; fence round, hedge round; picket; corral.

enfold, bury, incase, pack up, enshrine, inclasp *or* enclasp; wrap up etc. (*invest*) 225; embay, embosom.

adj. **circumscribed** etc. *v.;* begirt, circumambient, girt, cinct [*rare*], circumcinct [*rare*], lapt; buried in, immersed in; embosomed, in the bosom of, imbedded, encysted, mewed up; imprisoned etc. 751; landlocked, in a ring fence.

230. Outline

n. **outline**, circumference; perimeter, periphery; ambit, circuit, lines, *tournure* [*F.*], contour, profile, silhouette, relief, lineaments; bounds; coast line.

zone, belt, girth, band, baldric, zodiac, girdle, tire, cingle [*rare*], clasp, girt, girth; cordon etc. (*inclosure*) 232; circlet etc. 247.

v. **outline**, contour, delineate, silhouette, block, sketch, profile; circumscribe etc. 229.

adj. **outlined** etc. *v.;* circumferential, perimetric, perimetrical, peripheral.

231. Edge

n. **edge**, verge, brink, brow, brim, margin, border, confine, skirt, rim, flange, side, mouth; jaws, chops, chaps, fauces; lip, muzzle.

shore, coast, strand, bank; bunder, bund [*both Oriental*], quay, wharf, dock, mole, landing.

fringe, flounce, frill, list, trimming, edging, skirting, hem, selvage *or* selvedge, welt; furbelow, valance; frame; exergue.

threshold, door, porch; portal etc. (*opening*) 260.

v. **edge**, border, skirt, fringe, marginate.

adj. **border**, marginal, skirting; labial, labiated, marginated.

232. Inclosure

n. **inclosure** *or* enclosure, envelope; case etc. (*receptacle*) 191; wrapper; girdle etc. 230.

pen, fold; sty, penfold, sheepfold; paddock, croft, pasture, wood lot; pound; corral; yard, compound; net, seine net.

fence etc. (*defense*) 717; pale, paling, balustrade, rail, railing, quickset hedge, park paling, circumvallation, *enceinte* [*F.*]; ring fence; wall; hedge, hedgerow; espalier.

barrier, barricade; gate, gateway; weir; bent, dingle; door, hatch, cordon; prison etc. 752.

dike, ditch, fosse, trench, drain, dugout, *tranchée* [*F.*], *coupure* [*F.*], moat.

v. **inclose** *or* enclose; circumscribe etc. 229.

233. Limit

n. **limit**, boundary, bounds, confine, enclave, term, bourn *or* bourne, verge, curbstone, but [*Scot.*], pale; termination, terminus, terminal; stint, stent; frontier, precinct, marches; backwoods.

boundary line, landmark; line of -demarcation, -circumvallation; pillars of Hercules; Rubicon, turning point; *ne plus ultra* [*L.*]; sluice, floodgate.

v. **limit**, bound, compass, confine, define, circumscribe, demarcate, delimit.

adj. **definite**; conterminate [*obs.*], conterminable; terminable, limitable; terminal, frontier; bordering, border, limitary, boundary, limital [*rare*].

adv. **thus far**, —and no further.

234. Front

n. **front**; fore, fore part *or* forepart; foreground, forefront; face, disk *or* disc, frontage, façade, proscenium, facia, frontispiece; priority, anteriority; obverse (*of a medal*).

van, vanguard; advanced guard; forerank, front rank; outpost; first line; scout.

brow, forehead, visage, physiognomy, phiz [*colloq.*], features, countenance, mug [*slang*]; metoposcopy; chin, mentum; rostrum, beak, bow, stem, prow, prore, jib, bowsprit.

pioneer etc. (*precursor*) 64; metoposcopist, physiognomist

v. **front**, face, confront, breast, buck [*slang*], brave, dare, defy oppose, outbrazen; bend forwards; come to the front, come to the fore; be *or* stand in front etc. *adj.*

adj. **fore**, forward, anterior, front, frontal; metopic

adv. **before** in front, in the van, in advance; ahead right ahead; foremost, headmost in the foreground, in the lee of; before one's -face, –eyes: face to face, *vis-à-vis* [*F.*]; *front à front* [*F.*].

235. Rear

n. **rear**, back, posteriority; rear rank, rear guard, rearward [*archaic*]; background, hinterland. occiput, nape; heels.
spine, backbone, rachis, spinal column, chine.
tail, scut, brush, appendage [*humorous*].
rump, croup, buttock, posteriors, fundament, bottom [*colloq.*], stern [*colloq.*], seat, backside [*vulgar*], breech, dorsum, tergum, loin; dorsal–, lumbar-region; hind quarters; aitchbone.
stern, poop, counter, mizzenmast, postern door, tailpiece, after-part, heel-piece, crupper.
wake; train etc. (*sequence*) 281.
reverse; other side of the shield.

v. **be behind** etc. *adv.;* fall astern; bend backwards; bring up the rear; heel, tag, shadow, follow etc. (*pursue*) 622.

adj. **back**, rear; hind, hinder, hindmost, hindermost; sternmost; postern, posterior; dorsal, after; caudal, tergal, neural, spinal, vertebral, lumbar; mizzen.

adv. **behind**; in the -rear, –background; behind one's back; at the -heels, –tail, –back- of; back to back.
after, aft, abaft, baft, astern, aback, rearward, hindward, backward.

236. Laterality

n. **laterality** [*rare*]; side, flank, quarter, lee; hand; cheek, jowl *or* jole, wing; profile; temple, paries (*pl.* parietes), loin, haunch, hip; beam.
gable, gable-end; broadside; lee side.
points of the compass; East, sunrise, Orient, Levant; West, Occident, sunset; orientation.

v. **flank**, outflank; sidle; skirt, border, wing; orientate; be on one side etc. *adv.*

adj. **lateral**, sidelong; collateral; parietal, flanking, skirting; flanked; sideling.
many-sided; multilateral, bilateral, trilateral, quadrilateral.
eastern, eastward, east, orient, oriental, auroral *or* aurorean; Levantine.

western, west, westerly, westward, occidental, Hesperian.

adv. **sideways** *or* sideway, sidewise, sideling, sidelong; broadside on; on one side, abreast, alongside, beside, aside; by, by the side of; side by side; cheek by jowl etc. (*near*) 197; to windward, to leeward; laterally etc. *adj.;* right and left; on her beam ends.

237. Contraposition

n. **contraposition**, opposition; polarity; inversion etc. 218; opposite side; reverse, inverse; counterpart; antithesis.
antipodes, opposite poles, North and South.

v. **be opposite** etc. *adj.;* subtend.

adj. **opposite**; reverse, inverse; converse; antipodal, diametrical, antithetic, counter, subcontrary; fronting, facing, diametrically opposite.
northern, north, northerly, northward, hyperborean, septentrional, boreal, polar, arctic.
southern, south, southerly, meridional, southward, Austral, antarctic.

adv. **over**, over the way, over against; against; face to face, *vis-à-vis* [*F.*]; as poles asunder.

238. Dextrality

n. **dextrality**; right, right hand; dexter, offside, starboard.

adj. **dextral**, dexterous *or* dextrous, right-handed; dexter, dextrorsal, dextrorse.
ambidexter, ambidextrous, ambidextral.

adv. **dextrad**, dextrally; ambidextrously.

239. Sinistrality

n. **sinistrality**, sinistration; left, left hand, southpaw; *sinistra or sinistra mano* [*music, It.*]; nearside, larboard, port.

adj. **left-handed**, sinister-handed [*obs.*], sinister, sinistral, sinistrorsal, sinistrorse, sinistrous, ambilevous [*rare*]; sinistrogyrate, sinistrogyric.

adv. **sinistrad**, sinistrally, sinistrously.

Section 3. Form

240. Form

n. **form**, figure, shape; conformation, configuration; make, formation, frame, construction, cut, set, build, *tournure* [*F.*], outline, get-up [*colloq.*], trim, cut of one's jib [*colloq.*]; stamp, type, cast, mold *or* mould; fashion; contour etc. (*outline*) 230; structure etc. 329; plasmature [*obs.*].

feature, lineament, turn; phase etc. (*aspect*) 448; posture, attitude, pose.

[science of form] morphology.

[similarity of form] isomorphism; isomorph.

formation, figuration, efformation [*rare*]; forming etc. *v.;* sculpture; plasmation [*rare*].

v. **form**, shape, figure, fashion, efform [*rare*], carve, cut, chisel, hew, cast; roughhew, roughcast; sketch; block out, hammer out; trim; lick–, put-into shape; model, knead, work up into, set, mold, sculpture; cast, stamp; build etc. (*construct*) 161.

adj. **formed** etc. *v.;* structural, morphologic *or* morphological.

shapely, well-proportioned, symmetrical, well-made, well-formed, comely, trim, neat.

[receiving form] plastic, fictile; formative, impressible, creative.

[giving form] plasmatic, plasmic; protoplasmic.

[similar in form] isomorphic, isomorphous.

241. Amorphism
[absence of form]

n. **amorphism**, misproportion, informity [*rare*]; uncouthness; rough diamond; unlicked cub; *rudis indigestaque moles* [*L.*]; disorder etc. 59; deformity etc. 243.

disfigurement, defacement; mutilation; deforming.

v. [destroy form] deface, disfigure, deform, mutilate, truncate; derange etc. 61; blemish, mar.

adj. **shapeless**, amorphous, formless; unshapely, misshapen, unsymmetrical, malformed, unformed, unhewn, unfashioned, unshapen; anomalous.

rough, rude, Gothic, barbarous, rugged, scraggy, vandalic; in the rough.

242. Symmetry
[regularity of form]

n. **symmetry**, shapeliness, finish; beauty etc. 845; proportion, eurythmy *or* eurhythmy, eurythmics *or* eurhythmics, uniformity, parallelism; bilateral–, trilateral–, multilateral-symmetry; centrality etc. 222; radiation, regularity, evenness.

arborescence, branching, ramification; arbor vitae; peloria.

adj. **symmetrical**, shapely, well set, finished; beautiful etc. 845; classic, chaste, severe.

regular, uniform, radiate, radiated, balanced; equal etc. 27; parallel, coextensive.

arborescent, arboriform; dendriform, dendroid *or* dendroidal; branching; ramous, ramose; fern-shaped, filiciform, filicoid; subarborescent; papilionaceous.

243. Distortion
[irregularity of form]

n. **distortion**, detortion [*rare*], contortion, contortuosity, knot, warp, buckle, screw, twist; crookedness etc. (*obliquity*) 217; grimace; deformity; malformation, malconformation; harelip; monstrosity, misproportion, want of symmetry, anamorphosy, anamorphosis; ugliness etc. 846; talipes, club-foot; teratology.

v. **distort**, contort, twist, warp, buckle, screw, wrench, writhe, gnarl, wrest, writhe, make faces, deform, misshape.

adj. **distorted** etc. *v.;* out of shape, irregular, unsymmetric, anamorphous, awry, wry, askew, crooked; not true, not straight; on one side, crump [*obs.*], deformed; harelipped; misshapen, misbegotten; misproportioned, ill-proportioned; ill-made; grotesque, crooked as a ram's horn; camelbacked, humpbacked, hunchbacked, bunchbacked, crook-backed; bandy; bandylegged, bowlegged; bowkneed, knock-kneed; splayfooted, taliped *or* talipedic, club-footed; round-shouldered; snub-nosed; curtailed of one's fair proportions; stumpy etc. (*short*) 201; gaunt (*thin*) etc. 203; bloated etc. 194; scalene; simous.

adv. all manner of ways.

244. Angularity

n. **angularity**, angularness; aduncity; angle, cusp, bend; fold etc. 258; notch etc. 257; fork, furculum, bifurcation.

elbow, knee, knuckle, ankle, groin, crotch, crutch; crane, fluke, scythe, sickle; zigzag.

corner, nook, recess, niche, oriel, coign (*as in* "coign of vantage").

right angle etc. (*perpendicular*) 212; obliquity etc. 217; angle of 45 degrees, miter; acute–, obtuse–, salient–, reëntering –, spherical-angle.

angular -measurement, –elevation, –distance, –velocity; trigonometry, goniometry; altimeter, pantometer, altimetry; clinometer, graphometer, goniometer; theodolite; transit *or* transit theodolite, sextant, quadrant; dichotomy.

triangle, trigon, wedge; rectangle, square, lozenge, diamond; rhomb, rhombus, rhomboid, rhombohedron, quadrangle, quadrilateral; parallelogram; quadrature; polygon, pentagon, hexagon, heptagon, octagon, oxygon, decagon.

Platonic bodies; cube, rhomboid; tetrahedron, pentahedron, hexahedron, octahedron, dodecahedron, icosahedron; prism, pyramid; parallelepiped *or* parallelepipedon; curb–, gambrel–, French–, mansard- roof.

v. **fork**, furcate, divaricate, branch, ramify, bifurcate, bend, crinkle.

adj. **angular**, bent, crooked, aduncous, adunc *or* aduncal, aduncate *or* aduncated, uncinated, aquiline, jagged, serrated; falciform, falcated; furcal, furcate, furcated, forked, bifurcate, crotched, zigzag, furcular, hooked; dove-tailed; knockkneed, crinkled, akimbo, kimbo [*obs.*], geniculated; oblique etc. 217.

wedge-shaped, cuneiform; cuneate, multangular, oxygonal; triangular, trigonal, trilateral; quadrangular, quadrilateral, foursquare, rectangular, square; multilateral; polygonal etc. *n.;* cubical, rhombic *or* rhombical, rhomboidal, pyramidal.

245. Curvature

n. **curvature**, curvity [*rare*], curvation; incurvature, incurvity [*obs.*], incurvation; bend; flexure, flexion; conflexure [*obs.*]; crook, hook, bought [*obs.*], bending; deflexion, inflexion; concameration; arcuation, devexity [*obs.*], turn; deviation, detour or *détour* [*F.*], sweep; curl, curling; bough; recurvity [*rare*], recurvation [*rare*]; sinuosity etc. 248; aduncity.

curve, arc, arch, arcade, vault, bow, crescent, meniscus, half-moon, lunule, horseshoe, loop, crane neck; parabola, hyperbola; catacaustic, diacaustic; geanticline, geosyncline; catenarian, catenary, festoon; conchoid, cardioid; caustic; tracery; arched- ceiling, –roof; bay window, bow window.

v. **be curved** etc. *adj.;* sweep, swag [*obs. or dial.*], sag; deviate etc. 279; turn; reënter.

render curved etc. *adj.;* bend, curve, incurvate; deflect, inflect; crook; turn, round, arch, arcuate, arch over, embow, recurvate [*rare*], concamerate [*rare*]; bow, coil, curl, recurve, frizzle, friz *or* frizz.

adj. **curved** etc. *v.;* curvate *or* curvated, lobiform; curviform, curvilineal *or* curvilinear; devex [*obs.*], devious; recurved, recurvous; crump [*obs.*]; bowed etc. *v.;* vaulted; geanticlinal, geosynclinal; bow-legged etc. (*distorted*) 243; oblique etc. 217; circular etc. 247.

beak-shaped, beaked, rostrate, rostriform, rostroid, rhamphoid.

bell-shaped, campaniform, campanular, campanulous, campanulate.

boat-shaped, navicular, cymbiform, naviform, scaphoid.

bow-shaped, arcuate *or* arcuated, arcual; arciform, arclike, embowed.

crescent-shaped, crescent, crescentiform, crescentic, convexo-concave, sigmoid, semilunar, horned, meniscal, bicorn, bicornute *or* bicornuate, bicornuous [*rare*], bicorned *or* bicornous, semicircular.

heart-shaped, cordiform, cardioid, cordate.

helmet-shaped, galeiform, galeate, galeated, cassidiform.

hook-shaped, hooked, hooklike, unciform, uncate, uncinal, uncinate, hamulate, hamate, hamiform, hamose *or* hamous [*both rare*]; unguiform, unguiculate *or* unguiculated; curvated, aduncate, aduncous, adunc.

kidney-shaped, reniform.

lens-shaped, lenticular, lentoid, lentiform, meniscal, meniscoid.

moon-shaped, lunar, lunate *or* lunated, luniform, lunular, lunulate *or* lunulated, crescent-shaped (*q. v.*); Cynthian.

oar-shaped, remiform [*rare*].

pear-shaped, pyriform; obconic.

shell-shaped, conchate, conchiform, conchylaceous [*rare*], conchoidal [*min.*].

shield-shaped, scutate, scutiform, peltate, clypeate *or* clypeated, clypeiform.

sickle-shaped, falcate, falciform, falculate [*rare*].

tongue-shaped, linguiform, lingulate, ligulate.

turnip-shaped, napiform.

246. Straightness

n. **straightness**, rectilinearity, rectilinearness; directness; inflexibility etc. (*stiffness*) 323; straight–, bee–, right–, direct- line; short cut.

v. **be straight** etc. *adj.;* have no turning; not -incline, –bend, –turn, –deviate- to either side; go straight; steer for etc. (*direction*) 278.

render straight, straighten, rectify; set–, put-straight; unbend, unfold, uncurl etc. 248; unravel etc. 219, unwrap.

adj. **straight**; rectilinear, rectilineal; direct, even, right, true, in a line; virgate, unbent etc. *v.;* undeviating, unturned, undistorted, unswerving; straight-lined, straight as an arrow etc. (*direct*) 278; inflexible etc. 323.

perpendicular, plumb, vertical, upright, erect.

247. Circularity
[simple circularity]

n. **circularity**, roundness; rotundity etc. 249.

circle, circlet, ring, areola, hoop, roundlet, annulus, annulet, bracelet, armlet; ringlet; eye, loop, wheel; cycle, orb, orbit, rundle, zone, belt, cordon, band; contrate–, crown- wheel; hub, nave; sash, girdle, cestus, cest *or* ceste, cincture, baldric, fillet, fascia, wreath, garland; crown, corona, coronet, chaplet, snood, necklace, collar; noose, lasso.

ellipse, oval, ovule; ellipsoid, cycloid, epicycloid, epicycle.

semicircle; quadrant, sextant, sector.

v. **make round** etc. *adj.;* round.

go round; encircle etc. 227; describe a circle etc. 311.

adj. **round**, rounded, circular, annular, orbicular, orbiculate *or* orbiculated; oval, ovate, obovate, ovoid, ovoidal [*rare*], elliptic, elliptical, egg-shaped; pear-shaped etc. 245; cycloidal etc. *n.;* spherical etc. 249; fasciate *or* fasciated.

248. Convolution
[complex circularity]

n. **convolution**, involution, circumvolution; winding etc. *v.;* wave, undulation, tortuosity, anfractuosity; sinuosity, sinuation, sinuousness, flexuosity, tortility; meandering, circuit, circumbendibus [*humorous*], twist, twirl, windings and turnings, ambagiousness, ambages; torsion; inosculation; reticulation etc. (*crossing*) 219; rivulation.

coil, roll, curl, buckle, spiral, helix, corkscrew, worm, volute, whorl, rundle; tendril; scollop, scallop, escalop *or* escallop; kink; ammonite, snakestone.

serpent, snake, eel; maze, labyrinth.

v. **be convoluted** etc. *adj.;* wind, twine, turn and twist, twirl; wave, undulate, meander; inosculate; entwine *or* intwine; twist, coil, roll; wrinkle, curl, crisp, twill; frizz, frizzle; crimp, crape, indent, scollop, scallop; wring, intort; contort; wreathe etc. (*cross*) 219.

adj. **convoluted**; winding, twisted etc. *v.;* tortile, tortive [*obs.*]; wavy; undate *or* undated [*rare*], undulatory; circling, snaky, snakelike, serpentine, serpentiform, anguilliform, anguiform, anguilloid, anguillous, vermiform, vermicular; mazy, tortuous, sinuose, sinuous, sinuate, flexuous; undulating, undulated, wavy; anfractuous, reclivate [*rare*], rivulose, scolecoid; sigmoid, sigmoidal; spiriferous, spiroid.

wreathy, frizzly, *crêpé* [*F.*], buckled; raveled etc. (*in disorder*) 59.

involved, intricate, complicated, perplexed; labyrinthic, labyrinthian, labyrinthine; circuitous, ambagious; peristaltic; Daedalian; kinky, curly.

spiral, coiled, helical; cochlear, cochleate, cochleous [*rare*]; screw-shaped; turbinated, turbiniform, turbinoid, turbinal.

adv. in and out, round and round.

249. Rotundity

n. **rotundity**; roundness etc. *adj.;* cylindricity; sphericality, sphericity, spheroidicity *or* spheroidity, globoseness, globosity, globularity, annularity, orotundity, orbiculation.

cylinder, cylindroid; barrel, drum; roll, roller; rouleau, column, rolling-pin, rundle.

cone, conoid; pear-shape, egg-shape, bell-shape.

sphere, globe, ball, bowlder *or* boulder; spheroid, geoid, globoid, ellipsoid; oblong–, oblate-spheroid; drop, spherule, globule, vesicle, bulb, bullet, pellet, clew, pill, marble, pea, knob, pommel, horn, knot; oval etc. 247.

v. **render spherical** etc. *adj.;* form into a sphere, sphere, roll into a ball; give rotundity etc. *n.;* round.

adj. **rotund**; round etc. (*circular*) 247; cylindric *or* cylindrical, cylindroid *or* cylindroidal, columnar, vermiform, lumbriciform; conic, conical; spherical, spheroidal; globular, globous, globose; gibbous; fungiform, bulbous; *teres atque rotundus* [*L.*]; round as -an orange, –an apple, –a ball, –a billiard ball, –a cannon ball.

bead-shaped, beadlike, moniliform, monilated.

bell-shaped, campaniform, campanulate, campanulous, campanular.

egg-shaped, ovoid, oviform, ovoidal, ovate, globoid, globate *or* globated; obovate, obovoid [*both bot.*].

pear-shaped, pyriform.

rice-shaped, riziform.

250. Convexity

n. **convexity**, prominence, projection, swelling, gibbosity, bilge, bulge, protuberance, protrusion, excrescency; camber, swell.

intumescence, tumidity; tumor *or* tumour; tubercle, tuberousness, tuberosity, carunculation, bubo.

excrescence, hump, hunch, bunch; knob, knur, knurl, gnarl, knot; bow, boss, embossment, bump, mamelon, clump; bulb, node, nodule, nodosity.

tooth, molar; lip, flange; tongue; withers, shoulder, back, dorsum; elbow.

process, apophysis, condyle.

wheel, hub, hubble.

peg; button, stud; ridge, rib, trunnion, snag; sugar loaf etc. (*sharpness*) 253.

pimple, wen, whelk, papula, papule, pustule, pock, proud flesh, growth, sarcoma, caruncle, corn, wart, verruca, furuncle, polypus, fungus, fungosity, exostosis, bleb, blister, bulla, blain; boil etc. (*disease*) 655; air bubble, blob.

papilla, nipple, teat, pap, breast, dug, mammilla.

proboscis, nose, olfactory organ, neb, beak, snout, nozzle.

belly, corporation [*colloq.*], paunch, epigastrium, abdomen.

arch, cupola, dome, vault, beehive; balcony; eaves.

relief, relievo, cameo; low relief, bas-relief, basso-relievo *or basso-rilievo* [*It.*]; half relief, mezzo-relievo *or mezzo-rilievo* [*It.*]; high relief, alto-relievo *or alto-rilievo* [*It.*]; pilaster.

point of land, hill etc. (*height*) 206; cape, promontory, mull; foreland, headland; hummock, ledge, spur; naze, ness; mole, jetty, jutty.

v. **be prominent** etc. *adj.;* project, bulge, protrude, bag, belly, carunculate, pout, bouge [*obs.*], bunch; jut out, stand out, stick out, poke out; stick up, bristle up, start up, cock up, shoot up; swell over, hang over, bend over; beetle.

render prominent etc. *adj.;* raise 307; emboss, chase.

adj. **prominent**, protuberant, protrusile, protrusive; undershot, underhung; projecting etc. *v.;* bossed, bossy, nodular, convex, bunchy; clavate, clavated, claviform; hummocky, *moutonné* [*F.*]; caruncular *or* carunculous, carunculate *or* carunculated; furuncular, furunculous, furunculoid; mammiform; papulous, papulose; hemispheric, bulbous; bowed, arched; bold; bellied; tuberous, tuberculous; tumorous; cornute, odontoid; lentiform, lenticular; gibbous; club-shaped, hubby, hubbly, knobby, papillose; saddle-shaped, selliform; subclavate, torose, ventricose, verrucose; excrescential.

salient, in relief, raised, *repoussé* [*F.*]; bloated etc. (*expanded*) 194.

251. Flatness

n. **flatness** etc. *adj.;* smoothness etc. 255.

plane; level etc. 213; plate, platter, table, tablet, slab.

v. **flatten**; render flat; squelch, squash, fell; level etc. 213.

adj. **flat**, plane, even, flush, scutiform, discoid; complanate, flattish, homaloid; level etc. (*horizontal*) 213; flat as -a pancake, –a fluke, –a flounder, –a board, –my hand; smooth.

adv. **flat**, flatly [*rare*], flatways, flatwise, lengthwise, horizontally.

252. Concavity

n. **concavity**, depression, dip; hollow, hollowness; indentation, intaglio, cavity, vug *or* vugg *or* vugh, dent, dint, dimple, follicle, pit, sinus, antrum, alveolus, lacuna; honeycomb.

excavation, pit, sap, mine, shaft, colliery; caisson, *fougasse* [*F.*], countermine; trough etc. (*furrow*) 259; bay etc. (*of the sea*) 343.

cup, basin, crater, punch bowl; cell etc. (*receptacle*) 191; socket.

valley, vale, dale, dell, dingle, coomb *or* combe, bottom, slade [*obs.*], strath [*Scot.*], gill *or* ghyll [*Scot. & dial. Eng.*], glade, grove, glen, donga [*S. Africa*], nullah [*India*], park.

cave, subterrane, cavern, cove; grot, grotto; alcove, blind alley, *cul-de-sac* [*F.*], hole, burrow, kennel, tunnel; gully etc. 198; arch etc. (*curve*) 245.

excavator, sapper, miner.

v. **be concave** etc. *adj.;* retire, cave in.

render concave etc. *adj.;* depress, dish, hollow; scoop, scoop out; gouge, dig, delve, excavate, dent, dint, mine, sap, undermine, burrow, tunnel, stave in.

adj. **depressed** etc. *v.;* alveolate, alveolar, calathiform, cup-shaped, dishing; favaginous, faveolate, favose; scyphiform, scyphose; concave, hollow, vuggy, stove in; retiring; retreating; cavernous; porous etc. (*with holes*) 260; cellular, spongy, spongious; honey-combed; infundibular, infundibuliform, funnel-shaped, bell-shaped, campani-form, capsular; vaulted, arched.

253. Sharpness

n. **sharpness** etc. *adj.;* acuity, acumination, mucronation; spinosity.

point, spike, spine, spiculum; needle, pin; prick, prickle; spur, rowel, barb; spit, cusp; horn, antler; snag; tag; thorn, bristle; Adam's needle, bear grass, tine, yucca.

nib, tooth, tusk; spoke, cog, ratchet.

beard, cheval-de-frise (*pl.* chevaux-de-frise), porcupine, hedgehog, brier, bramble, thistle; comb; awn, beggar's lice, bur *or* burr, catchweed, cleavers *or* clivers, goose grass, hairif or hariff [*dial. Eng.*], flax comb, hatchel *or* hackle *or* heckle.

peak, crag, crest, *arête* [*F.*], cone, sugar loaf, pike, aiguille; spire, pyramid, steeple.

cutting-edge, knife-edge, blade, edge tool, cutlery, knife, penknife, whittle, razor; scalpel, bistoury, lancet; plowshare, colter; hatchet, ax *or* axe, pickax, mattock, pick, adz *or* adze, bill; billhook, cleaver, cutter; scythe, sickle, scissors, shears; sword etc. (*arms*) 727; wedge; bodkin etc. (*perforator*) 262; *belduque* [*F.*], bowie knife, paring knife; bushwhacker; drawing knife *or* drawknife, drawshave.

sharpener, hone, strop; grindstone, whetstone; novaculite; steel, emery.

v. **be sharp** etc. *adj.;* taper to a point; bristle with, acuminate.

render sharp etc. *adj.;* sharpen, point, aculeate, acuminate, whet, barb, spiculate, set, strop, grind.

cut etc. (*sunder*) 44.

adj. **sharp**, keen; acute; acicular, aciform; aculeate *or* aculeated, acuminate *or* acuminated, pointed; tapering; mucronate *or* mucronated, mucronulate; spiked, spiky, peaked, salient; cusped, cuspidate *or* cuspidated; prickly, echinate *or* echinated, acanaceous, acanthophorous, spiny, spinous, spinulose, spinulescent, spinuliferous; apiculate *or* apiculated; thorny, bristling, muricate *or* muricated, corniculate, pectinate *or* pectinated, studded, thistly, briery; craggy etc. (*rough*) 256; snaggy, digitate *or* digitated, two-edged.

arrow-shaped, arrowheaded, arrowy, sagittal, sagittate, sagittated, sagittiform.

barbed, glochidiate, spurred, aristate, awned, awny, bearded, barbate, crestate, setarious, subulate, tetrahedral.

cone-shaped, conic, conical, coniform [*rare*], pyramidal.

horn-shaped, corniform, cornute *or* cornuted; crescent-shaped; horned, corniculate.

lance-shaped, lanceolate, lanciform.

reed-shaped, calamiform [*rare*], arundinaceous, reedy.

scimitar-shaped, acinaciform.

spear-shaped, hastate, hastiform [*rare*], lance-shaped (*q.v.*).

spindle-shaped, fusiform.

star-shaped, stellate *or* stellated, stelliform, stellular, starlike, starry.

sword-shaped, gladiate, ensate, ensiform, xiphoid.

tooth-shaped, dentiform, toothlike, odontoid, dentoid.

keen-edged, cutting; sharp-edged, knife-edged; sharp–, keen- as a razor; sharp as a needle; sharpened etc. *v.;* set.

254. Bluntness

n. **bluntness** etc. *adj.*

v. **be** *or* **render blunt** etc. *adj.;* obtund, dull; take off the -point, –edge; unedge [*rare*], turn.

adj. **blunt**, obtuse, dull, dullish, pointless, unpointed; unsharpened, bluff; edentate, toothless.

255. Smoothness

n. **smoothness** etc. *adj.;* polish, gloss; lubricity, lubrication.

[smooth surfaces] bowling green etc. (*level*) 213; glass, ice, slide; asphalt, granolithic pavement, wood pavement, flags; down, velvet, silk, taffeta, satin, velveteen, velumen.

smoother; roller, steam roller; sandpaper, emery paper; flatiron, sadiron; burnisher, chamois *or* shammy, turpentine and beeswax.

v. **smooth**, smoothen [*rare*]; plane; file; mow, shave; level, roll; macadamize; polish, burnish, sleek, planish, levigate, calendar, glaze; iron, hotpress, mangle; lubricate etc. (*oil*) 332.

adj. **smooth**; polished etc. *v.;* leiodermatous, slick [*colloq.*], velutinous; even; level etc. 213; plane etc. (*flat*) 251; sleek, glossy; silken, silky; lanate, downy, velvety; glabrous, slippery, glassy, lubricious *or* lubricous, oily, soft; unwrinkled; smooth as -glass, –ice, –monumental alabaster, –ivory, –satin, –velvet, –oil; slippery as an eel; woolly etc. (*feathery*) 256.

256. Roughness

n. **roughness** etc. *adj.;* tooth, grain, texture, ripple; asperity, rugosity, salebrosity [*obs.*], corrugation, nodosity, nodulation; arborescence etc. 242; pilosity.

hair, brush, beard, shag, mane, whiskers, moustache, imperial, trees, lock, curl, ringlet, fimbria, eyelashes, lashes, cilia, villi; lovelock; beaucatcher; curl paper; goatee; papillote, scalp lock, scolding locks [*colloq.*], elf locks, mop, mat, thatch; fringe, toupee; hair shirt.

plumage, plumosity; plume, panache, crest; feather, tuft.

nap, pile, floss, velvet, plush, fur, down, wool, fluff; byssus, moss, bur *or* burr.

v. **be rough** etc. *adj.;* go against the grain.

render rough etc. *adj.;* roughen, knurl, crinkle, ruffle, crisp, crumple, corrugate, engrail;

roughcast; set on edge, stroke the wrong way, rub the fur the wrong way, rumple.

adj. **rough**, uneven; scabrous, knotted; rugged, rugose, rugous, rugulose; nodose, nodular, nodulated; knurled, cross-grained, knurly; asperous [*obs.*], crisp, salebrous [*obs.*], gnarled, gnarly, scraggly, scragged, scraggy; jagged; unkempt, unpolished, unsmooth, rough-hewn; craggy, cragged; crankling [*obs.*]; prickly etc. (*sharp*) 253; arborescent etc. 242; leafy, well-wooded.

feathery, plumose, plumigerous.

hairy, bristly, hirsute, hispid, pappous *or* pappose, pileous, pilose, pilous; trichogenous, trichoid; tufted, ciliated, filamentous; crinose, crinite; bushy; villous, nappy; bearded, shaggy, shagged; setous [*obs.*], setose, setaceous, setiferous, setigerous, setiform; "like quills upon the fretful porcupine" [*Hamlet*]; rough as a -nutmeg grater, -bear.

downy, velvety, flocculent, woolly, lanate, lanated, lanuginous, lanuginose; tomentose; fluffy.

fringed, befringed, fimbriate, fimbriated, fimbricate, laciniate *or* laciniated, laciniform, laciniose.

adv. **against the grain**; the wrong way of the goods; in the rough; on edge.

257. Notch

n. **notch**, dent, nick, cut; dimple; scotch, indent, indentation, denticulation, serration, serrature.
saw, tooth, crenel *or* crenelle, scallop *or* scollop; rickrack, picot edge, vandyke; depression, jag.
embrasure, battlement, machicolation.

v. **notch**, nick, pink, mill, score, cut, dent, indent, jag, scarify, scotch, crimp, scallop *or* scollop, crenulate, crenelate *or* crenellate, vandyke.

adj. **notched** etc. *v.;* crenate *or* crenated; dentate *or* dentated, denticulate *or* denticulated, crenelated *or* crenellated, toothed, palmate *or* palmated, serriform, serrate *or* serrated, serrulate.

258. Fold

n. **fold**, plicature, plication, pleat, plait, ply, crease; knife-pleat, knife-plait, box-pleat, box-plait; accordion pleat, accordion plait; tuck, gather; flexion, flexure, joint, elbow, double, doubling, duplicature, gather, wrinkle, rimple, crinkle, crankle, crumple, rumple, rivel [*archaic*], ruck, ruffle, dog's-ear, corrugation, frounce [*obs.*], flounce, lapel; pucker, crow's-feet.

v. **fold**, double, plicate, pleat, plait, crease, wrinkle, crinkle, crankle, curl, smock, shrivel, cockle up, cocker [*dial.*], rimple, rumple, frizzle, frounce [*archaic*], rivel [*archaic*], twill, corrugate, ruffle, crimple [*obs.*], crumple, pucker; turn-, double- -down, -under; dog's-ear, tuck, ruck, hem, gather.

adj. **folded** etc. *v.*

259. Furrow

n. **furrow**, groove, rut, sulcus, scratch, streak, striae, crack, score, incision, slit; chamfer, fluting; corduroy road, cradle hole [*sleighing*].
trench, ditch, dike *or* dyke, moat, fosse, trough, channel, gutter, ravine etc. (*interval*) 198; depression, tajo.

v. **furrow** etc. *n.;* flute, groove, chamfer, carve, corrugate, cut, chisel, plow; incise, engrave, etch, enchase, mezzotint, crosshatch, hatch, grave, bite in.

adj. **furrowed** etc. *v.;* ribbed, striated, sulcated, fluted, caniculate *or* caniculated; bisulcous *or* bisulcate *or* bisulcated; canaliferous; unisulcate; trisulcate; corduroy; costate, rimiform [*rare*].

260. Opening

n. **opening**, aperture, apertness [*archaic*]; hiation [*rare*], yawning, oscitance *or* oscitancy, dehiscence, patefaction [*obs.*], pandiculation; chasm etc. (*interval*) 198.
outlet, inlet; vent, venthole, blow-hole, airhole, spiracle; vomitory [*Rom. arch.*]; embouchure; orifice, mouth, sucker, muzzle, throat, gullet, weasand, wizen [*dial.*], nozzle; placket.
window, casement; embrasure, *abatjour* [*F.*]; light; skylight, fanlight; lattice; bay window, bow window, oriel, dormer; lantern.
portal, porch, gate, ostiary [*obs.*], postern, wicket, trapdoor, hatch, door; arcade; cellarway, driveway, gateway, doorway, hatchway, gangway; lich gate *or* lych gate [*archaic*].
way, path etc. 627; thoroughfare; channel, gully; passage, passageway.
tube, pipe, main; water pipe etc. 350; air pipe etc. 351; vessel, tubule, canal, gut, fistula; ajutage *or* adjutage; ostium; smokestack; chimney, flue, tap, funnel.
tunnel, mine, pit, adit, drift, shaft; gallery.
alley, lane, mall, aisle, glade, vista.
bore, caliber *or* calibre; pore; blind orifice; fulgurite, thunder tube.

hole, foramen; puncture, perforation; fontane *or* fontanelle; transforation; pinhole, keyhole, loophole, porthole, peephole, mousehole, pigeonhole; eye, eye of a needle; eyelet; slot.

porousness, porosity; sieve, strainer, colander *or* cullender; cribble, riddle, screen; honeycomb.

performation, apertion [*archaic*]; piercing etc. *v.;* terebration, empalement, pertusion [*obs.*], puncture, acupuncture, penetration.

opener, key, master key, *passepartout* [*F.*], clavis, open-sesame.

v. **open**, ope [*poetic*], gape, yawn, hiate [*rare*], dehisce, bilge; fly open.

perforate, pierce, empierce [*obs.*], tap, bore, drill; mine etc. (*scoop out*) 252; tunnel; transpierce, transfix; enfilade, impale, spike, spear, gore, spit, stab, pink, puncture, lance; trepan, trephine; stick, prick, riddle, punch; stave in.
cut a passage through; make way for, make room for.

uncover, unclose, unrip, rip; lay–, cut–, rip–, throw- open.

adj. **open**; perforated etc. *v.;* perforate; wide open, patulous, agape, dehiscent, ringent; ajar, unclosed, unstopped; oscitant, gaping, yawning; patent.

tubular, cannular, fistulous; pervious, permeable; foraminous; vesicular, vascular; porous, follicular, cribriform, honeycombed, infundibular *or* infundibulate, riddled; tubulose *or* tubulous, tubulate *or* tubulated; piped, tubate, tubiform.

opening etc. *v.;* aperient.

int. open sesame! gangway! passageway!

261. Closure

n. **closure**, occlusion, blockade; shutting up etc. *v.;* obstruction etc. (*hindrance*) 706; embolism, embolus; contraction etc. 195; infarct, infarction; constipation, obstipation; blind -alley, –corner; keddah [*India*], cul-de-sac [*F.*]; cecum *or* caecum; imperforation, imperviousness etc. *adj.;* impermeability; stopper etc. 263; operculum.

v. **close**, occlude, plug; block up, stop up, fill up, bung up, cork up, button up, stuff up, shut up, dam up; blockade; obstruct etc. (*hinder*) 706; bar, bolt, stop, seal, plumb; choke, throttle; ram down, dam, cram; trap, clinch; put to–, shut-the door; slam, clap, snap.

adj. **closed** etc. *v.;* shut, operculated; unopened, blank.

unpierced, imporous, caecal; embolic; infarcted, imperforate, impervious, impermeable; impenetrable; impassable, unpassable, invious [*obs.*]; pathless, wayless; untrodden.

tight, unventilated, air-tight, water-tight, hermetically sealed; snug.

262. Perforator

n. **performator**, piercer, borer, auger, chisel, gimlet, drill, wimble, awl, bradawl, scoop, terrier [*obs.*], corkscrew, dibble, trocar, trepan, trephine, probe, bodkin, needle, stylet, stiletto, broach, reamer, rimer, lancet; punch, puncheon; spikebit, gouge; spear etc. (*weapon*) 727; puncher; punching machine, punching press; punch pliers.

263. Stopper

n. **stopper**, stopple; plug, cork, bung, spike, spill, spile, stopcock, tap, faucet; rammer; ram, ramrod; piston; stop-gap; wadding, stuffing, padding, stopping, dossil, pledget, sponge [*surg.*], tampion *or* tompion, tourniquet.

valve, vent peg, spigot, slide valve, cover etc. 223.

doorkeeper, gatekeeper, janitor, janitress [*fem.*], janitrix [*fem.*], *concierge* [*F.*], porter, portress [*fem.*], warder, beadle, tiler *or* tyler [*Freemasonry*], durwaun [*Hind.*], usher, guard, sentinel; beefeater, yeoman of the guard [*Eng.*]; Cerberus, watch dog, ostiary.

Section 4. Motion

264. Motion

[successive change of place]

n. **motion**, movement, motility, motivity; move; going etc. *v.;* mobility; movableness, motive power, motorium; laws of motion; mobilization. stream, flow, flux, run, course, stir; conduction; evolution; kinematics; telekinesis.

rate, pace, tread, step, stride, gait, port, footfall, cadence, carriage, velocity, angular velocity; clip [*colloq.*], progress, locomotion; journey etc. 266; voyage etc. 267; transit etc. 270.

restlessness etc. (*changeableness*) 149; unrest.

v. **be in motion** etc. *adj.;* move, go, hie, gang [*Scot. & dial. Eng.*], budge, stir, pass, slit; hover -round, –about; shift, slide, glide; roll, roll on; flow, stream, run, drift, sweep along; wander etc. (*deviate*) 279; walk etc. 266; change–, shift-one's -place, –quarters; dodge; keep going, keep moving.

put in motion, set in motion; move; impel etc. 276; propel etc. 284; render movable, mobilize.

adj. **moving** etc. *v.;* in motion; traveling, transitional, metabatic; motory [*rare*], motive; shifting, movable, mobile, motiferous, motile, motific [*rare*], motor, motorial, quicksilver, mercurial, unquiet; restless etc. (*changeable*) 149; nomadic etc. 266; erratic etc. 279.

telekinetic, kinematic *or* kinematical, evolutionary.

adv. **under way**; on the -move, –wing, –fly, –tramp, –march.

265. Quiescence

n. **rest**; stillness etc. *adj.;* quiescence; stagnation, stagnancy; fixity, immobility, catalepsy; indisturbance [*rare*]; quietism.

quiet, tranquillity, calm; repose etc. 687; peace; dead calm, anticyclone; statue-like repose; silence etc. 403; not a breath of air, not a mouse stirring; not a leaf stirring; sleep etc. (*inactivity*) 683.

pause, lull etc. (*cessation*) 142; stand, standstill; standing still etc. *v.;* lock; deadlock, dead stop, dead stand; full stop; fix; embargo.

resting place; *gîte* [*F.*]; bivouac; home etc. (*abode*) 189; pillow etc. (*support*) 215; haven etc. (*refuge*) 666; goal etc. (*arrival*) 292.

v. **be quiescent** etc. *adj.;* stand still, stand fast, stand firm, lie still; keep quiet, repose, rest one's bonnet on a chair [*dial.*], rest one's face and hands [*dial.*], hold the breath.

remain, stay; stand, lie to, ride at anchor, remain *in situ,* tarry, mark time; bring to, heave to, lay to; pull up, draw up; hold, halt; stop, stop short; rest, pause, anchor; cast anchor, come to anchor; rest on one's oars; repose–, rest- on one's laurels; lie back on one's record; take breath; stop etc. (*discontinue*) 142.

vegetate, stagnate; *quieta non movere* [*L.*]; let alone, let well enough alone; abide, rest and be thankful; keep within doors, stay at home, go to bed, live the life of a claim.

dwell etc. (*be present*) 186; settle etc. (*be located*) 184; alight etc. (*arrive*) 292; stick, stick fast; stand, stand like a post; not stir a -peg, –step; stand like a stuck pig [*colloq.*]; be at a stand etc. *n.*

quell, becalm, hush, calm, still, stay, lull to sleep, lay an embargo on, put the brakes on.

adj. **quiescent**, still; motionless, moveless; fixed; stationary; immotile; at rest, at a stand, at a standstill, at anchor; stock-still; standing still etc.

v.; sedentary, untraveled, stay-at-home; becalmed, stagnant, quiet; unmoved, undisturbed, unruffled; calm, restful; cataleptic; immovable etc. (*stable*) 150; sleeping etc. (*inactive*) 683; silent etc. 403; still as - a statue, –a post, –a stone, –a mouse, –death.

adv. **at a stand** etc. *adj.; tout court* [*F.*]; at the halt.

int. **stop!** stay! avast! [*naut.*], halt! hold hard! whoa! hold! *sabr karo!* [*Hind.*], *arrêtez!* [*F.*], *halte!* [*F.*].

266. Journey
[locomotion by land]

n. **travel**; traveling etc. *v.;* wayfaring, campaigning, nomadization.

excursion, journey, expedition, tour, trip, grand tour, *Wanderjahr* [*Ger.*], circuit, peregrination, discursion [*obs.*], ramble, pilgrimage, hadj *or* hajj [*Ar.*], trek [*S. Africa*], course, ambulation, march, walk, promenade, constitutional [*colloq.*], stroll, saunter, hike [*colloq.*], tramp, jog trot, turn, stalk, perambulation; outing, ride, drive, airing, jaunt.

nightwalking, noctambulation, noctambulism; somnambulism, sleep walking, somnambulation.

riding, equitation, horsemanship, manège, manage [*archaic*], ride and tie.

roving, vagrancy, pereration [*obs.*]; marching and countermarching; nomadism; vagabondism, vagabondage; hoboism; gadding; flit, flitting; migration; emigration, immigration, demigration [*obs.*], intermigration; *Wanderlust* [*Ger.*].

itinerary, plan, guide; handbook, travel guide, roadbook; Baedeker, Bradshaw, Michelin, Murray.

procession, parade, cavalcade, caravan, file, *cortège* [*F.*], column.

organs and instruments of locomotion] cycle, automobile, motor car etc. (*vehicle*) 272; trolley, locomotive; palanquin *or* palankeen, litter, dandy *or* dandi [*India*], jinrikisha *or* jinricksha; roller skates, skates, skis, snowshoes; legs, shanks, feet; pegs, pins, trotters [*colloq.*].

traveler etc. 268.

station, stop, stopping place, terminal, terminus, depot, railway station, *gare* [*F.*].

v. **travel**, journey, course; take–, go- a journey; railroad [*U. S.*]; flit, take wing; migrate, emigrate, immigrate; trek [*S. Africa*]; scour–, traverse- the country; peragrate [*obs.*]; perambulate, circumambulate; tour, peregrinate, itinerate [*rare*], nomadize.

motor, motorcycle, bicycle, cycle, spin, speed, burn up the road; trolley; go by -car, –trolley, –automobile, –rail, –train etc.

motorize, electrify.

wander, roam, range, prowl, rove, jaunt, ramble, stroll, saunter, hover, go one's rounds, straggle; gad, gad about; expatiate [*rare*]; patrol, pace up and down, traverse; take a walk etc. *n.;* go out for a walk etc. *n.;* have a run, take the air; noctambulate; somnambulate.

take horse, ride, drive, trot, amble, canter, prance, fisk [*obs.*], frisk, *caracoler* [*F.*], caracole; gallop etc. (*move quickly*) 274.

walk, march, step, tread, pace, plod, wend [*archaic*]; promenade; trudge, track, hoof it [*slang*], hike [*colloq.*], tramp; stalk, stride, straddle, strut, foot it, stump, bundle, bowl along, toddle; paddle; tread–, follow–, pursue- a path.

peg on, jog on, wag on, shuffle on; stir one's stumps [*colloq.*]; bend one's -steps, –course; make–, find–, wend–, pick–, thread–, plow- one's way.

glide, slide, coast, skim, skate.

file off, march in procession, defile.

go to, repair to, resort to, hie to, betake oneself to.

adj. **traveling** etc. *v.;* ambulatory, itinerant, peripatetic, perambulatory, mundivagant [*rare*], roving, rambling, gadding, discursive, vagrant, migratory, nomadic; circumforanean [*obs.*], circumforaneous.

night-wandering, noctivagant [*rare*], noctambulistic, noctivagous, somnambulistic *or* somnambular, somnambulant.

self-moving, automobile, automotive, locomotive, locomobile, automatic.

wayfaring, wayworn; travel-stained.

adv. on foot, on horseback, on shanks' mare; by the Marrowbone stage; *in transitu* etc. 270; *en route* etc. 282.

Int. come along! step on it!

267. Navigation

[locomotion by water or air]

n. **navigation**; volatility; aquatics; boating, yachting, cruising; ship etc. 273.

oar, scull, sweep, pole; paddle, screw, turbine; sail, canvas.

nation, swimming; fin, flipper, fish's tail.

aeronautics, aerostatics, aerostation, aerodonetics, aerial navigation, aeronautism; aeromechanics, aerodynamics, balloonery; balloon etc. 273; ballooning; aviation, airmanship; flying,

flight, volitation; volplaning, planing [*colloq.*], hydroplaning, volplane, glide, dive, nose-dive, spin, looping the loop; wing' pinion, aileron.

voyage, sail, cruise, passage, circumnavigation, periplus; headway, sternway, leeway; fairway.

mariner etc. 269; **aeronaut** etc. 269a.

v. **sail**; put to sea etc. (*depart*) 293; take ship, weigh anchor, get under way; spread -sail, –canvas; gather way, have way on; make–, carry- sail; plow the -waves, –deep, –main, –ocean; ride the waves, ride the storm, buffet the waves, walk the waters.

navigate, warp, luff, scud, boom, kedge; drift, course, cruise, steam, coast; hug the -shore, –land; circumnavigate.

row, paddle, ply the oar, pull, scull, punt.

float, swim, skim, *effleurer* [*F.*], dive, wade.

[in aeronautics] fly, soar, drift, hover, be wafted, aviate, volplane, plane [*colloq.*], glide, dive, fly over, nose-dive, spin, loop the loop, land; take wing, take a flight; wing one's flight, wing one's way.

adj. **sailing** etc. *v.;* seafaring, nautical, maritime, naval; seagoing, coasting; afloat; navigable; grallatorial *or* grallatory.

aeronautic, aeronautical, aerostatic, *or* aerostatical, aeromechanic *or* aeromechanical, aerodynamic, aerial, volant, volitant, volatile, volitational.

aquatic, natatory, natatorial, natational.

adv. **under -way**, –sail, –canvas, –steam; on the wing.

268. Traveler

n. **traveler**, wayfarer, voyager, itinerant, passenger, transient, commuter, straphanger [*colloq.*].

tourist, excursionist, explorer, adventurer, mountaineer, Alpine Club; peregrinator, wanderer, rover, straggler, rambler; landsman, landlubber, horse marine; bird of passage; gadabout [*colloq.*], gadling [*obs.*]; vagrant, scattering [*obs.*], landlouper *or* landloper, waifs and estrays, wastrel, stray; loafer, swagman *or* swagsman [*Australia*], tramp, vagabond, nomad, Bohemian, gypsy, Arab, Wandering Jew, hadji *or* hajji [*Ar.*], pilgrim, palmer; peripatetic; comers and goers, immigrant; *émigré* [*F.*], emigrant; runagate, runaway, renegade, fugitive, refugee; beachcomber; booly [*Irish hist.*]; globe-girdler, globetrotter [*colloq.*]; hobo [*U. S.*], runabout, trekker [*S. Africa*], camper, *zingaro* (*pl. zingari*) [*It.*].

sleepwalker, somnambulist, somnambulator [*rare*], nightwalker, noctambulist.

courier, messenger, express, *estafette* [*F.*], runner; Mercury, Iris, Ariel; comet.

pedestrian, walker, foot passenger, hiker [*colloq.*], perigrinator [*rare*], tramper.

rider, horseman, horsewoman [*fem.*], equestrian, equestrienne [*fem.*], cavalier, jockey, roughrider, trainer, breaker, huntsman, whip, postilion *or* postillion, postboy.

driver, coachman, Jehu [*humorous*], charioteer, carter, wagoner, drayman; cabman, cabdriver; *voiturier* [*F.*], *vetturino* [*It.*], *condottiere* [*It.*], gharry-wallah *or* gari-wala [*Hind.*], hackman, syce [*India*], truckman.

[railroad] engine driver [*Brit.*], engineer, fireman, stoker, conductor, guard [*Brit.*], motorman.

[automobile] driver, chauffeur, chauffeuse [*fem.*], automobilist, motorist, truck driver, mechanician; scorcher [*slang*], speed maniac, road hog [*slang*].

269. Mariner

n. **mariner**, sailor, navigator; seaman, seafarer, seafaring man, sea dog [*colloq.*], hand, water dog [*colloq.*], shellback [*slang*]; Ancient Mariner, Flying Dutchman; dock walloper [*slang*]; Jack, Jack Tar *or* jack-tar, tar, jacky (*pl.* jackies) [*landsman's term*], shipman [*obs. or poet.*], gob [*slang*]; salt, able seaman, A. B.; man-of-war's man, bluejacket, galiongee *or* galionji, marine, devil-dog [*slang*], jolly [*slang*]; midshipman, middy [*colloq.*]; lascar, *mangee* or *manjhi* [*Hind.*], *matelot* [*F.*], captain, commander, master mariner, skipper; mate; boatman, ferryman, waterman, lighterman, bargeman, longshoreman; bargee, gondolier; oar, oarsman; rower; boatswain.

steersman, coxswain *or* cockswain, cox [*colloq.*], helmsman, wheelman, pilot, *patron* [*F.*]; crew.

269a. Aeronaut

n. **aeronaut**, aviator, aeroplanist, airman, airwoman, flyer, birdman [*colloq.*], birdwoman [*colloq.*], aviatress *or* aviatrix, navigator, manbird [*colloq.*], wizard of the air, monoplanist; pilot, observer, spotter, scout, bombardier *or* bomber, ace; balloonist, Icarus.

270. Transference

n. **transfer**, transference; translocation, elocation [*obs.*]; displacement; metastasis, metathesis; removal; remotion; amotion; relegation; deportation, asportation, extradition, conveyance, draft; carrying, carriage; convection, conduc-

tion, contagion, infection; transfusion; transfer etc. (*of property*) 783.

transit, transition; passage, ferry, gestation; portage, porterage, freightage, carting, cartage; shoveling etc. *v.;* vection [*obs.*], vecture [*obs.*], vectitation [*obs.*]; shipment, freight, waftage; transmission, transport, transporation, transumption [*rare*], transplantation, translation; shifting, dodging; dispersion etc. 73; transposition etc. (*interchange*) 148; traction etc. 285; *portamento* [*music, It.*].

[thing transferred] drift, alluvion, alluvium, detritus, deposit, moraine; deed, gift, bequest, legacy, lease; quitclaim; freight, cargo, mail, baggage, luggage, goods.

transferee, grantee, assignee; donee, legatee, consignee, indorsee, devisee.

v. **transfer**, transmit, transport, transplace, transplant, transfuse; convey, carry, bear, fetch and carry; carry over, ferry over; hand, pass, forward; shift; conduct, convoy, bring, fetch, reach; tote.

send, delegate, consign, relegate, turn over to, deliver; ship, freight, embark; waft; shunt; transpose etc. (*interchange*) 148; displace etc. 185; throw etc. 284; drag etc. 285; mail, post.

ladle, bail *or* bale, bucket, lade, dip, drip; shovel, decant, draft off.

adj. **transferred** etc. *v.;* drifted, movable; portable, portative; conductive, contagious, infectious; metastatic, metathetic *or* metathetical; transumptive [*rare*].

transferable, assignable, conveyable, devisable, bequeathable, negotiable, transmittible, transmissible; mailable.

adv. from hand to hand, from pillar to post; by freight, by rail, by steamer, by aeroplane, by trolley, by motor truck, by express, by mail, by special delivery.

on the way, by the way; on the road, on the wing; as one goes; *in transitu* [*L.*], *en route* [*F.*], *chemin faisant* [*F.*], *en passant* [*F.*], in mid-progress.

271. Carrier

n. **carrier**, porter, red cap, bearer, tranter [*obs.*], conveyer; *cargador* [*P.I.*], freighter, express, expressman; stevedore; coolie; conductor, chauffeur, truck driver; letter carrier, postman, man of letters [*humorous*], aerial mail-carrier.

beast of burden, beast, cattle, horse, steed, nag, palfrey, Arab, blood horse, thoroughbred, galloway, charger, courser, racer, hunter, jument [*obs.*], pony; Shetland, –pony; filly, colt, foal, barb, roan, jade, hack, bidet, pad, cob, tit [*dial.*], punch [*dial.*], roadster, goer; race–, pack–, draft–, cart–, dray–, post- horse; shelty *or* sheltie; garran *or* garron [*Brit.*], jennet *or* genet, bayard, mare, stallion, gelding; broncho *or* bronco, cayuse; creature, critter; cow pony, mustang, Narragansett, waler; stud.

ass, donkey, jackass, burro, cuddy [*Scot. & dial. Eng.*], moke [*slang*]; wild ass, onager.

mule, hinny; sumpter -horse, –mule; ladino.

reindeer; camel, dromedary, llama, elephant; carrier pigeon.

Pegasus, Bucephalus, Rosinante *or* Rocinante, Alborak, Bayard, Incitatus, Kantaha, Veillantif, Vindictive, Black Bess, Kelpie *or* Kelpy.

[means of transport] locomotive, motor, trolley, carriage etc. (*vehicle*) 272; ship etc. 273.

adj. equine, asinine; electric, motor, express.

272. Vehicle

n. **Vehicle,** conveyance, carriage, caravan, car, van; wagon *or* waggon, wain [*archaic*], dray, cart, lorry.

cariole *or* carriole; truck, tram; limber, tumbrel *or* tumbril, pontoon; barrow; wheelbarrow, handbarrow; perambulator; Bath–, wheelchair; chaise; police van, patrol wagon, black Maria [*colloq.*]; conestoga wagon *or* wain; jinrikisha *or* jinricksha, ricksha [*colloq.*], dearborn, dump cart, hack, jigger, horse car; kittereen, mail stage, manumotor, rig, rockaway, prairie schooner, shay [*colloq.*], sloven [*Can.*], team, tonga [*India*], Cape cart [*S. Africa*], hackery [*India*], ekka [*India*]; gharri *or* gharry *or* gari [*India*]; gocart.

equipage, turnout [*colloq.*]; coach, chariot, phaeton, mail phaeton, wagonette, break *or* brake, drag, curricle, tilbury, whiskey [*obs.*], landau, barouche, victoria, brougham, clarence, calash, *calèche* [*F.*], britzka, araba [*Oriental*], kibitka; berlin; sulky, *désobligeant* [*F.*], sociable, *vis-à-vis* [*F.*], *dormeuse* [*F.*], jaunting–, outside- car; runabout; *vettura* [*It.*].

post chaise; diligence [*F.*], stage, stagecoach; mail–, hackney–, glasscoach; stage wagon; car, omnibus, bus [*colloq.*]; fly [*Eng.*], cabriolet, cab, hansom, four-wheeler, growler [*slang, Eng.*]; droshki *or* drosky.

dogcart, trap [*colloq.*], whitechapel, buggy, *char-à-bancs* (*pl. chars-à-bancs*) [*F.*], shandrydan *or* shandradan [*Scot., Ir., & dial. Eng.*].

team, pair, span, tandem, random; spike team *or* spike, unicorn; four-in-hand.

litter, palanquin *or* palankeen, sedan *or* sedan chair; palki, jampan, dandy *or* dandi, dooly

or doolie, munchil [*all India*]; cacolet [*F.*]; tonjon [*Ceylon*], brancard, horse litter; stretcher, hurdle; ambulance.

sled, bob, bobsled *or* bobsleigh; cutter; doubleripper, doublerunner; jumper [*U. S. & Can.*], sledge, sleigh, toboggan, cariole *or* carriole [*Can.*], pung; ski (*pl.* ski *or* skis), snowshoes, skates, roller skates.

cycle, monocycle, bicycle, bicycle built for two, tricycle, quadricycle, hydrocycle, tandem; machine [*colloq.*], wheel [*colloq.*], bike [*slang*], safety bicycle *or* safety [*colloq.*], motor cycle *or* motorcycle; velocipede, hobbyhorse, draisine *or* draisene.

automobile, motor car *or* motorcar, limousine, sedan, touring car, roadster, coupé, motor, machine, car, auto, locomobile, autocar, steamer, electric, runabout, couplet, racer, torpedo; truck, tractor; taxicab, taxi, taxicoach, bus, motor bus *or* motorbus; flivver [*slang*], jitney [*colloq.*], tacot [*F. mil. slang*].

[allied automobile terms] tonneau, trunk, chassis, hood, top, ignition, spark plug, trunk, generator, distributor, magneto, self-starter, gear, gear box, differential, cylinder, manifold, intake, exhaust, carburetor ; four–, six–, eight–, twelve-cylinder; twin six, ammeter, speedometer, oil gauge, primer, clutch, universal joint, crank shaft, transmission, tire, rim; gasoline, petrol [*Brit.*]; trailer; garage; chauffeur etc. 268.

train; express, mail; accommodation–, passenger–, express–, special–, limited–, mail–, corridor–, parliamentary–, luggage [*Brit.*] –, freight–, train; 1st-, 2d-, 3d-class- -train, –carriage, –compartment; rolling stock; cattle truck; car, coach, carriage [*Brit.*]; baggage–, freight–, chair–, drawing- room–, parlor–, Pullman–, sleeping-car; surface–, tram- car; trolley *or* trolley car [*U. S. & Can.*], electric car, electric [*colloq.*]; trollibus, trackless trolley; box car, box wagon; horse box [*Brit.*], horse car; lightning express; mail car, mail van [*Brit.*]; baggage car, luggage van [*Brit.*].

hand car, trolley *or* trolley.

[utensils & implements] spoon, spatula, ladle, hod, hoe; spade, shovel, spaddle [*obs.*], boy [*Ir.*]; spud; pitchfork.

adj. **vehicular,** curricular [*rare*], vehiculatory [*rare*]; ambulatory etc. (*traveling*) 266.

273. Ship

n. **ship,** vessel, sail; craft, bottom.

navy, marine, fleet, flotilla.

shipping, man-of-war etc. (*combatant*) 726; transport, tender, storeship; merchant ship, merchantman; packet, liner; whaler, slaver, collier, coaster, freight-steamer, freighter, lighter; fishing–, pilot- boat; trawler, hulk; yacht; baggala; floating -hotel, –palace; ocean greyhound [*colloq.*].

ship, bark *or* barque; shipentine, four-masted bark *or* barque; brig, snow, hermaphrodite brig; brigantine, barkentine *or* barquentine, schooner; topsail–, fore-and-aft- schooner; fore-and-after [*colloq.*]; three–, four–, five–, six- masted schooner; *chasse-marée* [*F.*], sloop, cutter, corvet *or* corvette, clipper, foist [*obs.*], yawl, dandy, ketch, smack, lugger, barge, hoy, cat, catboat, buss; sailer, sailing vessel; windjammer; steamer, steamboat, steamship; mail–, paddle–, turbine–, screw- steamer; tug; line of steamers etc.

boat, pinnace, launch; lifeboat, long-boat, jollyboat, bumboat, flyboat, cockboat, ferry-boat, canal boat; ark, bully [*N fld.*], bateau [*Can.*], broadhorn, dory, drogher, dugout, Durham boat, galiot *or* galliot, flatboat, shallop, gig, funny [*Eng.*], skiff, dinghy *or* dingey *or* dingy, scow, cockleshell, wherry, coble, punt, cog, lerret [*dial. Eng.*]; eight–, four–, pair- oar; randan; outrigger; float, raft, pontoon; ice-boat, ice-canoe, ice-yacht.

catamaran, coracle, gondola, caravel *or* carvel, felucca, caique, canoe; galley, bilander, dogger, hooker *or* howker [*obs.*]; argosy, carack *or* carrack [*hist.*], galleass *or* galliass, galleon; polacre *or* polacca, corsair, piragua, bunderboat [*India*], tartane, junk, lorcha, praam, proa *or* prahu, saic, sampan, xebec, dhow; dahabeah; nuggar; kayak, keel boat, canoe, pirogue; quadrireme, trireme; stern-wheeler; wanigan *or* wangan, wharf boat; derelict.

[aeronautics] balloon; airship, aeroplane, airplane, monoplane, biplane, triplane; *avion* [*F.*], aeronat, dirigible, zeppelin, zepp [*colloq.*]; air cruiser, battle–, bombing–, combatplane; two-seater, *biplace* [*F.*]; single-seater, *monoplace* [*F.*], aeroboat, aerobus, aero-hydroplane, aeroyacht, flying boat; aircraft; hydroplane, aerodrome [*obsoles.*], air–, pilot–, captive–, fire-balloon; aerostat, Montgolfier; kite, parachute.

[allied aeronautical terms] fuselage, gondola, wings, *ailes* [*F.*], controls, aileron, lifting power, camouflage, rudder; tail, *empennage* [*F.*]; cabane, hangar; aeronaut etc. 269a.

adj. **marine**, maritime, naval, nautical, seafaring, ocean-going; A1, A1 at Lloyd's; seaworthy.

aeronautic *or* aeronautical, aerial; airworthy; volant etc. 267.

adv. **afloat**, aboard; on board, on ship board; hard-a -lee, –port, –starboard, –weather.

274. Velocity

n. **velocity**, speed, celerity; swiftness etc. *adj.;* rapidity, eagle speed, lightning speed; expedition etc. (*activity*) 682; pernicity [*obs.*], acceleration; haste etc. 684.

spurt, sprint, rush, dash, race, steeple chase; automobile race; Marathon race *or* Marathon; smart–, lively–, swift etc. *adj.* -, rattling [*colloq.*] -, spanking [*slang*] -, strapping [*colloq.*]- -rate, –pace; round pace; flying, flight.

pace, gallop, canter, trot, round trot, run, scamper; hand–, full- gallop; swoop.

[comparisons] lightning, light, electricity, wind; cannon ball, rocket, arrow, dart, hydrargyrum, quicksilver, Mercury; wireless, telegraph, express train; swallow flight; torrent.

eagle, antelope, courser, race horse, barb, gazelle, greyhound, hare, doe, squirrel, camel bird, swallow, chickaree, chipmunk, hackee, ostrich.

scorcher [*slang*], joy rider, speedster, speed maniac.

Mercury, Ariel, Puck, Camilla, Harlequin.

[measurement of velocity] velocimeter, speedometer, patent log, log, log line.

v. **move quickly**, trip, fisk [*obs.*]; speed, hie, hasten, spurt, sprint, post, spank, scuttle; scud, scuddle [*obs. or Scot.*], scurry, whiz; thunder -by, –on; scour, scour the plain; scamper; run, run like mad [*colloq.*], fly, race, run a race, cut away, shoot, tear, whisk, sweep, skim, brush; skedaddle [*colloq.*], cut and run [*colloq.*], cut along [*colloq.*], bowl along; scorch [*colloq.*]; rush etc. (*be violent*) 173; dash on, dash off, dash forward; bolt; trot, gallop, bound, flit, spring, dart, boom; march in -quick, –double- time; ride hard, get over the ground; give her the gas, step on her tail, run wide open.

hurry etc. (*hasten*) 684; bundle, bundle along; bundle on; accelerate, put on; quicken; quicken–, mend -one's pace; clap spurs to one's horse; make haste, make rapid strides, make forced marches, wing one's way, set off at a score; carry sail, crowd sail; go off like a shot, go ahead, gain ground; outstrip the wind, fly on the wings of the wind.

keep up with, keep pace with.

outstrip etc. 303; outmarch.

adj. **fast**, speedy, swift, rapid, quick, fleet; nimble, agile, expeditious; express; active etc. 682; flying, galloping etc. *v.;* light-footed, nimblefooted; winged, eagle-winged, mercurial, electric, telegraphic; light-legged, light of heel;

swift as an arrow etc. *n.;* quick as lightning etc. *n.;* quick as thought.

adv. **swiftly** etc. *adj.;* with speed etc.*n.;* apace; at a great rate, at full speed, at railway speed; full drive, full gallop; posthaste, in full sail, tantivy; like a shot [*colloq.*], like greased lightning [*colloq.*]; trippingly; instantaneously etc. 113.

under press of -sail, −canvas, −sail and steam; *velis et remis* [*L.*], on eagle's wing, in double-quick time; with rapid strides, with giant strides, *à pas de géant* [*F.*], in seven-league boots; whip and spur; *ventre à terre* [*F.*]; as fast as one's -legs, −heels- will carry one; as fast as one can lay feet to the ground, at the top of one's speed; by leaps and bounds; with haste etc. 684; in high (gear *or* speed).

275. Slowness

n. **slowness** etc. *adj.;* languor etc. (*inactivity*) 683; drawl; creeping etc. *v.*, lentor [*rare*].

jog-trot, dog-trot; amble, rack, pace, single-foot, walk; mincing steps; dead march, slow march, slow time.

retardation; slackening etc. *v.;* delay etc. (*lateness*) 133; claudication [*obs.*].

slow goer, slow coach [*colloq.*]; lingerer, loiterer, sluggard, tortoise, snail; slow poke [*slang*]; dawdle etc. (*inactive*) 683.

v. **move slowly** etc. *adv.;* creep, crawl, lag, slug [*dial.*], walk, drawl, linger, loiter, saunter; plod, trudge, stump along, lumber; trail, drag; dawdle etc. (*be inactive*) 683; grovel, worm one's way, inch, inch along, steal along; jog on, rub on, toddle, waddle, wabble *or* wobble, wamble, traipse [*dial. or colloq.*], slouch, shuffle, halt, hobble, limp, claudicate [*obs.*], shamble: flag, falter, totter, stagger; mince, step short; march in slow time, march in funeral procession; take one's time; hang fire etc. (*be late*) 133.

retard, relax, slacken, check, moderate, rein in, curb; reef; strike−, shorten−, take in- sail; put on the drag, brake, apply the brake; clip the wings; reduce the speed; slacken speed, slacken one's pace, backwater, back pedal, throttle down, lose ground.

adj. **slow**, slack; tardy; dilatory etc. (*inactive*) 683; gentle, easy; leisurely; deliberate, gradual; insensible, imperceptible; languid, sluggish, apathetic, phlegmatic, lymphatic; moderate, slowpaced, tardigrade [*rare*], snail-like; creeping etc. *v.;* reptatorial *or* reptatory.

dull, slow [*colloq.*], prosaic, unentertaining, boresome, wearisome, uninteresting etc. (*dull*) 843.

adv. **slowly** etc. *adj.;* leisurely; *piano* [*It.*], *adagio* [*It.*], *largo* [*It.*], *larghetto* [*It.*], at half speed, under easy sail; at a -foot's, −snail's, −funeral-pace; dead slow [*colloq.*]; slower than- death, −cold molasses [*colloq.*], −a funeral; in slow time; with mincing steps, with clipped wings; in low (gear *or* speed).

gradually etc. *adj.;* gradatim; by degrees, by slow degrees, by inches, by little and little; step by step; inch by inch, bit by bit, little by little, *seriatim* [*L.*], consecutively.

276. Impulse

n. **impulse**, impulsion, impetus; momentum; push, pulsion, thrust, shove, jog, jolt, brunt, boom, booming, boost, throw; explosion etc. (*violence*) 173; propulsion etc. 284.

clash, collision, occursion [*obs.*], encounter, appulsion, appulse, shock, crash, bump; impact; *élan* [*F.*]; charge etc. (*attack*) 716; percussion, concussion; beating etc. (*punishment*) 972.

blow, dint, stroke, knock, tap, rap, slap, smack, pat, dab; fillip; slam, bang; hit, whack, thwack; cuff etc. 972; squash, douse *or* dowse, whap [*dial.*], swap [*obs.*], punch, thump, pelt, kick, punce [*obs.*], calcitration; *ruade* [*F.*]; arietation [*obs.*]; cut, thrust, lunge, yerk [*obs.*]; carom *or* carrom, clip [*slang*], jab, plug [*slang*], sidewinder [*slang*], sidewipe [*slang*].

hammer, sledge hammer, mall, maul, mallet, flail; ram, rammer; ramrod; battering-ram, monkey, tamper, tamping iron, pile driver, pile-driving engine, punch, bat; cant hook; cudgel etc. (*weapon*) 727; ax etc. (*sharp*) 253.

[science of mechanical forces] mechanics, dynamics; kinematics, kinetics; dynamograph, dynamometer; seismometer.

v. **impel**, give an impetus etc. *n.;* push; start, give a start to, set going; drive, urge, boom; thrust, prod, foin [*archaic*]; cant; elbow, shoulder, jostle *or* justle, hustle, hurtle, shove, jog, jolt, encounter; run−, bump−, butt- against; knock−, run- one's head against; impinge; boost; bunt, carom *or* carrom, clip [*slang*]; fan, −out; jab, plug [*slang*].

strike, knock, hit, tap, rap, slap, flap, dab, pat, thump, beat, bang, slam, dash; punch, thwack, whack; hit−, strike- hard; swap [*obs.*], batter, douse *or* dowse [*obs.*], tamp, baste, paste [*slang*], pelt, patter, buffet, belabor; fetch one a blow; poke at, pink, lunge, yerk [*obs.*]; kick, calcitrate; butt, strike at etc. (*attack*) 716; whip etc. (*punish*) 972.

collide; come−, enter- into collision; foul; fall−, run- foul of; telescope, throw etc. (*propel*) 284.

adj. **impulsive**, impellent, propulsive, pulsive [*rare*], booming; dynamic, dynamical; kinetic, kine-

matic *or* kinematical; impelled etc. *v.;* impelling
etc. *v.*

277. Recoil

n. **recoil**; reaction, retroaction; revulsion; rebound,
ricochet, backlash, repercussion, recalcitration:
kick, *contrecoup* [*F.*]; springing back etc. *v.;*
elasticity etc. 325; reflexion, reflex, reflux; reverberation etc. (*resonance*) 408; rebuff, repulse; return.

ducks and drakes; boomerang; spring.

reactionary, reactionist, recalcitrant.

v. **recoil**, react; balk, jib; spring–, fly–, bound-back;
rebound, reverberate, repercuss, recalcitrate;
echo, ricochet.

adj. **recoiling** etc. *v.;* refluent, repercussive, recalcitrant, reactionary, revulsive, retroactive.

adv. on the recoil etc. *n.*

278. Direction

n. **direction**, bearing, course, set, trend, run, drift,
tenor; tendency etc. 176; incidence; bending,
trending etc. *v.;* dip, tack, aim, collimation;
steering, steerage.

points of the compass, cardinal points; north, east,
south, west; NNE, NE, ENE, E, etc.

rhumb, azimuth, line of collimation.

line, path, road, range, quarter, line of march;
alignment; air line, bee line; straight shot.

v. **tend toward**, bend toward, point toward; conduct to, go to; point -to, –at; bend, trend, verge,
incline, dip, determine.

steer for, steer towards, make for, make toward;
aim at, level at; take aim; keep–, hold- a course;
be bound for; bend one's steps toward; direct–, steer–, bend–, shape- one's course;
align one's march; go straight, –to the point;
make a bee line; march -on, –on a point.

ascertain one's direction etc. *n.; s'orienter* [*F.*], see
which way the wind blows; box the compass;
take the air line.

adj. **directed** etc. *v.,* - toward; pointing toward etc.
v.; bound for; aligned with; direct, straight; undeviating, unswerving; straightforward; north,
northern, northerly, etc. *n.*

directable, steerable, leadable, dirigible, guid-
able, aimable, determinable.

adv. **towards**; on the -road, –high road- to; *en
avant* [*F.*]; *versus* [*L.*], to; hither, thither,
whither; directly; straight, –forwards, –as
an arrow; point-blank; in a -bee, –direct,
–straight- line -to, –for, –with; in a line with;
full tilt at, as the crow flies.

before–, near–, close to–, against-the wind;
windward, in the wind's eye.

through, *via* [*L.*], by way of; in all -directions,
–manner of ways; *quaqua-versum* [*L.*], from
the four winds.

279. Deviation

n. **deviation**; swerving etc. *v.;* obliquation [*obs.*],
warp, refraction; flection *or* flexion; sweep; de-
flection, deflexure; declination.

diversion, digression, departure from, aberration, drift, sheer, divergence etc. 291; zigzag;
detour etc. (*circuit*) 629; divagation, disorientation, exorbitation [*rare*].

[desultory motion] wandering etc. *v.;* vagrancy,
evagation [*obs.*]; bypaths and crooked ways; by-
road.

[motion sideways, oblique motion] sidling etc.
v.; jibe, tack, yaw [*all naut.*]; passage, right
passage, left passage [*manège*]; echelon [*mil.*];
knight's move at chess.

v. **deviate**, alter one's course, depart from, turn,
trend; bend, curve etc. 245; swerve, heel, bear
off; jibe, break, yaw, wear, sheer, tack [*all
naut.*].

deflect; intervert [*obs.*]; divert, divert from its
course; put on a new scent; shift, shunt, switch,
draw aside, crook, warp.

stray, straggle; sidle, edge; diverge etc. 291; tra-
lineate [*obs.*], digress, wander; wind, twist, meander; veer, divagate; go astray, go adrift; lose
one's way; ramble, rove, drift.

sidetrack; turn aside, turn a corner, turn away
from; wheel, steer clear of; dodge; step aside,
ease off, make way for, shy, jib.

glance off, fly off at a tangent; wheel about, face
about; turn–, face-to the right-about; echelon
[*mil.*]; waddle etc. (*oscillate*) 314; go out of
one's way etc. (*perform a circuit*) 629.

adj. **deviating** etc. *v.;* aberrant, errant; excursive, discursive; devious, desultory, loose; rambling;
stray, erratic, vagrant, undirected; circuitous,
round-about, crooked, sidelong, indirect, zigzag; crab-like.

adv. **astray from**, round about, wide of the mark; to
the right about; all manner of ways; circuitously
etc. 629.

obliquely, sideling, sidelong, like the knight's
move [*chess*].

280. Precession
[going before]

n. **precession**, leading, heading; precedence etc. 62;
priority etc. 116; the lead, *le pas* [*F.*]; van etc.
(*front*) 234; precursor etc. 64.

v. **precede**, go before, go ahead, go in the van, go in
advance; forerun, forego [*archaic*]; usher in,

introduce, herald, head, take the lead; lead, lead the way, lead the dance; get–, have– a start; steal a march; get before, get ahead, get in front of; outstrip etc. 303; take precedence etc. (*first in order*) 62.

adj. **leading**, precedent etc. *v.;* first, foremost.

adv. **in advance**, before, ahead, in the van; foremost, headmost; in front.

281. Sequence

[going after]

n. **sequence**; sequel; coming after etc. (*order*) 63, (*time*) 117; following; pursuit etc. 622; run [*cards*].

follower, attendant, satellite, pursuer, shadow, dangler, train.

v. **follow**; pursue etc. 622; go after, fly after.

attend, beset, dance attendance on, dog; tread in the steps of, tread close upon; be–, go–, follow– in the -wake, –trail, –rear- of; follow as a shadow, hang on the skirts of; tread–, follow-on the heels of; camp on the trail.

lag, loiter, linger, get behind.

adj. **following** etc. *v.*

adv. **behind**; in the rear etc. 235, in the train of, in the wake of; after etc. (*order*) 63, (*time*) 117.

282. Progression

[motion forward; progressive motion]

n. **progression**, progress, progressiveness; advancing etc. *v.;* advance, advancement; ongoing; flood tide, headway; march etc. 266; rise; improvement etc. 658.

v. **advance**; proceed, progress; get on, get along, get over the ground; gain ground; forge ahead; jog on, rub on, wag on [*obs.*], go with the stream; keep–, hold on- one's course; go–, move–, come–, get–, pass–, push–, press--on, –forward, –forwards, –ahead; press onward *or* onwards, step forward; make–, work–, carve–, push–, force–, edge–, elbow-one's way; make -progress, –head, –way, –headway, –advances, –strides, –rapid strides etc. (*velocity*) 274; go ahead, shoot ahead; drive -on, –ahead; go full steam ahead; distance; make up leeway.

adj. **advancing** etc. *v.;* ongoing; progressive, profluent; advanced.

adv. **forward**, onward; forth, on, ahead, under way, *en route* for, on -one's way, –the way, –the road, –the high road- to; in progress, in mid-progress; *in transitu* [*L.*] etc. 270.

283. Regression

[motion backward]

n. **regression**, regress, retrocession, retrogression, retrogradation, retroaction; *reculade* [*F.*], retreat, withdrawal, retirement, remigration; recession etc. (*motion from*) 287; recess [*obs.*]; crab-like motion.

reflux, refluence, backwater, regurgitation, ebb, return; resilience, resiliency; reflexion (*recoil*) 277; *volte-face* [*F.*].

countermotion, countermovement, countermarch; veering, tergiversation, recidivation [*obs. exc. in criminology*], backsliding, fall; deterioration etc. 659; recidivism *or* recidivity, relapse.

turning point etc. (*reversion*) 145; climax.

v. **recede**, regrade, return, revert, retreat, remigrate, retire; retrograde, retrocede; back, back out [*colloq.*], back down [*colloq.*], balk; crawfish [*slang*], crawl [*slang*]; withdraw; rebound etc. 277; go–, come–, turn–, hark–, draw–, fall–, break–, get–, put–, run- back; lose ground; fall astern, drop astern; backwater, put about [*naut.*], take the back track; veer, veer round; double, wheel, countermarch; ebb, regurgitate; jib, shrink, shy.

turn tail, turn round, turn upon one's heel, turn one's back upon; retrace one's steps, dance the back step; sound–, beat- a retreat; go home.

adj. **receding** etc. *v.;* retrograde, retrogressive; regressive, refluent, reflex, recidivous, resilient; crab-like; contraclockwise, counterclockwise; balky; reactionary etc. 277.

adv. **back**, backward; reflexively, to the right-about; *à reculons* [*F.*], *à rebours* [*F.*].

284. Propulsion

[motion given to an object situated in front]

n. **propulsion**, projection; propelment; *vis a tergo* [*L.*], push etc. (*impulse*) 276; jaculation, ejaculation; ejection etc. 297; throw, fling, toss, shot, discharge, shy.

[science of propulsion] gunnery, ballistics, archery.

propeller, screw, twin-screws, turbine.

missile, projectile, ball, shot; spear, arrow; gun etc. (*arms*) 727; discus, quoit; brickbat.

shooter, shot; archer, toxophilite; bowman, rifleman, marksman, gun [*cant*], gunner, good shot, dead shot, crack shot; sharpshooter etc. (*combatant*) 726.

v. **propel**, project, throw, fling, cast, pitch, chuck, toss, jerk, heave, shy, hurl; flirt, fillip.

dart, lance, tilt; ejaculate, jaculate [*rare*], fulminate, bolt, drive, sling, pitchfork.

send; send off, let off, fire off; discharge, shoot; launch, send forth, let fly; dash.

start; put–, set- in motion; set agoing, give a start to, give an impulse to; bundle, bundle off; impel etc. 276; trundle etc. (*set in rotation*) 312; expel etc. 297.

carry one off one's legs; put to flight.

adj. propelled etc. *v.;* propelling etc. *v.;* propulsive, projectile, ballistic.

285. Traction

[motion given to an object situated behind]

n. **traction**; drawing etc. *v.;* draft *or* draught, pull, haul; rake; "a long pull, a strong pull, and a pull all together"; towage, haulage.

v. **draw**, pull, haul, lug, rake, snake [*slang*], trawl, draggle, drag, tug, tow, trail, train; take in tow.

wrench, jerk, twitch; yank [*U.S.*].

adj. **drawing** etc. *v.;* tractile, tractive, tractional, ductile.

286. Approach

[motion toward]

n. **approach**, approximation, approximateness, appropinquation; access; appulse, appulsion; afflux, affluxion; advent etc. (*approach of time*) 121; pursuit etc. 622.

v. **approach**, approximate [*archaic*], appropinquate [*rare*]; near; get–, go–, draw- near; come, –near, –to close quarters; move towards, set in towards; drift; make up to [*dial. or slang*]; gain upon; pursue etc. 622; tread on the heels of; bear up; make land; hug the shore, hug the land.

adj. **approaching** etc. *v.;* approximate, approximative; affluent; converging, connivent, convergent; impending, imminent etc. (*destined*) 152.

adv. on the road.

int. **approach**! come hither! here! come! come near! forward!

287. Recession

[motion from]

n. **recession**, retirement, withdrawal; retreat; regression, regress, retrogradation, retrocession etc. 283; departure, etc. 293; recoil etc. 277; flight etc. (*avoidance*) 623.

switch, by-pass, shunt.

v. **recede**, go, move back, move from, retire, withdraw, retrograde, retrogress, regress, ebb; shrink; come–, move–, go–, get–, drift- away; depart etc. 293; retreat etc. 283; move off, stand off, sheer off, swerve from; fall back, stand aside; run away etc. (*avoid*) 623.

switch, shunt, sidetrack, turn, remove.

adj. **receding** etc. *v.;* recessive, retrogressive, regressive.

288. Attraction

[motion toward, actively]

n. **attraction**, attractiveness; attractivity; pull, drawing to, pulling towards, attrahent, adduction, magnetism, gravity, attraction of gravitation.

loadstone *or* lodestone, lodestar *or* loadstar, polestar, lode [*archaic*]; magnet, magnetite, siderite.

lure, bait, charm, decoy.

v. **attract**, adduct; draw–, pull–, drag- towards; pull, draw, magnetize, bait, trap, decoy, charm; adduce.

adj. **attracting** etc. *v.;* attrahent, attractive, adducent, adductive.

289. Repulsion

[motion from, actively]

n. **repulsion**; driving from etc. *v.;* repulse, abduction, retrusion [*rare*].

v. **repel**; push from, drive from etc. 276; chase, dispel; retrude [*rare*]; abduce [*obs.*], abduct; send away; repulse; repercuss.

keep at arm's length, turn one's back upon, give the cold shoulder; send -off, –away- with a flea in one's ear [*colloq.*]; send about one's business; send packing.

adj. **repellent**, repulsive; repelling etc. *v.;* abducent, abductive, repercussive.

290. Convergence

[motion nearer to]

n. **convergence** *or* convergency, confluence, concourse, conflux, congress, concurrence, concentration; appulse, meeting; corradiation [*rare*].

assemblage etc. 72; resort etc. (*focus*) 74; asymptote.

v. **converge**, concur; come together, unite, meet, fall in with; close with, close in upon; center *or* centre, center round, center in; enter in; pour in.

89

concentrate, bring into a focus; gather together, unite.

adj. **converging** etc. *v.;* convergent, confluent, concurrent; centripetal; asymptotic *or* asymptotical; confluxible [*rare*].

291. Divergence
[motion further off]

n. **divergence** *or* divergency, divarication, ramification, forking; radiation; separation etc. (*disjunction*) 44; dispersion etc. 73; deviation etc. 279; aberration, declination.

v. **diverge**, divaricate, radiate; ramify; branch off, glance off, file off; fly off, fly off at a tangent; spread, scatter, disperse etc. 73; deviate etc. 279; part etc. (*separate*) 44.

adj. **diverging** etc. *v.;* divergent, divaricate, radiant, radial, centrifugal; aberrant; broadcast.

adv. broadcast; *passim* [*L.*].

292. Arrival
[terminal motion at]

n. **arrival**, advent; landing; debarkation, disembarkation.

reception, welcome; *vin d'honneur* [*F.*].

destination, bourn *or* bourne, goal; landing -place, –stage; bunder *or* bandar [*Pers. & India*]; resting place; harbor, haven, port; terminus, terminal; halting -place, –ground; home, journey's end; anchorage etc. (*refuge*) 666; completion etc. 729.

return, recursion [*obs.*], remigration, reëntry.

meeting, joining, recounter, encounter, rejoining.

v. **arrive**; get to, come to; come; reach, attain; come up, –with, –to; overtake; make, fetch; come from, hail from; complete etc. 729; join, rejoin.

visit, pitch one's tent; sit down etc. (*be located*) 184; get to one's journey's end; be in at the death; come-, get- -back, –home; return; come in etc. (*ingress*) 294; make one's appearance etc. (*appear*) 446; drop in; detrain; out-span, offsaddle [*both S. Africa*].

light, alight, dismount.

land, make land, cast anchor, put in, put into; go ashore, debark, disbark [*rare*], disembark

meet; encounter, rencounter [*rare*], come in contact; come to hand; come at, come across; hit; come-, light-, pop [*colloq.*] -, bounce [*colloq.*] -, plump [*colloq.*]-, burst-, pitch- upon.

adj. **arriving** etc. *v.;* homeward bound, terminal.

adv. **here**, hither.

int. **welcome**! hail! all hail! good-day! good-morrow! come in and rest your bonnet on a chair! [*Southern U. S.*], bienvenu! [*F.*].

293. Departure
[initial motion from]

n. **departure**, decession [*rare*], decampment; embarkation; outset, start, headway, inspan [*S. Africa*], debouchment, debouch *or* débouché [*F.*]; removal; exit etc. (*egress*) 295; congé [*F.*], exodus, hegira, flight.

leave-taking, valediction, adieu, farewell, goodby *or* good-bye, Godspeed, stirrup cup; valedictorian.

starting point, starting post; point–, place- of -departure, –embarkation; port of embarkation.

v. **depart**; go, go away, part [*archaic*], take one's departure, set out; set-, march-, put-, start-, be-, move-, get-, whip-, pack-, go-, take oneself-off; start, boun [*archaic*], issue, march out, debouch; go forth, sally forth; sally, set forward; be gone.

leave a place, quit, vacate, evacuate, abandon; go off the stage, make one's exit; retire, withdraw, remove; "use your legs" [*Merchant of Venice*]; vamose *or* vamoose [*slang, U. S.*], mizzle [*slang*], skip [*slang*], cut [*colloq. or slang*], go one's way, go along, go from home; take flight, take wing; spring, fly, flit, wing one's flight; fly away, whip away; strike tents, decamp; break camp, break away, break ground, walk one's chalks [*slang*], cut one's stick *or* cut stick [*slang*], cut and run [*colloq.*]; take leave; say–, bid- good-by etc. *n.;* disappear etc. 449; abscond etc. (*avoid*) 623; entrain; saddle, bridle, harness up, hitch up [*colloq.*], inspan [*S. Africa*]; "speed the parting guest" [*Pope*].

embark; go on board, go aboard; set sail; put to sea, go to sea; sail, take ship; hoist the blue Peter; get under way, weigh anchor.

adj. **departing** etc. *v.;* valedictory; outward bound.

adv. **hence**, whence, thence; with a foot in the stirrup; on the wing, on the move.

int. **begone**! etc. (*ejection*) 297; cut! cut away! cut off! [*all colloq.*], away! to horse! boot! saddle! all aboard! busk and boun ye! [*archaic*].

farewell! adieu! good-by *or* goodbye! good-day! *au revoir!* [*F.*], *vale!* [*L.*], fare you well! God bless you! Godspeed! *auf Wiedersehen!* [*G.*], *au plaisir de vous revoir!* [*F.*], bon voyage! [*F.*], *glückliche Reise!* [*G.*], *vive valeque!* [*L.*], byebye! [*colloq.*], be good! [*slang*], so long! [*slang*], come again!

294. Ingress

[motion into]

n. **ingress**; entrance, entry; introgression, ingressiveness, influx, intrusion, inroad, incursion, invasion, irruption; ingression; penetration, interpenetration; illapse [*rare*], infiltration; insinuation etc. (*interjacence*) 228; insertion etc. 300.

immigration, incoming, foreign influx; admission etc. (*reception*) 296.

import, importation; imports.

immigrant, visitor, incomer, newcomer, comeling [*archaic*], colonist, Buttinsky [*humorous*].

inlet; way in; mouth, door, etc. (*opening*) 260; barway; path etc. (*way*) 627; conduit etc. 350.

v. **enter**; go–, come–, pour–, flow–, creep–, slip–, pop–, break–, burst- -into, –in; have the entrée; set foot on; ingress [*obs.*]; burst–, break-in upon; invade, insinuate itself; interpenetrate, penetrate; infiltrate; find one's way–, wriggle–, worm oneself- into; intrude, butt in [*slang*] horn in [*slang, U. S.*].

give entrance to etc. (*receive*) 296, insert etc. 300

adj. **incoming**, inbound, ingressive, inward, entrant [*rare*]; entering etc. *v.*

295. Egress

[motion out of]

n. **egress**, exit, issue; emersion, emergence; outbreak, outburst, proruption [*rare*], eruption; emanation; egression; evacuation, disemboguement, exudation, transudation; extravasation, perspiration, sweating, leakage, percolation, lixiviation, leaching, distillation, seep, oozing; gush etc. (*water in motion*) 348; outpour, outpouring; effluence, effusion; efflux, effluxion; drain; dribbling etc. *v.;* defluxion; drainage; outcome, output; outflow, discharge etc. (*excretion*) 299.

export, exportation; exports, shipments.

emigration, exodus etc. (*departure*) 293; expatriation, remigration.

emigrant, migrant, redemptioner, colonist, émigré [*F.*].

outlet, vent, spout, tap, sluice, flood-gate; vomitory, outgate, sallyport; debouch [*mil.*], débouché [*F.*]; way out; mouth, door etc. (*opening*) 260; path etc. (*way*) 627; conduit etc. 350; airpipe etc. 351; pore, emunctory.

v. **emerge**, emanate, issue; egress; go–, come–, move–, pass–, pour–, flow-out of; pass off, evacuate.

exude, transude; leak; run, –out, –through; lixiviate, leach, percolate, transcolate [*obs.*]; egur-

gitate [*rare*]; strain, distill; perspire, sweat, drain, seep, ooze; filter, infiltrate, filtrate; dribble, gush, spout, flow out; well, –out; pour, trickle, etc. (*water in motion*) 348; effuse, extravasate, disembogue, discharge itself, debouch; come–, break forth; burst -out, –through; find vent; escape etc. 671.

adj. **emergent**, emerging, erumpent, eruptive, emanant, emanational, emanative, exudative, porous, pervious, leaky, sweaty, transudatory; effused etc. *v.;* outgoing, outbound, outwardbound.

percolative, oozing, gushing, transuding etc. *v.;* effluent, emunctory, effusive, excretory.

296. Reception

[motion into, actively]

n. **reception**; admission, admittance, entrée, importation; initiation, introduction, intromission; immission, ingestion, imbibition, introception, absorption, resorbence, engorgement, ingurgitation, inhalation; suction, sucking; eating, drinking etc. (*food*) 298; insertion etc. 300; interjection etc. 228; introit.

v. **give entrance to**, give admittance to, give the entrée; introduce, usher, admit, initiate, intromit [*rare*], receive, import, bring in, immit [*rare*], open the door to, throw open, ingest, absorb, imbibe, instill, implant, infiltrate, induct, inhale; let in, take in, suck in; readmit, resorb, reabsorb; snuff up.

swallow, ingurgitate; engulf, engorge; gulp; eat, drink etc. (*food*) 298.

adj. **introductory**, introductive, initiatory, initiary [*rare*], preliminary, ingestive; imbibitory, introceptive, intromittent, intromissive; admissible; absorbent, resorbent; admitting etc. *v.*, admitted etc. *v.*

297. Ejection

[motion out of, actively]

n. **ejection**, emission, effusion, rejection, expulsion, eviction, extrusion, detrusion, trajection; discharge.

egestion, evacuation, vomition; emesis, eruption, eruptiveness, eruptivity, voidance, disgorgement; ructation, eructation; bloodletting, venesection, phlebotomy, extravasation, paracentesis; expuition [*rare*], exspuition [*rare*]; tapping, drainage; emetic; vomiting, excretion etc. 299; clearance, clearage.

dislodgment; deportation; banishment etc. (*punishment*) 972; rogue's march; relegation; extradition.

ejector, bouncer [*slang, U. S.*], chucker-out [*slang*].

v. **eject,** reject; expel, discard; cut [*colloq.*], ostracize, send to Coventry, boycott; *chasser* [*F.*], banish etc. (*punish*) 972; bounce [*slang*]; fire [*slang*]; throw etc. (284) -out, –up, –off, –away, –aside; push etc. (276) -out, –off, –away, –aside; shovel–, sweep- -out, –away; brush–, whisk–, turn–, send- -off, –away; discharge; send–, turn–, cast- adrift; turn out, bundle out; throw overboard; give the sack to [*slang*]; send packing, send about one's business, send to the right-about; strike off the roll etc. (*abrogate*) 756; turn out -neck and heels [*colloq.*], –head and shoulders, –neck and crop [*colloq.*]; pack off; send away with a flea in the ear [*colloq.*]; send to Jericho [*colloq.*]; bow out, show the door to.

evict, oust, dislodge; turn out of -doors, –house and home; unhouse, unkennel; unpeople, dispeople; depopulate; relegate, deport.

let out, give out, pour out, send out; dispatch *or* despatch, exhale, excern [*obs.*], excrete; embogue [*obs.*], disembogue; extravasate, shed, void, egest, evacuate; emit; open the -sluices, –floodgates; turn on the tap; give exit to, give vent to; extrude, detrude; effuse, spend, expend; pour forth; squirt, spurt *or* spirt, spill, slop; perspire etc. (*exude*) 295; breathe, blow etc. (*wind*) 349.

tap, draw off; bale out, lade out; let blood, broach.

empty; drain, –to the dregs; sweep off; clear, –off, –out, –away; suck, draw off; clean out, make a clean sweep of, clear decks, purge.

disembowel, embowel [*rare*], disbowel [*rare*], eviscerate, gut.

root out, root up, unearth; eradicate, averruncate [*obs.*]; weed out, get out; eliminate, get rid of, do away with, shake off; exenterate [*rare*].

vomit, spew, puke]*vulgar*], keck, retch, upchuck [*colloq.*]; cast up, bring up; disgorge.

salivate, ptyalize, expectorate, clear the throat, hawk, spit, sputter, splutter, slobber, drivel, slaver, slabber, drool.

belch, eruct, eructate.

unpack, unlade, unload, unship; break bulk; dump.

emerge, ooze etc. 295; be let out.

adj. **ejective,** emissive, extrusive; egestive; salivant; vomitive, vomitory; emitting, emitted etc. *v.*

int. **begone!** get you gone! get–, go- -away, –along, –along with you! go your way! away, –with! off with you! go! go about your business! be off! avaunt! aroint *or* aroynt! [*archaic*], allez-vous-en! [*F.*], jao! [*Hind.*], va-t'en! [*F.*], scoot! [*colloq.*], shoo! "get thee behind me, Satan!" [*Bible*].

298. Food
[eating]

n. **eating** etc. *v.;* deglutition, gulp, epulation [*rare*], mastication, manducation [*rare*], rumination; gastronomy, gastrology, pantophagy, hippophagy, carnivorism, carnivorousness, herbivority [*rare*], vegetarianism, ichthyophagy; gluttony etc. 957.

carnivore; herbivore, vegetarian.

mouth, jaws, gob [*slang*], mandible, mazard, chaps, chops.

drinking etc. *v.;* potation, draft *or* draught, libation; compotation, symposium; carousal etc. (*amusement*) 840; drunkenness etc. 959.

food, pabulum; aliment, nourishment, nutriment; sustenance, sustentation; nurture, subsistence, provender, corn, feed, fodder, provision, ration, keep, commons, board; commissariat etc. (*provisions*) 637; prey, forage, pasture, pasturage; fare, cheer; diet, dietary; regimen; belly timber [*facetious, dial.*], staff of life; bread, –and cheese; liquid diet, spoon victuals.

eatables, comestibles, victuals, edibles, ingesta; grub [*slang*], prog [*slang*], meat; bread, breadstuffs; cereals, viands, cates [*obs.*], delicacy, dainty, creature comforts, creature, contents of the larder, fleshpots; festal board; ambrosia; good cheer, good living.

[breadstuffs and desserts] biscuit, cracker, bun, cooky *or* cookie, doughnut, cruller, hard-tack, pilot bread, sea biscuit, pilot biscuit, ship biscuit, hoecake, ashcake, corncake, corndodgers, corndabs, shortbread, scone, rusk, matzo [*Jewish*], chupatty [*India*], damper [*Australia*], flapjack, waffle, pancake, griddlecake, pastry, *pâtisserie* [*F.*], pie, *pâté* [*F.*], pasty, patty, turnover, *vol-au-vent* [*F.*], apple dumpling, apple slump, apple dowdy, pandowdy, mince pie, pudding, supawn, apple pie, blueberry pie, custard pie, lemon pie, pumpkin pie, squash pie, charlotte russe, plum pudding, tart, compote, apple fritters, *beignets de pommes* [*F.*], banana fritters, macaroon, meringue, marchpane *or* marzipan, *massepain* [*F.*], whipped cream, *crème fouettée* [*F.*], cake, *gâteau* [*F.*], stewed prunes, *pruneaux* [*F.*], stewed apples, *compote de pommes* [*F.*], blancmange, cornstarch, jam, *confiture* [*F.*], Bar-le-Duc, red currant jelly, *gelée de groseilles* [*F.*], ice cream, *crème glacée* [*F.*], ice, sundae; vanilla–, strawberry–, chocolate–, coffee–, Neapolitan–, country club-ice cream; banana royal, water ice, sherbet; sweets etc. 396; see **fruit**.

[cereals] hominy, oatmeal, mush, hasty pudding, porridge, gruel, crowdie *or* crowdy [*Scot. & dial. Eng.*], *atole* [*Mex. Sp.*], samp, hulled corn, frumenty.

[soups] *potage* [*F.*], pottage, broth, *bouillon* [*F.*], gravy soup, *consommé* [*F.*], thick soup, *purée* [*F.*], bisque, mulligatawny, turtle soup, mock-turtle soup, oyster stew, oyster chowder, clam chowder, fish chowder, *julienne* [*F.*], *potage à la julienne* [*F.*], vermicelli soup, *potage au vermicelle* [*F.*], chowder, spoon-meat, trepang, ox-tail soup, gumbo, okra soup, stock, *bouillabaisse* [*F.*].

[fish] *poisson* [*F.*], salmon, *saumon* [*F.*], sole, fried sole, *sole frite* [*F.*], shad, plaice, bluefish, whiting, *merlan* [*F.*], trout, *truite* [*F.*], mackerel, *maquereau* [*F.*], herring, *hareng* [*F.*], bloater, kipper, kippered herring, cod, *morue* [*F.*], sturgeon ("Albany beef"), sardines, haddock, *aiglefin* [*F.*], finnan haddie *or* haddock, scrod, sturgeon roe, caviar *or* caviare, shad roe, tarpon, tuna, lobster, *homard* [*F.*], lobster à la King, lobster Newburg, periwinkles, prawns, shrimps, *crevettes* [*F.*], oysters, *huitres* [*F.*], oyster stew, blue points, sea slug, *bêche de mer* [*F.*], clams, eel, *anguille* [*F.*], crab, crab meat, soft-shell crab, crawfish *or* crayfish, *écrevisse* [*F.*].

[meats] *rôti* [*F.*], joint, *pièce de résistance* [*F.*], *relevé* [*F.*], hash, *réchauffé* [*F.*], stew, ragout, fricassee, mince, chow mein, chop suey, salmis, fatling, barbecue, kickshaws, mincemeat, forcemeat, meat balls, croquettes, goulash *or* Hungarian goulash; condiment etc. 393; haggis [*Scot.*], bubble and squeak, pilau *or* pilaw [*India*], curry, aspic jelly; turtle, terrapin, diamond-back terrapin.

beef, *boeuf* [*F.*], porterhouse steak, boiled beef, bouilli, beef à la mode, beefsteak, roast beef, *rosbif* [*F.*], *bifteck* [*F.*], sirloin, rump, chuck.

veal, *veau* [*F.*], fricandeau, calf's head, *tête de veau* [*F.*], tongue, *langue* [*F.*], fried brains, *cervelle frite* [*F.*], sweetbread, *ris de veau* [*F.*], calf's liver, *foie de veau* [*F.*].

mutton, *mouton* [*F.*], mutton chop, *côtelette de mouton* [*F.*], plain chop, *côtelette au naturel* [*F.*], *côtelette à la maître d'hôtel* [*F.*], *côtellette à la jardinière* [*F.*], broiled kidneys, *rognons à la brochette* [*F.*], lamb, *agneau* [*F.*], saddle, *selle* [*F.*]

pork, *porc* [*F.*], pork chop, *côtelette de porc frais* [*F.*], sausage, *saucisson* [*F.*], frankfurter, hot dog [*slang, U. S.*], bacon, ham, *jambon* [*F.*], sucking pig, *cochon de lait* [*F.*], pig's knuckles, pig's feet, trotters, *pieds de cochon* [*F.*], crackling.

poultry, *volaille* [*F.*], capon, *chapon* [*F.*], *poularde* [*F.*], pigeon, fowl, broiler, chicken, *poulet* [*F.*], duck, *canard* [*F.*], muscovy duck, roast duck, *canard rôti* [*F.*], goose, *oie* [*F.*], turkey, *dinde* (*masc. dindon*) [*F.*], wing, *ailc* [*F.*], leg, *cuisse* [*F.*], breast, *filet* (of a goose) [*F.*], *blanc* (of a fowl) [*F.*], drumstick.

game, venison, *chevreuil* [*F.*], hare, *lièvre* [*F.*], jugged hare, *civet* [*F.*], rabbit, *lapin* [*F.*], pheasant, *faisan* [*F.*], partridge, *perdrix* [*F.*], snipe, *bécasse* [*F.*], quail, *caille* [*F.*], wild duck, *canard sauvage* [*F.*], canvasback, teal, *sarcelle* [*F.*], grouse, ricebird [*Southern U. S.*], pigeon, squab.

[eggs] *oeufs* [*F.*], boiled eggs, *oeufs à la coque* [*F.*], fried eggs, *oeufs sur le plat* [*F.*], poached eggs, *oeufs pochés* [*F.*], scrambled eggs, *oeufs brouillés* [*F.*], new-laid eggs, *oeufs frais* [*F.*], buttered eggs, dropped eggs, shirred eggs, stuffed eggs, omelet, *omelette* [*F.*], *soufflé* or *soufflée* [*F.*].

[cheese dishes] cheese, *fromage* [*F.*], cheesecake, *talmouse* [*F.*], cheese-mold, *moule à fromage* [*F.*], Welsh rabbit *or* Welsh rarebit [*an erroneous form*], *rôtie au fromage* [*F.*], golden buck, cheese straws, cheese fondue; cream–, cottage–, Neuchatel–, Swiss (*Schweizerkäse* or *Schweitzerkäse* or *Schweitzer*) –, Gruyère –, Emmenthaler–, Dutch–, Edam–, Roquefort–, Brie–, Limburg *or* Limburger–, Wensleydale-cheese.

[vegetables] *légumes* [*F.*], greens, asparagus, *asperge* [*F.*], green peas, *petits pois* [*F.*], artichoke, *artichaut* [*F.*], cabbage, *chou* [*F.*], coleslaw, Brussels sprouts, *choux de Bruxelles* [*F.*], cauliflower, *chou-fleur* (*pl. choux-fleurs*) [*F.*], lettuce, *laitue* [*F.*], romaine, cos lettuce, *laitue romaine* [*F.*], lima beans, string beans, French beans, *haricots verts* [*F.*], kidney beans, *haricots blancs* [*F.*], baked beans, potatoes, *pommes de terre* [*F.*], yams, sweet potatoes, *patates* [*F.*], spinach, *épinards* [*F.*], endive, *chicorée* [*F.*], pumpkin, squash, sauerkraut, *choucroute* [*F.*], eggplant, oyster plant, salsify, *salsifis* [*F.*], tomato, *tomate* [*F.*], celery, *céleri* [*F.*], cress, *cresson* [*F.*], watercress, *cresson de fontaine* [*F.*], beets, beetroot [*Brit.*], *betterave* [*F.*], parsnips, *panais* [*F.*], turnip, *navet*

[F.], radish, *radis* or *rave* [F.], horse radish, *raifort* [F.], onion, *oignon* [F.], scallion, shalot, *échalote* [F.], cucumber, *concombre* [F.], mushrooms, *champignons* [F.], rhubarb, truffles, succotash.

[fruit] figs, *figues* [F.], raisins, nuts, *noisettes* [F.], almonds: *les quatres mendiants* [F.]; apple, *pomme* [F.], pear, *poire* [F.], alligator pear, avocado, apricot, *abricot* [F.], peach, *pêche* [F.], plantain, banana, breadfruit, grapefruit, mango, mangosteen, grapes, pineapple, *ananas* [F.], walnuts, *noix* [F.], orange, lemon, lime, cherries, *cerises* [F.], watermelon, currants, cranberry, loganberry, blueberry, blackberry, gooseberry, whortleberry, huckleberry, raspberry, strawberry.

table, *cuisine*, bill of fare, menu, *table d'hôte* [F.], ordinary, *à la carte* [F.], cover, *couvert* [F.]; American plan, European plan.

meal, repast, feed [*archaic or colloq.*], spread [*colloq.*]; mess; dish, plate, course; side dish, *hors-d'oeuvre* [F.], entrée, *entremets* [F.], remove, dessert [*in U. S., often includes pastry or pudding*]; regale; regalement, refreshment, entertainment; refection, collation, picnic, feast, banquet, junket; breakfast; lunch, luncheon, *déjeuner* [F.], *déjeuner à la fourchette* [F.]; bever [*dial.*], tiffin, dinner, supper, snack [*colloq.*], whet, bait [*dial.*]; potluck; hearty–, square–, substantial–, full- meal; blowout [*slang*]; light refreshment; *chota hazri, bara hazri, bara khana* [*all Hind.*].

mouthful, bolus, gobbet [*archaic*], tidbit, kickshaw, morsel, sop, sippet.

drink, beverage, liquor, broth, soup; potion, dram, draft *or* draught, drench, swill [*slang*]; nip, sip, sup, gulp.

[beverages] wine, spirits, liqueur, beer, ale, malt liquor, (Sir) John Barleycorn, stingo [*old slang*]; heavy wet [*slang, Eng.*]; grog, toddy, flip, purl, punch, negus, cup, bishop, wassail; hooch [*slang*], whisky *or* whiskey, the creature [*humorous*]; gin etc. (*intoxicating liquor*) 959; coffee, chocolate, cocoa, tea, "the cup that cheers but not inebriates"; bock–, lager–, Pilsener–, schenk–, near- beer; Brazil tea, cider, claret, ice water, maté, mint julep.

restaurant, eating house etc. 189.

v. **eat**, feed, fare, devour, swallow, take; gulp, bolt, snap; fall to; dispatch *or* despatch, discuss [*colloq.*]; take–, get–, gulp- down; lay in, lick, pick, peck; tuck in [*slang*], gormandize etc. 957; bite, champ, munch, craunch *or* cranch, crunch, chew, masticate, nibble, gnaw, mumble.

live on; feed–, batten–, fatten–, feast- upon; browse, graze, crop, regale; carouse etc. (*make merry*) 840; lick one's chops [*colloq.*], make one's mouth water; eat heartily, do justice to, play a good knife and fork [*dial. Eng.*], banquet.

break bread, break one's fast; breakfast, lunch, dine, take tea, sup.

drink, –in, –up, –one's fill; quaff, sip, sup; suck, –up; lap; swig [*dial. or colloq.*], swill [*slang*], tipple etc. (*be drunken*) 959; empty one's glass, drain the cup; toss off, toss one's glass; wash down, crack a bottle [*colloq.*], wet one's whistle [*colloq.*].

cater, purvey etc. 637.

adj. **eatable**, edible, esculent, comestible, gustable, alimentary; cereal, cibarious [*rare*]; dietetic; culinary; nutritive, nutritious; gastric; succulent.

underdone, rare, *saignant* [F.]; well-done, *bien cuit* [F.]; overdone; with gravy, *au jus* [F.]; high [*of game*]; ripe [*of cheese*].

drinkable, potable, potulent [*obs.*]; bibulous.

omnivorous, carnivorous, herbivorous, granivorous, graminivorous, phytivorous, phytophagous, ichthyophagous; omophagic, omophagous; pantophagous, xylophagous.

299. Excretion

n. **excretion**, discharge, emanation, ejection; exhalation, exudation, extrusion, secretion, effusion, extravasation, ecchymosis, evacuation, dejection, feces, defecation, cacation, excrement; bloody flux; celiac *or* coeliac, flux; dysentery; perspiration, sweat; subation [*obs.*], exudation; diaphoresis; sewage; eccrinology.

hemorrhage, bleeding; outpouring etc. (*egress*) 295; menses, menstrual discharge, menstrual flow, catamenial discharge; leucorrhea *or* leucorrhoea, the whites.

ejecta (*pl.*), saliva, spittle, sputum (*pl.* sputa); spit, rheum; ptyalism, salivation, catarrh; diarrhea *or* diarrhoea; egesta (*pl.*), excreta; lava; exuviae etc. (*uncleanness*) 653.

v. **excrete** etc. (*eject*) 297; secrete, secern; emanate etc. (*come out*) 295.

adj. **excretory**, fecal, feculent, secretory.
ejective, eliminative, eliminant.

300. Insertion

[forcible ingress]

n. **insertion**, infixion, implantation, introduction; embolism, interpolation, intercalation, interlineation, insinuation etc. (*intervention*) 228; planting etc. v.; injection, inoculation, importation, infusion; forcible ingress etc. 294; immersion; submersion, submergence, dip, plunge; bath etc. (*water*) 337; interment etc. 363.

enema, clyster, glyster, lavage, lavement.

v. **insert**, introduce, intromit, put into, run into; import; inject; imbed, inlay, inweave; interject etc. 228; infuse, instill *or* instil, inoculate, impregnate, imbue, imbrue.

insert etc. itself; plunge *in medias res* [*L.*].

graft, ingraft, engraft, bud, plant, implant; dovetail.

obtrude; thrust in, stick in, ram in, stuff in, tuck in, press in, drive in, pop in, whip in, drop in, put in: impact; pierce etc. (*make a hole*) 260.

immerse, immerge, merge; bathe, soak etc. (*water*) 337; dip, plunge etc. 310.

bury etc. (*inter*) 363.

adj. **inserted** etc. *v.*

301. Extraction
[forcible egress]

n. **extraction**; extracting etc. *v.;* removal, elimination, extrication, eradication, evulsion, extirpation, extermination; ejection etc. 297; export etc. (*egress*) 295; avulsion, wrench, forcible separation.

expression, squeezing; distillation.

extractor, corkscrew, forceps, pliers.

v. **extract**, draw; take out, draw out, pull out, tear out, pluck out, pick out, get out; wring from, wrench; extort; root-, weed-, grub-, rake--up, −out; eradicate; pull-, pluck- up by the roots; averruncate [*obs.*]; unroot; uproot, pull up, extirpate, dredge.

educe, elicit, evolve, bring forth, draw forth; extricate.

eliminate etc. (*eject*) 297; eviscerate etc. 297; remove.

express, squeeze out, press out, distill *or* distil.

adj. **extracted** etc. *v.*

302. Passage
[motion through]

n. **passage**, transmission; permeation; penetration, interpenetration; transudation, infiltration; exosmosis *or* exosmose; osmosis *or* osmose, endosmosis, endosmose; intercurrence; ingress etc. 294; egress etc. 295; path etc. 627; conduit etc. 350; opening etc. 260; journey etc. 266; voyage etc. 267.

v. **pass**, pass through; perforate etc. (*hole*) 260; penetrate, permeate, thread, thrid [*archaic or dial.*], enfilade; go through, go across; go over, pass over; cut across; ford, cross; pass and repass, work; make-, thread-, worm-, force-

one's way; make−, force- a passage; cut one's way through; find its -way, −vent; transmit, make way, clear the course; traverse, go over the ground.

adj. **passing** etc. *v.;* intercurrent; endosmosmic, endosmotic, exosmotic *or* exosmic, osmotic.

adv. *en passant* [*F.*] etc. (*transit*) 270.

303. Overrun
[motion beyond]

n. **overrun**, transcursion [*obs.*], transilience *or* transiliency [*rare*], transgression; trespass; inroad, advancement, intrusion, infraction, encroachment, infringement; extravagation [*obs.*], transcendence; redundance etc. 641.

v. **surpass**, transgress, pass; go beyond, go by; show in front, come to the front; shoot ahead of; steal a march upon, gain upon.

overstep, overpass, overreach, overgo, override, overleap, overjump, overskip, overlap, overshoot the mark; outstrip, outleap, outjump, outgo, outstep, outrun, outride, outrival, outdo; beat, beat hollow [*colloq.*]; distance; leave in the -lurch, −rear; throw into the shade; exceed, transcend, surmount; soar etc. (*rise*) 305.

encroach, trespass, infringe, intrude, invade, accroach [*rare*], advance upon, trench upon, intrench on; strain; stretch−, strain- a point; pass the Rubicon.

adj. **surpassing** etc. *v.*

adv. **ahead**, beyond the mark.

304. Shortcoming
[motion short of]

n. **shortcoming**, failure; falling short etc. *v.;* default, defalcation, delinquency; leeway; labor in vain, no go [*colloq.*]; fizzle [*colloq.*], dud [*slang*], slump [*colloq.*]; flash in the pan.

incompleteness etc. 53; imperfection etc. 651; insufficiency etc. 640; noncompletion etc. 730; failure etc. 732.

v. **fall short**, −of; come short, −of; stop short, −of; not reach; want; keep within -bounds, −the mark, −compass.

collapse, fail, break down, stick in the mud, flat out, come to nothing; fall down, slump, fizzle out [*all colloq.*]; fall through, fall to the ground; cave in [*colloq.*], end in smoke, miss the mark; lose ground; miss stays [*naut.*]; miss one's moorings.

adj. **unreached**; deficient; short, short of; minus; out of depth; perfunctory etc. (*neglect*) 460.

adv. **within the mark**, within compass, within bounds; behindhand; *re infecta* [*L.*]; to no purpose; far from it.

305. Ascent

[motion upwards]

n. **ascent,** ascension; rising etc. *v.;* rise, upgrowth, upward flight, upgrade; leap etc. 309; grade, gradient [*Eng.*], ramp, acclivity, hill etc. 217.

stairway, staircase, stair [*esp. in Scot.*], stairs; flight of -steps, -stairs; ladder, scaling ladder; Jacob's ladder, companionway, companion, companion ladder [*all naut.*]; escalator, elevator etc. 307.

[comparisons] rocket, skyrocket, lark, skylark; Alpine Club.

v. **ascend,** rise, mount, arise, uprise; go up, get up, work one's way up, start up, spring up, shoot up; aspire, aim high.

plane, swim, float.

climb, shin [*colloq.*], swarm [*colloq.*], clamber, ramp [*rare*], scramble, escalade, surmount; wind upward; scale, -the heights.

tower, soar, hover, spire, go-, fly- aloft; surge; leap etc. 309.

adj. **rising** etc. *v.;* upcast; scandent, buoyant; supernatant, superfluitant; excelsior.

adv. **up,** upward *or* upwards, skyward. heavenward, toward the empyrean; upturned; uphill.

306. Descent

[motion downwards]

n. **descent,** descension [*rare*], inclination, declension, declination; decurrence [*rare*], downcome, comedown, downcast, setback, fall; falling etc. *v.;* slump [*colloq.*], drop, cadence; subsidence, lapse; downfall, tumble, slip, tilt, trip, lurch; *culbute* [*F.*], titubation, stumble; fate of -Icarus, -Phaëthon, -Lucifer.

avalanche, debacle, *débâcle* [*F.*], landslip [*Eng.*], landslide, slide, snowslip, snowslide, glissade.

declivity, dip, decline, pitch, drop, down-grade.

elevator etc. 307.

stairway etc. 305.

v. **descend;** go-, drop-, come- down; fall, gravitate. drop, slip, slide, settle; decline, set, sink, droop, come down a peg [*colloq.*], slump [*colloq.*].

get down, dismount, alight, light; swoop, souse; stoop etc. 308; fall prostrate, precipitate oneself; let fall etc. 308.

tumble, trip, stumble, titubate [*rare*], lurch, pitch, swag, topple; topple-, tumble- -down, -over; tilt, sprawl, plump, plump down; come-, fall-, get- a cropper [*colloq. or slang*].

adj. **steep,** sloping, declivitous, declivous; beetling etc. (*high*) 206; bottomless etc. (*deep*) 208.

descending etc. *v.;* down, downcast; descendent; decurrent, decursive; labent [*rare*], deciduous; nodding to its fall.

adv. **downward** *or* downwards, downhill.

307. Elevation

n. **elevation;** raising etc. *v.;* erection, lift; sublevation, upheaval; sublimation, exaltation; prominence etc. (*convexity*) 250.

lever etc. 633; crane, derrick, windlass, capstan, winch; dredge, dredger, dredging machine.

elevator, *ascenseur* [*F.*], lift [*chiefly Eng.*], dumbwaiter, escalator.

v. **elevate,** raise, heighten, lift, erect; set up, stick up, perch up, perk up, tilt up; rear, hoist, heave; uplift, upraise, uprear, upbear, upcast, uphoist, upheave; buoy, weigh, mount, give a lift; exalt; sublimate; place-, set- on a pedestal.

take up, drag up, fish up; dredge.

stand up, rise up, get up, jump up; spring to one's feet; hold oneself up, hold one's head up; draw oneself up to his full height.

adj. **elevated** etc. *v.;* upturned, *retroussé* [*F.*]; stilted, attollent, rampant.

adv. on stilts, on the shoulders of, on one's legs, on one's hind legs [*colloq.*].

308. Depression

n. **depression;** lowering etc. *v.;* dip etc. (*concavity*) 252; abasement; detrusion; reduction.

overthrow, overset, overturn; upset; prostration, subversion, precipitation.

bow; curtsy *or* curtsey, dip [*colloq.*], bob, obedience [*archaic*], duck, genuflexion, kotow *or* kowtow [*Chinese*]. obeisance, salaam *or* salam.

v. **depress,** lower; let-, take- -down, -down a peg [*colloq.*]; cast; let drop, let fall; sink, debase, bring low, abase, reduce, detrude, pitch, precipitate.

overthrow, overturn, overset; upset, subvert, prostrate, level, fell; down [*archaic or colloq.*], cast down, take down, throw down, fling down, dash down, pull down, cut down, knock down, hew down; raze, raze to the ground; trample in the dust, pull about one's ears; come off-, pull off- one's high horse [*slang*]; come off-, get off- one's perch [*slang*].

sit, sit down, couch, squat; recline etc. 213.

crouch, stoop, bend, cower.

bow; curtsy *or* curtsey, genuflect, kotow [*Chinese*], duck, bob, dip, kneel; bend-, bow- the

-head, −knee; incline, make obeisance, salaam *or* salam, prostrate oneself, bow down.

adj. **depressed** etc. *v.;* at a low ebb; prostrate etc. (*horizontal*) 213; detrusive.

309. Leap

n. **leap**, jump, hop, spring, bound, vault, pole vault, leaping, saltation [*rare*].

caper; dance, curvet, caracole *or* caracol; gambade, gambado, gambol, frisk, prance, dido, capriole, demivolt; buck, −jump; hop skip and jump; falcade.

[comparisons] kangaroo, jerboa, chamois, goat, frog, grasshopper, flea; buckjumper; wallaby.

v. **leap**; jump -up, −over the moon; hop, spring, bound, vault, negotiate [*cant*], clear, ramp, trip, skip.

prance, dance, caper; buck, buck-jump; curvet, caracole *or* caracol; foot it, bob, bounce, flounce, start; frisk etc. (*amusement*) 840; jump about etc. (*agitation*) 315; cut capers [*colloq.*], cut a dido [*colloq.*]; trip it on the light fantastic toe, dance oneself off one's legs, dance the soles off one's feet.

adj. **leaping** etc. *v.;* saltatorial, saltatoric *or* saltatory; frisky, lively.

adv. on the light fantastic toe.

310. Plunge

n. **plunge**, dip, dive, nose dive [*aviation*], header [*colloq.*]; ducking etc. *v.*

submergence, submersion, immersion, engulfment [*rare*].

diver; diving bird, loon, auk, penguin, grebe, sea duck etc.

v. **plunge**, dip, souse, duck; dive, plump; take a -plunge, −header [*colloq.*]; make a plunge; bathe etc. (*water*) 337; pitch.

submerge, submerse; immerse; douse *or* dowse, sink, engulf, send to the bottom; send to -Davy Jones's locker, −feed the fishes.

founder, welter, wallow; get out of one's depth; go to the bottom, go down like a stone.

adj. **plunging** etc. *v.;* submergible, submersible; soundable.

311. Circuition

[curvilinear motion]

n. **circuition** [*archaic*], circulation, volutation; turn, curvet; excursion; circumvention, circumnavigation, circumambulation, circumambience *or* circumambiency, circumflexion, circumfluence [*rare*], circummigration, circumvolation [*rare*]; Northwest Passage; wheel, gyre, ambit, compass, lap, circuit etc. 629.

turning etc. *v.;* wrench; evolution; coil, spiral, corkscrew.

v. **turn**, bend, wheel; go about, put about [*both naut.*]; heel; go−, turn- -round, −to the right-about; turn on one's heel.

circle, encircle, circumscribe; circuit; make−, describe- a -circle, −complete circle; go−, pass-through -180°, - 360°; circumnavigate, circumambulate, circumvent; "put a girdle round about the earth" [*Midsummer Night's Dream*]; go the round, make the round of, circumvolate [*rare*], circumflex.

round; turn−, round- a corner; double a point [*naut.*]; make a detour etc. (*circuit*) 629.

wind, circulate, meander; whisk, twirl; twist etc. (*convolution*) 248.

wallow, welter, roll, volutate.

adj. **circuitous**; turning etc. *v.;* circumforaneous, circumfluent, roundabout; devious, deviatory; circumambient, circumflex, circumfluent, circumfluous, circumvolant, circumnavigable.

adv. round about.

312. Rotation

[motion in a continued circle]

n. **rotation**, revolution, gyration, circulation, roll; circumrotation, circumvolution [*rare*], circumgyration; circumfusion, circination [*obs.*], turbination, pirouette, convolution.

eddy, vortex, whirlpool, swirl, gurge [*rare*]; verticity [*obs.*]; vertiginousness; whir, whirl; countercurrent; cyclone, tornado; surge; vertigo, dizzy round; maelstrom, Charybdis.

Ixion; Wheel of Fortune.

[comparisons] wheel, screw, propeller, turbine, whirligig, rolling stone, windmill; treadmill, top, teetotum; roller; cogwheel, gear, gearwheel, flywheel; jack, smokejack, turnspit; gyroplane, gyroscope, gyrostat, gyrocar; caster.

axis, axle, spindle, pivot, pin, hinge, pole, swivel, gimbals, arbor, bobbin, spool, reel, mandrel.

[science of rotatory motion] trochilics, gyrostatics.

v. **rotate**; roll, roll along; revolve, spin; turn, turn round; circumvolve [*rare*], circumgyrate [*rare*], circumvolute, circumfuse, turbinate [*rare*], encircle; circulate, gurge [*rare*], swirl, gyre, gyrate, wheel, whirl, twirl, trundle, troll, bowl, roll up, furl.

box the compass; spin like a -top, −teetotum.

adj. **rotating** etc. *v.;* rotatory, rotary; circumrotatory, trochilic, vertiginous, gyral, circumgyratory, circumvolutory, gyratory, gulfy; vorticular, vortical, vorticose; gyrostatic, gyroscopic.

adv. **round and round**, head over heels, like a horse in a mill, in circles, clockwise.

313. Evolution
[motion in a reverse circle]

n. **evolution**, unfolding, development; evolvement; unfoldment; eversion etc. (*inversion*) 218.

v. **evolve**; unfold, unroll, unwind, uncoil, untwist, unfurl, untwine, unravel; disentangle; develop.

adj. **evolutional**, evolutionary; evolving etc. *v.;* evolved etc. *v.*

314. Oscillation
[reciprocating motion, motion to and fro]

n. **oscillation**; vibration, vibratility, libration; motion of a pendulum; nutation, circumnutation; undulation; pulsation; pulse, beat, throb; seismicity, seismism, seismology.

alternation; coming and going etc. *v.;* ebb and flow, flux and reflux, systole and diastole; libration -of the moon, −in latitude; ups and downs; crossruff [*in cards*].

fluctuation; vacillation etc. (*irresolution*) 605.

swing, wave, vibratiuncle [*rare*], beat, shake, wag, seesaw, teeter; dance, lurch, dodge.

rocking stone, logan (*or* loggan) stone.

[instruments] vibroscope, vibrograph; seismograph, seismoscope.

v. **oscillate**; nutate, vibrate, librate; undulate, wave; rock, sway, swing; pulsate, beat; wag, waggle; nod, bob, curtsy *or* curtsey, tick; play; wamble, wabble; dangle, swag [*obs. or dial.*].

fluctuate, dance, curvet, reel, quake; quiver, quaver; shake, flicker; wriggle; roll, toss, pitch; flounder, stagger, totter; move−, bob- up and down etc. *adv.*

alternate, pass and repass, shuttle, ebb and flow, come and go; vacillate etc. 605.

brandish, shake, flourish; agitate etc. 315.

adj. **oscillating** etc. *v.;* oscillatory, undulatory, pulsatory, libratory; vibratory, vibrative, vibratile; seismic *or* seismical, seismal, seismographic, seismological; pendulous; shuttlewise.

adv. **to and fro**, up and down, backwards and forwards, back and forth, in and out, seesaw, zigzag, wibble-wabble [*colloq.*], in and out, from side to side, like buckets in a well.

315. Agitation
[irregular motion]

n. **agitation**, stir, tremor, shake, ripple, jog, jolt, jar, jerk, shock, succussion, trepidation, quiver, quaver, dance, tarantella, tarantism; vellication, jactation, jactitation, quassation [*rare*]; shuffling etc. *v.;* twitter, flicker, flutter.

disquiet, perturbation, commotion, turmoil, turbulence; tumult, tumultuation [*obs.*]; hubbub, rout, bustle, fuss, racket.

twitching, subsultus, floccillation, carphology *or* carphologia; staggers, megrims, epilepsy, fits; chorea, the jerks [*colloq.*], St. Vitus's dance, tilmus.

spasm, throe, throb, palpitation, pitapatation [*humorous*], convulsion, paroxysm, seizure, grip, cramp.

disturbance etc. (*disorder*) 59; restlessness etc. (*changeableness*) 149.

ferment, fermentation; ebullition, effervescence, hurly-burly, *cahotage or cahotement* [*F.*], cahot [*Can.*]; tempest, storm, ground swell, heavy sea, whirlpool, vortex etc. 312; whirlwind etc. (*wind*) 349.

v. **be agitated** etc.; shake; tremble, −like an aspen leaf; shake like a jelly, quiver, quaver, quake, shiver, twitter, twire [*obs.*], writhe, toss, jactitate [*rare*], shuffle, tumble, stagger, bob, reel, sway; wag, waggle; wriggle, −like an eel; dance, stumble, shamble, flounder, totter, flounce, flop, curvet, prance, cavort; squirm; bustle.

toss about, jump about; jump like a parched pea; shake like an aspen leaf; shake to its -center, −foundations; be the sport of the winds and waves; reel to and fro like a drunken man; move−, drive- from post to pillar and from pillar to post; keep between hawk and buzzard.

throb, pulsate, beat, palpitate, go pitapat.

flutter, flitter [*archaic*], flicker, bicker; twitch, vellicate.

ferment, effervesce, foam; boil, boil over; bubble, bubble up; simmer.

agitate, shake, convulse, toss, tumble, bandy, wield, brandish, flap, flourish, whisk, jerk, hitch, jolt, jog, joggle; jostle, buffet, hustle, disturb, stir, shake up, churn, jounce, wallop [*dial.*], whip.

adj. **agitated**, tremulous; subsultory [*obs.*], desultory, successive, saltatorial, saltant, saltatoric *or* saltatory; quassative [*rare*]; shambling; giddy-paced, convulsive, jerky; effervescent, effervescive, vellicative, unquiet, restless, all of a twitter [*colloq.*], all of a flutter; shaking etc. *v.*

adv. by fits and starts; subsultorily [*obs.*] etc. *adj.; per saltum* [*L.*]; hop, skip, and jump; in convulsions, in fits, in a flutter.

Class 3. Matter

Section 1. Matter in General

316. Materiality

n.   **materiality**, materialness; corporeity, corporality; substantiality, substantialness, materialization, material existence, incarnation, flesh and blood, plenum; physical condition.

matter, body, substance, brute matter, protoplasm, plasma, stuff, element, principle, parenchyma, material, substratum, hyle, *corpus* [*L.*], pabulum; frame.

object, article, thing, something; still life; stocks and stones; *matériel* [*F.*]; materials etc. 635.

[science of matter] physics; somatology, somatics; natural–, experimental- philosophy; physicism; physical science, *philosophie positive* [*F.*], materialism, hylism, hylicism, hylotheism, somatism, substantialism.

materialist; physicist; somatologist, somatist, corporealist [*rare*], hylicist, hylotheist, substantialist.

v.   **materialize**, incorporate, substantiate, substantialize, insubstantiate [*rare*], incorporate, embody, incarnate, corporify [*obs.*].

adj.   **material**, bodily; corporeal, corporal; physical; somatic, somatoscopic; mundane etc. (*terrestrial*) 318; sensible, tangible, ponderable, palpable, substantial, somatologic *or* somatological; embodied, fleshy.

neuter, unspiritual, materialistic *or* materialistical, hylic, hylotheistic *or* hylotheistical, parenchymatous.

objective, impersonal, nonsubjective.

317. Immateriality

n.   **immateriality**, immaterialness; incorporeity, dematerialization, insubstantiality, incorporality, decarnation [*obs.*], unsubstantiation, unsubstantiality, spirituality; inextension; astral plane.

personality; I, myself, me.

ego, spirit etc. (*soul*) 450; astral body, etheric double, subliminal self, subconscious self, higher self.

immaterialism; spiritualism, spiritism, animism, Platonism; Platonic -Idea, –Ideal.

immaterialist, spiritualist, spiritist, animist, Platonist.

v.   **immaterialize**, dematerialize, unsubstantialize [*rare*]; disembody, spiritualize.

adj.   **immaterial**, immateriate, incorporeal, incorporal, incorporate, unsubstantial, insubstantial, immateriate [*obs.*], spiritistic, animistic; unfleshly; supersensible; asomatous, unextended; unembodied, discarnate, bodiless, decarnate *or* decarnated, disembodied; extramundane, unearthly; pneumatoscopic; spiritual etc. (*psychical*) 450; Platonistic.

subjective, personal, nonobjective.

318. World

n.   **world**, creation, nature, universe; earth, globe, wide world; cosmos; Midgard; terraqueous globe, sphere; macrocosm, megacosm; music of the spheres.

heavens, sky, welkin [*archaic*], empyrean; starry -cope, –heaven, –host; firmament, *caelum* [*L.*], hyaline, supersensible regions; *varuna* [*Skr.*]; vault–, canopy- of heaven; celestial spaces.

heavenly bodies, luminaries, stars, asteroids; nebulae; galaxy, Milky Way, galactic circle, *via lactea* [*L.*].

sun, orb of day, day-star [*poetic*], Helios, Apollo, Phoebus etc. (*sun god*) 423; photosphere, chromosphere; solar system; planet, planetoid; Venus, Aphrodite Urania, Hyades; comet; satellite; moon, orb of night, Diana, Luna, Phoebe, Cynthia, Selene, "glimpses of the moon" [*Hamlet*], silver-footed queen; aerolite, meteor; falling–, shooting-star; meteorite, uranolite.

constellation, zodiac, signs of the zodiac; Charles's Wain, The Dipper; Great Bear, Ursa Major; Little Bear, Ursa Minor; Southern Cross, Orion's Belt, Cassiopeia's Chair, Pleiades.

colures, equator, ecliptic, orbit.

[science of heavenly bodies] astronomy; uranography, uranology; uranometry, cosmology, cosmography, cosmogony; eidouranion, orrery; geodesy etc. (*measurement*) 466; star-gazing; observatory; planetarium.

cosmologist, cosmographer, cosmogonist, geodesist, geographer; astronomer, star-gazer.

adj.   **cosmic** *or* cosmical, mundane; terrestrial, terrestrious [*obs.*], terraqueous, terrene, terrenous, [*obs.*]; fluvioterrestrial, geodesic *or* geodesical, geodetic *or* geodetical, cosmogonal, cosmogonic, cosmographic *or* cosmographical; telluric, earthly, under the sun; sublunary, subastral.

solar, heliacal; lunar; empyreal, celestial, heavenly, sphery; starry, stellar, stellary, bespangled, sidereal; sideral, astral; nebular; uranic.

adv. in all creation, on the face of the globe, here below, under the sun.

319. Gravity

n. **gravity**, gravitation; weight; heft, heaviness etc. *adj.;* specific gravity; ponderation [*rare*], ponderousness, ponderance [*rare*], ponderosity, pressure, load; burden *or* burthen; ballast, counterpoise; mass; lump-, mass-, weight-of.
[comparisons] lead, millstone, mountain; Ossa on Pelion.

weighing, ponderation, trutination [*obs.*]; weights; avoirdupois-, troy-, apothecaries'-weight; grain, scruple, drachma, dram *or* drachm, ounce, pound, lb., arroba, load, stone, hundred-weight, cwt., ton, quintal, carat, penny-weight, tod; gram *or* gramme, decagram, hectogram, kilogram *or* kilo, myriagram, decigram, centigram, milligram.
[weighing instrument] balance, scales steelyard, beam, weighbridge, spring balance.
[science of gravity] statics.

v. **be heavy** etc. *adj.;* gravitate, weigh, press, cumber, load.
[measure the weight of] weigh, counterweigh, scale [*rare*], poise.

adj. **weighty**; weighing etc. *v.;* heavy, –as lead; ponderous, ponderable; lumpish, lumpy, cumbersome, burdensome; cumbrous, unwieldy, massive; static *or* statical.
incumbent, superincumbent.

320. Levity

n. **levity**; lightness etc. *adj.;* imponderability, buoyancy, volatility; imponderables [*tech.*].
[comparisons] feather, dust, mote, down, thistledown, flue, fluff, cobweb, gossamer, straw, cork, bubble; float, buoy; ether, air.
ferment, leaven, barm, yeast, zyme, enzyme, pepsin, diastase.

v. **be light** etc. *adj.;* float, swim, be buoyed up.
render light etc. *adj.;* lighten.
ferment, work, raise, leaven.

adj. **light**, subtile, subtle, airy; imponderous, imponderable; astatic, weightless, ethereal, sublimated; gossamery; suberose *or* suberous, subereous; uncompressed, volatile; buoyant, floating etc. *v.;* foamy, frothy; portable.
light as -a feather, –thistledown, –air.
fermenting, fermentative, zymogenic, zymologic *or* zymological, diastatic, yeasty.

Section 2. Inorganic Matter

321. Density

n. **density**, solidity; solidness etc. *adj.;* impenetrability, impermeability; incompressibility; imporosity; cohesion etc. 46; costiveness, constipation, consistence, spissitude.
specific gravity; hydrometer, areometer.
condensation; caseation; solidation [*obs.*], solidification, consolidation, concretion, coagulation; petrification etc. (*hardening*) 323; crystallinity, crystallizability, crystallization, precipitation; deposit, precipitate; inspissation; incrassation, crassitude; thickening etc. *v.*
indivisibility, indiscerptibility, indissolvableness [*rare*], infrangibility, infrangibleness, indissolubility, indissolubleness.
solid body, mass, block, knot, lump; concretion, concrete, conglomerate; cake, stone, bone, gristle, cartilage.
clot, coagulum, casein, crassament [*obs.*], crassamentum, legumin, curd; clabber, bonnyclabber, clotted cream, Devonshire cream, grume.
sediment, lees, dregs, settlings.

v. **be dense** etc. *adj.;* become *or* render solid etc. *adj.;* solidify, solidate; concrete, set, take a set, consolidate, congeal, coagulate; curd, curdle, cruddle [*dial.*], lopper; fix, clot, cake, candy, precipitate, deposit, cohere, crystallize; petrify etc. (*harden*) 323.
condense, thicken, inspissate, incrassate.
compress, squeeze, ram down, constipate [*rare*].

adj. **dense**, solid; solidified etc. *v.;* caseate, caseous; pucka *or* pakka [*Hind.*], coherent, cohesive etc. 46; compact, close, serried, thickset; substantial, massive, lumpish; impenetrable, impermeable, imporous; incompressible; constipated, costive; crass, spiss [*obs.*], clabber, kern [*chiefly dial.*]; concrete etc. (*hard*) 323; knotted, knotty; gnarled; crystallitic, crystalline, crystallizable; thick, grumose, grumous, stuffy.
undissolved, unmelted, unliquefied, unthawed.
indivisible, indiscerptible, infrangible, indissolvable [*rare*], indissoluble, insoluble, infusible.

322. Rarity

n. **rarity**; tenuity; absence of solidity etc. 321; subtility; subtilty; sponginess, compressibility.
rarefaction, rarefication [*rare*], expansion, dilatation, inflation, subtilization.
ether etc. (*gas*) 334.

v. **rarefy**, expand, dilate, subtilize [*rare*], attenuate, thin.

adj. **rare**, subtile [*now rare*], subtle, thin, fine, tenuous, compressible, flimsy, slight; light etc. 320; cavernous, porous, spongy etc. (*hollow*) 252.

rarefied etc. v.; unsubstantial; uncompact, uncompressed; rarefiable, rarefactive, rarefactional.

323. Hardness

n. **hardness** etc. *adj.;* rigidity; renitency *or* renitence; inflexibility, temper, callosity, durity [*obs.*].

induration, petrifactioon; lapidification, lapidescence [*rare*]; cornification, chondrification, vitrification, vitrescence, ossification; crystallization.

[comparisons] stone, pebble, flint, marble, rock, fossil, crag, crystal, quartz, granite, adamant; bone, cartilage; calculus; hardware; heart of oak, block, board, deal board; iron, steel; cast–, decarbonized–, wrought- iron; nail; brick, concrete; cement; osmiridium, iridosmine *or* iridosmium.

v. **harden**; render hard etc. *adj.;* stiffen, indurate, petrify, temper, ossify, vitrify, lithify, lapidify, cement.

adj. **hard**, rigid, stubborn, stiff, firm; starch, starched; stark, unbending, unlimber, renitent, unyielding; inflexible, tense; indurate, indurated; gritty, proof.

adamantine, adamantean; concrete, stony, rocky, granitic, calculous, lithic, vitrescent, vitrifiable, vitrescible, vitreous; horny, cornified, callous, corneous; bony, ossipid, osseous, ossific; cartilaginous; lapideous, lapidific *or* lapidifical [*rare*]; crystallized, crystalloid; hard as a -stone etc. *n.;* stiff as -buckram, –a poker.

324. Softness

n. **softness**, pliableness etc. *adj.;* flexibility; pliancy, pliability; sequacity [*obs. in this sense*], malleability, ductility, ductibility, tractability, tractility, extensibility, extendibility; plasticity; inelasticity, flaccidity, laxity, flabbiness, flocculence; mollescence, mollification; softening etc. *v.*

[comparisons] clay, alumina, argil; wax, putty, butter, dough, pudding; cushion, pillow, feather bed, down, eider down, padding, wadding.

v. **soften**; render soft etc. *adj.;* mollify, mellow, milden, tender [*rare*], gentle [*rare*], dulcify; relax, temper; mash, knead, massage, squash [*colloq.*].

bend, yield, relent, relax, give.

adj. **soft**, tender, supple; pliant, pliable; flexible, flexile; lithe, lithesome; lissom, limber, plastic; ductile, ductible [*rare*], tractile, tractable; malleable, extensile, extensible, lax, sequacious [*obs. in this sense*], inelastic; aluminous; remollient [*obs.*], mollient, mollescent, mollitious, mollified.

yielding etc. *v.;* flabby, limp, flimsy.

flaccid, flocculent, downy; spongy, oedematous *or* edematous, medullary, doughy, clayey, argillaceous, mellow.

soft as -butter, –down, –silk, –putty, –a feather bed; yielding as wax; tender as a chicken.

325. Elasticity

n. **elasticity**, springiness, spring, resilience *or* resiliency, renitency, buoyancy, tensibility, tensibleness, tensility, extensibility; recoil, rebound, reflex.

[comparisons] India rubber *or* india-rubber, caoutchouc, gum elastic, whalebone, baleen; turf, moss; balloon, battledore.

v. **be elastic** etc. *adj.;* spring back etc. (*recoil*) 277.

adj. **elastic**, tensile, tensible, springy, resilient, renitent, ductile, extensible, buoyant.

326. Inelasticity

n. **inelasticity** etc. (*softness*) 324; want of–, absence of- elasticity etc. 325; irresilience.

adj. **inelastic** etc. (*soft*) 324; irresilient.

327. Tenacity

n. **tenacity**, toughness, strength; cohesiveness, cohesion etc. 46; sequacity, sequaciousness [*both obs. in this sense*]; stubbornness etc. (*obstinacy*) 606; gumminess, glutinousness, viscidity etc. 352.

[comparisons] leather; white leather *or* whitleather, tawed leather; gristle, cartilage.

claw, talon, pincers, nippers, vise; bulldog.

v. **be tenacious** etc. *adj.;* resist fracture.

adj. **tenacious**, cohesive, tough, strong, resisting, adhesive, stringy, viscid, gummy, glutinous, gristly, cartilaginous, leathery, coriaceous, tough as whiteleather; stubborn etc. (*obstinate*) 606.

328. Brittleness

n. **brittleness** etc. *adj.;* fragility, friability, frangibility, fissility [*rare*], frailty, cold-shortness; house of -cards, –glass.

v. **be brittle** etc. *adj.;* live in a glass house.

break, crack, snap, split, shiver, splinter, crumble, crash, crush, break short, burst, fly, give way; fall to pieces; fall to dust; crumble -to, –into- dust.

adj. **brittle**, brash, frangible, breakable, friable, delicate, shattery [*rare*], fragile, frail, gimcrack, shivery, fissile; splitting etc. *v.*; lacerable, splintery, crisp, crimp, short, brittle as glass, cold-short; crisp as celery.

329. Texture
[structure]

n. **structure**, organization, anatomy, frame, mold *or* mould, fabric, construction; framework, carcass, architecture; stratification, cleavage.

substance, stuff, compages, parenchyma; constitution, staple, organism.

[science of structures] organology, osteology, myology, splanchnology, neurology, angiology, adenology; angiography, adenography, organography.

texture, intertexture, contexture; tissue, grain, web, surface; warp and -woof, –weft; gossamer, homespun, linsey-woolsey, frieze, fustian; satin, velvet; tooth, nap etc. (*roughness*) 256; fineness–, coarseness- of grain; dry goods.

[science of textures] histology.

adj. **structural**, organic; anatomic *or* anatomical; splanchnic, splanchnological, visceral, adenological.

textural, textile; fine-grained, coarse-grained, ingrained, ingrain; fine, delicate, subtle, subtle, gossamer, gossamery, filmy; coarse; homespun, linsey-woolsey.

330. Pulverulence

n. [state of powder] **pulverulence**; sandiness etc. *adj.*; efflorescence; friability, friableness, arenosity, sabulosity.

particle etc. (*smallness*) 32; powder, dust, sand, shingle; sawdust; grit; meal, bran, flour, farina, rice, paddy, spore, sporule; crumb, seed, grain; limature [*obs.*], filings, *débris* [*F.*], detritus, scobs, magistery, fine powder; flocculi.

smoke; cloud of -dust, –sand, –smoke; puff–, volume- of smoke; sand storm, dust storm.

[reduction to powder] pulverization, comminution, attenuation, granulation, disintegration, subaction, contusion, trituration, levigation, abrasion, detrition, multure limitation; tripsis; filing etc. *v.*

[instruments for pulverization] mill, arrastra, gristmill, grater, rasp, file, pestle and mortar, nutmeg grater, teeth, grinder, grindstone, kern [*dial.*], quern, quernstone, millstone.

[science] koniology.

v. **come to dust**; be disintegrated, be reduced to powder etc.

pulverize, comminute, granulate, triturate, levigate; reduce *or* grind to powder; scrape, file, abrade, rub down, grind, grate, rasp, pound, bray, bruise, contuse, contund [*rare*]; beat, crush, craunch *or* cranch, crunch, scranch [*colloq.*], crumble, disintegrate; attenuate etc. 195.

adj. **powdery**, pulverulent, granular, mealy, floury, farinaceous, branny, furfuraceous, flocculent, dusty, sandy, sabulous, psammous; detrital, arenaceous, arenose, arenarious, gritty; efflorescent, impalpable; lentiginous, lepidote, sabuline; sporaceous, sporous.

pulverable *or* pulverizable; friable, crumbly, shivery; pulverized etc. *v.*; attrite; in pieces.

331. Friction

n. **friction**, attrition; rubbing etc. *v.*; attriteness, attritus, erasure; confrication [*obs.*], contrition [*obs.*]; affriction [*obs.*], abrasion, arrosion [*obs.*], limature [*obs.*], anatripsis, anatripsology, frication, rub; elbow grease [*colloq.*]; rosin; massage.

masseur (*fem. masseuse*) [*F.*], massagist, rubber.

v. **rub**, abrade, scratch, scrape, scrub, fray, rasp, graze, curry, scour, polish, rub out, raze, erase, gnaw; file, grind etc. (*reduce to powder*) 330; rosin; massage.

set one's teeth on edge.

adj. **abrasive**, anatriptic; attrite [*rare*], attritive [*obs.*].

332. Lubrication
[absence of friction. prevention of friction]

n. **lubrication**, lubrification [*rare*], lubricity; anointment; oiling etc. *v.*

smoothness etc. 255; unctuousness etc. 355.

lubricant, lubricator, synovia; glycerin, oil etc. 356; saliva; lather; ointment, salve, balm, unguent, unguentum [*pharm.*], lenitive, unction.

v. **lubricate**, lubricitate [*obs.*]; oil, grease, lather, soap; wax; anoint; salivate.

adj. **lubricated** etc. *v.*; lubricous, lubricant, lubric [*rare*]; lenitive, synovial.

333. Fluidity

n. **fluidity**, liquidity, liquefaction; liquidness etc. *adj.*; gaseity etc. 334; solution, chylifaction, serosity.

fluid, inelastic fluid; liquid, liquor; lymph, humor, juice, sap, serum, blood, gravy, rheum, ichor, sanies; chyle.

solubility, solubleness.

[science of liquids at rest] hydrology, hydrostatics, hydrodynamics, hydrometry, hydrokinetics.

hydrometer, hydrophone, hydrostat, meter.

v. **be fluid** etc. *adj.;* flow etc. (*water in motion*) 348; liquefy etc. 335.

adj. **liquid**, fluid, serous, juicy, succulent, sappy; ichorous; rheumy, chylous, sanious, lymphatic; fluent etc. (*flowing*) 348.

liquefied etc. 335; uncongealed; soluble.

hydrological, hydrostatic *or* hydrostatical, hydrodynamic *or* hydrodynamical, hydrometric *or* hydrometrical.

334. Gaseity

n. **gaseity**, gaseousness, vaporousness etc. *adj.;* flatulence *or* flatulency; volatility; aeration, aerification; gasification.

elastic fluid, gas, air, vapor *or* vapour, ether, steam, fume, reek, effluvium, flatus; cloud etc. 353; ammonia, ammoniacal gas; volatile alkali.

[science of elastic fluids] pneumatics, pneumatology, pneumatonomy, pneumatostatics; aerostatics, aerodynamics, aeroscopy, aerography, aerology, aeromechanics.

pneumatoscope, pneumatometer, gasometer, gas meter; air–, swimming-bladder, sound (*of a fish*).

v. **gasify**, aërify, aërate; emit vapor etc. 336.

adj. **gaseous**, gasiform, aeriferous, aëriform, ethereal, aery, aerial, airy, vaporous, volatile, evaporable, flatulent.

pneumatolytic, aerostatic *or* aerostatical, aerodynamic, aeromechanic.

335. Liquefaction

n. **liquefaction**; liquescence, liquescency; deliquescence; melting etc. (*heat*) 384; colliquation [*obs.*], colliquefaction [*obs.*]; thaw; solubleness, deliquation [*obs.*], liquation; lixiviation, dissolution.

solution, decoction, apozem [*rare*], infusion, flux; alloy; lixivium.

solvent, diluent, resolvent, dissolvent, menstruum, alkahest.

v. **render liquid** etc. 333; liquefy, run; deliquesce; melt etc. (*heat*) 384; solve; dissolve, resolve; liquate; hold in solution.

leach, lixiviate, percolate.

adj. **liquefied** etc. *v.,* liquescent, liquefiable; deliquescent, soluble, dissoluble, dissolvable, colliquative; leachy, porous.

solvent, diluent, resolutive, resolvent, dissolvent.

336. Vaporization

n. **vaporization**, volatilization; gasification; evaporation, vaporation [*rare*], vaporishness, vaporosity, atomization, distillation, cupellation, cohobation, sublimation, exhalation; volatility.

fumigation, steaming.

vaporizer, atomizer, spray, evaporator, cohobator, finestill, still, retort.

bay salt, chloride of sodium.

v. **render gaseous** etc. 334; vaporize, volatilize, atomize. spray; distill, sublime, sublimate, evaporate, exhale, smoke, transpire, emit vapor, fume, reek, steam, fumigate; cohobate; finestill.

adj. **volatile**, evaporable, vaporizable, vaporific, vapory, vaporous, gaseous; volatilized etc. *v.;* reeking etc. *v.*

337. Water

n. **water**, lymph; aqua [*L.*], eau [*F.*], flood, crystal [*poetic*], Adam's ale [*humorous*], agua [*Sp.*], pani [*Hind.*]; diluent, serum etc. 333.

washing etc. *v.;* immersion, mersion [*obs.*]; dilution, maceration, lotion; humectation, infiltration, spargefaction [*obs.*], affusion, irrigation, seepage, balneation, bath.

deluge etc. (*water in motion*) 348; high water, flood tide, springtide.

sprinkler, sparger, aspergillum *or* aspergill, shower *or* shower bath, douche, enema; nozzle; atomizer etc. 336.

v. **be watery** etc. *adj.;* reek.

water, wet; moisten etc. 339; dilute, add water, dip, immerse; merge; soak, drouk [*Scot.*]; affuse [*rare*], immerge, douse *or* dowse, submerge; plunge, souse, duck, drown; steep, macerate, wash, sprinkle, sparge, humect *or* humectate [*rare*], lave, bathe, splash, swash, drench; dabble, slop, slobber, irrigate, inundate, deluge; infiltrate, percolate, seep; slosh; marinate *or* marinade, pickle.

inject, gargle; syringe, douche.

adj. watery, aqueous, aquatic, hydrous, lymphatic; balneal; diluent, solvent, hydrotic *or* hydrotical; infiltrative, seepy; drenching etc. *v.;* diluted etc. *v.;* weak; wet etc. (*moist*) 339.

338. Air

n. **air** etc. (*gas*) 334; common–, atmospheric- air; atmosphere; aerosphere [*rare*].

the open, –air; sky, lift [*archaic*], welkin [*archaic*], the blue, blue serene, blue sky; cloud etc. 353.

weather, climate; rise and fall of the -barometer, −mercury.

isopiestic line, isobar.

exposure to the -air, −weather; ventilation.

[science of air] aerology, aerometry, aeroscopy, aerography; meteorology, climatology; pneumatics; aeronautics; eudiometry; eudiometer, barometer, vacuometer, climatometer, aerometer, aeroscope; aneroid, baroscope, weatherglass, weathergauge, barograph.

aerostation etc. (*aeronautics*) 267; aeronaut etc. 269*a*.

weathervane, weathercock, vane, cock.

v. **air,** ventilate, perflate [*rare*]; fan etc. (*wind*) 349.

fly, soar, drift, hover; aviate etc. (*aeronautics*) 267.

adj. **containing air,** flatulent, effervescent; windy etc. 349.

atmospheric, airy; aerial, aeriform; aery, pneumatic.

meteorologic *or* meteorological, aerological, aerometric, eudiometric *or* eudiometrical, barometric *or* barometrical, barographic, baroscopic *or* baroscopical; isobaric, isopiestic; aerographic *or* aerographical; weatherwise.

adv. **in the open air,** *à la belle étoile* [*F.*], in the open, out of the blue, under the stars, out of doors, outdoors; *al fresco* [*It.*]; *sub Jove* [*L.*], *sub dio* [*L.*].

339. Moisture

n. **moisture;** moistness etc. *adj.;* humidity, humectation; madefaction [*obs.*], dew; *serein* [*F.*]; marsh etc. 345.

hygrometry, hygrometer.

v. **moisten,** wet; humect *or* humectate [*rare*]; sponge, damp, bedew; imbue, imbrue, infiltrate, saturate; soak, sodden, seethe, sop, dampen; drench etc. (*water*) 337.

be moist etc. *adj.;* not have a dry thread; perspire etc. (*exude*) 295.

adj. **moist,** damp; watery etc. 337; madid [*now rare*], undried, humid, wet, dank, muggy, dewy; roric; roriferous, rorifluent [*both rare*], roral [*obs.*], rorid [*obs.*]; roscid [*rare*]; juicy.

saturated etc. *v.;* wringing wet; wet through, wet to the skin.

sodden, swashy [*dial.*], soppy, soggy, dabbled; reeking, dripping, soaking, droukit [*Scot.*], soft, sloppy, muddy; swampy etc. (*marshy*) 345; irriguous.

340. Dryness

n. **dryness** etc. *adj.;* siccity [*rare*], siccation, aridness, aridity, drought *or* drouth.

ebb tide, low water.

desiccation, exsiccation [*rare*], dehydration, insolation, anhydration, anhydromyelia [*med.*], evaporation, arefaction [*rare*], dephlegmation, drainage.

drier, desiccative, desiccator.

v. **be** *or* **render dry** etc. *adj.;* dry; dry up, soak up; sponge, swab, wipe. drain, parch, sear.

be fine, hold up; be bright and fair.

desiccate, exsiccate, dehydrate, anhydrate, evaporate, insolate, infumate, torrefy, siccate [*rare*], arefy.

adj. **dry,** arid; droughty, waterless, siccaneous [*rare*], siccate [*obs.*], aneroid, sear *or* sere, siccant [*rare*], siccific, desiccatory; adjust, arescent; dried etc. *v.;* undamped; dephlegmatory; juiceless, sapless; corky; husky; rainless, without rain, fine; dry as -a bone, −dust, −a stick, −a mummy, −a biscuit; waterproof, watertight.

anhydrous, desiccated, desiccate, anhydric, dehydrated, insolated.

341. Ocean

n. **ocean,** sea, main, deep, blue, brine, salt water, waters, waves, billows, high seas, offing, great waters, watery waste, "vasty deep" "briny deep," "swan-bath" [*A.-S.*], "swan-road" [*A.-S.*], "whale-path" [*A.-S.*], mere [*archaic*], herring pond *or* pond [*humorous for Atlantic*], hyaline, the Seven Seas, *kala pani* [*Hind.*]; wave, tide etc. (*water in motion*) 348; ocean basin; ocean lane, steamer track.

Neptune, Poseidon, Oceanus, Thetis, Triton, Naiad, Nereid; sea nymph, Siren, mermaid, merman; trident, dolphin.

oceanography, hydrography; oceanographer, hydrographer.

adj. **oceanic,** marine, maritime; pelagic; seaworthy, seagoing; hydrographic *or* hydrographical, oceanographic *or* oceanographical; bathybic, cotidal.

adv. at sea, on sea; afloat; oversea *or* overseas, oceanward *or* oceanwards.

342. Land

n. **land,** earth, ground, soil, dry land, *terra firma* [*L.*].

continent, mainland, main, peninsula, chersonese, delta; tongue−, neck- of land; isthmus, oasis; promontory etc. (*projection*) 250; highland etc. (*height*) 206.

realty, real estate etc. (*property*) 780; acres.

coast, shore, scar *or* scaur, strand, beach; *playa* [*Sp.*]; bank, lea; seaboard, seaside, sea bank, seacoast, seabeach; seashore, rock-bound coast, iron-bound coast; loom of the land; derelict; innings; reclamation, made land, alluvium, alluvion; ancon [*S. W. U. S.*].

region etc. 181; home, fatherland etc. (*abode*) 189.

soil, glebe, clay, loam, marl, cledge [*dial. Eng.*], chalk, gravel, mold *or* mould, subsoil, clod, clot [*dial.*].

rock, crag, cliff.

geography, geodesy, geology, geognosy, geogony, agriculture, agronomics, agronomy, geoponics, georgics.

geographer, geodesist, geologist, geognost.

landsman, landlubber, tiller of the soil; agriculturist etc. 371.

v. **land**, disembark, debark, come to land; set foot on -the soil, –dry land; come–, go- ashore.

adj. **earthy**; continental, midland; terrene etc. (*world*) 318.

littoral, riparian, riparial, riparious, ripicolous, ripuarian; alluvial.

landed, predial, territorial; geophilous.

geographic *or* geographical, geodesic *or* geodesical, geodetic *or* geodetical, geognostic *or* geognostical, geologic *or* geological, geoponic; agricultural etc. 371.

adv. **ashore**; on shore, on land, on dry land, on *terra firma* [*L.*].

343. Gulf. Lake

n. **gulf**, gulph, bay, inlet, bight, estuary, arm of the sea, bayou, fiord, armlet; frith *or* firth, ostiary [*obs.*], mouth; lagoon *or* lagune; indraft *or* indraught [*obs.*], cove, creek; natural harbor; roads; strait; narrows; euripus; sound, belt, gut, kyle [*Scot.*].

lake, loch [*Scot.*], lough, [*Ir.*], mere, tarn, plash, broad [*Eng.*], pond, pool, sump [*Scot. or dial. Eng.*], slab [*dial.*], linn *or* lin [*Scot.*], tank, puddle, well, artesian well; standing–, dead–, sheet of- water; fish–, mill- pond; ditch, dike *or* dyke, dam, race, mill race; reservoir etc. (*store*) 636; *alberca* [*Sp. Amer.*], hog wallow, buffalo wallow.

adj. **lacustrine**, lacustral.

344. Plain

n. **plain**, tableland, face of the country; open–, champaign-country; basin, downs, waste, weary waste, desert, wild, steppe, tundra, peneplain, pampas, savanna, prairie etc. (*grassland*) 367; heath, common, wold, veldt *or* veld, moor, moorland; bush, plateau etc. (*level*) 213;

campagna [*obs. as Eng.*], champaign, uplands, fell [*Brit.*]; reach, stretch, expanse; alkali flat, llano; mesa, mesilla, *playa* [*Sp.*]; shaking–, trembling- prairie; *vega* [*Sp. Amer.*].

meadow, mead, haugh [*Scot. & dial. Eng.*], pasture, lea, ley *or* lay [*dial.*], pasturage, field.

lawn, green, plat, plot, grassplat.

greensward, sward, turf, sod, grass; heather.

grounds; *maidan* [*India*], park, common, campus, *agostadero* [*Sp.*].

adj. **champaign**, campestral, campestrial [*obs.*], campestrian, campestrine.

alluvial, fluvio-marine.

adv. in the bush.

345. Marsh

n. **marsh**, swamp, morass, marish [*archaic*], peat bog, moss, fen, bog, quagmire, slough, sump [*Scot. or dial. Eng.*], bottoms, holm [*Eng.*], wash; mud, squash, slush; baygall, *ciénaga* [*Sp.*], *jhil* [*India*], *vlei* [*S. Africa*].

adj. **marsh**, marshy, swampy, boggy, plashy, poachy, quaggy, soft; muddy, sloppy, squashy, spongy; paludal; moorish, moory; fenny, marish [*archaic*].

346. Island

n. **island**, isle, islet, ait *or* eyot, holm, reef, atoll; archipelago; islander.

v. **insulate**, island, enisle [*rare*], isle [*rare*].

adj. **insular**, insulary [*rare*], seagirt; archipelagic.

347. Stream
[fluid in motion]

n. **stream** etc. (*of water*) 348, (*of air*) 349.

v. **flow** etc. 348; **blow** etc. 349.

348. River
[water in motion]

n. running water.

jet, swash, spurt *or* spirt, squirt, spout, splash, rush, gush, *jet d'eau* [*F.*]; sluice.

waterspout, waterfall; fall, cascade, force *or* foss [*dial. Eng.*], linn *or* lin [*Scot.*], gill *or* ghyll; Niagara; cataract, catadupe [*obs.*], cataclysm; debacle, inundation, deluge; chute, washout.

rain, rainfall; *serein* [*F.*]; plash, shower, scud [*dial.*]; downpour; downflow, pour, cloudburst, drencher; driving–, drenching- rain; predominance of Aquarius, reign of St. Swithin; drisk, brash [*dial.*], mizzle [*dial.*], drizzle, stillicidium, dropping etc. *v.*; rains, rainy season, monsoon, *bursat* *or* *barsat* [*Hind.*]; falling weather [*colloq.*].

hyetology, hyetography; hyetograph, rain chart.

stream, course, flux, flow, profluence; effluence etc. (*egress*) 295; defluxion; flowing etc. *v.;* current, tide, race, mill race, tide race.

spring; fount, fountain; rill, rivulet, rillet; streamlet, brooklet; branch; runnel, runlet; sike, burn [*both dial. Eng. & Scot.*], beck [*Eng.*], brook, river; reach; tributary.

body of water, torrent, rapids, flush, flood, swash; spring–, high–, flood–, full- tide; bore, eagre *or* hygre; fresh, freshet; indraft *or* indraught; ebb, refluence, reflux, undercurrent, undertow, eddy, vortex, gurge [*rare*], whirlpool, Charybdis, Maelstrom (*also* maelstrom), regurgitation, overflow, alluvion; confluence, corrivation [*obs.*].

wave, billow, surge, swell, ripple, *anerithmon gelasma* [*Gr.*]; beachcomber, riffle, tidal wave, comber, chop, choppiness, roll, rollers, ground swell, surf, breakers, white horses; rough–, heavy–, cross–, long–, short–, choppy–, chopping- sea.

[science of fluids in motion] hydrodynamics; hydraulics, hydrostatics, hydrokinetics, hydromechanics, pegology, pluviometry.

[measures] hyetometer, hyetometrograph, hydrodynamometer, nilometer, fluviometer, fluviograph, marigraph, hydrometer, hydrometrograph, udometer, ombrometer, rain gauge *or* gage, pluviometer, pluviograph.

irrigation etc. (*water*) 337; pump; watering- pot, –cart; hydrant, standpipe, syringe, siphon, *mussuk* [*Hind.*].

water carrier, bheesty *or* bheestie [*India*], Water Bearer, Aquarius.

v. flow, run; meander; gush, pour, spout, roll, jet, well, issue; drop, drip, dribble, plash, spirtle, trill, trickle, distill, percolate; stream, gurge [*rare*], surge, swirl, overflow, inundate, deluge, flow over, splash, swash; guggle, murmur, babble, bubble, purl, gurgle, sputter, spurt, regurgitate; ooze, flow out etc. (*egress*) 295.

flow into, fall into, open into, drain into; discharge itself, disembogue.

[cause a flow] pour; pour out etc. (*discharge*) 297; shower down; irrigate, drench etc. (*wet*) 337; spill, splash.

[stop a flow] stanch *or* staunch; dam, dam up etc. (*close*) 261; obstruct etc. 706.

rain, –hard, –in torrents, –cats and dogs, –pitchforks [*both colloq.*]; pour, shower, sprinkle, pour with rain, drizzle, spit [*colloq.*], set in; mizzle.

adj. fluent, deliquescent, defluent, profluent [*rare*], diffluent, affluent; tidal; flowing etc. *v.;* mean-

dering, meandrous, meandry [*obs.*], flexuous, fluvial, fluviatile; streamy, streamful; choppy, rolling; stillicidious [*obs.*], stillatitious [*rare*]; hydragogue [*med.*].

rainy, showery, pluvial [*rare*], pluvious, pluviose [*rare*], drizzly, drizzling, mizzly, wet; pluviometric *or* pluviometrical.

349. Wind
[air in motion]

n. wind, draught, flatus, afflatus, sufflation [*rare*], insufflation, perflation, inflation, afflation, indraft *or* indraught, efflation; air; breath, –of air; puff, whiff, whiffet, zephyr, blow, drift; aura; stream, current; undercurrent.

Aeolus *or* Eolus, Boreas, Euroclydon, Eurus, Notus [*rare*], Zephyr *or* Zephyrus, Favonius; cave of Aeolus *or* Eolus; Wabun (east wind), Kabibonokka (north wind), Shawondasee (south wind), Mudjekeewis (west wind) [*all four from Hiawatha*].

gust, blast, breeze, capful of wind, fresh breeze, stiff breeze, keen blast, squall, half a gale, gale.

trade wind, trades, monsoon.

storm, tempest, hurricane, whirlwind, tornado, samiel, cyclone, typhoon, simoom *or* simoon, harmattan, sirocco, mistral, *bise* [*F.*], *tramontana* [*It.*], tramontane, levant, levanter; blizzard, barber [*Can.*], *candelia* [*Sp. Am.*], chinook, foehn, khamsin, norther, northeaster, northeast gale, *vendaval* [*Sp.*], wuther [*dial.*], willy-willy [*Austral.*].

windiness etc. *adj.;* ventosity [*obs.*]; rough–, dirty–, ugly–, wicked–, foul–, stress of-weather; dirty sky, mare's-tail, mackerel sky; cloud etc. 353; thick–, black–, white- squall.

anemography, anemology, anemometry, aerology, aerography, aerodynamics.

wind-gauge, anemometer, anemoscope, anemograph, anemometrograph; weathercock, weathervane, vane.

breathing, respiration, inspiration, inhalation, expiration, exhalation; blowing, fanning, etc. *v.;* ventilation; sneezing etc. *v.;* errhine; sternutation; hiccup *or* hiccough, eructation, catching of the breath; inspirator, respirator, ejector.

air pump, lungs, bellows, pulmotor, blowpipe; branchiae, gills.

fan, punkah *or* punka [*India*], flabellum, thermantidote, electric fan; *ventilabrum* [*L.*].

ventilator, louver, aerator [*rare*], transom; air-pipe etc. 351; hygrometer, psychrometer.

v. **blow**, waft; blow -hard, –great guns, –a hurricane etc. *n.;* storm; wuther [*dial.*], stream, issue.

respire, breathe, inhale, exhale; inspire, expire; puff; whiff, whiffle; gasp, wheeze; snuff, snuffle; sniff, sniffle; sneeze, cough, hiccup *or* hiccough; belch, eruct [*rare*].

fan, ventilate; inflate, pump, perflate [*obs.*]; blow up.

whistle, scream, roar, howl, sing, sing in the shrouds, growl.

adj. **windy**, airy, aeolian *or* eolian, borean, favonian; ventilative; blowing etc. *v.;* breezy, gusty, squally.

stormy, tempestuous, blustering, cyclonic, typhonic; boisterous etc. (*violent*) 173.

anemographic, anemological, anemometric *or* anemometrical, aerologic *or* aerological, aerographic *or* aerographical, aerodynamic.

pulmonic, pulmonary, pulmonate.

nasal, errhine; sternutative, sternutatory.

flatulent, gassy, windy, ventose.

350. Conduit
[channel for the passage of water]

n. **conduit**, channel, duct, watercourse, cañon *or* canyon, coulee *or* coulée [*geol.*], water gap, gorge, ravine, chasm; race; head–, tail- race; abito [*F. Amer.*], aboideau *or* aboiteau [*local Can.*], bito [*dial., U. S.*]; acequia [*Sp. Amer.*], acequiador [*Sp. Amer.*], arroyo; adit, aqueduct, canal, trough, gutter, pantile; flume, dike, main; gully, gullet [*rare*], gulch, moat, ditch, drain, sewer, culvert, cloaca, sough [*dial. Eng.*], kennel, siphon; piscine, piscina; pipe etc. (*tube*) 260; funnel; tunnel etc. (*passage*) 627; water–, waste- pipe; emunctory, gully hole, spout, scupper; ajutage; hose; gargoyle *or* gurgoyle; penstock, pentrough, weir, lock weir, floodgate, water gate, sluice, lock, valve; rose, rosehead; waterworks.

[for metal] ingate, runner, tedge.

[anatomy] artery, vein, *vena* [*L.*], blood vessel, lymphatic, pore; aorta; intestines, bowels; small intestine, duodenum, jejunum, ileum; large intestine, cecum or caecum, colon, rectum; esophagus, gullet; throat.

adj. **vascular** etc. (*with holes*) 260.

excretory, eliminative.

351. Air Pipe
[channel for the passage of air]

n. **air pipe**, air tube, air hole, blowhole, breathing hole, spiracle, touchhole, vent hole, spile hole, bung, bunghole; shaft, airway, air shaft, smoke- shaft, flue, chimney, funnel, vent, ventage; ventiduct, ventilator; pipe etc. (*tube*) 260; blowpipe etc. (*wind*) 349.

nostril, nozzle, throat, weasand, bronchus (*pl.* bronchi), larynx, tonsils, windpipe, trachea.

louver, Venetian blind, Venetian shutter, *jalousie* [*F.*], *jhilmil* [*India*].

352. Semiliquidity

n. **semiliquidity**; stickiness etc. *adj.;* viscidity, viscosity, mucidness, gummosis, emulsification, jellification; gummosity [*rare*], glutinosity [*rare*], mucosity; crassitude, spissitude; lentor [*now rare*]; pastiness; adhesiveness etc. (*cohesion*) 46; succulence *or* succulency; lactescence.

inspissation, incrassation, crassamentum, coagulum; thickening.

[comparisons] jelly, gelatin, carlock, ichthyocol, ichthyocolla, isinglass; mucus, pus, phlegm, pituite; lava; paste; library–, flour- paste; glair, starch, gluten, albumen, milk, cream, protein; treacle, rob, syrup, molasses; gum, size, glue, varnish, mastic, mucilage, fish glue; wax, beeswax; emulsion; gruel, porridge; *purée* [*F.*], soup.

squash, mud, slush, slime, ooze; moisture etc. 339; marsh etc. 345.

v. **inspissate**, incrassate; coagulate, gelatinate, gelatinize; jellify, jelly, jell; emulsify, thicken; mash, squash, churn, beat up.

adj. **semifluid**, semiliquid; half-melted, half-frozen; milky, muddy etc. *n.;* lacteal, lactean [*rare*], lacteous, lactescent, lactiferous; emulsive, curdled, thick, succulent, uliginose *or* uliginous.

gelatinous, albuminous, mucilaginous, glutinous; gummous, spissated [*rare*], crass, tremelloid, tremellose, amylaceous, ropy, clammy, clotted; viscid, viscous; sticky, tacky; slab [*dial.*], slabby; lentous [*obs.*], pituitous; mucid, muculent, mucous.

353. Bubble. Cloud
[mixture of air and water]

n. **bubble**; foam, froth, head, spume, scum, fume, lather, suds, spray, surf, yeast, barm, spoondrift *or* spindrift.

effervescence, fermentation; bubbling etc. *v.;* evaporation, exhalation, emanation.

cloudiness etc. (*opacity*) 426; nebulosity etc. (*dimness*) 422.

cloud, vapor, fog, mist, haze, steam; scud, rack, nimbus; cumulus, nebula, meteor, woolpack, cirrus, curl cloud, thunderhead, stratus; cirro-

107

stratus, cumulo-stratus; cirro-cumulus; mackerel sky, mare's-tail, colt's-tail, cat's-tail, cocktail, dirty sky; frost smoke.

[science of clouds] nephology, nephelognosy, meteorology; nephoscope, nephelometer, nephograph.

v. **bubble**, boil, foam, spume, froth, mantle, sparkle, guggle, gurgle; effervesce, pop, ferment, fizzle; aerate.

cloud, overcast, overcloud, befog, becloud, adumbrate [*rare*], mist, fog, overshadow, shadow.

adj. **bubbling** etc. v.; frothy, nappy [*obs.*], effervescent, sparkling, *mousseux* [*F.*], fizzy, heady, with a head on, with a collar on [*slang*], up [*colloq.*].

cloudy etc. n.; cirrous, cirrose; nubiferous, cumulous, thunderheaded; vaporous, nebulous, overcast.

nephological, nepheloscopic, nephelometric, meteorologic *or* meteorological.

354. Pulpiness

n. **pulpiness** etc. adj.; pulp, paste, dough, sponge, batter, clotted cream, curd, pap, jam, pudding, poultice, grume.

v. **pulp**, pulpify [*rare*], mash, squash [*colloq.*], masticate, macerate; coagulate etc. 352.

adj. **pulpy** etc. n.; pultaceous, grumous; baccate; [*of fruit*] fleshy, succulent.

355. Unctuousness

n. **unctuousness** etc. adj.; unctiousness [*rare*], unguent, unctuosity, lubricity; salve, cerate; ointment etc. (*oil*) 356; anointment; lubrication etc. 332.

v. **oil**, anoint, lubricate etc. 332; smear, salve, grease, lard, pinguefy.

adj. **unctuous**, unctious [*rare*], unguentary, unguentous, oily, oleaginous, adipose, sebaceous, unguinous, fat, fatty, greasy; waxy, butyraceous, soapy, saponaceous, pinguid, lardaceous; slippery.

356. Oil

n. **oil**, fat, butter, cream, grease, tallow, suet, lard, dripping, exunge [*obs.*], blubber; glycerin *or* glycerine, stearin, elain *or* elaine, olein, oleagine; coconut butter; soap; soft soap, wax, cerement; paraffin, benzine, gasoline, petrol, spermaceti, adipocere; petroleum, mineral–, rock–, crystal- oil; vegetable–, colza–, olive–, salad–, linseed–, cottonseed–, coconut–, palm–, nut- oil; animal–, neat's-foot–, train-

oil; ointment, pomade, pomatum, unguent, liniment; amole, Barbados tar; fusel–, grain–, rape–, seneca-oil; hydrate of amyl, ghee *or* ghi [*India*], kerosene, naphtha.

356a. Resin

n. **resin**, rosin, colophony, gum; lac, shellac, sealing wax; amber, ambergris; bitumen, pitch, tar; asphalt *or* asphaltum; camphor; varnish, copal, mastic, megilp *or* magilp, lacquer, japan, Brunswick black.

v. **varnish** etc. (*overlay*) 223; rosin, resin.

adj. **resinous**, resiny, rosinous [*rare*], lacquered, japanned, camphorated, tarred, tarry, pitched, pitchy, gummed, gummy, gummous, waxed; bituminous, asphaltic, asphaltite.

Section 3. Organic Matter

357. Organization

n. **organization**, organized world, organized nature, living nature, animated nature; living beings; organic remains; organism, bion [*physiological individual*]; morphon [*morphological individual*]; biota, animal and plant life, fauna and flora.

fossils, fossilization, lapidification, petrification, petrifaction, paleontology *or* palaeontology, paleozoölogy *or* paleozoölogy; paleontologist.

[science of living beings] biology, natural history; zoölogy etc. 368; botany etc. 369; physiology, anatomy, cytology, embryology, organic chemistry, morphology; promorphology, tectology; cell theory *or* cellular theory, evolution, metabolism; abiogenesis, spontaneous generation; archigenesis etc. (*production*) 161; biotaxy, ecology, ontogeny, phylogeny, polymorphism, oxidation, invagination, vertebration.

Darwinism, Lamarckism, neo-Lamarckism, Weismannism.

naturalist, biologist, zoölogist, botanist, bacteriologist, embryologist, Darwinian.

protoplasm, plasma *or* plasm, cytoplasm, metaplasm, karyoplasm, bioplasm, trophoplasm, idioplasm; cell, proteid, protein, albumen, albumin, albuminoid; structure etc. 329; chromatin; centrosome, nucleolus, karyosome, vacuole, chromosome; protoplast, protozoan, amoeba; karyaster, erythroblast, dysmeromorph, antherozoid.

ovum, oösperm, zygote, oösphere, oöcyte, ooecium, ovicell, oögonium; oöphyte, oöspore, oögamy, heterogamy, isogamy, oögenesis; gamete, gametophore, gametophyte, sporophyte,

360. Death

sporocyte, sporocyst, sporocarp, cystocarp, sporogonium, sporozoite, gametangium, antheridium *or* antherid; macrospore, megasporangium; microspore, microsporangium; biophore; spermatozoid, zoöspore, macrogamete, microgamete, spermatozoön, spermatium, spermatia, spermatocyte, spermatogenesis, spermatophore, spermatozoid, spermatozooid; spermogonium, spermary, sperm gland, testis, testicle, ovary; germ cell, blastoderm, mesoblast *or* mesoplast, meroblast (*opp. to* holoblast); germinal matter, biogenesis *or* biogeny, germ plasm, zooid.

v. **organize**, systematize, form, arrange, construct.
fossilize, petrify, lapidify, mummify.

adj. **organic**, organized; biotic, zooid, zooidal.
fossilized, petrified, petrifactive, lapidined; paleontologic, paleontological *or* palaeontological, paleozoölogical *or* palaeozoölogical.

protoplasmic, plasmatic *or* plasmic, cytoplasmic, metaplasmic, karyoplasmic, bioplasmic, trophoplasmic, idioplasmic; cellular, cellulous; proteid, proteinaceous, albuminous *or* albuminose, albuminoidal, structural; nuclear, nucleate, nucleolar, nucleolate *or* nucleolated; vacuolar, protoplastic, protozoan, amoebic, amoeboid.

ovarian, oviferous, oviparous (*opp. to* viviparous), ovicular; oöphytic, oösporic, oösporous, oögamous, heterogamous (*opp. to* autogamous *or* isogamous); gamic, sporogenous; spermatic, spermatogenetic, spermatoid, spermatophoral, spermatozoal; blastodermic, mesoblastic (*opp. to* holoblastic), biogenetic, germinal; zoögleic, zoögleoid; unsegmentic, dioecious *or* diecious (*opp. to* monoecious *or* monecious).

358. Inorganization

n. **mineral kingdom**, mineral world; unorganized-, inorganic-, brute-, inanimate- matter.
[science of the mineral kingdom] mineralogy, geology, geognosy, geoscopy, metallurgy, metallography, lithology, petrology, oryctology [*obs.*], oryctography [*obs.*].

v. **mineralize**; pulverize, turn to dust.

adj. **inorganic**, inanimate, unorganized *or* inorganized, lithoid, *or* lithoidal; azoic; mineral.

359. Life

n. **life**; vitality, viableness, viability; animation.
vital spark, vital flame, Promethean spark, lifeblood; respiration, wind; breath of life, breath of one's nostrils; Archeus *or* Archaeus; *anima* [*L.*], *anima bruta* [*L.*], *anima divina*

[*L.*], *anima mundi* [*L.*]; world -soul, –spirit, –principle; existence etc. 1.
vivification; oxygen; vital -air, –force; life force; vitalization; revival; revivification etc. 163; Prometheus; Deucalion and Pyrrha; life to come etc. (*destiny*) 152.
"a short summer" [Johnson]; "a bubble" [Browne]; "a battle" [Aurelius]; "one dem'd horrid grind" [Dickens].
[science of life] physiology, biology, etiology, embryology; animal economy.
nourishment, staff of life etc. (*food*) 298.

v. **live**; be alive etc. *adj.;* breathe, respire, suspire; subsist etc. (*exist*) 1; walk the earth; (a poor player that) "struts and frets his hour upon the stage" [*Macbeth*]; be spared.
be born, see the light, come into the world; fetch-, draw- -breath, –the breath of life; breathe the vital air; quicken; revive; come to, –life.
give birth to etc. (*produce*) 161; bring to life, put into life, vitalize; vivify, vivificate [*rare*]; reanimate etc. (*restore*) 660.
keep alive, keep body and soul together, keep the wolf from the door; support life.
have nine lives like a cat.

adj. **living**, alive; in life, in the flesh, in the land of the living; on this side of the grave, above ground, breathing, quick, animated; animative; lively etc. (*active*) 682; alive and kicking [*colloq.*]; tenacious of life.
vital, vitalic; vivifying, vivified etc. *v.;* viable, zoëtic; Promethean.

adv. *vivendi causa* [*L.*].

360. Death

n. **death**; decease, demise; mortality; dying; passing -away, –of the soul; dissolution, departure, obit, release, rest, eternal rest, quietus, fall; loss, bereavement.
end etc. 67-, cessation etc. 142-, loss-, extinction-, ebb- of life etc. 359.
death-warrant, deathwatch, death rattle, deathbed; stroke-, agonies-, shades-, valley of the shadow-, summons-, jaws-, hand-, bridge-, river- of death; Jordan, Jordan's bank, "one more river to cross"; last -breath, –gasp, –agonies; dying -day, –breath. –agonies; swan song, *chant du cygne* [*F.*]; *rigor mortis* [*L.*]; Stygian shore; "crossing the bar" [Tennyson]; the great adventure.
euthanasia, euthanasy [*rare*]; happy release, *bona mors* [*L.*]; break-up of the system; natural -death, –decay; sudden-, violent- death; un-

109

timely end, taking off [*colloq.*], watery grave; debt of nature; mortification, heart failure, suffocation, asphyxia; fatal disease etc. (*disease*) 655; deathblow etc. (*killing*) 361.

angel of death, death's bright angel, Azrael; King -of terrors, –Death; Death, doom etc. (*necessity*) 601; "Hell's grim Tyrant" [*Pope*].

necrology, bills of mortality, obituary.

death song etc. (*lamentation*) 839.

v. **die**, expire, perish; meet one's -death, –end; pass away, pass over, be taken; yield–, resign- one's breath; resign one's -being, –life; end one's -days, –life, –earthly career; breathe one's last; cease to -live, –breathe; depart this life; be no more etc. *adj.;* go off [*colloq.*], drop off [*colloq.*], pop off [*slang*]; lose–, lay down–, relinquish–, surrender- one's life; drop–, sink- into the grave; close one's eyes; fall–, drop- -dead, –down dead; break one's neck; give–, yield- up the ghost; be all over with one.

pay the debt to nature, shuffle off this mortal coil, take one's last sleep; go the way of all flesh; hand–, pass- -in one's checks, –in one's chips [*all slang*]; go over to the–, join the- -greater number, –majority, –great majority; join the choir invisible; awake to life immortal; come–, turn- to dust; give an obolus to Charon; cross the Stygian ferry; go to one's long account, go to one's last home, go to Davy Jones's locker, go to glory [*colloq.*]; receive one's death warrant, make one's will, step out [*colloq.*], die a natural death, go out like the snuff of a candle; come to an untimely end; catch one's death; go off the hooks, kick the bucket, hop the twig, turn up one's toes [*all slang*]; die a violent death etc. (*be killed*) 361.

die for one's country, make the supreme sacrifice, go West [*World War I euphemism*].

adj. **dead**, lifeless; deceased, demised, departed, defunct; late, gone, no more; exanimate [*rare*], inanimate; out of the world, taken off, released; bereft of life; stone dead; departed this life etc. *v.;* dead and gone; dead as -a doornail, –a doorpost, –mutton, –a herring, –nits [*all slang or colloq.*]; launched into eternity, gathered to one's fathers, numbered with the dead; born into a better world, born into the next world; gone to a better land; dying–, dead- in the Lord; asleep in Jesus; with the saints.

stillborn; mortuary; deadly etc. (*killing*) 361.

dying etc. *v.;* moribund, morient [*obs.*]; Hippocratic; *in articulo* [*L.*], *in extremis* [*L.*]; in the -jaws, –agony- of death; going, –off; *aux abois* [*F.*]; on one's -last legs [*colloq.*], –death-

bed; at the point of death, at death's door, at the last gasp; near one's end, given up, given over, booked [*slang*]; with one foot in–, tottering on the brink of- the grave.

adv. *post obit* [*L.*], *post mortem* [*L.*].

361. Killing

[destruction of life; violent death]

n. **killing** etc. *v.;* homicide, manslaughter, murder, assassination, trucidation [*obs.*], occision [*obs.*]; effusion of blood; blood, bloodshed; gore, slaughter, carnage, butchery; *battue* [*F.*]; bomb explosion, electrocution, shipwreck; gladiatorial combat; lapidation.

massacre; fusillade, *noyade* [*F.*]; thuggism, thuggee, thuggery; saturnalia of blood, sacrifice to Moloch; organized massacre, *pogrom* [*Russia*].

war, warfare, "organized murder," *horrida bella* [*L.*], crusade, jihad *or* jehad [*Moham.*]; battle; war to the death etc. (*warfare*) 722; Armageddon; gigantomachy; deadly weapon etc. (*arms*) 727.

deathblow, finishing stroke, *coup de grâce* [*F.*], quietus; execution etc. (*capital punishment*) 972; judicial murder; martyrdom.

suffocation, strangulation, garrote *or* garrotte; hanging etc. *v.*

slayer, butcher, murderer, Cain, assassin, cutthroat, garroter *or* garrotter, bravo, Thug *or* thug, Moloch, matador, *sabreur* [*F.*]; *guetapens* [*F.*]; gallows, executioner etc. (*punishment*) 975; man-eater, Apache, hatchet man, highbinder, gunman, bandit, lapidator [*rare*].

regicide, parricide, fratricide, infanticide; feticide, aborticide; uxoricide, vaticide [*these words ending in* -cide *refer to both doer and deed*].

suicide, self-murder, self-destruction, *felo-de-se* (*pl. felos-de-se*), seppuku [*Jap.*], hara-kiri [*Jap.*], suttee, sutteeism, car of Jagannath *or* Juggernaut [*an erroneous assumption*]; immolation, holocaust.

fatal accident, violent death, casualty, disaster, calamity.

Aceldama (*often l.c.*), potter's field, field of blood.

[destruction of animals] slaughtering; phthiozoics; sport, sporting; the chase, venery; hunting, coursing, shooting, fishing; pig-sticking.

sportsman, huntsman, fisherman; hunter, Nimrod.

shambles, slaughterhouse, *abattoir* [*F.*].

v. **kill**, put to death, slay, shed blood; murder, assassinate, butcher, slaughter, victimize, immolate; massacre; take away–, deprive of- life; make away with, put an end to; dispatch *or* despatch; burke, settle [*colloq.*], do to death, do for [*colloq.*]; hunt.

shoot, –dead; blow one's brains out; brain, knock on the head, blackjack; drop in one's tracks; stone, lapidate; give–, deal- a deathblow; give the -quietus, –*coup de grâce* [*F.*].

strangle, garrote *or* garrotte, hang, throttle, choke, stifle, suffocate, stop the breath, smother, asphyxiate, drown.

saber *or* sabre; cut -down, –to pieces, –the throat; jugulate; stab, run through the body, bayonet; put to the -sword, –edge of the sword.

execute, behead, guillotine, hang, electrocute; bowstring etc. (*execute*) 972.

cut off, nip in the bud, launch into eternity, send to one's last account, sign one's death warrant, strike the death knell of.

give no quarter, pour out blood like water; decimate; run amuck *or* amok; wade knee-deep in blood; dye-, imbrue- one's hands in blood.

die a violent death, welter in one's blood; dash–, blow- out one's brains; commit suicide; kill–, make away with–, put an end to- oneself; suicide [*colloq.*]; disembowel, commit hara-kiri.

adj. **murderous**, slaughterous, sanguinary, sanguinolent, blood-stained, blood-thirsty; killing etc. *v.;* homicidal, red-handed; bloody, bloody-minded; ensanguined, gory, sanguineous.

mortal, fatal, lethal; deadly, deathly; mortiferous [*obs.*], lethiferous; unhealthy etc. 657; mutually destructive, internecine; suicidal.

sporting; piscatorial, piscatory.

int. thumbs down! *habet! hoc habet!* [*L.*], let him have it!

362. Corpse

n. **corpse**, corse [*archaic*], carcass, cadaver, bones, skeleton, dry bones; defunct, relics, reliquiae, remains, mortal remains, dust, ashes, earth, clay; mummy; carrion; food for -worms, –fishes; tenement of clay, "this mortal coil" [*Hamlet*]; "this too, too solid flesh" [*Hamlet*].

ghost, shade, manes, phantom, specter *or* spectre, apparition, spirit, revenant, sprite [*archaic*], spook [*colloq.*].

organic remains, fossils.

adj. **cadaverous**, cadaveric, corpse-like; unburied etc. 363.

363. Interment

n. **interment**, burial, sepulture, entombment *or* intombment, inhumation, humation [*obs.*]; obsequies, exequies; funeral, wake.

cremation, burning; pyre, funeral pile.

funeral rite, funeral solemnity; knell, passing bell, death bell, funeral ring, tolling; dirge etc. (*lamentation*) 839; cypress; obit, dead march, muffled drum; elegy; funeral -oration, –sermon.

undertaker, mortician, funeral director.

mourner, mute, keener [*Ireland*], lamenter; pall-bearer, bearer.

graveclothes, shroud, winding sheet, cerecloth; cerements.

coffin, casket, shell, sarcophagus.

urn, cinerary urn; pall, bier, litter, hearse, catafalque.

burial place, grave, pit, sepulcher *or* sepulchre, tomb, vault, crypt, catacomb, mausoleum, cenotaph, golgotha, house of death, narrow house, low green tent, low house, long home, last home; cemetery, necropolis; burial ground; graveyard, churchyard; God's acre; potter's field; cromlech, barrow, tumulus, cairn; ossuary; bonehouse, charnel-house, deadhouse; morgue, mortuary; lich gate; burning ghât *or* ghaut [*India*]; crematorium, crematory; mastaba *or* mastabah [*Egypt*], tope *or* stupa [*Buddhist*]; dokhma, Tower of Silence [*Parsee*].

gravedigger, sexton, *fossoyeur* [*F.*].

monument, cenotaph, shrine; gravestone, headstone, tombstone; *memento mori* [*L.*]; hatchment, stone, marker, cross; epitaph, inscription.

necropsy, necroscopy, autopsy, *post mortem* examination *or* *post mortem* [*L.*].

exhumation, disinterment.

v. **inter**, bury; lay in–, consign to- the -grave, –tomb; entomb *or* intomb; inhume; hold–, conduct- a funeral; put to bed with a shovel [*colloq.*]; inurn; cremate.

lay out; embalm, mummify; toll the knell.

exhume, disinter, unearth.

adj. **funereal**, funebrial [*now rare*], funeral, funerary, mortuary, sepulchral, cinerary; buried etc. *v.;* burial; elegiac; necroscopic *or* necroscopical.

adv. *hic jacet* [*L.*], *ci-gît* [*F.*], *R. I. P.;* in memoriam [*L.*]; *post obit* [*L.*], *post mortem* [*L.*]; beneath the sod, under the sod, underground; at rest.

364. Animality

n. **animality**, animalism, animal life; animation, animalization, animalness.

corporeal nature, human system; breath; flesh, flesh and blood; physique; strength etc. 159.

v. **animalize**; incarnate, incarn [*rare*], incorporate.

adj. **fleshly**, carnal, human, corporeal.

365. Vegetation

n. **vegetation**, vegetable life, vegetability [*obs.*], vegetativeness, vegetism, vegetality [*rare*]; herbage, flowerage.

v. **vegetate**, germinate, sprout, grow, shoot up, luxuriate, fungate; grow -rank, –lush, –like a weed; flourish etc. 367; cultivate.

adj. **vegetative**, vegetal, vegetable; leguminous etc. 367.

luxuriant, rank, dense, lush, wild, jungly.

366. Animal

n. **animal kingdom**, fauna, brute creation.

animal, creature, created being; creeping thing, living thing; dumb animal, dumb friend, dumb creature; brute, beast.

mammal, quadruped, bird, reptile, fish, crustacean, shellfish, mollusk, worm, insect, zoöphyte; plankton, nekton, benthos; animalcule etc. 193.

beasts of the field, fowls of the air, denizens of the day; flocks and herds, live stock, domestic animals; wild animals, *ferae naturae* [*L.*], game.

[domestic animals] horse etc. (*beast of burden*) 271; cattle, kine, ox; bull, bullock; cow, milch cow, Alderney, Guernsey, Holstein, Jersey, calf, heifer, shorthorn, yearling, steer, stot [*prov. Eng.*]; sheep; lamb, lambkin, ewe lamb, pet lamb; ewe, ram, tup, wether, tag [*prov. Eng.*], teg [*prov. Eng.*]; pig, swine, boar, hog, sow; yak, zebu, Indian buffalo.

dog, hound, canine; pup, puppy; whelp, cur [*contemptuous*].

house–, watch–, sheep–, shepherd's–, sporting–, hunting–, fancy–, lap–, toy- dog; collie; mastiff; bulldog, English bulldog, Boston bull, bull terrier, French bull; police dog, bloodhound, greyhound, staghound, deerhound, foxhound, coach dog, bandog, lurcher, Russian *or* Siberian wolfhound, boarhound, St. Bernard, husky *or* Eskimo dog; otter-hound; harrier, beagle, spaniel, pointer, setter, retriever, Newfoundland; water -dog, –spaniel; pug, poodle; turnspit; terrier; fox–, Airedale–, Yorkshire–, Irish–, Skye–, toy-terrier; Dandie Dinmont; dachshund, badger dog; brindle; Pomeranian, cocker spaniel, King Charles spaniel, toy spaniel, spitz dog; chow *or* chow-dog, Japanese poodle.

pariah dog, pye-dog *or* pie-dog [*India*]; mongrel, mutt [*slang*].

female, bitch, slut, brach, brachet, lady [*euphemistic*].

cat, feline, puss, pussy, grimalkin, tomcat *or* tom, gib [*rare*], Angora, Persian, Maltese, tortoise-shell, mouser; tabby; kitten, kit, catling, kitling [*dial.*].

[wild animals] **deer**, buck, doe, fawn, stag, hart, hind, roe, roebuck, caribou, elk, moose, reindeer, sambar, wapiti *or* American elk, mule deer, black-tailed deer *or* Virginia deer, fallow deer, red deer.

antelope, gazelle, nilghau, eland, gnu, hartebeest, springbok *or* springbuck, oryx, steinbok, ibex; American antelope *or* pronghorn, chamois, koodoo *or* kudu.

armadillo, peba, poyou, tatouay; wild ass, kiang, dziggetai, onager; bear, polar bear, grizzly bear, brown bear; beaver; bison, buffalo; musk ox, giraffe, okapi, tapir; wild boar; babiroussa *or* babirussa; ape, monkey, gorilla, marmoset, chimpanzee, lemur, baboon, orang-utan *or* orang-outang; kangaroo, opossum; wild horse, zebra; elephant, *hathi* [*Hind.*]; fox, reynard, Reynard, vixen [*fem.*], varmin *or* varmint [*dial.*], prairie fox, gray fox, red fox, arctic fox; dingo, coyote; wildcat, lynx, bobcat; skunk; hippopotamus, rhinoceros, lion, tiger etc. (*wild beast*) 913; squirrel, chipmunk, gopher, prairie dog, ferret, stoat, weasel, mongoose, raccoon *or* coon, bandicoot, rat, mouse; bat, flying mouse, flying phalanger, flying squirrel; flying fox, flying lemur, colugo.

lizard, saurian, iguana, eft, newt, chameleon, gecko, Gila monster, dragon, horned toad, horned lizard.

crocodilian, crocodile, mugger *or* magar [*India*], gavial [*India*], alligator, cayman, American crocodile.

whale, sperm whale, baleen whale; shark, porpoise, walrus, seal, octopus, devilfish; swordfish; pike; salmon etc. (*food*) 298.

[birds] feathered tribes, feathered songster, singing bird, warbler, dickybird [*colloq.*].

canary, vireo, linnet, finch, goldfinch, brown thrasher, siskin, crossbill, aberdevine, chewink, peewee, lapwing [*Scot.*], titmouse *or* chickadee, nightingale, lark; magpie, cuckoo, mocking bird, catbird, laughing jackass, starling, myna *or* mina; bobolink, reedbird, ricebird, cardinal, cowbird, crow, rook, jackdaw, raven; pigeon, dove, cushat, ringdove, wood pigeon; swan, cygnet, goose, gander, duck, drake, wild duck, mallard; flamingo, heron, crane, stork, eagle, kingfisher, sandpiper, lyre bird, robin, thrush, hermit thrush, veery, mavis, missel thrush, ouzel *or* ousel, blackbird, red-winged blackbird; kingbird, fly-catcher; woodpecker, flicker; sparrow, song sparrow, chipping sparrow, vesper sparrow; swallow, swift, martin, sand martin, oriole, bluebird, meadow lark; bird of paradise, parrot, parrakeet *or* parakeet; penguin, pelican; gull, sea gull, albatross, petrel, stormy petrel *or* Mother Carey's chicken, fulmar *or* Mother Carey's goose; ostrich, emu; owl, bird of night; hawk, vulture, buzzard, turkey buzzard; eagle, bird of freedom, bird of Jove.

game, black game, black grouse, ruffed grouse, grouse, blackcock, duck, plover, rail, snipe; pheasant etc. 298.

poultry, fowl, cock, rooster, chanticleer, dunghill fowl, barndoor fowl, barnyard fowl, hen, Partlet, chicken, chick, chickabiddy; guinea fowl, guinea hen; peafowl, peacock, bird of Minerva, peahen.

[insects] ant, bee, honeybee, queen bee, drone; ant, white ant, termite; wasp, sawfly, locust, grasshopper, cicada, cicala, cricket; dragon fly, June fly, caddis fly; beetle; butterfly, moth; fly, May fly, thrips, aphid, bug; ant lion, hellgramite *or* hellgamite, earwig; springtail, podura, lepisma; buffalo bug, buffalo carpet beetle etc. (*injurious insects*) 913.

vermin, lice, cooties [*slang*], flies, fleas, cockroaches *or* roaches, water bugs *or* Croton bugs, bugs, bedbugs, Norfolk Howards [*slang*], mosquitoes; rats, mice, weasels.

snake, serpent, viper; asp, adder, copperhead, coral snake *or* harlequin snake, sidewinder, krait [*India*], viper, cobra, cobra de capello, king cobra, rattlesnake *or* rattler, copperhead, constrictor, boa constrictor, boa, python, Kaa [Kipling], ophidian.

[mythological] dipsas (*pl.* dipsades), basilisk, cockatrice, amphiobaena, Python, Hydra.

salamander; griffin *or* griffon *or* gryfon; chimaera; Cerberus.

adj. **animal**, zoic, zooid *or* zooidal, zoölogical.

equine; bovine, vaccine; canine; feline; fishy, piscatory, piscatorial; molluscous, vermicular; gallinaceous, rasorial, solidungulate, soliped; planktonic, nekteric, benthonic.

ophidian, ophiologic, ophiomorphous, reptilian, anguine, ophic [*rare*], snakelike, serpentiform [*rare*], viperine, colubrine.

367. Vegetable

n. **vegetable**, vegetable kingdom; flora.

organism, plant, tree, shrub, bush, creeper, vine; herb, seedling, plantlet, exotic, annual, perennial, biennial, triennial; legume, pulse, vetch, greens; asparagus etc. (*vegetables*) 298.

foliage, leafage, verdure, foliation, frondescence [*rare*]; prefoliation, vernation; branch, bough, ramage, stem, tigella *or* tigelle *or* tigellum *or* tigellus; leaf, spray, leaflet, frond, foliole, bract, bractlet, bracteole, cotyledon, pad, flag, petal, needle, sepal; spray etc. 51; petiole, petiolule, bine; shoot, tendril.

flower, blossom, bud, burgeon, blow, blowth [*rare*]; floweret, floret, floscule, flowering plant; inflorescence, flowerage.

tree, sapling, seedling, stand, pollard, dryad [*fig.*]; oak, elm, beech, birch, timber tree, pine, palm, spruce, fir, hemlock, yew, larch, cedar, savin *or* savine, juniper, chestnut, maple, alder, ash, myrtle, magnolia, walnut, olive, poplar, willow, linden, lime; apple etc. (*fruit trees*) 298; arboretum etc. 371.

banyan, teak, acacia, deodar, pipal *or* pipal tree; fig tree, eucalyptus, gum tree.

woodlands, virgin forest, forest primeval, forest, wood, timberland, timber, wood lot; hurst, frith, holt [*poetic or dial.*], weald, wold [*obs.*], park, chase [*Eng.*], greenwood, grove, copse, coppice, bocage [*F.*], tope [*India*], clump of trees, thicket, spinet [*obs.*], spinney [*Eng.*], bosk, chaparral, ceja [*Texas*], motte [*local, U. S.*]; jungle, bush.

undergrowth, underwood, brushwood, brake, "the mid-forest brake" [Keats], boscage, scrub, palmetto barrens, bosch [*Dutch*]; heath, heather, fern, bracken, furze, gorse, whin, broom, genista, sedge, rush, bulrush, bamboo; weed, moss, foggage [*Scot.*], lichen, Iceland moss, mushroom, toadstool, fungus; turf, turbary, mold *or* mould.

grass, fog, second growth, second crop; herbage.

alfalfa, lucern *or* lucerne, alfilaria, clover, bent *or* bent grass, timothy, redtop *or* English grass, switch grass *or* black bent, blue grass, Kentucky blue grass, ribbon grass, meadow grass, spear grass, wire grass, blue joint, crab grass, bunch grass, meadow fescue, meadow foxtail, grama *or* mesquite grass, gama *or* sesame grass, sheep's fescue; cereal, wheat, barley, buckwheat, maize *or* Indian corn, oats, rice, rye.

grassland, greensward, green, lawn, sward, common, maidan [*India*], mead, meadow, pasture, pasturage, prairie, pampas, steppe, llano, savanna, campo, plain, field, campus.

seaweed, alga (*pl.* algae), fucus, fucoid, conferva (*pl.* confervae), confervoid, wrack, dulse, kelp, rockweed, sea lettuce, gulfweed, sargasso, sargassum; plankton, benthos; Sargasso Sea.

v. **vegetate,** grow, flourish, bloom, flower, blossom; bud etc. (*expand*) 194; timber, retimber, coppice, copse; bush, plant, trim, cut.

adj. **vegetable,** vegetal, vegetive [*obs.*], vegetative, vegetarian; leguminous, herbaceous, herbal, botanic *or* botanical; arborary, arboreous, arborescent, arborical [*obs.*], arboreal, arboral; silvan *or* sylvan; treelike, dendriform, dendritic *or* dendritical, dendroid; grassy, verdant, verdurous; floral, floreal [*rare*], lignose *or* lignous [*rare*], ligneous, lignescent, wooden, woody; bosky, cespitose, copsy; mossy, turfy, turf-like; fungous, fungiform, fungoid; tigellate, radiculose, radicular, radiciform, radiciflorous, rhizanthous, radicated; endogenous, exogenous; deciduous, evergreen.

native, domestic, indigenous, native-grown, home-grown.

algal, fucoid, confervoid; planktonic, benthonic.

368. Zoology
[science of animals]

n. **zoology,** zoonomy, zoography, zootomy; morphology, anatomy, histology, embryology; comparative anatomy, animal physiology, comparative physiology; mammalogy.

anthropology, anthropotomy, ornithology, ornithotomy, ichthyology, ichthyotomy, herpetology, herpetotomy, ophiology, malaeology, helminthology, entomology, entomotomy; oryctology [*obs.*], paleontology *or* palaeontology; mastology, vermeology; taxidermy.

zoologist, zoographer, zoographist, zootomist, anatomist, anthropotomist, morphologist, promorphologist, anthropologist, ornithologist, ornithotomist, ichthyologist, ichthyotomist, herpetologist, herpetotomist, ophiliologist, malacologist, helminthologist, entomologist, entomotomist; oryctologist [*obs.*], paleontologist *or* palaeontologist; vermeologist, taxidermist.

[principal groups] **protozoa** (the simplest animals): Rhizopoda, rhizopod; Foraminifera, foraminifer; Radiolaria, radiolarian; Flagellata, Infusoria, infusorian; Gregarinae, gregarine.

coelentera *or* **coelenterata** (sponges, corals, jellyfishes): Porifera, poriferan; Cnidaria, cnida; Spongiae *or* Spongiaria *or* Spongiozoa, sponge, calcareous sponges, siliceous sponges; Anthozoa, anthozoan, coral polyps; Hydrozoa, hydrozoön, hydroid, medusa.

echinodermata (crinoids, starfishes, and sea urchins): Pelmatozoa, Asterozoa, Echinozoa; Cystidea *or* Cystoidea, cystid, cystidean; Crinoidea, stone lilies, crinoidean; Blastoidea, blastoid; Ophiuroidea *or* Ophiurioidea, brittle stars, ophiuroid *or* ophiurid; Asterioidea *or* Asteridea, starfishes, asteridian; Echinoidea, sea urchins, echinoid; Holothurioidea, sea cucumbers, holothurian, holothure.

vermes (worms): Platyhelminthes *or* Plathelminthes, flatworms, platyhelminth; Rotifera, rotifer; Nemathelminthes *or* Nematelminthes, roundworms; Gephyrea, marine annelids, gephyrean, gephyreoid; Annelida, annelid, annelidan, anneloid.

molluscoidea (mollusk-like animals): Bryozoa *or* Polyzoa, sea mosses, bryozoan; Brachiopoda, lamp shells, brachiopod.

mollusca (mollusks): Pelecypoda *or* Lamellibranchia, bivalves, lamellibranch; Scaphopoda, tooth-shells *or* tusk-shells, scaphopod; Amphineura, chitons; Gastropoda, univalves, snails, gastropod; Cephalopoda, nautilus, cuttlefish, squid, octopus, cephalopod *or* cephalopode.

arthropoda (articulates): Branchiata, Tracheata; Crustacea, crustacean; Trilobita, trilobite; Limuloidea *or* Xiphosura, horseshoe crab, limulus; Entomostraca, ostracoids, barnacles, entomostracan; Malacostraca, lobsters, crabs, malacostracan; Myriapoda, centipedes, galleyworms, millipeds, myriapod; Arachnida *or* Arachnoidea, spiders, scorpions, mites, ticks, arachnid, arachnidan; Insecta, insects.

vertebrata (vertebrate animals): Cyclostomata *or* Cyclostoma, lampreys; Pisces, fishes; Selachii, sharks, rays, selachian; Holocephali *or* Holocephala, chimaeras, spooks; Dipnoi, lungfishes; Teleostomi, ordinary fishes, ganoids, teleost, teleostean; Amphibia, amphibians, batrachians; Reptilia, reptiles; Aves, birds; Mammalia, mammals; Monotremata *or* Prototheria, monotremes; Marsupialia, marsupials, marsupialian *or* marsupian; Placentalia, placentals.

adj. **zoological,** zoologic; zoonomic; zoographical etc. *n.*

protozoan, rhizopodous; foraminiferous, foraminous, foraminated; radiolarian; flagellate; infusorial, infusory; gregarine.

coelenterate, poriferan, spongiose *or* spongious, spongoid, spongiform; anthozoan, anthozoic, corallaceous, coralliferous, coralliform, coralligenous, coralligerous, coralloid, coralloidal; polyparous, polypean; hydrozoal, hydroid; medusiform, medusoid.

echinodermatous, echinodermal; pelmatozoan; crinoidal, crinoid; ophiuran, ophiuroid; asteridian; echinoid, holothurian.

vermicious, vermicular, vermiculate, vermiculose *or* vermiculous, vermiform; gephyrean, gephyreoid; annelid *or* annelidan, annelidous.

molluscoid, molluscoidal; bryozoan; brachiopod.

molluscan, molluscoid, molluscous; lamellibranch, lamellibranchiate, bivalvular, bivalvous, bivalved; gastropodous, univalve *or* univalved, univalvular; cephalopodic, cephalopodous, nautiloid.

arthropodal, articulate; branchial, branchiate, branchiferous; tracheate; crustacean, crustaceous; arachnoid, arachnoidal, arachnidan, arachnidial; insectile, insected.

vertebrate, vertebrated, vertebral; cyclostome, cyclostomous; piscatorial *or* piscatory, pisciform, piscine; amphibian, amphibial [*rare*], amphibious; batrachian, batrachoid; reptilian; avicular; mammalian, mammiferous.

369. Botany
[science of plants]

n. **botany**; physiological–, structural–, systematic-botany; phytography, phytology, phytotomy, phytobiology, phytogenesis *or* phytogeny, phytonomy, phytopathology; phytochemistry, phytochimy [*obsoles.*], vegetable chemistry; pomology; vegetable physiology, herborization, dendrology, mycology, fungology, algology; flora, Flora, Pomona; botanic garden etc. (*garden*) 371; *hortus siccus* [*L.*]; herbarium, herbal [*obs.*].

phyton, phytomer *or* phytomeron.

[principal groups] **thallogens** *or* **thallophytes** (thallus plants): algae and algoid forms: Cyanophyceae, blue-green algae; Chlorophyceae, green algae; Phaeophyceae, brown algae; Rhodophyceae, red algae.

fungi and fungoid forms: Schizomycetes, fission fungi, bacteria; Myxomycetes, slime molds; Phycomycetes, algae fungi, water molds; As-comycetes, sac fungi, lichen fungi; Basidiomycetes, basidium fungi, rusts, mushrooms.

bryophytes (moss plants): Hepaticae, liverworts; Musci, mosses.

pteridophytes (fern plants): Lycopodiales: Sigillaria, Stigmaria, Lepidodendra, fossil trees, lepidodendrid, lepidodendroid; Lycopodiaceae; club mosses: Equisetales, calamites, Equisetacae, horsetails, equisetum; Filicales: Cycadofilices, cycad ferns; Filices, ferns, filicoid.

spermatophytes (seed plants): Gymnospermae (naked-seeded plants): gymnosperm. Cycadales, cycads; Gnetales, gnetums; Ginkgoales, ginkgo (*pl.* ginkgoes); Coniferae, conebearing evergreens, conifer.

Angiospermae (covered-seeded plants): angiosperm; Monocotyledones, monocotyledon, cereals, palms, lilies, orchids, banana, pineapple etc., endogens; Dicotyledones: oak, apple, sunflower, pea, dicotyledon.

botanist, phytologist, phytotomist, phytobiologist, dendrologist; mycologist, fungologist; phytopathologist, horticulturist etc. 371; herbalist, herbist, herbarist [*obs.*], herborist, herbarian; pomologist.

v. **botanize**, herborize.

adj. **botanic** *or* botanical, phytoid, dendroid *or* dendroidal, herbose *or* herbous, dendriform, dendritic *or* dendritical, dendrologous, herby, herbal; fungoid, fungous, mycologic *or* mycological, mycetoid, phytobiological, phytochemical, phytogenetic *or* phytogenous, pomological, horticultural.

thalloid, thalline; hepatic, musciform, muscoid, lycopodiaceous, lepidodendroid, equisetaceous, equisetiform, filicoid, filiciform, gymnospermous, cycadaceous, coniferous, angiospermous, angiospermatous, monocotyledonous, endogenous, dicotyledonous.

370. Cicuration
[economy or management of animals]

n. **cicuration** [*obs.*], taming etc. *v.;* zoohygiantics; domestication, domesticity; manège *or* manege, veterinary art; farriery; breeding; pisciculture; apiculture.

menagerie, vivarium, zoological garden, zoo [*colloq.*]; bear pit; aviary; apiary, alvearium, alveary, beehive, hive; aquarium, fishery, fish hatchery, fish pond; swan pond, duck pond; incubator.

[destruction of animals] phthisozoics etc. (*killing*) 361.

[keeper] herder, oxherd, neatherd (*obs.*), cowherd, grazier, drover, cowkeeper; shepherd, shepherdess; keeper, gamekeeper; trainer, breeder; bull whacker, cowboy, cow puncher, *vaquero* [*Sp. Amer.*]; horse trainer, bronchobuster [*slang*]; apiarian [*rare*], apiarist, apiculturist.

veterinarian, veterinary surgeon, vet [*colloq.*], horse doctor, horse leech [*rare*]; farrier [*obsoles. as veterinarian*], horseshoer.

inclosure, stable, barn, byre; cage etc. (*prison*) 752; hencoop, bird cage, coif, cauf; sheepfold etc. 232.

v. **tame,** domesticate, domesticize, acclimatize, breed, tend, corral, round up, break in, gentle, cicurate [*obs.*], break, bust [*slang*], break to harness, train; ride, drive etc. (*take horse*) 266; cage, bridle, etc. (*restrain*) 751; guide, spur, prick, lash, goad, whip; trot, gallop etc. (*move quickly*) 274; bolt; yoke, harness, harness up [*colloq.*], hitch, hitch up [*colloq.*], cinch.

groom, rub down, brush, currycomb; water, feed, fodder; bed, bed down, litter; drench, embrocate.

tend stock, milk, shear; water etc. (*groom*) *v.*; herd; raise, bring up, bring up by hand.

hatch, incubate, sit, brood, cover.

swarm, hive.

adj. **pastoral,** bucolic, rural; agricultural etc. 371.

tame, domestic, domesticated, broken, gentle, docile.

371. Agriculture
[economy or management of plants]

n. **agriculture,** cultivation, husbandry, farming; georgics, geoponics; agronomy, agronomics, tillage, tilth, gardening, spade husbandry, vintage; horticulture, arboriculture, silviculture, forestry; floriculture; landscape gardening; viticulture.

husbandman, horticulturist, gardener, florist; agricultor [*rare*], agriculturist, agronomist, yeoman, farmer, cultivator, tiller of the soil, plowman *or* ploughman, reaper, sower; logger, lumberman, lumberjack, forester, woodcutter, pioneer, backwoodsman; granger, habitant, *vigneron* [*F.*], viniculturist, vine-grower, vintager, viticulturist; Triptolemus.

garden; botanic-, winter-, ornamental-, flower-, kitchen-, market-, truck-, hop- garden; nursery; greenhouse, hothouse; conservatory, forcing house, cold-frame; bed, border,

seed plot; grassplot *or* grassplat, lawn; parterre; shrubbery, plantation, avenue, arboretum, pinery, pinetum, orchard; vineyard, vinery, orangery.

field, meadow, mead, green, common, maidan [*India*]; park etc. (*pleasure ground*) 840; farm etc. (*abode*) 189.

v. **cultivate,** till, till the soil, farm, garden, sow, plant; reap, mow, cut; manure, dress the ground, dig, spade, delve, dibble, hoe, plow *or* plough, harrow, rake, weed, lop and top; backset; force, seed, turf, transplant, thin out, bed, prune, graft.

adj. **agricultural,** agronomic, geoponic, georgic, agrestical [*obs.*], agrestian, praedial *or* predial; horticultural, viticultural.

arable, plowable *or* ploughable, tillable.

rural, rustic, country, agrarian, pastoral, bucolic, Arcadian.

372. Mankind

n. **mankind,** man; human -race, −species, −kind, −nature; humanity, mortality, flesh, generation.

[science of man] anthropology, anthropogeny, anthropography, anthroposophy; ethnology, ethnography; anthropotomy, androtomy; humanitarianism.

human being; person, personage; individual, creature, fellow creature, mortal, body, somebody, one; such a one, some one; soul, living soul; earthling; party, head, hand; member, members of the cast, *dramatis personae* [*L.*]; *quidam* [*L.*].

people, persons, folk, public, society, world; community, −at large; general public; nation, nationality; state, realm; commonweal, commonwealth; republic, body politic; million etc. (*commonalty*) 876; population etc. (*inhabitant*) 188.

cosmopolite; lords of creation; ourselves.

adj. **human,** mortal, personal, individual, national, civic, public, social; cosmopolitan; anthropoid.

372a. Anthropology

n. **anthropology;** physical anthropology, anthropometry, human evolution, human paleontology; cultural anthropology *or* social anthropology, ethnology, ethnography, archaeology, linguistics.

[eras of recent life] Cenozoic era; Tertiary period *or* Age of Mammals (Paleocene epoch, Eocene epoch, Oligocene epoch, Miocene epoch, Pliocene epoch), Quaternary period *or* Age of Man (Pleistocene epoch, Holocene epoch).

[fossil primates] Parapithecus; Propliopithecus; Dryopithecus, Dryopithecus fontani, Dryopithecus rhenanus, Dryopithecus darwini; Proconsul africanus; Pliopithecus; Australopithecus africanus, Paranthropus robustus, Plesianthropus transvaalensis.

[fossil races of man] Gigantanthropus *or* Gigantopithecus blacki, Meganthropus paleojavanicus; Pithecanthropus robustus, Pithecanthropus erectus, Pithecanthropus modjokertensis; Sinanthropus pekinensis *or* Peking man; Homo soloensis *or* Solo man; Homo Africanthropus; Homo heidelbergensis *or* Heidelberg man; Homo neanderthalensis *or* Neanderthal man, Rhodesian group, Mousterian group, Ehringsdorf group (Ehringsdorf forms, Tabun Mt. Carmel forms, Steinheim forms), Skhul Mt. Carmel forms, Galilee forms; Homo Sapiens, Galley Hill man, London man, Swanscombe man, Fontechevade man; Cro-Magnon man, Grimaldi man, Predmost man, Brünn man, Chancelade man, Ofnet man; Wadjak man, Keilor man, Talgai man; Oldoway man, Boskop man, Springbok man, Fish Hoek man; Eoanthropus dawsoni *or* Piltdown "man."

[prehistoric cultural eras] Eolithic *or* Dawn Stone Age; Paleolithic *or* Old Stone Age, Lower Paleolithic Age (pre-Chellean stage, Chellean stage, Acheulean stage), Middle Paleolithic Age *or* Mousterian stage, Upper Paleolithic Age (Aurignacian stage, Solutrean stage, Magdalenian stage); Epipaleolithic *or* Mesolithic Age *or* Azilian-Tardenoisian stage; Neolithic or New Stone Age; Metal Age; Bronze Age, Early Bronze Age, Middle Bronze Age, Late Bronze Age; Iron Age.

[races] Caucasoid (Ainu, Australoid, Dravidian, Vedda; Alpine, Armenoid, Mediterranean, Nordic; Dinaric, East Baltic, Polynesian); Mongoloid (Asiatic, Indonesian-Malay, American Indian); Negroid (Forest Negro, Negrito; Hottentot-Bushman, Nilote *or* Nilotic Negro, Oceanic Negro).

index; acrocranic index, acromiocristal index, bodily fullness index, brachial index, cephalic index (dolichocephalic index, mesocephalic index, brachycephalic index), cranial index, cranial breadth-height index, cranial length-height index, crural index, facial index (euryprosopic index, mesoprosopic index, leptoprosopic index), femorohumeral index, forearm-hand index, gnathic index, hand index, intermembral index, ischium-pubis index, length-breadth sacral index, lower leg-foot index, maxillo-alveolar index, morphological *or* Naccarati's index, nasal index (platyrrhine index, mesorrhine index, leptorrhine index), orbital index, palatal index, pelvic breadth-height index, pelvic inlet index, pilastric index, platycnemic index, platymeric index, sicklemia index, stem-leg length *or* Manouvrier's skelic index, thoracic index, tibiofemoral index, tibio-radial index, total facial index, transverse fronto-parietal index, trunk index, upper facial index, vertical lumbar index; Frankfort line *or* Frankfort plane; Mongoloid eye; epicanthic *or* Mongoloid fold, external epicanthic fold, internal epicanthic fold; Negroid lip; prognathism; peppercorn hair; steatopygy *or* steatopygia; genotype, phenotype; blood type *or* group; constitutional type, pyknic type, leptosome type, athletic type; ectomorphy, mesomorphy, endomorphy.

culture; culture pattern, ideal pattern, behavioral pattern; integration of culture; function, theme, configuration, drive, postulate, affirmation; Apollonian configuration, Dionysian configuration; culture trait *or* element; trait complex *or* culture complex; age area, culture area, culture center *or* nucleus, marginal area; cultural evolution, savagery, barbarism, civilization; invention, discovery; convergence, parallelism; cultural transmission *or* borrowing; diffusion, stimulus diffusion; assimilation; acculturation, antagonistic acculturation, marginal acculturation, planitational acculturation; evolutionism, diffusionism (heliolithic diffusionism, culture-historical diffusionism), Kulturkreis, functionalism.

folkway; custom; mos; moral; law, collective responsibility; tort *or* private wrong crime *or* public wrong; sanction, legal *or* organized sanction; oath, compurgation; ordeal.

kinship; kin group; consanguine kinship, affinal kinship; unilateral kinship *or* descent, bilateral kinship *or* descent, mixed kinship *or* descent; patrilineal *or* agnatic kinship, matrilineal *or* uterine kinship; sibling; cross-cousin, parallel cousin *or* ortho-cousin; family; nuclear family, stem family, elementary family, composite family, extended family, joint family (patrilocal joint family, matrilocal joint family); conjugal *or* biological *or* small family, consanguineal family; patriarchal family; paternal family, maternal family; sib; clan; complex *or* genealogical clan, equalitarian clan; patrilineal clan, matrilineal clan; gens; lineage, unilocal lineage, multilocal lineage; phratry; moiety, simple moiety, compound moiety; tribe; familiarity *or* privileged familiarity, kin familiarity (avunculate, amitate), joking relationship; kin avoidance.

373. Man

n. **man**, male, he; manhood etc. (*adolescence*) 131; gentleman, sir, master, dan [*archaic*], don, huzur [*India*], sahib [*India*]; yeoman, chap [*colloq.*], wight [*now chiefly jocose*], swain, fellow, blade, beau, gaffer [*dial. Eng.*], goodman [*archaic*]; husband etc. (*married man*) 903; boy etc. (*youth*) 129.

mister, Mr., *monsieur* (abbr. M., *pl.* MM. *or* Messrs.) [*F.*], *Herr* [*Ger.*], *signor* [*It., used before name*], *signore* [*It.*], *signorino* [*It., dim. of signore*], signior [*Eng. form*], seignior, *señor* [*Sp.*], *senhor* [*Pg.*]

[male animal] cock, drake, gander, dog, boar, stag, hart, buck, horse, entire horse, stallion; gib [*rare*], tom, tomcat; he-goat, billy-goat [*colloq.*]; ram, tup; bull, bullock; capon; ox, gelding; steer, stot [*prov. Eng.*].

adj. **male**, he, masculine; manly, virile; unwomanly, unfeminine.

374. Woman

n. **woman**, she, female, petticoat; skirt, jane [*both slang*].

feminality, femininity, femineity, feminacy, feminity, muliebrity; gynics.

womankind; womanhood etc. (*adolescence*) 131; the sex, the fair; fair sex, softer sex; weaker vessel.

dame [*archaic except as an elderly woman*], madam, mastress [Chaucer, *obs.*], lady, Donna, belle, matron, dowager, goody, grammer [*dial. Eng.*], memsahib [*Anglo-Ind.*], sahiba [*Hind.*], *bibi* [*Hind.*], frow, *vrouw* [*Du.*], good woman, good wife [*archaic*]; squaw; wife etc. (*marriage*) 903; matronage, matronhood.

bachelor girl, new woman, feminist, suffragist, suffragette; spinster, old maid.

nymph, houri, wench, grisette; girl etc. (*youth*) 129.

mistress, Mrs., *madame* (*pl. mesdames*) [*F.*], *Frau* [*Ger.*], *signora* [*It.*], *señora* [*Sp.*], *senhora* [*Pg.*]; Ms.; miss, *mademoiselle* (*pl. mesdemoiselles*) [*F.*], *Fräulein* [*Ger.*], *signorina* [*It.*], *señorita* [*Sp.*], *senhorita* [*Pg.*].

[effeminacy] betty, cot betty, cotquean, henhussy, molly, mollycoddle, muff, old woman, tame cat [*all contemptuous*].

[female animal] hen; bitch, slut, brach, brachet; sow, doe, roe, mare; she-goat, nanny-goat [*colloq.*], nanny [*colloq.*]; ewe, cow; lioness, tigress; vixen.

harem, gynaeceum *or* gynaecium, seraglio, zenana [*India*], purdah [*India*].

adj. **female**, she; feminine, womanly, ladylike, matronly, girlish, maidenly; womanish, effeminate, unmanly; gynecic *or* gynaecic.

375. Physical Sensibility

n. **sensibility**; sensitiveness etc. *adj.;* physical sensibility, feeling, impressibility, perceptivity, susceptibility, aesthetics *or* esthetics; moral sensibility etc. 822.

sensation, impression; consciousness etc. (*knowledge*) 490.

external senses.

v. **be sensible of** etc. *adj.;* feel, perceive; feel-keenly, −exquisitely.

render sensible etc. *adj.;* sharpen, refine, excite, stir, cultivate, tutor.

impress, cause sensation; excite−, produce- an impression.

adj. **sensible**, sensitive, sensuous; aesthetic *or* esthetic, perceptive, sentient; conscious etc. (*aware*) 490; alive, alive to impressions, answering quickly to, impressionable, responsive, easily affected, quick in response.

acute, sharp, keen, vivid, lively, impressive, thin-skinned.

adv. **to the quick**; on the raw [*slang*].

376. Physical Insensibility

n. **insensibility**, physical insensibility; obtuseness etc. *adj.;* palsy, paralysis, anaesthesia *or* anesthesia, narcosis, narcotization, hypnosis, stupor, coma; twilight sleep, *Dämmerschlaf* [*Ger.*]; sleep etc. (*inactivity*) 683; moral insensibility etc. 823; hemiplegia, motor paralysis.

anaesthetic *or* anesthetic, anaesthetic agent; local−, general- anaesthetic; opium, ether, chloroform, chloral; nitrous oxide, laughing gas; exhilarating gas, protoxide of nitrogen; cocaine, novocain; refrigeration.

v. **be insensible** etc. *adj.;* have a -thick skin, −rhinoceros hide.

render insensible etc. *adj.;* blunt, cloy, satiate, pall, obtund, benumb, numb, deaden, freeze, paralyze; anaesthetize *or* anesthetize, put under the influence of chloroform etc. *n.;* put to sleep, hypnotize, stupefy, stun.

adj. **insensible**, unfeeling, senseless, impercipient, callous, thick-skinned, pachydermatous; hard,

118

hardened; case-hardened; proof; obtuse, dull; anaesthetic *or* anesthetic; paralytic, palsied, numb, dead.

377. Physical Pleasure

n. **pleasure**; physical–, sensual–, sensuous - pleasure; bodily enjoyment, animal gratification, delight, sensual delight, hedonism, sensuality; luxuriousness etc. *adj.;* dissipation, round of pleasure; titillation, gusto, creature comforts, comfort, ease; pillow etc. (*support*) 215; luxury, lap of luxury; purple and fine linen; bed of -down. –roses; velvet, clover; cup of Circe etc. (*intemperance*) 954.

treat; diversion, entertainment, banquet, regalement, refreshment, regale; feast; delice [*obs.*]; dainty etc. 394; *bonne bouche* [*F.*].

source of pleasure etc. 829; happiness, felicity, bliss, beatitude etc. (*mental enjoyment*) 827.

v. **enjoy**, pleasure [*rare*]; feel–, experience–, receive- pleasure; relish; luxuriate–, revel–, riot–, bask–, swim–, wallow- in; feast on; gloat -over, –on; smack the lips; roll under the tongue.

live on the fat of the land, live in comfort etc. *adv.;* bask in the sunshine, *faire ses choux gras* [*F.*].

give pleasure etc. 829; charm, delight, enchant.

adj. **enjoying** etc. *v.;* luxurious, voluptuous, sensual, comfortable, cosy, snug, in comfort, at ease, in clover [*colloq.*].

agreeable etc. 829; grateful, refreshing, comforting, cordial, genial; gratifying, titillative, sensous; apolaustic, hedonic, hedonistic, palatable etc. 394; sweet etc. (*sugar*) 396; fragrant etc. 400; melodious etc. 413; lovely etc. (*beautiful*) 845.

adv. **in comfort** etc. *n.;* on a bed of roses etc. *n.;* at one's ease; on flowery beds of ease.

378. Physical Pain

n. **pain**; suffering, sufferance [*rare*]; bodily–, physical- -pain, –suffering; mental suffering etc. 828; dolor *or* dolour, ache; aching etc. *v.;* smart; shoot, shooting; twinge, twitch, gripe, hurt, cut; sore, soreness; discomfort; headache, *malaise* [*F.*], megrim, migraine, cephalalgy, cephalalgia; otalgia, earache, ischiagra, lumbago, arthritis, neuritis, gout, podagra, rheumatism, sciatica, ischialgia, neuralgia, tic douloureux, toothache, odontalgia; stiffneck, torticollis.

spasm, cramp; nightmare, ephialtes; kink, crick, stitch; convulsion, throe; throb etc. (*agitation*) 315; pang; colic; tormina, gripes.

sharp–, piercing–, throbbing–, grinding–, stabbing–, shooting–, gnawing–, burning-pain.

torment, torture, agony, anguish, lancination, rack, cruciation, crucifixion, martyrdom; vivisection.

martyr, sufferer; toad under a harrow.

v. **suffer**; feel–, experience–, suffer–, undergo-pain etc. *n.;* ache, smart, bleed; tingle, shoot; twinge, twitch, lancinate; writhe, wince, make a wry face; sit on -thorns, –pins and needles.

pain, give pain, inflict pain; lacerate; hurt, chafe, sting, bite, gnaw, stab, grind, gripe, pinch, tweak; grate, gall, fret, prick, pierce, wring, convulse; torment, torture; rack, agonize; crucify; cruciate [*obs.*], excruciate, break on the wheel, put to the rack; flog etc. (*punish*) 972; grate on the ear etc. (*harsh sound*) 410.

adj. **in pain** etc. *n.,* in a state of pain; under the harrow; pained etc. *v.;* gouty, podagric, torminous, torminal.

painful; aching etc. *v.;* poignant, pungent, torturous, baleful [*rare*], biting; with exposed nerves, sore, raw.

379. Touch
[sensation of pressure]

n. **touch**; tact, taction, tactility; contact, tangency, tangence [*rare*], impact, attain [*archaic*]; feeling, kiss, osculation, graze, glance, brush; lick, licking, lambency, palpation, palpability; contrectation [*rare*]; manipulation, palmation [*obs.*], contaction [*obs.*]; stereognosis; rubbing, kneading, massage.

[organ of touch] hand, palm, finger, forefinger, thumb, paw, feeler, antenna; tongue, palpus.

v. **touch**, feel, handle, finger, thumb, paw, fumble, grope, grabble; twiddle, tweedle [*obs. or dial.*]; pass–, run- the fingers over; stroke, palpate, palm, massage, rub, knead, manipulate, wield; throw out a feeler.

adj. **tactual**, tactile; tangible, palpable, tangent, contactual [*rare*], lambent; touching etc. *v.;* stereognostic.

380. Sensations of Touch

n. **itching** etc. *v.;* formication; aura [*med.*].
tickling, titillation.
itch, scabies, psora, pruritus, prurigo [*all med.*]; mange.

v. **itch**, tingle, creep, thrill, sting; prick, prickle.
tickle, titillate.

adj. **itching**, tingling etc. *v.*
ticklish, titillative.

itchy, psoric, scabious, mangy; creepy, crawly; prurient.

381. Numbness

[insensibility to touch]

n. **numbness** etc. (*physical insensibility*) 376; anaesthesia *or* anesthesia, narcosis, narcotization; pins and needles [*colloq.*].

v. **benumb** etc. 376; stupefy, narcotize, drug, deaden, paralyze.

adj. **numb**; benumbed etc. *v.;* insensible, unfeeling, anaesthetic *or* anesthetic, deadened; intangible, impalpable; dazed, dazy [*rare*], comatose, torporific, narcotic, carotic.

382. Heat

n. **heat**, caloric; temperature, warmth, fervor, calidity [*obs.*], torridity; incalescence *or* incalescency [*rare*], incandescence; recalescence, decalescence; adiathermancy, athermancy, diathermacy, diathermance *or* diathermancy *or* diathermaneity; phlogiston [*old chem.*], phlogisis; thermogenesis; liquation.

summer, dog days, canicule, canicular days; baking etc. 384–, white–, tropical–, Afric–, Indian–, Bengal–, summer–, blood- heat; sirocco, simoom *or* simoon, hot wave, sun at noon, "the bloody Sun, at noon" [Coleridge], vertical rays, broiling sun; insolation; warming etc. 384.

flush, glow, blush, bloom, redness; rubicundity; fever, hectic; febricity, pyrexia.

fire, spark, scintillation, flash, flame, blaze; bonfire; firework, pyrotechny; wildfire; sheet of fire, lambent flame; devouring element; pyrotechnics.

sun etc. (*luminary*) 423.

hot springs, geysers; thermae, hot baths; sauna, hot tub; Turkish–, electric–, Russian-bath; steam.

fire worship, pyrolatry, sun worship, heliolatry, Sabaeanism *or* Sabeanism *or* Sabeism, Parsiism *or* Parseeism, Zoroastrianism; pyrolator, heliolator, Sabaean *or* Sabean, Parsi *or* Parsee, Zoroastrian.

[science of heat] pyrology; thermology, thermotics; thermometer etc. 389.

v. **be hot** etc. *adj.;* glow, flush, sweat, swelter, bask, smoke, reek, stew, simmer, seethe, boil, burn, singe, scorch, scald, grill, broil, blaze, flame; smolder *or* smoulder; parch, fume, pant.

heat etc. (*make hot*) 384; insolate, incandesce, recalesce.

thaw, fuse, melt, liquate, liquefy; give.

adj. **warm**, mild, genial, tepid, lukewarm, unfrozen; calid; warm as -toast, –wool.

hot, heated, fervid, fervent; roasting, sweltry; reeking etc. *v.;* ardent, aglow; baking etc. 384; sunny, sunshiny, aestival *or* estival, canicular, torrid, tropical; thermal, thermic; calorific.

red–, white–, smoking–, burning etc. *v.* –, piping- hot; like -a furnace, –an oven; hot as -fire, –pepper; hot enough to roast an ox.

close, sultry, stifling, stuffy, suffocating, oppressive.

fiery; incandescent, incalescent [*rare*]; candent, ebullient, glowing, smoking; live; on fire; blazing etc. *v.;* in flames, in a blaze; alight, afire, ablaze; unquenched; unextinguished; smoldering *or* smouldering; in a -heat, –glow, –perspiration, –sweat; sudorific; sweltering, sweltered; blood-hot, blood-warm; recalescent, decalescent, thermogenic, thermogenous, thermogenetic, thermotic *or* thermotical; pyrotechnic *or* pyrotechnical; phlogotic *or* phlogistic; pyrological.

[transmitting radiant heat] diathermic, diathermal, diathermanous.

[not transmitting radiant heat] athermanous, adiathermal, adiathermanous, adiathermic.

volcanic, plutonic, igneous.

isothermal, isothermic, isothermical.

feverish, febrile, febricose [*rare*], febrific, febrifacient, pyretic, pyrexic [*rare*], inflamed, burning; in a fever.

383. Cold

n. **cold**, coldness etc. *adj.;* frigidity, gelidity, algidity, glaciation, gelidness [*rare*], frore [*poetic*], inclemency, fresco [*obs.*]; "a hard, dull bitterness of cold" [Whittier].

winter; depth of–, hard- winter; Siberia, Nova Zembla; Arctic, North Pole; Antarctic, South Pole.

ice; sleet; hail, hailstone; frost, rime, hoarfrost; rime–, white–, hard–, black–, sharp-frost; *barf* [*Hind.*], glaze, lolly [*N. Amer.*]; icicle, thick-ribbed ice; iceberg, floe, berg, ice field, ice float *or* ice floe, ice pack, glacier; *nevé* [*F.*], *sérac* [*F.*]; *pruina* [*L. & It.*]; icequake.

snow, snowflake, snowdrift, fall of snow, snowstorm, heavy fall; snowball, snowslide, snowslip, snow avalanche.

[sensation of cold] chilliness etc. *adj.;* chill; shivering etc. *v.;* goose flesh, goose skin, rigor, horripilation, aching, ache, chilblains, frostbite, chattering of teeth.

v. **be cold** etc. *adj.;* shiver, starve [*rare in U. S.*], quake, shake, tremble, shudder, didder, quiver; perish with cold; chill etc. (*render cold*) 385; horripilate, glaciate [*obs.*].

adj. **cold**, cool; chill, chilly; gelid, frigid, frore [*poet.*], algid; fresh, keen, bleak, raw, inclement, bitter, biting, cutting, nipping, piercing, pinching; clay-cold; starved etc. (*made cold*) 385; shivering etc. *v.;* aguish, *transi de froid* [*F.*], frostbitten, frost-bound, frost-nipped.

cold as - a stone, −marble, −lead, −iron, -a frog, −charity, −Christmas; cool as -a cucumber, −custard.

icy, glacial, ice-built, frosty, freezing, wintry, brumal, hibernal, boreal, arctic, Siberian, hiemal *or* hyemal; hyperborean, hyperboreal [*rare*]; snow-bound, ice-bound; frozen out.

unwarmed, unheated; unthawed.

lukewarm, tepid; warm etc. *adj.* 382.

isocheimal, isocheimenal, isocheimic.

adv. **coldly**, bitterly etc. *adj.; à pierre fendre* [*F.*]; with chattering teeth.

384. Calefaction

n. **calefaction**, tepefaction, torrefaction; increase of temperature; heating etc. *v.;* melting, fusion; liquefaction etc. 335; burning etc. *v.;* combustion; incension [*obs.*], accension [*archaic*]; concremation, cremation; scorification; cautery, cauterization; ustulation [*rare*], calcination; incineration; carbonization; cupellation.

ignition, kindling, inflammation, adustion [*rare*], flagration [*obs.*], deflagration, conflagration; empyrosis, incendiarism; arson; *auto-da-fé* [*Pg.*], *auto-de-fe* [*Sp.*], the stake, burning at the stake; suttee.

incendiary, arsonist, arsonite, *pétroleur (fem. pétroleuse)* [*F.*], pyromaniac, fire bug, macher [*slang*].

boiling etc. *v.;* coction, ebullition, ebullience *or* ebulliency, aestuation *or* estuation, elixation [*obs.*], decoction; ebullioscope, ebulliometer; hot spring, geyser.

crematory, crematorium, burning ghat [*India*], incinerator, calcinatory; cupel; furnace etc. 386.

wrap, blanket, flannel, wool, fur; muff, mittens, wristers; muffler, fascinator, comforter, comfortable; ear-muffs, ear-flaps; shawl; wadding etc. (*lining*) 224; clothing etc. 225.

cauterant, scorifier; match etc. (*fuel*) 388; caustic, lunar caustic, apozem, moxa; aqua fortis, aqua regia; catheretic, nitric acid, nitrochlorhydric acid, nitromuriatic acid, radium.

sunstroke, *coup de soleil* [*F.*]; insolation [*rare*], siriasis, [*med.*]; sunburn, burn, tan, suntan, ambustion [*rare*].

pottery, ceramics, crockery, porcelain, china; earthenware, stoneware; pot, mug, terra cotta, brick.

[products of combustion] cinder, ash, scoriae; embers, slag, cinders, clinker, coke, carbon, charcoal.

inflammability, combustibility, accendibility.

[transmission of heat] diathermance *or* diathermancy etc. 382; transcalency.

v. **heat**, warm, chafe, foment; make hot etc. 382; sun oneself, bask in the sun.

fire, set fire to, set on fire; kindle, enkindle, light, ignite, strike a light; apply the -match, −torch-to; rekindle, relume; fan-, add fuel to- the flame; poke-, stir-, blow- the fire; make a bonfire of; build a campfire.

melt, thaw, fuse; liquefy etc. 335.

burn, inflame, roast, toast, fry, grill, incinerate, singe, parch, bake, torch [*slang*], torrefy, scorch; brand, cauterize, sear, burn in; corrode, char, carbonize, calcine, incinerate, calefy, calcinate [*rare*], tepefy, cupel, cupellate [*rare*], deflagrate [*chem.*]; smelt, scorify; reduce to ashes; burn to a cinder; commit-, consign- to the flames.

take-, catch- fire; blaze etc. (*flame*) 382.

boil, digest, stew, cook, seethe, ebullate [*rare*], scald, parboil, simmer; do to rags [*colloq.*].

adj. **heated** etc. *v.;* molten, sodden; *réchauffé* [*F.*]; heating etc. *v.;* adjust; ambustial [*rare*], calefactive, deflagrable [*chem.*], ustulate; calcinatory, cauterant; aestuous [*rare*]; apozemial, scoriaceous; transcalent; burnt etc. *v.;* volcanic.

inflammable, burnable, inflammatory, accendible, combustible.

diathermic, diathermal, diathermanous.

radioactive; salamandrine.

385. Refrigeration

n. **refrigeration**, infrigidation, reduction of temperature; cooling etc. *v.;* congelation, conglaciation [*obs.*], glaciation, regelation; ice etc. 383; solidification etc. (*density*), 321; ice box, cooler, ice chest; refrigerator, freezer, etc. 387.

fire-extinguisher, *extincteur* [*F.*]; fire annihilator; amianthus, amianth, earth flax, mountain flax; asbestos, flexible asbestos; fireman, fire brigade, fire department, fire engine.

incombustibility, incombustibleness etc. *adj.*

v. **cool**, fan, refrigerate, infrigidate, refresh, ice; congeal, freeze, glaciate; benumb, starve [*rare in U. S.*], pinch, chill, petrify, chill to the marrow, regelate, nip, cut, pierce, bite, make one's teeth chatter.

damp, slack; quench; put out, stamp out; extinguish.

go out, burn out, die.

adj. **cooled** etc. *v.;* frozen out; cooling etc. *v.;* frigorific, infrigidative [*rare*], refrigerative [*rare*].

incombustible, asbestic, nonflammable, unflammable, uninflammable; fireproof; amianthine, amianthoid *or* amianthoidal.

386. Furnace

n. **furnace**, stove; air-tight-, Franklin-, Dutch-, gas-, oil-, electric- stove; cookstove, cooker, oven, brick oven, tin oven, Dutch oven, range, kitchener [*Eng.*]; fireless- heater, -cooker; forge, fiery furnace; kiln, brickkiln, limekiln; tuyère, brasier, salamander, heater, warming pan, foot-stove, foot-warmer; radiator, register, coil; boiler, caldron *or* cauldron, seething caldron, pot; urn, kettle, frying pan, stew pan, spider, broiler, skillet, tripod, chafing dish; retort, crucible, alembic, still; waffle irons; flatiron, sadiron; curling tongs; toasting fork, toaster.

galley, caboose *or* camboose; hothouse, conservatory, bakehouse, washhouse, laundry; athanor, hypocaust, reverberatory; volcano.

fireplace, hearth, grate, firebox, andiron, firedog, fire-irons; poker, tongs, shovel, hob, trivet; damper, crane, pothooks, chains, turnspit, spit, gridiron.

hot bath; thermae, calidarium, tepidarium, vaporarium, sudatorium [*all L.*]; sudatory; Turkish-, Russian -vapor-, electric-, sitz-, hip-, shower-, warm - bath; tub, hot tub, sauna; lavatory.

387. Refrigeratory

n. **refrigeratory**, refrigerator; frigidarium; cold storage; ice-, freezing-, refrigerating-machine; refrigerating plant; icehouse, ice pail, ice bag, ice box, ice chest, ice pack, cold pack; cooler, wine cooler.

refrigerant, freezing mixture, ice, ammonia.

388. Fuel

n. **fuel**, firing, combustible, coal, wallsend [*Eng.*], anthracite, blind coal, glance coal; bituminous-, egg-, stove-, nut-, pea- coal; culm, coke, carbon, briquette, slack, cannel coal *or* cannel, lignite, charcoal; turf, peat; oil, gas, natural gas, electricity; ember, cinder etc. (*products*

of combustion) 384; ingle; port-fire; fire-barrel, fireball, firebrand.

log, backlog, yule log *or* yule clog, firewood, fagot *or* faggot, kindling wood, kindlings, brushwood, bavin [*dial. Eng.*].

tinder, touchwood; punk, German tinder, amadou; smudge [*U. S. & Can.*], pyrotechnic sponge.

fumigator, incense, joss-stick; sulphur, brimstone, disinfectant.

[*illuminants*] candle etc. (*luminary*) 423; oil etc. (*grease*) 356.

brand, torch, fuse *or* fuze, wick; spill, match, safety match, lights [*chiefly Eng.*], light, lucifer, congreve, vesuvian, vesta, fusee *or* fuzee, locofoco [*obs.*], linstock [*obs. or hist.*].

v. coal, stoke; feed, fire etc. 384.

adj. carbonaceous; combustible, inflammable; slow-burning, free-burning.

389. Thermometer

n. **thermometer**, thermocouple, thermometrograph, thermopile, thermostat, thermoscope; differential thermometer, telethermometer, pyrometer, calorimeter, radiomicrometer.

390. Taste

n. **taste**, flavor, gust [*archaic*], gusto, savor; *goût* [*F.*], relish; sapor [*obs.*], sapidity; twang [*dial. Eng.*], smack, smatch [*dial. Eng.*]; aftertaste, tang.

tasting; degustation, gustation.

palate; tongue; tooth; stomach.

v. **taste**, savor, smatch [*dial. Eng.*], smack, flavor; tickle the palate etc. (*savory*) 394; smack the lips.

adj. **sapid**, saporific, gustable, gustatory, gustative, tastable, savory, gustful, tasty; strong; flavored, spiced, tanged [*obs.*]; palatable etc. 394.

391. Insipidity

n. **insipidity**; tastelessness etc. *adj.;* jejuneness.

v. **be tasteless** etc. *adj.*

adj. **insipid**; void of taste etc. 390; tasteless, gustless [*obs.*], unsavory, unflavored, jejune, savorless; ingustible [*obs.*], mawkish, milk and water, weak, stale, flat, vapid, *fade* [*F.*], wishy-washy [*colloq.*], mild; untasted.

392. Pungency

n. **pungency**, piquancy, poignancy, *haut-goût* [*F.*], acrity [*obs.*], strong taste, twang [*dial. Eng.*], race, tang, nip, kick [*slang*].

sharpness etc. *adj.;* acrimony, acridity; roughness etc. (*sour*) 392; unsavoriness etc. 395.

[pungent articles] niter, saltpeter; mustard, cayenne, caviare; seasoning etc. (*condiment*) 393; brine; carbonate of ammonia; sal-ammoniac, sal-volatile; smelling salts; hartshorn.

dram, cordial, nip, toothful [*colloq.*], tickler [*colloq.*], bracer [*colloq.*], pick-me-up [*colloq.*], potion, liqueur, *pousse-café* [*F.*].

tobacco, Lady Nicotine, Nicotiana, nicotian [*rare*], nicotine; snuff, quid; cigar *or* segar, cigarette, fag [*slang*], cheroot, Trichinopoli cheroot, Trichi [*colloq.*], Havana *or* Habana [*Sp.*], Cuban tobacco; weed [*colloq.*]; fragrant–, Indianweed; Cavendish, fid [*dial.*], rappee, stogy, old soldier [*slang*].

v. **be pungent** etc. *adj.;* bite the tongue.

render pungent etc. *adj.;* season, spice, bespice, salt, pepper, pickle, brine, devil, curry.

use tobacco, smoke, chew, inhale, take snuff.

adj. **pungent**, strong; high-flavored, full-flavored; high-tasted, high-seasoned; gamy, high; sharp, stinging, rough, piquant, racy; biting, mordant; spicy; seasoned etc. *v.;* hot, –as pepper; peppery, vellicative, vellicating, escharotic, meracious [*obs.*]; acrid, acrimonious, bitter; rough etc. (*sour*) 397; unsavory etc. 395.

salt, saline, brackish, briny; salt as -brine, –a herring, –Lot's wife.

393. Condiment

n. **condiment**, flavoring, salt, ketchup *or* catsup, mustard, pepper, cayenne, cinnamon, nutmeg, curry, seasoning, sauce, spice, relish, *sauce piquante* [*F.*], *sauce tartare* [*F.*], caviare, pot herbs, onion, sauce-alone, hedge garlic, garlic, pickle; *achar* [*Hind.*], allspice, appetizer; bell–, Jamaica–, red- pepper; horseradish, capsicum, chutney, tabasco; cubeb, pimento.

v. **season** etc. (*render pungent*) 392.

394. Savoriness

n. **savoriness** etc. *adj.;* nectareousness; relish, zest.

appetizer, *apéritif* [*F.*], *hors d'oeuvre* [*F.*]

delicacy, titbit, dainty, ambrosia, nectar, delice [*obs.*], *bonne-bouche* [*F.*]; game, turtle, venison; delicatessen.

v. **be savory** etc. *adj.;* tickle the -palate, –appetite; tempt the appetite, taste good, taste of something; flatter the palate.

render palatable etc. *adj.*

relish, like, smack the lips.

adj. **savory**, to one's taste, tasty, good, palatable, good-tasting, pleasing, nice, dainty, delectable; toothful [*obs.*], toothsome; gustful, appetizing, lickerish *or* liquorish [*rare*], delicate, delicious,

exquisite, rich, luscious, ambrosial, ambrosian, nectareous, distinctive.

adv. *per amusare la bocca* [*It.*].

395. Unsavoriness

n. **unsavoriness** etc. *adj.;* amaritude [*rare*], acrimony, acritude [*obs.*], acridity, acridness, roughness etc. (*sour*) 397; acerbity, austerity.

gall and wormwood, rue, quassia, aloes, asafetida *or* asafoetida; hemlock; sickener; Marah.

v. **be unpalatable** etc. *adj.;* sicken, disgust, nauseate, pall, turn the stomach.

adj. **unsavory**, unpalatable, unsweet; ill-flavored; bitter, bitter as gall; amarulent [*obs.*], acrid, acrimonious; rough.

offensive, repulsive, nasty; sickening etc. *v.;* nauseous; loathsome, fulsome; unpleasant etc. 830.

396. Sweetness

n. **sweetness**, dulcitude, saccharinity.

sugar, saccharin *or* saccharine, saccharose, crystallose; cane–, beet–, loaf–, lump–, granulated- sugar.

preserve, conserve, confiture [*obs.*], jam, julep; sugar candy, sugarplum; marmalade.

sweets, confectionery, caramel, lolly [*colloq.*], lollipop, bonbon, licorice, jujube, comfit, sweetmeat, confection, confectionery; honey, manna; apple butter, glucose, sucrose, dulcin [*chem.*], dulcite [*chem.*]; sirup *or* syrup, treacle, molasses, maple sirup *or* syrup, maple sugar; *mithai* [*India*], sorghum, taffy, butterscotch.

[sweet beverages] nectar; hydromel, mead, metheglin, liqueur, sweet wine, *eau sucrée* [*F.*].

pastry, cake, pie, tart, puff, pudding.

dulcification, dulcoration [*obs.*], saccharification, saccharization, edulcoration.

v. **be sweet** etc. *adj.*

render sweet etc. *adj.;* sweeten, sugar, saccharize, saccharify, sugar off [*local, U. S. & Can.*]; edulcorate; dulcorate [*obs.*], dulcify [*obs.*]; candy; mull.

adj. **sweet**, sugary, saccharine, sacchariferous, saccharoid *or* saccharoidal; dulcet, candied, honied, luscious, cloying, honey-sweet, nectarious [*rare*], nectareous, nectareal, nectarous, nectarean, nectarian; melliferous; sweetened etc. *v.*

sweet as -sugar, –honey.

397. Sourness

n. **sourness** etc., *adj.;* acid, acetosity, acerbity, acidity. subacidity; acescence *or* acescency; acetous fermentation.

[sour articles] vinegar, acetum, tartar, verjuice, crab, alum; acetic acid; lime, lemon, crab apple, chokeberry, chokecherry; unripe–, green fruit.

v. **be sour**, turn sour etc. *adj.;* set the teeth on edge.
render sour etc. *adj.;* acidify, acidulate, acetify, acetize [*are*], tartarize, ferment.

adj. **sour**; acid, acidulous, acidulated; tart, crab, crabbed; acetous, acetose, acerb, acetic; sour as vinegar, sourish; acescent, subacid; hard, rough, unripe, green; astringent, styptic.

398. Odor

n. **odor** or odour, smell, odorament [*obs.*], scent, effluvium; emanation, exhalation; fume, essence, trail, nidor [*obs.*], redolence.
scent; sense of smell; act of smelling etc. *v.;* olfaction, olfactories.

v. **have an odor** etc. *n.;* smell, –of, –strong of; exhale, effluviate [*rare*]; give out a smell etc. *n.;* scent.
smell, scent; snuff, –up; sniff, nose, inhale.

adj. **odorous**, odorant [*rare*], odoriferous; smelling, strong-scented, effluvious, redolent, nidorous, pungent.
[relating to the sense of smell] olfactory, olfactive, olfactible *or* olfactable; quick-scented.

399. Inodorousness

n. **inodorousness**; absence–, want- of smell.
deodorization; deodorizer, deodorant.

v. **be inodorous** etc. *adj.;* not smell.
deodorize.

adj. **inodorous**, inodorate [*obs.*], scentless; without–, wanting- smell etc. 398.
deodorized, deodorizing.

400. Fragrance

n. **fragrance**, aroma, redolence, incensation, thurification [*rare*], perfume, bouquet; sweet smell, sweet odor *or* odour, aromatic perfume, scent.
[comparisons] agalloch *or* agallochum, agalwood, eaglewood, aloes wood, sandalwood, cedar, champak, calambac *or* calambour, lign-aloes, linaloa; bayberry, bay leaf, balsam, fir balsam; wild clove, wild cinnamon, Jamaica bayberry, oil of myrcia, bay rum; horehound, Marrubium, mint, musk root, muskrat, napha water, olibanum.
perfumery; incense, frankincense; musk, pastil *or* pastille; myrrh, perfumes of Arabia; attar *or* ottar *or* otto; bergamot, balm, civet, potpourri, pulvil [*obs.*]; tuberose, hyacinth, heliotrope, rose, jasmine, lily, lily of the valley, violet, arbutus, carnation, sweet pea, sweet

grass, new-mown hay, lilac; pomade, pomatum, pomander, toilet water; *eau de cologne* [*F.*], cologne, cologne water.
bouquet, nosegay, posy [*archaic or colloq.*], boughpot *or* bowpot; *boutonnière* [*F.*], buttonhole [*colloq.*].
spray; wreath, garland, chaplet.
[scent containers] smelling bottle, scent bottle, vinaigrette; scent bag, sachet; thurible, censer, incense burner, incensorium, incensory; atomizer, spray.
perfumer, *parfumeur* [*F.*]; thurifer.

v. **be fragrant** etc. *adj.;* have a perfume etc. *n.;* smell sweet, scent, perfume; embalm.
incense, cense, thurificate, thurify [*rare*]; aromatize.

adj. **fragrant**, aromatic, redolent, spicy, balmy, scented; sweet-smelling, sweet-scented; perfumed, perfumatory [*rare*], perfumy, incense-breathing, thuriferous; fragrant–, sweet- as a rose, muscadine, ambrosial.

401. Fetor

n. **fetor** *or* foetor; bad etc. *adj.* -smell, –odor *or* odour; stench, stink; foul odor, malodor *or* malodour, fetidness, mephitis, empyreuma; fustiness, mustiness etc. *adj.;* rancidity, reastiness *or* reasiness [*dial. Eng.*]; foulness etc. (*uncleanness*) 653.
[comparisons] stoat, polecat, skunk, zoril; foumart *or* foulmart, fitchew, fitchet, peccary; asafetida *or* assafoetida; fungus, garlic, onion, leek, skunk cabbage; stinkpot, stinkball, stinker, stinkhorn, stinkbush, stinkstone, stinkweed, stinkwood.

v. **have a bad smell** etc. *n.;* smell, empyreumatize; stink, –in the nostrils, –like a polecat; smell strong etc. *adj.*, smell to heaven, stench [*obs.*], smell offensively.

adj. **fetid**; strong-smelling; high, bad, strong, fulsome, offensive, graveolent, noisome, rank, rancid, reasty *or* reasy [*dial. Eng.*], moldy *or* mouldy, tainted, musty, frowsty [*dial. Eng.*], fusty, frowsy *or* frouzy; olid, olidous [*obs.*]; nidorous [*rare*], smelling, stinking; putrid etc. 653; suffocating, mephitic; empyreumatic *or* empyreumatical.

402. Sound

n. **sound**, noise; sonority, sonorosity [*obs.*], sonification, strain; accent, twang, intonation, tune, cadence; sonorescence, sonorousness etc. *adj.;* audibility; resonance etc. 408; voice etc. 580; phonation; aspirate; phonogram, ideophone; rough breathing.

[science of sound] acoustics, acoumetry, diacoustics, catacoustics, diaphonics, cataphonics, polycoustics, phonics, phonetics, phonology, phonography; telephony, radiophony, photophony; polyphony, homophony; phonetism; acoustician.

v. **produce sound**; sound, make a noise; give out sound, emit sound; phonate, consonate [*rare*], resound etc. 408.

phoneticize, phonetize [*rare*].

adj. **sounding**; soniferous; sonorous, sonorescent; sonorific [*rare*]; sonorant, sonoric; resonant, audible, distinct; auditory, acoustic, acoustical, diacoustic, polycoustic; stertorous, ear-splitting.

phonic, phonetic; homophonic *or* homophonous (*opp. to* polyphonic), monodic, monophonic; sonant; ideophonous; phonocamptic [*rare*].

403. Silence

n. **silence**; stillness etc. (*quiet*) 265; peace, hush, lull; rest [*music*]; muteness etc. 581; solemn–, awful–, dead–, deathlike- silence; silence of the -tomb, –grave.

v. **be silent** etc. *adj.;* hold one's tongue etc. (*not speak*) 585; whist [*dial. Eng.*].

render silent etc. *adj.;* silence, still, hush; stifle, muffle, gag, stop; muzzle, put to silence etc. (*render mute*) 581.

adj. **silent**; still, stilly; noiseless, quiet, calm, hush [*archaic*], echoless, speechless, soundless; hushed etc. *v.;* aphonic, surd, mute etc. 581.

solemn, soft, awful, deathlike; silent as the -tomb, –grave; inaudible etc. (*faint*) 405.

adv. **silently** etc. *adj.; sub silentio* [*L.*]; in–, in dead–, in perfect- silence.

int. **hush**! silence! soft! whist! mum! sh! chut! tut! *pax!* [*L.*], *tais-toi!* [*F.*], hold your tongue! shut up! [*colloq.*], be quiet! be silent! be still! *chup!* [*Hind.*], *chup rao!* [*Hind.*], *tace!* [*L.*].

404. Loudness

n. **loudness**, power; vociferation, uproariousness.

din, loud noise, clang, clangor, clatter, noise, bombilation, roar, uproar, racket, clutter, hullabaloo, pandemonium, hell let loose; outcry etc. 411; hubbub; explosion, detonation; bobbery, fracas, charivari.

blare, trumpet blast, flourish of trumpets, fanfare, tintamarre [*archaic*]; blast; peal, swell, larum [*archaic*], alarum, boom; resonance etc. 408.

lungs; stentor; megaphone; calliope, steam siren, steam whistle; watchman's rattle.

[comparisons] artillery, cannon, guns, bombs, shells, barrage; thunder.

v. **be loud** etc. *adj.;* peal, swell, clang, boom, thunder, fulminate, bombilate [*rare*], roar; resound etc. 408; speak up, shout etc. (*vociferate*) 411; bellow etc. (*cry as an animal*) 412.

clatter, clutter, racket, uproar [*rare*].

rend the air, rend the skies; fill the air; din–, ring–, thunder- in the ear; pierce–, split–, rend-the-ears, –head; deafen, stun; *faire le diable à quatre* [*F.*]; make one's windows shake; awake the echoes, startle the echoes; give tongue.

adj. **loud**, sonorous; high-sounding, big-sounding; deep, full, powerful, noisy, blatant, clangorous, multisonous; thundering, deafening etc. *v.;* trumpet-tongued; ear-splitting, ear-rending, ear-deafening; piercing; shrill etc. 410; obstreperous, rackety, uproarious; enough to wake the -dead, –seven sleepers; clamorous etc. (*vociferous*) 411; stentorian, stentorophonic [*obs.*].

adv. **loudly** etc. *adj.;* aloud; with one wild yell; at the top of one's -lungs, –voice; lustily, in full cry.

405. Faintness

n. **faintness** etc. *adj.;* faint sound, whisper, breath; undertone, underbreath; murmur, hum, buzz, purr, lap [*of waves*], plash; sough, moan, rustle, susurration [*rare*], tinkle; "still small voice."

hoarseness etc. *adj.*

silencer, muffler; soft pedal, damper, mute, *sordino* [*It.*], sordine [*all music*].

v. **whisper**, breathe; mutter etc. (*speak imperfectly*) 583; susurrate [*rare*].

murmur, purl, hum, gurgle, ripple, babble, flow; rustle, tinkle.

steal on the ear, melt in the air, float on the air.

muffle, deaden, mute, subdue.

adj. **faint**, scarcely–, barely–, just-audible; low, dull; stifled, muffled; inaudible; hoarse, husky; gentle, soft; floating; purling, flowing etc. *v.;* muttered; whispered etc. *v.;* liquid; soothing; dulcet etc. (*melodious*) 413; susurrant [*rare*], susurrous [*rare*].

adv. **in a whisper**, with bated breath, *sotto voce* [*It.*], between the teeth, aside; piano, pianissimo [*both music*], *sordamente* [*It.*], *sordo* [*It.*], *à la sourdine* [*F.*]; out of earshot; inaudibly etc. *adj.*

406. Snap

[sudden and violent sounds]

n. **snap** etc. *v.;* toot, shout, yell, yap [*dial.*], yelp, bark; rapping etc. *v.*

2000

report, decrepitation, crepitation; thump, knock, clap, thud; burst, thunderclap, thunderburst, eruption, blowout [*tire*], explosion, discharge, detonation, firing, salvo, volley.

detonator, bomb, gun, rifle; torpedo, squib, cracker, firecracker, popgun, rattle.

v. **snap**, rap, tap, knock; click; clash; crack, crackle; crash; pop; slam, bang, clap; thump, toot, yap [*dial.*], yelp, bark, fire, explode, rattle, burst on the ear; crepitate, flump.

adj. rapping etc. *v.;* crepitant.

adv. **slap-bang** or slam-bang [*colloq.*], bang [*colloq.*].

int. **bang!** crash!

407. Roll

[repeated and protracted sounds]

n. **roll** etc. *v.;* drumming etc. *v.; berloque* [*F.*], ululation, howl, bombilation, bombination, rumbling; dingdong; tantara, rataplan, ratatat, rubadub, tattoo; pitapat; quaver, clutter, brustle [*dial.*], charivari, racket; cuckoo; repetition etc. 104; peal of bells, devil's tattoo; drum fire, barrage; whirr, rattle, drone; reverberation etc. 408.

v. **roll**, drum, rataplan, boom; whirr, rustle, tootle, clutter, roar, drone, rumble, rattle, clatter, patter, clack; bombinate, bombilate [*rare*].

hum, trill, shake; chime, peal, toll; tick, beat.

drum in the ear, din in the ear.

adj. **rolling**, etc. *v.;* monotonous etc. (*repeated*) 104; like a bee in a bottle.

408. Resonance

n. **resonance**; ring etc. *v.;* ringing etc. *v.;* reflection *or* reflexion; clangor, bell-note, tintinnabulation, vibration, reverberation.

low-, base-, bass-, flat-, grave-, deep- note; bass; *basso* [*It.*], *basso profondo* [*It.*]; barytone *or* baritone, contralto; pedal point, organ point.

v. **resound**, reverberate, reëcho; ring, sound, jingle *or* gingle, chink, clink; tink, tinkle; chime; gurgle etc. 405; plash, guggle, echo, ring in the ear.

adj. **resonant**, reverberant, resounding etc. *v.;* tinnient [*obs.*], tintinnabula *or* tintinnabulary; deep-toned, -sounding, -mouthed; hollow, sepulchral; gruff etc. (*harsh*) 410.

408a. Nonresonance

n. **nonresonance**; mutescence; thud, thump, dead sound; muffled drums, cracked bell; damper, *sordino* [*It.*], sordine, mute; muffler, silencer.

v. **muffle**, deaden, mute; sound dead; stop-, damp-, deaden-, the -sound, -reverberations; use *or* employ the *sordino* [*It.*] etc. *n.*

adj. **nonresonant**, dead, mute; muffled etc. *v.*

409. Sibilation

[hissing sounds]

n. **sibilation**; zip; hiss etc. *v.;* sternutation; high note etc. 410.

goose, serpent, snake.

v. **hiss**, buzz, whiz, rustle; fizz, fizzle; wheeze, whistle, snuffle; squash; sneeze; sizz [*colloq.*], sizzle, swish.

adj. **sibilant**; hissing etc. *v.;* wheezy; sternutative.

410. Stridor

[harsh or high sounds]

n. **stridor**, harshness, roughness, sharpness etc. *adj.;* raucousness, raucity; creak etc. *v.;* creaking etc. *v.;* discord, etc. 414; cacophony; cacoëpy.

high note, acute note; soprano, treble, tenor, alto, falsetto; *voce di testa* [*It.*], head voice, head tone; shriek, yell; cry etc. 411.

penny trumpet, piccolo, fife, whistle; penny-, willow- whistle; Panpipes, syrinx; pipes, bagpipes, doodlesack [*Scot.*].

v. **grate**, creak, saw, snore, jar, burr, pipe, twang, jangle, clank, clink; scream etc. (*cry*) 411; yelp etc. (*animal sound*) 412; buzz etc. (*hiss*) 409.

set the teeth on edge, *écorcher les oreilles* [*F.*]; pierce-, split- the -ears, -head; offend-, grate upon-, jar upon- the ear.

adj. **grating**, creaking etc. *v.;* stridulous, strident, harsh, coarse, hoarse, horrisonant [*obs.*], raucous, metallic, horrisonous [*obs.*], rough, rude, jangly [*rare*], gruff, grum, sepulchral, hollow.

high, sharp, acute, shrill; trumpet-toned; piercing, ear-piercing, high-pitched, high-toned; cracked; discordant etc. 414; cacophonous.

411. Cry

n. **cry** etc. *v.;* voice etc. (*human*) 580; view halloo, yoicks [*both hunting*]; hubbub; bark etc. (*animal*) 412.

outcry, vociferation, hullabaloo, chorus, clamor *or* clamour, hue and cry, plaint; lungs; Stentor, stentor.

v. **cry**, roar, shout, bawl, brawl, halloo, halloa, yo-ho, yoick, whoop *or* hoop [*rare*], yell, bellow, howl, scream, screech, screak, shriek, shrill, squeak, squeal, squall, whine, pule, pipe, yap, yaup *or* yawp.

cheer, huzza, hurrah; hoot.

moan, grumble, groan.

snort, snore; grunt etc. (*animal sounds*) 412.

vociferate; raise-, lift up- the voice; yell out, call out, sing out, cry out; exclaim; rend the air;

make the welkin ring; split the -throat, −lungs; thunder−, shout- at the -top of one's voice, −pitch of one's breath; *s'égosiller* [*F.*]; strain the -throat, −voice, −lungs; give cry; give a cry etc.; clamor *or* clamour.

adj. **clamant**, clamorous; crying etc. *v.;* vociferous; stentorian etc. (*loud*) 404; open-mouthed; full-mouthed.

412. Ululation
[animal sounds]

n. **ululation**, howling, mugiency [*obs.*], reboation [*rare*]; cry etc. *v.;* crying etc. *v.;* call, note, howl, bark, yelp, bow-wow, latration, belling; woodnote; insect cry, twittering, fritiniancy [*obs.*], drone; cuckoo.

v. **ululate**, howl, cry, roar, bellow, blare, rebellow, latrate, bark, yelp; bay, bay the moon; yap, growl, yarr [*obs.*], yawl [*dial.*], yaup *or* yawp, snarl, howl; grunt, gruntle; snort, squeak; neigh, bray; mew, mewl, purr, caterwaul, miaow; bleat, low, moo; troat [*rare*], croak, crow, screech, caw, coo, gobble, quack, cackle, gaggle, guggle; chuck, chuckle; cluck, clack; chirp, cheep, chirrup, chirk [*obs.*], peep, sing, pule, twitter, chatter, hoot, wail, cuckoo; hum, buzz; hiss, blatter, blat [*colloq.*].

adj. **ululant**, crying etc. *v.;* blatant, latrant, remugient [*obs.*], mugient; deep-mouthed, full-mouthed; rebellowing, reboant [*rare*].

adv. in full cry.

413. Melody. Concord

n. **melody**, rhythm, measure; rime *or* rhyme etc. (*poetry*) 597.

[musical terms] pitch, timbre, intonation, tone, overtone.

orchestration, harmonization, modulation, phrasing, temperament, syncope, syncopation, preparation, suspension, solution, resolution.

staff *or* stave, line, space, brace; bar, rest; *appoggiato* [*It.*], *appoggiatura* [*It.*]; *acciaccatura* [*It.*], trill *or* shake, turn, *arpeggio* [*It.*].

note, musical note, notes of a scale; sharp, flat, natural; high note etc. (*shrillness*) 410; low note etc. 408; interval; semitone; second, third, fourth etc.; diatessaron [*ancient music*].

breve, semibreve *or* whole note, minim *or* half note, crotchet *or* quarter note, quaver *or* eighth note, semiquaver *or* sixteenth note, demisemiquaver *or* thirty-second note, hemidemisemiquaver *or* sixty-fourth note; sustained note, drone, bourdon, burden.

scale, gamut; diapason; diatonic−, chromatic−, enharmonic- scale; key, clef, chords.

tonic; key−, leading−, fundamental- note; supertonic, mediant, dominant; pedal point, organ point; submediant, subdominant; octave, tetrachord; Dorian *or* Doric - mode, −tetrachord; major−, minor- -mode, −scale, −key; passage, phrase.

harmony, concord, emmeleia; euphony, euphonism; tonality; consonance; concent [*archaic*], concentus; part.

unison, unisonance; chime, homophony.

[science of harmony] harmony, harmonics; thorough bass, fundamental bass; counterpoint; faburden [*medieval music*].

opus (*pl.* opera) [*L.*], piece of music etc. 415.

composer, harmonist, contrapuntist.

v. **harmonize**, chime, symphonize, transpose, orchestrate; blend, put in tune, tune, accord, string; be harmonious etc. *adj.*

adj. **harmonious**, harmonic, harmonical; in concord etc. *n.,* in tune, in concert, in unison; unisonant, concentual *or* concentuous [*rare*], symphonizing, isotonic, homophonous, assonant; ariose, consonant.

measured, rhythmic *or* rhythmical, diatonic, chromatic, enharmonic.

melodious, musical; melic; tuneful, tunable; sweet, dulcet, canorous; mellow, mellifluous; soft; clear, −as a bell; silvery; euphonious, euphonic *or* euphonical, symphonious; enchanting etc. (*pleasure-giving*) 829; fine-toned, silver-toned, full-toned, deep-toned.

adv. **harmoniously** etc. *adj.*

414. Discord

n. **discord**, discordance; dissonance, cacophony, want of harmony, caterwauling; harshness etc. 410; charivari, shivaree [*dial., U. S.*], racket; consecutive fifths.

[confused sounds] Babel, pandemonium; Dutch concert, cat's concert, marrowbones and cleavers [*all colloq.*].

v. **be discordant** etc. *adj.;* jar etc. (*sound harshly*) 410; shivaree [*dial., U. S.*].

adj. **discordant**, dissonant, absonant; out of tune, tuneless; unmusical, untunable; immelodious, unmelodious, unharmonious, inharmonious, unsweet [*rare*], singsong; cacophonous; harsh etc. 410; jarring.

415. Music

n. **music**; strain, tune, air; melody etc. 413; piece of music, *morceau* [*F.*], rondo, rondeau, *pas-*

torale [*It.*], pastoral, cavatina, fantasia, *toccata* [*It.*], *toccatella* [*It.*], *toccatina* [*It.*], *capriccio* [*It.*], fugue, canon; potpourri, medley, incidental music; variations, roulade, cadenza, cadence, trill; serenade, *notturno* [*It.*], nocturne; *passamezzo* [*It.*]; staff *or* stave etc. 413.

instrumental music; orchestral score, full score; minstrelsy, tweedledum and tweedledee [*applied by John Byrom to the feuds between Handel and Bononcini*]; band, orchestra etc. 416; composition, *opus* (*pl. opera*) [*L.*], movement, concert piece, concerted piece, symphony, *concerto* [*It.*], sonata, symphonic poem, tone poem; chamber music; overture, prelude, voluntary, *Vorspiel* [*Ger.*]; string quartet *or* quartette.

lively music, polka, reel etc. (*dance*) 848; ragtime, disco, reggae, rock, hard rock, acid rock, punk rock, jazz; syncopation; *allegro* etc. *adv.*

slow music, slow movement, Lydian measures; *adagio* etc. *adv.*; minuet; siren strains, soft music; lullaby, cradle song, *berceuse* [*F.*]; dump [*obs.*]; dirge etc. (*lament*) 839; pibroch, coronach [*Scot. & Ir.*], dead march, martial music, march; waltz etc. (*dance*) 840.

vocal music, vocalism; chaunt [*archaic*], chant; psalm, psalmody, hymnology; hymn; song etc. (*poem*) 597; oratorio, opera, operetta; canticle, cantata, lay, ballad, ditty, carol, pastoral, recitative *or* recitativo, *aria parlante* [*It.*], aria, arietta *or* ariette, canzonet; bravura, *coloratura* [*It.*], coloraure; virtuoso music, cantabile.

solo, duet, *duo* [*It.*], trio, terzetto, quartet *or* quartette, quintet *or* quintette, sestet *or* sextet, septet, double quartet, chorus; part song, descant, glee, madrigal, catch, round, chorale; antiphon, antiphony; accompaniment; inside part, second, alto, tenor, bass; score, piano score, vocal score; burden, bourdon, drone.

concert, musicale, musical [*colloq.*], recital, chamber concert, popular concert *or* pop [*colloq.*], open-air concert, rock concert, serenade, *aubade* [*F.*]; community singing, singsong [*colloq.*].

method, *solfeggio* [*It.*], tonic sol-fa, solmization; sight -singing, -reading; reading at sight.

composer etc. 413; **musician** etc. 416.

v. **compose**, write, set to music, arrange etc. 416; attune.

perform, execute, play etc. 416.

adj. **musical**; instrumental, vocal, choral, lyric, melodic, pure, operatic; classic, modern, orchestral, symphonic, contrapuntal, program; imitative, falsetto; harmonious etc. 413; Wagnerian.

adv. adagio; largo, larghetto, andante, andantino; alla cappella; maestoso, moderato; allegro, allegretto; spiritoso, vivace, veloce; presto, prestissimo; con brio; capriccioso; scherzo, scherzando; legato, staccato, crescendo, diminuendo, rallentando, affettuoso; arioso, parlante, cantabile; obbligato; pizzicato; desto [*all It.*].

416. Musician
[performance of music]

n. **musician**, artiste [*F.*], virtuoso, performer, player, minstrel; bard etc. (*poet*) 597; accompanist, instrumentalist, organist, pianist, violinist, tweedledee [*Scot.*], fiddler, catgut scraper [*slang*]; flutist *or* flautist; harpist *or* harper, fifer, trumpeter, cornetist, piper, drummer; accordionist.

orchestra; string -orchestra, -quartet; strings, woodwind, brass; band, brass band, military band, German band, jazz band; street musicians, waits.

vocalist, melodist, singer, warbler; songster, chanter *or* chaunter [*archaic*]; *cantatore* [*It.*], *cantatrice* [*F.*], improvisator, *improvvisatore or improvisatore* [*It.*]; *improvvisatrice or improvisatrice* [*It.*], songstress, chantress *or* chauntress [*archaic*]; chorister; chorus singer.

choir *or* quire [*archaic*]; chorus; *Liedertafel* [*Ger.*], *Liederkranz* [*Ger.*]; choral -club, -society; singing -club, -society; festival chorus, eisteddfod [*Welsh*].

song bird, nightingale, philomel, lark, ringdove, bulbul, cuckoo, thrush, mavis.

[patrons] Orpheus, Apollo, Apollo Musagetes, the Muses, Polyhymnia, Erato, Euterpe, Terpsichore; Pierides, sacred nine, tuneful nine, tuneful quire [*archaic*]; Siren.

composer etc. 413.

conductor, choirmaster, bandmaster, concert master *or* Konzertmeister [*Ger.*], drum major, song leader, precentor.

performance, execution, touch, expression.

v. **play**, tune, tune up, pipe, pipe up, strike up, sweep the chords, fiddle, scrape [*derog.*], strike the lyre, beat the drum; blow-, sound-, wind- the horn; doodle [*Scot. or colloq.*]; toot, tootle, grind the organ; touch the guitar etc. (*instruments*) 417; twang, pluck, pick, paw the ivories [*slang*]; pound, thump; drum, thrum, strum, beat time.

execute, perform; accompany; sing-, play- a second.

compose, set to music, arrange, harmonize, orchestrate.

sing, chant *or* chaunt [*archaic*], intone, hum, warble, carol, yodel, chirp, chirrup, lilt, purl, quaver, trill, shake, twitter, whistle; sol-fa; do-re-mi.

have an ear for music, have a musical ear, have a correct ear, have absolute pitch.

adj. **musical**; lyric, dramatic; *coloratura* [*It.*], bravura, florid, brilliant; playing etc. *v.*

adv. adagio [*It.*], andante [*It.*] etc. (*music*) 415.

417. Musical Instruments

n. **musical instruments**; orchestra, band; string band, military band, brass band; orchestrion, orchestrina.

[stringed instruments] polychord, harp, lyre, lute, archlute, theorbo, cithara, cither, cittern *or* cithern, gittern, zither, psaltery, guitar, banjo, banjo-zither; rebec *or* rebeck, mandola, mandolin *or* mandoline, ukulele [*Hawaii*]; *bandurria* [*It.*], samisen [*Jap.*]; bina, vina [*India*].

violin, Cremona, Stradivarius; fiddle, kit; viol, vielle; viola, *–d'amore, –di gamba;* tenor, violoncello, bass viol *or* base viol; double bass, *contrabasso* [*It.*], *violone* [*It.*]; bow, fiddlestick, strings, catgut.

piano *or* pianoforte; grand–, concert-grand–, baby-grand–, square–, upright - piano; harpsichord, monochord [*hist.*], clavichord, clarichord, manichord *or* manichordon, clavier, spinet, virginals, dulcimer; hurdy-gurdy, street piano, piano organ; pianette, pianino, piano player, player piano, player; Aeolian (*or* Eolian) harp.

[wind instruments] organ; church–, pipe–, reed-organ; seraphine *or* seraphina, harmonium, cabinet organ, American organ; harmoniphon [*obs.*], barrel organ, hand organ, melodeon, accordion, concertina; humming top.

flute, fife, piccolo, flageolet, clarinet *or* clarionet, bass clarinet, basset horn, *corno di bassetto* [*It.*], musette, oboe *or* hautboy, *cor anglais* [*F.*], English horn, *corno inglese* [*It.*], bassoon, double bassoon, *contrafagotto* [*It.*], serpent, bag-pipes, union pipes, doodlesack [*Scot.*]; ocarina, Panpipes *or* Pandean pipes; reed instrument; pipe, pitch-pipe; whistle; willow–, penny- whistle; calliope, siren *or* sirene; cat-call.

horn, bugle, cornet, cornet-à-pistons, cornopean [*obs.*], clarion [*now chiefly poetic*], trumpet, trombone, tuba, bombardon, bass tuba, ophicleide; French horn, bugle horn, post horn, sax-horn, *Flügelhorn* [*Ger.*], alt horn *or* althorn, tenor horn, sackbut, euphonium.

[vibrating surfaces] cymbals, bell, gong; drum, tambour, snare drum, side drum, tabor *or* tabour, taboret *or* tabouret, kettle drum, timpano (*pl.* timpani), timbal *or* tymbal, tom-tom *or* tam-tam, timbrel, tambourine, castanet, bones; musical glasses, musical stones; mouth organ, harmonica; sounding-board, *abatvoix* [*F.*]; rattle, watchman's rattle; phonograph, graphophone, gramophone, stereo, victrola [*trade-mark name*]; *zambomba* [*Sp.*].

[vibrating bars] reed, tuning fork, triangle, jew's-harp, music box *or* musical box, harmonicon, xylophone.

mute, sourdine, *sordino* [*It.*], sordine, sordet, sourdet.

418. Hearing
[sense of sound]

n. **hearing** etc. *v.;* audition, auscultation; audibility; acoustics etc. 402; eavesdropping.

acute–, nice–, delicate–, quick–, sharp–, correct–, musical- ear; ear for music.

ear, auricle, pinna, concha, labyrinth, lug [*Scot.*], lobule *or* lobe, acoustic organs, auditory apparatus, eardrum, tympanum; malleus, incus, stapes, vestibule, cochlea, auditory nerve, Eustachian tube.

ear trumpet, speaking trumpet; telephone, phonograph, microphone; gramophone, phonograph, victrola [*trademark name*], megaphone, phonorganon; dictagraph *or* dictograph [*trade-mark name*], dictophone [*trade-mark name*], audiphone, dentiphone; stethoscope; telephone etc. 527.

hearer, auditor, auditory, audience, listener, eavesdropper.

otology, otoscopy, auriscopy; otoscope, auriscope; otopathy, otography, otoplasty; otorrhea, tympanitis; otologist, aurist.

v. **hear**, overhear; hark, hearken *or* harken; list, listen; give–, lend–, bend- an ear; strain one's ears, attend to, give attention, catch a sound, prick up one's ears; give ear, give a hearing to, give audience to.

hang upon the lips of, be all ear, listen with both ears.

become audible; meet–, fall upon–, catch–, reach- the ear; be heard; ring in the ear etc. (*resound*) 408.

adj. **hearing** etc. *v.;* auditory, otic, aural, acoustic, acoustical, phonic; auriculate, auricular; auricled, eared; auditive.

adv. arrectis auribus [*L.*]; all ears.

int. **hark**! hark ye! hear! list! listen! oyez *or* oyes! attend! attention! lend me your ears!

419. Deafness

n. **deafness**, hardness of hearing, surdity [*obs.*], deaf ears; inaudibility, inaudibleness.
adder, beetle, slowworm, blindworm; deaf-mute.
dactylology, deaf-and-dumb alphabet.

v. **be deaf** etc. *adj.;* have no ear; shut–, stop–, close- one's ears; turn a deaf ear to.
render deaf, stun, deafen; split the -ears, –eardrum.

adj. **deaf**, earless, surd; hard–, dull- of hearing; deaf-mute; stunned, deafened; stone deaf; deaf as -a post, –an adder, –a beetle, –a trunkmaker; inattentive etc. 458.
inaudible, out of -earshot, –hearing.

420. Light

n. **light**, ray, beam, stream, gleam, streak, pencil; sunbeam, moonbeam; aurora, dawn.
day; sunshine; light of -day, –heaven; sun etc. (*luminary*) 423, daylight, broad daylight, noontide light; noontide, noonday.
glow etc. *v.;* afterglow, sunset glow; glimmering etc. *v.;* glint; glare; play–, glare–, flood- of light; phosphorescence, lambent flame.
halo, glory, nimbus, aureola, aureole, gloriole [*rare*], aura.
spark, scintilla; facula; sparkling etc. *v.;* emication [*obs.*], scintillation, flash, blaze, coruscation, fulguration [*now rare*]; flame etc. (*fire*) 382; lightning, levin; *ignis fatuus* [*L.*] etc. (*luminary*) 423.
luster *or* lustre, sheen, shimmer, reflection *or* reflexion; gloss, tinsel, spangle, brightness, brilliancy, splendor *or* splendour, effulgence, refulgence; fulgor, fulgidity [*rare*]; dazzlement, resplendence *or* resplendency, transplendency [*rare*], luminousness etc. *adj.;* luminosity; lucidity; nitency [*rare*]; radiance, radiation; irradiation, illumination.
[science of light] optics; photology, photics; actinology, actinometry, radiology, heliology, radiometry, radioscopy, photometry, dioptrics, catoptrics; photography, photolithography, photomicography, phototelegraphy, radiotelegraphy; phototherapy, heliotherapy, radiotherapy; heliometry, heliography.
actinic rays, actinism; radioactivity, radium emanation, exradio; Röntgen *or* Roentgen rays, X-rays, ultra-violet rays; photometer etc. 445; heliometer, refractometer.

[distribution of light] *chiaroscuro* or *chiaro-oscuro* [*It.*], clair-obscure, *clair-obscure* [*F.*], mezzotint, mezzotinto, half tone *or* half-tone, demitint, half tint; breadth, light and shade, black and white, tonality.
reflection, refraction, dispersion; refractivity.
illuminant, artificial light; gas etc. 423.

v. **shine**, glow, beam, glitter; glister; glisten; twinkle, gleam; flare, flare up; glare, shimmer, glimmer, flicker, sparkle, scintillate, coruscate, flash, blaze; be bright etc. *adj.;* reflect light, daze, dazzle, bedazzle, radiate, shoot out beams; fulgurate, phosphoresce.
clear up, brighten.
lighten, enlighten; levin; light, light up; irradiate, shine upon; give–, hang out a - light; cast–, throw–, shed-luster, –light- upon; illume, illumine, illuminate; relume, strike a light; kindle etc. (*set fire to*) 384.

adj. **luminous**, luminiferous; shining etc. *v.;* lucid, lucent, luculent, luciferous [*rare*], lucific [*rare*]; illuminate [*archaic*], illuminant, light, lightsome; bright, vivid, splendent, nitid, lustrous, shiny, beamy, scintillant, fulgurant, radiant, lambent; sheen, sheeny; glossy, burnished, glassy, sunny, orient, meridian; noonday, noontide; cloudless, clear; unclouded, unobscured.
garish; resplendent, transplendent [*rare*]; refulgent, effulgent, fulgid, fulgent, relucent, splendorous *or* splendrous, splendid, blazing, in a blaze, ablaze, rutilant, meteoric, phosphorescent; aglow.
bright as silver; light–, bright- as -day, –noonday, –the sun at noonday.
[scientific] actinic, radioactive; optic, optical, photologic *or* photological, heliological; photogenic, photographic; heliographic; heliophagous.

421. Darkness

n. **darkness** etc. *adj.;* tenebrosity, umbrageousness, dunness [*rare*], caliginousness, lightlessness, sootiness; blackness etc. (*dark color*) 431; obscurity, gloom, murk *or* mirk, murkiness *or* mirkiness, darksomeness; dusk etc. (*dimness*) 422.
Cimmerian–, Stygian–, Egyptian-darkness; night; midnight; dead of–, witching hour of–, witching time of- night; darkness visible; "darkness which may be felt" [*Bible*]; "the palpable obscure" [Milton]; "embalmèd darkness" [Keats]; Erebus; "the jaws of darkness" [*Midsummer Night's Dream*]; "sable-vested Night" [Milton].

shadow, shade, umbra, penumbra; skiagraphy *or* sciagraphy; skiagram *or* sciagram, skiagraph *or* sciagraph; radiograph.

obscuration; obumbration [*rare*]; obtenebration [*rare*], offuscation [*obs.*], caligation [*obs.*], adumbration; extinction; eclipse, total eclipse; gathering of the clouds.

shading; distribution of shade; *chiaroscuro* [*It.*] etc. (*light*) 420.

v. **be dark** etc. *adj.;* be in darkness etc. *n.*

darken, obscure, shade; dim; tone down, lower; overcast, overshadow; cloud, cloud over, darken over, murk *or* mirk; eclipse; offuscate [*obs.*], obumbrate, obtenebrate [*rare*], obfuscate; adumbrate; cast into the shade; becloud, bedim, bedarken; cast-, throw-, spread- a -shade, -shadow, -gloom; "walk in darkness and in the shadow of death" [*Book of Common Prayer*].

extinguish, put out, blow out, snuff out, dout [*obs. or dial. Eng.*]

adj. **dark**, darksome, darkling; obscure, tenebrious, tenebrous, sombrous, pitch dark, pitchy; caliginous [*archaic*]; black etc. (*in color*) 431.

dark as -pitch, -the pit, -Erebus.

sunless, lightless etc. (*see* sun, light, etc. 423); somber, dusky; unilluminated etc. (*see* illuminate etc. 420); nocturnal; dingy, lurid, gloomy; murky *or* mirky, murksome *or* mirksome, sooty, shady, umbrageous; overcast etc. (*dim*) 422; cloudy etc. (*opaque*) 426; darkened etc. *v.*

benighted; noctivagant, noctivagous.

adv. in the -dark, -shade; at night, by night, through the night; darkling, darklings [*rare*].

422. Dimness

n. **dimness** etc. *adj.;* darkness etc. 421; paleness etc. (*light color*) 429.

half light, *demi-jour* [*F.*]; partial shadow, partial eclipse; "shadow of a shade" [Aeschylus]; "shadows numberless" [Keats]; glimmer, glimmering; nebulosity, nebulousness, obnubilation [*rare*]; cloud etc. 353; eclipse.

twilight, aurora, dusk, nightfall, gloaming, gloam [*rare*], blind man's holiday, *entre chien et loup* [*F.*], *inter canem et lupem* [*L.*], shades of evening, crepuscule, cockshut time [*obs.*]; break of day, daybreak, dawn.

moonlight, moonbeam, moonglade, moonshine; owl's-light, starlight, candlelight, rushlight, firelight; farthing candle.

v. **be** *or* **grow dim** etc. *adj.;* gloom; cloud over; flicker, twinkle, glimmer, loom, lower; fade; pale, "pale his uneffectual fire" [*Hamlet*].

render dim etc. *adj.;* dim, bedim, obscure, shade, shadow; encompass with -gloom, -shadow; darken, dark [*archaic*], cloud, becloud, darkle.

adj. **dim**, dull, lackluster, dingy, darkish, dusky, shorn of its beams; dark etc. 421.

faint, shadowed forth; glassy; cloudy; misty etc. (*opaque*) 426; blear; fuliginous; nebulous, nebular, obnubilated [*rare*], obnubilous [*obs.*].

lurid, leaden, dun, dirty; overcast, muddy; looming etc. *v.*

twilight, crepuscular, crepusculous [*rare*], crepusculine [*rare*].

pale etc. (*colorless*) 429; confused etc. (*invisible*) 447.

423. Luminary

[source of light]

n. **luminary**; light etc. 420; flame etc. (*fire*) 382.

spark, scintilla; phosphorescence.

[heavenly bodies] sun, orb of day, day-star [*poetic*], Aurora; star, orb, meteor; falling star, shooting star; blazing star, dog star, canicula, Sirius, Aldebaran; constellation, galaxy, Milky Way; pole star, Polaris; Cynosure; anthelion; morning star, Lucifer, Phosphor, Phosphorus; Venus, Hesperus, evening star; mock sun, parhelion, sun dog *or* sundog, moon etc. 318.

sun god, Helios, Titan, Phaëthon, Phoebus, Apollo, Hyperion, Ra *or* Re [*Egypt*], Shamash [*Babylon & Assyria*].

lightning, levin; chain-, fork-, sheet-, summer-lightning.

phosphorus; *ignis fatuus* [*L.*]; Jack o'-, Friar's-lantern; will-o'-the-wisp, firedrake, Fata Morgana, St. Elmo's fire, Castor and Pollux [*naut.*], corposant.

glowworm, firefly.

polar lights, northern lights, *aurora borealis* [*L.*], *aurora australis* [*L.*]; aurora; zodiacal light.

[artificial light] gas, gaslight, electric light; headlight, searchlight, spotlight, flashlight, limelight, calcium light, lamplight, lamp; lantern, lanthorn [*archaic*]; electric torch, dark lantern, bull's-eye; candle; wax-, tallow-, bayberry-candle; farthing dip, tallow dip [*colloq.*]; bougie, taper, rushlight; oil etc. (*grease*) 356; wick, burner; Argand, moderator, duplex; torch, flambeau, link, brand; gaselier, chandelier, electrolier; candelabrum, girandole, sconce, luster *or* lustre, candlestick.

firework, Catherine wheel, Roman candle, fizgig; pyrotechnics.

signal light, rocket, balefire, beacon fire; light-house etc. (*signal*) 550.

pyre, funeral pyre; death fire; corpse candle.

v. **illuminate** etc. (*light*) 420.

adj. **self-luminous;** phosphoric, phosphorescent; radiant etc. (*light*) 420.

424. Shade

n. **shade;** awning etc. (*cover*) 223; parasol, sunshade, umbrella.

screen, curtain, chick [*India*], purdah [*India*], *portière* [*F.*]; shutter, blind, Venetian blind, *jalousie* [*F.*].

gauze, veil, mantle, mask, yashmak [*Turk.*].

cloud, mist; gathering of clouds; smoke screen [*mil.*].

umbrage [*archaic*], glade; shadow etc. 421; ambush, covert.

blinkers, blinders; smoked glasses, colored spectacles.

v. **veil** etc. *v.;* draw a curtain; put up–, close- a shutter; cast a shadow etc. (*darken*) 421.

adj. **shady,** umbrageous, shadowy, bowery.

425. Transparency

n. **transparency,** transparence, translucence, translucency, diaphaneity, diaphanousness; lucidity, pellucidity, limpidity; fluorescence; transillumination, translumination.

transparent medium, glass, crystal, lymph, water, hyalite, hyaline.

v. **be transparent** etc. *adj.;* transmit light.

adj. **transparent,** pellucid, lucid, diaphanous; translucent, tralucent [*obs.*], limpid, clear, serene, crystalline, clear as crystal, pervious [*rare*], vitreous, transpicuous [*rare*], glassy, hyaline, hyaloid [*rare*], vitreform.

426. Opacity

n. **opacity;** opaqueness etc. *adj.;* obfuscation, fuliginosity, nubilation.

film; cloud etc. 353.

v. **be opaque** etc. *adj.;* obstruct the passage of light; obfuscate, offuscate [*obs.*].

adj. **opaque,** impervious to light; adiaphanous; dim etc. 422; turbid, thick, muddy, opacous [*obs.*], obfuscated, fuliginous, cloudy, nubilous, nubilose [*obs.*], foggy, vaporous, nubiferous.

smoky, fumid [*obs.*], murky *or* mirky, smeared, dirty.

427. Semitransparency

n. **semitransparency,** opalescence, milkiness, pearliness.

[comparisons] gauze, muslin, cypress *or* cyprus [*hist.*], bombyx, thin silk; film; mica, mother-of-pearl, nacre, opal glass, opaline, frosted glass; mist etc. (*cloud*) 353.

adj. **semitransparent,** semipellucid, semidiaphanous, semiopacous [*obs.*], semiopaque; opalescent, opaline; pearly, milky, frosted, nacreous; hazy, misty.

v. **cloud,** frost, cloud over, frost over; become -pearly, –milky, –misty.

be opalescent etc. *adj.;* opalesce.

428. Color

n. **color** *or* colour, hue, tint, tinct [*archaic*], tinction, tinge, dye, complexion, shade, tincture, cast, livery, coloration, chromatism *or* chromism, glow, flush; tone, key.

pure–, positive–, primary–, primitive–, complementary- color; three primaries; spectrum, chromatic dispersion; broken–, secondary–, tertiary- color.

local color, coloring, keeping, tone, value, aerial perspective.

[science of color] chromatics, spectrum analysis; chromatography, chromatology, chromatoscopy; chromatograph, chromatometer, chromatoscope, chromoscope, chromatrope, chromometer, colorimeter; prism, spectroscope, kaleidoscope.

pigment, coloring matter, paint, dye, wash, distemper, stain, chromogen; medium; mordant; oil paint etc. (*painting*) 556.

v. **color** *or* colour, dye, tinge, stain, tint, tinct [*archaic*], hue, tone, complexion [*rare*]; paint, wash, distemper, ingrain, grain, illuminate, emblazon, imbue; paint etc. (*fine art*) 556.

adj. **colored** etc. *v.;* colorific, tingent [*rare*], tinctorial; chromatic, prismatic; full–, high–, rich–, deep- colored; double-dyed; polychromatic; chromatogenous; chromatophoric, chromatophorous; tingible.

bright, vivid, intense, deep; fresh, unfaded; rich, gorgeous; bright-colored, gay.

gaudy, florid; garish; showy, flaunting; flashy; many-colored, party-colored *or* parti-colored, variegated; raw, crude; glaring, flaring; discordant, inharmonious.

mellow, harmonious, pearly, sweet, delicate, subtle, tender.

dull, sad, somber *or* sombre, sad-colored, grave, gray, dark.

429. Achromatism

[absence of color]

n. **achromatism,** achromatization; decoloration, decolorization, discoloration; pallor, pallidity; paleness etc. *adj.;* etiolation.

neutral tint, monochrome, black and white.

v. **lose color** etc. 428; fade, fly, go, become colorless etc. *adj.;* turn pale; pale, fade out, bleach out; wan; fly, go.

deprive of color, decolor *or* decolour, decolorize *or* decolourize, whiten, bleach, tarnish, achromatize, blanch, etiolate, wash out, tone down.

adj. **colorless**; achromatic; uncolored etc. (*see* color etc. 428); etiolated; hueless, pale, pallid; pale-faced, anemic, tallow-faced; faint, dull, cold, muddy, leaden, dun, wan, sallow, dead, dingy, ashy, ashen, ghastly, cadaverous, glassy, lackluster; discolored etc. *v.*

pale as -death, −ashes, −a witch, −a ghost, −a corpse.

light-colored, fair, blond, ash-blond; white etc. 430; tow-headed, tow-haired.

430. Whiteness

n. **whiteness** etc. *adj.;* whitishness, canescence; argent, argentine.

albification, albication, albinism, albinoism; leucopathy, leucoderma *or* leucodermia [*med.*], dealbation, albescence, etiolation; lactescence.

[comparisons] snow, paper, chalk, milk, lily, ivory, silver, alabaster; albata, eburin *or* eburine *or* eburite, German silver, white metal, barium sulphate, *blanc fixe* [*F.*], pearl white; white lead, ceruse, carbonate of lead, Paris white, zinc white, flake white, Chinese white.

whitewash, whiting, whitening, calcimine.

v. **be white** etc. *adj.*

render white etc. *adj.;* whiten, bleach, blanch, etiolate, silver, besnow, dealbate [*obs.*], albify [*rare*], frost.

whitewash, calcimine, white.

adj. **white**; snow-white; snowy, niveous; candent, candid [*archaic*], frosted, hoar, hoary; silvery, silver, argent, argentine; canescent, chalky, cretaceous; lactescent, milk-white, milky, marmoreal *or* marmorean; albificative, albicant, albescent; albinistic.

white as -a sheet, −driven snow, −a lily, −silver; like ivory etc. *n.*

whitish, creamy, pearly, ivory, fair, blond, ash-blond; blanched etc. *v.;* high in tone, light.

431. Blackness

n. **blackness** etc. *adj.;* darkness etc. (*want of light*) 421; swarthiness, swartness; lividity; dark -color, −tone; *chiaroscuro* [*It.*] etc. 420.

nigrification [*rare*], nigrefaction [*obs.*], nigrescence, denigration, infuscation [*rare*].

[comparisons] jet, ink, ebony, ebon [*now poetic*], coal, pitch, soot, charcoal, sloe; smut, smutch, smudge, smirch; raven, crow.

negro, negress, blackamoor, man of color, colored man, colored woman, black, Black, Ethiop, Ethiopian, buck [*colloq.*], *kala admi* [*Hind.*], Melanesian, Hottentot, Pygmy, Bushman, Negrillo [*African Pygmy*], Negrito [*Asiatic Pygmy*], African, Mandingo, Senegambian, Sudanese, Papuan, blackfellow, Australian aborigine.

[pigments] lamp−, ivory−, blue-black; writing−, printing−, printer's−, Indian- ink.

v. **be black** etc. *adj.*

render black etc. *adj.;* black, blacken, infuscate [*rare*], denigrate, nigrify; blot, blotch, smut, smudge, smutch, smirch; darken etc. 421.

adj. **black,** sable, somber *or* sombre, livid, dark, inky, ebon, atramentous, jetty; coal-black, jet-black; fuliginous, pitchy, sooty; *dhu* [*Ir. & Gaelic*], swart, swarthy, dusky, dingy, murky *or* mirky; blotchy, smudgy, smutty; nigrine [*rare*], nigricant, nigrescent, Ethiopian, Ethiopic; low-toned, low in tone; of the deepest dye.

black as -jet etc. *n.,* − my hat, −a shoe, −a tinker's pot, −November, −the ace of spades, −thunder, −midnight; nocturnal etc. (*dark*) 421; gray etc. 432; obscure etc. 421.

adv. in mourning.

432. Gray

n. **gray** *or* grey etc. *adj.;* neutral tint, silver, dove-color, pepper and salt, *chiaroscuro* [*It.*], grisaille.

grayness *or* greyness etc. *adj.*

[pigments] Payne's gray; black etc. 431.

v. **render gray** etc. *adj.;* gray *or* grey.

adj. **gray** *or* grey; iron-gray, dun, drab, dingy, leaden, livid, somber, sad, pearly, calcareous, limy, silver, silvery, silvered; French−, steel−, Quaker−, dapple- gray; dappled; dove-colored, *gorge-de-pigeon* [*F.*]; ashen, ashy, favillous; cinereous, cineritious; grizzly, grizzled; slate-colored, stone-colored, mouse-colored, ash-colored; cool.

433. Brown

n. **brown** etc. *adj.;* brownness.

[pigments] bister *or* bistre, brown ocher *or* ochre, mummy, sepia, Vandyke brown.

v. **render brown** etc. *adj.;* brown, tan, embrown, imbrown, bronze.

adj. **brown,** adust [*rare*], castaneous, toast-brown, nut-brown, seal-brown, cinnamon, hazel, fawn, puce, musteline, musteloid, écru, *feuille-morte* [*F.*], tawny, fuscous, chocolate, maroon, tan, brunette, whitey-brown; fawn-colored, snuff-colored, liver-colored; brown as -a berry, –mahogany, –oak leaves; khaki.

reddish-brown, terra cotta, rufous, russet, russety, russetish, ferruginous, rust, foxy, bronze, coppery, copperish, copper-colored; bay, bayard, roan, sorrel, henna, auburn, chestnut, mahogany; rubiginous, rubiginose, rust-colored; lurid.

sun-burnt; tanned etc. *v.*

434. Redness

n. **red**, scarlet, cardinal, cardinal red, vermilion, carmine, crimson, pink, rose, cerise, cherry, rouge, coquelicot, salmon, lake, maroon, carnation, *couleur de rose* [*F.*], *rose du Barry* [*F.*]; magenta, solferino, damask, flesh -color, –tint; color; fresh–, high-color; warmth; gules [*her.*].

redness etc. *adj.;* rubescence, rubicundity, ruddiness, rubefaction, rubrication, rubification; erubescence, blush.

[comparisons] ruby, *grenat* [*F.*], garnet, carbuncle; rust, iron mold *or* mould; rose, cardinal flower, lobelia; cardinal-bird, –grosbeak; redstart.

[dyes and pigments] cinnabar, cochineal, red ocher *or* ochre, stammel, fuchsine *or* fuchsin, vermilion; ruddle, madder; Indian red, palladium red, light red, Venetian red; red ink, annatto *or* annotto, realgar, minium, red lead.

v. **be** *or* **become red** etc. *adj.;* blush, flush, color, color up, mantle, redden.

render red etc. *adj.;* redden, rouge, crimson, encrimson [*rare*], empurple; rubify [*rare*], rubricate; incarnadine; ruddle, rust.

adj. **red** etc. *n.,* reddish; incarnadine, sanguine, sanguineous, bloody, gory; coral, coralline, rosy, roseate; stammel, blood-red, laky, wine-red, wine-colored, vinaceous; incarmined [*rare*], rubiform [*rare*], rufous, rufulous, murrey, bricky, lateritious [*rare*]; rubineous, rubious, rubricate, rubricose; Pompeiian red; reddish-brown etc. 433.

rose–, ruby–, cherry–, claret–, flame–, flesh–, peach–, salmon–, brick–, rust-colored.

red as -fire, –blood, –scarlet, –a turkey cock, –a lobster; warm, hot.

red-complexioned, red-faced, florid, burnt, rubicund, ruddy, red, blowzed, blowzy, glowing, sanguine, blooming, rosy, hectic, flushed, inflamed; blushing etc. *v.;* erubescent, rubescent; reddened etc. *v.*

[of hair] sandy, carroty, brick-red, Titian red, auburn, chestnut.

435. Greenness

n. **green** etc. *adj.;* blue and yellow; vert [*her.*].
greenness, verdancy, verdure, viridescence, viridity.

[comparisons] emerald, malachite, chrysoprase, jasper, chrysolite *or* olivine, beryl; verd antique, verdigris, aquamarine; reseda, mignonette, absinthe, *crème de menthe* [*F.*].

[pigments] *terre verte* [*F.*], viridian, bice, verditer, verdine, celadon.

v. **render green** etc. *adj.;* green.

adj. **green**, verdant; glaucous, olive; green as grass; verdurous, citrine *or* citrinous, porraceous, olivaceous, smaragdine [*rare*].

emerald–, pea–, grass–, apple–, sea–, olive–, cucumber–, leaf–, Irish–, Nile–, Kelly–, bottle- green.

greenish, virent [*rare*], virescent, viridescent [*rare*], chlorine; aquamarine, blue-green.

436. Yellowness

n. **yellow** etc. *adj.;* or [*her.*]; yellowness etc. *adj.;* xanthocyanopia *or* xanthocyanopsia, xanthochroia.

[comparisons] crocus, jonquil, saffron, topaz; xanthite; gold, gilding, gilt; yolk; jaundice, icterus; London fog.

[pigments] gamboge, fustic, massicot; cadmium–, chrome–, Indian–, king's–, lemon-yellow; orpiment, yellow ocher, Claude tint, aureolin; xanthein, xanthin; xanthophyll.

v. **render yellow** etc. *adj.;* yellow, gild; jaundice.

adj. **yellow**, aureate, golden, gold, gilt, gilded, flavous [*obs.*], citrine, citreous, lemon, fallow; fulvous, fulvescent, fulvid [*rare*]; sallow, lutescent, luteolous, luteous, tawny, cream, creamy, sandy; xanthic, xanthous; jaundiced; auricomous, ocherous *or* ochreous, ochery *or* ochry, flaxen, yellowish, buff, écru; icterine, icteritious *or* icteritous, icteroid; xanthochroid, yellow complexioned.

gold–, saffron–, citron–, lemon–, sulphur–, amber–, straw–, primrose–, cream-colored; xanthocarpous, xanthopous [*bot., rare*].

yellow as a -quincy, –crow's foot; yellow as saffron.

437. Purple

n. **purple** etc. *adj.;* blue and red, bishop's purple; gridelin, amethyst; damson, heliotrope; purpure [*her.*].

lividness, lividity.

v. **render purple** etc. *adj.;* purple, empurple.

adj. **purple**, violet, plum-colored, lavender, lilac, puce, mauve, purplish, purpurate [*archaic*], violaceous, hyacinthine, amethystine, magenta, solferino, heliotrope; livid.

438. Blueness

n. **blue** etc. *adj.;* garter-blue; watchet [*obs.*]; blueness, bluishness; bloom.

[comparisons] *lapis lazuli* [*L.*], sapphire, turquoise; indicolite.

[pigments] ultramarine, smalt, cobalt, cyanogen; Prussian-, syenite- blue; bice, indigo; zaffer.

v. **render blue** etc. *adj.;* blue.

adj. **blue**, azure, cerulean, cyanic; sky-blue, sky-colored, sky-dyed; navy blue, midnight blue, cadet blue, robin's-egg blue, baby blue, ultramarine, aquamarine, electric blue *or* electric, steel blue *or* steel; cerulescent; bluish; atmospheric, retiring; cold.

439. Orange

n. **orange**, red and yellow; old gold; gold color etc. *adj.*

[pigments] ocher *or* ochre, Mars orange, cadmium.

v. **gild**, engild, deaurate [*rare*], warm.

adj. **orange**; ocherous *or* ochreous, ochery *or* ochry; henna, burnt orange; orange-, gold-, brass-, apricot- colored; warm, hot, glowing, flame-colored.

440. Variegation

n. **variegation**; dichroism, trichroism; iridescence, irisation, play of colors, polychrome, maculation, spottiness, striae.

[comparisons] spectrum, rainbow, iris, tulip, peacock, chameleon, butterfly, zebra, leopard, jaguar, panther, cheetah, ocelot, ophite, nacre, mother-of-pearl, tortoise shell; opal, cymophane, marble; mackerel, mackerel sky; harlequin; Joseph's coat; tricolor.

check, plaid, tartan, patchwork; marquetry, parquet, parquetry, mosaic, tesserae, tessellation, checkerwork; chessboard, checkers *or* chequers.

v. **variegate**, stripe, streak, checker *or* chequer, fleck, bespeckle, speckle, besprinkle, sprinkle; stipple, maculate, dot, bespot; tattoo, inlay, tessellate. damascene; embroider, braid, quilt. be variegated etc. *adj.*

adj. **variegated** etc. *v.;* many-colored, many-hued; divers-colored, party-colored *or* parti-colored,

dichromatic, polychromatic; bicolor, tricolor; versi-color; of all the colors of the rainbow, of all manner of colors; kaleidoscopic, naevose *or* nevose, daedal.

iridescent, opaline, opalescent, prismatic, nacreous, pearly, shot, *gorge-de-pigeon* [*F.*], chatoyant; irised, irisated, pavonine; tortoise-shell.

mottled, pied, piebald, skewbald; motley, marbled, pepper-and-salt, paned, dappled, clouded, cymophanous.

checkered *or* chequered, mosaic, tessellated, plaid.

spotted, spotty; punctate *or* punctuated [*rare*], powdered; speckled etc. *v.;* freckled, flea-bitten, studded; flecked, fleckered.

striated, barred, veined; brinded, brindled, tabby; watered; strigose, strigillose, strigate, striolate; listed; embroidered etc. *v.*

441. Vision

n. **vision**, sight, optics, eyesight.

view, look, espial, glance, ken, *coup d'oeil* [*F.*]; glimpse, glint, peep, peek; gaze, stare, leer; perlustration [*rare*], contemplation; conspection [*obs.*], conspectuity [*obs.*]; regard, survey; inspection, introspection; reconnoissance, reconnaissance, speculation, watch, espionage, *espionnage* [*F.*]; autopsy; ocular -inspection, -demonstration; sight-seeing, globe-trotting.

viewpoint, standpoint, point of view; gazebo, loophole, belvedere, watchtower.

field of view; theater *or* theatre, amphitheater *or* amphitheatre, arena, vista, horizon; commanding view, bird's-eye view, panoramic view.

visual organ, organ of vision; eye; naked eye, unassisted eye; retina, pupil, iris, cornea, white; optics, orbs; saucer-, goggle-, gooseberry-eyes.

short sight etc. 443; clear-, sharp-, quick-, eagle-, piercing-, penetrating-sight, -glance, -eye; perspicacity, discernment; catopsis.

[comparison] eagle, hawk; cat, lynx, weasel; Argus.

evil eye, blighting glance; basilisk, cockatrice.

[optical devices] spectacles, eyeglass, lorgnette, monocle, reading glass, field glass, opera glass; telescope etc. 445; microscope, periscope.

v. **see**, behold, discern, perceive, have in sight, descry, sight, make out, discover, distinguish, recognize, spy, espy, ken [*archaic*]; get-, have-, catch- a -sight, -glimpse -of; command a view of; witness, contemplate, speculate; cast-, set-the eyes on; be a spectator of etc. 444; look on etc. (*be present*) 186; see sights etc. 455; see at a glance etc. 498.

look, view, eye; lift up the eyes, open one's eye; look -at, −on, −upon, −over, −about one, −round; survey, scan, inspect; run the eye -over, −through; reconnoiter *or* reconnoitre, glance- round, −on, −over; turn−, bend- one's looks upon; direct the eyes to, turn the eyes on, cast a glance.

observe etc. (*attend to*) 457; watch etc. (*care*) 459; see with one's own eyes; watch for etc. (*expect*) 507; peep, peek, peer, pry, take a peep; play at bopeep.

look full in the face, look hard at, look intently; strain one's eyes; fix−, rivet- the eyes upon; stare, gaze; pore over, gloat on, gloat over; leer, ogle, glare; goggle; cock the eye, squint, gloat, look askance *or* askant.

adj. **ocular**; seeing etc. *v.;* visual, optic *or* optical; ophthalmic.

clear-sighted etc. *n.;* clear-eyed, far-sighted; eagle−, hawk−, lynx−, keen−, Argus-eyed.

visible etc. 446.

adv. **visibly** etc. 446; in sight of, with one's eyes open.

at sight, at first sight, at a glance, at the first blush; *prima facie* [*L.*].

int. **look**! etc. (*attention*) 457.

442. Blindness

n. **blindness**, sightlessness, benightedness, anopsia *or* anopsy, cecity, excecation [*obs.*], cataract, ablepsia *or* ablepsy [*rare*], prestriction [*obs.*]; dim-sightedness etc. 443; amaurosis, *gutta serena* ["drop serene" *of Milton*], teichopsia.

[type for the blind] Braille *or* Braille type, New York point, Gall's serrated type, Howe's American type *or* Boston type, Moon's type; Alston's Glasgow type, Lucas's type, Frere's type; string alphabet, writing stamps, noctograph.

v. **be blind** etc. *adj.;* not see; lose sight of; have the eyes bandaged; grope in the dark.

not look; close−, shut−, turn away−, avert- the eyes; look another way; wink etc. (*limited vision*) 443; shut the eyes to, be blind to; wink at, blink at.

render blind etc. *adj.;* excecate [*obs.*], blind, blindfold; hoodwink, dazzle; put one's eyes out; throw dust into one's eyes; *jeter de la poudre aux yeux* [*F.*]; screen from sight etc. (*hide*) 528.

adj. **blind**; eyeless, sightless, visionless; dark; stone-blind, stark-blind, sand-blind [*archaic*]; undiscerning; dimsighted etc. 443.

blind as -a bat, −a buzzard, −a beetle, −a mole, −an owl; wall-eyed.

blinded etc. *v.*

adv. **blindly**, blindfold; darkly.

443. Dim-sightedness
[imperfect vision]

n. dim−, dull−, half−, short−, near−, long−, double−, astigmatic−, failing- sight; dim etc. -sightedness; purblindness, monocularity, blearedness, lippitude; myopia, presbyopia; confusion of vision; astigmatism; color blindness, chromato-pseudoblepsis, Daltonism; day blindness, hemeralopia; snow blindness; xanthocyanopia *or* xanthocyanopsia; ophthalmia; cataract; nyctalopia, moon blindness.

squint, cross-eye, strabismus, strabism, nystagmus; cast in the eye, swivel eye, cockeye, goggle-eyes; obliquity of vision.

winking etc. *v.;* nictitation, nictation; blinkard, albino.

dizziness, swimming, scotomy *or* scotoma [*med.*].

[limitation of vision] blinker, blinder; screen etc. (*hider*) 530.

[fallacies of vision] *deceptio visus* [*L.*]; refraction, distortion, illusion, false light, anamorphosis, virtual image, spectrum, mirage, looming, phasma [*obs.*]; phantasm, phantasma, phantom; vision; specter *or* spectre, apparition, ghost; *ignis fatuus* [*L.*] etc. (*luminary*) 423; specter of the Brocken; magic mirror; magic lantern etc. (*show*) 448; mirror, lens etc. (*instrument*) 445.

v. **be dim-sighted** etc. *n.;* see double; "see men as trees walking" [*Bible*]; have a mote in the eye, have a mist before the eyes, have a film over the eyes; see through a -prism, −glass darkly; wink, blink, nictitate, nictate; squint; look askance *or* askant, screw up the eyes, glare, glower.

dazzle, glare, swim, blur, loom.

adj. **dim-sighted** etc., myopic, nearsighted, shortsighted; presbyopic; astigmatic; moon−, blear−, goggle−, gooseberry−, one- eyed; blind of one eye, monoculous *or* monocular *or* monoculate; half-blind, purblind; cockeyed [*colloq.*], dim-eyed, mole-eyed, mope-eyed [*obs.*]; dichroic.

blind as a bat etc. (*blind*) 442; winking etc. *v.*

444. Spectator

n. **spectator**, beholder, observer, looker-on, onlooker, *assistant* [*F.*], viewer, gazer, witness, eye-witness, bystander, passer-by; sightseer; rubberneck.

spy, scout; sentinel etc. (*warning*) 668.

grandstand [*fig.*], bleachers, gallery, the gods [*slang*].

v. **witness,** behold etc. (*see*) 441; look on etc. (*be present*) 186; rubber *or* rubberneck.

445. Optical Instruments

n. **optical instruments**; lens, meniscus, magnifier; microscope, simple microscope *or* single microscope, compound microscope, projecting microscope, ultramicroscope; spectacles, glasses, barnacles [*colloq., Eng.*], gig lamps [*slang*], goggles, eyeglass, *pince-nez* [*F.*]; periscopic lens; telescope, glass, teinoscope, prism telescope; lorgnette, binocular; spyglass, opera glass, field glass; burning glass, convex lens.

prism; camera, hand camera, kodak [*trade name*], moving-picture machine; camera-lucida, camera-obscura; magic lantern etc. (*show*) 448; megascope; stereopticon; chromatrope, thaumatrope; stereoscope, pseudoscope, polyscope, kaleidoscope, kaleidophon *or* kaleidophone.

photometer, optometer, eriometer, actinometer, lucimeter, radiometer; abdominoscope, gastroscope, helioscope, polariscope, polemoscope, spectroscope, spectrometer.

mirror, reflector, speculum; looking-glass, pier-glass, cheval-glass; hand mirror.

optics, optician; photography, photographer; optometry, optometrist; abdominoscopy; gastroscopy; microscopy, microscopist.

446. Visibility

n. **visibility,** perceptibility, perceivability; conspicuousness, distinctness etc. *adj.;* conspicuity [*rare*]; appearance etc. 448; basset [*geol.*]; exposure; manifestation etc. 525; ocular-proof, –evidence, –demonstration; field of view etc. (*vision*) 441; periscopism.

v. **be** *or* **become visible** etc. *adj.;* appear, open to the view; meet–, catch-the eye; basset [*geol.*], crop out; present–, show–, manifest–, produce–, discover–, reveal–, expose–, betray-itself; stand forth, stand out; materialize; show; arise; peep out, peer out; start up, spring up, show up [*colloq.*], turn up, crop up; glimmer, gleam, glitter, glow, loom; glare; burst forth; burst upon the -view, –sight; heave in sight [*naut. or colloq.*]; come in sight, come into view, come out, come forth, come forward; see the light of day; break through the clouds; make its appearance, show its face, appear to one's eyes,

come upon the stage, float before the eyes, speak for itself etc. (*manifest*) 525; attract the attention etc. 457; reappear; live in a glass house.

expose to view etc. 525.

adj. **visible,** perceptible, perceivable, discernible, apparent; in view, in full view, in sight; exposed to view, *en évidence* [*F.*]; unclouded.

distinct, plain, clear, definite; obvious etc. (*manifest*) 525; well-defined, well-marked; in focus; recognizable, palpable, autoptic *or* autoptical; glaring, staring, conspicuous; stereoscopic *or* stereoscopical; in bold relief, in strong relief, in high relief.

periscopic *or* periscopical, panoramic.

adv. **before one**; under one's -nose, –very eyes; before–, under- one's eyes; *à vue d'oeil* [*F.*], in one's eye, *oculis subjecta fidelibus* [*L.*]; visibly etc. *adj.;* in sight of; *veluti in speculum* [*L.*].

447. Invisibility

n. **invisibility,** invisibleness, nonappearance, imperceptibility; indistinctness etc. *adj.;* mystery, delitescence *or* delitescency.

concealment etc. 528; latency etc. 526.

v. **be invisible** etc. *adj.;* be hidden etc. (*hide*) 528; lurk etc. (*lie hidden*) 526; escape notice.

render invisible etc. *adj.;* conceal etc. 528; put out of sight.

not see etc. (*be blind*) 442; lose sight of.

adj. **invisible,** imperceptible; undiscernible, indiscernible; unapparent, nonapparent; out of sight, not in sight; *à perte de vue* [*F.*], behind the -scenes, –curtain; viewless, sightless; unconspicuous, inconspicuous; unseen etc. (*see see* etc. 441); covert etc. (*latent*) 526; eclipsed, under an eclipse.

indistinct; dim etc. (*faint*) 422; mysterious, dark, obscure, confused; indistinguishable, undiscernible *or* undiscernable, shadowy, indefinite, undefined; ill-defined, ill-marked; blurred, blurry, fuzzy, out of focus; misty etc. (*opaque*) 426; veiled etc. (*concealed*) 528; delitescent.

448. Appearance

n. **appearance,** phenomenon, sight, spectacle, show, premonstration [*obs.*], scene, species, view, *coup d'oeil* [*F.*]; lookout, outlook, prospect, vista, perspective, bird's-eye view, scenery, landscape, seascape, picture, tableau; display, exposure, *mise en scène* [*F.*], rising of the curtain.

phantasm, phantom etc. (*fallacy of vision*) 443.

spectacle, pageant; peep show, raree-show, galanty (*or* gallanty) show; *ombres chinoises* [*F.*]; magic lantern, phantasmagoria, dissolving views; biograph, cinematograph, cinema, moving pictures, movies, photoplay, photodrama; panorama, diorama, cosmorama, georama; *coup de théâtre* [*F.*], *jeu de théâtre* [*F.*]; pageantry etc. (*ostentation*) 882; insignia etc. (*indication*) 550.

aspect, angle, phase, phasis, seeming; shape etc. (*form*) 240; guise, look, complexion, color, image, mien, air, cast, carriage, port, demeanor; presence, expression, first blush, face of the thing; point of view, light.

lineament, feature, trait, lines; outline, outside; contour, silhouette, face, countenance, visage, phiz [*colloq.*], cast of countenance, profile, *tournure* [*F.*], cut of one's jib [*colloq.*], outside etc. 220.

physiognomy, metoposcopy, phrenology; physiognomist, metoposcopist, phrenologist.

v. **appear**; be *or* become visible etc., 446; seem, look, show; present–, wear–, carry–, have–, bear–, exhibit–, take–, take on–, assume- the -appearance, –semblance- of; look like; cut a

figure, figure; present to the view; show etc. (*make manifest*) 525.

adj. **apparent**, seeming, ostensible; on view.

adv. **apparently**; to all seeming, to all appearance; ostensibly, seemingly, as it seems, on the face of it, *prima facie* [*L.*]; at the first blush, at first sight; in the eyes of; to the eye.

449. Disappearance

n. **disappearance**, evanescence, eclipse, occultation; insubstantiality.

departure etc. 293; exit; vanishing, vanishment, vanishing point; dissolving views.

v. **disappear**, vanish, dissolve, fade, melt away, pass, go, avaunt [*obs.*]; be gone etc. *adj.;* leave no trace, "leave not a rack behind" [*Tempest*]; go off the stage etc. (*depart*) 293; suffer–, undergo-an eclipse; retire from sight; be lost to view, be lost to sight, see no longer, fade away [*slang*], pass out of sight.

lose sight of.

efface etc. 552.

adj. **disappearing** etc. *v.;* evanescent; missing, lost; lost to sight, lost to view; gone.

int. **vanish!** disappear! fade! [*slang*], beat it! [*slang*], avaunt! etc. (*ejection*) 297.

Class 4. Intellect
Division 1. Formation of Ideas

Section 1. Operations of Intellect in General

450. Intellect

n. **intellect**, mind, understanding, reason, thinking principle; rationality; cogitative–, cognitive–, discursive–, reasoning–, intellectual-faculties; faculties, senses, consciousness, observation, percipience *or* percipiency, apperception, mentality, intelligence, intellection [*obs.*], intuition, association of ideas, instinct, conception, judgment, wits, parts, capacity, intellectuality, genius; brains, cognitive–, intellectual-powers; wit etc. 498; ability etc. (*skill*) 698; wisdom etc. 498; *Vernunft* [*Ger.*], *Verstand* [*Ger.*].

ego, soul, spirit, ghost [*archaic*], inner man, heart, breast, bosom, *penetralia mentis* [*L.*], *divina particula aurae* [*L.*], *anima divina* [*L.*], heart's

core; psyche, pneuma, subconscious self, subliminal consciousness, supreme principle, the Absolute.

seat of thought, organ of thought, sensorium, sensory, brain; head, headpiece; pate [*colloq.*], noodle [*colloq.*], noddle [*slang*], skull, pericranium, cerebrum, cranium, brain pan, brain box, brain case, sconce [*colloq.*], upper story [*colloq.*].

[science of mind] metaphysics; philosophy etc. 451; psychics; pneumatology, psychology, psychogenesis; noölogy, noöscopics, ideology; mental–, moral-philosophy; philosophy of the mind.

phrenology; craniology, cranioscopy; psychometry, psychophysics, psycho-analysis.

ideality, idealism; transcendentalism, immateriality etc. 317; universal -concept, –conception; mahat [*theos.*].

psychical research; telepathy, thought transference, thought reading; clairaudience; clairvoyance, mediumship; spiritualism etc. 992*a*.

metaphysician, philosopher, psychiatrist, psychologist, psychometer, psychopath, psychophysicist psychotherapist; psychic, medium, spiritist; adept, mahatma, yogi [*Hinduism*].

v.   **reason**, understand, think, reflect, cogitate, excogitate, conceive. judge, contemplate, meditate; ruminate etc. (*think*) 451.

note, notice, mark; take -notice, −cognizance- of; be aware of, be conscious of; realize; appreciate; fancy etc. (*imagine*) 515.

adj. **[relating to intellect]** intellectual, mental, rational, endowed with reason; subjective, noöscopic, psychological; cerebral; percipient, appercipient, animastic; brainy [*colloq.*].

hyperphysical, superphysical; subconscious, subliminal; telepathic, clairaudient, clairvoyant; psychic *or* psychical, spiritual, ghostly; metaphysical, transcendental.

immaterial etc. 317.

450a. Absence or want of Intellect

n.   **absence of intellect**, want of intellect etc. 450; apartments to let [*slang*], nobody home [*slang*], nobody home upstairs [*slang*], *non compos mentis* [*L.*], unintellectuality; imbecility etc. 499; brutality, brute instinct, brute force.

adj. unendowed with−, void of- reason; unintelligent etc. (*imbecile*) 499.

451. Thought

n.   **thought**; exercitation−, exercise- of the intellect; intellection; reflection, cogitation, consideration, meditation, study, lucubration, speculation, deliberation, pondering; head work, brainwork; cerebration; mentation, deep reflection; close study, application etc. (*attention*) 457.

association−, succession−, flow−, train−, current- of -thought, −ideas.

mature thought; afterthought, reconsideration, second thoughts; retrospection etc. (*memory*) 505; excogitation; examination etc. (*inquiry*) 461; invention etc. (*imagination*) 515.

thoughtfulness etc. *adj.*

abstraction, abstract thought, contemplation, musing; brown study etc. (*inattention*) 458; reverie *or* revery, depth of thought, workings of the mind, thoughts, inmost thoughts; self-counsel, self-communing, self-consultation.

[philosophy] philosophical -opinions, −systems, −schools; the handmaid of theology, *ancilla theologioe* [*L.*].

oriental philosophy: Vedânta *or* Uttara-Mîmâmsâ ["later investigation"]; Pûrva-Mîmâmsâ ["prior investigation"]; Sâmkhyas−, Yoga−, Nyâya−, Vaisheshika- philosophy.

greek and greco-roman philosophy: Ionian−, Pythagorean−, Eleatic- school; Atomism; Sophism *or* Sophistic philosophy.

Socratic−, Megarian *or* Eristic−, Elean- school; Cynic philosophy; Cyrenaic *or* Hedonistic school, Hedonism; Platonism; philosophy of the -Absolute, −Academy; Aristotelianism, philosophy of the Lyceum; Peripatetic school [historical formula: *concept, Idea, essence*].

Stoic philosophy, Stoicism, philosophy of the Porch; Epicureanism, philosophy of the Garden; Scepticism; Eclecticism.

Neo-Phythagoreanism; Neo-Platonism.

patristic philosophy: Gnosticism, Manicheism; Alexandrian school; philosophy of the Ante-Nicene Fathers, philosophy of the Post-Nicene Fathers.

scholastic philosophy: Scholasticism; Eclecticism; Mysticism, Mystic philosophy; Pantheistic school, pantheism; Thomism, Scotism, voluntarism; Averroism.

modern philosophy: Post-Reformation philosophy; Humanism, rationalism, political philosophy; Cartesianism; Spinozism; empiricism, moralism; idealistic philosophy, idealism; Leibnitzianism *or* Leibnizianism, Berkeleian philosophy, Berkeleyism; pan-phenomenalism.

modern German philosophy: Kantianism, Fichteanism, Schelling's philosophy, Hegelianism, Herbartianism, Schopenhauer's philosophy; neocriticism; Freudianism, Freudian theory; Einstein theory, relativism.

modern French philosophy: traditionalism; psychologico-spiritualistic school; Positivism; sociological school; Bergsonism.

modern English philosophy: associational psychology, utilitarianism, Darwinism, evolutionistic ethics; Spencerian philosophy; agnosticism, idealism, Neo-Hegelianism.

modern Italian philosophy: Vicoism, sensism, empiricism, criticism, idealism, ontologism, Neo-Scholasticism.

American philosophy: Transcendentalism, pragmatism, neo-voluntarism, new ethical movement; Neo-Hegelianism, Neo-Hegelian movement.

v. **think,** reflect, cogitate, excogitate, consider, reason, deliberate; bestow -thought, –consideration -upon; speculate, contemplate, meditate, ponder, muse, dream, ruminate; brood over, con over, study; mouse over, mull over, sweat over [*colloq.*]; bend–, apply- the mind etc. (*attend*) 457; digest, discuss, hammer at, hammer out, weigh, perpend [*archaic*]; realize, appreciate; fancy etc. (*imagine*) 515; trow [*archaic*].

rack–, ransack–, crack–, beat–, cudgel- one's brains; set one's -brain, –wits- to work; cerebrate, mentalize [*rare*].

harbor–, entertain–, cherish–, nurture- an idea etc. 453, take into one's head; bear in mind; reconsider.

take into consideration; take counsel etc. (*be advised*) 695; commune with oneself, bethink oneself; collect one's thoughts; revolve–, turn over–, run over-in the mind; chew the cud upon [*colloq.*], sleep upon; take counsel of–, advise with- one's pillow.

suggest itself, present itself, occur; come–, get-into one's head; strike one, flit across the view, come uppermost, run in one's head; enter–, pass in–, cross, –, flash on–, flash across–, float in–, fasten itself on–, be uppermost in–, occupy- the mind; have in one's mind.

make an impression; sink–, penetrate- into the mind; engross the thoughts.

adj. **thoughtful,** pensive, meditative, reflective, cogitative, excogitative, museful, wistful, contemplative, speculative, deliberative, studious, sedate, introspective, Platonic, philosophical; thinking etc. *v.*

under consideration, in contemplation, under advisement.

absorbed, rapt; lost in thought etc. (*inattentive*) 458; engrossed in etc. (*intent*) 457.

adv. all things considered, taking everything into -account, –consideration.

452. Incogitance
[absence or want of thought]

n. **incogitance** *or* incogitancy, vacancy, inunderstanding, vacancy of mind, poverty of intellect etc. 499; thoughtlessness etc. (*inattention*) 458; inanity, fatuity, vacuity.

v. **not think** etc. 451; not think of; dismiss from the -mind, –thoughts etc. 451.

indulge in reverie etc. (*be inattentive*) 458.

put away thought; unbend–, relax–, divert- the mind; make the mind a blank, let the mind lie fallow.

adj. **vacant,** inane, unintellectual, nonunderstanding, unideal, unoccupied, unthinking, incogitant, incogitative, unreasoning, inconsiderate, thoughtless; absent etc. (*inattentive*) 458; diverted; irrational etc. 499; narrow-minded etc. 481.

unthought of, undreamt of, unconsidered; off one's mind; incogitable, inconceivable, not to be thought of.

453. Idea
[object of thought]

n. **idea,** notion, conception, thought, apprehension, impression, perception, image, eidolon, sentiment, reflection, observation, consideration; abstract idea; archetype, formative notion; guiding–, organizing- conception; image in the mind, regulative principle.

view etc. (*opinion*) 484; theory etc. 514; conceit, fancy; phantasy etc. (*imagination*) 515.

viewpoint, point of view; aspect etc. 448; field of view.

454. Topic
[subject of thought]

n. **subject of thought,** material for thought; food for the mind, mental pabulum.

subject, subject matter; matter, *motif* [*F.*], theme, *noemata* [*Gr.*], topic, what it is about, thesis, text, business, affair, matter in hand, argument; motion, resolution; head, chapter; case, point; proposition, theorem; field of inquiry; moot point, debatable point, point at issue, point in question; problem etc. (*question*) 461.

v. float–, pass- in the mind etc. 451.

adj. **thought of;** uppermost in the mind; *in petto* [*It.*].

adv. **under consideration,** under advisement; in question, in the mind; at issue, up for discussion, before the house, on foot, on the docket, on the carpet, on the tapis, *sur le tapis* [*F.*]; relative to etc. 9.

Section 2. Precursory Conditions and Operations

455. Curiosity
[desire of knowledge]

n. **curiosity,** curiousness; interest, thirst for knowledge, mental acquisitiveness; newsmongery, inquiring mind; inquisitiveness.

questioner, *enfant terrible* [*F.*], walking question mark [*humorous*], quidnunc.

busybody, newsmonger; Peeping Tom, Paul Pry, eavesdropper; gossip etc. (*news*) 532.

sight-seer, rubberneck.

v. **be curious** etc. *adj.;* take an interest in, stare, gape; prick up the ears, see sights, lionize; rubber *or* rubberneck.

pry, nose, search, ferret out, poke one's nose into.

adj. **curious**, inquisitive, burning with curiosity, over-curious, nosey [*colloq.*]; inquiring etc. 461; prying; inquisitorial; agape etc. (*expectant*) 507.

456. Incuriosity
[absence of curiosity]

n. **incuriosity**; incuriousness etc. *adj.;* apathy, insouciance etc. 866; indifference.

v. **be incurious** etc. *adj.;* have no curiosity etc. 455; be bored by, take no interest in etc. 823; mind one's own business, pursue the even tenor of one's way, glance neither to the right hand nor to the left.

adj. **incurious**, uninquisitive, indifferent; impassive etc. 823; uninterested, bored.

457. Attention

n. **attention**; mindfulness etc. *adj.;* intentness, intentiveness [*rare*]; alertness; thought etc. 451; advertence *or* advertency; observance, observation; consideration, reflection, perpension [*obs.*]; heed; heedfulness; particularity; notice, regard etc. *v.;* circumspection etc. (*care*) 459; study, scrutiny; inspection, introspection; revision, revisal.

active-, diligent-, exclusive-, minute-, close-, intense-, deep-, profound-, abstract-, labored-, deliberate- -thought, -attention, -application, -study.

absorption of mind etc. (*abstraction*) 458.

minuteness, meticulosity, meticulousness, finicality, finicalness; circumstantiality, attention to detail.

indication, calling attention to etc. *v.*

v. **be attentive** etc. *adj.;* attend, advert to, observe, look, see, view, remark, notice, regard, take notice, mark; give-, pay- -attention, -heed- to; know what time it is [*colloq.*], know the time of day [*colloq.*]; incline-, lend- an ear to; trouble one's head about; give a thought to, animadvert; occupy oneself with; contemplate etc. (*think of*) 451; look -at, -to, -after, -into, -over; see to; turn-, bend-, apply-, direct-, give- the -mind, -eye, -attention -to; have an eye to, have in one's eye; bear in mind; take into -account, -consideration; keep in -sight, -view; have regard to, heed, mind, take cogni-

zance of, entertain, recognize; make-, take-note of; note.

examine, -closely, -intently; scan, scrutinize, consider; give-, bend- one's mind to; overhaul, revise, pore over; inspect, review, pass under review; take stock of; get the gist of; fix-, rivet-, devote- the -eye, -mind, -thoughts, -attention- on *or* to; hear out, think out; mind one's business, attend to one's business.

examine cursorily; glance -at, -upon, -over; cast-, pass- the eyes over; run over, turn over the leaves, dip into, perstringe [*obs.*]; skim etc. (*neglect*) 460; take a cursory view of.

revert to, hark back to; watch etc. (*expect*) 507, (*take care of*) 459; hearken *or* harken to, listen to; prick up the ears; have-, keep- the eyes open; come to the point.

meet with attention; fall under one's -notice, -observation; be under consideration etc. (*topic*) 454.

catch-, strike- the eye; attract notice; catch-, awaken-, wake-, invite-, solicit-, attract-, claim-, excite-, engage-, occupy-, strike-, arrest-, fix-, engross-, absorb-, rivet- the -attention, -mind, -thoughts; be present to the mind, be uppermost in the mind.

call attention to, bring under one's notice; point -out, -to, -at, -the finger at; lay the finger on, indigitate [*obs.*], indicate; direct attention to; show; put a mark upon etc. (*sign*) 550; call soldiers to "attention"; bring forward etc. (*make manifest*) 525.

adj. **attentive**, mindful, heedful, intentive [*rare*], advertent, all eyes and ears, observant, regardful; alive to, awake to; on the job [*colloq.*]; there with the goods [*colloq.*], with it [*slang*]; observing etc. *v.;* alert; taken up with, occupied with; engaged in, engrossed in, wrapped in; absorbed, rapt; breathless; preoccupied etc. (*inattentive*) 458; watchful etc. (*careful*) 459; intent on, all eyes [*colloq.*], open-eyed; breathless, undistracted, upon the stretch; on the watch etc. (*expectant*) 507.

steadfast etc. (*persevering*) 604a.

int. **see**! look! look you! look to it! mark! lo! behold! soho! hark! hark ye! mind! look out! look alive! [*colloq.*]; look here! [*colloq.*]; halloo! observe! lo and behold! attention! *nota bene* [*L.*]; **n.b.;** ★, †; I'd have you know! notice! O yes! Oyez! *dekko!* [*Hind.*], *ecco!* [*It.*], yo-ho! ho!

458. Inattention

n. **inattention**, inconsideration, want of consideration; inconsiderateness etc. *adj.;* oversight; in-

141

advertence *or* inadvertency, nonobservance, disregard.

supineness etc. (*inactivity*) 683; *étourderie* [*F.*]; want of thought; heedlessness etc. (*neglect*) 460; insouciance etc. (*indifference*) 866.

abstraction; absence of mind, absorption of mind; preoccupation, distraction, reverie *or* revery, brown study [*colloq.*], woolgathering, moonraking [*dial. Eng.*], pipe dream [*colloq.*], castle in the air, *château en Espagne* [*F.*], fancy, deep musing, fit of abstraction.

v. **be inattentive** etc. *adj.;* overlook, disregard; pass by etc. (*neglect*) 460; not observe etc. 457; think little of.

close–, shut- one's eyes to; pay no attention to; dismiss–, discard–, discharge- from one's -thoughts, –mind; drop the subject, think no more of; set–, turn–, put- aside: turn away from, turn one's attention from, turn a deaf ear to, turn one's back upon.

abstract oneself, dream, be somewhere else, be absent, be woolgathering, indulge in reverie *or* revery.

escape notice, escape attention; come in at one ear and go out at the other; forget etc. (*have no remembrance*) 506.

call off–, draw off–, call away–, divert–, distract- the -attention, –thoughts, –mind; put out of one's head.

confuse, disconcert, discompose, put out, perplex, bewilder, moider [*dial. Eng.*], fluster, flurry, rattle [*colloq.*], muddle, dazzle.

adj. **inattentive**; unobservant, unmindful, unheeding, undiscerning; inadvertent; mindless, regardless, respectless; listless etc. (*indifferent*) 866; blind, deaf; hen-headed [*colloq.*], flighty, giddy-pated, giddy-headed, bird-witted; hand over head [*rare*]; cursory, percursory [*rare*], volatile, scatter-brained, hare-brained; unreflecting, *écervelé* [*F.*], inconsiderate, offhand, thoughtless, dizzy, muzzy [*colloq.*], brainsick; giddy, –as a goose; wild, harum-scarum [*colloq.*], rantipole, heedless, careless etc. (*neglectful*) 460.

abstracted, absent, *distrait* [*F.*], woolgathering, moonraking [*dial. Eng.*], dazed, absent-minded, lost; lost–, wrapped- in thought; rapt, in the clouds, bemused, day-dreaming; dreaming of–, musing on- other things; preoccupied, engrossed etc. (*attentive*) 457; in a reverie etc. *n.;* off one's guard etc. (*inexpectant*) 508; napping; dreamy; caught napping.

disconcerted, put out etc. *v.;* rattled [*colloq.*].

adv. **inattentively**, inadvertently etc. *adj.;* per incuriam [*L.*], sub silentio [*L.*].

459. Care

[vigilance]

n. **care**, solicitude, heed, concern, reck [*poetic*], heedfulness etc. *adj.;* scruple etc. (*conscientiousness*) 939.

vigilance; watchfulness etc. *adj.;* surveillance, eyes of a lynx, eyes of Argus, watch, vigil, lookout, watch and ward, *l'oeil du maître* [*F.*].

espionage etc. (*reconnoitering*) 461; invigilation, watching.

alertness etc. (*activity*) 682; attention etc. 457; prudence etc., circumspection etc. (*caution*) 864; anxiety; forethought etc. 510; precaution etc. (*preparation*) 673; tidiness etc. (*order*) 58, (*cleanliness*) 652; accuracy etc. (*exactness*) 494; minuteness, meticulousness, meticulosity, circumstantiality, attention to detail.

watcher, watchdog etc. 664.

v. **be careful** etc. *adj.;* reck [*archaic*]; take care etc. (*be cautious*) 864; pay attention to etc. 457; take care of; look–, see- -to, –after; keep an eye upon, keep a sharp eye upon; chaperon, matronize, play gooseberry; keep watch, keep watch and ward; mount guard, set watch, watch; keep in -sight, –view; mind, mind one's business.

look sharp, look about one; look with one's own eyes; keep a -good, –sharp-lookout; have all one's -wits, –eyes-about one; watch for etc. (*expect*) 507; keep one's eyes open, have the eyes open, sleep with one eye open; catch a weasel asleep.

do one's best etc. 682; mind one's Ps and Qs [*colloq.*], speak by the card, pick one's steps.

take precautions etc. 673; protect etc. (*render safe*) 664.

adj. **careful**, regardful, heedful; taking care etc. *v.;* particular; prudent etc. (*cautious*) 864; considerate; thoughtful etc. (*deliberative*) 451; provident etc. (*prepared*) 673; alert etc. (*active*) 682; sure-footed.

guarded, on one's guard; on the *-qui vive* [*F.*], –alert, –watch, –lookout; awake, broad awake, vigilant; watchful, wakeful, Argus-eyed, lynx-eyed; wide awake etc. (*intelligent*) 498; on the watch for etc. (*expectant*) 507.

scrupulous etc. (*conscientious*) 939; tidy etc. (*orderly*) 58, (*clean*) 652; accurate etc. (*exact*) 494; *cavendo tutus* [*L.*] etc. (*safe*) 664.

adv. **carefully** etc. *adj.;* with care, gingerly.

460. Neglect

n. **neglect**; carelessness etc. *adj.;* trifling etc. *v.;* negligence; omission, laches [*obs.*], deferment, cunctation, procrastination, default; supineness etc. (*inactivity*) 683; conspiracy of silence; inattention etc. 458; nonchalance etc. (*insensibility*) 823; imprudence, recklessness etc. 863; slovenliness etc. (*disorder*) 59, (*dirt*) 653; improvidence etc. 674; noncompletion etc. 730; inexactness etc. (*error*) 495.

paraleipsis *or* paralipsis *or* paralepsis [*rhet.*].

trifler, waiter on Providence; Micawber; waster [*colloq.*], wastrel [*dial. Eng.*], drifter [*colloq.*], bum [*slang*], hobo, tramp, Knight of the Road [*humorous*], down-and-outer [*colloq.*], deadbeat, dead one [*slang*], stiff [*slang*], roustabout, sundowner [*Australia*]; slacker.

v. **be negligent** etc. *adj.;* take no care of etc. (take care of etc. 459); neglect; let slip, let go; lay–, set–, cast–, put- aside; keep–, leave- out of sight; lose sight of.

delay, defer, procrastinate, postpone, adjourn, pigeonhole, tie up with red tape, shelve, stay, suspend, table, lay on the table.

overlook, disregard; pass over, pass by; let pass; blink; wink at, connive at; gloss over; take no -note, –notice, –thought, –account- of; pay no regard to; *laisser aller* [*F.*].

scamp; trifle, fribble; do by halves; slight etc. (*despise*) 930; play with, trifle with; slur; skimp [*dial. & colloq.*]; skim, –the surface; *effleurer* [*F.*]; take a cursory view of etc. 457; slur–, slip–, skip–, jump- over; pretermit, miss, skip, jump, cut [*colloq.*], omit, push aside, throw into the background, sink.

ignore, refuse to notice, shut one's eyes to, refuse to hear, turn a deaf ear to, leave out of one's calculation; not attend to etc. 457, not mind; not trouble -oneself, –one's head- -with, –about: forget etc. 506.

be caught napping etc. (*not expect*) 508; leave a loose thread; let the grass grow under one's feet.

render neglectful etc. *adj.;* put *or* throw off one's guard.

adj. **neglecting** etc. *v.;* unmindful, negligent, neglectful; heedless, careless, thoughtless, inconsiderate; perfunctory, remiss.

unwary, unwatchful, unguarded, incircumspect [*rare*], uncircumspect, off one's guard, offhand.

supine etc. (*inactive*) 683; inattentive etc. 458; insouciant etc. (*indifferent*) 823; imprudent, reckless etc. 863; slovenly etc. (*disorderly*) 59, (*dirty*) 653; inexact etc. (*erroneous*) 495; improvident etc. 674.

neglected etc. *v.;* unheeded, uncared for, unperceived, unseen, unobserved, unnoticed, unnoted, unmarked, unattended to, unthought of, unregarded, unremarked, unmissed; shunted, shelved.

unexamined, unstudied, unsearched, unscanned, unweighed, unsifted, unexplored.

abandoned; buried in a napkin; hid under a bushel.

adv. **negligently** etc. *adj.;* hand over head [*obs.*], in any old way [*colloq.*], anyhow; in an unguarded moment etc. (*unexpectedly*) 508; *per incuriam* [*L.*]; when the cat is away.

int. **never mind**, no matter, let it pass; it will be all the same a hundred from now; *mañana* [*Sp.*].

461. Inquiry

[subject of inquiry. question]

n. **inquiry**; request etc. 765; search, research, quest; pursuit etc. 622.

examination, review, scrutiny, investigation, indagation [*obs.*]; perquisition, perscrutation [*rare*], pervestigation [*obs.*]; inquest, inquisition; exploration; exploitation, ventilation.

sifting; calculation, analysis, dissection, resolution, induction; Baconian method.

strict–, close–, searching–, exhaustive- inquiry; narrow–, strict-search; study etc. (*consideration*) 451.

scire facias [*L.*], *ad referendum* [*L.*]; trial.

questioning etc. *v.;* interrogation, interrogatory; interpellation; challenge, examination, third degree [*colloq.*], cross-examination, catechism, catechesis; feeler, Socratic method, zetetic philosophy; leading question; discussion etc. (*reasoning*) 476.

reconnoitering, reconnaissance *or* reconnoissance, prying etc. *v.;* espionage, *espionage* [*F.*]; domiciliary visit, peep behind the curtain; lantern of Diogenes.

question, query, problem, poser, desideratum, point to be solved, porism; subject–, field- of -inquiry, –controversy; point–, matter- in dispute; moot point; issue, question at issue; bone of contention etc. (*discord*) 713; plain–, fair–, open- question; enigma etc. (*secret*) 533; knotty point etc. (*difficulty*) 704; *quodlibet* [*L.*]; threshold of an inquiry.

inquirer, investigator, inquisitor, inspector, querist, examiner, probator, catechist; scrutator, scrutineer, scrutinizer; analyst; quidnunc etc. (*curiosity*) 455.

v. **inquire**, seek, search; make inquiry etc. *n.;* look -for, –about for, –out for; scan, reconnoiter *or* reconnoitre, explore, sound, rummage, ransack, pry, peer, look round; look–, go- -over, –through; give the once-over [*slang*]; spy, overhaul.

scratch the head, slap the forehead.

look–, peer–, pry- into every hole and corner; visit–, look- behind the scenes; nose, nose out, trace up; hunt out, fish out, ferret out; unearth; leave no stone unturned.

track, seek a clew *or* clue; hunt, trail, shadow, mouse, dodge, trace; follow the -trail, –scent; pursue etc. 662; beat up one's quarters; fish for; feel for etc. (*experiment*) 463.

investigate; take up–, institute–, pursue–, follow up–, conduct–, carry on–, prosecute- an inquiry etc. *n.;* look at, look into; pre-examine; discuss, canvass, agitate.

examine, mouse over, study, consider, calculate; dip–, dive–, delve–, go deep- into; make sure of, probe, sound, fathom; probe to the -bottom, –quick; scrutinize, analyze, anatomize, dissect, parse, resolve, sift, winnow; view–, try- in all its phases; thresh out.

bring in question, subject to examination, pose; put to the proof etc. (*experiment*) 463; audit, tax, pass in review; take into consideration etc. (*think over*) 451; take counsel etc. 695.

question, ask, demand; put–, propose–, propound–, moot–, start–, raise–, stir–, suggest–, put forth–, ventilate–, grapple with–, go into- a question.

interrogate, put to the question, catechize, pump; cross-question, cross-examine; roast [*colloq.*], grill [*colloq.*], put through the third degree [*colloq.*]; dodge; require an answer; pick–, suck- the brains of; feel the pulse.

be in question etc. *adj.;* undergo examination.

adj. **inquiring** etc. *v.;* inquisitive etc. (*curious*) 455; requisitive [*obs.*], requisitory; catechetical, inquisitorial, analytic; in search of, in quest of; on the lookout for, interrogative, zetetic; all-searching.

undetermined, untried, undecided, tentative; in question, in dispute, in issue, in course of inquiry; under -discussion, –consideration, –investigation etc. *n.;* sub judice [*L.*], moot, proposed; doubtful etc. (*uncertain*) 475.

adv. **what?** why? wherefore? *pourquoi?* [*F.*], *warum?* [*Ger.*], whence? whither? where? *quoere?* [*L.*]; how comes it? how does it happen?

how is it? what is the reason? what's the matter? what's in the wind? what's afoot? what's up? what's in the air? what is it all about? what on earth? when? who? *nicht wahr?* [*Ger.*].

462. Answer

n. **answer**, response, reply, replication, riposte *or* ripost, subjoinder, rejoinder, retort, repartee; rescript, rescription [*archaic*]; antiphon, antiphony; acknowledgment; password; echo; counterstatement, counterblast, countercharge, contradiction.

[*law*] defense, plea, surrebutter, surrejoinder, reply, rejoinder, rebutter.

solution etc. (*explanation*) 522; discovery etc. 480*a;* rationale etc. (*cause*) 153; clew *or* clue etc. (*indication*) 550.

Oedipus; oracle etc. 513; return etc. (*record*) 551.

v. **answer**, respond, reply, rebut, riposte *or* ripost, retort, rejoin; give answer, return for answer; acknowledge, echo.

[*law*] defend, plead, surrebut, surrejoin, rebut, reply.

explain etc. (*interpret*) 522; solve etc. (*unriddle*) 522; discover etc. 480*a;* fathom, hunt out etc. (*inquire*) 461; satisfy, set at rest, determine.

adj. **answering** etc. *v.;* responsive, respondent; antiphonal; Oedipean, oracular; conclusive.

adv. **for this reason**; because etc. (*cause*) 153; on the scent, on the right scent.

int. eureka.

463. Experiment

n. **experiment**; essay etc. (*attempt*) 675; analysis etc. (*investigation*) 461; docimasy, trial, tentative method, *tâtonnement* [*F.*].

verification, probation, *experimentum crucis* [*L.*], proof, criterion, diagnostic, test, crucial test; assay, ordeal.

reagent, crucible, check, touchstone, pyx *or* pix [*Brit. mint*], curcuma paper, turmeric paper.

empiricism, rule of thumb.

feeler; pilot–, messenger- balloon; pilot engine; scout; straw to show the wind.

speculation, random shot, leap in the dark.

experimenter, experimentist, experimentalist, assayer, analyst, analyzer; prospector *or* prospector, Forty-Niner, adventurer; speculator, gambler, stock gambler, plunger [*slang*].

v. **experiment**; essay etc. (*endeavor*) 675; try, assay; make an experiment, make trial of; give a trial to; put upon–, subject to- trial; experiment upon; rehearse; put–, bring–, submit- to the

-test, −proof; prove, verify, test, touch, practice upon, try one's strength.

grope; feel−, grope- -for, −one's way; fumble, *tâtonner* [*F.*], *aller à tâtons* [*F.*]; put−, throw-out a feeler; send up a pilot balloon; see how the -land lies, −wind blows; consult the barometer; feel the pulse; fish for, bob for; cast−, beat-about for; angle, trawl, cast one's net, beat the bushes.

venture; try one's fortune etc. (*adventure*) 675; explore etc. (*inquire*) 461.

adj. **experimental**, probative, probatory, probation-ary; analytic, docimastic *or* docimastical, spec-ulative, tentative; empirical.

tried, tested, proved.

on trial, on examination, on *or* under probation, "on suspicion," under suspicion; on one's trial.

464. Comparison

n. **comparison**, collation, contrast, parallelism, bal-ance; identification; comparative−, relative- es-timate.

simile, similitude, parallelization [*rare*]; allegory etc. (*metaphor*) 521.

v. **compare**, −to, −with; collate, confront; place side by side etc. (*near*) 197; set−, pit- against one another; contrast, balance.

compare notes; institute a comparison; *parva com-ponere magnis* [*L.*].

parallel, parallelize; draw a parallel.

adj. **comparative**, relative, contrastive; metaphorical etc. 521.

compared with etc. *v.;* comparable; judged by comparison.

adv. **relatively** etc. (*relation*) 9; as compared with etc. *v.*

465. Discrimination

n. **discrimination**, distinction, differentiation, di-agnosis, diorism; nice perception; perception−, appreciation- of difference; estimation etc. 466; nicety, refinement; taste etc. 850; critique, judgment; tact; discernment etc. (*intelligence*) 498; acuteness, penetration; *nuances* [*F.*].

tip, pointer, dope [*slang*]; past performances, re-cord.

v. **discriminate**, distinguish, severalize [*obs.*]; sepa-rate; draw the line, sift; separate−, winnow- the chaff from the wheat; separate the wheat from the tares; separate the sheep from the goats; split hairs.

estimate etc. (*measure*) 466; tip, tip off, sum up, criticize; know which is which, know what's what [*colloq.*], know one's way about, know a

thing or two, know what o'clock it is, know the time of day, have cut one's eyeteeth, know the ways of the world [*all colloq.*]; "know a hawk from a handsaw" [*Hamlet*].

take into -account, −consideration; give−, allow-due weight to; weigh carefully.

adj. **discriminating** etc. *v.;* dioristic *or* dioristical [*obs.*], critical, diagnostic, perceptive, dis-criminative, distinctive; nice, acute.

465a. Indiscrimination

n. **indiscrimination**; indistinctness, indistinction; want of distinction, want of discernment, ina-bility to discriminate; uncertainty etc. (*doubt*) 475.

v. **not discriminate** etc. 465; overlook etc. (*ne-glect*) 460- a distinction; confound, confuse, jumble, jumble together, heap indiscriminately; swallow whole, judge in a lump, use loosely.

adj. **indiscriminate**, indistinguishable, lacking dis-tinction, undistinguished, undistinguishable; unmeasured; promiscuous, undiscriminating.

466. Measurement

n. **measurement**, admeasurement, mensuration, metage, survey, valuation, appraisement, as-sessment, assize; estimate, estimation; dead reckoning [*naut.*]; reckoning etc. (*numera-tion*) 85; gauging etc. *v.;* horse power, candle power, candle foot, foot candle, volt ampere, kilowatt; foot pound, foot poundal, foot ton.

metrology, weights and measures, compound arithmetic.

measure, yard measure, standard, rule, foot rule, spirit level, plumb line; square, T-square, steel square, compass, dividers, calipers; gauge *or* gage, standard gauge, broad *or* wide gauge, nar-row gauge; log, log-line, patent log [*naut.*]; meter, line, rod, check.

flood mark, high-water mark, load-line mark, Plimsoll mark; index etc. 550.

scale; graduation, graduated scale; nonius; vernier etc. (*minuteness*) 193; quadrant, theodolite, transit *or* transit theodolite, viagraph; scale, beam, steelyard, weighing machine, balance etc. (*weight*) 319; anemometer etc. (*wind*) 349; ba-rometer etc. (*air*) 338; bathometer etc. (*depth*) 208; dynamometer etc. (*force*) 276; galvanome-ter etc. (*power*) 157; goniometer etc. (*angle*) 244; hyetometer etc. (*fluids in motion*) 348; landmark etc. (*limit*) 233; pedometer etc. (*length*) 200; photometer etc. (*optical instruments*) 445; radi-ometer etc. (*light*) 420; stethoscope etc. (*medi-cal*) 662; thermometer etc. 389.

145

coordinates, ordinate and abscissa, polar coordinates, latitude and longitude, declination and right ascension, altitude and azimuth.

geometry, stereometry, planimetry, hypsometry, altimetry, hypsography, chorometry, chorography, topography, cartography; surveying, land surveying, geodesy, geodetics, geodaesia *or* geodesia, orthometry; cadastre *or* cadaster; cadastral survey, cadastration.

astrolabe, armillary sphere.

surveyor, land surveyor; geometer, chorographer, topographer, cartographer.

v. **measure,** meter, mete; value, assess, rate, appraise, estimate, form an estimate, set a value on; appreciate; standardize.

span, pace, step, inch, dial; caliper, divide, apply the compass etc. *n.;* gauge *or* gage; balance, poise, hold the scales, place in the beam, kick the beam; plumb, probe, sound, fathom; heave the -log, –lead; survey, plot, block in, block out, rule, draw to scale.

take an average etc. 29; graduate, calibrate.

adj. **measuring** etc. *v.;* metric, metrical; measurable; geodetical, cadastral, hypsographic *or* hypsographical, hypsometric *or* hypsometrical, chorographic *or* chorographical, topographic *or* topographical, cartographic *or* cartographical.

Section 3. Materials for Reasoning

467. Evidence
[on one side]

n. **evidence;** facts, premises, data, praecognitum (*pl.* praecognita), grounds; indication etc. 550; criterion etc. (*test*) 463.

testimony, testification; attestation; affirmation, declaration; deposition etc. 535; examination.

authority, warrant, credential, diploma, voucher, certificate, docket; *testamur* [*L.*]; record etc. 551; muniments; document; *pièce justificative* [*F.*]; deed, warranty etc. (*security*) 771; autograph, handwriting, signature, seal etc. (*identification*) 550; exhibit; citation, reference, quotation; admission etc. (*assent*) 488.

witness, indicator, eyewitness, earwitness, deponent; sponsor; cojuror, oath-helper [*hist.*], compurgator [*hist.*].

evidence in chief; oral–, documentary–, hearsay–, external–, extrinsic–, internal–, intrinsic–, circumstantial–, cumulative–, *ex parte* [*L.*]–, presumptive–, collateral–, constructive- evidence; proof etc. (*demonstration*) 478; finger print, thumb print.

secondary evidence; confirmation, corroboration, support; ratification etc. (*assent*) 488; authentication; compurgation [*hist.*], wager of law [*hist.*], comprobation [*obs.*].

writ, summons etc. (*lawsuit*) 696.

v. **be evidence** etc. *n.;* evince, show, betoken, tell of; indicate etc. (*denote*) 550; imply, involve, argue, bespeak, breathe.

have weight, carry weight; tell, speak volumes; speak for itself etc. (*manifest*) 525.

rest upon, depend upon; repose on.

bear witness etc. *n.;* give evidence etc. *n.;* testify, depose, witness, vouch for; sign, seal, undersign, set one's hand and seal, sign and seal, deliver as one's act and deed, certify, attest; acknowledge etc. (*assent*) 488.

confirm, make absolute, ratify, corroborate, indorse *or* endorse, countersign, support, bear out, vindicate, uphold, warrant.

adduce, attest, evidence, cite, quote; refer to, appeal to; call, call to witness; bring forward, bring on, bring into court; allege, plead; produce–, confront- witnesses; collect–, bring together–, rake up- evidence.

establish; have–, make out- a case; authenticate, circumstantiate, substantiate, verify, make good, quote chapter and verse; bring home to, bring to book, bring off.

adj. **evidential;** showing etc. *v.;* indicative, indicatory; deducible etc. 478; grounded on, founded on, based on; first-hand, authentic, verificative, verifiable, veridical, cumulative, corroborative, confirmatory; significant, weighty, overwhelming, damning, conclusive.

oral, documentary, hearsay etc. (*evidence in chief*) *n.*

adv. **by inference;** according to, witness, *a fortiori* [*L.*]; still more, still less; *raison de plus* [*F.*]; in corroboration of etc. *n.;* *valeat quantum* [*L.*]; under seal, under one's hand and seal; at first hand, at second hand.

468. Counterevidence
[evidence on the other side]

n. **counterevidence;** evidence on the other -side, –hand; disproof; refutation etc. 479; negation etc. 536; conflicting evidence.

plea etc. 617; vindication etc. 937; counter-protest; *tu quoque* [*L.*] argument; other side–, reverse- of the shield; *reductio ad absurdum* [*L.*].

v. **countervail**, oppose; rebut etc. (*refute*) 479; subvert etc. (*destroy*) 162; check, weaken; contravene; run counter; contradict etc. (*deny*) 536; tell another story, turn the scale, alter the case; turn the tables; cut both ways; prove a negative. *audire alteram partem* [*L.*].

adj. **countervailing** etc. *v.;* contradictory, in rebuttal.

unattested, unauthenticated, unsupported by evidence; supposititious, trumped up.

adv. **conversely**, on the other hand, on the other side, in opposition; *per contra* [*L.*].

469. Qualification

n. **qualification**, limitation, modification, coloring. **allowance**, grains of allowance, consideration, extenuating circumstances; mitigation. **condition**, proviso, exception; exemption; salvo [*rare*], saving clause; discount etc. 813; restriction.

v. **qualify**, limit, modify, affect, leaven, take color from, give a color to, introduce new conditions, narrow, temper. **allow for**, make allowance for; admit exceptions, take into account; modulate. **take exception**, file exceptions, object, raise objections, rise to a point of order.

adj. **qualifying** etc. *v.;* modificatory, extenuatory, mitigatory, lenitive, palliative; conditional; exceptional etc. (*unconformable*) 83. **hypothetical** etc. (*supposed*) 514; contingent etc. (*uncertain*) 475.

adv. **provided**, –always; if, unless, but, yet; according as; conditionally, admitting, supposing; on the supposition of etc. (*theoretically*) 514; with the understanding, even, although, though, for all that, after all, at all events. **if possible** etc. 470; with grains of allowance, *cum grano salis* [*L.*]; *exceptis excipiendis* [*L.*], wind and weather permitting. **subject to**; with this proviso etc. *n.*

470. Possibility

n. **possibility**, potentiality, potency; what may be, what is possible etc. *adj.;* compatibility etc. (*agreement*) 23. **practicability**, feasibility, workability, workableness; practicableness etc. *adj.* **contingency**, chance etc. 156.

v. **be possible** etc. *adj.;* stand a chance; have a leg to stand on; admit of, bear.

render possible etc. *adj.;* put in the way of, bring to bear, bring together.

adj. **possible**; on the -cards, –dice; *in posse* [*L.*], within the bounds of possibility, conceivable, imaginable, credible; compatible etc. 23; likely. **practicable**, feasible, workable, performable, achievable; within -reach, –measurable distance; accessible, superable, surmountable; attainable, obtainable; contingent etc. (*doubtful*) 475.

adv. **possibly**, by any possibility; perhaps, perchance, peradventure; may be, it may be, haply, mayhap. **if possible**, wind and weather permitting, God willing, *Deo volente* [*L.*], D. V.; as luck may have it.

471. Impossibility

n. **impossibility** etc. *adj.;* what cannot be, what can never be; sour grapes; hopelessness etc. 859; infeasibility, infeasibleness, impracticality; discrepancy etc. (*disagreement*) 241. [comparisons] Canute (commanding the tide), Mrs. Partington (and her mop).

v. **be impossible** etc. *adj.;* have no chance whatever. **attempt impossibilities**; square the circle, find the elixir of life, discover the philosopher's stone, discover the grand panacea, find the fountain of youth, discover the secret of perpetual motion; wash a blackamoor white; skin a flint; make a silk purse out of a sow's ear, make bricks without straw; have nothing to go upon; weave a rope of sand, build castles in the air, *prendre la lune avec les dents* [*F.*], extract sunbeams from cucumbers, milk a he-goat into a sieve, catch a weasel asleep, *rompre l'anguille au genou* [*F.*], be in two places at once; gather grapes from thorns, fetch water in a sieve, catch wind in cabbage nets, fling eels by the tail, make cheese of chalk.

adj. **impossible**; not possible etc. 470; absurd, contrary to reason; at variance with the facts; unlikely; unreasonable etc. 477; incredible etc. 485; beyond the bounds of -reason, –possibility; from which reason recoils; visionary; inconceivable etc. (*improbable*) 473; prodigious etc. (*wonderful*) 870; unimaginable, inimaginable [*obs.*], not to be thought of, unthinkable. **impracticable**, unachievable; unfeasible, infeasible; insuperable; insurmountable *or* unsurmountable, unattainable, unobtainable; out of reach, out of the question; not to be had; beyond control; desperate etc. (*hopeless*) 859; incompatible etc. 24; inaccessible, uncomeatable [*colloq.*], impassable, impervious, innavigable, inextricable; self-contradictory.

out of-, beyond- one's -power, –depth, –reach, –grasp; too much for; *ultra crepidam* [*L.*].

472. Probability

n. **probability**, likelihood; credibleness; likeliness etc. *adj.; vraisemblance* [*F.*], verisimilitude, plausibility; color, semblance, show of; presumption; presumptive-, circumstantial- evidence; credibility.

reasonable-, fair-, good-, favorable- -chance, –prospect; prospect, well-grounded hope; chance etc. 156.

v. **be probable** etc. *adj.;* give-, lend- color to; point to; imply etc. (*evidence*) 467; bid fair etc. (*promise*) 511; stand fair for; stand a chance; stand-, run- a good chance; stand-, run- an even chance.

presume, infer, venture, suppose, take for granted, think likely, dare say, flatter oneself; expect etc. 507; count upon etc. (*believe*) 484.

adj. **probable**, likely, hopeful, to be expected, in a fair way.

plausible, specious, ostensible, colorable, *ben trovato* [*It.*], well-founded, reasonable, credible, easy of belief, presumable, presumptive, apparent.

adv. **probably** etc. *adj.;* belike [*archaic*]; in all probability, in all likelihood; very-, most- likely; like enough; very like; ten etc. to one; apparently, seemingly, to all seeming, as like as not [*colloq.*], according to every reasonable expectation; *prima facie* [*L.*]; to all appearance etc. (*to the eye*) 448.

473. Improbability

n. **improbability**, unlikelihood; unfavorable-, bad-, ghost of a-, little-, small-, poor-, scarcely any-, no- chance; bare possibility; long odds; incredibility etc. 485.

v. **be improbable** etc. *adj.;* violate-, stretch- the probabilities; go beyond reason, strain one's credulity; run counter to the laws of nature; have a small chance etc. *n.;* stand a poor show [*colloq.*].

adj. **improbable**, unlikely, contrary to all reasonable expectation; contrary to -fact, –experience; implausible, rare etc. (*infrequent*) 137; unheard of, inconceivable; unimaginable, inimaginable [*obs.*]; incredible etc. 485; more than doubtful.

int. **not likely**! no fear! [*chiefly Eng.*]; I ask you! [*slang*]; catch me! [*slang*].

474. Certainty

n. **certainty**; necessity etc. 601; certitude, sureness, surety, assurance; dead-, moral- certainty; infallibleness etc. *adj.;* infallibility, reliability, reliableness; indubitableness, inevitableness, unquestionableness.

gospel, scripture, church, pope, court of final appeal; *res adjudicata*, [*L.*], *res judicata* [*L.*]; ultimatum.

fact; positive fact, matter of fact; *fait accompli* [*F.*].

bigotry, positiveness, dogmatism, dogmatization; fanaticism.

dogmatist, dogmatizer, doctrinaire, bigot, opinionist, Sir Oracle; dogmatic theorist; zealot, fanatic; *ipse dixit* [*L.*].

v. **be certain** etc. *adj.;* stand to reason.

render certain etc. *adj.;* insure *or* ensure, assure; clinch, make sure; determine, find out once for all, decide, set at rest, "make assurance double sure" [*Macbeth*]; know etc. (*believe*) 484; dismiss all doubt, admit of no doubt.

dogmatize, lay down the law.

adj. **certain**, sure; assured etc. *v.;* solid, well-founded.

unqualified, absolute, positive, determinate, definite, clear, unequivocal, categorical, unmistakable, decisive, decided, ascertained.

inevitable, unavoidable, avoidless; ineluctable.

conclusive, unimpeachable, undeniable, unquestionable; indefeasible, indisputable, incontestable, incontrovertible, indubitable; irrefutable etc. (*proven*) 478; without power of appeal, inappealable, final.

indubious; without-, beyond a-, without a shade or shadow of- -doubt, –question; past dispute; clear as day; beyond all -question, –dispute; undoubted, uncontested, unquestioned, undisputed; questionless, doubtless.

authoritative, authentic, official, governmental, curule.

sure as -fate, –death and taxes, –a gun [*colloq.*].

evident, self-evident, axiomatic; clear, –as day, –as the sun at noonday; apparent etc. (*manifest*) 525.

infallible, unerring; unchangeable etc. 150; to be depended on, trustworthy, reliable, bound.

dogmatic, opinionative, opinionated, dictatorial, doctrinaire; fanatical, bigoted.

adv. **certainly** etc. *adj.;* for certain, certes [*archaic*], sure, no doubt, doubtless, and no mistake [*colloq.*], *flagrante delicto* [*L.*]; sure enough, to be sure, of course, as a matter of course, *a coup sûr* [*F.*], *sans doute* [*F.*], questionless [*rare*], for a certainty, of a certainty, to a certainty; in truth etc. (*truly*) 494; at any rate, at all events; without fail; *coûte que coûte* [*F.*], *coûte qu'il coûte* [*F.*]; whatever may happen, if the worse come to the worst; come what may, come what will, happen what may, happen what will; sink or swim; rain or shine, live or die.

475. Uncertainty

n. **uncertainty**, incertitude, doubt; doubtfulness etc. *adj.;* dubiety, dubitation, dubitancy [*obs.*], dubiosity, dubiousness.

hesitation, suspense, state of suspense; perplexity, embarrassment, dilemma, Morton's fork [*hist.*], bewilderment; botheration [*colloq.*]; puzzle, quandary; timidity etc. (*fear*) 860; vacillation etc. 605; aporia, diaporesis, indetermination; sealed orders.

vagueness etc. *adj.;* haze, fog; obscurity etc. (*darkness*) 421; ambiguity etc. (*double meaning*) 520; contingency, double contingency, possibility upon a possibility; open question etc. (*question*) 461; *onus probandi* [*L.*], blind bargain, pig in a poke, leap in the dark, something or other; needle in a haystack; roving commission.

fallibility; unreliability, unreliableness, untrustworthiness; precariousness etc. *adj.*

v. **be uncertain** etc. *adj.;* wonder whether.

lose the -clew *or* clue, -scent; miss one's way, wander aimlessly, beat about, hang around.

not know -what to make of etc. (*unintelligibility*) 519, -which way to turn, -whether one stands on one's head or one's heels; float in a sea of doubt, hesitate, flounder; lose oneself, lose one's head; muddle one's brains.

render uncertain etc. *adj.;* put out, pose, puzzle, perplex, embarrass; muddle, confuse, confound, fluster; bewilder, bother, moider [*dial.*], rattle [*colloq.*], nonplus, addle the wits, throw off the scent, keep in suspense, keep one guessing.

doubt, etc. (*disbelieve*) 485; hang in the balance, tremble in the balance; depend.

adj. **uncertain**, unsure; casual; random etc. (*aimless*) 621; changeable, changeful etc. 149.

doubtful, dubious; dazed; insecure, unstable, indecisive; unsettled, undecided, undetermined; in suspense, open to discussion; controvertible; in question etc. (*inquiry*) 461.

vague; indeterminate, indefinite; ambiguous, equivocal; undefined, undefinable, confused etc. (*indistinct*) 447; mysterious, cryptic, veiled, obscure, oracular.

perplexing etc. *v.;* enigmatic, paradoxical, apocryphal, problematical, hypothetical; experimental etc. 463.

fallible, questionable, precarious, slippery, ticklish, debatable, disputable; unreliable, untrustworthy.

unauthentic, unauthenticated, unauthoritative; unascertained, unconfirmed; undemonstrated; untold, uncounted.

contingent, contingent on, dependent on; subject to; dependent on circumstances; occasional; provisional.

in a state of uncertainty, on the horns of a dilemma, in a cloud, in a maze; bushed, off the track; derailed; ignorant etc. 491; afraid to say; out of one's reckoning, out of one's bearings, astray, adrift; at sea, at fault, at a loss, at one's wit's end, at a non-plus; puzzled etc. *v.;* lost, abroad, *désorienté* [*F.*]; distrait, distracted, distraught.

adv. **uncertainly** etc. *adj.;* at random, until things straighten out, while things are so uncertain, in this state of suspense; *pendente lite* [*L.*]; *sub spe rati* [*L.*].

Section 4. Reasoning Processes

476. Reasoning

n. **reasoning**; ratiocination, rationalism; dialectics, dialecticism, induction, generalization.

discussion, comment; ventilation; inquiry etc. 461.

argumentation, controversy, debate; polemics, wrangling; contention etc. 720; logomachy, disputation, disceptation [*archaic*]; paper war.

logic, art of reasoning.

process-, train-, chain- of reasoning; deduction, induction; synthesis, analysis.

argument; case, plea, *plaidoyer* [*F.*], opening; premise *or* premiss; lemma, proposition, terms, premises; postulate, data, starting point, principle; inference etc. (*judgment*) 480.

prosyllogism, syllogism; enthymeme, sorites, dilemma, *a fortiori* reasoning, *a priori* reasoning, *reductio ad absurdum* [*L.*], horns of a dilemma, *argumentum ad hominem* [*L.*], comprehensive argument; empirema, epagoge.

logical sequence; good case; correct-, just-, sound-, valid-, cogent-, irrefutable-, logical-, forcible-, persuasive-, persuasory [*rare*]-, consectary [*obs.*]-, conclusive etc. 478-, subtle- reasoning; force of argument; strong -point, -argument.

arguments, reasons, pros and cons.

reasoner, logician, dialectician; disputant; controversialist, controvertist; wrangler, arguer, debater, devil's disciple, polemic, casuist, rationalist; scientist; eristic.

v. **reason**, argue, discuss, debate, dispute, wrangle; argufy *or* argify [*dial.*], bandy -words, -arguments; chop logic; hold-, carry on- an argument; controvert etc. (*deny*) 536; canvass; comment-, moralize- upon; consider etc. (*examine*) 461.

try conclusions; open a -discussion, -case; join-, be at- issue; moot; come to the point; stir-, agitate-, ventilate-, torture- a question; take up a -side, -case.

contend, take one's stand upon, insist, lay stress on; infer etc. 480.

follow from etc. (*demonstration*) 478.

adj. **reasoning** etc. *v.;* rational, ratiocinative, rationalistic; argumentative, controversial, dialectic, polemical; discursory, discursive; disputatious; logomachic *or* logomachical; Aristotelian, eristic *or* eristical.

debatable, controvertible.

logical; syllogistic, soritical, epagogic, inductive, deductive, synthetic *or* synthetical, analytic *or* analytical; relevant etc. 23.

adv. **for**, because, hence, whence, seeing that, since, sith [*archaic*], then, thence, so; for -that, -this, -which- reason; for as much as *or* forasmuch as, in as much as *or* inasmuch as; whereas, *ex concesso* [*L.*], considering, in consideration of; therefore, argal [*archaic*], wherefore; consequently, *ergo* [*L.*], thus, accordingly; *a priori* [*L.*]; *a fortiori* [*L.*].

finally, in conclusion, in fine; after all, *au bout du compte* [*F.*], on the whole, taking one thing with another; pro and con; rationally etc. *adj.*

477. Intuition

[absence of reasoning]

Sophistry

[specious reasoning]

n. **intuition**, instinct, association; presentiment; rule of thumb.

sophistry, paralogy, perversion, casuistry, jesuitry, equivocation, evasion, mental reserva- tion; chicane, chicanery; quiddit [*obs.*], quiddity; mystification; special pleading; speciousness etc. *adj.;* nonsense etc. 497; word fence, tongue fence; overrefinement, hairsplitting, quibbling etc. *v.*

false-, fallacious-, specious-, vicious- reasoning; begging of the question, *petitio principii* [*L.*], *ignoratio elenchi* [*L.*]; *post hoc ergo propter hoc* [*L.*]; *non sequitur* [*L.*], *ignotum per ignotius* [*L.*].

misjudgment etc. 481; false teaching etc. 538.

sophism, solecism, paralogism; quibble, quirk, elench, elenchus, fallacy, *quodlibet* [*L.*], subterfuge, shift, subtlety, quillet [*archaic*]; inconsistency, antilogy; claptrap, mere words; "lame and impotent conclusion" [*Othello*].

meshes-, cobwebs- of sophistry; flaw in an argument; weak point, bad case.

sophist, casuist, paralogist.

v. **judge intuitively**, judge by intuition; hazard a proposition, talk at random.

pervert, quibble; equivocate, mystify, evade, elude; gloss over, varnish; misteach etc. 538; mislead etc. (*error*) 495; cavil, refine, subtilize, split hairs; misrepresent etc. (*lie*) 544.

reason ill, reason falsely etc. *adj.;* misjudge etc. 481; paralogize.

beg the question, reason in a circle, cut blocks with a razor, beat about the bush, play fast and loose, blow hot and cold, prove that black is white and white black, travel out of the record, *parler à tort et à travers* [*F.*], put oneself out of court, not have a leg to stand on.

adj. **intuitive**, instinctive, impulsive; independent of-, anterior to- reason; gratuitous, hazarded; unconnected.

illogical, unreasonable, false, unsound, invalid; unwarranted, not following, incongruous, inconsequent, inconsequential; inconsistent; absonous [*obs.*], absonant, unscientific; untenable, inconclusive, incorrect; fallacious, fallible; groundless, unproved.

specious, sophistic *or* sophistical, jesuitic *or* jesuitical, casuistic *or* casuistical, paralogistic, paralogical; deceptive, illusive, illusory; hollow, plausible, *ad captandum* [*L.*], evasive; irrelevant etc. 10.

weak, feeble, poor, flimsy, loose, vague, irrational; nonsensical etc. (*absurd*) 497; foolish etc. (*imbecile*) 499; frivolous, pettifogging, quibbling; finespun, overrefined.

at the end of one's tether, *au bout de son latin* [*F.*].

adv. **intuitively** etc. *adj.;* by intuition.

illogically etc. *adj.*

478. Demonstration

n. **demonstration**, proof, irrefragability; conclusiveness etc. *adj.;* apodeixis *or* apodixis, probation, comprobation [*obs.*].

logic of facts etc. (*evidence*) 467; *experimentum crucis* [*L.*] etc. (*test*) 463; argument etc. 476; rigorous–, absolute- establishment.

v. **demonstrate**, prove, establish, make good; show, evince etc. (*be evidence of*) 467; verify etc. 467; settle the question, reduce to demonstration, set the question at rest.

make out, –a case; prove one's point, have the best of the argument; draw a conclusion etc. (*judge*) 480.

follow, –of course; stand to reason; hold good, hold water [*colloq.*].

adj. **demonstrating** etc. *v.;* demonstrative, demonstrable; probative, unanswerable, conclusive, convincing; apodeictic *or* apodictic, apodeictical *or* apodictical; irresistible, irrefutable, irrefragable, undeniable.

categorical, decisive, crucial.

demonstrated etc. *v.;* proven; unconfuted, unanswered, unrefuted; evident etc. 474.

deducible, consequential, consectary [*obs.*], inferential, following.

adv. **of course**, in consequence, consequently, as a matter of course.

479. Confutation

n. **confutation**, refutation; answer, complete answer; disproof, conviction, redargution, invalidation; exposure, exposition, *exposé* [*F.*], clincher [*colloq.*], retort, *reductio ad absurdum* [*L.*]; knock-down-; *tu quoque-* argument; sockdolager [*slang*].

v. **confute**, refute; parry, negative, disprove, redargue, expose, show up, show the fallacy of, rebut, defeat; demolish etc. (*destroy*) 162; overthrow, overturn; scatter to the winds, explode, invalidate;. silence; put–, reduce- to silence; clinch -an argument, –a question; stop the mouth, shut up; have, have on the hip, have the better of; confound, convince.

not leave a leg to stand on, cut the ground from under one's feet; smash all opposition; knock the bottom out of an argument [*colloq.*].

be confuted etc.; fail; expose–, show- one's weak point.

adj. **confutable**, confutative, refutable; confuting, confuted, etc. *v.;* capable of refutation.

condemned -on one's own showing, –out of one's own mouth; "hoist with his own petar" [*Hamlet*].

Section 5. Results of Reasoning

480. Judgment
[conclusion]

n. **judgment**, decision, determination, finding, verdict, sentence, decree; *res adjudicata* [*L.*], *res judicata* [*L.*]; opinion etc. (*belief*) 484; good judgment etc. (*wisdom*) 498.

result, conclusion, upshot; deduction, inference, ergotism [*obs.*], illation; corollary, porism; moral.

estimation, valuation, appreciation, judication; dijudication, adjudication; arbitrament, arbitrement, arbitration; assessment, ponderation [*rare*]; valorization.

estimate, award; review, criticism, critique, notice, report.

plebiscite, plebiscitum, voice, casting vote; vote etc. (*choice*) 609.

arbiter, arbitrator; judge, umpire; assessor, referee; inspector, inspecting officer; censor.

reviewer, critic; connoisseur; commentator etc. 524.

v. **judge**, conclude, opine; come to–, draw–, arrive at- a conclusion; ascertain, determine, make up one's mind.

deduce, derive, gather, collect, infer, draw an inference, make a deduction, weet [*obs.*], ween [*archaic*].

estimate, form an estimate, appreciate, value, count, assess, rate, rank, account; regard, consider, think of; look upon etc. (*believe*) 484; review; size up [*colloq.*].

decide, settle; pass–, give- an opinion; try, pronounce, rule; pass -judgment, –sentence; sentence, doom, decree; find; give–, deliver- judgment; adjudge, adjudicate, judicate [*rare*]; arbitrate, award, report; bring in a verdict; make absolute, set a question at rest; confirm etc. (*assent*) 488.

hold the scales, sit in judgment; try a cause, hear a cause.

review, comment, criticize; pass under review etc. (*examine*) 457; investigate etc. (*inquire*) 461.

adj. **judging** etc. *v.;* judicious etc. (*wise*) 498; determinate, conclusive, confirmatory.

critical, hypercritical, hairsplitting, censorious.

adv. **on the whole**, all things considered, taking all this into consideration, this being so, *quae cum ita sint* [*L.*], therefore, wherefore.

480a. Discovery

[result of search or inquiry]

n. **discovery**, detection, disenchantment; ascertainment, disclosure, find, revelation.

trover etc. 775.

v. **discover**, find, determine, evolve; fix upon; find-, trace-, make-, hunt-, fish-, worm-, ferret-, dig-, root- out; fathom; bring out, draw out; educe, elicit, bring to light; dig up, grub up, fish up; unearth, disinter.

solve, resolve; unriddle, unravel, ravel, ravel out, unlock; pick-, open- the lock; find a clew *or* clue to; interpret etc. 522; disclose etc. 529.

trace, get at; hit it, have it; lay one's -finger, -hands- upon; spot [*colloq.*], see through a millstone [*colloq.*]; get-, arrive- at the -truth etc. 494; put the saddle on the right horse, hit the right nail on the head.

scent, be near the truth, be warm [*colloq.*], burn [*colloq.*]; smoke, sniff, smell out, smell a rat [*colloq.*].

see through, see daylight, see in its true colors, see the cloven foot; open the eyes to; detect; catch, catch tripping.

meet with; pitch-, fall-, light-, hit-, stumble-, pop- upon; come across; fall in with.

recognize, realize, verify, make certain of, identify.

int. eureka! I have it! at last!

481. Misjudgment

n. **misjudgment**, obliquity of judgment, warped judgment; miscalculation, miscomputation, misconception etc. (*error*) 495, hasty conclusion.

preconception, prejudgment, prejudication [*rare*], prejudice; foregone conclusion; prenotion, prevention [*Gallicism*], predilection, prepossession, preapprehension, presumption, presentiment, foreboding; fixed idea; *idée fixe* [*F.*], obsession, preconceived idea, *mentis gratissimus error* [*L.*]; fool's paradise.

partisanship, *esprit de corps* [*F.*], party spirit, mob spirit, class prejudice, class consciousness, race prejudice, provincialism, clannishness, prestige.

quirk, shift, quibble, equivocation, evasion, subterfuge.

bias, warp, twist; hobby, whim, craze, fad, crotchet, partiality, infatuation, blind side, blind spot, mote in the eye.

one-sided-, partial-, narrow-, confined-, superficial- -views, -ideas, -conceptions, -notions; purblindness, *entêtement* [*F.*]; narrow mind; bigotry etc. (*obstinacy*) 606; *odium theologicum* [*L.*]; pedantry; hypercriticism.

doctrinaire etc. (*positive*) 474.

v. **misjudge**, misestimate, misesteem, misthink, misconjecture, misconceive etc. (*error*) 495; fly in the face of facts; miscalculate, misreckon, miscompute.

overestimate etc. 482; underestimate etc. 483.

prejudge, forejudge; presuppose, presume, prejudicate [*rare*], dogmatize; have a bias etc. n.; have only one idea; *jurare in verba magistri* [*L.*], run away with the notion; jump-, rush- to a conclusion; go off half-cocked [*colloq.*]; look only at one side of the shield; view with jaundiced eye, view through distorting spectacles; not see beyond one's nose; *dare pondus fumo* [*L.*]; get the wrong sow by the ear etc. (*blunder*) 699.

bias, warp, twist; give a -bias, -twist; prejudice, prepossess.

adj. **misjudging** etc. v.; ill-judging, wrong-headed; prejudiced, prepossessed; jaundiced; short-sighted, purblind; partial, one-sided, superficial.

narrow, narrow-minded, narrow-souled; provincial, parochial, insular; mean-spirited; confined, illiberal, intolerant, besotted, infatuated, fanatical, *entêté* [*F.*], positive, dogmatic, dictatorial; pragmatic *or* pragmatical, egotistical, conceited, opinioned, opinionated, opinionate [*rare*], opinionative [*rare*], opinative [*obs.*], opiniative [*obs.*]; self-opinionated; self-opinioned, wedded to an opinion, *opiniâtre* [*F.*]; bigoted etc. (*obstinate*) 606; crotchety, fussy, impracticable; unreasonable, stupid etc. 499; credulous etc. 486; warped.

misjudged etc. v.

adv. *ex parte* [*L.*].

482. Overestimation

n. **overestimation** etc. v.; exaggeration etc. 549; vanity etc. 880; optimism, pessimism.

much cry and little wool, much ado about nothing; storm in a teacup; fine talking; fine writing, rodomontade, gush [*colloq.*], hot air [*slang*].

egoism, egotism, bombast, conceit, swelled head [*slang*], megalomania.

egoist, egotist, megalomaniac; optimist, booster, pessimist; Rodomont, Braggadochio, braggart, boaster, braggadocio, swaggerer; hot-air artist [*slang*], gas-bag [*slang*], wind-bag [*slang*].

v. **overestimate**, overrate, overvalue, overprize, overweigh, overreckon, overstrain, overpraise;

estimate too highly, attach too much importance to, make mountains of molehills, catch at straws; strain, magnify; exaggerate etc. 549; set too high a value upon; think–, make- -much, –too much- of; out-reckon.

have too high an opinion of oneself etc. (*vanity*) 880.

    eulogize, panegyrize, optimize, gush [*colloq.*], gush over [*colloq.*], boost; puff *or* puff up [*colloq.*]; extol, –to the skies; make the -most, –best, –worst- of; make two bites of a cherry.

adj. overestimated etc. *v.;* oversensitive etc. (*sensibility*) 822.

    inflated, puffed up; grandiose, stilted, pompous, pretentious, megalomaniacal, braggart, bombastic.

483. Underestimation

n.   **underestimation**; depreciation etc. (*detraction*) 934; pessimism; self-detraction, self-depreciation; undervaluation, miosis, litotes [*rhet.*]; undervaluing etc. *v.;* modesty etc. 881.

    pessimist, depreciator, knocker [*slang*], crapehanger [*slang*].

v.   **underrate**, underestimate, undervalue, underreckon; depreciate; disparage etc. (*detract*) 934; not do justice to; misprize, disprize; ridicule etc. 856; pessimize; slight etc. (*despise*) 930; neglect etc. 460; slur over.

make -light, –little, –nothing, –no account- of; belittle, knock [*slang*], slam [*slang*], run down [*colloq.*], minimize, think nothing of; set no store by, set at naught; shake off like water from a duck's back, shake off as dewdrops from the lion's mane.

adj. **depreciating** etc. *v.;* depreciative, depreciatory.

    depreciated etc. *v.;* unappreciated, unvalued, unprized.

484. Belief

n.   **belief**; credence; credit; assurance; faith, trust, troth, confidence, presumption, sanguine expectation etc. (*hope*) 858; dependence on, reliance on.

    conviction, persuasion, convincement, plerophory [*rare*], self-conviction; certainty etc. 474; opinion, mind, view; conception, thinking; impression etc. (*idea*) 453; surmise etc. 514; conclusion etc. (*judgment*) 480.

    tenet, dogma, principle, persuasion, views, way of thinking; popular belief etc. (*assent*) 488.

firm–, implicit–, settled–, fixed–, rooted–, deep-rooted–, staunch–, unshaken–, stead-fast–, inveterate–, calm–, sober–, dispassionate–, impartial–, well-founded- -belief, –opinion etc.; *uberrima fides* [*L.*].

    doctrine, system of opinions, school, articles, canons; article–, declaration–, profession- of faith; tenets, credenda, creed, credo, thirty-nine articles etc. (*orthodoxy*) 983a; gospel, gospel truth; catechism; assent etc. 488; propaganda etc. (*teaching*) 537.

    credibility etc. (*probability*) 472.

v.   **believe**, credit; give -faith, –credit, –credence- to; see, realize; assume, receive; set down for, take for; have it, take it; consider, esteem, presume.

count–, depend–, calculate–, pin one's faith–, reckon–, lean–, build–, rely–, rest- upon; cast one's bread upon the waters; lay one's account for; make sure of.

make oneself easy -about, –on that score; take on -trust, –credit; take for -granted, –gospel; allow–, attach- some weight to.

    know, –for certain; be in the know [*slang*]; have–, make- no doubt; doubt not; be–, rest- -assured etc. *adj.;* persuade–, assure–, satisfy- oneself; make up one's mind.

    confide in, believe in, put one's trust in; give one credit for; place–, repose- implicit confidence in; take one's word for, take at one's word; place reliance on, rely upon, swear by, regard to.

    think, hold; take, take it; opine, be of opinion, conceive, trow [*archaic*], ween [*archaic*], fancy, apprehend; have–, hold–, possess–, entertain–, adopt–, imbibe–, embrace–, get hold of–, hazard–, foster–, nurture–, cherish- -a belief, –an opinion etc. *n.*

view as, consider as, take as, hold as, conceive as, regard as, esteem as, deem as, look upon as, account as, set down as; surmise etc. 514.

get–, take- it into one's head; come round to an opinion; swallow etc. (*credulity*) 486.

    persuade; cause to be believed etc. *v.;* satisfy, bring to reason, have the ear of, gain the confidence of, assure; convince, convict, convert; wean, bring round; bring–, win- over; indoctrinate etc. (*teach*) 537; cram down the throat; produce–, carry- conviction; bring–, drive- home to.

    find credence, go down, pass current; be received etc. *v.*, be current etc. *adj.;* possess–, take hold of–, take possession of- the mind.

adj. **believing** etc. *v.;* certain, sure, assured, positive, cocksure [*colloq.*], satisfied, confident, unhesitating, convinced, secure.

under the impression; impressed–, imbued–, penetrated- with.

confiding, trustful, suspectless [*obs.*], unsuspecting, unsuspicious, void of suspicion; credulous etc. 486; wedded to.

believed etc. *v.;* accredited, putative; unsuspected, trusted, undoubted.

worthy of–, deserving of–, commanding- -belief, –confidence; credible, reliable, trustworthy, to be depended on; satisfactory; probable etc. 472; fiducial, fiduciary; persuasive, impressive.

doctrinal, relating to belief.

adv. **in the opinion of**, in the eyes of; *me judice* [*L.*]; meseems [*archaic*], methinks [*archaic*]; to the best of one's belief; in my opinion, in my judgment, according to my belief; I dare say, I doubt not, I have no doubt, I am sure; cocksure, sure enough etc. (*certainty*) 474; depend–, rely- upon it; be–, rest-assured; I'll warrant you etc. (*affirmation*) 535.

485. Unbelief. Doubt

n. **unbelief**, disbelief, misbelief; discredit, miscreance *or* miscreancy [*archaic*]; infidelity etc. (*irreligion*) 989; wrangling, ergotism [*rare*]; dissent etc. 489; change of opinion etc. 484; retractation etc. 607.

doubt etc. (*uncertainty*) 475; skepticism *or* scepticism, misgiving, demur; distrust, mistrust; misdoubt, suspicion, jealousy, scruple, qualm; *onus probandi* [*L.*].

incredibility, incredibleness, incredulity, unbelievability.

agnostic, skeptic *or* sceptic; unbeliever etc. 487.

v. **disbelieve**, discredit; not believe etc. 484; misbelieve; refuse to admit etc. (*dissent*) 489; refuse to believe etc. (*incredulity*) 487.

doubt; be doubtful etc. (*uncertain*) 475; doubt the truth of; be skeptical as to etc. *adj.;* diffide [*obs.*], distrust, mistrust; suspect, smoke, scent, smell, smell a rat [*colloq.*], have–, harbor–, entertain- -doubts, –suspicions; have one's doubts.

throw doubt upon, raise a question; bring–, call- in question; question, challenge; dispute; deny etc. 536; cause–, raise–, start–, suggest–, awake- a -doubt, –suspicion; cavil, wrangle, ergotize [*rare*].

demur, stick at, pause, hesitate, shy at, scruple; stop to consider, waver.

hang in suspense, hang in doubt.

stagger, startle; shake–, stagger- one's -faith, –belief.

adj. **unbelieving**; skeptical *or* sceptical, incredulous–, skeptical- as to; distrustful of, shy of, suspicious of; doubting etc. *v.*

doubtful etc. (*uncertain*) 475; disputable; unworthy–, undeserving- of -belief etc. 484; questionable; suspect [*archaic*], suspicious; open to -suspicion -doubt; staggering, hard to believe, incredible, unbelievable, not to be believed, inconceivable.

fallible etc. (*uncertain*) 475; undemonstrable; controvertible etc. (*untrue*) 495.

adv. **with caution**, *cum grano salis* [*L.*]; with grains of allowance.

486. Credulity

n. **credulity**, credulousness etc. *adj.*; gullibility, cullibility [*obs.*]; gross credulity, infatuation; self-delusion, self-deception; superstition; one's blind side; bigotry etc. (*obstinacy*) 606; hyperorthodoxy etc. 984; misjudgment etc. 481.

credulous person etc. (*dupe*) 547.

v. **be credulous** etc. *adj.*; *jurare in verba magistri* [*L.*]; follow implicitly; swallow, swallow whole, gulp down; take on trust; take for -granted, –gospel; take on faith; run away with -a notion, –an idea; jump–, rush- to a conclusion; think the moon is made of green cheese; take–, grasp- the shadow for the substance; catch at straws.

impose upon etc. (*deceive*) 545.

adj. **credulous**, gullible; easily deceived etc. 545; simple, green, soft, childish, silly, stupid; easily convinced; overcredulous, overconfident, overtrustful; infatuated, superstitious; confiding etc. (*believing*) 484.

487. Incredulity

n. **incredulity**. incredulousness; skepticism, free thought, Pyrrhonism; want of faith etc. (*irreligion*) 989; minimifidianism; unbelief etc. 485.

suspiciousness etc. *adj.*; scrupulosity; suspicion etc. (*unbelief*) 485; inconvincibility.

unbeliever, skeptic *or* sceptic, miscreant [*archaic*], doubting Thomas, disbeliever, agnostic, infidel, misbeliever, nullifidian, minimifidian, zendik [*Oriental*], freethinker, Pyrrhonist etc. (*irreligion*) 989; heretic etc. (*heterodox*) 984.

v. **be incredulous** etc. *adj.*; distrust etc. (*disbelieve*) 485; refuse to believe; shut one's eyes to, shut one's ears to; turn a deaf ear to; hold aloof; ignore, *nullius jurare in verba magistri* [*L.*].

adj. **incredulous**, skeptical *or* sceptical, dissenting, unbelieving, inconvincible; hard of belief, shy of belief; suspicious, scrupulous, distrustful, disposed to doubt, indisposed to believe; heterodox.

488. Assent

n. **assent**, assentment [*archaic*]; acquiescence, admission; nod; accord, concord, concordance; agreement etc. 23; affirmance, affirmation; recognition, acknowledgment, avowal, recognizance [*rare*], confession, confession of faith.

unanimity, common consent, consensus, acclamation, chorus, *vox populi* [*L.*]; popular-, current- -belief, -opinion; public opinion; concurrence etc. (*of causes*) 178; cooperation etc. (*voluntary*) 709.

ratification, confirmation, corroboration, approval, acceptance, visa, *visé* [*F.*]; indorsement etc. (*record*) 551.

consent etc. (*compliance*) 762.

affirmant, assentant [*obs.*], professor [*esp. in relig.*], confirmist, consenter, covenantor, subscriber, indorser *or* endorser; upholder etc. (*auxiliary*) 711.

v. **assent**; give-, yield-, nod- assent; acquiesce; agree etc. 23; receive, accept, accede, accord, concur, lend oneself to, consent, coincide, reciprocate, go with; be at one with etc. *adj.;* go along with, chime in with, strike in with, close with; echo, enter into one's views, agree in opinion; vote for, give one's voice for; recognize; subscribe-, conform-, defer- to; say -yes, -ditto, -amen, -aye- to.

go-, float-, swim- with the stream; float with the current; get on the band wagon [*slang*]; be in the fashion, join in the chorus; be in every mouth.

arrive at-, come to- -an understanding, -terms, -an agreement.

acknowledge, own, admit, allow, avow, confess; concede etc. (*yield*) 762; come round to; abide by; permit etc. 760.

confirm, affirm; ratify, approve, indorse, visa, *visé* [*F.*], countersign; corroborate etc. 467.

adj. **assenting** etc. *v.;* of one -accord, -mind; of the same mind, affirmant, assentaneous [*rare*], assentant [*obs.*], at one with, agreed, acquiescent, content; willing etc. 602.

uncontradicted, unchallenged, unquestioned, uncontroverted.

carried-, agreed- *-nem. con.* [*L.*] etc. *adv.;* unanimous; agreed on all hands, carried by acclamation.

affirmative etc. 535.

adv. **yes**, yea, aye *or* ay, true; good; well; how true, very -well, -true; well and good; granted; even so, just so; to be sure, as you say, sure, surely, assuredly, "thou hast said"; truly, exactly, precisely, that's just it, indeed, certainly, certes [*archaic*], *ex concesso* [*L.*], of course, unquestionably, no doubt, doubtless.

be it so; so be it, so let it be; so mote it be, with all one's heart; amen; willingly etc. 602.

affirmatively, in the affirmative.

unanimously, *unâ voce* [*L.*], by common consent, in chorus, to a man; with one -consent, -voice, -accord; *nem. con.* [*L.*]; *nemine contradicente* [*L.*], *nemine dissentiente* [*L.*], without a dissentient voice; as one man, one and all, on all hands.

489. Dissent

n. **dissent**, nonconsent, discordance etc. (*disagreement*) 24; difference-, diversity- of opinion.

nonconformity etc. (*heterodoxy*) 984; protestantism, recusancy, schism; disaffection; secession etc. 624; recantation etc. 607.

dissension etc. (*discord*) 713; discontent etc. 832; caviling, wrangling, ergotism [*rare*].

protest; contradiction etc. (*denial*) 536; noncompliance etc. (*rejection*) 764.

dissentient, dissenter, nonconformist; sectary, separatist, recusant, schismatic, protestant; heretic etc. (*heterodoxy*) 984.

v. **dissent**, nonconsent, demur; call in question etc. (*doubt*) 485; differ in opinion, disagree, agree to differ; say no etc. 536; refuse -assent, -to admit; cavil, wrangle, ergotize [*rare*], protest, raise one's voice against, repudiate; contradict etc. (*deny*) 536.

have no notion of, differ *toto coelo* [*L.*], revolt at, revolt from the idea.

shake the head, shrug the shoulders; look askance *or* askant.

secede; recant etc. 607.

adj. **dissenting** etc. *v.;* negative etc. 536; dissident, dissentient; unconsenting etc. (*refusing*) 764; noncontent, nonjuring; protestant, recusant; unconvinced, unconverted.

unavowed, unacknowledged; out of the question.

unwilling etc. 603; extorted; discontented etc. 832.

sectarian, sectary [*rare*], denominational, schismatic; heterodox; intolerant.

adv. **no** etc. 536; at variance with, at issue with; under protest.

int. **God forbid**! not for the world! I'll be hanged if! [*colloq.*]; not another word! no, sirree!; not if I know it! I beg to differ; never tell me! pardon me.

490. Knowledge

n. **knowledge**; cognizance, cognition, cognoscence [*obs.*]; acquaintance, experience, ken, privity, insight, familiarity; comprehension, apprehension; recognition; appreciation etc. (*judgment*) 480; intuition; conscience, consciousness; perception, apperception, precognition; acroamatics.

system–, body- of knowledge; science, philosophy, pansophism, pansophy; acroama; theory, aetiology *or* etiology; circle of the sciences; pandect, doctrine, body of doctrine; cyclopedia *or* cyclopaedia, encyclopedia *or* encyclopaedia, circle of knowledge; school etc. (*system of opinions*) 484.

tree of knowledge; republic of letters etc. (*language*) 560.

enlightenment, light; glimpse, inkling, glimmer, glimmering, dawn; scent, suspicion; impression etc. (*idea*) 453; discovery etc. 480a.

learning, erudition, lore, scholarship, reading, letters; literature; book madness; book learning, bookishness; bibliomania, bibliolatry; information, general information; store of knowledge etc.; education etc. (*teaching*) 537; culture, *Kultur* [*Ger.*], cultivation, menticulture, attainments; acquirements, mental acquisitions; accomplishments; proficiency; practical knowledge etc. (*skill*) 698; liberal education, higher education; dilettantism; rudiments etc. (*beginning*) 66.

deep–, profound–, solid–, accurate–, acroatic–, acroamatic–, vast–, extensive–, encyclopedic- -knowledge, –learning; omniscience, pantology.

march of intellect; progress–, advance- of -science, –learning; schoolmaster abroad.

v. **know**, ken [*dial.*], scan, wot [*archaic*]; wot of [*archaic*], be aware of etc. *adj.;* ween [*archaic*], weet [*obs.*], trow [*archaic*]; have, possess.

conceive; apprehend, comprehend; take, realize, understand, savvy [*slang*], be wise to [*slang*], appreciate; fathom, make out; recognize, discern, perceive, see, get a sight of, experience.

know full well; have–, possess- some knowledge of; be *au courant* [*F.*] etc. *adj.;* have in one's head, have at one's fingers' ends; know by -heart, –rote; be master of; *connaître le dessous*

des cartes [*F.*], know what's what [*colloq.*] etc. 698.

discover etc. 480a; see one's way.

learn, come to one's knowledge etc. (*information*) 527.

adj. **knowing** etc. *v.;* cognitive; acroamatic *or* acroamatical, apperceptive, appercipient.

aware of, cognizant of, conscious of; acquainted with, made acquainted with; privy to, no stranger to; *au fait* [*F.*], *au courant* [*F.*]; in the secret; up to [*colloq.*], alive to; behind the -scenes, –curtain; let into; apprised of, informed of; undeceived.

proficient in, versed in, read in, forward in, strong in, at home in; conversant with, familiar with.

educated, erudite, instructed, learned, lettered; well-informed, well-versed, well-read, well-grounded, well-educated; enlightened, shrewd, *savant* [*F.*], bluestocking, high-brow [*slang*], bookish, scholastic, solid, profound, deep-read, book-learned, aetiological *or* etiological, pansophic *or* pansophical; accomplished etc. (*skillful*) 698; omniscient; self-taught, self-educated, autodidactic; self-made.

known etc. *v.;* ascertained, well-known, recognized, received, notorious, noted; proverbial; familiar, –as household words, –to every schoolboy; hackneyed, trite, commonplace.

knowable, cognizable, cognoscible.

adv. to–, to the best of- one's knowledge; as every schoolboy knows.

490a. Astronomy

n. **astronomy**, cosmogony, interpretational astronomy, observational astronomy, descriptive astronomy, astrometry, geometrical astronomy, celestial mechanics; astrophysics, astrionics, radio astronomy, solar radio astronomy; astrobiology; planetology, heliography, actinometry, areography, cometography, astrography; celestial navigation, astrogation, nautical astronomy.

Ptolemaic system; Copernican system; evolutionary theory of the universe, expanding universe hypothesis, nebular hypothesis, collision hypothesis; planetismal hypothesis, protoplanet hypothesis; Lorentz-Fitzgerald contraction theory; infinity of the universe; Newton's universal laws of motion; Bode's law; Kepler's laws; Fechner's law; fission theory.

universe, cosmos, metagalaxy; firmament, space, deep space, interplanetary space, intergalactic space, interstellar space; lunar space, solar space.

solar system; planet; inner planets, outer planets; minor planets, major planets; inferior planets, superior planets; Mercury, Venus, Earth, Mars, Jupiter, Saturn, Uranus, Neptune, Pluto; evening star, morning star; satellite; asteroid, planetoid; comet (nucleus, coma, tail), periodic comets (Encke, Giacobini-Zinner, Pons-Winnecke, Biela, Faye, Arend, Westphal, Olbers, Halley, Herschel-Rigollet), comet group, comet family.

meteor, fire ball, bolide; meteor shower, Aquarids, Arietids, Draconids, Geminids, Leonids, Perseids; micrometeorite; meteorite, aerolite, achrondite, siderite, ataxite, siderolite.

sun; photosphere, sunspots, granules, faculae, plages, maculae; M regions; reversing layer; chromosphere, flocculi, spicules; corona, K corona, F corona; prominences, jets; limb; aureole; halo; Zeeman effect.

moon, new moon, first quarter, crescent moon, half-moon, last quarter gibbous moon, full moon; harvest moon, hunter's moon; lunar plains or maria or seas (Mare Foecunditatis, Mare Nectaris, Mare Crisium, Mare Tranquillitatis, Mare Serenitatis, Mare Imbrium, Oceanus Procellarum, Mare Nubium, Mare Humorum), lunar mountain ranges, lunar rays, lunar rills, lunar craters (Alphonsus, Archimedes, Aristarchus, Aristoteles, Arzachel, Bullialdus, Catharina, Clavius, Copernicus, Cyrillus, Eratosthenes, Furnerius, Gassendi, Grimaldi, Kepler, Langrenus, Maginus, Maurolycus, Petavius, Plato, Proclus, Ptolemaeus, Schickard, Theophilus, Tycho).

star, circumpolar star, double star, binary star, lucid star, lucida, faint companion star, astrometric companion, multiple star, nova, supernova, Kepler's star; Population I stars, Population II stars; main sequence stars; dwarf, subdwarf, white dwarf, subgiant, giant, red giant, blue giant, supergiant; variable star, Cepheid variables, RR Lyrae variables, irregular variables, eclipsing variables, Mira-type stars; high velocity stars; star cluster, galactic cluster, globular cluster, moving cluster; Hertzsprung-Russell diagram, color-magnitude diagram, color index; magnitude, apparent magnitude, absolute magnitude, bolometric magnitude; absolute luminosity, period-luminosity relation; Messier number.

[stars] Achernar, Acrux, Adhara, Albireo, Alcor, Aldebaran, Algol, Alioth, Alkaid, Alphard, Alphecca, Alpheratz, Altair, Antares, Arcturus, Bellatrix, Benetnasch, Betelgeuse, Canopus, Capella, Caph, Castor, Cor Caroli, Deneb,

Deneb Kaitos, Denebola, Dubhe, Fomalhaut, Hamal, Kaus Australis, Kochab, Marfak, Markab, Megrez, Merak, Mira, Mizar, Phad, Polaris, Pollux, Procyon, Rasalhague, Regulus, Rigel, Rigil Kentaurus, Saiph, Shaula, Sirius, Spica, Thuban, Vega; (constellations) Andromeda, Aquarius, Aquila, Ara, Aries, Auriga, Boötes, Canes Venatici, Canis Major, Canis Minor, Capricornus, Carina, Cassiopeia, Centaurus, Cepheus, Cetus, Columba, Corona Borealis, Corvus, Crux, Cygnus, Delphinus, Draco, Eridanus, Gemini, Grus, Hercules, Hydra, Hydrus, Leo, Lepus, Libra, Lupus, Lyra, Musca, Ophiuchus, Orion, Pavo, Pegasus, Perseus, Phoenix, Puppis, Sagitta, Sagittarius, Scorpius, Serpens, Taurus, Triangulum, Triangulum Australe, Tucana, Ursa Major, Ursa Minor, Vela, Virgo.

nebulae, galactic nebulae, bright nebulae, dark nebulae, planetary nebulae, diffuse nebulae; Orion Nebula, Coal Sack Nebula, Loop Nebula; extragalactic nebulae, external galaxy, galaxy, spiral galaxy, barred spiral galaxy, elliptical galaxy, irregular galaxy; galactic cluster; galactic window; Milky Way; Magellanic Clouds, Andromeda Nebula.

celestial sphere; celestial equator, celestial poles, celestial meridian, antimeridian, zenith, nadir, vertical circle, diurnal circle, horizon, azimuth; hour angle, hour circle; amplitude; altitude, altitude circle, altitude difference; declination; apex, antapex; culmination; astronomical latitude, celestial latitude, astronomical longitude, celestial longitude; ecliptic; right ascension; equinox, autumnal equinox, vernal equinox; solstice, summer solstice, winter solstice.

celestial motion; proper motion; rotation; revolution; orbit, perihelion, aphelion, apogee, perigee; inclination, perturbation; libration; precession, nutation; acceleration, deceleration; antecedence; arc of progression, arc of retrogression; anomaly; inequality; daily aberration, annual aberration.

transit; occultation; immersion; eclipse, annular eclipse, partial eclipse, total eclipse, umbra, penumbra; conjunction, inferior conjunction, synodic period, sidereal period.

gravity; acceleration of gravity, g; antigravity; barycenter; galactic center; atmospheric tides.

[instruments] accelerometer; astrolabe; astronomical triangle; barograph, barometer; chronometer, chronograph, astronomical clock; helioscope, spectrohelioscope, spectroheliograph, coronagraph, heliometer, magnetograph; illuminometer; sextant; thermocouple;

157

spectroscope, spectrograph, spectrobolometer, micrometer; telescope, astronomical telescope, meridian circle telescope, equatorial telescope; reflecting telescope, Newtonian telescope, coelostat; refracting telescope; radio telescope; astronomical observatory; planetarium.

490b. Chemistry

n. **chemistry**, general chemistry, inorganic chemistry, organic chemistry, analytical chemistry (qualitative analysis, quantitative analysis), biological chemistry or biochemistry, radiochemistry or nuclear chemistry, theoretical chemistry or physical chemistry.

matter, organic matter, inorganic matter; homogeneous matter, substance, stable substance, unstable substance, volatile substance, amorphous substance, crystalline substance; element, active element, inactive element, nonmetal, metal, alkali metal, alkaline earth metal, amphoteric element; free state, combined state; allotropic forms, allotropy.

[chemical notation] symbol, coefficient, subscript, radical; formula, equation, word equation, skeleton equation, balanced equation, ionic equation; molecular weight, formula weight; valence, negative valence, positive valence, zero valence.

mixture; compound, binary compound, ternary compound, electrovalent compound, ionic compound, chain compound, covalent compound; covalent linkage; law of definite proportions; heat of formation, heat of neutralization.

chemical change, chemical reaction, chemical combination, decomposition, displacement, double decomposition; irreversible reaction, completion, reversible reaction, complete reaction, incomplete reaction; endothermic reaction, exothermic reaction, photochemical reaction; dynamic equilibrium, equilibrium constant, ionization constant, solubility product constant; common ion effect; catalyst or catalytic agent; law of conservation of matter, law of mass action.

ionization or dissociation, nonionization, electrolytic dissociation; electrolyte, nonelectrolyte; electrolysis; ion, positive ion or cation, negative ion or anion; positive electrode or anode, negative electrode or cathode; Ionization Theory or Theory of Electrolytic Dissociation; activity coefficient.

acid, binary acid, ternary acid, monobasic acid, dibasic acid, tribasic acid; weak acid (or base), strong acid (or base); base, alkali, monoacid

base, diacid base, triacid base; salt, binary salt, ternary salt, acid salt, basic salt, normal salt, double salt, complex salt; neutralization, hydrolysis, titration; indicators, litmus, phenolphthalein, methyl orange, methyl violet, alizarin yellow; hydrogen ion concentration or pH.

ascorbic acid, benzoic acid, boric acid, butyric acid, carbolic acid, citric acid, formic acid, gallic acid, hydrochloric acid, hydrofluoric acid, lactic acid, malic acid, nitric acid, oleic acid, oxalic acid, phosphoric acid, picric acid, prussic acid, salicylic acid, stearic acid, sulfuric acid, tannic acid, tartaric acid; (bases) ammonium hydroxide, calcium hydroxide, magnesium hydroxide, potassium hydroxide, sodium hydroxide; (salts) ammonium chloride, bismuth subnitrate, calcium carbonate, potassium chloride, potassium nitrate, sodium acetate, sodium acid phosphate, sodium bicarbonate, sodium bisulfite, sodium chloride.

solution, gaseous solution, liquid solution, solid solution, dilute solution, concentrated solution, unsaturated solution, supersaturated solution; molar solution, molal solution, normal solution, standard solution; solute, solvent; seeding, precipitate, filtration; suspension.

crystal, ionic crystal, atom crystal, molecule crystal; crystal symmetry, isometric crystal (cube), hexagonal crystal, tetragonal crystal, orthorhombic crystal, monoclinic crystal, triclinic crystal; water of crystallization or water of hydration; hydrate, anhydrous compound; decrepitation, sublimation; deliquescent substance, hygroscopic substance, efflorescent substance.

oxide, metallic oxide or basic anhydride, nonmetallic oxide or acid anhydride, amphoteric oxide, neutral oxide, suboxide, saline oxide, peroxide; oxidation, rapid oxidation, combustion, spontaneous combustion, slow oxidation, organic oxidation, inorganic oxidation; oxidizing agent; reduction, reducing agent; kindling temperature, temperature of combustion, heat of combustion.

hydrocarbons; aliphatic hydrocarbons, saturated or methane series (methane, ethane, propane), unsaturated series, ethylene series (ethylene, propylene, butylene), acetylene series (acetylene, allylene); aromatic hydrocarbons, benzene series (benzene, toluene, xylene), naphthalene series (naphthalene), anthracene series (anthracene).

[hydrocarbon derivatives] halogen substitution products (chloroform or trichloromethane); alcohols, monohydroxy alcohols, dihydroxy alcohols (methyl alcohol, ethyl alcohol); aldehydes (formaldehyde, acetaldehyde); ketones (acetone, butanone); organic acids; ethers (diethyl ether); esters (methyl acetate); carbohydrates (sugars, starches, cellulose); proteins (albumin, globulin, glutelin).

colloid, natural colloid, lyophobic colloid, hydrophobic colloidal system, lyophilic colloid, hydrophilic colloidal system; sol, gel; dispersed medium, dispersing medium; condensation *or* coagulation method, dispersion method (mechanical disintegration, peptization, emulsification); emulsion, temporary emulsion, permanent emulsion; emulsifying agent *or* protective colloid; miscible liquids, nonmiscible liquids; dialysis, adsorption, flotation process, Cottrell process, cataphoresis, electroendosmosis.

[apparatus] aspirator, blowpipe, Büchner funnel, Bunsen burner, burette *or* buret, crucible, disiccator, distiller, etna, Kipp apparatus, matrass, mortar, pestle, reagent bottle, receiver, retort, ring, ring stand, still, test tube.

490c. Geology

n. **geology**, mineralogy, petrology, stratigraphy, paleontology, structural geology, glacial geology, geomorphology, oceanography, meteorology, geophysics, terrestrial magnetism, seismology, geodesy, geochemistry, petroleum geology, economic geology, engineering geology, hydrology.

crystal, crystallization; euhedral crystal, subhedral crystal, anhedral crystal; crystal symmetry, isometric system, hexagonal system, tetragonal system, orthorhombic system, monoclinic system, triclinic system.

minerals, amphibole group, feldspar group, mica group, pyroxene group; hornblende, apatite, azurite, bauxite, bornite, calcite, carnotite, cassiterite, chalcopyrite, chert, chlorite, chromite, copper, corundum, diamond, dolomite, epidote, microcline, orthoclase, albite, labradorite, anorthite, fluorite, galena, garnet, gold, graphite, gypsum, halite, hematite, kyanite, limonite, magnetite, malachite, biotite, lepidolite, muscovite, olivine, pyrite, augite, pyrrhotite, quartz, serpentine, sillimanite, sphalerite, staurolite, sulfur, talc, tourmaline.

[properties of minerals], specific gravity, cleavage, hardness, fracture, luster (adamantine luster, vitreous luster, resinous luster, greasy luster, pearly luster, silky luster), color, streak, taste, radio-activity, magnetism, opalescence, fluorescence; twinning.

[gross features of earth's crust] continent, continental shield, young folded mountain belt; zone of transition, continental margin, continental shelf, continental slope, continental rise; island arcs; ocean basin, deep oceanic crust, mid-ocean ridges; ocean currents; drift, tide, tidal current, wave, breaker, surf, sea, ground swell.

earthquake, shallow earthquake, intermediate earthquake, deep earthquake, volcanic earthquake; seismism; elastic rebound, foreshock, aftershock; shock wave, P wave *or* dilational wave *or* compressional wave *or* longitudinal wave, S wave *or* shear wave *or* transverse wave; Rayleigh wave; seismograph, seismometer, seismogram, accelerograph.

[deformation of earth's crust] isostasy; epeirogeny, uplifting, downwarping; orogeny, mountain building; diastrophism, confining pressure, stress, strain; fold, anticline, sycline, dome, basin, monocline; fault, fault plane, slickensides, hanging-wall side, foot-wall side, strike-slip movement, dip-slip movement, oblique-slip movement, normal fault, reverse fault, scissors fault, transverse fault, thrust fault, fault scarp, graben, horst, klippe, nappe *or* decke; fracture, tension fracture, shear fracture, rock cleavage; unconformity.

metamorphism, rock flowage; granulation, recrystallization, recombination; contact metamorphism, dynamic metamorphism; foliated metamorphic rock, nonfoliated metamorphic rock; slates, schists, gneisses, phyllites, marble, quartzite, hornfels, amphiboles.

volcano, cinder cone, lava cone, composite cone; shield volcano, flood basalt; vent, fumarole, solfatara, spatter cone, caldera; volcanism, eruption, explosion, expulsion, lava flow; (pyroclastic materials) blocks, bombs, lapilli, ash, volcanic dust; gases; lava, basalt lavas, rhyolite lavas, andesite lavas.

igneous rock, magmas, basaltic magma, granitic magma; (discordant igneous intrusions) batholith, stock, dike; (concordant igneous intrusions) sill, laccolith, lopolith; aphanitic rock, phaneritic rock, porphyritic rock, glassy rock; granite, graphic granite, granite pegmatite, orbicular granite, syenite, diorite, gabbro, peridotite, dunite, pyroxene, hornblendite, felsite, basalt, dolerite, obsidian, pitchstone, pumice, scoria; pyroclastic debris, tuff, agglomerate, volcanic breccia.

sedimentary rock; marine environment, transitional environment, continental environment; residual deposits, transported deposits; mechanical deposition, chemical deposition, organic deposition; rudaceous rocks, arenaceous rocks, silty rocks, argillaceous rocks, chemically deposited siliceous rocks, carbonate rocks, chemically deposited ferruginous rocks, salt rocks, organically deposited siliceous rocks, calcareous rocks, phosphatic rocks, organically deposited ferruginous rocks, carbonaceous rocks; conglomerate, breccia; sandstone, arkose, graywacke; siltstone, loess; mudstone, shale; sinter, chert-flint; tufa, travertine, oölitic limestone, dolostone, lithographic limestone; ironstone, caliche, gypsum, anhydrite, halite; radiolarian ooze, diatom ooze; fossiliferous limestone, chalk, marl; rock phosphates, guano; bog iron ore; coal.

erosion, weathering; mechanical weathering, thermal contraction *and* expansion, unloading, crystal growth, freezing; chemical weathering, oxidation, hydration, carbonation; (specialized erosion) deflation, corrasion, abrasion, impact, corrosion, hydraulicking, quarrying, plucking, solution, slump, rolling, sliding, dislodgement, falling; transportation; deposition.

[wind erosion] undercut hill, cave rock, table, mushroom rock, ventifact, desert pavement, lag gravel; (running water erosion) river valley, pediment, peneplain, river terrace, wadi, pothole; (glacial erosion) striation, groove, drumlin, crescentic mark, u-shaped valley, truncated spur, hanging valley, cirque, fiord, col, arête, horn; (ground water erosion) cave, sinkhole, karst topography; (mass movement erosion) slide scar, surface subsidence; (ocean erosion) cliff, terrace, guyot, stack, arch, sea cave, notch.

geologic time, era, period, epoch, age; rock system, rock series, rock stage; Precambrian Era; Paleozoic Era, Cambrian Period, Ordovician Period, Silurian Period, Devonian Period, Mississippian Period, Pennsylvanian Period, Permian Period; Mesozoic Era, Triassic Period, Jurassic Period, Cretaceous Period; Cenozoic Era, Paleogene Period, Paleocene Epoch, Eocene Epoch, Oligocene Epoch, Neogene Period, Miocene Epoch, Pliocene Epoch, Pleistocene Epoch.

490d. Physics

n. **physics**, classical physics, modern physics; mechanics (kinematics, dynamics, statics, hydrostatics, hydrodynamics, hydraulics), heat (thermometry, calorimetry, thermodynamics), sound, acoustics, light, optics, spectroscopy, electricity (electrostatics, electronics), magnetism; high-energy physics *or* elementary-particle physics, nuclear physics, atomic physics, molecular physics, solid-state physics, physics of liquids, physics of gases, plasma physics, biophysics, low-temperature physics, mathematical physics, theoretical physics, space physics.

atom, neutral atom, ion, nucleus, atomic number, atomic weight, mass number, isobar, isotope; elementary particles *or* subatomic particles; hyperons, nucleons, mesons, leptons, photons; proton, neutron, electron, positron; element; molecule; chemical change, nuclear change, physical change.

matter; solid, liquid, gas, extension *or* volume, mass, weight, density, fluid; specific gravity, impenetrability; elasticity, stress, strain, elastic limit; malleability, ductility; adhesion, cohesion, surface tension, capillarity, diffusion, osmosis, Brownian movement, buoyancy, viscosity; pressure, atmospheric pressure, air pressure; Hooke's law, kinetic theory of matter *or* molecular theory of matter, Pascal's law, Archimedes' principle, Bernoulli's principle; pycnometer, hydrometer, barometer, aneroid barometer, barograph, altimeter, manometer.

fusion, heat of fusion, melting, melting point; freezing, freezing point; regelation; vaporization, heat of vaporization; boiling, boiling point; evaporation, dew point, humidity, absolute humidity, relative humidity; sublimation, volatile liquid *or* solid; condensation *or* liquefaction, critical temperature, critical pressure, vapor; distillation, fractional distillation, distillate.

motion, rectilinear motion, curvilinear motion, circular motion, projectile motion, rotation *or* rotary motion, precession, revolution; velocity, terminal velocity, acceleration, speed, momentum, impulse, inertia; Newton's laws of motion; projectile, trajectory; pendulum, simple pendulum, compound pendulum, compensation pendulum, seconds pendulum; center of percussion; oscillation *or* vibration, amplitude, period, frequency.

force, centrifugal force, centripetal force, parallel forces, couple, component forces, effective component, ineffective component, resultant force; friction, coefficient of friction; equilibrant, equilibrium; resolution of forces, composition of forces, moment of force *or* torque; vector, vector quantity, scalar quantity; dyne, poundal, slug, newton; gravitation, gravity; free fall; Newton's law of universal gravitation.

work; foot-pound, foot-poundal; gram-centimeter, kilogram-meter; erg, joule; power, horsepower; energy, potential energy, kinetic energy; law of conservation of energy.

machines, simple machine, compound machine; inclined plane, screw, wedge, lever and fulcrum, wheel and axle, pulley; mechanical advantage, ideal mechanical advantage, actual mechanical advantage; efficiency, input, output.

[heat] conduction, conductor, conductometer; insulator, convection; radiation; law of heat exchange, Newton's law of cooling; expansion, linear expansion, coefficient of linear expansion, differential expansion; bimetallic bar, compound bar, thermostat; pressure coefficient of gases, general gas law, Boyle's law, Charles's law, Gay-Lussac's law; standard conditions, standard pressure, standard temperature; absolute zero; heat engine, internal-combustion engine, external-combustion engine, turbine; Joule's equivalent; temperature, degree; thermometer, absolute scale, Kelvin scale, Fahrenheit scale, centigrade scale; foot-pound-second system, centimeter-gram-second system; British thermal unit, btu; calorie, kilogram-caloric; specific heat.

[sound] wave, wavelength, sound wave, longitudinal wave (condensation, rarefaction); transverse wave (crest, trough); pitch, intensity, loudness; bel, decibel; beat, echo, reverberation; interference, resonance; frequency, audio frequency, ultrasonic frequency, infrasonic frequency.

[musical sound] tone, fundamental tone, overtone, quality, major chord, musical interval; consonance, dissonance; noise; musical scale, chromatic scale or tempered scale, diatonic scale; standing wave, node, antinode, loop, segment.

[light] luminosity, incandescence, fluorescence, illuminated body; opaque body, translucent body, transparent body; shadow, umbra, penumbra; photometry, photometer; luminous intensity, candle power, candle, foot-candle, lumen, illumination; quantum, quantum theory; Einstein's special theory of relativity, Einstein's general theory of relativity; Doppler effect.

reflection, diffusion, angle of reflection, angle of incidence; image, real image, virtual image; magnification; mirror, concave mirror, convex mirror; center of curvature, radius of curvature, principal axis; focus, virtual focus, focal length, principal focus, focal plane; spherical aberration.

refraction, angle of refraction, index of refraction, critical angle; diffraction; convex lens or positive lens, concave lens or negative lens; optical center, optical density; achromatic lens, chromatic aberration; diopter.

color, primary colors, complementary colors; pigments, primary pigments; complementary pigments; monochromatic light, polychromatic light, polarized light, polarization; polarizer, analyzer.

spectrum; dispersion; electromagnetic spectrum, electromagnetic radiations (infrared rays, ultraviolet rays, X-rays, gamma rays); angstrom; continuous spectrum, absorption spectrum (Fraunhofer lines); bright-line spectrum, dark-line spectrum; spectroscope.

[magnetism], induced magnetism, residual magnetism; magnet, saturated magnet, temporary magnet, permanent magnet; lodestone, magnetic compass, dipping needle; magnetic retentivity; magnetic poles, south-seeking pole, north-seeking pole; magnetic line of force, magnetic field, magnetic flux, magnetic permeability, magnetic transparency; magnetic delination, isogonic line, agonic line; magnetic inclination, isoclinic line, magnetic equator, aclinic line.

[electricity], static electricity; electric current, direct current, D.C., alternating current, A.C.; induced current; eddy current; electromagnetism; electric field; circuit, parallel circuit, series circuit; electromotive force or e.m.f.; resistance, specific resistance or resistivity; reactance, inductive reactance, capacitive reactance; impedance; conduction, conductance, conductor; induction, electromagnetic induction, inductance; self-inductance; capacitance; electrolysis; dissociation; electroplating; electrolyte, nonelectrolyte, Ohm's law, Coulomb's law, inverse-square law, Lenz's law.

generator, motor; armature or keeper, commutator, brush, slip rings; electrophorus; capacitor or condenser; insulator or dielectric; transformer; primary coil, secondary coil; rectifier; rheostat, galvanoscope; oscillator, relay; shunt; electrode, anode or plate, cathode; electrolytic cell; Leyden jar, voltaic cell, storage cell.

coulomb, ohm, ampere, volt, henry, farad, watt; watt-hour, kilowatt-hour; electroscope, ammeter, galvanometer, voltmeter.

diode, triode, vacuum tube; cathode-ray tube, cathode rays; photoelectric cell, photoelectric effect; transistor.

[radioactivity], alpha particle, beta particle, gamma rays, cosmic rays; isotope, radioactive isotope; transmutation of elements; particle accelerator *or* atom smasher, betatron, cyclotron, synchrotron; nuclear reactor, uranium-graphite pile; atomic energy, nuclear energy; fission, chain reaction, critical mass; fusion, thermonuclear reaction.

491. Ignorance

n.   **ignorance**, nescience, *tabula rasa* [*L.*], illiteracy, unlearnedness, crass ignorance, *ignorance crasse* [*F.*]; unacquaintance; unconsciousness etc. *adj.;* darkness, blindness; incomprehension, inexperience, simplicity.

sealed book, *terra incognita* [*L.*], virgin soil, unexplored ground; dark ages.

unknown quantities; *x, y, z.*

[imperfect knowledge] smattering, superficiality, half-learning, shallowness, sciolism, glimmering; bewilderment etc. (*uncertainty*) 475; incapacity.

[affectation of knowledge] pedantry, charlatanry, charlatanism; Philistine, *Philister* [*Ger.*].

v.   **be ignorant** etc. *adj.;* not know etc. 490; know -not, −not what, −nothing of; have no -idea, −notion, −conception; not have the remotest idea.

ignore, be blind to; keep in ignorance etc. (*conceal*) 528.

see through a glass darkly; have a film over the eyes, have a glimmering etc. *n.;* wonder whether; not know what to make of etc. (*unintelligibility*) 519; not pretend to say, not take upon oneself to say.

adj.   **ignorant**; nescient; unknowing, unaware, unacquainted, unapprised, unwitting, unweeting [*obs.*], unconscious; witless, weetless [*obs.*]; a stranger to; unconversant.

uninformed, uncultivated, unversed, uninstructed, untaught, uninitiated, untutored, unschooled, unscholarly, unguided, unenlightened; Philistine; behind the age.

shallow, superficial, green, rude, empty, half-learned, half-baked [*colloq.*], low-brow [*slang*]; illiterate; unread, uninformed, uneducated, unlearned, unlettered, unbookish; empty-headed; pedantic.

in the dark; benighted, belated; blinded, blindfold; hoodwinked; misinformed; *au bout de son latin* [*F.*], at the end of his tether, at fault; at

sea etc. (*uncertain*) 475; caught tripping, caught napping.

unknown, unapprehended, unexplained, unascertained, uninvestigated, unexplored, unheard of, unperceived; concealed etc. 528; novel.

adv.   **ignorantly** etc. *adj.;* unawares; for anything one knows, for aught one knows; not that one knows.

int.   God−, Heaven−, the Lord−, nobody- knows!

492. Scholar

n.   **scholar**, savant [*F.*], pundit *or* pandit [*India*], schoolman, professor, graduate, wrangler [*Cambridge Univ., Eng.*], academician, academist [*obs.*], doctor, fellow, don [*Eng. Univ. cant*], graduate, postgraduate, clerk [*archaic*]; *Artium Magister* [*L.*], A.M. *or* M.A., master of arts; *Artium Baccalaureus,* A.B. *or* B.A., bachelor of arts; bookman [*rare*], classicist, licentiate, gownsman; philosopher, philomath; scientist, connoisseur, sophist, sophister; linguist; etymologist, philologist; philologer [*now rare*]; lexicographer, glossographer, glossologist, lexicologist, scholiast, commentator, annotator; grammarian; *littérateur* [*F.*], *literati* [*L.*], *dilettanti* [*It.*], illuminati; mayven [*Jew.*], munshi *or* moonshee [*India*], mullah [*Moslem*], moolvi [*India*], guru [*India*]; Hebraist, Hellenist, Graecist, Sanskritist; sinologist, sinologue.

bookworm, *helluo librorum* [*L.*], bibliophile, bibliophilist, bibliomaniac, blue-stocking [*colloq.*], *bas-bleu* [*F.*], high-brow [*slang*].

Admirable Crichton, Mezzofanti, "learned Theban" [*King Lear*], Dominie Sampson [*Guy Mannering*], Socrates.

learned man, literary man; *homo multarum literarum* [*L.*]; man of -learning, −letters, −education, −genius; giant of learning, colossus of knowledge, prodigy.

antiquarian, antiquary, archaeologist, Assyriologist, Egyptologist, sage etc. (*wise man*) 500.

pedant, doctrinaire; pedagogue, Dr. Pangloss; pantologist; instructor etc. (*teacher*) 540.

student, learner, classman, senior, junior, sophomore, freshman, pupil, schoolboy etc. (*learner*) 541.

adj.   **learned** etc. 490; brought up at the feet of Gamaliel.

493. Ignoramus

n.   **ignoramus**, illiterate, dunce, duffer, woodenhead [*colloq.*], bonehead [*slang*], solid ivory [*slang*], numskull [*colloq.*], wooden spoon [*Cambridge Univ., Eng., cant*]; no scholar.

sciolist, smatterer, dabbler, half scholar; charlatan; wiseacre.

novice, tenderfoot; greenhorn etc. (*dupe*) 547; plebe *or* pleb [*cant, U. S.*]; tyro etc. (*learner*) 541; lubber etc. (*bungler*) 701; fool etc. 501.

adj. **bookless**, shallow, simple, lumpish, dull, dumb [*colloq.*], dense, crass, imbecile; wise in his own conceit; ignorant etc. 491.

494. Truth
[object of knowledge]

n. **truth**, verity; fact, reality etc. (*existence*) 1; plain matter of fact; nature etc. (*principle*) 5; gospel; orthodoxy etc. 983*a;* authenticity; veracity etc. 543.

plain-, honest-, sober-, naked-, unalloyed-, unvarnished-, unqualified-, stern-, exact-, intrinsic- truth; *nuda veritas* [*L.*]; the very thing; not an illusion etc. 495; real Simon Pure; unvarnished tale; the truth, the whole truth and nothing but the truth; just the thing.

accuracy, exactitude; exactness, preciseness etc. *adj.;* precision, delicacy; rigor, mathematical precision, fidelity; clockwork precision etc. (*regularity*) 80; conformity to rule; nicety.

orthology; *ipsissima verba* [*L.*], the very words; realism.

v. **be true** etc. *adj.,* be the case; stand the test; have the true ring; hold good, hold true, hold water.

render true, prove true etc. *adj.;* substantiate etc. (*evidence*) 467.

get at the truth etc. (*discover*) 480*a.*

adj. **true**, real, actual etc. (*existing*) 1; veritable; certain etc.; 474; substantially-, categorically-true etc.; true -to the letter, -as gospel, -as steel, -to life, -to the facts; unimpeachable; veracious etc. 543; unrefuted, unconfuted; unideal, unimagined; realistic.

exact, accurate, definite, precise, well-defined, just, right, correct, strict, severe; close etc. (*similar*) 17; orthological, literal; rigid, rigorous; scrupulous etc. (*conscientious*) 939; religiously exact, punctual, punctilious, mathematical, scientific; faithful, constant, unerring; curious, particular, nice, meticulous, delicate, fine; clean-cut, clear-cut.

authentic, genuine, legitimate; orthodox etc. 983*a;* official, *ex officio* [*L.*].

pure, natural, sound, sterling, true-blue; unsophisticated, unadulterated, Simon-Pure [*colloq.*], unvarnished, uncolored; in its true colors.

valid, well-grounded, well-founded; solid, substantial, pukka *or* pucka *or* pakka [*Hind.*], tan-

gible; undistorted, undisguised; unaffected, unexaggerated, unromantic, unflattering.

adv. **truly** etc. *adj.;* verily, indeed, in reality; in very truth, in fact, as a matter of fact, to state the facts; beyond -doubt, -question; with truth etc. (*veracity*) 543; certainly etc. (*certain*) 474; actually etc. (*existence*) 1; in effect etc. (*intrinsically*) 5.

exactly etc. *adj.; ad amussim or adamussim* [*L*], verbatim, *verbatim et literatim* [*L.*]; word for word, literally, *literatim* [*L.*], *totidem verbis* [*L.*], *sic* [*L.*], to the letter, chapter and verse, *ipsissimis verbis* [*L.*]; *ad unguem* [*L.*]; to an inch; to a -nicety, -hair, -tittle, -turn, -T; *au pied de la lettre* [*F.*]; neither more nor less; in every respect, in all respects; *sous tous les rapports* [*F.*]; at any rate, at all events; strictly speaking.

495. Error

n. **error**, fallacy; misconception, misapprehension, misunderstanding; aberration, aberrance *or* aberrancy; inexactness etc. *adj.;* laxity; misconstruction etc. (*misinterpretation*) 523; anachronism; miscomputation etc. (*misjudgment*) 481; *non sequitur* [*L.*] etc. 477; misstatement, misreport; mumpsimus.

mistake; miss, fault, blunder, cross-purposes, oversight, misprint, erratum, corrigendum, slip, blot, flaw, loose thread; trip, stumble etc. (*failure*) 732; botchery etc. (*want of skill*) 699; slip of the tongue, *lapsus linguae* [*L.*]; slip of the pen, *lapsus calami* [*L.*], clerical error; bull etc. (*absurdity*) 497; Spoonerism, Malapropism, Leiterism [*U. S.*], Mrs. Partington; haplography.

delusion, illusion; false-, warped-, distorted-impression, -idea; bubble; self-deceit, self-deception; mists of error; exploded -notion, -idea, -superstition.

heresy etc. (*heterodoxy*) 984; hallucination etc. (*insanity*) 503; false light etc. (*fallacy of vision*) 443; dream etc. (*fancy*) 515; fable etc. (*untruth*) 546; bias etc. (*misjudgment*) 481; misleading etc. *v.*

v. **be erroneous** etc. *adj.*

mislead, misguide; lead astray, lead into error; cause error; beguile, misinform etc. (*misteach*) 538; delude; give a false -impression, -idea; falsify, misstate; deceive etc. 545; lie etc. 544.

err; be in error etc. *adj.,* be mistaken etc. *v.;* be deceived etc. (*duped*) 547; mistake, receive a false impression, deceive oneself; fall into-, lie

163

under–, labor under- an error etc. *n.;* be in the wrong, blunder; misapprehend, misconceive, misunderstand, misreckon, miscount, miscalculate etc. (*misjudge*) 481.

play–, be- at cross purposes etc. (*misinterpret*) 523.

trip, stumble; lose oneself etc. (*uncertainty*) 475; go astray; fail etc. 732; be in the wrong box; take the wrong sow by the ear etc. (*mismanage*) 699; put the saddle on the wrong horse; reckon without one's host; take the shadow for the substance etc. (*credulity*) 486; dream etc. (*imagine*) 515.

adj. **erroneous**, untrue, false, devoid of truth, faulty, erring, fallacious, apocryphal, unreal, ungrounded, groundless; unsubstantial etc. 4; heretical etc. (*heterodox*) 984; unsound; illogical etc. 477.

inexact, unexact, inaccurate, incorrect; indefinite etc. (*uncertain*) 475.

illusive, illusory, delusive; mock, ideal etc. (*imaginary*) 515; spurious etc. 545; deceitful etc. 544; perverted.

controvertible, unsustainable, unsustained, unauthentic, unauthenticated, untrustworthy.

exploded, refuted, discarded.

mistaken etc. *v.;* in error, under an error etc. *n.;* tripping etc. *v.;* out, out in one's reckoning; aberrant; beside–, wide of- -the mark, –the truth; astray etc. (*at fault*) 475; on -a false, –the wrong- -scent, –trail; in the wrong box; at cross-purposes, all in the wrong; at sea, bewildered.

adv. more or less.

496. Maxim

n. **maxim**, aphorism; apothegm *or* apophthegm; dictum, saying, adage, saw, proverb, epigram, gnomic saying, gnome, sentence, mot [*Gallicism*], motto, word, byword, bromide, bromidium [*slang*], commonplace, moral, phylactery, protasis [*rare*].

wise–, sage–, received–, admitted–, recognized- maxim etc.; true–, common–, hackneyed–, trite–, commonplace- saying etc.

axiom, theorem, scholium, truism, postulate.

principle, principia; profession of faith etc. (*belief*) 484; settled principle, formula; reflection etc. (*idea*) 453; conclusion etc. (*judgment*) 480; golden rule etc. (*precept*) 697.

adj. **aphoristic**, aphorismic, aphorismatic, proverbial, phylacteric; axiomatic *or* axiomatical, gnomic *or* gnomical.

adv. as the saying is, as they say, as it was said by them of old.

497. Absurdity

n. **absurdity**, absurdness etc. *adj.;* imbecility etc. 499; alogy [*obs.*], comicality, nonsense, paradox, inconsistency; stultiloquy [*rare*], stultiloquence [*rare*], stultification, futility, nugacity.

blunder, muddle, bull; Irishism, Hibernicism; anticlimax, bathos; sophism etc. 477.

farce, galimatias, burlesque, parody, fiddle-faddle [*colloq.*], amphigory *or* amphigouri, rhapsody; farrago etc. (*disorder*) 59; bêtise [*F.*]; extravagance, romance; sciamachy.

pun, sell [*colloq.*], catch [*colloq.*], verbal quibble, macaronic composition, limerick, joke.

jargon, slipslop [*colloq.*], gibberish, balderdash, bombast, claptrap, fustian, twaddle etc. (*no meaning*) 517; exaggeration etc. 549; moonshine, stuff; mare's-nest, quibble, self-delusion.

tomfoolery, vagary, mummery, monkeyshine, monkey trick, boutade [*F.*], frisk, practical joke, escapade.

v. **play the fool** etc. 499; stultify, blunder, muddle; employ absurdity etc. *n.;* rhapsodize; romance, sell [*slang*], fiddle-faddle [*colloq.*]; talk nonsense, parler à tort et à travers [*F.*]; battre la campagne [*F.*]; anemolia bazein [*Gr.*]; be absurd etc. *adj.;* frisk, caper, joke, play practical jokes.

be the fool, be the goat [*colloq.*], bite [*colloq.*].

adj. **absurd**, nonsensical, farcical, preposterous, egregious, senseless, inconsistent, stultiloquent [*rare*], stulty [*obs.*], ridiculous, extravagant, quibbling; self-annulling, self-contradictory; paradoxical, macaronic *or* maccaronic, punning.

burlesque, foolish etc. 499; sophistical etc. 477; unmeaning etc. 517; amphigoric; without rhyme or reason; fantastic *or* fantastical, rhapsodic *or* rhapsodical, bombastic, high-flown.

int. fiddledeedee! pish! pooh! pooh-pooh! bah! stuff and nonsense! fiddle-faddle! bosh! come off! [*slang*].

498. Intelligence. Wisdom

n. **intelligence**, capacity, comprehension, understanding; cuteness [*colloq.*], sabe [*slang*], savvy [*slang*]; intellect etc. 450; nous [*colloq.*], docity [*dial.*], parts, sagacity, mother wit, wit, esprit [*F.*], gumption [*colloq.*], quick parts, grasp of intellect; acuteness etc. *adj.;* acumen, longheadedness, arguteness, subtility, subtlety, penetration, perspicacy [*obs.*], perspicacity, discernment, due sense of, good judgment; discrimination etc. 465; cunning etc. 702; refinement etc. (*taste*) 850.

head, brains, gray matter [colloq.], brain-stuff [colloq.], headpiece, upper story [colloq.], long head.

eagle -eye, –glance; eye of a lynx, eye of a hawk.

wisdom, sapience, sense; good-, common-, horse - [colloq.], plainsense; clear thinking, rationality, reason; reasonableness etc. adj.; judgment, solidity, depth, profundity, caliber or calibre; enlarged views; reach-, compass- of thought; enlargement of mind.

genius, lambent flame of intellect, inspiration, Geist [Ger.], fire of genius, heaven-born genius, soul; talent etc. (aptitude) 698.

[wisdom in action] prudence etc. 864; vigilance etc. 459; tact etc. 698; foresight etc. 510; sobriety, self-possession, aplomb [F.], ballast, mental poise, balance.

a bright thought, an inspiration, not a bad idea.

v. **be intelligent** etc. adj.; have all one's wits about one; be brilliant, be witty, scintillate, coruscate; understand etc. (intelligible) 518; catch-, take in- an idea; take a -joke, –hint.

penetrate; see through, see at a glance, see with half an eye, see far into, see through a millstone [colloq.]; discern etc. (descry) 441; foresee etc. 510.

discriminate etc. 465; know what's what [colloq.] etc. 698; listen to reason.

adj. [applied to persons] **intelligent**, quick of apprehension, keen, acute, alive, brainy [colloq.], awake, bright, quick, sharp; quick-, keen-, clear-, sharp- -eyed, –sighted, –witted; wide-awake; canny, sly, pawky [dial.], shrewd, astute; clear-headed; farsighted etc. 510; discerning, perspicacious, penetrating, piercing; argute; nimble-witted, needle-witted; sharp as a tack; alive to etc. (cognizant) 490; clever etc. (apt) 698; arch etc. (cunning) 702; pas is bête [F.]; acute etc. 682.

wise, sage, sapient [often in irony], sagacious, reasonable, rational, sound, in one's right mind, sensible, abnormis sapiens [L.], judicious, strong-minded.

impartial, unprejudiced, unbiased, unbigoted, unprepossessed; undazzled, unperplexed; of unwarped judgment, equitable, fair.

cool; cool-, long-, hard-, strong-headed; long-sighted, calculating, thoughtful, reflecting; solid, deep, profound.

prudent etc. (cautious) 864; sober, staid, solid; considerate, politic, wise in one's generation; watchful etc. 459; provident etc. (prepared) 673; in advance of one's age; wise as -a serpent, –Solomon, –Solon, –Nestor, –Mentor.

oracular; heaven-directed, heaven-born.

[applied to actions] **wise**, sensible, reasonable, judicious; well-judged, well-advised; prudent, politic; expedient etc. 646.

499. Imbecility. Folly

n. **imbecility**; want of intelligence etc. 498, want of intellect etc. 450; shallowness, unwisdom, silliness, foolishness etc. adj.; morosis, incapacity, vacancy of mind, poverty of intellect, clouded perception, poor head; apartments-, rooms-, space- to let [all slang]; nobody home [slang]; stupidity, insulsity [rare], stolidity; hebetude, dull understanding, meanest capacity, short-sightedness; incompetence etc. (unskillfulness) 699.

bias etc. 481; infatuation etc. (insanity) 503; one's weak side.

simplicity, puerility, babyhood; senility, dotage, anility, second childishness, fatuousness, fatuity; idiocy, idiotism, jobbernowlism [colloq., Eng.], driveling, driveling idiocy; senile dementia.

folly, frivolity, irrationality, trifling, ineptitude, nugacity, futility, inconsistency, lip wisdom, conceit; sophistry etc. 477; giddiness etc. (inattention) 458; eccentricity etc. 503; extravagance etc. (absurdity) 497; rashness etc. 863.

act of folly etc. 699.

v. **be imbecile** etc. adj.; have no -brains, –sense etc. 498; have a screw loose [colloq.].

trifle, drivel, radoter [F.], dote, ramble etc. (madness) 503; play the -fool, –monkey; take leave of one's senses; not see an inch beyond one's nose; stultify oneself etc. 699; talk nonsense etc. 497.

adj. [applied to persons] **unintelligent**, unintellectual, unreasoning; mindless, witless, reasonless, brainless; half-baked [colloq.], having no head etc. 498; not bright etc. 498; inapprehensive, thick [colloq.].

blockish, unteachable; Boeotian, Boeotic; bovine; ungifted, undiscerning, unenlightened, unwise, unphilosophical; apish, simious, simian.

weak-, addle-, puzzle-, blunder-, muddle- [colloq.], jolter-, jolt-, chowder-, pig-, beetle-, buffle- [obs.], chuckle-, mutton-, gross-headed; maggot-pated [obs.], beef-headed, beef-witted, fat-headed, fat-witted.

weak-minded, feeble-minded; dull-, shallow-, lack- brained; rattle- brained, –headed; saphead [colloq.], muddy-brained, addle-brained; half-, lean-, short-, shallow-, dull-, blunt-witted; shallow-, clod-, addle- pated; dim-, short- sighted; thick-skulled; thick-headed;

weak in the upper story [*colloq.*], inapprehensible, nutty [*slang*], batty [*slang*], loony [*slang*].

shallow, *borné* [*F.*], weak, wanting, soft [*colloq.*], sappy, spoony *or* spooney [*slang*]; dull,
—as a beetle.

stupid, heavy, insulse [*rare*], obtuse, blunt, stolid,
doltish; asinine; inapt etc. 699; prosaic etc. 843;
hebetudinous, hebetate, hebete [*rare*].

childish, childlike; infantine, infantile, babyish,
babish; puerile, senile, anile; simple etc.
(*credulous*) 486; old-womanish.

imbecile, fatuous, idiotic, driveling; blatant, babbling; vacant; sottish; bewildered etc. 475.

foolish, silly, senseless, irrational, insensate, nonsensical, inept; maudlin.

narrow-minded etc. 481; bigoted etc. (*obstinate*) 606; giddy etc. (*thoughtless*) 458; rash etc.
863; eccentric etc. (*crazed*) 503.

[applied to actions] **foolish**, unwise, injudicious,
improper, unreasonable, without reason, ridiculous, silly, stupid, asinine; ill-imagined, ill-
advised, ill-judged, ill-devised; *mal entendu*
[*F.*]; inconsistent, irrational, unphilosophical;
extravagant etc. (*nonsensical*) 497; sleeveless
[*obs.*], idle; useless etc. 645; inexpedient etc.
647; frivolous etc. (*trivial*) 643.

500. Sage

n. **sage**, wise man; master mind, master spirit of the
age; longhead, thinker, philosopher.

authority, oracle, mentor, luminary, shining
light, *esprit fort* [*F.*], *magnus Apollo* [*L.*], Solon,
Solomon, Buddha, Confucius, Mentor, Nestor,
the Magi; Seven Wise Men of Greece, Seven
Sages, Philosophical Pleiad; "second Daniel."

savant [*F.*], pundit etc. (*scholar*) 492; wiseacre
[*archaic or ironical*]; expert etc. 700; wizard etc.
994.

adj. **venerable**, venerated, reverenced, revered, honored, looked up to; authoritative, wise, oracular; erudite etc. (*knowledge*) 490; *emeritus*
[*L.*].

501. Fool

n. **fool**, idiot, tomfool, wiseacre, simpleton, Simple
Simon, moron, gaby [*colloq.*], witling, dizzard
[*obs.*], donkey, ass; ninny, ninny hammer,
chowderhead [*dial.*], jolterhead *or* jolthead,
chucklehead [*colloq.*], dolt, booby, tomnoddy,
loony [*slang*], looby, hoddy-doddy [*obs.*],
noddy, nonny [*dial.*], noodle, nizy [*obs.*], owl,
goose, imbecile; *radoteur* [*F.*], nincompoop
[*colloq.*], *badaud* [*F.*], zany; trifler, babbler;
pretty fellow; natural, *niais* [*F.*].

child, baby, infant, innocent, milksop, sop.

oaf, lout, loon *or* lown [*dial.*]; bullhead, blunderhead, addle-pate, addlebrain, addlehead
[*all colloq.*]; blockhead, dullhead, bonehead
[*slang*], rattlepate, dullard, doodle [*obs.*], calf
[*colloq.*], colt, buzzard [*obs.*], block, put, stick
[*colloq.*], stock, numps [*obs.*], tony [*obs.*]; log-
gerhead, beetlehead, grosshead [*obs.*], mut-
tonhead [*colloq.*], noodlehead, giddyhead
[*colloq.*], numskull [*colloq.*], thickhead [*colloq.*], thick skull; lackbrain, shallowbrain; half-
wit, lackwit; dunderpate; lunkhead.

sawney [*dial. Eng.*], clod, clodhopper; clodpoll,
clodpate, clotpole *or* clotpoll [*obs.*], clotpate
[*obs.*], soft *or* softy [*colloq. or slang*], saphead
[*slang*], bull calf [*colloq.*], spoony *or* spooney
[*slang*], gawk, gawky, gowk, Gothamite, lummox [*dial.*], rube; men of Boeotia, wise men of
Gotham.

un sot à triple étage [*F.*], sot [*Scot.*], jobbernowl
[*colloq., Eng.*], changeling [*archaic*], mooncalf,
gobe-mouches [*F.*].

greenhorn etc. (*dupe*) 547; dunce etc. (*ignoramus*) 493; lubber etc. (*bungler*) 701; madman
etc. 504; solid ivory.

one who -will not set the Thames on fire, —did not
invent gunpowder, —does not exactly scintillate; *qui n'a pas inventé la poudre* [*F.*]; no con-
jurer; no Solomon.

dotard, driveler; old fogy *or* fogey [*colloq.*], old
woman; crone, grandmother; cotquean [*ar-
chaic*], henhussy, betty [*contempt*].

502. Sanity

n. **sanity**; soundness etc. *adj.*; rationality, normalcy,
normality, sobriety, lucidity, lucid interval;
senses, sober senses, common sense, horse
sense [*colloq.*], sound mind, *mens sana* [*L.*].

v. **be sane** etc. *adj.*; retain one's senses, —reason.

become sane etc. *adj.*; come to one's senses,
sober down, cool down, get things into proportion, see things in proper perspective.

render sane etc. *adj.*; bring to one's senses,
sober, bring to reason.

adj. **sane**, rational, normal, wholesome, right-minded,
reasonable, *compos mentis* [*L.*], of sound mind;
sound, sound-minded; lucid.

self-possessed; sober, sober-minded.

in one's -sober senses, —right mind; in possession
of one's faculties.

adv. **sanely** etc. *adj.*; in reason, within reason, within
bounds; according to the dictates of -reason,
—common sense; in the name of common
sense.

503. Insanity

n. **insanity**, lunacy; madness etc. *adj.,* mania, rabies, furor, mental alienation, aberration, amentia, paranoia; dementation, dementia, demency [*rare*], morosis, idiocy; *dementia a potu* [*L.*], delirium tremens, d.t.'s, the horrors [*colloq.*]; phrenitis, frenzy, raving, incoherence, wandering, delirium, calenture of the brain, delusion, hallucination; lycanthropy.

derangement; disordered -reason, –intellect; diseased–, unsound–, abnormal- mind; unsoundness.

vertigo, dizziness, swimming, sunstroke, *coup de soleil* [*F.*], siriasis.

oddity, eccentricity, twist, monomania; fanaticism, infatuation, craze; kleptomania, dipsomania; hypochondriasis etc. (*low spirits*) 837; melancholia, hysteria.

screw-, tile-, slate-loose; bee in one's bonnet, rats in the upper story, bats in the belfry, bee in the head [*all colloq.*].

dotage etc. (*imbecility*) 499.

v. **be** *or* **become insane** etc. *adj.;* lose one's senses, –reason, –faculties, –wits; go mad, run mad; rave, dote, ramble, wander; drivel etc. (*be imbecile*) 499; have a screw loose etc. *n.,* have a devil; *avoir le diable au corps* [*F.*]; lose one's head etc. (*be uncertain*) 475.

derange; render *or* drive mad etc. *adj.;* madden, dementate [*rare*], addle the wits, derange the head, infatuate, befool; turn the brain, turn one's head.

adj. **insane**, mad, lunatic; crazy, crazed, *aliéné* [*F.*], *non compos mentis* [*L.*], not right, dement [*rare*], dementate, cracked [*colloq.*], touched; bereft of reason; all-possessed, unhinged, unsettled in one's mind; insensate, reasonless, beside oneself, demented, maniacal, daft; frenzied, frenetic *or* frenetical; possessed, –with a devil; deranged, far gone, maddened, moonstruck; shatterpated, shatterbrained; madbrained, scatterbrained, crack-brained; off one's head.

Corybantic, dithyrambic; rabid, giddy, vertiginous, wild; haggard, mazed; flighty; distracted, distraught; bewildered etc. (*uncertain*) 475.

mad as a -March hare, –hatter; of unsound mind etc. *n.;* touched-, wrong-, not right- in one's -head, –mind, –wits, –upper story [*colloq.*]; out of one's -mind, –senses, –wits; not in one's right mind; nutty [*slang*].

odd, fanatical, infatuated, eccentric; hypochondriac, hyppish [*rare*], hipped *or* hypped [*colloq.*], hippish [*colloq.*].

delirious, light-headed, incoherent, rambling, doting, wandering; frantic, raving, stark mad, stark staring mad.

imbecile, silly, etc. 499.

adv. like one possessed.

504. Madman

n. **madman**, lunatic, maniac, bedlamite, candidate for Bedlam, raver, phrenetic, madcap; energumen [*eccl. antiq.*]; automaniac, monomaniac, dipsomaniac, kleptomaniac, paranoiac; hypochondriac etc. (*low spirits*) 837; crank, Tom o' Bedlam; nut [*slang*].

dreamer etc. 515; rhapsodist, seer, highflyer *or* highflier [*obs.*], enthusiast, fanatic, *fanatico* [*It.*], *exalté* [*F.*], Don Quixote, Ophelia, Madge Wildfire.

idiot etc. 501.

Section 6. Extension of Thought

505. Memory

n. **memory**, remembrance; retentivity, retention, retentiveness; tenacity; tablets of the memory; readiness.

retentive–, tenacious–, trustworthy–, capacious–, faithful–, correct–, exact–, ready–, prompt- memory; Memory's halls, Memory's pictures.

recollection, reminiscence, recognition, recurrence, rememoration [*rare*], rememorance [*rare*]; retrospect, retrospection; "that inward eye" [Wordsworth]; afterthought.

reminder; suggestion etc. (*information*) 527; prompting etc. *v.;* hint, token of remembrance, memento, souvenir, keepsake, relic, memorandum (*pl.* memoranda); remembrancer, flapper; memorial etc. (*record*) 551; commemoration etc. (*celebration*) 883.

things to be remembered, memorabilia.

mnemonics, art of–, artificial- memory; *memoria technica* [*L.*]; mnemotechnics, mnemotechny; Mnemosyne.

aids to memory, jogger [*colloq.*], memorandum book, notebook, promptbook, engagement book.

fame, celebrity, renown, reputation etc. (*repute*) 873.

v. **remember**, mind [*obsoles.*], rememorate [*rare*]; retain the -memory, –remembrance- of; keep in view.

have-, hold-, bear-, carry-, keep-, retain- in *or* in the -thoughts, –mind, –memory,

–remembrance; be in–, live in–, remain in–, dwell in–, haunt–, impress- one's -memory, -thoughts, -mind.

sink in the mind; run in the head; not be able to get it out of one's head; be deeply impressed with; rankle etc. (*revenge*) 919.

recognize, bethink oneself, recall, call up, conjure up, retrace; look–, trace- -back, –backwards; think upon, look back upon; review; call–, recall–, bring- to -mind, –remembrance; carry one's thoughts back; rake up the past.

redeem from oblivion; keep the -memory alive, –wound green; *tangere ulcus* [*L.*]; keep the memory green, keep up the memory of; commemorate etc. (*celebrate*) 883.

recollect, recur to the mind; flash on the mind, flash across the memory.

remind; suggest etc. (*inform*) 527; prompt; put–, keep- in mind; fan the embers; call up, summon up; renew; *infandum renovare dolorem* [*L.*]; task–, tax–, jog–, flap–, refresh–, rub up–, awaken- the memory; pull by the sleeve; bring back to the memory, put in remembrance, memorialize.

memorize, commit to memory; con, –over; fix–, rivet–, imprint–, impress–, stamp–, grave–, engrave–, store–, treasure up–, bottle up–, embalm–, bury–, enshrine- in the memory; load–, store–, stuff–, burden- the memory with; get–, have–, learn–, know–, say–, repeat- by -heart, –rote; get–, drive- into one's head; bury in the mind; say one's lesson; repeat, –like a parrot; have at one's fingers' ends.

make a note of etc. (*record*) 551.

adj. **remembering,** remembered etc. *v.;* mindful, reminiscential; alive in memory; retained in the memory etc. *v.;* pent up in one's memory; fresh; green, –in remembrance; still vivid, rememorant [*rare*]; not–, never -to be erased, –to be forgotten; unforgettable *or* unforgetable; enduring, –in memory; unforgotten, present to the mind; within one's memory etc. *n.;* indelible; uppermost in one's thoughts; memorable etc. (*important*) 642; suggestive.

adv. **by heart,** *par coeur* [*F.*], by rote; without book, *memoriter* [*L.*].

in memory of; *in memoriam* [*L.*]; *memoria in aeterna* [*L.*].

506. Oblivion

n. **oblivion;** forgetfulness etc. *adj.;* obliteration etc. (552) of–, insensibility etc. (823) to- the past.

short–, treacherous–, loose–, slippery–, failing- memory; decay–, failure–, lapse- of memory;

mind–, memory- like a sieve; untrustworthy memory; waters of -Lethe, –oblivion; amnesia.

amnesty, general pardon.

v. **forget;** be forgetful etc. *adj.;* fall–, sink- into oblivion; have a short memory etc. *n.,* have no head.

forget one's own name, have on the tip of one's tongue, come in one ear and go out the other.

slip–, escape–, fade from–, die away from- the memory; lose, lose sight of.

efface etc. (552)–, discharge- from the memory; unlearn; consign to -oblivion, –the tomb of the Capulets; think no more of etc. (*turn the attention from*) 458; cast behind one's back, wean one's thoughts from; let bygones be bygones etc. (*forgive*) 918.

adj. **forgotten** etc. *v.;* unremembered, past recollection, bygone, out of mind; buried–, sunk- in oblivion; clean forgotten; gone out of one's -head, –recollection.

forgetful, oblivious, mindless, Lethean; insensible etc. (823) to the past; heedless.

507. Expectation

n. **expectation,** expectance, expectancy; anticipation, contingency, contingent, reckoning, calculation; foresight etc. 510; contemplation, prospection.

prospect, lookout [*chiefly Eng.*], perspective, horizon, vista; destiny etc. 152; futures [*stock exchange*].

suspense, waiting, abeyance; curiosity etc. 455; anxious–, ardent–, eager–, breathless–, sanguine- expectation; torment of Tantalus.

assurance, confidence, presumption, reliance; hope etc. 858; trust etc. (*belief*) 484; prognosis [*med.*], prognostic, prognostication; auspices etc. (*prediction*) 511.

v. **expect;** look -for, –out for, –forward to; hope for, anticipate; have in -prospect, –contemplation; keep in view; contemplate, promise oneself; not wonder at *or* if etc. 870.

wait for, tarry for, lie in wait for, watch for, bargain for; keep a -good, –sharp -lookout for; await; stand at "attention," abide, mark time, bide one's time, watch.

prick up one's ears, hold one's breath.

foresee etc. 510; prepare for etc. 673; forestall etc. (*be early*) 132; count upon etc. (*believe in*) 484; think likely etc. (*probability*) 472; bargain for; make one's mouth water.

predict, prognosticate, forecast; lead one to expect etc. (*predict*) 511; have in store for etc. (*destiny*) 152.

adj. **expectant**; expecting etc. *v.;* in expectation etc. *n.;* on the watch etc. (*vigilant*) 459; open-eyed, open-mouthed; agape, gaping, all agog; on tenterhooks, on tiptoe, on the tiptoe of expectation; *aux aguets* [*F.*]; ready, prepared, provided for, provisional, provident; curious etc. 455; looking forward to; on the rack.

expected etc. *v.;* long expected, foreseen; in prospect etc. *n.;* prospective, future, coming; in one's eye, in view, on the horizon; impending etc. (*destiny*) 152.

adv. **expectantly**; on the watch etc. *adj.;* in the event of; as a possible contingency; with muscles tense, on edge [*colloq.*]; with eyes–, with ears -strained; with ears pricked forward; *arrectis auribus* [*L.*]; with breathless expectation etc. *n.,* with bated breath.

soon, shortly, forthwith, anon [*archaic*], presently; prospectively etc. 121.

508. Inexpectation

n. **inexpectation** [*rare*], nonexpectation; unforeseen contingency, the unforeseen; false expectation etc. (*disappointment*) 509; miscalculation etc. 481.

surprise, sudden burst, thunderclap, blow, shock; bolt out of the blue; astoundment [*rare*], astonishment, mazement [*rare*], amazement; wonder etc. 870; eye opener.

v. **not expect** etc. 507; be taken by surprise; start; miscalculate etc. 481; not bargain for; come–, fall- upon.

be unexpected etc. *adj.;* come unawares etc. *adv.;* turn up, pop [*colloq.*], drop from the clouds; come–, burst–, flash–, bounce–, steal–, creep- upon one; come–, burst- like a -thunderclap, –thunderbolt; take–, catch- -by surprise, –unawares; catch napping, catch off one's guard; yach [*S. Africa*].

surprise, startle, take aback [*colloq.*], electrify, stun, stagger, take away one's breath, throw off one's guard; pounce upon, spring, spring upon, spring a mine upon; stound [*archaic*], astound; astonish etc. (*strike with wonder*) 870.

adj. **nonexpectant**, inexpectant; surprised etc. *v.;* unwarned, unaware; off one's guard; inattentive etc. 458.

unexpected, unanticipated, unlooked for, unforeseen, unhoped for; dropped from the clouds; beyond–, contrary to–, against- expectation; out of one's reckoning; unheard of etc. (*exceptional*) 83, startling; sudden etc. (*instantaneous*) 113.

adv. **unexpectedly**, abruptly, plump, pop, *à l'improviste* [*F.*], unawares; without -notice, –warning, –saying "by your leave"; like a thief in the night, like a thunderbolt; like a lightning flash; in an unguarded moment; suddenly etc. (*instantaneously*) 113.

int. heydey! etc. (*wonder*) 870; do tell!

509. Disappointment
[failure of expectation]

n. **disappointment**; blighted hope, disillusion, balk; blow; slip 'twixt cup and lip; nonfulfillment of one's hopes; sad–, bitter- disappointment; trick of fortune; afterclap; false–, vain- expectation; miscalculation etc. 481; fool's paradise; much cry and little wool.

v. **be disappointed**; look blank, look blue [*colloq.*]; look *or* stand aghast etc. (*wonder*) 870; find to one's cost; laugh on the wrong side of one's mouth [*colloq.*], laugh out of the other corner of the mouth [*colloq.*]; find one a false prophet.

disappoint; crush–, dash–, balk–, disappoint–, blight–, falsify–, defeat–, not realize- one's -hope, –expectation; balk, jilt, bilk; play one -false, –a trick; dash the cup from the lips; tantalize; dumfounder *or* dumbfounder, dumfound *or* dumbfound, disillusion, disillusionize; come short of; dissatisfy, make dissatisfied, disgruntle.

adj. **disappointed** etc. *v.;* disconcerted, aghast; disgruntled; out of one's reckoning; short of expectations.

510. Foresight

n. **foresight**, prospicience, prevision, long-sightedness, farsightedness; anticipation; providence etc. (*preparation*) 673.

forethought, forecast; predeliberation, presurmise; foregone conclusion etc. (*prejudgment*) 481; prudence etc. (*caution*) 864.

foreknowledge, precognition, prescience, prenotion, presentiment; second sight; sagacity etc. (*intelligence*) 498; antepast, prelibation; prophasis [*med.*], prognosis [*med.*].

prospect etc. (*expectation*) 507; foretaste; prospectus etc. (*plan*) 626.

v. **foresee**; look -forward to, –ahead, –beyond; scent from afar; feel it in one's bones [*colloq.*]; look–, pry–, peep- into the future.

see one's way; see how the -land lies, –wind blows, –cat jumps [*colloq.*].

anticipate; expect etc. 507; be beforehand etc. (*early*) 132; predict etc. 511; foreknow, forejudge, forecast; surmise; have an eye to the -future, –main chance; *respicere finem* [*L.*]; keep a sharp lookout etc. (*vigilance*) 459; forewarn etc. 668.

adj. **foreseeing** etc. *v.;* prescient, anticipatory; farseeing, farsighted, long-sighted; sagacious etc. (*intelligent*) 498; weatherwise; provident etc. (*prepared*) 673; on the lookout, –for; prospective etc. 507.

adv. against the time when; for a rainy day.

511. Prediction

n. **prediction**, announcement; program *or* programme etc. (*plan*) 626; premonition etc. (*warning*) 668; prognosis, prognostic, presage, presagement, precurse [*obs.*], prophecy, vaticination, mantology [*rare*], prognostication, premonstration [*obs.*]; augury, auguration [*obs.*], ariolation [*obs.*], hariolation [*obs.*], foreboding, aboding [*obs.*], abode [*obs.*], bode [*obs.*], bodement, abodement; omniation [*obs.*], auspice (*pl.* auspices), forecast; omen etc. 512; horoscope, nativity; sooth [*obs.*], soothsaying, fortune-telling; divination.

adytum, oak of Dodona; cave of the Cumaean Sibyl, Sibylline leaves, Sibylline books; tripod of the Pythia.

prefiguration, prefigurement; prototype, type.

[divination by the stars] astrology, astromancy, horoscopy, genethlialogy, judicial *or* mundane astrology.

oracle, prophet, seer etc. 513.

[means of divination] crystal, ink, tea leaves, cards; Hallowe'en -nuts, mirror; divining-rod, witch-hazel; hand of glory; wax image; teraphim; shadows etc. [*see footnote*]; spell, charm etc. 993.

sorcery, magic, necromancy etc. 992; heteroscopic divination.[1]

v. **predict**, prognosticate, prophesy, vaticinate, divine, foretell, soothsay, augurate, tell fortunes; cast a horoscope, cast a nativity; advise; forewarn, prewarn etc. 668.

presage, augur, bode, abode [*obs.*], forebode; foretoken, betoken; prefigure, prefigurate, augurate [*rare*], ariolate [*rare*], figure [*obs.*], forecast, precurse, portend; preshow, foreshow, foreshadow; shadow forth, typify, pretypify, ominate [*obs.*], signify, point to.

hold out–, raise–, excite- -expectation, –hope; bid fair, promise, lead one to expect; be the precursor etc. 64.

herald, usher in, premise, announce; lower.

adj. **predicting** etc. *v.;* predictive, prophetic, fatidic *or* fatidical, precursal, precurrent, presageful, vaticinal, oracular, fatiloquent [*rare*], haruspical; Sibylline; weatherwise.

ominous, portentous; augurous, augurial, augural, precursive, precursory, auspicial, auspicious; prescious [*rare*], prescient, monitory, extispicious [*obs.*], premonitory, significant of, pregnant with, big with the fate of.

[1]The following terms, expressive of different forms of divination, have been collected from various sources, and are here given as a curious illustration of bygone superstitions:

Divination *by oracles*, theomancy; *by the Bible*, Bibliomancy; *by ghosts*, psychomancy; *by crystal gazing*, crystallomancy; *by shadows or manes*, sciomancy; *by appearances in the air*, aeromancy, chaomancy; *by the stars at birth*, genethliacs; *by meteors*, meteoromancy; *by winds*, austromancy; *by sacrificial appearances*, aruspicy (*or* haruspicy), hieromancy, hieroscopy; *by the entrails of animals sacrificed*, extispicy, hieromancy; *by the entrails of a human sacrifice*, anthropomancy; *by the entrails of fishes*, ichthyomancy; *by sacrificial fire*, pyromancy; *by redhot iron*, sideromancy; *by the smoke from the altar*, capnomancy; *by mice*, myomancy; *by birds*, orniscopy, ornithomancy; *by a cock picking up grains*, alectryomancy (*or* alectoromancy); *by snakes*, ophiomancy; *by herbs*, botanomancy; *by water*, hydromancy; *by fountains*, pegomancy; *by a wand*, rhabdomancy; *by dough of cakes*, crithomancy; *by meal*, aleuromancy, alphitomancy; *by salt*, halomancy; *by lead*, molybdomancy; *by dice*, cleromancy; *by arrows*, belomancy; *by a balanced hatchet*, axinomancy; *by a balanced sieve*, coscinomancy; *by a suspended ring*, dactyliomancy; *by dots made at random on paper*, geomancy; *by precious stones*, lithomancy; *by pebbles*, pessomancy; *by pebbles drawn from a heap*, psephomancy; *by mirrors*, catoptromancy; *by writings in ashes*, tephramancy; *by dreams*, oneiromancy; *by the hand*, palmistry, chiromancy; *by nails reflecting the sun's rays*, onychomancy; *by finger rings*, dactylomancy; *by numbers*, arithmancy; *by drawing lots*, sortilege; *by passages in books*, stichomancy; *by the letters forming the name of the person*, onomancy, nomancy; *by the features*, anthroposcopy; *by the mode of laughing*, geloscopy; *by ventriloquism*, gastromancy; *by walking in a circle*, gyromancy; *by dropping melted wax into water*, ceromancy; *by currents*, bletonism; *by the color and peculiarities of wine*, oenomancy; *by the shoulder blade*, scapulimancy *or* scapulomancy, omoplatoscopy.

512. Omen

n. **omen**, portent, presage, prognostic, augury, auspice; sign etc. (*indication*) 550; harbinger etc. (*precursor*) 64; yule candle, yule log *or* clog.

bird of ill omen; halcyon birds; signs of the times; gathering clouds, thunder, lightning, rainbow, comet, shooting star; rain of blood, warning etc. 668.

prefigurement etc. 511; adytum etc. 511.

adj. **ill-boding**, ill-omened, inauspicious.

513. Oracle

n. **oracle**; prophet, seer, soothsayer, augur, medium, clairvoyant, palmist, fortune teller, prophetess, sibyl, witch, geomancer, haruspice *or* aruspice, haruspex *or* aruspex; Sibyl; python, pythoness, Pythia; Pythian oracle, Delphian (*or* Delphic) oracle; Monitor, Sphinx, Tiresias, Cassandra, Sibylline leaves; oak–, oracle- of Dodona; sorcerer etc. 994; interpreter etc. 524.

weather prophet, weather sharp [*slang*], weather bureau, Old Probabilities *or* Old Prob. [*humorous nickname for U. S. weather bureau*]; Old Moore, Zadkiel.

Section 7. Creative Thought

514. Supposition

n. **supposition**, assumption, supposal, supposableness [*rare*], supposality [*obs.*], postulation [*rare*], condition, presupposition, hypothesis, postulate, postulatum, theory, data; proposition, position; thesis, theorem; proposal etc. (*plan*) 626; assumed position.

bare–, vague–, loose- -supposition, –suggestion; conceit; conjecture; guess, guesswork; rough guess, shot [*colloq.*]; conjecturality [*rare*], suggestiveness, presurmise, surmise, suspicion, inkling, suggestion, association of ideas, hint; presumption etc. (*belief*) 484; divination, speculation, shot in the dark.

theorist, theorizer, speculatist [*rare*], speculator, notionalist, hypothesist, hypothetist [*rare*], doctrinaire, doctrinarian.

v. **suppose**, conjecture, surmise, suspect, guess, divine; theorize; presume, presuppose; assume, fancy, wis [*archaic*], take it; give a guess, speculate, believe, dare say, take it into one's head, take for granted.

propound, propose, put forth; start, put a case, submit, move, make a motion; hazard–, venture–, throw out–, put forward- a -suggestion, –conjecture, –supposition; hypothesize.

suggest, allude to, hint, put it into one's head.

suggest itself etc. (*thought*) 451; run in the head etc. (*memory*) 505; marvel - wonder- -if, –whether.

adj. **supposing** etc. *v.;* given, mooted, postulatory [*now rare*]; assumed etc. *v.;* suppositive, supposititious; gratuitous, speculative, conjectural, conjecturable, hypothetical, theoretical, academic, supposable, presumptive, putative; suppositional, suppositionary.

suggestive, allusive, stimulating.

adv. **if**, if so be; an [*archaic*]; on the supposition etc. *n.; ex hypothesi* [*L.*], in case, in the event of; if that [*archaic*], so that, whether; quasi, as if, provided; perhaps etc. (*by possibility*) 470; for aught one knows.

515. Imagination

n. **imagination**, originality, invention; fancy; inspiration; verve.

warm–, heated–, excited–, sanguine–, ardent–, fiery–, boiling–, wild–, bold–, daring–, playful–, lively–, fertile- -imagination, –fancy.

"mind's eye" [*Hamlet*]; "the mind's internal heaven" [Wordsworth]; "such stuff as dreams are made on" [*Tempest*].

ideality, idealism; romanticism, utopianism, castle-building; dreaming; frenzy, ecstasy; calenture etc. (*delirium*) 503; reverie *or* revery, brown study, pipe dream, daydream, trance; somnambulism.

conception, *Vorstellung* [*Ger.*], excogitation, "a fine frenzy" [*Midsummer Night's Dream*]; cloudland, dreamland; flight–, fumes- of fancy; "thick-coming fancies" [*Macbeth*]; creation–, coinage- of the brain; imagery; word painting.

fantasy, conceit, figment, myth, dream, vision, shadow, chimera; phantasm, phantasy, fancy; maggot, whim, whimwham, whimsey *or* whimsy, vagary, rhapsody, romance, gest *or* geste, extravaganza; "air-drawn dagger" [*Macbeth*], bugbear, nightmare; flying Dutchman, great sea serpent, man in the moon, castle in the air, castle in Spain, *château en Espagne* [*F.*], pleasure dome of Kubla Khan, Utopia; Heavenly City, New Jerusalem; Atlantis, Happy Valley [Johnson], millennium, fairyland; land of Prester John, kingdom of Micomicon; Estotiland *or* Estotilandia [Milton]; Laputa; Cockagne, Lubberland; Arabian nights; *le pot au lait* [*F.*]; pot of gold at the end of the rainbow; dream of Alnaschar etc. (*hope*) 858; golden dream.

[creative works] work of fiction etc. (*novel*) 594; poetry etc. 597; play, tragedy, comedy etc. (*drama*) 599; sonata etc. (*music*) 415.

illusion etc. (*error*) 495; phantom etc. (*fallacy of vision*) 443; *Fata Morgana* [*L.*] etc. (*ignis* *fatuus*) 423; vapor etc. (*cloud*) 353; stretch of the imagination etc. (*exaggeration*) 549; mythogenesis.

idealist, romanticist, visionary; mopus [*slang*], romancer, daydreamer, dreamer; somnambulist; rhapsodist etc. (*fanatic*) 504; castle-builder, fanciful projector; "sweetest Shakespeare, Fancy's child" [Milton].

v. **imagine**, fancy, conceive; idealize, realize; dream, –of; "gives to airy nothing a local habitation and a name" [*Midsummer Night's Dream*].

set one's wits to work; strain–, crack- one's invention; rack–, ransack–, cudgel- one's brains; excogitate.

give -play, –the reins, –a loose [*obs.*]- to the--imagination, –fancy; tilt at windmills; indulge in reverie.

conjure up a vision; fancy–, represent–, picture–, figure- to oneself; *vorstellen* [*Ger.*]; "see visions and dream dreams" [*Bible*].

float in the mind; suggest itself etc. (*thought*) 451.

create, originate, devise, invent, make up, coin, fabricate; improvise, strike out something new.

adj. **imagined** etc. *v.; ben trovato* [*It.*]; air-drawn, air-built.

imaginative; imagining etc. *v.;* original, inventive, creative, fertile, productive, ingenious.

extravagant, romantic, high-flown, flighty, preposterous; rhapsodic *or* rhapsodical; fanatic, enthusiastic, Utopian, Quixotic.

ideal, unreal; in the clouds, *in nubibus* [*L.*]; unsubstantial etc. 4; illusory etc. (*fallacious*) 495; fictitious, theoretical, hypothetical.

fanciful; fabulous, legendary, mythic *or* mythical, mythological, chimerical; imaginary, visionary; dream-beset, dream-ridden, dreamy, entranced, notional, fancy, fantastical, high-fantastical, fantasied, maggoty, made of empty air, vaporous, whimsical; fairy, fairylike.

Division 2. Communication of Ideas

Section 1. Nature of Ideas Communicated

516. Meaning

[idea to be conveyed]

[thing signified]

n. **meaning**; signification, significance; sense, expression; import, purport; implication, connotation, essence, force; drift, tenor, spirit, bearing, coloring; scope.

allusion etc. (*latency*) 526; suggestion etc. (*information*) 527; interpretation, acceptation etc. 522; acceptance [*rare*].

general–, broad–, substantial–, colloquial–, literal–, primary–, accepted–, essential–, plain–, simple–, natural–, unstrained–, true etc. (*exact*) 494–, honest etc. 543–, *prima facie* [*L.*] etc. (*manifest*) 525- meaning.

literality; literal–, obvious–, real- -meaning, –sense, –interpretation.

equivalent meaning; interchangeable word, figure of speech etc. 521; equivalent, synonym etc. 522.

thing signified, matter, subject, subject matter, substance, sum and substance; gist etc. 5; argument, text.

v. **mean**, signify, connote, denote, express; import, purport; convey, imply, breathe, indicate, bespeak, bear a meaning, bear a sense; tell of, speak of; touch on; point to, allude to; drive at; involve etc. (*latency*) 526; declare etc. (*affirm*) 535.

understand by etc. (*interpret*) 522.

synonymize, express by a synonym; paraphrase, state differently.

adj. **meaning** etc. *v.;* expressive, suggestive, allusive; significant, significative, significatory; pithy; meaningful; full of–, pregnant with- meaning; explicit etc. 525.

declaratory etc. 535; intelligible etc. 518.

literal, metaphrastic *or* metaphrastical, word-for-word, verbatim; exact, real.

synonymous; tantamount etc. (*equivalent*) 27.

implied etc. (*latent*) 526; understood, tacit.

adv. **to that effect**; that is to say etc. (*being interpreted*) 522.

verbatim, literally; evidently, apparently, from the context.

517. Unmeaningness

[absence of meaning]

n. **unmeaningness** etc. *adj.;* scrabble, scribble, scrawl, pothooks.

empty sound, dead letter, *vox et praeterea nihil* [*L.*]; "a tale told by an idiot, full of sound and fury, signifying nothing" [*Macbeth*]; "weasel words" [Roosevelt]; "sounding brass or a tinkling cymbal" [*Bible*].

nonsense, jargon, gibberish, jabber, mere words, hocus-pocus, fustian, rant, bombast, balderdash, palaver, patter, flummery, verbiage, babble, *bavardage* [*F.*], *baragouin* [*F.*], platitude, *niaiserie* [*F.*]; inanity; flapdoodle [*colloq.*]; rigmarole, rodomontade; truism; twaddle, twattle, fudge, trash; poppy-cock; stuff, –and nonsense; bosh [*colloq.*], rubbish, moonshine, wish-wash [*slang*], fiddle-faddle [*colloq.*]; absurdity etc. 497; imbecility, folly etc. 499; unintelligibleness, ambiguity, vagueness etc. (*unintelligibility*) 519.

v. **mean nothing**; be unmeaning etc. *adj.;* twaddle, quibble, jabber, rant, rodomontade, palaver, babble, fiddle-faddle [*colloq.*].

scribble, scrawl, scrabble, scratch.

adj. **unmeaning**; meaningless, senseless; nonsensical etc. 497; void of sense etc. 516.

inexpressive, unexpressive; vacant; not significant etc. 516; insignificant.

trashy, washy, wishy-washy [*colloq.*], inane, wash [*obs.*], rubbishy, vague, trumpery, trivial, fiddle-faddle [*colloq.*], twaddling, quibbling.

unmeant, not expressed; tacit etc. (*latent*) 526.

inexpressible, undefinable, ineffable, unutterable, incommunicable.

int. **fudge**! stuff! stuff and nonsense! bosh! fiddle-faddle! [*colloq.*]; poppycock! *oh! la-la!* [*F.*]; rubbish! fiddledee-dee! etc. 497.

518. Intelligibility

n. **intelligibility**; clearness, clarity, explicitness etc. *adj.;* lucidity, comprehensibility, perspicuity; legibility, plain speaking etc. (*manifestation*) 525; precision etc. 494; *phonanta sunetoisi* [*Gr.*], a word to the wise.

v. **be intelligible** etc. *adj.;* speak for itself, speak volumes; tell its own tale, lie on the surface.

render intelligible etc. *adj.;* popularize, simplify, clear up; elucidate etc. (*explain*) 522.

understand, comprehend; take, –in; catch, grasp, follow, collect, master, make out; see with half an eye, see daylight, see one's way [*all colloq.*]; enter into the ideas of; come to an understanding.

adj. **intelligible**; clear, clear as -day, –noonday, –crystal; lucid; perspicuous, transpicuous; luminous, transparent.

easily understood, easy to understand, for the million, intelligible to the meanest capacity, popularized.

plain, distinct, clear-cut, hard-hitting, to the point, explicit; positive; definite etc. (*precise*) 494.

unambiguous, unequivocal, unmistakable etc. (*manifest*) 525, unconfused; legible, recognizable; obvious etc. 525.

graphic, telling, vivid; expressive etc. (*meaning*) 516; illustrative etc. (*explanatory*) 522.

adv. in plain -terms, –words, –English; hitting the nail on the head.

519. Unintelligibility

n. **unintelligibility**, incomprehensibility, imperspicuity [*rare*]; inconceivableness, unknowability, unknowableness, vagueness etc. *adj.;* obscurity; ambiguity etc. 520; doubtful meaning; uncertainty etc. 475; perplexity etc. (*confusion*) 59; spinosity; *obscurum per obscurius* [*L.*]; mystification etc. (*concealment*) 528; latency etc. 526; transcendentalism.

pons asinorum [*L.*], asses' bridge; double Dutch, high Dutch [*slang*], Greek, Hebrew, Choctaw; jargon etc. (*unmeaning*) 517.

enigma, riddle etc. (*secret*) 533; paradox; *dignus vindice nodus* [*L.*]; sealed book; steganography, cryptography, freemasonry.

v. **be unintelligible** etc. *adj.;* require explanation etc. 522; have a doubtful meaning, pass comprehension.

render unintelligible etc. *adj.;* conceal etc. 528; darken etc. 421; confuse etc. (*derange*) 61; mystify, perplex etc. (*bewilder*) 475.

not understand etc. 518; lose, –the clew; miss; not know what to make of, be able to make nothing of, give it up; not be able to -account for, –make head or tail of; be at sea etc. (*uncertain*) 475; wonder etc. 870; see through a glass darkly etc. (*ignorance*) 491.

not understand one another; play at cross-purposes etc. (*misinterpret*) 523.

adj. **unintelligible**, unaccountable, undecipherable, undiscoverable, unknowable, unfathomable; incognizable, inexplicable, inscrutable; inapprehensible, incomprehensible; insolvable, insoluble; impenetrable.

puzzling, as Greek to one, unexplained, paradoxical, enigmatic *or* enigmatical, indecipherable, illegible.

obscure, crabbed, imperspicuous [*rare*], dark, muddy, clear as mud [*colloq.*], seen through a mist, dim, nebulous, shrouded in mystery; undiscernible etc. (*invisible*) 447; misty etc. (*opaque*) 426; hidden etc. 528; latent etc. 526; mysterious; mystic, mystical, acroamatic *or* acroamatical, metempiric *or* metempirical; transcendental; occult, esoteric, recondite, abstruse.

indefinite etc. (*indistinct*) 447; perplexed etc. (*confused*) 59; undetermined, vague, loose, ambiguous.

inconceivable, inconceptible [*obs.*]; searchless; above–, beyond–, past-comprehension; beyond one's depth; unconceived.

inexpressible, unutterable, ineffable, undefinable, incommunicable.

520. Equivocalness
[having a double sense]

n. **equivocalness** etc. *adj.;* equivocation; double meaning etc. 516; ambiguity, *double entente* [*F.*], double-entendre, pun, paragram [*rare*], *calembour* [*F.*], quibble, equivoque *or* equivoke, anagram; conundrum etc. (*riddle*) 533; word play etc. (*wit*) 842; homonym, homonymy; amphiboly, amphibologism, amphilogism *or* amphilogy [*rare*], anagrammatism, ambilogy, ambiloquy [*obs.*].

Sphinx, Delphic oracle.

equivocation etc. (*duplicity*) 544; white lie, mental reservation etc. (*concealment*) 528; paltering.

v. **equivocate** etc. (*palter*) 544; anagrammatize; be equivocal etc. *adj.;* have two meanings etc. 516.

adj. **equivocal**, ambiguous, amphibolous [*obs.*], doubtful, amphibolic, ambiloquent [*obs.*], ambiloquous, homonymic, homonymous; double-tongued etc. (*lying*) 544; enigmatical, indeterminate.

521. Metaphor

n. **figure of speech**; *façon de parler* [*F.*], way of speaking, colloquialism.

phrase etc. 566; figure, trope, metaphor, tralatition, metonymy, enallage, catachresis, synecdoche, antonomasia; satire, irony, figurativeness etc. *adj.;* image, imagery, metathesis, metalepsis, type, anagoge, simile.

personification, prosopopoeia, allegory, allegorization, apologue, parable, fable.

inference, implication, deduction, allusion, adumbration; euphemism, euphuism, application.

v. **employ metaphor** etc. *n.;* personify, allegorize, fable, adumbrate, shadow forth, apply, allude to.

adj. **metaphorical**, tropical, tralatitious, figurative, catachrestic *or* catachrestical, antonomastic *or* antonomastical, typical, parabolic *or* parabolical, allegoric *or* allegorical, allusive, referential, anagogic *or* anagogical; euphuistic *or* euphuistical, euphemistic *or* euphemistical, ironic, ironical; colloquial.

adv. **as it were**, so to -speak, –say, –express oneself; in a manner of speaking [*colloq.*].

522. Interpretation

n. **interpretation**, definition; explanation, explication; solution, answer; rationale; plain-, simple-, strict- interpretation; meaning etc. 516; *mot d'énigme* [*F.*]; clew etc. (*indication*) 550.

symptomatology, semeiology *or* semiology, diagnosis, prognosis; metoposcopy, physiognomy; paleography etc. (*philology*) 560; oneirology.

translation; rendering, rendition; reddition; literal-, free- translation; key; secret; *clavis* [*L.*], crib, pony, trot [*Eng.*].

comment, commentary; exegesis; expounding, exposition; hermeneutics; inference etc. (*deduction*) 480; illustration, exemplification; gloss, annotation, scholium, note; enucleation, elucidation, dilucidation [*obs.*]; *éclaircissement* [*F.*].

acception [*obs.*], acceptation, acceptance; light, reading, lection, construction, version.

equivalent, –meaning etc. 516; synonym, poecilonym, polyonym [*rare*]; paraphrase, metaphrase; convertible terms, apposition.

dictionary etc. 562; polyglot.

prediction etc. 511; chiromancy *or* cheiromancy, palmistry; astrology.

v. **interpret**, explain, define, construe, translate, render; do into, turn into; transfuse the sense of.

find out etc. (480*a*)- -the meaning of etc. 516; read; spell out, make out; decipher, unravel, disentangle; find the key of, enucleate, resolve, solve; consignify [*rare*]; read between the lines, read into.

elucidate, account for; find-, tell- the cause of etc. 153; throw-, shed- -light, –new light, –fresh light- upon; clear up.

illustrate, exemplify; unfold, expound, comment upon, annotate; popularize etc. (*render intelligible*) 518.

understand by; take-, understand-, receive-, accept- in a particular sense; put a construction on, be given to understand.

adj. **explanatory**, expository; explicative, explicatory; exegetical; construable; hermeneutic *or* hermeneutical, interpretive, interpretative, commentarial, commentatorial, inferential, illustrative, exemplificative, exemplificational, annotative, scholiastic, elucidative; symptomatological; paleographic *or* paleographical.

equivalent etc. 27; paraphrastic, consignificative [*rare*], consignificant, synonymous, poecilonymic, polyonymal [*rare*], polyonymic [*rare*].

metaphrastic, literal etc. 516; polyglot.

adv. **in explanation** etc. *n.;* that is to say, *id est* [*L.*], *videlicet* [*L.*], to wit, namely, in other words.

literally, strictly speaking: in -plain, -plainer--terms, -words, -English; more simply.

523. Misinterpretation

n. **misinterpretation**, misapprehension, misdoubt, misconception, misunderstanding, misacceptation [*obs.*], misconstruction, misapplication; catachresis; eisegesis; cross-reading, cross-purposes; mistake etc. 495.

misrepresentation, perversion, misstatement, exaggeration etc. 549; false -coloring, -construction; abuse of terms; play upon words, *jeu de mots* [*F.*], pun, parody, travesty; double-talk; falsification etc. (*lying*) 544.

v. **misinterpret**, misapprehend, misunderstand, misconceive, misjudge, misdeem, misdoubt, misspell, mistranslate, misconstrue, misapply; mistake etc. 495.

misrepresent, pervert; explain wrongly, misstate; garble etc. (*falsify*) 544; distort, detort [*obs.*]; travesty, play upon words; stretch-, strain-, twist-, wrench-, wring-, wrest- the -sense, -meaning; explain away; put a -bad, -wrong, -erroneous, -false- construction on; give a false coloring; look through dark-, rose-colored- spectacles.

be out; be-, play- at cross-purposes; be off [*slang*], be 'way off [*slang*], be off base [*slang*].

adj. **misinterpreted** etc. *v.;* eisegetical, catachrestic *or* catachrestical; untranslated, untranslatable.

confused, tangled, snarled, mixed, dazed, perplexed, bewildered, rattled [*slang*], benighted.

adv. **at cross-purposes**, at sixes and sevens [*colloq.*]; *à tort et à travers* [*F.*]; all balled up [*colloq.*], in a maze, all fouled up [*slang*].

524. Interpreter

n. **interpreter** (*fem.* interpretress), translator, expositor, expounder, exponent, explainer; demonstrator.

commentator, scholiast, annotator; metaphrast, paraphrast; glossarist, prolocutor.

spokesman, speaker, mouthpiece, foreman of the jury; mediator, delegate, exponent, representative, diplomatic agent, ambassador, plenipotentiary; advocate, judge, Supreme Court.

guide, dragoman, courier, *valet de place* [*F.*], cicerone, showman, barker [*colloq.*], oneirocritic; Oedipus, Joseph; oracle etc. 513.

Section 2. Modes of Communication

525. Manifestation

n. **manifestation**, unfoldment, unfolding; plainness etc. *adj.;* plain speaking; expression; showing etc. *v.;* exposition, demonstration, séance, materialization; exhibition, production; display, show-down [*slang*], show, showing off [*colloq.*]; premonstration [*obs.*].

[thing shown] exhibit, exhibition, exposition, show [*colloq.*], performance.

indication etc. (*calling attention to*) 457; publicity etc. 531; disclosure etc. 529; openness etc. (*honesty*) 543, (*artlessness*) 703; *épanchement* [*F.*]; saliency, prominence.

v. **make** *or* **render manifest** etc. *adj.;* materialize; bring -forth, -forward, -to the front, -into view; give notice; express; represent, set forth, evidence, exhibit; show, -up; expose; produce; hold up-, expose- to view; set-, place-, lay- before -one, -one's eyes; tell to one's face; trot out [*colloq.*], put through one's paces [*colloq.*], show one's paces, show off [*colloq.*]; show forth, unveil, bring to light, display, demonstrate, unroll; lay open; draw out, bring out; bring out in strong relief; call-, bring- into notice; hold up the mirror to; wear one's heart upon his sleeve; show one's -face, -colors; manifest oneself; speak out; make no -mystery, -secret- of; unfurl the flag; proclaim etc. (*publish*) 531.

indicate etc. (*direct attention to*) 457; disclose etc. 529; translate, transcribe, decipher, decode; elicit etc. 480a.

be manifest etc. *adj.;* appear etc. (*be visible*) 446; transpire etc. (*be disclosed*) 529; speak for itself, stand to reason; stare one in the face, loom large, appear on the horizon, rear its head; give -token, -sign, -indication of; tell its own tale etc. (*intelligible*) 518; go without saying, be self-evident.

adj. **manifest**, apparent; salient, striking, demonstrative, prominent, in the foreground, notable, pronounced.

> **flagrant**; notorious etc. (*public*) 531; arrant; stark-staring; unshaded, glaring.

> **plain**, clear, defined, definite, distinct, conspicuous etc. (*visible*) 446; obvious, evident, unmistakable, conclusive, indubitable, not to be mistaken, palpable, self-evident, autoptic *or* autoptical; intelligible etc. 518; clear as -day, –daylight, –noonday; plain as -a pikestaff [*colloq.*], –the sun at noonday, –the nose on one's face [*colloq.*], –way to parish church [*colloq.*].

> ostensible; open, –as day; overt, patent, express, explicit; naked, bare, literal, downright, undisguised, exoteric.

> **unreserved**; frank, plain-spoken etc. (*artless*) 703.

> **barefaced**, brazen, bold, shameless, daring, flaunting, *risqué* [*F.*], loud.

> **manifested** etc. *v.;* disclosed etc. 529; capable of being shown, producible; unconcealable.

adv. **manifestly**, openly etc. *adj.;* before one's eyes, under one's nose [*colloq.*], under one's very eyes, to one's face, face to face, above board, cards on the table, *cartes sur table* [*F.*], on the stage, in open court, in the open streets, in plain sight, in the open, at the cross-roads, in the market place, in market overt; in the face of -day, –heaven; in- broad-, open- daylight; without reserve; at first blush, *prima facie* [*L.*], on the face of; in set terms.

526. Latency

n. **latency**, inexpression; hidden–, occult- meaning; obscurity etc. (*unintelligibility*) 519; occultness, mystery, cabala *or* cabbala, cabalism, occultism, mysticism, symbolism, anagoge; silence etc. (*taciturnity*) 585; concealment etc. 528; more than meets the -eye, –ear; Delphic oracle; *le dessous des cartes* [*F.*], undercurrent; "something rotten in the state of Denmark" [*Hamlet*].

> snake in the grass etc. (*pitfall*) 667; secret etc. 533.
> darkness, invisibility, imperceptibility.

> **allusion**, insinuation, inference, implication; innuendo etc. 527; adumbration.

> **latent influence**, invisible government, power behind the throne, friend at court, wire-puller [*colloq.*], king-maker; "a destiny that shapes our ends" [*Hamlet*].

v. **be latent** etc. *adj.;* lurk, smolder *or* smoulder, underlie, make no sign; escape -observation, –detection, –recognition; lie hid etc. 528.

laugh up one's sleeve; keep back etc. (*conceal*) 528.

> **involve**, imply, implicate, connote, import, understand, allude to, infer, leave an inference; mysticize [*rare*], symbolize; whisper etc. (*conceal*) 528.

adj. **latent**; lurking etc. *v.;* secret, occult, anagogic *or* anagogical, cabalistic *or* cabalistical, symbolic, esoteric, recondite, veiled, symbolic, cryptic *or* cryptical; mystic, mystical; implied etc. *v.;* dormant; abeyant.

> unapparent, unknown, unseen etc. 441; in the background; invisible etc. 447; indiscoverable, dark; impenetrable etc. (*unintelligible*) 519; unspied, unsuspected.

> undeveloped, unsolved, unexplained, untraced, undiscovered etc. 480*a*, untracked, unexplored, uninvented.

> **unexpressed**, unmentioned, unpronounced, unsaid, unwritten, unpublished, unbreathed, untalked of, untold etc. 527, unsung, unexposed, unproclaimed, undisclosed etc. 529, not expressed, tacit.

> **indirect**, crooked, inferential; by inference, by implication; implicit; constructive; allusive, covert, muffled; steganographic; understood, underhand, underground; concealed; under cover etc. 528; delitescent.

adv. **secretly** etc. 528; by a side wind; *sub silentio* [*L.*]; in the background; behind the scenes, behind one's back; on the tip of one's tongue; between the lines; by a mutual understanding; *sub rosa* [*L.*]; below the surface.

527. Information

n. **information**, advisement [*archaic*], enlightenment, acquaintance, knowledge etc. 490; publicity etc. 531.

> mention; acquainting etc. *v.;* instruction etc. (*teaching*) 537; outpouring; intercommunication, communicativeness.

> **intimation**, communication, notice, notification, enunciation, annunciation, announcement, *communiqué* [*F.*]; representation, round robin, presentment.

> **report**, advice, monition; news etc. 532; return etc. (*record*) 551; account etc. (*description*) 594; statement etc. (*affirmation*) 535; case, estimate, specification.

> **dispatch** *or* despatch, message, wire [*colloq.*], cable, telegram, telex etc. (*news*) 532; telephone, phone [*colloq.*], radiophone, wireless telephone, telegraphone.

> **informant**, authority, teller, annunciator, harbinger, herald, intelligencer [*now rare*], re-

porter, exponent, mouthpiece; spokesman etc. (*interpreter*) 524; informer, eavesdropper, delator, detective, bull [*slang, U. S.*], sleuth [*colloq.*]; *mouchard* [*F.*], spy, newsmonger; messenger etc. 534; *amicus curiae* [*L.*].

guide, *valet de place* [*F.*], cicerone, pilot, guidebook, handbook; *vade mecum* [*L.*], manual; map, plan, chart, gazetteer; itinerary etc. (*journey*) 266.

hint, suggestion, innuendo, inkling, whisper, passing word, word in the ear, subaudition, subauditur, cue, byplay; gesture etc. (*indication*) 550; gentle-, broad- hint; *verbum sapienti* [*L.*]; word to the wise; insinuation etc. (*latency*) 526.

v. **tell**; inform, -of; acquaint, -with; impart, -to; make acquainted with, apprise, advise, enlighten, awaken.

let fall, mention, express, intimate, represent, communicate, make known; publish etc. 531; notify, signify, specify, convey the knowledge of; retail, render an account; give an account etc. (*describe*) 594; state etc. (*affirm*) 535.

let one know, have one know; give one to understand; give notice; set-, lay-, put- before; point out, put into one's head; put one in possession of; instruct etc. (*teach*) 537; direct the attention to etc. 457.

announce, annunciate; report, -progress; bring-, send-, leave-, write- word; telegraph, wire [*colloq.*], telephone, telex, phone [*colloq.*].

disclose etc. 529; show cause; explain etc. (*interpret*) 522.

hint; give an inkling of; give-, drop-, throw out- a hint; insinuate; allude to, make allusion to; glance at; tip off [*slang*], give one a tip [*colloq.*]; tip the wink [*slang*] etc. (*indicate*) 550; suggest, prompt, give the cue, breathe; whisper, -in the ear.

berate, scold, chide, strafe [*colloq.*], score [*colloq.*], dress down [*colloq.*], reprove, trim [*slang*], rate; give one a -bit, -piece- of one's mind; tell one -plainly, -once for all; speak volumes.

undeceive, unbeguile; set right, correct, open the eyes of, disabuse.

be informed of etc.; know etc. 490; learn etc. 539; get scent of, gather from; sleuth [*colloq.*]; awaken to, open one's eyes to; become -alive, -awake- to; hear, understand; come to one's -ears, -knowledge; reach one's ears; overhear etc. (*hear*) 418; get wise to [*slang*].

adj. **informed** etc. *v.;* *communiqué* [*F.*]; informational, advisory, intelligential; reported etc. *v.;* published etc. 531.

expressive etc. 516; explicit etc. (*open*) 525, (*clear*) 518; plain-spoken etc. (*artless*) 703.

declaratory, declarative, enunciative, nunciative [*rare*], annunciative [*rare*], enunciatory, insinuant [*rare*]; oral, nuncupative [*said of oral wills*], nuncupative [*said of oral wills*], nuncupatory [*obs.*]; expository; communicative, communicatory.

adv. **from information received**; according to -reports, -suggestion, -rumor; from notice given; by the underground route; as a matter of -general information, -common report; in the air; according to-, from- what one can gather.

528. Concealment

n. **concealment**; hiding etc. *v.;* occultation, mystification.

reticence, reserve, reservation; mental reservation, aside; *arrière pensée* [*F.*], suppression, evasion, white lie, misprision; silence etc. (*taciturnity*) 585; suppression of truth etc. 544; underhand dealing; closeness, secretiveness etc. *adj.;* mystery.

seal of secrecy; freemasonry; screen etc. 530; disguise etc. 530; masquerade; masked battery; hiding place etc. 530.

cryptography, steganography; cipher, code, cable code; sympathetic ink, palimpsest.

stalking, still-hunt, hunt.

stealth, stealthiness; obreption [*obs.*]; slyness etc. (*cunning*) 702.

secrecy, latitancy [*rare*], latitation [*obs.*]; seclusion etc. 893; privacy, secretness, hugger-mugger [*archaic*]; disguise, incognito (*fem.* incognita).

mysticism, occultism, supernaturalism; esotericism, esoterics, esotery.

latency etc. 526; snake in the grass; secret etc. 533; stowaway; blind baggage [*slang*].

masquerader, masker, mask, domino.

v. **conceal**, hide, secrete, put out of sight; lock up, seal up, bottle up.

cover, screen, cloak, veil, shroud; cover up one's tracks; screen from -sight, -observation; draw the veil; draw-, close- the curtain; curtain, shade, eclipse, throw a veil over; becloud, bemask; mask, camouflage, disguise, ensconce, muffle; befog; whisper.

keep- from, -back, -to oneself; keep -snug, -close, -secret, -dark; bury; sink, suppress; keep -from, -out of- view, -sight; keep in-, throw into- the -shade, -background; stifle, hush up, smother, withhold, reserve; fence with a question; ignore etc. 460.

code, codify; use a -code, -cipher.

keep a secret, keep one's own counsel; hold one's tongue etc. (*silence*) 585; make no sign, not let it go further; not breathe a -word, –syllable- about; not let the right hand know what the left is doing; hide one's light under a bushel, bury one's talent in a napkin.

hoodwink; keep–, leave- in -the dark, –ignorance; blind, -the eyes; blindfold, mystify; puzzle etc. (*render uncertain*) 475; bamboozle etc. (*deceive*) 545.

be concealed etc. *v.;* suffer an eclipse; occult, retire from sight, couch; hide oneself; lie -hid, –in ambush, –perdu, –snug, –low [*colloq.*], –close; latitate [*obs.*]; seclude oneself etc. 893; lurk, sneak, skulk, slink, prowl, gumshoe [*slang*]; steal -into, –out of, –by, –along; play at -bopeep, –hide and seek; hide in holes and corners; still-hunt.

adj. **concealed** etc. *v.;* hidden; secret, latitant [*rare*], recondite, mystic, mystical, cabalistic *or* cabalistical, occult, dark; cryptic *or* cyptical, private, privy, *in petto* [*It.*], auricular, clandestine, close, close-mouthed, inviolate; tortuous.

behind a screen etc. 530; under -cover, –an eclipse; in ambush, in hiding, in disguise; in a -cloud, –fog, –mist, –haze, –dark corner; in the -shade, –dark; clouded, wrapt in clouds; invisible etc. 447; buried, underground, perdu; secluded etc. 893.

undisclosed etc. 529, untold etc. 527; covert etc. (*latent*) 526; mysterious etc. (*unintelligible*) 519.

inviolable, irrevealable, confidential; esoteric; not to be spoken of.

furtive, obreptitious, stealthy, feline; skulking etc. *v.;* surreptitious, underhand, hole and corner [*colloq.*]; sly etc. (*cunning*) 702; secretive, clandestine, evasive; reserved, reticent, uncommunicative, buttoned up; close, –as wax; taciturn etc. 585.

adv. **secretly** etc. *adj.;* in secret, in private, in one's sleeve, in holes and corners [*colloq.*]; in the dark etc. *adj.*

januis clausis [*L.*], with closed doors, *à huis clos* [*F.*]; hugger-mugger, in hugger-mugger [*archaic*], *à la dérobée* [*F.*], under the -cloak of, –rose, –table; *sub rosa* [*L.*], *en tapinois* [*F.*], in the background, aside, on the sly [*colloq.*], with bated breath, sotto voce, in a whisper, without beat of drum, *à la sourdine* [*F.*].

behind the veil; beyond -mortal ken, –the grave, –the veil; hid from mortal vision; into the -eternal secret, –realms supersensible, –supreme mystery.

confidentially etc. *adj.;* in–, in strict- confidence; between -ourselves, –you and me; *entre nous* [*F.*], *inter nos* [*L.*], under the seal of secrecy; *à couvert* [*F.*].

underhand, by stealth, like a thief in the night; stealthily etc. *adj.;* behind -the scenes, –the curtain, –one's back, –a screen etc. 530; incognito; *in camera* [*L.*].

529. Disclosure

n. **disclosure**; retection [*obs.*]; unveiling etc. *v.;* deterration [*obs.*], revealment, revelation; divulgement, divulgation [*rare*], divulgence, exposition, exposure, publication, *exposé* [*F.*], whole truth; telltale etc. (*news*) 532.

bursting of a bubble; *dénouement* [*F.*].

acknowledgment, avowance, avowal; confession, confessional; shrift.

narrator etc. 594; talebearer etc. 532.

v. **disclose**, discover, dismask [*obs.*]; draw–, draw aside–, lift–, raise–, lift up–, remove–, tear- the -veil, –curtain; unmask, unveil, unfold, uncover, unseal, unkennel; take off–, break- the seal; lay open, lay bare; expose; open, –up; bare, bring to light; evidence; make -clear, –evident, –manifest; evince.

raise–, drop–, lift–, remove–, throw off- the mask; expose; lay open; undeceive, unbeguile; disabuse, set right, correct, open the eyes of; *désillusionner* [*F.*].

divulge, reveal, break [*obs.*]; let into the secret; reveal the secrets of the prison house; tell etc. (*inform*) 527; rat [*slang*], squeal [*slang*]; breathe, utter, blab, peach [*slang*]; let -out, –fall, –drop, –slip, –the cat out of the bag [*colloq.*], come out with it [*colloq.*], come it [*slang*], betray; tell tales, –out of school; come out with; give vent to, give utterance to; open the lips, blurt out, vent, whisper about; speak out etc. (*make manifest*) 525; break the news; make public etc. 531; unriddle etc. (*find out*) 480a; split.

acknowledge, allow, concede, grant, admit, own, confess, avow, throw off all disguise, turn inside out, make a clean breast; show one's -hand, –cards; unburden–, disburden- one's mind, –conscience, –heart; open–, lay bare–, give one a piece of [*colloq.*]- one's mind; unbosom oneself, "own the soft impeachment" [Sheridan]; say–, speak- the truth; turn informer; turn -King's, –Queen's, –State's- evidence.

be disclosed etc.; transpire, come to light; come in sight etc. (*be visible*) 446; become known, escape the lips; come out, ooze out, creep out, leak out, peep out, crop out, crop forth, crop up; show its -face, –colors; discover etc. itself; break through the clouds, flash on the mind; come to one's ears etc. 527.

adj. **disclosed** etc. *v.;* revelative, revelatory, revelational, expository, confessional, confessionary, confessory.

int. out with it! 'fess up! [*slang*]; open up! [*colloq*].

530. Ambush
[means of concealment]

n. **ambush,** ambuscade; stalking-horse; lurking-hole, –place; secret path, back stairs; retreat etc. (*refuge*) 666.

hiding place, hidlings [*Scot. & dial. Eng.*]; secret -place, –drawer; recess, hole, cubbyhole, hidie-hole [*Scot.*], holes and corners; closet, crypt, adytum, abditory [*rare*], *oubliette* [*F.*]; safe, safe-deposit box, safety-deposit box.

screen, cover, shade, blinker; veil, curtain, blind, purdah [*India*], cloak, cloud.

mask, visor *or* vizor, vizard [*archaic*], disguise, masquerade dress, domino.

pitfall etc. (*source of danger*) 667; trap etc. (*snare*) 545.

v. **ambush,** ambuscade; lie in ambush etc. (*hide oneself*) 528; lie in wait for; set a trap for etc. (*deceive*) 545.

adv. *aux aguets* [*F.*]; *januis clausis* [*L.*] etc. 528.

531. Publication

n. **publication;** public announcement etc. 527; promulgation, propagation, proclamation, pronouncement, *pronunciamiento* [*Sp.*], pronunciamento, edict, encyclical; circulation, indiction [*rare*], edition, impression, imprint.

publicity, notoriety, currency, flagrancy, cry, hue and cry, *bruit* [*F.*]; bruit, oyez *or* oyes, *vox populi* [*L.*]; report etc. (*news*) 532; telegram, cable [*colloq.*] etc. 532; telegraphy; publisher etc. *v.*

the press, the Fourth Estate, public press, newspaper, tabloid, journal, gazette, daily, weekly, monthly, quarterly, annual; magazine.

advertisement, ad., placard, bill, flyer [*cant*], leaflet, handbill, *affiche* [*F.*], broadside, broadsheet, poster; circular, –letter; manifesto; notice etc. 527; program *or* programme.

v. **publish;** make -public, –known etc. (*information*) 527; speak of, talk of; broach, utter; put forward; circulate, propagate, promulgate; spread, –abroad; rumor, diffuse, disseminate, evulgate [*obs.*]; put-, give-, send- forth; emit, edit, get out; issue; bring-, lay-, drag- before the public; give -out, –to the world; report, cover [*newspaper cant*]; put-, bandy-, hawk-, buzz-, whisper-, bruit-, blaze- about; drag into the -open day, –limelight [*colloq.*], throw the spotlight on [*colloq.*]; voice, bruit.

proclaim, herald, blazon; blaze–, noise- abroad; sound a trumpet; trumpet-, thunder- forth; give tongue; announce with -beat of drum, –flourish of trumpets; proclaim -from the housetops, –at Charing Cross, –at the cross-roads, –at the market cross.

raise a -cry, –hue and cry, –report; set news afloat.

telegraph, cable, wireless [*colloq.*], broadcast, telecast, televise, wire [*colloq.*].

advertise, placard; post, –up; *afficher* [*F.*], publish in the Gazette, send round the crier, cry abroad.

be published etc.; be *or* become public etc. *adj.;* come out; go–, fly–, buzz–, blow- about; get -about, –abroad, –afloat, –wind; find vent; see the light; go forth, take air, acquire currency, pass current; go the rounds, go the round of the newspapers, go through the length and breadth of the land; *virum volitare per ora* [*L.*]; pass from mouth to mouth; spread; run–, spread- like wildfire.

adj. **published** etc. *v.;* current etc. (*news*) 532; in circulation, public; notorious; flagrant, arrant; open etc. 525; trumpet-tongued; encyclic *or* encyclical, proclamatory, annunciatory, promulgatory; exoteric.

telegraphic, cabled, radiotelegraphic, telegraphed, wireless; radiophonic.

adv. **publicly** etc. *adj.;* in public, in open court, with open doors; in the -limelight, –spotlight [*both colloq.*]; for publication.

int. Oyez! Oyes! notice! flash!

532. News

n. **news;** information etc. 527; piece-, budget- of -news, –information; intelligence, tidings; beat *or* scoop [*newspaper cant*], story, copy [*cant*], print, letterpress.

fresh–, stirring–, old–, stale- news; glad tidings; old–, stale- story; chestnut [*slang*].

message, word, advice, aviso, dispatch *or* despatch; telegram, cable [*colloq.*], wire [*colloq.*], radio [*colloq.*], radiogram, wireless telegram, wireless [*colloq.*], marconigram, pneumatogram, communication, errand, embassy; bulletin; broadcast.

report, rumor, hearsay, on-dit, flying rumor, news stirring, cry, buzz, bruit, fame; talk, *ouï-dire* [*F.*], scandal, eavesdropping; town–, table- -talk, –gossip; tittle-tattle; canard, topic of the day, idea afloat.

narrator etc. (*describe*) 594; newsmonger, scandalmonger; busybody, talebearer, telltale, gossip, tattler, blab, babbler, tattletale, chatterer; informer, squealer [*slang*].

v. **transpire** etc. (*be disclosed*) 529; rumor etc. (*publish*) 531.

adj. **rumored**; publicly–, currently- -rumored, –reported; many-tongued; rife, current, floating, afloat, going about, in circulation, in every one's mouth, all over the town.

having news value, newsy [*colloq.*], snappy [*slang*].

adv. **as they say**; as the story -goes, –runs; it is said.

by telegraph, by cable, by radio [*colloq.*], by television, by wireless [*colloq.*].

533. Secret

n. **secret**; dead–, profound- secret; arcanum, mystery; latency etc. 526; Asian mystery; sealed book, secrets of the prison house; *le dessous des cartes* [*F.*].

enigma, riddle, puzzle, nut to crack, conundrum, charade, rebus, logogriph; monogram, anagram, anagrammatism; Sphinx; *crux criticorum* [*L.*].

maze, labyrinth, meander [*usually in pl.*], Hyrcynian wood; intricacy.

problem etc. (*question*) 461; paradox etc. (*difficulty*) 704; unintelligibility etc. 519; *terra incognita* [*L.*] etc. (*ignorance*) 491.

adj. **secret** etc. (*concealed*) 528; involved etc. 248; labyrinthian, labyrinthine, labyrinthic *or* labyrinthical, mazy, meandrous.

enigmatic *or* enigmatical, anagrammatic *or* anagrammatical, monogrammatic, logogriphic, cryptic *or* cryptical.

534. Messenger

n. **messenger**, angel, envoy, emissary, legate, delegate, nuncio, internuncio, intermediary, go-between; ambassador etc. (*diplomatist*) 758.
Gabriel, Hermes, Mercury, Iris, Ariel.
marshal, flag bearer, herald, crier, trumpeter, bellman, pursuivant, *parlementaire* [*F.*], apparitor.

courier, runner, dak *or* dawk [*India*], estafette *or* estafet, commissionaire; errand boy, chore boy, newsboy.

mail; post, post office; letter bag, mail bag; postman, mail-man, letter carrier; mail train, mail boat, mailer; aërial mail; carrier pigeon.

telegraph, cable [*colloq.*], wire [*colloq.*], radiotelegraph, wireless telegraph, wireless [*colloq.*], radio [*colloq.*], television [*colloq.*].

telephone, phone [*colloq.*], radio-telephone, radiophone, wireless telephone.

reporter, newspaperman, journalist; gentleman–, representative- of the Press; penny-a-liner; hack writer, special–, war–, own-correspondent; spy, scout; informer etc. 527.

535. Affirmation

n. **affirmation**, affirmance, statement, allegation, assertion, predication, predicate [*logic*], declaration, word, averment; confirmation.

asseveration, adjuration, swearing, oath, affidavit; deposition etc. (*record*) 551; avouchment, avouch [*rare*], assurance; protest, protestation; profession; acknowledgment etc. (*assent*) 488; legal pledge, pronouncement; solemn -averment, –avowal, –declaration.

vote, voice; ballot, suffrage; *vox populi* [*L.*].

remark, observation; position etc. (*proposition*) 514; saying, dictum, sentence, *ipse dixit* [*L.*].

positiveness, emphasis, peremptoriness; dogmatism etc. (*certainty*) 474; weight.

dogmatist etc. 887.

v. **assert**; make an assertion etc. *n.;* have one's say; say, affirm, predicate, declare, state; protest, profess; acknowledge etc. (*assent*) 488.
put forth, put forward; advance, allege, propose, propound; announce etc. 527; enunciate, broach, set forth, hold out, maintain, contend, pronounce, pretend.

depose, depone, aver, avow, avouch, asseverate, swear, rap [*archaic slang*], affirm; make–, take one's- oath; make–, swear–, put in- an affidavit; take one's Bible oath, kiss the book, vow, *vitam impendere vero* [*L.*]; swear till -one is black in the face, –all's blue [*both colloq.*]; be sworn, call Heaven to witness; vouch, warrant, certify, assure; swear by bell, book, and candle; attest etc. (*evidence*) 467; adjure etc. (*put to one's oath*) 768.

emphasize; swear by etc. (*believe*) 484; insist upon, take one's stand upon; lay stress on; assert -roundly, –positively; lay down, –the law; raise one's voice, dogmatize, have the last word; rap out; repeat; reassert, reaffirm.

adj. **affirmative**; asserting etc. *v.;* declaratory, predicatory, predicative, predicational, pronunciatory, pronunciative, *soi-disant* [*F.*]; positive; unmistakable; clear; certain etc. 474; express, explicit etc. (*patent*) 525; absolute, emphatic, flat, broad, round, pointed, marked, distinct, decided, assertive, insistent, confident, trenchant, dogmatic, definitive, formal, solemn, categorical, peremptory; unretracted.

predicable, affirmable, attributable.

adv. **affirmatively** etc. *adj.;* in the affirmative.

with emphasis, ex-cathedra, without fear of contradiction.

I must say, indeed, i' faith, let me tell you, why, give me leave to say, marry [*archaic*], you may be sure, I'd have you know; upon my -word, –honor; by my troth, egad [*euphemism*], I assure you; by jingo, by Jove, by George etc. [*all colloq.*]; troth, seriously, sadly [*obs.*]; in–, in sober- -sadness, –truth, –earnest; of a truth, truly, pardie *or* perdy [*archaic*]; in all conscience, upon oath; be assured etc. (*belief*) 484; yes etc. (*assent*) 488; I'll -warrant, –warrant you, –engage, –answer for it, –be bound, –venture to say, –take my oath; in fact, forsooth, joking -aside, –apart; in all -soberness, –seriousness; so help me God; not to mince the matter.

536. Negation

n. **negation**, abnegation; denial; disavowal, disclaimer; abjuration; contradiction, contravention; recusation, protest; recusancy etc. (*dissent*) 489; flat-, emphatic- -contradiction, –denial; *démenti* [*F.*].

qualification etc. 469; repudiation etc. 610; recantation, revocation; retractation etc. 607; rebuttal; confutation etc. 479; refusal etc. 764; prohibition etc. 761.

v. **deny**; contradict, contravene; controvert, give denial to, gainsay, negative, shake the head; take the Fifth [*slang*].

deny -flatly, –peremptorily, –emphatically, –absolutely, –wholly, –entirely; give the lie to, belie.

disclaim, disown, disaffirm, disavow, abjure, forswear, abnegate, renounce; recant etc. 607; revoke etc. (*abrogate*) 756.

dispute, impugn, traverse, rebut, join issue upon; bring *or* call in question etc. (*doubt*) 485; give (one) the lie in his throat.

repudiate etc. 610; set aside, ignore etc. 460; rebut etc. (*confute*) 479; qualify etc. 469; refuse etc. 764.

adj. **denying** etc. *v.;* denied etc. *v.;* revocatory, abjuratory, abnegative [*rare*], contradictory; negative, negatory; recusant etc. (*dissenting*) 489; at issue upon.

adv. **no**, nay, not, nowise, no way [*colloq.*], noways; not a -bit, –whit, –jot; not at all, not in the least,

not so; no such thing; nothing of the -kind, –sort; quite the contrary, *tout au contraire* [*F.*], far from it; *tant s'en faut* [*F.*]; on no account, in no respect; by no means, by no manner of means; negatively.

537. Teaching

n. **teaching** etc. *v.;* pedagogics, pedagogy; instruction; edification; education; tuition; tutorship, tutorage, tutelage; direction, guidance; opsimathy [*rare*].

preparation, qualification, training, schooling etc. *v.;* discipline; exercise, exercitation, drill, practice.

persuasion, proselytism, propagandism, propaganda; indoctrination, inculcation, inoculation, initiation.

lesson, lecture, sermon, homily, harangue, disquisition; apologue, parable; discourse, prelection, preachment; explanation etc. (*interpretation*) 522; chalk talk [*colloq.*].

Chautauqua -system, –course; lyceum.

exercise, task; curriculum; course, –of study; grammar, three R's; A. B. C. etc. (*beginning*) 66.

[education] elementary–, primary–, grammar school–, common school–, high school–, secondary–, technical–, college–, collegiate–, military–, university–, liberal–, classical–, academic–, religious–, denominational–, moral–, secular- education; propaedeutics, moral tuition; the humanities, humanism, humane studies.

normal–, kindergarten- -course, –training; vocational -training, –therapeutics; Montessori system.

physical education, physical drill, gymnastics, calisthenics, eurythmics *or* eurhythmics; sloyd.

v. **teach**, instruct, edify, school, tutor; cram [*colloq.*], grind [*colloq.*], prime, coach; enlighten etc. (*inform*) 527.

inculcate, indoctrinate, inoculate, infuse, instill, infix, ingraft *or* engraft, infiltrate; imbue, impregnate, implant; graft, sow the seeds of, disseminate, propagate.

give an idea of; put up to [*slang*]; put in the way of; set right.

sharpen the wits, enlarge the mind; give new ideas, open the eyes, bring forward, "teach the young idea how to shoot" [Thomson]; improve etc. 658.

direct, guide; direct attention to etc. (*attention*) 457; impress upon the -mind, –memory; beat into, –the head; convince etc. (*belief*) 484.

expound etc. (*interpret*) 522; lecture; read–, give– a -lesson, –lecture, –sermon, –discourse; incept [*Cambridge Univ., Eng.*]; hold forth, preach; prelect, sermonize, moralize; point a moral.

train, discipline; bring up, –to; educate, form, ground, prepare, qualify, drill, exercise, practice, habituate, familiarize with, nurture, dry-nurse, breed, rear, take in hand; break, –in; tame; preinstruct; initiate, graduate; inure etc. (*habituate*) 613.

put to nurse, send to school.

adj. **educational**; scholastic, academic, doctrinal; disciplinal, disciplinary, instructive, instructional, hortatory, homiletic *or* homiletical, pedagogic *or* pedagogical, didactic; teaching etc. *v.;* taught etc. *v.;* propaedeutic *or* propaedeutical; propagative; cultural, humanistic, humane; pragmatic *or* pragmatical, practical, utilitarian; naturalistic, psychological, scientific, sociological, eclectic, coeducational.

538. Misteaching

n. **misteaching**, misinformation, misintelligence, misguidance, misdirection, mispersuasion [*archaic*], misinstruction, misleading etc. *v.;* perversion; false–, dangerous- teaching; sophistry etc. 477; college of Laputa; the blind leading the blind.

v. **misinform**, misteach, misdescribe, misdirect, misguide, misinstruct, miscorrect; pervert; put on a false–, throw off the- scent; deceive etc. 545; mislead etc. (*error*) 495; misrepresent; lie etc. 544; *spargere voces in vulgum ambiguas* [*Virgil*], preach to the wise, teach one's grandmother to suck eggs [*colloq.*].

render unintelligible etc. 519; bewilder etc. (*uncertainty*) 475; mystify etc. (*conceal*) 528; unteach [*archaic*].

adj. **misteaching** etc. *v.;* unedifying.

539. Learning

n. **learning**; acquisition of -knowledge etc. 490, –skill etc. 698; acquirement, attainment; mental cultivation, edification, scholarship, erudition; acquired knowledge, lore; wide–, general-information; wide reading; self-instruction; study, grind [*colloq.*], reading, perusal; inquiry etc. 461.

docility etc. (*willingness*) 602; aptitude etc. 698.

apprenticeship, prenticeship [*obs. or colloq.*], pupilage, tutelage, novitiate.

examination, matriculation; responsions *or* smalls [*Oxford Univ.*], previous examination

or little go [*Cambridge Univ., Eng.*], moderations *or* mods. [*Oxford Univ.*], final examination, finals, greats [*Oxford Univ.*], great go, tripos [*both Cambridge Univ., Eng.*].

translation, crib [*student cant*]; pony, trot, horse [*all student slang*].

v. **learn**; acquire–, gain–, receive–, take in–, drink in–, imbibe–, pick up–, gather–, get–, obtain–, collect–, glean- knowledge, –information, –learning.

acquaint oneself with, master; make oneself -master of, –acquainted with; grind [*college slang*], cram *or* cram up [*colloq.*], get up, coach up [*colloq.*]; learn by -heart, –rote.

read, spell, peruse; con; run–, pore–, thumb-over; wade through, run through, plunge into, dip into; glance–, run the eye- -over, –through; turn over the leaves.

study; be studious etc. *adj.;* consume–, burn- -the midnight oil; mind one's book, bury oneself in.

go to -school, –college, –the university; serve an (*or* one's) apprenticeship, serve one's time; learn one's trade; be informed etc. 527; be taught etc. 537.

adj. **studious**; industrious etc. 682; scholastic, scholarly, well read, widely read, well posted [*colloq.*], erudite, learned; full of -information, –learning, –lore.

teachable; docile etc. (*willing*) 602; apt etc. 698.

adv. at one's books; *in statu pupillari* [*L.*] etc. (*learner*) 541.

540. Teacher

n. **teacher**, trainer, perceptor, instructor, institutor [*obs.*], master, tutor, director, coryphaeus [*Oxford Univ.*], dry nurse [*slang*], coach [*colloq.*], crammer [*colloq.*], grinder [*college slang, Eng.*], don [*Univ. cant*]; governor [*obs.*], bear leader [*humorous*]; governess, duenna; disciplinarian.

professor, lecturer, reader, prelector *or* praelector, prolocutor, preacher; chalk talker, *khoja* [*Turk.*], munshi *or* moonshee [*Moham.*]; pastor etc. (*clergy*) 996; schoolmaster, dominie, usher [*Brit.*], pedagogue, abecedarian; schoolmistress, dame [*rare*], kindergartner, monitor, pupil teacher.

guide; docent, coach, expositor etc. 524; guru [*Hindu*]; mentor etc. (*adviser*) 695; pioneer, apostle, missionary, propagandist; example etc. 22.

professorship etc. (*school*) 542.

tutelage etc. (*teaching*) 537.

adj. **pedagogic** *or* pedagogical, preceptorial, tutorial, professorial; scholastic etc. 537.

541. Learner

n. **learner**, scholar, student, alumnus (*fem.* alumna, *pl.* alumni), *élève* [*F.*], pupil, schoolboy, schoolgirl; questionist, questioner, inquirer; monitor, prefect; beginner, tyro, abecedarian, alphabetarian.

undergraduate, undergrad. [*colloq.*], freshman, fresh *or* freshie *or* frosh [*slang*], plebe [*West Point cant*], sophomore, soph [*colloq.*], junior, senior; commoner; pensioner, sizar [*both Cambridge Univ., Eng.*]; exhibitioner, scholar [*winner of a scholarship*], fellow commoner [*Eng. Univ.*], demy [*Magdalene Coll., Oxford*]; junior, sophister *or* soph, senior sophister *or* soph, sophister, questionist [*all Eng. Univ.*].

graduate student, post-graduate student, post-doctoral fellow.

class, form, grade, room; promotion, graduation, remove; pupilage etc. (*learning*) 539.

disciple, chela [*India*], follower, apostle, proselyte.

fellow student, *condiscipulus* [*L.*], condisciple, classmate, schoolmate, schoolfellow, fellow pupil.

novice, recruit, tenderfoot [*slang*], neophyte, inceptor, *débutant* [*F.*], catechumen, probationer; apprentice, prentice [*obs. or colloq.*], articled clerk.

adj. *in statu pupillari* [*L.*], in leading strings, pupillary, monitorial; abecedarian, rudimentary; probationary, probatory, probational; sophomoric *or* sophomoral.

542. School

n. **school**, academy, lyceum, *Gymnasium* [*Ger.*], *lycée* [*F.*], palaestra *or* palestra, seminary, college, educational institution, institute; university, 'varsity [*colloq.*], *Alma Mater* [*L.*].

[general] day–, boarding–, preparatory *or* prep [*colloq.*], –, elementary–, common–, denominational–, secondary–, endowed–, free–, continuation–, convent–, art–, music–, military–, naval–, technical–, library–, secretarial–, business–, correspondence– school; kindergarten, nursery, day nursery, nursery school, *crèche* [*F.*]; Sunday–, Sabbath–, Bible-school; reform school, reformatory; teachers' training college; university extension -lectures, –course.

[british] primary–, infant–, dame [*hist.*]–, voluntary–, government–, Board–, higher grade–, National–, mission–, missionary–, British and Foreign–, state-aided–, grant-in-aid–, middle-class–, County Council–, training–, normal–, grammar–, collegiate–, high–, upper–, modern–, lower–, County–, County high–, Cathedral–, municipal secondary–, municipal technical–, Friends'–, coeducational *or* dual–, Polytechnic–, King Henry VIII's–, King Edward's–, Queen Elizabeth's–, Queen Mary's–, merchant guild–, Blue-Coat- school; Christ's Hospital; public school (*as* Eton, Harrow, Rugby etc.); school of art, school of arts and crafts, trade school; Royal Naval College, Royal Military Academy (Woolwich), Royal Military College (Sandhurst); training ship for -royal navy, –mercantile marine; College of Preceptors; Royal Academy–, London College–, Trinity College- of Music; Royal College of Organists.

[united states] district–, grade–, parochial–, public–, primary–, grammar–, junior high–, high–, Latin- school; private–, technological–, normal–, kindergarten training- school; summer school; military academy (West Point); naval academy (Annapolis); college, freshwater college [*slang*], jerk water college [*slang*], State university; graduate school, post-graduate school.

class, division, form etc. 541; seminar *or* seminary.

class room, room, school room, recitation room, lecture room, lecture hall, theater *or* theatre, amphitheater *or* amphitheatre.

desk, reading desk, ambo, pulpit, forum, stage, rostrum, platform, hustings, tribune.

schoolbook, textbook, hornbook; grammar, primer, abecedary [*rare*], abecedarium, New England Primer, rudiments, manual, *vade mecum* [*L.*]; encyclopedia *or* encyclopaedia; cyclopedia *or* cyclopaedia; Lindley Murray, Cocker; dictionary, lexicon, thesaurus.

professorship, associate professorship, lectureship, readership, fellowship, preceptorship, tutorship, instructorship; chair.

directorate, board, syndicate; College Board, Board of Regents (N. Y.), School Board, Council of Education; Board of Education; Board–, Prefect- of Studies; Textbook Committee; propaganda.

adj. **scholastic**, academic, collegiate; educational, palaestral *or* palestral, cultural; gymnastic, athletic, physical, eurythmic.

adv. ex-cathedra.

543. Veracity

n. **veracity**; truthfulness, frankness etc. *adj.;* truth, soothfastness [*archaic*], smooth [*archaic*], veridicality, sincerity, candor, honesty, fidelity; plain dealing, *bona fides* [*L.*]; love of truth; probity etc. 939; ingenuousness etc. (*artlessness*) 703.

the truth the whole truth and nothing but the truth; honest–, unvarnished–, sober- truth etc. (*fact*) 494; unvarnished tale; light of truth.

v. **speak the truth**, tell the truth; speak on oath; speak without -equivocation, –mental reservation; speak by the card; paint in its–, show oneself in one's- true colors; make a clean breast, let it all hang out [*slang*] etc. (*disclose*) 529; speak one's mind etc. (*be blunt*) 703; not lie etc. 544, not deceive etc. 545.

adj. **truthful**, true; veracious, veridical; scrupulous etc. (*honorable*) 939; sincere, candid, frank, open, straightforward, unreserved; open–, frank–, true–, simple- hearted; soothfast [*archaic*], truth-telling, honest, trustworthy; undissembling etc. (dissemble etc. 544); guileless, pure; truth-loving; unperjured; true-blue, as good as one's word; one's word one's bond; unaffected, unfeigned, *bona fide* [*L.*]; outspoken, ingenuous etc. (*artless*) 703; undisguised etc. (*real*) 494.

adv. **truly** etc. (*really*) 494; in plain words etc. 703; in–, with–, of a–, in good- truth; as the dial to the sun, as the needle to the pole; honor bright [*colloq.*]; troth; in good -sooth, –earnest; soothfast [*archaic*], unfeignedly, with no nonsense, in sooth, sooth to say, *bona fide* [*L.*], *in foro conscientiae* [*L.*]; without equivocation; *cartes sur table* [*F.*], from the bottom of one's heart; by my troth etc. (*affirmation*) 535.

544. Falsehood

n. **falsehood**, falseness; falsity, falsification; deception etc. 545; untruthfulness; untruth etc. 546; guile; lying etc. *v.*, misrepresentation; mendacity, perjury, false swearing; forgery, invention, fabrication; subreption; covin [*archaic*].

perversion–, suppression- of truth; *suppressio veri* [*L.*]; perversion, distortion, false coloring; exaggeration etc. 549; prevarication, equivocation, shuffling, fencing, evasion, fraud; *suggestio falsi* [*L.*] etc. (*lie*) 546; mystification etc. (*concealment*) 528; simulation etc. (*imitation*) 19; dissimulation, dissembling, deceit; *blague* [*F.*].

sham, pretense, scam [*slang*], pretending, malingering.

duplicity, double dealing, insincerity, tartufism *or* tartuffism, hypocrisy, cant, humbug, fake [*slang*]; casuistry, jesuitism, jesuitry; pharisaism; Machiavelism, "organized hypocrisy"; lip -homage, –service; mouth honor; hollowness; mere -show, –outside; crocodile tears, mealymouthedness, quackery; charlatanism, charlatanry; gammon [*Eng. colloq.*], buncombe *or* bunkum *or* bunk, flam: bam [*slang*], flimflam, cajolery, flattery; Judas kiss; perfidy etc. (*bad faith*) 940; *il volto sciolto i pensieri stretti* [*It.*].

unfairness etc. (*dishonesty*) 940; artfulness etc. (*cunning*) 702; missatement etc. (*error*) 495.

v. **be false** etc. *adj.*, be a liar etc. 548; speak falsely etc. *adv.;* tell a lie etc. 546; lie, fib; lie like a trooper; swear falsely, forswear, perjure oneself, bear false witness.

falsify, misstate, misquote, miscite, misreport, misrepresent; belie, pervert, distort; put a false construction upon etc. (*misinterpret*) 523.

prevaricate, equivocate, quibble; palter, –to the understanding; *répondre en Normand* [*F.*]; trim, shuffle, fence, mince the truth, beat about the bush, blow hot and cold [*colloq.*], play fast and loose.

garble, gloss over, disguise, give a color to; give–, put- a -gloss, –false coloring- upon; color, varnish, cook [*colloq.*], doctor [*colloq.*], dress up, embroider; exaggerate etc. 549; *blague* [*F.*].

fabricate, invent, trump up, get up; forge, fake [*slang*], hatch, concoct; romance etc. (*imagine*) 515; cry "wolf!"

dissemble, dissimulate; feign, assume, put on, pretend, make believe; act the old soldier [*colloq.*], play possum; play -false, –a double game; coquet; act–, play- a part; affect etc. 855; simulate, pass off for; counterfeit, sham, make a show of; malinger; say the grapes are sour.

cant [*dial. Eng.*], play the hypocrite, sham Abram *or* Abraham, *faire pattes de velours* [*F.*], put on the mask, clean the outside of the platter, lie like a thief, lie through one's teeth; hand out–, hold out–, sail under- false colors; "commend the poisoned chalice to the lips" [*Macbeth*]; *spargere voces in vulgum ambiguas* [Virgil]; deceive etc. 545.

adj. **false**, deceitful, mendacious, unveracious, fraudulent, dishonest; faithless, truthless, untruthful, trothless [*archaic*]; unfair, uncandid; hollowhearted; evasive; uningenuous, disingenuous; hollow, insincere, *Parthis mendacior* [*L.*]; forsworn.

collusive, collusory [*obs.*]; artful etc. (*cunning*) 702; perfidious etc. 940; spurious etc. (*deceptive*) 545; untrue etc. 546; falsified etc. *v.;* covinous.

hypocritical, canting, jesuitical, pharisaical; tartufish *or* tartuffish; Machiavellic, Machiavellian *or* Machiavelian; double, –tongued, –handed, –minded, –hearted, –dealing; two-faced, double-faced; Janus-faced; smooth-faced, –spoken, –tongued; plausible; mealy-mouthed; affected etc. 855.

adv. **falsely** etc. *adj.; à la Tartufe* [*F.*], with a double tongue; slily etc. (*cunning*) 702.

545. Deception

n. **deception**; falseness etc. 544; untruth etc. 546; imposition, imposture; fraud, deceit, guile; fraudulence, fraudulency; covin [*archaic*]; knavery etc. (*cunning*) 702; misrepresentation etc. (*falsehood*) 544; bluff; straw-bail, straw-bid; spoof [*slang*]; hocus-pocus, *escamoterie* [*F.*], jockeyship; trickery, coggery [*obs.*], pettifoggery, sharp practice, chicanery; *supercherie* [*F.*], cozenage, circumvention, ingannation [*obs.*], collusiveness, collusion; treachery etc. 940; practical joke.

delusion, gullery [*archaic*]; juggling, jugglery; sleight of hand, legerdemain; prestigiation [*obs.*], prestidigitation; magic etc. 992; conjuring, conjuration.

trick, cheat, wile, blind, feint, plant [*slang*], bubble, fetch, catch [*dial.*], chicane, artifice, reach [*obs.*], bite [*obs., colloq.*], juggle, hocus [*archaic*]; thimble-rig, card sharping, artful dodge, swindle; tricks upon travelers; trapan *or* trepan [*archaic*]; stratagem etc. (*artifice*) 702; fake [*colloq. or slang*], hoax; theft etc. 791; ballot-box stuffing, barney [*slang*], bunko *or* bunco, bunko game; confidence -trick, –game; brace–, drop–, gum–, panel–, shell–, skin- game [*all slang*]; gold brick [*colloq.*].

snare, trap, pitfall, Cornish hug, decoy, gin; springe, springle [*obs.*]; noose, hook; bait, decoy duck, stool pigeon, tub to the whale, baited trap, *guet-apens* [*F.*]; cobweb, net, meshes, toils, mouse trap, birdlime; Dionaea, Venus's flytrap; ambush etc. 530; trapdoor, sliding panel, false bottom; spring net, spring gun; mask, masked battery; mine; flytrap; green goods; panel house.

disguise, disguisement; false colors, masquerade, mummery, borrowed plumes; wolf in sheep's clothing etc. (*deceiver*) 548; *pattes de velours* [*F.*].

sham; mockery etc. (*imitation*) 19; copy etc. 21; counterfeit, make-believe, forgery, fraud; lie etc. 546; "a delusion, a mockery, and a snare" [Denman], hollow mockery; whited–, painted-sepulcher; jerry-building, jerryism [*builders' cant*]; man of straw.

tinsel, paste, false jewelry, scagliola, ormolu, mosaic gold, brummagem, German silver, albata, paktong, white metal, Britannia metal, paint.

illusion etc. (*error*) 495; *ignis fatuus* [*L.*] etc. 423; mirage etc. 443.

v. **deceive,** take in, Machiavellize; defraud, cheat, jockey, do [*slang*], escamoter [*F.*], cozen, diddle [*dial.*], nab [*slang*], chouse [*colloq.*], bite [*colloq.*], play one false, bilk, cully, jilt [*obs.*], pluck [*rare*], swindle, victimize; abuse; mystify; blind, –one's eyes; blindfold, hoodwink; throw dust into the eyes, "keep the word of promise to the ear and break it to the hope" [*Macbeth*].

impose–, practice–, play–, put–, palm–, foist-upon; snatch a verdict; bluff, –off; bunko *or* bunco, four-flush [*slang*]; gum [*slang*], spoof [*slang*], stuff (a ballot box) [*U. S.*].

circumvent, overreach; outreach, outwit, outmaneuver *or* outmanoeuvre, steal a march upon, give the go-by to [*slang*], leave in the lurch.

insnare, ensnare; set–, lay- a -trap, –snare- for; bait the hook, forelay [*obs.*], spread the toils, lime; decoy, waylay, lure, beguile, delude, inveigle; trapan *or* trepan [*archaic*]; kidnap; let in, hook in; trick; entrap *or* intrap, nick, springe [*rare*], nousel *or* nousle [*obs.*]; blind a trail, enmesh *or* immesh; shanghai, crimp; catch, –in a trap; sniggle, entangle, illaqueate [*rare*], balk, trip up; throw a tub to a whale, hocus.

fool, befool, practice on one's credulity, dupe, gull, hoax, bamboozle [*colloq.*]; hum [*slang or colloq.*], humbug, gammon [*Eng. colloq.*], stuff up [*slang*], stuff [*slang*], sell [*slang*]; play a -trick, –practical joke- upon one; fool to the top of one's bent, send on a fool's errand; make -game, –a fool, –an April fool, –an ass- of; trifle with, cajole, flatter; come over etc. (*influence*) 615; gild the pill, make things pleasant, divert, put a good face upon; dissemble etc. 544.

live by one's wits; cog [*rare*], cog the dice; play at hide and seek; obtain money under false pretenses etc. (*steal*) 791; conjure, juggle, practice chicanery; deacon; jerry-build; pass by trickery, play off, palm off, foist off, fob off [*archaic*].

mislead etc. (*error*) 495; lie etc. 544; misinform etc. 538; betray etc. 940.

be deceived etc. 547.

adj. **deceptive**, deceptious [*rare*], deceitful, covinous [*law*]; delusive, delusory; illusive, illusory; deceived etc. *v.*; deceiving etc. *v.*; cunning etc. 702; prestigious [*obs.*], prestigiatory [*obs.*]; elusive, insidious, *ad captandum vulgus* [*L.*].

make-believe; untrue etc. 546; mock, sham, counterfeit, snide [*slang*], pseudo, spurious, so-called, pretended, feigned, trumped-up, bogus [*colloq.*], scamped, fraudulent, tricky, factitious, artificial, bastard; surreptitious, illegitimate, contraband, adulterated, sophisticated; unsound, rotten at the core; colorable; disguised; meretricious; jerry-built, jerry [*builders' cant*]; tinsel, pinchbeck, plated; catchpenny; brummagem; simulated etc. 544.

adv. under -false colors, –the garb of, –cover of; over the left [*slang*].

546. Untruth

n. **untruth**, falsehood, lie, story, thing that is not, fib, bounce, crammer [*slang*], tarradiddle *or* taradiddle [*colloq.*], whopper *or* whapper [*colloq.*], *jhuth* [*Hind.*].

fabrication, forgery, invention; misstatement, misrepresentation, perversion, falsification, gloss, *suggestio falsi* [*L.*]; exaggeration etc. 549.

fiction; fable, nursery tale; romance etc. (*imagination*) 515; absurd-, untrue-, false-, trumped up- -story, –statement; thing devised by the enemy; canard; shave [*slang, Eng.*], sell [*colloq.*], hum, [*slang*], whopper [*colloq.*], yarn [*colloq.*], fish story [*colloq.*], tall tale, traveler's tale, Canterbury tale, cock-and-bull story, fairy tale, fake, press-agent's yarn [*colloq.*], hot air [*slang*], claptrap.

myth, moonshine, bosh [*colloq.*], all my eye and Betty Martin [*colloq.*], all my eye [*colloq.*], mare's-nest, farce.

half truth, white lie, pious fraud; mental reservation etc. (*concealment*) 528; irony.

pretense, pretext; false plea etc. 617; subterfuge, evasion, shift, shuffle, make-believe; sham etc. (*deception*) 545; profession, empty words; Judas kiss etc. (*hypocrisy*) 544; disguise etc. (*mask*) 530.

v. **ring untrue**; have a -false meaning, –hidden meaning, –false appearance; be an untruth etc. *n.*; lie etc. 544.

feign, pretend, sham, counterfeit, gammon [*Eng. colloq.*], make-believe.

adj. **untrue**, false, trumped up; void of-, without-foundation; fictive, far from the truth, false as dicer's oaths; unfounded, *ben trovato* [*It.*], invented, fabulous, fabricated, fraudulent, forged; fictitious, factitious, supposititious, surreptitious; illusory, elusory; evasive, satiric *or* satirical, ironical; *soi-disant* [*F.*] etc. (*misnamed*) 565.

547. Dupe

n. **dupe**, gull, gudgeon, *gobemouche* [*F.*], cully, victim, April fool; jay, sucker, pigeon, cull [*all slang*]; laughingstock etc. 857; simple Simon, flat [*colloq.*], greenhorn; fool etc. 501; puppet, cat's-paw.

v. **be deceived** etc. 545, be the dupe of; fall into a trap; swallow-, nibble at- the bait; bite; catch a Tartar.

adj. **credulous** etc. 486.

mistaken etc. (*error*) 495.

548. Deceiver

n. **deceiver** etc. (deceive etc. 545); dissembler, hypocrite; sophist, Pharisee, Jesuit, Mawworm, Pecksniff, Joseph Surface, Tartufe *or* Tartuffe, Janus; serpent, snake in the grass, cockatrice, Judas, wolf in sheep's clothing; jilt; shuffler.

liar etc. (*lie* etc. 544); Tom Pepper, Machiavel, Machiavelist; story-teller, perjurer, false witness, *menteur à triple étage* [*F.*], Scapin; bunko artist, bunko steerer, carpetbagger, capper [*all slang, U. S.*], faker [*slang*], fraud, four-flusher [*slang*], confidence man, grifter, horse coper [*Eng.*], ringer [*slang*], spieler [*colloq.*]; straw bidder; crimp; decoy duck, stool pigeon; rogue, knave, cheat; swindler etc. (*thief*) 792; jobber, gypsy.

impostor, pretender, malingerer, humbug; adventurer, adventuress; Cagliostro, Fernam Mendex Pinto; ass in lion's skin etc. (*bungler*) 701; actor etc. (*stage player*) 599.

quack, charlatan, mountebank, saltimbanco [*obs.*], *saltimbanque* [*F.*], *blagueur* [*F.*], empiric, quacksalver [*now rare*], medicaster.

conjuror, juggler, trickster, prestidigitator, necromancer, sorcerer, magician, wizard, mage [*archaic*], medicine man, shaman.

549. Exaggeration

n. **exaggeration**; expansion etc. 194; hyperbole, stretch, strain, coloring; high coloring, caricature, *caricatura* [*It.*]; extravagance etc. (*nonsense*) 497; Baron Munchausen; Munchausenism; men in buckram, big one, yarn [*colloq.*], fringe, embroidery, tall tale, traveler's tale; fish story [*colloq.*], gooseberry [*slang*].

storm–, tempest- in a teacup; much ado about nothing etc. (*overestimation*) 482; puffery etc. (*boasting*) 884; rant etc. (*turgescence*) 577.

false coloring etc. (*falsehood*) 544; aggravation etc. 835.

figure of speech, *façon de parler* [*F.*]; stretch of -fancy, –the imagination; flight of fancy etc. (*imagination*) 515.

v. **exaggerate,** magnify, pile up, aggravate; amplify etc. (*expand*) 194; optimize; overestimate etc. 482; hyperbolize; overcharge, overstate, overdraw, overlay, overshoot the mark, overpraise; make much of, make the most of; strain, –a point; stretch, –a point; go great lengths; spin a long yarn [*colloq.*]; draw–, pull–, use–, shoot with- a (*or* the) longbow [*colloq.*]; deal in the marvelous.

out-Herod Herod, run riot, talk at random.

overcolor, heighten; color -highly, –too highly; *broder* [*F.*], embroider, be flowery; flourish; color etc. (*misrepresent*) 544; puff etc. (*boast*) 884.

underrate, pessimize, underestimate etc. 483.

adj. **exaggerated** etc. *v.;* overwrought; bombastic etc. (*magniloquent*) 577; hyperbolical, on stilts; fabulous, extravagant, preposterous, egregious, *outré* [*F.*], highflying.

Section 3. Means of Communication

550. Indication

n. **indication;** symbolism, symbolization; symptomatology, semeiology *or* semiology, semeiotics *or* semiotics, pathognomy; *Zeitgeist* [*Ger.*], sign of the times.

means of recognition; lineament, feature, trait, trick, carmark, characteristic, diagnostic; diving rod; cloven hoof; footfall.

sign, symbol; index, indice [*obs.*], indicator, point, pointer; exponent, note, token, symptom; dollar mark; type, figure, emblem, cipher, device; representation etc. 554.

motto, epigraph, epitaph, posy [*archaic*].

gesture, gesticulation; pantomime; wink, glance, leer; nod, shrug, beck; touch, cudge; grip, freemasonry; telegraphy, byplay, dumb show; cue; hint etc. 527.

track, spoor, trail, footprint, scent; clew *or* clue, key.

dactylology, dactylography, dactylonomy, dactyliomancy, chirology [*rare*], chiromancy, palmistry; finger print, Bertillon system.

signal, signal post, rocket, blue light, red light; watch fire, watchtower; telegraph, semaphore, flagstaff; fiery cross; calumet, peace pipe; heliograph; guidon; headlight, searchlight, flashlight, spotlight.

mark, line, stroke, score, stripe, streak, scratch, tick, dot, point, notch, nick, blaze; red letter, sublineation, underlining, jotting; print; imprint, impress, impression; note, annotation.

[map drawing] hachure, contour line; isobar, isopiestic line, isobaric line; isotherm, isothermal line; latitude, longitude, meridian, equator.

[typography] dash, hyphen, parentheses, brackets *or* crotchets, apostrophe, question mark, exclamation *or* exclamation point; acute–, grave- accent; long *or* macron, short *or* breve, dieresis, caret, brace, ellipsis, leaders, asterisk, dagger *or* obelisk, double dagger, section, parallels, paragraph, index, asterism, cedilla, guillemets [*rare*], quotation marks *or* quotes [*colloq.*], tilde, circumflex.

[for identification] badge, criterion; countercheck, countermark, countersign, counterfoil, stub, duplicate, tally; label, ticket, billet, letter, counter, check, chip, chop [*Oriental*], dib [*slang*]; broad arrow; government mark; totem; tessera, card, bill; witness, voucher; stamp; *cachet* [*F.*]; trade–, hall- mark; signature; address–, visiting- card; *carte de visite* [*F.*]; credentials etc. (*evidence*) 467; attestation; hand, handwriting, sign manual; cipher; monogram; seal, sigil, signet; autograph, autography; finger print; paraph, brand; superscription; indorsement *or* endorsement; title, heading, docket; tonsure, scalp lock; mortar board [*colloq.*], cap and gown, hood; caste mark; *mot de passe* [*F.*], *mot du guet* [*F.*], passeparole *or* passparole [*obs.*], shibboleth; watchword, catchword, password; sign, countersign, pass, dueguard, grip; open-sesame; timbrology [*rare*].

insignia; banner, banneret; banderole, bandrol *or* bannerol; flag, colors, streamer, standard, eagle, vexillum, labarum, oriflamme *or* oriflamb; figurehead; ensign; pennant, whip *or* coach-whip, pennon, burgee, blue peter, jack, ancient [*rare*], gonfalon, union jack; "Old Glory" [*colloq.*], quarantine flag; yellow flag, yellow jack; tricolor, *drapeau tricolore* [*F.*], stars and stripes; stars and bars; half-masted flag, union down; red flag; bunting.

heraldry, crest; arms, coat of arms; armorial bearings, hatchment; escutcheon *or* scutcheon, achievement, shield, supporters; livery, uniform; cockade, brassard, epaulet, chevron; garland, chaplet, fillet [*antiq.*], love knot, favor.

[of locality] beacon, beacon fire, cresset, cairn, post, staff, flagstaff, hand, pointer, vane, cock, weathercock, weathervane; guide-, hand-, finger-, directing-, sign- post; pillars of Hercules, pharos; balefire, signal fire; *l'Etoile du Nord* [*F.*], North Star, polestar, Polaris; landmark, seamark; lighthouse, balize [*rare*], lodestar *or* loadstar; cynosure, guide; address, direction, name; sign, signboard.

[of the future] warning etc. 668; omen etc. 512; prefigurement etc. 511.

[of the past] trace, record etc. 551.

[of danger] warning etc. 668; fire alarm, burglar alarm; alarm etc. 669.

[of authority] scepter etc. 747.

[of triumph] trophy etc. 733.

[of quantity] gauge etc. 466.

[of distance] milestone, milepost; mileage ticket; milliary [*Rom. antiq.*].

[of disgrace] brand, fool's cap, mark of Cain, stigma, stripes, broad arrow.

[for detection] check, time clock, telltale; test etc. (*experiment*) 463.

notification etc. (*information*) 527; advertisement etc. (*publication*) 531.

call, word of command; bugle call, trumpet call; bell, alarum, cry; battle-, rallying- cry; reveille, taps, last post; sacring bell, Sanctus bell, angelus; pibroch, keen [*Ir.*], coronach [*Scot. & Ir.*], dirge.

v. **indicate**; be the sign of etc. *n.;* denote, betoken; argue, testify etc. (*evidence*) 467; bear the impress of etc. *n.;* connote, connotate, signify.

represent, stand for; typify etc. (*prefigure*) 511; symbolize.

mark; put an indication, put a mark etc. *n.;* note, tick, stamp, nick, earmark; blaze; label, ticket, docket; dot, spot, score, dash, trace, chalk.

print, imprint, impress; engrave, stereotype, electrotype, lithograph; prove, pull, reprint.

make a sign etc. *n.;* signalize; give-, hang out- a signal; beck [*archaic*], beckon; nod; wink, glance, leer, nudge, shrug, tip the wink [*slang*]; gesture, gesticulate; raise-, hold up- the -finger, -hand; saw the air, "suit the action to the word" [*Hamlet*].

wave-, unfurl-, hoist-, hang out- a banner etc. *n.;* wave -the hand, -a kerchief; give the cue etc. (*inform*) 527; show one's colors; give-,

sound- an alarm; beat the drum, sound the trumpets, raise a cry.

sign, seal, attest etc. (*evidence*) 467; underscore, underline etc. (*give importance to*) 642; call attention to etc. (*attention*) 457; give notice etc. (*inform*) 527.

adj. **indicative**, indicatory; indicating etc. *v.* connotative, denotative; diacritical, representative, typical, symbolic *or* symbolical, pantomimic, pathognomonic *or* pathognomonical, symptomatic, semeiotic *or* semiotic, sematic, ominous, characteristic, significant, significative, demonstrative, diagnostic, exponential, emblematic, armorial; individual etc. (*special*) 79.

known by, recognizable by; indicated etc. *v.;* pointed, marked.

[capable of being denoted] denotable; indelible.

adv. **symbolically** etc. *adj.;* in token of; in dumb show, in pantomime.

551. Record

n. **trace**, vestige, relic, remains; scar, cicatrix; footstep, footmark, footprint; pug [*India*], track, mark, wake, trail, scent, *piste* [*F.*].

monument, hatchment, achievement; escutcheon *or* scutcheon; slab, tablet, trophy, obelisk, pillar, column, monolith; memorial; memento etc. (*memory*) 505; testimonial, medal, Congressional medal; cross, Victoria cross *or* V. C., iron cross [*Ger.*]; ribbon, garter; commemoration etc. (*celebration*) 883.

record, note, minute; register, registry; roll etc. (*list*) 86; chartulary *or* cartulary, diptych, Domesday book; *catalogue raisonné* [*F.*]; entry, memorandum, indorsement *or* endorsement, inscription, copy, duplicate, docket; notch etc. (*mark*) 550; muniments; deed etc. (*security*) 771; document; deposition, *procés verbal* [*F.*]; affidavit; certificate etc. (*evidence*) 467.

notebook, memorandum book, pocketbook, commonplace book, portfolio; bulletin, bulletin board, score board, score sheet, totalizator [*racing*] tote board [*colloq.*]; card index, file, letter file, pigeonholes; *excerpta* [*L.*], excerpt, extract, adversaria, jottings, dottings.

newspaper, daily, gazette etc. (*publication*) 531; magazine.

calendar, ephemeris, diary, log, log book *or* logbook, journal, daybook, ledger, cashbook, petty cashbook.

archive, scroll, state paper, return, bluebook *or* blue book; almanac *or* almanack, gazetteer, Almanach de Gotha, Statesman's Year-book, Whitaker's Almanack; census report; statistics etc. 86; *compte rendu* [*F.*]; Acts–, Transactions–, Proceedings- of; Hansard's Debates; Congressional Records; minutes, chronicle, annals; legend; history, biography etc. 594.

registration; registry, enrollment *or* enrolment, tabulation; entry, booking; signature etc. (*identification*) 550; recorder etc. 553; journalism.

mechanical record, recording instrument; gramophone, phonograph etc. 418; seismograph, seismometer; speedometer, pedometer, patent log [*naut.*]; ticker, tape; time clock; anemometer etc. (*measurement*) 466; turnstile; cash register; votograph.

v. **record**; put–, place- upon record; chronicle, calendar, excerpt, hand down to posterity; keep up the memory etc. (*remember*) 505; commemorate etc. (*celebrate*) 883; report etc. (*inform*) 527; commit to–, reduce to- writing; put–, set down- -in writing, –in black and white; put–, jot–, take–, write–, note–, set-down; note, minute, put on paper; take–, make- a -note, –minute, –memorandum; summarize, make a return; mark etc. (*indicate*) 550; sign etc. (*attest*) 467.

enter, book; post, post up; insert, make an entry of; mark off, tick off; register, list, docket, enroll, inscroll; file etc. (*store*) 636.

adv. **on record**, on file; in one's -good books, –bad books.

552. Obliteration
[suppression of sign]

n. **obliteration**, erasure, rasure [*rare*]; cancel, cancellation; circumduction [*rare*], deletion, blot; *tabula rasa* [*L.*]; effacement, extinction.

v. **efface**, obliterate, erase, rase [*rare*], expunge, cancel, dele; blot–, take–, rub–, scratch–, strike–, wipe–, wash–, sponge- out; wipe off, rub off; wipe away; deface, render illegible; draw the pen through, rule out, apply the sponge.

be effaced etc.; leave no trace etc. 550; "leave not a rack behind" [*Tempest*].

adj. **obliterated** etc. *v.;* leaving no trace; intestate; unrecorded, unregistered, unwritten; printless, out of print.

int. dele; out with it!

553. Recorder

n. **recorder**, notary, clerk; registrar, registrary [*obs.*], register; prothonotary; amanuensis, secretary, recording secretary, stenographer, scribe, babu [*India*], remembrancer, book-

keeper, *custos rotulorum* [*L.*], Master of the Rolls.

annalist, historian, historiographer, chronicler; biographer etc. (*narrator*) 594; antiquary etc. (*antiquity*) 122; memorialist.

journalist, newspaperman, reporter, interviewer, pressman, publicist, author, editor.

554. Representation

n. **representation**, depiction, depicture; imitation etc. 19; illustration, delineation, depictment; imagery, portraiture, iconography; design, designing; art, fine arts; painting etc. 556; sculpture etc. 557; engraving etc. 558.

photography; radiography, X-ray photography, skiagraphy; spectroheliography, photospectroheliography.

personation, personification; impersonation; drama etc. 599.

drawing, picture, sketch, draft *or* draught; tracing; copy etc. 21.

photograph, photo [*colloq.*], daguerreotype, talbotype, calotype; heliotype, heliograph; print, cabinet, *carte de visite* (*pl. cartes de visite*) [*F.*], ping-pong [*cant*], snapshot.

image, likeness, icon, portrait; striking likeness, speaking likeness; spitting image [*colloq.*]; very image; effigy, facsimile.

figure, figurehead; puppet, doll, figurine, aglet *or* aiglet, manikin, mannequin, lay figure, model, marionette, fantoccini, waxwork, bust; statue, statuette, hieroglyph.

hieroglyphic, anaglyph, diagram, monogram.

map, plan, chart; ground plan, projection, elevation; atlas; outline, scheme; view etc. (*painting*) 556; ichnography, cartography.

radiograph, radiogram, scotograph, skiagraph *or* sciagraph, skiagram *or* sciagram, CAT scan, ultrasound image, X-ray photograph, X-ray [*colloq.*]; spectrogram, spectroheliogram, photospectroheliogram.

delineator, draftsman *or* draughtsman; artist etc. 559; photographer, radiographer, X-ray photographer, skiagrapher, daguerreotypist.

v. **represent**, delineate, depict, depicture, portray, picture, limn, take–, catch- a likeness etc. *n.;* hit off, photograph, daguerreotype; snapshot; figure; shadow -forth, –out; adumbrate; body forth; describe etc. 594; trace, copy; mold *or* mould.

illustrate, symbolize; paint etc. 556; carve etc. 557; engrave etc. 558.

personate, personify, impersonate, dress up [*colloq.*], assume a character, pose as, act; play etc. (*drama*) 599; mimic etc. (*imitate*) 19; hold the mirror up to nature.

adj. **representing** etc. *v.,* representative; illustrative; represented etc. *v.;* imitative, figurative; iconic, like etc. 17; graphic etc. (*descriptive*) 594.
Renaissance, trecento, quattrocento, cinquecento, Directoire, Moyen Age.

555. Misrepresentation

n. **misrepresentation**, misstatement, falsification, caricatura [*obs.*], exaggeration; daubing etc. *v.;* bad likeness, daub, scratch; imitation, effigy.
distortion, anamorphosis, anamorphoscope; Claude Lorrain–, concave–, convex- mirror.
burlesque, travesty, parody, takeoff, caricature, extravaganza.

v. **misrepresent**, distort, overdraw, exaggerate, daub; falsify, understate, overstate, stretch.
burlesque, travesty, parody, caricature.

adj. **misrepresented** etc. *v.;* bluesky.

556. Painting and Black and White

n. **painting**; depicting; drawing etc. *v.;* design; perspective; *chiaroscuro* etc. (*light*) 420; composition; treatment; arrangement, values, atmosphere, tone, technique.
historical–, portrait–, miniature–, landscape–, marine–, flower–, poster–, interior–, scene- painting; scenography.
pallet, palette; easel; brush, pencil, stump; black lead, charcoal, crayons, chalk, pastel; paint etc. (*coloring matter*) 428; water–, body–, oil- color; oils, oil paint; varnish etc. 356a; priming; *gouache* [*F.*], tempera, distemper, fresco, water glass; enamel; encaustic painting; mosaic; tapestry, batik; sun painting.
style, school; the grand style, high art, *genre* [*F.*], portraiture; futurist, cubist, vorticist; ornamental art etc. 847; monochrome, polychrome; grisaille.
[schools of painting] Italian–, Bolognese–, Florentine–, Milanese–, Modena–, Parma–, Neapolitan–, Paduan–, Roman–, Umbrian–, Venetian–, British–, Dutch–, Flemish–, French–, German–, Spanish- School; School of Raphael etc.
picture, painting, piece, tableau, canvas; oil painting etc.; fresco, cartoon; easel–, cabinet-picture; drawing, draft *or* draught; pencil etc. drawing, water-color drawing; still life; sketch, outline, study.
portrait etc. (*representation*) 554; whole–, full–, half- length; three-quarters profile; head; miniature; shade, silhouette; profile.

view, landscape, seascape, sea view, seapiece; scene, prospect; interior; panorama, bird's-eye view, diorama.
picture gallery, art gallery, art museum, pinacotheca; studio, *atelier* [*F.*].
photography, skiagraphy, radiography etc. 554; photograph, radiograph etc. 554; scenograph.

v. **paint**, design, limn, draw, sketch, pencil, scratch, shade, stipple, hatch, dash off, chalk out, square up; color, dead color, wash, varnish; draw in pencil etc. *n.;* paint in oils etc. *n.;* stencil; depict etc. (*represent*) 554.

adj. **pictorial**, graphic; painted etc. *v.;* picturesque, genre; historical etc. *n.;* monochrome, polychrome; scenographic; futurist, cubist, vorticist; in the grand style; painty, pastose.
pencil, oil etc. *n.*

adv. in pencil etc. *n.*

557. Sculpture

n. **sculpture**, insculpture [*obs.*]; carving etc. *v.;* statuary, anaglyptics, cermaics.
marble, bronze, terra cotta; ceramic ware, pottery, porcelain, china, earthenware; cloisonné, enamel, faïence, satsuma.
relief, relievo; basso-relievo *or* bassorilievo [*It.*], low relief, bas-relief; alto-relievo *or* alto-rilievo [*It.*], high relief; mezzo-relievo *or* mezzo-rilievo [*It.*]; glyph, intaglio, anaglyph; medal, medallion; cameo.
[schools of sculpture] Aeginetan–, Attic–, Chian–, Pergamene–, Rhodian–, Samian–, Sicyonian- School.
statute etc. (*image*) 554; cast etc. (*copy*) 21; glyptotheca.
[statues] Apollo Belvedere, Venus of Melos *or* Milo, Cnidian Aphrodite, Venus de' Medici, Dying Gaul, Farnese Hercules, Laocoön, Niobe, Silenus and Infant Bacchus, Theseus, Centaur and Eros, Niké *or* Winged Victory of Samothrace, The Wrestlers, Michelangelo's David, Mercury taking Flight, Rodin's The Thinker.

v. **sculpture**, carve, cut, chisel, model, mold; cast.

adj. **sculptured** etc. *v.;* in relief, glyptic, anaglyphic, anaglyptic, ceroplastic. ceramic; Parian; marble etc. *n.;* xanthian.

558. Engraving

n. **engraving**, chalcography, glyptography; line–, mezzotint–, stipple–, chalk- engraving; dry point, bur; etching, aquatint *or* aquatinta; chiseling; plate–, copperplate–, steel–, halftone–, process–, wood- engraving; xylography, lignography, glyptography, cerography, lithography, chromolithography, photolithography, zincography, glyphography, xerography.

graver, burin, etching point, style; plate, stone, wood block, negative; die, punch, stamp.

printing; plate-, copperplate-, anastatic-, color-, lithographic- printing; type printing etc. 591; three-color process.

impression, print, engraving, plate; steel-plate, copperplate; etching; aquatint, mezzotint, lithotint; cut, woodcut; stereotype, graphotype, autotype, heliotype; xylograph, lignograph, glyptograph, cerograph, lithograph, chromolithograph, photolithograph, zincograph, glyphograph; process.

illustration, illumination; half tone; photogravure; rotogravure [*trade name*]; vignette, initial letter, *cul de lampe* [*F.*], tailpiece.

v. **engrave**, grave, insculp [*rare*], stipple, scrape, etch; bite, bite in; lithograph etc. *n.;* print.

adj. **engraved** etc. *v.;* insculptured, glyptographic; "insculp'd upon" [*Merchant of Venice*].

559. Artist

n. **artist**; painter, limner, drawer, sketcher, designer, engraver, chalcographer, glyptographer, graver, line engraver, draftsman *or* draughtsman copyist; enameler *or* enameller, enamelist *or* enamellist; cartoonist, caricaturist.

historical-, landscape-, marine-, flower-, portrait-, genre-, miniature-, scene- painter; carver, chaser, modeler, *figuriste* [*F.*], statuary, sculptor.

Phidias, Praxiteles, Apelles, Raphael, Michelangelo, Titian; Royal Academician.

560. Language

n. **language**; phraseology etc. 569; speech etc. 582; tongue, lingo [*chiefly humorous*], vernacular; mother-, vulgar-, native- tongue; household words; King's *or* Queen's English; dialect, brogue, gobbledegook, patois etc. 563; idiom, idiotism.

confusion of tongues, Babel; *pasigraphie* [*F.*], pasigraphy; universal language, Volapük, Esperanto, Ido; pantomime etc. (*signs*) 550.

linguistics, lexicology, philology, glossology, glottology, comparative philology; Grimm's law, Verner's law; comparative grammar, phonetics; chrestomathy; paleology *or* palaeology, paleography *or* palaeography.

onomatopoeia, betacism, mimmation, myatism, nunnation.

literature, letters, polite literature, *belles lettres* [*F.*], muses, humanities, *litterae humaniores* [*L.*], republic of letters, dead languages,

classics; genius-, spirit-, idiom- of a language; scholarship etc. (*knowledge*) 490.

linguist etc. (*scholar*) 492.

v. **express**, say, express by words etc. 566.

adj. **lingual**, linguistic; dialectic; vernacular, current; bilingual; diglot, hexaglot, polyglot; literary; colloquial, slangy.

561. Letter

n. **letter**; character; hieroglyphic etc. (*writing*) 590; type etc. (*printing*) 591; capitals; digraph, trigraph; ideogram, ideograph; majuscule, *majusculoe* [*L.*]; minuscule, *minusculae* [*L.*]; alphabet, ABC, abecedary, christcrossrow *or* crisscross-row [*obs. or dial. Eng.*].

consonant, vowel; diphthong, triphthong; mute, surd, sonant, liquid, labial, palatal, cerebral, dental, guttural; guna, vriddhi [*Skr. gram.*].

syllable; monosyllable, dissyllable, polysyllable; affix, prefix, suffix.

spelling, orthography; phonography, phonetic spelling, phonetics; anagrammatism, metagrammatism.

cipher, monogram, anagram; acrostic, double acrostic, double crostic.

v. spell, orthographize [*rare*]; gunate; transliterate.

cipher, decipher; code, decode; make-, construct- acrostics; design monograms; play anagrams; use-, invent- ciphers.

adj. **literal**; alphabetical, abecedarian; syllabic; majuscular, minuscular; uncial etc. (*writing*) 590.

phonetic, voiced, tonic, sonant; voiceless, surd; mute, labial, palatal, cerebral, dental, guttural, liquid.

562. Word

n. **word**, term, vocable; name etc. 564; phrase etc. 566; root, etymon; derivative; part of speech etc. (*grammar*) 567; ideophone, ideogram, ideograph.

dictionary, lexicon, vocabulary, word book, index, glossary, thesaurus, gradus, delectus, concordance; Rosetta stone.

[science of language] etymology, derivation, glottology *or* glossology, semantics, linguistics; terminology, orismology; translation; pronunciation, orthoëpy; paleology etc. (*philology*) 560; lexicography.

lexicographer, lexicologist, etymologist, linguist, orthoëpist, verbarian; semanticist, glossographer etc. (*scholar*) 492.

verbosity, verbiage, wordiness; loquacity etc. 584.

v. vocalize; etymologize, derive, philologize; index; translate.

adj. **verbal**, literal; titular, nominal.

[similarly derived] conjugate, paronymous; derivative.

verbose, wordy etc. 573; loquacious etc. 584.

adv. **verbally** etc. *adj.; verbatim* [*L.*] etc. (*exactly*) 494.

563. Neology

n. **neology**, neologism; newfangled expression; caconym; barbarism; archaism, black letter, monkish Latin; corruption, missaying, antiphrasis; pseudology; idioticon.

play upon words, paronomasia; word play etc. (*wit*) 842; *double-entente* [*F.*] etc. (*ambiguity*) 520; palindrome, paragram, clinch [*now rare*], double entendre pun; abuse of -language, – terms.

dialect, brogue, patois, provincialism, broken English, Anglicism, Briticism, Gallicism, Scotticism, Hibernicism, Americanism; Gypsy lingo, Romany.

lingua franca, pidgin *or* pigeon English; Chinook, Hindustani, kitchen Kaffir, Swahili, Haussa, Volapük, Esperanto, Ido.

jargon, dog Latin, gibberish; confusion of tongues, Babel; babu English, chi-chi [*Anglo-India*].

colloquialism etc. (*figure of speech*) 521; byword; technicality, lingo, slang, cant, argot, *bat* [*Hind.*], macaronics, rhyming slang, St. Giles's Greek, thieves' Latin, peddler's French, flash tongue, Billingsgate, Franglais.

pseudonym etc. (*misnomer*) 565; Mr. So-and-so; "Sergeant What-is-name" [Kipling]; what d'ye call 'em, what's his name, thingummy, thingamabob, thingummybob [*all colloq.*]; *je ne sais quoi* [*F.*].

neologist, coiner of words.

v. coin words; Americanize, Anglicize, Gallicize; sling the bat [*slang, Anglo-Ind.*].

adj. neologic, neological; archaic, rare, obsolescent; obsolete etc. (*old*) 124; colloquial, dialectal, dialectic *or* dialectical; slang, cant, flash, barbarous; *Anglice* [*NL.*].

564. Nomenclature

n. **nomenclature**; naming etc. *v.;* nuncupation [*obs.*], nomination [*obs.*], baptism; orismology; onomatopoeia; antonomasia.

name; appellation, appellative; designation; title; head, heading; caption; denomination; byname; nickname etc. 565; epithet; what one may -well, –fairly, –properly, –fitly- call.

style, proper name; praenomen, agnomen, cognomen; patronymic, surname; cognomination;

eponym; compellation, description, synonym, antonym; empty -title, –name; title, handle to one's name; namesake.

term, expression, noun; byword; convertible terms etc. 522; technical term; cant etc. 563.

v. **name**, call, term, denominate, designate, style, entitle, clepe [*archaic*], dub [*colloq. or humorous*], christen, baptize, nickname, characterize, specify, define, distinguish by the name of; label etc. (*mark*) 550.

be called etc. *v.;* take–, bear–, go (*or* be known) by–, go (*or* pass) under–, rejoice in- the name of; hight [*archaic*], yclept *or* ycleped [*archaic or humorous*].

adj. **named** etc. *v.;* known as; nuncupatory [*obs.*], nuncupative [*obs.*]; cognominal, titular, nominal, orismological.

565. Misnomer

n. **misnomer**; *lucus a non lucendo* [*L.*]; Mrs. Malaprop; what d'ye call 'em etc. (*neologism*) 563.

nickname, *sobriquet* [*F.*] *or* soubriquet, pet name, little name, by-name; assumed -name, –title; alias; *nom de course* [*F.*], *nom de théâtre* [*F.*], stage name; *nom de guerre* [*F.*], *nom de plume* [*English formation*], pen name, pseudonym; pseudonymity, pseudonymousness.

v. **misname**, miscall, misterm; call out of one's name [*colloq.*], nickname; assume -a name, –an alias; take an -alias, –assumed name.

adj. **misnamed** etc. *v.;* pseudonymous; *soi-disant* [*F.*]; self-called, self-styled, self-christened; so-called, quasi.

nameless, anonymous; without a–, having no-name; innominate, unnamed; unacknowledged; pseudo, bastard.

adv. in no sense; by whatever name, under any name.

566. Phrase

n. **phrase**, expression, locution, set phrase; sentence, paragraph; figure of speech etc. 521; idiom, idiotism; turn of expression; style.

paraphrase etc. (*synonym*) 522; euphemism; euphuism; periphrase etc. (*circumlocution*) 573; motto etc. (*proverb*) 496; phraseology etc. 569.

v. **express**, phrase; word, word it; give -words, –expression -to; voice; arrange in–, clothe in–, put into–, express by- words; couch in terms; find words to express; speak by the card; call, denominate, designate, dub.

adj. expressed etc. *v.;* idiomatic; stylistic.

adv. in -round, –set, -good set- terms; in set phrases; by the card.

567. Grammar

n. **grammar**, accidence, syntax, analysis, praxis, punctuation; parts of speech; jussive; syllabication *or* syllabification, paradigm, syllepsis, synopsis; inflection, case, declension, conjugation; *jus et norma loquendi* [*L.*]; Lindley Murray etc. (*schoolbook*) 542; correct style, philology etc. (*language*) 560.

v. parse, analyze *or* analyse, conjugate, decline; punctuate, syllabicate, syllabize.

adj. grammatical, syntactic *or* syntactical, inflectional; synoptic.

568. Solecism

n. **solecism**; bad–, false–, faulty-grammar; grammatical blunder; *faux pas* [*F.*], error, slip; slip of the pen, *lapsus calami* [*L.*]; slip of the tongue, *lapsus linguae* [*L.*]; slipslop; bull, Hibernianism; barbarism, impropriety.

v. **solecize** *or* solecise, commit a solecism; use –bad, –faulty- grammar; murder the King's (*or* Queen's) English; speak–, write-out of the idiom; break Priscian's head.

adj. **ungrammatical**; incorrect, inaccurate, faulty; improper, incongruous; solecistic *or* solecistical; slipslop.

569. Style

n. **style**, diction, phraseology, wording; manner, strain; composition; mode of expression, idiom, choice of words; mode of speech, literary power, ready pen, pen of a ready writer; grand style, grand manner; command of language etc. (*eloquence*) 582; authorship, artistry; *la morgue littéraire* [*F.*].

v. **word**; express by words etc. 566; write; apply–, employ- the file.

570. Perspicuity

n. **perspicuity** etc. (*intelligibility*) 518; plain speaking etc. (*manifestation*) 525; definiteness, definition; exactness etc. 494; explicitness, lucidness, lucidity, limpidity, clearness.

adj. **lucid** etc. (*intelligible*) 518; limpid, pellucid, clear; explicit etc. (*manifest*) 525; exact etc. 494.

571. Obscurity

n. **obscurity** etc. (*unintelligibility*) 519; involution, crabbedness, confusion; hard words; ambiguity etc. 520; unintelligibility, unintelligibleness; vagueness etc. 475, inexactness etc. 495; what d'ye call 'em etc. (*neologism*) 563; darkness of meaning.

adj. **obscure** etc. *n.*; crabbed; involved, confused.

572. Conciseness

n. **conciseness** etc. *adj.*; brevity, "the soul of wit," laconicism *or* laconism; ellipsis; syncope; abridgment etc. (*shortening*) 201; compression etc. 195; epitome etc. 596; monostich; Spartans; Tacitus.

portmanteau-word [Lewis Carroll]; brunch [breakfast+lunch], squarson [squire+parson]; slithy, *adj.* [slimy+lithe], torrible, *adj.* [torrid +horrible], crowzy, *adj.* [crowded+cozy], motel, *n.* [motor+hotel].

v. **be concise** etc. *adj.*; telescope, laconize; condense etc. 195; abridge etc. 201; abstract etc. 596; come to the point.

adj. **concise**, brief, short, terse, close; to the point, exact; neat, compact; compressed, condensed, pointed; laconic, curt, pithy, trenchant, summary; pregnant; compendious etc. (*compendium*) 596; succinct; elliptical, epigrammatic, crisp; sententious.

adv. **concisely** etc. *adj.*; briefly, summarily; in brief, in short, in a word, in few words; for the sake of brevity, for shortness' sake; to come to the point, to make a long story short, to cut the matter short, to be brief; it comes to this, the long and short of it is, the gist is.

573. Diffuseness

n. **diffuseness** etc. *adj.*; amplification etc. *v.*; dilating etc. *v.*; verbosity, wordiness; verbiage, cloud of words, *copia verborum* [*L.*]; flow of words etc. (*loquacity*) 584; looseness.

tautology, battology, polylogy [*obs.*], perissology [*obs.*]; pleonasm, exuberance, redundance; thrice-told tale; prolixity, longiloquence, longsomeness, circumlocution, ambages [*rare*], periphrase, periphrasis, roundabout phrases; episode; expletive; penny-a-lining; richness etc. 577; padding; drivel, twaddle, drool.

v. **be diffuse** etc. *adj.*; run out on, descant, expatiate, enlarge, dilate, amplify, expand, inflate, pad [*editor's cant*], launch out, branch out; rant.

maunder, prose; harp upon etc. (*repeat*) 104; dwell on, insist upon.

digress, ramble, *battre la campagne* [*F.*], beat about the bush, perorate, spin a long yarn, protract; spin–, swell–, draw- out; battologize *or* battalogize; drivel, twaddle, drool.

adj. **diffuse**, profuse; wordy, verbose, largiloquent [*obs.*], copious, exuberant, pleonastic, lengthy; long, longsome, long-winded, longspun, long drawn out; spun out, protracted, prolix, diffusive, prosing, maundering; circumlocutory, periphrastic, ambagious *or* ambaguious, ambagitory, roundabout; digressive; discursive, excursive; loose; rambling, episodic; flatulent, frothy.

adv. **diffusely** etc. *adj.;* at large, *in extenso* [*L.*]; about it and about.

574. Vigor

n. **vigor**, power, force; boldness, raciness etc. *adj.;* intellectual force; spirit, punch [*slang*], point, piquancy; verve, ardor, enthusiasm, glow, fire, warmth; strong language; gravity, weight, sententiousness.

loftiness, elevation, sublimity, grandeur.

eloquence; command of words, command of language.

adj. **vigorous**, nervous, powerful, forcible, forceful, mordant, biting, trenchant, incisive, graphic, impressive; sensational.

spirited, lively, glowing, sparkling, racy, bold, slashing, crushing; pungent, piquant, full of beans [*slang*], full of pep [*slang*], having punch [*slang*], full of point, pointed, pithy; sententious.

lofty, elevated, sublime, poetic, grand, weighty, ponderous; eloquent.

vehement, petulant, passionate, burning, impassioned.

adv. in -glowing, −good set, −no measured- terms; with his heart on fire; like a ton of bricks [*colloq.*].

575. Feebleness

n. **feebleness** etc. *adj.;* enervation, flaccidity, vapidity, poverty, frigidity.

adj. **feeble**, bald, tame, meager *or* meagre, insipid, watery, nerveless, jejune, vapid, trashy, cold, frigid, poor, dull, dry, languid; colorless, enervated; prosing, prosy, prosaic, unvaried, monotonous, weak, washy, wishy-washy [*colloq.*], sloppy, sketchy, slight; careless, slovenly, loose, disjointed, disconnected, lax; slipshod, slipslop; inexact; puerile, childish; flatulent; rambling etc. (*diffuse*) 573.

576. Plainness

n. **plainness** etc. *adj.;* simplicity, *simplex munditiis* [Hor.], lack of ornamentation, severity; plain talk; plain -terms, −English; Saxon English; household words.

v. **speak plainly**, waste no words, call a spade a spade; plunge *in medias res* [*L.*]; come to the point.

adj. **plain**, simple; unornamented, unadorned, unvarnished; homely, homespun; neat; severe, chaste, pure, Saxon; commonplace, matter-of-fact, natural, prosaic, sober, unimaginative.

dry, unvaried, monotonous etc. 575.

adv. **point-blank**; in plain -terms, words, −English; in common parlance.

577. Ornament

n. **ornament**; floridness etc. *adj.;* turgidity, turgescence *or* turgescency; altiloquence [*obs.*], grandiloquence, magniloquence, declamation, teratology [*obs.*]; well-rounded periods; elegance etc. 578; orotundity.

inversion, antithesis, alliteration, paronomasia; trope; figurativeness etc. (*metaphor*) 521.

flourish; flowers of -speech, −rhetoric; frills, −of style; euphuism, euphemism.

bombast, big-sounding words, high-sounding words; macrology, *sesquipedalia verba* [*L.*], sesquipedalian words, sesquipedality, sesquipedalianism, Alexandrine; inflation, pretension; rant, fustian, highfalutin' [*slang*], buncombe *or* bunkum *or* bunk, balderdash; prose run mad; fine writing; purple patches; Minerva press.

phrasemonger, euphuist, euphemist; word coiner.

v. **ornament**, overlay with ornament, overcharge, overload; euphuize, euphemize; buncomize [*colloq.*]; smell of the lamp.

adj. **ornate**; ornamented etc. *v.;* beautified etc. 847; florid, rich, flowery; euphuistic, euphemistic; sonorous; high- big- sounding; inflated, swelling, tumid; turgid, turgescent; pedantic, pompous, stilted; orotund; high-flown, high-flowing, highfalutin' [*slang*]; sententious, rhetorical, declamatory; grandiose; grandiloquent; magniloquent; altiloquent [*obs.*]; sesquipedal, sesquipedalian; Johnsonian, mouthy; bombastic; fustian; frothy, flashy, flamboyant.

antithetical, alliterative; figurative etc. 521; artificial etc. (*inelegant*) 579.

adv. *ore rotundo* [*L.*], with rounded phrase.

578. Elegance

n. **elegance**, distinction, clarity, purity, grace, felicity, ease; gracefulness, readiness etc. *adj.;* concinnity, concinnation [*rare*], euphony; balance, rhythm, symmetry, proportion, taste, good taste, restraint, nice discrimination, propriety, correctness; Attic salt, Atticism, classicalism, classicism.

well-rounded–, well-turned–, flowing- periods; the right word in the right place; antithesis etc. 577.

purist, classicist, stylist.

v. **flow -smoothly,** –with ease; discriminate nicely, display elegance etc. *n.;* point an antithesis, round a period.

adj. **elegant,** polished, classic *or* classical, classicistic, concinnous [*rare*], correct, Attic, Ciceronian, artistic; chaste, pure, Saxon, academic *or* academical.

graceful, easy, readable, fluent, flowing, tripping; unaffected, natural, unlabored; mellifluous, euphonious; euphemistic; symmetrical, balanced, restrained; rhythmic *or* rhythmical.

felicitous, happy, neat; well–, neatly- -put, –expressed.

579. Inelegance

n. **inelegance,** impurity, vulgarity; want of–, poor–, bad- taste; stiffness etc. *adj.;* "unlettered Muse" [Gray]; cacology, cacography, poor diction, poor choice of words; loose–, slipshod- construction; want of balance, ill-balanced sentences; barbarism; slang etc. 563; solecism etc. 568; mannerism etc. (*affectation*) 855; euphuism, Marinism, Gongorism; fustian etc. 577; cacophony; words that -break the teeth, –dislocate the jaw.

cacographer, barbarian; euphuist, Marinist, Gongorist.

v. **be inelegant** etc. *adj.;* employ inelegance etc. *n.*

adj. **inelegant,** graceless, ungraceful; harsh, abrupt; dry, stiff, cramped, formal, *guindé* [*F.*]; forced, labored; artificial, mannered, ponderous; awkward, uncourtly, unpolished; turgid etc. 577; affected, euphuistic; barbarous, uncouth, grotesque, rude, crude, halting, cacographic *or* cacographical; offensive to ears polite; vulgar, tasteless.

580. Voice

n. **voice;** vocality; organ, lungs, bellows; good–, fine–, powerful etc. (*loud*) 404–, musical etc. 413- voice; intonation; tone etc. (*sound*) 402- of voice.

utterance; vocalization; cry etc. 411; strain, prolation [*archaic*]; exclamation, ejaculation, vociferation, ecphonesis; enunciation, articulation; articulate sound, distinctness; clearness, –of articulation; stage whisper; delivery, attack.

accent, accentuation; emphasis, stress; broad–, strong–, pure–, native–, foreign- accent; pronunciation; orthoëpy; euphony etc. (*melody*) 413; polyphonism, polyphony.

[words similarly pronounced] homonyms.

ventriloquism *or* ventriloquy, ventrilocution, gastriloquism *or* gastriloquy [*rare*]; ventriloquist, gastriloquist [*rare*].

[science of voice], phonology; etc. (*sound*) 402.

v. **speak,** utter, breathe; give utterance, give tongue; cry etc. (*shout*) 411; ejaculate, rap out; vocalize, prolate [*obs.*], articulate, enunciate, pronounce, accentuate, aspirate, deliver, emit; whisper, murmur, whisper in the ear; ventriloquize.

adj. **vocal,** phonetic, oral; ejaculatory, articulate, articulated, distinct, enunciative, accentuated, aspirated; euphonious etc. (*melodious*) 413; whispered.

ventriloquous, ventriloquistic, gastriloquial [*rare*], gastriloquous [*rare*].

581. Aphonia

n. **aphonia** *or* aphony; dumbness etc. *adj.;* obmutescence [*rare*]; absence–, want- of voice; dysphonia *or* dysphony; silence etc. (*taciturnity*) 585; raucity; harsh voice etc. 410, unmusical voice etc. 414; quaver, quavering; falsetto, "childish treble"; deaf-mutism, deaf-muteness, deaf-dumbness, mute, dummy, deaf-mute.

v. **speak low,** speak softly; whisper etc. (*faintness*) 405; keep silence etc. 585.

silence; render -mute, –silent; muzzle, muffle, suppress, smother, gag, strike dumb, dumfound *or* dumbfound dumfounder *or* dumbfounder, mum [*obs.*], drown the voice, put to silence, stop one's mouth, cut one short.

stick in the throat.

adj. **aphonous,** nonvocal, aphonic, dumb, mute, deaf and dumb, deaf-dumb; mum; obmutescent [*rare*], tongue-tied; breathless, tongueless, voiceless, speechless, wordless; mute as a -fish, –stockfish, –mackerel; silent etc. (*taciturn*) 585; muzzled; inarticulate, inaudible.

croaking, raucous, hoarse, husky, dry, hollow, sepulchral, hoarse as a raven; rough.

adv. **with bated breath,** with the finger on the lips; *sotto voce* [*It.*]; in a -low tone, –cracked voice, –broken voice; in broken tones, aside, in an aside.

int. **mum!** hush! sh! silence! whist! whisht! [*dial.*]; *chut!* etc. (*silence*) 403.

582. Speech

n. **speech**, faculty of speech; locution, talk, parlance, verbal intercourse, prolation [*archaic*], oral communication, word of mouth, parole, palaver, prattle.

oration, recitation, delivery, say [*colloq.*], speech, lecture, prelection *or* praelection, harangue, sermon, tirade, formal speech, peroration; speechifying; soliloquy etc. 589; allocution etc. 586; interlocution etc. 588; salutatory [*U. S.*]; screed; valedictory [*U. S.*].

oratory, elocution, eloquence, rhetoric, declamation; grandiloquence, multiloquence, talkativeness; burst of eloquence; facundity [*obs.*]; flow–, command- of -words, –language; *copia verborum* [*L.*]; power of speech, gift of gab [*colloq.*]; *usus loquendi* [*L.*].

speaker etc. *v.;* spokesman; prolocutor, interlocutor; mouthpiece, Hermes; orator, oratrix, oratress; Demosthenes, Cicero; rhetorician, lecturer, preacher, prelector *or* praelector; elocutionist, reciter, reader; spellbinder; stump–, platform- orator; speechmaker, patterer, monologist, monologuist, improvisator, *improvvisatore or improvisatore* [*It.*], *improvvisatrice or improvisatrice* [*It.*].

v. **speak**, –of; say, utter, pronounce, deliver, give utterance to; utter–, pour- forth; breathe, let fall, come out with; rap out, blurt out; have on one's lips; have at the -end, –tip-of one's tongue.

soliloquize etc. 589; tell etc. (*inform*) 527; speak to etc. 586; talk together etc. 588.

break silence; open one's -lips, –mouth; lift–, raise- one's voice; give tongue, wag the tongue [*colloq.*]; talk, outspeak; put in a word or two.

declaim, hold forth; make–, deliver- a speech etc. *n.;* speechify [*derisive or humorous*], harangue, stump [*colloq.*], flourish, spout, rant, recite, lecture, prelect *or* praelect, sermonize, discourse, be on one's legs; have–, say- one's say; expatiate etc. (*speak at length*) 573; speak one's mind, go on the–, take the-stump [*U. S.*].

be eloquent etc. *adj.;* have a tongue in one's head, have the gift of gab [*colloq.*] etc. *n.*

pass one's lips, escape one's lips; fall from the -lips, –mouth.

adj. **oral**, lingual, phonetic, not written, nuncupative [*of wills*], unwritten; speaking etc., spoken etc. *v.;* outspoken, facund [*archaic*].

eloquent, oratorical, rhetorical, elocutionary, declamatory; grandiloquent etc. 577; talkative etc. 584; Ciceronian, Tullian.

adv. **orally** etc. *adj.;* by word of mouth, *viva voce* [*L.*], from the lips of; from his own mouth.

583. Stammering
[imperfect speech]

n. **inarticulateness**; stammering etc. *v.;* hesitation etc. *v.;* impediment in one's speech; titubancy [*obs.*], traulism [*obs.*]; whisper etc. (*faint sound*) 405; lisp, drawl, tardiloquence [*rare*]; nasal -tone, –accent; twang; falsetto etc. (*want of voice*) 581; cacology, cacoëpy; broken -voice, –accents, –sentences; brogue etc. 563.

slip of the tongue, *lapsus linguae* [*L.*].

v. **stammer**, stutter, hesitate, falter, hammer [*obs. or dial. Eng.*], balbutiate [*obs.*], balbucinate [*obs.*], haw, hem and haw, be unable to put two words together.

mumble, mutter, maund [*obs.*], maunder; whisper etc. 405; mince, lisp; jabber, gabble, gibber; splutter, sputter; muffle, mump; drawl, mouth; croak; speak thick, speak through the nose; talk incoherently, quaver, snuffle, clip one's words.

murder the language, murder the King's (*or* Queen's) English; mispronounce, missay [*rare*].

adj. **inarticulate**; stammering etc. *v.;* guttural, throaty, nasal; tremulous; affected; stertorous; cacoëpistic.

adv. *sotto voce* etc. (*faintly*) 405.

584. Loquacity

n. **loquacity**, loquaciousness, effusion; talkativeness etc. *adj.;* garrulity; multiloquence, much speaking.

gabble, gab [*colloq.*], jaw [*colloq.*], hot air [*slang*]; jabber, chatter; prate, prattle, cackle, clack; twaddle, twattle, rattle, *caquet* [*F.*], *caqueterie* [*F.*], blabber, *bavardage* [*F.*], bibble-babble, gibble-gabble; small talk etc. (*converse*) 588; Babel.

fluency, flippancy, volubility, flowing tongue; flow, –of words; *flux de -bouche, –mots* [*F.*]; *copia verborum* [*L.*], *cacoëthes loquendi* [*L.*]; *furor loquendi* [*L.*]; verbosity etc. (*diffuseness*) 573; gift of the gab etc. (*eloquence*) 582.

talker; chatterer, chatterbox; babbler etc. *v.;* rattle; "agreeable rattle" [Goldsmith]; ranter; sermonizer, proser, driveler *or* driveller, blatherskite [*colloq.*], blab, jaw-box [*slang*], gas-bag [*slang*], wind-bag [*slang*], hot-air artist [*slang*]; gossip etc. (*converse*) 588; magpie, jay, parrot, poll *or* polly; *moulin à paroles* [*F.*].

v. **be loquacious** etc. *adj.;* talk glibly, pour forth, patter; prate, palaver, prose, maunder, chatter, blab, gush, prattle, clack, jabber, jaw [*low*], shoot one's mouth off [*slang*]; blather, blatter, blether; rattle, –on; twaddle, twattle; babble, gabble; outtalk; talk oneself -out of breath, –hoarse; talk–, run on- like a mill race; have one's tongue hanging in the middle and wagging at both ends; talk the hind legs off a mule, talk one deaf and dumb, clack like a hen, go on forever; expatiate etc. (*speak at length*) 573; gossip etc. (*converse*) 588; din in the ears etc. (*repeat*) 104; talk at random, talk nonsense etc. 497; be hoarse with talking.

adj. **loquacious**, talkative, garrulous, linguacious [*obs.*], multiloquent *or* multiloquous; chattering etc. *v.;* chatty etc. (*sociable*) 892; declamatory etc. 582; open-mouthed.

fluent, voluble, glib, flippant; long-tongued, long-winded etc. (*diffuse*) 573.

adv. **glibly** etc. *adj.;* trippingly on the tongue.

585. Taciturnity

n. **silence**, muteness, obmutescence [*rare*], laconism, laconicism, taciturnity, pauciloquy, costiveness [*obs.*], curtness; reserve, reticence etc. (*concealment*) 528.

man of few words; Spartan, Laconian.

v. **be silent** etc. *adj.;* keep silence; hold one's -tongue, –peace; not speak etc. 582; say nothing; seal–, close–, put a padlock on- the -lips, –mouth; put a bridle on one's tongue; keep one's tongue between one's teeth; make no sign, not let a word escape one; keep a secret etc. 528; have not a word to throw at a dog, not have a word to say; lay–, place- the finger on the lips; render mute etc. 581.

stick in one's throat.

adj. **silent**, mute, mum; silent as a -post, –stone, –the grave etc. (*still*) 403; dumb etc. 581; unconversable.

taciturn, laconic, pauciloquent, concise, sententious, sparing of words; close, close-mouthed, close-tongued; costive [*obs.*], inconversable [*obs.*], curt; reserved; reticent etc. (*concealing*) 528.

int. **silence**! tush! mum! hush! *chut!* [*F.*], hist! tut! not another word! shut up! stop right there! be still! *chup!* [*Hind.*].

586. Allocution

n. **allocution**, alloquy [*obs.*], address; smoke talk, chalk talk [*both colloq.*]; speech etc. 582; apostrophe, interpellation, appeal, invocation, salutation, salutatory; word in the ear.

platform etc. 542; plank [*politics*].

audience etc. (*interview*) 588.

[feigned dialogue] dialogism.

v. **address**, speak to, accost, make up to [*colloq.*], apostrophize, appeal to, invoke; hail, salute; call to, halloo.

lecture etc. (*make a speech*) 582; preach, sermonize, harangue, spellbind.

take aside, take by the button; talk to in private.

int. soho! halloo! hey! hist! hi!

587. Response

etc. *see* Answer 462.

588. Interlocution

n. **interlocution**; collocution, colloquy, converse, conversation, confabulation, confab [*colloq.*], chin-music [*slang*], talk, discourse, verbal intercourse; oral communication, commerce; dialogue, duologue, trialogue.

"the feast of reason and the flow of soul" [Pope]; *mollia tempora fandi* [*L.*].

chat, causerie [*F.*], chitchat; small–, table–, tea-table–, town–, village–, idle-talk; tattle, gossip, tittle-tattle; babble, babblement; *tripotage* [*F.*], cackle, prittle-prattle, *on dit* [*F.*]; talk of the -town, –village.

conference, parley, interview, audience, *pourparler* [*F.*]; *tête-à-tête* [*F.*]; reception, *conversazione* [*It.*]; congress etc. (*council*) 696; powwow.

hall of audience, durbar [*India*], auditorium, assembly room.

debate, palaver, logomachy, war of words, controversy, newspaper war.

talker, gossip, tattler; Paul Pry; tabby [*colloq.*], chatterer etc. (*loquacity*) 584; interlocutor etc. (*spokesman*) 582; conversationist, conversationalist, dialogist.

v. **converse**, talk together, confabulate; dialogue, dialogize; hold–, carry on–, join in–, engage in- a conversation; put in a word; shine in conversation; bandy words; parley; palaver; chat, gossip, tattle; prate etc. (*loquacity*) 584; powwow.

confer with, discourse with, commune with, commerce with; hold -converse, –conference,

–intercourse; talk it over; be closeted with; talk with one in private, talk with one *tête-à-tête* [*F.*].

adj. **conversing** etc. *v.;* interlocutory; conversational, conversable; discursive *or* discoursive [*obs.*]; chatty etc. (*sociable*) 892; colloquial, confabulatory, *tête-à-tête* [*F.*].

589. Soliloquy

n. **soliloquy**, monology, monologue, apostrophe; monology.
soliloquist, monologist, monologuist, monologian, soliloquizer; speaker etc. 582; Dr. Johnson, Coleridge.

v. **soliloquize**, monologize, monologuize, say–, talk- to oneself; rehearse a speech, address an imaginary audience; address the four walls; say aside, think aloud, apostrophize.

adj. **soliloquizing** etc. *v.;* monologic *or* monological; apostrophic, apostrophal [*rare*].

adv. **aside**, apart.

590. Writing

n. **writing** etc. *v.;* chirography, stelography [*rare*], monography, stylography, cerography, graphology; pencraft, penmanship; quill driving [*humorous*]; typewriting.
stroke–, dash- of the pen; *coup de plume* [*F.*]; line; headline; pen and ink.
manuscript, MS., writing, *litterae scriptae* [*L.*]; these presents [*law*].
character, letter etc. 561; uncial writing, cuneiform character, arrowhead, contraction; Ogham, runes; hieroglyphic, hieratic, demotic, Hebrew, Greek, Cyrillic, Roman; Arabic, Persian, Naskhi *or* Neskhi, Shikasta, Nasta'lik *or* Ta'lik; Brahmi, Devanagari, Nagari; Chinese; script.
shorthand; stenography, brachygraphy, tachygraphy; secret writing, writing in cipher; cryptography, steganography; phonography, pasigraphy, polygraphy [*rare*], logography.
copy; transcript, rescript; rough–, fair- copy; rough draft.
handwriting; signature, sign manual, mark, autograph, monograph, holograph; hand, fist [*colloq.*].
calligraphy; good–, running–, flowing–, cursive–, Italian–, slanting–, perpendicular–, round–, copybook–, fine–, legible–, bold-hand.
cacography, *griffonage* [*F.*], *barbouillage* [*F.*]; bad–, cramped–, crabbed–, illegible- hand;

scribble etc. *v.; pattes de mouche* [*F.*], fly tracks; ill-formed letters; pothooks and hangers.
stationery; pen, reed, quill, goose quill; pencil, style, stylograph, stylographic pen, fountain pen; paper, foolscap, parchment, vellum, papyrus, tablet, block, pad, notebook, memorandum book, copybook, commonplace-book; slate, marble, pillar, table; blackboard; ink-bottle, inkhorn, inkpot, inkstand, inkwell; typewriter.
composition, authorship; *cacoëthes scribendi* [*L.*]; graphomania; lucubration, production, work, preparation; screed, article, paper, pamphlet; book etc. 593; essay, theme, thesis; novel, textbook, poem, book of poems, book of verse; compilation, anthology; piece of music, *morceau* [*F.*] etc. (*musical composition*) 415.
transcription etc. (*copy*) 21; inscription etc. (*record*) 551; superscription etc. (*indication*) 550.
writer, scribe, amanuensis, scrivener, secretary, clerk, penman, copyist, transcriber, quill driver [*humorous*]; stenographer, brachygrapher, tachygrapher, phonographer, logographer, cipherer, cryptographer *or* cryptographist, steganographist; typewriter, typist; writer for the press etc. (*author*) 593; chirographer, cerographist; monographist, graphomaniac; calligraphist, calligrapher; cacographer; graphologist.

v. **write**, pen, typewrite, type [*colloq.*]; copy, engross; write out, –fair; transcribe; scribble, scrawl, scrabble, scratch; interline; take down in -shorthand, –longhand; spoil–, stain- paper [*humorous*]; note down; write down etc. (*record*) 551; sign etc. (*attest*) 467; enface.
compose, indite, draw up, draft, formulate; dictate; inscribe, throw on paper, dash off; manifold.
take up the pen, take pen in hand; shed–, spill–, dip one's pen in- ink.

adj. writing etc. *v.;* written etc. *v.;* in writing, in black and white; under one's hand.
uncial, runic, cuneiform, hieroglyphic *or* hieroglyphical, arrowhead etc. *n.*
stenographic, phonographic, brachygraphic, cryptographic, pasigraphic, logographic, tachygraphic; stenographical etc.

adv. *currente calamo* [*L.*]; pen in hand; with the pen of a ready writer; that "the wayfaring men, though fools, shall not err therein" [*Bible*].

591. Printing

n. **printing**; block–, type- printing; linotype, monotype; plate printing etc. (*engraving*) 558; the press etc. (*publication*) 531; composition.

print, letterpress, text, matter; live–, standing–, dead- matter; copy; context, page, column, note, section; catch-word; running head, running title; signature; justification; dummy.

folio etc. (*book*) 593; copy, impression. pull, proof, revise, advance sheets; author's–, galley–, page–, plate–, press- proof; press revise.

typography; stereotype, electrotype; matrix; font *or* fount; pi *or* pie; roman, italics; capitals etc. (*letters*) 561, caps., small caps., upper case, lower case; logotype; type-bar, type-slug; type-body; em, en; type measure, type scale; type casting, type metal, type mold, typograph; type foundry, letter foundry; composing stick, stick; composing -frame. -rule, –stand; foot stick; chase, form, galley, measure, scale, case, boxes; gauge, gauge pin, feed gauge, guide, dabber, gutter, gutter stick; brayer, boss, batter, bank; bearer, guard; bed, blanket, tympan, turtle, platen, bevel, burr, frame, frisket, gripper; quadrat, quad; quoin, slug, slur, ratchet, reglet; guillotine, rounce, cylinder; overlay, underlay, sinkage, macule; platen press, perfecting machine; printing-press, printing-machine; press-work; sheet work; off-cut, off-print; set-off; off-set, smut; turn, turned letter; bookplate, bookstamp, colophon; composing room, press room.

space, 3-em, thick space; 4-em, 5-em, thin space; 6-em, hair space; patent space.

metal type, body, shank, face, shoulder, counter, serif *or* ceriph, stem, beard, groove, feet.

styles of type: Old English, Black Letter, German Text, Gothic, Antique, Clarendon, Bold-face *or* Full-face, French Elzevir, Caslon Old Style, Ionic, Script, Typewriter.

point system: 4½ point (diamond), 5 pt. (pearl), 5½ pt. (agate *or* ruby), 6 pt. (nonpareil); 7 pt. (minion), 8 pt. (brevier), 9 pt. (bourgeois), 10 pt. (long primer), 11 pt. (small pica), 12 pt. (pica), 14 pt. (English), 16 pt. (Columbian), 18 pt. (great primer).

printer, compositor, reader, proof reader;- printer's devil; copyholder.

v. print; compose; put–, go- to press; pass–, see-through the press; publish etc. 531; bring out; appear in–, rush into- print; set up, stick, make-up, impose, justify, macule *or* mackle, mortise, offset, overrun, rout.

distribute, pi *or* pie, pi a form.

adj. typographical etc. *n.;* printed etc. *v.;* in type; solid in galleys; kerned, deckle-edged; bold-faced *or* full-faced; pied.

592. Correspondence

n. correspondence, letter, epistle, note, billet, written communication, post card *or* postcard, postal, postal card; missive, circular, favor, *billet-doux* [*F.*]; chit *or* chitty [*India*], letter card [*Brit.*], picture post card; dispatch *or* despatch; bulletin, these presents [*law*]; rescript, rescription [*archaic*]; post etc. (*messenger*) 534.

letter writer, epistolarian, correspondent, writer, communicator; author, contributor.

v. correspond, –with; write to, send a letter to; drop a line to [*colloq.*]; start–, begin–, keep up- a correspondence; deluge with -letters, –post cards; communicate by -writing, –letter; let one know by -post, –mail; dispatch *or* despatch, circularize, follow up, bombard; reply, reply by return mail, communicate.

adj. epistolary, epistolarian.

593. Book

n. book, booklet; writing, work, volume, tome, opuscule *or* opuscle, opusculum; tract, tractate, treatise, *livret* [*F.*], brochure, monograph, pamphlet, codex, libretto; handbook, manual, enchiridion; novel etc. (*composition*) 590; circular, publication; the press etc. 531; chapbook.

part, issue, number, *livraison* [*F.*]; album, portfolio; periodical, serial, magazine, ephemeris, annual, journal.

paper, bill, sheet, broadsheet; leaf, leaflet; fly leaf, page; quire, ream.

pasteboard, cardboard, strawboard, millboard, binder's board; carton.

make-up, bastard title, title, printer's imprint, subtitles, dedication, preface, contents, list of plates *or* illustrations, errata, introduction, text; chapter, section, head, article, paragraph, passage, clause; recto, verso *or* reverso; supplement, appendix, index.

[sizes] folio, quarto (4to *or* 4°); octavo (8vo), cap 8vo, demy 8vo, imperial 8vo, medium 8vo, royal 8vo, post 8vo, pott 8vo, crown 8vo, foolscap 8vo; duodecimo, twelvemo *or* 12mo; sextodecimo, sixteenmo *or* 16mo; octodecimo, eighteenmo *or* 18mo.

bookbinding, bibliopegy; folding, stitching, wire-stitching; tooling; blind–, gold- tooling; binder's title; case, cover; quarter–, half–, three-quarters- bound book; full leather.

[binding materials] paper, paper boards, buckram, cloth, skiver, roan, pigskin, Russia, Turkey morocco, levant morocco, seal, parchment, vellum.

work of reference, encyclopedia *or* encyclopaedia, cyclopedia *or* cyclopaedia, dictionary, thesaurus, concordance, anthology; compilation.

writer, author, *littérateur* [*F.*], essayist; pen, scribbler, the scribbling race; free lance; literary hack, Grub-street writer; adjective jerker [*slang*], hack writer, hack, ghost [*cant.*], ghost writer, ink slinger [*slang*]; journalist, publicist, writer for–, gentleman of–, representative of– the press; reporter, correspondent; war–, special- correspondent; knight of the -plume, –pen, –quill [*all humorous*]; penny-a-liner; editor, subeditor, reviser, diaskeuast; scribe etc. 590; playwright etc. 599; poet etc. 597.

the trade, publisher, bookseller; book -salesman, –agent, –canvasser, –solicitor.

bibliopole, bibliopolist, book collector; bookbinder, bibliopegist; bookworm etc. 492; bibliologist, bibliographer, bibliophile, bibliognost, librarian, bibliothec.

bookstore, bookshop, bookseller's shop, *librairie* [*F.*], publishing house.

library, bibliotheca, public library, lending library.

knowledge of books, bibliography, bibliology; book learning etc. (*knowledge*) 490; bookselling, bibliopolism.

594. Description

n. **description**, account, statement, report; *exposé* [*F.*] etc. (*disclosure*) 529; specification, particulars; summary of facts; brief etc. (*abstract*) 596; return etc. (*record*) 551; *catalogue raisonné* [*F.*] etc. (*list*) 86; guidebook etc. (*information*) 527.

delineation etc. (*representation*) 554; sketch, pastel, vignette, monograph; minute–, detailed–, particular–, circumstantial–, graphic- account; narration, recital, rehearsal, relation.

narrative, history; memoir, memorials; annals etc. (*chronicle*) 551; saga; tradition, legend, story, tale, historiette; personal narrative, journal, letters, biography, autobiography, life; obituary, orbit [*cant.*], necrology; adventures, fortunes, experiences, confessions; anecdote, ana.

historiography, chronography; historic Muse, Clio.

work of fiction, novel, romance, short story; detective -story, –yarn; "grue" [Stevenson]; fairy–, nursery- tale; fable, parable, apologue, allegory; dime novel, penny dreadful, shilling shocker [*slang*].

relator etc. *v.; raconteur* [*F.*]; historiographer, chronographer, historian etc. (*recorder*) 553; biographer, fabulist, novelist, story-teller, romancer, spinner of yarns, teller of tales, anecdotist, word-painter; writer etc. 593.

v. **describe**; set forth etc. (*state*) 535; draw a picture, picture; portray etc. (*represent*) 554; characterize, analyze, give words to, narrate, relate, recite, recount, sum up, run over, recapitulate, rehearse, fight one's battles over again; harrow up the soul, hold one breathless, novelize, romance.

unfold etc. (*disclose*) 529- a tale; tell; give–, render- an account of; report, make a report, draw up a statement; throw into -essay form, –book form; stick to the facts, show life as it is; historicize.

detail, particularize, itemize; enter into–, descend to- -particulars, –details.

adj. **descriptive**, graphic, narrative, epic, suggestive, well-drawn; historic *or* historical, historiographical, chronographic *or* chronographical, biographic *or* biographical, autobiographical; traditive [*esp., from ancestors to descendants*], traditional, traditionary; legendary, mythical, fabulous; anecdotic, storied; described etc. *v.;* romantic, idealistic; realistic, true to life; expository.

595. Dissertation

n. **dissertation**, treatise, essay; thesis, theme; tract, tractate, tractation [*obs.*]; discourse, memoir, disquisition, lecture, sermon, homily, pandect, digest; excursus.

investigation etc. (*inquiry*) 461; study etc. (*consideration*) 451; discussion etc. (*reasoning*) 476; exposition etc. (*explanation*) 522.

commentary, commentation, review, critique, criticism, article; leader, leading article; editorial; running commentary.

commentator, critic, essayist, pamphleteer, publicist, reviewer, leader writer, editor, annotator.

v. **comment**, explain, interpret, criticize, illuminate; dissert [*rare*]–, descant–, write–, touch upon a subject; treat of–, take up–, ventilate–, discuss–, deal with–, go into–, canvass–, handle–, do justice to- a subject; show the true inwardness of.

adj. **disquisitional**, disquisitive, disquisitionary [*rare*]; expository, commentarial, commentatorial, critical.

discursive, discoursive, digressive, desultory.

596. Compendium

n. **compendium**, compend, abstract, *précis* [*F.*], epitome, *multum in parvo* [*L.*], analysis, pandect, digest, sum and substance, brief, abridgment, *abrégé* [*F.*], summary, *aperçu* [*F.*], draft, minute, note; excerpt, extract; synopsis, textbook, conspectus, outlines, syllabus, contents, heads, prospectus.

album; scrap-, note-, memorandum-, commonplace- book.

fragments, ana, extracts, *excerpta* [*L.*], cuttings; fugitive -pieces, −writings; *spicilegium* [*L.*], flowers, anthology, miscellany, collectanea, analects *or* analecta; compilation.

recapitulation, *résumé* [*F.*], review.

abbreviation, abbreviature; contraction; shortening etc. 201; compression etc. 195.

v. **abridge**, abstract, epitomize, summarize; make-, prepare-, draw-, compile- an abstract etc. *n.;* abbreviate etc. (*shorten*) 201; condense etc. (*compress*) 195.

compile etc. (*collect*) 72; note down, collect, edit.

recapitulate, review, skim, run over, sum up.

adj. **compendious**, synoptic, analectic; *abrégé* [*F.*], abridged etc. *v.;* abbreviatory; analytic *or* analytical; variorum.

adv. **in short**, in epitome, in substance, in few words.

597. Poetry

n. **poetry**, poetics, poesy, Muse, tuneful Nine, Apollo, Apollo Musagetes, Calliope, Parnassus, Helicon, Pierides, Pierian spring; inspiration, fire of genius, coal from off the altar.

poem; epic, epic poem; epopee *or* epopoeia, epos, ode, epode, idyl *or* idyll, lyric, eclogue, pastoral, bucolic, georgic, dithyramb *or* dithyrambus, anacreontic, sonnet, roundelay, rondeau, rondel, roundel, rondelet; triolet, sestina, virelay, ballade, cento, ghazal *or* ghazel, madrigal, monody, elegy; amoebaeum, palinode.

dramatic-, didactic-, narrative-, lyric-, satirical- poetry; satire, opera.

anthology, posy [*archaic*], garland, miscellany, *disjecta membra poetae* [*L.*].

song, ballad, lay; love-, drinking-, war-, seasong; lullaby, *aubade* [*F.*]; music etc. 415; nursery rhymes.

[bad poetry] doggerel, Hudibrastic verse; macaronics, macaronic verse; "not poetry, but prose run mad" [Pope].

versification, riming *or* rhyming, making verses; prosody; scansion, scanning, orthometry [*rare*].

canto, stanza, distich, verse, line, couplet, triplet, quatrain; strophe, antistrophe; refrain, chorus, burden; octave, sextet.

verse, rime *or* rhyme, assonance, crambo [*contemptuous*], meter, measure, foot, numbers, strain, rhythm; ictus, beat, accent; accentuation etc. (*voice*) 580; iambus, iambic, iamb; dactyl, spondee, trochee, anapest etc.; hexameter, pentameter; Alexandrine; anacrusis, antispast, blank verse, Leonine verse, runes, alliteration; *bout-rimé* [*F.*].

elegiacs etc. *adj.;* elegiac etc. *adj.* -verse, −meter *or* metre, −poetry.

poet, minor poet; genius, maker [*obs.*], creator; poet laureate; laureate; bard, lyrist, scald *or* skald, scop [*hist.*], idylist *or* idyllist, sonneteer, rhapsodist, epic [*obs.*], epic poet, dithyrambic, satirist, troubadour, trouvère; minstrel; minnesinger, Meistersinger; jongleur, improvisator *or* improvvisatore [*It.*] *or* improvisatore; versifier, rimer *or* rhymer, rimester *or* rhymester; ballad monger, runer; poetaster; *genus irritabile vatum* [*L.*].

v. **poetize**, sing, "lisp in numbers" [Pope], build the stately rime, sing deathless songs, make immortal by verse; satirize; compose epic etc. *adj.* -poetry; string verses together, cap rimes, poeticize, versify, make verses, rime *or* rhyme, scan.

produce -lame verses, −limping meters, −halting rime.

adj. **poetic** *or* poetical; lyric *or* lyrical; tuneful; epic; dithyrambic etc. *n.;* metrical; acatalectic, catalectic; elegiac, iambic, dactylic, spondaic *or* spondaical, trochaic, anapestic; amoebaeic, Melibean, scaldic *or* skaldic; Ionic, Sapphic, Alcaic, Pindaric, Pierian.

598. Prose

n. **prose**, prosaism, prosaicness, prosaicism [*rare*]; poetic prose; history etc. (*description*) 594.

prose writer, essayist, monographer, monographist, novelist; *raconteur* [*F.*] etc. 594.

v. **prose**; write -prose, −in prose.

adj. **prosaic**, prosy, prosal [*obs.*]; unpoetical.

rimeless *or* rhymeless, unrimed *or* unrhymed, in prose, not in verse.

599. The Drama

n. **the drama**, the stage, the theater *or* theatre, the play; theatricals, dramaturgy, histrionic art, mimography, buskin, sock, cothurnus, Melpomene and Thalia, Thespis.

play, drama, stageplay, piece, five-act play, tragedy, comedy, opera, vaudeville, comedietta, *lever de rideau* [*F.*], curtain raiser, interlude, afterpiece, exode [*Rom. antiq.*], farce, *divertissement* [*F.*], extravaganza, burletta, harlequinade, pantomime, burlesque, *opéra bouffe* [*F.*], ballet, spectacle, masque, *drame* [*F.*], *comédie drame* [*F.*]; melodrama; *comédie larmoyante* [*F.*]; emotional -drama, –play; sensation drama; tragi-comedy; light–, genteel–, low–, farce- comedy, comedy of manners, farcical-comedy; monodrama, monodram *or* monodrame, monologue, duologue, dialogue; trilogy; charade, *proverbe* [*F.*]; mystery, miracle play, morality play.

act, scene, tableau, curtain; introduction, induction [*archaic*], exposition, expository scenes; prologue, epilogue; libretto, book, text, prompter's copy.

performance, representation, show [*colloq.*], *mise en scène* [*F.*], stage setting, stagery [*obs.*], stagecraft, *jeu de théâtre* [*F.*]; acting; gesture etc. 550; impersonation etc. 554; stage business, gag, patter, slap-stick [*slang*], buffoonery.

theater *or* theatre, playhouse, opera house; music hall; amphitheater *or* amphitheatre, circus, hippodrome; moving-picture theater, moving pictures, movies [*colloq.*], films, cinematograph *or* cinema [*colloq., Brit.*]; puppet show, fantoccini; marionettes. Punch and Judy.

auditory, auditorium, front of the house, front [*colloq. and professional*], stalls [*chiefly Eng.*], orchestra seats *or* orchestra, pit [*chiefly Eng.*], parquet, orchestra circle, boxes, balcony, gallery, peanut gallery [*slang*]; dressing rooms, greenroom.

scenery; back scene, flat; drop, drop scene; wing, screen, coulisse, side scene, transformation scene, curtain, act drop; proscenium; fire curtain, asbestos curtain.

stage, movable stage, scene, the boards; trap, mezzanine floor; flies; floats, footlights; limelight, spotlight, colored light; klieg light; orchestra.

theatrical costume, theatrical properties, props [*theat. cant*].

cast, *dramatis personae* [*L.*], persons in the play; role, part, character; repertoire, repertory, *répertoire* [*F.*].

actor, player; stage–, strolling- player; barnstormer, stager [*rare*], old stager; masker, masquer [*rare*], mime, mimer, mimic, mimester [*rare*]; *artiste* [*F.*], performer, star, headliner;

comedian, tragedian, *tragédienne* [*F.*], Thespian, Roscius, ham [*slang*], hamfatter [*slang*]; utility, general utility, utility man.

buffoon, pantomimist, clown, *farceur* [*F.*], *buffo* (*pl. buffi*) [*It.*], grimacer, pantaloon, harlequin, columbine; punch, punchinello, *pulcinella* [*It.*].

mummer, guiser [*Eng. & Scot.*], guisard [*Scot.*], gysart [*obs.*], masque [*obs.*], mask.

mountebank, Jack Pudding; tumbler, posture master, acrobat; contortionist; ballet dancer, ballet girl; *coryphée* [*F.*], *danseuse* [*F.*]; chorus girl, chorus singer.

company; first tragedian, prima donna, leading lady; lead; leading man, protagonist; *jeune premier* [*F.*], *débutant* (*fem. débutante*) [*F.*]; light–, genteel–, low- comedian; walking gentleman *or* lady [*obsoles.*], amoroso [*It.*], juvenile lead, juvenile; heavy lead, heavy; heavy father, ingenue, *ingénue* [*F.*], *jeune veuve* [*F.*], soubrette, *farceur* (*fem. farceuse*) [*F.*].

mute, figurant, figurante, walking part, supernumerary, super [*theat. cant*], supe [*theat. cant*].

manager; stage–, actor–, acting- manager; *entrepreneur* [*F.*], impresario; angel [*slang*].

[theater staff] property man, prop [*theat. cant*]; costumer, costumier, wig-maker, make-up artist; sceneshifter, grip, stage hand, stage carpenter, machinist, electrician, chief electrician; prompter, call boy; advance agent, publicity agent.

dramatist, playwright, playwriter; dramatic -author, –writer; mimographer, mimist [*obs.*]; dramatic critic.

audience, auditory, house; orchestra etc. *n.*; gallery, the gods [*colloq.*], gallery gods [*collow.*].

v. **act**, play, perform; put on the stage, dramatize, stage, produce, set; personate etc. 554; mimic etc. (*imitate*) 19; enact; play–, act–, go through–, perform-a part; rehearse, spout, gag [*slang*], patter [*slang*], rant; strut and fret one's hour upon the stage; tread the -stage, –boards; make one's début, take a part, come out; star; supe [*slang*].

adj. **dramatic**; theatric *or* theatrical; scenic, histrionic, comic, tragic, buskined, cothurned; farcical, tragi-comic, melodramatic, operatic; stagy *or* stagey; spectacular, stellar, all-star [*cant*]; stagestruck.

adv. **on the stage**, on the boards; in the limelight, in the spotlight; before the floats, before the footlights, before the curtain, before an audience; behind the scenes.

Class 5. Volition

Division 1. Individual Volition

Section 1. Volition in General

600. Will

n. **will,** volition, conation, volitiency, velleity; *liberum arbitrium* [*L.*]; will and pleasure, free will; freedom etc. 748; discretion; choice, inclination, intent, purpose, voluntarism; option etc. (*choice*) 609; voluntariness; spontaneity, spontaneousness; originality.

wish, desire, pleasure, mind, frame of mind etc. (*inclination*) 602; intention etc. 620; predetermination etc. 611; self-control etc. determination etc. (*resolution*) 604; force of will, will power, autocracy, bossiness [*colloq.*].

v. **will,** list [*archaic*]; see fit, think fit; determine etc. (*resolve*) 604; enjoin; settle etc. (*choose*) 609; volunteer.

have a will of one's own; do what one chooses etc. (*freedom*) 748; have it all one's own way; have one's will, have one's own way; use-, exercise- one's discretion; take -upon oneself, –one's own course, –the law into one's own hands; do of one's own accord, do upon one's own authority, do upon one's own responsibility; take responsibility, boss [*colloq.*], take the bit between one's teeth; originate etc. (*cause*) 153.

adj. **voluntary,** volitional, willful *or* wilful; free etc. 748; optional; discretional, discretionary; volitient, volitive; volunteer, voluntaristic; dictatorial, bossy [*colloq.*].

minded etc. (*willing*) 602; prepense etc. (*predetermined*) 611; intended etc. 620; autocratic; unbidden etc. (bid etc. 741); spontaneous; original etc. (*causal*) 153; unconstrained.

adv. **voluntarily** etc. *adj.;* at will, at pleasure; *à volonté* [*F.*], *à discrétion* [*F.*]; *al piacere* [*It.*]; *ad libitum* [*L.*], *ad arbitrium* [*L.*]; as one thinks proper, as it seems good to; *a beneplacito* [*It*].

of one's own -accord, –free will; on one's own responsibility; *proprio-, suo-, ex mero- motu* [*L.*]; out of one's own head; by choice etc. 609; purposely etc. (*intentionally*) 620; deliberately etc. 611.

601. Necessity

n. **involuntariness;** instinct, blind impulse; inborn-, innate- proclivity; native-, natural- tendency; natural impulse, predetermination.

necessity, necessitation, necessitarianism, obligation; compulsion etc. 744; subjection etc. 749; stern-, hard-, dire-, imperious-, inexorable-, iron-, adverse- -necessity, –fate; *anagke* [*Gr.*], what must be.

destiny, destination; fatality, fate, kismet, doom, foredoom, election, predestination; preordination, foreordination; lot, fortune; fatalism; inevitableness etc. *adj.;* spell etc. 993.

fates, Parcae, Sisters three, book of fate; God's will, Heaven, will of Heaven; star, stars; planet, planets; astral influence; wheel of Fortune, Ides of March, Hobson's choice.

last shift, last resort; *dernier ressort* [*F.*]; *pis aller* etc. (*substitute*) 147; necessaries etc. (*requirement*) 630.

necessarian, necessitarian; fatalist; automaton, pawn.

v. **lie under a necessity;** be fated, be doomed, be destined etc., be in for, be under the necessity of; be obliged, be forced, be driven; have no -choice, –alternative; be one's fate to etc. *n.;* be pushed to the wall, be driven into a corner, be unable to help, be swept on, be drawn irresistibly.

destine, doom, foredoom, devote; predestine, preordain; cast a spell etc. 992; necessitate; compel etc. 744.

be decreed, be determined, be destined etc., be written; be written in the -book of fate, –stars.

adj. **necessary,** necessarian, necessitarian; needful etc. (*requisite*) 630.

fated; destined etc. *v.;* fateful, big with fate; set apart, devoted, elect.

compulsory etc. (*compel*) 744; uncontrollable, inevitable, unavoidable, indefeasible, irresistible, irrevocable, inexorable, binding; avoidless, resistless.

involuntary, instinctive, automatic, blind, mechanical; unconscious, unwitting, unthinking; unintentional etc. (*undesigned*) 621; spellbound; impulsive etc. 612.

adv. **necessarily** etc. *adj.;* of necessity, of course; *ex necessitate rei* [*L.*]; needs must; perforce etc. 744; *nolens volens* [*L.*]; will he nil he, will I nill I, willy-nilly, *bon gré mal gré* [*F.*]; willing or unwilling, *coûte que coûte* [*F.*]; compulsorily, by compulsion, by force.

faute de mieux [*F.*]; by stress of; if need be; *que faire?* [*F.*].

602. Willingness

n. **willingness**, voluntariness etc. *adj.;* willing mind, heart.

disposition, inclination, liking, turn, propensity, propension, propenseness, leaning, animus; frame of mind, humor, mood, vein; bent etc. (*turn of mind*) 820; *penchant* [*F.*] etc. (*desire*) 865; aptitude etc. 698.

docility, docibleness [*rare*], docibility [*rare*], appetency, tractability, tractableness, persuadability, persuadableness, persuasibleness, persuasibility; pliability etc. (*softness*) 324.

geniality, cordiality; goodwill; alacrity, readiness, zeal, enthusiasm, earnestness, forwardness; eagerness etc. (*desire*) 865.

assent etc. 488; compliance etc. 762; pleasure etc. (*will*) 600.

labor of love, self-appointed task, volunteering; gratuitous service; social service, welfare work.

volunteer, unpaid worker, amateur, voluntary [*rare*]; social worker, welfare worker.

v. **be willing** etc. *adj.;* incline, lean to, mind, propend [*rare*], had as lief, would as lief; lend-, give-, turn- a willing ear; have -a, –half a, –a great- mind to; hold to, cling to; desire etc. 865.

acquiesce etc. (*assent*) 488; see think- -good, –fit, –proper; comply with etc. 762.

swallow-, nibble at- the bait; swallow bait, hook, and sinker; swallow bait and all; gorge the hook; have-, make- no scruple of; make no bones of [*colloq.*]; jump at, catch at; go in for, go in at [*both colloq.*]; take up, plunge into, have a go at [*colloq.*]; meet halfway.

volunteer, offer, proffer; offer oneself etc. 763.

adj. **willing**, minded, fain, disposed, inclined, favorable; favorably -minded, –inclined, –disposed; well-disposed, lief [*archaic*], nothing loth; in the -vein, –mood, –humor, –mind.

ready, forward, earnest, eager, zealous, enthusiastic; bent upon etc. (*desirous*) 865; predisposed, desirous, propense.

docile; persuadable, persuasible; suasible, amenable, easily persuaded, facile, easy-going; tractable etc. (*pliant*) 324; genial, gracious, cor-

dial, cheering, hearty; content etc. (*assenting*) 488.

voluntary, gratuitous, spontaneous; unasked etc. (*ask* etc. 765); unforced etc. (*free*) 748.

adv. **willingly** etc. *adj.;* fain, freely, as lief, heart and soul; with pleasure, with all one's heart, with open arms; with good will, with right good will; *de bonne volonté* [*F.*], *ex animo* [*L.*], *con amore* [*It.*], heart in hand, nothing loath, without reluctance, of one's own accord, graciously, with a good grace; without demur.

à la bonne heure [*F.*]; by all means, by all manner of means; to one's heart's content; yes etc. (*assent*) 488.

int. **surely**! sure! with pleasure! of course! delighted!

603. Unwillingness

n. **unwillingness** etc. *adj.;* indisposition, indisposedness, disinclination, aversation [*rare*], aversion; averseness etc. (*dislike*) 867; nolleity [*rare*], nolition [*rare*]; renitence *or* renitency; reluctance; indifference etc. 866; backwardness etc. *adj.;* slowness etc. 275; want of -alacrity, –readiness; indocility etc. (*obstinacy*) 606.

scrupulousness, scrupulosity; qualms-, twinge- of conscience; delicacy, demur, scruple, qualm, shrinking, recoil; hesitation etc. (*irresolution*) 605; fastidiousness etc. 868.

dissent etc. 489; refusal etc. 764.

forced labor, unwilling service, peonage; compulsion etc. 744; slacker.

v. **be unwilling** etc. *adj.;* nill [*archaic*]; dislike etc. 867; grudge, begrudge; not find it in one's heart to, not have the stomach to.

demur, stick at, scruple, stickle; hang fire, run rusty [*colloq.*], go stale; give up, let down [*slang*]; pull back, be a dead weight, be a passenger in the boat, not pull fair, shirk, slack, shy [*dial. Eng.*], fight shy of, get by [*slang*], duck [*slang*]; recoil, shrink, swerve; hesitate etc. 605; avoid etc. 623.

oppose etc. 708; dissent etc. 489; refuse etc. 764.

adj. **unwilling**; not in the vein, loath *or* loth, shy of, disinclined, indisposed, averse, reluctant, not content; renitent, opposed; adverse etc. (*opposed*) 708; laggard, backward, remiss, slack, slow to; indifferent etc. 866; scrupulous; squeamish etc. (*fastidious*) 868; repugnant etc. (*dislike*) 867; restiff [*obs.*], restive; demurring etc. *v.;* unconsenting etc. (*refusing*) 764; involuntary etc. 601; grudging, forced; irreconcilable.

adv. **unwillingly** etc. *adj.;* grudgingly, with a heavy heart; with -a bad, –an ill- grace; against-, sore against- one's wishes, –one's will, –the grain;

invita Minerva [*L.*]; *à contre coeur* [*F.*]; *malgré soi* [*F.*]; in spite of -one's teeth, −oneself; *nolens volens* [*L.*] etc. (*necessity*) 601; perforce etc. 744; under protest; no etc. 536; if I must I must; not if one can help it; not for the world; far be it from me.

604. Resolution

n. **determination**, will; iron will, unconquerable will; will of one's own, decision, resolution; backbone; clear grit, grit [*U. S. & Can.*]; sand [*slang*]; strength of -mind, −will; resolve etc. (*intent*) 620; intransigence *or* intransigency, *intransigeance* [*F.*]; firmness etc. (*stability*) 150; energy, manliness, vigor; resoluteness etc. (*courage*) 861; zeal etc. 682; desperation; devotion, devotedness.

self-control, *aplomb* [*F.*], mastery over self, self-mastery, self-command, self-possession, self-reliance, self-government, self-restraint, self-conquest, self-denial; moral -courage, −fiber, −strength.

tenacity, perseverance etc. 604*a;* obstinacy etc. 606; game, pluck; fighting cock, game cock; bulldog; British lion.

irreconcilable, intransigent, *intransigeant* [*F.*], bitter-ender [*colloq.*]; fighting minority, militant remnant.

v. **have determination** etc. *n.;* know one's own mind; be resolved etc. *adj.;* make up one's mind; will, resolve, determine; decide etc. (*judgment*) 480; form−, come to- a -determination, −resolution, −resolve; conclude, fix, seal, determine once for all, bring to a crisis, drive matters to an extremity; take a decisive step etc. (*choice*) 609; take upon oneself etc. (*undertake*) 676.

steel oneself, devote oneself to, give oneself up to; throw away the scabbard, kick down the ladder, nail one's colors to the mast, set one's back against the wall, burn one's bridges, grit one's teeth, set one's teeth, set one's jaw, take the bit in one's mouth, put one's foot down, take one's stand, stand firm etc. (*stability*) 150; stand no nonsense, not listen to the voice of the charmer; insist upon, make a point of; set one's heart upon, set one's mind upon.

buckle to; buckle oneself; put−, lay−, set- one's shoulder to the wheel; put one's heart into; run the gauntlet, make a dash at, take the bull by the horns; rush−, plunge- *in medias res* [*L.*]; go in for [*colloq.*].

stick at nothing; make short work of etc. (*activity*) 682; not stick at trifles; go all lengths,

go the limit [*slang*], go the whole hog [*slang*], go it blind [*slang*]; go down with one's colors flying; die game; persist etc. (*persevere*) 604 *a;* go through fire and water, "ride in the whirl-wind and direct the storm" [Addison].

adj. **resolved** etc. *v.;* determined; strong-willed, strong-minded; resolute etc. (*brave*) 861; self-possessed, earnest, serious; decided, definitive, peremptory, unhesitating, unflinching, un-shrinking; firm, iron, game, plucky, tenacious, gritty, indomitable, game to the backbone, game to the last; inexorable, relentless, not to be -shaken, −put down; *tenax propositi* [*L.*]; obstinate etc. 606; steady etc. (*persevering*) 604*a.*

unbending, unyielding; set−, bent−, intent-upon; grim, stern; inflexible etc. (*hard*) 323; cast-iron, irrevocable, irreversible; not to be de-flected; firm as Gibraltar.

steeled−, proof- against; *in utrumque paratus* [*L.*].

adv. **resolutely** etc. *adj.;* in earnest, in good earnest; seriously, joking apart, earnestly, heart and soul; on one's mettle; manfully, like a man; with a high -heart, −courage, −hand; with a strong hand etc. (*exertion*) 686.

at all risks, at all hazards, at all events; at any -rate, −risk, −hazard, −price, −cost, −sacrifice; *à bis ou à blanc* [*F.*], cost what it may; *coûte que coûte* [*F.*]; *à tort et à travers* [*F.*]; once for all; neck or nothing; survive or perish, live or die; rain or shine.

604a. Perseverance

n. **perseverance**; continuance etc. (*inaction*) 143; permanence etc. (*absence of change*) 141; firmness etc. (*stability*) 150.

constancy, steadiness; singleness−, tenacity- of purpose; persistence, plodding, patience; sedulity [*rare*] etc. (*industry*) 682; pertinacy [*obs.*], pertinacity, pertinaciousness; iteration etc. 104.

grit, bottom, game, pluck, stamina, backbone, sand [*slang*]; indefatigability, indefatigableness; tenacity, staying power, endurance; bulldog courage.

v. **persevere**, persist; hold -on, −out; die in the last ditch, be in at the death; stick to, cling to, ad-here to; stick to one's text; keep on, carry on, hold on; keep to−, maintain- one's -course, −ground; go all lengths, go through fire and water; bear up, keep up, hold up; plod; stick to work etc. (*work*) 686; continue etc. 143; follow up; die in harness, die at one's post.

adj. **persevering**, constant; steady, steadfast; undeviating, unwavering, unfaltering, unswerving, unflinching, unsleeping, unflagging, undrooping; steady as time; unintermitting, unremitting; plodding; industrious etc. 682; strenuous etc. 686; pertinacious; persisting, persistent.

solid, sturdy, stanch *or* staunch, true to oneself; unchangeable etc. 150; unconquerable etc. (*strong*) 159; indomitable, game to the last, indefatigable, untiring, unwearied, never tiring.

adv. **without fail**; through evil report and good report, through thick and thin, through fire and water; *per fas et nefas* [*L.*]; sink or swim, at any price, *vogue la galère* [*F.*]; rain or shine, fair or foul, in sickness and in health.

605. Irresolution

n. **irresolution**, infirmity of purpose, indecision, indetermination, undetermination [*rare*], instability; loss of will power, abulia, abulomania; unsettlement; uncertainty etc. 475; demur, suspense; hesitating etc. *v.*, hesitation, hesitancy; wabble *or* wobble; revocability, vacillation; changeableness etc. 149; fluctuation; alternation etc. (*oscillation*) 314; caprice etc. 608; lukewarmness, Laodiceanism.

fickleness, levity, *légèreté* [*F.*]; pliancy etc. (*softness*) 324; weakness; timidity etc. 860; cowardice etc. 862; half measures.

waverer, shilly-shally, ass between two bundles of hay; shuttlecock, butterfly, feather, piece of thistledown; house built on sand; doughface; turncoat, opportunist, Vicar of Bray, Dite Deuchars; Laodicean; timeserver etc. 607.

v. **be irresolute** etc. *adj.*; hang–, keep- in suspense; leave *ad referendum;* think twice about, pause; dawdle etc. (*inactivity*) 683; remain neuter; dilly-dally, hesitate, boggle, hover, dacker *or* daiker [*dial. Eng. & Scot.*], wabble *or* wobble [*colloq.*], shilly-shally, hem and haw, demur, not know one's own mind; debate, balance; dally with, coquet with; will and will not, *chasser-balancer* [*F.*]; go halfway, compromise, make a compromise; be thrown off one's balance, stagger like a drunken man; be afraid etc. 860; let "I dare not" wait upon "I would" [*Macbeth*]; falter, waver.

vacillate etc. 149; change etc. 140; retract etc. 607; fluctuate; pendulate; alternate etc. (*oscillate*) 314; keep off and on, play fast and loose; blow hot and cold etc. (*caprice*) 608; turn one's coat.

shuffle, palter, blink, shirk, trim.

adj. **irresolute**, infirm of purpose, palsied, drifting, double-minded, half-hearted; undecided, unresolved, undetermined; shilly-shally, wabbly *or* wobbly; fidgety, tremulous; hesitating etc. *v.*; off one's balance; abulic; at a loss etc. (*uncertain*) 475.

vacillating etc. *v.*; unsteady etc. (*changeable*) 149; unsteadfast, fickle, unreliable, irresponsible, unstable, unstable as water, without ballast; capricious etc. 608; volatile, frothy; light, lightsome, lightminded; giddy; fast and loose.

weak, feeble-minded, frail; timid etc. 860; cowardly etc. 862; dough-faced; facile; pliant etc. (*soft*) 324; unable to say "no," easy-going.

revocable, reversible.

adv. **irresolutely** etc. *adj.*; irresolvedly; in faltering accents; off and on; on the sands; from pillar to post; seesaw etc. 314.

606. Obstinacy

n. **obstinateness** etc. *adj.*; obstinacy, tenacity; cussedness; perseverance etc. 604a; immovability; old school; inflexibility etc. (*hardness*) 323; obduracy, obduration [*rare*], obdurateness, doggedness, dogged resolution; resolution etc. 604; ruling passion; blind side.

self-will, contumacy, perversity; pervicaciousness [*rare*], pervicacy [*obs.*], pervicacity [*obs.*]; indocility [*obs.*].

bigotry, intolerance, dogmatism; opiniatry [*obs.*], opiniativeness [*rare*]; impersuasibility, impersuadableness; intractableness, incorrigibility; fixed idea etc. (*prejudgment*) 481; fanaticism, zealotry, infatuation, monomania; opinionatedness, opinionativeness.

bigot, opinionist [*obs.*], opinionatist [*obs.*], opiniator [*obs.*], opinator [*obs.*]; stickler, dogmatist, zealot, enthusiast, fanatic, bitter-ender [*colloq.*]; mule.

v. **be obstinate** etc. *adj.*; stickle, take no denial, fly in the face of facts; opinionate [*rare*], be wedded to an opinion, hug a belief; have one's own way etc. (*will*) 600; persist etc. (*persevere*) 604a; have–, insist on having- the last word.

die hard, die fighting, fight to the last ditch, fight against destiny, not yield an inch, stand out.

adj. obstinate, tenacious, stubborn, obdurate, case-hardened; inflexible etc. (*hard*) 323; balky; immovable, not to be moved; inert etc. 172; unchangeable etc. 150; inexorable etc. (*determined*) 604; mulish, obstinate as a mule, pig-headed.

dogged; sullen, sulky; unmoved, uninfluenced, unaffected.

willful or wilful, self-willed, perverse; resty [*dial. Eng.*], restive, pervicacious [*rare*], ungovernable, wayward, refractory, unruly; heady, headstrong; *entêté* [*F.*]; contumacious; cross-grained.

arbitrary, dogmatic, positive, bigoted, opinionated, opinionative, opinionate [*obs.*], opinioned, opiniative [*rare*]; prejudiced etc. 481; creed-bound; prepossessed, infatuated; stiff-backed, stiff-necked, stiff-hearted; hard-mouthed, hidebound; unyielding; impervious, impracticable, impersuasible, impersuadable, unpersuadable; untractable, intractable; incorrigible, deaf to advice, impervious to reason; crotchety etc. 608.

adv. obstinately etc. *adj.;* with set jaw, with sullen mouth; no surrender.

607. Tergiversation

n. **tergiversation**, tergiversating, recantation; palinode, palinody [*rare*]; renunciation; abjuration, abjurement; defection etc. (*relinquishment*) 624; going over etc. *v.;* apostasy; retraction, retractation; withdrawal; disavowal etc. (*negation*) 536; revocation, revokement [*rare*], reversal; repentance etc. 950; *redintegratio amoris* [*L.*].

change of -mind, -intention, -purpose; afterthought.

coquetry, flirtation; vacillation etc. 605.

recidivism, recidivation, backsliding; *volte-face* [*F.*].

turncoat, turn-tippet [*obs.*]; rat [*cant*], apostate, renegade, pervert, deserter, backslider; recidivist; crawfish [*slang*], mugwump; blackleg, scab [*slang*]; proselyte, convert.

timeserver, time-pleaser; timist [*obs.*], Vicar of Bray, trimmer, ambidexter; double dealer; weathercock etc. (*changeable*) 149; Janus; coquet, flirt.

v. **tergiversate**, veer round, wheel round, turn round; change one's- mind, -intention, -purpose, -note; abjure, renounce; withdraw from etc. (*relinquish*) 624; turn a pirouette; go over-, pass-, change-, skip- from one side to another; go to the right-about; box the compass, shift one's ground, go upon another tack.

apostatize, change sides, go over, rat [*cant*], *tourner casaque* [*F.*], recant, retract; revoke; rescind etc. (*abrogate*) 756; recall; forswear, unsay; come -over, -round- to an opinion.

back down, draw in one's horns, eat one's words; eat-, swallow- the leek; swerve, flinch, back out of, retrace one's steps, crawfish, crawl [*both slang*]; think better of it; come back-, return- to one's first love; turn over a new leaf etc. (*repent*) 950.

trim, shuffle, play fast and loose, blow hot and cold, coquet, flirt, be on the fence, straddle, hold with the hare but run with the hounds; *nager entre deux eaux* [*F.*], wait to see how the -cat jumps, -wind blows.

adj. **changeful** etc. 149; irresolute etc. 605; ductile, slippery as an eel, trimming, ambidextrous, timeserving; coquetting etc. *v.*

revocatory, reactionary.

608. Caprice

n. **caprice**, fancy, humor; whim, whimsey or whimsy, whim-wham, crotchet, *capriccio* [*It.*], quirk, freak, maggot, fad, vagary, prank, fit, flimflam, escapade, boutade [*obs.*], wild-goose chase; capriciousness etc. *adj.;* kink.

v. **be capricious** etc. *adj.;* have a maggot in the brain; take it into one's head, take the bit in one's teeth; strain at a gnat and swallow a camel; blow hot and cold; play fast and loose, play fantastic tricks; *tourner casaque* [*F.*].

adj. **capricious**; erratic, eccentric, fitful, hysterical; full of whims etc. *n.;* maggoty; inconsistent, fanciful, fantastic, whimsical, crotchety, kinky, particular, humorsome, freakish, skittish, wanton, wayward; contrary; captious; unreasonable, unrestrained, undisciplined, not amenable to reason, arbitrary; unconformable etc. 83; penny wise and pound foolish; fickle etc. (*irresolute*) 605; frivolous, sleeveless [*obs.*], giddy, volatile.

adv. **by fits**, by fits and starts, without rime or reason, at one's own sweet will; without counting the cost.

609. Choice

n. **choice**, option; discretion etc. (*volition*) 600; preoption; alternative; dilemma, *embarras de choix* [*F.*]; adoption, coöptation; novation [*law*]; decision etc. (*judgment*) 480.

election, poll, ballot, vote, division, voice, suffrage, cumulative vote; plebiscitum, plebiscite, *vox populi* [*L.*], popular decision, referendum; electioneering; voting etc. *v.;* elective franchise; straight ticket, ticket; ballot box.

selection, excerption, gleaning, eclecticism; *excerpta* [*L.*]; gleanings, cuttings, scissors and paste; pick etc. (*best*) 650.

preference, prelation [*rare*]; predilection etc. (*desire*) 865; Apple of Discord; choice of Hercules; Scylla and Charybdis; good and evil.

v. **offer for one's choice**, set before; hold out–, present–, offer- the alternative; put to the vote.

choose, elect; coöpt, coöptate [*rare*]; take–, make- one's choice; make choice of, fix upon; use–, exercise–, one's- -discretion, -option; adopt, take up, embrace, espouse.

settle; decide etc. (*adjudge*) 480; list etc. (*will*) 600; make up one's mind etc. (*resolve*) 604.

vote, poll, hold up one's hand, give a (*or* the) voting sign; divide.

select; pick, –and choose; pick–, single- out; excerpt, cull, glean, winnow; sift–, separate–, winnow- the chaff from the wheat; pick up, pitch upon; pick one's way; indulge one's fancy.

set apart, mark out for; mark etc. 550.

prefer; have rather, had (*or* would) as lief; fancy etc. (*desire*) 865; reserve, set one's seal upon; be persuaded etc. 615.

take a decided step, take a decisive step; commit oneself to a course; pass–, cross- the Rubicon; cast in one's lot with; take for better or for worse.

adj. **optional**; coöptative; discretional etc. (*voluntary*) 600; at choice, on approval.

choosing etc. *v.;* eclectic; preferential.

chosen etc. *v.;* choice etc. (*good*) 648; elect, select, popular.

adv. **optionally** etc. *adj.;* at pleasure etc. (*will*) 600; either, –the one or the other; or; at the option of; whether or not; once for all; for one's money.

by choice, by preference; in preference; rather, before.

609a. Absence of Choice

n. **no choice**, Hobson's choice; first come first served; necessity etc. 601; not a pin to choose etc. (*equality*) 27; any, the first that comes; that or nothing.

neutrality, indifference; indecision etc. (*irresolution*) 605.

v. **be neutral** etc. *adj.;* have no -preference, –choice; waive, not vote; abstain–, refrain, –from voting; leave undecided; "make a virtue of necessity" [*Two Gentlemen from Verona*].

adj. **neutral**, neuter; indifferent; undecided etc. (*irresolute*) 605.

adv. **either** etc. (*choice*) 609.

610. Rejection

n. **rejection**, repudiation, exclusion; refusal etc. 764; declination, declinature, withdrawal; averseness.

v. **reject**; set–, lay- aside; give up; decline etc. (*refuse*) 764; exclude, except; pluck up, spurn, cast out.

repudiate, scout, set at naught; fling–, cast–, throw–, toss- -to the winds, –to the dogs, –overboard, –away; send to the right-about; disclaim etc. (*deny*) 536; discard etc. (*eject*) 297, (*have done with*) 678.

adj. **rejected** etc. *v.;* rejectaneous [*obs.*], rejectitious [*obs.*], declinatory; not chosen etc. 609, not to be thought of; out of the question; "declined with thanks."

adv. **neither**, neither the one nor the other; no etc. 536.

611. Predetermination

n. **predetermination**, predestination, preordination, premeditation, predeliberation; foregone conclusion; *parti pris* [*F.*]; resolve, propendency [*obs.*]; intention etc. 620; project etc. 626; fate, foredoom, necessity.

schedule, list, calendar, docket, slate, register, roster, poll, muster, draft, *cadre* [*F.*], panel.

v. **predetermine**, predestine, preordain, premeditate, preresolve, preconcert; resolve beforehand.

list, schedule, docket, slate, register, poll, empanel, draft.

adj. **premeditated** etc. *v.;* predesigned; prepense, advised, studied, designed, calculated; aforethought; intended etc. 620; foregone.

well-laid, well-devised, well-weighed; maturely considered; cut-and-dried, slated; cunning.

adv. **advisedly** etc. *adj.;* with premeditation, deliberately, all things considered, with eyes open, in cold blood; intentionally etc. 620.

612. Impulse

n. **impulse**, sudden thought; impromptu, improvisation; inspiration, flash, spurt.

improvisor, extemporizer, *improvvisatore or improvisatore* [*It.*]; creature of impulse.

v. flash on the mind.

improvise, extemporize; say what comes uppermost, say what comes first into one's head; act on the spur of the moment, rise to the occasion; spurt.

adj. **extemporaneous**, impulsive, indeliberate [*rare*]; snap; improvised, improvisate, improviso, improvisatory; unpremeditated; unmeditated, improvisatorial, improvisatory, *improvisé* [*F.*]; unprompted, unguided; natural, unguarded; spontaneous etc. (*voluntary*) 600; instinctive etc. 601.

adv. **extempore**, extemporaneously; offhand, impromptu, *a l'improviste* [*F.*]; on the spur of the -moment, −occasion.

613. Habit

n. **habit**, habitude, habituation, assuetude [*obs.*], assuefaction [*obs.*]; wont; run, way; habitual attitude, habitual state of mind, habitual course.

common−, general−, natural−, ordinary--course, −run, −state- of things; matter of course; beaten -path, −track, −ground.

cacoëthes; bad−, confirmed−, inveterate−, intrinsic etc. (5)- habit; addictedness, addiction, trick.

custom, use, usage, prescription, immemorial usage, practice; prevalence, observance; conventionalism, conventionality; mode, fashion, vogue; etiquette etc. (*gentility*) 852; order of the day, cry; conformity etc. 82; consuetude, dastur *or* dustoor [*India*].

one's old way, old school, *veteris vestigia flammae* [*L.*]; *laudator temporis acti* [*L.*].

rule, standing order, precedent, routine; red tape, red-tapism; pipe clay; rut, groove.

addict, habitué, habitual [*colloq.*], frequenter, case [*slang*], hard case [*slang*], the limit [*slang*].

inurement; training etc. (*education*) 537; seasoning, hardening; radication; second nature, acclimatization; knack etc. (*skill*) 698.

v. **be wont** etc. *adj.*

fall into a custom etc. (*conform to*) 82; tread−, follow- the beaten -track, −path; *stare super antiquas vias* [*L.*]; move in a rut, run on in a groove, go round like a horse in a mill, go on in the old jog-trot way; get wound up in red tape.

habituate, inure, harden, season, caseharden; accustom, familiarize; naturalize, acclimatize; keep one's hand in; train etc. (*educate*) 537.

get into the -way, −knack- of; learn etc. 539; cling to, adhere to; repeat etc. 104; acquire−, contract−, fall into- a -habit, −trick; addict oneself to, take to, accustom oneself to.

be habitual etc. *adj.;* prevail; come into use, become a habit, take root; gain upon one, grow upon one.

adj. **habitual**; accustomary, customary; prescriptive; accustomed etc. *v.;* of -daily, −everyday- occurrence; consuetudinary; wonted, usual, general, ordinary, common, frequent, every day, household, jog-trot; well-trodden, well-known; familiar, vernacular, trite, commonplace, conventional, regular, set, stock, established, stereotyped; prevailing, prevalent; current, received, acknowledged, recognized, accredited; of course, admitted, understood.

conformable etc. 82; according to -use, −custom, −routine; in vogue, in fashion; fashionable etc. (*genteel*) 852.

wont; used to, given to, addicted to, attuned to, habituated to etc. *v.;* in the habit of; *habitué* [*F.*]; at home in etc. (*skillful*) 698; seasoned; imbued with, soaked in, permeated with, never free from; devoted to, wedded to.

hackneyed, fixed, rooted, deep-rooted, ingrafted *or* engrafted, permanent, inveterate, besetting, naturalized; ingrained etc. (*intrinsic*) 5.

adv. **habitually** etc. *adj.;* always etc. (*uniformly*) 16.

as usual, as is one's wont, as things go, as the world goes, as the sparks fly upwards; as you were [*mil.*]; *more suo* [*L.*], *more solito* [*L.*]; *ex more* [*L.*].

as a rule, for the most part; generally etc. *adj.;* most -often, −frequently.

614. Desuetude

n. **desuetude**, disusage; obsolescence, disuse etc. 678; want of -habit, −use, −practice; insitation [*rare*]; newness to; new brooms.

nonprevalence; infraction of usage etc. (*unconformity*) 83; "a custom more honored in the breach than the observance" [*Hamlet*].

v. **be unaccustomed** etc. *adj.;* leave off−, cast off−, break off−, cure oneself of−, wean oneself from−, shake off−, violate−, break through−, infringe- a habit, −a custom, −a usage; break one's -chains, −fetters; do old things in a new way, give an original touch, give a new dress to old ideas; disuse etc. 678; wear off.

adj. **unaccustomed**, unused, unwonted, unseasoned, uninured, unhabituated, untrained; new, fresh, original; impulsive etc. *adj.* 612; green etc. (*unskilled*) 699; unhackneyed.

unconventional, unfashionable; dissident, protestant; unusual etc. (*unconformable*) 83; nonobservant; disused etc. 678.

adv. **contrary to -custom**, −usage, −convention; for once, just once; "this time doesn't count."

615. Motive

n. **motive**, springs of action.

reason, ground, call, principle; by-end, by-purpose; mainspring, *primum mobile* [*L.*], keystone; the why and the wherefore; *pro* and *con*, reason why; secret motive, ulterior motive; *arrière pensée* [*F.*]; intention etc. 620.

209

inducement, consideration; attraction; load-stone; magnet, magnetism, magnetic force; allectation [obs.], allective [obs.], temptation, enticement, agacerie [F.], allurement, witchery; bewitchment, bewitchery; charm; spell etc. 993; fascination, blandishment, cajolery; seduction, seducement; honeyed words, voice of the tempter, song of the Sirens; forbidden fruit, golden apple.

persuasibility, persuasibleness, persuadability, persuadableness; attractability; impressibility, susceptibility; softness; persuasiveness, attractiveness; tantalization.

influence, prompting, dictate, instance; impulse, impulsion; incitement, incitation; press, insistence, urge [rare], instigation; provocation etc. (excitation of feeling) 824; inspiration; persuasion, suasion; encouragement, advocacy; exhortation, hortation; advice etc. 695; solicitation etc. (request) 765; lobbyism; pull [slang].

incentive, stimulus, spur, fillip, whip, goad, ankus [India], rowel, provocative, whet, dram.

bribe, lure; decoy, decoy duck; bait, trail of a red herring; bribery and corruption; sop, sop to Cerberus.

tempter, seducer, seductor, seductress; prompter, suggester, coaxer, wheedler, Siren, Circe, vampire [colloq.], vamp [slang]; instigator, agent provocateur [F.]; lobbyist; firebrand, incendiary.

v. **induce**, move; draw, draw on; bring in its train, give an impulse to etc. n.; inspire; put up to [slang], prompt, call up; attract, beckon.

stimulate etc. (excite) 824; spirit, spirit up, inspirit; rouse, arouse, animate, incite, provoke, instigate, set on, actuate; act upon, work upon, operate upon; encourage; pat-, clap- on the -back, -shoulder.

set an example, set the fashion; keep in countenance, back up.

influence, weigh with, bias, sway, incline, dispose, predispose, turn the scale, inoculate; lead, -by the nose; have-, exercise-, influence--with, -over, -upon; go-, come- round one [colloq.]; turn the head, magnetize; lobby [chiefly U.S.].

persuade; prevail -with, -upon; overcome, carry; bring round, bring to one's senses; draw-, win-, gain-, talk- over; come over [colloq.]; procure, enlist, engage; invite, court.

tempt, seduce, overpersuade, entice, allure, captivate, fascinate, bewitch, carry away, charm, conciliate, wheedle, coax, lure, vamp [slang]; inveigle; tantalize; cajole etc. (deceive) 545.

bribe, tamper with, suborn, grease the palm, bait with a silver hook, gild the pill, make things pleasant, put a sop into the pan, throw a sop to, bait the hook.

enforce, force; impel etc. (push) 276; propel etc. 284; whip, lash, goad, spur, prick, urge; egg on, hound on, hurry on; drag etc. 285; exhort; advise etc. 695; call upon etc., press etc. (request) 765; advocate.

be persuaded etc.; yield to temptation, come round [colloq.]; concede etc. (consent) 762; obey a call; follow -advice, -the bent, -the dictates of; act on principle.

adj. **impulsive**, motive; persuasive, persuasory [rare], hortative, hortatory; protreptical [obs.]; inviting, tempting, etc. v.; suasive, suasory [obs.], irresistible, seductive, attractive; fascinating etc. (pleasing) 829; provocative etc. (exciting) 824.

induced etc. v.; disposed; persuadable etc. (docile) 602; spellbound; instinct-, taken-, smitten- with; inspired by etc. v.

adv. **because**, therefore etc. (cause) 155; from this motive, from that motive; for this reason, for that reason; for; by reason of, for the sake of, on the score of, on account of; out of, from, as, forasmuch as.

for all the world; on principle.

615a. Absence of Motive

n. **absence of motive**; caprice etc. 608; chance etc. (absence of design) 621.

v. **scruple** etc. (be unwilling) 603; have no motive.

adj. **aimless** etc. (chance) 621; without rhyme or reason.

adv. **capriciously**, out of mere caprice.

616. Dissuasion

n. **dissuasion**, dehortation [rare], expostulation, remonstrance; deprecation etc. 766.

discouragement, dehortative [rare], monitory, damper, wet blanket; contraindicant.

curb etc. (means of restraint) 752; constraint etc. (restraint) 751; check etc. (hindrance) 706.

reluctance etc. (unwillingness) 603; contraindication.

v. **dissuade**, dehort [rare], cry out against, remonstrate, expostulate, warn, contraindicate.

disincline, indispose, shake, stagger; dispirit; discourage, dishearten, disenchant; deter; hold back, keep back etc. (restrain) 751; render averse etc. 603; repel; turn aside etc. (deviation) 279; wean from; act as a drag etc. (hinder) 706; throw cold water on, damp, cool, chill, blunt, calm, quiet, quench; deprecate etc. 766.

adj. **dissuading** etc. *v.;* dissuasive; dehortatory [*rare*], dehortative [*rare*], expostulatory; monitive [*obs.*], monitory, monitorial.

dissuaded etc. *v.;* admonitory; uninduced etc. (induce etc. 615); unpersuadable etc. (*obstinate*) 606; averse etc. (*unwilling*) 603; repugnant etc. (*dislike*) 867.

617. Plea

[ostensible motive, ground, or reason]

n. **plea,** pretext; allegation, advocation [*archaic*]; ostensible -motive, –ground, –reason; excuse etc. (*vindication*) 937; color; gloss, guise.

handle, peg to hang on; room, *locus standi* [*L.*]; stalking-horse, *cheval de bataille* [*F.*], cue.

loophole, starting-hole [*obs.*]; hole to creep out of, come-off [*colloq.*], way of escape.

pretense etc. (*untruth*) 546; put-off, subterfuge, dust thrown in the eye; blind; moonshine; mere–, shallow- pretext; lame -excuse, –apology; tub to a whale; false plea, sour grapes; makeshift, shift, white lie; special pleading etc. (*sophistry*) 477; soft sawder [*slang*] etc. (*flattery*) 933.

v. **plead,** allege; shelter oneself under the plea of; creep out of; tell a white lie; excuse etc. (*vindicate*) 937; color, gloss over, lend a color to; furnish a handle etc. *n.;* make a pretext of, make a handle of; use as a plea etc. *n.;* take one's stand upon, make capital out of; pretend etc. (*lie*) 544.

adj. **advocatory** [*rare*], excusing; **ostensible** etc. (*manifest*) 525; alleged, apologetic; pretended etc. 545.

adv. **ostensibly;** under the plea of, under the pretense of.

618. Good

n. **good,** benefit, advantage; improvement etc. 658; greatest–, supreme- good; interest, service, behoof, behalf; weal [*archaic*]; main chance, *summum bonum* [*L.*]; commonwealth [*now rare*], commonweal *or* common weal; "consummation devoutly to be wished" [*Hamlet*]; gain, boot [*archaic*]; profit, harvest.

boon etc. (*gift*) 784; good turn; blessing, benison; world of good; piece of good -luck, –fortune; nuts [*now Eng. slang*], prize, windfall, godsend, waif, treasure-trove.

good fortune etc. (*prosperity*) 734; happiness etc. 827.

[source of good] goodness etc. 648; utility etc. 644; remedy etc. 662; pleasure giving etc. 829.

v. **benefit,** profit, advantage, serve, help, avail, boot [*archaic*], good [*obs.*], do good to.

gain, prosper, flourish, thrive etc. 734.

adj. **commendable** etc. 931; useful etc. 644; good etc., beneficial etc. 648.

adv. **well,** aright, satisfactorily, favorably, not amiss; all for the best; to one's advantage etc. *n.;* in one's favor, in one's interest etc. *n.*

619. Evil

n. **evil,** ill, harm, hurt, mischief, nuisance; machinations of the devil, Pandora's box, ills that flesh is heir to; mental suffering etc. (*pain*) 828.

[evil spirit] demon etc. 980.

[cause of evil] bane etc. 663.

[production of evil] badness etc. 649; painfulness etc. 830; evildoer etc. 913.

blow, buffet, stroke, scratch, bruise, wound, gash, mutilation; mortal -blow, –wound; *immedicabile vulnus* [*L.*]; damage, loss etc. (*deterioration*) 659.

disadvantage, prejudice, drawback.

disaster, accident, casualty; mishap etc. (*misfortune*) 735; bad job [*colloq.*], devil to pay [*colloq.*]; calamity, bale [*chiefly poetic*], woe, fatal mischief, catastrophe, tragedy; ruin etc. (*destruction*) 162; adversity etc. 735.

outrage, wrong, injury, foul play; bad turn, ill turn; disservice; spoliation etc. 791; grievance, crying evil.

v. **disserve,** do disservice to, harm, injure, hurt.

be in trouble etc. (*adversity*) 735.

adj. **disastrous,** bad etc. 649; awry, out of joint; disadvantageous; disserviceable, injurious, harmful.

adv. **amiss,** wrong, ill, to one's cost.

Section 2. Prospective Volition

620. Intention

n. **intention,** intent, intentionality; purpose; *quo animo* [*L.*]; project etc. 626; undertaking etc. 676; predetermination etc. 611; design, ambition.

contemplation, mind, animus, view, purview [*law*], proposal; study; lookout.

object, aim, end; final cause; *raisòn d'être* [*F.*]; *cui bono* [*L.*]; "the be-all and the end-all" [*Macbeth*]; drift etc. (*meaning*) 516; tendency etc. 176; destination, mark, point, butt, goal, target, bull's-eye, quintain; prey, quarry, game.

211

decision, determination, resolve; fixed-, set-, settled- purpose; ultimatum; resolution etc. 604; wish etc. 865; *arrière pensée* [*F.*]; motive etc. 615.

[study of final causes] teleology.

v. **intend**, purpose, design, mean; have to; propose to oneself; harbor a design; have in -view, -contemplation, -one's eye; have *in petto* [*It.*]; have an eye to.

bid for, labor for; be after, aspire to *or* after, endeavor after; be at, aim at, drive at, point at, level at; take aim; set before oneself; study to.

contemplate, meditate; take upon oneself etc. (*undertake*) 676; take into one's head; think of, dream of, talk of; premeditate etc. 611; compass [*legal*], calculate; destine, destinate; propose.

project etc. (*plan*) 626; have a mind to etc. (*be willing*) 602; desire etc. 865; pursue etc. 622.

adj. **intended** etc. *v.;* intentional, advised, express, determinate; prepense etc. 611; bound for; intending etc. *v.;* disposed, inclined, minded; bent upon etc. (*earnest*) 604; at stake; on the -anvil, -tapis; in view, in prospect, in the breast of; *in petto* [*It.*]; teleological.

adv. **intentionally** etc. *adj.;* advisedly, wittingly, knowingly, designedly, purposely, on purpose, by design, studiously, pointedly; with intent etc. *n.;* deliberately etc. (*with premeditation*) 611; with one's eyes open, in cold blood.

for; with a view to, with an eye to; in order -to, -that; to the end that, with the intent that; for the purpose of, with the view of, in contemplation of, on account of.

in pursuance of, pursuant to; *quo animo* [*L.*]; to all intents and purposes.

621. Chance

[absence of purpose]

n. **chance** etc. 156; lot, fate etc. (*necessity*) 601; luck; good luck etc. (*good*) 618; hoodoo, jinx [*slang*], jadoo *or* jadu [*Hind.*]; voodoo, voodooism; swastika *or* swastica, fylfot, gammadion; wheel of chance, Fortune's wheel; mascot.

speculation, venture, mere-, random- shot; blind bargain, leap in the dark; pig in a poke etc. (*uncertainty*) 475; fluke [*sporting cant*], potluck, flyer [*slang*], flutter [*Eng. slang*]; futures.

gambling, game of chance; drawing lots; sortilegy, sortition [*obs.*]; *rouge et noir* [*F.*], hazard, ante, chuck-a-luck *or* chuck-luck, crack-loo; craps; faro, faro bank; roulette, pitch and toss, chuck-farthing, cup tossing, heads or tails, cross and pile [*archaic*], dice, dice box, poker-dice; fan-tan [*Chinese*].

wager; gamble, risk, stake, pyramid, plunge; bet, betting; gambling; the turf.

gambling house, gaming house, gambling den, pool room, betting-house; bucket shop; joint [*slang*]; parimutuel, totalizator, totalizer tote board; hell; betting ring; Wall Street, Stock Exchange, curb, curb market.

gambler, gamester, dicer, sport [*cant*], punter, plunger, speculator, hazarder, sucker, bookmaker, bookie [*colloq.*], man of the turf; pool shark [*colloq.*], shark, adventurer.

v. **chance** etc. (*hap*) 156; stand a chance etc. (*be possible*) 470.

toss up; cast-, draw- lots; leave-, trust- -to chance, -to the chapter of accidents; tempt fortune; chance it, take one's chance; run-, incur-, encounter- the -risk, -chance; stand the hazard of the die.

speculate, try one's luck, set on a cast, raffle, put into a lottery, buy a pig in a poke, shuffle the cards.

risk, venture, hazard, stake; ante; lay, -a wager; make a bet, wager, bet, gamble, game, play for; play at chuck-farthing; play the ponies, play the bangtails [*both slang*]; play-, shoot-craps etc.

adj. **fortuitous** etc. 156; unintentional, unintended; accidental; not meant; undesigned, unpurposed; unpremeditated etc. 612; never thought of.

indiscriminate, promiscuous; undirected, random; aimless, driftless, designless, purposeless, causeless; without purpose.

possible etc. 470.

adv. **casually** etc. 156; unintentionally etc. *adj.;* unwittingly.

incidentally, *en passant* [*F.*], by the way.

at random, at a venture, at haphazard; as luck would have it; in luck; out of luck; by chance, by good fortune; as it may happen.

int. what luck! better luck next time!

622. Pursuit

[purpose in action]

n. **pursuit**; pursuing etc. *v.;* prosecution; pursuance; enterprise etc. (*undertaking*) 676; business etc. 625; adventure etc. (*essay*) 675; quest etc. (*search*) 461; scramble, hue and cry, game; hobby; still-hunt.

chase, hunt, *battue* [*F.*], race, steeplechase, hunting, coursing; venation [*obs.*], venery; fox chase, fox hunting; sport, sporting; shooting, angling, fishing, hawking; shikar [*India*].

pursuer; hunter, huntsman, the field; shikari [*India*], sportman, Nimrod; hound etc. 366.

v. **pursue**, prosecute, follow; run–, make–, be–, hunt–, prowl- after; shadow; carry on etc. (*do*) 680; be absorbed in; engage in etc. (*undertake*) 676; set about etc. (*begin*) 66; endeavor etc. 675; court etc. (*request*) 765; seek etc. (*search*) 461; aim at etc. (*intention*) 620; follow the trail etc. (*trace*) 461; fish for etc. (*experiment*) 463; press on etc. (*haste*) 684; run a race etc. (*velocity*) 274.

tread a path; take–, hold- a course; shape–, direct–, bend- one's -steps, –course; play a game; fight–, elbow- one's way; follow up; take to, take up; go in for; ride one's hobby.

chase, give chase, still-hunt, stalk, shikar [*India*], course, dog, hunt, hound; tread–, follow- on the heels of, etc. (*sequence*) 281; start game.

rush upon; rush headlong etc. (*violence*) 173; ride at, run full tilt at; make a leap at, jump at, snatch at; run down.

adj. **pursuing** etc. *v.;* in quest of etc. (*inquiry*) 461; in pursuit, in full cry, in hot pursuit; on the scent.

adv. **after**; in pursuance of etc. (*intention*) 620.

int. tallyho! yoicks! soho!

623. Avoidance

[absence of pursuit]

n. **avoidance**, evasion, elusion; seclusion etc. 893. avolation [*obs.*], flight; escape etc. 671; retreat etc. 287; recoil etc. 277; departure etc. 293; rejection etc. 610.

abstention, abstinence; forbearance; refraining etc. *v.;* inaction etc. 681; neutrality.

shirker etc. *v.;* slacker, shirk, quitter, eye servant, truant; fugitive, refugee, runaway, runagate, deserter, renegade, backslider; maroon.

v. **abstain**, refrain, spare, not attempt; not do etc. 681; maintain the even tenor of one's way.

eschew, keep from, let alone, have nothing to do with; keep–, stand–, hold- -aloof, –off; take no part in, have no hand in.

avoid, shun; steer–, keep- clear of; fight shy of; keep one's distance, keep at a respectful distance; keep–, get- out of the way; evade, elude, turn away from; set one's face against etc. (*oppose*) 708; deny oneself.

shrink; hang–, hold–, draw- back; recoil etc. 277; retire etc. (*recede*) 287; flinch, blink, blench, shy, shirk, dodge, parry, make way for, give place to.

beat a retreat; turn tail, turn one's back; take to one's heels; run, run away, run for one's life; maroon; cut and run [*colloq.*]; be off, –like a shot; fly, flee, fly–, flee–, run away- from; take flight, take to flight; desert, elope; make off,

scamper off, sneak off, shuffle off, sheer off; break–, burst–, tear oneself–, slip–, slink–, steal- -away, –away from; slip cable, part company, turn on one's heel; sneak out of, play truant, give one the go-by [*slang*], give leg bail [*slang*], take French leave, slope [*slang*], decamp, flit, bolt, abscond, levant [*slang, Eng.*], skedaddle [*dial.*], absquatulate, cut one's stick [*slang*], walk one's chalks [*slang*], show the heels, show a clean (*or* light) pair of heels, make oneself scarce [*slang*]; escape etc. 671; go away etc. (*depart*) 293; abandon etc. 624; reject etc. 610.

lead one a dance, lead one a pretty dance; throw off the scent, play at hide and seek.

adj. **avoiding** etc. *v.;* neutral; unsought, unattempted; shy of etc. (*unwilling*) 603; elusive, evasive; fugitive, runaway; shy, wild.

adv. **lest**, in order to avoid.

int. forbear! keep off! hands off! *sauve qui peut!* [*F.*], devil take the hindmost!

624. Relinquishment

n. **relinquishment**, abandonment; desertion, defection, secession, withdrawal; cave of Adullam; *nolle prosequi* [*L.*].

discontinuance etc. (*cessation*) 142; renunciation etc. (*recantation*) 607; abrogation etc. 756; resignation etc. (*retirement*) 757; desuetude etc. 614; cession etc. (*of property*) 782.

v. **relinquish**, give up, abandon, desert, forsake, leave in the lurch; go back on [*colloq.*]; depart–, secede - withdraw- from; back out of [*colloq.*], back down from [*colloq.*]; leave, quit, take leave of, bid a long farewell; vacate etc. (*resign*) 757.

renounce etc. (*abjure*) 607; forego, have done with, drop; nol-pros [*law*]; disuse etc. 678; discard etc. 782; wash one's hands of; drop all idea of.

break off, leave off; desist; stop etc. (*cease*) 142; hold one's hand, stay one's hand; quit one's hold; give over, shut up shop; throw up the -game, –cards.

give up the -point, –argument; pass to the order of the day, move the previous question, table, table the motion.

adj. **unpursued**; relinquished etc. *v.;* relinquishing etc. *v.*

int. avast! etc. (*stop*) 142.

625. Business

n. **business**, occupation, employment, undertaking; pursuit etc. 622; what one is doing, what one is about; affair, concern, matter, case.

task, matter in hand, irons in the fire; thing to do, agendum (*pl.* agenda), work, job, chore, errand, commission, mission, charge, care; duty etc. 926.

exercise; work etc. (*action*) 680; avocation, hobby; press of business etc. (*activity*) 682.

function, part, role, cue; province, lookout [*colloq.*], department, capacity, sphere, orb [*now rare*], field, line; walk, −of life; beat, round, routine; race, career.

office, place, post, chargeship, incumbency, living; situation, berth, billet, appointment, employ [*rare*], service etc. (*servitude*) 749; engagement; undertaking etc. 676.

vocation, calling, profession, cloth, faculty; industry, art; industrial arts; craft, mystery [*obs.*], handicraft; trade etc. (*commerce*) 794.

v. **occupy oneself with**; pass−, employ−, spend− one's time in; employ oneself -in, −upon; concern oneself with; make it one's business etc. *n.;* undertake etc. 676; enter a profession; betake oneself to, turn one's hand to; have to do with etc. (*do*) 680.

be about, be doing, be engaged in, be employed in, be occupied with, be at work on; have one's hands in, have in hand; have on one's -hands, −shoulders; bear the burden; have one's hands full etc. (*activity*) 682.

ply one's task, ply one's trade; drive a trade; carry on−, do−, transact- -business, −a trade etc. *n.;* keep a shop; labor in one's vocation; pursue the even tenor of one's way; attend to business, attend to one's work.

officiate, serve, act; act one's part, play one's part; do duty; serve−, discharge−, perform- the -office, −duties, −functions- of; hold−, fill- -an office, −a place, −a situation; hold a portfolio.

be in the hands of, be on the stocks, be on the anvil; pass through one's hands.

adj. **businesslike**; workaday; professional, vocational; official, functional; humming, busy etc. (*actively employed*) 682.

in hand, on hand; on *or* in one's hands; afoot; on foot, on the anvil; going on; acting.

adv. **in the course of business**, all in the day's work; professionally etc. *adj.*

626. Plan

n. **plan**, scheme, design, project, proposal, proposition, suggestion; resolution, motion; precaution etc. (*provision*) 673; deep-laid etc. (*premeditated*) 611- plan etc.; germ etc. (*cause*) 153.

system etc. (*order*) 58; organization etc. (*arrangement*) 60.

outline, sketch, skeleton, draft *or* draught, ébauche [*F.*], brouillon [*F.*]; rough -cast, −draft *or* draught, −copy; copy; proof, revise.

forecast, program *or* programme, prospectus; carte du pays [*F.*]; card; bill, protocol; order of the day, memoranda, list of agenda; bill of fare etc. (*food*) 298; base of operations; platform, plank, slate, ticket.

role; policy etc. (*line of conduct*) 692.

contrivance, invention, expedient, receipt, nostrum, artifice, device; pipelaying; stratagem etc. (*cunning*) 702; trick etc. (*deception*) 545; alternative, loop-hole; shift etc. (*substitute*) 147; last shift etc. (*necessity*) 601, gadget.

measure, step; stroke, −of policy; masterstroke; trump, trump card, courtcard; cheval de bataille [*F.*], great gun; coup, - d'état [*F.*]; clever−, bold−, good- -move, −hit, −stroke; bright -thought, −idea; great idea.

intrigue, cabal, plot, conspiracy, complot, machination; underplot, counterplot; mine, countermine.

schemer, schemist [*rare*], schematist [*obs.*]; strategist, machinator; Machiavellian, Machiavellist, conspirator; intrigant etc. (*cunning*) 702.

projector, promoter, designer etc. *v.;* organizer, founder (*fem.* foundress), author, artist, builder.

v. **plan**, scheme, design, frame, contrive, project, forecast, sketch; devise, invent etc. (*imagine*) 515; set one's wits to work etc. 515; spring a project; fall upon, hit upon; strike−, chalk−, cut−, lay−, map- out; lay down a plan; shape−, mark-out a course; predetermine etc. 611; concert, preconcert, preëstablish; prepare etc. 673; hatch, −a plot; concoct; take -steps, −measures.

systematize, organize; cast, recast, arrange etc. 60; digest, mature.

plot; counterplot, mine, countermine, dig a mine; lay a train; intrigue etc. (*cunning*) 702.

adj. **planned** etc. *v.;* strategic *or* strategical.

planning etc. *v.;* in course of preparation etc. 673; under consideration, on the tapis, on the carpet, on the table.

627. Method

[path]

n. **method**, way, manner, wise [*rare, exc. in phrases*], gait, form, mode, fashion, tone, guise; modus operandi [*L.*]; procedure etc. (*line of conduct*) 692.

path, road, route, course; line of way, line of road; trajectory, orbit, track, beat, tack.

steps; stair, staircase; flight of -steps, –stairs; ladder, stile; perron.

bridge, footbridge, viaduct, pontoon, stepping-stone, plank, gangway; draw-bridge.

pass, ford, ferry, tunnel; pipe etc. 260.

means of access, adit, entrance, approach, passage, cloister, covered way, lobby, corridor, aisle; alley, lane, vennel [*Scot. & dial. Eng.*], avenue, artery, channel; gateway etc. (*opening*) 260; door, backdoor, backstairs; secret passage; covert way.

roadway, express; thoroughfare; highway, macadam, parkway, boulevard; turnpike–, royal–, state–, coach- road; broad–, King's–, Queen's- highway; beaten -track, –path; horse–, bridle- -road, –track, –path; walk, *trottoir* [*F.*], footpath, pathway, pavement, flags, sidewalk, by-road, crossroad; by–, cross- -path, –way; cut; short cut & (*mid-course*) 628; *carrefour* [*F.*]; private–, occupation- road; highways and byways; railroad, railway, trolley track, tramroad, tramway; towpath; causeway; street etc. (*abode*) 189; stairway, gangway; speedway; canal etc. (*conduit*) 350.

adv. **how**; in what way, in what manner; by what mode; so, thus, in this way, after this fashion.

one way or another, anyhow; somehow or other etc. (*instrumentality*) 631; by way of; *via* [*L.*]; *in transitu* [*L.*] etc. 270; on the high road to, on the way to.

628. Mid-course

n. **mid-course**, midway [*rare*], middle way, middle course; moderation; mean etc. 29; middle etc. 68; *juste milieu* [*F.*], *mezzo termine* [*L.*], golden mean, *ariston metron* [*Gr.*], *aurea mediocritas* [*L.*]; fifty-fifty [*colloq.*].

shortcut, crosscut; straight etc. (*direct*) 278 -course, –path; great-circle sailing.

compromise, half measures, half-and-half measures; neutrality.

v. **keep the golden mean**; keep in–, steer–, preserve- -a middle, –an even- course; avoid both Scylla and Charybdis; go straight etc. (*direct*) 278.

compromise, make a compromise, go fifty-fifty [*colloq.*], concede half, go half-way.

adj. **neutral**, average, even, evenly balanced; impartial, moderate; straight etc. (*direct*) 278.

adv. **midway**, in the mean; in moderation.

629. Circuit

n **circuit**, round-about way, digression, detour, circumbendibus [*humorous*], circumambience, circumambiency, circumambulation, ambages,

loop; winding etc. (*circuition*) 311; zigzag etc. (*deviation*) 279.

v. **go round about**, circumambulate, perform a circuit, make a circuit, go out of one's way; make a detour; meander etc. (*deviate*) 279.

lead a pretty dance; beat about, –the bush; make two bites of a cherry.

adj. **circuitous**, circumambient, circumambulatory, indirect, roundabout; zigzag etc. (*deviating*) 279; backhanded.

adv. **in a roundabout way**; by a side wind, by an indirect course; from pillar to post.

630. Requirement

n. **requirement**, need, wants, necessities; necessaries, –of life; stress, exigency, pinch, *sine qua non* [*L.*], matter of necessity; case of need, case of life or death.

desideratum etc. (*desire*) 865; want etc. (*deficiency*) 640.

needfulness, essentiality, necessity, indispensability, urgency, prerequisite; the least one can -do, –require.

requisition etc. (*request*) 765 (*exaction*) 741; run; demand for, call for.

charge, claim, command, injunction, mandate, order, precept, ultimatum.

v. **require**, need, want, have occasion for; not be able to do without, not able to dispense with; prerequire.

be necessary etc. *adj.;* stand in need of; lack etc. 640; desiderate; desire etc. 865.

render necessary, necessitate, create a necessity for, call for, put in requisition; make a requisition etc. (*ask for*) 765, (*demand*) 741.

adj. **necessary**; required etc. *v.;* requisite, needful, imperative, essential, indispensable, prerequisite; called for; in demand, in request.

in want of; destitute of etc. 640.

urgent, exigent, pressing, instant, crying, absorbing.

adv. **of necessity**; *ex necessitate rei* [*L.*] etc. (*necessarily*) 601; out of -stern necessity, –bitter need; in a pinch.

631. Instrumentality

n. **instrumentality**; aid etc. 707; subservience *or* subserviency, intermediacy, intermediation, mediation, intervention, medium, intermedium, intermediary, interagent, intermediate, mediating agency, vehicle, hand; agency etc. 170.

minister, handmaid; midwife, *accoucheur* [*F.*], *accoucheuse* [*fem., F.*], obstetrician; servant, slave, maid, valet; friend at court; go-between; cat's-paw; stepping-stone.

key, master–, pass–, latch- key; "open sesame"; passport, *passe-partout* [*F.*], safe-conduct; pull [*slang*], influence.

instrument etc. 633; expedient etc. (*plan*) 626; means etc. 632.

v. **subserve**, minister, mediate, intervene, intermediate, come–, go- between; interpose; pull the -strings, –wires; use one's influence; be instrumental etc. *adj.;* pander to; officiate; tend.

adj. **instrumental**; useful etc. 644; ministerial, subservient, serviceable; mediatorial, intermedial, intermediary, intermediate, intervening; conducive.

adv. **through**, by, *per* [*L.*]; whereby, thereby, hereby; by the agency of etc. 170; by dint of; by *or* in virtue of; through the medium of etc. *n.;* along with; on the shoulders of; by means of etc. 632; by *or* with the aid of etc. (*assistance*) 707.

somehow; *per fas et nefas* [*L.*]; by fair means or foul; somehow or other; by hook or by crook.

632. Means

n. **means**, resources, wherewithal, ways and means; capital etc. (*money*) 800; revenue, income; stock in trade etc. 636; provision etc. 637; reserve, remnant, last resource, a shot in the locker [*colloq.*]; appliances etc. (*machinery*) 633; means and appliances; conveniences; cards to play; expedients etc. (*measures*) 626; two strings to one's bow; wheels within wheels; sheet anchor etc. (*safety*) 666; aid etc. 707; medium etc. 631.

v. **provide the wherewithal**; find–, have–, possess- means etc. *n.;* have something laid by, –for a rainy day; have powerful friends, have friends at court; have something to draw on; beg, borrow, or steal.

adj. **instrumental** etc. 631; **mechanical** etc. 633.

reliable, trustworthy, efficient; honorable etc. (*upright*) 939.

adv. **by means of**, with; by -what, –all, –any, –some- means; wherewith, herewith, therewith; wherewithal.

how etc. (*in what manner*) 627; through etc. (*by the instrumentality of*) 631; with *or* by the aid of etc. (*assistance*) 707; by the agency of etc. 170.

633. Instrument

n. **machinery**, mechanism, engineering.

instrument, organ, tool, implement, utensil, machine, engine, lathe, gin, mill; air–, caloric–,

heat–, steam–, internal-combustion- engine; motor.

equipment, gear, tackle, tackling; rigging, apparatus, appliances; plant, *matériel* [*F.*]; harness, trappings, fittings, accouterments *or* accoutrements, impedimenta; equipment, equipage; appointments, furniture, upholstery; chattels; paraphernalia etc. (*belongings*) 780.

mechanical powers; mechanical -advantage, –movements, –contrivances; leverage; fulcrum lever, crow, crowbar, gavelock [*Scot. & dial. Eng.*], jemmy, jimmy, marline spike *or* marlinspike, handspike, arm, limb, wing; oar, paddle etc. (*navigation*) 267.

wheel and axle; wheelwork, clockwork; rolling contact; epicyclic train; revolving lever; wheels within wheels; pinion, crank, winch; cam; capstan etc. (*lift*) 307; wheel etc. (*rotation*) 312; bevel gearing, spur gearing, universal joint; fly wheel, governor, turbine, water wheel; pump, lift-pump, force-pump, hydraulic ram.

pulley, crane, derrick; belt, open belt, crossed belt; cone pulley, stepped speed pulley.

inclined plane; wedge; screw; jack; spring, mainspring; can hook, glut, heald, heddle, loom, shuttle, jenny, parbuckle, sprag.

[tools etc.] hammer etc. (*impulse*) 276; edge tool etc. (*cut*) 253; turnscrew, screw driver *or* screwdriver; borer etc. 262; vise, teeth, etc. (*hold*) 781; nail, rope etc. (*join*) 45; peg etc. (*hang*) 214; support etc. 215; spoon etc. (*vehicle*) 272; arms etc. 727.

handle, hilt, haft *or* heft, shaft, shank, blade, trigger, tiller, rudder, helm, treadle, pedal, key; knocker.

adj. **instrumental** etc. 631.

mechanical, machinal [*rare*]; brachial; propulsive, driving, hoisting, elevating, lifting.

useful, labor-saving, ingenious; simple; complicated; well made, well fitted, sharp, in good order, well equipped.

634. Substitute

n. **substitute** etc. 147; proxy, alternate, stand-in [*colloq.*], understudy; deputy etc. 759; *badli* [*Hind.*].

635. Materials

n. **material**, raw material, stuff, stock, staple; ore.

[building material] marble, granite, limestone, freestone, sandstone, brown stone; stone, metal, brick, bricks and mortar; chinking, mortar, lime, chunam [*India*], clay, plaster, daubing, concrete, cement, reinforced concrete; unburnt brick, adobe; composition, compo; slates, tiles; whitewash etc. 223.

wood, timber, clapboard, shingle, shake, puncheon, log, rafter, beam, joist; two-by-four, four-by-four; post, upright, stud, lath; wall board.

materials; supplies, munition, fuel, grist, household stuff; crockery etc. 384; pabulum etc. (*food*) 298; oilcloth, linoleum; ammunition etc. (*arms*) 727; contingents; relay, reënforcement; baggage etc. (*personal property*) 780; means etc. 632.

fabrics, calico, cambric, cashmere, linen, cotton, wool, silk; muslin, lawn, voile, gingham, dimity, broadcloth, homespun, serge, tweed, crêpe de chine, chiffon, satin, velvet.

adj. raw etc. (*unprepared*) 674; finished; wooden etc. *n.;* adobe.

636. Store

n. **stock**, fund, mine, vein, lode, quarry; spring; fount, fountain; well, wellspring [*obs. exc. fig.*]; orchard, garden, farm; milch cow; hen.

stock in trade, supply; heap etc. (*collection*) 72; treasure; reserve, *corps de réserve* [*F.*], reserve fund, nest egg, savings, *bonne bouche* [*F.*].

crop, harvest, vintage, yield, product, gleaning.

store, accumulation, hoard; mow, rick, stack; lumber; relay etc. (*provision*) 637.

storehouse, storeroom, store closet; depository, depot, cache, repository, reservatory [*obs.*], repertory; repertorium [*rare*]; promptuary, warehouse, godown [*Oriental*], entrepôt [*F.*], magazine; buttery, larder, spence [*dial. Eng.*]; garner, granary, grain elevator, silo; cannery, safe-deposit vault, stillroom, bank etc. (*treasury*) 802; armory; arsenal; dock; freight yard, train shed, carbarn, power station; stable, barn, byre, cowhouse; piggery; hen house; fish hatchery; hothouse, conservatory.

quiver, bandolier *or* bandoleer; coffer etc. (*receptacle*) 191.

reservoir, cistern, *aljibar* [*Sp. Am.*], tank, pond, mill pond; gasometer.

[collections] library, public library, library of Congress, British Museum, Bodleian, Bibliothek; gallery, art gallery, picture gallery, Louvre, museum, Madame Tussaud's, zoölogical garden, zoo [*colloq.*], aquarium, menagerie.

work of reference, dictionary, lexicon, encyclopedia *or* encyclopaedia, cyclopedia *or* cyclopaedia, thesaurus, atlas, concordance, anthology.

conservation; storing etc. *v.;* storage.

file, letter file, card index, portfolio, budget; photographic -plate, –film; memory.

v. **store**; put by, lay by, set by; stow away; set apart, lay apart; store up, hoard up, treasure up, lay up, heap up, put up, garner up, save up; bank; cache; accumulate, amass, hoard, fund, garner, save.

reserve; keep back, hold back; husband, –one's resources.

deposit; stow, stack, load; harvest; heap, collect etc. 72; lay in store etc. *adj.;* keep, file [papers]; lay in etc. (*provide*) 637; preserve etc. 670.

adj. **stored** etc. *v.;* in store, in reserve, in ordinary; spare, supernumerary.

adv. for a rainy day, for a nest egg, to fall back upon; on deposit.

637. Provision

n. **provision**, supply; grist, –to the mill; subvention etc. (*aid*) 707; resources etc. (*means*) 632; groceries, grocery.

providing etc. *v.;* purveyance; reenforcement; commissariat.

provender etc. (*food*) 298; ensilage; viaticum; ration; emergency–, iron-ration.

caterer, purveyor, provider, commissary, quartermaster, steward, purser, housekeeper, manciple, feeder, batman, victualer *or* victualler, comprador *or* compradore [*China*], innkeeper, landlord, innholder, mine host, khansamah [*India*], *restaurateur* [*F.*]; grocer, green grocer, huckster, fishmonger, provision merchant; sutler etc. (*merchant*) 797.

provision shop, provision store, meat shop, fish store; market, supermarket, public market; grocery, grocery store.

v. **provide**; make -provision, –due provision for; lay in, –a stock, –a store.

supply, suppeditate [*obs.*]; furnish; find, find one in; arm.

cater, victual, provision, purvey, forage; beat up for; stock, –with; make good, replenish; fill, –up; recruit, feed.

store, have in -store, –reserve; keep, keep by one; have to fall back upon; store etc. 636; provide against a rainy day etc. (*economy*) 817; conserve, keep, preserve, lay by, gather into barns.

638. Waste

n. **consumption**, expenditure, exhaustion; dispersion etc. 73; ebb; leakage etc. (*exudation*) 295; loss etc. 776; wear and tear; waste; prodigality etc. 818; misuse etc. 679; wasting etc. *v.;* rubbish etc. (*useless*) 645.

v. **consume**, spend, expend, use, swallow up; exhaust; impoverish; spill, drain, empty, deplete; disperse etc. 73.

cast–, fool–, muddle–, throw–, fling–, fritter-away; burn the candle at both ends, waste; squander etc. 818.

labor in vain etc. (*useless*) 645; "waste its sweetness on the desert air" [Gray]; cast pearls before swine; employ a steam engine to crack a nut, waste powder and shot, break a butterfly on a wheel; cut blocks with a razor, pour water into a sieve, tilt at windmills.

run to waste; ebb; leak etc. (*run out*) 295; melt away, run dry, dry up; spoil.

adj. **wasted** etc. *v.;* gone to waste, useless, rendered useless, made unavailable; run to seed; dried up; at a low ebb.

wasteful etc. (*prodigal*) 818; penny wise and pound foolish.

639. Sufficiency

n. **sufficiency**, adequacy, enough, wherewithal, *quantum sufficit* [*L.*], satisfaction, competence; no less.

mediocrity etc. (*average*) 29.

fill; fullness etc. (*completeness*) 52; plenitude, plenty; abundance; copiousness etc. *adj.;* amplitude, galore [*rare*], lots [*colloq.*], profusion; full measure; "good measure, pressed down, and shaken together, and running over" [*Bible*].

luxuriance etc. (*fertility*) 168; affluence etc. (*wealth*) 803; fat of the land; "a land flowing with milk and honey" [*Bible*]; cornucopia; horn of -plenty, –Amalthaea; mine etc. (*stock*) 636.

outpouring; flood etc. (*great quantity*) 31; tide etc. (*river*) 348; repletion etc. (*redundance*) 641; satiety etc. 869.

rich man etc. (*wealth*) 803; financier, banker, creditor etc. 805; plutocrat.

v. **be sufficient** etc. *adj.;* suffice; do, just do [*both colloq.*], satisfy, pass muster; have enough etc. *n.;* eat–, drink–, have- one's fill; roll in, swim in; wallow in etc. (*superabundance*) 641; wanton.

abound, exuberate, teem, flow, stream, rain, shower down; pour, pour in; swarm; bristle with; superabound.

render sufficient etc. *adj.;* replenish etc. (*fill*) 52.

adj. **sufficient**, enough, adequate, up to the mark, commensurate, competent, satisfactory, valid, tangible.

moderate etc. (*temperate*) 953; measured.

ample; full etc. (*complete*) 52; plenty, plentiful, plenteous; plenty as blackberries; copious, abundant; abounding etc. *v.;* replete, enough and to spare, flush; chock-full *or* choke-full; well-stocked, well-provided; liberal; unstinted, unstinting; stintless; without stint; unsparing, unmeasured; lavish etc. 641; wholesale.

unexhausted, unwasted; exhaustless, inexhaustible.

rich; luxuriant etc. (*fertile*) 168; affluent etc. (*wealthy*) 803; wantless; big with etc. (*pregnant*) 161.

adv. **sufficiently**, amply etc. *adj.;* full; in abundance etc. *n.;* with no sparing hand; to one's heart's content, *ad libitum* [*L.*], without stint; to the good.

640. Insufficiency

n. **insufficiency**, inadequacy, inadequateness; incompetence etc. (*impotence*) 158; deficiency etc. (*incompleteness*) 53; imperfection etc. 651; shortcoming etc. 304; paucity; stint; scantiness etc. (*smallness*) 32; none to spare; bare subsistence.

scarcity, dearth; want, need, lack, poverty, exigency; inanition, starvation, famine, drought *or* drouth.

dole, mite, pittance; short -allowance, –commons; half rations; banyan day; fast day, Lent.

depletion, emptiness, poorness etc. *adj.;* vacancy, flaccidity; ebb tide; low water; "a beggarly account of empty boxes" [*Romeo and Juliet*]; indigence etc. 804; insolvency etc. (*nonpayment*) 808.

poor man, pauper etc. 804; bankrupt etc. (*nonpayment*) 808.

miser, niggard etc. (*parsimony*) 819.

v. **be insufficient** etc. *adj.;* not suffice etc. 639; kick the beam; come short of etc. 304; run dry.

want, lack, need, require; *caret* [*L.*]; be in want etc. (*poor*) 804; live from hand to mouth.

render insufficient etc. *adj.;* drain of resources; impoverish etc. (*waste*) 638; stint etc. (*begrudge*) 819; put on short -allowance, –commons.

do insufficiently etc. *adv.;* scotch the snake.

adj. **insufficient**, inadequate; too little etc. 32; not enough etc. 639; unequal to; incompetent etc. (*impotent*) 158; perfunctory etc. (*neglect*) 460; deficient etc. (*incomplete*) 53; wanting etc. *v.;* imperfect etc. 651; ill-furnished, ill-provided, ill-stored, ill-off.

short of, out of, destitute of, devoid of, bereft of etc. 789, denuded of; slack, at a low ebb; empty, vacant, bare; dry, drained.

unprovided, unsupplied, unfurnished; unreplenished, unfed; unstored, untreasured; empty-handed.

meager *or* meagre, poor, thin, scrimp, sparing, stunted, spare, stinted; starved, starveling, emaciated, undernourished, underfed, half-starved, famine-stricken, famished; jejune.

scarce; not to be had, –for love or money, –at any price; scurvy; stingy etc. 819; at the end of one's tether; without resources etc. 632; in want etc. (*poor*) 804; in debt etc. 806; scant etc. (*small*) 32.

adv. insufficiently etc. *adj.;* in default of, for want of; failing.

641. Redundance

n. **redundance;** too much, too many; superabundance, superfluity, superfluence [*obs.*], supersaturation; nimiety [*rare*], transcendency, exuberance, profuseness; profusion etc. (*plenty*) 639; repletion, enough in all conscience, *satis superque* [*L.*], lion's share; more than enough etc. 639; plethora, engorgement, congestion, load, surfeit, sickener; turgescence etc. (*expansion*) 194; overdose, overmeasure, oversupply, overflow; inundation etc. (*water*) 348; avalanche, deluge.

pleonasm etc. (*diffuseness*) 573; too many irons in the fire; *embarras de richesses* [*F.*]; embarrassment of riches; money to burn [*colloq.*].

accumulation etc. (*store*) 636; heap etc. 72; drug, –in the market; glut; crowd; burden.

excess, surplus, overplus; epact; margin; remainder etc. 40; duplicate; surplusage, expletive; work of supererogation; bonus, bonanza.

luxury; extravagance etc. (*prodigality*) 818; exorbitance, lavishment; intemperance etc. 954.

v. **superabound,** overabound; know no bounds, swarm; meet one at every turn; creep with, bristle with; overflow; run–, flow–, well–, brim-over; run riot; overrun, overstock, overlay, overcharge, overdose, overfeed, overburden, overload, overdo, overwhelm, overshoot the mark etc. (*go beyond*) 303; surcharge, supersaturate, gorge, glut, load, drench, whelm, inundate, deluge, flood; drug, –the market; hepatize.

send–, carry- -coals to Newcastle, –owls to Athens; teach one's grandmother to suck eggs [*colloq.*]; *pisces natare docere* [*L.*]; kill the slain, butter one's bread on both sides, put butter upon bacon; employ a steam engine to crack a nut etc. (*waste*) 638.

wallow in; roll in etc. (*plenty*) 639; remain on one's hands, hang heavy on hand, go a-begging *or* go begging; exaggerate etc. 549.

cloy, choke, accloy [*archaic*], suffocate; pile up, lay on thick; lay it on, –with a trowel; impregnate with; lavish etc. (*squander*) 818.

adj. **redundant;** too much, too many; exuberant, inordinate, superabundant, excess, overmuch, replete, profuse, lavish; prodigal etc. 818; exorbitant; overweening; extravagant; overcharged etc. *v.;* supersaturated, drenched, overflowing; running -over, –to waste, –down.

crammed–, filled- to overflowing; gorged, stuffed, smothered, ready to burst; dropsical, turgid, plethoric; full-blooded, haematose *or* hematose; obese etc. 194.

superfluous, unnecessary, needless, supervacaneous [*obs.*], uncalled for, to spare, in excess; over and above etc. (*remainder*) 40; *de trop* [*F.*]; adscititious etc. (*additional*) 37; supernumerary etc. (*reserve*) 636; on one's hands, spare, duplicate, supererogatory, expletory, expletive; *un peu fort* [*F.*].

adv. **over and above;** over much, too much; too far; over, too; without–, beyond–, out of- measure; with . . . to spare; over head and ears; over one's head; up to one's -eyes, –ears; extra; beyond the mark etc. (*overrun*) 303; *acervatim* [*L.*].

642. Importance

n. **importance,** consequence, moment, prominence, consideration, mark, materialness, materiality.

greatness etc. 31; superiority etc. 33; notability etc. (*repute*) 873; weight etc. (*influence*) 175; value etc. (*goodness*) 648; usefulness etc. 644.

import, significance, concern; emphasis, interest.

gravity, seriousness, solemnity; no joke, no laughing matter; pressure, urgency, stress; matter of life and death.

memorabilia, notabilia, great doings; red-letter day.

salient point, outstanding feature; great -thing, –point; main chance, "the be-all and the end-all" [*Macbeth*]; cardinal point; substance, gist etc. (*essence*) 5; sum and substance, gravamen, head and front; important–, principal–, prominent–, essential- part; half the battle; *sine qua non* [*L.*]; breath of one's nostrils etc. (*life*) 359; cream, salt, core, kernel, heart, nucleus; key, keynote; keystone; corner stone; trump card etc. (*device*) 626.

chief, top sawyer, first fiddle, top banana [*cant*], prima donna, triton among the minnows; "it"; the only pebble on the beach; burra (*or* bara) sahib [*India*]; bigwig etc. 875.

v. **be important** etc. *adj.;* be somebody, be something; import, signify, matter, be an object; carry weight etc. (*influence*) 175; make a figure etc. (*repute*) 873; be in the ascendant, come to the front, lead the way, take the lead, play first fiddle, throw all else into the shade; lie at the root of; deserve–, merit–, be worthy of- -notice, –regard, –consideration.

value; attach–, ascribe–, give- importance etc. *n.*- to; care for; set store -upon, –by; mark etc. 550; mark with a white stone, underline; write–, put–, print- in -italics, –capitals, –large letters, –large type, –bold-faced type, -letters of gold; accentuate, emphasize, lay stress on.

make much of; make -a fuss, –a stir, –a piece of work, –much ado- about.

adj. **important**; of importance etc. *n.;* momentous, material; to the point; not to be -overlooked, –despised, –sneezed at [*colloq.*]; egregious; weighty etc. (*influential*) 175; of note etc. (*repute*) 873; notable, prominent, salient, signal; memorable, remarkable; worthy of -remark, –notice; never to be forgotten; stirring, eventful.

in the front rank, first-rate, A1 *or* A number 1 [*colloq.*], first chop [*Anglo-Ind. & colloq.*]; superior etc. 33; considerable etc. (*great*) 31; marked etc. *v.;* rare etc. 137.

grave, serious, earnest, noble, grand, solemn, impressive, commanding, imposing.

urgent, pressing, critical, instant.

paramount, essential, vital, all-absorbing, radical, cardinal, chief, main, prime, primary, principal, leading, capital, foremost, overruling; of vital etc. importance.

significant, telling, trenchant, emphatic, pregnant; *tanti* [*L.*].

adv. **in the main**; materially etc. *adj.;* above all, in the first place, before everything else; *kat' exochen* [*Gr.*], *par excellence* [*F.*], to crown all.

643. Unimportance

n. **unimportance**, insignificance, nothingness, immateriality.

triviality, levity, frivolity, fribble; paltriness etc. *adj.;* poverty; smallness etc. 32; vanity etc. (*uselessness*) 645; matter of indifference etc. 866; no object.

nothing, –to signify, –worth speaking of, –particular, –to boast of, –to speak of; small–, no great–, trifling etc. *adj.*- matter; mere joke, mere nothing; hardly–, scarcely- anything; nonentity, small beer, cipher; no great shakes [*colloq.*], *peu de chose* [*F.*]; child's play.

toy, plaything, popgun, paper pellet, gimcrack, gewgaw, bauble, trinket, bagatelle, kickshaw, knickknack, whimwham, trifle, "trifles light as air" [*Othello*].

trumpery, trash, rubbish, stuff, *fatras* [*F.*], frippery; "leather or prunello" [Pope]; fiddle-faddle [*colloq.*], fingle-fangle; chaff, drug, froth, bubble, smoke, cobweb; weed; refuse etc. (*inutility*) 645; scum etc. (*dirt*) 653.

joke, jest, snap of the fingers, snap of one's thumb; fudge etc. (*unmeaning*) 517; fiddlestick, pack of nonsense, mere farce.

trifle, straw, pin, fig, fico [*archaic*], button, rush; bulrush, feather, half-penny, farthing, brass farthing, doit, peppercorn, iota, tinker's dam (*or* damn), continental, jot, mote, rap, pinch of snuff, old song; cent, mill, picayune; pai, pice [*both India*]; pistareen, red cent.

nine days' wonder, *ridiculus mus* [*L.*]; flash in the pan etc. (*impotence*) 158; much ado about nothing etc. (*overestimation*) 482; tempest–, storm- in a teapot.

minutiae, details, minor details, small fry; dust in the balance, feather in the scale, drop in the ocean, fleabite, pin prick, molehill.

v. **be unimportant** etc. *adj.;* not matter etc. 642; go for–, matter–, signify- -little, –nothing, –little or nothing; not matter a straw etc. *n.*

make light of etc. (*underestimate*) 483; catch at straws etc. (*overestimate*) 482; tumble–, stumble- over one's shadow; make mountains out of molehills, make much ado about nothing.

adj. **unimportant**; of -little, –small, –no- -account, –importance etc. 642; immaterial; nonessential, unessential, irrelevant, not vital, uninteresting; indifferent, amateurish.

subordinate etc. (*inferior*) 34; mediocre etc. (*average*) 29; passable, fair, respectable, tolerable, commonplace; uneventful, mere, common; ordinary etc. (*habitual*) 613; inconsiderable, soso *or* so-so, insignificant, nugatory, inappreciable.

trifling, trivial; slight, slender, light, flimsy, frothy, idle; puerile etc. (*fool-*ish) 499; airy, shallow; weak etc. 160; powerless etc. 158; frivolous, petty, niggling; peddling, piddling, fribbling, fribble, inane, ridiculous, farcical; finical, finicking *or* finicky *or* finikin, mincing, fiddle-faddle [*colloq.*], namby-pamby, wishy-washy [*colloq.*], milk and water, insipid.

paltry, poor, pitiful; contemptible etc. (*contempt*) 930; sorry, mean, meager *or* meagre, shabby, miserable, wretched, vile, scrubby, scrannel [*archaic*], weedy, niggardly, scurvy, beggarly, worthless, twopenny-halfpenny, two-for-a-cent, two-bit, two-by-four, cheap, trashy, catchpenny, gimcrack, trumpery; one-horse.

not worth -the pains, −while, −mentioning, −speaking of, −a thought, −a curse, −a cent, −a rap, −a hair, −a straw etc. *n.;* beneath contempt, below par; not up to -sample, −specification; beneath−, unworthy of- -notice, −regard - consideration; *de lana caprina* [*L.*]; vain etc. (*useless*) 645.

adv. **slightly** etc. *adj.;* rather, somewhat, pretty well, fairly, fairly well, tolerably.

for aught one cares; it matters not, it does not signify; it is of no -consequence, −importance.

int. **no matter**! pish! tush! tut! pshaw! pugh! pooh, −pooh! fudge! bosh! humbug! fiddlestick, −end! fiddledeedee! never mind! *n'importe!* [*F.*]; what signifies! what matter! what boots it! what of that! what's the odds! a fig for! stuff! nonsense! stuff and nonsense!

644. Utility

n. **utility**; usefulness etc. *adj.;* efficacy, efficiency, adequacy; service, use, stead, avail, boot [*archaic*]; help etc. (*aid*) 707; applicability etc. *adj.;* subservience etc. (*instrumentality*) 631; function etc. (*business*) 625; value; worth etc. (*goodness*) 648; money's worth; productiveness etc. 168; *cui bono* etc. (*intention*) 620; utilization etc. (*use*) 677; step in the right direction.

commonweal *or* common weal; commonwealth; public -good, −service, −interest; utilitarianism etc. (*philanthropy*) 910; public servant.

v. **be useful** etc. *adj.;* avail, serve; subserve [*rare*] etc. (*be instrumental to*) 631; conduce etc. (*tend*) 176; answer−, serve- -one's turn, −a purpose.

act a part etc. (*action*) 680; perform−, discharge -a function etc. 625; do−, render- -a service, −good service, −yeoman's service; bestead, stand one in good stead; be the making of; help etc. 707.

benefit etc. (*do good*) 648; bear fruit etc. (*produce*) 161; bring grist to the mill; profit, remunerate.

find one's -account, −advantage- in; reap the benefit of etc. (*be better for*) 658.

render useful etc. (*use*) 677.

adj. **useful**; of use etc. *n.;* serviceable, proficuous [*obs.*], good for; subservient etc. (*instrumental*) 631; conducive etc. (*tending*) 176; subsidiary etc. (*helping*) 707.

advantageous etc. (*beneficial*) 648; profitable, gainful, remunerative, worth one's salt; valuable; invaluable, beyond price, of general utility; prolific etc. (*productive*) 168.

adequate; efficient, efficacious; effective, effectual; expedient etc. 646.

applicable, usable, available, ready, handy, at hand, tangible; commodious, adaptable; of all work.

adv. **usefully** etc. *adj.*

for use, for service; in the public service; for the good of the -people, −public, −service; *pro bono publico* [*L.*].

645. Inutility

n. **inutility**; uselessness etc. *adj.;* inefficacy, futility; ineptitude, inaptitude; inadequacy etc. (*insufficiency*) 640; unfitness; inefficiency etc. (*incompetence*) 158; unskillfulness etc. 699; disservice; unfruitfulness etc. (*unproductiveness*) 169; labor -in vain, −lost, -of Sisyphus; lost -trouble, −labor; work of Penelope; Penelope's web; sleeveless [*obs.*]−, bootless- errand; wild-goose chase, mere farce.

redundance, supererogation etc. 641; tautology etc. (*repetition*) 104.

worthlessness; vanity, *vanitas vanitatum* [*L.*], inanity, nugacity; triviality etc. (*unimportance*) 643.

worthless residue, *caput mortuum* [*L., old chem.*]; waste paper, dead letter; blunt tool.

rubbish, junk, lumber, litter, odds and ends, cast-off clothes; button top; shoddy; rags, orts [*archaic*], leavings, dross, trash, refuse, sweepings, scourings, offscourings, waste, rubble, *débris* [*F.*]; chaff, stubble, broken meat; dregs etc. (*dirt*) 653; weeds, tares; rubbish heap, dust hole; *rudera* [*L.*], deads, slag.

idler; *fruges consumere natus* [Horace] etc. (*drone*) 683.

v. **be useless** etc. *adj.;* go a-begging etc. (*redundant*) 641; fail etc. 732.

labor in vain; seek−, strive- after impossibilities; use vain efforts, roll the stone of Sisyphus, beat the air, lash the waves, *battre l'eau avec un bâton* [*F.*], *donner un coup d'épée dans l'eau* [*F.*], fish in the air, milk the ram, drop a bucket into an empty well, pour water into a sieve, sow the sand; bay the moon; preach−, speak- to the winds; whistle jigs to a milestone; kick against the pricks, *se battre contre des moulins* [*F.*]; lock the stable door when the steed is stolen etc. (*too late*) 135; hold a farthing candle to the sun; cast pearls before swine etc. (*waste*) 638; carry coals to Newcastle etc. (*redundance*) 641; wash a blackamoor white etc. (*impossible*) 471.

render useless etc. *adj.;* dismantle, dismast, dismount, disqualify, disable; unrig [*chiefly naut.*]; hamstring, hock *or* hough, cripple, lame etc. (*injure*) 659; spike guns, clip the wings; put out of gear; throw a wrench in the machinery, throw a monkey-wrench into the works.

adj. **useless**, inutile, nugatory, inefficacious, futile, unavailing, bootless; inoperative etc. 158; inadequate etc. (*insufficient*) 640; inservient [*obs.*], inept, inefficient etc. (*impotent*) 158; of no avail etc. (*use*) 644; ineffectual etc. (*failure*) 732; incompetent etc. (*unskillful*) 699; "weary, stale, flat, and unprofitable" [*Hamlet*]; superfluous etc. (*redundant*) 641; dispensable; thrown away etc. (*wasted*) 638; abortive etc. (*immature*) 674.

worthless, valueless, unsalable; not worth a straw etc. (*trifling*) 643; dear at any price.

vain, empty, inane; gainless, profitless, fruitless; unserviceable, unprofitable; ill-spent; effete, barren, sterile, impotent, worn out; unproductive etc. 169; *hors de combat* [*F.*], past work etc. (*impaired*) 659; obsolete etc. (*old*) 124; fit for the dust hole; good for nothing; of no earthly use; not worth -having, −powder and shot; leading to no end, uncalled for; unnecessary, unneeded, superfluous.

adv. **uselessly** etc. *adj.;* to -little, −no, −little or no-purpose.

int. *cui bono?* [*L.*]; what's the good! what's the use!

646. Expedience

[specific subservience]

n. **expedience** *or* expediency, desirability, desirableness etc. *adj.;* fitness etc. (*agreement*) 23; utility etc. 644; propriety; opportunism; advantage, opportunity; pragmatism, pragmaticism; a working proposition.

high time etc. (*occasion*) 134; suitable time *or* season, tempestivity [*obs.*].

v. **be expedient** etc. *adj.;* suit etc. (*agree*) 23; befit; suit-, befit- the -time, −season, −occasion; produce the goods [*colloq.*].

conform etc. 82.

adj. **expedient**; desirable, advisable, acceptable; convenient; worth while, meet; fit, fitting; due, proper, eligible, seemly, becoming; befitting etc. *v.;* opportune etc. (*in season*) 134; in

loco [*L.*]; suitable etc. (*accordant*) 23; applicable etc. (*useful*) 644.

practical, practicable, effective, pragmatic, pragmatical.

adv. **conveniently** etc. *adj.;* in the nick of time; in the right place.

647. Inexpedience

n. **inexpedience** *or* inexpediency, undesirability, undesirableness etc. *adj.;* discommodity, impropriety; unfitness etc. (*disagreement*) 24; inutility etc. 645; disadvantage, disadvantageousness, inconvenience, inadvisability.

v. **be inexpedient** etc. *adj.;* come amiss etc. (*disagree*) 24; embarrass etc. (*hinder*) 706; put to inconvenience.

adj. **inexpedient**, undesirable; unadvisable [*rare*], inadvisable, unsuitable, troublesome, objectionable; inapt, ineligible, inadmissible, inconvenient; incommodious, discommodious; disadvantageous; inappropriate, unfit etc. (*inconsonant*) 24.

ill-contrived, ill-advised; unsatisfactory; unprofitable etc., inept etc. (*useless*) 645; inopportune etc. (*unseasonable*) 135; out of-, in the wrong- place; improper, unseemly.

clumsy, awkward; cumbrous, cumbersome; lumbering, unwieldy, hulky; unmanageable etc. (*impracticable*) 704; impedient etc. (*in the way*) 706.

unnecessary etc. (*redundant*) 641.

648. Goodness

[capability of producing good, good qualities]

n. **goodness** etc. *adj.;* excellence, merit; virtue etc. 944; value, worth, price.

superexcellence, supereminence, quintessence; superiority etc. 33; perfection etc. 650; *coup de maître* [*F.*]; masterpiece, *chef d'oeuvre* [*F.*], prime, flower, cream, *élite* [*F.*], pick, nonesuch [*now rare*], A1 *or* A number 1 [*colloq.*], *nonpareil* [*F.*], *crème de la crème* [*F.*], flower of the flock, cock of the walk, salt of the earth; champion; prodigy, wonder, best ever [*colloq.*].

gem, −of the first water; *bijou* [*F.*], precious stone, jewel, pearl, diamond, ruby, brilliant, treasure; tidbit, good thing; *rara avis* [*L.*], one in a thousand.

beneficence etc. 906.

good man etc. 948.

v. **be beneficial** etc. *adj.;* produce *or* do good etc. 618; profit etc. (*be of use*) 644; benefit; confer a benefit etc. 618.

produce a good effect; be the making of, do a world of good, make a man of; do a good turn, confer an obligation; improve etc. 658.

do no harm, break no bones.

be good etc. *adj.;* be pure gold, be all wool; be the real -thing, −article; look good to [*colloq.*]; excel, transcend etc. (*be superior*) 33; bear away the bell.

stand the -proof, −test; pass muster, pass an examination.

vie, challenge comparison, emulate, rival.

adj. **beneficial**, valuable, of value; serviceable etc. (*useful*) 644; advantageous, profitable, edifying; salutary etc. (*healthful*) 656.

harmless, hurtless; unobnoxious; innocuous, innocent, inoffensive.

favorable; propitious etc. (*hopegiving*) 858; fair.

good, good as gold; excellent; better; superior etc. 33; above par; nice, fine; genuine etc. (*true*) 494.

choice, best, select, picked, elect, *recherché* [*F.*], rare, priceless; unparagoned [*rare*], matchless, peerless, unequaled *or* unequalled, unparalleled etc. (*supreme*) 33; superlatively etc. (33)- good; bully [*slang*], crackerjack [*slang*], gilt-edge *or* gilt-edged [*colloq.*]; superfine, superexcellent; of the first water; first-rate, first-class; high-wrought, exquisite, very best, crack [*colloq.*], prime, tip-top [*colloq.*], capital, cardinal; standard etc. (*perfect*) 650; inimitable.

admirable, estimable; praiseworthy etc. (*approve*) 931; pleasing etc. 829; *couleur de rose* [*F.*], precious, of great price; costly etc. (*dear*) 814; worth -its weight in gold, −a king's ransom; priceless, invaluable, inestimable, precious as the apple of the eye.

satisfactory, up to the mark, unexceptionable, unobjectionable; tidy [*colloq.*].

in -good, −fair- condition; unspoiled, fresh; sound etc. (*perfect*) 650.

adv. **beneficially** etc. *adj.;* well etc. 618; for one's benefit.

649. Badness

[capability of producing evil, bad qualities]

n. **hurtfulness** etc. *adj.;* virulence.

bane etc. 663; plague spot etc. (*insalubrity*) 657; evil star, ill wind; hoodoo [*colloq.*], jinx [*slang*], *jadu* [*Hind.*], Jonah; snake in the grass, skeleton in the closet; *amari aliquid* [*L.*]; thorn in the -side, −flesh.

malignity, damnability, damnification, damnifying; malevolence etc. 907; tender mercies [*irony*].

ill-treatment, annoyance, molestation, abuse, oppression, persecution, outrage; misusage etc. 679; *damnum* [*L.*], scathe; injury etc. (*damage*) 659; Mickey, Mickey Finn [*both slang*], knockout drops.

badness etc. *adj.;* peccancy, abomination; painfulness etc. 830; pestilence etc. (*disease*) 655; guilt etc. 947; depravity etc. 945.

bad man etc. 949; evildoer etc. 913.

v. **be hurtful** etc. *adj.;* cause-, produce-, inflict-, work-, do- evil etc. 619; damnify, endamage, hurt, harm, scathe; injure etc. (*damage*) 659; pain etc. 830.

wrong, aggrieve, oppress, persecute; trample-, tread-, bear hard-, put-upon; overburden; weigh -down, −heavy on; victimize; run down, run hard; thwart; molest etc. 830.

maltreat, abuse; ill-use, illtreat; buffet, bruise, scratch, maul; smite etc. (*scourge*) 972; do violence, do a mischief; stab, pierce, outrage.

do mischief, do harm, make mischief, bring-, lead-, get- into trouble; hex, hoodoo [*colloq.*].

destroy etc. 162.

adj. **hurtful**, harmful, scathful [*obs. or dial.*], scatheful, baneful, baleful, injurious, deleterious, detrimental, noxious, pernicious, mischievous, full of mischief, mischief-making, malefic, malignant, nocuous, noisome; prejudicial; disserviceable, disadvantageous; wide-wasting.

unlucky, sinister; obnoxious; untoward, disastrous.

oppressive, burdensome, onerous; malign etc. (*malevolent*) 907.

corrupting etc. (*corrupt* etc. 659); virulent, venomous, envenomed, corrosive; poisonous etc. (*morbific*) 657; deadly etc. (*killing*) 361; destructive etc. (*destroying*) 162; inauspicious etc. 859.

bad, ill, arrant, as bad as bad can be, dreadful; horrid, horrible; dire; rank, peccant, foul, fulsome; rotten, rotten at the core.

unsatisfactory, indifferent; injured etc. deteriorated etc. 659; exceptionable, below par etc. (*imperfect*) 651; ill-contrived, ill-disposed, ill-conditioned.

deplorable, wretched, sad, grievous, lamentable, pitiful, pitiable, woeful etc. (*painful*) 830; mean etc. (*paltry*) 643.

evil, wrong; depraved etc. 945; shocking; reprehensible etc. (*disapproved*) 932.

hateful, −as a toad; abominable, vile, base, villainous, detestable, execrable, cursed, accursed, confounded; damned, damnable,

223

damnatory, damnific [*rare*]; infernal; diabolic etc. (*malevolent*) 907.

inadvisable, unadvisable [*rare*] etc. (*inexpedient*) 647; unprofitable etc. (*useless*) 645; incompetent etc. (*unskillful*) 699; irremediable etc. (*hopeless*) 859.

adv. **badly** etc. *adj.;* wrong, ill; to one's cost; where the shoe pinches; with malignity etc. *n.*

650. Perfection

n. **perfection**; perfectness etc. *adj.;* indefectibility; impeccancy, impeccability.

paragon, pink, *beau ideal* [*F.*]; pink–, acme– of perfection; *ne plus ultra* [*L.*]; summit etc. 210. [comparisons] *cygne noir* [*F.*]; Phoenix *or* Phenix; black tulip, *tulipe noir* [*F.*]; philosopher's stone; Koh-i-noor.

model, standard, pattern, mirror, Admirable Crichton; trump, brick, corker, caution, humdinger [*all slang*]; "the observed of all observers" [*Hamlet*], very prince of.

Bayard, *chevalier sans peur et sans reproche* [*F.*]; Roland, Sidney.

masterpiece, masterstroke, prize-winner, prize; superexcellence etc. (*goodness*) 648; transcendence etc. (*superiority*) 33.

v. **be perfect** etc. *adj.;* transcend etc. (*be supreme*) 33.

perfect, bring to perfection, ripen, mature; consummate, crown, put the finishing touch to (*or* upon); complete etc. 729; put in trim etc. (*prepare*) 673; maturate [*rare*].

adj. **perfect**, faultless; indefective [*rare*], indeficient [*rare*], indefectible; immaculate, spotless, impeccable; free from imperfection etc. 651; unblemished, uninjured etc. 659; sound, –as a roach; in perfect condition; scathless [*obs. or dial.*], scatheless, intact, harmless; seaworthy etc. (*safe*) 644; right as a trivet; *in se ipso totus teres atque rotundus* [Hor.]; consummate etc. (*complete*) 52; finished etc. 729; complete in itself; well-rounded.

best etc. (*good*) 648; model, standard; inimitable, unparagoned [*rare*], unparalleled etc. (*supreme*) 33; superhuman, divine; beyond all praise etc. (*approbation*) 931; *sans peur et sans reproche* [*F.*].

adv. **to perfection**; perfectly etc. *adj.; ad unguem* [*L.*]; clean, –as a whistle; with a finish; to the limit.

651. Imperfection

n. **imperfection**; imperfectness etc. *adj.;* deficiency; inadequacy etc. (*insufficiency*) 640; pec-

cability, defection, peccancy etc. (*badness*) 649; immaturity etc. 674.

fault, defect, "little rift within the lute" [Tennyson], weak point; screw loose; flaw etc. (*break*) 70; gap etc. 198; twist etc. 243; taint, attainder; *mésalliance* [*F.*], bar sinister; hole in one's coat; blemish etc. 848; weakness etc. 160; shortcoming etc. 304; drawback; seamy side.

half blood, drop of black blood, touch of the tar-brush [*colloq.*].

mediocrity; no great -shakes, –catch [*both colloq.*]; not much to boast of; one-horse shay; one-horse town; peanut -politics, –policy.

v. **be imperfect** etc. *adj.;* rot before it ripens, bear within it the seeds of decay; have a defect etc. *n.;* lie under a disadvantage; spring a leak.

not pass muster, barely pass muster; fall short etc. 304.

adj. **imperfect**; not perfect etc. 650; deficient, defective; faulty, unsound, tainted, specked; mutilated; out of order; out of tune, cracked; leaky; sprung; warped etc. (*distort*) 243; lame; injured etc. (*deteriorated*) 659; peccant etc. (*bad*) 649; frail etc. (*weak*) 160; inadequate etc. (*insufficient*) 640; crude etc. (*unprepared*) 674; incomplete etc. 53; found wanting; below par; short-handed; below–, under– its full -strength, –complement.

indifferent, middling, ordinary, mediocre; average etc. 29; soso *or* so-so; *couci-couci* [*F.*], milk-and-water; tolerable, fair, passable; pretty -well, –good; rather–, moderately- good; good–, well- enough; decent; not bad, not amiss; unobjectionable, admissible, bearable, better than nothing.

secondary, inferior; second-rate, second best; one-horse; two-bit, two-by-four.

adv. **almost** etc.; to a limited extent, rather etc. 32; pretty, moderately; only, considering, all things considered, enough; might be worse.

652. Cleanness

n. **cleanness** etc. *adj.;* purity; cleaning etc. *v.;* purification, defecation etc. *v.;* purgation, lustration; abstersion [*rare*], detersion; aspersion, asperges [*R. C. Ch.*]; epuration [*rare*], mundation [*obs.*], ablution, lavation, colature [*obs.*]; disinfection etc. *v.;* drainage, sewerage.

bath, bathroom, swimming pool, natatorium, swimming bath, public bath, baths, bathhouse, hot bath, sauna etc. 386; lavatory; laundry, washhouse.

cleaner, washerwoman, laundress, dhobi [*India*], laundryman, washerman; scavenger, sweeper; mehtar (*fem.* mehtrani), bhangi [*all India*]; mud lark [*slang*]; sanitation worker, crossing–, street- sweeper, white wings; dustman; sweep.

brush; broom, besom, vacuum cleaner, carpet sweeper; mop, swab, hose; scraper; rake, shovel; sieve, riddle, screen, filter; blotter.

napkin, serviette, cloth, maukin [*obs.*], malkin [*obs.*], handkerchief, towel, sudary, sudarium, face cloth, wash cloth; doily *or* doyley, bib; carving cloth, tablecloth; duster, sponge.

mat, doormat, rug, drugget, cover.

[cleansing agents] wash, lotion, detergent, soap, purifier etc. *v.;* disinfectant; benzene, benzine, benzol, benzolin; bleaching powder, chloride of lime; lye, buck.

dentifrice, tooth paste, tooth powder; mouth wash.

cathartic, purgative, aperient, deobstruent, laxative.

v. **be** *or* **render clean** etc. *adj.*

clean, cleanse; mundify [*obs.*], rinse, wring, flush, full, wipe, mop, sponge, scour, swab, scrub.

wash, lave etc. (*water*) 337; launder, buck; absterge [*rare*], deterge; decrassify; clear, purify; depurate, spurate [*rare*], despumate, defecate; purge, expurgate, elutriate, lixiviate, edulcorate, clarify, refine, rack; percolate, separate, strain, filter, filtrate, drain.

sift, winnow, sieve, bolt, screen, riddle; pick, weed.

comb, rake, scrape, rasp; hackle, heckle, card.

sweep, brush, brush up, whisk, broom, vacuum [*colloq.*].

rout–, clear–, sweep etc.- out; make a clean sweep of, clean house, spruce up [*colloq.*].

disinfect, fumigate, ventilate, deodorize; whitewash.

adj. **clean**, cleanly; pure; immaculate; spotless, stainless, taintless, trig [*dial.*], without a stain, unstained, unspotted, unsoiled, unsullied, untainted, uninfected; sweet, –as a nut.

neat, spruce, tidy, trim, jimp *or* gimp [*Scot. & dial. Eng.*], clean as a new penny, like a cat in pattens; cleaned etc. *v.;* kempt [*archaic*].

abstergent, detergent, depurative, abstersive [*rare*], cathartic, cleansing, purifying.

adv. **neatly** etc. *adj.;* clean as a whistle.

653. Uncleanness

n. **uncleanness** etc. *adj.;* impurity; immundity [*rare*], immundicity [*rare*], mucidness, impurity etc. (of mind) 961.

defilement, contamination etc. *v.;* defoedation [*obs.*]; soilure, soiliness [*obs.*]; abomination; taint, tainture [*obs.*]; fetor etc. 401.

lousiness, pediculosis, pediculation, phthiriasis [*med.*].

decay; putrescence, putrefaction; corruption; mold *or* mould, must, mildew, dry rot, mucor [*rare*], caries [*med.*], rubigo [*obs.*].

slovenry; slovenliness etc. *adj.;* squalor.

dowdy, drab, slut, malkin *or* mawkin [*obs. or dial. Eng.*], slattern, sloven, slammerkin [*obs.*], slammock *or* slummock [*dial.*], drabble-tail, draggle-tail, mud lark [*slang*], dustman, sweep; beast, pig.

dirt, filth, soil, slop; dust, cobweb, flue; smoke, soot, smudge, smut, grime, raff [*dial.*], riffraff; sossle *or* sozzle [*dial.*].

dregs, sordes, grounds, lees; argol; sediment, settlement; heeltap; dross, drossiness; mother [*obs.*], precipitate, *scoriae* [*L.*], ashes, cinders, recrement, slag; scum, froth.

useless refuse, hogwash [*colloq.*], swill, garbage, ditch water, dishwater, bilge-water; rinsings, cheeseparings; sweepings etc. 645; outscourings, offscourings, offscum; *caput mortuum* [*L.*], residuum, sprue, dross, clinker, draff; scurf, scurfiness; exuviae; furfur, dandruff; tartar, fur.

spawn, offal, gurry; carrion; slough, peccant humor, pus, matter, suppuration.

dung, ordure, lienteria; feces *or* faeces, excrement, feculence; excreta etc. 299; sewage, sewerage [*rare in this sense*]; fertilizer, muck; coprolite; guano, manure, compost.

[receptacles] dunghill, colluvies [*med.*]; mixen, midden [*both archaic or dial. Eng.*], bog, laystall [*obs.*]; cesspool; sump [*Scot. & dial. Eng.*], sough [*dial. Eng.*], cloaca, Cloaca Maxima; sink, drain, sewer, common sewer; Cloacina; dust hole; glory hole [*colloq.*].

water-closet, w. c., toilet [*colloq.*], *cabinet d'aisance* [*F.*], latrine, backhouse, necessary, privy, jakes [*rare*], Mrs. Jones; head [*naval slang*].

sty, pigsty, lair, den, Augean stable, sink of corruption; slum, rookery.

mud, mire, quagmire, alluvium, silt, sludge, slime, slush, slosh [*dial.*], sposh.

vermin, louse, flea, nit, bug, chinch; lice etc. 366.

v. **be** *or* **become unclean** etc. *adj.;* rot, putrefy, fester, rankle, reek; stink etc. 401; mold *or* mould, molder *or* moulder; go bad etc. *adj.*

wallow in the mire; slobber, slabber.

render unclean etc. *adj.;* dirt, dirty; soil, smoke, tarnish, slaver, spot, smear; daub, blot, blur, smudge, smutch, smirch; begrease; drabble, dabble, daggle, spatter, slubber [*dial.*]; besmear etc., bemire, beslime, begrime, befoul; splash, stain, distain [*archaic*], maculate, sully, pollute,

defile, debase, contaminate, taint, leaven; corrupt etc. (*injure*) 659; cover with dust etc.
n.; drabble in the mud; roil.

adj. **unclean**, dirty, filthy, grimy; soiled etc. *v.;* not to
be handled -without gloves, –with kid gloves;
dusty, snuffy, smutty, sooty, smoky; thick, turbid, dreggy; slimy; mussy.

lousy, pedicular, pediculous.

uncleanly, slovenly, slatternly, untidy, sluttish,
dowdy, draggle-tailed, drabble-tailed; uncombed, unkempt, unscoured, unswept, un-
wiped, unwashed, unstrained, unpurified;
squalid; lutose, slammocky *or* slummocky
[*dial.*], sossly *or* sozzly [*dial.*], sloppy [*colloq.*].

offensive, nasty, coarse, foul, impure, abominable, beastly, reeky, reechy [*dial. Eng.*]; fetid etc.
401.

moldy *or* mouldy, musty, fusty, mildewed, rusty,
moth-eaten, mucid, rancid, bad, gone bad, lentiginous *or* lentiginose, touched, reasty [*dial.
Eng.*], rotten, corrupt, tainted, high, flyblown,
maggoty; putrid, putrefactive, putrescent, pu-
trefied; saprogenic *or* saprogenous; purulent,
carious, peccant; fecal, feculent; stercoraceous,
excrementitious; scurfy, impetiginous; gory,
bloody; rotting etc. *v.;* rotten as -a pear,
–cheese.

crapulous etc. (*intemperate*) 954; beastlike; gross
etc. (*impure in mind*) 961; fimetarious, fimicolous.

int. pah! faugh! ugh!

654. Health

n. **health**, sanity; soundness etc. *adj.;* vigor;
good-, perfect-, excellent-, rude-, robust-
health; bloom, *mens sana in corpore sano*
[*L.*]; Hygeia; incorruption, incorruptibility;
valetude [*obs.*]; good state-, clean bill- of
health; eupepsia *or* eupepsy, euphoria *or* eu-
phory; convalescence, upgrade; strength, poise.

v. **be in health** etc. *adj.;* be bursting with -vigor,
–pep [*slang*]; never feel better; bloom, flourish.

keep body and soul together, keep on one's legs;
enjoy -good, –a good state of- health; have a
clean bill of health.

return to health; recover etc. 660; get better etc.
(*improve*) 658; take a -new, –fresh- lease of life;
convalesce, be convalescent; add years to one's
life; recruit; restore to health; cure etc. (*restore*) 660.

adj. **healthy**, healthful; in health etc. *n.;* well, sound,
whole, strong, blooming, hearty, hale, fresh,
green, florid, flush, hardy, stanch *or* staunch,
brave, robust, vigorous, weatherproof.

on one's legs; sound as a -roach, –bell; fresh as -a
daisy, –a rose, –April; walking on air; hearty as
a buck; in -fine, –high- feather; in good case,
in full bloom; pretty bobbish [*Eng. dial. or
slang*]; bursting with -health, –vigor; in fine
fettle; chipper [*colloq.*]; tolerably well, as well as
can be expected.

unscathed, uninjured, unmaimed, unmarred, untainted; sound of wind and limb, without a
scratch, safe and sound.

sanitary etc. (*health-giving*) 656; sanatory etc.
(*remedial*) 662.

655. Disease

n. **disease**; illness, sickness etc. *adj.;* ailing etc.
v.; "the thousand natural shocks That flesh is
heir to" [*Hamlet*]; "all ills that men endure"
[*Cowley*]; morbidity, morbosity [*obs.*]; infirmity, ailment, indisposition; complaint, disorder,
malady, distemperature [*archaic*]; valetudinarianism; loss of health, delicacy, delicate health,
invalidity, invalidism, invalescence [*rare*]; mal-
nutrition, want of nourishment, cachexia *or*
cachexy; prostration, decline, collapse; decay
etc. 659.

visitation, attack, seizure, stroke, fit, epilepsy,
apoplexy, bloodstroke; palsy, paralysis, motor
paralysis, sensory paralysis, hemiplegia, paraplegia *or* paraplegy; *paralysis agitans* [*L.*],
shaking palsy, Parkinson's disease; shock; shell-
shock [*World War I*].

taint, virus, pollution, infection, contagion; sep-
ticaemia *or* septicemia, blood poisoning, pya-
emia *or* pyemia, septicity; epidemic; sporadic,
endemic; plague, pestilence.

fever, calenture; inflammation; ague; intermit-
tent-, remittent-, congestive-, pernicious-
fever; malaria, malarial fever; dengue *or* dandy
fever, breakbone fever; yellow fever, yellow
jack; typhoid *or* typhoid fever, enteric fever;
typhus; eruptive fever; scarlet fever, scarlatina;
smallpox, variola; varioloid; vaccinia, cow pox;
varicella, chicken pox; rubeola, measles.

eruption, rash, brash, breaking out; canker rash;
dartre, exanthema *or* exanthem; scabies, itch,
psora; pox; eczema, tetter, psoriasis; lichen,
papular rash; lichen tropicus, prickly heat; im-
petigo; erythema; erysipelas, St. Anthony's fire;
urticaria, hives, nettlerash; herpes; herpes
zoster, shingles; herpes simplex *and* circinatus,
ringworm; miliaria, pemphigus, rupia.

sore, canker, ulcer, fester, boil, gumboil; pimple
etc. (*swelling*) 250; carbuncle; gathering; abscess, impostume *or* imposthume [*obsoles.*],

apodeme; Rigg's disease, pyorrhea or pyorrhoea; chancre; peccant humor; proud flesh; corruption; enanthem or enanthema, gangrene; mortification, sphacelus, sphacelation; slough, caries, necrosis; cancer, carcinoma; tumor, leprosy.

heart disease, carditis, pericarditis, endocarditis, valvular lesion; hypertrophy–, dilatation–, atrophy–, fatty degeneration- of the heart; angina pectoris.

wasting disease, marasmus, emaciation, atrophy; consumption, white plague, tuberculosis, T.B. [med. cant], phthisis; pulmonary–, galloping- consumption; pulmonary phthisis, phthisi-pneumonia, pneumonia; chlorosis, green sickness; anaemia or anemia; leucocythaenia or leucocythenia.

throat disease, laryngitis, tonsillitis, quinsy, cynanche; bronchitis, diphtheria, whooping cough, pertussis; thrush, canker.

cold, cough; rheum; catarrh, hay fever; influenza, grippe or grip; rose cold.

indigestion, dyspepsia, poor digestion, pyrosis, water qualm; cardialgia, heartburn; seasickness, mal de mer [F.]; nausea; giddiness, vertigo; constipation, autointoxication.

eye disease, trachoma, conjunctivitis, pink eye; cataract, caligo, pin-and-web, gutta serena [L.].

veneral disease, pox, syphilis; gonorrhea or gonorrhoea, blennorrhea or blennorrhoea, blennorrhagia.

[various diseases] headache etc. (physical pain) 378; goiter or goitre, bronchocele, struma, tracheocele; lockjaw, tetanus, trismus; diarrhea or diarrhoea, dysentery, bloody flux, flux, issue, hemorrhage; hemorrhoids, piles; cholera, cholera morbus, Asiatic cholera, cholera infantum, summer complaint; colic; jaundice, icterus; apnea; asthma; king's evil, scrofula; rickets, rachitis; appendicitis; gall-stones, biliary calculus, stone; hernia, rupture; varicosis, varicose veins; arteriosclerosis, hardening of the arteries; neuritis; nervous prostration; St. Vitus's dance, chorea; neurasthenia; sciatica; rheumatism, arthritis, lumbago; dropsy, edema; elephantiasis; beriberi; locomotor ataxia; paresis, softening of the brain; bubonic plague; black death; leprosy, elephantiasis; sleeping sickness.

fatal etc. (hopeless) 859 -disease etc.; dangerous illness, churchyard cough; general breaking up, break-up of the system.

[disease of mind] idiocy etc. 499; insanity etc. 503.

martyr to disease; cripple; "the halt, the lame, and the blind"; valetudinary, valetudinarian; invalid, patient, case.

sick-room, sick-chamber; hospital etc. 662.

[science of disease] pathology, pathogeny, etiology, nosology, nosography, nosogeny, therapeutics; diagnostics, symptomatology, semeiology, semeiography, prognosis, diagnosis; clinic, polyclinic.

[veterinary] anthrax, splenic fever, woolsorter's disease, charbon, milzbrand, malignant pustule, quarter evil, quarter ill, Texas fever, blackwater, murrain, bighead; blackleg, black quarter; cattle plague, glanders, milk sickness; rinderpest, foot-and-mouth disease, hog cholera; epizoötic; heaves, rot, sheep rot; scabies, mange, distemper.

v. **be or feel ill** etc. adj.; ail, suffer, labor under, be affected with, complain of; droop, flag, languish, halt; sicken, peak, pine, dwindle; gasp; drop down in one's tracks; waste away, fail, lose strength, lose one's grip.

keep one's bed; lay by, lay up; be laid by the heels; lie helpless, –on one's back.

fall a victim to–, be stricken by–, take–, catch- -a disease etc. n., - an infection; break out.

malinger, feign sickness etc. (falsehood) 544.

adj. **ailing** etc. v.; ill, ill of; taken ill, seized with; indisposed, unwell, sick, squeamish, poorly, seedy [colloq.]; affected–, afflicted- with illness; laid up, confined, bedridden, invalided, in hospital, on the sick list; out of health, out of sorts [colloq.], under the weather; valetudinary.

unsound, unhealthy; morbose [obs.], healthless, infirm, chlorotic, unbraced, cranky [dial. Eng.], sickly, weakly, weakened etc. (weak) 160; drooping, flagging; lame, halt, crippled, halting; hors de combat [F.] etc. (useless) 645.

touched in the wind, broken-winded, spavined, gasping.

diseased, morbid, tainted, vitiated, peccant, contaminated, poisoned, septic, septical, tabetic, tabid, mangy, leprous, cankered; rotten, –to, –at- the core; withered; palsied, paralytic; dyspeptic; luetic, pneumonic, pulmonic, phthisic or phthisical, consumptive, tubercular, tuberculous, rachitic; syntectic or syntectical, varicose.

decrepit; decayed etc. (deteriorated) 659; incurable etc. (hopeless) 859; in declining health; in a bad way, in danger, prostrate; moribund etc. (death) 360.

epidemic, epizoötic [of animals]; zymotic, contagious; morbific etc. 657.

656. Salubrity

n. **salubrity**, salubriousness, wholesomeness, healthfulness; healthiness etc. *adj.;* Hygeia, Aesculapius.

fine -air, -climate; eudiometer.

[preservation of health] hygiene; valetudinarianism; pure air, exercise, nourishment, tonic; immunity; sanitarium, sanatorium; valetudinarian, sanitarian.

v. **be salubrious** etc. *adj.;* make for health, conduce to health; be good for, agree with; assimilate etc. 23.

adj. **salubrious**, salutary, salutiferous [*rare*]; wholesome; healthy, healthful; sanitary, prophylactic; benign, bracing, tonic, invigorating, good for, nutritious; hygeian, hygienic; Hygeian.

sanative etc. (*remedial*) 662; restorative etc. (*reinstate*) 660; useful etc. 644.

innoxious, innocuous, innocent; harmless, uninjurious, uninfectious; immune.

657. Insalubrity

n. **insalubrity**, insalubriousness; unhealthiness etc. *adj.;* plague spot; malaria etc. (*poison*) 663; death in the pot, contagion; poisonousness, toxicity.

v. **be insalubrious** etc. *adj.;* disagree with; shorten one's days.

adj. **insalubrious**; unhealthy, unwholesome; noxious, noisome; morbific *or* morbifical, morbiferous; mephitic, septic, azotic, deleterious; pestilent, pestiferous, pestilential; virulent, venomous; envenomed, poisonous, toxic, toxiferous, narcotic; deadly etc. (*killing*) 361.

innutritious, unnutritious [*rare*], undigestible [*rare*], indigestible, ungenial; uncongenial etc. (*disagreeing*) 24.

contagious, infectious, catching, taking, communicable, inoculable, epidemic, zymotic, sporadic, endemic, pandemic; epizoötic [*of animals*].

658. Improvement

n. **improvement**, amelioration, melioration, betterment; mend, amendment, emendation; mending etc. *v.;* advancement; advance etc. (*progress*) 282; ascent etc. 305; promotion, preferment; elevation etc. 307; increase etc. 35.

cultivation, culture, march of intellect, menticulture; race-culture, acculturation, civilization; culture zone; eugenics.

reform, reformation; revision, radical reform; second thoughts, correction, refinement, elaboration; purification etc. 652; repair etc. (*restoration*) 660; recovery etc. 660.

revise, revised edition, new edition, new issue.

reformer, reformist, progressive, radical.

v. **improve**; be-, become-, get- better; mend, amend.

advance etc. (*progress*) 282; ascend etc. 305; increase etc. 35; fructify, ripen, mature; pick up, come about, rally, take a favorable turn; turn over a new leaf, turn the corner; raise one's head, have sown one's wild oats; recover etc. 660.

profit by; be better etc. *adj.,* be improved by; turn to -right, -good, -best- account; reap the benefit of; make good use of, make capital out of; place to good account.

render better, improve, mend, amend, better; ameliorate, meliorate, relieve; correct; repair etc. (*restore*) 660; doctor etc. (*remedy*) 662; purify etc. 652; decrassify.

improve-, refine- upon; rectify; enrich, mellow, elaborate, fatten.

refresh, revive; put-, infuse- new blood into; invigorate etc. (*strengthen*) 159; reinvigorate, recruit, renew, make over, revivify, freshen.

promote, cultivate, advance, forward, enhance; bring forward, bring on; foster etc. 707.

touch up, rub up, brush up, furbish up, bolster up, vamp up, brighten up, warm up; polish, cook, make the most of, set off to advantage; prune; put in order etc. (*arrange*) 60.

revise, edit, redact, digest, review, make corrections, make improvements etc. *n.*

reform, remodel, reorganize; build -afresh, -anew; reclaim, civilize; lift, uplift, inspire; new-model.

view in a new light, think better of, appeal from Philip drunk to Philip sober.

palliate, mitigate; lessen etc. (36) an evil.

adj. **better**, -off, -for; all the better for; better advised; improving etc. *v.;* progressive, improved etc. *v.*

reformatory, emendatory; reparatory etc. (*restorative*) 660; remedial etc. 662.

corrigible, improvable, curable; accultural.

adv. **on consideration**, on reconsideration, on second thoughts, on better advice; on the mend, on the upgrade; *ad melius inquirendum* [*L.*].

659. Deterioration

n. **deterioration**, debasement; wane, ebb; recession etc. 287; retrogradation etc. 283; decrease etc. 36.

degeneracy, degeneration, degenerateness; degradation; depravation, depravement [*rare*], depravedness; devolution; depravity etc. 945; demoralization, retrogression; masochism.

impairment, inquination [*obs.*], injury, damage, loss, detriment, delaceration [*obs.*], outrage, havoc, inroad, ravage, scathe, scath [*dial.*], perversion, prostitution, vitiation, discoloration, pollution, defoedation, poisoning, venenation [*rare*], leaven, contamination, canker, corruption, adulteration, alloy.

decline, declension, declination; decadence *or* decadency; falling off etc. *v.;* caducity [*rare*], senility, decrepitude.

decay, dilapidation, ravages of time, wear and tear; erosion, corrosion, moldiness *or* mouldiness; rottenness; moth and rust, dry rot, blight, marcescence, marasmus, atrophy, collapse; disorganization; *délabrement* [*F.*] etc. (*destruction*) 162; aphid, aphis (*pl.* aphides), plant louse; vine fretter, vine grub; gypsy (*or* gipsy) moth; buffalo carpet beetle etc. (*injurious insects*) 913.

wreck, mere wreck, honeycomb, *magni nominis umbra* [*L.*], jade, rackabones, skate; tacky *or* tackey, plug [*slang*].

v. **deteriorate**; be–, become- -worse, –deteriorated etc. *adj.;* have seen better days, degenerate, fall off; wane etc. (*decrease*) 36; ebb; retrograde etc. 283; decline, droop; go down etc. (*sink*) 306; go downhill, go on from bad to worse, go farther and fare worse; jump out of the frying pan into the fire; avoid Scylla and fall into Charybdis.

run to -seed, –waste; swale [*obs.*], sweal [*obs.*]; lapse, be the worse for; sphacelate; break, break down; spring a leak, crack, start; shrivel etc. (*contract*) 195; fade, go off, wither, molder *or* moulder, rot, rankle, decay, go bad; go to–, fall into- decay; fall "into the sere, the yellow leaf" [*Macbeth*]; rust, crumble, shake; totter, –to its fall; perish etc. 162; die etc. 360.

[render less good] deteriorate; weaken etc. 160; put back; taint, infect, contaminate, poison, empoison, envenom, canker, corrupt, exulcerate [*obs.*], pollute, vitiate, inquinate [*obs.*], debase, embase [*obs.*]; denaturalize, leaven; deflower, debauch, defile, deprave, degrade; ulcerate; stain etc. (*dirt*) 653; discolor; alloy, adulterate, sophisticate, tamper with, prejudice.

pervert, prostitute, demoralize, brutalize; render vicious etc. 945.

embitter, acerbate, exacerbate, aggravate.

injure, impair, labefy [*rare*], damage, harm, hurt, shend, scath [*dial.*], scathe, spoil, mar, despoil, dilapidate, waste; overrun; ravage; pillage etc. 791.

wound, stab, pierce, maim, lame, surbate [*obs.*], cripple, hock *or* hough, hamstring, hit between

wind and water, scotch, mangle, mutilate, disfigure, blemish, deface, warp.

blight, rot; corrode, erode; wear away, wear out; gnaw, — at the root of; sap, mine, undermine, shake, sap the foundations of, break up; disorganize, dismantle, dismast; destroy etc. 162.

damnify etc. (*aggrieve*) 649; do one's worst; knock down; deal a blow to; play -havoc, — sad havoc, –the mischief [*colloq.*], –the deuce [*colloq.*], — the very devil [*colloq.*]- -with, — among; decimate.

adj. **deteriorated** etc. *v.;* altered, — for the worse; unimproved etc. (improve etc. 658); injured etc. *v.;* sprung; withering, spoiling etc. *v.;* on the -wane, –decline; tabid; degenerate; worse; the —, all the- worse for; out of -repair, — tune; imperfect etc. 651; the worse for wear; battered; weathered, weather-beaten; stale, *passé* [*F.*], shaken, dilapidated, frayed, faded, wilted, shabby, secondhand, threadbare; worn, –to- -a thread, — a shadow, — the stump, — rags; reduced, — to a skeleton; far-gone; tacky.

decayed etc. *v.;* moth-eaten, worm-eaten; mildewed, rusty, moldy *or* mouldy, spotted, seedy, time-worn, moss-grown; discolored; effete, wasted, crumbling, moldering *or* mouldering, rotten, cankered, blighted, marcescent, tainted; depraved etc. (*vicious*) 945; decrepit; broken-down; done, — for, — up [*all colloq.*]; worn-out, used up [*colloq.*]; fit for the -dust hole, — waste-paper basket; past work etc. (*useless*) 645.

at a low ebb, in a bad way, on one's last legs; undermined, deciduous; nodding to its fall etc. (*destruction*) 162; tottering etc. (*dangerous*) 665; past cure etc. (*hopeless*) 859; washed out, run down; fatigued etc. 688; unprogressive, improgressive [*rare*], backward, stagnant, behind the times; retrograde etc. (*retrogressive*) 283; deleterious etc. 649.

adv. **on the down grade**, on the downward track; beyond hope.

660. Restoration

n. **restoration**, restoral [*rare*], restorance [*obs.*]; reinstatement, replacement, rehabilitation, reëstablishment, reconstitution, reconstruction; reproduction etc. 163; renovation, renewal; revival, revivement [*rare*], reviviscence *or* revivescence; refreshment etc. 689; resuscitation, reanimation, revivification, reviction [*obs.*]; reorganization.

reaction; redemption etc. (*deliverance*) 672; restitution etc. 790; relief etc. 834.

recurrence etc. (*repetition*) 104; *réchauffé* [*F.*], *rifacimento* [*It.*].

renaissance, renascence, rebirth, second youth, rejuvenescence, rejuvenation, new birth; regeneration, regeneracy, regenerateness, regenesis, palingenesis, reconversion; resurgence, resurrection.

redress, retrieval, reclamation, recovery; convalescence; resumption, *résumption* [*F.*]; sanativeness.

cure, recure [*obs.*], sanation [*obs.*]; healing etc. *v.;* redintegration; rectification; instauration; cicatrization; disinfection; delousing, delousement.

repair, repairing, reparation, mending; recruiting etc. *v.;* tinkering.

mender, doctor, physician, surgeon; priest, clergyman, pastor; carpenter, joiner, plumber, tinker, cobbler; reviver, revivor [*rare*], renewer, *vis medicatrix* [*L.*] etc. (*remedy*) 662.

curableness, curability, reparability, restorableness, retrievability, recoverability, recoverableness.

v. **return to the original state**; recover, rally, revive; come to, come round, come to oneself; pull through, weather the storm, be oneself again; get -well, — round, — the better of, — over —, up, — about; rise from -one's ashes, — the grave; resurge, resurrect; survive etc. (*outlive*) 110; resume, reappear; come to, — life again; live again, rise again.

heal, heal over, skin over, cicatrize; right itself, heal itself.

restore, put back, place *in statu quo* [*L.*]; reinstate, replace, reseat, rehabilitate, reëstablish, reëstate, reinstall.

reconstruct, rebuild, reorganize, reconstitute; convert, reconvert; recondition, renew, renovate; regenerate; rejuvenate.

redeem, reclaim, recover, retrieve; rescue etc. (*deliver*) 672.

cure, heal, remedy, doctor, physic, medicate; redress, recure; break of; bring round, set on one's legs.

resuscitate, revive, reanimate, revivify, recall to life; reproduce etc. 163; warm up; reinvigorate, refresh etc. 689.

redintegrate, make whole; recoup etc. 790; make good, make all square; rectify; put —, set- -right, — to rights, — straight; set up, correct; put in order etc. (*arrange*) 60; refit, recruit; fill up, — the ranks; reinforce.

repair, mend; put in repair, put in thorough repair; retouch, botch, vamp, tinker, cobble; do up, patch up, plaster up, vamp up; darn, finedraw, heelpiece; stop a gap, stanch *or* staunch, calk *or* caulk, careen, splice, bind up wounds.

adj. **restored** etc. *v.;* redivivus, redivivous [*rare*], reviviscible, convalescent; in a fair way; none the worse; rejuvenated; renascent.

restoring etc. *v.;* restorative, recuperative; sanative, sanatory; reparative, reparatory; curative, remedial.

restorable, recoverable, remediable, retrievable, curable, sanable [*rare*].

adv. *in statu quo* [*L.*]; as you were.

661. Relapse

n. **relapse**, lapse; falling back etc. *v.;* retrogradation etc. (*retrogression*) 283; deterioration etc. 659. [return to, or recurrence of, a bad state] backsliding, recidivation [*obs.*]; recidivism, recidivity; recrudescence.

v. **relapse**, lapse; fall —, slide —, slip —, sink-back; have a relapse, be overcome, be overtaken, yield again to, fall again into; return; retrograde etc. 283; recidivate [*rare*]; fall off etc. 659- again.

adj. **backsliding**, relapsing etc. *v.;* recidivous, recidivistic, recrudescent, retrograde.

662. Remedy

n. **remedy**, help, redress; anthelmintic, vermifuge, helminthagogue; antifebrile, febrifuge; antipoison, antidote, mithridate [*old pharm.*], theriaca *or* theriac, counterpoison; antispasmodic; lithagogue; bracer, pick-me-up [*colloq.*], stimulant, tonic; abirritant, prophylactic, antiseptic, germicide, bactericide, corrective, restorative; alterant, alterative; cathartic etc. 652; specific; emetic, carminative.

materia medica, pharmacy, pharmacology, pharmaceutics, acology, posology, dosology [*rare*]; pathology etc. 655; pharmacopoeia.

narcotic, nepenthe *or* nepenthes, opium, morphine, cocaine, hashish, methadone, bhang, ganja; dope, speed, grass, crystal, angel dust, acid, horse, coke [*all slang*]; sedative etc. 174.

cure; partial —, attempted —, radical —, perfect —, certain- cure; sovereign remedy, panacea, cure-all, catholicon.

physic, medicine, simples, drug, potion, draft *or* draught, dose, pill, bolus, electuary; lincture *or* linctus; medicament; pharmacon.

nostrum, recipe, receipt, prescription; elixir, *elixir vitae* [*L.*], balm, balsam, cordial, tisane, ptisan.

agueweed, boneset; arnica, benzoin, cream of tartar, bitartrate of potash, calomel, mercurous chloride; catnip, catmint; Epsom salts; fever-root or feverwort, feverweed, friar's balsam, Indian sage; ipecac or ipecacuanha; Peruvian bark, Jesuits' bark, cinchona, quinine or quinin, sassafras, yarrow.

salve, ointment, cerate, oil, lenitive, palliative, lotion, embrocation, liniment.

harquebusade or arquebusade, traumatic, vulnerary, pepastic, maturative, maturant, suppurative; eyewater, collyrium; cosmetic; depilatory.

poultice, cataplasm, vesicatory, plaster, *emplastrum* [*L.*], epithem, sinapism.

compress, pledget; bandage etc. (*support*) 215.

treatment, medical treatment, regimen, diet; dietary, dietetics; *vis medicatrix* [*L.*]; *vis naturae* [*L.*]; *médecine expectante* [*F.*]; bloodletting, bleeding, venesection, phlebotomy, cupping, sanguisuge, leeches; operation, the knife [*colloq.*], surgical operation; major operation; electrolysis, electrolyzation.

healing art, leechcraft [*archaic*], practice of medicine, therapeutics; allopathy, homeopathy, osteopathy, eclecticism, heteropathy; gynecology, gyniatrics, gynecological therapeutics; pediatrics; surgery, chirurgery [*archaic*]; orthopedics, orthopedia or orthopaedia, orthopraxy, orthopraxis, orthopedic surgery; sarcology, organotherapy; hydrotherapy, hydropathy, cold-water cure; faith cure, faith healing, mind cure, psychotherapy, psychotherapeutics; Christian Science, Eddyism; radiotherapy, heliotherapy, serotherapy, serum therapy; aerotherapy, pneumatotherapy; occupational or vocational therapy; dentistry, surgical dentistry; midwifery, obstetrics, tocology.

hospital, infirmary, clinic, *hôpital* [*F.*], general hospital, *hotel-Dieu* [*F.*]; special hospital (cancer, children's, dental, fever, maternity or lying-in, ophthalmic etc); pesthouse, lazarhouse, lazaretto, lazaret; lock hospital [*Eng.*]; *maison de santé* [*F.*]; *Hôtel des Invalides* [*F.*]; sanatarium, sanitarium, sanatorium, springs, baths, spa, pump room, well; hospice; asylum, home; Red Cross; ambulance.

dispensary, dispensatory, drug store, chemist's shop [*Brit.*].

doctor, physician, leech [*archaic*], medical man, disciple of Aesculapius; medical —, general-practitioner; medical attendant, specialist; surgeon, chirurgeon [*archaic*].

consultant, operator; resident, interne; anaesthetist or anesthetist; aurist, oculist, dentist, dental surgeon; osteopath, osteopathist; orthopedist; gynecologist, obstetrician; Christian Science practitioner, faith healer; medical student, medic [*colloq.*]; *accoucheur (fem. accoucheuse)* [*F.*], midwife; nurse; registered —, graduate —, trained —, district —, practical —, monthly–, visiting —, nurse; sister, nursing sister; dresser, bonesetter, apothecary, druggist, chemist [*Brit.*], pharmacopolist, pharmaceutist, pharmacist, pharmaceutical chemist, pharmacologist; Aesculapius, Hippocrates, Galen; *masseur (fem. masseuse)* [*F.*], massagist, rubber.

[instruments] stethoscope, stethometer, stethograph, respirometer, spirometer, pneumometer, spirograph, pneumatograph, pneumatometer, pulmotor.

v. **apply a remedy** etc. *n.;* doctor [*colloq.*], dose, physic, nurse, minister to, attend, dress the wounds, plaster, poultice; strap, splint, bandage; prevent etc. 706; relieve etc. 834; palliate etc. 658; heal, cure, "kill or cure," work a cure, remedy, stay (disease), snatch from the jaws of death; restore etc. 660; drench with physic; consult, specialize, operate, anaesthetize or anesthetize; straighten, mold or mould; deliver; extract, fill, stop; transfuse, bleed, cup, let blood; electrolyze.

manicure; pedicure; shampoo; massage, rub.

adj. **remedial**; restorative etc. 660; corrective, palliative, healing; sanatory, sanative; prophylactic; salutiferous etc. (*salutary*) 656; medical, medicinal; therapeutic, hypnotic, neurotic, chirurgical [*archaic*], surgical, epulotic [*obs.*], paregoric, tonic, corroborant, roborant; analeptic, balsamic, anodyne, narcotic, sedative, lenitive, demulcent, emollient; detersive, detergent; abstersive, disinfectant; febrifugal, antifebrile; alternative; traumatic, vulnerary.

allopathic, homeopathic, eclectic, hydropathic, heteropathic; aperient, laxative, cathartic, purgative; septic; aseptic, antiseptic; antiluetic, antisyphilitic; anthelmintic, vermifugal; chalybeate, deobstruent; purifying, cleansing, depurative, depuratory; electrolytic or electrolytical.

dietetic, dietary, alimentary; nutritious, nutritive; digestive, digestible, peptic.

remediable, curable; antidotal, alexipharmic, alexiteric.

663. Bane

n. **bane**, curse, hereditary evil, thorn in the flesh; *bête noir* [*F.*], bugbear; evil etc. 619; hurtfulness etc. (*badness*) 649; painfulness etc. (*cause of pain*) 830; scourge etc. (*punishment*) 975; *damnosa hereditas* [*L.*]; white elephant.

rust, worm, helminth, moth, "moth and rust" [*Bible*], fungus, mildew; dry rot; canker, cankerworm; cancer; viper etc. (*evildoer*) 913; demon etc. 980.

sting, fang, thorn, tang [*dial. Eng.*], bramble, brier *or* briar, nettle.

poison, leaven, virus, venom; arsenic, Prussic acid, antimony, tartar emetic, strychnine, tannin *or* tannic acid, nicotine; miasma *or* miasm, effluvium, mephitis, stench; fetor etc. 401; malaria, azote [*rare*], nitrogen, coal gas, illuminating gas, natural gas, gas, poison gas, mustard gas, chlorine, tear gas, lachrymose gas; sewer gas; pest.

Albany hemp, arsenious -oxide, — acid; bichloride of mercury; carbonic acid, — gas; choke damp, black damp, fire damp, afterdamp, marsh gas, methane; cyanide of potassium, carbolic acid, corrosive sublimate; hydrocyanic acid, hydrocyanide; nux vomica, ratsbane.

toxicant, intoxicant, deliriant, delirifacient, hemlock, hellebore, nightshade, deadly nightshade, belladonna, henbane, aconite; banewort, opium, bhang [*India*], ganja [*India*], hemp, cannabin, cannabis, marijuana, hashish; Upas tree.

[science of poisons] toxicology.

adj. **baneful** etc. (*bad*) 649; poisonous etc. (*unwholesome*) 657.

664. Safety

n. **safety**, security, surety, impregnability; invulnerability, invulnerableness etc. *adj.*; danger -past, — over; storm blown over; coast clear; escape etc. 671; means of escape; blow-, safety-, snifting- valve; safeguard, palladium; sheet anchor; rock, tower.

guardianship, wardship, wardenship; tutelage, custody, safe-keeping; preservation etc. 670; guardship [*obs.*], protection, auspices.

protector, guardian; warden, warder; preserver, life saver, custodian, duenna, chaperon, third person.

safe-conduct, escort, convoy; guard, shield etc. (*defense*) 717; guardian angel; tutelary -god, — deity, — saint; *genius loci* [*L.*].

watchdog, bandog; Cerberus.

watchman, patrolman, policeman, police officer, officer, "the finest"; cop, copper, peeler, bobby [*all slang*], blue coat [*colloq.*], constable, roundsman, *gendarme* [*F.*], military police; detective, tec [*slang*], bull [*slang*], spotter [*slang*]; sheriff, deputy; sentinel, sentry, scout etc. (*warning*) 668.

armed force, garrison, life guard, State guard, militia, regular army, navy; volunteer; marine etc. 726; battleship, man-of-war etc. 726.

[means of safety] refuge etc., anchor etc. 666; precaution etc. (*preparation*) 673; guard, guard rail, hand rail; bulkhead, watertight compartment, safety appliance; bolt, hasp etc. (*pin*) 45; cyclone cellar, dugout, bombproof dug-out; quarantine, *cordon sanitaire* [*F.*].

[sense of security] confidence etc. 858.

judge, justice, judiciary, magistrate, beak [*slang, Eng.*], justice of the peace, J. P.; deemster [*Isle of Man*], hakim [*Oriental*]; chancellor etc. 967.

v. **be safe** etc. *adj.*; keep one's head above water, tide over, save one's bacon [*colloq.*]; ride out —, weather- the storm; light upon one's feet; bear a charmed life; escape etc. 671; possess nine lives.

protect, watch over; make *or* render safe etc. *adj.*; take care of etc. (*care*) 459; preserve etc. 670; cover, screen, shelter, shroud, flank, ward; take charge of; guard etc. (*defend*) 717; garrison; man the -garrison, — lifeboat; secure etc. (*restrain*) 751; intrench *or* entrench, mine, countermine; dig in; fence round etc. (*circumscribe*) 229; house, nestle, ensconce.

escort, support, accompany, convoy.

watch, mount guard, patrol, go on one's beat; do —, perform- sentry go; scout, spy.

take precautions etc. (*prepare for*) 673; "make assurance double sure" [*Macbeth*] etc. (*caution*) 864; take up a loose thread; reef, take in a reef, make all snug, have an anchor to windward, double reef topsails.

seek safety; take —, find- shelter etc. 666; run into port.

adj. **safe**, secure, sure; in safety, in security; in shelter, in harbor, in port; in the shadow of a rock; on *terra firma* [*L.*]; on the safe side; under the -shield of, — shade of, — wing of, — shadow of one's wing; under cover, under lock and key; out of -danger, — the meshes, — harm's way; on sure ground, at anchor, high and dry, above water; unthreatened, unmolested; protected etc. *v.*; *cavendo tutus* [*L.*]; panoplied etc. (*defended*) 717.

safe and sound etc. (*preserved*) 670; harmless; scatheless etc. (*perfect*) 650; unhazarded; not dangerous etc. 665.

snug, seaworthy, airworthy; watertight, weathertight, weatherproof, waterproof, fireproof; bombproof, shellproof.

defensible, tenable, proof against, invulnerable; unassailable, unattackable; "founded upon a rock" [*Bible*], impregnable, imperdible [*obs.*]; inexpugnable.

protecting etc. *v.;* guardian, tutelary; preservative etc. 670; trustworthy etc. 939.

adv. *ex abundante cautela* [*L.*]; with impunity.

int. **all's well**! all clear! all serene! [*slang*]; safety first! at rest! at ease!

665. Danger

n. **danger**, peril, insecurity, jeopardy, risk, hazard, venture, precariousness, slipperiness; instability etc. 149; defenselessness etc. *adj.*

exposure etc. (*liability*) 177; vulnerability; vulnerable point, heel of Achilles; forlorn hope etc. (*hopelessness*) 859.

[dangerous course] leap in the dark etc. (*rashness*) 863; road to ruin, *facilis descensus Averni* [Vergil], hairbreadth escape.

[approach of danger] cause for alarm; source of danger etc. 667; rock —, breakers- ahead; storm brewing; clouds -in the horizon, — gathering; warning etc. 668; alarm etc. 669.

[sense of danger] apprehension etc. 860.

v. **be in danger** etc. *adj.;* be exposed to —, run into —, incur —, encounter- danger etc. *n.;* run a risk; lay oneself open to etc. (*liability*) 177; lean on —, trust to- a broken reed; feel the ground sliding from under one, have to run for it; have the -chances, — odds- against one.

hang by a thread, totter; tremble on the verge; totter on the brink; sleep —, stand- on a volcano; sit on a barrel of gunpowder, live in a glass house.

endanger; bring —, place —, put- in -danger etc. *n.;* expose to danger, imperil; be proscribed; have one's name on the danger list; be overdue [*naut.*], be despaired of; be under sentence of death; jeopard, jeopardize; put one's head in the lion's mouth; beard the lion in his den; compromise; sail too near the wind etc. (*rash*) 863.

threaten etc. (909) danger; run one hard; lay a trap for etc. (*deceive*) 545.

adventure, risk, hazard, venture, stake, set at hazard; run the gauntlet etc. (*dare*) 861; engage in a forlorn hope.

adj. **in danger** etc. *n.;* endangered etc. *v.;* fraught with danger; dangerous, hazardous, perilous, periculous [*obs.*], parlous [*archaic*], unsafe, unprotected etc. (safe, protect etc. 664); insecure, untrustworthy, unreliable; built upon sand, on a sandy basis; unsound, speculative, wild-cat.

defenseless, guardless, fenceless [*archaic*], harborless, unsheltered, unshielded; vulnerable, expugnable, exposed; open to etc. (*liable*) 177.

aux abois [*F.*], at bay, with one's back to the wall; on the wrong side of the wall, on a lee shore, on the rocks.

precarious, critical, ticklish; slippery, slippy; hanging by a thread etc. *v.;* with a halter round one's neck; between -the hammer and the anvil, — Scylla and Charybdis, — two fires; on the edge, brink, *or* verge of -a precipice, — a volcano, — an abyss, —a pit; in the lion's den, on slippery ground, under fire; not out of the wood; in the condemned cell, under sentence of death; at stake, in question.

unwarned, unadmonished, unadvised; unprepared etc. 674; off one's guard etc. (*inexpectant*) 508.

tottering, unstable, unsteady; shaky, top-heavy, tumble-down, ramshackle, crumbling, waterlogged; helpless, guideless; in a bad way; reduced to —, at- the last extremity; trembling in the balance; nodding to its fall etc. (*destruction*) 162.

threatening etc. 909; ominous, ill-omened; alarming etc. (*fear*) 860; explosive; poisonous; venomous etc. (*insalubrious*) 657; rotten at the core.

adventurous etc. (*rash*) 863, (*bold*) 861.

int. **stop**! look! listen! look out! watch your step! look alive! look slippy! [*colloq.*]; below there! 'ware heads! beware! take care! *prenez garde!* [*F.*].

666. Refuge
[means of safety]

n. **refuge**, sanctuary, retreat, fastness, stronghold, fortress, castle, acropolis; keep, last resort; ward; prison etc. 752; asylum, ark, home, refuge for the destitute; almshouse; hiding place &. (*ambush*) 530; *sanctum sanctorum* [*L.*] etc. (*privacy*) 893.

anchorage, roadstead; breakwater, mole, port, haven; harbor, — of refuge; seaport; pier, jetty, embankment, quay, wharf, landing place; bund, bunder [*both Oriental*]; water wing [*arch.*].

covert, shelter, screen, lee wall, wing, shield, umbrella; dashboard, dasher, splashboard, mud guard *or* mudguard, wheel guard.

wall etc. (*inclosure*) 232; fort etc. (*defense*) 717.

anchor, sheet anchor, sacred anchor [*Gr. & Rom. antiq.*], kedge *or* kedge anchor; Trotman's —, Martin's —, mushroom- anchor; killick; grapnel, grappling iron; mainstay; support etc. 215; check etc. 706; ballast.

means of escape etc. (*escape*) 671; lifeboat, swimming belt, cork jacket, life preserver, buoy, breeches buoy; parachute, plank, stepping-stone.

safeguard etc. (*protection*) 664.

jury mast; vent-peg; safety -valve, — lamp; lightning -rod, — conductor.

v. **seek** *or* **find safety** etc. 664; seek —, take —, find- refuge etc. *n.;* claim sanctuary; head for the hills, take to the high ground; throw oneself into the arms of; break for the tall timber, break for the woods; fly to, reach in time; make port, make the harbor; anchor in the roadstead; crouch in the lee of; reach -shelter, — home, — running water.

bar the gate, let the portcullis down; lock —, bolt —, make fast- the door; raise the drawbridge.

667. Pitfall

[source of danger]

n. rocks, reefs, coral reef, sunken rocks, snags; sands, quicksands; syrt [*rare*], syrtis [*rare*]; Goodwin sands, sandy foundation; slippery ground; breakers, shoals, shallows, bank, shelf, flat, lee shore, ironbound coast, rockbound coast; rock —, breakers- ahead; derelict.

abyss, abysm, pit, void, chasm, crevasse.

whirlpool, eddy, vortex, gurge [*rare*], rapids, undertow; current, tide gate, tide race, maelstrom; eagre, bore, tidal wave.

pitfall; ambush etc. 530; trapdoor; trap etc. (*snare*) 545; mine, masked battery, spring-gun.

pest, ugly customer, dangerous person, *le chat qui dort* [*F.*]; crouching tiger; incendiary, firebug [*slang*]; firebrand; hornet's nest.

sword of Damocles; wolf at the door, snake in the grass, snake in one's bosom, death in the -cup, — pot; latency etc. 526.

668. Warning

n. **warning,** caution, caveat; notice etc. (*information*) 257; premonition, premonishment [*rare*]; prediction etc. 511; symptom, contraindication, lesson, dehortation; admonition, monition; alarm etc. 669.

handwriting on the wall, *tekel upharsin* [*Heb.*], yellow flag; red flag, red light, fog-signal, foghorn; siren; monitor, warning voice, Cassandra, signs of the times, Mother Cary's chickens, stormy petrel, bird of ill omen, gathering clouds, cloud no bigger than a man's hand, clouds in the horizon, death watch, death lights etc. (*premonitions*) 992a.

watchtower, beacon, signal post; lighthouse etc. (*indication of locality*) 550.

sentinel, sentry; watch, watchman; watch and ward; watchdog, bandog, house dog; patrol, vedette, picket, bivouac, scout, spy, spial [*obs.*]; advanced —, rear- guard; lookout, flagman.

cautiousness etc. 864.

v. **warn,** caution; forewarn, prewarn; admonish, forebode, premonish [*rare*]; give -notice, — warning; menace etc. (*threaten*) 909; put on one's guard; sound the alarm etc. 669; croak.

beware, ware [*dial.*]; take -warning, — heed at one's peril; look out, keep one's wits about one; keep watch and ward etc. (*care*) 459.

adj. **warning** etc. *v.;* premonitory, monitory, cautionary, admonitory, admonitive [*rare*]; ominous, threatening, lowering, minatory etc. (*threat*) 909; symptomatic, sematic [*biol.*].

warned etc. *v.;* on one's guard etc. (*careful*) 459, (*cautious*) 864.

adv. with alarm, on guard, after due warning, with one's eyes open; *in terrorem* [*L.*].

int. **beware!** ware! take care! mind —, take care- what you are about! mind! look out! watch your step!

669. Alarm

[indication of danger]

n. **alarm**; alarum, larum [*archaic*], alarm bell, tocsin, *alerte* [*F.*], beat of drum, sound of trumpet, note of alarm, hue and cry, fiery cross; signal of distress; flag at -half-mast, — half-staff; blue lights; war cry, war whoop; warning etc. 668; fog signal, fog bell, fog horn, siren; yellow flag; danger signal; red light, red flag; fire bell, fire alarm, still alarm; burglar alarm; watchman's rattle, police whistle.

false alarm, cry of wolf; bugbear, bugaboo.

v. **alarm**; give —, raise —, sound —, turn in —, beat- the *or* an -alarm etc. *n.;* warn etc. 668; ring the tocsin; *battre la générale* [*F.*]; cry wolf; half-mast.

adj. **alarmed**; warned; alarming etc. *v.*

int. *sauve qui peut!* [*F.*]; *qui vive?* [*F.*]; who goes there?

670. Preservation

n. **preservation**; safe-keeping; conservation etc. (*storage*) 636; maintenance, support, sustentation [*rare*], conservatism; economy; *vis conervatrix* [*L.*]; salvation etc. (*deliverance*) 672.

[means of preservation] prophylaxis; preserver, preservative; hygiastics, hygiantics [*both rare*]; hygiene, hygienics; cover, drugget; *cordon sanitaire* [*F.*]; ensilage; dehydration, anhydration, evaporation; drying, putting up, canning, pickling; tinned goods [*chiefly Brit.*], canned goods; hyanization.

[superstitious remedies] charm etc. 993.

v. **preserve**, maintain, keep, sustain, support; keep -up, — alive; not willingly let die; nurse; cure etc. (*restore*) 660; save, rescue; be —, make- safe etc. 664; take care of etc. (*care*) 459; guard etc. (*defend*) 717; bank, bank up, shore up.

embalm, dry, cure, salt, pickle, season, kyanize, bottle, pot, tin [*chiefly Brit.*], can; dehydrate, anhydrate, evaporate; husband etc. (*store*) 636.

hold one's own; *stare super antiquas vias* [Bacon]; hold —, stand- one's ground etc. (*resist*) 719.

adj. **preserving** etc. *v.;* conservative; prophylactic; preservatory, preservative; hygienic.

preserved etc. *v.;* unimpaired, unbroken, unin- jured, unhurt, unsinged, unmarred; safe, — and sound; intact, with a whole skin, without a scratch.

671. Escape

n. **escape**, scape [*obs.*]; avolation [*obs.*], elopement, flight; evasion etc. (*avoidance*) 623; retreat; nar- row —, hairbreadth- escape; close call [*col- loq.*], close shave, near shave [*colloq.*]; come off, impunity.

[means of escape] loophole etc. (*opening*) 260; path etc. 627; secret -chamber, passage; refuge etc. 666; vent, — peg; safety valve; drawbridge, fire escape.

reprieve etc. (*deliverance*) 672; liberation etc. 750. **refugee** etc. (*fugitive*) 623.

v. **escape**, scape [*archaic*]; make —, effect —, make good- one's escape; break jail; get off, get clear off, get well out of; *échapper belle* [*F.*], save one's bacon [*colloq.*], make a get-away [*slang*]; weather the storm etc. (*safe*) 664; es- cape scot-free.

elude etc., make off etc. (*avoid*) 623; march off etc. (*go away*) 293; give one the slip; slip through the -hands, — fingers; slip the collar, wriggle out of; break loose, break from prison; break — slip —, get- away; find vent, find a hole to creep out of.

adj. escaping, escaped etc. *v.;* stolen away, fled; scot- free.

672. Deliverance

n. **deliverance**, extrication, rescue, ransom; re- prieve, reprieval [*rare*], respite; armistice, truce; liberation etc. 750; emancipation; re- demption, redeemableness, salvation; exemp-

tion; day of grace; riddance; jail (*Brit.* gaol) delivery.

v. **deliver**, extricate, rescue, save, free, liberate, set free, release, emancipate, redeem, ransom; bring -off, — through; *tirer d'affaire* [*F.*], get the wheel out of the rut, snatch from the jaws of death, come to the rescue; rid; retrieve etc. (*restore*) 660; be —, get- rid of.

adj. saved etc. *v.;* extricable, redeemable, rescuable.

int. to the rescue! a rescue! saved!

673. Preparation

n. **preparation**; providing etc. *v.;* provision, provi- dence; anticipation etc. (*foresight*) 510; pre- caution, preconcertedness, preconcertion, predisposition; forecast etc. (*plan*) 626; re- hearsal, note of preparation; dissemination, propaganda.

groundwork, first stone, cradle, stepping-stone; foundation, first rung, scaffold etc. (*support*) 215; scaffolding, *échafaudage* [*F.*].

elaboration; ripening etc. *v.;* maturation, evolu- tion; perfection; concoction, digestion; gesta- tion, hatching, incubation, sitting.

[putting in order] arrangement etc. 60; clearance; adjustment etc. 23; tuning; equipment, outfit, accouterment *or* accoutrement, armament, array.

[preparation of men] training etc. (*education*) 537; inurement etc. (*habit*) 613; novitiate.

[preparation of food] cooking, cookery, culinary art; brewing.

[preparation of the soil] tilling, plowing *or* ploughing, sowing, semination, cultivation.

[state of being prepared] preparedness, readiness, ripeness, mellowness; maturity; *un impromptu fait à loisir* [*F.*].

[preparer] preparer, trainer, coach; teacher etc. 540; pioneer; *avant-courrier* [*F.*], *avant- coureur* [*F.*]; *voortrekker* [*Dutch*]; prophet; forerunner etc. (*precursor*) 64; sappers and min- ers, pavior, navvy; packer, stevedore, long- shoreman; warming pan.

v. **prepare**; get —, make- ready; predispose, ad- dress oneself to, get under weigh; make prepa- rations, settle preliminaries, get up, sound the note of preparation.

set *or* put in order etc. (*arrange*) 60; forecast etc. (*plan*) 626; prepare —, plow —, dress- the ground; till —, cultivate- the soil; sow the seed, lay a train, dig a mine; lay —, fix- the -founda- tions, — basis, — groundwork; dig the foun- dations, erect the scaffolding; lay the first stone etc. (*begin*) 66.

roughhew; cut out work; block out, hammer out; lick into shape etc. (*form*) 240.

elaborate, mature, ripen, mellow, season, bring to maturity; nurture etc. (*aid*) 707; hatch, cook, brew; temper, anneal, smelt; barbecue; dry, cure, salt, smoke, infumate [*rare*]; maturate.

equip, arm, man; fit out, fit up; furnish, rig, dress, garnish, betrim, accouter *or* accoutre, array, fettle, fledge; dress up, furbish up, brush up, vamp up; refurbish; sharpen one's tools, trim one's -tackle, — foils; set, prime, attune; whet the -knife, — sword; wind up, screw up; adjust etc. (*fit*) 27; put in -trim, — train, — gear, — working order, — tune, — a groove for, — harness; pack, stow away, stow down, stow, load, store.

prepare for etc.; train etc. (*teach*) 537; inure etc. (*habituate*) 613; breed; rehearse; make provision for; take -steps, — measures, — precautions; provide, provide against; beat up for recruits; open the door to etc. (*facilitate*) 705.

set one's house in order, make all snug; clear decks, clear for action; close one's ranks; shuffle the cards.

prepare oneself; serve an apprenticeship etc. (*learn*) 539; lay oneself out for, get into harness, gird up one's loins, buckle on one's armor, *reculer pour mieux sauter* [*F.*], prime and load, shoulder arms, get up steam; put the horses to, harness, harness up [*colloq.*], hitch up [*colloq.*].

guard against, make sure against; forearm, make sure, prepare for the evil day, have a rod in pickle, have a bone to pick, provide against a rainy day, feather one's nest; lay in provisions etc. 637; make investments; keep on foot, keep going.

be prepared, be ready etc. *adj.;* hold oneself in readiness, watch and pray, keep one's powder dry, lie in wait for etc. (*expect*) 507; anticipate etc. (*foresee*) 510; *principiis obstare* [*L.*]; *venienti occurrere morbo* [*L.*].

adj. **preparing** etc. *v.;* in preparation, in course of preparation, in agitation, in embryo, in hand, in train; afoot, afloat; on foot, on the stocks, on the anvil; under consideration etc. (*plan*) 626; in consultation; brewing, hatching, forthcoming, brooding; in store for, in reserve.

precautionary, provident; preparative, preparatory; provisional, inchoate, under revision; under advisement; preliminary etc. (*precedent*) 62.

prepared etc. *v.;* in readiness; ready, — to one's hand, ready made; cut and dried; made to one's hand, ready cut, made to order, at one's elbow, ready for use, all ready; handy, on the table; in gear; running -smoothly, — sweetly; in working -order, — gear; snug; in practice.

in full feather, in best bib and tucker [*colloq.*]; in —, at- harness; in the saddle, in arms, in battle array, in war paint; up in arms; armed -at all points, — to the teeth, — *cap à pie* [*F.*]; sword in hand; booted and spurred.

in utrumque paratus [Virgil], *semper paratus* [*L.*]; on the alert etc. (*vigilant*) 459; at one's post.

ripe, mature, mellow; pucka *or* pukka *or* pakka [*Hind.*]; practiced etc. (*skilled*) 698; labored, elaborate, high-wrought, smelling of the lamp, worked up.

adv. **in preparation**, in anticipation of; afoot, astir, abroad; abroach; in fine fettle.

674. Nonpreparation

n. **nonpreparation**, unpreparedness; absence of —, want of- preparation; inculture [*obs.*], inconcoction [*obs.*], improvidence.

immaturity, crudity; rawness etc. *adj.;* abortion; disqualification.

[absence of art] nature, state of nature; virgin soil, unweeded garden; rough diamond; neglect etc. 460.

rough copy etc. (*plan*) 626; germ etc. 153; raw material etc. 635.

improvisation etc. (*impulse*) 612.

v. **be unprepared** etc. *adj.;* want —, lack- preparation; lie fallow; *s'embarquer sans biscuits* [*F.*]; live from hand to mouth.

[render unprepared] dismantle etc. (*render useless*) 645; undress etc. 226.

extemporize, improvise; cook up, fix up, vamp.

surprise, drop in on [*colloq.*], pay a surprise visit, drop in [*colloq.*], give a surprise party, take potluck with; take —, catch- unawares; take by surprise, call informally.

adj. **unprepared** etc. (prepare etc. 673); without preparation etc. 673; incomplete etc. 53; rudimental, embryonic, abortive; immature, unripe, *kutcha or kachcha* [*Hind.*]; callow, unfledged, unhatched, unnurtured, raw, green, crude; coarse; rough, roughcast, roughhewn; in the rough; rough-edged, unhewn, unformed, unfashioned, unwrought, unlabored, unblown; indigested, undigested; unmellowed, unseasoned, unleavened; uncooked, unboiled, unconcocted; unpolished, uncut, deckle-edged.

untaught, uneducated, untrained, untutored, undrilled, unexercised; unlicked; precocious, premature.

fallow, unsown, untilled, uncultivated.

natural, *in puris naturalibus* [*L.*], in a state of nature; undressed; in dishabille, *en déshabillé* [*F.*], in negligee.

unfitted, disqualified, unqualified, ill-digested; unbegun, unready, unarranged, unorganized, unfurnished, unprovided, unequipped, untrimmed; out of -gear, — kilter *or* kelter [*colloq.*], — order; dismantled etc. *v.*

shiftless, improvident, unthrifty, thriftless, thoughtless, unguarded; happy-go-lucky; slack, remiss; caught napping etc. (*inexpectant*) 508; unpremeditated etc. 612.

adv. **inadvertently**, by surprise, without premeditation; extempore etc. 612.

675. Essay

n. **essay**, trial, endeavor, attempt; aim, struggle, venture, adventure, speculation, *coup d'essai* [*F.*], *début* [*F.*]; probation etc. (*experiment*) 463.

v. **try**, essay; experiment etc. 463; endeavor, strive; tempt, attempt, make an attempt; venture, adventure, speculate, take one's chance, tempt fortune; try one's -fortune, — luck, — hand; use one's endeavor; feel —, grope —, pick one's way.

try hard, push, make a bold push, use one's best endeavor; do one's best etc. (*exertion*) 686.

adj. **essaying** etc. *v.*; experimental etc. 463; tentative, empirical, problematic *or* problematical, probationary.

adv. **experimentally** etc. *adj.*; on trial, at a venture; by rule of thumb.

if one may be so bold.

676. Undertaking

n. **undertaking**; compact etc. 769; adventure, venture; engagement etc. (*promise*) 768; enterprise, emprise *or* emprize [*archaic*]; pilgrimage; matter in hand etc. (*business*) 625; move; first move etc. (*beginning*) 66.

v. **undertake**; engage —, embark- in; launch —, plunge- into; volunteer; apprentice oneself to; engage etc. (*promise*) 768; contract etc. 769; take upon -oneself, — one's shoulders; devote oneself to etc. (*determination*) 604.

take up, take on, take in hand; tackle [*colloq.*]; set —, go- about; set —, fall- -to, — to work; launch forth; break the ice; set up shop; put in -hand, — execution; set forward; break the neck of a -day's work, — business; be in for [*colloq.*]; put one's hand to; betake oneself to, turn one's hand to, go to do; be in the midst of; begin etc. 66; broach, institute etc. (*originate*) 153; put —, lay- one's -hand to the plow, — shoulder to the wheel.

have in hand etc. (*business*) 625; have many irons in the fire etc. (*activity*) 682.

adj. **undertaking** etc. *v.*; on the anvil etc. 625; available, receptive; full of pep [*colloq.*], peppy [*colloq.*], energetic; adventurous, venturesome.

int. here goes! shoot! [*colloq.*].

677. Use

n. **use**, employ; exercise, exercitation; application, appliance; adhibition, disposal; consumption; agency etc. (*physical*) 170; usufruct; usefulness etc. 644; benefit; recourse, resort, avail; pragmatism, pragmaticism.

[conversion to use] utilization, utility, service, wear.

[way of using] usage, employment, *modus operandi* [*L.*].

user, consumer, purchasing public, buying public; market, public demand, popular demand, demand.

v. **use**, make use of, employ, put to use; apply; put in -action, — operation, — practice; set in motion, set to work.

ply, work, wield, handle, manipulate; play, play off; exert, exercise, practice, avail oneself of, profit by; resort to, lay one's hand to, fall back upon, have recourse to, recur to, take to, take up, betake oneself to; take up with, take advantage of; lay one's hands on, try.

render useful etc. 644; mold *or* mould; turn to -account, — use; convert to use, utilize; administer; work up; call —, bring- into play; put into requisition; call —, draw- forth; press —, enlist- into the service; task, tax, put to task; bring to bear upon, devote, dedicate, consecrate, apply, adhibit, dispose of; make a handle of, make a cat's-paw of.

fall back upon, make a shift with; make the most of, make the best of.

consume, use up, devour, swallow up; absorb, expend; wear, outwear.

adj. **in use**; used etc. *v.*; well-worn, well-trodden.

useful etc. 644; subservient etc. (*instrumental*) 631; utilitarian, pragmatic *or* pragmatical.

678. Disuse

n. **disuse**; forbearance, abstinence; relinquishment etc. 782; desuetude etc. (*want of habit*) 614; disusage.

v. **not use**; do without, dispense with, let alone, not touch, forbear, abstain, spare, waive, neglect; keep back, reserve.

disuse; lay up, lay by, lay on the shelf, lay up in a napkin; shelve; set —, put —, lay- aside;

leave off, have done with; supersede; discard etc. (*eject*) 297; dismiss, give warning.

throw aside etc. (*relinquish*) 782; make away with etc. (*destroy*) 162; cast —, heave —, throw- overboard; cast to the -dogs, — winds; dismantle etc. (*render useless*) 645.

lie —, remain- unemployed etc. *adj.*

adj. **not used** etc. *v.;* unemployed, unapplied, undisposed of, unspent, unexercised, untouched, untrodden, unessayed, ungathered, unculled; uncalled for, not required.

disused etc. *v.;* done with, run down, worn out, not worth saving.

int. no use!

679. Misuse

n. **misuse**, misusage, misemployment, misapplication, misappropriation.

abuse, profanation, prostitution, desecration; waste etc. 638.

v. **misuse**, misemploy, misapply, misappropriate.

desecrate, abuse, profane, prostitute.

overtask, overtax, overwork, overdrive; squander etc. 818; waste etc. 638.

cut blocks with a razor, employ a steam engine to crack a nut; catch at a straw.

adj. **misused** etc. *v.*

Section 3. Action

680. Action

n. **action**, performance; doing etc. *v.;* perpetration; exercise, exercitation; movement, operation, evolution, work, employment; labor etc. (*exertion*) 686; *praxis* [*L.*], execution; procedure etc. (*conduct*) 692; handicraft; business etc. 625; agency etc. (*power at work*) 170.

deed, act, overt act, stitch, touch, gest *or* geste; transaction, job, doings, dealings, proceeding, measure, step, maneuver *or* maneuvre, manoeuver *or* manoeuvre, bout, passage, move, stroke, blow; *coup*, — *de main*, — *d'état* [*F.*]; *tour de force* [*F.*] etc. (*display*) 882; feat, exploit; achievement etc. (*completion*) 729; handiwork, craftsmanship, workmanship; manufacture; stroke of policy etc. (*plan*) 626.

actor etc. (*doer*) 690.

v. **do**, perform, execute; achieve etc. (*complete*) 729; transact, enact; commit, perpetrate, inflict; exercise, prosecute, carry on, work, practice, play.

employ oneself, ply one's task; officiate, have in hand etc. (*business*) 625; labor etc. 686; be at

work; pursue a course; shape one's course etc. (*conduct*) 692.

act, operate; take action, take steps; strike a blow, mix it up with [*slang*], lift a finger, stretch forth one's hand; take in hand etc. (*undertake*) 676; put oneself in motion; put in practice; carry into execution etc. (*complete*) 729; act upon.

be an actor etc. 690; take —, act —, play —, perform- a part in; participate in; have a -hand in, — finger in the pie; have to do with; be a party to, be a participator in; bear —, lend- a hand; pull an oar, run in a race; mix oneself up with etc. (*meddle*) 682.

be in action; come into operation etc. (*power at work*) 170.

adj. **in action**; doing etc. *v.;* acting; in harness; up to one's ears in work; in the midst of things; on duty; at work; operative; in operation etc. 170.

adv. in the -act, — midst of, — thick of; red-handed, *in flagrante delicto* [*L.*]; while one's hand is in; while one is at it.

681. Inaction

n. **inaction**, passiveness, abstinence from action; watchful waiting; noninterference; Fabian —, *laisser-aller* [*F.*], *laisser-faire* [*F.*] —, conservative- policy; neglect etc. 460.

inactivity etc. 683; stagnation, vegetation, loafing, loaf; rest etc. (*repose*) 687; quiescence etc. 265; want of occupation, unemployment, inoccupation; idle hours, idle hands, time hanging on one's hands, *dolce far niente* [*It.*]; shore duty; interregnum; sinecure; soft snap, soft thing, soft touch, cinch [*all four slang*].

v. **not do**, not act, not attempt; be inactive etc. 683; abstain from doing, do nothing, hold, spare; not stir —, not move —, not lift- a -finger, — hand, — foot, — peg; fold one's -arms, — hands; leave —, let- alone; let be, let pass, let things take their course, let it have its way, let well alone, let well enough alone; *quieta non movere* [*L.*]; *stare super antiquas vias* [*L.*]; rest and be thankful, live and let live; lie —, rest- upon one's oars; *laisser aller* [*F.*], *laisser faire* [*F.*]; stand aloof; refrain etc. (*avoid*) 623; keep oneself from doing; remit —, relax- one's efforts; desist etc. (*relinquish*) 624; stop etc. (*cease*) 142; pause etc. (*be quiet*) 265.

wait, lie in wait, bide one's time, take time, tide it over.

cool —, kick- one's heels; while away the -time, — tedious hours; pass —, fill up —, beguile- the time; talk against time; waste time etc. (*inactive*) 683.

lie by, lie on the shelf, lie idle, lie to, lie fallow; keep quiet, slug [*obs.*]; have nothing to do, whistle for want of thought; twiddle one's thumbs.

undo, do away with; take down, take to pieces; destroy etc. 162.

adj. **not doing** etc. *v.;* not done etc. *v.;* undone; passive; unoccupied, unemployed; out of -employ, — work, — a job; uncultivated, fallow; *désoeuvré* [*F.*].

adv. **at a stand,** *re infecta* [*L.*], *les bras croisés* [*F.*], with folded arms; with the hands -in the pockets, — behind one's back; *pour passer le temps* [*F.*].

int. **stop**! etc. 142; hands off! so let it be! enough! no more! *bas!* [*Hind.*], *basta!* [*It.*].

682. Activity

n. **activity**; briskness, liveliness etc. *adj.;* animation, life, vivacity, spirit, verve, pep [*slang*], dash, go [*colloq.*], energy; snap, vim.

smartness, nimbleness, agility; quickness etc. *adj.;* velocity etc. 274; alacrity, promptitude; dispatch *or* despatch, expedition; haste etc. 684; punctuality etc. (*early*) 132.

eagerness, zeal, ardor, enthusiasm, *perfervidum ingenium* [*L.*], *empressement* [*F.*], earnestness, intentness; *abandon* [*F.*]; vigor etc. (*physical energy*) 171; devotion etc. (*resolution*) 604; exertion etc. 686.

industry, assiduity; assiduousness etc. *adj.;* sedulity [*rare*], sedulousness; laboriousness; drudgery etc. (*labor*) 686; painstaking, diligence; perseverance etc. 604a; indefatigation [*obs.*]; businesslike habits, habits of business.

vigilance etc. 459; wakefulness; sleeplessness, restlessness; insomnia; pervigilium, *insomnium* [*L.*]; racketing.

bustle, hustle [*colloq.*], movement, stir, fuss, ado, bother, fidget, fidgetiness; flurry etc. (*haste*) 684.

officiousness; dabbling, meddling; interference, interposition, intermeddling; butting in [*slang*], horning in [*slang*], intrusiveness, minding others' business, not minding one's own business; tampering with, intrigue.

press of business, no sinecure, plenty to do, a great deal doing [*colloq.*], a lot going on [*colloq.*], many irons in the fire, great doings, busy hum of men, the madding crowd, the thick of things, battle of life, thick of the action.

man of action, busy bee; new broom; sharp fellow, blade; devotee, enthusiast, fanatic, zealot, hummer [*slang*], hustler [*colloq.*], humdinger [*slang*], rustler [*slang*]; live wire, human dynamo [*both colloq.*], live man.

meddler, intermeddler, intriguer, intrigant *or* intriguant, telltale, busybody, pickthank [*archaic*].

v. **be active** etc. *adj.;* busy oneself in; stir, stir about, stir one's stumps [*colloq.*]; bestir —, rouse oneself; speed, hasten, peg away, lay about one, bustle, fuss; raise —, kick up- a dust; push; make a -fuss, — stir; go ahead, push forward; fight —, elbow- one's way; make progress etc. 282; toil etc. (*labor*) 686; moil, drudge, plod, persist etc. (*persevere*) 604a; keep up the ball; keep the pot boiling.

look sharp; have all one's eyes about one etc. (*vigilance*) 459; rise, arouse oneself, hustle [*colloq.*], push [*colloq.*], get up early, be about, keep moving, steal a march, catch a weasel asleep, kill two birds with one stone; seize the opportunity etc. 134; lose no time, not lose a moment, make the most of one's time, not suffer the grass to grow under one's feet, improve the shining hour, make short work of; dash off; make haste etc. 684; do one's best, take pains etc. (*exert oneself*) 686; do —, work- wonders; have a lot of -kick [*colloq.*], — pep [*slang*].

have many irons in the fire, have one's hands full, have much on one's hands; have other -things to do, — fish to fry; be busy; not have a moment -to spare, — that one can call one's own.

have one's fling, run the round of; go all lengths, stick at nothing, run riot.

outdo; overdo, overact, overlay, weigh down, overshoot the mark; make a toil of a pleasure.

have a hand in etc. (*act in*) 680; take an active part, put in one's oar, have a finger in the pie, mix oneself up with, trouble one's head about, intrigue; agitate.

meddle, tamper with, intermeddle, interfere, interpose; obtrude; poke —, thrust- one's nose in; butt in, horn in [*both slang*].

adj. **active,** brisk, — as a lark, — as a bee; lively, animated, vivacious; alive, — and kicking [*colloq.*]; frisky, spirited, stirring.

nimble, — as a squirrel; agile; light-footed, nimble-footed; featly tripping.

quick, prompt, yare [*archaic*], instant, ready, alert, spry, sharp, smart; fast etc. (*swift*) 274; capable, smart as a steel trap, no sooner said than done etc. (*early*) 132; quick as a lamplighter, expeditious; awake, broad awake; go-ahead, live, hustling [*colloq.*]; wide-awake etc. (*intelligent*) 498.

forward, eager, ardent, strenuous, zealous, enterprising, in earnest; resolute etc. 604.

industrious, assiduous, diligent, sedulous, notable [obsoles. in this sense], painstaking; intent etc. (attention) 457; indefatigable etc. (persevering) 604a; unwearied, never weary, sleepless, unsleeping, never tired; plodding, hard-working etc. 686; businesslike.

bustling; restless, — as a hyena; fussy, fidgety, pottering; busy as a hen with one chicken.

working, at work, on duty, in harness; up in arms; on one's legs, at call; up and -doing, — stirring; laboring, workday, workaday.

busy, occupied; hard at work, hard at it; up to one's ears in, full of business; busy as a -bee, — housewife.

meddling etc. v.; meddlesome, pushing, officious, overofficious, intrigant [F.].

astir, stirring; agoing, afoot; on foot; in full swing; eventful; on the alert etc. (vigilant) 459.

adv. **actively** etc. adj.; featly [archaic]; with life and spirit, with might and main etc. 686, with haste etc. 684, with wings; full tilt, in mediis rebus [L.].

int. be —, look- -alive, — sharp! move on! push on! keep moving! go ahead! stir your stumps! [colloq.]; age quod agis! [L.], jaldi! [Hind.], jaldi karo! [Hind.], step lively! get a move on!

683. Inactivity

n. **inactivity**; inaction etc. 681; inertness etc. 172; obstinacy etc. 606.

lull etc. (cessation) 142; quiescence etc. 265; rust, rustiness.

idleness, remissness etc. adj.; sloth, indolence, indiligence [rare]; dawdling etc. v.; ergophobia, otiosity, hoboism.

dull work; pottering; relaxation etc. (loosening) 47; Castle of Indolence.

languor; dullness etc. adj.; segnity [obs.], segnitude [obs.], lentor; sluggishness etc. (slowness) 275; procrastination etc. (delay) 133; torpor, torpidity, torpescence; stupor etc. (insensibility) 823; somnolence; drowsiness etc. adj.; nodding etc. v.; oscitation, oscitancy; pandiculation, hypnotism, lethargy; statuvolence or statuvolism; sand in the eyes, heaviness, heavy eyelids.

sleep, slumber; sound —, heavy —, balmy-sleep; Morpheus; Somnus; coma, trance, catalepsy; hypnosis, ecstasis, dream; hibernation; nap, doze, snooze [colloq.], siesta, wink of sleep, forty winks [colloq.]; snore; hypnology.

[cause of inactivity] lullaby, berceuse [F.],

Schlummerlied [Ger.]; anaesthesia or anesthesia, anaesthetic or anesthetic, opiate, sedative etc. 174.

idler, drone, dawdle [rare], dawdler; dead head, stiff, dead one [all slang], mopus [obs.], dolittle, fainéant [F.], dummy, sleeping partner; afternoon farmer; truant etc. (runaway) 623; bummer, bum [slang], Weary Willie [colloq.], tramp, sundowner [slang, Austral.], hobo, fakir or fakeer [Moham.], sunyasi [Hind.]; beggar, cadger [slang], lounge lizard [slang], lounger, lazzarone, loafer; lubber, lubbard [rare]; slow coach etc. (slow) 275; opium —, lotus- eater; slug; laggard, sluggard; slumberer, the Dustman, the Sandman; the Fat Boy in Pickwick; dormouse, marmot; waiter on Providence, fruges consumere natus [L.]; Mr. Micawber.

v. **be inactive** etc. adj.; do nothing etc. 681; move slowly etc. 275; let the grass grow under one's feet; take one's time, dawdle, drawl, lag, hang back, slouch; loll, lollop [colloq., Brit.], lounge, poke, loaf, loiter; go to sleep over; sleep at one's post, ne battre que d'une aile [F.].

take it easy, take things as they come; lead an easy life, vegetate, swim with the stream, eat the bread of idleness, goof off [slang]; loll in the lap of -luxury, — indolence; waste —, consume —, kill —, lose- time; burn daylight, waste the precious hours.

dally, dilly-dally; idle —, trifle —, fritter —, fool- away time; spend —, take- time in; peddle, piddle; potter, putter, dabble, faddle [dial. Eng.], fribble, fiddle-faddle.

sleep, slumber, be asleep; hibernate; oversleep; sleep like a -top, — log, — dormouse; sleep -soundly, — heavily; doze, drowse, snooze [colloq.], nap; take a nap etc. n.; dream; snore; settle —, go —, go off- to sleep; drop off [colloq.]; fall asleep, drop asleep; get some shuteye [slang], close —, seal up- -the -eyes, — eyelids; weigh down the eyelids; get sleepy, nod, yawn; go to bed, turn in, hit the hay [slang], hit the sack [slang], rest in the arms of Morpheus.

languish, expend itself, flag, hang fire; relax.

render idle etc. adj.; sluggardize; mitigate etc. 174.

adj. **inactive**; motionless etc. 265; unoccupied etc. (doing nothing) 681.

indolent, lazy, slothful, idle, lusk [obs.], remiss, slack, inert, torpid, torpescent, sluggish, otiose, languid, supine, heavy, dull, leaden, lumpish; drony, dronish; lazy as Ludlam's dog.

dilatory, laggard; lagging etc. v.; slow etc. 275; rusty, flagging; fiddle-faddle; pottering etc. v.; shilly-shally etc. (irresolute) 605.

exanimate [*now rare*], soulless; listless; lackadaisical, maudlin.

sleeping etc. *v.;* asleep; fast —, dead —, sound-asleep; in a sound sleep; sound as a top, dormant, comatose; in the -arms, — lap- of Morpheus.

sleepy, sleepful [*rare*], full of sleep, oscitant, dozy, drowsy, somnolent, torpescent; lethargic *or* lethargical, somnifacient; statuvolent, statuvolic; heavy, heavy with sleep; nappy, somnific, somniferous; soporose *or* soporous, soporific, soporiferous; hypnotic; balmy, dreamy; unawakened, unwakened.

sedative etc. 174.

adv. **inactively** etc. *adj.;* at leisure etc. 685; with half-shut eyes, half asleep; in dreams, in dreamland.

684. Haste

n. **haste**, urgency, dispatch *or* despatch, acceleration, spurt *or* spirt, forced march, rush, scurry *or* skurry, scuttle, dash; velocity etc. 274; precipitancy, precipitation, precipitousness etc. *adj.;* impetuosity; *brusquerie* [*F.*]; hurry, drive, scramble, bustle, fuss, fidget, flurry, flutter, splutter.

v. **haste**, hasten; make haste, make a dash etc. *n.;* hurry —, dash —, whip —, push —, press- -on, — forward; hurry, scurry *or* skurry, scuttle along, bundle on, dart to and fro, bustle, flutter, scramble; plunge, — headlong; dash off; rush etc. (*violence*) 173; express, railroad [*colloq.*].

bestir oneself etc. (*be active*) 682; lose -no time, — not a moment, — not an instant; make short work of; make the best of one's -time, — way.

be precipitate etc. *adj.;* jump at, be in haste, be in a hurry etc. *n.;* have -no time —, have not a moment- -to lose, — to spare; work against time, work under pressure.

quicken etc. 274; accelerate, expedite, put on, precipitate, urge, whip, spur, flog, goad.

adj. **hasty**, hurried, brusque; scrambling, cursory, precipitate, headlong, furious, boisterous, impetuous, hot-headed; feverish, fussy; pushing.

in haste, in a hurry etc. *n.;* in hot haste, in all haste; breathless, pressed for time, hard pressed, urgent.

adv. **with haste**, with all haste, with breathless speed; in haste etc. *adj.;* apace etc. (*swiftly*) 274; amain; all at once etc. (*instantaneously*) 113; at short notice etc., immediately etc. (*early*) 132; posthaste; by cable, by telegraph, by wireless [*colloq.*], by airmail, by air, by return mail, by steam [*colloq.*], by forced marches.

hastily, precipitately etc. *adj.;* helter-skelter, hurry-skurry, holus-bolus; slap-dash, slap-bang; full-tilt, full-drive; heels over head, head and shoulders, headlong, *à corps perdu* [*F.*].

by fits and starts, by spurts; hop skip and jump.

int. **rush!** immediate! urgent! look alive! *jaldi karo!* [*Hind.*]; get with it [*colloq.*], get a move on! [*colloq.*], get a wiggle on! [*colloq.*]; quickmarch! [*mil.*], double! [*mil.*]; gallop! charge! [*mil.*].

685. Leisure

n. **leisure**; convenience; spare -time, — hours, –moments; vacant hour; time, — to spare, — to burn [*slang*], — on one's hands; holiday etc. (*rest*) 687; *otium cum dignitate;* ease.

v. **have leisure** etc. *n.;* take one's -time, — leisure, — ease; repose etc. 687; move slowly etc. 275; while away the time etc. (*inaction*) 681; be master of one's time, be an idle man; *desipere in loco* [*L.*].

686. Exertion

n. **exertion**, effort, strain, tug, pull, stress, throw, stretch, struggle, spell, spurt *or* spirt; stroke —, stitch- of work.

"a long pull, a strong pull, and a pull all together"; dead lift; heft [*dial.*]; wear and tear; ado; toil and trouble; uphill —, hard —, warm- work; harvest time.

exercise, exercitation, practice, play, gymnastics, field sports; breather [*colloq.*], racing, running, jumping, riding etc.

labor, work, toil, travail [*rare*], manual labor, sweat of one's brow, swink [*obs.*], operoseness, drudgery, slavery, fag [*colloq., Eng.*], faggery, fagging, hammering; *limae labor* [*L.*]; operosity [*obs.*], operoseness.

trouble, pains, duty; resolution etc. 604; energy etc. (*physical*) 171.

worker, plodder, laborer, drudge, fagger, fag [*Eng. schools*], slave; man of action etc. 682; agent etc. 690; Samson, Hercules.

v. **exert oneself**; exert —, tax- one's energies; use exertion.

labor, work, toil, moil, sweat, fag, swink [*archaic*], toil and moil, drudge, slave, drag a lengthened chain, wade through, strive, strain; make —, stretch- a long arm; pull, tug, ply; ply —, tug at- the oar; do the work; take the laboring oar.

bestir oneself (*be active*) 682; take trouble, trouble oneself.

work hard; rough it; put forth -one's strength, — a strong arm; fall to work, bend the bow; buckle to, set one's shoulder to the wheel etc.

(*resolution*) 604; work like a -horse, — cart horse, — dog, — galley slave, — coal heaver, — Briton; labor —, work- day and night; redouble one's efforts; do double duty; work double -hours, — tides; sit up, burn the candle at both ends, burn the midnight oil; stick to etc. (*persevere*) 604a; work —, fight- one's way; lay about one, hammer at.

do one's best, do one's level best, do one's utmost; take pains; do the best one can, do all one can, do all in one's power, do as much as in one lies, do what lies in one's power; use one's -best, — utmost- endeavor; try one's- best, — utmost; play one's best card; put one's -best, — right- leg foremost; put one's best foot foremost; have one's whole soul in his work, put all one's strength into, strain every nerve; spare no -efforts, —pains; go all lengths; go through fire and water etc. (*resolution*) 604; move heaven and earth, leave no stone unturned.

adj. laboring etc. *v.*

laborious, hefty [*colloq.*], operose, elaborate; strained; toilsome, troublesome, wearisome, burdensome; uphill; herculean, gymnastic, palaestric *or* palestric, athletic.

hardworking, painstaking, strenuous, energetic, never idle.

hard at work, on the stretch, on the move, on the jump, on the dead jump, on the run.

adv. **laboriously** etc. *adj.;* lustily; *pugnis et calcibus* [*L.*]; with might and main, with all one's might, with a strong hand, with sledge hammer, with much ado; to the best of one's abilities, *totis viribus* [*L.*], *vi et armis* [*L.*], *manibus pedibusque* [*L.*], tooth and nail, *unguibus et rostro* [*L.*], hammer and tongs, heart and soul; through thick and thin etc. (*perseverance*) 604a.

by the sweat of one's brow, *suo Marte* [*L.*].

687. Repose

n. **repose**, rest, silken repose; sleep etc. 683.

relaxation, breathing time; halt, stay, pause etc. (*cessation*) 142; respite.

day of rest, *dies non* [*L.*], Sabbath, Lord's day, Sunday, First Day, holiday, red-letter day; gala day etc. (*amusement*) 840; vacation, recess.

v. **repose**; rest, rest and be thankful; take rest, take one's ease.

lie down; recline, recline on a bed of down, recline on an easychair; go to -rest, — bed, — sleep etc. 683.

relax, unbend, slacken; take breath etc. (*refresh*) 689; rest upon one's oars; pause etc. (*cease*) 142; stay one's hand.

take a holiday, shut up shop; lie fallow etc. (*inaction*) 681.

adj. **reposing** etc. *v.;* unstrained.

holiday, festal, ferial [*rare*]; sabbatic *or* sabbatical.

adv. at rest.

688. Fatigue

n. **fatigue**; weariness etc. 841; yawning, drowsiness etc. 683; lassitude, tiredness, fatigation [*obs.*], sweat.

shortness of breath; anhelation [*rare*], dyspnea, panting, labored breathing.

faintness, fainting, swoon, goneness, exhaustion, collapse, prostration, deliquium, syncope, lipothymy.

v. **be fatigued** etc. *adj.;* yawn etc. (*get sleepy*) 683; droop, sink, flag; lose breath, lose wind; gasp, pant, puff, blow, drop, swoon, faint, succumb.

fatigue, tire, bore, weary, irk [*chiefly impersonal, as,* it irks me], flag, jade, harass, exhaust, knock up, wear out, bleed white, prostrate.

tax, task, strain; overtask, overwork, overburden, overtax, overstrain, fag, fag out.

adj. **fatigued** etc. *v.;* weary etc. 841; drowsy etc. 683; drooping etc. *v.;* haggard; toilworn, wayworn; footsore, surbated [*obs.*], weather-beaten; faint; done, done up, knocked up [*all Brit. colloq.*]; bushed [*slang*], done in; exhausted, used up [*colloq.*], prostrate, spent; overtired, overspent, overfatigued; unrefreshed, unrestored.

ready to drop, all in [*slang*], more dead than alive, dog-weary, dog-tired, walked off one's legs, tired to death, on one's last legs, played out, *hors de combat* [*F.*].

worn, worn out; battered, shattered, pulled down, seedy [*colloq.*], enfeebled, altered.

breathless, windless; short of —, out of -breath, — wind; blown, puffing and blowing; short-breathed; anhelose; broken-winded, short-winded; dyspneal, dyspneic.

689. Refreshment

n. **recuperation**; recovery of strength etc. 159; refreshing, bracing etc. *v.;* restoration, revival etc. 660; repair, refection, refocillation [*obs.*], refreshment, regale, regalement, bait; relief etc. 834.

v. **refresh**; brace etc. (*strengthen*) 159; reinvigorate; air, freshen up, recruit; repair etc. (*restore*) 660; fan, refocillate [*obs.*]; refresh the inner man; get better, raise one's head; recover —, regain —, renew- one's strength etc. 159; perk up.

breathe, respire; drink in the ozone; draw —, take —, gather —, take a long —, regain —, recover- breath.

recuperate; come to oneself etc. (*revive*) 660; feel like a giant refreshed.

adj. refreshing etc. *v.;* recuperative etc. 660.

refreshed etc. *v.;* untired, unwearied.

690. Agent

n. agent, doer, actor, performer, perpetrator, operator; executor, executrix; practitioner, worker, old stager; mediary, medium, reagent.

minister etc. (*instrument*) 631; representative etc. (*commissioner*) 758, (*deputy*) 759; factor, steward.

servant etc. 746; factotum, general, maid-of-all-work, servant-of-all-work, do-all [*colloq.*].

[comparisons] bee, ant, working bee, termite, white ant; laboring oar; shaft horse.

workman, artisan; craftsman, handicraftsman; mechanic, operative; workingman, laboring man; hewers of wood and drawers of water, laborer, navvy [*Eng.*]; hand, man, day laborer, journeyman, hack; mere tool etc. 633; beast of burden, drudge, fag; lumper, stevedore, roustabout.

maker, artificer, *artifex* [*L.*], artist, wright, manufacturer, architect, contractor, builder, mason, bricklayer, smith, forger, Vulcan; carpenter; platelayer; blacksmith, locksmith, sailmaker, tailor, cordwainer, wheelwright.

machinist, mechanician, engineer, electrician, plumber, gasfitter.

workwoman, charwoman, seamstress *or* sempstress, needlewoman, laundress, washerwoman, "Madonna of the tubs" [Phelps].

coworker, associate, fellow worker, cooperator, colleague, *confrère* [*F.*]; party to, participator in, *particeps criminis* [*L.*], *dramatis personae* [*L.*]; *personnel* [*F.*].

691. Workshop

n. workshop, workhouse; laboratory, manufactory, armory, arsenal, mill, factory, *usine* [*F.*], mint, loom; cabinet, bureau, studio, *atelier* [*F.*]; hive, hive of industry; plant; hothouse, hotbed; kitchen; alveary, beehive; bindery, forcing pit, nailery, dock, dockyard, slip, yard, wharf; foundry *or* foundery, forge, furnace; vineyard, orchard, nursery, truck garden, truck farm, farm.

melting pot, crucible, caldron *or* cauldron, mortar, alembic; matrix.

692. Conduct

n. conduct, behavior; deportment, comportment; carriage, *maintien* [*F.*], demeanor, guise, bearing, manner, observance.

course —, line- of -conduct, — action, — proceeding; role; process, ways, practice, procedure, *modus operandi* [*L.*]; method etc., path etc. 627.

dealing, transaction etc. (*action*) 680; business etc. 625.

policy, polity; tactics, game, generalship, statesmanship, seamanship; strategy, strategics; plan etc. 626.

management; government etc. (*direction*) 693; stewardship, husbandry; housekeeping, housewifery; *ménage or* menage; *régime or* regime, regimen, economy, economics; political economy.

career, life, course, walk, province, race, record; execution, manipulation, treatment; campaign.

v. transact, execute; dispatch *or* despatch, proceed with, discharge; carry -on, — through, — out, — into effect; work out; go through, get through; enact; put into practice; officiate etc. 625.

bear —, behave —, comport —, demean —, carry —, conduct —, acquit- oneself.

run a race, lead a life, play a game; take —, adopt- a course; steer —, shape- one's course; play one's part, play one's cards; shift for oneself; paddle one's own canoe; bail one's own boat.

conduct; manage etc. (*direct*) 693.

deal with, have to do with; treat, handle a case; take -steps, — measures.

adj. conducting etc. *v.;* directive, strategic *or* strategical, methodical, business-like, practical, executive; economic.

693. Direction

n. direction; management, managery [*obs.*]; government, gubernation [*obs.*], conduct, legislation, regulation, guidance; bossism; legislature; steerage, pilotage; reins, — of government; helm, rudder, needle, compass; guiding star, lodestar *or* loadstar, polestar; cynosure.

ministry, ministration; administration; stewardship, proctorship; chair; agency.

supervision, superintendence; surveillance, oversight; eye of the master; control, charge; auspices; board of control etc. (*council*) 696; command etc. (*authority*) 737.

statesmanship; statecraft, kingcraft, queencraft; premiership, senatorship; director etc. 694; seat, portfolio.

v. **direct**, manage, govern, conduct; order, prescribe, cut out work for; head, lead; lead the way, show the way; take the lead, lead on; regulate, guide, steer, pilot; take the helm, be at the helm; have —, handle —, hold —, take- the reins; drive, tool [*cant*], tackle.

superintend, supervise; overlook, oversee, control, keep in order, look after, see to, legislate for; administer, ministrate [*obs.*]; matronize; patronize; have the -care, — charge- of; have —, take- the direction; pull the -strings, — wires; rule etc. (*command*) 737; be the guiding force; have —, hold- -office, — the portfolio; preside, — at the board; take —, occupy —, be in- the chair; pull the stroke oar.

adj. **directing** etc. *v.;* executive, gubernatorial, supervisory; hegemonic *or* hegemonical, predominant; statesmanlike.

adv. **in charge of**, under the guidance of, under the auspices of; in control of, at the helm, at the head of.

694. Director

n. **director**, manager, governor, rector [*rare*], controller, comptroller; superintendent, supervisor; intendant; overseer, overlooker; supercargo, husband [*archaic*], inspector, foreman, ganger [*Eng.*], visitor, ranger, surveyor, aedile *or* edile [*Rom. hist.*], moderator, monitor, taskmaster; master etc. 745; leader, ringleader, agitator, demagogue, corypheus, conductor, fugleman, precentor, bellwether; *caporal* [*F.*], choregus, collector, file leader, flugelman, linkboy.

guiding star etc. (*guidance*) 693; adviser etc. 695; guide etc. (*information*) 527; pilot; helmsman; steersman, steersmate [*obs.*]; wire-puller.

driver, whip, jehu [*humorous*], charioteer; coachman, carman, cabman; postilion, *vetturino* [*It.*], muleteer, *arriero* [*Sp.*], teamster; whipper-in; chauffeur, motorman, engine-driver.

head, headman, chief, principal, president, speaker; chair, chairman; captain etc. (*master*) 745; superior; mayor etc. (*civil authority*) 745; vice-president, prime minister, premier, vizier *or* vizir, grand vizier, eparch.

officer, functionary, minister, official, red-tape, red-tapist, bureaucrat; Jack in office; office bearer, office holder; person in authority etc. 745.

statesman, strategist, legislator, lawgiver, politician, statist [*rare*], statemonger; Minos, Draco; arbiter etc. (*judge*) 967; boss, political dictator, dictator, power behind the throne, kingmaker;

secretary, — of state; Reis Effendi; vicar etc. (*deputy*) 759; board etc. (*council*) 696.

steward, factor; agent etc. 758; bailiff, middleman; clerk of works; landreeve; factotum, major-domo, seneschal, housekeeper, shepherd; croupier; proctor, procurator, curator, librarian.

adv. **ex officio**.

695. Advice

n. **advice**, counsel, adhortation [*obs.*]; word to the wise; suggestion, submonition [*obs.*], recommendation, advocacy; advisement [*archaic*]; consultation.

exhortation etc. (*persuasion*) 615; expostulation etc. (*dissuasion*) 616; admonition etc. (*warning*) 668; guidance etc. (*direction*) 693.

instruction, charge, injunction; Governor's —, President's- message; King's —, Queen's- speech; message, speech from the throne.

adviser, prompter; counsel, counselor; monitor, mentor, Nestor, sage, wise man, wise woman; *magnus Apollo* [*L.*], senator; teacher etc. 540; yogi *or* yogin; physician, leech [*archaic*]; archiater; arbiter etc. (*judge*) 967.

guide, manual, chart etc. (*information*) 527.

consultation, conference, *pourparler* [*F.*], parley, powwow; reference, referment.

v. **advise**, counsel; give -advice, — counsel, — a piece of advice; suggest, prompt, submonish [*obs.*], recommend, prescribe, advocate; exhort etc. (*persuade*) 615.

enjoin, enforce, charge, instruct, call; call upon etc. (*request*) 765; dictate.

expostulate etc. (*dissuade*) 616; admonish etc. (*warn*) 668.

advise with; lay heads —,consult- together; compare notes; hold a council, deliberate, be closeted with.

confer, consult, refer to, call in; follow, follow implicitly; take —, follow- advice; be advised by, have at one's elbow, take one's cue from.

adj. **recommendatory**; hortative etc. (*persuasive*) 615; dehortatory etc. (*dissuasive*) 616; admonitory etc. (*warning*) 668; consultative; dictatory, dictatorial; didactic.

int. go to!

696. Council

n. **council**, committee, subcommittee, comitia [*Rom. hist.*], privy council, court, chamber, cabinet, board, bench, staff.

junta, divan, musnud, sanhedrin *or* sanhedrim [*Jewish antiq.*], amphictyonic council [*Gr.*

hist.]; syndicate; court of appeal etc. (*tribunal*) 966; board of -control, — works; county council, local board, parish council, common council, town meeting; board of overseers; *zemstvo* [*Russ.*].

[ecclesiastical] convocation, synod, congregation, church, chapter, directory, vestry, consistory, conventicle, conclave, convention, classis.

legislature, parliament, congress, national council, states-general, diet.

Duma [*Russia*], Storthing *or* Storting [*Norway*], Rigsdag [*Denmark*], Riksdag [*Sweden*], Knesset [*Israel*], Cortes [*Spain*], Reichsrath *or* Reichsrat [*Austria*], Volksraad [*Dutch*]; Dail Eireann [*Ireland*]; witan, witenagemot *or* witenagemote [*Anglo-Saxon hist.*].

upper house, upper chamber, first chamber, senate, *senatus* [*Rom. hist.*], legislative council, House of Lords, House of Peers; Bundesrath *or* Bundesrat [*Ger.*], federal council, Lagting [*Nor.*], Landsthing [*Den.*].

lower house, lower chamber, second chamber, house of representatives, House of Commons, the house, legislative assembly, chamber of deputies; Odelsting [*Nor.*], Folkething [*Den.*], Reichstag [*Ger.*].

assembly, plenum, caucus, clique; meeting, sitting, séance, *camarilla* [*Sp.*], conference, hearing, session, palaver, *pourparler* [*F.*], durbar [*India*]; quorum; council fire [*N. Am.*], pow-wow.

[representatives] congressman, M. C., senator, representative; member, — of parliament, M. P.; representative of the people; assemblyman, councilor.

adj. curule, congressional, senatorial, parliamentary; synodic *or* synodical.

697. Precept

n. **precept**, direction, instruction, charge; prescript, prescription; recipe, receipt; golden rule; maxim etc. 496.

rule, canon, law, code, *corpus juris* [*L.*], *lex scripta* [*L.*], convention; unwritten law; canon law; act, statute, rubric, stage direction, regulation; model, form, formula, formulary; technicality; nice point, fine point, norm.

order etc. (*command*) 741.

698. Skill

n. **skill**, skillfulness *or* skilfulness, address; dexterity, dexterousness *or* dextrousness, adroitness, expertness etc. *adj.;* proficiency, competence, craft; callidity [*rare*], callidness, facility, knack,

trick, sleight; mastery, mastership; excellence, panurgy [*rare*]; ambidexterity, ambidextrousness; sleight of hand etc. (*deception*) 545.

seamanship, airmanship, marksmanship, horsemanship; rope-dancing; tight-rope —, slack-rope- walking.

accomplishment, acquirement, attainment; art, science; finish, finished execution, technique, technique, practical —, technical- knowledge; technology.

world wisdom, knowledge of the world, *savoir faire* [*F.*]; tact; mother wit etc. (*sagacity*) 498; discretion etc. (*caution*) 864; finesse; craftiness etc. (*cunning*) 702; management etc. (*conduct*) 692; self-help.

cleverness, talent, ability, ingenuity, capacity, parts, talents, faculty, endowment, forte, turn, gift, genius; intelligence etc. 498; sharpness, readiness etc. (*activity*) 682; invention etc. 515; aptness, aptitude; turn for, capacity for, genius for; felicity, capability, *curiosa felicitas* [*L.*], qualification, habilitation.

proficient, expert, adept etc. 700.

masterpiece, masterwork, *coup de maître* [*F.,*] *chef d'oeuvre* [*F.*], *tour de force* [*F.*]; good stroke etc. (*plan*) 626.

v. **be skillful** etc. *adj.;* excel in, be master of; have a turn for etc. *n.*

know what's what, know- a hawk from a handsaw, — what one is about, — on which side one's bread is buttered, — what's o'clock, — what o'clock it is, — what's up, — the time of day, — a thing or two, — the ropes; have cut one's -eyeteeth, — wisdom teeth; see through a millstone; be up to [*all colloq.*]

see one's way, see where the wind lies, see which way the wind blows; have all one's wits about one, have one's hand in; *savoir vivre* [*F.*]; *scire quid valeant humeri quid ferre recusent* [*L*].

look after the main chance; cut one's coat according to one's cloth; live by one's wits; exercise one's discretion, feather the oar, sail near the wind; stoop to conquer etc. (*cunning*) 702; play one's cards well, play one's best card; hit the nail on the head, put the saddle on the right horse.

take advantage of, make the most of; profit by etc. (*use*) 677; make a hit etc. (*succeed*) 731; make a virtue of necessity; make hay while the sun shines etc. (*occasion*) 134.

adj. **skillful** *or* skilful, dexterous *or* dextrous, adroit, expert, apt, handy, quick, deft, ready, slick [*slang*], smart etc. (*active*) 682; proficient, good at, up to, at home in, master of, a good hand at, *au fait* [*F.*], thoroughbred, masterly, crack [*colloq.*], crackerjack [*slang*], accomplished; conversant etc. (*knowing*) 490.

experienced, practiced, skilled; up in, well up in; in practice; competent, efficient, qualified, capable, fitted, fit for, up to the mark, up and coming, trained, initiated, prepared, primed, finished.

clever, cute [*colloq.*], able, ingenious, felicitous, gifted, talented, endowed; inventive etc. 515; shrewd, sharp etc. (*intelligent*) 498; cunning etc. 702; alive to, up to snuff [*slang*], not to be caught with chaff; discreet.

neat-handed, fine-fingered, nimble-fingered, ambidextrous, sure-footed; cut out for [*colloq.*], fitted for.

technical, artistic, scientific, daedalian, shipshapelike, workmanlike, businesslike, statesmanlike.

adv. **skillfully** or skilfully etc. *adj.;* well etc. 618; artistically; with skill, with fine technique, with consummate skill; *secundum artem* [*L.*], *suo Marte* [*L.*]; to the best of one's abilities etc. (*exertion*) 686; like a machine.

699. Unskillfulness

n. **unskillfulness** or unskilfulness etc. *adj.;* want of skill etc. 698; incompetence *or* incompetency; inability, infelicity, indexterity [*rare*], clumsiness, inaptitude etc. *adj.;* inexperience; disqualification, unproficiency; quackery.

folly, stupidity etc. 499; indiscretion etc. (*rashness*) 863; thoughtlessness etc. (*inattention*) 458, (*neglect*) 460; *sabotage* [*F.*].

mismanagement, misconduct, misfeasance; inexpedience, bad policy, impolicy; maladministration; misrule, misgovernment, misapplication, misdirection.

absence of rule, rule of thumb; bungling etc. *v.;* failure etc. 732; screw loose; too many cooks.

blunder etc. (*mistake*) 495; *étourderie* [*F.*], *gaucherie* [*F.*], act of folly, *balourdise* [*F.*], bungle, botch, botchery; bad job, sad work.

sprat sent out to catch a whale, butterfly broken on a wheel, tempest in a teacup, storm in a teacup, much ado about nothing, wild-goose chase.

bungler etc. 701; fool etc. 501; hen with its head cut off [*colloq.*].

v. **be unskillful** *or* unskilful, etc. *adj.;* not see an inch beyond one's nose; blunder, bungle, muff [*esp., baseball*], boggle, fumble, botch, mar, spoil, bitch [*obs.*], flounder, stumble, trip; hob-

ble etc. 275; put one's foot in it [*colloq.*]; make a -mess, — hash, — sad work- of [*all colloq.*]; overshoot the mark.

play tricks with, play Puck; mismanage, misconduct, misdirect, misapply, missend.

act foolishly; stultify —, make a fool of —, commit- oneself; play the fool; put oneself out of court; lose one's -head, — senses, — cunning; begin at the wrong end; do things by halves etc. (*not complete*) 730; make two bites of a cherry; play at cross-purposes; strain at a gnat and swallow a camel etc. (*caprice*) 608; put the cart before the horse; lock the stable door when the horse is stolen etc. (*too late*) 135.

not know what one is about, not know one's own interest, not know on which side one's bread is buttered; stand in one's own light, quarrel with one's bread and butter, throw a stone in one's own garden, kill the goose which lays the golden eggs, pay dear for one's whistle, cut one's own throat, burn one's fingers; knock —, run- one's head against a stone wall; bring the house about one's ears; have too many -eggs in one basket (*imprudent*) 863, — irons in the fire.

cut blocks with a razor; hold a farthing candle to the sun etc. (*useless*) 645; fight with —, grasp at- a shadow; catch at straws, lean on a broken reed, reckon without one's host, go on a wild-goose chase; go on a fool's errand, go on a sleeveless errand [*obs.*]; go further and fare worse; fail etc. 732.

mistake etc. 495; take the shadow for the substance etc. (*credulity*) 486; bark up the wrong tree; be in the wrong box, aim at a pigeon and kill a crow; take —, get- -the wrong pig by the tail, — the wrong sow by the ear, — the dirty end of the stick [*all colloq.*]; put the saddle on the wrong horse, put a square thing into a round hole, put new wine into old bottles; lose one's way, miss one's way; fall into a trap, catch a Tartar.

adj. **unskillful** or unskilful etc. 698; unskilled, inexpert; bungling etc. *v.;* awkward, clumsy, unhandy, lubberly, *gauche* [*F.*], maladroit; left-handed, heavy-handed; slovenly, slatternly; gawky.

adrift, at fault.

inapt, unapt; *inhabile* [*obs.*]; untractable, unteachable; giddy etc. (*inattentive*) 458; inconsiderate etc. (*neglectful*) 460; stupid etc. 499; inactive etc. 683; incompetent; unqualified, disqualified, ill-qualified; unfit; quackish; raw, green, inexperienced, rusty, out of practice.

unaccustomed, unused, untrained etc. 537, un-initiated, unconversant etc. (*ignorant*) 491; unbusinesslike, unpractical, shiftless; unstatesmanlike.

ill-advised, unadvised, misadvised; ill-devised, ill-imagined, ill-judged, ill-contrived, ill-conducted; unguided, misguided; misconducted, foolish, wild; infelicitous; penny wise and pound foolish etc. (*inconsistent*) 608.

700. Proficient

n. **proficient**, expert, adept; dab, dabster [*both colloq. or dial.*], connoisseur etc. (*scholar*) 492; master, — hand; top sawyer, top banana [*cant*], prima donna, *première danseuse* [*F.*], first fiddle, *chef de cuisine* [*F.*]; protagonist; past master; mahatma.

nice —, good —, clean- hand; practiced —, experienced- -eye, — hand; marksman; good —, dead —, crack- shot [*colloq.*]; ropedancer, ropewalker, funambulist; contortionist, acrobat; conjuror etc. (*deceiver*) 548; wizard etc. 994.

picked man; medallist, prizeman, honorsman.

veteran; old -stager, — campaigner, — soldier, — file, — hand; man of business, man of the world.

genius; master -mind, — head, — spirit.

pantologist, Admirable Crichton, Jack of all trades; prodigy of learning, quiz kid [*colloq.*], walking encyclopedia, mine of information.

man of cunning; cunning —, sharp- -blade, — fellow; diplomatist, diplomat, Machiavellian; politician, jobber; tactician, strategist.

peculator, forger, coiner; cracksman etc. 792.

701. Bungler

n. **bungler**; blunderer, blunderhead; marplot, fumbler, lubber, clown, lout, duffer [*colloq.*]; stick, poor stick, odd stick [*all colloq.*]; bad —, poor--hand, — shot; butterfingers [*colloq.*], fumble-fist [*colloq.*].

no conjuror; flat, muff, muffer, slow coach [*all colloq.*]; looby, swab [*slang & dial.*], doit, yokel [*Eng.*], clod; awkward squad, novice, greenhorn, *blanc-bec* [*F.*], galoot [*slang*].

fish out of water, ass in lion's skin, jackdaw in peacock's feathers; quack etc. (*deceiver*) 548; Lord of Misrule, Abbot of Unreason [*both obs. or hist.*].

landlubber, fresh-water sailor, fair-weather sailor, horse marine.

sloven, slattern, traipse *or* trapes [*obs. or dial. Eng.*], slut.

702. Cunning

n. **cunning**, craft; cunningness, craftiness etc. *adj.*; subtlety, subtilty, subtility [*rare*]; the cunning of the -serpent, — Old Boy [*slang*]; artificiality; maneuvering *or* manoeuvring etc. *v.*; temporization; circumvention.

chicane, chicanery; sharp practice, knavery, jugglery; concealment etc. 528; guile [*colloq.*], doubling, duplicity etc. (*falsehood*) 544; foul play.

diplomacy, politics; Machiavellianism *or* Machiavellism; gerrymander, jobbery, back-stairs influence.

artifice, art, device, machination; plot etc. (*plan*) 626; maneuver, stratagem, dodge, artful dodge, wile; trick, trickery etc. (*deception*) 545; ruse, *ruse de guerre* [*F.*]; finesse, side blow, thin end of the wedge, shift, go-by [*colloq.*], subterfuge, evasion; white lie etc. (*untruth*) 546; juggle, *tour de force* [*F.*]; tricks -of the trade, — upon travelers; gold brick [*colloq.*], imposture, deception; *espièglerie* [*F.*]; net, trap etc. 545.

schemer, trickster, keener [*Western U. S.*], Philadelphia lawyer [*colloq.*]; sly boots [*humorous*], fox, reynard; intriguer, intrigant; repeater, floater; man of cunning etc. 700; horse trader; Indian giver [*colloq.*].

Ulysses, Machiavelli *or* Machiavel.

v. **be cunning** etc. *adj.*; have cut one's eyeteeth; contrive etc. (*plan*) 626; live by one's wits; maneuver *or* manoeuvre; intrigue, gerrymander, finesse, double, temporize, stoop to conquer, *reculer pour mieux sauter* [*F.*], circumvent, steal a march upon; outdo, get the better of, snatch a thing from under one's nose; overreach etc. 545; throw off one's guard; surprise etc. 508; snatch a verdict; waylay, undermine, introduce the thin end of the wedge; be too much for, be too deep for, sell a gold brick to [*colloq.*], give the go-by to [*slang*]; play a deep game, play tricks with; flatter, make things pleasant; have an ax to grind.

adj. **cunning**, crafty, artful; skillful *or* skilful etc. 698; subtle, subtile, feline, vulpine; cunning as a -fox, — serpent; deep, — laid; profound; designing, contriving; intriguing etc. *v.*; strategic, diplomatic, politic, Machiavellian *or* Machiavelian, timeserving; artificial; tricky, tricksy [*rare*], wily, sly, slim [*S. Africa*], insidious, stealthy; underhand etc. (*hidden*) 528; subdolous [*obs.*], double-faced, double-tongued, shifty, deceptive; deceitful etc. 545; crooked; arch, pawky [*Scot. & dial. Eng.*], shrewd, acute; sharp, — as a needle; canny *or* cannie, astute,

leery [*slang*], knowing, up to snuff [*slang*], too
clever by half, not to be caught with chaff.

adv. **cunningly** etc. *adj.;* slily, on the sly [*colloq.*], by
a side wind.

703. Artlessness

n. **artlessness** etc. *adj.;* inartificiality, unsophistica-
tion; nature, simplicity; innocence etc. 946;
bonhomie [*F.*], *naïveté* [*F.*], *abandon* [*F.*], candor, sincerity; singleness of -purpose, –heart;
honesty etc. 939; plain speaking; *épanchement* [*F.*].
rough diamond, matter-of-fact man; *le palais de
vérité* [*F.*]; *enfant terrible* [*F.*].

v. **be artless** etc. *adj.;* be round with one [Shakes-
peare]; look one in the face; wear one's heart
upon one's sleeve for daws to peck at; think
aloud; speak -out, –one's mind; be free with
one, call a spade a spade; tell the truth, the
whole truth, and nothing but the truth.

adj. **artless**, natural, pure, native, confiding, simple,
plain, inartificial, untutored, unsophisticated,
ingénu [*F.*], unaffected, naïve; sincere, frank;
open, –as day; candid, ingenuous, guileless; unsuspicious, honest etc. 939; childlike;
innocent etc. 946; Arcadian; undesigning,
straightforward, unreserved, above-board; simple-minded, single-minded; frank–, open–,
single–, simple- hearted.

matter-of-fact, free-spoken, plainspoken, outspoken; blunt, downright, direct, unpoetical;
unflattering, untrimmed, unvarnished.

adv. **in plain -words**, –English; without mincing the
matter; not to mince the matter etc. (*affirmation*) 535.

Section 4. Antagonism

704. Difficulty

n. **difficulty**; hardness etc. *adj.;* impracticability etc.
(*impossibility*) 471; tough–, hard–, uphill-
work; hard–, Herculean–, Augean- task; task
of Sisyphus, Sisyphean labor, tough job
[*colloq.*], tough proposition [*colloq.*], teaser
[*colloq.*], rasper [*slang*], dead weight, dead lift.

dilemma, embarrassment; deadlock; perplexity
etc. (*uncertainty*) 475; intricacy; entanglement
etc. 59; cross fire; awkwardness, delicacy; delicate ground, thin ice, ticklish card to play, knot,
Gordian knot, *dignus vindice nodus* [*L.*], net,
meshes, maze; coil etc. (*convolution*) 248;
crooked path; involvement; hard road to travel.

vexed question, *vexata quoestio* [*L.*], poser; puzzle etc. (*riddle*) 533; nice–, delicate–, subtle–,
knotty- point; paradox; hard–, nut to crack;
bone to pick, crux, *pons asinorum* [*L.*], where
the shoe pinches.

quandary, nonplus, strait, pass, pinch, rub,
pretty pass, stress, brunt; critical situation, crisis; trial, emergency, exigency, scramble.

scrape, hobble, slough, quagmire, hot water
[*colloq.*], hornet's nest; sea–, peck- of troubles;
pretty kettle of fish [*colloq.*]; pickle, stew, imbroglio, mess, muddle, botch, fuss, bustle, ado;
false position; stand; deadlock, dead set; fix,
horns of a dilemma, *cul de sac* [*F.*], blind alley;
hitch; stumblingblock etc. (*hindrance*) 706.

v. **be difficult** etc. *adj.;* run one hard, go against the
grain, try one's patience, put one out; put to
one's -shifts, –wit's end; go hard with one, try
one; pose, perplex etc. (*uncertain*) 475; pother,
bother, nonplus, gravel [*colloq.*], bring to a
deadlock; be impossible etc. 471; be in the way
of etc. (*hinder*) 706.

be in difficulty etc. *n.;* meet with–, labor
under–, get into–, plunge into–, struggle
with–, contend with–, grapple with- difficulties; labor under a disadvantage; fish in troubled waters, buffet the waves; swim against the
-current, –stream; scud under bare poles; have
much ado with, have a hard time of it; come to
the -push, –pinch; bear the brunt; grope in the
dark, lose one's way, weave a tangled web, walk
on eggshells, walk among eggs.

get into a scrape etc. *n.;* bring a hornet's nest
about one's ears; be put to one's shifts;
flounder, boggle, struggle; not know which way
to turn etc. (*uncertain*) 475; *perdre son latin*
[*F.*]; stick -at, –in the mud, –fast; come to a
-stand, –deadlock; get all -balled up [*slang*],
–snarled up, –tangled up, –wound up; hold the
wolf by the ears.

render difficult etc. *adj.;* enmesh, encumber,
embarrass, ravel, entangle; put a spoke in the
wheel etc. (*hinder*) 706; spike one's guns; lead
a wild-goose chase, lead a pretty dance.

adj. **difficult**, not easy, hard, tough [*colloq.*]; troublesome, toilsome, irksome; operose, laborious,
onerous, arduous, Herculean, formidable;
sooner–, more easily- said than done; difficult–, hard- to deal with; ill-conditioned,
crabbed; not to be handled with kid gloves, not
made with rose water.

awkward, unwieldy, unmanageable; intractable,
stubborn etc. (*obstinate*) 606; perverse, refractory, plaguy [*colloq.*], trying, thorny, rugged;

knotted, knotty; invious [*obs.*]; pathless, track-less; labyrinthine etc. (*convoluted*) 248; intri-cate, complicated etc. (*tangled*) 59; impracticable etc. (*impossible*) 471; not feasible etc. 470; desperate etc. (*hopeless*) 859.

embarrassing, perplexing etc. (*uncertain*) 475; delicate, ticklish, critical, uncertain, thorny, set with thorns; beset with−, full of−, surrounded by−, entangled by−, encompassed with- difficulties.

under a difficulty; in a box; in difficulty, in hot water [*colloq.*], in the suds [*colloq.*], in the soup [*slang*], in a cleft stick, in a fix [*colloq.*], in the wrong box, in a scrape etc. *n.,* in deep water, in a fine pickle [*colloq.*], *in extremis* [*L.*]; between -two stools, −Scylla and Charybdis; on the horns of a dilemma; on the rocks; sur-rounded by -shoals, −breakers, −quicksands; at cross-purposes; not out of the wood.

reduced to straits; hard−, sorely- pressed; run hard; pinched, put to it, straightened; hard up [*slang*]; hard put to it, hard set [*both colloq.*]; put to one's shifts; puzzled, at a loss, etc. (*uncertain*) 475; at the end of one's tether, at one's wits' end, at a nonplus, at a standstill; graveled, nonplused *or* nonplussed, stranded, aground; stuck−, set- fast; out, put out, out in one's reck-oning; up a tree, at bay, *aux abois* [*F.*], driven -into a corner, −from post to pillar, −to ex-tremity, −to one's wit's end, −to the wall; *au bout de son Latin* [*F.*]; out of one's depth; thrown out.

accomplished with difficulty; hard-fought, hard-earned.

adv. **with difficulty**, with much ado; hardly etc. *adj.;* uphill; upstream; against the -stream, −grain; *à rebours* [*F.*]; *invita Minerva* [*L.*]; in the teeth of; at a pinch, upon a pinch; at long odds.

705. Facility

n. **facility**, ease; easiness etc. *adj.;* capability; feasi-bility etc. (*practicability*) 470; flexibility, pli-ancy etc. 324; smoothness etc. 255; disencum-brance, disentanglement; deoppilation [*obs.*]; permission etc. 760.

plain−, smooth−, straight- sailing; mere child's play, holiday task; cinch, snap [*both slang*].

all clear, smooth water, fair wind; smooth−, roy-al- road; clear -coast, −stage, −course; straight course; *tabula rasa* [*L.*]; full play etc. (*free-dom*) 748.

v. **be easy** etc. *adj.;* go on−, run- smoothly; have full play etc. *n.;* go−, run- on all fours [*colloq.*]; hit on all -four, −six, −eight, −twelve (cylinders) [*automobile cant*]; obey the helm, work well, work smoothly, work like a machine.

flow−, swim−, drift−, go- with the- -stream, −tide; see one's way; have it all one's own way, have the game in one's own hands; walk over the course, win at a canter, win at a walk, win hands down [*colloq.*]; make little of, make light of, make nothing of; be at home in etc. (*skill-ful*) 698.

render easy etc. *adj.;* facilitate, smooth, ease, popularize; lighten, −the labor; free, clear; disencumber, disembarrass, disentangle, disen-gage; deobstruct, unclog, extricate, unravel, unknot, get the kinks out of; untie−, cut- the knot; disburden, unload, exonerate, emanci-pate, free from, deoppilate [*obs.*]; humor etc. (*aid*) 707; lubricate etc. 332; relieve etc. 834.

leave a hole to creep out of, leave a loophole, leave a way out, leave the matter open; give the reins to, give full play, give full swing; make way for; open the -door to, −way; prepare−, smooth−, clear- the -ground, −way, −path, −road; make all clear for, pave the way, bridge over; permit etc. 760.

adj. **easy**, facile; feasible etc. (*practicable*) 470; easily -managed, −accomplished; within reach, ac-cessible, easy of access, for the million, open to.

manageable, wieldy [*rare*], toward, towardly, tractable; submissive; yielding, ductile; suant *or* suent [*local U. S. & prov. Eng.*]; tractable etc. (*docile*) 602, pliant etc. (*soft*) 324; glib [*obs.*], slippery; smooth etc. 255; on friction wheels, on velvet.

unburdened, disburdened, disencumbered, disembarrassed; exonerated; unloaded, unob-structed, untrammeled; unrestrained etc. (*free*) 748; at ease, light.

at home, quite at home; in one's element, in smooth water.

adv. **easily** etc. *adj.;* readily, smoothly, swimmingly, with no effort, on easy terms, single-handed, with one hand tied behind one's back.

706. Hindrance

n. **prevention**, preclusion, obstruction, stoppage; embolus, clot, embolism; interruption, inter-ception, interclusion [*obs.*], hindrance, im-pedition [*obs.*]; retardment, retardation; embarrassment, oppilation [*obs.*], striction, constriction, coarctation, stricture, restriction; infarct, infarction; restraint etc. 751; inhibition etc. 761; blockade etc. (*closure*) 261.

interference, interposition; obtrusion; discouragement, discountenance; disapproval, disapprobation, opposition.

impediment, let [archaic], obstacle, obstruction, knot, knag; check, hitch, contretemps [F.], screw loose, grit in the oil; stumbling-block, stumbling-stone; lion in the path; snag; snags and sawyers, sawyer, planter [local, U. S.]

bar, stile, barrier; turnstile, turnpike; gate, portcullis; beaver dam; barricade etc. (defense) 717; wall, dead wall, breakwater, groin or groyne; bulkhead, block, buffer; stopper etc. 263; boom, dam, weir.

check; encumbrance or incumbrance; clog, skid, shoe, spoke, brake; drag anchor, drag sail, drag sheet, drift sail, sea anchor, floating anchor; anchor; mushroom–, sheet–, kedge- anchor; kedge, bower; checkrein, bearing rein; bit, snaffle, curb, curb bit; drag, –chain, –weight; load, burden, fardel [obs.], onus, millstone round one's neck, impedimenta; dead weight; lumber, pack; nightmare, ephialtes, incubus, old man of the sea; remora [surg.]; stay, stop; preventive, prophylactic.

drawback, objection; difficulty etc. 704; insuperable etc. (471) obstacle; trail of a red herring; estoppel [law]; ill wind; head wind etc. (opposition) 708; trammel, tether etc. (means of restraint) 752; holdback, counterpoise.

damper, wet blanket, hinderer, marplot, kill-joy, crape-hanger [slang], dog in the manger, Nosy Parker [colloq.], buttinsky [humorous]; usurper, interloper; opponent etc. 710; filibusterer.

v. hinder, impede, filibuster [U. S.], impedite [obs.], embarrass.

avert, keep off, stave off, ward off; obviate; antevert [obs.]; turn aside, draw off, prevent, forfend or forefend [archaic], nip in the bud; retard, slacken, check, let [archaic]; counteract, countercheck; preclude, debar, foreclose, estop [law]; inhibit etc. 761; shackle etc. (restrain) 751; restrict.

obstruct, stop, stay, bar, bolt, lock; block, –up; choke off; belay, barricade; block–, stop- the way; forlay or forelay [obs.], dam up etc. (close) 261; put on the brake etc. n.; scotch–, lock–, put a spoke in- the wheel; put a stop to etc. 142; traverse, contravene; interrupt, intercept; oppose etc. 708; hedge -in, –round; cut off; interclude [obs.].

interfere, interpose, intermeddle etc. 682.

encumber or incumber; cramp, hamper; clog, –the wheels; cumber; handicap; choke; saddle with, load with; overload, overlay, overwhelm;

lumber, trammel, tie one's hands, put to inconvenience; incommode, discommode; discompose; hustle [colloq.], corner, drive into a corner.

run foul of, fall foul of; cross the path of, break in upon.

thwart, frustrate, disconcert, balk, foil; faze, feeze or feaze; baffle, snub, override, circumvent; defeat etc. 731; spike guns etc. (render useless) 645; spoil, mar, clip the wings of; cripple etc. (injure) 659; put an extinguisher on; damp; dishearten etc. (dissuade) 616; discountenance, throw cold water on, spoil sport; lay–, throw- a wet blanket on; steal one's thunder; cut the ground from under one, take the wind out of one's sails, undermine; be–, stand-in the way of; act as a drag; hang like a millstone round one's neck.

adj. hindering etc. v.; obstructive, obstruent; intrusive, meddlesome; impeditive, impedient; intercipient [obs.]; prophylactic etc. (remedial) 662; impedimentary, impedimental.

in the way of, unfavorable; onerous, burdensome; cumbrous, cumbersome; obtrusive.

hindered etc. v.; windbound, water-logged, heavy laden; hard pressed.

unassisted etc. (see assist etc. 707); single-handed, alone; deserted etc. 624; unseconded.

adv. in the way, with everything against one, with one's wheels clogged, through all obstacles; with many difficulties, under many difficulties.

707. Aid

n. aid, aidance, assistance, help, opitulation [obs.], succor; support, lift, advance, furtherance, promotion; coadjuvancy etc. (cooperation) 709.

patronage, auspices, championship, countenance, favor, interest, advocacy.

sustenance, sustentation [rare], maintenance, alimentation, nutrition, nourishment; eutrophy; manna in the wilderness; food etc. 298; means etc. 632; subsidy, bounty, subvention.

ministry, ministration; subministration [obs.], accommodation.

relief, rescue; help at a dead lift; supernatural aid; deus ex machina [L.].

supplies, reënforcements, succors, contingents, recruits; support etc. (physical) 215; adjunct, ally etc. (helper) 711.

v. aid, assist, help, succor, lend one's aid; come to the aid of etc. n.; contribute, subscribe to; bring–, give–, furnish–, afford–, supply aid etc. n.; give–, stretch–, lend–, bear–, hold out- a -hand, –helping hand; give one a -lift,

–cast, –turn; take by the hand, take in tow; help a lame dog over a stile, lend wings to.

relieve, rescue; set up, set agoing, set on one's legs; bear–, pull– through; give new life to, be the making of; reënforce, recruit; set–, put–, push– forward; give -a lift, –a shove, –an impulse- to; promote, further, forward, advance; speed, expedite, quicken, hasten.

support, sustain, uphold, prop, hold up, bolster.

nourish, nurture, nurse, cradle, dry nurse, suckle, foster, cherish, put out to nurse; manure, cultivate, force; foment; feed–, fan- the flame.

serve; do service to, tender to, pander to; administer to, subminister to [*obs.*], minister to; tend, attend, wait on; take care of etc. 459; entertain; smooth the bed of sickness.

oblige, accommodate, consult the wishes of; humor, cheer, encourage.

second, stand by; back, –up; pay the piper, abet; work for, make interest for, stick up for [*colloq.*], stick by, take up the cudgels for; take up–, espouse–, adopt- the cause of; advocate, beat up for recruits, press into the service; squire [*colloq.*], give moral support to, keep in countenance, countenance, patronize, take up; lend one's name to; lend oneself to, lend one's countenance to; smile upon, shine upon; favor, befriend, take in hand, enlist under the banners of; side with etc. (*cooperate*) 709.

be of use to; subserve etc. (*instrument*) 631; benefit etc. 648; render a service etc. (*utility*) 644; conduce etc. (*tend*) 176.

adj. **aiding** etc. v.; auxiliary, adjuvant, helpful; coadjuvant etc. 709; subservient, ministrant, ancillary, accessary, accessory, subsidiary.

friendly, amicable, favorable, propitious, well-disposed; neighborly; obliging etc. (*benevolent*) 906; at one's beck.

adv. **with** *or* **by the aid of** etc. *n.;* on–, in- behalf of; in aid of, in the service of, in favor of, in the name of, in furtherance of; on account of; **for** the sake of, on the part of; *non obstante* [*L.*].

int. **help**! save us! to the rescue! this way! *à moi!* [*F.*].

708. Opposition

n. **opposition**, antagonism; oppugnancy, oppugnation [*rare*]; impugnation, impugnment, contrariousness [*rare*], contrariness, contrariety; contravention; counteraction etc. 179; counterplot.

resistance etc. 719; restraint etc. 751; hindrance etc. 706; absence of aid etc. 707.

cross fire, cross current, undercurrent, head wind.

clashing, collision, conflict, discord, want of harmony; filibuster, filibusterism.

competition, two of a trade, rivalry, emulation, race, contest; tug of war.

v. **oppose**, counteract, run counter to; withstand etc. (*resist*) 719; control etc. (*restrain*) 751; hinder etc. 706; antagonize, oppugn, fly in the face of, go dead against, kick against, cross, kick at, fall out with, fall foul of; set–, pit- against; face, confront, cope with; make a -stand, –dead set- against; set -oneself, –one's face- against; protest–, vote–, raise one's voice- against; disfavor, turn one's back upon; set at naught, slap in the face, slam the door in one's face.

thwart, be–, play- at cross-purposes; counterwork, countermine; over-thwart.

encounter, stem, breast; stem–, breast- the -tide, –current, –flood; buffet the waves; beat up against, make head against; grapple with; kick against the pricks etc. (*resist*) 719; contend with *or* against etc. 720; do battle with *or* against etc. (*warfare*) 722.

contradict, contravene; belie; go–, run–, beat–, militate- against; come in conflict with.

compete, emulate etc., 720; rival, spoil one's trade, force out, drive one out of business.

adj. **opposing**, opposed etc. v.; adverse, antagonistic, oppugnant, overthwart; contrary etc. 14; at variance etc. 24; at issue, at war with, in controversy with, in opposition; "agin' the government."

in hostile array, front to front, with crossed bayonets, at daggers drawn; up in arms; resistant etc. 719.

unfavorable, unpropitious, unfriendly, hostile, inimical, cross; filibusterous.

competitive, emulous, cut-throat; in rivalry with, in friendly rivalry.

adv. **against**, *versus* [*L.*], counter to, in conflict with, at cross-purposes, cross, contrariwise, unfavorably.

against the -grain, –current, –stream, –wind, –tide; with a head-wind; with the wind -ahead, –in one's teeth.

in spite, in despite, in defiance; in the -way, –teeth, –face- of; across; athwart, overthwart; where the shoe pinches; in one's teeth.

though etc. 30; even; *quand même* [*F.*]; *per contra* [*L.*].

709. Cooperation

n. **cooperation**; coadjuvancy, coadjutorship, coadjument [*rare*], coagency, coefficiency; concert, concurrence, complicity, coadministration, coaction; participation; union etc. 43; coefficacy; combination etc. 48; collusion, collusiveness.

association, alliance, colleagueship, joint stock, copartnership, pool, gentleman's agreement; cartel; confederation etc. (*party*) 712; coalition, federation, fusion; a long pull a strong pull and a pull all together; logrolling, *quid pro quo* [*L.*], freemasonry.

unanimity etc. (*assent*) 488; *esprit de corps* [*F.*], party spirit; clanship, partisanship; concord etc. 714; synergy, synergism.

v. **cooperate**, concur; conduce etc. 178; combine, coadjute, coadjuvate, coact [*rare*], unite one's efforts; keep-, draw-, pull-, club-, hand-, hold-, league-, band-, be banded- together; pool; stand-, put- shoulder to shoulder; act in concert, join forces, fraternize, cling to one another; vote solidly, vote in blocks; conspire, concert, lay one's heads together; confederate, make an agreement with, be in league with; collude, understand one another, play into the hands of, hunt in couples.

side with, take sides with, go along with, go hand in hand with, join hands with, make common cause with, strike in with, unite with, join with, mix oneself up with, take part with, cast in one's lot with; join-, enter into- partnership with; rally round, flock to, follow the lead of; come to, pass over to, come into the views of; be-, row-, sail- in the same boat; sail on the same tack.

participate, be a party to, lend oneself to; chip in [*colloq.*], have a -hand in, -finger in the pie; take-, bear- part in; second etc. (*aid*) 707; take the part of, play the game of; espouse a -cause, -quarrel.

adj. **cooperating** etc. *v.;* in cooperation etc. *n.,* in league etc. (*party*) 712; coadjuvant, coadjutant, coadjutive, coactive, coalitional, hand in glove with; dyed in the wool; synergetic, synergistic.

favorable to etc. 707; unopposed etc. 708.

adv. **unanimously**, as one man etc. 488; shoulder to shoulder, in cooperation with.

710. Opponent

n. **opponent**, antagonist, adversary, oppugnant [*rare*]; adverse party, opposition; enemy etc. 891; assailant.

oppositionist, obstructive; brawler, wrangler, brangler [*rare*], disputant; filibuster, filibusterer, extremist, bitter-ender, irreconcilable, obstructionist, "willful men."

malcontent; demagogue, reactionist; anarchist, anarch; Jacobin, Fenian, Sinn Feiner, Red; Industrial Workers of the World, I. W. W.

rival, competitor, contestant, entrant; the field.

711. Auxiliary

n. **auxiliary**; recruit; assistant; adjuvant, adjutant; *ayudante* [*Sp. Amer.*], co-aid; adjunct; help, helper, helpmate, helping hand; colleague, partner, mate, confrère, cooperator; coadjuvant, coadjutant, coadjutator [*rare*], coadjutor, coadjutrix, collaborator.

ally; friend etc. 890; confidant (*fem.* confidante), *fidus Achates* [*L.*], *alter ego* [*L.*], pal [*slang*], chum [*colloq.*], mate, comate.

aide-de-camp [*F.*], secretary, clerk, associate, marshal; right-hand, right-hand man; candleholder, bottle-holder [*colloq.*]; handmaid; servant etc. 746.

puppet, cat's-paw, creature, jack-straw, tool; jackal; *âme damnée* [*F.*]; satellite, adherent; parasite, dependent, client [*Rom. hist.*].

confederate; complice [*archaic*], accomplice; accessory, -after the fact; *particeps criminis* [*L.*]; *socius criminis* [*L.*].

upholder; votary; sectarian, sectary; seconder, backer, supporter, abettor, advocate, partisan, champion, patron, friend at court, mediator; angel [*slang*].

friend in need, jack at a pinch, special providence, *deus ex machina* [*L.*], guardian angel, fairy godmother, tutelary genius.

712. Party

n. **party**, faction, denomination, class, communion, side, crew, team; band, horde, posse, phalanx; caste, family, gens [*Rom. hist.*], clan etc. 166.

Confederates, Conservatives, Democrats, Federalists, Federals, Liberals, Libertarians, Radicals, Republicans, Socialists, Tories, Whigs etc.

community, body, fellowship, solidarity; freemasonry; party spirit etc. (*cooperation*) 709; fraternity, sodality, confraternity, sorority; *familistère* [*F.*], familistery; brotherhood, sisterhood.

fraternal order, Elks, Freemasons, Knights Templars, Odd Fellows, Knights of Pythias; Royal Arcanum etc.

gang, tong [*Chin.*]; Camorra, Kuklux, Kuklux Klan, Molly Maguires, Fenians, Sinn Feiners,

Bolsheviki, Bolshevists, Industrial Workers of the World, I. W. W., Luddites; ring, machine; Tammany, –Hall; junto, cabal, camarilla, brigue [*obs.*].

clique, knot, circle, set, coterie; club, casino.

corporation, corporate body, guild; establishment, company, copartnership, partnership, cahoot [*slang*]; firm, house; joint concern, joint-stock company; cartel, combine [*colloq.*], trust; holding company, consortium, merger.

society, association; institute, institution; union; trades union; league, syndicate, alliance; *Verein, Bund, Zollverein* [*all Ger.*]; combination; *Turnverein* [*Ger.*]; *Liedertafel* etc. (*singing societies*) 416; league–, alliance– offensive and defensive; coalition; federation; confederation, confederacy.

staff; cast, *dramatis personae* [*L.*].

v. **unite**, join; band together; club together etc. (*cooperate*) 709; found a –firm, –house; cement–, form– a party etc. *n.;* associate etc. (*assemble*) 72; federate, federalize, go cahoots [*slang*], go fifty-fifty [*slang*].

adj. **in league**, in partnership, in alliance etc. *n.* bonded–, banded–, linked etc. (*joined*) 43- together; embattled; confederated, federative, joint, corporate, organized, enleagued, leagued, syndicated; clubbable *or* clubable, fraternal, Masonic, institutional, denominational; cliquish, cliquy *or* cliquey; union-made.

adv. **side by side**, hand in hand, shoulder to shoulder, *en masse* [*F.*], in the same boat.

713. Discord

n. **discord**, disaccord, dissidence, dissonance; disagreement etc. 24; jar, clash, break, shock; jarring, jostling etc. *v.;* screw loose.

variance, difference, dissension, misunderstanding, cross-purposes, odds, *brouillerie* [*F.*]; division, split, rupture, disruption, division in the camp, house divided against itself, "rift within the lute" [*Tennyson*], disunion, breach; schism etc. (*dissent*) 489; feud, faction.

polemics; litigation; strife etc. (*contention*) 720; warfare etc. 722; outbreak, open rupture, breaking off of negotiations, recall of ambassadors, declaration of war.

quarrel, dispute, tiff, bicker, *tracasserie* [*F.*], squabble, altercation, barney [*slang*], *démêlé* [*F.*], snarl, spat [*colloq. or dial.*], towrow [*Scot. & dial Eng.*], words, high words; wrangling etc. *v.;* jangle, brabble [*archaic*], brabblement [*archaic*], cross questions and crooked answers, snip-snap [*rare*]; family jars.

broil, brawl, row [*colloq.*], racket, hubbub, rixation [*obs.*]; embroilment, embranglement, imbroglio, fracas, breach of the peace, piece of work, scrimmage, rumpus [*colloq.*]; breeze [*colloq.*], squall; riot, disturbance etc. (*disorder*) 59; commotion etc. (*agitation*) 315; bear garden, Donnybrook.

subject of dispute, ground of quarrel, battle ground, disputed point; bone -of contention, –to pick; apple of discord, *casus belli* [*L.*]; question at issue etc. (*subject of inquiry*) 461; vexed question, *vexata quaestio* [*L.*], brand of discord.

contentiousness etc. *adj.;* enmity etc. 889; hate etc. 898; troublous times; cat-and-dog life; Kilkenny cats; disputant etc. 710; strange bedfellows.

v. **disagree**; be discordant etc. *adj.;* disaccord, come amiss etc. 24; clash, jar, jostle, pull different ways, conflict, have no measures with, misunderstand one another; live like cat and dog; differ; dissent etc. 489; have a bone to pick with, have a crow to pluck with.

quarrel, fall out, dispute; litigate; controvert etc. (*deny*) 536; squabble, tiff, spat, altercate, row [*colloq.*], brabble, wrangle, jangle, brangle, bicker, nag; spar etc. (*contend*) 720; have words with etc. *n.;* fall foul of.

split; break–, break squares–, part company- with; declare war, try conclusions; join–, put in- issue; pick a quarrel, fasten a quarrel on; sow–, stir up- dissension etc. *n.;* embroil, entangle, disunite, widen the breach; rub one's fur the wrong way; get one all het up [*dial.*]; get one hot under the collar [*colloq.*]; set at odds, set together by the ears; set–, pit- against.

get into hot water, fish in troubled waters, brawl; kick up a -row, –dust [*colloq.*]; turn the house out of window.

adj. **discordant**, dissident; disagreeing etc. *v.;* out of tune, dissonant, harsh, grating, jangling, unmelodious, inharmonious, ajar; on bad terms, dissentient etc. 489; unreconciled, unpacified; inconsistent, contradictory, incongruous, discrepant.

quarrelsome, unpacific; gladiatorial, controversial, polemic, disputatious; factious; litigious, litigant.

at strife, at odds, at loggerheads, at daggers drawn, at variance, at issue, at cross-purposes, at sixes and sevens, at feud, at high words; up in arms, heated, het up [*dial.*], hot under the collar [*colloq.*], together by the ears, in hot water, embroiled; torn, disunited.

714. Concord

n. **concord**, accord, harmony, symphony; homologue, homology, correspondence; agreement etc. 23; sympathy etc. (*love*) 897; response; union, unison, unity; bonds of harmony; peace etc. 721; unanimity etc. (*assent*) 488; league etc. 712; happy family.

rapprochement [*F.*], reunion; amity etc. (*friendship*) 888; alliance, *entente cordiale* [*F.*], good understanding, conciliation, arbitration.

peacemaker, intercessor, interceder, propitiator, mediator.

v. **agree** etc. 23; accord, harmonize with, blend in with; fraternize; be concordant etc. *adj.;* go hand in hand; run parallel etc. (*concur*) 178; understand one another; pull together etc. (*cooperate*) 709; put up one's horses together, sing in chorus.

side with, sympathize with, go with, chime in with, fall in with; come round [*colloq.*]; be pacified etc. 723; assent etc. 488; enter into the -ideas, -feelings- of; reciprocate.

hurler avec les loups [*F.*]; go-, swim- with the stream; get on the band wagon [*slang*].

smooth, pour oil on the troubled waters; keep in good humor, render accordant, put in tune; come to an understanding, meet halfway; keep the peace, remain at peace; mediate, intercede.

adj. **concordant**, congenial; agreeing etc. *v.;* in accord etc. *n.;* harmonious, united, cemented; banded together etc. 712; allied; friendly etc. 888; fraternal; conciliatory; at one with; of one mind etc. (*assent*) 488.

at peace, in still water; tranquil etc. (*pacific*) 721.

adv. **unanimously**, without a dissentient voice; with one voice etc. (*assent*) 488; in concert with, hand in hand; on one's side.

int. make it unanimous! are you with us?

715. Defiance

n. **defiance**; daring etc. *v.;* dare, defial, defi [*slang*]; "dare, dare, and double-dare" [*child's challenge*]; challenge, cartel; threat etc. 909; war cry, war whoop.

v. **defy**, dare, beard; brave etc. (*courage*) 861; bid defiance to; bite the thumb at; set at defiance, set at naught; hurl defiance at; dance the war dance; snap the fingers at, laugh to scorn; disobey etc. 742.

show -fight, -one's teeth, -a bold front; bluster, look big, stand with arms akimbo; double-, shake- the fist; threaten etc. 909.

challenge, call out; throw-, fling- down the -gauntlet, -gage, -glove.

adj. **defiant**; defying etc. *v.;* with arms akimbo; rebellious, bold, insolent, reckless, contemptuous, greatly daring, regardless of consequences.

adv. **in defiance of**, in the teeth of; under one's very nose; in open rebellion.

int. do your worst! come if you dare! come on! just try it! marry come up! [*archaic or dial.*], hoity toity!

716. Attack

n. **attack**; assault, -and battery; onset, onslaught, charge.

base of operations, point of attack; echelon; open order; close formation.

aggression, offense; incursion, inroad, invasion; irruption; outbreak; bucking, estapade [*manège*], *ruade* [*F.*], kicking, kick; punch etc. (*impulse*) 276; *coup de main* [*F.*]; sally, sortie, camisade *or* camisado [*archaic*], raid, foray; run at, run against; dead set at.

storm, storming; boarding, escalade; siege, investment, obsession [*obs.*], bombardment, cannonade, barrage; zero hour.

battue [*F.*], razzia, dragonnade *or* dragoonade; devastation etc. 162; *éboulement* [*F.*].

fire, volley; direct-, ricochet-, plunging-, rolling-, horizontal-, vertical-, platoon-, file-fire; fusilade; fire of demolition, percussion fire; sharpshooting, broadside; raking-, cross-fire; volley of grapeshot, *feu d'enfer* [*F.*].

cut, thrust, lunge, pass, passado [*obs.*], stoccado *or* stoccata [*archaic*], carte (*or* quarte) and tierce, home thrust; *coup de bec* [*F.*].

assailant, aggressor, invader; sharpshooter, dead shot, fusilier, dragoon, Uhlan.

v. **attack**, assault, assail; set upon, fall upon; charge, impugn, break a lance with, enter the lists.

show fight, come on; assume-, take- the offensive; be-, become- the aggressor; strike the first blow, throw the first stone at, fire the first shot; lift a hand-, draw the sword- against; take up the cudgels; advance-, march- against; march upon, invade, harry.

strike at, poke at, thrust at; aim-, deal- a blow at; give-, fetch- one a -blow, -kick; have a -cut, -shot, -fling, -shy- at; be down upon, pounce upon; fall foul of, light into [*colloq.*], pitch into [*colloq.*], launch out against; bait, slap on the face; make a -thrust, -pass, -set, -dead set- at; bear down upon.

close with, come to close quarters, bring to bay, come to blows.

ride full tilt against; let fly at, dash at, run a tilt at, rush at, tilt at, run at, fly at, hawk at, have at, let out at; make a -dash, -rush at; attack tooth and nail; strike home; drive–, press- one hard; be hard upon, run down, strike at the root of.

lay about one, run amuck.

fire upon, fire at, fire a shot at; draw a bead on; shoot at, pop at, level at, let off a gun at; open fire, pepper, bombard, shell, pour a broadside into; fire a volley, fire red-hot shot; spring a mine.

stone, lapidate, pelt; throw - a stone, –stones - at; hurl -at, –against, –at the head of; rock.

beset, besiege, beleaguer; lay siege to, invest, open the trenches, plant a battery, sap, mine; storm, board, scale the walls, go over the top.

cut and thrust, bayonet, give one the bayonet; butt; kick, strike etc. (*impulse*) 276; horsewhip, whip etc. (*punish*) 972.

adj. **attacking** etc. *v.;* aggressive, offensive, incursive, invasive, irruptive, obsidional.

up in arms.

adv. **on the offensive**, on the warpath, amuck, amok. over the top; at bay.

int. "up and at them!"

717. Defense

n. **defense** or defence, protection, guard, ward; shielding etc. *v.;* propugnation [*obs.*]; preservation etc. 670; guardianship.

self-defense, self-preservation; resistance etc. 719.

safeguard etc. (*safety*) 664; screen etc. (*shelter*) 666, (*concealment*) 350; fortification; munition, muniment; bulwark, fosse, trench, mine, countermine, dugout; moat, ditch, intrenchment or entrenchment, vallation, rampart, scarp, escarp, counterscarp, vanfoss; dike or dyke; parapet, sunk fence, haha, embankment, mound, mole, bank; earthwork, fieldwork; fence, wall, dead wall, contravallation or countervallation; paling etc. (*inclosure*) 232; palisade, stockade, stoccado [*obs.*], laager [*S. Africa*], sangar [*India*]; barrier, barricade; boom; portcullis, *chevaux de frise* [*F.*]; abatis or abattis, barbed wire entanglements, vallum [*Rom. antiq.*], circumvallation, merlon, battlement, glacis; casemate; buttress, abutment; shore etc. (*support*) 215.

breastwork, banquette, mantelet or mantlet, tenaille or tenail, ravelin, curtain, demilune, half-moon; bastion, demibastion, redan; vauntmure [*rare*], faussebraie or faussebraye, advanced work, hornwork, lunette, outwork; barbican, redoubt, sconce, fortalice; lines.

machicolation, bartizan, loophole, balistraria [*ancient fortification*]; postern gate, sally port.

stronghold, hold, fastness; asylum etc. (*refuge*) 666; keep, donjon, citadel, capitol, castle; tower, –of strength; fortress, propugnaculum, fort, kila [*India*]; barracoon, barrack; pah or pa [*N. Z.*]; peel, peel tower, peelhouse; rath [*Ir. antiq.*]; martello tower, blockhouse, wooden walls.

[protective devices] buffer, fender, cowcatcher; apron, mask, gauntlet, thimble; armor or armour, shield, buckler, scutum [*Rom. antiq.*], target, targe [*archaic*], aegis, breastplate, cuirass, backplate, habergeon, mail, coat of mail, brigandine, hauberk, lorica, helm [*archaic*], armet, basinet or bassinet, sallet or salade, greave, jambe, heaume, morion, cabasset, beaver, visor or vizor; face guard, helmet, casque, casquetel, siege cap, headpiece; steel helmet, tin -helmet, –hat [*soldiers' cant*]; camail, neckguard; *Pickelhaube* [*Ger.*]; spiked helmet; shako etc. (*dress*) 225; bearskin; vambrace, rerebrace, cubitière; sollerets, pédieux; panoply, caparison, housings; chamfron or chamfrain; truncheon etc. (*weapon*) 727; carapace, shell; spines, needles.

defender, protector; Defender of the Faith, *fidei defensor* [*L.*], guardian etc. (*safety*) 664; bodyguard, champion; knight-errant, Paladin; propugnator or propugner or propugnor [*obs.*]; picket; garrison.

v. **defend**, forfend or forefend [*archaic*], fend; shield, screen, shroud; engarrison, garrison, man; fence round etc. (*circumscribe*) 229; fence, intrench or entrench; arm, harness [*archaic*], accouter or accoutre; guard etc. (*keep safe*) 664; guard against; take care of etc. (*vigilance*) 459; bear harmless; fend–, keep–, ward–, beat- off; hinder etc. 706.

repel, parry, propugn [*obs.*], put to flight; give a warm reception to [*ironical*]; hold - keep- at -bay, –arm's length.

resist invasion, stand siege; be–, stand–, act- on the defensive; show fight; maintain–, stand- one's ground; stand by; hold one's own; bear–, stand- the brunt; fall back upon, hold, stand in the gap.

adj. **defending** etc. *v.;* defensive; mural; armed, –at all points, –cap-a-pie, –to the teeth; panoplied; accoutered or accoutred, harnessed [*archaic*], "in complete steel" [*Hamlet*]; iron-plated, ironclad; loopholed, castellated, machicolated, casemated; defended etc. *v.;* proof against, ball-proof, bullet-proof; protective.

adv. **defensively**; on the defensive; in defense; in self-defense; at bay, *pro aris et focis* [*L.*].

int. **no surrender**! *"ils ne passeront pas!"* "they shall not pass!" [*the French at Verdun*].

718. Retaliation

n. **retaliation**, reprisal, talion [*rare*], retort; counterstroke, counterblast, counterplot, counterproject; retribution, *lex talionis* [*L.*]; reciprocation etc. (*reciprocity*) 12.

requital, desert; tit for tat, give and take, blow for blow, *quid pro quo* [*L.*], a Roland for an Oliver, measure for measure, diamond cut diamond, an eye for an eye, boomerang, the biter bit, a game at which two can play; reproof valiant, retort courteous.

recrimination etc. (*accusation*) 938; revenge etc. 919; compensation etc. 30; reaction etc. (*recoil*) 277.

v. **retaliate**, retort, turn upon; pay, pay off, pay back; pay in -one's own, –the same- coin; cap, match; reciprocate etc. 148; turn the tables upon, return the compliment; give a *quid pro quo* etc. *n.*, give as much as one takes; give as good as was sent; exchange blows; give and take, exchange fisticuffs; be quits, be even with; pay off old scores.

serve one right, be hoist on one's own petard, throw a stone in one's own garden, catch a Tartar.

adj. **retaliating** etc. *v.;* retaliatory, retaliative, retributive, recriminatory, reciprocal; talionic [*rare*].

adv. **in retaliation**; *en revanche* [*F.*].

719. Resistance

n. **resistance**, stand, front, oppugnation [*rare*], oppugnance, oppugnancy; opposition etc. 708; renitency, renitence, reluctance [*archaic*], reluctation [*rare*], recalcitrance *or* recalcitrancy, recalcitration; repugnance, repulsion; kicking etc. *v.*

repulse, rebuff, snub.

insurrection etc. (*disobedience*) 742; strike; turnout [*colloq.*], lockout; barring-out; *levée en masse* [*F.*], *Jacquerie* [*F. hist.*]; rebellion; boycott; riot etc. (*disorder*) 59.

v. **resist**; not submit etc. 725; repugn [*obs.*], reluctate [*rare*], oppugn, withstand; stand up–, strive–, bear up–, be proof–, make head-against; stand, –firm, –fast, –one's ground, –the brunt of, –out; hold -one's ground, –one's own, –out; stick it out [*colloq.*].

face, confront, breast the -wave, –current; stem the -tide, –torrent; grapple with; show a bold front etc. (*courage*) 861; present a front, make a stand, take one's stand.

oppose etc. 708; kick, –against; recalcitrate, kick against the pricks; fly in the face of; lift the hand against etc. (*attack*) 716; withstand -an attack, –a siege, –the onset; rise up in arms etc. (*war*) 722; strike, turn out; draw up a round robin etc. (*remonstrate*) 932; put one's foot down; boycott; revolt etc. (*disobey*) 742; make a riot.

prendre le mors aux dents [*F.*], take the bit between the teeth; sell one's life dearly, die hard, keep at bay; repel, repulse.

adj. **resisting** etc. *v.;* oppugnant, resistive, resistant; refractory etc. (*disobedient*) 742; repugnant; recalcitrant, renitent, repulsive, repellent; up in arms.

proof against; unconquerable etc. (*strong*) 159; stubborn, unconquered; indomitable etc. (*persevering*) 604*a*; unyielding etc. (*obstinate*) 606.

int. **hands off**! keep off!

never say die! stick it! [*colloq.*]; show what you're made of! give 'em hell! [*colloq.*]; "up, Guards, and at them!" [*Wellington—at Waterloo, as alleged*].

720. Contention

n. **contention**, strife; contest, contestation; struggle; belligerency; opposition etc. 708.

controversy, polemics; debate etc. (*discussion*) 476; war of words, logomachy, litigation; paper war; high words etc. (*quarrel*) 713; sparring etc. *v.*

competition, rivalry; corrivalry, corrivalship; agonism [*obs.*], *concours* [*F.*], match, race, tug of war, horse racing, heat, dash, steeple chase, point-to-point race, handicap; regatta; field day; sham fight, Derby day; turf, sporting, bullfight, tauromachy [*rare*], gymkhana [*orig. Anglo-Indian*]; boat race, torpids [*Oxford Univ.*].

pugilism, boxing, fisticuffs, spar, mill [*cant*], set-to [*colloq.*], round, bout, event; prize fighting; quarterstaff, single stick; gladiatorship, gymnastics; wrestling; catch-as-catch-can–, Greco-Roman (*or* Graeco-Roman)–, Cornish–, Westmorland and Cumberland- style [of wrestling]; jujutsu (*also* jujitsu, jiujutsu, jiujitsu), *samo* [*Jap.*], *kooshti* [*Hind.*]; karate; athletics, athletic sports; games of skill etc. 840.

fracas etc. (*discord*) 713; clash of arms; tussle, scuffle, broil, fray; affray, affrayment [*obs.*]; velitation [*obs.*]; luctation [*rare*], colluctation

256

[*obs.*], shindy [*Brit. colloq.*], brigue [*obs.*], brabble, scramble, *mêlée* [*F.*], scrimmage, stramash [*dial. or slang*], free-for-all [*cant*]; free-, stand up-, hand to hand-, running- fight.

conflict, skirmish; encounter, rencounter, rencontre, collision, affair, brush, fight; sharp contest, hard knocks; battle, −royal; combat, action, engagement, just *or* joust, tournament; tilt, tilting; tourney, lists; pitched battle; guerrilla (*or* guerilla)−, irregular- warfare; bush-fighting.

deeds−, feats- of arms; pugnacity; combativeness etc. *adj.;* bone of contention etc. 713.

death struggle, struggle for life or death, Armageddon.

naval engagement, naumachia *or* naumachy, sea fight.

duel, duello [*rare*], single combat, *monomachia* [*L.*] *or* monomachy, satisfaction, *passage d'armes* [*F.*], passage of arms, affair of honor; triangular duel; hostile meeting, digladiation [*archaic*]; appeal to arms etc. (*warfare*) 722.

v. **contend**; contest, strive, struggle, scramble, wrestle; spar, square [*colloq.*]; exchange -blows, −fisticuffs; fib [*slang, Eng.*], jostle *or* justle, tussle, tilt, box, stave [*obs. or dial.*], fence; skirmish; pickeer [*obs.*]; fight etc. (*war*) 722; wrangle etc. (*quarrel*) 713.

contend etc. with; grapple−, engage−, close−, buckle [*obs.*]−, bandy−, try conclusions−, have a brush etc. *n.* −, tilt- with; encounter, fall foul of, pitch into [*colloq.*], clapperclaw [*archaic or dial.*], run a tilt at; oppose etc. 708; reluct.

compete−, cope−, vie−, race- with; outvie, emulate, rival; run a race.

contend etc. for, stipulate for, stickle for; insist upon, make a point of.

join issue, come to blows; be at−, fall to−, go to- loggerheads; set to, come to the scratch, pull a gun [*slang*], exchange shots, measure swords, meet hand to hand; take up the -cudgels, −glove, −gauntlet; tourney, just *or* joust, enter the lists; couch one's lance; give satisfaction; appeal to arms etc. (*warfare*) 722.

lay about one; break the peace.

adj. **contending** etc. *v.;* at loggerheads, at war, at issue.

contentious, combative, bellicose, belligerent, unpeaceful; warlike etc. 722; quarrelsome etc. 901; pugnacious, pugilistic; tauromachian *or* tauromachic [*rare*]; gladiatorial.

athletic, gymnastic, palaestral *or* palestral, palaestric *or* palestric; competitive, rival.

721. Peace

n. **peace**; amity etc. (*friendship*) 888; pacifism; harmony etc. (*concord*) 714; tranquility etc. (*quiescence*) 265; truce etc. (*pacification*) 723; pipe of peace, calumet.

piping time of peace, quiet life; neutrality.

v. **be at peace**; keep the peace etc. (*concord*) 714; make peace etc. 723; pacify; be a pacifist.

adj. **pacific**; peaceable, peaceful; calm, tranquil, untroubled, halcyon; bloodless; neutral, pacifistic, "too proud to fight" [Woodrow Wilson].

722. Warfare

n. **warfare**; fighting etc. *v.;* hostilities; war, arms, the sword; Mars, Bellona, grim-visaged war, *horrida bella* [*L.*]; bloodshed.

appeal to -arms, −the sword; ordeal−, wager- of battle; *ultima ratio regum* [*L.*], arbitrament of the sword, declaration of war.

battle array, campaign, crusade, expedition; mobilization; state of siege; battlefield etc. (*arena*) 728; warpath.

art of war, rules of war, the war game, tactics, strategy, castrametation; generalship, soldiership; military evolutions, ballistics, gunnery; aviation; chivalry; gunpowder, shot, shell, poison gas.

battle, conflict etc. (*contention*) 720; service, campaigning, active service, tented field; kriegspiel *or Kriegsspiel* [*Ger.*], fiery cross, trumpet, clarion, bugle, pibroch, slogan; war cry, war whoop; battle cry, beat of drum, *rappel* [*F.*], tom-tom; word of command; password, watchword; *passage d'armes* [*F.*].

war to the -death, −knife; *guerre à -mort, −outrance* [*F.*]; open−, trench−, guerrilla (*or* guerilla)−, internecine−, civil- war (*or* warfare).

war medal, military medal, Congressional medal, Victoria Cross, V. C., *croix de guerre* [*F.*], *médaille militaire* [*F.*], iron cross [*Ger.*].

war news, war bulletin, war extra; war correspondent.

v. **arm**; prepare for war; raise−, mobilize- troops; raise up in arms; take up the udgels etc. 720; take up−, fly to−, appeal to- -arms, −the sword; draw−, unsheathe- the sword; dig up the -hatchet, −tomahawk.

war, make war, go to war, declare war, wage war, "let slip the dogs of war" [*Julius Caesar*]; cry havoc; kindle−, light- the torch of war; raise one's banner, send round the fiery cross, hoist the black flag; throw−, fling- away the scabbard; take the field; take the law into one's own hands; do−, give−, join−, engage in−, go to-battle; flesh one's sword; set to, fall to, engage, measure swords with, draw the trigger, cross swords; come to -blows, −close quarters; fight; combat; contend etc. 720; battle with, break a lance with.

serve; enroll, enlist; see−, be on- -service, −active service; campaign; wield the sword, shoulder a musket, smell powder, be under fire; spill blood, imbrue the hands in blood; be on the warpath.

carry on -war, −hostilities; keep the field; fight the good fight; take by storm; go over the top [*World War I*]; fight -it out, −like devils, −one's way, −hand to hand; cut one's way -out, −through; sell one's life dearly.

adj. **armed**, −to the teeth, −cap-a-pie; sword in hand; contending, contentious etc. 720; in−, under−, up in- arms; at war with; bristling with arms; in battle array, in open arms, in the field; embattled; battled.

warlike, belligerent, combative, armigerous, bellicose, martial, unpacific, unpeaceful; military, militant; soldier like, soldierly, chivalrous; strategical, civil, internecine; irregular, guerrilla *or* guerilla.

adv. *flagrante bello* [*L.*], in the thick of the fray, in the cannon's mouth; at the sword's point, at the point of the bayonet.

int. **to arms**! *vae victis!* [*L.*] to your tents O Israel! *c'est la guerre!* [*F.*].

723. Pacification

n. **pacification**, conciliation; reconciliation, reconcilement, shaking of hands, calumet, peace pipe; accommodation, arrangement, adjustment; terms, compromise; amnesty, deed of release.

peace offering; olive branch; calumet, −of peace; overture, preliminaries of peace.

truce, armistice; suspension of -arms, −hostilities; truce of God; breathing time; convention; *modus vivendi* [*L.*]; flag of truce, white flag, *parlementaire* [*F.*], cartel.

hollow truce, *pax in bello* [*L.*]; drawn battle.

v. **pacify**, tranquilize, compose; allay etc. (*moderate*) 174; reconcile, propitiate, placate, conciliate, meet halfway, hold out the olive branch, heal the breach, make peace, restore harmony, bring to terms.

make up a quarrel; settle−, arrange−, accommodate- -matters, −differences; set straight; *tantas componere lites* [*L.*]; come to -an understanding, −terms; bridge over, hush up; make it up, make matters up; shake hands; mend one's fences.

raise a siege; put up−, sheathe- the sword; bury the hatchet, lay down one's arms, turn swords into plowshares; smoke the calumet, close the temple of Janus; keep the peace etc. (*concord*) 714; be pacified etc.; come round.

adj. **conciliatory**, pacificatory; composing etc. *v.;* pacified etc. *v.;* accommodative.

724. Mediation

n. **mediation**, mediatorship, mediatization, mediatorialism; intervention, interposition, interference, intermeddling, intercession; parley, negotiation, arbitration; flag of truce etc. 723; good offices, peace offering; diplomatics [*rare*], diplomacy; compromise etc. 774.

mediator, intercessor, peacemaker, make-peace, negotiator, go-between; diplomatist etc. (*consignee*) 758; moderator; propitiator; umpire, arbitrator, referee.

v. **mediate**, mediatize; intercede, interpose, interfere, intervene; step in, negotiate; meet halfway; arbitrate, propitiate; agree to arbitration; submit; *componere lites* [*L.*].

adj. **mediatory**, mediatorial, negotiable; mediating etc. *v.;* propitiatory, diplomatic.

725. Submission

n. **submission**, yielding, acquiescence, compliance, submittal, submissiveness, deference, nonresistance; obedience etc. 743.

surrender, cession, capitulation, resignation, backdown [*colloq.*]; passing under the yoke, laying down one's arms, delivering up the keys (of the city etc.), handing over one's sword.

obeisance, homage, kneeling, genuflexion, curtsy *or* curtsey, kotow *or* kowtow [*Chinese*], salaam *or* salam [*Oriental*], prostration.

v. **submit**, succumb, yield, bend, stoop, accede, relent, resign, defer to.

surrender, −at discretion; cede, capitulate, come to terms, retreat, beat a retreat; lay down−, deliver up- one's arms; lower−, haul down−, strike- one's -flag, −colors; draw in one's horns etc. (*humility*) 879; give -way, −ground, −in, −up; cave in [*colloq.*]; suffer judgment by default; bend, −to one's yoke, −before the storm; reel back; bend−, knuckle- -down, −to, −under; knock under.

humble oneself; eat -dirt, −crow, −the leek, −humble pie; bite−, lick- the dust; be−, fall- at one's feet; crouch before, throw oneself at the feet of; swallow the -leek, −pill; kiss the rod; turn the other cheek; *avaler les couleuvres* [*F.*], gulp down.

pocket the affront; make the best of, make a virtue of necessity; grin and abide, grin and bear it, shrug the shoulders, resign oneself; submit with a good grace etc. (*bear with*) 826.

yield obeisance; obey etc. 743; kneel to, bow to, pay homage to, cringe to, truckle to; bend the -neck, –knee; kneel, fall on one's knees, bow submission, curtsy *or* curtsey, kotow *or* kowtow [*Chinese*].

adj. **submissive**, resigned, crouching, prostrate; downtrodden; surrendering etc. *v.;* down on one's marrowbones [*slang*]; on one's bended knee; nonresisting, unresisting; pliant etc. (*soft*) 324; humble etc. 879; undefended.

untenable, indefensible, insupportable, unsupportable.

726. Combatant

n. **combatant**; disputant, controversialist, polemic, litigant, belligerent; competitor, rival, corrival; fighter, assailant; champion, Paladin; moss-trooper, swashbuckler, fire eater, duelist, swordsman, *sabreur* [*F.*], *beau sabreur* [*F.*]; athlete, wrestler, boxer.

bully, bludgeon man, rough, rowdy, ruffian, tough [*colloq., U. S.*], gunman [*colloq.*], Thug *or* thug; terrorist etc. 887; fighting man, prize fighter, pugilist, bruiser, the fancy [*now rare*], gladiator, fighting-cock, gamecock.

soldier, warrior, brave, man at arms, guardsman, *gendarme* [*F.*]; campaigner, veteran; redcoat, military man, Rajput; armiger, esquire, knight; Amazon.

Janizary *or* Janissary; myrmidon; Mameluke *or* Mamaluke, spahi *or* spahee, bashi-bazouk [*Turk.*], Cossack, Croat, Pandor; irregular, free lance, franc-tireur, tirailleur, guerrilla *or* guerilla, *condottiere* [*It.*], mercenary; bushwhacker, companion; Hessian.

private, –soldier; Tommy Atkins [*Brit.*], doughboy [*slang*], grunt [*slang*], G.I. [*slang*], rank and file, peon, sepoy [*India*], *légionnaire* [*F.*], legionary, food for powder, fodder for cannon, cannon fodder, *Kannonenfutter* [*Ger.*]; spearman, pikeman; archer, bowman; halberdier; musketeer, carabineer, rifleman, sharpshooter, jäger *or* yager, skirmisher; grenadier, fusileer, infantryman, foot soldier, footman [*rare*], light infantryman, chasseur, zouave; artilleryman, gunner, cannoneer, bombardier [*hist.*], matross [*obs.*]; engineer, sapper, –and miner; cavalryman, trooper, sowar [*India*], dragoon; light–, heavy- dragoon; heavy, cuirassier, hussar, lancer; recruit, rookie [*slang*], conscript, drafted man, enlisted man.

officer etc. (*commander*) 745; subaltern, ensign, standard bearer.

horse and foot; cavalry, horse, light horse, mounted rifles; infantry, foot, light infantry, rifles; artillery, horse artillery, field artillery, gunners; military train.

armed force, troops, soldiery, military, forces, Sabaoth, host, the army, standing army, regulars, the line, troops of the line, militia, national guard, state guard, bodyguard, yeomanry, volunteers, trainband, fencibles [*hist.*]; auxiliary, *bersagliere* [*It.*]; *garde -nationale, –royale* [*F.*]; minuteman [*Am. hist.*]; auxiliary–, reserve- forces; reserves, *posse comitatus* [*L.*], posse; guards, yeomen of the guard, beefeaters [*Eng.*], life guards, household troops, Horse Guards, Foot Guards; Swiss guards.

levy, draft *or* draught; raw levies, awkward squad; Landwehr, Landsturm.

army, *crops d'armée* [*F.*], army corps; host, division, battalia [*rare*], sotnia [*Russ.*], column, wing, detachment, garrison, flying column, brigade, regiment, corps, battalion, squadron, company, battery, subdivision, section, platoon, squad; picket, guard, rank, file; legion, phalanx, cohort, maniple, manipulus [*Rom. hist.*]; cloud of skirmishers.

war horse, charger, destrer *or* destrier [*archaic*].

navy, first line of defense, wooden walls, naval forces, fleet, flotilla, armada, squadron; man-of-war's man etc. (*sailor*) 269; marines.

man-of-war, line-of-battle ship, ship of the line, battleship, warship, ironclad, war vessel, war castle, H.M.S., U.S.S.; superdreadnought, dreadnought, cruiser; armored–, protected-cruiser; torpedo-boat, –destroyer; destroyer, torpedo-catcher, gunboat; submarine, submersible, U-boat; submarine chaser; mine layer, sweeper; turret ship, ram, monitor, floating battery; first-rate, frigate, sloop of war, corvet *or* corvette; bomb vessel; flagship, guard ship, privateer; troopship, transport, tender, storeship, catamaran [*obs.*], fire boat.

aeroplane, airplane, *avion* [*F.*], Fokker, dirigible, blimp; zeppelin etc. (*aeronautics*) 273.

727. Arms

n. **arms**, arm, weapon, deadly weapon; armament, armature; panoply, stand of arms; armor etc. (*defense*) 717; armory etc. (*store*) 636; *apparatus belli* [*L.*]; gunnery; ballistics etc. (*propulsion*) 284.

side arms, *armes blanches* [*F.*], sword; good–, trusty–, naked- sword; cold steel, naked steel,

steel, blade, brand [archaic]; broadsword, Toledo, Ferrara, claymore, glaive [archaic] or glave [obs.]; saber or sabre, cutlass, hanger, bilbo, falchion, scimitar or cimeter [obs.], whinyard [obs.], rapier, tuck [hist.], foil, yataghan (also ataghan, attaghan); dagger, poniard, baselard, dirk, stiletto, katar or kuttar [India], stylet; skean, skean dhu [Scot.]; creese or kris; dudgeon [archaic], bowie knife; bayonet, sword bayonet, sword stick.

ax or **axe**, battle ax, Lochaber ax, adaga, poleax or poleaxe, halberd or halbert, gisarme, tomahawk, bill, black bill, brown bill, partisan.

spear, lance, pike, spontoon, assagai or assegai, javelin, jereed or jerid, dart, shaft, bolt, reed, arrow; harpoon, gaff, eelspear; weet-weet, womerah, throwing stick, throw stick, boomerang; oxgoad, ankus.

club, war club, waddy [Austral.], mace, truncheon, staff, bludgeon, cudgel, shillalah or shillelagh, handstaff, quarterstaff; bat, cane, stick, walking-stick, knuckle duster; billy, life-preserver, blackjack, sandbag.

bow, crossbow, arbalest, ballista or balista, balister [obs.], trebuchet or trebucket, catapult, sling; battering-ram etc. (impulse) 276.

firearms; gun, piece; artillery, ordnance; siege–, battering- train; park, battery; cannon, gun of position, heavy gun, fieldpiece, field gun, mountain gun, siege gun, seacoast gun; mortar, howitzer, carronade, culverin, basilisk [obs.]; falconet, jingal swivel, swivel gun, pedrero or pederero, bouche à feu [F.], smooth bore, rifled cannon; Armstrong–, Lancaster–, Paixhans–, Whitworth–, Parrott–, Krupp–, Vickers–, Benet-Mercié–, Gatling–, Maxim–, machine- gun; pompom, mitrailleuse [F.]; "seventy-five" [French rapid-fire 75 mm. field gun]; Lewis gun; auto-rifle, ten-pounder; bazooka; flame-thrower, Flammenwerfer [Ger.], lance-flamme [F.].

small arms; musketry; musket, firelock, fowling piece, rifle, fusil [obs. or hist.], escopette or escopet, carbine, blunderbuss, musketoon, Brown Bess, matchlock, harquebus or arquebus, caliver, hackbut or hagbut, shotgun, petronel [hist.]; small bore; breechloader, muzzle-loader; gunflint, gunlock; Minié–, Enfield–, Flobert–, Westley Richards–, Snider–, Martini-Henry–, Lee-Metford–, Lee-Enfield–, Mauser–, Mannlicher–, Springfield–, magazine- rifle; needle gun, chassepot [F.]; wind gun, air gun; automatic -gun, –pistol; automatic; revolver, repeater; shooting iron [slang],

shooter [colloq.], six-shooter, gun, pistol, pistolet [obs.].

missile, bolt, projectile, shot, ball; grape; grape–, canister–, bar–, cannon–, langrage or langrel–, round–, chain- shot; slung shot; shrapnel, mitraille [F.], grenade, hand grenade, rifle grenade; shell, high-explosive shell, obus explosif [F.], bomb, depth bomb, smoke bomb, gas bomb; bullet; dumdum–, man-stopping–, explosive–, expanding- bullet; petard; infernal machine, torpedo; carcass, rocket; congreve, –rocket; slug, stone, rock, brickbat.

thunderbolt, levin- -bolt, –brand; stroke, stroke of lightning, thunderstone [obs. or dial. Eng.].

ammunition; powder, –and shot; explosive; gunpowder, "villanous saltpetre" (villainous saltpeter) [Henry IV.]; guncotton, pyroxylin or pyroxyline, dynamite, melinite, cordite, gelignite, lyddite, nitroglycerin or nitrogylcerine, trinitrotoluol, trinitrotoluene, T.N.T.; cartridge; ball cartridge, cartouche, fireball; poison gas, mustard gas, chlorine gas, tear gas etc.

728. Arena

n. **arena**, field, platform; scene of action, theater or theatre, walk, course; hustings; stage, boards etc. (playhouse) 599; amphitheater or amphitheatre, Coliseum, Colosseum; Flavian amphitheater, hippodrome, circus, race course, corso [It.], turf, cockpit, bear garden, gymnasium, palaestra or palestra, ring, lists; tilt-yard, tilting ground; Campus Martius [L.], Champ de Mars [F.]; campus, playing field, playground.

battle field, battle ground; field of -battle, –slaughter; No Man's Land [World War I]; "over there" [used in America, esp. of the Western Front in World War I], "out there" [corresponding term in Eng.]; theater–, seat- of war; Aceldama, camp; the enemy's camp.

trysting place etc. (place of meeting) 74.

Section 5. Results of Action

729. Completion

n. **completion**; accomplishment, achievement, fulfillment or fulfilment; performance, execution; dispatch or despatch, consummation, culmination; finish, conclusion; limit, effectuation; close etc. (end) 67; terminus etc. (arrival) 292; winding up; finale [It.], dénouement [F.], catastrophe, issue, upshot, result; final–, last–, crowning–, finishing- touch, –stroke; last finish, coup de grâce [F.]; crowning of the edifice; coping stone, copestone, keystone; missing link etc. 53; superstructure, *ne plus ultra* [*L.*], work done, *fait accompli* [*F.*]. elaboration; finality; completeness etc. 52.

v. **complete**, perfect; effect, effectuate; accomplish, achieve, compass, consummate, hammer out; bring to -maturity, −perfection; elaborate.

do, execute, make; go−, get- through; work out, enact; bring -about, −to bear, −to pass, −through, −to a head.

dispatch *or* despatch, knock off [*colloq.*], finish off, polish off; make short work of; dispose of, set at rest; perform, discharge fulfill *or* fulfil, realize; put in -practice, −force; carry -out, −into effect, −into execution; make good; be as good as one's word.

do thoroughly, not do by halves, go the whole hog [*colloq.*]; drive home, be in at the death etc. (*persevere*) 604a; carry through, deliver the goods [*colloq.*], play out, exhaust; fill the bill [*colloq.*].

finish, bring to a close etc. (*end*) 67; wind up, stamp, clinch, seal, set the seal on, put the seal to; give the final touch etc. *n.* to; put the -last, −finishing- touch to; crown, crown all; cap.

ripen, culminate; come to a -head, −crisis; come to its end; die a natural death, die of old age; run its course, run one's race; touch−, reach−, attain- the goal; reach etc. (*arrive*) 292; get in the harvest.

adj. **completing**, final; concluding, conclusive; crowning etc. *v.;* exhaustive, elaborate, complete, mature, perfect, consummate, thorough.

done, completed etc. *v.;* done for [*colloq.*], sped, wrought out; highly wrought etc. (*preparation*) 673; thorough etc. 52; ripe etc. (*ready*) 673.

adv. **completely** etc. (*thoroughly*) 52; to crown all, out of hand; with absolute -perfection, −finish; as a last stroke; as a fitting climax.

730. Noncompletion

n. **noncompletion**, nonfulfillment *or* nonfulfilment, shortcoming etc. 304; incompleteness etc. 53; drawn -battle, −game; work of Penelope; Sisyphean -labor, −toil, −task.

nonperformance, inexecution; neglect of execution; neglect etc. 460.

v. **not complete** etc. 729; leave unfinished etc. *adj.,* leave undone; neglect etc. 460; let alone, let slip; lose sight of.

fall short of etc. 304; do things by halves, scotch the snake not kill it; hang fire; be slow to; collapse etc. 304.

adj. **incomplete** etc. 53; not completed etc. *v.;* uncompleted, unfinished, unaccomplished, unperformed, unexecuted; sketchy; addle, muddled, sterile.

in progress, in hand, on the stocks, in preparation, moving, getting along, going on, proceeding; on one's hands; on the anvil.

adv. *re infecta* [*L.*]; without−, lacking- -the final touches, −the finishing stroke.

731. Success

n. **success**, successfulness; speed; advance etc. (*progress*) 282.

trump card; hit, stroke; lucky−, fortunate−, good- -hit, −stroke; bold stroke, masterstroke; ten-strike [*colloq.*]; *coup de maître* [*F.*], checkmate; half the battle, prize; profit etc. (*acquisition*) 775.

continued success; good fortune etc. (*prosperity*) 734; time well spent.

mastery, advantage over; upper hand, whip hand; ascendancy, expugnation [*obs.*], conquest, victory, walkover [*colloq.*], subdual; subjugation etc. (*subjection*) 749; triumph etc. (*exultation*) 884; proficiency etc. (*skill*) 698; a feather in one's cap [*colloq.*].

victor, victress [*rare*], victrix [*rare*], conqueror, master, champion, winner; master of the -situation, −position.

v. **succeed**; be successful etc. *adj.;* gain one's -end, −ends; crown with success.

gain−, attain−, carry−, secure−, win- -a point, −an object; get there [*colloq.*]; manage to, contrive to; accomplish etc. (*effect, complete*) 729; do−, work- wonders; make a go of it [*colloq.*].

come off -well, −successfully, −with flying colors; make short work of; take−, carry- by storm; bear away the bell; win one's spurs, win the battle; win−, carry−, gain- the -day, −prize, −palm; have the best of it, have it all one's own way, have the game in one's own hands, have the ball at one's feet, have one on the hip; walk over the course; carry all before one, remain in possession of the field; socre a success, strike it rich, hit pay dirt.

make progress etc. (*advance*) 282; win−, make−, work−, find- one's way; speed; strive to some purpose; prosper etc. 734; drive a roaring trade; make profit etc. (*acquire*) 775; reap−, gather- the -fruits, −benefit of, −harvest; strike oil [*slang*], make one's fortune, get in the harvest, turn to good account; turn to account etc. (*use*) 677.

triumph, be triumphant; gain–, obtain- a victory, –an advantage; chain victory to one's car.

surmount–, overcome–, get over–, –an obstacle etc. 706; *se tirer d'affaire* [*F.*]; make head against; stem the -torrent, –tide, –current; weather -the storm, –a point; turn a corner, keep one's head above water, tide over; master; get–, have–, gain- the -better of, –best of, –upper hand, –ascendancy, –whip hand, –start of; distance; surpass etc. (*superiority*) 33.

defeat, conquer, vanquish, discomfit; euchre [*slang*]; overcome, overthrow, overpower, overmaster, overmatch, overset, override, overreach; outwit, outdo, outflank, outmaneuver *or* outmanoeuvre, outgeneral, outvote; take the wind out of one's adversary's sails; beat, beat hollow [*colloq.*], lick [*colloq.*], rout, drub, floor, worst, lick to a frazzle [*colloq.*]; put -down, –to flight, –to the rout, –*hors de combat* [*F.*], –out of court.

settle [*colloq.*], do for [*colloq.*], break the -neck of, –back of; capsize, sink, shipwreck, drown, swamp; subdue; subjugate etc. (*subject*) 749; reduce; make the enemy bite the dust; victimize, roll in the dust, trample under foot, put an extinguisher upon.

checkmate, silence, quell, nonsuit, upset, confound, nonplus, stalemate, trump; baffle etc. (*hinder*) 706; circumvent, elude; trip up, –the heels of; drive -into a corner, –to the wall; run hard, put one's nose out of joint [*colloq.*].

avail; answer, –the purpose; prevail, take effect, do, turn out well, work well, take [*colloq.*], tell, bear fruit; hit it, hit the mark, hit the nail on the head; nick it; turn up trumps, make a hit; find one's account in.

adj. **successful**; prosperous etc. 734; succeeding etc. *v.*; triumphant; flushed–, crowned- with success; victorious; set up [*colloq.*]; in the ascendant; unbeaten etc. (*see* beat etc. *v.*); well-spent; felicitous, effective, in full swing.

adv. **successfully** etc. *adj.*; with flying colors, in triumph, swimmingly; *à merveille* [*F.*], beyond all hope; to some–, to good- purpose; to one's heart's content.

732. Failure

n. **failure**, unsuccess, nonsuccess, nonfulfillment *or* nonfulfilment; dead failure, successlessness; abortion, miscarriage; *brutum fulmen* [*L.*] etc. 158; labor in vain etc. (*inutility*) 645; no go [*colloq.*]; inefficacy; inefficaciousness etc.

adj.; vain–, ineffectual–, abortive- -attempt, –efforts, flash in the pan, "lame and impotent conclusion" [*Othello*]; frustration; slip 'twixt cup and lip etc. (*disappointment*) 509.

blunder etc. (*mistake*) 495; fault, omission, miss, oversight, slip, trip, stumble, claudication [*obs.*] footfall; false–, wrong- step; *faux pas* [*F.*], titubation, *bévue* [*F.*], *faute* [*F.*], lurch; botchery etc. (*want of skill*) 699; scrape, mess, muddle, botch, fiasco, breakdown; flunk [*colloq.*].

mishap etc. (*misfortune*) 735; split, collapse, smash, blow, explosion.

repulse, rebuff, defeat, rout, overthrow, discomfiture; beating, drubbing; quietus, nonsuit, subjugation; checkmate, stalemate, fool's mate.

losing game, *affaire flambée* [*F.*]

fall, downfall, ruin, perdition; wreck etc. (*destruction*) 162; deathblow; bankruptcy etc. (*nonpayment*) 808.

victim, prey; bankrupt; flunker [*colloq.*], flunky *or* flunkey [*cant*].

v. **fail**; be unsuccessful etc. *adj.*; not succeed etc. 731; make vain efforts etc. *n.*; do–, labor–, toil- in vain; flunk [*colloq.*]; lose one's labor, take nothing by one's motion; bring to naught, make nothing of; wash a black-amoor white etc. (*impossible*) 471; roll the stone of Sisyphus etc. (*useless*) 645; do by halves etc. (*not complete*) 730; lose ground etc. (*recede*) 283; fall short of etc. 304; go to -the wall, –the dogs, –pot [*colloq.*], lick–, bite- the dust; be defeated etc. 731; have the worst of it, lose the day, come off second best, lose; not have a leg to stand on; fall a prey to; succumb etc. (*submit*) 725.

miss, –one's aim, –the mark, –one's footing, –stays [*naut.*]; slip, trip, stumble; make a slip etc., *n.*; make a blunder etc. 495, make a mess of, make a botch of; bitch it [*obs.*], miscarry, abort, go up like a rocket and come down like the stick, reckon without one's host; get the wrong -pig by the tail, –sow by the ear [*colloq.*] etc. (*blunder, mismanage*) 699.

flounder, falter; limp, halt, hobble, titubate; fall, tumble; lose one's balance; fall to the ground, fall between two stools; stick in the mud, run aground, split upon a rock; run–, knock–, dash- one's head against a stone wall; break one's back; break down, sink, drown, founder, have the ground cut from under one; get into -trouble, –a mess, –a scrape; come to grief etc. (*adversity*) 735.

come to nothing, end in smoke; flat out [*colloq.*]; fall -to the ground, –through, –dead, –stillborn, –flat; slip through one's fingers; hang fire, misfire, flash in the pan, collapse;

topple down etc. (*descent*) 305; go to wrack and ruin etc. (*destruction*) 162.

go amiss, go wrong, go cross, go hard with, go on a wrong tack; go on–, come off–, turn out–, work- ill; take a wrong turn, take an ugly turn, be all over with, be all up with; explode; dash one's hopes etc. (*disappoint*) 509; defeat the purpose; sow the wind and reap the whirlwind, jump out of the frying pan into the fire.

adj. **unsuccessful**, successless, stick-it [*Scot.*]; failing, tripping etc. *v.;* at fault; unfortunate etc. 735.

abortive, sterile, impotent, addle, stillborn; fruitless, bootless; ineffectual, ineffective; inefficient etc. (*impotent*) 158; inefficacious; lame, hobbling, *décousu* [*F.*]; insufficient etc. 640; unavailing etc. (*useless*) 645; of no effect.

stranded, aground, grounded, swamped, cast away, wrecked, foundered, capsized, shipwrecked, nonsuited; foiled; defeated etc. 731; struck–, borne–, broken- down; downtrodden; overborne, overwhelmed; all up with [*colloq.*]; plowed *or* ploughed [*Eng. Univ. cant*], plucked [*college cant*].

undone, lost, ruined, broken; bankrupt etc. (*not paying*) 808; played out; done up, done for [*both colloq.*]; deadbeat [*colloq.*], ruined root and branch, *flambé* [*F.*], knocked on the head; destroyed etc. 162.

frustrated, thwarted, crossed, unhinged, disconcerted, dashed; thrown -off one's balance, –on one's back, –on one's beam ends; unhorsed, in a sorry plight; hard hit; stultified, befooled, dished [*colloq.*], hoist on one's own petard; victimized, sacrificed.

wide of the mark etc. (*error*) 495; out of one's reckoning etc. (*inexpectation*) 508; left in the lurch; thrown away etc. (*wasted*) 638; unattained; uncompleted etc. 730.

adv. **unsuccessfully** etc. *adj.;* to little or no purpose, in vain, *re infecta* [*L.*].

733. Trophy

n. **trophy**; medal, prize, palm, laurel, laurels, bays, crown, chaplet, wreath, civic crown; insignia etc. 550; eulogy, citation; fellowship, scholarship; feather in one's cap etc. (*honor*) 873; garland; triumphal arch; Victoria Cross, Congressional medal, *croix de guerre* [*F.*], *médaille militaire* [*F.*], Iron Cross; Pulitzer Prize, Oscar, Emmy; Carnegie medal, Nobel prize; blue ribbon; red ribbon of the Legion of Honor; decoration etc. 877.

triumph etc. (*celebration*) 883; flying colors etc. (*show*) 882.

734. Prosperity

n. **prosperity**, welfare, well-being; affluence etc. (*wealth*) 803; success etc. 731; thrift, roaring trade; good–, smiles of - fortune; blessings; godsend; bed of roses; fat of the land, milk and honey, loaves and fishes, fleshpots of Egypt.

luck; good–, run of- luck; sunshine; fair -weather, –wind; fair wind and no favor; palmy–, bright–, halcyon-days; piping times, tide, flood, high tide.

golden age, golden time, *Saturnia regna* [*L.*], Saturnian age.

man of substance, made man, lucky dog, *enfant gâté* [*F.*], spoiled child of fortune.

upstart, parvenu, *nouveau riche* [*F.*], narikin [*Jap.*], skipjack [*dial. Eng.*], mushroom.

v. **prosper**, thrive, flourish; be prosperous etc. *adj.;* drive a roaring trade; go on -well, –smoothly, –swimmingly; sail before the wind, swim with the tide; run -smooth, –smoothly, – on all fours [*colloq.*].

rise–, get on- in the world; work–, make- one's way; look up; lift–, raise-one's head, make one's fortune, feather one's nest, make one's pile [*slang*].

flower, blow, blossom, bloom, fructify, bear fruit, fatten, batten.

keep oneself afloat; keep–, hold-one's head above water; light–, fall-on one's -legs, –feet; drop into a good thing; bear a charmed life; bask in the sunshine; have a good (*or* fine) time of it; have a run, –of luck; have the good fortune etc. *n.* to; take a favorable turn; live -on the fat of the land, –in clover, –on velvet.

adj. **prosperous**; thriving etc. *v.;* in a fair way, buoyant; well off, well to do, well to live [*archaic*], set up [*colloq.*], well to do in the world; at one's ease; rich etc. 803; in good case; in full feather, in high feather; fortunate, lucky, in luck; born with a silver spoon in one's mouth, born under a lucky star; on the sunny side of the hedge.

palmy, halcyon; agreeable etc. 829; *couleur de rose* [*F.*].

auspicious, propitious, providential.

adv. **prosperously** etc. *adj.;* swimmingly; as good luck would have it; beyond all -expectation, –hope; beyond one's deserts; beyond the dreams of avarice.

735. Adversity

n. **adversity**, evil etc. 619; failure etc. 732; bad -ill–, evil–, adverse–, hard- -fortune, –hap, –luck, –lot; frowns of fortune; evil -dispensation, −star, −genius; ups and downs of life; the sport of fortune; broken fortunes; hard -case, −lines, −life; sea−, peck- of troubles; hell upon earth; slough of despond.

pressure of the times, iron age, evil day, time out of joint; hard−, bad−, sad- times; rainy day, cloud, dark cloud, gathering clouds, ill wind; affliction etc. (*painfulness*) 830; bitter -pill, −draft (*or* draught), −cup; care.

trouble, hardship, curse, blight, blast, load, pressure, humiliation.

misfortune, misventure [*archaic*], mishap, mischance, misadventure, disaster, calamity, catastrophe; accident, casualty, cross, blow, trial, sorrow, visitation, infliction, reverse, check, *contretemps* [*F.*], pinch, rub; backset, comedown, setback.

downfall, fall; losing game; falling etc. *v.;* ruination, ruinousness, undoing; extremity; ruin etc. (*destruction*) 162.

v.   **be ill of** etc. *adj.;* go hard with; fall on evil, −days; go on ill; not prosper etc. 734.

come to grief, go downhill, go to rack and ruin etc. (*destruction*) 162, go to the dogs [*colloq.*]; fall, −from one's high estate; decay, sink, decline, go down in the world; have seen better days; bring down one's gray hairs with sorrow to the grave; be all over with, be all up with [*colloq.*]; bring a wasp's (*or* hornet's) nest about one's ears.

adj.   **unfortunate,** unblest, unhappy, unlucky, unprosperous, improsperous [*obs.*]; hoodooed [*colloq.*], Jonahed [*slang*], jinxed [*slang*], luck-

less, hapless; out of luck; in trouble, in a bad way, in an evil plight; under a cloud; clouded; ill off, badly off; in adverse circumstances; poor etc. 804; behindhand, down in the world, decayed, undone; on the road to ruin, on its last legs, on the wane; in one's utmost need; up the creek without a paddle [*colloq.*].

ill-fated, ill-starred, ill-omened; planet-struck, devoted, doomed; inauspicious, unauspicious [*rare*], ominous, sinister, unpropitious; unfavorable; born -under an evil star, −with a wooden ladle in one's mouth.

adverse, untoward; disastrous, calamitous, ruinous, dire, deplorable.

adv.   if the worst come to the worst, as ill luck would have it, from bad to worse, out of the frying pan into the fire.

736. Mediocrity

n.   **mediocrity;** golden mean etc. (*mid-course*) 628, (*moderation*) 174; moderate−, average- circumstances; respectability.

middle classes, *bourgeoisie* [*F.*].

v.   strike the golden mean; preserve a middle course etc. 628.

jog on, get along [*colloq.*], get by [*slang*]; go−, get on- -fairly, −quietly, −peaceably, −tolerably, −respectably.

adj.   **middling,** *comme ci comme ça* [*F.*], so-so, fair, fair to middling [*colloq.*], medium, moderate, mediocre, ordinary; second−, third−, fourth-rate.

adv.   with nothing to brag about.

Division 2. Intersocial Volition

Section 1. General

737. Authority

n.   **authority;** influence, patronage, power, preponderance, credit, prestige, prerogative, jurisdiction; right etc. (*title*) 924.

divine right, dynastic rights, authoritativeness; royalty, regality, imperiality [*rare*]; absoluteness, absolutism, despotism, tyranny; *jus nocendi* [*L.*]; *jus divinum* [*L.*].

command, empire, sway, rule; dominion, domination; sovereignty, supremacy, suzerainty; kinghood, kingship; lordship, headship; chiefdom; patriarchy, patriarchate; leadership,

hegemony; seigniory; mastery, mastership, masterdom; government etc. (*direction*) 693; dictation, control.

hold, grasp; grip, gripe; reach; iron sway etc. (*severity*) 739; fangs, clutches, talons; rod of empire etc. (*scepter*) 747.

reign, *régime* [*F.*], dynasty; directorship, dictatorship; protectorate, protectorship; caliphate, pashalic, electorate; presidency, presidentship; administration; consulship, proconsulship; prefecture; seneschalship; magistrature, magistracy.

[governments] empire; monarchy; limited−, constitutional- monarchy; aristarchy, aristocracy; oligarchy, democracy, demagogy; heteronomy;

republic; thearchy; diarchy, duarchy, duumvirate; triarchy, triumvirate; heterarchy [*obs.*]; autocracy, monocracy.

representative government, constitutional government, *vox populi* [*L.*], home rule, dominion rule [*Brit.*], colonial government; self-government, autonomy, self-determination; republicanism, federalism; socialism; collectivism; pantisocracy; *imperium in imperio* [*L.*]; bureaucracy; beadledom, Bumbledom; stratocracy [*rare*], martial law; military -power, –government; feodality, feodatory, feudal system, feudalism.

gynocracy, gynarchy, gynecocracy, matriarchy, matriarchate, metrocracy; petticoat government.

[vicarious authority] commission etc. 755; deputy etc. 759; permission etc. 760.

state, realm, commonwealth, country, power, polity, body politic, *posse comitatus* [*L.*]; toparchy.

ruler; person in authority etc. (*master*) 745; judicature etc. 965; cabinet etc. (*council*) 696; seat of -government, –authority; headquarters.

usurper, tyrant, jack-in-office.

[acquisition of authority] accession; installation etc. 755; usurpation.

v. **authorize** etc. (*permit*) 760; warrant etc. (*right*) 924; dictate etc. (*order*) 741; have–, hold–, possess–, exercise–, exert–, grasp–, seize–, wrest–, wield- -authority etc. *n.*

rule, sway, command, control, administer; govern etc. (*direct*) 693; lead, preside over, reign; possess–, be seated on–, occupy–, seize- the throne; sway–, wield- the scepter *or* sceptre; wear the crown.

be at the head of etc. *adj.;* hold–, be in–, fill an office; hold–, occupy- a post; be master etc. 745.

dominate; have–, get- the -upper, –whip-hand; gain a hold upon, preponderate, dominate, rule the roast; boss [*colloq.*]; override, overrule, overawe; lord it over, hold in hand, keep under, make a puppet of, lead by the nose, turn round one's little finger, bend to one's will, hold one's own, wear the breeches [*colloq.*]; have the ball at one's feet, have it all one's own way, have the game in one's own hand, have on the hip, have under one's thumb; be master of the situation; take the lead, play first fiddle, set the fashion; give the law to; carry with a high hand; lay down the law; "ride in the whirlwind and direct the storm" [*adapted from* Addison]; rule with a rod of iron etc. (*severity*) 739.

assume authority etc. *n.;* ascend–, mount- the throne; take the reins, –into one's hand; assume the reins of government; take–, assume the- command.

be governed by, be in the power of; be under the -rule of, –dominion of.

adj. **ruling** etc. *v.;* regnant, at the head, dominant, paramount, supreme, predominant, preponderant, in the ascendant, influential; gubernatorial; imperious; authoritative, executive, administrative, clothed with authority, official, bureaucratic, departmental, *ex officio* [*L.*], imperative, peremptory, overruling, absolute; hegemonic *or* hegemonical; arbitrary; compulsory etc. 744; stringent.

at one's command; in one's power, in one's grasp; under control; authorized etc. (*due*) 924.

sovereign; regal, royal, royalist, monarchical, kingly; dynastic, imperial, imperialistic; princely; feudal; aristocratic, autocratic; oligarchic etc. *n.;* democratic, republican.

adv. in the name of, by the authority of, at one's command, *de par le Roi* [*F.*], in virtue of; under the auspices of, in the hands of.

at one's pleasure; by a dash (*or* stroke) of the pen; at one's nod; by lifting one's finger; *ex mero motu* [*L.*]; *ex cathedra* [*L.*].

738. Laxity
[absence of authority]

n. **laxity**; laxness, looseness, slackness; toleration etc. (*lenity*) 740; freedom etc. 748.

anarchy, interregnum; relaxation; loosening etc. *v.;* remission; dead letter, *brutum fulmen* [*L.*]; misrule; license, licentiousness; insubordination etc. (*disobedience*) 742; mob rule, mob law, mobocracy, ochlocracy; lynch law etc. (*illegality*) 964, nihilism, reign of violence.

[deprivation of power] dethronement, impeachment, deposition, abdication; usurpation.

v. **be lax** etc. *adj.; laisser faire* [*F.*], *laisser aller* [*F.*]; hold a loose rein; give the reins to, give rope enough, give a loose to [*obs.*], give a free course to, give free rein to; tolerate; relax; misrule.

go beyond the length of one's tether; have one's -swing, –fling; act without -instructions, –authority; act on one's own responsibility, usurp authority, undermine the authority of.

dethrone, depose; abdicate.

adj. **lax**, loose; slack; remiss etc. (*careless*) 460; weak.

relaxed; licensed; reinless, unbridled; anarchic *or* anarchical, nihilistic; "agin the government"; unauthorized etc. (*unwarranted*) 925; adespotic, undespotic; not imperious etc. (*ruling*) 737.

739. Severity

n. **severity**; strictness, harshness etc. *adj.;* rigor, stringency, austerity; inclemency etc. (*pitilessness*) 914a; arrogance etc. 885; precisianism, formalism.

arbitrary power; absolutism, despotism; dictatorship, autocracy, tyranny, domineering, domination, oppression; assumption, usurpation; inquisition, reign of terror, martial law; iron -heel, –rule, –hand, –sway; tight grasp; brute -force, –strength; coercion etc. 744; strong–, tight- hand.

bureaucracy, red-tapism, pipe-clay, officialism; hard -lines, –measure; tender mercies [*ironical*]; sharp practice.

tyrant, disciplinarian, precisian, martinet, stickler, bashaw, despot, the Grand Panjandrum himself, hard master, Draco, oppressor, inquisitor, extortioner, harpy, vulture; Accipitres, Raptores, raptors [*obs.*], birds of prey.

v. **be severe** etc. *adj.*

arrogate, assume, usurp, take liberties; domineer, bully etc. 885; tyrannize; wrest the law to one's advantage; inflict, wreak, stretch a point, put on the screw; be hard upon; bear–, lay- a heavy hand on; be down upon [*slang*], come down upon [*colloq.*]; illtreat; deal hardly with, deal hard measure to; rule with a rod of iron, chastise with scorpions; dye with blood; oppress, override; trample–, tread- down, –upon, –under foot; crush under an iron heel, ride roughshod over; rivet the yoke; hold–, keep- a tight hand; force down the throat; coerce etc. 744; give no quarter etc. (*pitiless*) 914a.

adj. **severe**; strict, hard, harsh, dour [*Scot.*], rigid, stiff, stern, rigorous, uncompromising, exacting, exigent, *exigeant* [*F.*], inexorable, inflexible, obdurate, austere, hard-headed, hard-shell [*colloq.*], relentless, Spartan, Draconian, stringent, strict, prudish, precise, puritanical, straitlaced, searching, unsparing, iron-handed, peremptory, absolute, positive, arbitrary, imperative; coercive etc. 744; tyrannical, extortionate, grinding, withering, oppressive, inquisitorial; inclement etc. (*ruthless*) 914a; cruel etc. (*malevolent*) 907; haughty, arrogant etc. 885; precisian, formal, punctilious.

adv. **severely** etc. *adj.;* with a -high, –strong, –tight, –heavy- hand.

at the point of the -sword, –bayonet.

740. Lenity

n. **lenity**, lenitence, lenitency; moderation etc. 174; tolerance, toleration; mildness, gentleness; favor; indulgence, indulgency [*rare*], clemence [*obs.*], clemency, mercy, forbearance, quarter; compassion etc. 914.

v. **be lenient** etc. *adj.;* tolerate, bear with; *parcere subjectis* [*L.*], spare the vanquished, give quarter.

indulge; allow one to -go his own gait, –have his own way, spoil.

adj. **lenient**; mild, –as milk; gentle, soft; tolerant, indulgent, easy, moderate, complaisant, unconcerned, easy-going; clement etc. (*compassionate*) 914; forbearing; long-suffering.

741. Command

n. **command**, order, ordinance, act, fiat, *hukm* [*Hind.*], bidding, dictum, hest, behest, call, beck, nod.

dispatch *or* despatch, message, direction, injunction, charge, instructions; appointment, fixture.

demand, exaction, imposition, requisition, claim, reclamation, revendication [*rare*]; ultimatum etc. (*terms*) 770; request etc. 765; requirement.

decree, dictate, dictation, mandate, caveat, *senatus consultum* [*L.*]; precept; prescript, rescript, writ, ordination, bull, edict, decretal, dispensation, prescription, brevet, placet, *placitum* [*L.*], ukase, firman, hatti-sherif, hatti-humayoun (*or* humayun), warrant, passport, mittimus, mandamus, summons, subpoena, *nisi prius* [*L.*], interpellation, citation; word, –of command; *mot d'ordre* [*F.*]; bugle–, trumpet-call; beat of drum, tattoo; order of the day; enactment etc. (*law*) 963; plebiscite etc. (*choice*) 609.

v. **command**, order, decree, enact, ordain, dictate, direct, give orders.

issue a command; make–, issue–, promulgate- -a requisition, –a decree, –an order etc. *n.;* give the -word of command, –word, –signal; call to order; give–, lay down- the law; assume the command etc. (*authority*) 737; remand.

prescribe, set, appoint, mark out; set–, prescribe–, impose- a task; set to work, put in requisition.

bid, enjoin, charge, call upon, instruct; require, –at the hands of; exact, impose, tax, task; demand; insist on etc. (*compel*) 744.

claim, lay claim to, revendicate [*rare*], reclaim.
cite, summon, avoke; call for, send for; subpoena; beckon.
be ordered etc.; receive an order etc. *n.*

adj. **commanding** etc. *v.;* authoritative etc. 737; decretory, decretive, decretal; callable; imperative, jussive; decisive, final, without appeal; interpellative, demanded, commanded etc. *v.*

adv. in a commanding tone; by a -stroke, –dash- of the pen; by order, at beat of drum, on the first summons, to order, at the word of command; by -command, –order, –decree- of; as required, as requested, as ordered, as commanded.

742. Disobedience

n. **disobedience**, insubordination, contumacy; infraction, infringement; violation, noncompliance; nonobservance etc. 773.
revolt, rebellion, mutiny, outbreak, rising, uprising, insurrection, *émeute* [*F.*], riot, tumult etc. (*disorder*) 59; strike etc. (*resistance*) 719; barring out; defiance etc. 715.
mutinousness etc. *adj.;* mutineering; sedition, treason; high–, petty–, misprison of- treason; praemunire *or* premunire; *lèse-majesté* [*F.*]; violation of law etc. 964; defection, secession, Sinn Fein; revolution; overthrow–, overturn- of -government, –authority; *sabotage* [*F.*], sansculottism, bolshevism.
insurgent, mutineer, rebel, revolter, rioter, traitor, *Carbonaro* [*It.*], sansculotte, red republican, *bonnet rouge* [*F.*], communist, Fenian, Sinn Feiner, Red, Bolshevist, *frondeur* [*F.*], seceder, Secessionist [*esp., U. S. hist.*] *or* Secesh [*colloq. or slang*]; apostate, renegade, runaway, runagate; brawler, anarchist, demagogue; Spartacus, Masaniello, Wat Tyler, Jack Cade; ringleader.

v. **disobey**, violate, infringe; shirk, slide out of, slack; set at defiance etc. (*defy*) 715; set authority at naught, run riot, fly in the face of; take the law into one's own hands; kick over the traces; refuse to support, bolt.
turn–, run- restive; champ the bit; strike etc. (*resist*) 719; rise, –in arms; secede; mutiny, rebel.

adj. **disobedient**; uncomplying, uncompliant; unsubmissive, unruly, ungovernable; breachy, insubordinate, impatient of control; restive, restiff [*obs.*], refractory, contumacious; recusant etc. (*refuse*) 764; recalcitrant; resisting etc. 719; lawless, riotous, mutinous, seditious, insurgent, revolutionary, sansculottic, secessionist.
unobeyed, disobeyed; unbidden.

743. Obedience

n. **obedience**; observance etc. 772; compliance; submission etc. 725; subjection etc. 749; nonresistance; passiveness, passivity, resignation.
allegiance, loyalty, fealty, homage, deference, devotion; constancy, fidelity.
submissiveness, submissness [*obs.*]; ductility etc. (*softness*) 324; obsequiousness etc. (*servility*) 886.

v. **be obedient** etc. *adj.;* obey, bear obedience to; submit etc. 725; comply, answer the helm, come at one's call; do one's bidding, do what one is told, do suit and service; attend to orders; serve -faithfully, –loyally, –devotedly, –without question; give -loyal, –devoted-service; be resigned to, be submissive to.
follow, –the lead of, –to the world's end; serve etc. 746; play second fiddle.

adj. **obedient**, law-abiding, complying, compliant; loyal, faithful, devoted; at one's -call, –command, –orders, –beck and call; under beck and call, under control.
restrainable; resigned, passive; submissive etc. 725; henpecked; pliant etc. (*soft*) 324.
unresisted, unresisting.

adv. **obediently** etc. *adj.;* as you please, if you please; in compliance with, in obedience to; at your -command, –orders, –service.

744. Compulsion

n. **compulsion**, coercion, coaction, constraint; restraint etc. 751; duress, enforcement, press, conscription; eminent domain.
force; brute–, main–, physical- force; the sword, *ultima ratio* [*L.*]; club–, lynch–, mob- law, *argumentum baculinum* [*L.*], *le droit du plus fort* [*F.*]; the force of -might, –right; martial law.
necessity etc. 601; *force majeure* [*F.*], spur of necessity, Hobson's choice.

v. **compel**, force, make, drive, coerce, constrain, enforce, necessitate, oblige.
force upon, press; cram–, thrust–, force- down the throat; say it must be done, make a point of, insist upon, take no denial; put down, dragoon.
extort, wring from; put–, turn- on the screw; drag into; bind, –over; pin–, tie- down; require, tax, put in force; commandeer; restrain etc. 751.

adj. **compelling** etc. *v.;* coercive, coactive; inexorable etc. 739; compulsory, compulsatory; obligatory, stringent, peremptory, binding.
forcible, not to be trifled with; irresistible etc. 601; compelled etc. *v.;* fain to.

adv. **forcibly**; by force etc. *n.*, by force of arms; on compulsion, perforce; *vi et armis* [*L.*], under the lash; at the point of the -sword, –bayonet; by a strong arm.

under protest, in spite of, in one's teeth; against one's will etc. 603; *nolens volens* [*L.*] etc. (*of necessity*) 601; by stress of -circumstances, –weather; under press of; *de rigueur* [*F.*].

745. Master

n. **master**, *padrone* [*It.*], lord, –paramount; commander, commandant, captain, chief, chieftain; paterfamilias [*Rom. law*], patriarch; sahib [*India*], bara (*or* burra) sahib [*India*], sirdar, sheik; head, senior, governor, ruler, dictator; leader etc. (*director*) 694; boss, baas [*Dutch*]; cockarouse [*obs.*], sachem, sagamore, werowance.

lord of the ascendant; cock of the -walk, –loft, –midden [*archaic*], –roost; gray mare; mistress.

potentate; liege, –lord; suzerain, overlord, overking, sovereign, monarch, autocrat, despot, tyrant, oligarch; boss of bosses [*slang*], godfather [*slang*].

crowned head, emperor, king, anointed king, majesty, imperator, protector, president, stadholder *or* stadtholder, judge.

caesar, kaiser, czar *or* tsar, sultan, soldan [*obs.*], grand Turk, caliph, imam *or* imaum, shah, padishah, sophi, mogul, great mogul, khan, lama, pendragon, tycoon, mikado, inca, cazique; voivode *or* waywode, hospodar, landamman; sayid *or* sayyid, cacique, czarevitch, grand seignior.

prince, duke etc. (*nobility*) 875; archduke, doge, elector; seignior; landgrave, margrave; maharajah, rajah, emir, nizam, nawab etc. (*Indian ruling chiefs*) 875.

empress, queen, sultana, czarina *or* tsarina, princess, infanta, duchess, margravine; czarevna *or* tsarevna, czarina; maharani, rani [*both Hindu*], begum [*Moham.*]; rectoress *or* rectress, rectrix.

regent, viceroy, exarch, palatine, khedive, beglerbeg *or* beylerbey, three-tailed bashaw, pasha *or* bashaw, bey *or* beg, dey, shereef *or* sherif, tetrarch, satrap, mandarin, nabob, burgrave; laird etc. (*proprietor*) 779; commissioner, deputy commissioner, collector, woon *or* wun [*Burmese*].

the authorities, the powers that be, the government, "them above" [Eliot]; staff, *état major* [*F.*], aga, official, man in office, person in authority; sirkar *or* sircar; Sublime Porte.

[*military authorities*] marshal, field marshal, *maréchal* [*F.*], generalissimo; commander-in-chief, seraskier [*Turk.*], hetman [*Cossack*]; general, brigadier general, brigadier, lieutenant general, major general, colonel, lieutenant colonel, major, captain, ressaldar *or* risaldar [*India*], subahdar *or* subadar [*India*]; centurion, lieutenant, jemadar [*India*], sublieutenant, officer, staff officer, aide-de-camp, brigade major, adjutant, ensign, cornet, cadet, subaltern; non-commissioned officer; sergeant, –major; color sergeant; top-sergeant [*U.S.*], havildar [*India*]; corporal, –major; lance corporal, acting corporal; naik [*India*]; drum major; captain general, knight marshal.

[**civil authorities**] mayor, mayoralty; *maire* [*F.*], prefect, chancellor, archon [*Gr.*], provost, magistrate, syndic; alcalde [*Sp.*], alcaide *or* alcaid; burgomaster, *corregidor* [*Sp.*], seneschal, alderman, warden, constable, portreeve; lord mayor; officer etc. (*executive*) 965; diwan *or* dewan [*India*]; hakim; *fonctionnaire* [*F.*].

[*naval authorities*] admiral, admiralty; rear–, vice–, port- admiral; commodore, captain, commander, lieutenant; skipper, master, mate, navarch [*Gr. antiq.*].

746. Servant

n. **servant**, retainer, follower, henchman, servitor, domestic, menial, help, lady help [*Brit.*], employee *or* employé; *attaché* [*F.*], official.

subject, liege, liegeman; people, "my people."

retinue, suite, *cortège* [*F.*], staff, court; office force, clerical staff, clerical force, workers, associate workers, employees, the help.

attendant, squire, usher, donzel [*obs.*], apprentice, prentice [*colloq. or dial.*]; page, buttons [*colloq.*], footboy; trainbearer, cupbearer; waiter, tapster, butler, livery servant, lackey, footman, flunky *or* flunkey [*colloq.*]; bearer [*Anglo-Ind.*], boy; hamal [*India*], scout [*Oxford Univ.*], gyp [*Camb. Univ.*], valet, *valet de chambre* [*F.*]; equerry, groom; jockey, hostler *or* ostler, orderly, messenger, gillie *or* gilly, caddie *or* caddy, herdsman, swineherd; barkeeper, bartender, barkeep; boots [*Brit.*]; cad [*Eng. Univ. cant*], bell boy, bellhop [*slang*], tiger, chokra [*India*], boy; counterjumper [*colloq.*]; khansamah *or* khansaman [*India*], khitmutgar [*India*]; yardman, journeyman.

bailiff, castellan *or* castellain, seneschal, chamberlain, major-domo, groom of the chambers.

secretary; under–, assistant- secretary; stenographer, clerk; subsidiary; agent etc. 758; subaltern; underling, understrapper; man.

maid, maidservant; girl, help, handmaid; confidant (*fem.* confidante), *confident* (*fem. confidente*) [*F.*]; lady's maid, abigail, soubrette, amah [*Oriental*], biddy [*colloq.*], *bonne* [*F.*], ayah [*India*]; nurse–, nursery–, house–, parlor–, waiting–, chamber–, kitchen–, scullery-maid; *femme* –, *fille*- *de chambre* [*F.*]; *chef de cuisine* [*F.*], *cordon bleu* [*F.*], chef, cook, scullion, Cinderella; pot-walloper; maid–, servant-of all work; slavey [*slang, Eng.*], general servant [*Brit.*], general housework maid, general [*colloq.*]; washerwoman, laundress, bedmaker; charwoman etc. (*worker*) 690.

dependent *or* dependant, hanger-on, led friend [*obs.*], satellite; parasite etc. (*servility*) 886; led captain; *protégé* [*F.*], ward, hireling, mercenary, puppet, man of straw, creature; serf, vassal, slave, negro, helot; bondsman, bondswoman; bondslave; *âme damnée* [*F.*], odalisque *or* odalisk, ryot, *adscriptus gleboe* [*L.*], villein *or* villain [*hist.*], churl *or* ceorl [*hist.*]; beadsman *or* bedesman; sizar *or* sizer [*Camb. & Dublin Univs.*], pensioner, pensionary; client.

badge of slavery; bonds etc. 752.

v. **serve,** minister to, help, coöperate; wait–, attend–, dance attendance–, fasten oneself–, pin oneself- upon; squire, valet, tend, hang on the sleeve of; chore [*dial.*], do the chores [*colloq.*], char [*dial. Eng.*], do for [*colloq.*], fag.

adj. **serviceable,** useful, helpful; cooperative.

serving etc. *v.*; in the train of; in one's -pay, –employ; at one's call etc. (*obedient*) 743; in bonds.

servile, slavish, vernile [*rare*]; subject, thrall, bond; subservient, obsequious, base, fawning, truckling, sycophantic *or* sycophantical, sycophantish [*rare*], parasitic, cringing.

747. Scepter

[insignia of authority]

n. [*regal*] scepter *or* sceptre, rod of empire; orb; pall; robes of -state, –royalty; ermine, purple; crown, coronet, diadem, cap of maintenance; triple plume, Prince of Wales's feathers; uraeus, flail [*both Egyptian*]; signet, seal.

[*ecclesiastical*] tiara, triple crown; ring, keys; miter *or* mitre, crozier, crook, staff; cardinal's hat; bishop's -apron, –sleeves, –lawn, –gaiters, –shovel hat; fillet.

[*military*] epaulet *or* epaulette, star, bar, eagle, crown [*Brit.*], oak leaf, Sam Browne belt; chevron, stripe.

caduceus; Mercury's -staff, –rod, –wand; mace, fasces, ax *or* axe, truncheon, staff, baton, wand, rod; staff–, rod- of office, –of authority; in-

signia–, ensign–, emblem–, badge- of authority; flag etc. (*insignia*) 550; regalia; toga, mantle, decoration; title etc. 877; portfolio.

throne, Peacock throne [*Chinese*], musnud *or* masnad [*Ar.*]; raj-gaddi, gaddi *or* guddee [*India*], divan; wool-sack, chair; dais etc. (*seat*) 215.

talisman, amulet, charm, sign.

helm; reins etc. (*means of restraint*) 752.

748. Freedom

n. **freedom,** liberty, independence; license etc. (*permission*) 760; eleutherism [*rare*]; facility etc. 705.

scope, range, latitude, play; free–, full- -play, -scope; free field and no favor; swing, full swing, elbowroom, margin, rope, wide berth; Liberty Hall.

franchise, denization; prerogative etc. (*dueness*) 924.

freeman, freedman, liveryman [*London guilds*], citizen, denizen.

immunity, exemption; emancipation etc. (*liberation*) 750; affranchisement, enfranchisement; right, privilege.

autonomy, self-government, liberalism, free trade; self-determination; noninterference etc. 706; Monroe Doctrine.

free land, freehold; alod *or* allod, alodium *or* allodium; frankalmoign *or* frankalmoigne [*Eng. law*], tenure in (*or* by) free alms [*Eng. law*]; dead hand, mortmain [*law*].

independent, free lance, freethinker, free trader *or* freetrader; bushwhacker.

v. **be free** etc. *adj.*; have -scope etc. *n.*, - the run of, –one's own way, –a will of one's own, –one's fling; do what one -likes, –wishes, –pleases, –chooses; go at large, feel at home, paddle one's own canoe; stand on one's rights; stand on one's own legs; shift for oneself.

take a liberty; make free with, make oneself quite at home; use a freedom; take leave, take French leave.

free, liberate, set free etc. 750; give the reins to etc. (*permit*) 760; allow–, give -scope etc. *n.* to; give a horse his head.

make free of; give the -freedom of, –franchise; enfranchise, affranchise.

laisser faire [*F.*], *laisser aller* [*F.*]; live and let live; leave to oneself; leave *or* let alone, mind one's own business.

adj. **free,** –as air; out of harness, independent, at large, loose, scot-free; left -alone, –to oneself.

unconstrained, unbuttoned, unconfined, unrestrained, unchecked, unprevented, unhindered, unobstructed, unbound, uncontrolled, untrammeled, uncaught; in full swing.

unsubject, ungoverned, unenslaved, unenthralled, unchained, unshackled, unfettered, unreined, unbridled, uncurbed, unmuzzled, unvanquished.

unrestricted, unlimited, unconditional; absolute; with unlimited -power, −opportunity; discretionary etc. (*optional*) 600.

unassailed, unforced, uncompelled.

unbiased, unprejudiced, uninfluenced; spontaneous.

free and easy; at−, at one's- ease; *dégagé* [*F.*], quite at home; beyond all bounds; wanton, rampant, irrepressible.

exempt; freed etc. 750; freeborn; autonomous, freehold, alodial *or* allodial; eleutherian [*rare*].

gratuitous, gratis etc. 815; for nothing, for love.

unclaimed, going a-begging.

adv. freely etc. *adj.; ad libitum* [*L.*] etc. (*at will*) 600; with no restraint etc. 751.

749. Subjection

n. **subjection**; dependence, dependency; subordination; thrall, thralldom *or* thraldom, enthrallment *or* enthralment, subjugation, bondage, serfdom; feudalism, feudality; vassalage, villenage *or* villeinage, slavery, enslavement, involuntary servitude; conquest.

service; servitude, servitorship; tendence, employ, tutelage, clientship; liability etc. 177; constraint etc. 751; oppression etc. (*severity*) 739; yoke etc. (*means of restraint*) 752; submission etc. 725; obedience etc. 743.

v. **be subject** etc. *adj.;* be *or* lie at the mercy of; depend−, lean−, hang- upon; fall a prey to, fall under; play second fiddle.

be a -mere machine, −puppet, −doormat, −football; not dare to say one's soul is his own; drag a chain.

serve etc. 746; obey etc. 743; submit etc. 725.

subjugate, subject, tame, break in; master etc. 731; tread -down, −under foot; weigh down; drag at one's chariot wheel; reduce to -subjection, −slavery; enthrall *or* enthral, inthrall *or* inthral, bethrall, enslave, lead captive; take into custody etc. (*restrain*) 751; rule etc. 737; drive into a corner, hold at the sword's point; keep under; hold in -bondage, −leading strings, −swaddling clothes; have at one's -apron strings, −beck and call; have in one's pocket.

adj. **subject**, dependent, subordinate; feudal, feudatory; in subjection to, servitorial [*rare*], under control; in leading strings, in harness; subjected, thrall [*archaic*]; servile, slavish etc. 746; enslaved etc. *v.;* constrained etc. 751; downtrodden; overborne, overwhelmed; under the lash, on the hip, led by the nose, henpecked; the -puppet, −sport, −plaything- of; under one's -orders, −command, −thumb; used as a doormat, treated like dirt under one's feet; a slave to; at the mercy of; in the -power, −hands, −clutches- of; at the feet of; in one's pocket; tied to one's apron strings; uxorious; at one's beck and call etc. (*obedient*) 743; liable etc. 177; parasitical; stipendiary.

adv. **under**; under -orders, −the heel, −command; at one's orders; with no -mind, −will, −soul- of one's own.

750. Liberation

n. **liberation**, disengagement, release, enlargement, emancipation, disenthrallment *or* disenthralment, Emancipation Proclamation; affranchisement, enfranchisement; manumission; discharge, dismissal.

deliverance etc. 672; redemption, extrication, acquittance, absolution; acquittal etc. 970; escape etc. 671.

v. **liberate**, free; set free, set at liberty; render free, emancipate, release; enfranchise, affranchise; manumit; enlarge; demobilize, disband, discharge, disenthrall *or* disenthral, disinthrall *or* disinthral, dismiss; let go, let loose, let out, let slip; cast−, turn- adrift; deliver etc. 672; absolve etc. (*acquit*) 970.

unfetter etc. 751, untie etc. 43; loose etc. (*disjoin*) 44; loosen, relax; unbolt, unbar, unclose, uncork, unclog, unhand, unbind, unchain, unharness; disengage, disentangle; clear, extricate, unloose; reprieve.

become free; gain−, obtain−, acquire- one's -liberty etc. 748; get rid of, get clear of; deliver oneself from; shake off the yoke, slip the collar; break loose, break prison; tear asunder one's bonds, cast off trammels; escape etc. 671.

adj. **liberated** etc. *v.;* out of harness etc. (*free*) 748; foot-loose; breathing free air again; one's own master again.

adv. **at large**, at liberty; adrift.

int. unhand me! let me go! reprieve! go in peace! free!

751. Restraint

n. **restraint**; hindrance etc. 706; coercion etc. (*compulsion*) 744; cohibition [*rare*], constraint, repression; discipline, control.

270

limitation, restriction, protection, monopoly; prohibition etc. 761; economic pressure.

confinement, restringency [*obs.*], durance, duress; imprisonment; incarceration, coarctation [*obs.*], entombment, mancipation [*obs.*], thrall; thralldom etc. (*subjection*) 749; durance vile, limbo, captivity; blockade; detention camp; quarantine station.

arrest, arrestation [*rare*], arrestment, custody.

keep, care, charge, ward.

curb etc. (*means of restraint*) 752; *lettres de cachet* [*F.*].

repressionist, monopolist, protectionist.

prisoner etc. 754.

v. **restrain,** check; put-, lay- under restraint, put under arrest; enthrall *or* enthral, inthrall *or* inthral, bethrall *or* bethral; restrict; debar etc. (*hinder*) 706; constrain; coerce etc. (*compel*) 744; curb, control; hold-, keep- -back, -from, -in, -in check, -within bounds; hold in -leash, -leading strings; withhold.

repress, suppress; keep under; smother; pull in, rein in; hold, -fast; keep a tight hand on; prohibit etc. 761; inhibit, cohibit.

fasten etc. (*join*) 43; enchain, fetter, shackle; entrammel, trammel; bridle, muzzle, hopple, gag, pinion, manacle, handcuff, tie one's hands, hobble, bind, bind hand and foot; swathe, swaddle; pin down, tether; picket; tie, -up, -down; peg -out, -down; keep [*archaic*], secure; forge fetters.

confine; shut -up, -in; clap up, lock up, box up, mew up, bottle up, cork up, seal up, button up; hem in, bolt in, wall in, rail in; impound, pen, coop; inclose etc. (*circumscribe*) 229; cage; incage *or* encage; close the door upon, cloister; imprison, jug [*slang*], immure; incarcerate, entomb; clap-, lay- under hatches; put in -irons, -a strait-waistcoat; throw-, cast- into prison; put into bilboes.

arrest; take -up, -charge of, -into custody; restringe [*rare*], cohibit [*rare*]; take-, make--prisoner, -captive; captivate [*rare*]; lead -captive, -into captivity; send-, commit-to prison; commit; give in -charge, -custody; subjugate etc. 749.

adj. **restrained,** constrained; imprisoned etc. *v.;* pent up; jammed in, packed in, wedged in; under -restraint, -lock and key, -hatches; in swaddling clothes; on parole; serving-, doing- time [*colloq. or slang*]; in irons, in the guardhouse; in custody etc. (*prisoner*) 754; cohibitive [*rare*]; mancipatory [*Rom. law*]; coactive etc. (*compulsory*) 744.

icebound, windbound, weatherbound; "cabined, cribbed, confined" [*Macbeth*]; in lob's pound, laid by the heels.

stiff, restringent [*obs.*], narrow, prudish, straitlaced, hidebound, barkbound.

adv. **under restraint,** under discipline; in prison, in jail, in durance vile, in confinement; behind bars; in captivity, during captivity; under arrest; under prohibition; within limits, within bounds.

752. Prison
[means of restraint]

n. **prison,** prisonhouse; jail *or* gaol, cage, coop, den, cell; stronghold, fortress, keep, donjon, dungeon, Bastille, *oubliette* [*F.*], bridewell [*Eng.*], jug [*slang*], house of correction, hulks, tollbooth, panopticon, penitentiary, state prison, guardroom, lockup, roundhouse [*archaic*], watch-house [*obs. or Scot.*], station house, station [*colloq.*], sponging house; house of detention, poky [*slang*], black hole, pen [*also slang for penitentiary*], fold, pinfold *or* penfold, pound; inclosure etc. 232; penal settlement; bilboes, stocks, limbo *or* limbus, quod [*slang*]; hoosegow [*slang*], calaboose [*local*], choky *or* chokey [*Anglo-Ind. or slang, Eng.*]; *chauki, thana* [*both India*]; workhouse [*U.S.; in England, a workhouse is a poorhouse*], reformatory, reform school; debtor's prison, college [*slang, Eng.*].

Tower, Newgate, Fleet, Marshalsea; King's (*or* Queen's) Bench; Alcatraz, Sing Sing, the Tombs.

[restraining devices] shackle, bond, gyve, fetter, trammel, irons, pinion, manacle, handcuff, strait-waistcoat, hopples; vise *or* vice; bandage, splint, strap.

yoke, collar, halter, harness; muzzle, gag, bit, curb, snaffle, bridle; rein, reins; bearing rein; martingale; leading string; tether, picket, band, guy, chain; cord etc. (*fastening*) 45; cavesson, hackamore [*Western U.S.*], jaquima [*S. W. U. S.*], headstall, lines [*U.S. & dial. Eng.*], ribbons [*colloq.*]; brake.

bar, bolt, lock, padlock; rail, paling, palisade; wall, fence, barrier, barricade.

drag etc. (*hindrance*) 706.

adj. imprisoned etc. (*restrained*) 751.

753. Keeper

n. **keeper,** custodian, *custos* [*L.*], ranger, gamekeeper, warder, jailer *or* gaoler, turnkey, castellan, guard; watch, watchdog, watchman, night watchman, Charley *or* Charlie [*Brit.*]; chokidar

[*Anglo-Ind.*], durwan [*Anglo-Ind.*], hayward; sentry, sentinel, watch and ward; *concierge* [*F.*], coastguard.

escort, bodyguard; convoy.

guardian, protector, governor, duenna; governess etc. (*teacher*) 540; nurse, *bonne* [*F.*], amah [*Oriental*], ayah [*India*].

754. Prisoner

n. **prisoner**, convict, captive, *détenu* [*F.*], collegian [*slang*], close prisoner.

jailbird or gaolbird, ticket-of-leave man [*Brit.*], *chevronné* [*F.*].

v. stand committed, be imprisoned etc. 751.

adj. **imprisoned** etc. 751; in prison, in quod [*slang*], in durance vile, in limbo, in custody, in charge, in chains; behind bars; under lock and key, under hatches.

on parole.

755. Commission

[*vicarious authority*]

n. **commission**, delegation; consignment, assignment; proxy, power of attorney, procuration; deputation, legation, mission, embassy; agency, agentship; clerkship.

errand, charge, brevet, diploma, exequatur, permit etc. (*permission*) 760.

appointment, nomination, return; charter; ordination; installation, inauguration, investiture; accession, coronation, enthronement.

regency, regentship; vicegerency.

viceroy etc. 745; consignee etc. 758; deputy etc. 759.

v. **commission**, delegate, depute; consign, assign; charge; intrust *or* entrust; commit, –to the hands of; authorize etc. (*permit*) 760.

put in commission, accredit, engage, hire, bespeak, appoint, name, nominate, return, ordain; install, induct, inaugurate, invest, crown; enroll, enlist; give power of attorney to; employ, empower; set–, place- over; send out.

be commissioned, be accredited; represent, stand for; stand in the -stead, –place, –shoes- of.

adj. commissioned etc. *v.*

adv. **instead of**; in one's -stead, –place; as proxy for; *per procurationem* [*L.*], *in loco parentis* [*L.*].

756. Abrogation

n. **abrogation**, annulment, nullification; *vacatur* [*L.*]; *nolle prosequi* [*L., law*]; canceling etc. *v.*; cancel; revocation, revokement; repeal, rescission, defeasance.

dismissal, *congé* [*F.*], demission [*obs.*]; bounce [*slang*]; deposal, deposition; dethronement;

disestablishment, disendowment; secularization, deconsecration; sack [*slang*], walking-papers, walking-ticket [*both colloq.*], yellow cover [*slang*].

abolition, abolishment; dissolution.

counterorder, countermand; repudiation, retractation; recantation etc. (*tergiversation*) 607.

abolitionist, prohibitionist.

v. **abrogate**, annul, cancel; destroy etc. 162; abolish; revoke, repeal, rescind, reverse, retract, recall; overrule, override; set aside; disannul, dissolve, quash, nullify, make void, nol-pros [*law*], declare null and void; disestablish, disendow; deconsecrate.

countermand, counterorder; do away with; sweep–, brush- away; throw overboard, throw to the dogs; scatter to the winds, cast behind.

disclaim etc. (*deny*) 536; ignore, repudiate; recant etc. 607; divest oneself, break off.

dismiss, discard; cast–, turn- -off, –out, –adrift, –out of doors, –aside, –away; send off, send away, send about one's business; discharge, get rid of etc. (*eject*) 297; bounce [*slang*]; fire, fire out, sack [*all slang*].

cashier; break; oust; unseat, unsaddle; unthrone, dethrone, disenthrone, depose, uncrown; unfrock, strike off the roll; disbar, disbench.

be abrogated etc.; receive its quietus.

adj. **abrogated** etc. *v.*; *functus officio* [*L.*].

int. get along with you! begone! go about your business! away with!

757. Resignation

n. **resignation**, retirement, abdication; renunciation, retractation, retraction, renunciance [*rare*], disclamation, disclaimer, abjuration; abandonment, relinquishment.

v. **resign**; give up, throw up; lay down, throw up the cards, wash one's hands of, abjure, renounce, forego, disclaim, retract; deny etc. 536.

abrogate etc. 756; desert etc. (*relinquish*) 624; get rid of etc. 782.

vacate, –one's seat; abdicate; accept the stewardship of the Chiltern Hundreds [*Eng.*]; retire; tender–, pass in–, hand in- one's resignation.

adj. **abdicant**; resigning etc. *v.*; renunciatory, renunciant [*rare*], abjuratory, disclamatory [*rare*], retractive.

758. Consignee

n. **consignee**, trustee, nominee; committee.

functionary, placeman, curator; treasurer etc. 801; agent, factor, reeve [*Eng. hist.*], steward, gomashta [*India*], bailiff, clerk, secretary, attorney, solicitor, proctor, broker, dalal

[*India*], dubash [*India*]; insurer, underwriter, commission agent, auctioneer, one's man of business; factotum etc. (*director*) 694; caretaker; garnishee; under agent, employé; servant etc. 746.

negotiator, go-between; middleman; shop steward *and* walking delegate [*labor unions*].

delegate; commissary, commissioner; emissary, envoy, commissionaire; messenger etc. 534.

diplomatist, diplomat *or* diplomate, *corps diplomatique* [*F.*], embassy; ambassador *or* embassador, diplomatic agent, representative, resident, consul, legate, nuncio, internuncio, *chargé d'affaires* [*F.*], *attaché* [*F.*]; vicegerent etc. (*deputy*) 759; plenipotentiary.

salesman, traveler, bagman, *commis voyageur* [*F.*], traveling salesman, commercial traveler, drummer [*U. S.*], traveling man; agent for (firm *or* commodity); touter [*colloq.*], barker [*colloq*].

reporter; newspaper–, own–, foreign–, war–, special- correspondent.

759. Deputy

n. **deputy**, substitute, proxy, *locum tenens* [*L.*], *badli* [*Hind.*], delegate, representative, next friend [*law*], pinch hitter [*cant*], *prochein ami* [*F. law*], surrogate, secondary; vice-president, vice-chairman, vice [*colloq.*].

regent, vicegerent, vizier, minister, vicar; premier etc. (*director*) 694; chancellor, prefect, provost, warden, lieutenant, archon [*antiq.*], consul, proconsul [*Rom. antiq.*]; viceroy etc. (*governor*) 745; ambassador; commissioner etc. 758; plenipotentiary, plenipotent; *alter ego* [*L.*].

team, eight, nine, eleven; captain, champion.

v. **be deputy** etc. *n.;* stand–, appear–, hold a brief–, answer- for; represent; stand–, walk- in the shoes of; stand in the stead of.

delegate, depute, empower, commission, substitute, ablegate [*R. C. Ch.*], accredit.

adj. **acting**; vice, viceregal; accredited to; delegated etc. *v.;* representative, plenipotent [*rare*], consular, proconsular.

adv. **in behalf of**, in the place of, as representing, by proxy.

Section 2. Special

760. Permission

n. **permission**, leave; allowance, sufferance; tolerance, toleration; liberty, law, license, concession, grace; indulgence etc. (*lenity*) 740; favor, dispensation, exemption, release; connivance; vouchsafement.

authorization, warranty [*law*], accordance, admission.

permit, warrant, brevet, precept, sanction, authority, firman; *hukm* [*Hind.*]; pass, passport; furlough, license, *carte blanche* [*F.*], ticket of leave; grant, charter, patent.

v. **permit**; give permission etc. *n.*, give power; let, allow, admit; suffer, bear with, tolerate, recognize; concede etc. 762; accord, vouchsafe, favor, humor, gratify, indulge, stretch a point; wink at, connive at; shut one's eyes to.

grant, empower, charter, enfranchise, privilege, confer a privilege, license, authorize, warrant; sanction; intrust etc. (*commission*) 755.

give *carte blanche* [*F.*], give the reins to, give scope to etc. (*freedom*) 748; leave -alone, –it to one, –the door open; open the -door to, –floodgates; give a loose to [*obs.*].

ask–, beg–, crave–, request- -leave, –permission.

let off; absolve etc. (*acquit*) 970; release, exonerate, dispense with.

adj. **permitting** etc. *v.;* permissive, indulgent.

permitted etc. *v.;* patent, chartered, permissible, allowable, lawful, legitimate, legal; legalized etc. (*law*) 963; licit; unforbid [*archaic*], unforbidden; unconditional.

adv. **permissibly**, licitly; by–, with–, on- leave etc. *n.; speciali gratia* [*L.*]; under favor of; *pace* [*L.*]; *ad libitum* [*L.*] etc. (*freely*) 748, (*at will*) 600; by all means etc. (*willingly*) 602; yes etc. (*assent*) 488.

761. Prohibition

n. **prohibition**, inhibition; veto, disallowance; interdict, interdiction; injunction; embargo, ban, taboo *or* tabu, proscription; *index expurgatorius* [*L.*], restriction etc. (*restraint*) 751; hindrance etc. 706; forbidden fruit; Maine law, Volstead Act, 18th amendment.

v. prohibit, inhibit; forbid, put one's veto upon, disallow; bar; debar etc. (*hinder*) 706, forfend *or* forefend [*archaic*].

restrain etc. 751; keep -in, –within bounds; cohibit [*rare*], withhold, limit, circumscribe, clip the wings of, restrict; interdict, taboo *or* tabu; put–, place- under -an interdiction, –the ban; proscribe; exclude, shut out; shut–, bolt–, show- the door; warn off; dash the cup from one's lips; forbid the banns.

adj. **prohibitive**, prohibitory; proscriptive; restrictive, exclusive; forbidding etc. *v.*

prohibited etc. *v.;* not permitted etc. 760; unlicensed, contraband, under the ban of, taboo *or* tabu; illegal etc. 964; unauthorized, not to be thought of.

adv. on no account etc. (*no*) 536.

int. forbid it heaven! heaven forbid! etc. (*deprecation*) 766.

hands off! keep off! hold! stop! avast!

762. Consent

n. **consent**; assent etc. 488; acquiescence; approval etc. 931; compliance, agreement, concession; yieldance [*obs.*], yieldingness; accession, acknowledgment, acceptance, agnition [*obs.*].

settlement, adjustment, ratification, confirmation.

permit etc. (*permission*) 760; promise etc. 768.

v. **consent**; assent etc. 488; yield assent, admit, allow, concede, grant, yield; come over, come round; give into, acknowledge, agnize [*archaic*], give consent, comply with, acquiesce, agree to, fall in with, accede, accept, embrace an offer, close with, take at one's word, have no objection.

satisfy, meet one's wishes, settle, come to terms etc. 488; not refuse etc. 764; turn a willing ear etc. (*willingness*) 602; jump at; deign, vouchsafe; promise etc. 768.

adj. **consenting** etc. *v.;* complaint, agreeable [*colloq.*], willing, eager; agreed etc. (*assent*) 488; unconditional.

adv. **yes** etc. (*assent*) 488; by all means etc. (*willingly*) 602; if you please, as you please; be it so, so be it, well and good, of course.

763. Offer

n. **offer**, proffer, presentation, tender, bid, overture; proposal, proposition; motion, invitation; candidature, candidacy; offering etc. (*gift*) 784.

v. **offer**, proffer, present, tender; bid; propose, move; make a motion, make advances; start; invite, hold out, place in one's way; put-, place- at one's disposal; put in one's power, make possible, put forward.

hawk about; offer for sale etc. 796; press etc. (*request*) 765; go a-begging; lay at one's feet.

volunteer, come forward, be a candidate; offer-, present- oneself; stand for, bid for; seek; be at one's service.

bribe etc. (*give*) 784; grease the palm [*slang*].

adj. **offering**, offered etc. *v.;* in the market, for sale, to let, disengaged, on hire; at one's disposal.

764. Refusal

n. **refusal**, rejection; noncompliance, incompliance; denial; declining etc. *v.;* declension; declinature; peremptory-, flat-, point blank- refusal;

repulse, rebuff; discountenance, disapprobation.

negation, recusancy, abnegation, protest, disclamation, renunciation, disclaimer; dissent etc. 489; revocation etc. 756.

v. **refuse**, reject, deny, decline; nill [*archaic*], turn down [*slang*], abnegate, negate, negative; refuse-, withhold- one's assent; shake the head; close the -hand, -purse; grudge, begrudge, be slow to, hang fire; pass [*at cards*].

stand aloof, be deaf to; turn a deaf ear to, turn one's back upon; set one's face against, discountenance, not hear of, have nothing to do with, wash one's hands of, forswear, set aside, cast behind one; not yield an inch etc. (*obstinacy*) 606.

resist, cross; not grant etc. 762; repel, repulse; shut-, slam- the door in one's face; rebuff; send -back, -to the right about, -away with a flea in the ear [*colloq.*]; deny oneself, not be at home to; discard etc. (*repudiate*) 610; rescind etc. (*revoke*) 756; disclaim, protest; dissent etc. 489.

adj. **refusing** etc. *v.;* restive, restiff [*obs.*]; recusant; uncomplying, noncompliant, incompliant, unconsenting; declinatory, uncomplaisant, disclamatory [*rare*], negatory, protestant; not willing to hear of, deaf to.

refused etc. *v.;* ungranted, out of the question, not to be thought of, impossible.

adv. **no** etc. 536; on no account, not for the world; no thank you; your humble servant [*ironically*], *bien obligé* [*F.*], not on your life!

765. Request

n. **request**, requisition; claim etc. (*demand*) 741; petition, suit, prayer; begging letter, round robin.

motion, overture, application, canvass, address, appeal, apostrophe; imprecation; rogation [*eccl.*]; proposal, proposition.

orison etc. (*worship*) 990; incantation etc. (*spell*) 993.

mendicancy, mendication [*rare*]; asking, begging etc. *v.;* postulation, solicitation, invitation, entreaty, importunity, supplication, instance, impetration, imploration, obsecration, obtestation, invocation, interpellation.

v. **request**, ask, beg, crave, sue, pray, petition, solicit, invite, pop the question [*colloq.*], make bold to ask; beg leave, beg a boon; apply to, call to, put to; call upon, call for; make-, address-, prefer-, put up- a -request, -prayer, -petition; make -application, -a requisition; ask-, trouble- one for; claim etc. (*demand*) 741;

offer up prayers etc. (*worship*) 990; whistle for [*colloq.*].

bespeak, canvass, tout [*cant, Eng.*], make interest, court; seek; bid for etc. (*offer*) 763; publish the banns.

entreat, beseech, plead, supplicate, beg hard, implore; conjure, adjure; obsecrate [*rare*], apostrophize, obtest [*rare*]; cry to, kneel to, appeal to; invoke, evoke; impetrate, imprecate, ply, press, urge, beset, importune, dun, tax, clamor for; cry aloud, cry for help; fall on one's knees; throw oneself at the feet of; come down on one's marrowbones [*slang or humorous*].

beg from door to door, send the hat round, go a-begging; mendicate [*rare*], mump, cadge [*dial. or slang, Eng.*], beg one's bread.

dance attendance on, besiege, knock at the door.

adj. **requesting** etc. *v.*, precatory, supplant, supplicant, supplicatory, invocative, invocatory, invitatory, imprecatory, rogatory; postulatory [*rare*], postulant; obsecratory [*rare*], obsecrationary [*rare*]; imploratory [*rare*], mendicant, mendicatory [*obs.*].

importunate, clamorous, urgent, solicitous; cap in hand; on one's -knees, –bended knees, –marrowbones [*slang or humorous*].

adv. **please,** prithee, do, pray; be so good as, be good enough; have the goodness, vouchsafe, will you, I pray thee, if you please.

int. for- God's, –heaven's - goodness', –mercy's- sake! we beseech thee to hear us! help! save me!

766. Deprecation
[negative request]

n. **deprecation,** expostulation; intercession, mediation, protest, remonstrance.

v. **deprecate,** protest, expostulate, enter a protest, intercede for; remonstrate.

adj. **deprecatory,** expostulatory, intercessory, mediatorial.

deprecated, protested.

unsought, unbesought; unasked etc. (*see* ask etc. 765).

Int. **God forbid!** cry you mercy! forbid it Heaven! Heaven forfend (*or* forefend)! Heaven forbid! far be it from! hands off! etc. (*prohibition*) 761.

767. Petitioner

n. **petitioner,** solicitor, applicant, suppliant, supplicant, suitor, candidate, claimant, postulant, aspirant, competitor, bidder; place hunter, pothunter, prizer [*archaic*].

salesman, drummer [*archaic*]; bagman etc. 758; canvasser.

beggar, mendicant, mumper, sturdy beggar, panhandler [*slang*], cadger.

hotel runner [*cant*] touter [*colloq.*], runner [*cant*], steerer, tout [*cant, Eng.*]; barker [*colloq.*].

sycophant, parasite etc. (servility) 886.

Section 3. Conditional

768. Promise

n. **promise,** undertaking, word, troth, plight, pledge, parole, word of honor, vow; oath etc. (*affirmation*) 535; profession, assurance, warranty, guarantee, insurance, obligation; contract etc. 769; stipulation.

engagement, preengagement; affiance; betrothal, betrothment; marriage -contract, –vow; plighted faith, troth-plight [*Scot. or dial.*], *gage d'amour* [*F.*].

v. **promise;** give a promise etc. *n.;* undertake, engage; make–, form- an engagement; enter into *or* on an engagement; bind–, tie–, pledge–, commit–, take upon- oneself; vow; swear etc. (*affirm*) 535, give–, pass–, pledge–, plight- one's -word, –honor, –credit, –troth; betroth, plight faith, take the vows, trothplight [*Scot. or dial.*].

assure, warrant, guarantee; covenant etc. 769; avouch, vouch for; attest etc. (*bear witness*) 467.

hold out an expectation; contract an obligation; become bound to, become sponsor for; answer for, be answerable for; secure; give security etc. 771; underwrite.

adjure, administer an oath, put to one's oath, swear a witness.

adj. **promising** etc. *v.;* promissory; votive; under hand and seal, upon oath, upon the Book; upon–, on- affirmation.

promised etc. *v.;* affianced, pledged, bound; committed, compromised; in for it [*colloq.*].

adv. as true as I live; in all soberness; upon my honor; my word for it; my head upon it; I call God to witness; as one's head shall answer for; *ex voto* [*L.*].

768a. Release from engagement

n. **release** etc. (*liberation*) 750.

adj. **absolute;** unconditional etc. (*free*) 748.

769. Compact

n. **compact,** contract, specialty, bundobast [*India*], deal [*colloq.*], agreement, bargain; affidation [*rare*], pact, paction [*chiefly Scot.*], bond, covenant, indenture [*law*].

stipulation, settlement, convention; compromise, cartel.

negotiation etc. (*bargaining*) 794; diplomacy etc. (*mediation*) 724; negotiator etc. (*agent*) 758.

treaty, protocol, concordat, *Zollverein* [*Ger.*], *Sonderbund* [*Ger.*], charter, Magna Charta *or* Magna Carta, pragmatic sanction.

ratification, completion, signature, seal, sigil, signet, bond.

v. **contract**, covenant, agree for; engage etc. (*promise*) 768; indent.

negotiate, treat, stipulate, make terms; bargain etc. (*barter*) 794.

conclude, close, close with, complete; make–, strike- a bargain; come to -terms, –an understanding; compromise etc. 774; set at rest; settle; confirm, ratify, clinch *or* clench, subscribe, underwrite; indorse, endorse, put the seal to; sign on the dotted line; sign, seal etc. (*attest*) 467; take one at one's word, bargain by inch of candle.

adj. **contractual**, complete; agreed etc. *v.;* conventional; under hand and seal; signed, sealed, and delivered.

adv. **as agreed upon**, as promised, as contracted for; according to the -contract, –bargain, –agreement, on the dotted line [*slang*].

770. Conditions

n. **conditions**, terms; articles, –of agreement; memorandum; clauses, provisions; proviso etc. (*qualification*) 469; covenant, stipulation, obligation, ultimatum, *sine qua non* [*L.*]; *casus foederis* [*L.*].

v. **condition**, make it a condition, stipulate, insist upon, make a point of; bind, tie up; fence in, hedge in, have a string to it [*colloq.*]; make–, come to- -terms etc. (*contract*) 769.

adj. **conditional**, provisional, guarded, fenced, hedged in.

adv. **conditionally** etc. (*with qualification*) 469; provisionally, *pro re nata* [*L.*], on condition; with a string to it [*colloq.*], with strings attached [*colloq.*], with a reservation.

771. Security

n. **security**; guaranty, guarantee; gage, warranty, bond, tie, pledge, *vadium vivum* [*L.*], plight [*rare*], mortgage, *vadium mortuum* [*L.*], debenture, hypothec [*Rom. & civil law*], hypothecation, bill of sale, lien, pawn, pignoration; real security; vadium, collateral, bail; parole etc. (*promise*) 768.

stake, deposit, earnest, handsel *or* hansel, handsale, caution [*Scot. law*].

promissory note; bill, –of exchange; I.O.U.; personal security, covenant.

acceptance, indorsement *or* endorsement, signature, execution, stamp, seal.

sponsor, surety, bail, replevin; mainpernor, mainprise *or* mainprize [*hist. law*]; hostage; godchild, godfather, godmother; sponsion, sponsorship.

recognizance; deed–, covenant- of indemnity.

authentication, verification, warrant, certificate, voucher, docket *or* doquet [*obs.*]; record etc. 551; probate, attested copy.

acquittance, quittance; discharge, release; receipt.

muniments, title deed, instrument; deed, deed poll, indenture; specialty; insurance; charter etc. (*compact*) 769; charter poll; paper, parchment, settlement, will, testament, last will and testament, codicil.

v. **give security**, give bail, give substantial bail; go bail; handsel *or* hansel, pawn, put in pawn, pledge, put up the spout [*slang*], hock [*slang*], impawn *or* empawn [*obs.*], spout [*slang*], impignorate, mortgage, hypothecate.

guarantee, warrant, assure; accept, indorse *or* endorse, underwrite, insure.

execute, stamp; sign, seal etc. (*evidence*) 467.

let, set *or* sett [*Scot. law*]; grant-, take-, hold- a lease; hold in pledge; lend on security etc. 787.

adj. **pledged**, pawned etc. *v.;* secure; impignorate, pignorative [*rare*], in pawn, up the spout [*slang*]; at stake, on deposit, as earnest.

sponsorial, sponsional [*rare*]; as sponsor etc. *n.*

let, leased; held in pledge.

772. Observance

n. **observance**, performance, compliance, acquiescence, concurrence; obedience etc. 743; fulfillment *or* fulfilment, satisfaction, discharge; acquittance, acquittal.

adhesion, acknowledgment; fidelity etc. (*probity*) 939; exact etc. 494- observance; unserving fidelity to.

v. **observe**, comply with, respect, acknowledge, abide by; cling to, adhere to, be faithful to, act up to; meet, fulfill *or* fulfil; carry out, carry into execution; execute, perform, keep, satisfy, discharge; do one's office.

keep faith with; perform–, fulfill–, discharge–, acquit oneself of- an obligation; make good; make good–, keep- one's -word, –promise; redeem one's pledge; stand to one's engagement.

adj. **observant**, faithful, true, loyal; honorable etc. 939; true as the dial to the sun, true as the needle to the pole; punctual, punctilious, scrupulous, meticulous; literal etc. (*exact*) 494; as good as one's word.

adv. **faithfully** etc. *adj.;* to the letter.

773. Nonobservance

n. **nonobservance** etc. 772; evasion, inobservance, failure, omission, neglect, laches [*law*], casualness, slackness, laxness, laxity, informality.

lawlessness; disobedience etc. 742; bad faith etc. 940.

infringement, infraction; violation, transgression; piracy.

retractation, repudiation, nullification; protest; forfeiture.

v. **evade**, fail, neglect, omit, elude, give the go-by to [*slang*], cut [*colloq.*], set aside, ignore; shut–, close- one's eyes to.

infringe, transgress, violate, pirate, break, trample under foot, do violence to, drive a coach and four (*or* six) through.

discard, protest, repudiate, fling to the winds, set at naught, nullify, declare null and void; cancel etc. (*wipe off*) 552.

retract, go back from, be off, forfeit, go from one's word, palter; stretch a point, strain a point.

adj. **violating** etc. *v.;* lawless, transgressive; elusive, evasive, slack, lax, casual, slippery; nonobservant.

unfulfilled etc. (*see* fulfill etc. 772).

774. Compromise

n. **compromise**, commutation, composition; middle term, *mezzo termine* [*It.*]; compensation etc. 30; abatement of differences, adjustment, mutual concession.

v. **compromise**, commute, compound; take the mean; split the difference, meet one halfway, give and take; come to terms etc. (*contact*) 769; submit to arbitration, abide by arbitration; patch up, bridge over, arrange; straighten out, adjust, adjust differences; agree; cut a deal [*slang*]; make the best of, make a virtue of necessity; take the will for the deed.

Section 4. Possessive Relations

775. Acquisition

n. **acquisition**; gaining etc. *v.;* obtainment, procuration, procurement; purchase, descent, inheritance; gift etc. 784.

recovery, retrieval, revendication [*rare*], replevin; redemption, salvage, trover; find, *trouvaille* [*F.*], foundling.

gain, thrift; money-making, money-grubbing; lucre, filthy lucre, loaves and fishes, fleshpots of Egypt, the main chance, pelf; emolument etc. (*remuneration*) 973.

profit, earnings, winnings, innings, pickings, perquisite, accruement [*obs.*], net profit; avails; income etc. (*receipt*) 810; proceeds, produce, product; outcome, output; return, fruit, crop, harvest; second crop, aftermath; benefit etc. (*good*) 618.

prize, sweepstakes, trick, pool; kitty, jackpot, pot; wealth etc. 803.

[fraudulent acquisition] subreption; obreption; stealing etc. 791.

v. **acquire**, get, gain, win, earn, obtain, procure, gather; collect etc. (*assemble*) 72; pick, pick up; glean.

find; come-, pitch-, light- upon; come across, come at; scrape -up, –together; get in, reap and carry, net, bag, sack, bring home, secure; derive, draw, get in the harvest.

get hold of, get between one's finger and thumb, get into one's hand, get at; take–, come into–, enter into- possession.

profit; make-, draw- profit; turn to -profit, –account; make capital out of, make money by; obtain a return, reap the fruits of; reap–, gain- an advantage; turn -a penny, –an honest penny; hit the jackpot [*colloq.*], strike it rich; make the pot boil, bring grist to the mill; make-, coin-, raise- money; raise funds, raise the wind [*slang*]; fill one's pocket etc. (*wealth*) 803.

realize, clear; treasure up etc. (*store*) 636; produce etc. 161; take etc. 789.

receive etc. 785; come by, come in for; inherit; step into, –a fortune, –the shoes of; succeed to.

recover, get back, regain, retrieve, revendicate [*rare*], replevin, replevy, redeem, come by one's own.

be profitable etc. *adj.;* pay, answer.
accrue etc. (*be received*) 785.

adj. **acquisitive**, productive, profitable, advantageous, gainful, remunerative, paying, lucrative, acquiring, acquired etc. *v.*

adv. in the way of gain; for money; at interest.

776. Loss

n. **loss**, perdition, deperdition [*archaic*]; forfeiture, lapse.

privation, bereavement; deprivation etc. (*dispossession*) 789; riddance; damage, squandering, waste.

v. **lose**; incur–, experience–, meet with- a loss; miss; mislay, let slip, allow to slip through the fingers; be deprived of; be without etc. (*exempt*) 777a; forfeit, pay with.

squander; get rid of etc. 782; waste etc. 638.

be lost, lapse.

adj. **losing** etc. *v.;* not having etc. 777a.

    deprived of; shorn of, deperdite [*rare*], denuded, bereaved, bereft, minus [*colloq., exc. in math.*], cut off; dispossessed etc. 789; rid of, quit of; out of pocket.

    lost etc. *v.;* long lost; irretrievable etc. (*hopeless*) 859; off one's hands.

int. **farewell to**! adieu to! good riddance.

777. Possession

n. **possession**, seizin *or* seisin; ownership etc. 780; occupancy; hold, holding; tenure, tenancy, feodality, feodatory, feud *or* feod, fief, fee, fee tail, fee simple; dependency; villenage *or* villeinage; socage, chivalry, knight service.

    bird in hand, *uti possidetis* [*L.*], chose in possession [*rare*].

    exclusive possession, impropriation, monopoly, retention etc. 781; prepossession, preoccupancy; nine points of the law; corner, usucapion *or* usucaption [*Rom. law*], prescription.

    future possession, heritage, inheritance, heirship, reversion, fee; primogeniture, ultimogeniture.

v. **possess**, have, hold, occupy, enjoy; be possessed of etc. *adj.;* have in hand etc. *adj.;* own etc. 780; command.

    inherit; come to, come in for.

    monopolize, engross, forestall, regrate, impropriate, appropriate, usucapt [*Rom. law*], have all to oneself; corner; have a firm hold of etc. (*retain*) 781; get into one's hand etc. (*acquire*) 775.

    belong to, appertain to, pertain to; be in one's possession etc. *adj.;* vest in.

adj. **possessing** etc. *v.;* worth; possessed of, seized of, master of, usucapient [*Rom. law*]; in possession of; endowed–, blest–, instinct–, fraught–, laden–, charged- with.

    possessed etc. *v.;* on hand, by one; in hand, in store, in stock; unsold, unshared; in one's -hands, –grasp, –possession; at one's command, at one's disposal; one's own etc. (*property*) 780.

777a. Exemption

n. **exemption**; absence etc. 187; exception, immunity, privilege, release.

v. **not have** etc. 777; be without etc. *adj.;* excuse.

adj. **devoid of**, exempt from, without, unpossessed of, unblest with; immune from.

    not having etc. 777; unpossessed; untenuated etc. (*vacant*) 187; without an owner.

    unobtained, unacquired.

778. Participation

[joint possession]

n. **participation**; condominium, cotenancy, joint tenancy; occupancy–, possession–, tenancy- in common; joint–, common- stock; limited partnership, copartnership, partnership; communion; community of -possessions, –goods; communication, communalization; communism, communalism, collectivism, socialism; cooperation etc. 709.

    snacks [*obs.*], coportion [*obs.*], picnic, hotchpot *or* hotchpotch, hodgepodge; coheirship, coparcenary *or* coparceny; gavelkind.

    participator, sharer, copartner, partner; shareholder; cotenant, joint tenant; tenants in common; coheir, coparcener.

    communist, communitarian, communalist, collectivist, socialist.

v. **participate**, partake; share, share in; come in for a share; go shares, go snacks [*obs.*], go cahoots [*slang*], halve; share and share alike.

    join in; have a hand in etc. (*coöperate*) 709.

    communize, communalize; have–, possess–, be seized- -in common, –as joint tenants etc. *n.*

adj. **partaking** etc. *v.*

    communistic, communalistic, socialistic; cooperative, profit-sharing.

adv. **in common**, share and share alike; on shares; in cahoots [*slang*].

779. Possessor

n. **possessor**, holder; occupant, occupier; tenant; person *or* man in possession etc. 777; renter, lodger, lessee, underlessee; zamindar *or* zemindar [*India*]; ryot [*India*]; tenant -on sufferance, –at will, –from year to year, –for years, –for life.

    owner; proprietor, proprietress, proprietary; impropriator, master, mistress, lord.

    landholder, landowner, landlord, landlady; lord -of the manor, –paramount; heritor [*Scots law*], laird [*Scot.*], vavasor *or* vavasour [*feud. law*]; landed gentry, mesne lord; planter.

    beneficiary, *cestui que* (or *qui*) *trust* [*law*], mortgagor.

    grantee, feoffee, feoffee in trust, releasee, devisee; legatee, legatary [*rare*].

trustee; holder etc. of the legal estate; mortgagee. right owner, rightful owner.

[future possessor] heir, –apparent, –presumptive; inheritor, reversioner; remainder-man; heiress, inheritress, inheritrix.

780. Property

n. **property,** possession, seizin *or* seisin; tenure etc. (*possession*) 777; *suum cuique* [*L.*], *meum et tuum* [*L.*].

ownership, proprietorship, lordship; seigniory *or* seignory *or* seigneury, seignoralty; empire etc. (*dominion*) 737.

estate, interest, stake, right, title, claim, demand, holding; vested–, contingent–, beneficial–, equitable- interest; use, trust, benefit; legal–, equitable- estate.

absolute interest, paramount estate, freehold; fee, –simple, –tail; estate -in fee, –in tail, –tail; estate in tail -male, –female, –general.

term, limitation, lease, settlement, strict settlement, particular estate; estate -for life, –for years, –*pur autre vie* [*F.*]; remainder, reversion, expectancy, possibility.

dower, dowry, jointure, appanage *or* apanage, inheritance, heritage, patrimony, alimony; legacy etc. (*gift*) 784; Falcidian law, paternal estate, thirds.

assets, belongings, means, resources, circumstances; wealth etc. 803; money etc. 800; what one -is worth, –will cut up for [*colloq.*]; estate and effects.

realty, land, lands; landed–, real- estate, –property; tenements; hereditaments; corporeal–, incorporeal- hereditaments; acres; ground etc. (*earth*) 342; acquest, mesestead [*archaic*], messuage, toft [*Scot. & dial. Eng.*].

manor, honor [*Eng. feudal law*], domain, demesne; farm, plantation, hacienda [*Sp. Am.*]; alodium *or* allodium etc. (*free*) 748; feoff, fief, feud *or* feod, zamindari *or* zemindari [*India*], arado [*S. W. U. S.*], rancho [*S. W. U. S.*], ranch, spread.

freeholds, copyholds, leaseholds; folkland [*O. Eng. law*].

chattels real; fixtures, plant, heirloom; easement; right of -common, –user.

territory, state, kingdom, principality, realm, empire, protectorate, dependency, sphere of influence, mandate.

personalty; personal -property, –estate, –effects; chattels, goods, effects, movables; stock, –in trade; things, traps [*colloq.*], chattels personal, rattletraps, paraphernalia; equipage etc. 633; parcels [*Eng.*], appurtenances.

impedimenta; luggage, baggage; bag and baggage; pelf; cargo, lading.

income etc. (*receipts*) 810; rent roll; maul and wedges [*U. S.*].

patent, copyright; chose in action; credit etc. 805; debt etc. 806.

v. **possess** etc. 777; be the possessor of etc. 779; own; have for one's -own, –very own; come in for, inherit; enfeoff.

savor of the realty.

belong to; be one's property etc. *n.;* pertain to, appertain to.

adj. **one's own;** landed, praedial *or* predial, manorial, alodial *or* allodial; seigniorial *or* seigneurial; freehold, copyhold, leasehold; feudal *or* feodal; hereditary, entailed, real, personal.

adv. **to one's credit,** to one's account; to the good.

to one and -his heirs for ever, –the heirs of his body, –his heirs and assigns, –his executors, administrators and assigns.

781. Retention

n. **retention;** retaining etc. *v.;* keep [*archaic*], detention, custody; tenacity, firm hold, grasp, gripe, grip, iron grip; bond etc. (*vinculum*) 45.

clutches, tongs, forceps, tenaculum, pincers, nippers, pliers, vise, hook.

fangs, teeth, claws, talons, nail, unguis, tentacle.

paw, hand, finger, wrist, fist, nieve *or* nief [*archaic or dial.*].

captive etc. 754; bird in hand.

v. **retain,** keep; hold, –fast, –tight, –one's own, –one's ground; clinch, clench, clutch, grasp, gripe, hug, have a firm hold of.

secure, withhold, detain; hold–, keep- back; keep close; husband etc. (*store*) 636; reserve; have–, keep- in stock etc. (*possess*) 777; entail, tie up, settle.

adj. **retentive,** tenacious; retaining etc. *v.*

unforfeited, undeprived, undisposed, uncommunicated.

incommunicable, inalienable; in mortmain; in strict settlement.

782. Relinquishment

n. **relinquishment,** abandonment etc. (*of a course*) 624; renunciation, expropriation, dereliction; cession, surrender, dispensation; resignation etc. 757; riddance.

derelict etc. *adj.;* jetsam *or* jettison; abandoned farm; waif, foundling.

v. **relinquish**, give up, surrender, yield, cede; let go, let slip; spare, drop, resign, forego, renounce, abandon, expropriate, give away, dispose of, part with; lay -aside, –apart, –down, –on the shelf & (*disuse*) 678; set aside, put aside; make away with, cast behind; discard, cast off, dismiss; maroon.

cast-, throw-, pitch-, fling- -away, –aside, –overboard, –to the dogs; cast-, throw-, sweep- to the winds; put-, turn-, sweep- away; jettison.

quit one's hold.

supersede, give notice to quit, give warning; be *or* get rid of; be *or* get quit of; eject etc. 297.

rid–, disburden–, divest–, dispossess- oneself of; wash one's hands of.

divorce, unmarry [*rare*]; cut off, desert, disinherit; separate.

adj. **relinquished** etc. *v.;* cast off, derelict; unowned, disowned, disinherited, divorced; unappropriated, unculled; left etc. (*residuary*) 40.

int. away with!

783. Transfer

n. **transfer**, conveyance, assignment, alienation, abalienation; demise, limitation; conveyancing; transmission etc. (*transference*) 270; enfeoffment, bargain and sale, lease and release; exchange etc. (*interchange*) 148; barter etc. 794; substitution etc. 147.

succession, reversion; shifting use, shifting trust; devolution.

v. **transfer**, convey; alien, alienate; assign; enfeoff; grant etc. (*confer*) 784; consign; make over, hand over; pass, hand, transmit, negotiate; hand down; exchange etc. (*interchange*) 148.

change hands, change from one to another; devolve, revert, succeed; come into possession etc. (*acquire*) 775.

disinherit; abalienate [*rare*]; dispossess etc. 789; substitute etc. 147.

adj. **alienable**, negotiable, transferable, reversional, transmissive; inherited.

adv. **by transfer** etc. *n.;* on lease.

784 Giving

n. **giving** etc. *v.;* bestowal, bestowment, donation; presentation, presentment; accordance; concession, cession; delivery, consignment, dispensation, communication, endowment; investment, investiture; award.

charity, almsgiving, liberality, generosity.

[thing given] gift, donation, present, *cadeau* [*F.*]; fairing; free gift, boon, favor, benefaction, grant, offering, oblation, sacrifice, immolation.

grace, act of grace, bonus.

allowance, contribution, subscription, subsidy, tribute, subvention.

bequest, legacy, devise, will, dotation, dot, appanage *or* apanage, dowry, dower; voluntary -settlement, –conveyance etc. 783; amortization.

gratuity, lagniappe *or* lagnappe [*Louisiana*], pilon [*S. W. U. S.*]; alms, largess, bounty, dole, sportule [*obs.*], donative, help, oblation, offertory, honorarium, Peter pence, sportula, Christmas box, Easter offering, vails [*rare*], *douceur* [*F.*], drink money, tip, hand out [*slang*], *pourboire* [*F.*], *Trinkgeld* [*G*], baksheesh *or* bakshish, cumshaw [China], dash *or* dashee [Africa]; fee etc. (*recompense*) 973; consideration.

bribe, bait, ground bait; peace offering; handsel *or* hansel; boodle [*slang*], graft [*colloq.*], grease [*slang*].

giver, grantor etc. *v.;* donor, almoner, testator, feoffer, settlor [*law*]; investor, subscriber, contributor; Fairy Godmother [*or l. c.*].

v. **deliver**, hand, pass, put into the hands of; hand–, make–, deliver–, pass–, turn- over; assign dower.

present, give away, dispense, dispose of; give–, deal–, dole–, mete–, squeeze-out; fork over, fork out, shell out [*all slang*].

make a present; allow, contribute, subscribe, furnish its quota.

pay etc. 807; render, impart, communicate.

concede, cede, yield, part with, shed, cast; spend etc. 809; sacrifice, immolate.

give, bestow, donate, confer, grant, accord, award, assign; offer etc. 763.

intrust, consign, vest in.

invest, endow, settle upon; bequeath, leave, devise.

furnish, supply, help; administer to, minister to; afford, spare; accommodate with, indulge with, favor with; shower down upon; lavish, pour on, thrust upon.

bribe, tip; tickle–, grease- the palm [*slang*].

adj. **giving** etc. *v.;* given etc. *v.;* allowed, allowable; concessional; communicable.

charitable, eleemosynary, sportulary [*obs.*], tributary; gratis etc. 815; donative.

adv. **as a free gift** etc. *n.;* in charity; toward the endowment fund.

int. don't mention it! not another word! glad to do it!

785. Receiving

n. **receiving** etc. *v.;* acquisition etc. 775; reception etc. (*introduction*) 296; suscipiency [*rare*], acceptance, admission.

recipient, receiver, suscipient [*rare*], accipient; assignee, devisee; legatee, legatary; grantee, feoffee, donee, relessee, lessee.

beneficiary, sportulary [*obs.*], stipendiary; pensioner, pensionary; almsman.

income etc. (*receipt*) 810.

v. **receive**; take etc. 789; acquire etc. 775; admit.

pocket; take in, catch, touch; put into one's -pocket, −purse; accept; take off one's hands.

be received; come in, come to hand; pass−, fall- into one's hand; go into one's pocket; fall to one's -lot, −share; come−, fall- to one; accrue; have given etc. (784) to one.

adj. **receiving** etc. *v.;* recipient, suscipient [*rare*]; stipendiary, stipendarian, pensionary.

received etc. *v.;* given etc. 784; secondhand.

not given, unbestowed etc. (*see* give, bestow etc. 784).

786. Apportionment

n. **apportionment**, allotment, consignment, assignment, allocation, appointment; appropriation; dispensation, distribution; division, deal; partition, repartition, administration.

portion, dividend, contingent, share, allotment, lot, measure, dose; dole, meed, pittance; *quantum* [*L.*], ration; ratio, proportion, quota, modicum, mess, allowance.

v. **apportion**, divide; distribute, administer, dispense; billet, allot, allocate, detail, cast, share, mete; portion−, parcel−, dole- out; deal, carve.

partition, assign, appropriate, appoint.

participate, come in for one's share etc. 778.

adj. **apportioning** etc. *v.;* apportioned etc. *v.;* respective.

adv. respectively, each to each; by lot; in equal shares.

787. Lending

n. **lending** etc. *v.;* loan, advance, accommodation, feneration [*obs.*]; mortgage etc. (*security*) 771; investment.

pawnshop, spout [*slang*], *mont de piété* [*F.*], my uncle's [*slang*].

lender, pawnbroker, money lender, usurer, Shylock.

v. **lend**, advance, accommodate with; lend on security; loan; pawn etc. (*security*) 771.

invest; intrust; place−, put- out to interest; place, put; embark, risk, venture, sink, fund.

let, lease, set *or* sett [*Scot. law*], sublet, sublease, underlet; demise.

adj. **lending** etc. *v.;* lent etc. *v.;* come across (*or* down) with the needful [*slang*].

adv. in advance; on loan, on security.

788. Borrowing

n. **borrowing**, pledging, pawning, putting up the spout [*slang*].

borrowed plumes; plagiarism etc. (*thieving*) 791.

v. **borrow**, desume [*obs.*]; pawn, put up the spout [*slang*], patronize my uncle [*slang*].

raise−, take up- money; raise the wind [*slang*]; get the -dough, −needful [*both slang*]; fly a kite, borrow from Peter to pay Paul; run into debt etc. (*debt*) 806.

hire, rent, farm; take a -lease, −demise; take−, hire- by the -hour, −mile, −year etc.

appropriate, adopt, apply, imitate, make use of, take; plagiarize, pirate.

replevy.

adj. borrowed etc. *v.*

789. Taking

n. **taking** etc. *v.;* reception etc. (*taking in*) 296; deglutition etc. (*taking food*) 298; appropriation, prehension [*chiefly zoöl.*], prensation [*obs.*]; capture, caption; apprehension, deprehension [*obs.*]; abreption [*obs.*], seizure; abduction, ablation; subtraction etc. (*subduction*) 38; abstraction, ademption; androlepsia *or* androlepsy.

dispossession; deprivation, deprivement; bereavement; divestment; disinheritance, dishersion; distraint, distress, attachment, execution; sequestration, confiscation; eviction etc. 297.

rapacity, rapaciousness, extortion, predacity; bloodsucking, vampirism; theft etc. 791.

resumption; reprises [*law*], reprisal; recovery etc. 775.

clutch, swoop, wrench; grip etc. (*retention*) 781; haul, take, catch; scramble.

taker, captor, capturer; extortioner *or* extortionist; vampire.

v. **take**, catch, hook, nab [*slang*], bag, sack, pocket, put into one's pocket; receive; accept.

reap, crop, cull, pluck; gather etc. (*get*) 775; draw.

appropriate, impropriate [*Eng. eccl. law*]; assume, possess oneself of; take possession of; commandeer [*colloq.*]; lay–, clap- one's hands on [*colloq.*]; help oneself to; make free with, dip one's hands into, lay under contribution; intercept; scramble for; deprive of.

seize, abstract; take–, carry–, bear- -away, –off; adeem [*law*]; hurry off–, run away- with; abduct; steal etc. 791; ravish; pounce–, spring- upon; swoop to, swoop down upon; take by -storm, –assault; snatch, reave [*archaic*].

snap up, nip up, whip up, catch up; kidnap, crimp, capture, lay violent hands on.

get–, lay–, take–, catch–, lay fast–, take firm- hold of; lay by the heels, take prisoner; fasten upon, grapple, embrace, grip, gripe, clasp, grab [*colloq.*], make away with, clutch, collar, throttle, take by the throat, claw, clinch, clench, make sure of.

catch at, jump at, make a grab at, snap at, snatch at; reach, make a long arm [*colloq.*], stretch forth one's hand.

disseize *or* disseise; take from, take away from; deduct etc. 38; retrench etc. (*curtail*) 201; dispossess, ease one of, snatch from one's grasp; tear–, tear away–, wrench–, wrest–, wring- from; extort; deprive of, bereave; disinherit, cut off with a shilling; oust etc. (*eject*) 297; divest; levy, distrain, confiscate; sequester, sequestrate; accroach; usurp; despoil, strip, fleece, shear, displume.

absorb etc. (*suck in*) 296; draw off; suck, –like a leach, –the blood of; impoverish, eat out of house and home; drain, –to the dregs; gut, dry, exhaust, swallow up.

retake, resume; recover etc. 775.

adj. **taking** etc. *v.;* privative, prehensile; predacious *or* predaceous, predal [*obs.*], predatory, wolfish, lupine, rapacious, raptorial; ravening, ravenous; parasitic; all-devouring, all-engulfing.

bereft etc. 776.

adv. at one fell swoop.

790. Restitution

n. **restitution**, return; rendition, reddition; restoration, reinstatement, reinvestment, recuperation; rehabilitation etc. (*reconstruction*) 660; reparation, atonement; compensation, indemnification.

recovery etc. (*getting back*) 775; release, replevin, replevy, redemption; reversion; remitter.

v. **restore**, return; give–, carry–, bring- back; render–, –up; give up; let go, unclutch; disgorge, regorge; regurgitate; recoup, reimburse, com- pensate, indemnify, reinvest, reinstate, remit, rehabilitate; repair etc. (*make good*) 660.

recover etc. (*get back*) 775; redeem; take back again; revest, revert.

adj. **restoring** etc. *v.;* recuperative etc. 660; compensatory, indemnificatory; reversionary, redemptive, revertible.

adv. in full restitution; as partial compensation; to atone for.

791. Stealing

n. **stealing** etc. *v.;* theft, thievery, robbery, direption [*rare*]; abstraction, appropriation; plagiary [*rare*], plagiarism, autoplagiarism; rape, depredation; kidnaping *or* kidnapping.

pillage, spoliation, plunder, sack, sackage [*rare*], rapine, brigandage, latrociny [*obs.*], latrocinium [*Rom. law*], highway robbery, holdup [*slang*]; raid, foray, razzia; piracy, privateering, buccaneering; filibustering, filibusterism; burglary, housebreaking; abaction, cattle stealing, cattle lifting [*colloq.*], cattle rustling horse stealing; automobile–, car- stealing.

blackmail, badger game [*cant*], Black Hand [*U. S.*].

peculation, embezzlement; fraud etc. 545; larceny, petty larceny, pilfering, shoplifting.

thievishness, rapacity, predacity, predaciousness; kleptomania.

Alsatia; Whitefriars; den of Cacus, den of thieves.

license to plunder, letters of marque.

v. **steal**, thieve, rob, purloin, pilfer, filch, prig [*Brit. cant*], bag, nim [*obs.*], crib [*colloq.*], cabbage, palm; abstract; appropriate, plagiarize.

disregard the distinction between *meum* and *tuum*.

abduct, convey away, carry off, kidnap, crimp, impress, press [*rare*]; make–, walk–, run- off with; run away with; spirit away, seize etc. (*lay violent hands on*) 789.

plunder, pillage, rifle, sack, loot, ransack, spoil, spoliate, despoil, strip, sweep, gut, forage, levy blackmail, pirate, pickeer [*obs.*], maraud, lift cattle [*colloq.*], poach, rustle, smuggle, run; badger [*cant*], bunko *or* bunco; hold up; bail up, stick up [*both colloq. or slang, Austral.*], filibuster.

swindle, peculate, embezzle; sponge, mulct, rook, bilk, pluck, pigeon [*slang*], thimblerig; diddle [*colloq. or dial.*], fleece; defraud etc. 545; obtain under false pretenses; live by one's wits.

rob–, borrow from- Peter to pay Paul; set a thief to catch a thief.

adj. **thieving** etc. *v.;* thievish, light-fingered, furacious [*rare*]; furtive; piratical; predacious *or*
predaceous, predal [*obs.*], predatory; raptorial
etc. (*rapacious*) 789.

stolen etc. *v.*

792. Thief

n. **thief**, robber, *homo trium literarum* [*L.*], spoiler,
depredator, pillager, marauder; pilferer, rifler,
filcher, plagiarist; harpy, shark [*slang*], land rat
[*cant*], land pirate, land shark, falcon; smug-
gler, poacher; abductor, badger [*cant*], kid-
naper *or* kidnapper; *chor* [*Hind.*], crook
[*slang*], lifter, skin [*slang*], contrabandist, hawk;
hold-up, jackleg, rustler [*all three slang*]; spieler
[*colloq., Austral.*], sandbagger, sneak thief,
strong-arm man.

pirate, corsair, viking, sea king, buccaneer, privateer; Paul Jones.

brigand, bandit, freebooter, thug, dacoit
[*India*]; rover, ranger, pickeerer [*obs.*], pica-
roon, filibuster, rapparee [*Ir.*]; cattle thief,
abactor; bushranger, mosstrooper [*hist.*], Bed-
ouin; wrecker; highwayman, footpad, sturdy
beggar, knight of the road.

Dick Turpin, Claude Duval, Jonathan Wild,
Macheath, Nevison, Jesse James.

pickpocket, dip [*slang*], cutpurse, pickpurse
[*rare*], light-fingered gentry; sharper; card
sharper, card cheat, Greek; thimblerigger; bun-
koman *or* buncoman, rook [*slang*], welsher
[*slang*], blackleg [*colloq.*], leg [*slang, Eng.*], diddler [*colloq. or slang*], defaulter; Autolycus,
Jeremy Diddler, Robert Macaire, Artful
Dodger, trickster; swell mob [*slang*], *chevalier
d'industrie* [*F.*]; shoplifter.

swindler, duffer [*Eng.*], peculator; forger, coiner,
smasher [*cant, Eng.*], counterfeiter; fence, receiver of stolen goods.

burglar, housebreaker, yeggman *or* yegg
[*slang*], cracksman [*slang*], magsman [*slang*],
sneak thief; second-story -thief, –man; Bill
Sikes, Jack Sheppard.

793. Booty

n. **booty**, spoil, plunder, prize, loot, swag [*cant*];
perquisite, boodle [*polit. cant*], graft [*colloq.*],
pork barrel [*polit. cant*], pickings; *spolia
opima* [*L.*], prey; blackmail; stolen goods.

adj. **looting**, plundering, spoliative, manubial [*obs.*].

794. Barter

n. **barter**, exchange, scorse [*obs.*], truck system; interchange etc. 148.

a Roland for an Oliver, *quid pro quo* [*L.*], commutation, composition; Indian gift [*colloq.*].

trade, commerce, mercature [*obs.*], buying and
selling, bargain and sale; traffic, business, nun-
dination [*obs.*], custom, shopping; commercial
enterprise, speculation, jobbing, stockjobbing,
agiotage, brokery.

dealing, transaction, negotiation, bargain.

free trade [*opp. to* protection].

v. **barter**, exchange, truck, scorse [*obs.*], swap *or*
swop [*colloq. & dial.*]; interchange etc. 148;
commutate etc. (*sub titute*) 147; compound for.

trade, traffic, buy and sell, give and take, nundi-
nate [*obs.*]; carry on–, ply–, drive- a trade; be
in -business, –the city; keep a shop, deal in,
employ one's capital in.

trade–, deal–, have dealings- with; put through a
deal with; have truck with; transact–, do- business with; open–, have–, keep- an account
with.

bargain; drive–, make- a bargain; negotiate, bid
for; haggle, stickle, –for; higgle, dicker, chaffer,
huckster, cheapen, beat down; underbid;
outbid; ask, charge; strike a bargain etc.
(*contract*) 769.

speculate; give–, bait with- a sprat to catch a
-herring, –mackerel; buy low and sell high, buy
in the cheapest and sell in the dearest market;
stag the market [*London Stock Exchange*], rig
the market [*Exchange cant*].

adj. **commercial**, mercantile, trading; interchangeable, marketable, staple, in the market, for sale;
at a bargain, marked down.

wholesale, retail.

adv. over the counter; in the marts of trade; on the
Rialto, on 'change.

795. Purchase

n. **purchase**, emption [*rare*]; buying, purchasing,
shopping; preëmption, refusal.

coemption [*Rom. law*]; bribery; slave trade.

buyer, purchaser, emptor [*law*], coemptor, vendee; client, customer, clientele, clientage; patron, employer.

v. **buy**, purchase, invest in, regrate, procure; rent
etc. (*hire*) 788; repurchase, buy in.

make–, complete- a purchase; buy over the
counter; pay cash for; charge, –to one's account.

shop, market, go a-shopping.

keep in one's pay, bribe, suborn; pay etc. 807;
spend etc. 809.

adj. **purchased** etc. *v.;* emptorial, coemptional, co-
emptive; cliental.

796. Sale

n. **sale**, vent [*rare*], vend [*Eng.*], disposal; auction, roup [*Scot.*], outcry, vendue, Dutch auction; custom etc. (*traffic*) 794.

salableness, salability, marketability, vendibility, vendibleness.

seller, vender, vendor; consigner; *institor* [*L.*]; rouping wife [*Scot.*]; merchant etc. 797; auctioneer.

salesmanship, selling ability.

v. **sell**, vend, dispose of, make a sale, effect a sale; sell over the counter, sell at auction, sell by [*esp. Brit.*] auction, auction, roup [*Scot.*], outcry; put up to (*or* at) auction; bring to (*or* under) the hammer; offer-, put up- for sale; hawk, bring to market; wholesale; dump, unload, place; offer etc. 763; undersell; dispense, retail; deal in etc. 794; sell -off, –out; turn into money, realize.

let; mortgage etc. (*security*) 771.

adj. **for sale**, under the hammer, in the market.

salable, marketable, vendible, staple, merchantable; in demand, popular.

unsalable etc., unpurchased, unbought; on the shelves, shelved, on one's hands.

797. Merchant

n. **merchant**, trader, dealer, monger, chandler, salesman; money changer, changer [*archaic*]; regrater; shopkeeper, shopman; tradesman, tradespeople, tradesfolk.

retailer; chapman, hawker, huckster, higgler; peddler *or* pedlar, colporteur, cadger, Autolycus; sutler, vivandière; costerman, costermonger; tallyman [*rare*], canvasser, solicitor; cheap Jack, *camelot* [*F.*]; faker [*slang*]; vintner; greengrocer, groceryman, haberdasher.

money-lender, cambist, usurer, moneyer [*obs.*], banker; money-changer, money-broker.

jobber; broker etc. (*agent*) 758; buyer etc. 795; seller etc. 796; bear, bull [*Stock Exchange*].

concern, house, corporation; firm etc. (*partnership*) 712.

798. Merchandise

n. **merchandise**, ware, commodity, effects, goods, article, stock, produce, staple commodity; stock in trade etc. (*store*) 636; cargo etc. (*contents*) 190.

799. Mart

n. **mart**, market, marketplace; fair, bazaar, staple, exchange, stock exchange, Wheat Pit [*Chi-cago*]; 'change, bourse, curb, hall, guildhall; tollbooth [*Scot. & dial. Eng.*], customhouse; Tattersall's.

shop, stall, booth; wharf; office, chambers, countinghouse, bureau; counter *or* compter [*obs.*].

store etc. 636; department store, finding store [*U. S.*], grindery warehouse, warehouse, wareroom; depot, interposit [*rare*], entrepôt [*F.*], emporium, establishment.

market overt, open market.

800. Money

n. **money**, finance; money -matters, –market; accounts etc. 811; funds, treasure; capital, stock; assets etc. (*property*) 780; wealth etc. 803; supplies, ways and means, wherewithal *or* wherewith, sinews of war, almighty dollar, cash.

solvency, responsibility, reliability, solidity, soundness.

sum, amount; balance, balance sheet; sum total; proceeds etc. (*receipts*) 810.

currency, circulating medium, specie, coin, piece, hard cash; dollar, sterling; pounds, shillings, and pence, £ s. d.; guinea; gold mohur [*India*]; eagle, double eagle; pocket, breeches pocket [*colloq.*], wallet, roll, purse; money in hand; *argent comptant* [*F.*], ready [*colloq.*], ready money; Federal-, fractional-, postal-currency; bottom dollar [*colloq.*]; checks, chips. [*slang terms*] the needful, rhino, brass, blunt, dust, mopus, tin, salt, chink, dough, jack, moss, rock, dibs, slug [*Calif.* 1849]; buzzard dollar, spondulics, long green; barrel, pile, wad; dough, bread, long green.

precious metals, gold, silver, copper, bullion, ingot, bar, nugget.

petty cash, pocket money, pin money, spending money, change, small coin; long bit, short bit, two bits, quarter [*all U. S.*]; dime, nickel, cent, red cent [*colloq., U.S.*]; doit, stiver, rap, mite, farthing, sou, penny, shilling, tester, groat, rouleau.

wampum, wampumpeag, seawan *or* seawant, roanoke, cowrie.

great wealth, money to burn [*colloq.*]; power-, mint-, barrel-, raft- of money [*all colloq.*]; good-, round-, lump- sum; plum (=£100,-000) [*rare slang*]; million, millions, thousands; crore (= ten million rupees, written *Rs.* 1,00,00,000) [*India*]; lac *or* lakh, lac of rupees (= 100,000 rupees, written *Rs.* 1,00,000) [*India*].

[*science of coins*] numismatics, numismatology, chrysology.

paper money; money–, postal–, post office-order; note, –of hand; bank–, promissory-note; I O U, bond; bill, –of exchange; draft, check [*esp. U.S.*] or cheque [*esp. Brit.*], hundi [*India*], order, warrant, coupon, debenture, exchequer bill, assignat, greenback; blueback, shinplaster [*slang*].

remittance etc. (*payment*) 807; credit etc. 805; liability etc. 806.

drawer, drawee; obligor, obligee.

counterfeit–, false–, bad- money; queer [*slang*], base coin, flash note, slip [*obs.*], kite [*slang*]; fancy stocks; Bank of Elegance.

counterfeiter, coiner, moneyer, forger.

v. **total**, amount to, come to, mount up to.

touch the pocket; draw, draw upon; back; indorse etc. (*security*) 771; discount etc. 813.

issue, utter, circulate; fiscalize, monetize, remonetize.

demonetize, deprive of standard value; cease to issue.

coin, counterfeit, forge; circulate bad money, shove the queer [*slang*].

adj. **monetary**, pecuniary, crumenal [*obs.*], fiscal, financial, sumptuary, numismatical; sterling; nummary.

solvent, sound, substantial, good, reliable, responsible, solid, having a good rating; able to pay -20 shillings to the pound, –100 cents on the dollar.

801. Treasurer

n. **treasurer**; bursar, purser, purse bearer; cash keeper, banker; depositary; questor or quaestor [*Rom.*], receiver, liquidator, steward, trustee, accountant, expert accountant, Accountant General, almoner or almner, paymaster, cashier, teller; cambist; money changer etc. (*merchant*) 797.

financier, Chancellor of the Exchequer, Secretary of the Treasury, minister of finance.

802. Treasury

n. **treasury**, bank, exchequer, almonry, fisc or fiscus, hanaper; kutcherry or cutcherry or kachahri [*India*], bursary; strong box, stronghold, strong room; coffer; chest etc. (*receptacle*) 191; safe; depository etc. 636; cash register, cash box, money-box, till, tiller.

purse, moneybag, portemonnaie, pocketbook, wallet; purse strings; pocket, breeches pocket.

sinking fund; stocks; public–, parliamentary--stocks, –funds, –securities; Consols, *crédit mobilier* [*F.*]; bonds, government bonds, Lib-

erty bonds, savings bonds, three per cents; gilt-edged securities.

803. Wealth

n. **wealth**, riches, fortune, handsome fortune, opulence, affluence; good–, easy- circumstances; independence; competence etc. (*sufficiency*) 639; solvency etc. 800.

capital, money; round sum; great wealth etc. (*treasure*) 800; mint of money, mine of wealth, bonanza, El Dorado, Pactolus, Golconda, Potosi, Philosopher's Stone; the Golden Touch.

long–, full–, well lined–, heavy- purse; purse of Fortunatus; *embarras de richesses* [*F.*].

pelf, Mammon, lucre, filthy lucre; loaves and fishes, fleshpots of Egypt.

means, resources, substance, command of money; property etc. 780; income etc. 810.

provision, maintenance, livelihood; dowry, alimony.

rich man, moneyed man, warm man [*old slang*], man of substance; capitalist, millionaire, tippybob [*slang*], Nabob, Croesus, Midas, Plutus, Dives, Timon of Athens; Danaë.

timocracy, plutocracy.

v. **be rich** etc. *adj.;* roll–, wallow- in -wealth, –riches; have money to burn [*colloq.*].

afford, well afford; command -money, –a sum; make both ends meet, hold one's head above water.

become rich etc. *adj.;* fill one's pocket etc. (*treasury*) 802; feather one's nest, make a fortune; make money etc. (*acquire*) 775.

enrich, imburse [*rare*].

worship Mammon, worship the golden calf.

adj. **wealthy**, rich, affluent, opulent, moneyed, worth a great deal; well-to-do, well off; warm [*old slang*]; well–, provided for.

made of money; rich as - Croesus; rolling in -riches, –wealth; having a power of money etc. (*great wealth*) 800.

flush, –of -cash, –money, –tin [*slang*]; in funds, in cash, in full feather.

solvent etc., 800; pecunious [*rare*], out of debt, all straight.

804. Poverty

n. **poverty**, indigence, penury, pauperism, destitution, want; need, neediness; lack, necessity, privation, distress, difficulties, wolf at the door.

straits; bad–, poor–, needy–, embarrassed–, reduced–, straightened- circumstances; slender–, narrow- means; hand-to-mouth existence, *res angusta domi* [*L.*], low water [*slang*], impecuniosity.

mendicity, beggary, mendicancy; broken–, loss of– fortune; insolvency etc. (*nonpayment*) 808.

empty -purse, –pocket; light purse; "a beggarly account of empty boxes" [*Romeo and Juliet*].

poor man, pauper, mumper, mendicant, beggar, starveling; *pauvre diable* [*F.*], fakir *or* fakeer [*India*], sunyasi [*India*], schnorrer [*Yiddish*].

v. **be poor** etc. *adj.;* want, lack, starve, live from hand to mouth, have seen better days, go down in the world, come upon the parish; go to -the dogs, –the almshouse, –the poorhouse, –rack and ruin; not have a -penny etc. (*money*) 800, –shot in one's locker; beg one's bread, –from door to door; *tirer le diable par la queue* [*F.*]; run into debt etc. (*debt*) 806.

render poor etc. *adj.;* impoverish; reduce, –to poverty; pauperize, fleece, ruin, bring on the parish.

adj. **poor**, indigent; poverty-stricken; badly–, poorly–, ill- off; poor as -a rat, –a church mouse, –Job, –Job's turkey [*colloq.*]; fortune-less, dowerless, moneyless, penniless; unportioned, unmoneyed; impecunious; out–, short-of -money, –cash; without–, not- worth- a rap etc. (*money*) 800; *qui n'a pas le sou* [*F.*], out of pocket, hard up; out at -elbows, –heels; seedy [*colloq.*], in rags, barefooted; beggarly, beggared, destitute; fleeced, stripped; bereft, bereaved; reduced.

in want etc. *n.;* needy, necessitous, distressed, pinched, straitened; put to one's -shifts, –last shifts; unable to -keep the wolf from the door, –make both ends meet; embarrassed, under hatches; involved etc. (*in debt*) 806; insolvent etc. (*not paying*) 808.

adv. *in forma pauperis* [*L.*].

805. Credit

n. **credit**, trust, tick [*colloq.*], strap [*slang*], score, tally, account.

paper credit, letter of credit, circular note; duplicate; mortgage, lien, debenture, floating capital; draft, *lettre de créance* [*F.*], securities.

creditor, lender, lessor, mortgagee; dun, dunner; usurer.

v. **credit**, accredit, intrust *or* entrust; keep–, run up- an account with.

place to one's -credit, –account; give–, take-credit; fly a kite [*com. slang*]; have one's credit good for.

adj. **accredited**; of good credit, of unlimited credit; well rated; credited, crediting.

adv. on credit etc. *n.;* to the account of, to the credit of; *à compte* [*F.*].

806. Debt

n. **debt**, obligation, liability, indebtment, debit, score.

arrears, deferred payment, deficit, default; insolvency etc. (*nonpayment*) 808; bad debt.

interest; premium; usance [*obs.*], usury; floating -debt, –capital.

debtor, debitor [*obs.*], mortgagor; defaulter etc. 808; borrower.

v. **be in debt** etc. *adj.;* owe; incur–, contract- a debt etc. *n.;* run up -a bill, –a score, –an account; go on tick [*colloq.*]; borrow etc. 788; run–, get-into debt; be over head and ears in debt; be in difficulties; outrun the constable.

answer for, go bail for; back one's note.

adj. **liable**, chargeable, answerable for.

indebted, in debt, in embarrassed circumstances, in difficulties; encumbered *or* incumbered, involved; involved–, plunged–, deep–, over head and ears- in debt; deeply involved; fast tied up; insolvent etc. (*not paying*) 808; minus [*colloq.*], out of pocket.

unpaid; unrequited, unrewarded; owing, due, in arrear, outstanding.

807. Payment

n. **payment**, defrayment; discharge; acquittance, quittance; settlement, clearance, liquidation, satisfaction, reckoning, arrangement.

acknowledgment, release; receipt, –in full, –in full of all demands; voucher.

repayment, reimbursement, retribution; pay etc. (*reward*) 973; money paid etc. (*expenditure*) 809.

ready money etc. (*cash*) 800; stake, remittance, installment *or* instalment.

payer, liquidator etc. 801.

v. **pay**, defray, make payment; pay -down, –on the nail [*slang*], –ready money, –at sight, –in advance; cash, honor a bill, acknowledge; redeem; pay in kind.

pay one's -way, –shot, –footing; pay -the piper, –sauce for all [*both colloq.*], –costs; come down with the needful [*slang*]; shell–, fork- out [*both slang*]; come down with, –the dust [*both slang*]; tickle–, grease- the palm [*both colloq.*]; expend etc. 809; put down, lay down.

discharge, settle, quit [*archaic*], acquit oneself of; foot the bill [*colloq.*]; account with, reckon with, settle with, be even with, be quits with; strike a balance; settle–, balance–, square- accounts with; quit scores [*archaic*]; wipe–, clear- off old scores; satisfy; pay in full; satisfy–, pay in full- all demands; clear, liquidate; pay -up, –old debts.

repay, refund, reimburse, retribute [*obs.*]; make compensation etc. 30; disgorge, make repayment.

adj. **paying** etc. paid etc. *v.;* owing nothing, out of debt, all straight, all clear, clear of encumbrance, clear of debt, above water; unowed, never indebted; solvent etc. 800.

adv. to the tune of [*colloq.*]; on the nail [*slang*], money down, cash down, cash on delivery, C.O.D.

808. Nonpayment

n. **nonpayment**; default, defalcation; protest, repudiation; application of the sponge; whitewashing.

insolvency, bankruptcy, failure; insufficiency etc. 640; run upon a bank; overdrawn account.

waste paper bonds; dishonored–, protested- bills; bogus check *or* cheque, rubber check [*colloq.*].

defaulter, bankrupt, insolvent debtor, lame duck [*slang*], man of straw; welsher *or* welcher, stag [*obs.*], levanter, absconder.

v. **not pay** etc. 807; fail, break, stop payment; become -insolvent, –bankrupt; be gazetted; have one's check -dishonored, –protested.

pay under protest; button up one's pockets, draw the purse strings; apply the sponge; pay over the left shoulder [*colloq.*], get whitewashed; swindle etc. 791; run up bills, fly kites [*com. slang*].

protest, dishonor, repudiate, nullify.

adj. **not paying**; in debt etc. 806; behindhand, in arrear; beggared etc., (*poor*) 804; unable to make both ends meet, minus [*colloq.*], worse than nothing.

insolvent, bankrupt, in the gazette, gazetted, ruined.

unpaid etc. (*outstanding*) 806; gratis etc. 815; unremunerated.

809. Expenditure

n. **expenditure**, money going out; outgoings, outlay; expenses, disbursement; prime cost etc. (*price*) 812; circulation; run upon a bank.

[money paid] payment etc. 807; pay etc. (*remuneration*) 973; bribe etc. 973; fee, footing, garnish [*obs.*]; subsidy; tribute; contingent, quota; donation, gift etc. 784.

investment; purchase etc. 795.

deposit, pay in advance, earnest, handsel *or* hansel, installment *or* instalment.

v. **expend**, spend; run–, get- through; pay, disburse; ante, ante up [*both poker*]; pony up [*slang*]; open–, loose–, untie- the purse strings, lay out, shell out [*slang*], fork out [*slang*]; bleed; make up a sum, invest, sink money.

fee etc. (*reward*) 973; pay one's way etc. (*pay*) 807; subscribe etc. (*give*) 784; subsidize; bribe.

adj. **expending**, expended etc. *v.;* sumptuary, lavish, free, free with one's money, liberal; beyond one's income.

expensive, costly, dear, high-priced, precious, high.

810. Receipt

n. **receipt**, value received, money coming in; income, incomings [*rare*], revenue, return, proceeds; gross receipts, net profit; earnings etc. (*gain*) 775; accepta [*L.*], avails.

rent, rent roll; rental, rentage [*obs.*], rack-rent.

premium, bonus; sweepstakes, tontine, prize, drawings, hand-out [*slang*].

pension, annuity; jointure etc. (*property*) 780; alimony, pittance; emolument etc. (*remuneration*) 973.

v. **receive** etc. 785; get, have an income of, be in receipt of, have coming in; take money; draw from, derive from; acquire etc. 775; take etc. 789; have in prospect.

yield, bring in, afford, pay, return; accrue etc. (*be received from*) 785.

adj. **receiving**, received etc. *v.;* well-paying, remunerative, interest-bearing; well–, profitably- invested; profitable etc. (*gainful*) 775.

adv. at interest; within one's income.

811. Accounts

n. **accounts**, accompts [*archaic*]; business–, commercial–, monetary- arithmetic; statistics etc. (*numeration*) 85; money matters, finance, budget, bill, score, reckoning, account.

bookkeeping, audit, single entry, double entry; computation, calculation, casting up.

account book, books, ledger; day–, cash–, petty-cash–, pass- book; journal; debtor and creditor–, cash–, running- account; account current; balance, –sheet; *compte rendu* [*F.*], account settled; *acquit* [*F.*], assets, expenditure, liabilities, outstanding accounts; profit and loss -account, –statement; receipts; receipt -in full, –in part, –on account; spread sheet.

accountant, auditor, actuary, bookkeeper; financier etc. 801; accounting party; chartered accountant [*Eng.*], certified public accountant [*U. S.*], C.P.A., bank examiner, bank auditor.

v. **keep accounts**, enter, post, post up, book, credit, debit, carry over; take stock; tot up [*colloq.*], add, add up; balance–, make up–, square–, settle–, wind up–, cast up- accounts; make accounts square.

bring to book, audit, examine the books, tax.

falsify, surcharge; falsify–, garble- an account; cook–, doctor- an account [*both colloq.*]; cook–, doctor- the books [*both colloq.*].

adj. monetary etc. 800; accountable, accounting; statistical; entered etc. *v.*

812. Price

n. **price**, amount, cost, expense, prime cost, charge, figure, demand, damage [*colloq.*], fare, hire; wages etc. (*remuneration*) 973.

dues, duty, toll, tax, impost, tariff, cess, sess [*obs.*], tallage *or* tailage [*Old Eng. law*], levy; *abkari* [*India*], capitation, capitation tax, poll tax; doomage, *likin* [*Chinese*], gabel *or* gabelle, salt tax; gavel [*Old Eng. law*], octroi [*F.*], custom, excise, assessment, taxation, benevolence [*hist.*], forced loan; tenths [*hist.*], tithe, exactment, ransom, salvage, towage; brokerage, wharfage, freightage.

worth, rate, value, par value, valuation, appraisement, money's worth; penny etc. -worth; price current, market price, quotation, current quotation; what it will fetch etc. *v.*

bill etc. (*account*) 811; shot, scot, scot and lot.

v. **price**; bear–, set–, fix- a price; appraise, assess, doom, charge, demand, ask, require, exact, run up; distrain; run up a bill etc. (*debt*) 806; have one's price; liquidate.

amount to, come to, mount up to; stand one in [*colloq.*], put one back [*slang*].

fetch, sell for, cost, bring in, yield, afford.

adj. **priced** etc. *v.;* to the tune of, *ad valorem* [*L.*]; dutiable, taxable, assessable; mercenary, venal.

813. Discount

n. **discount**, abatement, concession, reduction, depreciation, allowance, qualification, set-off, drawback, poundage, agio, percentage; rebate, rebatement, backwardization [*Eng.*], backwardation [*Eng.*], contango [*Eng. Stock Exchange*]; salvage; tare [*com.*], tare and tret.

v. **discount**, bate, rebate, abate, deduct, strike off, mark down, reduce, take off, allow, give, make allowance; depreciate.

adj. **discounting** etc. *v.;* concessional; marked down; depreciative.

adv. **at a discount**, at a bargain, below par, on sale.

814. Dearness

n. **dearness** etc. *adj.;* high–, famine–, fancy- price; overcharge; extravagance; exorbitance, extortion; heavy pull upon the purse.

v. **be dear** etc. *adj.;* cost much, cost a pretty penny [*colloq.*]; rise in price, look up.

overcharge, bleed [*colloq.*], skin [*slang*], fleece, extort.

pay too much, pay through the nose [*colloq.*], pay too dear for one's whistle [*colloq.*].

adj. **dear**; high, –priced; of great price, expensive, costly, precious, dear bought; unreasonable, extravagant, exorbitant, extortionate.

at a premium; not to be had, –for love or money; beyond price, above price; priceless, of priceless value.

adv. **dear**, dearly; at great cost, at heavy cost, at a high price, *à grands frais* [*F.*].

815. Cheapness

n. **cheapness**, low price; depreciation; bargain, *bon marché* [*F.*]; good penny etc. -worth; drug in the market.

[absence of charge] gratuity; free -quarters, –seats, –admission; free lunch; run of one's teeth [*slang*]; nominal price, peppercorn rent; labor of love.

deadhead [*colloq.*], dead beat [*slang*], beat [*slang*], sponger.

v. **be cheap** etc. *adj.;* cost little; come down–, fall-in price; be marked down.

buy for a mere nothing, buy at a bargain, buy dirt-cheap, buy for an old song; have one's money's worth; beat down, cheapen.

adj. **cheap**; low, –priced; moderate, reasonable; inexpensive *or* unexpensive; well–, worth the money; *magnifique et pas cher* [*F.*]; good–, cheap- at the price; dirt-cheap, dog-cheap; cheap as dirt, cheap and nasty [*colloq.*]; peppercorn; catchpenny.

reduced, half-price, depreciated, shopworn, marked down, unsalable.

gratuitous, gratis, free, for nothing; costless, expenseless; without charge, not charged, untaxed; scot-free, shot-free, rent-free; free of -cost, –expense; complimentary, honorary, unbought, unpaid for.

adv. **at a bargain**, for a mere song; at cost price, at prime cost, at a reduction; on the cheap [*colloq., Eng.*]; *bon marché or à bon marché* [*F.*].

816. Liberality

n. **liberality**, generosity, munificence; bounty, bounteousness, bountifulness; hospitableness, hospitality; charity etc. (*beneficence*) 906; open–, free- hand; open–, large–, free- heart; enough and to spare.

cheerful giver, free giver, patron; benefactor etc. 912.

v. **be liberal** etc. *adj.;* spend–, bleed- freely; shower down upon; open one's purse strings etc. (*disburse*) 809; spare no expense, give *carte blanche* [*F.*]; give with both hands; give the coat off one's back; keep open house, fill one's house with guests.

adj. **liberal**, free, generous; charitable etc. (*beneficent*) 906; hospitable; bountiful, bounteous, ample, handsome; unsparing, ungrudging; unselfish; open–, free–, full- handed; open–, large–, free-hearted; munificent, princely.

adv. **liberally** etc. *adj.;* ungrudgingly; with open hands, with both hands.

817. Economy

n. **economy**, frugality; thrift, thriftiness; care, husbandry, good housewifery, savingness, retrenchment.

savings; prevention of waste, save-all; parsimony etc. 819.

v. **be economical** etc. *adj.;* practice economy, economize, save; retrench, cut down expenses; cut one's coat according to one's cloth, make both ends meet, keep within compass, meet one's expenses, keep one's head above water, pay one's way; husband etc. (*lay by*) 636; save–, invest- money; put out to interest; provide–, save- -for, –against- a rainy day; feather one's nest; look after the main chance [*colloq.*].

adj. **economical**, frugal, careful, thrifty, saving, chary, spare, sparing; parsimonious etc. 819; sufficient; plain.

adv. **sparingly** etc. *adj.; ne quid nimis* [*L.*].

818. Prodigality

n. **prodigality**, prodigence [*obs.*], wastefulness, wastry *or* wastrie [*Scot.*], unthriftiness, waste; profusion, profuseness; extravagance; squandering etc. *v.;* lavishness.

pound-foolishness, pound-folly, penny wisdom.

prodigal, spendthrift, wastethrift, wastrel [*dial. Eng.*], waster, high roller [*slang*], squanderer, spender, spendall, scattergood [*archaic*]; locust; Prodigal Son; Timon of Athens.

v. **be prodigal** etc. *adj.;* squander, lavish, sow broadcast; blow in [*slang*]; pay through the nose etc. (*dear*) 814; spill, waste, dissipate, ex-

haust, drain, eat out of house and home, overdraw, outrun the constable; run out, run through; misspend; throw good money after bad, throw the helve after the hatchet; burn the candle at both ends; make ducks and drakes of one's money; fool–, potter–, muddle–, fritter–, throw- away one's money; squander one's substance in riotous living; spend money like water; pour water into a sieve, kill the goose that lays the golden eggs; *manger son blé en herbe* [*F.*].

adj. **prodigal**, profuse, thriftless, unthrifty, improvident, wasteful, losel, extravagant, lavish, dissipated, over-liberal; full-handed etc. (*liberal*) 816; overpaid.

penny-wise and pound-foolish.

adv. with an unsparing hand; money burning one's pocket.

int. keep the change! hang the expense!

819. Parsimony

n. **parsimony**, parcity [*obs.*]; parsimoniousness, stinginess etc. *adj.;* stint; illiberality, avarice, tenacity, avidity, rapacity, extortion, malversation, venality, cupidity; lack of prodigality etc. 818; selfishness etc. 943; *auri sacra fames* [*L.*]; cheeseparings and candle ends.

miser, niggard, churl, screw, skin-flint, skin [*slang*], codger [*dial. Eng.*], money-grub [*slang*], muckworm, scrimp [*colloq.*], pinchgut [*obs. or vulgar*], lick-penny, hunks [*colloq.*], curmudgeon, harpy, extortioner, usurer, Hessian [*U.S.*]; pinchfist, pinchpenny [*obs.*].

Harpagon, Euclio, Silas Marner, Daniel Dancer.

v. **be parsimonious** etc. *adj.;* grudge, begrudge, stint, pinch, gripe, screw, dole out, hold back, withhold, starve, famish, live upon nothing, skin a flint [*colloq.*], pinch a sixpence till it squeaks.

drive a bargain, cheapen, beat down; stop one hole in a sieve; have an itching palm, grasp, grab.

adj. **parsimonious**, penurious, stingy, miserly, mean, shabby, peddling, penny wise, near, near as the bark on a tree, niggardly, close; close-handed, close-fisted, fast-handed [*obs.*], hard-fisted, straithanded [*obs.*], tight-fisted; tight [*colloq.*], sparing, chary; grudging, gripping etc. *v.;* illiberal, ungenerous, churlish, hidebound, sordid, mercenary, venal, covetous, usurious, avaricious; greedy, extortionate, rapacious; underpaid.

adv. with a sparing hand.

Class 6. Affections

Section 1. Affections in General

820. Affections

n. **character**, qualities, disposition, affections, nature, spirit, tone; temper, temperament; diathesis, idiosyncrasy; cast-, habit-, frame- of -mind, -soul; predilection, turn; natural-, turn of mind; bent, bias, predisposition, proneness, proclivity, propensity, propenseness, propension, propendency [*obs.*]; vein, humor, mood, grain, mettle, backbone; sympathy etc. (*love*) 897.

soul, heart, breast, bosom, inner man; heart's -core, -strings, -blood; heart of hearts, *penetralia mentis* [*L.*]; secret and inmost recesses of the heart, cockles of one's heart; inmost- heart, -soul.

passion, pervading spirit; ruling-, master- passion; *furore* [*It.*], furor; fullness of the heart, heyday of the blood, flesh and blood, flow of soul.

energy, fervor, fire, verve, force.

v. have *or* possess character etc. *n.;* be of a character etc. *n.;* be affected etc. *adj.;* breathe energy etc. *n.*

adj. **characterized**, affected, formed, molded *or* moulded, cast; attemperate, attempered, tempered; framed.

prone, predisposed, disposed, inclined; having a bias etc. *n.;* tinctured-, imbued-, penetrated-, eaten up- with.

inborn, inbred, ingrained; deep-rooted, ineffaceable, inveterate; congenital, dyed in the wool, implanted by nature, inherent, in the grain.

adv. in one's heart etc. *n.;* at heart; heart and soul etc. 821; in the vein, in the mood.

821. Feeling

n. **feeling**; suffering etc. *v.;* endurance, tolerance, sufferance, experience, response; sympathy etc. (*love*) 897; impression, inspiration, affection, sensation, emotion, pathos, deep sense.

warmth, glow, unction, gusto, vehemence, fervor, fervency; heartiness, cordiality; earnestness, eagerness; *empressement* [*F.*], gush [*colloq.*], ardor, zeal, passion, enthusiasm, verve, *furore* [*It.*], furor, fanaticism; excitation of feeling etc. 824; fullness of the heart etc.

(*disposition*) 820; passion etc. (*state of excitability*) 825; ecstasy etc. (*pleasure*) 827.

state of excitement; blush, suffusion, flush; hectic, hectic fever, hectic flush; tingling, thrill, turn, shock; agitation etc. (*irregular motion*) 315; quiver, heaving, flutter, flurry, fluster, twitter, tremor; throb, throbbing; pulsation, palpitation, panting; trepidation, perturbation, ruffle, hurry of spirits, pother, stew [*colloq.*], ferment.

v. **feel**; receive an impression etc. *n.;* be impressed with etc. *adj.;* entertain-, harbor-, cherish- -feeling etc. *n.*

respond; catch the -flame, -infection; enter into the spirit of.

bear, suffer, support, sustain, endure, thole [*obs. or dial.*], aby *or* abye; brook; abide etc. (*be composed*) 826; experience etc. (*meet with*) 151; taste, prove; labor-, smart- under; bear the brunt of, brave, stand.

be agitated, be excited etc, 824; swell, glow, warm, flush, blush, crimson, change color, mantle; darken, whiten, pale; turn -color, -pale, -red, -black in the face; tingle, thrill, heave, pant, throb, palpitate, go pitapat, tremble, quiver, flutter, twitter; shake etc. 315; blench, stagger, reel; look -blue, -black; wince, draw a deep breath.

impress etc. (*excite the feelings*) 824.

adj. **feeling** etc. *v.;* sentient; sensuous, sensorial, sensory; emotive, emotional; of *or* with feeling etc. *n.*

lively, quick, smart, strong, sharp, acute, cutting, piercing, incisive; keen, -as a razor; trenchant, pungent, racy, piquant, poignant, caustic.

impressive, deep, profound, indelible; deep-felt, homefelt, heartfelt; swelling, soul-stirring, heart-expanding, electric, thrilling, rapturous, ecstatic; pervading, penetrating, absorbing.

earnest, wistful, eager, breathless; fervent, fervid, gushing [*colloq.*], warm, passionate, warmhearted, hearty, cordial, sincere, zealous, enthusiastic, glowing, ardent, burning, red-hot, fiery, flaming; boiling, -over.

rabid, raving, feverish, fanatical, hysterical; impetuous etc. (*excitable*) 825; overmastering.

impressed-, moved-, touched-, affected-, penetrated-, seized-, imbued etc. 820- with; devoured by; wrought up etc. (*excited*) 824; struck all of a heap [*colloq.*]; rapt; in a quiver etc. *n.;* enraptured etc. 829.

290

the heart -big, –full, –swelling, –beating, –pulsating, –throbbing, –thumping, –beating high, –melting, –overflowing, –bursting, –breaking.

adv. **heartily**, heart and soul, from the bottom of one's heart, *ab imo pectore* [*L.*], *de profundis* [*L.*]; at heart, *con amore* [*It.*], devoutly, over head and ears.

821a. Psychology and Psychotherapy

n. **psychology**, psychonomics, abnormal psychology, applied psychology, animal psychology, child psychology, clinical psychology, comparative psychology, differential psychology, dynamic psychology, experimental psychology, existential psychology, faculty psychology, functional psychology, genetic psychology, individual psychology, industrial psychology, parapsychology, rational psychology, self-psychology, structural psychology; physiological psychology, psychobiochemistry, psychobiology, psychophysics; psychoasthenics, psychostatics, psychogenetics; psychotechnics, psychotechnology.

[systems] Freudian psychology; Gestalt psychology *or* configurationism; behavior psychology *or* Watson's psychology; association psychology, mental chemistry.

psychiatry, psychiatrics, neuropsychiatry; prophylactic psychiatry, mental hygiene; psychosomatic medicine; psychosocial medicine.

psychotherapy; group therapy; occupational therapy; recreational therapy; narcotherapy, narcoanalysis, amytal *or* pentothal interview; hypnotherapy, hypnoanalysis; psychosurgery; suggestion therapy; hypnotic suggestion, posthypnotic suggestion; autosuggestion; sleep treatment; shock therapy, electroshock therapy, protein shock therapy, metrazol shock therapy, hypoglycemic shock therapy, insulin shock therapy, insulin coma therapy, convulsive shock therapy; psychoanalysis, depth interview; psychoanalytic therapy, depth psychology; psychognosis; dream analysis, interpretation of dreams, dream symbolism.

psychological test; aptitude test, Oseretsky test, Stanford scientific aptitude test; personality test, Bernreuter personality inventory, Minnesota multiplastic personality inventory; association test, controlled association test, free association test; apperception test, card test; Rorschach test, ink-blot test; intelligence test, I.Q. test; alpha test, beta test, Babcock-Levy test, Binet-Simon test, Goldstein-Sheerer test,

Kent mental test, aussage test; Wechsler-Bellevue intelligence scale, Gesell's development schedule, Minnesota preschool scale, Cattell's infant intelligence scale.

psyche, mind; preconscious, foreconscious, coconscious; subconscious, unconscious, submerged mind; libido, libidinal energy, libidinal object; id, ego, superego; ego-ideal, ego-id conflict.

[pathological personality types] neurotic, psychoneurotic, neuropath; maladjusted personality, hostile personality; antisocial personality, sociopath; escapist; psychotic personality; mental defective, ament; hypochondriac; alcoholic.

neurosis, psychoneurosis, functional nervous disorder; pathoneurosis, actual neurosis, anxiety neurosis, blast neurosis, fright neurosis, traumatic neurosis, transference neurosis; compulsion neurosis, obsessional neurosis, obsessive-compulsion neurosis; occupational neurosis, professional neurasthenia; combat *or* war neurosis, battle fatigue, shell-shock; nervous breakdown.

psychosis, psychopathy, psychopathic condition; schizophrenia, functional disintegration, dissociation of personality, split personality, multiple personality; dementia praecox, paranoia, catatonia; hebephrenia, paraphrenia, schizophasia, schizothymia; melancholia, manic-depressive insanity, affective psychosis, cyclothymia; Korsakoff's psychosis, polyneuritic psychosis; amentia, fugue; dementia paralytica; senile dementia, senile psychosis, degenerative psychosis; presenile dementia; psychopathia sexualis, psychosexuality; pharmacopsychosis; arteriosclerotic psychosis, climacteric psychosis, exhaustive psychosis, gestational psychosis, involuntary psychosis, involutional psychosis, metabolic psychosis, organic psychosis, postinfectious psychosis, psychasthenia, psycholepsy, psychokinesia, psychorhythmia, toxic psychosis; moral insanity, psychopathic personality; rabies, hydrophobia.

[neurotic symptoms] anxiety, precordial anxiety, free-floating anxiety; asthenia; hysteria, conversion hysteria, anxiety hysteria; dissociation, emotional instability, flight reaction, immaturity; depression; detachment; passive aggression, passive dependence; phobia, morbid fear, astraphobia (lightning and thunder), acrophobia (heights), agoraphobia (open places), ailurophobia (cats), claustrophobia (confined places), hematophobia (blood), hydrophobia (water), pyrophobia (fire), scotophobia (darkness), toxiphobia (being poisoned), xenophobia (strangers); unresponsiveness, apathy; stupor, catatonic stupor, euphoria, elation.

mania, obsession, compulsion; megalomania, monomania, kleptomania, pyromania, erotomania, dipsomania.

complex, inferiority complex, superiority complex, Oedipus or nuclear complex, Electra complex, persecution complex, castration complex; fixation, libido fixation, arrested development; infantile fixation, pregenital fixation; regression.

defense mechanism, psychological or sociological adjustive reaction; negativism; escape mechanism; withdrawal; isolation, emotional insulation; autistic thinking; compensation, overcompensation, decompensation; substitution; sublimation; projection; displacement; rationalization; suppression, repression, inhibition, reaction formation.

822. Sensibility

n. **sensibility**, sensibleness, sensitiveness; moral sensibility; impressibility, affectibility; susceptibleness, susceptibility, susceptivity; mobility; vivacity, vivaciousness; tenderness, softness; sentimentality, sentimentalism.

excitability etc. 825; fastidiousness etc. 868; physical sensibility etc. 375; sensitive plant.

sore point, sore place; quick, raw; where the shoe pinches.

v. **be sensible** etc. *adj.;* have a tender, –warm, –sensitive- heart; be all heart.

take to heart, treasure up in the heart; shrink, wince, blench, quiver.

"die of a rose in aromatic pain" [Pope]; touch to the quick; touch–, flick one- on the raw.

adj. **sensible**, sensitive; impressible, impressionable; susceptive, susceptible; alive to, impassionable, gushing [*colloq.*]; warm-hearted, tender-hearted, soft-hearted; tender, soft, maudlin, sentimental, romantic; enthusiastic, impassioned, highflying, spirited, mettlesome, vivacious, lively, expressive, mobile, tremblingly alive; excitable etc. 825; oversensitive, without skin, thin-skinned; fastidious etc. 868.

adv. **sensibly** etc. *adj.;* to the quick, on the raw, to the inmost core.

823. Insensibility

n. **insensibility**, insensibleness; want of sensibility etc. 823; moral insensibility; inertness, inertia, *vis inertiae* [*L.*]; impassibility, impassibleness;

inappetency, apathy, phlegm, dullness, hebetude, supineness, insusceptibility, unimpressibility, luke-warmness.

coldness; cold -fit, –blood, –heart; coolness; frigidity, *sang-froid* [*F.*], stoicism, imperturbation etc. (*inexcitability*) 826; nonchalance, unconcern, dry eyes; insouciance etc. (*indifference*) 866; recklessness etc. 863; callousness, callosity, obtundity, brutification; heart of stone, blood and iron, stock and stone, marble, deadness.

neutrality; quietism, vegetation.

torpor, torpidity; obstupefaction [*obs.*], lethargy, coma, trance; sleep etc. 683; inanimation [*rare*], suspended animation; stupor, stupefaction; paralysis, palsy; numbness etc. (*physical insensibility*) 376; analgesia.

stoic, Indian, man of iron, pococurante, pococurantist; the Fat Boy in Pickwick.

trifler, dabbler, dilettante, sciolist etc. 493.

v. **be insensible** etc. *adj.;* have a rhinoceros hide; show insensibility etc. *n.;* not mind, not care, not be affected by; have no desire for etc. 866; have–, feel–, take- no interest in; *nil admirari* [*L.*]; not care a straw etc. (*unimportance*) 643 for; disregard etc. (*neglect*) 460; set at naught etc. (*make light of*) 483; turn a deaf ear to etc. (*inattention*) 458; vegetate.

render insensible, render callous; blunt, obtund, numb, benumb, paralyze, chloroform, deaden, hebetate, stun, stupefy; brutify, brutalize.

insure; harden, harden the heart; steel, case-harden, sear.

adj. **insensible**, unconscious; impassive, impassible; blind to, deaf to, dead to; obtundent, insusceptible *or* unsusceptible, unimpressionable, unimpressible; passionless, spiritless, heartless, soulless, unfeeling; unmoral.

apathetic, unemotional, leucophlegmatic [*obs.*], phlegmatic; dull, frigid; cold cold-blooded, cold-hearted; cold as charity; flat, obtuse, inert, supine, sluggish, torpid, torpedinous [*rare*], torporific; sleepy etc. (*inactive*) 683; languid, half-hearted, tame; numb, numbed; comatose; anaesthetic etc. 376; stupefied, chloroformed, palsy-stricken.

indifferent, lukewarm, Laodicean, careless, mindless, regardless; inattentive etc. 458; neglectful etc. 460; disregarding.

unconcerned, nonchalant, pococurante, insouciant, *sans souci* [*F.*]; unambitious etc. 866.

unaffected, unruffled, unimpressed, uninspired, unexcited, unmoved, unstirred, untouched, unshocked, unstruck; unblushing etc. (*shameless*) 885; unanimated; vegetative.

callous, thick-skinned, pachydermatous, impervious; hard, hardened; inured, casehardened; steeled-, proof- against; imperturbable etc. (*inexcitable*) 826; unfelt.

adv. **insensibly** etc. *adj.; aequo animo* [*L.*], without being -moved, -touched, -impressed; in cold blood; with dry eyes, with withers unwrung.

int. never mind! it is of no consequence etc. (*unimportant*) 642; it cannot be helped! it is all the same!

824. Excitation

n. **excitation of feeling**; mental-, excitement; suscitation [*obs.*], suscitability [*obs.*], galvanism, high pressure, stimulation, piquancy, provocation, inspiration, calling forth, infection; animation, agitation, perturbation; subjugation, fascination, intoxication, enravishment, ravishment, entrancement; unction, impressiveness etc. *adj.*

trial of temper, *casus belli* [*L.*], irritation etc. (*anger*) 900; passion etc. (*state of excitability*) 825; thrill etc. (*feeling*) 821; repression of feeling etc. 826.

emotional appeal, melodrama; great moment, crisis; sensationalism, yellow journalism.

v. **excite**, affect, touch, move, impress, strike, interest, animate, inspire, impassion, smite, infect; stir-, fire-, warm- the blood; set astir; awake, wake; awaken, waken; call forth; evoke, provoke; raise up, summon up, call up, wake up, blow up, get up, light up; raise; get up the steam, rouse, arouse, stir, fire, kindle, enkindle, illumine, illuminate, apply the torch, set on fire, inflame.

stimulate; exuscitate *or* exsuscitate [*both obs.*], suscitate [*obs.*]; inspirit; spirit up, stir up, work up; infuse life into, give new life to; bring-, introduce- new blood; quicken; sharpen, whet; work upon etc. (*incite*) 615; hurry on, give a fillip, fillip, put on one's mettle.

fan the -fire, -flame; blow the coals, stir the embers; fan, fan into a flame; foster, heat, warm, foment, raise to a fever heat; keep up, keep the pot boiling; revive, rekindle; rake up, rip up.

intoxicate, overwhelm, overpower, *bouleverser* [*F.*], upset, turn one's head; send [*slang*], fascinate; enrapture etc. (*give pleasure*) 829.

penetrate, pierce; stir-, play on-, come home to- the feelings; touch -a string, -a chord, -the soul, -the heart; go to one's heart, go through one, open the wound, turn the knife in the wound; touch to the quick; possess-, pervade-, imbue-, penetrate-, imbrue [*obs.*]-, absorb-, affect-, disturb- the soul; rivet the attention; sink into the -mind, -heart; absorb; prey on the mind.

agitate, perturb, ruffle, fluster, flutter, flurry, shake, disturb, startle, shock, stagger; give one a -shock, -turn; strike all of a heap [*colloq.*], strike dumb, stun, astound, electrify, galvanize, petrify.

irritate, sting; cut; cut to the -heart, -quick; try one's temper; fool to the top of one's bent, pique; infuriate, madden, make one's blood boil; lash into fury etc. (*wrath*) 900.

be excited etc. *adj.;* flash up, flare up; catch the infection; thrill etc. (*feel*) 821; mantle; work oneself up; seethe, boil, simmer, foam, fume, flame, rage, rave; run mad etc. (*passion*) 825; run amuck *or* amok.

adj. **excited** etc. *v.;* wrought up, on the *qui vive*, astir, sparkling; in a -quiver etc. 821, -fever, -ferment, -blaze, -state of excitement; in hysterics; black in the face, overwrought; hot, red-hot, flushed, feverish; all of a -flutter, -twitter; all in a pucker [*colloq.*]; with quivering lips, with trembling lips, with twitching lips, with tears in one's eyes.

raging, flaming; boiling, -over; ebullient, seething; foaming, -at the mouth; fuming; stung to the quick; on one's high ropes; on one's high horse; carried away by passion, wild, raving, frantic, mad, amuck, distracted, beside oneself, out of one's wits, ready to burst, *bouleversé* [*F.*], demoniacal.

lost, *éperdu* [*F.*], tempest-tossed; haggard; ready to sink.

exciting etc. *v.;* impressive, warm, glowing, fervid, swelling, imposing, spirit-stirring, thrilling; high-wrought; soul-stirring, soul-subduing; heart-stirring, heart-swelling, heart-thrilling; agonizing etc. (*painful*) 830; telling, sensational, melodramatic, hysterical; overpowering, overwhelming; more than flesh and blood can bear; yellow.

piquant etc. (*pungent*) 392; spicy, appetizing, stinging, provocative, *provoquant* [*F.*], tantalizing.

adv. at a critical -moment, -period, -point; under a sudden strain; with heart-interest [*cant*]; with plenty of pep [*slang*], with a punch [*slang*]; till one is blue in the face.

825. Excitability

[excess of sensitiveness]

n. **excitability**, impetuosity, vehemence; boisterousness etc. *adj.;* turbulence; impatience, intolerance, non-endurance; irritability etc. (*irascibility*) 901; itching etc. (*desire*) 865; wincing; disquiet, disquietude; restlessness; fidgets, fidgetiness; agitation etc. (*irregular motion*) 315.

trepidation, perturbation, ruffle, hurry, fuss, flurry, fluster, flutter; pother, stew [*colloq.*], ferment; whirl; buck fever [*colloq.*]; stage fright; hurry-scurry *or* hurry-skurry; thrill etc. (*feeling*) 821; state–, fever- of excitement; transport.

passion, excitement, flush, heat; fever, fever-heat; fire, flame, fume, blood boiling; tumult; effervescence, ebullition; boiling, –over; whiff, gust, storm, tempest; scene, breaking out, burst, fit, paroxysm, explosion, outbreak, outburst; agony.

fury; violence etc. 173; fierceness etc. *adj.;* rage, furor, *furore* [*It.*], desperation, madness, distraction, raving, delirium; frenzy *or* phrensy, hysterics; intoxication; tearing–, raging- passion; towering rage; anger etc. 900.

fixed idea, *l'idée fixe* [*F.*], monomania; fascination, infatuation, fanaticism; Quixotism, Quixotry; *tête montée* [*F.*].

v. **be impatient** etc. *adj.;* not be able to bear etc. 826; bear ill, wince, chafe, champ the bit; be in a stew [*colloq.*] etc. *n.;* be out of all patience, fidget, fuss, not have a wink of sleep; toss, –on one's pillow.

fume, rage, foam; lose one's temper etc. 900; break out, burst out, fly out; go–, fly- -off, –off at a tangent; explode; flare up, flame up, fire up, burst into a flame, take fire, fire, burn; stew [*colloq.*]; boil, –over; rave, rant, tear; go–, run--wild, –mad; go into hysterics; run riot, run amuck *or* amok; *battre la campagne* [*F.*], *faire le diable à quatre* [*F.*]; play the deuce [*slang*]; raise -Cain, –the mischief, –the devil [*all slang*].

adj. **excitable**, easily excited, in an excitable state; startlish, mettlesome, high-mettled, skittish; high-strung; irritable etc. (*irascible*) 901; impatient, intolerant; moody, maggoty-headed.

feverish, febrile, hysterical; delirious, mad.

unquiet, mercurial, electric, galvanic, hasty, hurried, restless, fidgety, fussy; chafing etc. *v.*

vehement, demonstrative, violent, wild, furious, fierce, fiery, hot-headed, madcap.

overzealous, enthusiastic, impassioned, fanatical; rabid etc. (*eager*) 865.

rampant, clamorous, uproarious, turbulent, tempestuous, tumultuary, boisterous.

impulsive, impetuous, passionate, uncontrolled, uncontrollable, ungovernable, irrepressible, stanchless *or* staunchless, inextinguishable, burning, simmering, volcanic, ready to burst forth.

excited, exciting etc. 824.

adv. in confusion, pell-mell; in trepidation etc. *n.*

int. pish! pshaw! horrors!

826. Inexcitability

n. **inexcitability**, imperturbability, inirritability; even temper, tranquil mind, dispassion; toleration, tolerance, patience.

passiveness etc. (*physical inertness*) 172; hebetude, hebetation; impassibility etc. (*insensibility*) 823; stupefaction.

calmness etc. *adj.;* composure, placidity, indisturbance, imperturbation, *sang-froid* [*F.*], coolness, tranquillity, serenity; quiet, quietude; peace of mind, mental calmness.

equanimity, poise, staidness etc. *adj.;* gravity, sobriety, quietism, Quakerism; philosophy, stoicism, command of temper; self-possession, self-control, self-command, self-restraint; presence of mind.

resignation, submission etc. 725; sufferance, supportance, endurance, longsufferance, forbearance, longanimity, fortitude; patience of Job, "patience on a monument" [*Twelfth Night*], "patience sovereign o'er transmuted ill" [Johnson]; moderation; repression–, subjugation- of feeling; restraint etc. 751; tranquilization etc. (*moderation*) 174.

v. **be composed** etc. *adj.*

laisser faire [*F.*], *laisser aller* [*F.*]; take things -easily, –as they come; take it easy, rub on [*colloq.*], live and let live; take -easily, –coolly, –in good part; *aequam servare mentem* [*L.*].

endure; bear, –well, –the brunt; go through, support, brave, disregard; tolerate, suffer, stand, bide; abide, aby *or* abye; bear with, put up with, take up with, abide with; acquiesce; submit etc. (*yield*) 725; submit with a good grace; resign–, reconcile- oneself to; brook, digest, eat, swallow, pocket, stomach; carry on, carry through; make light of, make the best of, make "a virtue of necessity" [Chaucer]; put a good face on, keep one's countenance; check etc. 751- oneself.

compose, appease etc. (*moderate*) 174; propitiate; repress etc. (*restrain*) 751; render insensible etc. 823; overcome–, allay–, repress- one's excitability etc. 825; master one's feelings; make -one-self, –one's mind- easy; set one's mind at -ease, –rest; calm–, cool- down; gentle, tame, thaw, grow cool.

be borne, be endured, be swallowed; go down.

adj. **inexcitable**, imperturbable; unsusceptible etc. (*insensible*) 823; dispassionate, unpassionate, cold-blooded, unirritable, inirritable; enduring etc. *v.;* stoical, Platonic, philosophic, staid, stayed [*obs.*], sober, –minded; grave; sober–, grave- as a judge; sedate, demure, cool-headed, level-headed.

easy-going, peaceful, placid, calm; quiet, –as a mouse; tranquil, serene; cool, –as -a cucumber, –custard [*both colloq.*]; undemonstrative.

composed, collected; temperate etc. (*moderate*) 174; unexcited, unstirred, unruffled, undisturbed, unperturbed, unimpassioned.

meek, tolerant; patient, –as Job; unoffended; unresisting; submissive etc. 725; tame; content, resigned, chastened, subdued, lamblike; gentle, –as a lamb; *suaviter in modo* [*L.*]; mild, –as mother's milk; soft as peppermint; armed with patience, bearing with, clement, long-suffering, forbearant, longanimous.

adv. "like patience on a monument smiling at grief" [*Twelfth Night*]; *aequo animo* [*L.*], in cold blood etc. 823; more in sorrow than in anger.

int. patience! and shuffle the cards.

Section 2. Personal

827. Pleasure

n. **pleasure,** gratification, enjoyment, fruition, delectation, oblectation [*rare*]; relish, zest; gusto etc. (*physical pleasure*) 377; satisfaction etc. (*content*) 831; complacency.

well-being; good etc. 618; snugness, comfort, ease; cushion etc. 215; *sans souci* [*F.*], mind at ease.

joy, gladness, delight, glee, cheer, sunshine; cheerfulness etc. 836.

treat, refreshment; amusement etc. 840; luxury etc. 377.

happiness, felicity, bliss; beatitude, beatification; enchantment, transport, rapture, ravishment, ecstasy; *summum bonum* [*L.*]; paradise, elysium etc. (*heaven*) 981; third–, seventh- heaven; unalloyed happiness etc.; hedonics, hedonism.

mens sana in corpore sano [Juvenal].

honeymoon; palmy–, halcyon- days; golden -age, –time; Eden, Paradise; Dixie, Dixie land *or* Dixie's land; *Saturnia regna* [*L.*], Arcadia, Cockaigne, happy valley, Agapemone.

v. **be pleased** etc. 829; oblectate [*rare*]; feel–, experience- pleasure etc. *n.;* joy; enjoy–, hug- oneself; be in clover [*colloq.*] etc. 377, be in elysium etc. 981; tread on enchanted ground; fall–, go- into raptures.

feel at home, breathe freely, bask in the sunshine.

enjoy, like, relish; be pleased with etc. 829; receive–, derive- pleasure etc. *n.-* from; take pleasure etc. *n.-* in; delight in, rejoice in, indulge in, luxuriate in; gloat over etc. (*physical pleasure*) 377; love etc. 897; fall for [*slang*]; take to, take a fancy to [*both colloq.*]; have a liking for; enter into the spirit of; take in good part; treat oneself to, solace oneself with.

adj. **pleased** etc. 829; not sorry; glad, gladsome; pleased as Punch; pleased as a child with a new toy.

happy, blest, blessed, blissful, beatified; happy as -a clam at high water [*U. S.*], –a king, –the day is long; thrice happy, *ter quaterque beatus* [*L.*]; enjoying etc. *v.;* joyful etc. (*in spirits*) 836; hedonic.

in a blissful state, in paradise etc. 981, in raptures, in ecstasies, in a transport of delight.

comfortable etc. (*physical pleasure*) 377; at ease; in clover [*colloq.*]; content etc. 831; *sans souci* [*F.*].

overjoyed, entranced, enchanted; raptured, enraptured, enravished, ravished, transported; fascinated, captivated.

with a joyful face, with sparkling eyes.

pleasing etc. 829; ecstatic, beatific *or* beaitifical; painless, unalloyed, without alloy, cloudless.

adv. **happily** etc. *adj.;* with pleasure etc. (*willingly*) 602; with glee etc. *n.*

828. Pain

n. **pain,** mental suffering, dolor, suffering, sufferance [*rare*], ache; smart etc. (*physical pain*) 378; passion.

displeasure, dissatisfaction, discomfort, discomposure, disquiet; *malaise* [*F.*], inquietude, uneasiness, vexation of spirit; taking [*colloq.*]; discontent etc. 832.

dejection etc. 837; weariness etc. 841; anhedonia.

annoyance, irritation, worry, infliction, visitation; plague, bore; bother, botheration [*colloq.*], stew [*colloq.*], vexation, mortification, chagrin, *esclandre* [*F.*]; *mauvais quart d'heure* [*F.*].

care, anxiety, solicitude, trouble, trial, ordeal, fiery ordeal, shock, blow, cark [*archaic*], dole [*archaic*], fret, burden, load.

grief, sorrow, distress, affliction, woe, bitterness, heartache; carking cares [*archaic*]; concern; heavy–, aching–, bleeding–, broken- heart; heavy affliction, gnawing grief.

misery, unhappiness, infelicity, tribulation, wretchedness, desolation; despair etc. 859; extremity, prostration, depth of misery; slough of despond etc. (*adversity*) 735; peck–, sea– of troubles; "the thousand natural shocks that flesh is heir to" [*Hamlet*] etc. (*evil*) 616; miseries of human life; the iron entering the soul; "unkindest cut of all' [*Julius Caesar*].

nightmare, ephialtes, incubus.

anguish, pang, agony, torture, torment; crucifixion, martyrdom, rack; purgatory etc. (*hell*) 982; hell upon earth; iron age, reign of terror.

sufferer, victim, prey, martyr, object of compassion, wretch, shorn lamb.

v. **suffer**, ail; feel–, suffer–, experience–, undergo–, bear–, endure– pain etc. *n.*, smart, ache etc. (*physical pain*) 378; bleed; be the victim of.

labor under afflictions; bear–, stagger under–, take up- the cross; quaff the bitter cup, have a bad time of it; fall on evil days etc. (*adversity*) 735; go hard with, come to grief, fall a sacrifice to, drain the cup of misery to the dregs, "sup full of horrors" [*Macbeth*].

fret, chafe, sit on thorns, be on pins and needles, wince, worry oneself, be in a taking [*colloq.*], fret and fume; take on [*colloq.*], take to heart; cark [*archaic*].

grieve; mourn etc. (*lament*) 839; yearn, repine, pine, droop, languish, sink; give way; despair etc. 859; heart-scald [*dial. Eng.*]; break one's heart; weigh upon the heart etc. (*inflict pain*) 830.

adj. **pained**, afflicted; in–, in a state of–, full of- pain etc. *n.;* suffering etc. *v.;* worried, displeased etc. 830; aching, griped, sore etc. (*physical pain*) 378; on the rack, in limbo; between hawk and buzzard.

uneasy, uncomfortable, ill at ease; in a taking, in a way [*both colloq.*]; disturbed; discontented etc. 832; out of humor etc. 901a; weary etc. 841.

unfortunate etc. (*hapless*) 735; to be pitied, doomed, devoted, accursed, undone, lost, stranded; fey [*obs.*]; victimized, a prey to, ill-used.

unhappy, infelicitous, poor, wretched, miserable, woe-begone; cheerless etc. (*dejected*) 837; care-worn; heavy laden, stricken, crushed.

concerned, sorry; sorrowing, sorrowful; cut up [*colloq.*], chagrined, horrified, horror-stricken; in–, plunged in–, a prey to- grief etc. *n.;* in tears etc. (*lamenting*) 839; steeped to the lips in misery; heartstricken, heartbroken, heart-scalded [*dial. Eng.*]; broken-hearted; in despair etc. 859.

829. Pleasurableness
[capability of giving pleasure]

n. **pleasurableness**, pleasantness, agreeableness etc. *adj.;* pleasure giving, jucundity [*rare*], jocundity, delectability; amusement etc. 840; goodness etc. 648; manna in the wilderness, land flowing with milk and honey, "the shadow of a great rock in a weary land" [*Bible*]; flowery beds of ease; fair weather.

treat; regale etc. (*physical pleasure*) 377; sweets etc. (*sugar*) 396; dainty, *bonne bouche* [*F.*], titbit *or* tidbit; sweets, sweetmeats, nuts, *sauce piquante* [*F.*], salt, savor; a sight for sore eyes [*colloq.*].

attraction etc. (*motive*) 615; attractiveness, attractability [*rare*], attractableness; invitingness etc. *adj.;* charm, fascination, captivation, enchantment, witchery, seduction, winning ways, amenity, amiability; winsomeness; loveliness etc. (*beauty*) 845; sunny side, bright side.

v. **delight**, charm, becharm, imparadise; gladden etc. (*make cheerful*) 836; win–, gladden–, rejoice–, warm the cockles of- the heart; do one's heart good; bless, beatify; take, captivate, fascinate; enchant, entrance, enrapture, transport, bewitch, ravish, enravish.

cause–, produce–, create–, give–, afford–, procure–, offer–, present–, yield- pleasure etc. 827.

please, satisfy, gratify, –desire etc. 865; slake, satiate, quench; indulge, humor, flatter, tickle; tickle the palate etc. (*savory*) 394; regale, refresh; enliven; treat; amuse etc. 840; take–, tickle–, hit- one's fancy; meet one's wishes.

attract, allure etc. (*move*) 615; stimulate etc. (*excite*) 824; interest.

make things pleasant, make everyone feel happy, popularize, gild the pill, sweeten; smooth–, pour oil upon- the troubled waters.

adj. **pleasurable**, causing pleasure etc. *v.;* laetificant; pleasure-giving; pleasing, pleasant, amiable, agreeable, grateful, gratifying; lief *or* leef [*obs.*], acceptable; dear, beloved; welcome, –as the roses in May; welcomed; favorite; to one's taste, –mind, –liking; satisfactory etc. (*good*) 648.

refreshing; comfortable; cordial; genial; glad, gladsome; sweet, delectable, nice, dainty; delicate, delicious; dulcet; luscious etc. 396; palatable etc. 394.

luxurious, voluptuous; sensual etc. 377.

attractive etc. 615; inviting, prepossessing, engaging; winning, winsome; taking, fascinating, captivating, killing [*colloq.*]; seducing, seductive; heart-robbing; alluring, enticing; appetizing etc. (*exciting*) 824; cheering etc. 836; bewitching; enchanting, entrancing, enravishing.

delightful, charming, felicitous, exquisite; lovely etc. (*beautiful* 845; ravishing, rapturous; heartfelt, thrilling, ecstatic, beatific *or* beatifical, seraphic; empyrean; paradisaic *or* paradisaical; elysian etc. (*heavenly*) 981.

palmy, halcyon, Saturnian.

adv. **to one's delight**, to one's heart's content, in utter satisfaction; at one's ease; in clover; in heaven, in paradise, in elysium; from a full heart.

830. Painfulness
[capability of giving pain]

n. **painfulness** etc. *adj.;* trouble, care etc. (*pain*) 828; trial, affliction, infliction; cross, blow, stroke, burden, load, curse; bitter -pill, -draft *or* draught, -cup; cup-, waters- of bitterness.

annoyance, grievance, nuisance, vexation, mortification, sickener [*rare*], worry, bore, bother, pother, hot water, "sea of troubles" [*Hamlet*], hornet's nest, plague, pest.

source of -irritation, -annoyance; wound, sore subject, skeleton in the closet; thorn in -the flesh, -one's side; where the shoe pinches, gall and wormwood; fly in the ointment; worm at the heart of the rose; crumpled rose-leaf; pea in the shoe.

cancer, ulcer, sting, thorn; canker etc. (*bane*) 663; scorpion etc. (*evildoer*) 913; dagger etc. (*arms*) 727; scourge etc. (*instrument of punishment*) 975; carking care [*archaic*], canker worm of care.

mishap, misfortune etc. (*adversity*) 735; désagrément [*F.*], esclandre [*F.*], rub.

sorry sight, heavy news, provocation; affront etc. 929; "head and front of one's offending" [*Othello*].

infestation, molestation; malignity etc. (*malevolence*) 907.

v. **pain**, hurt, wound; cause-, occasion-, give-, bring-, induce-, produce-, create-, inflict- pain etc. 828.

pinch, prick, gripe etc. (*physical pain*) 378; pierce, lancinate, cut.

hurt-, wound-, grate upon-, jar upon- the feelings; wring-, pierce-, lacerate-, break-, rend- the heart; make the heart bleed; tear-, rend- the heartstrings; draw tears from the eyes; add a nail to one's coffin.

sadden; make unhappy etc. 828; plunge into sorrow, grieve, fash [*Scot.*], afflict, distress; cut up [*colloq.*], cut to the heart.

annoy, incommode, displease, discompose, trouble, disquiet; faze [*U. S.*], feeze *or* feaze [*colloq., U. S. & dial. Eng.*], disturb, cross, thwart, perplex, molest; tease, tire, irk, vex, mortify, wherret [*obs.*], worry, plague, bother, pester, bore, pother, harass, harry, badger, heckle, bait, beset, infest, persecute, importune.

torment, wring, harrow, torture; bullyrag; put to the -rack, -question; break on the wheel, rack, scarify; cruciate [*obs.*], crucify; convulse, agonize; barb the dart; plant a - dagger in the breast, -thorn in one's side.

irritate, provoke, sting, nettle, try the patience, pique, fret, roil rile [*colloq. & dial.*], tweak the nose, chafe, gall; sting-, wound-, cut- to the quick; aggrieve, affront, enchafe [*obs.*], enrage, ruffle, sour the temper; give offense etc. (*resentment*) 900.

maltreat, bite, snap at, assail; smite etc. (*punish*) 972; bite the hand that feeds one.

repel, revolt; sicken, disgust, nauseate; disenchant, offend, shock, stink in the nostrils; go against-, turn- the stomach; make one sick, set the teeth on edge, go against the grain, grate on the ear; stick in one's -throat, -gizzard [*colloq.*]; rankle, gnaw, corrode, horrify, appal, freeze the blood; make the flesh creep, make the hair stand on end; make the blood -curdle, -run cold; make one shudder.

haunt, haunt the memory; weigh-, prey- on the -heart, -mind, -spirits; bring one's gray hairs with sorrow to the grave.

adj. **painful**, causing pain, hurting etc. *v.;* hurtful etc. (*bad*) 649; dolorific *or* dolorifical, dolorous.

unpleasant, unpleasing, displeasing, disagreeable, unpalatable, bitter, distasteful, unpleasing, uninviting, unwelcome, undesirable, undesired; obnoxious; unacceptable, unpopular, thankless.

untoward, unsatisfactory, unlucky, inauspicious, ill-starred, uncomfortable.

distressing; afflicting, afflictive; joyless, cheerless, comfortless, dismal, disheartening; depressing, depressive; dreary, melancholy, grievous, piteous, woeful, rueful, mournful; deplorable, pitiable, lamentable, sad, affecting, touching, pathetic.

irritating, provoking, stinging, annoying, aggravating [*colloq.*], exasperating, mortifying, galling; unaccommodating, invidious, vexatious; troublesome, tiresome, irksome, wearisome; plaguing, plaguesome, plaguy [*colloq.*]; awkward.

importunate; teasing, pestering, bothering, harassing, worrying, tormenting, carking [*archaic*].

insufferable, intolerable, insupportable, unbearable, unendurable; past bearing; not to be -borne, −endured; more than flesh and blood can bear; enough to -drive one mad, −provoke a saint, −make a parson swear [*colloq.*], −try the patience of Job.

shocking, terrific, grim, appalling, crushing; dreadful, fearful, frightful; thrilling, tremendous, dire; heartbreaking, heart-rending, heart-wounding, heart-corroding, heart-sickening; harrowing, rending.

odious, hateful, execrable, repulsive, repellent, abhorrent; horrid, horrible, horrific, horrifying; offensive; nauseous, nauseating; disgusting, sickening, revolting; nasty; loathsome, loathful; fulsome; vile etc. (*bad*) 649; hideous etc. 846.

acute, sharp, sore, severe, grave, hard, harsh, cruel, biting, caustic; cutting, corroding, consuming, racking, excruciating, searching, searing, grinding, grating, agonizing; envenomed; catheretic, pyrotic.

cumbrous, cumbersome, burdensome, onerous, oppressive.

desolating, withering, tragical, disastrous, calamitous, ruinous.

adv. **painfully** etc. *adj.;* with pain etc. 828; deuced *or* deucedly [*slang*]; under torture, in agony, out of the depths.

int. woe's me! alas! that I had ever been born! *hinc illae lacrimae!* [Terence].

831. Content

n. **content**, contentment, contentedness; complacency, satisfaction, entire satisfaction, ease, heart's ease, peace of mind; serenity etc. 826; cheerfulness etc. 836; ray of comfort; comfort etc. (*well-being*) 827.

patience, moderation, endurance; conciliation, reconciliation; resignation etc. (*patience*) 826; quietism.

waiter on Providence; quietist.

v. **be content** etc. *adj.;* rest satisfied, rest and be thankful; take the good the gods provide, let well enough alone, feel oneself at home, hug oneself, lay the flattering unction to one's soul.

take up with, take in good part; assent etc. 488; be reconciled to, make one's peace with; get over it; take heart, take comfort; put up with etc. (*bear*) 826.

render content etc. *adj.;* set at ease, comfort; set one's -heart, −mind- at -ease, −rest; speak peace; conciliate, reconcile, win over, propitiate, disarm, beguile; content, satisfy; gratify etc. 829.

be tolerated etc. 826; go down, go down with [*colloq.*], do.

adj. **content**, contented; satisfied etc. *v.;* at ease, at one's ease, at home; with the mind at ease, *sans souci* [*F.*], *sine curâ* [*L.*], easy-going, not particular; conciliatory; unrepining, of good comfort; resigned etc. (*patient*) 826; cheerful etc. 836.

serene etc. 826; unafflicted, unvexed, unmolested, unplagued; at rest; snug, comfortable; in one's element; not easily perturbed; imperturbable.

satisfactory, adequate, commensurate, sufficient, ample, equal to; satisfying.

adv. to one's heart's content; à la bonne heure [*F.*]; all for the best.

int. amen etc. (*assent*) 488; very well! all the better! so much the better! well and good! it will do! that will do! it cannot be helped! done! content! i' faith! [*archaic*]; better and better! good! good for you! put it thar, pard! [*colloq.*].

832. Discontent

n. **discontent**, discontentment; dissatisfaction; "the winter of our discontent" [*Henry VI*]; dissent etc. 489; querulousness etc. (*lamentation*) 839; hypercriticism.

disappointment, mortification; cold comfort; regret etc. 833; repining, taking on [*colloq.*] etc. *v.;* inquietude, vexation of spirit, soreness; heartburning, heart-grief.

malcontent, grumbler, growler, grouch [*slang*], croaker, *laudator temporis acti* [*L.*]; censurer, complainer, faultfinder, murmurer.

The Opposition; Bitter-Enders [*U. S. politics*], Die-Hards; cave of Adullam; indignation meeting.

v. **be discontented** etc. *adj.;* quarrel with one's bread and butter; repine; regret etc. 833; wish one to Jericho, wish one at the bottom of the Red Sea; take on [*colloq.*], take to heart; shrug the shoulders; make a wry face, pull a long face; knit one's brows; look blue, look black, look black as thunder, look blank, look glum.

grumble, take ill, take in bad part; fret, chafe, make a piece of work [*colloq.*], croak; lament etc. 839.

cause discontent etc. *n.;* dissatisfy, disappoint, mortify, put out [*colloq.*], disconcert; cut up; dishearten.

adj. **discontented**; dissatisfied etc. *v.;* unsatisfied, ungratified; dissident; dissentient etc. 489; malcontent, exigent, exacting, hypercritical.

repining etc. *v.;* regretful etc. 833; down in the mouth etc. (*dejected*) 837.

glum, sulky; in high dudgeon, in a fume, in the sulks, in the dumps, in bad humor; sour, sour as a crab; sore as a crab [*colloq.*]; soured, sore; out of humor, out of temper.

disappointing etc. *v.;* unsatisfactory.

adv. **from bad to worse**, out of the frying pan into the fire, in the depths of despair.

int. so much the worse! that's bad! couldn't be worse! worse and worse!

833. Regret

n. **regret**, repining; homesickness, nostalgia; *mal du pays* [*F.*], *maladie du pays* [*F.*]; lamentation etc. 839; penitence etc. 950.

bitterness, heartburning.

laudator temporis acti [*L.*] etc. (*discontent*) 832.

v. **regret**, deplore; bewail etc. (*lament*) 839; repine, cast a longing lingering look behind; rue, rue the day; repent etc. 950; *infandum renovare dolorem* [*L.*].

prey−, weigh−, have a weight- on the mind; leave an aching void.

adj. **regretting** etc. *v.;* regretful; homesick.

regretted etc. *v.;* much to be regretted, regrettable; lamentable etc. (*bad*) 649.

int. what a pity! hang it *or* hang it all! [*colloq.*].

834. Relief

n. **relief**; deliverance; refreshment etc. 689; easement, softening, alleviation, mitigation, palliation, soothing; lullaby, cradle-song, *berceuse* [*F.*].

solace, consolation, comfort, encouragement; crumb of comfort, balm in Gilead.

lenitive, palliative, restorative etc. (*remedy*) 662; stupe, poultice, fomentation, assuasive; cushion etc. 215.

v. **relieve**, ease, alleviate, mitigate, palliate, soothe; salve; soften, −down; forment, stupe, poultice; assuage, allay, abirritate.

remedy; cure etc. (*restore*) 660; refresh; pour balm into, pour oil on.

smooth the ruffled brow of care, temper the wind to the shorn lamb, lay the flattering unction to one's soul.

cheer, comfort, console; enliven; encourage, bear up, pat on the back, give comfort, set at ease; gladden−, cheer- the heart; inspirit, invigorate.

disburden etc. (*free*) 705; take off a load of care.

be relieved; breathe more freely, draw a long breath; take comfort; dry the eyes, dry the tears, wipe the eyes, wipe away the tears; pull oneself together.

adj. **relieving** etc. *v.;* consolatory, soothing; assuaging, assuasive; balmy, balsamic; lenitive, palliative; anodyne etc. (*remedial*) 662; curative etc. 660.

835. Aggravation

n. **aggravation**, heightening; exacerbation; exasperation; overestimation etc. 482; exaggeration etc. 549.

v. **aggravate**, render worse, heighten, embitter, sour; exacerbate, acerbate, exasperate, envenom; enrage, provoke, tease.

add fuel to the -fire, −flame; fan the flame etc. (*excite*) 824; go from bad to worse etc. (*deteriorate*) 659.

adj. **aggravated** etc. *v.;* worse, unrelieved; aggravable [*obs.*], aggravative, aggravating etc. *v.*

adv. out of the frying pan into the fire, from bad to worse, worse and worse.

int. so much the worse! *tant pis!* [*F.*].

836. Cheerfulness

n. **cheerfulness** etc. *adj.;* geniality, gayety, *L'Allegro* [*It.*], cheer, good humor, spirits; high spirits, animal spirits, flow of spirits; glee, high glee, light heart; sunshine of the -mind, −breast; *gaieté de coeur* [*F.*], *bon naturel* [*F.*].

liveliness etc. *adj.;* life, alacrity, vivacity, animation, *allégresse* [*F.*]; jocundity, joviality, jollity; levity; jocularity etc. (*wit*) 842.

mirth, merriment, hilarity, exhilaration; laughter etc. 838; merrymaking etc. (*amusement*) 840; heyday, rejoicing etc. 838; marriage bell.

nepenthe *or* nepenthes, lotus; Euphrosyne.

optimism etc. (*hopefulness*) 858; self-complacency; hedonics, hedonism.

v. **be cheerful** etc. *adj.;* have the mind at ease, smile, put a good face upon, keep up one's spirits; view the bright side of the picture, view things *en couleur de rose* [*F.*]; look through rose-colored spectacles; *ridentem dicere verum* [*L.*], cheer up, brighten up, light up, bear up; take heart, cast away care, drive dull care away, perk up; keep a stiff upper lip [*slang*].

rejoice etc.; 838; carol, chirp, chirrup, lilt; frisk, rollic, give a loose to mirth [*obs.*].

cheer, enliven, elate, exhilarate, gladden, inspirit, animate, raise the spirits, inspire; put in good humor; cheer−, rejoice- the heart; delight etc. (*give pleasure*) 829.

adj. **cheerful**; happy etc. 827; cheery, of good cheer, smiling; blithe; in spirits, in good spirits; breezy, bully [*slang*], chipper [*colloq.*]; in high -spirits, −feather; happy as -the day is long, −a king; gay, gay as a lark; *allegro* [*It.*]; debonair *or* debonaire, light, lightsome, lighthearted; buoyant, bright, free and easy, airy; jaunty *or* janty, rollicky [*colloq.*], canty [*Scot. & dial. Eng.*], "crouse an' canty" [*Burns*]; hedonic; riant; sprightly, sprightful; spry; spirited, spiritful [*rare*], lively, animated, vivacious; brisk, −as a bee; sparkling; sportive; full of -play, −spirit; all alive.

sunny, palmy; hopeful etc. 858.

merry, −as a -cricket, −grig, −marriage bell; joyful, joyous, jocund, jovial; jolly, −as a thrush, −as a sand-boy; blithesome; gleeful, gleesome; hilarious, rattling [*colloq.*].

winsome, bonny, hearty, buxom.

playful, playsome; *folâtre* [*F.*], playful as a kitten, tricksy, frisky, frolicsome; gamesome; jocose, jocular, waggish; mirth-loving, laughter-loving, abderian; mirthful, rollicking.

elate, elated; exulting, jubilant, flushed; rejoicing etc. 838; cock-a-hoop.

cheering, inspiriting, exhilarating; cardiac *or* cardiacal; pleasing etc. 829; palmy, flourishing, halcyon.

adv. **cheerfully** etc. *adj.;* cheerily, with good cheer; with a cheerful etc. heart; with relish, with zest; on the crest of the wave.

int. **never say die**! come! cheer up! hurrah! etc. 838; "hence loathed melancholy!" begone dull care! away with melancholy!

837. Dejection

n. **dejection**; dejectedness etc. *adj.;* depression, prosternation [*obs.*], mopishness, damp; lowness−, depression- of spirits; weight−, oppression−, damp- on the spirits; low−, bad−, drooping−, depressed- spirits; heart sinking; heaviness−, failure- of heart.

heaviness etc. *adj.;* infestivity, gloom; weariness etc. 841; *taedium vitae* [*L.*], disgust of life; *mal du pays* [*F.*] etc. (*regret*) 833; anhedonia.

melancholy; sadness etc. *adj.; Il Penseroso* [*Old It.*], melancholia, dismals, blue devils [*colloq.*], blues [*colloq.*], mopes, lachrymals *or* lacrimals, mumps, dumps [*chiefly humorous*], doldrums, vapors [*archaic*], megrims, spleen [*obsoles.*], horros, hypochondriasis, hypochondria, jawfall [*rare*], pessimism; *la maladie sans maladie* [*F.*], despondency, slough of Despond; disconsolateness etc. *adj.;* hope deferred, blank despondency; voiceless woe.

prostration, prostration of soul; broken heart; despair etc. 859; cave of despair, cave of Trophonius.

gravity; demureness etc. *adj.;* solemnity; long face, grave face.

hypochondriac, seek-sorrow, self-tormentor, *heautontimorumenos* [*Gr.*], *malade imaginaire* [*F.*], *médecin tant pis* [*F.*]; croaker, pessimist; mope, mopus [*dial. Eng. & slang*], damper, wet blanket crape-hanger [*slang*], Job's comforter.

[cause of dejection] affliction etc. 830; sorry sight; *memento mori* [*L.*]; deathwatch, death's-head, skeleton at the feast.

v. **be dejected** etc. *adj.;* grieve; mourn etc. (*lament*) 839; take on [*colloq.*], give way, lose heart, despond, droop, sink.

lower, look downcast, frown, pout; hang down the head; pull−, make- a long face; laugh on the wrong side of the mouth; grin a ghastly smile; look blue, look like a drowned man; lay to heart, take to heart.

mope, brood over; fret; sulk; pine, pine away; yearn; repine etc. (*regret*) 833; despair etc. 859.

refrain from laughter, keep one's countenance; be *or* look grave etc. *adj.;* repress a smile, keep a straight face.

depress, discourage, dishearten, dispirit; damp, dull, deject, lower, sink, dash, knock down, unman, prostrate, break one's heart; frown upon; cast a gloom on, cast a shade on; sadden; damp−, dash−, wither- one's hopes; weight−, lie heavy−, prey- on the -mind, −spirits; damp−, dampen−, depress- the spirits.

adj. **cheerless**, joyless, spiritless, uncheerful, uncheery, unlively; unhappy etc. 828; melancholy, dismal, somber, dark, gloomy, *triste* [*F.*], clouded, murky, lowering, frowning, lugubrious, funereal, mournful, lamentable, dreadful.

dreary, flat; dull, −as -a beetle, −ditchwater; depressing etc. *v.;* damp [*archaic*].

downcast, downhearted, mopy [*colloq.*], "melancholy as a gib cat" [*Henry IV Part I*]; a prey to melancholy; "besieged with sable-coloured melancholy" [*Love's Labour Lost*]; down in the mouth [*colloq.*], down on one's luck [*colloq.*]; heavy-hearted; in the -dumps, −suds [*colloq.*], −sulks, −doldrums; in doleful dumps, in bad humor; sullen; mumpish, dumpish, mopish, moping; moody, glum; sulky etc. (*discontented*) 832; out of -sorts, −humor, −heart, −spirits; ill at ease, low-spirited, in low spirits, a cup too low; weary etc. 841; discouraged, disheartened, desponding, chapfallen *or* chopfallen, jawfallen [*rare*]; crestfallen.

sad, pensive, *pensieroso* [*It.*], tristful; dolesome, doleful; woe-begone, lachry-mose, in tears, melancholic, hypochondriacal, bilious, jaundiced, atrabilious, saturnine, splenetic; lackadaisical.

serious, sedate, staid, earnest; grave, –as -a judge, –an undertaker, –a mustard pot [*colloq.*]; sober, solemn, demure; grim, grim-faced, grim-visaged; rueful, wan, long-faced.

disconsolate, inconsolable, forlorn, comfortless, desolate, *désolé* [*F.*], sick at heart; soul-sick, heartsick; *au désespoir* [*F.*]; in despair etc. 859; lost.

overcome; broken-down, borne-down, bowed-down; heartstricken etc. (*mental suffering*) 828; cut up [*colloq.*], dashed, sunk; unnerved, unmanned; downfallen, downtrodden; broken-hearted; careworn.

adv. **sadly** etc. *adj.*; with a long face, with tears in one's eyes.

838. Rejoicing

[expression of pleasure]

n. **rejoicing**, exultation, triumph, jubilation, heyday, flush, reveling *or* revelling; merrymaking etc. (*amusement*) 840; jubilee etc. (*celebration*) 883; paean, *Te Deum* [*L.*] etc. (*thanksgiving*) 990; congratulation etc. 896.

smile, simper, smirk, grin; broad grin, sardonic grin.

laughter, giggle, titter, snicker, snigger, crow, cheer, chuckle, shout; Homeric laughter; horse–, hearty- laugh; guffaw; burst–, fit–, shout–, roar–, peal- of laughter; cachinnation; Kentish fire.

risibility; derision etc. 856; "sport that wrinkled Care derides" [Milton].

Momus; Democritus the Abderite; rollicker.

cheer, huzza, hurrah *or* hurra, cheering; shout, yell, college yell; tiger [*colloq.*].

v. **rejoice**; thank–, bless- one's stars; congratulate oneself, hug oneself; rub–, clap- one's hands; smack the lips, fling up one's cap; dance, skip; sing, carol, chirrup, chirp; hurrah *or* hurra; cry for joy, leap with joy, skip for joy; exult etc. (*boast*) 884; triumph; hold jubilee etc. (*celebrate*) 883; sing a *Te Deum,* sing a paean of triumph; make merry etc. (*sport*) 840.

smile, simper, smirk; grin, –like a Cheshire cat [*colloq.*]; mock, laugh in one's sleeve.

laugh, –outright; giggle, titter, snigger, snicker, crow, smicker [*obs.*], chuckle, cackle; burst out; burst into a roar of laughter, burst into a fit of laughter; shout, split [*colloq.*], roar.

shake–, split–, hold both- one's sides; roar–, shake–, nearly die–, die- with laughter.

raise laughter etc. (*amuse*) 840.

adj. **rejoicing** etc. *v.*; jubilant, exultant, triumphant; flushed, elated; laughing etc. *v.*; risible; ready to -burst, –split, –die with laughter [*all colloq.*]; convulsed with laughter; shaking like a jelly with -laughter, –suppressed merriment [*both colloq.*].

laughable etc. (*ludicrous*) 853.

adv. **laughingly**; on a broad grin, in fits of laughter, amid peals of laughter; in triumph; in mockery; with a -roar, –peal, –outburst- of laughter.

int. **hurrah**! huzza! three cheers! right on! hip, hip, hurrah! aha! hail! tolderolloll! Heaven be praised! *tant mieux!* [*F.*], so much the better! good enough! tra-la-la!

839. Lamentation

[expression of pain]

n. **lamentation**, lament, wail, complaint, plaint, murmur, mutter, grumble, groan, moan, whine, whimper, sob, sigh, suspiration, deep sigh; frown, scowl.

cry etc. (*vociferation*) 411; scream, howl; outcry, wail, wail of woe.

weeping etc. *v.*; tear; flood of tears, fit of crying, lachrymation [*rare*], crying; melting mood; "weeping and gnashing of teeth" [*Bible*].

plaintiveness etc. *adj.*; languishment; condolence etc. 915.

mourning, weeds [*colloq.*], widow's weeds, willow, cypress, crape, deep mourning; sackcloth and ashes; lachrymatory, tear bottle, lachrymals *or* lacrimals; knell etc. 363; dump [*obs.*], death song, dirge, coronach [*Scot. & Ir.*], nenia, requiem, elegy, epicedium; threne [*rare*], menody, threnody; jeremiad *or* jeremiade, ululation, keen [*Ir.*], ullalulla [*Ir.*].

mourner, keener [*Ir.*]; grumbler etc. (*discontent*) 832; Niobe; Heraclitus, Jeremiah, Mrs. Gummidge.

v. **lament**, mourn, deplore, grieve, keen [*Ir.*], weep over; bewail, bemoan; condole with etc. 915; fret etc. (*suffer*) 828; wear–, go into–, put on- mourning; wear -the willow, –sackcloth and ashes; *infandum renovare dolorem* [Virgil] etc. (*regret*) 833; give sorrow words.

sigh; give–, heave–, fetch- a sigh; "waft a sigh from Indus to the pole" [Pope]; sigh "like furnace" [*As You Like It*]; wail.

cry, weep, sob, greet [*archaic or Scot.*], blubber, snivel, bibber, whimper, pule; pipe, pipe one's eye [*both slang, orig. naut.*]; drop–, shed- -tears,

–a tear; melt–, burst- into tears; *fondre en larmes* [*F.*], cry oneself blind, cry one's eyes out; yammer [*dial.*].

scream etc. (*cry out*) 411; mew etc. (*animal sounds*) 412; groan, moan, whine, yelp, howl, yell, ululate; roar; roar–, bellow- like a bull; cry out lustily, rend the air.

show signs of grief; frown, scowl, make a wry face, gnash one's teeth, wring one's hands, tear one's hair, beat one's breast, roll on the ground, burst with grief.

complain, murmur, mutter, grumble, growl, clamor, make a fuss about, croak, grunt, maunder [*obs.*]; deprecate etc. (*disapprove*) 932.

cry out before one is hurt, complain without cause.

adj. **lamenting** etc. *v.;* in mourning, in sackcloth and ashes; ululant, ululative [*obs.*], clamorous; crying–, lamenting- to high heaven, sorrowing, sorrowful etc. (*unhappy*) 828; mournful, tearful; lachrymose, lachrymal *or* lacrimal, lachrymatory, plaintive, plaintful; querulous, querimonious; in the melting mood.

in tears, with tears in one's eyes; with moistened eyes, with watery eyes; bathed–, dissolved- in tears; "like Niobe, all tears" [*Hamlet*].

elegiac, epicedial, threnetic *or* threnetical.

adv. *de profundis* [*L.*], *les larmes aux yeux* [*F.*].

int. **alas**! alack! heigh-ho! O dear! ah me! woe is me! lackadaisy! well a day! lack a day! alack a day! wellaway! alas the day! *O tempora, O mores!* [*L.*]; what a pity! *miserabile dictu!* [*L.*]; too true!

840. Amusement

n. **amusement**, entertainment, diversion, divertisement, *divertissement* [*F.*]; reaction, relaxation, solace; pastime, *passe-temps* [*F.*], sport; labor of love; pleasure etc. 827.

fun, frolic, merriment, jollity, joviality, jovialness; heyday; laughter etc. 838; jocosity, jocoseness; drollery, buffoonery, tomfoolery; mummery, mumming, masquing, pageant; pleasantry; wit etc. 842; quip, quirk.

play; game, game of romps; gambol, romp, prank, antic, frisk, rig [*obs. or dial.*], lark [*colloq.*], spree, skylarking, vagary, monkey trick, *fredaine* [*F.*], escapade, *échappée* [*F.*], bout, *espièglerie* [*F.*]; practical joke etc. (*ridicule*) 856.

[dance steps] *gambade* [*F.*], gambado, *pas* [*F.*]; pigeonwing, heel-and-toe, buck-and-wing, shuffle, double shuffle; *chassé* [*F.*], *coupé* [*F.*], grapevine, etc.

[dances] dance, hop [*colloq.*], stag dance, shindig [*slang*]; ball; *bal, bal masqué, bal costumé*

[*all F.*], masquerade, masquerade ball, cornwallis [*U. S.*]; mistletoe-bough dance; Dance of Death, *danse macabre* [*F.*]; interpretative dance, step dance, sand dance, *pas seul* [*F.*], skirt dance, folk dance; Morisco *or* morice [*obs.*], morris dance, saraband, fandango, bolero, tarantella, boutade, gavot *or* gavotte, minuet, *allemande* [*F.*], rigadoon, fling, Highland fling, Highland schottische, strathspey, reel, jig, hornpipe, sword dance, breakdown, cakewalk; kantikoy, snake dance; country dance, Scotch reel, Virginia reel, Sir Roger de Coverley, Portland fancy; ballet etc. (*drama*) 599; ragtime [*colloq.*] etc. (*music*) 415; jazz [*slang*]; nautch [*India*].

square dance, quadrille, Lancers, cotillion *or* cotillon [*F.*], German.

round dance, waltz, *valse* [*F.*], polka, mazurka, galop, gallopade *or* galopade, schottische, one-step, two-step, fox-trot, turkey-trot; shimmy.

danse du ventre [*F.*], belly dance, break dance, *chonchina* [*Jap.*], cancan.

dancer, *danseur (fem. danseuse)* [*F.*], *première danseuse* [*F.*], ballet dancer; geisha [*Jap.*]; nautch girl, bayadere [*both India*]; clog–, step–, skirt–, figure-dancer; figurant (*fem.* figurante), Morisco [*obs.*], morris dancer; terpsichorean [*colloq.*]; Terpsichore.

festivity, merrymaking; party etc. (*social gathering*) 892; revels, revelry, reveling *or* revelling, carnival, Saturnalia, jollification [*colloq.*], junket, picnic.

fête champêtre [*F.*], lawn party, garden party, regatta, field day, *fête* [*F.*], festival, gala, gala day; feast, banquet etc. (*food*) 298; regale, symposium, high jinks [*colloq.*], carouse, carousal, brawl; wassail; wake; bust [*slang*], tear [*slang*]; *Turnerfest* [*Ger.*]; gymkhana [*orig. Anglo-Ind.*]; treat; *ridotto* [*It.*], drum [*obs. or hist.*], kettledrum [*colloq.*], rout [*archaic*]; tea party, tea, tea fight [*slang*]; *Kaffee-Klatsch* [*Ger.*]; concert etc. (*music*) 415; show [*colloq.*]; play etc. (*drama*) 599; randy [*dial.*]; clambake, fish fry, beefsteak fry, squantum, donation party [*all U. S.*]; bat, bum [*both slang*], jamboree [*slang*].

round of pleasure, dissipation, a short life and a merry one, racketing, holiday making.

rejoicing etc. 838; jubilee etc. (*celebration*) 883.

fireworks, *feu-de-joie* [*F.*], firecrackers, bonfire.

holiday; red-letter day, play day; high days and holidays; high holiday, Bank holiday [*Eng.*]; May day, Derby day [*Eng.*]; Easter Monday, Whitmonday, Twelfth Night, Halloween;

Christmas etc. 138; Dewali [*Hindu*], Holi *or* Hoolee [*Hindu*]; Bairam, Muharram [*both Moham.*]; wayzgoose [*Printers*], beanfeast [*Eng.*]; Arbor–, Declaration–, Independence–, Labor–, Memorial *or* Decoration–, Thanksgiving- Day; Washington's–, Lincoln's–, King's- birthday; Empire Day [*Brit.*]; Mardi gras, *mi-carême* [*F.*], *feria* [*S. W. U. S.*], *fiesta* [*Sp.*].

place of amusement, theater *or* theatre; concert -hall, –room; ballroom, dance hall, assembly room; moving-picture–, cinema- theater; movies [*colloq.*]; music hall; vaudeville -theater, –show; circus, hippodrome.

park, pleasance *or* plaisance [*archaic*]; arbor; garden etc. (*horticulture*) 371; pleasure–, play–, cricket–, croquet- archery–, polo–, hunting-ground; tennis–, racket–, squash–, badminton-court; bowling- green, –alley; croquet lawn, rink, glaciarium, ice rink, skating rink; golf links, race course, athletic field, stadium; gymnasium, swimming -pool, –bath; billiard room, pool room, casino, shooting gallery; flying horses, roundabout, merry-go-round; swing; *montagne Russe* [*F.*]; aërial railway, scenic railway, roller coaster, chutes, flying boats, etc.

Vauxhall, Ranelagh, Hurlingham; Lord's, Epsom, Newmarket, Doncaster, Sandown Park, Henley, Cowes, Mortlake [*all in Eng.*]; Coney Island; Brooklands, Sheepshead Bay, Belmont Park, Saratoga; New London, Forest Hills, Longwood [*all in U. S.*]; Monte Carlo; Longchamps [*France*]; Flemington [*Melbourne, Australia*].

[sports and games] athletic sports, track events, gymnastics; archery, rifle shooting; tournament, pugilis m etc. (*contention*) 720; sporting etc. 622; horse racing, the turf; water polo; aquatics etc. 267.

skating, ice skating, roller skating, sliding; cricket, tennis, lawn tennis, pallone, rackets, squash, fives, trap bat and ball, badminton, battledore and shuttlecock, pall-mall, croquet, golf, curling, hockey, shinny *or* shinney; polo, football, Rugby, rugger [*colloq.*]; association, soccer [*colloq.*]; tent pegging, tilting at the ring, quintain, greasy pole; knur (*or* knurr) and spell [*Eng.*]; quoits, discus; hammer–, horseshoe-throwing; putting the -weight, –shot; hurdling; leapfrog; sack–, potato–, obstacle–, three-legged- race; hop skip and jump; French and English, tug of war; rounders, baseball, basket ball, pushball, captain ball; lacrosse; tobogganing.

blind-man's buff, hunt the slipper, hide and seek, kiss in the ring; snapdragon; cross questions and crooked answers, twenty questions, what's my thought? charades, crambo, dumb crambo, crisscross, proverbs, *bouts rimés* [*F.*]; hopscotch, jackstones, mumble-the-peg *or* mumblety-peg; ping-pong, tiddledywinks, tipcat.

billiards, pool, pyramids, bagatelle; bowls, skittles, ninepins, American bowls; tenpins, bowling, tivoli.

chess, draughts, checkers *or* chequers, backgammon, dominoes, halma, dice, craps, crap shooting, crap game, "negro golf," "indoor golf" [*both humorous*]; merelles, nine men's morris, gobang, "the royal game of goose" [Goldsmith]; fox and geese; lotto *or* loto etc.

cards; whist, rubber; round game; loo, cribbage, *bésique* [*F.*], euchre, cutthroat euchre, railroad euchre; drole, *écarté*, picquet, all fours, quadrille, omber *or* ombre, reverse, Pope Joan, commit; boston, *vingt et un* [*F.*], quinze, thirty-one, put, speculation, connections, brag, cassino, lottery, commerce, snip-snap-snorem, lift smoke, blind hookey, Polish bank, Earl of Coventry, napoleon *or* nap [*colloq.*]; banker, penny-ante, poker, jack pot; blind–, draw–, straight–, stud–, poker; bluff; bridge, –whist; auction; monte, reversis, squeezers, old maid, fan-tan, fright, beggar-my-neighbor, goat, hearts, patience, solitaire, pairs.

court cards; ace, king, queen, knave, jack, joker; bower; right–, left- bower; dummy; hand; trump; face cards, diamonds, hearts, clubs, spades; pack, deck; flush, full-house, straight, three of a kind, pair, *misère* [*F.*] etc.

toy, plaything, bauble; doll etc. (*puppet*) 554; teetotum; knickknack etc. (*trifle*) 643; magic lantern etc. (*show*) 448; peep–, puppet–, raree–, galanty *or* gallanty–, Punch-and-Judy-show; marionettes; toy-shop; "quips and cranks and wanton wiles, nods and becks and wreathed smiles" [Milton].

sportsman (*fem.* sportswoman), hunter, Nimrod. archer, toxophilite; cricketer, footballer, ball-players etc.

gamester (*fem.* gamestress), sport, gambler; dicer, punter, plunger.

reveler *or* reveller, carouser; master of the -ceremonies, –revels; *arbiter elegantiarum* [*L.*]; *arbiter bibendi* [*L.*].

devotee, enthusiast, follower, fan [*slang*], rooter [*slang*]; turfman.

v. **amuse,** entertain, divert, enliven; tickle, –the fancy; titillate, raise a smile, put in good humor;

cause–, create–, occasion–, raise–, excite–, produce–, convulse with- laughter; set the table in a roar, be the death of one.

cheer, rejoice; recreate, solace; please etc. 829; interest; treat, regale.

amuse oneself; game; play, –a game, –pranks, –tricks; sport, disport, toy, wanton, revel, junket, feast, carouse, banquet, make merry, drown care; drive dull care away; frolic, gambol, frisk, romp; caper; dance etc. (*leap*) 309; keep up the ball; run a rig, sow one's wild oats, have one's fling, take one's pleasure; paint the town red [*slang*]; see life; *desipere in loco* [Horace], play the fool.

make–, keep- holiday; go a-Maying.

while away–, beguile- the time; kill time, dally.

adj. **amusing,** entertaining, diverting etc. *v.;* recreative, lusory; pleasant etc. (*pleasing*) 829; laughable etc. (*ludicrous*) 853; witty etc. 842; festive, festal; jovial, jolly, jocund, roguish, rompish; playful, –as a kitten; sportive, ludibrious [*obs.*].

amused etc. *v.;* "pleased with a rattle, tickled with a straw" [Pope].

adv. "on the light fantastic toe" [Milton], at play, in sport.

int. *vive la bagatelle!* [*F.*], *vogue la galère!* [*F.*], come on fellows! "hail, hail, the gang's all here!" some party! [*slang*].

841. Weariness

n. **weariness,** defatigation [*obs.*], ennui, boredom; lassitude etc. (*fatigue*) 688; drowsiness etc. 683.

disgust, nausea, loathing, sickness; satiety etc. 869; *taedium vitae* [*L.*] etc. (*dejection*) 837.

tedium, wearisomeness, tediousness etc. *adj.;* heavy hours, dull work, monotony, twice-told tale; "the enemy" [time].

bore, buttonholer, proser, dry-as-dust, fossil [*colloq.*], wet blanket; pill, stiff [*both slang*].

v. **weary;** tire etc. (*fatigue*) 688; bore; bore–, weary–, tire- -to death, –out of one's life, –out of all patience; set–, send- to sleep; buttonhole.

pall, sicken, nauseate, disgust; harp on the same string; drag its -slow, –weary- length along.

never hear the last of; be tired etc. *adj.* of *or* with; yawn; die with *ennui.*

adj. **wearying** etc. *v.;* wearing; wearisome, tiresome, irksome; uninteresting, stupid, bald, devoid of interest, jejune, dry, monotonous, dull, arid, tedious, humdrum, mortal [*colloq.*], flat; prosy, prosing; slow; soporific, somniferous, dormitive, opiate.

disgusting etc. *v.;* unenjoyed.

weary; tired etc. *v.;* drowsy etc. (*sleepy*) 683; uninterested, flagging, used up, worn out, *blasé* [*F.*], life-weary, weary of life; sick of.

adv. **wearily** etc. *adj.; usque ad nauseam* [*L.*].

842. Wit

n. **wit,** wittiness; Attic -wit, –salt; Atticism; salt, *esprit* [*F.*], point, fancy, whim, humor *or* humour, drollery, pleasantry.

buffoonery, fooling, farce, tom-foolery; shenanigan [*slang*], harlequinade etc. 599; broad -farce, –humor; fun, *espiéglerie* [*F.*]; *vis comica* [*L.*].

jocularity; jocosity, jocoseness; facetiousness; waggery, waggishness; whimsicality; comicality etc. 853.

smartness, ready wit, banter, persiflage, *badinage* [*F.*], retort, repartee, *quid pro quo* [*L.*]; ridicule etc. 856.

facetlae, quips and cranks; jest, joke, capital joke; *canorae nugae* [*L.*]; standing -jest, –joke; conceit, quip, quirk, crank, quiddity [*rare*], *concetto* [*It.*], *plaisanterie* [*F.*], brilliant idea; merry–, bright–, happy- thought; sally; flash, –of wit, –of merriment; scintillation; *mot*, –*pour rire* [*F.*]; witticism, smart saying, *bon mot* [*F.*], *jeu d'esprit* [*F.*], epigram; jest book; dry joke, *quodlibet* [*L.*], cream of the jest.

word-play, *jeu de mots* [*F.*], play upon words; pun, punning; *double entente* [*F.*] etc. (*ambiguity*) 520; quibble, verbal quibble; conundrum etc. (*riddle*) 533; anagram, acrostic, double acrostic, trifling, idle conceit, turlupinade [*obs.*].

old joke, Joe Miller, chestnut [*slang*]; hoary-headed -joke, –jest; joke–, jest- with whiskers [*humorous*].

v. **joke,** jest, cut jokes; crack a joke, get off a joke; pun; perpetrate a -joke, –pun; make fun of, make merry with; set the table in a roar etc. (*amuse*) 840; tell a good -story, –yarn.

retort, flash back, flash, scintillate; banter etc. (*ridicule*) 856; *ridentem dicere verum* [*L.*]; joke at one's expense.

adj. **witty,** Attic; clever, keen, keen-witted, brilliant, pungent; quick-witted, nimble-witted; smart; jocular, jocose, funny, waggish, facetious, whimsical, humorous; playful etc. 840; merry and wise; pleasant, sprightly, cute [*colloq.*], *spirituel* [*F.*], sparkling, epigrammatic, full of point, *ben trovato* [*It.*]; comic etc. 853.

adv. in joke, in jest, for the jest's sake, in sport, in play.

843. Dullness

n. **dullness** *or* dulness, heaviness, flatness; infestivity etc. 837, stupidity etc. 499; want of originality; dearth of ideas.

prose, matter of fact; heavy book, *conte à dormir debout* [*F.*]; commonplace, platitude.

v. **be dull** etc. *adj.;* hang fire, fall flat; platitudinize, prose, take *au sérieux* [*F.*], be caught napping.

render dull etc. *adj.;* damp, depress, throw cold water on, lay a wet blanket on; fall flat upon the ear.

adj. **dull**, –as ditch water; jejune, dry, unentertaining, uninteresting, unlively, heavy-footed, elephantine; slow of comprehension; insipid, tasteless, slow as molasses [*colloq.*], logy; unimaginative; insulse; dry as dust; prosy, prosing, prosaic; matter-of-fact, commonplace, platitudinous, pointless; "weary, stale, flat, and unprofitable" [*Hamlet*].

stupid, slow, flat, humdrum, monotonous; melancholic etc. 837; stolid etc. 499; plodding.

844. Humorist

n. **humorist**, wag, wit, reparteeist, epigrammatist, punster; *bel esprit* [*F.*], life of the party; joker, jester, Joe Miller, *drôle de corps* [*F.*], galliard *or* gaillard [*archaic*], spark; *bon diable* [*F.*]; *persifleur* [*F.*], banterer, "Agreeable Rattle" [Goldsmith].

buffoon, *farceur* [*F.*], merry-andrew, mime, tumbler, acrobat, mountebank, charlatan, posture master, harlequin, punch, punchinello, *pulcinella* [*It.*], Scaramouch, clown; wearer of the -cap and bells, –motley; motley fool; pantaloon, gypsy; jack-pudding [*archaic*], Jack-in-the-green; jack-a-dandy; zany; madcap, pickle-herring, witling, caricaturist, grimacer, grimacier.

845. Beauty

n. **beauty**, beautifulness, pulchritude; the beautiful, *to kalon* [*Gr.*].

beauty unadorned; form, elegance, grace, *belle tournure* [*F.*]; symmetry etc. 242; concinnity, delicacy, refinement, charm, *je ne sais quoi* [*F.*], *nescio quid* [*L.*], style.

comeliness, fairness etc. *adj.;* polish, gloss; good effect, good looks; trigness.

bloom, brilliancy, radiance, splendor *or* splendour, gorgeousness, magnificence; sublimity, sublimification [*obs.*].

beau ideal, *le beau idéal* [*F.*]; Venus, Aphrodite, Hebe, the Graces, Peri, Houri, Cupid, Apollo, Hyperion, Adonis, Antinous, Narcissus, As-tarte; Helen of Troy, Cleopatra; Venus of Milo, Apollo Belvedere.

[comparisons] butterfly; flower, flow'ret gay; garden, anemone, asphodel, buttercup, crane's-bill, daffodil, lily, lily of the valley, ranunculus, rose, rhododendron, windflower.

the flower of, the pink of; *bijou* [*F.*]; jewel etc. (*ornament*) 847; work of art.

loveliness, pleasurableness etc. 829.

beautifying, beautification [*rare*]; landscape gardening; decoration etc. etc. 847; calisthenics, physical culture.

[science of the perception of beauty] callaesthetics.

v. **be beautiful** etc. *adj.;* shine, beam, bloom; become one etc. (*accord*) 23; set off, become, grace.

render beautiful etc. *adj.;* beautify; polish, burnish; gild etc. (*decorate*) 847; set out.

"snatch a grace beyond the reach of art" [Pope].

adj. **beautiful**, beauteous, handsome; pretty; lovely, graceful, elegant, exquisite, flowerlike, delicate, dainty, refined.

comely, fair, personable, seemly [*obs.*], decent [*archaic*], proper, bonny, good-looking; well-favored, well-made, well-formed, well-proportioned, shapely, zaftig [*colloq.*]; symmetrical etc. (*regular*) 242; harmonious etc. (*color*) 428; sightly, fit to be seen.

bright, bright-eyed; rosy-cheeked, cherry-cheeked; rosy, ruddy; blooming, in full bloom.

goodly, dapper, tight, jimp *or* gimp [*Scot. & dial. Eng.*], jaunty *or* janty, trig, natty [*orig. slang*], quaint [*archaic*], trim, tidy, neat, spruce, smart, tricksy [*rare*].

brilliant, shining; beamy, beaming; sparkling, radiant, splendid, resplendent, dazzling, glowing; glossy, sleek; rich, gorgeous, superb, magnificent, grand, fine, sublime.

artistic *or* artistical, aesthetic; picturesque, pictorial; *fait à peindre* [*F.*], paintable, well-composed, well-grouped, well-varied; curious.

enchanting etc. (*pleasure-giving*) 829; attractive etc. (*inviting*) 615; becoming etc. (*accordant*) 23; ornamental etc. 847; of consummate art.

perfect, unspotted, spotless etc. 650; immaculate; undeformed, undefaced.

passable, presentable, tolerable, not amiss.

846. Ugliness

n. **ugliness** etc. *adj.;* deformity, inelegance; acomia, baldness, alopecia; disfigurement etc. (*blemish*) 848; want of symmetry, inconcinnity

[rare], "uglification" [Carroll]; distortion etc. 243; squalor etc. (uncleanness) 653.

forbidding countenance, vinegar aspect, hanging look, wry face, face that would stop a clock [colloq.]; spretae injuria formae [Virgil].

eyesore, object, figure, sight [colloq.], fright, octopus. specter or spectre. scarecrow, hag, harridan, satyr, witch, toad, baboon, monster, Caliban, Aesop; monstrum horrendum informe ingens cui lumen ademptum [Virgil].

v. **be ugly** etc. adj.; look ill, grin horribly a ghastly smile, grin through a horse collar [colloq.], make faces.

render ugly etc. adj.; deface; disfigure, defigure [obs.], deform, uglify [rare], spoil; distort etc. 243; blemish etc. (injure) 659; soil etc. (render unclean) 653.

adj. **ugly**, –as –sin, –a toad, –a scarecrow, –a dead monkey; plain, coarse; homely etc. (unadorned) 849; ordinary, unornamental, inartistic; unsightly, unseemly, uncomely, unshapely, unlovely; sightless [obs.], seemless [obs.], not fit to be seen; unbeauteous, unbeautiful, beautiless.

bald, bald-headed, acomous, hairless, chauve [F.], depilous [rare], glabrous [bot.]; smooth-faced, beardless, whiskerless, clean-shaven.

misshapen, misproportioned; shapeless etc. (amorphous) 241; monstrous; gaunt etc. (thin) 203; dumpy etc. (short) 201; curtailed of its fair proportions; ill-made, ill-shaped, ill-proportioned; crooked etc. (distorted) 243.

unprepossessing, hard-featured, hard-visaged; ill-favored, hard-favored, evil-favored; ill-looking; squalid, haggard; grim, grim-faced, grim-visaged; grisly, ghastly; ghostlike, death-like; cadaverous, gruesome or grewsome.

uncouth, ungainly, graceless, inelegant; ungraceful, stiff; rugged, rough, gross, rude, awkward, clumsy, slouching, rickety, gawky, lumping, lumpish, lumbering, hulking or hulky, unwieldy.

repellent, forbidding, frightful, hideous, odious, uncanny, repulsive; horrid, horrible; shocking etc. (painful) 830.

foul etc. (dirty) 653; dingy etc. (colorless) 429; gaudy etc. (color) 428; tarnished, smeared, besmeared, bedaubed; disfigured etc. v.; discolored, spotted, spotty.

showy, specious, pretentious, garish etc. (ostentatious) 882.

847. Ornament

n. **ornament**, ornamentation, ornamental art; ornature [rare], ornateness, ornation [rare], adornment, decoration, embellishment; architecture.

garnish, polish, varnish, French polish, gilding, japanning, lacquer, ormolu, enamel; champlevé ware, cloisonné ware; cosmetics.

[ornamentation] pattern, diaper, powdering, paneling, graining, inlaid work, pargeting; detail; texture etc. 329; richness; tracery, molding or moulding, fillet, listel, strapwork, coquillage [F.], flourish, fleur-de-lis [F.], arabesque, fret, anthemion; egg and -tongue, –dart; astragal, zigzag, acanthus, cartouche; pilaster etc. (projection) 250; bead, beading; frostwork, tooling; Moresque, Morisco.

embroidery, broidery [archaic], needlework, brocade, brocatel or brocatelle, bugles, beads, galloon, lace, fringe, border, insertion, motif [F.], edging, trimming; trappings; drapery, over-drapery, hanging, tapestry, arras; millinery, ermine; drap d'or [F.].

wreath, festoon, garland, chaplet, flower, nosegay, bouquet, posy; "daisies pied and violets blue" [Love's Labour Lost].

tassel, knot; shoulder knot, epaulet or epaulette, aglet or aiglet, aigulet [rare], frog; star, rosette, bow; feather, plume, panache, aigret or aigrette; fillet, snood.

jewelry or jewellery, bijouterie [F.] or bijoutry; tiara, crown, coronet, diadem; jewel, bijou [F.], trinket, locket, necklace, bracelet, bangle; armlet, anklet, earring, nose-ring, carcanet [archaic], chain, chatelaine, brooch, torque.

gem, precious stone; diamond, brilliant; pearl; sapphire, Oriental topaz, lapis lazuli; ruby, balas or balais or balas ruby; emerald, beryl, aquamarine, alexandrite; opal, fire opal, girasol or girasole; garnet, carbuncle; amethyst, plasma; turquoise or turquois; topaz; coral; chalcedony, agate, onyx, sard, sardonyx, chrysoprase, carnelian, cat's-eye, jasper; heliotrope, bloodstone; hyacinth, jacinth, zircon, jargon or jargoon; chrysolite, peridot; spinel or spinelle, spinel ruby; moonstone, sunstone.

frippery, finery, gewgaw, knickknack, gimcrack, tinsel, spangle, clinquant, pinchbeck, paste; excess of ornament etc. (vulgarity) 851; gaud, pride, show, ostentation.

illustration, illumination, vignette; fleuron [F.]; headpiece, tailpiece, cul-de-lampe [F.]; purple patches, flowers of rhetoric etc. 577.

virtu, article of virtu, piece of virtu, work of art, bric-a-brac, curio; rarity, a find.

v. **ornament**, embellish, enrich, decorate, adorn, beautify; adonize [rare], dandify.

garnish, furbish, polish, gild, varnish, whitewash, enamel, japan, lacquer, paint, grain.

spangle, bespangle, bead, embroider, work; chase, tool, emboss, fret; emblazon, blazon, illuminate; illustrate.

smarten, trim, dizen, bedizen, prink, prank; trick up, trick out, fig out; deck, bedeck, dight [*archaic*], bedight [*archaic*], array; titivate *or* tittivate [*colloq.*], spruce up [*colloq.*]; smarten up, dress, dress up; powder.

become etc. (*accord with*) 23.

adj. **ornamented**, beautified etc. *v.;* ornate, rich, gilt, begilt, tessellated, inlaid, festooned; *champlevé* [*F.*], *cloisonné* [*F.*], topiary [*rare*].

smart, gay, tricksy [*rare*], flowery, glittering; new-gilt, new-spangled; fine; fine as -a Mayday queen, –fivepence, –a carrot fresh scraped, –a fiddle [*all colloq.*]; pranked out, bedight [*archaic*], well-groomed.

in full dress etc. (*fashion*) 852; *en grande -tenue, –toilette* [*F.*]; in one's best bib and tucker, in Sunday best, *endimanché* [*F.*]; dressed to advantage.

showy, flashy; gaudy etc. (*vulgar*) 851; garish *or* gairish, splendiferous [*humorous*], gorgeous.

ornamental, decorative; becoming etc. (*accordant*) 23.

848. Blemish

n. **blemish**, disfigurement, deformity; adactylism; defect etc. (*imperfection*) 651; flaw, maculation; injury etc. (*deterioration*) 659; spots on the sun; eyesore.

stain, blot, spot, spottiness; speck, speckle, blur, freckle, mole, macula, macule, patch, blotch, birthmark; blobber lip, blubber lip, harelip; blain, tarnish, smudge; dirt etc. 653; scar, wem [*obs.*], wen; pustule; whelk; excrescence, pimple etc. (*protuberance*) 250; burn, blister, roughness.

v. **disfigure** etc. (*injure*) 659; uglify [*rare*]; render ugly etc. 846.

adj. **disfigured**; discolored; imperfect etc. 651; blobber-lipped *or* blubber-lipped, harelipped; chapped, specked, speckled, freckled, pitted, bloodshot, bruised; injured etc. (*deteriorated*) 659.

849. Simplicity

n. **simplicity**; plainness, homeliness; undress, nudity, beauty unadorned; chasteness, chastity, restraint, severity, naturalness, unaffectedness.

v. **be simple** etc. *adj.*

render simple etc. *adj.;* simplify, reduce to simplicity, strip of ornament, chasten, restrain.

adj. **simple**, plain, homelike, homish, homely, homespun [*fig.*], ordinary, household.

unaffected, natural, native; inartificial etc. (*artless*) 703; free from -affectation, –ornament; *simplex munditiis* [Horace]; *sans façon* [*F.*], *en déshabillé* [*F.*].

chaste, inornate, severe.

unadorned, unornamented, undecked, ungarnished, unarranged, untrimmed, unvarnished.

bald, flat, blank, dull.

simple-minded, childish, credulous etc. 486.

850. Taste

[good taste]

n. **taste**; good–, refined–, cultivated- taste; delicacy, refinement, fine feeling, gust, gusto, tact, finesse; nicety etc. (*discrimination*) 465; *to prepon* [*Gr.*], polish, elegance, grace.

artistic quality, virtu; dilettanteism, virtuosity, connoisseurship, fine art of living; fine art; culture, cultivation.

"caviare to the general" [*Hamlet*].

[science of taste] aesthetics.

man of taste etc.; connoisseur, judge, critic, conoscente, virtuoso, amateur, dilettante; Aristarchus, Corinthian; Aristotle, Stagirite; Petronius, *arbiter elegantiae* [*L.*], *arbiter elegantiarum* [*L.*].

euphemist, purist, precisian.

v. **display taste** etc. *n.;* appreciate, judge, criticize, discriminate etc. 465.

adj. **in good taste**, tasteful, unaffected, pure, chaste, classical, Attic, cultivated; attractive, charming, dainty; aesthetic, artistic.

refined, tasty [*colloq.*]; prim, precise, formal, prudish; elegant etc. 578; euphemistic.

to one's taste, to one's mind; after one's fancy; *comme il faut* [*F.*]; *tiré à quatre épingles* [*F.*].

adv. **elegantly** etc. *adj.;* with quiet elegance; with elegant simplicity; without ostentation.

851. Vulgarity

[bad taste]

n. **vulgarity**, vulgarism; barbarism, Vandalism, Gothicism; *mauvais goût* [*F.*], bad taste; want of tact; ungentlemanliness, ungentlemanlikeness; ill-breeding etc. (*discourtesy*) 895.

coarseness etc. *adj.;* indecorum, loud behavior [*colloq.*], misbehavior; *gaucherie* [*F.*], awkwardness; boorishness etc. *adj.;* homeliness, rusticity.

lowness, low life, *mauvais ton* [*F.*]; brutality; blackguardism, rowdyism, ruffianism; ribaldry; slang etc. (*neology*) 563.

bad joke, *mauvaise plaisanterie* [*F.*], poor joke, joke in bad taste; practical joke.

[excess of ornament] gaudiness, tawdriness, gingerbread, false ornament, cheap jewelry; flashy -clothes, –dress; finery, frippery, trickery, tinsel, gewgaw, clinquant.

vulgarian, rough diamond; clown etc. (*commonalty*) 876; Goth, Vandal, Boeotian; snob, cad [*colloq.*], gent [*humorous*]; parvenu etc. 876; frump [*colloq.*], dowdy; slut, slattern etc. 653; tomboy, hoyden, cub, unlicked cub.

v. be vulgar etc. *adj.;* misbehave; talk–, smell of the-shop; show a want of -tact, –consideration; be a vulgarian etc. *n.*

adj. **in bad taste**, vulgar, unrefined, coarse, indecorous, ribald, gross; unseemly, unbeseeming, unpresentable; *contra bonos mores* [*L.*]; ungraceful etc. (*ugly*) 846; dowdy; slovenly etc. (*dirty*) 653; ungenteel, shabby genteel; low etc. (*plebeian*) 876.

extravagant, monstrous, horrid; shocking etc. (*painful*) 830.

ill-mannered, ill-bred, underbred, snobbish, uncourtly; uncivil etc. (*discourteous* 895; ungentlemanly, ungentlemanlike; unladylike, unfeminine; wild, wild as a hawk, wild as an unbacked colt.

uncouth, unkempt, uncombed, untamed, unlicked, unpolished, plebeian; incondite [*rare*]; heavy, rude, awkward; homely, homespun, homebred; provincial, countrified, rustic; boorish, clownish; savage, brutish, blackguard, blackguardly, rowdyish, rowdy.

barbarous, barbaric, Gothic, heathenish, tramontane, outlandish; uncultivated; Bohemian; unclassical, doggerel *or* doggrel.

obsolete etc. (*antiquated*) 124; out of fashion, old-fashioned, out of date, unfashionable.

newfangled etc. (*unfamiliar*) 83; fantastic, fantastical, odd etc. (*ridiculous*) 853; particular; affected etc. 855.

tawdry, gaudy, meretricious, brummagem [*slang*], bedizened, tricked out; obtrusive, flaunting, loud, crass, showy, flashy, garish.

852. Fashion

n. **fashion**, style, *ton* [*F.*], *bon ton* [*F.*], society; good–, polite- society; *monde* [*F.*]; drawing-room, civilized life, civilization, town, *beau monde* [*F.*], high life, court; world; fashionable–, gay- world; height–, pink–, star–, glass- of fashion; "the glass of fashion and the mould of form" [*Hamlet*]; Vanity Fair; Mayfair; show etc. (*ostentation*) 822.

manners, breeding etc. (*politeness*) 894; air, demeanor etc. (*appearance*) 448; *savoir faire* [*F.*]; gentlemanliness, gentility, decorum, propriety, *bienséance* [*F.*]; conventions of society; Mrs. Grundy; dictates of -Society, –Mrs. Grundy; convention, conventionality, the proprieties; punctiliousness, punctilio, form, formality; etiquette, point of etiquette.

mode, vogue, style, the latest thing, *dernier cri* [*F.*], the go [*colloq.*], the rage etc. (*desire*) 865; prevailing taste; dress etc. 225; custom etc. 613.

leader of fashion; *arbiter elegantiarum* [*L.*] etc. (*taste*) 850; man–, woman- of -fashion, –the world; clubman, clubwoman; upper ten thousand etc. (*nobility*) 875; upper ten [*colloq.*]; *élite* [*F.*] etc. (*distinction*) 873; smart set [*colloq.*]; the four hundred.

v. **be fashionable** etc. *adj.*, be the rage etc. *n.;* have a run, pass current.

follow–, keep up with–, conform to–, fall in with- the fashion etc. *n.;* go with the stream etc. (*conform*) 82; be on (*or* get on) the band wagon [*slang*], be in the swim [*colloq.*]; *savoir -vivre, –faire* [*F.*]; keep up appearances, behave oneself.

set the fashion, bring into fashion; give a tone to society, cut a figure in society [*colloq.*]; brush shoulders with -the nobility, –royalty; appear–, be presented- at court.

keep one's -automobile, –car, –carriage, –yacht, –house in town [*Eng.*], –cottage at Newport; be a member of the best clubs.

adj. **fashionable**; in fashion etc. *n.; à la mode* [*F.*], *comme il faut* [*F.*]; admitted–, admissible- in society etc. *n.;* presentable; punctilious, decorous, conventional etc. (*customary*) 613; genteel; well-bred, well-mannered, well-behaved, well-spoken; gentlemanlike, gentlemanly; ladylike; civil, polite etc. (*courteous*) 894.

dashing, jaunty *or* janty, showy, spirited, fast.

polished, refined, thoroughbred, gently bred, courtly; *distingué* [*F.*], distinguished, aristocratic *or* aristocratical; unselfconscious, self-possessed, poised, easy, frank, unconstrained, unembarrassed, *dégagé* [*F.*].

modish, stylish, swell [*slang*], recherché, *récherché* [*F.*]; newfangled etc. (*unfamiliar*) 83; all the rage, all the go [*colloq.*].

in -court, –full, –evening- dress; *en grande tenue* [*F.*] etc. (*ornament*) 847.

adv. **fashionably** etc. *adj.;* for fashion's sake; in fear of Mrs. Grundy; in the latest -style, –mode.

int. it isn't done!

853. Ridiculousness

n. **ridiculousness** etc. *adj.;* comicality, oddity etc. *adj.;* drollery; farce, comedy; burlesque etc. (*ridicule*) 856; buffoonery etc. (*fun*) 840; frippery; amphigory *or* amphigouri, doggerel (*or* doggrel) verses; bull, Irish bull, Hibernicism, Hibernianism, Spoonerism; absurdity etc. 497.

fustian, extravagance, bombast etc. (*unmeaning*) 517; anticlimax, bathos; monstrosity etc. (*unconformity*) 83; laughingstock etc. 857; screamer *or* scream [*slang*].

v. **be ridiculous** etc. *adj.;* pass from the sublime to the ridiculous; make one laugh; play the fool, make a fool of oneself, commit an absurdity; ride–, play- the goat [*colloq.*].

make ridiculous, make a goat of [*colloq.*], make a fool of, play a joke on.

adj. **ridiculous,** ludicrous, comic *or* comical, drollish, waggish, quizzical, droll, funny, laughable, risible, farcical, screaming; serio-comic, serio-comical; tragi-comic, tragi-comical; *pour rire* [*F.*].

odd, grotesque; whimsical, –as a dancing bear; fanciful, fantastic, queer, rum [*slang*], quaint, bizarre; eccentric etc. (*unconformable*) 83; strange, outlandish, out-of-the-way, baroque, rococo; awkward etc. (*ugly*) 846.

extravagant, *outré* [*F.*], monstrous, preposterous, absurd, bombastic, inflated, stilted, burlesque, mock heroic.

trivial, doggerel *or* doggrel, gimcrack, contemptible etc. (*unimportant*) 643.

derisive, ironical etc. 856.

854. Fop

n. **fine gentleman,** fop, swell [*colloq.*], dandy, exquisite, coxcomb, beau, macaroni [*hist.*]; blade, blood, buck [*archaic*], man about town, fast man, *roué* [*F.*]; fribble, jemmy [*obs.*], spark, popinjay, puppy [*contemptuous*], prig, *petit maître* [*F.*]; jackanapes, jack-a-dandy, jessamy [*obs.*], man milliner; carpet knight; masher [*slang*], dude [*colloq.*].

fine lady, belle, flirt, coquette, toast.

855. Affectation

n. **affectation;** affectedness etc. *adj.;* acting a part etc. *v.;* pretense etc. (*falsehood*) 544, (*ostentation*) 882; boasting etc. 884; charlatanism, quackery, shallow profundity.

pretension, airs, pedantry, pedantism, purism, precisianism, stiffness, formality, buckram; prunes and prisms; euphuism; teratology etc. (*altiloquence*) 577.

prudery, demureness, mock modesty, *minauderie* [*F.*], sentimentalism; *mauvaise honte* [*F.*], false shame.

mannerism, *simagrée* [*F.*], grimace.

foppery, dandyism, man millinery, coxcombry, coquetry, puppyism, conceit.

affecter *or* affector, performer, actor; pedant, pedagogue, doctrinaire, purist, euphuist, mannerist; grimacier [*rare*]; lump of affectation, *précieuse ridicule* [*F.*], *bas bleu* [*F.*], blue stocking, poetaster; prig; charlatan etc. (*deceiver*) 548; *petit maître* [*F.*] etc. (*fop*) 854; flatterer etc. 935; coquette, prude, puritan, precisian, formalist.

v. **affect,** act a part, put on; give oneself airs etc. (*arrogance*) 885; boast etc. 884; coquet; simper, mince, attitudinize, pose; flirt a fan; languish; euphuize; overact, overdo.

adj. **affected,** full of affectation, pretentious, pedantic, stilted, stagy, theatrical, big-sounding, *ad captandum* [*L.*]; canting, insincere; not natural, unnatural; self-conscious; mannered, *maniéré* [*F.*]; artificial; overwrought, overdone, overacted; euphuistic etc. 577.

stiff, starch, formal, prim, smug, demure, *tiré à quatre épingles* [*F.*], quakerish, puritanical, prudish, pragmatical.

priggish, conceited, coxcomical, foppish, dandified, finical, finicking *or* finicky *or* finikin; mincing, simpering, namby-pamby, sentimental, languishing.

856. Ridicule

n. **ridicule,** derision; sardonic -smile, –grin; irrision [*obs.*], snicker *or* snigger, grin, twit [*rare*]; scoffing etc. (*disrespect*) 929; mockery, quiz, banter, irony, persiflage, raillery, chaff, *badinage* [*F.*]; quizzing etc. *v.;* asteism.

squib, satire, skit, quip, quib [*obs.*].

burlesque, parody, travesty, *travestie* [*F.*]; farce etc. (*drama*) 599; caricature.

buffoonery etc. (*fun*) 840; practical joke, horseplay, roughhouse [*slang*].

v. **ridicule,** deride; laugh at, grin at, smile at; snicker *or* snigger; laugh in one's sleeve; banter, rally, chaff, joke, twit, quiz, poke fun at, roast [*slang*], guy [*colloq.*], jolly [*colloq.*], rag [*slang, Eng.*]; haze; tehee *or* teehee; fleer; play upon, play tricks upon; get the laugh on [*slang*]; fool, –to the top of one's bent; show up.

turn into ridicule; make merry with; make -fun, –game, –a fool, –an April fool- of; rally; scoff etc. (*disrespect*) 929.

burlesque, satirize, parody, caricature, travesty.

be **ridiculous** etc. 853; raise a laugh etc. (*amuse*) 840; play the fool, make a fool of oneself.

adj. **derisive**, derisory, mock; sarcastic, ironical, quizzical, burlesque, Hudibrastic, Rabelaisian; scurrilous etc. (*disrespectful*) 929.

adv. **in ridicule** etc. *n.;* as a joke, to raise a laugh.

int. "What fools these mortals be!" [*Midsummer Night's Dream*].

857. Laughingstock
[object and cause of ridicule]

n. **laughingstock**, jesting-stock, gazing-stock; butt, game, fair game; April fool etc. (*dupe*) 547, original, oddity; queer–, odd- fish [*colloq.*], figure of fun [*colloq.*]; quiz, square toes; old fogy *or* fogey [*colloq.*].

monkey; buffoon etc. (*jester*) 844; pantomimist etc. (*actor*) 599.

jest etc. (*wit*) 842.

858. Hope

n. **hope**, hopes; desire etc. 865; fervent hope, sanguine expectation, trust, confidence, reliance; faith etc. (*belief*) 484; affiance, assurance; secureness, security; reassurance.

good -omen, –auspices; promise, well-grounded hopes; good–, bright-prospect; clear sky.

hopefulness, buoyancy, optimism, enthusiasm, heart of grace, aspiration; assumption, presumption; anticipation etc. (*expectation*) 507.

optimist, utopist [*rare*], utopian.

daydream, castles in the air, castles in Spain, *châteaux en Espagne* [*F.*], *le pot au lait* [*F.*], Utopia, millennium; golden dream; dream of Alnaschar; airy hopes, fool's paradise; mirage etc. (*fallacies of vision*) 443; fond hope.

ray of hope; beam–, gleam–, glimmer–, dawn–, flash–, star- of hope; cheer; bit of blue sky, silver lining of the cloud, bottom of Pandora's box, balm in Gilead.

mainstay, anchor, sheet anchor; staff etc. (*support*) 215; heaven etc. 981.

v. **hope**, trust, confide, rely on, put one's trust in, lean upon; pin one's hope upon, pin one's faith upon etc. (*believe*) 484.

feel–, entertain–, harbor–, indulge–, cherish–, feed–, foster–, nourish–, encourage–, cling to–, live in- hope etc. *n.;* see land; feel–, rest- -assured, –confident etc. *adj.*

hope for etc. (*desire*) 865; anticipate; presume; promise oneself; expect etc. (*look forward to*) 507.

be **hopeful** etc. *adj.;* look on the bright side of, view on the sunny side, *voir en couleur de rose* [*F.*], make the best of it, hope for the best; hope against hope; put -a good, –a bold, –the best- face upon; keep one's spirits up; take heart, –of grace; be of good -heart, –cheer; flatter oneself, "lay the flattering unction to one's soul" [*Hamlet*].

catch at a straw, hope against hope, count one's chickens before they are hatched.

encourage, hearten, inspirit; give–, inspire–, raise–, hold out- hope etc. *n.;* raise expectations; encourage, cheer, assure, reassure, buoy up, embolden; promise, bid fair, augur well, be in a fair way, look up, flatter, tell a flattering tale.

adj. **hopeful**, confident; hoping etc. *v.;* in hopes etc. *n.;* secure etc. (*certain*) 484; sanguine, in good heart, buoyed up, buoyant, elated, flushed, exultant, enthusiastic; heartsome [*chiefly Scot.*]; utopian.

fearless; free from–, exempt from- fear, –suspicion, –distrust, –despair; unsuspecting, unsuspicious, undespairing, self-reliant; dauntless etc. (*courageous*) 861.

propitious, promising; probable, on the high road to; within sight of -shore, –land; of–, full of- promise; of good omen; auspicious, *de bon augure* [*F.*]; reassuring; encouraging, cheering, inspiriting, looking up, bright, roseate, *couleur de rose* [*F.*], rose-colored.

adv. hopefully etc. *adj.*

int. God speed! good luck!

859. Hopelessness
[absence, want, or loss of hope]

n. **hopelessness** etc. *adj.;* despair, desperation; despondency etc. (*dejection*) 837; pessimism.

hope deferred, dashed hopes; vain expectation etc. (*disappointment*) 509.

airy hopes etc. 858; bad -job, –business; gloomy–, clouds on the–, black spots in the- horizon; dark future; slough of Despond, cave of Despair; *immedicabile vulnus* [*L.*].

forlorn hope, *enfant perdu* (*pl. enfants perdus*) [*F.*]; goner [*slang*]; gone -case, –coon [*slang*].

pessimist, Job's comforter; hypochondriac etc. 837; bird of bad omen, bird of ill omen.

v. **despair**; lose–, give up–, abandon–, relinquish- -all hope, –the hope of; give up, give over; yield to despair; falter; despond etc. (*be dejected*) 837; *jeter le manche après la cognée* [*F.*].

shatter one's hopes; inspire–, drive to- despair etc. *n.;* disconcert; dash–, crush–, destroy-one's hopes; dash the cup from one's lips; undermine one's foundation; take away one's last hope.

adj. **hopeless**, desperate, despairing, gone, in despair, *au désespoir* [*F.*], forlorn; inconsolable etc. (*dejected*) 837; broken-hearted.

out of the question, not to be thought of; impracticable etc. 471; past -hope, –cure, –mending, –recall; at one's last gasp etc. (*death*) 360; given up, given over.

undone, ruined; incurable, cureless, immedicable, remediless, beyond remedy; incorrigible; irreparable, irremediable, irrecoverable, irreversible, irretrievable, irreclaimable, irredeemable, irrevocable, immitigable.

unpropitious, unpromising, inauspicious, ill-omened, threatening, clouded over, lowering, ominous.

860. Fear

n. **fear**, timidity, diffidence, want of confidence; apprehensiveness, fearfulness etc. *adj.;* solicitude, anxiety, care, apprehension, misgiving; feeze [*colloq., U. S.*]; mistrust etc. (*doubt*) 485; suspicion, qualm; hesitation etc. (*irresolution*) 605.

trepidation, flutter, fear and trembling, perturbation, tremor, quivering, shaking, trembling, throbbing heart, palpitation, ague fit, cold sweat; nervousness, restlessness etc. *adj.;* inquietude, disquietude, heartquake; abject fear etc. (*cowardice*) 862; mortal funk [*colloq.*], heartsinking, despondency; despair etc. 859.

batophobia, hypsophobia; claustrophobia; agoraphobia.

fright, affright [*archaic*], affrightment [*archaic*], boof [*slang*], alarm, dread, awe, terror, horror, dismay, consternation, panic, scare, panic fear, panic terror; "terror by night" [*Bible*]; chute [*N. U. S.*], stampede [*of horses*].

intimidation, terrorism, reign of terror; terrorist. [object of fear] bugbear, bugaboo, scarecrow; hobgoblin etc. (*demon*) 980; nightmare, Gorgon, mormo [*obs.*], ogre, Hurlothrumbo, raw head and bloody bones, fee-faw-fum, *bête noire* [*F.*], *enfant terrible* [*F.*].

alarmist etc. (*coward*) 862.

v. **fear**, stand in awe of; be afraid etc. *adj.;* have qualms etc. *n.;* apprehend, sit upon thorns, eye askance; distrust etc. (*disbelieve*) 485.

hesitate etc. (*be irresolute*) 605; falter, funk [*colloq.*], cower, crouch; skulk etc. (*cowardice*) 862; take fright, take alarm; start, wince, flinch, shy, shrink, blench; fly etc. (*avoid*) 623.

grow pale, turn pale, stand aghast; be in a daze; not dare to say one's soul is one's own.

tremble, shake; shiver, –in one's shoes; shudder, flutter; shake–, tremble- like an aspen leaf, –all over; quake, quaver, quiver, quail.

frighten, fright, affright, terrify; inspire–, excite- -fear, –awe; raise apprehensions; bulldoze [*colloq.*], faze [*colloq.*], feeze *or* feaze [*colloq.*]; give–, raise–, sound- an alarm; alarm, startle, scare, cry "wolf," disquiet, dismay, astound; frighten from one's propriety; frighten out of one's -wits, –senses, –seven senses; awe; strike all of a heap [*colloq.*], strike an awe into, strike terror; harrow up the soul, appall *or* appal, unman, petrify, horrify; pile on the agony.

make one's -flesh creep, –hair stand on end, –blood run cold, –teeth chatter; take away–, stop- one's breath; make one tremble etc.

daunt, put in fear, intimidate, cow, daunt, overawe, abash, deter, discourage; browbeat, bully; threaten etc. 909; terrorize, put in bodily fear.

haunt, obsess, beset, besiege; prey–, weigh- on the mind.

adj. **afraid**, fearful, timid, timorous, nervous, diffident, coy, faint-hearted, tremulous, shaky, afraid of one's shadow, apprehensive, restless, fidgety; more frightened than hurt.

fearing etc. *v.;* frightened etc. *v.;* in fear, in a fright etc. *n.;* haunted with the fear of etc. *n.;* afeard [*dial.*].

aghast; awe-struck, awe-stricken; horror-struck, horror-stricken; terror-struck, terror-stricken; panic-struck, panic-stricken; frightened to death, white as a sheet; pale, -as -death, –ashes, –a ghost; breathless, in hysterics.

inspiring fear etc. *v.;* alarming; formidable, redoubtable; perilous etc. (*danger*) 665; portentous; fearful, dread, dreadful, fell, dire, direful, shocking, frightful, terrible, terrific, tremendous; horrid, horrible, horrific, ghastly, awful, awe-inspiring; revolting etc. (*painful*) 830; Gorgonian, Gorgon-like.

adv. *in terrorem* [*L.*].

int. "angels and ministers of grace defend us!" [*Hamlet*].

861. Courage

[absence of fear]

n. **courage**, bravery, valor *or* valour; resoluteness, boldness etc. *adj.;* spirit, daring, gallantry, intrepidity, prowess, heroism, chivalry; contempt-, defiance- of danger; derring-do [*pseudoarchaic*]; audacity; rashness etc. 863; dash; defiance etc. 715; confidence, self-reliance.

manhood, manliness, nerve, pluck, mettle, game; heart, −of grace; spunk [*colloq.*], grit, virtue, hardihood, fortitude; firmness etc. (*stability*) 150; heart of oak; bottom, backbone etc. (*perseverance*) 604a; resolution etc. (*determination*) 604; tenacity, bulldog courage.

exploit, feat, deed, act, achievement; heroic, −deed, −act; bold stroke.

brave man, man of courage, man of mettle; a man; hero, demigod, paladin; Hercules, Theseus, Perseus, Achilles, Hector; Bayard, *chevalier sans peur et sans reproche;* Lancelot, Sir Galahad.

brave woman, heroine, Amazon, Joan of Arc.

[comparisons] lion, tiger, panther, bulldog; gamecock, fighting-cock.

dare-devil, fire eater etc. 863.

v. **be courageous** etc. *adj.;* dare, venture, make bold; face−, front−, affront−, confront−, brave−, defy−, despise−, mock- danger; look in the face; look -full, −boldly, −danger- in the face; face; meet, meet in front; brave, beard; defy etc. 715.

bell the cat, take the bull by the horns, beard the lion in his den, march up to the cannon's mouth, go through fire and water, run the gantlet *or* gauntlet.

nerve oneself; take−, muster−, summon up−, pluck up- courage; take heart; take−, pluck up- heart of grace; hold up one's head, screw one's courage to the sticking place; come -to, −up to- the scratch; stand, −to one's guns, −fire, −against; bear up, −against; hold out etc. (*persevere*) 604a.

put a bold face upon; show−, present- a bold front; show fight; face the music.

hearten; give−, infuse−, inspire- courage; reassure, encourage, embolden, inspirit, cheer, nerve, put upon one's mettle, rally, raise a rallying cry; pat on the back, make a man of, keep in countenance.

adj. **courageous**, brave, valiant, valorous, gallant, intrepid, spirited, spiritful; high-spirited, high-mettled, mettlesome, plucky; manly, manful, resolute, stout, stout-hearted; iron-hearted, lion-hearted; heart of oak; Penthesilean.

bold, bold-spirited; daring, audacious; fearless, dauntless, aweless, dreadless [*obs.*]; undaunted, unappalled, undismayed, unawed, unblenched, unabashed, unalarmed, unflinching, unshrinking, unblenching, unapprehensive; confident, self-reliant; bold as -a lion, −brass [*colloq.*].

enterprising, adventurous, venturous, venturesome, dashing, chivalrous; soldierly etc. (*warlike*) 722; heroic.

fierce, savage; pugnacious etc. (*bellicose*) 720.

strong-minded, strong-willed, hardy, doughty [*archaic or humorous*]; firm etc. (*stable*) 150; determined etc. (*resolved*) 604; dogged, indomitable etc. (*persevering*) 604a.

upon one's mettle; up to the scratch; reassured etc. *v.;* unfeared, undreaded.

862. Cowardice

[excess of fear]

n. **cowardice**, pusillanimity; cowardliness etc. *adj.;* timidity, effeminacy.

poltroonery, baseness, dastardness, dastardy, abject fear, funk [*colloq.*]; Dutch courage [*colloq.*]; fear etc. 860; white feather, faint heart; cold feet [*slang*], yellow streak [*slang*].

coward, poltroon, dastard, sneak, recreant; shy−, dunghill- cock; coistrel *or* coistril [*archaic*], milksop, white-liver [*colloq.*], nidget [*obs.*]; slink [*Scot. & dial. Eng.*], cur [*contemptuous*], craven, caitiff; Bob Acres, Jerry Sneak.

alarmist, terrorist, pessimist; sheep in wolf's clothing.

shirker, slacker; runagate etc. (*fugitive*) 623.

v. **quail** etc. (*fear*) 860; be cowardly etc. *adj.,* be a coward etc. *n.;* funk [*colloq.*], cower, skulk, sneak; flinch, shy, fight shy, slink, turn tail; run away etc. (*avoid*) 623; show the white feather.

adj. **cowardly**, coward, fearful, shy, timid, timorous, skittish; poor-spirited, spiritless, soft, effeminate; weak-minded; infirm of purpose etc. 605; weak−, faint−, chicken−, hen−, pigeon-hearted; white−, lily−, milk- livered; smock-faced.

dastard, dastardly, base, craven, sneaking, dunghill, recreant; unwarlike, unsoldierlike; "in face a lion but in heart a deer"; "more like a rabbit than a robber."

unmanned; frightened etc. 860.

adv. with fear and trembling, in fear of one's life, in a blue funk [*colloq.*]; "with groanings that cannot be uttered" [*Bible*].

int. sauve qui peut! [*F.*], devil take the hindmost!

863. Rashness

n. **rashness** etc. *adj.;* temerity, want of caution, imprudence, indiscretion; overconfidence, presumption, audacity; precipitancy, precipitation, impetuosity; levity; foolhardihood, foolhardiness; heedlessness, thoughtlessness etc. (*inattention*) 458; carelessness etc. (*neglect*) 460; desperation; Quixotism, knight-errantry; fire eating.

gaming, gambling; blind bargain, leap in the dark, fool's paradise; too many eggs in one basket.

desperado, rashling [*obs.*], madcap, daredevil, Hotspur, Hector; scapegrace, *enfant perdu* [*F.*]; Don Quixote, knight-errant, Icarus; adventurer; dynamiter *or* dynamitard; fire eater, bully, bravo.

gambler, gamester etc. (*chance*) 621.

v. **be rash** etc. *adj.;* stick at nothing, play a desperate game; run into danger etc. 665; play with -fire, -edge tools; *donner tête baissée* [*F.*]; knock one's head against a wall etc. (*be unskillful*) 699; kick against the pricks; rush on destruction; tempt Providence, go on a forlorn hope.

carry too much sail, sail too near the wind, ride at single anchor, go out of one's depth; go to sea in a sieve.

take a leap in the dark; buy a pig in a poke; bet against a dead certainty.

count one's chickens before they are hatched; reckon without one's host; catch at straws; trust to-, lean on- a broken reed.

adj. **rash**, incautious, indiscreet, injudicious, imprudent, improvident, temerarious; uncalculating, impulsive; heedless; careless etc. (*neglectful*) 460; without ballast, head over heels, heels over head; giddy etc. (*inattentive*) 458.

reckless, wanton, wild, madcap, desperate, devil-may-care, death-defying; hot-blooded, hot-headed, hot-brained; headlong, headstrong; breakneck, foolhardy, harebrained, precipitate.

overconfident, overweening; venturesome, venturous, adventurous, Quixotic; fire-eating.

unexpected; off one's guard etc. (*inexpectant*) 508.

adv. posthaste, *à corps perdu* [*F.*], hand over head [*rare*], *tête baissée* [*F.*], headforemost; happen what may.

864. Caution

n. **caution**; cautiousness etc. *adj.;* discretion, prudence, cautel [*obs.*], heed, circumspection, calculation, deliberation.

foresight etc. 510; vigilance etc. 459; warning etc. 668.

worldly wisdom; "safety first," Fabian policy, "watchful waiting."

coolness etc. *adj.;* self-possession, self-command; presence of mind, *sang-froid* [*F.*], well-regulated mind.

v. **be cautious** etc. *adj.;* take -care, -heed, -good care; have a care; mind, mind what one is about; be on one's guard etc. (*keep watch*) 459; "make assurance double sure" [*Macbeth*].

think twice, look before one leaps, keep one's eye peeled [*slang*], keep one's weather eye open [*colloq.*]; count the cost, look to the main chance; cut one's coat according to one's cloth; feel one's -ground, -way; see how the land lies etc. (*foresight*) 510; pussy-foot; wait to see how the cat jumps; bridle one's tongue; *reculer pour mieux sauter* [*F.*] etc. (*prepare*) 673; let well enough alone, *ne pas reveiller le chat qui dort* [*F.*]; let sleeping dogs lie.

keep out of -harm's way, -troubled waters; keep at a respectful distance, stand aloof; keep-, be- on the safe side.

anticipate; bespeak etc. (*be early*) 132.

lay by; husband one's resources etc. 636.

warn, caution etc. 668.

adj. **cautious**, wary, guarded, guardful [*rare*]; on one's guard etc. (*watchful*) 459; gingerly, precautious [*rare*], suspicious, leery [*slang*]; *cavendo tutus* [*L.*]; *in medio tutissimus* [*L.*]; vigilant; careful, heedful, cautelous [*obs.*], stealthy, chary, shy of, circumspect, prudent, canny [*Scot.*], safe, noncommittal, discreet, politic; sure-footed etc. (*skillful*) 698.

unenterprising, unadventurous, cool, steady, self-possessed; overcautious.

adv. cautiously etc. *adj.*

int. have a care! look out! danger! mind your eye! [*colloq.*]; stop! look! listen! *cave canem!* [*L.*].

865. Desire

n. **desire**, wish, fancy, fantasy; inclination, leaning, bent, mind, animus, partiality, *penchant* [*F.*], predilection; propensity etc. 820; willingness etc. 602; liking, love, fondness, relish.

longing, hankering, yearning, coveting; aspiration, ambition, vaulting ambition; eagerness, zeal, ardor, *empressement* [*F.*], breathless impatience, solicitude, anxiety, overanxiety; impetuosity etc. 825.

need, want, exigency, urgency, necessity.

appetite, appetition, appetence, appetency; sharp appetite, keenness, hunger, stomach, twist; thirst, thirstiness; drought *or* drouth, mouth-watering.

edge of -appetite, -hunger; torment of Tantalus; sweet tooth [*colloq.*], lickerish (*or* liquorish) tooth; longing-, wistful-, sheep's- eyes.

avidity, greed, greediness, covetousness, ravenousness etc. *adj.;* grasping, craving, canine appetite, rapacity; voracity etc. (*gluttony*) 957.

passion, rage, furor, frenzy, mania, manie [*obs.*]; itching palm; inextinguishable desire; itch, itching, prurience, cacoëthes, cupidity,

313

lust, concupiscence; kleptomania, dipsomania; monomania, *idée fixe* [*F.*].

[of animals] heat, rut, oestrus.

[person desiring] lover, amateur, votary, devotee, aspirant, solicitant, candidate; cormorant etc. 957; parasite, sycophant.

[object of desire] desideratum, desideration; want etc. (*requirement*) 630; "a consummation devoutly to be wish'd" [*Hamlet*]; attraction, magnet, loadstone, lure, allurement, fancy, temptation, seduction, fascination, prestige, height of one's ambition, idol; whim, whimsey *or* whimsy, whim-wham; maggot; hobby, hobbyhorse [*rare*].

Fortunatus's cap; wishing -cap, -stone, -well; love potion; aphrodisiac.

v. **desire**; wish, wish for; be desirous etc. *adj.;* have a longing etc. *n.;* hope etc. 858.

care for, affect, like, list [*archaic*]; take to, cling to, take a fancy to; fancy; prefer etc. (*choose*) 609; have an eye to, have a mind to; find it in one's heart etc. (*be willing*) 602; have a fancy for, set one's eyes upon; cast sheep's eyes upon, look sweet on [*colloq.*]; take into one's head, have at heart, be bent upon; set one's cap at [*colloq.*], set one's heart upon, set one's mind upon; covet.

hunger-, thirst-, crave-, lust-, itch-, hanker-, run mad- after; raven for, die for; burn to; sigh-, cry-, gape-, gasp-, pine-, pant-, languish-, yearn-, long-, be on thorns-, hope- for; aspire after; catch at, grasp at, jump at.

woo, court, ogle, solicit; fish for, whistle for, put up for [*slang*].

want, miss, need, lack, desiderate, feel the want of; would fain -have, -do; would be glad of.

hunger; be hungry etc. *adj.;* have a good appetite, play a good knife and fork [*colloq.*].

attract, allure; cause-, create-, raise-, excite-, provoke- desire; whet the appetite; appetize, titillate, take one's fancy, tempt; hold out -temptation, -allurement; tantalize, make one's mouth water, *faire venir l'eau à la bouche* [*F.*].

gratify desire etc. (*give pleasure*) 829.

adj. **desirous**; desiring etc. *v.;* orectic, appetitive; inclined etc. (*willing*) 602; partial to [*colloq.*]; fain, wishful, longing, wistful; optative; anxious, curious; at a loss for, sedulous, solicitous.

eager, avid, keen; burning, fervent, ardent; agog; all agog; breathless; impatient etc. (*impetu-*

ous) 825; bent-, intent-, set- -on, -upon; mad after, *enragé* [*F.*], rabid, dying for, devoured by desire.

aspiring, ambitious, vaulting, sky-aspiring, high-reaching.

craving, hungry, sharp-set, peckish [*colloq.*], ravening, with an empty stomach, esurient, lickerish, thirsty, athirst, parched with thirst, pinched with hunger, famished, dry, droughty *or* drouthy; hungry as a -hunter, -hawk, -horse, -church mouse.

greedy, -as a hog; overeager, voracious; ravenous, -as a wolf; open-mouthed, covetous, rapacious, grasping, extortionate, exacting, sordid, *alieni appetens* [*L.*]; insatiable, insatiate, unquenchable, quenchless; omnivorous.

unsatisfied, unsated, unslaked.

desirable; desired etc. *v.;* in demand, popular; pleasing etc. (*giving pleasure*) 829; appetizing, appetible; tantalizing.

adv. **fain**; with eager appetite; wistfully etc. *adj.*

int. would that! would it were! O for! if only! *esto perpetua!* [*L.*].

866. Indifference

n. **indifference**, neutrality; unconcern, insouciance, nonchalance; want of -interest, -earnestness; anorexia *or* anorexy, inappetence *or* inappetency; apathy etc. (*insensibility*) 823; supineness etc. (*inactivity*) 683; disdain etc. 930; recklessness etc. 863; inattention etc. 458; coldness etc. *adj.;* anaphrodisia.

anaphrodisiac *or* antaphrodisiac; lust-quencher, passion-queller.

v. **be indifferent** etc. *adj.;* stand neuter; take no interest in etc. (*insensibility*) 823; have no desire for etc. 865, have no taste for, have no relish for; not care for; care nothing -for, -about; not care a -straw etc. (*unimportance*) 643 -about, -for; not mind.

set at naught etc. (*make light of*) 483; spurn etc. (*disdain*) 930.

adj. **indifferent**, cold, frigid, luke-warm; cool, -as a cucumber; neutral, unconcerned, insouciant, phlegmatic, pococurantish, pococurante, easy-going, devil-may-care, careless, listless, lackadaisical; half-hearted, unambitious, unaspiring, undesirous, unsolicitous, unattracted, inappetent, all one to.

unattractive, unalluring, undesired, undesirable, uncared for, unwished, unvalued.

insipid etc. 391.

adv. for aught one cares; with utter indifference.

int. **never mind**! who cares! it's all one to me!

867. Dislike

n. **dislike**, distaste, disrelish, disinclination, displacency [*rare*].

reluctance; backwardness etc. (*unwillingness*) 603.

repugnance, disgust, queasiness, nausea, loathing, loathfulness [*rare*], aversion, averseness, aversation [*obs.*], abomination, antipathy, abhorrence, horror; mortal-, rooted- -antipathy, -horror; hatred, detestation; hate etc. 898; animosity etc. 900.

hydrophobia, canine madness; xenophobia, batophobia etc. (*nervousness*) 860; Anglophobia, Germanophobia, Slavophobia etc.

sickener; gall and wormwood etc. (*unsavory*) 395; shuddering, cold sweat.

v. **dislike**, mislike, disrelish; mind, object to; would rather not, not care for; have-, conceive-, entertain-, take- -a dislike, -an aversion- to; have no -taste, -stomach- for; shrug the shoulders at, shudder at, turn up the nose at, look askance at; make a -mouth, -wry face, -grimace; make faces.

shun, avoid etc. 623; eschew; withdraw-, shrink-, recoil - from; not be able to -bear, -abide, -endure.

loathe, nauseate, wamble [*obs. or dial. Eng.*], abominate, detest, abhor; hate etc. 898; take amiss etc. 900; have enough of etc. (*be satiated*) 869.

cause dislike, excite dislike; disincline, repel, sicken; make sick, render sick; turn one's stomach, nauseate, disgust, shock, stink in the nostrils; go against the -grain, -stomach; stick in the throat; make one's blood run cold etc. (*give pain*) 830; pall.

adj. **disliking** etc. *v.;* averse to, loath *or* loth, adverse; shy of, sick of, out of conceit with; disinclined; heartsick, dogsick; queasy.

disliked etc. *v.;* uncared for, unpopular, out of favor; repulsive, repugnant, repellent; abhorrent, insufferable, fulsome, nauseous, loathsome, loathful [*rare*], offensive; disgusting etc. *v.;* disagreeable etc. (*painful*) 830.

uneatable, inedible, inesculent [*rare*], unappetizing, unsavory.

adv. **to satiety**, to one's disgust; *usque ad nauseam* [*L.*].

int. faugh! foh! ugh!

868. Fastidiousness

n. **fastidiousness** etc. *adj.;* nicety, meticulosity, hypercriticism, difficulty in being pleased; *friandise* [*F.*], epicurism, *omnia suspendens naso* [*L.*].

discrimination, discernment, perspicacity, perspicaciousness [*rare*], keenness, sharpness, insight.

epicure, gourmet.

[excess of delicacy] prudery, prudishness, primness.

v. **be fastidious** etc. *adj.;* split hairs; hunt for the crumpled rose-leaf.

mince the matter; turn up one's nose at etc. (*disdain*) 930; look a gift horse in the mouth, see spots on the sun; see the mote in one's brother's eye.

discriminate, have nice discrimination; have exquisite taste; be discriminative etc. *adj.*

adj. **fastidious**, nice, delicate, *délicat* [*F.*]; meticulous, finicking *or* finicky *or* finikin, exacting, finical; difficult, dainty, lickerish, squeamish, thin-skinned; queasy; hard-, difficult- to please; querulous; particular, scrupulous; censorious etc. 932; hypercritical; overcritical.

prudish, strait-laced, prim.

discriminative, discriminating, discerning, discriminant [*rare*], judicious, keen, sharp, perspicacious.

869. Satiety

n. **satiety**, satisfaction, saturation, repletion, glut, surfeit; cloyment [*obs.*], satiation; weariness etc. 841.

spoiled child; *enfant gâté* [*F.*]; too much of a good thing, *toujours perdrix* [*F.*]; a diet of cake; *crambe repetita* [Juvenal].

v. **sate**, satiate, satisfy, saturate; cloy, quench, slake, pall, glut, gorge, surfeit; bore etc. (*weary*) 841; tire etc. (*fatigue*) 688; spoil.

have enough of, have quite enough of, have one's fill, have too much of; be satiated etc. *adj.*

adj. **satiated** etc. *v.;* overgorged; gorged with plenty, overfed; *blasé* [*F.*], used up [*colloq.*], sick of, heartsick.

int. **enough!** hold! *eheu jam satis!* [*L.*].

870. Wonder

n. **wonder**, marvel; astonishment, amazement, wonderment, bewilderment; amazedness etc. *adj.;* admiration, awe; stupor, stupefaction, stound [*obs.*], fascination; sensation; surprise etc. (*inexpectation*) 508.

note of admiration; thaumaturgy etc. (*sorcery*) 992.

v. **wonder**, marvel, admire; be surprised etc. *adj.;* start; stare; open-, rub-, turn up- one's eyes; gloar [*obs.*]; gape, open one's mouth, hold one's breath; look-, stand- -aghast, -agog;

315

look blank etc. (*disappointment*) 509; *tomber des nues* [*F.*]; not believe one's -eyes, −ears, −senses; not be able to account for etc. (*unintelligible*) 519; not know whether one stands on one's head or one's heels.

astonish, surprise, amaze, astound; dumfound *or* dumbfound, dumfounder *or* dumbfounder, startle, dazzle; daze; strike, −with - wonder, −awe; electrify; stun, stupefy, petrify, confound, bewilder, flabbergast [*colloq.*]; stagger, throw on one's beam ends, fascinate, turn the head, take away one's breath, strike dumb; make one's -hair stand on end, −tongue cleave to the roof of one's mouth; make one stare.

take by surprise, take unawares etc. (*be unexpected*) 508.

be wonderful etc. *adj.;* beggar−, baffle- description; stagger belief.

adj. **astonished**, surprised etc. *v.;* aghast, all agog, breathless, agape; open-mouthed; awe−, thunder−, moon−, planet- struck; spellbound; lost in -amazement, −wonder, −astonishment; struck all of a heap [*colloq.*], unable to believe one's senses; like a duck in -a fit, −thunder [*both colloq.*].

wonderful, wondrous; surprising etc. *v.;* unexpected etc. 508; unheard of; mysterious etc. (*inexplicable*) 519; miraculous.

monstrous, prodigious, stupendous, marvelous; inconceivable, incredible, inimaginable [*obs.*], unimaginable; strange etc. (*uncommon*) 83; passing strange.

striking etc. *v.;* overwhelming; wonder-working.

indescribable, inexpressible, ineffable; unutterable, unspeakable.

adv. **wonderfully** etc. *adj.;* fearfully; for a wonder, in the name of wonder; strange to say; *mirabile dictu* [*L.*], *mirabile visu* [*L.*]; to one's great surprise.

with wonder etc. *n.,* with gaping mouth, with open eyes, with upturned eyes; with the eyes starting out of one's head.

int. **lo**! lo and behold! O! heyday! halloo! what! indeed! really! surely! humph! hem! good -lack, −heavens, −gracious! gad so! welladay! dear me! only think! lackadaisy! my stars! my goodness! gracious goodness! goodness gracious! mercy on us! heavens and earth! God bless me! bless us! bless my heart! odzookens! *O gemini!* adzooks! hoity-toity! strong! Heaven save−, bless- the mark! can such things be! zounds! 'sdeath! what on earth! what in the world! who would have thought it! etc. (*inexpectation*) 508; you don't say so! what do you

say to that! *nous verrons!* [*F.*], how now! where am I? fancy! do tell! *Ciel!* [*F.*]; what do you know! [*slang*]; what do you know about that! [*slang*], well, I'll be jiggered! [*colloq.*].

871. Expectance
[absence of wonder]

n. **expectance**, expectancy etc. (*expectation*) 507.

imperturbability. imperturbableness, imperturbation, *sang-froid* [*F.*], calmness, unruffled calm, coolness, coldbloodedness, hardheadedness, steadiness, lack of nerves, want of imagination, practicality.

nothing out of the ordinary.

v. **expect** etc. 507; not be surprised, not wonder etc. 870; *nil admirari* [*L.*], make nothing of; take it coolly; be unamazed etc. *adj.;* display imperturbability etc. *n.*

adj. **expecting** etc. *v.;* unamazed, astonished at nothing; *blasé* [*F.*] etc. (*weary*) 841; expected etc. *v.;* foreseen.

imperturbable, nerveless, cool, cool-headed, unruffled, calm, steady, hard-headed, practical, unimaginative.

common, ordinary etc. (*habitual*) 613.

int. no wonder! of course! why not?

872. Prodigy

n. **prodigy**, phenomenon, wonder, wonderment, marvel, miracle; freak, freak of nature, *lusus naturae* [*L.*], monstrosity; monster etc. (*unconformity*) 83; curiosity, infant prodigy, lion, sight, spectacle; *jeu−, coup- de théâtre* [*F.*]; gazingstock; sign; St. Elmo's -fire, −light; portent etc. 512.

what no words can paint; wonders of the world; *annus mirabilis* [*L.*]; *dignus vindice nodus* [*L.*].

detonation; bursting of a -shell, −bomb, −mine; volcanic eruption, peal of thunder; thunderclap, thunderbolt, thunderstone [*obs. or dial. Eng.*].

873. Repute

n. **repute**, reputation; distinction, mark, name, figure; good−, high- repute; note, notability, notoriety, éclat, "the bubble reputation" [*As You Like It*], vogue, celebrity; fame, famousness; renown; popularity, *aura popularis* [*L.*]; approbation etc. 931; credit, *succès d'estime* [*F.*], prestige, talk of the town; name to conjure with.

account, regard, respect; reputability [*rare*], reputableness etc. *adj.;* respectability etc. (*probity*) 939; good -name, −report; fair name.

dignity; stateliness etc. *adj.;* solemnity, grandeur, splendor, nobility, majesty, sublimity; glory, honor; luster etc. (*light*) 420; illustriousness etc. *adj.*

rank, standing, brevet rank, precedence, *pas* [*F.*], station, place, status; position, –in society; order, degree, *locus standi* [*L.*], caste, condition.

graduation, university degree, baccalaureate, doctorate, doctorship; scholarship, fellowship.

eminence; greatness etc. *adj.;* height etc. 206; importance etc. 642; preëminence, supereminence; high mightiness, primacy; top of the -ladder, –tree; elevation; ascent etc. 305; superexaltation, exaltation, dignification [*rare*], aggrandizement; dedication, consecration, enthronement.

celebrity, worthy, hero, man of mark, great card, lion, *rara avis* [*L.*], notability, somebody; "the observed of all observers" [*Hamlet*]; classman; man of rank etc. (*nobleman*) 875; pillar of the -state, –church; "a mother in Israel" [*Bible*].

chief etc. (*master*) 745; first fiddle etc. (*proficient*) 700; scholar, *savant* [*F.*] etc. 492; cynosure, mirror; flower, pink, pearl; paragon etc. (*perfection*) 650; "the choice and master spirits of this age" [*Julius Caesar*]; *élite* [*F.*]; star, sun, constellation, galaxy.

ornament, honor, feather in one's cap, halo, aureole, nimbus; halo–, blaze- of glory; "blushing honors" [*Henry VIII*]; laurels etc. (*trophy*) 733.

posthumous fame, memory, niche in the temple of fame; celebration, canonization, enshrinement, glorification; immortality, immortal name; *magni nominis umbra* [Lucan].

v. **glory in**; be conscious of glory; be proud of etc. (*pride*) 878; exult etc. (*boast*) 884; be vain of etc. (*vanity*) 880.

be distinguished etc. *adj.;* shine etc. (*light*) 420; shine forth, figure; cut a figure, cut a dash [*colloq.*], make a splash [*colloq.*].

surpass, outshine, outrival, outvie, outjump, eclipse; throw–, cast- into the shade; overshadow.

rival, emulate, vie with.

gain *or* **acquire honor** etc. *n.;* live, flourish, glitter; flaunt; play first fiddle etc. (*be of importance*) 642; bear the -palm, –bell; lead the way, take precedence, take the wall of [*obs.*]; gain–, win- -laurels, –spurs, –golden opinions etc. (*approbation*) 931; graduate, take one's degree, pass one's examination; win a -scholarship, –fellowship.

make -a, –some- -noise, –noise in the world; leave one's mark, exalt one's horn, star, have a run, be run after; be lionized, come into vogue, come to the front; raise one's head.

honor; give–, do–, pay–, render- honor to; accredit, pay regard to, dignify, glorify; sing praises to etc. (*approve*) 931; look up to; exalt, aggrandize, elevate, nobilitate [*archaic*]; enthrone, signalize, immortalize, deify, exalt to the skies; hand one's name down to posterity.

consecrate; dedicate to, devote to; enshrine, inscribe, blazon, lionize, blow the trumpet, crown with laurel.

confer *or* reflect honor on etc. *n.;* shed a luster on; redound to one's honor, ennoble.

adj. **distinguished**, *distingué* [*F.*], noted; of note etc. *n.;* honored etc. *v.;* popular; fashionable etc. 852; remarkable etc. (*important*) 642; notable, notorious; celebrated, renowned, in every one's mouth, talked of, famous, famed, far-famed; conspicuous, to the front; foremost; in the -front rank, –ascendant.

in good odor; in favor, in high favor; reputable, respectable, creditable.

imperishable, deathless, immortal, never fading, fadeless, *aere perennius* [*L.*], time-honored.

illustrious, glorious, splendid, brilliant, radiant; bright etc. 420; full-blown; honorific.

eminent, prominent; high etc. 206; in the zenith; at the -head of, –top of the tree; peerless, of the first water; superior etc. 33; supereminent, preëminent.

great, dignified, proud, noble, honorable, worshipful, lordly, grand, stately, august, princely, imposing, solemn, transcendent, majestic, sacred, sublime, heaven-born, heroic, *sans peur et sans reproche* [*F.*]; sacrosanct.

int. **hail**! all hail! *ave!* [*L.*], *viva!* [*It.*], *vive!* [*F.*], long life to! glory–, honor- be to!

874. Disrepute

n. **disrepute**, discredit; ill–, bad- -repute, –name, –odor, –favor; disapprobation etc. 932; ingloriousness, derogation, abasement, debasement; abjectness etc. *adj.;* degradation, dedecoration [*rare*]; "a long farewell to all my greatness" [*Henry VIII*]; odium, obloquy, opprobrium, ignominy.

dishonor, disgrace, shame, crying–, burning-shame; humiliation; scandal, baseness, vileness; turpitude etc. (*improbity*) 940; infamy.

stigma, brand, reproach, imputation, slur, stain, blot, spot, blur; *scandalum magnatum* [*L.*], badge of infamy, blot in one's escutcheon; bend sinister, bar sinister, champain, point champain [*her.*]; byword of reproach; object of scorn, hissing [*archaic*]; Ichabod.

tarnish, taint, defilement, pollution.

argumentum ad verecundiam [*L.*]; sense of shame etc. 879.

v. **be inglorious** etc. *adj.;* incur disgrace etc. *n.;* have–, earn- a bad name; put–, wear- a halter round one's neck; disgrace–, expose- oneself.

play second fiddle; lose caste; "pale his uneffectual fire" [*Hamlet*]; recede into the shade; fall from one's high estate; keep in the background etc. (*modesty*) 881; be conscious of disgrace etc. (*humility*) 879; look -blue, –foolish, –like a fool; cut a -poor, –sorry- figure; laugh on the wrong side of the mouth [*colloq.*]; make a sorry face, go away with a flea in one's ear [*colloq.*], slink away.

cause shame etc. *n.;* shame, disgrace, put to shame, dishonor; throw–, cast–, fling–, reflect- dishonor etc. *n.* upon; be a reproach to etc. *n.;* derogate from.

tarnish, stain, blot, sully, taint; discredit; degrade, debase, defile; beggar; expel etc. (*punish*) 972.

stigmatize, vilify, defame, slur, cast a slur upon, impute shame to, brand, post, hold up to shame, send to Coventry; tread–, trample- under foot; show up [*colloq.*], drag through the mud, drag through the mire, heap dirt upon; reprehend etc. 932.

bring low, put down, snub; take down; take down a peg, –lower, –or two [*colloq.*].

obscure, eclipse, outshine, take the shine out of [*colloq.*]; throw–, cast- into the shade; overshadow; leave–, put- in the background; push into a corner, put one's nose out of joint [*colloq.*]; put out, put out of countenance.

disconcert, upset, throw off one's center, discompose; put to the blush etc. (*humble*) 879.

adj. **disgraced** etc. *v.;* blown upon; "shorn of its beams" [Milton], shorn of one's glory; overcome, downtrodden; loaded with shame etc. *n.;* in bad repute etc. *n.;* out of -repute, –favor, –fashion, –countenance; at a discount; under -a cloud, –an eclipse; unable to show one's face; in the -shade, –background; out at elbows, down in the world, down on one's uppers [*colloq.*], down and out.

inglorious, nameless, renownless, obscure, unknown to fame, unnoticed, unnoted, unhonored, unglorified.

discreditable, shameful, disgraceful, disreputable, despicable; questionable; unbecoming, unworthy, derogatory; degrading, humiliating, *infra dignitatem* [*L.*], dedecorous [*rare*]; scandalous, infamous, too bad, unmentionable, ribald, opprobrious; arrant, shocking, outrageous, notorious.

ignominious, scrubby, dirty, abject, vile, beggarly, pitiful, low, mean, petty, shabby; base etc. (*dishonorable*) 940.

adv. to one's shame be it spoken.

int. **shame!** fie! for shame! *proh pudor!* [*L.*]; *O tempora! O mores!* [*L.*]; ough! *sic transit gloria mundi!* [*L.*].

875. Nobility

n. **nobility**, rank, condition, distinction, optimacy [*rare*], blood, *pur sang* [*F.*], birth, high descent, order; quality, gentility; blue blood of Castile; "all the blood of all the Howards" [Pope]; caste of "Vere de Vere" [Tennyson]; *ancien régime* [*F.*].

high life, *haut monde* [*F.*]; upper classes, upper ten [*colloq.*], upper ten thousand; the four hundred; *élite* [*F.*], aristocracy, great folks; fashionable world etc. (*fashion*) 852.

personage–, man- of -distinction, –mark, –rank; notables, notabilities; celebrity, bigwig [*humorous*], magnate, great man, star; big bug, big gun, great gun [*colloq.*]; gilded rooster [*slang*]; *magni nominis umbra* [Lucan]; "every inch a king" [*Lear*].

[the nobility] peerage, baronage; house of -lords, –peers; lords, –temporal and spiritual; noblesse; knightage.

peer, noble, nobleman; lord, lording [*archaic*], lordling; grandee, magnifico, hidalgo; daimio, samurai, *shizoku* [*Jap.*]; don; aristocrat, swell [*colloq.*], three-tailed bashaw; gentleman, squire, squireen [*humorous, Eng.*], patrician; laureate.

gentry, gentlefolk; squirarchy *or* squirearchy, better sort, magnates, primates, optimates; pantisocracy.

king etc. (*master*) 745; atheling [*hist.*]; prince, duke, marquis, earl, viscount, baron, thane [*hist.*], banneret, baronet, knight, chevalier, count, armiger, esquire, laird [*Scot.*]; signior, seignior; *signor* [*It.*], *señor* [*Sp.*], *senhor* [*Pg.*]; boyar *or* boyard [*Russ.*]; effendi, sheik *or* sheikh, emir, shereef *or* sherif, pasha, sahib; palsgrave [*Ger. hist.*], waldgrave, margrave; vavasor [*feudal law*].

empress, queen, princess, duchess, marchioness, viscountess, countess; lady, *doña* [*Sp.*], *dona* [*Pg.*]; *signora* [*It.*], *señora* [*Sp.*], *senhora* [*Pg.*]; dame; memsahib.

[indian ruling chiefs] raja, rana, rao, rawal, rawat, rai, raikwar, raikbar, raikat; maharaja, maharana, maharao etc.; Gackwar [*lit.* cowherd; *Baroda*]; maharaja bahadur, raja bahadur, rai (*or* rao) bahadur; rai (*or* rao) sahib; jám, thakur [*all Hindu titles*].

nawab, wali, sultan, ameer *or* amir, mir, mirza, mian, khan; Nizam, nawab bahadur, khan bahadur, khan sahib [*all Moham. titles*].

sirdar *or* sardar, diwan *or* dewan [*both Hindu and Moham. titles*].

[honorifics] shahzada ["King's son"], kumar *or* kunwar ["prince"]; mirza [*when appended it signifies* "prince"; *when prefixed,* "Mr."]; arbab ["lord"]; malik ["master"]; khanzada ["son of a khan"]; huzur *or* huzoor ["the presence"].

[female titles] rani, maharani [*Hindu*]; sultana, malikah, begum *or* begam [*Moham.*].

shahzadi, kumari *or* kunwari, raj-kumari, malikzadi, khanam [*all equivalent to* "princess"].

[rank or office] kingship, dukedom, marquisate, earldom; viscountship, viscounty, viscountcy; lordship, baronetcy, knighthood, donship.

v. be noble etc. *adj.*

adj. **noble**, exalted; of rank etc. *n.;* princely, titled, patrician, aristocratic; highborn, well-born; of gentle blood; genteel, *comme il faut* [*F.*], gentlemanlike, courtly etc. (*fashionable*) 852; highly respectable.

adv. in high quarters.

876. Commonalty

n. **commonalty**, democracy; obscurity; low -condition, –life, –society, –company; *bourgeoisie* [*F.*]; mass of -the people, –society; Brown, Jones, and Robinson; Tom, Dick, and Harry; "the four million" [O. Henry]; the peepul [*humorous*]; lower–, humbler- -classes, –orders; vulgar–, common- herd; rank and file, *hoc genus omne* [*L.*]; the -many, –general, –crowd, –people, –populace, –multitude, –million, –masses, –mobility [*humorous*], –other half, –peasantry; king Mob; proletariat; *fruges consumere nati* [*L.*], *demos* [*Gr.*], *hoi polloi* [*Gr.*], great unwashed; man in the street.

rabble, –rout; chaff, rout, horde, canaille; scum–, residuum–, dregs- of -the people, –society; mob, swinish multitude, *foex populi* [*L.*]; trash; *profanum–, ignobile- vulgus* [*L.*]; vermin, raff, riffraff, rag-tag and bobtail; small fry.

commoner, one of the people, democrat, plebeian, republican, proletary, proletarian, proletaire, *roturier* [*F.*], John Smith, Mr.

Snooks, *bourgeois* [*F.*], *épicier* [*F.*], Philistine, cockney; grisette, demimonde, demimondaine.

peasant, countryman, boor, carl *or* carle [*Scot. or archaic*], churl; villain *or* villein [*obs. or rare*], serf; *terrae filius* [*L.*], kern *or* kerne [*Ir.*], gossoon [*Anglo-Ir.*]; tike *or* tyke [*archaic or dial.*], ryot [*India*], fellah [*Ar. pl.* fellahin *or* fellaheen]; docker, stevedore, longshoreman; swain, clown, hind [*Eng.*], clod, clodhopper, hobnail, yokel, bogtrotter, bumpkin; plowman *or* ploughman, plowboy *or* ploughboy; chuff, hayseed [*slang*], rustic, lunkhead [*colloq.*], loon [*archaic*], rube [*slang*], chaw-bacon [*slang*], tiller of the soil; hewers of wood and drawers of water; sons of Martha; groundling [*obs.*], gaffer, put, cub, Tony Lumpkin [Goldsmith], looby, lout, underling; gamin, street Arab, mudlark.

rough, rowdy, roughneck [*slang*], ruffian, tough [*colloq.*], pot-walloper [*slang*], scullion, slubberdegullion [*obs.*], vulgar–, low- fellow; cad.

upstart, parvenu, skipjack [*dial. Eng.*]; nobody, –one knows; *hesterni quirites* [*L.*], *pessoribus orti* [*L.*]; *bourgeois gentilhomme* [*F.*]; *novus homo* [*L.*], snob, gent [*vulgar or humorous*], mushroom, no one knows who, adventurer; *nouveau riche (pl. nouveaux riches; fem. nouvelles riches)* [*F.*].

vagabond, beggar, gaberlunzie [*Scot.*], beadsman *or* bedesman [*Scot.*], muckworm, *sans-culotte* [*F.*], tatterdemalion, caitiff, ragamuffin, pariah, outcast of society, tramp, bezonian [Shakespeare], panhandler [*slang*], sundowner [*Austral.*], bum [*slang*], hobo; chiffonier *or* chiffonnier [*rare*], ragman, ragpicker, sweeper, sweep, scrub.

wench, slut, quean, Cinderella.

barbarian, Goth, Vandal, Hottentot, Zulu, savage, Yahoo; unlicked cub, rough diamond.

barbarousness, barbarism, savagery; Boeotia; Philistinism; parvenuism, parvenudom.

v. **be ignoble** etc. *adj.,* be nobody etc. *n.;* be of (*or* belong to) the common herd etc. *n.*

adj. **ignoble**, common, mean, low, base, vile, sorry, scrubby, beggarly; below par; no great shakes etc. (*unimportant*) 643; homely, homespun, vulgar, low-minded; snobbish, parvenu, low bred; menial, underling, servile.

plebeian, proletarian; of -low, –mean- -parentage, –origin, –extraction; lowborn, baseborn, earthborn; mushroom, dunghill, risen from the ranks; unknown to fame, obscure, untitled.

rustic, country, uncivilized; loutish, boorish, clownish, churlish, brutish, raffish; rude, unpolished, unlicked.

barbarous, barbarian, barbaric, barbaresque [De Quincey].

cockney, born within sound of Bow bells.

adv. below the salt.

877. Title

n. **title**, honor; knighthood etc. (*nobility*) 875.

highness, excellency, grace, lordship, worship; reverence; reverend; esquire, sir, master, Mr., *signor* [*It.*], *señor* [*Sp.*], etc. 373; *Mein Herr* [*Ger.*], mynheer; your–, his- honor; serene highness.

madam, *madame* [*F.*] etc. (*mistress*) 374; empress, queen etc. 875.

decoration, laurel, palm, wreath, garland, bays, medal, ribbon, riband, blue ribbon, red ribbon, cordon, cross, crown, coronet, star, garter, fleece; feather, –in one's cap; epaulet *or* epaulette, chevron, *fourragère* [*F.*], colors, cockade; livery; order, arms, coat of arms, shield, escutcheon *or* scutcheon, crest; reward etc. 973; handle to one's name.

878. Pride

n. **pride**; haughtiness etc. *adj.;* high notions, hauteur; vainglory, crest; arrogance etc. (*assumption*) 885; self-importance, pomposity, pompousness; side [*slang*], swank, swagger, toploftiness [*colloq.*].

proud man, highflyer *or* highflier; fine gentleman; fine lady, *grande dame* [*F.*].

dignity, self-respect, *mens sibi conscia recti* [Virgil].

v. **be proud** etc. *adj.;* put a good face on; look in the face; stalk abroad, perk, perk up, perk oneself up; think no small beer of oneself [*colloq.*]; think no small potatoes of oneself [*colloq.*]; presume, swagger, strut; rear–, lift up–, hold up- one's head; hold one's head high, look big, take the wall; "bear like the Turk no rival near the throne" [Pope]; carry with a high hand; ride the–, mount on one's- high horse; set one's back up, bridle, toss the head; give oneself airs etc. (*assume*) 885; boast etc. 884.

pride oneself on; glory in, take a pride in; pique–, plume–, hug- oneself; stand upon, be proud of; not hide one's light under a bushel, not put one's talent in a napkin; not think small beer of oneself [*colloq.*] etc. (*vanity*) 880.

adj. **dignified**; stately, proud-crested, lordly, baronial; lofty-minded, high-souled, high-minded, high-mettled, high-plumed, high-flown, high-toned.

proud, haughty, lofty, high, mighty, swollen, puffed up, flushed, blown; vainglorious; purse-proud, fine; proud as -a peacock, –Lucifer; bloated with pride.

supercilious, disdainful, bumptious, magisterial, imperious, high-handed, high and mighty, overweening, consequential; pompous, toplofty [*colloq.*]; arrogant etc. 885; unblushing etc. 880.

stiff, stiff-necked; starched, perked up, stuck up [*colloq.*]; in buckram, strait-laced; prim etc. (*affected*) 855.

on one's dignity; on one's -high horse, –tight ropes, –high ropes; on stilts; *en grand seigneur* [*F.*].

adv. with head erect; *de haut en bas* [*F.*]; with nose in air, with nose turned up; with a sneer, with curling lip.

879. Humility

n. **humility**, humbleness, meekness, lowness, lowliness, lowlihood; abasement, self-abasement; submission etc. 725; resignation.

modesty, timidity etc. 881; verecundity [*obs.*], blush, suffusion, confusion; sense of -shame, –disgrace; humiliation, mortification; letdown, setdown.

condescension; affability etc. (*courtesy*) 894.

v. **be humble** etc. *adj.;* deign, vouchsafe, condescend; humble oneself, demean oneself [*colloq.*]; stoop, –to conquer; carry coals; submit etc. 725; submit with a good grace etc. (*brook*) 826; yield the palm.

lower one's -tone, –note; sing small [*colloq.*], draw in one's horns [*colloq.*], sober down; hide one's -face, –diminished head; not dare to show one's face, take shame to oneself, not have a word to say for oneself; feel–, be conscious of- -shame, –disgrace; be humiliated, be put out of countenance, be shamed, be put to the blush etc. *v.;* receive a snub; eat humble pie, eat crow, eat dirt; drink the cup of humiliation to the dregs.

blush for, blush up to the eyes; redden, change color; color up; hang one's head, look foolish, feel small.

render humble; humble, humiliate; let–, set–, take–, tread–, frown-down; snub, abash, abase, make one sing small [*colloq.*], strike dumb; teach one his distance; take down a peg, –lower; throw–, cast- into the shade etc. 874; stare–, put- out of countenance; put to the blush; confuse, ashame [*rare*], shame, mortify,

320

disgrace, crush; send away with a flea in one's ear [*colloq.*].

get a setdown.

adj. **humble**, lowly, meek; modest etc. 881; humble-minded, sober-minded; unoffended; submissive etc. 725; servile etc. 886.

condescending; affable etc. (*courteous*) 894.

humbled etc. *v.;* bowed down, resigned; abashed, ashamed, dashed; out of countenance; down in the mouth; down on one's -knees, −marrow-bones [*colloq.*], −uppers [*colloq.*]; humbled in the dust, brow-beaten; chapfallen, crestfallen; dumfoundered *or* dumbfoundered, flabber-gasted [*colloq.*], struck all of a heap [*colloq.*]; shorn of one's glory etc. (*disrepute*) 874.

adv. **humbly**; with downcast eyes, with bated breath, on bended knee; on all fours; with one's tail between one's legs.

under correction, with due deference.

880. Vanity

n. **vanity**; conceit, conceitedness; self-conceit, self-complacency, self-confidence, self-sufficiency, self-esteem, self-love, self-approbation, self-praise, self-glorification, self-laudation, self-gratulation, self-applause, self-admiration; *amour propre* [*F.*]; selfishness etc. 943.

pretensions, airs, affected manner, mannerism; egoism, egotism, priggism, priggishness; cox-combery, gaudery, vain-glory, elation; pride etc. 878; ostentation etc. 882; assurance etc. 885.

vox et praeterea nihil [*L.*].

egoist, egotist; peacock; coxcomb etc. 854; Sir Oracle etc. 887.

v. **be vain** etc. *adj.;* be vain of; pique oneself etc. (*pride*) 878; lay the flattering unction to one's soul.

have -too high, −an overweening- opinion of -oneself, −one's talents; blind oneself as to one's own merit; not think small beer of oneself [*colloq.*]; strut; put oneself forward; fish for compliments; give oneself airs etc. (*assume*) 885; boast etc. 884.

render vain etc. *adj.;* inspire with vanity etc. *n.;* inflate, puff up, turn one's head.

adj. **vain**, −as a peacock; conceited, overweening, pert, forward; vainglorious, high-flown; ostentatious etc. 882; puffed up, inflated, flushed.

self-satisfied, self-confident, self-sufficient, self-flattering, self-admiring, self-applauding, self-glorious, self-opinionated; *entêté* [*F.*] etc. (*wrong-headed*) 481; wise in one's own conceit, pragmatical [*rare*], overwise, pretentious, prig-

gish; egotistic *or* egotistical; *soidisant* [*F.*] etc. (*boastful*) 884; arrogant etc. 885; assured.

unabashed, unblushing, unconstrained, un-ceremonious; free and easy.

adv. **vainly** etc. *adj.*

881. Modesty

n. **modesty**; humility etc. 879; diffidence, timidity; retiring disposition; unobtrusiveness; bashful-ness etc. *adj.; mauvaise honte* [*F.*]; blush, blush-ing; verecundity [*obs.*]; self-knowledge.

reserve, constraint; demureness etc. *adj.;* "blush-ing honors" [*Henry VIII*].

[comparison] violet.

v. **be modest** etc. *adj.;* retire, reserve oneself; give way to; draw in one's horns etc. 879; hide one's face.

keep private, keep in the background, keep one's distance; pursue the noiseless tenor of one's way, "do good by stealth and blush to find it fame" [Pope], hide one's light under a bushel; cast sheep's eyes.

adj. **modest**, diffident; humble etc. 879; timid, timor-ous, bashful; shy, nervous, skittish, coy, sheep-ish, shame-faced, blushing, overmodest.

unpretending, unpretentious; unobtrusive, unas-suming, unostentatious, unboastful, unaspir-ing; poor in spirit; deprecative, deprecatory.

reserved, constrained, demure.

abashed, ashamed; out of countenance etc. (*humbled*) 879.

adv. **modestly** etc. *adj.;* quietly, privately; without -ceremony, −beat of drum; *sans façon* [*F.*].

882. Ostentation

n. **ostentation**, display, show, *coup d' oeil* [*F.*], flourish, parade, *étalage* [*F.*], pomp, magnifi-cence, splendor, pageantry, array, state, solem-nity; dash [*colloq.*], splash [*colloq.*], splurge [*colloq.*], glitter, strut, pomposity, pompous-ness; pretense, pretensions, showing off; fuss; grand doings.

demonstration, flying colors; flourish of trum-pets etc. (*celebration*) 883; pageant, spectacle, exhibition, exposition, procession, turnout [*colloq.*], set out; grand function; fête, gala, field day, review, march past, promenade, "insub-stantial pageant" [*Tempest*].

coup de théâtre [*F.*], stage effect, stage trick; clap-trap; *mise en scène* [*F.*], *tour de force* [*F.*], *chic* [*colloq., F.*].

dress; court-, full-, evening−, ball−, fancy-dress; tailoring, millinery, man millinery, frip-pery; foppery, equipage.

ceremony, ceremonial, ritual, form, formality, etiquette, puncto [obs.], punctilio, punctiliousness, starchedness, stateliness.

mummery, solemn mockery, mouth honor; tomfoolery; attitudinarianism.

attitudinarian; fop etc. 854; no modest violet.

v. **be ostentatious** etc. adj.; come forward, put oneself forward, attract attention, star; make–, cut- a -figure, –dash, –splash, –splurge [all colloq.]; strut; blow one's own trumpet; have no false modesty; figure; make a show, –display; glitter.

show off, show one's paces; parade, march past; display, exhibit, put forward, hold up; trot out [slang], hand out; sport [colloq.], brandish, blazon forth; dangle, –before the eyes; cry up etc. (praise) 931; prôner [F.], flaunt, emblazon, prink, set off, mount, have framed and glazed.

put on the mask; put a -good, –smiling- face upon; clean the outside of the platter etc. (disguise) 544.

adj. **ostentatious,** showy, dashing, pretentious, jaunty or janty, grand, pompous, high-sounding; turgid etc. (big-sounding) 577; garish or gairish; gaudy, –as a -peacock, –butterfly, –tulip; flaunting, flashing, flaming, glittering; gay etc. (ornate) 847.

splendid, magnificent, sumptuous, palatial.

theatrical, theatric, dramatic, spectacular, scenic, scenical; dramaturgic or dramaturgical.

ceremonial, ritual, ritualistic; solemn, stately, majestic, formal, stiff, ceremonious, punctilious, starched, starchy.

en grande tenue [F.], in one's best bib and tucker [colloq.], in one's Sunday best, endimanché [F.], chic [colloq., F.].

adv. with flourish of trumpet, with beat of drum, with flying colors, with a brass band; at the head of the procession; with no false modesty.

endimanché ad captandum vulgus [L.].

883. Celebration

n. **celebration,** solemnization, commemoration, ovation, triumph; lionization.

inauguration, installation, presentation; coronation; début [F.], coming out [colloq.]; Lord Mayor's show [London, Eng.]; harvest-home, husking bee, quilting bee; birthday, anniversary, biennial, triennial etc.; centenary, centennial; bicentenary, bicentennial; tercentenary, tercentennial etc.; "the day we celebrate"; redletter day; trophy etc. 733; jubilation, laudation, paean or pean; Te Deum etc. (thanksgiving) 990; festivity, festival, fête etc.

882; Forefathers' Day [U. S.], Independence Day, "the Glorious Fourth"; holiday etc. 840.

triumphal arch, bonfire; salute, salvo, salvo of artillery; feu de joie [F.], flourish of trumpets, fanfare, colors flying, illuminations.

[wedding anniversaries] wooden wedding [5th], tin wedding [10th], crystal wedding [15th], china wedding [20th], silver wedding [25th], golden wedding [50th], diamond wedding [60th].

jubilee, 50th anniversary; diamond jubilee, 60th anniversary.

v. **celebrate,** keep, signalize, do honor to, commemorate, solemnize, hallow; keep high festival, keep holiday; mark with a red letter.

pledge, drink to, toast; hob and nob, hobnob with; present.

inaugurate, install, instate, induct, chair.

rejoice etc. 838; kill the fatted calf, hold jubilee; roast an ox, serve up the Thanksgiving turkey, serve up the Christmas goose; fire a salute, dip the colors, present arms; paint the town red [colloq.]; maffick [colloq., Eng.].

adj. **celebrating** etc. v.; commemorative, celebrated, immortal; solemn, jubilant; kept, kept in remembrance.

adv. **in honor of,** in commemoration of, in celebration of, in memory of; as a toast.

int. **hail!** all hail! "see the conquering hero comes!" "Hail! hail! the gang's all here!"

884. Boasting

n. **boasting** etc. v.; boast, vaunt, crake [obs.], pretense, pretensions, cock-a-hoopness, braggadocio, braggadocianism, puff [colloq.], puffery; flourish, fanfaronade; gasconade, bluff, highfaluting or highfalutin, blague [F.]; side [slang, Eng.], swagger, jingoism, spread-eagleism; brag, braggartism or braggardism, braggartry, bounce, rant, bluster, bravado, bunk or buncombe or bunkum; jactation, jactitation, jactancy; venditation [obs.], vaporing, rodomontade, bombast, gas [slang], hot air [slang], fine talking, tall talk, tall story [both colloq.], fish story [humorous]; magniloquence, teratology [obs.], heroics; chauvinism; exaggeration etc. 549; vanity etc. 880; vox et praeterea nihil [L.]; much cry and little wool, brutum fulmen [L.].

exultation, gloriation [obs.], glorification; flourish of trumpets; triumph etc. 883.

boaster, braggart, braggadocio, fanfaron, pretender, bluffer, blower [slang], blower of his own trumpet, windbag [slang], hot-air artist [*slang*], Fourth of July orator; Thraso, Gascon; chauvinist, jingo, jingoist; blusterer, swaggerer etc. 887; charlatan, trumpeter; puppy etc. (*fop*) 854.

v. **boast**, make a boast of, brag, vaunt, puff, show off, flourish, crake [*obs.*], crack, trumpet, strut, swagger, *blague* [*F.*], gasconade, vapor; blow [*slang*], four-flush [*slang*], bluff; talk big, draw the long bow, speak for Buncombe; *faire claquer son fouet* [*F.*], blow one's own trumpet; put on side [*slang, Eng.*], swank [*dial. Eng.*]; let the American eagle scream, sing "Rule, Britannia," indulge in jingoism; *se faire valoir* [*F.*], take merit to oneself, make a merit of; holloa before one is out of the wood.

exult; crow, crow over [*both colloq.*], triumph, glory, jubilate, rejoice, maffick [*colloq., Eng.*], throw up one's cap, yell oneself hoarse, cheer. gloat, gloat over; chuckle; neigh.

adj. **boasting** etc. *v.;* magniloquent, flaming, thrasonic [*rare*], thrasonical, stilted, gasconading, braggart, boastful, pretentious; vainglorious etc. (*conceited*) 880; highfaluting *or* highfalutin; spread-eagle [*colloq. & humorous*].

elate, elated, jubilant, triumphant, exultant; in high feather; flushed, –with victory; cock-a-hoop, cock-a-hoopish; on stilts [*colloq.*]. vaunted etc. *v.*

adv. **vauntingly** etc. *adj.;* in triumph; with a blare of trumpets.

885. Insolence
[undue assumption of superiority]

n. **insolence**, brashness, brazenness, malapertness; haughtiness etc. *adj.;* arrogance, airs; bumptiousness, toploftiness [*colloq.*], assumption, presumption; assumption of infallibility; contumely, disdain, insult; overbearance, domineering etc. *v.;* bluster, swagger, swaggering etc. *v.;* bounce; terrorism; tyranny etc. 739; beggar on horseback; usurpation.

impertinence, cheek [*colloq. or slang*], nerve [*slang*], nerviness [*slang*], sauce [*colloq.*], abuse; sauciness etc. *adj.;* flippancy, dicacity [*obs.*], petulance [*rare in this sense*], procacity [*rare*].

impudence, self-assertion, assurance, audacity, hardihood; front, face, brass, gall [*slang*]; shamelessness etc. *adj.;* effrontery, hardened front, face of brass.

jingoism, chauvinism; *Kultur* [*Ger.*], "might is right," *Macht ist Recht* [*Ger.*].

malapert, saucebox etc. (*blusterer*) 887.

jingo, jingoist, chauvinist; fire eater [*colloq.*]; boaster etc. 884.

v. **be insolent** etc. *adj.;* bluster, vapor, swagger, swell, give oneself airs, snap one's fingers, kick up a dust [*colloq.*]; swear etc. (*affirm*) 535; rap out oaths; roister.

arrogate, assume, presume; make bold, make free; take a liberty, give an inch and take an ell.

outface, outlook, outstare, outbrazen, outbrave; stare out of countenance; brazen out; lay down the law; teach one's grandmother to suck eggs [*colloq.*]; assume a lofty bearing; talk big, look big, put on big looks, act the *grand seigneur;* mount–, ride- the high horse; toss the head, carry with a high hand; tempt Providence; want snuffing [*colloq.*].

domineer, bully, dictate, hector; lord it over; *traiter–, regarder- de haut en bas* [*F.*]; exact; snub, huff, beard, fly in the face of; put to the blush; bear–, beat- down; browbeat, intimidate; trample–, tread- -down, –under foot; dragoon, ride roughshod over; bulldoze [*colloq.*], terrorize.

adj. **insolent**, haughty, arrogant, imperious, magisterial, dictatorial, arbitrary; high-handed, high and mighty; contumelious, supercilious, overbearing, toplofty [*colloq.*], toploftical [*rare*], intolerant, domineering, overweening, high-flown; precocious, assuming, would-be, bumptious.

pert, flippant, fresh [*slang*], brash, cavalier, saucy, forward, impertinent, malapert; impudent, audacious, presumptuous.

brazen, bluff, shameless, aweless, unblushing, unabashed; bold-faced, bare-faced, brazen-faced; dead–, lost- to shame.

blustering, swaggering, hectoring, rollicking, roistering, vaporing, free and easy, devil-may-care, jaunty *or* janty; thrasonic [*rare*], thrasonical, fire-eating [*colloq.*]; "full of sound and fury" [*Macbeth*].

jingo, jingoistic, chauvinistic.

adv. **insolently** etc. *adj.;* with nose in air; with arms akimbo; *de haut en bas* [*F.*]; with a high hand; *ex cathedra* [*L.*].

886. Servility

n. **servility**; slavery etc. (*subjection*) 749; obsequiousness etc. *adj.;* subserviency; abasement, prostration, prosternation [*obs.*]; genuflection etc. (*worship*) 990; toadeating; fawning etc. *v.;* tufthunting, timeserving, flunkyism *or* flunkeyism; sycophancy etc. (*flattery*) 933; humility etc. 879.

sycophant, parasite; toad, toady, toadeater, tufthunter; snob, flunky *or* flunkey, lapdog, spaniel, lick-spit, lick-spittle, smell-feast, *Graeculus esuriens* [*L.*], hanger on, *cavalier (or cavaliere) servente* [*It.*], led captain, carpet knight; timeserver, fortune hunter, Vicar of Bray, Sir Pertinax MacSycophant, pickthank; flatterer etc. 935; doer of dirty work; *âme damnée* [*F.*], tool; reptile; slave etc. (*servant*) 746; *homme de cour* [*F.*], courtier; beat [*slang*], dead beat [*slang*], doughface [*slang*]; heeler, ward heeler [*both polit. cant*]; jackal, sponge, sponger, sucker [*slang*], tagtail, truckler.

v. **cringe**, bow, stoop, kneel, bend the knee; fall on one's knees, prostrate oneself; worship etc. 990.

fawn, crouch, cower, sneak, crawl, sponge, truckle, toady, truckle to, grovel, lick the feet of, lick one's shoes, make a doormat of oneself, kiss the hem of one's garment; be servile etc. *adj.*

pay court to; feed on, fatten on, batten on, dance attendance on, follow at heel, pin oneself upon, hang on the sleeve of, *avaler les couleuvres* [*F.*], keep time to, fetch and carry, do the dirty work of.

go with the stream, follow the crowd, worship the rising sun, hold with the hare and run with the hounds; get on the band wagon; be a timeserver etc. *n.*

adj. **servile**, obsequious; supple, –as a glove; soapy [*slang*], oily, pliant, cringing, abased, doughfaced [*colloq.*], fawning, slavish, groveling, reptilian, sniveling, mealy-mouthed; beggarly, sycophantic, parasitical; abject, prostrate, down on one's marrowbones [*jocular or slang*]; base, mean, sneaking; crouching etc. *v.;* timeserving.

adv. **with servility** etc. *n.;* hat-, cap- in hand; "in a bondman's key" [*Merchant of Venice*]; "with bated breath and whispering humbleness" [*ibid.*].

int. so please you! as my lord wills! don't mind me!

887. Blusterer

n. **blusterer**, swaggerer, vaporer, roisterer, brawler; fanfaron; braggart etc. (*boaster*) 884; bully, terrorist, rough, ruffian, rough-neck [*slang*], tough [*colloq.*], rowdy, bulldozer [*colloq.*], roarer [*slang, obs.*], slang-whanger [*slang*], larrikin [*Austral. & Eng.*]; hoodlum [*colloq.*], hooligan [*slang*], Mohock, Mohawk [*rare*], Drawcansir, swashbuckler, Captain Bobadil, Sir Lucius O'-Trigger, Thraso, Pistol, Parolles, Bombastes Furioso, Hector, Chrononhotonthologos; jingo; desperado, dare-devil, fire eater [*colloq.*]; fury etc. (*violent person*) 173.

puppy etc. (*fop*) 854, jackanapes, bantam-cock; malapert, saucebox [*colloq.*]; minx, hussy.

dogmatist, doctrinaire, Sir Oracle, stump orator etc. 582; prig, Jack-in-office.

Section 3. Sympathetic

888. Friendship

n. **friendship**, amity; friendliness etc. *adj.;* brotherhood, fraternity, sodality, confraternity; sorority, sorosis, sisterhood; harmony etc. (*concord*) 714; peace etc. 721.

firm–, staunch–, intimate–, familiar–, bosom–, cordial–, tried–, devoted–, lasting–, fast–, sincere–, warm–, ardent- friendship.

cordiality, fraternization, association, *entente cordiale* [*F.*], good understanding, *rapprochement* [*F.*], sympathy, fellow-feeling, response, welcomeness; affection etc. (*love*) 897; partiality, favoritism; good will etc. (*benevolence*) 906.

acquaintance, introduction, familiarity, intimacy, intercourse, fellowship, knowledge of.

v. **be friendly** etc. *adj.*, be friends etc. 890, be acquainted with etc. *adj.;* know; have the ear of; keep company with etc. (*sociality*) 892; hold communication with, have dealings with, sympathize with; have a leaning to; bear good will etc. (*benevolent*) 906; love etc. 897; make much of; befriend etc. (*aid*) 707; introduce to.

set one's horses together; have the latchstring out; hold out–, extend- the right hand of -friendship, –fellowship; become friendly etc. *adj.;* make friends etc. (890) with; break the ice, be introduced to; pick up acquaintance; make–, scrape- acquaintance with; get into favor, gain the friendship of.

shake hands with, strike hands with, fraternize, sororize [*rare*], embrace; receive with open arms, throw oneself into the arms of; meet halfway, take in good part.

adj. **friendly**, amicable, amical; well-affected, unhostile, neighborly; brotherly, fraternal, sisterly, sororal [*rare*]; ardent, devoted, sympathetic, harmonious, hearty, cordial, warm-hearted.

friends with, at home with, hand in hand with; on -good, –friendly, –amicable, –cordial, –familiar, –intimate- -terms, –footing; on speaking terms, on visiting terms, on one's visiting list; in one's good -graces, –books.

acquainted, familiar, intimate, thick, hand and glove, hail fellow well met, free and easy; welcome.

adv. **amicably** etc. *adj.;* with open arms, *à bras ouverts* [*F.*]; *sans cérémonie* [*F.*]; arm in arm.

889. Enmity

n. **enmity**, hostility, antagonism; unfriendliness etc. *adj.;* discord etc. 713; bitterness, rancor; heartburning; animosity etc. 900; malevolence etc. 907.

alienation, estrangement; dislike etc. 867; aversion, hate etc. 898.

v. **be unfriendly** etc. *adj.;* keep–, hold- at arm's length; be at loggerheads; bear malice etc. 907; fall out; take umbrage etc. 900; harden the heart, alienate, estrange.

adj. **unfriendly**, inimical, hostile; at enmity, at variance, at daggers drawn, at open war with; up in arms against; in bad odor with.

on bad terms, not on speaking terms; cool, cold, cold-hearted; estranged, alienated, disaffected, irreconcilable.

890. Friend

n. **friend**, –of one's bosom; *alter ego* [*L.*], other self; intimate, confidant (*masc.*), confidante (*fem.*), confident; best–, bosom–, fast-friend; *amicus usque ad aras* [*L.*], *fidus Achates* [*L.*]; *persona grata* [*L.*]; well-wisher; neighbor *or* neighbour, acquaintance.

favorer, fautor [*rare*], patron, backer, Maecenas; tutelary saint, good genius, advocate, partisan, sympathizer; ally; friend in need etc. (*auxiliary*) 711.

associate, consociate, compeer, comrade, mate, companion, *camarade* [*F.*], *confrère* [*F.*], colleague, comate, copemate *or* copesmate [*obs.*]; partner; side-partner, copartner, consort; old–, crony; chum [*colloq.*], pal [*slang*], buddy [*slang*]; playfellow, playmate, schoolfellow; bedfellow, bunkie [*colloq.*], bedmate, chamberfellow; classfellow, classman, classmate; roommate, shopmate, shipmate, messmate; fellow–, boon–, pot- companion; fellow-man, stable companion; best man, bridesmaid, maid of honor.

[famous friendships] Pylades and Orestes, Castor and Pollux, Achilles and Patroclus, Diomedes and Sthenalus, Hercules and Iolaus, Theseus and Pirithoüs, Epaminondas and Pelopidas, Nisus and Euryalus, Damon and Pythias, David and Jonathan, Christ and the beloved disciple; Soldiers Three, the Three Musketeers.

par nobile fratrum [*L., often ironical*]; *Arcades ambo* [*L.*].

host, hostess (*fem.*), Amphitryon, Boniface.

guest, visitor, frequenter, habitué, *protégé* [*F.*].

compatriot; fellow–, countryman; fellow townsman, townie [*slang*].

int. "Thank God for a trusty chum!" [Kipling].

891. Enemy

n. **enemy**; antagonist; foe, foeman; open–, bitter-enemy; opponent etc. 710; backfriend [*obs.*], copemate *or* copesmate [*obs.*], "dearest foe"; mortal -aversion, –antipathy; snake in the grass.

public enemy, enemy to society; anarchist, seditionist, traitor, traitress (*fem.*).

892. Sociality

n. **sociality**, sociability, sociableness etc. *adj.;* social intercourse, consociation, intercourse, intercommunion; consortship, companionship, comradeship, fellowship; urbanity etc. (*courtesy*) 894; intimacy, familiarity; clubbability *or* clubability [*colloq.*], clubbism; *esprit de corps* [*F.*]; *morale* [*F.*].

conviviality; good- fellowship, –company; joviality, jollity, *savoir vivre* [*F.*], *joie de vivre* [*F.*], festivity, festive board, walnuts and wine, merrymaking; loving cup; hospitality, heartiness; cheer; "the feast of reason and the flow of soul" [Pope].

welcome, welcomeness, greeting; hearty–, warm–, welcome- reception; hearty welcome; hearty–, warm- greeting; the glad hand [*slang*].

boon companion; good–, jolly-fellow; *bon enfant* [*F.*], bawcock [*archaic*], crony, *bon vivant* [*F.*]; a good mixer [*colloq.*].

social–, family- circle; family hearth; circle of acquaintance, coterie, society, company; club etc. (*association*) 712.

social gathering, social reunion; assembly etc. (*assemblage*) 72; barbecue; bee; corn-husking, corn-shucking; husking, husking-bee; hen party [*colloq.*]; house raising, house-warming, hanging of the crane; infare *or* infair [*Scot. & dial., U. S.*]; smoker, –party [*both colloq.*]; Dutch treat [*colloq.*]; stag, –party [*both colloq.*]; sociable, tamasha [*Hind.*], party, entertainment, reception, levee, at home, *conversazione* [*It.*], *soirée* [*F.*], matinée; evening–, morning–, afternoon–, garden–, coming-out–, surprise- party; *partie carrée* [*F.*]; kettledrum, drum, drum major, rout [*archaic*], tempest, hurricane; *ridotto* [*It.*]; ball, hunt ball, dance, dinner dance, festival etc. (*amusement*) 840.

[social meals] breakfast, wedding breakfast, hunt breakfast; luncheon, lunch; picnic lunch, basket lunch, picnic; tea, afternoon tea, five o'clock tea, cup of tea, dish of tea [*esp. Brit.*], *thé dansant* [*F.*], coming-out tea [*colloq.*]; tea party, tea fight [*slang*]; dinner, potluck, bachelor dinner, stag dinner [*colloq.*], hunt dinner; church supper, high tea; banquet etc. 298.

visit, visiting; round of visits; call, morning call; interview etc. (*interlocution*) 588; assignation; tryst, trysting place; appointment.

v. be sociable etc. *adj.;* know; be acquainted etc. *adj.;* associate with, sort with, consort with, keep company with, walk hand in hand with; eat off the same trencher, club together, consort, bear one company, join; consociate [*rare*], intercommunicate, intercommune [*rare*], make acquaintance with etc. (*friendship*) 888; make advances, fraternize, embrace.

visit, pay a visit; interchange -visits, –cards; call at, call upon; leave a card; drop in, look in, look one up, beat up one's quarters [*colloq.*].

receive hospitality; be–, feel–, make oneself- at home with; make free with; crack a bottle with; take potluck with; live at free quarters; find the latchstring out.

entertain; give a party etc. *n.;* be at home, see one's friends, keep open house, do the honors; receive, –with open arms; welcome; give a warm reception etc. *n.* to; kill the fatted calf.

adj. **sociable**, companionable, clubbable *or* clubable [*colloq.*], clubbish; conversable, cozy *or* cosy *or* cosey, chatty, conversational; convivial, festive, festal, jovial, jolly, hospitable.

welcome, –as roses in May; fêted, entertained.

free and easy, hail fellow well met, familiar, intimate, consociate, consociated; associated with etc. *v.;* on visiting terms, acquainted; social, neighborly.

international, cosmopolitan; gregarious.

adv. **sociably** etc. *adj.;* *en famille* [*F.*], in the family circle; on terms of intimacy; in the social whirl; *sans -façon, –cérémonie* [*F.*], arm in arm.

893. Seclusion. Exclusion

n. **seclusion**, privacy, retirement, eremitism, anchoretism, anchoritism, reclusion, recess; suspension; snugness etc. *adj.;* concealment, delitescence; rustication, *rus in urbe* [*L.*], ruralism, rurality [*rare*], solitude; solitariness etc. (*singleness*) 87; isolation; "splendid isolation"; loneliness etc. *adj.;* estrangement from the world, voluntary exile; aloofness.

depopulation, desertion, desolation; wilderness etc. (*unproductive*) 169; howling wilderness; rotten borough, Old Sarum [*Eng.*].

retreat, cell, hermitage, cloister; convent etc. 1000; *sanctum sanctorum* [*L.*], study, library, den [*colloq.*].

exclusion, excommunication, banishment, exile, ostracism, proscription; economic pressure; cut, cut direct; dead cut.

unsociability, unsociableness, dissociability, dissociality; inhospitality, inhospitableness etc. *adj.;* domesticity, self-sufficiency, Darby and Joan.

recluse, hermit, eremite, anchoret *or* anchorite, anchorist [*obs.*]; santon; stylite, pillarist, pillar-saint [*all Ch. hist.*]; St. Simeon Stylites; caveman, cave-dweller, troglodyte, Timon of Athens, solitarian [*obs.*], solitaire, ruralist [*obs.*], disciple of Zimmermann, closet cynic, cynic, Diogenes.

outcast, pariah, leper; outsider, rank outsider; castaway, pilgarlic [*low*], wastrel [*dial. Eng.*], losel, foundling; wilding.

v. **be** *or* **live secluded** etc. *adj.;* keep–, stand–, hold oneself- -aloof, –in the background; keep snug; shut oneself up; deny oneself, seclude oneself; creep into a corner, rusticate, dissocialize; retire, –from the world; hermitize; take the veil; abandon etc. 624; sport one's oak [*Univ. slang, Eng.*].

exclude, repel; cut, –dead; refuse to -associate with, –acknowledge; send to Coventry, look cool–, turn one's back–, shut the door- upon; blackball, excommunicate, exile, expatriate; banish, outlaw, maroon, ostracize, proscribe, cut off from, keep at arm's length, draw a cordon round, boycott, embargo, blockade, isolate.

depopulate, dispeople, unpeople; desolate, devastate.

adj. **secluded**, sequestered, retired, delitescent, private, by; in a backwater; out of the world, out of the way; "the world forgetting by the world forgot" [*Pope*].

unsociable, unsocial, dissocial, inhospitable, cynical, inconversable [*obs.*], unclubbable *or* unclubable [*colloq.*], *sauvage* [*F.*]; hermitical, eremitic *or* eremitical, anchoretic *or* anchoretical, anchoritic *or* anchoritical, anchoretish, anchoritish, troglodytic.

snug, domestic, stay-at-home.

excluded etc. *v.;* unfrequented, unvisited, unintroduced, uninvited, unwelcome; on the fringe of society; under a cloud, left to shift for oneself; deserted, –in one's utmost need; unfriended, friendless, kithless, homeless, desolate, lorn, forlorn; solitary, lonely, lonesome, isolated, single, estranged; derelict, outcast, outside the gates, "yammering at the bars"; banished etc. *v.;* under an embargo.

uninhabited, unoccupied, untenanted, tenantless, abandoned; uninhabitable.

894. Courtesy

n. **courtesy;** respect etc. 928; good- manners, –behavior, –breeding; manners; politeness etc. *adj.; bienséance* [F.], urbanity, comity, gentility, breeding, gentle breeding, cultivation, culture, polish, presence; civility, civilization; amenity, suavity; good temper, good humor, amiability, easy temper, complacency, soft tongue, mansuetude [*archaic*]; condescension etc. (*humility*) 879; affability, complaisance, compliance, *prévenance* [F.], amiability, gallantry, chivalry; fine flower of -courtesy, –chivalry.

pink of courtesy, pink of politeness; flower of knighthood, *chevalier sans peur et sans reproche,* Bayard, Sidney, "a verray parfit gentil knight" [Chaucer], Chesterfield; Launcelot, Gawaine, Colonel Newcome; "gentle Shakespeare" [Ben Jonson].

compliment; fair-, soft-, sweet- words; honeyed phrases, ceremonial; salutation, reception, presentation, introduction, *accueil* [F.], greeting, recognition; welcome, abord [*obs.*], respects, *devoir* [F.], duty [*archaic*], regards, remembrances; kind -regards, –remembrances; deference, love, best love, empty encomium, flattering remark, hollow commendation; salaams.

[forms of greeting] obeisance etc. (*reverence*) 928; bow, curtsy *or* curtsey, scrape, salaam, kotow *or* kowtow [*China*], bowing and scraping; kneeling; genuflection etc. (*worship*) 990; obsequiousness etc. 886; capping, pulling the forelock, making a leg [*colloq.*], shaking hands, etc. *v.;* grip of the hand; embrace, hug, squeeze, kiss, buss, smack; salute, accolade; loving cup, *vin d'honneur* [F.], pledge; love token etc. (*endearment*) 902.

mark of recognition, nod; "nods and becks and wreathed smiles" [Milton]; valediction etc. 293; condolence etc. 915.

v. **be courteous** etc. *adj.;* show courtesy etc. *n.*

mind one's P's and Q's [*colloq.*], behave oneself, be all things to all men, conciliate, speak one fair, take in good part; do the amiable [*colloq.*]; look as if butter would not melt in one's mouth; mend-, mind- one's manners.

do the honors, usher, usher in, receive, greet, hail, bid welcome; welcome, –with open arms; shake hands; hold out-, press-, squeeze- the hand; bid Godspeed; speed the parting guest; cheer, serenade.

visit, wait upon, present oneself, pay one's respects, pay a visit etc. (*sociability*) 892; dance attendance on etc. (*servility*) 886; pay attentions to; do homage to etc. (*respect*) 928; give *or* send one's regards to etc. *n.*

salute; embrace etc. (*endearment*) 902; kiss, –hands; drink to, pledge, hob and nob; move to [*colloq.*], nod to; smile upon.

uncover, cap; touch-, raise-, lift-, take off- the hat; doff the cap; tip the hat to [*slang*]; pull the forelock; present arms; make way for; bow, make one's bow, make a leg scrape, curtsy *or* curtsey, bow and scrape, bob a curtsy, kneel; bow-, bend- the knee; salaam, kotow *or* kowtow [*China*]; prostrate oneself etc. (*worship*) 990.

render polite etc. *adj.;* polish, rub off the -corners, –rough edges; cultivate, civilize, humanize.

adj. **courteous,** polite, civil, mannerly, urbane; well-behaved, well-mannered, well-bred, well-brought up; gently bred; of gentle -manners, –breeding; good-mannered, polished, civilized, cultivated; refined etc. (*taste*) 850; gentlemanlike etc. (*fashion*) 852; gallant, chivalrous, chivalric; on one's good (*or* best) behavior.

ingratiating, winning; gentle, mild; good-humored, cordial, gracious, amiable, tactful, affable, familiar; neighborly; obliging, complaisant, complacent, conciliatory.

bland, suave; fine-, fair-, soft- spoken; honey-mouthed, honey-tongued; oily, oily-tongued, unctuous; obsequious etc. 886.

adv. **courteously** etc. *adj.;* with a good grace; with open arms, with outstretched arms, *à bras ouverts* [F.]; *suaviter in modo* [L.], with perfect courtesy, in good humor.

int. **hail!** welcome! well met! *ave!* [L.]; all hail! good -day, –morrow, –morning, –evening, –afternoon, –night! sweet dreams! Godspeed! *pax vobiscum!* [L.]; all good go with you! may your shadow never be less!

895. Discourtesy

n. **discourtesy;** ill-breeding; ill-, bad-, ungainly- manners; tactlessness; uncourteousness etc. *adj.;* rusticity, inurbanity, illiberality, incivility, displacency [*obs.*]; lack *or* want of courtesy etc. 894; disrespect etc. 929; procacity [*obs.*], impudence, misbehavior, barbarism, barbarity; brutality, brutishness, brutification, blackguardism, conduct unbecoming a gentleman, *grossièreté* [*F.*], *brusquerie* [*F.*], vulgarity etc. 851.

bad temper, ill temper; peevishness, surliness; churlishness etc. *adj.;* spinosity, perversity; moroseness etc. (*sullenness*) 901*a*.

sternness etc. *adj.;* austerity; moodishness, captiousness etc. 901; cynicism; tartness etc. *adj.;* acrimony, acerbity, virulence, asperity.

scowl, black looks, frown; sulks, short answer, rebuff; hard words, contumely; unparliamentary language, personality.

bear, bruin, grizzly, grizzly bear; brute, blackguard, beast; unlicked cub; frump [*colloq.*], crosspatch [*colloq.*]; grouch, old grouch; saucebox etc. 887; crooked stick.

v. **be rude** etc. *adj.;* insult etc. 929; treat with discourtesy; take a name in vain; make bold with, make free with; take a liberty; stare out of countenance, ogle, point at, put to the blush.

cut; turn one's back upon, turn on one's heel; give the cold shoulder; keep at -a distance, −arm's length; look -cool, −coldly, −black- upon; show the door to, send away with a flea in the ear [*colloq.*].

lose one's temper etc. (*resentment*) 900; mump [*dial.*], sulk etc. 901*a;* frown, scowl, glower, pout; snap, snarl, growl.

render rude etc. *adj.;* brutalize, brutify.

adj. **discourteous**, uncourteous, uncourtly; ill-bred, ill-mannered, ill-behaved, ill-conditioned, unbred; unmannerly, unmannered, impolite, unpolite, uncivil, ungracious, unceremonious, cool; unpolished, uncivilized, ungenteel, ungentlemanlike, ungentlemanly; unladylike; blackguard; vulgar etc. 851; dedecorous [*obs.*]; foul-mouthed, foul-spoken; abusive.

pert, forward, obtrusive, impudent, rude, saucy, procacious [*archaic*], brash; flippant etc. (*insolent*) 885.

repulsive; uncomplaisant, unaccommodating, unneighborly, ungallant; inaffable; ungentle, ungainly, rough, rugged, bluff, blunt, gruff; churlish, boorish, bearish; brutal, brusque, stern, harsh, austere; cavalier.

bad-tempered, ill-tempered, ill-humored; out of -temper, −humor; crusty, tart, sour, crabbed, sharp, short, trenchant, sarcastic, biting, doggish, currish, caustic, virulent, bitter, acrimonious, venomous, contumelious; snarling etc. *v.;* surly, −as a bear; perverse; grim, sullen etc. 901*a;* peevish etc. (*irascible*) 901; bristling, thorny, spinose, spinous.

adv. **discourteously** etc. *adj.;* with discourtesy etc. *n.*, with a bad grace.

896. Congratulation

n. **congratulation**, gratulation, felicitation; salute etc. 894; condolence etc. 915; compliments of the season; good wishes, best wishes.

v. **congratulate**, gratulate, felicitate; give joy, wish one joy; compliment; tender−, offer- one's congratulations; wish many happy returns of the day, wish a merry Christmas and a happy new year.

congratulate oneself etc. (*rejoice*) 838.

adj. **congratulatory**, gratulatory.

897. Love

n. **love**, affection, sympathy, fellow-feeling; tenderness etc. *adj.;* heart, brotherly love; charity, good will; benevolence etc. 906; attachment; fondness etc. *adj.;* liking; inclination etc. (*desire*) 865; regard, dilection [*obs.*], admiration, fancy.

yearning, *eros* [*Gr.*], tender passion, amour; gyneolatry; gallantry, passion, flame, devotion, fervor, enthusiasm, transport of love, rapture, enchantment, infatuation, adoration, idolatry.

mother love, maternal love, natural affection, *storge* [*Gr.*].

attractiveness, charm; popularity; idol, favorite etc. 899.

god of love, Cupid, Venus, Eros, Kama [*Hindu*]; myrtle; turtle dove, sparrow; cupid amoretto; true lover's knot; love -token, −suit, −affair, −tale, −story; the old story, plighted love; courtship etc. 902; amourette; free-love.

lover, suitor, *fiancé* [*F.*], follower [*colloq.*], admirer, adorer, wooer, amoret [*obs.*], amorist, beau, sweetheart, inamorato, swain, young man [*colloq.*], flame [*colloq.*], love, truelove; leman [*archaic*], Lothario, gallant, paramour, captive; *amoroso, cavaliere servente, cicisbeo, caro sposo* [*all It.*].

ladylove, sweetheart, mistress, inamorata, idol, darling, duck, Dulcinea, angel, goddess, *cara sposa* [*It.*]; betrothed, affianced, *fiancée* [*F.*].

flirt, coquette, amorette.

pair of turtledoves; abode of love; Agapemone [*Ch. hist.*].

v. **love**, like, affect, fancy, care for, take an interest in, be partial to, sympathize with; affection; be in love with etc. *adj.;* have−, entertain−, harbor−, cherish- a love for etc. *n.;* regard, revere; take to, bear love to, be wedded to; set one's affections on; burn; adore, idolize, love to distraction, *aimer éperdument* [*F.*]; dote- on, −upon.

make much of, feast one's eyes on; hold dear, prize; hug, cling to, cherish, caress, fondle, pet.

take a fancy to, look sweet upon [*colloq.*]; become enamored etc. *adj.;* fall in love with, lose one's heart; desire etc. 865.

excite love; win–, gain–, secure–, engage- the -love, –affections, –heart; take the fancy of; have a place in–, wind round- the heart; attract, attach, endear, charm, fascinate, captivate, bewitch, seduce, enamor, enrapture, turn the head.

get into favor; ingratiate–, insinuate–, worm- oneself; propitiate, curry favor with, pay one's court to, *faire l'aimable* [*F.*], set one's cap at [*colloq.*], coquet, flirt.

adj. **loving** etc. *v.;* fond of; taken with [*colloq.*], struck with [*colloq.*], smitten, bitten [*colloq.*]; attached to, wedded to; enamored; charmed etc. *v.;* in love; love-sick; over head and ears in love.

affectionate, tender, sweet upon [*colloq.*], sympathetic, amorous, amatory; fond, erotic, uxorious, ardent, passionate, rapturous, devoted, motherly.

loved etc. *v.;* beloved, well beloved, dearly beloved; dear as the apple of one's eye, nearest to one's heart; dear, precious, darling, pet, little; favorite, popular.

congenial; to–, after- one's -mind, -taste, -fancy, –own heart; in one's good graces etc. (*friendly*) 888.

lovable, adorable, lovely, sweet, attractive, seductive, winning, winsome, charming, engaging, interesting, enchanting, captivating, fascinating, bewitching, amiable; seraphic *or* seraphical, angelic, like an angel.

898. Hate

n. **hate**, hatred, vials of hate; "Hymn of Hate."

disaffection, disfavor; alienation, estrangement, coolness; enmity etc. 889; animosity etc. 900; malice etc. 907; implacability etc. (*revenge*) 919.

umbrage, pique, grudge, dudgeon, spleen, bitterness, bitterness of feeling; ill blood, bad blood; acrimony.

repugnance etc. (*dislike*) 867; odium, unpopularity; detestation, abhorrence, loathing, execration, abomination, aversion, antipathy; demonophobia, gynephobia, negrophobia; Anglophobia etc. 867.

object of hatred, an abomination, an aversion, *bête noire* [*F.*]; enemy etc. 891; bitter pill; source of annoyance etc. 830.

v. **hate**, detest, abominate, abhor, loathe; recoil at, shudder at; shrink from, view with horror, hold

in abomination, revolt against, execrate; scowl etc. 895; disrelish etc. (*dislike*) 867.

owe a grudge; bear spleen, bear a grudge, bear malice etc. (*malevolence*) 907; conceive an aversion to.

excite hatred, provoke hatred etc. *n.;* be hateful etc. *adj.;* stink in the nostrils; estrange, alienate, repel, set against, sow dissension, set by the ears, envenom, incense, irritate, rile [*dial. or colloq.*], ruffle, vex, roil; horrify etc. 830.

adj. **hating** etc. *v.;* abhorrent; averse from etc. (*disliking*) 867; set against; bitter etc. (*acrimonious*) 895; implacable etc. (*revengeful*) 919.

unloved, unbeloved, unlamented, undeplored, unmourned, uncared for, unendeared, unvalued; disliked etc. 867.

crossed in love, forsaken, rejected, lovelorn, jilted.

hateful, obnoxious, odious, abominable, repulsive, offensive, shocking; disgusting etc. (*disagreeable*) 830; reprehensible.

invidious, spiteful; malicious etc. 907.

insulting, irritating, provoking.

[mutual hate] at daggers drawn; not on speaking terms etc. (*enmity*) 889; at loggerheads.

899. Favorite

n. **favorite**, pet, fondling, cosset, minion [*rare*], idol, jewel, spoiled child, *enfant gâté* [*F.*]; led captain; crony; apple of one's eye, man after one's own heart; *persona grata* [*L.*].

love, dear, darling, duck, honey, jewel; mopsy *or* mopsey, moppet; sweetheart etc. (*love*) 897.

general–, universal- favorite; idol of the people; matinée idol.

900. Resentment

n. **resentment**, displeasure, animosity, anger, wrath, ire, indignation; exasperation, vexation, bitter resentment, wrathful indignation.

pique, umbrage, huff, miff [*colloq.*], soreness, dudgeon, acerbity, virulence, bitterness, acrimony, asperity, spleen, gall; heartburning, heartswelling; rankling.

ill–, bad- -humor, –temper; irascibility etc. 901; scowl etc. 895; sulks etc. 901*a;* ill blood etc. (*hate*) 898; revenge etc. 919.

irritation; warmth, bile, choler, fume, pucker [*colloq.*], dander [*colloq.*], ferment, excitement, ebullition; angry mood, taking [*colloq.*], pet, tiff, passion, fit, tantrum.

rage, fury; towering -rage, –passion; *acharnement* [*F.*], desperation, burst, explosion, paroxysm, storm; violence etc. 173; fire and fury; viais of wrath; gnashing of teeth, hot blood, high words.

furies, Erinyes (*sing.* Erinys), Eumenides; Alecto, Megaera, Tisiphone.

[cause of umbrage] affront, provocation, offense; indignity etc. (*insult*) 929; grudge; crow to -pluck, -pick, -pull; red rag, last straw, sore subject, *casus belli* [*L.*]; ill turn, outrage.

buffet, blow, slap in the face, box on the ear, rap on the knuckles.

v. **resent;** take -amiss, -ill, -to heart, -offense, -umbrage, -huff, -exception; not take it as a joke; *ne pas entendre raillerie* [*F.*]; take in bad part, take in ill part.

pout, knit the brow, frown, scowl, lower, snarl, growl, gnarl, gnash, snap; redden, color; look black, look black as thunder, look daggers; bite one's thumb; show-, grind- one's teeth; champ the bit.

be angry; fly-, fall-, get- into a -rage, -passion; fly off the handle, fly off at a tangent; let one's angry passions rise; bridle up, bristle up, froth up, fire up, flare up; foam at the mouth; open-, pour out- the vials of one's wrath.

chafe, mantle, fume, kindle, fly out, take fire; boil, -over; boil with- indignation, -rage; rage, storm, foam; hector, bully, bluster; vent one's -rage, spleen; lose one's temper; have a fling at; kick up a -row, -dust, -shindy [*all slang*]; cut up rough [*slang*], stand on one's hind legs, stamp the foot; stamp-, quiver-, swell-, foam- with rage; burst with anger; raise -Cain, -the devil, -Ned, -the mischief, -the roof [*all slang*]; breathe fire and fury; breathe revenge.

bear malice etc. (*revenge*) 919.

cause anger, raise anger; affront, offend; give -offense, -umbrage; anger; hurt the feelings; insult, discompose, fret, ruffle, roil, heckle, nettle, huff, pique; excite etc. 824; irritate, stir the blood, stir up bile; sting, -to the quick; rile, provoke, chafe, wound, incense, inflame, wrath [*obs.*], make one hot under the collar [*slang*], enrage, aggravate, add fuel to the flame, fan into a flame, widen the breach, envenom, embitter, exasperate, infuriate, kindle wrath; stick in one's craw *or* crop *or* gizzard [*colloq.*]; rankle etc. 919; hit-, rub-, sting-, strike- on the raw.

put out of -countenance, -humor; put (*or* get) one's monkey up [*colloq.*], put (*or* get) one's back up; raise one's -gorge, -dander [*colloq.*], -choler; work up into a passion, make one's blood boil, make the ears tingle, throw into a ferment, madden, drive one mad; lash into -fury, -madness; fool to the top of one's bent; set by the ears; bring a hornet's nest about one's ears.

adj. **angry,** wroth, irate, ireful, wrathful; cross etc. (*irascible*) 901; Achillean; sulky etc. 901*a;* bitter, virulent; acrimonious etc. (*discourteous*) etc. 895; offended etc. *v.;* waxy [*slang, Eng.*], wrought, worked up; indignant, hurt, sore; set against.

warm, burning; boiling, -over; fuming, raging, hot under the collar [*slang*]; *acharné* [*F.*]; foaming, -at the mouth; convulsed with rage; fierce, wild, rageful, furious, mad with rage, fiery, infuriate, rabid, savage; relentless etc. 919; violent etc. 173.

flushed with -anger, -rage; in a- huff, -stew [*colloq.*], -fume, -pucker [*dial. or colloq.*], -wax [*slang*], -passion, -rage, -fury, -taking [*colloq.*]; on one's high ropes [*colloq.*], up in arms; in high dudgeon.

adv. **angrily** etc. *adj.;* in the height of passion; in the heat of -passion, -the moment; in an ecstasy of rage.

int. *tantaene animis caelestibus irae!* [Virgil]; marry come up! zounds! 'sdeath!

901. Irascibility

n. **irascibility,** irascibleness, temper; crossness etc. *adj.;* susceptibility, procacity [*rare*], petulance, irritability, tartness, acerbity, acrimony, asperity, protervity [*rare*]; huff etc. (*resentment*) 900; a word and a blow; pugnacity etc. (*contentiousness*) 720; excitability etc. 825; bad-, fiery-, crooked-, irritable etc. *adj.* -temper; *genus irritabile* [*L.*], hot blood.

ill humor etc. (*sullenness*) 901*a;* churlishness etc. (*discourtesy*) 895.

Sir Fretful Plagiary; brabbler, Tartar; shrew, vixen, virago, termagant, dragon, scold, Xanthippe *or* Xantippe, Kate the Shrew; porcupine; spitfire; fire eater etc. (*blusterer*) 887; fury etc. (*violent person*) 173.

v. **be irascible** etc. *adj.;* have a temper etc. *n.,* have a devil in one, be possessed of the devil, have the temper of a fiend; brabble [*archaic or dial.*]; fire up etc. (*be angry*) 900.

adj. **irascible,** bad-tempered, ill-tempered, irritable, susceptible; excitable etc. 825; thin-skinned etc. (*sensitive*) 822; fretful, fidgety; on the fret.

hasty, overhasty, quick, warm, hot, testy, touchy, techy *or* tetchy; like -touch- wood, -tinder, -a barrel of gunpowder; huffy, pettish, petulant, querulous, captious, moody, moodish; fractious, peevish, *acariâtre* [*F.*].

quarrelsome, contentious, disputatious; pugnacious etc. (*bellicose*) 720; cantankerous [*colloq.*], exceptious [*rare*], cross-grained; waspish, snappish, peppery, fiery, passionate, choleric, shrewish, "sudden and quick in quarrel" [*As You Like It*]; restive etc. (*perverse*) 901 *a*; churlish etc. (*discourteous*) 895; cross, −as −crabs, −a bear with a sore head, −a cat, −a dog, −two sticks, −the tongs [*all colloq.*]; sore, sore as a crab [*colloq.*].

in a bad temper; sulky etc. 901*a*; angry etc. 900; resentful, resentive; vindictive etc. 919.

int. pish!

901a. Sullenness

n. **sullenness** etc. *adj.*; morosity, spleen; churlishness etc. (*discourtesy*) 895; irascibility etc. 901; moodiness etc. *adj.*; perversity; obstinacy etc. 606; torvity [*obs.*], thorniness, spinosity; crabbedness etc. *adj.*

ill-, bad- -temper, −humor; sulks, dudgeon, mumps, dumps [*humorous*], doleful dumps [*colloq. or humorous*], vapors [*archaic*], glooming, doldrums, fit of the sulks, bouderie, black looks, scowl; grouch [*slang*]; huff etc. (*resentment*) 900.

v. **be sullen** etc. *adj.*; sulk; frown, scowl, lower, glower, pout, have a hangdog look, glout [*rare or dial.*], grouch, grout.

adj. **sullen**, sulky; ill-tempered, ill-humored, ill-affected, ill-disposed; grouty; in -an ill, −a bad, −a shocking- -temper, −humor; out of - temper, −humor; naggy [*colloq.*], torvous [*obs.*], crusty, crabbed, sour, sore, sore as a crab; surly etc. (*discourteous*) 895.

moody, moodish, spleenish, spleeny, spleenful, splenetic, cankered; cross, cross-grained; perverse, wayward, humorsome; restive, restiff [*rare*], malignant, refractory, ungovernable, cantankerous, intractable, exceptious [*rare*], sinistrous [*obs.*], deaf to reason, unaccommodating, rusty [*dial. Eng.*], froward, cussed [*vulgar*], curst [*archaic or dial.*].

grumpy, glum, grim, grum, morose, frumpish [*obs.*]; in the sulks etc. *n.*; out of sorts; scowling, glowering, growling, grouchy; peevish etc. (*irascible*) 901; dogged etc. (*stubborn*) 606.

902. Endearment
[expression of affection]

n. **endearment**, caress, blandishment, blandiment [*obs.*]; *épanchement* [*F.*], fondling, billing and cooing, dalliance, caressing, embrace, salute, kiss, buss, smack, osculation, deosculation [*obs.*].

courtship, wooing, suit, addresses, the soft impeachment; love-making; calf love [*colloq.*];

amorous glances, ogle, side-glance, sheep's eyes, goo-goo eyes [*slang*]; serenading, caterwauling.

flirting etc. *v.*; flirtation, gallantry; coquetry, spooning [*slang*].

true lover's knot, plighted love, engagement, betrothal; marriage etc. 903; honeymoon; love tale, love token; love letter, *billet-doux* [*F.*]; posy [*archaic*]; valentine.

Strephon and Chloe, 'Arry and 'Arriet.

flirt, coquette; male flirt, philanderer; spoon [*slang*].

v. **caress**, fondle, pet, dandle; pat, −on the -head, −cheek; chuck under the chin, smile upon, coax, wheedle, cosset, coddle, cocker, make much of, cherish, foster, kill with kindness.

clasp, hug, cuddle; fold to the heart, press to the bosom; fold-, strain- in one's arms; take to one's arms; snuggle, nestle, nuzzle; embrace, kiss, buss, smack, blow a kiss; salute etc. (*courtesy*) 894.

make love, bill and coo, spoon [*slang*], toy, dally, flirt, coquet, gallivant *or* galavant; philander; pay one's -court, −addresses, −attentions- to; serenade; court, sweetheart [*colloq. or dial.*], woo; set one's cap at *or* for [*colloq.*]; be *or* look sweet upon [*colloq.*]; ogle, cast sheep's eyes upon, make goo-goo eyes at [*slang*], *faire les yeux doux* [*F.*].

fall in love with, fall over head and ears in love with; win the affections etc. (*love*) 897; die for.

propose; make−, have- an offer; pop the question [*colloq.*]; become engaged, become betrothed; plight one's -troth, −faith.

adj. **caressing** etc. *v.*; "sighing like furnace" [*As You Like It*]; love-sick, spoony *or* spooney [*slang*].
caressed etc. *v.*

903. Marriage

n. **marriage**, matrimony, wedlock, union, intermarriage, miscegenation, marriageability; *vinculum matrimonii* [*L.*], nuptial tie, nuptial knot; match; betrothment etc. (*promise*) 768.

married state, coverture, bed, cohabitation.

wedding, nuptials, Hymen, bridal, espousals, spousals; leading to the altar etc. *v.*; nuptial benediction, epithalamium; sealing.

torch−, temple- of Hymen; saffron -veil, −robe; hymeneal altar; honeymoon.

bridesmaid, maid of honor, matron of honor; usher, best man, bridesman, groomsman; bride, bridegroom.

married man, neogamist [*obs.*], Benedict, partner, spouse, mate, yokemate, husband, man, consort, baron [*old law & her.*], goodman [*archaic or dial.*], old man.

married woman, wife, wife of one's bosom, wedded wife, rib [*dial. & sportive*], helpmeet, helpmate, better half, ball and chain [*slang*], gray mare, goodwife [*archaic or dial.*], old lady *or* old woman [*vulgar*].

feme, –covert [*law*]; lady [*obs. or uncultivated*]; squaw; matron, matronship, matronage, matronhood.

married couple, man and wife, wedded pair, wedded couple, Darby and Joan, Philemon and Baucis.

affinity, soul-mate; spiritual wife, spiritual husband.

[kinds of marriage] monogamy, monogyny; bigamy, digamy, deuterogamy; trigamy; polygamy, polygyny, polyandry, polyandrism; Mormonism, spiritual wifery (*or* wifeism); levirate.

harem, seraglio; Mormon.

monogamist, monogynist, bigamist etc.; Turk, Bluebeard.

unlawful–, left-handed–, morganatic–, ill-assorted- marriage; *mésalliance* [*F.*], *mariage de convenance* [*F.*].

marriage broker, matchmaker, professional matchmaker, schatchen [*Yiddish*]; matrimonial -agency, –agent, –bureau.

v. **marry**, wive, take to oneself a wife; be married, be spliced [*colloq.*]; go off, go to the world [*obs.*], pair off; wed, espouse, lead to the hymeneal altar, take "for better for worse," give one's hand to, bestow one's hand upon.

marry, join, handfast [*archaic*]; couple etc. (*unite*) 43; be made one; tie the nuptial knot; give away, give in marriage; seal; affy, affiance; betroth etc. (*promise*) 768; publish–, call–, proclaim–, bid- the banns, be asked in church.

remarry, rewed; intermarry, interwed.

adj. **married** etc. *v.;* one, one bone and one flesh.

marriageable, nubile.

engaged, betrothed, affianced.

matrimonial, marital, conjugal, connubial, wedded; nuptial, hymeneal, spousal, bridal; monogamous etc.

904. Celibacy

n. **celibacy**, singleness, single blessedness; bachelorhood, bachelorship; misogamy, misogyny.

virginity, pucelage [*rare*], maidhood [*rare*], maidenhood, maidenhead.

unmarried man, bachelor, Coelebs, agamist, old bachelor; misogamist, misogynist; monk, priest, celibate, religious.

unmarried woman, spinster, maid, maiden; virgin, *feme sole* [*law*], old maid; bachelor-girl, girl-bachelor; nun, sister, vestal, vestal virgin; Diana, St. Agnes.

v. live single, enjoy single blessedness, keep bachelor hall.

adj. **unmarried**, unwedded; wifeless, spouseless; single, celibate, virgin.

905. Divorce. Widowhood

n. **divorce**, divorcement; separation, judicial separation, separate maintenance; *separatio a -mensa et thoro, –vinculo matrimonii* [*L.*].

widowhood, viduity [*rare*], viduage, viduation, weeds; viduate [*eccl.*].

widow, relict, dowager; divorcée; grass widow.

widower; grass widower; cuckold.

v. live separate; separate, divorce, disespouse [*obs.*], put away; cheat on [*slang*]; wear the horns.

906. Benevolence

n. **benevolence**, Christian charity; God's love, God's grace; good will; philanthropy etc. 910; unselfishness etc. 942.

good -nature, –feeling, –wishes; kindness, kindliness etc. *adj.;* loving-kindness, benignity, brotherly love, charity, humanity, kindly feelings, fellow-feeling, sympathy; goodness–, warmth- of heart; warm-heartedness, bonhomie *or* bonhommie, kind-heartedness; amiability, milk of human kindness, tenderness; love etc. 897; friendship etc. 888; toleration, consideration; mercy etc. (*pity*) 914.

charitableness etc. *adj.;* bounty, almsgiving; good works, beneficence, generosity; "the luxury of doing good" [Goldsmith].

acts of kindness, a good turn; good–, kind-offices, –treatment.

philanthropist, "one who loves his fellow-men" [Hunt], salt of the earth; good Samaritan, sympathizer, well-wisher, *bon enfant* [*F.*]; altruist.

v. **be benevolent** etc. *adj.;* have one's heart in the right place, bear good will; wish well, wish Godspeed; view–, regard - with an eye of favor; take in good part; take–, feel - an interest in; be–, feel- interested- in; have a fellow-feeling for, sympathize with, feel for; fraternize etc. (*be friendly*) 888.

enter into the feelings of others, practice the Golden Rule, do as you would be done by, meet halfway.

treat well; give comfort, smooth the bed of death; do good, do a good turn; benefit etc. (*good-*

ness) 648; render a service, render assistance, give one a hand, be of use; aid etc. 707.

adj. **benevolent**, kind, kindly, well-meaning, amiable, cordial; obliging, accommodating, indulgent, gracious, complacent, good-humored; tender, considerate; warm-hearted, kind-hearted, tender-hearted, large-hearted, broad-hearted, soft-hearted; merciful etc. 914.

good-natured, well-natured, spleenless [*rare*]; sympathizing, sympathetic; complaisant etc. (*courteous*) 894; well-meant, well-intentioned, kindly meant.

full of natural affection, fatherly, motherly, brotherly, sisterly; paternal, maternal, fraternal; sororal [*rare*]; friendly etc. 888.

charitable, beneficent, philanthropical, generous, humane, benignant, bounteous, bountiful.

adv. **with good will**, with a good intention [*rare*], with the best intentions; out of deepest sympathy; in a burst of generosity.

int. **godspeed**! good luck! all good luck go with you! count on me!

907. Malevolence

n. **malevolence**, bad intent, bad intention, unkindness, diskindness [*obs.*]; ill-nature, ill-will, ill-blood, bad blood; enmity etc. 889; hate etc. 898; malice, –prepense, –aforethought; malignance, malignancy, malignity; maliciousness etc. *adj.*; spite, despite, resentment etc. 900.

uncharitableness etc. *adj.*; incompassion [*rare*], incompassionateness [*rare*] etc. 914a; gall, venom, rancor, rankling, virulence, mordacity, acerbity; churlishness etc. (*discourtesy*) 895; hardness of heart, heart of stone, obduracy; evil eye, cloven -foot, –hoof.

ill turn, bad turn; affront etc. (*disrespect*) 929; bigotry, intolerance, tender mercies [*ironical*]; "unkindest cut of all" [*Julius Caesar*].

cruelty, cruelness etc. *adj.*; brutality, savagery, ferity, ferocity; outrage, atrocity, ill-usage, persecution; barbarity, inhumanity, immanity [*obs.*], truculence, ruffianism; Inquisition, torture, vivisection.

v. **be malevolent** etc. *adj.*; bear-, harbor- -spleen, –a grudge, –malice; betray–, show- the cloven foot; hurt etc. (*physical pain*) 378; annoy etc. 830; injure, harm, wrong; do harm to, do an ill office to; outrage; disoblige, malign, plant a thorn in the breast; turn and rend one.

molest, worry, harass, haunt, harry, bait, tease; throw stones at; play the devil with; hunt down, dragoon, hound; persecute, oppress, grind, maltreat, ill-treat, ill-use, misuse.

wreak one's malice on, do one's worst, break a butterfly on the wheel; dip–, imbrue- one's hands in blood; show no quarter, have no mercy etc. 914a.

adj. **malevolent**, unbenevolent, unbenign; ill-disposed, ill-intentioned, ill-natured, ill-conditioned, ill-contrived; evil-minded, evil-disposed, black-browed; malicious, malign, malignant; rancorous, spiteful, despiteful, treacherous, mordacious, caustic, bitter, envenomed, acrimonious, virulent; unamiable, uncharitable; maleficent, venomous, grinding, galling.

harsh, disobliging, unkind, unfriendly, ungracious, inofficious [*obs.*], invidious; churlish etc. (*uncourteous*) 895; surly, sullen etc. 901a.

cold-blooded, cold-hearted; black-hearted, hard-hearted, flint-hearted, marble-hearted, stony-hearted, hard of heart, cold, unnatural; ruthless etc. (*unmerciful*) 914a; relentless etc. (*revengeful*) 919.

cruel, brutal, brutish, savage; savage as a -bear, –tiger; ferine, ferocious, feral, inhuman; barbarous, fell, untamed, tameless, truculent, incendiary; blood-thirsty etc. (*murderous*) 361; atrocious; bloody-minded; fiendish, fiendlike; demoniac *or* demoniacal; diabolic *or* diabolical, devilish, infernal, hellish, Tartarean *or* Tartareous, Satanic.

adv. **malevolently** etc. *adj.*; with bad intent etc. *n.*; with the ferocity of a tiger.

908. Malediction

n. **malediction**, malison, curse, imprecation, denunciation, execration; anathema, –maranatha; maranatha [*a misinterpretation*]; ban, proscription, excommunication, commination, thunders of the Vatican, fulmination; aspersion, disparagement, vilification, vituperation.

abuse; foul–, bad–, strong–, unparliamentary- language; billingsgate, sauce [*colloq.*]; blackguardism etc. (*discourtesy*) 895; evil speaking; cursing etc. *v.*; profane swearing, oath; foul invective, ribaldry, rude reproach, scurrility, threat etc. 909; more bark than bite; invective etc. (*disapprobation*) 932.

v. **curse**, accurse, imprecate, damn; curse with bell, book, and candle; invoke–, call down- curses on the head of; call down curses upon one's devoted head; devote to destruction.

execrate, beshrew [*archaic*], scold; anathematize etc. (*censure*) 932; hold up to execration, denounce, proscribe, excommunicate, fulminate, thunder against; curse up hill and down dale; threaten etc. 909.

swear, curse and swear; swear like a trooper; fall a-cursing, rap out an oath, swear at, damn.

adj. **maledictory**, imprecatory; cursing, cursed etc. *v.*

int. woe to! beshrew! [*archaic*], *ruat coelum!* [*L.*], woe betide! ill betide! confusion seize! damn! confound! blast! curse! devil take! hang! out with! a plague upon! out upon! aroynt! *honi soit!* [*F.*], *parbleu!* [*F.*].

909. Threat

n. **threat**, menace; defiance etc. 715; abuse, minacity [*rare*], minaciousness, intimidation; denunciation; fulmination; commination etc. (*curse*) 908; gathering clouds etc. (*warning*) 668.

v. **threaten**, threat, menace; snarl, growl, gnarl, mutter, bark, bully.

defy etc. 715; intimidate etc. 860; keep–, hold up–, hold out- *in terrorem* [*L.*]; shake–, double–, clinch- the fist at; thunder, talk big, fulminate, use big words, bluster, look daggers.

adj. **threatening**, menacing, mínatory, minacious, comminatory, abusive; *in terrorem* [*L.*]; ominous etc. (*predicting*) 511; defiant etc. 715; under the ban.

int. *vae victis!* at your peril! do your worst! look out!

910. Philanthropy

n. **philanthropy**, altruism, humanity, humanitarianism, universal benevolence, eudaemonism *or* eudemonism, *deliciae humani generis* [*L.*].

public welfare, commonwealth [*now rare*], commonweal *or* common weal [*now rare*]; socialism, communism; Fourierism, phalansterism *or* phalansterianism, Saint Simonianism; cosmopolitanism, utilitarianism, the greatest happiness of the greatest number, social science, sociology.

public spirit, patriotism, civism, nationality, love of country, *amor patriae* [*L.*].

chivalry, knight errantry; generosity etc. 942.

philanthropist, eudaemonist *or* eudemonist, utilitarian, Benthamite, socialist, communist, cosmopolite, citizen of the world, *amicus humani generis* [*L.*]; altruist etc. 906; "little friend of all the world" [Kipling]; knight errant; patriot.

adj. **philanthropic**, altruistic, humanitarian, utilitarian, cosmopolitan; public-spirited, patriotic; humane, large-hearted etc. (*benevolent*) 906; chivalric, chivalrous; generous etc. 942.

adv. *pro bono publico* [*L.*]; *pro aris et focis* [Cicero].

911. Misanthropy

n. **misanthropy**, incivism; egotism etc. (*selfishness*) 943; moroseness etc. 901*a;* cynicism; want of patriotism etc. 910.

misanthrope, misanthropist, egotist, cynic, man hater, Timon, Diogenes.

woman hater, misogynist.

adj. **misanthropic**, antisocial, unpatriotic; egotistical etc. (*selfish*) 943; morose etc. 901*a*.

912. Benefactor

n. **benefactor**, savior, protector, good genius, tutelary saint, guardian angel, good Samaritan; friend in need, "a very present help in time of trouble" [*Bible*]; fairy godmother; *pater patriae* [*L.*]; salt of the earth etc. (*good man*) 948; auxiliary etc. 711.

913. Evildoer
[maleficent being]

n. **evildoer**, evil worker, malfeasor; wrongdoer etc. 949; mischiefmaker, marplot; oppressor, tyrant; firebrand, incendiary, fire bug, macher *or* torch [*slang*], pyromaniac, arsonist etc. 384; anarchist, nihilist, destroyer, Vandal, iconoclast, terrorist; Attila, scourge of the human race.

bane etc. 963; torpedo, bomb, U-boat.

savage, brute, ruffian, barbarian, semibarbarian, caitiff, desperado; Apache, gunman, hoodlum [*colloq.*], plug-ugly [*slang*], Redskin, tough [*colloq.*], Mohock, Mohawk [*rare*], bludgeon man, bully, rough, hooligan [*slang*], larrikin [*Austral. & Eng.*], ugly customer, dangerous classes; thief etc. 792; butcher, hangman; cutthroat etc. (*killer*) 361.

wild beast, tiger, leopard, panther, hyena, catamount, catamountain, lynx, cougar, jaguar, puma; bloodhound, hellhound, sleuth-hound; gorilla; vulture.

cockatrice, adder; snake, –in the grass; serpent, cobra, asp, rattlesnake, anaconda; boa; viper etc. (*snake*) 366; *alacrán* [*Sp. Amer.*], alligator, cayman, crocodile, mugger *or* magar [*Hind.*]; Gila monster; octopus.

[injurious insects] buffalo carpet beetle, cucumber flea beetle, elm-tree beetle, striped cucumber beetle, Japanese beetle, gypsy (*or* gipsy) moth, brown-tail moth, flat-headed apple-tree borer, peach-tree borer, round-headed apple-tree borer, squash vine borer, bedbug, harlequin cabbage bug, potato bug, buffalo bug, rose bug, squash bug, tent caterpillar; curculio, weevil, snout beetle, billbeetle, billbug, plum curculio; horn fly, white grub, San José scale, onion maggot, clover-seed midge, grain weevil, bollworm, cankerworm, cutworm, fall web-worm, tobacco worm, tomato worm, wireworm; white ant, scorpion, hornet, mosquito, locust, Colorado beetle.

hag, hellhag, beldam, Jezebel.

monster; fiend etc. (*demon*) 980; devil incarnate, demon in human shape; Frankenstein's monster; cannibal, anthropophagus, anthropophagist; bloodsucker, vampire, ogre, ghoul.

harpy, siren, vampire [*colloq.*], vamp [*slang*]; Furies, Eumenides.

914. Pity

n. **pity**, compassion, commiseration; bowels, –of compassion; sympathy, fellow-feeling, tenderness, soft-heartedness, yearning, forbearance, humanity, mercy, clemency; leniency etc. (*lenity*) 740; exorability, exorableness; charity, ruth, long-suffering.

melting mood; *argumentum ad misericordiam* [*L.*]; quarter, grace, *locus poenitentiae* [*L.*].

sympathizer; advocate, friend, partisan, patron, wellwisher, defender, champion.

v. **pity**; have–, show–, take- pity etc. *n.;* commiserate, compassionate; condole etc. 915; sympathize; feel for, be sorry for, yearn over; weep, melt, thaw, enter into the feelings of.

forbear, relent, relax, give quarter, wipe the tears, *parcere subjectis* [*L.*]; give a *coup de grâce* [*F.*], put out of one's misery; be cruel to be kind.

raise *or* **excite pity** etc. *n.;* touch, soften, melt, melt the heart; appeal, –to one's better feelings; propitiate, disarm.

supplicate etc. (*request*) 765; ask for mercy etc. *n.;* cry for quarter, beg one's life, kneel; deprecate.

adj. **pitying** etc. *v.;* pitiful, compassionate, sympathetic, touched.

merciful, clement, ruthful; humane; humanitarian etc. (*philanthropic*) 910; tender, tender-hearted; soft, soft-hearted; unhardened; lenient etc. 740; exorable, forbearing; melting etc. *v.;* weak.

int. for pity's sake! mercy! have–, cry you- mercy! God help you! poor -thing, –dear, –fellow! woe betide! *quis talia fando temperet a lachrymis!* [Virgil].

914a. Pitilessness

n. **pitilessness** etc. *adj.;* inclemency, inexorability, inflexibility, incompassion [*rare*], hardness of heart; want of pity etc. 914; severity etc. 739; malevolence etc. 907.

v. **be pitiless** etc. *adj.;* turn a deaf ear to; claim one's "pound of flesh" [Merchant of Venice]; have no–, shut the gates of- mercy etc. 914; give no quarter.

adj. **pitiless**, merciless, ruthless, bowelless; unpitying, unmerciful, inclement; grim-faced, grim-visaged; uncompassionate, incompassionate [*rare*], uncompassioned; inflexible, relentless, inexorable; unrelenting etc. 919; harsh etc. 739; cruel etc. 907.

915. Condolence

n. **condolence**; lamentation etc. 839; sympathy, consolation.

v. **condole with**, console, sympathize; express–, testify- pity; afford–, supply- consolation; lament with etc. 839; express sympathy for, feel for, send one's condolences; feel -grief, –sorrow- in common with; share one's sorrow.

916. Gratitude

n. **gratitude**, gratefulness, thankfulness; feeling of–, sense of- obligation.

acknowledgment, recognition, thanksgiving, giving thanks; thankful good will.

thanks, praise, benediction; paean; *Te Deum* etc. (*worship*) 990; grace, –before meat, –after meat; thank offering; requital.

v. **be grateful** etc. *adj.;* thank; give–, render–, return–, offer–, tender-thanks etc. *n.;* acknowledge, requite.

feel–, be–, lie- under an obligation; *savoir gré* [*F.*]; not look a gift horse in the mouth; never forget, overflow with gratitude; thank–, bless- one's stars; fall on one's knees.

adj. **grateful**, thankful, obliged, beholden, indebted to, under obligation

int. **thanks**! many thanks! gramercy! much obliged! thank you! thank Heaven! Heaven be praised!

917. Ingratitude

n. **ingratitude**, thanklessness, oblivion of benefits, unthankfulness.

"benefits forgot" [*As You Like It*]; thankless task, thankless office.

v. **be ungrateful** etc. *adj.;* feel no obligation, owe one no thanks, forget benefits; look a gift horse in the mouth.

adj. **ungrateful**, unmindful, unthankful; thankless, ingrate, wanting in gratitude, insensible of benefits.

forgotten; unacknowledged, unthanked, unrequited, unrewarded; ill-requited; ill-rewarded.

int. thank you for nothing! *"et tu Brute!"* [*Julius Caesar*].

918. Forgiveness

n. **forgiveness**, pardon, condonation, grace, remission, absolution, amnesty, oblivion; indulgence; reprieve.

conciliation; reconcilement; reconciliation etc. (*pacification*) 723; propitiation.

longanimity, placability; *amantium iroe* [*L.*]; *locus poenitentiae* [*L.*]; forbearance.

exoneration, excuse, quittance, release, indemnity; bill–, act–, covenant–, deed– of indemnity; exculpation etc. (*acquittal*) 970.

v. **forgive**, –and forget; pardon, condone, think no more of, let bygones be bygones, shake hands; forget an injury; bury the hatchet; drown all unkindness; start afresh, make a new start.

let off [*colloq.*], remit, absolve, give absolution; blot out one's -sins, –offenses, –transgressions, –debts; wipe the slate clean; reprieve; acquit etc. 970.

excuse, pass over, overlook; wink at etc. (*neglect*) 460; bear with; allow for, make allowances for; let one down easily, not be too hard upon, pocket the affront.

conciliate, propitiate, placate; beg–, ask–, implore- pardon etc. *n.;* make up a quarrel etc. (*pacify*) 723; let the wound heal.

adj. **forgiving**, placable, conciliatory.

forgiven etc. *v.;* unresented, unavenged, unrevenged.

int. have mercy! cry you mercy! forgive and forget!

919. Revenge

n. **revenge**, revengement [*rare*], vengeance; avengement, avengeance [*obs.*], sweet revenge, vendetta, death feud, blood for blood; eye for an eye, tooth for a tooth, *lex talionis* [*L.*], retaliation etc. 718; day of reckoning.

rancor, vindictiveness, immitigability; implacability; malevolence etc. 907; ruthlessness etc. 914*a*.

avenger, vindicator [*obs.*], Nemesis, Eumenides.

v. **revenge**, avenge, vindicate [*obs.*]; take revenge, have one's revenge; breathe -revenge, –vengeance; wreak one's - vengeance, –anger; cry quittance; give no quarter, take no prisoners.

have accounts to settle, have a crow to pluck, have a rod in pickle.

keep the wound green; nurse one's revenge, harbor -revenge, –vindictive feeling; bear malice; rankle, rankle in the breast.

have at a disadvantage, have on the hip, have the upper hand, have at one's mercy.

adj. **revengeful**, vengeful, vindictive, rancorous; pitiless etc. 914*a;* ruthless, rigorous, avenging, retaliative, grudgeful [*rare*].

unforgiving, unrelenting; inexorable, stony-hearted, implacable, relentless, remorseless.

rankling, immitigable; *aeternum servans sub pectore vulnus* [*L.*].

920. Jealousy

n. **jealousy**, jealousness; jaundiced eye; distrust, mistrust, misdoubt, heartburn; envy etc. 921; doubt, envious suspicion, suspicion; "green-eyed monster" [*Othello*]; yellows; Juno.

v. **be jealous** etc. *adj.;* view with jealousy, view with a jealous eye, view with a jaundiced eye; grudge, begrudge.

doubt, distrust, mistrust, suspect, misdoubt, heartburn [*obs.*]; jealouse [*obs. or Scot. & dial. Eng.*].

adj. **jealous**, jealous as a Barbary pigeon; jaundiced, yellow-eyed, envious; beside oneself with -jealousy, –envy.

921. Envy

n. **envy**; enviousness etc. *adj.;* rivalry; *jalousie de métier* [*F.*]; ill-will, spite; jealousy etc. 920.

v. **envy**, covet, grudge, begrudge, burst with envy, break the tenth commandment.

adj. **envious**, individious, covetous, grudging, begrudged; belittling; *alieni appetens* [*L.*].

Section 4. Moral

922. Right

n. **right**; what ought to be, what should be; what is fit etc. *adj.;* fitness etc. *adj.; summum jus* [*L.*].

justice, equity; equitableness etc. *adj.;* propriety; fair play, square deal [*colloq.*], impartiality, measure for measure, give and take, *lex talionis* [*L.*].

scales of justice, evenhanded justice, karma; *suum cuique* [*L.*]; clear stage–, fair field- and no favor; retributive justice, nemesis.

Astraea, Nemesis, Themis, Rhadamanthus.

morals etc. (*duty*) 926; law etc. 963; honor etc. (*probity*) 939; virtue etc. 944.

v. **be right** etc. *adj.;* stand to reason.

see justice done, see one righted, see fair play; do justice to; recompense etc. (*reward*) 973; hold the scales even, give and take; serve one right, put the saddle on the right horse; give every one his due, give the devil his due; *audire alteram partem* [*L.*].

deserve etc. (*be entitled to*) 924.

adj. **right**, good; just, reasonable; fit etc. 924; equal, equable, equitable; evenhanded, fair, square, fair and square.

legitimate, justifiable, rightful; as it should be, as it ought to be; lawful etc. (*permitted*) 760, (*legal*) 963.

deserved etc. 924.

adv. **rightly** etc. *adj.; à−, au- bon droit* [*F.*], in justice, in equity, in reason.

without -distinction of, −regard to, −respect to- persons; upon even terms.

int. all right!

923. Wrong

n. **wrong**; what ought not to be, what should not be *malum in se* [*L.*]; unreasonableness grievance; shame.

injustice; unfairness etc. *adj.;* iniquity, foul play, partiality, leaning, favor, favoritism, nepotism; partisanship, party spirit; undueness etc. 925; unlawfulness etc. 964.

robbing Peter to pay Paul etc. *v.;* the wolf and the lamb; vice etc. 945.

v. **be wrong** etc. *adj.;* cry to heaven for vengeance.

do wrong etc. *n.;* be inequitable etc. *adj.;* favor, lean towards; encroach; impose upon; reap where one has not sown; give an inch and take an ell; rob Peter to pay Paul.

adj. **wrong,** wrongful; bad, too bad; unjust, unfair, inequitable, unequitable, unequal, partial, one-sided; injurious.

unjustifiable, unreasonable, unallowable, unwarrantable, objectionable, improper, unfit; unjustified etc. 925; illegal etc. 964; iniquitous; immoral etc. 945.

in the wrong, −box; in bad [*slang*], in wrong [*slang*].

adv. **wrongly** etc. *adj.*

int. this is too bad! it will not do!

924. Dueness

n. **dueness,** right, droit [*law*], due, privilege, prerogative, prescription, title, claim, pretension, demand, birthright.

immunity, license, liberty, franchise; vested -interest, −right.

sanction, authority, warranty [*law*], charter, licitness, warrant etc. (*permission*) 760; constitution etc. (*law*) 963; tenure; bond etc. (*security*) 771.

deserts, merits, dues; all that is coming to one [*colloq.*].

claimant, appellant; plaintiff etc. 938.

v. **be due to** etc. *adj.;* be the due of etc. *n.;* have -right, −title, −claim- to; be entitled to; have a claim upon; belong to etc. (*property*) 780.

deserve, merit, be worthy of, richly deserve.

demand, claim; call upon one for, come upon one for, appeal to for; revendicate [*rare*], revindicate, reclaim; exact; insist -on, −upon; challenge; take one's stand, make a point of, require, lay claim to; assert, assume, arrogate.

make good; substantiate; vindicate a -claim, −right; fit-, qualify- for; make out a case.

use a right, assert, enforce, put in force, lay under contribution.

entitle; give *or* confer a right; authorize etc. 760; sanction, sanctify, legalize, ordain, prescribe, allot.

give every one his due etc. 922; pay one's dues; have one's -due, −rights; stand upon one's rights.

adj. **having a right to** etc. *v.;* entitled to; claiming; deserving, meriting, worthy of.

privileged, allowed, sanctioned, warranted, authorized; ordained, prescribed, constitutional, chartered, enfranchised.

prescriptive, presumptive, absolute, indefeasible, unalienable, inalienable, imprescriptible, inviolable, unimpeachable, unchallenged; sacrosanct.

due to, merited, deserved, condign [*archaic, except of punishment*], richly deserved.

right, fit, fitting, correct, proper, meet, befitting, becoming, seemly; decorous; creditable, up to the mark, right as a trivet; just-, quite- the thing; *selon les règles* [*F.*]; square, unexceptionable, equitable etc. 922; due, *en règle* [*F.*].

lawful, licit, legitimate, legal; legalized etc. (*law*) 963; allowable etc. (*permitted*) 760.

adv. **duly**; as is -right, −fitting, −just; unexceptionably; *ex officio* [*L.*], *de jure* [*L.*]; by right, by divine right; *jure divino* [*L.*], *Dei gratia* [*L.*], in the name of.

925. Undueness
[absence of right]

n. **undueness** etc. *adj.; malum prohibitum* [*L.*]; impropriety; illegality etc. 964.

falseness etc. *adj.;* emptiness−, invalidity- of title; illegitimacy.

loss of right, disfranchisement, forfeiture.

assumption, usurpation, tort [*law*], violation, breach, encroachment, presumption, seizure; stretch, exaction, imposition, lion's share.

usurper, pretender, impostor.

v. **be undue** etc. *adj.;* not be due etc. 924.

infringe, encroach, trench on, exact; arrogate, −to oneself; give an inch and take an ell; stretch−, strain- a point; usurp, violate, do violence to; get under false pretenses, sail under false colors.

disentitle, disfranchise, disqualify; invalidate.

relax etc. (*be lax*) 738; misbehave etc. (*vice*) 945; misbecome.

adj. **undue**; unlawful etc. (*illegal*) 964; unconstitutional, illicit, unauthorized, unwarranted, unallowed, unsanctioned, unjustified; disentitled, unentitled; disqualified, unqualified; unprivileged, unchartered.

undeserved, unmerited, unearned; unfulfilled. forfeited, disfranchised.

illegitimate, bastard, spurious, false; usurped, tortious [*law*].

improper; unmeet, unfit, unbefitting, unseemly, unbecoming, misbecoming, seemless [*obs.*]; *contra bonos mores* [*L.*]; not the thing, out of the question, not to be thought of; preposterous, pretentious, would-be.

926. Duty

n. **duty**, what ought to be done, moral obligation, accountableness, liability, onus, responsibility; bounden-, imperative- duty; call, -of duty; accountability.

allegiance, fealty, tie; engagement etc. (*promise*) 768; part; function, calling etc. (*business*) 625.

observance, fulfillment, discharge, performance, acquittal, satisfaction, redemption; good behavior.

morality, morals, decalogue; case of conscience; conscientiousness etc. (*probity*) 939; conscience, inward monitor, still small voice within, sense of duty, tender conscience; the hell within [*P.L.*].

propriety, fitness; dueness etc. 924; seemliness, amenableness, amenability, decorum, *to prepon* [*Gr.*]; the thing, the proper thing; the -right, -proper- thing to do.

[science of morals] ethics, ethology [*obs. in this sense*]; deontology, aretology [*obs.*]; moral-, ethical- philosophy; casuistry, polity.

v. **be the duty of**, be incumbent on etc. *adj.;* be responsible etc. *adj.;* behoove, become, befit, beseem; belong to, pertain to; fall to one's lot; devolve on; lie upon, lie on one's head, lie at one's door; rest with, rest on the shoulders of.

take upon oneself etc. (*promise*) 768; be-, become- -bound to, -sponsor for; incur a responsibility etc. *n.;* be-, stand-, lie- under an obligation; stand responsible for; have to answer for; owe it to oneself.

enter upon-, perform-, observe-, fulfill-, discharge-, adhere to-, acquit oneself of-, satisfy- -a duty, -an obligation; act one's part, redeem one's pledge, do justice to, be at one's post; do duty; do one's duty etc. (*be virtuous*) 944.

be on one's good behavior, mind one's P's and Q's; walk the straight path.

impose a duty etc. *n.;* enjoin, require, exact; bind, -over; saddle with, prescribe, assign, call upon, look to, oblige.

adj. **obligatory**, binding; imperative, peremptory; stringent etc. (*severe*) 739; behooving etc. *v.;* incumbent on, chargeable on; under obligation; obliged by, bound by, tied by; saddled with.

due to, beholden to, bound to, indebted to; tied down; compromised etc. (*promised*) 768; in duty bound.

amenable, liable, accountable, responsible, answerable.

right, meet etc. (*due*) 924; moral, ethical, casuistical, conscientious, ethological.

adv. with a safe conscience, as in duty bound on good behavior, on one's own responsibility, at one's own risk, *suo periculo* [*L.*]; *in foro conscientiae* [*L.*]; *quamdiu se bene gesserit* [*L.*]; at one's post.

927. Dereliction of Duty

n. **dereliction of duty**; fault etc. (*guilt*) 947; sin etc. (*vice*) 945; nonobservance, nonperformance, noncoöperation; indolence, neglect, relaxation, infraction, violation, transgression, failure, evasion; eyeservice; dead letter.

slacker, loafer, time-killer; eyeserver, eyeservant; striker; noncoöperator.

v. **violate**; break, break through; infringe; set aside, set at naught; encroach upon, trench upon; trample -on, -under foot; slight, get by [*slang*], neglect, evade, renounce, forswear, repudiate; wash one's hands of; escape. transgress, fail.

call to account etc. (*disapprobation*) 932.

927a. Exemption

n. **exemption**, freedom, irresponsibility, immunity, liberty, license, release, quitclaim [*law*]; exoneration, excuse, dispensation, absolution, franchise [*obs.*], renunciation, discharge; exculpation etc. 970.

v. **exempt**, release, acquit, discharge, quitclaim [*law*], remise, remit; free, set at liberty, let off [*colloq.*], pass over, spare, excuse, dispense with, give dispensation, license; stretch a point; absolve etc. (*forgive*) 918; exonerate etc. (*exculpate*) 970; save the necessity.

be exempt etc. *adj.*

adj. **exempt**, free, immune, at liberty, scot-free; released etc. *v.;* unbound, unencumbered; irresponsible, not responsible, unaccountable, not answerable; excusable.

928. Respect

n. **respect**, regard, consideration; courtesy etc. 894; attention, deference, reverence, honor, esteem, estimation, veneration, admiration; approbation etc. 931.

homage, fealty, obeisance, genuflection, kneeling, prostration; obsequiousness etc. 886; salaam, kotow *or* kowtow [*Chinese*], bow, presenting arms, salute.

respects, regards, duty, *devoirs* [*F.*], *égards* [*F.*].

devotion etc. (*piety*) 987.

v. **respect**, regard; revere, reverence; hold in reverence, honor, venerate, hallow; esteem etc. (*approve of*) 931; think much of; entertain–, bear– respect for; look up to, defer to; have–, hold– a high opinion of; pay attention to, pay respect to etc. *n.;* do *or* render honor to; do the honors, hail; show courtesy etc. 894; salute, present arms.

do *or* pay homage to; pay tribute to, kneel to, bow to, bend the knee to; fall down before, prostrate oneself, kiss the hem of one's garment; worship etc. 990.

keep one's distance, make room, observe due decorum, stand on ceremony.

command respect, inspire respect; awe, impose, overawe, dazzle.

adj. **respecting** etc. *v.;* respectful, deferential, decorous, reverential, obsequious, ceremonious, bareheaded, cap in hand, on one's knees; prostrate etc. (*servile*) 886.

respected etc. *v.;* in high -esteem, –estimation; time-honored, venerable, *emeritus* [*L.*].

adv. **in deference to**; with all respect, with due respect, with the highest respect; with submission.

excusing the liberty; saving your -grace, –presence; *salva sit reverentia* [*L.*]; *pace tanti nominis* [*L.*].

int. hail! all hail! *hoch!* [*Ger.*]; *esto perpetua!* [*L.*], may your shadow never be less!

929. Disrespect

n. **disrespect**, disesteem, disestimation; disfavor, disrepute, want of esteem, low estimation, disparagement etc. (*dispraise*) 932, (*detraction*) 934; irreverence; slight, neglect; superciliousness etc. (*contempt*) 930.

indignity, vilipendency [*obs.*], contumely, affront, dishonor, insult, outrage, discourtesy etc. 895; practical joking; scurrility, scoffing; sibilation, hiss, hissing, hoot, irrision [*rare*], derision; mockery; irony etc. (*ridicule*) 856; sarcasm.

gibe *or* jibe, flout, jeer, scoff, gleek [*obs.*], fleer, taunt, sneer, quip, fling, twit, wipe [*dial. or slang*], slap in the face.

v. **treat with disrespect** etc. *n.;* hold in disrespect etc. (*despise*) 930; misprize, disregard, slight, undervalue, humiliate, depreciate, trifle with, set at naught, pass by, push aside, overlook, turn one's back upon, laugh in one's sleeve; be disrespectful etc. *adj.;* be discourteous etc. 895; set down, browbeat.

dishonor, desecrate; insult, affront, outrage.

speak slightingly of; disparage etc. (*dispraise*) 932; vilipend, call names; throw–, fling- dirt; throw mud at; make ride the rail, drag through the mud, point at, indulge in personalities; make mouths [*archaic*], make faces; bite the thumb; take–, pluck- by the beard; toss in a blanket, tar and feather.

deride, have *or* hold in derision; scoff, barrack [*dial. Eng. & Austral.*], sneer, laugh at, snigger, ridicule, gibe *or* jibe, mock, jeer, taunt, twit, niggle, gleek [*obs.*], gird, flout, fleer; roast [*colloq.*], guy [*colloq.*], rag [*dial. Eng. & college slang*] smoke [*old slang*]; turn into ridicule; burlesque etc. 856; laugh to scorn etc. (*contempt*) 930; lead one a dance, have a fling at, scout, hiss, hoot, mob.

fool; make game of, make a fool of, make an April fool of; play a practical joke.

adj. **disrespectful**; aweless, irreverent; disparaging etc. 934; insulting etc. *v.;* supercilious etc. (*scornful*) 930; rude, derisive, sarcastic; scurrile, scurrilous, contumelious, contemptuous, insolent, disdainful.

unrespected, unworshiped, unenvied, unsaluted; unregarded, disregarded.

adv. **disrespectfully** etc. *adj.*

930. Contempt

n. **contempt**, disdain, scorn, sovereign contempt; despisal [*rare*], despiciency [*obs.*], despisement [*rare*]; vilipendency [*obs.*], contumely; slight, sneer, spurn, byword; despect [*rare*].

contemptuousness etc. *adj.;* scornful eye; smile of contempt; derision etc. (*disrespect*) 929.

[state of being despised] despisedness.

v. **despise**, contemn, scorn, disdain, feel contempt for, view with a scornful eye; disregard, slight, not mind; pass by etc. (*neglect*) 460; look down upon; hold - cheap, –in contempt, –in disrespect; think nothing of, think small beer of [*colloq.*]; make light of; underestimate etc. 483; esteem slightly, esteem of small or no account; take no account of, care nothing for; set no store by; not care a straw etc. (*unimportance*) 643; set at naught, laugh in one's sleeve, snap one's fingers at, shrug one's shoulders, turn up one's nose at, pooh-pooh, "damn with faint praise" [*Pope*].

sneeze at, whistle at, sneer at; curl up one's lip, toss the head, *traiter de haut en bas* [*F.*]; laugh at etc. (*be disrespectful*) 929; point the finger of–, hold up to–, laugh to- scorn; scout, hoot, flout, hiss, scoff at.

spurn, turn one's back upon, turn a cold shoulder upon; tread–, trample- -upon, –under foot; kick; fling to the winds etc. (*repudiate*) 610; send away with a flea in the ear [*colloq.*].

adj. **contemptuous**, disdainful, scornful, withering, contumelious, supercilious, cynical, haughty, cavalier; derisive; with the nose in air, *de haut en bas* [*F.*].

contemptible, despicable; pitiable; pitiful etc. (*unimportant*) 643; despised etc. *v.;* downtrodden; unenvied.

adv. **contemptuously** etc. *adj.*

int. a fig for etc. (*unimportant*) 643; bah! pooh! pshaw! never mind! away with! hang it! fiddledeedee!

931. Approbation

n. **approbation**, approval, approvement [*obs.*], bepraisement, sanction, advocacy; nod of approbation; esteem, estimation, good opinion, golden opinions, admiration; love etc. 897; appreciation, regard, account, popularity, *kudos* [*Gr.*], credit; repute etc. 873.

commendation, praise, laud, laudation; good word; meed–, tribute- of praise; encomium, eulogy, eulogium, *éloge* [*F.*], panegyric, blurb [*slang*]; homage, hero worship; benediction, blessing, benison.

applause, plaudit, clap; clapping, –of hands; acclaim, acclamation; cheer; paean, hosanna; shout–, peal–, chorus–, thunders- of -applause etc.; prytaneum.

winner, prize winner, best seller, corker [*slang*], peach [*slang*], oner [*slang*], the real thing [*colloq.*], the goods [*slang*].

v. **approve**, approbate, think good of, think much of, think well of, think highly of; esteem, value, prize; set great store by.

honor, hold in esteem, look up to, admire; like etc. 897; be in favor of, wish Godspeed; hail, hail with satisfaction, do justice to, appreciate.

stand up for, stick up for [*colloq.*], uphold, hold up, countenance, sanction; clap–, pat- on the back; keep in countenance, indorse *or* endorse; give credit, recommend; mark with a white -mark, –stone.

commend, belaud, praise, laud, compliment, pay a tribute, bepraise; clap, –the hands; applaud, cheer, acclaim, acclamate [*rare*], encore; panegyrize, eulogize, boost [*colloq.*], root for [*slang*], cry up, *prôner* [*F.*], puff; extol, –to the skies; magnify, glorify, exalt, swell, make much of; flatter etc. 933; bless, give a blessing to; have–, say- a good word for; speak - well, –highly, –in high terms- of; sing–, sound–, chant–, resound- the praises of; sing praises to; cheer–, applaud- to the -echo, –very echo.

redound to the -honor, –praise, –credit- of; do credit to; deserve -praise etc. *n.;* recommend itself; pass muster.

be praised etc.; receive honorable mention; be in favor with, be in high favor with; ring with the praises of, win golden opinions, gain credit, find favor with, stand well in the opinion of; *laudari a laudato viro* [*L.*].

adj. **approving** etc. *v.;* in favor of; lost in admiration; commendatory, complimentary, benedictory, laudatory, panegyrical, eulogistic, encomiastic, acclamatory, lavish of praise, uncritical.

approved, praised etc. *v.;* uncensured, unimpeached; popular, in good odor; in high esteem etc. (*respected*) 928; in favor, in high favor.

praiseworthy, commendable, of estimation; deserving–, worthy of- praise etc. *n.;* good etc. 648; meritorious, estimable, creditable, unimpeachable; beyond all praise.

adv. **commendably**, with credit, to admiration; well etc. 618; with three times three.

int. hear hear! good for you! do it again! bully for you! [*slang*], well done! fine! bravo! *bravissimo!* [*It.*], euge! [*Gr. & L.*], *macte virtute!* [*L.*], so far so good! that's right! quite right! one cheer more! may your shadow never be less! *esto perpetua!* [*L.*], long life to! *viva!* [*It.*], *evviva!* [*It.*], Godspeed! *valete et plaudite!* [*L.*], encore! [*F.*], bis! [*L. & F.*].

932. Disapprobation

n. **disapprobation**, disapproval, improbation [*obs.*], disesteem, displacency [*rare*]; odium; dislike etc. 867; black list, blackball, ostracism, boycott; index expurgatorius.

disparagement, depreciation, disvaluation, dispraise, discommendation; detraction etc. 934; denunciation; condemnation etc. 971; animadversion, reflection, stricture, objection, exception, criticism; blame, censure, obloquy; sardonic -grin, –laugh; sarcasm, satire, insinuation, innuendo; bad–, poor–, left-handed-compliment.

sneer etc. (contempt) 930; taunt etc. (disrespect) 929; cavil, carping, censoriousness; hypercriticism etc. (fastidiousness) 868.

reprehension, remonstrance, expostulation, reproof, reprobation, admonition, increpation [archaic], reproach; rebuke, reprimand, castigation, jobation [colloq.], lecture, curtain lecture, blowup [colloq.]; blowing up, trimming, wigging, dressing, dressing down [all colloq.]; rating, scolding, correction, set down, rap on the knuckles, coup de bec [F.], rebuff; slap, slap on the face; home thrust, hit; frown, scowl, black look.

diatribe, jeremiad or jeremiade, tirade, philippic.

chiding, upbraiding etc. v.; exprobration [rare], personal remarks, abuse, vituperation, invective, objurgation, contumely; hard–, cutting–, bitter- words; evil-speaking; bad language etc. 908; personality.

clamor, outcry, hue and cry; hiss, hissing, sibilation, catcall; execration etc. 908.

v. **disapprove**; dislike etc. 867; lament etc. 839; object to, take exception to; be scandalized at, think ill of; view with -disfavor, –dark eyes, –jaundiced eyes; nil admirari [L.], disvalue, improbate [obs.].

frown upon, look grave; bend–, knit- the brows; shake the head at, shrug the shoulders; turn up the nose etc. (contempt) 930; look askance, look black upon; look with an evil eye; make a wry face at, make a face at, make a mouth at [archaic], set one's face against.

blame; lay–, cast- blame upon; censure, fronder [F.], reproach, pass censure on, reprobate, impugn, impeach; disbar, unfrock.

accuse etc. 938; impeach, denounce; hold up to -reprobation, –execration; expose, brand, gibbet, stigmatize; show up, pull up [both colloq.]; take up; cry "shame" upon; be outspoken; raise a hue and cry against.

reprehend, chide, admonish; berate, betongue; bring–, call- to account, –over the coals [colloq.], –to order; take to task, haul over the coals [colloq.], reprove, lecture, bring to book; read a -lesson, –lecture- to; rebuke, correct; reprimand, chastise, castigate, lash, trounce; trim, blow up, give it to, give one fits, give it to one, lay out [all six colloq.]; laver la tête [F.], overhaul.

remonstrate, expostulate, recriminate.

execrate etc. 908; exprobate [rare], speak daggers, vituperate; abuse, –like a pickpocket; tongue-lash [colloq.], scold, rate, objurgate, upbraid, fall foul of; jaw [low]; rail, –at, –in good set terms; bark at, yelp at, anathematize, call names; call by -hard, –ugly- names; avile [obs.], revile, vilify, vilipend, bespatter; clapperclaw [archaic]; rave–, thunder–, fulminate-against; load with reproaches.

decry, cry down, run down, frown down; exclaim–, protest–, inveigh–, declaim–, cry out–, raise one's voice- against; clamor, hiss, hoot, –catcall, mob; backbite; ostracize, blacklist, boycott, blackball; draw up–, sign- a round robin.

take down, set down; snub, snap one up, give a rap on the knuckles; throw a stone -at, –in one's garden; have a fling at, have a snap at; have words with, pluck a crow with; give one a wipe [dial. or slang]; give one a lick with the rough side of the tongue [colloq.].

animadvert upon, reflect upon; glance at; cast -reflection, –reproach a slur- upon; insinuate, "damn with faint praise" [Pope]; "hint a fault and hesitate dislike" [Pope]; not to be able to say much for.

disparage, depreciate, knock [colloq.], dispraise, discommend [rare], deprecate, speak ill of, not speak well of; condemn etc. (find guilty) 971; scoff at, point at; twit, taunt etc. (disrespect) 929; sneer at etc. (despise) 230; satirize, lampoon; defame etc. (detract) 934; depreciate, find fault with, criticize, cut up; pull–, pick- to pieces; take exception; cavil; peck at, nibble at, carp at; be censorious etc. adj.; pick -holes, –a hole, –a hole in one's coat; poke holes in; make a fuss about.

incur blame, excite disapprobation, scandalize, shock, revolt; get a bad name, forfeit one's good opinion, be under a cloud, come under the ferule, bring a hornet's nest about one's ears.

take blame, stand corrected; have to answer for.

adj. **disapproving** etc. v.; disparaging, condemnatory, damnatory, denunciatory, reproachful, abusive, objurgatory, clamorous, vituperative; defamatory etc. 934.

satirical, sarcastic, sardonic, cynical, dry, sharp, cutting, biting, severe, withering, trenchant, hard upon; censorious, critical, captious, carping, hypercritical; scandalized; fastidious etc. 868; sparing of–, grudging -praise.

disapproved, chid etc. v.; in bad odor, blown upon, unapproved; unblest; at a discount, exploded; weighed in the balance and found wanting.

unlamented, unbewailed, unpitied.

blameworthy, reprehensible etc. *(guilt)* 947; to-, worthy of- blame; answerable, uncommendable, exceptionable, not to be thought of; bad etc. 649; vicious etc. 945.

adv. **reproachfully** etc. *adj.;* with a wry face.

int. it is too bad! it won't do! it will never do! it isn't done! marry come up! [*archaic or dial.*], Oh! come! 'sdeath! [*archaic*].

forbid it Heaven! God forbid! Heaven forbid! out upon it! fie upon it! away with! tut! *O tempora! O mores!* [*L.*]; shame! fie, –for shame! out on you!

tell it not in Gath!

933. Flattery

n. **flattery**, adulation, gloze [*rare*]; blandishment [*rare*], blandiloquence; cajolery; fawning, wheedling etc. *v.;* captation, coquetry, obsequiousness, sycophancy, flunkeyism, toadyism, toadeating, tufthunting; snobbishness.

incense, honeyed words, flummery, buncombe *or* bunkum [*cant or slang*]; blarney, butter, soft soap, soft sawder [*all colloq.*]; rose water.

voice of the charmer, mouth honor; lip homage; euphemism; unctuousness etc. *adj.*

v. **flatter**, praise to the skies, puff; wheedle, cajole, glaver [*obs. or dial.*], coax; fawn, –upon; humor, gloze [*now rare*], soothe, pet, coquet, slaver, butter [*colloq.*], jolly [*colloq.*]; bespatter, beslubber, beplaster, beslaver; lay it on thick, overpraise; cog [*obs.*], collogue [*obs. in this sense*]; truckle to, pander *or* pandar to, pay court to; court; creep into the good graces of, curry favor with, hang on the sleeve of; fool to the top of one's bent; lick the dust.

lay the flattering unction to one's soul, gild the pill, make things pleasant.

overestimate etc. 482; exaggerate etc. 549.

adj. **flattering** etc. *v.;* adulatory; mealy-mouthed, honey-mouthed, honeyed, smooth, smooth-tongued; soapy [*slang*], oily, unctuous, blandiloquous, specious; fine–, fair– spoken; plausible, servile, sycophantic, fulsome; courtierly, courtierlike.

adv. **ad captandum**.

934. Detraction

n. **detraction**, disparagement, depreciation, vilification, obloquy, scurrility, scandal, defamation, aspersion, traducement [*rare*], slander, calumny, obtrectation [*obs.*], evil-speaking, backbiting, *scandalum magnatum* [*L.*].

sarcasm, cynicism; criticism *(disapprobation)* 932; invective etc. 932; envenomed tongue; *spretae injuria formae* [*L.*].

personality, libel, lampoon, skit [*Scot. & dial.*], squib, pasquil, pasquinade; *chronique scandaleuse* [*F.*], roorback.

detractor etc. 936.

v. **detract**, derogate, decry, depreciate, disparage; run down, cry down; back-cap; belittle; pessimize [*obs.*]; sneer at etc. *(contemn)* 930; criticize, pull to pieces, pick a hole in one's coat, asperse, cast aspersions, blow upon, bespatter, blacken, vilify, vilipend, avile [*obs.*]; give a dog a bad name, brand, malign; backbite, libel, lampoon, traduce, slander, defame, caluminate, bear false witness against; speak ill of behind one's back.

muckrake; fling dirt etc. *(disrespect)* 929; anathematize etc. 932; dip the pen in gall, view in a bad light.

adj. **detracting** etc. *v.;* defamatory, traducent [*rare*], detractory, derogatory, disparaging, libelous; scurrile, scurrilous, abusive; foul-spoken, foul-tongued, foul-mouthed; slanderous, calumnious, calumniatory; sarcastic, sardonic, satirical, cynical.

935. Flatterer

n. **flatterer**, adulator, eulogist, euphemist; optimist, encomiast, laudator, booster [*colloq.*], whitewasher.

today, toadeater, sycophant, courtier, flattercap [*obs. or dial. Eng.*], pickthank [*archaic or dial.*], Damocles, Sir Pertinax MacSycophant; *flatteur* [*F.*], *prôneur* [*F.*]; puffer, *claquer* [*F.*], claquer; tout, touter [*both colloq.*], clawback [*obs. or dial. Eng.*], slaverer; doer of dirty work; parasite, hanger-on etc. *(servility)* 886.

adj. flattering etc. 933.

936. Detractor

n. **detractor**, reprover; censor, censurer; cynic, critic, caviler, carper, word-catcher, *frondeur* [*F.*], barracker [*dial. Eng. & Austral.*].

defamer, knocker [*colloq.*], backbiter, slanderer, Sir Benjamin Backbite, lampooner, satirist, traducer, libeler, caluminator, dearest foe, Thersites; Zoilus; good-natured friend [*satirical*]; reviler, vituperator, castigator; shrew etc. 901; muckraker.

disapprover, *laudator temporis acti* [Horace].

adj. black-mouthed, abusive etc. 934.

937. Vindication

n. **vindication**, justification, warrant; exoneration, exculpation, disculpation; acquittal etc. 970; whitewashing.

extenuation, palliation, palliative, softening, mitigation.

plea etc. 617; apology, gloss, varnish; salvo [*rare*], excuse, extenuating circumstances; allowance, −to be made; *locus poenitentiae* [*L.*]; reply, defense *or* defence; recrimination etc. 938.

apologist, vindicator, justifier; defendant etc. 938.

true bill, justifiable charge.

v. **justify**, warrant; be an excuse for etc. *n.;* lend a color, furnish a handle; vindicate, exculpate, disculpate [*rare*]; acquit etc. 970; clear, set right, exonerate, whitewash; clear the skirts of.

extenuate, palliate, excuse, soften, apologize, varnish, slur, gloze; put a -gloss, −good face-upon; mince; gloss over, bolster up, help a lame dog over a stile.

advocate, defend, plead one's cause; stand up for, stick up for [*colloq.*], speak up for; contend for, speak for; bear out, keep in countenance, support; plead etc. 617; say in defense; plead ignorance; confess and avoid, propugn [*obs.*], put in a good word for.

take the will for the deed, make allowance for, do justice to; give one his due, give the Devil his due.

make good; prove the truth of, prove one's case; be justified by the event.

adj. **vindicative**, vindicatory, vindicated, vindicating etc. *v.;* palliative; exculpatory, disculpatory, apologetic.

excusable, defensible, pardonable; venial, veniable [*obs.*]; specious, plausible, justifiable.

938. Accusation

n. **accusation**, charge, imputation, slur, inculpation, exprobration [*rare*], delation; crimination, incrimination, accrimination [*obs.*], recrimination; *tu quoque* argument; invective etc. 932.

denunciation, denouncement [*archaic*]; libel, challenge, citation, arraignment, impeachment, appeachment [*obs.*], indictment, bill of indictment, true bill; lawsuit etc. 969; condemnation etc. 971.

gravamen of a charge, head and front of one's offending, *argumentum ad hominem* [*L.*]; scandal etc. (*detraction*) 934; *scandalum magnatum* [*L.*].

accuser, prosecutor, plaintiff, complainant, libelant, delator, informant, informer.

accused, defendant, prisoner, respondent, corespondent; litigant; panel.

v. **accuse**, charge, tax, impute, twit, taunt with, reproach; brand with reproach; stigmatize, slur; cast a stone at, cast a slur on; criminate, incriminate, inculpate, implicate; call to account etc. (*censure*) 932; take to -blame, −task; put in the black book.

inform against, indict, denounce, arraign; impeach, appeach [*obs.*]; have up, show up [*colloq.*], pull up [*colloq.*]; challenge, cite, lodge a complaint; prosecute, bring an action against etc. 969; blow upon [*colloq.*], squeal [*slang*].

charge with, saddle with; lay to one's -door, −charge; lay the blame on, bring home to; cast−, throw- in one's teeth; cast the first stone at.

have−, keep- a rod in pickle for; have a crow to pluck with.

trump up a charge.

adj. **accusing** etc. *v.;* accusatory, accusative, imputative, denunciatory, recriminatory, criminatory.

accused etc. *v.;* suspected; under -suspicion, −a cloud, −surveillance.

in custody, in detention, in the lockup, in the watch-house, in the jug [*slang*], in stir [*slang*], in the house of detention.

accusable, imputable, indefensible, inexcusable, unpardonable, unjustifiable; vicious etc. 845.

int. look at home! *tu quoque* [*L.*] etc. (*retaliation*) 718.

939. Probity

n. **probity**, integrity, rectitude; uprightness etc. *adj.;* honesty, faith; honor; *bonne foi* [*F.*], good faith, *bona fides* [*L.*]; purity, grace; clean hands.

constancy; faithfulness etc. *adj.;* fidelity, loyalty, incorruption [*archaic*], incorruptibility; trustworthiness etc. *adj.;* truth, candor, singleness of heart; veracity etc. 543; tender conscience etc. (*sense of duty*) 926.

fairness etc. *adj.;* fair play, justice, equity, impartiality, principle.

court of honor, a fair field and no favor; *argumentum ad verecundiam* [*L.*].

punctiliousness, punctilio, delicacy, nicety, scrupulosity, scrupulousness etc. *adj.;* scruple; point, −of honor; punctuality [*rare in this sense*].

dignity etc. (*repute*) 873; respectability, respectableness etc. *adj.*

man of honor, man of his word, gentleman, *gentilhomme* [*F.*], *fidus Achates* [*L.*], *preux* *chevalier* [*F.*], *galantuomo* [*It.*]; true-penny, trump [*slang*], brick [*slang or colloq.*], true Briton.

v. **be honorable** etc. *adj.;* deal -honorably, –squarely, –impartially, –fairly; speak the truth etc. (*veracity*) 543; draw a straight furrow; tell the truth and shame the Devil, *vitam impendere vero* [*L.*]; show a proper spirit, make a point of; do one's duty etc. (*virtue*) 944; play the game [*colloq.*].

redeem one's pledge etc. 926; keep–, be as good as- one's -promise, –word; keep faith with, not fail.

give and take, *audire alteram partem* [*L.*], give the Devil his due, put the saddle on the right horse.

redound to one's honor.

adj. **upright**; honest, –as daylight; veracious etc. 543; virtuous etc. 944; noble, honorable, reputable, respectable; fair, right, just, equitable, impartial, evenhanded, square; fair–, open- and aboveboard; white [*slang*].

inviolable, inviolate, unviolated, unbroken, unbetrayed; unbought, unbribed.

constant, –as the northern star; faithful, loyal, staunch; true, –blue, –to one's colors, –to the core, –as the needle to the pole; "marble-constant" [*Antony and Cleopatra*]; true-hearted, trusty, trustworthy; as good as one's word, to be depended on, incorruptible, honest as the day.

manly, straightforward etc. (*ingenuous*) 703; frank, candid, open-hearted.

conscientious, tender-conscienced, right-minded, high-principled, high-minded, scrupulous, religious, strict; nice, punctilious, overscrupulous, correct, punctual.

stainless, unstained, untarnished, unsullied, untainted, unperjured, uncorrupt, uncorrupted; innocent etc. 946; pure, undefiled, undepraved, undebauched; *integer vitae scelerisque purus* [Horace]; *justus et tenax propositi* [Horace]; supramundane, unworldly.

chivalrous, jealous of honor, *sans peur et sans reproche* [*F.*]; high-spirited.

adv. **honorably** etc. *adj.; bona fide* [*L.*]; on the square [*colloq.*], in good faith, in all honor, by fair means, *foro conscientiae* [*L.*], with clean hands.

int. on my honor! honor bright! [*colloq.*]; by my faith!

940. Improbity

n. **improbity**, dishonesty, dishonor; deviation from rectitude; disgrace etc. (*disrepute*) 874; fraud etc. (*deception*) 545; lying etc. 544; mouth honor etc. (*flattery*) 933; bad faith, *mala fides* [*L.*], Punic faith, *Punica fides* [*L.*]; infidelity; faith-

lessness etc. *adj.;* Judas kiss, betrayal; perfidy; perfidiousness etc. *adj.;* treachery, double dealing; unfairness etc. *adj.*

breach of -promise, –trust, –faith; prodition [*obs.*], disloyalty, divided allegiance, hyphenated allegiance [*cant*], treason, high treason; apostasy etc. (*tergiversation*) 607; nonobservance etc. 773.

shabbiness etc. *adj.;* villainy; baseness etc. *adj.;* abjection, debasement, degradation, turpitude, moral turpitude, laxity, trimming, shuffling.

knavery, roguery, rascality, foulplay; jobbing, jobbery, graft [*colloq.*], venality, nepotism; corruption, job, shuffle, fishy transaction; barratry [*law*], sharp practice, heads I win tails you lose.

v. **be dishonest** etc. *adj.;* play false; break one's -word, –faith, –promise; jilt, betray, forswear; shuffle etc. (*lie*) 544; play with marked cards, cheat at cards, live by one's wits, sail near the wind.

disgrace–, dishonor–, lower–, demean–, degrade- oneself; derogate, stoop, grovel, sneak, lose caste; sell oneself, squeal [*slang*], go back on [*colloq.*], go over to the enemy; seal one's infamy.

adj. **dishonest**, dishonorable; unconscientious, unscrupulous; fraudulent etc. 545; knavish; disgraceful etc. (*disreputable*) 974; wicked etc. 945.

false-hearted, disingenuous; unfair, one-sided; double, double-hearted, double-tongued, double-faced; time-serving, crooked, tortuous, insidious, Machiavellian, dark, slippery; fishy [*colloq.*], questionable.

infamous, arrant, foul, base, vile, low, ignominious, blackguard, perfidious, treacherous, perjured; hyphenated [*cant*].

contemptible, abject, mean, shabby, little, paltry, dirty, scurvy, scabby, sneaking, groveling, scrubby, rascally, barratrous [*law*], pettifogging; corrupt, venal; debased, mongrel; beneath one.

low-minded, low-thoughted, base-minded.

derogatory, degrading, undignified, indign [*obs.*], unbecoming, unbeseeming, unbefitting, *infra dignitatem* [*L.*], ungentlemanly, ungentlemanlike; unknightly, unchivalric, unmanly, unhandsome; recreant, inglorious.

faithless, of bad faith, false, unfaithful, disloyal; untrustworthy; trustless, trothless [*archaic*], lost to shame, dead to honor.

adv. **dishonestly** etc. *adj.; mala fide* [*L.*]; like a thief in the night, by crooked paths, by foul means.

int. *O tempora! O mores!* [Cicero].

941. Knave

n. **knave**, rogue, villain; Scapin, rascal; Lazarillo de Tormes; bad man etc. 949; blackguard etc. 949; barrator *or* barrater [*law*], shyster.

traitor, betrayer, archtraitor, conspirator, Judas, Catiline; reptile, serpent, snake in the grass, wolf in sheep's clothing, sneak, Jerry Sneak, squealer [*slang*], telltale, mischief-maker; trimmer, renegade etc. (*tergiversation*) 607; truant, recreant, slacker; sycophant etc. (*servility*) 886.

942. Disinterestedness

n. **disinterestedness** etc. *adj.;* generosity; liberality, liberalism; altruism; benevolence etc. 906; elevation, loftiness of purpose, exaltation, magnanimity; chivalry, chivalrous spirit, heroism, sublimity.

self-denial, self-abnegation, self-sacrifice, self-devotion, self-immolation, self-control etc. (*resolution*) 604; stoicism, devotion; martyrdom, suttee.

labor of love.

[comparisons] Good Shepherd, Good Samaritan, Bishop Bienvenu [Victor Hugo], Great Heart.

v. **be disinterested** etc. *adj.;* make a sacrifice, lay one's head on the block; put oneself in the place of others, do as one would be done by, do unto others as we would men should do unto us.

adj. **disinterested**, unselfish, self-denying, self-sacrificing, self-devotional.

magnanimous, noble-minded, high-minded; princely, handsome, great, high, elevated, lofty, exalted, spirited, stoical, great-hearted, large-hearted; generous, liberal; chivalrous, heroic, sublime.

unbought, unbribed; uncorrupted etc. (*upright*) 939.

943. Selfishness

n. **selfishness** etc. *adj.;* self-love, self-indulgence, self-worship, self-seeking, self-interest; egotism, egoism; *amour propre* [*F.*] etc. (*vanity*) 880; nepotism; charity that begins at home.

worldliness etc. *adj.;* world wisdom.

illiberality; meanness etc. *adj.*

self-seeker, timeserver, time-pleaser, tufthunter, fortune hunter; jobber, worldling; egotist, egoist, monopolist, nepotist; dog in the manger, *canis in praesepi* [*L.*], "foes to nobleness," temporizer, hyphenate [*cant*], trimmer; hog, road-hog, end-seat hog [*colloq.*].

v. **be selfish** etc. *adj.;* please–, indulge–, pamper–, coddle- oneself; consult one's own -wishes, –pleasure; look after one's own interest; feather one's nest; take care of number one, have an eye to the main chance, know on which side one's bread is buttered; give an inch and take an ell.

adj. **selfish**, self-seeking, self-indulgent, self-interested; wrapt up in self, centered in self; egotistic *or* egotistical, egotistic *or* egotistical.

illiberal, mean, ungenerous, narrowminded; mercenary, venal; covetous etc. 819.

worldly, unspiritual, earthly, earthly -minded, mundane, worldly-minded, worldly-wise; time-serving.

interested; *alieni appetens sui profusus* [Sallust].

adv. **ungenerously** etc. *adj.;* to gain some private ends, from selfish motives, from interested motives.

944. Virtue

n. **virtue**; virtuousness etc. *adj.;* morality; moral rectitude; integrity etc. (*probity*) 939; nobleness etc. 873.

merit, worth, desert, excellence, credit; self-control etc. (*resolution*) 604; self-denial etc. (*temperance*) 953.

well-doing; good actions, good behavior; discharge–, fulfillment–, performance- of duty; well-spent life; innocence etc. 946.

morals; ethics etc. (*duty*) 926; cardinal virtues.

[science of virtue] aretaics (*contrasted with* eudemonism); aretology.

v. **be virtuous** etc. *adj.;* practice virtue etc. *n.;* do–, fulfill–, perform–, discharge- one's duty; redeem one's pledge etc. 926; act well, –one's part; fight the good fight; acquit oneself well; command–, master- one's passions; keep in the right path, keep on the straight and narrow way.

set an example, set a good example; be on one's -good, –best- behavior.

adj. **virtuous**, good; innocent etc. 646; meritorious, deserving, worthy, desertful [*rare*], correct; dutiful, duteous; moral, right, righteous, right-minded; well-intentioned, creditable, laudable, commendable, praiseworthy; above praise, beyond all praise; excellent, admirable; sterling, pure, noble; whole-souled.

exemplary; matchless, peerless; saintly, saintlike; heaven-born, angelic, seraphic, godlike.

adv. **virtuously** etc. *adj.;* *e merito* [*L.*].

945. Vice

n. **vice**; evildoing, evil courses; wrongdoing; wickedness, viciousness etc. *adj.;* hardness of heart;

iniquity, peccability, demerit; sin, Adam, old
Adam, offending Adam.

immorality, impropriety, indecorum, scandal,
laxity, looseness of morals; want of -principle
-ballast; knavery, etc. (*improbity*) 940; atrocity,
brutality etc. (*malevolence*) 907; obliquity,
backsliding, infamy.

depravity, demoralization, pravity, pollution;
corruption etc. (*debasement*) 659; profligacy;
flagrancy, unnatural desires, unnatural habits,
Sadism, Lesbianism, sodomy; lust etc. 961.

lowest dregs of vice, sink of iniquity, Alsatian den;
gusto picaresco [*L.*].

cannibalism, endocannibalism, endophagy; ex-
ocannibalism, exophagy; "long pig" [*humorous*].

weakness etc. *adj.;* infirmity, weakness of the
flesh, frailty, imperfection, error; weak side;
foible; failing, failure; crying sin, besetting sin;
defect, deficiency; cloven foot.

fault, crime; criminality etc. (*guilt*) 947.

reprobate; sinner etc. 949.

[resorts] brothel etc. 961; gambling house etc.
621; joint [*slang*], opium den.

v. **be vicious** etc. *adj.;* sin, commit sin, do amiss, err,
transgress; misdemean–, forget–, misconduct-
oneself; misdo [*rare*], misbehave; fall, lapse,
slip, trip, offend, trespass; deviate from the
-line of duty, –path of virtue etc. 944; take a
wrong course, go astray; hug a sin, hug a fault;
sow one's wild oats.

render vicious etc. *adj.;* demoralize, brutalize;
corrupt etc. (*degrade*) 659.

adj. **vicious**; sinful; sinning etc. *v.;* wicked, iniquitous,
immoral, unrighteous, wrong, criminal; unprin-
cipled, lawless, disorderly, dissolute, profligate,
scampish; worthless, desertless [*rare*], disgraceful, recreant, disreputable; demoralizing, degrading.

miscreated, misbegotten; demoralized, corrupt,
depraved; Sadistic, degenerate.

evil-minded, evil-disposed; ill-conditioned; malevolent etc. 907; heartless, graceless, shameless, virtueless, abandoned, lost to virtue;
unconscionable; sunk–, lost–, deep–, steeped-
in iniquity.

base, sinister, scurvy, foul, gross, vile, black,
grave, facinorous [*obs.*], felonious, nefarious,
shameful, scandalous, infamous, villainous, of a
deep dye, heinous; flagrant, flagitious, atrocious, incarnate, accursed.

diabolic *or* diabolical, Mephistophelian, satanic,
hellish, infernal, stygian, fiendlike, hellborn,
demoniacal, devilish, fiendish.

incorrigible, irreclaimable, obdurate, reprobate,
past praying for; culpable, reprehensible etc.
(*guilty*) 947.

unjustifiable, indefensible, inexcusable, inexpiable, unpardonable, irremissible.

improper, unseemly, indecorous, indiscreet, *contra bonos mores* [*L.*], unworthy, blameworthy,
reprehensible, uncommendable, discreditable;
naughty, incorrect, unduteous, undutiful.

weak, frail, lax, infirm, imperfect; spineless, invertebrate [*both fig.*]; dotty [*slang*].

adv. wrong; sinfully etc. *adj.;* without excuse.

int. fie upon! it smells to heaven!

946. Innocence

n. **innocence**; guiltlessness etc. *adj.;* incorruption,
impeccability, inerrability, inerrableness.

clean hands, clear conscience, *mens sibi conscia
recti* [Virgil].

innocent, new-born babe; lamb, dove.

v. **be innocent** etc. *adj.; nil conscire sibi nulla palles-
cere culpa* [Horace].

acquit etc. 970; exculpate etc. (*vindicate*) 937.

adj. **innocent**, not guilty; unguilty; guiltless, faultless,
sinless, stainless, bloodless, spotless; clear, immaculate; *rectus in curia* [*L.*]; unspotted, unblemished, unerring; undefiled etc. 939;
unhardened, Saturnian; Arcadian etc. (*artless*) 703; paradisaic *or* paradisaical, paradisiac
or paradisiacal.

inculpable, unculpable [*rare*], unblamed, unblamable, blameless, unfallen, inerrable, above suspicion, irreproachable, irreprovable [*rare*],
irreprehensible; unexceptionable, unobjectionable, unimpeachable; salvable; venial etc.
937.

virtuous etc. 944; unreproved, unimpeached, un-
reproached.

harmless, inoffensive, innoxious [*obs.*], innocuous; dovelike, lamblike; pure, harmless as
doves; innocent as -a lamb, –the babe unborn;
"more sinned against than sinning" [*Lear*].

adv. **innocently** etc. *adj.;* with clean hands; with a
-clear, –safe- conscience.

947. Guilt

n. **guilt**, guiltiness, culpability, criminality, crimi-
nousness [*obs.*]; deviation from rectitude etc.
(*improbity*) 940; sinfulness etc. (*vice*) 945; peccability.

misconduct, misbehavior, misdoing, misdeed;
fault, sin, error, transgression; dereliction, delinquency.

indiscretion, lapse, slip, trip, *faux pas* [*F.*], peccadillo; flaw, blot, omission, failing, failure; blunder, break *or* bad break [*colloq.*].

offense, trespass; misdemeanor, tort [*law*], delict, *delictum* [*L.*]; misfeasance [*law*], misprision, misprision of treason *or* felony [*law*]; malfeasance [*law*], official misconduct, nonfeasance [*law*]; malefaction, malversation, corruption, malpractice; crime, felony, capital crime.

enormity, atrocity, outrage; unpardonable sin, deadly sin, mortal sin; "deed without a name" [*Macbeth*].

corpus delicit [*L.*], body of the crime, substantial facts, fundamental facts, damning evidence.

adj. **guilty**, blamable, culpable, peccable, in fault, censurable, reprehensible, blameworthy.

objectionable, exceptionable, uncommendable, illaudable; weighed in the balance and found wanting.

adv. **in the very act**, *in flagrante delicto* [*L.*], redhanded.

948. Good Man
[good woman]

n. **good man**, worthy.

model, paragon etc. (*perfection*) 650; good example; hero, demigod, seraph, angel; saint etc. (*piety*) 987; benefactor etc. 912; philanthropist etc. 910; Aristides; noble liver, pattern.

salt of the earth; one in ten thousand; a man among men, white man [*slang*]; brick [*slang*], trump [*slang*], rough diamond.

good woman, virgin, innocent; goddess, queen, Madonna, ministering angel, heaven's noblest gift; "a perfect woman, nobly planned" [Wordsworth].

949. Bad Man
[bad woman]

n. **bad man**, wrongdoer, worker of iniquity; evildoer etc. 913; sinner, transgressor; the wicked etc. 945; bad example.

rascal, scoundrel, villain, miscreant, budmash [*India*], caitiff, wretch, reptile, viper, serpent, cockatrice, basilisk; tiger, monster; devil etc. (*demon*) 980; devil incarnate; demon in human shape, Nana Sahib; hellhound, rakehell.

roué [*F.*], rake; Sadist, one who has sold himself to the devil, fallen angel, *âme damnée* [*F.*], *vaurien* [*F.*], *mauvais sujet* [*F.*], loose fish [*colloq.*], rounder [*slang*]; lost sheep, black sheep; castaway, recreant, defaulter; prodigal etc. 818.

bad woman, jade, Jezebel, hell-cat, quean, wench, slut; adultress etc. 962.

rough, rowdy, ugly customer, ruffian, bully, tough [*colloq.*], hoodlum etc. 886; Jonathan Wild; hangman; incendiary, fire bug; thief etc. 792; murderer etc. 361.

culprit, delinquent, criminal, malefactor, misdemeanant; felon; convict, jailbird *or* gaolbird, ticket-of-leave man [*Brit.*]; outlaw.

riffraff, scum of the earth; blackguard, *polisson* [*F.*], loafer, sneak, rascalion *or* rascallion; cullion, mean wretch, varlet [*archaic*], kern [*obs.*], *âme-de-boue* [*F.*], *drôle* [*F.*]; cur, dog, hound, whelp, mongrel; losel [*archaic or dial.*], loon *or* lown [*obs. or dial. variant*], ronion *or* ronyon *or* runnion [*obs. or rare*]; outcast, vagabond, runagate; rogue etc. (*knave*) 941.

scamp, scapegrace, rip [*colloq.*], ne'er-do-well, good for nothing, reprobate, scalawag *or* scallawag [*colloq.*], sad dog [*colloq.*], limb [*colloq.*], rapscallion [*all the words in this paragraph are commonly applied jocularly or lightly*].

int. sirrah!

950. Penitence

n. **penitence**, contrition, compunction, repentance, remorse; regret etc. 833.

self-reproach, self-reproof, self-accusation, self-condemnation, self-humiliation; stings–, pangs–, qualms–, prickings–, twinge–, twitch–, touch–, voice- of conscience; "compunctious visitings of nature" [*Macbeth*].

acknowledgment, confession etc. (*disclosure*) 529; apology etc. 952; recantation etc. 607; penance etc. 952; resipiscence [*rare*].

awakened conscience, deathbed repentance, *locus poenitentiae* [*L.*], stool of repentance, cutty stool [*Scot.*], mourners' bench [*local*].

penitent, repentant [*rare*], Magdalen, prodigal son, returned prodigal, "a sadder and a wiser man" [Coleridge].

v. **repent**, be sorry for; be penitent etc. *adj.*; rue; regret etc. 833; think better of; recant etc. 607; knock under etc. (*submit*) 725; plead guilty; sing -miserere, -de profundis [*L.*]; cry *peccavi* [*L.*]; say *culpa mea* [*L.*], own oneself in the wrong; acknowledge, confess etc. (*disclose*) 529; humble oneself; beg pardon etc. (*apologize*) 952; turn over a new leaf, put on the new man, turn from sin; repent in sackcloth and ashes etc. (*do penance*) 952; learn by experience.

reclaim, reform, regenerate, redeem, convert, amend, set straight again, make a new man of, restore self-respect.

adj. **penitent**; repenting etc. *v.;* repentant, contrite, softened, melted, touched; conscience-smitten, conscience-stricken; self-accusing, self-convicted.

penitential, penitentiary; reclaimed; not hardened: unhardened.

adv. *mea culpa* [*L.*]; *de profundis* [*L.*].

951. Impenitence

n. **impenitence**, irrepentance, recusancy, recusance; lack of contrition.

hardness of heart, heart of stone, seared conscience, induration, obduracy; deaf ears.

v. **be impenitent** etc. *adj.;* steel the heart, harden the heart; turn away from the light; die game, die and make no sign.

adj. **impenitent**, uncontrite, obdurate, hard, hardened, seared, recusant, unrepentant; relentless, remorseless, graceless, shriftless.

lost, incorrigible, irreclaimable.

unreclaimed, unreformed; unrepented, unatoned.

952. Atonement

n. **atonement**, reparation; compromise, composition; compensation etc. 30; quittance, quits [*rare*], expiation, redemption, reclamation, conciliation, propitiation; indemnification, redress.

amends, apology, *amende honorable* [*F.*], satisfaction; peace–, sin–, burnt- offering; scapegoat, sacrifice.

penance, fasting, maceration, sackcloth and ashes, white sheet, shrift, flagellation, lustration; purgation, purgatory.

v. **atone**, atone for; expiate; propitiate; make amends, make good; reclaim, redeem, repair, ransom, absolve, purge, shrive, do penance, stand in a white sheet, repent in sackcloth and ahses.

set one's house in order, wipe off old scores, make matters up; pay the forfeit, pay the penalty.

apologize, express regret, beg pardon, *faire l'amende honorable* [*F.*], give satisfaction; get–, fall- down on one's knees, –marrowbones [*slang or jocular*].

adj. **propitiatory**, expiatory, sacrifice, sacrificial, sacrificatory [*rare*]; piacular, piaculous [*rare*].

953. Temperance

n. **temperance**, moderation, sobriety, soberness.

forbearance, abnegation; self-denial, self-restraint, self-control etc. (*resolution*) 604.

abstinence, abstemiousness, asceticism; Encratism, prohibition; frugality; vegetarianism, teetotalism, total abstinence; system of -Pythagoras, –Cornaro; Pythagorism; Stoicism.

abstainer, Pythagorean, gymnosophist; nephalist, teetotaler etc. 958; Encratite, vegetarian, fruitarian, hydropot [*rare*]; ascetic etc. 995.

v. **be temperate** etc. *adj.*; abstain, forbear, refrain, deny oneself, spare; know when one has had enough; take the pledge; prohibit; control the -old Adam, –carnal man, –fleshly lusts; refrain from indulgence, look not upon the wine when it is red.

adj. **temperate**, moderate, sober, frugal, sparing, abstemious, abstinent; within compass; measured etc. (*sufficient*) 639.

Pythagorean; vegetarian, fruitarian; teetotal.

954. Intemperance

n. **intemperance**, sensuality, rakery [*rare*], animalism, carnality; tragalism; pleasure; effeminacy, silkiness; luxury, luxuriousness; lap of -pleasure, –luxury; free-living.

indulgence; high living, inabstinence, self-indulgence; voluptuousness etc. *adj.;* epicurism, epicureanism, sybaritism.

dissipation; licentiousness etc. *adj.;* debauchery; crapulence.

revel, revels, revelry, orgy; drunkenness etc. 959; debauch, carousal, jollification [*colloq.*], high old time [*colloq.*], drinking bout, wassail, saturnalia, excess, too much.

drug habit; Circean cup; bhang, hashish, opium, hop [*slang*], dope [*slang*], cocaine; drug fiend, dope fiend [*slang*].

v. **be intemperate** etc. *adj.;* indulge, exceed; live -well, –high, –on the fat of the land; eat drink and be merry, look upon the wine when it is red, dine not wisely but too well; give free rein to indulgence etc. *n.;* wallow in voluptuousness etc. *n.;* plunge into dissipation; sensualize, brutify, carnalize.

revel, rake, live hard, run riot, sow one's wild oats; slake one's -appetite, –thirst; swill; pamper.

adj. **intemperate**, inabstinent, excessive; sensual, self-indulgent; voluptuous, licentious, wild, dissolute, rakish, fast, debauched; orgiastic, Corybantic, Paphian.

brutish, crapulous, swinish, piggish, hoggish, beastlike, theroid [*med.*].

luxurious, Epicurean, Sybaritical; bred–, nursed- in the lap of luxury; indulged, pampered; full fed, high fed.

intoxicated, drunk etc. 959.

954a. Sensualist

n. **sensualist**, Sybarite, voluptuary, Sardanapalus, man of pleasure, carpet knight; epicure, epicurean, *gourmet* [*F.*]; gourmand; glutton etc. 957; pig, hog; votary–, swine- of Epicurus; Heliogabalus; free liver, hard liver; libertine etc. 962; hedonist; tragalist.

955. Asceticism

n. **asceticism**, puritanism, sabbatarianism; cynicism, austerity; total abstinence; nephalism; Yoga.

mortification, maceration, sackcloth and ashes, flagellation; penance etc. 952; fasting etc. 956; martyrdom.

ascetic, anchoret *or* anchorite, *Heautontimorumenos* [*Gr.*]; hermit etc. (*recluse*) 893; puritan, sabbatarian, cynic; bhikshu, sannyasi *or* sanyasi, yogi [*all Hindu*]; dervish, fakir [*both Moham.*]; martyr.

adj. **ascetic**, austere, puritanical; cynical; over-religious; acerb, acerbic.

956. Fasting

n. **fasting**; xerophagy; famishment, starvation.

fast, *jour maigre* [*F.*]; fast day, banyan day; Lent, quadragesima; Ramadan *or* Ramazan [*Moham.*]; spare–, meager- diet; lenten -diet, –entertainment; *soupe maigre* [*F.*], short commons, Barmecide feast; short rations; punishment of Tantalus.

v. **fast**, starve, clem [*obs.*], famish, perish with hunger; dine with Duke Humphrey; make two bites of a cherry; "keep the larder lean."

adj. **fasting** etc.*v.;* lenten, quadragesimal; unfed; starved etc. *v.;* half-starved; hungry etc. 865.

957. Gluttony

n. **gluttony**; greed; greediness etc. *adj.;* voracity.

epicurism, gastronomy; good–, high-living; edacity, gulosity [*rare*], crapulence; guttling, guzzle [*rare*], guzzling; pantophagy.

feast etc. (*food*) 298; good cheer, blow out [*slang*]; *batterie de cuisine* [*F.*].

glutton, gormandizer, gourmand, cormorant, pig, hog etc. (*sensualist*) 954a; guttler, pantophagist; belly-god, Apicius, gastronome.

epicure, *bon vivant* [*F.*], gourmand *gourmet* [*F.*], gourmet.

v. **gormandize**, gorge; overgorge oneself, overeat oneself, glut, satiate, engorge, eat one's fill, cram, stuff, guttle, guzzle, bolt, devour, gobble up; overindulge; gulp etc. (*swallow food*) 298; raven, eat out of house and home; have the stomach of an ostrich; play a good knife and fork etc. (*appetite*) 865; have a capacious -gorge, –maw.

pamper [*obs. as* glut], indulge.

adj. **gluttonous**, greedy; gormandizing etc. *v.;* edacious, omnivorous, pantophagic, pantophagous, voracious, devouring, all-devouring, crapulent, swinish.

pampered [*obs. as* fed to excess]; overfed, overgorged, overindulged.

958. Sobriety

n. **sobriety**; teetotalism, nephalism.

water-drinker; hydropot [*rare*], prohibitionist; teetotaler *or* teetotaller, abstainer, nephalist, Good Templar, band of hope, W. C. T. U. (Women's Christian Temperance Union).

v. take the pledge, swear off.

adj. **sober**, –as a judge; temperate, moderate.

959. Drunkenness

n. **drunkenness** etc. *adj.;* intemperance; drinking etc. *v.;* inebriety, inebriation, ebriety [*rare*], ebriosity [*rare*], insobriety, intoxication; temulence [*rare*], bibacity, wine-bibbing; compotation, potation; deep potations, bacchanals, bacchanalia, bacchanalianism, libations; bender [*slang*].

alcoholism, oinomania, dipsomania; delirium tremens, D. T.'s [*colloq.*]; *mania a potu* [*L.*].

drink, alcoholic drinks, alcohol, blue ruin [*slang*], booze *or* bouse [*colloq.*], "the luscious liquor" [Milton]; grog, port wine, punch; punchbowl, cup, rosy wine, flowing bowl; drop, –too much; dram; beer etc. (*beverage*) 298; *aguardiente* [*Sp.*]; apple-brandy, apple-jack; bourbon; brandy, brandy smesh; chain lightning [*slang*], champagne, cocktail; gin, gin-sling; highball, peg [*slang, orig. India*]; burra (*or* bara) peg, chota peg [*both India*]; rum, schnapps, sherry, xeres, sling, usquebaugh, vodka, whisky *or* whiskey, rye; stirrup cup, parting cup, doch-an-dorrach *or* doch-an-dorris [*Scot.*].

illicit distilling; moonshining, moonshine *or* moonshine whisky [*colloq.*], hooch [*slang*], home-brew; white lightning; moonshiner [*colloq.*], bootlegger [*slang*].

drunkard, sot, toper, tippler, bibber, winebibber; hard–, gin–, dram- drinker; soaker [*slang*], sponge [*slang*], tun [*jocose*], love-pot, tosspot, guzzler, guzzle [*rare*], barfly, boozer *or* bouser [*colloq.*], bum [*slang*], tavern haunter, thirsty soul, reveler, carouser, Bacchanal, Bacchanalian; Bacchae, bacchante, maenad; devotee to Bacchus.

v. **get** *or* **be drunk** etc. *adj.;* see double; take a -drop, −glass- too much; get smashed [*slang*]; drink, tipple, tope [*colloq.*], booze *or* bouse [*colloq.*], guzzle, swill [*slang*], soak [*slang*], sot [*rare*], bum [*slang*], besot, have a jag on [*slang*], lush [*slang*], bib [*obs. or dial.*], swig [*dial. or colloq.*], carouse; sacrifice at the shrine of Bacchus; take to drinking; drink -hard, −deep, −like a fish; have one's swill [*slang*], drain the cup, splice the main brace [*slang*], take a hair of the dog that bit you.

liquor, liquor up [*both slang*], wet one's -whistle, −clay, −swallow [*colloq. or humorous*]; wet the red lane [*humorous*]; raise the elbow, raise the little finger, hit the booze [*slang*], take a whet; crack a−, pass the- bottle; toss off etc. (*drink up*) 298; go to the -alehouse, −public house, −saloon.

make one drunk etc. *adj.;* inebriate, fuddle [*colloq.*], befuddle, fuzzle [*obs.*], get into one's head.

sell illicitly, bootleg [*slang*].

adj. **drunk,** tipsy, intoxicated, bibacious, inebrious, inebriate, inebriated; in one's cups; in a state of intoxication etc. *n.;* temulent, temulentive [*both rare*]; fuddled [*colloq.*], mellow, cut [*slang*], boozy *or* bousy [*colloq.*], full [*vulgar*], fou [*Scot.*], lit up [*slang*], glorious [*humorous*], fresh [*slang*], merry, elevated; flush, flushed, flustered, disguised [*archaic*], groggy [*colloq.*], beery; top-heavy; pot-valiant, potulent [*obs.*], squiffy [*slang*]; overcome, overtaken [*obs.*], whittled [*obs.*]; screwed, tight, primed, corned, raddled, smashed, stoned, sewed up, lushy [*all slang*], muzzy [*colloq.*], nappy [*rare*], muddled, obfuscated, maudlin; crapulous, blind drunk, dead drunk.

inter pocula [*L.*], in liquor, the worse for liquor; having had a drop too much, half-seas over [*slang*], three sheets in the wind [*sailors' slang*], under the table.

drunk as -a piper, −a fiddler, −a lord, −Chloe, −an owl, −David's sow, −a wheelbarrow [*all colloq.*].

drunken, bibacious, sottish; given−, addicted- to -drink, −the bottle; toping etc. *v.;* primed, −on the hip; heeled [*slang*].

960. Purity

n. **purity;** decency, decorum, delicacy; continence, chastity, honesty, virtue, modesty, shame; pudicity, pucelage [*rare*], virginity.

virgin, vestal, prude; Lucretia, Diana, Athena Parthenos; Joseph, Hippolytus.

adj. **pure,** undefiled, modest, delicate, decent, decorous; *virginibus puerisque* [*L.*]; chaste, continent, virtuous, honest, Platonic.

961. Impurity

n. **impurity;** uncleanness etc. (*filth*) 653; immodesty; grossness etc. *adj.;* indelicacy, indecency, impudicity, obscenity, ribaldry, smut, bawdry, *double entente, équivoque* [*F.*]; pornography.

incontinence, debauchery, libertinism, libertinage, fornication, wenching, venery, dissipation.

concupiscence, lust, carnality, flesh, salacity; pruriency, lechery, lasciviousness, lewdness, lasciviency [*obs.*], lubricity; Sadism, Sapphism, Lesbianism, nymphomania, aphrodisia, satyriasis.

seduction; defloration, defilement, abuse, violation, stupration, rape; incest.

social evil, harlotry, whoredom, concubinage, cuckoldom, adultery, advoutry [*obs.*], crim. con.; free-love.

intrigue, amour, amourette, *liaison* [*F.*], *faux pas* [*F.*], entanglement; gallantry.

[*resorts*] brothel, bagnio, stew, bawdyhouse, lupanar, house of ill fame, bordel [*obs.*]; Yoshiwara [*Jap.*], red-light district.

harem, seraglio, zenana [*India*].

v. **be impure** etc. *adj.;* debauch, defile, seduce; prostitute; abuse, violate, rape, stuprate [*rare*], deflower; commit adultery etc. *n.;* intrigue.

adj. **impure;** unclean etc. (*dirty*) 653; not to be mentioned to ears polite; immodest, shameless, indecorous, indelicate, indecent, Fescennine; loose, *risqué* [*F.*], coarse, gross, broad, free, equivocal, smutty, fulsome, ribald, obscene, bawdy, pornographic.

concupiscent, prurient, lickerish, rampant, lustful; carnal, carnal-minded; lewd, lascivious, lecherous, libidinous, erotic, ruttish, must *or* musty [*said of elephants*]; salacious, Paphian, voluptuous; goatish, beastly, bestial, incestuous.

unchaste, light, wanton, licentious, adulterous, debauched, dissolute; of loose character, of easy virtue; frail, gay, riggish [*obs.*], incontinent, meretricious, rakish, gallant, dissipated; no better than she should be; on the town, on the streets, on the *pavé* [*F.*], on the loose [*colloq.*].

962. Libertine

n. **libertine**; voluptuary etc. 954a; rake, debauchee, loose fish [*colloq.*], rip [*colloq.*], rakehell, fast man; intrigant, gallant, seducer, fornicator, lecher, satyr, goat, whoremonger, *paillard* [*F.*], advocater [*obs.*], adulterer, gay deceiver, Lothario, Don Juan, Bluebeard; chartered libertine.

adultress, advoutress [*obs.*], courtesan, prostitute, strumpet, harlot, whore, hooker [*slang*], punk [*obsoles.*], *fille de joie* [*F.*], woman, woman of the town, streetwalker, Cyprian, miss [*obs.*], piece [*slang*], demirep, wench, trollop, trull, baggage, hussy, drab, bitch [*low*], jade, skit [*obs.*], rig [*obs.*], quean, mopsy [*dial. Eng.*], slut, minx, harridan; unfortunate, –female, –woman; woman -of easy virtue etc. (*unchaste*) 961; wanton, fornicatress; *lorette* [*F.*], *cocotte* [*F.*], *petite dame* [*F.*], grisette; demimondaine; chippy [*slang*]; Sapphist; white slave.

Jezebel, Messalina, Delilah, Thais, Phryne, Aspasia, Lais.

demimonde, erring sisters, fallen women, frail sisterhood.

mistress, concubine, kept woman, doxy, *chère amie* [*F.*]; *bona roba* [*It.*]; spiritual wife.

procurer, pimp, pander *or* pandar, bawd, *conciliatrix* [*L.*], procuress, mackerel [*archaic*], wittol [*obs.*].

963. Legality

n. **legality**, legitimacy, legitimateness; legitimatization, legitimization.

law, code, *corpus juris* [*L.*], constitution, pandect, charter, act, enactment, statute, rule; canon etc. (*precept*) 697; ordinance, institution, regulation; bylaw *or* bye-law; rescript, decree etc. (*order*) 741; ordonnance; standing order; plebiscite etc. (*choice*) 609; legislature.

legal process; form, formula, formality, rite, arm of the law; *habeas corpus* [*L.*]; *fieri facias* [*L.*].

equity, common law; *lex scripta* [*L.*]; *lex non scripta* [*L.*], unwritten law; law of nations, *droit des gens* [*F.*], international law, *just gentium* [*L.*]; *just civile* [*L.*]; civil–, canon–, crown–, criminal–, statute–, ecclesiastical- law; *lex mercatoria* [*L.*].

constitutionalism, constitutionality; justice etc. 922.

[science of law] jurisprudence, nomology; legislation, codification, nomography.

v. **legalize**, legitimate, legitimize, legitimatize; enact, ordain; decree etc. (*order*) 741; pass a law, legislate; codify, formulate, formalize, regularize, authorize.

adj. **legal**, legitimate; according to law; vested, constitutional, chartered, legalized; lawful etc. (*permitted*) 760; statutable, statutory; legislatorial, legislative; judicial, juridical; nomistic, nomothetical.

adv. **legally** etc. *adj.;* in the eye of the law; *de jure* [*L.*].

964. Illegality
[absence or violation of law]

n. **lawlessness**; illicitness; breach–, violation- of law; disobedience etc. 742; unconformity etc. 83; arbitrariness etc. *adj.;* antinomy, violence, brute force, despotism, tyranny, outlawry.

mob–, lynch–, club–, Lydford–, martial–, drumhead- law; *coup d'état* [*F.*]; *le droit du plus fort* [*F.*]; *argumentum baculinum* [*L.*].

illegality, informality, unlawfulness, illegitimacy, bar sinister.

trover and conversion; smuggling, bootlegging [*slang*], illicit distilling etc. 959; poaching; simony.

v. **violate the law**, offend against the law, set the law at defiance, ride roughshod over, drive a coach and six through a statute; make the law a dead letter, take the law into one's own hands. smuggle, run, poach, bootleg [*slang*].

adj. **illegal**; prohibited etc. 761; not allowed, unlawful, illegitimate, illicit, contraband, actionable. unchartered, unconstitutional; unwarranted, unwarrantable, unauthorized; informal, unofficial, injudicial [*rare*], extra-judicial.

lawless, arbitrary, despotic, despotical; summary, irresponsible; unanswerable, unaccountable. null and void; a dead letter.

adv. **illegally** etc. *adj.;* with a high hand, in violation of law.

965. Jurisdiction
[executive]

n. **jurisdiction**, judicature, administration of justice; soc, soke [*both A. S. & early Eng. law*]; executive, commission of the peace; magistracy etc. (*authority*) 737; judge etc. 967; tribunal etc. 966.

city government, municipal government, commission government, Oregon plan; municipality, corporation, bailiwick, shrievalty; police, police force; constabulary, Bumbledom.

executive officer, officer, commissioner, lord
lieutenant [*Brit.*], collector [*India*]; city manager, mayor, alderman, councilor *or* councillor,
selectman; bailiff, tipstaff, bumbailiff [*Eng.*],
catchpole *or* catchpoll, beadle; sheriff, shrieve
[*obs.*], bailie [*Scot.*], constable; policeman, police constable, police sergeant, patrolman etc.
664; *sbirro* [*It.*], alguazil, *gendarme* [*F.*], kavass
[*Turk.*], lictor, mace bearer, *huissier* [*F.*], tith-
ingman; excise man, gauger *or* gager, customhouse officer, *douanier* [*F.*]; press gang *or*
pressgang.

coroner, aedile *or* edile; reeve, portreeve [*early
Eng. hist.*], paritor [*obs.*], *posse comitatus*
[*L.*].

bureau, cutcherry [*India*], department, portfolio, secretariat.

v. **judge,** sit in judgment; have jurisdiction over.

adj. **executive,** administrative, judicative, municipal;
inquisitorial, causidical; judicatory, judiciary,
judicial, juridical.

adv. *coram judice* [*L.*].

966. Tribunal

n. **tribunal,** court, curia, board, bench, judicature,
judicatory; court of -justice, −law, −arbitra-
tion; inquisition; guild; durbar [*India*], divan
[*Oriental*], Areopagus.

justice−, judgment−, mercy-seat; woolsack; bar,
bar of justice; dock; forum, hustings, bureau,
drumhead; jury-box; witness box, witness
stand.

senate-house, town hall, theater *or* theatre; House
of Commons, House of Lords; statehouse,
townhouse, courthouse.

[British courts], sessions; petty−, quarter−, spe-
cial−, general- sessions [*Eng. law*]; assizes;
eyre, justices in eyre, wardmote, burghmote,
barmote, courtleet, court-baron, court of pie-
poudre [*all old Eng. law*]; superior courts of
Westminster; court of -record, −oyer and terminer, −assize, −appeal, −error; High court of
-Judicature, −Appeal; Judicial Committee of
the Privy Council; Star Chamber; Court of
-Chancery, −King's *or* Queen's Bench, −Ex-
chequer, −Common Pleas, −Probate,
−Admiralty; Lords Justices'−, Rolls−, Vice
Chancellor's−, Stannary−, Divorce−, Pala-
tine−, county−, police- court; Court of Criminal Appeal; Court of Small Causes [*India*];
court of common council; board of green cloth.

[United States courts] United States -Supreme
Court, −District Court, −Circuit Court of Appeal; Federal Court of Claims, Court of Private

Land Claims; Supreme Court, court of sessions, criminal court, police court, juvenile
court, night court [*colloq.*], municipal court.

court-martial (*pl.* courts-martial), drumhead
court-martial.

ecclesiastical court, Rota *or* Rota Romana
[*R. C. Ch.*]; Court of Arches [*Eng.*].
Papal Court, Curia.

adj. **judicial** etc. 965; appellate; curial.

967. Judge

n. **judge,** justice; justiciar [*Eng. [Scot. hist.*]; justici-
ary [*Eng. & Scot. hist.*]; chancellor; justice−,
judge- of assize; recorder, common serjeant;
puisne−, assistant−, county court- judge;
conservator−, justice- of the peace; J.P.; "the
Great Unpaid" [*Eng.*]; court etc. (*tribunal*)
966; deemster [*Isle of Man & archaic*], moderator, bencher [*archaic*], jurat, magistrate, police
magistrate, beak [*slang*]; his worship, his honor,
his lordship; the court.

Lord Chancellor, Lord Justice; Master of the
Rolls, Vice Chancellor; Lord Chief -Justice,
−Baron; Chief Justice; Mr. Justice; Baron, −of
the Exchequer.

assessor; arbiter, arbitrator, doomsman *or* domes-
man [*obs.*], umpire, referee, referendary
[*rare*]; revising barrister [*Eng.*], receiver, official receiver; censor etc. (*critic*) 480; barmaster
[*Eng.*].

archon, tribune, praetor, ephor, syndic, podesta
[*It.*]; mollah, ulema, hakim, mufti, cadi *or* kadi
[*all Moham.*]; alcalde [*Sp.*]; Rhadamanthus,
Minos, Solomon.

jury, grand jury, petty jury, inquest, panel, country; twelve men in a box.

juror, juryman, talesman; grand-juror, grand-
juryman, recognitor; petty-juror, petty-jury-
man.

litigant etc. (*accusation*) 938.

v. **adjudge** etc. (*determine*) 480; try a case, try a
prisoner.

adj. judicial etc. 965.

968. Lawyer

n. **lawyer,** jurist, legist, pundit [*India*], civilian,
publicist, jurisconsult, legal adviser, advocate;
barrister, barrister-at-law; counsel, counselor
or counsellor, King's *or* Queen's counsel; K. C.;
Q. C.; silk *or* silk gown; junior counsel, stuff
or stuff gown; leader, serjeant-at-law, bencher,
pleader, special pleader; tubman [*Eng. law*],
judge etc. 967.

solicitor, attorney, vakil *or* vakeel [*India*], proctor; equity draftsman, conveyancer, notary, –public; scrivener, cursitor [*Eng. law*]; writer, –to the signet; S.S.C.; limb of the law; pettifogger, shyster.

bar, legal profession, gentlemen of the long robe; junior–, outer–, inner- bar; Inns of Court [*Eng.*].

v. **practice law**; practice at (*or* within) the bar, plead; call to (*or* within) the bar, be called to (*or* within) the bar; admitted to the bar, take silk.

disbar, disbench [*Eng. law*], degrade.

adj. learned in the law; at the bar; forensic.

969. Lawsuit

n. **lawsuit**, suit, action, cause; litigation; suit in law; dispute etc. 713.

writ, summons, subpoena, citation, latitat [*Eng. law*]; *nisi prius, venire, venire facias, habeas corpus* [*all L.*].

arraignment, prosecution, impeachment; accusation etc. 938; presentment, true bill, indictment.

arrest, apprehension, committal, commitment; imprisonment etc. (*restraint*) 751.

pleadings; declaration, bill, claim; *procès-verbal* [*F.*], bill of right, information, *corpus delicti* [*L.*]; affidavit, state of facts, libel; answer, replication, plea, demurrer, rebutter, rejoinder; surrebutter, surrejoinder.

suitor, libelant *or* libellant, party to a suit; litigant etc. 938.

hearing, trial; judgment, sentence, finding, verdict etc. 480; appeal, –motion; writ of error; certiorari.

case, decision, precedent; decided case, reports.

v. **go to law**, appeal to the law; bring to -justice, –trial, –the bar; put on trial, pull up; accuse etc. 938; prefer *or* file a claim etc. *n.;* take the law of [*colloq.*], inform against.

cite, summon, summons, serve with a writ, arraign, sue, prosecute, bring an action against, indict, impeach, attach, distrain, commit; apprehend, arrest; give in charge etc. (*restrain*) 751.

empanel a jury, challenge the jurors; implead, join issue; close the pleadings; set down for hearing.

try, hear a cause; sit in judgment; adjudicate etc. 480.

adj. **litigious** etc. (*quarrelsome*) 713; *qui tam, coram judice, sub judice* [*all L.*].

adv. pendente lite [*L.*].

970. Acquittal

n. **acquittal**, acquitment [*obs.*]; exculpation, acquittance, clearance, exoneration; discharge etc. (*release*) 750; *quietus* [*L.*], absolution, compurgation, reprieve, respite; pardon etc. (*forgiveness*) 918.

[exemption from punishment] impunity, immunity.

v. **acquit**, exculpate, exonerate, clear; absolve, whitewash, assoil [*archaic*], assoilzie [*Scot.*]; discharge, release; liberate etc. 750.

reprieve, respite; pardon etc. (*forgive*) 918; let off, let off scot-free.

adj. **acquitted** etc. *v.;* uncondemned, unpunished, unchastised; recommended to mercy.

971. Condemnation

n. **condemnation**, conviction, judgment, penalty, sentence; proscription, damnation; death warrant.

attainder, attainture, attaintment.

v. **condemn**, convict, cast [*obs. or dial.*], bring home to, find guilty, damn, doom, sign the death warrant, sentence, pass sentence on, attaint, confiscate, proscribe, sequestrate; nonsuit.

disapprove etc. 932; accuse etc. 938.

stand condemned, be convicted.

adj. **condemnatory**, damnatory; condemned etc. *v.;* nonsuited etc. (*failure*) 732; self-convicted.

972. Punishment

n. **punishment**, punition, chastisement, chastening, correction, castigation; discipline, infliction, trial; judgment; penalty etc. 974; retribution; thunderbolt, Nemesis, Eumenides, the Furies; requital etc. (*reward*) 973; retributive justice; penology.

[forms of punishment] lash, scaffold etc. (*instrument of punishment*) 975; imprisonment etc. (*restraint*) 751; transportation, banishment, expulsion, exile, involuntary exile, ostracism; penal servitude, hard labor; galleys etc. 975; beating etc. *v.;* flagellation, fustigation, cudgeling, gantlet, strappado, estrapade, bastinado, *argumentum baculinum* [*L.*], stick law, rap on the knuckles, box on the ear; blow etc. (*impulse*) 276; stripe, cuff, kick, buffet, pummel; slap, –in the face; wipe [*dial. or slang*], douse *or* dowse [*rare*]; torture, rack; rail-riding, scarpines; picket [*obs.*], picketing; dragonnade.

capital punishment, execution; hanging, shooting etc. *v.;* electrocution, decapitation, decollation, dismemberment; strangling, strangulation, garrote *or* garrotte; crucifixion, impalement; martyrdom, *auto-da-fé* (*pl. autos-da-fé*) [*Pg.*], *auto-de-fe* [*Sp.*], *noyade* [*F.*], harakiri [*Jap.*], seppuku [*Jap.*], happy dispatch [*jocular*], lethal chamber, hemlock.

v. **punish**, chastise, chasten, castigate, correct, inflict punishment, administer correction, deal retributive justice; tar and feather; masthead, keelhaul.

visit upon, pay; pay out [*colloq.*], serve out [*colloq.*], settle, settle with, do for [*colloq.*], get even with, get one's own back [*slang*], make short work of, give a lesson to, serve one right, make an example of; have a rod in pickle for; give it to, give it one [*both colloq.*].

strike etc. 276; deal a blow to, administer the lash, smite; slap, –the face; smack, cuff, box the ears, spank, thwack, thump, beat, lay on, swinge, buffet; thresh, thrash, pummel, drub, leather [*slang*], trounce, baste, belabor; lace, –one's jacket; dress, dress down, give a dressing, trim [*colloq.*], warm [*dial.*], warm one's jacket [*colloq.*], wipe [*slang*], tund [*obs.*], cob [*dial., Eng.*], bang, strap, comb [*humorous*], lick, larrup [*both colloq.*], wallop [*Scot., dial. Eng. & colloq., U. S*]., cowhide, lambaste [*slang*], lash, whop [*obs.*], flog, scourge, whip, birch, cane, give the stick, switch, flagellate, horsewhip, bastinado, towel [*slang*], rub down with an oaken towel [*slang*], ribroast [*slang*], dust one's jacket [*slang*], fustigate, pitch into [*colloq.*], lay about one, beat black and blue; beat to a -pulp, –mummy, –jelly; give a black eye; hit on the head, crack on the bean [*slang*], sandbag, blackjack, put away [*slang*]; pelt, stone, lapidate.

execute; bring to the -block, –gallows; behead, decapitate, decollate, guillotine; hang, turn off [*slang*], gibbet, bowstring, dismember, hang draw and quarter; shoot; burn; break on the wheel, crucify; impale *or* empale, flay; lynch; electrocute.

torture, agonize, rack, put on (*or* to) the rack, martyr, martyrize, picket [*obs. or hist.*]; prolong the agony, kill by inches.

banish, exile, transport, deport, expel, ostracize; rusticate; drum out; dismiss, disbar, disbench [*Eng. law*]; strike off the roll, unfrock; post.

suffer, suffer for, suffer punishment; be flogged, be hanged etc.; come to the gallows, dance upon nothing [*ironical*], die in one's shoes; be rightly served.

adj. **punishing** etc. *v.*; penal, punitory, punitive, inflictive, castigatory; punished etc. *v.*

int. *à la lanterne!* [*F.*].

973. Reward

n. **reward**, recompense, remuneration, prize, meed, guerdon, reguerdon [*obs.*]; price; indemnity, indemnification; quittance, compensation, reparation, redress, retribution, reckoning, acknowledgment, requital, amends, sop; atonement; consideration, return, *quid pro quo* [*L.*]; salvage.

perquisite, perks [*slang*]; vail etc. (*donation*) 784; *douceur* [*F.*], tip; bribe, bait etc. 784; hush-money, smart-money, blackmail; carcelage [*obs.*]; solatium.

allowance, salary, stipend, wages; pay, payment; emolument; tribute; batta [*India*], shot, scot; premium, fee, honorarium; hire; dasturi *or* dustoori [*India*]; mileage.

crown etc. (*decoration of honor*) 877.

v. **reward**, recompense, repay, requite; remunerate, munerate [*obs.*]; compensate; fee, tip, bribe; pay one's footing etc. (*pay*) 807; make amends, indemnify, atone; satisfy, acknowledge.

get for one's pains, reap the fruits of.

adj. remunerative, remuneratory [*rare*], munerary [*obs.*], compensatory, retributive, reparatory [*rare*], reparative.

974. Penalty

n. **penalty**; retribution etc. (*punishment*) 972; pain, pains and penalties; wergild *or* weregild [*hist.*], bloodwite *or* bloodwit [*early Eng. law*]; *peine forte et dure* [*F.*]; penance etc. (*atonement*) 952; the devil to pay.

fine, mulct, amercement, sconce [*Oxford Univ., Eng.*], forfeit, forfeiture, escheat, damages, deodand, sequestration, confiscation, praemunire *or* premunire; domage.

v. **penalize**, fine, mulct, amerce, sconce, confiscate, sequestrate, sequester, escheat, estreat, forfeit.

975. Scourge

[instrument of punishment]

n. **scourge**, whip, lash, strap, thong, cowhide, knout, cat, cat-o'-nine-tails; rope's end; *azote* [*Sp. Am.*], black-snake, bullwhack, kurbash [*Turk.*], chabuk [*Hind.*], quirt, rawhide, sjambok [*S. Africa*].

rod, cane, stick, rattan *or* ratan, birch, birch rod; rod in pickle; switch, ferule, cudgetl, truncheon.

[various instruments] pillory, stocks, whipping post; cucking stool, ducking stool, brank, trebuchet *or* trebucket; triangle, wooden horse, maiden; thumbscrew, boot, rack, wheel, iron heel; treadmill, crank, galleys; bed of Procrustes.

scaffold; block, ax, guillotine; stake; cross, gallows, gibbet, tree, drop; noose, rope, halter, bowstring; death chair, electric chair; *mecate* [*Sp.*].

prison, house of correction etc. 752; jailer *or* gaoler.

executioner; electrocutioner; lyncher, garroter *or* garrotter, torturer; headsman, hangman, topsman *or* topping cove [*slang*], Jack Ketch.

malefactor, criminal, culprit, felon, evildoer, misdemeanant; victim, gallows-bird [*slang*], Jack Ketch's pippin [*old slang*].

Section 5. Religious

976. Deity

n. **deity**, Divinity, Godhead, Godship, Omnipotence, Omniscience, Providence.

[quality of being divine] divineness, divinity.

GOD, Lord, Jehovah, The King of Kings, The Lord of Lords, The Almighty, The Supreme Being, The Eternal Being, The Absolute Being, The First Cause; I AM, The All-Father, *Ens Entium* [*L.*], Author of all things, Creator of all things, Author of our being; Cosmoplast, Demiurge; The Infinite, The Eternal; The All-powerful, The Omnipotent, The All-wise, The All-merciful, The All-holy, The All-knowing, The Omniscient.

Deus [*L.*], *Theos* [*Gr.*], *Dieu* [*F.*], *Gott* [*Ger.*], *Dio* [*It.*], *Dios* [*Sp.*], *Deos* [*Pg.*], *Gud* [*Nor., Sw., & Dan.*], *God* [*Du.*], *Bog'* [*Russ.*], *Brahmă* [*Skr.*], *Deva* [*Skr.*], *Khuda* [*Hind.*], *Allah* [*Ar.*], *Kami* [*Jap.*], *Ten-shu* [*Jap., Christian*], *Jahweh* [*Heb.*].

[attributes and perfections] infinite -power, −wisdom, −goodness, −justice, −truth, −love, −mercy; omnipotence, omniscience, omnipresence; unity, immutability, holiness, glory, light, majesty, sovereignty; infinity, eternity etc. (*perpetuity*) 112.

THE TRINITY, The Holy Trinity, The Trinity in Unity, The Triune God, Triunity, Threefold Unity, "Three in One and One in Three."

I. GOD THE FATHER, The Maker, The Creator, The Preserver.

[functions] creation, preservation, divine government, Theocracy, Thearchy; Providence; ways−, dealings−, dispensations−, visitations- of Providence.

II. GOD THE SON, Jesus Christ; The Messiah, The Anointed, The Saviour, The Redeemer, The Mediator, The Intercessor, The Advocate, The Judge; The Son of God, The Son of Man, The Son of David; The Only-Begotten, The Lamb of God, The Word, Logos; The Man of Sorrows, Jesus of Nazareth, King of the Jews, The Son of Mary, The Risen, Immanuel, Emmanuel, The King of Kings and Lord of Lords, The King of Glory, The Prince of Peace, The Good Shepherd, The Way, The Door, The Truth, The Life, The Bread of Life, The Light of the World, The Vine, The True Vine; The Lord our Righteousness, The Sun of Righteousness.

The Incarnation, The Hypostatic Union, The Word made Flesh.

[functions] salvation, redemption, atonement, propitiation, mediation, intercession, judgment; soteriology.

III. GOD THE HOLY GHOST, The Holy Spirit, Paraclete, The Comforter, The Consoler, The Intercessor, The Spirit of God, The Spirit of Truth, The Dove.

[functions] inspiration, unction, regeneration, sanctification, consolation, grace.

[the deity in other religions] **brahmanism** *or* **hinduism**: Brahm *or* Brahmā (*neuter*), the Supreme Soul *or* Essence of the Universe; Trimurti *or* Hindu trinity *or* Hindu triad: (1) Brahmā (*masc.*), the Creator; (2) Vishnu, the Preserver, (3) Siva *or* Shiva, the Destroyer and Regenerator. For other Hindu deities see 979.

buddhism: the Protestantism of the East; Buddha, the Blessed One, the Teacher, the Lord Buddha.

zoroastrianism: Zerâna-Akerana, the Infinite Being; Ahuramazda *or* Ormazd, the Creator, the Lord of Wisdom, the Wise Lord, the Wise One, the King of Light, the Guardian of Mankind (*opposed by* Ahriman, the King of Darkness).

mohammedanism *or* **islam**: Allah.

judaism: Jehovah.

v. **create**, fashion, make, form, mold *or* mould, manifest.

preserve, uphold, keep, perpetuate, immortalize.

atone, redeem, save, propitiate, expiate; intercede, mediate.

predestinate, predestine, foreordain, preordain; elect, call, ordain.

bless, sanctify, hallow, justify, absolve, glorify.

355

adj. **almighty**, all-powerful, omnipotent; omnipresent, all-wise, all-seeing, all-knowing, omniscient, supreme.

divine, heavenly, celestial; holy, hallowed, sacred, sacrosanct.

supernatural, superhuman, hyperphysical, superphysical, spiritual, ghostly, supramundane, supersensuous, supersensitive, supersensual, supernormal, unearthly.

theistic; theocratic; deistic; anointed; soterial.

adv. **under God**, by God's will, by God's help, *Deo volente* [*L.*], D. V., God willing; in Jesus' name, in His name, in His fear, to His glory; *jure divino* [*L.*], by divine right.

977. Angel
[beneficient spirits]

n. **angel**, archangel, Messenger of God, guardian angel, ministering spirits, invisible helpers, Choir Invisible, heavenly host, host of heaven, sons of God; morning star; saint.

[celestial hierarchy of pseudo-dionysius] (1) Seraphim (*sing.* seraph, *E. pl.* seraphs), Cherubim (*sing.* cherub, *E. pl.* cherubs; cherubim *or* cherubin *are often treated as sing.*), Thrones; (2) Dominions, Virtues, Powers; (3) Principalities, Archangels, Angels.

Michael, Gabriel, Raphael, Uriel, Chamuel, Jophiel, Zadkiel; Abdiel, Azrael.

madonna, Our Lady, *Notre Dame* [*F.*], Holy Mary, The Virgin, The Blessed Virgin, The Virgin Mary; *Dei Mater* [*L.*], Mother of God; *Regina Coeli* [*L.*], Queen of Heaven; *Regina Angelorum* [*L.*], Queen of Angels; *Stella Maris* [*L.*], Star of the Sea; *Mater Dolorosa* [*L.*]; Zion's Lily; *Alma Mater Redemptoris, Virgo Gloriosa, Virgo Sponsa Dei, Virgo Potens, Virgo Veneranda, Virgo Proedicanda, Virgo Clemens, Virgo Sapientissima, Sancta Virgo Virginum* [*all L.*]; *La Vergine Gloriosa* [*It.*]; *La Grande Vierge* [*F.*].

adj. **angelic**, seraphic, cherubic, archangelic.

978. Satan
[maleficent spirits]

n. **satan**, the Devil, Lucifer, Belial, Beëlzebub, Eblis [*Ar.*], Ahriman [*Zoroastrianism*], Mephistopheles, Mephisto, Shaitan [*Hind.*], Samael, Asmodeus, Satanas [*archaic*], Abaddon [*Heb.*], Apollyon, *le Diable* [*F.*], Deil [*Scot.*], Teufel [*Ger.*], *Diabolus* [*L.*].

his Satanic Majesty, the Prince of the Devils, the Prince of Darkness, the Prince of this world, the Prince of the power of the air; the Tempter, the Adversary, the Evil One, the Evil Spirit, the Archenemy, the Archfiend, the Foul Fiend, the Devil Incarnate, the Father of Lies, the Author of Evil, the Father of Evil, the Old Serpent, the Wicked One, the Common Enemy, the angel of the bottomless pit; the Deuce, the Dickens, the Old Gentleman, Old Nick, Old Scratch, Old Horny, Old Harry, Old Gooseberry [*all slang*].

fallen angels, unclean spirits, devils; the rulers of darkness, the powers of darkness; inhabitants of Pandemonium; demon etc. 980.

moloch, Mammon, Azazel [*Milton*]; Belial [*P. L.*], Beëlzebub [*in P. L., the fallen angel next to Satan*], Loki [*Norse myth.*]

diabolism, devil worship, devil lore, diablerie *or* diablery, diabolology *or* diabology, Satanism, devilism; devilship, devildom; demonry, demonism, demonology, Manichaeism *or* Manicheism; Black Mass, Black Magic, demonolatry, demonomagy; witchcraft etc. (*sorcery*) 992; the cloven hoof; hoofs and horns; demonomy.

diabolist, demonologist, demonologer, demonolater, demonist, demonographer [*rare*], demonomist; Manichaean *or* Manichean.

v. **diabolize** [*rare*], demonize; bewitch, bedevil etc. (*sorcery*) 992; possess, obsess.

adj. **satanic**, diabolic *or* diabolical, devilish, demoniac *or* demoniacal, infernal, hellborn.

979. Mythic and pagan deities

n. **god**, goddess; *deus* [*L.*], *dea* [*L.*]; deva (*fem.* devi) ["the shining ones," *Skr.*]; heathen gods and goddesses; pantheon; theogony.

[Greek and Latin] Zeus, Jupiter *or* Jove (*King*); Apollon, Apollo (*the sun*); Ares, Mars (*war*); Hermes, Mercury (*messenger*); Poseidon, Neptune (*ocean*); Hephaistos, Vulcan (*smith*); Dionysus, Bacchus (*wine*); Pluton *or* Hades [*Gr.*], Pluto *or* Dis [*L.*] (*King of the lower world*); Kronos, Saturn (*time*); Eros, Cupid (*love*); Pan, Faunus (*flocks, herds, forests, and wild life*).

Hera, Juno (*Queen*); Demeter, Ceres (*fruitfulness*); Persephone, Proserpina *or* Proserpine (*Queen of the lower world*); Artemis, Diana (*the moon and hunting*); Athena, Minerva (*wisdom*); Aphrodite, Venus (*love and beauty*); Hestia, Vesta (*the hearth*); Rhea *or* Cybele ("Mother of the gods," *identified with* Ops, *wife of Saturn*); Gaea *or* Ge, Tellus (*earth goddess, mother of the Titans*).

[Norse] Ymir (*primeval giant*), Reimthursen (*frost giants*), Bori (*fashioner of the world*), Bor (*father of Odin*), Odin *or* Woden (*the All-father,*

= *Zeus*); the Aesir *or* Asas; Thor (*the Thunderer*), Balder *or* Baldr (= *Apollo*), Freyr (*fruitfulness*), Tyr *or* Tyrr (*war*), Bragi (*poetry and eloquence*), Höder *or* Hödr (*blind god of the winter*), Heimdall (*warder of Asgard*), Vidar (= *Pan*), Uller *or* Ullr (*the chase*), Forseti (*peacemaker*), Vali (*knowledge and eternal light*), Loki (*evil*).

the Vanir *or* Vans: Njorth *or* Njord (*the winds and the sea*), Frey *or* Freyr (*prosperity and love*), Freya *or* Freyja (*goddess of love and beauty,* = *Venus*).

Frigg *or* Frigga (*wife of Odin*), Hel (*goddess of death,* = *Persephone*), Sif (*wife of Thor*), Nanna (*wife of Balder*), Idun (*goddess of spring, wife of Bragi*), Sigyn (*wife of Loki*).

[Hindu] **vedic gods**: Dyaus (*the Heaven*), Indra (*cloud-compeller*), Varuna (*the sky, also the waters*), Surya (*the sun,* = *Gr.* Helios), Savitar ("*the Inciter,*" *a sun god*), Soma (*the sustainer*), Agni (*fire*), Vavu (*the winds*), the Marutas (*storm gods*), Ushas ("*the Dawn,*" *goddess of wisdom*).

brahmanic gods: Brahmâ, Vishnu, Siva *or* Shiva etc. (*Brahmanism*) 976; avatars of Vishnu: (1) Matsya, the fish; (2) Karma, the turtle; (3) Varah, the boar; (4) Narsinh, man-lion; (5) Vaman, the dwarf; (6) Parshuram, a Brahman; (7) Rama; (8) Krishna; (9) Buddha; (10) Kalki; Jagannath *or* Juggernaut (*Krishna*); Ganesha *or* Ganpati (*wisdom*), Hanuman (*monkey god*), Yama (*judge of the dead*).

Sarasvati (*sakti or wife of Brahmâ; goddess of poetry, wisdom, and fine art*), Lakshmi (*wife of Vishnu; goddess of wealth, and prosperity*), Durga *or* Kali (*wife of Siva, conceived as a malignant deity*); Devi ("*the goddess*") *or* Uma ("*light*") *or* Gauri ("*the brilliant*") *or* Parvati ("*the mountaineer,*" *wife of Siva, conceived as a beneficient deity*).

[Egyptian] Ra *or* Amun-Ra (*the sun god*), Neph *or* Nef (*spirit or breath*), Pthah (*demiurge*), Khem (*reproduction*), Mut *or* Maut (= *Gr.* Demeter), Osiris (*judge of the dead*), Isis (*wife of Osiris*), Horus (*the morning sun; son of Osiris and Isis*), Anubis (*jackal-god, brother of Horus, a conductor of the dead*), Nephthys (*sister of Isis*), Set (*evil deity, brother of Osiris*), Thoth (*clerk of the underworld*), Bast *or* Bubastis (*a goddess with head of a cat*), the Sphinx (*wisdom*).

[various] Baal (*Heb. pl.* Baalim) [*Semitic*]; Astarte *or* Ashtoreth (*goddess of fertility and love*) [*Phoenician*]; Bel *Babylonian*]; The Great Spirit [*N. Amer Indian*]; Mumbo Jumbo [*Sudanese Negroes, an idol or bugaboo*].

nymph, dryad, hamadryad, alseid, wood nymph; naiad, fresh-water nymph; oread, mountain nymph; nereid, sea nymph; limoniad *or* leimoniad, meadow nymph *or* flower nymph; Oceanid, ocean nymph; napaea, glen nymph; potamid, river nymph; Pleiades *or* Atlantides, Hyades, Dodonides.

fairy, fay, sprite *or* spright [*archaic*]; nix (*fem.* nixie), water sprite; the Good Folk, brownie *or* browny, pixy, elf (*pl.* elves), banshee *or* banshie; the Fates *or* Moerae, *Clotho* (Spinner), *Lachesis* (Disposer of Lots), *Atropos* (Inflexible One); gnome, kelpie; faun; peri, nis, kobold, sylph, sylphid; undine, sea maid, sea nymph, mermaid (*masc.* merman); Mab, Oberon, Titania, Ariel; Puck, Robin Goodfellow, Hobgoblin; Leprechaun; denizens of the air; afreet etc. (*bad spirit*) 980.

familiar spirit, familiar, genius, guide, good genius, tutelary genius, daimon, demon *or* daemon, guardian.

mythology, mythical lore, heathen mythology, folklore, fairyism, fairy mythology.

adj. **mythical**, mythic, mythological, fabulous, legendary etc. 515.

fairylike, sylphlike, sylphine, sylphish, sylphidine; elfin, elflike, elfish, nymphlike.

980. Evil Spirits

n. demon, fiend, devil etc. (*Satan*) 978; evil genius, familiar, familiar spirit; bad–, unclean- spirit; cacodaemon *or* cacodemon, incubus, succubus *and* succuba; daeva *or* deev, bad peri, afreet, lamia, barghest *or* barguest; ogre, ogress, ghoul, vampire, harpy; Fury, the Furies, the Erinyes, the Eumenides; Titan; Friar Rush.

imp, bad fairy, sprite, jinni *or* jinnee (*pl.* jin), genius (*pl.* genii), flibberti-gibbet, ouphe, dwarf, troll, urchin, Cluricaune.

changeling, elf-child, auf, oaf; werewolf, *loup-garou* [*F.*]; satyr.

elemental, sylph, gnome, salamander, nymph [*Rosicrucian*].

siren, nixie, undine, Lorelei.

bugbear, bugaboo, bogy *or* bogey *or* bogie, bug [*obs.*], poker [*rare*], goblin, hobgoblin, boggart *or* boggard.

demonology, demonry etc. (*diabolism*) 978.

adj. demoniac, demoniacal, fiendish, fiendlike, evil, ghoulish; pokerish [*colloq.*], bewitched.

980a. Specter

n. **specter** *or* spectre, ghost, revenant, apparition, spirit, sprite, shade, shadow, wraith, spook [*now humorous*], phantom, phantasm, fantasm [*rare*], idolum; materialization [*Spiritualism*], ectoplasmic manifestation; double, etheric body, etheric self, aura, auric egg, astral body, *mayavi rupa*, ego [*all Theos. and Occultism*]; vision, theophany.

banshee, White Lady, the White Ladies of Normandy, the White Lady of Avenel [*Scott*]; lemures, larva *or* larve [*Roman relig.*].

will-o'-the-wisp, Friar's lantern etc. 423.

adj. **spectral**, ghostly, ghostlike, spiritual, wraithlike, weird, uncanny, eerie *or* eery, spooky *or* spookish [*colloq.*], haunted; unearthly, supernatural.

981. Heaven

n. **heaven**; kingdom of -heaven, -God; heavenly kingdom; heaven of heavens, God's throne, throne of God, presence of God; inheritance of the saints in light.

paradise, Eden, Zion, Holy City, New Jerusalem, Heavenly City, City Celestial, abode of the blessed; celestial bliss, eternal bliss, unending bliss, glory, never-ending day.

[mythological heaven or paradise] Olympus; Elysium, Elysian fields, Islands (*or* Isles) of the Blessed, Happy Isles, Fortunate Isles, Arcadia, bowers of bliss, garden of the Hesperides, third heaven, seventh heaven; Valhalla *or* Walhalla [*Scandinavian*]; Nirvana [*Buddhist*]; happy hunting grounds [*N. Amer. Indian*]; *Alfardaws, Assama; Falak al aflak,* ("the highest heaven") [*Mohammedan*].

future state, life after death, eternal home, resurrection, translation; resuscitation etc. 660; apotheosis, deification.

[theosophy] Devachan *or* Devaloka, the land of the Gods.

adj. **heavenly**, celestial, supernal, unearthly, from on high, paradisaic *or* paradisaical, paradisiac *or* paradisiacal, beatific, elysian, Olympian, Arcadian.

982. Hell

n. **hell**, bottomless pit, place of torment; habitation of fallen angels; Pandemonium, Abaddon, Domdaniel; *jahannan* [*Hind.*], Sheol.

hell fire; everlasting -fire, -torment; lake of fire and brimstone; fire that is never quenched, worm that never dies.

purgatory, limbo, gehenna, abyss, Tophet.

[mythological hell] Tartarus, Hades, Avernus, Styx, Stygian creek, pit of Acheron, Cocytus; infernal regions, inferno, shades below, realms of Pluto.

pluto, Rhadamanthus, Erebus, Charon, Cerberus; Persephone, Proserpina *or* Proserpine; Minos, Osiris.

rivers of hell: Styx, Acheron, Cocytus, Phlegethon, Lethe.

adj. **hellish**, infernal, stygian.

983. Theology
[religious knowledge]

n. **theology** (natural and revealed), theosophy, divine wisdom, divinity, hagiology, hagiography, hierography; Caucasian mystery; monotheism, theism, religion; religious -persuasion, -sect, -denomination, -affiliation; creed etc. (*belief*) 484; articles-, declaration-, profession-, confession- of faith.

theologian, theologue [*now rare*], scholastic, divine, schoolman, canonist, theologist [*now rare*], theologus; monotheist, theist; Homoousian (*opp. to* Homoiousian); the Fathers.

adj. **theological**, religious, divine, canonical; denominational; sectarian etc. 984.

983a. Orthodoxy

n. **orthodoxy**; strictness, soundness, religious, truth, true faith; truth etc. 494; soundness of doctrine.

christianity, Christianism; Catholicism, Catholicity; "the faith once delivered to the saints"; hyperorthodoxy etc. 984.

the church, Holy Church, Church Militant, Church Triumphant; Catholic-, Universal-, Apostolic-, Established- Church; the Bride of the Lamb; temple of the Holy Ghost; Church-, body-, members-, disciples-, followers- of Christ; Christians.

true believer; textualist, textuary; canonist etc. (*theologian*) 983; the Orthodox; Christian community; Christendom, collective body of Christians.

canons etc. (*belief*) 484; thirty-nine articles; Apostles'-, Nicene-, Athanasian- Creed; Church Catechism.

adj. **orthodox**, sound, strict, faithful, catholic, schismless, Christian, evangelical, scriptural, literal, divine, monotheistic, theistic; true etc. 494; true blue.

984. Heterodoxy
[sectarianism]

n. **heterodoxy**; error etc. 495; false doctrine, heresy, schism, schismaticism, schismaticalness; recusancy, backsliding, apostasy; materialism, hylotheism; atheism etc. (*irreligion*) 989.

anthropomorphism, anthropopathism, anthropopathy; idolatry etc. 991; superstition etc. (*credulity*) 486.

bigotry etc. (*obstinacy*) 606; fanaticism, iconoclasm; hyperorthodoxy, precisianism; bibliolatry, hagiolatry; sabbatarianism, puritanism.

sectarianism, sectarism [*obs.*], nonconformity; dissent etc. 489; secularism; syncretism; religious sects, the clash of creeds.

protestantism, Arianism, Adventism, Jansenism, Stundism, Erastianism, Calvinism, Quakerism, Methodism, Anabaptism, Puseyism, tractarianism, ritualism, Origenism, Sabellianism, Socinianism, Gnosticism, Mormonism, Second Adventism, materialism, positivism, latitudinarianism, ethicism, deism, higher pantheism, henotheism; monism, philosophical unitarianism etc.; the isms.

anglicanism, Church of England; High–, Low–, Broad–, Free-Church; ultramontanism; monasticism, monkery; Catholicism, Romanism, popery, papism, papistry, papacy, Maryolatry [*usually opprobrious*], Scarlet Woman, Church of Rome; Greek Church. [*Generally speaking, each sect is* orthodox *to itself and* heterodox *to others.*]

judaism; Mohammedanism, Islam, Islamism.

theosophy, New Thought, ethical culture, mental science, mental healing; Christian Science, Eddyism; Spiritualism, Spiritism, occultism; Swedenborgianism.

paganism, heathenism, heathendom; mythology; animism, polytheism, ditheism, tritheism, pantheism; dualism.

gentilism, Babism, Sufiism, Neoplatonism, Brahmanism, Hinduism, Vedantism, Buddhism, Lamaism; Sikhism, Jainism; Confucianism, Taoism; Shintoism, Sabaeanism *or* Sabeanism *or* Sabeism.

pagan, heathen, paynim; *giaour* [*Turk.*], Gheber *or* Ghebre, kafir, non-Mohammedan; gentile; pantheist, polytheist, animist.

misbeliever, heretic, apostate; backslider; antichrist; idolater; skeptic etc. 989.

bigot etc. (*obstinacy*) 606; fanatic, abdal, dervish, iconoclast.

sectarian, sectary, sectarist [*rare*], schismatic; seceder, separatist, recusant, dissenter, nonconformist, nonjuror.

Huguenot, Protestant, Episcopalian; Trinitarian; latitudinarian; limitarian; orthodox dissenter, Puritan, Unitarian, Congregationalist, Independent; Presbyterian; Lutheran, Ubiquitarian, Calvinist, Methodist, Wesleyan; Anabaptist, Baptist; Mormon, Latter-day Saint; Irvingite, Sandemanian, Glassite, Erastian, Sublapsarian, Supralapsarian; Gentoo, Antinomian, Swedenborgian; Adventist, Second Adventist, Bible Christian, Bryanite, Brownian, Dunker, Ebionite, Eusebian; Faith Curer, Faith Christ, Faith Healer, Mental Healer, Christian Scientist; Familist, Jovinianist, Libadist, Restitutionist, Quaker, Shaker, Quietist, Stundist, Tunker etc.

catholic, Roman Catholic, Romanist, Papist, ultramontane; Anglican, Oxford School; tractarian, Puseyite, ritualist; High Churchman.

jew, Hebrew, Rabbinist; Mohammedan, Mussulman, Moslem, Islamite, Osmanli, Motazilite, Shiah, Sunni, Wahabi; Brahman *or* Brahmin; Brahmo; Vedantist, Jain *or* Jaina, Sikh, Parsi *or* Parsee, fire worshiper, Zoroastrian [*erron. called fire worshiper*]; Sufi, Babist, Buddhist; Confucianist, Taoist, Shintoist; Magi, Gymnosophist, Sabian, henotheist, Gnostic, Sadducee, Rosicrucian, Mystic, Occultist, Theosophist, Spiritualist, Spiritist etc.

materialist, hylotheist; positivist, deist, agnostic, atheist etc. 989.

adj. **heterodox**, heretical, unorthodox, unscriptural, uncanonical, unchristian, antiscriptural, apocryphal; antichristian; schismatic, recusant, iconoclastic; sectarian, dissenting, dissident [*now rare*]; Protestant etc. *n.;* secular etc. (*lay*) 997; deistic, agnostic, atheistic; skeptical etc. 989.

bigoted etc. (*prejudiced*) 481, (*obstinate*) 606; superstitious etc. (*credulous*) 486; fanatical; idolatrous etc. 991; visionary etc. (*imaginative*) 515.

judaical; Mohammedan, Islamic *or* Islamitic, Moslem; Brahmanic *or* Brahmanical, Brahminic *or* Brahminical; Buddhist etc. *n.*

popish, papish, papistic *or* papistical, Romish.

pagan, heathen, heathenish, ethnic, ethnical; gentile, paynim; polytheistic, pantheistic, animistic.

985. Revelation

[biblical]

n. **revelation**, inspiration, *afflatus* [*L.*]; theophany, theopneusty.

the bible, the Book, the Book of Books, the Good Book, the Word, the Word of God, Scripture, the Scriptures, Holy Writ, Holy Scriptures, inspired writings, Gospel.

old testament, Septuagint, Vulgate, Pentateuch; Octateuch; the Law, the Jewish Law; the Prophets; major–, minor- Prophets; Hagiographa, Hierographa; Apocrypha.

new testament; Gospels, Evangelists, Synoptic Gospels, Acts, Epistles, Apocalypse, Revelation; Good Tidings, Glad Tidings.

[hebrew] Talmud, Torah, Mishna, Gemara; Masora or Masorah.

inspired writers, inspired penmen; prophet etc. (*seer*) 513; evangelist, apostle, disciple, saint; the Fathers, the Apostolic Fathers; Holy Men of old.

adj. scriptural, biblical, sacred, prophetic; evangelical, evangelistic, apostolic, apostolical; inspired, theopneustic, theopneusted [*rare*], apocalyptic, revealed; ecclesiastical, canonical, textuary; Talmudic.

986. Sacred Writings
[non-biblical]

n. The Vedas (Rig-Veda, Yajur-Veda, Sama-Veda, Atharva-Veda), the Upanishads, the Puranas, Sutras, Sastra or Shastra, Tantra, Bhagavad Gita [*all Brahmanic*]; Zenda-vesta, A vesta [*Zoroastrian*]; The Koran or Alcoran [*Mohammedan*]; Tripitaka, Dhammapada [*Buddhist*]; Granth, Adigranth [*Sikh*]; the Agamas [*Jain*]; the Kings [*Chinese*]; the Eddas [*Scandinavia*].

arcana Coelestia etc. [*Swedenborgian*]; Book of Mormon; "Science and Health with Key to the Scriptures" [*Christian Science*].

[non-biblical prophets and religious founders] Gautama (Buddha); Zoroaster, Confucius, Lao-tse [*Taoism*], Mohammed, Nanak Shah [*Sikhism*], Vaddhamana, "Maha-vira" [*Jainism*], Mirza Ali Mohammed, "Bab-ud-Din" (*Per.* "Gate of the Faith") [*Babism*], Ram Mohun Roy [*Brahmo-Samaj*].

swedenborg, Joseph Smith [*Mormonism*], Mary Baker Eddy [*Christian Science*].

987. Piety

n. piety, religion, theism, faith; religiousness, religiosity, holiness etc. *adj.;* saintship; religionism; sanctimony etc. (*assumed piety*) 988; reverence etc. (*respect*) 928; humility, veneration, devotion; prostration etc. (*worship*) 990; grace, unction, edification; sanctity, sanctitude [*rare*]; consecration.

spiritual existence, odor of sanctity, beauty of holiness.

theopathy, beautification, adoption, regeneration, conversion, justification, theodicy, sanctification, salvation, inspiration, bread of life; Body and Blood of Christ.

believer, convert, theist, Christian, devotee, pietist, Saint.

the -good, −righteous, −just, −believing, −elect; the children of -God, −Our Father, −the kingdom, −light.

v. be pious etc. *adj.;* have faith etc. *n.;* believe, receive Christ; venerate, adore, worship, perform the acts of devotion; revere etc. 928; be converted etc.; experience the divine illumination [*Mysticism*]; be at one with God, be on God's side, stand up for Jesus, fight the good fight, keep the faith, let one's light shine.

regenerate, convert, edify, sanctify, hallow, keep holy, beatify, inspire, consecrate, enshrine.

adj. pious, religious, devout, devoted, reverent, godly, heavenly-minded, humble, pure, pure in heart, holy, spiritual, pietistic, saintly, saintlike; seraphic, sacred, solemn.

believing, faithful, Christian, Catholic.

regenerated; inspired, born-again, consecrated, converted, unearthly, not of the earth, in the world not of it.

elected, adopted, justified, sanctified.

988. Impiety

n. impiety; sin etc. 945; irreverence; profaneness etc. *adj.*, profanity, profanation; blasphemy, desecration, sacrilege; scoffing etc. *v.*

[assumed piety] hypocrisy etc. (*falsehood*) 544; pietism, cant, pious fraud; lip-devotion, lip-service, lip-reverence; misdevotion, formalism, austerity; sanctimony, sanctimoniousness etc. *adj.;* pharisaism, precisianism; sabbatism, sabbatarianism; *odium theologicum* [*L.*], sacerdotalism; bigotry etc. (*obstinacy*) 606, (*prejudice*) 481; blue laws.

apostasy, recusancy, hardening, backsliding, declension, perversion, reprobation.

hypocrite etc. (*dissembler*) 548; "Scribes and Pharisees" [*Bible*]; *Rawana-sannyasi* [*Hind.*]; Tartufe, Mawworm, Holy Willie [*Burns*].

bigot, saint [*ironical*]; Pharisee, sabbatarian, formalist, methodist, puritan, pietist, precisian, religionist, devotee, ranter, fanatic; juramentado [*Moro*].

sinner etc. 949; scoffer, blasphemer, sacrilegist [*rare*], sabbath breaker; worldling.

the wicked, the evil, the unjust, the reprobate; sons of -men, −Belial, −the wicked one; children of -the devil, −darkness.

v. be impious etc. *adj.;* profane, desecrate, blaspheme, revile, scoff; swear etc. (*malediction*) 908; commit sacrilege.

dissemble, simulate, play the hypocrite, hypocrify [*obs.*], hypocrize [*rare*], snuffle, talk through the nose, talk nasally, hold up the hands in horror, turn up the whites of the eyes; sing psalms for a pretense, make long prayers.

adj. **impious**; irreligious etc. 989; desecrating etc. *v.;* profane, irreverent, sacrilegious, blasphemous.

unhallowed, unsanctified, unregenerate; hardened, perverted, reprobate.

hypocritical etc. (*false*) 544; canting, pietistical, sanctimonious, unctuous, pharisaical, overrighteous, righteous over much.

bigoted, fanatical, hidebound, narrow, illiberal, prejudiced, little; provincial, parochial, insular; priest-ridden.

adv. under the -mask, −cloak, −pretense, −form, −guise- of religion; in blasphemy.

989. Irreligion

n. **irreligion**, indevotion, impiety; ungodliness etc. *adj.;* laxity, apathy, indifference; quietism, passiveness, passivity.

skepticism, doubt; unbelief, disbelief, incredulity, incredulousness etc. *adj.;* want of -faith, −belief; pyrrhonism; doubt etc. 485; agnosticism, freethinking; deism; hylotheism; materialism, rationalism, positivism; nihilism.

infidelity, antichristianity, antichristianism, atheism.

unbeliever, infidel, atheist, antichristian; *giaour* [*Turk.*], heretic, miscreant [*archaic*], heathen, alien, gentile, Nazarene; *espirit fort* [*F.*], freethinker, skeptic, pyrrhonist, deist, latitudinarian, rationalist; materialist, positivist, nihilist, agnostic, somatist, theophobist.

v. **be irreligious** etc. *adj.;* disbelieve, lack faith; doubt, question etc. 485.

dechristianize, antichristianize [*rare*]; serve Mammon, contend against the light, love darkness rather than light, deny the truth.

adj. **irreligious**; indevout, undevout, devoutless, godless, graceless, ungodly; unholy, unsanctified, unhallowed; atheistic, without God.

skeptical, freethinking, unbelieving, unconverted; incredulous, faithless, lacking faith; deistic, deistical; antichristian, unchristian.

worldly, mundane, earthly, carnal; worldly etc. worldly-minded, unspiritual.

adv. **irreligiously** etc. *adj.*

990. Worship

n. **worship**, adoration, devotion, cult, aspiration, homage, service, humiliation; kneeling, genuflection, prostration; latria, dulia, hyperdulia.

prayer, invocation, supplication, rogation, intercession, orison, holy breathing, petition etc. (*request*) 765; collect, litany, Lord's prayer, paternoster; *Ave Maria* [*L.*]; Hail, Mary; rosary, bead-roll.

revival; anxious−, revival−, camp- meeting.

thanksgiving; giving−, returning- thanks; grace, praise, glorification, paean, benediction, doxology, hosanna, hallelujah *or* halleluiah, alleluia *or* alleluiah; *Te Deum, non nobis Domine, nunc dimittis; O Salutaris* [*all L.*]; Sanctus, *Agnus Dei* [*L.*], *Kyrie Eleison* [*Gr.*], *Gloria* [*L.*], The Annunciation, Tersanctus, Trisagion.

psalm, psalmody; hymn, plain song, chant, chaunt [*archaic*], response, anthem, motet, antiphon, antiphony.

oblation, sacrifice, incense, libation, offering; burnt−, heave−, thank−, votive- offering; offeratory, collection.

discipline, self-discipline, self-examination, self-denial; fasting, penance, confession.

divine service, office, duty; exercises; morning prayer; Mass, matins, nones, complin *or* compline, evensong, vespers, vigils, lauds; undersong, tierce; holyday etc. (*rites*) 998.

prayer book, missal, breviary, Virginal; ritual etc. 998.

worshiper, congregation, communicant, celebrant.

v. **worship**, lift up the heart, aspire; revere etc. 928; adore, do service, pay homage; humble oneself, kneel; bow−, bend- the knee; throw oneself on one's knees, fall down, fall on one's knees; prostrate oneself, bow down and worship; beat the breast.

intone, chant, deacon *or* deacon off [*colloq.*], lead the choir, sing.

pray, invoke, supplicate; put−, offer- up -prayers, −petitions; beseech etc. (*ask*) 765; say one's prayers, tell one's beads, recite the rosary.

give thanks, return thanks, say grace, bless, praise, laud, glorify, magnify, sing praises; give benediction.

propitiate, offer sacrifice, fast, deny oneself; vow, offer vows, give alms.

attend service, attend Mass, go to church, attend divine service; communicate etc. (*rite*) 998; work out one's salvation.

adj. **worshiping** etc. *v.;* devout, devotional, reverent, pure, solemn; fervid etc. (*heartfelt*) 821.

int. **hallelujah** *or* halleluiah! alleluia *or* alleluiah! hosanna! glory be to God! *sursum corda* [*L.*], *Deo gratias* [*L.*].

o Lord! pray God that! God -grant, −bless, −save, −forbid!

991. Idolatry

n. **idolatry**, idolatrousness, idololatry, idolism, idolodoulia, demonism, demonolatry, demonology; idol–, chthonian–, demon–, devil–, fire-worship; zoölatry, fetishism *or* fetichism; ecclesiolatry, heliolatry, bibliolatry, hierolatry [*rare*].

idolization, deification, apotheosis, canonization; hero worship.

sacrifice, idolothyte, hecatomb, holocaust; human sacrifices, immolation, mactation, infanticide, self-immolation, suttee.

idol, golden calf, graven image, fetish *or* fetich, eidolon, *thakur* [*Hind.*], joss [*Chinese*], *lares et penates* [*L.*]; god (*or* goddess) of one's idolatry; Baal, Moloch, Dagon, Juggernaut.

idolater, idolatress, demonolater *or* demonolator, chthonian, fetishist *or* fetichist; idolatrizer, idolizer, idolant [*obs.*], idolaster [*obs.*]; ecclesiolater, heliolater, zoölater, bibliolater.

v. **idolatrize**, idolize; *adorer le veau d'or* [*F.*]; worship -idols, –pictures, –relics; apotheosize, worship, put on a pedestal, prostrate oneself before; make sacrifice to, immolate before; deify, canonize.

adj. **idolatrous**, idololatric [*rare*], idolatric [*rare*], idolistic, chthonian, demonolatrous, fetishic [*rare*], fetishistic *or* fetichistic, idolothyte; worshiping *or* worshipping, prone before, prostrate before, in the dust before, at the feet of; heliolatrous, zoölatrous.

992. Sorcery

n. **sorcery**; occult -art, –sciences; magic, black magic, the black art, necromancy, theurgy, thaumaturgy; demonology, demonomy [*obs.*], demonomancy, demonship; diablerie, bedevilment, witchcraft, witchery; fetishism *or* fetichism; ghost dance, hoodoo, voodoo, voodooism; fire worship, heliolatry; obi *or* obiism, shamanism, vampirism; conjuration, incantation, bewitchment, glamour, enchantment; obsession, possession; exorcism.

divination etc. (*prediction*) 511; sortilege, ordeal, *sortes Vergilianae;* hocuspocus etc. (*deception*) 545.

v. **practice sorcery** etc. *n.;* cast a nativity, cast a horoscope, conjure, exorcise *or* exorcize [*rare in the sense of* conjure], charm, enchant, bewitch, bedevil, overlook, look on with the evil eye, witch, voodoo, hoodoo [*colloq.*]; entrance, fascinate etc. (*influence*) 615; taboo *or* tabu; wave a wand; rub the -ring, –lamp; cast a spell; call up spirits; raise spirits from the dead; raise ghosts, lay ghosts; command jinn *or* genii.

adj. **magic**, magical; witching, weird, cabalistic, talismanic, phylacteric, incantatory; charmed etc. *v.;* Circean; voodoo.

992a. Psychical Research

n. **psychical research**, psychical (*or* psychic) investigation; abnormal psychology; abnormal–, supernormal–, mediumistic-phenomena; mysticism; psychophysics; "psychologist's fallacy" [William James].

the subconscious, the subconscious self, the subliminal self, the higher self; ego etc. 980 *a;* subconsciousness, subliminal consciousness; dual personality, mental duality, secondary consciousness, intuition; multiple personality, mental dissociation, dissociation of personality, functional disintegration; impersonation, obsession, possession.

psychotherapy, psychotherapeutics, psychoanalysis; hysteria, neurasthenia, psychasthenia; over-stimulation; dreams, visions, apparitions, hallucinations, veridical hallucinations; Freud's theory.

mesmerism, animal magnetism; od, odyl *or* odylic force [*obsoles.*], electrobiology; mesmeric trance; hypnotism; hypnosis, hypnoidal state.

[phenomena] **telepathy**, thought transference, thought transmission, telepathic transmission; "malicious animal magnetism" *or* "M. A. P."; telepathic dreams; second sight, clairvoyance, clairaudience, psychometry.

premonitions, previsions, telepathic hallucinations; premonitory apparition, fetch, wraith, double; symbolic hallucinations; death lights, ominous dreams, ominous animals.

automatism, automatic writing, planchette, ouija board, trance writing, spirit writing, psychography; trance speaking, inspirational speaking.

crystal gazing, crystallomancy, crystal vision; hydromancy, lecanomancy, catoptromancy, onychomancy.

spiritualism, spiritism, spirit rapping, "Rochester knockings," table-turning, Poltergeist; spirit manifestations; ghost, specter etc. 980*a;* haunted houses; trance, spirit control, spirit possession; mediumistic communications; séance; materialization.

[theosophy and occultism] astral body etc. 980*a,* *kamarupa* [*Skr.*], desire body; etheric body; *linga sharira* [*Skr.*]; dense body, *sthula sharira* [*Skr.*]; mental body; causal body; bliss body, Buddhic body.

seven principles of man: (1) spirit *or atma* [*Skr.*], (2) spiritual mind, (3) intellect, (4) instinctive mind, (5) prana *or* vital force, (6) astral body, (7) physical body [*Yogi philosophy*].

medium, ecstatica [*rare*], seer, clairvoyant, clairaudient, telepathist; guide, control; mesmerist, hypnotist.

v. **psychologize;** investigate the -abnormal, −suprarational, −supernormal, −the subconscious, −the subliminal; search beyond the threshold, traverse the borderland, know oneself.

mesmerize, magnetize, hypnotize, place under control, subject to suggestion, place in a trance, induce hypnosis.

hold a séance, call up spirits, summon familiar spirits, "call spirits from the vasty deep" [*I Henry IV*]; hold spirit communications; materialize.

adj. **psychical,** psychic, psychal [*rare*], psychological; spiritistic, spiritualistic, spiritual; subconscious, "coconscious" [Morton Prince], subliminal (*opp. to* supraliminal); supernormal, abnormal, suprarational; mystic *or* mystical.

mediumistic, clairvoyant, clairaudient, telepathic; psychometric; hypnoidal, hypnagogic.

993. Spell

n. **spell,** charm, incantation, exorcism, weird [*obs. or Scot.*], cabala *or* cabbala, exsufflation [*obs.*], cantrip *or* contraip *or* contrap [*chiefly Scot.*], runes, abracadabra, open sesame, *or* open-sesame, hocus-pocus, counter-charm, Ephesian letters, bell book and candle, Mumbo Jumbo, evil eye.

talisman, amulet, madstone, periapt, telesm [*archaic*], phylactery, philter *or* philtre, fetish *or* fetich, manito *or* manitou *or* manitu; furcula, furculum, wishbone, merrythought; mascot *or* mascotte, rabbit's foot, hoodoo [*colloq.*], jinx [*slang*], scarabaeus *or* scarab; Om *or* Aum, *Om mani padme hum* [*Buddhist*]; sudarium, veronica, triskelion; swastika, fylfot, gammadion.

wand, caduceus, rod, divining rod, witch hazel, Aaron's rod.

[magic wish-givers] Aladdin's lamp, Aladdin's casket, magic casket, magic ring, magic belt, magic spectacles, wishing cap, Fortunatus's cap; seven-league boots; cap of darkness, Tarnkappe, Tarnhelm.

[fairy lore] fairy ring, fairy circle, fairy round; fernseed, rowan tree, quicken tree [*dial. Eng.*].

994. Sorcerer

n. **sorcerer,** magician, wizard, warlock, necromancer, conjuror, prestidigitator, *prestidigitateur* [*F.*], charmer, exorcist, voodoo,

thaumaturge, thaumaturgist, theurgist, image [*poetic*], Magi (*sing.* Magus); diviner, dowser.

sorceress, witch, hag.

medicine man *or* medicine, witch doctor, shaman, shamanist.

vampire, lamia, ghoul; siren, harpy; incubus etc. 980.

astrologer, figure caster [*obs.*], figure flinger [*obs.*]; soothsayer etc. 513.

Katerfelto, Cagliostro, Merlin, Comus; Circe, weird sisters, Graeae *or* Graiae, witch of Endor.

995. Churchdom

n. **churchdom;** church, ministry, apostleship, priesthood, prelacy, hierarchy, church government, pale of the church, christendom.

clericalism, sacerdotalism, episcopalianism, ultramontanism; ecclesiology; theocracy; priestcraft, *odium theologicum* [*L.*]; religious sects etc. 984.

monasticism, monkhood, monachism; celibacy.

[ecclesiastical offices and dignities] cardinalate, cardinalship; primacy, archbishopric, archiepiscopacy; prelacy, bishopric, bishopdom, episcopate, episcopacy, see, diocese; deanery, stall; canonry, canonicate; prebend, prebendaryship, prebendal stall; benefice, incumbency, glebe, advowson, living, cure, charge, cure of souls; rectorship, vicariate, vicarship; pastorate, pastorship, pastoral charge; deaconry, deaconship; curacy; chaplaincy, chaplainship, chaplainry *or* chaplanry [*Scot.*]; abbacy, presbytery.

holy orders, ordination, institution, consecration, induction, reading in [*Eng.*], preferment, translation, presentation.

papacy, pontificate, popedom, See of Rome, the Vatican, the apostolic see.

council etc. 696; conclave, college of cardinals, convocation, conference [*Meth.*], session, synod, consistory, chapter, vestry, presbytery, standing committee; sanhedrin, *congé d'élire* [*F.*].

ecclesiastical courts, consistorial court, court of Arches.

v. **call,** ordain, induct, prefer [*rare*], translate, consecrate, present, elect, bestow

take orders, take the veil, take vows.

adj. **ecclesiastical,** ecclesiological; clerical, sacerdotal, priestly, prelatical, pastoral, ministerial, capitular, theocratic; hierarchical, archiepiscopal; episcopal, episcopalian; canonical; monastic, monachal, monkish; abbatial, abbatical; Anglican; Aaronic, levitical, pontifical, papal, apostolic; ultramontane; priestridden.

996. Clergy

n. **clergy**, clericals, ministry, priesthood, presbytery, the cloth, the pulpit, the desk.

clergyman, divine, ecclesiastic, churchman, priest, presbyter, hierophant, pastor, shepherd, minister, clerk in holy orders, parson, sky pilot [*slang*]; father, –in Christ; padre, abbé [*F.*], curé [*F.*]; reverend; black coat; confessor.

[dignitaries of the church] ecclesiarch, sacrist, hierarch; patriarch [*Eastern Ch.*]; Abba Salamah, Abuna [*Abyssinian Ch.*]; eminence, reverence, primate, metropolitan, archbishop, bishop, angel [*as in the Cath. Apostolic Ch.*], prelate, diocesan, suffragan, bishop coadjutor, dean, subdean, archdeacon, prebendary, canon, rural dean, rector, vicar, perpetual curate, residentiary, beneficiary, incumbent, chaplain, curate; elder, deacon, deaconess; preacher, reader, Bible reader, lay reader, lecturer; capitular; missionary, propagandist, Jesuit, revivalist, field preacher, colporteur.

churchwarden, deacon, questman [*hist.*], sidesman; clerk, precentor, choir; almoner, suisse [*F.*], verger, beadle, sexton, sacristan; acolyte, thurifer, censor-bearer; choirster, choir boy, member of the choir; soloist, quartet *or* quartette; organist.

[roman catholic priesthood] Pope, Holy Father, papa [*obs. or rare*], pontiff, high priest, cardinal; archbishop, bishop, bishop coadjutor; canon-regular, canon-secular, confessor, penitentiary, Grand Penitentiary, spiritual director.

religious, monastic, cenobite, conventual, abbot, prior, monk, friar, lay brother, beadsman *or* bedesman, mendicant, pilgrim, palmer; Jesuit, Franciscan, Friars minor, Minorites; Observant, Capuchin, Dominican, Carmelite; Augustinian; Gilbertine; Austin–, Black–, White–, Gray–, Crossed–, Crutched- Friars; Bonhomme, Carthusian, Benedictine, Cistercian, Trappist, Cluniac, Premonstratensian, Maturine; Templar, Hospitaler; Bernardine, Lorettine, pillarist, stylite; caloyer, hieromonach [*both Eastern Ch.*].

nun, sister, religieuse [*F.*]; priestess, abbess, prioress, canoness; mother superior, superioress, the reverend mother; novice, postulant.

[jewish] prophet, priest, high priest, Levite; Rabbi, Rabbin, scribe.

[mohammedan] imam *or* imaum, kahin, kasis, sheik; mullah, murshid, mufti; hadji *or* haji, muezzin [*all Ar.*]; dervish *or* darvesh [*Pers.*], abdal (*pl.* abdali) [*Pers.*], fakir *or* faquir [*Ar.*], beshara [*Hind.*], bashara [*Hind.*], santon [*Turkey*].

[hindu] Brahman *or* Brahmin, pujari, purohit [*family priest*]; pundit *or* pandit, guru; yogi, sannyasi *or* sanyasi; bhikshu, bhikhari, vairagi *or* bairagi, Ramwat, Ramanandi [*all Hind.*].

[buddhist] poonghie *or* poonghee [*Burma*], talapoin [*Ceylon & Indo-China*], bonze; lama, Grand Lama *or* Dalai Lama [*Tibet*].

[various] druid, druidness [*ancient Celts*]; flamen [*Rom. relig. and ancient Britain*]; hierus, hierophant [*Gr. relig.*]; daduchus *or* dadouchos, mystae, epoptae [*Eleusinian Mysteries*].

v. take orders etc. 995.

adj. **ordained**, in orders, in holy orders, called to the ministry; the Reverend, the very Reverend, the Right Reverend.

997. Laity

n. **laity**, flock, fold, congregation, assembly, brethren, people; society; class [*Meth.*], meeting.

layman, civilian [*obs.*], laic, parishioner, catechumen; secularist.

v. **laicize**, secularize.

adj. **secular**, lay, laic *or* laical, congregational, civil, temporal, profane.

998. Rite

n. **rite**, ceremony, ceremonial, ordinance, observance, function, duty; form, formulary; solemnity, sacrament; incantation etc. (*spell*) 993; service, ministry, ministration; liturgics.

sermon, preaching, preachment, predication [*obs. or Scot.*], exhortation, religious harangue, homily, lecture, discourse, pastoral.

[seven sacraments] **baptism**, immersion, christening, chrism; baptismal regeneration; font.

confirmation, imposition of hands, laying on of hands.

eucharist, Lord's supper, communion; the sacrament, the holy sacrament; consecrated elements, bread and wine; intinction; celebration, high celebration; missa cantata [*L.*]; asperges [*L.*]; offertory; introit; consecration; consubstantiation, impanation, subpanation, transubstantiation; real presence; elements; Mass; high–, low–, dry- mass; hunter's (*or* hunting) mass [*obs.*].

penance etc. (*atonement*) 952; flagellation, maceration, fasting, sackcloth and ashes.

extreme unction, last rites, viaticum.

holy orders, ordination etc. (*churchdom*) 995.

matrimony, marriage, wedlock etc. 903.

worship etc. 990; invocation of saints, canonization, transfiguration, auricular confession, the confessional; absolution; reciting the rosary, telling of beads; processional; thurification, incense, holy water, aspersion.

circumcision; purification; visitation of the sick; burial etc. 363.

[sacred articles] relics, rosary, beads, reliquary, host, cross, rood, crucifix; pyx, pix [obs.]; pax, *Agnus Dei* [L.], censer, thurible, incensory, patera; urceus, urceole; prayer wheel, prayer machine; Sangraal *or* Sangrael, Holy Grail.

ritual, rubric, canon, ordinal, missal, breviary, Mass book, beadroll; farse; liturgy, prayer book, Book of Common Prayer, *Pietà* [*It.*], euchologion *or* euchology [*Eastern Ch.*], litany, lectionary.

psalter, psalm book, hymn book, hymnal; hymnology, psalmody.

ritualism, ceremonialism; sabbatism, sabbatarianism; ritualist, sabbatarian.

holyday, feast, fast; Sabbath, Passover, Pentecost; Advent, Christmas, Epiphany, Lent; Passion Week, Holy Week; Good Friday, Easter; Ascension Day, Holy Thursday; Whitsuntide, Whitsunday *or* Whit-Sunday [*erroneously,* Whitsun Day]; Trinity Sunday, Corpus Christi; All Saints *or* All Saints' Day, All Souls' Day; love feast, agape; Candlemas *or* Candlemas Day; Lammas, Lammas Day, Lammastide; Michaelmas, Martinmas.

v. **perform service**, do duty, minister, officiate; baptize, dip, sprinkle; confirm, lay hands on; give–, administer–, take–, receive–, attend–, partake of- the -sacrament, –communion, –Holy Eucharist; communicate; celebrate Mass, celebrate; administer–, receive- extreme unction; anele [*obs.*], shrive, absolve; administer–, receive- absolution; confess, make confession; do–, perform–, receive–, inflict-penance; tell one's beads; genuflect; make the sign of the Cross.

excommunicate, ban with bell book and candle.

preach, sermonize, predicate, lecture, address the congregation.

adj. **ritual**, ritualistic, ceremonial; liturgic *or* liturgical; baptismal, eucharistical; paschal.

999. Canonicals

n. **canonicals**, vestments; robe, gown, Geneva gown, frock, pallium, surplice, cotta, cassock; communion cloth, eileton [*Eastern Ch.*], corporal [*Western Ch.*]; scapular *or* scapulary, cope, mozetta *or* mozzetta, amice, scarf, fanon *or* fannel, bands, chasuble, tunicle, dalmatic, alb *or* alba, stole; tonsure, cowl, hood, capuche, calotte; vagas *or* vakas *or* vakass; apron, lawn sleeves, pontificals, pall; miter *or* mitre, tiara, triple crown; shovel–, cardinal's-hat; biretta *or* berretta; crosier *or* crozier, cross staff, pastoral staff; Sanctus bell, sacring bell; seven-branched candlestick; monstrance; censer etc. 998; costume etc. 225.

1000. Temple

n. **temple**, place of worship; house of God, house of prayer; cathedral, minister, church, kirk [*Scot. & dial. Eng.*], chapel, meeting-house, bethel, ebenezer [*Eng.*], conventicle, basilica, fane, holy place, chantry, oratory.

synagogue, tabernacle; mosque, masjid [*Moham.*]; dewal, kan-pati [*both Hindu*], girja [*Hind., Christian*]; pagoda, pagod [*archaic*], kiack [*Buddhist*]; Chinese temple, joss house [*colloq.*]; pantheon.

shrine, dagoba [*India*]; tope, stupa [*Buddhist*], Marabout [*Moham.*].

[interior] altar, sanctuary, Holy of Holies, *sanctum sanctorum* [*L.*], sacristy; sacrarium; communion–, holy–, Lord's- table; table of the Lord; pyx; baptistery, font; piscina; stoup; holy-water stoup, holy-water basin; ambry, aumbry [*archaic*]; sedile; reredos; rood screen, rood beam, chapel screen, jube; rood loft.

chancel, apse, choir, quire [*archaic*], nave, triforium, blindstory, aisle, transept, crypt, porch, cloisters; churchyard, golgotha; calvary, Easter sepulcher; stall, pew, seat, seating; pulpit, ambo, lectern, reading desk; confessional; prothesis, table (*or* altar) of prothesis, chapel of prothesis [*Eastern Ch.*]; credence, baldachin *or* baldaquin; belfry; vestry, chapter house; presbytery; diaconicon *or* diaconicum; mourners' bench, mourners' seat; anxious bench, anxious seat, penitent form.

monastery, priory, abbey, friary, convent, nunnery, cloister.

parsonage, rectory, vicarage, manse, deanery, clergy house; glebe; Vatican; bishop's palace; Lambeth.

adj. **churchly**, claustral, cloistered, monastic, monasterial, monachal, conventual; cruciform.

Index Guide

The numbers refer to the headings under which the words or phrases occur. When the same word or phrase can be used in various senses, the several headings under which it, or its synonyms, will be found are indicated by *italics*. These words in italics are not intended to explain the meaning of the word or phrase to which they are annexed, but only to assist in the required reference.

Italicized references within parentheses are merely suggestive, the parentheses indicating that the term itself is not included in the list referred to.

When the word given in the Index Guide is itself the title or heading of a category, the reference number is printed in bold-face type, thus: **abode 189.**

To keep the Index Guide—necessarily very large—from becoming unwieldy, a considerable number of obsolete, rare, foreign, dialectic, and slang terms have been omitted. Such words, while useful in the text, are not the ones for which synonyms would ordinarily be sought.

Derivatives likewise have been sparingly admitted, since the allied or basic term will serve as a key to the various derived forms; thus, *cold* is given, but not *coldness* or *coldly*. By such means, unnecessary duplication is avoided.

IMPORTANT NOTE

The numbers following all references in this Index Guide refer to the *section numbers* in the text, and *not* to pages. Thus "Aaronic 995" refers to *section* 995, under which the citation will be found. For further ease of reference, the *section* numbers will be found at the *top* of every page.

A

A 1 273, 648
  –at Lloyd's 273
Aaronic 995
A. B. 269
abacist 85
aback 235 take–508
abaction 791
abacus 85
Abaddon 978, 982
abaft 235
abalienate 783
abandon
  depart from 293
  –*a purpose* 624
  –*property* 782
  –*hope* 859
  –*society* 893
abandon *lively* 682
  artless 703
abandoned
  neglected 460
  forsaken 893
  vicious 945
  –*farm* 782
abandonment 757
abase *depress* 308
  degrade 879
abased 886
abasement
  disrepute 874
  servility 886
abash *daunt* 860
  humiliate 879

abashed *modest* 881
abate *lessen* 36
  –*a price* 813
abatement 36
  –*of differences* 774
abatjour 260
abattis 717
abattoir 361
abat–voix 417
abba 166
abbacy 995
abbatial 995
abbatis 717
abbess 996
abbey 1000
abbot 996
abbreviation
  shortening 201
  compendium 596
abbreviatory
  short 201
  compendious 596
abbreviature 596
A B C *beginning* 66
  teaching 537
  letters 561
abdal *fanatic* 984
  clergy 996
abderian 836
abdicant 757
abdicate
  –*a throne* 738
  resign 757
abditory 530
abdomen 221, 250
abdominal 221, 250

abdominoscope 445
abdominous 194
abducent 289
abduct *repel* 289
  take 789
  steal 791
abduction 289
abductor 792
abecedarian
  teacher 540
  learner 541
abecedary *school* 542
  letter 561
aberdevine 366
aberrant
  exceptional 83
  deviating 279
  divergent 291
  erroneous 495
aberration
  (*see* aberrant)
  variation 20a
  mental –503
abet 707
abettor 711
abeyance *extinction* 2
  suspense 142
  expectation 507
  in–172
abeyant 526
abhor *dislike* 867
  hate 898
abhorrence
  (*see* abhor)
abhorrent
  painful 830

abide *endure* 1, 106
  remain 110
  continue 141, 143
  dwell 186
  quiet 265
  expect 507
  –*by assent* 488
  observe 772
  –*with*
   be composed 826
   not–867
abigail 746
abilities
  to the best of one's
   –686
ability *power* 157
  skill 698
abiogenesis 161, 357
abirritate 834
abito 350
abject *vile* 874, 940
  servile 886
  –*fear* 862
abjunction 44
abjuratory 536, 757
abjure *deny* 536
  renounce 607
  resign 757
abkari 812
ablation
  subduction 38
  taking 789
ablaze *heat* 382
  light 420
able *capable* 157
  skillful 698

  –*seaman* 269
able–bodied 159
ablegate *displace* 185
  depute 759
ablepsia 442
ablude 15
ablution 652
abnegation
  denial 536
  refusal 764
  forbearance 953
  self–942
abnormal 83
  –*mind* 503
abnormalize 83
aboard *present* 186
  ship 273
  go–293
abode 189 *presage* 511
  take up one's
  –*settle* 150
  locate oneself 184
abodement 511
aboideau 350
abolish (*see* abolition)
abolition *destroy* 162
  abrogate 756
abolitionist 756
abolitionize 756
abomasum 191
abominable *bad* 649
  foul 653
  hateful 898
abominate
  dislike 867
  hate 898

actual *existing* 1
  present 118
  real 494
  (*identical* 13)
actuality (*see* actual)
actualize 220
actuary 85, 811
actuate *influence* 175
  incite 615
acuity 253
aculeated 253
acumen 498
acuminated 253
acupuncture 260
acute *energetic* 171
  physically violent 173
  pointed 253
  physically sensible 375
  musical tone 410
  discriminative 465
  perspicacious 498
  cunning 702
  strong feeling 821
  morally painful 830
  –*angle* 244
  –*ear* 418
  –*note* 410
acutely 31
acuteness 465
A. D. 106
adactylism 848
adaga 727
adage 496
adagio *music* 415
  slow 275
Adam *sin* 945
adamant *strong* 159
  hard 323
Adam's ale 337
Adam's needle 253
adapt *agree* 23
  equalize 27
  –*oneself to*
  conform 82
adaptable
  conformable 82
  useful 644
adaptation
  (*see* adapt)
add *increase* 35
  join 37
  numerically 85
  accounts 811
addendum 39
adder 366, 913
  deafness 419
addict *habit* 613
adding machine 85
additament 39
addition (*see* add)
  adjunction **37**
  thing added 39
  arithmetical 85
addle *barren* 169

  incomplete 730
  abortive 732
  –*the wits*
  bewilder 475
  craze 503
addle–head 501
addle–headed 499
address *compose* 54
  residence 189
  direction 550
  speak to 586
  skill 698
  request 765
addressee 188
addresses
  courtship 902
adduce *bring to* 288
  evidence 467
adduct 288
adeem 789
adelomorphous 83
ademption 789
adenology 329
  intellectual 450
  proficient 698, 700
adept
adequate *power* 157
  sufficient 639
  for a purpose 644
  content 831
adespotic 738
adhere *stick* 46
  –*to persevere* 604a
  habit 613
  –*to a duty* 926
  –*to an obligation* 772
adherent 65, 711
adhesive *sticking* 46
  tenacious 327
  sticky 352
adhibit 677
adhortation 695
adiaphanous 426
adiathermancy 382
adieu *departure* 293
  loss 776
adipocere 356
adipose 355
adit *orifice* 260
  conduit 350
  passage 627
adjacent 197
adjection 37
adjective 39
  –*jerker* 593
adjoin *near* 197
  contact 199
adjourn *postpone* 133
  neglect 460
adjudge 480
adjudicate 480
adjunct *addition* 37
  thing added **39**
  accompaniment 88
  aid 707
  auxiliary 711

adjuration
  affirmation 535
  negation 536
adjure *request* 765
  promise 768
adjust *adapt* 23
  equalize 27
  regulate 58
  prepare 673
  settle 723
  –*differences* 774
adjustment 762, 774
adjutant
  auxiliary 711
  military 745
adjuvant *helping* 707
  auxiliary 711
admeasurement 466
administer
  utilize 677
  conduct 693
  exercise authority 737
  distribute 786
  –*correction* 972
  –*oath* 768
  –*sacrament* 998
  –*to aid* 707
  give 784
administration of justice 965
administrative
  official 737
  judicial 965
admirable
  excellent 648
  virtuous 944
admiral 745
Admiralty, court of – 966
admiration
  wonder 870
  love 897
  respect 928
  approval 931
admirer 897
admissible
  relevant 23
  receivable 296
  tolerable 651
  –*in society* 852
admission (*see* admit)
admit *composition* 54
  include 76
  let in 296
  assent 488
  acknowledge 529
  permit 760
  concede 762
  accept 785
  –*exceptions* 469
  –*of* 470
admitted
  customary 613
  –*maxim etc.* 496
admixture 41

admonish *warn* 668
  advise 695
  reprove 932
admonitory 616
ado *activity* 682
  exertion 686
  difficulty 704
  make much–about important 642
  much–about nothing
  overestimate 482
  unimportant 643
  unskillful 699
adobe 635
adolescence 131
Adonis 845
adonize 847
adopt *naturalize* 184
  choose 609
  appropriate 788
  –*a cause aid* 707
  –*a course* 692
  –*an opinion* 484
adoption *religious* 987
adore *love* 897
  worship 990
adorn 847
adown 207
adrift *unrelated* 10
  disjoined 44
  dispersed 73
  uncertain 475
  unapt 699
  liberated 750
  go–deviate 279
  turn–disperse 73
  liberate 750
  dismiss 756
adroit 698
adscititious
  extrinsic 6
  added 37
  redundant 641
adulation 933
adulator 935
Adullam, cave of–
  desertion 624
  discontent 832
adult 131
adulterate *mix* 41
  deteriorate 659
adulterated
  sham 545
adulterer 962
adultery 961
adulthood 131
adultism 131
adumbrate
  darkness 421
  allegorize 521
  represent 554
adumbration
  semblance 21
  darkness 421
  allusion 526

aduncate 245
aduncity 244
adust *arid* 340
  heated 384
  brown 433
adustion 384
advance *increase* 35
  course 109
  progress 282
  assert 535
  improve 658
  aid 707
  succeed 731
  lend 787
  –*against* 716
  –*agent* 599
  –*guard* 234
  –*of learning etc.* 490
  –*upon* 303
  in–precedence 62
  front 234
  precession 280
  in–of superior 33
  in–of one's age 498
advanced 282
  –*in life* 128
  –*work* 717
advancement
  (*see* advance)
  infringement 303
advances, make–
  offer 763
  social 892
advantage
  superiority 33
  increase 35
  influence 175
  benefit 618
  expedience 646
  –*over success* 731
  *dressed to–*847
  find one's–in 644
  *gain an–*775
  *mechanical–*633
  *set off to–*658
  take–of use 677
  make the most of 698
advantageous
  beneficial 648
  profitable 775
advene 37
Advent 998
advent *futurity* 121
  event 151
  approach 286
  arrival 292
Adventist 984
adventitious
  extrinsic 6
  casual 156
adventive 156
adventure *event* 151
  chance 156
  pursuit 622
  danger 665

trial 675
undertaking 676
adventurer
traveler 268
experimenter 463
deceiver 548
gambler 621
rash 863
ignoble 876
adventures
history 594
adventuress 548
adventurous
undertaking 676
bold 861
rash 863
adversaria 551
adversary 710
Adversary, the–978
adverse *contrary* 14
opposed 708
unprosperous 735
disliking 867
–party 710
adversity 735
advert 457
advertent 457
advertise 531
advice *notice* 527
news 532
counsel **695**
good–695
advisable 646
advise *predict* 511
inform 527
counsel 695
–with one's pillow 451
advised
predetermined 611
intended 620
better–658
advisement
advice 695
(see advise)
under–453
adviser *teacher* 540
counselor 695
advisory 527
advocacy
approbation 931
advocate
interpreter 524
prompt 615
recommend 695
aid 707
auxiliary 711
friend 890, 914
vindicate 937
counselor 968
Advocate, the–
Savior 976
advocation *plea* 617
advoutress 962
advoutry 961
advowson 995

adynamic 160
adytum *room* 191
prediction 511
secret place 530
aedile 965
aegis 717
Aeolian 349
–harp 417
Aeolus 349
aeon 109, 110
aerate 334, 353
aeration 334
aerial *elevated* 206
navigation 267, 273
gas 334
air 338
–mail 534
–mail–carrier 271
–navigator 269
–perspective 428
–railway 840
aerie 189
aeriferous 334
aerification 334
aeriform 334
aerify 334
aeroboat 273
aerobus 273
aerodonetics 267
aerodrome 273
aerodynamics
navigation 267
gas 334
wind 349
aerography 334, 349
aero-hydroplane 273
aerolite 318
aerology *gaseity* 334
air 338
wind 349
aeromancy 511
aeromechanic 267, 334
aerometer 338
aerometric 338
aeronat 273
aeronaut 269a
aeronautic 273
(see aeronautics)
aeronautics
navigation 267
air 338
aeroplane 273
combatant 726
by–684
aeroplanist 269
aeroscope 338
aeroscopy 334
aerosphere 338
aerostat *balloon* 273
aerostatics 267 334
aerostation 338
aerotherapy 662
aeroyacht 273
aery *gaseous* 334

atmospheric 338
Aesculapius 662
Aesop 846
aesthetic
sensibility 375
beauty 845
taste 850
aestival 125
aestivation 384
aetiology *causes* 155
life 359
knowledge 490
disease 655
afar 196
afeard 860
affable
condescending 879
courteous 894
affair *event* 151
topic 454
business 625
battle 720
–of honor 720
affaires, chargé d'–
758
affect *relate to* 9
tend to 176
qualify 469
feign 544
touch 824
desire 865
love 897
affectation 855
affected 583
–manner 880
affected with
feeling 821
disease 655
affectibility 822
affecting *pathetic* 830
affection *feeling* 821
love 897
affectionate 821, 897
affections 820
affettuoso *music* 415
affiance *promise* 768
trust 858
affianced *love* 897
marriage 903
affiche 531
affidation 769
affidavit
affirmation 535
record 551
lawsuit 969
affiliation *relation* 9
kindred 11
attribution 155
affinal 11
affinitive 9
affinity *relation* 9
similarity 17
affirmant 488
affirmation
evidence 467
assent 488

assert **535**
affirmative 535
affix *add* 37
sequel 39
fasten 43
precedence 62
letter 561
afflation 349
afflatus *wind* 349
inspiration 985
afflict 830
–with illness 655
affliction *pain* 828
infliction 830
adversity 735
affluence
sufficiency 639
prosperity 734
wealth 803
affluent *river* 348
afflux 286
afford *supply* 784
wealth 803
yield 810
sell for 812
–aid etc. 707
affranchise
make free of 748
liberate 750
affray 720
affriction 331
affright 860
affront *molest* 830
provocation 900
insult 929
–danger 861
affuse 337
affusion 73
afield 186
afire 382
afloat *extant* 1
unstable 149
going on 151
ship 273
navigation 267
ocean 341
news 532
preparing 673
keep oneself–734
set–publish 531
afoot *on hand* 625
ready 673
astir 682
afore 116
aforegoing 116
aforehand 116
aforementioned 62, 116
aforesaid
preceding 62
repeated 104
prior 116
aforesighted 116
aforethought 116, 611, 907
aforetime 116

a fortiori
superiority 33
evidence 467
reasoning 476
afraid 860–*to say*
uncertain 4
be–irresolute 605
afreet 980
afresh *repeated* 104
new 123
African 431
Afric heat 382
Afrikander 57
aft 235
after *in order* 63
in time 117
too late 135
rear 235
pursuit 622
–all for all that 30
qualification 469
on the whole 476
–time 133
be–intention 620
pursuit 622
go–follow 281
after acceptation 516
after–age 124
afterbirth 63
afterburden 63
afterclap 63, 154, 509
aftercome 65, 154
aftercrop 63, 154, 168
afterdamp 663
afterdinner 117
afterglow
decrement 40a
sequence 63
light 420
aftergrass 63
aftergrowth 65, 154
afterlife 152
aftermath
sequence 63
effect 154
fertile 168
profit 775
afternoon 126
–farmer 683
afterpain 63
after–part *sequel* 65
rear 235
afterpiece 63, 599
aftertaste 63, 390
afterthought
thought 451
memory 505
change of mind 607
aftertime 121, 133
afterwards 117
aga 745
again *duplicate* 90
repeated 104

antedate 115
antediluvian 124
antelope 274, 360
antemundane 124
antenna 379
antepast 510
anteposition 62
anterior *in order* 62
  in time 116
  in place 234
  –to reason 477
anteroom 191
antevert 706
anthelion 423
anthelmintic 662
anthem 990
anthemion 847
antherozoid 357
anthology
  writing 590
  book 593
  collection 596
  poem 597
  store 636
anthracite 388
anthrax 655
anthropod 193
anthropogeny 372
anthropoid 372
anthropology
  zoology 368
  mankind 372
anthropomancy 511
anthropomorphism
  984
anthropophagus 913
anthroposcopy 511
anthroposophy 372
anthropotomy 372
antic 840
antichristian
  heterodox 984
  irreligious 989
antichronism 115
anticipant 120
anticipate
  anachronism 115
  priority 116
  future 121
  early 132
  expect 507
  foresee 510
  prepare 673
  hope 858
  caution 864
anticipation 120
  (*see* anticipate)
anticlimax
  decrease 36
  bathos 497, 853
anticlinal 217
anticyclone 265
antidote 662
antigropelos 225
antifebrile 662
antilogarithm 84

antilogy 477
antiluetic 662
antimacassar 223
antimony 663, 490a
Antinomian 984
antinomy 964
Antinous 845
antiorgastic 174
antiparallel 217
antipathy
  contrariety 14
  dislike 867
  hate 898
antiphon *music* 415
  answer 462
  worship 990
antiphonal 462
antiphrasis 563
antipodes
  difference 14
  distance 196
  contraposition 237
antipoison 662
antiquary
  past times 122
  scholar 492
  historian 553
antiquated *aged* 128
  (*out of fashion* 851)
antique 124
antiquity 122
antiscriptural 984
antiseptic 662
antisocial 911
antispasmodic 174,
  662
antispast 597
antistrophe 597
antithesis *contrast* 14
  difference 15
  contraposition 237
  style 577
antithesize 14
antitype 22
antler 253
antonomasia
  metaphor 521
  nomenclature 564
antrum 252
anvil *conversion* 144
  support 215
  on the–
    intended 620
    in hand 625, 730
    preparing 673
anxiety *solicitude* 459
  pain 828
  fear 860
  desire 865
anxious (*see* anxiety)
  –bench 1000
  –expectation 507
  –meeting 1000
  –seat 1000
any *some* 25
  part 51

no choice 609a
at–rate *certain* 474
  true 494
at all hazards 604
anybody 78
anyhow *careless* 460
  in some way 627
aorist 109, 119
aorta 350
apace *early* 132
  swift 274
Apache 913
apache *assassin* 361
aparejo 215
apart *irrelative* 10
  separate 44
  singleness 87
  soliloquy 589
  set–636
  wide–196
apartment 191
  –house 189
  –s to let
    imbecile 450a, 499
apathetic 275
apathy
  incuriosity 456
  insensibility 823
  irreligion 989
ape *monkey* 366
  imitate 19
aperient 652, 662
apéritif 394
aperture 260
apery 19
apex *height* 206
  summit 210
aphelion 196
aphid 366, 659
Aphis 659
aphonic 403, 581
aphonia 581
aphorism 496
aphrodisia 173, 961
aphrodisiac 865
Aphrodite 845
apiarism 370
apiarist 370
apiary 370
apical 210
apiculate 253
apiculture 370
apiece 79
apish 19, 499
apishamore 223
aplomb *stability* 150
  verticality 212
  self–possession 498
  resolution 604
Apocalypse 985
Apocrypha 985
apocryphal
  uncertain 475
  erroneous 495
  heterodox 984
apodeictic 478

apodeixis 478
apodosis 67
apogee 490a
apograph 21
apolaustic 377
Apollo *sun* 318
  music 416
  luminary 423
  beauty 845
  –Musagetes 416
  magnus–*sage* 500
  adviser 695
apologue
  metaphor 521
  teaching 537
  description 594
apology
  substitution 147
  excuse 617
  vindication 937
  penitence 950
  atonement 952
apophysis 250
apoplexy 158
aporia 475
apostasy
  recantation 607
  dishonor 940
  heterodoxy 984
  impiety 988
apostate *convert* 144
  turncoat 607
  seceder 742
  heretic 984
  (*recreant* 941)
apostatize 607
apostle *teacher* 540
  disciple 541
  inspired 985
  –'s creed 983a
apostolic 985
  –church 983a
  –see 995
apostrophe
  typography 550
  address 586
  soliloquy 589
  appeal 765
apostrophize 765
apothecary 662
  –'s weight 319
apothegm 496
apotheosis
  resuscitation 163
  heaven 981
  hero worship 991
apozem *liquefy* 335
  fuse 384
apozemial 384
appal *pain* 830
  terrify 860
appanage
  property 780
  gift 784
apparatus 633
apparel 225

apparent *visible* 446
  appearing 448
  probable 472
  manifest 525
  heir–779
apparition *shade* 362
  fallacy of vision 443
  spirit 980a
  psychical research
    992a
  (*appearance* 448)
apparitor
  precursor 64
  messenger 534
appeach 938
appeal *address* 586
  request 765
  –motion 969
  –to
    call to witness 467
  –to arms 722
  –to for (*claim*) 924
  court of–966
appear
  come in sight 446
  show itself 525
  (*come into being* 1)
  –for 759
  –in print 591
appearance 448
  make one's–
    arrive 292
  to all–*to the eye* 448
  probable 472
appearances
  keep up–852
appease 174
appellant
  claimant 924
appellate 966
appellation 564
append *add* 37
  sequence 63
  hang 214
appendage
  addition 37
  adjunct 39
  accompaniment 88
  rear 235
appendicitis 655
appendix 65, 67
apperception 450,
  490
appercipient 450
appertain *related to* 9
  component 56
  belong 777
  property 780
appetence 865
appetency 602
appetite 865
  tickle the–
  savory 394
appetitive 865
appetizer 393, 394
appetizing 865

repute 873
lord of the–745
one's star in the–
prosperity 734
ascension
(see ascend)
calefaction 384
Ascension Day 998
ascent (see ascend)
gradient 217
rise **305**
glory 873
ascertain fix 150
determine 480
ascertained
certain 474
known 490
ascertainment 480a
ascetic 955
asceticism 953, **955**
ascititious intrinsic 6
additional 37
supplementary 52
ascribe 155
ascription
(see ascribe)
aseptic 662
ash 367, 384
–blond 429
–colored 432
ashamed 879, 881
ash cake 298
ashen 429
ashes corpse 362
dirt 653
lay in–162
pale as–
colorless 429
fear 860
ashore 342 go
–arrive 292
Ash Wednesday 138
ashy 429
Asian mystery 533
aside laterally 236
whisper 405
private 528
–from the purpose
10
say–589
set–displace 185
neglect 460
negative 536
reject 610
disuse 678
abrogate 756
discard 782
step–279
asinine ass 271
fool 499
ask inquire 461
request 765
for sale 794
price 812
(invoke 990)
–leave 760

askance 217 eye
–fear 860
look
–vision 441, 443
dissent 489
dislike 867
disapproval 932
asked in church 903
askew oblique 217
distorted 243
asking (see ask)
aslant 217
asleep 683
aslope 217
Asmodeus 978
asomatous 317
asp animal 366
evil doer 913
asparagus 298, 367
Aspasia 962
aspect feature 5
state 7
situation 183
appearance 448
aspen leaf
shake like an–
motion 315
fear 860
asperges 998
aspergillum 337
asperity
roughness 256
discourtesy 895
anger 900
irascibility 901
asperse 934
aspersion
nonassemblage 73
cleanness 652
malediction 908
rite 998
asphalt smooth 255
resin 356a
asphodel 845
asphyxia 360
asphyxiate 361
aspirant
candidate 767
desire 865
aspirate 402, 580
aspirated 681
aspire rise 305
project 620
hope 858
desire 865
worship 990
asportation 270
asquint 217
ass
beast of burden 271
fool 501
–'s bridge
unintelligible 519
cheat 548
bungler 701
make an–of

delude 545
assafetida 401
assagai 727
assail attack 716
pain 830
assailant
opponent 710
attacker 726
assassin,–ate 361
assault 716
take by–789
assay 463
assayer 463
assemblage **72**
assembly council 696
society 892
religious 997
assemblyman 696
assembly room 189,
588
assent belief 484
agree **488**
willing 602
consent 762
content 831
assert affirm 535
claim as a right 924
assess measure 466
determine 480
tax 812
assessor judge 967
assets property 780
money 800
accounts 811
asseverate 535
assiduous 682
assign commission 755
transfer 783
give 784
allot 786
–a duty 926
–as cause 155
–dower 784
–places 60
assignable 270
assignat 800
assignation tryst 892
place of–74
assignee transfer 270
donee 785
assignment 155
assimilate uniform 16
resemble 17
imitate 19
agree 23
transmute 144
assimilation 161
assist 707
assistant 711
assize measure 466
tribunal 966
justice of–967
associate mix 41
unite 43
combine 48
collect 72

accompany 88
colleague 690
auxiliary 711
friend 890
–professorship 542
–with sociality 892
association
(see associate)
relation 9
cooperation 709
partnership 712
friendship 888
–of ideas intellect 450
thought 451
intuition 477
hint 514
associational
psychology 457
assoil acquit 970
(liberate 750)
assoilzie 970
assonance
agreement 23
music 413
poetry 597
assort arrange 60
assortment
collection 72
class 75
assuage moderate 174
relieve 834
(–morally 826)
assuasive 174, 834
assuetude 613
assume believe 484
suppose 514
falsehood 544
take 789
insolent 885
right 924
–a character 554
–a form 144
–authority 737
–command 741
–the offensive 716
assumed–name 565
–position 514
assuming
insolent 885
assumption
(see assume)
severity 739
hope 858
insolence 885
seizure 925
assurance
speculation 156
certainty 474
belief 484
confidence 507
assertion 535
promise 768
security 771
hope 858
vanity 880
insolence 885

make–double sure
safe 664
caution 864
assure
render certain 474
believe 484
certify 535
promise 768
secure 771
give hope 858
assured
self–satisfied 880
assuredly assent 488
astatic 320
asteism 856
asterisk 550
astern 235 fall–283
asteroid 318
asthenia 160
astigmatism 443
astir ready 673
active 682
set–824
astonish 870
astonishing great 31
astonishment 508,
870
astound
be unexpected 508
excite 824
fear 860
surprise 870
astraddle 215
astragal 847
astral 318
–body 317, 992a
–influence 601
–plane 317
astray at fault 475
error 495
go–deviate 279
sin 945
astriction 43, 195
astride 215
astringent 195, 397
astrolabe 466, 490a
astrology 511, 522
astronomy **490a,** 318
astute wise 498
cunning 702
asunder separate 44
distant 196
as poles–237
asylum hospital 662
retreat 666
defense 717
asymptote 290
ataghan 727
atajo 72
atavism 145
atelier studio 556
workshop 691
athanasia 112
Athanasian creed
983a
athanor 386

production 161
style 569
writing 590
autistic thinking
821a
auto 272
autobiography 594
autocar 272
autochthonous 188
autocracy *will* 600
authority 737
severity 739
autocrat 745
autocratic *will* 600
ruling 737
auto–da–fe
burning 384
execution 972
autodidactic 490
autograph
evidence 467
signature 550
writing 590
autography 550
autointoxication 655
Autolycus *thief* 792
peddler 797
automaniac 504
automatic 266, 601
pistol 727
–*gun* 727
–*writing* 992a
automatism 992a
automaton 1
automobile 266, 272
–*race* 274
automobilist 268
automotive 266
autonomy *rule* 737
free 748
autoplagiarism 791
autopsy
post–mortem 363
vision 441
autoptical *visible* 446
manifest 525
auto–rifle 727
autotype 558
autumn 126
auxiliary 711
extra 37
aid 707
–*forces* 726
avail *benefit* 618
useful 644
succeed 731
–*oneself of* 677
of no–645
available 676
avails 775, 810
avalanche *fall* 306
redundance 641
avant–courier
precursor 64
pioneer 673
avarice 819

avast! *stop* 142, 265
desist 624
forbid 761
avatar *change* 140
Vishnu 979
avaunt! *eject* 297
disappear 449
ave! *honor* 873
courtesy 894
Ave Maria 900
avenge 919
avenger 919
avenue *plantation* 371
way 627
aver 535
average *mean* 29
neutral 628
mediocre 651
–*circumstances* 736
take an–466
Avernus 982
averruncate *eject* 297
extract 301
averse *contrary* 14
unwilling 603
averseness
unwillingness 603
rejection 610
aversion *dislike* 867
enmity 889
hate 898
avert 706
–*the eyes* 442
Avesta 986
aviary 370
aviate 267
aviation 267
aviator 269
avidity *avarice* 819
desire 865
avile 932, 934
avion 273, 726
aviso 532
avocado 298
avocation 625
avoid 623
avoidance 623
avoidless *certain* 474
necessary 601
avoirdupois 319
avoke 741
avolation *avoid* 623
escape 671
avouch 535
avow *assent* 488
disclose 529
assert 535
avowal (*see* avow)
avulsion
separation 44
extraction 301
await *future* 121
be kept waiting 133
impend 152
expect 507
awake *attentive* 457

careful 459
intelligent 498
active 682
excite 824
awaken *inform* 527
excite 824
–*the attention* 457
–*the memory* 505
award *adjudge* 480
give 784
aware 490
away *absent* 187
distant 196
depart 293
–*from unrelated* 10
–*with!* 930, 932
break–623
do–with undo 681
abrogate 756
fly–293
get–671
move–287
awayness 187
awe *fear* 860
wonder 870
respect 928
aweless *fearless* 861
insolent 885
disrespectful 929
awe–struck 870
awful *great* 31
fearful 860
–*silence* 403
awhile 111
awkward *uncouth* 579
inexpedient 647
unskillful 699
difficult 704
painful 830
ugly 846
vulgar 851
ridiculous 853
–*squad* 701, 726
awkwardness
(*see* awkward)
awl 262–*shaped* 253
awned 253
awning *tent* 223
shade 424
awry *oblique* 217
distorted 243
evil 619
ax *edge tool* 253
impulse 276
weapon 727
for beheading 975
axial 222
axinomancy 511
axiom 496
axiomatic 474
axis *support* 215
center 222
rotation 212
axle 312
wheel and–633
axletree 215

ay 488
ayah *servant* 746
nurse 753
aye *ever* 112
yes 488
ayudante 711
azimuth
horizontal 213
direction 278
measurement 466
–*circle* 212
azoic 358
azote 663 *whip* 975
azotic 657
Azrael 360
azure 438
azurite 490c
azygous *single* 87

B

Baal *divinity* 979
idol 986
baas *master* 745
babble *rivulet* 348
faint sound 405
unmeaning 517
talk 584, 588
babbler 501 532
babbling *foolish* 499
babe 129
Babel *confusion* 59
discord 414
tongues 560
jargon 563
loquacity 584
Babism 984
Babist 984
baboon 366, 846
babu 553
–*English* 563
Bab–ud–Din 986
baby *infant* 129
posterity 167
fool 501
–*blue* 438
–*grand piano* 417
–*linen* 225
babyhood 127
babyish 499
baccalaureate 873
baccarat 840
baccate 354
bacchanals 959
Bacchus *drink* 959
bachelor 904
bachelor girl 374,
904
back *rear* 235
shoulder 250
aid 707
indorse 800
–*and forth* 148, 314
–*down recede* 283
apostatize 607

–*out retire* 283
change sides 607
relinquish 624
–*pedal* 275
–*to back* 235
–*up support* 215
aid 707
behind one's–
latent 526
hidden 528
come–292
fall–relapse 661
give–790
go–283
go–from retract 773
have at one's–215
hold–avoid 623
keep–reserve 636
look–505
on one's
–*impotent* 158
horizontal 213
failure 732
pat on the–
incite 615
encourage 861
approve 931
pay–retaliate 718
put–deteriorate 659
restore 660
send–764
set one's–against
the wall 604
set one's–up
pride 878
some time–122
spring–277
take–again 790
trace–505
turn–283
turn one's–
retire 283
turn one's–upon
repel 289
inattention 458
avoid 623
oppose 708
seclusion 893
discourtesy 895
disrespect 929
contempt 930
backbite *traduce* 932
detract 934
backbiter 936
backbone *intrinsic* 5
energy 171
frame 215
center 222
grit 604
persevere 604a
soul 820
game to the–604
backcap 934
back door 627
backdown 725
backer 711

backfriend 891
backgammon 840
background
  distance 196
  rear 235
  in the–*latent* 526
  ignoble 874
  keep in the
  –*hide* 528
  modest 881
  seclusion 893
  throw into the–460
backhanded 217, 629
backlash 277
backlog 386, 388
backplate 717
backset
  agriculture 371
  reverse 735
backsettler 188
backside 235
backslider
  turncoat 607
  shirker 623
  apostate 984
backsliding
  regression 283
  tergiversation 607
  relapse 661
  vice 945
  heterodox 984
  impiety 988
backstairs
  ambush 530
  way 627
  –*influence* 702
backward *tardy* 133
  rear 235
  regression 283
  unwilling 603
  unprogressive 659
backwardation 813
backwards 283
  –and forwards
  interchange 148
  oscillation 314
  bend–325
backwater
  cessation 142
  slowness 275
  regression 283
backwoods 233
backwoodsman
  inhabitant 188
  agriculture 371
bacon 298
  save one's–
  safety 644
  escape 671
Baconian method
  461
bacteria 193, 369
bactericide 662
bacteriologist 357
bad 649 *unclean* 653
  wrong 923

–blood *hate* 898
  malevolence 907
–break 947
–business 859
–case 477
–chance 473
–debt 806
–fairy 980
–faith 940
–grace 895
–habit 613
–hand 701
–humor
  discontent 832
  dejection 837
  anger 900
  sullen 901a
–intent 907
–job *evil* 619
  botch 699
  hopeless 859
–joke 851
–language 908
–luck etc. 735
–man 949
–name 932, 934
–repute 874
–smell 401
–spirit 980
–spirits 837
–taste 851
–temper
  discourtesy 895
  resentment 900
  irascibility 901
  sullenness 901a
–time of it 828
–turn *evil* 619
  malevolence 907
–woman 949
  from–to worse
  aggravation 835
  go–*decay* 853
  deteriorate 659
  in a–*way*
  disease 655
  worse 659
  danger 665
  adversity 735
  in–odor 889
  not a–*idea* 498
  on–terms
  discord 713
  enmity 889
  put a–construction
  on 523
  take in–part
  discontent 832
  anger 900
  view in a–light 934
badaud 501
badge 550
–of authority 747
–of infamy 874
–of slavery 746
badger 830

  stealing 791, 792
–dog 366
–game 791
badinage *wit* 842
  ridicule 856
badli 634, 759
badly off
  adversity 735
  poor 804
badness 649
Baedeker 266
baffle *hinder* 706
  defeat 731
–description
  unconformable 83
  wonder 870
baft 235
bag *put up* 184
  receptacle 191
  protrude 250
  acquire 775
  take 789
  steal 791
–and baggage 780
bagatelle *trifle* 643
  pastime 840
baggage
  endearment 129
  transference 270
  materials 635
  property 780
  hussy 962
–car 272
baggala 273
baggy 47
bagman 758, 767
bagnio 961
bagpipes 410, 417
bah! 497, 930
bail *receptacle* 191
  transference 270
  security 771
–one's own boat 692
–up 791
  go–806
  leg–623
bailiff *director* 694
  servant 746
  factor 758
  officer 965
bailiwick *region* 181
  jurisdiction 965
Bairam 138, 840
bairn 129, 167
bait *fulcrum* 215
  draw 288
  food 298
  trap 545
  lure 615
  refresh 689
  attack 716
  bribe 784
  harass 830
  reward 973
  swallow the–547
bake 384

baked beans 298
bakehouse 386
baker's dozen 98
baking heat 382
bakshish 784
bal 840
balais 847
balaklava helmet
  225
balance *equal* 27
  mean 29
  compensate 30
  remainder 40
  numeration 85
  weigh 319
  compare 464
  measurement 466
  intelligence 498
  elegance 578
  hesitate 605
  money 800
  accounts 811
–accounts with
  pay 807
  in the–475
  off one's–
  irresolute 605
  fail 732
  the mind losing its–
  503
balanced *stable* 150
  symmetrical 242
  graceful 578
balbucinate 583
balbutiate 583
balcony 250
  theater 599
bald *bare* 226
  style 575
  uninteresting 841
  ugly 846
  plain 849
baldachin 223, 1000
balderdash 497, 517
baldness (*see* bald)
baldric *belt* 230
  ring 247
bale *bundle* 72
  load 190
  evil 619
–out 297
baleen 325
balefire 423, 550
baleful 649
balista 727
balister 727
balistraria 717
balize 550
balk *deviate* 279
  disappoint 509
  deceive 545
  hinder 706
balky 283, 606
ball *globe* 249
  missile 284
  shot 727

  dance 840
  party 892
–at one's feet
  success 731
  power 737
  keep up the–
  continue 143
  active 682
ballad *song* 415
  poem 597
–monger 597
ballast
  compensation 30
  weight 319
  wisdom 498
  safety 666
  without–*rash* 863
  vicious 945
ballet *drama* 599
  dance 840
ballet dancer 599
ballista 727
ballistics
  projectiles 284
  war 722
  arms 727
balloon 273, 325
balloonery 267
ballooning 267
balloonist 269
ballot 535, 609
–box stuffing 545
ball player 840
ballproof 717
ballroom 840
balm *moderate* 174
  lubrication 332
  fragrance 400
  remedy 662
  relief 834
Balmoral *boot* 225
balmy *sleep* 683
balneal 337
balourdise 699
balsam 400, 662
balsamic
  salubrious 834
balustrade
  support 215
  inclosure 232
bam 544
bambino 129
bamboo 367
bamboozle 545
ban *prohibit* 761
  denounce 908
–with bell, book, and
  candle 998
  under the–906
banana 298, 369
banco regis 968
band *ligature* 45
  assemblage 72
  filament 205
  belt 230
  ring 247

music 415, 416, 417
party 712
shackle 752
–of hope 958
–s *canonicals* 999
–together 709
–with 720
bandage *tie* 43
ligature 45
support 215
cover 223
remedy 662
restraint 752
the eyes–d 442
bandbox 191
banded together
concurring 178
party 712
banderole 550
bandit *slayer* 361
brigand 792
bandmaster 416
bandobast
(*see* bundobust)
bandog *animal* 366
safeguard 664
warning 668
bandolier 636
bandrol 550
bandurria 417
bandy *exchange* 148
agitate 315
–about *publish* 531
–legged 243
–words *discuss* 476
converse 588
bane *evil* 619
source of evil 663
baneful 649
banewort 663
bang *impel* 276
sound 406
beat 972
banish *eject* 297
seclude 893
punish 972
(*exclude* 55)
banister 215
banjo 417
bank *acclivity* 217
side of lake 342
store 636
sand 667
fence 717
money 802
–examiner 811
–holiday 840
–of Elegance 800
–up 670
sea–342
banker
man of means 639
merchant 797
treasurer 801
card game 840
bank note 800

bankrupt 640
–of life 683
bankruptcy
failure 732
nonpayment 808
banlieue *near* 197
circumjacent 227
banner 550
enlist under the–s
of 707
raise one's–722
banneret 875
banns forbid the–761
publish the–
ask 765
marriage 903
banquet *meal* 298
pleasure 377
feast 840
banquette 717
banshee 979, 980*a*
bant 38
bantam cock 887
banter *wit* 842
ridicule 856
banterer 844
bantling *child* 129
scion 167
Bantu 372*a*
banyan *tree* 367
stint 640
fast 956
baptize 564, 998
baptism *name* 564
rite 998
Baptist 984
baptistery 1000
bar *except* 38
fastening 45
exclude 55
hotel 189
line 200
support 215
inclosure 232
close 261
music 413
hindrance 706
insignia 747
prison 752
prohibit 761
tribunal 966
legal profession 968
–room 189
–sinister *flaw* 651
disrepute 874
illegal 964
–tender 746
baragouin 517
bara hazri 298
bara khana 298
bara sahib 642, 745
barb *spike* 253
nag 271
velocity 274
–the dart *pain* 830
Barbados tar 356

barbarian *alien* 57
inelegance 579
uncivilized 876
evildoer 913
barbaric
extraneous 57
vulgar 851
rude 876
barbarism
neology 563
solecism 568
bad style 579
vulgarity 851
discourtesy 895
barbarous
unformed 241
neologic 563
plebeian 876
maleficent 907
barbate 205, 253
barbecue
repast 298, 892
cook 673
barbed 225
–wire entanglements
717
barbel 205
barber *wind* 349
barbican 206, 717
barbouillage 590
bard *musician* 416
poet 597
barded 225
bare *mere* 32
nude 226
manifest 525
disclose 529
scanty 640
–possibility 473
–supposition 514
bareback 226
barebone 203
barefaced 885
barefoot 226
poor 804
bareheaded *respect* 928
bargain *compact* 769
barter 794
cheap 815
–and sale
transfer of property
783
–for 507
into the–37
barge 273
bargee 269
barghest 980
barf 383
baritone 408
barium sulphate 430
bark *rind* 223
flay 226
ship 273
yelp 406, 412
–at *threaten* 909
censure 932

–up the wrong tree 699
–worse than bite 885
more–than bite 908
barkbound 751
barkeep 746
barkeeper 746
barkentine 273
barker *guide* 524
tout 758
petitioner 767
barley 367
barleycorn *little* 193
Barleycorn, Sir John
298
barm *leaven* 320
bubbles 353
barmaster 967
Barmecide feast 956
barmote 966
barn 189, 370, 636
barnacles 368, 445
barndoor fowl 366
barney 545, 713
barograph 338, 490*a*
barometer *air* 338
measure 466, 490*a*
consult the–463
baron *peer* 875
husband 903
–of the Exchequer 967
court–966
baronage 875
baronet 875
baronial 878
baroque 853
baroscope 338
barouche 272
barque 273
barrack
encampment 184
abode 189
shed 223
jibe 929
defense 717
barracker 936
barracoon 717
barrage *loudness* 404
drumming 407
attack 716
barranco 198
barrator 941
barratrous 940
barratry 940
barred *crossed* 219
striped 440
barrel *vessel* 191
cylinder 249
–organ 417
barrel house 189
barren 169
barricade *fence* 232
obstacle 706
defense 717
prison 752
barrier
(*see* barricade)

barring *save* 38
excluding 55
except 83
–out *resist* 719
disobey 742
barrister 968
revising–967
barrow *mound* 206
vehicle 272
grave 363
barter *reciprocate* 12
interchange 148
commerce 794
barway 294
basalt 490*c*
bas bleu *scholar* 492
affectation 855
base *low* 207
lowest part 211
support 215
evil 649
menial 746
cowardly 862
shameful 874
servile 886
dishonorable 940
vicious 945
–coin 800
–note 408
–of operations
plan 626
attack 716
baseball 840
baseboard 211
baseborn 876
based on
ground of belief 467
baselard 727
baseless *unreal* 2
unsubstantial 4
basement *cellar* 191
lowest part 207, 211
baseness (*see* base)
inferiority 34
bashaw *tyrant* 739
ruler 745
bashful 881
bashfulness 881
bashi-bazouk 726
basilica 1000
basilisk
unconformity 83
sight 441
cannon 737
serpent 366, 949
basin *dock* 189
vessel 191, 211
hollow 252
plain 344
basis *lowest part* 211
support 215
preparation 673
bask
physical enjoyment
377
warmth 382

prosperity 734
moral enjoyment 827
–in the sun 384
basket 191–of 190
basket ball 840
bas–relief *convex* 250
sculpture 557
bass *music* 415
–clarinet 417
–note 408
–tuba 417
–viol 417
basset 446
basset horn 417
bassinet *cradle* 191
helmet 717
bassoon 417
basso profondo 408
basso–rilievo
convex 250
sculpture 557
bastard *spurious* 545
nameless 565
illegitimate 925
baste *beat* 276
punish 972
Bastille 752
bastinado 972
bastion 717
bat *strike* 276
club 727
spree 840
batch *quantity* 25
collection 72
bate *diminish* 36
subtract 38
reduce price 813
bateau 273
bated breath with
–*faint sound* 405
expecting 507
hiding 528
whisper 581
humble 879
bath 337, 652–s
remedy 662
warm–386
Bath chair 272
bathe *immerse* 300
plunge 310
water 337
bathhouse 652
batholith 490c
bathometer 208, 341, 466
bathos *anticlimax* 497
(*ridiculous* 853)
bathroom 191, 652
bathybic 341
bathycolpian 208
bathymeter 208
bathymetry 208
bathypelagic 208
bathysmal 208
batik 556
bating 55

batman 637
baton *support* 215
scepter 747
batophobia 206, 860, 867
batrachians 368
batta 973
battalia 726
battalion 726
batten 298–on 886
batter *destroy* 162
beat 276
pulpiness 354
battered
worse for wear 659
tired 688
battering–ram 276
battering train 727
battery *artillery* 726
guns 727
floating–726
plant a–716
battle *killing* 361
contention 720
warfare 722
–*array order* 60
prepare 673
war 722
–ax 727
–cruiser 273
–cry *sign* 550
war 722
–field *arena* 728
–ground *discord* 713
–with *oppose* 708
half the–642
win the–731
battled 722
battledore 325
–and shuttlecock
interchange 148
game 840
battlement
embrasure 257
defense 717
battleship 664, 726
battologize 573
battology *repeat* 104
diffuse style 573
battue *kill* 361
pursuit 622
attack 716
bauble *trifle* 643
toy 840
bauxite 490c
bavardage
unmeaning 517
chatter 584
bavin 388
bawarchi–khana 191
bawcock 892
bawd 962
bawdy,–house 961
bawl 411
bawn 189
bay *concave* 252

gulf 343
cry 412
brown 433
at–*danger* 665
difficulty 604
defense 717, 719
–*leaf* 400
–the moon
useless 645
bring to–716
bayadere 840
Bayard 271
bayard *bay* 433
bayberry 400
–*candle* 423
baygall 345
bayonet *kill* 361
attack 716
weapon 727
at the point of the–
war 722
severity 739
coercion 744
crossed–s 708
bayou 343
bay rum 400
bays *trophy* 733
crown 877
baysalt 336
bay window 245, 260
bazaar 799
B.C. 106
be 1–*alive with* 102
–*all and end all*
whole 50
intention 620
importance 642
–*all up with* 162
–*off depart* 293
eject 297
retract 773
–*it so* 488
–*that as it may* 30
beach 342
beach comber 268, 348
beacon *sign* 550
warning 668
(*light* 423)
–*fire* 423, 550
bead 249, 847
beading 847
beadle *janitor* 263
law officer 965
church 996
beadledom 737
beadroll *list* 86
prayers 990
ritual 998
beads 847
tell one's–990, 998
beadsman
servant 746
clergy 996
beagle 366
beak *face* 234

nose 250
magistrate 967
beaked 245
beaker 191
beam *support* 215
quarter 236
weigh 319
light 420
measurement 466
on–*ends*
powerless 158
horizontal 213
side 236
fail 732
wonder 870
beaming
beautiful 845
beanfeast 840
beans 298
bear *produce* 161
sustain 215
carry 270
animal 366
admit of 470
stock exchange 797
suffer 821
endure 826
–*a hand* 680
–*a sense* 516
–*away* 789
–*away the bell*
best 648
success 731
–*company* 88
–*date* 114
–*down violent* 173
insolent 885
–*down upon* 716
–*false witness* 544
–*fruit produce* 161
useful 644
success 731
prosper 734
–*hard upon* 649
–*harmless* 717
–*ill* 825
–*off deviate* 279
–*on* 215
–*oneself* 692
–*out evidence* 467
vindicate 937
–*pain* 828
–*the brunt*
difficult 704
defense 717
–*the burden* 625
–*the cross* 828
–*the palm supreme* 33
–*through* 707
–*up approach* 286
persevere 604a
relieve 834
cheerful 836
–*up against resist* 719
brave 861
–*upon relevant* 9, 23

influence 175
–*with tolerate* 740
permit 760
take coolly 826
forgive 918
bring to–677
more than flesh and
blood can–824
unable to–
excited 825
dislike 867
bear *savage* 907
surly 895
–*garden disorder* 59
discord 713
arena 728
–*leader* 540
–*pit* 370
–*skin cap* 225
helmet 717
bearable 651
beard *hair* 205
prickles 253
rough 256
defy 715
brave 861
insolence 885
pluck by the–
disrespect 929
bearded *hairy* 256
beardless 127, 226
bearer 271
funeral 363
servant 746
bear grass 253
bearing *relation* 9
support 215
direction 278
meaning 516
demeanor 692
–*rein* 706, 752
bearings
circumstances 8
situation 183
bearish 895
beast *animal* 366
unclean 653
discourteous 895
–*of burden*
carrier 271
laborer 690
beastlike *unclean* 653
beastly *unclean* 653
impure 961
beat *be superior* 33
periodic 138
region 181
impulse 276
surpass 303
oscillate 314
agitation 315
crush 330
sound 407
verse 597
line of pursuit 625
path 627

Bel 979
belabor *buffet* 276
  thump 972
belated *late* 133
  ignorant 491
belaud 931
belay *join* 43
  restrain 706
belch *eject* 297
  emit gas 349
beldam
  grandmother 130
  hag 173, 913
belduque 253
beleaguer, 227, 716
belfry 206, 1000
Belial 978
  sons of–988
belie *deny* 536
  falsify 544
  contradict 708
belief *credence* **484**
  religious creed 983
  easy of–472
  hug a–606
believe (*see* belief)
  suppose 514
  –*who may* 485
  not–*one's senses* 870
  reason to–472
believer *religious* 987
  true–983*a*
belike 472
belittle *decrease* 36
  underestimate 483
  detract 934
belittling *envy* 921
bell *time* 106
  sound 417
  sign 550
  alarm–669
  bear away the–
  goodness 648
  success 731
  repute 873
  –*book, and candle*
  swear 535
  curse 908
  spell 993
  rite 998
  –*boy* 746
  –*mare* 64
  –*note* 408
  –*pepper* 393
  –*the cat* 861
  cracked–408*a*
  passing–363
  peal of–*s* 407
belladonna 663
belle 374, 854
belles–lettres 560
bellicose
  contentious 720
  warlike 722
bellied 250

belligerent
  contentious 720
  warlike 722
  combatant 726
belling 412
bellman 534
Bellona 722
bellow *loud* 404
  cry 411
  animal cry 412
  wail 839
bellows *wind* 349
  lungs 580
bell–shaped
  globose 249
  concave 252
bellwether *go first* 64
  direct 694
belly *inside* 221
  convex 250
  –*god* 957
bellyful *complete* 52
  enough 639
belomancy 511
belong to *related* 9
  component 56
  included 76
  attribute 157
  property 777, 780
  duty 926
beloved 897
below 207
  –*its full strength* 651
  –*par inferior* 34
  at a low ebb 207
  contempt 643
  bad 649
  indifferent 651
  discount 813
  ignoble 876
  –*stairs* 207
  –*the mark* 32
  here–318
belt *inclose* 227
  outline 230
  ring 247
  strait 343
  swimming–666
belvedere 441
bemask 528
bemingle 41
bemire 653
bemoan 839
bemused 458
bench *support* 215
  council 696
  tribunal 966
Bench, King's–752
bencher 967, 968
bend *oblique* 217
  angle 244
  curve 245
  incline 278
  deviate 279
  depression 308
  circuit 311

  give 324
  submit 725
  –*backward* 235
  –*one's course* 278
  –*one's looks upon* 441
  –*one's steps* 622
  –*over* 250
  –*sinister* 874
  –*the bow* 686
  –*the brows* 932
  –*the knee*
  bow down 308
  submit 725
  humble 879
  servile 886
  courtesy 894
  respect 928
  worship 990
  –*the mind* 457
  –*to tend* 176
  –*to one's will* 737
  –*to rules etc.* 82
  –*towards* 278
bender 959
beneath 207
  –*contempt* 643
  –*notice* 643
  –*one* 940
Benedick 903
Benedictine 996
benediction
  gratitude 916
  approval 931
  worship 990
  nuptial–903
benefaction 784
benefactor 816, **912**
benefice 995
beneficent 906
beneficial *good* 648
  (*useful* 644)
  –*interest* 780
beneficiary
  possessor 779
  receive 785
  clergy 996
benefit *profit* 618
  use 644, 677
  do good 648
  aid 707
  acquisition 775
  property 780
  benevolence 906
  (*improve* 658)
  –*s forgot* 917
  reap the–*of* 731
benevolence *tax* 812
  love 897
  kindness **906**
  universal 910
Bengal heat 382
benighted *dark* 421
  ignorant 491
benightedness 442
benign 656

benignant 906
benison 931
Benjamin's mess
  greater 33
  chief part 50
bent *tendency* 176
  framework 232
  angle 244
  grass 367
  turn of mind 820
  desire 865
  –*on willing* 602
  resolved 604
  intention 620
  desirous 865
  fool to the top of one's–856
benthal 208
Benthamite 910
benthopelagic 208
benthos 208, 366, 367
ben trovato
  likely 472
  imagination 515
  untruth 546
  wit 842
benumb
  insensible 376
  cold 385
  deaden affections 823
benzine 356, 652
benzoin 662
benzolin 652
beplaster 933
bepraise 931
bequeath 784
bequeathable 270
bequest *gift* 270, 784
  (*acquisition* 775)
berate 527, 932
Berber 372*a*
berceuse 415
bereavement
  death 360
  loss 776
  take away 789
bereft *poor* 804
  –*of life* 360
  –*of reason* 503
berg *iceberg* 383
bergamot 400
Bergsonism 451
beriberi 655
Berkeleyism 451
berlin 272
berloque 407
Bernardine 996
Bernoulli's principle 490*d*
bersagliere 726
berserk 173
berth *lodging* 189
  bed 215
  office 625
Bertillon system 550
beryl *green* 435

  jewel 847
beseech *request* 765
  pray 900
beseem 926
beset *surround* 227
  follow 281
  attack 716
  entreat 765
  annoy 830
  fear 860
  –*with difficulties* 704
besetting *general* 78
  habit 613
  –*sin* 945
beshrew 908
beside *except* 83
  near 197
  alongside 236
  –*oneself mad* 503
  excited 824
  –*the mark*
  irrelevant 10
  error 495
besides 37
besiege *surround* 227
  attack 716
  solicit 765
  fear 860
bésique 840
beslaver 933
beslime 653
beslubber 933
besmear *cover* 223
  dirt 653
besnow 430
besom 652
besot 959
besotted 481
bespangle 847
bespangled 318
bespatter *dirt* 653
  disapprove 932
  flatter 933
  detract 934
bespeak *early* 132
  evidence 467
  indicate 516
  engage 755
  ask for 765
bespeckle 440
bespot 440
besprinkle *mix* 41
  variegate 440
best *good* 648
  perfect 650
  all for the–
  good 618
  prosper 734
  content 831
  hope 858
  bad is the–649
  –*bib and tucker*
  prepared 673
  ornament 847
  ostentation 882
  –*ever* 646

bluestocking
pedant 491
scholar 492
affectation 855
bluff *violent* 173
high 206
cliff 212
blunt 254
deceive 545
brag 884
card game 840
insolent 885
discourteous 895
–off 545
bluffer *boaster* 884
blunder *error* 495
absurdity 497
awkward 699
failure 732
indiscretion 947
–upon 156
blunderbuss 727
blunderhead 701
blunderheaded 499
blunt *weaken* 160
inert 172
to moderate 174
obtuse 254
benumb 376
to damp 616
plain–spoken 703
cash 800
deaden feelings 823
discourteous 895
–tool 645
–witted 499
bluntness 254
blur *dim* 443
dirt 653
blemish 848
stigma 874
blurb 931
blurred *invisible* 477
blurt out *disclose* 529
speak 582
blush *heat* 382
redden 434
feel 821
humbled 879
modest 881
at first–see 441
appear 448
manifest 525
put to the–
humble 879
browbeat 885
discourtesy 895
blushing honors
repute 873
modesty 881
bluster *violent* 173
defiant 715
insolent 885
resent 900
threaten 909
blusterer 887

blustering
(*see* bluster)
windy 349
Blut und Eisen 159
boa 225
–constrictor 366
boar *animal* 366
male 373
*wild–*366
board *layer* 204
support 215
food 298
hard 323
directorate 542
council 696
attack 716
tribunal 966
–of education 542
–of Regents 542
–of studies 542
–school 542
*festive–*892
go by the–
powerless 158
destruction 162
*go on–*293
on–present 186
ship 273
*preside at the–*693
boarder 188
boards *theater* 599
arena 728
boardwalk 189
boast 884
not much to–of 651
boaster 884 *jingo* 885
boastful 884
boasting 884
boat 273–*race* 720
in the same–
accompany 88
party 712
boating 267
boatman 269
boat–shaped 245
boatswain 269
bob *depress* 308
leap 309
oscillate 314
agitate 315
–*a courtesy* 894
–*for fish* 463
Bobadil, Captain–
887
bobbery 404
bobbin 312
bobbish 654
bobcat 366
bobsled 272
bobtailed 53
bocage 367
bock beer 298
bode 511
bodice 225
bodiless 317
bodily *substantially* 3

wholly 50
material 316
–enjoyment 377
–fear 860
–pain 378
bodkin
go between 228
perforator 262
body *substance* 3
whole 50
assemblage 72
matter 316
party 712
–and blood of Christ
987
–clothes 225
–color 556
–forth 554
–of doctrine 490
–of knowledge 490
–of water 348
–politic *mankind* 372
authority 737
in a–together 88
keep–and soul
together 654
bodyguard
defense 717
combatant 726
keeper 753
Boeotian *small* 32
stupid 499
fool 501
vulgar 851
ignoble 876
bog *swamp* 345
dunghill 653
–trotter 876
boggart 980a
boggle *hesitate* 605
awkward 699
difficulty 704
bogie 980
bogle 980
bogus 545–*check* 808
Bohemian
unconformity 83
traveler 268
ungenteel 851
boil *violence* 173
effervesce 315
bubble 353
heat 382, 384
ulceration 655
excitement 824, 825
anger 900
–down 195
boiled (*see* boil)
–beef 298
–eggs 298
boiler 386
boisterous
violent 173
hasty 684
excitable 825
bold *prominent* 250

unreserved 525
vigorous 574
defiant 715
brave 861
–push *essay* 675
–relief *visible* 446
–stroke *plan* 626
success 731
make–with
discourtesy 895
show a–front
defy 715
brave 861
bold face *type* 591
boldfaced
insolent 885
printing 591
bole 50
bolero 840
boldness (*see* bold)
bolshevism 146, 742
bolshevist 146, 712
bolster *support* 215
repair 658
aid 707
–up *vindicate* 937
bolt *sift* 42, 652
fasten 43
fastening 45
close 261
move rapidly 274
propel 284
run away 370, 623
safety 664
escape 671
hindrance 706
shaft 727
shackle 752
–food *swallow* 298
gormandize 957
–in 751
–out of the blue 508
–the door 761
–upright 212
bolthead 191
bolus *mouthful* 298
remedy 662
bomb 404, 406, 727
–explosion 361
–vessel 726
bombard 716
circularize 592
bombardier 726
bombardon 417
bombast
overestimation 482
absurdity 497
unmeaning 517
magniloquence 577
ridiculous 853
boasting 884
(*exaggeration* 549)
bombastic
(*see* bombast)
bomber 269a
bombilation 404, 407

bombinate 407
bombing cruiser 273
bombproof 664
bon:–diable 844
–enfant *social* 892
kindly 906
–mot 842
–ton 852
–vivant 957
voyage 267
bona fides
veracity 543
probity 939
bonanza *extra* 641
wealth 803
bonbon 396
bond *tie* 45
servile 746
compact 769
security 771
money 800
right 924
–of union 9, 45
bondage 749
bonded together 712
bonds (*see* bond)
fetters 752
securities 802
–of harmony 714
in–service 746
bondsman 746
bone *dense* 321
hard 323
strength 159
–of contention 713,
720
–to pick
difficulty 704
discord 713
*bred in the–*5
one–and one flesh
903
bonehouse 363
bones (*see* bone)
corpse 362
music 417
*break no–*648
make no
–willing 602
bonesetter 662
bonfire 382
festivity 840
celebration 883
make a–of 384
bonhomie *candor* 703
kindness 906
bonhomme 996
Boniface 890
bonne *servant* 746
nurse 753
–bouche *treat* 377
savory 394
saving 636
pleasant 829
bonnet 225
–rouge 742

theater 599
fight 720
-car 272
-pleat 258
-the compass
  direction 278
  rotation 312
  change of mind 607
-the ear *anger* 900
  strike 972
-up 751
  horse-272
  in a-704
  musical-417
  wrong-*error* 495
  unskillful 699
  dilemma 704
boxer 726
boy 129 *servant* 746
boyage 127
boyar 875
boycott *eject* 297
  resist 719
  seclude 893
  disapprove 893
boyhood 127
Boyle's Law 490d
boylike 129
brabble *discord* 713
  contest 720
brabbler 901
brace *tie* 43
  fasten 45
  two 89
  strengthen 159
  support 215
  music 413
  typography 550
  refresh 689
  -game 545
bracelet *circle* 247
  ornament 847
bracer 392, 662
brachial 633
brachycephalic
  index 372a
brachygraphy 590
bracing
  salubrious 656
bracken 367
bracket *tie* 43, 45
  couple 89
  support 215
  -s *typography* 550
brackish 392
bract 367
brad 45
bradawl 262
Bradshaw 266
brae 206
brag *cards* 840
  boast 884
braggadocio 482, 884
braggart 482, 884
Brahma 976
Brahman *religion* 984

priest 996
Brahmanism 976
Brahmi 590
Brahmo 984
braid *tie* 43
  ligature 45
  net 219
  variegate 440
Braille 442
brain *kill* 361
  intellect 450
  skill 498
  rack one's-s 451,
    515
  suck one's-s 461
brainless 499
brainpan 450
brainsick 458
brainwork 451
brainy 450, 498
brake *slowness* 275
  copse 367
  check 706
  curb 752
  apply the
  -*slower* 275
  hinder 706
  put the-s on 265
  (*see also* break)
bramble *thorn* 253
  bane 663
bran 330
brancard 272
branch *member* 51
  posterity 167
  ramify 244
  stream 348
  tree 367
  -off *bifurcate* 91
  diverge 291
  -out *ramify* 91
  diffuse style 573
branchiae 349
branching
  ramous **242**
brand *burn* 384
  fuel 388
  torch 423
  mark 550
  sword 727
  disrepute 874
  censure 932
  stigmatize 934
  -new 123
  -of discord 713
  -with reproach 938
brandish *oscillate* 314
  flourish 315
  display 882
brandy smash 959
brangle 713
brangler 710
brank 975
brash *brittle* 328
  downpour 348
  sickness 655

brashness 885
brasier 386
brass *alloy* 41
  music 416
  insolence 885
  bold as-861
  -band 416, 417
  -colored 439
  -farthing 643
brassard 550
brassière 225
brat 129, 167
brattice 224, 228
bravado 884
brave *healthy* 654
  defy 234, 715
  warrior 726
  bear 821, 826
  courage 861
bravery (*see* brave)
bravo *assassin* 361
  desperado 863
  applause 931
bravura 415, 416
brawl *cry* 411
  discord 713
  revel 840
brawler *disputant* 710
  rioter 742
  blusterer 887
brawny *strong* 159
  stout 192
bray *grind* 330
  cry 412
Bray, Vicar of-
  tergiversation 607
  servility 886
braze 43
brazen *unreserved* 525
  insolent 885
brazier 191
Brazil tea 298
breach *crack* 44
  gap 198
  quarrel 713
  violation 925
  -of faith 940
  -of law
    unconformity 83
    illegal 964
  -of the peace 713
    custom honored in
    the-614
breachy 198
  unruly 742
bread 298 beg-765
  selfish 943
  -of idleness 683
  -of life *Christ* 976
  piety 987
  -upon the waters 484
breadbasket 191
breadfruit 298
breadstuffs 298
breadth 202
  chiaroscuro 420

break *fracture* 44
  discontinuity 70
  change 140
  gap 198
  carriage 272
  deviate 279
  crumble 328
  train animals 370
  disclose 529
  discord 713
  cashier 756
  violate 773, 927
  bankrupt 808
  faux pas 947
  -a habit 614
  -a lance *attack* 716
  battle 722
  -a law 83
  -away *depart* 293
  avoid 623
  -bread 298
  -bulk 297
  -camp 293
  -down *destroy* 162
  fall short 304
  decay 659
  fail 732
  -for taller timber 666
  -forth 295
  -ground *begin* 66
  depart 293
  -in *ingress* 294
  domesticate 370
  teach 537
  tame 749
  -in upon *derange* 61
  inopportune 135
  hinder 706
  -jail 671
  -loose *escape* 671
  get free 750
  -no bones 648
  -of 660
  -of day *morning* 125
  twilight 422
  -off *cease* 70, 142
  relinquish 624
  abrogate 756
  -one's neck
  powerless 158
  die 360
  -on the wheel
  physical pain 378
  mental pain 830
  punishment 972
  -open 173
  -out *begin* 66
  violent 173
  disease 655
  excited 825
  -Priscian's head 568
  -prison 750
  -short 328
  -silence 582
  -the heart
  pain 828, 830

  dejection 837
  -the ice 888
  -the neck of *task* 676
  success 731
  -the peace
  violence 173
  contest 720
  -the ranks 61
  -the teeth
  hard words 579
  -the thread 70
  -through a custom
    614
  -through the clouds
  visible 446
  disclose 529
  -up *disjoin* 44
  decompose 49
  end 67
  revolution 146
  destroy 162
  -up of the system
  death 360
  disease 655
  -with 713
  -with the past 146
  -word *deceive* 545
  improbity 940
breakable 328
breakbone fever 655
breakdown 840
breaker *of horses* 268
  wave 348
breakers *surf* 348
  shallow 667
  -ahead 665
  surrounded by-704
breakfast 298
breakneck
  precipice 217
  rash 863
breakwater
  refuge 666
  obstruction 706
breast *interior* 221
  confront 234
  convex 250
  meat 298
  mind 450
  oppose 708
  soul 820
  at the-129
  -high 206
  -the current 719
  in the-of 620
breastplate 717
breastwork 717
breath *instant* 113
  breeze 349
  life 359
  animality 364
  faint sound 405
  -of accusation 938
  expect 507
  wonder 870
  in the same-120

not a–of air
quiet 265
hot 382
out of–688
shortness of–688
take away one's–
unexpected 508
fear 860
wonder 870
take–*rest* 265
refresh 689
with bated–581
breathe *exist* 1
blow 349
live 359
faint sound 405
evince 467
mean 516
inform 527
disclose 529
utter 580
speak 582
refresh 689
–freely *pleasure* 827
relief 834
–one's last 360
–the vital air 359
not–a word 528
breathing *time* 106
air 349
–time *repose* 687
truce 723
breathing–hole 351
breathless
voiceless 581
out of breath 688
feeling 821
fear 860
eager 865
wonder 870
–attention 457
–expectation 507
–impatience 865
–speed 684
breech *invest* 225
rear 235
breeches 225
–maker 225
–pocket
money 800, 802
wear the–737
breechloader 727
breed *race* 11
kind 75
multiply 161
progeny 167
animals 370
rear 537
(*prepare* 673)
breeding
production 161
style 852
politeness 894
–place 153
breeze *wind* 349
discord 713

breezy 836
brethren 997
breve 413
brevet *warrant* 741
commission 755
permit 760
–rank 873
breviary 990, 998
brevier 591
brevipennate 193
brevity *short* 201
concise 572
brew *mix* 41
prepare 673
brewing
impending 152
Briarean 102, 159
Briareus 159, 192
bribe *equivalent* 30
tempt 615
offer 763
gift 784
buy 795
reward 809, 973
bribery (*see* bribe)
bric-a-brac 847
brick *hard* 323
pottery 384
material 635
trump 939, 948
–color 434
–over 386
–red 434
make–s without
straw 471
brickbat 727
brickkiln 386
bricklayer 690
bricky 434
bridal 903
bride 903
bridegroom 903
bridesmaid 890, 903
bridesman 903
bridewell 752
bridge
intermedium 45
way 627
card game 840
–of death 360
–over *join* 43
facilitate 705
make peace 723
compromise 774
bridle *depart* 293
restrain 751
rein 752
–one's tongue
silent 585
cautious 864
–road 627
–up 900
brief *time* 111
space 201
concise 572
compendium 596

–case 191
hold a–for 759
briefly *anon* 132
brier *sharp* 253
bane 663
brig 273
brigade *arrange* 60
military 726
brigadier 745
brigand 792
brigandage 791
brigandine 717
brigantine 273
bright *shine* 420
color 428
intelligent 498
cheery 836
beauty 845
glory 873
–colored 428
–days 734
–prospect 858
–side 829
–thought *sharp* 498
good stroke 626
wit 842
look at the–side
cheer 836
hope 858
brighten up
furbish 658
bright-eyed 845
brigue *party* 712
contention 720
brilliant *shining* 420
music 416
good 648
witty 842
beautiful 845
gem 847
glorious 873
be–*intellectual* 498
–idea 842
brim 231–over 641
brimful 52
brimstone 388
brindled 440
brine *sea* 341
salt 392
bring 270–about
cause 153
achieve 729
–back 790
–back to the memory
505
–forth *produce* 161
extract 301
–forward
evidence 467
manifest 525
teach 537
improve 658
–gray hairs to the
grave
adversity 735
pain 830

–grist to the mill 644
–home 775
–home to 155
–in *receive* 296
income 810
price 812
–in a verdict 480
–in its train 88
–in question 461
–into being 161
–into play 677
–low 874
–off 672
–out *discover* 480a
manifest 525
publish 531
–over *persuade* 484
–round *persuade* 615
restore 660
–to *convert* 144
halt 265
–to a crisis 604
–to a point 74
–to bear 470
–to bear upon
relation 9
action 170
–together *assemble* 72
–to life 359
–to light 480a
–to maturity
prepare 673
complete 729
–to mind 505
–to perfection 677
–to terms 723
–to trial 969
–under one's notice
457
–up *develop* 161
vomit 297
train 370
educate 537
–up the rear 235
–word 527
brink 231
–of the grave 360
on the–*almost* 32
coming 121
near 197
briny 392–*deep* 341
brio *music* 415
briquette 388
brisk *prompt* 111
energetic 171
active 682
cheery 836
–with *plenty* 639
too much 641
–with arms 722
bristle 253–up
stick up 250
angry 900
–with *plenty* 639
too much 641
–with arms 722
bristling *thorny* 253
discourtesy 895
bristly *rough* 256

Britannia metal 545
Briticism 563
British 188
–courts 966
–lion 604
Britisher 188
Briton 188 true–939
brittle 328
brittleness **328**
britzka 272
broach *begin* 66
found 153
perforate 262
tap 297
publish 531
assert 535
broad *general* 78
space 202
lake 343
emphatic 535
indelicate 961
–accent 580
–arrow 550
–awake *vigilant* 459
brisk 682
–daylight *light* 420
manifest 525
–farce 842
–gauge 466
–grin 838
–highway 627
–hint 527
–meaning 516
broadcast
disperse 73, 291
publish 531
news 532
sow–818
broadcloth 219, 635
broaden 78
broadhearted 906
broadhorn 273
broadsheet 531, 593
broad-shouldered
159
broadside *lateral* 236
publication 531
cannonade 716
broadsword 727
Brobdingnagian 159,
192
brocade 847
brocatelle 847
brochure 593
broder 549
brogan 225
brogue *boot* 225
dialect 560, 563
broidery 847
broil *heat* 382
fry 384
fray 713, 720
broiler *fowl* 298
broken *divided* 51
discontinuous 70
weak 160

of horses 370
−color 428
−down *decrepit* 659
failing 732
dejected 837
−English 563
−fortune
adversity 735
poverty 804
−heart *pain* 828
dejected 837
hopeless 859
−meat 645
−reed 665
−voice 581, 583
−winded *disease* 655
fatigue 688
broker *agent* 758
merchant 797
brokerage *pay* 812
brokery 794
bromide
conventionalist 82
bromidium 496
bronchia 351
broncho 271
−buster 370
bronchocele 655
bronze *brown* 433
sculpture 557
brooch 847
brood *multitude* 102
family 167
hatch 370
−over *think* 451
mope 837
brooding
preparing 673
brook *stream* 348
bear 826
broom
undergrowth 367
sweep 652
broomstick 491
broth 298
brothel 945, 961
brother *kin* 11
similar 17
equal 27
−Jonathan 188
brotherhood 712
brotherly
friendship 888
love 897
benevolence 906
brougham 272
brought to bed 161
brouillerie 713
brouillon 626
brow *top* 210
edge 231
front 234
browbeat
intimidate 860
swagger 885
disrespect 929

−en *humbled* 879
brown 433−Bess 727
−ocher 433
−stone 635
−stone house 189, 831
−study *thought* 451
inattention 458
imagination 515
Brownian 984
brownie 979
brownness 433
browse 298
bruin 895
bruise *powder* 330
hurt 619
injure 649
bruised *blemished* 848
bruiser 726
bruit 531, 532
brumal 383
brummagem 545
brunch 572
brunette 433
Brünn man 372a
Brunswick black 356a
brunt *beginning* 66
impulse 276
bear the−
difficulty 704
defense 717
endure 821, 826
(*resist* 719)
brush *tail* 235
rough 256
rapid motion 274
groom 370
touch 379
clean 652
fight 720
−away *reject* 297
abrogate 756
−up *clean* 652
furbish 658
prepare 673
paint−556
brushwood 367, 388
brusque *violent* 173
haste 684
discourtesy 895
Brussels sprouts 298
brustle 407
brutal *vulgar* 851
rude 895
savage 907
brutalize (*see* brutal)
corrupt 659
deaden 823
vice 945
brute *animal* 366
rude 895
maleficent 913
−force *strength* 159
violence 173
animal 450a

severe 739
compulsion 744
lawless 964
−matter *matter* 316
inorganic 358
brutify 954
brutish (*see* brute)
vulgar 851
ignoble 876
intemperate 954
Bryanite 984
bryophites 369
bubble
unsubstantial 4
transient 111
little 193
light 320
water 348
air **353**
error 495
deceit 545
trifle 643
−burst *fall short* 304
disappoint 509
fail 732
−reputation 873
−up *agitation* 315
bubbling 353
bubo 250
bubonic plague 655
buccaneer 791, 792
Bucephalus 271
buck *confront* 234
leap 309
stag 366
male 373
negro 431
wash 652
fop 854
−basket 191
−fever 825
−jump 309
−nigger 431
bucket *receptacle* 191
load 270
−shop 621
kick the−360
bucking *attack* 716
buckle *tie* 43
fastening 45
distort 243
curl 248
−oneself 604
−on one's armor 673
−to *resolution* 604
exertion 686
−with *grapple* 720
buckler 717
buckram
affectation 855
pride 878
men in−549
buckwheat 367
bucolic
pastoral 370, 371
poem 597

bud *beginning* 66
germ 153
expand 194
graft 300
blossom 367
−from 154
Buddha 976, 986
Buddhism 976, 984
Buddhist 984
−priests 996
−temple 1000
budding *young* 127
expansion 194
buddy *chum* 890
budge 264
budget *heap* 72
bag 191
store 636
finance 811
−of news 532
budmash 949
buff *skin* 223
color 436
native−226
buffalo 366−bug 366
−robe 223
−wallow 343
buffer *hindrance* 706
defense 717
buffet *strike* 276
agitate 315
evil 619
bad 649
affront 900
smite 972
−the waves
difficulty 704
opposition 708
buffet *bar* 189
cupboard 191
buffle−headed 499
buffo 599
buffoon *actor* 599
humorist 844
butt 857
buffoonery
amusement 840
humor 842
bug *littleness* 193
insect 366, 653
bugaboo *alarm* 669
fear 860
bugbear
imaginary 515
alarm 669
fear 860, 980
buggy 272
bugle *instrument* 417
war cry 722
−call *sign* 550
command 741
bugles *ornament* 847
build *construct* 161
form 240
−a campfire 384
−up *compose* 54

−upon *belief* 484
−upon a rock 150
builder 626, 690
building material 635
buildings 189
built on *basis* 211
bulb *knob* 249
projection 250
bulbul 416
bulge 250
bulk *be great* 31
whole 50
size 192
bulkhead
covering 223
interjacence 228
safety 664
hindrance 706
bulky 31
bull *animal* 366
male 373
error 495
absurdity 497
solecism 568
detective 664
ordinance 741
stock exchange 797
−in a china shop 59
take the−by the
horns
resolution 604
courage 861
Bull, John− 188
bulla 250
bull calf 501
bulldog
animal 327, 366
pluck 604, 604a
courage 861
bulldoze 860, 885
bulldozer 887
bullet *ball* 249
arms 727
(*missile* 284)
−proof 717
bulletin *list* 86
news 532
record 551
letter 592
−board 551
bullfight 720
bullhead 501
bullion 800
bull's−eye *center* 222
lantern 423
aim 620
bullwhack 975
bullwhacker 370
bully *boat* 273
first−rate 648
fighter 726
jovial 836
frighten 860
rashness 863
bluster 885

-up one's pockets
808
  take by the-586
buttoned-up
  reserved 528
buttonhole *flower* 400
  bore 841
buttonholer 841
buttons *page* 746
button-top
  useless 645
buttress *strength* 159
  support 215
  defense 717
butyraceous 355
buxom 836
buy 795-and sell 794
  -a pig in a poke 621
buzz *hiss* 409
  insect cry 412
  publish 531
  news 532
  -saw 44
buzzard *bird* 366
  fool 501
  between hawk and-
  agitation 315
  worry 828
  blind as a-442
  -dollar 800
by *alongside* 236
  instrumental 631
  sequestered 893
  -and by 121, 132
  -itself 87
  -means of 632
  -my troth etc. 535
  -no means 32
  -telegraph 532
  -the by 134
  -the card 82
  -the hour etc.
  hire 788
  -the way *à propos* 9
  beside the purpose 10
  parenthetical 134
  -wireless 532
  go-*pass* 303
  have-one
  provide 637
  possess 777
bye *departure* 293
by-end 615
bygone *past* 122
  forgotten 506
  let-s be bygones
  918
bylaw 963
byname 565
by-pass 287
bypast 122
bypath 279
byplay *hint* 527
  gesture 550
by-purpose 615
byre 189, 370, 636

byroad 278, 627
by-room 191
byssus 256
bystander *near* 197
  spectator 444
byway 627
byword *maxim* 496
  cant term 563, 564
  reproach 874
  contempt 930

C

cab 272
cabal *plan* 626
  confederacy 712
cabala *latency* 526
  spell 993
cabalism 526
cabalistic *hidden* 528
  sorcery 992
cabane 273
cabaret 189
cabasset 717
cabbage 298, 791
cabestro 45
cabin *room* 189
  receptacle 191
cabined 751
cabinet *receptacle* 191
  workshop 691
  council 696
  -picture 556
cable *link* 45
  dispatch 527
  news 531, 532
  telegraph 534
  by-684
  -code 528
  slip-623
  telegraphic-534
cabled *telegraphic* 531
cabman *traveler* 268
  director 694
caboose 386
cabriolet 272
cacation 299
cachalot 192
cache 636
cachet 550
  lettre de-751
cachexia
  weakness 160
  disease 655
cachinnation 838
cacique 745
cackle *of geese* 412
  chatter 584
  talk 588
  laugh 838
cacodemon 980
cacoëpy 410, 583
cacoëthes *habit* 613
  itch 865
  -loquendi 584

-scribendi 590
cacographer 579
cacographic 579
cacography 590
cacology 579, 583
caconym 563
cacophonous
  (see cacophony)
cacophony
  stridor 410
  discord 414
  style 579
Cacus, den of- 791
cad *servant* 746
  vulgar 851
  plebeian 876
cadastral survey 466
cadastration 466
cadastre *list* 86
  measurement 466
cadaverous
  corpse 362
  pale 429
  hideous 846
caddy 191
cadeau 784
cadence *pace* 264
  fall 306
  sound 402
  music 415
cadenza 415
cadet *junior* 129
  soldier 726
  officer 745
  -blue 438
cadge 765
cadger *beggar* 767
  huckster 797
cadi 967
cadmium 439
caduceus *insignia* 747
  wand 215, 993
caducity *fugacity* 111
  age 128
  impotence 158
  decay 659
caducous 111
caecal 261
caecum 221, 350
Caesar 745
caesura
  disjunction 44
  discontinuity 70
  cessation 142
  interval 198
café 189
caftan 225
cafuzo 41
cage *receptacle* 191
  restrain 751
  prison 752
Cagliostro
  impostor 548
  sorcerer 994
cahoot 712, 778
cahot 250, 315

cahotage *disorder* 59
  agitation 315
Cain 361
caique 273
cairn *grave* 363
  sign 550
caisson 191, 252
caitiff *churl* 876
  ruffian 913
  villain 949
cajole *flatter* 933
  (see cajolery)
cajolery
  imposition 544, 545
  persuasion 615
  flattery 933
cake *stick* 46
  pastry 298, 396
  consolidate 321
  -walk 840
calabash 191
calaboose 752
calambac 400
calambour 400
calamiform 253
calamitous
  adverse 935
  disastrous 830
calamity *killing* 361
  evil 619
  adversity 735
  suffering 830
calash *cap* 225
  vehicle 272
calathiform 252
calcareous 432
calcimine 430
calcinatory 384
calcine 384
calcitrate 276
calcium light 423
calculate *reckon* 85
  investigate 461
  expect 507
  intend 620
  -upon 484
calculated
  tending 176
  premeditated 611
calculating
  prudent 498
  -machine 85
calculation
  (see calculate)
  accounts 811
  caution 864
calculous 323
calculus 85, 323
caldron
  (see cauldron)
calèche 272
Caledonian 188
calefaction 384
calefy 384
calembour 520
calendar *list* 86

chronicle 114
  record 551
  schedule 611
calender 255
calenture
  delirium 503
  disease 655
calf *young* 129
  animals 366
  fool 501
  -love 902
  golden-986, 991
Caliban 846
caliber *degree* 26
  size 192
  breadth 202
  opening 260
  intellectual capacity
  498
calibrate *degree* 26
  breadth 202
  measure 466
caliche 490a
calico 635
calid 382
calidarium 386
calidity 382
caliginous 421
calipers 466
caliph 745
caliphate 737
calisthenics
  training 537
  beauty 845
caliver 727
calk 660
call *signal* 550
  name 564
  express 566
  motive 615
  visit 892
  sanctify 976
  ordain 995
  at one's- *alert* 682
  obedient 743
  -attention to 457
  -for *require* 630
  order 741
  ask 765
  -forth *resort to* 677
  excite 824
  -in *advice* 695
  -in question 485
  -into being 161
  -into notice 525
  -into play 677
  -names 929, 932
  -of duty 926
  -off the attention
  458
  -out *cry* 411
  challenge 715
  -over *number* 85
  -to 586
  -to account 932
  -to mind 505

charger *carrier* 271
  fighter 726
chargeship 625
chariot 272
  drag at one's–
    wheels 749
charioteer *driver* 268
  pilot 694
charitable
  (*see* charity)
charity *give* 784
  liberal 816
  beneficient 906
  pity 914
  –that begins at home
    943
  cold as
    –*insensible* 823
charivari *loud* 404
  clatter 407
  discord 414
charlatan
  ignoramus 493
  impostor 548
  mountebank 844
  boaster 884
charlatanism
  ignorance 491
  falsehood 544
  affectation 855
Charles's wain 318
Charley 753
charm *draw* 288
  motive 615
  talisman 747
  please 829
  beauty 845
  love 897
  attraction 928
  conjure 992
  spell 993
  bear a–d life
  safe 664
  prosperous 734
charmer *sorcerer* 994
  voice of the–
  flattery 933
charming *taste* 850
  (*see* charm)
charnel house 363
chart *inform* 527
  represent 554
charter
  commission 755
  permit 760
  compact 769
  security 771
  privilege 924
chartered *legal* 963
  –accountant 811
  –libertine 962
chartulary 86
charwoman
  worker 690
  servant 746
chary *economical* 817

stingy 819
  cautious 864
Charybdis
  whirlpool 312, 346
  danger 665
chase *emboss* 250
  drive away 289
  killing 361
  forest 367
  pursue 622
  ornament 847
  wild goose–645
chaser 559
chasm *interval* 198
  opening 260
  gully 350
  abyss 667
  (*discontinuity* 70)
chassepot 727
chasser 297
  –*balancer* 605
chasseur 726
chassis 272
chaste *shapely* 242
  language 576, 578
  simple 849
  good taste 850
  pure 960
chasten *moderate* 174
  punish 972
chastened
  subdued spirit 826
chasteness
  (*see* chaste)
chastise *censure* 932
  punish 972
  –with scorpions 739
chastity 960
chasuble 999
chat 588
château 189
châtelaine 847
chatoyant 440
chattels
  furniture 633
  property 780
chatter 412, 584
chatterbox 584
chattering of teeth
  cold 383
chatti 191
chatty *talkative* 584
  sociable 892
chauffeur 268, 271,
  694
chauki 752
chaunt (*see* chant)
chaussé 225
Chautauqua 537
chauvinism 884, 885
chauvinist 885
chawbacon 876
cheap *worthless* 643
  low price 815
  hold–930
cheapen *haggle* 794

begrudge 819
cheapness 815
cheat *deceive* 545
  deceiver 548
check *numerical* 85
  cessation 142
  moderate 174
  counteract 179
  slacken 275
  plaid 440
  experiment 463
  measure 466
  evidence 468
  ticket 550
  dissuade 616
  hinder 706
  misfortune 735
  restrain 751
  money order 800
  –in full career 142
  –oneself 829
  –the growth 201
checkered
  diversified 16a
  changeable 149
  variegated 440
checkers 440
  game 840
checkmate
  deadlock 142
  success 731
  failure 732
checkrein 706
checkroll 86
checkstring
  pull the–142
cheek *side* 236
  –by jowl *with* 88
  near 197
cheeks *dual* 89
cheep 412
cheer *repast* 298
  cry 411
  aid 707
  pleasure 827
  relief 834
  mirth 836
  rejoicing 838
  amusement 840
  courage 861
  exult 884
  sociality 892
  welcome 894
  applaud 931
  (*please* 829)
  good–*hope* 858
  high living 957
cheerful 836
  –giver 816
cheerfulness **836**
cheering 602
cheerless
  unpleasing 830
  dejected 837
cheese 298
cheesecake 298

cheeseparings
  remains 40
  dirt 653
  parsimony 819
cheetah 440
chef de cuisine
  proficient 700
  servant 746
chef–d'oeuvre
  masterpiece 648
  master stroke 698
cheiromancy 522
chela 541
chemical 144
chemical apparatus
  490b
chemise 225
chemisette 225
chemistry 490b, 144
  organic–357
cheque 800
chequer 440–roll 86
cherish *aid* 707
  love 897
  endearment 902
  –a belief 484
  –an idea etc. 451
  –feelings etc. 821
cheroot 392
cherry 298, 434
  two bites of a–
  overrate 482
  roundabout 629
  clumsy 699
cherry–cheeked 845
cherry–colored 434
chersonese 342
cherub 167, 977
Cherubim 977
Cheshire cat 838
chess 840
chessboard 440
chest *box* 191
  money coffer 802
chestnut
  stale joke 105, 532
  fruit 367
  red 434
chestnut–color 433
cheval–de–bataille
  plea 617
  plan 626
cheval glass 445
chevalier 875
  –d'industrie 792
chevaux de frise
  spikes 253
  defense 717
chevron *obliquity* 217
  rank 550, 747, 877
chevronné 754
chew 298 *tobacco* 392
  –the cud 451
chiaroscuro *light* 420
  gray 432
  painting 556

chiasm 43, 219
chiasmal 219
chic *show* 882
chicane *sophistry* 477
  deceit 545
  cunning 702
chicanery
  (*see* chicane)
chi–chi 563
chick 424
chickaree 274
chicken *young* 129
  fowl 298, 366
  reckon–s before
    hatched *hope* 858
  rash 863
  tender as a–*soft* 324
  sensitive 822
  compassionate 914
chicken–hearted 862
chide 527, 932
chief *principal* 642
  master 745
  –part 31
  evidence in–467
chiefdom 737
Chief Justice 967
chieftain 745
chiffon 635
chiffonier 876
chiffonnière 191
chignon 225
chilblains 383
child *infant* 129
  offspring 167
  fool 501
  –of God 987
  –'s play *trifling* 643
  easy 705
childbirth 161
childhood 127
childish *credulous* 486
  foolish 499
  feeble 575
  –treble 581
childlike *artless* 703
childly 129
children 167
chiliad 98, 120
chill *cold* 383
  render cold 385
  indispose 616
chilly 383
Chiltern Hundreds
  757
chimaera *fish* 368
chime *repetition* 104
  roll 407
  resonance 408
  melody 413
  –in with *agree* 23
  conform 82
  assent 488
  concord 714
chimera *monster* 83
  imaginary 515

(error 495)
chimney opening 260
  airpipe 351
  (egress 295)
  –corner 189
chin 234
china ceramic 384
  art 557
  –wedding 883
Chinaman 188
chinch 653
chine 235
Chinese 188
  –temple 1000
chink gap 198
  sound 408
  money 800
chinking 635
Chinook 349, 563
chip small 32
  detach 44
  bit 51
  reduce 195
  counter 550
  –in 709
  –off the old block
  similar 17
  copy 21
  offspring 167
chipmunk 274, 366
chipper 654, 836
chippy 962
chirography 590
chirology 550
chiromancy 511, 550
chirp bird–note 412
  sing 416
  cheerful 836
  rejoice 838
chirrup (see chirp)
chirurgery 662
chisel fabricate 161
  form 240
  furrow 259
  tool 262
  sculpture 557
chiseling 558
chit infant 129, 167
  small 193
  letter 592
chit–chat 588
chitterlings 221
chivalrous 894
  (see chivalry)
chivalry war 722
  tenure 777
  courage 861
  philanthropy 910
  honor 939
  generosity 942
chivarras 225
chlamys 225
chloral 376
chloride–of lime 652
  –of sodium 336
chlorine 435, 663

–gas 727
chloroform
  opiate 174
  anaesthetic 376
  mental insensibility
  823
chlorosis 655
chlorotic 655
chock–full
  complete 52
  replete 639
chocolate food 298
  color 433
choice will 600
  election **609**
  excellent 648
  absence of–**609a**
  by–600
  –of words 569
  –spirits 873
choir sing 416
  church music 996
  church 1000
Choir Invisible 977
choirmaster 416
choke close 261
  stifle 361
  redundant 641
  hinder 706
  –off 706
chokeberry 397
choke damp 663
choke–full
  (see chock–full)
chokidar 753
chokra 746
choky 752
choler 900
cholera 655
choleric 901
chondrification 323
choose 609
  do what one–s 748
chop disjoin 44
  change 140
  water in motion 348
  indication 550
  –and change 140
  –logic 476
  –up 201
chopfallen 837
chophouse 189
choppiness 348
chopping large 192
  –sea 348
choppy 348
chops mouth 66
  jaws 231
  food 298
chop–suey 298
chor 792
choral 415–club 416
  –society 416
chord 413
chore 625, 746
  –boy 534

chorea 315, 655
choregus 694
chorister singer 416
  church singer 996
chorographer 466
chorography 183,
  466
chorometer 466
chorus shout 411
  song 415
  singers 416
  unanimity 488
  poetry 597
  opera 599
  concord 714
  –girl 599
chose–in action 780
  –in possession 777
chosen 609
chota hazri 298
chouse 545
chowchow 41
chowder 298
chowderhead 501
chow dog 366
chrestomathy 560
chrism 998
Christ 976
  Church of–983a
  receive–987
Christcross 219
Christcross–row 561
christen name 564
  rite 998
Christendom 983a,
  995
Christian 983a, 987
  –charity 906
  –Science 984
Christmas period 138
  Church festival 998
Christmas box 784
chromatic color 428
  –scale music 413
chromation 357
chromatism 428
chromatogenous 428
chromatograph 428
chromatography 428
chromatology 428
chromatometer 428
chromato–pseudo-
  blepsis 443
chromatoscope 428
chromatoscopy 428
chromatrope 428,
  445
chrome 436
chromium 490b
chromogen 428
chromolithograph
  558
chromometer 428
chromoscope 428
chromosome 357
chromosphere 318

chronic 110, 143
chronicle
  measure time 114
  annals 551
chronicler 553
chronogram 114
chronographer 594
chronography
  measure time 114
  description 594
chronolithograph
  558
chronologic 114
chronologize 114
chronology 114
chronometry 114
chrononhoton-
  thologos 887
chrysalis 129
chrysolite
  greenness 435
  perfection 650
  jewel 847
chrysology 800
chrysoprase 435
chthonian 991
chubby 192
chuck throw 284
  beef 298
  animal cry 412
  –under chin 902
chucker–out 297
chuck farthing 621
chuckle
  animal cry 412
  laugh 838
  exult 884
chucklehead 501
chuddar 225
chuff 876
chum 711, 890
chummery 189
chunk 51
chunky 201
chupatty 298
Church building 189
  infallible 474
  orthodox 983a
  Christendom 995
  temple 1000
  –of Christ 983a
  dignitaries of–996
  go to–990
  High–, Low–, etc.
  984
churchdom 995
churchman 996
churchwarden 996
churchyard
  burial 363
  church 1000
  –cough 655
churl boor 876
churlish niggard 819
  rude 895
  sulky 901a

  malevolent 907
churn agitate 315
  butter 352
chute 348
chutney 393
chyle 333
chylification 333
chylous 333
cibarious 298
cicada 366
cicatrix 551
cicatrize 660
Cicero 582
cicerone 524, 527
Ciceronian 578, 582
cicisbeo 897
cicuration 370
cider 298
cienaga 345
cigar 392
cilia hairs 205
  rough 256
ciliolum 205
cimeter 727
Cimmerian 421
cinch girth 45, 370
  facility 705
cinchona 662
cinct 229
cincture 247
cinder combustion 384
  dirt 653
  (remains 40)
Cinderella
  servant 746
  commonalty 876
cinema 448, 840
cinematograph 448,
  559
cinerary 363
cineration 384
cinereous 432
cingle 230
cinnabar 434
cinnamon 393, 433
cinque 98
cinquecento 114, 554
cipher unsubstantial 4
  number 84
  compute 85
  zero 101
  concealment 528
  mark 550
  letter 561
  unimportant 643
  writing in–590
Circe seductor 615
  sorcerer 994
Circean 992–cup
  pleasure 377
  intemperance 954
circination 312
circle region 181
  encompass 227
  form 247
  party 712

under a–
  insane 503
  adversity 735
  disrepute 874
  secluded 893
  censured 932
  accused 938
cloud–built 4
cloudburst 348
clouded
  variegated 440
  dejected 837
  hopeless 859
  –*perception* 499
cloudland 515
cloudless *light* 420
  happy 827
cloudy *dim* 422
  opaque 426
clough 206
clove 198
cloven 91
cloven foot *mark* 550
  malevolence 907
  vice 945
  Satan 978
  see the–480*a*
  show the–907
clover *grass* 367
  luxury 377
  prosperity 734
  comfort 827
  in–377, 827
clown *pantomime* 599
  buffoon 844
  vulgar 851
  rustic 876
cloy *pall* 376
  redundance 641
  satiety 869
cloying 396
cloyment 869
club *combine* 48
  place of meeting 74
  house 189
  association 712
  weapon 727
  sociality 892
  –*law compulsion* 744
  lawless 964
  –together
  coöperate 709
clubbability 892
clubbable 712
club–footed 243
clubman 852
club–shaped 250
clubwoman 852
cluck 412
clue (*see* clew)
clump *assemblage* 72
  projecting mass 250
  –*of trees* 367
clumsiness
  (*see* clumsy)
clumsy *unfit* 647

awkward 699
ugly 846
Cluniac 996
cluricaune 980
cluster 72
clutch *automobile* 272
  retain 781
  seize 789
clutches 737
  in the–of 749
clutter *be loud* 404
  roll 407
clypeate 245
clypeiform 245
clyster 300
coacervation 72
coach *carriage* 272
  teach 537
  tutor 540, 673
  –*road* 627
  –up 539
  drive a–and six
    through 964
coach house 191
coachman *travel* 268
  pilot 694
coaction
  concurrence 178
  cooperation 709
  compulsion 744
coactive 709
coadjutant 709, 711
coadjutive 709
coadjutor 711
coadjuvancy 709
coadjuvant 711
coadjuvate 709
coadministration
  709
coadunate 178
coagency *concur* 178
  cooperate 709
coagmentation 72
coagulate *cohere* 46
  densify 321
  thicken 352
  pulpy 354
coagulum 321, 352
co–aid 711
coal 388 *carry–s* 879
  carry–s to
    Newcastle 641
  haul over the–s 932
coal–black 431
coalesce *identity* 13
  combine 48
coalheaver
  work like a–686
coalition
  cooperate 709
  party 712
coaptation 23
coarctate 195, 203
coarctation
  decrease 36
  contraction 195

narrow 203
impede 706
restraint 751
(*compulsion* 744)
coarse *harsh* 410
  dirty 653
  unpolished 674
  vulgar 851
  impure 961
  –*grain* 329
coast *border* 231
  glide 266
  navigate 267
  land 342
  –*line* 230
coaster 273
coastguard 753
coat *layer* 204
  paint 223
  habit 225
  (*surface* 220)
  –*of arms* 550
  –*of mail* 717
  cut–according to
    cloth 698
coatee 225
coating, inner–224
coax *persuade* 615
  endearment 902
  flatter 933
coaxer 615
cob *horse* 271
  punish 972
cobalt 438
cobble *mend* 660
cobbler
  shoemaker 225
coble 273
cobra 366, 913
cobweb *filament* 205
  light 320
  fiction 545
  flimsy 643
  dirt 653
  –*s of antiquity* 124
  –*s of sophistry* 477
cocaine 376, 662, 954
cochineal 434
cochlea 418
cochleate 248
cock *vane* 338
  bird 366
  male 373
  –*and–bull story* 546
  –*of the walk best* 648
  master 745
  –*the eye* 441
  –*up vertical* 212
  convex 250
  game–861
cockade *badge* 550
  title 877
cock–a–hoop
  gay 836
  exulting 884
cockarouse 745

cockatrice *monster* 83
  serpent 366
  piercing eye 548
  evildoer 913
  miscreant 949
cockboat 273
cockcrow 125
Cocker
  school book 542
  according to–82
cocker *fold* 258
  dog 366
  caress 902
cock–eyed 443
cockle *pucker* 195
  fold 258
  –*s of one's heart* 820
cockleshell 273
cockloft 191
cockney
  Londoner 188
  plebeian 876
cockpit *hold* 191
  arena 728
cockroach 366
cockshut *evening* 126
  dusk 422
cocksure 484
cockswain 269
cocktail 959
cocoa 298
co–conscious 992*a*
coconut–*butter*
  –oil 356
cocoon 129
cocotte 962
coction 384
Cocytus 982
C. O. D. *receipt* 810
cod *fish* 298
  shell 223
coddle 902
  –*oneself* 943
code *concealment* 528
  cipher 561
  precept 697
  law 963
  (*compendium* 596)
codex 593
codger 819
codicil *addition* 37
  sequel 65
  testament 771
  (*adjunct* 39)
codification 60
codify *arrange* 60
  conceal 528
  legalize 963
codlin 129
coecum 261
coeducational 537
coefficacy 709
coefficient *factor* 84
  accompany 88
  cooperate 709
Caelebs 904

Coelentera 368
coeliac 221–*flux* 299
coemption 795
coequal 27
coequality 27
coerce *compel* 744
  restrain 751
coetaneous 120
coeternal
  perpetual 112
  synchronous 120
coeternity 110, 112
coeval 120
  –*with birth* 5
coevality 27
coexist *exist* 1
  accompany 88
  synchronism 120
  continguity 199
coexistence
  (*see* coexist)
coextension
  equality 27
  parallelism 216
  symmetry 242
coextensive 216, 242
coffee 298
coffeepot 191
coffeehouse 189
coffer *chest* 191
  store 636
  money chest 802
cofferdam 55
coffin 363
  add a nail to one's–
    830
cog *tooth* 253
  boat 273
  deceive 545
  flatter 933
cogency 157
cogent *powerful* 157
  –*reasoning* 476
coggery 545
cogitate 450, 451
cogitative 451
  –*faculties*–450
cognate *related* 9
  consanguineous 11
  similar 17
cognation 11
cognition 490
cognitive
  –*faculties* 450
cognizance 490
  take–*of intellect* 490
  attention 457
cognomen 564
cognoscence 490
cogwheel 312
cohabitation
  location 184
  marriage 903
coheir 778
cohere 46
coherence *unite* **46**

-off *loose* 44
event 151
escape 671
-off well 731
-on *future* 121
destiny 152
I defy you 715
attack 716
-out *disclosure* 529
publication 531
on the stage 599
-out of *effect* 154
egress 295
-out with
disclose 529
speak 582
-over *influence* 615
consent 762
-round *period* 138
conversion 144
belief 484
assent 488
change of mind 607
influence 615
restoration 660
be pacified 723
consent 762
-short of *inferior* 34
fall short 304
-to *equal* 27
whole 50
arithmetic 85
future 121
become 144
destiny 152
effect 154
inherit 777
money 800
price 812
-to a determination
604
-to a head *climax* 33
complete 52
-to a stand 142
-together *assemble* 72
converge 290
-to hand 785
-to life 359
-to nothing
unproductive 169
fail 732
-to oneself 660
-to one's knowledge
527
-to one's senses 502
-to pass *state* 7
event 151
-to pieces 44
-to terms *assent* 488
contract 769
-to the point
specialty 79
attention 457
concise 572
-to the front 303
-to the rescue 672

-to the same thing
27
-under 76
-upon *unexpected* 508
acquire 775
claim 924
-what may 474
cut and-again 639
it-s to this
concisely 572
comedown 306, 735
comedy *drama* 599
comic 853
comely 240, 845
come-off
loophole 617
comestible 298
comet *wanderer* 268
star 318
omen 512
cometary 111
comfit 396
comfort *pleasure* 377
delight 827
content 831
relief 834
a man of-834
give-906
comfortable
pleasing 829
Comforter 976
comforter
wrap 223, 384
comfortless
painful 830
dejected 837
comic *wit* 842
ridiculous 853
coming (*see* come)
impending 152
-events
prediction 511
-out *celebration* 883
-time 121
comitia 696
comity 894
comma 142
command *high* 206
requirement 630
authority 737
order **741**
possess 777
at one's-
obedient 743
-a view of 441
-belief 484
-of language
writing 574
speaking 582
-of money 803
-one's passions 944
-one's temper 826
-respect 928
commandant 745
commandeer 744,
789

commander
mariner 269
chief 745
**commander-in-
chief** 745
commanding
(*see* command)
important 642
comme il faut
taste 850
fashion 852
genteel 875
commemorate 883
commence 66
commend 931
-the poisoned chalice
544
commendable 944
commendably 931
commensurate
accordant 23
numeral 85
adequate 639
content 831
comment *reason* 476
judgment 480
interpretation 522
explain 595
commentary 595
commentator 492,
524
commerce
conversation 588
barter 794
cards 840
commercial
-arithmetic 811
-traveler 758
commination 908,
909
commingle 41
comminute 330
commiserate 914
commissariat 637
commissary
consignee 758
commission *task* 625
delegate **755**, 759
-of the peace 965
commissioner 745,
758
commissionnaire
messenger 534
consignee 758
commissure 43
commis-voyageur
758
commit *do* 680
delegate 755
cards 840
arrest 969
-an absurdity 853
-oneself *clumsy* 699
promise 768
-oneself to a course
609

-to memory 505
-to prison 751
-to sin 945
-to the flames 384
-to writing 551
commitment 969
committee
council 696
consignee 758
(*director* 694)
commix 41
commode 191
commodious 644
commodity 798
commodore 745
common *general* 78
ordinary 82
plain 344
grass 367
agriculture 371
habitual 613
trifling 643
base 876
-consent 488
-council 966
-course 613
-herd 876
-law *old* 124
law 963
-measure 84
-origin 153
-parlance 576
-run 78, 613
-saying 496
-school 537
-sense 498, 502
-sewer 653
-stock 778
-weal *mankind* 372
good 618
utility 644
philanthropy 910
in-*related* 9
participate 778
make-*cause* 709
right of-780
tenant in-778
commonalty 876
commoner 541, **876**
commonplace
usual 82
known 490
maxim 496
plain 576
habit 613
unimportant 643
dull 843
-book *record* 551
compendium 596
**Common Pleas,
Court of**-966
commons 298
commonweal
mankind 372
good 618
utility 644

philanthropy 910
commonwealth
region 181
mankind 372
utility 644
state 737
commorant 188
commotion 315
communalism 778
commune
township 181
commune with 588
-oneself 451
communicable 784
communicant 990
communicate *join* 43
tell 527
give 784
sacrament 998
communication
news 532
oral-582, 588
communicative 527
communion
society 712
participation 778
sacrament 998
-table 1000
hold-with 888
communiqué 527
communist *rebel* 742
participation 778
philanthropy 910
communitarian 778
community
party 712
-at large 372
-of goods 778
-singing 415
commutation
difference 15
compensation 30
substitution 147
interchange 148
compromise 774
barter 794
commuter 268
commutual 12
compact *joined* 43
united 87
compressed 195
compendious 201
dense 321
bargain **769**
compactness
(*see* compact)
compages *whole* 50
structure 329
compagination 43
companion *match* 17
accompaniment 88
stairway 305
friend 890
companionable 892
companionless 87
companionship 892

care 459
business 625
importance 642
firm 797
grief 828
−oneself with 625
concerning
  relative to 9
  (*topic* 454)
concert *agreement* 23
  synchronous 120
  music 415
  act in−709
  −hall 189
  −master 416
  −measures 626
  −piece 415
  in−*musical* 413
  concord 714
concertina 417
concerto 415
concert room 840
concession
  permission 760
  consent 762
  giving 784
  discount 813
concetto 842
conch 204, 215
concha 418
conchate 245
conchiform 245
conchoid 245
conchology 223
concierge 263, 753
conciliate
  talk over 615
  pacify 723
  satisfy 831
  courtesy 894
  atonement 952
conciliatory
  (*see* conciliate)
  concord 714
  courteous 894
  forgiving 918
conciliatrix 962
concinnity
  agreement 23
  style 578
  beauty 845
concise 572
  taciturn 585
conciseness 572
concision 201
conclave *assembly* 72
  council 696
  church 995
conclude *end* 67
  infer 480
  resolve 604
  complete 729
  compact 769
conclusion
  (*see* conclude)
  sequel 65

eventuality 151
effect 154
judgment 480
*foregone−*611
*hasty−*481
try−s 476
conclusive
  (*see* conclude)
  final 67
  answer 462
  evidential 467
  certain 474
  proof 478
  manifest 525
  −*reasoning* 476
concoct *lie* 544
  plan 626
  prepare 673
concomitant
  accompany 88
  same time 120
  concurrence 178
concord *agree* 23
  music **413**
  assent 488
  harmony **714**
  (*amity* 888)
concordance
  dictionary 562, 593,
    636
concordant 178
concordat 769
concours 720
concourse
  assemblage 72
  convergence 290
  −*of atoms* 621
concremation 384
concrete *mass* 46
  density 321
  hardness 323
  materials 635
concretion 46
concubinage 961
concubine 926
concupiscence
  desire 865
  impurity 961
concur *coexist* 120
  causation 178
  converge 290
  assent 488
  concert 709
concurrence *crisis* 43
  coagency **178**
  observance 772
concurrent 178, 216
concussion 276
condemn 971
condemnation
  censure 932
  conviction **971**
condemnatory 971
condesation
  brevity 201
  (*see* condense)

condense
  compress 195
  dense 321
condensed 572
condescend 879
condescension 879
condign 924
condiment 393
condisciple 541
condition *state* 7
  modification 469
  supposition 514
  term 770
  repute 873
  rank 875
  in−*plump* 192
  in good−648
  in perfect−650
  on−770
  physical−316
conditional 8
conditions 770
condolence 914, **915**
condone 918
condottiere
  traveler 268
  fighter 726
conduce
  contribute 153
  tend 176
  concur 178
  avail 644
conducent 176
conducive 631
conduct *transfer* 270
  procedure **692**
  lead 693
  −an inquiry 461
  −to 278
  safe−*passport* 631
  safety 664
conduction 264
conductivity 157
conductor *guard* 268
  conveyer 271
  music 416
  director 694
  lightning−666
conduit 350
conduplicate 89
condyle 250
cone *round* 249
  pointed 253
cone−shaped 253
conestoga wagon 272
confab 588
confabulation 588,
  821a
confection 396
  confectionery 396
confederacy
  cooperation 709
  party 712
confederate
  combine 48
  auxiliary 711

Confederates 712
confer *advise* 695
  give 784
  −benefit 648
  −power 157
  −privilege 760
  −right 924
  −with 588
conference
  (*see* confer)
  council 696
  churchdom 995
conferva 367
confess *assent* 488
  avow 529
  penitence 950
  −and avoid 937
confession
  (*see* confess)
  worship 990
  auricular−998
  −of faith 983
confessional
  disclosure 529
  rite 998
  temple 1000
confessions
  biography 594
confessor 996
confidant
  auxiliary 711
  maid 746
  friend 890
confidante
  servant 746
  friend 890
confidence *trust* 484
  expectation 507
  deception 545
  hope 858
  courage 861
  −man 548
  −trick 545
  in−528
confident
  (*see* confidence)
  affirm 535
confidential 528
confiding 703
configuration 240
confine *place* 182
  circumscribe 229
  border 231
  limit 233
  imprison 751
confined
  narrow judgment
    481
  ill 655
confinement
  childbed 161
confines of
  on the−197
confirm
  corroborate 467
  assent 488

consent 762
compact 769
rite 998
confirmation 535
confirmatory 480
confirmed 150
  −habit 613
confirmist 488
confiscate *take* 789
  condemn 971
  penalty 974
confiture 298, 396
conflagration 384
conflation 54
conflexure 245
conflict
  disagreement 24
  opposition 708
  discord 713
  contention 720
  warfare 722
conflicting
  contrary 14
  counteracting 179
  −evidence 468
confluence
  junction 43
  convergence 290
  river 348
confluent 290
conflux *assemblage* 72
  convergence 290
conform *assent* 488
conformable
  agreeing 23
  concurrent 178
conformation 240
conformity 82
  concurrence 178
  −to rule 494
confound *disorder* 61
  destroy 162
  not discriminate
    465a
  perplex 475
  confute 479
  defeat 731
  astonish 870
  curse 908
confounded *great* 31
  bad 649
confraternity
  party 712
  friendship 888
confrère *colleague* 711
  friend 890
confrication 331
confront *face* 234
  compare 464
  oppose 708
  resist 719
  −danger 861
  −witnesses 467
Confucius 986
confuse *derange* 61
  perplex 458

governor 745
officer 965
constancy 743
constant *uniform* 16
  continuous 69
  regular 80
  frequent 136
  periodic 138
  immutable 150
  exact 494
  persevering 604a
  faithful 939
  –*flow* 69
constellation
  stars 318
  luminary 423
  glory 873
consternation 860
constipate 321
constipation
  closure 261
  density 321
constituency 609
constituent 56, 609
constitute
  compose 54, 56
  produce 161
constituted by 1
constitution *nature* 5
  state 7
  composition 54
  structure 329
  charter 924
  law 963
  higher *law* than–
  926
constitutional
  walk 266
  –*government* 737
constitutive 153
constrain *compel* 744
  restrain 751
  abash 881
constraint
  contraction 195
  [*see* constrain]
constrict 195
constriction 706
constringe 195
constringency 195
construct *compose* 54
  produce 161
  organize 357
construction
  production 161
  form 240
  structure 329
  meaning 522
  put a false–upon
  523
constructive
  creative 161
  latent 526
  –*evidence* 467
constructor 164
construe 522

consubstantiation
998
consuetude 613
consul 758, 759
consular 759
consulship 737
consult *remedy* 662
  advise 695
  –one's own wishes
  943
  –one's pillow 133
  –the wishes of 707
consultant 662
consultation 695
consume *decay* 49
  destroy 162
  waste 638
  use 677
  time *time* 106
  inactivity 683
consumer *user* 677
consuming 830
consummate *great* 31
  complete 52
  be perfect 650
  completed 729
  –*skill* 698
consummation
  end 67
  completion 729
  –devoutly to be
  wished *good* 618
  desire 865
consumption
  [*see* consume]
  decrease 36
  shrinking 195
  disease 655
consumptive 655
contact *contiguity* 199
  touch 379
  come in–
  arrive 292
contagion
  transfer 270
  unhealthy 657
contagious 655, 657
contain
  be composed of 54
  include 76
contained in 1
container
  receptacle 191
contaminate *soil* 653
  spoil 659
contaminated
  diseased 655
contamination 653,
  659
contango 813
contemn 930
contemper 48, 174
contemplate
  view 441
  intellect 450
  think 451

expect 507
purpose 620
contemplation
  [*see* contemplate]
contemporaneous
120
contemporary 120
contemporation 174
contempt 930
  –of danger 861
contemptible
  unimportant 643
  dishonorable 940
contemptuous
  defiant 715
  disrespectful 929
  disdainful 930
contend *reason* 476
  assert 535
  fight 720
  –for *vindicate* 937
  –with difficulties 704
content *assenting* 488
  willing 602
  calm 826
  satisfied 831
  to one's heart's–
  sufficient 639
  success 731
contention 720
contentious 901
contents
  ingredients 56
  list 86
  components 190
  book 593
  synopsis 596
conterminate *end* 67
  limit 233
conterminous 199
contesseration 72
contest 708, 720
contestant 710
context 591
contexture 329
  (*state* 7)
contiguity 199
contiguous 197
continence 960
continent 342
continental *trifle* 643
continentals 225
contingency
  junction 43
  event 151
  uncertainty 475
  expectation 507
contingent *extrinsic* 6
  conditional 8
  casual 156
  liable 177
  possible 470
  uncertain 475
  supply 635
  aid 707
  allotted 786

donation 809
–*duration* 108a
–*interest* 780
continual
  perpetual 112
  frequent 136
continuance 117, 143
continuation *affix* 37
  adjunct 39
  sequence 63
  sequel 65
  –*school* 542
continuations
  trousers 225
continue *exist* 1
  endure 106, 110
  persist 143
continued 69
  –*existence* 112
  –*success* 731
continuing 143
continuity 16, 69
continuous 69
contortion
  distortion 243
  convolution 248
  (*ugliness* 846)
contortionist 599
contortuosity 243
contour *outline* 230
  appearance 448
  –*line* 550
contra 14 per–708
contraband
  deceitful 545
  prohibited 761
  illicit 964
contrabandist 792
contrabasso 417
contraclockwise 283
contract *shrink* 195
  narrow 203
  promise 768
  bargain 769
  (*decrease* 36)
  (*curtail* 201)
  –a *debt* 806
  –a *habit* 613
  –an *obligation* 768
contractible 195
contractility 195
  (*elasticity* 325)
contraction 195
  shorthand 590
  compendium 596
contractive 36, 464
contractor 690
contractual 769
contradict
  contrary 14
  dissent 489
  deny 536
  oppose 708
contradiction
  difference 15
  answer 462

contradictoriness 15
contradictory
  evidence 468
  discordant 713
contradistinction 15
contrafagotto 417
contraindicant 616
contraindicate
  dissuade 616
  warning 668
contralto 408
contraposition
  inversion 218
  reversion 237
contrapuntal 415
contrapuntist 413
contrariety 14, 15,
  708
contrariness 708
contrariwise 148,
  708
contrary *opposite* 14
  antagonistic 179
  captious 608
  opposing 708
  –to expectation
  improbable 473
  unexpected 508
  –to reason 471
  quite the–536
contrast
  contrariety 14
  difference 15
  comparison 464
contrastive 15
contrate wheel 247
contravallation 717
contravene
  contrary 14
  counteract 179
  counterevidence 468
  deny 536
  hinder 706
  oppose 708
contre–coup 277
contrectation 379
contretemps
  ill timed 135
  hindrance 706
  misfortune 735
contribute *cause* 153
  tend 176
  concur 178
  aid 707
  give 784
contribution 784
  lay under– *take* 789
  due 924
contributor
  correspondent 592
  giver 784
contributory *extra* 37
contrition
  abrasion 331
  penitence 950
contrivance 626

up *destroy* 162
crush 195
crunch *shatter* **44**
chew 298
pulverize 330
crupper 235
crusade 361, 722
cruse 191
crush *crowd* 72
destroy 162
compress 195
shatter 328
pulverize 330
humble 879
(*injure* 649)
–one's hopes
disappoint 509
hopeless 859
–under an iron heel
739
crushed *unhappy* 828
crush hat 225
crushing *vigorous* 574
painful 830
crust 223
crustacean 366, 368
crusty
discourteous 895
sullen 901a
crutch *support* 215
angle 244
crux *cross* 219
difficulty 704
Crux 490a
cry *stridor* 410
human **411**
animal 412
publish 531, 532
call 550
voice 580
vogue 613
weep 839
–aloud *implore* 765
–and little wool
overrate 482
boast 884
disappoint 509
–before hurt 839
–down 932, 934
–for 865
–for joy 838
–for vengeance 923
–out against
dissuade 616
censure 932
–shame 932
–to *beseech* 765
–up 931
–wolf *false* 544
alarm 669
–you mercy
depreciate 766
pity 914
forgive 918
far–to 196
full–*loud* 404

raise a–550
crying (*see* cry)
urgent 630
–evil 619
–shame 874
–sin 945
crypt *cell* 191
grave 363
ambush 530
altar 1000
cryptic *uncertain* 475
concealed 528
secret 533
cryptography
unintelligibility 519
hidden 528
writing 590
crystal *hard* 323
water 337
transparent 425
–gazing 992a
–oil 356
snow–383
crystalline *dense* 321
transparent 425
crystallinity 321
crystallization 321, 323
crystallize 321
crystallomancy 511
crystallose 396
cub *young* 129
offspring 167
vulgar 851
clown 876
unlicked–241
cubby–hole 191, 530
cube
three dimensions 92, 93
form 244
cubeb 393
cubicle 191
cubist 556
cubit 200
cucking stool 975
cuckold 905
cuckoldom 961
cuckoo *imitation* 19
repetition 104
bird 366
sound 407
cry 412
songbird 416
cucullate 223
cucumber 298
–green 435
cuddle 902
cuddy 271
cudgel *beat* 276
weapon 727
punish 975
–one's brains
think 451
imagine 515
take up the–s

aid 707
attack 716
contention 720
cudgeling
punishment 972
cue *humor* 5
role 51, 625
hint 527
watchword 550
plea 617
take one's–from
695
cue rest 215
cuff *sleeve* 225
blow 276
punishment 972
cuirass 717
cuirassier 726
cuisine 298
culbute *inversion* 218
fall 306
cul–de–lampe
engraving 558
ornament 847
cul–de–sac
concave 252
closed 261
difficulty 704
culet 211
culinary 298–art 673
cull *dupe* 547
choose 609
take 789
cullender 260
cullibility 486
cullion 949
cully *deceive* 545
dupe 547
culm 388
culminate
maximum 33
height 206
top 210
complete 729
culpability *vice* 945
guilt 947
culprit 949, 975
cult 990
cultivate *till* 365, 371
sharpen 375
improve 658
prepare 673
aid 707
courtesy 894
cultivated
courteous 894
–taste 850
cultivation
(*see* cultivate)
knowledge 490
cultivator 371
cultural 537, 542
cultural
anthropology 372a
culture *knowledge* 490
improvement 658

taste 850
courtesy 894
culverin 727
culvert 350
cumber *load* 319
obstruct 706
cumbersome
incommodious 647
disagreeable 830
cumbrous 830
cummerbund 225
cumshaw 784
cumulative
assembled 72
evidential 467
–evidence 467
–vote 609
cumulous 353
cumulus 353
cunctation *delay* 133
(*inactivity* 683)
cuneate 244
cuneiform 244, 372a
–character 590
cunning *prepense* 611
sagacious 698
artful 702
–fellow 700
cup *vessel* 191
hollow 252
beverage 298
remedy 662
tipple 959
between–and lip
111
bitter–828
–of humiliation 879
–that cheers etc. 298
–too low 837
–tossing 621
dash the–from
one's lips 509
in one's–s 959
cupbearer 746
cupboard 191
cupel 384
cupellation 336, 384
Cupid *beauty* 845
love 897
cupidity *avarice* 819
desire 865
cupola *height* 206
dome 223, 250
cupping 662
cup–shaped 252
cur *dog* 366
sneak 949
curable 658, 660, 662
curacy 995
curate 996
curative 660
curator 694, 758
curb *moderate* 174
slacken 275
dissuade 616
chance 621

check 706
restrain 751
shackle 752
mart 799
–bit 706
–roof 244
curcuma paper 463
curd *density* 321
pulp 354
(*cohere* 46)
curdle *condense* 321
make the blood–
830
curdled 352
cure *reinstate* 660
remedy 662
preserve 670
benefice 995
curé 996
cure–all 662
cureless 859
curfew 126
curia 966
curio 847
curiosity
unconformity 83
inquiring 455
phenomenon 872
curious *exceptional* 83
inquisitive 455
true 494
beautiful 845
desirous 865
curiously *very* 31
curl *bend* 245
convolution 248
hair 256
cockle up 258
–cloud 353
–paper 256
–up one's lip 930
curling *game* 840
curling tongs 386
curly 248
curmudgeon
miser 819
currants 298
currency
publicity 531
money 800
current *existing* 1
general 78
present 118
happening 151
of water 348
of air 349
rife 531, 532
language 560
habit 613
danger 667
–account 811
against the–708
–belief 488
–of events 151
–of ideas 451
–of time 109

dabbler 493, 823
dabster 700
dachshund 366
dacker 605
dacoit 792
dactyl 597
dactyliomancy 511
dactylography 550
dactylology 419, 550
dactylonomy
  numeration 85
  symbol 550
dad 166
dado 211
daedal *various* 15
  diversified 16a
  variegated 440
Daedalian
  convoluted 248
  artistic 698
daeva 980
daft 503
daffodil 845
dagger
  typography 550
  weapon 727
  air drawn–515
  at–s drawn
  opposed 708
  discord 713
  enmity 889
  hate 898
  –of the mind 860
  looks–s *anger* 900
  threat 909
  plant–in breast
  give pain 830
  speak–s 932
daggle *hang* 214
  dirty 653
dagoba 1000
Dagon 991
daguerreotype
  represent 554
dahabeah 273
Dail Eireann 696
daily *frequent* 136
  periodic 138
  newspaper 531
  –occurrence
  normal 82
  habitual 613
daimio 875
dainty *food* 298
  savoring 394
  pleasing 829
  delicate 845
  tasty 850
  fastidious 868
dairy 191
dais *support* 215
  throne 747
daisy–pied 847
  fresh as a–654
dak 534
  –bungalow 189

dalal 758
dale *valley* 252
dally *delay* 133
  irresolute 605
  inactive 683
  amuse 640
  fondle 902
dalmatic 999
Daltonism 443
dam *parent* 166
  close 261
  pond 343
  obstruct 706
damage *evil* 619
  injure, spoil 659
  loss 776
  price 812
damages 974
damascene 440
damask 434
dame *woman* 374
  teacher 540
  lady 875
damn *malediction* 908
  condemn 971
  –with faint praise
  932, 934
damnability 649
damnable 649
damnatory *evil* 649
  disapprove 932
  condemn 971
damnify *damage* 649
  spoil 659
Damocles
  –sword of–667
damoiseau 129
damoiselle 129
Damon and Pythias
  890
damp *moderate* 174
  moist 339
  cold 385
  dissuade 616
  hinder 706
  depress 837
  dull 843
  –the sound 408a
dampen 339
damper *cake* 298
  furnace 386
  faintness 405
damsel *youth* 129
  female 374
damson 437
Danaë 803
dance *jump* 309
  oscillate 314
  agitate 315
  rejoice 838
  sport 840
  –attendance
  waiting 133
  follow 281
  servant 746
  petition 765

  servility 886
  –music 415
  –steps 840
  –the back step 283
  –the war dance 715
  –upon nothing 972
  lead one a–
  run away 623
  circuit 629
  difficult 704
  practical joke 929
  lead the–175
dancer 840
dander 900
dandi 272
Dandie Dinmont
  366
dandify 847
dandiprat 193
dandle 902
dandruff 653
dandy *litter* 266, 272
  ship 273
  fop 854
dandyism 855
danger 665–*past* 664
  –signal 669
  in–*liable* 177
  –source of–667
dangerous
  (*see* danger)
  –classes 913
  –illness 655
  –person 667
dangle *hang* 214
  swing 314
  display 882
dangler 281
Daniel *sage* 500
  judge 967
  –come to judgment
  480
dank 339
danseuse 599
Dan to Beersheba
  complete 52
  extent 180
dapper *little* 193
  elegant 845
dapple-gray 432
dappled 432, 440
Darby and Joan
  secluded 893
  married 903
dare *confront* 234
  defy 715
  face danger 861
  –not 860
  –say *probable* 472
  believe 484
  suppose 514
dare-devil
  courage 861
  rash 863
  bluster 887
daring *unreserved* 525

  courageous 861
  –imagination 515
dark *obscure* 421
  dim 422
  color 428
  black 431
  blind 442
  invisible 447
  unintelligible 519
  latent 526
  joyless 837
  insidious 940
  –ages 491
  –amid the blaze of
  noon 442
  –cloud 735
  –lantern 423
  in the–*ignorant* 491
  keep–*hide* 528
  leap in the–
  experiment 463
  chance 621
  rash 863
  view with–eyes 932
darken *obscure* 422
  look black 821
  –over 421
darkened 421
darkle 422
darkling 421
darkly
  see through a glass–
  443
darkness
  (*see* dark) **421**
  children of–988
  –of meaning 571
  powers of–978
darksomeness 421
darky 431
darling *beloved* 897
  favorite 599
darn 660
dart *swift* 274
  propel 284
  missile 727
  –to and fro 684
dartre 655
Darwinian 357
Darwinism 357
dash
  small quantity 32
  mix 41
  start 146
  swift 276
  fling 284
  mark 550
  courage 861
  cut a–*repute* 873
  display 882
  –at *resolution* 604
  attack 716
  –cup from lips 761
  –down 308
  –hopes
  disappoint 509

  fail 732
  dejected 837
  despair 859
  –off *compose* 54
  paint 556
  write 590
  active 682
  haste 684
  –of the pen 590
  –on 274
dashboard 666
dashed (*see* dash)
  humbled 879
dasher 666
dashing
  fashionable 852
  brave 861
  ostentatious 882
dastard 862
dasturi 973
data *evidence* 467
  reasoning 476
  supposition 514
datal 114
date *time* 106
  chronology 114
  to this–118
  up to–123
dateless 124
datum (*see* data)
daub *cover* 223
  bad painting 555
  dirt 653
daubing 635
daughter 167
daunt 860
dauntless 858, 861
davenport 191, 215
dawdle *tardy* 133
  slow 275
  inactive 683
dawn *precursor* 64
  begin 66
  priority 116
  morning 125
  light 420
  dim 422
  glimpse 490
day *period* 108
  present time 118
  light 420
  all–110
  all in–'s work 625
  clear as–
  certain 474
  intelligible 518
  manifest 525
  close of–126
  –after day
  diuturnal 110
  frequent 136
  –after the fair 135
  –after to–morrow
  121
  –and night
  frequent 136

decimal
  numeration 84
  tenth 98, 99
decimalize 99
decimate *subtract* 38
  tenth 99
  few 103
  weaken 160
  kill 361
  play havoc 659
decipher 522, 525, 561
decision
  judgment 480
  resolution 604
  intention 620
  law case 969
decisive *certain* 474
  proof 478
  commanding 741
  take a—step 609
deck *floor* 211
  cards 840
  beautify 847
deckle—edged 674
declaim 582
  —against 932
declamatory
  style 577
  speech 582
declaration
  evidence 467
  affirmation 535
  law pleadings 969
  —of faith belief 484
  theology 983
  —of war 713, 722
declarative 527
declaratory
  meaning 516
  inform 527
declare 535
declension
  (see decline)
  grammar 567
  backsliding 988
declensions 5
declination
  (see decline)
  deviation 279
  divergence 291
  measurement 466
  rejection 610
declinatory 764
declinature 764
decline *decrease* 36
  old 124
  weaken 160
  descent 306
  grammar 567
  be unwilling 603
  reject 610
  disease 655
  become worse 659
  adversity 735
  refuse 764

  —of day 126
  —of life 128
declivitous 217, 306
declivity *slope* 217
  descent 306
declivous 306
decoction 335, 384
decode 525, 561
decollate 972
décolletée 225
decolor 429
decoloration 429
decolorize 429
decompose 49
decomposition 49
decompound 49
deconsecrate 756
decoloration
  trophy 733
  insignia 747
  ornament 847
  title 877
Decoration Day 840
decorous
  (see decorum)
  proper 924
  respectful 928
decorticate 226
decorum *fashion* 852
  duty 926
  purity 960
decoy *draw* 288
  deceive 545
  deceiver 548
  entice 615
decrassify 652, 658
decrease *in degree* 36
  in size 195
decree *judgment* 480
  order 741
  law 963, 969
decrement
  decrease 36
  thing deducted 40a
  contraction 195
decrepit *old* 128
  impotent 158
  weak 160
  disease 655
  decayed 659
decrepitate 406
decrepitation 490b
decrepitude
  (see decrepit)
decrescence 36
decrescendo 36
decretal 741
decretive 741
decry *underrate* 483
  censure 932
  detract 934
decumbent 213, 214
decuple 98
decursive 306
decurtation 201
decussate 219

decussation 219
dedecorous
  disreputable 874
  discourteous 895
dedicate *use* 677
  inscribe 873
dedication *book* 593
  (see dedicate)
deduce *deduct* 38
  infer 480
deducible
  evidence 467
  proof 478
deduct *retrench* 38
  deprive 789
deduction
  (see deduce)
  decrement 40a
  reasoning 476
  inference 521
deductive 476
deed *transference* 270
  evidence 467
  record 551
  act 680
  security 771
  —s of arms 720
  —without a name 947
deem 484
deemster 664, 967
deep *great* 31
  profound 208
  sea 341
  sonorous 404
  cunning 702
  —color 428
  —game 702
  —in debt 806
  —knowledge 490
  —mourning 839
  —note 408
  —potations 959
  —reflection 451
  —sea 208
  —sense 821
  —sigh 839
  —study 457
  —toned 413
  in—water 704
  plough the— 267
deep—dyed
  intense 171
  black 431
  vicious 945
deepen *increase* 35
deep—felt 821
deep—laid *plan* 626
deeply (see deep)
deep—mouthed
  resonant 408
  bark 412
deep musing 458
deep—read 490
deep—rooted
  stable 150
  strong 159

  belief 484
  habit 613
  affections 820
deep—seated 208
  interior 221
deer 366
  in heart a— 862
deev 980
deface
  destroy form 241
  obliterate 552
  injure 659
  render ugly 846
defalcation
  incomplete 53
  contraction 195
  shortcoming 304
  nonpayment 808
defamation
  (see defame)
defamatory 932, 934
defame *shame* 874
  censure 932
  detract 934
defamer 936
defatigation 841
default *incomplete* 53
  shortcoming 304
  neglect 460
  insufficiency 640
  debt 806
  nonpayment 808
  in—of 187
  judgment by— 725
defaulter *thief* 792
  nonpayer 808
  rogue 949
defeasance 756
defeat *confute* 479
  succeed 731
  failure 732
  —one's hope 509
defecate 652
defecation 299
defect *decrement* 40a
  incomplete 53
  imperfect 651
  failing 945
defection
  relinquishment 624
  imperfection 651
  disobedience 742
defective
  incomplete 53
  insufficient 640
  imperfect 651
defend (see defense)
defendant 938
  defender 914
defense *answer* 462
  resist 717
  vindication 937
defenseless
  impotent 158
  weak 160
  exposed 665

defense mechanism 821a
defensible *safe* 664
  excusable 937
defensive alliance 712
defer *put off* 133
  neglect 460
  —to assent 488
  submit 725
  respect 928
deference
  submission 725
  obedience 743
  humility 879
  courtesy 894
  respect 928
deferment 460
defial 715
defiance 715
  threat 909
  —of danger 861
  in—opposition 708
  set at—disobey 742
defiant 715
deficiency
  (see deficient)
  vice 945
  —of blood 160
deficient *inferior* 34
  incomplete 53
  shortcoming 304
  insufficient 640
  imperfect 651
deficit
  incompleteness 53
  debt 806
defigure 846
defile *interval* 198
  march 266
  dirt 653
  spoil 659
  shame 874
  impure 961
define *limit* 233
  explain 522
  name 564
definite *special* 79
  limited 233
  visible 446
  certain 474
  exact 494
  intelligible 518
  manifest 525
  perspicuous 570
definition
  interpretation 521
definitive *final* 67
  affirmative 535
  decided 604
deflagration 384
deflate 195
deflect *curve* 245
  deviate 279
deflower *spoil* 659
  violate 961

sect 712
religious–983
denominational
dissent 489
party 712
theological 983
–education 537
denominator 84
denotative 550
denote *specify* 79
mean 516
indicate 550
dénouement *end* 67
result 154
disclosure 529
completion 729
denounce *curse* 908
disapprove 932
accuse 938
dense *crowded* 72
close 321
vegetation 365
ignorant 493
density 321
dent *hollow* 252
notch 257
dental 561
dentate 257
denticulated
sharp 253
notched 257
denticulation 257
dentifrice 652
dentiphone 418
dentist 662
dentistry 662
denude 226
denuded *loss* 776
–of *insufficient* 640
denunciation 909
(*see* denounce)
deny *dissent* 489
negative 536
refuse 764
–oneself *avoid* 623
seclude 893
temperate 953
ascetic 990
deobstruct 705
deobstruent 652, 662
deodand 974
deodorant 399
deodorize 399
clean 652
deodorizer 399
deontology 926
deoppilation 705
deorganization 61
deosculation 902
deoxidation 140
deoxidization 140
depart 293 –from
differ 15
deviate 279
relinquish 624
–this life 360

departed
nonexistent 2
department *class* 75
region 181
business 625
bureau 965
–store 799
departmental 737
departure 293
new–66
point of–293
depend *hang* 214
contingent 475
–on circumstances 475
–upon
be the effect of 154
evidence 467
trust 484
to be–ed on
certain 474
reliable 484
honorable 939
dependence 46
dependency
relation 9
property 777, 780
dependent *effect* 154
liable 177
hanging 214
puppet 711
servant 746
subject 749
deperdition 776
dephlegmation 340
dephlegmatory 340
depict 554, 556
describe 594
depiction (*see* depict)
depilation 226
depilatory 662
depilous 226
deplete 638
depletion 640
deplorable *bad* 649
disastrous 735
painful 830
deplore *regret* 833
complain 839
remorse 950
deploy 194
depone 535
deponent 467
depopulate *eject* 297
desert 893
deport 972
deportation
removal 270
emigration 297
deportment 692
depose *evidence* 467
declare 535
dethrone 738, 756
deposit *place* 184
transference 270
precipitate 321

store 636
security 771
payment 809
depositary 801
deposition
see depose, deposit
record 551
depository 636
depot *station* 266
store 636
shop 799
depotentiate 158
deprave *spoil* 659
depraved *bad* 649
vicious 945
depravity 945
depreciation 766
pity 914
disapprove 932
deprecative 881
deprecatory 766, 881
depreciate
disrespect 929
(*see* depreciation)
depreciation 766
decrease 36
underestimate 483
discount 813
cheap 815
censure 932
detraction 934
accusation 938
depreciator 483
depredation 791
depredator 792
deprehension 789
depress
(*see* depression)
depressing
painful 830
depression
lowness 207
depth 208
concavity 252
dent 257
furrow 259
lowering 308
dejection 837
dullness 843
deprivation 789
deprive *subduct* 38
take 789
–of life 361
–of power 158
–of property 789
–of strength 160
deprived of 776
de profundis
lamentation 839
penitence 950
depth *physical* 208
mental 498
–beyond depth 104
–bomb 208, 727
–of misery 828
–of thought 451

–of winter 383
out of one's–304, 310
depthless 209
depurate *clean* 652
improve 658
depurative 652
depuratory 662
deputation 755
depute 755, 759
deputies, chamber of–696
deputy 759 *police* 664
–commissioner 745
dequantitate 36
deracinate 2
derail 142
derange *insane* 503
deranged 503
derangement 61
mental–503
derby *hat* 225
Derby–day 720
derelict *ship* 273
land 342
source of danger 667
relinquished 782
outcast 893
dereliction
relinquishment 624, 782
guilt 947
–of duty 927
deride *ridicule* 856
disrespect 929
contempt 930
derisive 582, 853
(*see* deride)
derivate 155
derivation
origin 153, 154, 155
verbal 562
derivative 562
derive *attribute* 155
deduce 480
word 562
acquire 775
income 810
derm 223
dermal 223
dermatogen 223
dermatography 223
dermatoid 223
dermatology 223
dermatopathy 223
dermatophyte 223
dermatoplasty 223
dermic 223
dermis 223
dermoid 223
dernier cri 123
derogate
underrate 483
disparage 934
dishonor 940
–from 874

derogatory
shame 874
dishonor 940
derrick 307, 633
derring–do 861
dervish 955, 984, 996
descant *precursor* 64
music 415
diffuseness 573
loquacity 584
dissent 595
descend *slope* 217
go down 306
–to particulars
special 79
describe 594
descendant 120, 167
descent 69
lineage 166
fall **306**
inheritance 775
describe 594
description *kind* 75
name 564
narration 594
descriptive 594
descry 441
desecrate *misuse* 679
disrespect 929
profane 988
desert
unproductive 169
space 180
empty 187
plain 344
run away 623
relinquish 624
retaliation 718
divorce 782
merit 924, 944
deserted *outcast* 893
deserter 607, 623
desertion (*see* desert)
desertless 945
deserve
be entitled to 924
merit 944
–belief 484
–notice 642
deserving 924
déshabille
(*see* dishabille)
desiccate 340
desiccator 340
desiderate *need* 630
desire 865
desideratum
inquiry 461
requirement 630
desire 865
design *prototype* 22
composition 54
delineation 554
painting 556
intention 620
plan 626

contract 195
–the number 103
diminuendo
  music 415
diminution 36, 195
diminutive *degree* 32
  size 193
dimity 635
dimness 422
dimple *concavity* 252
  notch 257
dim–sightedness 443
  unwise 499
din 404–in the ear
  repeat 104
  drum 407
  loquacity 584
  –of arms 716
dine 298
  –with Duke
    Humphrey 956
dingdong 407
dinghy 273
dingle 252 *door* 232
dingy *dark* 421, 422
  colorless 429
  black 431
  gray 432
dining room 191
dinner 298
  –jacket 225
dint *power* 157
  concavity 252
  blow 276
  by–of
  instrumentality 631
diocesan 996
diocese 181, 995
Diogenes
  recluse 893
  cynic 911
  lantern of–
  inquiry 461
Dionaea 545
dioptrics 420
diorama *view* 448
  painting 556
diorism 465
dip *slope* 217
  concavity 252
  load 270
  direction 278
  insert 300
  descent 306
  depression 308
  plunge 310
  water 337
  baptize 998
  –into *glance at* 457
  inquire 461
  learn 539
  –one's hands into
    take 789
diphthong 561
diphyletic 89, 167
diploma *evidence* 467

commission 755
diplomacy
  artfulness 702
  mediation 724
  negotiation 769
diplomatic
  (see diplomacy)
  –agent 758
diplomatist
  messenger 534
  consignee 758
dipper 191
Dipper 318
dipsomania
  insanity 503
  desire 865
  drunkeness 959
dipsomaniac 504
diptych *list* 86
  record 551
dire *hateful* 649
  disastrous 735
  grievous 830
  fearful 860
direct *straight* 246
  teach 537
  artless 703
  command 741
  –attention to 457
  –one's course
    motion 278
    pursuit 622
  –the eyes to 441
directable 278
direction (see direct)
  tendency 278
  indication 550
  management 693
  precept 697
directive 692
directly *soon* 132
director *teacher* 540
  college 542
  manager **694**
  master 745
directorship 737
directory *list* 86
  council 696
diremption 44
direption 791
dirge *funeral* 363
  song 415
  lament 839
dirigible
  balloon 273, 726
  direction 278
dirk 727
dirt 653–cheap 815
  throw–*defame* 874
  disrespect 929
dirtiness (see dirty)
dirty *dim* 222
  opaque 426
  unclean 653
  disreputable 874
  dishonorable 940

–end of stick 699
–sky 353
–weather 349
  do–work *servile* 886
  flatterer 935
diruption 162
disability
  impotence 158
disable 158
  weaken 160
disabled 158
disabuse *inform* 527
  disclose 529
disaccord 713
  –with 15
disadvantage
  evil 619
  inexperience 647
  at a–34
  lie under a–651
disadvantageous
  disastrous 619
  inexpedient 647
  bad 649
disaffection
  dissent 489
  enmity 889
  hate 898
disaffirm 536
disagree
  (see disagreement)
disagreeable
  unpleasing 830
  dislike 867
disagreement
  difference 15
  incongruity 24
  dissent 489
  discord 713
disallow 761
disannul 756
disappear 449
disappearance 449
disappointment
  balk **509**
  fail 732
  discontent 832
disapprobation
  hindrance 706
  refusal 764
  disapproval 932
disapprove 932
disapprover 936
disarm *disable* 158
  weaken 160
  reconcile 831
  propitiate 914
disarrange 61
disarray *disorder* 59
  undress 226
disaster *killing* 361
  evil 619
  failure 732
  adversity 735
  calamity 830
disastrous *bad* 649

disavow 536
disband *separate* 44
  disperse 73
  liberate 750
disbar *abrogate* 756
  disapprove 932
  punish 968, 972
disbelief 485
  religious 989
disbelieve 485, 989
disbench
  abrogate 756
  disbar 968
  punish 972
disbowel 297
disbranch 44
disburden
  facilitate 705
  –oneself of 782
  –one's mind 529
disburse 809
disc *surface* 220
  front 234
discard *eject* 297
  relinquish 624
  disuse 678
  abrogate 756
  refuse 764
  repudiate 773
  surrender 782
  –from one's thoughts
    458
discarded 495
discarnate 317
disceptation 476
discern *see* 441
  know 490
discernible 446
discerning 498
discernment 498,
  868
discerptible 51
discerption 44
discharge
  violence 173
  propel 284
  emit 297
  excrete 299
  sound 406
  acquit oneself 692
  complete 729
  liberate 750
  abrogate 756
  pay 807
  exempt 927a
  acquit 970
  –a duty 926, 944
  –a function
    business 625
    utility 644
  –an obligation 772
  –from the memory
    506
  –from the mind 458
  –itself *egress* 295
    river 348

discind 44
disciple *pupil* 541
  Christian 985
disciplinarian
  master 540
  martinet 739
discipline *order* 58
  follower 65
  teaching 537
  training 673
  restraint 751
  punishment 972
  religious 990
disclaim *deny* 536
  repudiate 756
  objure 757
  refuse 764
disclaimer 536
disclamation
  (see disclaim)
disclose 529
disclosure 529
  discovery 480a
discoid *broad* 202
  layer 204
  frontal 220
  flat 251
discoloration 429
discolored
  shabby 659
  ugly 846
  blemish 848
discomfit 731
discomfiture 732
discomfort
  physical 378
  mental 828
discommend 932
discommode
  hinder 706
discommodious
  useless 645
  inexpedient 647
discompose
  derange 61
  put out 458
  hinder 706
  pain 830
  disconcert 874
  anger 900
discomposure 828
disconcert *derange* 61
  distract 458
  disappoint 509
  hinder 706
  discontent 832
  confuse 874
disconcerted
  hopeless 859
  (failure 732)
disconformity 83
discongruity 15, 24
disconnect 44, 70
disconnected
  divided 51
  feeble 575

disconnection
irrelation 19
disjunction 44
discontinuity 70
disconsolate 837
discontent 832
discontinuance
cessation 142
relinquishment 624
discontinuity 70
discontinuous 70
discord
disagreement 24
of sound 414
of color 428
dissension 713
discordance
(*see* discord)
discount *decrease* 36
decrement 40*a*
money 813
at a–*disrepute* 874
disapproved 932
discountenance
disfavor 706
refuse 764
discourage
dissuade 616
sadden 837
frighten 860
(*disfavor* 706)
discourse *teach* 537
speech 582
talk 588
dissert 595
sermon 998
discourtesy 895
discouse 202
discover *perceive* 441
solve 462
find 480*a*
disclose 529
–itself *be seen* 446
discovery 480*a*
discredit *disbelief* 485
dishonor 874
discreditable
vicious 945
discreet *careful* 459
cautious 864
(*clever* 698)
discrepancy 20*a*, 471
discrepant
differing 15
disagreeing 24
discordant 713
discrepate 15
discrete *separate* 44
disjunctive 70
single 87
discretion *will* 600
choice 609
skill 698
caution 864
surrender at–725
years of–131
discriminate
(*see* discrimination)
discrimination
difference 15
nice perception 465
wisdom 498
taste 850
fastidiousness 868
disculpate 937
discumbency 213
discursion 266
discursive
moving 264
migratory 266
wandering 279
–faculties 450
argumentative 476
diffuse style 573
conversable 588
disserting 595
discus 840
discuss *eat* 298
reflect 451
inquire 461
reason 476
dissert 595
discussion
(*see* discuss)
open to–475
under–461
discutient 73
disdain
indifference 866
fastidious 868
pride 878
insolence 885
contempt 930
disdainful
(*see* disdain)
disrespectful 929
disease 655
diseased 655
–mind 503
disembark 292, 342
disembarrass 705
disembodied 317
disembody
decompose 49
disperse 73
spiritualize 317
disembogue *emit* 295
eject 297
flow out 348
disembowel 297, 301, 361
disembroil 60
disenable 158
disenchant
discover 480*a*
dissuade 616
displease 830
disencumber 705
disendow 756
disengage *detach* 44
facilitate 705
liberate 750
disengaged *to let* 763
disentangle
separate 44
arrange 60
unroll 313
decipher 522
facilitate 705
liberate 750
disenthrall 750
disenthrone 756
disentitle 925
disespouse 905
disestablish
displace 185
abrogate 756
disesteem
disrespect 929
censure 932
disfavor *oppose* 708
hate 898
disrespect 929
view with–932
disfigure *deface* 241
injure 659
deform 846
blemish 848
disfranchise 925
disfurnish 226
disgorge *emit* 297
flow out 348
restore 790
pay 807
disgrace *shame* 874
dishonor 940
sense of–879
disgraceful *vice* 945
disgruntle 509
disgruntled 509
disguise *conceal* 528
mask 530
falsify 544
untruth 546
disguised
(*see* disguise)
–in drink 959
disgust *taste* 395
offensive 830
weary 841
dislike 867
hatred 898
–of life 837
disgusting
(*see* disgust)
dish *destroy* 162
plate 191
scoop out 252
food 298
–of tea 892
dishabille
undress 225
unprepared 674
dishearten
dissuade 616
pain 830
discontent 832
deject 837
dished 732
disherison 789
dishevel *loose* 47
disorder 61
disperse 73
intermix 219
dishevelment 59
(*see* dishevel)
dishing 252
dishonest *false* 544
base 940
dishonor
disrepute 874
disrespect 929
baseness 940
–bills 808
dishwater 653
disillusion 509
disinclination 867
disincline
dissuade 616
dislike 867
disinclined 603
disinfect *purify* 652
restore 660
disinfectant 388, 662
disingenuous
false 544
dishonorable 940
disinherit 782, 783, 789
disinheritance 789
disintegrate
separate 44
decompose 49
pulverize 330
disintegration 49
disinter *exhume* 363
discover 480*a*
disinterested 942
disinvigorate 158
disjoin 44
disjointed *disorder* 59
powerless 158
feeble 575
disjointure 44
disjunction 44
disjunctive 70
disk (*see* disc)
diskindness 907
dislike 867
reluctance 603
hate 898
dislimb 44
dislocate *separate* 44
put out of joint 61
dislocated *disorder* 59
dislodge
displace 185
eject 297
disloyal 940
dismal *depressing* 830
dejected 837
–universal hiss 930
dismantle *destroy* 162
divest 226
render useless 645
injure 659
disuse 678
dismask 529
dismast
render useless 645
injure 659
disuse 678
dismay 860
dismember
separate 44
disperse 73
execute 972
dismemberment 972
dismiss *discard* 678
liberate 750
abrogate 756
relinquish 782
punish 972
–from the mind 452, 458
dismount *arrive* 292
descend 306
render useless 645
disniche 185
disobedience 742
nonobservance 773
disoblige 907
disomatous 90
disorder *confusion* 59
derange 61
turbulent 173
disease 655
–ed intellect 503
disorderly
unprincipled 945
disorganize
derange 61
destroy 162
spoil 659
disorganized 59
disorientation 279
disown 536
disowned 782
dispansion 194
disparage
underrate 483
disrespect 929
dispraise 932
detract 934
disparagement 908
disparate 15
disparity *different* 15
dissimilar 18
disagreeing 24
unequal 28
isolated 44
dispart 44
dispassionate 826
–opinion 484
dispatch *eject* 297
eat 298
kill 361
message 527
news 532
epistle 592

distrain *take* 789
  appraise 812
  attach 969
distrait 458
distraught 475, 503
distress *distraint* 789
  poverty 804
  affliction 828
  cause pain 830
  signal of–669
distribute *arrange* 60
  disperse 73
  type 591
  allot 786
distribution
  (*see* distribute)
distributor
  electrical 272
district
  to partition 44
  area 181
  –*court* 966
distrust *disbelief* 485
  fear 860
distrustful 487
disturb *derange* 61
  change 140
  displace 185
  agitate 315
  excite 824
  distress 828, 830
disturbance
  disorder 59
disunion
  disagreement 24
  separation 44
  disorder 59
  discord 713
disunite *separate* 44
  break with 713
disunity 24
disuse *desuetude* 614
  relinquish 624
  unemploy **678**
disused 124, 678
disvaluation 932
disvalue 932
ditch *inclosure* 232
  hollow 252
  trench 259
  water 343
  conduit 350
  defense 717
ditch water 653
ditheism 984
dithyramb *poetry* 597
dithyrambic
  wild 503
ditto *identity* 13
  repetition 104
  say–*to* 488
ditty 415–*bag* 191
diurnal 138
diuturnal 110
diuturnity 110
divagate 279

divan *sofa* 215
  council 696
  throne 747
  tribunal 966
divaricate *differ* 15
  bifurcate 91
  fork 244
  diverge 291
divarication 16a
dive *resort* 189
  swim 267
  plunge 310
  –*into inquire* 461
divellicate 44
diverge
  (*see* divergence)
divergence
  nonuniformity 16a
  difference 15
  dissimilarity 18
  variation 20a
  disagreement 24
  deviation 279
  separation **291**
divers *different* 15
  multiform 81
  many 102
  –*colored* 440
diverse 15
diversiform 81
diversify
  (*see* diversity)
  vary 20a
  change 140
diversion *change* 140
  deviation 279
  pleasure 377
  amusement 840
diversity *difference* 15
  irregular 16a
  dissimilar 18
  multiform 81
  –*of opinion* 489
divert *turn* 279
  deceive 545
  amuse 840
  –*the mind* 452, 458
divertissement
  drama 599
  amusement 840
Dives 803
divest *denude* 226
  take 789
  –*oneself of*
  abrogate 756
  relinquish 782
divestment 226
divide *separate* 44
  part 51
  arrange 60
  arithmetic 85
  bisect 91
  measure 466
  vote 609
  apportion 786
dividend *part* 51

  number 84
  portion 786
dividers 466
divination
  prediction 511
  sorcery 992
divine *predict* 511
  guess 514
  perfect 650
  of God 976, 983,
    983a
  clergyman 996
  –*right authority* 737
  due 924
  –*service* 990
diviner 994
diving 267–*bird* 310
divining rod *sign* 550
  magic 993
Divinity *God* 976
  theology 983
divisible (*see* divide)
  number 84
division (*see* divide)
  part 51
  class 75
  arithmetic 85
  school 542
  election 609
  discord 713
  military 726
divisor 84
divorce *separation* 44
  relinquish 782
  matrimonial **905**
Divorce Court 966
divorcée 905
divulge 529
divulsion 44
diwan 745
dixi 535
Dixie's land 827
dizen 225, 847
dizzard 501
dizziness (*see* dizzy)
dizzy *dim*–*sighted* 443
  confused 458
  vertigo 503
  –*height* 206
  –*round* 312
do *fare* 7
  suit 23
  produce 161
  cheat 545
  act 680
  complete 729
  succeed 731
  I beg 765
  all one can–686
  –*as done by* 906, 942
  –*a service useful* 644
  aid 707
  –*as one pleases* 748
  –*as others do* 82
  –*away with*
    destroy 162

  eject 297
  abrogate 756
  –*battle* 722
  –*business* 625
  –*for destroy* 162
  kill 261
  conquer 731
  punish 972
  –*good* 906
  –*harm* 907
  –*honor* 873
  –*into translate* 522
  –*justice to* 595
  –*like* 19
  –*little* 683
  –*no harm* 648
  –*nothing* 681
  –*nothing but* 136
  –*one's bidding* 743
  –*one's office* 772
  –*over* 223
  –*tell* 508
  –*the work* 686
  –*up* 660
  –*without* 678
  –*wrong* 923
    have to–*with* 680,
      692
    plenty to–682
    thing to–625
doch–an–dorrach
  959
docile *of horses* 370
  learning 539
  willing 602
docimastic 463
docimasy 463
dock *diminish* 36
  cut off 38
  port 189
  shorten 201
  store 636
  tribunal 966
  –*walloper* 269
docked
  incomplete 53
docket *list* 69, 86
  evidence 467
  note 550
  record 551
  schedule 611
  security 771
  on the–454
dockyard 691
doctor
  learned man 492
  prevaricate 544
  improve 658
  restore 660
  remedy 662
  after death the–135
  –*accounts* 811
  when –*s disagree*
    475
doctorate 873
doctorship 873

doctrinaire
  positive 474
  pedant 492
  theorist 514
  affectation 855
  blusterer 887
doctrinal 537
doctrine *tenet* 484
  knowledge 490
document 551
documentary 467
  –*evidence* 467
dodder 160
dodecahedron 244
dodge *follow* 63
  change 140
  shift 264
  deviate 279
  oscillate 314
  pursue 461
  avoid 623
  stratagem 702
  (*deceive* 545)
doe *swift* 274
  deer 366
  female 374
doer *originator* 164
  agent 690
doff 226–*the cap* 894
dog *follow* 63, 281
  animal 366
  male 373
  pursue 622
  wretch 949
  cast to the–s
    destroy 162
  reject 610
  disuse 678
  abrogate 756
  relinquish 782
  –*in manager* 943
  –*in office* 737
  –*s of war* 722
  go to the–s
    destruction 162
  fail 732
  adversity 735
  poverty 804
  hair of–*that bit you*
    959
dogcart 272
dog–cheap 815
dog days 382
doge 745
dogged *obstinate* 606
  valor 861
  sullen 901a
doggedness 606
  (*see* dogged)
dogger 273
doggerel *verse* 597
  ridiculous 851, 853
doggish 895
doghole 189
dog Latin 563
dogma *tenet* 484

431

–on one's
 marrowbones 886
–on one's uppers 879
 get–306
 go–*sink* 306
 calm 826
 go–like a stone 310
 money–807
 take–*lower* 308
 rebuff 874
 humble 879
downcast
 descendent 306
 dejected 837
 –eyes 879
downcome 306
down-easter 188
downfall
 destruction 162
 fall 306
 earth 342
 failure 732
 misfortune 735
down-grade 306
down-hearted 837
downhill *sloping* 217
 descent 306
 go–*adversity* 735
downpour 348
down-reaching 208
downright *absolute* 31
 manifest 525
 sincere 703
downs *uplands* 180
 heights 206
 wolds 344
down-trodden
 submission 725
 vanquished 732
 subject 749
 dejected 837
 disrepute 874
 contempt 930
downwards 306
downy *smooth* 255
 plumose 256
 soft 324
dowry *property* 780
 bequest 784
 provision 803
dowse 276
dowser 994
doxology 990
doxy 962
doyen 128, 130
doyley 652
doze 683
dozen 98
drab *color* 432
 slut 59, 653
 hussy 962
drabble 653
drachm 319
Draco *ruler* 694
 severe 739
draff 653

draft
 (*see also* draught)
 decrement 40a
 traction 285
 drawing 554, 556
 write 590
 abstract 596
 list 611
 plan 626
 physic 662
 combatant 726
 check 800, 805
 –off *displace* 185
 transfer 270
drafted man 726
draft-horse 271
drag *elapse* 109
 carriage 272
 crawl 275
 traction 285
 impediment 706
 –a chain *tedious* 110
 exertion 686
 subjection 749
 –along 106
 –anchor 706
 –into *implicate* 54
 compel 744
 –into open day 531
 –on *endure* 106, 110
 continue 143
 –sail *check* 706
 –sheet 706
 –slow *length*
  long 200
  weary 841
 –through mire
  disrepute 874
  disrespect 929
 –towards *attract* 288
 put on the–275
draggle 285, 653
draggle-tail 59
drag-net *all sorts* 78
dragoman 524
dragon
 monster 83, 366
 violent 173
 irascible 901
dragon fly 366
dragonnade
 attack 716
 punish 972
dragoon *attack* 716
 soldier 726
 compel 744
 insolent 885
 worry 907
drain *dike* 232
 flow out 295
 empty 297
 dry 340
 conduit 350
 waste 638
 clean 652
 unclean 653

 exhaust 789
 dissipate 818
 –into 348
 –of resources 640
 –the cup *drink* 298
 drunken 959
 –the cup of misery
  828
drainage (*see* drain)
drake *male* 373
 fire–423
dram *drink* 298
 weight 319
 pungent 392
 stimulus 615
 –drinking 959
drama 599
dramatic
 musician 416
 drama 599
 ostentation 882
 –author 599
 –poetry 597
dramatis personae
 mankind 372
 play 599
 agents 690
 party 712
dramatist 599
dramatize 599
dramaturgic 882
dramaturgy 599
drap d'or 847
drape 225
draper 225
drapery 225
drastic 171
draught
 (*see also* draft)
 depth 208
 traction 285
 drink 298
 stream of air 349
 delineation 554, 556
 plan 626
 physic 662
 troops 726
 –off 73
draughts *game* 840
draughtsman
 artist 559
Dravidian 372a
draw *compose* 54
 pull 285
 delineate 554, 556
 money 800
 –a bead on 716
 –a curtain 424
 –and quarter 972
 –an inference 480
 –a parallel 9
 –a picture 594
 –aside 279
 –a straight furrow
  939
 –back *regret* 283

 avoid 623
 –breath *refresh* 689
 feeling 821
 relief 834
 –down 153
 –forth *extract* 301
 use 677
 –from 810
 –in 195
 –in one's horns
  tergiversation 607
  humility 879
 –lots 621
 –near *time* 121
 approach 286
 –off *eject* 297
 hinder 706
 take 789
 –off the attention
  458
 –on *time* 121
 event 151
 induce 615
 –on futurity 132
 –out *protract* 110
 late 133
 prlong 200
 extract 301
 discover 480a
 exhibit 525
 diffuse style 573
 –over *induce* 615
 –poker 840
 –profit 775
 –the line 465
 –the pen through
  552
 –the sword
  attack 716
  war 722
 –the teeth of 158
 –the veil 528
 –together *assemble* 72
 cooperate 709
 –towards 288
 –up *order* 58
 stop 265
 write 590
 –up a statement 594
 –upon *money* 800
drawback
 decrement 40a
 evil 619
 imperfection 651
 hindrance 706
 discount 813
drawbridge *way* 627
 escape 671
drawcansir 887
drawee 800
drawer *receptacle* 191
 artist 559
 –of water 690
drawers *garment* 225
drawing
 delineation 554, 556

drawing knife 253
drawing-room
 assembly 72
 room 191
 fashion 852
 –car 272
drawl *prolong* 200
 creep 275
 in speech 583
 sluggish 683
drawn *equated* 27
 –battle
  pacification 723
  incomplete 730
dray 272
dray horse 271
drayman 268
dread 860
dreadful *great* 31
 bad 649
 dire 830
 depressing 837
 fearful 860
dreadless 861
dreadnought
 coat 225
 battleship 726
dream *unsubstantial* 4
 error 495
 fancy 515
 sleep 683
 psychotherapy 992a
 –of *think* 451
 intend 620
 –on other things 458
 golden–858
dreamer
 madman 504
 imaginative 515
dreamlike 4
dreamy
 unsubstantial 4
 inattentive 458
 imaginative 515
 sleepy 683
drear 16
drearisome 16
dreary *uniform* 16
 solitary 87
 melancholy 830, 837
dredge *collect* 72
 extract 301
 raise 307
dredging machine
 307
dregs *remainder* 40
 density 321
 refuse 645
 dirt 653
 –of the people 876
 –of vice 945
drench *drink* 298
 water 337
 physic 370
 redundance 641
 –with physic 662

enhance *increase* 35
   improve 658
enhancement 35
enharmonic 413
enigma *question* 461
   unintelligibility 519
   secret 533
enigmatic
   uncertain 475
   obscure 519
   (*hidden* 528)
enigmatical 520
enjoin 600 *advise* 695
   command 741
   prescribe 926
enjoy *physically* 377
   possess 777
   morally 827
   –a state 7
   –health 654
enjoyment (*see* enjoy)
enkindle *heat* 384
   excite 824
   (*induce* 615)
enlarge *increase* 35
   swell 194
   in writing 573
   liberate 750
   –the mind 537
enlarged views 498
enlighten
   illumine 420
   inform 527
   teach 537
enlightened
   knowledge 490
enlist *engage* 615
   war 722
   commission 755
   –into the service 677
   –under the banners
     of 707
enlisted man 726
enliven *delight* 829
   inspirit 834
   cheer 836
   amuse 840
enmesh 545, 704
enmity 889
ennead 98
enneahedral 98
enneastyle 98
ennoble 873
ennui 841
enormity *crime* 947
enormous *great* 31
   bid 192
   –number 102
enough *much* 31
   no more! 142
   sufficient 639
   moderately 651
   satiety 869
   –and to spare 639
   –in all conscience
     641

–to drive one mad
   830
know when one has
   had–953
enrage *provoke* 830
   aggravate 835
   incense 900
enragé 865
enrapture *excite* 824
   beautify 829
   love 897
enraptured 827
enravish *beatify* 829
enravished 827
enravishment 824
enrich *improve* 658
   wealth 803
   ornament 847
enrobe 225
enroll *list* 86
   record 551
   enlist 722
   commission 755
   –troops 722
ens *essence* 1
ensample 22
ensanguined 361
ensate 253
ensconce *conceal* 528
   safety 664
ensconced
   located 184
ensemble 50
Ens Entium 976
enshrine
   circumscribe 229
   repute 873
   sanctify 987
   –in the memory 505
ensiform 253
ensign *standard* 550
   officer 726
   master 745
   –of authority 747
ensilage 637, 670
enslave 749
ensnare 545
ensphere 227
ens rationis 1, 451
ensue *follow* 63, 117
   happen 151
ensure 474
entablature 210
entail *cause* 153
   tie up property 781
entangle *interlink* 43
   derange 61
   ravel 219
   entrap 545
   embroil 713
entangled *disorder* 59
   –by difficulties 704
entanglement
   (*see* entangle)
   impurity 961
entelechy 161

entente cordiale
   agreement 23
   alliance 714
   friendship 888
enter *list* 86
   go in 294
   note 551
   account 811
   –a profession 625
   –in *converge* 290
   –into an engagement
     768
   –into details
     special 79
     describe 594
   –into the
     composition of 56
   –into the feelings of
     914
   –into the ideas of
     understand 518
     concord 714
   –into the spirit of
     feel 821
     delight 827
   –into one's views 488
   –the lists *attack* 716
     contention 720
   –the mind 451
   –upon 66
enteritis 221
enterology 221
enteropathy 221
enterotomy 221
enterprise
   pursuit 622
   undertaking 676
   commercial–794
enterprising
   energetic 171
   active 682
   courageous 861
entertain
   bear in mind 457
   support 707
   amuse 840
   sociality 892
   –an idea 451
   –an opinion 484
   –doubts 485
   –feeling 821
entertainment
   (*see* entertain)
   repast 298
   pleasure 377
enthrall
   subjection 749
   restraint 751
enthrone 873
enthronement 755
enthusiasm *vigor* 574
   willingness 602
   eagerness 682
   feeling 821
   hope 858
   love 897

enthusiast
   madman 504
   obstinate 606
   active 682
   sports 840
enthusiastic
   imaginative 515
   willing 602
   sensitive 822
   excitable 825
   sanguine 858
enthymeme 476
entice 615
enticement 615
enticing 829
entire *whole* 50
   complete 52
   continuous 69
   –horse 373
entirely *much* 31
entirety (*see* entire)
entitle *name* 564
   give a right 924
entity 1
entomb *inter* 363
   imprison 751
entombment 363
entomology 368
entourage
   situation 183
   surroundings 227
entozoön 193
entrails 221
entrain 293
entrammel 751
entrance
   beginning 66
   ingress 294
   means of access 627
   enrapture 827, 829
   magic 992
   give-to 296
entranced 515
entrancement 824
entrant 710
entrap *deceive* 545
   (*imperil* 665)
entreat 765
entrée *reception* 296
   dish 298
   give the–296
   have the–294
entremet 298
entrepôt *store* 636
   mart 799
entrepreneur 599
entre–sol 191
entrust
   commission 755
   give 784
   credit 805
entry *beginning* 66
   ingress 294
   record 551
entwine *join* 43
   intersect 219

convolve 248
enucleate 522
enumerate 85
   –among 76
enunciate *inform* 527
   affirm 535
   voice 580
envelop 225
envelope *covering* 223
   inclosure 232
envenom *deprave* 659
   exasperate 835
   hate 898
   anger 900
envenomed *bad* 649
   insalubrious 657
   painful 830
   malevolent 907
   –tongue 934
envious 920
   –suspicion 920
environ 227
environment 183,
   227
environs 197
   in such and such
     183
envisage 220
envoy *messenger* 534
   consignee 758
envy 921
enwrap 225
enzyme 320
Eolian harp 417
Eolus 349
eon 106, 110
epacme 62
epact 641
epagoge 476
eparch 694
epact 108
epaulet *badge* 550
   insignia 747
   ornament 847
   decoration 877
epergne 191
ephemera 193
ephemeral 111
ephemerality 111
ephemerid 193
ephemeris
   calendar 114
   record 551
   book 593
ephemeron 111
Ephesian letters 993
ephialtes
   physical pain 378
   hindrance 706
   mental pain 828
ephor 967
epic *descriptive* 594
   poetry 597
epicarp 223
epicedium 839
epicene *multiform* 81

demonstraté 478
−equilibrium 27
established
 permanent 141
 habit 613
−church 983*a*
establishment
 party 712
 shop 799
estafette 268, 534
estaminet 189
estate *condition* 7
 kind 75
 property 780
 come to man's−131
esteem *believe* 484
 approve 931
 in high−928
estimable 648
estimate *number* 85
 measure 466
 adjudge 480
 information 527
−too highly 482
estimation
 (*see* esteem,
 estimate)
estival 382
estop 706
estrade 213
estrange *disjoin* 44
 alienate 889
 hate 898
estranged
 secluded 893
estrapade *attack* 716
 punishment 972
estreat 974
estuary 343
estuation 384
esurient 865
et cetera *add* 37
 include 76
 plural 100
état major 745
etch *furrow* 259
 engraving 558
etching 54, 558
Eternal, The−976
eternal 112
−home 981
−rest 360
 into the−secret 528
eternalize 112
eterne 112
eternity 112 an−110
 launch into−360,
 361
 palace of−543
ether *space* 180
 lightness 320
 rarity 322
 vapor 334
 anesthetic 376
ethereal 4
etheric body 980*a*

etheric double 317
ethical 926
−culture 984
ethicism 984
ethics 926
Ethiop *black* 431
Ethiopian 431
−'s skin
 unchangeable 150
ethnic 984
ethnography 372*a*
ethnology 372
ethology 926
etiolate *bleach* 429
 whiten 430
etiology
 (*see* aetiology)
etiquette *custom* 613
 fashion 852
 ceremony 882
etymologist 492, 562
etymologize 562
etymology 562
etymon *origin* 153
 verbal 562
Eucharist 998
euchology 998
euchre 840 *defeat* 731
eucrasy 41
eudaemonism 910,
 944
eudaemonist 910
eudiometer *air* 338
 salubrity 656
eudiometry 338
eugenics 658
eulogist 935
eulogize 482
eulogy 733, 931
Eumenides
 violence 173
 fury 900
 evildoers 913
 revenge 919
eumerogenesis 161
eunuch 158
eunuchize 158
eupepsia 654
euphemism
 metaphor 521
 affirmation 535
 phrase 566
 style 577, 578
 flattery 933
euphemist
 man of taste 850
 flatterer 935
euphonium 417
euphony *melody* 413
 elegant style 578
euphoria 654
Euphrosyne 836
euphuism
 metaphor 521
 elegant style 577
 affected style 579

affectation 855
euphuize 855
Eurasian 41
eureka! *answer* 462
 discovery 480*a*
Euripus 343
European plan 298
eurythmic 542
eurythmics 242, 537
eurythmy 242
Eusebian 984
Eustachian tube 418
Euterpe 416
euthanasia 360
eutrophy 707
evacuate *quit* 293
 excrete 295
 emit 297
evacuation 299
evade *sophistry* 477
 avoid 623
 not observe 773
 exempt 927
evagation 279
evanescent *small* 32
 transient 111
 little 193
 disappearing 449
evangelical 983*a*,
 985
Evangelists 985
evanid 160
evaporable 334
evaporate
 unsubstantial 4
 transient 111
 vaporize 336
 dry up 340
evaporation
 vaporization 336
 dryness 340
 cloud 353
 preserving 670
evaporator 336
evasion *sophistry* 477
 quirk 481
 concealment 528
 falsehood 544
 untruth 546
 avoidance 623
 escape 671
 cunning 702
 nonobservance 773
 dereliction 927
evasive (*see* evasion)
eve 126 on the−of
 transient 111
 prior 116
 future 121
evection 61
even *uniform* 16
 equal 27
 still more 33
 level 213
 parallel 216
 straight 246

 flat 251
 smooth 255
 although 469
 neutral 628
 in spite of 708
 be−with
 retaliate 718
 pay 807
−course 628
−now 118
−off 27
−so *for all that* 30
 yes 488
−temper 826
−tenor *uniform* 16
 order 58
 regularity 80
−terms 922
 pursue the−tenor
 continue 143
 avoid 623
 business 625
even−handed
 just 922
 honorable 939
evening 126
−dress 225
−star 423
 shades of−422
evenness (*see* even)
 symmetry 242
evensong 126, 990
event 151 *bout* 720
 in the−of
 circumstance 8
 eventuality 151
 destiny 152
 supposition 514
 justified by the−937
eventful 151
 remarkable 642
 stirring 682
eventide 126
eventual *future* 121
eventuality **151**
eventually *effect* 154
eventuate 151
ever *invariable* 16
 perpetually 112
−and anon 136
−changing 149
−recurring 104
−so little 32
−so long 110
−so many 102
everduring 112
evergreen
 continuous 69
 lasting 110
 always 112
 fresh 123
 plant 367, 369
everlasting
 perpetual 112
 destined 152
−fire 982

−life 152
evermore 112
eversible 140
eversion 140, 218
evert 140, 218
every *general* 78
 periodic 138
 at−turn 186
−day *conformity* 82
 frequent 136
 habit 613
−description 81
−hand against one
 891
−inch 50
−other 138
−whit 52
 in−mouth
 assent 488
 news 532
 repute 873
 in−quarter 180
 in−respect 194
 on−side 22
everybody 78
every one 78
−his due 922
−in his turn 148
everywhere *space* 180
 presence 186
evict 297
evidence **467**
 manifestation 525
 disclosure 529
 ocular−446
evident *visible* 446
 certain 474
 manifest 525
evidential 467
evil *harm* **619**
 badness 649
 demoniac 980
 impious 988
−day *adversity* 735
−eye *vision* 441
 malevolence 907
 disapprobation 932
 spell 993
−favored 846
−fortune 735
−genius 980
−hour 135
−one 978
−plight 735
−spirits **980**
−star 649
 prepare for−673
 through−report etc.
 604*a*
evildoer 913, 975
evildoing 945
evil−minded
 malevolent 907
 vicious 945
evil speaking
 malediction 908

censure 932
detraction 934
evince *show* 467
prove 478
disclose 529
evirate 158
eviscerate *eject* 297
extract 301
eviscerated 4
eviternal 112
evoke *cause* 153
call upon 765
excite 824
evolution
numerical 85
production 161
motion 264
circuition 311
turning out **313**
organization 357
training 673
action 680
military –s 722
evolutionary 264,
313
evolve *discover* 480a
evolved from 154
(*and see* evolution)
evolvement 313
evulgate 531
evulsion 301
evviva! 931
ewe *sheep* 366
female 374
ewer 191
ex–animo 602
–dono 784
–more 613
–officio *officer* 694
authority 737
duty 924
–parte 467
–post facto 122, 133
–tempore *instant* 113
occasion 134
–voto 768
exacerbate
increase 35
exasperate 173
pervert 659
aggravate 835
exact *similar* 17
copy 21
true 494
literal 516
style 572
require 741
tax 812
insolence 885
claim 924, 926
–meaning 516
–memory 505
–observance 772
–truth 494
exacting *severe* 739
discontented 832

grasping 865
exaction (*see* exact)
undue 925
exactly *literally* 19
just so 488
exactness (*see* exact)
exaggeration
increase 35
expand 194
overestimate 482
magnify **549**
misrepresent 555
exalt *increase* 35
elevate 307
extol 931
(*boast* 884)
–one's horn 873
exalted *high* 206
repute 873
noble 875
magnanimous 942
examination
(*see* examine)
evidence 467
on–463
undergo–461
examine
attend to 457
inquire 461
–the books
accounts 811
example *pattern* 22
instance 82
bad–949
good–948
make an–of 974
set a good–944
exanimate *dead* 360
supine 683
exanthema 655
exarch 745
exasperate
exacerbate 173
aggravate 835
enrage 900
excavate 252
excavation 252
execation 442
exceed *surpass* 33
remain 40
transgress 303
intemperance 954
exceedingly
(*greatly* 31)
excel *surpass* 33
–in *skillful* 698
excellence
goodness 648
virtue 944
excellency *title* 877
excelsior 305
except *subduct* 38
exclude 55
reject 610
exception
unconformity 83

qualification 469
exemption 777a
disapproval 932
take–qualify 469
resent 900
exceptionable
bad 649
guilty 947
exceptional
unimitated 20
extraneous 57
uncomfortable 83
in an–degree 31
exceptions 901, 901a
excern 297
excerpt 551, 609
excerpta *parts* 51
compendium 596
selections 609
excerption 609
excess *remainder* 40
redundance 641
intemperance 954
excessive *great* 31
exchange
reciprocity 12
interchange 148
saloon 189
transfer 783
barter 794
mart 799
bill of–771
–blows etc.
retaliation 718
battle 720
Exchequer 802
Baron of–967
Court of–966
–bill 800
excise 812
exciseman 965
excision 38
excitability
excitement **825**
irascibility 901
excitant 171
excitation 824
excitative 171
excite *energy* 171
violence 173
impassion 824
–an impression 375
–attention 457
–desire 865
–hope 811
–love 897
excited 173
–fancy 515
excitement 824, 825
anger 900
exclaim 411
–against 932
exclamation
typography 550
utterance 580
exclude *sift* 42

leave out 55
reject 610
prohibit 761
banish 893
exclusion 55, 57
exclusive *simple* 42
omitting 55
special 79
irregular 83
forbidding 761
–of 38
–possession 777
–thought 457
excogitate
ruminate 450
thought 451
imagination 515
excommunicate
banish 893
curse 908
rite 998
(*exclude* 55)
excoriate 226
excrement
excretion 299
dirt 653
excrescence
projection 250
blemish 848
excreta *excretion* 299
dirt 653
excretion 297, **299**
excretory 295, 299,
350
excruciating
physical pain 378
mental pain 830
exculpate *forgive* 918
vindicate 937
acquit 970
excursion 266, 311
excursionist 268
excursive
deviating 279
–style 573
excursus 595
excuse *plea* 617
exempt 777a
forgive 918
exempt 927a
vindicate 937
execrable *bad* 649
offensive 830
execrate *hate* 898
curse 908
execute *kill* 361
(*see* execution)
execution *music* 416
action 680
conduct 692
signing 771
observance 772
punishment 972
carry into–
complete 729
put in–

undertaking 676
executioner 975
executive *conduct* 692
directing 693
authority 737
judicature 965
executor 690
to one and his–s
etc. *property* 780
exegesis 522
exegetical 522
exemplar 22
exemplary 944
exemplify *quote* 82
illustrate 522
exempt *free* 748
dispensation 927a
–from *absent* 187
unpossessed 777a
exemption
exception 83
qualification 469
deliverance 672
permission 760
nonpossession **777a**
nonliability **927a**
exenterate 297
exequatur 755
exequies 363
exercise
operation 170
teach 537
task 625
use 677
act 680
exert 686
(*prepare* 673)
–authority 737
–discretion 600
–power 157
–the intellect 451
exercises 990
exercitation
(*see* exercise)
exergue 231
exert *use* 677
–authority 737
–oneself 686
exertion *physical* 171
effort **686**
exertive 170
exfoliate 226
exhalation
ejection 297
excretion 299
vapor 336
breathing 349, 353
odor 398
exhale 349
exhaust *paralyze* 158
deflate 195
of an automobile 272
waste 638
fatigue 688
complete 729
drain 789

to one's–525
wry–378
face cloth
  cleanness 652
face guard 717
facet 220
facetiae 842
facetious 842
facia 234
facile *willing* 602
  irresolute 605
  easy 705
facile princeps 33
facilitate 705
facility *skill* 698
  easy **705**
facing *covering* 223
  lining 224
facinorous 945
façon de parler
  figure of speech 521
  exaggeration 549
facsimile *copy* 21
  duplication 90
  representation 554
fact *existence* 1
  event 151
  certainty 474
  truth 494
  in–535
faction *company* 72
  party 712
  feud 713
factious 24, 713
factitious 545, 546
factor *numerical* 84
  agent 690
  director 694
  consignee 758
  (*merchant* 797)
factory 691
factotum *agent* 690
  manager 694
  employé 758
facts *evidence* 467
  summary of–594
factual 1
facula 420
faculties 450
  in possession of
  one's–502
faculty *power* 157
  profession 625
  skill 698
facundity 582
fad *bias* 481
  caprice 608
faddle 683
fade *vanish* 4
  transient 111
  become old 124
  droop 160
  grow dim 422
  lose color 429
  disappear 449
  spoil 659

–away *cease* 142
  disappear 449
–from the memory
  506
–out 129
fadeless 873
fadge 23
faeces [*see* feces]
fag *labor* 686
  fatigue 688
  drudge 690
  –end *remainder* 40
  end 67
fagot *bundle* 72
  fuel 388
  –voter 4
Fahrenheit scale
  490d
faïence 557
fail *droop* 160, 655
  shortcoming 304
  be confuted 479
  not succeed 732
  not observe 773
  not pay 808
  dereliction 927
failing (*see* fail)
  incomplete 53
  insufficient 640
  vice 945
  guilt 947
  –heart 837
  –luck 735
  –memory 506
  –sight 443
  –strength 160
failure 732
fain *willing* 602
  compulsive 744
  wish 865
fainéant 683
faint
  small in degree 32
  impotent 158
  weak 160
  sound 405
  dim 422
  color 429
  swoon 688
  damn with–praise
  930, 932, 934
  –heart *fear* 860
  cowardice 862
  wooing 902
faintness *sound* **405**
  (*see* faint)
fair *in degree* 31
  pale 429
  white 430
  wise 498
  important 643
  good 648
  moderate 651
  mart 799
  beautiful 845
  just 922

honorable 939
  by–*means or foul*
  631
  –chance 472
  –copy *copy* 21
  writing 590
  –field *occasion* 134
  freedom 748
  –game 857
  –name 873
  –play 922, 923
  –question 461
  –sex 374
  –weather 734
  pleasurableness 829
  –weather sailor 701
  –wind 705
  –words 894
  in a–way
  tending 176
  probable 472
  convalescent 658
  prosperous 734
  hopeful 858
fairing 784
fairly *intrinsically* 5
  slightly 643
  get on–736
fair–spoken
  courtesy 894
  flattery 933
fairway 267
fairy *fanciful* 515
  fay 979
  imp 980
  –lore 993
  –tale 594
  fabrication 546
fairyism 979
fairyland 515
fait accompli
  certain 474
  complete 729
faith *belief* 484
  hope 858
  honor 939
  piety 987
  declaration of–983
  –cure 662
  –curer 984
  –healing 662
  i'–535
  keep–with
  observe 772
  plight–*promise* 768
  love 902
  true–*orthodox* 983a
  want of–
  incredulity 487
  irreligious 989
faithful (*see* faith)
  like 17
  copy 21
  exact 494
  obedient 743
  –memory 505

faithless *false* 544
  dishonorable 940
  skeptical 989
fake *imitation* 19
  concoct 544
  swindle 545
  untruth 546
faker 548, 683, 797
fakir 804, 955, 996
falcade 309
falcate *pointed* 244
  carved 245
falchion 727
Falcidian law 780
falciform (*see* falcate)
falcon 792
falconet 727
faldstool 215
fall *autumn* 126
  happen 151
  perish 162
  slope 217
  regression 283
  descend 306
  die 360
  fail 732
  adversity 735
  vice 945
  –a cursing 908
  –a prey to
  defeated 732
  subject 749
  –asleep 683
  –astern *rear* 235
  regress 283
  –at one's feet 725
  –away 195
  –back *return* 283
  recede 287
  relapse 661
  –back upon *use* 677
  defense 717
  –dead *die* 360
  –down *collapse* 304
  worship 990
  –down before 928
  –flat on the ear 843
  –foul of *blow* 276
  hinder 706
  oppose 708
  discord 713
  attack 716
  contention 720
  censure 932
  –from one's high
  estate
  adversity 735
  disrepute 874
  –from the lips 582
  –in *order* 58
  continuity 69
  event 151
  –in love with 897
  –in price 815
  –in the way of 186

–in with *agree* 23
  conform 82
  converge 290
  discover 480a
  concord 714
  consent 762
  –into *conversion* 144
  river 348
  –into a custom
  conform to 82
  –into a habit 613
  –into a passion 900
  –into a trap 547
  –into decay 659
  –into oblivion 506
  –into raptures 827
  –of day 125
  –off *decrease* 36
  deteriorate 659
  –off again 661
  –of snow 383
  –of the curtain 67
  –of the leaf 126
  –of the mercury 338
  –on one's knees
  submit 725
  servile 886
  gratitude 916
  worship 990
  –out *happen* 151
  quarrel 713
  enmity 889
  –short *inferior* 34
  contract 195
  shortcoming 304
  –through *fail* 732
  –to *eat* 298
  take in hand 676
  do battle 722
  –to dust 328
  –to one's lot
  event 151
  chance 156
  receive 785
  duty 926
  –to pieces
  disjunction 44
  destruction 162
  brittle 328
  –to the ground
  be confuted 479
  fail 732
  –to work 686
  –under *inclusion* 76
  subjection 749
  –under one's notice
  457
  –upon *discover* 480a
  unexpected 508
  devise 626
  attack 716
  –upon the ear 418
  have to–back upon
  provision 637
  let–*lower* 308
  inform 527

water–348
fallacy *sophistry* 477
  error 495
  show the–of 497
fallen angel
  bad man 949
  Satan 978
fallible *uncertain* 475
  sophistical 477
falling–action 154
  –star *world* 318
  luminary 423
  –weather 348
fallow
  unproductive 169
  yellow 436
  unready 674
  inactive 681
false *sophistry* 477
  error 495
  untrue 544, 546
  spurious 925
  dishonorable 940
  –alarm 669
  –coloring
    misinterpretation 523
    falsehood 544
  –construction 523, 544
  –doctrine 984
  –expectation 509
  –hearted 940
  –impression 495
  –light *vision* 443
  –money 800
  –ornament 851
  –plea *untruth* 546
    plea 617
  –position 704
  –pretenses *steal* 791
  –prophet
    disappoint 509
    (pseudo–revelation) 986
  –reasoning 477
  –scent *error* 495
    mislead 538
  –shame 855
  –statement 546
  –step 732
  –teaching 538
  –witness *deceiver* 548
    detraction 934
falsehood 544, 546
falsetto *squeak* 410
  music 415
  want of voice 581
falsification 555
falsify *error* 495
  falsehood 544, 546
  misrepresent 555
  –accounts 811
  –one's hope 509
falsity (*see* false)
falter *slow* 275

stammer 583
  hesitate 605
  slip 732
  hopeless 859
  fear 860
fame *greatness* 31
  memory 505
  renown 873
familiar *known* 490
  habitual 613
  sociable 892
  affable 894
  spirit 979, 980
  on–terms 888
familiarity
  (*see* familiar)
familiarize *teach* 537
  habit 613
Familist 984
familistery 712
family *kin* 11
  pedigree 69
  class 75
  ancestors 166
  posterity 167
  domestic 221
  party 712
  –circle 892
  –jars 713
  –likeness 17
  –tie 11
  –tree 166
  happy–714
  in the bosom of one's–221
  in the–way 161
famine 640
  –price 814
famine–stricken 640
famish *stingy* 819
  fasting 956
famished
  insufficient 640
  hungry 865
famous 873
famously *much* 31
fan *strike* 276
  blow 349
  cool 385
  refresh 689
  stimulate 824
  enthusiast 840
  –into a flame
    anger 900
  –the embers 505
  –the flame
    violence 173
    heat 384
    aid 707
    excite 824
  flirt a–855
fanatic *dogmatist* 474
  madman 504
  imaginative 515
  zealot 682
  religious–988

fanatical
  dogmatic 474
  misjudging 481
  insane 503
  emotional 821
  excitable 825
  heterodox 984
  overrighteous 988
fanaticism
  dogmatism 474
  obstinacy 606
  (*see* fanatical)
fanciful
  imaginative 515
  capricious 608
  ridiculous 853
  –projector 515
fancy *think* 451
  idea 453
  believe 484
  suppose 514
  imagine 515
  caprice 608
  choice 609
  pugilism 726
  wit 842
  desire 865
  love 897
  after one's–850
  –dog 366
  –price 814
  –stocks 800
  indulge one's–609
  take a–to
    delight in 827
    desire 865
  take one's
    –*please* 829
fandango 840
fane 1000
fanfare *loudness* 404
  celebration 883
fanfaron 887
fanfaronade 884
fangs *venom* 663
  rule 737
  retention 781
fanlight 260
fanlike 202
fannel 999
fanon 999
fan–shaped 194
fantasia 415
fantastic *odd* 83
  absurd 497
  imaginative 515
  capricious 608
  bad taste 851
  ridiculous 853
fantasy
  imagination 515
  desire 865
fantoccini
  representation 554
  drama 599
faquir (*see* fakir)

far–and near 180
  –and wide 31, 180, 196
  –as the eye can see 180
  –away 196
  –be it from
    unwilling 603
    deprecation 766
  –between
    disjunction 44
    few 103
    interval 198
  –from it *unlike* 18
    shortcoming 304
    no 536
  –from the truth 546
  –off 196
farad 490d
farce *absurdity* 497
  untruth 546
  drama 599
  wit 842
  ridiculous 853
  mere–
    unimportant 643
    useless 645
farceur *actor* 599
  humorist 844
farcical *absurd* 497
  ridiculous 853
fardel *bundle* 72
  hindrance 706
fare *state* 7
  food 298
  price 812
  bill of–*list* 86
farewell
  departure 293
  relinquishment 624
  loss 776
  –to greatness 874
far–famed 31, 873
far–fetched 10
far–flung 180
far–gone *much* 31
  insane 503
  spoiled 654
farina 330
farinaceous 330
farm *till* 371
  productiveness 636
  property 780
  rent 788
farmer 371
  afternoon–683
farmhouse 189
faro 621–bank 621
farrago 59
farrier 370
farrow *produce* 161
  litter 167
  multitude 102
farse 998
far–sighted
  vision 441

foresight 510
farther 196
  (*see* further)
farthing *quarter* 97
  worthless 643
  coin 800
  –candle 422
farthingale 225
fasces 747
fascia *band* 205
  circle 247
fasciate 247
fascicle 51, 72
fasciculated 72
fascinate
  influence 615
  excite 824
  please 829
  astonish 870
  love 897
  conjure 992
fascinated
  pleased 827
fascination
  (*see* fascinate)
  infatuation 825
  desire 870
  (*spell* 993)
fascinator *wrap* 384
fascine 72
fash 830
fashion *state* 7
  form 240
  custom 613
  method 627
  ton **852**
  create 976
  after a–*middling* 32
  after this–627
  be in the–488
  follow the–82
  for–'s sake 852
  man of–852
  set the
    –*influence* 175
    authority 737
fast *joined* 43
  steadfast 150
  rapid 274
  fashionable 852
  intemperate 954
  not eat 956
  worship 990
  rite 998
  –and loose
    sophistry 477
    falsehood 544
    irresolute 605
    tergiversation 607
    caprice 608
  –asleep 683
  –by 197
  –day 640, 956
  –friend 890
  –man *fop* 854
    libertine 962

446

stick–704
fasten *join* 43
  hang 214
  restrain 751
–a quarrel upon 713
–on the mind 451
–upon 789
fastening 45
fast–handed 819
fastidious 868
  censorious 932
fastidiousness 868
fastigium 210
fasting *worship* 990
  penance 952
  abstinence **956**
fastness *asylum* 666
  defense 717
fat *corpulent* 192
  expansion 194
  unctuous 355
  oleaginous 356
  in the fire
  disorder 59
  violence 173
–of the land
  pleasure 377
  enough 639
  prosperity 734
  intemperance 95
  kill the–ted calf
  celebration 883
  sociality 892
fata Morgana
  ignis fatuus 423
fatal 361–*disease* 655
–gift of beauty 845
fatalism 601
fatality 601
fate *end* 67
  necessity 601
  predetermination
  611
  chance 621
  be one's–156
  sure as–474
fateful 601
Fates 601
fat–headed 499
father *eldest* 128
  paternity 166
  priest 996
  Apostolical–s 985
–upon 155
  gathered to one's–s
  360
  heavy–599
Father, God the–976
fatherhood 166
fatherland 181, 189,
  342
fatherless 158
fatherly 906
fathership 166
Fathers, the–983
fathom *length* 200

investigate 461
  solve 462
  measure 466
  discover 480a
  knowledge 490
fathomless 208
fatidical 511
fatigation 688
fatigue **688**
  (*weariness* 841)
fatihah 66
fatiloquent 511
fatling 298
fatness (see fat)
fatras 643
fatten *expand* 194
  improve 658
  prosperous 734
–on *parasite* 886
–upon *feed* 298
fatuity 499
fat–witted 499
faubourg 227
fauces 231
faucet 263
faugh! 867
fault *break* 70
  rift 198
  error 495
  imperfection 651
  failure 732
  vice 945
  guilt 947
  at–*uncertain* 475
  ignorant 491
  unskillful 699
  find–with 932
fault–finder 832
faultless *perfect* 650
  innocent 946
faulty *imperfect* 651
faun 978
fauna 366
fault: comme il–
  taste 850
  fashion 852
fauteuil 215
fautor 890
faux pas *failure* 732
  misconduct 947
  intrigue 961
favaginous 252
faveolate 252
favilious 432
favonian 349
favor *resemble* 17
  badge 550
  letter 592
  aid 707
  indulgence 740
  permit 760
  gift 784
  partiality 923
  appearances in–of
  472
–with 784

  get into–
  friendship 888
  love 897
  in–*repute* 873
  approbation 931
  in–of *approve* 931
  under–of 760
  view with–906
favorable
  occasion 134
  willing 602
  good 648
  aid 707
–*prospect* 472
–to 709
  take a–turn
  improve 658
  prosperity 734
favorably *well* 618
favorer 890
favorite *pleasing* 829
  beloved 897, **899**
favoritism
  friendship 888
  wrong 923
favose 252
fawn *animal* 366
  brown 433
  cringe 886
  flatter 933
fawn–colored 433
fawning *servile* 746
fay 979
faze *disconcert* 706
  bother 830
  daunt 860
fealty *obedience* 743
  duty 926
  respect 928
fear **860**
fearful *incredible* 31
  painful 830
  timid 862
fearfully *much* 31
  wonderfully 870
fearless *hope* 858
  courage 861
feasible *possible* 470
  easy 705
feast *period* 138
  repast 298
  pleasure 377
  revel 840
  rite 998
–one's eyes 897
feast of reason
  conversation 588
–and flow of soul
  sociality 892
feat *action* 680
  courage **861**
–of arms 720
–of strength 159
feather *class* 75
  tuft 256
  light 320

  irresolution 605
  trifle 643
  ornament 847
  decoration 877
–in one's cap
  honor 873
  decoration 877
–in the scale 643
–in one's nest
  prepare 673
  prosperity 734
  wealth 803
  economy 817
  selfish 943
–the oar 698
  hear a–drop 403
  in full–*prepared* 673
  prosperous 734
  rich 803
  in high–*health* 654
  cheerful 884
  pleased with a–840
feather bed 324
feathered tribes 366
feathery 149, 256
featly 682
feature *character* 5
  component 56
  form 240
  appearance 448
  lineament 234, 550
feaze 60
  (see also faze)
febricity 382
febrifacient 383
febrific 382
febrifuge 662
febrile 382, 825
fecal 299, 653
feces *excretion* 299
  foulness 653
feculence 653
fecund 168
fecundate 161
federal 48
–currency 800
federalism 737
federalists 712
federate 48, 712
federation 712
fee *possession* 777
  property 780
  pay 809
  reward 973
feeble *weak* 160
  illogical 477
  (*scanty* 32)
feeble–minded
  imbecile 499
  irresolute 605
feebleness *style* **575**
feed *eat* 298
  fodder 370
  fuel 388
  supply 637
–the flame 707

fee–faw–fum
  bugbear 860
feel *sense* 375
  touch 379
  emotion 821
–for *try* 463
  benevolence 906
  pity 914
–*grief* 915
–one's way *essay* 675
  caution 864
–the pulse 461
–the want of 865
feeler 379
  inquiry 461
  experiment 463
feeling 821
–of sense 916
feet *low* 207
  walkers 266
  at one's–*near* 197
  subjection 749
  humility 879
  fall at one's–
  submit 725
  fall on one's–
  prosper 734
  lick the–of
  servile 886
  light upon one's–
  safe 664
  spring to one's–307
  throw oneself at
  the–
  of *entreat* 765
feign 544, 546
feigned 545
feint 545
felicitate 896
felicitious *agreeing* 23
–*style* 23
  skillful 698
  successful 731
  pleasant 829
felicity *elegance* 578
  happiness 827
feline *cat* 366
  stealthy 528
  cunning 702
fell *destroy* 162
  mountain 206
  lay flat 213
  skin 223
  knock flat 251
  lay low 308
  plain 344
  dire 860
  malevolent 907
fellah 876
fellow *similar* 17
  equal 27
  companion 88
  dual 89
  man 373
  scholar 492
–*commoner* 541

ugly 846
cut a–*repute* 873
display 882
–to oneself 515
–of speech 521
exaggeration 549
poor–874
figure flinger 994
figurehead *sign* 550
representation 554
figurine 554
figuriste 559
filaceous 205
filament 205
filamentiferous 205
filamentous 256
filch 791
filcher 762
file *subduct* 38
arrange 60
row 69
assemblage 72
list 86
reduce 195
smooth 255
pulverize 330
record 551
store 636
soldiers 726
–a claim 969
–exceptions 469
–leader 694
–off *march* 266
diverge 291
on–551
file–fire 716
filgurate 420
filial 167
filiality 155
filiate 155
filiation
consanguinity 11
attribution 155
posterity 167
filibeg 225
filibuster *delay* 133
impede 706
obstructionist 710
plunder 791
thief 792
filibusterer 707, 710
filibustering 791
filibusterous 708
filiciform 242
filicoid 242
filiform 205
filigree 219
filings 330
filius nullius 925
filius terrae 876
fill *complete* 52
occupy 186
contents 190
stuff 224
provision 637
remedy 662

eat one's–957
–an office
business 625
government 737
–ed to overflowing
641
–one's pocket 803
–out *expand* 194
–the bill 729
–time 106
–up *compensate* 30
compose 54
close 261
restore 660
–up the time
inaction 681
have one's–
enough 639
satiety 869
fille–de chambre 746
–de joie 962
filled
–to overflowing 641
fillet *band* 45
filament 205
circle 247
indication 550
ornament 847
filling *stuffing* 224
fillip *impulse* 276
propulsion 284
stimulus 615
excite 824
filly 271
film *layer* 204
opaque 426
semitransparent 427
–over the eyes
dim sight 443
ignorant 491
filmy *texture* 329
filter *percolate* 295
clean 652
filth 653
filthy 653
filtrate 652
filtration 490d
fimbria 256
fimbriated 256
fimetarious 653
fimicolous 653
fin 267
final *ending* 67
completing 729
commanding 741
court of–appeal 474
–cause 620
–stroke 729
–touch 729
have the–word 153
finale *end* 67
completion 729
finality 67, 729
finally *for good* 141
eventually 151
on the whole 476

finance *money* 800
account 811
minister of–801
financier 639, 801
finch 366
find *eventuality* 151
adjudge 480
discover 480a
acquire 775
–a clue to 480a
–credence 484
–in *provide* 637
–it in one's heart 602
–means 632
–one's account in
644
–oneself *be* 1
present 186
–one's way 731
–one's way into 294
–out 480a
–the cause of 522
–the key of 522
–the meaning 522
–to one's cost 509
–vent 671
fin–de–siècle 123
finding *judgment* 480
lawsuit 959
–store 799
fine *small* 32
large 192
thin 203
rare 322
not raining 340
exact 494
good 648
beautiful 845
adorned 847
proud 878
mulct 974
–air 656
–arts 554
–by degrees 30
–feather *strong* 159
healthy 654
–feeling 850
–frenzy 515
–gentleman *fop* 854
proud 878
–grain 329
–lady 854, 878
–powder 330
–talking *overrate* 482
boast 884
–time of it 734
–voice 580
–writing 482, 577
in–*end* 67
after all 476
one–morning 106
some–morning 119
finedraw 660
fine–fingered 698
fineness (see fine)
finery *ornament* 847

vulgarity 851
fine–spoken
courtesy 894
flattery 933
finespun *thin* 203
sophistry 477
finesse *tact* 698
artifice 702
taste 850
(*deception* 545)
finest the–*police* 664
finestill 336
fine–toned 413
finger *touch* 379
hold 781
at one's–s' end
near 197
know 490
remember 505
–in the pie *cause* 153
interfere 228
act 680
active 682
cooperate 709
–on the lips
aphony 581
taciturnity 585
–'s breadth 203
lay the–on
point out 457
discover 480a
life a–680
not lift a–681
point the–at 457
turn round one's
little–737
fingerling 193
finger post 550
finger print
evidence 467
dactylology 550
finger stall 223
fingle–fangle 643
finical *trifling* 643
affected 855
fastidious 868
finicality 457
finicking *trifling* 643
affected 855
fastidious 868
finis 67
finish *end* 67
symmetry 242
skill 698
complete 729
finished *absolute* 31
perfect 650
skilled 698
finishing–stroke 361
–touch 729
finite 32
finnan haddie 298
Finno–Ugric 372a
fiord 343, 490a
fir *tree* 367
–balsam 400

fire *energy* 171
eject 297
heat 382
make hot 384
fuel 388
shoot 406
dismiss 756
excite 834, 825
between two–s 665
catch–384
passion 820
–and fury 900
–and sword 162
–at 716
–a volley 716
–off 284
–of genius 498
–the blood 824
–up *excite* 825
anger 900
go through–and
water
resolution 604
perseverance 604a
courage 861
hell–982
on–382
open–*begin* 66
play with–863
take–*excitable* 825
angry 900
under–*danger* 665
war 722
fire alarm 550, 669
fire annihilator 385
firearms 727
fireball *fuel* 388
arms 727
fire balloon 273
fire barrel 388
fire bell 669
firebox 386
firebrand *fuel* 388
instigator 615
dangerous man 667
incendiary 913
fire brigade 385
fire bug 384, 913, 949
firecracker 406, 840
fire curtain
theater 599
firedamp 663
fire department 385
firedog 386
firedrake 423
fire–eater
courage 861
fighter 726
jingo 885
blusterer 887
fire–eating
rashness 863
insolence 885
fire engine 385
fire escape 671
fire extinguisher 385

firefly 423
fireless cooker 386
fire light 422
firelock 727
fireman *stoker* 268
  extinguisher 385
fire-new 123
fireplace 386
fireproof 385 *safe* 664
fireside 189
firewood 388
firework *fire* 382
  luminary 423
  amusement 840
fire worship 382, 991
fire worshipper 984
firing *fuel* 388
  explosion 406
firkin 191
firm *junction* 43
  stable 150
  hard 323
  resolute 604
  partnership 712
  merchant 797
  brave 861
  -belief 484
  -hold 781
  stand-719
firman *decree* 741
  permit 760
firmness (*see* firm)
first 66 at-sight 448
  come back to-love
   607
  -and foremost 66
  -and last 87
  -blow 716
  -blush *morning* 125
  vision 441
  appearance 448
  manifest 525
  -cause 976
  -come first served
   609a
  -fiddle
  importance 642
  proficient 700
  authority 737
  -impression 66
  -line 234
  -move 66
  -opportunity 132
  -stage 66
  -stone
  preparation 673
  attack 716
  -that comes 609a
  great-Cause 976
  in the-place 153
  of the-water
  best 648
  repute 873
  on the-summons
   741
firstborn 124, 128

first-class *best* 648
first fruits 154
firstling *eldest* 128
  effect 154
first-rate
  important 642
  excellent 648
  man-of-war 726
firth 343
fisc 802
fiscal 800
fiscalize 800
fish *food* 298
  sport 361, 622
  animal 366
  zoology 368
  -for *seek* 461
  experiment 463
  desire 865
  -for compliments
   880
  -fry 840
  -glue 352
  -hatchery 370, 636
  -in the air 645
  -in troubled waters
  difficult 704
  discord 713
  -out *inquire* 461
  discover 480a
  -out of water
  disagree 24
  unconformable 83
  displaced 185
  bungler 701
  -story 546, 549
  -up *raise* 307
  find 480a
  food for-es 362
  other-to fry
  ill-timed 135
  busy 682
  queer-857
fisherman 361
fishery 370
fishing *kill* 361
  pursue 622
fishing boat 273
fishmonger 637
fish pond *pool* 343
  pisciculture 370
fish-tail 267
fishy transaction 940
fisk *run* 266
  speed 274
fissile 328
fission 44
fissure *break* 44
  chink 198
fist *handwriting* 590
  grip 781
  shake the-*defy* 715
  threat 909
fisticuffs 720
fistula 260
fit *state* 7

agreeing 23
  equal 27
  paroxysm 173
  agitation 315
  caprice 608
  expedient 646
  disease 655
  excitement 825
  anger 900
  right 922
  due 924
  duty 926
  by-s and starts
  irregular 59
  discontinuous 70
  agitated 315
  capricious 608
  haste 684
  -for 698, 924
  -of abstraction 458
  -of crying 839
  -out *dress* 225
  prepare 673
  -to be seen 845
  in-s 315
  think-600
fitchet 401
fitchew 401
fitful *irregular* 139
  changeable 149
  capricious 608
fittings 633
five 98 division by-99
  -act play 599
  -and twenty 98
fives *game* 840
fix *dilemma* 7
  join 43
  arrange 60
  establish 150
  place 184
  immovable 265
  solidify 321
  resolve 604
  difficulty 704
  -the eyes upon 441
  -the foundations 673
  -the memory 505
  -the thoughts 457
  -the time 114
  -upon *discover* 480a
  choose 609
fixed *intrinsic* 5
  durable 110
  permanent 141
  stable 150
  quiescent 265
  habitual 613
  -idea 481, 825
  -opinion 484
  -periods 138
  -purpose 620
fixity 141, 265
fixture
  appointment 741
  property 780

fizgig 423
fizz 409
fizzle 304, 353
  -out 304
fizzy 353
flabbergast
  astonish 870
flabbergasted
  humbled 879
flabby 324
flabelliform 194
flabellum 349
flaccid *weak* 160
  soft 324
  empty 640
flaccidity (*see* flaccid)
  feeble style 575
flag *weak* 160
  flat stone 204
  floor 211
  smoothness 255
  slow 275
  plant 367
  sign 550
  path 627
  infirm 655
  inactive 683
  tired 688
  insignia 747
  weary 841
  -of truce 723
  -ship 726
  lower one's-725
  red-*alarm* 669
  yellow-
  warning 668
  alarm 669
flag bearer 534
flagellation
  penance 952
  asceticism 955
  flogging 972
  rite 998
flagelliform 205
flageolet 417
flagitious 945
flagman 668
flagon 191
flagrant *great* 31
  manifest 525
  notorious 531
  atrocious 945
flagration 384
flagstaff *tall* 206
  signal 550
flagstone 204
flail 276
flake 204 snow-383
flam 544
flambé 732
flambeau 423
flamboyant 577
flame *fire* 382
  light 420
  luminary 423
  passion 824, 825

  love 897
  add fuel to the-173
  catch the-
  emotion 821
  consign to the-s
   384
  -colored *red* 434
  orange 439
  -thrower 727
  -up 825
  in-s 382
flamen 996
flaming *violent* 173
  feeling 821
  excited 824
  ostentatious 882
  boasting 884
flamingo 366
flange *support* **215**
  rim 231
  projection 250
flank *side* 236
  protect 664
flannel 384
flap *adjunct* 39
  hanging 214
  move to and fro 315
  -the memory 505
flapdoodle 517
flapjack 298
flapper *girl* 129
flapping *loose* 47
flare *violent* 173
  glare 420
  -up *excited* 824, 825
  angry 900
flaring *color* 428
flash *instant* 113
  violent 173
  fire 382
  light 420
  wit 842
  eyes-fire 900
  -across the memory
   505
  -back 842
  -in the pan
  unsubstantial 4
  impotent 158
  unproductive 169
  failure 732
  -note 800
  -of wit 842
  -on the mind
  thought 451
  disclose 529
  impulse 612
  -tongue 563
  -up *excited* 824
  -upon *unexpected* 508
flashing
  ostentatious 882
flashlight 423, 550
flashy *gaudy color* 428
  -style 577
  ornament 847

tawdry 851
flask 191
flat *inert* 172
  story 191
  low 207
  horizontal 213
  paint 223
  vapid 391
  low tone 408
  musical note 413
  positive 535
  dupe 547
  back–scene 599
  shoal 667
  bungler 701
  insensible 823
  dejected 837
  weary 841
  dull 843
  simple 849
  fall–732
  –*contradiction* 536
  –*house* 189
  –*out* 304, 732
  –*refusal* 764
flatboat 273
flatiron 255, 386
flatness 251
flatsided 203
flatten 251
flatter *deceive* 545
  cunning 702
  please 829
  encourage 858
  approbation 931
  adulation 933
  –*oneself probable* 472
  hope 858
  –*the palate* 394
flatterer 935
flattering
  –*remark* 894
  –*tale hope* 858
  –*unction to one's*
    soul content 831
  vain 880
  flattery 933
flattery *falsehood* 544
  adulation **933**
flattish 251
flatulent *gaseous* 334
  air 338
  wind 349
  –*style* 573, 575
flatus *gas* 334
  wind 349
flaunt *flourish* 873
  display 882
flaunting *gaudy* 428
  unreserved 525
  ridiculous 853
flautist 416
flavor 390
flavoring 393
flavous 436
flaw *break* 70

crack 198
error 495
imperfection 651
blemish 848
fault 947
–*in an argument* 477
flax comb 253
flaxen 436
flay *divest* 226
  punish 972
flea *jumper* 309
  insect 366
  dirt 653
  –*in one's ear*
  repel 289
  eject 297
  refuse 764
  disrepute 874
  abashed 879
  discourteous 895
  contempt 930
flea–bite 643
flea–bitten 440
fleck 440
flecked 440
flection 279
fled *escaped* 671
fledge 673
flee *avoid* 623
fleece *tegument* 223
  strip 789
  rob 791
  impoverish 804
  surcharge 814
fleer *ridicule* 856
  insult 929
fleet *unsubstantial* 4
  transient 111
  ships 273
  swift 274
  navy 726
Fleet *prison* 752
fleeting 111
flesh *bulk* 192
  animal 364
  mankind 372
  carnal 961
  –*and blood*
  substance 3
  materiality 316
  animality 364
  affections 820
  gain–194
  ills that–*is heir to*
  evil 619
  disease 655
  in the–359
  make the–*creep*
  pain 830
  fear 860
  one–903
  way of all–360
  weakness of the–
    945
flesh color 434
fleshly 316

fleshpots 298
fleshy *of fruit* 354
fleur–de–lis 847
fleuron 847
flexible *pliant* 324
  easy 705
flexion *curvature* 245
  fold 258
  deviation 279
flexuosity 248
flexuous 248, 348
flexure *curve* 245
  fold 258
flibbertigibber 980
flicker *changing* 149
  waver 314
  flutter 315
  light 420
  dim 422
flickering
  irregular 139
flies *insects* 366
  theater 599
flight *flock* 102
  volitation 267
  swiftness 274
  departure 293
  avoidance 623
  escape 671
  –*of fancy* 515
  –*of stairs ascent* 305
  way 627
  –*of time* 109
  put to–*propel* 284
  repel 717
  vanquish 731
flighty *inattentive* 458
  mad 503
  fanciful 515
flimflam *lie* 544
  caprice 608
flimsy *copy* 21
  weak 160
  rarity 322
  soft 324
  sophistical 477
  trifling 643
flinch *swerve* 607
  avoid 623
  fear 860
  cowardice 862
fling *propel* 284
  jig 840
  jeer 929
  –*aside* 782
  –*away reject* 610
  waste 638
  relinquish **782**
  –*down* 308
  –*to the winds*
  destroy 162
  not observe 773
  have a–*at*
  attack 716
  resent 900
  disrespect 929

censure 932
have one's–
active 682
laxity 738
freedom 748
amusement 840
flint *hard* 323
flint–hearted 907
flip *beverage* 298
flippant *fluent* 584
  pert 885
  discourteous 895
flipper *paddle* 267
flirt *propel* 284
  changer 607
  coquette 854, 902
  love 897
  endearment 902
  –*a fan affectation* 855
flirtation 902
flit *elapse* 109
  changeable 149
  move 264
  travel 266
  swift 274
  depart 293
  run away 623
flitter *small part* 32
  changeable 149
  flutter 315
flitting *evanescent* 111
flivver 272
float *establish* 150
  navigate 267
  boat 273
  buoy up 305
  lightness 320
  before the–*s*
  on the stage 599
  –*before the eyes* 446
  –*in the mind*
  thought 451
  imagination 515
  –*on the air* 405
floater *schemer* 702
floating (*see* float)
  rumored 532
  –*anchor* 706
  –*battery* 726
  –*capital* 805
  –*debt* 806
  –*hotel* 273
floccillation 315
flocculence 324
flocculent *woolly* 256
  soft 324
  pulverulent 330
flock *assemblage* 72
  multitude 102
  laity 997
  –*s and herds* 366
  –*together* **72**
floe *ice* 383
flog 684, 972
flood *much* 31
  crowd 72

water 337
river 348
abundance 639
redundance 641
prosperity 734
–*of light* 420
–*of tears* 839
stem the–708
floodgate *limit* 233
  egress 295
  conduit 350
  open the–*s*
  eject 297
  permit 760
flood mark 466
flood tide *increase* 35
  complete 52
  height 206
  advance 282
  water 337
floor *level* 204
  base 211
  horizontal 213
  support 215
  overthrow 731
  ground–191
flop 315
flora 369
floral 367
floret 367
floriculture 371
florid *music* 416
  color 428
  red 434
  –*style* 577
  health 654
florist 371
floss 256
flotation (*see* float)
flotilla *ships* 273
  navy 726
flotsam and jetsam
  73
flounce *trimming* 231
  jump 309
  agitation 315
  (*move quickly* 274)
flounder *change* 149
  toss 315
  uncertain 475
  bungle 699
  difficulty 704
  fail 732
  (*blunder* 495)
flour 330
flourish
  brandish 314, 315
  vegetate 365, 367
  exaggerate 549
  language 577
  speech 582
  gain 618
  healthy 654
  prosperous 734
  ornament 847
  repute 873

trump up 544
foundry 691
–ahead 282
–fetters 751
forged *false* 546
forger *maker* 690
  thief 792
  counterfeiter 800
forgery *deception* 545
forget 506
  –benefits 917
  –injury 918
  –oneself 945
  hand–cunning 699
forgetful 506
forgive 918
forgiveness 918
forgo (*see* forego)
forgotten *past* 122
  ingratitude 917
  –by the world 893
fork *bifid* 91
  pointed 244
  –lightning 423
  –out *give* 784
  pay 807
  expenditure 809
forking 291
forlay 706
forlorn *dejected* 837
  hopeless 859
  deserted 893
  –hope *danger* 665
  hopelessness 859
  rashness 863
form *state* 7
  likeness 21
  make up 54
  order 58
  arrange 60
  convert 144
  produce 161
  bench 215
  shape **240**
  organization 357
  educate 537
  pupils 541
  school 542
  manner 627
  beauty 845
  fashion 852
  etiquette 882
  law 963
  create 976
  rite 998
  –a party 712
  –a resolution 604
  –part of 56
formal (*see* form)
  regular 82
  definitive 535
  style 579
  severe 739
  taste 850
  affected 855
  stately 882

–speech 582
formaldehyde 490b
formalism 739, 988
formalist 82, 988
formality (*see* formal)
  ceremony 852
  affectation 855
  law 963
formalize 963
formation
  composition 54
  production 161
  shape 240
formative *causal* 153
  form 240
  –notion 453
formed (*see* form)
  attempered 820
former *in order* 62
  prior in time 116
  past 122
formerly 66, 119
formic acid 490b
formication 380
formidable
  difficult 704
  terrible 860
formless 241
formula *rule* 80
  arithmetic 84
  maxim 496
  precept 697
  law 963
formulary 998
formulate 590
fornication 961
fornicator 962
forsake 624
forsaken 898
forsooth 535
forswear *deny* 536
  lie 544
  tergiversation 607
  refuse 764
  transgress 927
  improbity 940
fort *refuge* 666
  defense 717
fortalice 717
forte 698
forth 282 come
  –egress 295
  visible 446
  go–*depart* 293
forthcoming
  destiny 152
  preparing 673
forthright 113, 132
forthwith 132, 507
fortification
  defense 717
fortify *strengthen* 159
fortitude
  endurance 826
  courage 861
fortnightly 138

fortress *refuge* 666
  defense 717
  prison 752
fortuitous
  adventitious 6
  chance 156
  undesigned 621
  –combination of
    circumstances 621
  –concourse of atoms
    59
fortuity 156
fortunate
  opportune 134
  successful 731
  prosperous 734
Fortunatus's–cap
  wish 865
  spell 993
  –purse 803
fortune *chance* 156
  fate 601
  wealth 803
  be one's–151
  evil–735
  –s *narrative* 594
  good–734
  make one's–
  succeed 731
  wealth 803
  tempt–*hazard* 621
  essay 675
  trick of–509
  try one's–675
  wheel of–601
fortune hunter
  servile 886
  selfish 943
fortuneless 804
fortune teller 513
fortune telling 51
forty 98–winks 683
Forty–Niner 463
forum *place* 182
  school 542
  tribunal 966
forward *early* 132
  front 234
  transmit 270
  advance 282
  interjection 286
  willing 602
  improve 658
  active 682
  help 707
  vain 880
  insolent 885
  uncourteous 895
  bend–234
  come–*in sight* 446
  offer 763
  display 882
  –in *knowledge* 490
  move–282
  press–*haste* 684
  put–*aid* 707

offer 763
  put oneself–88
  set–676
foss 348
fosse *inclosure* 232
  ditch 259
  defense 717
  (*interval* 198)
fossil *remains* 40
  ancient 124
  hard 323
  organic 357
  dry bones 362
fossilization 357
fossilize 357
foster *aid* 707
  excite 824
  caress 902
  –a belief 484
fou 959
foul *collide* 276
  bad 649
  dirty 653
  ugly 846
  base 940
  vicious 945
  fall–of *oppose* 708
  quarrel 713
  attack 716
  fight 720
  censure 932
  –fiend 978
  –invective 908
  –language
    malediction 908
  –odor 401
  –play *evil* 619
  cunning 702
  wrong 923
  improbity 940
  run–of *impede* 706
foul–mouthed
  uncourteous 895
foulness (*see* foul)
foul–spoken
  detraction 934
foumart 401
found *cause* 153
  support 215
foundation
  stability 150
  base 211
  support 215
  lay the–s 673
  sandy–667
  shake to its–s 315
founded–on *base* 211
  evidence 467
  well–472
founder
  originator 164
  sink 310
  projector 626
  fail 732
  religious–s 986
foundling *trover* 775

derelict 782
  outcast 893
foundry 691
fount *type* 591
fountain *source* 153
  river 348
  store 636
  –pen 590
fountainhead 210
four 95–in hand 272
  –score etc. 98
  –times 96
  from the–winds 278
  on all–s *identity* 13
  agreement 23
  horizontal 213
  easy 705
  prosperous 734
  humble 879
four–flush 545, 884
fourfold 96
Four Hundred 852,
  875
Fourierism 910
four–oar 273
four–poster 215
fourragère 877
foursquare 244
fourth 96, 97
  musical 413
Fourth Estate 531
four–wheeler 272
fowl 298, 366
fowling piece 727
fox *animal* 366
  cunning 702
  –chase 622
  –hunting 622
foxhound 366
foxy *brown* 433
fox terrier 366
fox trot *dance* 840
fracas *disorder* 59
  noise 404
  discord 713
  contention 720
fraction *part* 51
  numerical 84
  less than one **100a**
Foxy Quiller 804
fractional 100a
  –currency 800
fractious 901
fracture
  disjunction 44
  discontinuity 70
  fissure 198
fragile *weak* 160
  brittle 328
fragment *small* 32
  part 51
  little 193
  extract 596
fragmentary 100a
fragrance 400
fragrant 400

-weed 392
frail *weak* 160
  brittle 328
  irresolute 605
  imperfect 651
  failing 945
  impure 961
  -sisterhood 962
frailty (*see* frail)
frame *intrinsicality* 5
  condition 7
  make 161
  support 215
  border 231
  form 240
  substance 316
  structure 329
  contrive 626
 -of mind
  inclination 602
  disposition 820
  have--d and glazed
   822
frame house 189
framework
  support 215
  structure 329
franchise *freedom* 748
  right 924
  exemption 927a
Franciscan 996
franc--tireur 726
frangible 328
frank *open* 525
  sincere 543
  artless 703
  honorable 939
 -as rain 703
frankalmoigne 748
Frankenstein 913
Frankfurter 298
frankincense 400
frantic *violent* 173
  delirious 503
  excited 824
fraternal *brother* 11
  leagued 712
  concord 714
  friendly 888
  (*benevolent* 906)
 -order 711
fraternity *brothers* 11
  party 712
  friends 888
fraternize *combine* 48
  cooperate 709
  agree 714
  sympathize 888
  associate 892
fratricide 361
Frau 374
fraud *falsehood* 544
  deception 545
  impostor 548
  dishonor 940
  pious--988

fraudulent
  (*see* fraud)
  untruth 546
fraught *full* 52
  pregnant 161
  possessing 777
  (*sufficient* 639)
 -with danger 665
fray *rub* 331
  battle 720
  in the thick of the-
   722
frayed *worn* 659
freak 608
 -of nature 83
freckle 848
freckled 440, 848
fredaine 840
free *detached* 44, 47
  unconditional 52
  deliver 672
  unobstructed 705
  liberate 748, 750
  expending 809
  gratis 815
  liberal 816
  insolent 885
  exempt 927a
  impure 961
 -and easy
  cheerful 836
  vain 880
  insolent 885
  friendly 888
  sociable 892
 -companion 726
 -fight 720
 -from *simple* 42
 -from imperfection
  650
 -gift 784
 -giver 816
 -lance 523, 726, 748
 -land 748
 -liver 954a
 -living 954
 -love 897, 961
 -lunch 815
 -play 170, 748
 -quarters *cheap* 815
  hospitality 892
 -space 180
 -stage 748
 -trade *commerce* 794
 -translation 522
 -will 600
  make--of 748
  make--with
  frank 703
  take 789
  sociable 892
  uncourteous 895
freebooter 792
freeborn 748
free--burning 388
freedman 748

freedom 748
free--handed 816
freehold 780
freely *willingly* 602
freeman 748
Freemason 711
freemasonry
  unintelligible 519
  secret 528
  sign 550
  cooperation 709
  party 712
free--spoken 703
freestone 635
freethinker 487, 748,
  989
free thought 487
free trader 748
freeze 376, 385
 -the blood 830
freezing 383
 -machine 387
 -mixture 387
freight *lade* 184
  cargo 190
  transfer 270
 -train 272
 -yard 636
freightage 270, 812
freighter *carrier* 271
  vessel 273
French 188
 -beans 298
 -gray 432
 -horn 417
 -leave *avoid* 623
  freedom 748
 -philosophy 451
 -polish 847
  peddler's-563
Frenchman 188
frenetic 503
frenzy *madness* 503
  imagination 515
  excitement 825
frequency 136
frequent
  in number 104
  in time 136
  in space 186
  habitual 613
frequenter 613
fresco *cold* 383
  painting 556
  al-*out of doors* 220
  in the air 338
fresh *extra* 37
  new 123
  flood 348
  cold 383
  color 428
  remembered 505
  novice 541
  unaccustomed 614
  good 648
  healthy 654

  pert 885
  tipsy 959
 -breeze 349
 -color 434
 -news 532
freshen 689
freshet 348
freshman 492, 541
freshness (*see* fresh)
fresh--water
 -college 542
 -sailor 701
fret *suffer* 378
  grieve 828
  gall 830
  discontent 832
  sad 837
  ornament 847
  irritate 900
 -and fume 828
fretful 901
fretwork 219
Freud's theory 992a
friable *brittle* 328
  pulverulent 330
friandice 868
friar 996 Black--s 996
 -Rush 980
 -'s balsam 662
 -'s lantern 423
friary 1000
fribble *slur over* 460
  trifle 643
  dawdle 683
  fop 854
fricassee 298
frication 331
friction *force* 157
  obstacle 179
  rubbing **331**
  on--wheels 705
fried--brains 298
 -eggs 298
 -sole 298
friend *auxiliary* 711
  wellwisher **890**
  sympathizer 914
  be--s 888
 -at court 631
  next--759
  see one's--s 892
friendless 893
friendliness 888
friendly *amicable* 714
friendship 888
frieze 210, 329
frigate
  man--of--war 726
  (*ship* 273)
fright *cards* 840
  alarm 860
frighten 860
frightful *dreadful* 830
  ugly 846
frightfully *much* 31
frigid *cold* 383

 -style 575
  callous 823
  indifferent 866
frigidarium 387
frigorific 385
frill *border* 231
  convolution 248
frills 577
 -of style 577
fringe *border* 231
  lace 256
  exaggeration 549
  ornament 847
frippery *trifle* 643
  ornament 847
  finery 851
  ridiculous 853
  ostentation 882
  (*dress* 225)
friseur 225
frisk *prance* 266
  leap 309
  absurdity 497
  gay 836
  amusement 840
frisky *brisk* 682
  in spirits 836
frith *chasm* 198
  strait 343
  forest 367
fritiniancy 412
fritter *small* 32
 -away *lessen* 36
  waste 638
  (*misuse* 679)
 -away time 683
frivolity
  (*see* frivolous)
frivolous
  unreasonable 477
  foolish 499
  capricious 608
  trivial 643
friz *curl* 245, 248
  fold 258
frock *dress* 225
  canonicals 999
 -coat 225
frog *leaper* 309
  ornament 847
frolic 840
frolicsome 836
from *motive* 615
 -day to day 106, 138
 -end to end 52
 -that time 117
 -this cause 155
 -time immemorial
  122
 -time to time 136
frond 367
fronder *censure* 932
frondeur *disobey* 742
  detract 936
front *first* 66
  wig 225

fore part **234**
resist 719
insolence 885
bring to the–
manifest 525
come to the–
surpass 303
important 642
repute 873
–*danger* 861
–of the house 599
–rank 234
–to front 708
in–280
in the–rank
important 642
repute 873
present a–719
frontage 234
frontal 220
frontier *vicinity* 199
limit 233
fronting *opposite* 237
frontispiece 64
frost *cold* 383
semitransparent 427
whiten 430
–over 427
frost–bite 383
frosted 427, 430
–glass 427
frost smoke 353
frostwork 847
froth *bubble* 353
trifle 643
dirt 653
–up *angry* 900
frothy 353
–*style* 573, 577
irresolute 605
frounce 258
frow 374
froward 901a
frown *lower* 837
scowl 839
discourteous 895
angry 900
sulky 901a
disapprove 932
–*down abash* 879
–s of fortune 735
frowzy 401
frozen 383, 385
fructiferous 168
fructify *produce* 161
be productive 168
improve 658
prosper 734
fructuous 168
frugal *economical* 817
temperate 953
fruit *result* 154
produce 161
profit 775
forbidden–615
–*tree* 367

reap the–s
succeed 731
reward 973
fruitarian 953
fruit–bearing 168
fruitful 168
fruition 161, 827
fruitless
unproductive 169
useless 645
failure 732
frumenty 298
frump *vulgar* 851
unmannerly 895
frumpish *sulky* 901a
frustrate
counteract 179
prevent 706
(*defeat* 731)
frustrated 732
frustum 51
fry *shoal* 102
child 129
heat 384
small–
unimportant 643
commonalty 876
frying pan 386
out of–into fire
worse 659
clumsy 699
failure 732
misfortune 735
aggravation 835
fuchsine 434
fucoid 367
fuddled 959
fudge *unmeaning* 517
trivial 643
(*nonsense* 497)
fuel *combustible* **388**
materials 635
add–to the flame
increase 35
heat 384
aggravate 835
anger 900
fugacious 111
fugitive *transient* 111
emigrant 268
avoiding 623
(*escape* 671)
–*writings* 596
fugleman *pattern* 22
director 694
fugue 415
fulciment 215
fulcrum *support* 215
mechanical power
633
(*leverage* 175)
fulfill *complete* 729
–a *duty* 926
–an *obligation* 772
fulgent 420
fulgurant 420

fulgurite 260
fuliginosity 426
fuliginous *dim* 422
opaque 426
black 431
full *circumstantial* 8
much 31
complete 52
large 192
loud 404
abundant 639
cleanse 652
–age 131
–bloom *health* 654
beauty 845
–colored 428
–cry *aloud* 404
bark 412
pursuit 622
–dress *dress* 225
ornament 847
fashion 852
show 882
–drive 274
–feather *prepared* 673
–force 159
–gallop 274
–heart 820
–house *cards* 840
–many 102
–measure 639
–of business 682
–of incident 151
–of meaning 516
–of people 186
–of point 842
–of whims 608
–play *facility* 705
freedom 748
–scope 748
–score 415
–size 192
–speed 274
–steam ahead **282**
–stop *cease* 142
rest 265
–swing *strong* 159
active 682
successful 731
free 748
–tide 348
–tilt *active* 682
haste 684
–view 446
hands–*active* 682
receipt in–807
full–blown
expanded 194
glorious 873
full–blooded 641
full–fed 954
full–flavored 392
full–grown
adolescent 131
large 192
(*expanded* 194)

full–handed
liberal 816
prodigal 818
full–length 556
full–mouthed 411,
412
fullness (*see* full)
in the–of time 109
full–toned 413
fully 31
fulminate *violent* 173
propel 284
loud 404
malediction 908
threat 909
–against *accuse* 932
fulsome
nauseous 395
fetid 401
bad 649
abhorrent 867
adulatory 933
impure 961
fulvescent 436
fulvid 436
fulvous 436
fumarole 490c
fumble *derange* 61
handle 379
grope 463
awkward 699
fumbler 701
fume *violent* 173
exhalation 334, 336
air pipe 351
heat 382
odor 398
excitement 824
be impatient 825
anger 900
–s of fancy 515
in a
–*discontented* 832
fumid 426
fumigate
vaporize 336
cleanse 652
fumigator 388
fun *amusement* 840
humor 842
make–of 856
funambulist 700
function *algebra* 84
office 170
business 625
utility 644
pomp 882
duty 926
functionary
director 694
consignee 758
fund *store* 636
invest 787
(*abundance* 639)
sinking–802
fundament 235

fundamental
intrinsic 5
base 211
support 215
–bass 413
–note 413
fundamentally
very 31
funds 800 in–803
public–802
funebrial 363
funeral *procession* 69
interment 363
–director 363
–pace 275
–pyre 423
–ring 363
funerary 363
funereal
interment 363
dismal 837
fungate 365
fungi 369
fungiform 249
fungoid 369
fungologist 369
fungology 369
fungosity
projection 250
fungous 367, 369
fungus *projection* 250
vegetable 367
fetor 401
bane 663
funicle 205
funk *fear* 860
cowardice 862
funnel *opening* 260
conduit 350
air pipe 351
funnel–shaped 252
funny *odd* 83
boat 273
humorous 842
comic 853
fur *covering* 223
hair 256
warm 384
dirt 653
furacious 791
furbelow 231
furbish *improve* 658
prepare 673
adorn 847
furcate 244
furcation 91
furcula 993
furcular 91, 244
furculum 91, 244
furfur 653
furfuraceous 330
Furies *anger* 900
evildoers 913
furiosity 173
furious *violent* 173
haste 684

457

chasm 198
stand in the—717
gape *open* 260
  curiosity 455
  wonder 870
  —for *desire* 865
gaping (*see* gape)
  expectant 507
gar 161
garage 191, 272
garb 225
  under the—of 545
garbage 653
garble *take from* 38
  exclude 55
  misinterpret 523
  falsify 544
  —*accounts* 811
garbled *incomplete* 53
garde—nationale 726
  —royale 726
garden *grounds* 189
  horticulture 371
  source of supply 636
  beautiful 845
  botanic—371
  zoological—370
gardener 371
gardens *street* 189
gare 266
gargle 337
gargoyle 350
garish *light* 420
  color 428
  ornament 847
  gay 845
  tawdry 851
  display 882
gari—wala 268
garland *circle* 247
  fragrance 400
  sign 550
  poetry 597
  trophy 733
  ornament 847
  decoration 877
garlic *condiment* 393
  fetid 401
garment 225
garner *store* 636
  (*collect* 72)
garnet 434, 847
garnish *addition* 39
  prepare 673
  fee 809
  ornament 847
garnishee 758
garniture *dress* 225
garran 271
garret *room* 191
  top 210
garrison
  occupant 188
  safety 664
  defense 717
  soldiers 726

garron 271
garrote
  render powerless 158
  kill 361
  punishment 972
garrulity 584
garter *fastening* 45
  decoration 877
  —blue 438
garth 181
gas *gaseity* 334
  fuel 388
  light 420
  bombast 884
  —bomb 727
  —meter 334
  —stove 386
gasconade 884
gaseity 334
gaseous
  unsubstantial 4
  of gas 324
  vaporous 336
gash *cut* 44
  interval 198
  wound 619
gasification 334, 336
gasiform 334
gasify 334
gaskins 225
gaslight 423
gasoline 272, 356
gasometer 636
gasp *blow* 349
  droop 655
  poison 663
  fatigue 688
  at the last—360
  —for *desire* 865
gassy 349
gastric 191, 298
gastriloquism 580
gastromancy 511
gastronomy 298, 957
gastroscope 445
gate *beginning* 66
  inclosure 232
  mouth 260
  barrier 706
  —way *way* 627
  water—350
gâteau 298
gatekeeper 263
Gath, tell it not in—
  conceal 528
  disapprove 932
gather *collect* 72
  expand 194
  fold 258
  conclude 480
  acquire 775
  take 789
  —breath 689
  —flesh 194
  —from one
    information 527

—fruits 731
—grapes from thorns
  471
gathered
  —to one's fathers 360
gathering
  assemblage 72
  abscess 655
  —clouds *dark* 421
  shade 424
  omen 512
  danger 665
  warning 668
  adversity 735
gathering place 74
Gatling gun 727
gauche *clumsy* 699
gaucherie 699
  vulgarity 851
gaud *ornament* 847
gaudery *vanity* 880
gaudy *color* 428
  vulgar 851
  showy 882
gauge 466 rain—348
  wind—349
gauger 965
gaunt *bulky* 192
  lean 203
  ugly 846
gauntlet *glove* 225
  armor 717
  fling down the—715
  take up the—720
Gautama 986
gauze *shade* 424
  semitransparent 427
gavel *worth* 812
  sheaf 72
gavelkind 778
gavelock 633
gavot 840
gawk 501
gawky *awkward* 699
  ugly 846
  (*ridiculous* 853)
gay *color* 428
  cheerful 836
  adorned 847
  showy 882
  dissipated 961
  —deceiver 962
  —world 852
gayety (*see* gay) 836
Gay—Lussac's law
  490d
gaze 441
gazebo 441
gazelle *swift* 274
  animal 366
gazer *spectator* 444
gazette
  publication 531
  record 551
  in the—
  bankrupt 808

gazetteer *list* 86
  information 527
  record 551
gazingstock
  ridiculous 857
  wondrous 872
geanticline 245
gear *clothes* 225
  automobile 272
  cogwheel 312
  harness 633
  in—673
  out of—*disjoin* 44
  derange 61
  useless 645
  unprepared 674
gearwheel 312
gehenna 982
Geist 982
gelatin 352
gelatinize 352
gelatinous 352
geld *subduct* 38
  impotence 158
gelding *horse* 271
  male 373
gelid 383
gelidity 383
gelignite 727
geloscopy 511
gem *excellence* 648
  ornament 847
  (*perfect* 650)
geminate 90
gemination 161
Gemini *twins* 89
  O—! 870
gemma 153
gemmation 194
gemmule 153
gemot 72
gendarme *safety* 664
  soldier 726
  police 965
gender 75
genealogy *line* 69
  paternity 166
general *whole* 50
  generic 78
  habitual 613
  servant 690, 746
  officer 745
  —breaking up 655
  —conception 25
  —favorite 899
  —information 490
  —meaning 516
  —public 372
  —run 613
  the
  —commonalty 876
  things in—151
generalissimo 745
generality *mean* 29
  universal 78
generalize 476

generally 16
  —speaking 613
generalship
  tactics 692
  warfare 722
generate *produce* 161
  productive 168
generation
  consanguinity 11
  period 108
  production 161
  mankind 372
  rising—167
  spontaneous—161
  wise in one's—498
generative 153, 161
generator
  producer 164
  of automobile 272
generic 78
generosity
  greatness 31
  giving 784
  liberality 816
  benevolence 906
  disinterestedness 942
generous
  (*see* generosity)
genesis *beginning* 66
  production 161
genet 271
Genethliacs 511
genetic 5, 161
genetous 5
Geneva gown 999
genial *productive* 161
  sensuous 377
  warm 382
  willing 602
  delightful 829
  (*renascent* 163)
geniality (*see* genial)
  cheerfulness 836
geniculated 244
genital 161
genitor 166
geniture 161
genius *intellect* 450
  talent 498
  poet 597
  skill 698
  proficient 700
  familiar spirit 979
  evil—980
  —borrows nobly 19
  —for 698
  —loci 664
  —of a language 560
  good—*friend* 898
  benefactor 912
  spirit 979
  man of—492
  tulelary—711
genre *painting* 556
gens 712
gent *vulgar* 851

strain at a—etc.
caprice 608
gnaw *eat* 298
  rub 331
  injure 659
gnawing
  —*grief* 828, 830
  —*pain* 378
gnome 496, 980
gnomic 496
gnomon 114
Gnostic 984
Gnosticism 451
gnu 366
go *cease to exist* 2
  energy 171, 682
  move 264
  recede 287
  depart 293
  jade 429
  disappear 449
  fashion 852
  as things—613
  come and—314
  give the—by to
  neglect 460
  deceive 545
  avoid 623
  not observe 773
  —about
    turn round 311
    published 531
    undertake 676
  —about your business
    ejection 297
    dismissal 756
  —across 302
  —after *in time* 117
    in motion 281
  —against 708
  —ahead *precede* 280
    advance 282
    active 682
  —all lengths 604*a*
    complete 52
    resolve 604
    exertion 686
  —aloft 305
  —astray 495
  —away 293
  —back 283
  —back on 624
  —bad 659
  —bail 771
  —before 280
  —beyond 303
  —by *conform to* 82
    elapse 109
    past 122
    outrun 303
    subterfuge 702
  —by the board 158
  —by the name of 564
  —cahoots 712
  —deep into 461
  —down *sink* 306

decline 659
—down with
  believed 484
  tolerated 826
  content 831
—farther and fare
  worse 659
—for nothing
  sophistry 477
  unimportant 643
—forth *depart* 293
  publish 531
—from one's word
  773
—halves 91
—hand in hand
  accompany 88
  same time 120
—hard 704
—in 294
—in for *resolution* 604
  pursuit 622
—into *ingress* 294
  inquire 461
  dissert 595
—mad 503
—near 286
—no further
  keep secret 528
—off *explode* 173
  depart 293
  die 360
  wither 659
  marry 903
—on *time* 106
  continue 143
  advance 282
—on for ever 112
—on ill 735
—on the stump 582
—out *cease* 142
  egress 295
  extinct 385
—out of one's head
  506
—over *passage* 302
  explore 461
  apostate 607
  faithless 940
—round 311
—shares 778
—the limit 52, 604
—through
  meet with 151
  pass 302
  explore 461
  perform 599
  conduct 692
  complete 729
  endure 826
—through fire and
  water 604*a*
—to *extend* 196
  travel 266
  direction 278
  remonstrance 695

—to glory 162, 360
—to pieces 162
—to sleep 683
—to war 722
—under 162
—up 305
—West *die* 360
—with *assent* 488
  concord 714
—with the stream
  conform 82
  servile 886
goad *for oxen* 370
  motive 615
  quicken 684
go-ahead 171, 682
goal *end* 67
  reach 292 *object* 620
  reach the—
  complete 729
goat *jumper* 309
  lecher 962
  he—*male* 373
goatee 256
goatish 961
gob *sailor* 269
  jaws 298
gobang 840
gobbet *small piece* 32
  food 298
gobble *cry* 412
  gormandize 957
  eat 298
gobemouche *fool* 501
  dupe 547
go-between
  interjacent 226
  instrumental 631
  mediate 724
  agent 758
goblet 191
goblin 980
  (*bugbear* 860)
gocart 272
GOD 976
  for—'s sake 765
  —bless me! 870
  —bless you
    farewell 293
  —forbid 766
  —forsaken 196
  —grant 990
  —knows 491
  —'s acre 363
  —'s grace 906
  —'s love 906
  —'s own country 189
  —'s will 601
  —willing 470
  house of—1000
  kingdom of—981
  sons of—977
  to—be true 772
god 979
  household—s 189
  the—s

gallery 444, 599
  tutelary—664
godchild 771
goddess *love* 897
  good woman 948
  heathen 979
  she moves a—374
godfather 771
Godhead 976
godlike 987
godly 944
godmother 771
godown 636
godsend *good* 618
  prosperity 734
Godspeed
  farewell 293
  hope 858
  courtesy 894
  benevolence 906
  approbation 931
goer *horse* 271
goes (*see* go)
  as one—270
  here—676
goggle 441
goggle-eyed 443
goggles 445
going (*see* go)
  general 78
  rumor 532
  —on
    incomplete 53, 730
    current 151
    transacting 625
  —to happen 152
goiter 655
Golconda 803
gold *yellow* 436
  orange 439
  money 800
  all is not—486
  —brick 545, 702
  —mohur 800
  worth its weight in—
    648
  write in letters of—
    642
golden (*see* gold)
  —age *prosperity* 734
    pleasure 827
  —apple 615
  —calf *wealth* 803
    idolatry 991
  —dream
    imagination 515
    hope 858
  —mean
    moderation 174
    mid-course 628
  —opinions 931
  —opportunity 134
  —rule *precept* 697
  —season of life 127
  —wedding 883
  music's—tongue 415

golf 840
Golgotha *burial* 363
  churchyard 1000
Goliath *strength* 159
  size 192
gomashta 758
gondola 273
gondolier 269
gone (*see* go) *past* 122
  absent 187
  dead 360
  hopeless 859
  —bad 653
  —by *antiquated* 124
  —case 859
  —coon 859
  —out of one's
    recollection 506
  —where the woodbine
    twineth 771
goneness 688
goner 859
gonfalon 550
gong 417
goniometer *angle* 244
  measure 466
gonorrhea 655
good *complete* 52
  palatable 394
  assent 488
  benefit **618**
  beneficial 648
  right 922
  virtuous 944
  pious 987
  as—as 197
  be—enough 765
  be so—as 765
  do— 906
  for—*diuturnal* 110
  permanent 141
  —actions 944
  —as one's word
    veracity 543
    observance 772
    probity 939
  —at 698
  —at the price 815
  —auspices 858
  —behavior
    contingent 108*a*
    duty 926
    virtue 944
  —bye 293
  —chance 472
  —cheer *food* 298
    cheerful 826
  —circumstances 803
  —condition 192
  —day *arrival* 292
    departure 293
    courtesy 894
  —effect *goodness* 648
    beauty 845
  —enough
    not perfect 651

–fellow 892
–fight *war* 722
  virtue 944
–for *useful* 644
  salubrious 656
–fortune 734
–Friday 138, 998
–genius *friend* 890
  benefactor 912
  god 979
–hand 700
–humor *concord* 714
  cheerfulness 836
  amuse 840
  courtesy 894
  kindly 906
–intention 906
–judgment 498
–lack! 870
–living *food* 298
  gluttony 957
–look out 459
–looks 845
–luck 734
–man *man* 373
  husband 903
  worthy **948**
–manners 894
–morrow 292
–name 873
–nature 906
–offices
  mediation 724
  kind 906
–old time 122
–omen 858
–opinion 931
–pennyworth 815
–repute 873
–sense 498
–society 852
–taste 850
–tasting 394
–temper 894
–thing 648
–time *early* 132
  opportune 134
  prosperous 734
–turn *kindness* 906
–understanding 714
–wife *woman* 374
  spouse 903
–will *willingness* 602
  benevolence 906
–woman 948
–word *approval* 931
  vindication 927
–works 906
  in–case 192
  in–odor *repute* 873
  approbation 931
  in one's–books 888
  in one's–graces 888
  make–*evidence* 467
  provide 637
  restore 660

complete 729
substantiate 924
vindicate 937
atone for 952
put a–face upon
cheerful 836
proud 878
so far so–931
take in–part
pleased 827
courteous 894
kind 906
think–931
to–purpose 731
to the–780
turn to–account
  731
what's the–645
good–for–nothing
impotence 158
useless 645
good–looking 845
goodly *great* 31
large 192
handsome 845
good–natured 906
goodness
(*see* good) **648**
virtue 944
–gracious! 870
–of heart 906
have the
  –*request* 765
goods *effects* 780
merchandise 798
Goodwin sands 667
goody 374
goose *bird* 298, 366
hiss 409
game of–840
giddy as a–458
–egg *zero* 101
–flesh 383
–grass 253
kill the–with golden
  eggs *bungler* 699
prodigal 818
gooseberry *fruit* 298
yarn 549
–eyes 441, 443
old–978
goosecap 501
goosequill 590
goose–skin 383
Gordian knot
tangled 59
difficulty 704
(*problem* 461)
gore *gusset* 43
stab 260
blood 361
gorge *ravine* 198, 350
fill 641
satiety 869
gluttony 957
(*eat* 298)

–the hook 602
raise one's–900
gorge–de–pigeon
432, 440
gorgeous *color* 428
beauty 845
ornament 847
Gorgon 860
gorilla 366, 913
gormandize *eat* 298
gluttony 957
gorse 367
gory *murderous* 361
red 434
unclean 653
gospel *certainty* 474
doctrine 484
truth 494
take for–484
Gospels 985
gossamer
filament 205
light 320
texture 329
gossamery
unsubstantial 4
weak 160
light 320
gossip *news* 532
babbler 584
conversation 588
gossoon 876
Goth *vulgar* 851
barbarian 876
gothamite 501
**Gotham, wise men
of** 501
gothic *amorphous* 241
Gothicism 851
gouache 556
gouge *concave* 252
perforator 262
goulash 298
gourmand
sensualist 954a
glutton 957
gourmet
fastidious 868
sybarite 954a
gout 378
goût 390
govern *direct* 693
authority 737
governess 540
government
(*see* govern)
ruling power 745
divine–976
–bonds 802
–mark 550
–s *authority* 737
–school 542
petticoat–699
governor *father* 166
tutor 540
director 694

ruler 745
keeper 753
–'s message 695
gowk 501
gown *dress* 225
canonicals 999
gownsman 492
grab *take* 789
miser 819
grabble 379
grace *style* 578
permission 760
concession 784
elegance 845
polish 850
title 877
pity 914
forgiveness 918
honor 939
piety 987
worship 990
act of–784
God's–906
–before meat 916
heart of–861
in one's good–s 888
say–990
submit with a good
  –826
with a bad–603
with a good–
willing 602
courteous 894
graceful *elegant* 578
beautiful 845
tasteful 850
graceless
inelegant 579
ugly 846
vicious 945
impenitent 951
irreligious 989
Graces 845
gracile 203
gracious *willing* 602
courteous 894
kind 906
good–870
gradatim *in order* 58
continuous 69
slow 275
gradation *degree* 26
order 58
continuity 69
gradatory 69
grade *degree* 26
classify 60
term 71
obliquity 217
ascent 305
class 541, (75)
at–219
–crossing 219
gradient 217, 305
gradual *degree* 26
continuous 69

slow 275
graduate *adjust* 23
degree 26
divide 44
arrange 60
series 69
measure 466
scholar 492
teaching 537
rank 873
–school 542
graduated scale 466
graduation *class* 541
rank 873
gradus 86, 562
Graecist 492
graft *join* 43
locate 184
insert 300
–a *plant* 371
teach 537
bribe 784
improbity 940
grain *essence* 5
small 32
tendency 176
little 193
rough 256
weight 319
texture 329
powder 330
paint 428
temper 820
ornament 847
against the–
rough 256
unwilling 603
opposing 708
–elevator 636
–oil 356
–s of allowance
qualification 469
doubt 485
in the–820
like–s of sand
incoherent 47
grallatory 267
gramercy 916
gram–fed 192
graminivorous 298
grammar
beginning 66
teaching 537
school 542
language **567**
bad–568
comparative–560
–school 537
grammarian 492
grammatical 567
–blunder 568
grammatism 561
gramophone 417,
418, 551
granary 636
grand *august* 31

slow 275
–the battle
  important 642
  success 731
–tint 421
–truth 546
  see with–an eye
  intelligent 498
  intelligible 518
  manifest 525
half–baked
  ignorant 491
  imbecile 499
half–blind 443
half blood *mixture* 41
  unconformity 83
  imperfect 651
half–breed 41
half–frozen 352
half–hearted
  irresolute 605
  insensible 823
  indifferent 866
half–learned 491
half–learning 491
half–melted 352
halfpenny *trifle* 643
half–starved
  insufficient 640
  fasting 956
half–tone 421, 558
half–way *small* 32
  middle 68
  between 228
  go–*irresolute* 605
  mid–course 628
  meet–*willing* 602
  compromise 774
half–witted 499, 501
hall *chamber* 189
  receptacle 191
  mart 799
  –mark 550
  –of audience 588
  –s of time 109
  music–599
hallelujah 990
Halley 490a
halloo *cry* 411
  look here! 457
  call 586
  wonder 870
hallow *celebrate* 883
  respect 928
hallowed 976
Halloween 138
Hallowmas 138
hallucination
  error 495
  insanity 503
  psychical research
    992a
halo *light* 420
  glory 873
halomancy 511
halser 45

halt *cease* 142
  weak 160
  rest 265
  go slowly 275
  lame 655
  fail 732
  at the–265
halter *rope* 45
  restraint 752
  punishment 975
  wear a–874
  with a–round one's
    neck 665
halting *style* 579
  –place 292
halve (*see* half)
halves do by–
  neglect 460
  not complete 730
  go–778
  not do by–729
ham *house* 189
  meat 298
hamadryad 979
hamal 746
hamfatter 599
hamiform 245
Hamitic 372a
hamlet 189
hammer *repeat* 104
  knock 276
  stammer 583
  between the–and
    the anvil 665
  –at *think* 451
  work 686
  –out *form* 240
  thought 451
  prepare 673
  complete 729
  under the–
  auction 796
hammock 215
hamous 245
hamper *basket* 191
  obstruct 706
hamstring
  incapacitate 158
  render useless 645
  injure 659
hamulate 245
hanaper 802
hand
  measure of length
    200
  side 236
  mariner 269
  transfer 270
  man 372
  organ of touch 379
  indicator 550
  writing 590
  medium 631
  agent 690
  grasp 781
  cards 840

transfer 783
at–*present* 118
future 121
destined 152
near 197
useful 644
bad–590
bird in–781
come to–*arrive* 292
received 785
fold one's–s 681
give one's–to
  marry 903
good–*writing* 590
skill 698
proficiency 700
–and glove 888
–back 683
–down *record* 551
transfer 783
–in hand *joined* 43
  accompanying 88
  same time 120
  concur 178
  coöperate 709
  party 712
  concord 714
  friend 888
  social 892
–in one's chips 360
–of death 360
–organ 417
–over *transfer* 783
  give 784
–over head
  inattention 458
  neglect 460
  reckless 863
–s off! *avoid* 623
  leave alone 681
  prohibition 761
–to hand
  touching 199
  transfer 270
  fight 720, 722
have a–in *cause* 153
  act 680
  cooperate 709
have one's–in
  skill 698
have one's–s full
  682
helping–707, 711
hold in–*rule* 737
hold out the
  –*courtesy* 894
hold up the
  –*vote* 609
in–*incomplete* 53
  business 625
  preparing 673
  not finished 730
  possessed 777
  money 800
  in the–s of
  authority 737

subjection 749
keep one's–in 613
lay–s on
discover 480a
use 677
take 789
rite 998
live from–to mouth
insufficient 640
unprepared 674
poor 804
much on one's–s
  682
no–in 623
on one's–s
  business 625
redundant 641
not finished 730
for sale 796
on the other–468
poor–701
put into one's–s
  784
put one's–to 676
ready to one's–673
shake–s 918
stretch forth one's–
  680
take by the–707
take in–*teach* 537
undertake 676
time hanging on
  one's–
  inaction 681
  leisure 685
  weary 841
try one's–675
turn one's–to 625
under one's–
  in writing 590
  promise 768
  compact 769
with the –s in the
  pockets 681
hand–bag 191
hand–barrow 272
handbill 531
handbook *travel* 266
  information 527
  book 593
handbreadth 200
hand camera 445
hand car 272
handfast 903
handful *quantity* 25
  small 32
  few 103
hand gallop 274
hand grenade 727
handicap *equalize* 27
  incumber 706
  race 720
handicraft
  business 625
  working 680
handicraftsman 690

handiwork *effect* 154
  doing 680
handkerchief
  clothes 225
  cleaner 652
handle *feel, touch* 379
  dissert 595
  plea 617
  instrument 633
  use 677
  manage 693
  furnish a–937
  –a case 692
  –to one's name
  name 564
  honor 877
  make a–of 677
handmaid
  instrumentality 631
  auxiliary 711
  servant 746
hand mirror 445
hand post 550
handsel *begin* 66
  security 771
  gift 784
  pay 809
handsome *liberal* 816
  beautiful 845
  disinterested 942
  –fortune 803
  –is that handsome
    does 816
handspike 633
handstaff 727
handwriting
  evidence 467
  signature 550
  autograph 590
  –on the wall
  warning 668
handy *near* 197
  useful 644
  ready 673
  dexterous 698
hang *lateness* 133
  pendency 214
  kill 361
  curse 908
  execute 972
  –about 133, 197
  –back 133, 623
  –by a thread 665
  –down the head 837
  –fire *late* 133
  cease 142
  unproductive 169
  inert 172
  slow 275
  reluctance 603
  inactive 683
  not finish 730
  fail 732
  refuse 764
  –in doubt 485
  –in suspense 605

hedgerow 232
hedonic 827, 836
hedonism 377, 451, 827
hedonist 954a
hedonistic 377
heed *attend* 457
  care 459
  beware 668
  caution 864
heedful 457
heedless
  inattentive 458
  neglectful 460
  forgetful 506
  rash 863
heel *follow* 63
  support 215
  lean 217
  tag 235
  deviate 279
  go round 311
  –of Achilles 665
  iron–975
  turn on one's–
    go back 283
    go round 311
    avoid 623
heeler 886
heelpiece *sequel* 65
  back 235
  repair 660
heeltap *remainder* 40
  dress 653
heels *lowness* 207
  at the–of *near* 197
  behind 235
  cool one's–681
  follow on the–of
    281
  –over head
  inverted 218
  hasty 684
  rash 863
  laid by the–751
  lay by the–789
  show a light pair of
    –623
  take to one's–623
  tread on the–of
  near 197
  follow 281
  approach 286
heft *weight* 319
  handle 633
  exertion 686
hefty *laborious* 686
Hegelianism 451
hegemonic 33
hegemony
  influence 175
  direction 693
  authority 737
hegira 293
Heidelberg man
  372a

heifer 366
heigho! 839
height *degree* 26
  altitude **206**
  summit 210
  at its–*great* 31
  supreme 33
  draw oneself up to
    his full–307
heighten *increase* 35
  elevate 307
  exaggerate 549
  aggravate 835
heinous 945
heir *futurity* 121
  posterity 167
  inheritor 779
heirloom 780
heirship 777
heliacal 318
helical 248
Helicon 597
Heliogabalus 954a
heliograph *signal* 550
  picture 554
heliography *light* 420
  painting 556
heliolater 382
heliolatry 382, 991
heliology 420
heliometer 420
heliometry 420
Heliophagous 420
Helios 318, 423
helioscope 445
heliotherapy 420,
  662
heliotrope *purple* 437
  ornament 847
heliotype 437, 554,
  558
helium 490*b*
helix 248
hell *abyss* 208
  gaming house 621
  gehenna **982**
  –broke loose 59
  –upon earth
  misfortune 735
  pain 828
  –within 926
hellborn *vicious* 945
  satanic 978
hellebore 663
hell–cat 949
Hellenist 492
hellhag 913
hellhound
  evildoer 913
  bad man 949
hellish
  malevolent 907
  vicious 945
  hell 982
  (*bad* 649)
helm *handle* 633

  scepter 747
  (*authority* 737)
  answer the–743
  at the–693
  obey the–705
  take the–693
helmet *hat* 225
  armor 717
helminth 663
helminthagogue 662
helminthology 368
helmsman 269, 694
helot 746
help *benefit* 618
  utility 644
  remedy 662
  aid 707
  servant **746**
  give 784
  –oneself to 789
  it can't be–ed
  submission 725
  never mind 823
  content 831
  God–you 914
  so–me God 535
helper 711
helpful 746
helpless
  incapable 158
  exposed 665
helpmate
  auxiliary **711**
  wife 903
helpmeet 903
helter–skelter
  disorder 59
  haste 684
hem *edge* 231
  fold 258
  indeed! 870
  –in *inclose* 229
  restrain 751
  kiss the–of one's
    garment 886
hematite 490*c*
hemeralopia 443
hemi– 91
hemiplegia 376
hemisphere 181
hemispheric 250
hemlock *herb* 367
  unsavoriness 395
  bane 663
  punishment 972
hemorrhage 299
hemorrhoids 655
hemp *filament* 205
  poison 663
hen *bird* 366
  female 374
  source of supply 636
  –party 892
  –with one chicken
  busy 682
henbane 663

hence
  arising from 155
  departure 293
  deduction 476
henceforth 121
henchman 746
hencoop 370
hen–headed 458
hen–hearted 862
henhussy 374, 501
henna 433, 439
henotheism 984
henpecked
  obedient 743
  subject 749
hepatize 641
heptad 98, 193
heptagon 98, 244
heptahedral 98
heptamerous 98
heptangular 98
herald *precursor* 64
  precede 116
  precession 280
  predict 511
  informant 527
  proclaim 531
  messenger 534
heraldry 550
herb 367
herbaceous 367
herbage 367
herbal 369
Herbartianism 451
herbivore 298
herbivorous 298
herborize 369
herculean *great* 31
  strong 159
  exertion 686
  difficult 704
Hercules
  strength 159
  size 192
  support 215
  pillars of– *limit* 233
  mark 550
herd *assemblage* 72
  multitude 102
herder 370
herdsman 746
here *situation* 183
  presence 186
  arrival 292
  come–! 286
  –and there
  dispersed 73
  few 103
  place 182, 183
  –below 318
  –goes 676
  –there and
    everywhere
  diversity 16a
  space 180
  omnipresence 186

  –to–day and gone
    tomorrow 111
hereabouts *site* 183
  near 197
hereafter 121
  destiny 152
hereby 631
hereditament 780
hereditary *intrinsic* 5
  derivative 154, 167
  property 780
heredity 154, 167
herein 221
heresy *error* 495
  religious 984
heretic 489, 984
heretical 495, 984
heretofore 122
hereupon 106
herewith
  accompanying 88
  means 632
heritage *futurity* 121
  possession 777
  property 780
heritor 779
hermaphrodite 83
  –brig 273
hermeneutics 522
Hermes 582
hermetically 261
hermit *recluse* 893
  ascetic 955
hermitage *house* 189
  cell 191
  seclusion 893
hermitize 893
hernia 655
hero *brave* 861
  glory 873
  good man 948
  –worship
  approbation 931
  idolatry 991
Herod, out–Herod–
  549
heroic (*see* hero)
  magnanimous 942
  mock–853
heroics 884
heroism 861
heron 366
herpes 655
herpetology 368
herring *fish* 298
  pungent 392
  –pond 341
  trail of a red–615,
    706
herring–gutted 203
hesitate
  uncertain 475
  skeptical 485
  stammer 583
  reluctant 603
  irresolute 605

fearful 860
Hesperian 236
Hesperides
garden of the–981
Hesperus 423
Hessian 726, 819
Hessian boot 225
hest 741
heterarchy 737
heteroclite 83, 139
heterodox 487, 489
heterodoxy 984
heterogamy 161, 357
heterogeneity 15,
16a
heterogeneous
unrelated 10
different 15
mixed 41
multiform 81
exceptional 83
heterogenesis 161
heteromorphism
16a
heteronomy 737
heteropathy 662
heterotopy 185
hetman 745
hew *cut* 44
shorten 201
fashion 240
–down 213, 308
hewers of wood
workers 690
commonalty 876
hexad 98, 193
hexaglot 560
hexagon 98, 244
hexahedral 98
hexahedron 98, 244
hexameter 98, 597
hexangular 98
hexastyle 98
heyday
exultation 836, 838
festivity 840
wonder 870
–of the blood 820
–of youth 127
hiation 260
hiatus *interval* 198
(*discontinuity* 70)
hibernal 383
hibernate 683
Hibernian 188
Hibernicism
absurdity 497
neology 563
hiccup 349
hickory shirt 225
hid
–under a bushel 460
hidalgo 875
hidden 528
–meaning 526
hide *skin* 223

conceal 528
–and seek
deception 545
avoid 623
game 840
–diminished head
inferior 34
decrease 36
humility 879
–one's face
modesty 881
hidebound
strait–laced 751
stingy 819
bigoted 988
hideous 846
hiding place
abode 189
ambush 530
refuge 666
hie *go* 264
speed 274
–to 266
hiemal 383
hierarch 996
hierarchy 995
hieratic 372a
hieroglyphic
representation 554
letter 561
writing 590
hierographa 985
hierography 983
hierolatry 991
hieromancy 511
hierophant 996
hieroscopy 511
higgle 794
higgledy–piggledy
59
higgler 797
high *much* 31
lofty 206
of game 298
fetid 401
treble 410
foul 653
noted 873
proud 878
from on–981
–and dry *stable* 150
safe 664
–and mighty
pride 878
insolence 885
–art 556
–as heaven 67
–celebration 998
–color *color* 428
red 434
exaggerate 549
–days and holidays
840
–descent 875
–glee 836
–hand *violent* 173

resolved 604
authority 737
severe 739
pride 878
insolence 885
lawless 964
–in tone *white* 430
–life *fashion* 852
rank 875
–living
intemperance 954
gluttony 957
–mass 998
–mightiness 873
–note 410
–notions 878
–places 210
–pressure *power* 157
energy 171
excitation of feeling
824
–price 814
–priest 996
–principled 939
–repute 873
–school 542
–seas 341
–tide *wave* 348
prosperity 734
–time *late* 133
occasion 134
–treason
disobedience 742
dishonor 940
–words *quarrel* 713
anger 900
in a–degree 31
in–*automobile* 274
in–esteem 928
in–feather
strong 159
health 654
cheerful 836
boasting 884
in–quarters 875
in–spirits 836
on–206
on one's–ropes
excitation 824
pride 878
anger 900
on the–road to
way 627
hope 858
ride the–horse 878
think–ly of 931
highball 959
highbinder 361
highborn 875
high–brow
pedantry 491
higher 33, 206
–education 490
–pantheism 984
highest 210
–heaven 981

highfaluting 577, 884
high–fed 954
high–flavored 392
highflier
madman 504
proud 878
high–flown
absurd 497
imaginative 515
style 577
proud 878
vain 880
insolent 885
highflyer
madman 504
highflying
exaggerated 549
ostentatious 822
highlands 206
high–low 225
high–mettled
excitable 825
brave 861
high–minded
honorable 939
magnanimous 942
highness *title* 877
high–pitched 410
high–plumed 878
high–priced 809
high–reaching 206,
865
high–roller 818
high–seasoned 392
high–souled 878
high–sounding
loud 404
words 577
display 882
high–spirited
brave 861
honorable 939
high–strung 825
hight 564
high–toned 410, 878
highwater
completeness 52
height 206
crater 337
–mark *measure* 466
highway 627
–s and byways 627
highwayman 792
high–wrought
good 648
prepared 673
excited 824
hike 260
hiker 268
hilarity 836
hill *height* 206
convexity 250
ascent 305
–station 189
hill–dwelling 206
hillock 206

hilly 206
hilt 633
hind *back* 235
deer 366
clown 876
on one's–legs
elevation 307
anger 900
hinder *impede* 706
(*counteract* 179)
(*prohibit* 761)
hindermost *end* 67
back 235
hind quarters 235
Hindu *deities* 979
priests 996
temples 1000
Hinduism 976, 984
Hindustani 563
hindrance 706
hindward 235
hinge *fasten* 43
fastening 45
cause 153
depend upon 154
rotate 312
hinny 271
hint *reminder* 505
suppose 514
inform 527
–a fault etc. 932
take a–498
hinterland 235
hip 236 have on the–
confute 479
success 731
authority 737
subjection 749
hip bath 386
hipped *deranged* 503
hippish 503
hippocentaur 80
Hippocrates 219, 662
hippocratic 360
hippodrome
drama 599
arena 728
hippogriff 83
Hippolytus 960
hippophagy 298
hippopotamus 192,
366
hip rafter, 215
hip roof 223
hire *commission* 755
borrowing 788
price 812
reward 973
(*purchase* 795)
on–763
hireling 746
hirsute 256
hispid 256
hiss *sound* 409
animal cry 412
disrespect 929

471

contempt 930
disapprobation 932
hist *hush!* 585, 586
histogenesis 161
histology 329, 368
historian 553
historic 594
historical 594
−*painter* 559
−*painting* 556
historicize 594
historiette 594
historiographer 553, 594
historiography 594
history *pedigree* 69
  the past 122
  record 551
  narrative 594
  prose 598
  natural−357
histrionic 599
hit *chance* 156
  strike 276
  reach 292
  succeed 731
  censure 932
  (*punish* 972)
  good−626
−*off* 554
−*one's fancy* 829
−*on the raw* 900
−*the mark* 731
−*upon chance* 156
  discover 480a
  plan 626
  make a−731
  palpable−276
hitch *fasten* 43
  cessation 142
  concurrence 178
  hang 214
  jerk 315
−*a horse* 370
  difficulty 704
  hindrance 706
hither *direction* 278
  arrival 292
  come−286
hitherto 122
Hittite 372a
hive *multitude* 102
  location 184
  abode 189
  apiary 370
  workshop 691
H. M. S. 726
hoar *aged* 128
  white 430
−*frost* 383
hoard 636
−s *after*−s 819
hoarse *husky* 405
  harsh 410
  voiceless 581
  talk oneself−584

hoary (*see* hoar)
  old 124
hoax 545
hob *support* 215
  stove 386
−*and nob*
  celebration 883
  courtesy 894
hobble *limp* 275
  awkward 699
  difficulty 704
  fail 732
  shackle 751
hobbledehoy 129
hobby *crotchet* 481
  pursuit 622
  avocation 625
  desire 865
hobbyhorse 272
hobgoblin *fearful* 860
  demon 980
hobnail 876
hobo *tramp* 268
  neglect 460
  idler 683
  vagabond 876
hoboism 266, 683
Hobson's choice
  necessity 601
  no choice 609a
  compulsion 744
hock *maim* 645
hockey 840
hocus 545
hocus−pocus
  interchange 148
  unmeaning 517
  cheat 545
  conjuration 992
  spell 993
hod *receptacle* 191
  vehicle 272
hoddy−doddy 501
hodgepodge 41, 59
hoe *vehicle* 272
  agriculture 371
hoecake 298
hog *animal* 366
  selfishness 943
  sensualist 954a
  glutton 957
  go the whole−604
  greedy as a−865
hog's back 206
hog wallow 343
hog wash 653
hoist 307−*a flag* 550
−*on one's own petard*
  retaliation 718
  failure 732
−*the black flag* 722
hoity−toity
  defiance 715
  wonder 870
hold *cohere* 46
  contain 54

remain 141
cease 142
go on 143
happen 151
receptacle 191
cellar 207
base 211
support 215
halt 265
believe 484
be passive 681
defend 717
power 737
restrain 751
prohibit 761
possess 777
retain 781
enough! 869
gain a−*upon* 737
get−*of* 789
have a firm−781
have a−*upon* 175
−*a council* 695
−*a high opinion of*
  928
−*a lease* 771
−*aloof absence* 187
  distrust 487
  avoid 623
−*a meeting* 72
−*an argument* 476
−*a situation* 625
−*authority* 737
−*back avoid* 623
  store 636
  restrain 751
  retain 781
  miserly 819
−*both one's sides* 838
−*converse* 588
−*fast restrain* 751
  retain 781
−*forth teach* 537
  speak 582
−*good*
  demonstration 478
  truth 494
−*hard* 265
−*in hand* 737
−*in remembrance* 505
−*in solution* 335
−*off* 623
−*office* 693
−*on*
  continue 141, 143
  persevere 604a
−*one's breath*
  wonder 870
−*oneself in readiness*
  673
−*oneself up* 307
−*one's ground* 141
−*one's hand*
  cease 142
  relinquish 624
−*one's own*

preserve 670
defend 717
resist 719
−*one's tongue* 585
−*out*
  (*see below*)
−*the scales* 466
−*to* 602
−*together junction* 43
  cooperate 709
−*up*
  (*see below*)
−*up one's head* 861
  quit one's−782
  take−175
holdback 706
holder 779
holdfast 45
holding *tenancy* 777
  property 780
−*company* 712
hold out *continue* 106
  affirm 535
  persevere 604a
  resist 719
  offer 763
  brave 861
−*expectation*
  predict 511
  promise 768
−*temptation* 865
hold up *continue* 143
  support 215
  not rain 340
  aid 707
  display 882
  extol 931
−*one's hand sign* 550
  threat 600
−*the mirror* 525
−*to execration*
  curse 908
  censure 932
−*to scorn* 930
−*to shame* 874
−*to view* 525
hold−up 791, 792
hole *state* 7
  place 182
  hovel 189
  receptacle 191
  cave 251
  opening 260
  ambush 530
−*and corner*
  place 182
  peer into−461
  hiding 528, 530
−*in one's coat* 651
−*to creep out of*
  plea 617
  escape 671
  facility 705
Holi 138
holiday *leisure* 685
  repose 687

amusement 840
celebration 883
−*task easy* 706
holiness *God* 976
  piety 987
holloa 411
−*before one is out of*
  the wood 884
hollow *unsubstantial* 4
  completely 52
  incomplete 53
  depth 208
  concavity 252
−*sound* 408 *gruff* 410
  specious 477
  voiceless 581
  beat−731
−*commendation* 894
−*truce* 723
hollow−hearted 544
hollowness
  (*see* hollow)
holm 345, 346
holocaust *kill* 361
  sacrifice 991
  (*destruction* 162)
holograph 590
holt 367
holus−bolus 684
Holy *of God* 976
  pious 987
−*breathing* 990
−*day* 998
−*Ghost* 976
−*Grail* 998
−*men of old* 985
−*orders* 995
−*place* 1000
−*Scriptures* 985
−*Spirit* 976
−*Thursday* 998
−*water* 998
−*week* 998
  keep−987
  temple of the−
  Ghost 983a
homage
  submission 725
  fealty 743
  reverence 928
  approbation 931
  worship 990
homaloid 251
home *focus* 74
  habitation 189
  near 197
  interior 221
  arrival 292
  country 342
  hospital 662
  refuge 666
  at−*party* 72
  present 186
  within 221
  at ease 705
  social gathering 892

at–in *knowledge* 490
skill 698
at–with
friendship 888
be at–*to visitors* 892
bring–to
evidence 467
belief 484
accuse 938
condemn 971
come–292
drive–729
eternal–98
feel at–*freedom* 748
pleasure 827
content 831
from–187
get–292
go from–293
go–283
–rule 737
–stroke 170
–thrust *attack* 716
censure 932
look at–
accusation 938
make oneself at–
free 748
sociable 892
not be at–764
stay at–265
strike–*energy* 171
attack 716
home–bred 851
home–felt 821, 824
home–grown 367
homeless
unhoused 185
banished 893
homelike 849
homeliness 851
(*see* homely)
homely *language* 576
unadorned 849
common 851, 876
homeopathic
small 32
little 193
homeopathy 662
homesick 833
homespun *simple* 42
texture 219, 329, 635
homestall 189
homestead 189
homeward bound 292
homicide 361
homiletical 537
homily *teaching* 537
advice 595
sermon 998
hominy 298
homish 849
homme de cour 886
homocentric 68

homogeneity
relation 9
identity 13
uniformity 16
simplicity 42
homogenesis 161
homoiousia 17
homoiousian 983
homologate 23
homologue 714
homology *relation* 9
uniformity 16
equality 27
concord 714
homonym
equivocal 520
vocal sound 580
homonymy 520
homoousia 13
homoousian 983
homophonic 402
homophony 402, 413
homunculus 193
hone 253
honest *veracious* 543
honorable 939
pure 960
–*meaning* 516
–*truth* 494
turn an–*penny* 775
honey *sweet* 396
favorite 899
–*sweet* 396
milk and–734
honeybee 366
honeycomb
concave 252
opening 260
deterioration 659
honeyed–*phrases* 894
–*words*
allurement 615
flattery 933
honeymoon
pleasure 827
endearment 902
marriage 903
honey–mouthed
courteous 894
flatter 933
honor *demesne* 780
glory 873
title 877
respect 928
approbation 931
probity 939
affair of–720
do–to 883
do the–s
sociality 892
courtesy 894
respect 928
his–*judge* 967
–a bill 807
–be to 873
–bright *veracity* 543

probity 939
in–of 883
man of–939
upon my–535
word of–768
honorable (*see* honor)
reliable 632
honorarium *gift* 784
reward 973
honorary 815
honored 500
(*see* honor)
hooch 298
hood *cap* 225
automobile 272
distinction 550
cowl 999
hooded 223
hoodlum 887, 913
hoodoo *chance* 621
bane 649
sorcery 992
hoodooed 735
hoodwink *ignore* 491
blind 442
hide 528
deceive 545
hoof 211
hook *fasten* 43
fastening 45
hang 214
curve 245
deceive 545
retain 781
take 789
by–or by crook 631
hooked 244, 245
hooker *ship* 273
Hooke's law 490*d*
hookey, blind–840
hooklike 245
hook–shaped 245
hooligan 887, 913
hoop *circle* 247
cry 411
hoot *cry* 411, 412
deride 929
contempt 930
censure 932
hop *leap* 309
dance 840
–skip and jump
leap 309
agitation 315
haste 684
game 840
–the twig 360
hope 858
band of–958
beyond all–734
dash one's–s 837
excite–511
foster–858
–against hope 858
–deferred
dejection 837

lamentation 859
–for *expect* 507
desire 865
–for the best 858
well grounded–472
hopeful *infant* 129
probable 472
hope 858
hopelessness 471, **859**
hop garden 371
hop–o'–my–thumb 193
hopper 191
hopple 751
hopples 752
hopscotch 840
horary 108
horde *assemblage* 72
party 712
commonalty 876
horehound 400
horizon *distance* 196
view 441
expectation 507
(*future* 121)
gloomy–859
horizontality 213
horizontally 213, 251
horn *receptacle* 191
pommel 215, 249
sharp 253
music 417
draw in one's–s
recant 607
submit 725
humility 879
exalt one's–873
–in 294
–of plenty 639
–s of a dilemma
reasoning 476
difficulty 704
wear the–s 905
hornbook 542
horned 245
hornet *evildoer* 913
–'s nest *pitfall* 667
difficulty 704
adversity 735
painful 830
resentment 900
censure 932
hornpipe 840
horn–shaped 253
hornwork 717
horny 323
Horny, old–978
horologer 114
horology 114
horoscope 511
horrible *great* 31
noxious 649
dire 830
ugly 846
fearful 860

horrid (*see* horrible)
vulgar 851
horrific (*see* horrible)
horrified *pain* 828
fear 860
horrify *pain* 830
terrify 860
horripilation 383
horrisonous 410
horror *fear* 860
dislike 867
view with–898
horrors *dejection* 837
cup full of–828
horror–stricken 828
hors de combat
impotent 158
useless 645
tired out 688
put–731
hors d'oeuvre 298, 394
horse *hang on* 214
stand 215
carrier 271
animal 366
male 373
translation 539
cavalry 726
–and foot 726
–artillery 726
–box 272
–car 272
–cloth 225
–coper 548
–doctor 370
–guards 726
–laugh 838
–leech 370
–litter 272
–marine 268, 701
–racing–*pastime* 840
contention 720
–sense 498
–soldier 726
–stealing 791
–track 627
–trainer 370
like a–in a mill 613
put thes to 673
put up one's–s at 184
put up one's–s together
concord 714
friendship 888
ride the high–885
take–266
war–726
work like a–686
horseback 266
horseman 268
horsemanship
riding 266
skill 698
horseplay 856

implanted
ingrained 5
adventitious 6
–by nature 820
implausible 473
implead 969
implement 633
impletion 52
implex 41
implicate
involve 54, 526
accuse 938
implicated
related 9
component 56
implication
disorder 59
meaning 516
metaphor 521
latency 526
implicit 526
–belief 484
implied (*see* imply)
implore 765
imply *evidence* 467
mean 516
involve 526
(*metaphor* 521)
impolicy 699
impolite 895
imponderable 4, 320
imporous *closed* 261
dense 321
import
put between 228
ingress 294
take in 296
insert 300
mean 516
involve 526
be of consequence
642
importance
greatness 31
consequence **642**
attach–to 642
attach too much–to
482
of no–643
important 642
importune *ask* 765
pester 830
impose *print* 591
order 741
awe 928
–upon *credulity* 486
deceive 545
be unjust 923
imposing
important 642
exciting 824
glorious 873
imposition
(*see* impose)
undue 925
–of hands 998

impossibilities
seek after–645
impossibility 471
impossible 471
deception 702
refusal 764
(*difficulty* 704)
–quantity *algebra* 84
impost 812
impostor 548, 925
impostume 655
imposture 545
impotence 158
impotent 732
–conclusion 732
–to rise 158
impound
imprison 751
(*inclose* 229)
impoverish
weaken 160
waste 638
despoil 789
render poor 804
impracticable
impossible 471
misjudging 481
obstinate 606
difficulty 704
impracticality 471
imprecation
prayer 765
curse 908
imprecatory 765, 908
impregnable
strong 159
safe 664
impregnate *mix* 41
combine 48
fecundate 161, 168
insert 300
teach 537
–with *cloy* 641
impresario 599
imprescriptible 924
impress *effect* 154
cause sensation 375
mark 550
excite feeling 824
–upon the mind
memory 505
teach 537
impressed with
belief 484
feeling 821
impressibility 375
impressible
motive 615
sensibility 822
impression *effect* 154
sensation 375
idea 453
belief 484
publication 531
mark 550
engraving 558

print 591
emotion 821
make an *act* 171
thought 451
impressionable 375,
822
impressive
language 574
important 642
feeling 821, 824
imprimis 558
imprimus 66
imprint *publisher* 531
indication 550
–in the memory 505
imprison
circumscribe 229
restrain 751
punish 972
improbability 473
improbate 932
improbity 940
impromptu 612
improper
incongruous 24
foolish 499
solecistic 568
inexpedient 647
wrong 923
unmeet 925
vicious 945
–time 135
impropriate
possess 777
take 789
impropriator 779
impropriety
(*see* improper)
improve 658
–the occasion 134
–the shining hour
682
–upon 658
improvement **658**
improvident
careless 460
not preparing 674
prodigal 818
rash 863
improvisator 416,
582
improvisatore
speech 582
poetry 597
impulse 612
improvise
imagination 515
extemporize 612
unprepared 674
improviser 612
imprudent
neglectful 460
rash 863
(*unwise* 699)
impudence
insolence 885

discourtesy 895
impudent
insolent 885
discourteous 895
impudicity 961
impugn *deny* 536
attack 716
blame 932
impugnation 708
impugnment 708
impuisance 158
impulse *push* 276
sudden thought **612**
motive 615
blind–601
creature of–612
give an–to
propel 284
aid 707
impulsive
(*see* impulse)
intuitive 477
unaccustomed 604
excitable 825
rash 863
impunctual 133
impunity
escape 671
acquittal 970
with–*safely* 664
impurity
inelegance 579
foul 653
licentious **961**
imputation
ascribe 155
slur 874
accuse 938
in 221 go–294
–a jiffy 113
–and out 314
–a rut 16
–as much as
relation 9
degree 26
–for *undertake* 676
promise 768
–s and outs 182
in–camera 528
–*extenso whole* 50
diffuse 573
–*loco* 23
–*medias res* 68
–*propria persona* 79,
186
–*re* 9
–*statu quo* 141
–*statu quo ante*
bellum 140
–*toto* 52
–*transitu*
transient 111
transfer 270
inability
want of power 158
want of skill 699

–to discriminate
465a
inabstinent 954
inaccessible
distant 196
impossible 471
inaccordant 24
inaccurate *error* 495
solecism 568
inacquiescent 24
inaction *inertness* 172
not doing **681**
inactivity **683**
inertness 172
inadequacy
(*see* inadequate)
inadequate
unequal 28
powerless 158
insufficient 640
useless 645
imperfect 651
(*weak* 160)
inadmissible
incongruous 24
excluded 55
extraneous 57
inexpedient 647
inadvertence 458
inadvisable 647, 649
inaffable 895
inalienable
retention 781
right 924
inamorata 897
inane *void* 4
incogitancy 452
unmeaning 517
insufficient 640
trivial 643
useless 645
inanimate 360
–matter 358
inanition 158
inanity (*see* inane)
inappetency
insensibility 823
indifference 866
inapplicable
irrelation 10
disagreement 24
inapposite
irrelation 10
disagreement 24
inappreciable
in degree 32
in size 193
unimportant 643
inapprehensible
stolid 499
unintelligible 519
inappropriate
unconsonant 24
inexpedient 647
inapt *incongruous* 24
impotent 158

useless 645
inexpedient 647
unskillful 699
inarticulate 581, 583
inartificial 703
inartistic 846
inasmuch *whereas* 9
however 26
because 476
inattention 458
inattentive 419, 458
inaudible *silence* 403
faint sound 405
deaf 419
voiceless 581
inaugural
precursor 64
inaugurate *begin* 66
install 755
celebrate 883
inauguratory 66
inauspicious
untimely 135
untoward 649
adverse 735
hopeless 859
inbeing 5
inborn *intrinsic* 5
affections 820
(*habit* 613)
−*proclivity* 601
inbound 294
inbred (*see* inborn)
inca 745
incage 751
incalculable *much* 31
infinite 105
incalescence 382
incandescence 382
incantation
invocation 765
spell 993
incantatory 992
incapable
impotent 158
(*weak* 160)
incapacious 203
incapacitate 158
incapacity
impotence 158
ignorance 491
stupidity 499
(*weakness* 160)
incarcerate
imprison 751
(*surround* 229)
incarnadine 434
incarnate *intrinsic* 5
materiality 316
to incorporate 364
vicious 945
devil−bad man 949
Satan 978
incarnation 316, 976
incase *cover* 223
surround 229

incautious *rash* 863
(*neglect* 460)
incendiary
destroy 162
burn 384
influence 615
pitfall 667
malevolent 907
evildoer 913
bad man 949
incensation 400
incense *fuel* 388
fragrant 400
hate 898
anger 900
flatter 933
worship 990
rite 998
−*breathing* 400
−*burner* 400
incension
burning 384
incensorium 400
incentive 615
incept 66, 537
inception 66
inceptive
beginning 66
causal 153
generative 168
inceptor 541
incertitude 475
incessant
repeated 104
ceaseless 112
frequent 136
incest 961
inch *small* 32
length 200
move slowly 275
measure 466
by−es 275
*give an−and take
an ell* 789
−*by inch*
by degrees 26
in parts 51
slowly 275
*not see an−beyond
one's nose* 699
*not yield an−*606
*to an−*494
inchoation
beginning 66
preparation 673
incide 44
incidence 278
incident 151
*full of−*151
incidental *extrinsic* 6
circumstance 8
irrelative 10
occurring 151
casual 156
liable 177
chance 621

−*music* 415
incinerate 384
incinerator 384
incipience 66
incircumspect 460
incise *cut* 44
furrow 259
incision *cut* 44
furrow 259
incisive *energy* 171
vigor 574
feeling 821
incite *exasperate* 173
urge 615
incitement
(*see* incite)
incivility 895
incivism 911
inclasp 229
inclement
violent 173
cold 383
severe 739
pitiless 914a
inclination
(*see* incline)
descent 306
will 600
affection 820
desire 865
love 897
incline *tendency* 179
slope 217
direction 278
willing 602
induce 615
−*an ear to* 457
inclined *oblique* 217
intended 620
−*plane* 633
inclose
place within 221
surround 227
hem in 229
inclosure *region* 181
envelope **232**
fence 752
include
composition 54
−*in a class* 76
inclusion 76
inclusive *additive* 37
component 56
class 76
inclusory 56
incogitance 452
incognito 528
incognizable 519
incoherence
physical **47**
mental 503
incombustible 385
income *means* 632
profit 775
property 780
wealth 803

receipt 810
incomer
immigrant 294
incoming *ingress* 294
receipt 810
incommensurable
irrelation 10
(*disagreeing* 24)
−*quantity* 84, 85
incommode
hinder 706
(*trouble* 830)
(*incommodious* 647)
incommodious 647
incommunicable
unmeaning 517
unintelligible 519
retention 781
incommutable 150
incomparable
superior 33
(*good* 648)
incompassionate
914a
incompatibility 15
incompatible 24
incompetence
inability 158
incapacity 499
unskillful 699
incomplete
fractional 51
not complete 53, 730
incompleteness 53
noncompletion 730
incomplex 42
incompliance 764
incomprehensible
infinite 105
unintelligible 519
incomprehension
491
incompressible 321
inconceivable
unthought of 452
impossible 471
improbable 473
incredible 485
unintelligible 519
wonder 870
inconceptible 519
inconcinnity
disagreement 24
ugliness 846
inconclusive 477
inconcoction 674
incondite 851
inconformity 15
incongruous
differing 15
disagreeing 24
faulty 568
discordant 713
inconnection
irrelation 10
disjunction 44

inconsequence
irrelation 10
inconsequential
illogical 477
inconsiderable
small 32
fractional 100a
unimportant 643
inconsiderate
thoughtless 452
inattentive 458
neglectful 460
foolish 699
inconsistent
contrary 14
disagreeing 24
illogical 477
absurd 497
foolish 499
discordant 713
capricious 608
inconsolable 837
inconsonant
disagreeing 24
fitful 149
inconspicuous 447
inconstant 149
incontestable
strong 159
certain 474
incontiguous 196
incontinent 961
incontinently 132
incontrollable 173
incontrovertible
certain 474
(*stable* 150)
inconvenience 647
*put to−*706
inconvenient 135,
647
inconversable
taciturn 585
unsociable 893
inconvertible
continuing 143
(*stable* 150)
inconvincible 487
incorporality 317
incorporate
combine 48
include 76
materialize 316
immaterial 317
animality 364
incorporation
(*see* incorporate)
incorporeal 317
−*hereditaments* 780
incorrect *illogical* 477
erroneous 495
solecism 568
vicious 945
incorrigible
obstinate 606
hopeless 859

−one's fancy 609
−with *give* 784
indulgence
  (*see* indulge)
  absolution 918
indulgent *kind* 906
induration
  hardening 323
  impenitence 951
industrious
  studious 539
  (*see* industry)
industry *business* 625
  activity 682
  hive of−691
indweller 188
indwelling 5
inebriety 959
inedible 867
ineffable *great* 31
  unmeaning 517
  wonderful 870
ineffaceable 820
ineffectual
  incapable 158
  useless 645
  failing 732
  −attempt 732
  pale its−fire 422
inefficacious
  incapable 158
  useless 645
  failing 732
inefficient 158
inelastic *soft* 324
  −fluid 333
inelasticity 326
inelegance
  in language 579
  ugly 846
ineluctable 474
inept *incapable* 158
  useless 645
  (*inexpedient* 647)
inequality 24, 28
inequation 28
inequitable 923
ineradicable
  intrinsic 5
  stable 150
inerrable 946
inert (*see* inertness)
inertia 172
inertness
  physical 172
  inactive 683
  moral 823
inessential 10
inestimable 648
inevitable *certain* 474
  destiny 601
inexact *erroneous* 495
  feeble 575
inexcitability 826
inexcusable
  accusable 938

vicious 945
inexecution 730
inexhaustibility 105
inexhaustible 104, 639
inexistence 2
inexorable
  unavoidable 601
  resolved 604
  stern 739
  compelling 744
  pitiless 914a
  revengeful 919
  (*wrathful* 900)
  (*malevolent* 907)
inexpectation 508
inexpedience 647, 699
inexpensive 815
inexperience
  ignorant 491
  unskillful 699
inexpert 699
inexpiable 945
inexplicable 519
inexpressible
  great 31
  unmeaning 517
  unintelligible 519
  wonderful 870
inexpressibles 225
inexpression
  latency 526
inexpressive 517
inexpugnable 664
inextension 180a
  littleness 193
  immateriality 317
inextinguishable
  stable 150
  strong 159
  excitable 825
  −desire 865
inextricable
  coherent 46
  disorder 59
  impossible 471
  (*difficult* 704)
infallibility 474
  assumption of−885
infallible 474
infamy *shame* 874
  dishonor 940
  vice 945
infancy
  beginning 66
  youth 127
infant 129 *fool* 501
Infanta 745
infanticide
  killing 361
  sacrifice 991
infantine 129
  foolish 499
infantry 726
infarct 261, 706

infarction 261, 706
infare 892
infatuation
  misjudgment 481
  credulity 486
  folly 499
  insanity 503
  obstinacy 606
  passion 825
  love 897
infeasible 471
infect *mix with* 41
  contaminate 659
  excite 824
infection
  transference 270
  disease 655
infectious 270, 657
infecund 169
infelicitous 24, 828
infelicity
  inexpertness 699
  misery 828
infer *presume* 472
  deduce 480
  imply 526
inference
  reasoning 476
  judgment 480
  implication 521
  latency 526
  by−467
inferential
  demonstrative 478
  construable 522
  latent 526
inferior
  (*see* inferiority)
  low 207
inferiority
  in degree 34
  in size 195
  imperfection 651
  personal−34
infernal *bad* 649
  malevolent 907
  wicked 945
  satanic 978
  −machine 727
  −regions 982
infertility 169
infest 830
infestivity *sad* 837
  dull 843
infibulation 43
infidel 487, 989
infidelity
  dishonor 940
  irreligion 989
infiltrate *mix* 41
  intervene 228
  interpenetrate 294
  ooze 295
  receive 296
  moisten 337, 339
  teach 537

infiltration
  passage 302
  (*see* infiltrate)
infinite 105
  −goodness 976
Infinite, the− 976
infinitely *great* 31
infinitesimal
  small 32
  little 193
  −calculus 85
infinity 105
infirm *weak* 160
  disease 655
  vicious 945
  −of purpose 605
infirmary 662
infirmity (*see* infirm)
infix 537
infixion 300
inflame
  render violent 173
  burn 384
  excite 824
  anger 900
  (*incite* 615)
inflamed *red* 434
  (*see* inflame)
inflammable
  burn 384
  fuel 388
inflammation
  heating 384
  disease 655
inflammatory
  heated 384
  (*see* inflame)
inflate *increase* 35
  expand 194
  blow 349
inflated *style* 573, 577
  ridiculous 853
  vain 880
inflation (*see* inflate)
  rarefaction 322
inflect 245
inflection *change* 140
  curvature 245
  grammar 567
inflectional 567
inflexible *hard* 323
  resolved 604
  obstinate 606
  stern 739
  a will−906
  −in faith 159
inflexion
  (*see* inflection)
inflict *act upon* 680
  severity 739
  −evil 649
  −pain *bodily pain* 378
    mental pain 830
  −punishment 972
infliction
  adversity 735

mental pain 828, 830
  punishment 972
inflorescence 161
influence *cause* 153
  change 140
  physical−175
  tendency 176
  inducement 615
  instrumentality 631
  authority 737
  (*importance* 642)
  absence of−175a
  make one's−felt 175
  sphere of−780
influenza 655
influx 294
inform 527−against
  accuse 938
  go to law 969
informal *irregular* 83
  lawless 964
informality
  nonobservance 773
informant 527, 938
information
  knowledge 490
  communication 527
  lawsuit 969
  pick up−539
  wide−539
informed 527
informity 241
infraction
  infringement 303
  disobedience 742
  nonobservance 773
  exemption 927
  −of usage
    unconformity 83
    desuetude 614
infrangible
  combined 46
  dense 321
infrequency 137
infrequent 137
infrigidation 385
infringe
  transgress 303
  disobey 742
  not observe 773
  undueness 925
  dereliction 927
  −a law 83
infructuose 169
infumate 340, 673
infundibular
  concave 252
  hole 260
infuriate *violent* 173
  excite 824
  anger 900
infuscate 431
infuse *mix* 41
  insert 300
  teach 537

love 897
take no—in
insensibility 823
indifference 866
want of—866
interested *selfish* 943
interesting
lovable 897
interfacial 228
interfere *disagree* 24
counteract 179
intervene 228
activity 682
thwart 706
mediate 724
interferometer 193
interfuse 48
interfusion 41
intergrowth 228
interim *time* 106
short time 111
interior 221
painting 556
interiority 221
interjacence
middle 68
coming between **228**
interject *interpose* 228
insert 300
interlace *join* 43
combine 48
twine 219
interlacement 41
interlard *mix* 41
combine 48
interpolate 228
interleave 228
interline
interpolate 288
write 590
interlineal 228
interlineation 37, 300
interlink *join* 43
twine 219
interlobular 228
interlocation 228
interlocular 228
interlocution 588
interlocutor 582
interloper
extraneous 57
intervene 228
obstruct 706
interlude *time* 106
dramatic 599
intermarriage 903
intermarry 903
intermaxillary 228
intermeddle
interfere 682
hinder 706
intermeddling 724
intermedial 228, 631
intermediary 534, 631

intermediate
mean 29
middle 68
intervening 228
ministerial 631
—*time* 106
intermediation
agency 170
intermedium
mean 29
link 45
intervention 228
instrument 631
(means 632)
interment 363
insertion 300
intermigration 266
interminable
infinite 105
eternal 112
long 200
intermingle 41
intermission
time 106
discontinuance 142
intermit *interrupt* 70
recur 138
discontinue 142
intermittence
time 106
periodicity 138
intermittent 138
intermix 41, 48
intermolecular 228
intermundane 228
intermutation 148
intern 221
internal *intrinsic* 5
interior 221
—*evidence* 467
internasal 228
international
reciprocal 12
interchange 148
sociality 892
—*law* 963
interne 662
internecine 361
—*war* 722
interneural 228
internodal 228
internuncio
messenger 534
diplomatist 758
interoceanic 228
interosseal 228
interpel 142
interpellation
inquiry 461
address 586
summons 471
command 741
appeal 765
interpenetration
interjacence 228
ingress 294

passage 302
interplanetary 228
interpolar 228
interpolation
analytical 85
interpose 228
insertion 300
interpose
intervene 228
act 682
hinder 706
mediate 724
interposit 799
interposition
(see interpose)
interpret 522, 595
interpretation 516, **522** *(answer* 462)
interpreter 524
interradial 228
interregnum
intermission 106
transient 111
discontinuance 142
interval 198
inaction 681
laxity 738
(discontinuity 70)
interrelation 9, 12
interrenal 228
interrogate 461
interrogation 461
typography 550
interrupt
discontinuity 70
cessation 142
hinder 706
interruption
derangement 61
interval 198
interscapular 228
interscholastic 148
intersect 219
intersection 198, 219
interseptal 228
interspace
interval 198
interior 221
intersperse *diffuse* 73
interpose 228
(music 41)
interstate 148
interstellar 228
interstice 198
interstitial
internal 221
interjacent 228
intertanglement 41
intertexture
mixture 41
intersection 219
tissue 329
intertribal 148
intertwine *unite* 43
cross 219
intertwist 43, 219

interurban 148
interval *degree* 26
—*of time* 106
—*of space* **198**
—*in music* 413
at—s
discontinuously 70
at regular—s 138
intervalvular 228
intervascular 228
intervene
—*in order* 70
—*in time* 106
—*in space* 228
be instrumental 631
mediate 724
(agent 758)
intervener 228
interventricular 228
intervert *change* 140
deviate 279
intervertebral 228
interview
conference 588
society 892
interviewer 553, 554
intervolved 43
interweave *join* 43
cross 219
interjacence 228
interwork 148
interworking 170
intestate 552
intestine 221, 350
inthrall
subjection 749
restraint 751
intimacy 888
intimate *special* 79
close 197
tell 527
friendly 888
friend 890
intimately *joined* 43
intimation 527
intimidate
frighten 860
insolence 885
threat 909
intinction 998
into go—294
put—300
run—300
intolerable 830
intolerance
prejudice 481
obstinacy 606
impatience 825
insolence 885
malevolence 907
intolerant 489
intomb 363
intonation *sound* 402
musical 413
voice 580
intone *sing* 416

worship 990
intort 248
intoxicant *bane* 663
intoxicated 959
intoxication
excitement 824, 825
inebriation 959
intracanal 221
intracellular 221
intractable
obstinate 606
difficult 704
sullen 901a
intrados 221
intralobular 221
intramarginal 221
intramolecular 221
intramundane 221
intramural 221
intransient 110
intransigence 604
intransigent 604
intransitive 110
intransmutable
diuturnal 110
stable 150
intraocular 221
intrap 545
intraregarding 221
intraseptal 221
intratelluric 221
intrauterine 221
intravascular 221
intravenous 221
intraventricular 221
intrench *safety* 664
defend 717
—*on* 303
intrepid 861
intricacy 533
intricate *confused* 59
convoluted 248
difficult 704
intrigant
meddlesome 682
cunning 702
libertine 962
intrigue *plot* 626
activity 682
cunning 702
licentiousness 961
intriguer *activity* 682
cunning 702
intrinsic 5 *forming* 56
—*evidence* 467
—*habit* 613
—*truth* 494
intrinsicality 5
introception 296
introduce *lead* 62
interpose 228
precede 280
insert 300
—*new blood* 140
—*new conditions* 469
—*to* 888

introducer 164
introduction
  (see introduce)
  preface 64
  reception 296
  drama 599
  friendship 888
  courtesy 894
introductory
  precursor 64
  beginning 66
  priority 116
  receptive 296
introgression 294
introit 296, 998
intromissive 296
intromit *receive* 296
intromittent 296
introspection
  look into 441
  attend to 457
introspective 451
introvert 218
intrude *interfere* 24
  inopportune 135
  intervene 228
  enter 294
  trespass 303
intruder 57
intrusion
  (see intrude)
intrusive 706
intrusiveness 682
intrust *commit* 755
  lend 787
intuition *mind* 450
  unreasoning **477**
  knowledge 490
  subconsciousness
    992a
intumescence
  swell 194
  convex 250
intussuscept 14, 218
intwine *join* 43
  twist 248
inunction 223
inundate *effusion* 337
  flow 348
  redundance 641
inurbanity 895
inure *habituate* 613
  train 673
inured *insensible* 823
inurn 363
inusitate 20
inusitation 614
inutility **645**
invade *ingress* 294
  trespass 303
  attack 713
invaginate 14, 218
invagination 218,
  357
invalid *powerless* 158
  illogical 477

diseased 655
undue 925
invalidate *disable* 158
  weaken 160
  confute 479
invalidity *disease* 655
invaluable 644, 648
invariable *intrinsic* 5
  uniform 16
  conformable 82
  stable 150
invasion *ingress* 294
  attack 716
invective 932
inveigh 932
inveigle *deceive* 545
  seduce 615
invent *imagine* 515
  lie 544
  devise 626
invented *untrue* 546
invention (see invent)
  composition 54
inventive *skillful* 698
inventor 164
inventory 86
inverse *contrary* 14
  upside down 218
inversion
  derangement 61
  change 140
  of position **218**
  contraposition 237
  reversion 145
  language 577
invertebracy 158
invertebrate
  impotent 158
  frail 945
invest *impower* 157
  clothe 225
  surround 227
  besiege 716
  commission 755
  give 784
  lend 787
  expend 809
  –*in locate* 184
  purchase 795
  –*money* 817
  –*with ascribe* 155
investigate 461
investiture
  appointment 755
investment
  clothing 225
  (see invest)
  make–s 673
investor 784
inveterate *old* 124
  established 150
  inborn 820
  –*belief* 484
  –*habit* 613
invidious *painful* 830
  hatred 898

spite 907
envy 921
invigilation 459
invigorate
  strengthen 159
  improve 658
  inspirit 834
invigorating
  healthy 656
invincible 159
inviolable *secret* 528
  right 924
  honor 939
inviolate
  permanent 141
  secret 528
  honorable 939
invious *closed* 261
  pathless 704
invisibility **447**
invisible *small* 193
  not to be seen 447
  concealed 526
  –*government* 526
  –*helpers* 977
invitation (see invite)
invitatory 765
invite *induce* 615
  offer 763
  ask 765
  –*the attention* 457
inviting (see invite)
  pleasing 829
invocation
  (see invoke)
invocative 765
invoice 86
invoke *address* 586
  implore 765
  pray 990
  –*curses* 908
  –*saints* 998
involucrum 223
involuntary
  necessary 601
  unwilling 603
  –*servitude* 749
involution
  (see involve)
  algebra 85
involutional
  psychosis 821a
involve *include* 54
  derange 61
  wrap 225
  evince 467
  mean 516
  latency 526
involved *disorder* 59
  convoluted 248
  secret 533
  obscure style 571
  in debt 806
involvement 61, 704
invulnerable 664
inward *intrinsic* 5

inside 221
incoming 294
–*monitor* 926
inweave 219, 300
inwrap 225
inwrought 5
ion 490d
Ionian school 451
Ionic 597
iota *small* 32
  trifle 643
  (*minute* 193)
I O U *security* 771
  money 800
ipecacuanha 662
ipse dixit
  certainty 474
  affirmation 535
ipso facto 1
irascibility **901**
irate 900
iridescent 440
iridosmine 323
Iris *traveler* 268
  messenger 534
iris *rainbow* 440
  eye 441
irisated 440
irisation 440
Irish 188–*green* 435
Irishism 497
Irishman 188
irk 688, 830
irksome *tiresome* 688
  difficult 704
  painful 830
  weary 841
iron *strength* 159
  smooth 255
  hard 323
  resolution 604
  –*age adversity* 735
  pain 828
  –*cross* 551, 733
  –*entering into the*
    soul 828, 830
  –*gray* 432
  –*grip* 159
  –*gripe* 781
  –*heel* 739
  –*necessity* 601
  –*rule* 739
  –*sway* 739
  –*will* 604
  rule with a rod of–
    739
iron–bound coast
  land 342
  danger 667
ironclad *covering* 223
  defense 717
  man of war 726
iron–handed 739
iron–hearted 861
ironic (see irony)
iron mold 434

irons 752 *fire*–386
  –*in the fire*
  business 625
  redundance 641
  active 682
  unskillful 699
  put in–751
irony
  figure of speech 521
  untruth 546
  ridicule 856
irradiate 420
irrational *number* 84
  illogical 477
  silly 499
irreclaimable
  hopeless 859
  vicious 945
  impenitent 951
irreconcilable
  unrelated 10
  discordant 24
  unwilling 603
  intransigent 604
  opponent 710
  enmity 889
irrecoverable
  past 122
  hopeless 859
  (*lost* 776)
irredeemable
  hopeless 859
  (*lost* 776)
irreducible
  discordant 24
  out of order 59
  unchangeable 150
irrefragable 478
irrefutable
  certain 474
  proved 478
irregular *diverse* 16a
  out of order 59
  multiform 81
  against rule 83
  –*in recurrence* 139
  distorted 243
  guerrilla 722
  combatant 726
irregularity **139**
irrelation 10
irrelevant
  unrelated 10
  unaccordant 24
  sophistical 477
  unimportant 643
irreligion **989**
irremediable
  bad 649
  hopeless 859
  (*spoiled* 659)
  (*lost* 776)
irremissible 945
irremovable 141, 150
irreparable
  hopeless 859

landsman 268, 342
Landsturm 726
landsurveying 466
Landwehr 726
lane *street* 189
  opening 260
  way 627
langrage shot 727
langrel 727
Langrenus 490a
langsyne 122
language 560
  command of–582
  strong– *vigor* 574
  malediction 908
languid *weak* 160
  inert 172
  slow 275
  –*style* 575
  inactive 683
  torpid 823
languish *decrease* 36
  ill 655
  inactive 683
  repine 828
  affect 855
  –for 865
languishing 160
languishment
  lament 839
languor (*see* languid)
laniate 162
lank *long* 200
lanky *thin* 203
  tall 200, 206
lantern *window* 260
  lamp 423
  –jaws 203
  –of Diogenes 461
  magic–448
lanthanide series
  490b
lanuginous 256
Laocoön 557
Laodicean 823
lap *flap* 39
  abode 189
  eager 204
  support 215
  interior 221
  wrap 225
  encompass 227, 229
  drink 298
  circuition 311
  –*of waves* 405
  –of luxury
   pleasure 377
   inactivity 683
   voluptuousness 954
lapdog *animal* 366
  servile 886
lapel 39, 258
lapidate *kill* 361
  attack 716
  punish 972
lapideous 323

lapidescence 323
lapidify 323, 357
lapis lazuli *blue* 438
  jewel 847
lappet 39
lapse *course* 109
  past 122
  conversion 144
  fall 306
  degeneracy 659
  relapse 661
  loss 776
  vice 945
  guilt 947
  –of memory 506
  –of time 109
lapsus linguae
  mistake 495
  solecism 568
  stammering 583
larboard 239
larceny 791
larch 367
lard 355, 356
lardaceous 355
larder 636
  contents of the–298
lares et penates
  home 189
  idols 991
large *quantity* 31
  size 192
  at–*diffuse* 573
  free 748
  liberated 750
  become–194
  –number 102
  –type 642
large-hearted
  liberal 816
  benevolent 906
  disinterested 942
larger 194
largess 785
largest 784
largest portion 192
larghetto *slow* 275
  music 415
largiloquent
  verbose 573
largo *slow* 275
  music 415
lariat 45
larigo 45
lark *ascent* 305
  bird 366
  musician 416
  spree 840
  with the–
   morning 125
larmier 210
larrigan 225
larrikin 887, 913
larrup 972
larum *loud* 404
  alarm 669

larva 129, 193
larynx 351
lascar 269
lascivious 961
lash *tie together* 43
  violence 173
  whip 370
  incite 615
  censure 932
  punish 972
  scourge 975
  –into fury 900
  –the waves 645
  under the
   –compelled 744
   subject 749
lashes *hair* 256
lass *girl* 129
  (*woman* 374)
lassitude *fatigue* 688
  weariness 841
lasso *tie* 45
  loop 247
last *abide* 1
  model 22
  –*in order* 67
  endure 106
  durable 110
  –*in time* 122
  continue 141
  at–133
  at the–extremity
   665
  breathe one's–360
  die in the–ditch
   604a
  game to the–604a
  go to one's–home
   360
  –but one etc. 67
  –finish 729
  –for ever 112
  –gasp 360
  –home 363
  –post 550
  –resort 666
  –shift 601
  –sleep 360
  –stage 67
  –straw 153
  –stroke 729
  –touch 729
  –word
   affirmation 535
   obstinacy 606
  –year etc. 122
  never hear the–of
   104
  on–legs *weak* 160
  dying 360
  spoiled 659
  adversity 735
lastingness 141
latch *fasten* 43
  fastening 45
latchet 45

latchkey 631
latchstring
  find the–out 892
  have the–out 888
late *past* 122
  new 123
  tardy 133
  dead 360
  too–135
lately *formerly* 122
  recently 123
latency 526
lateness **133**
latent *inert* 172
  concealed 526
  influence 526
later 117
laterality **236**
lateritious 434
latest 118
lateward 132, 133
lath 205, 635
  thin as a–203
lathe *region* 181
  conversion 144
  machine 633
lather *lubrication* 332
  bubble 353
lathi 215
lathy 203
latifoliate 202
Latin–deities 979
  thieves'–563
latitancy 528
latitat 969
latitude *extent* 180
  region 181
  breadth 202
  measurement 466
  map drawing 550
  freedom 748
  –and longitude
   situation 183
latitudinarian
  heterodox 984
  irreligious 989
latration 412
latria 990
latrine 653
latrocinium 791
latrociny 791
latter *sequent* 63
  past 122
Latter-day Saint
  984
latterly 123
lattice *crossing* 219
  opening 160
  opening 260
laud *praise* 931
  worship 990
laudable 944
laudanum 174
laudation 883
laudator 935
laudatory 931

laugh 838–at
  ridicule 856
  sneer 929
  (*undervalue* 483)
  –in one's sleeve
   latent 526
   ridicule 856
   disrespect 929
   contempt 930
  –on the wrong side
   of one's mouth
   disappointed 509
   dejected 837
   in disrepute 874
  –to scorn *defy* 715
   despise 930
  make one–853
  raise a–840
laughable 853
laughing-gas 376
  no–matter 642
laughingstock **857**
laughter (*see* laugh)
  –holding both his
   sides 838
laughter-loving 836
launch *begin* 66
  boat 273
  propel 284
  –forth 676
  –into 676
  –into eternity 360,
   361
  –out 573
  –out against 716
laundress
  washerwoman 652
  agent 690
  servant 746
laundry *room* 191
  heat 386
  clean 652
laundryman 652
laureate 875
  poet–597
laurel *trophy* 733
  glory 873
  decoration 877
  (*reward* 973)
  repose on one's–s
   265
lava *excretion* 299
  semiliquid 352
lavage 300
lavatory 386, 652
lave *water* 337
  clean 652
lavement 300
lavender *color* 437
laver la tête 932
lavish *profuse* 641
  give 784
  expend 809
  squander 818
  –of praise 931
law *regularity* 80

haste 684
–one's balance 732
–one's cunning 699
–one's head
  bewildered 475
–one's heart 897
–one's life 360
–oneself
  uncertain 475
–one's reason 503
–one's temper 900
–one's way
–sight of blind 442
  disappear 449
  neglect 460
  oblivion 506
  not complete 730
–the clew
  uncertain 475
  unintelligible 519
–the day 732
–time 683
  wander 279
  unskillful 699
  difficulty 704
  no time to–684
losel 893, 949
losing game
  failure 732
  misfortune 735
loss decrement 40a
  death 360
  evil 619
  deterioration 659
  privation **776**
  at a–uncertain 475
  at a–for
  desiring 865
–of fortune 804
–of health 655
–of life 360
–of right 925
–of strength 160
lost nonexisting 2
  absent 187
  invisible 449
  abstracted 458
  uncertain 475
  failure 732
  loss 776
  over–excited 824
  pain 828
  dejection 837
  impenitent 951
–in admiration 931
–in astonishment 870
–in iniquity 945
–in thought 458
–labor 645
–to shame
  insolent 885
  improbity 940
  bad man 949
–to sight 449
–to view 449
–to virtue 945

lot state 7
  quantity 25
  group 72
  multitude 102
  necessity 601
  chance 621
  sufficient 639
  allotment 786
  be one's–151
  cast in one's–with
  choose 609
  cooperate 709
  cast–s 621
  fall to one's–156
  in–s 51
  where one's–is cast
    189
lota 191
loth (see loath)
Lothario lover 897
  libertine 962
lotion liquid 337
  clean 652
  remedy 662
loto 840
lotto 156, 840
lottery chance 156
  cards 840
  put into a–621
lotus–eater 683
loud noisy 404
  unreserved 525
  bad taste 851
loudness **404**
lough 343
lounge chamber 191
  inactive 683
  (quiet 275)
–lizard 683
loup garou 980
louse 653
lousiness 653
lousy 653
lout fool 501
  clown 876
louver 349, 351
lovable 897
love desire 865
  courtesy 894
  affection **897**
  favorite 899
  abode of–897
  God's–906
  labor of–
  willing 602
  inexpensive 815
  amusement 840
  disinterested 942
–affair 897
–all trust a few 864
–of country 910
  make–902
  no–lost 713
  not for–or money
  scarce 640
  dear 814

love knot token 550
loveliness (see lovely)
lovelock 256
lovelorn 898
lovely beautiful 845
  lovable 897
love making 902
love pot 959
lover (see love)
love–sick 897, 902
love story 897, 902
love token 897, 902
loving cup social 892
  courteous 894
loving–kindness 906
low small 32
  not high 207
–sound 405
  moo 412
  vulgar 851
  disreputable 874
  common 876
  ata–ebb small 32
  inferior 34
  depressed 308
  waste 638
  deteriorated 659
  bring–308
  in–automobile 275
–comedy 599
–condition 876
–estimation 929
–fellow 876
–green tent 363
–life 851
–note 408
–origin 876
–price 815
–spirits 837
–tide 207
–tone black 431
  mutter 581
–water low 207
  dry 340
  insufficient 640
  poor 804
lowborn 876
low–brow
  ignorance 491
lower inferior 34
  decrease 36
  hang 214
  depress 207, 308
  dark 421
  dim 422
  predict 511
  sad 837
  irate 900
  sulky 901a
–case 591
–one's flag 725
–one's note 879
–orders 876
–quality 34
lowering hanging 214
  ominous 668

hopeless 859
lowermost 207
lowlands 207
lowliness 879
lowly 879
low–minded
  vulgar 876
  base 940
lown fool 501
  knave 949
lowness (see low) **207**
  humility 879
loxic 217
loxodromic 217
loy 272
loyal obedient 743
  observant 772
  honorable 939
lozenge 244
lubbard (see lubber)
lubber slow 683
  bungler 701
lubberly huge 192
  awkward 699
lubricant 332
lubricate oil 332, 355
  smooth 255
lubrication
  smooth 255
  oil **332**
lubricity slippery 255
  lubrication 332
  unctuous 355
  impure 961
lubricous 332
lucent 420
lucid luminous 420
  transparent 425
  intelligible 518
  rational 502
–style 570
–interval 502
lucidity (see lucid)
lucifer 388
Lucifer 306, 423, 978
lucimeter 445
luck chance 156, 621
  prosperity 734
  as–may have it 470
luckless 735
lucky occasion 134
  successful 731
lucrative 775
lucre gain 775
  wealth 803
Lucretia 960
luctation 720
lucubration 451, 590
luculent 420
lucus a non lucendo
  dissimilar 18
  misnomer 565
Luddites 712
ludibrous 840
ludicrous 853
luetic 655

luff 267
lug flap 39
  pull 285
  ear 418
luggage 270, 780
–van 272
lugger 273
lugubrious 837
lukewarm
  temperate 382, 383
  torpid 823
  indifferent 866
lukewarmness
  irresolution 605
  (see lukewarm)
lull cessation 142
  mitigate 174
  silence 403
–by soft zephyrs 349
–to sleep 265
lullaby moderate 174
  song 415
  verses 597
  inactivity 683
  relief 834
lumbago 378
lumbar 235
lumber disorder 59
  slow 275
  store 636
  useless 645
  hindrance 706
lumbering unfit 647
  ugly 846
lumber house
–of books 539
lumberjack 371
lumberman 371
lumber room 191
lumbriciform 249
lumen 490d
luminary star 318
  light **423**
  sage 500
luminosity 420
luminous light 420
  intelligible 518
lummox 501
lump whole 50
  chief part 51
  amass 72
  mass 192
  projection 250
  weight 319
  density 321
  in the–50
–of affection 855
–sugar 396
–sum 800
–together join 43
  combine 48
  assemble 72
lumper 690
lumpish (see lump)
  ignorant 493
  inactive 683

market *provision* 637
  consumer 677
  buy 795
  mart 799
  bring to—796
  buy in the cheapest
    etc.—794
  in the—*offered* 763
  barter 794
  sale 796
  —garden 371
  —overt *manifest* 525
  —place *street* 189
  mart 799
  —price 812
  public—637
  rig the—794
marketable 794, 796
marksman 700
marksmanship 698
marl 342
marmalade 396
marmoreal 430
marmot 683
maroon *brown* 433
  red 434
  fugitive 623
  abandon 782
  outlaw 893
marplot *bungler* 701
  obstacle 706
  malicious 913
marque, letters of— 791
marquee 223
marquetry
  variegated 440
marquis 875
marquisate 877
marriable 131
marriage 903
  ill—assorted—904
  —bell 836
  —broker 903
marriageable
  adolescent 131
  nubile 903
married 903
  —man 903
  —woman 903
marrow *essence* 5
  interior 221
  central 222
  (*meaning* 516)
  (*importance* 642)
  chill to the—385
marrowbones, one's
  — *submit* 725
  beg 765
  humble 879
  servile 886
  atonement 952
marrowless 158
Marrubium 400
marry *combine* 48
  assertion 535

wed 903
—come up
  defiance 715
  anger 900
  censure 932
Mars 722—orange 439
marsh 345—gas 663
marshal *arrange* 60
  messenger 534
  auxiliary 711
  officer 745
Marshalsea 752
marshy 345
marsupial 191, 368
mart 799
martello tower 206, 717
martial 722
  court—966
  —law *severe* 739
  compulsory 744
  illegal 964
  —music 415
martinet 739
martingale 752
Martinmas 998
martyr
  bodily pain 378
  mental pain 828
  ascetic 955
  punishment 972
  —to disease 655
martyrdom
  killing 361
  agony 378, 828
  unselfish 942
  punishment 972
marvel *wonder* 870
  prodigy 872
  —whether 514
marvelous *great* 31
  wonderful 870
  deal in the—549
Masaniello 742
mascot 621, 993
masculine *strong* 159
  male 373
mash *mix* 41
  disorder 59
  soft 324
  semiliquid 352
  pulpiness 354
masher 854
masjid 1000
mask *dress* 225
  shade 424
  concealment 528
  ambush 530
  deceit 545
  shield 717
  put on the—544
masked *concealed* 528
  —battery 667
masker 599
masochism 659
mason 690

Masonic 712
Masorah 985
masque 599
masquerade
  dress 225
  concealment 528
  deception 545
  frolic 840
  —dress 530
masquerader 528
Mass *worship* 990
  Eucharist 998
  —book 998
mass *quantity* 25
  much 31
  whole 50
  heap 72
  size 192
  gravity 319
  density 321
  in the—50
  —of society 876
massacre 361
massage 324, 331, 379, 662
masses, the—876
masseur 331, 662
massicot 436
massive *huge* 192
  heavy 319
  dense 321
mast 206
mastaba 363
master, Master
  boy 129
  influence 175
  man 373
  know 490
  understand 518
  learn 539
  teacher 540
  director 694
  proficient 698, 700
  succeed, conquer 731
  ruler 745
  possession 777
  possessor 779
  title 877
  eye of the—693
  hard—739
  —hand 700
  —key *open* 260
  instrument 631
  —mariner 269
  —mind *sage* 500
  proficient 700
  —of Arts 492
  —of one's time 685
  —of self 604
  —of the position 731
  —of the revels 840
  —of the Rolls
  recorder 553
  judge 967
  —of the situation
  success 731

authority 737
  —one's feelings 826
  —one's passions 944
  —passion 820
  —spirit of the age
  sage 500
  repute 873
  past—700
masterdom 737
masterpiece *good* 648
  perfect 650
  skill 698
masterstroke
  plan 626
  masterpiece 650
  success 731
masterwork 698
mastery *success* 731
  authority 737
  get the—of 175
masthead *punish* 972
mastic *viscid* 352
  resin 356a
masticate 298, 354
mastiff 366
mastology 368
mat *support* 215
  woven 219
  roughness 256
  doormat 652
matador 361
match *similar* 17
  copy 19
  equal 27
  fuel 388
  retaliate 718
  contest 720
  marriage 903
matchless *unequal* 28
  supreme 33
  virtuous 944
  best 648
  (*perfect* 650)
matchlock 727
matchmaker
  marriage 903
mate *similar* 17
  equal 27
  duality 89
  auxiliary 711
  master 745
  friend 890
  wife 903
  check—732
maté 298
mater, alma—542
  —familias 166
material
  substance 316
  stuff 635
  important 642
  —existence 316
  —for thought 454
  —point 32
materialism
  matter 316

heterodoxy 984
  irreligion 989
materiality
  substantiality 3
  matter **316**
  importance 642
materialization
  materiality 316
  manifestation 525
  spiritualism 992a
materialize 316, 446
materials **635**
materia medica 662
matériel 316, 633
maternal
  parental 166
  benevolent 906
  —love 897
maternity 166
mathematical
  precise 494
  —point 193
mathematician 85
mathematics 25
mathesis 25
matin 125
matinée 892
  —idol 899
matins 125, 990
matrass 191
matriarch 166
matriarchy 737
matriculate 539
matrimonial 903
  —agency 903
matrimony
  mixture 41
  wedlock 903
matrix *mold* 22
  printing 591
  workshop 691
matron *woman* 374
  married 903
  —of honor
  marriage 903
matronize 459, 693
matronly *age* 128
  adolescent 131
matross 726
matter *substance* 3
  copy 21
  material world 316
  topic 454
  meaning 516
  printing 591
  business 625
  importance 642
  pus 653
  in the—of 9
  —in dispute 461
  —in hand *topic* 454
  business 625
  —nothing 643
  —of course
  conformity 82
  certain 474

melancholia
  insanity 503, 821a
  dejection 837
melancholy
  distressing 830
  dejection 837
  away with–836
Melanesian 431
mélange 41
melée *disorder* 59
  contention 720
Melibean 597
melic 413
melinite 727
meliorate 658
melliferous
  sweet 396
mellifluous
  music 413
  –*language* 478
mellow *old* 128
  grow into 144
  soft 324
  sound 413
  color 428
  improve 658
  prepare 673
  tipsy 959
melodeon 417
melodic 415
melodious 413
melodist 416
melodrama 599, 824
melody 413
Melpomene 599
melt *vanish* 111
  convert 144
  liquefy 335
  heat 382
  fuse 384
  pity 914
  –away *cease to exist* 2
  unsubstantial 4
  decrease 36
  disappear 449
  waste 638
  –in the air 405
  –into one 48
  –into tears 839
  –the heart 914
melting pot 691
member *part* 51
  component 56
  mankind 372
  councilor 696
  –of the cast 372
membranaceous 204
membrane 204
membranous 204
memento 505
memoir 594, 595
memorabilia
  affairs 151
  reminiscences 505
  important 642
memorable 151, 642

memorandum
  memory 505
  record 551
  system 626
  conditions 770
  –book 551, 590
  compendium 596
memorial record
  551
Memorial Day 138,
  840
memorialist 553
memorialize 505
memorials 594
memoriam, in–
  tomb 363
  memory 505
memoria technica
  505
memory 505
  store 636
  fame 873
  alive in–506
  failing–506
  in the–of man 122
  –runneth not to the
    contrary 124
  short–506
memsahib 374, 875
men–may come 348
menace 909
ménage 692
menagerie
  collection 72
  animals 370
  store 636
mend *improve* 658
  repair 660
  –one's fences 723
  –one's manners 894
mendacity 544
mendicancy
  begging 765
  poverty 804
mendicant
  beggar 765, 767
  poor 804
  monk 996
mendicity 804
menhir 372a
menial *servant* 746
  rustic 876
meniscal 245
meniscus 245, 445
menses 138, 299
menstrual 138
menstruum 335
mensuration 466
mental 450
  –acquisitiveness 455
  –calm 826
  –cultivation 539
  –excitement 824
  –healing 984
  –pabulum 454
  –philosophy 450

  –poise 498
  –reservation 528, 543
  –suffering 828
mentality 450
mentalize 451
mentation 451
menticulture 490,
  658
mention 527
  above–ed 104
  not worth–ing 543
mentor *sage* 500
  teacher 540
  adviser 695
mentum 234
menu *list* 86
  food 298
Mephistopheles 978
Mephistophelian 945
mephitic *fetid* 401
  deleterious 654
mephitis 663
meracious 392
mercantile 794
mercatoria, lex–963
mercature 794
mercenary
  soldier 726
  servant 746
  price 812
  parsimonious 819
  selfish 943
mercer 225
merchandise 798
merchant 797
merchantable 795
merchantman 273
merciful 914
merciless 914a
mercurial
  changeable 149
  mobile 264
  quick 274
  excitable 825
mercurous chloride
  662
Mercury *traveler* 268
  quick 274
  messenger 534
  –'s rod 747
mercy *lenity* 740
  pity 914
  at the–of *liable* 177
  subject 749
  cry you–766
  for–'s sake 765
  have no–914a
  –on us! 870
  –seat 966
mere *simple* 32
  lake 343
  trifling 643
  buy for a–nothing
    815
  –nothing *small* 32
  trifle 643

  –pretext 617
  –words 477
  –wreck 659
merelles 840
meretricious
  false 495
  vulgar 851
  licentious 961
merge *combine* 48
  include 76
  insert 300
  plunge 337
  –in 56
  –into *become* 144
merged 228
merger 712
meridian *region* 181
  room 125
  summit 210
  light 420
  map drawing 550
  –of life 131
meridional 125, 237
meringue 298
merit *goodness* 648
  due 924
  virtue 944
  make a–of 884
  –notice 642
merito, e–944
meritorious 931
mermaid *monster* 83
  ocean 341
  mythology 979
merman 341
meroblast 357
merogenesis 161
merriment
  cheerful 836
  amusement 840
merry *cheerful* 836
  drunk 959
  make–*sport* 840
  make–with *wit* 842
  ridicule 856
  –and wise 842
  –as the day is long
    836
  –heart 836
  wish a–Christmas
    etc. 896
merry–andrew 844
merry–go–round
  840
merrymaking
  revel 840
  sociality 892
merrythought 842,
  993
mersion 337
mesa 344
mésalliance
  ill–assorted 24
  marriage 903
meseems 484
mesh *interstices* 198

  crossing 219
meshes *trap* 545
  difficulty 704
  –of sophistry 477
mesial *middle* 68
  (*central* 222)
mesilla 344
mesmerism 992
mesmerist 992a
mesne 228–lord 779
mesoblast 357
mesocephalic index
  372a
mesons 490d
Mesozoic Era 490c
mess *mixture* 41
  disorder 59
  derangement 61
  meal 298
  difficulty 704
  portion 786
  make a
  –*unskillful* 699
  fail 732
message *dispatch* 527
  intelligence 532
  command 741
Messalina 962
messenger
  traveler 268
  cloud 353
  envoy **534**
  servant 746
  –balloon 463
Messiah 976
messmate 890
messuage 189, 780
mestee 41
mestizo 41
metabatic 264
metabola 140
metabolism 140, 357
metabolize 140
metacenter 222
metachronism 115
metage 466
metagenesis 140
metagrammatism
  561
metal 635
  Britannia–545
metalepsis 521
metallic *harsh* 410
metallurgy 358
metamorphosis 140
metamorphotic 81
metaphor
  comparison 464
  figure **521**
  (*analogy* 17)
metaphrase 522
metaphrast 524
metaphrastic 516
metaphysics 450
metaplasm 357
metasomatism 140

will 600
willing 602
purpose 620
warning 668
desire 865
dislike 867
bear in–*thought* 451
attention 457
bit of one's–527
food for the–454
give one a piece of
 one's–529
give the–to 457
have a–to
willing 602
desire 865
in the–*thought* 451
topic 454
willing 602
make one's–easy
 826
make up one's–
opinion 484
resolve 604
–at ease 827
–cure 662
–one's book 539
–one's business
incurious 456
attentive 457
–'s eye 515
–what one is about
 864
never–*neglect* 460
unimportant 643
not know one's own
 –605
not–866
out of–506
set one's–upon 604
speak one's
–*say* 582
blunt 703
to one's–*taste* 850
love 897
the public–488
willing–602
minded *willing* 602
intending 620
mindful *attentive* 457
memory 505
mindless
inattentive 458
imbecile 499
forgetful 506
insensible 823
mine *sap* 162
hollow 252
open 260
snare 545
intrigue 626
store 636
abundance 639
damage 659
intrench 664
pitfall 667

attack 716
defense 717
dig a–*plan* 626
prepare 673
–layer 726
–of wealth 803
spring a–
unexpected 508
attack 716
miner 252
sapper and–726
mineral 358–oil 356
mineralize 358
mineralogy 358
Minerva invita
unwilling 603
difficult 704
Minerva press
fustian 577
mingle 41
miniature
small 32, 193
portrait 556
–painter 559
Minié rifle 727
minikin 32, 193
minim *small* 32
music 413
minimifidian 487
minimize 36, 483
minimum *small* 32
inferior 34
minion 899
minister
instrumentality 631
remedy 662
agent 690
director 694
aid 707
deputy 759
give 784
clergy 996
rites 998
–to *help* 746
ministerial
clerical 995
ministering–angel
948–*spirit* 977
ministration
direction 693
aid 707
rite 998
ministry
direction 693
aid 707
church 995
clergy 996
rite 998
minimum 434
miniver 223
minnesinger 597
minnow 193
minor *inferior* 34
infant 129
–key 413
–poet 597

Minorites 996
minority *few* 103
youth 127
Minos 694
minotaur 83
minster 1000
minstrel
musician 416
poet 597
minstrelsy 415
mint *mold* 22
fragrance 400
workshop 691
wealth 803
–julep 298
minuend 38
minuet *music* 415
dance 840
minus *inexistent* 2
less 34
subtracted 38
absent 187
deficient 304
loss 776
in debt 806
nonpayment 808
minusculae 561
minute
circumstantial 8
–in degree 32
special 79
–of time 108
instant 113
–in size 193
record 551
compendium 596
(*unimportant* 643)
–account 594
–attention 457
to the–132
minutemen 726
minuteness *care* 459
minutiae *small* 32
details 79
unimportant 643
minx *girl* 129
malapert 887
wanton 962
miosis 483
mir 188
Mira 490a
miracle
exceptional 83
prodigy 872
–play 599
miraculous
wonderful 870
mirage 443
mire 653
mirror *imitate* 19
reflector 445
perfection 650
glory 873
hold the–up to
 nature 554
hold up the–525

magic–443
mirth 836
misacceptation 523
misadventure
contretemps 135
adversity 735
(*evil* 619)
(*failure* 732)
misadvised 699
misanthropy 911
misapply
misinterpret 523
misuse 679
mismanage 699
misapprehend
mistake 495
misinterpret 523
misappropriate 679
misarrange 61
misbecome 925
misbegotten
crooked 243
vicious 945
misbehave
vulgar 851
vice 945
misbehavior
discourtesy 895
guilt 947
misbelief 485
misbeliever 487, 984
miscalculate
misjudge 481
err 495
disappoint 509
miscall 565
miscarry 732
miscegenation 41,
903
miscellany
mixture 41
collection 72
generality 78
compendium 596
poetry 597
mischance *evil* 619
misfortune 735
(*failure* 732)
mischief 619 do–649
make–649
mischief–maker
evildoer 913
knave 941
mischievous 649
miscible 41
miscite 544
miscompute
misjudge 481
mistake 495
misconceive
mistake 495
misinterpret 523
misconception 495,
523
misconduct
bungling 699

guilt 947
–oneself 945
misconjecture 481
misconstrue 523
miscorrect 538
miscount 495
miscreance 485
miscreant 487, 949
miscreated 945
misdate 115
misdeed 947
misdemean 945
misdemeanant 949,
975
misdemeanor 947
misdescribe 538
misdevotion 988
misdirect
misteach 538
unskillful 699
misdo 945
misdoing 947
misdoubt 485, 523
mise en scène
appearance 448
drama 599
display 882
misemploy 679
miser 640, 819
miserable *small* 32
contemptible 943
unhappy 828
miserably *very* 31
misère 840
miserere *sing*–950
misericordia
Domini 470
miserly 819
misery 828
put out of one's–
 914
misesteem 481
misestimate
misjudge 481
(*mistake* 495)
misfeasance
bungling 699
guilt 947
misfire 732
misfortune
adversity 735
unhappiness 830
(*evil* 619)
(*failure* 732)
misgiving *doubt* 485
fear 860
misgovern 699
misguide *error* 495
misteaching 538
misguided 699
mishap *evil* 619
failure 732
misfortune 735
painful 830
mishmash 59
Mishna 985

-back 287
-forward 282
-from 287
-heaven and earth
  686
-in a groove 82
-off 293
-on *progress* 282
  activity 682
-out of 295
-quickly 274
-slowly 275
-to 894
  on the-293
moved with 821
moveless 265
movement
  motion 264
  music 415
  action 680
  activity 682
mover 164
movies
  theater 448, 599,
    840
moving 185
  keep-682
-pictures 448, 599
-picture machine 445
mow *shorten* 201
  smooth 255
  agriculture 371
  store 636
-down *destroy* 162
  level 213
moxa 384
mozetta 999
M. P. 696
Mr. *man* 373
  gentleman 877
Mrs. 374
M. S. 590
much 31 make-of
  important 642
  friends 888
  love 897
  endearment 902
  approval 931
-ado *exertion* 686
  difficulty 704
-ado about nothing
  overestimate 482
  exaggerate 549
  unimportant 643
  unskillful 699
-cry and little wool
    884
-speaking 584
-the same *identity* 13
  similarity 17
  equality 27
  not say-for 932
  think-of *respect* 928
  approbation 931
muchness 31
mucid *semiliquid* 352

unclean 653
mucilage 352
muck 653
muckle 31
muckrake 934
muckraker 936
muckworm *miser* 819
  lowborn 876
mucor 653
mucosity 352
mucous 352
mucronate 253
mucronulate 253
muculent 352
mucus 352
mud *marsh* 345
  semiliquid 352
  dirt 653
  clear as-519
  stick in the-704
muddle *disorder* 59
  derange 61
  inattention 458
  render uncertain 475
  absurd 497
  difficulty 704
  blunder 732
-away 638
-one's brains 475
muddled 730, 959
muddle-headed 499
muddy *moist* 339
  dim 422
  opaque 426
  color 429
mudguard 666
mud lark *dirty* 653
  commonalty 876
muezzin 996
muff *incapable* 158
  dress 225
  effeminacy 374
  warmth 384
  bungle 699
  bungler 701
muffer *bungler* 701
muffle *wrap* 225
  silent 403
  faint 405
  nonresonant 408a
  conceal 528
  voiceless 581
  stammer 583
muffled *faint* 405
  latent 526
-drums *funeral* 363
  nonresonance 408a
muffler *dress* 225
  wrap 384
  silencer 405, 408a
mufti *undress* 225
  judge 967
  priest 996
mug *cup* 191
  face 234
  pottery 384

mugger 913
muggy *moist* 339
mughouse 189
mugient 412
mugwump 607
Muharram 138
mulada 72
mulatto *mixture* 41
  exception 83
mulct *steal* 791
  fine 974
mule *mongrel* 83
  beast of burden 271
  obstinate 606
muleteer 694
muliebrity 374
mulish 606
mull
  prominence 250
  sweeten 396
-over 451
mullah 492, 996
mulligatawny 298
mullion 215
multangular 244
multifarious
  irrelevant 10
  diverse 16a
  multiform 81
multifid *divided* 51
multifold 81, 102
multiformity 81
multigenerous 81
multilateral
  sides 236
  angles 244
multilocular 191
multiloquence
  speech 582
  loquacity 584
multinominal 102
multiparity 168
multiparous 168
multipartite 44
multiphase 81
multiple *product* 84
  numerous 102
multiplex 81
multiplicand 84
multiplication
  arithmetic 85
  multitude 102
  reproduction 163
  productiveness 168
multiplicator 84
multiplicity 102
multiplier 84
multiply
  (*see* multiplication)
multipotent 157
multisonous 404
multitude
  number **102**
  (*assemblage* 72)
  many-headed-102
  the-876

multum in parvo
  596
multure 330
mum *mute* 581
  taciturn 585
mumble *chew* 298
  mutter 583
mumble peg 840
mumblety 840
Mumbo Jumbo
  god 979
  spell 993
mummer 599
mummery
  absurdity 497
  imposture 545
  masquerade 840
  parade 882
  (*ridicule* 856)
mummify 357, 363
mumming 840
mummy *dry* 340
  corpse 362
  brown 433
  beat to a-972
mump *mutter* 583
  beg 765
mumper *beggar* 767
  pauper 804
mumpish *sad* 837
mumps *dejection* 837
  sullenness 901a
mumpsimus 495
munch 298
Munchausen 549
munchil 272
mundane *world* 318
  selfish 943
  irreligious 989
mundation 652
mundivagant 266
munerary 973
munerate 973
municipal 965
munificent 816
muniment
  evidence 467
  record 551
  defense 717
  security 771
munition
  materials 635
  defense 717
munshi
  learned man 493
  teacher 540
muon 32
mural 717
murder 361
-the King's English
  solecism 568
  stammering 583
  the-is out 529
murderer 361
muricated 253
murky *dark* 421

opaque 426
  black 431
  gloomy 837
murmur *purl* 348
  sound 405
  voice 580
  complain 839
murmurer 832
murrain 655
Murray *travel* 266
  Lindley-542
murrey 434
muscadine 400
muscle 159
muscular 159
muse 451
  (*see* musing)
Muse *poetry* 597
  historic-594
-of fire 597
  unlettered-579
museology 72
Muses, the-416
musette 417
museum *collection* 72
  store 636
mush *food* 298
mushroom
  unsubstantial 4
  new 123
  fungus 367
  upstart 734
  lowborn 876
-anchor 706
-s *food* 298
  fungi 369
  spring up like-s
    163
music **415**-box 417
-of the spheres
  order 58
  universe 318
  set to-416
musical 413, 415, 416
-ear *musician* 416
  hearing 418
-instruments **417**
-note 413
-voice 580
musicale 415
music hall
  playhouse 599
  amusement 840
musician **416**
musing
  thought 451
-on other things 458
  thick-eyed-837
musk 400
musket 727
  shoulder a-722
musketeer 726
musketry 727
musk ox 366
muskrat 400
musk root 400

510

set at–
make light of 483
opposition 708
disobey 742
not observe 773
disrespect 929
contempt 930
naughty 945
naumachia 720
nausea *weariness* 841
disgust 867
nauseate
unsavory 395
give pain 830
nauseous
unsavory 395
unpleasant 830
disgusting 867
nautch 840
nautch girl 840
nautical 267, 273
–almanac 86
nautilus 368
naval 267, 273
–authorities 745
–engagement 720
–forces 627
–school 542
navarch 745
nave *middle* 68
center 222
circularity 247
church 1000
navel *middle* 68
center 222
navicular 245
naviform 245
navigation **267**
navigator 269
navvy *pioneer* 673
laborer 690
navy *ships* 273
fighters 664, 726
–blue 438
–list 86
nawab 745, 875
nay 536–rather 14
Nazarene 989
naze 250
ne plus ultra
supreme 33
complete 52
distance 196
summit ?
limit 210
perfection 650
completion 729
neap
going down 195
low 207
–tide 36
near *like* 17, 19
–*in space* 197
–*in time* 121
soon 132
impending 152

approach 286
stingy 819
bring–17
come–286
draw–197
–at hand 132
–one's end 360
–run 32
–side 239
–sight 443
–the mark 32
–the truth 480a
–upon 32
sail–the wind
skillful 698
rash 863
nearly 32–all 50
nearness 9, **197**
nearsighted 443
neat *simple* 42
order 58
form 240
in writing 572, 576,
578
clean 652
spruce 845
–'s foot oil 356
neat-handed 698
neatherd 370
neb 250
nebula *stars* 318
mist 353
nebular *dim* 422
nebulous *misty* 353
obscure 519
necessarian 601
necessaries 630
necessarily
cause and effect 154
necessary
(*see* necessity)
necessitarianism 601
necessitate 630
necessity *fate* **601**
predetermination
611
requirement 630
impulsion 744
indigence 804
need 865
make a virtue of–
698
neck *contraction* 195
narrow 203
break one's–360
–and crop
completely 52
turn out –297
–and neck 27
–of land 342
–or nothing
resolute 604
rash 863
neckcloth 225
necklace *circle* 247
ornament 847

necrology
obituary 360
biography 594
necromancer 548,
994
necromancy 511, 992
necrophilia 821a
necropolis 363
necropsy 363
necroscopic 363
necrosis 655
nectar *savory* 394
sweet 396
nectareous 394, 396
need *necessity* 601
requirement 630
insufficiency 640
indigence 804
desire 865
friend in–711
in one's utmost–735
needful *necessary* 601
requisite 630
money 800
do the–*pay* 807
needle *sharp* 253
perforator 262
compass 693
foliage 367
as the–to the pole
veracity 543
observance 772
honor 939
–in a bottle of hay
475
needle gun 727
needle-shaped 253
needless 641
needle-witted 498
needlewoman 690
needlework 847
ne'er 107
ne'er-do-well 949
nefarious 945
negation **536**, 764
negatory 764
negative
inexisting 2
contrary 14
prototype 22
quantity 84
confute 479
deny 536
photograph 558
refuse 764
prove a–468
neglect **460**
disuse 678
leave undone 730
omit 773
evade 927
disrespect 929
–of time 115
négligé 225
negligence 460
negligent 460

negotiable
transferable 270
mediatory 724
negotiate *leap* 309
mediate 724
bargain 769
transfer 783
traffic 794
negotiator
go-between 724
agent 758
negress 431
Negrillo 193, 431
Negrito 193, 431
negro *black* 431
slave 746
negrophobia 898
negus 298
neif 781
neigh *cry* 412
boast 884
neighbor
near 197, 199
friend 890
neighborhood 197,
227
neighborly *aid* 707
friendly 888
social 892
courteous 894
neither 610
–here nor there
irrelevant 10
absent 187
–more nor less
equal 27
true 494
–one thing nor
another 83
nekton 366
nem. con. 488
Nemesis
vengeance 919
justice 922
punishment 972
nenia 839
neo-criticism 451
neogamist 903
Neo-Hegelianism
451
Neo-Lamarckism
357
neologism 123
neologist 123
neology **563**
neophyte 144, 541
Neoplatonism 451,
984
neoteric 123
neo-voluntarism
451
nepenthe *remedy* 662
cheer 836
nephalism 953, 955
nephelognosy 353
nephelometer 353

nephew 11
nephograph 353
nephology 353
nephoscope 353
nepotism *nephew* 11
wrong 923
dishonest 940
selfish 943
Neptune 341, 490a
Nereid *ocean* 341
mythology 979
nerve *strength* 159
courage 861
with exposed–s 378
nerveless
impotent 158
–style 575
imperturbable 871
nervous *weak* 160
style 574
timid 860
modest 881
nescience 491
ness 250
nest *cradle* 153
lodging 189
–of boxes 204
nest egg 636
nestle *lodge* 186
safety 664
endearment 902
nestling 129, 167
Nestor *veteran* 130
sage 500
advice 695
net *remainder* 40
receptacle 191
intersection 219
inclosure 232
snare 545
difficulty 704
gain 775
–profit *gain* 775
receipt 810
nether 207
nethermost 207, 211
netlike 219
netting 219
nettle *bane* 663
sting 830
incense 900
network *disorder* 59
crossing 219
neural 235
neuralgia 378
neurasthenia 158,
655, 992a
neurology 329
neuropsychiatry
821a
neurosis 821a
neurotic 662
neuter *matter* 316
no choice 609a
remain
–irresolute 605

nuptials 903
nurse *remedy* 662
  preserve 670
  help 707
  servant 746
  custodian 753
  put to—537
nursery *infancy* 127
  nest 153
  room 191
  garden 371
  school 542
  plants 691
  —rhymes 597
  —tale *fiction* 546
  narrative 594
nursling 129
nurture *feed* 298
  educate 537
  prepare 673
  aid 707
  —a belief 484
  —an idea 451
nut 298 *madman* 504
  —to crack *riddle* 533
  difficulty 704
  —oil 365
nutation 314
nut—brown 433
nutmeg 393
  —grater 330
nuts *good* 618
  pleasing 829
nutshell *small* 32
  lie in a— *little* 193
  compendium 596
nutriment 298
nutrition 707
nutritious *food* 298
  healthy 656
  remedy 662
nux vomica 663
nuzzle 902
nyctalopia 443
nymph *child* 129
  woman 374
  mythology 979
  elemental 980
  sea—341
nympha 129
nymphomania 821a
nystagmus 443

O

O! *wonder* 870
  discontent 932
  —for *desire* 865
oaf *fool* 501
oak *strong* 159
  tree 367, 369
  heart of—*hard* 323
  brave 861
oakleaf *insignia* 747
oakum 205

oar *paddle* 267
  oarsman 269
  instrument 633
  laboring—686
  lie upon one's—s
    681
  ply the—
  navigate 267
  exert 686
  pull an—680
  put in an—
  interpose 228
  busy 682
  rest on one's—
  cease 142
  quiescence 265
  repose 687
  stroke—693
oar—shaped 245
oarsman 269
oasis *separate* 44
  land 342
oath *assertion* 535
  bad language 908
  —helper 467
  rap out—s 885
  upon—768
oatmeal 298
oats 367
obbligato
  accompaniment 88
  music 415
obconic 245
obduction 223
obdurate
  obstinate 606
  severe 739
  malevolent 907
  graceless 945
  impenitent 951
obedience 743
obeisance *bow* 308
  submission 725
  courtesy 894
  reverence 928
obelisk *tall* 206
  monument 551
Oberon 979
obese 194
obesity 192
obey 743
  be subject to 749
  —a call 615
  —rules 82
  —the helm 705
obfuscate *dark* 421
  opaque 426
obfuscated *drunk* 959
obi 992
obiism 992
obit *death* 360
  interment 363
  post—360, 363
obiter dictum
  irrelevant 10
  occasion 134

  interjacent 228
obituary *death* 360
  biography 594
object *thing* 3
  matter 316
  intention 620
  ugly 846
  disapprove 932
  be an—
  important 642
  —lesson 82
  —to *dislike* 867
objectify 220
objection
  hindrance 706
  disapproval 932
  no—762
objectionable
  inexpedient 647
  wrong 923
  guilty 947
objective *extrinsic* 6
  material 316
objectize 220
objurgate 932
oblate 201
  —spheroid 249
oblation *gift* 784
  religious—990
  (*offer* 763)
oblectation 827
obligation
  necessity 601
  promise 768
  conditions 770
  debt 806
  confer an—
  good 648
  feeling of—916
  under an—
  gratitude 916
  duty 926
oblige *benefit* 707
  compel 744
  duty 926
obliged *grateful* 916
  duty 926
  be—601
obligee 800
obliging *helping* 707
  courteous 894
  kind 906
obliquation 279
obliquity *slope* **217**
  vice 945
  —of judgment 481
  —of vision 443
obliterate 2, 162
obliteration **552**
  —of the past 506
oblivion **506**
  inexistence 2
  forgiveness 918
  —of benefits 917
  —of time 115
  redeem from—505

oblivious 506
oblong 200
  —spheroid 249
obloquy *disrepute* 874
  disapprobation 932
  detraction 934
obmutescence
  voiceless 581
  taciturn 585
obnoxious
  pernicious 649
  unpleasing 830
  hateful 898
  —to *liable* 177
obnubilated 422
oboe 417
obovate 247
obreption 528, 775
obscene *dirty* 653
  indecent 961
obscure *dark* 421
  dim 422
  unseen 447
  uncertain 475
  unintelligible 519
  eclipse 874
  ignoble 876
obscurity
  (see obscure)
  unsubstantiality 4
  latency 526
  style **571**
obsecration 765
obsecratory 765
obsequies 363
obsequious
  servile 746, 886
  courteous 894
  respectful 928
obsequiousness 933
observance *rule* 82
  attention 457
  habit 613
  practice 692
  fulfillment **772**
  duty 926
  rite 998
Observant *friar* 996
observation
  intellect 450
  idea 453
  attention 457
  assertion 535
observatory 318
observe
  (see observance,
    observation)
  —a duty 926
  —rules 82
observer
  aviator 269a
  spectator 444
obsess *haunt* 860
  bedevil 978
  sorcery 992
obsession (*see* obsess)

  siege 716
obsidional 716
obsolescence 614
obsolescent 563
obsolete *old* 124
  words 563
  effete 645
obstacle *moral*—706
  (*physical*—179)
obstetrician 631
obstetrics
  production 161
  surgery 662
obstinacy **606**
  prejudice 481
obstipation 261
obstreperous
  violent 173
  loud 404
obstruct *close* 261
  hinder 706
  —the passage of light
    426
obstructionist 710
obstructive
  opponent 710
obstruent 706
obstupefaction 823
obtain *exist* 1
  get 775
  —under false pretense
    791
obtainable 470
obtenebration 421
obtestation
  entreaty 765
obtrectation 934
obtrude *interfere* 228
  insert 300
  meddle 682
  (*obstruct* 706)
obtruncate 201
obtrusion
  interference 228
  obstruction 706
obtrusive
  interfering 228
  vulgar 851
  rude 895
obtund *mitigate* 174
  blunt 254
  deaden 376
  paralyze 823
obtundent 823
obtundity 823
obtuse *blunt* 253
  insensible 376
  imbecile 499
  dull 823
  —angle 244
obumbrate 421
obverse 234
obviate 706
obvious *visible* 446
  clear 518
  manifest 525

in–*store* 636
–condition *rule* 80
–course of things 613
ordinate 466
ordination
  arrangement 60
  measurement 466
  command 741
  commission 755
  church 995
  rite 998
ordnance 727
ordonnance 963
ordure 653
ore 635
oread 979
orectic 865
organ *music* 417
  voice 580
  instrument 633
  –of the soul 580
  –point 408, 413
organic *state* 7
  structural 329
  protoplastic 357
  –change 146
  –chemistry 357, 490a
  –remains 357
  dead 362
organism 329, 366
organist 416, 996
organization
  arrangement 60
  production 161
  structure 329
  animated nature 357
organize *arrange* 60
  produce 161
  animated nature 357
  plan 626
  (*prepare* 673)
organized
  (*see* organize)
  –hypocrisy 544
  –massacre 361
  –murder 361
organizer 626
organography 329
organology 329
organotherapy 662
orgasm 173
orgiastic 954
orgies 954
oriel *recess* 191
  corner 244
  window 260
  chapel 1000
Orient *East* 236
  sunrise 420
Oriental 236
  –philosophy 451
orientate 236
orifice *beginning* 66
  opening 260
oriflamme 550
Origenism 984

origin *beginning* 66
  cause 153
  derive its–154
original *dissimilar* 18
  not imitated 20
  model 22
  individual 79
  exceptional 83
  cause 153
  invented 515
  unaccustomed 614
  laughingstock 857
  return to–*state* 660
originality *will* 600
  want of–843
originate *begin* 66
  cause 153
  invent 515
  –in 154
originative 153, 168
originator 164
Orion 490a
Orion's belt 318
orismology *word* 562
  name 564
orison *request* 765
  worship 990
ormolu *sham* 545
  ornament 847
Ormazd 976
ornament
  in writing **577**
  adornment **847**
  glory 873
  excess of–851
ornamental art 847
  painting 556
ornamentation 847
ornate–*writing* 577
  ornamental 847
orniscopy 511
ornithology 368
ornithomancy 511
orotund 577
orotundity 249, 577
Orpheus 416
orpiment 436
orrery 318
orthodox
  comfortable 82
  –*religion* 983a
  –*dissenter* 984
orthodoxy **983a**
orthoepist 562
orthoepy 562, 580
orthogonal 212
orthography 561
orthology 494
orthometry
  measurement 466
  prosody 597
orthopedist 662
orthopraxy 662
orts *remnants* 40
  useless 645
  (*trifles* 643)

oryctology
  minerals 358
  organic remains 368
O Salutaris 990
oscillation
  change 149
  motion **314**
  center of–222
oscitancy *opening* 260
  sleepy 683
osculation
  contact 199
  touch 379
  endearment 902
osculature 43
Osiris 979
Osmanli 984
osmiridium 323
osmosis 302
Ossa on Pelion
  heap 72
  weight 319
osseous 323
ossify 323
ossuary 363
ostensible
  appearance 448
  probable 472
  manifest 525
  plea 617
ostentation 847, **882**
ostentatious 845, 882
osteology 329
osteopathy 662
ostiary *mouth* 260
  doorkeeper 263
  estuary 343
ostium 260
ostler 746
ostracism
  (*see* ostracize)
ostracize *exclude* 55
  eject 297
  banish 893
  censure 932
  punish 972
ostrich 274, 366
  stomach of an–957
otalgia 378
other *different* 15
  extra 37
  do unto–s as we
    would men
    should do unto
    us 942
  enter into the
    feelings of–s 906
  every–138
  in–words 522
  just the–way 14
  –extreme 14
  –self *friend* 890
  –side of the shield
    468
  –than 18
  –things to do 683

–time 119
  the–day 123
otherwise 18
otic 418
otiose 169, 683
otiosity 683
otography 418
otologist 418
otology 418
otopathy 418
otoplasty 418
otorrhea 418
otoscope 418
otoscopy 418
ottar, otto (*see* attar)
otter hound 366
ottoman 215
oubliette *ambush* 530
  prison 752
ough! 874
ought–to be 922
  –to be done 926
ouija board 992a
ounce *weight* 319
ouphe 980
Our Lady 977
ourselves 372
oust *eject* 297
  dismiss 756
  deprive 789
out *exterior* 220
  in error 495
  come–446
  go–*egress* 295
  cool 385
  –and out 52
  –at elbows 874
  –at heels 804
  –in one's reckoning
    495
  –of
    (*see below*)
  –upon it
    malediction 908
    censure 932
  –with it *disclose* 529
    obliterate 552
    play–729
    send–297
    time–of joint 735
    waters–337
outbalance
  compensate 30
  superiority 33
outbid 794
outbound 295
outbrave 885
out–brazen 234, 885
outbreak
  beginning 66
  violence 173
  egress 295
  discord 713
  attack 716
  revolt 742
  passion 825

outburst *violence* 173
  egress 295
  revolt 825
outcast
  unconformable 83
  Pariah 876
  secluded 893
  bad man 949
outcome *effect* 154
  egress 295
  produce 775
outcry *noise* 404, 411
  auction 796
  complaint 839
  censure 932
outdo *superior* 33
  transcursion 303
  activity 682
  conquer 731
outdoor 220
outdoors 338
outer 220
outermost 220
outface 885
outfit *clothes* 225
  equipment 673
outflank *flank* 236
  defeat 731
outflow 295
outgate 295
outgeneral 731
outgo 303
outgoing 295
outgoings 809
outgrow 194
outgrowth 65, 154
out–Herod
  superior 33
  bluster 174
  (*exaggerate* 549)
outhouse 191
outing 266
outjump
  transcursion 303
  repute 873
outlandish *foreign* 10
  extraneous 57
  irregular 83
  barbarous 851
  ridiculous 853
outlast 110
outlaw *irregular* 83
  secluded 893
  reprobate 949
outlawry 964
outlay 809
outleap 303
outlet *opening* 260
  egress 295
outlie 196
outline *contour* **230**
  form 240
  features 448
  sketch 554
  painting 556
  plan 626

overfeed 641
overflow *stream* 348
  redundance 641
  –with gratitude 916
overgo 303
overgorged
  satiety 869
  gluttony 957
overgrown *much* 31
  large 192
  expanded 194
overhang *high* 206
  pendency 214
overhanging
  destiny 152
  pendency 214
overhasty 901
overhaul *count* 85
  attend to 457
  inquire 461
  censure 932
overhead 206
overhear *hear* 418
  be informed 527
overjoyed 827
overjump 303
overlap *inwrap* 225
  go beyond 303
overlay *layer* 204
  cover 223
  exaggerate 549
  excess 641
  overdo 682
  hinder 706
  –with ornament
  writing 577
overleap 303
overliberal 818
overlie 223
overload
  ornament 577
  redundance 641
  hinder 706
overlook *slight* 458
  neglect 460
  superintend 693
  forgive 918
  disparage 929
  bewitch 992
overlooked 642
  not to be–642
overlooker 694
overlord 745
overlying 206
overman 33
overmaster 731
overmastering 821
overmatch
  unequal 28
  superior 33
  strength 159
  conquer 731
overmeasure 641
overmodest 881
overmost 210
overmuch 641

overnight 122
overofficious 682
overpaid 816
overpass *exceed* 33
  transgress 303
overpersuade 615
overplus
  remainder 40
  excess 641
overpoise 179
overpower
  counteract 179
  subdue 731
  emotion 824
overpowering
  strong 159
overpraise
  overrate 482
  exaggerate 549
  flatter 933
overprize 482
overrate 482
overreach *pass* 303
  deceive 545
  baffle 545
overreckon 482
overrefinement 477
over-religious 955
override *superior* 33
  influence 175
  pass 303
  hinder 706
  defeat 731
  authority 737
  severity 739
  abrogate 756
overrighteous 988
overrule *control* 737
  cancel 756
overruling
  important 642
overrun *presence* 186
  spread 194
  motion beyond **303**
  printing 591
  redundance 641
  despoil 659
overscrupulous 939
oversea 57, 341
overseas cap 225
oversee 693
overseer 694
oversensitive 822
overset
  invert 218
  level 308
  subvert 731
overshadow
  darken 353, 421
  repute 873
  disrepute 874
overshoot the mark
  go beyond 303
  exaggerate 549
  overdo 682
  clumsy 699

oversight
  inattention 458
  error 495
  superintendence 693
  failure 732
overskip 303
oversleep 683
overspent 688
overspread
  disperse 73
  be present 186
  cover 233
overstate 549, 555
overstep 303
overstock 641
overstrain *extol* 482
  fatigue 688
oversupply 641
overt 525–*act* 680
overtake 292
overtaken *tipsy* 959
overtask *misuse* 679
  fatigue 688
overtax 679, 688
overthrow
  revolution 146
  destroy 162
  level 308
  confute 479
  vanquish 751
overthrown
  vanquished 732
overthwart 708
overtired 688
overtone 413
overtop *surpass* 33
  height 206
  (*perfection* 650)
overtrustful 486
overture
  precursor 62, 64
  music 415
  offer 763
  request 765
overturn
  revolution 146
  destroy 162
  invert 218
  level 308
  confute 479
overvalue 482
overweening
  excess 641
  rash 863
  pride 878
  conceit 880
  insolence 885
overweigh *exceed* 33
  influence 175
  overrate 482
overwhelm *ruin* 162
  redundant 641
  thwart 706
  affect 824
overwhelmed
  defeated 732

  subjection 749
overwhelming
  strong 159
  wonderful 870
overwise 880
overwork *misuse* 679
  fatigue 688
overwrought
  exaggerated 549
  emotion 824
  affectation 855
overzealous 825
ovicell 357
oviform 249
ovo, in–153
ovoid 247, 249
ovule 247
ovum 357
owe 806
  –it to oneself 926
owelty 27
owing *debt* 806
  attribution 155
owl *bird* 366
  fool 501
  –'s light 422
  –s to Athens 641
  screech–412
own *assent* 488
  divulge 529
  possess 777
  property 780
  act on one's–
   responsibility 738
  after one's–heart
   897
  at one's–risk 926
  come by one's–775
  condemned out of
   one's–mouth 479
  hold one's–737
  look after one's–
   interest 943
  look with one's–
   eyes 459
  out of one's–head
   600
  –flesh and blood
   consanguinity 11
owner
  possessor 779
  without an–777*a*
ownership
  property 780
ox *animal* 366
  male 373
  hot enough to roast
   an–382
Oxford school 984
Oxford shoe 225
oxgoad 727
oxidation 357
oxreim 45
ox–tail soup 298
oxygen 359
oxygon 244

oyer and terminer,
  court of–966
oyes 531
oyez! *hear* 418
  publication 531
oyster 298–plant 298
  –stew 298

P

P mind one's–'s and Q's
  care 459
  polite 894
  duty 926
pabulum *food* 298
  material 316
  mental–454
pace *walk* 264
  journey 266
  measure 466
  keep–with
  concur 178
  velocity 274
  –up and down 266
  put through one's–s
   525
  show one's–s
  ostentation 882
pace *permission* 760
  –tanti nominis 928
pachydermatous
  physically–376
  morally–823
pacific 721
pacification 723
pacifism 721
pacify *allay* 174
  (*compose* 823)
  (*forgive* 918)
pack *arrange* 60
  assemblage 72
  locate 184
  squeeze 195
  prepare 673
  burden 706
  –off *depart* 293
  eject 297
  –of nonsense 643
  –up 229
  send–ing 297
package
  assemblage 72
packer 673
packet
  assemblage 72
  ship 273
pack horse 271
pack saddle 215
pack thread 205
pact 769
Pactolus 803
pad *thicken* 194
  line 224
  horse 271
  diffuseness 573

writing 590
padding *lining* 224
  stopper 263
  soft 324
  diffuseness 573
paddle *walk* 266
  row 267
  oar 633
  —one's own canoe
    conduct 692
    free 748
  —steamer 273
paddock 232
Paddy *Irishman* 188
paddy *rice* 330
padishah 745
padlock *fastening* 45
  fetter 752
  put a—on one's lips
    585
padre 996
padrone 745
paean *rejoicing* 838
  celebration 883
  gratitude 916
  approbation 931
  worship 990
pagan 984
  —deities **979**
paganism 984
page *numeration* 85
  printing 591
  book 593
  attendant 746
pageant *spectacle* 448
  amusement 840
  show 882
pagination 85
pagoda 206, 1000
pagri 225
pah 717
pai 643
pail 191
paillard 962
paillasse 215
pain *physical* **–378**
  moral **–828**
  penalty 974
painfulness 830
painfully *very* 31
painless 827
pains 686
  get for one's—973
  —and penalties 974
  take—686
painstaking
  active 682
  laborious 686
paint *coat* 223
  color 428
  deceive 545
  delineate 556
  ornament 847
  —the lily 641
  —the town red 840
painter *rope* 45

artist 559
painting 54, **556**
painty 556
pair *similar* 17
  combine 48
  couple 89
  —horses 272
  —off *average* 29
    marry 903
pair–oar 273
pairs *cards* 840
pajamas 225
pakka (*see* pucka)
paktong 545
pal *ally* 711
  chum 890
palace 189
  bishop's—1000
  —car 272
Paladin *defense* 717
  combatant 726
palaeocrystic 124
palaeology
  (*see* paleology etc.)
palaestra *school* 542
  arena 728
palaestral
  strength 159
  school 542
  contention 720
palaestric
  exertion 686
  (*see* palaestral)
palang 215
palanquin 266, 272
palatable *savory* 394
  pleasant 829
palatal *phonetic* 561
palate 390
  tickle the—394
palatial *palace* 189
  ostentatious 882
palatinate 181
palatine 745
Palatine Court 966
palaver
  unmeaning 517
  speech 582
  loquacity 584
  colloquy 588
  council 696
pale *region* 181
  inclosure 232
  limit 233
  dim 422
  colorless 429
  frightened 860
  —its ineffectual fire
  dim 422
  out of repute 874
  —of the church 995
  turn—*lose color* 429
  emotion 821
  fear 860
pale–faced 429
paleoanthropic 124

paleography *past* 122
  philology 560
Paleolithic Age 372a
paleology *past* 122
  language 160
paleontology 357,
  368
paleozoic 124, 372a
paleozoology 357
palestra
  (*see* palaestra etc.)
paletot 225
palette 556
palfrey 271
palimpsest 147, 528
palindrome
  inversion 218
  neology 563
paling *fence* 232
  prison 752
palingenesis 163, 660
palinody 607
palisade *defense* 717
  prison 752
  —s *cliff* 212
palki 272
pall *mantle* 225
  funeral 363
  disgust 395
  insignia 747
  weary 841
  dislike 867
  satiety 869
  canonicals 999
  —bearer 363
palladium *safety* 664
  (*defense* 717)
pallet *support* 215
  painter's —556
palliament 225
palliate *moderate* 174
  mind 658
  relieve 834
  extenuate 937
  moderation 174
palliative 174
  qualification 469
  remedy 662
pallid 429
pallium 999
pall–mall 840
pallone 840
pallor 429
palm
  measure of length
    200
  tree 367, 369
  touch 379
  trophy 733
  steal 791
  laurel 877
  bear the—873
  grease the
  —*induce* 615
  give 784
  itching—865

—off 545
—upon 545
  win the—731
palmated 257
palmer *traveler* 268
  clergy 996
palmiped 219
palmist 513
palmistry 500, 511,
  522
palm oil 356
palmy *prosperous* 734
  pleasant 829
  joyous 836
  —days *prosperity* 734
  pleasure 827
palpable *material* 316
  tactile 379
  obvious 446
  manifest 525
  (*intelligible* 518)
  —obscure 421
palpate 379
palpation 379
palpitate *tremble* 315
  emotion 821
  fear 860
palpus 379
palsgrave 875
palsied (*see* palsy)
  irresolute 605
palsy *impotence* 158
  physical insensibility
    376
  disease 655
  mental insensibility
    823
  (*weakness* 160)
palter *falsehood* 544
  shift 605
  elude 773
paltering 520
paltry *small* 32
  unimportant 643
  mean 940
paludal 345
pampas 344, 367
pamper *indulge* 954
  gorge 957
pamphlet 590, 593
pamphleteer 595
pan 191
panacea 662
panache *plume* 256
  ornament 847
panama *hat* 225
Pan–American 78
Pan–Anglican 78
pancake 298
pancratiast 159
pandar (*see* pander)
Pandean pipes 417
pandect
  knowledge 490
  dissertation 595
  compendium 596

code 963
pandemic 657
Pandemonium 982
  inhabitants of—978
pandemonium 59,
  404, 414
pander *pimp* 962
  —to *instrument* 631
  help 707
  flatter 933
pandiculation
  expansion 194
  opening 260
  sleepy 683
Pandoor 726
Pandora's box 619
  bottom of—858
pan–dowdy 298
paned 440
panegyric 931
panegyrize 482
panel *list* 86
  partition 228
  accused 938
  jury 967
  —game 545
  sliding—545
paneling 847
pang *physical* —378
  moral 828
Pan–Germanic 78
Pangloss 492
panhandler 876
panharmonic 78
Pan–Hellenic 78
pani 337
panic 860—*fear* 860
panier 225
pannel 213
pannier 191
panoply 490
  defense 717
  arms 727
panopticon 752
panorama *view* 448
  painting 556
panoramic 78, 446
  —view 441
pan–
  phenomenalism
    451
Panpipes 417
Panslavic 78
pansophism 490
pant *heat* 382
  fatigue 688
  emotion 821
  —for 865
pantaloon
  old man 130
  pantomimist 599
  buffoon 844
pantaloons 225
pantheism 451, 984
Pantheon *gods* 979
  temple 1000

–of the sacrament 998
parterre *level* 213
 cultivation 371
 (*vegetation* 367)
parthenogenesis 161
partial *unequal* 28
 part 51
 special 79
 fractional 100a
 misjudging 481
 unjust 923
 –shadow 422
partiality
 preponderance 33
 desire 865
 friendship 888
 love 897
partially *a little* 32
 partly 51
partibility 44
particeps criminis
 doer 690
 auxiliary 711
participate
 cooperate 709
 share 778
 –in *be a doer* 680
participation 778
participator
 agent 690
particle *small* 32
 grain 333
particular *item* 51
 event 151
 attentive 457
 careful 459
 exact 494
 capricious 608
 odd 851
 fastidious 868
 in–79
 –account 594
 –estate 780
particularization 75
particularize
 special 79
 describe 594
Pascal's law 490d
particularly *very* 31
 more 33
particulars
 speciality 79
 description 594
parting 44 –cup 959
Partington, Mrs. 471
parti pris 611
partisan *follower* 65
 auxiliary 711
 weapon 727
 friend 890
 sympathizer 914
partisanship
 warped judgment 481
 cooperation 709
 wrong 923

partition *divide* 44
 wall 228
 allot 786
partlet 366
partly 51
partner *companion* 88
 auxiliary 711
 sharer 778
 friend 890
 spouse 903
 sleeping–683
partnership
 party 712
 join–with 709
partridge 298
parts *intellect* 450
 skill 698
 wisdom 498
parturient 161
parturition 161
party *assemblage* 72
 special 79
 person 372
 association 712
 sociality 892
 –spirit
 warped judgment 481
 cooperation 709
 wrong 923
 –to *action* 680
 agent 690
 cooperate 709
 –to a suit 969
 –wall 228
party–colored 428, 440
parvenu *new* 123
 successful 734
 vulgar 851
 lowborn 876
parvenuism 876
parvitude 193
pas *precedence* 62
 term 71
 precession 280
 rank 873
paschal 998
pasha 745, 875
pashalic 737
pasigraphy 560, 590
pasquil 934
pasquinade 934
pass *predicament* 7
 conjuncture 8
 be superior 33
 course 109
 lapse 122
 happen 151
 interval 198
 defile 203
 move 264
 transfer 270
 move through 302
 exceed 303

vanish 449
indication 550
way 627
difficulty 704
thrust 716
passport 760
 at cards 764
–as *property* 783, 784
 barely–651
 barely–muster 651
 let it–460
 make a–at 716
 –a law 963
 –and repass 302
 oscillate 314
 –an examination
 goodness 648
 repute 873
 –an opinion 480
 –away *cease to exist* 2
 end 67
 transient 111
 past 122
 cease 142
 die 360
 –by *course* 109
 inattention 458
 neglect 460
 deception 545
 disrespectful 929
 –comprehension 519
 –current 484
 –in one's checks 360
 –in review
 attention 457
 inquiry 461
 –in the mind 451
 –into 144
 –into one's hand 785
 –judgment 480
 –muster
 conform to 82
 sufficient 639
 good 648
 approbation 931
 –off *be past* 122
 egress 295
 –off for 544
 –on 282
 –one's time in 625
 –one's word 768
 –out of 295
 –out of sight 449
 –over *exclude* 55
 cross 302
 die 360
 give 784
 forgive 918
 exemption 927a
 –over to 709
 –sentence on 971
 –the eyes over 457
 –the fingers over 379
 –the Rubicon 609
 –through *event* 151
 motion 302

–through one's hands 625
–time *exist* 1
 time 106
 do nothing 681
 –to 144
 –to the order of the day 624
 –under the name of 564
 pretty–704
passability 174
passable *small* 32
 unimportant 643
 imperfect 651
 pretty 845
passado 716
passage (see pass)
 part 51
 conversion 144
 street 189
 corridor 191
 opening 260
 navigation 267
 deviation 279
 moving through 302
 music 413
 –in a book 593
 means of access 627
 action 680
 cut a–260
 force a–302
 –of arms 720
passage d'armes 722
passamezzo 415
pass book 811
passé *antiquated* 124
 aged 128
 spoiled 659
passed away 122
passenger 268
 –train 272
passeparole 550
passe partout
 key 260
 instrument 631
passer-by 444
passetemps 840
passim *dispersed* 73
 place 182
 situation 183
passing *very* 31
 transient 111
 –away *death* 360
 –bell 363
 –strange 870
 –word 527
passion
 emotion 820, 821
 excitability 825
 pain 828
 desire 865
 love 897
 anger 900
 –queller 866
 ruling–606

passionate *style* 575
 warm 825
 irascible 901
passionless 823
Passion week 998
passive *inert* 172
 inaction 681
 obedient 743
 inexcitable 826
passiveness
 irreligion 989
pass–key 631
Passover 998
passport
 instrumentality 631
 order 741
 permission 760
password *answer* 461
 sign 550
 military 722
past 122, 124
 danger–664
 insensibility to the–506
 obliteration of the–506
 –bearing 830
 –comprehension 519
 –cure 859
 –dispute 474
 –one's prime 128
 –perfect 122
 –performances 465
 –praying for 945
 –recollection 506
 –work *useless* 645
 impaired 659
 thing of the–124
paste *cement* 45
 to cement 46
 pulp 352, 354
 sham 545
 tinsel 847
 scissors and–609
pasteboard 593
pastel 556, 594
pasticcio
 imitation 21
 mixture 41
pastil 400
pastime 840
pastiness (see pasty)
pastor 996
pastoral
 bucolic 370, 371
 music 415
 poem 597
 religious 995
 sermon 998
pastorale 415
pastose 556
pastry *food* 298
 sweets 396
pasturage
 meadow 344
 herbage 367

–a funeral 363
–an obligation 772
–a part *drama* 599
  action 680
–a service 998
–the duties of 625
performable 470
performance
  (*see* perform)
  effect 154
performer
  musician 416
  actor 599
  agent 690
  affectation 855
perfume 400
perfumery 400
perfunctory
  incomplete 53
  neglect 460
perhaps *possibly* 470
  supposition 514
  (*chance* 156)
peri *beauty* 845
  mythology 979
periapt 993
pericarp 191
pericranium 450
periculous 665
peridot 847
perigee 490a
perihelion 197, 490a
peril 665 at your–909
  take heed at one's–
  668
perimeter 230
period *end* 67
  point 71
  –*of time* 106, **108**
  recurrence 138
  at fixed–s 138
  well rounded–s
  577, 578
periodical
  recurring 138
  book 593
periodicity 138
peripatetic
  journey 266
  traveler 268
Peripatetic school
  451
periphery 230
periphrase
  phrase 566
  diffuse 573
periplus 267
periscope 441
periscopic 446
  –*lens* 445
perish *cease to exist* 2
  be destroyed 162
  die 360
  decay 659
  –*with cold* 383
  –*with hunger* 956

perishable 111
perissology
  diffuseness 573
  (*loquacity* 584)
peristalsis 221
peristaltic 248
peristyle 189
periwig 225
periwinkles 298
perjured 940
perjurer 548
perjury 544
perk *dress* 225
  –*up elevate* 307
  revive 689
  cheer 836
perked up *proud* 878
perlustration 441
permanence
  uniformity 16
  durability 110
  unchanging **141**
  unchangeable 150
permanent
  habitual 613
permeable 260
permeate
  insinuate 228
  pervade 186
  pass through 302
permissible
  permitted 760
  (*lawful* 924)
permission 760
permissive 760
permit 760
permitting 760
  weather etc.–469,
  470
permutation
  numerical–84
  change 140
  interchange 148
pernicious 649
pernicity 274
perorate *end* 67
  diffuse style 573
peroration *sequel* 65
  end 67
  speech 582
perpend *partition* 228
  think 451
perpendicular 212,
  246
perpension
  attention 457
perpetrate 680
  –*a pun etc.* 842
perpetrator 690
perpetual 112
  frequent 136
  –*curate* 996
perpetually 16, 112
perpetuate 112
  continue 143
  establish 150

preserve 976
perpetuity 112
perplex *derange* 61
  distract 458
  uncertainty 475
  bother 830
perplexed
  confused 59, 523
  convoluted 248
perplexity *disorder* 59
  uncertainty 475
  unintelligibility 519
  difficulty 704
  (*ignorance* 491)
perquisite 775, 973
perquisition 461
perron 627
perscrutation 461
persecute *oppress* 649
  annoy 830
  malevolence 907
persecution complex
  821a
Perseids 490a
perseverance
  continuance 143
  persistence **604a**
persevere 143, 604a
persiflage 842, 856
persifleur 844
persist *duration* 106
  permanence 141
  continue 143
  persevere 604a
persistence 110
persistent 110, 143
person
  substantiality 3
  man 372
  without distinction
  of–s 922
personable 845
personage 372
persona grata
  friend 890
  favorite 899
personal (*see* person)
  special 79
  subjective 317
  –*narrative* 594
  –*property* 780
  –*security* 771
personality
  (*see* personal)
  discourtesy 895
  disrespect 929
  censure 932
  detraction 934
personalty 780
personate *imitate* 19
  represent 554
personify
  allegory 521
  represent 554
personnel
  constituent 56

doer 690
perspective *view* 448
  expectation 507
  painting 556
  aerial–428
  in–200
perspicacity
  sight 441
  intelligence 498
  fastidiousness 868
perspicuity
  intelligibility 518
  style **570**
perspiration
  exudation 295
  excretion 299
  in a–382
perstringe 457
persuadability 602,
  615
persuadable 602
persuade *belief* 484
  induce 615
  (*advise* 695)
persuasibility
  willingness 602
persuasion
  opinion 484
  teaching 537
  inducement 615
  religious–983
persuasive 615
  –*reasoning* 476
pert *vain* 880
  insolent 885
  discourteous 895
pertain to *relate to* 9
  included under 76
  power 157
  belong 777
  property 780
  duty 926
pertinacity 604a
pertinent *relative* 9
  congruous 23
  (*applicable* 644)
pertingent 199
perturbation
  derange 61
  ferment 171
  agitation 315
  emotion 821
  excitation 824, 825
  fear 860
pertusion 260
pertussis 655
peruke 225
peruse 539
Peruvian bark 662
pervade *influence* 175
  extend 186
  affect 821
  –*the soul* 824
pervading spirit 820
perverse
  obstinate 606

difficult 704
  churlish 895
  sulky 901a
perversion
  sophistry 477
  misinterpretation
  523
  misteaching 538
  falsehood 544
  untruth 546
  injury 659
  impiety 988
perversity
  (*see* perverse)
pervert
  (*see* perversion)
  convert 144
  recant 607
perverted
  in error 495
pervestigation 461
pervicacious 606
pervigilium 682
pervious 260, 295
pessimism
  overrate 482
  underrate 483
  dejection 837
  hopeless 859
pessimist 482, 862,
  859
pessimize 549, 934
pessomancy 511
pest *bane* 663
  painfulness 830
pester 830
pesthouse 662
pestiferous 657
pestilence 655
pestle 330
pet *love* 897
  favorite 899
  anger 900
  fondle 902
  flatter 933
petal 367
petard 727
  hoist on one's own–
  retaliation 718
  failure 732
Peter pence 784
petiole 367
petition *ask* 765
  pray 990
petitioner 767
petitio principii 477
petit maitre 854
petname 565
petrel *warning* 668
petrify *dense* 321
  hard 323
  organization 357
  freeze 385
  thrill 824
  affright 860
  astonish 870

529

pie *food* 298
  sweet 396
  printing 591
piebald 440
piece *adjunct* 39
  bit 51
  change 140
  painting 556
  drama 599
  cannon 727
  coin 800
  courtesan 962
  fall to—s 162
  give a—of advice 695
  in—s 330
  make a—of work about 642
  of a—42
  —of a good fortune 618
  —of music 415
  —of news 532
  —of work *discord* 713
  —out 52
  —together 43
  pull to—s 162
pièce
  —de résistance 298
  —justificative 467
piecemeal 51
pied 440
pier 666
pierce *perforate* 260
  insert 300
  bodily pain 378
  chill 385
  hurt 649
  wound 659
  affect 824
  mental pain 830
  —the head 410
  —the heart 830
piercer 262
piercing *cold* 383
  loud 404
  shrill 410
  intelligent 498
  feeling 821
  —eye 441
  —pain 378
pier glass 445
Pierian spring 597
Pierides 416
pietas 998
pietism 988
pietist 987, 988
piety 987
pig *animal* 366
  sensual 954a
  —in a poke
  uncertain 475
  chance 621
  rash 863
  —together 72
pigeon *bird* 298, 366

  dupe 547
  steal 791
  gorge de—440
pigeon—hearted 862
pigeonhole
  receptacle 191
  hole 260
  shelve 460
piggery 636
piggin 191
piggish 954
pig—headed
  foolish 499
  obstinate 606
pigment 428
pigmy (*see* pygmy)
pignoration 771
pig—sticking 361
pigsty 653
pigtail 214
Pigwiggen 193
pike *hill* 206
  sharp 253
  fish 366
  weapon 727
pikeman 726
pikestaff *tall* 206
  plain 525
pilaster *support* 215
  projection 250
  ornament 847
pile *heap* 72
  multitude 102
  edifice 161
  velvet 256
  store 636
  money 800
  (*house* 189)
  funeral—363
  —on the agony 860
  —up *exaggeration* 549
  redundance 641
pile—driver 276
pile—dwelling 189
pileous 256
piles 655
pilfer *steal* 791
pilferer 792
pilgarlic *outcast* 893
pilgrim *traveler* 268
  palmer 996
pilgrimage
  journey 266
  undertaking 676
pill *sphere* 249
  medicine 662
  bore 841
  bitter—735
pillage *injury* 659
  theft 791
pillager 792
pillar *stable* 150
  lofty 206
  support 215
  monument 551
  tablet 590

  from—to post
  transfer 270
  agitation 315
  irresolute 505
  circuit 629
  —of the state etc. 873
  —s of Hercules 550
pillarist 996
pillion 215
pillory 975
pillow *support* **215**
  soft 324
  consult one's—
  temporize 133
  reflect 451
pillowcase 223
pilon 784
pilose 256
pilot *mariner* 269
  inform 527
  guide 693
  director 694
pilot balloon
  experiment 463
pilot boat 273
pilot bread 298
pilot jacket 225
Pilsener beer 298
pimento 393
pimp 962
pimple *tumor* 250
  blemish 848
pin *fasten* 43
  fastening 45
  locate 184
  sharp 253
  axis 312
  trifle 643
  might hear a—drop 403
  not a—to choose
  equal 27
  no choice 609a
  —down
  compulsion 744
  restraint 751
  —oneself upon
  serve 746
  servile 886
  —one's faith upon **484**
  point of a—193
pinacotheca 556
pinafore 225
pince—nez 445
pincers 781
pinch *emergency* 8
  contract 195
  pain 378
  chill 385
  need 630
  difficulty 704
  grudge 819
  hurt morally 830
  (*insufficiency* 640)
  in a—704

  jack at a—711
  —of snuff 643
  where the shoe—es 830
pinchbeck *sham* 545
  jewelry 847
pinched (*see* pinch)
  thin 203
  poor 804
  —with hunger 865
pinchfist 819
pinchgut 819
pinching *cold* 383
  miserly 819
Pindaric 597
pine *tree* 367
  disease 655
  dejection 837
  suffer in mind 828
  —away 837
  —for 865
pineapple 298, 369
pinery 371
pingpong
  photograph 554
  game 840
pin grass 367
pinguid 355
pinguify 355
pinhole 260
pinion *fasten* 43
  wing 267
  instrument 633
  restrain 751
  fetter 752
pink *indent* 257
  pierce 260
  thrust 276
  color 434
  perfection 650
  glory 873
pink of *beauty* 845
  —courtesy 894
  —fashion 852
  —perfection 650
  —politeness 894
pin money 800
pinna 418
pinnace 273
pinnacle 210
pinprick 180a, 643
pins *legs* 266
  —and needles
  bodily pain 378
  numb 381
  mental pain 828
pioneer *precursor* 64
  leader 234
  agriculture 371
  teacher 540
  prepare 673
pious 987—fraud
  untruth 546
  false piety 988
pipe *tube* 260
  conduit 350

  vent 351
  sound 410
  cry 411
  music 416, 417
  weep 839
  no—no dance 812
  —of peace 721
  —one's eye 839
  —s *stridor* 410
pipe clay *habit* 613
  strictness 739
piped 260
pipe dream 458, 515
pipelaying 626
piper 416 pay the —aid 707
  payment 807
piping—hot 382—time
  peace 721
  prosperity 734
pipkin 191
piquant *pungent* 392
  —style 574
  impressive 821
pique *excite* 824
  pain 830
  hate 898
  anger 900
  —oneself *pride* 878
piracy 773
piragua 273
pirate *plagiarize* 788
  steal 791
  thief 792
pirogue 273
pirouette
  inversion 218
  evolution 312
  turn a—607
Pisa, tower of—217
pis—aller
  substitute 147
piscatorial 366
pisciculture 370
piscina *drain* 350
  altar 1000
piscine 350
pish! *absurd* 497
  trifling 643
  excitable 825
  irascible 901
pistareen 643
piste 551
pistol 727
Pistol 887
pistol shot 197
piston 263
pit *deep* 208
  hole 252
  opening 260
  grave 363
  theater 599
  abyss 667
  bottomless—982
  —against
  opposition 708

discord 713
–against one another 464
–of Acheron 982
pitapat *agitation* 315
  rattle 407
  feeling 821
  excitation 824
pitapatation 315
pitch *degree* 26
  term 71
  location 184
  height 206
  summit 210
  verticality 212
  obliquity 217
  throw 284
  descent 306
  depression 308
  reel 314
  resin 356a
  musical –413
  black 431
  have absolute–416
–and toss 621
–dark 421
–into *attack* 716
  contend 720
  punish 972
–of one's breath 411
–one's tent 292
–overboard 782
–upon *reach* 292
  discover 480a
  choose 609
  get 775
  touch–653
pitched battle 720
pitcher 191
pitchfork *vehicle* 273
  throw 284
  rain–s 348
pitch pipe 417
piteous *painful* 830
piteously *much* 31
pitfall *snare* 545
  danger **667**
pith *gist* 5
  strength 159
  interior 221
  center 222
  meaning 516
  important part 642
pithless 158
pithy *meaning* 516
  concise 572
  vigorous 574
pitiable *bad* 649
  painful 830
  contemptible 930
pitied, to be–828
pitiful
  unimportant 643
  bad 649
  disrepute 874
  pity 914

pitiless 914a
  revengeful 919
  (*malevolent* 907)
pittance *quantity* 25
  dole 640
  allotment 786
  income 810
pitted *blemish* 848
pituitous 352
pity 914 express–915
  for–'s sake 914
  what a–*regret* 833
  lament 839
pivot *junction* 43
  cause 153
  support 215
  axis 312
pivotal 222
pix *box* 191
  assay 563
  rites 998
pixy 979
pizzicato 415
placable 918
placard 531
placate *pacify* 723
  forgive 918
place *circumstances* 8
  order 58
  arrange 60
  term 71
  occasion 134
  situation **182**, 183
  locate 184
  abode 189
  office 625
  invest 787
  sell 796
  rank 873
  give–to 623
  have–1
  in–183
  in–of 147
  make a–for 184
  out of–185
–in order 60
–itself 58
–to one's credit 805
–upon record 551
–under *include* 76
  take–151
place hunter 767
placeman 758
placenta 63
placentals 368
placet 741
placid 826
placket 260
plafond 223
plagiarism
  imitation 19
  borrowing 788
  theft 791
plagiarist 792
plagiarize
  (*see* plagiarism)

plagihedral 217
plague *disease* 655
  pain 828
  worry 830
–of sighing and grief 837
plague spot 657
plaguy *difficult* 704
  troublesome 830
plaice 298, 367
plaid *shawl* 225
  variegation 440
plaidoyer 476
plain *horizontal* 213
  country **344**
  obvious 446
  meaning 518
  manifest 525
  style 576
  artless 703
  economical 817
  ugly 846
  simple 849
–dealing 543
–English 576
–interpretation 522
–question 461
–sailing 705
–sense 498
–speaking
  manifest 525
  frank 703
–terms *intelligble* 518
  interpreted 522
  language 576
  –truth 494
–words 703
plainly 525
  tell one–527
plainness 576
plains, lunar 490a
plain song 990
plain-spoken
  manifest 525
  frank 703
plaint *cry* 411
  lament 839
plaintiff 938
plaintive 839
plaisance
  (*see* pleasance)
plaisanterie 842
plaister 223
plait *weave* 219
  fold 258
plan *itinerary* 266
  information 527
  representation 554
  scheme **626**
planchette 992a
planchment 223
plane *horizontal* 213
  flat 251
  smooth 255
  soar 305
  inclined–633

planet *world* 318
  fate 601
planetarium 318, 490a
planet-struck
  adversity 735
  wonder 870
planimetry 466
planing 267
plank *board* 204
  platform 586, 626
  path 627
  safety 666
plankton 366, 367
plant *place* 184
  insert 300
  vegetable 367
  agriculture 371
  trick 545
  tools 633
  property 780
–a battery 716
–a dagger in the breast 830
–a thorn in the side 830
–oneself 184
plantain *banana* 298
plantation
  location 184
  agriculture 371
  estate 780
planter 188, 779
  snag 706
plant house 659
plash *lake* 343
  stream 348
  faintness 405
  sound 408
plashy 345
plasm 22
plasma 357, 847
plasmatic 240
plasmature 240
plasmic 240
plaster *cement* 45
  covering 223
  remedy 662
–up *repair* 660
plasterwork 223
plastic *alterable* 149
  form 240
  soft 324
  (*facile* 705)
plat *weave* 219
  ground 344
plate *dish* 191
  layer 204
  covering **223**
  flat 251
  food 298
  engraving 558
  printing 558, 591
plateau *level* 213
  plain 344
plated 545

plate layer 690
platform
  horizontal 213
  support 215
  stage 542
  scheme 626
  arena 728
  –orator 582
platitude
  unmeaning 517
  dull 843
  (*absurdity* 497)
Plato 490a
Platonic
  contemplative 451
  inexcitable 826
  chaste 960
–bodies 244
–Idea 317
–Ideal 317
Platonism 317, 451
Platonist 317
platoon *army* 726
  (*assemblage* 72)
–fire 716
platter *receptacle* 191
  layer 204
  flat 251
  clean the outside of the–544
plaudit 931
plausible
  probable 472
  sophistical 477
  false 544
  flattery 933
  vindication 937
play *operation* 170
  influence 175
  scope 180
  oscillation 314
  music 416
  drama 599
  use 677
  action 680
  exertion 686
  freedom 748
  amusement 840
  at–840
  bring into–677
  full of–836
  full–175
  give–to the imagination 515
  in–842
–a deep game 702
–a game *pursue* 622
  conduct 692
  pastime 840
–a part *false* 544
  drama 599
  action 680
–at cross purposes
  confusion 59
  misinterpret 523
–fast and loose

—one's task 680
—one's trade 625
plytophagous 298
p. m. 126
pneuma 450
pneumatics 334, 338
pneumatogram 532
pneumatograph 662
pneumatology 334, 450
pneumatolytic 334
pneumatometer 334, 662
pneumatonomy 334
pneumatoscope 334
pneumatoscopic 317
pneumatotherapy 662
pneumometer 662
pneumonia 655
poach *steal* 791
  illegality 964
poached eggs 298
poacher 792
poachy 345
pock 250
pocket *place* 184
  pouch 191
  diminutive 193
  receive 785
  take 789
  money 800
  treasury 802
  brook 826
  button up one's—808
  out of—*loss* 776
  debt 806
  —the affront
  submit 725
  forgive 918
  touch the—800
pocketbook 551
  purse 802
pocket handkerchief 225
pocket money 800
pocket pistol
  bottle 191
pococurante
  insensible 823
  indifferent 866
pod *receptacle* 191
  covering 223
podagra 378
podesta 967
poem 597
poesy 597
poet 597
poetaster *poet* 597
  affectation 855
poetic *style* 574
  —*vigor* 574
  —*prose* 598
poetize 597
poeticize 597

poetry 597
pogrom 361
poignancy
  physical energy 171
  pungency 392
  feeling 821
poignant 378
  (*see* poignancy)
poignard
  (*see* poniard)
point *condition* 8
  degree 26
  small 32
  end 67
  term 71
  integer 87
  time 106
  poignancy 171
  no magnitude 180a
  place 182
  speck 193
  sharp 253
  topic 454
  mark 550
  vigor 574
  intention 620
  wit 842
  punctilio 939
  at the—of 197
  at the—of the
    bayonet 173
  at the—of the sword
  violence 173
  severity 739
  compulsion 744
  come to the—
  special 79
  attention 457
  reasoning 476
  plain language 576
  culminating—210
  disputed—713
  from all—s 180
  full of—574
  give—s to 27
  go straight to the—278
  in—*relative* 9
  agreeing 23
  conformable 82
  in—of fact 1
  knotty—704
  make a—of
  resolution 604
  contention 720
  compulsion 744
  conditions 770
  due 924
  honor 939
  on the—of
  transient 111
  future 121
  —a moral 537
  —an antithesis 578
  —at *direction* 278
  direct attention 457

  intend 620
  discourtesy 895
  disrespect 929
  censure 932
  —at issue 454
  —in dispute 461
  —of attack 716
  —of convergence 74
  —of death 360
  —of etiquette 852
  —of honor 939
  —of land 250
  —of the compass 278
  —of view *view* 441
  aspect 448
  —out *indicate* 79
  —*the reason* 155
  draw attention 457
  inform 527
  —system 591
  —the finger of scorn 930
  —to *attribute* 155
  direction 278
  probable 472
  predict 511
  mean 516
  to the—*concise* 572
  material 642
point-blank
  direct 278
  plain language 576
  refusal 764
point champain 874
point d'appui 215
pointed *great* 31
  sharp 253
  affirmation 535
  marked 550
  concise 572
  language 574
pointedly
  intention 620
pointer *dog* 366
  discrimination 465
  indicator 550
pointless 254, 843
point-to-point race 720
poise *balance* 27
  weight 319
  measurement 466
  health 654
  inexcitability 826
poison *injure* 659
  bane 663
  —*gas* 663, 722, 727
poisoned 655
  commend the—
    chalice 544
poisonous 657, 665
poke *pocket* 191
  loiterer 275
  dawdle 683
  pig in a—
  uncertain 475

  chance 621
  rash 863
  —at *thrust* 276
  attack 716
  —fun at 856
  —one's nose in 455, 682
  —out *project* 250
  —the fire 384
poker 386 *cards* 840
poker dice 621
pokerish 980
polacca 273
polacre 273
polar 210
  —coordinates 466
  —lights 423
Polaris 423, 490a
polariscope 445
polarity *duality* 89
  counteraction 179
  contraposition 237
polarization 490d
pole
  measure of length 200
  tall 206
  summit 210
  axis 222
  oar 267
  rotation 312
  from—to pole 180
  greasy—840
  opposite—s 237
  —*vault* 309
poleax 727
polecat 401
polemic
  discussion 476
  discord 713
  contention 720
  combatant 726
polemoscope 445
polestar
  attraction 288
  luminary 423
  indication 550
  direction 693
  (*guide* 695)
police *regulate* 58
  guardian 965
  —court 966
  —dog 366
  —officer 664
  —magistrate 967
  —van 272
  —whistle 669
policeman
  safeguard 664
  jurisdiction 965
policy *plan* 626
  conduct 692
polish *smooth* 255
  rub 331
  furbish 658
  beauty 845

  ornament 847
  taste 850
  politeness 894
  —off *finish* 729
Polish bank 840
polished
  —*language* 578
  fashionable 852
  polite 894
polisson 949
polite 894
  offensive to ears—579
  —*literature* 560
  —society 852
politeness 894
politic *wise* 498
  cunning 702
  cautious 864
  (*skillful* 698)
  body—*mankind* 372
  government 737
political economy 692
politician
  director 694
  proficient 700
politics 702
polity *conduct* 692
  state 737
  duty 926
polka 415, 840
poll *count* 85
  list 86
  vote 609
  schedule 611
pollard *little* 193
  short 201
  tree 367
polloi, hoi 876
poll tax 812
pollute *soil* 653
  corrupt 659
  disgrace 874
  (*dishonor* 940)
pollution *disease* 655
  vice 945
Pollux 490a
polo 840
Poltergeist 992a
poltroon 862
polyandry 903
polychord 417
polychromatic
  colored 428
  variegated 440
polychrome 440
  painting 556
polyclinic 655
polycoustics 402
polygamy 903
polygastric 191
polyglot
  translation 522
  language 560
polygon *buildings* 189

posteriority 117
posterity *futurity* 121
  descendants 167
  hand down to-
    record 551
  fame 873
postern *portal* 66
  back 235
  opening 260
postexist 1
postexistence 152
postfix 37
postgraduate 492
  -school 542
posthaste *swift* 274
  haste 684
  rash 863
post–horse 271
posthumous
  subsequent 117
  late 133
  -fame 873
posthypnotic
  suggestion 821a
postilion *rider* 268
  guide 694
postliminary
  subsequent 117
  late 133
postlude 65
postman 271, 534
postmeridian 126
post–mortem
  death 360
  interment 363
postnate 117
post–obit 360, 363
post office 534
  -order 800
postpone 133, 460
postprandial 117
postscript 37, 65
postulant *asking* 765
  petitioner 767
  nun 996
postulate
  reasoning 476
  axiom 496
  supposition 514
postulation
  supposition 514
  request 765
postulatory 765
posture
  circumstances 8
  situation 183
  form 240
posture master
  player 599
  buffoon 844
posy *bouquet* 400
  motto 550
  poem 597
  flowers 847
pot *much* 31
  mug 191

heat 384
saucepan 386
preserve 670
stakes 775
death in the-657
go to-
  destruction 162
failure 732
keep the-boiling
continue 143
active 682
le–au lait
imagination 515
hope 858
make the-boil 775
potable 298
potage 298
potager 191
Potomac
  all quiet on-721
potation *beverage* 298
  tippling 959
potato 298
pot–bellied 194
pot companion 890
potency 157, 175, 470
potent 157, 159, 175
potentate 745
potential *inexistent* 2
  powerful 157
potentiality
  power 157
  possibility 470
potentialize 171
pother *disorder* 59
  difficult 704
  feeling 821
  excitement 825
  annoyance 830
pot herbs 393
pothooks 386, 517,
  590
pothouse 189
pot hunter 767
potion *beverage* 298
  pungency 392
  medicine 662
potluck *eating* 298
  chance 621
  sociality 892
Potosi 803
potpourri *mixture* 41
  fragrance 400
  music 415
pottage 298
pottering
  faddling 683
potter's field 361,
  363
potter's wheel 144
pottery *baked* 384
  art 557
pottle 191
potulent *drink* 298
  drunken 959
pot–valiant 959

pot–walloper
  voter 609
  servant 746
  commoner 876
pouch 191
poultice *pulp* 354
  remedy 662
  relief 834
poultry 366
pounce upon
  unexpected 508
  attack 716
  seize 789
pound–*inclose* 232
  weight 319
  bruise 330
  -the piano 416
  imprison 752
  -together 41
poundage 813
pounds shillings and
  pence 800
pour *emerge* 295
  rain 348
  sufficient 639
  it never rains but it
    -s 641
  -a broadside into 716
  -forth *eject* 297
  speak 582
  loquacity 584
  -in *converge* 290
  ingress 294
  sufficiency 639
  -on *lavish* 784
  -out 295, 297
  -out blood like water
    361
  -water into a sieve
    waste 638
  prodigality 818
  -with rain 348
pourboire 784
pourparler
  interlocution 588
  advice 695
  council 696
pousse–café 392
pout *project* 250
  sad 837
  discourteous 895
  irate 900
  sulky 901a
poverty *style* 575
  insufficiency 640
  unimportance 643
  indigence **804**
  -of blood 160
  -of intellect 452, 499
powder 330
  food for-726
  gun-727
  keep one's-dry 673
  not worth-645
  -and shot 727
  smell-722

waste-638
powdered
  variegated 440
powdering
  ornament 847
powdery 330
power *much* 31
  numerical 84
  multitude 102
  efficacy 157
  influence 175
  loud 404
  -of style 574
  authority 737
  do all in one's-686
  give-760
  in the-of
    authority 737
    subjection 749
  literary-569
  -of attorney 755
  -of money 800
  -station 636
powerful *strong* 159
  -voice 580
powerless
  impotent 158
  weak 160
powerlessness 175a
powers that be 745
powwow 696
  palaver 588
pox 655
praam 273
practicable
  possible 470
  practical 646
  (easy 705)
practical *substantial* 3
  acting 170
  teaching 537
  practicable 646
  executive 692
  imperturbable 871
  -joke *absurdity* 497
  deception 545
  ridicule 856
  disrespect 929
  -knowledge 698
practicality
  (see practical)
practically
  intrinsically 5
practice *arithmetic* 85
  training 537
  habit 613
  exertion 686
  conduct 692
  in–prepared 673
  skilled 698
  out of-699
  -law 968
  put in–use 677
  action 680
  conduct 692
  complete 729

practice *train* 537
  use 677
  act 680
  -at the bar 968
  -on one's credulity
    545
  -upon
    experiment 463
    deceive 545
practiced *skilled* 698
  -eye 700
  -hand 700
practitioner
  medical-662
  doer 690
praecognita 467
praedial 342, 371
praemunire 742, 974
praenomen 564
praetor 967
pragmatic
  narrow 481
  teaching 537
  practical 646
  -sanction 769
pragmatical
  pedantic 855
  vain 880
pragmatism
  philosophy 451
  expedience 646
  use 677
prahu 273
prairie *space* 180
  plain 344
  vegetation 367
  -dog 366
  -schooner 272
praise *thanks* 916
  commendation 931
  worship 990
praiseworthy
  commendable 931
  virtue 944
prance *move* 266
  leap 309
  dance 315
prank *caprice* 608
  amusement 840
  adorn 847
prate 584
prattle *talk* 582
  chatter 584
pravity 945
prawns 298
praxis *grammar* 567
  action 680
Praxiteles 559
pray *beg* 765
  worship 990
prayer *request* 765
  worship 990
  house of-1000
  -of Ajax 421
prayer book 990, 998
prayer wheel 998

preach *teach* 537
  allocution 586
  predication 998
  –to the winds 645
  –to the wise 538
preacher *teacher* 540
  speaker 582
  priest 996
preachment 998
preadamite
  antique 124
  veteran 130
preamble 62, 64
preapprehension 481
prebend 995
prebendary 996
precarious
  transient 111
  uncertain 475
  dangerous 665
precatory 765
precaution *care* 459
  expedient 626
  safety 664
  preparation 673
precede *superior* 33
  –*in order* 62
  –*in time* 116
  –*in motion* 280
precedence 62
  rank 873
  (*see* precede)
precedent
  (*see* precede)
  prototype 22
  precursor 64
  priority 116
  habit 613
  legal decision 969
  follow–s 82
precentor
  musician 416
  leader 694
  priest 996
precept
  requirement 630
  maxim 697
  order 641
  permit 760
preceptor 540
precession
  –*in order* 62
  –*in motion* 280
précieuse ridicule
  855
precinct *region* 181
  place 182
  environs 227
  boundary 233
precious *great* 31
  excellent 648
  expending 809
  valuable 814
  beloved 897
  –metals 800
  –stone *goodness* 648

  ornament 847
precipice *vertical* 212
  slope 217
  dangerous 667
  on the verge of a–
    665
precipitancy
  haste 684
  rashness 863
precipitate *early* 132
  sink 308
  consolidate 321
  refuse 653
  haste 684
  rash 863
  –oneself 306
precipitous 217
précis 596
precise *exact* 494
  severe 739
  taste 850
precisely *imitation* 19
  assent 488
precisian 739, 850
precisianism
  affectation 855
  heterodoxy 984
  overreligious 988
preclude 706
preclusion 55
preclusive 55
precocious *early* 132
  immature 674
  pert 885
precognition
  forethought 490
  knowledge 510
precompose 56
preconception 481
preconcert
  predetermination
    611
  plan 626
precursal 511
precurse 511
precursor
  –*in order* 62, **64**
  –*in time* 116
  (*predict* 511)
  (*presage* 512)
predacious 789, 791
predacity 789
predatory *taking* 789
  thieving 791
predecessor 64
predeliberation
  foresight 510
  predetermination
    611
predella 215
predesigned 611
predestination
  fate 152
  necessity 601
  predetermination
    611

  Deity 976
predetermination
  601, **611**
predial *land* 342
  agriculture 371
  manorial 780
predicament *state* 7
  circumstances 8
  junction 43
  character 75
predicate *forecast* 507
  affirm 535
  preach 998
predict 511
prediction 511
predilection *bias* 481
  affection 820
  desire 865
  (*love* 897)
predispose
  motive 615
  prepare 673
predisposed
  willing 602
predisposition
  tendency 176
  affection 820
predominance 157
  (*see* predominant)
predominant
  influence 175
  directing 693
  authority 737
predominate
  superior 33
preeminent
  superior 33
  celebrated 873
preemption 795
preengage *early* 132
preengagement 768
preestablish 626
preexamine 461
preexist *existence* 1
  priority 116
  (*past* 122)
preface *precedence* 62
  precursor 64
  book 593
prefect *learner* 541
  ruler 745
  deputy 759
  –of studies 542
prefecture 737
prefer *choose* 609
  –a claim 969
  –a petition 765
preference 62
preferment
  improvement 658
  ecclesiastical–995
prefigure
  prediction 511
  (*indication* 550)
prefix 62, 64
preglacial 124

pregnable 158
pregnant
  producing 161
  productive 168
  predicting 511
  –*style* 572
  important 642
  –with meaning 516
prehensile 789
prehension 789
prehistoric 124
preinstruct 537
prejudge 481
prejudicate 481
prejudice
  misjudge 481
  evil 619
  detriment 659
prejudicial 649
prelacy 995
prelate 996
prelation 609
prelect *expound* 531
  teach 537
  speech 582
prelection 537, 582
prelector 540, 582
prelibation 510
preliminaries
  –of peace 723
  settle–673
preliminary
  preceding 62
  precursor 64
  reception 296
  (*prior* 116)
prelude *prefix* 62
  precursor 64
  beginning 66
  music 415
  (*priority* 116)
premature *early* 132
  unripe 674
premeditate
  predetermine 611
  intend 620
premices 154
premier *director* 694
  vicegerent 759
  –pas 66
premiership 693
premise *prefix* 62
  announce 511
premises
  precursor 64
  prior 116
  ground 182
  evidence 467
  logic 476
premium *debt* 806
  receipt 810
  reward 973
  at a–814
premonish 668
premonition 668,
  992a

premonitory
  prediction 511
  warning 668
Premonstratensian
  996
premonstration
  appearance 448
  prediction 511
  manifestation 525
premunire
  (*see* praemunire)
prenotion
  misjudgment 481
  foresight 510
prensation 789
prentice 541
prenticeship 539
preoccupancy
  possession 777
preoccupation
  inattention 458
preoption 609
preordain 611
  destiny 152
  necessity 601
  Deity 976
preparation 673
  music 413
  instruction 537
  writing 590
  in course of
  –*plan* 626
preparatory
  preceding 62
prepare 673
  –the way 705
prepared *predict* 507
  deft 698
preparedness 673
preparing
  destined 152
prepense
  spontaneous 600
  predetermined 611
  intended 620
  malice–907
prepollence 157
preponderance
  superiority 33
  influence 175
  dominance 737
  (*importance* 642)
prepossessed
  obstinate 606
prepossessing 829
prepossession
  prejudice 481
  possession 777
preposterous
  great 31
  absurd 497
  imaginative 515
  exaggerated 549
  ridiculous 853
  undue 925
prepotency 157

Pre-Raphaelite 122, 124
prerequire 630
prerequisite 630
preresolve 611
prerogative
  authority 737
  right 924
presage *predict* 511
  omen 512
presbyopia 443
presbyter 996
Presbyterian 984
presbytery 995, 996, 1000
prescience 510
prescient 510, 511
prescious 511
prescribe *direct* 693
  advice 695
  order 741
  entitle 924
  enjoin 926
prescript *precept* 697
  decree 741
prescription
  remedy 662
prescriptive *old* 124
  unchanged 141
  habitual 613
  due 924
presence *in space* **186**
  appearance 448
  breeding 824
  in the-*of near* 197
  -chamber 191
  -of God 981
  -of mind *calm* 826
  cautious 864
  real-998
  saving one's-928
present-*in time* 118
  -*in space* 186
  offer 763
  give 784
  church preferment 995
  at-118
  -a bold front 861
  -a front 719
  -arms *courtesy* 894
  respect 928
  -in spirit 187
  -itself *event* 151
  visible 446
  thought 451
  -oneself *presence* 186
  offer 763
  courtesy 894
  -time **118**
  instant 113
  -to the mind
  attention 457
  memory 505
  -to the view 448
  these-s *writing* 590

epistle 592
presentable 845, 852
presentation
  (*see* present)
  celebration 883
  courtesy 894
presentiment
  instinct 477
  prejudgment 481
  foresight 510
presently 132
presentment
  information 527
  law proceeding 969
preservation
  continuance 141
  conservation **670**
  Divine attributes 976
preserve *sweets* 396
  provision 637
  (*see* preservation)
  -a middle course 628
preserver
  safeguard 664
preshow 511
preside-at the board
  direction 693
  -over *authority* 737
presidency 737
president *director* 694
  master 745
  -'s message 695
press *crowd* 72
  closet 191
  weight 319
  public -531
  printing 591
  book 593
  move 615
  compel 744
  offer 763
  solicit 765
  go to-591
  -agent's yarn 546
  -in 300
  -into the service
  use 677
  aid 707
  -of business 682
  -on *course* 109
  progression 282
  haste 684
  -one hard 716
  -out 301
  -proof 591
  -to the bosom 902
  under-*of* 744
  writer for the-593
pressed , hard-704
  -for time 684
pressgang 965
pressing *need* 630
  urgent 642
pressman 554
press room 591

pressure *power* 157
  influence 175
  weight 319
  urgency 642
  adversity 735
  center of-222
  high-824
presswork 591
Prester John 515
prestidigitation 545
prestidigitator 548
prestige *bias* 481
  authority 737
  fascination 865
  fame 873
prestigiation 545
prestissimo 415
presto *instantly* 113
  music 415
prestriction 442
presumable 472
presume
  probability 472
  misjudge 481
  believe 484
  suppose 514
  hope 858
  pride 878
presumption
  (*see* presume)
  probability 472
  expectation 607
  rashness 863
  arrogance 885
  unlawfulness 925
presumptive
  probable 472
  supposed 514
  due 924
  heir-779
  -evidence
  evidence 467
  probability 472
presumptuous 885
presuppose
  misjudge 481
  suppose 514
presurmise
  foresee 510
  suppose 514
pretend *assert* 535
  simulate 544
  untruth 546
pretended 545
pretender
  deceiver 548
  braggart 884
  unentitled 925
pretending 544
pretense
  imitation 19
  falsehood 544
  untruth 546
  excuse 617
  ostentation 882
  boast 884

pretension
  ornament 577
  affectation 855
  due 924
pretentious
  inflated 482
  specious 846
  affected 855
  vain 880
  ostentatious 882
  boasting 884
  undue 925
preterience 111
preterit 122
preterition **122**
preterlapsed 122
pretermit 460
preternatural 83
pretext *untruth* 546
  plea 617
pretty *much* 31
  imperfectly 651
  beautiful 845
  -fellow 501
  -good 651
  -kettle of fish, pass, etc. *disorder* 59
  difficulty 704
  -quarrel 720
  -well *much* 31
  little 32
  trifling 643
preux chevalier 939
prevail *exist* 1
  superior 33
  general 78
  influence 175
  habit 613
  succeed 731
  -upon 615
prevailing 78
  -taste 852
prevalence
  (*see* prevail)
prevaricate
  falsehood 544
  (*equivocate* 520)
prévenance 894
prevene 116
prevenient
  precedent 62
  early 132
prevent 706
prevention
  prejudice 481
  hindrance 706
  -of waste 817
preventive 55
previous-*in time* 116
  (-*in order* 62)
  move the-question 624
  not within-experience 137
prevision 510
prewarn 668

prey *food* 298
  quarry 620
  booty 793
  victim 828
  fall a-to
  be defeated 732
  subjection 749
  -on the mind
  excite 824
  regret 833
  fear 860
  -on the spirits 837
  -to grief 828
  -to melancholy 837
price
  consideration 147
  value 648
  money **812**
  at any-604a
  beyond-814
  cheap at the-815
  have one's-812
  of great-*good* 648
  dear 814
  reward 973
price current 812
priceless *valuable* 648
  dear 814
prick *sharp* 253
  hole 260
  sting 378
  sensation of touch 380
  incite 615
  mental suffering 830
  kick against the-s
  useless 645
  resistance 719
  -up one's ears
  hear 418
  curiosity 455
  attention 457
  expect 507
prickle *sharp* 253
  sensation of touch 380
prickly 253
pride *ornament* 847
  loftiness **878**
  take a-in 878
prie-dieu 215
priest 904, 996
priestcraft 995
priestess 996
priesthood 995, 996
priest-ridden
  false piety 988
  churchdom 995
prig *steal* 791
  puppy 854
  affected 855
  blusterer 887
priggish *affected* 855
  vain 880
prim *taste* 850
  affected 855

writing 590
(*see* produce)
productive *cause* 153
  power 157
  imagination 515
  acquiring 775
productiveness 168
proem 64, 66
proemial
  preceding in order
    62
  beginning 66
profane *desecrate* 679
  impious 988
  laical 997
  −*swearing* 908
profess
  (*see* profession)
profession
  assertion 535
  pretense 546
  business 625
  promise 768
  enter a−625
  −*of faith belief* 484
  theology 983
professional
  business 625
  −*matchmaker* 903
professor
  learned man 492
  teacher 540
professorship 542
proffer 602, 763
proficient
  knowledge 490
  skill 698
  adept **700**
proficuous 644
profile *outline* 230
  side 236
  appearance 448
  portraiture 556
profit *increase* 35
  advantage 618
  utility 644
  acquisition 775
  −*and loss account*
    811
  −*by use* 677
profitable *useful* 644
  good 648
  gainful 775
  (*receipts* 810)
profitless 646
profligacy 945
profluent
  progressive 282
  stream 348
profound *great* 31
  deep 208
  learned 490
  wise 498
  sagacious 702
  feeling 821
  −*attention* 457

−*knowledge* 490
−*secret* 533
profundity
  (*see* profound)
profuse
  diffuse style 573
  redundant 641
  prodigal 818
profusion
  multitude 102
  plenty 639
prog 298
progenerate 161
progenitive 163
progenitor 166
progeny 167
prognathism 372a
prognosis
  foresight 510
  prediction 511
  interpretation 522
  disease 655
prognostic 507, 511,
  512
prognosticate 511
program *catalogue* 86
  music 415
  publication 531
  plan 626
progress *growth* 144
  motion 264
  advance 282
  (*improvement* 658)
  in
  −*incomplete* 53, 730
  in mid−270
  make−282
  −*of science* 490
  −*of time* 109
progression
  gradation 58
  series 69
  numerical−84
  motion **282**
progressive
  continuous 69
  course 109
  advancing 282
  improving 658
prohibition 761
  exclusion 55
  temperance 953
prohibitionist 756,
  958
prohibitive 55, 761
project *bulge* 250
  impel 284
  intend 620
  plan 626
projectile 727
projecting 214
projection *map* 554
projector
  promoter 626
prolation *voice* 580
  speech 582

prolegomena 64
prolepsis *precursor* 64
  anachronism 115
proletarian 876
proliferous 163, 168
prolific 168
proligerous 163
prolix 573
prolixity 573
prolocutor
  interpreter 524
  teacher 540
  speaker 582
prologue *precursor* 64
  drama 599
  what's past is−122
prolong *protract* 110
  late 133
  continue 143
  lengthen 200
prolongation
  sequence 63
  protraction 110
  posterity 117
  continuance 143
prolusion 64
promenade *walk* 266
  display 882
Promethean 359
  −*spark* 359
prominence
  (*see* prominent)
prominent
  convex 250
  manifest 525
  important 642
  eminent 873
prominently
  much 31
  more 33
promiscuous
  mixed 41
  irregular 59
  indiscriminate 465a
  casual 621
promise *predict* 511
  engage **768**
  hope 858
  keep one's−939
  keep−*to ear and*
    break to hope
    545
  −*of celestial worth*
    511
  −*oneself expect* 507
  hope 858
promissory 768−*note*
  security 771
  money 800
promontory
  height 206
  projection 250
  land 342
promorphology 357
promote *improve* 658
  aid 707

promoter
  planner 626
promotion *class* 541
  improvement 658
prompt *early* 132
  remind 505
  tell 527
  induce 615
  active 682
  advise 695
  (*quick* 274)
  −*book* 505
  −*memory* 505
prompter *theater* 599
  tempter 615
  adviser 695
promptuary 636
promulgate 531
  −*a decree* 741
pronation and
  supination 218
prone *horizontal* 213
proneness
  tendency 176
  disposition 820
prôner
  ostentation 882
  praise 931
prôneur 935
prong 91
pronounce
  judge 480
  assert 535
  voice 580
  speak 582
pronounced 31, 525
pronouncement 531,
  535
pronunciation 562,
  580
pronunciative 535
proof *hard* 323
  insensible 376
  test 463
  demonstration 478
  indication 550
  printing 591
  draft 626
  ocular−446
  −*against strong* 159
  resolute 604
  safe 664
  defense 717
  resistance 719
  insensible 823
proof reader 591
prop *support* 215
  help 707
propaedeutic 537
propaedeutics 537
propagable 168
propaganda
  teaching 537
  school 542
  preparation 673
propagandism 537

propagandist
  teacher 540
  priest 996
propagate
  droduce 161
  be productive 168
  publish 531
  teach 537
propel 284
propeller 284, 312
propend 602
propendency
  predetermination
    611
  inclination 820
propense 602
propension 820
propensity
  tendency 176
  willingness 602
  inclination 820
proper *special* 79
  expedient 646
  handsome 845
  due 924
  (*right* 922)
  in its−*place* 58
  −*name* 564
  −*time* 134
  show a−*spirit* 939
  the−*thing duty* 926
properties,
  theatrical−
  costume 225
  drama 599
property *power* 157
  possessions **780**
  wealth 803
property−man 599
prophasis 510
prophecy 511
prophet *oracle* 511
  seer 513
  preparer 673
  priest 996
  non−*Biblical*−*s* 986
prophetess 513
prophetic *predict* 511
  revelation 985
Prophets, the−985
prophylactic
  healthful 656
  remedy 662
  preservative 670
  hindrance 706
prophylaxis 670
propinquity 197
propitiate *pacify* 723
  mediate 724
  calm 826
  content 831
  love 897
  pity 914
  forgive 918
  atone 952
  worship 990

(*skillful* 698)

prudery
  affectation 855
  fastidiousness 868
prudish *severe* 739
  stiff 751
  taste 850
  (*see* prudery)
pruina 383
prune *take away* 38
  lop 201, 371
  repair 658
  –s and prisms 855
prunello
  leather or–643
prurience *desire* 865
  lust 961
prurient 380, 961
Prussian blue 438
Prussic acid 663
pry *look* 441
  curiosity 455
  inquire 461
  –into the future 510
  –open 173
prytaneum 931
psalm *music* 415
  worship 990
psalm book 998
psalmody 415
psalter 998
psaltery 417
psammous 330
psephomancy 511
pseudo *simulated* 17
  imitative 19
  sham 545
  misnomer 565
pseudoblepsis 443
pseudology 563
pseudonym 565
pseudonymity 565
pseudoscope 445
pshaw *trifling* 643
  excitement 825
psora 380, 655
psychasthenia 992a
psyche 450, 821a
psychic 450
psychical 450
  –research 450, **992a**
psychoanalysis 450
psychogenesis 450
psychological 450,
  537
psychologico-
  spiritualistic
  school 451
psychologize 992a
psychology 821a, 450
psychomancy 511
psychometry 450
psychoneurosis 821a
psychopath 450
psychophysicist 450
psychophysics 450

psychosis 821a
psychotherapy 821a,
  662, 992a
psychrometer 349
pteridophytes 369
ptisan 662
ptyalism 299
ptyalize 297
puberty 127
pubescent 131
public , general–372
  make–531
  –demand 677
  –enemy 891
  –good 644
  –library 593
  –mind 593
  –opinion 488
  –press 531
  –school 542
  –servant 644
  –spirit 910
  –welfare 910
  purchasing–677
publication
  production 161
  disclosure 529
  promulgation **531**
  book 593
public house 189
  go to the–959
publicist 554, 593,
  968
publicity 531
publish 531
  –the banns 765
publisher 593
puce 433, 437
pucelage *youth* 127
  celibacy 904
  purity 960
Puck 274, 979
  play–699
pucka *permanent* 141
  solid 321
  valid 494
  ripe 673
pucker *contracted* 195
  fold 258
  anger 900
  in a–*excited* 824
pudder *disorder* 59
pudding *food* 298
  soft 324
  pulpy 354
  sweets 396
  in–time 132
puddle 343
pudgy 201
pudicity 960
puerile *boyish* 129
  foolish 499
  feeble 575
  trifling 643
puerperal 161
puff *inflate* 194

  wind 349
  tartlet 396
  pant 688
  boast 884
  praise 931
  flatter 933
  –of smoke 330
  –up *vanity* 880
puffed up
  inflated 482
  pride 878
puffer 935
puffery 884
puffy 194
pug *short* 201
  dog 366
  footprint 551
puggaree 225
pugilism 720
pugilist 726
pugilistic 720
pugnacity
  contentiousness 720
  irascibility 901
puisne *young* 127
puissant *powerful* 157
  strong 159
puke 297
pulchritude 845
pulcinella *actor* 599
  buffoon 844
pule *cry* 411, 412
  weep 839
pull *superiority* 33
  power 157
  influence 175, 615,
    631
  row 267
  draw 285
  attraction 288
  indicate 550
  printing 591
  a long and a strong
    – *cooperate* 709
  –about one's ears 308
  –an oar 680
  –by the sleeve 505
  –different ways 713
  –down *destroy* 162
  lay low 308
  –in 751
  –out 301
  –the check string 142
  –the wires 693
  –through
    restoration 660
    aid 707
  –together 709
  –to pieces
    separate 44
    destroy 162
    censure 932
    detract 934
  –towards *attract* 288
  –up *stop* 142
    rest 265

  root out 301
  reprimand 932
  accuse 969
  –upon the purse 814
  strong–exertion 686
pulled down
  weak 160
  fatigued 688
pullet 129
pulley 633
Pullman car 272
pullulate
  produce 161, 168
  multiply 168
  grow 194
pulmonary 349
pulmonate 349
pulmonic 655
pulmotor 349, 662
pulp 354
pulpiness 354
pulpit *rostrum* 542
  clergy 996
  church 1000
pulsate *periodic* 138
  oscillate 314
  agitate 315
pulsation *feeling* 821
pulse (*see* pulsate)
  vegetable 367
  feel the–*inquire* 461
  test 463
pulsion 276
pultaceous 354
pulverable 330
pulverize 330, 358
pulverulence 330
pulvil 400
puma 913
pummel (*see* pommel)
pump *shoe* 225
  water supply 348
  inflate 349
  inquire 461
  instrument 633
pumpkin 298
pump room
  house 189
  remedy 662
pun *similarity* 17
  absurdity 497
  ambiguity 520
  misinterpretation
    523
  neology 563
  wit 842
punce 276
Punch *buffoon* 844
  –and Judy 599
punch *mold* 22
  perforate 260
  perforator 262
  nag 271
  strike 276, 716
  beverage 298
  engrave 558

  vigor 574
punchbowl *vessel* 191
  hollow 252
  tippling 959
puncheon 635
  vessel 191
  perforator 262
puncher 262
punchinello 599, 844
punctated 440
punctilio *fashion* 852
punctilious *exact* 494
  severe 739
  observant 772
  ostentation 882
  scrupulous 939
puncto 882
punctual *early* 132
  periodical 138
  exact 494
  observance 772
  scrupulous 939
punctuation 567
puncture 260
pundit
  learned man 492
  sage 500
  lawyer 968
pung 272
pungency 392
  physical energy 171
  taste 392
pungent *pain* 378
  taste 392
  odor 398
  vigor 574
  feeling 821
punish 972
punishment 972
punition 972
punitive 972
punk 962 *fuel* 388
punkah 349
punster 844
punt *row* 267
  boat 273
punter 840
puny 193
pup *infant* 129
  give birth 161
  dog 366
pupa 129
pupil–*of the eye* 441
  student 492
  learner 541
pupilage
  youth 127
  learning 539
pupillary 541
puppet *little* 193
  dupe 547
  effigy 554
  auxiliary 711
  tool 746
  be the–of 749
  make a–of 737

   measure 466
   estimation 480
   berate 527
   price, tax 812
   abuse 932
   at a great–274
rath *early* 132
   fort 717
rather *a little* 32
   trifling 643
   have–609
   have–not 867
–good 651
ratification
   confirm 467
   affirm 488
   consent 762
   compact 769
ratio *relation* 9
   degree 26
   proportion 84
   apportionment 786
ratiocination 476
ration *food* 298
   provision 637
   allotment 786
rational–*quantity* 84
   intellectual 450
   reasoning 476
   judicious 498
   sane 502
rationale *cause* 153
   attribution 155
   answer 462
   interpretation 522
rationalism
   philosophy 451
   reasoning 476
   irreligion 989
rationalization 821a
ratlings 215
ratsbane 663
rattan 975
ratten 158
rattle *noise* 406, 407
   music 417
   confuse 458
   prattle 584
   death–360
–on 584
rattle–brained 499
rattled
   inattentive 458
   confused 523
rattle–headed 499
rattlesnake 366, 913
rattletraps 780
rattling 836
–pace 274
raucity 410
raucous *strident* 410
   hoarse 581
ravage *destroy* 162
   despoil 659
–s of time 659
rave *madness* 503

   excitement 824, 825
–against 932
ravel *untwist* 60
   derange 61
   entangle 219
   solve 480a
   difficulty 704
raveled 59
ravelin 717
raven *bird* 366
   black 431
   hoarse 581
   gorge 957
–for 865
ravening *violent* 173
   desire 865
ravenous
   grasping 789
   desirous 865
raver 504
ravine *interval* 198
   narrow 203
   dike 259, 350
raving *mad* 503
   feeling 821
   excitement 824, 825
ravish *seize* 789
   please 829
ravished *pleased* 827
ravishment 824
raw *immature* 123
   sensitive 378
   cold 383
   color 428
   unprepared 674
   unskilled 699
   sensibility 822
   on the–375
–head and bloody
    bones 860
–levies 726
–material 635
rawboned 203
rawhide 975
ray *fish* 368
   light 420
–of comfort 831
   thou living–450
rayah 745
Rayleigh wave 490c
rayless 421
raze *destroy* 162
   level 213
   friction 331
–to the ground
   lower 308
razor 253
   cut blocks with a–
   waste 638
   misuse 679
   unskillful 699
   keen as a–821
razzia *destruction* 162
   attack 716
   plunder 791
reabsorb 296

reach *degree* 26
   equal 27
   distance 196
   fetch 270
   arrive at 292
   plain 344
   river 348
   deceive 545
   grasp 737
   take 789
–of thought 498
–the ear *hearing* 418
   information 527
–to *distance* 196
   length 200
   within–*near* 197
   possible 470
reaction
   compensation 30
   counteraction 179
   recoil 277
   restoration 660
reactionary
   reversion 145
   tergiversation 607
reactionist
   opponent 710
read *interpret* 522
   learn 539
–a lecture 537
   well–490
readable 578
reader *teacher* 540
   speaker 582
   printer 591
   clergyman 996
readership 542
readily 705
reading *specialty* 79
   knowledge 490
   interpretation 522
   learning 539
–at sight *music* 415
–in 995
reading desk 1000
readjust *agree* 23
   equalize 27
readmit 296
ready *expecting* 507
   willing 602
   useful 644
   prepare 673
   active 682
   skillful 698
   cash 800
   get–673
   make–673
–made 673
–memory 505
–money 800
–pen 569
–to burst forth 825
–to sink 824
–wit 842
reaffirm 535
reagent 463, 690

real *existing* 1
–*number* 84
   true 494
   liberal 516
   property 780
–*estate* 780
–*property* 780
–*security* 771
realgar 434
realism 494
realistic 494, 594
realize *speciality* 79
   intellect 450
   think 451
   discover 480a
   believe 484
   conceive 490
   imagine 515
   accomplish 729
   acquire 775
   sell 796
really *wonder* 870
   (*very* 31)
realm *region* 181
   people 372
   government 737
   property 780
realty 342, 780
ream 593
reamer 262
reanimate
   reproduce 163
   life 359
   resuscitate 660
reap *shorten* 201
   agriculture 371
   take 789
–and carry 775
–the benefit of
   be better for 658
–the fruits
   succeed 731
   acquire 775
   reward 973
–the whirlwind
   product 154
   failure 732
–where one has not
   sown 154, 923
reaper 371
reappear
   repetition 104
   reproduce 163
   visible 446
   restore 660
   (*frequent* 136)
rear *sequel* 65
   end 67
   bring up 161
   erect 212
   back 235
   elevate 307
   teach 537
   in the–281
–its head
   manifest 525

–one's head
   pride 878
rear admiral 745
reason *cause* 153
   intellect 450
   thought 451
   argue 476
   wisdom 498
   motive 615
   by–of 615
   feast of–588
   for this–462
   in–*moderate* 174
   sanity 502
   right 922
   listen to–498
–in a circle 477
–why *cause* 153
   motive 615
   stand to
–*certain* 474
   proof 478
   manifest 525
   what's the–? 461
   without rime or–
    615a
reasonable
   moderate 174
   probable 472
   judicious 498
   sane 502
   cheap 815
   right 922
–prospect 472
reasoner 476
reasoning 476
–faculties 450
reasonless 499
reasons 476
reassemble 72
reassert 535
reassure *hope* 858
   courage 861
reasty *fetid* 401
   unclean 653
reave 789
rebate *deduction* 38
   discount 40a
   moderate 174
   discount 813
rebatement 36, 813
rebec 417
rebel *revolution* 146
   disobedience 742
   (*resistance* 719)
rebellion
   revolution 146
   insurrection 719
   revolt 742
rebellious *defiant* 715
   (see rebellion)
rebellow 412
rebirth 660
reboation 412
rebound *recoil* 277
   regression 283

(counteraction 179)
on the–145
rebuff *recoil* 277
  resist 719
  repulse 732
  refuse 764
  discourtesy 895
  censure 932
rebuild 660
rebuke 932
rebus 533
rebut *answer* 462
  counter evidence 468
  confute 479
  deny 536
rebuttal *(see* rebut)
rebutter *ansswer* 462
  law pleadings 969
recalcitrance 719
recalcitrant 742
recalcitrate
  recoil 277
  resist 719
recalesce 382
recall *recollect* 505
  recant 607
  cancel 756
  –to life 660
recant *deny* 536
  retract 607
  resign 756
recapitulate
  enumerate 85
  repeat 104
  describe 594
  summarize 596
recast *revolution* 146
  scheme 626
recede *move back* 283
  move from 287
  –into the shade 874
receipt *scheme* 626
  prescription 662
  precept 697
  security 771
  payment 807
  –of *money* 810
  –in full 807
  –s *accounts* 811
receive *include* 76
  admit 296
  belief 484
  assent 488
  acquire 775
  take in 785
  take 789
  –*money* 810
  welcome 892, 894
  –Christ 987
received *known* 490
  habitual 613
  (conformable 82)
  –*maxim* 496
receiver *vessel* 191
  assignee 785, 967
  treasurer 801

–of stolen goods 792
receiving 785
recension 85
recent *lately* 122
  new 123
receptacle 191
  (storehouse 636)
reception
  comprehension 54
  inclusion 76
  arrival 292
  ingestion 296
  interview 588
  receiving 785
  welcome 892, 894
  warm–892
reception room 191
receptive
  undertaking 676
  (see reception)
recess *receptacle* 191
  corner 244
  regression 283
  ambush 530
  vacation 687
  retirement 893
recesses *interior* 221
  secret–of one's
    heart 820
recession
  motion from 287
recessive 287
réchauffé *copy* 21
  repetition 104
  food 298
  made hot 384
  restored 660
recherché
  unimitated 20
  good 648
  fashionable 852
recidivation
  regression 283
  relapse 661
recidivism 607
recidivist 607
recipe *remedy* 662
  precept 697
recipient
  receptacle 191
  receiving 785
reciprocal *mutual* 12
  –*quantity* 84
  retaliation 718
reciprocate
  correlation 12
  interchange 148
  assent 488
  concord 714
  retaliate 718
reciprocitist 12
reciprocity 12, 148
recision 38
recital *music* 415
recitation *(see* recite)
recitativo 415

recite *enumerate* 85
  speak 582
  narrate 594
reciter 582
reck 459
reckless *careless* 460
  defiant 715
  rash 863
reckon *count* 85
  –among 76
  –upon *believe* 484
  expect 507
  –with 807
  –without one's host
    unskillful 699
  fail 732
  rash 863
reckoning
  numeration 85
  measure 466
  expectation 507
  payment 807
  accounts 811
  reward 973
  day of–919
reclaim *improve* 658
  restore 660
  command 741
  due 924
  atonement 952
reclaimed
  penitent 950
reclamation *land* 342
  (see reclaim)
recline *lie flat* 213
  depress 308
  response 687
  –on 215
reclivate 248
recluse 893
recognition
  (see recognize)
  courtesy 894
  thanks 916
  means of–550
recognitor 967
recognizable
  visible 446
  intelligible 518
  –by 550
recognizance 771
recognize *see* 441
  attention 457
  discover 480a
  assent 488
  know 490
  remember 505
  permit 760
  (affirm 535)
recognized
  influential 175
  customary 613
  (conformable 82)
  –*maxim* 496
recoil *reaction* 179
  repercussion 277

reluctance 603
  shun 623
  from which
    reason–s 471
  –at *hate* 898
  –from *dislike* 867
recollect 505
recommence 66
recommend
  advise 695
  approve 931
  (induce 15)
  –itself
  approbation 931
recompense
  reward 973
  (pay 809)
recompose
  combine 56
reconcile *agree* 23
  pacify 723
  content 831
  forgive 918
  –oneself to 826
recondite *obscure* 519
  hidden 528
recondition 660
reconnoissance 441
reconnoiter *see* 441
  inquire 461
reconsideration 451
  on–658
reconstitute 660
reconstruct 660
reconvert 660
record 551
  discrimination 465
  career 692
  break the–33
  Congressional–s
    551
  court of–966
recorder 553
  judge 967
recording
  –*instrument* 551
  –*secretary* 554
recount 594
recoup 30, 790
recourse 677
recovery
  improvement 658
  reinstatement 660
  getting back 775
  restitution 790
  –of strength 689
recreant
  coward 862
  base 940
  knave 941
  vicious 945
  bad man 949
recreation 840
recrement 653
recriminate 932
recrimination 938

recriminatory 718,
  938
recrudescence 661
recruit *alien* 57
  strength 159
  learner 541
  provision 637
  health 654
  repair 658
  reinstate 660
  refresh 689
  aid 707
  auxiliary 711
  soldier 726
  beat up for–s
  prepare 673
  aid 707
rectal 221
rectangle 244
rectangular
  perpendicular 212
  angle 244
rectify *degree* 26
  straighten 246
  improve 658
  reëstablish 660
rectilinear 246
rectitude *probity* 939
  virtue 944
rector *director* 694
  clergyman 996
rectorship 995
rectory 1000
rectrix 745
rectum 221, 350
recubant 213, 217
recueil 54
recumbent
  horizontal 213
  oblique 217
recuperation 689,
  790
recuperative 660
recur *repeat* 104
  frequent 136
  periodic 138
  –to 677
  –to the mind 505
recure 660
recurrence
  (see recur)
recursion 292
recurvity 245
recusancy
  impiety 988
  (see recusant)
recusant
  dissenting 489
  denying 536
  disobedient 742
  refusing 764
  impenitent 951
  heterodox 984
  (unwilling 603)
Red
  anarchist 146, 710

red 434
  –and yellow 439
  –book *list* 86
  –cap *porter* 271
  –cent 643, 800
  –cross 662
  –flag 550, 668
  –hot *great* 31
    violent 173
    hot 382
    emotion 821
    excited 824
  –lead 434
  –letter *mark* 550
    celebrate 883
  –letter day
    important 642
    rest 687
    amusement 840
    celebration 883
  –light 550, 668
  –light district 961
  –ocher 434
  –pepper 393
  –republican 742
  –tape 613, 694
  –with mirth 892
  turn–*feeling* 821
redact 54, 658
redan 717
redargue 479
redcoat 726
red–complexioned 434
redden *color* 434
  humble 879
  angry 900
reddish–brown 433, 434
reddition
  interpretation 522
  restitution 790
redeem
  compensate 30
  substitute 147
  reinstate 660
  deliver 672
  regain 775
  restore 790
  pay 807
  penitent 950
  atone 952
  –from oblivion 505
  –one's pledge
    observe 772
    duty 926
Redeemer 976
redemption
  (*see* redeem)
  liberation 750
  duty 926
  salvation 976
  (*preservation* 676)
redemptioner 295
red–faced 434
red giant 490a

red–handed
  murder 361
  in the act 680
  guilty 947
redict 905
redintegrate 660
redivivus 660
redness 382, 434
redolence *odor* 398
  fragrance 400
redouble *increase* 356
  duplication 90
  repeat 104
  –one's efforts 686
redoubt 717
redoubtable 860
redound to
  conduce 176
  –one's honor
    glory 873
    approbation 931
    honor 939
redress *restore* 660
  remedy 662
  atonement 952
  reward 973
Redskin 913
red–tapist 694
redtop *grass* 367
reduce *lessen* 36
  pare 38
  –in number 103
  weaken 160
  contract 195
  shorten 201
  lower 308
  subdue 731
  discount 813
  –in strength 160
  –the speed 275
  –to convert 144
  –to a mean 29
  –to ashes 384
  –to demonstration 478
  –to order 60
  –to poverty 804
  –to powder 330
  –to subjection 749
  –to writing 551
reduced (*see* reduce)
  impoverished 804
  –to a skeleton 659
  –to straits 704
  –to the last extremity 665
reductio ad absurdum
  reasoning 476
  confutation 479
reduction
  (*see* reduce)
  arithmetical 85
  conversion 144
  at a–815
  –of temperature 385

reductive 36
redundance
  superiority 33
  diffuseness 573
  too much 641
  inutility 645
  (*remainder* 40)
redundancy 104
reduplication
  imitation 19
  doubling 90
  repetition 104
reecho *imitate* 19
  repeat 104
  resonance 408
reechy 653
reed *weak* 160
  writing 590
  arrow 727
  –instrument 417
  trust to a broken–699
reed–shaped 253
reedy 253
reef *slacken* 275
  shoal 346
  make safe 664
  danger 667
  double–topsails 664
reek *gas* 334
  vaporize 336
  liquid 337
  hot 382
  fester 653
reeking *moist* 339
  unclean 653
reel *rock* 314
  spool 312
  agitate 315
  music 415
  dance 840
  –back *yield* 725
reembody *junction* 43
  combination 48
reenforce *add* 37
  strengthen 159
  restore 660
  aid 707
reinforcement
  increase 35
  addition 37
  adjunct 39
  materials 635
  provision 637
  aid 707
reenter 245
reentering angle 244
reentry 292
reestablish 660
refashion 163
refect *strengthen* 159
refection *meal* 298
  refreshment 689
  (*restoration* 660)
refectory 191
refer to *relate* 98

  include 76
  attribute 155
  cite 467
  take advice 695
referable *relative* 9
  attributable 155
referee *judgment* 480
  judge 967
  mediation 724
reference (*see* refer)
referendary 967
referendum 609
referential 521
refine *sensibility* 375
  clean 652
  –upon 658
refined *taste* 850
  fashionable 852
refinement
  discrimination 465
  wisdom 498
  improvement 658
  elegance 845
  taste 850
  over–477
refit 660
reflect *imitate* 19
  think 450, 451
  –dishonor 874
  –light 420
  –upon *censure* 932
reflecting
  thoughtful 498
reflection (*see* reflect)
  light 420
  idea 453
  cool–came 498
reflector *mirror* 445
reflex *copy* 21
  recoil 277
  regressive 283
reflexion 21, 277
  resonance 408
  light 420
refluence *recoil* 277
  regress 283
  reflux 348
reflux *decrease* 36
  recoil 277
  regress 283
  current 348
refocillate
  strengthen 159
  refresh 689
reform *convert* 144
  improve 658
  –school 542, 752
reformation 658
reformatory
  school 542
  prison 752
reformer 658
reformist 658
refound 144
refraction
  deviation 279

  light 420
  fallacy of vision 443
refractivity 420
refractometer 420
refractory
  obstinate 606
  difficult 704
  mutinous 742
  sullen 901a
refrain *repetition* 104
  poetry 597
  avoid 623
  do nothing 681
  temperate 953
  (*unwilling* 603)
  (*reject* 610)
  –from laughter 837
  –from voting 609a
refresh *strengthen* 159
  cool 385
  refit 658
  restore 660
  recruit 689
  relieve 834
  –the inner man 689
  –the memory 505
refreshing
  bodily pleasure 377
  mental delight 829
refreshment *food* 298
  recruiting 689
  delight 827
refrigerant 387
refrigeration
  anaesthetic 376
  making cold 385
refrigerator 385
refrigeratory 387
reft 44
refuge 666
refugee *emigrant* 268
  fugitive 623
refulgence 420
refund *pay* 807
  (*restore* 790)
refurbish 673
refusal 764
  preemption 795
refuse *remains* 40
  useless 645
  not consent 764
  –assent 489
  –to associate with 893
  –to believe 487
  –to hear 460
refute 479
refuted 495
regain 775
  –breath 689
regal 737
regale *feast* 298
  physical pleasure 377
  refresh 689
  pleasing 829
  amusement 840

regalia 747
regality 737
regard *relation* 9
  view 441
  attention 457
  judge 480
  credit 873
  love 897
  respect 928
  approbation 931
  have–to 457
  merit–642
  pay–to *believe* 484
  honor 873
  –as 484
regardful
  attentive 457
  careful 459
regardless
  inattentive 458
  insensible 823
regards *courtesy* 894
  respect 928
regatta
  contention 720
  amusement 840
regelate 385
regency 755
regenerate
  reproduce 163
  restore 660
  penitence 950
  piety 987
regeneration
  conversion 144
  divine function 976
  baptismal–998
regent *governor* 745
  deputy 759
regicide 361
régime
  circumstances 8
  conduct 692
  authority 737
  ancien–875
regimen *diet* 298
  remedy 662
regiment
  assemblage 72
  army 726
regimentals 225
region 181, 342
regional 181, 189
register *arrange* 60
  list 86
  chronicle 114
  furnace 386
  record 551
  recorder 553
  schedule 611
registrar 553
registration 551
registry 114
  record 551
reglet 591
regnant *influence* 175

authority 737
regorge 790
regrade 283
regrate 777, 795
regrater 797
regress 287
regression 283, 287
regret *sorrow* 833
  penitence 950
regretted, to be–833
regrowth 163
reguerdon 973
regular *uniform* 16
  complete 52
  order 58
  arrangement 60
  rule 80
  conformity 82
  periodic 138
  symmetric 242
  habitual 613
  by–*intervals* 58
  –*return* 138
regularity
  (*see* regular)
regularize *legal* 963
regulars 726
regulate *adjust* 23
  order 58
  arrange 60
  direct 693
regulated by
  conformity 82
regulation
  precept 697
  law 963
  (*command* 741)
regulative principle
  453
Regulus 490a
regurgitate
  return 283
  flow 348
  restore 790
rehabilitate
  reconstruct 660
  restore 790
rehearse *repeat* 104
  try 463
  describe 594
  drama 599
  prepare 673
Reichsrath 696
reign *influence* 175
  government 737
  –of terror
  severity 739
  fear 860
  –of violence 738
reimburse *restore* 790
  pay 807
rein
  means of restraint
  752
  (*moderate* 174)
  (*counteract* 179)

–in *retard* 275
  restrain 751
reindeer 271, 366
reinforce
  (*see* reënforce)
reinforcement
  (*see* reenforcement)
reinless 738
reins (*see* rein)
  direction 693
  give–to the
    imagination 515
  give the–to
  facilitate 705
  lax 738
  permit 760
  hold the–693
  take the–
  authority 737
reinstall 660
reinstate 660, 790
reinvest 790
reinvigorate 689
reiterate 104
reject *exclude* 55
  eject 297
  refuse 764
rejected *hateful* 898
rejection 610
rejoice *exult* 838
  amuse 840
  –in 827
  –in the name of 564
  –the heart
  gratify 829
  cheer 836
rejoicing 838
rejoin *assemble* 72
  arrive 292
rejoinder *answer* 462
  law pleadings 969
rejoining *meeting* 292
rejuvenescence 660
rekindle *ignite* 384
  excite 824
  (*incite* 615)
relapse *turn back* 145
  regression 283
  fall back 661
relate *narrate* 594
  –to *refer* 9
related *kin* 11
relation 9 *kin* 11
  narrative 594
relationship 9
relative
  comparative 464
  –*position* 9
relativism 451
relax *loose* 47
  weaken 160
  moderate 174
  slacken speed 275
  soften 324
  inactive 683
  repose 687

misrule 738
  liberate 750
  relent 914
  –one's efforts 681
  –the mind 452
relaxation (*see* relax)
  amusement 840
  dereliction 927
relaxed *weak* 160
relay *materials* 635
  provision 637
release *death* 360
  deliver 672
  liberate 750
  exempt 760
  from engagement
  768a
  security 771
  exemption 777a
  restore 790
  repay 807
  forgive 918
  exempt 927a
  discharge 970
  deed of–723
relegate *banish* 55
  transfer 270
  remove 297
relent *moderate* 274
  soften 324
  submit 725
  pity 914
relentless *resolute* 604
  severe 739
  wrathful 900
  malevolent 907
  revenge 919
  impenitent 951
relessee *possessor* 779
  receiver 785
relevancy
  pertinence 9
  congruity 23
relevé 298
reliability
  (*see* reliable)
  solvency 800
reliable *certain* 474
  trustworthy 632
reliance
  confidence 484
  expectation 507
  hope 858
relic *remainder* 40
  reminiscence 505
  token 551
relics *corpse* 362
  sacred 998
relict 905
relief *composition* 54
  silhouette 230
  prominence 250
  aid 707
  comfort **834**
  bas–*convex* 250
  sculpture 557

in strong
  –*visible* 446
  manifest 525
relieve *improve* 658
  aid 707
  comfort 834
relievo *convex* 250
  sculpture 557
religieuse 996
religion *theology* 983
  piety 987
  under the mask of
    988
religionist 988
religious *celibacy* 904
  honorable 939
  theological 983
  pious 987
  over–955
  –education 537
  –persuasion 983
  –sects 984
relinquish 624, 782
  –a purpose 624
  recant 607
  –*hope* 859
  –*life* 360
  –*property* 782
relinquishment 624,
  782 *resignation* 757
reliquary *box* 191
  sacred 998
reliquiae 362
relish *pleasure* 377
  taste 390
  condiment 393
  savory 394
  delight 827
  desire 865
relucent *light* 420
reluct 720
reluctance
  dissuasion 616
  unwilling 603
  dislike 867
reluctation 719
relume *ignite* 384
  light 420
rely *believe* 484
  hope 858
  (*expect* 507)
remain *abide* 1
  be left 40
  endure 106
  long time 110
  continue 141
  be present 186
  stand 265
  –*firm* 150
  –in one's mind 505
  –in possession of the
    field 731
  –*neuter* 605
  –on one's hands 641
remainder 40
  estate 780

pardon 918
respite 970
reprimand 932
reprint *copy* 21
  reproduce 163
  indicate 550
reprisal
  retaliation 718
  resumption 789
reprise *decrement* 40a
reproach *disgrace* 874
  blame 932
  accusation 938
reprobate
  disapproved 932
  vicious 945
  bad man 949
  sinner 988
reprobation
  censure 932
  sin 988
reproduce *match* 17
  imitate 19
  repeat 104
  renovate 163
reproduction 163
  copy 21
  (*see* reproduce)
reproductive 163
reproof 932
  –*valiant* 718
reprove *berate* 527
  disapprove 932
reprover 936
reptatorial 275
reptile
  animal 366, 368
  servile 886
  knave 941
  miscreant 949
republic *people* 372
  government 737
  –*of letters* 560
republican
  government 737
  commonalty 876
republicanism 737
Republicans 712
repudiate *exclude* 55
  deny 489
  reject 610
  abrogate 756
  violate 773
  not pay 808
  evade 927
repugn 719
repugnance
  contrariety 14
  incongruity 24
  resistance 719
  dislike 867
  hate 898
  (*unwillingness* 603)
repulse *recoil* 277
  repel 289
  resist 719

failure 732
refusal 764
repulsion 289, 719
repulsive
  (*see* repulse)
  unsavory 395
  painful 830
  ugly 846
  disliked 867
  discourteous 895
  hateful 898
repurchase 795
reputable
  honored 873
  honorable 939
reputation 505, 873
repute 873
request 765 in–630
  –*permission* 760
requiem *lament* 839
  (*funeral* 363)
  (*music* 415)
require *need* 630
  insufficient 640
  exact 741
  compel 744
  price 812
  due 924
  duty 926
  –*explanation* 519
requirement 630
requisite 630
requisition
  exaction 741
  request 765
  put in–use 677
  order 741
requital
  retaliation 718
  gratitude 916
  punishment 972
  reward 973
requite 148
reredos 1000
rescind *cut off* 44
  abrogate 756
  refuse 764
rescission 44, 756
rescript *answer* 462
  transcript 590
  letter 592
  order 741
rescriptive
  prohibition 761
rescue
  preserve 670
  deliver 672
  aid 707
research 461
reseat 660
resection 44
reseda 435
resemblance 17, 21
resent 900
resentful 901
resentment 900

reservation
  concealment 528
  mental–528
  equivocation 520
  untruth 546
  with a–38
reservatory
  receptacle 191
  store 636
reserve
  concealment 528
  silence 585
  choice 609
  means 632
  store 636
  disuse 678
  retain 781
  shyness 881
  in–*destined* 152
  prepared 673
  –*forces* 726
  –*oneself* 881
reservoir 153, 636
resiance 189
resiant 186
reside 186
residence 189
  have one's legal–at
  184
resident
  consignee 758
  present 186
  inhabitant 188
residential 186
residentiary 186, 188
  clergy 996
residue 40
residuum
  remainder 40
  dregs 653
  commonalty 876
resign *give up* 757
  relinquish 782
  –*one's being* 360
  –*one's breath* 360
  –*oneself submit* 725
  not mind 826
resignation
  (*see* resign)
  submission 725
  obedience 743
  abdication **757**
  renunciation 782
  endurance 826
  humility 879
resilience
  regression 283
  elasticity 325
resin 356a
resipiscence 950
resist *oppose* 179
  withstand 719
  disobey 742
  refuse 764
  –*invasion* 717
resistance 708, 719

(*see* resist)
résistance, pièce de–
  298
resisting
  tenacious 327
resistivity 490d
resistless *strong* 159
  necessity 601
resolute
  determined 604
  brave 861
resolution
  (*see* resolve)
  decomposition 49
  conversion 144
  music 413
  topic 454
  investigation 461
  mental energy **604**
  intention 620
  scheme 626
  courage 861
resolvable into
  equal 27
  convertible 144
resolve *change* 140
  liquefy 335
  investigate 461
  discover 480a
  interpret 522
  determine 604
  predetermine 611
  intend 620
  –*into convert* 144
  –*into elements* 49
resolvent
  decomposition 49
  dispersion 73
  liquefaction 335
resonance *sound* 402
  ringing **408**
resorb 296
resorbent 296
resort *assemble* 72
  focus 74
  dwelling 189
  converge 290
  last–601
  –*to be present* 186
  travel 266
  employ 677
resound *loud* 404
  ring 408
  –*praises* 931
resources *means* 632
  property 780
  wealth 803
respect *relation* 9
  observe 772
  fame 873
  salutation 894
  deference **928**
  in no–536
  with–to 9
respectability
  mediocrity 736

repute 873
probity 939
respectable
  unimportant 643
  distinguished 873
  upright 939
  highly–875
respectful 928
  –*distance avoid* 623
  cautious 864
respective *special* 79
  apportioned 786
respectless 458
respects *courtesy* 894
  deference 928
resperse 73
respiration 349
respirator 349
respire *breathe* 349
  live 359
  refresh 689
respirometer 662
respite
  intermission 106
  defer 133
  pause 142
  deliver 672
  repose 687
  reprieve 970
  (*escape* 671)
resplendent
  luminous 420
  splendid 845
respond *accord* 23
  answer 462
  feel 821
respondent 462
  accused 938
response
  answer 462, **587**
  concord 714
  feeling 821
  friendship 888
  worship 990
responsibility
  solvency 800
  duty 926
responsible 177, 926
responsions 539
responsive 375
rest *remainder* 40
  pause 141
  cessation 142
  support 215
  quiescence 265
  death 360
  music 403, 413
  inaction 681
  repose 687
  at–interment 363
  repose 687
  content 831
  –*and be thankful*
  inaction 681
  repose 687
  –*assured belief* 484

reversis 840
revert *repeat* 104
 return 145
 turn back 283
 revest 790
 –to 457
revest 790
reviction 660
review *consider* 457
 inquiry 461
 judge 480
 recall 505
 dissertation 595
 compendium 596
 revise 658
 parade 882
reviewer 480, 595
revile *abuse* 932
 blaspheme 988
reviler 936
revise *copy* 21
 consider 457
 printing 591
 plan 626
 edit 658
revising barrister
 967
revision 658
 under–673
revisit 186
revival
 reproduction 163
 life 359
 restoration 660
 worship 990
revivalist 996
revive *reproduce* 163
 refresh 658
 resuscitate 660
 excite 824
revivify *reproduce* 163
 life 359
 resuscitate 660
revocable 605
revocation 536
revoke *recant* 607
 cancel 756
 (*deny* 536)
 (*refuse* 764)
revolt *contrariety* 14
 revolution 146
 resist 719
 disobey 742
 shock 830
 disapproval 932
 –*against hate* 898
 –*at the idea*
 dissent 489
revolting
 painful 830
revolution
 periodicity 138
 change 146
 rotation 312
revolutionary 146,
 742

revolutionize 140,
 146
revolve
 (*see* revolution)
 –*in the mind* 451
revolver 727
revulsion
 reversion 145
 revolution 146
 inversion 218
 recoil 277
revulsive 276
revulsively 145
reward 30, **973**
reword 104
rewriting 21
Reynard *animal* 366
 cunning 702
rez de chaussée
 room 191
 low 207
rhabdology 85
rhabdomancy 511
rhadamanthus
 judge 967
 hell 982
rhamphoid 245
rhapsodical
 irregular 139
rhapsodist
 fanatic 504
 poet 597
rhapsodize 497
rhapsody
 discontinuity 70
 nonsense 497
 fancy 515
rheometer 157
rheostat 490d
rhetoric *speech* 582
 flowers of–577
rheum *excretion* 299
 fluidity 333
rheumatism 378
rhino 800
rhinoceros 366–hide
 physically insensible
 376
 morally insensible
 823
rhipidate 194
rhizanthous 367
rhododendron 845
rhomb 244
rhomboid 244
rhubarb 298
rhumb 278
rhyme (*see* rime etc.)
rhythm
 periodicity 138
 melody 413
 elegance 578
 verse 597
rhythmic 413, 578
rhythmical–*style* 578
riant 836

rib *support* 215
 ridge 250
 wife 903
ribald *vulgar* 851
 disreputable 874
 impure 961
ribaldry 908
ribband (*see* ribbon)
ribbed *furrowed* 259
ribbon *tie* 45
 filament 205
 record 551
 decoration 877
ribbons *reins* 752
ribroast 972
rice 330, 367
ricebird 298
rich *savory* 394
 color 428
 language 577
 abundant 639
 wealthy 803
 beautiful 845
 ornament 847
 –*gifts wax poor* 907
 –*man* 639, 803
riches 803
richly *much* 31
 –*deserve* 924
rick *accumulation* 72
 store 636
rickety *weak* 160
 ugly 846
 imperfect 651
rickrack 257
ricksha 272
ricochet 277
rid *deliver* 672
 get–*of eject* 297
 liberation 750
 loose 776
 relinquish 782
riddance 672, 776,
 782
riddle *arrange* 60
 crossing 219
 sieve 260
 secret 533
 sift 652
 (*question* 461)
ride *get above* 206
 move 266
 –*a horse* 370
 –*and tie*
 periodicity 138
 journey 266
 –*at anchor* 265
 –*full tilt at*
 pursue 622
 attack 716
 –*hard* 274
 –*in the whirlwind*
 will 604
 rule 737
 –*one's hobby* 622
 –*out the storm* 664

–*roughshod*
 violence 173
 severity 739
 insolence 885
 illegality 964
 –*the waves* 267
rider *affix* 37
 appendix 39
 equestrian 268
ridge *narrow* 203
 height 206
 prominence 250
ridicule 856
 disrespect 929
ridiculous *absurd* 497
 foolish 499
 trifling 643
 grotesque 853
ridiculousness 853
riding *district* 181
 journey 266
ridotto *gala* 840
 rout 892
rifacimento
 repetition 104
 resuscitation 660
rife *general* 78
 influence 175
riffle 348
riffraff *dirt* 653
 commonalty 876
 bad folk 949
rifle *musket* 406, 727
 plunder 791
 –*grenade* 727
rifled cannon 727
rifleman 726
rifler 792
rifles 726
rifle shooting 840
rift *separation* 44
 fissure 198
rig *dress* 225
 vehicle 272
 prepare 673
 frolic 840
 strumpet 962
 –*the market* 794
 run the–*upon* 929
rigadoon 840
rigging *ropes* 45
 gear 225
 instrument 633
riggish 961
right *dextral* 238
 straight 246*true* 494
 freedom 748
 property 780
 just **922**
 privilege 924
 duty 926
 honor 939
 virtuous 944
 bill of–969
 by–924
 have a–*to* 924

hit the–*nail on the*
 head
 discover 480a
 skill 698
 in one's–*mind*
 wise 498
 sane 502
 in the–*place* 646
 keep the–*path* 944
 –*about*
 (*see below*)
 –*ahead* 234
 –*and left space* 180
 circumjacence 227
 lateral 236
 –*angle* 212
 –*as a trevet* 650
 –*ascension* 466
 –*away* 113, 143
 –*bower* 840
 divine–*of kings* 737
 –*establishment* 478
 –*hand*
 (*see below*)
 –*itself* 660
 –*line* 246
 –*man in the right*
  place 23
 –*owner* 779
 –*passage* 279
 –*thing to do* 926
 –*word in the right*
  place 578
 set–*inform* 527
 disclose 529
 step in the–
  direction 644
 that's–931
right–**about**
 go to the–
  circuit 311
 tergiversation 607
 send to the
 –*eject* 297
 reject 610
 refuse 764
 to the–283
 turn to the–
 inversion 218
 deviation 279
righteous
 virtuous 944
 –*overmuch* 988
 the–987
Righteousness
 Lord our–976
 Sun of–976
rightful 922
 –*owner* 779
right hand *power* 157
 dextrality 238
 help 711
 not let the–*know*
  what the left is
  doing 528
 –*of friendship* 888

secondly 90
second-rate 651
secrecy (see secret)
secret key 522
  latent 526
  hidden 528
  riddle **533**
  in the–490
  keep a–silent 585
  –motive 615
  –passage 627
  –place 530
  –writing 590
secretariat 965
secretary desk 191
  recorder 553
  writer 590
  director 694
  auxiliary 711
  servant 746
  consignee 758
secrete 299
  conceal 528
secretion 299
secretive 528
secretory 299
sect 75
  religious–983, 984
sectarian dissent 489
  ally 711
  heterodox 984
sectary 65
section division 44
  part 51
  class 75
  indication 550
  printing 591
  chapter 593
  troops 726
sector part 51
  circle 247
secular centenary 98
  periodic 138
  laity 997
  –education 537
secularism 984
secularization 756
secundines 63
secundum artem
  conformable 82
  skillful 698
secure fasten 43
  bespeak 132
  belief 484
  safe 664
  restrain 751
  engage 768
  gain 775
  confident 858
  –an object
    success 731
securities 805
security safety 664
  pledge **771**
  hope 858
  lend on–787

sedan 272
sedan chair 272
sedate thoughtful 451
  calm 826
  grave 837
sedative calming 174
  remedy 662
sedentary 265
sedge 367
sedile 1000
sediment 321, 653
sedimentary
  remainder 40
sedition 742
seditionist 891
seduce entice 615
  love 897
  debauch 961
seducer 962
seduction
  pleasing 829
  desire 865
seductress 615
sedulous active 682
  desirous 865
see view 441
  look 457
  believe 484
  know 490
  bishopric 995
  –after 459
  –at a glance 498
  –daylight 480a
  –double 959
  –fit 600, 602
  –justice done 922
  –life amusement 840
  –one's way
    foresight 510
    intelligible 518
    skill 698
    easy 705
  –service 722
  –sights 455
  –the light born 359
  published 531
  –through
    discover 480a
    intelligence 498
  –to attention 457
    care 459
    direction 693
  we shall–507
seed small 32
  cause 153
  posterity 167
  grain 330
  agriculture 371
  run to–age 128
  lose health 659
  –plants 369
  sow the–673
seedling 129, 367
seed plot
  productive 168
  agriculture 371

seedtime of life 127
seedy weak 160
  disease 655
  deteriorated 659
  exhausted 688
  needy 804
seeing 441–that
  circumstance 8
  reasoning 476
seek inquire 461
  pursue 622
  offer 763
  request 765
  –safety 664
seek-sorrow 837
seel 217
seem 448
  as it–s good to 600
seeming 488
seemingly 472
seemless ugly 846
  undue 925
seemliness duty 926
seemly expedient 646
  handsome 845
  due 924
seep 295, 337
seepage 337
seer veteran 130
  madman 504
  oracle 511, 513
  sorcerer 994
seesaw 12, 314
seethe moisture 339
  hot 382
  make hot 384
  excitement 824
seething caldron 386
segar 392
segment 44, 51
segnitude 683
segregate
  not related 10
  separate 44
  exclude 55
segregated
  incoherent 47
seignior master 745
  nobility 875
seigniory
  authority 737
  property 780
seine net 232
seisin (see seizin)
seismic 314
seismograph 314,
  551
seismology 314, 490c
seismometer 276,
  490c
seismoscope 314
seize take 789
  rob 791
  –an opportunity 134
  –the present hour
    134

seized with
  disease 655
  feeling 821
seizin possession 777
  property 780
seizure 315, 925
sejunction 44
seldom 137
select specify 79
  choose 609
  good 648
selection 75
selectman 965
Selene 318
self identity 13
  specialty 79
  –abasement 879
  –accusing 950
  –admiration 880
  –annulling 497
  –applause 880
  –assertion 885
  –called 565
  –command
    resolution 604
    caution 864
    (temperance 953)
  –communing 451
  –complacency
    cheerful 836
    vanity 880
  –confidence 880
  –conquest
    resolution 604
    (temperance 953)
  –conscious 855
  –consultation 451
  –contradictory 471,
    497
  –control 604
  –convicted 950
  –conviction belief 484
    penitent 950
    condemned 971
  –council 451
  –deceit error 495
  –deception
    credulity 486
  –defense 717
  –delusion 486, 347
  –denial
    disinterested 942
    temperance 953
    penance 990
  –depreciation 483
  –determination 737,
    748
  –detraction 483
  –discipline 990
  –educated 490
  –esteem 880
  –evident certain 474
    manifest 525
  –examination 990
  –existing 1
  –government

    authority 737
    freedom 748
    (virtue 944)
  –help 698
  –immolation 991
  –importance 878
  –indulgence
    selfishness 943
    intemperance 954
  –instruction 539
  –interest 943
  –knowledge 881
  –love 943
  –luminous 423
  –made 490
  –opinionated 481
  –opinioned
    narrow–minded 481
    (foolish 499)
    (obstinate 606)
  –possessed 852
  –possession
    sanity 502
    resolution 604
    inexcitability 826
    caution 864
  –praise 880
  –preservation 717
  –reliance
    resolution 604
    hope 858
    courage 861
  –reproach 950
  –respect pride 878
  –restraint 826, 953
  –sacrifice 942
  –satisfied 880
  –seeker 943
  –seeking 943
  –starter
    automobile 272
  –styled 565
  –sufficiency 893
  –sufficient 880
  –taught 490
  –tormentor 837
  –will 606
selfish 943
selfishness **943**
selfsame 13
sell absurdity 497
  deception 545
  untruth 546
  sale 796
  –for 812
  –off 796
  –oneself 940
  –one's life dearly
    resist 719
    fight 722
  –out 796
seller 796
selliform 250
selling ability 796
selvage 231
semaphore 550

useful 644
good 648
servant 746
servile *servant* 746
 subject 749
 ignoble 876
 obsequious 886
servility
 obsequious **886**
 (*flattery* 933)
 (*see* servile)
servitor 746
servitorship 749
servitude 749
 penal–972
sesame, open–
 opening 260
 watchword 550
 spell 993
sesqui–87
sesquipedalian
 long 200
sess 812
sessile 46
session *council* 696
 churchdom 995
sessions *law* 966
sestet 415
set *condition* 7
 join 43
 coherence 46
 compose 54
 group 72
 class 75
 firm 150
 tendency 176
 situation 183
 place 184
 form 240
 sharpen 253
 direction 278
 go down 306
 dense 321
 stage 599
 habit 613
 prepare 673
 gang 712
 impose 741
 make a dead–*at* 716
 –about *begin* 66
 undertake 676
 –abroach 73
 –afloat *originate* 153
 publish 531
 oppose 708
 quarrel 713
 hate 898
 angry 900
 (*counteract* 179)
 –against one another
  464
 –agoing *impulse* 276
 propulsion 284
 aid 707
 –an example
 model 22

motive 615
 –apart *separate* 44
 exclude 55
 select 609
 –a price 812
 –aside *displace* 185
 disregard 458
 neglect 460
 negative 536
 reject 610
 disuse 678
 annul 756
 refuse 764
 not observe 773
 relinquish 782
 dereliction 927
 –at ease 831
 –at hazard 665
 –at naught
 make light of 483
 reject 610
 oppose 708
 defy 715
 disobey 742
 not observe 773
 dereliction 927
 –at trap for 545
 –at rest *end* 67
 answer 462
 adjudge 480
 complete 729
 compact 769
 –before *inform* 527
 choice 609
 –before oneself 620
 –by 636
 –by the ears 898
 –down
 (*see below*)
 –foot on 294
 –forth *show* 525
 assert 535
 describe 594
 –forward 293
 –free 750
 –going (*see* –agoing)
 –in *begin* 66
 rain 348
 –in motion *move* 264
 use 677
 –in order 60
 –in towards 286
 –no store by
 make light of 483
 despise 930
 –off *compensation* 30
 depart 293
 improve 658
 discount 813
 adorn 845
 display 882
 –on 615
 –on a cast 621
 –one's affections on
  897
 –one's back up 878

–one's cap at
 love 897
 endearment 902
 –one's face against
 oppose 708
 refuse 764
 disapprove 932
 –one's hand to 467
 –one's heart upon
 resolve 604
 desire 865
 –one's seal to 467
 –one's teeth 604
 –one's wits to work
 think 451
 imagine 515
 plan 626
 –on fire *ignite* 384
 excite 824
 –on foot 66
 –on its legs
 establish 150
 –on one's legs
 strengthen 159
 restore 669
 –out *arrange* 60
 begin 66
 depart 293
 decorate 845
 display 882
 –over 755
 –phrase 566
 –purpose 620
 –right *inform* 527
 disclose 529
 teach 537
 reinstate 660
 vindicate 937
 –sail 293
 –store by 642
 –straight
 straighten 246
 pacify 723
 –terms *manifest* 525
 phrase 566
 style 574
 –the eyes on 441
 –the fashion
 influence 175
 authority 737
 fashion 852
 –the seal on 729
 –the table in a roar
  840
 –to *contend* 720
 war 722
 –to music 416
 –too high a value
  upon 482
 –to rights 60
 –to work
 undertake 676
 impose 741
 –up *originate* 153
 strengthen 159
 produce 161

upright 212
 raise 307
 successful 731
 prosperous 734
 –upon *resolved* 604
 attack 716
 desirous 865
 (*intending* 620)
 –up shop 676
 –watch 459
setaceous 256
setarious 253
setback 306, 735
set down *record* 551
 humiliate 879
 slight 929
 censure 932
 give one a–
 confute 479
 –a cause for hearing
  969
 –as 484
 –for 484
 –in writing 551
 –to 155
setiferous 256
set–off *printing* 591
setose 256
sett *lease* 771, 787
settee 215
setter 366
settle *regulate* 60
 establish 150
 be located 184
 bench 215
 come to rest 265
 subside 306
 kill 361
 decide 480
 choose 609
 vanquish 731
 consent 762
 compact 769
 pay 807
 –accounts *pay* 807
 accounts 811
 –down
 adolescence 131
 stability 150
 moderate 174
 locate onseelf 184
 –into 144
 –matters 723
 –preliminaries 673
 –property 781
 –the question 478
 –to sleep 683
 –upon *give* 784
 –with *pay* 807
settled (*see* settle)
 ended 67
 account–811
 –opinion 484
 –principle 496
 –purpose 620
settlement (*see* settle)

location 184
 colony 188
 dregs 653
 compact 769
 deed 771
 property 780
 strict–781
settler 188
settlings 321
settlor 784
seven 98
 in–league boots 274
 wake the–sleepers
  404
Seven Seas 341
seventy 98
seventy–five *gun* 727
sever 44
severable 44
several *special* 79
 plural 100
 many 102
 –times 104
severalize 465
severally *divided* 44
 respectively 79
severalty 44
severe *energetic* 171
 symmetry 242
 exact 494
 –*style* 576
 harsh 739
 painful 830
 simple 849
 critical 932
severely *very* 31
severity **739**
 (*see* severe)
sew 43
sewage *excretion* 299
 filth 653
sewed up
 drunk 959
sewer *drain* 350
 cloaca 653
sewerage
 drainage 652
 filth 653
sewer gas 663
sewing silk 205
sex *kind* 75
 women 374
 fair–374
sexagenarian 130
sexagenary 98, 99
sexagesimal 98
sextan 98
sextant *angle* 244
 circle 247
sextennial 138
sextet 98 *verse* 597
sextodecimo 593
sexton *interment* 363
 clergy 996
sextuple 98
sexual congress 43

-cut *straight* 246
 mid–course 628
-distance 197
-life and merry 840
-measure 53
-of *small* 32
 inferior 34
 subtraction 38
 incomplete 53
 shortcoming 304
 insufficient 640
-of cash 804
-rations 956
-sea 348
shortage 53
shortbread 298
shortcoming
 inequality 28
 inferiority 34
 motion short of **304**
 noncompletion 730
shorten 201–sail 275
shorthand 590
short–handed 651
shorthorn 366
short–lived 111
shortly *soon* 132, 507
shortness 201
 for–sake 572
shorts 225
shortsighted
 myopic 443
 misjudging 481
 foolish 499
short–winded
 weak 160
 fatigue 688
short–witted 499
shot *missile* 284
 variegated 440
 guess 514
 war material 722,
  727
 price 812
 reward 973
 bad–701
 exchange–s 720
 good–700
 have a–at 716
 like a–113
 not have a–in one's
  locker 804
 off like a–623
 random
 –experiment 463
 chance 621
 round–727
 –in the locker 632
shot–free 815
shotgun 727
should be
 no better than she–
  961
 what–922
shoulder *support* 215
 projection 250

shove 276
 printing 591
 broad–ed 159
 cold–289
 have on one's–s
  625
 on the–s of
 high 206
 elevated 307
 instrumentality 631
 rest on the–s of
  926
 –a musket 722
 –arms 673
 –to shoulder
 cooperate 709
 party 712
 –to the wheel
 resolution 604
 undertaking 676
 shrug the–s
 (*see* shrug)
 take upon one's–s
  676
shoulder knot 847
shout *loud* 404
 cry 406, 411
 rejoice 838
 (*voice* 580)
shove 276 give a–to
 aid 707
shovel *receptacle* 191
 transfer 270
 vehicle 272
 fire iron 386
 cleanness 652
 –away 297
shovel hat 999
show *occasion* 134
 visible 446
 appear 448
 draw attention 457
 evidence 467
 demonstrate 478
 manifest 525
 drama 599, 840
 ornament 847
 parade 882
 dumb–550
 make a–544
 mere–544
 peep–840
 –a light pair of heels
  623
 –cause 527
 –fight *defy* 715
 attack 716
 defend 717
 brave 861
 –forth 525
 –in front 303
 –itself 446
 –of *similarity* 17
 probability 472
 –off *display* 882
 boast 884

–one's cards 529
–one's colors 550
–one's face
 presence 186
 manifest 525
 disclose 529
–one's hand 529
–one's teeth 715
–up *visible* 446
 manifest 525
 ridicule 856
 degrade 874
 censure 932
 accuse 938
show–down 525
shower *assemblage* 72
 shower bath 337
 rain 348
 –bath 337, 386
 –down
 abundance 639
 –down upon *give* 784
 liberal 816
showman 524
showy *color* 428
 ugliness 846
 ornament 847
 tawdry 851
 fashionable 852
 ostentatious 882
shrapnel 727
shred *small* 32
 filament 205
 (*part* 51)
shrew 901
shrewd *knowing* 490
 wise 498
 cunning 702
 (*clever* 698)
shriek 410, 411
shrievalty 965
shrieve 965
shrift *confession* 529
 absolution 952
shriftless 951
shrill *loud* 404, 410
 cry 411
shrimp 193, 298
shrine *receptacle* 191
 tomb 363
 temple 998, 1000
shrink *decrease* 36
 shrivel 195
 go back 283, 287
 unwilling 603
 avoid 623
 sensitive 822
 –from *fear* 860
 dislike 867
 hate 898
shrive 952
shrivel *contract* 195
 fold 258
 (*decrease* 36)
shriveled *thin* 203
 (*small* 193)

shroud *covering* 223
 invest 225
 funeral 363
 hide 528
 safety 664
 defend 717
 –ed in mystery 519
shrub *plant* 367
 plantation 371
shrug *sign* 550
 (*hint* 527)
 –the shoulders
 dissent 489
 submit 725
 discontent 832
 dislike 867
 contempt 930
 disapprobation 932
shrunk *little* 193
 shrink 195
shudder *cold* 383
 fear 860
 make one
 –*painful* 830
 –at *aversion* 867
 hate 898
shuffle *mix* 41
 derange 61
 change 140
 interchange 148
 changeable 149
 move slowly 275
 agitate 315
 falsehood 544
 untruth 546
 irresolute 605
 recant 607
 improbity 940
 patience and–the
  cards 826
 –off *run away* 623
 –off this mortal coil
  360
 –on 266
 –the cards
 begin again 66
 change 140
 chance 621
 prepare 673
shuffler 548
shun *avoid* 623
 dislike 867
shunt *transfer* 270
 deviate 279
 remove 287
shunted *shelved* 460
shut 261–in 751
 –one's ears *deaf* 419
 not believe 487
 –oneself up 893
 –one's eyes to
 not attend to 458
 neglect 460
 not believe 487
 permit 760
 not observe 773

–out *exclude* 55
 prohibit 761
 –the eyes 442
 –the door 761
 –the door in one's
  face 764
 –the door upon 893
 –the gates of mercy
  914a
 –up *close* 261
 confute 479
 imprison 751
 (*inclose* 229)
 taciturnity 585
 –up shop *end* 67
 cease 142
 relinquish 624
 repose 687
shutter 424
shuttle
 correlation 12
 oscillate 314
 instrument 633
shuttlecock 605
shuttlewise 314
shy *deviate* 279
 draw back 283
 propel 284
 avoid 623
 fearful 860
 cowardly 862
 modest 881
 fight–of 623
 have a–at 716
 –cock 862
 –of *doubtful* 485
 unwilling 603
 cautious 864
 dislike 867
 –of belief 487
Shylock 787
shyster 941, 968
Siamese 372a
Siamese twins 89
sib 11
Siberia 383
sibilation *hiss* **409**
 disrespect 929
 disapprobation 932
sibling 372a
sibyl *oracle* 513
 ugly 846
sibylline 511
 –leaves 513
sic *imitation* 19
 exact 494
siccation 340
siccity 340
sick *ill* 655
 make one–
 painful 830
 aversion 867
 –at heart 837
 –of *weary* 841
 dislike 867
 satiated 869

slabsided 200, 203
slack *loose* 47
 weak 160
 inert 172
 slow 275
 cool 385
 coal 388
 unwilling 603
 insufficient 640
 unprepared 674
 inactive 683
 lax 738
 nonobservant 773
slacken *loosen* 47
 moderate 174
 neglect 460
 repose 687
 hinder 706
 one's pace 275
slacker 623, 927
slade 252
slag *embers* 384
 rubbish 645
 dirt 653
 (*remains* 40)
slake *quench* 174
 gratify 829
 satiate 869
 (*content* 831)
 —one's appetite
 intemperance 954
slam *shut* 261
 slap 276
 snap 406
 —the door in one's
 face *oppose* 708
 refuse 764
slammerkin 653
slammock 653
slander 934
slanderer 936
slang 563
slang–whanger 887
slangy 560
slant 217
slap *instantly* 113
 strike 276
 censure 932
 punish 972
 —in the face
 opposition 708
 attack 716
 anger 900
 disrespect 929
 disapprobation 932
 —the forehead 461
slap–bang 406
slap–dash 684
slap–stick 599
slash 44
slashing *style* 574
slate *list* 86
 writing tablet 590
 schedule 611
 plan 626
 —loose *mad* 503

slate–colored 432
slates *roof* 223
slattern *disorder* 59
 dirty 653
 bungler 701
 vulgar 851
 (*negligent* 460)
slatternly
 (*see* slattern)
 unskillful 699
slaughter 361
slaughterhouse 361
slave *servant* 631, 746
 worker 686
 a–to 749
 —to no sect 984
 —trade 795
slaver *ship* 273
 slobber 297
 dirt 653
 flatter 933
slavery *toil* 686
 subjection 749
slavish
 servile 746, 886
 subject 749
slay 361
slave 59
sleazy 160
sled 272
sledge 272
sledge hammer 276
 with a–*destroy* 162
 exertion 686
sleek *smooth* 255
 pretty 845
sleep *inactivity* 683
 balmy–683
 last–360
 not have a wink of–
 825
 put to–376
 rock to–*smooth* 174
 send to–841
 —at one's post 683
 —upon *defer* 133
 consider 451
 —with one eye open
 459
sleeper *support* 215
 wake the seven–s
 404
sleeping car 272
sleeping partner 683
sleepless *active* 682
sleepwalker 268
sleepwalking 266
sleepy 683
sleet 383
sleeve *skein* 219
 dress 225
 hang on the–of 746
 in one's–*hidden* 528
 laugh in one's–
 latency 526
 rejoice 838

 hope 856
 wear one's heart
 upon one's
 —*manifest* 525
 artless 703
sleeveless *foolish* 499
 unreasonable 608
 —errand *useless* 645
 unskillful 699
sleigh 272
sleight *skill* 698
 —of hand
 deception 545
 (*interchange* 146)
slender *small* 32
 thin 203
 trifling 643
 —means 804
sleuth 527
 —hound 913
slice *cut* 44
 piece 51
 layer 204
slick *smooth* 255
 smart 698
slicker 225
slide *elapse* 109
 smooth 255
 pass 264
 locomotion 266
 descend 306
 —back 661
 —in 228
 —into 144
slide valve 263
sliding
 amusement 840
sliding panel 545
sliding rule 85
slight *small* 32
 shallow 209
 rare 322
 neglect 460
 disparage 483
 feeble 575
 trifle 643
 dereliction 927
 disrespect 929
 contempt 930
slight–made 203
slily
 surreptitiously 544
 craftily 702
slim 203 *cunning* 702
slime *viscous* 352
 dirt 653
sling *hang* 214
 project 284
 weapon 727
 drink 959
slink *hide* 528
 cowardice 862
 —away *avoid* 623
 disrepute 874
 (*escape* 671)
slinky 203

slip *small* 32
 elapse 109
 child 129
 strip 205
 descend 306
 error 495
 workshop 691
 fail 732
 false coin 800
 vice 945
 guilt 947
 give one the–671
 let–*liberate* 750
 lose 776
 relinquish 782
 let–the dogs of war
 722
 —away 187, 623
 —cable 623
 —in (*or*–into) 294
 —of the pen 495, 568
 —of the tongue
 solecism 568
 stammering 583
 —on 225
 —over *neglect* 460
 —the collar
 escape 671
 free oneself 750
 —the memory 506
 —through the fingers
 miss an opportunity
 135
 escape 671
 fail 732
 —'twixt cup and lip
 509
slipper 225
 hunt the–840
slippery *transient* 111
 smooth 255
 greasy 355
 uncertain 475
 vacillating 607
 dangerous 665
 facile 705
 nonobservant 773
 faithless 940
 —ground 667
slipshod 575
slipslop *absurdity* 497
 solecism 568
 weak language 575
slit *divide* 44
 chink 198
 furrow 259
sliver 51
slobber *drivel* 297
 slop 337
 dirt 653
sloe *black* 431
slogan 722
sloop 273
 —of–war 726
slop *spill* 297
 water 337

 dirt 653
slope *oblique* 217
 run away 623
sloping 306
sloppy *moist* 339
 marsh 345
 style 575
slops *clothes* 225
slosh 337, 653
slot 260
sloth 683
slouch *low* 207
 oblique 217
 move slowly 275
 inactive 683
slouching *ugly* 846
slough *covering* 223
 divest 226
 quagmire 345
 dirt 653
 difficulty 704
 adversity 735
 (*remains* 40)
 —of Despond 859
sloughy 226
sloven *untidy* 59
 bungler 701
 vehicle 272
slovenly *untidy* 59
 careless 460
 style 575
 dirty 653
 awkward 699
 vulgar 851
slow *tardy* 133
 inert 172
 moderate 174
 motion 275
 inactive 683
 wearisome 841
 dull 843
 be–to *unwilling* 603
 not finish 730
 refuse 764
 by–degrees 26
 march in–time 275
 —down 174
 —movement
 music 415
slow–burning 388
slow coach 701
slowness 275
slowworm 419
sloyd 537
slubber *unclean* 653
 (*inactive* 683)
slubberdegullion 876
sludge 653
slug *slow* 275
 printing 591
 inaction 681
 inactivity 683
 bullet 727
 money 800
sluggard 275, 683
sluggish *inert* 172

snippet 32
snip–snap 713
snivel *weep* 839
sniveling *servile* 886
snob *vulgar* 851
  plebeian 876
  servile 886
snobbishness
  flattery 933
snood *headdress* 225
  circle 247
snooze 683
snore *noise* 441
  sleep 683
snort 411, 412
snorter 83
snout 250
snow *ship* 273
  ice 383
  white 430
snow avalanche 383
snow ball 72, 383
snow blindness 443
snow–bound 383
snowdrift 72
snowshoes 225, 266,
272
snowslide 306, 383
snowslip 306, 383
snowstorm 383
snub *short* 201
  hinder 706
  cast a slur 874
  humiliate 879
  bluster 885
  censure 932
snub–nosed
  distortion 243
  (ugly 846)
snuff *blow* 349
  pungent 392
  odor 398
  go out like the–of a
  candle 360
–out *destroy* 162
  dark 421
–up *inhale* 296
  smell 398
  up to–*skillful* 698
  cunning 702
snuff–color 433
snuffle *blow* 349
  hiss 409
  stammer 583
  hypocrisy 988
snuffy 653
snug *closed* 261
  comfortable 377
  safe 664
  prepared 673
  content 831
  secluded 893
  keep–*conceal* 528
  seclude 893
  make all
–prepare 673

snuggery 189
snuggle 902
snugness 827
so *similar* 17
  very 31
  therefore 476
  method 627
–be it *assent* 488
  consent 762
–far so good 618
–let it be 681
–much the better
  content 831
  rejoicing 838
–much the worse
  discontent 832
  aggravation 835
–to speak *similar* 17
  metaphor 521
soak *immerse* 300
  water 337
  moist 339
  drunkenness 959
–up 340
soap *lubricate* 332
  oil 356
soapy *unctuous* 355
  service 886
  flattery 933
soar *great* 31
  height 206
  fly 267
  rise 305
  air 338
sob 839
sober *substantial* 3
  moderate 174
  wise 498
  sane 502
  plain 576
  grave 837
  temperate 953
  abstinent 958
  in–sadness
  affirmation 535
–down 174, 502
  humility 879
–senses 502
–truth *fact* 494
sober–minded 502
  calm 826
  humble 879
soberness 953
sobriety 958
sobriquet 565
soc *jurisdiction* 965
socage 777
so–called
  deception 545
  misnomer 565
sociable *carriage* 272
  sociality 892
social *mankind* 372
  sociable 892
–circle 892
–evil 961

–gathering 892
–science 910
–service 602
–smile 906
–worker 602
socialism
  government 737
  participation 778
  philanthropy 910
Socialists 712
sociality 892
society *mankind* 372
  party 712
  fashion 852
  sociality 892
  laity 997
  position in–873
sociological 537
–school 451
sociology 910
sociopath 821a
socius criminis 711
sock *hosiery* 225
  drama 599
sockdolager 67, 479
socket *receptacle* 191
  concave 252
socle 215
Socratic method 461
Socratic school 451
sod 344
  beneath the–363
sodality *party* 712
  friendship 888
  (sociality 892)
sodden *moist* 339
  boiled 384
sofa 215
soft *stop!* 142
  weak 160
  moderate 174
  smooth 255
  not hard 324
  moist 339
  marsh 345
  silence! 403
–sound 405
  dulcet 413
  credulous 486
  silly 499
  lenient 740
  tender 822
  timid 862
  (docile 602)
  (irresolute 605)
  own the–
  impeachment 529
–buzzing slander 934
–music 415
–pedal 405
–sawder *plea* 617
  flattery 933
–snap 681
–soap *oil* 356
  flattery 933
–thing 681

–tongue,–words 894
soften (*see* soft)
  moderate 174
  relieve 834
  pity 914
  palliate 937
  penitent 950
–down 834
softening 324
–of the brain 158
softer sex 374
soft–hearted 914
softling 160
softness 324
  persuasibility 615
soft–spoken 894
soggy 339
soho *attention* 457
  parley 586
  hunting 622
soi–distant
  asserting 535
  misnomer 565
  vain 880
soil *region* 181
  land 342
  dirt 653
  deface 846
  (spoil 659)
  (blemish 848)
  till the–
  agriculture 371
  prepare 673
soilure 653
soirée 892
sojourn *dwell* 186
  abode 189
  (rest 265)
sojourner 188
soke 181
solace *relief* 834
  recreation 840
–oneself with
  pleasure 827
solar 318–system 318
solatium 973
sola topi 225
soldan 745
solder *join* 43
  cement 45
  cohere 46
soldier 726
soldierlike *war* 722
  brave 861
sole *alone* 87
  base 211
  support 215
  fish 298
  feme–904
solecism
  ungrammatical **568**
  (sophistry 477)
solemn
  affirmation 535
  important 642
  grave 837

  glorious 873
  ostentatious 882
  commemoration 883
  religious 987
  worship 990
–avowal 535
–declaration 535
–mockery 882
–silence 403
solemnity *rite* 998
solemnization 883
sol–fa 416
solfeggio 415
solferino 434, 437
solicit *induce* 615
  request 765
  desire 865
–the attention 457
solicitor *agent* 758
  petitioner 767
  merchant 797
  lawyer 968
solicitous 765, 865
solicitude *care* 459
  pain 828
  anxiety 860
  desire 865
solid *complete* 52
  dense 321
  certain 474
  learned 490
  exact 494
  wise 498
  persevering 604a
–in galleys 591
solidarity *party* 712
solidify 48, 321
solidity (*see* solid)
  solvency 800
solidungulate 366
soliloquist 589
soliloquy 589
soliped 366
solitaire *game* 840
  hermit 893
solitary *alone* 87
  secluded 893
solitude 87, 893
solmization 415
solo 415
soloist 996
Solomon 498, 500
Solon 498, 500
solstice dance 372a
soluble *fluid* 333
  liquefy 335
solus 87
solution *fluid* 333
  liquefaction 335
  music 413
  answer 462
  explanation 522
–of continuity 70
solve *liquefy* 335
  discover 480a
  unriddle 522

strings
  music 416, 417
  leading–541
  pull the
  –*influence* 175
  direct 693
  two–to one's bow
      632
stringy
  filamentous 205
  tough 327
striolate 440
strip *narrow* 203
  filament 205
  divest 226
  take 789
  rob 791
stripe *length* 200
  variegation 440
  mark 550
  insignia 747
  blow 972
stripling 129
stripped *poor* 804
strive *endeavor* 675
  exert 686
  contend 720
  –*against* 720
stroke *impulse* 276
  touch 379
  mark 550
  evil 619
  expedient 626
  disease 655
  action 680
  success 731
  painful 830
  at a–113
  good–626
  –of death 360
  –of policy 626
  –of the pen
    writing 590
    command 741
  –of time 113
  –of word 686
  –the wrong way 256
stroll 266
strolling player 599
strong *great* 31
  powerful 159
  energetic 171
  tough 327
  taste 390
  pungent 392
  fetid 401
  resolved 604
  healthy 654
  feeling 821
  wonderful! 870
  by a–arm 744
  smell–of 398
  –accent 580
  –argument 476
  –arm man 792
  –box 802

  –language 574
  –point 476
  –pull 686
    with a–hand
    resolution 604
    exertion 686
    severity 739
strong–headed 498
stronghold *refuge* 666
  defense 717
  prison 752
strong–minded
  wisdom 498
  courage 861
strong–room 802
strong–scented 398
strong–willed 604,
    861
strop 253
strophe 597
strow 73
struck
  (*see* stricken, strike)
  awe–860
  –all of a heap
    emotion 821
    wonder 870
  –down *defeated* 732
  –with *love* 897
structural 7, 240
structure
  production 161
  form 240
  texture 329
  organization 357
  (*house* 189)
struggle *essay* 675
  exert 686
  difficulty 704
  contend 720
strum 416
struma 655
strumpet 962
strut *walk* 266
  pride 878
  parade 882
  boast 884
  –and fret one's hour
    upon the stage
    life 359
    drama 599
strychnine 663
stub 550
stubbed 201
stubble *remains* 40
  useless 645
stubborn *strong* 159
  hard 323
  obstinate 606
  resistance 719
stubby 201
stucco *cement* 45
  covering 223
stuck (*see* stick)
  –fast *firm* 150
  difficulty 704

stuck–up 878
stud *hanging peg* 214
  knob 250
  horses 271
  –poker 840
studded *many* 102
  spiked 253
  variegated 440
student 492, 541
studied
  predetermined 611
  (*willful* 600)
studio *room* 191
  painting 556
  workshop 691
studious
  thoughtful 451
  docile 539
  intending 620
study *copy* 21
  room 191
  thought 451
  attention 457
  research 461
  learning 539
  painting 556
  intention 620
  seclusion 893
  –in anatomy 203
stuff *substance* 3
  contents 190
  expand 194
  line 224
  matter 316
  texture 329
  absurdity 497
  unmeaning 517
  deceive 545
  material 635
  trifle 643
  overeat 957
  –and nonsense
    unsubstantial 4
    unmeaning 517
  –in 300
  –the memory with
      505
  –up *close* 261
  hoax 545
  such–as dreams are
      made of 515
stuffed *crammed* 641
  –eggs 298
stuffing *contents* 190
  lining 224
  stopper 263
stuffy *dense* 321
  sultry 382
stultified *failure* 732
stultify 497
  –oneself 699
stultiloquy 497
stumble *fall* 306
  flounder 315
  error 495
  unskillful 699

  failure 732
  –on *chance* 556
  discover 480a
stumblingblock
  difficulty 704
  hindrance 706
stump *remainder* 40
  trunk 51
  walk 266
  drawing 556
  speak 582
  stir your–s
  active 682
  –along *slow* 275
  worn to the–659
stump orator 582
stumpy *short* 201
stun
  physically insensible
      376
  loud 404
  deafen 419
  unexpected 508
  morally insensible
      823
  affect 824
  astonish 870
Stundist 984
stung (*see* sting)
  –to the quick 824
stunt *shorten* 201
stunted *small* 193
  contracted 195
  meager 640
stupa 363
stupe 834
stupefaction 826
stupefy
  –*physically* 376
  –*morally* 823
  astonish 870
stupendous *great* 31
  large 192
  wonderful 870
stupid *misjudging* 481
  credulous 486
  unintelligent 499
  tiresome 841
  dull 843
stupor
  insensibility 376,
      823
  wonder 870
stupration 961
sturdy *strong* 159
  persevering 604a
  –beggar *beggar* 767
  thief 792
sturgeon 298
stutter 583
sty *inclosure* 189, 232
  dirt 653
Stygian *dark* 421
  diabolic 945
  infernal 982
  cross the–ferry

  die 360
  –shore *death* 360
style *state* 7
  time 114
  painting 556
  graver 558
  name 564
  phrase 566
  diction 569
  writing 590
  beauty 845
  fashion 852
stylet *awl* 262
  dagger 727
stylish 852
stylist 578
stylite 996
Stylites, Simeon–
    893
stylography 590
styptic 397
Styx 982
suanpan 85
suant 705
suasible 602
suasion 615
suave 894
suavity 894
sub 34
subacid 397
subacidity 397
subaction 330
subahdar 745
subalpine 206
subaltern *inferior* 34
  soldier 726
  officer 745
  servant 746
subaqueous 208
subarborescent 242
subastral 318
subaudition 527
subclavate 250
subcommittee 696
subconscious 450,
    992a –self 317, 450
subcontrary 237
subcutaneous 221,
    223
subdean 996
subdichotomy 91
subditious 147
subdivide 44
subdivision *part* 51
  military 726
subdolous 702
subdominant 413
subdual 731
subduction
  subtraction 38
  (*taking* 789)
subdue *calm* 174
  faint sound 405
  succeed 731
subdued *morally* 826
subeditor 593

suberose 320
subitaneous 113
subito 113
subjacency 34, 207
subjacent 207
subject *influence* 175
  liable 177
  topic 454
  meaning 516
  servant 746
  enthrall 749
  be–ed to 177
  –matter 516
  –of dispute 713
  –to examination 461
  –of inquiry 461
  –of thought 454
  –to *qualification* 469
  uncertain 475
subjection **749**
subjective *intrinsic* 5
  immaterial 317
  intellectual 450
subjoin 37, 63
subjoinder 462
subjugate
  conquer 731
  subject 749
subjugation
  defeat 732
  moral impression
    824
subjunction 43
subjunctive 37
Sublapsarian 984
sublation 38
sublet 787
sublease 787
sublevation 307
sublieutenant 745
sublimate *elevate* 307
  lighten 320
  vaporize 336
sublime *greatness* 31
  high 206
  language 574
  beauty 845
  glory 873
  magnanimous 942
  from the–to the
    ridiculous 853
Sublime Porte 745
subliminal 450
  –consciousness 450,
    992a
  –self 317
sublimity
  (*see* sublime)
sublineation 550
sublunary 318
submarine 208
  boat 726
  –chaser 726
submediant 413
submerge *destroy* 162
  immerse 300

plunge 310
  steep 337
submergible 310
submersible 310, 726
submersion
  depth 208
  plunge 310
subministration 707
submission 725
  obedience 643
  with–928
submissive
  tractable 705
  enduring 826
  humble 879
  (*penitent* 950)
submit *propound* 514
  mediate 724
  yield 725
  –to arbitration 774
submittal 725
submonish 695
submultiple 84
subordinacy 34
subordinate
  inferior 34
  unimportant 643
  subject 749
subordination
  order 58
  (*obedience* 743)
suborn *induce* 615
  purchase 795
  bride 784)
subpanation 998
subpoena
  command 741
  lawsuit 969
subreption
  falsehood 544
  acquisition 775
subrogate 147
subscribe *assent* 488
  aid 707
  agree to 769
  give 784
subscriber
  (*see* subscribe)
subscript 37, 65
subscription *gift* 784
subsequent
  –*in order* 63
  –*in time* 117
  –time 121
subserviency
  servility 886
subservient
  instrumental 631
  aid 707
  servile 746
subside *decrease* 36
  sink 306
subsidiary *extrinsic* 6
  aid 707
  servant 746
  (*tending* 176)

subsidy *aid* 707
  gift 784
  pay 809
subsist *exist* 1
  continue 141, 106
  live 359
subsistence *food* 298
subsoil *interior* 221
  earth 342
substance *thing* 3
  intrinsicality 5
  quantity 25
  inside 221
  matter 316
  texture 329
  meaning 516
  important part 642
  wealth 803
  in–596
  man of–803
substantial *existing* 1
  hypostatic 3
  material 316
  dense 321
  true 494
  –meaning 516
substantialism 316
substantialist 316
substantiality 3
substantialize 316
substantially
  intrinsically 5
  –true 494
substantiate
  materialize 316
  evidence 467
  make good 924
substantive *existing* 1
  substantial 3
substitute *change* 147
  means **634**
  deputy 759
substitution **147**
substratum
  substance 3
  layer 204
  base 211
  support 215
  interior 221
  materiality 316
substructure 211
subsultory 315
subsultus 315
subsume 76
subtend 237
subterfuge
  sophistry 477
  quirk 481
  lie 546
  pretense 617
  cunning 702
subterrane 252
subterranean 208
subtile *light* 320
  rare 322
  –*texture* 329

subtility 498
subtilize *rarefy* 322
  sophistry 477
subtilty 322
subtle *slight* 32
  light 320
  rarity 322
  texture 329
  color 428
  cunning 702
  –point 704
  –reasoning 476
subtlety *sophistry* 477
  wisdom 498
subtraction
  subduction 38
  arithmetic 85
  taking 789
subtrahend
  subtract 38
  number 84
subulate 253
suburb *town* 189
  near 197
  environs 227
subvention
  support 215
  aid 707
  gift 784
subversion
  revolution 146
subvert *destroy* 162
  invert 218
  depress 308
succedaneum 147
succeed *follow* 63
  posterior 117
  success 731
  transfer 783
  –to *acquire* 775
success 731
succession
  sequence 63
  continuity 69
  repetition 104
  posteriority 117
  transfer 783
  in quick–136
  in regular–138
  –of ideas 451
  –of time 109
successless 732
successor *sequel* 65
  posterior 117
succinct 572
succor 707
succotash 298
succubus 980
succulent
  nutritive 298
  juicy 333
  semiliquid 352
  pulpy 354
succumb *fatigue* 688
  yield 725
  fail 732

(*obey* 743)
succussion 315
such– a one 372
  –as 17
  –being the case 8
  –like 17
suchwise 8
suck *draw off* 297
  drink 298
  take 789
  –in 296
  –the blood of 789
sucker 260 *dupe* 547
  servility 886
sucking pig 298
suckle 707
suckling *infant* 129
sucrose 386
suction *force* 157
  reception 296
Sudanic 372a
sudarium 652, 993
sudary 652
sudation 299
sudatorium 386
sudatory 386
sudden *transient* 111
  instantaneous 113
  soon 132
  unexpected 508
  –and quick in quarrel
    901
  –burst 508
  –death 360
  –thought 612
sudorific 382
suds *froth* 353
  in the–*difficulty* 704
  dejected 837
sue *demand* 765
  go to law 969
suet 356
suffer
  physical pain 378
  disease 655
  allow 760
  feel 821
  endure 826
  moral pain 828
  –for 972
  –punishment 972
sufferance 826
  tenant on–779
suffice 639
sufficiency **639**
sufficient *enough* 639
  economical 817
  satisfactory 831
suffix *adjunct* 39
  sequence 63
  sequel 65
  letter 561
sufflation 349
suffocate *kill* 361
  excess 641
suffocating *hot* 382

supervene
  be added 37
  succeed 117
  happen 151
supervise 693
supervisor 694
supervisory 693
supination 213
supine *horizontal* 213
  inverted 218
  sluggish 683
  mentally torpid 823
suppeditate 637
supper 298
  *full of—*954a
supplant 147
supple *soft* 324
  servile 886
supplement
  addition 37
  adjunct 39
  completion 52
suppletory 37
suppliant *begging* 765
  beggar 767
supplicate *beg* 765
  pity 914
  worship 990
supplies
  materials 635
  aid 707
  money 800
supply *store* 636
  provide 637
  give 784
  —aid 707
  —deficiencies 52
  —the place of 147
support *perform* 170
  sustain 215
  evidence 467
  escort 664
  preserve 670
  aid 707
  feel 821
  endure 826
  vindicate 937
  —life 359
supporter
  auxiliary 711
supporters
  heraldic 550
suppose 472, 514
supposing
  provided 469
supposition 514
supposititious
  unattested 468
  untrue 546
suppress *destroy* 162
  conceal 528
  silent 581
  restrain 751
suppression
  (*see* suppress)
  —of truth 544

suppuration 653
suppurative 663
suppute 85
supralapsarian 984
supramundane 939
supremacy
  superior 33
  authority 737
supreme 33
  summit 210
  authority 737
  almighty 976
  in a—degree 31
  —good 618
  —principle 450
Supreme Being 976
surbate 659
surbated 688
surcease 142
surcharge
  redundance 641
  (*dear* 814)
  falsify 811
surcingle 45
surcost 225
surd *number* 84
  silent 403
  deaf 419
  phonetic 561
sure *certain* 474
  belief 484
  assent 488
  safe 664
  make—against 673
  make—of
  inquire 461
  take 789
  on—ground 664
  security 771
  to be—assent 488
  you may be—
    affirmation 535
sure—footed
  careful 459
  skillful 698
  cautious 864
surely 870
sureness (*see* sure)
surety *certainty* 474
  safety 664
surf *tide* 348
  foam 353
surface *outside* 220
  texture 329
  lie on the—
  intelligible 518
  manifest 525
  skim the—
  slur over 460
  —car 272
surfeit
  redundance 641
  satiety 869
surge *swarm* 72
  swell 305
  rotation 312

  wave 348
surgeon 662
surgery 662
surly *gruff* 895
  sullen 901a
  unkind 907
surmise 510, 514
surmount *tower* 206
  summit 210
  transcursion 303
  ascent 305
  —a difficulty 731
surmountable 470
surname 564
surpass *be superior* 33
  grow 194
  go beyond 303
  outshine 873
surplice 999
surplus *remainder* 40
  redundance 641
surplusage 641
surprise
  nonexpectation 508
  take unawares 674
  wonder 870
  —party 892
surprisingly 31
surrebut 462
surrebutter
  answer 462
  pleadings 969
surrejoin 462
surrejoinder 462
surrender *submit* 725
  relinquish 782
  (*obey* 743)
  no—obstinate 606
  defense 717
  —one's life 360
surreptitious
  furtive 528
  deceptive 545
  untrue 546
surrogate 147, 759
surround
  circumjacent 227
  circumscribe 229
  surroundings 227
surtout *coat* 225
surveillance *care* 459
  direction 693
  *under—*938
survene 151
survey *view* 441
  measure 466
surveyor 466, 694
survive *remain* 40
  long time 110
  permanent 141
susceptibility
  power 157
  tendency 176
  liability 177
  sensibility 375
  motive 615

  impressibility 822
  irascibility 901
susceptive 177
suscipient 785
suscitate *cause* 153
  produce 161
  stir up 173
  excite 824
suspect *doubt* 485
  suppose 514
suspected *accused* 938
suspectless 484
suspend *defer* 133
  discontinue 142
  hang 214
  neglect 460
suspended
  animation 823
suspenders 45
suspense
  cessation 142
  uncertainty 475
  expectation 507
  irresolution 605
  in—inert 172
suspension
  lateness 133
  cessation 142
  hanging 214
  music 413
  seclusion 893
  —of arms 723
suspicion *doubt* 485
  incredulity 487
  knowledge 490
  supposition 514
  fear 860
  cautious 864
  jealousy 920
  *under—*938
suspiration 839
suspire 359
sustain *continue* 143
  strength 159
  perform 170
  support 215
  preserve 670
  aid 707
  endure 821
sustained note 413
sustaining power
  170
sustenance 298, 707
sustentation
  (*see* sustain)
  food 298
sustentative 215
sustention 215
susurration 405
sutler *purveyor* 637
  merchant 797
suttee *killing* 361
  burning 384
  unselfishness 942
  idolatry 991
sutteeism 361

suture 43
suzerain 745
suzerainty 737
swab *dry* 340
  clean 652
  lubber 701
swaddle *clothe* 225
  restrain 751
swaddling clothes in
  —infant 129
  subjection 749
swag *hang* 214
  lean 217
  curve 245
  drop 306
  oscillate 314
  booty 793
swage 174
swagger *pride* 878
  boast 884
  bluster 885
swaggerer 482, 884,
  887
swagsman 268
swain *man* 373
  rustic 876
  lover 897
swale 659
swallow *swift* 274
  gulp 296
  eat 298
  bird 366
  believe 484
  credulous 486
  brook 826
  —flight 274
  —the bait dupe 547
  willing 602
  —the leek recant 607
  submit 725
  —up destroy 162
  store 636
  use 677
  take 789
  —whole 465a
swallow—tailed coat
  225
swamp *destroy* 162
  marsh 345
  defeat 731
swamped *failure* 732
swampy *moist* 339
swan 366—*bath* 341
  —road 341
  —song 360
swap *exchange* 148
  blow 276
  barter 794
sward 344, 367
swarm *crowd* 72
  multitude 102
  climb 305
  bees 370
  sufficiency 639
  redundance 641
swarthy 431

585

arrogate 885
–the appetite 394
temptation
–hath a music 615
tempter 615
  Satan 978
  voice of the–615
temulence 959
ten 98–*thousand* 98
–*to one* 472
tenable 664
tenacity *coherence* 46
  toughness **327**
  memory 505
  resolution 604
  perservance 604a
  obstinacy 606
  retention 781
  avarice 819
–*of life* 357
–*of purpose* 604a
tenaculum 781
tenancy 777
tenant *present* 186
  occupier 188
  possessor 779
tenantless
  absence 187
  seclusion 893
tenax propositi
  determined 204
  honorable 939
tend *conduce* 176
–*animals* 370
  minister 631
  aid 707
  serve 746
–*stock* 370
–*towards*
  direction 278
tendence 176, 749
tendency **176**
tender *slight* 32
  ship 273
  soft 324
  color 428
  war vessel 726
  offer 763
  susceptible 822
  affectionate 897
  benevolent 906
  compassionate 914
–*age* 127
–*conscience duty* 926
  (*honor* 939)
–*heart susceptible* 822
  kind 906
  compassionate 914
–*mercies*
  (*ironical*)
  badness 649
  severity 739
  cruelty 907
–*one's resignation*
  757
–*passion* 897

–*to* 707
tenderfoot 57, 541
tenderling 158
tendon 45
tendril *fastening* 45
  runner 51, 367
  infant 129
  filament 205
  convoluted 248
tenebrous 421
tenement *house* 189
  apartment 191
  property 780
–*of clay* 362
tenet *belief* 484
  (*theology* 983)
tenez 142
tenfold 98
tennis 840
tenor *course* 7
  degree 26
  directions 278
  high note 410
  violin 417
  meaning 516
  (*musician* 416)
  pursue the noiseless
  –*of one's way*
  881
–*horn* 417
tenpins 840
ten pounder 727
tense *hard* 323
tensibility 325
tensile 325
tension *strength* 159
  length 200
ten–strike 731
tensure 200
tent *abode* 189
  covering 223
  pitch one's–
  locate 184
  arrive 292
tentacle 781
tentative *inquiry* 461
  experimental 463
  essaying 675
tented field 722
tenter–hook 214
  on–s 507
tenth 99
tenths *lithe* 812
tent pegging 840
tenuity *smallness* 32
  thinness 203
  rarity 322
tenuous (*see* tenuity)
  unsubstantial 4
tenure *possession* 777
  property 780
  due 924
tepee 189, 223
tepefaction 384
tepefy 384
tephramancy 511

tepid *warm* 382
  half cold 383
tepidarium 386
teratism 83
teratogenic 83
teratology
  unconformity 83
  distortion 243
  altiloquence 577
  boasting 884
tercentenary 98, 883
terceron 41
terebration
  opening 260
  (*passage through*
  302)
tergal 235
tergiversate 140, 607
tergiversation
  regress 283
  change of mind **607**
tergum 235
term *end* 67
  place in series **71**
  period of time 106
  limit 233
  word 562
  name 564
  lease 780
termagant 901
terminable 233
terminal *end* 67
  limit 233
terminate *end* 67
  limit 233, 292
  journey 266
termination 67, 151
terminology 562
terminus *end* 67
  limit 233
  journey 266
  arrival 292
termite 366, 690
termless 105
terms (*see* term)
  circumstances 8
  reasoning 476
  pacification 723
  conditions 770
  bring to–723
  come to–*assent* 488
  pacify 723
  submit 725
  consent 762
  compact 769
  couch in–566
  in no measured–
  574
  on friendly–888
ternal 94
ternary 93, 490a
ternion 92
Terpsichore
  music 416
  dancing 840
terra cotta *baked* 384

brown 433
  sculpture 557
terra firma
  support 215
  land 342
terra incognita 491
terrace *houses* 189
  level 213
terrain 181
terraqueous 318
terrene *world* 318
  land 342
terrestrial 318
terret 45
terre verte 435
terrible *vast* 31
  fearful 860
terribly *greatly* 31
terrier *list* 86
  auger 262
  dog 366
terrific *painful* 830
  fearful 860
terrify 860
terrine 191
territorial *land* 342
territory *region* 181
  property 780
terror 860
  King of–s 360
  reign of
  –*severity* 739
  pain 828
terrorism 860
  insolence 885
terrorist
  combatant 726
  intimidator 860
  coward 862
  blusterer 887
  evildoer 913
terrorize 860, 885
Tersanctus 900
terse 572
tertian *periodic* 138
tertiary 92, 93
tertium quid
  dissimilar 18
  mixture 41
  combination 48
  unconformable 83
terza 93
terzetto 415
tessellated
  variegated 440
  ornament 847
tessellation 440
tesserae *mosaic* 440
  counters 550
test 463
testa 223
testaceology 223
testaceous 223
testament
  security 771
  (*record* 551)

Testament 985
testamur 467
testator 784
tester *bedspread* 215
  sixpence 800
testicle 357
testify *evidence* 467
  sign 550
testimonial 551
testimony 467
testy 901
tetanus 655
tetchy 901
tête-à-tête *two* 89
  near 197
  confer 588
tether *fasten* 43
  locate 184
  restrain 751
  means of restraint
  752
  go beyond the
  length of one's–
  738
tethered *firm* 150
tetrachord 413
tetract 95
tetrad 95, 193
tetragon 95
tetragram 95
tetrahedral 253
tetrahedron 95, 244
tetrarch 745
tetter 655
Texas fever 655
text *prototype* 22
  topic 454
  meaning 516
  printing 591
  book 593
  libretto 599
textbook *school* 542
  synopsis 596
  (*teaching* 537)
–*committee* 542
textile *woven* 219
  texture 329
textuary
  orthodox 983a
  revelation 985
texture *mixture* 41
  roughness 256
  fabric **329**
  (*condition* 7)
Thais 962
Thalia 599
thallogens 369
Thames
  never set the–*on*
  fire fool 501
  bungler 701
thana 752
thane *nobility* 875
  (*master* 745)
thank 916
  no–*you* 764

-the palm *give* 784
pay 807
tickler *pungency* 392
tickling 380
ticklish *touch* 380
uncertain 475
dangerous 665
difficult 704
tidal wave 348, 667
tidbit *food* 298
gem 646
good 648
pleasing 829
tide *time* 106
ocean 341
wave 348
abundance 639
prosperity 734
against the-708
drift with the-
facile 705
go with the-
conformity 82
high etc.-348
stem the-708
swim with the-
prosperity 734
-of eloquence 582
-of events 151
-of time 109
-over *time* 106
defer 133
safe 664
inaction 681
succeed 731
-race 348, 667
turn of the-210
tidings 532
tidy *orderly* 58
arrange 60
covering 223
good 648
clean 652
pretty 845
tie *relation* 9
equality 27
fasten 43
fastening 45
neckcloth 225
security 771
obligation 926
nuptial-903
ride and-266
-down *hinder* 706
compel 744
restrain 751
-oneself *promise* 768
-the hands
render powerless 158
restrain 751
-s of blood 11
-up *restrain* 751
condition 770
entail 771
tiebeam 45
tied up *in debt* 806

tier *continuity* 69
layer 204
tierce *triality* 92
worship 990
carte and-716
tiff *quarrel* 713
anger 900
tiffin 298
tigella 367
tiger *violent* 173
servant 746
cheer 838
courage 861
savage 907
evildoer 913
bad man 949
tight *fast* 43
closed 261
smart 845
drunk 959
keep a-hand on
751
on one's-ropes 878
-grasp 739
-hand 739
tighten 43
contract 195
tight-fisted 819
tights 225
tigress 374
tike 876
tilbury 272
tilde 550
tile *roof* 223
hat 225
-loose *insane* 503
tiler *sentinel* 263
till *up to the time* 106
coffer 191
cultivate 371
treasury 802
-doomsday 112
-now 122
-the soil *prepare* 673
tillable 371
tiller *instrument* 633
money-box 802
-of the soil
agriculture 342, 371
clown 876
tilmus 315
tilpah 223
tilt *slope* 217
cover 223
propel 284
fall 306
contention 720
full-*direct* 278
active 682
haste 684
ride full-at
pursue 622
attack 716
run a-at 716
-over 218
-up 307

-with 720
tilth 371
tilting 720
-at the ring 840
tilt-yard 728
timbal 417
timber *trees* 367
materials 635
timbre 413
timbrel 417
timbrology 550
time 106
adjust 58
instant 113
leisure 685
against-*haste* 684
at-s 136
course of-109
employ one's-in
625
glass of-106
in-*course* 109
early 132
destiny 152
measure-114
no-*instantly* 113
soon 132
no-to lose *need* 630
haste 684
no-to spare 684
ravages of-659
slow-275
take-*slow* 275
inaction 681
inactive 683
there being-s when
136
-after time 104
-and again 104
-being 118
-clock 550, 551
-drawing on 121
-enough 132
-gone by 135
-hanging on one's
hands
inaction 681
leisure 685
weariness 841
-has been 122
-immemorial 122
-is out of joint 106
-of day 113
-of life *duration* 106
now 118
age 128
-out of mind 122
-to come 121
-to spare 685
-up *transient* 111
occasion 134
-was 122
-wasted 106
true-113
waste-683
timeful 134

time-honored
old 124
repute 873
respected 928
timekeeper 114
timeless 135
timely *early* 132
opportune 134
timeous 134
timepiece 114
timepleaser 607, 943
times *present* 118
events 151
hard-735
many-136
timeserver 607, 943
timeserving
tergiversation 607
cunning 702
servility 886
improbity 940
selfishness 943
time-worn *old* 124
age 128
deteriorated 659
timid *fearful* 860
cowardly 862
humble 881
timidity (see timid)
humility 879
timist 607
timocracy 803
Timon of Athens
wealth 803
seclusion 893
misanthrope 911
timorous (see timid)
timothy 367
timpano 417
tin *preserve* 670
money 800
-oven 386
-wedding 883
tinct 428
tinction 428
tinctorial 428
tincture
small quantity 32
mixture 41
color 428
tinctured
disposition 820
tinder *fuel* 388
irascible 901
tine 253
tinge
small quantity 32
mix 41
color 428
tingent 428
tingible 428
tingle *pain* 378
touch 380
emotion 821
make the ears-900
tink 408

tinker *repair* 660
(improve 658)
tinkle *faint sound* 405
resonance 408
tinkling cymbal 517
tinned goods 670
tinnient 408
tinsel *glitter* 420
sham 545
ornament 847
frippery 851
tint 428
tintamarre 404
tintinnabulary 408
tintinnabulation 408
tiny 193
tip *end* 67
summit 210
cover 223
discrimination 465
give 784
(pay 807)
on-toe *high* 206
expect 507
-off 465
-the wink 550
tipcat 840
tippet 214, 225
tipple *drink* 298
tope 959
tippler 959
tippybob 803
tipstaff 965
tipsy 959
tiptop *summit* 210
good 648
tirade *speech* 582
censure 932
tirailleur 726
tire *invest* 225
automobile 272
fatigue 688
worry 830
weary 841
tiresome (see tire)
tisane 662
Tisiphone 173
tissue *whole* 50
assemblage 72
matted 219
texture 329
tit *small* 193
pony 271
Titan *strength* 159
size 192
sun god 423
demon 980
Titaness 192
Titanic 159
titanic 31, 192
titbit *savory* 394
pleasing 829
tit for tat 718
tithe *tenth* 99
tax 812
tithing 181

topek 189
toper 959
topfull 52
top–gallant mast
  height 206
  summit 210
top–heavy
  unbalanced 28
  inverted 218
  dangerous 665
  tipsy 959
Tophet 982
topiary 847
topic 454
  –of the day 532
topical 183
toploftiness 878, 885
topmast 206
topmost 210
topographer 466
topography 183, 466, 550
topple unbalanced 28
  perish 162
  decay 659
  –down fall 306
  –over 28, 306
topsail schooner 273
top sawyer 700
top–sergeant 745
topsy–turvy 59, 218
tor 206
torch fuel 388
  luminary 423
  apply the–824
  light the–of war 722
  –of Hymen 903
Tories 712
torment physical 378
  moral 828, 830
  place of–982
tormina 378
torminous 378
torn (see tear)
  discord 713
tornado whirl 312
  wind 349
  (violence 173)
torose 250
torpedinous 823
torpedo vehicle 272
  detonator 406
  weapon 727
  evildoer 913
torpedo boat 726
torpescent 683
torpid inert 172
  inactive 683
  insensible 823
torpor (see torpid)
torpids 720
torporific 823
torque 847
torrefy 340, 384
torrent violence 173

rapid 274
flow 348
rain in–s 348
torrid 382
torsion 248
torso 50
tort 925, 947
torticollis 378
tortile 248
tortious 925
tortive 248
tortoise 275
tortoise–shell 440
tortuous twisted 248
  concealed 528
  dishonorable 940
torture physical 378
  moral 828, 830
  cruelty 907
  punishment 972
  –a question 476
torturer 975
torturous 378
torvity 901a
toss derange 61
  throw 284
  oscillate 314
  agitate 315
  –in a blanket 929
  –off drink 298
  –on one's pillow 825
  –overboard 610
  –the head pride 878
  insolence 885
  contempt 930
  –up 156, 621
tosspot 959
tot child 129, 167
  –up 811
total add 37
  whole 50
  number 84, 85
  –abstinence
  temperate 953
  ascetic 955
  –eclipse 421
  sum–800
totality 52
totalizator 551, 621
totally 52
tote 270
totem 550
totemism 372a
totient 84
totitive 84
totter changeable 149
  weak 160
  limp 275
  oscillate 314
  agitate 315
  decay 659
  danger 665
  –to its fall 162
touch relate to 9
  small quantity 32
  mixture 41

contact 199
sensation **379, 380**
music 416
test 463
indication 550
act 680
receive 785
excite 824
pity 914
in–with 9
some–of nature's glow 318
–and go instant 113
soon 132
changeable 149
easy 705
–on 516
–on the raw 822
–the guitar 416
–the hat 894
–the heart 824
–to the quick 822
–up 658
–upon treat on 595
touched crazy 503
  tainted 653
  compassion 914
  penitent 950
  –in the wind 655
  –with feeling 821
touchhole 351
touching 830
touchstone 463
touchwood fuel 388
  irascible 901
touchy 901
tough coherent 46
  violence 173
  tenacious 327
  difficult 704
  ruffian 726, 876
  larrikin 887
  bully 913
toupee 256
tour 266
tour de force
  skill 698
  stratagem 702
  display 882
touring car 272
tourist 268
tournament 720
tourney 720
tourniquet 263
tournure outline 230
  form 240
  appearance 448
tousle 61
tout solicit 765
  petitioner 767
  flatterer 935
tout ensemble 226
touter agent 758
  solicitor 767
  eulogist 935
tow 285 take in

–aid 707
towardly 705
towards 278
  draw–288
  move–286
towel clean 652
  flog 972
tower stability 150
  edifice 161
  abode 189
  height 206
  soar 305
  safety 664
  check 706
  defense 717
  prison 752
  –above 31
  –of silence 363
  –of strength
  strong 159
  influential 175
towering great 31
  violent 173
  large 192
  high 206
  –passion 900
  –rage 825
tow–headed 429
town city 189
  fashion 852
  all over the–532
  man about–854
  on the–961
  talk of the–873
townhall 966
townhouse 189, 966
township 181
townsman 188
town talk news 532
  gossip 588
towpath 627
towrow 713
toxic 657
toxicant 663
toxicology 663
toxiferous 657
toxophilite 840
toy trifle 643
  amusement 840
  fondle 902
toy dog 366
toyshop 840
tracasserie 713
trace follow 63
  inquire 461
  discover 480a
  mark 550
  record 551
  delineate 554
  –back 122
  –out 480a
  –to 155
  –up 461
tracery lattice 219
  curve 245
  ornament 847

traces harness 45
trachea 351
tracheocele 655
trachoma 655
tracing 21
track travel 266
  trace 461
  spoor 550
  record 551
  way 627
  in one's–s 113
  –events 840
trackless space 180
  difficult 704
  –trolley 273
tract region 181
  book 593
  dissertation 595
  –of time 109
tractable
  malleable 324
  willing 602
  easy 705
tractarian 984
tractate 595
tractile traction **285**
  soft 324
traction 285
tractive 285
tractor 272
trade business 625
  traffic 794
  drive a–625
  learn one's–539
  the–booksellers 593
  –with 794
  tricks of the–702
  two of a–708
trader 797
trademark 550
tradesman 797
trade union 712
trade wind 349
tradition old 124
  description 594
traditionalism 451
traditive 594
traduce 934
traducer 936
traffic 794
tragalism 954
tragalist 954a
tragedian 599
tragedy drama 599
  evil 619
tragic drama 599
tragical 830
tragi–comedy 599
tragi–comic 853
trail sequel 65
  pendent 214
  slow 275
  traction 285
  odor 398
  inquiry 461
  track 550

(wonderful 870)
unaccustomed
unusual 83
unused 614
unskillful 699
unachievable 471
unacknowledged
ignored 489
nameless 565
unrequited 917
unacquainted 491
unacquired 777a
unactuated (616)
unadmonished 665
unadorned *style* 576
simple 849
beauty – 845
unadulterated
simple 42
genuine 494
(good 648)
unadventurous 864
unadvisable 647
unadvised
dangerous 665
unskillful 699
unaffected
genuine 494
sincere 543
– *style* 578
obstinate 606
artless 703
insensible 823
simple 849
taste 850
(physically callous 376)
unafflicted 831
unaided
weak 160
(unsupported 706)
unalarmed 861
unalienable 924
unallayed 159
unallied 10
unallowable 923
unallowed 925
unalloyed 42
– *happiness* 827
– *truth* 494
unalluring 866
unalterable 150
unaltered
identical 13
stable 150
(unchanged 141)
unamazed 871
unambiguous 518
unambitious 866
unamiable 907
unanimated 823
unanimity
agreement 23
assent 488
accord 714
unannexed 44

unanswerable
demonstrative 478
irresponsible 927a
arbitrary 964
(certain 474)
unanswered 478
unanticipated 508
unappalled 861
unappareled 226
unapparent
latent 526
(invisible 447)
unappeasable 173
unappetizing 867
unapplied 678
unappreciated 483
unapprehended 491
unapprehensive 861
unapprised 491
unapproachable
great 31
infinite 105
distant 196
unapproached
unequal 28
superior 33
unappropriated 782
unapproved 932
unapt *incongruous* 24
impotent 158
unskillful 699
(inexpedient 647)
unarmed 158
unarranged
disorder 59
unprepared 674
unarrayed 226, 849
unartificial 849
unascertained
uncertain 475
ignorant 491
unasked
voluntary 602
not asked 766
unaspiring
indifferent 866
modest 881
unassailable 664
unassailed 748
unassembled 73
unassisted *weak* 160
unaided 706
– *eye* 441
unassociated 44
unassuming 881
unatoned 951
unattached 44
unattackable 664
unattainable 471
unattained 732
unattempted 623
unattended 87
– *to* 460
unattested
not evidence 468
(unrecorded 552)

unattracted
indifferent 866 (616)
unattractive 866
unauthenticated
improved 468
uncertain 475
inexact 495
unauthoritative
uncertain 475
unauthorized
prohibited 761
undue 925
lawless 964
unavailing *useless* 645
failure 732
unavenged 918
unavoidable
certain 474
necessary 601
unavowed 489
unawakened 683
unaware *ignorant* 491
unexpecting 508
unawed 861
unbalanced 28
unbar 750
unbearable 830
unbeaten 123
unbeauteous 846
unbecoming
incongruous 24
disreputable 874
undue 925
dishonorable 940
– *a gentleman* 895
unbefitting *inapt* 24
undue 925
improbity 940
(see unbecoming)
unbegotten 2
unbeguile *inform* 527
disclose 529
unbegun
unprepared 674
unbeheld (447)
unbelief 485
irreligion 989
(incredulity 487)
unbelievable 485
unbeliever *infidel* 989
unbelieving 485
unbeloved 898
unbend *straighten* 246
repose 687
– *the mind* 452
unbending *hard* 323
resolute 604
unbenevolent 907
unbenign 907
unbent 246
unbeseeming
vulgar 851
dishonorable 940
unbesought
not ask 766
(spontaneous 602)

unbestowed (785)
unbetrayed 939
unbewailed 932
unbiased *wise* 498
free 748
(spontaneous 602a)
unbidden *willful* 600
disobedient 742
unbigoted 498
unbind *detach* 44
release 750
unblamable 946
unblamed 946
unblemished
perfect 650
innocent 946
unblenching 861
unblended 42
unblest
unfortunate 735
not approved 932
– *with* 777a
unblown 674
unblushing
proud 878
vain 880
imprudent 885
unboastful 881
unbodied 317
unboiled 674
unbolt *liberate* 750
(unfasten 44)
unbookish 491
unborn *not existing* 2
destined 152
(future 121)
unbosom oneself 529
unbought
not bought 796
honorary 815
honorable 939
unselfish 942
unbound *free* 748
exempt 927a
unbounded
infinite 105
(great 31)
(large 192)
(space 180)
unbrace *weaken* 160
relax 655
unbreathed 526
unbred 895
unbribed
honorable 939
disinterested 942
unbridled *violent* 173
lax 738
free 748
unbroken *entire* 50
continuous 69
preserved 670
unviolated 939
– *extent* 69
unbruised 50
unbuckle 44

unburden
– *one's mind* 529
unburdened 705
unburied 362
unbuttoned 748
uncalculating 863
uncalled for
redundant 641
useless 645
not used 678
uncandid
insincere 544
morose 907
uncanny *ugly* 846
spectral 980a
uncanonical 984
uncared for
neglected 460
indifferent 866
disliked 867
hated 898
uncase (226)
uncate 245
uncaught *free* 748
uncaused 156
unceasing 112, 143
uncensured 931
unceremonious
vain 880
discourteous 895
uncertain
irregular 139
not certain 475
doubtful 485
embarrassing 704
in an – *degree* 32
uncertainty 475
unchain *unfasten* 44
liberate 750
unchained *free* 748
unchallenged
assent 488
due 924
unchangeable
stable 150
persevering 604a
unchanged 16, 141
unchangingly 136
uncharitable 907
unchartered
undue 925
illegal 964
unchaste 961
unchastised 970
unchecked 748
uncheckered 141
uncheerful 837
unchivalric 940
unchristian
heterodox 984
irreligious 989
uncial 590
unciform 245
uncinated 244
uncircumscribed 180
uncircumspect 460

603

uninfluential
 inert 172
 no influence 175a
uninformed 491
uningenuous 544
uninhabit
 absence 187
 secluded 893
uninhabitable 187,
 893
uninhabited 187, 893
uninitiated
 ignorant 491
 unskillful 699
uninjured *perfect* 650
 healthy 654
 preserved 670
uninjurious 656
uninquisitive 456
uninspired
 unexcited 823
 (*unactuated* 616)
uninstructed 491
unintellectual
 incogitant 452
 inbecile 499
unintellectuality
 450a
unintelligent 32, 499
unintelligibility 519,
 571
unintelligible 519
 -style 571
 render-538
unintended 621
unintentional
 necessary 601
 undesigned 621
uninterested
 incurious 456
 weary 841
 dull 843
uninteresting 643
unintermitting
 unbroken 69
 durable 110
 continuing 143
 persevering 604a
uninterrupted
 continuous 69
 perpetual 112
 unremitting 893
 -*existence* 112
unintroduced 893
uninured
 unaccustomed 614
 (*unprepared* 674)
uninvented 526
uninvestigated 491
uninvited 893
uninviting 830
union *agreement* 23
 junction 43
 combination 48
 concurrence 178
 party 712

 concord 714
 marriage 903
 -*down flag* 550
union jack 550
union pipes 417
unique *dissimilar* 18
 original 20
 unequal 28
 exceptional 83
 alone 87
unirritable 826
unirritating 174
unison *agreement* 23
 melody 413
 concord 714
 (*uniform* 16)
 in-*melody* 413
unisulcate 259
unit 87
Unitarian 984
unitary 87
unite *join* 43
 combine 48
 component 56
 assemble 72
 concur 178
 converge 290
 party 712
 (*agree* 23)
 -in pairs 89
 -one's efforts 709
 -with coöperate 709
united *coherent* 46
 concord 714
United States courts
 966
unity *identity* 13
 uniformity 16
 whole 50
 complete 52
 single **87**
 concord 714
 -of time 120
Unity, Trinity in-
 976
universal 78
 -Church 983a
 -concept 450
 -favorite 899
 -joint 272, 633
 -language 560
 -ly present 186
 -predicament 25
universality 52
universalize 78
universe 318
university 542
 go to the-539
 -degree 873
 -education 537
unjust *wrong* 923
 impious 988
unjustifiable
 wrong 923
 inexcusable 938
 wicked 945

unjustified 923
 undue 925
unkempt *rough* 256
 unclean 653
 vulgar 851
unkennel *eject* 297
 disclose 529
unkind 907
 -est cut of all 828
unkindness hard-907
unknightly 940
unknit (44)
unknot 705
unknowable 519
unknowing 491
unknown
 ignorant 491
 latent 526
 -quantities 491
 -to fame
  inglorious 874
  lowborn 876
unlabored-*style* 578
 unprepared 674
unlace (44)
unlade 297
unladylike
 vulgar 851
 rude 895
unlamented
 hated 898
 disapproved 932
unlatch 44
unlawful *undue* 925
 illegal 964
unlearn 506
unlearned 491
unleavened 674
unless *circumstances* 8
 except 83
 qualification 469
 (*condition* 770)
unlettered 491
 -Muse 579
unlicensed 761
unlicked
 unprepared 674
 vulgar 851
 clownish 876
 -cub *shapeless* 241
  unmannerly 895
unlike 18
unlikely 471, 473
unlimber 323
unlimited *great* 31
 infinite 105
 free 748
 -space 180
unlink (44)
unliquefied 321
unlively *grave* 837
 dull 843
unload *displace* 185
 eject 297
 disencumber 705
 sell 796

unlock *unfasten* 44
 discover 480a
 (*explain* 462)
unlooked for 508
unloose *unfasten* 44
 liberate 750
unloved 898
unlovely 846
unlucky
 inopportune 135
 bad 649
 unfortunate 735
 in pain 830
unmade 2
unmaimed 654
unmake 145
unman *castrate* 38
 render powerless 158
 madden 837
 frighten 860
unmanageable
 unwieldy 647
 perverse 704
unmanly
 effeminate 374
 dishonorable 940
unmanned
 dejected 837
 cowardly 862
unmannered 895
unmannerly 895
unmarked 460
unmarred *sound* 654
 preserved 670
unmarried 904
unmask
 disclose 529
 (*show* 525)
unmatched
 different 15
 dissimilar 18
 unparalleled 20
 unequal 28
unmeaningness 517
unmeant 517
unmeasured
 infinite 105
 undistinguished
  465a
 abundant 639
unmeditated
 impulsive 612
 (*undesigned* 621)
unmeet 925
unmellowed 674
unmelodious 414,
 713
unmelted 321
unmentionable 874
unmentionables 225
unmentioned 526
unmerciful
 pitiless 914a
 (*malevolent* 907)
unmerited 925
unmethodical 59

unmindful
 inattentive 458
 neglectful 460
 ungrateful 917
unmingled 42
unmissed 460
unmistakable
 certain 474
 intelligible 518
 manifest 525
 affirmation 535
 (*visible* 446)
unmitigable 173
unmitigated *great* 31
 complete 52
 violent 173
unmixed 42
unmodified (141)
unmolested *safe* 664
 content 831
unmoneyed 804
unmoral 823
unmourned 898
unmoved
 quiescent 265
 obstinate 606
 insensible 823
 (*resolute* 604)
 (*uninduced* 616)
unmusical 414
 -voice 581
unmuzzle 748
unnamed 565
unnatural
 exceptional 83
 affected 855
 spiteful 907
unnecessary
 redundant 641
 useless 645
 inexpedient 647
unneeded 645
unneighborly 895
unnerved
 powerless 158
 weak 160
 dejected 837
unnoted *neglected* 460
 ignoble 874
unnoticed 460, 874
unnumbered 105
unnurtured 674
unobeyed 742
unobjectionable
 good 648
 pretty good 651
 innocent 946
unobnoxious 648
unobscured 420
unobservant 458
unobserved 460
unobstructed
 clear 705
 free 749
 (*unopposed* 709)
unobtainable 471

611

vindicate
  evidence 467
  avenge 919
  justify 937
  –a right 924
vindication 937
vindicator
  revenge 919
vindictive
  irascible 901
  revengeful 919
vine 367
vinegar 397
  –aspect 846
vine–grower 371
vinegrub 659
vineyard *tillage* 371
  workshop 691
vingt et un 840
viniculturist 371
vintage
  agriculture 371
  store 636
vintner 797
viol 417
violaceous 437
violate *disobey* 742
  nonobservance 773
  undue 925
  dereliction 927
  ravish 961
  –a law 83
  –a usage 614
  –the law 964
violence 173
  arbitrary 964
  do–to *bad* 649
  nonobservance 773
  undue 925
violent 173
  excitable 825
  in a–degree 31
  lay–hands on 789
  –death *death* 360
  kill 361
violet 437
  modesty 881
violin 417
violinist 416
violoncello 417
violone 417
viper *snake* 366
  bane 663
  evildoer 913
  bad man 949
viperine 366
virago 901
virent 435
virescence 435
virgate 246
virgin *new* 123
  girl 129
  spinster 904
  good woman 948
  pure 960
  –soil *ignorance* 491

  untilled 674
virginal 900
virginals 417
Virginia
  crooked as–fence
  243
  –reel 840
viridian 435
viridity 435
virile *adolescent* 131
  strong 159
  manly 373
virtu 847, 850
virtual *inexistent* 2
  unsubstantial 5
  –image 443
virtually 5
  (*truly* 494)
virtue *power* 157
  courage 861
  goodness 944
  purity 960
  by–of *power* 157
  instrumentality 631
  in–of *authority* 737
  make a–of necessity
  no choice 609a
  skill 698
  submit 725
  compromise 774
  bear 826
virtueless 945
virtuosity *taste* 850
virtuoso 415, 416,
  850
virtuous *virtue* 944
  purity 960
virulence *energy* 171
  noxiousness 649
  insalubrity 657
  discourtesy 895
  anger 900
  malevolence 907
virus *disease* 655
  poison 663
vis inertiae
  power 157
  inertness 172
  insensibility 823
visa 488
visage *front* 234
  appearance 448
vis–à–vis
  contrariety 14
  front 234
  opposite 237
  carriage 272
viscera 221
visceral 221, 329
viscid 327, 352
viscidity 327
viscount 875
viscountship 877
viscous 352
viscum 45
vise 327, 752, 781

Vishnu 979
visibility 446
visible 446
  (*intelligible* 518)
  become–448
  be–448
  darkness–421
vision *sight* 441
  phantasm 443
  dream 515
  specter 980a
  psychical research
  992a
  organ of–441
visionary *inexistent* 2
  unsubstantial 4
  impossible 471
  imaginary 515
  heterodox 984
  (*untrue* 495)
visionless 442
visit *arrival* 292
  social 892
  courtesy 894
  –behind the scenes
  461
  –upon 972
visitation *disease* 655
  adversity 735
  suffering 828
  (*evil* 619)
  –of the sick 998
  –s of Providence 976
visiting 892
  on–terms
  friendship 888
  sociality 892
  –card 550
visitor *immigrant* 294
  director 694
  friend 890
visor 530
vista *convergence* 260
  sight 441
  appearance 448
  expectation 507
  –of time 109
visual 441–organ 441
visualize 220
vitability 359
vital *life* 359
  important 642
  –air 359
  –force 359
  –part 3
  –principle 1
vitalic 359
vitality *stability* 150
  strength 159
  life 359
vitalize 359
vitals 221
vitiate *deteriorate* 659
vitiated *diseased* 655
viticulture 371
vitreform 425

vitreous *hard* 323
  transparent 425
vitrescent 323
vitrics 191
vitrify 323
vitrine 191
vituperate 932
vituperation 908
vituperator 936
viva! *glory* 873
  praise 931
vivace *music* 415
vivacious *active* 682
  sensitive 822
  cheerful 836
vivandière 797
vivarium 370
viva voce 582
vive *glory be to* 873
  on the qui–824
vivid *energetic* 171
  sensibility 375
  light 420
  color 428
  graphic 518
  (*powerful* 157)
  still–
  remembering 506
vivify *strength* 159
  life 359
vivisection *pain* 378
  cruelty 907
vixen *fox* 366
  female 374
  shrew 901
viz. (*see videlicet*)
vizier *director* 694
  deputy 759
vizor *mask* 530
  shield 717
vlei 345
vocable 562
vocabulary 562
vocal *music* 415
  voice 580
  –score 415
vocalist 416
vocalize 562, 580
vocation *business* 625
  (*duty* 926)
vocational 625
  –therapy 662
  –training 537
vociferation *loud* 404
  cry 411
  voice 580
vogue *custom* 613
  fashion 852
  fame 873
voice *sound* 402
  cry 411
  judgment 480
  promulgate 531
  affirmation 535
  express 566
  human–580

  choice 609
  (*belief* 484)
  give one's–for 488
  make one's–heard
  175
  raise one's
  –shout 411
  speak 582
  still small–
  faint sound 405
  conscience 926
  want of–581
  warning–668
  –against *dissent* 489
  oppose 708
  –of the charmer 933
  –of the tempter 615
voiceless 561, 581
  –woe 837
void *unsubstantial* 4
  absence 187
  emit 297
  abyss 667
  (*inexistence* 2)
  null and–964
  –of foundation 546
  –of reason 450a
  –of suspicion 484
voidance 297
voile 635
voiturier 268
voivode 745
volant 267
Volapük 560, 563
volatile *transient* 111
  light 320
  gaseous 334
  vaporizable 336
  assent 488
  irresolute 605
  capricious 608
  –alkali 334
vol–au–vent 298
volcanic *violent* 173
  heat 382
  burnt 388
  excitable 825
volcanism 490c
volcano *violence* 173
  furnace 386
  pitfall 667
  on a–*danger* 665
volition 267
volitient 600
volksraad 696
volley *collection* 72
  violence 173
  report 406
  attack 716
  (*impulse* 276)
volplane 267
volplaning 267
Volstead Act 761
volt 490d
voltaic 157
  –electricity 157

616

means 632
(*joined* 43)
go–178
–all its parts 52
–a sting to it 770
–a vengeance
great 31
complete 52
–a witness 31
–regard to 9
withal *in addition* 37
accompanying 88
withdraw *subduct* 38
absent 187
turn back 283
recede 287
depart 293
–from *recant* 607
relinquish 624
dislike 867
withdrawal
(*see* withdraw)
rejection 610
withe 45
wither *shrink* 195
decay 659
–one's hopes 837
withered *weak* 160
disease 655
withering *harsh* 739
painful 830
contempt 930
censure 932
withers 250–unwrung
strong 159
insensible 323
withhold *hide* 528
restrain 751
prohibit 761
retain 781
stint 819
–one's assent 764
within 221
derived from–5
keep–221
place–221
–an ace 32
–bounds *small* 32
shortcoming 304
restraint 751
–call 197
–compass
shortcoming 304
temperate 953
–one's memory 505
–reach *near* 197
easy 705
–the mark 304
without *unless* 8
subduction 38
exception 83
absence 187
exterior 220
circumjacent 227
exemption 777*a*
derived from–6
not be able to do–
630
–a dissentient voice
488
–a leg to stand on
158
–alloy 827
–a rap 804
–a shadow of turning
141
–ballast *irresolute* 605
unprincipled 945
–ceasing 136
–ceremony 881
–charge 815
–end *infinite* 105
perpetual 112
–exception 16
–excuse 945
–fail *certain* 474
persevering 604*a*
–fear of
contradiction 535
–God 989
–limit 105
–measure 105
–notice 508
–number 105
–parallel 33
–reason 499
–regard to 10
–reluctance 602
–reserve 525
–rhyme or reason
615*a*
–stint 639
–warning 508
withstand *oppose* 708
resist 719
(*counteract* 179)
withy 45
witless 491
witling *fool* 501
wag 844
witness *see* 441
spectator 444
evidence 467
voucher 550
call to–467
witness box 966
wits 450
all one's–about one
care 459
intelligence 498
skin 698
live by one's–
deceive 545
skill 698
cunning 702
steal 791
dishonorable 940
one's–gone a wool-
gathering 458
set one's–to work
think 451
invent 515
plan 626
witsnapper 844
witticism 842
wittingly 620
wittol 962
witty 842, 844
be–498
wive 903
wivern 83
wizard *sage* 500
deceiver 548
proficient 700
sorcerer 994
–of the air 269
wizen *wither* 195
throat 260
woe *pain* 828
evil 619
–betide
malediction 908
pity 914
–is me 839
–to 908
woebegone 828
sad 837
woeful *bad* 649
painful 830
woefully *very* 31
wold 344
wolf *ravenous* 865
cry–*false* 544
alarm 669
fear 860
hold the–by the
ears 704
keep the–from the
door 359
unable to keep the–
from the door
804
–and the lamb 923
–at the door
source of danger 667
poverty 804
–in sheep's clothing
deceiver 548
knave 941
wolfish 789
woman *adult* 131
human **374**
–of the town 962
–perfected 374
–the lesser man 374
woman hater 911
womanhood 131, 374
womanish 374
womankind 374
womanly
adolescent 131
feminine 374
womb *cause* 153
interior 221
–of time *future* 121
destiny 152
womerah 727
wonder *exception* 83
superexcellence 646
astonishment **870**
prodigy 872
do–s *activity* 682
succeed 731
for a–870
nine days'–643
not–507
–s of the world 872
–whether
uncertain 475
ignorant 491
suppose 514
wonderfully
greatly 31
wonderworking 870
wondrous 870
wont *habitual* 613
(*conformity* 82)
won't do, it–
disapproval 932
woo *desire* 865
courtship 902
wooer 897
wood *trees* 367
material 635
not out of the–
danger 665
difficulty 704
–lot 232
woodbine
gone where the–
twineth 771
woodchuck day 138
woodcut 558
woodcutter 371
wooded, well–256
wooden 635
–horse 975
–spoon 493
–walls *defense* 717
men–of–war 726
wood engraving 558
woodlands 367
wood–note 412
wood nymph 979
wood pavement 255
wood pigeon 366
woodwind 416
woody 367
woof 329
wool *flocculent* 256
warm 382
wrap 384
fabric 635
much cry and little
–482
woolgathering 458
woolly 255, 256
woolpack *cloud* 353
woolsack *pillow* 215
authority 747
tribunal 966
woon 745
word *maxim* 496
intelligence 532
assertion 535
volable **562**
phrase 566
command 741
promise 768
give the–741
good as one's–
veracious 543
complete 729
probity 939
in a–572
keep one's–939
man of his–939
not a–to say
silent 585
humble 879
pass–550
put in a–582
take at one's–
believe 484
consent 762
upon my–535
watch–*military* 722
–and a blow
hasty 684
contentious 720
irascible 901
–for word
imitation 19
truth 494
–it 566
–of command
indication 550
military 722
command 741
–in the ear
information 527
allocution 586
–of honor 768
–of mouth 582
–to the wise
intelligible 518
advice 695
Word *Deity* 573
–of God 985
wordbook 86
word–catcher 936
wordiness 562, 573
wording 569
wordless 581
word painter 594
word painting 515
word play
equivocal 520
neology 563
wit 842
words *quarrel* 713
bandy–588
bitter–932
choice of–569
command of–574
express by–566
flow of
–*eloquence* 582
loquacity 584
mere–*sophistry* 477